THE CHURCH CYCLOPÆDIA.

A DICTIONARY

OF

CHURCH DOCTRINE, HISTORY,

ORGANIZATION AND RITUAL,

AND CONTAINING ORIGINAL ARTICLES ON SPECIAL TOPICS, WRITTEN EXPRESSLY
FOR THIS WORK BY BISHOPS, PRESBYTERS, AND LAYMEN.

DESIGNED ESPECIALLY FOR THE USE OF
THE LAITY OF THE PROTESTANT EPISCOPAL CHURCH
IN THE UNITED STATES OF AMERICA.

EDITED BY
REV. A. A. BENTON, M.A.,
PROFESSOR OF MATHEMATICS IN DELAWARE COLLEGE.

SEVENTH THOUSAND.

NEW YORK:
M. H. MALLORY & CO.,
47 LAFAYETTE PLACE.

Republished by Gale Research Company, Book Tower, Detroit, 1975

Copyright, 1883, by L. R. HAMERSLY & Co.

Library of Congress Cataloging in Publication Data

Benton, Angelo Ames, 1837-1912, ed.
 The church cyclopaedia.

  Reprint of the ed. published by M.H. Mallory,
New York.
  1. Theology--Dictionaries. 2. Protestant Episcopal
Church in the U.S.A.--Dictionaries. I. Title.
BR95.B5   1975   283'.03   74-31499
ISBN 0-8103-4204-9

PREFACE.

THIS Cyclopædia is designed to fill a void which still exists in our general literature. It is especially intended to give the Laity, in a condensed and handy form, a great variety of information, culled from many elaborate volumes, and written by a great diversity of men, as to the constitution, nature, and practical working of the Church of CHRIST. It is to enable them to judge for themselves, upon the many questions of fact, and doctrine, and government, in our Communion, furnishing them the materials for forming such judgments, and for holding correct views thereon.

The importance of having the Laity intelligently taught concerning these things, cannot be overrated in our Church, where the Lay element is so conspicuous and powerful.

Nor would we wish it less prominent. The Church gains largely by the wisdom and sound counsel of its Laity. Hence the more accessible ecclesiastical information is made to them, the wiser will be their action, the more loyal their support, and the more conservative their influence.

While this Cyclopædia will be of much use to the Clergy who have not the advantage of libraries, yet it was not prepared for them, as they are supposed to have already a certain basis of information on these topics, and also opportunities of prosecuting their researches in any special line of history or doctrine.

Hence, only the outside, as it were, of many questions is shown here; for many of the subjects here introduced require volumes, rather than pages, and many minds, rather than one mind, to do them justice. As furnishing heads and data of thought and fact concerning the large circle of topics here introduced, this volume, then, will be of the greatest service to all Lay people, as well as furnish a convenient reference book for the Clergy.

In preparing this volume, the Editor, himself a scholar of much ripeness and breadth, has called to his aid writers of varying shades of opinion, so as to reflect, as far as possible, the many-sidedness of the Church's views on some of the practical questions of ritual and discipline. It does not represent one party or school, but gives fair and candid expression to many different minds and opinions, which are tolerated within the wideness of the outstretched arms of the Church of the living GOD. It is well that it should be so. In an age when no asserted truth goes unchallenged, and no opinion is uttered without subjecting it to the crucible of heated criticism, we want to know how these points are viewed by divergent, yet representative, minds, in the several departments of sacred learning. The names of the contributors show the range of minds, as the number of the different subjects treated show the range of topics embraced in the volume. The plan has been to let each man speak for himself, and so be responsible alone for his opinions.

Whatever will enlarge the area of knowledge, or give shape and definiteness to floating opinions, or throw light upon obscure points, or stimulate deeper investigation in this broad department of learning, cannot but prove a great blessing to all thinking and Christian men. This Cyclopædia will, it is hoped, fulfill all, or nearly all, these conditions, and it ought, therefore, to be hailed with favor, especially by the Laity, as a marked help to them in seeking after a deeper knowledge and wider views of the person and glory of CHRIST our LORD, as seen in "the Church which is His body, the fullness of Him that filleth all in all."

WILLIAM BACON STEVENS.

# THE
CHURCH CYCLOPÆDIA.

A.

A and Ω (Rev. i. 8, xxi. 6, xxii. 13; *cf.* Is. xii. 4, xliv. 6). The first and last letters of the Greek alphabet, used to express the eternity of GOD. Its form belongs to St. John's Revelation, but its meaning is found already in Isaiah. It was used by the Jews later to express the comprehensive nature of GOD. The symbol is generally assigned to our LORD. In the first passage, the symbol may refer to the TRINITY, but it is better (in view of the fact that in xxii. 13, our LORD gives this title to Himself) to hold that it is one of our LORD'S titles, implying for Him all the attributes of the Godhead, as being the Source, Upholder, and End of all things. These two letters passed into early Christian use, being found in the catacombs; and into ecclesiastical Latin poetry (*vide* Prudentius, Cathem. ix. 10), and so into liturgical use. It is often used as a monogram in church decorations. (*Vide* Bishop Wordsworth's New Testament, Archbishop Trench's Commentary on the Epistles to the Seven Churches, for thorough discussion of the meaning of AΩ in the Revelation.)

Aaron, the brother of Moses and the first High-Priest under the Law. His father was Amram, and his mother was Jochebed; his wife was Elisheba, daughter of Nahshon, of the tribe of Judah. He was three years older than Moses, and apparently, since GOD Himself called him "the Levite," he was of priestly dignity in his family. His was a far weaker character than his brother's. Able to speak well, ready, and not wanting in courage, he was given to Moses to be his mouth-piece, as Moses was the mouth-piece of GOD, *i.e.*, the Prophet. In then his being first the Prophet and then the High-Priest Aaron becomes a type of CHRIST. He went willingly with Moses upon the mission. They twain went to the people and gathered their elders. Aaron apparently does the evidential signs before them instead of Moses, and after they had been acknowledged by the people, the two brothers go before Pharaoh. Throughout the first part Aaron acts for Moses: Aaron casts down the rod that becomes a serpent; he smites the Nile, stretches the rod over the streams, smites the dust. The two sprinkle the ashes of the furnace. Thence till the last stroke Moses acts. He stretches the rod toward heaven, for the storm of hail; over the land, for swarms of locusts. But the LORD reserved to Himself without stroke of rod or word of prophet the two death-plagues at the set time: the murrain wasted the herds of Egypt; at midnight there was the great cry. Aaron is withdrawn from the prominent place in the narrative till the Israelites reach the wilderness of Sin. Moses bids him prepare the people for the miracle of the manna. Aaron bears up Moses' hand with the rod till Amalek is discomfited. He draws near with Moses to the summit of Sinai, but does not enter the Fire and the Cloud. Now left to himself, he shows the weakness of his character. The murmuring of the people upon the long absence of Moses, and their cry for some god to go up before them, led him to collect the offerings of their golden ear-rings and to cast the molten calf. It shows him to be a facile and popular leader rather than a deeply-principled master of men. The worship of the molten calf with the rites due to the LORD perversely offered before it led to the sin of licentiousness. The end of it was the shame and shrinking on Aaron's part, the indignant discipline inflicted by Moses, and then his wonderful, loving intercession for the sinning people and his erring brother. The forgiveness was complete, for Aaron was immediately consecrated to the High-Priesthood, and it was conferred by a perpetual grant to his family alone. Here we have to call attention to the typical character of his office. It was his right to enter into the Holy of Holies once in the year, on the great Day of Atonement, with the blood of the goat and the bullock. He made the atonement when he stood between the living and the dead, and stayed the fire that burst from the LORD'S anger. It was his right to offer asylum for his lifetime to the manslayer fled to the city of refuge. He could not share in funeral rites. The intercessory, expiatory, and ever-living work of our LORD are typified in these rites. Whatever defects in his private character marred its evenness, in his official character he was between JEHOVAH and JEHOVAH'S people. Aaron appears again when he murmured against his brother. His commission, its grandeur, and its awful duties dazzled him. His sister presuming upon her office as prophetess showed herself jealous of Moses also. In fact, Miriam was the chief in the resistance to the Lawgiver's authority. Its vindication by GOD Himself was a severe lesson. Again, when Korah's rebellion ended in his destruction and Aaron had used his priestly function of making an atonement, then, as a further attestation to his office, the LORD chose to give the people the sign of his rod, with buds, blooms, and fruit,—a sign that was laid up together with the pot of manna before the ark testimony. Then GOD gave a special charge to Aaron that he and his sons, and his father's house, should "bear the iniquity" of the sanctuary, and he and his sons should "bear the iniquity" of the priesthood (*cf*. Ps. lxxxix. 50, 51, and the Agony in the Garden). His were to be the tithes, the peace-offerings, the wave-offerings, the first fruits, the devoted, the redemption-money of the first-born, of man and beast, for he and his sons were to have no inheritance in the land, but to be separate to the LORD. Aaron's character appears again markedly in sharing his brother's impatience at the rock, when he smote when he should have only spoken. Miriam by this time was dead, and the weary journeying was drawing to a close; now at the very end when the longed-for land was almost in sight, to be forbidden. He seems to have acquiesced in the decree. And when the command came for him to climb the Mount Hor, and there upon its top to have his priestly garments taken from him and put upon his son, and then to lie down and die there, in the sight of the congregation, his submission did not fail him. The Lawgiver, the faithful servant, despoiled his loved brother of the sacred vestments with which he had, at the outset of their journeyings so many years before, adorned him, "And Aaron died then in the top of the mount, and Moses and Eleazar came down from the mount." The real greatness of Aaron's character is overshadowed by the splendor of his brother's, but he was, with all the weaknesses so faithfully recorded in Holy Scripture, a far more perfect man than many others who are in their careers more prominently, not more really, types of CHRIST. His own shortcomings may have taught him that compassion which our Great High-Priest had learned, not from taint of sin, but by contact with and suffering from its loathsome effects. In Aaron's descendants flowed the blood of their mother, a daughter of the tribe from which our LORD took His Flesh.

Abaddon (Job xxxi. 12, Destruction). In Job xxvi. 6, the Chaldee paraphrast makes it mean the "house of destruction;" in Job xxviii. 22, its Chaldee equivalent is the angel of Death. It was also applied later by the Jews to the Christian schools Be'Abidan. In Rev. ix. 11 it is a title of the "Angel of the bottomless pit," whose name in the Hebrew tongue is Abaddon, but in the Greek tongue hath his name Apollyon (*i.e.*, destroyer). There is much Jewish trifling upon the name. It is, however, one of the titles of Satan. The woe in Rev. ix., where Abaddon is spoken of, is interpreted usually of the Saracens, and he is named as their king.

Abba (Syriac). A peculiarly tender form of FATHER. Our LORD (Mark xiv. 36) uses it in His Prayer in the Garden. St. Paul uses it twice (Rom. viii. 15; Gal. iv. 6), in referring to our adoption as Sons through the HOLY GHOST (*vide* Confirmation). Selden and other writers say that the Jews had a law which forbade bondservants to use the term father to their masters, so Paul used a term tender and expressive of filial reverence. In the Palestinian and Egyptian Churches it became an ecclesiastical title, and so probably passed into the West as Abbot.

Abbess. The Mother or Superior of an abbey of nuns, or female persons living under religious vows and discipline.

Abbey. The building in which a society devoted to religion dwelt; a monastery whose head was an Abbot or Abbess. They were quite numerous in England before the Reformation, and the title still clings to some of the churches. Westminster is better known as Westminster Abbey than as St. Peter's. In Cathedral Abbeys the Bishop was the Abbot, and the presbyteral Superiors of these establishments were styled Priors. Cranmer and Latimer tried hard, at the dissolution of the monasteries, to save some of the abbeys from confiscation to put them to reformed use, but did not succeed.

Abbot. The Father or Superior of a body of men living under religious vows. The derivation of the word is from *Abba* (Med. Lat. *Abbas*). The word Father, in its forms Abbas, Papa, Father, has been ever applied to the Christian presbyter as a title of respect, except in the later history of the English Church. An Abbot was elected either by all the members of the monastery, or by a part of them as a chapter. Abbots were divided into two ranks, Abbots and Mitred Abbots. There were in England twenty-five Mitred Abbots, who sat and voted in the House of Lords. Abbots were subject to their diocesan; but special exemptions were granted, for favors or by purchase, to many monasteries,—some owning obedience to the See of Rome, others to the Crown, and so exempted from episcopal visitation and reformation. The Abbot received confirmation of his office and benediction from his diocesan, and vowed canonical obedience to him. (Dugdale's Monasticon, Willis's Mitred Abbots, Encyclopædia Britannica, *sub voce*.)

Abjuration. A solemn act of renouncing all false or heretical doctrines which a person had formerly held. There is no authorized form in use in the English Church, though public abjuration has been made by persons at different times. A form was put forth by one of the houses of Convocation, 1714, but it did not receive royal sanction.

Ablution. A liturgical term for any ceremonial washing of the person or of sacred vessels. I. *Person.*—The washings of the priests in the Mosaic Law previous to consecration, and after it frequently in their ministration. The washing of the feet, after our LORD's example, and according to St. Paul's question as to the character of a widow needing church aid if she have washed the feet of strangers; also the early ritual use of washing the hands before and after the celebration of the Holy Communion. II. *Things.* —So the ablutions in the ceremonial of the law. In early liturgic use a reverent ablution of the vessels with a little water for the consumption of every portion of the consecrated elements.

Abraham. The Father of the Faithful (Rom. iv. 16). The Friend of GOD (Is. xli. 8). The Heir of the World (Rom. iv. 13). The Solitary in the religion and worship of JEHOVAH. The grandest of the men of the Old Testament save his great descendant, Moses. The man through whose faith the world has received the blessings of CHRIST the LORD. The man whose name was changed by GOD as a sign of His blessing. He in his life and conduct stands forth as almost unapproached in true courtesy, noble loftiness, and simplicity. The patriarchal life he led is accurately portrayed in Holy Scripture, and can be, even yet, verified in the customs and habits of the Arabs, some of whom are his descendants.

He was the son of Terah, an idolater. Though Abram's name is first in the list, he was probably the second son. The sons of Terah were Haran, who died before the migration, Abram, and Nahor, who remained in Ur. Terah died in Haran, and Abram became the head of the family. The life of the patriarch is divided into four chief eras:

I. The migration from Ur to Haran (Charran, Gen. xi. 31; *cf.* Acts vii. 2-4). Here Terah died, and then (Gen. xii.) the command was given to Abram to remove from Haran to a land GOD would show him, and then he would be blessed, and of his descendants should be made a great nation, and a solemn promise of protection was added. He obeyed, and removed with Lot, his nephew. He first settled near Bethel, and there built an altar to the LORD; thence he went down to Egypt. It is strange as we read it, but in reality it was most natural, that he should have unconsciously distrusted the full meaning of the promise of protection. He was afraid that his wife would be taken from him, and he framed a deceit by having her say she was his sister. Sarah was taken from him, but Pharaoh was plagued of the LORD because of her, and restored her to him, and he was dismissed. From Egypt he returned to Bethel, and there upon the altar he had built he renewed his worship of JEHOVAH (Gen. xiii. 1-4). A wealthy, prospering man, with a large retinue, and a kinsman with him who also was wealthy, he was sufficiently strong to be safe from attack. But this very wealth, and the need of room, caused a strife between their followers, and they found it prudent to separate. Lot chose the plain of Jordan, near Sodom, and Abram remained in the hilly region. Here he received a renewal of the promise, which was a little more clearly and fully expressed, and he was directed to walk through the length and breadth of the land, for it should be his. Upon this command he removed to Mamre (Hebron), and there built an altar and worshipped. At this point occurs one of the most vivid of the incidents of his life. While crushing the revolt of the subject Sodomites Chedorlaomer carried off Lot and his family. Abram, with his three hundred and eighteen servants, planned a night surprise, which was completely successful. He apparently slew the king in the fight. Upon his victorious return, Melchizedec, the mysterious king of Salem, priest of the Most High GOD, met him with bread and wine, and blessed him. Abram paid him tithes and received his blessing as from a superior. Abram's refusal to receive any part of the spoil was a nobly proud act on his part.

II. The second period of his life is from this event and the renewed promise which followed till the third covenanted promise with direct promise of Isaac. This second renewal was still more full, and was sealed with a sacrifice and a solemn sign of a horror of great darkness in his sleep. He was told of the servitude in Egypt, of the deliverance and the establishment of his descendants in the land GOD promised him. To accomplish this promise Sarah persuaded him to take her Egyptian maid as a concubine; but the act was both a proof of his yet defective trust and of the evil of taking accomplishments into his hands. Hagar's insolence and Sarah's jealousy drove the concubine to run away from her mistress. Hagar was ordered to return and to submit to Sarah. She became the mother of Ishmael.

III. And yet again the promise was renewed when Abram was ninety-nine years old. GOD appeared to him, promised that Sarah should bear him a son, changed his name to Abraham, and gave him the covenant sign of circumcision. Still its fulfilment was delayed. Here occurred the touching visit of the JEHOVAH Angel with two attendants to Abraham, their warning him of the impending destruction of Sodom, and his earnest, persistent plea in its behalf. It was a proof of his growth in faith and in a trusting confidence. Again, however, he shows his distrust when among the Philistines. Afraid of being deprived of her (despite GOD'S promise that Sarah should give him a son), he called her his sister, and King Abimelech sent and took her. GOD protected her, and warned the king of his error, who restored Sarah, with a just reproach to Abraham for his deceit. After this Sarah bore Abraham a son, and she called him Isaac, or Laughter, in reference to Sarah's laugh of joy when she heard the promise that she in her old age should have a son and also to his own happiness.

IV. The last main period begins with the great trial of faith to which Abraham was subjected. He was tempted, was proved in the highest form in the command to offer up Isaac. How could the promise be fulfilled if Isaac was offered, and how could a human sacrifice be acceptable to the GOD of Life? The command was couched in words which showed how precious Isaac must be: "Take now thy son, thine only son Isaac, whom thou lovest." The Patriarch had learned that nothing could fail of all that JEHOVAH had promised, and he obeyed. His obedience and its result were thenceforth the very crown of faith and of the truth of GOD'S promises, and became the type of the sacrifice of His sinless Son upon the Cross. It was so wonderful a proof of His trust that the gift was given him that the spiritual blessing he had should be given to all nations upon earth, and the Son of Abraham is the heir of the world, by that act in verity upon the Cross, which was done by figure upon the altar in the Mount Moriah. It was done, it is well to note, when Isaac could understand what was to be transacted, and his obedience, therefore, must not be overlooked. Was it now that Abraham saw the day of CHRIST and was glad?

Sarah died at an advanced age at Kerjath Arba, to which Abraham removed from Beersheba, some time after the offering of Isaac. The whole account of the death, the purchase of a burying-place in the land which had all been given to him, his courtesy and stately mode of preferring his request, and the high respect paid to him by the Hittites, and the simplicity of the whole narrative, make it one of the most touching passages in the record of his life.

He lived nearly thirty years longer, and married Keturah. It was, perhaps, not, we should suppose, fit for so holy and exalted a personage,—one so blessed and prospered,—but Abraham was living at a different era, with ideas current around him far other than those we are habitually using and living in. He is a person, to us, so conjoined to the faith that he displayed that we cannot think of him as a man who, in that Eastern life, needed the care of some woman's hand to minister to him. At the age of a hundred and seventy-five years he died, and was buried by his sons, Isaac and Ishmael. Abraham is for us the type of the solitariness of the man of faith. Others, as Job, as Melchizedec, were servants of GOD and of great holiness, but he had still greater and more enduring blessings because of his faith. And this faith grew; it was disciplined and developed. The clash between this faith and his conduct that occurs in his career was rather the result of not seeing how trustfulness must penetrate the lower planes of our daily life and work. He believed that GOD would not forsake him; still, the emergencies seemed so pressing that he deemed he must do something, and he acted as he did. The consequences bore evil fruit for him and his children in the first instance, as the Egyptian maid gave him so much trouble, and a thousand years later Ishmael sorely distressed Israel. And, too, the daily life and authority of a man of lordly means, while it was a constant proof of GOD'S blessing, tended to withdraw him from the finer, subtler interconnection of his religious life with the slightest parts of his daily life. But this he evidently outgrew. Again, to him we owe our salvation. To him, more than to any one man, we owe our Christian privileges. The children of Abraham (according the faith he had, before circumcision) we are heirs with him of the world, not only of this visible, but of the world unseen. From him came the LORD JESUS CHRIST, through whom he, as well as we, received all the promises, and in whom they are fulfilled.

The more Abraham's life and conduct are studied the more thoroughly human do they appear. He was a great man, endowed with large capacities, with deeply religious and meditative characteristics, with power of will to rise to the height of the demands made upon him, and with a loving and a sympathetic strain throughout. His abilities and weight were early acknowledged by the peoples in whose neighborhood he dwelt. It was only by deep pondering and prayer that he could have been strengthened to meet the discipline GOD put upon him. The influence Sarah had over him and his deep affection for Isaac are proof enough of that best of all domestic bonds,—a loving nature.

Absolute. In theology, a perfect unalterable condition, e.g., Divine goodness is absolute; so Divine justice and mercy, without imperfection or defect. The absolute gift of redemption will be at the resurrection. Its gift is conditional here and now.

Absolution. The authoritative act of declaring GOD'S forgiveness of a penitent. Cf. P. B., "Hath given power and commandment to His ministers to declare and pronounce to His people being penitent the absolution and remission of their sins. He pardoneth and absolveth all those who truly repent and unfeignedly believe His Holy Word." The use of this authority is confined only to the bishops and the priests. It is formed upon the authority our LORD gave His Church (St. Matt. xvi. 19, xviii. 18; St. John xx. 23). A charge thrice repeated at different times, first while preparing the Apostles for their work and then immediately after His resurrection. It is an integral part of the ministry of the Church to men, as it is involved in the sacraments of Baptism and the Eucharist. But its practical use was also long before involved in all sacrifices in the Levitical dispensation; and a notable instance of the declaration of absolution is in Nathan's reply to King David,—"The LORD also hath put away thy sin" (2 Sam. xii. 13). Our LORD making all forgiveness flow from His own person pronounced His absolution authoritatively. "Son, thy sins be forgiven thee. . . . That ye may know that the Son of man hath power on earth to forgive sins." So to the sinful woman, "Thy sins are forgiven." Then it was a development into Christian use of the germ which lay in the Mosaic dispensation, and was ordained by our LORD for the comfort of His own. As all power is His in heaven and in earth, and as He is ever with His Church to the end of the world, and has by a direct gift of the HOLY GHOST for that end endowed the Apostolate with the Commission, it must be of continuous and continual use in His Church.

"The special acts or ways in which the ministers of CHRIST are commissioned or authorized to exemplify this their power of retaining or remitting sins appear to be four acts of the ministry whereby the benefit of absolution is ordinarily dispensed unto men.

"The power of administering the two sacraments of Baptism and the Lord's Supper to all such as are qualified to receive them, which is, therefore, called 'sacramental absolution.'

"The power of declaring or publishing the terms or conditions upon which the Gospel promises pardon and remission of sins, which is called the 'declaratory absolution of the word and doctrine.'

"The power of interceding with GOD for pardon of sins through the merits of CHRIST, which is the 'absolution of prayer.'

"The power of executing Church discipline and censures upon delinquents, which consists in excluding flagitious and scandalous sinners from the communion of the Church, and receiving penitents again into her communion when they have given just evidence of a sincere repentance.

"In these four acts, regularly exercised, consists the ministerial power of retaining or remitting sins, so far as the delegated authority of man can be concerned in it." (Bingh. Chr. Ant., bk. viii.)

"The minister can only lend his mouth or his hand toward the external act of absolution; but he cannot absolve internally, much less the unqualified sinner. CHRIST Himself has assured us, that unless men repent, they must inevitably perish; and that unless they forgive men their trespasses, their heavenly Father will not forgive them their trespasses. Now, it would be absurd to think, after this, that a sinner who performs neither of these conditions should, notwithstanding, be pardoned by GOD, continuing impenitent still; and only because he chances surreptitiously to be loosed on earth by some error or fraud, that, therefore, he should be also most certainly loosed in heaven. This were to imagine one of the vainest things in the world, that CHRIST, to make His priests' words true, would make His own words false, as they must needs be if any outward absolution, given by a fallible and mistaken man, could translate an impenitent sinner into the kingdom of heaven." (Bingh. Chr. Ant., bk. iii.)

The very formal words which our Church requires to be used in the ordination of a minister are these: "Whose sins thou dost forgive, they are forgiven; and whose sins thou dost retain, they are retained." (The Form of Ordering of Priests.) We acknowledge most willingly that the principal part of the priest's ministry is exercised in the matter of "forgiveness of sins,"—the question only is of the manner, how this part of their function is executed by them, and of the bounds and limits thereof.

That we may therefore give unto the priest the things that are the priest's, and to GOD the things that are GOD's, and not communicate unto any creature the power that properly belongs to the Creator, who "will not give His glory unto another" (Isaiah xlviii. 11), we must, in the first place, lay this down for a sure ground, that to forgive sins properly, directly, and absolutely, is a privilege only appertaining unto the Most High. "I, even I, am He that blotteth out thy transgressions for mine own sake, and will not remember thy sins" (Isaiah xliii. 25). "Who is a GOD like unto thee, that pardoneth iniquity?" says the prophet Micah (vii.18); which in effect is the same with that of the scribes (Mark ii. 7, and Luke v. 21): "Who can forgive sins but GOD alone?" And therefore, when David says unto GOD, "Thou forgavest the iniquity of my sins" (Ps. xxxii. 5), Gregory, surnamed the Great, the first Bishop of Rome of that name, thought this to be a sound paraphrase of his words: "Thou, who alone sparest, who alone forgivest sins. For who can forgive sins but GOD alone?" (Gregor. Exposit. xi., Ps. Pœnit.) Irenæus tells us that our SAVIOUR in this place, "forgiving sins, did both cure the man and manifestly discover who He was. For if none," says he, "can forgive sins but GOD alone, and our LORD did forgive them, and cured them, it is manifest that He was the Word of GOD made the Son of man; and that, as man, He was touched with compassion of us, as GOD He hath mercy on us, and forgiveth us our debts which we do owe unto our Maker" (Irenæus, adv. Hæres., lib. v. cap. 17). Tertullian (lib. iv. adv. Marcion, cap. 10) says, that "when the Jews, beholding only His humanity, and not being yet certain of His deity, did deservedly reason that a man could not forgive sins, but GOD alone, He, by answering of them, that 'the Son of man had authority to forgive sins,' would by this remission of sins have them call to mind that He was 'that only Son of man prophesied of in Daniel, who received power of judging, and thereby also of forgiving sins'" (Dan. vii. 13, 14). St. Ambrose also observes, upon the history of the woman taken in adultery (John viii. 9), that "JESUS being about to pardon sin, remaineth alone. For it is not the ambassador," says he, "nor the messenger, but the LORD Himself that hath saved His people. He remaineth alone, because it cannot be common to any man with CHRIST to forgive sins. This is the office of CHRIST alone, who 'taketh away the sin of the world'" (Ambros. Epist. lxxvi., ad. Studium). So, too, St. Chrysostom is careful to preserve GOD'S privilege entire, by often interposing such sentences as these: "None can forgive sins but GOD alone" (Chrysost. in 2 Cor. iii., Hom. vi.). "To forgive sins belongeth to no other" (Id. in John viii., Hom. liv., ed. Græc., vel liii., Latin). "To forgive sins is possible to GOD only" (Id. in 1 Cor. 'xv, Hom. xl.). "GOD alone doth this; which also He worketh in the washing of the new birth" (Id. ib.). Whence it is seen that the work of cleansing the soul is wholly GOD'S, and the minister hath no hand at all in effecting any part of it. Having thus, therefore, reserved unto GOD His sacred rights, we give unto His underofficers their due, when we "account of them as of the ministers of CHRIST, and stewards of the mysteries of GOD" (1 Cor. iv. 1, 2), not as lords, that have power to dispose of spiritual graces as they please (Chrysost. in 1 Cor. iv., Hom. x.), but as servants that are bid to follow their master's prescriptions therein (Id. in 2 Cor. iv., Hom. viii. circa init.); and in following thereof do but bring their external ministry, for which itself also they are beholden to GOD's mercy and goodness, GOD conferring the inward blessing of His Spirit thereupon, when and where He will. "Who then is Paul?" says St. Paul, "and who is Apollos, but ministers by whom ye believed, even as the LORD gave to every man?" (1 Cor. iii. 5.) "Therefore," says Optatus (lib. v.), "in all the servants there is no dominion but a ministry." "It is He who is believed that giveth the things which is believed, not he by whom we do believe" (Id. ib. Similiter et Chrysost. in 1 Cor. iii., Hom. viii.). Whereas our SAVIOUR then said unto His apostles, "Receive the HOLY GHOST; whose sins you forgive shall be forgiven" (John xx.). St. Bazil (lib. v. adv. Eunom, p. 113, ed. Græco-Latin), Ambrose (de Spir. Sanct., lib. iii. cap. 19), Augustine (contra Epist. Parmenian, lib. ii. cap. ii. et Hom. xxiii. Ex. 50), Chrysostom. (in 2 Cor. iii., Hom. vi.), and Cyril. Alexand. (in Joh., lib. xii. cap. 56), make this observation thereupon: that this is not their work properly, but the work of the HOLY GHOST, who remitteth by them, and therein performeth the work of the true GOD. "For indeed," says St. Cyril (Id. ib.), "it belongeth to the true GOD alone to be able to loose men from their sins. For who else can free the transgressors of the law from sin but He who is the author of the law itself?" "The LORD," says St. Augustine (Hom. xxiii. Ex. 50), "was to give unto men the HOLY GHOST; and He would have it to be understood, that by the HOLY GHOST Himself sins should be forgiven to the faithful, and not that by the merits of men, sins should be forgiven. For what art thou, O man, but a sick man that hast need to be healed? Wilt thou be a physician to me? Seek the physician together with me." So St. Ambrose (de Spir. Sanct., lib. iii. cap. 19), "Behold, that by the HOLY GHOST sins are forgiven. But men to the remission of sins bring their ministry; they exercise not the authority of any power." St. Chrysostom, though he makes this to be the exercise of a great power, yet in the main accords fully with St. Ambrose, that "it remains in GOD alone to bestow the things wherein the priest's service is employed" (Id. in Joh. xx. Hom. lxxxvi., ed. Græc., vol. lxxxv. Latin). "And what speak I of priests?" says he (Id. ib.). "Neither angel nor arch angel can do aught in those things which are given by GOD; but the Father and the Son and the HOLY GHOST do dispense all. The priest lendeth his tongue, and putteth to his hand." "His part only is to open his mouth; but it is GOD that worketh all" (Id. in 2 Tim., cap. i. Hom. xi.). And the reasons whereby both he and Theophylact (Id. in Joh. viii., Hom. liv., Græc., vel liii., Latin) after him do prove that the priests of the law had no power to forgive sins, are of as great force to take the same power from the ministers of the Gospel. First, because (Theophylact in Joh. viii.) it is GOD's part only to forgive sins, which is the moral that Haymo (Halberstat in Evang. Domin., xv., post Pentecost) makes of that part of the history of the Gospel, wherein the lepers are cleansed by our SAVIOUR before they be commanded to show themselves unto the priest, "because (Theophylact in Joh. viii.) the priests were servants, yea, servants of sin, and therefore had no power to forgive sins unto others; but the SON is the LORD of the house, who was manifested to take away our sins, says St. John (1 John iii. 5)." Upon which saying of his, St. Augustine writes: "It is He in whom there is no sin that came to take away sin. For if there had been sin in Him too, it must have been taken away from Him; He could not take it away Himself" (August., Tract. iv., in 1 John iii.). There then follows another part of the ministry of reconciliation, consisting in the due administration of the sacraments, which being the proper seals of the promises of the Gospel, as the censures are of the threats, must therefore necessarily also have reference to the "remission of sins" (Acts ii. 38; Matt. xxvi. 28). And so we see the ancient fathers held that (Cyprian, Epist. lxxvi. sec. 4, ed. Pamelii, 8 Goulartii; Cyril. Alexand., in Joh., lib. xii. c. 56; Ambros. de Pœnit. lib. i. c. 7; Chrysost. de Sacerdot., lib. iii. tom. vi., ed. Savil., p. 17, lin. 25; vide et tom. vii. p. 268, lin. 37) the commission, "Whosoever sins remit, they are remitted unto them" (John xx. 23), is executed by the ministers of CHRIST, as well in the conferring of baptism as in the reconciling of penitents; yet so in both these, and in all the sacraments likewise of both the testaments, that (August. Quæst. in Levit. clxxxiv.; Optat. lib. v. contra Donat.; Chrysost. in Matt. xxvi., Hom. lxxvii., edit. Græc., vel lxxxiii., Latin; in 1 Cor. iii., Hom. viii.; et in 2 Tim. i., Hom. ii. circa finem) the ministry only is to be accounted man's, but the power GOD'S. "For," as St. Augustine observes, "it is one thing to baptize by way of ministry, another thing to baptize by way of power" (Aug. in Evang. Joh., Tract. v.): "the power of baptizing the LORD retaineth to Himself, the ministry He hath given to His servants" (Id. ib.): "the power of the LORD'S baptism was to pass from the LORD to no man, but the ministry was; the power was to be transferred from the LORD unto none of His ministers; the ministry was both unto the good and unto the bad" (Id. ib.). And the reason which he assigns is, "that the hope of the baptized might be in Him by whom they did acknowledge themselves to have been baptized. The LORD, therefore, would not have a servant to put his hope in a servant" (Id. ib.). And therefore those schoolmen argued, "It is a matter of equal power to baptize inwardly, and to absolve from mortal sin; but it was not fit that GOD should communicate the power of baptizing unto any, lest our hope should be reposed in man. Therefore, by the same reason, it was not fit that He should communicate the power of absolving from actual sin unto any" (Alexand. de Hales, Summ., part iv. quæst. xxi. Memb. i.). Our SAVIOUR, therefore, must still have the privilege reserved unto Him of being the absolute LORD over His own house. It is sufficient for His officers that they be esteemed, as Moses was, "faithful in all His house as servants" (Heb. x. 5, 6). The place wherein they serve is a steward's place; and the Apostle tells them that "it is required in stewards, that a man be found faithful" (Cor. iv. 2). They may not, therefore, carry themselves in their office as the unjust steward did, and presume to strike out their Master's debt without His direction, and contrary to His liking (Luke xvi. 6-8). But our LORD has given no authority unto His stewards to grant an acquittance unto any of His debtors that bring not unfeigned faith and repentance with them. "Neither angel nor archangel" can; "neither yet the LORD Himself (who alone can say, 'I am with you') when we have sinned, doth release us, unless we bring repentance with us," writes St. Ambrose (Epist. xxviii. ad Theodosium Imp.); and Eligius, Bishop of Noyon, in his sermon unto the penitents, "Before all things, it is necessary you should know that howsoever you desire to receive the imposition of our hands, yet you cannot obtain the absolution of your sins before the divine piety shall vouchsafe to absolve you by the grace of compunction" (Eligius Noviamens, Hom. xi. tom. vii., Biblioth. Partr., p. 248, ed. Colon). To think, therefore, that it lies in the power of any priest truly to absolve a man from his sins, without implying the condition of his "believing and repenting as he ought to do," is both presumption and madness in the highest degree.

And Cardinal Bellarmine, who censures this conditional absolution in us for idle and superfluous, is driven to confess that when the priest (Bellarmin, de Pœnitent., lib. ii. c. 4, sect. penult.) says, "I absolve thee," he "doth not affirm that he doth absolve absolutely, as not being ignorant that it may many ways come to pass that he doth not absolve, although he pronounce those words; namely, if he who seemeth to receive this sacrament" (for so they call it) "peradventure hath no intention to receive it, or is not rightly disposed, or putteth some block in the way. Therefore the minister," says he, "signifieth nothing else by those words but that he, as much as in him lieth, conferreth the sacrament of reconciliation or absolution, which, in a man rightly disposed, hath virtue to forgive all his sins."

"Evil and wicked, carnal, natural, and devilish men," says St. Augustine (de Baptism, contra Donatist., lib. iii. cap. ult.), "imagine those things to be given unto them by their seducers, which are only the gifts of GOD, whether sacraments or any other spiritual works concerning their present salvation." But such as are thus deceived ought to listen to this grave admonition of St. Cyprian (de Laps., sec. 7, ed. Pamel, 14 Goulart): "Let no man deceive, let no man beguile himself; it is the LORD alone that can show mercy. He alone can grant pardon to the sins committed against Him, who did Himself bear our sins, who suffered grief for us, whom GOD did deliver for our sins. Man cannot be greater than GOD, neither can the servant by his indulgence remit or pardon that which by heinous trespass is committed against the LORD; lest to him that is fallen this yet be added as a further crime, if he be ignorant of that which is said, ' Cursed is the man that putteth his trust in man.'" Whereupon St. Augustine (in Evang. Joh., Tract. v.) writes, that good ministers do consider that "they are but ministers; they would not be held for judges; they abhor that any trust should be put in them; and that the power of remitting and retaining sins is committed unto the Church, to be dispensed therein, "but according to the arbitrament of GOD" (*Id.* de Baptism, contra Donatist., lib. iii. c. 18). Repentance from dead works is one of the foundations and principles of the doctrine of CHRIST (Heb. vi. 1). "Nothing maketh repentance certain but the hatred of sin and the love of GOD" (August. Serm. vii., de Tempore). And without true repentance all the priests under heaven are not able to give us a discharge from our sins and deliver us from the wrath to come. " Except ye be converted, ye shall not enter into the kingdom of heaven" (Matt. xviii. 3). "Except ye repent, ye shall all perish" (Luke xiii. 3, 5), is the LORD'S saying in the New Testament. And in the Old, " Repent, and turn from all your transgressions; so iniquity shall not be your ruin. Cast away from you all your transgressions, whereby ye have transgressed, and make you a new heart and a new spirit; for why will ye die, O house of Israel?" (Ezek. xviii. 30, 31). (Dr. Stephens's Notes to Book of Common Prayer.)

Abstinence. A reduction of food for the sake of self-discipline. It implies a certain degree of voluntariness on the part of him who practices it, and also a power to determine how far he will or will not abstain. It is not to be confounded with fasting, though it is so often. As for total abstinence, *i.e.* from "alcoholic liquids," no Christian can take the vow in its fullest sense, as he must receive for his soul's health the Holy Communion. But St. Paul gives us the only true principle in, "It is good neither to eat flesh nor to drink wine, nor anything whereby thy brother stumbleth or is offended or is made weak."

Accidents. This term of ancient philosophy, which referred to the changeable parts of matter, as form, color, taste, as opposed to substance, proper, and the immutable properties of matter, was appropriated by later mediæval theologians to the alleged change in the elements after consecration at the Eucharist. The "species," or "accidents," were said to remain of bread and wine, but the substance was transubstantiated. It was a mere subterfuge for a logical difficulty in endeavoring to explain what is given us as a mystery.

Accommodation. A word used to express the manner in which Divine teachings convey and adapt Divine truths to our comprehension. These, it is evident, must be fitted to the capacity, development, and circumstances of those receiving these truths. Abraham, with his surroundings, could not receive what was given to David, or Isaiah, or Daniel, though he was the Father of the Faithful. So, again, the use of parables is an instance of accommodation. But, again, it is an accommodation to our limited power to speak to us of GOD'S anger or jealousy, or that His Eye is upon us, His Hand upholds us. It would be impossible for us to understand many things revealed to us of GOD without some such accommodation from Him. But while fitted to our dwarfed power, yet they are themselves truths, which we are gradually enabled to understand better and to throw aside grosser, materialistic conceptions which the mere words would teach. Another form of accommodation is in the gradual additions to the fundamental elementary truths first revealed. Eve received a prophecy of CHRIST, but a fuller one was given to Abraham, and a still fuller to David, and so on. We practice this mode, rather of development than of accommodation, in teaching children. So St. Paul gave the Corinthians milk rather than meat. But a *positive* accommodation perverts the truth and therefore it is inadmissible, and any attempt to explain difficult passages upon such a principle must be condemned.

Acephali (without a head). Certain heretics who separated from the Church, following Nestorius, or who held Eutychian principles and were condemned by the Synod at Constantinople 536 A.D. The Church in Cyprus was autocephalous as not under the jurisdiction of the Patriarch. But those priests who refused to be under a bishop were said to be acephali.

Acolyte. A sub-officer assisting in Divine service in the Latin and Greek Churches. His duty is to light the candles, hand the bread and wine, the water, etc., to the priest. In the Greek Church it is another name for a sub-deacon. In the English Church, before the Reformation, the name was corrupted into Collet.

Acrostic Psalms. Certain Psalms in Holy Scripture begin with the several successive letters of the alphabet, each stanza beginning with each letter in its order. There are twelve such poems in the Old Testament: Psalms xxv., xxxiv., xxxvii., cxi., cxii., cxix., cxlv., a part of Prov. xxxi., Lamentations i.-iv. But Psalm cxix. is the most remarkable of these compositions. It is divided into twenty-two sections, of eight couplets each; each division beginning with that letter of the alphabet in its order, and every couplet in the division beginning with the letter of its division, *e.g.*, the first division begins with *Ashre*, etc., and each couplet begins with the letter A. Psalms xxv., xxxiv., and cxv. are of twenty-two stanzas each, the first line only of each couplet being acrostical. Psalm xxxvii. is in twenty quatrains, the first line of each quatrain being acrostical. Psalms cxi. and cxii. are of twenty-two lines each, and each line begins with a new letter in alphabetical order. But Proverbs xxxi. is in twenty-two couplets; Lamentations chs. i. ii. in twenty-two triplets, the first line of each triplet being acrostical. Lamentations ch. iii. is in twenty-two triplets, each triplet being in each line acrostical, while Lamentations ch. iv. is in twenty-two couplets, each couplet, in its first line, being acrostical. These remarkable poems exhibit well the rhythmical and antithetical character of Hebrew poetry, and its peculiar style of parallelisms.

Acts of the Apostles (The). Probably St. Luke did not give any title to his work further than would be implied in the term by which he designates this gospel,—"the former treatise" (Acts i. 1). In this, then, as in nearly all the other books of the Bible, there was no title or name supplied or prefixed by the writer. And as the heading Acts of the Apostles does not literally conform to the contents of the history, it would be better to give it its truer meaning, "Practice of the Apostles," which is probably nearer the idea intended by those who supplied the title. For the treatise only records, and, too, partially records, the Acts and the Practice of four Apostles, SS. Peter, John, Paul, and Barnabas, with scarcely more than a reference to St. James. In fact, SS. John and Barnabas appear only in connection with, or in relation to, SS. Peter and Paul. The history, then, may be considered as the inspired record of what should be the Apostolic policy and practice historically illustrated by the actions of these representative Apostles; also as unfolding the expansion of the Gospel from Jerusalem to Samaria, and thence to the Gentiles; as beside in a peculiar way declaring the controlling power of the ascended LORD JESUS.

It is no lessening of the authenticity and inspired accuracy of St. Luke to suppose that he may have used written documents, easily accessible to one so situated as himself, for his earlier facts, and to have recorded what came within his own personal knowledge later in his attendance on St. Paul. But the whole tone of the Acts implies that though he may not have taken an active part, yet he was not only an eye-witness of the general course of the events he records, but had intimate relations with some of the principal actors. The minute touches in his narrative prove this, *e.g.*, the description of St. Stephen before the Sanhedrim, and the spirited condensation of his speech; the mention of significant surnames; the detailed account of St. Peter's deliverance from prison, and his reception at the house of Mary, the mother of Mark, whose surname is John. Even the narrative of the conversion of Cornelius renders it probable that he was one of the brethren who went with St. Peter from Joppa to Cæsarea. Of course in the journeys of St. Paul we have the record of an actual companionship, though St. Luke was often separated from the Apostle by the exigencies of the mission work, as is clearly marked by the pronoun "*we*" used in many places, and then (when St. Luke was away) dropped for "they."

The plan of the book, while the narrative passes on in a perfectly natural way from event to event, is not always evident to ordinary readers. But when we remember that the HOLY SPIRIT caused certain facts to be set down, and others seemingly even more important to be omitted, and that there is no waste or uncertainty in His purposes, His purpose, we may reverently say, is to record the work given to the Church to do, not the achievements of His servants. With this clue we can well see that it is an outline, sufficient, clear, definite, but very concise, of the work to be done, of the lines upon which the future officers in the Church were to move forward. It contains in its history the true solution of the problems which can be presented to the Church in the several epochs of her career. It is (to borrow the illustration of Bishop Wordsworth) the journal of the movements, directed by the Captain of our Salvation, of His officers leading His army to its final victory. The Apostles had much the same difficulties to encounter. And their mode of surmounting obstacles and their strategy and tactics are lessons to us in the present day. The plan of the Acts is simply a development of our LORD'S direction, "But ye shall receive power, after that the HOLY GHOST is come upon you, and ye shall be witnesses unto me, both in Jerusalem and in all Judæa, and in Samaria, and unto the uttermost part of the earth."

Beginning with the Ascension (ch. i. 1–12), St. Luke goes on to record the continuance of the company of the one hundred and twenty faithful in prayer and supplication (vs. 13, 14), and the election of Matthias into the place of Judas (vs. 15–26); then the wondrous outpouring of the HOLY GHOST (ch. ii. 1–4), and the attention it attracted, and the resulting conversion of the three thousand (vs. 5–41). Thereupon he describes the practice of the new community (vs. 42–47). Chapter iii. narrates the miracle of healing the lame beggar at Solomon's Gate, and St. Peter's appeal, and ch. iv. the arrest and imprisonment by "the priests, the Captain of the Temple, and the Sadducees," with St. Peter's manly boldness, and their dismissal (vs. 1–22), and the thanksgiving, and their renewed courage by the grace of the HOLY GHOST (vs. 23–31). Then the community life is described (vs. 32–37), with the stern retribution that fell upon Ananias and Sapphira (ch. v. 1–11); the continued growth of the Church through the signs and wonders wrought by the Apostles (vs. 12–16); the indignation this produced in the Jewish rulers; the arrest of the Apostles and their defense; the private consultation and the counsel given by Gamaliel; their illegal stripes and release (vs. 17–42).

Then the narrative relates for us another step in the Church's development. It has nearly outgrown the swathing-bands of a mere community life. The increase of their number demanded a new arrangement for the government of the rapidly-growing

Church, and this led to the establishment of the Diaconate and the special reservation to themselves by the Apostles of the duties of prayer and the ministry of the Word (ch. vi. 1-8). The new Order, however, shared in the work of preaching ; specially Stephen (vs. 9, 10), who was arrested and placed before the council (vs. 11-15). Then follows St. Stephen's most characteristic speech (ch. vii. vs. 1-53), and glorious martyrdom (vs. 54-60). Out of the change in the interior organization grew this first martyrdom, and then the persecution (ch. viii. 1-3), which, without breaking up the Church, drove those who were active in the work of conversion to the third step in her work. The deacon Philip goes down to Samaria, and there (vs. 4-13) gathers in many of the Samaritans, but as yet no Gentile was admitted. Since only the Apostles could confirm, the College of Apostles sent SS. Peter and John down to give them the HOLY GHOST by the laying on of hands (vs. 14-34), and took the opportunity (v. 25) to preach in the neighboring Samaritan villages. Then follows the sending Philip to gather in the first convert for Africa (vs. 26-40). Then (ch. ix.) succeeds the narrative of St. Paul's conversion (vs. 1-22) his escape from the Jews, who lay in wait for him (vs. 23-31). St. Peter's mission work in lower Syria (vs. 32-43) brought him to Joppa, whence he was called to fulfill his work part in laying the foundation of the Church for the Gentiles by the baptism of the centurion Cornelius (ch. x.).

This brought on the second dissension within the Church (ch. xi. 1-18), which was settled by St. Peter's account. Henceforth, whatever temporary or local prejudice there might be, there was no contention about it. But this work was transferred, as soon as it began to be important, to Barnabas, who soon took Saul to labor with him (vs. 19-30). St. James's martyrdom and the imprisonment of St. Peter follow in the narrative (ch. xii. 1-19), which, however, soon reverts to Barnabas and Saul. But the Church has overstepped her narrow bounds. The mission, by command of the HOLY GHOST, of Barnabas and Saul to their work (ch. xiii. 1-3) inaugurates a new work. Henceforth, while the Jews are first appealed to, the Gentiles have the Gospel preached to them. This first missionary journey beyond the limits of Syria (chs. xiii. 4 ; xiv.) was important in its results, but really it led the way to greater changes. Saul becomes Paul, and is the leading speaker. Ch. xv. records the third and last struggle within the Church. The Judaic party made their last resistance upon circumcision. This was also settled ; and now whatever bickering might arise, the policy of the Church was settled by this Council at Jerusalem in its Encyclical.

From this time forward the narrative is of St. Paul alone with the company he gathered about him (ch. xv. 36-99). But there is also a significant change in the policy of carrying forward the Gospel. St. Paul does not trust to his personal influence and constant supervision, nor pause for minute attention to comparatively unimportant fields. That is trusted in true faith to his companions, or to those chosen out of the new converts to be their ministers. He seeks centres and influential towns with the instinct of a general who plans his strategy and leaves tactical dispositions to his trusty subordinates. Only in Corinth and in Ephesus did he make voluntarily any long stay, and both were most important posts for the Church to hold firmly. His first journey is recited in chs. xiii. and xiv. His second in chs. xv. 36 ; xviii. 23. His third journey is recounted in chs. xviii. 26 ; xxi. 14. His labors are henceforth from a prison or a guard-house, ever in the presence of, if not chained to, a soldier, or else upon a storm-driven ship, till he is at last permitted, though a state prisoner, to dwell in his own hired house through two quiet years. These last chapters (from ch. xiii. to the end) are most precious to us Gentiles. With the direction of our LORD clearly set before us, they are the only record of the fulfillment of His command. This Book of the Acts, then, bears upon its front the stamp of consistent truthfulness. It is a faithful account, scrupulously accurate, of the chief and to us most important facts connected with the Apostolic founding, nurture, organization, and proclamation of the Church as the Body of CHRIST, which He purchased with His own blood. Its title, "The Practice of the Apostles," gives with concise clearness its purpose. When we question it we find that it gives us the Threefold order,—Apostles, Presbyters, Deacons. It sets before us the Sacrament of Baptism ; the necessity of Confirmation ; the daily celebration of the Communion ; the observance of the LORD'S Day. In it we learn the true Financial policy of the Church ; the Apostolic authority for Episcopal visitation ; the tone and policy of our missionary work ; the power of sermons ; the use of forms of prayer. In it is given us naturally, incidentally as a part of the narrative, the usages or practice of those who had the mind of CHRIST, and who had been instructed by Him for the forty days He was with them in the things pertaining to the Kingdom of Heaven.

This, as with every other book of the Scripture, has been subjected to the wildest, vaguest criticism, which is best replied to by pointing out that, as in so many other cases, the critics cannot agree upon any one common ground. Its text, which, of course, was copied out by writers in successive ages, has undergone some mutilation, and some slight variations have crept in, but there is nothing to throw the slightest shadow of doubt upon its genuineness or its inspiration. Nor is there any material variation in the best critically restored form of the text that can affect the sense of our Authorized Version.

Adiaphoristic Controversy. (*Adiaphoi*,

or things indifferent.) A dispute which arose and continued for some time between the followers of Luther and of Melancthon about the traditions and ceremonies of the Church. Melancthon was disposed to surrender them as indifferent for the sake of peace and unity. The chief opponent in the controversy was the Hebrew professor at Wittenberg, Illyrius Flaccus.

Adjuration. The binding of, or solemn appeal to, a person by an invocation of the Divine name, as the High-Priest to our LORD: "I adjure Thee by the living GOD that Thou tell us whether Thou be the CHRIST the SON OF GOD." To this adjuration our LORD, hitherto silent, at once replied. Adjuration was a part of the form of exorcism which anciently was the precedent office to baptism.

Administration. The performance of a duty, or office, or function. It is used several times in the Prayer-book, as in the title to the Office of the Holy Communion, the prayer for those to be ordained, and in the Ordinal. In ecclesiastical law it refers to the distribution of the effects of intestates.

Admonition. Advice or warning. A word used to assert the advisory authority of a Bishop over his clergy, when they promise to follow with a glad mind his godly admonition. But it is also in the charge to the priest at his ordination. It is, however, now used in a harsher sense, meaning the first step of warning, which, if persistently rejected, must lead on to excommunication; following St. Paul's direction, "A man that is an heretic after the first and second admonition reject" (Titus iii. 10).

Admonition, Godly. The earliest form of an examination of a candidate for orders during the process of ordination is found in an Ordinal of the eleventh century, though questions were asked of Bishops, at the time of their consecration, at an earlier period. The questions propounded in our Ordinal are peculiar to the English service, and were framed by the reformers of our Liturgy in 1549-50. They seem, as Palmer has said, "to have been modeled in a great degree after the parallel formularies used in the ordination of Bishops." The last question is probably the most ancient of them all, and is found in manuscript Ordinals, written eight hundred years ago, where it is placed in exactly the position which it holds in our service, at the beginning. In the English Prayer-book the phrase used is, "Will you reverently obey your Ordinary and other chief ministers?" The Ordinary, according to Canon Law, is the Bishop, and the "other chief ministers" are such officers as are established by law,—the Archdeacon, Dean, or Commissary of the Bishop. But in our Ordinal is inserted after "chief ministers" the words, "who according to the Canons of the Church may have the charge over you." The reason of this change is found in the fact that on the introduction of the Episcopate into this country, it was not deemed best at that time to introduce those other offices and titles, such as Archdeacons, Deans, and Rural Deans, which have so long existed in England. It will be noticed that the only chief ministers other than the Bishop whose admonitions and judgment the Deacon and Priest are to follow are those who are invested with such authority by the "Canons of the Church." This must mean the Canons of *this* Church, because the Canons of the English Church recognized these several offices and dignities; and its use here was evidently to restrict this vow of obedience to those whom the American branch of the Church by its Canons might appoint over them.

The only chief ministers recognized by our Canons as invested with any governing or controlling authority are those elected by the several Standing Committees, which Standing Committees, under certain circumstances, exercise "the powers and duties to be performed by a Bishop." For in case there is a vacancy in the Episcopate, the Standing Committee is the ecclesiastical authority of the diocese for all purposes declared in the Canons of the Church. And this authority is exercised by them when acting in their corporate capacity as members of that committee. There is but little doubt that the phraseology of the question was so framed in order to meet just such a development as is now seen in some of the dioceses where the Cathedral and Decanal institutions and usages obtain more or less, and which, perhaps, it was conjectured might in the future, in the great growth of the Church, arise as a practical necessity.

Confining ourselves simply to the American Ordinal, what is promised here? Reverent obedience; conformity to godly admonitions; submission to godly judgment—of the "Bishop and other chief ministers who, according to the Canons of the Church, may have the charge and government over you." But here the question arises, What is meant by the phrases "godly admonition; godly judgment"? This must be interpreted by the tenor of the office in which the terms are found, and by the general usage and explanation of it in recognized authorities. It is that admonition and that judgment which as a reverend father in GOD in the fullness of his Episcopal office he delivers in questions of conduct and duty in carrying out the provisions of the Church's law and worship. It is an "admonition" delivered in the fear of GOD, to whom the Bishop is amenable for all his acts, in reference to some course or practice which the Bishop, acting as an authorized ruler in GOD's house, deems wrong. It is a "judgment" made in the fear of GOD, and with a full recognition of his being judged of GOD; as to the right or wrong, the propriety or impropriety of some act or ceremony which, in the estimation of the Bishop, contravenes the letter or the spirit of the promise of conformity to the doctrine, discipline, and worship of the Protestant Episcopal Church.

It is not meant that a godly admonition or a godly judgment should be a perfectly holy and perfectly just admonition or judgment such as GOD Himself would give, because the admonition and judgment, being human, must necessarily partake of human infirmity and imperfection. Neither does it mean that such an admonition or judgment will be such as shall be sustained by process of law, because decisions of law are ever varying both in time and place, and the conflict of laws is a fact recognized by the most eminent jurists.

Neither does it mean that such an admonition and judgment shall always be wise and productive, for as "to err is human," so Bishops are not exempt from such errancy, and with the most devout aspirations and earnest endeavors to do right they may yet miss the marks of wisdom and prudence. But it does mean that when a Bishop under the realizing sense of his consecration vows to "banish and drive away from the Church all erroneous and strange doctrine contrary to GOD'S Word," and "both privately and openly call upon and encourage others to do the same," and "diligently exercise such discipline as by the authority of GOD'S Word and by the order of this Church is commended to Him ;" does, on questions of conduct which he believes to be reprehensible or on points of ritual of doubtful interpretation and authority, give his official admonition and judgment touching these things, it is the duty of the clergy to reverently obey such godly admonition and submit themselves to such godly judgment. Yet this submission to obedience does not debar them the privilege or weaken the duty of testing the right of the clergy to their course and views by the process of Canon Law. For such admonition and judgment but takes the place of a temporary injunction in civil law, whereby a course of conduct is arrested and made stationary until judicial decision shall be had in the premises. So in these cases, if the clergyman feels aggrieved by the admonition of the Bishop or that he has been wronged by the judgment, he has redress in law. The ecclesiastical courts are open to him, and questions of fact, of interpretation, of issue, can be then and there settled.

Bishop Mant, in his "Discourses upon the Church and Her Ministrations," says in reference to these words: "The rule and limits of the respect and deference due may be judged to be that in all matters of spiritual or ecclesiastical concern, in all matters which affect the welfare of religion or of the Church, it is the duty of the clergy to comply with the advice and to acquiesce in the decision of their Ordinary, unless his authority be suspended by a paramount or superior power. If the Law of GOD or the law o⸺ the country clearly and indisputably presc⸺:e a different course, their authority surpasses that of the Bishop and ought to be preferred. If neither of these authorities clearly interferes with it, then I apprehend they concur in sustaining and supporting it, and it becomes the duty of the clergy to follow with a glad mind and will the admonition of their lawful governor, though abstractedly their inclinations may lead them in a different course, and to submit their judgment to the judgment of their official superior, though abstractedly they may not be convinced of the correctness of his decision." (The Church and Her Ministrations, p. 236.) "It may be noted also," says Dean Comber, "that the candidates promise *gladly to obey*, that is, readily and willingly, without murmuring or too nice disputing, unless the thing enjoined be notoriously evil; for to be very scrupulous proceeds from the pride of inferiors and tends to overthrow the superior's authority. Yet this doth not give superiors any unlimited powers to command anything that is evil, for they only promise to obey *their godly admonitions*, so that such as govern in the Church must take heed they do not enjoin anything but that which is either good in itself or apparently tends to promote piety and virtue and is not evil." (On the Ordination Offices, p. 214.) Canon James (Comment on the Ordination Services, p. 270) says "The Episcopal admonition which the clergy are to follow, and the like judgments to which they are to submit themselves, must be 'godly admonitions' and 'godly judgments.' Now this caution by which the vow is accompanied, like every other cautionary counsel and guarded command given by the Church, is used not as doubting either the godliness of the Bishop or the due obedience of his clergy, but because this or any other vow is required to be *solemnly* made, and because all the services, and particularly the ordination services, are written as unto fallible men, and there can be no sound legislation either in Church or State where all is not based on this principle. The framers, therefore, of these services wisely so acted. They remembered that St. Paul scrupled not to avow of himself that he was a man of like passions, as well with those he ordained as with those among whom he ministered. A frank avowal this that he was liable to error. It is only in this view of the case that the term can be considered appropriate, for to suppose that the admonitions of a Bishop to be other than godly would appear impossible, and it is equally impossible to conceive otherwise of his judgment in matters of religion than that it should be *godly* according to the written Word of GOD declared in His Gospel and adopted by the Church."

The venerable Bishop White, in his "Comment on the Ordination Offices," a book unanimously approved by the whole House of Bishops in 1833, speaking of these promises, after stating that these "godly admonitions must have respect to some standard by which they are directed, and that this standard must be the various established institutions of the Church and not the private opinions of the Bishop," he adds, "that injudicious or even impertinent interference is possible ought not to be denied, and cannot be justified." But there are two descriptions of cases in which no such censure is applicable. One is where an offense against morals, the other where an offense against order is the subject. In either of these cases indeed the admonition of the Bishop would be unseasonable unless the offense were notorious and admitted, because he would be in danger of making himself an accuser when he is appointed to be a judge. But if either of the species of offense is acknowledged by the offending party, and especially if it be justified and persevered in, then is here claimed to the Bishop the right in question, not only on the ground of ecclesiastical law, but on that of the consent of the party in the answer to the question last read, which may be considered as a personal contract binding him to submission under reproof for past fault, and to amendment under exhortation relative to the time to come.

When, therefore, a Bishop acting as a Father in GOD of a family over which the HOLY GHOST has made him overseer, moved by an honest and zealous love for GOD'S truth, and sustained by the specific decisions of the established and recognized Ecclesiastical tribunals of the Church of England, a Church from which ours has not departed "in any essential point of Doctrine, Discipline, or Worship," and by the decisions and Canons of our own Church, issues his admonition and gives his judgment upon questions of usage and ritual, especially when the points objected to are innovations upon the established services of this Church, as carried on since its foundation nearly a century ago, such admonitions and judgment are those recognized by the Ordinal as godly. They proceed from godly motives, are directed to godly ends, and concern things pertaining to the worship of GOD in His Holy Temple.

To disobey, then, is an act of self-will and subversive of all authority. In the case of a Deacon, we see at once that subordination to the Presbyter which makes that Presbyter, specially the one under whom he serves, one of the chief ministers set over him, to whose admonitions and judgment he must conform himself as a true *Diaconos;* and if to a Presbyter set over him in a particular parish or missionary station, much more to his Bishop, to whose direction and authority he is canonically bound.

RT. REV. WM. BACON STEVENS, D.D.,
Bishop of Pennsylvania.

Adonai. One of the titles of GOD (*q. v.*); My LORD. It was pronounced by the Jews for the word JEHOVAH, which was only uttered by the priests in the sanctuary when blessing the people (Numb. vi. 22), and by the High-Priest on the Day of Atonement when before the mercy-seat. The true pronunciation was said to be lost. The Jews refuse, generally, to utter the "Incommunicable Name," and for it substituted the phrase Shem Hammephorash, *i.e.*, the name of four letters, Yod He Vav He. The Alexandrian translators of the Scriptures into Greek (Septuagint) used the word Kyrios as its equivalent, and thus it passed into the New Testament as the title of our LORD. The word Adon, LORD, is found in many names, as in Adonijah, Adonizebek, Nebuchadon-ezer, and in Greek mythology the Syrian Adon is Adonis.

Adoption. A term of Roman law which St. Paul used to express the relation of the Christian to his heavenly Father. The Roman law ran thus: "When aliens were to be taken into a family or into the place of children, the ceremony was either before a prætor or before the people. If it were done through the prætor it was called adoption." The parallel is accurate. Our adoption is not created by our will or choice, but is by the gift of GOD. We may choose whether we shall accept it, but it is still His gift, and not ours by any claim or merit. It is granted to us in and through our LORD JESUS CHRIST, therefore by His incarnation and the grace thereby accruing to the human race from Him. It is conveyed in baptism, and reversing the order of the verses, "As many of you as have been baptized into CHRIST have put on CHRIST" (v. 27); "For ye are all the children of GOD by faith in CHRIST JESUS" (v. 26), and then "And if ye be CHRIST'S then are ye Abraham's seed, and heirs according to the promise" (Gal. iii. 29); and the Apostle proceeds in his argument (ch. iv. 4-7): "But when the fulness of the time was come, GOD sent forth His Son, made of a woman, made under the law, to redeem them that were under the law, that we might receive the adoption of sons. And because ye are sons, GOD hath sent forth the Spirit of His Son into your hearts, crying Abba, Father. Wherefore thou art no more a servant, but a son; and if a son, then an heir of GOD through CHRIST." So, too, in the Apostle's argument in the eighth chapter of Romans. St. Paul uses the word adoption in Rom. viii. 15, 23, ix. 4; Gal. iv. 5; and Ephesians i. 5.

Adoptionist. Heresy. A heresy which taught that CHRIST was not the Son of GOD by His eternal generation, but by adoption. It was broached as early as the later Arian controversies, 380 A.D., but did not take a distinct shape, though combated by the early fathers (as Ambrose, Gregory, Naz. Ep. ad Cled., i.), till the eighth century, and in Spain, Elipandus, Archbishop of Toledo, and Felix, Bishop of Urgel. It was probably hit upon by Elipandus as a theory to conciliate the Mohammedans among whom his province was placed. Felix was a subject of Charlemagne. They taught that CHRIST JESUS as man was adopted, though as the Word of GOD eternally begotten, thus practically dividing the Person of CHRIST, for they denied that the man CHRIST JESUS from the beginning of His Incarnation perfectly united with the Word the eternal and only-begotten SON of GOD. It was but another form of Nestorianism. Several theologians at once combated it, as Beatus and Bishop Etherius, of Osma, but Charlemagne sent fdr Alcuin, who refuted the heresy in several works and letters written both to Felix and to Elipandus, founding his argument not only upon the opposing silence of Scripture, but upon the contradiction in the nature of the Unity of Person in CHRIST, that He could be the SON of GOD by nature and the SON of GOD by adoption. His two natures cannot make Him two Sons, for they are perfectly conjoined in His one Person.

Felix recanted his heresy at the Council at Ratisbon, 792 A.D., but was sent to Rome by Charlemagne, where he had to make a second still more formal abjuration of his error in full orthodox terms, but when he regained his diocese he relapsed. Being summoned anew, and his tenets condemned at Frankfort (796 A.D.), he sought refuge with Elipandus within the Mohammedan rule. Adoptionism was again condemned at Friule (796 A.D.).

The heresy was condemned again at Aix-la-Chapelle, 799 A.D., and was abjured by Felix, but Elipandus steadily adhered to it to the last. They sought in vain to prove their error by appeals to the Liturgy, which appeals are valuable to us now as settling the date of parts of the Mozarabic Liturgy.

Adoration. A synonym for devout, reverent worship. Its origin is from the Latin *manus ad os mittere*, to put the hand to the mouth in token of silent awe. It is used exclusively to mean the worship paid to GOD, and is in act both outward and inward; outward in such kneeling or bowing and singing or speaking words of praise; interior, of the heart and mind in such devout affections as raise the soul in adoring thought. The outward is empty form if it be not conjoined and informed by the interior adoration, which make it acceptable as a personal offering to GOD.

Adultery. Criminal intercourse of a married person of either sex with another of the other sex, whether married or not. The moral sin of adultery is implied in the inspired words with which Adam received Eve, and is set forth in the Seventh Commandment. CHRIST confirmed the binding force of Adam's declaration in emphatic terms (Mark x. 6-9), and expounded the force of the Commandment in His Sermon on the Mount (Matt. v. 27-32). In all countries the crime has been branded as a heinous one, and often and earlier was punishable with death, and if the injured husband should slay the guilty parties *flagrante delictu* even now, the homicide does not receive the condemnation it should. Our LORD'S forgiveness of the guilty woman (John viii. 11) is taken as a mitigation of the death-sentence under the Mosaic dispensation; but the guilt of it, both as to the moral and spiritual death of the sinning ones, and as to the sin against society, is not thereby extenuated, and the severest enactments have always stood upon the Church's Canon Law against the guilty parties. This and fornication are the only causes allowed by our LORD to justify divorce. It is a sin that is absolutely heinous in the sight of GOD and in His Law. But moral theologians sometimes distinguish between degrees of heinousness in reference to the destructive results to society. A petition against the sin stands in the English Prayer-book in the Litany, which petition has been softened by hardly equivalent phrases in the American form.

Advent. There is no certainty of the date when the season of Advent was appointed. The early Sacramentary of Leo I. does not mention any Sundays in Advent. The Comes of St. Jerome, and later the Sacramentary of Gelasius I. (496 A.D.), ascribe Collects, Epistles, and Gospels to five Sundays in Advent. These documents are probably much interpolated. But Maximus of Tours (450 A.D.) makes the earliest certain mention of Advent, and Cæsarius of Arles (501-42 A.D.) has left the first set of Advent sermons we have (those ascribed to St. Ambrose and St. Augustine are spurious). In the Ambrosian and Mozarabic Liturgies the Advent season dates from St. Martin's day (November 11), and includes forty days, which were accounted as a lesser fast among the religious. But the first of these five Sundays was really counted as preceding the Sundays in Advent, so that there were only four Sundays counted. The Gallican Church (Maçon, 581 A.D.) ordered Monday, Wednesday, and Friday to be observed as fasts in Advent, but the rule was disregarded. In the Prereformed English Uses, as in the Gallican and Mozarabic Rites, we find special Epistles and Gospels for these days. The observance of Advent in the Greek Church was probably much later, for Balsamon (1200 A.D.) says " the others (besides the Lenten fast), as the fast of the Nativity, are each of seven days only. Those monks who fast forty days, viz., from St. Philip (September 14), are bound to this by their rule. Such laics as do the like are to be praised therefor."

Advowson. The right, in England, of patronage to a church or an ecclesiastical benefice, and he who has the right of Advowson is called the Patron of the Church, from his obligation to defend the rights of the Church from oppression and violence. For when lords of manors first built churches upon their own demesnes and appointed the tithes of these manors to be paid to the officiating ministers which were before given to the clergy in common, the lord who thus built a church and endowed it with glebe or land had, of common right, a power annexed of nominating such minister as he pleased (provided he were canonically qualified) to officiate in that church of which he was the founder, endower, maintainer, or, in one word, the patron. This patronage is heritable, and is subject to many curious and intricate rules. (*Vide* Burn's Ecclesiastical Law.)

Æon. This is a word which has two separate uses; the true one, in connection with the future life and eternity, and the other, in which the Gnostics used it, personifying and deifying their imagined succession of ages. Borrowing some phrases from Christian Revelation and adding to them the wildest imaginings, the Gnostics, who were either Orientals or Egyptians, pretended to a deeper Gnosis than that the Apostles taught. Their origin must have been in the years nearly contemporary with the close of the Apostolic century, for we find Ignatius alluding to this word shortly after the death of St. John.

Aerians. A small sect, founded by Aerius, a Presbyter of Sebaste, about 355 A.D. Aerius, it is said, was disappointed in not obtaining the Episcopate, and in consequence seceded from the Church and denied that there was any difference between the office of a Bishop and that of a Presbyter. In contrast to the care that all other schismatical or heretical bodies had taken to procure at the outset Episcopal consecration for their ministers, Aerius, by this, gave the best proof possible that hitherto an unbroken succession from the Apostles was ever deemed essential to a true ministry, even by those who were attacking that very authority of the ministry itself. The sect did not last very long.

Affections. The Affections, as love, joy, grief, anger, jealousy, are also called the Feelings. In later religious teaching they are made the basis of theologic systems to a much larger extent than the New Testament warrants. Feeling cannot be called into proper activity without a use (rightly or wrongly) of the Reason. As then reason must precede, to base religion upon feeling, which may or may not have any true depth in separate individual natures, is to build upon the shifting sand. The value of the Affections or Feelings cannot be overestimated in their true place, but they must be subordinated to the reason, and must not warp the free action of conscience, a danger which is very imminent in all enthusiastic forms of religion. The inspired teachers never appealed in the first instance to the Affections; nay, they speak very strongly upon the need of controlling them. The popular confusion of the principles and doctrines of Christianity, and the enthused reception of them, leads to a false comprehension of the true Christian state. According to a very common confusion, a person is not a true Christian unless he has certain experiences or feelings overlooking the true basis in the gifts and adoption by GOD in the Church. A German school of Pietism has endeavored to shelter religion from the attacks of opponents by withdrawing it into the province of Feeling. The folly of making Religion wholly a state of experience or spiritual judgment is evident by instituting the slightest comparison between the dogmas and history of the New Testament and the fanciful notions of the Pietist.

Affinity. The relationship contracted between a husband and his wife's blood relations. By the old Canons illicit intercourse also resulted in affinity. Within certain degrees the Divine Law (in the 18th ch. of Leviticus) has forbidden marriage with a wife's relations. The Table of Kindred and Affinity, which is Canon Law in England, does not bind the Church in America, though various efforts have been made to make it so, and the House of Bishops declared (General Convention of 1808) that it ought to be observed By the old Law (Just. Cod.) a kind of spiritual affinity was created between the sponsors and the adult or the infant baptized and marriage was consequently forbidden.

Affusion. *Vide* BAPTISM.

Agapæ. The feasts of charity, St. Jude v. 12; St. Peter ii. 13. They had their rise in the community of goods mentioned in Acts ii. 44, and as the sharing of all things in common could not be continued when the society became too numerous, such a feast for the poorer members would become a substitute which could express well the fellowship and love between Christians of all ranks. St. Paul describes but does not so designate a feast of this kind. It became very popular and spread throughout the Church. Pliny may refer to it in his famous letter to Trajan . . . "that they, later in the day, partook in common of a simple and innocent meal." Ignatius speaks of it. Tertullian also, in the next century; Clement (192 A.D.) also speaks of the luxury which was introduced into the feasts which were intended to be for the poor, and as simple and temperate as became Christians. Meat, wine, fish, cheese, bread, milk, poultry, made up the articles usually furnished by the richer for the poorer brethren. The real use of the feast was not the relief to the needy, for that could be and was attained by other agencies, but as a living proof of the common brotherhood. This common bond was lost sight of as the Church grew in wealth and drew into it the wealthy upper classes. Ascetic ideas, too, and the practice of fasting before Communion, and the abuses readily growing up about these Feasts of Charity, would lead to their disuse and abolishment. When they finally disappeared is not probably to be ascertained now, but traces of the practice survived in Egypt till near the close of the fifth century, and the Council in Trullo (692 A.D.) forbids them, though no other notice of them at that date is found.

Agenda. A term meaning Things to be

done, in distinction from Things to be believed. It usually means the divine offices, as in the Council of Carthage (390 A.D.) and Innocent I. (Ep ad Decentium, though its genuineness is now questioned.) Latterly, as in Bede, it meant specially commemoration of the dead.

Agnosticism (from the negative particle *a* and γιγνώσκω, I know) is a modern word representing a form of philosophy which has attained a wide acceptance with some men of cultivated intellect. It is fairly described in the following sentences taken from Prebendary Row's "Revelation and Modern Theology Contrasted," London, 1883, p. 338: "This philosophy maintains that while belief in the existence of a first cause of the universe, which it designates GOD, is a necessity of thought, yet this first cause, or GOD, owing to the limitations of the human intellect, must forever remain unknown and unknowable to man. In other words, that it is impossible to affirm of it a single attribute; and that to assert that it possesses personality, volition, intelligence, or a moral character is nothing else than anthropomorphism, by which is meant that to ascribe such conceptions, *being purely human*, to the first cause of the universe is simply to manufacture a GOD after our own likeness. The GOD of this system, therefore, while the assumption of this existence satisfies an intellectual necessity, is precisely the same for all moral purposes as if He existed not. (*Vide* ATHEISM.) For anything that we can know, He is incapable of caring for us or regarding our conduct, and we, in like manner, may both live and die without any regard for Him." While this subtle philosophy is apparently more modest than atheism, and to that degree less offensive to the cultivated taste of intellectual men, it is plain from the above description that it is absolutely anti-Christian. (*Vide* ATHEISM. See also "Agnosticism: A Doctrine of Despair," by President Porter, of Yale College, in the series of "Present-Day Tracts." London, The Religious Tract Society.)

REV. HALL HARRISON.

Agnus Dei. I. The words with which St. John Baptist pointed out JESUS to His disciples—"Behold the Lamb of GOD which taketh away the sin of the world"—was very naturally and devoutly used in the liturgic worship. It was incorporated into the glorious hymn "Gloria in Excelsis," found at the end of St. Clement of Alexandria's works (192 A.D.), and now in our Prayer-Book. It was also used as a versicle during the celebration of the Holy Communion, at the time of consecrating the elements, and became common during the mediæval ages. But the English Use dropped it, though it is being revived in many places.

II. A medallion of wax stamped with the effigy of a lamb. It was an ancient custom to distribute to worshipers on the first Sunday after Easter particles of wax taken from the Paschal taper, which had been solemnly blessed on the Easter-eve of the previous year. These particles were burned in houses, fields, or vineyards to secure them against evil influence or thunder-strokes. In Rome itself, however, instead of a Paschal taper, the archdeacon was accustomed to pronounce a benediction over a mixture of oil and wax, from which small medallions were made bearing the figure of a lamb, to be distributed to the people on the first Sunday after Easter, especially to the newly baptized. In modern times this benediction of the *Agnus Dei* is reserved to the Pope himself, and takes place in the first year of his pontificate and every seventh year following.

Alabama, Diocese of. On Monday, January 25, 1830, a meeting of the members and friends of the Protestant Episcopal Church in the State of Alabama was held in the city of Mobile, for "the purpose of giving a more efficient and permanent character to its institutions, and for the better administration of its rites and ordinances." This seems to have been the first step taken towards organizing the Diocese. Two clergymen of the Church were then living in the State,—the Rev. Mr. Shaw in Mobile, and the Rev. Mr. Muller in Tuskaloosa,—and both were present at this meeting. It also appears that the Rt. Rev. Bishop Brownell, of Connecticut, and the Rev. William Richmond, of New York, were in Mobile at that time, and were invited to be present. Bishop Brownell, by special request, presided over the meeting.

The Diocese was formally organized by the adoption of a constitution, which recognized the authority of the Church in the United States. After this was done, a resolution was passed looking to the formation of a Southwestern Diocese, to be composed of the Dioceses of Mississippi, Louisiana, and Alabama. After correspondence between the parties interested in this, a number of clergy and laity, duly elected to represent these several States, assembled in Christ Church, New Orleans, on the 4th of March, 1835. Their object was to secure the privilege granted by a Canon of the General Convention of 1832, which Canon was expressed in the following words: "The Dioceses of Mississippi and Alabama, and the Clergy and Churches in the State of Louisiana, are hereby authorized to associate and join in the election of a Bishop, anything in the Canons of this Church to the contrary notwithstanding; the said association to be dissolved on the demise of the Bishop, and not before, unless by the consent of General Convention." Acting under the authority of such Canon, this Convention unanimously elected the Rev. Francis L. Hawks, D.D., of St. Thomas' Church, New York, Bishop of this Southwestern Diocese; but, in consequence of the repeal of said Canon by a succeeding General Convention, this plan was abandoned.

The Convention of Alabama which

met in Tuskaloosa, on the 3d of January, 1831, invited Bishop Brownell to take charge of parishes in this State, under the provisions of Canon 20 of the Church in the United States, and to perform such Episcopal services as might be required. This invitation was accepted, and the Bishop remained in official charge of this Diocese until 1840, at which time he requested to be relieved. Between 1831 and 1840 Bishop Brownell paid at least two visits to Alabama. He presided at the Convention which met in Tuskaloosa in 1835, confirmed several persons, and consecrated the church in that city; and again in 1837, administered confirmation in the city of Mobile.

In 1836, Bishop Otey, of Tennessee, acting for Bishop Brownell, visited the State; and in 1838, Bishop Kemper, at the invitation of Bishop Otey, performed several Episcopal acts in the Diocese.

In 1840 the Diocese was placed under the official charge of the Rt. Rev. Bishop Polk, who made two visits to the Diocese, and presided at the Convention of 1843.

In the year 1842 the Rev. Martin P. Parks, of Virginia, at that time Chaplain at the Military Academy at West Point, was elected Bishop, but declined to take charge of the Diocese. In 1843 the Rev. James T. Johnston, of Virginia, was duly elected Bishop, but declined to accept the position.

At a Convention held in Greensboro', Alabama, in 1844, the Rev. N. H. Cobbs, D.D., of the Diocese of Ohio, was elected Bishop of Alabama. The Rev. Dr. Cobbs accepted the election, was consecrated in October, 1844, and came at once to his work in the Diocese.

At the Convention of 1845, the first one held after Bishop Cobbs took charge of the Diocese, the number of clergy entitled to seats was 17; at the Convention of 1860, the last one at which this Bishop was present, the number canonically connected with the Diocese was 32. The labors of this Bishop were very greatly blessed; the number of his clergy rapidly increased, and his Diocese was always a household at unity with itself.

Bishop Cobbs died in January, 1861, and on May 2, 1861, the Annual Convention of the Diocese assembled in St. John's Church, Montgomery. Failing to agree in the choice of a Bishop the Convention adjourned to meet in Selma, on Thursday, November 21, 1861; and reassembling at the time and place appointed, the Rev. Richard Hooker Wilmer, D.D., of the Diocese of Virginia, was unanimously elected Bishop of Alabama. The Rev. Dr. Wilmer accepted this election, and was consecrated in St. Paul's Church, Richmond, Va., March 6, 1862, the Rt. Rev. William Meade, D.D., Bishop of Virginia, the Rt. Rev. John Johns, Assistant Bishop of Virginia, and the Rt. Rev. Stephen Elliott, D.D., Bishop of Georgia, uniting in this consecration. When the war ended this consecration was fully recognized by the Protestant Episcopal Church in the United States, and the Bishop of Alabama took his seat with his brethren in the House of Bishops.

Bishop Wilmer came at once to his Diocese, and in God's providence has been spared to labor continuously in this portion of the Master's vineyard.

In 1857 the subject of a Diocesan School for Girls was brought before the Convention in the Bishop's address, and the action which then began resulted in the purchase of a lot near the city of Montgomery, and the erection of a suitable building, called Hamner Hall. This property was managed for a time by a separate board of trustees, then by St. John's Parish, Montgomery, and finally came into the possession of the Diocese. The school is now in a very flourishing condition, under the charge of Rev. George M. Everhart, D.D.

On the same lot is a large and handsome brick house, known formerly as the Bishop Cobbs Home for Orphans, which house is also the property of the Diocese, and is reserved as the residence of the future Bishops of Alabama.

In 1864, Bishop Wilmer issued a Pastoral Letter urging upon the Diocese the establishment of a Home for Widows and Orphans, which should be under the care of a Sisterhood of Deaconesses. The plan was approved by the Convention, and steps were taken to carry it into effect. A few orphans were collected at Tuskaloosa, but they were soon removed to Mobile, and to this number were added the inmates of the Bishop Cobbs Home at Montgomery. A building was purchased in which were placed a number of orphan girls. As necessity required it, a similar Home was furnished for boys, both Homes being under the care of the Deaconesses. The liberality of Church people, almost exclusively of Mobile, has enabled the managers not only to provide comfortably for these orphans from day to day, but also to lay up funds for future use; the property of the Home amounting, in 1883, to $15,769.29.

In 1846 there was formed a Society for the Relief of Disabled Clergymen, and of the Widows and Orphans of Deceased Clergymen. This society has preserved its existence under several changes of constitution, and seems destined to be the means of doing much good. It holds property to the amount of $13,108.42.

In 1836 an effort was made to secure a Bishop's Fund. Three trustees were appointed to receive a gift of land offered by Jacob Lorillard, Esq., of New York City, for the benefit of a fund whose annual interest would in time be sufficient to support the Bishop of the Diocese. This fund is managed by three trustees, who are elected annually by the Convention, and its property now amounts to $29,862.

From 1830 to 1844 the various reports show the following statistics: baptisms, 836;

confirmations, 168; marriages, 194; funerals, 314.

From 1844 to 1861, baptisms, 6493; confirmations, 2351; marriages, 1082; funerals, 2287.

From 1861 to 1883, baptisms, 10,739; confirmations, 6768; marriages, 2558; funerals, 5134.

Total baptisms, 18,068; confirmations, 9287; marriages, 3834; funerals, 7735.

Deacons ordained from 1845 to 1861, 28.
Priests   "   "   "   "   26.
Churches consecrated "   "   "   14.
Deacons ordained   " 1861 to 1883, 26.
Priests   "   "   "   "   17.
Churches consecrated "   "   "   19.
Total deacons ordained,   54.
"   priests   "   43.
"   churches consecrated, 33.

The present condition of the Diocese is best explained by citing some words from the address of Bishop Wilmer to the Convention of 1882:

"We have passed through a grand revolution, socially and politically. In view of all that has taken place during the last twenty years, the wonder with me is that so much has been accomplished by our people, under every possible disadvantage and discouragement. We have lost a large number of our people by emigration to more fertile territories. Compare the number of confirmations reported for the last twenty years with the number of communicants at present reported, and it will be seen how large a number must have emigrated from the State. And the clergy, finding no sufficient maintenance, have followed the tide of population.

"The statement following will show, at a glance, how the clergy have been affected by the fluctuations of the times:

No. of clergy canonically resident in the Diocese March 6, 1862	34
No. of clergy since added by transfer from other Dioceses	49
No. of clergy since added by Ordination to Deaconate	22
	— 71
No. of clergy at any time connected with Diocese since above date	105
No. of clergy died whilst resident in Diocese	8
No. of clergy transferred to other Dioceses since date	66
No. of clergy deposed since above date	3
	— 77
	28
One under suspension, name not reported	1
Present number reported	27"

There has been a strong tendency on the part of the people to leave the country and make their homes in the cities, and in consequence, while the city parishes have rapidly increased in numbers, the country parishes have languished. With the return of prosperity the Church will go forward, with fresh vigor, in the discharge of her work.

Statistics for 1886 A.D.: Clergy, 30; parishes, 33; missions, 25; candidates for H. O., 2; ord., D. 1; baptisms, 164; con., 369; com.,

4216; S. S. teachers, 315; S. S. scholars, 2533; contr., $92,721.92. RICHARD H. COBBS, D.D.

Alb. *Vide* VESTMENTS.

Albany, Diocese of. *History.*—The Diocese of Albany, forming a part of the State of New York, consists of nineteen counties, which comprised the old Northern Convocation. These counties are Albany, Clinton, Columbia, Delaware, Essex, Franklin, Fulton, Greene, Hamilton, Herkimer, Montgomery, Otsego, Rensselaer, Saratoga, Schenectady, Schoharie, St. Lawrence, Warren, and Washington. It embraces within its limits 20,888 square miles, and, according to the census of 1880, has a population of 949,545 souls. Its territory is diversified by lake and river, mountain and valley, forest and plain; while the great Adirondack Wilderness, with its wonderful resources, lies in its bosom. It has also such famous summer resorts as Lebanon and Richfield Springs, Luzerne and Scharon, Lake George and Saratoga. The Diocese takes its name from the capital of the State, which is also the residence of the Bishop. It was carved out of the Diocese of New York, together with Long Island, in the year 1868, by act of the General Convention. Its primary Convention, pursuant to the call of the Rt. Rev. Horatio Potter, D.D., LL.D., D.C.L., Bishop of New York, met in the city of Albany, in St. Peter's Church, on December 2, 1868. The Bishop of New York presided and preached the sermon. Among the visiting clergy was the Rt. Rev. Henry Lascelles Jenner, D.D., Lord Bishop of Dunedin, New Zealand. On the second day of the Convention, December 3, the Rev. William Croswell Doane, S.T.D., Rector of St. Peter's Church, Albany, was chosen Bishop. His consecration took place in the same church on the Feast of the Purification in 1869, the preacher being Rt. Rev. W. H. Odenheimer, D.D, Bishop of New Jersey. The Bishop of New York was the Consecrator, and was assisted by the Bishops of New Jersey, Maine, Missouri, and Long Island. Under the wise management of Bishop Doane the Diocese of Albany has been steadily increasing in strength and influence. At the time of its organization in 1868 there were 78 clergymen belonging to it. In 1878 there were 117, and in 1883 there were 123. In 1868 there were 95 churches, in 1878 there were 113, and in 1883 there were 122.

There were reported from 75 churches:

	Baptisms.	Confirmations.	Communicants.
In 1868	1137	795	6561
In 1878	1800	1356	10,617
In 1883	1799	937	13,018

In 1868 the offerings were $118,433.87; in 1878, $236,400.05; and in 1883 they were $296,928.52. In some parishes new churches have taken the place of old ones, while in others the old have been renovated. Church property also of great value has been acquired for mission work and other religious purposes. Offerings are made for the following objects, as required by Canon: Diocesan Fund, Missions of the Diocese, Aged and Infirm Clergy, Widows and Orphans of Deceased Clergymen, Bible and Common Prayer-Book Society of Albany, Episcopal Fund, salary of the Bishop, Education of Young Men for the Ministry, Orphan House of the Holy Saviour, Domestic Missions, Foreign Missions. Offerings are also presented by the Sunday-schools of the Diocese for the Child's Hospital.

Missions.—The chief glory of the Diocese is its mission work. Under the energetic leadership of the Bishop, who must be the great missionary, the Church is extended far and wide, and the things that remain are strengthened. There are about ninety mission stations receiving aid from the Board of Missions, and the sum of $10,000 is appropriated annually for this work. The Board is composed of the Bishop, *ex-officio* president, and five other clergymen, and five laymen chosen by the Convention.

Convention.—The Convention meets annually on the first Tuesday after the first Sunday after the Epiphany. Where, the Bishop determines. Hitherto the cities of Albany and Troy have shared the honors of the meetings. This body is composed, first, of the Bishop; secondly, of all clergymen canonically resident within the Diocese for six months previous to Convention, restriction of time not to apply to rectors duly elected, or missionaries duly appointed; and, thirdly, to three lay delegates from the Cathedral and three lay delegates from each Church in union with the Convention. The delegates must be, in all cases, communicants. The sessions usually last two days. The permanent officers of the Diocese are the Bishop, a Standing Committee, a Secretary, a Treasurer, and a Registrar.

Convocations.—The Diocese is divided into districts called Convocations, the titles and limits of which are as follows: The Convocation of Albany comprises the counties of Albany, Greene, Columbia, Schenectady, Montgomery, Fulton, Hamilton, and Herkimer; the Convocation of Troy, the counties of Rensselaer, Saratoga, Washington, Warren, Clinton, and Essex; the Convocation of Susquehanna, the counties of Delaware, Otsego, and Schoharie; the Convocation of Ogdensburg, the counties of St. Lawrence and Franklin. The Bishop is head of each Convocation *ex-officio*, and the executive officer is an Archdeacon, appointed annually by the Bishop, on the nomination of the Convocation, from among its clergy. Two meetings are required each year by Canon. Others may be held by order of Convocation. The work of the Convocations is specially missionary in its character.

Other Institutions of the Diocese are the Bible and Common Prayer-Book Society of Albany and its vicinity, incorporated in 1820. St. Agnes' School for Girls, located in Albany, with the Bishop as Rector, and twenty-six teachers and officers; the Child's Hospital, Albany, with branch Home for Convalescents at Saratoga in the summer; the Orphan House of the Holy Saviour, Cooperstown; St. John's Clergy House, East Line, incorporated in 1881; Home of the Good Shepherd, Saratoga Springs, incorporated in 1869; the Church Home, Troy.

The Sisterhood of the Holy Child Jesus has its headquarters at Albany, and is under the direction of the Bishop of Albany. The Sisters are at work in St. Agnes' School, and in charge of the Child's Hospital, Albany, and the Child's Convalescent Home, Saratoga Springs. The Cathedral Building of All-Saints, which has been the dream of the Bishop for years, will soon crown the commanding site chosen for it. A large lot has been secured in the city of Albany, north of the Capitol, and near St. Agnes' School and the old chapel, which has done good service. About $75,000 are in hand, and the work is to be diligently prosecuted. The grand edifice, which will be built of stone, will be an enduring monument of the zeal and labors of the first Bishop of Albany. Bishop Doane, on whom has fallen the mantle-spirit of his sainted father, a former Bishop of New Jersey, is in his vigor and manly prime, and is noted for his ripe scholarship, his facile pen, his gifts as a presiding officer, his eloquence as a preacher, and his largeness of heart. He received the degree of Doctor of Laws a few years ago from Union University,—a just recognition of his ability and superior talents.

Statistics for 1886 A.D.: Clergy, 130; parishes, 100; missions, 40; candidates for H. O., 18; ordinations, D. 2, P. 2; baptisms, 1343; confirmed, 1135; com., 14,340; S. S. teachers, 1172; S. S. scholars, 9981; contr., $218,248.98. Rev. Joseph Carey, D.D.

Albate. A sort of Christian hermits, so called from the white linen they wore.

Alexandria. *Vide* Eastern Churches.

Alexandria, School of. Every church had its catechetical school, somewhat corresponding to our confirmation classes, but with more definiteness of organization, and some provision was made for the education of Christian children, but no church ever possessed as famous a school as that at Alexandria. Its foundation is obscure, though ascribed to St. Mark, and the list of its earliest masters is very doubtful till we reach Pantænus, who was at its head about 179 A.D. He was as a heathen an eclectic, but brought his philosophical studies to the service of the Church. In such a city as Alexandria his ability would be very useful in attracting many to his lectures. When he was sent on his mission to the Indians (probably to Lybia), Clement, who was most likely of Roman extraction, himself in early life an enthusiastic student of philosophy, and later a devout Christian, succeeded him. His works, the "Cohortatio," "Pædagogus," and the "Stromata," discursive collections of his lectures, probably based upon a loose outline of the Apostolic constitutions, are a valuable picture of how far a public lecturer upon Christian topics could go before a mixed audience. The administrative ability of the Bishop Demetrius used both Pantænus and his two successors with great wisdom till Demetrius fell out with Origen. It is said that before Demetrius's time the Church of Alexandria had no dependencies, but from the date of Pantænus's mission, and from the fame and success of the school, soon Sees were added upon Sees, till Alexandria was at the head of a large province. Origen, who succeeded to Pantænus, who resumed his post upon his return, brought, perhaps, the loftiest abilities yet used for the task. Adamantine in endurance, with a mind capacious of all instruction, a master of the Scriptures, no mean critic, he was devoted to his school. His peculiar notions, probably more speculatively held than otherwise, gave a notoriety that pained him, since they were rather questions for debate in his school than formulated dogmas. At any rate, they were fastened upon him. In an hour of enthused fear for himself and his influence in the school he mutilated himself, giving a wrong interpretation to our LORD'S words (Matt. xix. 12). The act disabled him from ordination. When, then, he received ordination on a visit to Palestine, contrary to the Canons, his Bishop took his office as catechist from him. The school became of less importance later as the adults to be prepared for baptism and confirmation grew rarer, but it nurtured a spirit of dispute which produced Arius, the famous heretic, who, however, had received his dialectic training from Lucian, of Antioch. The school was finally closed by becoming a mere nursing-school for the young to be prepared for baptism and confirmation. It is not worth the while to give the names of its later masters save one, Didymus, who was totally blind (340–395 A.D.).

Alienation is, in church matters, the improper disposal of such lands or goods as have been given to the Church for sacred and devout uses. It has always been deemed sinful to apply such means or property to other than direct Church needs. It was hardly an alienation in this sense, when, for the ransom of Christian captives, Bishops sold the Church's plate, or lands even. The like was done in cases of severe famine. But this does not justify the act under other circumstances. The Bishops were only the stewards, and not the owners, and many Canons were necessary throughout the history of every part of the Church restraining them from wasting and for private purposes parting with Church property.

Alienation in Mortmain. The conveying of real estate to any corporate body; in this case, for religious purposes.

Allegory (Gal. iv. 24). An allegory sums up in itself the separate purposes of the Type, Parable, or Metaphor, using either one of these three as a leading form at varying times. The Canticles are filled with types of CHRIST and His Church, but the whole is allegorical. It expresses one thing under words that, upon the surface, are the expression of another. So Ps. lxxx. 8–16, are an allegory. But the same imagery in Is. v. is there a parable. St. Paul uses the allegory in 1 Cor. x. 4, and in Gal. iv. 16–21. The use of allegories is peculiarly Oriental. It is a form adapted to the conveyance of religious truth in very attractive shapes. Allegorical interpretations became a favorite mode of explaining the obscurities in Holy Scripture. The example of St. Paul, as above quoted, was imitated, and a devout spirit, seeing CHRIST everywhere in the Scripture, was tempted to drag into line many texts which could not possibly contain any direct reference to Him. Theologians claimed for the interpretation of Scripture several modes of treating the text, some of them enumerating sixteen, but three were generally admitted,—the Moral, the Allegorical, and the Mystical Sense, apart from the historical or grammatical sense. But the striving to torture new significations and to find new allegories soon brought on a reaction. However, these methods of interpretation held precedence till the Reformation, when the reaction went too far, producing a temper which empties Holy Scripture of much of its true meaning.

Alleluia. A formula, or proclamation, "Praise ye the LORD," found in Ps. cxvii., and as a heading to several other Psalms, especially cxiii.–cxviii., the great Hallel. Psalms sung at all the greater Jewish festivals. The word has been transferred into all languages. It was recorded by St. John, as used by the Angel Host (Rev. xix. 6, 7). Of course it passed immediately into Christian usage. There is the story of the Hallelujah victory by the Christian Britons over the pagan Picts and Scots (429 A.D.). It was used as a watch-cry of encouragement. It was introduced into the Liturgy in both East and West. It is in the Liturgy of St. James, as the earliest instance. In the West, the Mozarabic (which is of Eastern parentage, however), it was freely used; but in the other Western Churches it was very sparingly used, being used most freely during the Easter and Whitsun feasts. Our own Church bears as one of the marks of Eastern influence the use of the Hallelujah in the Versicles, "Praise ye the LORD, the LORD'S name be praised," in the Morning and Evening Prayers.

All-Saints. In the Eastern Church this was a very ancient feast, St. Chrysostom speaking of it under the name All-Martyrs. It falls upon our Trinity Sunday, crowning the Church's year with a joyful commemoration of all saints of GOD.

In the Western Church this feast had its rise much later, in the consecration into Christian Churches of heathen temples. This practice began in the latter part of Pope

Gregory's life, and when (607 A.D.) Boniface III. procured from the emperor a recognition of his supremacy, his successor, Boniface IV., consecrated the Pantheon to the Virgin and all martyrs (May 13). It is not certain when the commemoration was transferred to November 1. It was not observed in Gaul till later; in England, Bede speaks of it; nor was it general till Louis the Pious, under advice from Gregory IV., ordered it. The Collect, Epistle, and Gospel were of later date.

All-Souls. A festival falling on the next day after All-Saints' Day. It had its origin in the continuous commemoration at the Holy Communion of "the souls of all those who have died in the communion of the body and blood of our LORD." But beside this Eucharistic commemoration, there were anniversary observances, probably by the surviving relatives. In 837, Amalarius of Metz writes of the annual commemoration of the dead. The festival was at once very popular, after an ordinance by Odilo, Abbot of Clugny, for the abbacies under him.

Almighty. Synonymous with Hebrew LORD GOD of Hosts; the Mighty GOD; Omnipotent. A title which GOD gives Himself in His covenant with Abraham (Gen. xvii. 1). It is continuously used afterwards adown the stream of Revelation. It was taken at once into the Creed, and has maintained its place there ever since as an integral part of the first clause. It is a most important title, for it may be considered (a) as Comprehensive, containing all things; (b) Originative, as creating all things; (c) Preservative of all things. It is fitly used, therefore, by the Church in her Creed, in her Prayers, at the Holy Communion, and in her Hymns, the "Te Deum" and the "Gloria in Excelsis." But this power being of the essential attributes of the Divine Nature belongs equally to the THREE PERSONS of the TRINITY, and so the Athanasian Hymn, "So, likewise, the FATHER is Almighty, the SON is Almighty, the HOLY GHOST is Almighty, and yet there are not *Three* Almighties but One ALMIGHTY."

Alms. In Job's solemn protestation of his integrity he places the sharing of his bread with the poor as one of his righteous customs (Job xxxi. 17). From the earliest ages almsgiving and relief of the poor and needy has had a special promise and pledge attached. The Israelite when given the land was ordered to leave the gleaning. He was to share the tithe of his produce every third year with not only the Levite, but also the stranger, the fatherless, and the widow. From the Law the Israelite had this enjoined upon him, and he received the promises of prosperity (Prov. xix. 17; Ps. xii. 1). Our LORD assumes it as a right and duty in His Sermon on the Mount, and Himself, though ministered to by others, was a Giver of alms. It was the first popular duty in the Church, and it grew so rapidly that the Diaconate was established to superintend the work. When St. Peter and St. Paul arranged their missionary jurisdictions, St. Paul was enjoined to be mindful of the poor. And it received from him much attention, as we gather from his directions to the Corinthians and elsewhere. He went up to Jerusalem with the collections made for the saints there. When there was a famine threatened in Judæa, alms were sent to the poor from other parts of Syria. In the course of time this almsgiving took more systematic shape. The offertory included food as well as money, and it was shared by the ministers with the poor. The moneys gathered into the treasury were divided into three parts,—one for the ministry, one for the repairing and building churches, and the third for the widows and poor. The offertory now should take this latter place to a far larger extent than it has done, especially as the Rubric makes the alms for the poor its chief use. In England extraordinary collections have been taken up from time to time upon royal briefs, but latterly, as the machinery for such a gathering was very expensive,—taking up above half the amount collected,—it has not been often used. After reforms under Anne, and again under George IV., it gradually fell into disuse, though a royal brief was issued as late as 1854.

There should be some system devised and faithfully carried out in each Diocese that shall teach the duty of almsgiving, and show how much good it effects. Alms should be put into the hands of the Bishop of the Diocese for use oftener than they are.

Altar. A structure of stone or wood, upon which the elements of the Holy Communion are consecrated. The more usual name in the Prayer-Book is the LORD's Table, but the term Altar is used in the office of Institution. The word occurs in the Epistle to the Hebrews, "We have an altar, whereof they have no right to eat which serve the tabernacle" (Heb. xiii. 10), and is best referred to the Christian Table. The altar of the Old Testament was one on which bloody sacrifices were offered, though there was also the Altar of Incense. The first altar was built by Noah. The altar was usually placed in some spot deemed for some reason hallowed: as where GOD appeared to Jacob. The material of which they were made was, according to the Mosaic Law, either of earth or of "stones, upon which no tool had been lifted." It was contrary to the Law to build an altar elsewhere than in the Tabernacle, and afterwards in the Temple, though this was frequently violated: as when David built an altar at the threshing-floor of Araunah. Altars, not for sacrifice, were often built, as when the tribes of Reuben and Manasseh, and Gad, put up an Altar of Witness. There was the altar for burnt sacrifice in the Tabernacle made of wood and overlaid with brass; a second larger one made wholly of brass was erected in the first Temple; a third, of unhewn stones (at least the one that replaced it under Judas Maccabeus, when he cleansed the polluted Temple after Antiochus Epiphanes had desecrated it, was so), was placed in the second Temple on the spot where the brazen altar had stood. In the Temple, as restored by Herod, the altar was also of unhewn stone. There was also the Altar of Incense, which, however, was not properly so, since no sacrifices were offered upon it. As for Christian altars, they have been made of various materials, in early times, generally of wood, but very often of marble, and in one or two instances of gold. Often the wood was decorated or covered with gold or silver plating or chased work and adorned with gems. The form varies from the Table to the Tomb form. In the Greek Liturgical language the term used is trapeza,—table, but with some epithet, as "the spiritual," "the mystical," "the royal," "the holy," or "the divine."

In this country there is no rule, and an altar may be made of either wood or stone, and in either of the forms above described. There can be no real objection to using the term altar for the Holy Table, since both terms are used in the Prayer-Book, and upon it are placed the oblations for the memorial our LORD commanded us to make of His one, full, perfect, and sufficient sacrifice once offered.

Altar-Cloth. The cloths with which the Holy Table is vested, either as permanent coverings, or for the celebration of the Holy Communion. The earliest unquestionable reference to altar-cloths other than for the celebration is found in St. Chrysostom's Homily on Matthew xiv. 23, 24, wherein he contrasts the costly silken embroidered covering given for the Holy Table with the scanty clothing often grudgingly given to the poor. In his time (390–405 A.D.) we see that such costly altar-cloths were usual. The symbolic use of colors in altar vestments for the several seasons of the Christian year is not more than seven or eight centuries old. (*Vide* COLORS.)

Altar-Piece. This was a picture or carved bas-relief placed behind and over the altar. This practice of placing pictures in churches, though very ancient, still won its way slowly, against much opposition. The danger that arose later was clearly seen by a few. The feeling that the house of GOD should be made as glorious as possible filled the devout hearts of the many. The earliest instance we have of a picture in a church is from St. Epiphanius (391 A.D.), who, when journeying through Palestine, found at Anablatha a veil hanging before the doors of the sanctuary of the church with a painting of CHRIST or some Saint upon it. This he had torn into pieces and given for a winding-sheet for the poor, and replaced it with a plain veil from his own home in Cyprus. Paulinus of Nola (402 A.D.) introduced pictures largely in his new church. They were of Scripture subjects, and were designed to instruct the illiterate. From this time on the decoration of churches with paintings became more common. These remarks apply to pictures proper, for we find symbolic decoration much earlier, but nothing that applies to paintings. But while frequent casual references are made to pictures, after this there is ever a note of warning sounded. The famous Gregory I., in condemning the misuse of pictures, urges that it would be wrong to remove them, as they were object-lessons in sacred history to the unlearned (Ep. ad Ser. Mass.). There was, at first, very much objection to producing any likeness of our LORD, but that, soon after the common introduction of art into the Church, was overcome.

Very early mosaics exist, the oldest of which are at Ravenna and at Thessalonica. The Cross was a symbol that was employed at a very early date, but the Crucifix was not used till very much later. The oldest frescoes are of Saints, in the catacombs at Naples, in the fifth, but the nearest in age after them are dated about the eighth, century. There were three styles, distinct in treatment of the same subjects,—the Roman, the Byzantine, and the Lombard, which developed upon different lines of church decoration. In the Greek Church the iconostasis is the space on which the greatest amount of painting is placed.

Altar-Rails are of modern arrangement, being due probably to Archbishop Laud, who had them erected to prevent the profanations and intrusions which frequently occurred. They have taken the place of the old open-work grating or screen which parted the choir from the nave. This latter separation was of ancient date, as may be shown by the frequent references and descriptions, as that by Eusebius (325–40 A.D.) of the Church in Tyre. It was open trellised work, often enriched by bronze or gilt or silver. The material was usually of wood or iron, but sometimes of stone. There was always some mode of marking the division between the nave of the church and the sanctuary. In the Eastern Church it was as above, till later, when the open-work was paneled and painted with pictures of CHRIST and the Apostles or Saints, and entered by doors, which therefore formed a complete partition between the two portions of the church (ICONOSTASIS). The material of which this iconostasis was made was usually of wood, though other material is used also. In the West, the partition was, as stated above, without railing and open-work.

Ambon, or Ambo. The desk or raised platform for the reader, from which the Epistle and Gospel were read, notices were published, and from which the inferior clergy preached. Its position varied. It probably occupied the same position relatively that the place for the readers did in the synagogue. It often stood in the middle of the nave, but sometimes to the right of the front of what we now call the choir.

In large churches there were often two Ambons, one on the right for the Gospel, the other on the left for the Epistle. The Ambon was probably movable. It preceded the pulpit, which was later. (*Vide* PULPIT.) It was frequently ornamented with carved work on its panels, and in some examples still surviving it was supported upon a pillar. That at St. Sophia (536 A.D.) had two flights of steps, the one on the east, the other on the west. The Bishop generally preached from his chair (Cathedra), but sometimes from a desk in front of the altar. St. Chrysostom preached from the Ambon that he might be heard the better. At Ravenna exists still an Ambon which may date from the building of the church (493–525 A.D.).

Ambrosian Rite. *Vide* LITURGIES.

Amen. Faithful, True, Firm (Heb. and Gr.). The response of the people to every prayer. It is a strong asseveration of either faith in or consent to the contents of the prayer. The people gave their consent to the binding power of the curses pronounced upon Mt. Ebal (Deut. xxvii. 15) by their Amen. It was a title GOD by Isaiah (lxv. 16) gave Himself,—" the GOD of *Amen*." It had the force of an oath, as when the accused woman was to reply to the Priest, reciting the curse upon perjury, Amen, Amen, in the trial for jealousy (Num. v. 22). It, of course, passed into Christian use at once (1 Cor. xiv. 16), but our LORD gave it a significance which we undervalue. The enunciation of solemn central truths of His Revelation was always preceded by an Amen, Amen (Verily, Verily), as in St. John iii. 3, 5, 11; v. 19, 24, 25; vi. 32, 47, 53; viii. 51, 58, etc. Compare with this and with Is. lxv. 16; Rev. iii. 14. The response was always made loud and full. The Amen should be printed in other type when it is a response than when it is an invocation. In the one case (in *Italics*) the congregation alone respond, as in the prayers generally, but when it is also for the minister to use, it should be always printed in Roman.

American Church, The (officially, "The Protestant Episcopal Church in the United States of America"), is that branch of the One, Holy, Catholic, Apostolic Church in America which traces its Apostolic origin through the Church of England. It is in communion and in agreement in doctrine, discipline, and worship with the Church of England, which it venerates as its mother-Church, while being at the same time as entirely independent of it as any daughter can be who has left her mother's home and is mistress of a house and family of her own.

Through the Church of England this Church has affiliations with the whole Church of the West. In its Creeds and Liturgy and Discipline it occupies the ground which is common to all the churches of CHRIST from the beginning. As having cast off the errors of Rome, it is so far in sympathy with those bodies of Christians who, since the Reformation of the sixteenth century, have been known as Protestant and Reformed.

The history of the Church in America is a story of full three hundred years, for it was in the year 1578 that on the shores of Frobisher's Straits (named in honor of the admiral in command) "Master Wolfall celebrated a communion upon land, at the partaking whereof were the captain and many others with him. The celebration of the Divine mystery was the first sign, seal, and confirmation of CHRIST'S death and passion ever known in these quarters." The first known baptisms in English America were those of Virginia Dare, the granddaughter of Governor White, and "Manteo the savage," both baptized on shipboard off Roanoke Island, on the coast of North Carolina, both baptized by White, the governor of Raleigh's second colony. Another layman, Sir Thomas Hariat, records his use of the Prayer-Book among "the poor infidels" in 1585,—one of "the first lay-readers in the American Church." The next date takes us north again. In 1605 an expedition sailed from Bristol, under Captain Richard Weymouth, whose declared object was "the promulgating of GOD'S holy Church by planting Christianity," and which sailed up the Penobscot and erected a cross near the site of the present town of Belfast. This attempt failed, but two years later another effort promised better results. In August, 1607, a company, among whom was the Rev. Richard Seymour, landed on an island at the mouth of the Sagadahock, or Kennebec, and, besides fifty houses and a fort and store-house, built a church. The severity of the climate, and a fire that destroyed their store-house and church, disheartened them, and they returned to England the next season. This was thirteen years before the celebrated Pilgrim Fathers landed on Plymouth Rock. The same year, 1607, the first permanent settlement was effected in Virginia. In May, 1607, under Mr. Robert Hunt, a priest of the Church of England, the first services were held, and a church begun at Jamestown in Virginia. Services were held at first "under an awning and in an old cotton tent. This," says Captain John Smith, "was our church till we built a homely thing like a barn, where we had daily common prayer morning and evening, every Sunday two sermons, and every three months the Holy Communion till our minister died. But our prayers daily, with an homily on Sundays, we continued till more preachers came." With liberal gifts of money and land the Church in Virginia was in a fair way to prosper, though the disturbances at home told upon the colonies, and the clergy who came out were by no means all that they should have been. Among those who deserve to be remembered were Buck and Whitaker, who succeeded Mr. Hunt. Whitaker has been named the Apostle of Virginia. He it was who baptized Pocahontas. In the mean time settlements were being established all along the coast under different religious influences, and some of them, as in New England, distinctly hostile to the Church. Among them were here and there Churchmen and Church colonies, though the Church was never so strong, even in Virginia and Maryland, as is often supposed. Elsewhere it was very weak.

The case of Maryland is peculiar and not generally understood. The Charter of 1634 and the Act of 1649 are represented as a noble instance of religious toleration on the part of Roman Catholics, but without sufficient ground. Those acts, it is true, were obtained by Roman Catholics, but they were granted not by them, but to them. They were obtained from Charles and his advisers for the special benefit of Roman Catholics, and Roman Catholics took advantage of them, as it was intended that they should. That liberty and protection which was granted was all they asked for, and all they could have obtained. But neither in Maryland nor anywhere else did Roman authority ever regard the doctrine "that in conscience and in worship men should be free" as anything but insanity (*deliramentum*). In Maryland from the first the Church of England was "protected," and the Rev. Richard James, a clergyman of the Church of England, came on with the first Lord Baltimore and with his flock settled on Kent Island, opposite Annapolis. In 1623, Governor Robert Gorges brought with him the Rev. William Morrell, a Church of England clergyman, to his colony on Massachusetts Bay. In 1630 the Rev. William Blackstone sold his farm in Shawmut, where Boston now stands, and removed to Providence. In 1629, John and Samuel Brown, two of the original patentees, were banished from Salem for using the Prayer-Book. In 1646 and 1664 petitions were presented in Boston for permission to use the Prayer-Book; and the petitioners were punished for sedition. The first church services were held in Boston in 1686. None are known to have been held within the limits of New York before 1678, nor in Pennsylvania before 1695. When the Independents became the masters in Maryland, they at once repealed the laws of toleration and proscribed "popery and prelacy," as they had from the first in New England.

The Church grew, however, slowly, but it was without head or chief pastors until 1685, when Dr. Blair was sent to Virginia as Commissary of the Bishop of London; there was no authority over the Presbyters of the Church, who too often were just the men who needed overlooking. Soon afterwards Dr. Bray was sent out as Commissary to Maryland, and they did what good men could who were clothed with such authority as a Bishop can delegate, but who still were not Bishops. The Church in America for another hundred years was an Episcopal Church without a Bishop. Dr. Blair was Commissary of Virginia for fifty-three years. Dr. Bray entered upon the field of his labors in 1700, and a result of his missionary zeal was the founding of two societies which have done so much for the cause of the Gospel, the Society for promoting Christian Knowledge, and the Society for the Propagation of the Gospel in Foreign Parts. When after a few years he returned home, the majority of the colony of Maryland were accounted of the communion of the Church. In 1667 New Amsterdam was ceded to the English, and in 1696 "Trinity Church," in New York, was built and endowed. In 1679 King's Chapel, in Boston, was erected "for the exercise of religion according to the Church of England."

At the time of the foundation of the S. P. G. "in South Carolina were 7000 souls, besides negroes and Indians, living without any minister of the Church, and above half regardless of any religion. In North Carolina above 5000 without any minister. Virginia containing 40,000, divided into 40 parishes, but wanting near half the number of clergymen. Maryland containing 25,000, in 26 parishes, wanting half the number of clergymen. In Pennsylvania at least 20,000 souls, of which not above 700 frequent the church, and not above 250 are communicants. In New York the numbers are 30,000, 1200, 450. In Connecticut, 30,800, 150, 35. In other colonies of New England, 90,000, 750, 150." And the writer adds, "This is the true though melancholy state of our Church in North America."

The missionaries of the S. P. G. were sent into the provinces in which the Church had no establishment, as it had in Virginia and Maryland, and fruit was not wanting to their labors, though it was not gathered without opposition. In New England the movement Churchward began within the very walls of Yale College, when Dr. Cutler the rector of the college, and Messrs. Johnson and Brown, two of the tutors, through reading of works of the English divines in the college library, were brought to resign their positions, and in 1723 went over to England for ordination. Mr. Brown died in England of smallpox, but Dr. Cutler in Boston, and Mr. Johnson at Stratford, labored many years, and exerted a powerful influence for the Church. Many more would have followed them into the priesthood, but were deterred by the dangers of the sea-voyage and "the unhappy fate of Mr. Brown." "The fountain of all our misery is the want of a Bishop." They were bitterly opposed and persecuted, but nowhere in the country were there so many native clergy, and nowhere was the Church more firmly planted, at the breaking out of the Revolution, than in Connecticut. On the other hand, in Virginia and Maryland the Church, though comparatively strong in numbers, was weak in influence. There was no Episcopal authority, and the whole system of the Church was gradually dissolved. "Certainly," says Bishop White, "the different Episcopalian congregations knew of no union before the Revolution : except what was the result of the connection which they in common had with the Bishop of London. That authority being withdrawn, the clergy and people of any district might, without unlawfulness, have acted for themselves, and in some departments such a proceeding would not have been surprising."

There could be no confirmations and no ordinations, and the supply of clergy fell off, and the authority which belonged to a Bishop was usurped or lost altogether.

Many causes were at work to prevent the appointment of a Bishop, and to make that which was not altogether easy at first more and more difficult. The primary obstacle lay in the eighteenth century idea, which friends and enemies shared alike, that a Bishop was partly an ecclesiastical function-ary and at least half a State dignitary. Many who would not have objected to a "purely religious Episcopacy" did object to a "political Episcopacy." So general had this apprehension become that Bishop White declares his belief that a few years before the Revolutionary war it would have been "impossible to have obtained the concurrence of a respectable number of laymen in any measure for the obtaining of an American Bishop," and that when all were ready to avow "their preference of Episcopacy and of a form of prayer." To add force to this apprehension came in the understanding that this dignitary required a large endowment to support him. But more than all other causes was the prevailing ignorance and coldness which prevailed even among professed friends of the Church in the colonies.

A writer in 1735 expresses the feeling of a great many, who writes that "considering how long a time it is since the establishment (of the S. P. G.), the colonies may by this time be provided with ministers among themselves, and likewise be of sufficient abilities to support them if they were inclined to it." And still more when he adds, "in effect I know hardly any here that are disposed to do much for promoting or advancing religion, or that seems to be much concerned what becomes of it either abroad or at home." Efforts were made, but they failed. At one time matters went so far that a palace was purchased for the Bishop at Burlington, and considerable bequests were received for the endowment of the See, but the death of the queen in 1712 put a stop to all proceedings. In 1727, chiefly through the exertions of Berkeley (afterwards Bishop), a charter and a grant were obtained, but before the broad seal was attached the king died. Once the Church came near obtaining Bishops in spite of opposition, when Dr. Welton ard Mr. Talbot were consecrated by one of the non-juring Bishops. But the matter went no further. Dr. Welton was summoned home, and Mr. Talbot dismissed from his post as missionary of the S. P. G. Archbishop Secker renewed the effort in 1761, and the New England clergy joined in strong representations, but all in vain.

But GOD was preparing for His Church a deliverance in His own way. England's statesmen in neglecting the Church in America had neglected the strongest of all bonds between the colonies and the mother-country, and England owes in no small degree to that neglect the loss of these colonies. When the war of the Revolution came, while in the North the Church clergy were generally loyal to the mother-country, they were weak in numbers and in influence. For a time it seemed as though the war, with its consequent hatred of England, would work the destruction of the Church. But instead, it gave her freedom. The close of the war saw most of the clergy exiles, their churches desecrated or destroyed, and their congregations broken up. In Pennsylvania only one church was left,—Christ Church, in Philadelphia, under the Rev. (afterwards Bishop) William White. Virginia entered on the war with 164 churches and chapels and 91 clergymen. At the close of the contest a large "number of her churches were destroyed, 95 parishes were extinct or forsaken, and only 28 clergymen remained, and the Church was so depressed and so little zeal was found in her members that Dr. Griffith was unable to go over, with Drs. White and Provoost, to be consecrated Bishop of Virginia, because funds could not be raised to defray his expenses."

The number of those in "English America" who belonged to the Church was never so large as would be and is naturally supposed, partly owing to the fact that some of the colonies were settled by those disaffected and hostile to the Church, partly because of the immigration of those of other nations. At the beginning of the Revolutionary war there were only about eighty clergymen of the Church to the north and east of Maryland, and those, except in Boston, Newport, New York, and Philadelphia, principally supported by the S. P. G. Outside of Philadelphia there were never more than six in Pennsylvania. In Maryland and Virginia the Church was more numerous, and supported by legal establishments. Farther south they were less than in these provinces, but more than in the North. And besides this paucity of numbers, the very connection and name of England was a disadvantage. But the greatest disadvantage of all lay in its very organization, which required Bishops, who were denied.

The difficulties which stand in the way of the Church are illustrated by the fact that Mr. Adams took up the case of some candidates for orders, and through the Danish minister at the court of St. James made application for their ordination to the Danish Church, which was favorably received but never acted upon. Indeed, those who sought to supply the exigency had no idea of having recourse to any others besides the English Bishops, at least until that hope failed.

In 1784 occurred a correspondence which needs no comment to illustrate the condition of the Church. Two young men had braved the dangers of the sea to obtain ordination in England, but had been refused because the Bishops could not dispense with the oaths of uniformity, and they applied to Franklin for assistance. His answer is dated " Passy, near Paris," and with a refreshing innocence he informs them that he had applied to the Pope's Nuncio on their behalf, but advised them to give up the thought of England and go to the Church of Ireland, and if that application failed, to act as though England and Ireland were sunk in the sea; and expresses his wonder " that men in America qualified to pray for and instruct their neighbors should not be permitted to do it till they have voyaged 6000 miles to ask leave of a cross old gentleman at Canterbury, who seems, by your own account, to have as little regard for your souls as did Attorney-General Seymour for those of Virginia. Commissary Blair begged him to consider that the people of Virginia had souls to be saved. 'Souls!' (said he); '—— your souls! make tobacco.' "

One curious result of the want of Bishops may well be noticed. In 1784, John Wesley ordained and sent out Dr. Coke to be Superintendent of the Methodist Societies in America, and afterwards joined Mr. Asbury with him in office. Partly as a result of this action, the Methodists were separated from the Church. For this action, so opposed to his former conduct and teaching, Mr. Wesley gave the reason that while at home he would not suffer it, inasmuch as there were in America " no Bishops with legal jurisdiction, his scruples were at an end." The excuse is a sufficiently weak one, and it is Dr. Coke's own testimony that he went further in separation than Mr. Wesley intended, as he did in calling himself a Bishop; but such as the excuse is, it suggests some interesting questions as to the possibilities in case even this had been wanting. It was only in November of the same year that Bishop Seabury was consecrated. In 1791, Dr. Coke applied to Bishop White for the ordination of the Methodist ministers and for the consecration of himself and Mr. Asbury, and expressed a strong regret for his past action and desire of reunion. The effort came to naught, but when the question of separation turned upon such points, it is hardly possible to avoid saying to ourselves, What might have been if a Bishop had been here! So hopeless did the prospect seem of obtaining Bishops and continuing the proper ministry of the Church, that Dr. White put forth a scheme of presbyterian and provisional ordination, in order that the duty of worship and of preaching the Gospel might not utterly lapse. But the peace of 1783 opened a better prospect, and in 1784 several conferences were held in Brunswick, N. J., in Philadelphia and New York, which resulted in a General Convention in Philadelphia in 1785. But in the mean time the clergy of Connecticut had acted for themselves, and by their appointment Dr. Samuel Seabury sailed for England and applied for consecration as Bishop. But the English prelates could do nothing without the consent of the ministry, and the ministry would not give their consent without a formal request of Congress, which of course was out of the question; and after waiting some months in vain, at length following the instructions which he had received at home, and acting upon the advice of friends in England, Dr. Seabury turned his steps to Scotland, where was a Church which, if it was persecuted by the state; and its assemblies forbidden by law, was, at least, not hampered in its spiritual rights by state control. On the 14th of November, 1784, in a little upper room in Aberdeen, the first Bishop of the American Church was consecrated by three Bishops, Kilgour, Petre, and Skinner, and in June, 1785, he was at home. His consecration had a double good effect, encouraging the Churchmen of America and rousing the authorities in England, by the certainty that even if they were refused by England, Scotland could and would supply them with Bishops.

At the Convention in Philadelphia in October, 1785, seven States were represented. Dr. White presided, and it is to his meekness and wisdom that the Church owes its deliverance from the many dangers that encompassed it. There were grave differences on almost every conceivable subject. Some were afraid of a Bishop, and wanted his hands tied and himself made the creature of the Convention. Some would have excluded the laity from the Convention. Some would omit the opening petitions of the Litany. Bishop Seabury and his clergy declined to attend the Convention. By some Dr. White himself was charged with Socinianism. There were elements in the Church and in the Convention that boded neither any good, but out of them all the LORD delivered them.

The "proposed book" of 1785, which was by order of the Convention sent out into the different States for consideration, and which embodied many radical changes from the English Prayer-Book, fell flat. Correspondence with the English Prelates resulted in bringing the mind of the Church to a general agreement that the best thing to be done was to take the English book with as few changes as possible, and when, in 1786, Dr. White and Dr. Provoost, elected for Pennsylvania and New York, arrived in England, they were favorably received, and on February 4, 1787, were consecrated in Lambeth Chapel by the two Archbishops, and the Bishops of Bath and Wells, and Peterborough. In 1789 the union between the Dioceses was happily effected, Bishops White and Seabury constituting the House of Bishops in General Convention. When again the alterations in the Prayer-Book came under discussion, the influence of Bishop Seabury appears in the important alterations in the Communion office, by which that office follows the Scottish model. The prayers of invocation and oblation are those of the First Book of Edward VI., but the order is that of the Scottish and of the ancient Liturgies. It was a change that "lay very near to the heart of Bishop Seabury," who even doubted whether the form of the Church of England "strictly amounted to a consecration." When the proposed change came down to the lower house, by the influence of the President, Dr. William Smith, it was accepted without opposition. By it "the Holy Eucharist is restored to its ancient dignity and efficacy," and we have an office than which nothing more magnificent and worthy can be conceived. In comparison with this great gain, for which, under GOD, we have to thank Bishop Seabury, the other changes and omissions are small. The omission of the Athanasian Creed was the only important omission. Besides changes required by the changed political condition of the country, others were made. Selections from the Psalms were added to the Psalter. The Magnificat and Nunc Dimittis were omitted, the Venite and Benedictus shortened, and other alterations were made, some of them decided improvements, some decided losses, and some for which it would be hard to give a reason, but none of them affecting any doctrine or indicating any "essential departure from the doctrines, discipline, or worship of the Church of England."

The revolution, therefore, effected no break in the line of the Church's history. Nothing in her discipline, or worship, or practice is to be regarded as having a beginning at that time. There were portions of the Prayer-Book, as the Articles, for example, not finally acted upon until 1801, and even later, but there was no release from former obligations on that account, except from those political obligations which were affected by the war. The Church always had the Liturgy, and that which was not expressly changed simply continued in force. The declaration which was made in the Convention of 1811, that the Protestant Episcopal Church is the Church formerly known under the name of "the Church of England in America," a declaration called for by some disputes which had arisen about land-titles, expressed the universal understanding that in no respect was this a "new Church." We look back over the long struggle for existence which culminated so successfully, and we are more and more impressed with the greatness of the leaders of the Church, of the two especially who made up the House of Bishops in 1789, and on whom so much depended; but of those two we must give the palm to one. Bishop Seabury's zeal and devotion to Church principles supplied what was lacking in the character of Bishop White, and we owe him a great debt of admiration and gratitude But the gentle and firm hand that guided the frail bark of the Church through the dangers that beset her on every side, the one man who was to the Church what Washington was to the State, was WILLIAM WHITE.

The life was still very feeble. In 1790, one hundred and eighty-four years after the first planting of the Church of England in Virginia, Dr. Madison went over to England and was consecrated Bishop of Virginia. But nineteen years after, when the General Convention was held in Baltimore, the Bishop of Virginia considered that his duties to the college of which he was president were sufficient excuse for his absence from Convention, and the Diocese was not represented. At that Convention only Bishops White and Claggett were present, and, as Bishop Claggett was just recovering from a severe illness, it was a question not unlikely to present itself whether a single Bishop could constitute a house. Special reasons doubtless existed in some Dioceses for the weakness of the Church. In Virginia the immediate and apparent reason was the withdrawal of the stipends and seizure of the glebes by the Legislature. Patrick Henry resisted the act to the last, and as long as he lived it could never be obtained, and it was declared unconstitutional by the Supreme Court of the United States; but, aside from the illegality of the act, such was the character of many of the clergy who received the stipends and held the glebes, that, in the opinion of Bishop Meade, the loss of them was the saving of the Church, by relieving her of the burden of unworthy ministers and throwing her upon her own resources, though for a time her condition was deplorable.

The Convention of 1811 met in New Haven under serious difficulties, since out of seven Bishops in the Church there were but two present,—Bishops White and Jarvis. Bishop Claggett was prevented from attendance by sickness; Bishop Madison by the duties of his college. Bishop Provoost was in ill health. The consecration of Drs. Hobart and Griswold was necessarily postponed, and, after the Bishops had gone down to New York, it was till the last minute doubtful whether the assistance of Bishop Provoost could be obtained. He, however, "finally found himself strong enough to give his attendance, and thus the business was happily accomplished."

The Church in America was in more ways than one hampered by its English origin. The branch had been bound, and choked almost to death by long neglect before it was broken off and planted in the American soil, and it inherited many of the defects and deformities of worship and discipline of the mother-Church at that time. In its earliest dealing with its own proper missionary work it rivaled its teacher. In 1801 several clergy of Western Pennsylvania and Virginia, which were largely settled by Church people, made an effort to have the Western country organized into a separate Diocese. It was not till 1808 that General Convention gave the desired permission, which, in effect, was repeated in 1811. In 1819, Philander Chase was consecrated for Ohio; but it was not till 1825 that a Bishop was seen in Pennsylvania west of the Alleghanies. From 1800 to 1823 the clergy in Pennsylvania had only increased from 16 to 34. It is only natural to add that the Church in the western part of the State had been for many years in a state of decline, while the disposition to fraternize with those who in doctrine and discipline were the Church's enemies, and to "oppose the received properties of our Communion, or to undermine them insidiously and by degrees," saddened the last years of Bishop White's life, and made him fear, while he prayed, for the Church's existence.

In Maryland, party spirit ran so high that at Dr. Kemp's election a party endeavored to create a schism in the Church, and after the death of Bishop Stone, in 1838, it was three years, and after two elected had declined the See, that a successful choice was made.

In Virginia, the Convention which assembled to elect Bishop Moore, after Bishop Madison's death, numbered only 7 clergy and 17 laymen, and was the first which had met for seven years. In Richmond "Episcopacy was almost dead." Churchmen assured Dr. Moore that "no man could carry out our forms in all their rubrical sign;" but the man of their choice had had a different training and held different views, and acted upon them, though he was not able to carry the body of his clergy with him. The Church in Virginia, through his efforts and those of his successor, was roused from its slumbers that were almost death. Only three years before the election of Bishop Moore to Virginia, John Henry Hobart had been chosen Assistant Bishop of New York, and along with Dr. Griswold had been consecrated at a time when the Episcopate could with the greatest difficulty muster the necessary three for a consecration. He did not find the Church or the Churchmanship of New York what he left it, or what it has been ever since, but he roused his own Diocese from its slumbers, and the influence of his writing and preaching, and of his laborious and holy life, was felt in the State as well as the Diocese, and went out over the whole country and through the whole Church. •His motto was "the Gospel in the Church," and he shrunk from no labor and from no contest in behalf of his belief. Bishop White looked forward to the future of his son in the faith with the keenest hope "that he would not cease to be efficient in extending the Church and preserving her integrity," and it was fulfilled. Schools and seminaries were established, publication societies incorporated, the Board of Missions was organized, the old apologetic tone was laid aside, and the Church claimed her place and her right. It is one indication of the rapid turn of the tide that the Diocese which at his consecration contained 40 clergy, twenty-four years afterwards—five years after his death —contained 198. Not till 1819 was the first "Western" Bishop consecrated,—Philander Chase for Ohio. In 1835, the last Convention at which Bishop White presided, Jackson Kemper was consecrated the first Missionary Bishop of the Northwest, and in his sermon at the consecration Bishop Doane spoke for the Church, which was wakening to new life, when he laid down the principle that this "Church is to be a Missionary Church, that her Bishops are true Apostles, and that of this missionary body every Christian by the terms of his baptismal vow is a member."

The difference between the Church of then and now is greater than appears by any mere comparison of numbers. We read in reports of General Convention, "so many Bishops present, so many Dioceses represented;" but the bodies which they represented were smaller still. In Illinois, in 1835, "three clergymen met for organization," and "this Convention unanimously appoint Philander Chase to the Episcopate of Illinois;" and at the seventh Annual Convention the Bishop reports "that neither as pioneer missionary, as a Diocesan Bishop, or as parish minister, has he received any salary except $20." In Delaware, in 1791, 3 clergymen and 11 laymen met to frame a constitution and organize the Church. In the Peninsula of which Delaware forms part, in 1827, there were only 15 clergy, while there were 40 churches in a fit state for worship. In Kentucky the "organization of the Diocese was thus happily effected, there being 16 lay delegates and 3 of the clerical order," only one of whom was "settled." In North Carolina, where, in 1770, a list is given of 18 settled clergy, and which was organized in 1817, at Bishop Ravenscroft's death, in 1830, the clergy only numbered 11. In South Carolina, where 153 clergy are recorded as laboring from 1700 to 1800, in 1786 only 9 parishes are represented. On the other hand, South Carolina, in 1882, reports 45 clergy; North Carolina, 73, and in 1883 asks for a division; Kentucky 36 clergy; and Illinois is a province including 3 Dioceses, with 60, 26, and 45 clergy respectively.

Bishop Doane was elected to New Jersey in 1832, and died in 1858. During his Episcopate the number of communicants in New Jersey increased from 800 to 4500, the clergy from 14 to 94, and the parishes from 31 to 79. In 1882 the two Dioceses of New Jersey and Northern New Jersey report 99 clergy and nearly 8000 communicants, and 80 clergy and 8700 communicants.

The first Convention of New York, in 1785, consisted of 5 clergy and delegates from 7 parishes. In 1811, the year of Bishop Hobart's consecration, the number of clergy was 40. In 1835, five years after his death, the number was 194.

In 1882 the Dioceses of New York, Albany, Western New York, Central New York, and Long Island contained 743 clergy and 87,364 communicants.

Pennsylvania, which, in 1811, contained 20 clergy, in 1882 reports in the three Dioceses of Pennsylvania, Pittsburg, and Central Pennsylvania 352 clergy and 39,251 communicants.

Some figures presented at the General Convention of 1883 will give an idea of the general growth of the Church. In 1790 there were 7 Dioceses and 190 clergy; in 1800, 12,000 communicants. In 1832, 18 Dioceses, 592 clergy, 30,939 communicants. In 1883, 48 Dioceses and 15 missionary jurisdictions, with 67 Bishops, 3575 clergy, 4348 parishes and missions, 373,000 communicants. Between 1865 and 1883 the revenue of the Church increased from $6,471,669 to $23,217,765.

When the venerable Bishop Green took leave of the Convention of 1883, he said, "Of the Convention of 1823, which met in this city, I alone am alive. When I went into holy orders, sixty-three years ago, there were nine Bishops in the Church. When I looked around me to-day in the House of Bishops I cast my eyes upon more than seven times that number. How hath God wrought! His blessing hath been upon the Church and she hath prospered." Since 1800, when the first report is made of communicants, the increase has been over 30 to 1, while the population of the country has increased as 10 or 12 to 1.

If, however, the American Church suffered from the deadness of the English Church in the last century and in the first part of this century, it has felt in no less a degree the movement of life which has wrought such a reformation and restoration in that Church in the last forty years, and it is still feeling it. There was "in the forties" the same panic—cry of "popery"—here as in England, and the same folly has been repeated on occasion since; but wisdom has come with advancing years: only a weak handful has gone over to Rome to justify the fears, while in respect of knowledge of the Church and faith in her as a true branch of the Church Catholic, of the doctrine and practice of worship, of belief in her mission in America, there has been a general education and elevation that has brought whole "parties" forward upon ground which, forty years ago, they were almost ready to condemn as heretical. The Convention of 1844 came to the conclusion of far-sighted wisdom when, after days of excited discussion, the effort of some to procure a condemnation of the doctrine of the Oxford Tracts resulted in a vote of confidence in the "Liturgy, officers, and Articles and Canons of the Church as sufficient exponents of the sense of Holy Scripture, and affording ample means of discipline and correction." A similar result was reached in 1868, and again in 1871, when, after a protracted and brilliant discussion, the conclusion was in effect a vote of general condemnation of all ceremonies fitted to express a doctrine foreign to that set forth in the authorized standards of the Church, and expressing confidence in the paternal counsel and advice of the Right Reverend Fathers.

Some untoward events require to be noticed. The trial and suspension of the two brothers, Bishop Henry W. Onderdonk, of Pennsylvania, in 1844, and of Bishop Benjamin T. Onderdonk, of New York, in 1846, demonstrated at least the power of discipline that existed in the Church. The attempted "trial" of Bishop Doane (1849–53) resulted not only in his triumphant acquittal, and in "making the trial of a Bishop hard," but established firmly the principles of order upon which an Episcopal Church must stand. Bishop Ives, in 1853, set the only example of a Bishop of this Church perverting to Rome. In 1873, Bishop Cummins became the leader of the only schism which has rent the Church, and which has effectually taught us the lesson that all the treachery and danger does not lurk on one side of the camp. The "Reformed Episcopal Church," commonly known as the "Cumminsite movement," still continues to exist for our warning.

A real danger was escaped at the close of the civil war of 1861–65. During the war the Southern Dioceses had organized themselves under the title of the "Church in the Confederate States," and in the General Convention of 1862, which met in the midst of the war, none of them were represented. But in 1865, at the close of the war, two Southern Bishops presented themselves at the General Convention, and the reunion of the once politically-divided Church was happily and thoroughly effected. All signs of that division have long passed away, and no others appear to disturb us or to hinder our progress.

At the Convention of 1880 the new arrangement went into operation, by which the Convention is made the Board of Missions, and the session was marked by a new interest in the subject of missions. Three new missionary jurisdictions were set off and Bishops elected. The special work of the Convention of 1883 was dealing with the report of the committee on enrichment of the Prayer-Book. To some this work, and that of missions, seem to partake of the same character of catholicity with the final action upon doctrine and ritual in former Conventions, and either are a far more worthy subject of the attention of the Convention than the length of a cassock, or the conversation in a seminary student's room. It is believed that the development of the missionary work of the Church and the work of enrichment of the Prayer-Book will make the Conventions of 1880 and 1883, in the future judgment of the Church, among the most important Conventions that have been held.

The American Church is not without weak points in her constitution, some of which she inherited, and for some of which the neglect and exposure of her early existence are responsible.

The pew-system, which makes it a possible and not improbable thing that the poor shall be excluded from the house of the Lord; the vestry system and delegate system of most Dioceses, which makes it not impossible that the body on which depends the calling and supporting of a rector, and the lay portion of that body which elects the Bishop, may be composed of unbaptized unbelievers; the want of endowments, which makes the living of the clergy a precarious hire; the small salaries which hinder young men from entering the ministry, and which produce frequent changes of parishes; the disposition of the lay-power and the purse-power to tyrannize over the clergy;—these are some of the special forms of evil in our constitution, though not one of them is peculiar to us. On the other hand, there are some advantages which are the result of the independence of Church and State in this country which it would be difficult to overestimate. The Church in America is absolutely free from state control. She has only to speak the word to be absolutely free from the control of official worldliness. She is free to carry on her own affairs in her own way. Her failures and successes are her own. She has a fair field and no favor. Her relation to the state is that of the primitive Church, with the added advantage of being respected instead of persecuted. She is in the midst of a hundred different religious bodies, and in the eye of the state she is one among the hundred. But her real position in her own eyes is that she offers a centre of union for them all, and occupies the ground of apostolic order and evangelic truth, towards which all of them are tending, and where all can stand together. Her past history furnishes no ground for boasting, but much for gratitude and encouragement. The days of doubt and darkness have passed away; she no longer apologizes for existence or hesitates to assert her claims. Let us hope that the days of division and doubting each other have passed away also. The present is full of encouragement. The future is in the hands of them that believe and lay hold of it.

Authorities: Wilberforce's American Church, S. P. G. Documents, Bp. Perry's Hand-book of Gen. Conv., Bp. White's Memoirs, Bp. Meade's Churches of Virginia, Life of Bp. Hopkins, Sermon of Bp. Morris. REV. L. W. GIBSON.

Amice. A vestment worn on the shoulders over the cassock and covering the neck. Apparently it was a sort of cape which could be drawn over the head. It was in use in pagan times, but the earliest use of it mentioned in England was in the tenth century. It was later a sort of fur cape. If, as is now held, the vestments were varieties of the usual dress which, being made of richer material and with more costly ornamentation, were used in the services, the amice was evidently used as a protection from the cold. When it was used as a distinct and sacred vestment, the mystical meaning of it was that it denoted the Helmet of Salvation, and a short prayer was recited when it was put on, imploring the overshadowing of the HOLY SPIRIT.

Amos, whose name signifies "burden," was of the herdsmen of Tekoah, a village not far from Bethlehem, and probably, though nowhere so recorded, a native of the place, as his tomb was shown there in the time of St. Jerome. It was in the days of Uzziah, King of Judah, and of Jeroboam II., King of Israel, that he was called to deliver GOD'S message against the nations neighboring to Israel and Judah, and especially against the northern kingdom of Israel. The date of his prophecy is variously assigned to the years between 808 B.C. and 784 B.C., during which period these kings were contemporary.

Amos declares of himself that he was not the son of a prophet, nor trained in any school of prophets (chap. vii. 14), but that it was from feeding his flocks and gathering the fruits of the sycamore (*Ficus Sycamorus*) that the LORD took him and said, "Go, prophesy unto my people Israel."

This statement of his occupation and manner of life is corroborated by many expressions in the prophecy, which show the author to be a man accustomed to out-door life, observant of nature and familiar with the care of cattle (see chap. ii. 9, 13; iii. 4, 5, 12; iv. 1, 2, 9; v. 8; vii. 1; ix. 9, 13). Yet this prophet's language is not that of an unlettered or ignorant man, as it exhibits great natural powers of thought, of observation, and experience, and further presupposes a popular acquaintance with the Pentateuch, and implies ceremonies of religion (though corrupted by Jeroboam) in accordance with the law of Moses. The prophecy displays a remarkable unity throughout, and was probably put into its present form by the author himself; it may be analyzed into four principal parts, viz.: I. Chap. i. to ii. 3. A general denunciation against various nations connected with Judah and Israel; II. Chap. ii. 4, to vi. 14. Prophecies against Judah, and especially against Israel; III. Chap. vii. to ix. 10. An account of the prophet's visit to Bethel, and a series of visions or prophetical symbols; IV. Chap. ix. 10 to end. An evangelical prophecy foretelling the day when the fallen tabernacle of David shall be raised up again, and the hope of the MESSIAH'S kingdom shall be fulfilled. The vigor, beauty, and freshness of the prophet's style have been acknowledged from the earliest times. It is true St. Jerome calls him " rude in speech, but not in knowledge," but the opinion of Bishop Lowth is far otherwise, as follows: "Let any person who has candor and perspicacity enough to judge, not from the man, but from his writings, open the volume of his predictions, and he will, I think, agree with me that our shepherd 'is not a whit behind the very chief of the prophets.' He will agree that as in sublimity and magnificence he is almost equal to the greatest, so in splendor of diction and elegance of expression he is scarcely inferior to any." (Lowth's Lectures on Hebrew Poetry.)

There is a tradition that Amos suffered martyrdom at the hands of his offended countrymen, but there is no sure foundation for the assertion, which might easily have been a development of Amaziah's complaint to Jeroboam, "Amos hath conspired against thee in the midst of the House of Israel ; the land is not able to bear all his words."

Authorities: Bible Commentary, Smith's Dictionary of Bible, Pusey's Minor Prophets.

Amphibalum. A name for a part of the ecclesiastical dress used in Gaul. Its Greek derivation is one of the minor proofs that the Gallican Church received so much of its details as well as its foundation from the East. The word was synonymous with *casula*, or *chasuble*, and was probably a heavy outer garment worn in bad weather; but as its texture and use were modified in course of time it passed into ecclesiastical use, and became a part of the vestments in the service. It was seamless, or rather united from top to bottom without any slit for the hands, without sleeves. It is probably identical with the phenoleon worn by the Eastern Bishops.

Analogy of Faith (Rom. xii. 6. A. V. "proportion of the faith"). It is evident that faith here is not the act of the mind, whether as a "saving faith" or merely belief. It must be compared (Eph. iv.) "with One Faith," and, Jude v. 3, "the Faith once delivered to the saints." It must therefore stand for the body of the doctrines whose contents are the object of faith. If so, it will be necessary to compare it with 2 Tim. i. 13, "the form of sound words." Now reverting to Rom. xii. 6, "Having therefore gifts differing according to the grace given us, whether prophecy, let us prophesy according to the proportion [analogy] of the Faith," the only fair conclusion that can be drawn is that there was a distinct body of doctrinal statements universally received, for St. Paul had no authority over the Christians at Rome, and therefore spoke of not what he might have ordained, but of what all received together, and to which the teacher was to conform his public teaching. It points to an apostolic form of the Creed; but without pressing this so far, this phrase of the Apostle's shows that already there was a criterion by which all teachers should be guided, and which was received as authoritative. It is clear that at that date, 58 A.D., there was no body of Christian literature such as the New Testament now is that could claim that position. Therefore if it was not a Creed, as we now mean by this word, it was something equivalent to it. Again, there follows the necessity for us now to use the same restraint, not selecting such texts as suit our views, but using them all fairly, *i.e.*, according to the proportion of the Faith. Compare Article XX. in the XXXIX. Articles : "The Church hath power to decree Rites or Ceremonies and authority in Controversies of Faith ; and yet it is not lawful for the Church to ordain anything that is contrary to GOD'S Word, written: *neither may it so expound one place of Scripture that it be repugnant to another.* Wherefore, although the Church be a Witness and a Keeper of Holy Writ, yet as it ought not to decree anything against the same, so besides the same it ought not to enforce anything to be believed for necessity of salvation."

Anaphora. (*Gr.* lifting up; offering; *cf.* Heb. vii. 27, offering sacrifices; thence the oblation at the Holy Communion.) The term Anaphora is, then, equivalent to our Lift up your hearts. The whole subject will come up under the word Liturgy, but it may be well here to compare the Eastern Liturgy with our own. Omitting the preparation, we have—

Preface.	Lift up your hearts.
Prayer of the Triumphal Hymn.	Preface.
Triumphal Hymn.	Sanctus.
Commemoration of our LORD'S Life.	All glory be to Thee, etc.
Commemoration of institution.	And did institute, etc.
Words of institution for the Bread.	He took bread.
Words of institution for the Wine.	Likewise.
Oblation of the Body and Blood.	Wherefore, O LORD, etc.
Prayer for the Descent of the HOLY GHOST. Prayer for the change of the Elements	And we most humbly, etc. " " " "
General intercession for Quick and Dead.	*Cf.* Prayer for CHRIST, Church Militant, and Here we offer and present, etc.
Prayer before the LORD'S Prayer. LORD'S Prayer. Embolismus. Prayer after LORD'S Prayer.	Nothing directly parallel in our Prayer-book
Prayer of inclination Holy things to Holy Persons.	
Fraction. Confession.	ALMIGHTY GOD Maker of all.
Communion.	Communion.
Antidoro, or Thanksgiving.	Almighty and ever Living GOD.

But this, though the general order, was not invariable. The preceding preparation (proanaphora) was far less changed than this which we now would shrink from changing. Our own Prayer-Book has, in the placing the Invocation in the office, drawn more nearly to the Eastern rule than have any other of the Western Churches

Anathema. (*Gr.* a devoted thing or offering. A cutting off from the offices and privileges of the Church of an obstinate offender.) Anathema was the greater, as Aphorismos or Separation was the lesser, excommunication. It is the extremest act of discipline that can be inflicted. It was based upon the words of our Lord, "If he will not hear the Church, let him be as an heathen man and a publican." "He must be a grievous and scandalous sinner, notorious, under accusation and conviction." St. Paul used the term five times, and always to express strong feeling of condemnation. It was derived from the Septuagint translation by the New Testament writers, and was understood by them in its deepest spiritual sense, not merely formal exclusion from the Church's privileges, but a most serious, nay, fatal loss to the soul. "If any man love not the Lord Jesus Christ let him be anathema." The anathema was directed against heresies, as they were the preaching of another Gospel. The form occurs in the declaration appended to the Nicene Creed. (*Vide* Nicene Creed.) "But those who say, 'Once He was not,' and, 'Before He was begotten He was not,' and, 'He came into existence out of nothing;' or who say that 'The Son of God is of another substance, or essence, or is created or mutable or changeable,' the Catholic and Apostolic Church anathematizes." The consent or the refusal to subscribe to this formed the test. The anathema was afterwards used in several enactments by succeeding Councils, but the most notable were the twelve anathemas launched by Cyril of Alexandria against Nestorius at the Council of Ephesus, 430 A.D., and the Canon then passed, and re-enacted at Chalcedon, 451 A.D., threatening the anathema against the layman who should issue a Creed in place of the Nicene, also the anathema against all past heresies enacted by the fifth General Council of Constantinople (553 A.D.).

But later it became fearfully abused. Of course its binding power is only as the anathema defends a truth of Holy Writ, or cuts off an offender against it. But the terror it inspired was so great that many times it was utterly perverted. It was launched against the offender with solemn tolling of bells. Its terms were recited by the Bishop sitting before the altar in full vestments, with twelve priests in attendance holding each a lighted candle, which, as the last terrible words of the curse were uttered, were dashed upon the pavement. Hence the phrase "Cursed with Bell, Book, and Candle." Its misuse, while it wrought great and often irreparable mischief, overreached itself, and it was often set at naught at later times.

But the English Church has been singularly cautious in pronouncing any anathema. It occurs once in the Article (XIII.) upon obtaining eternal salvation only by the name of Christ, following closely in temper the example of St. Paul.

Anchoret. A person who lives apart; a hermit. (*Vide* Hermit.)

Ancyra. In the year 314 A.D. a Council was held at Ancyra by some eighteen Bishops, among whom were Vitalis of Antioch, Marcellus of Ancyra, Lupus of Tarsus, and Amphion of Epiphania. Their consultations were embodied in 24 Canons, chiefly relating to the treatment of such as had fallen in times of persecution. Canon 10 allows those to marry who, on receiving Deacons' orders, declare their purpose to do so; but forbids marriage, under pain of deposition, to those who are ordained professing continenee; Canon 13 forbids Chorepiscopi to ordain without permission in writing, from the Bishop.

Another Council was held at Ancyra in 358 A.D. by Basil of Ancyra and George of Laodicea, with a party of Semi-Arian Bishops. This Council condemned the doctrine of the pure Arians, and put forth an exposition of their faith, in which they affirmed that the Son was of *like* substance with the Father; meaning it to be inferred that He was not of the *same* substance; they condemned the term *consubstantial*, and, on the other hand, they also condemned the Arian formulary of faith called the Second Creed of Sirmium.

Andrew, St., surnamed Protolectos, or first-called, was a native of Galilee. He was the son of Jona, and, together with his brother Simon, he followed the occupation of fishing. Bethsaida, a small town on the Sea of Galilee, was their birthplace. Little mention is made of St. Andrew individually in the Gospels, yet a good judgment of his character may be formed from that little. He was probably older than his brother Simon, since he first attended the preaching of John the Baptist. When he heard the declaration of John, "*Behold the Lamb of God*" as he saw Jesus approaching, Andrew (after his interview with Christ, in company with St. John) went first to his brother, to whom he told of his finding the Messiah, and whom as a brotherly duty he brought to Jesus. He was of a devotional turn of mind, seeking earnestly for the truth himself, and desiring to bring others to the knowledge of it. After this first interview with his future Lord it is conjectured that more than a year passed before the formal call to the two brothers took place, which was after the miraculous draught of fishes on the Sea of Galilee, when, with their partners, James and John, "they forsook all and followed Him" (St. Luke v. 11).

There are but two other circumstances in St. Andrew's life mentioned in the Gospels, the first in St. John's Gospel, ch. xii. 21, where he brings the inquiring Greeks to Jesus, and the other in St. Mark, ch. xiii. 9, when Peter, James, John, and Andrew inquire privately of their Lord concerning the destruction of Jerusalem.

Ecclesiastical history, however, gives an

account of the labors of St. Andrew. He went, after the dispersion of the Apostles, to Scythia, Cappadocia, and Bithynia, converting many to the faith and establishing Churches. From thence he went to Sarmatia, a portion of Russia that borders on the Black Sea, and for this he is called the Founder of the Russian Church, and is honored as their titular saint. Sinope and Sebastopol are both connected with the name of St. Andrew. Having suffered many persecutions he returned to Jerusalem. On his way he tarried at Byzantium, where he instructed the inhabitants in the religion of CHRIST and founded a Church, over which he consecrated "the beloved Stachys" as first Bishop.

He traveled after this into Thrace, Macedonia, and Achaia, where for many years he preached the faith, and at last gave his great testimony to its truth by laying down his life in its defense.

The account of his martyrdom is very affecting. At an advanced age he was called before the proconsul, at Patras, a city of Achaia, on the Gulf of Lepanto, and required to cease from preaching the Christian doctrine. Instead of complying he proclaimed CHRIST even before the judgment-seat of Ægeus, the proconsul, who was so enraged that he commanded the aged Apostle to be imprisoned and scourged seven times on his naked back, and then to be fastened to a cross with cords, that his sufferings might be prolonged. This cross differed from the upright cross, and was called the cross decussate, from the Roman numeral X.

When the suffering Apostle came near to this instrument of torture, he fell on his knees and addressed to it this famous invocation, "Hail, precious cross! thou hast been consecrated by the Body of my LORD and adorned with His limbs as with rich jewels. I come to thee exulting and glad; receive me into thine arms. Oh, good cross, I have ardently loved thee; long have I desired thee and sought thee; now thou art found by me and art made ready for my longing soul; receive me into thine arms, taking me from among men, and present me to my MASTER, that He who redeemed me *on* thee may receive me *by* thee." For two days the dying martyr preached to the people from the cross, at the end of which time the people importuned the proconsul that he might be taken down; but the blessed Apostle prayed earnestly to the LORD that he might at this time seal the truth with his blood, when he instantly expired, November 30, in the year 70 A.D.

The feast of St. Andrew, on which the beginning of Advent depends, is considered the beginning of the Christian year, and is of very ancient date, being one of those for which an Epistle and Gospel are provided in the Lectionary of St. Jerome, and which has also prayers provided for it in the Sacramentary of St. Gregory. The relics of St Andrew, which had been preserved in Constantinople for thirteen centuries, on the taking of that city by the Turks were dispersed throughout Christendom. He is called the patron saint of Scotland and Russia, and three orders of knighthood bear his emblem (the *Crux decussata*), the Scotch order of the Thistle, the Burgundian order of the Golden Fleece, and the Russian order of the Cross of St. Andrew, and for nearly three centuries this cross has been borne on the national banner of Great Britain.

Angels. "Which are spirits, immaterial and intellectual, the glorious inhabitants of those sacred palaces where nothing but light and blessed immortality, no shadow of matter for tears, discontentments, griefs, and uncomfortable passions to work upon, but all joy, tranquillity, and peace, never for ever and ever, doth dwell. As in number they are huge, mighty, and royal armies, so likewise in perfection of obedience unto that law which the Highest, whom they adore, love, and imitate, hath imposed upon them, such observants they are thereof, that our SAVIOUR Himself, being to set down the perfect idea of that which we are to pray and wish for on earth, did not teach to pray or wish for more, than only that here it might be with us, as with them it is in heaven. Beholding the face of GOD, they adore Him: being rapt with love of His beauty, they cleave unto Him: desiring to resemble Him, they long to do good unto all His creatures, and especially unto the children of men." (Hooker.)

" How oft do they their silver bowers leave
To come to succor us, that succor want!
How oft do they with golden pinions cleave
The flitting skies, like flying pursuivang,
Against foul fiends to aid us militant!
They for us fight, they watch and duly war,
And their bright squadrons round about us plant,
And all for love, and nothing for reward,—
O why should heavenly GOD to men have such regard?"
(Spencer.)

It certainly does not lessen the wonder, while perhaps it leads towards an answer to the question, if we believe that the appearances which are ascribed in the Old Testament to the Angel JEHOVAH (" the angel of the LORD") were Theophanies,—manifestations of GOD,—and that "the angel of the LORD" is the LORD of the angels, and not one of the angelic host. It is very evident that He who appears to Abraham in the plains of Mamre and in the land of Moriah, to Lot in Sodom, to Hagar in the Wilderness, to Jacob in Haran (Gen. xvi. 7; xviii. 1; xix. 1; xxii. 11; xxxi. 11, 13), to Moses in the bush, to Balaam, at Bochim to the people, to Gideon, to Manoah, to Elijah the Tishbite, is one who assumes the authority, exercises the power, and is called by the name of JEHOVAH and GOD (Num. xxii. 35; Judges ii. 1; vi. 11; xiii. 18; 2 Kings i. 3, 15). Other later cases there are where the angel is plainly the minister and messenger of JEHOVAH, as in the vision of David at the threshing floor, and at the destruction of the Assyrians and in the vision of Zachariah (2 Sam. xxiv

16; 2 Kings xix. 35; Zech. i. 12). But in the instances which have been cited, even where a distinction seems to be made, He whom JEHOVAH calls "Mine angel" is named by Isaiah "the angel of His presence" (Ex. xxiii. 20; xxxii. 34; Is. lxiii. 9), and by JEHOVAH Himself it is said "my presence shall go with thee, and I will give thee rest" (Ex. xxxiii. 14). And whether we understand with the earlier Fathers that "the angel of the Father is the LORD and GOD," or, with St. Augustine, that the Theophanies were "self-manifestations of GOD through a created being" (Liddon, Bamp. Lec.), the fact of those divine manifestations is the same. The Angel JEHOVAH is the LORD of the angels.

And they are His creatures and servants. We need not pause to consider the reasonableness of a belief, which all races and generations of men share, in the existence of orders of beings higher than man and between man and GOD, nearer to GOD than man is, holier and wiser, and, on the other hand, having relations of duty towards men,—the fact that all men do share it proves its reasonableness. What we have to consider, as servants of the same LORD, who has set them before us as our examples of obedience to His will, is, what He has revealed to us in His Word concerning them. And the instruction which He has given us is by no means so meagre as is sometimes supposed.

In the Old Testament, aside from those instances which have been cited, and which were with few exceptions evident manifestations of the Divine presence, the instances in which the angels are named are not many, but they are pregnant with meaning. Abraham saw three (Gen. xviii. 2, 3), of whom One was pre-eminent; Lot, two (ch. xix. 1). But He whom Joshua saw is Captain of the LORD's host (Josh. v. 4). The Psalmist names "the chariots of GOD, thousands of angels" (Ps. lxviii. 17), "whom He maketh spirits" (Ps. civ.), " whom He giveth charge concerning" His people, who "excel in strength" (Ps. xci 11; ciii. 20). Jacob saw them ascending and descending on the ladder from earth to heaven (Gen. xxviii. 12). Isaiah "saw the LORD high and lifted up, and His train filled the temple, and above it stood the seraphim, crying one to another, 'Holy, Holy, Holy'" (Is. vi. 1). Ezekiel saw "the cherubims of GOD," "the living creatures," "in the visions of GOD by the river of Chebar" (Ezek. x. 20). In Daniel's vision the angel Gabriel—"man of GOD"— is his teacher, and angels are the princes of the kingdoms, of whom Michael is one of the chief,—Michael, "who like GOD?" (Dan. ix. 16; x. 13).

In 2 Esdras the angel, who is sent to instruct the prophet, is named Uriel, "the flame of GOD" (Esd. iv. 1), one of "the innumerable multitude of angels gathered together" (ch. vi. 3), whose hosts stand trembling before the LORD (2 Esd. viii. 21). The angel's name in Tobit is Raphael, "one of the seven holy angels which present the prayers of the saints, and which go in and out before the Holy One" (ch. xii. 15), one not to be feared, but who served men "not of any favor of mine, but by the will of our GOD," as the angel who talked with St. John forbade his worship, "for I am thy fellow-servant" (Rev. xxii. 9).

But it is in the Christian Scriptures in the light of the "manifestation of GOD in the flesh" that we have the fullest evidence and doctrine of the angels of GOD. We can believe, we can almost understand, that His coming from heaven must have opened the way and brought the atmosphere and the angelic attendance of heaven with Him to the earth. An angel announced the birth of His forerunner (St. Luke i. 1, 27; ii. 10). The angel Gabriel saluted His virgin mother with the promise of His conception and birth. A multitude of the heavenly host attended the angel that announced His birth to the shepherds. An angel warned and guided Joseph (Matt. i. 20, 24). Angels delivered Him from the hand of Herod. Angels ministered to Him in His temptation (Matt. iv. 11). An angel comforted Him in Gethsemane (St. Luke xxii. 43). Legions of angels were at His bidding when He was betrayed (St. Matt. xxii. 53). Angels announced His resurrection (St. John xx. 14). Angels accompanied His ascension (Acts i. 10). Far above all angels He sitteth now. Before Him angels bow and veil their faces as they worship (Heb. i. 7). The voice of the archangel shall herald His coming to judgment (St. Luke iv. 16). With all holy angels He shall come (St. Matt. xxv. 31). Angels shall summon quick and dead before His throne (St. Luke xii. 8). Before angels He shall confess them that have confessed Him, and deny them that have denied Him. Angels shall be His ministers of reward and punishment (St. Matt. xiii. 39).

They differ from us and excel us, these glorious creatures of GOD, in many things, but most of all in holiness and obedience. They are wonderful in knowledge, in appearance glorious, great in power, in dignity exalted, in number "an innumerable company," "thousand thousands and ten thousand times ten thousand." These are they whom we understand by "the elect angels" (1 Tim. v. 21), who have passed the ordeal before which others fall, have "kept their first estate" (Jude 6), and will keep it forever. And yet these glorious and immortal beings are but creatures, and finite creatures. They are so far beyond us that the "worshiping of angels" (Col. ii. 18) would be the natural impulse of humility and of reverence for the infinite GOD. But they themselves forbid such worship. "Stand up," said St. Peter; "I also am a man" (Acts x. 26). And in the same spirit the angel forbade St. John, "I am thy fellow-servant, worship GOD" (Rev. xxii. 8). But, "let all the angels of GOD worship

Him," for "by Him, the SON, were all things created, that are in Heaven, and that are in earth, visible and invisible, whether they be thrones, or dominions, or principalities, or powers: all things were created by Him and for Him, and by Him all things consist" (Col. i. 16). Finite, therefore, in power, for they were created; finite in magnitude, for space contains them; finite in knowledge, "desiring to look into" (1 Pet. i. 12) the mysteries of CHRIST, so that the Apostles of the LORD are "a spectacle to them" (1 Cor. iv. 9), and "even to the principalities and powers in heavenly places is made known by the Church the manifold wisdom of GOD" (Eph. iii. 11), and of the future ignorant. As compared with us wise; but "He chargeth His angels with folly" (Job iv. 18). As compared with us Holy, but a great host of them has fallen. The great leader of that fallen host, so great that he could make "war in Heaven" (Rev. xii. 7-9), and on earth so divide the kingdom of GOD that in the very presence of the SON of GOD he could offer Him all the kingdoms of the earth and the glories of them, is a fallen angel (St. Matt. iv. 9; 2 Cor. iv. 4).

Of that glorious host of the elect Heaven is the home. Of them alone, there they alone—the judgment is not yet, and all men wait for it—worship and adore and do the will of their GOD. There they worship and adore Him that sitteth upon the throne and the Lamb. "When He bringeth the first-begotten into the world He saith, Let all the angels of GOD worship Him" (Heb. i. 6). And angels worship Him who sitteth upon the throne in human form, who "took not on Him the nature of angels, but He took on Him the seed of Abraham" (Heb. ii. 16), "the Man CHRIST JESUS" (1 Tim. iii. 5), "the SON of whom He saith Thy Throne, O GOD, is for ever and ever" (Heb. i. 8).

But their work is not all done in Heaven. "Are they not all ministering spirits, sent forth to minister to them that shall be heirs of salvation?" (Heb. i. 14) The existence of them that do the will of GOD in Heaven is no life of idleness. They are the fellow-servants of Him who is the LORD and the SAVIOUR of men. They are the agents of GOD and the means of intercourse between earth and Heaven. It is no novel interpretation to read, "He maketh His angels to be winds, and His ministers a flame of fire." The fires on Mount Sinai were the work of angels. An angel troubled the waters of Bethesda. In the Apocalypse we read of angels restraining the four winds. Works of vengeance, the destruction of Sodom and Gomorrah by the fiery lava of volcanoes, the destruction of Sennecharib's hosts by means, it is supposed, of a suffocating wind, the pestilence in Israel when David numbered the people, the smiting of the earth in the Apocalypse, are ascribed to angels. Nature is not inanimate. Its toils are duties. "For all things serve Thee." "And every breath of air, and every ray of heat and light, every beautiful prospect, is, as it were, the skirts of their garments, the waving of the robes of those gracious and holy beings, whose faces see GOD in Heaven. And I put it to any one whether it is not as philosophical, and as full of intellectual enjoyment, to refer the movements of the natural world to them as to attempt to explain them by certain theories of science, useful as these are, and capable of a religious application." (Newman.)

They guarded, led, and fed His Church in the wilderness (Ps. lxxviii. 25). They watch over nations. They watch over men. "The angel of the LORD campeth round about" (Ps. xxxiv. 7); "and lo! the whole mountain round about was full of horses and chariots of fire round about the prophet" (2 Kings vi. 17). They are the instruments of mercies and punishments (2 Sam. xxiv. 16). They bear the prayers of men up to GOD (Rev. viii. 3). They watch over little children (ch. xxvi.). "Of such is the kingdom of Heaven," and "their angels do always behold the face of my FATHER which is in Heaven" (St. Matt. xviii. 10). They are present in the assemblies of Christians; the reason for their decency and order is "because of the angels" (Eccl. v. 6; 1 Cor. xi. 10). They are GOD'S messengers to men (Acts viii. 26; x. 4), and under the guise of strangers and needy "some have entertained angels unawares" (Heb. xiii. 2). They watch over the living, and there is joy in the presence of the angels of GOD over one sinner that repenteth." And when Lazarus, the beggar, dies, they "carry his soul to Abraham's bosom" (St. Luke vii. 39; xv. 10).

Their work is of a kind that to our pride and envy (the devil's own sins) seem irksome and unworthy (1 Tim. iii. 6; Wis. ii. 24). But "the angelic life is passed between Heaven and earth" (Leighton), and in their eyes it is "Glory to GOD on high" where there is "peace on earth, good-will towards men," and nothing which is worthy of the care and love of GOD is beneath their attention. What we learn about them shows us that there is close connection between these two portions of the one kingdom,—the visible and the invisible. It is not without meaning that the Apostolic Liturgies repeat the very forms of words and of worship which the shepherds heard, and which were revealed to Isaiah and St. John (St. Luke ii. 14; Is. vi. 3; Rev. iv. 4-11). So Moses was bidden to "make all things according to the pattern showed to thee in the mount" (Heb. viii. 5). May it not be for a like reason that as the name of Malachi signifies "my Angel," and his prophecy of John the Baptist is "Behold, I send my angel before Thy face" (Mal. iii. 1), so in the letters to the Churches of Asia the LORD chooses to name the Chief Pastors not Apostles or Bishops, but by the very name of those ministering spirits which were about His throne? The men on earth officers in the Church visible, and the Spirits in Heaven officers of the Church invisible, are knit together in the same Communion of Saints, set to do the same will of GOD, and called by the same name of "Angels" (Rev. i. 20).

What St. John saw in Heaven it is for the Church to reflect on earth, and so to do the will of our Father. In their worship, its order, harmony, beauty, constancy, they show us who, and who alone, is the object of our worship,—not spirits of the dead and "souls yet under the altar" (Rev. vi. 9), not even their glorious selves, but "the LORD GOD ALMIGHTY, which was, and is, and is to come" (Rev. iv. 8), and how He is to be worshiped. And in their ministrations, making His will theirs, caring for what He cares for, seeking His glory because they are Holy and His, they show us what is to be the spirit and the manner of our work. The LORD tells us who they shall be that in the resurrection shall inherit the kingdom and be "as the angels" (St. Luke xx. 36), those who have like them ministered to "these his brethren" (St. Matt. xxv. 40). They have confessed Him here, and He shall confess them before the angels. They have followed and worshiped Him here, and there as here, "with angels and archangels and all the company of Heaven, they shall laud and magnify His glorious name, evermore praising Him and saying, Holy, Holy, Holy, LORD GOD of Hosts. Heaven and earth are full of Thy Glory. Glory be to Thee, O LORD, Most High."

REV. L. W. GIBSON.

Anglican. The Angles were one of the tribes of Teutonic sea-robbers that descended upon the coasts of England, drove the ancient Britons back to the mountains of Cornwall and Wales, and established themselves as permanent residents on the soil. For some occult reason, perhaps for its euphony, their name has been perpetuated in English and England.

The term Anglican is now commonly applied to the National Church of England, as the term Gallican is to the National Church of France,—the ancient Gaul,—Coptic to the Church of the Copts, or Russian to the Oriental Church in Russia.

These are national terms. They evince the important fact that while the Catholic Church is one over all Christendom and remains one and the same into whatever land her missionaries penetrate, still she conforms herself to national peculiarities. The customs, the tastes and habits, with the mode of thought and action, which distinguish the nations from each other, enter even into the national forms of religion. While the Anglican is, as she claims to be, the One, Holy, Catholic Church in England, she has her own English modes of Liturgical worship, and her special terms and ways of theological teaching. The Anglican Church was originated among the Britons in Apostolic times and was revived among the Anglo-Saxons, 598 A.D., by Augustine and his companion monks, who was induced by Gregory the Great, a Bishop of Rome, to enter upon a mission at Canterbury. The Roman Bishop pursued the same policy towards England that was so successful towards the other nations of Western Europe. His claim of supremacy was rejected at first by the British Christians, and was never tamely submitted to by the English Church or people. Even Hildebrand (Gregory VII.), while grinding under his heel the crown of the Holy Roman Empire in the person of Henry IV. of Germany, was careful not to turn the screws of his usurpations too tightly upon William of Normandy, conqueror of England. John was the first of the kings of England to acknowledge the temporal and spiritual lordship of the Pope, but even then the barons, who were the representative English people, wrung from him the Magna Charta, in which the phrase "our Church of England" shows that the nation itself rejected the uncatholic claims of the Roman Pontiff. At last, after many vicissitudes, the English Convocation, 1537 A.D., finally resisted successfully the Roman usurpations, and the National Church of England became, as she still remains, free from foreign control. She became only the more distinctly Catholic by rejecting the uncatholic assumptions of the Pope. The Gallican Church was at least equally restive under the Papal grip, but she now, like other National Churches of Western Europe, has been forced to succumb. The Anglican Church, however, maintains successfully her national autonomy. While recognizing the authority of the whole Church Catholic, and remaining ready to obey it should it ever be clearly and legitimately exercised, she supports the right of National Churches to conduct their peculiarly national affairs without foreign intervention.

What the Anglican Church claims for herself she allows to others. Both the Scottish and Irish Churches have their own Liturgies, canons of discipline, and general self-rule, while they keep up reciprocal communion with England. The English colonies being essentially parts of England, their Churches are branching outgrowths that still retain not only organic union with the "Church of England," but canonical conjunction with her.

The Church in America, though descending through both the English and Scottish lines of the Apostolic Episcopacy, is properly not Anglican. Here, as in England, in France, and in other countries, the Catholic Church is one in organic union with the universal Body of CHRIST, holding to the one succession under the one LORD, with the one faith and the one baptism, but she is already, and is more and more manifesting herself to be a distinctively national Church. She feels the current of progress, and while doing all she can to purify it and keep in the ways of truth and holiness, she does not madly and foolishly throw herself athwart it. Her mission is primarily and chiefly to the American people, and she is fast developing an American type of Catholic doctrine and practice.

The Anglican Church has no authority in the Church in the United States. She has rightfully great influence through the writings of her scholars living and dead, as well as through her noble example; but the daughter has a domain and household of her own which she holds directly under the one LORD, and by the grace of His presence she is bearing her witness to His name, winning souls to His glory, constructing forms of worship adapted to her time and sphere, and learning fast so to teach the one Faith that it shall take up into itself, after American methods, the best thought and purest life of the American people.

REV. B. FRANKLIN, D.D.

Annates. The revenues or profits of one year, and so far synonymous with first fruits. They were the revenues of the Bishopric for the first year after the consecration of the Bishop to his See. They were a tribute paid to the Papacy. They arose from the disposal made of the accruing rents, tithes, and payments due, though the Bishopric were vacant. Who was to enjoy them? The temptation to the Bishop over vacant benefices, and to the Metropolitan in the case of the vacant See, was to keep the See vacant and to appropriate the revenues, or else to require from the Bishop-elect the payment of the first year's incomes. This right, or rather, usurpation, passed on to the Pope. The beginning of the practice is said to have begun with Pope Gregory (600 A.D.), but it did not finally take the burdensome shape it attained till about 1253 A.D., when Innocent III., by granting to Henry III. the Episcopal revenues for three years, obtained the royal aid in fixing the claim upon the clergy for the Papacy. It formed part of the complaints made for centuries before the Reformation. It is estimated that in the forty-five years between 1486 and 1531 the equivalent of $225,000 a year was paid to the Popes by English Bishops in the form of annates alone. In 1531 the Convocation of Canterbury applied to the crown for relief, and a conditional act was passed, by which a compromise was offered to the Pope. As no notice was taken of it, the act was confirmed by letters patent two years later. Annates in a less burdensome shape have ever since been paid to the crown by every Bishop and every priest holding a benefice above a certain amount of annual value. But this revenue was applied to the benefit of the clergy by Queen Anne's Bounty Act, and is now chiefly used for building parsonages.

Annotine Easter. The meaning of the word is doubtful, but the most probable explanation is that it was the anniversary Sunday of those who had been baptized the previous years, as this was usually administered at Easter-tide; yet, if observed on the actual Sunday the year following, it might fall very much later, or before the Easter of that year. This will explain why it could fall on such varying dates. It does not appear to have been kept up, as it was obsolete (*antiquus*) in 1100 A.D., when Micrologus mentioned it in his treatise.

Annunciation. The Feast of the Annunciation of the Angel Gabriel to the Virgin Mary. The feast commemorating this event is said to date earlier than 492 A.D., for in the Sacramentary of Gelasius there is an Epistle, Gospel, and Collect, but the actual day observed varied. However, the Sacramentary has had interpolations, and no undoubted proof for the observance of the feast can be traced higher than the Spanish Council of Toledo (656 A.D.), which ordered that, as the feast day would fall in Lent, it should be observed in December, in accordance with the Laodicean Canon (51st), ordering that no festivals of Martyrs, *i.e.*, Holy Days, should be observed in Lent. But the Trullan Council (692 A.D.) ordered that this feast should be excepted from the prohibition and restored to its right place,—the 25th of March. The purpose of the festival is to commemorate the announcement made by the Angel Gabriel to the Virgin, that she should conceive and bring forth the promised MESSIAH, and the conception of our LORD, which followed that announcement.

Antelucan. (Before dawn.) In the primitive Church in time of persecution the Christians were wont to meet before dawn to escape detection. The custom was continued after persecution had ceased, but it was broken up later, as it led to some irreverence and disorder. In dangerous times, of course, the Holy Communion was then most safely and readily celebrated; but in times of quiet this was not necessary, and the custom was no longer imperative. Also there were irregularities connected with the celebrations at that hour, so that it was ordered that the Holy Communion should not be celebrated at night.

Antependium. A frontal vesting the front of the altar. The color of the antependium should vary with the season and the special day. The Holy Table in the Greek Church is always vested with special care, with altar-cloths which were consecrated at the time the altar or the church was consecrated.

Anthem. *Vide* ANTIPHON.

Anthropomorphism. (The likeness or form of man.) The gross error of some heretics,—Audeans,—who held that GOD had a human form. It was and is probably a natural hasty error which some may find it difficult to put away. At any rate, it has been supposed that many held it whose language, following the accommodations of Holy Scripture, has seemed to justify the charge. One of the earliest, Tertullian (180-202 A.D.), taught that GOD had a body, but being self-existent, was bound by very different and to us incomprehensible, laws of existence. The language, His Eye, His Hand, His creating man in His own Image, is only suited to our powers of comprehension, for we are distinctly and authoritatively taught (Is. xl. 18; Acts xvii. 20, et al.) that He is everywhere present, a SPIRIT whom no man hath seen nor can see, who cannot be delineated by man's art or device, or, as the Article hath it (Art. I.), "There is but one living and true GOD, everlasting, without body, parts, or passions, of infinite power, wisdom, and goodness." As we can only use Scripture language upon such lofty and insoluble subjects, it is well to use great care and devout thought in forming such conceptions. Anthropomorphism does not necessarily exclude a person from the Church Communion, though, as St. Augustine says of those who were misled in his own times, they are carnal and childish.

Antichrist. A word compounded from the Greek *anti* and *Christos*, and meaning "opposed to," or, "instead of CHRIST." There is probably no theological subject involved in greater obscurity, and from the earliest times the explanatory theories have been almost innumerable. The idea of Antichrist may be traced back almost as far as the Messianic idea, and is undoubtedly the Christian analogue of that dualism which characterizes all Oriental religious systems, and which is most familiar in the Persian Ormuzd and Ahriman, the personal opposing powers of Good and Evil. The simplest solution of these striking analogies is that the great truths of Christianity were foreshadowed in the primeval or patriarchal revelation and retained in purity only in the Old Testament prophecies, but lived on in one or other corrupted form in all the cognate heathen systems. The term Antichrist is found in the New Testament only in the 1st and 2d Epistles of St. John, although the idea is very clearly taught in St. Matthew xxiv. and St. Mark xiii. St. Paul, also, in 2 Thess. ii., speaks of "The man of sin," by whom it is generally believed he means Antichrist. Certainly St. John states positively that the coming of Antichrist was a doctrine well known to those to whom he wrote. The greatest diversity of opinion has prevailed as to whether is meant by Antichrist a person, or a system, or a corrupted Church, or a persecuting anti-Christian power; as to whether Antichrist has already come, or is yet to be expected, or is typical of a constant opposition of the world-power to that of CHRIST. In the Roman Church Antichrist is generally believed to mean heathen imperial Rome, though many interpret the prophecies in Revelation as pointing to a personal opponent of Christianity who is to appear immediately prior to the second coming of CHRIST. In the Greek Church Gregory VII. was called Antichrist by some, as Boniface III. had already been by Phocas; but the prevailing belief has pointed to Mohammed, as might naturally be expected. Among Protestants the almost universally accepted solution has been found either in the Pope or in the Church of Rome; while individual rulers, from Caligula to Napoleon III., have been claimed as meeting the most minute requirements of prophecy. It would be as unprofitable as impossible to allude, even, to all these beliefs and fancies. The sad divisions of Christianity have caused almost every Christian system to be regarded as Antichrist by some opposing system. The confusion has largely resulted from the many unsuccessful attempts to solve the mysterious prophecies of Daniel and the Revelation, especially those which concern "the number of the beast," and the "time, and times, and dividing of time," which are supposed to point to the name of the individual Antichrist and the duration of the anti-Christian power. This immense diversity of belief, together with the mystery in which the whole subject is involved, would seem to suggest that the matter, outside of the general principles taught by our LORD Himself, is of far less practical importance than has been assigned to it. The one essential point is that Christianity is in constant conflict with "the prince of this world," "the evil one" from whom the LORD has taught us to pray for daily deliverance, and that Antichrist is to be found in every concrete development or incarnation of his power. A close examination of St. Paul's language in 2 Thessalonians will show conclusively that the Roman emperors, of whom Nero was the type, fulfilled every particular of his description of the "Man of sin." They were in all respects personal Antichrists. They were "Christoi," "anointed" sovereigns; they were worshipped as God and declared themselves to be incarnations of the Supreme God, assuming the title "Divine;" they claimed "lying wonders" in support of their assumed divinity; they were monsters of iniquity such as the world has never seen before or since, and they were the relentless persecutors of all who confessed CHRIST, demanding the abjuration of His faith and the substitution for it of their own worship as the price of life from every apprehended Christian; and, finally, the great Arian apostasy immediately preceded the final destruction of Roman heathen imperialism by "the breath," or "spirit"— "pneuma"—of the LORD'S mouth, for the death of the half-converted Constantine ended forever the great centralization of the world-power which had been the uncompromising opponent of the kingdom of CHRIST, and thenceforth Christianity became the dominant power in the world. This view is greatly strengthened by St. Paul's reference to our LORD as having predicted the events which, for obvious reasons of safety to the Church as well as to Himself, He could mention only in figurative and obscure language. It was, doubtless, to this language of St. Paul, and other and more secret teachings to the same effect, that St. John alludes in his First Epistle, and his declaration that there were then "already *many* Antichrists" is most significant, as apparently designed to draw attention from the prevailing expectation of a personal Antichrist, and the immediate occurrence of the Second Advent, and fix it upon the doctrinal defection which had even then arisen, and which embodied the most important features of the prophecy. In regard to the bearing of the Revelation upon the subject, that book is yet too much an unsolved mystery to permit any definite conclusion to be drawn. How much of it is prophecy and how much the mystical description of events already past or then passing we cannot yet decide. Nor is the theory above advanced in any way inconsistent with the doctrine of a personal Antichrist, immediately to precede the final coming of the LORD in glory. Almost all prophecy is manifold in its fulfillment, having general and special significations, the teaching of some general truth being always the more important, and the prediction of events in most cases secondary. This is undoubtedly true of the prophecies of Antichrist. What we need to know and remember may be summed up in a very few words. No orthodox development of Christianity can possibly be meant as being a power hostile to CHRIST. But the world-power is *always* opposing the Christ-power and striving to set itself in its place, and the world-power is always assuming some concrete form to make its opposition tangible and effective. As faithful Christians we must be constant in maintaining the LORD's side in this ceaseless conflict, and in enduring the trials which that faithfulness involves, and doing so we need not to disturb our minds with looking for a personal Antichrist, but rather direct them in watchful hope to the coming of the LORD Himself in the full assurance that every opposing power will be destroyed before Him and every faithful watcher be rewarded.

REV. ROBERT WILSON, D.D.

Antidoron. The remaining unconsecrated bread which had been blessed in the service of the preparation of the Elements. Prothesis. Its name signifies "instead of the gift" (*i.e.*, the consecrated bread), given to non-communicants instead of the consecrated bread. There is, doubtless, a historic bond, though not very distinct, connecting the old love-feasts (1 Cor. xi. 20, 39), this Antidoron, the Eulogiæ of the Western Church, the "pain beni" of the Gallican, and the blessed bread of the older English Church, together.

Antinomianism. (Opposed to Law; in Church History, those opposed to the moral Law of GOD.) The earliest Antinomians were the Gnostics, whose wild speculations and gross imaginations led them into such a conclusion. Their profligate lives and absurd doctrines and high pretensions to Wisdom and inner Knowledge naturally led to the denial of any moral obligations at all. But in this they sought for some support from the strong and decided language of St. Paul upon Faith, and so misled those willing to be misled by their want of self-control. There is always an Antinomian principle in mere human nature, and this reappears in some form or other along the line of Church history, some leader in each age not being entirely free from some form of the error. But it reappeared with violence at the Reformation. In that age and in the whirl of that terrible breaking up it is not at all surprising that some were tempted to use more violent language than the truth would bear (as did Luther), and that others would fall into this heresy. John Agricola, at Wittenberg (1538 A.D.), became the leader of the sect. His tenets were repudiated by Luther and Melanchthon, and it is said that he himself recanted his error afterwards. It sprang up again under Cromwell in England, among the innumerable sectaries which swarmed in that country during the Great Rebellion (1640-56 A.D.). In every age, however, some sectaries have held it, though in a repressed way. The Holy Scriptures present, as is their wont, both sides, both Faith and Works, most strongly, and the Church's duty is to do the same. Logical consequences in such cases are to be measured by practical consequences. The true line is to fill out works with the Life of Faith and to clothe faith with the body of works. "Show me thy Faith without thy Works, and I will show thee my Faith by my Works" (*cf.* iii. 13; Jas. ii. 18).

Antioch. There were two Antiochs, the best known in Syria, where the disciples were first called Christians, where St. Peter labored so much, where St. Ignatius afterwards ruled; the other a large town in Pisidia, where St. Paul preached and suffered for the Gospel's sake. But the first Antioch deserves a longer notice, from the important events which took place there, and from the influence its School exercised at one time.

It was founded by Seleucus Nicator (300 B.C.), and a part of its population was Jewish. It grew apace, as its position was excellent both in a political and in a commercial sense. It was adorned by the Seleucid kings, the Romans favored it, and Herod the Great contributed to its adornment. Its population, like that of Alexandria, was witty, gay, and licentious, easily roused, and often (as in the famous case of the Statues) proceeding to excesses. Its fondness for giving nicknames possibly is noted in the fact that the disciples received there their future designation as Christians. Ignatius, upon the death of Evodius in a riot, became the Bishop of the Jewish, as he already was of the Gentile, congregations, and, having safely brought his flock through the persecution under Domitian (95-96 A.D.), bravely set the example of a good confession before Trajan. His letters are a precious result of his devotion, and the journey to Rome was unintentionally a better way of proclaiming the Gospel than if he had remained inhumed at home. Antioch became famous for its Catechetical School, under Lucian, who was martyred (311 A.D.). He was a clear, cool man, with a great deal of insight and originality. But he was hardly orthodox in his teaching. His pupils were nearly all afterwards Arians, under the lead of Arius, who was himself trained in this Antiochean school. Lucian's teaching seems to have been of a disputatious turn. He combated the Syrian mysticism and gnosticism, and in the effort brought out the plan of proposing problems on the Faith for debate. The sophistical style of argument was in vogue, and to his training in dialectics in such a school Arius owed much of his first successes. In this the school of Lucian did much more harm to Christian Truth than all the fancies of Origen. Lucian redeemed his own good name afterwards by a good confession at his martyrdom (311 A.D.), but he sowed seeds that bore poisoned fruit in the next twenty years. The history of Arianism belongs to another article, but here in Antioch were held some of its strongest Councils. Lucian's school soon died out, but his influence in urging more practical and grammatical criticism of the Bible long continued. From him really came the tone which influenced Diodorus of Tarsus in his exegesis, and through him Theodore.

A Council was held at Antioch in the year 340 or 341 A.D. Some historians affirm that there were two Councils, one in each year, but whether or not that was so, it will suffice to consider the things done as the acts of one Council. The Emperor Constantine had laid the foundations of a magnificent church at Antioch, which was finished about this time by his son Constantius; and Eusebius of Nicomedia gathered together a large number of Bishops (as many as 97, of whom 40 were Eusebians) to dedicate it; these organized themselves into a Council, which is often called the Council of the Dedication, and is the second Council of Antioch, if, as some think, another was held in 340 A.D. The Bishops assembled were from the East alone, no one from the Western Empire being present, nor any representative of the Pope; and Eusebian opinions seem to have prevailed, either through the retirement of the orthodox Bishops, or through the influence of Constantius, who was present in person. The charges against St. Athanasius, formerly preferred at the Synod of Tyre (of murder, sacrilege, and impurity), were renewed, in spite of having been plainly confuted; and he was condemned without a hearing. The Council then proceeded to elect and consecrate a Bishop of Alexandria in his place,—one Gregory of Cappadocia, a coarse and violent man, who presently took possession of his See by military force with many outrages and cruelties. They then drew up three or four creeds, which under ordinary circumstances would have been unobjectionable, but were suspicious from the careful omission of the term ὁμοούσιος (co-essential, consubstantial), which had become the test of orthodoxy. The second of these creeds is sometimes styled the *Formulary of Antioch*, or the *Creed of the Dedication*, but is ascribed to an earlier date than the Council. Besides these Creeds twenty-five Canons were passed, which, though technically rejected as the work of heretics, have actually been received into the Code of Church Canons, being confirmed by the Council of Chalcedon. Those of most interest now are the following: The 1st Canon establishes the decree of Nice concerning Easter; the 5th prescribes a rule for dealing with those who assemble private independent congregations; the 7th enjoins the use of letters of peace, or dismissary letters; the 12th (which was directed against Athanasius) deprives of all hope of restoration any one who being deposed shall carry his complaint to the emperor instead of to a Synod of Bishops; the 15th forbids appeal from the unanimous decision of a provincial Synod; the 21st forbids translations; and the 22d forbids one Bishop interfering in the Church of another. Other Councils or Synods were held at Antioch, as follows: in 345 A.D., when the Confession of faith called the μακρόστιχος was drawn up; in 360 A.D., when Meletius was elected Patriarch of Antioch, who, warmly espousing the defense of the Catholic faith, so provoked the Arians that they procured his banishment as a Sabellian; in 363 A.D., when the Creed of Nice was received as the exposition of the true faith; in 380 A.D., of which no records are preserved, though the Council is said to have received, unanimously, the Epistle of Pope Damasus; in 391 A.D., when the errors of the Massalians were condemned; in 417 A.D., against Pelagius; in 433 A.D., against Nestorius; and in 435 A.D., when the memory of Theodorus of Mopsuestia was defended.

REV. R. A. BENTON.

Antiphon (English form, *Anthem*). Antiphonal chanting, *i.e.*, responsive, as when two choirs respond to each other. Antiphonal reading, as in our reading the Psalter in the service, minister and congregation replying the one to the other. It was the Jewish mode. Indeed (Is. vi. 3, "this cried to this," Heb.), the Seraphim respond the one to the other. The arrangements of the choirs (1 Chron. vi. 31, *sq.*, and xxv.) necessarily involved antiphonal singing. Many of the Psalms (*e.g.* xxiv., cxviii., cxxxiv.) must have been so used: Miriam's Song at the Red Sea was choral and antiphonal. The dedication of the rebuilt walls of Jerusalem was evidently with antiphonal singing, as was also thus celebrated the founding of the second Temple (Neh. xii. 27, *sq.*: Ezra iii. 10, 16).

Pliny's famous letter to Trajan about the Christian implies in the phrase " *secum invicem,*" by turns among themselves, antiphonal singing. It is a very old tradition that Ignatius of Antioch introduced antiphonal singing into the Gentile Church because of a vision of antiphonal chanting in heaven. Most probably, as he united the Jewish and Gentile congregations under his jurisdiction, it may be a way of recording his argument from Isaiah to the Gentiles for such singing. East and West took it up, and it spread with great rapidity. The custom once taken up was not laid aside. But the term antiphon came later to have various meanings, springing out of the one central use of the Psalms: (*a*) The Psalms were so called from their use. (*b*) It came to mean later a section of a Psalm, or a compilation of several Psalms, or other selections from Scriptures. The use was in this case for one choir to sing each verse, and at its close the other choir responded with an unvarying versicle. Such arrangements are frequent in the old office-books. The Canticles used in English state services instead of the Venite are of this nature. (*c*) A further change took place in its meaning when it was the name for a single sentence from the Psalm, originally sung between the verses, but later only at the beginning and the close. (*d*) The last step was to make it mean the sentence taken by itself and sung alone. This antiphon might be from Scripture or from some other source. These antiphons are very common in the Greek services. The word anthem (antiphona, O. E. antefn, antem), found in Chaucer (Mod. E. anthem), means in English music such a verse most usually from Scripture, though often the composer made a single anthem out of two separate texts or passages from the Holy Writ. The antiphon forms a very notable part of the Liturgical services, especially in the Mozarabic and Eastern rites. (For the use of the Anthem in the service, see ANTHEM and MUSIC.)

Antiphonal. (Antiphonar.) The book which contains the invitatories, responsories, verses, collects, and whatever is sung in the choir, but not including the hymns peculiar to the Communion service, which are contained in the Graduale. It is a book that belongs to the Roman rite. The antiphonal was also used in the English service till tne compilation of the Prayer-Book did away with its use.

Antipope. Rival Popes were called antipopes. They were pretenders to the Papal throne, elected by partisans upon some pretext or claim. But several of them were elected under such circumstances that, had they been successful in their claims, they would have been acknowledged as legitimately chosen. The number of rival claimants has been variously stated, and probably cannot be completely given. But it has been estimated at about forty. Many began an opposition which maintained itself too short a time to require notice. Others again surrendered their claims by compromise. From the date 251 A.D. there was but one century (the thirteenth) which was not marked by an antipope. For over a century, from 1046 A.D. to 1180 A.D., there was a continuous series of antipopes; and at the outset (1046 A.D.) there were as many as four in the field. The Council of Pisa (1409 A.D.) deposed both the legitimate and the anti pope and elected a third. This but introduced three rivals. The Council of Constance (1414–18 A.D.) deposed two, the third abdicated, and a fourth was elected, who remained possessor of the See; but before he died there were two rival claimants (1425–26 A.D.). This, together with other historical facts, make a very significant commentary upon the doctrine of Papal infallibility.

Antitype. This word can be used in two distinct and opposing senses: (*a*) as opposed to mere representations of a reality as the substance is opposed to the shadow. CHRIST was the antitype; Moses, David, Solomon, were the types. It is also used (*b*) in a reverse sense, as twice in the New Testament (Heb. ix. 24): "For CHRIST is not entered unto the holy places made with hands, which are the figures (the antitypes) of the true; but unto heaven itself, now to appear in the presence of GOD for us," where the antitype means the shadow, while the type, as St. Chrysostom says, has the power of the reality. And again in 1 Pet. iii. 21, where the word antitype led to its use in the Liturgies: "The like figure whereunto (the antitype) baptism doth also now save us." The Fathers then used this word in the same way. Irenæus: "The HOLY SPIRIT is then invoked that the bread may be the body and the cup may be the blood of CHRIST, that they who receive these antitypes may obtain remission of sins and everlasting life." St. Basil uses this term antitype in reference to the human body. As at first glance the body would be called a simple substance, but subsequent reasoning would show that it was a complex thing, having color and shape, and antitype and magnitude, when, if the text be correct, it is difficult to translate it unless it be a reference to its prototype—GOD'S Image. It can be compared, therefore, with the phrase in his Liturgy: "We offering the antitypes of the Holy Body and Blood of CHRIST, beseech Thee that Thy HOLY SPIRIT may descend upon us and upon these gifts."

Apocrypha. This Greek word means "hidden, secret." It seems to be used for "spurious" in the latter part of the second century. Perhaps the name indicates a secret knowledge made known only to the initiated. The names of distinguished men, as Solomon and Ezra, Daniel and Jeremiah, were falsely given as authors of the various books. The introducing of Apocryphal books into the Septuagint gave them a certain weight, though Jerome speaks strongly against an undue valuation of them. The Church of Rome, at the Council of Trent, included the doubtful books in its definition of Canonical Scripture, excepting the two books of Esdras and the Prayer of Manasseh. The German and English Reformers followed the opinion of Jerome. In Luther's German Bible the title "Apocrypha" had this addition : "*i.e.*, Books which are not of like worth with Holy Scripture, yet are good and useful to be read." Wiclif used the term Apocrypha for the uncanonical books, and the judgment of St. Jerome is given in the VI. Article of the English Church. He admits them to be "read for example of life and instruction of manners," but not "to establish any doctrine." The Apocryphal books are interesting in their connection with the literature and history of the Jews. "They represent the period of transition and decay which followed on the return from Babylon, when the prophets, who were then the teachers of the people, had passed away and the age of scribes succeeded." "The alterations of the Jewish character, the different phases which Judaism presented in Palestine and Alexandria, the good and the evil which were called forth by contact with idolatry in Egypt, and by the struggle against it in Syria, all these present themselves to the reader of the Apocrypha with greater or less distinctness." These books lack the prophetic element, though there is some attempt to feign it. The Song of the Three Children is the only poetry in the Apocrypha. Where the writers are affected by Greek culture there is "the taste for rhetorical ornament which characterized the literature of Alexandria." In the Apocrypha works of fiction appear, which rest, or purport to rest, on "an historical foundation." The Jewish exiles had a reputation for music, and were asked to sing the "songs of Zion" (Ps. cxxxvii.). The trial of skill in wise sayings given in 1 Esdras iii. and iv. "implies a traditional belief" that the Persian kings honored those who possessed such gifts. The transition to story-telling was natural. The captivity, with its remoteness of scene and strange adventures, gave a wide field to the imagination. In Bel and the Dragon there is a love of the marvelous, and a scorn of the idolater. In Tobit and in Susanna there is a moral tendency. Jeremiah has a prominent place in the hopes of the Jews, and so in 2 Macc. xv. 13-16, he is represented as appearing to Judas Maccabæus and giving him "a sword as a gift from GOD." This may help to explain the rumor of the people in CHRIST'S day, that "Jeremias, or one of the prophets," had appeared on earth (Matt. xvi. 14). With regard to the false names given to Apocryphal writers, it is difficult at this day to know how much deception existed, if any was intended. Solomon's name may have been used to draw attention by personation. Later Jewish history shows this, however, to be a dangerous practice. There are inaccuracies in the history contained in the Apocrypha. This may be partly due to a want of "power to distinguish truth from falsehood." The influence against idolatry is strong, as in the story of the noble Maccabees, and in the books of Judith, Baruch, and Wisdom. The heroic death by martyrdom of the mother and her seven sons in 2 Macc. vii. is a wonderful narrative. A high idea of almsgiving appears in Tobit iv. 7-9, which form a part of the sentences used in the Offertory. In Tobit xii. 8, prayer, fasting, and alms are named as characteristics of a holy life. Our LORD explains their relation to true religion in St. Matt. vi. 1-18. The Wisdom of Solomon is a book of a very elevated tone of thought. Wisdom is beautifully styled "the brightness of the everlasting light, the unspotted mirror of the power of GOD, and the image of His goodness" (ch. vii. 26). "In all ages, entering into holy souls, she maketh them friends of GOD" (v. 27). This resembles Philo's teaching, and foreshadows St. John's description of CHRIST as the Word of GOD and "the true Light, which lighteth every man that cometh into the world" (John i. 1, 9). Eternal blessedness shines out in this book. How magnificently the following words sound in days of heathen darkness : "The souls of the righteous are in the hand of GOD" (Wisdom iii. 1), and, "In the sight of the unwise they seemed to die" (v. 2) ; "But they are in peace" (v. 3). See the final triumph of the righteous in ch. vi., with its figures of rapidly passing life, in the ship, the bird, and the arrow. In such a fleeting life the wicked cry, "We in like manner, as soon as we were born, began to draw to our end" (v. 13). The wide love of GOD is described in ch. xi. 23-26 : "Thou lovest all the things that are, and abhorrest nothing which Thou hast made" (v. 24) ; "O Lord, Thou lover of souls" (v. 26). The second book of Esdras, from the "allusions to JESUS CHRIST and to the phraseology of the New Testament," is supposed to be the work of a Jewish Christian. Ecclesiasticus is believed to be written by the son of Sirach, as it claims to be. Josephus excludes the Apocryphal books from the Canon of Scripture, and "Philo never quotes them as he does the Sacred Scriptures. By the Jews they were never viewed as part of the Canon." Still they form an "important link" in Jewish history, and narrate "the fulfillment of many of the Old Testament prophecies, especially those in the book of Daniel." They give accounts of customs and circumstances alluded to in the New Testament, and so help us to understand it. They contain, also, "pious reflections, written by devout men, who were waiting for the consolation of Israel." The Fathers often appealed to them and quoted them. In very early times "they were read in most Churches, at least in the West," not as Canonical Scripture, but as ancient and valuable for instruction, as a homily or sermon might be read. The Belgic Confession al-

'lowed them to be read in Churches. This passage occurs in Cecil's "Remains": "Man is a creature of extremes. The middle path is generally the wise path; but there are few wise enough to find it. Because Papists have made too much of some things, Protestants have made too little of them. . . . The Papist puts the Apocrypha into his Canon; the Protestant will scarcely regard it as an ancient record." While the English Church reads the Apocrypha in the public service, it is not read as Scripture. The Episcopal Church takes the middle ground of which Cecil speaks. While she, with the Jews themselves, excludes the Apocryphal books from Canonical Scripture, she is ready to draw from them such information as may be of benefit to her children. Bishop Ch. Wordsworth contends that if the early Church had claimed canonicity for them she would have impeded the entrance of the Jews into her fold; but all the Apostles were Jews, "the first fifteen Bishops of Jerusalem were of Hebrew extraction" (Euseb. H. E., iv. 5). The Greek Church, though not considering the Apocrypha inspired, venerates it, and by a proper use of it we keep in concord thus far with that ancient body. While the Apocrypha was allowed to be read for instruction in ancient Churches, Cyril's Catechetical Lectures show that the Church of Jerusalem was an exception, and the Council of Laodicea determined the case for some other Churches by forbidding all but the Canonical books to be read in the Church. The author of the Apostolic Constitutions, giving orders about the reading of Old Testament books, omits the Apocrypha.

Authorities: E. H. Plumptre in Wm. Smith's Dictionary of the Bible; Horne's Introduction; Bible Lore, by J. Comper Gray; Browne on the Articles; Wordsworth on the Canon; Bingham's Antiquities. For a list of works on the Apocrypha, see Introduction to the Old Testament in Lange's Genesis, Third Division, p. 64

REV. S. F. HOTCHKIN.

Apollinarianism. Apollinaris, Bishop of Laodicea (d. 390 A.D.), a very learned and influential Bishop, promulgated certain erroneous teachings concerning our LORD'S nature. The Nicene Council had determined Holy Scripture to teach that He was perfect man as well as Eternal SON of GOD. As perfect man His human nature must subsist of body and soul, or He would not be perfect man. But this Apollinaris denied. He did not deny the true body, but he did deny the soul in our LORD'S human nature. He was refuted by Athanasius (who, however, did not mention his name, for they were personal friends), by Gregory Nazianzen, Gregory of Nyssa, and others, and was condemned by a Council at Alexandria (362 A.D.), and by the second General Council at Constantinople (381 A.D.). His error led him to leave the Church and create a sect. Gregory Nazianzen states firmly the true doctrine of the Church (Ep. ad Cled.): " Let not men deceive nor be deceived," supposing "the lordly nature" (using this term instead of our LORD and GOD) " to be soulless. For we do not separate the manhood from His Divinity; but we confess that it is one and the same; not that the manhood was first, but, that He was GOD, the only SON, before all worlds, without a human body or its attributes. But in the fullness of time He took upon Him flesh for our salvation. He was capable of suffering according to the flesh. He was incapable of suffering according to His divinity, circumscribed according to His body; not to be circumscribed according to His divinity; at once earthly and heavenly, He was seen; he was known; He was in space (as to His human body); He was not bounded by space (as to His divinity, compare St. John iii. 13). That our whole manhood having fallen under sin might be reformed by Him who was wholly man as well as GOD."

Apostasy. (A falling away; a desertion from a cause or from a general.) A defection from the true faith of CHRIST. In times of persecution this sin was rife among Christians from fear of bodily peril especially, as generally the act itself was often proposed in the mildest way: a few grains of incense offered to an idol, or to the image of the emperor, or a renunciation easily ambiguously made, and certified to by a magistrate. But there have been other apostates, such as was the Emperor Julian, or renegades to the Mohammedan Faith. It was legislated upon by the Church, and the penitents had to undergo a long discipline of probation, in some places for twelve years, before they could be restored. But when the state took up apostasy into its Civil Code, its enactments were intolerant. The apostate to paganism was not allowed to bequeath by will or to inherit. At one time he was to be dismissed from all posts of civil dignity. And if the apostasy of a testator could be established within five years after his death, his will was null and void.

Apostle. One who is sent; a title given to the Twelve disciples by our blessed LORD when He chose them to be His messengers to all the world. As for the special traits of the individual Apostles we must turn to the short sketches under their names. Here their office is dwelt upon. They are called Apostles by St. Matthew, only when their appointment is recorded, and by St. Mark, when they return from their mission. But St. Luke gives them this title, from their appointment, in six places, evidently showing that the full value of their title was appreciated later. In St. John's Gospel the name is not given at all, but the Twelve are called disciples. Our LORD considered them as one body. He gave them the practical training His presence and mission work afforded. He seems rather to have trusted to His having them with Him, and to His personal influence, than to His many instructions (St. John xiv. 9). His words, His parables, His works, His example, were His instruction more than the imparting of doctrine. Indeed, His doctrine being so much the expansion and the enforcement of the Old Testament, except the prediction concerning Himself and His Atonement and Resurrection He gave them no secret doctrines. Out of the Twelve there appear to have been chosen to serve Him more closely SS. Peter, James, and John. These were taken up into the Mount of Transfiguration, were with Him in the Garden, as well as selected at other special occasions. Still, He made no further distinctions between them, and it would seem that the Three stood so closely to Him, because of their own love to Him. They all, however, were dull to see what His purposes were, and, with all their training and their zeal and perseverance, still failed to comprehend Him aright. It was not till after His resurrection, and then by a special gift from Him, that they understood all the Scripture about Him. But their office began properly after His Resurrection. The commission that had been given (St. Matt. xvi. 18, 19; xviii. 18, 21) was by anticipation, but now it was given fully and finally, yet not at once, but during the forty days previous to His Ascension. The first part given was on that evening, in the upper chamber, when he met them: (a) "Peace be unto you. As my FATHER hath sent me, even so send (Apostleize) I you." It was a plenary commission, with equal but delegated powers. Then follows: (b) "He breathed on them, and said, Receive ye the HOLY GHOST: whose soever sins ye remit, they are remitted unto them; and whose soever sins ye retain, they are retained." This is recorded in St. John's Gospel xx. 21-23. There appears to have been a pause in the conveyance of their commission. For the forty days that He was going in and out among them He was "speaking of the things pertaining to the Kingdom of GOD" (Acts i. 8). But here we must place the giving of the second part of the commission in His appearing to the Eleven as they sat at meat (St. Mark xvi. 14-18). The mission is now given: (c) "Go ye into all the world, and preach the Gospel to every creature. He that believeth and is baptized shall be saved; and he that believeth not shall be damned." At this point, too, we may add St. Luke's record as parallel and explanatory of St. Mark's: "And that repentance and remission of sins should be preached in His Name among all nations, beginning at Jerusalem. And ye are witnesses of these things" (St. Luke xxiv. 47, 48). In obedience to His command they meet Him in a mountain in Galilee, and then He claims His royal authority: "All power is given to ME in Heaven and in earth. Go ye, therefore, and make disciples of all nations, baptizing them in the Name of the FATHER, and of the SON, and of the HOLY GHOST; teaching them to observe all things whatsoever I have commanded you." And then He gives that solemn promise, now so strangely denied as possible, "And, lo, I am with you alway, even unto the end of the world. Amen" (St. Matt. xxviii. 19, 20). We see that the command to baptize is given twice, and the commission to absolve, which involves the effects of baptism, is given once with plenary and co-equal power as His own, and that this delegation rests upon the power given to Him, and He seals it with the gift of the HOLY GHOST for their official acts. St. Luke gives a note, too, in the Apostolic office, "And ye are witnesses of these things." The whole commission is given in perpetuity: "I am with you alway, even to the end of the world." We ascertain, then, that the Apostolic office was never to fail, and was to be a witness of Him and His Resurrection; that it was to convey to the repentant sinner the effect of His atonement, i.e., pardon, and forgiveness by baptism, and it was to use discipline; that its mission-field was the world.

The continuity of the office was shown by the election of Matthew (Acts i. 15-26), the condition being that the person elected must have been with the LORD JESUS from the beginning, that he might be a competent witness of the Resurrection. The co-equality in the office was shown by the co-equal gift of the HOLY GHOST to the Twelve, and in the fact that the College of the Apostles sent SS. Peter and John down to Samaria (Acts viii.), and that St. James presided at the Council of Jerusalem (Acts xv.), and that St. Paul admitted no superior to himself (Gal. i. 1). The perpetuity of the office was shown by the fact that Silvanus and Timothy and Epaphroditus and Titus were Apostles as well as Barnabas and Paul. Indeed, there were some who were false Apostles (2 Cor. xi. 13; Rev. ii. 2), which could not have been unless the office was widely spread. This we note was within Apostolic time. But as Timothy was an Apostle (comp. 1 Thess. i. 1 with ii. 6), he was led (2 Tim. ii. 1, 2) to commit to faithful men the commission that they might teach others also, a very direct command on the succession, which was of course implied in the directions about Bishops or Elders and Deacons. What, then, were the functions of the Apostle? He was primarily to Preach, and to Baptize, and to Confirm (Acts viii. and xix.; Heb. vi.), and to Discipline (cf. St. John xx. 23, with Acts viii. 20-23; 1 Cor. v. 1-5; 1 Tim. i. 18-20). Again, it is to be noted that not only did our LORD promise a perpetual presence with the holders of the office, but it was the only office He ordained, prayed for, and gave the HOLY GHOST to Himself, and sent it for them to use for the Church. They selected Elders in every Church, they ordained Deacons, but they alone were in the original sacred commission. This would be alone sufficient to prove its continuity did the New Testament give us no other facts. But in truth the whole work presupposes Apostolic authority. And continuance in the unity of the Apostles was from the first a proof of orthodoxy (Acts ii. 42 ; 2 Thess. ii. 15, iii. 4-9 ; 1 Cor. iv. 16-21 ; xi. ; Gal. i. ; Phil. iii. 17 ; 1 John i. 3; ii. 19; Rev. ii. 2, 3). In fact, Apostolic authority is so constantly presupposed that to quote any texts in proof is needless. All commands and directions are founded upon it. Now, the Apostolic office was to give real and true spiritual gifts, and to be the only appointed channel by which they were conveyed. Prophets and Teachers might be multiplied, but since Baptism and Absolution, and the Confirmation, and the LORD's Supper, and the Blessing of Peace are real and true gifts to be received and lived in, and are not conferred by merely preaching which opens the mind, or teaching which trains the disciples to receive ; and since these gifts are only to be received by these officers, the Apostolic office must be perpetual. It was and it must continue to be the witness of the Incarnation and Resurrection (1 John throughout), and it is a sad fact, but one which follows from the principles inherent in the commission, that wherever it has been dropped by any sect, and there has been no continuing Apostolic Church near it to enforce these doctrines, the body so rejecting the Apostolic office has also rejected the Divinity of CHRIST.

Apostolic Fathers. Clement, the companion of St. Paul, and later Bishop of Rome (97 A.D.), Ignatius (116 A.D.), and Polycarp (167 A.D.), companions of St. John, wrote certain letters which have come down to us, and are of great value. Clement's letter to the Corinthians is valuable not only for its own merits, but chiefly for its quotations from the New Testament, being an unconscious witness of the authenticity and general reception of the books he cites. Ignatius wrote six Epistles to the Churches of Ephesus, Tralles, Rome, Magnesia, Philadelphia, and Smyrna, and one to Polycarp, which give incidental but positive information on Episcopacy, and upon Church government, and which quote the New Testament very freely, enabling us to establish the early circulation of parts of the New Testament. There is also a cotemporary account of his martyrdom. Polycarp wrote a letter to the Philadelphians, and there is also a cotemporary narrative of his martyrdom. These are most valuable records from those who were trained by the Apostles. There are, besides, the Shepherd of Hermas (identified by some with the Hermas of Rom. xvi. 14, but very doubtful), which was at one time very popular, the very doubtful (but very early written) Epistle of St. Barnabas, and some fragments of the works of Papias, Bishop of Hierapolis, and a disciple of St. John. These had been taught by the Apostles St. John and St. Paul; and their writings, especially since their testimony cannot be doubted as true, are valuable not so much on the subjects they discussed as upon the facts of Church government they assumed or alluded to, and of the genuineness of such of the New Testament Scriptures as they quoted incidentally, doing so without hesitation, as if appealing to an inspired authority equal to the Old Testament Scripture.

Apostolic Succession. The real meaning of this term is but little appreciated even by many otherwise well-informed Churchmen. It is supposed to be, as it really is, a consecration of a person to Episcopal authority and office by those who have themselves received it from others tracing their authority by successive ascent back to some one of the Apostles. But harsh deductions are drawn from it, and the Church is accused of judging and "unchurching" those who from some prejudice or other reject it. She does not do this. She has a duty to do in asserting her right to be a part of the Holy Catholic Church, and this is one of the visible elements of her divine organization. She judges none. That is GOD's prerogative. If they reject her claims to their fealty, it is not her fault. If there is any unchurching, they do it themselves. But this Law of Apostolic Succession in the Church is only what she must have as a self-perpetuating Body. Its principle underlies all acknowledged government. Unless the exercise of supreme authority be received from some acknowledged and revered source, this authority is but usurpation. And the formal admission to wield this authority by the proper persons thereto appointed constitutes the person so admitted an officer clothed with this authority. The President of the United States is elected, but he is not President and cannot assume the authority of his office till the oath of office is administered to him by the officer appointed by the Constitution. It must be so in every organization. The Church is CHRIST's organized kingdom. It cannot break a law which He has put as fundamental to all government. It must derive its authority from Him. Spiritually He is present. The HOLY GHOST abides in it, and it is sustained and fed by Him. As He withdraws His visible Presence it must have a self-perpetuating government. As it is divine and miraculous it must be founded in miracles. Our LORD took not His office upon Himself, but was sent (Apostleized), even as Aaron was called of GOD. It was founded in miracles. In fact, it is a proper law in GOD's dealings with men, that every dispensation or covenant He makes is founded in miracles, rests upon them. For the Patriarchs, the miracles to Abraham were vouchers. For the Jew, from Moses' time forth, the wonders in the land of Ham, in the field of Zoan, at the Red Sea, and in the Wilderness were enough. And the authority of the High-Priest rested upon the miraculous call and the wonderful power given to Aaron. So our LORD had a public commission given Him, and was endowed by His FATHER (as well as by inherent right as GOD'S SON) to prove His doctrine by His miracles. And He sent His officers forth with that power. It was superadded, not essential. It was for proof, not for authority. The last High-Priest that entered within the veil was as much a High-Priest as was Aaron. But our LORD was sent, was His FATHER'S "APOSTLE" (Heb. iii. 1). He chose twelve, whom He called Apostles (St. Luke vi. 13), and when He commissioned them anew after His Resurrection He admitted them to His own rank. "As my FATHER has made me an apostle, even so I send you" (St. John xx. 21). For this reason the distinction between the Apostolate and the Presbyterate is clearly preserved throughout the New Testament. Again, as this office involves our LORD'S own office, He has promised an abiding perpetuating presence in it to the end of the world (St. Matt. xxviii. 20). He has Himself made unity with Him and His FATHER depend upon it. (I.) It is noticeable that He does not pray for unity till interceding first for the Apostles. He pleads, "Neither pray I for these alone, but for them also that believe on me through their word; that they all may be one, as Thou, FATHER, art in Me, and I in Thee, that they also may be one in us" (St. John xvii. 20, 21). When we remember the time of this prayer, the High-Priest sanctifying Himself as the one perfect victim, the unutterably solemn power of it will be felt. (II.) The Apostles claimed that fellowship with themselves was essential to the continuance of the members in the Church (Acts ii. 42; 1 John i. 1–7; ii. 19; 2 Thess. iii. 6, as in other like places). This authority resided in them to admit to their own rank upon the LORD'S own commission. Indeed, they admitted several,—St. Matthias, St. Barnabas, St. Paul. We know that St. Paul numbered with himself in rank St. Timothy, and Titus, and Silvanus (*vide* 1 Thess. ii.; comp. with ii. 6). Indeed, if these steps of the transmission can be proven it is useless to deny the fact or to explain away the principle. But we see our LORD, our Apostle, from His Father; the Twelve, the Apostles, from our LORD; St. Matthias, and Barnabas, and Paul (Acts xiii. 1, 2) from the Twelve; St. Timothy, and Titus, and Silvanus from St. Paul. The question of the Angels of the Churches (Rev. ii. and iii.) needs no discussion here, since the acceptance of the principle in the New Testament is sufficiently established. It is absurd to suppose that St. Timothy or St. Titus would break the commandment they had received so solemnly from St. Paul. The question is authoritatively decided by the Ignatian Epistles, since they accept and carry forward this line of succession.

It is absurd to claim that the line has been broken. For (*a*) the earliest Canon of post-Apostolic times orders that the consecrators shall be three. The purpose being that the consecration shall be most public and notorious. (*b*) The intercommunion of the different Churches kept any one Church from being imposed upon. It is significant that this was tried in the times of the Apostles. False Apostles, cried St. Paul. Our LORD commends the Angel of the Church in Ephesus, "and hast tried them which say they are Apostles and are not, and hast found them liars" (Rev. ii. 2). The chain can no more be broken than the descents of an ever-increasing family be denied. We ask no Jew to prove his descent from Abraham. The principle of the succession is well shown by the following occurrence, which shall be set down in the words of the venerated narrator:

"A doctrine is sometimes better illustrated by a story than by a dogmatic treatise. The character of true repentance, and the possibility of free pardon for transgressions against Heaven, are better exhibited by the parable of the Prodigal Son than they would be by a homiletical treatise. Bearing this in mind, we are inclined to believe that an anecdote of parochial experience will satisfy, if not convince, multitudes, better than more formal statements respecting Apostolical successions.

"A rector, who had gone to a railroad depot to see a clerical brother start upon a journey, encountered a lady who, though a Presbyterian, had for years belonged to his church-choir. She was much pleased to see him, for she was going from home permanently and was glad to bid him farewell. She thanked him for his ministrations, and confessed that her mind had become softened about many Episcopal peculiarities; but *one* she had never been able to admit or tolerate. Of course, the natural question was, to what do you allude? Oh, to the well-known theory of an Apostolic succession in the ministry. Why, the answer was, you yourself believe in a whole family of Apostolic successions, and surely a single specimen in the ministry ought not to give you any trouble. Oh, no; she had no faith in anything of the kind. Well, let us see. Do you, or do you not, believe in the Apostolic succession of the Christian religion? Why, she had never heard of such an idea before. But, it was pressed upon her, if you do not, then you must admit the charge of infidels that Christianity is an invention or an imposture, for it must be traced to its sources to be true to its own pretensions. So she admitted the point and consented to the most comprehensive of all Apostolic successions whatever.

"Then she was asked about the Apostolic succession of the Christian Church,—the grand outward institution of Christianity. Was there ever a time, since the days of CHRIST and His Apostles, when there was not a Christian Church upon the earth? Had this Church ever died out and vanished? Oh, no; she could allow nothing of the kind. Then you believe in the Apostolic succession of the Christian Church? Rather timorously (for she began to have an inkling of the journey she was traveling) she admitted that she did.

"Now, exclaimed her somewhat amused querist, here comes a formidable matter: Do you, or do you not, believe in the Apostolic succession of the Christian Scriptures? Remember, and remember well, here confronts us one of those awful gaps with which your friends so often threaten us. We have no manuscripts of such Scriptures which go back of about the middle of the fourth century, that is, say 350 A.D. And the last writer of Christian Scripture may be dated at 100 A.D. Here, then, is a prodigious gap of two hundred and fifty years to be bridged over, and unless you will cross it under the guidance of history and ancient authors, unless you will take the testimony of that institution whose continuity you have acknowledged, you have no Bible. You have lost it in that dark abyss which has swallowed up (as you affirm) our pretensions to a ministry whose line has never been broken. It was an awful alternative, and she surrendered without conditions.

"Then the question was followed up by one about visible sacraments. If such things had no Apostolic succession we must abandon the celebration of old-fashioned sacraments and join the Quakers. Infant baptism came next; and if this could not be traced by its Apostolic succession, we must march for the camping-ground of Anabaptists.

"From outward institutions the questioner went on to doctrines. If the doctrine of the Trinity had no Apostolic succession, we must acknowledge this doctrine a failure or a misconception, make fellowship with actual heretics, and adopt Socinianism. If the doctrine of the fall and original sin had no Apostolic succession, we must justify Pelagianism and avow ourselves our own redeemers. She now foresaw her destiny quite plainly, and bowed to the rector's postulate, that with him she believed in a family of successions which were truly Apostolic.

"But now, said he, comes the *crux* of this debated matter. You believe in the Apostolic succession of *a* Christian ministry. Was there ever a time when there was not such a ministry upon earth? when its continuity was broken and its existence was to be again begun? Oh, no; by no means. Then at last you believe with me in the steady existence of *an* Apostolic ministry, be its inward constitution what it might, and the difference between us is about the nature of an exceedingly long chain,—whether it has three strands in it or only one. Take Solomon's assurance about the reliability of a threefold cord, and you will come over to my side cordially. The difference between us has dwindled down to an affair so small that for safety's sake you should capitulate without a qualm. And to help you do so gracefully, let me beg you to remember that there is almost the same unanimity in Christendom about Episcopacy which even Gibbon was constrained to admit there is about the doctrine of the Trinity, which, of course, as a governing doctrine concerning the Godhead, is the pivot on which doctrinal orthodoxy has for ages turned. 'The consubstantiality of the FATHER and the SON,' says the skeptical historian, 'was established by the Council of Nice, and has been *unanimously* received as a fundamental article of the Christian Faith, by the consent of the Greek, the Latin, the Oriental, and the Protestant Churches.' (Dec. and Fall, ch. xvii. 12mo. ed., vol. ii. p. 317, 318; and comp. p. 312 at top.) The unanimity of Christendom about Episcopacy is nearly as complete as its unanimity about the Trinity; and with the Trinity for doctrine and Episcopacy for discipline, Christendom might begin to be, as in the primitive ages, a united whole, an unbroken communion of Saints." (Rev. T. W. Coit, D.D.)

The succession of the English Church from St. Polycarp, from the unknown founder of the Roman line, and from St. James, the first Bishop of Jerusalem, is here given. As this must have been an interlacing of the Churches in the East, which were founded by St. Peter at Antioch, and St. Paul at Ephesus, as well as by St. John in Asia Minor, doubtless the direct line of the Patriarchs of Jerusalem was bound up with these successions by acting upon the Canon requiring the three consecrators. So the English Episcopate has probably twined into one "cord" more of the separate successions than any other communion.*

EPHESUS.	A.D.	ROME.	A.D.	JERUSALEM.	A.D.
		SS. PAUL and PETER	65	ST. JAMES	35
After his exile		LINUS	58	SIMEON	65
ST. JOHN	96	ANACLETUS	78		
resides at Ephesus, and		CLEMENT	93		
his pupil at Smyrna is		EVARISTUS	100		
POLYCARP	107 to 169	ALEXANDER	109	JUSTUS I	107
				ZACHEUS	111
From Smyrna he sends				TOBIAS	112
out				BENJAMIN	117

* This list is much more fully traced in larger works, as in Dr. A. B. Chapin's Primitive Church.

EPHESUS.	A.D.	ROME.	A.D.	JERUSALEM.	A.D.
POTHINUS, who survived till	177	SEXTUS I	119	JOHN	119
				MATTHEW	121
				PHILIP	122
				SENECA	126
				JUSTUS II	127
				LEVI	128
		TELESPHORES	129	EPHRAIM	129
				JOSEPH	131
				JUDAS	132
		HYGINUS	138	MARCUS I	134
		PIUS	142	CASSIANUS	146
				PUBLIUS	154
		ANICETUS	157	MAXIMUS	159
				JULIAN	163
				CAIUS I	165
		SOTER	168	SYMMACHUS	168

LYONS.	A.D				
				CAIUS II	170
				JULIAN	173
POTHINUS	177	ELEUTHERIUS	177	MAXIMUS	178
				ANTONIUS	182
IRENÆUS	177 to 202			CAPITO	186
		VICTOR	192	VALENS	191
				DOLCHIANUS	194
				NARCISSUS	196
		ZEPHERINUS	201	DIUS	200
				GERMANIO	207
ZACHARIAS.				GORDIUS and NARCISSUS	211
		CALIXTUS	219		
ELIAS.		URBANUS	224		
FAUSTINUS.		PONTIANUS	231		
		ANTERUS	235		
		FABIANUS	236	ALEXANDER	237
VERUS.		CORNELIUS	250	MAZABENES	251
		LUCIUS	252		
		STEPHEN	253		
		SEXTUS II	257		
		DIONYSIUS	258		
JULIUS.				HYMENÆUS	265
		FELIX	271		
PTOLOMY.		EUTYCHIANUS	276		
		CAIUS	283		
		MARCELINUS	296	ZAMBDAS	298
				HERMAN	300
		MARCELLUS	308	MACARIUS I	310
VOCIUS.		EUSEBIUS	309		
		MELCHIADES	311		
MAXIMUS.		SYLVESTER	313	MAXIMUS III	315
TETRADUS.		MARK	335	CYRIL (expelled by the Arians)	330
		JULIUS	336		
VERISSIMUS.		LIBERIUS	352	HERENIUS	350
				CYRIL (restored, and again expelled)	361
		DAMASUS	366	HILARY	364
JUSTUS	374			CYRIL (again)	379
ALBINUS.		SIRICIUS	385	JOHN II	386
MARTIN.		ANASTASIUS	398		
ANTIOCHUS.		INNOCENTIUS	402		
ELPIDIUS.		ZOSIMUS	417	PRAGLIUS	416
SICHARIUS.		BONIFACE	418		
		CELESTINE	423	JUVENAL	424
		Consecrated PALLADIUS for the Irish.			
EUCHERIUS I	427	SEXTUS III	432		
PATIENS	451	LEO I	440		
		HILARY	461	ANASTASIUS	458
LUPICINUS.		SIMPLICIUS	467	MARTYRIUS	478
		FELIX II	483	SALUTIS	486
RUSTICIUS	494	GELASIUS	492	ELIAS	494
STEPHANUS	499	SYMMACHUS	498		

APOSTOLIC SUCCESSION

LYONS.	A.D.	ROME.	A.D.	JERUSALEM.	A.D.
VIVENTIOLUS	515	HORMISDAS	514	JOHN III	513
EUCHERIUS II	524	JOHN I	523	Consecrated DAVID of Wales, who therefore carried the succession of the Church of Jerusalem to Britain, whence it passed to the English succession.	
		FELIX III	526		
		BONIFACE II	530		
		JOHN II	532		
		AGAPETUS	535		
LUPUS	538	SYLVERIUS	536		
LICONTIUS	542	VIGILIUS	540		
SACERDOS	549				
NICETUS	552	PELAGIUS II	555		
		JOHN III	560		
PRISCUS	573	BENEDICT I	574		
		PELAGIUS III	578		
ETHERIUS	589	GREGORY	590		

Etherius, with Virgilius of Arles, consecrated the Monk Augustine (whom Gregory had sent out to the Saxons in Britain) as Archbishop of Canterbury. The English succession is by Augustine, through Etherius and Virgilius to St. John. It runs on thus:

CANTERBURY.	A.D.	ROME.	A.D.
1. AUGUSTINE	597		
2. LAURENTUS	604	SABIANUS	604
		BONIFACE III?	606
		BONIFACE IV	607
3. MELITUS	617	DEUSDEDIT	615
		BONIFACE V	618
4. TUSTUS	622	HONORIUS	624
5. HONORIUS	626	SEVERINUS	640
		JOHN IV	640
		THEODORE	642
		MARTIN	649
6. ADEODATUS	654	EUGENIUS	654
		VITALIAN	657

Vitalian being asked to aid the Saxons in selecting an Archbishop, selected Theodorus, a Greek of Tarsus, and consecrated him, and sent him to England. At this late point the Roman succession enters into the English line, which traced first to St. John.

7. THEODORE	668	42. HUBERT WALTER	1193
8. BRITHWALD	693	43. STEPHEN LANGTON	1207
9. TATWIN	731	44. RICHARD WETHERSHED	1229
10. NOTHELM	735	45. EDMUND RICH	1234
11. CUTHBERT	736	46. BONIFACE OF SAVOY	1245
12. BREGWIN	759	47. ROBERT KILWARBY	1273
13. LAMBERT	764	48. JOHN PECKHAM	1279
14. ATHELARD	793	49. ROBERT WINCHELSEY	1294
15. WULFRED	805	50. WALTER REYNOLDS	1313
16. THEOGILD	832	51. SIMON MEPEHAM	1328
17. CEOLNOTH	833	52. JOHN STRATFORD	1332
18. ETHELRED	870	53. JOHN DE UFFORD	1348
19. PLEGMUND	890	54. THOMAS BRADWARDINE	1349
20. ATHELM	914	55. SIMON ISLIP	1349
21. WULFHELM	923	56. SIMON LANGHAM	1366
22. ODO	942	57. WILLIAM WHITTLESEY	1368
23. DUNSTAN	960	58. SIMON SUDBURY	1375
24. ETHELGAR	988	59. WILLIAM COURTENAY	1381
25. SIRICIUS	990	60. THOMAS ARUNDEL	1397
26. ELFRIC	995	61. ROGER WALDEN	1398
27. ELPHEGE	1005	62. THOMAS ARUNDEL	1399
28. LIVINGUS	1013	63. HENRY CHICHELEY	1414
29. ETHELNOTH	1020	64. JOHN STAFFORD	1443
30. EADSINUS	1083	65. JOHN KEMPE	1452
31. ROBERT	1051	66. THOMAS BOURCHIER	1454
32. STIGAND	1052	67. JOHN MORTON	1486
33. LANFRANC	1070	68. HENRY DEANE	1501
34. ANSELM	1093	69. WILLIAM WAREHAM	1503
35. RALPH	1114	70. THOMAS CRANMER	1533
36. WILLIAM CORBEUIL	1123	71. CARDINAL POLE	1556
37. THEOBALD	1139	72. MATTHEW PARKER	1559
38. THOMAS À BECKET	1162	73. EDMUND GRINDAL	1576
39. RICHARD	1174	74. JOHN WHITGIFT	1583
40. BALDWIN	1185	75. RICHARD BANCROFT	1604
41. REGINALD FITZ-JOCELIN	1191	76. GEORGE ABBOT	1611

APOSTOLIC SUCCESSION

77. William **Laud**	1633
78. William Juxon	1660
79. Gilbert Sheldon	1663
80. William Sancroft	1678
81. John Tillotson	1691
82. Thomas Tenison	1695
83. William Wake	1716
84. John Potter	1737
85. Thomas Herring	1747
86. Matthew Hutton	1757
87. Thomas Secker	1758
88. Frederick Cornwallis	1768
89. John Moore	1783

Archbishop Moore, assisted by the Archbishop of York, and by the Bishops of Bath and Wells and of Peterborough, consecrated William White and Samuel Provoost, on February 4, 1787. Three years later he, with the Bishops of London and of Rochester, consecrated James Madison, on September 19, 1790. Already, Samuel Seabury had received consecration from the Bishops of Scotland, Robert Kilgour, Bishop of Aberdeen; Arthur Petrie, Bishop of Moray; and John Skinner, of Aberdeen, Primus of the Church of Scotland, on November 14, 1784.

The Scotch succession springs from the English succession, as Archbishop Sheldon, assisted by the Bishops of Carlisle, Worcester, and Llandaff, consecrated James Sharpe Archbishop of St. Andrew's; from them the consecrators of Bishop Seabury drew their authority.

The number of American Bishops from this beginning has become a total of one hundred and thirty-four.

Order.	Name of Bishop.	Name of See.	Date of Consecration.	Date of Decease.
1	Samuel Seabury (Presiding Bp.)	Connecticut	Nov. 14, 1784	Feb. 25, 1796
2	William White " "	Pennsylvania	Feb. 4, 1787	July 17, 1836
3	Samuel Provoost " "	New York	Feb. 4, 1787	Sept 6, 1815
4	James Madison	Virginia	Sept. 19, 1790	Mar 6, 1812
5	Thomas John Claggett	Maryland	Sept. 17, 1792	Aug. 2, 1816
6	Robert Smith	South Carolina	Sept. 13, 1795	Oct. 28, 1801
7	Edward Bass	Massachusetts	May 7, 1796	Sept 10, 1803
8	Abraham Jarvis	Connecticut	Sept. 18, 1797	May 3, 1813
9	Benjamin Moore	New York (*Assistant*)	Sept. 11, 1801	Feb. 27, 1816
10	Samuel Parker	Massachusetts	Sept. 14, 1804	Dec. 6, 1804
11	John Henry Hobart	New York (*Assistant*)	May 29, 1811	Sept. 12, 1830
12	Alexander Viets Griswold P. Bp.	Eastern Diocese	May 29, 1811	Feb. 15, 1843
13	Theodore Dehon	South Carolina	Oct. 15, 1812	Aug. 6, 1817
14	Richard Channing Moore	Virginia	May 18, 1814	Nov. 11, 1841
15	James Kemp	Maryland (*Suffragan*)	Sept. 1, 1814	Oct. 28, 1827
16	John Croes	New Jersey	Nov. 19, 1815	July 30, 1832
17	Nathaniel Bowen	South Carolina	Oct. 8, 1818	Aug. 25, 1839
18	Philander Chase (Presiding Bp.)*	Ohio	Feb. 11, 1819	Sept. 20, 1852
19	Thomas Church Brownell " ..	Connecticut	Oct. 27, 1819	Jan. 13, 1865
20	John Stark Ravenscroft	North Carolina	May 22, 1823	Mar. 5, 1830
21	Henry Ustick Onderdonk	Pennsylvania (*Assistant*)	Oct. 25, 1827	Dec. 6, 1858
22	William Meade	Virginia (*Assistant*)	Aug. 19, 1829	Mar. 14, 1862
23	William Murray Stone	Maryland	Oct. 21, 1830	Feb. 26, 1838
24	Benjamin Tredwell Onderdonk	New York	Nov. 26, 1830	April 30, 1861
25	Levi Silliman Ives†	North Carolina	Sept. 22, 1831	Oct. 13. 1867
26	John Henry Hopkins (Pres. Bp.)	Vermont	Oct. 31, 1832	Jan. 9, 1868
27	Benjamin B. Smith " "	Kentucky	Oct. 31, 1832	May 31, 1884
28	Charles Pettit McIlvaine	Ohio	Oct. 31, 1832	Mar. 12, 1873
29	George Washington Doane	New Jersey	Oct. 31, 1832	April 27, 1859
30	James Hervey Otey	Tennessee	Jan. 14, 1834	April 23, 1863
31	Jackson Kemper‡	Mo. and Ind. (*Miss.*)	Sept. 25, 1835	May 24, 1870
32	Samuel Allen McCoskry§	Michigan	July 7, 1836	
33	Leonidas Polk‖	Arkansas (*Missionary*)	Dec. 9, 1838	June 14, 1864
34	William Heathcote De Lancey	Western New York	May 9, 1839	April 4, 1865
35	Christopher Edwards Gadsden	South Carolina	June 21, 1840	June 23, 1852
36	William Rollinson Whittingham	Maryland	Sept. 17, 1840	Oct. 17, 1879
37	Stephen Elliott	Georgia	Feb. 28, 1841	Dec. 21, 1866
38	Alfred Lee (Presiding Bp.)	Delaware	Oct. 12, 1841	
39	John Johns	Virginia (*Assistant*)	Oct. 13, 1842	April 4, 1866
40	Manton Eastburn	Massachusetts (*Assistant*)	Dec. 29, 1842	Sept. 11, 1872
41	John Prentiss Kewly Henshaw	Rhode Island	Aug. 11, 1843	July 20, 1852
42	Carlton Chase	New Hampshire	Oct. 20, 1844	Jan. 18, 1870
43	Nicholas Hammer Cobbs	Alabama	Oct. 20, 1844	Jan. 11, 1861
44	Cicero Stephens Hawks	Missouri	Oct. 20, 1844	April 19, 1868

* Translated to Illinois, 1833.
‡ Accepted Bishopric of Wisconsin in 1854.
‖ Translated to Louisiana Oct. 16, 1841.

† Deposed Oct. 14, 1853.
§ Deposed Sept. 3, 1878.

APOSTOLIC SUCCESSION

Order	Name of Bishop	Name of See	Date of Consecration	Date of Decease
45	William Jones Boone	China (Missionary)	Oct. 26, 1844	July 17, 1864
46	George Washington Freeman	Arkansas "	Oct. 26, 1844	April 29, 1858
47	Horatio Southgate*	Turkey "	Oct. 26, 1844	
48	Alonzo Potter	Pennsylvania	Sept. 23, 1845	July 4, 1865
49	George Burgess	Maine	Oct. 31, 1847	April 23, 1866
50	George Upfold	Indiana	Dec. 16, 1849	Aug. 26, 1872
51	William Mercer Green	Mississippi	Feb. 24, 1850	Feb. 13, 1887
52	John Payne†	Africa (Missionary)	July 11, 1851	Oct. 23, 1874
53	Francis Huger Rutledge	Florida	Oct. 15, 1851	Nov. 6, 1866
54	John Williams	Connecticut (Assistant)	Oct. 29, 1851	
55	Henry John Whitehouse	Illinois (Assistant)	Nov. 20, 1851	Aug. 10, 1874
56	Jonathan Mayhew Wainwright	New York (Provisional)	Nov. 10, 1852	Sept. 21, 1854
57	Thomas Frederick Davis	South Carolina	Oct. 17, 1853	Dec. 2, 1871
58	Thomas Atkinson	North Carolina	Oct. 17, 1853	Jan. 4, 1881
59	William Ingraham Kip	California (Missionary)	Oct. 28, 1853	
60	Thomas Fielding Scott	Or. and Wash. (Miss.)	Jan. 8, 1854	July 14, 1867
61	Henry Washington Lee	Iowa	Oct. 18, 1854	Sept. 26, 1874
62	Horatio Potter	New York (Provisional)	Nov. 22, 1854	Jan. 2, 1887
63	Thomas March Clark	Rhode Island	Dec. 6, 1854	
64	Samuel Bowman	Pennsylvania (Assistant)	Aug. 25, 1858	Aug. 3, 1861
65	Alexander Gregg	Texas	Oct. 13, 1859	
66	William Henry Odenheimer‡	New Jersey	Oct. 13, 1859	Aug. 14, 1879
67	Gregory Thurston Bedell	Ohio (Assistant)	Oct. 13, 1859	
68	Henry Benjamin Whipple	Minnesota	Oct. 13, 1859	
69	Henry Champlin Lay§	Arkansas (Missionary)	Oct. 23, 1859	Sep. 17, 1885
70	Joseph Cruickshank Talbot‖	Northwest "	Feb. 15, 1860	Jan. 15, 1883
71	William Bacon Stevens	Pennsylvania (Assistant)	Jan. 2, 1862	
72	Richard Hooker Wilmer	Alabama	Mar. 6, 1862	
73	Thomas Hubbard Vail	Kansas	Dec. 15, 1864	
74	Arthur Cleveland Coxe	West New York (Assist.)	Jan. 4, 1865	
75	Charles Todd Quintard	Tennessee	Oct. 11, 1865	
76	Robert Harper Clarkson	Nebraska (Missionary)	Nov. 15, 1865	Mar. 10, 1884
77	George Maxwell Randall	Colorado "	Dec. 28, 1865	Sept. 28, 1873
78	John Barret Kerfoot	Pittsburg	Jan. 25, 1866	July 10, 1881
79	Channing Moore Williams	China and Japan (Miss.)	Oct. 3, 1866	
80	Joseph Pere Bell Wilmer	Louisiana	Nov. 7, 1866	Dec. 2, 1878
81	George David Cummins¶	Kentucky (Assistant)	Nov. 15, 1866	June 26, 1876
82	William Edmond Armitage	Wisconsin "	Dec. 6, 1866	Dec. 7, 1873
83	Henry Adams Neely	Maine	Jan. 25, 1867	
84	Daniel Sylvester Tuttle**	Montana (Missionary)	May 1, 1867	
85	John Freeman Young	Florida	July 25, 1867	Nov. 15, 1885
86	John Watrous Beckwith	Georgia	April 2, 1868	
87	Francis McNeece Whittle	Virginia (Assistant)	April 30, 1868	
88	William Henry Augustus Bissell	Vermont	June 3, 1868	
89	Charles Franklin Robertson	Missouri	Oct. 25, 1868	May 1, 1886
90	Benjamin Wistar Morris	Or. and Wash. (Miss.)	Dec. 3, 1868	
91	Abram Newkirk Littlejohn	Long Island	Jan. 27, 1869	
92	William Croswell Doane	Albany	Feb. 2, 1869	
93	Frederic Dan Huntington	Central New York	April 8, 1869	
94	Ozi William Whitaker††	Nev. and Ariz. (Miss.)	Oct. 13, 1869	
95	Henry Niles Pierce	Ark. and Ind. Ter. (Miss.)	Jan. 25, 1870	
96	William Woodruff Niles	New Hampshire	Sept. 21, 1870	
97	William Pinkney	Maryland (Assistant)	Oct. 6, 1870	July 4, 1883
98	William Bell White Howe	South Carolina (Assist.)	Oct. 8, 1871	
99	Mark Antony DeWolfe Howe	Central Pennsylvania	Dec. 28, 1871	
100	William Hobart Hare	Niobrara (Missionary)‡‡	Jan. 9, 1873	
101	John Gottlieb Auer	Africa "	April 17, 1873	Feb. 16, 1874
102	Benjamin Henry Paddock	Massachusetts	Sept. 17, 1873	
103	Theodore Benedict Lyman	North Carolina (Assist.)	Dec. 11, 1873	
104	John Franklin Spalding	Colorado (Missionary)	Dec. 31, 1873	
105	Edward Randolph Welles	Wisconsin	Oct. 25, 1874	
106	Robert W. B. Elliott	Western Texas (Miss.)	Nov. 15, 1874	
107	John Henry Ducachet Wingfield	North California "	Dec. 2, 1874	
108	Alexander Charles Garrett	Northern Texas "	Dec. 20, 1874	

* Resignation accepted by the House of Bishops, Oct. 12, 1850.
† Resignation accepted by the House of Bishops, Oct. 21, 1871.
‡ Elected the Diocese of Northern New Jersey Nov. 12, 1874.
§ Translated to Easton, 1869. ‖ Translated to Indiana, 1865.
¶ Deposed June 24, 1874.
** Translated to Missouri, 1886. †† Translated to Pennsylvania, 1886.
‡‡ Jurisdiction enlarged and title changed to Southern Dakota by the General Convention of 1883.

Order.	Name of Bishop.	Name of See.	Date of Consecration.	Date of Decease.
109	William Forbes Adams*	New Mexico (Missionary)	Jan. 17, 1875	
110	Thomas Underwood Dudley	Kentucky (Assistant)	Jan. 27, 1875	
111	John Scarborough	New Jersey	Feb. 2, 1875	
112	George DeNormandie Gillespie	Western Michigan	Feb. 24, 1875	
113	Thomas Augustus Jagger	Southern Ohio	April 28, 1875	
114	William Edward McLaren	Illinois	Dec. 8, 1875	
115	John Henry Hobart Brown	Fon du Lac	Dec. 15, 1875	
116	William Stevens Perry	Iowa	Sept. 10, 1876	
117	Charles Clifton Penick	Africa (Missionary)	Feb. 13, 1877	
118	Samuel I. J. Schereschewsky †	Shanghai "	Oct. 31, 1877	
119	Alexander Burgess	Quincy	May 15, 1878	
120	George William Peterkin	West Virginia	May 30, 1878	
121	George Franklin Seymour	Springfield	June 11, 1878	
122	Samuel Smith Harris	Michigan	Sept. 17, 1879	
123	Thomas Alfred Starkey	Northern New Jersey	Jan. 8, 1880	
124	John Nicholas Galleher	Louisiana	Feb. 5, 1880	
125	George K. Dunlop	New Mexico (Missionary)	Nov. 21, 1880	
126	Leigh Richmond Brewer	Montana "	Dec. 8, 1880	
127	John Adams Paddock	Washington Ter. "	Dec. 15, 1880	
128	Cortlandt Whitehead	Pittsburg	Jan. 25, 1882	
129	Hugh Miller Thompson	Mississippi (Assistant)	Feb. 24, 1883	
130	David Buel Knickerbacker	Indiana	Oct. 14, 1883	
131	Henry Codman Potter	New York (Assistant)	Oct. 20, 1883	
132	Alfred Magill Randolph	Virginia "	Oct. 21, 1883	
133	William D. Walker	North Dakota (Miss.)	Dec. 20, 1883	
134	A. A. Watson,	East Carolina	April 17, 1884	
135	William Jones Boone	Shanghai (Missionary)	Oct. 28, 1884	
136	Nelson S. Rulison, D.D	Central Penna. (Assist.)	Oct. 28, 1884	
137	William Paret, D.D	Maryland	Jan. 8, 1885	
138	George Worthington, D.D	Nebraska	Feb. 24, 1885	
139	Samuel D. Ferguson, D.D	Cape Palmas (Miss.)	June 24, 1885	
140	E. Gardner Weed, D.D	Florida	Aug. 11, 1886	
141	Mahlon N. Gilbert, D.D	Minnesota (Assistant)	Oct. 17, 1886	

* Resignation accepted by the House of Bishops, Oct. 15, 1877.
† Resignation accepted by the House of Bishops, Oct. 24, 1883.

The discussion on the Apostolic Succession has occupied so many pens there is no need to mention the many works that are easily accessible. The lists of the succession above given have been compiled from Chapin's "Primitive Church" and Bishop Seymour's List in the "Churchman's Calendar" for 1866.

Appellate Court. In all our Dioceses, except the three in Illinois, the system of Church courts, for the trial of priests, deacons, and laymen, is incomplete, providing, for the most part, for only one formal trial. In nearly all, no trial can be entered upon unless the Bishop consents. In nearly all, the Bishop has so large an agency in the formation of the Court,—which is a Court appointed for the special case,—that it is possible to organize it to convict or to acquit, as he may prefer. In some Dioceses the Court is a permanent body, elected annually by the Convention. Where there is a definite party predominance in any such Diocesan Convention, it will naturally be embodied in the *personnel* of the Court, and any trial marked with the slightest partisan tinge would merely be decided like any other party vote. In neither case is any appeal provided. If injustice were done, there could be no possible remedy. Even if a Bishop should be so extreme as to lay himself open to trial and conviction for the mode in which he might have secured the deposition of an obnoxious clergyman, still, the punishment of the Bishop would not operate to restore the poor clergyman. For *him* there is no remedy. His oppressor might be deposed, but he himself would not be in the slightest degree relieved from the consequences of that oppression.

Several attempts to establish an Appellate Court by General Convention have failed, for various reasons. Every such attempt has shown the cumbrousness and practical difficulty of constructing any *one* Appellate Court, which can receive appeals from the whole American Church; and it is as well that they have failed, for they were not reasonably workable. In the Canon for the trial of a Bishop we find an important recognition of the true principle, in the establishment of a Board of Inquiry, whose members are taken from the Diocese concerned and the three *adjoining Dioceses*. The *grouping* of Dioceses *conveniently situated* is the true solution of the difficulty. The other principle involved is, that whereas the probability of injustice in the first instance is due to the predominance of the will of one man, the appeal should be to the judgment of more than one. Individual prejudice is more likely to be remedied by collective fairness.

The "grouping of Dioceses conveniently situated" is only another description of what is known in Ecclesiastical language as a *Province*. And the first Province to be fully organized in this country is also the first to give us a reasonable Court of Appeal. We refer to Illinois, whose three Dioceses of "Chicago," "Quincy," and "Springfield" are united in the "Province of Illinois." The scrupulous obstructiveness of the General Convention had decided that a Court of Appeals, under Article VI. of the Constitution, could be established only by the action of the Dioceses as such, and *not* by the action of the Province as a Province. Accordingly, the Federate Council acted only as an informal committee in preparing the draft of a Canon, which, with substantial identity, was afterwards adopted by *each* of the three Diocesan Conventions. The leading principles of this Canon are as follows :

1. The Bishops of the Province are the judges of the Court of Appeal. As the possible prejudice or passion of the Bishop of the Diocese from which the appeal comes may be the leading feature in the case, it would be manifestly a departure from our established ideas for the official action of one Bishop to be officially reviewed and corrected, except by his peers,—his brethren in the same order. Moreover, this is the primitive rule,—the Bishops of the Province being the universal Court of Appeal in the earlier ages. It is wisely provided, however, that the Bishop whose judgment is appealed from shall not preside in the Court during the trial of that case. In all other cases, the Bishop who presides in the Federate Council (the *Metropolitan*, as he was called in ancient days) presides also in the Appellate Court.

2. But there are few of our Bishops who have been trained as lawyers; and to one who has not had that training, there are many legal points which may fail to be appreciated by the unlegal mind. The Illinois Canon, therefore, provides that there shall be *Assessors* in the Court of Appeal,—each Diocesan Convention shall elect one Clerical and one Lay Assessor. It may be taken for granted that each Convention will select a clergyman who is known for his familiarity with the Canons, and a layman who is learned in the law of the land. As occasions may arise when there will not be entire harmony between a Bishop and the majority in his Convention, and as it is his *right* that he should have the advice of those in whom he has confidence, it is properly added that, besides the elected Assessors,—who may be depended upon to protect the rights of clergy and laity,—each Bishop may, if he see fit, appoint one clerical or lay Assessor, or both. This power will, doubtless, be very seldom exercised; but it is quite proper that it should be secured.

3. In other Courts of Appeal, with Assessors, it has been a contested point whether the members of the Court should be bound to decide in accordance with the advice of the Assessors, or should have power to decide otherwise. In Illinois, the responsibility is accurately divided in the Canon itself. As the Assessors are supposed to be superior in the knowledge to be expected of experts, *they* are to decide all interlocutory questions, —all those questions of historical or professional interpretation, admissibility of evidence, etc., in which men without special training are most likely to make mistakes. In this way they protect the dignity of the Bishops from the danger of making an unhappy exhibit of insufficient information. But when all preliminary questions are thus settled, and nothing remains but the final decision as to whether the appeal shall be granted, or refused, or a new trial ordered, then the dignity of the Bishops is further secured by giving to *them alone* the right to vote. But a further safeguard for the rights of clergy and laity is secured in the provision that each Bishop shall give, in writing, *seriatim*, the *reasons* for his decision. When it is known beforehand that every such opinion must run the gauntlet of open and public criticism, it is the more likely to be fair.

4. The Illinois Canon is seriously defective in one point. It allows of no appeal except from an adverse decision in a Diocesan Court. This would limit the usefulness of the Court to the lowest possible minimum. Not one-tenth part of the grievances that arise ever come before an Ecclesiastical Court at all: and thus nine-tenths of our practical troubles would be left just where they are now,—with *no* remedy whatsoever. An appeal should be allowed to every person claiming to be aggrieved by any action on the part of any of the constituted authorities of the Church in any Diocese of the Province. In the primitive Church, this was carried so far as to include every case of suspension from the communion or of excommunication. The principle was, indeed, early recognized that an act of discipline by one Bishop could not be revoked by another Bishop. The one under discipline could be restored only by *his own* Bishop. But every such act was open to revision by the Bishops of the Province. For instance, the 5th Canon of the great Council of Nicæa provides as follows :

"Concerning those, whether of the *Clergy* or of the *Laity*, who have been excommunicated by the Bishops in the several Provinces, let the provision of that Canon prevail which provides that persons who have been cast out by one Bishop are not to be readmitted by another. Nevertheless, inquiry should be made whether they have been excommunicated through captiousness, or contentiousness, or any such like ungracious disposition, in the Bishop. And, that this matter may have due investigation, it is decreed that, in every Province, Synods shall be held twice every year ; in order that, all the Bishops of the Province being assembled together, such questions may by them be thoroughly examined; so that those who have confessedly offended against their Bishop may be seen to be, for just cause, excommunicated by all, until it shall seem fit to the common assembly of the Bishops to pronounce a milder sentence upon them," etc.

And the 6th Canon of Antioch (afterwards made œcumenical) provides in like manner: " If any one has been excommunicated by his own Bishop, let him not be received by others until he has either been restored by his own Bishop, or until, when a Synod is held, he shall have appeared and made his defense, and, having convinced the Synod, shall have received a different sentence. And let this decree apply to the Laity, and to Presbyters and Deacons, and all who are in the Canon" (*i.e.*, on the Sacerdotal List).

It is clear that if the exercise of the power of the keys—specifically given to each Bishop at his consecration—was thus open to appeal, and revision by other Bishops, there can be *no* official action of a Bishop secure from such revision. And if *all* the official acts of a Bishop are liable to revision and correction by his brethren, there are no inferior officers or organizations in the Church who can have the face to claim exemption.

The good example set by Illinois will, in course of time, it is to be hoped, be followed in other States of the Union, only with its imperfections remedied, so as to bring it into closer agreement with the example of the primitive Church, and with the requirements of justice and common sense. The true idea of the Episcopate is, *not* that each Bishop may be an irresponsible despot within his own territorial limits, liable to *no* correction until he is bad enough to be deposed, but that the entire order is One (*Episcopatus est unus*), in such wise that there is *no* official act of any Bishop which may not be submitted to the revision of his brethren. The strength of the *whole order* will thus rest in each act: while, on the other plan, the authority of the entire order will suffer from any manifestation of arbitrary caprice or infirmity on the part of any individual Bishop. Nothing short of the true system will realize St. Cyprian's description of the One Episcopate,—" *cujus a singulis* IN SOLIDUM *pars tenetur*."

REV. J. H. HOPKINS, D.D.

Archbishop. It at first probably meant what it now signifies,—Bishops over provinces, but themselves under Metropolitans or Patriarchs. About the time of the Council of Chalcedon, however, it came to mean the Patriarchs themselves. But later again it fell back to its original use, *i.e.*, the Bishop over other Bishops in a Province. The co-equality of spiritual power of his suffragans, and the superiority position for the discipline of the Church in the Archbishop, were both strenuously set forth. The Archbishops of the Western Church for centuries were independent, but about 514 A.D. the Popes began giving the pall (*vide* PALL), and from that in about two hundred and fifty years succeeded in enforcing that the gift of the pall was imperative, and that the Archbishop should swear fealty to the Pope on receiving it. This was thrown off by the Anglican Communion. In the English Communion there are four Archbishops,—Canterbury, York, Armagh, and Dublin. In the American Church the presiding Bishop, who is the eldest consecrated Bishop, has many Archepiscopal functions to perform. Through him must be made all official communications from foreign Churches. He presides in the House of Bishops, or convenes it for special meetings; either consecrates in person or appoints consecrators for a Bishop-elect; appoints the council of five Bishops to settle differences between a parish and the Diocesan; receives the resignation of a Bishop and communicates it to each of the Bishops having jurisdiction in the Church, and upon their advice accepts or refuses such resignation; and receives charges against, and arranges for the trial of, an accused Bishop.

Archdeacon. The Archdeacon was originally the presiding Deacon over the body of Deacons, either in a city or a Deanery, or a Diocese. Later, in the ninth century, the Archdeacon was in priests' orders. His functions were to look after the finances of the Church and the distribution of funds to the poor. He exercised a discipline over the Deacons and Presbyters under him in the Bishop's behalf, and he had a care over the property of the Church. He was the Bishop's business man, so to speak. In the East, when a See was vacant, he was one of the guardians of its rights and its property. The Diocese usually had several Archdeacons. In the English Church the Archdeacon looks after the condition of the church and of the parsonage, and is the proper person to order or to permit repairs. It is there an office of great weight, since the Archdeacon holds a court, at which cases of discipline of the laity are presented. The rights of the office vary much in the several Dioceses, but usually the Archdeacon visits for the Bishop the clergy, inspects the property, inducts parsons, receives the presentments of the Church-wardens, and holds a minor court.

The *title* has been revived in two of the Dioceses of the American Church,—Albany and Connecticut, but the office is probably identical with the title Dean of Convocation.

Archimandrite. (*Gr.* the leader of the fold.) The title of the ruler over several monasteries. It does not necessarily imply that the Archimandrite had several monasteries under him, but this was usually the case. The Hegumen was the chief over a single monastery, and consequently when several monasteries were under one rule he was subject to the Archimandrite. The Archimandrite was, of course, under the authority of the Bishop. It was a title which soon came into use after monastic bodies obtained some cohesion and lived by some acknowledged rule.

Architecture, Church. *Prefatory.*—Under this head an endeavor will be made to inquire into the nature and structure of the places of worship of the early Christians, their development from the upper room of the days of the Apostles, through the intervening centuries, to the magnificent structures of the Middle Ages, continuing thence to our own times. But a cursory glance can be given to the history of this subject in the limited space here allotted, the idea of this article being mainly to show what may be done in the way of improving the architecture and arrangement of our parish churches, adapting them not only to the wants of the congregation, but making them more houses of GOD, monuments and offerings of a grateful people to the great and unseen CREATOR of all things.

Early History.—What little is known of the places of worship of the early Christians is found in the patristic writings and among the writings of the early Christian historians, while much information is also obtainable from the early heathen writers of the age. In the earliest times, doubtless, there were no fixed edifices, services being held in the houses of Christians, sometimes, as we read in the Scriptures, in an upper room, as when Paul was stopping at Troas: "Upon the first day of the week, when the disciples came together to break bread (that is, to celebrate the Eucharist), Paul preached unto them, ready to depart on the morrow, and continued his speech until midnight. And there were many lights in the upper chamber, where they were gathered together. Now there sat in a window a certain young man named Eutychus, being fallen into a deep sleep, and as Paul was long preaching, he sunk down with sleep and fell down from the third loft and was taken up dead."

This is the most particular description of a house of worship that we find in the Scriptures. It will be noticed that this is an upper room, as was also that in which our SAVIOUR celebrated the Last Supper. These out-of-the-way places were doubtless selected because in those early days it was as much as a man's life was worth to proclaim himself a Christian. In Rome we find them worshiping in the houses of wealthy Christians, in underground chapels, and in other places where they were least liable to be disturbed.

Owing to the cruel persecutions to which the early Christians were subjected, both under the tyrant Nero, 64 A.D., and then under the Roman Emperor Domitian, 94 A.D., many have held that there were no structures set apart for the worship of GOD. Yet St. Paul says, "Have ye not houses to eat and drink in? or despise ye the Church of GOD?" Now it is shown that the ancient writers, St. Austin, St. Basil, St. Chrysostom, and St. Jerome, took this to mean the place set apart for Christian worship, and not the assembly of people. Then we know that the disciples often met together for prayer and worship after the death of our SAVIOUR.

In the second century, when the persecutions were still active against the Christians and it became necessary for them to band together, Ignatius writes to exhort them to meet together in one place, and in his Epistle to the Philadelphians says that at this time there was one altar in every church, and one Apostolic Bishop, or head, appointed with his Presbytery and Deacons. Some of the later Greek readings omit the word Church, but speak of the one altar, thus showing that there was a stated place of worship. Then history tells us of people turning their houses over to the Church in which to celebrate the divine offices of worship. We have record of forty churches in Rome at the date of the last persecution, and there were many in Africa.

As early as the middle of the third century Gregory of Neo Cæsarea writes describing the degrees of admission of penitents, according to the discipline of those days:

1st. *Weepers* (the first degree of penance) were without the porch of the oratory. There the mournful sinners stood and begged of all the faithful, as they went in, to pray for them.

2d. *Hearers* (the second degree) were within the porch, in the place called Narthex, where the penitent sinners might stand near the catechumens and hear the Scripture read and expounded, but were to go out before them.

3d. *Prostrantes,—lying down along the church-pavement.* These prostrate ones were admitted somewhat farther into the church and went out with the catechumens.

4th. *Stantes,—staying with the people or congregation.* These *consistentes* did not go out with the catechumens, but after they and the other penitents had left remained, and joined in prayer with the faithful.

5. *Participators in the Sacraments.*

About the beginning of the fourth century Constantine ascended the throne, and becoming fully convinced of the truth of the Christian religion, set about establishing it throughout his dominions, erecting churches everywhere. For some time before his reign, and even into it for twenty-five years, heathen temples were used to some extent for Christian worship, how much has never been determined. At this time, however (333 A.D.), Constantine ordered all the temples, altars, and images of the heathen to be destroyed, and in many instances these temples were demolished and their revenues confiscated. Some of the later emperors, however, instead of pulling down the temples, converted them to Christian uses. Honorius published in the Western Empire two laws forbidding the destruction of any more temples in the cities, as they might serve for ornament or public use, being once purged of their idols and altars. There can be no doubt of the antipathy of the Christians to the fine arts, because defiled by idolatrous uses, and that they destroyed everything that was beautiful that came in their way. Notwithstanding the later imperial decrees for the preservation of the heathen temples, nothing could induce the people to tolerate them or their contents, and it was only in a few out-of-the-way places, as at Palestine, they were allowed to remain. At Rome the only example that owes its preservation distinctively to the Christians is the Pantheon. They destroyed everything that they could lay their hands on, the more beautiful the quickest destroyed, it mattered not so long as it savored of the rites of the heathen Church. They worked, even as in later times the Puritans worked in England: whatever was beautiful, whatever pleased the eye, if it belonged to the earlier religion, must give way to the new.

We know that the Emperor Constantine gave orders, after a long search by the Empress Helena, which resulted in finding the Holy Sepulchre, that a church be erected over its site. The place had been desecrated by the pagans; they even had erected a statue of Venus over the place, and dedicated the spot to the heathen goddess. Constantine orders how the church shall be built, of what form, of what materials, and sets forth as to the decoration, etc. All in a most elaborate manner. There is even a plan of this Holy Sepulchre Church handed down by the Abbot Adamnan of Iona on his tablets, as he took it down from the description of Arculphus, a Gallican Bishop, who had visited the East. It was of "wonderful rotundity," entered by four doors; it contained three aisles, and was surrounded by twelve columns; hanging in it were twelve lamps, burning day and night, emblems of the twelve Apostles.

Although the Church of the Holy Sepulchre was evidently round, it had other parts attached, and there is little evidence of this form being employed elsewhere to any great extent, the usual form being that of a parallelogram. Baptisteries, however, were generally built either round or polygonal. It is evident that the churches, of whatever form, had other buildings attached, both for secular and religious purposes,—such as libraries, houses for the clergy, schools, etc., much the same as in the later cathedrals and in many of the mission churches of to-day in London, and occasionally in America. The entrance was at the west end, the church being placed east and west, with the altar at the east. There are exceptions to this custom; no more, however, than to prove the rule, the habit being to face to the east, so in this way it became natural to orientate the churches. Entering the western door, and passing through the porch, a large open court was reached, surrounded by a colonnade. In the centre, this court contained a fountain, used to wash the hands and face, sometimes the feet. This, perhaps, is the origin of the custom now in vogue in Roman churches, though perverted, of having a stoup of holy water at the door. This open court, or atrium, was used for penitents of the first order, those who were not allowed to enter the church; later it was used as a place of burial, particularly for the wealthy and those of distinction. Passing through this quadrangle the narthex was reached. Entrance to this was had through three gates, the central usually the larger. There were, sometimes, several narthexes to a church, even as many as four. The narthex formed the first division of the church, and contained the catechumens and the hearers. Jews, infidels, and heretics were admitted here. In front came the third class of penitents.

The narthex was separated from the nave or church proper by a wooden screen, or railing. The nave was entered through several gates, often called royal or beautiful gates. Here were congregated the main body of worshipers, those in full communion and under no censure.

The sexes were usually separated during service, a practice that is yet in use in some of the modern ritualistic Churches. St. Cyril says, "Let men be with men and women with women in the church." Then in the Apostolical constitutions, " Let the door-keepers stand at the gate of the men, and the deaconesses at the gate of the women." The women were usually placed on the north side of the church. The Greeks now put them in the galleries.

Not only was this order observed, but the virgins, matrons, and widows were given distinct places; then came the order of penitents not allowed to partake of the Holy Eucharist, but permitted to stay in the church and witness the celebration. East of the nave came the choir, the place for the singers. This was separated from the former by a screen or low wall. Here was placed the ambo, or pulpit, from which the gospel and epistle were read. The sermon, as a rule, was preached by the Bishop from the altar-steps, although St. Chrysostom, the better to be heard of the people, preached from the ambo.

Extending from the choir eastward, was the sanctuary, corresponding to the holy of holies of Jews. The Latins called it the sacrarium. Here were celebrated the Church's most sacred offices. The sacrarium was always elevated above the choir, and was often separated from it by a rail or low screen called cancelli, hence the word chancel. This was to keep out the multitude. The Council of Laodicea forbade lay persons entering the sanctuary, while the Council of Trullo says, " That no layman whatsoever be permitted to enter the place of the altar, excepting only the Emperor, when he makes his oblation to the CREATOR, according to ancient custom."

The sacrarium was usually semicircular in plan. In the centre was placed the altar, raised on several steps, and surmounted by a canopy supported by twelve columns, symbolical of the twelve Apostles. On the top of the canopy was a cross, while behind the altar was the Bishop's chair raised and facing west. Around the circumference of the apse were placed the seats for the priests. The early altars were of wood, but this material was not used long, as is evident from the decree of the Council of Epone, that no altars should be consecrated except such as be of stone. Gregory Nyssen says, "This altar whereat we stand is by nature only common stone, nothing different from other stones, whereof our walls are made and pavements formed; but after it is consecrated, and dedicated to the services of GOD, it becomes a holy table, an immaculate altar, which may not promiscuously be touched by all, but only by the priests in the time of divine service." All of which goes to show the sacred feeling for the church, and especially its more sacred altar, held even in the very early days of the Church. The spaces between the columns of the canopy to the altar were hung with curtains or veils to conceal the altar. St. Chrysostom says, "When you see the veils undrawn, then think you see heaven opened, and the angels descending from above." Hangings were placed in other parts of the church, sometimes richly worked in gold. They were placed between nave and chancel, and before doors, etc. The altar was covered with a linen cloth, emblem of purity. The sacred vessels were of various substances, usually of gold and silver, yet glass was used in the earlier times for chalices.

Often beside the altar in a recess on one side was a shelf to contain the offerings of bread and wine. On the opposite side from this was the priest's vestry.

Outside the main body of the church, and within an outer inclosure, were the various buildings connected with the church, such as the baptistery, which in those days was always a separate structure, the library, priests' houses, etc.

The interiors of these churches of the early Christians were, according to the writers of the time, quite elaborately decorated. The walls were often lined with marble, while the roofs were of mosaic or paneled, and covered with gold and color. The altars were inlaid with precious stones and gold and silver, while gates were set with silver and ivory, and columns were of rare marbles with capitals of bright gold.

It has been thought by some that the ancient Roman basilica, the seat of public justice of the time, suggested the form and arrangement of the Christian church. However true this may be, they certainly bore a close resemblance, and there are numerous instances of basilicæ being converted into churches. This plan of Trajan's Basilica will show how far the basilica was imitated in the arrangement of the Christian church (Fig. 1). The basilica was of the shape of a parallelogram, with a semicircular apse at one—sometimes at either—end

FIG. 1.

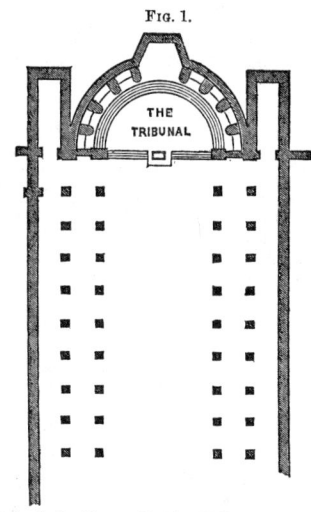

Trajan's Basilica or Justice Hall, Rome, 98 A.D.

In the centre of the apse was the seat of the prætor, and below and about him those of the assessors and other officers. These were separated from the main body of the building by a screen of lattice-work called cancelli. In the main body sat the people, while between them and the higher officers of the court sat the advocates and notaries. The main building was divided by two rows of columns into three aisles. These columns supported an arcade carrying a wall containing windows, forming a clear-story, the side aisles being lower. A better arrangement could not have been devised for a Christian church, and it is the form, with slight modifications, that is in use to this day throughout Western Christendom. However well adapted these heathen basilicæ were to the exigencies of Christian worship, they did not continue long in use. There is only one example remaining to us of a heathen basilica converted to a Christian church. A veneration for the graves of the martyrs and a distaste for edifices constructed for pagan uses caused, under Christian rule, the demolition of these ancient structures and their re-erection in other places made sacred by containing the remains of the martyrs. Here they were built again on much the same plan and on a yet grander scale. The martyrs were usually put to death outside the city walls, and were supposed to be buried on the spot of their execution, so that when the churches came to be erected on these spots they were very inconvenient of access, being so far from the centre of population.

A custom had grown up of worshiping underground in the catacombs among the graves of the martyrs, and this custom undoubtedly was the reason, when Christianity became legalized by Constantine, of the churches being set up in the same places, as instanced in Rome by Santa Agnese and San Lorenzo, and also at St. Peter's, which Constantine had placed near to the Circus of Nero, and whose altar was set over the remains of the Apostles. This custom of placing the churches without the city walls caused great inconvenience and was a matter of much moment in later times, when the incursions of northern barbarians prevented an attendance upon the churches and finally caused their desecration, and, in many instances, entire demolition.

The Basilica of St. Peter, however, contained certain additions and variations from the civil basilica. (Fig. 2.) It consisted of a

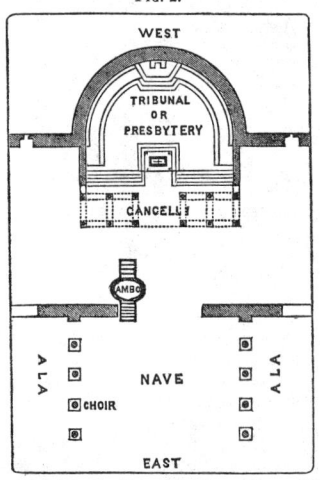

FIG. 2.

Plan of ancient Basilica of St. Peter, Rome, 330 A.D.

five-aisled church, extending east and west. At the end of the five aisles was an aisle running north and south; east of this came the apse, giving the plan the form of a cross. There were forty-eight columns of precious marbles inclosing the large aisle, and the lateral aisles contained forty-eight columns likewise. There were an hundred other columns surrounding the various chapels and shrines. The walls were covered with paintings of religious subjects. The flat wooden ceiling was covered with gilt metal and Corinthian brass taken from the temples of Romulus and Jupiter Capitolinus. In this magnificent structure was one candelabrum that alone contained 1360 lights. Beside this there were more than a thousand other lights. All this magnificence in less than three centuries after the death of CHRIST! This structure withstood the varied fortunes of Rome for twelve hundred years, being respected by all its invaders, finally falling away with age. On its site rose another basilica, grander and more beautiful still, that glory of modern times. When the seat of the Roman Empire was removed to Byzantium, Constantine set about erecting a grand church there, probably modeled on St. Peter's. This did not last long. Another was built on its site and partially destroyed, rebuilt and destroyed again, meeting with many disasters in the mean time. Finally, the most famous architects were called from all parts of the known world by Justinian, and the erection began of the great Church of St. Sophia. This church, unlike those of Rome, formed a Greek cross in plan, each arm being alike, while the Western churches had a Latin cross for a plan. At the intersection of the arms of the cross rose a great dome of peculiar construction. During the revival of learning, communication was established between Greece and Italy, and this last and most magnificent basilica of the Eastern Empire greatly influenced the form and architecture of the new buildings. The Church of St. Mark, at Venice, of the tenth century, was copied in many particulars from St. Sophia, and this influence extended throughout Italy. The modern Church of St. Peter at Rome owes much to this importation of the dome from the East. As did the ancient Basilica of St. Peter's furnish the form for the ancient St. Sophia, so did the later St. Sophia supply much that influenced the modern St. Peter's.

Some writers have held that Constantine removed his seat of empire from Rome to the East to have more freedom in the establishment of his new religion, to throw off all the trammels of an earlier paganism, to start anew and fresh. One of his first objects, of course, was the erection of churches, and having no example anywhere about, the architects were left to their own resources. They undoubtedly drew some from Rome,—the idea of the round arch, maybe, and a partial use of the basilica plan. The Eastern architecture developed from these efforts, however, is a distinct style of its own and essentially a Christian architecture, notwithstanding its early Roman influence. It grew out of the exigencies of the time, having no contact with the earlier pagan styles, and spread over the entire Eastern Empire. This is the style generally known as Byzantine. Its plan is usually the shape of a Greek cross, the eastern end terminating in a semicircular apse: a plan that might be effectually used in the present day, and of which more will be said farther on.

Many say that this work at Byzantium was but a debasement of the Romanesque, itself debased from the Roman and the classics.

It may have been so; allow it so, and yet still we have much to admire; perhaps more in the utilities, than in the beauties, of this style, a style which spread throughout the East, and in the fifth and sixth centuries even to North Italy, where, at Ravenna, are several types. These, and the much later examples at Venice, made mention of above, are the purest types of the style in the West. The Lombards, however, were greatly influenced in their building by Byzantium; and through the trade with the East this style crept into France, where a whole line of unmistakably Byzantine churches stretch across the southwestern corner of the country. Its correlative, the Romanesque, abounds throughout Southern and Central France, running into Normandy and England, where it is represented by what is called the Norman style.

Both the Romanesque and Byzantine are distinguishable by the round arch, the latter also by the dome. To show the potency of the influence of the dome, essentially a Byzantine production, we have only to be reminded of the name given to the cathedral, even to our day, in many European countries. In Germany we have the *Dom*, in Italy the *Duomo*, and, although now the terms are indiscriminately applied to the principal church of a city, they came from the habit of this church being domical. Running from Italy north, and down through the Rhine towns, is a line of round-arched domical churches, evidently owing their inspiration to the East, where the Byzantine maintained its sway until the supremacy of the Ottomans summarily checked its farther spread.

The other essentially Christian style is that now usually denominated Gothic. It may be said to have sprung up simultaneously throughout Europe, while it is certain that no one nation can claim any priority of introduction. Its main characteristic, as now generally understood, is the pointed arch, although many writers have held that the term Gothic included all styles in use after the debasement of the classics and the decline of Roman architecture, including the Lombardic, Romanesque, Byzantine, and Norman.

But the word has now, generally, come to be confined to the pointed arch of the Middle Ages, and in general use throughout Christendom. To be sure, there is the Saracenic, also pointed, but this style is easily distinguished from the Gothic. There are many theories as to the origin of the pointed arch, yet, the divergence of opinion being so great, scarcely any two writers agreeing on any one theory, it will be sufficient here to instance a few of the theories put forth, and a favorite one is that of the form presented by the overhanging boughs of an avenue of trees. Then we have interlaced wicker-work, and the bending of two twigs or wands to meet at the top. Still more plausible is that of the intersected groin of the ceilings of early churches, which formed a pointed arch, while the round arch was observable elsewhere throughout the structure. It is certain, also, that the ancients knew of this shape, as is seen in some of their underground passages and tombs, yet they had not arrived at the correct method of construction of the arch. Although some of these theories might account for the origin and growth of the pointed arch in a certain locality, yet they could not be held to favor its general and rapid introduction into so many countries at once. Simultaneously, on the return, in the twelfth century, of the Crusaders from the East, this style began to appear, buildings springing up rapidly in all directions. This fact of its springing up at such a time, and so rapidly, has led to the theory of its derivation from the pointed Saracenic arch, and some prejudiced writers have, in their efforts to prevent its use, called it the Saracenic style. Allowing the fact of the adoption of the pointed arch of the East, how are we to account for the wide divergence in the styles? for, although the pointed arch is a principal characteristic of the Gothic, it is not the only one. There are the great idea of verticality; the clustered columns, with their light and slender shafts; the lofty spires and towers; the tracery; the mullions; the cross vaulting.

Fortunately for this Saracenic theory, it has the advantage of chronological correctness, while the simultaneity of the growth of Gothic is the main objection to the adoption of the other theories. Some derive the use of tracery from the perforated fret-work of the Arabians.

The origin of the term Gothic lies shrouded in as much mystery as the source of the style. That the Goths had nothing to do with the introduction of the style which bears their name is now generally accepted, and the use of this pagan name to designate an essentially Christian architecture has annoyed and puzzled many. Other names have been suggested, such as Christian, Pointed, English; but all of them are objectionable and misleading. The Byzantine and Lombardic are as much outgrowths of Christianity as the Gothic, while there are other pointed styles. As for the last term, surely England cannot lay claim to the architecture of the Christian world.

Many writers used the name Gothic as one of reproach, meaning thereby to stigmatize the style as barbarous, outlandish, and uncivilized. The style had its growth in, and belongs essentially to, those countries that had been overrun and inhabited by the Goths, and for this reason, perhaps, it is as appropriate as any.

The Gothic with which we in America have had most to do is that known as English, and this is divided into three distinct periods, with transitions from one period to another, where the character of the work is of necessity more or less mixed. These three periods are designated Early English, Decorated, and Perpendicular. This is confining the definition of the term Gothic to Pointed Gothic. Saxon and Norman are often counted in as being Gothic, although round-arched. The arch of the Early English is quite sharp, the openings being narrow and high, a complete subversion of the preceding low round-arched Norman, while the character of the work was simpler than in the succeeding styles, the wall-spaces greater, and there was little carving or decoration. The decorated work is characterized by a somewhat flatter arch and wider openings, profuse carvings and ornamentations, and, in short, is the style in which Gothic reached its height of grandeur and magnificence. The Perpendicular has quite flat-headed openings, very broad, with many divisions by vertical bars, called mullions. In this style the windows often are larger than the surrounding wall-space. It represents the decline of Gothic architecture, and is characterized by all kinds of depravities, while much of it is very beautiful.

Most of the prominent cathedrals and churches contain examples of all the different styles, from the Norman of William the Conqueror down. Sometimes one part is Norman, another Early English, and so on. Again, one sees the division of styles in the different stories, the lower arcade being Norman, the blind-story Early English, and the clear-story decorated, thus showing when the different parts were built or rebuilt. It is not within the province of this article to say which is the proper style for to-day, each having its own merits. Nothing, however, can be more beautiful than an English parish church built in the true spirit of Gothic work. And this English parish church is where ordinarily we should look for our model; not but what this nation and age may be capable of developing a style of church architecture of its own, without reverting to the Middle Ages for enlightenment, yet it has so far been unable to do so. Not only the church architecture, but the whole architecture of this country has been but a continuous series of tentative experiments in the endeavor to create an American style. Each architect and church committee has started out on his or its own independent line, sometimes copying, in so far as their knowledge or ignorance allowed, the architecture of an earlier age, sometimes reaching out in a blind, groping, pitiable way for that which they were unable to reach, yet thought they had consummated.

Seemingly the more intelligent solution of the problem would be to adapt our churches to the wants and needs of the people, keeping in mind the variations of climate and temperature, not letting the utilitarianism of the age run away with us. Employing the best talent, using the best materials, and building in the most substantial, churchly, and beautiful manner. With the thousands of churches built in this country since its foundation, there stands in the city of New York, at the head of Wall Street, a church erected a half-century ago, that, to this day, is the best example of a thoroughly-appointed, well-adapted, and beautiful parish church that we have. However conventional it may be, however unoriginal, however faulty in detail, designed as it was by a man who, when he first came to this country from England, worked at a carpenter's bench, it yet stands to remind us of the beauties of an English parish church, and of the folly of striving for something new when one simple edifice can show us more of beauty and of use in its little conventions than all the scores and hundreds and thousands of other churches strewn over our land, and devoted to the worship of GOD. The main idea of this age is to get a large, ugly, ungainly assembly-room that might be used for a barn, skating-rink, or railway-station, with as much or more purpose than that for which it is built, erected in a spirit and form unknown in any age or country but this, without even the merit of beauty or originality, an unintelligent, illiterate attempt at an adaptation of a style once the glory of the Christian world, a style yet capable of as perfect and beautiful an interpretation and exposition as was ever given it in the summit of its power. And yet they call this style Gothic! Better that architecture had been relegated to the master-workman of the Middle Age ere it became thus debased. One may travel from one end of this great land to the other, from ocean to ocean, from gulf to gulf, and see scarce a beggarly dozen of churches worthy of the name, either as to appropriateness of plan, beauty of structure, or simplicity or monumental grandeur. For not only should a church be arranged for the economies and decencies of public worship, but it should be for a monument, standing through all time to the glory of the Triune GOD. Builded as of old, by loving and masterly hands, of the best of the earth, not cheaply nor niggardly, but, where poverty will allow no more, simply and substantially, then grandly, magnificently, and gloriously. It must keep in mind the character of the cause it is to serve, the name it is to commemorate, the GOD it is to glorify. Then will we have a structure worthy its holy name, not crumbling to dust, but serving its purpose through generation and generation, through the ages and centuries, as have the churches of old, and that, with the care of dutiful hands, may stand for all time.

Who can see the work of the ancients and say that they built not well nor strongly? It is only work done in the times of the debasement of the arts and sciences that crumbled and fell away. The simplest form of the parish church in England consisted of a nave and chancel, both long and narrow. When an enlargement was needed an aisle was added, first on one side and then on the other. Sometimes, to obtain more room, resort was had to transepts, but these, as a rule, were confined to cathedrals. The form of plan thus obtained was that of a Latin cross. Occasionally the aisles were extended along the sides of the chancel. The churches almost invariably faced the east, as did those of the early times. The tower was placed in various positions, at the west end; in the centre, at junction of nave and transepts; on the south side, in which case it was usually near the west end; and, in short, in any place that seemed best adapted or, in the opinion of the architect, most becoming. There was usually a porch on the south side, near the west end. Entrances were had also at other places, as when the tower was at the west end, an entrance was given through it. Then there was the priest's door in one side of the chancel, opposite to the vestry. The vestry was usually on the north side of the chancel, and was the only place in the church in which a chimney was permissible. Just inside the main door of the church was placed the font, the most conspicuous object on entering, sometimes almost blocking the way, an all-time reminder that the only entrance to CHRIST's Church was through baptism. It was invariably large enough for immersion of infants, and of a dignified and substantial character, not reminding one, as do some of the fonts often seen in our churches, of the vases of a flower-garden. Running up through the church was one wide, central alley or passage, with open benches on each side, while near the walls, on either side, were other alleys, giving easy access to the benches. At the head of the central alley, at the chancel steps, was the desk or stool for saying the Litany at; while the pulpit was placed at one side, either at the north or south. The chancel was raised several steps, and divided from the nave often by a screen, called the rood-screen, from its being directly under the rood-beam and holy-rood placed thereon. This rood-beam was a heavy piece of timber extending across the chancel, on which was placed a cross or crucifix, with figures of St. John and the Virgin on either side. Sometimes a stone or wooden gallery extended across the chancel to carry the rood, and was called a rood-loft. Just within the chancel were the seats or stalls for the clergy and singers. These stalls ran north and south, facing each other, and were equally divided on the two sides. The end stalls, at the west, were returned and faced the altar. Here the service was said or sung, and here the lectern stood, on which was placed the Bible. A wide passage extended between the stalls leading to the sanctuary or sacrarium. This was raised again, above the chancel, by one or more steps, and separated from it by a rail. Within this rail, and usually against the east wall, was placed the altar, which was raised on at least three steps; in a very large church the number was increased, that the altar might not be obscured. The top step, called the foot-pace, was wider than the others, in order that the priest might the better stand to celebrate the Eucharist. The altar was usually of stone, the top slab of which was incised with five crosses, one in the middle and one at each end, emblematic of the five wounds of CHRIST. Back of the altar, or on it, and raised slightly above it, was a shelf, called the retable, on which were placed the cross and candle-sticks.

The east end of the churches was usually square, although occasionally polygonal or round; the apsidal form, however, being confined principally to the Continent. If this apse form was used the altar was not placed against the east wall, as then it lost its dignity, but was set forward, usually to the chord of the apse, where it was often left exposed on all four sides, with a canopy over it, or was placed against an elaborate stone screen called the reredos. Even when it came against the wall it usually had this screen back of it. Within the chancel-rail on one side, generally the south, were placed seats for the clergy, generally three, called sedilia. Sometimes on the same side, sometimes on the other, was set the credence, a recessed shelf in the wall to contain the unconsecrated bread and wine. Here was often placed the piscina, in which the priest washed his hands before the celebration. With the exception of the latter, the above arrangement is that now used and generally accepted throughout the Anglican and American churches; the universality of the adoption and use depending much upon the knowledge of the clergy or laity having in charge the erection of churches, often upon their individual ideas as to the utility or importance of such customs, and sometimes, perhaps frequently, upon a curious prejudice as to the superstitions liable to be engendered by their use, and this because they were or are used and observed by that branch of the Church under the jurisdiction of the Bishop of Rome. The enlightenment of this age is a sufficient guard against the introduction of the superstitions of a period five centuries past. The Church decrees that everything be done decently and in order, and in pursuance of this the house of worship should be arranged decently and orderly.

In the erection of a church the plan, perhaps, is the first thing to consider. The simplest and best form for a small church is that of nave and chancel, both as narrow and long as may be consistent with economy of space and practicability of hearing and seating. The narrower and higher the church the better the effect, both architecturally and ecclesiastically. In the simplest and smallest churches the nave and chancel may be under one roof, and even of the same width, the division being marked by an arch or screen of open-work. Often in the country a very small church only is needed; this may have low, rough stone walls, and be built on the line of picturesqueness of effect, rather than that of grandeur and sublimity. The outline of all country churches had better be studied on this line of picturesqueness.

Next to the simple form of nave and chancel comes the church with the side aisles; these separated from the nave by a row of columns on either side. These columns or piers should be of brick or stone, and carry an arcaded masonry wall called the clear-

5

story wall. This wall should extend higher than the outer, or aisle walls, and be pierced with windows to light the nave. Much objection is made in this country to having side aisles, since the columns obstruct a clear view of the chancel. This may be obviated by making the aisles narrow, or by a judicious distribution of the seating, so that there need be no trouble on this score. Another method of enlarging the church is by transepts; this, however, should be resorted to only in large churches, as the form really belongs to the cathedral. Deep transepts are very objectionable, as they throw the people off to one side, often entirely out of view of the chancel. The better way to do if transepts are needed is to adopt the Byzantine plan of a Greek cross. Here the nave and transepts may be made wide, and the chancel large, and not so deep as by the English plan. In this way the entire congregation is thrown nearer together and nearer the chancel. But never use the Greek plan without its inseparable great round arch and Byzantine detail. For nothing looks more incongruous than to see Gothic, which is essentially an architecture of height and vertical lines, used where the main character of the work must of necessity be low and broad, and the lines more or less horizontal, often on account of the lack of sufficient funds to make the building of the necessary height. For the effect of all ecclesiastical architecture is increased by great verticality. Byzantine or Romanesque may be made as lofty as you like, but if a broad church is needed, the round arch is much easier adapted than the pointed.

Materials.—The materials of the edifice should be either brick or stone, or both. Avoid the use of wood as much as possible, except for temporary structures, or perhaps for small mission chapels on the frontier. Even then a more substantial material should be used if obtainable. Very pretty and inexpensive churches may be erected out of the round boulders of the fields, such as our ancestors in some of the more sterile and rocky parts of the country gathered into stone walls to fence their lands. The walls should always show the rock face, and be usually what is called rubble-work, laid in mortar, and showing as rough and mossy a face as possible. The window-openings may be of the same stone, squared and dressed, or of a better stone wrought and moulded. Buttresses should be placed about the walls wherever necessary, but no particular regularity should be observed in their distribution. If the funds will afford it, build a tower, or tower and spire. If not, let your money be expended in making what you do attempt substantial and lasting. If it is desirable or necessary to use wood, a very pretty effect may be got, with an idea of solidity, by using rubble-stone for the foundations, which may be extended up to the line of the window-sills, the structure above being of wood. Instead, however, of battening or clapboarding the wooden part, it may be covered with shingles, which should be stained, not painted, thus showing the natural grain of the wood. The inside, even, may be treated in this way with wonderful effect. Always have everything simple and real, not tawdry, sham, or finical. It will be found, no matter what the climate, that if the church is built of masonry with thick walls, the temperature will be much more even, and more easily kept so, than if the building is of wood. In the South it will be found necessary to have the windows large, and to extend them nearly to the floor for air and ventilation.

A good way, perhaps, to go about the erection of a church is to build a little at a time, as the early builders did; say the chancel first, which may be used as a chapel; then the nave; then the tower; and if an enlargement is needed, aisles may be added. Never try to put up a large church with insufficient funds.

Red or yellow bricks, either pressed or common, may be used, and in city churches of a simple character, especially those for mission purposes, brick may seem the more appropriate material. Most of the new churches throughout London are of brick, and very beautiful they are, too. Many new churches in the east of London are usually of red brick in a very severe round-arched style. What strikes an observer mostly in these churches is their simplicity, appropriateness, and solidity. They are invariably lined on the inside with bricks, and often have vaulted ceilings of the same. They consist of nave and chancel, with usually two, sometimes four, side aisles. By the side of the chancel is a morning chapel, in which is held the week-day or early morning service, at which few people are likely to be present. The church is usually seated with chairs, sometimes with open benches, pews never, and floored with tiles, which are sometimes of clay, encaustic, or even wood. This last material has the advantage of not being cold and damp.

As consonant with the simple, lasting monumental character of your church, always have the material of the interior, as well as the exterior, of the walls substantial, either brick or stone, never plaster. For this latter is liable to drop off in time, or to get spotted with water, or frozen, and has, withal, a very unsubstantial look for a church, while to plaster you must put flooring strips and laths on the walls, thus making the fire risk much greater. If you want to plaster the ceilings to obtain an evenness of temperature, endeavor to have them ceiled over afterwards in wood, or paneled. It is pleasing to see the idea of the monumental character of a church gaining ground in this country, especially in the East, where many, if not the most, of the churches erected in the last few years, in the larger towns at least, have their interior walls of a substantial material, usually brick.

Furniture.—The altar and font, perhaps the pulpit, should be of stone, and the lectern of brass, while the other furniture is of wood, always substantial, and designed in keeping with the church. The most of the furniture obtained at the ecclesiastical furnishers', so called, is but a mongrel Gothic, clumsy and poorly designed. The brasswork is sometimes better. It is more desirable, however, where the funds will allow, to have the furniture, including brasswork, designed and made to order. Your architect will advise you, and if he is an able one,—you should have none other,—let him design, or oversee the designing of, everything that is connected with the church, even to the stained-glass windows and the gas-fixtures, and attend to the selection of carpets, rugs, etc. He will not usually undertake the designing of stained-glass work, unless of a simple character, but will advise you where to look, or will obtain designs for you.

There has been of late years some excellent stained-glass work done in this country. It is mostly, however, of a different character from the ancient stained glass, and consequently from that produced by the best makers in London and Munich of to-day. In small churches that cannot afford figure-work, a very pleasing effect can be got by using cathedral glass, and at a very small expense. It is not advisable to have a window in the east end over the altar, precedent to the contrary notwithstanding, for unless it is made very dark indeed, it is sure to throw an unpleasant glare in the faces of the congregation, and to obscure almost entirely the altar and things about it. The better way is to place a window on one side only, which may be made as large as needed, thus obtaining a sufficiency of light without the confusion resulting from the multifarious rays of conflicting lights. Then it is not well to have too much light in a church,—a glare is exceedingly unpleasant and confusing to many worshipers. Almost as bad is the lack of light found in some churches. This latter fact is not always owing to small or insufficient windows, but often to the fact of the church being so wide that the light from the low windows will not strike across. This can be obviated by building the church with a nave and aisles, and getting most of the light from the clear-story windows. The clear-story may be as high as you like, the higher the better. Windows in the west end are permissible, but they should not be too bright or large, else the clergy will experience the same annoyance that an east window causes the congregation.

The altar should be of stone and a fixture in the church, resting on a stone foundation. It should be of the form of a tomb, at least six feet long, and be two and a half feet wide and three feet and three inches high. It should be placed against the east wall in a square chancel, while in an apsidal one it should be set forward, even to the chord, if the room can be afforded. It should always be raised on at least three steps,—three will answer for all ordinary purposes,—the top one being wider than the other. The sanctuary-rail should be of brass if possible; if not, a round wooden rail is sufficient, set on simple standards of metal as open as possible. A rail is not at all necessary, except to keep out the multitude. A cord will answer for the gate, unless a metal rail is used, when a smaller metal pipe may be made to slide into the other. This is better than a cumbrous gate that is continually getting out of order. Near the altar should be a credence to hold the elements before the service, and against the south wall should be two or three, usually three, seats, or sedilia, for the clergy. The chancel should contain the stalls or benches for the clergy and choir, consisting of two or three long benches on each side, running longitudinally; the front ones being low for the choir and the back ones high for the clergy. The organist also should sit here with his key-board, and face the same way as the choir, the organ being placed in a recess or gallery on either side, or at the west end. On a line between the nave and chancel should be placed the lectern, which ought to be of brass and in the shape of an eagle. A simple wooden lectern is often used in small churches; a very neat one may be made of metal to fold up, and have a canvas or cloth book-rest. The pulpit may be placed on the north or south side of the church, and be of wood or stone. The lectern must be on the opposite side from the pulpit. The pulpit should be in the nave, and as near the people as possible, even among them. The prayer should never be said or sung at the lectern, as is sometimes done, but in the stalls, or at a prayer-desk, and facing north or south, not west. At the head of the main alley or passage may be a small desk at which to say the Litany. Often dividing the chancel from the nave is an open screen of wood or metal called the rood-screen. St. Stephen's, Providence, has a very fine new wooden one; while the Church of the Advent, Boston, has an iron one of considerable height, and St. Stephen's, Lynn, Mass., is, I believe, to have one of brass.

If the church is a free or mission church in a town, it is better to seat with chairs, otherwise plain open benches may be used. They should be two feet and ten inches apart from back to back, while they are often made three feet, and even more, as at Trinity Church, Boston. Twenty inches in width may be allowed for each person. The main alley can be from four to six feet wide, and the side ones three to four feet. The font should be of stone and placed near the main entrance. It must be on a solid foundation, and be large enough for immersion. It ought to be raised on two or three steps, so that the clergyman may be seen while administering the rite of baptism. Whether the floor is of wood or not, it is better to have a line of matting down the alleys than to carpet the whole church, while rugs and mats may be used for the pews. This last, however, is more a matter of convenience and comfort, and is often determined by the climate and by the methods of heating used.

Sunday-School Chapels.—A Sunday-school chapel is often attached to a church, and it is always better to have it so; a separate building being far more preferable than to use the basement of the main structure.

Heating and Ventilation.—Great care should be taken in the matter of heating and ventilation, especially in the North, where it is very seldom that the temperature of a church in winter is at all satisfactory. Heating by furnaces is probably the most desirable way. The whole basement may be made a hot-air chamber, letting the air up in a multitude of places under the pews. In this way, by a judicious arrangement of the openings for the fresh warm air and of outlets for the foul air, a reasonably perfect system may be obtained. It is difficult to put forth any one system for all cases. Each problem should be worked out for itself and to meet the exigencies of the occasion.

Lich-Gates.—A pleasant sight about churches, especially in the country, is the well-kept church-yard,—the GOD'S acre,—where lie all the dead of the parish. At the entrance to this church-yard it was a goodly custom to erect a shelter over the gate-way, under which the mourners might stop and rest the corpse while waiting for the procession of clergy to come out from the church to meet them. This sheltered gate was thence called lich-gate or corpse-gate. This custom might be revived, the gate serving as a shelter from the weather at all times, besides being a picturesque ornament to the church-yard.

FIG. 3.

Semicircular. Segmental. Horseshoe.
Horseshoe. Equilateral. Lancet.
Segmental Pointed. Trefoil. Trefoil.
Multifoil. Cinquefoil.

GLOSSARY.

ABACUS. The upper part of the capital of a column or pier.

ABBEY. A term for a collection of conventual buildings, consisting of a church and other structures, presided over by an abbot or abbess.

ABUTMENT. The solid part of a wall or pier from which an arch springs or abuts.

AISLE. The wings at the sides of a church, separated from the nave by columns or piers, and roofed lower than the main body of the church. It is an architectural division of the structure, and not a passage or alley between the pews, as often used.

ALMERY. A recess in the wall near the altar used to contain the sacred vessels.

ALMONRY, or AUMBRY. A room where alms were distributed to the poor.

ALTAR. An elevated tomb-like structure for the celebration of the Eucharist, placed at the eastern end of the church, made at first of wood, but the Council of Epone, in France (509 A.D.), commanded that altars be made of stone.

ALURE. An alley or passage in a wall, as in the clear-story of a church.

AMBO. A kind of pulpit in the early church, originally a reading-desk.

AMBULATORY. A passage to walk in, such as cloisters.

ANTE-CHAPEL. A small chapel, forming the entrance to another.

APSE. The semicircular or polygonal termination to the chancel or aisles of a church, very little used in England, but common on the Continent.

ARCADE. A row or range of arches supported on piers or columns, either against a wall or detached.

ARCH. A construction of masonry spanning an opening, and so constructed that the stones or bricks by mutual pressure will support each other. The lower part is called the springing, the sides the haunches, and the top the crown. (Fig. 3.)

ASHLAR. Squared stones used for the facing of walls. The ashlar-line is that of the face of the building.

BALDACHINO. A canopy, supported on shafts, standing over the altar.

BAPTISTERY. A separate building or an addition to the church to contain the font for the rite of baptism.

BASE. The moulded lower part of a column or shaft.

BASILICA. A building used by the Greeks and Romans for public purposes, as for a justice hall, hall of exchange, etc.

BAY. The compartment of an arcade, or space or division between any two columns or piers.

BELFRY. Usually applied to the ringing-loft of a church. Properly, a detached campanile containing bells.

BELL-GABLE, BELL-COT. A gable or cot in small churches and chapels that have no tower, to contain one or more bells, usually placed at the west end. When placed over the chancel arch it is called sanctus bell-cot.

BLIND-STORY, or TRIFORIUM. A term applied to the space between the lower arcade of the wall and the clear-story.

BUTTRESS. A pier of masonry projecting from a wall and used to strengthen it.

CANOPY. An ornamental projection or covering over niches, doors, windows, seats, and altars.

CAP, or CAPITAL. The upper part of a column, pier, or pilaster; usually elaborately carved.

CATHEDRAL. The principal church of a diocese, where the Bishop has his seat. (Fig. 4.)

FIG. 4.

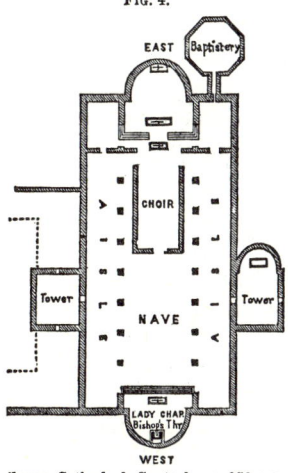

Saxon Cathedral, Canterbury, 950 A.D.

CHALICE. The cup used for the wine at the celebration of the Eucharist, at first made of wood and glass, then of gold and silver.

CHANCEL. The eastern end of a church, where the clergy and the choir are placed, and where the services are performed.

CHANTRY. A small chapel built out from a church, and often containing the tomb of the founder.

CHAPEL. A small building used in place of a church in a large parish; a building attached to a church or forming part of an institution, and used for the services of the church.

CHAPTER-HOUSE. The place of assembly for the chapter, or deans and canons, of a cathedral. The rooms are of various shapes, usually polygonal.

CHOIR. That part of a cathedral where the choir sits and where the service is sung. In a parish church this place is called the chancel, the term choir being confined to cathedrals; it was separated from the rest of the church by a screen.

CLEAR-STORY, or CLERE-STORY. An upper story or row of windows in a church above the blind-story. It is in the wall separating nave and aisle, which is usually called the clear-story wall.

CLOISTER. A covered ambulatory or walk about a quadrangle in a collegiate or monastic structure.

COLUMN. A vertical cylindrical shaft used to support a superincumbent weight. A clustered column is a collection of small slender shafts banded together.

COPING. The top or covering course of a wall, usually of stone, and weathered to throw off the rain-water.

CORBEL. A projecting stone or piece of timber jutting out from a wall and used as a support.

CREDENCE. A small table or recess in the wall near the altar, on which the bread and wine were placed before they were consecrated.

CROSS. The symbol of the Christian religion. The Greek cross has each of its arms alike, while the Latin has the lower arm longer than the others; this latter is the usual form of cross seen.

CRYPT. A vaulted apartment under a church or other building. In a church it is generally under the chancel.

CUSP. The point of meeting of the foliations of tracery as in a trefoil, where the three projecting points of meeting of the foils are called cusp.

DIAPER-WORK. A form of decorating of flat surfaces, such as walls, panels, etc., with a geometrical pattern, consisting of squares, lozenges, or other forms, filled with a flower or rosette design. The name is derived from a kind of cloth worked in similar patterns made at Ypres, Belgium, hence the name, Drap D'Ypres.

DOME. A cupola or inverted cup on the top of a building. The term is derived from the name given the Italian cathedral, "Il duomo," which usually had a dome.

DORSAL, or DOSSEL. The hangings behind the altar.

FALDSTOOL, or FOLDING-STOOL. A seat made to fold up like a camp-chair, and of wood or metal, carried about by a Bishop when away from his own church, a term erroneously applied to the Litany stool.

FINIAL. The ornament in which a spire, gable, pinnacle, or canopy terminates, consisting generally in a flower or bunch of flowers.

FLÈCHE. The small spire over the intersection of nave and transepts containing the sanctus bell.

FONT. The vessel used in the rite of baptism. It should be of stone, and of sufficient size to allow a child to be immersed.

FRITHSTOOL, or FREEDSTOOL. A seat placed near the altar, the last refuge for those who claimed the privilege of sanctuary. The seat of peace.

FRONTAL. The hanging of the front of the altar.

GABLE. The triangular-shaped upper part of a wall formed by the termination of a roof against it.

GALILEE. A chapel or porch at the western entrance to a church. Sometimes a part of the west end of the church, separated from the rest, and not considered so sacred as the rest of the edifice. Used chiefly for penitents not yet admitted to the body of the church.

GARGOYLE. An ornamental termination to a gutter or water-spout used to carry the water clear of the building. It is usually a grotesque, and supposed to be named from the gurgling sound made by the water passing through it.

GRILLE. The ornamental iron-work screen inclosing a chapel, tomb, or an opening, such as a window.

GROIN. The style of vaulting formed by the intersection of two vaults; a ceiling of this form is called a groined ceiling.

GROTESQUES. The light and fanciful ornaments used by the ancients; also gargoyles, corbels, and other ornaments carved in curious and grotesque forms are often thus called.

HAMMER-BEAM. A horizontal timber resting on the top of the wall and projecting into the church, forming part of a truss, and often carved; hence the name hammer-beam truss.

JAMB. The sides of a door or window-opening.

JOINTS. The interstices between the stones or bricks in masonry are called joints.

LADY-CHAPEL. A chapel placed to the eastward of the altar in large churches and dedicated to the Blessed Virgin, called Our Lady.

LANCET. A long, narrow window or opening with a narrow, pointed arch.

LANTERN. A term given to the light construction forming the top of a tower or dome, usually of a polygonal form; occasionally it is placed on a roof, and is used for purposes of light and air.

LECTERN. A movable desk of wood or metal used to hold the Bible, often made of brass in the form of an eagle, the Bible resting on the back of the eagle.

LICH-GATE. A covered gate-way at the entrance to a church-yard or cemetery, where the mourners rested the corpse while waiting for the clergy.

LOUVRE. An open structure on a roof, usually for ventilation, and consisting of a small lantern or cupola, the openings filled with slats or louvre boards.

MINSTER. A large church attached to an ecclesiastical establishment. If the fraternity be presided over by a Bishop it is called a *Cathedral*; if by an abbot, an *Abbey*; if by a prior, a *Priory*.

MISERERE. A projection on the under side of seats in the stalls of large churches. These seats were made to turn up during the long services, which were performed standing, and the misereres were projected enough to form a partial seat. They were elaborately carved in various grotesque forms.

MONASTERY. A group of buildings used for the habitation of an order of monks.

MOSAIC-WORK. Flat ornamental work formed by inlaying small pieces of stone, glass, enamel, or marble of various colors. Floors, walls, and ceilings are done in this manner.

MULLION. A vertical division of a window into two or more parts.

NARTHEX. The porch forming the entrance to the early Christian basilica.

NAVE. The main body or division of a church, so called from its fancied resemblance to a ship. On either side are the aisles, and at the east end is the chancel.

ORATORY. A small room or chapel attached usually to a private house and for individual or family devotions.

PACE, or FOOT-PACE. A broad step in front of the altar.

PATEN. A small plate or salver used in the celebration of the Eucharist; it was formed to fit the chalice as a cover.

PIER. That portion of a wall between windows or other openings, or a massive erection standing alone and used to support arches, etc.

PILLARS. The round or polygonal piers or columns that support the main arches of a building.

PINNACLE. A small turret or tall ornament, tapering to the top and usually elaborately carved, forming terminations to buttresses, corners, etc.

PISCINA. A small basin, either recessed in the wall, near the altar, or projecting from it, and used to carry off the water used in ablutions before the mass.

POPPY-HEADS. The finials, or ornaments, at the top of bench or stall ends.

PORCH. A covered shelter at the entrance of the church. Sometimes the lower story of the tower forms the porch. It is usually placed on the south side near the west end.

PULPIT. An elevated platform or desk from which sermons are preached. Sometimes of stone, but usually of wood, and polygonal or round in shape; placed at either the north or south side of nave near entrance to chancel.

REFECTORY. The dining-hall of a monastery or convent. It contained a desk or pulpit, from which one of the members read to the others during meals.

RELIQUARY. A small box, chest, or casket to contain relics.

REREDOS. The screen or other ornamental work at the back of the altar, either against the wall or detached.

RETABLE. A raised shelf at the back of the altar, on which are placed the cross, vases, and candlesticks.

RIDGE. The apex of the roof running the length of the building.

ROOD. The crucifix placed in the rood-loft, with figures of the Virgin Mary and St. John on either side.

ROOD-BEAM, or ROOD-LOFT. A heavy beam or gallery extending across the chancel at the junction with the nave, on which was placed the rood; underneath was often placed a screen or low wall, called rood-screen or rood-wall. These screens are made quite light and open.

ROOD-TOWER, ROOD STEEPLE. A name sometimes given to the great tower at the intersection of nave and transepts.

ROSE-WINDOW. A name given to a window of circular form filled with tracery; if the tracery is in the form of spokes it is called a wheel-window.

SACRARIUM. The inclosed space about the altar.

SACRISTY. A room attached to a church in which the priests robed, and in which the sacred vessels, vestments, etc., were kept.

SANCTUARY. The eastern end of the chancel, in which the altar is placed; called also sacrarium.

SANCTUS BELL-COT. A small gable or other structure on the roof, to contain a small bell called the sanctus-bell, which was used during various parts of the service, especially at the words "sanctus, sanctus, sanctus;" placed usually over the chancel arch; sometimes it is in a small spire called a flèche.

SEDILIA. Three seats placed near the altar, and against or recessed in one of the walls; used during parts of the service by the priest and his attendants, the deacon and subdeacon.

SEPULCHRE, THE EASTER. A recess, generally in the north wall of a Roman church, to contain the cross from Good-Friday to Easter.

SHAFTS. Slender columns, either standing alone or attached to walls, buttresses, etc.

SHRINE. A chest or box to contain relics; sometimes in the form of a church; often they were covered with jewels.

SILL, CILL. The horizontal stone forming the bottom of window-openings. In a wooden building the first timber put on the foundations and extending around the building.

SOFFIT. A ceiling; a term used only to designate subordinate parts and members of a building, as the ceiling or soffit, or an arch, doorway, stairway, cornice, etc.

SPAN. The width of an arch between the walls; also the width of a roof.

SPIRE. A sharply-pointed termination given to towers, and rising to a great height, forming the roof to the tower; usually built of masonry in the best work, sometimes of wood, and covered with shingles, tiles, or slates.

STALL. A fixed seat, partially inclosed, for the use of clergy and choir. The stalls are situated in the chancel or choir.

STANDARD. The term applied to the upright ends of stalls or benches.

STEEPLE. A general term used to include the whole structure of tower, belfry, and spire.

STOUP. A small vessel placed at the entrance to a Roman church to contain holy water.

SUPER ALTAR. A small portable stone altar.

TABERNACLE. A small cell or niche in which some holy or precious thing is placed; applied to the receptacle over the altar where the pix is placed; also a niche where an image may be placed.

TESSELLATED PAVEMENT. A pavement formed of small cubes of stone, marble, pottery, etc., of from an inch to a half-inch square, like dice.

TOWER. The large masonry structure used to mark the position of a church, usually square, sometimes round or polygonal; occasionally topped out with a flat roof, oftener, however, with a tall spire.

TRACERY. The ornamental filling in of circular windows, window-heads, and panels formed by the ramifications of the mullions. It should be of stone, and not of wood, as it often is.

TRANSEPT. That portion of a church that crosses transversely between nave and choir, extending beyond the nave on either side, and forming the arms of a cross.

TRANSOM. The horizontal cross-bars of wood or stone that divide a window or doorway in height, in contradistinction to mullions that run vertically.

TREFOIL. A panel, window, or window-head formed by cusping in the shape of a three-leafed flower; quatrefoil is four-leafed; cinquefoil, five-leafed; multifoil, many-leafed.

TRIFORIUM, or BLIND-STORY. The space of wall between the lower arcade and the clear-story.

TURRET. A small tower, usually round or octagonal; generally placed at corners of buildings or larger towers.

TYMPANUM. A name given to the space above the opening of a doorway, formed by the square head of the door and the form of the arch above it; often elaborately carved, or filled with mosaic.

VAULT. The arched ceiling of a roof; where the vaults intersect the ceiling is said to be groined.

VESICA PISCES. An oval-shaped ornament pointed at both ends; used for panels, windows, etc. It is the common form of the aureole, or glory, by which the representations of the persons of the Holy Trinity were surrounded in the Middle Ages. The name was given by Albert Durer.

VESTRY. *Vide* SACRISTY.

ION LEWIS, Chicago.

Ark of the Covenant. The coffer or chest of shittim or acacia wood, in which were placed the Tables of the Law. It was also called the Testimony. According to Heb. ix. 4, the pot of manna and Aaron's rod were within it. It was two and a half cubits long and one and a half cubits deep, and the same measurement in width. It was overlaid with gold within and without, and its lid was surrounded with a crown of gold. Four golden rings, one at each corner, were placed for the staves of acacia wood by which it was to be carried, and which were always to remain in place. It was the consecrated depository for the Tables of the LAW—GOD'S Testimony to His people. It therefore contained the stone tables, hewn by Moses, and written on by GOD for a Testimony before His people. It occupied the chief place in the Holy of Holies, and it was set before the mercy-seat, which was overshadowed by the cherubim. In the journeyings of the children of Israel it was always to be borne by the Kohathites, when the priests had covered it with the veil and pall of badger-skins. Upon the tent where the Testimony rested, the cloud, the glory of the LORD, hovered. It led the way in the three days of the first journey after leaving Sinai, and it was placed in the front of the advancing hosts with a solemn proclamation by Moses (Num. x. 33–36; *cf.* Ps. lxviii. 1). Its march was marked by the blast from two silver trumpets. It was never seen but by the High-Priest, for none could look upon it and live. It was thus in the central place in the Jewish worship, and was a perpetual witness of GOD'S covenant with His people. So Isaiah appeals to it: "To the Law (*i.e.*, the whole Levitical Law) and to the Testimony" (*i.e.*, the covenant in the Ark). (Is. viii. 20.) It excluded idolatry in the tabernacle, however much the heart of the people leaned to that sin.

Again, when Joshua was about to cross the Jordan, the Ark led the way, two thousand cubits in advance of the people (Josh. iii., iv.), and it was borne in front in the solemn processions about Jericho. It was at Gilgal, then removed to Shiloh, till the time of Samuel. It was taken by the Philistines when Hophni and Phinehas sacrilegiously carried it to the battle of Aphek, who kept it seven months. It was then returned (1 Sam. vi.), and remained at Kirjath Jearim twenty years, till it was left by David at the house of Obed Edom (1 Chron. xiii.); finally, it was carried to Jerusalem and placed in the tent David had prepared for it. Thence it was borne to the Temple by Solomon.

Arkansas and Indian Territory. This Diocese was organized in 1871 A.D. The population of the State is 802,564. Bishop Polk (born April 10, 1806 A.D.) was "consecrated Missionary Bishop of Arkansas and the Indian Territory south of 36° 30′, with provisional charge of Alabama, Mississippi, and the republic of Texas, December 9, 1838 A.D. At the General Convention held in Philadelphia, October 6 to 19, 1841 A.D., Bishop Polk was nominated by the House of Bishops to the Episcopate of Louisiana, agreeably to the request of that Diocese that the General Convention should elect its Bishop, in which action the House of Deputies unanimously concurred. Died June 14, 1864 A.D.

"Second Bishop, the Rt. Rev. George Washington Freeman, D.D. Born June 13, 1789 A.D. Consecrated Missionary Bishop of Arkansas and the Indian Territory south of 36½°, with supervision of the Church in Texas, October 26, 1844 A.D. Died April 29, 1858 A.D.

"Third Bishop, the Rt. Rev. Henry Champlain Lay, S.T.D., LL.D. Born December 6, 1813 A.D. Consecrated Missionary Bishop of Arkansas and the Indian Territory, October 23, 1859 A.D. Translated to Easton, 1869 A.D.

"Present Bishop, the Rt. Rev. Henry Niles Pierce, D.D., LL.D. Residence, Little Rock. Born in Pawtucket, Rhode Island, October 19, 1820 A.D. Graduated at Brown University 1842 A.D. Ordered Deacon April 23, 1843 A.D. Ordained Priest January 3, 1849 A.D. He was successively rector of St. John's, Mobile, Ala., St. Paul's, Springfield, Ill. (1850–70 A.D.). Received degree of D.D. from University of Alabama, and that of LL.D. from the College of William and Mary, Virginia, 1869 A.D. Consecrated Missionary Bishop of Arkansas and the Indian Territory in Mobile, Ala., January 25, 1870 A.D., by the Rt. Rev. Wm. M. Green, D.D., Rt. Rev. Henry J. Whitehouse, D.D., LL.D., D.C.L., Rt. Rev. R. H. Wilmer, D.D., Rt. Rev. C. J. Quintard, S.T.D., LL.D., Rt. Rev. Joseph P. B. Wilmer, D.D., Rt. Rev. J. F. Young, S.T.D. Writings: Occasional Sermons, Essays, Addresses, and Poems." (Living Church Annual, 1884.)

Bishop Freeman was rector of Immanuel Church, Newcastle, Del., before his elevation to the Episcopate, hence William T. Read, Esq., of New Castle, presented resolutions concerning his death in the Delaware Convention of 1858 A.D. They declare that "the Church has lost one of her brightest ornaments, a chief pastor eminently qualified for the exalted and responsible station to which the Church called him with considerable unanimity, and who discharged its duties with diligence, ability, uprightness, and zeal, directed by sound judgment, and animated by ardent love of God and man."

In 1835 A.D., Rev. Francis L. Hawks, D.D., was chosen by the General Convention as Missionary Bishop, to have jurisdiction in Louisiana and the Territories of Arkansas and Florida. He declined the position.

When Bishop Polk was elected by the General Convention of 1841 A.D. "to the Diocesan Episcopate of Louisiana, he resigned his previous charge, and Bishop Otey, of Tennessee, was made acting Bishop of Arkansas, etc. This state of things continued until 1844 A.D.," when Bishop Freeman was elected. Bishop Freeman was also to have jurisdiction in Texas, as well as the Indian Territory.

Bishop Lay reported to the General Convention of 1868 A.D. concerning Arkansas and the Indian Territory, that in the preceding three years he had licensed 6 lay-readers. There was 1 candidate for holy orders, and there were 8 Presbyters canonically resident, and 1 without a cure. There were 16 parishes, 5 churches, and 1 parsonage. Baptisms, 466; confirmations, 254; communicants, 605; Sunday-school teachers, 57; scholars, 520.

EDUCATIONAL INSTITUTIONS.

"*Academic.*—St. John's Associate Mission School, Fayetteville, Ark., C. A. Leverett, Principal. Went into operation the 1st of October, 1868 A.D."

Bishop Pierce's first annual report to the Board of Missions, in October, 1870 A.D., stated that 103 had received confirmation, and there had been 52 baptisms. The Bishop had traveled 5414 miles. "Two parishes were self-supporting, Little Rock and Helena." The Bishop was consecrated in January of this year.

Bishop Pierce reports to the Board of Missions in 1883 A.D. that he has been busily at work in his jurisdiction for the past four years, "having in that period allowed himself little or no time for simple recreation." He speaks with interest of a visit to the missions in the western part of the Indian Territory, under Rev. F. B. Wicks. Mr. Wicks was a rector in the State of New York, who took some Indian lads to educate, and afterwards entered on this missionary work. Progress has been made "in planting the Church among the Cheyennes, Arapahoes, Kiowas, and Comanches." The labors of Mr. Wicks have been aided by the help of the Cheyenne Deacon, Rev. David P. Okaharter. The Bishop confirmed at the Cheyenne school-house fifteen persons, all Cheyennes. They were young men and women, appearing very intelligent. The Bishop says that "they form a grand nucleus for a large work among these Indians." He adds, "I do not think that I was ever more deeply impressed with any religious services than I was by the baptism of three young men by Mr. Wicks on the Wednesday night previous to their confirmation, Sunday, October 5. There was a large congregation of Indians and whites present, and few eyes were seen in which no tear-drop glistened." At the Kiowa and Comanche school-house, Anadarko, Mr. Wicks baptized six Indian young men, and the Bishop confirmed twelve persons. At Anadarko the Kiowa Deacon, Rev. Paul C. Zotom, has assisted Mr. Wicks, and Mr. George W. Hunt, the superintendent of the Kiowa and Comanche school, has also given him valuable aid. Mr. Hunt has become a candidate for orders. Steps have been taken looking to the erection of a church at Anadarko. At Fort Sill the Bishop confirmed two persons, one of them being the wife of the commandant, Col. G. V. Hendry. The Bishop was pleased with the success of the plans of Mr. Wicks and his influence among the Indians, and thinks that the mission needs to be enlarged and developed under such wise leadership.

In Arkansas the Bishop reports a new church being pushed towards completion at Van Buren, and a new church soon to be commenced at Marianna. The Bishop is exceedingly anxious to establish a central mission and clergy-house, with a Board of Clergy at Little Rock. He has worked for years, steadily but gradually, "towards the establishment of this cathedral and clergy-house." He says, "I am now, and have been since the middle of June last, trying to raise the requisite funds. My success has not been up to this time great, and yet not discouraging. With $2000 in addition to what is now secured, I can begin to build this fall, and have much of my scheme in operation during the coming year. I consider this work one of so much importance and so vital to the Church in Arkansas that I shall place it second to nothing else till it is done. May God put it into the hearts of Churchmen everywhere to help me! The sum I ask is so little, that I ought not to be obliged to take months to raise it."

Statistics for 1886 A.D.: Clergy, 17; parishes, 19; missions, 10; ordination, priest, 1; baptisms, 177; confirmed, 149; com., 1364; contributions, $13,955.60.

REV. S. F. HOTCHKIN.

Arles. Of the numerous ecclesiastical conventions called Councils of Arles, the first only need be considered in any fullness. About the beginning of the fourth century, on occasions of violent persecution, much weakness had been exhibited by Christians, as well as much fortitude and zeal, which latter was sometimes carried to foolish fanaticism; and there had arisen, chiefly in Africa, two classes in the Church; one, of those inclined to treat forgivingly and leniently such as had fallen when sorely tried by persecution, and to discourage fanaticism which provoked persecution; the other, of those who thought they ought to take a severer view, and exclude the lapsed, often styled *traditors*, from Church privileges and communion, at least until the hour of death. The antagonism of these two parties took more definite form, and became open and violent, on the election of Cæcilian to the See of Carthage (311 A.D.). and a rival, Majorinus, was elected and consecrated to the same See, on the ground that Cæcilian's consecration was not valid, having been given by a traditor. The Emperor Constantine, who became master of the West about this time, gave some attention to these disputes, and authorized a meeting of Bishops at Rome to compose them (313 A.D.). Cæcilian was present at this conference, as was also the opposite party, headed by a certain Donatus; not, however, that one from whom the party shortly afterwards was named. The decision was in favor of Cæcilian, but Donatus and his brethren were not satisfied, and they applied to the Emperor for another hearing. This application issued in the Council of Arles, a general Council of the West assembled at Arelate, a city near the mouth of the Rhone (August 1, 314 A.D.). It is said as many as two hundred Bishops met at this time, among whom were three from Britain,—Eborius of York, Restitutus of London, and Adelfius of Lincoln. The result of the deliberations was again in favor of Cæcilian and the more moderate party, and a number of Canons were passed in the hope of ending the dissensions. Among other things it was decided that clergymen who were duly convicted as traditors should be deposed; that false accusers should be excommunicated until near death; that ordination by traditors, if otherwise unexceptionable, should be valid; that persons baptized by heretics in the Name of the Father, etc., and in the right form, should not be rebaptized, but received into the Church by imposition of hands; and that Easter should be observed on Sunday.

Articles, the XXXIX. "Articles of Religion" were an invention, in Western Europe, of the sixteenth century. The Eastern Church retains yet the Catholic practice of fifteen hundred years, and is satisfied with the Creed as the one formula of faith, with the Liturgy as the rule of worship, and with Canons for discipline. The latter tend to preserve good morals and promote the order of the Church. The second nourishes growth in grace, wisdom, and soundness of faith. The first maintains the primary facts respecting FATHER, SON, and HOLY GHOST, which are necessary to be believed in order to be saved. They are so necessary because salvation is a fact, and must, therefore, rest on facts. The only facts which make a sure foundation are those set forth in the formulas of the Creed. Though the Creed has two forms, one called the Apostles', and the other the Nicene, the latter is only an expansion of the former, containing no merely human opinions or explanations, but merely such enlargements of the old statements of facts as were known to have been accepted and taught from the beginning in all the Churches of Apostolic foundation and upgrowth.

In the sixteenth century, however, the resistance to the Bishop of Rome, which led to the convulsions of the Reformation, was accompanied by a fierce reaction against the mediæval theology. Indeed, the encroachments of the Pope upon the rights of the national Churches in Western Europe, and his usurpations of power based upon his uncatholic claims of "supremacy," had long proceeded, *pari passu*, with the development of novel and, therefore, erroneous theological doctrines. Practical corruptions followed from erroneous teaching, and induced an active, indignant, and sometimes violent resistance. The whole Church, in the West, had become so bound in the chains of a tyrannous papal rule, and so held captive by a powerful, well-organized, and minutely-divided ecclesiasticism, that when the inevitable reaction came, and the indestructible dignity of personal man—made in GOD'S image, and responsible directly to Him—was reasserted and defended, the rebound, like its occasion, became extreme.

Not only were the rights of man as man, free by nature and godlike, an impelling force under the Reformation, but the supremacy of Truth, as the Word of GOD, was naturally set forth as the only sure test of His will and ways. A general intellectual renaissance had prepared the way for a theological, as well as moral and religious revival. The theological revival led, of course, to doctrinal controversies. These disturbed the quiet of both Church and State. The rulers, in both Church and State, endeavored to check disorder. The Reformers were in earnest, and began to show something more than a mere spirit of endurance. They were not all ecclesiastics. Princes favored the Reformation. Both Pope and Emperor tried in vain to stamp out the movement. Huss and Jerome had been silenced, but Luther, Zwingle, Calvin, and the English Convocation were, both jointly and severally, too strong to be repressed, and too numerous to be confined.

Open controversy was, therefore, the only resort, and out of this controversy grew the invention of "Articles of Religion." Generally, though not always, especially at first, Articles of Religion were distinguished from the Articles of the Faith. The latter were contained in the Creed. The former, while claimed to be accordant with and based upon the Creed, treated largely the contemporary questions in dispute.

A body of Articles of Religion was presented by Luther, Melancthon, and their associates to the Germanic Diet at Augsburg, June 23, 1530 A.D., and is called "the Augsburg Confession." On October 3, 1529 A.D., a body of seventeen articles, known as the "Schwabach Articles," had been presented to a joint meeting of the followers of Luther and of Zwingle at Marburg, but were not accepted by the latter. Indeed, this conference seems to have settled the fact that Luther and Zwingle could not agree. The latter insisted that every point should be settled solely upon the express words of Holy Scripture, while the former claimed that the Church had at least some weight of authority as interpreter of Holy Scripture. Luther, therefore, wished to retain all existing doctrines and practices which were not against the express words of Holy Scripture. On this point they separated, and the German Reformers proceeded alone.

The first part of "The Augsburg Confession" consisted of XXII. Articles; the last of which "concludes . . . by declaring that there is nothing in the doctrine of the Lutheran body which differs either from the Scriptures or the ancient Church." (Hardwicke.)

The English Church 1534 A.D., by distinct convocational enactment, rejected the supremacy of the Pope. This was the first decisive act which involved the English Church in the flood of the Reformation. Naturally the Continental Reformers were conferred with; and a strong effort was made, in which both Henry VIII. and Cranmer joined, to induce Lutherans, and especially Melancthon, to meet and confer with the English Convocation. 1536 A.D. a series of English "Articles of Religion" were drawn up, but not actually authorized and set forth. The hands of both Gardiner and Cranmer appear in them, with not a little of the dash of Henry VIII. Meanwhile, the Smalcaldic League had organized in Germany a political as well as religious resistance to papal usurpations; and efforts were made to attach Henry VIII. to it. He and his Bishops were not, however, willing to adopt the Augsburg Confession. Embassies were interchanged, and conferences followed; until some time in the summer of 1538 A.D. a body of XIII. Articles were agreed upon. They were (1) of the Unity of GOD and Trinity of persons, (2) of Original Sin, (3) of the two natures of CHRIST, (4) of Justification, (5) of the Church, (6) of Baptism, (7) of the Eucharist, (8) of Penitence, (9) of use of Sacraments, (10) of Ministers of the Church, (11) of Ecclesiastical Rites, (12) of Things Civil, (13) of Resurrection of the Body and Last Judgment.

These Articles, though showing the influence of the Augsburg Confession, were full also of signs of those views which distinguished the English Reformation from that on the Continent.

The death of Henry VIII., 1547 A.D., placed the crown upon the head of the boy Edward VI. The Duke of Somerset—the Protector of King and realm—was a correspondent of Calvin. Both King and Protector were in close intimacy with Cranmer, who is regarded as the chief compiler and constructor of the XLII. Articles. These, though "agreed by the Bishops and other learned men in the Synod of London, 1552 A.D.," were set forth June 19, 1553 A.D., by "a mandate in the name of the King directed to the officials of the Archbishop of Canterbury, requiring them to see that the New Formulary should be subscribed;" i.e., by all the clergy, school-masters, and members of the university on admission to degrees. This was not, however, carried generally into effect.

The reign of Mary Tudor restored papal authority, and though nothing official was done with the XLII. Articles, they remained so in abeyance, that on the ascension to the throne of Elizabeth—November 17, 1558 A.D.,—they were not held to be of authority.

Indeed (1559 A.D.), "Archbishop Parker, with the sanction of the other Metropolitan and the rest of the English prelates," set forth XI. Articles of Religion; "and the clergy were required to make a public profession of it;" and it was "appointed to be taught and holden of all parsons, vicars, and curates, as 'well in testification of their common consent in the said doctrine, to the stopping of the mouths of them that go about to slander the ministers of the Church for diversity of judgment, as necessary for the instruction of their people.'" (Hardwicke.)

The XLII. Articles were, however, taken up and discussed by both houses of Convocation 1562 A.D. They were a remodeling of those set forth ten years before under Edward VI. Four were stricken out and several altered, but subscription to them was not at first required, although they were used sometimes as tests of orthodoxy. Now and then "men suspected of heterodoxy were called upon to subscribe as equivalent to recantation." The XXXIX. Articles were set forth by authority of Queen, Convocation, and Parliament 1571 A.D., and subscription to them was required by a Canon of the Convocation, assembled at that period, and by a contemporary enactment of the civil legislature." (Hardwicke.)

After the death of Luther, 1546 A.D., Calvin, who was then about thirty-seven years old, began to be felt as a power among the Continental Reformers. Geneva, in Switzerland, was his home, but his writings spread abroad. He was particularly noted for advocating, what is freely talked about though never clearly defined, viz., the "right of private judgment." This, at least, indicates the full evolution of one of the germinal forces of the Reformation, viz., the dignified position under GOD and before man of the free person. With a not unusual inconsistency Calvin added to this the theology of Predestination. These two incompatible propositions—human freedom and absolute decrees—worked strangely together, and exerted, indeed, still exert, a vast influence upon the Reformation and its development. English divines, and especially Whitgift, were captivated by Calvinism, and endeavored to get a series of Calvinistic articles established by authority. They put forth the Lambeth Articles, *nine* in number, which were "approved by John (Whitgift), Archbishop of Canterbury, Richard, Bishop of London, and other theologians. at Lambeth, November 20, 1595 A.D." The *first* reads: "GOD from eternity has predestinated some to life, and reprobated others to death." The *fourth:* "They who are not predestinated to salvation, necessarily on account of their own sins, are damned." The *ninth:* "It is not put in the will or power of every man to be saved."

XIX. Articles of Religion, containing one hundred and five paragraphs, "were agreed upon by the Archbishops and Bishops and the rest of the Cleargie of Ireland in the Convocation holden at Dublin 1615 A.D., for the avoiding of diversities of opinion, and the establishing of consent touching true Religion." They were not Calvinistic, but were strongly anti-Romish; and closed with a severe denunciation and decree of silence and deprival of office against whoever, "after due admonition, doe not conforme himselfe and cease to disturbe the peace of the Church."

Calvinism was rampant in England under Elizabeth. Presbyterianism became, both in Church and State, an aggressive force soon to be exceeded by Puritanism. The later was equally Calvinistic with, and more violent than, the former.

The Calvinists in France and Switzerland had drawn up several bodies of articles of religion, called Confessions.

When James I., 1603 A.D., came to the English throne he disappointed the Presbyterians by siding with the Church of England. He dabbled in theology, and was well disposed towards a reconciliation, *if possible*, with Calvinism. He sent "a private deputation of divines to the national Synod of Dort," 1619 A.D., but without avail. This Synod drew up the final Calvinistic confession, and manifested the irrepressible antagonism of that doctrine to the Catholic faith, as set forth in the formulas of worship in the Church of England. The "XXXIX. Articles of Religion" still carried the firm rejection, by the Church of England, both of the dogmas of Calvin and the usurpations of Rome. Neither were the peculiar tenets of Arminius, who held the opposite pole to Calvinism, sanctioned by the Articles. Though drawn in the prevalent theological language of the times, they were an earnest effort to express the peculiarly catholic position of the Church of England. Necessarily, with dangers on every hand, they had to be more or less negative in spirit and form. In denying errors they may not have escaped, in every case, the inevitable tendency towards overstatement.

The ferment in Western Europe stirred even the Roman Church to her depths. She was compelled to respond to the Reformation. Pope Paul III. convened the Council of Trent, 1545 A.D. It continued through his reign and that of Julius III., and came to a close December 3-4, 1563 A.D., under Pius IV. It made no concessions, but rather the contrary. It petrified many of the Roman corruptions, added new articles to the Faith, and confirmed that principle of "Development" which has now at last culminated in setting forth, as "Articles of Faith," the Immaculate Conception of the Blessed Virgin, and the Infallibility of the Pope.

James I. died 1625 A.D., and was succeeded by his son Charles I., who was beheaded January 30, 1648 A D. The preceding year the Assembly of Divines in Westminster set forth the well-known

"Westminster Confession," which is the authorized exponent of Presbyterian doctrine. The XXXIX. Articles, however, remained, and still continue with authority in the Church of England.

The Church in America did not at first adopt the XXXIX. Articles. They were not referred to even in the Preface to the American Prayer-Book, last paragraph but one, where it is stated "that this Church is far from intending to depart from the Church of England in any essential point of doctrine, discipline, or worship." This declaration had direct reference, as the context shows, only "to those alterations in the Liturgy which became necessary . . . in consequence of the Revolution." That it did not refer specifically to the XXXIX. Articles will appear in the proceedings of Convention, 1792 A.D., 1799 A.D., as referred to below.

The first action taken in the American Church on Articles of Religion was in General Convention, 1789 A.D., as follows: The House of Bishops, consisting of Seabury and White, "originated and sent to the House of Clerical and Lay Deputies . . . a proposed ratification of the Thirty-nine Articles, with an exception in regard to the Thirty-sixth and Thirty-seventh Articles." This was on the last day of the session. In the House of Deputies the "proposed ratification" was, "with the concurrence of the House of Bishops, referred to a future Convention."

At the General Convention of the Protestant Episcopal Church in the United States of North America, 1792 A.D., the matter was considered in the House of Deputies, but postponed "because the Churches in some of the States are not represented in this Convention and others only partially." The General Convention held 1795 A.D. again postponed the matter. At the Special General Convention, held in Philadelphia 1799 A.D., on Thursday, June 13, the Rev. Ashbel Baldwin, from Connecticut, moved in the House of Deputies, that "the House resolve itself into a committee of the whole to take into consideration the propriety of framing articles of religion." This was agreed to, and when the committee rose, "the chairman of the committee, Wm. Walter, D.D., of Massachusetts, reported the following resolution, viz.:

"*Resolved*, That the Articles of our faith and religion, as founded on the Holy Scriptures of the Old and New Testaments, are sufficiently declared in our Creeds and Liturgy as set forth in the Book of Common Prayer established for the use of this Church, and that further articles do not appear necessary."

"This resolution was disagreed to by the House."

On Saturday, June 15, "A resolution was proposed by Mr. Bisset,—Rev. John Bisset, of New York,—that the Convention now proceed to the framing of articles of religion for this Church." "The question was taken by yeas and nays," and "carried in the affirmative. Clergy: yea, Connecticut, Rhode Island, New York, New Jersey, Delaware, 5; nay, Massachusetts, Pennsylvania, Virginia, 3. Laity: yea, Connecticut, New Jersey, Pennsylvania, 3; nay, Virginia, 1." The committee was "chosen," and consisted of seven members, one from each State except Rhode Island.

On Tuesday, June 18, "The chairman of the Committee on the Articles reported seventeen articles of Religion, which were read. Whereupon, on motion of Mr. Bisset,

"*Resolved*, unanimously, That on account of the advanced period of the present session, and the thinness of the Convention, the consideration of the Articles now reported and read be postponed, and that the Secretary transcribe the Articles into the journal of this Convention, to lie over for the consideration of the next General Convention."

The XVII. Articles are printed in full in an appendix.

The House of Bishops do not appear to have taken action upon the subject. Its members present were Bishops White, Provoost, and Bass. Bishop Provoost was absent first and last day. Bishop Bass was absent on the first day. Session continued from Tuesday, June 11, to Tuesday, June 18, inclusive, except Sunday.

The General Convention, 1801 A.D., was opened in St. Michael's Church, Trenton, N. J., September 9, a sufficient quorum not appearing on the 8th, the day of call. The House of Bishops, consisting of Bishops White, Pennsylvania, Claggett, Maryland, and Jarvis, Connecticut, on Wednesday, September 9, "agreed on a form and manner of setting forth the Articles of Religion, and agreed that the same be sent to the House of Clerical and Lay Deputies for their concurrence."

It will thus be seen that the Bishops ignored, of course, the XVII. Articles, which had only passed in a committee of the lower house, and took the initiative in action. The Articles sent by them were the XXXIX. of the English Church, with such alterations as adapted them to the American Church. It will be observed that they call them "The Articles of Religion."

Conference between the houses and several action resulted in setting forth the so-called XXXIX. Articles, as now printed in the Prayer-Book, entitled "Articles of Religion as established by the Bishops, the Clergy, and the Laity of the Protestant Episcopal Church in the United States of America, in Convention, on the 12th day of September, in the year of our Lord 1801."

In Article VIII. all reference to the Athanasian Creed is left out. Article XXI. is omitted "because it is partly of local and civil nature, and is provided for as to the remaining parts of it in other Articles." Article XXXV. has a note modifying its recommendation of the Homilies. Article

XXXVI. "Of Consecration of Bishops and Ministers," is made to commend and defend "The book of Consecration of Bishops, and ordering of Priests and Deacons, as set forth by the General Convention of this Church in 1792." "Article XXXVII. to be omitted, and the following substituted in its place: 'Of the power of the Civil Magistrate.'"

Thus the American Church has thirty-eight Articles of Religion "set forth" by the General Convention 1801 A.D., and since acquiesced in.

"In the Church of England, the 36th Canon requires the candidate (for orders) after reference, first, to the royal supremacy; second, to the Book of Common Prayer with the Ordinal; and, third, to the XXXIX. Articles, to signify his assent as follows : I, N. N., do willingly and *ex animo* subscribe to those three Articles above mentioned, and to all things that are contained in them."

In the American Church, Article VII. of the Constitution requires, "Nor shall any person be ordained until he shall have subscribed the following declaration : " I do believe the Holy Scriptures of the Old and New Testaments to be the Word of God, and to contain all things necessary to salvation ; and I do solemnly engage to conform to the doctrines and worship of the Protestant Episcopal Church in the United States."

The authority of the "XXXIX. Articles" extends specifically to the clergy, and is set forth in the above forms of subscription. The laity, as such, even in England, are not bound to their terms, though some laymen —*e.g.*, members of the universities—have to subscribe them. In America the laity are only bound by the Creeds. They profess belief in the Apostles' Creed at baptism, and usually recite the Nicene Creed in the Liturgy proper, or, as it is designated in the Prayer-Book, " The Order for the Administration of the Lord's Supper, or Holy Communion." Their profession of faith, in the Holy Catholic Church, subjects the American laity to such Canons of Discipline as are or may be established by the American Church.

Authorities : Bishop Burnet on XXXIX. Articles, Hardwicke's History of the Articles, Bishop H. Browne on the XXXIX. Articles, Bishop Tomlines' Elements of Theology, etc.   Rev. B. Franklin, D.D.

Ascension. The article of the Creed declares that our Lord ascended into heaven. A creed properly states only facts to be believed. A Christian creed states the facts of the Christian religion. Therefore a fact linking the Resurrection with His continuous mediatorial acts and His gift of the Holy Ghost could not be omitted. But this fact, so briefly stated in the Creed, must also be vouched for in the inspired record. Therefore we have recorded by St. John that Christ foretold his Ascension (ch. xvi. 5 ; xx. 17), that He did ascend openly before His Apostles, by St. Mark (ch. xvi. 19), by St. Luke (ch. xxiv. 51 ; Acts i. 9–11). He was seen at His place in heaven by St. Stephen. His ascension was taught and inferences drawn from it by St. Paul (Eph. iv. 8–16 ; Col. ii. 15 ; 1 Tim. iii. 16), by St. Peter, who was also an eye-witness (1 Pet. iii. 22). Therefore it was in His very and true Body and Soul, now immortally conjoined to His Divinity, by which He hath entered into the Holiest. The Ascension was necessary for us, since He could not otherwise send to His Apostles, and therefore to His Church, and consequently to us, the gift of the Holy Ghost, nor those gifts which he received for men that the Lord God might dwell among us. It was necessary that He might take up His mediatorial work. It was necessary that our affections might ascend to Him (Col. iii. 1–4). These main facts are thus grandly summed up by Bishop Pearson : "Upon these considerations we may easily conclude what every Christian is obliged to confess in these words of our Creed, *He ascended into heaven;* for thereby he is understood to express thus much. I am fully persuaded that the only begotten and eternal Son of God, after He rose from the dead, did, with the same soul and body with which He rose, by a true and local translation, convey Himself from the earth on which He lived, through all the regions of the air, through all the celestial orbs, until He came unto the heaven of heavens, the most glorious Presence of the majesty of God ; and thus I believe in Jesus Christ who ascended into heaven." (Pearson on the Creed.)

Ascetics. (*Vide* Hermits.) The name ascetic is derived from the Greek word "asketikos," which means "exercised." Asceticism has been said to be a temperament, rather than a law of Christian life. The idea of the ancient ascetics was that solitude, extreme fasting, and self-denial, and hardening of the body and keeping it under, and bringing it into subjection (1 Cor. ix. 27), brought the spirit into better condition for constant contemplation of Divine things.

This style of life is first met with in the heathen world, and doubtless many good men among them have thus sought God according to their light. The East Indians, the Mohammedans, and the ancient Egyptian priests all practiced asceticism. The Therapeutæ (Worshipers) of Egypt, who endeavored to mingle the teachings of Moses and Plato, belonged to this school.

Among the Jews the Essenes were noted ascetics, and in the days of St. John the Baptist they were leading in their mountain valleys a life similar to his. Those who strive to trace the history of such communities see a forerunner of them in the prophet Elijah. Daniel the prophet, in his mourning, ate no pleasant bread (Dan. x. 3). In the Apocrypha, when Esdras prepares himself for his visions, he goes, according to commandment, into the field Ardath, "and did eat of the herbs of the field, and," he adds, "the meat of the same satisfied me"

(2 Esdras ix. 26). Anna, the prophetess, "served GOD with fastings and prayers night and day" (St. Luke ii. 36, 37).

The ascetic is older than the monk, and the term is a more general one. In the beginning he lived alone, or he could live in the busy city, distinguished by his zeal; the communities were an after-thought.

Egypt, "the mother of wonders," was the natural home of asceticism. The Eastern mind is naturally given to reflection. A warm climate allows men to live much in the open air, and the magnificent clear starlight nights of the East "declare the glory of GOD" to the silent watcher. About the close of the fourth century the mountains and deserts of Egypt were full of Christian brethren, whose self-denying lives astonished the world. The dwellers in the Roman empire, which was then rotting in vice, were allured to these seats of piety, and St. Jerome and others visited them. Noble Roman women gave up their property, and, tired of the effeminate, faithless life of the capital, sought the Egyptian desert. The question which met all was whether pleasure or virtue was the aim of life. From the Thebaid asceticism has spread over the world, and for centuries it was a mighty power among men.

The Essene by his mountain spring with his incessant washings was a type of all who have followed him. The Carthusians, with their rule to eat no flesh and keep perpetual silence and never go abroad, and the monks of La Trappe, who were to observe silence and dig their own graves, are lineal descendants of the ascetic Jew and the Egyptian Christian. The dark forests of Mount Athos contain the monasteries which gave Bishops to the Eastern Church, and thus its doctrine and worship were determined by men who knew not the education of public life.

Hallam, in the "Middle Ages," draws attention to the fact that the fasting and watching and hard lot of monks and hermits must lead men to conclude that they are living in hope of a better world in the future. The reality of heaven was a constant impulse in their life. "Jerusalem the Golden" is the composition of a monk. The worthlessness and uncertainty of earthly things led their minds above. The fasting, continued often for days, subdued the body to the spirit. If heaven was a reality, hell was also one. No wonder that the worn-out watcher heard the cries of devils in the night-birds' notes or in the yells of wild beasts among ruins. The sinfulness of sin on the one hand and the nearness of GOD on the other were constantly before the mind of the ascetic as he watched under the sky or tilled his little field.

A weariness of life, and a preparation for death, were the great stimulants to those who led so solitary and denying a life. Contemplation and prayer were the business of life. The Holy Scriptures were the guide, and those early ascetics who could not read committed them to memory.

In a busy age, when men must be in the world and yet not of the world, it is well sometimes to look upon the lives of men who gave up all for CHRIST, and who, with all their imperfections, were the salt of the earth in a godless age.

Authorities: Bingham's Antiquities, Hase, Burton's Anatomy of Melancholy, Farrar's Life of Christ, Geikie's Life of Christ, and Kingsley's Hermits. Kingsley refers to Gibbon, Montalembert's "Moines d'Occident," Dean Milman's "History of Christianity" and "Latin Christianity," and Ozanam's "Etudes Germaniques," and especially to Rosmeyde's "Lives of the Hermit Fathers."

REV. S. F. HOTCHKIN.

Assurance of Faith. The word assurance, in the first verse of St. Luke's Gospel and in St. Paul's Epistles, is a metaphor taken from the onward sweep of a ship before a favoring breeze. St. Luke means to say that outward historical facts have given us a full persuasion of the truth of what spiritual facts we teach in the Gospel. St. Paul means the same thing when writing to his converts (1 Thess. i. 5; Heb. vi. 11; x. 22; and Rom. iv. 21; xiv. 5). It is the conviction that comes from those proofs (as the gifts of sacramental life by the HOLY GHOST, cf. the texts cited), which He chooses to put before us as sufficient, and our action upon that conviction. It cannot refer to the inward conviction from emotion or excitement. The word assurance is used in connection either with historic proofs or with the power of the HOLY GHOST, shown by miracles or in connection with the sacraments, or with Abraham's faith (Rom. iv. 21), who had already outward demonstration of GOD's power. Therefore Hooker was right when he taught that the proofs of faith were not so strong as the assurance of the senses, from the certainty of evidence depending upon the proofs adduced; but there arises from this a certainty of adherence, which, itself, causes the heart to "cleave and stick to that which it doth believe. The reason is this: the faith of a Christian doth apprehend the words of the law, the promises of GOD not only as true but as good; and therefore even then when the evidence which he hath of the truth is so small that it grieveth him to feel his weakness in assenting thereto, yet is there in him such a sure adherence unto that which he doth but faintly and fearfully believe, that his spirit having once truly tasted the heavenly sweetness thereof, all the world is not able quite and clean to remove him from it, but he striveth with himself to hope against all reason of believing, being settled with holy Job upon this immovable resolution, 'Though GOD kill me I will not give over trusting in Him.' For why? this lesson remaineth forever imprinted in him, 'It is good for me to cleave unto GOD.'" (Hooker, Serm. i., p. 585, Keble's ed.) This, however, is very different from the presumptuous assurance of pardon sometimes taught by sectaries, but which has no warrant of Holy Scripture. Even St. Paul felt the need of constant active work for his Christian life (*cf.* 1 Cor. ix. 27, with 2 Tim. iv. 8).

Athanasian Creed. *Vide* CREEDS and QUICUMQUE VULT.

Atheism, from *a* and θέος, is the denial of the existence of a personal GOD. It thus includes pantheism, which teaches that everything is GOD. Atheism must be carefully distinguished from skepticism, which simply doubts, and from infidelity, which is the rejection of an organized faith or form of religion. Nor does it include the godlessness of savage tribes, if there be such, whose intellectual development is too low to form a conception of GOD. Avowed and consistent atheism is exceedingly rare, and is always individual, no sect or system having ever been willing to establish itself upon this basis. Even the positivism of Comte stops short of avowed atheism, content with holding the futility of all speculation beyond the data of positive experience. The charge of atheism has always been most abhorrent to those, even, who might be practical atheists. Among the Greeks and Romans it was punished with death, those convicted of it being regarded by the law as *hostes humani generis*,—enemies to the human race. A little thought will reveal the grounds of this universal repugnance. First, it is the deliberate rejection of the suggestions of consciousness, no argument being ever required to establish a belief in GOD, while atheism is always the result of some process of thought. Then the mind naturally recoils from what is contrary to reason, and atheism is so because it necessitates the recognition of effect without cause, of design without a designer, of law without a lawgiver, and of life without a source. A slight elaboration of the last two points may be sufficient for illustration. One of the first results of observation and experience is the necessary recognition of laws by which natural processes are governed, and which man can neither understand nor control. The recurrence of the seasons, the germination of seed, the reproduction of plants and animals each after its kind, with many more instances which will readily occur, are seen to be regular, systematic, and permanent. Man finds them necessary to his life, while he can neither alter nor restrain them, but he may rely upon them, and does rely upon them, with the absolute certainty of not being disappointed. Reason tells him that there must be a Mind greater than his to conceive laws which he cannot comprehend, and a Power greater than his to enforce them. This Mind and this Power he always finds greater than the grasp of his mind and power, and this supreme intelligent force is GOD. Again, man recognizes the fact and the phenomena of life, but finds no origin for them within his experience. But reason demands an origin, which must necessarily be beyond his experience. He finds, too, in close connection with life the phenomenon of death, and soon discovers that it is abnormal. There ought to be no death ; by the very nature of life the machines which it quickens should be permanent. But they are not so, and that systematically. Reason demands for this a controlling Will which restrains, as it originates, the phenomena of life. That originating and controlling will is GOD. Thus the rejecting of the existence of GOD is contrary to reason, and, therefore, abhorrent to human intellect. We sometimes meet the phrase " scientific atheism," but there can be no such thing as scientific atheism, because nothing could be more unscientific than to deny the existence of that which is undemonstrable. But the existence of a personal GOD is undemonstrable by science because science deals necessarily with finite data and causes ; but finite causes must lead to finite results, and GOD is of necessity infinite. Hence science can neither prove nor disprove the existence of GOD, because it must work with data which cannot lead beyond human experience, while GOD is beyond human experience. But to assume that which we cannot know is contrary to science, and therefore there can be no scientific atheism. Finally, atheism is repugnant to reason because it is illogical, logic being the perfection of the processes of reason. For logic is essentially the necessary sequence of cause and effect, and therefore to deny to any effect an antecedent cause is illogical. But the human mind must necessarily confine its processes to sequences, beginning within its own experience, and the ultimate attainment of human experience is always manifestly an effect. But atheism denies any antecedent cause beyond the possible attainment of human experience, and therefore atheism is illogical, and consequently repugnant to reason. Thus we may readily account for the abhorrence always manifested by individuals to the charge of atheism. But it is equally repugnant to morality, and consequently to the welfare of society, because it destroys the strongest and highest incentive to the control and restraint of those natural appetites and passions which in their unbridled indulgence are hostile to the interests of society. The first element of social order and welfare is the restriction of individual liberty for the common good, and the restraint within permitted limits of those dispositions and desires which are common to all animal nature. But the fear of human punishment and the desire of the good of others have never been found sufficient to accomplish these ends, unless aided and supported by a sense of responsibility and accountability unto a higher Power, whose vigilance cannot be escaped and whose authority cannot be defied, or whose love and kindness excites to reverence and obedience. But atheism destroys alike this fear and this reverence, and by removing all sense of danger beyond this life, or of compensating reward hereafter, directly fosters the commission of acts contrary to the common welfare. Hence society has ever regarded atheism as hostile to its best interests and subversive of its fundamental principles, and has punished it as a crime or made it a bar to social privileges and respect. The refusal to accept the oath of an atheist in a court of justice is a brand of disgrace, and the assertion of a distrust by his fellow-citizens, from which every man must shrink with horror. It is a powerful proof of the healthy tone of public sentiment upon this vital matter, that there is probably not a single society in the country organized for mutual benefits of any kind into which an avowed atheist could obtain admission.

Among those who have been classed as atheists are the Peripatetic and Epicurean philosophers of ancient times, and Hobbes, Hume, Kant, Spinoza, Blount, Vanini, and others in the modern period. We must remember, however, how inaccurate was the language and how intolerant the views of theological writers only a few years ago. Few, if any, of those named can be properly called atheists under the exact terminology and discriminating classifications of more recent philosophy, though most of them, wandering in the misty regions of metaphysical speculation, have trodden dangerously near to the fatal verge, and there are few minds strong enough to follow their teachings with safety.

REV. ROBERT WILSON, D.D.

Atonement. This word, as applied to the great work of CHRIST, has been used in two senses, differing according to the view taken of the Person of CHRIST and of His relation to the process of man's salvation. Those who deny the divinity of our LORD JESUS CHRIST commonly regard the Atonement as a mere restoration of friendly feeling between two alienated parties. It is, to use their own favorite etymology, an "*at-one-ment*,"—a *reconciliation* of the CREATOR and creature to each other. From this point of view, inasmuch as the CREATOR cannot be supposed to have contributed to the alienation,—and is not supposed to have raised any barrier to the restoration of the original amicable relations between Himself and His creature,—inasmuch, therefore, as both the original departure and the continued separation are exclusively on the part of the creature, the Atonement is regarded as a process not for reconciling the CREATOR to the creature, or the law to the offender, but only for reconciling the creature to the CREATOR. According to this view the work of CHRIST is reduced to the exercise of a mere persuasory influence upon the creature. First, persuading him to desire reconciliation, and then persuading him to take the steps of moral and spiritual reform necessary for the restoration of harmony. But in all this there is nothing of the nature of *expiation* or of satisfaction rendered for the offense.

But the Holy Catholic Church, while including this persuasory process in her idea of the Atonement, and understanding the language of St. Paul (2 Cor. v. 20) as expressing it, has, from the first, included much more. She holds that the fitness of things, their accurate adjustment, the eternal principles of justice and truth, and the permanent well-being of the universe demand that where law has been broken some adequate satisfaction for the offense shall be rendered, especially where a penalty has been attached beforehand to the infraction and made known to those under its authority.

1st. It is contrary to justice, to the essential *fitness* of things, and to the dignity of all law that the infraction of any law should have no evil consequences for the infringer; that the results of disobedience should be to him the same as those of obedience. Law is something more than a mere indication or suggestion of action. It is an *obligatory rule* of action, imposing respect for itself upon all; not only binding the person governed but existing as an authority in the universe, the maintenance of which becomes of *universal* obligation and interest. To be law in this sense it must be an *enforced* rule of action.

2d. The *controlling* power of law,—its value as an effective *regulator* of action is sacrificed when disobedience goes unpunished. Wherefore, when law is violated, its regulating efficiency, which is impaired by the violation, must be restored by some expiatory penalty. It is for the benefit of all for whom law is made, the law-breaker himself included, that the law shall not be rendered ineffective and contemptible by permitting its infraction with impunity.

This becomes more evident when the nature of Sin is considered: 1st. "Sin is transgression of Law." 2d. Sin is always the responsible act of a free agent. No being is responsible for what he cannot help. Therefore sinfulness is our common inherited nature. But Sin itself involves freedom of action,—action performed not by compulsion—however induced through the persuasive influence of *motives*,—but not the less free because the result of such persuasion. Hence the *rationale* and the importance of offsetting all temptation to law-breaking by corresponding penalty. This is an absolutely rational arrangement, and one of universal application,—in all worlds and forms of responsible existence,—one adapted to the nature of free agents, who, because they *are* free, must therefore be *able* to break the law, and who are therefore to be hindered from doing so not by compulsion, but by the persuasory power of motives. These motives may be of different sorts. They may be found in the love of the right, or in the love of the lawmaker. But these motives may be legitimately and effectively supported by another, viz., the apprehension of the evil *consequences* of breaking the law. The attachment of a penalty to law-breaking is therefore more than a measure of *justice*. It is a positive measure of mercy, since it supplies an additional protection of the universe against the disturbing influences of temptation and sin by protecting the free agent against himself. It is, therefore, also as much a measure of mercy for the law-breaker as for the law-keeper.

But in order that a penalty may have any useful effect its enforcement must be *assured*. This is—equally as the other, and for the same reasons—a measure of true mercy as well as of justice,—and for *all*—for the law-breaker as well as for the law-keeper. And all that might be said of the protective power of an enforced penalty in the case of a *first* offense would apply to all subsequent offenses. The *rationale* is the same.

But where a particular penalty has been beforehand attached to the breach of a law the *veracity* of the law-maker is also involved in its enforcement. It is of course conceivable that the terms of the penalty may be that the law-breaker shall only be *liable* to certain consequences. But whatever the actual terms of the penalty, the veracity of the law-maker requires that those terms be enforced. A *positive* threat is only a *promise* in another form. And it is a promise not only to the possible law-breaker, made with the merciful intent to deter him from the crime, but it is a promise to the rest of the universe also, whose peace is more or less endangered by any infraction of law. The actual enforcement of the penalty becomes, therefore, an obligation of *justice*, of *mercy*, and of *veracity*.

When man was placed in probation he was told that if he sinned he should die. It was a *promise* on the part of the Divine Law-maker, and, as made by Divine wisdom, one which must be held to have been in just proportion to the offense. Having been made, its fulfillment was required by the principles of absolute *justice*,—by the *interests* of the universe, those of the law-breaking race included, and by the *veracity* of the Creator.

It was necessary, therefore, from all these points of view, that man's offense should be punished by the actual infliction, in some way, of the promised penalty. And it must be observed that the penalty promised was a *positive* and *punitive* one. There was something more than a mere separation from GOD as a simple *effect* or resulting *fact*,—a fact which could be neutralized or extinguished by another simple fact, viz., by a mere bringing together again of the separated parties,—an *at-one-ment*. The penalty was not only consequential, but was also positively *punitive*, and was therefore something more than the offender could himself remove by simply returning. The offender could not reinstate himself. He must needs be reinstated. But inasmuch as it was due to absolute justice, as well as to the interests of the universe, that no reinstatement should take effect which should leave the sin unpunished or the broken influence of the law unrepaired or uncompensated, some adequate compensation, or satisfaction, or expiation was necessary, that the law-breaking might be properly offset or balanced, and the shattered influence of the law itself repaired. Could the human law-breaker make this expiation for himself either by subsequent obedience or by suffering? He could not do this by subsequent *obedience*, inasmuch as there was still due from him to his CREATOR a perpetually perfect service. All that he could do, therefore, at the best, would be not to break the law again. There could be no room or possibility for a superabundant or superfluous service or obedience. But not to offend again would offer no satisfaction for the breach already committed; nothing but suffering in such case could answer the purpose of expiation; and had the offender risen from his first fault to a continuously perfect obedience thereafter, it is conceivable that by his sufferings justice could have been satisfied and the law vindicated, and its influence sustained. But, unfortunately for him, his sin not only subjected him to punishment, but brought in a depravation of his nature. So that from the first he has gone on increasing in place of diminishing the fatal record against himself. Manifestly, therefore, he, being a *continuous* offender, could make no expiation for himself, either by obedience or by suffering.

At the same time it was not consistent with justice that the penalty should be borne by one absolutely unconnected with the offense. Besides which, the penalty having been denounced specifically upon the offender himself, the veracity of the Law maker was pledged for its infliction upon *him*. How, then, could expiation be made, or the reinstatement of the offender accomplished, if neither one himself an offender, nor one unconnected with the offense, could make it?

Just here an important fact must be noticed. Adam represented the race of man, and his act was a *representative* act. His offense was a *race-offense*, and so the penalty was a *race-penalty*. That this is so is evident from two facts, not to speak of others:

1st. The whole race, *as a race*, have inherited the taint of Adam's sin. The case is not one of a multitude of individual sinners, but one of a *race* or *stock* of sinners, in whom the sinfulness in the stock is congenital. There is absolutely never an exception.

2d. The penalty of mortality is equally universal and congenital. There is no exception in respect to it. It is, therefore, a *race-punishment*.

But here again another fact must be borne in mind, viz., that the human family is, after all, in a very real sense, only one continuous person. As the branches of a tree are a part of the one tree, and as, no matter how long the life of the tree, its continuity is preserved, so that it is, after all, but one and the same tree, and its latest branches are only a continuation of the wood which was in it as a sapling a hundred years before, so with the human stock. It has not been a series of successive creations; it has been but one continuous, uninterrupted individual, at least so far as body and brain are concerned, and so far as we may hold that mental and moral qualities are *inherited*, we may include the mind with the body in this statement (the will is perhaps the only separable part of the man). The child begins by being a living part of its parents before it sets out on its own independent career of will. There has never been a break or an interval in this human continuity, and so, in point of fact, there has been literally but one ever-developing, continuous *human being*. Its many branches, however separated after a time from the parent stem, are in their start as identical with the original stock as are the branches of a tree with its trunk.

This great, continuous, self-involving human being, now as many years old as have elapsed since the creation, sinned *as a whole*, was sentenced *as a whole*, and *as a whole* now lies under the penalty of the law. In this fact we find the beginning of the solution of our difficulty. To complete it another fact is necessary.

The Most High GOD, the SON, by causing Himself to be born of the Virgin Mary, entered into the human race and became a part of the same. Having thus become part of the human stock, He could, in His human nature, rightfully represent that stock in any transaction with Divine Justice. Punishment inflicted upon Him in His human nature would be punishment inflicted upon the human race. And as the pain inflicted upon any part of a human body is inflicted upon that body as a whole, so the penalty inflicted upon an individual of a race is inflicted upon the race. Thus, one person might become proxy for his race to the avenging law.

Yet a continuously sinful member of the race could not thus stand as proxy, seeing that he would have his own offenses to answer for. But one who had incurred no individual penalty might thus, by suffering, atone—*according to his measure*—for the offense of his race, so that in him his race might be punished.

But could any one person *adequately* atone for a whole race? Could the majesty of the law be thus sufficiently vindicated, the necessities of justice be maintained, the veracity of the law-maker be preserved, and the interests of the universe be sufficiently guarded?

When in human warfare a body of men having become liable to punishment certain of their number are selected as representatives of the rest, the punishment of a leader is accounted the equivalent of that of many private individuals. Natural reason accepts this as a principle. But GOD, the SON, by taking humanity did not put off His own Divinity. And so in standing proxy to justice for the human race, His value as an example or substitute for others was infinitely multiplied. By how much a Divine victim was of more value than a human one by so much the more did His suffering exceed in value that of any merely human victim in supplying a suitable satisfaction to the broken law and in restoring the power of the law as a preventive of future disobedience. Being a part of the human stock, the sentence of the law against that stock was literally executed in Him, and the veracity of the Law-giver was maintained. Being Divine, as well as human, *i.e.*, a *Divine man*, He could adequately represent any number of individuals in that race. Thus was solved the riddle. Eternal justice, the true honor and dignity of law, its availability as a barrier against sin, and the truth of GOD were made consistent with man's salvation.

Atonement, then, in the sense in which it is applied by the Holy Catholic Church to the work of CHRIST, is the expiation offered in the Person of the Divine man whereby He put Himself in the place of the rest of the condemned human race and suffered in its stead. As man, He paid the penalty adjudged against man; as GOD, He gave value to the substitution of Himself for the whole race.

Thus the Atonement, while including the idea of reconciliation or "*at-one-ment*," and indeed involving all the subsequent processes of reconciliation whereby the offender is brought to a better mind and into harmony again with the Divine will, yet contains also the principle of a *satisfaction* rendered for the breach of the law; and so a *ransom* paid for the deliverance of the offender.

In this sense the ancient sacrifices were measures of atonement. They were satisfactions or ransoms rendered, and being antetypes of the Atonement of CHRIST, imperfect themselves, they were said to effect an atonement through Him for those who offered them. Thus (to select one out of many passages) in Lev. iv. 35, it is said with respect to any one of the people who should sin and bring a sacrifice, "The priest shall make an atonement for his sin that he hath committed, and it shall be forgiven him." And so of the sacrifice of our LORD JESUS CHRIST, it is said (Rom. v. 11), "By Him we have received the atonement." That His Atonement was not a mere process of reconciliation, but an expiation by suffering, is evident from Eph. i. 7, *et al.*: " In whom we have redemption *through His blood*, the forgiveness of sins."

Correspondent to this view of the Atonement was the language of the Fathers. St. Clement of Rome (a contemporary of the

Apostles), 1 Epist. vii.: "Let us look steadfastly to the *blood* of CHRIST. . . . shed for our salvation." Epist. St. Barnabas (a very early document), ch. v.: "The remission of sins which is effected by His *blood* of sprinkling." Ignatius ad Smyrn., vi.: "If they believe not in the *blood* of CHRIST (they) shall incur condemnation." Epist. ad Diognetum, ix.: "He (GOD) took on Him the burden of our iniquities; He gave His SON to be a *ransom* for us." Justin Martyr, Dial. Tryph., lxiii., speaks of CHRIST as "delivered over to *death by* GOD for the *transgressions of the people."

The above are only a few specimens of the vast mass of patristic testimony to the doctrine held by the Holy Catholic Church upon this subject and confirmatory of the view we have presented.

Attributes of God. Those characteristics by which we can recognize Him and His dealing with us. "His property is always to have Mercy;" Justice is another; Love is more properly Himself. Holiness, Compassion, Omnipotence, Omnipresence, are attributes. In short, in the Divine nature, since we cannot comprehend it in itself, we can only recognize attributes. These may be grouped into those relating to His nature absolutely, and those displayed towards us. Of the first we may recite His Omnipotence, His Omniscience, His Omnipresence, His Wisdom, His Truth. Of the second, we may recite His Justice, His Mercy, His Love, His Compassion. These are evidently part of the Divine Essence. They coexist in Him and are inseparable from Him, but they are all cognizable by us, and in our own unaided speculations concerning the Divine nature are forced upon our recognition because there is some faint counterpart in our own human nature. They are so many cords to draw us to the Divine nature. Yet while they coexist and are inseparable from His Essence, it is something more, as our soul is an essence known to us by our capacities, yet it is something more. Therefore these several attributes that inhere in the very nature of GOD and belong to any conception we can form of Him yet do not describe His full nature.

Attrition. An attempt by the schoolmen to give an analysis of repentance led to a too curious and untenable series of subdivisions. Attrition is defined to be the first step towards repentance. It is akin to the worldly sorrow which worketh death; not a sorrow that arises from a hatred of sin, but a sorrow from the consequences of the act. It is a step towards true repentance which yet may never be attained. As a preliminary part to the series of acts in the heart of the sinner leading to a true hearty repentance, the distinction is useful enough for the theologian, but it is a very dangerous suggestion to the imperfectly taught layman, more especially since the Council of Trent (Sess. xiv. c. 4, de pœnit.) taught that contrition, confession, and satisfaction were sufficient, making contrition consist in the terrors of a stricken conscience, and a faith that the sins of the penitent are forgiven by CHRIST. It is evident that this is but a partial statement made more fully and accurately elsewhere, but certainly (as this is a canon complete in itself) very mistakenly here, since the other teaching would be lowered to this, not this lifted up to meet the truer definition.

Autocephali. Those Metropolitans who were not under a Patriarch were called Autocephali. Such were the Archbishop of Cyprus by the express recognition of the General Council of Ephesus, 431 A.D., and the Archbishops of Bulgaria and Georgia. The British Archbishop of Caerleon-upon-Usk was also autocephalous.

Ave Maria. The salutation of the Angel Gabriel to the Virgin Mary at the Annunciation (St. Luke i. 28). The words of the angel were simply "Hail! thou that art highly favored, the LORD is with thee. Blessed art thou among women." The modern Roman invocation following the Vulgate reads, "Hail Mary! full of grace," then adds from the salutation of St. Elizabeth, "blessed art thou among women, and blessed is the fruit of thy womb." The first part came into use about 1196 A.D., as is seen from the injunctions of Odo, Bishop of Paris, at that date. Its universal use was ordered by Urban IV. (1261 A.D.), together with the addition of Elizabeth's salutation. Later yet a precatory, "Holy Mary, mother of GOD, pray for us now and at the hour of our death," was added and ordered to be used, in the Breviary of Pius V. (1566 A.D.). The first clause was in use in England, but not the second, till nearly the date of the Reformation, and the precatory addition never. And in the "Institution of a Christian Man," 1530 A.D., the preachers were enjoined to teach that it was no prayer, but that it was a laud and thanksgiving for our LORD'S birth, with a remembrance that the Virgin humbly submitted and believed.

Azyme. (Unleavened bread.) The controversy between the Greek and Roman Churches upon the use by the latter of unleavened bread in the Eucharist. The earliest use was that of unleavened bread, and was so for several centuries (*vide* OBLATIONS), but the Roman Church gradually fell from the use of leavened bread after the close of the ninth century. The Greek Church has always used leavened bread. When, then, the various causes of division came to a focus about 1054 A.D., this use of unleavened bread became a bitter part of the furious disputes which raged over the differences and wrongs of the two Churches, and it continued to be a serious subject of controversy for a long time. (*Vide* Neale's Introduction to the History of the Eastern Church, vol. ii.; Scudamore's Notitia Eucharistica, pp. 749–65.)

B.

Baal. (Lord.) The name of a deity worshiped among the Semitic peoples of Syria and Mesopotamia. It is identified with the Babylonian Bel. The Baal-worship into which the Israelites fell when "they joined themselves to Baal-peor" when tempted by the Moabites, clung to them till late in their history. The minor prophets are full of references to it, and, in fact, they were only cured of it when finally all idolatrous tendencies were crushed out by the Babylonian captivity.

Balaam. The famous prophet who blessed Israel (Num. xxiii. and xxiv.). The whole history of his contact with Israel is recorded in these two chapters, with a necessary slight reference to him in a later chapter. He appears from the first as a prophet of GOD, and so acts and is so entitled in the Bible. It is not the place here to enter into the question how much knowledge of GOD the heathen really had, and how far He chose to have Himself witnessed to among them. For any knowledge given to them would be perverted into polytheistic teaching. The history of Balaam is short, but very instructive. Balak, the king of Moab, sends for him to come to curse the passing hosts of Israel, "for I wot that he whom thou blessest is blessed, and he whom thou cursest is cursed." It is not necessary to suppose that the rewards of divination in the hands of the elders of Moab were any other than the usual and courteous gifts from a prince to a prophet (cf. 1 Sam. ix. 7-9). Balaam, desirous to go, still inquired of GOD whether he could go. The LORD forbade him, "for thou shalt not curse the people, for they are blessed." The princes returned to Balak with the message, but Balak, unwilling to let the prophet put him off, as he thought, sent other and more honorable ambassadors. Balaam still professed utter inability to act without permission from the LORD. The permission was conditional,—"if the men come to call thee." Of this call nothing is said, only, "Balaam rose up early in the morning and saddled his ass and went with the princes of Moab." His willful conduct brought upon him the terrible rebuke,— the dumb ass, speaking with man's voice, forbade the madness of the prophet. Doubtless the bribe of political honors held out to Balaam was really irresistible, and was, as we know, yielded to, but he was at least nominally obedient to the inspiration of GOD. Despite Balak's entreaty he blessed the people, adding his prophecy of the MESSIAH, "There shall come a star out of Jacob and a sceptre shall rise out of Israel." It is not necessary to suppose that he could understand how far his prophecy reached; that he thought it only political is clear from the next verses: its spiritual truth was beyond his ken. After this Balaam returned home, but with the Midianite princes—who were leagued with Balak (Num. xxii. 4-7)—he plotted the licentious feast into which Israel fell, and for which Moses inflicted a fearful vengeance. Balaam himself thus helped to bring on a momentary fulfillment of his prophecy, "He shall smite the corners of Moab and destroy all the children of Sheth." He fell in the battle that broke the power of the Midianites (Num. xxxi. 1-10). His is a very fascinating history. A prophet of GOD though a heathen, using his influence for temporal good among his people, ambitious, self-willed, vain of his political sagacity, his was a character of mingled clay and gold, and was strong and weak in proportion. Not above the ideas of his day in his surroundings, though as prophet of the One GOD holding the clue to higher principles, he probably deemed his counsel to the Midianites a stroke of real policy, and did not at all enter into the peculiar purposes of GOD in the separation of Israel from among the Gentiles. This was far beyond all he had ever learned of GOD'S merciful dealings with men. Sharing the political views of his tribe, he fell from the pure height into a sin that brought him under the edge of the sword. He is a type of a large human nature touching many sides and appealing to our sympathies. In many respects, too, he typifies the character which, rising above demagogism, yet does not rank above the trickery of the politician when it has the opportunity to become a statesman.

But as one of those permitted to prophesy, no matter how obscurely, yet to prophesy of CHRIST, and to leave this prophecy among his people, which finally should bring the wise men to the cradle of the Star of Jacob, Balaam claims of us a special attention. It was not necessary that he should understand the full reach of his prophecy, but assuredly he understood much of its political bearing, and, therefore, it added to his responsibility in his after-action. To us it is a proof that GOD did not leave Himself without witness among the Gentiles.

Bands. A part of the clerical dress that has now almost entirely fallen into disuse. It is a remnant of the ancient *amice*. In reality it is a part of the full dress for lawyers, as well as clergymen in the English Church, but there, as well as here, it is hardly ever to be seen.

Banners are of late origin. In the Bible the "banner" appears to have been merely a pole with some device upon it, as a rallying-point for the squadron (or worked into the sail of the ship if used at sea). It was not a *flag*, whatever standards were used. Rabbinical writers state that the standards for the four divisions of the tribes upon their march (Numb. ii.) were, for Judah, a lion; for Reuben, a man; for Ephraim, an ox; for Dan, an eagle. But this is mere tradition; compare, however, the Vision of Ezekiel (ch. x.) and of the Revelation (ch. iv.). But the banner, as a flag, belongs rather to the age of Chivalry, and is a heraldic standard, and so it passed into Church usage. There is no authorization for its use in our services. In the Sunday-school celebrations it appears to be quite appropriate, and certainly most unobjectionable. Banners were formerly a part of the accustomed ornaments of the altar, and were suspended over it.

Banns; Banns of Marriage. The word "bann" comes from the Low Latin, signifying to proclaim an edict; hence the edict or proclamation itself, and thence, in the Church, a proclamation of marriage between parties then and there named. The publication of banns of marriage is not required in this country, though the custom is in many places still carried out.

The form in England is as follows: After the second lesson, at morning prayer (or if there be no morning prayer at evening prayer), for three several Sundays previous, "the curate shall say, after the accustomed manner, I publish the banns of marriage between M. of ―― and N. of ――. If any of you know cause or just impediment why these two persons should not be joined together in holy matrimony, ye are to declare it. This is the first (second, or third) time of asking." But now marriages may also be celebrated without either banns or license upon production of the superintendent registrar's certificate.

Baptism. One of the two great sacraments "generally necessary to salvation," "ordained by CHRIST Himself" (*vide* SACRAMENT) as a means of initiation into His Church, and "a sign of regeneration or new birth" (Article of Religion XXVII.); whereby we are made "members of CHRIST, children of GOD, and heirs of the Kingdom of Heaven" (Catechism).

In considering baptism we shall set forth (A) The history of the sacrament; (B) the outward sign and manner of administration; (c) The Covenant: (1) the inward grace, (2) the conditions required of those who come; (D) by whom and to whom it is to be administered.

(A) THE HISTORY.—The washing with water as an emblem of purity was of very ancient origin and of general use. It is specially to be found among Eastern nations. Classical writers, both Greek and Latin, frequently allude to it as a means of purification before offering sacrifices, and of removing ceremonial uncleanness. (See Smith's Bible Dictionary.)

In the Mosaic Ritual washing or bathing in water is constantly prescribed as a means of ceremonial purification. Numerous such commands are found in the Pentateuch, both for the priests and the people. Thus, before going into the sanctuary the priests were to wash their hands and their feet, "that they died not" (Ex. xxx. 20). For this purpose, and also for washing the vessels and things used in the sacrifices, Moses was ordered to place a laver of brass between the altar and the tabernacle. Solomon made ten lavers and "a molten sea" to be put before the Temple (2 Chron. iv. 1-6). It is these divers washings that are referred to in Mark vii. 4, and Heb. ix. 10; in both places the Greek word being "Baptisms."

That the deep spiritual signification of the ceremony was understood appears from many passages of the Old Testament: "Wash me thoroughly from mine iniquity and cleanse me from my sin" (Ps. li. 2); "I will wash mine hands in innocency, O Lord, and so will I go to Thine altar" (Ps. xxvi. 6); "Wash thine heart from wickedness" (Jer. iv. 14).

Jewish writers of a later date tell us that proselytes from the heathen received a baptism as well as circumcision as a sign of the putting away of the old life and admission into the new as GOD's people.

It is evident that the idea of spiritual purification was in the minds of the Jews connected with washing or baptism. And thus we can understand the readiness with which they came to John "preaching the baptism of repentance for remission of sins;" and that they at first saw in him the promised MESSIAH, who was to bring remission of sins. And when he denied this, they naturally asked, "Why baptizest thou, then?" His answer pointed to the higher baptism of which his was the preparation, the baptism of water and of the SPIRIT.

When the CHRIST instituted baptism as the great sacrament of forgiveness of sins, and initiation into His Church, He only adapted an old custom well known to the Jews and other people; though in so doing He gave it a wider use and deeper meaning. It does not appear that the CHRIST Himself ever baptized, but His disciples did; the character of this rite is not described. After His resurrection the commission given to the Apostles is clear: "Go ye therefore and teach (make disciples of) all nations, baptizing them" (Matt. xxviii. 19). And it is very certain that the disciples understood that this rite was the "outward visible sign" of remission of sins and reception into the Church, CHRIST's Body. For whenever men, convinced by their preaching that JESUS was the SON of GOD, the MESSIAS, asked, "What shall we do?" the uniform answer was, "Repent and be baptized for the remission of sins, and ye shall receive the gift of the HOLY GHOST" (Acts ii. 38. See also Acts viii. 12, 36; x. 47; xxii. 16). Thus baptism took the place of circumcision as the means of entering into covenant with GOD, and as all who were circumcised were called Israelites, so all baptized persons were called Christians. Nor had any a right to assume the name until admitted into the Church by baptism.

It is unnecessary to show further that from the Apostolic times baptism has been regarded by the Church as essential. However they may differ as to its meaning and modes of administration, all "who profess and call themselves Christian" agree in this.

(B) THE OUTWARD SIGN AND MANNER OF ADMINISTRATION. — The Catechism teaches that "the outward visible sign or form in baptism" is "water, wherein the person is baptized, *In the Name of the* FATHER, *and of the* SON, *and of the* HOLY GHOST." Two things, then, are to be considered, the WATER and the WORD.

(1) That WATER is an essential part of baptism we learn from the words of our LORD to Nicodemus: "Except a man be born of water, and of the SPIRIT, he cannot enter into the kingdom of GOD" (St. John iii. 5). So also St. Peter after that the HOLY GHOST had fallen upon Cornelius and those with him, said, "Can any man forbid water, that these should not be baptized?" (Acts x. 47). And the testimony of the Church is so clear as to the fact, and it is one so universally admitted, that it is unnecessary to take up space with quotations from the Fathers.

But while there is no doubt as to the use of water in this sacrament, there is a difference of opinion and custom as to the mode of administration; whether it should be by *sprinkling*, or *pouring*, or *immersion*.

As regards *sprinkling*, though it may be regarded as valid, yet is it irregular, there being no authority for its use. The rubric in the office in the American Prayer-Book orders that the minister taking the child "shall *dip* it in the water discreetly, or shall *pour* water upon it." In the English office there are two rubrics, the first ordering dipping in the water discreetly and warily, "provided that the sponsors shall certify that the child may well endure it." Another adds, "but if they certify that the child is weak, it shall suffice to pour water upon it." The same direction is given for the baptism of adults. Thus our Church allows as valid and regular either "dipping" or "pouring," giving precedence to the former. Blunt says (Annotated Prayer-Book): "There can be no question that affusion, if thoroughly performed, is amply sufficient for the due administration of the sacrament of baptism. In such a climate as ours, with such habits as those of modern times, and all its consequences considered, the dipping of infants could seldom be seemly, and would often be attended with danger. The 'weakness' of the rubric may justly be assumed as the normal condition of infants brought up under such conditions."

Thus *pouring* the water has come to be with us the usual form of administration. But great care should be taken that water be poured freely over the head of the child or person from the hollow of the minister's hand, so that there may be no possible doubt of the actual contact of the water with the person. To insure this no covering should be retained on the head at that time.

Trine Immersion,—*i.e.*, the dipping or the pouring of the water at the naming of each Person of the Trinity, making three times,— though not ordered by the rubric, is a very ancient custom, worthy to be observed as teaching the doctrine of the Holy Trinity, and rendering more certain the contact with the water.

Total Immersion.—As regards this, which some hold to be essential to baptism, we have seen that the Church does not require it. Is she right in allowing this discretion? There appears little doubt that the usual custom of the early Church was to lead the candidate into the water and there dip him three times while repeating the prescribed formula. And it is urged that St. Paul alludes to this in the well-known text, "Therefore we are buried with him by baptism into death" (Rom. vi. 4). Too much stress has been laid upon an argument drawn from a figurative passage, from which, if the whole be thus taken literally, we might also prove that we ought to be crucified as he was. Doubtless there is here an allusion to the usual manner of baptizing, but scarcely intended as making it essential. From old drawings in the catacombs at Rome, it appears that the candidate was led into the water, and he standing there, the water was poured over his head. But even if total immersion generally obtained in the early Church, it never was considered essential. What was called *clinic baptism*, or the baptism of the sick and weak, was by pouring, so also where water was scarce, as in prison or in the desert, and these were held so valid that Canons were passed forbidding the rebaptizing of such.

If we turn to the New Testament, we find that in many of the instances there recorded immersion would have been highly improbable if not impossible. How could the three thousand baptized on the day of Pentecost, or the five thousand afterwards added, have been immersed in Jerusalem? Nor is it probable that the jailer of Philippi could have been immersed in the prison. The word baptized does not always mean immersion; "the baptizing of tables" (Mark vii. 4), and the "divers baptizings" of the law, were really washings. The Israelites "were baptized unto Moses in the cloud and in the sea" (1 Cor. x. 2). Yet they went over dry-shod; the Egyptians, indeed, were immersed. St. Peter also declares baptism to be the "figure" of (literally, antitype, *i.e.*, "that which corresponds to and was figured by") the salvation of Noah in the Ark by water (1 Peter iii. 21). Yet

Noah was borne upon the water, and rained upon from heaven; he was not immersed, as were the unbelievers. Great stress has been laid upon the account of the baptism of the eunuch (Acts viii. 38): "And they went down both into the water, both Philip and the eunuch; and he baptized him. And when they were come up out of the water," etc. But this really proves nothing, except, indeed, the necessity of water. For, first, the Greek words translated "into" and "out of" (εις and εκ), mean also the place towards which and from which there is motion; second, one may "go down into" and "come up out of" a water without immersing the whole body; and, third, if total immersion be meant, then must Philip the minister as well as the eunuch have been immersed, for it reads, "they went down both into the water," which proves too much. Most probably both standing in the water, Philip taking up thereof in his hand or in a vessel, baptized by pouring over the head of the eunuch.

We assert, then, that Scripture and the Church prescribe nothing as to the precise manner of administering the water of baptism. It is therefore one of those ceremonies and rites which may be changed by particular Churches "according to the diversity of countries, times, and men's manners, so that nothing be ordained against GOD'S Word" (Art. XXXIV).

(2) THE FORM OF WORDS.—About this there can be no dispute. The dipping in or the pouring on of water must be accompanied by the words prescribed by our LORD: "*In the Name of the* FATHER, *and of the* SON, *and of the* HOLY GHOST." Without these no baptism is valid, "for these are essential parts of baptism." (See rubric at end of "Private Baptism of Children.")

But what is meant by "Baptizing in the Name"? Not only by the authority of, as His ministers, though this is meant, but also and especially "*into* the name," as it should be translated. For "the name" was put for the thing itself: thus, "His name shall be called JESUS (SAVIOUR), for He shall save;" "They shall call His name EMMANUEL," for He is "GOD with us." The sacred name FATHER, SON, and HOLY GHOST is put upon the baptized, as that of JEHOVAH was upon the children of Israel (Num. vi. 27), whereby they were made a holy, peculiar people. Thus to be baptized into "the name" means into the Holy Trinity, for "the name" of old meant GOD Himself, as in the revelation to Moses from the burning bush the name I AM, is GOD. Therefore the Hebrews always spoke with the deepest reverence of THE NAME. It was not "to be taken in vain;" "Incense was to be offered to it;" "In it men were to trust." The Old Testament is full of such expressions, by which we learn that "The Name" is GOD Himself, or, rather, the revelation of GOD. To know GOD'S name is to know Him; to do anything by or in His name is to do it by or in Him. So also in the New Testament we read: "Hallowed be Thy Name;" "His name, through faith in His name, hath made this man strong;" "At the name of JESUS every knee should bow." And numerous texts can be quoted where the name of JESUS is put for Himself.

Therefore, when He whose name is EMMANUEL, "GOD with us," is about to send forth His messengers to deliver men from bondage to sin and death, of which that of Egypt was the type, He speaks to them from the risen body, dead, yet alive, seeing no corruption, of which the Bush was the emblem, and gives them His new name to be put upon His people, as He did of old to Moses,—a new name expressing the fuller revelation of Himself, "FATHER, SON, and HOLY GHOST," not three names, but one, for He says not into the names, but into the Name expressing the unity of the Godhead in the Trinity of the Persons. This Holy Name is to be said over them, and into union with this Holy Trinity they are by baptism received.

This, we remark in passing, is also in brief the creed of the Church, as taught in our Catechism. For all Confessions of Faith are enlargements or developments or explanations of this divinely-given formula. With what reverence and awe should it be regarded!

(c) THE COVENANT.—As under the old dispensation GOD made a covenant with His people whereby they were made His, circumcision being the outward sign and seal thereof, so has He made the new covenant in JESUS (Hebrews xii. 24), whereof baptism is the outward sign and pledge. This was foretold by the prophet Ezekiel: "Then will I sprinkle clean water upon you, and ye shall be clean; from all your filthiness and from all your idols will I cleanse you. A new heart also will I give you, and a new spirit will I put within you, and I will take away the stony heart out of your flesh, and I will give you an heart of flesh" (Ezek. xxxvi. 25, 26).

In this covenant there are the two parties, GOD and man. What GOD offers is entirely a free gift or grace from Him; He annexes to its reception such conditions as He may please, but they are in no way of the nature of an equivalent; man cannot purchase them; so St. Paul writes, "By grace are ye saved through faith; and that not of yourselves it is the gift of GOD; not of works, lest any man should boast" (Eph. ii. 8). We are thus led to consider, first, GOD'S part, and, second, man's part in the covenant made in baptism.

(1) THE INWARD GRACE OF BAPTISM.—The Catechism defines this to be "a death unto sin, and a new birth unto righteousness; for, being by nature born in sin, and the children of wrath, we are hereby made the children of grace." And the child is taught that in baptism it "was made a member of CHRIST, the child of GOD, and

an inheritor of the kingdom of heaven." This is called REGENERATION (which see); according to our LORD'S Word, "Ye must be born again." "Except a man be born of water and of the SPIRIT, he cannot enter into the kingdom of GOD."

God gives in baptism, 1st. Remission of sins; as St. Peter said to the multitude asking, "What shall we do?" "Repent, and be baptized every one of you in the name of JESUS CHRIST for the remission of sins, and ye shall receive the gift of the HOLY GHOST" (Acts ii. 38); as also it was said unto Saul, "Arise and be baptized, and wash away thy sins" (Acts xxii. 16).

2d. Membership in His Church, the Body of CHRIST: "For by one Spirit are we all baptized into one body;" "Now ye are the body of CHRIST, and members in particular" (1 Cor. xii. 13, 27); "His body's sake, which is the Church" (Col. i. 24).

3d. Adoption as His children, and with this the gift of the HOLY SPIRIT and heirship of heaven : "For ye are all the children of GOD by faith in CHRIST JESUS, for as many of you as have been baptized into CHRIST have put on CHRIST;" "And because ye are sons, GOD hath sent forth the SPIRIT of His SON into your hearts, crying, Abba, Father. . . . And if a son, then an heir of GOD through CHRIST" (Gal. iii. 27 ; iv. 6, 7).

The Church, then, for her teaching has most certain warrant of Holy Scripture. Following this, in the baptismal service, she bids us pray GOD to "sanctify this water to the mystical washing away of sin." The sponsors are exhorted to pray for the person now to be baptized, "That our LORD JESUS CHRIST would vouchsafe to receive him, to release him from sin, to sanctify him with the HOLY GHOST, and to give him the Kingdom of Heaven and everlasting life." And the newly-baptized is spoken of as "regenerate and grafted into the body of CHRIST'S Church." The XXVII. Article of Religion declares that "Baptism . . . is also a sign of regeneration, or new birth, whereby they that receive baptism rightly are grafted into the Church, the promises of forgiveness of sin and of our adoption to be the sons of GOD by the HOLY GHOST are visibly signed and sealed." (*Vide* REGENERATION for further proofs.)

(2) THE CONDITIONS REQUIRED IN THOSE WHO COME TO BE BAPTIZED.—Though the benefits of baptism are entirely a free gift from GOD, yet has He seen fit to prescribe certain conditions with which man must comply before he can claim the promises. These are in the Catechism declared to be "Repentance, whereby they forsake sin ; and faith, whereby they steadfastly believe the promises of GOD made to them in that sacrament;" or, as it is set forth in the questions asked at the baptism, Renunciation of sin, belief in the Articles of the Christian Faith, and an honest purpose throughout life to keep GOD'S Commandments. Repentance and Faith have been called the hands stretched forth to take hold of GOD'S gifts. But even these are of Him, "for it is GOD that worketh in us both to will and to do." With the grace of baptism He gives the capacity for these, just as in the natural birth He gives the various faculties of mind and body. It is man's part to realize this and use the spiritual life and power thus given him "to work out his salvation." (*Vide* further in REGENERATION.)

(D) THE MINISTER AND SUBJECTS OF BAPTISM—*Lay Baptism.*—Ordinarily this sacrament is to be administered by one in holy orders, for it was in the original commission given to the Apostles that they should baptize. In the Acts of the Apostles we read of Philip the Deacon baptizing the Samaritans and the eunuch of Ethiopia. It certainly would seem right that the act of receiving into CHRIST'S Church should be by one duly commissioned as an ambassador for CHRIST. The Prayer-Book requires that it shall be by a minister ; a deacon may act in the absence of the priest. Notwithstanding this, the universal tradition and practice of the Church from the earliest ages has allowed the validity of lay baptism in cases of necessity, a rebaptism never being required for such persons. The question was fully discussed in the Church of Carthage, with the above conclusion. And, therefore, in our own Church, lay baptism is recognized by general custom, though there is no authority for it in the Prayer-Book, unless it be implied in the rubric appended to the "Office for Private Baptism," which limits the essentials of baptism to "water, in the Name," etc., but says nothing of the necessity of a lawful minister; the rubric in the service itself, however, requires "a lawful minister." It is well here to notice, as an historical fact, that in the first Prayer-Book, that of 1549 A.D., the rubric directed that "when great need shall compel them so to do," "one of them present" shall baptize the child. In 1603 A.D., after the Hampton Conference, to meet the prejudices of the Puritans (!), the words "lawful minister" were substituted for "one of them," and in the revision of 1662 A.D. the rubric took its present form. There is in this allowance of lay baptism, a departure from the strictness of the Church as regards orders ; but universal custom seems to sanction it; some writers take the ground that any irregularity or defect in such baptism is made good by confirmation. Others hold that there is a priesthood in every Christian sufficient to make his act valid ; these making a distinction between that which he has the power to do and that which he has the right to do.

Adult Baptism.—There is a special service provided for the baptism of those of riper years. The persons are required to answer for themselves, the sponsors being "their chosen witnesses." The rubric directs that "due care be taken for their examination, whether they be sufficiently instructed in the Principles of the Christian Religion; and that they be exhorted to prepare themselves with Prayer and Fasting for the receiving of this holy sacrament." There is also a rubric that "It is expedient that every person thus baptized should be confirmed by the Bishop so soon after his baptism as conveniently may be, that so he may be admitted to the Holy Communion."

Infant Baptism.—Though there is no direct command in the New Testament to baptize infants, yet the inference that it was done by the Apostles is so strong as to amount to proof. Baptism took the place of circumcision. Infants were circumcised, and so received into the old covenant; the Apostles naturally, unless forbidden, would baptize infants and receive them into the new covenant. So far from being forbidden, we read that the only time JESUS was "much displeased" was when the disciples rebuked those who brought to Him young children, saying, "Suffer the little children to come unto me, and forbid them not; for of such is the kingdom of GOD." If infants are of the kingdom, surely they may receive that rite which admits into the kingdom (St. Mark x. 13). St. Peter, commanding the Jews to be baptized, adds: "For the promise is unto you, and to your children" (Acts ii. 39). St. Paul on several occasions baptized whole households; there must have been children in some if not all of these.

But when we take the testimony of the Universal Church from the beginning, the proof is overwhelming. We have not space for quotations, suffice it to say "that all testimony of writers down to the twelfth century affirms its use," and "there is not one saying, quotation, or example that makes against it."

But we have seen that repentance and faith are required of those who come to baptism, and it is argued that as infants are incapable of these they should not be baptized. But for this the Church provides by requiring sureties or sponsors, who promise these both in the child's name. Their duty it is to see that it be taught, so soon as it be able to learn, what has been done for it, and to urge it at the proper time to fulfill the same by taking upon itself the baptismal obligatio˚ s, so that it may also enter upon the full baptismal privileges, just as the law allows children to hold property, but requires guardians to act for the minor until it comes of age, assumes full possession, and acts for itself.

Public Infant Baptism should be administered in church, either at Morning or Evening Prayer, immediately after the second lesson, both because it is an act in which the congregation are to take part, and also "for the better instructing of the People in the grounds of Infant Baptism." Nor ought baptism to be deferred till long after birth, as is too much the custom. The rubric says, not "longer than the first or second Sunday." It may not always be possible to comply with this, but there should be no unnecessary delay.

Private Infant Baptism is only allowed for "great cause and necessity:" a shortened form is provided to be used in such case. Though this be a lawful and sufficient baptism, still, if the child live, "it is expedient that it be brought into the Church," that "the Congregation may be certified of the true form of Baptism, and it be received publicly as one of the flock of true Christian People."

Authorities: Baptism tested by Scripture and History, by William Hodges, D.D.; Wall's History of Infant Baptism; Dr. W. Adams' Mercy to Babes; Wall and Jerriam on Infant Baptism. Indeed, the works on the subject of Baptism are many and easily accessible.

REV. E. B. BOGGS, D.D.

Baptism (Holy), Office of. The services in our Prayer-Book for the administration of baptism are taken almost word for word from those in the English book. The important changes are that permission is given for shortening the service for infant baptism in case it is used in the same church more than once a month, and that the sign of the cross may be omitted if the omission be specially desired, "although the Church knows no worthy cause of scruple concerning the same." The form of the service for infant baptism is not closely connected with that of ancient rituals, the reason being in great part, doubtless, because the Reformers thought it necessary to introduce exhortations, and to make the service a means of instruction to the congregation: and for this latter reason it is ordered that it shall be used in the midst of either Morning or Evening Prayer. Since 1552 A.D. the whole of the service has been said at the font; the book of 1549 A.D. ordered the first part, as far as the address to the godfathers and godmothers, to be said at the church-door and the rest at the font. This first part seems to correspond to the ancient form of making a catechumen, consisting of a call to prayer, a petition for GOD'S blessing on the child, a short Gospel, followed by a comment and exhortation based upon it, and a prayer which includes a thanksgiving. The minister then passes to the second part of the service, which is the special preparation for the sacrament. The sponsors are exhorted as to the meaning of the act, and are asked to answer in the child's name. The questions call for a renunciation (on which in early days great stress was laid), a profession of faith, an expression of desire for baptism, and a promise of obedience. Two of the answers in our service differ from those in the English book: the first, by the addition of all after the words "I renounce them all"; and the last, by the addition of the words "by GOD'S help." Then follow four short prayers for spiritual blessings, and a prayer for the blessing of the water. These prayers (or those which correspond to them) are not in the service of 1549 A.D., but will be found at the end of the form for private baptism, with a direction that when the water in the font is changed, which shall be once a month at the least, they shall be used before any child is baptized in it. Since 1552 A.D., the water has been put anew in the font at each baptism; this has been directed by rubric since 1662 A.D. The third part of the service consists of the baptism itself, which our Church allows to be either by immersion or by affusion (no permission is given for aspersion), and the making of the sign of the cross upon the child's forehead. Then in the fourth part the people are bidden to prayer, the LORD'S Prayer is used as the rightful utterance of the child of GOD, and it is followed by thanksgiving and prayer, and by exhortations to the sponsors to remember and to fulfill their duties to the child, and to see that in due time it is brought to the Bishop for confirmation. It does not belong to this article to speak of the doctrine of Baptism; but the historical fact may be stated that this last call to prayer and the prayer itself, both of which declare that the child is regenerate, were not in the first book of Edward VI. (1549 A.D.), but were inserted in his second book in 1552 A.D.

The service for private baptism, containing also a form for publicly receiving into the Church such as have been privately baptized, calls for no special notice. But with reference to the conditional form of baptism, which is placed at the end of the service, it may be of interest to quote two rubrics from the Prayer-Book which was set forth by Bishop Torry, of St. Andrew's, in 1848 A.D., as embodying a custom in the Scotch Church: "From the unhappy multiplicity of religious sects in this country, cases frequently occur in which persons, from conscientious motives, express a desire to separate themselves from such sects, and to unite themselves to the Church. In all such instances, when the applicants for admission into the Church, after due instruction, shall express a doubt of the validity of the Baptism which they have received from the Minister of the sect to which they formerly belonged, the clergyman to whom the application is made shall baptize the person in the hypothetical form prescribed in this office. In cases where such doubt does not exist, it shall suffice to receive the person into the Church in this manner: he first kneeling down, the Minister shall take him by the hand and say, *We receive this person*," etc. The former of these two rubrics was taken from the 17th of the former Canons of the Scotch Church; its substance, with the direction for the use of the hypothetical form of words, is in the 34th of the present Canons, § 4.

The English Church needed no office for the ministration of baptism to such as are of riper years until after the Great Rebellion. Then, in part because it was hoped that there would be great numbers of converts among the natives of America, and still more because so many had grown up unbaptized at home, a service was prepared (it is said by Bishop Griffith, of St. Asaph) and inserted in the book of 1662 A.D., from which it has passed into our own. Its outline is the same as that for infant baptism, and the changes which were made will readily explain themselves.

Authorities: Keeling's Liturgiæ Britannicæ, Bulley's Variations of the Communion and Baptismal Offices, Palmer's Origines Liturgicæ, Bishop Torry's Prayer-Book.

REV. PROF. S. HART.

Baptistery. The building or chamber set apart for the celebration of the sacrament of baptism. It was usually attached to the larger, or cathedral church, since the administration of the rite was usual there only. A spacious building was necessary, as the sacrament was administered by immersion, either simply or accompanied by aspersion. As many as three thousand were baptized on Easter-eve when St. Chrysostom was arrested, and many, both men and women, who had not yet received the sacrament, were dispersed. The oldest baptistery now in existence, at Ravenna, is older than 425-430 A.D. It is octagonal, about forty feet in diameter, with two niches, or apses. It has two stories. The font, which is in the centre and octagonal, has a semicircular indentation in the side, where the priest can stand to immerse without descending into the water. The walls are decorated with figures in low relief in stucco, but the dome is covered with mosaics; the central portion representing the baptism of our LORD. Baptisteries of later date are found in various parts of Europe, but as adult baptisms fell into disuse, the baptistery was not needed, and the font was transferred to the church. There it has happened that the canopy under which the font was placed was so enlarged and enriched as to be supported upon its own pillars, and so be almost a baptistery within the church. Examples of this occur in England.

Barnabas. (Son of prophecy or exhortation (Rev. Vers.); not so correctly in A.V., "of consolation.") A Levite by descent, a Cypriote by birth, and by some (Clem. Alex., Strom. ii. 176) said to be one of the seventy, was one of the earliest prominent members of the infant Church (Acts iv. 36). His real name, Joseph (or Joses), has been overshadowed by the name given him by the Apostles. His act of giving the price of a field which he had sold to the Church is the first notice we have of him. He takes Saul after his conversion (Acts ix. 27) to the Apostles as though there had been a previous friendship between them. When he saw the growth of the Gentile Church at Antioch he sought Saul at Tarsus and brought him there, as if knowing Saul's special mission to the Gentiles. With Saul he carried the relief the Church at Antioch sent to Jerusalem upon occasion of the famine (Acts xi. 30). Upon their return they were set apart by direction of the HOLY GHOST for their first missionary journey (Acts xiii., xiv.), which was first to Cyprus (where Saul took the name of Paul), and into Asia Minor as far as Derbe, in Lycaonia. Returning to Perga, they sailed to the port of Seleucia, and so returned home to Antioch. They were associated together in the struggle against the Judaizers in the question of circumcision, and were sent from the Council of Jerusalem with honor back to Antioch. When the second missionary journey was proposed, they disagreed as to the propriety of taking his nephew, John Mark, with them. "The contention was so sharp that they parted asunder." Since the brethren commended St. Paul to the grace of GOD, it has been inferred that Barnabas was in the wrong. This is the last notice in the Acts. St. Paul speaks of him in Gal. ii. St. Barnabas was emphatically a good man and full of the HOLY GHOST, but does not seem to have had that energetic determination that was so marked in St. Paul. He was impressed by St. Peter even when intimately associated with St. Paul (Gal. ii. 13). What his after-career was is not authentically told us. One tradition sends him to Milan, a later one gave him martyrdom upon his second visit to Cyprus.

An epistle under his name is extant. It has been held authentic by very many able scholars, but is not now admitted as genuine. However, it is a very ancient Christian writing, probably of the earlier part of the second century. It was evidently the work of a very devout but narrow Christian, who neither grasped the beauty of allegorical interpretation nor the true breadth of Christianity. It is a valuable writing, not for its contents, but for the inferences that may be drawn from it. (Feast-day, June 11.)

Bartholomew. Of him we have nothing but the name in the lists of the Apostles. In St. Matt. x. 5, we have Philip and Bartholomew the sixth in the list. In St. Mark iii. 18, with Philip, he is the sixth; as, too, in St. Luke vi. 14. If he is the same as Nathaniel, as some have thought with a great deal of plausibility, we have some clue to his character,—an Israelite indeed in whom is no guile. The arguments relied on are, briefly, (a) The call of St. Bartholomew is not recorded, while the address to Nathaniel is nearly equivalent. (b) The synoptists who mention Bartholomew do not allude to Nathaniel, while St. John does not name Bartholomew, but does Nathaniel. (c) Bar-tholmai is the same as Bar-Jona, St. Peter's other name, or Barnabas, and may be an appellative or a surname, as in the other two cases. But the concurrent tradition of the early Church is utterly silent upon this identification. Any certain tradition, too, about his career is wanting. It is supposed that he evangelized Northern India, leaving there a Hebrew copy of St. Matthew's Gospel, which afterwards was found by Pantænus, the great Alexandrian catechist (190 A.D.); that having once escaped crucifixion through the remorse of his persecutor, he was afterwards flayed alive by King Astyages, at Albanopolis, upon the Caspian Sea. But there is nothing to lead us to suppose that there is any substructure of fact for the tradition. It is only another example of the rule "principles, not men," which marks GOD's work in the world, while yet these principles are only for man's salvation. (Feast-day, August 24.)

Baruch. (Blessed.) The son of Neriah, and friend and amanuensis of Jeremiah (Jer. xxxii. 12; xxxvi. 10 sq.), was of courtly family. His brother Seriah held office under King Zedekiah. He was accused of urging Jeremiah in favor of the Chaldeans. Josephus says he was imprisoned with the prophet, but was permitted, after the fall of Jerusalem, by Nebuchadnezzar, to remain with Jeremiah, and was forced with him to go down to Egypt. This is the last certain information we have of him. He was a man of courage, as is shown by his steadfast adherence to Jeremiah, and by his acting as his amanuensis. The book attributed to him is apocryphal, though it was received by some of the Fathers, as Athanasius, Cyril of Jerusalem, and Nicephorus. Dr. Ginsburg's conjecture that it was written by some devout Jew about the middle of the second century before CHRIST is probably correct, but the value he puts upon it is as probably exaggerated. It is but a cento of passages from the prayer of Daniel (Dan. ix.), from Deut. xxviii., and from phrases to be found in the prophets, especially Isaiah. The first three chapters may be a translation from some Hebrew imitator, and the last two an addition by the translator, as has been conjectured. But beyond recording the hopes of the Jews under the Seleucidæ or the Ptolomies it is valueless.

Basin; for receiving the alms and other devotions of the congregation in the proanaphoral portion of the Communion service. The rubric runs:

"Whilst these sentences are in reading the Deacons, Church-wardens, or other fit persons appointed for that purpose, shall receive the Alms for the Poor and other Devotions of the people in a decent Basin to be provided by the Parish for that purpose; and reverently bring it to the Priest, who shall humbly present and place it upon the Holy Table."

Bath-kol. (Daughter of a voice.) Really, a sort of divination among the later Jews. It was pretended that after the inspiration of the prophets ceased devout men were guided by a voice (Bath-kol); in fact, they put such a construction upon the first words they accidentally heard, after devoutly asking for instruction. To give an instance:

"R. Iochanan and R. Simeon ben Lachish desiring to see the face of R. Samuel, a Babylonish doctor, said, Let us follow the hearing of Bath-kol. Traveling, therefore, near a school, they heard the voice of a boy reading these words out of the first book of Samuel: 'And Samuel died.' From thence the two Rabbis inferred that their friend Samuel was dead; and, indeed, Samuel of Babylon was just dead."

Beatific Vision. "As for me, I will behold Thy face in righteousness: and I shall be satisfied, when I awake, with Thy likeness" (Ps. xvii. 15). "Beloved, now are we the sons of GOD, and it doth not yet appear what we shall be: but we know that, when He shall appear, we shall be like Him; for we shall see Him as He is" (1 John iii. 2). These texts (and many others) contain the fullness of the doctrine of the highest and final state of blessedness. There is the blessedness of knowledge of GOD, the blessedness of a full Faith, the blessedness of seeing and hearing Him by every means vouchsafed to us here, but beside there will be the blessed joy of seeing Him face to face in holiness in His glory. It is not to be in this life. It was denied to Moses, St. John, and St. Paul; both declare "no man can see GOD." But in the hereafter we shall see Him face to face. "His servants shall serve Him, and they shall see His face; and His name shall be in their foreheads" (Rev. xxii. 3, 4). But the full glory of the vision of GOD will be, undoubtedly, after the Resurrection.

Beatification. The declaration by the Pope that such or such a holy person, whose life was notably holy and accompanied by miracles, is in eternal bliss, and in consequence permits religious honor to be paid him. In beatification the Pope does not *judicially* determine the state of the saint, but only so far as to free the religious honors paid to him from the charge of superstition. But in canonization the Pope does determine officially, *ex cathedra*, the condition of the new saint.

Bel and the Dragon,—Apocrypha. The Greek translations of Daniel contain additions to the original text. The most important are in the Apocrypha, and are the Song of the Three Holy Children, the History of Susanna, and the History of Bel and the Dragon. Bel and the Dragon is placed at the end of Daniel, and in the Septuagint is headed "Part of the prophecy of Habakkuk." There is no evidence that the additions ever formed a part of the Hebrew text. It is surmised that the translator of Daniel may have wrought up current traditions in these additions. The story of the Dragon appears like a "strange exaggeration" of the deliverance of Daniel from the lions (Dan. vi.). The story has received "embellishments in later times." It need not be regarded as a mere fable, but it was shaped for a moral purpose. While Calmet and the Port Royalists strive to trace the history in this work, it may be as well to consider rather its design, "to render idolatry ridiculous, and to exalt the true GOD." The idol Bel is represented as the object of the king's adoration, while Daniel is a worshiper of "the living GOD" (v. 5). The king speaks to him of the food which Bel eats, and Daniel declares that the idol is but brass and clay. A contest is brought on between Daniel and the idol priests, and when he shows their duplicity to the king they are slain, and Daniel destroys Bel and his temple. Then follows the killing of the Dragon by Daniel's skill, and the story of the den of lions, with an addition concerning Habakkuk's aid in feeding Daniel.

Authorities: B. F. Westcott, in Wm. Smith's Dictionary of the Bible, Horne's Introduction, Arnald's Commentary, in Patrick, Lowth, and Whitby.

REV. S. F. HOTCHKIN.

Belfry. *Vide* **Architecture.**

Bells, The. They are mentioned in the Bible as a part of the High-Priest's dress, fringing the lower edge of his robe, and by their tinkling the people might know when he went into the Holy Place, and when he came out, "that he die not." But in Christian times bells are used to summon the faithful to the services. The earliest bells in use were very small ones,—hand-bells, in fact,—and, trusting to the shape of several that still remain, shaped very much like our cow-bells. In times of persecution a messenger used to summon the congregation; in quiet times a Deacon announced the hours of service. Bells or their equivalents or substitutes were used after Christianity was formally recognized by the state. The oldest use of bells is attributed, but probably wrongly, to Paulinus, Bishop of Nola, in Campania (409 A.D.), but he does not speak of bells at all in his description of his Church. They soon became generally used in the West, and were of considerable size. Charlemagne (800 A.D.) encouraged the founding of bells, and employed skillful founders. Of these, Tancho, of St. Gall, was the chief, who cast a large bell for the great church at Aachen (Aix). He asked for one hundred pounds of silver as alloy for the copper, from which we may infer that the bells may have weighed four or five hundred pounds. In the East bells were introduced from Venice, and were becoming general (865 A.D.), till the Turks, through superstition, forbade their use. So now the summons to service is given by hammering upon a board suspended from a rope or chain (*Vide* SEMANTRON) or held by the centre in the hand. It was usually twelve feet long and from a foot to a foot and a half wide, and was reduced in the centre to a width sufficient to let it be grasped by the hand. It was struck with a hammer or mallet. Sometimes the semantron is made of iron or of brass.

Turketul, Abbot of Crowland (870 A.D.), gave seven bells to his monastery, probably the first peal in England. Kinsius of York (1051–61 A.D.) gave the Church of St. John, at Beverley, two great bells.

From the time that Church utensils were first used there was always some act of dedication of them to sacred and hallowed use. Forms for the benediction of bells are found in the later MSS. Sacramentarium of Gregory, and probably date from the time of Alcuin (790 A.D.). Upon many church-bells was placed the Latin doggerel,—

<small>Laudo Deum verum, Plebem voco, congrego clerum, Defunctos ploro, Pestem fugo, Festa decoro.</small>

A peal is of seven or more bells; a chime of three or more. For rules for ringing chimes and peals any hand-book on bells may be consulted.

For churches in the country the bell should be selected, if possible, with reference to the position of the church; if upon an eminence or on a plain, a bell of the lowest tone that can be heard the farthest (and it should be heard at least three miles) is the proper one to choose. From E to A should be the general range of the note.

Bema. The place of the Bishop's throne in the primitive Church, or, possibly, the whole apse itself. The Bishop's throne was anciently placed in the centre against the wall, and the sedilia for the Presbyters were ranged on either hand, while in the centre of the apse the altar was placed.

Benatura. A holy water stoup.

Benedicite. (The Song of the Three Children.) A hymn found in the Septuagint version of the book of Daniel, and also in the Apocrypha, but not occurring in the Hebrew Scripture. It is said to have been sung by Hananiah, Mishael, and Azariah after their miraculous deliverance from the fiery furnace, as recorded in Daniel iii. It resembles very much the 148th Psalm, and is said by many to be only an expansion of it. It was probably used in the Jewish synagogue worship, and so passed into early Christian usage. It was certainly in use in the days of St. Athanasius (325–60 A.D.). St. Chrysostom (425 A.D.) calls it "that admirable and marvelous song, which from that day to this has been sung everywhere throughout the world, and shall yet be sung by future generations." It was incorporated into the offices, common to both the English and Gallican Churches, and from thence it passed into its present place in the Prayer-Book of 1549 A.D., which it has kept ever since. In that Prayer-Book this rubric was prefixed to the *Te Deum:*

"After the first lesson shall follow *Te Deum laudamus* in English daily throughout the year except in Lent, all the which time in the place of *Te Deum* shall be used *Benedicite omnia Opera Domini Domino* in English, as followeth." (In the first Prayer-Book the hymn ran thus:

"O ALL ye works of the LORD speak good of the LORD: praise Him and set Him up forever."

In the second Prayer-Book (1552 A.D.) it was changed to the present form.) In 1552 this restriction was removed. However, the rule is often followed now, but it would be well to use it when Gen. i. is read. It has been commented on in a devotional tone by several recent writers, for which it is admirably adapted, bringing forth, as it can be well made to do, the glory of GOD in all His works.

Benediction. The act of blessing and the form of blessing. "And without all contradiction the less is blessed of the better" (Heb. vii. 7). In Patriarchal days the blessing of the children was a most sacred and important act. Abraham had his children blessed of GOD. Isaac was deceived into giving Jacob the greater blessing, but would not alter it. Jacob left a solemn prophetic blessing of his twelve sons. In the later history, Moses had given him the form of blessing the people, a form the Church has incorporated into her Office of Visitation of the Sick. It was a solemn threefold utterance of THE NAME, which was then put upon the children of Israel: "The LORD bless thee and keep thee. The LORD make His FACE shine upon thee and be gracious unto thee. The LORD lift up His countenance upon thee and give thee peace. And they shall put MY NAME upon the children of Israel and I will bless them."

In all lands and in all times the reception of a benediction has always been highly valued, and this formal putting of GOD'S blessing upon His people is of the highest importance. In the Prayer-Book there are six formulas of benediction and three prayers for special benediction. The first is the mutual benediction of both priest and people in the versicles: "The LORD be with you, R. and with thy spirit." The second is the benediction taken from 2 Cor. xiii. 14: "The grace of our LORD JESUS CHRIST and the love of GOD and the fellowship of the HOLY GHOST be with us all evermore," in which the variation of "us" for "you," though apparently slight when compared with the same benediction in St. James's Liturgy, hints at the possibility that St. Paul may have quoted from the Liturgy, and that our own use came not from the form in the New Testament, but from this ancient Liturgy. This blessing closes both Morning and Evening Prayer and the Burial service. The third form is the beautiful one formed by the English Church from an old Anglo-Saxon form and a benediction by St. Paul. The first part is from Phil. iv. 6, 7: "The peace of GOD which passeth all understanding shall keep your hearts and minds through JESUS CHRIST," but enlarged. The second part is also enlarged from this blessing in Leofric's Exeter Pontifical: "The blessing of GOD the FATHER, and of the SON, and of the HOLY GHOST, and the peace of the LORD be ever with you." This is used at the Holy Communion, at ordination, and at the consecration of a church. The latter part was also placed by the Caroline revisers (1662 A.D.) after the Confirmation Office. The fourth form is the one divinely commanded to be put upon the Holy People, and was incorporated into the Office for the Visitation of the Sick. The fifth form is the blessing (taken from Heb. xiii. 20, 21) in the Office of Institution. There is no alteration in this form. The sixth form is the one at the close of the Marriage service. It is modeled upon the one in the English Office, but differs from it materially. The English form is this: "ALMIGHTY GOD, who at the beginning did create our first parents, Adam and Eve, and did sanctify and join them together in marriage; Pour upon you the riches of His grace, sanctify and bless you, that ye may please Him both in body and soul, and live together in holy love unto your lives' end. Amen." Our American form is: "GOD the FATHER, GOD the SON, GOD the HOLY GHOST bless, preserve, and keep you. The LORD mercifully with His favor look upon you and fill you with all spiritual benediction and grace, that ye may so live together in this life that in the world to come ye may have life everlasting. Amen."

The three prayers of benediction are, first, the Invocation in the Holy Communion: "And we most humbly beseech Thee, O merciful Father, to hear us; and of Thy almighty goodness vouchsafe to bless and sanctify with Thy Word and Holy Spirit these Thy gifts and creatures of bread and wine." The second is the prayer for the blessing of the water in the Baptismal Office. The third is properly a series of prayers in the Form of Consecration of a Church or Chapel. The first being the prayer "O Eternal GOD," and the Collects following; the second, after the sentence of consecration is read, the prayer, "Blessed be Thy Name, O LORD," etc.; and after the Morning Prayer and Communion service the last prayer, "Blessed be Thy Name, O LORD GOD," etc. Of course the service closes with The Peace of GOD.

The acts of blessing are oft repeated, sometimes daily, as, for instance, grace at meat. In the primitive Church many forms of benediction were used; as of the utensils and furniture of a church, as well as of persons.

It were well if a little thought were spent upon the value and solemnity of benedictions, chiefly those given to us at the Church's services, but also on less solemn occasions. To have His name put upon us is no light thing, but of itself a rich and abiding gift, unless we cast it from us. Then as the acts of GOD'S officer are not mere forms, but true and effectual actions, we receive of GOD true and effectual blessing as we fit ourselves for it and give due heed to it.

Benedictus. The second of the two hymns after the second lesson at Morning Prayer. It is the hymn of Zacharias, the father of St. John Baptist, at his son's circumcision. The English places it first, and recites it at length; but the American Church places it second, and recites but four verses. If the tone of the hymn be noted carefully, it will be seen to be fitly used from Advent Sunday to Trinity Sunday, while the *Jubilate* is more proper for the Trinity season. It was intended in the English service to be used constantly, the *Jubilate* being given as an alternate, to avoid the repetition of the *Benedictus* when it should occur in the second lesson. Its ritual use has come to us from the Gallican and Salsbury uses.

Benefice. It was used to signify the gift of land given to the soldier out of conquered territory. "Hence, doubtless, came the word *benefice* to be applied to Church livings; for, besides that the ecclesiastics held for life, like the soldiers, the riches of the Church arose from the beneficence of princes." (Burns, Eccl. Law.) In the American Church no such thing as a benefice is properly known, since our parishes and churches are erected and supported under different conditions of life from those in which the Church in Europe grew. A benefice is the growth of different customs from ours. A benefice requires to be erected by Episcopal authority; to be founded for purely spiritual purposes; to be conferred upon a clerk in orders; it must be perpetual, and given to another per son than him who confers it. In obtaining a benefice, then, there must be, I. Presentation by the proper person to the Bishop of the nominee. II. Examination by the Bishop. III. Refusal (generally from want of learning); or, IV. Admission. V. Institution (when the nominee is presented by a patron to the Bishop or Collation (when the Bishop presents a benefice in his own gift). VI. Induction, usually by the Archdeacon. VII. Duty after induction. A benefice is a different thing from a cathedral preferment; for it has a cure of souls, which a cathedral preferment hath not.

Benefit of Clergy. A mediæval custom by which accused persons who proved themselves to be "clerks" by reading Latin could claim to be tried by the Bishop's, instead of the King's, Court. It was a privilege originally belonging only to those who were actually in holy orders, but it was gradually extended to those in minor orders and to every one who could read a verse in the Latin Bible. The privilege was grossly abused, and a hindrance to the execution of justice and a scandal and burden to the Church. It was modified and restrained at the Reformation, and the clergy were themselves subject to secular tribunals for crimes and misdemeanors at law, and finally the Benefit of Clergy was abolished in 1827 A.D.

Bible, The, is the popular collective title of the sacred books of the Christian Church. It includes the Old Testament, or the Hebrew Sacred Scriptures, the ecclesiastical books called "the Apocrypha," and the distinctively Christian books which compose the New Testament. The earliest collective title was the "Law," which embraced probably only the five books of Moses. Later the collection of the prophets was added, and later still the Hagiographa, or the Psalms. In our SAVIOUR's time the whole collection was spoken of as "the Law," "the Law and the Prophets," or "the Law, the Prophets, and the Psalms," or more generally, "the Scriptures," and "the Holy Scriptures," or "the Scripture." With one or two exceptions (2 Pet. iii. 16; 1 Tim. v. 18), whenever "the Scriptures" or "the Scripture" are mentioned in the New Testament, the reference is to the sacred books of the Old Testament (e.g., St. John ii. 22, v. 39; 2 Tim. iii. 15). St. Paul speaks of "the old covenant" or "testament" (2 Cor. iii. 14), and contrasts "the two Covenants" (Gal. iv. 24), so that very early these titles of "Old Covenant," or "Testament" and "New Testament," were in use. It was not till St. Jerome, in the fourth century, used the title "Bibliotheca divina" that any one term was used to include both. About the same time the Greeks began to use the plural Biblia, or "The Books," which was afterwards borrowed in the West and used as a singular, and so has passed into common use in the word Bible.

While, therefore, this use expresses a popular conviction and a great truth, St. Jerome's title, "the Divine Library," or that which is generally used in the Prayer-Book, is more strictly correct, inasmuch as the Bible is a collection of some sixty-six (or, including the Apocrypha, eighty) distinct books or documents, scattered over a period of fifteen hundred years, and written in different styles and for different purposes.

These are arranged in our Bibles, except so far as the threefold general division marks such a distinction, without regard to order of time. The Law of Moses comes first in order, followed by the historical books, and many of those which, in the Hebrew, are reckoned among the Psalms or Hagiographa, and those by the prophets The Hebrew Bible, after the Law of Moses, places two collections of "the Prophets," the first, *priores*, including Joshua, Judges, 1 and 2 Samuel, 1 and 2 Kings, and *posteriores*, including those that we name the prophets, except Daniel, who, along with David, as possessing the gift of prophecy but not exercising the pastoral office of the prophet, is reckoned among "the Writings," or "the Psalms." In the Septuagint version of the Old Testament, which has always been in use in the Eastern Church, the Apocryphal or Ecclesiastical books are interspersed among the books of the Prophets and Hagiographa as they are also in the Vulgate, which is used by the Roman Church and regarded as in every part of equal authority. Neither is the New Testament arranged chronologically. The general order is the Gospels and the book of Acts, which supplements St. Luke's Gospel, St. Paul's Epistles, the General Epistles, the Revelation of St. John.

The history of the Canon of the Old Testament is very meagre. The word Canon signifies a *rule* or *measuring line*, and is generally used to signify the collection of those books which came under the rule or definition of "inspired books," or "Holy Scriptures." Of the Canon of the Old Testament, it is conceded that up to the captivity only that portion which is called the Law (2 Kings xxii. 18; Isa. xxxiv. 16) was collected and reckoned as sacred and closed. A strong evidence of this is found in the fact that the Samaritans only receive the five books of Moses as sacred. After the return from the Captivity history ascribes the authoritative collection and use of "the Prophets" to Ezra, and after him to Nehemiah (2 Macc. ii. 13). Ezra organized "the great assembly" by which the collection of the Scriptures was carried on and completed. The last member of the great assembly was Simon the Just (290 B.C.), and after his time no new book was added to the Hebrew Canon. In Alexandria, however, in the third century B.C., the Greek version, called, it is said, from the number of the translators the Septuagint, or "the LXX.," had been made, and was in universal use among all Greek-speaking Jews in the world. To this additions were made, viz., those which are included in "the Apocrypha," and were received and used as part of the Holy Scriptures by the early Church. As has been said, they are still so received by the Eastern Church, and in spite of St. Jerome's protest and distinction, which is quoted in our VI. Article, the Roman Church declares all but three of them canonical and of equal value with the other books of the Old Testament, and those three being the two books of Esdras and the Prayer of Manasseh. Our own Church draws the distinction of St. Jerome between "the Canonical books of the Old and New Testament" and "the other books (as Hierome saith), which the Church doth read for example of life and instruction of manners, but yet doth not apply them to establish any doctrine."

The history of the Canon of the New Testament is of course much more complete. At first the Church had the living voice of Apostles, and with this to supplement and explain the Sacred Scriptures of the Old Covenant, it needed nothing more. But this state of things could not last, and partly by design (St. Luke i. 1-4; 2 Pet. i. 15), chiefly, it would appear, by the power of an overruling Providence, not only were the four Gospels written, but in a series of occasional letters the Apostles, and especially St. Paul, furnished a body of commentaries and instructions, which have been and will be the sacred legacy and the Sacred Scriptures of the Church for all time. Though these writings were at first the special property of different parts of the Church, and though at the very first not all Churches possessed them all, still as one body the Church possessed them all, and within another generation had gathered them all in one collection. The "Apostolic Fathers," St. Clement of Rome, St. Ignatius, St. Polycarp, St. Barnabas, frequently quote the Gospels and Epistles. Marcion the heretic, Irenæus, Tertullian, recognize the Gospel "comprising the four Gospels." Tatian's Diatessaron is a harmony of the four Gospels, and they quote "the Apostles" as collections of Epistles already known. Origen mentions the books of both the Old and the New Testaments by name, and comments on them. Other books of the Apostolic Fathers were read in churches, but were designated as "ecclesiastical," "read," or "disputed," though they were not forbidden till the Council of Laodicea, 360 A.D. The persecution of Diocletian, 303 A.D., was especially directed against the Churches and the Scriptures of the Christians, "that the Churches should be razed and the Scriptures consumed with fire," but it had the good effect to sharpen the distinction between "the Holy Scriptures" and all other writings, and the use of the word "Canonical," to distinguish those which were "inspired and sacred," may be said to date from this time. The controversies of the fourth century give frequent testimony to the fact that there was a general consent to the Canon of both the Old Testament and the New.

The earliest MSS. known date from that century and the following,—the Sinaitic and Vatican Codices (fourth century), and the Alexandrian and Ephræmic (fifth century). Many hundreds, more or less complete, are in existence and known, dating from every century since that time. These which have been named are evidently intended for public use, and, of course, represent older manuscripts which have perished. They contain more or less entirely both the Old and the New Testaments.

Attempts were made very early to divide the books into portions for convenience of use, but our present division into chapters dates only from the thirteenth century, and is the work of Cardinal Hugo, of Sancto Caro. The division into verses is later still, and the work of Stephens, the printer, in the sixteenth century.

The Scriptures were first received by the Church in Greek, and there is no known translation into Latin till Tertullian quotes that which was in use in Africa. The first attempt at translation into Anglo-Saxon was by Caedman, in the sixth century, and after him by the Venerable Bede. Wickliffe's version in the fourteenth century was the first complete English translation. The first printed edition of the New Testament in English was Tyndale's, probably printed at Worms. Coverdale's Bible was printed abroad in 1535 A.D. Cranmer's "Great Bible," in 1540 A.D., was the first appointed "to be read in Churches." The Genevan Bible of 1560 A.D. was for three-fourths of a century the popular Bible in England. The "Bishops' Bible" of 1568 A.D. is that from which the Prayer-Book version of the Psalms is taken. The authorized version, known as King James's Bible, dates from 1611 A.D., since which time till the year 1881 A.D. no revision by authority has been attempted.

II. This bald and imperfect sketch of the history of the Bible leaves upon the mind of the reader at first the impression of uncertainty and lack of the authority which we have been accustomed to associate with the Bible. The Bible is fragmentary instead of being one complete work, and the history is fragmentary and as incomplete. The authors of many books are not named. They do not plainly set forth claims of their own authority. The record of their origin is often not what we would desire or expect. The Canon was not established at once and finally. There is little apparent unity of time or place or purpose in the different books.

And yet out of these fragments, and under circumstances of the kingdom and people of Israel and of the early Church most unfavorable, grew and has been made up a collection which, without change of one part to adapt it to another, is so completely one that to many a reader of the Bible the knowledge comes with a kind of shock that it is not one in the same sense that a history or a treatise on arithmetic is one. The unity is so complete and acknowledged by friend and foe that it has passed into common speech and thought, and the bitterest enemy of the "Christian superstition" considers that when he has delivered a blow at Daniel or St. Peter's Epistle he has smitten the whole fabric, while many a diligent reader of the Bible "reads a chapter" without being compelled to recognize the difference between Gospel and Epistle, between history and poetry, or even between Old Testament and New. That is to say, in a true and deep sense the Bible is one book, and they who so regard it are not mistaken. It has grown with the growth of a living thing, and the life of it has been the Spirit who spake by the prophets.

The true character of this Divine Library can better be understood from another point of view. The Scriptures contain in themselves the record of the effect which they have had in the world, and their work is on record and in sight. The history of the people of Israel is the story of the education of a people from the lowest beginnings to the highest forms of civilization and enlightenment. In depth of thought, in pureness of morals, in lofty spiritual conceptions, and at the same time in the practical bearing of its wisdom upon daily life and upon society, no literature of any ancient nation compares with that of the people whom Moses led out of Egypt. And upon that foundation is built the structure of the New Testament. To compare the Christian Scriptures with the writings of their own time or of any other is impossible. Their character and their effect is one, and it is unique.

III. The Old Testament is therefore the history of a nation, and to be understood it must be read as a history. The story begins with the beginning of the whole race, and then is narrowed to the history of a family which becomes a great nation. That nation suffers reverses and is broken up, but it does not perish till its work is done. This history is not contained only in the historical books. The prophets are woven into it, and each of the other books and each portion of them falls into its place.

The first book tells the story of the earth from its creation "in the beginning," through successive changes until man's creation, and then goes on to relate the history of the race until the choice of one family, which henceforward becomes its almost exclusive subject. There is hardly a passage or a verse in the first part of the book of Genesis, *i.e.*, that part of it which relates the early history of the earth and of mankind, which has not been the object of attack and the subject of controversy. The accounts of the creation, of the fall, of the flood, the chronology, the theology,—everything in the book and everything about it has been denied and defended. Its Mosaic authorship has been impugned. It has been separated into two and three and an indefinite number of documents ascribed to as many authors. But still the book remains. Its account of the creation is declared to be "a remarkable anticipation of the conclusions of science." Its account of the fall of man is our only solution of the problem of evil in the world. The critics never have agreed in the results of their criticism. The Mosaic authorship is unshaken. And the historical character of the narrative rests on firmer ground than ever.

The remaining four books of the Pentateuch relate the history of that chosen people from the time of their great leader and lawgiver, Moses, down to the time of their establishment in the land which had been promised to them.

From Moses to David marks the trial and failure of the theocratic system, or rather the failure of the people to come up to the lofty ideal of that system. The three characters of prophet, priest, and king are remarkably blended in Samuel; but they are never reunited. He is the one chosen to anoint the king over the people, and to establish the line of the prophets which becomes from that time prominent. To this period belong the books of Joshua, Judges, Ruth. From David to the Captivity is the period of the kingdom, though in the second generation it was divided and continued as two kingdoms. The worship of JEHOVAH was established at Jerusalem. The prophets prophesied as special messengers of the LORD to both kingdoms. To this period belong the historical books of Samuel, Kings, and Chronicles, the prophecies of Isaiah, Jeremiah, the earlier of the minor prophets, the greater part of the Psalms, and the books of Solomon. During and after the Captivity, Ezekiel, Daniel, Haggai, Zechariah, Malachi, many of the Psalms, and the historical books of Ezra and Nehemiah. The book of Job is one of which the date and author are unknown, but apparently it is one of the earliest, if not the very earliest, of all.

These different books represent different stages of the national life and of the national education. The state of society in Genesis is patriarchal. When the children of Israel come prominently forward in Exodus, they are bondmen in Egypt. The Law is given to a people degraded by long bondage. Joshua, Judges, Ruth, depict a state of society of the rudest and most primitive. The books of the kingdom show us a nation highly cultivated and enlightened. From that condition they fell away, but the lofty spiritual conceptions and high moral purposes which had belonged to them at their best remained to them, and kept them from ever becoming really like the nations around them. There is in the history a distinct advance from time to time. The nation is being educated, as we can see very clearly.

IV. But while, say during the five centuries from Moses to Solomon, there is a continual progress and education of the people, evident in their customs, social, political, and even religious, in the evils that are rebuked and in the form of the rebukes, in the form of the instructions that are given to them, there is in the story from beginning to end one unchangeable element. He who in the beginning created the heavens and the earth is the LORD, who spake to Abraham and to Moses, who was revealed on Sinai, and who made the promise to David and to Solomon. The Law that He gave on Sinai embraced all the principles of all the law that He ever gave them. Higher conception of GOD, or of man's duty to Him, than was revealed then, and later in Deuteronomy,—"The LORD our GOD is one LORD: and thou shalt love the LORD thy GOD with all thine heart, and with all thy soul, and with all thy might" (Deut. vi. 4, 5), — was never revealed to them or to man. All that was taught them, and all that was given them, was involved in those first commandments. The priesthood as being nearer by their office to the source of truth, and as the teaching caste, no doubt were always somewhat in advance of the common people, but they had no secret knowledge, and nothing which did not belong alike to all and each of the "kingdom of priests" (Ex. xix. 6). Moses expressed the view of true wisdom and the view of the whole law when he rejoiced that some were prophesying in the camp, "would GOD that all the LORD's people were prophets." Our SAVIOUR appeals to the saying to Moses at the bush, "I am the GOD of Abraham and of Isaac and of Jacob," as proof of the resurrection of the dead. The progress and education of the nation was not in the way of discovery or development of new truth; but it was a progress and education up to a standard which was set for them on Sinai, and in the call of Moses and in the promise to Abraham, and never changed.

This thought of the perfectness and unity of the truth which was revealed gives us the key to the unity of the Scriptures. We can understand how the inspired words of the One GOD should be essentially one with each other. But we have an explanation more definite still. That explanation lies in the one purpose of GOD, which was first revealed in Eden, in the promise of the "seed of the woman who should bruise the serpent's head," which was repeated to Abraham, "in thy seed shall all the nations of the earth be blessed," and again to David of the SON, who should sit on his throne and reign forever. "Your father Abraham rejoiced to see my day," our SAVIOUR said. Of all the Law and the prophets He said, "I am not come to destroy but to fulfill." "The testimony of JESUS is the spirit of prophecy." The children of Israel were chosen and kept and taught and trained for the fulfillment of that one promise and purpose of Almighty GOD. What was true of the whole system was true of every part of it. Every sacrifice was a type of CHRIST. Every law and every prophecy foretold Him.

Still more evidently true is it of the Scriptures of the New Testament that they depend upon CHRIST and reveal Him. The Gospels are biographies of Him. The Epistles apply the truth as it is in Him, to establish and edify His Kingdom and to instruct and guide His followers. They are nothing without Him, and it is in vain to try to understand them without the presupposition of faith in Him.

The faith in CHRIST is therefore the bond of union between the Old Testament and the New. Out of the Old Testament had grown up at our SAVIOUR'S coming a strong and definite expectation of the CHRIST, the Son of David. And though many held that expectation along with such errors that they could not recognize the fulfillment, He did fulfill it, and it was the purpose of the Gospels and Epistles to show how He fulfilled it The Old and the New are, therefore, one "in Him." We could have neither without the other, but neither without Him.

V. The Bible is therefore a history, and a history which has one key, and which centres in one Person. But there is another view of its historical character which is involved in this one, and which is not less necessary in order to understand either the history which the Scriptures relate or their own history as books. It would be impossible for any man to understand the first sentence of the Old Testament who did not know who is *the* GOD who created, or to believe it who did not believe in Him. It would be impossible to form any idea of the connection of the different portions without some recognition of CHRIST our LORD as the object and fulfillment of the purpose of GOD.

But not less necessary than these two first principles of scriptural criticism is another,—the recognition of the kingdom of Israel and of its fulfillment, the Kingdom of Christ on earth, in their corporate and official capacity of the witness and keeper of Holy Scripture. The Old Testament Scriptures were written and committed to the Kingdom and Church of Israel (Rom. iii. 2) under all its varied circumstances. It is as necessary to keep this thought in mind in order to understand them as it is with regard to any history or public document of any nation. While they contain many things which are universally true and applicable to all times and peoples, they contain a great deal which is only directly true and applicable to this particular people and perhaps to this particular time, and even that universal truth must be seen to be understood through the medium of this "peculiar people."

This is one practical bearing of the principle. Another is no less important. These Scriptures are the inspired Word of GOD, and this chosen nation is the chosen people of GOD in the same sense and for the same purpose,—" an inspired nation" in Dean Stanley's words. To give any meaning to the words "inspired" or "chosen of GOD," is to suppose His overruling presence with them as a people in the reception and preservation of His words to them. He used men to write them. Who the men were or what the pen they wrote with or the material on which they wrote we do not know, but the fact that we have them proves that they were written, and proves also the fact of their preservation. The men and the names passed away, for they were acting officially,—the prophet is one who "speaks for GOD," —and what they spoke and wrote by virtue of their office, the whole living body acting by its various members, and through generations, tested, sifted, preserved by virtue of its office. When men neglected their duty GOD overruled their neglect, and when some reformation repairs the ruined Temple of the LORD, under the rubbish they find "the book of the Law of the LORD" (2 Chron. xxxiv. 14). The practical bearing of this principle as an answer to many of the attacks of unbelief is very evident. History and constitution and laws and poetry imply and prove the nation to which they belonged. The strong proof that the Scriptures of the Old Testament are all that we believe them to be lies in the testimony which the people of Israel supply us by their existence as a people. In this wider view many of the smaller questions and tests of words and styles and imagined probabilities of men who read the books of three thousand years ago with nineteenth century eyes simply sink out of sight.

We can see the bearing of this principle upon the Old Testament Scriptures. It is no less important to the understanding of the New Testament. The Scriptures of the New Testament were written and committed, not by chance, nor to all the world, nor to any miraculous agency, but to the Church of Christ, to which they stand related precisely as do the Scriptures of the Old Testament to the Church of Israel. It hardly needs to be suggested that the Epistle to the Church of GOD, which is at Corinth, supposes the existence of the Church of GOD at Corinth, and that one who would understand that Epistle must read it with the understanding of a Church thoroughly organized and possessing all that was needed for the full performance of the work of a Church: Creed, Sacraments, Liturgy, Psalms, and many other things not so desirable, but all indicative of corporate existence. What is true of this one letter is just as true, though not always so evident, of all the rest of the New Testament. No one can read and understand alike why some things are said, and some equally important are omitted, and many others only hinted at, who does not read these Scriptures with the understanding of the Church to which and for which they were written. The world receives them from the Church. It can only read them understandingly in the Church.

The same principle clears up many difficulties with regard to the history of the Canon of the New Testament. Written to and for the Church, that Church preserved them. Fathers and Councils were the voices, blending many in one, which spake the judgment of the living body in which the guiding Spirit had come to abide at Pentecost. We have an idea of what is meant by "public opinion," "the spirit of the age," etc. The Canon of Scripture expresses the matured judgment of the Church of GOD, whose office it is to be "the pillar and ground of the truth," and to which the Spirit was promised, and at Pentecost was sent to abide, who "shall guide you into all truth."

VI. In referring to these first principles of the truth about the Holy Scriptures we have not been unmindful of the recent attacks and the bold claims of modern criticism. We have had them constantly in mind, and this article has been shaped with reference to them, not with a view to avoid any of them, but to suggest the best way for the ordinary reader to meet them. There are two kinds of criticism,—one is the criticism of true, and therefore humble and faithful, scholarship, which regards no point of the truth beneath its notice, and so is not ashamed to busy itself with words and jots and points of the Scriptures, but which is not afraid of any truth wherever it finds it, but which, at the same time, recognizes the fact that there are weightier matters than these, and that there is truth which is higher and deeper than men can see or reach, and which is to be accepted not on evidence of sight, but of reason and faith. We need never fear such criticism or its results. There is another criticism which we need not so much fear as shun,—the dishonest and destructive criticism of determined unbelief, sometimes very learned, and sometimes very shallow and ignorant and boastful, which begins its investigations into the Scriptures in the spirit of the detective, with a mind warped and a heart hardened by determined prejudice. It says beforehand, There can be no such thing as a miracle; a real prophecy is impossible. There is no GOD, or if there is, He does not interfere with the order of nature and in the affairs of man; the supernatural is the work of imagination, the divine is the unknowable; and then in this spirit of "free inquiry" it proceeds to convict the Scriptures of folly and falsehood, and calls its conclusions "the results of the higher criticism." So another "sweeps the heavens with his telescope and finds no GOD there," and another "carves the living hound," and with knife and glass and unclean hand searches and finds no life in the carcass. Even so "their witness agrees not together," and the constant contradictions of the critics, both in their principles and in their conclusions, are enough to allay our fears if we had any. There is literally not a book of Holy Scripture which has not been the subject of such attacks, and it may be safely said that no book could possibly stand, and no evidence could be accepted, upon their principles. If the judge begins the trial of a case by declaring that all the witnesses are liars before he hears them, then no evidence can prove a case, and not only can no miracle and no prophecy be proved, but no ordinary event in life. If differences in style in the writings of one who prophesied during the reign of four kings proves that Isaiah could not have written all his prophecy, and demands a "great unknown" to supply his lack, and if the same reasons require two Zechariahs and two or more Daniels and two St. Johns, and two—the "Elohist" and the "Jehovist" —or a dozen writers of Genesis, and a forger of Deuteronomy, and even of St. Paul's Epistles, then no great poet or author who ever lived ever wrote his own writings, and no man who "now is old" could ever "have been young."

The truth about such attacks is that they are only new in form, they are old in spirit. They are the trials and tests not only of our faith, but of the truth. The final results have always been good. Small errors in the text have been detected and corrected, and there is a constant return to the very perfection of the original writings. But that we may not misunderstand the bearing of such an admission, let us understand just what it implies. Such a sifting and comparison of hundreds of old manuscripts, and the existence of such errors or any errors in some or other of them, proves two things,— in the first place, the vast number of other manuscripts which they represent, and therefore of other witnesses to the truth, and also proves the true existence of a common and perfect original as certainly as the converging of paths into roads, and of roads into a city, proves the existence of the city into which and out of which they lead. The finding and expunging of a word or a sentence or a passage (and especially one which has no special doctrinal significance, and which is, if not a copyist's error, at best a paraphrase or comment), so far from shaking our faith in the rest, only confirms our assurance. When the expert clerk in a bank discovers, by the aid of eye and glass, and scales, in packages of bills or a pile of gold and silver pieces, one which is counterfeit, but which, by its close imitation of the genuine, has escaped the ordinary eye, instead of rushing to the conclusion that all are therefore counterfeit, you are assured by the same tests that all the rest are true.

"I am not aware," says Professor Sanday, of Oxford, "of a single discovery of new documents or materials bearing, however indirectly, on New Testament criticism, that has tended in any way to shake the foundations of our faith, while by far the larger number have tended very positively to strengthen them. Nor is the prospect any less favorable as regards speculative, analytical, or reconstructive criticism. Here, perhaps, there is more reason for disquiet. Bold and revolutionary hypotheses have been thrown out, and will probably be thrown out again. But when we look back upon past controversies, we shall see indeed that they have left a residuum, but a residuum that leaves Christianity no weaker, but rather stronger, than it was before. Errors are corrected; exaggerations are modified; our understanding of the New Testament grows in depth and fullness. And in the mean time, as it seems to me, certain positions have been placed beyond the reach of controversy. They are so much secure ground from which we can look out in safety, even though there may be obscurity outside. It is only a matter of time, and in the end all will come out right again. One truth cannot permanently conflict with another truth."

There are "things hard to be understood in all the Holy Scriptures, which they that are unlearned and unstable wrest to their own destruction." But none the less we are commanded by our LORD to "search" them, only to read them in faith in Him if we would read them safely and profitably. They will be attacked, and many will deny and reject them. But we need neither be misled by their errors nor fear their attacks. Some of them proceed from ignorance. One is reminded of the anecdote of Franklin, who being in company with a number of French infidels, who were ridiculing the Bible, took from his pocket "an old book that he had picked up at a book-stall," and read to them, to their delight, the "Prayer of Habakkuk," and then compelled them to confess that they had never read the book on which they were sitting in judgment. Others proceed from other causes. But we need not fear them. We have endeavored to indicate some of the guards against them in those deeper and wider principles of scriptural criticism without which any student will go astray. With which we come down to these books from a wider view and a higher position.

It may be well to remind ourselves that one single fulfilled prophecy, such as the many that cluster about our SAVIOUR's coming, is decisive against the denials of prophecy and for the belief in it. One fact of definite, Messianic expectation, once so persistently denied and now so universally conceded, founded on the prophecy of Daniel, is enough to establish the truth of Daniel the prophet. One miracle, and above all the miracle of the Resurrection, justifies and establishes the belief in miracles. "If all the rest of the Christian Scriptures were lost or unauthentic, the four great undisputed Epistles of St. Paul furnish us with all the essentials of the Christian Faith." So that even against unbelieving criticism we are at liberty to choose our own ground, and to summon our enemy to stand upon it. But for our own purpose and advantage the true course is not even to take our stand at first even on such certain truth. We can come more safely and wisely to the examination even of such evidences — of which there is abundance — from above. Granted the being of GOD, and the supernatural is natural, things hard to be understood become matters of course. Prophecy is the necessary declaration of His will, and miracles the natural evidence and means by which He accomplishes it. If this is His will and His work, then these ways are such as are to be expected. Instead of fastening on some little point and testing the passage by a word, and the book by a misunderstood passage, and the whole by a darkened past, and so at every step shutting out the evidence and truth of GOD, we see in the Scriptures the Word of Him who is higher than the Scriptures, and who must be believed in, in order to understand His Word, the revelation of CHRIST the Incarnate Word without whom they are naught, and the message delivered to "the Church which is His Body." They are not, therefore, all our religion, nor the sum of the trust committed to us. They do not lose but gain to our view when we understand that they are not alone, but that they are as the law of the Kingdom, filling their place and fulfilling their work in the great system of the Kingdom of the great GOD and our SAVIOUR. Then we can read the books in their places, and each chapter and verse and word is magnified and enlightened by the light that falls upon it from the sun of the system. It is fully in accord with this principle that "the Article of the Sufficiency of the Holy Scriptures for Salvation was placed by our Anglican Fathers next after the Articles of the Trinity." "Holy Scripture containeth all things necessary to salvation, so that whatsoever is not read therein, nor may be proved thereby, is not to be required of any man that it should be believed as an article of the Faith, or be thought requisite or necessary to salvation." And it is in the same spirit that it goes on to define what is meant by Holy Scripture, with an appeal to the general judgment of the Church,—" those canonical books of the Old and New Testament of whose authority was never any doubt in the Church."

Authorities: Wordsworth's Commentary, The Bible in the Church, Westcott, Aids to Faith, Encyclopedia Britannica, Proceedings of Reading Church Congress.

REV. L. W. GIBSON.

Bidding Prayers. To bid not only meant to order, but also to pray (*cf.* German, beten). Bidding prayer, then, is a monition or call to prayer. It is retained in our " Let us pray." In the 55th Canon of 1603 A.D., the form of bidding prayer was given thus: " Before all sermons, lectures, and homilies the preachers and ministers shall move the people to join with them in prayer *in this form, or to this effect*, as briefly as conveniently they may: Ye shall pray for CHRIST'S Holy Catholic Church; that is, for the whole congregation of Christian people dispersed throughout the whole world, and especially for the Churches of England, Scotland, and Ireland. And herein I require you most especially to pray for the King's most excellent Majesty, our sovereign, Lord James, King of England, Scotland, France, and Ireland, defender of the faith and supreme governor in these his realms and all other his dominions and countries over all persons, in all causes as well ecclesiastical as temporal. Ye shall also pray for our gracious Queen Anne, the noble Prince Henry, and the rest of the King's and Queen's royal issue. Ye shall pray for the ministers of GOD'S Holy Word and sacraments, as well Archbishops and Bishops as other pastors and curates. Ye shall also pray for the King's most honorable Council and for all the nobility and magistrates of this realm, that all and every of these in their several callings may serve truly and faithfully to the glory of GOD and the edifying and well governing of His people, remembering the account they must make. Also ye shall pray for the whole Commons of this realm that they may live in the true faith and fear of GOD, in humble obedience to the King, and brotherly charity one to another. Finally, let us praise GOD for all those which are departed out of this life in the faith of CHRIST, and pray unto GOD that we may have grace to direct our lives after their good example, that this life ended we may be made partakers with them of the glorious resurrection in the life everlasting." It always concluded with the LORD'S Prayer. The names and estates are varied, of course, with the times and the sovereigns, but the bidding prayer is still used in England. As it often happens that it would be very convenient to deliver a lecture or sermon to a class or guild without the Evening Prayer preceding it, it is worth the while to consider whether it might not be advisable for the Church to permit some such form of bidding prayer to be used under due restrictions.

Bier. A portable carriage for the dead.

Bigamy. The crime of marrying a second wife while the first is still living. In the early Church it meant also the marrying of a second wife after the death of the first,—an act which was discouraged in every way, it being sometimes an impediment to holy orders. But the rule and the opposition varied in various parts of the Church and at different times.

Birretta. The square cap worn by foreign ecclesiastics over the zucchetto, or close skull-cap. It was probably a late introduction after tonsure was fully enforced.

Bishop, The Rights, Duties, and Privileges of a. Immediately before His ascension into Heaven, in a place apart where He had appointed, our LORD, in the presence of His eleven Apostles, asserting the plenitude of His power, " All power is given unto me in heaven and in earth" (St. Matthew xxviii. 18), made this the basis of the fullness of the functions with which He sent forth His Apostles to their work: " Go ye, therefore, and teach all nations. . . . and, lo, I am with you alway." " As ($καθως$) my Father has sent me, even so send I you" (St. John xx. 21). Of the fullness of the power with which He was Himself endued, according to this measure He invested His Apostles with authority to carry on the work which He had begun. Realizing the sole responsibility thus placed upon them, they fill up their number (Acts i. 26), and in due time constitute the subordinate orders of Deacon and Presbyter (Acts vi. 6; Titus i. 5), for the better execution of the task that at first rested wholly upon themselves. With the headship of the Church under CHRIST in this office always clearly indicated, but under varying names, it settled within the first century after CHRIST upon that designation of Bishop, which was used at times by the Apostles, and has been employed ever since. At first the oversight was in the body of the Apostles jointly. Then a single Apostle had the care of those whom he had been the means of converting to the Christian faith. Soon after this there arose naturally the Diocesan Episcopate, with the immediate authority of Bishops restricted to their several Dioceses, along with a joint responsibility on the part of each Bishop, as a part of the general Episcopate, for the welfare of the entire Church.

The duty of general oversight in the Bishop very soon compelled the designation of particular Presbyters to have the immediate spiritual care of the several districts or parishes as they were successively formed. These Presbyters at first were sent forth from the Bishop's Church, and acted with delegated authority. As the number of Christians and the distance from the Bishop increased, these Presbyters came gradually to act with greater independence, and the relation of their parishes with the cathedral became more indefinite. At the same time the connection of every baptized person with the Bishop was marked, and the significance of the sole office which was immediately created in the Church by our LORD was emphasized in the renewal before him of the baptismal vows, and the receiving from him in confirmation the seal of the HOLY GHOST.

The distinct purpose declared for which the number of the Apostles was completed was that the person so chosen might be a witness to the resurrection of our LORD. This office of the Episcopate, to hold, and hand on, and bear witness to, the purity of the faith, has always been very important. As different interpretations of the Holy Scriptures appeared, and questions arose about the faith which had been delivered, the Bishops from all parts of the Church were called together into Councils in order to bear witness to what had been held from the beginning, and to determine questions of discipline and order. This was the order in the Church with whom the decisions as to doctrine rested.

This witnessing function of the Episcopate, coming among the other reasons stated, from the fact that it never died, and could be distinctly traced in the history of the several Sees, was naturally joined with the executive function. Whatever others could do the Bishop could do, and more. All functions ended up in him. All appeals might finally come to him for settlement. He was the visible centre of communion. Through him the Diocese and its members were connected with the universal Church. He was the guardian of the rights and privileges of the several members of the Diocese as against each other.

This executive function of the Bishop manifested itself in several forms:

(1) Having a seat in all General Councils of the Church, he has the position of presidency in his own Diocese. He holds his own office in trust, being obliged to see that its powers and dignities suffer no diminution while they are in his hands. He is also the trustee of the traditional and immemorial immunities and privileges of all the clergymen and laymen in his jurisdiction. The interest and the greatest efficiency of the whole Church are involved in the development to the highest point of all the capacities which are in each office, and in the prevention of the dishonoring of any position or the diminution of its efficiency by the intrusion of other agencies out of their rightful place. This duty comes rightly on the Bishop.

Apostolic example shows that this rule of the Bishop is not designed to be autocratic, but to be shared and concurred in by the counsel of the Presbyters and Brethren (Acts xv. 23). In all forms of ecclesiastical action, whether in the adoption of Canons, or in the election of Bishops, or in the regulation of the minor business of the Church, this initiation of the Bishop along with the deliberate concurrence of the other orders in the Church has been seen.

(2) Outside of conciliar action the Bishop is responsible for the efficiency of the Church in all of the multiform activities of a living, aggressive body, all the time confronting new questions. Responsible for the spiritual interests of the Diocese, his original right of nomination of ministers to all parishes has yet its trace remaining in the need that he should concur in all elections of clergymen to cures, in order to the validity of the action. In case of differences between the minister and congregation, which may not otherwise be appeased, with him, either personally or by deputy, the business of final appeal and settlement lies. In case of fault of any sort alleged in the minister, the Bishop, on a formal presentation of the case to his notice, takes order for the constitution of the court, if he thinks that the matter should go to trial, and the pronouncement of sentence if guilt is found.

The Deacon is peculiarly under the Bishop's care. His studies, as are also those of the candidate for holy orders, are prosecuted under the Bishop's direction. The Deacon is also subject to the Bishop's control in officiating in the Diocese.

To the parish and the laity, from the Bishop, passed, in large degree, the power of nomination to the rectorship when the income of the parish went directly to the clergymen, instead of, as at first, coming to the Bishop for distribution. Where, however, the Bishop now does not nominate, he generally recommends for vacant positions, with an influence which is increased, not merely by the fact of his office, but also by his larger knowledge and the disinterestedness of his motives. In any event the choice of a rector has to be communicated to him and be approved by him.

(3) As the supreme executive officer of the Diocese, the distribution of the moneys of the Diocese is largely under his influence, if not his control. He, in consultation with others, distributes the money which is contributed for the missionary purposes of the Diocese, as well all the educational and eleemosynary funds which are at disposal. To him also, as having a better knowledge of the real condition and needs of the Diocese, are intrusted, from time to time, trust moneys for distribution according to his judgment, for church building and for personal and parochial aid.

The relation of the Bishop not merely with the Diocese, but with the general Church, is shown in the manner of his election and otherwise. It is required that he shall receive at least a majority of the votes of the clergymen and parishes having seats in the Convention; but his election is still incomplete until he receives the votes of a majority of the Dioceses, as represented by their Standing Committees or deputations in General Convention; and after this the evidence of the consent of a majority of the Bishops. He may not resign his office until he has not only the consent of the Diocese, but of the House of Bishops. If charged with fault, he is tried by the House of Bishops sitting as a court.

The official designation of the Bishop in this country, as recommended by the General Convention of 1785, was "The Right Reverend A. B., Bishop of the Protestant Episcopal Church in C. D."

It would not be strange that, from disuse on the part of the Bishop, or from ambition or excessive energy on the part of others, in the passage of time some of the original functions of the Episcopate may have lapsed or been intruded upon.

(1) The right of ordering the Liturgy and the Ritual of his Diocese, which originally belonged to the Bishop, has passed to the legislation of the national Church, to which the Bishop has virtually ceded a portion of his right. A disposition, also, practically to regulate the Ritual, without reference to the Bishop, has not infrequently appeared in certain ministers and parishes of a Diocese.

(2) The headship of the Diocese as represented in Council, and the possibility of rejecting all measures which did not meet with his approval, has in many instances shrunken to the honorary presidency of the body, and only such a voice in disapproval as belongs to any clergyman in the Diocese.

But his authority as being the chief officer, and his veto, which is inseparable from his right to legislate and to discipline, being inherent in the office of Bishop, are not forfeited when either not used or held in abeyance through force of circumstances.

(3) From non-residence and immersion in other interests the right of the Bishop in his cathedral has declined, in many cases, to the concession of but a formal visitation, and the privilege of an honorary seat in the choir.

(4) The right and the duty of giving holy orders, which is a primary office of the Episcopate, have in cases been so abridged by the excessive powers asserted by bodies having advisory functions, that it has been impossible for Bishops collectively or acting singly to give the Episcopate, or even approach the question of the fitness of the persons proposed for admission to the lower orders.

It is believed, however, that, with regard to these and many other functions of a like character, the disposition in the Church is to restore to the Bishop that which for the Divine regimen of the Church, and therefore the better efficiency of its work, rightly and originally belonged to him ; while providing that the wisdom and healthful influence of his work shall be increased by the counsel, the co-operation, and the necessary checks which come from the other constituent parts of the Church.

RT. REV. C. F. ROBERTSON, D.D.,
Bishop of Missouri.

Blasphemy. Blasphemy is sometimes confused with profanity. A profane person is one who uses evil language, oaths, and blasphemous phrases. But a person may be guilty of blasphemy without any profanity, for he may teach contrary to GOD'S honor or truth and yet use apparently reverent language. In the early Church there were three sorts of blasphemy distinguished : First, of apostates ; so St. Polycarp indignantly replied when required to deny CHRIST: "These eighty and six years have I served Him, and He never did me harm ; how, then, can I blaspheme my King and my SAVIOUR ?" Second, of heretics and schismatics, who yet may recommend their heresy by moral lives. The Church visited these with excommunication. The third sort of blasphemy was the sin against the HOLY GHOST. What this sin was, or is, was much debated. At the time when our LORD declared it, it was a denial of the evidence by miracles which He worked of the power of the HOLY GHOST. If, then, it was a sin then to deny the power of the HOLY GHOST, now it must be of the same kind. St. Athanasius and St. Ambrose defined it to be a denial of the Divinity of CHRIST, but St. Augustine defined it to be persistent and final impenitency. However this may be, the sin of blasphemy *is* committed with fearful frequency in this age. It is by a direct reviling of GOD a sin that marks the last age of the world (Rev. xvi. 9, 11, 21 ; 2 Tim. iii. 2). By willfully imputing to Him attributes or qualities which are not possible, as injustice, and creation of sin, or denying His attributes of love, mercy, truth, and such like. It may be also committed by reviling His creatures. Thus imprecations and profane swearing have the nature of blasphemy. By the Statute Law of England the denial of the persons of the TRINITY, of the Christian religion, of the Divine authority of the Holy Scriptures, is made blasphemy.

Blood. "But flesh with the life thereof, which is the blood thereof, ye shall not eat" (Gen. ix. 4). "And whatsoever man there be of the house of Israel, or of the strangers that sojourn among you, that eateth any manner of blood ; I will even set my face against that soul that eateth blood, and will cut him off from among his people" (Lev. xvii. 10). "That ye abstain from . . . blood" (Acts xv. 29).

It is very clear that in GOD'S sight blood has a sacred and significant character which is much disregarded. The command was strict, "he shall even pour out the blood thereof and cover it with dust." The Christians observed it under the directions of the Apostolic Letter, as quoted above. Blood was accounted the life, and modern science teaches us the same. "It is the life of all flesh ; the blood of it is for the life thereof."

The loss of blood is the loss of physical life, and this is typical of the death of the soul. So Holy Scripture speaks of the "pouring out of the soul," and "the offering of the soul." Blood, therefore, being the life, and as Atonement is based upon the life of one for the lives of all (Rom. v. and Heb. ix. 7 *sq*.), the bloody sacrifice was the type of the one full sufficient sacrifice of CHRIST. For the life of the flesh is in the blood: "and I have given it to you upon the altar to make an atonement for your souls: for it is the blood that maketh an atonement for the soul" (Lev. xvii. 11). If, then, the blood of the lamb, the heifer, or the dove could have such typical significance, of how much greater dignity must we devoutly count the redeeming blood of our LORD JESUS CHRIST, the Lamb of GOD, for whom were all previous sacrifices and in whom their meaning and efficacy centred! "The blood of JESUS CHRIST cleanseth us from all sin." "How much more shall the blood of CHRIST, who, through the eternal SPIRIT, offered Himself without spot to GOD, purge your conscience from dead works to serve the living GOD." "Unto Him that loved us and washed us from our sins in His own blood, and hath made us kings and priests unto GOD and His FATHER, to Him be glory and dominion for ever and ever. Amen." "These are they which came out of great tribulation and have washed their robes and made them white in the blood of the LAMB." Thence the blood of redemption upon the cross is made by Him our life. "This is my blood" which is shed for you and for many for the remission of sins. Do this as oft as ye shall drink it, for the LORD JESUS had already said, "Whoso eateth my Flesh, and drinketh my Blood, hath eternal life; and I will raise him up at the last day" (St. John vi. 54).

Body, Mystical. The union between CHRIST and His members is so real, so intimate, that St. Paul declares we are of His flesh and of His bones (Eph. v. 30). The Body into which we are so bound up is His Mystical Body the Church, which the Apostle declares we are. "Now ye are the Body of CHRIST, and members in particular (1 Cor. xii. 27), but this Body hath CHRIST as its Head, "And gave Him to be the Head over all things to the Church, which is His Body, the fullness of Him that filleth all in all" (Eph. i. 23). This Church, the souls and bodies of them that believe, He has purchased to Himself with His own Blood. It is a *mystical* Body, and our union in CHRIST is mystical, because it is now beyond our comprehension, but not contrary to the analogies which faith supplies from the experience we daily have given us. It is, therefore, to be believed and acted upon in our spiritual life, for the spiritual life of the Christian is the Life of CHRIST. The Church is not only the fullness of Him that filleth all in all: it is His Bride; it is His joy. Therefore the joining of ourselves to CHRIST by baptism, by the Communion, by the faith, love, and obedience which enter into the nature of our spiritual life, is such and so close a union with Him that it is properly mystical, beyond human knowledge, and is summed up in the strong words St. Paul uses: "Ye are dead, and your life is hid with CHRIST in GOD," and the still more mysterious language of St. Peter: "Whereby are given unto us exceeding great and precious promises, that by these ye might be partakers of the *Divine nature*, having escaped the corruption that is in the world through lust" (2 Pet. i. 4). The Church is the visible appointed Body for the giving and receiving of the gifts, graces, and influences which make up the mystical union of the Christian with his LORD. The inner mystical union of the life is the spiritual activity and healthy use of these means of grace in the man himself. This mystical union has been treated of in many ways, its study and practice having formed a school of thought in the Church, which finally led into vagaries not warranted by Holy Scripture.

Body, Natural. Our natural bodies, however they may be viewed under the investigations of modern science, can finally be treated simply as returning to that dust out of which we are formed. The teachings of the 1st and 2d chapters of Genesis are the basis, finally, of all that can be said of our mortal bodies. That we were made by GOD in His own Image, and received from Him a living soul from His breath, that this breath was the breath of *lives* (*vide* margin in A. V. and Heb.), and that the subdivision of our life into physical, intellectual, and spiritual life, of which every thinking man is thoroughly conscious, all these are postulates with the Christian. The analysis of materialists cannot overthrow these, for they are aside from the line of study he has marked out for himself, and the clashing comes from his effort to overpass the bounds between mind and matter. And the last analysis even of the materialist ends in a pre-existent ideal. That He can and did call our nature into existence by His own fiat is, of course, a fact that every believer in Revelation asserts. How far, in what way it may be said that our body is in His Image, has ever been a matter of much speculation, but will be ever one of those mysteries solved in the hereafter, when we shall know even as we are known. Of the creation of woman, it may be said to be wholly of the one nature of man, but derivatively, and subsisting as subordinate, and not by original creation. There are in our human nature three forms of existence, two of them in the historical past, the third in the continuous flow of human history: Adam by original creation, Eve by being formed out of Adam, and their descendants by conception and birth. And this human nature thus brought into existence is intimately bound up in a unity wonderful and reacting, and typical of the infinite and incomprehensible unity of the Divine Nature.

The Fall, by the introduction of sin by disobedience into our nature, produced disintegration where the principle of unity had been fundamental. Capacities and endowments fitted for immortality and perfect happiness were so tainted and stained, and the principle of harmonic life in GOD so ruined, that death was the inevitable result. "Dying thou shalt die" was the enouncing of a fact resulting from sin. Death is the final result of a prolonged disintegration that begins with the moment of birth. When reparation no longer exceeds the waste, then death begins to win the victory in the lengthened struggle. But since man had all things put in subjection to him, his fall tainted and soiled all the subordinate creation. Therefore St. Paul teaches us that "we know that the whole creation groaneth and travaileth in pain together until now." Our space does not permit us to point out the bearing of the whole passage (Rom. viii. 19–23) upon the Fall, the interconnection of the natural creation and man, and the restoration of the one by the redemption of the other through JESUS CHRIST, and by the continuous presence of the HOLY SPIRIT. But this outline statement of the scriptural facts will give the clue to a clear grasp of this subject. The capacity for eternal life will be discussed under the title of IMMORTALITY. The disastrous consequences of the Fall ruined the corporeal powers and beauty of the body, but we cannot know the height from which Adam fell. Dr. South's well-known saying, that an Aristotle was but the rubbish of an Adam, is possibly the best way that we can express the extent of the injury. Immortality belonged since then only to the sinless CHRIST, for "it was not possible that He should be holden of death" (Acts ii. 24). But as the second Adam, the Quickening Spirit, He restores to us this immortality. The forgiveness, then, of sin is the first step to the giving back to our natural bodies their original power of mortality, which re-endowment is to be completed at the Resurrection.

Body, Spiritual. St. Paul distinctly teaches that the body to be given us at our resurrection is to be spiritual. This difficulty always has been presented: how, then, shall we be judged in the spiritual body for the deeds done in the natural body? or, in other words, how shall that personal identity which we now wear be brought up at the judgment-seat? That we cannot now understand, but it is no greater difficulty to accept the future fact than it is to accept and act upon the present fact, that our souls and our bodies—two distinct and, in some respects, antagonistic entities—form but one person, though we can never understand the ultimate principle of their union. Indeed, it is less difficult to admit that in a perfect state of sinlessness a spiritual body, with spiritual capacities now beyond us, may be the only fit habitation for the redeemed soul. But the words of Scripture are to be accepted, and then explanation to be patiently waited for. The fuller discussion of this subject belongs to the title RESURRECTION.

Bowing, in the Creed. A reverent act of worship at the name of JESUS (Phil. ii. 10). The text upon which this bowing is based refers properly to a bending of the knee, which was an Oriental act of homage. It is only when His name, JESUS, is uttered that this reverent bowing is proper. JESUS is His name as man with us. CHRIST is His title, as anointed to His threefold office as Prophet, Priest, and King. Therefore St. Paul's arguments with the Thessalonians were accurately stated, "that this JESUS whom I proclaim unto you is the CHRIST." The 18th Canon of the Church of England makes bowing at the name of JESUS proper, not only in the Creed, but at all other times when it is mentioned. "When, in time of Divine service, the LORD JESUS shall be mentioned, due and lowly reverence shall be done by all persons present as hath been accustomed: testifying by these outward ceremonies and gestures their inward humility, Christian resolution, and due acknowledgment that the LORD JESUS CHRIST, the true eternal SON of GOD, is the only Saviour of the world, in whom alone all the mercies, graces, and promises of GOD to mankind for this life and the life to come are fully and wholly comprised." (Canons of 1603 A.D.)

Breviary. The Book of the Daily Offices of the Roman Church. The name belonged to the particular MSS. prepared by Gregory VII. (1085 A.D.), but the book, in principle, was in use in the Church many ages before. It was made up of the Psalms, of the Lessons from Holy Scripture, or from the works of the Fathers, sentences thrown into the form of Versicles, Responds, Antiphons, Prosas, and other similar forms. Every Bishop had, originally, the power to alter, arrange, or recompile the Liturgy in his Diocese, but from the fifth century there was a tendency to unify the services, and especially was this done in the Provinces. Still there was a large degree of variation for many ages. In the English Church there were varieties in the several leading Dioceses. The monasteries had their special Breviaries. The Roman office-books, Missal and Breviary, were and are forced upon the Dioceses which receive the papal authority, despite of very determined resistance. The present form of the Roman Breviary was made under Pius V. It is divided into four parts, called after the seasons, Pars Hiemalis, Vernalis, Æstivalis, Autumnalis. Each of these parts, in addition to the introductory rubrics, calendar, and other tables, has four subdivisions: (I.) The Psalter, comprising the Psalms and Canticles, arranged for weekly recitation, and also the unvarying parts of the offices. (II.) The Proper Offices for the season, which vary with the season. (III.) The Proper Offices for the Festivals of the Saints. (IV.) The Common (*i.e.*, unvarying) Office for the Festivals of the Saints.

Brief. Usually applied to Letters Apostolic of the Pope. It is distinguished from the Bull chiefly from the form and nature of the instrument. They both have the same authority, but the Brief is generally shorter and deals often with matters of less importance, and it may be recalled or repressed at will. It is ordinarily written in the Latin character, has a wax seal attached bearing the impress of the so called "fisherman's ring,"—a figure of St. Peter fishing from a boat,—and is signed by the Secretary of Briefs. The form of the Brief, though now fixed by language, has varied in times past. (*Vide* BULLS.) In England the crown has from time immemorial issued Briefs for charitable purposes, which briefs are directed to be read among the notices after the recitation of the Nicene Creed after the Gospel. As the cost of issuing these briefs, though reduced very much from the previous charges, is still very great, they are not so frequently issued.

British Church, The. When or by whom Christianity was brought to Britain is unknown. As it was under the dominion of the Roman emperors until 409 A.D., it is probable that the Gospel was preached there as in other parts of the empire at a very early period. Direct evidence is wanting until the end of the second century. Clement of Rome, 90 A.D., mentions that St. Paul, before his martyrdom, had visited the boundary of the West (τὸ τέρμα τῆς δύσεως), but the expression is too indefinite to found an argument upon it. The identification of Claudia and Pudens mentioned by St. Paul (2 Tim. iv. 21) with a Roman family connected with the government of Britain is also very doubtful. The story of St. Joseph of Arimathea and his twelve companions, their coming to Glastonbury, and the holy thorn which sprang from his planted staff, is a mediæval legend. The earliest undoubted testimony to the existence of Christianity in Britain is that of Tertullian (b. 160), and as he says that the Gospel had in his time penetrated regions in the island which the Romans had not visited, it is clear that it was no new thing. To that period (177 A.D.) belongs the account of a British chief, Lucius by name, applying to the Bishop of Rome for Christian instruction. Very little can be collected from our scanty records with regard to the state of the Church in its earliest period, its extension, mode of government, or life. There were Bishops in the principal Roman towns, in which places there may have been some churches of Roman brick, but in most cases, away from those centres, such buildings as existed for purposes of Christian worship were constructed of wands or wattles in the ancient British fashion. But it does not appear that much progress had been made during the Roman period in the conversion of the great body of the population. That the Church had her martyrs here as elsewhere is shown by the story of Alban, converted by the Christian priest to whom he had in pity given shelter, and in whose stead he gave himself up to the persecutors. With his name are associated many others at the same period, the beginning of the fourth century, under the merciless Emperor Maximian. Bishops from Britain were present at the Council of Arles in France, 314 A.D., from York, London, and (probably) Caerleon. During the Arian controversy in the fourth century the steadfastness of the British Church is frequently referred to, though British Bishops at the Council of Ariminum (359 A.D.) assented with those more learned than themselves to the uncatholic formulary there adopted. But like the mass of those who were there misled, their weakness was but temporary. St. Jerome speaks of the British Christians of his time as sharing in the common enthusiasm for pilgrimages to the Holy Land. We obtain at this period some interesting glimpses of British Christianity shortly before the withdrawal of the Romans. In North Britain, near Dumbarton, we read of the Deacon Calpurnius, whose father, Potitus, was a priest, and his son the famous St. Patrick. Ninian, from Cumberland, is educated at Rome and returns in Episcopal orders to establish a mission on the coast of Galloway. Here he built his church on the promontory of Whithorn, which, being of stone instead of the more common wood, became renowned as the White House,—Candida Casa. This mission was a centre of light throughout the Roman province of Valentia. The heresy of Pelagius, or Morgan, the Briton, deeply affected his native country, and occasioned the mission from Gaul of the famous St. German and his companion, Lupus, who succeeded in stemming the tide of heresy, and seem to have done much good of other kinds. In this connection comes the story of the "Alleluia Victory," when a British army, mostly converted from paganism and baptized by German at the Easter festival just past, rose from ambush shouting "Alleluia," and put to rout an army of Picts and Saxons without striking a blow. During his mission in Britain, which included two visits (429 and 447 A.D.), German is said to have founded schools in Wales, and some old religious customs were always referred to him. This mission of St. German, the still earlier one of Victricius of Rouen, the fact that a Briton was the first Bishop of Rouen, the character of the earliest Liturgical remains, are facts which point to a Gallican origin for the British Church. The supposed proofs of an Eastern origin are without foundation, as will be seen hereafter.

In the fifth century came the labors of St. Patrick and the conversion of Ireland. The infant Church, owing to the circumstances of the case, assumed in Ireland, and afterwards in Scotland, through the mission of St. Columba, a peculiar form. The country was peopled by wild clans, each attached to its own chieftain, a type which remained longest in the Highlands of Scotland. The missionaries were compelled to direct their efforts first to the conversion of the chiefs, for without this nothing could be effected. Almost of necessity the monastic system became predominant. The Abbot occupied with reference to his society a position parallel with that of the chief to his clan, and, in fact, both characters were sometimes united in the same person. The consequence of this system in a country in which other centres did not exist was, that the Abbot exercised the chief religious control of the district in which his house was situated, and the position of Bishops was inferior to that which they occupied generally in the Catholic Church. This, which grew out of the necessities of the earliest missions, long remained a striking feature of Celtic Christianity in Ireland and Scotland, but a little later we see it disappearing and the Bishop assuming his more appropriate functions, when these missions spread into the north of England. It would be a mistake, however, to suppose that the essential functions of the Bishop were at any time lost sight of or usurped by the Abbot. The Bishop was always called upon to ordain, to give confirmation and the more solemn benediction, and to consecrate churches. A Bishop might be a member of a religious house, advanced perhaps to the Episcopal order for pre-eminent piety or learning. He would be subject, like the rest, to the Abbot, yet the Abbot never ventured to exercise any of his Episcopal functions. It would appear that there were in Ireland a great number of "village Bishops." To such a one St. Columba was sent for ordination, and found the good man plowing in his field. From such a system as this went forth some of the grandest missionaries the Christian Church has ever produced, through whom the conversion of Germany was well begun, that of paganized England mainly accomplished. Such a system was, in fact, far better suited for mission work among wild and barbarous tribes than to be the permanent form under which Christianity should occupy the land. We can only mention here the names of Columban and Gall, who labored in the Vosges and in Switzerland, Kilian and Vergilius in Germany, and many others their companions and associates It was the foundation of St. Columba in Scotland which became the chief source of light for England, as we see in following the history of early English Christianity.

Reviewing the interesting though scanty records of British Christianity, we easily discern, (1) That the supremacy or even the primacy of Rome was unknown. St. Columba and the other Irish missionaries treated the Pope with the respect due to the Bishop of the most important See in the West, but nothing more; they hesitated not to differ with him and to rebuke him in no measured terms. (2) We see Christianity assuming a unique form of external organization among the Irish and Northern Celts, which, however, is not seen among the Britons of the south until the Saxon conquest drives them into Wales. (3) Such characteristic marks as can be made out indicate a probable Gallic origin for early British Christianity, while that of North Britain and Ireland is derived from South Britain.

The Saxon Period, the Conversion of England.—During the century and a quarter from 449-577 A.D. Britain becomes England, and with this change Christianity is driven from the land, and the worship of Thor and Odin reigns supreme. The only account of this momentous change, from the British side, is that of Gildas, who shows fully the weak and divided condition of the mingled heathen and Christian Britons, which made them on the whole the easy prey of desultory conquest. The remnants recover some degree of strength and maintain themselves long after the conquest in Wales, Cornwall, and Strathclyde along the western coast. Christianity here undergoes a revival of earnestness aided perhaps by closer relations with the vigorous life of the Irish Church. Colleges and monasteries were founded in which religion and learning were fostered and kept alive. Such were the famous Bangor Isceod in Flintshire; St. Asaph, founded by St. Mungo (Munghu); at Llancarfan the college founded by St. Cadoc, who resigned a princely heritage for the religious life. Elsewhere the Angles and Saxons had occupied the land. The old Episcopal Sees had become centres of pagan worship. Then came the mission of Augustine and his monks (597 A.D.), sent by Pope Gregory, the one great mission which came forth from Rome itself. The missionaries landed at Thanet, where the fierce Jute had first stepped upon British soil. Kent was soon conquered for the Church and the See of Canterbury established, with Augustine for its first occupant. Essex followed, with Mellitus as first Bishop of London, from which, however, he was soon driven, and paganism resumed its sway. Paulinus, another member of the mission, became the Apostle of Northumbria under the patronage of King Edwin, and showed himself a faithful and unwearied missionary, but on the death of the king he too was driven out. Birinus, who came later under the auspices of Pope Honorius, converted the West Saxons.

The Celtic Missions.—But while the good work of the Roman missionaries was thus proceeding with many vicissitudes, an independent movement of even greater strength was setting in from the northward, and ten years after Paulinus was driven from York St. Aidan arrived to take up the work, from the great monastery of St. Columba at Iona. He established himself not at York, but, after the Celtic custom, selected a retired spot upon the coast, and founded the new House of Lindisfarne, from which went forth the men who were to convert all North and Middle England, that is, the greater part of the land. It was not long before the two elements, that from Rome and that from Scotland, came into collision. Augustine, acting under the direction of St. Gregory, had made an endeavor to arrive at an understanding with the British Bishops of the west of England, but failed of success, partly through his own want of tact, partly through their obstinate adherence to their own customs. This was at the meeting at Augustine's Oak near the Severn (600 A.D.). Here the points of difference between the Roman Church and the Celtic first came into view, from which it plainly appears that the latter knew nothing of the supremacy of Rome. The principal ground of difference was the time of the observance of Easter. There was also some difficulty in regard to the mode of baptism, but precisely what we have no means of knowing. A third point had reference to the tonsure. The first and last of these have often been adduced as proofs of the Eastern origin of British Christianity, but (1) the Celtic Easter was not the same with the Quortodeciman practice of Asia Minor, ascribed to St. John, according to which the festival was celebrated on the 14th Nisan, which might fall on any day of the week. The Celtic Easter must always fall upon a Sunday, but the cycle employed was simply the uncorrected cycle of an earlier time. Neither (2) was their tonsure like that of the East. The Greek tonsure was total, that of Rome was coronal, the Celtic shaved the anterior half of the head.

The next great occasion when these points of difference came in question was at the conference of Whitby, 664 A.D. This was not so much a contest between men as principles, since the leaders of the discussion on both sides were men who had been trained originally in the Celtic system. On the Celtic side was Colman, the successor of Aidan; on the Roman side the famous Wilfrid, then Abbot of Ripon. Wilfrid was a native of Northumbria, trained first at Lindisfarne, but afterwards with Benedict Biscop, the earliest Englishman who appears as a promoter of religious art, he had visited Rome and become filled with an enthusiastic determination to bring his earlier friends into accord with the usages of the Church at large, especially as represented by the mother-Church of the West, as she now claimed to be. The conference was held at Whitby, the famous monastery of St. Hilda, who had become the counselor of kings. Wilfrid gained the victory, and Colman with a part of his monks from Lindisfarne, and other followers, withdrew to Iona and afterwards to Ireland, where he died in 676 A.D. This conference and its results constitute an epoch in the history of English Christianity. The single-mindedness and saintly lives of these Celtic missionaries, their utter unworldliness, as Bede, himself a strong Roman sympathizer, describes it, might make us regret the triumph of the Roman system. Looking at the later development of the papal claims, we might be tempted to dream of a Church which, taking its rise independent of Rome, never submitted to her domination, and thus in the far West might have presented a parallel to the orthodox Church of the East. But such a result was probably impossible, when we consider the difficulties which the future history of England had in store for the Church. The Celtic Church was "devoid of that unifying power, that wonderful gift of order and organization which was the strength of the Roman," therefore it would not have enabled England "to endure the tremendous strain of the next four hundred years." As it was, it was the Church which gave England unity and the strength which comes from unity. After the withdrawal of Colman, Wilfrid was appointed Bishop of York, and went into Gaul for consecration. During his prolonged absence the Celtic party obtained a temporary victory, by persuading the king to appoint to the vacant bishopric Chad, one of the original disciples of Aidan at Lindisfarne. His consecration, which took place at Winchester, is interesting from the circumstance that Bishop Wini of that See, who had been consecrated in Gaul, obtained the assistance of two Bishops of British race from Cornwall, and thus in the person of Chad the two lines were united.

Another epoch in the history of England and its Church was the arrival of Theodore of Tarsus, an Eastern monk (669 A.D.), appointed and consecrated Archbishop of Canterbury by the Pope himself after the death of the nominee of the English kings, who had gone to Rome for consecration. Theodore, taking his seat at Canterbury, commenced his work by making a careful visitation of his whole province. He was the first Archbishop to whom all England submitted. One result of his visitation was the establishment of Wilfrid in the See of York, Chad quietly withdrawing to become, later, Bishop of Lichfield. But the great work of Theodore was the extension and organization of the Episcopate. According to high authority, "by his arrangement of Dioceses and the way in which he grouped them around the See of Canterbury, in his national Synods and ecclesiastical Canons, Theodore did unconsciously a political work." The spectacle of a Church at one, under one Archbishop, prepared the way for a united state under one king. The union of England was, however, very gradual, and only effected long after this time, when danger threatened from abroad. Theodore is also thought to have taken the first steps towards the establishment of the parochial system.

Schools and Learning.—Learning followed in the wake of Christian enlightenment. At the school of Canterbury, under Theodore, Hebrew, Greek, and Latin were taught. Here was trained Adhelm, Abbot of Malmesbury and Bishop of Sherborne, who zealously promoted the cause of education in Wessex, and composed many re-'igious songs in ballad form and in the Saxon tongue. He is to be remembered as the first Englishman who cultivated classical learning with success. He died 709 A.D. The poetry of Cædmon, a lay brother of Whitby, the great St. Hilda's monastery in the north, enabled Biblical lore to spread among the common people of the lowest class. By casting the Sacred Story and the Creed of Christendom into the simplest vernacular speech, the Faith was brought home to the hearts of serf and shepherd. Learning flourished most in the schools of Northumbria, especially at Jarrow and York. It was at Jarrow that Bede, called the Venerable, passed his life (b. about 673 A.D.). He is the true father of English literature, and through his many treatises made accessible to his countrymen all the knowledge of his day, sacred and profane; the first theologian and the first cultivator of science the English race ever produced. From the school of York came in the next century (b. 735 A.D.) the famous Alcuin, who spent many years at the court of Charlemagne, and aided in the great educational designs of that enlightened emperor. In Alfred the Great Christianized England produced the perfect king. "Alfred was the noblest, as he was the most complete embodiment of all that is great, all that is loveable in the English temper" (Green's English People). The first in the line of ecclesiastical statesmen who have played such a large part in English history was St. Dunstan. As virtual ruler of Wessex from 950–979 A.D., he did much by his firmness and strict even-handed justice to fuse the English people into one nation.

The Effects of Monasticism.—In the later Saxon period the glory of the earlier Church is obscured. The galaxy of saints and learned men who appeared at the period of the conversion of England and in the next age left few successors. Gradually a certain feebleness crept over the whole people which made them the easy prey, first of the Danes, then of the Normans. The cause of this was undoubtedly the abnormal development of monasticism. England, like all Northern Europe, was converted by monks,—those of the rule of St. Columba on the one hand, and of St. Benedict on the other. It was inevitable that monasticism should be strong, and it soon pervaded the whole of Anglo-Saxon life. Immense donations of land were conferred upon the monasteries, more than thirty kings and queens ended their days in the cloister, and from other walks of life an innumerable company. The grandest and most successful of all missionary agencies, monasticism becomes a heavy burden and a grave evil when it dominates the whole life of a nation. Asceticism, which has and ever must have its place, and that a most important place, in the Christian Church, is a fruitful source of error and corruption when it is attempted to make it the only allowable form of Christian life. The strength of the nation forsaking the work of common life to serve GOD in the cloistered walls, and ultimately to avoid the burden of duty laid upon them, was putting an end to progress, both in Church and State. The condition of things is well expressed by Dean Milman: "The Anglo-Saxon clergy, since the days of Dunstan, had produced no remarkable man. The triumph of monasticism had enfeebled without sanctifying the secular clergy. . . . It might conceal much gentle and amiable goodness; but its outward character was that of timid and unworldly ignorance, unfit to rule, and exercising but feeble and unbeneficial influence."

England and the Papacy.—It is important to trace, however briefly, the relation of the Church in England to the Papacy. We have seen, in reviewing the history of British Christianity, that the Britons seem to have had no knowledge of any kind of papal jurisdiction. It would seem to be equally true that in the early English (Anglo-Saxon) Church there was but little notion of the rule of Rome over other Churches as a matter of right and law. They by no means submitted to the Pope as possessing the headship and universal dominion over the Catholic Church. Yet none the less they owned his sway. It is a popular error to represent the Anglo-Saxon Christians as asserting independence of Rome and maintaining their rights as a branch of the Church. The simple truth is that the relation between Rome and England at that period did not rest upon a basis of claims and concessions; it did not wear a legal aspect. Such words as these indicate the prevailing sentiment: "Gregory, our father, who sent us baptism," "Though he be not an apostle to others, yet he is to us, for the seal of his apostleship are we in the LORD." Notwithstanding the fact that the greater part of England had first received the Gospel from Iona and Lindisfarne, there was, after the reconciliation and fusion of the two elements under the influence of Wilfrid and the wise measures of Theodore, a remarkable lack of any consciousness of an independent origin among the Christian people of England. They leaned to Rome as colonists to the mother-country, without thinking of raising any question as to what might some time be claimed as a matter of right. Their loyalty to the mother-Church was romantic and childlike. A pilgrimage to Rome was the dream of every Christian Englishman's heart. "From no other land did there flow into the papal exchequer such rich contributions." Yet practically the independence of the Church was little interfered with. Bishops were chosen without the papal intervention, though sometimes that intervention was invited, as in the case of Archbishop Theodore. But in general all ecclesiastical appointments were in the hands of the king. If we compare the position of the Church in the Anglo-Saxon period with that under the Norman kings, the difference does not consist in the greater devotion shown to the Papacy at the later epoch. The contrary is true. Doubtless the foreign ecclesiastics who poured into England at this time, filling its Sees and Benefices, brought with them the latest forms and observances which the Catholic religion had assumed, and a perceptible change of tone. But as regards the Papacy, we find that the common practice of the earlier period, which had rested only on custom, became express law. The dependence of the Church on the royal power was strictly enforced. Prelates were practically chosen by the king. Moreover, William the Conqueror would allow no papal letters to be received into the realm without his assent. He met the demands of Gregory VII. with a stern refusal. "Fealty I have never willed to do, nor will I do it now. I have never promised it, nor do I find that my predecessors did it to yours." Such principles were maintained by William and his successors, not for the good of the Church, but to strengthen their own power. Yet the practical result was the comparative independence on Rome of the realm and Church of England, and at most periods a considerable jealousy of papal encroachments. It seemed to many noble and devoted men far more natural that the Church should lean on Rome than be subject to the tender mercies of a tyrant at home, and, very different from our view, they often identified the "liberties of the Church" with subjection to the Pope. Yet a deep, underlying feeling of independence resided in the English people. When the most powerful of Popes, Innocent III., deposed even so evil a man as King John, the bull might have remained ineffectual, so far as the main body of the people were concerned, notwithstanding the great encouragement which it gave to all his enemies, public and private. When the king yielded and knelt before the papal legate, "He has become the Pope's man; he has forfeited the very name of king," was said to have been the indignant outcry of his subjects. This was the highest point which papal aggression ever reached in England. With the growth of a strong national spirit came resistance, often renewed and gradually embodied in the laws of the kingdom, to the papal claims (1) of a right to exact pecuniary contributions, (2) of ecclesiastical jurisdiction, as exhibited in appointments to Bishoprics and other Benefices, and in appeals from English courts. The "Constitutions of Clarendon," 1164 A.D., provided that elections of Bishops or Abbots should take place in the presence of the king's officers, and have the king's assent, and that no appeals should go further than the Archbishop without his consent, and to these measures the prelates gave their indorsement. In Henry III.'s time there was a rising throughout the kingdom against the papal collectors, and the barons for their part refused to aid the Pope in his contest with Frederick II. It was at this time, says Green, "that the little rift first opened which was destined to widen into the gulf which parted one from the other at the Reformation." As Parliament rises into importance, the jealousy of papal aggression is exhibited from time to time in no uncertain tones. In the reign of Edward III. (1327-1377 A.D.) Parliament utters distinct protests against the corrupt and injurious interference of the Pope with the affairs of the Church of England, and supports the king against the Pope in the contest with Scotland. When a papal interdict was laid upon Flanders, English priests said mass in that country with bold defiance. Papal legates were threatened with stoning when they landed in England. In 1343 A.D. the Commons petitioned against papal appointments to vacant livings in despite of the rights of patrons or of the crown, and the king complained to the Pope of the appointment of "foreigners, mostly suspicious persons," and reminds his Holiness that the successor of the Apostles was set over the LORD'S sheep to feed and not to shear them. The Parliament declared that they "neither could nor would tolerate such things any longer."

In 1351 A.D. the Statute of Provisors forbade any one to receive a papal provision or appointment; that is, a grant of the Pope superseding the right acquired by election, and conferring afresh the spiritual and temporal administration of See or Benefice. This practice had commenced in 1300 A.D., but had constantly been resisted. In 1353 A.D. the first of the celebrated statutes of "Præmunire" was passed, forbidding any appeal from the English courts, under pain of outlawry, perpetual imprisonment, or banishment from the land. Both these laws were reiterated at later periods. By the enlarged statute of Præmunire, passed in 1390 A.D., it was enacted that all persons procuring in the Court of Rome or elsewhere translations, processes, sentences of excommunication, bulls, instruments, or other things which touch the king, his crown, regality, or realm, should suffer the penalties of præmunire. "This act is one of the strongest defensive measures taken during the Middle Ages against Rome" (Stubbs). When Pope Urban V. referred to King John's submission and oath of fealty as the ground of his demands, it was declared by Parliament that John's submission had been made "without their assent and against his coronation oath," and they pledged themselves to resist such claims with all their power. That was the last ever heard of a papal over-lordship in the feudal sense over England. These statutes of Præmunire and Provisors remained the law of England, though allowed to fall into disuse when the policy of the Papacy avoided direct conflict, until in the hands of Henry VIII. they proved a weapon of tremendous power, and hardly any new legislation was necessary, but simply the execution of laws already long existing, to complete the independence of the English Church. Whatever theories of the Papacy may have been held by many or few and acted upon from time to time in England, however far at some epochs the leaders of the Church may have committed themselves to Rome's extreme claims, history shows that the assertion of those claims was resisted whenever they came in conflict with the national spirit, that the general drift of English sentiment was towards independence, and that the steps needful to achieve that independence were almost all taken one hundred and eighty years before it was at last effected. While we may admit the subjection of the English Church to the Papacy in ways more or less defined and admitted through the Middle Ages, the facts show that such subjection was not looked upon as a matter of Divine right, and that the extremest claims of Hildebrand were not admitted. The Papacy had its part to play under Divine Providence, in aiding the Church to resist the tyranny of kings, and when that work was done its power ceased in England. Even Sir Thomas More and those who thought with him were not troubled at the rejection of papal control: their opposition was to the royal assumption of supremacy over the Church.

Conclusion.—We may fitly conclude in the words of Dean Church: " The lesson of history, I think, is this, *not* that all the good which might have been hoped for to society has followed from the appearance of the Christian religion in the forefront of human life; *not* that in this willful and blundering world, so full of misused gifts and wasted opportunities and disappointed promise, mistake and mischief have never been in its train; *not* that in the nations where it has gained a footing it has mastered their besetting sins, the falsehood of one, the ferocity of another, the characteristic sensuality, the characteristic arrogance of others. But history teaches us this: that in tracing back the course of human improvement we come, in one case after another, upon Christianity as the source from which improvement derived its principle and its motive; we find no other source adequate to account for the new spring of amendment; and, without it, no other sources of good could have been relied upon."

Authorities: Bede's Ecclesiastical History (trans. in Bohn's Library), Irish Primitive Church, by Daniel De Vinné, St. Patrick's Confession (Migne), Murray's Ireland and her Church, Bright's Early English Church, Archbishop Trench's Lectures on Mediæval Church History, Maclear's Conversion of the Celts, Maclear's Conversion of the English, Churton's Early English Church, Green's History of the English People, Stubbs' Constitutional History of England.

Rev. Prof. W. J. Gold.

Bull. The name given to the Letters of the Pope, whose authority, whether for temporary or constitutional purposes, is paramount. The name is taken from the leaden seal (*Bulla*) attached by a silken string (if it be a Bull of Grace) or by a hempen cord (if it be a Bull of Justice). This globular seal bears upon one side the representation of the Apostles SS. Peter and Paul, and on the other the name of the reigning Pontiff. The Bull is issued from the papal Chancery. There are also Consistorial Bulls; *i.e.*, those issued by the advice and consent of the Cardinals in Consistory, by whom they are signed. The matter of the Bull may be of comparatively private nature, or it may relate to public matters of a nation, or of an order, or it may be binding upon the whole Roman obedience, or it may lay down certain constitutional principles, as did the famous Bull *Unam Sanctam.*

Burial. While it was customary among the heathen, yet the whole surroundings accompanying the act of burial among Christians were so marked and so reverent, that they stamped the rite as Christian. Julian, the apostate emperor, 363 A.D., acknowledged that austerity of life, hospitality, and reverent burial of the dead were the powerful influences that gave Christians the conversion of the empire. It had its motive in the faith in the Resurrection, and, therefore, the body that God would so care for as to bring again from its dust must be reverently laid away. To attack this loving care of the Christian for the remains of his loved one was a controlling cause why so many martyrs were burnt by heathen magistrates. The honorable burial of our Lord's Body by Joseph of Arimathea was the pattern upon which the Christian based his care of his dead. But in times of persecution it was not always possible to bestow this care, and interment was often very hurried. Yet when Polycarp was burnt, his bones and ashes were gathered up, without hindrance, by the brethren. To be buried beside the remains of a martyr was always accounted honorable. At first burials were made anywhere it was most convenient outside of the city, as burials within were illegal. But care was had to obtain, whenever possible, a cemetery of their own, and their right to it was generally conceded. At Alexandria they had them openly. In Rome, where the soil was such that subterranean burial could be carried out, the Christians dug out those underground galleries—already begun by the heathen—for burial purposes, and these catacombs became places of refuge of safe meeting as well as of burial, since the tunnels as they were dug out ramified so as to form an underground labyrinth. When peace came, churches were frequently erected upon the tombs of saints. The early Christians, whenever they could do so, made their burial rites contrast notably with those of the heathen. The body was kept unburied as long as convenient. It was decently prepared for burial by the friends and relatives, not by hired persons, swathed in linen with decent orderliness. It was laid out either at the house or in the church. The watchers over it sang hymns and anthems. They buried in open day, with something of triumphal pomp, with hymns of hope and faith and scriptural anthems. When the grave was reached these hymns and prayers were renewed, and an address closed the service.

Burial rites must vary very much with the circumstances and with the development of the people, but the simpler and plainer a Christian burial can be conducted the better it is. Two chief things should be made prominent, the faith in the future Resurrection and the loving care which for CHRIST'S sake we should show the dead. The history of the Order for the Burial of the Dead is simple and clear. It has little relation to the ancient offices, taking from the Sarum use the first two opening sentences, and adding the third. The corpse was to be carried either to the church or the grave at once, apparently customarily to the grave. Then the noble anthem, "Man that is born of woman," was recited. Its use here was peculiar to the English Prayer-Book. It was to be said either by the priest alone or together with the clerks. The priest was to cast the earth upon the body in the first Prayer-Book (1549 A.D.); this was changed to the present use in the second Prayer-Book (1552 A.D.). The sentence of committal, as also the final prayer, expressed a strong hope in the blessedness of the deceased. In the first Prayer-Book, if the body was borne to the grave at once, the Psalms cxvi., cxxxix., cxlvi., were to be recited in the church afterwards, together with the Lesson (1 Cor. xv. 20 sq.), and then the suffrages and a final prayer were recited. The second Prayer-Book apparently, after the anthem, "I heard a voice," ordered the Lesson to be read at the grave, and then, with the Kyries and the LORD'S Prayer, closed with the final prayers nearly as in our Prayer-Book. The Prayer-Book of 1662 A.D. rearranged this material into the present order, which, with important verbal changes, we follow. These verbal changes consist in an entire omission of any reference to hopes especially for the deceased, the dropping of the Kyries, and the continuous recital of the two Psalms (xxxix. and xc.), whereas the Gloria is placed at the end of each Psalm in the English Prayer-Book.

This order for the Burial of the Dead is unapproached in simple and severe grandeur and lofty faith and perfect harmony with only what is revealed to us in Holy Scripture. Its clear proclamation of the RESURRECTION, its freedom from all that men may *wish* to believe, however naturally, yet without clear warrant, its solemn lesson to the living, make it a most noble office. And yet no office in the Prayer-Book has so many of its rubrics systematically violated, in ordinary cases at least. Comparatively little watchfulness is used to observe the rubric as to those who can have the office read over them. The anthem shall be said or sung *while* the corpse is made ready for the grave, not after it is placed. It is not incumbent on the minister to recite it by himself. The purpose evidently is to have the choir or the assembled friends recite it. This is true also of the other anthem, "I heard a voice." Then the minister *alone* should recite the LORD'S Prayer. Much of the impressiveness and solemnity of this beautiful office is lost by these infractions of the rubric.

Burse. The case for the fair linen cloth with which the elements are to be covered when all have communed.

C.

Cabala. The mystic theosophy of the later speculative Jewish schools. Its contents are much older than its written documents, which apparently date from the tenth century, though these are attributed to a much later age. The Cabala is based upon a mystic and allegorizing arithmetic, which is arbitrarily applied to the doctrine of the nature and attributes of GOD. It had its uses, doubtless, in counteracting the grosser anthropomorphic teachings of the Talmud, beside which it seems to have flowed in a parallel and distinct channel, though probably the Rabbi of the Talmud was also a master of the Cabala. It may indirectly have had a great influence in the allegorizing tendency in the interpretation of Holy Scripture, which overreached itself in the Church. The tendency to a mystical interpretation has always been very great in both the older Jewish, and in the Christian Church, based, indeed, upon the sanction and example of our LORD and of St. Paul, but running to a most absurd excess. The Cabala has many points of contact with Gnosticism. It was essentially pantheistic. That it should have some points of agreement with Christian doctrine is to be anticipated, yet they are very few. It supplied Philo, probably, with the idea of the Logos which prepared the way for understanding the revelation of the Word of GOD. It seems to hold to a triple condition of our soul,—the intellectual, the moral, and the spiritual energy of our life. The freedom of will in fallen man is asserted.

Calendar. A table of the order of days in the year, such as is prefixed to our Prayer-Book. The earliest tables of this class were very ancient, being civil as well as ecclesiastical. There is, however, combined with this calendar ecclesiastically a catalogue of the saints whose commemorations fall upon fixed days in the civil year. Our own calendar is a most admirably simple and clear arrangement for practical use. The following outline gives but the chief points. A thorough discussion would require a volume. The word calendar is derived from the Old Latin *caleo*, to call, from the custom of having the Pontifex announce to the people, called together, the holy days. Later the practice of posting in public places the proper holidays came in; hence the title *calendæ*, and in late Latin *calendarium*. The division of days was necessarily solar; that of weeks by Divine law. The months were originally lunar. Now it is remarkable that these three modes of marking time have no common divisor, yet are constantly commingled. It causes a great deal of embarrassment, and yet there is no means of making a change. By intercalations and arbitrary enactments points of time for new eras can be arranged as it was by Julius Cæsar or by Pope Gregory XIII. (1582 A.D.), or restorations effected as the several rectifications of the calculation for Easter; but these three incommensurable measures of time are unalterable.

To us the week is practically the most important, but as it is incommensurable with the 365 days 6 hrs. 48′ 46″ of the actual solar year, there must be some mode by which we can connect the two without confusing them. This was simply done by using the first seven letters of the alphabet for the days of the week, marking the 1st day of January as A, and so on. The letter for the 31st of December is A. Now as Sunday does not fall yearly in the same place, each letter becomes in its turn the Sunday letter. If Sunday fall on January 1, as it will in 1899 A.D., then A will be the Sunday letter. Again, if there be a leap-year, as the day intercalated falls between the 28th of February and the 1st of March, the Sunday letter with which the year begins, as, for instance, in 1896 A.D., E, will fall back, as in the date just given, to D, for the Sunday letter being E, and the 29th of February lettered D, as also March 1 is lettered D, the intercalated day is as it were a *dies non* in the calendar, but carries back the Sunday letter. So that the 23d of February being E in 1896, the eighth day after is March 1, which is lettered D, and this will be the letter for the rest of the year. Whenever the Sunday letter for any year is found, the date of any given day of the week can be readily found in the calendar by this simple contrivance.

The rule to find the Sunday letter for the remainder of this century is very clear, and is thus given in the first of the Tables for finding Easter-day: "To find the Dominical or Sunday Letter, according to the Calendar, until the year 1899, inclusive, add to the year of our LORD its fourth part, omitting fractions, divide the sum by 7, and if there be no remainder, then A is the Sunday Letter; but if any number remain, then the Letter standing against that number in the small annexed Table is the Sunday Letter.

0	A
1	G
2	F
3	E
4	D
5	C
6	B

"NOTE.—That in all Bissextile or Leap-Years, the Letter found as above will be the Sunday Letter from the intercalated day to the end of the year."

But it was a small part of the work to arrange the Dominical Letter. A more difficult work was to adjust the proper time for the celebration of Easter. Since Easter was the Christian Feast standing in historical relation to the Jewish Passover, it was necessarily governed by similar rules. Then Easter, as did the Passover, depended on the full moon, or, rather, on the fourteenth day of the moon. The Council of Nice, 325 A.D., laid down four postulates concerning it:

I. That the 21st of March must be taken as the day of the vernal equinox.

II. That the full moon happening upon or next after the 21st of March is to be taken for the full moon of the month Nisan.

III. That the next Lord's Day next after that full moon is to be observed as Easter Day.

IV. But if the full moon fall on a Sunday, the next Sunday is to be Easter Day.

But these are calendar, not astronomical full moons, since the lunar cycle being 29.5305 days, the equation proposed by the golden cycle of Meton of alternate twenty-nine and thirty days was not accurate enough after a lapse of time, and this slight error every nineteen years was sufficient to produce a serious inconvenience after a time. It was with some trouble that the corrections were effected. The Paschal term is that period within which the moon can pass through her lunation before and immediately after the vernal equinox. The Paschal moon is new at the earliest on March 8, so that it is full on the 21st (both days being counted),—that is, fourteen days after. But should the full moon fall after the 21st, the latest date is April 18, since from March 8 to April 5 is twenty-nine days, and April 18 is the latest full moon, so that the latest Sunday on which Easter can fall is April 25. Easter-day, then, may fall on any Sunday between March 22 and April 25, both inclusive, immediately after a full moon. Since, then, the calendar date of the full moon may be three days even different from the astronomical full moon, the two modes of calculation do not always coincide. The reason for this discrepancy is not far to seek, since the new moon from which both Jew and Christian counted was not the one obtained by calculation, but by observation. But the calculation of the calendar moon depended upon the Epact, which was the name given to the number of days' difference between the current *lunar* months and the solar year. The difference is eleven days. At the beginning of the cycle the year and the new moon coincide; but at the end of the solar year the moon is eleven days old. At the end of the second solar year the difference is twenty-two days. At the end of the third year it is only three days,—*i.e.*, thirty-three days minus the thirty days of a full lunation. At the end of the cycle of nineteen years the same order recurs. Since the true lunar month is 29.5308 days, to allow thirty days to a lunation is too much; therefore upon February, April, June, August, September, and November two epacts are assigned to a certain day in each of these months. This device serves to keep the error within bounds. The principal use of the Epact is to enable one to find the age of the moon at any required date of the given year, and of course its chief use is to determine the Paschal moon. The rule is, (1) Add together the day of the month given and the Epact, to be found in the third table in the Prayer-Book; (2) if the date given is after March, add the number of the month from March inclusive, and the sum is the required age of the moon. Let us take 1896 A.D. Easter-day for that year would be thus calculated: Since an Easter can fall between March 22 and April 25, let us choose April 1 on which to find the moon's age. The Epact for 1896 is 15; therefore,

April 1.............................	1
Epact................................	15
March and April.................	2
	—
	18

The moon will be eighteen days old on April 1. It was full, therefore, on March 29, and April 5 will be Easter-day.

The Golden Number was really the same cycle as the Epact, *i.e.*, one of nineteen years; but there was made no provision for the hour and a half of gain in each lunation, which amounted to about a day in three hundred and twelve years. Therefore, when the Calendar was rectified in the English Church in 1752, the Golden Number was set aside practically, and the Epact substituted. For the order of the Golden Number was fixed by law, and could not be moved to its true place in the column whenever the error by increment became serious; so it was dropped and the Epact was substituted, which could be placed opposite its true place in the cycle. The Golden Number is apparently different from the Epact, as will be seen:

Epact	0	11	22	3	14	25	6	17	28	9
Golden Number	1	2	3	4	5	6	7	8	9	10
Epact	20	1	12	23	4	15	26	7	18	
Golden Number	11	12	13	14	15	16	17	18	19	

But the fact is that the Golden Number needed the Epact originally; and if the Table of Lessons for March and April be examined a series of strangely arranged numbers will be noted. These are the Golden Numbers, marking the days upon which the full moons can fall in those months, so that the year on which the Golden Number points out the full moon being found, the Sunday letter following such Golden Number is Easter-day. Take, again, the year 1896 A.D. The Epact is 15, the Golden Number corresponding is 16. This is set opposite March 29 as the date of the full moon. Easter-day will, therefore, fall on April 5. These computations were necessary to procure an accurate mode for finding Easter-day; yet there will always be a variation from the astronomical full moon, since it is not possible in an ecclesiastical calendar to make provision for the minute errors which the loss of a few moments or seconds will produce in the lapse of centuries. Therefore a rectification must always be made at stated periods.

Easter determines the dates of all the Movable Feasts and Fasts which precede and follow it. Upon Easter depend the number of Sundays after Epiphany, the date of Septuagesima, Sexagesima, and Quinquagesima Sundays, Ash-Wednesday, Good-Friday, which precede, and Ascension-day, Whit-Sunday, and Trinity-Sunday, which follow, Easter-day, and necessarily the number of Sundays after Trinity are also thus determined. Except for the Immovable Feasts, which follow the solar calendar, all ecclesiastical calculations follow the Mosaic precept to regulate the feasts by the moon.

In fact, no proposed calendar can so well meet all the difficulties and nice adjustments required as the one we now use. It is a memorable example of the truth that GOD's ordinances are immutable. The French attempted to substitute a new calendar during the Revolution; but they had, in less than twelve years, to revert to the Church Calendar, which is based upon Jewish Law, which, again, is based upon the ordinance: "And GOD said, Let there be lights in the firmament of the heaven to divide the day from the night; and let them be for signs, and for seasons, and for days, and for years. . . . And GOD made two great lights" (Gen. i. 14, 16).

Under any system of chronology whatever each historian is inexorably bound by the conditions of Jewish computation, both because it is so universally received that he cannot escape it, and because, with all the difficulties attending calculations under it, it conforms to natural terms of time. Many facts of ancient history depend (to take but a single instance) upon the calculation of eclipses for their verification.

Calendar of Saints. *Vide* MARTYROLOGY.

California, Diocese of, 1850-1884. The first Convention was held in Trinity Church, San Francisco, in July (1850 A.D.), for the purpose of organizing the Diocese of California. The opening sermon was preached by the Rev. Dr. Ver Mehr, and the Rev. Flavel L. Mines was appointed chairman.

It is a fact in history that the early founders of the Church on this coast had no idea of uniting with the General Church at the East. There is no recognition of it in any of their proceedings. They ignored the name of "Protestant Episcopal," and called their organization the "Church in California." Knowing that while in this position no Bishop would be consecrated for them, the question was discussed of attempting to procure the Episcopate from the Greek Church. Abandoning this idea, the Convention elected as their Bishop the Rt. Rev. Bishop Southgate, who, having been consecrated to a foreign mission, had lately returned. He, however, declined the invitation. Three years passed away, during which time nothing further was done to organize the Church. In this time the Rev. Mr. Mines, the first minister to the coast and the first rector of Trinity, the mother-church of the Diocese, had been removed by death. The so-called parishes of Marysville, Stockton, and Sacramento had hardly an existence, and there were but two live parishes,—Trinity and Grace, of San Francisco, these constituting the "Diocese of California"

In October, 1853 A.D., the General Convention met in New York, and the wants of this coast soon claimed their attention. Ignoring most wisely the past action of the Diocese, which was not in accord with the majority of Churchmen in California, the General Convention decided to appoint a Missionary Bishop for California. The election was held in the House of Bishops, and the Rev. William Ingraham Kip, D.D., rector of St. Paul's Church, Albany, was nominated. The election was so unanimous, and the voice of the church so urgent, the Rev. Dr. Kip accepted the nomination, and was consecrated in Trinity Church, New York, on October 28, Festival of SS. Simon, Jude, 1853 A.D. The sermon was preached by Bishop Burgess, of Maine, and perhaps it will not be out of place in this brief history to give a few words or passages of that eloquent and touching sermon, for in the thirty years that have passed it seems like the fulfilling of prophecy:

"In this foremost temple of the great mart and metropolis of this new Western world we are assembled for a work which cannot be without fruit in distant days and in distant regions. From this spot, and from the act we are about to accomplish, the course, if Providence favors it, is straight to the Golden Gate, which opens towards Eastern Asia. He who shall enter there as the first Protestant Bishop will see before him the land which is the treasure-house of the republic. Behind it are the vales and rivers and snowy mountains, which are to our Far West the Farther West. And amidst them lie the seats of that abominable and sensual impiety, the cry of which goes up to heaven, like that of Sodom and Gomorrah from the valley of the Dead Salt Sea. Still beyond spread the deserts which divide, but which will not long divide, the Christians of this Continent.

"Upon the edge of the vast field he will stand when he shall place his foot on the shore of the Pacific. There he is to be occupied in laying the foundations of a Church which must be a pillar and ground of the truth for wide lands and for unborn millions.

"Few of the issues can he live to witness. But in the years to come, if years are given him, he must recall the prospects which opened upon him in this hour, and again when he first saw the coast of that Western ocean."

To the Bishop-elect: "Yours is an Episcopate to be exercised where fellow-laborers are still to be gathered, where seminaries are yet to be founded, where congregations are mostly to be begun. You go where thirst for gold, impatience of restraint, the vices of adventurers, and all the ills of unavoidable lawlessness have been before you; where the softening influence of old age and of childhood can as yet be little known, and where female piety throws but a small measure of its familiar light over the surface and face of society. A lover of the world, a pleaser of men, a reed shaken by the wind, has nowhere his place among the standard-bearers of CHRIST; but least of all on such an outpost beleaguered by temptations."

These passages help to show not only the magnitude of the work before the first Bishop of California, but the peculiar difficulties to encounter.

At the time of his arrival, January 29, 1854 A.D., there was but one clergyman, Rev. Dr. Wyat, rector of Trinity, actively engaged in parochial work. Rev. Dr. Clark was prevented by age from assuming the duties of a parish, and Dr. Ver Mehr, who was nominally rector of Grace Church, was engaged most of the time with his school at Sonoma.

At the first Convention held by the Bishop, three months after his arrival, there were but three parishes represented, Trinity and Grace, of San Francisco, and St. John's parish, Stockton, and the latter existed only on paper.

In December, 1856 A.D., the Diocese having strength enough to elect a Bishop, a special Convention was called for that purpose. It met in Sacramento, February 5, 1857 A.D. There were nine clergy present, and nine parishes represented, when the Rt. Rev. William Ingraham Kip, D.D., the

Missionary Bishop, was unanimously elected Bishop of the Diocese of California.

In 1874 A.D. the Diocese, by consent of General Convention, was divided, and the northern portion set off as the Missionary Jurisdiction of Northern California, of which the Rt. Rev. J. H. D. Wingfield, D.D., is its Missionary Bishop.

Instead of two parish ministers, as thirty years ago, now, with the northern portion of the State taken off, there are still about seventy on the list.

Never in its history has the Church in California been more prosperous than at the present. In sympathy, in Churchmanship, in loyalty, and devotion the clergy are united. Older parishes are awaking to the great work before them, while new missions, soon to be parishes, are springing up all over the Diocese.

To Eastern people trained in the Church and Church principles it might seem that the progress here has been slow, and that with all the reputed great wealth of California there should be Church institutions, largely endowed, springing up and reaching out aggressively all over the broad State. But very little of this great wealth is in the hands of Church people, and the Church is comparatively poor, and it has been a hand to hand struggle at times barely to exist.

In such a mixed population, the ends of the earth thrown together in a lump, as it were, with all shades of religion and no religion, one might well exclaim, "Who is sufficient for these things?" Yet amid the lawlessness, even in its early history, there have always been some noble souls doing valiant service for CHRIST and His Church. There have been earnest, self-denying souls going about doing good humbly, not to be seen of men, whose reward will one day come from Him in whose memory "no good deed is ever lost." Many a pioneer Churchman, of both clergy and laity, will be of those who shall be had "in everlasting remembrance."

The Women's Missionary Society of the Diocese (Auxiliary) is doing a good work, and many of our missionaries are cheered by their timely gifts and thoughtful care, while the little chapel is beautiful in its chancel furnished from the same source. With nearly every parish there is connected a Parish or Rectors' Aid Society, whose visits to the sick and sorrowing, together with substantial aid, do much to teach people of a living, loving CHRIST, as well as a living Church.

Trinity, the mother-parish, is a sort of rallying-point. Every year in our Diocesan Convention she welcomes the scattered children and bids them come once more around her altar. Beneath the chancel of this church rests all that is mortal of the first minister of our Church to the coast, the Rev. Flavel L. Mines.

Grace, formerly called the Cathedral, in which the Bishop labored for many years, and twice saved from the sheriff's hammer, stands upon what is called Grace Church or Nob Hill, and can be seen for many blocks around, as though inviting all to come and worship.

Advent, the down-town church, is next in age. It has its guilds, its brotherhoods, and its great army of choristers; its doors stand open to the weary laborer, as though saying, Come in and rest and pray, for this is the house of prayer.

St. John's, St. Paul's, St. Luke's, St. Stephen's, and St. Peter's,—this cluster of saints in these churches are in a certain way children of the older parishes, and are all doing good work for the Church.

Of the Church institutions, there is the Old Ladies' Home. The building was formerly used as St. Luke's Hospital; clean, bright, and truly home-like, it is admirably managed, some four ladies from each parish constituting the board. It is emphatically a Home, and its inmates, some forty in number, are tenderly cared for and their declining years made happy by watchful care and the comforting services of the Church.

The Diocese is well supplied with Church schools. I will not mention the very excellent institutions of Benicia, as they come under another head, viz., the Jurisdiction of Northern California. In this Diocese we have, as one of the oldest Church schools, St. Matthew's Hall, San Mateo, Rev. A. L. Brewer, Principal and Rector, founded in 1865 A.D. with but three pupils, until its rolls number about one hundred, and full. The school in all its appointments is well arranged; the stone church covered with ivy, the shaded walks and profusion of flowers, make a picture, one of the most *beautiful* in beautiful California. Independent of the thorough training, the thorough drill, and manly bearing of the cadets, the refining, Christianizing influence thrown around the boys is an education in itself.

Trinity School, in San Francisco, Rev. E. B. Spalding, Principal, though but five or six years in existence, has made splendid progress, and does great credit to its founder and instructors.

Irvin School for Young Ladies, in San Francisco, Rev. E. B. Church, Principal, is steadily growing in favor, as it so well deserves

There are also Church schools at San José, Santa Cruz, Alameda, and Oakland, so that our Diocese is not only well supplied with Church schools, but can be congratulated on their high character and efficiency.

Many of those who helped to lay the foundation of the Church in California have passed to their reward,—"they rest from their labor, and their works follow them." Our good Bishop, after thirty years of faithful doing, is still hale and erect, and as the years pass on is more and more beloved by his people. In "journeyings often" he visits every parish and mission in the Diocese every year, and some of them, as they call upon him, much more frequently, and among all the changes that have occurred in this changing population is a living oracle, a perpetual parish and diocesan register.

The future historian will look upon this little sketch of the Church in 1884 A.D. as in still greater contrast than in that first Convention thirty-one years ago.

Statistics for 1886 A.D. : Clergy, 65; parishes, 24; missions, 26; ordination diac., 2; priest, 1; baptisms, 826; confirmed, 502; com., 4892; contr., $134,944.75.

REV. W. L. GITHENS.

Call. *Vide* VOCATION.

Calvinism. The system of theology of John Calvin (1509-1564 A.D.). It was based upon Augustine's system of Predestination, but was far more systematic, and was based less upon the control of the Incarnation over men than the subordination of the Incarnation and Atonement to the logical exigencies of a strict dogma of Predestination. Calvin was a master of logic, and impressed his conclusions upon many who studied his works. His system affected many who did not agree with him in his ecclesiastical theories, and Calvinism is held by a great number who are by no means in sympathy with him, simply because it expresses most logically for them the conclusions to be drawn from GOD'S justice, prescience, and omniscience. The error lies, not in urging these, but in unconsciously subordinating to them the Atonement and its consequences to all men. In this as in so many other things, the Church does not interfere with any private opinions that are not pushed to the extent of breaking down the Articles of the Creed and to the practical denial of any part of the teachings of Holy Scripture upon the only true principle laid down in the XX. Article: "The Church hath power to decree Rules or Ceremonies and authority in controversies of Faith, and yet it is not lawful for the Church to ordain anything that is contrary to GOD'S Word written, neither may it so expound one place of Scripture that it be repugnant to another. Wherefore, although the Church be a witness and a keeper of Holy Writ, yet, as it ought not to decree anything against the same, so, besides, the same ought it not to enforce anything to be believed for necessity of salvation." Therefore, though men may by force of their individual temperaments need to form systems, the Church cannot form any system of theology other than the breadth of Scripture and the Creed allow. Calvin's extreme notions, or rather statements, are not now so tenaciously held as formerly. The Five Points of Calvinism, as they are called, are,—

I. That GOD has chosen a certain number in CHRIST to everlasting glory before the foundation of the world, according to His immutable purpose and of His free grace and love, without the least foresight of faith, good works, or any conditions performed by the creatures, and that the rest of mankind He was pleased to pass by and ordain them to dishonor and wrath for their sins, to the praise of His vindictive justice.

II. That JESUS CHRIST by His sufferings and death made an Atonement only for the sins of the elect.

III. That mankind are totally depraved in consequence of the Fall; and by virtue of Adam's being their public head the guilt of his sin was imputed, and a corrupt nature conveyed to his posterity, from which proceeds all actual transgression: and that by sin we are made subject to death, and all miseries, temporal, spiritual, and eternal.

IV. That all whom GOD has predestinated to life He is pleased in His appointed time effectually to call by His Word and Spirit out of that state of sin and death in which they are by nature to grace and salvation in JESUS CHRIST.

V. That those whom GOD has effectually called and sanctified by His Spirit shall never finally fall from a state of grace.

The older Calvinists strenuously defended these propositions, but at the present day they are held in a much modified form.

Candlemas. An old name for the Feast of the Purification of Saint Mary the Virgin (February 2). It was customary in the mediæval Church upon this feast to bear in procession, and to place in the church, a large number of lighted candles, typifying the description in the Song of Simeon of the LORD JESUS,—"a light to lighten the Gentiles, and the glory of Thy people Israel;" hence the name Candlemas-day. Alcuin (790 A.D.) speaks of the custom; St. Bernard also (1153 A.D.). (*Vide* FEASTS.)

Canon. Apparently it is a name given to an officer in the Cathedral staff—a member of the Chapter—who held the same general rank as the Prebend. They with the Prebends had their several duties in the services and care of the Cathedral. Possibly the Prebend enjoyed the income from a special endowment or estate, while the Canon was maintained out of the common income of the Cathedral. However that may have been, Canons and Prebends are now merged into the single title of Canons. They are members of, and vote in, the Cathedral Chapter. (*Vide* CHAPTER.) Minor Canons are not of the Chapter. They ought to be all priests, skilled in Church music, and are responsible for the decent and solemn celebration of divine service in daily rotation.

Canon. The term is from the Greek Canon, and means a rule or law, or the term is used generally for Canon Law,—*i.e.*, the rule of the Church; Canon of Scripture, *i.e.*, the books which the Church accepts as inspired and as binding; Canon of the Liturgy, *i.e.*, the rule for the celebration of the Holy Communion, which usually begins with the versicle, Lift up your hearts (*Sursum Corda*).

Canon Law. All the legislation of the Church, enacted by her own spiritual right, has from the first been embodied in *Canons*,— a word derived from the Greek, and signifying *Rules*. The earliest example of these Canons is found in the Acts of the Apostles, where by open consultation, free discussion, and joint action of Apostles, Elders, and Brethren (or, as we should now say, "Bishops, Clergy, and Laity"), the first Canons were made. At no time in the history of the Christian Church has any *individual*—not even the Pope—undertaken to enact *Canons* by his sole authority. The *collective* nature of the act, enduring to the present day, is an indisputable proof of the *collective* character of the law-making power from the beginning.

There are *three* distinct sources of Canon Law for us,—*Œcumenical, Anglican*, and *American*.

I. The Œcumenical Canons, besides those already alluded to in the Acts of the Apostles, include,—

1. The Apostolic Canons,—a body of eighty-five Canons, of unknown antiquity, but certainly in large measure embodying the rules of action taught everywhere by the Apostles themselves, though also with marks of later additions. The first two, brief as they are, have been the rule of all branches of the Apostolic Church in all ages: "Canon I. Let a Bishop be ordained by two or three Bishops." "Canon II. Let a Presbyter, or Deacon, and the other clergy, be ordained by one Bishop." These, as well as many others of the most important of these ancient Canons, are embodied in the "Digest" of the American Church.

2. The Canons passed by the undisputed General Councils. By the Council of Nice 20; by the first Council of Constantinople 7; by the Council of Ephesus 8; by the Council of Chalcedon 30;—these 65 Canons are of highest authority.

3. Besides these, the Council of Chalcedon gave Œcumenical approval to the Canons of several Provincial Synods, as follows: of Ancyra, 25 Canons; of Neo-Cæsarea, 15; of Gangra, 20; of Anticch, 25; of Laodicea, 60. The last of these Laodicean Canons is the earliest that settles the number of the books to be received as Holy Scripture. This entire body of Œcumenical law lies at the basis of the working system of the Church in all ages, though naturally some portions of these Canons have become obsolete through the many changes of time and circumstance.

II. The Anglican Canons. The Canons adopted in various Provincial Synods in England—Lyndwood enumerates *fifteen*—before the Reformation remained in force until 1603 A D., and *still* continue to be of force, except where subsequent legislation has expressly altered them. Of these Dr. Hook says, "The above Canons, made by our Church before the Reformation, are, of course, binding on our Church now, and are acted upon in the Ecclesiastical Courts, except where they are superseded by subsequent Canons, or by the provisions of an Act of Parliament." Blunt's "Book of Church Law" says, "The Canons passed up to the fifteenth century were collected by William Lyndwood (Archdeacon of Canterbury, and afterwards Bishop of St. David's) in a work called 'Provinciale,' of which the best edition is that printed at Oxford in 1679. They were published in English in Johnson's 'Collection of all the Ecclesiastical Laws, Canons, Answers, or Rescripts . . . of the Church of England,' the original edition of which was printed in 1720 A.D., and a revised one, edited by Baron, in 1850 A.D. Wilkins's 'Concilia Magnæ Britanniæ' contains all such documents down to 1717 A.D. Ayliffe's 'Parergon Juris Canonici Anglicani,' or, a Commentary by way of Supplement to the Canons and Constitutions of the Church of England,—a valuable work, the character of which is indicated by its title, was published in 1734 A.D. An entirely new and most trustworthy edition of Wilkins's 'Concilia' has lately been issued from the Clarendon Press under the editorship of Professor Stubbs and the Rev. A. W. Haddon."

Besides the above, there was the immense "Corpus Juris Canonici," the accumulated conglomeration of Church law as set forth by the Popes. In addition to the ancient Canons, it contains the decrees of Popes and Fathers of the Church, a large part of which are acknowledged forgeries. As edited under Gregory XIII. the bulk of the two massive folio volumes in fine print consists of the *Decretum* of Gratian, the *Decretals* of Gregory IX., the *Decretals* of Boniface VIII., the *Clementine Constitutions* (Clement V.), the *Extravagantes* of John XXII., and the *Extravagantes Communes*. In England the adoption of this Roman Canon Law was never unrestricted or unreserved. More than once the attempt to introduce it was successfully resisted; one such attempt bringing from the barons the famous reply, *Nolumus leges Angliæ mutari*. Subject to the admitted superiority of English law, however, many rules of the Roman Canon Law have been incorporated with the English, and the English courts have in recent times decided cases on no other authority than that of a Canon of the fourth Lateran Council, as accepted and recognized by English Ecclesiastical law.

At the Reformation settlement of this matter, which took place in the twenty-fifth year of Henry VIII., it was expressly provided that so much of the entire body of ecclesiastical legislation as did "not stand with GOD's laws and the laws of the realm, the same to be abrogated and taken away;" but "such of them as shall be seen . . . to stand with GOD's laws and the laws of the realm, to stand in full strength and power." A royal commission of thirty-two persons was to sift the whole, and put in tangible shape that which should continue in force. The "Reformatio Legum Ecclesiasticarum," issued in the reign of Edward VI., was the work of the commission contemplated; but it never received any legal sanction, so that the settlement of Henry VIII. still continues in force.

In 1603 A.D. a body of Canons was prepared by Convocation and approved by the king; but they were not adopted by Parliament, and therefore are not binding on the laity. In 1641 A.D. other Canons were put forth, but not with as high authority as those of 1603 A.D. One Canon, that concerning sponsors, has been altered since the revival of Convocation in our own day. Considerable portions of these English Canons are practically obsolete.

III. The Canons of the American Church (including the Constitution) are found in the "Digest," which is divided into four titles: Title I. is "*Of the Orders in the Ministry, and of the Doctrine and Worship of the Church,*" including general directions for the work of Priests, Deacons, and parishes; Title II. is devoted to "*Discipline,*" an abundance being provided for Bishops, Priests, and Deacons, and very little for anybody else; Title III. concerns the "*Organized Bodies and Officers of the Church;*" and Title IV. is occupied by "*Miscellaneous Provisions.*"

There is no restriction on the power of legislation possessed by the General Convention; but many things are left to the Diocesan Conventions, especially the *mode* of trying Priests and Deacons. Each Diocese, therefore, has a Constitution and Canons of its own, which are of subordinate authority to those of the General Convention.

As to the *present authority* of these three branches of Canon Law, it may be said:

I. Of the Œcumenical Canons, a pregnant recognition is embodied in our Ordinal, where the Presiding Bishop thus addresses the Bishop-elect: "Brother, forasmuch as the Holy Scripture and the ancient Canons *command*," etc. This recognizes a still abiding authority in those Canons, as well as in Holy Scripture. A very large proportion of those Canons, moreover, is embodied in our own "Digest." But no specific mention of them is made in that Canon which enumerates the causes for which a cleric may be presented and tried.

II. The Anglican Canons have, by many of our leading canonists, been declared to be still binding in this country, except where American Canons have covered the same ground differently; others deny it. The House of Bishops, in 1814 A.D., distinctly affirmed it.

This, at least, may be said, that both Œcumenical and Anglican Canons are a safe guide to the individual conscience or judgment, where American Canons are silent.

III. Among the charges for which a Bishop, Priest, or Deacon may be presented and tried, our American Canon specifies "Violation of the Constitution or Canons of the General Convention," and also "Violation of the Constitution or Canons of the Diocese to which he belongs."

It would not be safe to take for granted that an Ecclesiastical Court would carry its penal discipline beyond the two specifications here made.

It has been said that the first Canons were passed by the "Apostles, Elders, and Brethren." In the case of the Œcumenical Councils (as in all Provincial Synods), though only Bishops (or the representatives of absent Bishops) voted, yet the discussions were public, and the voice of the other orders of the ministry was freely heard, so that the result may fairly be said to be the voice of all. Nor had those Canons the force of *laws* until they received the official sanction of the emperor, the embodiment of the lay power. During the mediæval period no Council was held without some representation of the same secular element, either in the Council itself, or applied afterwards. The common rule was, that no bull of any Pope, and no Canon of any Council, could be published as binding in any country without the consent of the king. Under the Anglican system, where the Convocation includes only Bishops and clergy, their acts do not bind as law without the approval of Parliament. And, with us, no Canon can be enacted without the free vote of the order of the laity, as well as that of the Bishops and the clergy. The shape in which the principle is embodied in our American system is the fairest of all, and the least liable to any abuse.

REV. J. H. HOPKINS, D.D.

Canon of Scripture. A point of the highest importance from many points of view is the determination of the Canonical Scriptures. It has been urged latterly that the Scriptures are not of the essence of the Faith, but only inspired records of it. While it is very true that the Faith and the facts on which it rests are so woven into the very texture of the Christian polity that they would exist in all essentials without the record, yet the very constitution of our nature, our finite condition, and the relations of GOD dealing towards us, necessitating a Revelation, it follows that the preservation of this Revelation could not be left to chance, but being to men, for men, and deposited with men, for their instruction, it must be preserved by them under GOD's general guidance. A slight examination of the distortions of the original Divine communication which belonged to all men at the first, shows us that peculiar guards are needed for the accurate conservation of such a Revelation. When the family of Abraham was chosen there was at first a transmission of the Faith by tradition. It was a simple plain fact. The unity of GOD, and the blessed mission for which He had chosen them and the inheritance of the land of Canaan. Doubtless the doctrine of the unity of GOD was obscured by contaminating heathen communications, but the tradition was direct. But when Moses received a Revelation and a Law, and an order to write them down, then preparation was also made for their due preservation. They were put beside the Ark of the Covenant, and were kept with the care that watched over that. Then the records, not the full records of what we may call the state papers and public documents of their history, but the records that exhibit the direct line of GOD'S dealings with and care for His chosen people, as Joshua, Judges, Samuel, and Kings,—written by men whose names may be traditionally connected with them, or which may have been forgotten, but who nevertheless were recognized as the proper persons to do this,—were also published in some authentic way. So, too, of the prophetic writings, of Proverbs, and Ecclesiastes, and the Song of Songs,—the Psalms as belonging to the Temple ritual stands somewhat apart,—these were in some sense recognized as holy books, though not gathered into an authoritative collection as in the present Canon. The Law apparently was the only collection which received from the first full recognition. After the Captivity Ezra took up the work. He caused the Law to be read publicly. Jewish tradition assigns to him the collection and arrangement of all the books up to his time, and Nehemiah added what was wanting, save the books evidently later, as Malachi. This tradition of the Talmud shows the gradual forming of the collection of the sacred books. Later, as we know, the whole list underwent severe scrutiny, and some, as Esther and the Song of Solomon, were only received after sharp discussion. External testimony is not wanting. The translation of the Hebrew into Greek, though a work extending over a long period, may be assigned to about 270 A.D. While there are books in it which are not from Hebrew originals, and so are rejected, the list otherwise corresponds to the Palestinean Canon. In the ejected books in this Septuagint is a confused reference to the tradition of the Talmud. We have next the indirect testimony of the Alexandrian Philo, who quoted largely from some portions of the Old Testament, and referred to the laws and oracles uttered by prophets, and hymns and the other (books) by which knowledge and piety are perfected. This triple division into the books of "Moses, the Prophet, and the Psalms" (cf. Luke xxiv. 44) was common then, but the contents of the three parts varied, from thirteen prophets of Josephus to the eight that the prophets now contain, for the twelve minor prophets must be counted as one book. The usual number was arbitrarily made to consist of twenty-two books, to correspond with the twenty-two letters of the Hebrew alphabet. Thus Josephus classes them: The Law five books; the Prophets, Joshua, Judges with Ruth, Samuel, Kings, Isaiah, Jeremiah with Lamentations, Ezekiel, Daniel, Ezra with Nehemiah, Esther, Chronicles, the twelve minor prophets, and Job; and the Hagiographa Psalms, Proverbs, Ecclesiastes, and Song of Solomon. There was a gradual transference of separate books from the section of the Prophets to that of the Hagiographa, but the triple division was still the current one, and so accepted. It in truth represented not only the gathering of the books into one formal list, but the gradual growth of it among the Jews, and the appreciation of the relation of the Canon to their national history. But this is the state of the Old Testament at the time of our LORD. His references to it with approval, and His quotations from it, place its authority for us beyond any question; and, further, His quotations were not from every book, for from a few there is no quotation. Yet since He referred to this triple division, the Law of Moses and the Prophets and the Psalms, after His Resurrection as containing all things to be fulfilled, and as He opened their understanding to receive these Scriptures, we have a special seal placed upon their authenticity and authority. We have only to notice here that the lists given by Origen (220 A.D.), and Jerome (400 A.D.), and by the Talmud (550 A.D.), completely correspond. Other lists include some or all of the apocryphal books, but Origen, Jerome, and the Talmud adhered to the Hebrew text. These larger lists merely traced their lists through translations to the Septuagint, itself a translation, with additions, as we have seen. It follows that the Apocrypha is to be rejected as uninspired.

The history of the Canon of the New Testament is parallel. The Revelation of JESUS CHRIST, recorded by chosen men, was first published and authenticated and gathered into a Canon, after thorough testing. It holds precisely the same relation to the Christian Church that the Old Testament held to the Jewish Church. Through sixty years its writings were produced as the Hebrew writings were produced during the fourteen centuries of their production,—i.e., as the circumstances of the Church demanded. Persecution and difficulty of intercommunication for such purposes kept the formation of the Canon in abeyance. The Gospels and other writings were circulated, examined, used, tested and criticised, doubted of, and finally accepted as we now have them. The list as we now have it was the generally-accepted one made by the Council of Laodicea (363 A.D.). But there were complete collections made much earlier, though there were so many of the books which were still under doubt in one part or another of the Church that there was no general readiness to accept any one catalogue, till the cessation of persecution gave the Church leisure to examine this most necessary question; and when it was done satisfactorily, though by a Provincial Council only, it was at once received and restated by other Councils. It is out of place here to do more than to indicate the various lines of evidence which go to corroborate the genuineness of the several books so received as inspired and canonical. The first and most valued is the long series of quotations—made, as from books as inspired and of ultimate authority and of the highest value, to settle other points—to be found in the Christian writers, beginning with Clement, the fellow-worker of St. Paul, in his letter to the Corinthians, and continually increasing and widening till the date of the Council above referred to, later than which it would not be necessary to trace the quotations. Indeed, every verse in the New Testament, it is said, save one, can be found in the ante-Nicene Fathers,— *i.e.*, in the first two hundred and thirty years of Christian history. It is not that any one writer quoted from all the books, but all these writers together did do so. And this is the more remarkable not merely from the comparatively slight means of circulating those writings, but from the manifold difficulties which persecution created for the diffusion of the books, and the studied concealment and protection of them. The second line of evidence is the translations which were made at an early date, as the Peschito and the Itala. The third line is the use of them in the public services, showing how they were received as of inspired authority in the worship of the Church.

The 6th Article, after concisely stating the authority of Holy Scripture and the relation of the Apocryphal books to the inspired Scriptures, gives the lists of the books of the Old Testament. This was done because of the reverence which the Latin Church showed to the Apocryphal books, and to decide the question authoritatively.

Authorities: Browne on XXXIX. Articles, Smith's Dictionary, Wordsworth on the Canon, Wescott on the Canon of the New Testament, Schaff-Herzog Cyclopædia.

Canonization. The papal act of pronouncing upon the full sanctity of a holy person. In beatification the Pope only pronounces upon his (or her) blessedness, but does not decide whether he (or she) is a saint or not, and allows a certain cultus to be paid him. But in canonization the Pope *ex cathedra* announces the enrollment of the name upon the Calendar of Saints and the privilege to receive the cultus of the faithful in the Church.

In early times local fame for sanctity placed the name upon the roll. It was a continuation of the still more ancient rite of reciting the names of the faithful departed in the celebration of the Eucharist. (*Vide* DIPTYCHS.) But often, after the name was put upon the roll, papal sanction was sought. But the Roman See did not claim the exclusive right till the pontificate of Alexander III. (1181 A.D.). This right was not completely established till 1625 A.D., when Urban VIII. issued a bull (and a second 1634 A.D.) detailing the manner of procedure. The saint was entitled to the invocation and adoration of the whole Church. "The cultus of the beatified is permitted, the cultus of the canonized is enjoined."

Canticles. *Vide* THE SONG OF SOLOMON.

Cantor. The office of the singer was very anciently recognized in the Church, and he was set apart for his office with the charge, "See that thou believe in thy heart what thou sayest with thy mouth, and approve in thy works what thou believest in thy heart." The choir being divided into two parts, the Cantoris, or north side was the Precentors, or leaders, and was the leading side in the antiphonal singing, while the Decani side, in the opposite stalls, responded.

Capital. *Vide* ARCHITECTURE.

Capitulary. A name for a section of the laws enacted by the states-general which Charlemagne used to gather to advise upon the empire. The whole series was called The Capitularies, from capitula—chapters—of such a Diet. These capitularies of Charlemagne and his successors are well known, and are very important documents in the history of these times. They treated of every topic, from private matters to constitutional principles and ecclesiastical affairs, being often civil re-enactments of Provincial, and even Œcumenical, Canons.

Cardinal. The title of the highest dignitary under the Pope of the Roman Church. Its origin lies far back in the history of the Church in Rome, but in the form and rank it now holds it dates only from the sixteenth century. Each parish in the city had its own mother or baptismal church, and the incumbent was called *intitulatus incardinatus*, thence *cardinalis*. There were seven Deacons appointed for the charitable work in the several wards or parishes, a Deacon to each Church. These formed a council to the Bishop. Afterwards Stephen IV. (771 A.D.) added the suffragan Bishops of the neighbor cities. These, with the people, had the right to nominate the Bishop of Rome; but the right to confirm was exercised by the Franco-German emperors; finally, the right to *elect* was secured to the Cardinals only (1058 A.D.). The number of Cardinals varied. In the time of Innocent III. there were over thirty. Death, and political intrigues and difficulties in nominating, of course, all had their force. The Council of Basle fixed the number at twenty-four. In 1559 A.D., under Pius V., there were as many as seventy-six. Sixtus V. (1590 A.D.) fixed the number at seventy-six Bishops, fifty Priests, and fourteen Deacons. A Cardinal priest of a city church in Rome may also be a Bishop of a See elsewhere.

The Pope nominates the new Cardinal in one secret Consistory, who is confirmed in a second by vote of the Cardinals present; when the creation is publicly announced, installation with the red hat, the ring of office, etc., takes place. There must be some regard paid to the rights of other nationalities to a share in holding the office, but the majority of the Cardinals are Italians.

A Cardinal is alone eligible to election to the papal throne; his title is Eminentissimus. Offense against him ranks as treason. The oldest resident Cardinal Bishop is Dean of the College of Cardinals.

Carthage. The Councils of Carthage and the Councils of Africa are frequently interchanged by historians, and as they were often composed of the same Bishops and gathered in the same place, and even in the same year, it is possible that independent partial accounts of the same Council may have come to be reckoned as accounts of separate Synods. It will not be necessary to notice more than two or three in any detail. A Council was held at Carthage, or rather several Councils were held, in the year 255 A.D., on the question of baptizing those who had already been baptized by heretics. The uniform decision was that there was no valid baptism out of the Catholic Church, and that all who had once been baptized by heretics must be baptized again for admission to the Church. St. Cyprian maintained this opinion without wavering, and there was a long dispute between him and Pope Stephen on the matter of rebaptism, which was decided finally at the Council of Arles in 314 A.D. In the year 411 A.D. a Council, or perhaps a Conference, was held at Carthage on the schism of the Donatists. After considerable discussion, decision was made that the Donatists were entirely refuted by the arguments of the Catholics, and though their leaders appealed from this decision, it was in vain, and the sect from this time declined in number and influence. Several Councils were held in Carthage in the years 412, 416, 418, and 419 A.D. Some of these are called Africa, some Carthage, some by both names; and as they were composed largely of the same Bishops, they are more like several sessions of one Council than separate Councils. In the Councils of Carthage, held in 412, 416, and 418 A.D., the heresy of Pelagius was discussed and answered, and Pelagius and his disciple, Celestius, were condemned and excommunicated. From the last of these assemblies the Bishops addressed a very strong letter on the heresy of Pelagius to Zosimus, the Pope, who seems to have been imposed upon somewhat by Pelagius and Celestius. The Council of Africa, held in 419 A.D., is also called Carthage, and is numbered by some the fourth, by others the sixth, of Carthage. Aurelius, Bishop of Carthage, called the Council and presided over it. There were present two hundred and seventeen Bishops, among whom were the Primate of Numidia, St. Augustine, Bishop of Hippo, and St. Alypius, of Thagaste. A legate of the Pope was also present. The business of the Council was on the question of appeals to the Pope. Faustinus, the legate, produced a Canon, purporting to be one made at the Council of Nice, to show that all Bishops have a right of appeal to the Pope; it was denied that there was such a Canon, and in order to determine the dispute, authentic copies of the acts of Nice were sent for from Alexandria and Constantinople. In the mean while the affair of Apiarius, a priest of Sicca, was discussed. He had been deposed and excommunicated by his Bishop, but had appealed to Pope Zosimus, who had received the appeal, contrary to the decisions of several Councils, and readmitted him to communion. The African Bishops refused to admit this pretension of the Pope with regard to the right of appeal to Rome, and great contentions arose upon the subject. Five years later another assembly, or perhaps the same Bishops, came together on the business of Apiarius. It appears that he had been a second time excommunicated, and had afterwards fled to Rome, where he was received by Pope Celestine (for Zosimus was dead, and his successor Boniface), who gave credit to his statements, received him into communion, and gave him a letter to the Bishops of Africa. Accordingly, Apiarius appeared at this Council with Faustinus, who wished to have him received into communion. But the Council proceeding to inquire into his conduct, Apiarius confessed his crimes and was cut off from the body of the Church. By this time an answer had been received from Cyril of Alexandria and Atticus of Constantinople, certifying that the Canons cited by Zosimus were not made at Nice; so the Council addressed a letter to Pope Celestine, in which they complained of his conduct in the matter of Apiarius; begged him not to listen so easily to those who came to him from Africa; not to receive into communion those whom they had excommunicated, as this was contrary to Nice, which decided that all cases should be settled in the province where they arise, and could not be carried elsewhere without the especial direction of the Church; they added that the aid of the HOLY SPIRIT might be hoped for to assist several Bishops together as much as one alone; and finally they begged the Pope to send no more legates to Africa to execute his judgments, as likely to introduce too much of the pride of the world into the Church of CHRIST. A hundred years later, a Council was held at Carthage under Bonifacius, when certain Canons were passed forbidding without distinction all appeals beyond the sea. The Church of Africa maintained her right of judging her priests without appeal until the time of Gregory the Great.

Cassock. A long straight gown of some kind of stuff, or cloth. In the Church of Rome it varies in color with the dignity of the wearer. Priests wear black; Bishops, purple; Cardinals, scarlet, and Popes, white. In the Church of England black is worn by all the three orders of the clergy, but Bishops, upon state occasions, often wear purple coats. The lxxiv. English Canon enjoins that beneficed clergymen, etc., shall not go in public in their doublet and hose without coats or *cassocks. Jebb.* (Hook's Church Dictionary.)

Casuistry, or Cases of Conscience. Casuistry is the name that is given to that science which aims to show how to resolve "cases of conscience," as they are called. They are cases in which we are in doubt as to what is our duty, the doubt or hesitation arising from the fact that there are two or more duties, each of which has claims upon us, which are so situated that we can perform only one of them. The aim was legitimate and good; but the science, this branch of Moral Philosophy and Christian Ethics,— for it was included in both alike,—has fallen into neglect and some measure of disrepute, so that it is now seldom or never included in any treatises on these subjects. The disrepute into which it has fallen has resulted from two causes. In the first place, the views of Christian life and duty taken by Protestant denominations generally give but little occasion for the application of any of the principles of casuistry as it was taught by writers before the Reformation, and as it is still taught in the books of Roman Catholics on the subject. The other reason, which was perhaps much the most influential on the whole, was the fact that casuistry was too often used and regarded as a means of finding out how to escape the performance of some duty that was distasteful or inconvenient, rather than as a means for finding out in a conflict of several duties, which one of them was really *the* duty that ought to be performed.

Still, however, casuistry, properly regarded and properly treated, has its place and its use, and it ought not to be omitted from any work that undertakes to show a man what his duties are, or to help him to find out how he ought to deport himself, and what he ought to do under all conditions and in all the circumstances of life, whether it claims to be a treatise of Moral Philosophy based on reason and the light of nature alone, or a treatise on Christian Ethics based chiefly on the truths and doctrines of Revelation.

In the one case, that of Moral Philosophy, the rule is one of law, the fulfillment of which is exact and complete righteousness, with always a possibility of going beyond the requirements of duty and doing what will thus become works of "supererogation." In the other case,—Christian Ethics,—where the attention is directed both to the purity of heart and the uprightness of the motives, it is hardly recognized as a possibility that one can go beyond the requirement of the law— the law of liberty and of grace—and do more than is needed to fulfill one's obligations. Nay, only one Being in "the form of man" is supposed to have ever done so much as to fulfill the requirements of the law. In this code there are but two great duties,—love to GOD and love to man; these, when properly understood, can never be in conflict by any possibility or in any case. No human being can, in fact, come fully up to the requirements.

Still, however, there is a place and a sphere for casuistry even here. For although there can be no conflict between our duty to GOD and our duty to our fellow-men, when both are rightly understood, there will be many cases in the life of an earnest and conscientious man when he will be in doubt about his duty, even from a Christian point of view.

As specimens of the questions that have been discussed under the head of casuistry take the following. Under the head of the duty of truthfulness, " how far is one justifiable in withholding the truth and misleading others by telling what is known to be false, when the telling of the truth would put the man who tells it to inconvenience or loss, or damage to his friends, his country, or his Church?" Or, again, as coming under the head of honesty, "how far may a servant whose wages are either insufficient to support him and his family or below what they ought to be, take the property of his employer without his knowledge or consent to make up the deficiency?" It will readily be seen how and why the subject of casuistry should fall into disrepute when it is occupied with such questions.

Still, however, as we have already said, there will be occasions for the exercise of genuine casuistry in its proper and higher sense, whether we regard the matter as one purely of Moral Philosophy or as one of Christian Ethics.

As a matter of Moral Philosophy I think we may get a very important help from a recognition of the fact that our duties may be referred to those classes, with reference to their grade of importance or claim to preference in making our selection. In the first place, we may speak of those duties which each one of us may be said to *owe to himself;* second, those that he owes to *his fellow-men;* and, thirdly, those that he owes in the several orders to his country, to humanity, and to GOD.

Among the duties that one owes to himself are temperance, sobriety, care of health, moral and intellectual culture, and such like. Now it is hardly possible that there should occur any conflict between those duties one owes to himself and the duties of either of the higher grades. On the contrary, the performance and perfection of these duties are a help towards the performance of the higher duties. Health, temperance, purity, and a high state of culture make us more valuable to others and enable us to render duties of a higher grade, or to perform them more fully and more acceptably, than we could if we were deformed and degraded by the vices which are the opposites of those virtues and accomplishments. Then as between our duties to our families, our friends, and our country, humanity, and to GOD, there is less often a conflict than we are apt to imagine. But when there is really a conflict, there can be no doubt that the objects rise in superiority the one to the other, in the order in which they are named above. One who is fit to be a martyr for truth, for his country, and his GOD should have no hesitation about being a martyr. But no man of a mean or cowardly disposition has any such call, or any qualification for the calling. Men who are worthy to be martyrs are always the men who have the respect and esteem of their fellow-men, for their moral excellence and mental superiority. Of the foremost and most worthy of all the martyrs the world has ever had it was "He who has done nothing amiss," there was no cause of death in Him, "not even so much as a word of guile was ever found in His mouth." No one can render effective and acceptable service to any cause as a martyr who does not command the respect and confidence of his fellow-men.

We can well understand how one should enter upon a course of heroic devotion to his country or the service of GOD without even a regret for the comfort, the ease, and the occasions for selfish and sensual indulgence which the duties he undertakes to perform may compel him to sacrifice. But we cannot understand how any one should enter upon such a course without regret and pain at the thought of the sacrifices which others must make, or the losses which this course may entail upon them,—the loss of society and companionship, and, as it will often happen, the loss of much needed help and support. Hence one should well scan his motives before entering upon such duties, involving, as it does, the neglect or non-performance of other duties that are in a way and to a certain degree, at least, due to one's relatives and neighbors. He should carefully consider whether any help that *he* can render to the higher cause will compensate in the general balance for the loss of those duties which by a different course he could certainly perform for the good of man and the glory of GOD.

As a matter of Christian ethics the solution of questions of conscience or of duty becomes a very different thing. Here we have not only the Scriptures but also the Church in general, and each one his own immediate and particular Christian pastor, to inform, advise, and to guide him. But the Scriptures themselves have put the matter in such a light that the solution of such questions becomes comparatively easy. Christianity directs attention to the motives by which one is actuated in what he does as a chief and controlling element. It distinctly recognizes the fact that one may do from the best of motives what ought not to be done, and may, on the other hand, do from very bad motives the very thing that ought to be done. St. Paul will furnish us an example of both cases,—the one in his own person, and the other in that of some of the people with whom he was brought into contact in the course of his ministry. Before his conversion, and when he was persecuting the Christians, in a spirit of determined opposition to the very Gospel which he afterwards so effectively preached, he, as he himself informs us, did it from a zeal for GOD and the truth. The act was about the worst that could be done as he came to regard it afterwards, while the motive was of the highest order, and that one which of all others he regarded as the most holy and commendable. For an example of the other class of cases we may refer to his Epistle to the Philippians, chap. i. 15, where he says that some have preached CHRIST "of envy and strife," "not sincerely," but from mere "contention," supposing and intending to add "affliction to his bonds." "What then?" he asks, "notwithstanding, every way, whether in pretense, or in truth, CHRIST is preached; and I therein do rejoice, yea, I will rejoice." Hence manifestly the motive was bad, although the act was a very proper thing to be done. And so in fact in a large share of what we undertake there is always the possibility of some element of bad motive. However good and commendable the work in which we engage, the enforcement of law and the administration of discipline may be prompted or pursued more intensely than it would otherwise be from motives of anger or dislike towards those who are the objects of our activity and our zeal. So too in the highest, noblest works we can undertake,—even those that seem most noble and heroic, even in those cases where martyrdom may appear to be the inevitable result, there may be something of an unholy feeling, something of pride, of ambition, some thought of the halo of glory that will accompany our name in all the future generations of men.

Christianity does not teach, as it is sometimes claimed, that the character of our acts depends *wholly* and exclusively on our motives. It recognizes the fact, as we have just said and seen, that the motive may be bad while the act is good, and the reverse, which will happen far more frequently. The motive may be perfectly pure and good, while the act we perform is one that ought not to be done. And although we may hope for pardon from GOD, as St. Paul did, and obtain it, as he assures us he did, there are often certain *natural* consequences that will follow our acts which no repentance can avert, and from which, so far as we know, GOD will not grant us any exemption. The broken constitution that comes from a life of dissipation and vice will not be restored, although, as we may hope and believe, the final penalty for the transgression which is to follow in the next world will be remitted, and in fact many of the purely essential and psychical consequences may be averted by Divine grace, so that peace and hope will come as the result of the Divine favor and forgiveness.

We have spoken of three guides which the Christian believer has to a knowledge of his duty in the order of their authority and importance,—the Holy Scriptures, the Church, and the immediate pastor of each one as a member of some congregation of Christians. Ample provision is thus made for all classes and conditions of men. For the very lowest in the scale of culture, the most ignorant and least intellectual, perhaps, this order should be reversed, so as to put the pastor first, then the Church, and finally the Holy Scriptures; for, as a matter of fact, what these people learn of CHRIST and of duty they learn from their pastor, and through him they may come to know of the teachings of the Holy Scriptures or of the Church, without distinguishing or knowing any difference between the two elements, or in fact that these are the two sources from which this instruction has come to them. Such is the provision for the very lowest and those who have the least opportunity to learn and judge for themselves. Now we may well believe that for such persons GOD will not hold them responsible, to any considerable extent at least, for the errors that may be taught them, if any such should have entered into the instruction that has been given them. But for those of larger endowments there can be no doubt that GOD will hold them responsible for any errors they may hold, whether in doctrine or in regard to their duty, which they might have avoided by such a study of the Church and the Holy Scriptures as it was in their power to make. The Bible is for all, and all who can do so should read it. But it needs interpretation, and there are none, even the most learned and the wisest, who do not find in it many things that are "hard to be understood," and for the right understanding of which they would be glad of help that they have not yet received. But with regard to duty—the minor details of our actions—I think there are two principles or rules of the greatest importance. I speak now not of doctrine, or the doctrines of the faith, but of duty, what we are to do, and chiefly of those minor points of duty in regard to which there is most likely to be doubt, difficulty, or in which there may arise conflicts of duties, so that we are in doubt which to perform in order to serve GOD most acceptably.

1. The first principle is that it is always better to err, if we must err at all, or are in danger of erring, on the side of self-denial and generosity than in the direction of self-indulgence and selfishness. Most of us need restraint in the indulgence of our appetites and the enjoyment of our pleasures. Periods of prayer, abstinence, and self-denial are prescribed, and they are found necessary for most persons, and beneficial, I doubt not, for all. Now whenever a case of doubt occurs, in which it is merely a question of a little more enjoyment or ease on our part, and a duty of charity or of forbearance for the good of others, this principle will help us to a very ready solution. By abstinence and self-denial in order to do a deed of charity or to promote the happiness and welfare of some other person, we may be doing a double duty and conferring a twofold benefit,—one on ourselves and one on some brother in this common humanity of ours, on some one of those in reference to whom CHRIST has said, "Inasmuch as ye have done it unto one of those ye have done it unto me."

Of course there is a possibility of carrying our abstinence and self-surrender, not to say self-sacrifice, too far. There may be an abstinence and self-neglect that will impair the health or endanger the life. And there are cases of course in which one will have duties to perform that will require self-sacrifice to that extent. In the case of the parent and the professional nurse, as well as that of the physician, it sometimes becomes a clear duty to do what the case requires even at the risk of health and of life. And there are cases, as we cannot doubt, in which persons who are not supposed, and cannot be supposed on any *general* principles of duty to run such risks, have nevertheless done so, with the approval of GOD, and, as we doubt not, the approval of all right-minded persons and with, at any rate, the admiration of all subsequent ages.

And so with generosity. If in a matter of doubt whether I owe a man six pence or ten pence, on the principle I have stated it is safer, and, in a Christian point of view, it is better, to pay the ten pence. Most of us have constitutionally and naturally quite enough of selfishness. We need rather to check than to cultivate and encourage it. By acting on the rule suggested we may, and most likely we shall, be gaining more in a spiritual way than we lose in our temporal affairs.

This principle, however, should not be so understood and applied as to inculcate submission to wrong and extortion when the right is clearly known. We are speaking of cases of doubt, and not at all of those in which the right is clearly seen and known. How far we may submit to what is clearly wrong and unjust is another question, and one, too, that we are not considering now. There are cases, doubtless, in which it is a duty to resist wrong, not necessarily from any motives of self-interest or hope of gain or advantage to ourselves, but in the cause of truth, and of those great principles of righteousness without which there can be no peace on earth and on which happiness in the kingdom of heaven itself is founded.

2. The other great principle to which I referred is that of spiritual guidance in answer to prayer. In the state of nature our natural instincts are suggestive. In almost any circumstances, and in view of our duty before us, which is to be either done or to be left undone, those instincts will suggest, each one according to its nature, what we shall do. The instincts of a generous man will suggest and incline him to act generously, and he will decide and act accordingly; while the man of a different natural tendency in this respect will as readily choose and act in the other way under precisely the same circumstances. In this way we all show what is our *natural* disposition.

And these differences in natural disposition constitute the difference in natural character which we all exhibit in daily life, and which, to some extent, remain and underlie as a basis and the ground-soil the character that we carry or maintain through life, notwithstanding all the natural culture we may receive. But Christianity and Christian conversion changes our nature in this respect. It implants new instincts, gives new aims in life, and especially does it establish the idea of GOD, as omnipresent, knowing the very secrets of our thoughts and hearts, as a Being to be supremely loved and to be feared more than all else that we can have thought or conception of, and this puts its *natural* instincts and propensities to a very large extent into abeyance or into a state of inactivity, just as one may be so absorbed in some earthly pursuit that he becomes unconscious of pains, and even of bodily needs. One may even be so much overcome by fear as to be incapable of anger or of lust. Now, whatever of supernatural there may be in the religious experience, there is a change of this kind in our thoughts and feelings in consequence of the rise into activity of the religious emotions awakened in us by our Christian faith. Through the influence of this faith, and by perseverance in the acts and mode of life which Christianity prescribes and requires, these new motives become constantly prominent and predominating. They become habits, and supersede the old, constitutional, and natural instincts of the individual, so that after a period of confirmed experience and acquired habit, he acts as promptly, as unconsciously of his motives, and in a certain sense as *naturally* in the new way as he did in the old way—"after the flesh," as the Apostle calls it—before the change.

Now, the Bible teaches that in and along with this change the HOLY GHOST works on our hearts. And not only so, but Divine guidance, the sacred influence of the HOLY SPIRIT, will be given to guide us in all questions of doubt and uncertainty in answer to our prayers. When we pray for specific objects we are apt to confine our desires for those objects, and to encourage and strengthen our hopes of realizing them. But when we subordinate our wills to the will of GOD, and in praying for any object, pray also, and still more earnestly, that His will may be done, whatever may become of the object we desire, this is pretty sure to cause a clear, settled, and abiding conviction as to what we ought to do. On such a conviction we find that we may act, and have no cause to repent of our action; and seldom, perhaps never, if we want to see all the consequences of our act, shall we come to regret it or to wish that we had done otherwise, or in any respect differently from what we were led, as we shall believe, to do by the guidance of GOD, working within by His HOLY SPIRIT, and without and around us by His overruling providence. In the light of Christian Ethics, therefore, one does wrong only when (1) before the conscious adoption of the Christian Faith he follows those natural instincts which are bad, or in the degree and form in which they are bad, or (2) when, after having come under the influence of the Christian Faith and the guidance of the HOLY SPIRIT, he allows himself to choose an act without consulting and allowing himself to be guided by the Divine influence; and the only practical difficulty in this latter stage of our experience seems to be in silencing our own hearts and its promptings,—the promptings of that "corruption of our nature," "the infection of which doth remain even in those that are regenerate," and will remain until we are wholly transformed into the image of "Him who is our Resurrection and our Life."

REV. WM. D. WILSON, D.D.

Catechism. *To give instruction, to teach,* is an essential part of the spiritual teaching every Christian should receive. It was based upon the rule our LORD gave the Apostles: "Go ye, therefore, and make disciples of all the nations, baptizing them into the name of the FATHER, and of the SON, and of the HOLY GHOST: teaching them to observe all things whatsoever I commanded you" (St. Matt. xxviii. 19, 20). Whenever the Church made converts she instructed each specially in the doctrines of the Faith. From this grew up the Creed, and for this schools were everywhere established for the training of the *catechumens.* Several of these schools, or rather the teachers of them, became famous. The Alexandrian and Antiochean schools bore an important part in the early Church teaching, and most disastrously since Arius the heretic was trained in Antioch under Lucian the martyr, where he imbibed those principles of dialectics which resulted in his heretical doctrines, and was master for a time in the Alexandrian school, before his heresy became so flagrant. Pantænus, Clement of Alexandria, and Origen, were famous instructors in this school. Cyril of Jerusalem delivered in the Church of the Holy Sepulchre the valuable Catechetical Lectures that have come down to us. Everywhere the office of the Catechist was an important one, intrusted to him who was fittest. It was not properly confined to any order; a Layman, Deacon, Priest, or Bishop, as he had the gift and the opportunity, could fill it.

So St. Augustine wrote for a Deacon his elements of catechising (De. Rud. Catech.). There was ever a watchful care to see that children were properly catechised, and we have frequent enactments by Councils and Synods upon this important duty. The rough, strong missionary sermons of St. Boniface (740 A.D.) have a catechetic force and directness. So, too, in a missionary journey into Pomerania, Bishop Otho catechised the converts to the number of seven thousand, it is said (1124 A.D.). A great activity in this work was developed by the Reformation, and nearly every leading Reformer compiled a catechism which contained his own peculiar doctrinal views. Injunctions were made by Cranmer, and issued by Henry VIII. (1536 A.D.), enjoining the clergy anew to train the children in the Creed, LORD'S Prayer, and Ten Commandments. In Edward VI. Primer (1553 A.D.) a long catechism was set forth. In the Confirmation Office was prefixed the first half of our present Catechism. Who its author was is not certain. It has been claimed for Alexander Howell, second master in Westminster school in 1549 A.D., but Dean of St. Paul's from 1560 to 1602 A D.; also for Bishop Poynet, who was Bishop of Rochester in 1550 A.D. Bishop Goodrich, of Ely, has also been urged as its author, since the duty towards GOD and the duty towards my neighbor are on tablets in the walls of a spacious bow-window which he added to the Palace of Ely. The catechism in Edward's Prayer-Books ended with the explanation of the LORD'S Prayer. At the Hampton Court Conference, 1603 A.D., the Puritans complained that the Catechism was too short. In consequence the latter part, upon the Sacraments, was drawn up. Its author is claimed by Bishop Cosin to have been Bishop Overall, at that time Dean of St. Paul's. It is probable that he translated from some Latin catechism.

The present system of Sunday-schools usurps too much the place of proper catechetical instruction or thorough drill in the Catechism. It should be made a much more important part of the parochial work, in accordance with the plain language of the rubric at the end of the Catechism. The failure to do this lies of course mainly upon the rector, but the laity are not free. But little pains are taken to see that the children are so instructed at home that they can be profitably sent to the church to be catechised, and but little more care is taken to see that they do go at all whenever there is this duty discharged. Were the parents themselves to come, or were the open catechising directed by the Prayer-Book held after the second lesson in the evening service, when the parents and guardians could make it a duty to be present, there would be more energy and zeal shown. It is true that not all have the gift to catechise happily, but it can always be made most profitable to all engaged. The rubrics demand the earnest attention of every layman:

" ⁊ The minister of every Parish shall diligently, upon Sundays and Holy-days, or on some other convenient occasions, openly in the Church instruct or examine so many children of his Parish sent unto him as he shall think convenient in some part of this Catechism.

" ⁊ And all fathers, mothers, masters, and mistresses shall cause their children, servants, and apprentices who have not learned their Catechism, to come to the Church at the time appointed, and obediently to hear and to be ordered by the minister, until such time as they have learned all that is then appointed for them to learn.

" ⁊ So soon as children are come to a competent age and can say the Creed, the LORD'S Prayer, and the Ten Commandments, and can answer to the other questions of this short Catechism, they shall be brought to the Bishop.

" ⁊ And whensoever the Bishop shall give knowledge for children to be brought unto him for their Confirmation, the minister of every Parish shall either bring or send in writing, with his hand subscribed thereto, the names of all such persons within his Parish as he shall think fit to be presented to the Bishop to be confirmed."

The plan of the Catechism is very obvious. It is a most comprehensive summary, setting forth clearly the Baptismal Covenant, and our duty to assume it; the Creed and its summary; the Covenant of duty in the Ten Commandments, with a noble exposition of it; the Law of Prayer, and the grace of the Sacraments. As the Bishops at the Savoy Conference replied to Puritan objections, " The Catechism is not intended as a whole body of divinity, but as a comprehension of the Articles of Faith and other doctrines most necessary to salvation."

Catechumens. In the early Church those who were preparing for baptism, or who sought instruction in Christian doctrine for that end, were admitted into a class by some significant rite, by the laying on of hands and the sign of the cross. They were, besides receiving special instruction from the catechist, allowed to attend the public service and to listen to the Scriptures and to sermons, probably from some allotted place in the church. They were dismissed from the church with some special prayer, as this, from St. Chrysostom's Liturgy:

" LORD our GOD who dwellest on high and beholdest the humble, who didst send forth the salvation of the race of man, Thine only-begotten SON, our GOD and LORD JESUS CHRIST, look down upon Thy servants here the Catechumens who have bowed their necks unto Thee; and make them worthy, in due season, of the laver of regeneration, of the forgiveness of sins, of the robe of immortality; unite them to Thy Holy Catholic and Apostolic Church, and number them together with Thy elect flock, that they also together with us may glorify Thy honorable and majestic Name, FATHER, SON, and HOLY GHOST, now and ever and to ages of ages. Amen."

As they were better prepared they were instructed in the great facts and dogmatic truths, but were not intrusted with the words of either the Creed or the LORD'S Prayer till just before baptism. The teaching was clear and as full as the condition of the catechumen would permit. But if the catechumen was approaching death or was in danger of martyrdom, the regular season of baptism was anticipated, and he was baptized without hesitation or delay; or if baptism could not be administered in cases of martyrdom, the Church held that the baptism of blood supplied the grace of the laver.

Cathedral. Society in the first of the Christian centuries was urban, and the political organization was municipal. A man's country was not a region but a city; his patriotism did not embrace a whole nation of the same language and blood as himself, but those only who with him were shut up within the walls of a single town. A man was not a Greek or Italian, but an Athenian or a Roman. Within the walls of each city were the schools of philosophy, the political assembly, the sharp activities of commerce, the glorious works of art, and the magnificent temples and the worship of the gods. They who lived in the midst of all this urban culture, excitement, and strife could but grow in mental vigor, sensitiveness of spirit, and eagerness for what was new. On the other hand, they who were shut out and condemned to the drudgery of daily and endless toil, born to labor and with children doomed to the same hard lot, grew with the years and the generations more and more stolid, clinging unreasoningly to the past and unapt to adopt what was unwonted and new.

When they to whom the august command was given, to go into all the world and preach the Gospel to every creature, set about its obedience, they followed of necessity the lines on which they found society organized. They passed through the fields and villages, and the scanty and stolid populations there, into the city. They did so because here the multitudes were gathered. And these multitudes by education, culture, refinement, and long, daily, and anxious reasoning about the soul, its nature and destiny, had outgrown the mythology of their fathers and were ready to hear, heed, and accept a new solution of the mysteries of life, death, and immortality. But an itinerant apostleship, that blessed one city for a little while, and then, before what there had been won was well assured, was under the necessity of passing on to another, was unequal to the exigencies. As each city was a whole country unto its citizens, and commanded of them a patriotism as enthusiastic and narrow as the love of home, it followed that a local, stationary resident and municipal Episcopate was the only institution which could effectually work upon such populations. A Bishop of Greece or Italy was impossible. The autonomy of a Church in each city was a necessity by reason of the nature of every municipality. It was for this reason that the Apostles appointed elders in every city.

The actual work of obedience to the Divine command was conducted in the way we should expect. Going to his own city, the Bishop established himself in a certain place of residence and ministration. Here he gathered about him his Priests and Deacons in numbers according to circumstances; all living together, their hearts aflame with a common zeal, their intense activities devoted to a common life and work and destiny. Each of those whom he had gathered around him was assigned by him to some special task,—*e.g.*, labor among a class of the people whom he could more readily reach, or a section of the city which he could more conveniently serve, or a function of preaching or teaching or disputing or writing to which he was specially fitted. Each goes to his place and work, and returns to the Bishop with reports of what he has done and seen and heard, and to receive new orders, instructions, and assignments to duty. This common home of all his people, where all the ways of all their work begin and end, whither, after all toils and dangers and persecutions, they turn their weary feet for rest and their weary hearts for solace, is the Cathedral. It was not only the first Church in order of time: It was long the only Church, and it held its primacy among the institutions of the Christian state because it was the focus of all the work of the Diocese.

In Saxon England society was very differently organized. There were few towns. The population was sparsely scattered over the country. Each family, with its branches and dependents living by itself, held wide tracts of land, and much of the country lay vacant. The people were devoted to agriculture and pasturage. Their manners were rude and simple, and they were disinclined to the exactions of compact society. The polity was loose and easy; the country was divided among many tribes with indefinite, democratic institutions. Each had its king, but he was king in little else than name, except for purposes of defense and war.

The Bishop entering upon the work of converting a tribe fixed his seat, his Bishop's stool, as it was called, at any convenient place of his choice, and with no regard to population. Sometimes, as, for instance, at Ely, he planted it by itself in a vacant region, the religious colony afterwards drawing the people around it. Accordingly, he was the Bishop, not of a city, but of a tribe. This is illustrated by his title. On the Continent the Bishops were called after their city, as the Bishop of Jerusalem, of Antioch, of Rome. On the island, on the other hand, society being rural and the polity tribal, the Bishops took their style from their people. For instance, there was a tribe called the Somersaetas, from which the name Somerset comes. The Bishop, whose seat was at Wells, was the Bishop, not of Wells, but of the Somersaetas. There was also the tribe of the West Saxons, who had the royal city of Winchester. Their Bishop was not the Bishop of Winchester, but of the West Saxons.

But, however interesting this difference in circumstances, the work in Britain was the same as elsewhere, and was carried on in the same way. The Bishop having made choice of the place where he should live, built there the church, houses, gardens, farms, and all necessary conveniences for his clerical colony. Here he gathered about him his Priests and Deacons in considerable numbers, giving them homes in his own houses, and supporting them from his revenues. The life was not necessarily celibate, nor under one roof, nor at one table; but it was in community. He was the head of the family, and he ruled it as a father his household. He apportioned the work among his clergy, giving to each his place, office, and task. To this one he gave this circuit to travel in the country of the tribe, and to another that; to one he appointed this station or mission, and to another that; and so on through all the work of the Diocese. The sphere of duty whose centre was here embraced all ministrations, charities, instructions, and interests; and the service which went forth hence was circumscribed only by the boundaries of the whole Diocese. This centre of work was the Cathedral. For four centuries this was the polity of the Church, as well among rude and rural tribes of England as in the intense life of the great cities. Everywhere the polity of the primitive Church was the Diocesan system, just as everywhere the administration was Episcopal. The centre of the Diocese was the Cathedral, and from thence the work was conducted.

Throughout all the course of history, in all parts of the world, the polity of the primitive times has controlled the whole of the development of the constitution of the Christian Church. Its principles, modes, and administration have at all times been founded on what the Apostles and their immediate successors adopted and established. Under the pressure of circumstances there have been modifications in incidents and details, but never in what was essential and organic. When Christianity became the religion of the people, and the Cathedral could not contain them, nor be served directly from it, parishes sprang up as separate independent points of work. But the Bishop exercised his jurisdiction from his own Church as from the capitol of his Diocese. Thence proceeded the authority, the administration, the service by which the Diocese in city and country alike, and all the people, urban and rural, were ruled and served. The body of the clergy who hitherto had held a direct, personal, and constant relation to the Bishop, became now divided into two classes, one the Parochial, the other the Cathedral, clergy. The active work among the people was assumed by the former; the powers which all the Presbyters had exercised in assisting the Bishop in the administration of his office devolved upon the latter. The Diocesan system became accordingly separated into the Parochial and the Cathedral system; each of which was the complement of the other, and the whole still having a perfect union in the Episcopal function.

The Clergy of the Cathedral were now consolidated into a compact and highly-organized body. We shall define their duties and powers hereafter. We have now to direct our attention to their organization. They were first called Canons in the eighth century. Their corporation was called the Chapter. Their number differed at different Cathedrals and at different times. At Wells there were in the tenth century four or five.; in the twelfth at first ten, then twenty-two; afterwards the number was raised to fifty. At St. Paul's, London, there were thirty, and at Lincoln fifty-two. It was necessary that these great societies should have officers charged with special duties. The principal officer of the Cathedral body after the Bishop was called the Dean. Dean Milman in his Annals of St. Paul's, London (p. 132), thus defines his duties and office: " The Dean had supreme authority; was bound to defend the liberties of the Church; was bound by his oath to observe and to compel others, from the Canons down to the lowest officer and servants, to observe the laudable customs of the Church, to watch over all the possessions of the Church, and to recover what might have been lost or alienated. He had authority also over all who inhabited the manors and estates; an authority which singularly combined the seignorial and spiritual jurisdictions. He was the guardian at once of the rights and interests of the poorer tenants, and, it may also be said, vassals, as well as of their morals and religion. The Dean presided in all causes brought before the Chapter and determined them, with the advice of the Chapter. He corrected, with the advice of the Chapter, all excesses and contumacies. Lighter offenses of inferior persons were punished by the Chancellor. The Bishop had no authority in capitular affairs, except on appeal. The Dean, for more heinous offenses, could expel from the choir, and cut off all stipends and emoluments, with discretion, to the edification, not the destruction, of the Church. These words are in Colet's unaccepted code; but the same spirit prevails throughout the older statutes, only in different forms. The Dean had a Subdean to perform his functions when abroad or incapacitated from duty, with authority over all the inferior members of the Church except the Canons."

Next in rank to the Dean was the Precentor, who had charge of the choir of the Cathedral, and all the services which were performed in it, and the schools of music. He directed the music and had the discipline of all the choristers and singers. His deputy, where he had one, was called the Succentor.

Next after the Precentor came the Chancellor, who was charged with the care of the library, and the grammar and divinity schools. It was also his duty to lecture to the Cathedral clergy on divinity, and to organize theological instruction given by others. In some places, as at St. Paul's, he had " charge of education, not only for the Church, but for the whole city; all teachers of grammar are subject to him." His deputy was the Vice-Chancellor.

The last of the officers of the Chapter was the Treasurer. "The Treasurer was the responsible guardian of the treasures of the Church, and ample indeed they were. Reliques, first in value and importance; books, of which there is a curious catalogue; vessels of gold and silver, vestments, chalices, crosses, curtains, cushions, and palls. He was answerable to the Dean and Chapter for the safe custody of all these precious things, and could not lend any of them without the consent of the Dean and Chapter. Under the Treasurer was the Sacrist. His office was to superintend the tolling of the bells, to open the doors of the Church at the appointed times, to dress the altars, and take care that the vessels and vestments were clean and in good order. The Sacrist was to take care that there was in the Church, even on the festivals, no crowd, noise or singing, neither talking, quarreling, nor jesting, neither business nor sleeping. He was to maintain order and conduct every one to his proper place."

There was another body of the Cathedral clergy who cannot be passed over, namely, the Vicars. When non-residence became common it was required of each Canon that he provide a clergyman who should take his place in his absence; and the rule sprang up making it his duty to always have a deputy. Just as the Dean had his Subdean, the Precentor his Succentor, and so on, each Canon had his deputy, who was called his Vicar. There were therefore as many Vicars as there were Canons. When the Canons forsook the Cathedral for their prebends, the Vicars carried on the services and work perhaps as efficiently and decorously as those whom they represented. An old writer of those times, seeking to show the superiority of the monks over the secular Canons, says that the former praise GOD with their mouths, the latter through their Vicars. There is a story of Thomas à Becket, when Archbishop of Canterbury, sending a man with a bull of excommunication against the Bishop of London, who went to St. Paul's Cathedral on Ascension-day, and on that great festival found the officiating priest neither Bishop, Dean, nor Canon, but only a Vicar. The Vicars of each Cathedral having common employment, interests, and life, were naturally drawn together. First, they acquired estates separate from those of the Canons; then they had houses of their own, dormitories, refectories, and chapels; at last, unmarried and living a purely collegiate life, they were formed into a corporation, so that, as there was the corporation of the Dean and Canons, so there was a corporation of the Vicars. They were now no longer each the deputy of a Canon, but were the assistants of the residentiaries in the service and work of the Cathedral. Then a distinction came in,—there were priest Vicars and lay Vicars. But the latter were not merely singing men paid each as stipendiaries, but members of the college, with equal rights with their clerical brethren.

For many centuries all the Canons resided continuously at the Cathedral, and found their sole occupation in service there and in service proceeding therefrom. But after a time the Chapters acquired the right to appoint the Priests of certain Parishes, who received its tithes and other revenues, and naturally they appointed their own members to those places. Clergy holding such beneficiaries had thus two offices,—one, that of Canon; the other, that of Parish Priest, his title in the latter capacity being that of Prebend. The two functions were united in one person, but were distinct. By and by some of the Canons lived most of their time in their Parishes, leaving their duties at the Cathedral to their Vicars. Others lived most of the time at the Cathedrals, leaving their parochial duties to Priests whom they employed. At length the separation between the two classes became so fixed that the name of Canon was borne only by the Cathedral clergy, while that of Prebend was applied to those who remained on the beneficiaries. The distinction was further marked by the names residentiary Canons, that is, those who retained duties at the Cathedral, and non-residentiary Canons, that is, those who had only incidental or slight or no duties there.

The Chapters were composed only of the residentiaries. But there was also a general Chapter to which the non-residentiaries of most Cathedrals were summoned. The duties of this larger body were those of electing Bishops and representatives in Convocations.

This highly-organized system existed in its perfection in the twelfth, thirteenth, and fourteenth centuries throughout Europe and in Great Britain without material differences between them. But some of the Cathedrals were Monasteries, the Abbot holding the place of Dean, and the monks the places of the Canons.

When Henry VIII. suppressed the Monasteries in England he made no exceptions of the Cathedrals which were served by monks. These were Canterbury, Winchester, Worcester, Durham, Norwich, Rochester, Ely, and Carlisle. He found himself compelled to re-establish Chapters at these Cathedrals. The organization which he provided for them was much simpler than that which we have described. Each had a Dean and from four to twelve resident Canons, who formed the Chapter. Each also had honorary Canons, but this was only an empty title. Instead of Vicars there were Minor Canons, who performed the same duties. There were no Precentors, Chancellors, or Treasurers, but their duties were imposed on the Minor Canons. These Cathedrals are called Cathedrals of the new foundation. The others are called Cathedrals of the old foundation. The latter are London,

York, Exeter, Salisbury, Wells, Lincoln, Lichfield, Hereford, and Chichester.

In 1840 A.D. Parliament passed an act reducing the number of Canons at each Cathedral to four, except at Canterbury, Durham, and Ely, where there were to be six, and at Winchester, where there were to be five, and the endowments of all other Stalls were diverted to other purposes. The act also diverted the prebendal estates, leaving the Prebends in Cathedrals of the old foundation without compensation. The number of Minor Canons or Vicars was to be not more than six nor less than two. In 1874 A.D. an act was passed permitting the endowment of new Canonries by the munificence of private individuals and the appointment thereto of encumbents. The appointment of Deans is in the Crown, of the Canons, Prebends, and Honorary Canons, as a general rule, in the Bishop, and the Minor Canons in the Dean or the Chapter.

During the last fifteen years the attention of English Churchmen has been drawn to the Cathedrals, and an agitation has been going on with a view of giving them a larger place in the practical activities of the Church. A royal commission is now sitting. Its reports upon the several Cathedrals contain the statutes of their organization and government which are to be adopted by the Queen in Council, and are a vast body of interesting matter. Perhaps the most noticeable feature of the new statutes is the several provisions looking to a more direct and active relation of the Cathedrals with the Diocese and its administration.

In all except those for St. Paul's, London, provision is made for three Chapters; one called simply the Chapter, composed of residentiaries; one called the General Chapter, composed of the non-residentiaries, whether they are called Prependiaries or Honorary Canons, the Archdeacons, and (generally, but not always) of the Proctors in Convocation; and a third called the Diocesan Chapter, composed of the members of the General Chapter and all of the Diocesan officers. This latter body, newly created in these statutes, is a revival of the Chapters of the times when the Cathedrals were the most active and efficient agencies of the Church. It is so in its organization, and more especially in its functions. It is convened by the Bishop, and its duties are to advise and assist him in the administration of his office. In some of the statutes the same duties are enjoined upon the Chapters and the General Chapters; in others they are imposed on the General Chapters alone, but these provisions do not supersede the Diocesan Chapter. Provision is made for that body in all of the statutes except in those for St. Paul's, London, where the General Chapter is charged with the duties and service elsewhere committed to the Diocesan Chapter.

The importance of the introduction of these provisions into the statutes of the Cathedrals of England cannot be over-estimated. But they are only formulated statements of opinions which have been set forth in many writings of very eminent men, and especially in communications of Cathedral Authorities to the commission, which are appended to its reports. In these writings the contention has been earnest in behalf of the essentially Diocesan character of the Cathedrals.

In the statutes for Truro, provision is made for a force of men called Missioners, whose duty is to go up and down the Diocese assisting the parochial Clergy by preaching, lecturing, holding missions and other similar services. The first Bishop of Truro, now the Archbishop of Canterbury, originated the idea of this body, and speaks of them as the successors of the Prebendaries of the earlier times in the services above mentioned.

We pass now to consider the proper functions of the Cathedral and its Clergy. The first and most obvious of them is the maintenance of the constant, elaborate, and impressive worship of ALMIGHTY GOD. Speaking on this subject, Dean Goulburn, of Norwich, says,—

"I trust that I have opened a way by these remarks for the discernment of the true character of the *Cathedral* Church. It is a building specially and prominently dedicated to the glory of ALMIGHTY GOD. I say *specially* and *prominently;* and it is by this specialty and prominence that I believe a Cathedral to be distinguished from other Churches. All Churches are, of course, in one aspect of them, offerings to GOD for the honor of His Name. But then this is not the leading, but the subordinate idea in a parochial Church. The primary object there is the dealing with human souls, the converting and softening of human hearts, the stirring and awakening of human consciences, the initiating the worshiper into the knowledge of GOD, and the gradual drawing of him up into communion with GOD. Nor is this end in the least degree foreign to the functions of a Cathedral; rather it is a part of its functions, only not the most prominent part, not the great characterizing idea. The Cathedral is a place rather where GOD is worshiped than where man is impressed, though it is a most blessed thing indeed where the latter end is secured along with the former. The very core of its work is the daily office in the choir, solemn, effective, dignified; rendered as perfect as possible by the accessory of beautiful music, and ever striving and yearning to represent more perfectly upon earth the adoration which ceaselessly goes on in the courts of heaven. The anthem is quite in place in such worship; nor surely should anthems ever be discontinued in Cathedrals, though unsuited (in my judgment) to the worship of parochial Churches. To discard anthems from Cathedrals would be to discard some of the grandest efforts of music to praise the Creator, Redeemer, and Sanctifier, from those very houses of prayer which are, in a more especial manner, dedicated to the celebration of the glories of His Name." This is a service which has been always faithfully discharged by the Cathedrals and does not need further remark.

The second function of the Cathedral Chapter is to aid the Bishop by advice and labors in the administration of the Episcopal office. We have already seen how the Christian community was gathered by the Bishop about himself and directed and ruled by him in all their work. By the very circumstances of the situation it was a compact body: its members were all driven from the outside into the society for help and comfort and support. Without, society was unutterably corrupt and vile; sensuality, superstition, atheism, were on every hand. Popular amusements were altogether ungodly; the gravest thought, the noblest aspirations, were of the earth, earthy. The national religion, which multiplied the divinities, deified the emperors, and denied the one only and true GOD, was abhorrent. Against this wickedness it was the mission of the early Christians to protest with their lifeblood. Their Lord of Lords, and King of Kings, was the Eternal TRINITY worshiped through the Incarnate SON; and in proportion as the Roman state was leagued to uphold its adulterate *cultus*, so the Christian Commonwealth was banded around the universal Church of CHRIST. Their very depths of veneration and passionateness of devotion made these men and women recoil from the touch of the vile world, and drove them together and bound them by the most sacred ties. Their society, isolated in the midst of the multitudes, took a corporate character and had a polity of its own, and was in truth a *civitas Dei*.

In this sacred family the Bishop was the father, and all were his children. It was not only love they gave him for his tenderness and wisdom, but veneration also for his high office and his character, which the office sanctified. Now let us ask how this holy man must have carried himself among his brethren. He shared their intensity of devotion; he shrank with them from the sin without; he awaited the same destiny that they foresaw for themselves; and besides, ever in his ear rang the voice of JESUS, "Feed My Sheep"; "By this shall all men know that ye are My disciples, that ye love one another." He was their ruler. Did he lord it over them? Being what he was, and they what they were, all brethren together, he could not help but take them, or at least those who were competent, into his counsels, and listen patiently, respectfully, reverently, gladly, to what each had to say. There, in those first days, under the pressure of the sin without and the love within, this custom grew up, of the Bishop taking counsel of his Clergy.

When afterwards the purely Diocesan system became modified by the parochial system, the Clergy who were about the Bishop at his Cathedral succeeded to this right to share the Episcopal consultations, as they succeeded to almost all the other corporate rights of the whole clerical body. It became universal Canon Law that the Bishop must on certain subjects consult his Chapter before acting upon them.

Hence the Chapter has been called "the Senate of the Diocese," and the Canons have been called "Brothers of the Bishop." In some statutes the duty of the Chapter is declared to be, "to aid the Bishop when the See is full, to supply his place when it is vacant." One great writer on Ecclesiastical Law concludes from a mass of evidence, that everywhere "the Clergy of Cathedral Churches formed one body with the Bishop, and entered into their share of the anxiety and into some association with his sacred sway." Another speaking of the Canons says, "their principal duty was to assist the Bishop by their work and their counsels in the government of the Church." Reginald Pole says, "the rationale and ground of instituting Canonries and Prebends in Churches was, that they who are appointed to them, may assist the Bishop and aid him with counsel and work in the discharge of his office and divine things."

A third function of the Cathedral Clergy was to supplement and reinforce the parochial Clergy in their active and practical labors among the people. This includes the strictly missionary work, of which, as done by the Cathedral Clergy in the early days, enough has been already said. And of the assistance they did, and may render to the parochial Clergy, nothing need be added to the explanation of the society of Missioners formed by Archbishop Benson, at Truro, in the Diocesan Kalendar for 1881 A.D.

"Cathedral Missioners. *Sanctificatio in veritate.* The object of this association is to provide a staff of preachers, who, not being bound by parochial or other ties, may be entirely at the disposal of the Bishop for any work to which he may see fit to send them, at the call of the parochial Clergy. Besides undertaking and arranging for missions (technically so called), where the Bishop and parochial Clergy think desirable, they will endeavor, as far as their numbers may permit, to give courses of sermons or lectures at populous centres, to supply spiritual ministrations during the absence or sickness of encumbents, and to help in the gathering of Candidates for confirmation; in the formation of branches of the Church Society for the advancement of holy living, or other societies approved by the Bishop; in the instruction or supervision of Lay preachers; in the promotion of Mission Chapels, and in other works which aim at the spiritual and moral improvement of the people."

A fourth function of the Cathedral was the establishment and maintenance in close connection with it of institutions of charity and education. The custom has been universal to establish grammar schools for boys in connection with the Cathedrals. In England some of these schools have attained very great reputation. So, too, readerships and lectureships on divinity were general. The duty of hospitality was enjoined upon the Clergy, and this included care of the sick and unfortunate. These duties and services have devolved upon the modern institutions and cannot consistently be neglected. They are not essential, but they are practically so related to them that they ought to find a place in every scheme for their efficient organization.

After this review we are able to answer the question, what, then, is a Cathedral? How does it differ from any other Church? The name is derived from the Latin. The seat of a Bishop in a Church was his *Cathedra*. In and from this his seat he especially exercised his office. He had but one seat in his Diocese, which was in his Church; he had none in parish Churches. Soon what was peculiar to one Church gave it a distinctive name, and the Bishop's Church was called a Cathedral. Properly, the word is an adjective and qualifies Church. Speaking exactly we would say Cathedral Church, *Cathedralis ecclesia*. In common parlance the adjective is used as a noun, and dropping the word Church we say Cathedral.

The Cathedral, then, is the Church in which is the *Cathedra, Sedes*, See, or Seat of the Bishop. It is his Church. He is sometimes said to be the pastor, and sometimes the rector, of his Diocese. And his Cathedral has been called the parish Church, and the matrix of the Diocese. These words may be not always descriptive of the fact, but they convey one idea, that the Cathedral is the Bishop's Church and has relations of some sort to and connection in some way with the Diocese. Many suppose that it must be a large and beautiful building; that the services must be choral, and that the Clergy must be numerous. It is natural to expect all these of a Bishop's Church. But the Anglo-Saxon Bishops generally built their Churches of wood, small in size and rude in construction; and they were truly Cathedrals. The choral service has long since ceased to be peculiar to Cathedrals, and one priest serving at the altar with his Bishop may be the only clergyman. Size of building, mode of service, and number of Clergy are accidents, accessories, circumstances; they are not essential to the Cathedral. What is essential is that the Church should be the peculiar place of the Episcopal function.

But when the Bishop has planted his See in any Church, other things naturally and necessarily gather around it. Especially will be collected a number of Clergy to whom he will resort for aid and advice in carrying on his work. The Episcopal function is the primary, and a number of Clergy, larger or smaller, who assist him in the administration of the Diocese is the secondary, element of a Cathedral.

In the scheme upon which the Church in this country was organized the Cathedral had no place. Several reasons may be assigned for this departure from Catholic usage, but it is not within our purpose or our space to mention them. About thirty years ago an attempt was made to engraft the Cathedral upon the organization of the Church. Not long after he was sent out to California, Bishop Kip placed his Episcopal chair in Grace Church, of San Francisco, and called that Church his Cathedral. He did this in his right as rector of the parish, and when his incumbency ceased, the name of Cathedral was dropped. He afterwards held the rectorship of the Church of the Advent, and there again set up his Episcopal seat and gave its edifice the same name, and withdrew both when he resigned the position.

Afterwards other Bishops set up their Episcopal chair in parish Churches. Usually they have secured from the parochial organization the right to occupy the seat, to preach, to direct the ritual, and to use the building for Episcopal services. Examples of Cathedrals of this class are St. Paul's, Buffalo, and St. Paul's, Indianapolis. To the same class may also be referred other Cathedrals, such as St. Peter and St. Paul, Chicago, and Our Merciful Saviour, Faribault. At these institutions, the title to the property, and the entire power of administering it, and directing the services and work, are in the Bishop. But beyond this, these Churches have little to distinguish them from parish Churches. They have no Chapter or function not local to the building; nor organic relations to the Diocese. This is explained by Bishop Whipple in a letter to the writer. He says the Cathedral "should be solely in the Bishop's care, that he may set forth such a ritual as may be a model for the Diocese. It needs only such machinery as may help him."

A second class of Cathedrals have Chapters but no Diocesan relations. The Episcopate, as in the class first mentioned, is the primary, active, and central function, but not the sole and unqualified authority. The Bishop holds his office apart, sharing it with none, and aided in its exercise by none, but within the precincts of the Cathedral he has the aid of his Presbytery. All-Saints', Albany, and Davenport, Iowa, are examples of this class. In the institution at Albany there is a Chapter composed of the Bishop, Dean, Precentor, Chancellor, Treasurer, four Minor Canons, and six laymen. None of them except the Bishop has any Diocesan relations, duties, or rights other than those possessed by any clergyman or layman. The body has no care of the Missions of the Diocese, and whatever it attempts in that service is in subordination to the Diocesan Board of Missions. The funds and property of the Diocese are not in its hands, but in those of special Committees of the Diocesan Council. The Schools and Hospitals are independent of it; there is no duty on the part of the Bishop to ask the Chapter for advice in the administration of his office, nor on its part any duty to give him advice when asked for it. It is a body as local in its character and service as any parish Church. There is what is called a Greater Chapter, composed of the Archdeacons, the members of the Standing Committee, of the Board of Missions, and of the deputations to General Conventions, the officers of the Diocesan Council, and the rectors of the two oldest churches in the city. In its *personnel* it is Diocesan; but the only function of this body is to elect the members of the Chapter proper and to attend the Bishop upon certain special occasions. It has no direct and active relations with the Diocese.

The same is true of the scheme of the Cathedral at Davenport. Bishop Perry, retaining in his own hands the title to the property in order to preserve it as a Bishop's Church, has erected a Chapter, with a Dean, who is the head of the educational institutions, a Senior Canon, who has the pastoral care of the congregation, other Canons whose special duties are in the parish Churches of the city and in the schools, and Curators of the Cathedral, who are laymen charged with the temporalities. Its work is, first, to maintain the worship in the Cathedral in rich, abundant, and appropriate services; secondly, to conduct the work of the parish Churches and missions in the See city; thirdly, to carry on the schools there; fourthly, to extend missionary efforts into the Diocese as fully and as far as possible. But the Diocesan administration is here, as at Albany, distributed among the Board of Missions, the Trustees of the funds of the Diocese, and the Trustees of the Episcopate funds. It is not proposed to bring the powers and duties of these bodies within the jurisdiction of the Chapter.

Cathedrals of the third class are equally, with those last described, local as to the services or public worship and of charities; but they also have direct practical and constant relation with the Diocese. The Omaha Cathedral is an example. Its Chapter consists of the Bishop, Dean, three Canons, five honorary Canons, the Standing Committee, and all the other officers of the Diocese. It is charged with the care of the missions, funds, property, schools, and hospitals of the Diocese. It meets quarterly and deals with every subject of administration. In several Missionary Jurisdictions and also in several of the younger Dioceses it has been adopted. It comes much nearer to a restoration of the polity of the early Church than either of the two classes of institutions above described.

We have to-day in the American Church Cathedrals organized on three plans. The first are those based on the Episcopal office alone. The second are those based on the See principle, and have Chapters but no Diocesan relations. The third have the Episcopate as the primary element, with Chapters for the assistance of the Bishop in the administration of the Diocese.

In order to an intelligent view of the conditions in which the Cathedral in this country must be developed into a vigorous, efficient, and practicable agency in the American Church, something more than these descriptions are necessary. We have seen that the essential object of the Chapter is to provide from the Presbytery a competent body to assist the Bishop in the exercise of his office: which assistance is first by advice, and, secondly, by labors not parochial.

As the Cathedral was not recognized by those who framed the Constitution of the American Church, so nobody was provided for the assistance of the Bishop by advice. The need of such body was not felt at first. We need not concern ourselves with the reasons. But after a time it began generally to be felt that some authority ought to be provided to which the Bishop might resort, and which should also to a degree control the Episcopal function. Accordingly, in 1835 A.D. the General Convention by Canon provided that "in every Diocese where there is a Bishop the Standing Committee shall be a Council of Advice to the Bishop. They shall be summoned on the requisition of the Bishop whenever he shall wish for their advice, and they may meet of their own accord agreeably to their own rules when they may be disposed to advise the Bishop."

This was the restoration of the Chapter under another name. And if the functions of the Bishop extended to all the matters properly belonging to the Chapter, there would be little need of reviving it. But such is not the case. The duties of the Standing Committee are of the very highest and most solemn nature; but they are very limited. For instance, the Committee does not have the care of the missions of the Diocese. That is an interest the most active, urgent, and pressing of all. It is intrusted to the care of another separate, disconnected, and independent body called variously the Board of Missions, the Committee on Missions, or the Missionary Society. When a question touching missions has been determined by the body charged with their care, it would be not only unseemly, but mischievous in every way, for the Bishop to go to the Standing Committee for advice on the subject. It would be raising the Committee to an appellate jurisdiction, and subordinating to it all other bodies. Confusion and irritation would follow which would be intolerable. And what is true of missions and the Board charged with them, is true of all other interests of the Diocese, which are parceled out among different similar bodies. It thus appears that most of the administration of the Diocese being given into the hands of other bodies than the Standing Committees, it is impracticable for it to be a Council of Advice to the Bishop on only a modicum of the subjects in the discussion, consideration, and determination of which he needs assistance. It is very clear, therefore, that the Standing Committee of a Diocese does not answer all the needs which the Bishop may have for assistance in the way of advice. As his Council, as the Senate of the Diocese, it does not fill the place of the Chapter.

We pass on to consider the assistance which the Chapter may give the Bishop by clerical labors not within the province of the parochial Priest. A body of Clergy resident at the Cathedral, under the personal and active direction of the Bishop, going out to the missionary stations, serving them and returning to him for report and new orders, works in the same way as the forces by which the world was first conquered to the sway of the Church. It is a mode not only sanctified by primitive and Catholic usage, but in its nature fitted to the condition of modern missionary labor. Let this be explained by a view of the work done in this way. Suppose there were at the Cathedral a hall, and twice, or four times, or a dozen times a year, as should be appointed him, the Missionary should come up for a brief residence in it. Here he would meet and know and learn to love those who, like him, were devoted by vow and habit and zeal to the service of their common LORD; here he would find companionship and sympathy and affection and a freshened life and an animated spirit, such as come only from the warmth and fervor of association; here he would find the guidance and direction and counsel of his Bishop, and the elder and wiser of the Clergy; here he would see the need of reading to keep pace with the progress of others by whose conversation he would be stimulated to exertion; here, above all, he would have the altar at which to kneel in the highest act of worship and the splendid services of the temple. And so he would be strengthened against the trials of his lot among the people to whom he is sent, and against those other trials of the spirit. His stay need not be long; even a few days might suffice to return him to his work a new man.

But the Missionary is not the only person who would be blessed by this relief. Coming up at stated times, he would, either by express rule or in the natural course, report to the Bishop of his work, his field, and his life. The peculiar needs of the stations he serves, and his aptness to answer them, would become known; and he would be instructed by wise counsels and encouraged to go on, or be reinforced by others or withdrawn to some other place for which he would seem better fitted, as the case required. Missionaries thus organized and working from the Cathedral would in a very few years become a homogeneous body, having common interests, modes, sentiments, and aspirations. There would soon grow up among them an *esprit de corps*, without which no society was ever efficient.

The uses to which the Cathedral Clergy may be put in sections where the Church is well planted and rooted is admirably explained by Bishop Sweatman, of Toronto, in Canada, in his address to his Synod in 1881 A.D. He says, "Supposing that I had resident in Toronto, say four Canons, men of thorough practical parochial experience, of true missionary spirit, of a high order of pulpit power, of intense sympathy, and, above all, full of earnest spiritual life,—for they would need to be all this,—the value of such a body of men would be incalculable, as counselors and advisers. But—here is the point I wish to bring out—a mission in the Diocese is, for some cause, evidently in an unprosperous condition; the clergyman complains that he cannot obtain support from the people; or the Church is losing ground, and so forth. I direct one of my Canons to go to this place, to inquire into what is wrong, to stay a week, two weeks, or three weeks, to rouse up the people, and put new life into the Church's work. A young and inexperienced clergyman meets with difficulties he does not know how to deal with; he needs advice and guidance; another of the Chapter is sent to help him, to put him in the way of doing his work better; with the loving words and mature wisdom of an elder brother to give him confidence and cheer. Or a clergyman writes me for help in an emergency; his parish is invaded by a new sect, preaching strange doctrines and drawing his people away from the faith; he had spent himself in labors to counteract the mischief, but finds that it is an unequal task to cope with single-handed, or his arguments are exhausted, and he wants another mind to reinforce him with fresh arguments. Here is help for the emergency,—a well-learned, and well-equipped, and zealous member of the Cathedral Staff ready to go to the rescue. Have I justified my assertion? I feel sure that every earnest and faithful parish clergyman will confess that such a system, by which the clergy might occasionally be stirred up to more diligence, cheered in their isolation, aided in their difficulties, by a visit from a brother such as I have described, would go a long way to break down the congregationalism, to awaken the spiritual torpor of the people, to arouse to activity the missionary indifference, to systematize the inefficient diffusion of forces,—the chief difficulties and evils under which we suffer. To carry out this system fully will require means and time; but a small beginning may be made. I shall not touch this question of means; but I cannot forbear a concluding remark, that it is tantalizing to be taunted with aping titles and dignities, and at the same time to feel that no colonial Diocese ever had so nearly within its grasp the power to erect and maintain a real living Cathedral Establishment, with its active Chapter and Staff of officers, as the Diocese of Toronto with its richly endowed Church in the capital."

It needs no words to show the advantages of bringing the schools and charities of the Diocese together at the Cathedral, and conducting them by its Clergy under the eye of the Bishop.

It is a vision which may not be vouchsafed to us of this generation, but not beyond our reasonable hope: a Cathedral once more the Bishop's Church, in which the Episcopate shall be the primary function, but surrounded by a band of Clergy for its assistance, a body of well-learned, experienced, devout men, maintaining in its due dignity and beauty the worship of GOD; sharing the sacred sway and labors of the chief pastor in his administration in spreading the knowledge of the truth in new parts, and holding up the hands of those who are set among the people teaching and vindicating the great truths of the Gospel to those who are ignorant or perverse, training the children in the knowledge they need in this world, and the knowledge that fits them for another world, and serving the poor, sick, and unfortunate in Homes, Asylums, Hospitals, and Retreats of whatever sort.

The numbers vary according to the needs of each place, its organization as may be found convenient, the apportionment of work among them as their fitness and other conditions may require; but the whole forming a community co-operative, compact, efficient, with one heart and one mind, serving the great Bishop and Shepherd of souls with a holy fervency.

Authorities: "The Cathedral; its Necessary Place in the Life and Work of the Church," by Edward White Benson, Lord Bishop of Truro, late Chancellor of Lincoln. London, John Murray, Albemarle Street, 1878. "The Principles of the Cathedral System vindicated and enforced upon Numbers of Cathedral Foundations. Eight Sermons preached in the Cathedral Church of the Holy and Undivided Trinity of Norwich," by Edward Meyrick Goulburn, D.D., Dean of Norwich. Rivington's, London, Oxford, and Cambridge, 1870. "The English Cathedral of the Nineteenth Century," by A. J. B. Berresford Hope, M.P. D.C.L. With illustrations. London, John Murray, Albemarle Street, 1861. "Essays on Cathedrals by Various Writers," edited by the Very Reverend J. S. Howson, D.D., Dean of Chester. London, John Murray, Albemarle Street, 1872. "Annals of St. Paul's Cathedral," by Henry Hart Milman, D.D., late Dean of St. Paul's. John Murray, Albemarle Street, 1869. "The Cathedral in the American Church," by James M. Woolworth, LL.D., Chancellor of the Diocese of Nebraska. New York, E. P. Dutton & Co., 1883.

HON. JAS. M. WOOLWORTH, LL.D.

Catholic. The word Catholic, as its etymology shows, was of Greek origin. It is compounded of two words (*Kata* and *olos*, Καθ' ὅλου), and means literally "on the whole," or, as applied to the Church, "Universal." St. Cyril, Patriarch of Jerusalem, before the middle of the fourth century, and Alexander, Patriarch of Alexandria earlier in the same century, both used it. It probably came rapidly into use throughout the Church after the second General Council, held in Constantinople 381 A.D., which gives the whole article, as follows: "In One Holy Catholic and Apostolic Church."

Catholic was used commonly as one of the names of the Church from the time of the first General Council, held at Nice in Bithynia 325 A.D., though it does not appear in the original Creed of Nice. It designated those who adhered to the ancient faith as defined at Nice. They called themselves Catholics, but named the Heretics after their most prominent leaders,—*e.g.*, Cerinthians, Marcionites, Montanists, Arians, Nestorians, Eutychians, etc.

Catholic was not long coming into all forms of the Creed, and became a significant and distinguishing title of the Church in common use both among Greeks and Latins. It was and still is accepted as one of the *four* notes of the Church. "The Body of CHRIST," from its very nature and constitution, was, is, and ever must continue, One, Holy, Catholic, and Apostolic; One, as being the organic body in mystical but real union with "Him, who is Head over all things to the Church:" Holy, as the depositum of the truth and dispenser of the sacraments, by which holiness is begun, nurtured, and increased: Catholic, as sent into all the world to preach the Gospel, to baptize and feed with the "Bread of Heaven" every one, and all who would be saved: and, finally, Apostolic, as built upon the foundations of the Apostles and Prophets, JESUS CHRIST Himself being the chief cornerstone."

The word has been sadly misused in the course of history, and most signally by the assumptions of the Roman Church. In very early times the Bishop of Rome was accounted one of the five Patriarchs of the Catholic Church, each one officially equal to the other. These patriarchates differed in numbers and influence; those of Rome and Constantinople being the greatest. Indeed, so long as Christian emperors ruled the Roman Empire, from the throne in Byzantium, the See of Constantinople was the chief in power, though on account of the dignity of old Rome a kind of respectful priority was allotted to the Roman Bishop. Still the assumption of the exclusive right to the name Catholic was never made by Rome in early times, and is not yet even incidentally confessed, much less allowed, in the East. Incidentally it has come into common use in the West, so that sectarians and the world call the Roman Church Catholic; but no careful and well-taught English or American Churchman ever gives her that ancient, significant, and almost sacred title.

Although the Continental Reformers did not take the term Catholic to themselves, yet the Church of England and her daughter, the American Church, have adhered to it most tenaciously. It sets forth their claim to oneness with the primitive Church. It is the sign, warrant, and assurance that their ministry is derived in unbroken descent from the Apostles; that the faith they promulgate and bear witness to is the one faith which has been from the beginning; that the sacraments they administer are CHRIST'S own, wherewith He is ever present to bestow specifically the grace He attached to each; and that the HOLY SPIRIT continually indwells Her, making Her witness acceptable and Her ministrations effectual.

The term Catholic is so set forth among the gems of truth in the Creed that it demands solemn use. They who make it a designation of party, either do not recognize or feel its devotional significance, or do not perceive the fullness of its meaning. It may be contended for earnestly when denied us, as even the very name of our LORD may be; but its ordinary use is a devotional one. When spoken it should bring up in grateful souls the rich and dear consciousness that

"Living saints and dead
But one communion make,
All join in CHRIST, their living Head,
And of His *life* partake."

The ancient, though not primitive, application of the name Catholic to the Church and its universal use for more than fifteen hundred years, have induced the desire, which has been often warmly expressed on the floor of General Convention, to change the title of the American Church from the present "Protestant Episcopal" to "The Catholic Church in America." It is argued that we do not weakly protest against Rome, but that we firmly and resolutely reject her uncatholic assumptions. It is said that Episcopal, as a distinctive appellation, may be interpreted as a negative confession that the Episcopacy is not essential to the legitimate propagation of the Church. However the controversies about the name may fare, it is at least a fact that the American Church is, as the Creed she recites sets forth, a true and unsevered outgrowth from the stem of the One, Holy, Catholic, and Apostolic Church; and that she has the right, whether she exercise it or not, to call herself by the old name.

Her children are not disposed to lose the title to their own legitimacy. The growing knowledge and serious appreciation of the fact that they are born through and nurtured by the Bride of CHRIST is causing a wide and deep perception of the value of their Catholic heritage. They are more and more accounting the Church as in truth Catholic, and thereby perceiving more intelligently and feeling more profoundly their common union with all the early and late Christians, in life or death, who are in the immortal Catholic Church, of which CHRIST was, is, and ever will continue the Living Head.

Catholic Epistles. The Epistles of St. James, the two of St. Peter, the three of St. John, and the Epistle of St. Jude are so called. There is no very satisfactory reason for the title, which yet is felt to be most appropriate. Perhaps the title as it is translated in our Authorized Version gains its true explanation, The General Epistles, as encyclical and not to local Churches; and since it may be objected that this cannot apply to the second and third of St. John, it may be naturally not refused to these short epistles, since it is proper to the longer first epistle.

Celibacy. The virgin state; but the word is now used generally to denote the vow of never marrying exacted from members of the Roman Church, who enter either some monastic order, or take ecclesiastical office. It has no real defense, and is productive of much evil. It is true, however, that under some circumstances even St. Paul commended the unmarried state, but this has no true relation to the question. The New Testament says nothing that bears upon this except that several of the Apostles were married, and in the direction to Timothy (1 Tim. iii. 12), that the Bishop should be the husband of one wife. But there arose at an early date a strong feeling that the clergy should remain unmarried. Voluntary vows of virginity were common and increased as the Church grew, till the women were numerous enough to be put into a general organization under Episcopal rule. The tendency was strong to urge the clergy to remain unmarried. This increased so that the clergy were usually unmarried; but there was no imperative rule beyond continuous efforts by the Bishops, both East and West, to carry out this purpose, till the Civil Law forbade the priest to marry after ordination. It is needless here to recount the conditions permitted or the disabilities incurred. The Eastern Church was contented with this restriction; but the Latin Church went further, and after a long and severe struggle broke up the marriage of those in orders. It was disastrous in many ways, and the only gain was the dependence of the clergy upon the Church alone by the severance of all family ties. The Reformation was the only shock the system has received. The Church of England at once threw off the yoke, and permitted marriage to her clergy.

The person in the Roman Church who takes a monastic vow is bound by this promise, and so too every Deacon, Priest, and Bishop. It is probable that many clergy, living in apparent concubinage, were secretly bound by a marriage vow; at least, there is proof that many on their death-bed, by acknowledging the woman, attempted to establish a marriage and to salve their conscience.

Cemetery. A sleeping-place. This name was used by Christians to denote the place of burial. It was a new and beautiful use of a word that Christianity introduced. ("Death is not death among Christians, but is called a sleeping and a resting.") It was in use before the year 222 A.D. The early Church was very careful, if possible, to separate its dead from those of the heathen, and so acquired burial-grounds at the earliest opportunity. In Rome the burials were made in the underground galleries of the catacombs. The cemeteries were seized in times of persecution, but were very generally promptly restored. The word has long since lost its old sense, and now means simply a burial-place.

Censer. A light vessel, swung by chains, and in which incense is burnt. In mediæval and later times in the English Church, at the time of the celebration of the Holy Communion it is always used.

It was one of the vessels used in Jewish worship. It contained the live coals upon which incense was put to incense the altar and the sacrifice, morning and evening. The censer was specially used when the High-Priest, on the great day of Atonement, went into the Holy of Holies. Its use in the Christian Church, while indicated, is not defined at an early age. The earliest censers (thurible) mentioned weighed thirty and fifteen pounds respectively, and so could not have been swung. They were said to be gifts of Constantine to the Church of Rome.

Censures, Ecclesiastical. The penalties by which, for some notable sin, Christian laymen are deprived of communion, or clergymen are prohibited to execute their sacred office. These censures are excommunication, suspension, and interdict, and (lesser in rank) irregularity. All sentences incurred by any disobedience or sin are censures of the Church. They involve the withholding of those gifts for the spiritual life which she has to give; and if the sentence be justly incurred, the loss to the guilty party of all that they would convey. The Church may cut off from communion, or inflict lesser punishment, but she cannot expel from it and deprive the sinner of the entrance into the visible Church which the sacrament of baptism has given. She can discipline, and that, too, severely, but she cannot finally disinherit: that is the sole privilege of CHRIST alone at the day of judgment.

Central New York, Diocese of. In 1865 A.D., Bishop Coxe called the attention of his Convention to the need of greater provision for Episcopal work in the limits of his See. During 1866 A.D., the subject was further discussed, and in 1867 A.D. it was reported to the Convention by a committee appointed for that purpose that steps be taken to have the General Convention permit the erection of the counties of Broome, Cayuga, Chemung, Chenango, Cortland, Jefferson, Lewis, Madison, Oneida, Onondaga, Oswego, Seneca, Tioga, and Tompkins into a new See. A further resolution was offered looking to a Federate Council of the Dioceses in the State. The General Convention of 1868 A.D. concurred, and a primary Convention was called at Utica on November 10, 1868 A.D. Fifty clergy and eighty-seven lay deputies met in Trinity Church, Utica, to effect the organization. Rev. Dr. F. Rogers was chosen President, and Rev. A. B. Goodrich, Secretary. A minute upon the separation and cordially recognizing the pastoral care of Bishop Coxe in the past and tendering him their thanks was passed. On November 11 the election of Bishop was made the order of the day. After five ballots Rev. Dr. A. H. Littlejohn was duly elected. Dr. Littlejohn declined the election, and a special Convention was summoned on January 13, 1869 A.D. Bishop Coxe presided over fifty-seven clergy and one hundred and forty-seven lay deputies; Rev. Dr. Littlejohn preached the opening sermon. At the third ballot the Rev. Dr. F. D. Huntingdon was elected. He was consecrated in the parish church which he was leaving, Emmanuel, Boston, by Rt. Rev. Bishop Smith, on April 8, 1869 A.D. Bishops Eastburn, Potter, Clark, Coxe, Neely, and Doane joined in the act of consecration.

The Constitution which had been proposed and acted on in the previous special Convention was adopted June 14 at a special Convention in Grace Church, Utica, which Convention immediately adjourned and organized as the second Annual Convention. The reports at that Convention were chiefly upon the needs of the Diocese in the work of education, a work which has been pushed forward in that See with great energy. An excellent report was made upon Education in the Family, the Means of Church Education, the Practicability of Parochial Schools, and a statement of the resources of the Diocese in this important work. The following pregnant resolutions were adopted:

"*Resolved*, That the chief seminary of Christian education is the Christian family, and that all parents connected with the Church should endeavor to realize the privileges and obligations of the baptismal covenant, both as respects themselves and their children; should aim to fulfill its pledges by the faithful inculcation of those things which a Christian child ought to know and believe for its soul's health: by a watchful supervision over their children's studies, reading, and associations; and by such care, in reference to their places of resort for secular teaching, as may be necessary to guard them not only against contamination of morals, but also the undermining of their faith in the doctrines and practices of the Church.

"*Resolved*, That we recommend the establishment, whenever practicable, of parochial, infant, and grammar schools, at least for children from seven to twelve years of age.

"*Resolved*, That the clergy be requested

to take cognizance and to include in their parochial reports the mention of such private schools in their parishes as may be conducted or controlled by communicants of the Church, provided the proprietors of such schools shall give their consent to the publication of such statement.

"*Resolved*, That as the fear of the LORD is the beginning of wisdom, and all true morality is founded upon religion, in the judgment of this Convention any system of secular education that is not supplemented in some manner by an inculcation of the fundamental doctrines and precepts of Christianity, must in the end fail to secure the real welfare of society and the permanent prosperity of the State."

Principles as outspoken and as strongly stated as these show how thoroughly awake the Diocese of Central New York is to the current evils in the popular education, and how miserably the present system fails in meeting all the needs of a Christian commonwealth, and of giving what the Church is bound to try to give her children, the lambs of the flock of CHRIST. It is in this line that the Bishop has recently written upon the defects and dangers of the system of education the State attempts to provide. It is under such leadership that the educational efforts in the Diocese have increased and deepened.

In 1869 there were 98 parishes and missions; in 1883 there were 138; in 1869 there were a total of 83 clergy at work; in 1883 there were 96 clergy; in 1869 there were 8774 communicants; in 1883 there were 12,848; in 1869 there were 1074 confirmed; in 1883 there were 1880; in 1869 there was a total of $249,116.20 contributed; in 1883 there was a total of $292,564.75 offered for GOD's work.

Summary of Statistics (from **Living Church Annual**) for 1886 A.D.: Clergy, 95; parishes and missions, 140; lay readers, 10; deaconesses, 2; families, 7856; baptisms, infants, 969, adults, 393, total, 1362; confirmed, 852; communicants, 13,154; marriages, 455; burials, 851; Sunday-school teachers, 1072; scholars, 8427; contributions, $247.627.89.

Central Pennsylvania, History of the Diocese of, 1871–1883 A.D In 1866 A.D., at the next Convention after the formation of the Diocese of Pittsburg within the original limits of the Diocese of Pennsylvania, the subject of another division of the latter Diocese was brought up by a resolution and referred to a committee of seven, to report thereon at the next annual Convention. The report of the committee, when presented in 1867 A.D., showed that out of 75 parishes in the district proposed to be set off, only 29 wished division, and out of 58 clergymen, only 26 approved the measure.

At that Convention it was resolved, the Bishop of Pennsylvania concurring, that consent be given to the proposed division of the Diocese, on condition that two-thirds of the clergy and of the parishes now entitled to representation therein, and being in that portion of the Diocese proposed to be set off, do give official information to the Standing Committee of their desire for such division, and that they have provided sufficient means for the support of their Bishop, the proposed division being all that portion of the present Diocese of Pennsylvania which lies outside of the counties of Philadelphia, Chester, Delaware, Montgomery, and Bucks.

By the same Convention, all the documents touching the division of the Diocese were referred to the Committee on Division, appointed at the last Convention, and the said committee continued. It was also resolved that the committee confer with the Bishop of the Diocese of Pennsylvania and embody the result of their conference in a report to the Convention. This the committee did in 1868 A.D., and the consent of the Convention was given to a division in what is called the fourteen-county line upon certain conditions and restrictions. The conditions were not complied with, and the plan failed.

The Bishop of Pennsylvania, in the Convention of 1870 A.D., again called attention to the subject, and asked for a division of the Diocese, declaring that he should not withhold his consent from any line which the Convention, after full discussion, should in its wisdom fix upon, provided that it should leave in the Diocese of Pennsylvania not less than the five counties aforesaid.

In accordance with this portion of the Bishop's address the Convention of 1870 A.D. gave consent to the formation of a new Diocese to be thus composed; and also instructed their deputies to the next General Convention to present their resolution, duly authenticated, to that body, and request its consent to, and ratification of, the same. In June, 1871 A.D., the Bishop of the Diocese of Pennsylvania appointed the following gentlemen a Committee of Clergymen and Laymen to take charge of the preparation of the necessary documents concerning the division of the Diocese, and to lay the same before General Convention, viz.: The Rev. Messrs. A. A. Marple (chairman), Wm. P. Lewis, D.D., Leighton Coleman, R. J. Keeling, D.D., and Wm. P. Orrick; the Hon. Messrs. Frederick Watts, T. E. Franklin, Judge Elwell, Messrs. A. Ricketts and Henry Coppée, LL.D. (secretary).

In General Convention, held at Baltimore during the month of October, 1871 A.D., the House of Bishops and the House of Clerical and Lay Deputies duly concurred in giving consent to and ratifying the formation of the new Diocese from date of the 6th of October, 1871 A.D., admitting it into union with the General Convention from and after the 8th day of November, 1871 A.D., and directing that the name of the new Diocese be determined by the Primary Convention thereof, with the consent of the Bishop of Pennsylvania.

Canonical action being thus complete, the

Bishop of Pennsylvania issued a call for the assembling of the Primary Convention of the new Diocese at St. Stephen's Church, Harrisburg, on Wednesday, the 8th of November, for organization, and appointed Robert A. Lamberton, Esq., of Harrisburg, to act as temporary Secretary.

In the Primary Convention 59 of the clergy were entitled to seats, of whom 57 were present, and 193 of the laity, of whom 134 were present, representing 75 parishes, situated in 26 counties. The Rt. Rev. Wm. Bacon Stevens, D.D., LL.D., Bishop of Pennsylvania, was President. There were present also the following-named visitors from the Church of England: the Rt. Rev. Dr. Selwyn, Lord Bishop of Lichfield (the Apostle of New Zealand), with his son, the Rev. John R. Selwyn, and the Very Rev. Dr. Howson, Dean of Chester, and the Rev. J. H. Iles, Rector of Wolverhampton. The Bishop of Lichfield delivered the sermon, and divine service being concluded, the clergy and lay delegates present and claiming seats in the Convention were called to order by Bishop Stevens, who introduced the English Churchmen, the Convention rising to receive them. On proceeding to name the new Diocese, the following designations were put forward by various members, viz., Central Pennsylvania, Harrisburg, Williamsport, Bethlehem, Eastern Pennsylvania, Lichfield, and Middle Diocese of Pennsylvania. On the fourth ballot the first name was chosen by a concurrence of both orders, and received the consent of the Bishop of Pennsylvania. On the evening of the first day the Lord Bishop of Lichfield and Dean Howson addressed the Convention on " The Work of Women in the Church."

The Committee on the Endowment of the Episcopate of the Diocese made report that they had obtained $41,000 in cash and pledges; that they considered it expedient to raise the sum to the amount of $75,000. The Convention resolved that until the income from the Endowment Fund should fully meet the Bishop's salary (which was fixed at $4500), an equitable assessment should be made upon the parishes for the whole amount of the same, each parish being credited upon the said assessment with the interest accruing on its subscription to the Endowment Fund; and the committee was requested to solicit additional subscriptions to that Fund.

Nominations for a Bishop being in order, the Rev. Dr. Keeling nominated the Rev. Mark Antony DeWolfe Howe, D.D., rector of St. Luke's Church, Philadelphia; the Rev. Dr. Paret nominated the Rev. George Leeds, rector of Grace Church, Baltimore. The vote of the clergy having been taken, on the first ballot the Rev. Dr. Howe was declared duly nominated by the clergy to the laity; and on the first vote of the laity, a majority having voted for approval, the Chair declared that the Rev. Mark Antony DeWolfe Howe, D.D., was the choice of the Convention for Bishop of Central Pennsylvania. Whereupon the Rev. Dr. Paret moved and it was

"*Resolved*, That the members of this Convention, clerical and lay, do unanimously accept the election of the Rev. M. A. DeWolfe Howe, D.D., to be the first Bishop of this Diocese; and do, without exception or reserve, earnestly entreat his acceptance of the same, pledging him in his work for CHRIST and the Church their zealous and loving co-operation."

The Convention also elected the following Standing Committee of the Diocese: Clerical members—the Rev. Messrs. A. A. Marple, D. Washburn, William P. Orrick, William C. Leverett, and R. J. Keeling, D.D. Lay members—the Hon. Messrs. J. W. Maynard, V. L. Maxwell, E. O. Parry, Asa Packer, and Mr. R. A. Lamberton.

The Constitution and Canons of the Diocese of Pennsylvania were adopted by this Diocese with such few alterations as were necessary or expedient.

The Standing Committee having been instructed by the Primary Convention to take the necessary steps for the consecration of the Rev. Dr. Howe, appointed the Rev. Dr. Keeling to make the proper communications to the Standing Committees of all the Dioceses in the United States, and to the presiding Bishop. When the canonical consents had been received, the presiding Bishop, the Rt. Rev. Benjamin Bosworth Smith, D.D. (a maternal uncle of the Bishop-elect), appointed his consecration to take place on the Feast of the Innocents, in St. Luke's Church, Philadelphia. Of the House of Bishops there were present and taking part in the consecration on that day the presiding Bishop and Bishop of Kentucky, the Rt. Rev. Drs. Lee, of Delaware, McIlvaine, of Ohio, Bedell, assistant Bishop of Ohio, Potter, of New York, Kerfoot, of Pittsburg, Clark, of Rhode Island, and Morris, Missionary Bishop of Oregon and Washington Territory. The attendant Presbyters of the Bishop-elect were the Rev. Mr. Washburn and the Rev. Dr. Paret. The sermon was delivered by the Assistant and Bishop of Ohio, and the presentment made by the Bishops of Rhode Island and of Pittsburg. The Rev. Mr. Marple read the testimonial of the Convention of Central Pennsylvania, the Rev. Mr. Leverett, the certificate of the consent of the majority of the Standing Committees, and the Rev. Benjamin I. Haight, D.D., that of the majority of the Bishops.

During the twelve years of its existence the Diocese has increased in the number of its clergy from 59 to 96. Twenty-eight new church buildings have been consecrated, some of which stand noted among the rural Dioceses of the United States for their costliness and remarkable beauty. In the same period 13,945 baptisms have been administered by the parochial and mission clergy, and Bishop Howe has confirmed 8217 persons within his own jurisdiction. The whole number of parishes and mission stations is 114, containing 7486 communicants, and 12,063 Bible-class attendants and Sunday-school pupils. Forty-eight of the parishes possess rectory-houses, 12 have also school-houses, and 10 own cemeteries. In the same twelve years the total sum of offerings made in the young Diocese for all Church objects is $2,531,790.10. So vastly has the work of this jurisdiction increased that in consideration thereof, joined with the advanced age of the Bishop, who has declared his inability to fulfill all the duties of his office without the help of a coadjutor, the last Annual Convention, 1883 A.D., appointed a committee to report at the next Convention on the subject of the election of an Assistant Bishop.

Central Pennsylvania is divided into four Convocations, named respectively the Reading, the Harrisburg, the Williamsport, and the Northeastern; the Presidents of which constitute the clerical members of the Board of Diocesan Missions. The Secretary of Convention is Mr. R. A. Lamberton, LL.D.; the Treasurer of the Convention and Episcopal Funds is Mr. P. R. Stetson; of the Board of Missions, Mr. Robt. H. Sayre; the Registrar of the Diocese is Mr. Wm. H. Chandler, Ph.D.; and the Chancellor, Hon. Thomas E. Franklin.

The Diocese has seven Church institutions, viz.: the Lehigh University, at South Bethlehem, founded and endowed by the Hon. Asa Packer, of Mauch Chunk, in 1866 A.D., of which Robt. A. Lamberton, LL.D., is President, with a faculty of thirteen members. The library building, which is one of the finest and most substantial in the country, was built by Judge Packer in memory of a deceased daughter, Mrs. Lucy E. Lindeman, and is called the "Lucy Packer Library." It contains at present 35,000 volumes, and is endowed with $500,000. Judge Packer also endowed the university with $1,500,000. St. Luke's Hospital, at South Bethlehem, incorporated in 1872 A.D., received from the same great benefactor of the Diocese an endowment of $300,000. The Bishopthorpe School for Girls, also situated at South Bethlehem, was founded in 1867 A.D. Selwyn Hall, at Reading, is the Diocesan school for boys. Cottage Hill Seminary, York, is a home school for young ladies and children. The Yeates Institute is a Church school for boys, at Lancaster. The Church Home and Orphanage, the latest established institution, is at Jonestown, Lebanon Co.

The Bishop resides at Reading, where he has a Cathedral church, the front elevation of which is regarded as being one of striking beauty.

Statistics for 1886 A.D.: Clergy, 98; par., 90; miss., 31; can. for H. O., 4; ord., D. 1, P. 3; bap., 1415; con., 886; com., 8260; contr., $228,475.68. REV. W. B. MORROW.

Ceremony. The primary meaning is that of a corporeal act giving expression to a spiritual act. For instance, in marriage, the whole office is a series of ceremonies, but is itself a rite. In Confirmation the imposition of hands is the ceremony, but the whole conduct or action of the office is a rite. So of the other offices and sacramental acts of the Church. But this distinction cannot be always accurately followed from the lax usage of the proper terms; and the ritual is often called the ceremonial of worship. These rites, or ceremonies, are properly completely under the control of the Church, and while we may not alter aught that CHRIST has instituted by word and example, yet the Church, as a living power, and ministering to the spiritual needs of all men, must have power to alter, amend, or control rites and ceremonies suitable to the tendency of the peoples she ministers to. The ceremonial of one part of the Holy Catholic Church may be an example for, but is not an authority to, another independent part, ministering to a population with totally different habitudes.

The charge so often made, that the Church seized upon and used pagan festivals, while much exaggerated as to the facts, is rather a mark of her wisdom and adaptability, that she is to save men, not to cast them through some single mould. This rule holds under all circumstances. Therefore, however much individual tastes may regret the departures made in our Prayer-Book from the exact English order, the changes themselves were made upon this first and proper principle, and the fathers of the first General Convention, which adopted our present book, are to be commended for their wisdom and moderation, and were surely under the guidance of the HOLY SPIRIT.

Chaldee. The language spoken by the peoples inhabiting the alluvial plains of the Euphrates and Tigris. It was a cognate language, or more nearly a dialect of that family of the Shemitic language to which the Aramaic and the Hebrew belonged. It could not be readily understood by the Hebrews (2 Kings xviii. 26, 28). They came in direct and continuous contact with it during the Captivity. Parts of Jeremiah (ch. x. 11), of Daniel (ch. ii. 4; vii. 28), and Ezra (ch. iv. 7; vi. 18; vii. 12-26) are pure Chaldee, but many words and phrases are to be found in the later portions of Holy Scripture which are closely connected with the Chaldee.

Chalice. The Cup used in the administration of the wine in the LORD'S Supper. The word is from the Latin calyx. It was made of any material accessible. At first, of glass, of wood, of silver, or of gold; but soon wood was forbidden (though still used in places till a late date), and glass, pewter, gold, silver, bronze were used. These chalices were often of very beautiful workmanship, finely polished and chased, and in many cases incrusted with precious stones.

Chancel. The space in a church which contains the choir and sanctuary, and which was generally separated from the nave by a rail or grating (cancelli), from which it derives its name. It is a characteristic difference between the Eastern and Western Churches that in the former the distinction between the bema, or sanctuary, and the choir is so much more strongly marked than that between the choir and the nave, in the latter the distinction between the nave and the choir is much more strongly marked than that between the choir and the sanctuary. (Dictionary of Christian Antiquities, Smith & Cheetham, *sub voc.*) Legally, the chancel is the parson's freehold, and he is obliged to keep it in repair by English Ecclesiastical Law.

Chancellor. In England he is the law officer to the Bishop, advising him in all legal matters and holding courts for him. He may be either a layman or a clergyman (Blackstone, i. 382). It was not of very ancient introduction into the English Church, being rather an imitation of the like title by the state. It includes two other offices,— Official Principal and Vicar-General. "The Official hears causes between party and party concerning wills, legacies, marriages, and the like . . . The proper work of the Vicar-General is the exercise and administration of jurisdiction, purely spiritual, by the authority and under the direction of the Bishop, as visitation, correction of manners, granting institutions, and the like, with a general inspection of men and things, in order to the preserving of discipline and good government in the Church." (Burns, Ecclesiastical Law, vol. i. 289.)

In fifteen of our Dioceses there is a law officer bearing this official title of Chancellor, who is appointed or elected to advise the Bishop and the Standing Committee upon all legal matters which affect the interests of the Church as his professional counsel may be asked or required. But his duties are by broad construction often so extended as to make him also law adviser to the Diocesan Conventions

Chant. *Vide* MUSIC.

Chantry. In the English Pre-reformation Church, the endowment or founding of a small chapel or separated place in the church, for saying Masses for the soul of some person departed this life. Wolsey was in the beginning of his career a chantry priest. When such foundations were given by act of Parliament to the king, in the last year of Henry VIII. (1545 A.D.), at his death Cranmer tried to obtain from Edward VI. the remnant that had not been confiscated for the relief of the poor parochial clergy, but failed.

Chapel. The derivation of the word is very doubtful. It may be from the fact that the kings of France upon their campaigns carried with them St. Martin's cloak (cappa), and the tent in which it was kept and where service was held was called the Capella. The English Church distinguishes between chapels royal, domestic chapels, collegiate chapel, chapels of ease for those parishioners who live at a great distance from the parish church, parochial chapels, which are endowed apart from the mother-church, free chapels,—*i.e.*, exempt from Episcopal jurisdiction,— chapels belonging to guilds and corporations, and chapels which were built adjoining to the church building.

Chaplain. Originally a Priest attached to a chapel. Then a Minister rendering service to some person empowered to employ one, as an Archbishop, who may have eight chaplains, and so too others who according to their rank may maintain a proper number. Clergymen officiating in the army and navy, or in prisons, hospitals, or public corporations, who are serving Legislative bodies, are called Chaplains. So too the clergy who are appointed to examine candidates for Holy Orders are called Examining Chaplains. In fact, it is a general title applied to any clergyman serving any corporate body in his ministerial capacity.

Chapter. (*Vide* BIBLE.) The word is derived from the Latin *Caput*. It is the name for one of the principal divisions of a book;—in the Bible, one of the larger sections into which the separate books are divided. It was the work of Cardinal Hugo (1240 A.D.), who divided the Bible into convenient sections for the purposes of a Comment which he wrote upon it, and his division has been the one followed ever since.

Chapter. *Vide* DEAN, and CATHEDRAL.

Character. In theological language "the seal." The special graces stamped upon the soul by the gifts and graces of the various means of salvation given to us in the Church. The seal of the SPIRIT of the LORD is spoken of in such connection by St. Paul, and in one or two places in the Revelation. (Compare 2 Cor. i. 22; Eph. i. 13; iv. 30; Romans iv. 11; Rev. vii. 3-8; Rev. ix. 4; 2 Tim. ii. 19; in all of which a spiritual impress of some indelible character is more or less clearly asserted. Of these, 2 Cor. i. 22; Eph. i. 13; and iv. 30, refer clearly to confirmation.) It is not to be doubted that there is an impress made upon our spiritual nature by the gifts of Baptism, of Confirmation, and of Ordination. If the grace is given, it is bestowed once for all, however we may afterwards misuse it or abuse it.

Charge. The address of the Bishop to his Clergy and Laity. In the English Church Archdeacons do also deliver charges. In the American Church it is usually a weighty discussion of some important question relating either to the Church at large or to the Diocese. It is generally delivered separately, but is sometimes read, together with the address, containing his report of work done during the conventional year, to the Clergy and Laity in convention. Often, apart from their ability, these charges make a step forward in the Church's work.

Chasuble. An ancient vestment which was and is often worn by the Priest at the celebration of the Holy Communion. The chasuble was at first the out-of-door dress of the ecclesiastic when it had become distinctively a Church garb. But by the ninth century it became a part of the Vestment worn at a solemn service. It was circular, with an aperture in the centre by which, slipped over the head, it could be worn upon the shoulders, and it was wide enough when falling from the shoulders to cover the hands. It is one of the Vestments ordered by the famous Ornaments Rubric of Edward VI. to be worn at the celebration of the Holy Communion. It was laid aside for a long time, but has in recent years been revived. The use of it is not very general in this country.

Cherub. The wondrous spirits of Ezekiel's vision who spake not, though the beat of their wings was as the voice of speech; but there was a Voice from the firmament above them. The number in Ezekiel is four. The Cherubim were set in front of the Garden of Eden to keep it. Two were imaged over the mercy-seat of the Ark in the Tabernacle. Two of colossal size overshadowed it in Solomon's Temple. The Cherubim are first mentioned as guarding the gates of Eden. Their images were to be put upon the mercy-seat, probably in solid wrought-work. They were spoken of in the Psalms xviii. 10; lxxx. 1. In Ezekiel's first vision they are called Living Creatures and described as similar to the four Living Creatures in Rev. iv., but are identified both as Cherubim and as the Living Creatures of the first vision in Ezekiel's second vision (ch. x. 20). Mysterious and incomparable, yet likened to creatures of earth, the bearers of the Throne, voiceless, yet with harmonious flight, whose beat is as the voice of a mighty host.

Cherubic Hymn. This name is often given to the Tersanctus. But, in fact, it is a hymn which has no parallel in the Western Church. The Hymn and its preface, as it stands in the Liturgy of St. Chrysostom, is this: " Let us who mystically represent the Cherubim, and sing the hymn to the quickening TRINITY, lay by at this time all worldly cares, that we may receive the KING OF GLORY invisibly attended by the angelic orders. Alleluia! Alleluia! Alleluia!" It really is later than St. Chrysostom's day, and is an insertion, as it was composed in the time of Justinian (530 A.D.). It also has its place in the service of the protheses, and therefore cannot be identical with the Tersanctus which is sung in the Canon.

Chimere. The upper robe of a Bishop. (*Vide* VESTMENTS.)

Choir. In the Church, the place of the choristers without the chancel-rail, but upon the dais between the nave and the chancel. But the name is transferred popularly with us to the band of singers who have charge of the music of the Sanctuary. They have a long history behind them, for they are the representatives of the organization of the singers and musicians under David (1 Chron. xxv.) and under Solomon. They were reorganized by Nehemiah (ch. xii. *passim*). Every choir, properly appointed, should be large enough to be divided into two parts, that whenever necessary there may be antiphonal singing. Its members, if possible, should be communicants, and should have set before them, very clearly, the duty and the glory of their work in the worship. It was customary in the early Church to set apart the singers with the charge, " What thou believest in thine heart that sing with thy lips." There are two or three fundamental principles too often lost sight of that should rule the conduct of the music by the choir. *They are the leaders of the musical part of the service of* GOD'S *Sanctuary;* therefore they should lead in such music only as the congregation can follow. *They are under the authority of the Rector*, and his will should be their wish. When they are ready to keep out all light and unseemly music, and to repress all indecency and irreverence in the performance of it, they will find his authority but a name. The music, at least of the hymns and chants, should be only from some one well-known book, with which such of the congregation as choose to do so can provide themselves. It is sometimes allowed the choir to select an elaborate setting for the TE DEUM, and to sing an anthem or an offertory sentence as an offering of their musical skill to the Giver of their talent,—a very appropriate and devout custom when it is kept within due limits.

The composition of the choir is often so difficult to arrange satisfactorily that it may be impossible to put any hint here given into practice. But it would be well, whenever it can be done, to select boys with a musical ear and good voice for the choir. Two men and four or six boys would make a good basis, though it is the least number that could be used. Sixteen voices form such a mass of sound that, whenever sufficient enthusiasm is shown, the congregation will always join in. But if not, devout women can more readily be obtained who will make an offering of their work and skill. There are two or three *desiderata* which should be attended to in country choirs,—to have but one Hymnal from which to sing; to be taught the responsibility resting upon them; to have full punctual attendance at practice; to feel that it is little short of an insult to Him, before Whom the innumerable choirs of heaven are ever singing, to offer a hasty, ill-prepared, irreverently-performed service of song.

Chorepiscopus. Local Bishops in the ancient Church. They were Bishops having a jurisdiction in the country under the Bishop of the city who had supreme jurisdiction, but was himself under the Metropolitan. It was, in fact, a local missionary extension of the Episcopate. Its powers were defined to be nearly what our Bishops now practically exercise upon a Visitation. They confirmed, consecrated churches, appointed readers and subdeacons, but could only ordain by license from the Bishop,—*i.e.*, they had spiritual authority, but by the terms of their work and jurisdiction only exercised it by special license. They could not administer the affairs of the Diocese, and could not intrude for any official work into a city Parish. Individual chorepiscopi assumed so much at times, and gave so much trouble latterly in the West, that they were suppressed. In the East, the Council of Laodicea (360 A.D.) dealt a blow which was followed up, till in about a century or a little more they disappeared. But there was a long, stout struggle in the West, and finally they were destroyed as an order by the tenth century, though there are instances of the office as late as the thirteenth century. Theirs was essentially a missionary extension of the Episcopate, which was suppressed with more or less difficulty when the Church became National. But an attempt to establish this order, the memory of which seems to have lingered in England, was made under Henry VIII. (1534 A.D.) by appointing several towns as seats for such Bishops, entitled Suffragan Bishops. The act, after slumbering nearly three hundred and fifty years, has been revived and has been acted upon. There are four Suffragans,—Dr. Parry, of Dover, under the Archbishop of Canterbury; Dr. How, of Bedford, under the Bishop of London; Dr. Trollope, of Nottingham, under the Bishop of Lincoln; and Dr. Bloomfield, of Colchester, under the Bishop of St. Albans.

Chrism. An anointing oil used from early time in the Church in Baptism and in Confirmation. It was more prominently used in mediæval times in the Oriental and Latin Churches. In Confirmation it has often been held by Latin ritualists that chrism is of the essence of the rite; but from the inspired record (Acts viii. 18, 19; xix. 6; Heb. vi. 2) it is certain that prayer and imposition of hands are only essential. In the Oriental Church the Priest confirms with the chrism blessed by the Bishop.

Chrisome. In the office of Baptism it was a white vesture which the priest put upon the child, saying, "Take this white vesture for a token of innocency," etc. It was ordered in the Anglo-Saxon Church (736 A.D.) that chrisomes be used for mending surplices or for the wrapping of chalices. The Prayer-Book of 1549 A.D. orders that the woman shall offer the chrisome when she comes to be churched. But if the child died before her churching she was excused from offering it. It was the custom to bury the child in the chrisome, but by an abuse of words the chrisome child meant a child that died *before* it was baptized.

Christian. The name given (possibly in jest) by the people of Antioch to the Disciples; but it was so perfectly appropriate that it supplanted the earlier name entirely. A Christian is a baptized member of CHRIST'S Holy Church. He can only become so by Baptism, for Baptism is the sacrament of entrance, the Door, by which we are admitted. But there has arisen a too common perversion of the term Christian in modern times, referring to the unchristian, inconsistent conduct of too many who bear the name but practically deny its power. Baptism makes a person the Child of GOD whether he is an obedient or a disobedient child, as birth makes a child a citizen of the state whether he prove to be a good citizen or not; or as the oath of allegiance makes an alien a citizen and gives him the protection of the state whether he prove faithful to his oath or not. Therefore to say, as many Christian people do, when bewailing their short-comings, "I wish I were a Christian," is a serious misleading phrase at least, if not involving much more. To say, "Would I were a better Christian!" is but a confession that we all should devoutly utter.

Christianity is usually defined as the Religion of the LORD JESUS CHRIST. This is correct, but not in the same sense as when we say the Religion of Buddha or of Mohammed. The origin of Christianity was, in fact, the founding of the organized Church from which, in its beginnings and in its continuance, it is not rationally separable. There can be no greater error than to regard Christianity as derived from the Bible, or the Church as a development of Christianity. It is strange that these relations are not generally or clearly understood, so patent are they to any thoughtful examination. Even the elementary doctrines common to all orthodox believers, those contained in the Apostles' Creed, were not all originally taught by the Divine Founder of Christianity in any recorded words. His birth of the Virgin Mary He does not allude to, and the great facts of His life, death, resurrection, and ascension were at most only predicted by Him. He never substituted Christianity for Judaism, nor declared the formal repeal of the law of Moses. What He did was to choose twelve men, organize them as a corporation in perpetuity, endow them with a charter, authorize them to teach certain doctrines which He had *privately* taught them, and which the HOLY GHOST was to recall, and intrust them with the mysterious sacramental rites of initiation (Baptism) and full membership (Holy Communion) in the society thus formed. He then made them a promise, to be and co-operate with them until the end of the world. "Receive ye the HOLY GHOST. As my FATHER has sent ME, even so send I you." There was the Charter with its enabling act. "Go ye into all the world and make disciples of all nations, baptizing them," etc. These were the mission and authority to initiate. "Lo, I am with you alway, even unto the end of the world." There was the promise of perpetuity and continued authority. *That* was Christianity when He left the world. Nothing more whatever. But that was the Church. It is clear that if all this was said to the Apostles only as individuals, no other individuals could ever lay claim to any rights or privileges under it, or to any promises made only to them. It is equally clear that if it was said to them as a chartered corporation, the rights, privileges, and promises so given can belong only to "them, their heirs and assigns," on condition of the charter not being vitiated and the corporation not lapsing. It is clear also that as the *individuals* were not to exist until the end of the world, the promise to be with them until the end of the world *must* have been made to them as a perpetual corporation. It is thus evident that all authorized and authoritative Christianity is necessarily bound up in that corporation, which is the Church. But further, it was this corporation, and this only, that formulated, elaborated, and propagated Christianity, and upon this authority alone its doctrines have been accepted. A very singular and solemn authority had been conferred upon it: "Whosoever sins ye remit, they are remitted unto them; and whosesoever sins ye retain, they are retained." It matters not what the exact meaning of these words may have been. They certainly conveyed a most solemn and unique authority of some kind upon those to whom they were said. That authority was to withhold or inflict some penalties upon those who should become members of the organization. But the individuals did not at once proceed to exercise such functions or to perform the duties assigned. They passed fifty days in close consultation, during which, as a recognized duty, they elected a new member to complete their corporate number. Then, always acting together, they perfected the organization of the society by selecting and ordaining Deacons, Presbyters, and Apostles (as Timothy and Titus), and by instructing these and sending them out with authority to teach doctrines and initiate members. These new Apostles were authorized to proceed in the same way to perpetuate the corporation, the original twelve exercising discipline, organizing and administering the Church, and putting into writing, personally and by the aid of two authorized assistants, the whole body of Truth now accepted as Christianity. In this organization, therefore, Christianity consisted, and must continue to consist. If the corporation has lapsed,—if the original organization has ceased to exist, or become essentially altered in its form and methods,—there can be no authorized or authoritative Christianity now among men. All this is recorded in the Bible. But it amounts to nothing unless we remember that Christianity *is not derived from the Bible*, and further remember how it is that we know the Bible to be true. The simple fact is, that when the Church of CHRIST was organized the Bible did not exist. Even the Old Testament, as accepted by the Jewish Church of our LORD'S time, was not the Old Testament of the "Protestant" Bible. It contained what is known as the "Apocrypha;" not all together in separate books, but dispersed among the Canonical Books, and in some cases interpolating their text. It is to be carefully noted that our LORD Himself used and quoted this interpolated Septuagint Version without one recorded word of dissent. The New Testament Scriptures were not yet written. These consist of Four Gospels, written by two Apostles and two Evangelists working under their immediate oversight; the book of "Acts," written by one of these Evangelists to record the doings of the Apostles; twenty-one Epistles, being letters addressed by five of the Apostles at various times to organized Churches, or to individuals, or to the Christian society at large; and one book of "Revelation," whether a poem, a prophecy, or a rhapsody has never been fully determined. This also by the last of the original Apostles. But these "Books" were written during a period comprising at least forty years, and after probably twenty years of oral teaching. In this period there were extant (as St. Luke tells us) "many" other Gospels, and at least one other Epistle, *i.e.*, that to the Laodiceans. Thus there was certainly no "Bible" up to the time when the last Apostle died. But there *was* Christianity. Hence Christianity is *not* derived from the Bible. But *after* that last Apostle was dead some organized authority—certainly not the simple agreement of the mass of Christian people—determined what was and what was not GOD's revealed truth to man; rejected all the Apocryphal books and passages of the Old Testament,—which our LORD Himself had not done,—all extant "Gospels" save four, and all Apostolic Epistles except twenty-one. The same authority determined the "Revelation" to be inspired Scripture. Could that authority be aught else than the continued Corporation, the Church? Not possibly. Could any higher power be claimed or exercised by a human organization, or could such organization thus act except by a conceded Divine authorization? Clearly, then, it is the Church which is acknowledged by all Christian people to have given the Bible to the world, and the terms Christianity and "the Church" are convertible. But this being so, the definition of Christianity is not complete until we determine what is meant by "the Church." About this there can be no uncertainty or indefiniteness. It *must* be the perpetuated Corporation established and chartered by our LORD in person, which has come down in unbroken succession from the original Corporators, with its charter unvitiated and its constitution diligently observed and regarded. It must possess the essential form of the original organization; it must hold and practice the faith and sacraments intrusted to the Apostles for preservation, dissemination, and perpetuation; it must show its authority and that of its officers derived in unbroken succession and in the prescribed form from those Apostles; and it must prove its faithful performance of all the objects for which it was organized and perpetuated. Otherwise there can be no Christianity and no divinely-administered religion or reliable Divine promises left to mankind. Wherever these notes are found there is the historic Church of CHRIST, which in its universal organization is identical with Christianity, and upon the unbroken testimony of which rests the only authority for believing and accepting the Christian Bible with *all* that it contains. No Christian sect or communion which lacks the Apostolic form and constitution of Bishops (or Apostles), Priests (or Presbyters), and Deacons, no properly organized Church which has vitiated the Creed or abandoned the two original sacraments of Baptism and the LORD'S Supper, nor any single and separate part of the Corporation, whether Roman, Greek, or Anglican, can justly claim to be that Church whose charter and mission was "to all nations." The Church Universal in her integrity, in her authoritative Episcopal order, in her orthodox and pure faith, and in her duly administered sacraments is the perpetuated corporation in which Christianity consists, and thus when we express our belief in Christianity we only express our belief in the ONE, HOLY, CATHOLIC CHURCH.

REV. ROBERT WILSON, D.D.

Christmas. This Feast falls on December 25. Though this date is now universally observed, yet at first there was a diversity of practice. In Egypt April 20 and May 20 were observed. In Palestine, and the East generally, the 5th of January was kept, while the West observed the present day. But about the first part of the fifth century the East accepted the Western feast-day, and it became universal. St. Chrysostom has a homily which is very important upon this topic. The outline of the reasons for supposing the 25th of December to be the true date is this: Most probably Zacharias took the place of the High-Priest upon the great day of Atonement (such substitution, when some unforeseen accident prevented the High-Priest from executing his office himself, has been abundantly proven out of Josephus and Maimonides), which fell that year upon September 23. It was while he was within the veil the message of the angel came to him. This would place the nativity of St. John Baptist on June 24; and as he was six months older than our LORD, his cousin according to the flesh, it places the nativity of our LORD upon December 25. The celebration has always been observed with great solemnity and rejoicing, though too frequently with other than sacred and festal customs. There are in other than the English Church two celebrations of the Communion, with separate Collects, Epistles, and Gospels. Whenever there are two with us, it is because of the convenience of the communicants and to shorten the length of the services. Three festivals stand in immediate connection with it: those of St Stephen (December 26), the first martyr; of St. John (December 27), "whom JESUS loved;" of the Innocents' day (December 28), the *coætanei* of our LORD.

Christology is the doctrine contained in the Scriptures concerning the Person and office of CHRIST. The subject may be conveniently considered under two heads; the first containing the prophecies of the MESSIAH in the Old Testament, and the Messianic hopes of the Jew based upon them; and the second the revelation of the CHRIST made by JESUS in the New Testament, and the teaching of the Church upon the relation of the divine and human natures in His Person, together with some mention of the heresies which were the occasion of the more exact definition of this teaching.

1. The Christology of the Old Testament falls naturally into the three divisions of Patriarchal, Legal, and Prophetic Christology; just as the history of the chosen people presents the same stages, and just as the history advancing along these stages passes from outlines covering long intervals to more minute details of shorter periods, so does the doctrine of the MESSIAH in the successive divisions become more frequent, more definite, and more precise. To treat this topic at any length would require a volume, and it must suffice here merely to mention some of the chief passages of Scripture which are understood to form a connected chain of promise and prophecy concerning the CHRIST, and to indicate the outlines of the conception of the MESSIAH and His office inferred from them. The first of these passages is found in the story of the fall of man, where, with the curse pronounced upon the serpent, is joined the promise of the seed of the woman to be at enmity with the serpent: "it shall bruise thy head, and thou shalt bruise his heel." This promise of a deliverer, which, no doubt, had a fuller and deeper meaning (than its form now conveys) to those who received it, was for them the basis of faith and hope in a SAVIOUR to come, until the promise was renewed in the blessing pronounced upon Shem, "blessed be the LORD GOD of Shem" (Gen. ix.), and in the blessing of Abraham, "in thee shall all families of the earth be blessed" (Gen. xii.), which are remarkable as having their fulfillment not at the time spoken, nor for those to whom they were addressed, but in the far future and for others, even the whole family of man. But the promise becomes much clearer in the inspired words of the dying Jacob addressed to Judah, "The sceptre shall not depart from Judah, nor a lawgiver from between his feet until Shiloh come; and unto him shall the gathering of the people be" (Gen. xlix.), centering as it

does in one Person, who is to be a man of peace (Shiloh), to be a prince, and to whom the nations shall be obedient. The prophecy of Balaam (Numbers xxiv.), and the passages of the Pentateuch, which relate to the angel of the LORD (Gen. xii. 7; xviii. 1, etc.), have been thought also to refer to the MESSIAH. But the next step in the revelation of the MESSIAH, is the typical meaning of the Mosaic law of sacrifices, and of the High-Priest who offered them. Sacrifices were not a new thing with Moses, and no doubt the patriarchs who offered them did so with a sufficient conception of their hidden meaning; but the full system and elaborate ritual appointed by Moses were designed to be a shadow of the good things to come (as St. Paul declares), and to serve unto the example and shadow of heavenly things. Again, after a long interval, probably because primitive tradition was forgotten, and typical meanings had become obscure, the promise is renewed by messages to the prophets continually more definite and precise. In the Psalms (xxii., lxxii., etc.), and in the prophets (Isaiah xi., liii., lxiii.; Jer. xxiii.; Zech. ix., xiii., etc.), we read fuller and more personal descriptions of the MESSIAH, which, joined with the former revelations, furnish a conception of Him as a Person who should rescue His people from sin by making an expiatory offering for it, Himself at once Priest and Victim, and after triumphing over the enemy of righteousness, and destroying his power, should rule forever as the Prince of Peace. But in this conception there were such contradictory points that the Jews, despairing of reconciling them in one person, came to the conclusion that the prophets foretold two MESSIAHS, one to suffer and the other to triumph; and missing the true sense of their Scriptures, it is probable that in time they came to look for an earthly king only, who should triumph over the nations which had conquered and oppressed them, and restore again a temporal kingdom to Israel.

2. But in the fullness of time GOD sent forth His SON, made of a woman, made under the Law, to fulfill all the FATHER'S promises, and to reconcile in His own Person the conflicting predictions of the birth, rank, and appearance, of the reception and treatment, of the death and burial of the MESSIAH. Him the Jews rejected, refusing to see how He made true in Himself all the words of promise; but Him have Christians —His faithful followers—ever honored with divine worship as the MESSIAH, the CHRIST of GOD, yet GOD Himself; as the SAVIOUR of men, yet a true Man. The New Testament, *i.e.* the words of our LORD in the Gospels, the doctrines published by St. Paul and his brother Apostles in their Epistles, supplement the revelation contained in the Old Testament, and furnish the key to the true interpretation of the prophets, as well as the basis for the Christian doctrine of the Person of CHRIST, of the SON of GOD become the Son of Man. The reader will not need any reference to these Scriptures, nor any analysis of their contents, before admitting this statement; and he will as readily admit that they contain the premises from which follow as logical consequences the decrees of the first general Councils defining the right faith concerning the Person of CHRIST. The definition of this faith, in the first days of Christianity, was negative rather than positive; the earlier Fathers contenting themselves with combating the errors of heretics on the one hand or on the other, and denying that the doctrine of the CHRIST was not as stated by them; while they did not undertake to set forth exactly what the true doctrine was, more fully than in the words of St. John, "the Word was made Flesh." Still the process of logical inference and development went on, and men saw more and more clearly how to sum up the separate assertions of Scripture—the faith once delivered to the saints—in a carefully defined philosophical statement. This, however, was not done at once, but as it were step by step, as the vagaries of heresy made more explicit definitions necessary; so that it was six or seven hundred years before the Person of CHRIST ceased to form the chief question in the Councils of the Church. The decisions of the first six general Councils (Nice against Arius, 325 A.D.; Constantinople against Macedonius, 381 A.D., Ephesus against Nestorius, 431 A.D.; Chalcedon against Eutyches, 451 A.D.; Constantinople supplementary of Ephesus, 553 A.D.; and Constantinople supplementary of Chalcedon, 680 A.D.), the substance of which is expressed by the (so-called) Nicene Creed, set forth the Person of CHRIST as embracing truly and perfectly both the nature of GOD and the nature of man, inseparably and without confusion. It will be observed that this was the work of the Eastern Church; in the West, however, thinking men were not idle, and in like manner as the faith of the Church concerning the Person of CHRIST was thus gradually expressed with accuracy and precision, so the doctrine of His office and work was from time to time more clearly defined, as philosophical speculations ending in heresy made it desirable to do so, until the Christology of the Church was completed by the doctrine of CHRIST in His office as the Atonement for sin, the Restorer of man to the original dignity of his nature lost in Adam, and by the doctrine of Divine grace repairing human sinfulness. The subject of Christology, the doctrine of the Person of CHRIST, is sometimes treated as the development of a purely natural Messianic idea, of subjective or self-originated conception, to which there was no correspondent Divine Promise. Or it is discussed as the development of a Messianic idea which was both natural and supernatural, which was not purely subjective or self-originated, but had its origin in a Divine reality, and was fostered by a supernatural Provi-

dence until the revelation of that reality in the Incarnation,—GOD manifest in the flesh. Add to this second mode of considering Christology the teaching that the doctrine of the Person of CHRIST was made known to the patriarchs and prophets from the earliest ages by some knowledge of what His work should be, and the third and true method is reached; a method which has been called dogmatic, and is that commonly adopted by theological writers on Christology. For anything like a proper treatment of this subject the reader must turn to special works on Christology (Dorner, Hengstenberg), and on such subdivisions of it as the Atonement (Magee), or the Divinity of CHRIST (Liddon's Bampton Lectures): but the articles in Smith's "Dictionary of the Bible" on MESSIAH, JESUS CHRIST, SON of GOD, SON of Man, etc., may be consulted with advantage.

Authorities: Dictionary of the Bible, Hagenbach's History of Doctrines, Chambers' Cyclopædia, Blunt's Dictionary of Historical and Doctrinal Theology.

Chronicles, First and Second Books of. These two books, like those of the Kings, were in the Hebrew originally but a single book, but in the Greek translation they were divided for convenience, and so the Vulgate received them; thence they passed into the modern translations as two books. They have been attributed, with almost positive certainty, to Ezra; and all the circumstances and the contents of the books agree very well with this. They contain genealogies, especially those of the Priests and Levites. They have much of a national tone in them; they give other and parallel accounts to those in the books of the Kings of the same events. In these we may see Ezra's purpose to infuse a national tone in the remnant brought back from Babylon, and the need of exact genealogical records of the Levitical families, that the details of the Temple worship may be restored to those who alone were competent to conduct them; and also to give independent and corroborative narratives of the facts recorded by Jeremiah in the books of the Kings. These facts have stood much in the way of those who wish to show that the books of Moses were an invention of a forger after the "Captivity;" for if this were so, then the books of the Chronicles are still later. To destroy the credibility of the Chronicles the date of their composition would have to be placed later still. But the date and probable authorship have been abundantly established by competent critics. The authenticity of the Chronicles has been, then, the pivot upon which a great deal of critical acumen has been expended with an equivalently valuable result. The contents begin with the genealogies from Adam; and, after a rapid outline, come on to the later history of the two kingdoms; and while not always identical with, still traverse much the same ground as those of the books of the Kings. They are not supplementary or intentionally explanatory of the Kings, having another purpose in view; but they do indirectly throw much light upon them.

Chronology is the art of recording historical events in their proper order and succession, by expressing the interval of time which has elapsed between their occurrence and the occurrence of some other event chosen as a standard of reference. To treat this subject fully some explanation of the calendar, or mode of measuring time, and regulating the year, would be proper, but limited space forbids any such digression, and attention will be given here only to a brief mention of those systems of chronology most commonly met with in history. By a system of chronology is understood a scheme of historical events arranged in their proper sequence, and at their proper intervals, either before or after a chosen standard of reference; and it is easy to see how different systems may have been suggested and adopted in ancient times. For as tribes of men at first loosely associated together gradually developed a common national life, a need would arise of some fixed point of reckoning to which to refer in recording or comparing events. The most important characteristic of such a fixed point of time would be some event associated with it, of such moment as to be generally known and long remembered. Hence we find events referred to earthquakes or eclipses, the accession of kings and other like occasions commonly known, or of common interest. Different nations would naturally have their own standards of reference, and their own systems of chronology based upon them; hence, as is well known in ancient history, the Greeks used one method of recording events, the Romans another, and the nations of the East, and of Egypt, used various systems at different times; while in modern history, Christians, Mohammedans, Hindoos, and Chinese all have their own peculiar systems of chronology. As some six or eight of these are frequently mentioned in history, it will be well to notice them more particularly, and to explain how they may be connected with the Vulgar or Christian era.

In Greece the common life of the Hellenic race was kept alive and fostered by the four great national games, of which those at Olympia seem to have become prominent at an early day. It was the custom to name these games, which were celebrated every fourth year, early in July, from the winner of the foot-race; and at a later time to record his name in the gymnasium of Olympia. The first to be distinguished by this last honor was Coræbus; and naturally the event of his triumph having a fixed name of its own, and being brought regularly to the attention of the whole people every four years, became a ready standard to which all other events might be referred. Thus originated the era of the Olympiads, which are computed to have begun 776 years before the Christian era. But as the year of the Olympiads begins in July, it is necessary in reducing Olympiads to years before CHRIST, to subtract the year of the Olympiad from 777 if the event befell from July to December, but from 776 if from January to June. For example, Rome was founded in the third year of the sixth Olympiad, in April; then taking $5 \times 4 + 3 = 23$ from 776, we have 753 B.C. for the date of the foundation of the city; but if the year of the Olympiad is greater than 776, to find the year of the Christian era subtract from it 776 if the event befell from July to December, 777 if from January to June.

The Roman system of chronology refers all events to the founding of the city of Rome, which is generally fixed in April, 753 B.C., though it is also placed in the years 752, 751, 750, and 747 B.C. A simple subtraction of the year of the city from 753 should give the year before CHRIST of any event recorded in the era of Rome; but owing to the different dates assigned for the beginning of that era, the reduction is not always attended with certainty; nor is the difficulty lessened by the fact that the Romans employed two sorts of years, the civil year and the consular year, and further that the year of Rome does not coincide with the civil year, the latter beginning January 1, the other April 21.

The era of Nabonassar is that used by Ptolemy in his records of Assyrian and Babylonian history. Its chief merit is that it begins at a definite moment of time, viz., Wednesday at noon, February 26, 747 B.C., and for that reason is famous in astronomy; but on account of a difference in length of the Julian and Babylonian years, it is no easy matter to convert dates from the era of Nabonassar to the Christian era.

Before the Exodus the Jews began their year in September; but to commemorate that event the beginning of the year was changed to about the time of the vernal equinox (Exodus xii. 2) for ecclesiastical matters, the former year being still retained in civil affairs. There is reason to believe that the Exodus formed a chronological era with the Israelites (1 Kings vi. 1), but it is well known that they recorded historical events by referring them to the year of the reigning king or conqueror. In the later history of the Jews, and until comparatively modern times, they used the Macedonian era, which they styled the Era of Contracts, because their Syrian governors compelled them to use it in making contracts. They are said, however, to use now a Mundane era, reckoning from the creation of the world, which they set about 3760 years before CHRIST. (*Vide* article Chronology in Dr. Smith's Dictionary of the Bible.)

The Macedonian era, just spoken of, called also the Era of the Seleucidæ, was reckoned from the occupation of Babylon by Seleucus Nicator (311 B.C.). It was for a long time in general use in all the Greek countries bordering on the Levant; but as those who used it varied much in their time of beginning the year, it is hard to determine with readiness dates recorded in it.

The Vulgar or Christian era is that in common use in Europe and America, and largely in Asia. It was proposed some 500 years after CHRIST by Dionysius Exiguus, and gradually came into use by all Christians. Being designed to reckon from the Incarnation of CHRIST, its author chose March 25 in the year of Rome 752 B.C. (?) as its initial point, but after a time this was deferred to the following January; and the Vulgar era now begins January 1 in the year of Rome 753 B.C. Besides the 25th of March and the 1st of January, the 25th of December has been taken as the beginning of the year; a fact to be remembered in reckoning and comparing dates in early Christian ages, and in late history, too, for that matter, because the 25th of March was retained as New Year's Day in England, together with the Old Style, until 1752 A.D., at which time a change of both year and style was made; hence, though we now say that George Washington was born February 22, 1732 A.D., those who recorded that event wrote it February 11, 1731 A.D. However, historical writers had already reckoned the year to begin at January 1. For an explanation of these matters, and for rules for avoiding error and confusion in dates, the reader must refer to the subject of the Calendar as treated in the various cyclopædias.

The era of the Hegira is that used by the Mohammedans, and dates from the flight of Mohammed (the Hegira) from Mecca, or rather from a day shortly before the actual flight; so that it begins July 16, 622 A.D. But it is not used in Persia, where time is reckoned from the accession to the throne of Yezdegird, June 16, 632 A.D.

It remains now to speak of an important, and at the same time very difficult, branch of chronology, viz., that of Biblical chronology. The basis of such a system is of course the text of the Bible; and it might seem at first a simple matter to reduce its records to a tabulated scheme, but there are difficulties presented by the text itself, and in addition the Septuagint, or ancient Greek version, differs from the Hebrew text; and again, the Samaritan Pentateuch differs from both these. Now two of these must have been altered, and as certain alterations are suspected in the Hebrew text, whether by design or by accident, it has become impossible to determine which of the three is right on those points where they differ. Hence there have been so many discrepant opinions and contradictory conclusions among those who have given attention to this subject, that from over-confidence in treating it in a positive manner, men have gone apparently to the opposite extreme of thinking that nothing whatever can be done with it. These remarks apply of course only to that part of Biblical chronology which cannot be corroborated by contemporary profane history; but the truth about it, as in so many other cases, lies probably between two extremes, and a careful digest of the records of the Bible will afford a system of chronology which may be accepted as final; because, though not absolutely certain for the earliest ages, it is better than any other yet obtained; and in later times is confirmed by contemporary history, and especially by the wonderful disclosures of modern research and discovery.

The different systems of Bible chronology which have been advocated by the most learned and able men may be arranged (to take no notice of the Rabbinical systems) in two classes, the long systems and the short systems; though all long systems do not agree with one another, neither do all short systems agree together. The advocates of the short systems base their calculations on the genealogies of the antediluvians and patriarchs as given in the Hebrew text (and in our version of the Bible), while those who prefer the long systems choose the corresponding genealogies in the Septuagint, which are greater by one hundred years in the age of nearly every patriarch at the time when his successor was born. For this reason, and for certain other peculiarities of interpretation and reckoning, there is a very considerable difference between the two classes of chronologies, until they practically agree in the date of the destruction of Solomon's Temple. Taking Hales as a representative of the long systems and Ussher of the short, the two may be compared by the following table of six principal dates:

	Hales.	Ussher.
Destruction of Solomon's Temple	586 B.C.	588 B.C.
Foundation " " "	1027	1012
Exodus	1648	1491
Call of Abram	2078	1921
Flood	3155	2348
Creation	5411	4004

Out of all the many systems which have been published and advocated, that of Ussher, Archbishop of Ireland, has received the most favor, and is best known, at least to English-speaking men; owing, no doubt, to the fact that it is inserted in the margin of the Authorized Version of the Scriptures, completed and published under James I. of England; and the dates of such events as the Creation, the Flood, the Exodus, etc., are commonly given in accordance with it. Perhaps it is as well to adopt it as any, both because it is based upon the Hebrew text of the Bible, and because it has been so long received and used. But there are many able advocates of the long system, and in particular the learned writer of the article Chronology in Smith's "Dictionary of the Bible," to which reference has already been made, appears to favor the long system; and he suggests a scheme nearly the same as that of Hales as the most probable, making, however, a correction of four years in the date of the Exodus (and of the preceding dates), based upon a theory that the 14th day of the month Abib (when the Passover was instituted) corresponded to the 14th day of an Egyptian month, Phameneth, and upon the fact, as shown by astronomy, that a full moon fell upon the 14th of Phameneth in the year 1652 B.C. His statement of the dates above given would therefore be,—

Destruction of the Temple	586 B.C.
Foundation of the Temple	?
Exodus	1652
Abram	2082
Flood	3159 or 3099
Creation	5421 or 5361

The article spoken of must be again referred to for the explanation of the writer's grounds for his conclusions; and in it also will be found a full consideration of the whole subject of Biblical chronology. For the more general subject, the "Chronological Introduction to the History of the Church" and the "Church of the Redeemed," by the late Dr. Samuel F. Jarvis, may be consulted.

Authorities: Chronology and Calendar in Chambers's, Appleton's, and Metropolitan Encyclopædias.

REV. R. A. BENTON.

Church. The word has usually been derived from the Greek adjective *Kyriake*, belonging to the LORD, through the Teutonic changes of (Anglo-Saxon) *Circ, Cyric;* O.Germ. *Chirichu;* Icelandic, *Kyrkia;* while the Latin races usually retained the other Greek word, *Ecclesia.* The deviation has been challenged, but not on probably accurate grounds. It has three broad uses which are quite distinct: (A) the church building; (B) the Church in a city or a Diocese (in the New Testament in a household); (C) the Mystical Body of CHRIST in its Unity; these are quite distinct and definite uses and are generally well understood. It is only to the last two that this article refers. And, first, of the Mystical Body of CHRIST, which he purchased with His Blood (Acts xx. 28). Its Founder and Foundation is the LORD Himself. "Upon this Rock I will build my Church" (Matt. xvi. 18), and that Rock is CHRIST. Before its foundation He describes it, and calls it a Kingdom, His Kingdom, His FATHER'S Kingdom, the Kingdom of GOD, of Heaven, which He appoints to His Apostles. Men are bidden to enter it; it suffers violence and the violent take it by force; it is an open organization, yet it works as leaven in the soul. Parables best foreshadow its varied extent, power, and gifts. A net to gather all men, good and bad; a pearl, a treasure worth all else; the service of a great King which has great responsibilities and eternal rewards; a tree which shall shadow and lodge many. It is to be in the world, not of the world, but to lift men out of the world. It is a power in the heart and life. It is a kingdom with a Divine policy and bestowing an immortal citizenship. It admits without distinction babes and old men, bond and free, simple and learned, rich and poor. It is founded on love and in love, and its citizenship is retained by loving obedience. These intimations of it are part of the training the Apostles receive. Then offering the redemption on the Cross, He rises from the dead, and upon Himself as Eternal GOD and Immortal Man He founds His Church. It is a Covenant through Him, a union with Him, a worship of Him. Emphatically, it is the Church of CHRIST our GOD, who has bought it with His blood.

But in many ways CHRIST'S Church is not governed as secular kingdoms are. He governs it as its Head (Eph. i. 22, 23; iv. 1-16; Col. i. 15-22). By the HOLY GHOST (St. John xv. 7-15); by the Apostolic office (Eph. iv. 11, 12; St. Matt. xxviii. 20). For its purpose is to reconcile sinful man to the FATHER through the SON (2 Cor. v. 18, 19) by the pleading of the HOLY GHOST (Rom. viii. 26) in our hearts. It follows that the ministry of reconciliation in the Church is in CHRIST'S office as Apostle (Heb. iii. 1) and High-Priest, and He must appoint His own officers, who share in His authority (St. John xx. 21). He gives gifts and offers salvation. He must select His own messengers (St. Mark iii. 13; St. John xv. 16). This Apostolic office continues while the world lasts (St. Matt. xxviii. 20). But it exists only for His purposes and His work (St. John xv. 14; St. Mark xvi. 15, 16; St. Matt. xxviii. 18-20). But again, the work is for men. It reaches from the Throne of GOD the FATHER, from the Holiest Presence of CHRIST'S unceasing intercession, to the life and happiness of the least of His loved race of men. This wondrous organization is for the salvation of men, soul and body (Eph. ii.). This King has laid down certain conditions on which He receives our allegiance in baptism. He assigns duties and responsibilities upon His citizens. He governs by eternal law of love, mercy, and justice. He has rights, privileges, and immunities to confer, offices to grant, defenses to place about them. The conditions are faith (St. Mark xvi. 16; Rom. x. 9; Heb. xi. 6; Acts viii. 36, 37) and repentance (Acts ii. 38; St. Luke xxiv. 27; 2 Peter iii. 9). The oath of allegiance in *baptism* is the renunciation of the world, the flesh, and the devil, the vow of Faith and of obedience. The gifts are forgiveness (Luke xxiv. 47; Acts xxii. 16), cleansing (1 Cor. vi. 11; Titus iii. 5), a new creature (Gal. iii. 27; Col. iii. 10; Eph. iv. 24), and life immortal (Rom. vi.). This is the first sacrament (military oath) to the Captain of our salvation (Heb. ii.). By it we become citizens of His kingdom (Eph. ii. 17-22; Phil. iii. 20, 21), sons of GOD (Rom. viii. 14-17; 1 John iii. 1, 2; St. John i. 12), heritors of his royal rights (Gal. iv. 1-7; Rev. iii. 21; Eph. ii. 6). These are the privileges and gifts with which His citizens are clothed. But in a second act He conveys His HOLY SPIRIT for guidance and help (Heb. vi. 2; Acts ii. 38; viii. 17; xix. 1-6; Eph. iv. 30), whereby we become sanctified and are temples of the HOLY GHOST (1 Cor. iii. 16, 17; vi. 19; Eph. i. 13, 14). And a renewal of our vows is appointed in the Holy Communion (St. John vi. 51, 57; 1 Cor. xi. 23-26) for forgiveness (St. Matt. xxvi. 26-28); and direct power of absolution is given to His officers (St. John xx. 22, 23), or of discipline (1 Cor. v. 4, 5; 1 Tim. i. 20) and of blessing (Heb. xiii. 20, 21; 2 Cor. xii. 14). And He governs according to a Law part of which is revealed, and part lies behind the veil of eternal life. For He cannot govern but by Law, being the fount and source of all Law to us; and by perfect purity, holiness, and justice He governs us. The Law of CHRIST is drawn in part from the Law He gave on Mount Sinai, and whose principles are immutable, and in part from His own revelation of mercy and of justice (Gal. vi. 3; St. Matt. v., vii., x.; St. Luke vi.; St. John xiii. 34, 35; xiv., xv., xvi.). As the visible Church is, as it were, a polity and a colony from the eternal kingdom in heaven, it is governed not by laws of this world, but by Laws from thence (Phil. iii. 20, 21, and the Epistles in the New Testament generally); and the Law of Faith, of Righteousness, of Sanctification, the Law of Love and Forgiveness, the Law of Justice and of Good Works, are intermingled in the sacred writings left to His Church, that they become the rule of our daily life as citizens governed by Him in His kingdom.

But this citizenship, here probationary and disciplinary, involves certain responsibilities and duties. The conditions of entrance never cease to be binding. Faith in Him as a Person having power of life and death (St. John v. 20-27; St. Matt. xi. 27-30; St. John xi. 25, 26; xiv. 6; St. Matt. xxviii. 18), as one with GOD (St. John, i. 1, 2; x. 28-30; xiv. 9-11), as to be worshiped (St. John ix. 35-38; St. Luke xxiv. 52). Daily repenting. Increasing life in holiness (Gal. v. 22-25; Rom. viii.; Phil. iv. 8; Rom. xii.; 1 Cor. iii. 11-23). Good works (Rom. xii.-xv. 7; Eph. ii. 10; Phil. ii. 12-15). Service to others (St. John xiii. 34, 35; St. Matt. xxv. 31-46; Rom. xii. 18-21; Gal. v. 9, 10). Service of worship (Heb. x. 24-31; 1 Tim. ii. 1-4; Phil. iv. 6, 7; Eph. v. 19, 20). We have traced out the conditions of admission, the sacraments and their gifts, the rights and privileges, the heirship, the duties, the responsibilities, the blessing, and the strength, with an abundant reference to the Scripture, which is yet infinitely fuller of all of these. But again, all these gifts are contained in one Body. Our LORD'S prayer for unity (St. John xvii.) cannot be meaningless. The Scripture is full of this unity, ONE NET, ONE NARROW WAY. For there is but one Atonement, one Resurrection, one Mediator, one King, one kingdom, one citizenship, one LORD, one Faith, one baptism. For GOD is one, and our calling is one in the unity of the HOLY GHOST.

This kingdom so created, so governed, composed of such citizens and having aims not of this earth, and a certainty of duration beyond the continuance of this earth, more,—expecting only its completion when this earth shall pass away, dependent upon an immortal King who holds eternal power, who is planning, shaping, fitting together by so many modes so many diverse lower interests, sanctifying men and giving them immortal hopes, must not merely give its gifts to us upon our consent to join it, but this consent must express, on our part, a deep conviction of our needs, of our fatal danger in rejecting it and Him it represents, and of the glorious benefits it confers upon every one belonging to it. For it is a peculiar kingdom; it exists in the subjects of earthly kingdoms, a spiritual state within a secular one, lifting up and purifying the secular state; a state that binds into one all the kindreds of the earth, yet does not interfere with, nay, sanctions their political condition (Rom. xiii. 1–7; St. Matt. xxii. 21); yet binds them by an oath and by mutual pledges to the Person of their King, who rules them by the law of love and obedience. It is therefore a bounden duty to become citizens of it.

But this organization, so compacted, governed, and equipped, must be considered as a polity, having definite ends and employing definite instruments. But, it must have historic continuity. This is essential to it. It must have it, for it is part of GOD'S plan for the world throughout time as well as for all men; and, too, it cannot fail. It may be maimed and injured at times, but it must be perpetual, and have power of self-perpetuation in its visible organization. Its assured perpetuity rests in the Person of CHRIST, its visible perpetuity in the Apostolic office, which perpetuates itself. These facts of its historic continuity, of its perpetuity under all disasters, must be necessarily noted and accepted as fundamental: first, for our own faith (Heb. xi. 10; 1 Pet. v. 4), and, secondly, as relating to the general proof of the certainty of this kingdom (Matt. xxiv.; St. Mark xiii.; 1 Cor. xv.). For its doctrines have been and are borrowed, its authority imitated, its polity copied, its laws transferred, its citizenship promised. But in the past such organizations have failed, and all similar present ones we may be assured will fail also as soon as the forces so borrowed, not being self-sustaining, shall be expended. This Body, this Church, this visible kingdom, this Divine organization, this state within all, and permeating all earthly states, yet not of them, endowed with supremal vitality, inheriting a perpetuity, must have granted to it, as a body, certain powers, both because of its Founder and because of the abiding presence of the HOLY GHOST. Its Founder had a definite purpose, the HOLY SPIRIT has a definite mission in and through the Church. Therefore it becomes a *politeia* in the fullest sense of the word. Every state is founded to express some mighty political truth in behalf of and through the people who compose it. This heavenly kingdom is founded that men might know the only true GOD and JESUS CHRIST whom He has sent (John xvii. 2). It is therefore Trinitarian, (Athan. 2 Ep. ad Serapion), because of the baptismal words, which are the germ of this principle. It must, for itself and for its citizens, obtain the defense and continual blessing of the Holy Trinity; it is the public depository and the sole defender of this Faith. Its polity is framed for that end. It involves the use of all the means which can set forth before men the truth of the doctrine, its vital relation to the lives of men, and the necessity of believing in and therefore acting on all the consequences that flow from it. It must be the keeper and defender of this Faith, neither adding to it nor subtracting from it. It must proclaim before all men this Faith, and it must not exaggerate nor yet weaken the conditions of acceptance and the gifts that shall flow from it. As its government is framed upon this fact, the Holy Scriptures are given to it as an inspired record of it, and its historic development and continuity, the history of GOD'S teachings by it, and the results of its being received or rejected extending over a long section of its career, (a) in the Patriarchal, (b) the Mosaic, (c) the Christian revelation. This sacred inspired series of documents must be held and defended intact; and under the lines of action suggested by and contained in them, its policy must be carried out. This involves the arrangement of a Creed (Apostles', Nicene, the Psalm Quicunque Vult), the formation of a worship,—divinely indicated,—with rites and ceremonies and a ritual which shall offer to the king the renewed homage of his subjects, and also serve as an instruction and a teaching, and a public confession of this Faith in ways that shall attract all men. For as these rites, this Creed, and these documents, each, rightly used, shall train men, they mould their lives into a heavenly type, and so lift them up above other men, therefore the lives of the citizens of this kingdom should show the truth and sanctifying power of its laws, and the glorious love and mercy of its King. But the very fact of such a deposit made in a state so founded, and having its increase by a spiritual birth and given such a polity, determines for it another characteristic. It must be aggressive, for it is missionary, and this aggressiveness flows from the purest source—love. Its Founder was aggressive from utter love. The HOLY SPIRIT abiding in it is an aggressive love, and it is the sole and magnificent peculiarity of the Church to be aggressive, to seek to gather all in its fold through love.

Again, the extension throughout all races and in all states leads to another peculiarity in its Divine constitution. Intrusted with a positive Faith, having a special law, governed by a mode which possesses the greatest flexibility and power of adaptation, having a universally accepted Creed and broad foundations of a common ritual, it has points of unity and community among all these, and it is joined together by many bands and sinews to its, for the present, unseen Head. The Church as a state within other states is peculiarly placed. It has to protest boldly against sin. It has to be aggressive. These are points of moral antagonism. If, then, these widely spread parts of the Church were to be gathered as one body under a *visible* head, the friction, to call it by no stronger name, thus created would be a hindrance almost fatal to the discharge of its true functions. The fear of this, when as yet it could not possibly exist, led heathen emperors upon political principles of mistaken self-defense to persecute it, a danger that threatened its existence, but was divinely turned into a means of strength and of greater growth. When such an organization was effected contrary to all the traditions of its Divine founding, it has awakened the jealousy and antagonism of the several secular kingdoms, and has in itself led to assertions of the faith unwarranted, unfounded, and, were they logically carried out, subversive of its existence. This, then, leads us to the second and equally correct use of the title Church used with reference to the Church in each secular state. (B) To appoint a single visible Head when its Founder appointed none, and left no provision in its constitution for such Headship, is then opposed to and wellnigh fatal to the lofty ends for which the Church is established. But, on the contrary, in the Apostolic College together, He established this Headship; to them all in common He gave his own Apostolate (St. John xx. 21) in full. They were to be, as they yet are, in a common bond, yet as sufficiently independent to care for the necessarily separate interests of the Church in each nationality. They were to have the power of holding counsel. Nor yet was the Church solely vested in them, but also the people were to be an integral part of it. The interdependence of the several parts of the Church by their nationalities was secured through the Apostolate; the independence of the several nationalities was secured through their race or tribal peculiarities and customs,—non-essential in themselves, but the outgrowth of their mental dispositions, and of their forms of life and of government, and therefore antagonistic and creating jealousies and bickerings, were they to clash through the too close proximity of their diverse interests. So there was at the first the greatest freedom of play allowed the several portions of the Church in their own regions. Every portion was allowed to have its own modes of acting and of legislating within the great lines of a common Faith. Causes arose which providentially drew the different parts of the Church together, when it became so widely spread as to appear in danger of falling apart by its mere extent. Heresies occasioned Councils, and Councils bound the Churches together in the defense of a common Faith and in the unity of a common worship. So that it was not, it is not now, permitted us to admit a visible Head, but a visible common executive office. A bond of unity in the common Faith, common Law, which results from the needs of the time, a common worship of our one LORD. It also follows that as it exists whole and complete in each and every part, that the Episcopate held in common is equally present in each one of its members, that the Faith is complete in the Creed and the Scriptures, and the Law of government and identity of policy, both of aggression and conservation, and unity of worship, are complete in each part of the Church. So it is not arrogance, not presumption for any part of the Church to say that it is the Church as regards the nation to which it is established, and that it must be so as regards the necessity for each man to be within its pale, and the responsibility of the Church to gather into its pale all who are yet without. It follows that missionaries from one nation to another not having the Faith, when they have established the Church and given to it what instrumentalities and officers the Head of the Church has left, have thereby effected an extension of the old historic Church, and it must become national and independent, yet in closest union of all the common traditions which belong to that Church. This was precisely the principle of the national Church of America at the close of the Revolution, when, by 1789 A.D., it had received the Episcopate from the English line. Whatever the English Church had of the common Catholic Faith and use became ours as heirs taking from a common estate under a common will which had made provision for our inheriting. "Go ye into all the world." "Make disciples of all the nations." Therefore we, though but a century old, justly claim from our Founder a historic continuity in the EPISCOPATE, in the DEPOSIT of the Scriptures, in the COMMON CREEDS, in the broad unity of the LITURGIES, in the government under the CANON LAW of the universal Church. We hold these by the right of a common heritage. If it be the duty of the One, Holy, Catholic, and Apostolic Church to make disciples of all nations, that portion of it becomes the national Church in that country which it enters under this historic law of independence.

The topic broadens at every step, and we must stop here, for much which could be properly said here will be found under other headings,—EPISCOPACY, BISHOP, APOSTOLIC SUCCESSION, APOSTLE, BRITISH and ANGLICAN Churches. To these the reader must go for further information. But we cannot close without repeating that CHRIST'S Church is founded upon Himself by Himself, in His Resurrection, officered by His appointment, equipped by His gifts, sent by

His mission, and having His own continual presence and the abiding indwelling of the HOLY GHOST, that He might present it to Himself a glorious Church, not having spot or wrinkle or any such thing, but that it should be holy and without blemish; and in it He cherishes each of us. "For we are members of His body, of His flesh, of His bones"

Church Congress. The Church Congress in the Protestant Episcopal Church in the United States is a voluntary organization, in its membership co-extensive with the communion of that Church. In the main features of its purpose and plan similar to the kindred institution in the Church of England, its history also, although measured by fewer years than that of the former, like that has been one of half-doubtful experiment, eventually illustrated and vindicated by signal success. Originating in a small conference of clergy and laity, held in Trinity Church, New Haven, some ten years since, it took permanent form and title at a succeeding meeting, held in the parish of Christ Church, "Riverdale," New York City. At the latter meeting permanent officers were elected, as also the members of the General and Executive Committees. Sub-committees also were appointed, for the selection of topics, writers, and speakers for the first annual session, to be held in Association Hall, New York. On that occasion, in October, 1875 A.D., memorable for the Churchly order of its proceedings, the scholarly and eloquent character of the papers and addresses, and, as at all succeeding sessions, the thoroughly catholic comprehensiveness of opinion and representation at the several discussions, it wrought conviction, even in the minds of its earlier opponents, of the rightfulness, the wisdom, and expediency of such a *deliberative* organization within the Church in the United States.

Inclusive of the first meeting in New York, and excepting, as is now the rule of the Congress, the years in which a General Convention is held, eight sessions of the Congress, each occupying four or more days, have been held. Two of these have been in New York, and others in Philadelphia, Boston, Cincinnati, Albany, Providence, and Richmond. The opening service is uniformly that of Holy Communion, with an address by some one of the Bishops. On the same day, and at the place appointed for the discussion of topics, the Bishop of the Diocese has, with one exception, delivered the inaugural address. This has been followed by a service, memorial of deceased officials, with an address by the General Secretary.

The presiding officer at any meeting is the Bishop of the Diocese in which any Congress is held. The permanent officers are all the Bishops, thirteen of other clergy and of the laity, thirty-one as Vice-Presidents, together with a General Committee of forty, and an Executive Committee of twenty, clerical members. This latter, for convenience, is in the main composed of gentlemen residing in the city of New York, and holds its meetings semi-monthly during the greater part of the year. Vice-Presidents and members of the General Committee are, to a considerable extent, representatives of the different Dioceses throughout the country. Two Honorary Vice-Presidents, by election, are the Very Rev. Canon E. H. Plumptre, D.D., and the Rev. Archdeacon Emery, both of the English Church, and the latter one of the founders, and the present Honorary Secretary of the English Congress. The General Secretary, Rev. Geo. D. Wildes, D.D., of New York, is assisted by four clerical Secretaries, one of whom is the Secretary of the Executive Committee. A permanent Treasurer, whose office, with that of the Congress, is at 2 Bible House, completes the list of officials.

The annual meetings extend over four days, with three daily sessions, and a distinct topic, selected by the Executive Committee. Usually two writers, three appointed speakers, and such volunteers as may present cards, occupy the time of the session. All these are limited as to length; the rule is in every instance unvaried, and the expiration of the limit is signified by the bell of the Secretary. By the rules none but members of the Protestant Episcopal Church, or of Churches in communion with the same, can address the Congress, and no person is permitted to speak twice upon the same subject. All questions of order are in the discretion of the Chairman, and his decision is final. Persons offering themselves as volunteer speakers are required to send their cards to the General Secretary, and are called upon in the order in which these are received. The Chairman only is to be addressed in speaking, and no question arising out of any paper or subject can be put to vote. The rules, so fitted for public deliberation, and realized as admirable in their working, embrace also some minor specialties, completing a system of order unexceptionable in the regulation of debate.

The several daily sessions are opened with Collects and the singing of a hymn. Three of the latter are used on every occasion. Printed, as are the hymns, on programmes, with the Collects also, the large audiences, filling the music-halls or opera-houses in the various cities, have been enabled to join in response and singing with a grandeur of effect seldom realized in any other assembly of Church people.

A Local Committee appointed by the Bishop and others in the Diocese in which any Congress convenes, initiates and takes charge of the immediate local arrangements through sub-committees. The hospitalities of Church and other Christian people have been uniformly abounding and cheerfully dispensed. Not the least worthy among noticeable things is the fact that families connected with other Christian bodies have, as in England, extended generous welcomes to their homes to large numbers of attendants at the various meetings.

The Church Congress in the United States, while thus manifesting its thorough loyalty to the Church in her seemly order and rightful authority, is also a voluntary association for the free discussion of great questions pertaining to both Church and State. It lays no claim to official authority or responsibility. It takes no votes, it passes no resolutions, it seeks no influence in legislation. Represented in its membership, its debates, and its working forces by a large proportion of distinguished and influential laymen, it thus becomes representative also of the *whole* Church. A chief feature in its aim, and a foremost and healthful characteristic of its history, has been illustrated in bringing together men of diverse and opposing schools of thought within the bounds of the Church. Such have found themselves drawn nearer together by the close contact of the Congress platform, and, as a distinguished Bishop has well said, " The discussions, instead of widening the breach between brethren, have tended to narrow it."

The proceedings, papers, addresses, and speeches of the several sessions are embodied in annual reports, under the editorship of the General Secretary. These form a *thesaurus* of ripe learning, vigorous thought, and eloquent utterance upon great questions of the times, of which the Protestant Episcopal Church may well be proud. To the student in theology and its cognate topics, no less than to the clergyman and thoughtful layman, these volumes will be found most valuable.

The Ninth Church Congress is to be held in October, 1884 A.D. in Detroit, Michigan, under the Presidency of the Bishop of Michigan, the Rt. Rev. S. S. Harris, D.D., L.L.D.

REV. GEORGE D. WILDES, D.D.

Churching Office. (The thanksgiving of women after childbirth, commonly called the Churching of Women.) A deep sense of the protection of Providence in her great peril has always filled the hearts of devout mothers. While this office, then, may be founded upon the Jewish law, and continued in imitation of the purification of the Holy Virgin Mary, yet it really lies farther back, in the thankfulness of deliverance from danger. The service as it stands in our Prayer-Book is somewhat changed, but in no material point, from the English office. The Kyries are omitted, and only one Psalm (cxvi.) in place of two (the cxxvii. also) in the English book. The "decently appareled," meant coming in with a veil of white material, but this is disused. The convenient place, or as the ordinary shall direct, is all that is left of the early office, before the church door. Bishop Andrews directed before the choir, Bishop Wren at the chancel rails. There is less change from the old Salisbury use than in many other services.

There should always be an offering made, whether the prayer alone is used in behalf of the woman at the place of the thanksgivings, or whether this office is used.

Circumcision. The Jewish Covenant rite of cutting off the foreskin of the male child upon the eighth day, when also the child received its name (Gen. xvii. 23; xxi. 4; Ex. xii. 48; Lev. xii. 3; Josh. v. 2).

Circumcision, Feast of. The day was kept as the octave of the Nativity at first. Of the feast of the circumcision there is early observance, but after the seventh century there appear distinct directions for it. As it fell upon the 1st of January, which was a festival of mad riot among the heathen, it was natural that it should not be kept as a feast among Christians when the excesses of the heathen were so uncontrolled. There should be a celebration of the Holy Communion upon this feast, as upon all days when any part of our LORD's life and actions are commemorated.

Circumincession. The indwelling of the Three Divine Persons of the HOLY TRINITY in each other. It is expressly taught (St. John xiv. 10-11), "Believest thou not that I am in the FATHER and the FATHER in me? ... but the FATHER that dwelleth in me. He doeth the works. Believe me that I am in the FATHER, and the FATHER in me." So in xvii. 11, 21-23, and often implied, as in i. 1; Col. ii. 9. For in Him dwelleth all the fullness of the Godhead bodily. But it is a reasonable sequence from the mysterious doctrine of the HOLY TRINITY. For though the Three Persons are distinct and separate, they are One in the Divine Nature, and the Divine Nature is entire in each Person, yet there is but one GOD; which necessarily follows from the immutability and indivisibility of the Godhead. Yet the distinction of Persons is shown by it, while the deep mystery of the Divine Unity is kept, for, saith Bishop Bull, "in order to that mutual existence (in each other) which is discerned in the FATHER, SON, and HOLY GHOST, it is absolutely necessary that there should be some distinction between those who are thus joined together,—*i.e.*, that those who mutually exist in each other should be different in reality and not in mode of conception only, for that which is simply one is not said to exist in itself or to interpenetrate itself. ... No similitude can be devised which shall be in every respect apt to illustrate it; no language avails worthily to set it forth, seeing that it is a union which far transcends all other unions." (Bull's Defense of the Nicene Creed, L. iv. ch. iv. ? 13, 14.)

Citation. A precept or a summons from the proper officer or Ecclesiastical judge, citing the person against whom complaint is made to appear before him on a certain day at a certain place to answer to the complaints made against him.

Clergy. (Clergy, from *kleros*, a lot, as men having chosen GOD for their heritage.)

They were also called Canonici, from being under a rule or a canon. The name was made to include readers, acolytes, subdeacons. The title, however, properly belongs only to the three orders, the Bishops, Priests, and Deacons. In the Scriptures St. Paul, in the Epistle to the Hebrews, implies theirs to be an office of authority; so in his Epistles to Timothy and Titus. And again, St. Peter (1 Pet.v. 3) warns the clergy against a vainglorious use of their office. This rank comes out clearly immediately after Apostolic times. In the Epistles of St. Ignatius, "without these (the Bishops, Presbyters, and Deacons) it cannot be called a Church" (to the Trallians, c. ix.), and Clement of Alexandria (Stro., l. vi. c. v. in fin.). "For I suppose that the developments in the Church of the Bishops, Priests, and Deacons are imitated from the angelic glory, and of that economy which the Scriptures declare belong to those who live in the footsteps of the Apostles, in perfection of righteousness according to the Gospel." The appointment of Timothy and Titus over the Churches of Ephesus and of Crete to order and ordain, is an early proof of the development of Episcopal order in the footsteps of the Apostles. For if the Presbyters thus were competent to arrange these things and to perpetuate their order by ordination, why give Timothy and Titus such special instructions? why send them at all?" (But *vide* articles BISHOP, PRESBYTER, DEACON, ORDINATION.) The clergy were from the Apostolic times regarded as a separate order, with special responsibilities and special immunities. In the Acts of the Apostles (xv. 23), "The Apostles and Elders-brethren," seems to be the soundest form of the words, segregating them from the laity. The Bishop exercised the highest administrative and spiritual office, held in himself all the minor offices, and was (Rev. ii., iii.) held personally responsible for the growth, purity, discipline and orthodoxy of the Church committed to him. Certain of his prerogatives he reserved to himself, chief of which were the ordination of fit persons to the Diaconate and to the Presbyterate; and the admission by consecration of the elect to the office, to his own Episcopal rank; confirmation, excommunication. As administrator of jurisdiction he gave letters dimissory to Presbyters going to other Dioceses, administered the revenues, enforced the discipline of the Canons upon his clergy and laity, and was the officer with whom lay the last appeal in all Ecclesiastical cases in his Diocese; but if he were too arbitrary other Bishops could interfere. He sat as presiding officer in his Diocesan Synod, and had his place according to the precedence of his See (usually according to its political importance) in the Provincial Synod.

The Presbyter shared with the Bishop, or had committed to him, the right to celebrate the Eucharist, to administer baptism, to give the benediction and the absolution, to consecrate churches, and, in case of great need, to reconcile penitents. He was also Counselor to his Bishop upon all Diocesan matters.

The Deacon had the collection and dispensing of the moneys of the Diocese; he could baptize, assist in divine service, administer the cup at the Commun'on, could preach and aid in parochial work; but of these offices, baptizing and preaching were exercised when neither Bishop nor Presbyter were present. The clergy were supported at first, and for many centuries, from the common fund of the Diocese, which was divided usually every month. This common fund came from tithes and gifts, bequests and endowments, which were often made; the Bishop or Presbyter, if rich, often giving all of his property into the common treasury, as did Cyprian and many others.

The clergy had many immunities. Before the Empire was Christianized their immunities were only within the Church. They were supported by the Church, and were forbidden any secular employment. They received the respect and honor due to their office. After the Empire became Christian the civil law gave the Bishops certain prerogatives, as a share in municipal affairs and a power to pardon criminals, and also gave donations and revenues from the public treasury for the building of churches and the support of charitable work, till finally Bishops had their own Courts, and at last withdrew the inferior clergy from the secular jurisdiction of the courts for crimes or misdemeanors. It was one of the causes of the Reformation to do away with the abuses that flowed from the exemption of the clergy from secular trial for secular causes. The power of the clergy was always very great, as with their monopoly, as it were, of the learning of the Middle Ages, and with their authority under the laws, civil and feudal, the churches and religious houses were the seats both of learning and of asylum.

To-day, with the impressions that Independentism has made upon the minds of the majority of people, there is less than proper regard paid to the office of the clergy. While the cleric must, so far as his personal ability and character reach, only receive the consideration due him from them, yet his office and his teaching in that office need to be more reverentially received than they are. Surely something of the force of our LORD'S solemn words still rests upon His officers: "He that heareth you heareth Me, and he that despiseth you despiseth Me, and he that despiseth Me despiseth Him that sent Me."

Clerk. (From *clercus*, a clergyman.) It is sometimes used to designate a clergyman, but has gradually received the meaning of the lay clerk, who, in the English Church, does yet, and many years ago did in the Church in this country, lead the responses and otherwise assist in the due conduct of divine service.

Clinic Baptism. Baptism administered upon a sick-bed, or to one in imminent danger of death. But since it often happened that baptism so administered was given to one who, through fear of persecution, had deferred it, the person so baptized, if he recovered, could not be admitted to any sacred office. It was one of the charges against Novatus that he had deferred baptism till he was perilously sick, and yet on his recovery, being debarred from clerical office, he procured his consecration by deceitful practices.

Cloveshoo. A Council was assembled at Cloveshoo by Ethelbald, king of the Mercians. There is considerable difficulty in determining the date, and more in identifying the place, which is thought to be Rochester or Abingdon, or, perhaps, Tewksbury. The date is given 742 or 747 A.D.; it is possible there may have been two Councils; and if so, the first was chiefly concerned in inquiring how matters of religion, especially the Creed, were ordered in the early Church in Britain, and in confirming the privileges of the Church. In the Council of 747 A.D. two letters were read from Zacharias, " the Pontiff and Apostolic lord to be venerated throughout the world," and it is " acknowledged that the recital of these documents, in which he exhorts the English of every degree to reformation, under the threat of an anathema, was in obedience to his ' Apostolical authority.'" Thirty Canons were passed at this Council, in which clergy and laity are enjoined to more careful living, and greater diligence in public worship and in the observance of holy-days.

Not long after this Council certain Dioceses were taken from the Province of Canterbury and joined together into a new Province for an Archbishop of Lichfield. But Kenulf having annexed Kent to the kingdom of Mercia, and wishing to conciliate the clergy of his new territory, seconded Athelhard, the Archbishop of Canterbury, in his wish to recover these Dioceses to his Province. The matter was pressed at Rome, and Leo III., on attaining the popedom, gave his consent that the new archbishopric should be abolished. This was done accordingly by a Council held at Cloveshoo in 803 A.D., which decreed " that the Archiepiscopal See, from this time forward, should never be in the monastery of Lichfield, nor in any other place but the city of Canterbury." Two other Councils were held in Cloveshoo in 822 and 824 A.D.

Coadjutor. He was a Bishop ordained to assist another Bishop in case of infirmity or old age, was to assist him as long as he lived, and to succeed him when he died. In our Church he bears the title of Assistant Bishop.

Cœna Domini. The Supper of the LORD,—*i.e.*, the Holy Communion.

Collect. Collects are short, comprehensive prayers, which are found in all known Liturgies and public devotional offices. There is no certain explanation to be given of the origin of the word, only that it is very ancient, as is the Collect itself.

(*a*) The oldest Liturgies contain prayers upon this model, but in the Greek Liturgies it is called the Ectene—intense prayer—or the Exapostellaria. The latter being originally a kind of precatory hymn invoking the grace of GOD, which is a characteristic of the Collect. The oldest collections of offices contain numerous short prayers. These sacramentaries of Leo I., Gelasius, and Gregory I. contain the originals of the major part of our present Collects, with some notable exceptions. As for the model on which they are framed, we may compare them with the two short prayers recorded in the Acts (i. 24, 25; iv. 24 *sq.*), to which they bear much resemblance, but they may be compared at an humble distance with the compactness and terseness of the LORD'S Prayer. There is so definite and concise a structure in the Collect that it may be reduced as it were to rule. The Collect is said to contain,—

First, a single period; forming a single intense sentence.

Secondly, only a single petition is offered in it.

Thirdly, our LORD'S mediation or atonement is pleaded; or, it closes with an ascription of praise to GOD.

These mark its difference from the long rhetorical prayers with which the Eastern Liturgies are filled, and their intensity and terse pointedness make them very marked. They are the arrows of prayer which Tertullian says Christians shot towards heaven.

The structure of the Collect may be seen by studying the similar points of two beautiful ones composed—the first by St. Gregory, about 600 A.D., and the other by Bishop Cosin, 1660 A.D.—a thousand years apart,— the Collect for Whitsunday by St. Gregory, and the Collect for the sixth Sunday after Epiphany by Bishop Cosin. They are both noble prayers, worthy of the holy men who composed them.

Invocation.	GOD,	O GOD,
Reason on which the petition is founded.	who as at this time didst teach the hearts of Thy faithful people by sending to them the light of Thy HOLY SPIRIT,	whose blessed SON was manifested that He might destroy the works of the devil and make us the Sons of GOD and heirs of eternal life,
Petition.	grant us by the same SPIRIT to have a right judgment in all things,	grant us, we beseech Thee, that having this hope we may purify ourselves even as He is pure,
Benefit.	and ever more to rejoice in His holy comfort,	that when He shall appear again with power and great glory, we may be made like Him in His eternal and glorious kingdom,

Ascription or merits pleaded. through the merits of CHRIST JESUS our SAVIOUR, who liveth and reigneth with Thee in the Unity of the same SPIRIT, one GOD, world without end. where with Thee, O FATHER, and Thee, O HOLY GHOST. He liveth and reigneth, ever one GOD, world without end.

(*b*) The title Collect does not belong only to the proper Collect for the Sunday or holy-day, but is also given to the two prayers immediately after the Creed in morning and evening prayer, to the five at the end of the Communion office, and also to the special prayers in the several offices in the Prayer-Book as may be rubrically noted therein. There are one hundred and eleven Collects in our Prayer-Book. Eighty-five belong to special Sundays and holy-days, with Epistle and Gospel, and therefore imply a Communion. Seven others, for occasional services, have also Epistle and Gospel for the same end. The remaining nineteen belong to special services, but without any Epistle or Gospel following.

College. (From the Latin *collegium*, a community.) It was an old Roman rule that not fewer than three persons could form a college. Hence it needs at least three Bishops to form a house competent to transact business and to administer affairs. Corporations are in England often called colleges. The House of Bishops is also the College of Bishops.

Color. Colors were not used in the Church at first with any but the most general reference to their symbolism. The reference to the spiritual meaning attached to the several hues in common use was of the most general way. The modern use seems to date from the time when vestments and altar-cloths and Ecclesiastical decoration received a remarkable development, 850–1300 A.D. It was also the date of the greatest development of Church architecture. In the Mosaic ritual GOD directed the use of color: The blue and the white, the purple and the scarlet, of the Tabernacle hangings, and of the veil of the Most Holy Place; the gold, the blue, the purple, scarlet, and white of the Ephod; the gold chains, the many-hued breastplate, the mitre of blue, the curious girdle of the dress of the High-Priest; the white robes of the ministering Priests. Occasional allusions to the purity of white (Ps. cxxxii.) and the symbolic hues in Ezekiel's vision (Ezek. i.) occur. But there and in the New Testament there is little allusion to symbolism of color, except in the Revelation (ch. iv. 3–5; xxi. 19–22). Color was used as a matter of course, but there was apparently no figurative, but only a decorative use of it at the different seasons of the Church's year. Of course vestments were of some color, but apparently of white, seldom of any other hue. But from the ninth to the thirteenth century there was a development of the meaning to be assigned to colors. Throughout Europe there was a great variety of usages, some of which may be preserved in the Sarum use. However, there is no law or authoritative rule upon the use of colors in the Church of the Anglican communion. The inventories of Edward VI.'s Commission show a variety of usages in the colors of the vestments and in the altar-cloths. The Sarum use had probably a larger influence than any other in England, but its rubrics were not rigidly enforced. So we may suppose that in reality the earlier English Church practically continued the earliest prominent use of white, at least in her vestments. After the Reformation white was ordered for the vestments of the Holy Communion. The Bishops wore a white rochet and a scarlet chimere. But as good old Bishop Hooper thought scarlet too gay a color for a Bishop,—probably connecting it with the scarlet woman of Revelation,—black was afterwards substituted. The stoles are usually of black. The old Sarum colors, which prevailed in the English Church till the Reformation, and were in use in very many places after till 1640 A.D., were as follows:

From Christmas to Septuagesima, for Sundays, white.

From Septuagesima to Easter-eve, for Sundays, red.

From Easter to Whit-Sunday, for Sundays, white.

From Whit-Sunday to Christmas, for Sundays, red.

All-Saints' days not martyrs, and festivals of our LORD, white.

Martyrs, Invention of the Cross, etc., red.

Black was not used, at least by order, except in services for the dead. White and red are the only colors spoken of in the rubric of the Sarum missal. The inventories of the vestments in the return made in 1549 A.D., give blue as the color next frequently used, but green and yellow are also found. The colors for the altar-cloths very probably followed the sequence of the colors of the vestments ordered for the seasons. That some series of colors appropriate to, and symbolic of, each season of the Christian year should be used is reasonable enough. It is used with much variation, indeed, everywhere in other parts of the Church, and such a usage is not contrary to, or interfered with by, any rubric or order in the Prayer-Book. The white linen for the vesting of the Holy Table for the Holy Communion is the proper and rubrical color at the celebration of that sacrament. Whether Sarum or Rome, or the Eastern use, or the caprice or taste of influential individuals be the rule followed, as taste develops and more surely as reverence for GOD's house, and care for its decent order and the honor to be paid Him in it, deepens, there must be a desire to use all proper and fit symbolism. As GOD Himself has indicated the law of its uses, we can safely follow its suggestions, under our constituted authorities. It has already found expression in the generally correct, though wholly unauthoritative, directions found in many of the Church almanacs. It is a feeling which should be guided and trained rather than discouraged or repressed, or it may fall under the direction of some undisciplined taste or aimless caprice, or ignorant wilfulness. Either of these tempers lead to disorder, and might possibly lead to disobedience to lawful authority.

Appended is a part of the temperate statements made in Scudamore's "Notitia Eucharistica":

"The English colors appear to have been as follows:

"*White*, daily from the eve of the Nativity to the octave of the Epiphany inclusive, except when another color is especially appointed, as below; also daily from Evensong to the Friday before Whitsuntide inclusive; on Trinity Sunday and its Eve; the conversion of St. Paul, the Purification of St. Mary; the Annunciation, St. John Baptist, St. Michael, and all Saints, with their Eves; and the colors retained when they fall on a Sunday.

"*Red*, on all Sundays except those for which white is ordered, as above; on Ash-Wednesday, Maundy-Thursday, Good-Friday, Holy Saturday, till Evensong, all Whits week, with the Saturday before; the Festivals of Martyrs, whose death is commemorated unless falling between Easter and Pentecost.

"*Orange tawney (croceus)* was prescribed for the Festivals of all Confessors.

"*Green*, or *blue*, on week-days from the octave of the Epiphany to Septuagesima Sunday; from Trinity Sunday to Advent, except on Festivals, their Eves and Vigils.

"*Violet, brown,* or *gray,* on week-days from Septuagesima Sunday to Maundy-Thursday, and throughout Advent, except on Festivals and their Eves; also on the Ember-days and the Vigils of the Purification, the Annunciation, the Ascension, and the fasted Vigils of Saints' days." (Scudamore's Notitia Eucharistica, p. 108 *sq. q v.*)

It is said that cloth of gold supersedes all other colors.

Authorities: Blunt's Annotated Prayer-Book, Stephen's Sealed Books, vol. i., Smith's Dictionary of Antiquities.

Colorado, The Missionary Jurisdiction of. Colorado, Wyoming, and New Mexico were part of the jurisdiction of the Northwest under Bishop Talbot, 1859-65 A.D. Bishop Randall was elected for these Territories in October, 1865 A.D. The name of Colorado was, popularly, Pike's Peak. Settlements began in 1859 A.D. Wyoming was not known under that name till after Bishop Randall took charge. These three Territories formed one jurisdiction during Bishop Randall's eight years' Episcopate. The following year, October, 1874 A.D., New Mexico and Arizona were made a separate missionary district, the Bishop of Colorado continuing to have jurisdiction in Wyoming. During Bishop Talbot's six years' charge of the Northwest the Church was established in Denver, 1860 A.D., Rev. J. H. Kehler, rector; in Central City, 1864 A.D., Rev. Francis Granger, rector; and in Idaho Springs, 1864 A.D., Rev. William O. Jarvis, missionary. The two former parishes had secured church buildings. Of course other points were visited by the Bishop and his clergy.

Bishop Randall began his work (consecrated December 28, 1865 A.D.) with characteristic energy in the spring of 1866 A.D. With an increase of missionaries he pushed on the work of the Church at new points,—Nevadaville, Black Hawk, Georgetown, Pueblo, etc. In 1867 A.D. he took steps looking to the establishment of a school for girls. In 1868 A.D. he began like efforts for a boys' school. The former was built in Denver in 1868 A.D. The latter at Golden in 1869 A.D. In 1870 A.D. he built, in connection with the boys' school, a school of mines, the Territory contributing most of the cost of its erection, afterwards deeded back to the Territory, and now one of the best of the State institutions. In 1871 A.D. he secured the means, $10,000, from Nathan Matthews, Esq., for the erection of Matthews Hall for a divinity school at Golden. The girls' and the boys' schools were named respectively for Mr. John D. Wolfe and Mr. Geo. A. Jarvis, who largely aided in their foundation. In 1873 A.D. a wing was added to Wolfe Hall, and an Episcopal residence erected in Denver. Bishop Randall, during his active Episcopate, increased the number of parishes and missions to nineteen or twenty, and erected twelve churches. Besides these he bought and converted into chapels two or three saloons or "stores," for temporary use, in places that subsequently became depopulated. In 1881 A.D. work was begun on behalf of the Christian education of the Shoshone Indians in Wyoming, and a teacher, a layman, was employed. He had resigned, however, before the Bishop's death, on September 28, 1873 A.D., and the work was temporarily suspended.

Bishop Spalding (consecrated December 31, 1873 A.D.) entered upon the work in February following. Some of the clergy had left or had abandoned their posts; there were *seven* at work. Matthews Hall had seven divinity students under a competent instructor, with nothing to support them. Debts to a considerable amount had accrued against the school, and the income from pupils was greatly deficient. The financial panic beginning in the fall of 1873 A.D. was severely felt here from 1874 to 1878 A.D. It was with no little difficulty and not without the generous aid of friends of missions that all indebtedness was met and the schools put upon a better basis. Wolfe Hall from

1876 to 1882 A.D. was more than self-supporting. By liberal aid from Miss Wolfe and others, and the earnings of the school, enlargements were made in 1878-80 A.D., costing $18,000. Jarvis Hall and Matthews Hall were both destroyed by fire in May, 1878 A.D. The insurance, $8903.72 on Jarvis Hall, $6430.51 on Matthews Hall, and $989.34 on the library, was all that was left us. The site was abandoned and reverted to the donor under the terms of the deed.

These schools were the next year removed to Denver. Jarvis Hall rebuilt here has had much better success. It is under the most effective organization and discipline under the wardenship of Dean Hart of the Cathedral, assisted by five masters. Its specialty is the fitting of boys for the best colleges. The girls' school is one of the best in the country; the principal, Miss F. M. Buchan, is assisted by a corps of ten teachers. The studies embrace all those usual in such seminaries, music and art being specialties. Both schools greatly need better and ampler buildings, and libraries and apparatus for scientific studies.

When the present Bishop took charge the work was confined to the two principal towns in Wyoming, Cheyenne and Laramie City, and to the eight or nine principal places east of the main range of the Rocky Mountains. For four or five years, during the "hard times," the growth of population though steady was not rapid. The Church was making real progress, though the first object was to strengthen the foundations already laid, and to set in order the things that were wanting. A memorial church to Bishop Randall, Trinity, was built in Denver, 1874 A.D., churches in West Denver, Greeley, Cañon City, Boulder, Rosita, were erected, and the churches at Colorado Springs and Central City were completed. All inhabited parts of the jurisdiction were often visited and missions established wherever practicable. In 1878 A.D., with the discovery of the silver mines of Leadville and the impetus given to railway building, a new era of temporal prosperity was dawning. The church built in that city cost $15,000, on which a debt remained of $3000. The Church has been planted in Ouray, La Plata, San Juan, Rio Grande, Conejos, Custer, Saguache, Gunnison, and other counties, and strengthened in Pueblo, El Paso, Boulder, Wild, and Arapahoe Counties in the more eastern parts of the State. Seven parishes are self-sustaining. In Wyoming three new missions are well established on the Union Pacific Railroad, and at Lander, in Sweetwater County, while the parishes of Cheyenne and Laramie City are self-supporting. The Indian Mission at the Shoshone and northern Arapahoe Agency is under the charge of an able missionary, who is about to build a chapel. The government is building a school costing $12,000. Three more churches are to be built in Wyoming and several in Colorado, if the means can be secured, in 1884 A.D.

The Cathedral was begun in Denver in 1880 A.D., and ready for use in November, 1881 A.D. It will seat 1200. Its cost was $90,000, some $25,000 of which came from the sale of lots owned by the congregation. The Bishop secured and gave the site, its value at the time being $12,000. The corporation, which is the board of trustees of the schools and mission and most parish and other property, the title of which is "The Bishop and Chapter of the Cathedral of St. John the Evangelist, Denver, Colorado," was organized as early as 1879 A.D. The Cathedral organization is practical and effective.

In February, 1879 A.D., St. Luke's Hospital, Denver, Colorado, was organized. A suitable block of four acres, with a large frame building originally used as a hotel, was purchased and put in order, with accommodations for thirty-five to forty patients. The property is valued at $12,000, and the debt thereon is $4000. The hospital is under strictly Church management, and its benefits are extended to all without regard to sect or religion. It has treated over seven hundred patients and is under excellent management. It will long need aid in its charitable work. It has strong claims on Eastern communities, whence many of its patients come.

Bishop Spalding has been in charge of the jurisdiction ten years. The gains are as follows:

The population of Colorado and Wyoming in 1870 A.D. was 50,000, in 1880 A.D. 214,000. The per cent. of increase was 328. It was hardly to be expected that in so new and rapidly growing a frontier country we could keep pace with the secular growth. In some respects we have fallen short. In other important respects our statistics show a greater proportionate growth of the Church than of the Territories.

In 1873 A.D. the number of Church families reported was 360. In 1883 A.D. it was 1921; increase, 433 per cent. The number of souls for whom the clergy were caring was, at the respective dates, 620 and 13,141; increase, 2019 per cent. The infants baptized were, in 1873 A.D. 117; in 1883 A.D. 390; increase 233 per cent. Of adults in the years respectively, 17 and 61; increase 258 per cent. In 1873 A.D. there were confirmed 48; in 1883 A.D. 127. Since June 1, 20 more have been confirmed, making the number for the last year 147; but these are not counted, not being yet reported. Without these the increase is 164 per cent. In the ten years previous to 1874 A.D. 466 were confirmed. From then to June 1, 1883 A.D., 1081; increase, 131 per cent. The gain in the number of communicants is also especially gratifying. There were reported, in 1873 A.D. 550; in 1883 A.D. 2112; an increase of 284 per cent. So of Sunday-school teachers and scholars; in 1873 A.D. the report gave 658; in 1883 A.D. 2082; a gain of 216 per cent.

The ordinations to the priesthood and diaconate number 32. There had been previously ordained in and for Colorado 13; an increase of 146 per cent. There were here 12 churches; the report now shows 32; increase, 166 per cent. Three of those built before 1874 A.D. are unused; not one built since is unserviceable. The usual proportion—not greater than in Eastern dioceses—will, in time, from decay of towns and changes of population, become useless. There were, ten years ago, 2 rectories, omitting 1 that was subsequently alienated and lost by the vestry; there are now 16; a gain of 700 per cent. The number of sittings in the churches at the former date was 1600; at the latter date, 8281; an increase of 417 per cent. There were 7 clergymen at work in the jurisdiction. There were two or three others not belonging here or not employed. The report now shows 28; a gain of 300 per cent. The number of parishes and missions was 19. It is now 53; per cent. of increase, 179. There were 2 self-supporting. There are now 9; increase, 250 per cent. The offerings for all purposes of the jurisdiction have increased in much greater proportion. They were, 1873 A.D. $5086; in 1883 A.D. $52,509; a gain of 932 per cent. The value of churches and rectories was, at the first date, $26,300; at the present, $249,350; increase, 848 per cent. The Episcopal residence was worth $9000. Its value now is $25,000; increase, 177 per cent. Wolfe Hall (building, grounds, and furniture) was valued at $30,000. Its value now is $80,000; an increase of 166 per cent. Jarvis Hall had cost, with its furniture and apparatus, $19,781. Notwithstanding the disastrous fire, which left only the insurance of $8903.72, the value of its present lands and buildings is $50,000; an increase of 310 per cent. Matthews Hall, at Golden, cost $10,000. Matthews Hall, in Denver, is worth $15,000; increase, 50 per cent. Jarvis Hall endowment for theological education was estimated, in 1874, at $12,000. Nine years later its value is $75,000; an increase of 477 per cent. The increase in value of all our school property is from $73,000 to $220,000,—201 per cent.

Such have been some of our gains. It is a fair showing. It gives good grounds for encouragement and confidence as to future growth and prosperity. There is much that cannot be gathered from statistics. The great results for which we should be, above all things, solicitous, the coming of CHRIST'S spiritual kingdom, the souls gathered in and saved in CHRIST and built up in Him and edified, the fulfilling of the number of His elect,—no figures can tabulate these more substantial gains.

Very little special aid has been received during the last three years from individuals or parishes at the East. And yet the missionary ground now open to us and inviting us is four times as large as it was ten years ago. To keep our present missionaries will require $1000 more than the Board of Missions appropriates, and with several mission chapels to build at once, and many in the near future, there are no funds available but such as may be secured by solicitations. Mistake is made in withholding assistance that may, unless corrected, be fatal to our continuing to lead in pioneer work as in the past—to our becoming strong as heretofore, relatively to all other Christian bodies, in the vast wildernesses that are yet to be evangelized within the limits of the two jurisdictions. We are not receiving more than a fourth part of the amount of aid that is given to each of two or three leading denominations for Colorado and Wyoming. And we are expected to be even more successful than they! Whether our friends who have hitherto helped the work in this portion of the great New West come to see and rectify the mistake or not, it is clearly our interest and our duty to rely more and more for the support of all our work upon the active efforts and generous offerings of our own people. Our strength is in what *we do* and in what *we are*.

We cannot expect the same proportionate increases as in the past. There is much in the immediate outlook that is discouraging. The times are again becoming hard. There is no sale for mines. Owners of valuable properties are unable to develop them. We are discovering by sad experience that the work in all our mining districts, and these embrace a large portion of the country, must always be of a missionary character. The population in mining districts is migratory. Miners are hard-working men; dependent for daily bread upon daily wages. The few who acquire wealth move to lower altitudes and to cities that promise greater comforts and advantages. Still we shall have for generations good towns in the mining regions, and it is in these that much of our best work must be done.

The jurisdiction of Wyoming, as separate from Colorado, was established by the House of Bishops in October, 1883 A.D. The Missionary Bishop of Colorado is the Provisional Bishop. It is now the latest formed of the missionary districts; it is to be hoped that its needs will excite new interest.

Statistics for 1886 A.D.: Clergy, 34; missions, 40; baptisms, 392; confirmed, 175; com., 2075; candidates for H. O., 1; ordinations diac., 3; pr., 1; contr., $32,465.13

RT. REV. J. F. SPALDING, D.D.

Colossians. This Epistle to the Colossians—one of the three doctrinal Epistles which St. Paul sent out to the Churches from his own hired house in his first imprisonment — forms a strong link in the chain of doctrinal statements he makes concerning the Church as the body of CHRIST, the fullness of Him that filleth all things. It is not merely a restating of what had been eloquently put forth in the Epistles to the Ephesians, but it was something more, or rather different. The dangers of the Church at Colossæ required him to warn them of their being misled and drawn from the unity of the Faith (*cf.* ch. i. 23, with ii. 8 and 18-23), dangers which have not ceased to assail the members of the Church, to alienate them from their true LORD and Head. In it he uses terms which passed into early Liturgic usage (ch. ii. 13-15 and St James' Liturgy). There is considerable resemblance upon many points in this Epistle compared with the doctrines and the directions upon our social duties which occupy the Epistle to the Ephesians. These are largely repeated in this Epistle; indeed, there are nearly forty places where the two Epistles coincide and mutually illustrate each other; but the Church at Colossæ had many evils of a local character to contend with. Under a pretended philosophy and spiritual wisdom, the heresies of will-worship and of worship of angels, and a pretense to pierce into things hidden, some claimed a false humility and made a show of asceticism. A claim to supernatural powers and to a supernatural knowledge is ever most attractive to many minds, and the Colossian Christians were in great danger of being greatly misled. St. Paul wisely and boldly meets the danger by using the words which might have, and afterwards did, become freighted with false meaning, such as the word "fullness," and by setting forth the true supernatural teaching of CHRIST. He recounts his own former preaching upon the fullness of the reconciliation our LORD has effected. He warns them that these teachers do not hold fast by the "Head from which all the body by joints and bands, having nourishment ministered and knit together, increaseth with the increase of GOD."

He foresaw so much of the later Gnostic vagaries, and met them by using the word "fullness" (pleroma), and by reciting the heavenly orders and ranks, so anticipating the æons of these Gnostics; the will-worship, the claim to an esoteric knowledge, the vain deceits of later heresies, are all, as it were, provided for by the Apostle's peculiar phraseology.

The Epistle bears every mark of the Apostle's own hand. It is within the broad scope of the Apostle's thoughts and teachings before alluded to and elsewhere implied, but here in the leisure of the prison brought together and set forth with his own peculiar enthusiastic energy. The Apostle, chained to his guards, has lost none of the energy and force which he possessed when free, and he was as fully alive to the needs of the Colossians as though he were present and ministering to them. The practical hortatory portion, which occupies the last two chapters, is Pauline throughout in the clearness, directness, and delicacy with which sin is reproved and love, forbearance, and forgiveness are urged. The salutation and messages are all unmistakably from him who forgot no friend and overlooked no need of the Church to which he was writing.

Comes. An old collection of Epistles and Gospels, which has been ascribed to St. Jerome (380 A.D.), but may be probably later. It contains the Epistles and Gospels very nearly as we now use them, and whenever it disagrees from the Roman rite it agrees with the English use, except when the Reformers (1549-52 A.D.) or Reviser (1662 A.D.) may have arbitrarily changed. The Comes is mentioned as far back as 471 A.D. Its arrangement corresponds to the Salisbury use so very closely, and differs from the Roman use in so many ways, as to show that it was received and appropriated independently of any Roman influence. Several slight circumstances point to the probability that it belongs to St. Jerome's time at least. Before his time there was no special series of selected Scriptures; after the date above given the Scriptures begin to be cited as though such a lectionary were in use, by St. Ambrose, Augustine, Leo, etc. In the part appropriated to the saints none are commemorated after St. Jerome's day. Therefore it is exceedingly probable that this selection of Epistles and Gospels came to us from the East through the Gallican Church, and may have been in use before the days of Augustine of Canterbury.

Commemorations. (*Vide* DIPTYCHS.) In England, at Oxford and Cambridge, certain commemoration days are kept, on which the names of all known benefactors to the universities are proclaimed, special psalms and lessons appointed, and special collects and versicles recited. These days were observed before the Reformation.

Commendam. A living given in charge to a clergyman till a proper pastor is appointed. A living is then held in commendam. They are held by Bishops whose incomes are of small amount.

Commendatory Letters are very ancient in use. Such were the letters Apollos brought from Ephesus to the Church in Corinth and Achaia, and such that St. Paul referred to in 2 Cor. iii. 1, as well known and of constant use (*cf.* 1 Cor. xvi. 3). (For further notices, see LITERÆ FORMATÆ.)

Commentaries. Expositions or explanations of Holy Scriptures. It is one of the most difficult tasks ever set before men, since it is so difficult to grasp the whole nexus of revelation, to understand its exceeding breadth and yet its positiveness, to reach up to its strictness and yet its love, its unswerving statements yet its tenderness to all mankind. The task requires a prayerful, submissive mind, and a thoroughly trained logical power, and a full command of all the important learning that can illustrate or explain the Holy Scriptures. It demands that Scripture shall be diligently compared with Scripture and not against Scripture, and that there should be no prepossessions, no theories formed to be narrowly carried out, and above all that the expositor should lay down for himself and strictly adhere to the rule that the Church is the keeper and witness of Holy Writ.

For this purpose much of the ancient commentaries is most useful. St. Chrysostom and Augustine and Jerome form a valued series. Origen has some very valuable expositions, but is not to be trusted. Theophylact has compressed much of St. Chrysostom and added useful comments of his own. The "Critici Sacri" is the work of Bishop Pearson and other English divines. But it is useless to go on with the list, so many new and valuable commentaries have appeared. Perhaps for general use the Cambridge Bible for the use of schools, published in separate volumes, on each book of the Old and New Testaments, is the best for those who wish for special commentaries upon single books.

Burgon's "Plain Commentary" and Isaac Williams's "Devotional Commentary" are beyond praise. The "Speaker's Commentary," and Alford on the New Testament, are excellent. But while admitting the excellence of separate writers, it will be well to take only those who adhere most strictly to what has ever been received in the Church.

Commination Office. An office in the English Prayer-Book appointed for Ash-Wednesday. It is one of the last remnants left of the older penitential offices that carried out the disciplinary system of the early ages. Then offenders were deprived for a given length of time of their rights and privileges in the Church, not only till they proved their repentance but till the set time was expired. The English office has adapted the very old Salisbury service for Ash-Wednesday, prefacing it with an address and a recital of the curses of Mount Ebal, and then with an exhortation uses the older service very nearly as it stood. It was an endeavor to preserve something of the old disciplinary system and to remind men, by its reciting the denouncing of God's anger and judgments against sinners, that justice has not lost its stern vigor. The service was dropped out of our Prayer-Book, but the three last prayers were transferred to their present place after the Ash-Wednesday Collect, and the seven Penitential Psalms (with the oversight of omitting the 51st Psalm) were ordered for the proper Psalms for the day. The oversight occurred by not noting that it was used at length in the Commination, and therefore was not put into the table for proper Psalms for Ash-Wednesday.

Commissary. An officer sent by a Bishop to make inspections of parishes for him and to report thereon.

Common Prayer. In its proper place will be found the history of the Prayer-Book. But here it is well to mark the meaning of the word Common, what belongs to, and is to be used by, also that it may be joined in and understood by the congregation; not only that, but that all have a common share in its petitions, so that none are left out, of all estates and conditions of men, and that there are in it no petitions that any one may refuse to say Amen to, and that there are in it all the parts of worship and praise and confession, as well as of prayer, which all can join in, and in which, as Christians holding a common heritage, all can claim a portion. It is COMMON in the highest and noblest sense of the word.

Communion. *Vide* LORD'S SUPPER.

Communion (Holy), Office of. The earliest descriptions which we have of the Communion office of the early Church prove that from the beginning it contained these parts: The reading of Holy Scripture, with exhortation based upon it; the kiss of peace, with prayer for all men; the offering of bread and wine; the thanksgiving, ending with the Triumphal Hymn ("Holy, holy, holy"); the recital of the words of Institution; the Oblation of the elements to GOD, and the Invocation of the HOLY GHOST upon them; the administration of the consecrated elements in both kinds; the dismissal of the people (presumably after a thanksgiving). There is no ancient Liturgy* in which these parts do not appear, whatever else may be added, and no description of one which does not seem to imply them all. And, besides, they are always found in the order in which they have just been mentioned, the only variation of importance being that the great Intercession for all men, and especially for the whole Church, occupies different parts of the service. In the Liturgy of the Greek Church it has stood for many centuries after the Invocation of the HOLY GHOST,—that is to say, at the end of the consecration; in the ancient Liturgy of Gaul and Spain, which is believed to have been brought almost in Apostolic times from Ephesus, it stands early in the service, soon after the lessons from Scripture; in the Roman Liturgy, which, though much older than the doctrine of transubstantiation, and bearing in its text no indication of it, yet shows many traces of being mutilated and confused, it is divided. One other difference may be noted here as of interest in the study of our own service: the Greek Liturgy has no proper Prefaces to the Triumphal Hymn; the Gallic or Ephesine (so called) has more than a hundred and fifty for different occasions; the Roman was once as rich in its variations, though now it has but eleven.

Our Liturgy came to us from the Churches of England and Scotland, and it was theirs by descent from the Church of ancient days in England, modified in Scotland by Eastern influences. It is impossible to go into its early history here. It must suffice to say that the Liturgy of the Church of England

---

* This word is used in this article in its strict sense, as applying only to the office of the Holy Communion.

was never identical with that of the Church of Rome, and that it always showed that it was in part an inheritance from the Church of Gaul, which had, in its turn, taken its form of Eucharistic worship from the East. At the time cf the Reformation there was first added to the Latin form of Consecration an English form for the preparation of the communicants, and for administration to them; then a complete service was published in English (in 1549 A.D.), adding to the defective Roman form certain things from the ancient Liturgies, though not in the ancient order, together with certain others peculiar to itself; and then (in 1552 A.D.) the service was put into nearly its present shape, the form of the prayer of consecration being carried back more nearly into conformity with the Roman, in part, as it seems to the writer, from a feeling that a wrong order had been adopted three years before. The American Liturgy is taken almost exactly from that in the English Prayer-Book, with the important exception that the Prayer of Consecration follows the Scotch form,—not that in the Scotch book of 1637 A.D., which never went into use, but that which was taken from primitive sources by the non-jurors in 1718 A.D., and which was borrowed from them by the Scotch Bishops.

These things being premised, the meaning of the several parts of the service may be readily seen. First, after this recital of the LORD'S Prayer, and the Collect for Purity as preparatory to the whole service, comes, as in the earliest days, the reading of Holy Scriptures. The lesson from the Old Testament (called in some services the Prophecy) is with us invariable throughout the year, consisting of the Ten Commandments, which also serves, a proper response being provided to lead to a confession of sin and a prayer for grace. The Epistles and the Gospel are two lessons from the two parts of the New Testament, and are read by us in accordance with a very ancient calendar, which the Church of Rome has confused, as she has almost everything else in the Liturgy. To these the Collects, most of which are also very ancient, serve as a fitting and devout introduction. The Creed is the profession of our Faith as based on the Scriptures, parts of which have just been read, and the Sermon is an explanation of them and an exhortation based upon them. The offering of alms shows our charity, corresponding to the kiss of peace; and the offering of bread and wine is like the ancient presentation of the first fruits of the earth. The Prayer for the Church Militant is our great Intercession, keeping the position which it had in the old Liturgy of Gaul, and reminding us that English Christianity came in part from the East, and very probably from Ephesus and from St. John. The Exhortation is a continuation of the Sermon, having for its purpose to begin the special preparation of the people for receiving the Holy Sacrament.

It leads to the Invitation, which is followed most naturally, we may say necessarily, by a humble Confession of sins and an Absolution, the latter having its most solemn form —that of a prayer. The Comfortable Words which follow are peculiar to our office and to those from which it was taken, and are in a translation made (it is thought) by Archbishop Cranmer expressly for the first English Prayer-Book; they serve to confirm the faith of the worshipers in GOD'S promises of pardon. Then comes a form of words which can be traced back to the very earliest days, brief versicles and responses preparing the way for the Angelic or Triumphal Hymn (it is not strictly correct to call this the Trisagion); and in certain days the form of thanksgiving is made longer and adapted to the special commemoration, our number of proper prefaces being, however, probably owing to Roman influences, very small. The Prayer of Humble Access comes in as a parenthesis, though very suitably, between the Triumphal Hymn and the lofty strain of praise with which the Prayer of Consecration begins (which, by the way, first appears in the Scotch service of 1764 A.D.). The essential parts of this prayer are, through GOD'S good providence, in their proper order, in our book, as they were in every ancient Liturgy, as they are to-day in those of the Greek Church, and as so many of the earnest divines of the Church of England have wished that they might be in hers. The Words of Institution are followed by an Oblation of the elements to GOD, as a memorial of the one sacrifice of CHRIST; and after it is the Invocation of the HOLY SPIRIT, which completes the Consecration. But the prayer goes on with a brief intercession, which reminds us of that in the Greek Liturgy, an offering of the souls and the bodies of the worshipers to GOD, a prayer that their sins may not prevent the acceptance of their worship, and a doxology, which latter is prolonged and echoed in a hymn. Then comes the administration in both kinds, according to CHRIST'S institution. The Post-Communion, as it is called, is more elaborate in our offices than in almost any other. It includes the LORD'S Prayer as offered by those who have now renewed their covenant with GOD, a prayer of Thanksgiving, the venerable *Gloria in Excelsis*, and the Blessing of Peace. No other service than the English and our own has the LORD'S Prayer in this part of the service, all others placing it before the Communion. The other peculiarities of our Liturgy, which we share with those from which it is derived, are the Comfortable Words (a peculiarity of which we have no need to be ashamed), and the position of the *Gloria in Excelsis;* and in regard to the latter, though there are reasons for placing it as the Hymn of the Incarnation, at the beginning of the offices, as in the English service of 1549 A.D., use seems to commend its present position very strongly. The place of the Prayer of Humble Access in our books, as to which we follow the English, makes a break in the strain of thanksgiving, which is not found in the ancient offices; but it is, as has been said, of the nature of a parenthesis, and most fittingly expresses the feeling of humility with which we take upon our lips the praises of GOD.

It does not come within the scope of this article to speak of the rubrics of the service or of the doctrines of the Eucharist.

Authorities: Hammond's Liturgies, Eastern and Western; Keeling's Liturgæ Britannicæ, Freeman's Principles of Divine Service, Marshall's Ancient Liturgies of the Church of England, Hall's Fragmenta Liturgica.   REV. PROF. S. HART.

Communion in One Kind. The administration only of the bread and not the wine in the LORD's Supper. This practice, which is contrary to the express command, "Drink ye all," and to the continual usage of the Church everywhere else, has been the rule of the Roman Church for the last seven hundred years only.

Communion of Saints. The latter part of the IX. Article of the Creed. It forms a complement to the former part,—the Holy Catholic Church, and serves to partly explain it. It was a later addition to this Article. It adds to and carries on the confession of the outer visible union with CHRIST in the Holy Catholic Church, and confesses the inner mystical union with Him. It is best understood in this connection with the first verses of the first Epistle general of St. John, and adds the doctrine of the union of all his saints living and departed, which is brought out so nobly in the eleventh and twelfth chapters of the Epistle to the Hebrews, especially in the 22d and 24th verses of the twelfth chapter, which form an inspired exposition of its true meaning in the Creed.

Communion-Table. The name synonymous with the altar in the Christian Church. The Order for the Holy Communion in the Prayer-Book calls it, as does the Greek Church, the Holy Table and the LORD's Table, and so in the Ordinal. In the form for the Consecration of a Church or Chapel, which was compiled by the Bishops of this Church in 1799 A.D., the altar is called the Communion-Table. In the Office of Institution, framed in 1804 A.D. and revised in 1808 A.D., it is called Altar. It is both an altar and table, for as the place for offering the oblation of bread and wine it is an altar, and with respect to the feast it is a table. In the New Testament the use is indifferent in the few allusions made to it. Heb. xiii. 10: "We have an *Altar* whereof they have no right *to eat* which serve the Tabernacle." 1 Cor. x. 21: "Ye cannot be partakers of the LORD's Table and the table of devils," "where what was on the table of devils was from the altar of devils." And throughout table and altar are used indifferently. In strictness the table is the LORD's Table, the Holy Table, not the Communicant's Table so that the term Communion-Table is incorrect.

Compline, in the English Church, before the Reformation, was the last service of the day. When the two services of Morning and Evening Prayer were arranged, the services of the first hours were joined together to form the morning services, and the Vesper and Compline of the last hours were conjoined into a fixed form for the Evening Prayer. It was not intended that the public worship should interfere with the use of private prayer, an idea which has often been put forth, but she intended that the public worship should be common, and "understanded of the people."

Conception. The truth of the conception of CHRIST by the operation of the HOLY GHOST is of fundamental importance to the Christian. Unless it be so, the ancient prophecy (Is. vii. 14) has failed, the records of the Evangelists St. Matthew and St. Mark are false, the first chapter of St. John meaningless, and our faith vain; not merely this, but the whole career of the Christian Church an effect without a cause, if CHRIST is not the pre-existing Eternal SON of GOD, of one substance with His FATHER, begotten of His FATHER before all worlds.

Conclave. A room that can be locked, then an assembly-room, and, lastly, the assembly itself, generally the assembly of Cardinals, and more especially that assembly convened for the purpose of electing a new Pope. Up to the eleventh century the people as well as the clergy had a voice in the election, but under the guidance, it is said, of Hildebrand, afterwards the famous Gregory VII., Pope Nicholas II. arranged that the Cardinals, *i.e.*, the Presbyters of the Cardinal Churches, should hold the election to the exclusion of the rights of the other parties to the election, 1059 A.D. The election is conducted under certain very minute rules, the chief of which is the absolute seclusion of the Cardinals from all external communication.

Concomitance. The doctrine that in transubstantiation the Blood inheres in the Body in the Eucharist, and therefore that there is practically no withholding of the grace and value of the Cup in the Communion. This strange and erroneous doctrine was invented to parry the proofs that the Cup must by the New Testament rule be given to the laity in the administration of the LORD's Supper.

Concordance. (From *concordare,* to agree.) A dictionary and reference book of all the words which occur in an author. It is most generally applied to a verbal concordance of the Bible. There are many concordances, some of subjects (topical) and others of words (verbal), in the Hebrew, Greek (Septuagint), Latin (Vulgate), English, French, and German. Those in English claim our attention. The earlier concordances were quite defective, as they gave but the leading words. But they were superseded by the great work of ALEXANDER CRUDEN (1737 A.D.). It is in many repects the completest, and is arranged in very convenient form. It was incomplete in proper names, but that has been supplied in late editions. The most ambitious, and in many respects the most exhaustive, concordance is the recent one by Dr. Young, of Edinburgh, 1879 A.D. It gives the Hebrew and Greek words. It arranges these by subjects under the separate use of each word, not merely as noun or verb, etc., but in its several senses. It is probably the most perfect concordance that can be prepared.

Concordat. An agreement between powers relative to some subject. This word is usually restrained to agreements made between the Papacy and the contracting power acknowledging the Roman obedience, and it will be found that very often it was entered into to prevent the government from asserting and enforcing the just independence of the national Church. Such is the history of at least one concordat in France, the Pragmatic sanction (1516 A.D.), under Francis I., who was in correspondence with Melancthon. A second concordat was formed between Napoleon I. and Pius VII., which, however, did not give anything to the Roman See. It is now in force, after having been abrogated in 1817 A.D. to give place to a vain effort to restore the concordat of 1516 A.D. The interval between these concordats is filled with most instructive history. So in Spain the liberties of the Church were secured in the concordat of 1762 A.D., but in 1851 A.D. another not so favorable was made. But Portugal is noted upon the Peninsula for the firmness with which it has defended the practical independence of the Portuguese Church. In Germany the efforts of Joseph II. produced a great deal of excitement, but the intervention of the French Revolution and the treatment Napoleon inflicted upon Pius VI. produced a reaction in favor of the Roman See, and concordats were formed with the several states of Germany more or less favorable to the Roman See. The most favorable one (Austria in 1855 A.D.), proved to be a failure; many provisions in it could not be carried out, and those which were worked unfavorable results politically, so that in 1870 A.D. it was abolished. The history of the concordats from 1516 A.D. to the present day is the history of the effort to reconcile the National Historical Independence of the several Churches of Europe with the desire to remain, for varying, and often narrow, political reasons, in the obedience of the Roman See.

Condignity. A topic in the preformation discussion as to the relation of works done before, and those under the gracious influences of GOD. Some works, it was held by some, could be done so well that thereby a man could deserve salvation (congruity). On the other hand it was contended that a man under only divine influence could *deserve* eternal life (condignity). The error in each case was the insisting (whether wittingly or not) that man could deserve or merit eternal life. Compare the XIIIth of the Articles upon this.

Confession. A word used with a wide signification and many applications. It means an acknowledgment of either an act or a belief, therefore it may be used to signify (*a*) The acknowledgment of any sin or sins. (*b*) The avowal of a belief. (*c*) The public documents containing such avowals which have been put forth with authority. It often is used simply as meaning auricular confession of sins to a priest.

Confession of Faith. The great Confession of Faith is made in the Creed. The Church can recognize no other Confession of Faith, though documents bearing that title have been put forth, and the XXXIX. Articles of the English and American Churches are popularly so styled. It is really an error, though the XXXIX. Articles contain decisions upon theological points and protests upon errors in vogue at the time (1562 A.D.), and upon some points of Church Polity. *The* Confession of Faith is properly the one made at Baptism: "Dost thou believe all the Articles of the Christian Faith?" Anciently it was necessary to recite the Creed at that time. But this does not cover all that is now placed under this title. It refers now to those documents which were published during the first century of the Reformation (and is made to include those since), containing declarations upon points of faith, protests against errors, or malpractices in religion, and assertions upon controverted or undetermined articles. The first and most notable of these is the Confession of Augsburg, presented to the Emperor Charles V. (June 25, 1530 A.D.) in full diet at Augsburg. It was read to the Diet in German, and made a very deep impression. This and its Defense (Apologia) against the attempted refutations of Eck, Cochlæus, and other Roman theologians have become one of the standard authorities of the Lutheran Communion. The Calvinistic Confession of Basle, which took shape from a speech by Œcolampadius 1531 A.D., and was written out by Myconius in 1534 A.D.; the Helvetic Confession of 1536 A. D., in Basle, to unify the Swiss Reformers; the Genevan Catechism, the work of Calvin, 1536 A.D., takes rank as a confession,—are documents of this rank for the Calvinistic communion on the Continent; the Westminster Confession of Faith for the Presbyterians. These constitute only a very few of the many symbolic books,—*i.e.*, collections of standard Confessions of Faith of the various religious bodies which receive them.

Confession of Sin. It is one of the essentials of repentance. "I said, I will confess my transgressions unto the LORD; and thou forgavest the iniquity of my sin" (Ps. xxxii. 5). It is, however, a question as to manner and before whom this confession or sin is to be made. As to manner, it is to be complete and unreserved, so far as memory and conscience can render this confession; the Holy Scriptures are full of it, and so are the writings of all the best and holiest men of all times. This confession is to be unshrinking in owning the character and heinousness of sin. But *before* whom is this to be made? To GOD beyond a doubt; but David's confession, which was finally recorded so fully, and for all ages, in the 51st Psalm, was first before Nathan: "And David said unto Nathan, I have sinned against the LORD, and Nathan said unto David, The LORD also hath put away thy sin." Here we see confession before a Priest and absolution, but it is equally clear that it was open, and before all who were present in the Royal chamber, and that this was no secret confession, concealed, and never to be divulged. There is no example recorded of such auricular confession in the Bible; on the contrary, the most open and public acknowledgment of wrong-doing is urged, not only in the Psalms, the great Penitential authority for the Church, but also by the conduct of the Primitive Church during the first centuries, when she kept up her strict discipline (*vide* DISCIPLINE) in accordance with the precept of St. James: "Confess your faults one to another, and pray one for another that ye may be healed." With these and other directions before us (St. Matt. iii. 6-8; Acts xxx. 18, 19), we may compare (not contrast) our LORD'S commission in St. Matt. xvi. 19; xviii. 18; and most explicitly repeated in St. John xx. 23: "Receive ye the HOLY GHOST: whose soever sins ye remit, they are remitted unto them; and whose soever sins ye retain, they are retained," made to the eleven Apostles, as a committal of His own authority as Son of Man to forgive sins. This in nowise conflicts with the public confession, nay, rather agrees with it. Indeed, while it was clearly recognized that there *were* cases in which it were better that there should be no public confession,—we are not speaking of the ordinary wearing fretfulness of daily occurrence,—yet these were few and of rare occurrence, and they were exceptional cases. But we have full and clear information as to this. In this line and upon the best precedents the Church has given her children the public confessions of sin she places in her public formularies. They are three: the one in the Morning and Evening Prayer, the one in the Communion service, and the Prayer in the Ash-Wednesday service. Other confessions, in phrase, not in form, occur in the Collects; but these are the outlines upon which the Church instructs her children to frame their self-examination and confession, and she looks for an honest and devout desire on their part to give a hearty meaning to the lowly words she puts into their mouths. The public use of forms of confession was not intended to interfere with any private and devotional forms for the closet.

But while the Church thus publicly and openly avows her use of public confession, she does not interfere with the unburdening of the heart and its troubles to her ministers. Confession in private is urged upon the condemned convict in his cell, and at the close of the exhortation in the Communion service she uses these words: "And because it is requisite that no man should come to the Holy Communion but with a full trust in GOD'S mercy, and with a quiet conscience, therefore, if there be any of you who by this means cannot quiet his own conscience herein, but requireth further comfort or counsel, let him come to me or to some other minister of GOD's Word and open his grief, that he may receive such godly counsel and advice as may tend to the quieting of his conscience and the removing of all scruple and doubtfulness." So far she exhorts and advises the confidence which should ever exist between a faithful Priest and his people in any case of conscience or of scruple. The use of absolution under such cases must always be decided by the circumstances. (*Vide* ABSOLUTION.)

CONFESSION (AURICULAR), that is, confession into the ear of the Priest, who is bound to absolute secrecy, and who is at liberty to question the penitent in any way upon any part of his or her conduct. The practice arose upon the cessation of making public confession, and grew gradually till, after having been recognized by the Western Church, in several enactments of local Synods it was enjoined as a necessary preliminary to receiving the Communion and as obligatory on every one once a year on pain of excommunication, and therefore refusal of Christian burial. (IV. Council of Lateran, Can. 21, 1215 A.D.)

Confessor. One who at the risk of his life confesses his faith in CHRIST. For the use of the word, compare St. Matt. x. 32, and 1 Tim. vi. 13. The confessors were held in great esteem, and obtained so much influence that St. Cyprian, while admiring them and their constancy, had to oppose their ill-advised relaxations of the discipline of the lapsed. The title confessor properly belongs to him who at any time at the danger of his life because of it has confessed his faith in the LORD JESUS CHRIST.

Confessor. The title given to the Priest who hears confessions.

Confirmation. The imposition of the Bishop's hands, whereby the gift of the HOLY GHOST is given to the person confirmed; the strengthening of the soul by the graces of the SPIRIT. It bore several names in the works of the Fathers,—*e.g.*, the Seal, the Chrism, the Imposition of Hands. The seal from Eph. iv. 30; the chrism from 1 John ii. 27; the imposition of hands from Heb. vi. 2. The term confirmation or strengthening appears to come from Eph. iii. 16. The rite without doubt was typified by the descent of the HOLY SPIRIT upon Him at our LORD's baptism. He declared constantly that He came not only for the Redemptive acts which He alone could effect, but also to give the HOLY GHOST, which gift, including all other gifts in that, He gave to the Apostles when He breathed on them, and afterwards when at the day of Pentecost He sent Him upon the Apostles.

It was emphatically the Rite for that gift, as Baptism was the appointed Sacrament for our entrance and birth into CHRIST; so it was implied in St. Peter's words: " Repent, and be baptized every one of you in the name of JESUS CHRIST for the remission of sins, and ye shall receive the gift of the HOLY GHOST. For the promise is unto you, and to your children, and to all that are afar off, and to as many as the LORD our GOD shall call" (Acts ii. 38, 39). Now this promise is the pouring out of the SPIRIT, as St. Peter in the first part of his sermon had shown. The words of St. Peter imply then, that those who should be baptized were also to be confirmed. So, too, when Philip the evangelist went down to Samaria and baptized he could not confirm, but the Apostles sent Peter and John thither to confer that grace (Acts viii. 14–17). So, St. Paul confirmed the disciples at Ephesus (Acts xix. 6), a gift to which he repeatedly refers in his Epistle to the Ephesians (ch. i. 13, 14; iii. 16; iv. 4, 30). So laying on of hands is made a foundation act (Heb. vi. 2). So the anointing and sealing of the HOLY SPIRIT in 2 Cor. i. 21. There is a series of texts which derive their chief if not their full sense from this laying on of hands; the foremost places are the viii. chapter of Romans, Galatians vi. 6–8, and the references in 1 Corinthians to the body being the Temple of the HOLY GHOST. In the study of these passages comparison should also be made with the two leading prophecies, the text from Joel ii. 28, 32, and Isaiah xi. 1, 2.

It is not at all necessary to bring a long array of quotations from the Fathers to prove the fact that Confirmation—the laying on of hands—was the practice of the Church from the first. It may be necessary, however, to remark that Confirmation followed baptism immediately, and for that reason is the less often alluded to in the earliest Patristic writings, since it was, as it were, bound up in baptism. With baptism and Confirmation followed the receiving the Holy Communion, and so was not dwelt upon as discursively as other rites of the Church. The ancient formulas used both laying on of hands and the unction with consecrated oil. The laying on of hands was with the words, "Almighty Father of our LORD JESUS CHRIST, who hast regenerated Thy servants by water and the HOLY GHOST, who hast given them remission of all their sins, do Thou, O LORD, send upon them the HOLY GHOST, Thy Comforter; and give them the spirit of wisdom and understanding the spirit of counsel and grace, the spirit of knowledge and true godliness. Fill them with the spirit of the fear of GOD, in the name of our LORD JESUS CHRIST, with whom Thou livest and reignest ever GOD with the HOLY GHOST for ever and ever. Amen." Then the Bishop signed them on the forehead with the chrism, saying, "The sign of CHRIST to eternal life. Amen." (The Gelasian Sacramentary c. 500.) This form, as we see, is directly in the same line as our own service, with the one important omission of the chrism.

In our office the versicles are from the ancient Salisbury use. The words which accompany the act of the laying on of hands are drawn from several sentences of Holy Scripture. The Collect was framed after the pattern of one by Hermann, Archbishop of Cologne (1545 A.D.). The rubric on the admission of those ready and desirous of being confirmed to the Holy Communion was taken from a Constitution by Archbishop Peckham, 1281 A.D.

The blessings of Confirmation are to be received with a prepared and devout heart, not hastily or without instruction. To this end it is usual to deliver lectures upon Confirmation as a necessity in the Christian life, and because of its Apostolic appointment in the economy of the Christian Church, upon the duties of a devout and prayerful preparation, together with instruction about the Church and her office, and the duties laid upon the person confirmed in that act. These blessings and the position of this holy rite are well set forth in a homily dated before the Reformation: " In Baptism he was born again spiritually to live, in Confirmation he is made bold to fight. There he received remission of sin, here he receiveth increase of grace. There the Spirit of GOD did make him a new man, here the same Spirit doth defend him in his dangerous conflict. There he was washed and made clean, here he is nourished and made strong. In Baptism he was chosen to be GOD's son and an inheritor of His heavenly kingdom; in Confirmation GOD shall give him His HOLY SPIRIT to be his mentor, to instruct him and perfect him, that he lose not by his folly that inheritance which he is called unto. In Baptism he was called and chosen to be one of GOD's soldiers, and had his white coat of innocency delivered unto him, and also his badge, which was the red cross, the instrument of His Passion set upon his forehead and other parts of his body; in Confirmation he is encouraged to fight and take the armor of GOD put upon him, which be able to bear off the fiery darts of the devil and to defend him from all harm, if he will use them in his battle and not put himself in danger of his enemies by entering the field without them."

It is often asked, Is Confirmation as necessary to salvation as Baptism? A careful examination of the Scriptures quoted and referred to above—especially the viii. of Romans and the iv. of Ephesians—will show that it is, for it is part of the means of grace for our resurrection (*cf.* Rom. viii. 11; Eph. iv. 30).

Congregation. A word to which several meanings are attached. In the Old Testament it means (as does also the word Convocation) the whole people, whether in the wilderness, where they were always easily gathered, or in Canaan. It meant either a Congregation for worship, or a Congregation for deliberation, and so generally represented by the heads of the families. In the New Testament it meant the Ecclesia, whether merely a local congregation or the whole body of the Faithful. But except in one place the Ecclesia is translated Church in the A. V. In later Church usage it was restricted to the local gathering or to the organized body receiving ministration from a Pastor. It is a modern error, refuted by all early Church History, to give to the Congregation the formative voice, and to make it the source of authority to its officers. Throughout the New Testament, the Apostles exercised independent authority and ordained as men answerable to GOD for their authority. So, too, in the subapostolic record in Rev. ii. and iii. The Congregation had many privileges, which of need modified the action of the ruling body. The officers were not despots, but acting in GOD's behalf to the Congregation, and bearers and executants of His Covenant. They exist only for the sake of the Congregation, but from GOD. The Laity in Congregation had the right to nominate to the vacant Bishopric, to assent or object to the ordination of Deacons (Acts vi. 3) or Presbyters (1 Tim. iii.); as largely controlling the finances its influence was weighty. St. Cyprian's consultation of the Congregations in Carthage is a good illustration. But these primitive Congregations were not so wholly regulated as our own modern ones are; the clergy being more a body gathered around their Bishop, and directed by him, than a number of Presbyters and Deacons scattered over the Diocese and holding their Parochial cure at the hands of the Congregation. The Congregations themselves were not so markedly parted, even when much more scattered, and certainly in the city Churches, though there were many Churches and Congregations, they really formed for all minor legislative purposes but one body.

But our Congregations now are nearly identical with their Parishes. A Congregation may contain many individuals other than those in nonage, who cannot take any part in the management of the affairs of the Parish, or may be merely attendants on the services. But apart from these, generally a Congregation is made up of persons permanently members of the Parish, and for all proper purposes the two names apply to only one body. Yet in some particulars the modern Congregation is still endowed with the same privileges as the older. In an ordination the consent of the Congregation is had. The Congregation being offended by the scandalous conduct of a member he is proceeded against; and the Congregation has to be satisfied of his repentance and amendment. (Rubric to the Holy Communion.) In the Prayer-Book throughout, the people present at a service are distinguished from the Congregation. So properly at the office of Consecration of a Church or Chapel. As the Church is consecrated for the Parish, the *Congregation*, not the *People*, is the term used. So, too, in the office of Institution, in the Prayers and in the first of the two closing Rubrics.

In the Digest of Canons the words "Parish or Congregation" seem to imply a slight difference in the use of the two, the one not completely coinciding with the other. The Vestry sign testimonials as representatives of the Parish or Congregation (Tit. i., Can. ii., § 3; Can. vi., § 2). A clergyman can be rector of a Parish or Congregation (Tit. i., Can. xiv., § 2, § 4). The term "Congregation" is a broader term here than "Parish," for a Congregation must exist in a Parish, but a Congregation may not be organized into a Parish, therefore all general directions about music, about Congregations within the Territory of one Bishop placing themselves under the jurisdiction of another, use simply the term Congregation. The mere gathering of a Congregation needs the authority of no Canon, but when this Congregation attempts to organize, then it must take the steps pointed out by the Canons, both of the Church at large and the special ones of the Diocese, in order to become a Parish. Still, since the Parish is a regular organization, and the Congregation is a body with looser cohesion, and since for certain purposes the Church rightly speaks of the Congregation, the Parish, which can often act solely through its representatives, the Vestry, must in some capacities act as a Congregation also.

Connecticut, Diocese of. Connecticut was not, like some of her sister colonies, first settled by companies of Churchmen, nor had she, like others, royal governors who brought with them the forms of the national Church and in some sense established it within their jurisdiction. To be sure, the Rev. Messrs. Hooker and Stone, who led the settlers of Hartford in 1635 A.D., and the Rev. John Davenport, who was the founder of New Haven in 1638 A.D., had all received Holy Orders in the Church of England; but it was far from their purpose to build up in the forests of Connecticut and by the side of her pleasant waters a Church which should extend to a new land her doctrine, discipline, and worship. It need hardly be said that the colonists were of one mind with their teachers, that it was intended that each of the towns which were organized in the early days should contain (or, to use the words of the theory, should be) a "Church of Christ," of the pure Congregational type. Yet it was as early as

1664 A.D., a year before the New Haven colony was united to Connecticut,—Saybrook had been merged in this latter at an earlier date,—that William Pitkin and others petitioned the General Assembly in regard to privileges which they claimed as members of the Church of England, but which were withheld from them by the ecclesiastical authority here. But the first expression of a wish for the services of the Church seems to have come from a few Churchmen in Stratford about 1690 A.D., though it does not appear that any petition for a missionary was made till 1702 A.D., in which year two missionaries of the recently founded Society for the Propagation of the Gospel, the Rev. Messrs. George Keith and John Talbot, visited New London and preached there. Three years later, the Stratford Churchmen applied to the Rev. Mr. Vesey, rector of Trinity Church, New York, for his assistance, and in 1706 A.D. the Rev. George Muirson, missionary at Rye in New York colony, began to officiate for them, being ably encouraged by a layman whose name should always be held in honor, Col. Caleb Heathcote. In April, 1707 A.D., the parish of Christ Church, Stratford, was organized; but Mr. Muirson soon died, and it was left without a settled clergyman for more than fifteen years. In 1708 A.D. occurred two events of interest in the ecclesiastical history of Connecticut; the Congregational and the Presbyterian elements in the colony were united under the Saybrook platform of government, and the General Assembly included in the act which authorized it a clause for "the relief of sober dissenters," not freeing them from taxes for the support of the standing order, but removing the penalty for non-attendance at its services. But we do not hear of any sign of activity and hardly of life on the part of the Church until on Trinity Sunday, 1722 A.D., the Rev. George Pigot took charge of the parish at Stratford.

In this year (1722 A.D.) is properly dated the foundation of the Church in Connecticut; yet not from Mr. Pigot's labors, but from a most remarkable event, which is almost, if not quite, unparalleled in history, and which had its origin in the influence of "the first missionary of our Church in Connecticut, the Book of Common Prayer," and in particular of a copy of it which belonged to Mr. Smithson, of Guilford. That book had been studied, while he was yet a boy, by Samuel Johnson, who was graduated at Yale College and became for several years its tutor, and then Congregational pastor in West Haven, being held in high reputation for his abilities and his learning. With him other ministers of the standing order had joined in the study of the questions suggested by the Prayer-Book; and they had met in the college library to read and to discuss such books as Archbishop King's "Inventions of Men in the Worship of God," Scott's "Christian Life," and other writings of English divines. Among these ministers were Mr. Timothy Cutler, the Rector of the College, for ten years (1709–1719 A.D.) pastor at Stratford; Mr. Daniel Brown, its only other officer of instruction; Mr. James Wetmore, of North Haven; Mr. Jared Eliot, of Killingwood; Mr. John Hart, of East Guilford; and Mr. Samuel Whitlesey, of Wallingford. The result of their studies appeared on the day after the Commencement in 1722 A.D., when the seven ministers just named made a declaration that "some of them doubted of the validity, and the rest were more fully persuaded of the invalidity, of the Presbyterian ordination in opposition to the Episcopal." The declaration caused great consternation and excitement. A public disputation was held, which was moderated by Governor Salton stall, himself a Congregational minister, who had had great influence in the framing and adoption of the Saybrook platform, and who, it may be noted, had entertained Keith and Talbot at their visit to New London twenty years before. The result was that some of the doubters were persuaded to remain in their former positions; but Messrs. Johnson, Cutler, and Brown were not moved from their determination to seek holy orders at the hands of a Bishop; they sailed for England, where they were ordained in March, 1723, and they were soon followed by Mr. Wetmore. Mr. Brown died in England soon after his ordination, but the others returned as missionaries of the Society for the Propagation of the Gospel, Mr. Johnson being authorized to take up the work at Stratford, while Dr. Cutler (he had received the Divinity degree at Oxford) was sent to Boston, Mass., and Mr. Wetmore to Rye, New York. The progress of the Church in Connecticut was worthy of this wonderful beginning. Based on earnest conviction, fostered by earnest devotion, led by men of learning "well reported of among all the people," who testified their sincerity by giving up all they had and risking the dangers of six thousand miles of sea-voyage, besides the no less real dangers of pestilence and the violence of enemies, it was strong and courageous in itself, and it commanded the respect of its adversaries. With scarce an exception its clergy were natives of the colony and educated among their own people; at first they came from the ranks of the ministry of the Congregational order or from among those who were preparing for it; and all that was excellent in the character or in the religious convictions of the people was exhibited in them. In Connecticut, if anywhere, the Church was accepted on her own merits, and on her own merits she stood. Within eleven years after Johnson's return to Stratford five other parishes were organized: one at Fairfield in 1727 A.D., another at New London under Samuel Seabury (father of the Bishop) in 1732 A.D., at Newtown and Redding under John Beach, and at Hebron in 1734 A.D., and in 1736 A.D. it was estimated that there were seven hundred Church families in the colony. Meanwhile, in 1727 A.D., the Legislature had passed a law which allowed the members of any settled ecclesiastical society to pay their ecclesiastical taxes for the support of their own services instead of those of the standing order. The visit of Dean Berkeley to America had not been without its effects in Connecticut. He had resided in Rhode Island from 1729 A.D. to 1731 A.D., and though he was disappointed in his project of establishing a college in Bermuda and founding Bishoprics in the colonies, his influence had been great, and the books which he gave to Yale College and the scholarships which he endowed there extended that influence after his return. Soon great theological and religious controversies were rising in the colony. A period of irreligion and ungodliness had come upon the descendants of the pious settlers; and then in 1740 A.D. the great awakening began. In the midst of the excitement Mr. George Whitefield visited the eastern part of Connecticut and gave much encouragement to the " New Lights," as those were called who favored a change from the former religious beliefs and methods. Many irregularities attended the whole movement; and the strange speeches and actions of Whitefield and James Davenport, encouraging separation, and after a while finding it necessary to purify the separatists, distressed and alarmed devout people and threw many into a most unnatural and unhealthy frame of mind. The harm produced by the New Lights or feared from them was so great that in 1742 A.D. the law in favor of sober dissenters was repealed. In all these troubles the calm teaching of the Church was able to save many from undue enthusiasm or from utter recklessness, and her influence was constantly on the gain. Thirty years later, in 1774 A.D., the Congregationalists estimated that the Episcopalians, with their twenty clergymen and forty churches, were one-thirteenth part of all the inhabitants of the colony. It need hardly be said that all along the need of a Bishop was keenly felt, and petitions were sent again and again to the Bishops of the English Church,—formally as early as 1742, and in a more informal manner in the letters and reports of the missionaries. Many brave lives were sacrificed, one-fifth part of those who left Connecticut to apply for holy orders never returning. The cause of American Episcopacy had friends in England, but the constant reply to the petitions was *non possumus*. Then came the political troubles and the war of the Revolution. Most of the clergy were faithful to the British crown, as well from principle as from the obligation of their ordination vows, and persisted for a time in the use of the Prayer-Book with all the state prayers. Their sufferings were great and were patiently endured, and they suffered sometimes as much from the violence of the British troops as from the patriotism of the revolutionists. During the war two of the clergy died, three went within the British lines, and one to England, leaving thirteen within the limits of the State, and one in Great Barrington, Mass., which was reckoned ecclesiastically with Connecticut. Of these fourteen, it is worthy of mention, twelve were born in Connecticut, one in New Hampshire, and one in New York, and none of them had had any other than Episcopal ordination, though two had been Congregational licentiates.

A preliminary treaty of peace was signed November 30, 1782 A.D., and news of it was received on this side of the ocean early in 1783 A.D. The Connecticut clergy doubtless thought much on the course of events and consulted with each other; and they were ready to act. Moreover, they were alarmed at the tenor of a pamphlet published by the Rev. Dr. (afterwards Bishop) White in 1782 A.D., advocating, at least as a temporary expedient under their existing circumstances, the adoption by American Churchmen of a Presbyterian form of government. They therefore came together at the earliest possible day. Ten of the fourteen clergymen met at the rectory in Woodbury on the festival of the Annunciation in 1783 A.D., the rector, the Rev. John Rutgers Marshall, probably presiding, and the Rev. Abraham Jarvis acting as Secretary. They decided to do two things: to elect a Bishop and to reply to Dr. White's pamphlet. Their first choice for the Episcopate was the venerable and honored Rev. Jeremiah Leaming, till lately of Norwalk, a defender of the Church and a sufferer for her sake; and, in case (as seemed likely) his age and infirmities should force him to decline the burden, they decided to ask the Rev. Dr. Samuel Seabury to undertake it. Dr. Seabury was the son of a faithful clergyman, a native of New London, of strong and vigorous character, well known and highly esteemed in the State. The Secretary was to go to New York, to consult with Mr. Leaming and Dr. Seabury, and to arrange as to testimonials and letters of commendation; and the clergy directed him to instruct the one who should go to England to ask for consecration, that, if his petition was unsuccessful there, he should go to Scotland and seek the Episcopate at the hands of the bishops of the disestablished Church in that country. The clergy also authorized Mr. Jarvis to write a letter to Dr. White, pointing out the dangerous consequences of the ideas which he had advanced in his pamphlet, assuring him that they were utterly opposed to the principles of Connecticut Churchmen, and urging that at least nothing of the kind ought to be advanced until a request for the Episcopate had been made and rejected. It was found that Mr. Leaming felt it impossible for him to accept the election which was offered him; and Dr. Seabury sailed for England not far from the time when the formal proclamation of peace was made, and arrived in London July 7,

1783 A.D., several months before the evacuation of New York. The story of his sojourn in England cannot be told at length here. The English Bishops sought and obtained from Parliament permission to ordain Deacons and Priests for the United States; but the Erastian notions which prevailed in this Church, the machinations of English politicians, and the arguments of influential Congregationalists in Connecticut prevented the consecration of a Bishop. Yet Dr. Seabury waited for more than a year, till at last, losing all hope of an English consecration, he decided to act upon the instructions given him at the time of his election, seconded as they were by the advice of English friends, and to make application to the Bishops of the Scotch Church. The answer came from them almost at once, that they would freely give him what they had, "a free, valid, and purely Ecclesiastical Episcopacy," and he turned his steps to Aberdeen. There, on Sunday, November 14, 1784 A.D., in the chapel within Bishop Skinner's house in Long Acre, the worshiping-place of a large congregation, he was consecrated Bishop of Connecticut by three of the four Bishops of Scotland,—the Rt. Rev. Robert Kilgour, Bishop of Aberdeen and Primus, the Rt. Rev. Arthur Petrie, Bishop of Ross and Moray, and the Rt. Rev. John Skinner, Bishop Coadjutor of Aberdeen. On the following day Bishop Seabury signed a "Concordate" with his consecrators, in which they covenanted communion in faith and in ecclesiastical matters, and Bishop Seabury promised to use his influence for the introduction of the Scotch Eucharistic office into his Diocese. The Bishop returned to Connecticut to find but nine clergymen left, one having gone to another State and four having withdrawn, under British influence, to Nova Scotia. On the 2d of August, 1785 A.D., the clergy met their Bishop at Middletown; on the 3d they formally acknowledged and received him, and he ordained four candidates to the diaconate; on the following day he delivered his primary charge; and on the 5th a committee was appointed to act with the Bishop in setting forth such changes as should be thought necessary in the Prayer-Book, in consequence of which appointment a few amendments, relating to the State prayers, were duly published a week later. There was a strong disinclination to make any other changes in the services, and it does not appear that any action was taken upon the further recommendations of the committee. But almost immediately after the publication of the "Proposed Book" drawn up by the Philadelphia Convention of 1785 A.D., and probably in consequence of it, Bishop Seabury set forth and recommended for use a Communion office, almost identical with the Scotch office, differing from the English in matters of arrangement, and especially in having a distinct and formal Oblation and Invocation in their primitive order after the words of Institution. (This Scotch office must not be confused with that in the so-called Archbishop Laud's book of 1637 A.D., which was quite different; it is a lineal descendant of the Non-Jurors' office of 1718 A.D.) Many things seeming to prevent a union between Connecticut and the Dioceses to the south, the clergy, in February, 1786 A.D., decided to elect a coadjutor Bishop, thinking that it might be necessary to have a complete College of Bishops in the Scotch line; and Mr. Leaming and Mr. Mansfield both declining, Mr. Jarvis was elected. But he did not decide at once, and the whole project was abandoned, when, after much prayer, much correspondence, and much patience, a union was effected with the Dioceses which had secured Bishops from England. The Rev. Messrs. Bela Hubbard and Abraham Jarvis were chosen to accompany the Bishop to the Convention at Philadelphia at Michaelmas, 1789 A.D.; and on the 2d of October they became members of that body, Bishops Seabury and White organizing as the House of Bishops. At this Convention the Prayer-Book was revised, and the sound and moderate views of the Bishop of Connecticut had great weight in the revision. Especially do we owe it to him that the prayer of Consecration in the Communion office was taken almost exactly from the Scotch service. On the 30th of September, 1790 A.D., the clergy of Connecticut voted to confirm the doings of their proctors in the General Convention (the Rev. James Sayre being the only dissentient) and to adopt the new Prayer-Book; but the use of Bishop Seabury's Communion office was not altogether abandoned for some thirty years. In the same year a College of Doctors was established; but it is not mentioned after 1792 A.D., having been displaced by the Standing Committee, which was first chosen in 1791 A.D. The members of the Standing Committee were all clergymen; and it has been the uniform law of the Diocese to this day, with the exception of the year 1818 A.D., that they should all be chosen from the clerical order. Delegates of the laity had met with the clergy in 1788 A.D. to consult concerning the Bishop's salary; but the laity were not summoned to sit in Convention till 1792 A.D., when it was necessary to elect deputies of each order to the General Convention. This was, therefore, in one sense the first Convention of the Diocese; the convocations of the clergy began many years before a Bishop was elected, and continued to be held regularly for many years after. The revival of the Church in Connecticut under Bishop Seabury was most real and permanent. To increase and confirm its prosperity, he felt it necessary to establish an institution for Church education, and in 1788 A.D. steps were taken for the foundation of an Episcopal academy, which was permanently located at Cheshire in 1796 A.D. Though sometimes called Seabury College, a collegiate charter could not be obtained for it from the Legislature. In the midst of active work for the good of his diocese and of his parish in New London, Bishop Seabury died on the 25th of February, 1796 A.D. He had ordained forty-eight Deacons and forty-three Priests, and had confirmed a very large number of persons in Connecticut, Rhode Island, and elsewhere. It may be noted that he had been Bishop of Rhode Island since 1790 A.D., though there was no union of the Dioceses.

The Rev. Dr. Abraham Jarvis was chosen in May, 1796 A.D., to succeed Bishop Seabury, but he declined the Episcopate, as did also the Rev. John Bowden, principal of the Episcopal Academy. In June, 1797 A.D., Dr. Jarvis was again elected; and on the 18th of October he was consecrated in Trinity Church, New Haven, by Bishops White, Provoost, and Bass. His Episcopate of sixteen years was a quiet one, except for the persistent annoyance caused him by Ammi Rogers, whom he had deposed from the ministry. The establishment of the *Churchman's Magazine* in 1804 A.D. and the securing of additional facilities for the work of the academy at Cheshire, were among the signs of growth and prosperity. The trustees of the Bishop's Fund were chartered in 1799 A.D., though they were not organized till 1813 A.D. Bishop Jarvis died May 3, 1813 A.D., and, chiefly for financial reasons, there was much delay in the choice of a successor. In 1815 A.D., the Rev. John Croes was elected, but he was soon after chosen to New Jersey, and accepted that Diocese; and in the following year Bishop Hobart, of New York, was "requested to visit and perform the Episcopal offices in this Diocese," which he accordingly did, confirming very large numbers of persons in different places. Meanwhile, matters were ripening in Connecticut for the mixed political and religious revolution of 1818 A.D., in which year, by the adoption of a State Constitution (though by a small majority), the establishment of the Congregational order was broken. This event was preceded and followed by a long war of pamphlets, in which the champions of the Church showed zeal and ability. The revolution did much to strengthen the Church in material things, though it brought into the civil membership of its parishes many who did not become communicants. The Bishop's Fund was increased in part by a gift from the State of one-seventh of the amount repaid by the general government on account of money paid out during the war of independence, and in part by another grant from the Legislature, and on the 2d day of June, 1819 A.D., the Convention proceeded to the election of a Bishop. Thirty-three clergymen and fifty-four lay delegates were present, only five of the latter being from parishes on the east side of the Connecticut River. The choice fell upon the Rev. Dr. T. C. Brownell, an assistant minister of Trinity Church, New York, sometime professor in Union College, and he was consecrated in Trinity Church, New Haven, on the 27th of October, by Bishops White, Hobart, and Griswold. Bishop Brownell entered upon his work with vigor, and aided it by timely publications of much value. He was deeply interested in education, and in 1820 A.D. the General Theological Seminary was removed to New Haven, where it remained about two years. Renewed attempts were made to secure a charter for a college, and at last, in 1823 A.D., the religious bodies other than the Congregationalists uniting with the Church, Washington College was incorporated by the Legislature, and Bishop Brownell was chosen its first president. In 1845 A.D. its name was changed to Trinity College. A Christian Knowledge Society for diocesan missionary purposes had been chartered in 1818 A.D., and a Church Scholarship Society for assistance to young men in their studies for the ministry was founded in 1827 A.D., while in 1855 A.D. a charter was obtained for the Fund for Aged and Infirm Clergy and Clergymen's Widows. Bishop Brownell's Episcopate is a long record of faithful labor and wise counsel on his part, and of rapid growth following the blessing of GOD upon it. In 1831 A.D. he retired from the presidency of the college that he might devote all his time to the work of the Diocese. At the end of a quarter of a century from the time of his consecration the number of the clergy had increased to a hundred, and among them were many whose names were prominent in the church,—none more so than that of the learned Dr. S. F. Jarvis. At the Convention of 1851 A.D. the Bishop asked for an assistant, and the Convention elected the Rev. John Williams, President of Trinity College, who was consecrated in St. John's Church, Hartford, on the 29th day of October. Bishop Williams remained for three years at the head of the college, and a theological department grew up there under his supervision, which was removed in 1854 A.D., when he resigned the presidency, to Middletown, where it was incorporated as the Berkeley Divinity School, and it has been no unimportant part of the work of Bishop Williams's Episcopate that he has trained there so many of the clergy of the Church. The educational equipment of the Diocese was completed in 1875 A.D. by the establishment of St. Margaret's Diocesan School for Girls in Waterbury. After 1859 A.D., Bishop Brownell was not able to attend the Conventions, and on the 13th of January, 1865 A.D., he died, having held the Episcopate for more than forty-five years, during the latter twelve of which he had been presiding Bishop of the Church in the United States. During the thirty-two years which have passed since Bishop Williams's election the number of confirmations has been about 31,500, the proportional increase in the number of communicants has exceeded that of the population of the State and that of any other religious body within it, the present number being about 22,000, and the number of Deacons ordained has been 283, or about one-fifteenth of the whole number of the clergy now in the country. The number of clergy canonically resident in the Diocese at the time of the last Convention was 187. The contributions reported for the preceding year for parochial expenses and salaries were about $400,000; for diocesan missions and other charitable objects within the Diocese, $23,000; and for Church and charitable objects without the Diocese, $14,000. Until 1878 A.D the organization of all the parishes had been by State law under the Congregational form as ecclesiastical societies; in that year legislative authority was obtained for organization in a more churchly way and under the provisions of a Canon.

Two simple facts go a long ways in showing the influence of the Church in Connecticut. The one is, that, at least since 1790 A.D., the public fast has been annually appointed by the Governor of the State on Good-Friday; the other, that there are within the limits of the State but two houses of worship of the Unitarian denomination.

Statistics for 1886 A.D.: Clergy, 194; parishes, 144; missions, 28; candidates for H. O., 17; ordinations diac., 9; pr., 7; bap., 2103; con., 1436; com., 22,354; contr., $564,723.97.

REV. PROF. S. HART.

Consanguinity. Relationship by blood, as compared with AFFINITY, or relationship by marriage. Blood relationship within certain degrees has always been held an impediment to marriage. What those degrees are, beyond what the Civil Law has determined, has not been authoritatively settled by the Church in this country, though the Bishops have recommended, without endeavoring to bring the matter up in form, the adoption of the English Law, which is based upon the Levitical Table (Lev. xviii. 6-21).

Conscience. Few words in any language are used with a greater variety of meanings or with more indefiniteness of signification than the word *conscience*. When the translation of our Bible that is now in use was made, and for many years afterwards, we had but the one word conscience for the two classes of mental phenomena, which we now indicate by the two forms of the words,—*conscience* and *consciousness*. By the latter we mean, primarily and in the strictest sense, the means, or process rather, by which we know, immediately, what is going on in our own minds,—our thoughts and feelings, our purposes and aims, our hopes and fears,—as when we say I am conscious of perusing this paper, of remembering an event that occurred yesterday, and so forth. Thus, in a secondary sense, we mean by the word the knowledge itself, which we have by this means, and we speak of the knowledge as a matter of consciousness,—or as being "in consciousness,"—and finally, with a wider departure from the more strict and proper sense of the word, we often speak of the objects that are perceived or known as matters of consciousness. This is especially a view and a use of the word to which Sir William Hamilton has given rise and which he has brought into a certain degree of currency and recognition.

But by the word "conscious" we mean primarily our means of knowing what is right and our duty. Thus we denote the knowledge itself by the word; this latter use of the original word—that is, the significations that we *now* denote by *conscience*—prevailed in the earlier part of our history, and the latter—that is, what we now mean by *consciousness*—did not begin to attract any considerable amount of attention, and consequently did not need a separate term to denote it, until quite recently, and in fact not until after men had begun to study mental philosophy more carefully and more distinctly as a matter of observation and careful analysis. The word "conscience" occurs in our English Bible some thirty times, while the word "consciousness" does not occur at all. There are, however, several places in which this latter form of the word would better express the meaning than that one which is used; thus, St. Paul (1 Cor. viii. 7) says, "for some with conscience of the idol eat." It would be better "consciousness of the idol," or knowledge of the fact that it is an idol. So again (2 Cor. i. 12), St. Paul says, " the testimony of our conscience," when, in the more modern use, most persons would say consciousness,—that is, " we are conscious, or know from consciousness," "that in simplicity and godly sincerity we have had our conversation in the world, and more abundantly to you-ward."

It is hardly worth while to attempt, in this place, to describe or discuss all the theories that have been proposed with regard to the nature and functions of conscience, in this more restricted and most proper sense and use of the word. Bishop Butler, something more than a hundred years ago, gave great currency to the use of the word, and a far greater precision to its meaning, than it had had before. His view is that every created being has in its nature an indication of the end and purpose for which it was created, and, if a living being at all, it has certain faculties and instincts which, when taken together with a knowledge of its constitution, indicate very clearly how it should live and what it ought to do in order to accomplish the proper end of its being. Thus, as the eyes, ears, etc., of man not only enable him to see and to hear, so also they very clearly indicate that he *ought* to use these sense-organs, and take good heed to, and make proper use of, what he sees and hears, etc. This is an inward faculty to indicate what he ought to do with reference to the higher or moral qualities of the actions from among which he is to make his choice and determine what he will do. "Now," says the Bishop (Sermons on Human Nature, ser. ii.), "obligations of virtue shown, and motives to the practice of it enforced, from a review of the nature of man are to be considered as an appeal to each particular person's heart and natural conscience, as the external senses are appealed to for proof of things cognizable by them." And he claims that we have as much right "to argue from these inward feelings to conclusions about our duty as from what we learn by the eyes and ears in regard to objects in the outer world. A man can as little doubt," says he, "whether his eyes were given him to see with as he can doubt of the truth of the science of optics deduced from ocular experiments. And allowing the inward feeling, shame, a man can as little doubt whether it was given him to prevent his doing shameful actions as he can doubt whether his eyes were given him to guide his steps."

The question is sometimes raised and discussed, whether the conscience is a separate faculty of the mind or not. But the question itself implies a mistake with regard to the mind,—a misconception with regard to its nature and modes of operation. The mistake arises from the notion that the mind is made up of parts or "faculties," as the body is made up of organs, each one of them performing a separate task or function, as the heart, the lungs, the stomach, in the body; or that, as we have different organs of sense for the various kinds of knowledge that we get of the objects around us, as the eyes for their colors, the ears for their sounds, etc., so the mind must have faculties for each one of its kinds of activity, as one faculty for perception, another for imagination, and so on, including conscience among them as the faculty that sees and distinguishes between right and wrong. This, however, is acknowledged to be a mistaken view as soon as the attention is carefully drawn to the subject. The mind is one, and while it uses the eyes to see with and the ears for hearing, and the brain as its organ and instrument of thinking, remembering, etc., it is itself one, undivided and indivisible, so far as we know anything on the subject.

If, then, there is no *faculty of the mind* that can be called conscience *in this sense,* what we call conscience must be the result of *natural* instinct and education or acquired mental habit. There are those who would claim that conscience is "the voice of God within us," and in a certain sense,—and that, too, a very important sense,—which we will consider very soon, this view is undoubtedly correct. This was the view taken by Socrates, the first and the greatest of the Greek philosophers who distinctly considered the subject. He called it his "good spirit," that was always in him, guiding him to a knowledge of his duty and restraining him when he had a thought of doing what he ought not to do. I think there can be no doubt that St. Paul had very much the same view,—that is, St. Paul believed and taught that every man has within him a light and a guide to right and duty, which he regarded as the voice or influence of God, —the HOLY GHOST.

What we thus call conscience, in our modern use of the word, as it seems in the light of the latest and best discussions of the subject, is the result of three elements:

(1) There is a natural instinct in man which is analogous to the instincts that guide the brutes in all they do,—which in man is a guide in the higher walk of conscious motives and voluntary choice, into which the brutes can never enter. He feels a conscious approval of certain feelings, as love, good will, generosity, and, in fact, all the feelings and motives that we call good and virtuous; and, on the other hand, a conscious disapproval of their opposites, as enmity, spite, and such like. Here man approves or disapproves of himself and of his actions according as they proceed from motives of one or the other of these two classes. This is the foundation, the ineradicable and the indestructible basis of morality among men.

(2) There is, secondly, another element in conscience; for conscience is not *all* feeling,—it is insight or knowledge as well. It is very manifest that we have very early an insight into the nature and tendency of actions, we see what effect they will have, considered irrespective of any motives that may prompt us to perform them. Good *motives* sometimes lead to *wrong* actions. Hence we judge actions not only by the motives that they may proceed from, but also and as well by the consequences to which they may lead. And the two methods are usually and for the most part in harmony and lead to the same result. But it often happens, in the course of our experience, that our motives or feelings in regard to an act or a course of actions changes with our experience and a better knowledge of the consequences that flow from it. The first fruits or effects of an act may be such as we can approve, while a knowledge of the more remote consequences are such as to be vastly more important, and such in their character that no good man can choose the act with the motives which should actuate him or such as his conscience can approve.

(3) But, in the third place, a large element of what we ordinarily call conscience is the result of education and of acquired habit. We are told early in our lives that some things are wrong, and that we must not do them, and that others are right, and that we ought to do them. And thus we grow up with many principles or rules of action,— many of the dictates of our conscience, as we may call them,—which are the result of education and habit, without any clear insight or knowledge of the reasons why the course of action to which they lead ought to

be regarded as right, rather than avoided as wrong. What we thus learn to do as right and duty we grow up with the habit of regarding as right and part of our duty,—part of the dictates of conscience.

Of the three elements thus named as entering into what we call conscience, the first constitutes what we sometimes call man's moral nature, which was undoubtedly at first pure and upright. But it is a question to be considered, and one of great practical importance, how far it has been corrupted or depraved by the fall. That it has been corrupted or deadened by the inherited depravity of our nature admits of no doubt. But how far and in what respects it is to be distrusted on this account is a question that we need not now discuss or consider. The second element named above constitutes what we sometimes call "reason," or "the light of nature." And this most assuredly is never infallible in any one of us. Invaluable as a guide it is undoubtedly, and by means of it we are often able to rise above the notions and principles of action that prevail in the community where we live, and thus to do something towards introducing a better state of morals among our friends and neighbors. We become reformers and help to elevate the lives of men to a higher plane. The third element constitutes what we call education, and in this there is always one part that consists of the religious views that we have inherited, or rather have been taught as a part of our education. But the community where we live is never altogether perfect and our teachers are never infallible.

Now it is a question whether over and above these three elements, or as acting in and through the first and second named, there is any special Divine influence to be recognized and taken into the account. It would seem to be the teaching of St. Paul that there is such an influence even among the heathen who know not CHRIST. "For when the Gentiles, which have not the law, do by nature the things contained in the law, these, having not the law, are a law unto themselves: which *show the work of the law written in their hearts, their conscience also bearing witness*, and their thoughts the meanwhile accusing or else excusing one another" (Rom. ii. 14, 15). And then, too, in special cases, as that of Cornelius (Acts x.). And so likewise with the unconverted and the unregenerate in Christian lands, the disposition to faith and repentance that leads them to accept the Gospel would seem to be ascribed to the HOLY GHOST as something more and different from either of the natural elements of conscience that have been described above. But to those who have been admitted to the covenant relations with GOD there is promised a spiritual guidance in answer to prayer and obedience,—to those who will seek it and use it according to the terms and promises of GOD as revealed in His Holy Word. This influence comes, for the most part, if not wholly and exclusively, in and through what we call the conscience, and cannot always be discriminated from the other elements, especially the first and second that are named.

And if the Holy Scriptures speak of the influence of the HOLY GHOST leading us to think and to do those things that are right, they also speak of an Evil One who sometimes puts bad thoughts into our minds and leads us to do that which is wrong. Thus (Acts v. 3), "Peter, said Ananias, why hath Satan filled thine heart to lie to the HOLY GHOST?" And so also do the Scriptures speak of a "defiled conscience" (Titus i. 15), and of "a conscience" that is "seared with a hot iron" (2 Tim. iv. 2). Of the first we know nothing, perhaps, by the light of nature or reason alone, but of the latter we have abundant proof and illustration in the experience of life. The man who disregards his conscience soon comes to have no conscience at all, especially with reference to the wrong that he is doing. The conscience not only becomes "defiled," so as to guide us wrongly, and to evil, but it becomes dead,—seared as with a hot iron, so that it is insensible to guilt.

From these considerations it is very manifest that although conscience is both the voice of our nature—that nature which GOD hath given us—and also a special guiding influence of the HOLY GHOST, as the voice of GOD within us, it is not so distinct or unmixed with other influences and elements that it can be regarded as in all respects infallible. Hence the wisdom of the apparent paradox: "Man is always wrong when he does contrary to the dictates of his conscience; but he is not always right when he follows its dictates."

To understand and appreciate this paradox we must consider the difference between the guilt or innocence of the *man* on the one hand, and the rightness or wrongness of his *acts* on the other. Usually we regard a man as innocent who acts from proper and commendable motives, with due deliberation and caution, after having taken all the means in his power, or all that the occasion requires, to inform himself as to his duty, although, even under these circumstances, and with all these precautions, he may be so unfortunate as to do that which ought not to be done and which he may afterwards see occasion to regret. If, in this case, we regard the *man*, we should say that he was innocent and to be pitied, and we may believe that, in the sight of GOD, he is so; while, if we look at the act alone, and judge by its character and consequences, we should not hesitate to pronounce him guilty; he was guilty of the *act*, though guiltless of any bad intention or sinful motive.

With this understanding, the last part of the paradox is readily admitted as resulting from the fact that no one is infallible. He may think he is right when he is clearly in the wrong. He may be conscientious when he is actually doing a very bad thing;

as was St. Paul when, before his conversion, he persecuted the Church. He thought then, as he says, that he "ought to do many things contrary to the Name of JESUS of Nazareth" (Acts xxvi. 9), and he expects pardon and favor because he did it ignorantly.

The justice of the other part of the paradox appears from the fact that a man's conscience is not a mere part of himself, like his feet, his hands, or his eyes, but it is himself, acting, or rather thinking, in a certain way, and about a certain class of things. Hence, in this view of conscience, he who acts according to his conscience is doing what, with the best means of judging and deciding at his command, he thinks he ought to do; and he who acts contrary to his conscience is doing just that which he thinks he ought not to do. Hence in doing so he is wrong, not necessarily in regard to the act he performs,—that may be all right, just the thing one ought to do,—but wrong in that he is violating the conditions of his moral nature, the means of cultivating his conscience and of keeping it alive, sensitive and true to its duty and its functions. Hence, if he follows his conscience, although the act may be wrong, he is growing and gaining in the strength of his moral nature. And however *man* may regard his act, we may well believe that GOD looks upon it with favor and will forgive it, even if He does not reward the man for the good intentions he had, even though he falls into error and does the thing he ought not; for error it may be, but sin it can hardly be called, however man may regard it.

Conscience is thus seen to be a growing faculty or grace. It grows with our moral nature. It becomes not only clearer in its indications and directions with regard to what it is our duty to do, but it also becomes much stronger and more powerful as a motive. It becomes quick, too, in its actions, as quick as the lusts of the flesh or the passions of our baser nature. It becomes a realization of GOD'S law written and engraved on our hearts. It becomes the instinct of our second nature acquired through grace, and the struggle of the spirit against the flesh in this our warfare of life. And it may—and will finally if we go on faithful to the end—become stronger and more controlling, even as a mere matter of instinct, than any of the lusts or appetites of our baser natures.

REV. W. D. WILSON, D.D.

Consent of Antiquity. Generally refers to the evidence which the writers of any one age of the Church testify to any fact or series of facts or any doctrine. The rule which has been accepted as the true test by the controversial writers of the English Church is the ancient rule of St. Vincent of Lerins,—*Quod semper, quod ubique, quod ab omnibus*," "What has been always held, held everywhere, held by all." Very many doctrines and practices break down as binding everywhere. In fact, the Canon of Scripture is fairly included, since it was inherited from the Jewish Church, and so additions to it could not be binding while yet the true Canon, which was mixed up with the apocryphal books in so many places, was yet contained in the lists. But the Canon of Holy Scripture has a perfectly satisfactory history. The CREEDS satisfy perfectly this rule. The LORD's day has this seal. The Apostolic rule over the Church has this seal upon it. The doctrines bound up within the words of the Creed are sanctioned by it. The two sacraments of Baptism and the Lord's Supper, the rite of Confirmation, the use of Liturgies,—these all show the threefold stamp of the consent of Christian antiquity. Are they therefore binding? Yes. For while these have not the very words of CHRIST ordaining them,—apart from the two sacraments,—yet they are so interlaced and so dependent the one on the other, that the witness that they were in use and order from Apostolic times makes them binding. Since the Canon of Scripture is proven by this very consent, exhibited in this threefold way, and all else depends upon Scripture for its ultimate authority, there is a binding force in this consent. Other usages may be harmless, and may be accepted by some part of the Church, but they depend upon local authority, and may be laid aside by the exercise of the same authority that created them; but no interpretation of doctrine and no new teaching can be binding, no matter how universally accepted and enforced at some one time. We can show the date of the new teaching upon Purgatory, therefore it was not always held. We can show the date of the teaching of Transubstantiation. It too fails, for it was not always held. So of the government of the various sects. It was not known in antiquity. It is an innovation, therefore it has no authority.

Consistory. The Court of a Bishop, in which the principle is that he is surrounded by the representatives of the clergy of his Diocese. In modern times the Consistory Courts are held by deputy, the Chancellor of the Diocese, or the Commissary acting for him, being the sole representative of Bishop and clergy. The Pope's Council of Cardinals is so called. Many important actions can only be taken in Consistory.

Constitutions, Apostolical. A book of great value in the evidence it bears to the practices of the primitive Church, but whose actual date cannot be ascertained. A large portion of it—the first six books—was compiled, probably from materials of various dates, before the year 300 A.D. There are two different forms in which it appears, and quotations from it in Epiphanius and others do not agree with what we have in many places. It seems very likely that the compilation varied in several sections of Asia Minor. There is also a very old Syriac and an Æthiopic translation of these six books. They contain directions upon almost every topic of discipline and usage in the Church, and form a useful collection of evidence as to the practice in the third and fourth centuries. They claim to have been written or contributed to by the Apostles themselves. There is a parallel line of teaching (though but little direct similarity) in the "Pædagogus" and "Stromata" of St. Clement of Alexandria (190 A.D.). The seventh and eighth books were added later, and form a sort of Pontifical (*i.e.*, collection of offices of Episcopal ministration) for the Eastern Church. The Clementine Liturgy closes the eighth book. It is often supposed to have been the work of some ritualist, and never put in use, but Daniel (Codex Liturgeus, Onent. Fasc. i.) tries to show that it was in common use in Antioch in St. Chrysostom's time before he arranged his own Liturgy. The following outline gives some idea of the work. The Constitutions profess on the face of them to be the words of the Apostles themselves, written down by the hand of Clement of Rome. Book I. prescribes in great detail the manners and habits of the faithful laity. Book II. is concerned chiefly with the duties of the Episcopal office, and with assemblies for divine worship. Book III. relates partly to widows, partly to the clergy, and to the administration of baptism. Book IV. treats of sustentation of the poor, of domestic life, and of virgins. Book V. has mainly to do with the subjects of martyrs and martyrdom, and with the rules for feasts and fasts. Book VI. speaks of schismatics and heretics, and enters upon the question of the Jewish Law, and of the Apostolic discipline substituted for it, and refers incidentally to certain customs and traditions, both Jewish and Gentile. Book VII. describes the two paths, the one of life, the other of spiritual death, and follows out this idea into several points of daily Christian life. Then follow rules for the teaching and baptism of catechumens and liturgical precedents of prayer and praise, together with a list of Bishops said to have been appointed by the Apostles themselves. Book VIII. discusses the diversity of spiritual gifts, and gives the forms of public prayer and administration of the Communion, the election and ordination of Bishops and other orders in the Church, and adds various ecclesiastical regulations. (Smith's Dictionary of Christian Antiquities, p. 119, Am. ed.) "With much alloy there is much of the most venerable antiquity in these remains" (Prof. Blunt, Eccl. Hist.).

Constitution, Church. A constitution is a form of Church law passed by the authority of a single person. A canon is the result of legislative deliberation. Constitutions were common in the English Church, such as the Constitution of Lanfranc, 1078 A.D., the famous and important Constitutions of Clarendon, 1164 A.D., the Constitutions of Othobon, 1268 A.D. But the present sense of the word is borrowed from the political use common to England and America now. It means a charter containing all positive fundamental law needed for the creation, well-being, and government of the body enacting or receiving this charter. In the case of the Church, however, this charter of fundamental law has no *creative* force, for the Church has her foundations of GOD, and the Constitution is merely declarative of the Church's rights, privileges, immunities, and duties. So as she conforms so much in her adaptability to all conditions of men, she is here (as in no other country) governed by the Constitution of the General Convention in her national capacity and by the several Diocesan Constitutions in her local and diocesan work.

Constitution of the Church. In order to comprehend the scope and bearing of the Constitution of what by a strange misnomer is called the "Protestant Episcopal Church in the United States of America," it is essential to consider the *source* of all legislative and governmental authority in this and in every other National or Provincial Church; also in whom, and how, that authority is vested; and herein particularly whether any part or feature of that authority comes from Diocesan delegation, or, on the other hand, whether all such functions are not inherent in the Bishops by virtue of the commission granted by our dear LORD JESUS CHRIST to His holy Apostles and their successors "even unto the end of the world." And, in considering these propositions, there must be kept clearly in view the distinction between *inherent functions* themselves and the mere matter of arrangement of territorial lines within which to *exercise* the same. The Church was founded by ALMIGHTY GOD Himself; hence is Divine. From Adam to Jacob it was patriarchal and embraced in particular families. The external government was paternal, the father being by Divine appointment teacher and ruler of his household and descendants, dictating to them the true worship of GOD, transmitting His blessings, pronouncing His judgments, and, as prophet, declaring His promises and threatenings. The Fathers or Patriarchs were not only princes and governors, but also were Priests of the Church. Except when otherwise especially appointed of GOD, the eldest son of the Patriarchal family was by Him set apart and consecrated to be Priest in the Church, endowed with the princely prerogative of being lord over his brethren, and succeeding his father in chieftaincy and government.

After Jacob, GOD established the Levitical Priesthood, choosing out of the Twelve Tribes of Israel that of Levi to govern and minister in holy things; and in this tribe He likewise instituted superiors and inferiors, in respect both to declaring the sentence of the law and in serving at the altar. Not only were Priests set above the Levites, but Priests above Priests (Num. iii. 6, 9, 10; iv. 15, 19, 20, 27; xvi. 1, 10). The chiefest dignity was that of High-Priest. By Divine appointment he was "chief over the chief" of the " Levites," and had " the oversight of them that" " kept the charge of the sanctuary" (Num. iii. 32). He was ruler and was "over" both Priests and Judges in Jerusalem "in all matters of the Lord" (2 Chron. xix. 8, 11).

As the Patriarchal Church and ministry developed into the Jewish, so did the Jewish into the Christian, the latter, however, into a vastly more perfect condition. The Church is and always has been *one*. Its identity and perpetuity have been from the beginning. The functions and ministrations of the Priesthood have varied with the different dispensations, but, nevertheless, its identity has been preserved. The threefold orders of Bishops, Priests, and Deacons, of the New Dispensation, answer and, in some sort, are referable to the Divine Priesthood of High-Priests, Priests, and Levites under the Mosaic Law. The Christian Priesthood was foretold in the prophecy of Isaiah : " They shall declare my glory among the Gentiles, and I will also take of them (the Gentiles) for Priests and for Levites, saith the Lord" (Isaiah lxvi. 19, 21). The word " Priests" as here used, included the two orders of High-Priest and Priest. Aaron was High-Priest; yet he was sometimes called merely a " Priest" (Num. xvi. 37). St. Clement of Rome, the martyr, who lived and labored with the Apostles, who was a " fellow-laborer" with St. Paul, and whose "name is written in the Book of Life" (Phil. iv. 3), in speaking of the Christian ministry, identifies it with the Levitical. He says of the former: " To the Chief-Priest his peculiar offices are given ; and to the Priests their own proper place is appointed ; and to the Levites appertain their proper ministries" (1 Ep. Cor. c. xli.). Our blessed Lord came not to " destroy the law" " but to fulfill" (St. Matt. v. 17). The Law of Moses remains in full force except so far as in the new order of the Christian Dispensation it became essential to abrogate it. The law was abrogated as to circumcision (Acts xv.) and as to animal sacrifices (Heb. x. to verse 27), but not in regard to the orders of the Priesthood, nor as to the pre-eminence of the High-Priest. " The Law of Moses was observed by Jesus when on earth; neither were any precepts abolished afterwards, except those which had no inherent moral character in them. . . . That part of the law the necessity of which was taken away by Christ, did not contain in it anything of its own nature virtuous; but consisted of things indifferent in themselves and therefore not unalterable." (Grotius, De Veritate, lib. v. sec. vii.) Now the holy triplet of the Priesthood was an essential part of the system under the Old Dispensation. Christ came not to destroy this essential part, but to fulfill and render it more perfect. True, the Priesthood itself was changed under the Christian Dispensation, but not the *orders* of the Priesthood. " Perfection" did not come " by the Levitical Priesthood," and " the Priesthood being changed" (not the *orders* thereof) has now become "an *unchangeable* Priesthood" (Heb. vii. 11, 24). It follows that in fulfillment of the Law the Priesthood of Bishops, Priests, and Deacons, in their more perfect relation than that of the Levitical ministry, is to be perpetual " even unto the end of the world " These three orders, thus to be perpetual, involve *a priori* superiority and inferiority of functions ; which being true, the possessor of the superior must of necessity be the ruling or governing power.

Of the Christian ministry our dear Lord was the first and the great High-Priest. He was " the Apostle and High-Priest of our profession" (Heb. iii. 1). " He glorified not Himself to be made an High-Priest; but He that said unto Him, Thou art my Son ; to-day have I begotten Thee" (Heb. v. 5). But after Him the High-Priests were and are " taken from among men." " Every High-Priest *taken from among men* is ordained for men in things pertaining to God, that he may offer both gifts and sacrifices for sins : and by reason thereof he ought as for the people, so also for himself, to offer for sins. And no man taketh this honor unto himself, but he that is called of God, as was Aaron" (Heb. v. 1, 3, 4). Now the great High-Priest and Bishop of the Church, and in whom was and is merged or absorbed the Priesthood in all its grades, while He was fulfilling His visible ministry here on earth, reproduced the Priesthood in its three distinct orders, " taking of the Gentiles for Priests and for Levites." He Himself being the first order, " calleth unto Him whom He would ; and they came unto Him. And He ordained twelve that they should be with Him, and that He might send them forth to preach," etc. (St. Mark iii. 13, 14). Thus ordained, " they went out and preached that men should repent" (ch. vi. 12). And they baptized. " Jesus Himself baptized not, but His disciples" (St. John iv. 2). They afterwards " gathered themselves together unto Jesus and told Him all things, both what they had done and what they had taught" (St. Mark vi. 30). They were then further instructed in " the mysteries of the kingdom of God" (St. Luke viii. 10),—that is, the Church. Up to this time the "twelve" evidently had not been advanced beyond the second order in the ministry. " After these things the Lord appointed other seventy also" (St. Luke x. 1). They were not of equal degree with the twelve. Manifestly they were of the third order,—that of Levites or Deacons. Immediately before foreshadowing His death, our Lord, addressing St. Peter with the other disciples, promised " the Keys of Power" in these words · " I will give unto thee the keys of the kingdom of heaven : and whatsoever thou shalt bind on earth shall be bound in heaven ; and whatsoever thou shalt loose on earth shall be loosed in heaven" (St. Matt. xvi. 19). To all His disciples on another occasion He said, "Whatsoever ye shall bind on earth shall be bound in heaven, and whatsoever ye shall loose on earth shall be loosed in heaven" (St. Matt. xviii. 18). After His resurrection and just before the ascension, He commissioned the eleven (Judas had betrayed Him), "*As my Father hath sent me, even so send I you.* And when He had said this, He breathed on them and said unto them, Receive ye the HOLY GHOST; whose soever sins ye remit, they are remitted unto them; and whose soever sins ye retain, they are retained" (St. John xx. 21, 23). St. Matthew's account of the commission is, "And JESUS spake unto them saying, *All power* is given unto me in heaven and in earth. Go ye therefore and teach all nations, baptizing them in the name of the FATHER, and of the SON, and of the HOLY GHOST; teaching them to observe all things whatsoever I have commanded you; and lo, I am with you alway, even unto the end of the world" (St. Matt. xxviii. 18, 20).

By this commission the eleven were advanced from their former degree in the ministry to the Apostleship or Chief-Priesthood, not only endowed with "the power of the Keys," but having the Master's pledge to be with them and their successors "even unto the end of the world." Our LORD, having now relinquished His visible ministry, and the Apostles having been by Him further instructed "of the things pertaining to the kingdom of God" during the forty days between the Resurrection and the Ascension (Acts i. 3), their first official act was to start the line of Apostolical succession. Judas, who had been numbered with the twelve and "obtained part of this ministry," having "by transgression" fallen, it was commanded that "his Bishopric let another take." Accordingly, the Apostles, that another might "take part of this ministry and apostleship," "gave forth their lots; and the lot fell on Matthias; and he was numbered with the eleven Apostles" (Acts i. 15, 26).

The twelve Apostles correspond to the twelve Patriarchs; and they were promised by our LORD that they should "sit upon twelve *thrones*, judging the twelve tribes of Israel" (St. Matt. xix. 28; St. Luke xxii. 30). A "throne" is an emblem of power; and it will be noted that the Apostles were not only to sit on "thrones," but were to 'judge" the tribes of the Church. This same authority of "judging" the Church here on earth was also committed to their successors, as we have seen, "even unto the end of the world." Hooker has it that the "seventy" became Presbyters or Priests under the Apostles (Book v. c. lxxviii. 5). But whether so or not, the latter "ordained them Elders" (*i. e.*, Presbyters or Priests) "in every Church" (Acts xiv. 23), and "seven men of honest report full of the HOLY GHOST and wisdom," Stephen and Philip among them, were also chosen and "set before the Apostles," at their command, "and when they had prayed they laid their hands on them" and ordained them Deacons (Acts vi., and see also Acts viii. 5, 12, 13, 37, 38, and 1 Tim. iii. 8–13). Thus we have Apostles, Priests, and Deacons in the Christian ministry, upon the type of and answering to the High-Priests, Priests, and Levites of the Levitical Priesthood. St. Jerome, in the fourth century, wrote: "We know from Apostolic tradition taken from the Old Testament, that what Aaron and his sons and the Levites were in the Temple, the same the Bishop and the Presbyters and the Deacons may claim to themselves in the Church" (Epist. lxxxv., Hieron ad Evang., tom. ii. 311). Again he says, "What Aaron and his sons were, that the Bishops and Presbyters are" (Hieron ad Nepotianum, Epist. ii., tom. i. 5, 14). Tertullian, in the second century, speaks of the "High-Priest, who is the Bishop" (De Bap., c. 17). Isidore of Pelusium, in the fifth century, wrote, "The Bishops succeeded the Apostles,— they were constituted through the whole world in the place of the Apostles. Aaron, the High-Priest, was what the Bishop is; and Aaron's sons prefigured the Presbyters" (Lib. ii. c. 5).

That the Apostleship was not limited to the eleven is abundantly evidenced in the New Testament itself. Matthias, Paul, Epaphroditus, Timothy, Titus, Sylvanus (Silas), Barnabas, Andronicus, and Junia, if not others, are shown by the inspired Record to have filled the Apostolic office, in addition to the eleven. This line of succession, thus recorded in the Sacred Volume, has been continued in unbroken chain down through the ages, so that our American Bishops of the present day can trace their orders and authority, step by step, from SS. Peter and Paul, through the Roman and English channels, and from St. John, through the Gallican Bishops, and from St. James, Bishop of Jerusalem, down through Bishop David, of the Diocese of St. David, in England; all with just as much unerring certainty and precision as the line of the sovereigns of England or of the Presidents of the United States can be traced. (*Vide* Chapin's Primitive Church, ed. 1842, pp. 280–359, and article APOSTOLIC SUCCESSION.) The office of "Bishop," mentioned in the New Testament, was not primarily that of an Apostle. A "Bishop," as there signified, was merely a "Presbyter" or "Elder" with respect to his orders; though there is high authority for holding that such officer was possessed of a higher dignity than he who was designated merely as a "Presbyter" or "Elder," undoubtedly that of *primus inter pares*. But very soon after the original Apostles passed away, they who succeeded to their ordinary functions (not *extraordinary*, such as the power of working miracles), by way of fixing pre-eminent distinction upon those earlier Chief Priests of the Christian ministry, left the title of "Apostles" to those holy men, and assumed to themselves the *name* of " Bishop," though the ordinary functions of the office continued the same. The *office* continued,—the *name* only was changed. St. Hilary, the Deacon, in the fourth century, said, "They who are now called Bishops were originally called Apostles; but the holy Apostles, being dead, those who were ordained after them could not arrive at the excellency of the first; therefore they thought it not becoming to assume the *name* of Apostles; but dividing the name Presbyter and Bishop, they left the Presbytery the name of Presbyter, and they themselves were called 'Bishops'" (Comm. 1 Tim., iii.). Theodoret, about 420 A.D., wrote, "Epaphroditus was called the Apostle of the Philippians, because he was intrusted with the Episcopal *Government* as being Bishop. For those now called Bishops were anciently called Apostles; but in the process of time the *name* of Apostle was left to those who were truly Apostles, and the name of Bishop was restrained to those who were anciently called Apostles. Thus Epaphroditus was the Apostle of the Philippians, Titus of the Cretans, and Timothy of the Asiatics" (Theod. in 1 Tim., c. iii. 1). Eusebius, early in the fourth century, said, "St. Peter and St. John, though honored of the LORD, yet would not themselves be, but made St. James, surnamed the Just, *Bishop* of Jerusalem" (Eccl. Hist., lib. ii. c. 1). St. Cyprian said, "The LORD Himself chose the Apostles, that is, the Bishops" (Cyprian, lib. iii., Ep. 9). The early commentator, under the name of St. Ambrose, remarked, "The Apostles are Bishops" (in Ephes., c. iv. t. v. 354). Grotius, in his note on Acts xxi. 18, says, "He of the Apostles who was at Jerusalem performed the *office* which afterwards the Bishops did, and therefore he called together the Presbyters," etc.

The identity of the *office* of Bishop with that of Apostle being thus apparent, let us now consider the functions of the office, especially with reference to their law-making and governing aspect, with which this paper is more directly concerned.

The Apostles whose successors the Bishops are, and are to be, "even unto the end of the world," were commissioned by the blessed SAVIOUR Himself, as we have seen, unto whom was given " all power in heaven and in earth." After the promise to them of the "keys of the kingdom of heaven" and the pledge, "Whatsoever ye shall bind on earth shall be bound in heaven; and whatsoever ye shall loose on earth shall be loosed in heaven," and when the Great High-Priest relinquished His visible ministry, they were by Him solemnly commissioned in words before quoted: " As my FATHER hath sent me, even so send I you. . . . Receive ye the HOLY GHOST. Whose soever sins ye remit, they are remitted unto them; and whose soever sins ye retain, they are retained;" "And lo, I am with you alway, even unto the end of the world." He who had "all power" over His Church, which He was "sent" to establish, and over the subordinate ministry whom He was "sent" to appoint, and did appoint, declared to His Apostles, "As my FATHER hath sent me (to send you, etc.), even so I send you" (to send others, etc.). Can it be doubted, for one instant, that, under their commission, the Apostles (who, after our LORD's visible ministry, became the High-Priests of His Church) had authority over the subordinate ministry in all matters of discipline and government? It was through the Apostles (as it is now through their successors) that all official functions flowed to them whom they ordained; and upon every principle of right reason, they who confer official functions must necessarily possess authority, within their jurisdiction, to govern and discipline subordinates to whom such functions are so imparted.

Whatever else the words of the commission quoted may import, there can be no manner of question that they bear direct reference to government and discipline in the Church here on earth, both of the clergy and laity; and this authority, conferred upon the first Apostles, beyond all controversy was intended to flow down in and through their successors "even unto the end of the world." St. Paul consecrated Timothy to the Apostolic office, and gave him charge concerning his government of the Church of the Ephesians to "stir up the gift of GOD which is in thee by the putting on of my hands" (2 Tim. i. 6); "Preach the word; be instant in season, out of season: *reprove, rebuke*, exhort with all longsuffering and doctrine" (2 Tim. iv. 2); "*against an elder receive not an accusation*, but before two or three witnesses" (1 Tim. v. 19),—that is, receive not a *judicial complaint*, "but before two or three witnesses;" "lay hands suddenly on no man" (v. 22); "let the elders that rule well be counted worthy of double honor" (v. 17); "rebuke before all" (1 Tim. v. 20); "abide at Ephesus that *thou* mightest charge (command) some that they teach no other doctrine" (1 Tim. i. 3). That St. Timothy was an Apostle is shown by St. Paul's own words in 1 Thess. i. 1 and ii. 6. Eusebius says, "St. Luke, in the Acts of the Apostles, makes mention of several who were his companions, as of Timothy and Titus, of which the first was made Bishop of Ephesus, as Titus also was of the Churches in Crete" (Euseb. Hist. Eccl., lib. iii., c. 4, p. 58). The commentator, in St. Ambrose's name, in the fourth century, wrote: "St. Paul, having ordained him Bishop, writes his first epistle to him to give him instructions concerning his Episcopal office; and this epistle was written to instruct Timothy in his own person, *and all other Bishops in him* for their deportment in the Episcopal office." (Ambrosii in Ep. i. ad Tim., c. vi. See also, to substantially the same effect, Tertullian contra Marcion, lib. v., and St. Chrysostom in

Homil. 10 in Tim. t. IV. Op.) Epiphanius says, "The divine speech of the Apostle teacheth who is a Bishop, and who a Presbyter, in saying to Timothy, a Bishop, 'Rebuke not a Presbyter, but exhort him as a father.' 'How could a Bishop rebuke a Presbyter, if he had no power over a Presbyter?' As also, 'Receive not an accusation against a Presbyter, but under two or three witnesses'" (Epiphan. adv. Hæres., lib. iii.; Hæres., lxxv., Par. 1622, t. i. p. 909).

This chiefly in the highest order of the priesthood appears also in the case of Titus. St. Paul says to him, "For this cause left I thee in Crete, that thou shouldst set in order the things that are wanting, and ordain elders in every city as I had appointed thee" (Titus i. 5); "Speak and exhort and rebuke with all authority" (ch. ii. 15); "a man that is an heretic, after the first and second admonition, reject" (ch. iii. 10). St. Jerome says, "Timothy was ordained Bishop of Ephesus by blessed Paul; and Titus, Bishop of Crete, preached the Gospel there and in the islands round about" (Hieron. Catal. Scriptor Eccl., t. i., 265). The Ambrosian commentator remarks, "The Apostle had consecrated Titus to be a Bishop, and therefore he warned him to be careful in ecclesiastical ordination" (Ambrosii in Ep. ad Tit. Præfatio, t. v. 419). Theodoret writes, "Titus was a notable disciple of Paul, and ordained by Paul Bishop of Crete, and authorized to make the Bishops that were under him" (Theod. Apud Œcumen. in Præfat. Epist. ad Titum. Œcumen. Op. Lutet, Par. 1631, t. ii., 285). From St. Chrysostom's account it appears that Titus was Archbishop of Crete, having other Bishops under him. (An Archbishop has no greater spiritual authority than any other Bishop. His functions as Archbishop are such only as are conferred by legislation of the Church, and sometimes of the State also, where union of Church and State exists. They are merely supervisory. He is only "chief among equals,"—*i.e.*, equals in spiritual functions. *Vide* ARCHBISHOP.) St. Chrysostom says, "Titus, without doubt, was approved of for his worth, when the whole island of Crete, and the superintendency over all the Bishops thereof, was committed to his charge" (Chrysost. Homil. I. in Tit., t. iv. p. 384). Theophylact states, "That Titus was the most approved of any that attended on St. Paul, and on that account was made Bishop of the great island of Crete, and that he not only had the superintendency over all Crete, but the ordination of the Bishops thereof was committed to his care" (Theophylact in Arg. in Epist. ad Tit., 837 Op.).

As to the authority of Bishops as rulers and governors of the Church on earth, there never was any question for over fifteen hundred years after CHRIST. Sufficient already appears in this article to show this authority; but it will not be unprofitable to cite further authorities bearing on the subject. St. Ignatius was a companion of the Apostles and a disciple and pupil of St. John. About 70 A.D. he was made Bishop of Antioch, the metropolis of Syria, where the disciples were "first called Christians," and occupied that See for about thirty-seven years, when he suffered martyrdom at Rome, 107 A.D., only a very few years after the death of the Apostle St. John. This Apostolic saint and martyr wrote thus: "What is the Bishop but a one *who hath principality over all, so far forth as man can have it, being to his power a follower even of* GOD'S *own* CHRIST?" (Ignat. Ep. ad Trall., c. vii.)

Again: "It will become you to run together according to the will of your Bishop, as also ye do. For your famous Presbytery, worthy of GOD, is fitted as exactly to the Bishop as the strings are to the harp" (Ep. ad Eph.). Again: "It will therefore behoove you, with all sincerity, to *obey* your Bishop," . . . "because he that does not so, deceives not the Bishop whom he sees, but affronts Him that is invisible." . . . "some call indeed their Governor, Bishop; but do all things without him. But I can never think that such as these have a good conscience, seeing they are not gathered together thoroughly, according to GOD'S commandment" (Epis. ad Magn.). And again : "I exhort you that ye study to do all things in a Divine concord; your Bishop presiding in the place of GOD; your Presbyters in the place of the Council of Apostles, and your Deacons, most dear to me, being intrusted with the ministry of JESUS CHRIST" (Epis. ad Magnesians). Once more : "For whereas, ye are *subject to your Bishop* as to JESUS CHRIST, ye appear to me to live not after the manner of men, but according to JESUS CHRIST" (Ignat. Epis. ad Trall.).

St. Polycarp, the "Angel" or Bishop of Smyrna, referred to in Revelation ii. 8, was likewise a disciple of the Apostle St. John, and is said by his disciple St. Irenæus (lib. iii. c. 3, sec. 4) to have been made Bishop of Smyrna by the Apostles themselves. Between 107 and 116 A.D. he wrote his Epistle to the Philippians, subjoining the Epistles of St. Ignatius above referred to, with others, commending them as "treating of faith and patience, and of all things that pertain to edification in the LORD JESUS CHRIST" (Ep. Polyc. ad Phil.). St. Irenæus, in the second century, wrote: "We are able to enumerate those who were appointed by the Apostles Bishops in the Churches, and their successors, even down to ourselves, who never taught nor knew of such things as are madly dreamed of by these men" (*i.e.*, the heretics). . . . "If this had been so, then specially and chiefly would they (the Apostles) have delivered them *to those to whom they committed the Churches themselves*. For it was their wish that they should be eminently perfect and irreprehensible in all things, *whom also they left to be their successors*, delivering (*tradentes*) to them *their own office of* government," etc. (Irenæi adv. Hæres, lib. iii. c. 3). Speaking of the Church of Rome, Irenæus says, "The blessed Apostles, therefore, founding and instructing the Church, delivered to Linus the Bishopric, *to govern the Church*" (Idem). Tertullian, the latter part of the second century, said, "The High-Priest, who is the Bishop, possesses the right of conferring baptism, and after him the Presbyters; but not without the authority of the Bishop" (Tertull. de Baptismo, c. xvii., 263). Origen, early in the third century, remarked, "More is required of me (a Presbyter) than a Deacon; more of a Deacon than of a layman; but of *him to whom the ecclesiastical government over us all is committed*, more still is required" (Origen in Jerem., Homil. ii. t. i. Oper. 114). Again: "The power of the keys, as promised to St. Peter, in Matt. xvi. 18, 19, the Bishops of the primitive church apply to themselves. . . . It is orthodox for those Bishops so to do," etc. (Idem, tom. xii., 279.) St. Cyprian, the latter part of the first half of the third century, observed, "It is not a matter left to our own free choice *whether the Bishops shall rule over us or no*, but the *will of our* LORD *and* SAVIOUR *is*, that *every act* of the Church *be governed by her Bishops*. . . . *The Church is founded upon the Bishops*, by whom *every ecclesiastical act is governed*" (Cyp. Ep. 27, edit. Pamel., or Ep. 33, edit. Oxon., sec. 1). In another place he speaks of a Bishop as "the leader of the people, the pastor of the flock, the *Governor of the Church*, the Bishop of CHRIST and Priest of GOD" (Cyp. Ep. lxvi., ed. Erasm., lib. iv. Ep. 9).

Eusebius (who lived 270–340 A.D.) says, "Irenæus succeeded to the Bishopric of the Parish (*i.e.* Diocese) of Lyons, which Prometheus had ruled" (Eccl. Hist., Book v. c. 5). St. Jerome, in the last of the fourth or first of fifth century, wrote: "As with the King, so with the Bishop; or rather, still less to the Bishop than to the King, since one *rules over willing*, the other over unwilling, *subjects*" (Ep. ad Nepot., c. vii., 11). The Ambrosian commentator, writing in the fourth century, said in regard to St. Timothy, "With great vigilancy and providence doth the Apostle give precepts to the *ruler of the Church;* for in his person doth the safety of the people consist" (Ambros. in 1 Ep. ad Tim., c. vi. t. v. 410).

The "Ancient Canons," referred to in the office for "Ordaining or Consecrating a Bishop," and which were enacted during the purer days of the primitive Church, throw important light upon the subject under conderation. The "Apostolical Canons," so called, some ancient authors insist are genuine enactments of the Apostles themselves; but Beveridge and a majority of the most learned writers on the subject hold them to be a " collection of Canons enacted in different Synods, about the close of the second century and early part of the third." The XXXIXth of these reads thus: "Let not the Presbyters or Deacons do anything without the sanction of the Bishop; for *he it is who is intrusted with the people of the* LORD, and of whom will be required the account of their souls." The LVth is as follows: "If any of the clergy insult the Bishop, let him be deposed: for thou shalt not speak evil of the *Ruler* of the people." The Canons of the Undisputed General Councils are enactments which had the approval of the entire Christian world in the time of the primitive Church; which latter, according to our own Homilies, was "pure and uncorrupt." These and all other acts of such General Councils, and also all Canons of Provincial Councils during the period known as that of the primitive Church so far as they bear upon the matter at all, without a single exception, recognize the unquestioned power or authority inherent in the office of Bishop in all matters of government and discipline, including, of course, the enactment of laws. The Vth Canon of Nice relates to the "clergy or laity who have been excommunicated" or "cast out" by their own Bishops. The Vth of Ephesus makes provision concerning any "who have been condemned for their wrong practices . . . by their own Bishops." The IXth of Chalcedon recognizes the Bishop's judicial chieftany in ecclesiastical matters. The VIth Canon of Gangra (a Provincial Council) provides that "if any one shall . . . presume to perform ecclesiastical acts without . . . the judgment of the Bishop, let him be anathema." Many other Ecumenical Canons, and many of those of Provincial Synods having (like Gangra) Ecumenical sanction in the first Canon of Chalcedon, might be cited, showing the jurisdiction of Bishops in ecclesiastical government and discipline; but these will suffice.

Some additional authorities of later periods, however, may, in this connection, be consulted with profit. Gregory the Great says, "The Bishops now in the Church hold the places (of the Apostles). They which have that degree of regiment have authority to bind and loose" (Greg. M. in Evang., lib. ii. Homil. xxvi. t. i. Col. 1555, sec. 5). Theophylact remarks, "They have power to bind and loose, which have the grace of a Bishop's office, as Peter had" (Theophylac. in Matth. Com., cxvi. 24). Richard Hooker tells us, "In process of time the Apostles gave *Episcopal authority*, and that to continue always with them which had it. . . . The *Apostles*, therefore, *were the first which had such authority*, and all others who have it after them, in orderly sort, are their lawful successors. . . . They whom we now call Bishops were usually termed, at the first, Apostles, and so did carry their very names *in whose rooms of spiritual authority they succeeded*" (Hooker's Works, Book vii. c. iv., 3). Again: "The Bishop's pre-eminence, we say, therefore, was twofold: first, **he** excelled in latitude of order; secondly, in that of *power which belongeth unto jurisdiction.* Priests in the law had authority and power to do greater things than Levites, the High-Priests than inferior Priests might do; therefore the Levites were beneath the Priests, and Priests inferior to the High-Priest by reason of the very degree of dignity, and of worthiness in the nature of those functions which they did execute, and not only for that the one had *power to command and control the other.* In like sort Presbyters having a weightier and a worthier charge than Deacons had, the Deacon was in this sort the Presbyter's inferior; and where we say that a Bishop was likewise ever accounted a Presbyter's superior, even according unto this very power of order, we must of necessity declare what principal duties," etc. (Idem, Book vii. c. vi. 1, 3). Van Espen, the great Canonist, says, "III. It appears, also, from many testimonies gathered from antiquity, that Bishops, at that time, inquired into all crimes, even those concealed (*occulta*), and also instituted process, that they (the Bishops) might impose penalty according to the convicted crime. IV. But this is especially to be noted what Morinus says, that *Bishops exercised their jurisdiction then for all crimes, in a sacramental relation,* as we now say" (Van Espen's Canons and Laws of the Church, Part III. Title vi., 42). Again: "III. Therefore from Canon Law and our daily use in speaking, those are called *Judices Ordinarii* who do not receive their jurisdiction from any special delegation or commission, but by force of their own dignity or office. Hence the Canonists define the Ordinary as *one who has jurisdiction by his own right (jure suo),—a Bishop in his own Diocese*" (Idem, Part III. Tit. v. c. ii.,— De Judice Ordinario). "A Bishop is a minister of GOD, unto whom with permanent continuance there is given not only power of administering the Word and Sacraments which power the Presbyters have, but also a further power to ordain ecclesiastical persons, and *a power of chiefty in government over Presbyters as well as laymen,* a person to be, by way of jurisdiction, a pastor even unto pastors" (Eccles. Pol., Book vii. sec. 2; 1 Gibson's Codex, xvii.; Stillingfleet's Eccl. Cases, vi., *et seq.*). "The very office of Consecration warrants every Bishop, in the clearest and fullest terms, to obtain authority *by the Word of* GOD for the correcting and punishing such as be unquiet, disobedient, and criminous,—*i.e.,* for *the exercise of all manner of spiritual discipline* within his Diocese" (1 Gibson's Codex, xviii.). In the office for "the Consecration of Bishops," the Bishop-elect is required to promise that he will "diligently exercise such discipline as by the authority of GOD's Word and by the order of this Church is committed to" him. And in the same office is set forth a prayer for the Bishop-elect to ALMIGHTY GOD, that "he may faithfully serve Thee in this office to the glory of Thy Name, and the edifying and *well-governing* of Thy Church."

We have now seen how the Patriarchal Dispensation developed into the Mosaic, and the latter into the Christian; also how, in the matter of government and discipline, the Chief Priesthood of the Christian ministry is in harmony with, and in some sense took character from, that of each preceding dispensation. And we have likewise seen how the Commission of our blessed LORD to His beloved Apostles, and their successors in office, has been understood and construed and acted upon, in the Christian Church all through the ages, as constituting them chief rulers in matters ecclesiastical. But the functions exercised by a Bishop are not merely his own, but those of the College of Apostles, whereof he is one, whom he represents within his jurisdiction, and from or through whom he derives the authority of his office. "*Episcopatus unus est cujus a singulis in solidum pars tenetur.*" The government of a Bishop, however, was never intended to be arbitrary or irresponsible. He must answer to his peers for misconduct; but, to our shame be it said, there is no other branch of the Church on earth where practically he is under so little restraint against oppression and wrong as in this land of boasted justice; nor does the history of the Christian Church through all the centuries furnish another instance wherein the inferior clergy have been or are so powerless as are ours to resist the tyranny of a despotic Bishop, no provision for appeal being made, or other adequate remedy provided.

While the authority of the Episcopate *in solidum* is exercised by a single Bishop over the inferior clergy and the laity in his Diocese, yet the same authority subsists in the College of Bishops of a Provincial (which in this country is the National) Church over each individual Bishop thereof, and also, under the regulation of law, over his Diocese as well. Such Bishops have the inherent authority to make laws for the government of all the various Dioceses of their Province or organized jurisdiction, and the Bishops thereof, so far as the same may be consistent with Divine and Catholic law, notwithstanding the distinctive jurisdiction devolving upon each Bishop; and, by Ecclesiastical Law, no vacancy in a Bishopric can be filled except in virtue of their authority. Moreover, in a proper case, they may deprive one of their number of his individual jurisdiction. Thus it will be perceived that there is and can be no such thing as an independent Bishop or an independent Diocese, any more than a member of the human body can be independent of the particular body to which it belongs. The member being separated, its functions cease, and it must die.

For the more efficient exercise of the inherent authority and functions of the Universal Episcopate, the primitive Church (being that nearest to the time of the visible ministry of our LORD) established a distributive system or economy of Church government, which at a very early day was conformed, for its lines of territorial jurisdiction, to the civil divisions of the Roman Empire. This system was not only recognized by, but entered into the law of the Universal Church, as is evidenced by very many enactments of the Undisputed General Councils, and also by those of Provincial Synods having Ecumenical confirmation. It is not important, for the purposes of this article, to trace the details of this system; but it should be stated that the Province was an essential factor. It consisted of an aggregation of Sees (now also called Dioceses) having its Synod of Bishops, over which the Metropolitan presided, and which enacted laws, heard appeals, etc. Prior to the General Council of Nice, two or three Bishops might consecrate a Bishop, but, by the IVth Canon of Nicæa, it was decreed that "It is most proper that a Bishop should be constituted by all the Bishops of a Province; but if this be difficult on account of some urgent necessity, or because of distance, three at least should meet together, and the suffrages be taken, those of the absent Bishops also being communicated in writing, then the ordination should be made," etc. By the XXIIId Canon of Antioch (approved by the Ecumenical Council of Chalcedon) it was enacted that " It shall not be lawful for a Bishop, even at the close of life, to appoint another as successor to himself; and if any such thing should be done, the appointment shall be void. And the Ecclesiastical Law must be observed, that a Bishop must not be constituted otherwise than with a Synod and with the judgment of the Bishops, who, after the decease of a former Bishop, have the authority to promote the man who is worthy." The succession in the Episcopate, therefore, cannot be kept up, within the lines of law, by less than three Bishops acting in concurrence with the judgment of the other Bishops of the Province. Thus three Bishops are necessary to perpetuate their own order; and no perfect National or Provincial Church can exist with less than three.

In harmony with these propositions, and no doubt recognizing them as fundamental, those who acted in the matter did not formally adopt the Constitution of the " Protestant Episcopal Church in the United States" until after the requisite number of Bishops had been consecrated in order to the organization of a Provincial Church in this country. On the 5th day of August, 1789 A.D., the following resolutions were passed by the Convention, Bishop White presiding:

"*Resolved*, That a complete order of Bishops, derived as well under the English as the Scottish line of Episcopacy, doth now subsist within the United States of America, in the persons of the Right Rev. William White, D.D., the Right Rev. Samuel Provoost, D.D., and the Right Rev. Samuel Seabury, D.D.

"*Resolved*, That the said Bishops are fully competent to every act and duty of the Episcopal office and character in these United States, as well in respect to the consecration of other Bishops, and the ordering of Priests and Deacons, as for the *government of the Church*, according to such rules, canons, and institutions as now are, or hereafter may be duly made and ordained by the Church."

Three days thereafter the Constitution was formally adopted and signed by the members of the Convention; but it then had no operative effect except as an agreement by the consenting Dioceses to a National or Provincial union and jurisdiction on the terms and conditions expressed in the instrument. In other words, the Dioceses in effect thereby merely consented to provincial *jurisdiction* on the conditions indicated. The breath of life was afterwards infused into the Constitution by the assent thereto of the Bishops; without which assent the instrument would have had no vitality. There was no pretense of conferring functions on the Bishops. Any such attempt by the Dioceses or their representatives would have been gross impertinence. On the contrary, the effect of the Constitution was and is, by the voluntary assent thereto by the Bishops, to limit the exercise of their inherent functions in the aggregated or National jurisdiction, according to the terms of that instrument, and, among the rest, to bind them not to exercise their law-making authority without the advice and consent of the clergy and laity as represented in the House of Deputies, which latter body are, by the Constitution, in reality made the Bishop's Assessors, or Council of Advice, with permanent continuance as such, and with the right to initiate and veto measures. But no measure can have the force of law without the Bishop's assent.

As shown by the writings of St. Cyprian and other Fathers, and by the proofs in Van Espen, Provincial Councils of the Church were probably not held until about the middle of the second century; prior to which time, each Bishop made all the rules or laws for his Diocese. The clergy then formed his Council of Advice, and as such were convened whenever the Bishop desired; but they had no control. And a Bishop may still make rules for the government of his own Diocese, so far as the same may not be inconsistent with superior law, and except so far as by constitutional restriction, enacted by his own consent or that of a predecessor, he may be prevented from asserting this prerogative of his office. (See Stillingfleet's Eccl. Cases, 336.) Originally, when Provincial and other Councils came to be held in the early Church, Bishops only were received to membership; but afterwards others were admitted, only, however, as advisory members, and never being entitled to vote. No Canons or other measures were enacted except by the voice and vote of the Bishops; nor has there ever been to this day, nor can there be, any valid Church legislation without Episcopal sanction.

It will be perceived that constituting the House of Deputies as an advisory body to the House of Bishops in the General Convention is not out of harmony with the spirit of primitive custom ; but the negative on legislative action, which by concession the Bishops have accorded to that body, is a departure from such custom. Nevertheless, in this feature, the principle is not contravened that validity of ecclesiastical legislation depends upon the assent of Episcopal authority.

It follows from what has been said that the General Convention derives none of its powers by delegation from the Dioceses, and that the Constitution takes all its vitality through concession of the Bishops in respect to the *exercise* of their *inherent* functions within the National or Provincial jurisdiction consented to by the Dioceses, and under the limitations imposed. In the State, under our theory of government in this country, power ascends from the people ; whereas, in the Church, it descends from above. The Priest takes so much as he possesses of the power of the Keys and other functions (such as authority to administer the sacraments) by delegation from or through the Bishop ; but he is endowed with no inherent legislative function. Neither Priest nor layman possessing any inherent authority of legislation, no Diocese, in its own right, can have any such power. Whatever part it may take in making Diocesan law is by virtue of Episcopal consent, as in the case of the House of Deputies in General Convention ; and no enactment of a Diocesan Convention or Council can have validity without the Bishop's approval. The Dioceses, of their own right, possessing no functions of legislation, of course can impart none by delegation. In other words, they cannot impart what they do not possess.

Accordingly, and manifestly in recognition of the fundamental principles herein set forth, there is no attempt in the Constitution to delegate or even to enumerate powers. That instrument assumes that the needed powers exist, and in this regard, deals only with the manner of *exercising* them. The language is not in all cases felicitous. For instance, in the 3d Article it is provided that "The Bishops of this Church, when there shall be three or more, shall, whenever General Conventions are held, form a separate House, with a right to originate and propose acts for the concurrence of the House of Deputies," etc. At first blush, this would seem like an attempt to confer on the House of Bishops " a right ;" but, on reflection, it will be seen that the provision is simply an infelicitous expression of the method adopted for ascertaining the consent or " concurrence of the House of Deputies," without which, by operation of the Constitution, the Bishops have agreed that their legislative " acts" shall be inoperative. All laws must be construed in view of surrounding circumstances existing at the time of their enactment, particularly with reference to pre-existing laws *in pari materia ;* and especially must be construed in subordination to existing fundamental law. Therefore it would do violence to all rules of construction to hold that those who framed this provision intended by it to confer, in any degree, the right of legislation upon the Bishops, which already existed in virtue of law higher than any Constitution ever framed by man. The emphatic and objective point at which the provision is directed, therefore, is the concurrence of the " House of Deputies."

But another provision of this Article is of such a character as to require special notice. It is this : " And in all cases the House of Bishops shall signify to the Convention their approbation or disapprobation (the latter with their reasons in writing) within three days after the proposed act shall have been reported to them for concurrence ; and *in failure thereof, it shall have the operation of a law.*" This provision of the Constitution contemplates the *possibility* of an act having " the operation of law" without the approbation of the Bishops ; hence itself is " unconstitutional," as being in direct conflict with the fundamental or Higher Law by which our blessed LORD Himself commissioned the Apostles and their successors as the chief rulers and law-makers of His Church. As before stated, without the Bishops' approbation no law of the Church can be enacted ; hence this provision is *ultra vires* and void. It cannot be held that the provision acquires validity because the Bishops consented to the Constitution, and thus delegated to the House of Deputies the power of legislation in the contingency indicated ; for the exercise of such legislative functions cannot be delegated. As well might a Presbyter undertake to delegate his priestly functions to a layman ; and with stronger reason might it be argued that the Congress of the United States is capable of delegating its powers to the heads of Departments at Washington, or one house thereof its functions to the other.

From the philosophy of this article, and from the authorities cited, by which its propositions are sustained, it is believed that no impartial mind can do otherwise than conclude that the General Convention has plenary powers of ecclesiastical legislation, subject only to Divine and Catholic law and the limitations of the Provincial Constitution.

It was not the purpose, in preparing this paper, to discuss at large the details of the Constitution, but only to consider the general scope of that instrument and the underlying or fundamental principles that must govern its construction ; but there is one other feature, already alluded to in an incidental way, which may, in conclusion, appropriately be considered ; and that is, the *name* which the Constitution has given to our branch of the Holy Catholic Church. "Names are things," and sometimes *teaching* things, as in the present instance. Adjectives qualify the meaning of nouns; and, to the ordinary mind, "Protestant Episcopal" signifies the chief characteristics of the Church that bears the burden of such designation. The idea conveyed to the untutored by "Protestant," thus conspicuously occupying the foreground, is that the prime object of the Church so labeled is to "protest," instead of preaching the Gospel, ministering the sacraments, and saving souls. True, the Church protests against error in every form, be it Romish, Protestant, Agnostic, or otherwise, but her mission is affirmative, *objective*,—not that of negation. In solemn Creed we declare our belief in "the Holy Catholic Church" (or, in other words, the Church Universal),—not in a "Protestant Episcopal" sect. The title "Protestant Episcopal" does not surely describe the insignia of the Spouse of CHRIST and of that Faith which for more than fifteen hundred years was the *quod semper, ubique, et ab omnibus* of the Christian world.

The designation "Episcopal" implies that there can be a Church, in the proper meaning of the word, that does not hold to Episcopacy. One might as well speak of a man's gender as being that of a masculine male, or of a person skilled in treating diseases of the eye as an eye oculist. The Church—the Spouse of CHRIST—is *One*, and not divided into Episcopal and non-Episcopal fragments. "There is one Body . . . one LORD, one Faith, one Baptism" (Eph. iv. 4, 5). Our blessed LORD established only the one Church. If we are not of this fold,—if the Church of our love bears not the essentials that have characterized the Bride of CHRIST for nearly nineteen centuries,—if she cannot trace her ancestry, step by step, through all the ages, back to our LORD JESUS and His Apostles, —then duty to GOD and our souls requires of us the utmost haste in renouncing allegiance to her authority, and in seeking out and conforming to the true fold. Organized separation from the Church Catholic is schism; and schism is sin. That there are vast numbers of devoted Christian people living in such separation is only too true. It is not for us to judge them, but to pray ALMIGHTY GOD "to bring into the way of truth all such as have erred, and are deceived," and, at the last, to reward all faithful people in His everlasting kingdom. The Good Master prayed the FATHER "for the men Thou gavest me out of the world," adding, "Neither pray I for them alone, but for them also which shall believe on me through their word: that they all may be one; as Thou, FATHER, art in me, and I in Thee, that they also may be one in us" (St. John xvii. 6, 20, 21). But schismatic or dissenting societies are not of the "one fold" of the Good Shepherd, nor do they heed His prayer that believers in Him "all may be one." "And other sheep I have, which are not of this fold; them also I must bring, and they shall hear my voice; and there shall be one fold and one Shepherd" (St. John x. 16). For over fifteen hundred years after CHRIST'S visible ministry not one of these schismatic societies or organizations existed presuming to call itself a "Church"; nor during all that time was there any pretense of a "Church" existing in all the world, or that could exist, without the threefold ministry commissioned by our LORD, and in turn by His Apostles. It was St. Ignatius, the disciple and pupil of the Apostle St. John, who, in his epistle to the Trallians, said of Bishops, Priests, and Deacons, "without these there is no Church." Thus it appears that the maxim *Nulla Ecclesia sine Episcopo* is of no modern origin. And thus it also appears how tautological it is, and how unbecoming (at least for members of the one household of Faith) to designate our Mother as the "Episcopal" Church. But this tautology is less to be deplored than the narrowness and one-idea shallowness signified by "Protestant." No other branch of the Catholic Church has ever been, by her own children, subjected to the burden of such a dwarfing description.

HON. S. CORNING JUDD, LL.D.

Consubstantiation. A theory Luther held with regard to the Real Presence of CHRIST in the Eucharist. It was as to the *manner*, a part of the truth not revealed to us, and therefore the English Church wisely does not attempt to define, but simply and absolutely to declare her belief in His presence in the LORD's Supper. Luther used the illustration of the fire heating the iron to a white heat but not changing the nature or the weight of the iron. His view has not been accepted at all,—the Romanist defending transubstantiation, the English and Oriental Churches not defining, but accepting and declaring the Real Presence, and the Protestant denominations generally holding the Zwinglian theory of mere commemoration with more or less definiteness.

Contrition. The first essential step to a true repentance. Repentance is a state in which the soul must continue (as is also Faith), not a single act, which may then be dismissed. Attrition is merely the beginning of contrition. Attrition is rather a fear of consequences, not a sorrow for sin, and therefore is akin to the sorrow of the world which worketh death (2 Cor. vii 10). But contrition involves with the sorrow for sin also a hatred of it for itself, and an energetic casting it off. But this cannot be done at once. As sin in general is practiced and becomes habitual, and the soul is educated in it, so the soul, to throw it off, can only do so by patient habitual counter-action. It has to learn to hate what it once loved, and to love what it once hated, to become indifferent to the sins that once gave it pleasure, and to eagerly practice, till it does enjoy, the pure and holy thoughts and hopes to which it was once indifferent. The sorrow and the struggle together mark the true contrition, the broken heart. GOD can heal, but the sacrifice must be a truly broken heart. This share of contrition in the education of the heart is an essential factor in the Christian's development through the state of repentance. So St. Paul always was eagerly contrite for his persecution of the Church, and this sorrow inflamed his love to his LORD still more, while it abased him in his own sight. A true contrition never loses sight of the sins, whether of commission or omission, to be forsaken, and whose return is to be guarded against. A true contrition tries to fill the void left by the renunciation of evil habits or of sins by other and holy habits and acts. There is no greater danger to the soul than to be empty, swept, and garnished (St. Matt. xii. 44). And this contrition is also bound up in confession of the sin and satisfaction or reparation. These three require a continual practice and form the state of repentance. Therein is the real test of a true repentance.

Convent. A religious house, usually for nuns.

Conventicle. Properly, a little convent, a secret cabal of monks in a convent to make a party in the election of an Abbot. Hence a schismatical gathering, and so is used in England as the legal term to describe any place of worship used by dissenters. The wording of the 73d Canon of 1603 A.D. is clear, and includes meetings of the ministers of the Church as well as of those who reject her ministrations. "For as much as all *conventicles* and secret meetings of priests and ministers have ever been justly accounted very hateful to the state of the Church wherein they live, we do ordain that no priests or ministers of the Word of GOD, nor any other persons, shall meet together in any private house or elsewhere to consult upon any matter or course to be taken by them, or upon their motion or discretion by any other, which may any way tend to the impeaching or depraving of the doctrine of the Church of England, or the Book of Common Prayer, or any part of the government or discipline now established in the Church of England, under pain of excommunication *ipso facto*."

Convention. The meeting of the Bishops, clergy, and laity in council, generally but once in the year. This name for Diocesan Synods is peculiar to the American Church. It has been changed for the older and more appropriate name of Council in the Dioceses of Arkansas, Florida, Fond du Lac, Georgia, Kentucky, Louisiana, Minnesota, Mississippi, Nebraska, Texas, Virginia, West Virginia, and Wisconsin. The Diocese of Springfield uses the title Synod. The Province of Illinois has formed a Federate Council. Anciently the Diocesan Synods met twice a year.

The organization of the Convention demands the presence of the Bishop, with his clergy, in person, and the laity, by their delegates, from the several parishes of the Diocese having a right to representation. In truth, every parish being an integral part of the Diocese, has an inalienable right to representation, and every clergyman has a seat by right of office. So the phrase usual in the constitutional instruments and in the Canons of parishes, "in union with this Convention," is wrong in principle and fraught with possible mischief. The Bishop sits with, and presides over, the whole body by right of office; but frequently the practice is to elect a President out of the body of the Priests, who can preside as occasion serves. Sometimes a Bishop has claimed the right to act as a Bishop, and not as mere presiding officer, and in some instances he has claimed two votes upon this ground. The Convention is not a gathering of clergy and laity from a congeries of parishes, but is the legislative body of the Diocese, and therefore a representative body of the whole estate of the Church. The Diocese needs the Convention, the Convention does not create the Diocese, but merely organizes and harmonizes its work. A parish in propriety cannot be deprived of its seat so long as it is a parish, but it may be made amenable to discipline. The Convention meets at the appointed time, or, in case of emergence, is called into special session by the ecclesiastical authority, which is either the Bishop or, in the vacancy of the Diocese, the Standing Committee. The Convention takes cognizance of the conditions on which the members take their seats; elects its own officers, who are usually also Diocesan officers; directs how the several committees and delegations shall be constituted; in case of vacancy elects a Bishop; enacts Canons of discipline and of Diocesan organization and work; takes order on the finances of the Diocese; admits parishes and advises on the state of the Church; consents to or rejects all proposed changes in the rubrics and order of the Prayer-Book and in the Constitution of the General Convention, begun in or proposed to the General Convention. Its Canons are binding upon all the members of the Church alike,—Bishop, clergy, and laity,—and its decisions and resolutions demand heedful consideration from every member of the Diocese. Its functions, therefore, are those of a deliberative body, and it is conducted with all the gravity and decorum of, and under the same rules that obtain usually in, deliberative and legislative bodies.

Federate, or Council of the Dioceses within any State is authorized by Canon 7, Tit. III., of the "Digest." It sets forth the authorization in these terms:

"It is hereby declared lawful for the Dioceses now existing, or hereafter to exist within the limits of any State or Commonwealth, to establish for themselves a Federate Convention or Council representing such Dioceses, which may deliberate and decide upon the common interests of the Church within the limits aforesaid; but before any determined action of such Convention or Council shall be had, the powers proposed to be exercised thereby shall be submitted to the General Convention for its approval. Nothing in this Canon shall be construed as forbidding any Federate Council from taking such action as they may deem necessary to secure such legislative enactments as the common interests of the Church in the State may require."

The Dioceses in the State of Illinois have so far only formed themselves into a Federate Council, viz., Chicago, Quincy, and Springfield, under the Presidency of the Rt. Rev. Alex. Burgess, S.T.D. It is composed of the Bishops of the three Dioceses, and of five clerical and five lay delegates from each Diocese. It will meet on the second Tuesday in November, 1884 A.D., in St. Paul's Church, Springfield.

Conversion. A term that has had more meanings forced into it than it can bear, and for which meanings other accurate terms are used by the Church. In popular use conversion is made to stand, first, for REGENERATION, secondly, for SANCTIFICATION. It cannot bear these meanings, for its real root means a turning away,—*i.e.*, from one state to another. I. The conversion of the Gentiles from heathenism to Christianity. II. The conversion from a state of sin to a state of repentance. "There will I teach transgressors Thy way, and sinners shall be converted unto Thee" (Ps. li. 13). III. Conversion from a wavering character to one of firmness, as in St. Peter's case, where he was already a believer and a deeply religious man. IV. St. Paul's conversion was not from irreligion to Christianity, but from an enthusiastic zeal in behalf of Judaism, leading to persecution, to an equally enthusiastic zeal in behalf of Christianity, leading to lowly patience and forbearance, and energetic work.

These are the scriptural types of conversion, only one of which coincides with the state of repentance, but none of which at all coincide with its modern popular use to mean Regeneration, which is GOD'S own gift, and SANCTIFICATION, which is the gift of the HOLY GHOST working with our hearts. Conversion cannot be without the help of the HOLY SPIRIT, but it is only preparative to the reception of GOD'S gift of regeneration in baptism (*vide* REGENERATION), and is a state in which we should live, *i.e.*, of repentance; SANCTIFICATION is the gift of the HOLY GHOST, as by our humble use of the means of grace we are daily better fitted to receive and to live in it.

Convocation (in England). Convocation is an assembly of the spirituality of the realm of England, summoned by the Archbishops, pursuant to the queen's writ, whenever a Parliament is summoned, and it is continued or discharged at the same time that Parliament is prorogued or dissolved. The analogy is still further continued in the Constitution of Convocation, which consists of the Suffragan Bishops in the Upper House, and of the Deans, Archdeacons, a Proctor or proxy for each Chapter, and two from each Diocese in the Lower House of Convocation; and in respect of this Constitution it would appear to be of older date than Parliament itself, and to form like it an integral part of the body politic of England. The objects for which Convocation is summoned are to consult on matters which concern the crown, the security and defense of the Church of England, and the tranquillity, public good, and defense of the realm itself. Convocation formerly asserted and exercised the right of enacting ecclesiastical Canons, and of voting subsidies to the crown; but the former right was greatly restricted by Henry VIII., and by later acts of Parliament; and the latter was silently abandoned in 1664 A.D.; since which time the clergy have been taxed like other citizens. But this right had been little more than a nominal one, for after the time of Henry VIII. the votes of subsidies were always confirmed by Parliament. Certain Convocations are of great importance in the history of the State and Church of England; in particular that of 1529 A.D., establishing the king's supremacy; that of 1562 A.D., confirming the Articles of Religion; that of 1603 A.D., enacting certain Canons; and that of 1661 A.D., completing the revision of the Prayer-Book.

As there was little or nothing to do on ordinary occasions, the sessions of Convocation seldom occupied more than a few days, the meeting either adjourning itself or being prorogued by royal writ. But about the close of the seventeenth and the beginning of the eighteenth century a factious spirit so prevailed in the Lower House that the sittings were distinguished by unseemly contentions with the Bishops of the Upper House; and in 1717 A.D. Convocation was prorogued, and not again assembled for business for more than a hundred years, until, under Victoria, through the influence of Bishops Wilberforce, of Oxford, and Philpotts, of Exeter, it was again permitted to resume activity, both as a consultative and a deliberative body, but has not legislative powers restored. Convocation differs from an ordinary Provincial Council in that the latter is comprised of Bishops, and meets to consult on matters which concern the faith and peace of the Church as a religious body, while the former has other objects and is a representative body. Each Province, Canterbury and York, has its own Convocation.

Authorities: Encyclopædia Britannica, and Student's Hume.

Convocation of 1529 A.D., The. Henry VIII., of England, having determined at any cost to effect a divorce from Queen Catherine, summoned a Parliament to deal with that question and with other matters of equal importance. The Parliament assembled in 1529 A.D., and at the same time Convocation came together. Almost the first thing done in Parliament was to pass three acts regulating the probate of wills (which was a right of the Ecclesiastical Courts), the charge or fee of the clergy called "Mortuaries," and the obtaining license from Rome for holding pluralities; which acts amounted to a direct blow at the authority of the Pope in England. Convocation was far from pleased by them, and in response made an address to the king in behalf of their privileges. But it was of no avail, for the bills soon became law.

At the next session of Parliament in 1530 A.D., as there seemed no prospect of any assistance from the Pope in the matter of the king's divorce, steps were taken to decree it without reference to his authority, and a bill was brought into Parliament making it penal to introduce bulls from Rome; about the same time the whole clergy of England were declared guilty of breaking the statute of Præmunire (a law to restrain English ecclesiastics from acting under papal authority), and a heavy fine was imposed upon them as a penalty. Before accepting the fine to be levied, however, the clergy were informed that it must be accompanied by an acknowledgment that the king was the supreme head of the Church of England. Against this admission Convocation stood out for some time, but after considerable negotiation and discussion of phrases, the wording that the king is "the singular protector, the only and supreme lord, and as far as is permitted by the law of CHRIST, even the supreme head" of the Church, was fixed upon and passed by Convocation, apparently because not objected to when put to the vote. But the position of the clergy with reference to the crown and to Parliament was not yet sufficiently defined; and in 1532 A.D. the House of Commons brought an address to the king reciting many heavy charges against them. Against this address a reply was framed by Bishop Gardiner, and still another reply by a committee of the Lower House of Convocation; but the king was unyielding, and Convocation was required to subscribe the three following articles: (1) No constitution or ordinance should hereafter be enacted or put forth by the clergy without the king's consent. (2) That a committee of thirty-two persons be appointed to review the ancient Canons, and to abrogate such as shall be formed prejudicial to the king's prerogative and onerous to his highness's subjects. (3) That all such Canons as shall be approved shall stand good when ratified by the king's consent. To these articles the Lower House soon agreed; but the Bishops made more resistance, and would only agree to a form in which the third article was evaded, which was voted in May, 1532 A.D.; but even then not unanimously. By these acts was accomplished the abandoning of the Pope's supremacy and the establishment of that of the king, in the submission of the clergy. (See Perry's History of the Church of England.)

Convocations in the Church in the United States must not be confounded with the official assemblies of the same name in the Church of England, where they form a regularly authorized part of the Establishment under the laws of both Church and State. In the Protestant Episcopal Church in the United States there is no constitutional or canonical provision for the organization of any such bodies, but in most or all of the Dioceses the term Convocation has long been applied to stated assemblies of the clergy, with occasionally a lay element, regulated to some extent by the Diocesan Canons, but all more or less of a voluntary character. The constitution, duties, objects, and authority of Convocations differ widely in the various Dioceses, though there are a few prominent features common to all. The Diocese is usually territorially divided into such a number of Convocations as will insure the convenient assembling of a sufficient number of the clergy. The Bishop is, *ex officio*, the presiding officer of each when he is present. The meeting lasts two or three days, which are devoted to frequent public services, to private devotional exercises, to the discussion in public and among themselves by the clergy of timely and important topics of doctrinal or practical interest, and to social intercourse and relaxation. There is generally more or less of a missionary character given to all the exercises, and the opportunity is frequently used for doing mission work at outlying points in the neighborhood of the place of assembly. Efforts are made to stir up missionary zeal and to stimulate the work of Church extension. The meetings are thus of great value in discovering the missionary needs of the Diocese and developing methods of meeting them, though the Convocations are not the authorized Diocesan missionary organizations, special boards, elected by the Convocations, being intrusted with that work.

A custom has grown into use in some Dioceses, dating from the Lambeth Conference, of applying to the presiding Presbyter of each Convocation the title of Dean. There is in this a certain degree of convenience and appropriateness, but it may lead to confusion of ideas, unless we bear distinctly in mind the essential difference between these officers and the Deans of the Church of England. The latter belongs entirely to the organization of the Cathedral system, with some special exceptions, none of which bear any but the most remote analogy to the Presidents of the American Convocations. The analogies are equally remote in the case of Archdeacons, a title recently adopted in some American Dioceses. The nearest approach to the office is probably to be found in the English Rural Deans, although here, also, there are essential differences, as well in authority as in function. A Dean of Convocation holds his office either by the election of the clergy constituting the body, or by the appointment of the Bishop on their nomination. He may or may not be officially recognized by Diocesan Canon. His duties are determined in the same voluntary and irregular way. The office is therefore honorary, and of the most restricted character. It is evident that the possibilities of usefulness which are offered by Convocations have not yet been developed, nor can they be while these assemblies are mere voluntary gatherings of the clergy, with various and uncertain objects and authority. Systematized and unified in their Constitution and methods, and officially recognized as a part of the organization of the Church under the General and Diocesan Canons, they may become powerful instrumentalities for good. The following Constitution is suggested as a guide towards the accomplishment of this end, its principal features having been for years successfully tested in the Diocese of Easton.

The territorial division and the stated meetings three times a year are fixed by the Canons of the Diocese. The Bishop is *always* present, if possible, taking an active part in all the exercises, arranging, when necessary, his official visitation of the parishes to suit the time of meeting in each. The meetings are held in the various parishes in rotation, the times being fixed by the Bishop and Deans at each Annual Convention, and published with the journal. At each *anniversary* meeting a Secretary is elected and a Dean electively nominated to the Bishop for his appointment. The Bishop and the Deans, with two or more lay members, elected by the Convention, constitute the Diocesan Board of Missions, and, with the approval of the Convention, control the entire missionary work of the Diocese. Topics for discussion are carefully selected by the respective Deans in consultation with the Bishop, thoroughly syllabused and the parts assigned to selected speakers, and sent out in printed circulars one month before each stated meeting. These are discussed before the congregation after evening prayer, one of them being always of a missionary character. For example:

TOPIC.—THE CHRISTIAN LIFE.

I. Its Beginnings...................Rev. A. B.
II. Its Sustenance..................Rev. C. D.
III. Its Objects........................Rev. E. F.
IV. Its Reward......................The Bishop.

By this means unified, accurate, and systematic teaching is assured. The rector may suggest one of the topics upon which he specially desires his congregation to be instructed. These topics take the place of the sermon at evening service, the treatment being extempore or by short written papers, as the clergy assigned may elect or may be specially requested by the Bishop. Lay speakers are sometimes selected. A limit is usually assigned, and the exercises varied by the singing of hymns. There are three evening and two morning services, the latter with sermon and the Holy Communion at the first. There may be an offertory at each service to defray the expenses of the clergy, and there must be one for missionary purposes. In addition to these public exercises the clergy meet together in private, and after devotional services confer upon matters of current interest. A feature of great value has been the selection of some competent Presbyter as Preceptor, under whose guidance the other clergy carefully and critically study some previously assigned passage in the Greek Testament. In addition to all this there is opportunity for each rector or missionary to make a report of the special needs of his cure, of the prospects and best methods of Church extension therein, and of the probable amount of contributions to be expected. By these means the double object may be accomplished of stimulating interest in Church work and systematizing the methods of its performance.

REV. ROBERT WILSON, D.D.

Cope (*cappa*, whence *cape*). A cloak-shaped vestment which was originally a secular garment, worn as a protection against rain. As an ecclesiastical vestment it cannot be certainly traced earlier than St. Benedict's time (529 A.D.). As it was more withdrawn from common use it was made of costlier material and was more richly ornamented. Its modern form is a cloak of an exact semicircle with a border (osphrey) on the straight side, frequently very rich with figures and lambent work. The straight side should be ten feet in length, and when worn, the cope is fastened in front by a clasp called a morse. It was one of the vestments directed in the famous Ornaments Rubric in Edward VI. Prayer-Book; and in Cathedrals the cope is a very common vestment. (*Vide* VESTMENTS.)

Coptic Church. The Monophysite or Jacobite Christians of Egypt, who have since the seventh century maintained a schism, which at first comprised the larger part of the Egyptian Church, but which has been dwindling away. The Copts are the descendants of the ancient Egyptians, whose language passed into the present liturgic language of the Church. The Coptic was a spoken language, with much corruption and introduction of new terms, and was related to the Egyptian of the Pharaohs. It was a vernacular tongue till the sixteenth century, since which time it has disappeared, the last person who spoke it, so far as can be ascertained, dying in 1633 A.D.

The Copts refused to accept the deposition of Dioscorus, their Patriarch, by the Council of Chalcedon, and this led to the schism. Timothy (457 A.D.) was the first to usurp patriarchal functions. After various attempts at reconciling the orthodox (Melchites) and the Jacobites, the latter took final shape as a sect about 517 A.D. It was strengthened by the long vacancies which occurred in the orthodox See of Alexandria, and at one time was all-powerful. Now it numbers about one hundred thousand members, and, it is said, is losing ground before Mohammedanism. (*Vide* Neale's History of the Patriarchate of Alexandria.)

Corporal. The linen cloth spread over the consecrated bread after the communion. Its use, as directed in the rubric, "that a fair linen cloth shall be reverently placed over what remaineth of the consecrated Elements after all have communicated," can be traced directly to the fifth century, but from its nature must date from the earliest times that the Holy Tables were in use also. The term anciently meant both the fair white linen cloth which covered the Holy Table, and also the covering ordered for the Elements, and was to be always of pure white linen.

Corpus Christi. A feast instituted in 1264 A.D., and held on Thursday after Trinity Sunday. It is based upon the doctrine of Transubstantiation, when that was made an article of Faith.

Councils, Œcumenical. An Œcumenical or General Synod is an assembly which represents the universal Church, and not, like a Provincial or National Synod, only a particular region. It is not enough that such an assembly should be summoned from the whole Church, but it is also necessary that its decrees shall be universally accepted, and this is the only final proof of its œcumenical character. Its authority arises not from the number of Bishops present, but from the approbation of the Catholic Church dispersed throughout the world. If this condition is fulfilled, no defects in the composition of the Council or criticism of its procedure can avail to throw doubt upon its judgments.

Bishops alone had an authoritative voice, but Priests, Deacons, and even laymen might take part in the deliberations. Thus, at the Council of Nicæa, we are told that there was an "innumerable throng" of Priests, Deacons, and Acolytes. St. Athanasius, then only a Deacon, was the chief defender of the orthodox faith.

General Councils were only called when the integrity of the Faith was threatened. Their office was not to add to "the Faith once delivered to the Saints," but to *attest* it or *define* it as against heresy. Thus the Faith attains exact or dogmatic expression.

Six Synods alone have been universally received by the Catholic Church, as follows: 1, the Council of Nicæa, in Bithynia, 325 A.D.; 2, the first Council of Constantinople, 381 A.D.; 3, the Council of Ephesus, 431 A.D.; 4, the Council of Chalcedon, 451 A.D.; 5, the second Council of Constantinople, 553 A.D.; 6, the third Council of Constantinople, 680 A.D. The Oriental Church admits a second Council of Nicæa 787 A.D. The Roman Church asserts the œcumenical character of several others, but the number is not definitely agreed upon. Anglican, Roman, and Oriental alike acknowledge the six above enumerated.

The decrees of the six Œcumenical Councils were chiefly directed to the settlement of the doctrine of the Divinity and the Person of CHRIST.

The First Œcumenical Council.—Arius, one of the public preachers of Alexandria, began to teach that the SON of GOD was a creature, the first of all creatures; but still only a creature. He argued as follows: Since He is a son, (1) there was a time when He was not, (2) before He was begotten He was not, (3) and He was formed from what once was not. The reasoning was soon seen to be defective in that, starting from the relation of FATHER and SON, it conducted to the conclusion that He was not a son but a creature, and hence only a son by adoption. Afterwards it was argued that the existence of the SON resulted from an act of the FATHER'S will, and hence He must be essentially inferior. One of the inferences from these positions was that our LORD was tried as other moral agents and adopted on being found worthy: that His holiness was not essential but acquired. This heresy was promulgated first 319 A.D. It was condemned by a Synod held in Alexandria the following year; but the teachers of false doctrine obtained the countenance of several influential prelates in Asia Minor and Palestine, and the heresy soon obtained a wider currency.

Constantine, the first Christian emperor, on becoming master of the East, found this controversy troubling the Church, and, anxious for peace and harmony, summoned a General Council, which met accordingly at Nicæa, in Bithynia, in June, 325 A.D. It was attended by about three hundred Bishops, chiefly of the East. Either Hosius of Cordova, or Eustathius of Antioch, presided. Athanasius, about twenty-seven years old and still a Deacon, was the principal champion of the Catholic faith, and conducted public disputations with Arius and other heretical leaders. It appeared at once that in the minds of the overwhelming majority there was no doubt of the heretical character of the new teaching. It still remained to devise and agree upon a formula which would exclude such teaching. The proposed term Homoiousios, "of like substance," concealed the real question in dispute. The plain question was, whether our LORD was GOD in as full a sense as the FATHER, though not to be viewed as separable from Him, or whether He was a creature,—*i.e.*, of a substance which had a beginning.

The term Homoousios, "of the same essence or substance," was at length adopted. The Creed set forth by this Council embodying the doctrine of the Trinity and of the divinity of CHRIST in particular, agreed in its phraseology very closely with that now commonly called the Nicene Creed, but ended with the words, "And in the HOLY GHOST." The propositions of Arius were stated and condemned. This Synod also passed twenty Canons, one of which decreed that the feast of Easter should always be held on Sunday, and regulated its time by the vernal equinox; another contained the following words: "Let the ancient customs continue to exist in Egypt, and Libya, and Pentapolis; that is, that the Bishop of Alexandria should have jurisdiction over all these, for there is a similar relation for the Bishop of Rome." Anglican theologians have inferred from this that the authority of the Bishop of Rome was not considered at that time as extending beyond his own Patriarchate. All the decrees of the Council were published in a synodial epistle to the Universal Church.

The Second Œcumenical Council.—The decisions of Nicæa were followed by a determined and prolonged conflict, during which, at times, Arianism, backed by the persecuting arm of the civil power, almost gained the victory. Several of the successors of Constantine were Arians and one an apostate (Julian, 361–363 A.D.). Athanasius, who succeeded Alexander in the See of Alexandria, spent many years in exile, but never wavered in upholding the Nicene faith. Hosius of Cordova, in his hundredth year, yielded under great distress, and signed an heretical statement, which he afterwards recanted with bitter penitence. Liberius, Bishop of Rome, after a valiant and resolute defense of the faith, was banished, and in the homesickness of exile at last gave way. Many Conferences and Councils were held, some of high importance, especially that of Sardica, 347 A.D. The difficulties of the time were increased from two causes: first, a large body of Christian people, though orthodox at heart, could not for a long time reconcile themselves to the term Homoousios. It was only after a long controversy that all believers in the divinity of CHRIST came to see that no other term had the force requisite to exclude the heresy which would make Him only a creature. The other cause which obscured the true issue was the manner in which the Arians so often shifted their ground, proposing now one formula and now another.

At last, 380 A.D., in the person of Theodosius, an emperor at once Christian and orthodox ascended the throne of the Eastern Empire. His first care was to end this long strife, which had produced far more confusion in the East than in the West. The administration of the Church was deeply affected, Altar against Altar, Bishop against Bishop, thus Constantinople itself was in possession of the Arians, an Arian Bishop occupying its throne, but Gregory Nazianzen was leading an organized opposition. In Antioch, another of the great Patriarchal Sees, two Bishops, Meletius and Paulinus, claimed jurisdiction.

Theodosius resolved to summon a Council. In answer to his summons one hundred and fifty Bishops met at Constantinople. The Western Church was not represented. Meletius of Antioch, a man of holy life, was appointed to preside. Theodosius had already endeavored to regulate the ecclesiastical affairs of Constantinople by driving the Arian Bishop from the city and putting St. Gregory in possession of St. Sophia, the Cathedral church. It still remained to establish peace in Antioch. At this juncture Meletius died, universally lamented and revered as a saint by the Council of which he was president. The friends of peace proposed that the rival Bishop, Paulinus, should be recognized. St. Gregory strenuously advocated this course, and was bitterly disappointed when the Meletian party proceeded to elect a successor and thus perpetuated the schism. St. Gregory's possession of the See of Constantinople was now attacked on canonical grounds in the Council itself, he having been originally consecrated Bishop of another See, while the ancient rule forbade translations. Upon this he resigned, and withdrew also from the Council after an eloquent farewell address.

This Council enlarged the Creed of Nicæa by the insertion of several additional phrases, and of all the words which now stand after "HOLY GHOST," except the *filioque* clause (added at the Council of Toledo, 589 A.D.). The most important amendment was the amplification of the article on the HOLY GHOST. This was done to meet the heresy of Macedonius, an Arianizing Bishop of Alexandria, who denied the Divinity of the Third Person of the Blessed Trinity. They are placed here for comparison.

The Creeds of Nice and Constantinople, as they were recited at Chalcedon:

NICÆA.	CONSTANTINOPLE.
We believe in One GOD, the FATHER ALMIGHTY, Maker of [1] all things visible and invisible. And in One LORD JESUS CHRIST, the [2] SON OF GOD, begotten of the FATHER.	[1] heaven and earth, and of [2] Only-begotten SON OF GOD, begotten of the FATHER before all worlds,
Only begotten, that is of the substance of the FATHER; GOD OF GOD, Light of Light, Very GOD of Very GOD, Begotten, not made; being of One Substance with the FATHER; by Whom all things were made,[3] the things in heaven and things in earth. Who for us men and for our salvation came down[4] and was incarnate[5]	[3] *transposed to the beginning.*
and made Man,[6]	[4] from heaven, [5] of the HOLY GHOST and the Virgin Mary, [6] and was crucified for us under Pontius Pilate,
and suffered,[7] and rose again on the third day,[8]	[7] and was buried, [8] according to the Scriptures.
Who ascended into heaven,[9]	[9] and sitteth on the Right Hand of the FATHER.
and cometh again[10] to judge quick and dead,[11]	[10] in glory [11] of Whose Kingdom there shall be no end.

NICÆA.	CONSTANTINOPLE.
And in the HOLY GHOST,[12]	[12] the LORD, and Giver of Life, Who proceedeth from the FATHER, Who with the FATHER and the SON together is worshipped and glorified; Who spake by the Prophets; in One Holy Catholic and Apostolic Church; we acknowledge one Baptism for the remission of sins; and we look for the Resurrection of the dead, and the life of the world to come.

Four Canons were passed. The first pronounced the Creed inviolable and condemned seven heresies, the most important of which were the Arian, the Macedonian, and the Apollinarian. The latter was an error of an opposite kind to the Arian, Appollinaris having taught that our LORD had no "reasonable soul," but that the Word supplied the place of the mind or *nous*. The second guarded the bounds of territorial jurisdiction. The famous third Canon gave a "primacy of honor to the Bishop of Constantinople next after the Bishop of Rome, because Constantinople was new Rome." The fourth related to a recent intrusion into the See of Constantinople. This second General Council is a notable instance of a Council by no means representing the whole Church attaining the œcumenical character simply through its final acceptance by the Catholic Church. Arianism as a school within the Church was now at an end. From this time it only continued to exist as a sect without.

The Third Œcumenical Council.—About Christmas, 428 A.D., a priest named Anastasius, preaching in St. Sophia, Constantinople, used these words: "Let no one call Mary Theotokos (Mother of GOD); for she was a human creature, of whom GOD could not be born." The Archbishop, Nestorius, gave the sermon his emphatic sanction, and followed it with a course of sermons on the same theme. This was the starting-point of the Nestorian heresy. Such expressions as these were used: "It was not the Word that was born but the man JESUS," "that He who "held the circle of the earth" could not be wrapped in grave-clothes; that the sustainer of all things could not rise from the dead. Some of the immediate followers of Nestorius spoke of Mary as "the mother of *a* man united to GOD," "The son who suffered is one, GOD the Word is another." "For my part," said one, "I cannot say that a child of two or three months old was GOD." Superficially it was a criticism upon a term which in the sense they often attributed to it would be inadmissible, namely, if "Theotokos," or "Mother of GOD," be interpreted to mean, "Mother of the GODhead." But the expressions quoted above clearly show that the objection cut far deeper than this and resulted in dividing CHRIST into two Personalities, the Human and the Divine. It was not primarily the dignity of the Virgin-Mother which made the question important, but the reality of the Incarnation was involved, the truth of the grand declaration of St. John, "The Word was made Flesh and dwelt among us." "If the son of Mary were not literally GOD, He could not bring heaven and earth into unity; to have two SAVIOURS would be equivalent to having none" (Canon Bright). The great champion of the Faith as against Nestorius was Cyril of Alexandria. He is often accused of having used violent and arbitrary methods, though it is probable that the title of Saint awarded to him from ancient days at least indicates a general and wide-spread popular estimate of his character which can hardly fail to have had some substantial basis. He was, however, one of the foremost theologians in the history of the Christian Church, admirable for the clearness and precision of his thought and language. He took his stand upon the simple formula: "If our LORD JESUS CHRIST is GOD, how can our LORD'S Mother, the Holy Virgin, be *not* Mother of GOD?" He guarded himself against misinterpretation by clearly confessing a true manhood in CHRIST, and clearly denying that Mary could be Mother of GOD-*head*. The West was unmoved by the new heresy, and Pope Cœlestine (422–432 A.D.) accepting the doctrinal statements of Cyril, commissioned him to "join the authority of the Roman See to his own" and insist upon a recantation on the part of Nestorius. Accordingly, at a Council of Alexandria, 430 A.D., Cyril put forth a synodal letter containing an exposition of that portion of the Creed which concerns the Incarnation, and twelve "anathemas" or articles directed against the teaching of Nestorius. These anathemas express concisely and clearly the Catholic doctrine of the Person of CHRIST. At the height of the controversy, the emperor, Theodosius the Younger (408–450 A.D.), issued a call for a General Council to meet at Ephesus on the ensuing Pentecost (431 A.D.). Here accordingly met the third Œcumenical Council. Promptly at the time proposed Cyril arrived with fifty Bishops, and found Nestorius awaiting them with sixteen. Afterwards the Bishop of Jerusalem appeared and others from various places. But the Bishops of the Patriarchate of Antioch had not yet arrived when, a fortnight after the time appointed, the Council was organized under the influence of Cyril. That the Council should have proceeded to its work in the absence of the Antiochine prelates has been made an objection to its validity, inasmuch as they were known to be within five days' journey. Cyril presided as the chief Bishop present, and as representing not only his own See but that of Rome, and this notwithstanding the presence of two Bishops from Italy as papal legates. Nestorius and his party refused to attend until all the Bishops should reach the city. The Council, therefore, proceeded without him. The Creed of Nicæa was read and the recent statements compared with it. The writings of Cyril were read, and received a general approval. The doctrine of Nestorius was unanimously condemned and himself deposed. The Pelagian heresy, which had troubled the West in particular, was also condemned. The Council also published eight Canons of discipline. The decrees were signed by two hundred Bishops.

As in the case of the Council of Constantinople, the fact that it included only the East was covered by the final ratification and acceptance of its decrees throughout the Church, so any question of the regularity of the proceedings at Ephesus is met by the acceptance of its results.

The Fourth Œcumenical Council.—The orthodox doctrine of the Person of CHRIST, while denying the Nestorian statements which separated the One CHRIST into two Persons, GOD and a man, is equally careful to distinguish in the One Divine Personality two natures, the Human and the Divine. It is easy to see, however, that in zealous opposition to Nestorianism men were likely to fall into the opposite error, losing sight of the true humanity of our LORD, on which depends equally with His Divinity the redemption of the world; for it is only thus that He can be "the second Adam, a true example, a true sacrifice, a sympathizing and brotherly High-Priest, whose very manhood was the basis of the Church and the medium of his brethren's renewal" (Canon Bright). Accordingly, out of the controversies which still continued after the Council of Ephesus this opposite form of error soon emerged. It was distinctly formulated by Eutyches, a monk of Constantinople and a zealous admirer of St. Cyril (who died in 444 A.D.). In 448 A.D., at a Council of thirty Bishops in Constantinople, Eutyches was accused of renewing the Apollinarian heresy which had been condemned at the second General Council. On being examined before the Council, Eutyches declared that after the Incarnation he acknowledged but one nature in CHRIST, namely, the Divine. Upon this he was unanimously condemned. In the contest which followed a Council was called by the emperor, who sympathized with Eutyches. The meeting took place at Ephesus in 449 A.D. The President was Dioscorus, Bishop of Alexandria, an unscrupulous and fanatical partisan of Eutyches, who was aided by a military force. The proceedings were characterized by extreme violence, and resulted in favor of Eutyches. But the decisions of this assembly were immediately rejected at Rome, Constantinople, and elsewhere, and it was called by Pope Leo of Rome the Latrocinium, or Robber-Council, a name by which it has ever since been known. It is an example of a Council meant to be General and containing a representation from the West as well as the East, but repudiated by the consent of the Catholic Church.

This was followed by the grand Council of six hundred and thirty Bishops at Chalcedon in 451 A.D., called together by the Emperor Marcian (450-457 A.D.). The Roman legates sat in the highest place, though nineteen magistrates appointed by the emperor exercised a general control and acted as Moderators of the Assembly. The proceedings assumed in part the form of a trial of Dioscorus for heresy and violence. He was condemned and deposed. The most important work of the Council consisted in a careful examination of the Faith. The celebrated letter or treatise called the "tome" of St. Leo, Pope at this time, was adopted, and thus became part and parcel of Catholic teaching. It is a clear and profound exposition of the doctrine of the Incarnation. The epistles of St. Cyril were also approved, and thus the Faith was guarded on both sides. Finally the Council set forth a confession or definition of Faith and twenty-eight Canons of discipline. So thorough and complete was the work of this Council, so clearly was the Catholic Faith now defined as touching the Divinity and the Person of CHRIST, that ancient writers ranked the first four General Councils with the four Gospels. Some Anglican writers in like manner have spoken as if only four were to be counted as General. The universal Church, however, has accepted six, and the constant appeal of the English Church to the period of an undivided Christendom involves the acceptance on her part of all the six. It is nevertheless true that the last two may properly be termed supplementary, dealing as they did, not with new heresies, but with certain results of Nestorianism on the one hand, and of the Eutychian or Monophysite heresy on the other.

The Fifth Œcumenical Council.—The settlement of the doctrine of the Person of CHRIST in the Councils of Ephesus and Chalcedon did not prevent the two opposite extremes of Nestorianism and Monophysitism from continuing to exist in heretical sects, and in some modified forms, from affecting the views of many within the Church, especially in the East. In Alexandria some time after the Council of Chalcedon, the extreme Eutychians refusing to acknowledge the orthodox Patriarch, formed a separate sect, called the *Acephali*, as being without a head, and thus kept alive the heresy. In the next century it was represented to the Emperor Justinian (527-565 A.D.) that this schism might be healed by the condemnation of certain writings of three eminent theologians of the first half of the fifth century, who either had not been condemned or had been received with apparent favor in the Council of Chalcedon. These were Theodoret, Theodore of Mopsuestia, and Ibas of Edessa. Theodoret had opposed St. Cyril, but without altogether losing credit for orthodoxy. Theodore was undoubtedly heretical, and the work of Ibas to which exception was taken was a letter in which he was said to have denied the Incarnation. The collection made from the writings of these men was called the "Three Chapters" or "Articles." The emperor, who was a dabbler in theology, accepted the suggestion, and attempted to execute it by publishing an edict condemning the "Chapters" and anathematizing their authors. This led to a long contest, which was only settled by the calling of a General Council to meet at Constantinople in 553 A.D. A remarkable circumstance connected with this Council was the presence in Constantinople of Pope Vigilius of Rome. For refusing to subscribe to the emperor's edict he had been compelled to repair to Constantinople, where he was detained for seven years. By his vacillating course he had become an object of dislike to both parties in the controversy. When the Council met he refused to attend. There were present one hundred and sixty-five Bishops, including a very few from the West. The writings which had formed the subject of controversy were examined and condemned. At the same time the four earlier Councils were approved. It is also contended by some authors that in approving the theological edicts of the emperor certain writings of Origen, the celebrated Alexandrian theologian, were condemned. The Pope persisted in his refusal to attend the Council and condemned its proceedings, but some months afterwards retracted and accepted it as œcumenical, declaring that his previous course was instigated by Satan. This Council bears the title of the Second Council of Constantinople.

Sixth General Council, or Third Council of Constantinople.—As the fifth General Council completed the condemnation of Nestorianism and was thus supplementary to the Council of Ephesus, so the sixth and last met the final phase of the Eutychian or Monophysite heresy, and thus finishes the work of Chalcedon. A more refined form of the heresy of Eutyches arose in the early part of the seventh century. This was *Monothelism*, or the affirmation of one will alone,—*i.e.*, the Divine, in CHRIST. It was supposed by many that this doctrine might be safely held, and that it would form a compromise by means of which many monophysites might be brought back to the Church. It was promulgated in Constantinople by the Patriarch, about 616 A.D., enforced by a decree of the emperor, and for a while accepted by several of the Patriarchs. The chief opponent of the new doctrine was at first Sophronius, Bishop of Jerusalem, afterwards Maximus, a monk from Constantinople. In correspondence with the Bishop of Constantinople, Honorius, Pope from 625 to 638 A.D., clearly committed himself to monothelism. Attempts were made to stifle the controversy by imposing silence on both parties, but in vain. In the first Lateran Council (Rome, 649 A.D.) monothelism was condemned and an exposition of faith was published. At length the emperor, Constantine Pogonatus, summoned the sixth Œcumenical Council, which met at Constantinople in November, 680 A.D., and lasted about ten months. It was attended by two hundred Bishops. The controversy was carefully examined and a definition of Faith set forth, in which it was stated that, in accordance with the doctrine of the Incarnation, as previously defined, and the teachings of the Fathers, it follows that "In CHRIST there are two natural wills and two natural operations, without division, change, separation, or confusion; and these two natural wills are not contrary, as impious heretics pretend; but the human follows the divine and almighty will, not resisting or opposing it, but rather being subject to it." The preceding five Councils were confirmed, and the Creeds of Nice and Constantinople were accepted. The supporters of the monothelite heresy were condemned, among them Honorius, the monothelite Pope. Leo II. (682-83 A.D.) was a zealous champion of the Council, and expressly assented to the condemnation of Honorius, speaking of his teaching as a "profane betrayal of the Faith." Thus we see a Pope, for whom infallibility is claimed, condemned by a General Council and by another Pope.

Such, in brief, is the history of the Œcumenical Councils, by which the Faith of the Catholic Church as touching Our LORD and SAVIOUR JESUS CHRIST was defined for all time.

Authorities: Robertson's History of the Christian Church, Bright's History of the Church (313-451 A.D.), Hefele's Councils, Pusey's Councils, Palmer on the Church, etc. REV. PROF. W. J. GOLD.

Counsels of Perfection. A phrase much used to express the practice of what are called the three counsels of perfection,—chastity, poverty, and obedience. It is hard to see the full force of all that has been said about these counsels, for opposed to the way in which they are too often taught is the express direction of our LORD to say that we are unprofitable servants; we have done that which was our duty to do, when we have done all those things which were commanded us. This being so, the so-called counsel, "Be ye therefore perfect, even as your FATHER which is in heaven is perfect," is a command, and not a counsel. Doubtless there are better conditions and estates in which we can live than those in which we choose to live without being faulted for our choice. Marriage entangles the married couple more in the things of this world than does the unmarried state in those who are able to bear it, yet it does produce a loveliness of character, when holily used, not found otherwise. Wealth properly used is a means of grace, and can give greater scope for usefulness than poverty, yet each has its special blessing. But as obedience (the third law of these counsels) lies at the very root of all Christian faith and action, it is still more difficult to understand how there can be a superior obedience beyond what is absolutely bounden. The whole superstructure has too frail a foundation. Undoubtedly, as we push forward in the Christian race, we find many things lawful not expedient for our Christian characters, and these counsels of perfection should rather be called counsels for still deeper self-renunciation, as we are strengthened by the grace of the HOLY GHOST, to go forward and to endure a still straiter discipline.

Covenant comes from *con* and *venio*, and means coming together. It is the coming together of two persons, for an agreement or contract; whereas testament refers to one person only. And covenant is an affair, as well known to a Jewish mind, as anything in all sacred or social history. GOD made a covenant with Adam and his posterity in the Garden of Eden. On His part, He gave Adam not a body only, but " a living soul," with its inherent powers of thought, free-will, and self-government. On Adam's part, obedience to GOD'S wishes and inspirations was expected and demanded; and as a testimonial and proof of his obedience, he was to abstain from a selfish knowledge of good and evil, and learn the best way to use the powers intrusted to him, by partaking daily of the Tree of Life, GOD'S sacramental way of supplying his spiritual wants. A mode of perpetuating a sanctified existence which may be unceasing; for we read in the Revelation of St. John of " the Tree of Life, which is in the midst of the Paradise of GOD" (Rev. ii. 7).

But Adam chose his own way (as his descendants still do) of finding out and estimating good and evil; and the covenant between him and his all-wise CREATOR, with its conditional gift of life and its endowments, was forthwith at an end. Yet that CREATOR, as merciful as He is wise, allowed a renewal of the covenant on new requisitions. Life is represented by blood (Lev. xvii. 11), and lost or forfeited life by blood poured out, and seemingly gone to waste as worthless. The CREATOR would not renew the abdicated covenant unless (and the condition appears not natural only, but inevitable) man would acknowledge his terrible failure, would most significantly confess that his life was *now* forfeited and virtually thrown away, and was therefore to be held temporally and uncertainly, and no longer an endowment for immortality.

This was to be done by a sacrifice, emblematical of "a more excellent sacrifice," seen from afar, by an omniscient eye. It was to be a ceremony in which blood poured out, and, no longer life-giving, was to show, nay, to demonstrate, that man's fatal loss was freely admitted and acknowledged; and that he was to hold life thenceforth and always as, more than ever, a conditional gift, and one liable daily and hourly to be taken from him. Abel proved his submission to this new order of things by offering sacrifices in which life was taken away and blood poured out freely. Cain proved his insubmission by offering sacrifices from which blood was totally excluded, and which illustrated graphically his own choice, private judgment, and perversity of will. One sacrifice was accepted and made welcome, and the other rejected and set at naught. It repeated Adam's sin of judging for one's self; and the repeated sin has been reiterated from that day until now, making the yieldance of a human will to the Divine a moral miracle.

From this representation it is perfectly easy to comprehend that to a Jewish mind, accepting as historic verities the books of Moses, the ideas of a covenant, of a vacated covenant, of the renewal of a vacated covenant by sacrifices and the pouring forth of blood, life's closest emblem, must have become as familiar as matters of household economy. Talk to a Jew of a covenant, and of a covenant ratified by an offering of blood, and he would understand you as talking of what might be called (and is so called in a Judaico-Christian document, the Epistle to the Hebrews) one of " the first principles of the oracles of GOD." But talk to a Jew of a *testament*, and especially of a testament ratified by blood, and you would simply bewilder, astonish, or horrify him. He knew nothing of a last will and testament, for his religion disposed of all his property, and he could not make one (Numb. xxvii. 8-11). If our SAVIOUR meant to say what we mean by "this is my blood of the New Testament," His disciples would not have known what He intended, or would have supposed Him to speak in the dialect of Roman Law. Roman Law, and after a while Romish Theology, made the word *testament* a common word in Western countries, and the old Oriental word, *covenant*, became an excommunicate. The word *testament* is not to be found in our Common Version from Genesis to Malachi, while in the Hebrew it is to be found in the shape of noun, verb, etc., about three hundred times. In our Christian Scriptures the proper Greek word for *covenant* is found thirty-three times, and in twenty of them is translated covenant, and not testament; and yet we cling to the phrases Old Testament and New Testament as if the very existence of the Bible were wrapped up in them. Nevertheless, they have only thirteen precedents in their favor, while covenant and its correlatives have three hundred and twenty! Can history present another instance of a similar perversion in misusing and misnaming a word which GOD Himself has consecrated?

Notwithstanding, we are curtly asked, What are we to gain by exchanging *testament* for *covenant?* In the first place, we can understand our SAVIOUR's language in the institution of the Eucharist. He intended to say that by the outpouring of His blood on earth, and its oblation at the mercy-seat of the *real* Holy of Holies, a New Covenant could be established for fallen and death-stricken man. A testament has nothing to do with blood any more than a psalm-book. And, moreover, He never said the bread **was** the New Covenant in His body. He made the blood, the familiar emblem of a sacrifice, the immensely superior thing; and of course the wine the immensely superior element. If we withdraw the wine from the Eucharist we sadly depreciate, if we do not nullify it. The notion of concomitance is but a fetich of the schoolmen. It is dogma, but not doctrine.

Again, under a covenant everything becomes conditional instead of absolute; or, if absolute in terms, conditional in character. GOD's *promises* to us in baptism are under a covenant, and are therefore conditional, and completely so. If we fail in fulfilling *our* promises, we lose our title to the grace pledged to promises fulfilled, but never pledged to promises broken, neglected, or set at naught. It is insolent to expect that GOD will keep His word when we do not keep *our own*.

So GOD's *predictions* under a covenant are as conditional as His promises. There is a phalanx of predictions scattered through the Jewish prophecies which seem to have lost their virtue, since they never have been verified. Were those predictions insincere? Perish the evil thought! They were predictions under a covenant, the stipulations of that covenant were unfulfilled, and the predictions became suspended possibilities. They may, or may not be, demonstrations at another day.

And now comes something of profounder meaning, of intense significance. If promises and predictions are conditional under a covenant, so are *predestinations* also. Predestinations have nothing to do with metaphysics in the Bible - any more than promises and predictions. They are ecclesiastical, and not scholastic and dogmatic. And so St. Augustine understood them. He believed in the predestination to grace for all who were baptized reverentially. He believed that a baptism so begun, and properly carried on, was predestined to perseverance; and there he stopped. Calvin believed that his elect were predestined to absolute salvation, and his non-elect to absolute perdition, and rejected all conditions as an impertinence. It cannot take great acuteness to discern a heaven-wide difference between these separate systems, though it suits some to intermingle and confound them.

It is hoped, now, that few or none will persist in saying it is of no consequence whether the word *testament* or *covenant* be applied to what the first Council of Nice, in its very Creed, denominated The Scriptures; showing that to the file-leader of great Christian assemblies the word *testament* was unknown. Why, if this word is pettishly insisted on, the proper and annihilating answer is that it deprives us of a Bible. Look at Heb. ix. 16, 17, in the Common Version, or the Revisal of it. This passage informs us, magisterially, that "where a testament is, there must also of necessity be the death of the testator." Has, then, GOD our testator died? If not, we have no testament to go upon. And if He lives, we have no testament; for such a thing "is of no strength at all while the testator liveth." Either way we have no Bible; none, at least, which is available, while these verses are easily disposed of by using the word *covenant*. A covenant for the dead is firm; as of course it is, they having lived its term out with fidelity. But it has not reached this firmness while the covenanted liveth (not covenanter; the word is a participle, and not a noun), because he may lose everything by failing to keep its stipulations. This translation, too, is perfectly simple, and Hooker tells us that he holds it " for a most infallible rule in expositions of Sacred Scripture, that where a literal construction will stand, the farthest from the letter is commonly the worst" (Bk. v. ch. lix. sec. 2). No wonder, finally, that GOD should account it a peculiar satisfaction to have men take hold of His covenant with all their hearts (Isa. lvi. 4). The most unpromising may do so, as this text evinces, to their immortal joy. REV. T. W. COIT, D.D.

Creation. The manifestation of GOD's power: (*a*) in the physical world; (*b*) in the spiritual world. It is held that creation is the necessity in His nature. How, when, and where it shall be exhibited belongs to Him in His infinite wisdom, of His perfect will, and according to His perfect love. "Thou art worthy, O LORD, to receive glory and honor and power: for Thou hast created all things, and for Thy pleasure (*thelema*—the same word as will in the LORD's Prayer and in Hebrews x. 7, 10; so St. John vi. 39, and often) they are and were created" (Rev. iv. 11). We confess it, as His attribute, in the Creeds. Natural theology presents it to us as a deduction from the comparison of all the facts of the natural world. But inspiration sets this upon an unassailable basis for every one who receives the Revelation of Holy Writ. There the argument is always from the natural world directly to the spiritual world. So in Job, so in the 19th Psalm, and in innumerable other places.

The Persons present in the act of creation were the HOLY TRINITY. It was not framed by the hand of angels, but the Spirit of GOD brooded over the waters of chaos. The fiat of JEHOVAH went forth, Let there be. The Word of GOD, the wisdom was present (Prov. viii. 22-31; St. John i. 3; Col. i. 16; Eph. iii. 9; Heb. xi. 2).

Modern science has endeavored to pass beyond the study of the relation of things and of their constitution to ask how and why. In these discussions scientists are lost in their own imperfect grasp of the laws of nature, and despite all efforts they refute each other's theories, and have finally to fall back upon the statements concerning creation which the Divine wisdom has chosen to record. Religion has ever found that all clearly established facts are in full accord with inspiration, that when at first there appeared to be collision there was on the part of scientists a failure to see all the facts in their true relations, and on the part of devout Christians to abandon lightly teachings that had been accepted. But when these two had been adjusted there was ever a gain to the reception of the truth of Revelation. It is proper as well as natural that the Christian should refuse to readjust his already formed ideas about the natural world founded upon already established facts at the bidding of those who, having collected a fresh set, have formed them into crude, ill-balanced theories. Let us wait, and when a fact or series of facts have been indisputably interpreted and put into their natural and true position in the economy of nature, we will gladly accept them, knowing full well that they will prove to be in perfect accord with the records of Revelation. In the mean time, while hesitating to accept, it is not wise to sneer at what science has to suggest as to the true interpretation of these records.

Creationism. Controversies which were held in early ages as to the origin of the soul. Is it created and infused into the unborn infant, or is it propagated with the body as it is formed? These controversies were carried on for some time in the Church as different heresies had to be combated. St. Augustine's words state the doctrines, but do not determine the question raised. "As, therefore, both soul and body are alike punished unless what is born is purified by regeneration, certainly either both are derived in their corrupt state from man (Traducianism), or the one is corrupted in the other, as if in a corrupt vessel, where it is placed by the secret justice of the Divine Law (Creationism). But which of these is true I would rather learn than teach, lest I should presume to teach what I do not know." These wise words are practically accepted with this, as he says elsewhere: "if only that sentiment remain firm and unshaken, that the death of all is the fault of that one (Adam), and that in him we have all sinned." The instinctive belief is that of Creationism as being in better accord with all the Scripture teaches, and with our revealed knowledge of the immaterial and divine origin of the soul.

Credence-Table. The table, bracket, or slab on which the vessels and elements for the Holy Communion are placed till the proper time appointed in the rubric for them to be put upon the Holy Table. They were originally prepared and brought in from the sacristy, after the earliest custom of taking them directly at the time of the celebration from the offerings of the faithful. The term seems to come from the Italian, "to *taste beforehand;*" hence a plate on which anything is offered, thence a side table. It is of late introduction apparently in the English Church; it was a charge against Archbishop Laud that he used one, though after the example of Bishop Andrews and others. It has been declared a legal ornament in the English Church. Its proper position is upon the south side of the chancel. It may be a movable table, but more appropriately it should be a shelf properly supported against the wall.

Creed. The use of the very term "Creed" presupposes two assumptions, which are regarded as innate ideas that form the basis of all thought. They are considered as axioms because they are usually assented to without argument and must be determined before argument.

1st. The first is "I," or the conscious fact that every human being is a distinct person or entity, himself, not another. This conception of self, it is claimed, is simple, distinct, and universal. Every one regards himself as an uncompounded unit; a being possessed of faculties but not composed of them; having free-will, conscience, intelligence, tastes, appetites, passions, and the like; but being himself an indivisible unit to whom these characteristics belong, in which they naturally dwell, and all which he may rule and direct.

This person has an instinctive sense of freedom. He may be affected by internal impulse, or coerced by external powers, but his own assent or consent is essential to his own personal satisfaction. He cannot yield unwillingly to impulse without a feeling of degradation; nor submit to mere force without a sense of either shame or enslavement.

This person stands in natural connection with and reciprocal relation to all human nature, which has one origin and constitutes one organic race. This fact is also assumed in the very first word of every formal Creed. It is the assumption and confession of the unity of the human race; of which every human person is a constituent. It stands upon the fact, that what is common to all is essential to every one; and draws the conclusion that nothing shall be imposed upon any one (other things being equal) which is not equally required of all. Hence some creed-forms, especially the Oriental, begin with "We" instead of "I."

2d. The second fundamental concept and axiom contained in the very term "Creed" is "belief." In the singular form it is "I believe," and in the plural "We believe."

The assumption is, that belief is a primary necessity of every human person, and a like necessity for all the race. It is confidently claimed to be impossible for any conscious creature to escape the primary necessity of belief. The very consciousness of creaturehood, the conviction that one is not self-existent, that some power or person has caused him to be, make belief this primary necessity. While the common mind assents to this fact, the most searching analysis of the keenest thinking, and the profoundest searching of the most learned inquiry, have neither been able to reach a simpler element, nor discover a lower base than "belief." The spontaneous assent of the common mind is confirmed by all philosophy; hence belief is established as the primary source of all knowledge, the very first exercise of intelligence, as well as the ground of all duty and the support of all wisdom.

In granting this we confess that, logically considered, philosophy precedes faith. Whether formulated as distinct mental ideas, or merely accepted with more or less clearness of apprehension as axioms, the idea of personality, with its corollary, the unity in origin and continuance of the human race, together with the idea of necessary, primary universal belief, precede, underlie, support, and permeate every form of Creed.

The Creed of Christianity is not exempt from the confession of this philosophic basis. While in itself the Creed is not philosophic in construction, and from the nature of the case cannot be, yet it presumes a philosophic foundation, and acknowledges all the just rights of philosophy.

In fact, philosophy is simply the product of the reason which is natural to man. Christianity teaches that GOD is the author and finisher of nature. Hence Christianity acknowledges the rights, and not only allows, but encourages the honest use of all the powers of reason. Indeed, Christianity always respects and frequently appeals directly to human reason. The very assumptions of personality, common humanity, and necessarily primal belief, are a tacit confession that natural reason is a gift from and a trust under GOD.

If any one questions these axioms, included in the very term Creed, then they must be sustained. All axioms of Christianity philosophy may question, if it can. Should it do so in this case, then philosophic work must be done before Christianity may begin to be taught. Christianity asks no mere favors of philosophy. It stands only on the right and the true.

In point of fact, however, these fundamental concepts are never questioned by the common mind; and have never, even by the most acute or learned writers, been undermined, analytically divided, nor reduced to simpler elements. Hence Christianity takes one position, equally clear and strong, to either the lowly or the exalted, and both begins and prosecutes all its instructions, revelations, witnessings, and exhortations with "I, We believe."

The Apostles' Creed appeared so early in the devotional usage of the Church that its historic origin is unknown. The evidence is insufficient that ascribes it to the Apostles themselves. St. Paul, however, mentions "the form of sound words," which he exhorts Timothy to "hold fast." It is certain that our LORD JESUS Himself gave the essence of this Creed in the baptismal formula which He appointed: "Go ye therefore and make disciples of all nations, baptizing them into the name of the FATHER, and of the SON, and of the HOLY GHOST."

The Creed consists of three divisions, the first of which treats of the ALMIGHTY FATHER, the second of the SON, and the third of the HOLY GHOST. The special work of each of the three persons is named in this specific part of the Creed.

It is obvious that the Creed grew into form, probably in the very times of the Apostles, out of the necessity of instruction to the candidates for baptism. As they were to be baptized into the name of the FATHER, and of the SON, and of the HOLY GHOST, it was needful that they be well instructed in the points of their belief. As the belief was one and the same everywhere, —the One Faith,—some fixed form of its expression naturally arose and came into common use. Whether it thus grew naturally, or was actually a deliverance from the Apostles in person, severally and by agreement, cannot now be historically determined. In either case, however, its authority rests back upon antiquity. Whether given by the Apostles, or growing out of the necessity of baptismal occasions, it certainly appeared in the age of inspiration, has most sure warrant of Holy Scripture, has been sanctioned by universal acceptance in the Church of all ages, and stands now as the undoubtedly authorized summary of the facts necessary to be believed, and required to be confessed, by all who are to be made disciples of CHRIST.

Its present form, in universal use by the Church, is as follows:

"I believe in GOD the FATHER Almighty, Maker of heaven and earth:

"And in JESUS CHRIST His only SON our LORD; Who was conceived by the HOLY GHOST, Born of the Virgin Mary; Suffered under Pontius Pilate, Was crucified, dead, and buried; He descended into hell; The third day He rose from the dead; He ascended into heaven, And sitteth on the right hand of GOD the FATHER Almighty; From thence He shall come to judge the quick and the dead.

"I believe in the HOLY GHOST; The holy Catholic Church, The Communion of Saints; The Forgiveness of sins; The Resurrection of the body; And the Life everlasting. Amen."

This is the form in use throughout Western Europe, indeed, in all the Western Church, wherever the Latin language was formerly in vogue, and in all branches of the Church that have grown out of those which used the Latin in its Liturgies.

The Greek form, used in Russia, Turkey, Greece, and generally throughout the East, begins with the plural instead of the singular. Instead of "I believe" it has "We believe."

The two are essentially one, though supplemental to each other. They both carry the important truth, that there is only one Faith, which is obligatory alike upon every person. The idea, primarily in the mind of Western worshipers, is the faith of the person, the self; while the primary idea of the Eastern worshiper is the common faith, that which all together believe.

This merely shows the different habits of mind which pervade the distinct modes of progress and development which characterize and distinguish the West and the East. In the former the individual or person is the primary idea and pervading force. In the latter the organism—whether Church or State—is this idea and force. Each shows the strength and weakness of its own position. Apart they are weak. Only together are they strong. It is equally real and true that every human being is a person before GOD, and that he is a member of the human organism. Hence the salvation provided in CHRIST reaches persons both individually and in organized communion. One way of salvation is provided for all. "One LORD, one Faith, one Baptism!" What every one confesses as the Faith, all in like manner confess. The effect of the confession upon the individual confessors varies, but the confession itself is over one, comprehensive, and the same.

Two additions have been made to the Apostles' Creed since the Apostolic age, which, with some slight changes in the Nicene Creed, will be noticed when the articles of the Creed to which they are attached come up in order for consideration.

The Creed, commonly called the Nicene Creed, originated with the Council held in Nice, or Nicæa, in Bithynia, Asia Minor, 325 A.D. It is substantially the same as that now in use; except that it closed with, "We believe in the HOLY GHOST." The articles that follow were added by the Council of Constantinople, 381 A.D.

The whole Creed, as it now stands and is used in the Western Church, is as follows:

"I believe in one GOD, the FATHER Almighty, Maker of heaven and earth, and of all things visible and invisible:

"And in one LORD JESUS CHRIST, the only-Begotten SON OF GOD, Begotten of the FATHER before all worlds, GOD of GOD, Light of Light, Very GOD of Very GOD, Begotten, not made, Being of one substance with the FATHER; By Whom all things were made; Who for us men and for our salvation, came down from heaven, And was incarnate by the HOLY GHOST of the Virgin Mary, And was made Man, and was crucified for us under Pontius Pilate, He suffered and was buried, And the third day He rose again, according to the Scriptures, And ascended into heaven, And sitteth on the right hand of the FATHER, from thence He shall come to judge the quick and the dead, Whose kingdom shall have no end:

"I believe in the HOLY GHOST, the LORD and Giver of life; Who proceedeth from the FATHER, and the SON; Who with the FATHER and the SON together is worshiped and glorified; Who spake by the prophets: And I believe one Catholic and Apostolic Church; I acknowledge one Baptism for the remission of sins; And I look for the resurrection of the dead and the life of the world to come. Amen."

Before considering in order the different parts, or articles of the Creed, it may be well to remark that it is a short compendium of facts, rather than an elaborate definition of doctrines. Such definitions are drawn out, for example, in the XXXIX. Articles. These "Articles of Religion," as they are called, contain the opinions that prevailed in the Reformed Catholic Church, known as the Church of England, at the Reformation. They were finally signed by both the Houses of Convocation of Canterbury and York, 1571 A.D. They are even yet required to be signed by every clergyman in the English Church upon his ordination, although none of the laity, except the graduates of the Universities of Oxford and Cambridge, were ever required to sign them. The American Church does not require their signature, though she keeps them in her Prayer-Book, as sound expositions of the doctrines she teaches. She demands of her clergy their signature to a general declaration of conformity to the doctrines, discipline, and worship of the Protestant Episcopal Church in the United States of America.

The distinguishing characteristic of the Creed is that it sets forth the facts upon which the Gospel rests, and thereby points out the means generally—*i.e.*, for all persons—necessary to salvation. It will be observed that these are not only thoughts or ideas to be apprehended mentally and spiritually, and to be used devoutly, but they are also veritable, self-existing facts, not dependent upon human assent, but real and true in themselves; indeed, the one chain of facts, external to man, which a person must believe if he would enter and continue in the way of salvation. They are analogous in some respects to natural facts, which are also facts, whether men believe or disbelieve them. For example, fire burns; if a man believe it, he will use fire wisely; but if he do not believe it, fire will none the less scorch him or consume his houses, should he throw himself into it, or neglect precautions against it.

This point, therefore, is of the utmost practical importance to every human person, and to the whole human race. It is important that all who have reached "the age of understanding" should hold and confess the Creed; and that children should have all done for them that can be done according to the Creed, and that they should be diligently taught it so as soon as they are able to learn.

Differences of opinion, among even the wise and good, do not and cannot alter external facts. As facts they rest on their own verity, and are operative, whatever any person may think or not think about them.

Now the fact of personal identity, now existing and forever to continue, conjoined with the fact of the oneness of the human race, and this associated with the universal, primary and persistent, necessity of belief, can never be other than facts, however any person may choose, or fancy himself compelled to think about them. Every human person must take the consequences of his personality, and all the race the consequences of its unity, whatever opinions may be held individually or prevail with greater or less approach to generality.

Starting with personal identity, human unity, and the necessity of belief, the first succeeding fact of the Creed is "One GOD." Proof of this, if required, is to be sought outside the Creed. Of course the Bible or any revelation cannot be appealed to for primary proof of the existence of GOD, because revelation presupposes belief in the Revealer. The Creed itself presents no proof. It merely sets forth the fact. Here human philosophy comes in, and discussions arise. One school declares that belief in GOD is intuitive, born in all men, so that every human person has originally in himself belief in GOD. This school agrees that confirmatory, or rather definitive and strong, proofs of the Divine existence may be drawn from both conscious self-searching after one's own origin under the conviction of self-insufficience and consequent necessary dependence upon some supreme LORD of the universe and of men, and from the observation and study of other men and of nature. Here a wide and various philosophic field lies open; and, while Christianity enters this field and sustains itself therein, the Creed only formulates the conclusion in setting forth the fact of the "One GOD."

The next fact—the "FATHER Almighty" —is partly supported by reason, partly by intuition, and partly also by revelation. Reason, having perceived the One GOD and shown His necessary unity, declares that He is Almighty, as a necessary consequence, for the One GOD must from the very nature of the case be Almighty. He is FATHER,—*i.e.*, the Universal Father, the spring and source of love, the universal energy and assurance of love, the sweetest, purest, and strongest power in the universe, the person in whom love centres, whose essence is love. This fact accords with reason, but answers chiefly the longings and yearnings of human hearts. Hence there is intuitive response to the fact not only from the mind of man, but also from that deepest part of himself, whence springs the consciousness of what he is and what he needs. Revelation strengthens the human reason and satisfies human intuitions upon this point; not by originating the knowledge of the Divine Fatherhood, but by confirming it in every particular, and enlarging it beyond the utmost reach of human discovery.

That the One GOD, FATHER Almighty, is "Maker of heaven and earth, and of all things visible and invisible," follows as an irresistible deduction. He only can be this Maker. None other can be found, nor conceived of. The original self-existence only can be the Creator of the universe.

The Creed to this point may be attacked, and has been in every particular. Philosophy has called it in question, beginning even with dispute about personal identity and proceeding through the creation. It has been defended on philosophic grounds, as it should have been. In the future, philosophy must take this portion of the Creed to itself; and the learning, that will support it, must be based upon human reason and intuition. While it requires a high mental development to comprehend, and some learning to know the philosophic points involved in this first division of the Creed, it requires only the powers of reason and intuition that are common to all—even to children—to perceive the facts, to adopt them by belief, to make them means of comfortable assurance, and to use them solemnly in either trembling or joyful devotion.

The Creed gives them in concentrated form; they are placed in its beginning because they comprise the facts upon which all that follows is based. While Christian believers are enjoined to stand ready to defend this citadel of the faith, according to their ability and opportunity, they are permitted also to rest in it, as in a home of the soul, and to enjoy, every one, personal, sweet communion with GOD, addressing Him ever as "Our FATHER."

The Creed being established and accepted thus far, the conclusion springs up spontaneously and with great force, that this one GOD, FATHER Almighty, has surely manifested Himself to His creatures. He assuredly, from the force of His own essential love, has created them. Hence, in some way, He has surely revealed Himself unto them.

The Creed from this point sets forth the facts of revelation. It recognizes indeed, as truth always does, the rights of human reason. The facts that follow are held ever subject to question and proof. After the preliminary probability, which leads us to look for a revelation from GOD, comes the proof that what the Creed further contains is that revelation.

We can conceive of revelation coming in various ways. It might have been in the form of a voice from heaven proceeding continually or at intervals, heard of all men or heard of a few. It might have been in a still, small voice, or in no articulate form, but only by an internal influence or afflatus reaching one or many, and making itself known to the mind or the heart of men. We cannot limit the means, instruments, subjects, or objects of revelation. We can only ask, What had GOD said? What hath GOD wrought?

In point of fact, the Divine revelation all centres in one person, who is Himself both GOD and Man. The beginning of revelation points to Him, and the close of revelation clings to Him. Hence the Creed, being the formal Gospel concentrated, opens its revealed portions with setting forth the facts about JESUS.

Coming forth from the mysterious sanctuary wherein we have with our reason and intuitions worshiped GOD the FATHER, we apply the same powers to His word of revelation. We meet a Man who declares Himself to be the Son of GOD, who has come from His FATHER and our FATHER to make known the Divine person and declare the Divine will. We demand, as we have both the right and duty to do, His credentials. He gives them amply. He retires not from, but courts the criticism of men. He does not even confine Himself to the society of His friends. He meets His enemies openly, before audiences composed of those who are favorable or unfavorable to Him. He claims, with the very simplest and therefore most impressive boldness, to be the very Person pointed out in all the preceding Divine revelation. He declares that He is the very MESSIAH, the CHRIST, the anointed of GOD to whom all the prophets bore witness; and for whose advent the chosen and separate nation, which had kept alive the worship of the One GOD, had from age to age been waiting. He expounds, supports, and defends His stupendous claim, does the work that He says the FATHER had appointed Him to do, finishes it, and ascends openly towards heaven, going back, as it is declared, to the right hand of the Majesty on High.

The whole revelation of GOD therefore centres in JESUS. He is the corner-stone of the whole religion of the true GOD. The Gospel as an organism grows out of His person, and as a code of doctrine springs from His words. Divine truth at least, indeed, all truth, flows forth from Him as from a fountain. In Himself He is the Truth.

They who hold the Creed are not exempt from the necessity of proving all these points to the just satisfaction of human reason. They did so at first. They have done so in all the past. They are doing it in this age. They will do the same in the generations to come. The Creed itself, however, does not deal in argument. It only gives the facts, in the shortest possible form of full and sufficient words.

It proceeds with pronouncing JESUS LORD,—*i.e.*, the rightful ruler over every man, and over all mankind.

The ground of His lordship is His personal Divinity. He evidently is not the original Divine Person, whom we worship as one GOD, FATHER Almighty. He distinguishes Himself from the FATHER by speaking of Him as another person.

Here reason is baffled,—not confounded, only required to stand in awe. It is beyond human power to *comprehend* the existence of more than one personality in the unity of the GOD-head. What reason cannot comprehend the understanding may yet receive as a fact. Reason may demand that the fact be clearly set forth and duly authenticated. It can fairly demand no more. The proof has many branches, but they all grow out of the truth of JESUS, as from a root. That root being acknowledged, the whole Gospel proceeds and is evolved from it. The point now in view is the character and peculiar distinctiveness of the Deity of JESUS, with its relations to the one GOD-head.

We learn that He is the Only-Begotten of the FATHER. We take this fact into our understandings. We are fully capable of receiving it as a fact. It teaches us that the One GOD FATHER is father, not in a metaphorical but in a literal sense. He has existed from all eternity in unity of substance, that included distinct—not separate—persons, one of whom was, is, and forever will continue FATHER, and the other SON.

Hence the SON is GOD, not originally, in and of His own self, but GOD *of* GOD. He is of the very Divine essence, being in Himself Light, but Light *of* Light. He is in the superlative sense GOD, being therefore equal with the FATHER in power, glory, beauty, love, and all excellence, indeed, Very GOD; but Very GOD *of* GOD.

"Begotten, not made, being of one substance with the FATHER."

This is the peculiar clause that distinguished the Nicene Creed. The Council of Nice was called by Constantine I., the Roman emporor, and met at Nice 325 A.D. The chief occasion of its convention was the heresy called Arianism, which had arisen in Alexandria and was spreading through the Church. Arius, a Presbyter of Alexandria, in Egypt, taught that JESUS was a partaker of the Divine nature, but not of the veritable Divine substance. He was therefore a creature, the highest indeed of all creatures, the very nearest and dearest of all whom GOD had made, but still a creature. Arius was willing to confess that JESUS was of *like* substance, but not of the *very same* substance with the FATHER. In Greek, one single letter contains the whole controversy. If the Council of Nice had adopted the word *omoiousios* Arianism would not have been condemned. It refused the middle "*i*," and hence the dreadful controversy that afflicted the Church, and has not yet ceased. That JESUS was *omoousios*, of the very same substance with the FATHER, was the fact to which members of the Council bore testimony, not as their own opinion only, but as the witness of the Catholic Church to the orginally inspired truth, which from the beginning had been the Christian faith. Hence the true doctrine is that JESUS, as to His Divine nature, is begotten, not made, and is by nature GOD.

The Creed next declares that JESUS is the Creator of all things. The FATHER then is Creator in a sense analogous to that of

Architect, and the SON Creator in a sense analogous to Builder. This shows something of the practical relation between the FATHER and the SON, as what preceding shows of their essential relation. Each exercises the functions of His Own personality, with distinctiveness of will and act, though, of course, with the accord of entire unity in love.

Next follows the special work of JESUS for mankind. The love of the FATHER went, and ever goes, forth towards the world of His creation. Man, misusing his freedom, had fallen into sin. GOD in love sent his SON, who was called JESUS, *i.e.*, the SAVIOUR. JESUS, responding to this love and sharing it, "for us men and for our salvation came down from heaven."

This is a fact, not discovered nor discoverable by man, but to be received upon most sure warrant of the Divine revelation. JESUS laid aside His Divine manifestation of power and glory, took upon Himself the form of a servant, and came into that relation with human nature that was necessary to His work as man's SAVIOUR.

"He was incarnate by the HOLY GHOST of the Virgin Mary, and became Man."

This is all literal truth, a fact with all actual significance and force, real in itself and all its relations. The Incarnation was a true human conception, wrought, however, by the supernatural operation of the HOLY GHOST. Mary was the true Mother of JESUS, yet a very virgin.

He became man in the fullest possible sense. All that constitutes man He was, is, and henceforth will forever continue. And yet He remains the same person, who is Very GOD of Very GOD. The General Council of Ephesus, 431 A.D., and that of Chalcedon, 451 A.D., established the doctrine that JESUS is One Person, who at His Incarnation took human nature into Himself, so that He became very man, not by confusion of natures,—*i.e.*, not by compounding into a new commixture the human nature with the Divine,—but by so taking up the human with the Divine that His personality extended over the human; so that, remaining His very Divine self, He yet became man. Hence He enters into all essentially human relations, and from His Incarnation onward forever remains man.

Having thus set forth the SAVIOUR, in the singleness of His personality, and in the fullness of both His Divine and Human Natures, the Creed proceeds to declare His mission. It proceeds to show what He did in obedience to the will of the FATHER, who sent Him; and in accordance with His own coinciding love, which impelled Him; for the working out of the salvability of men, and for making salvation itself actual to all those who use their freedom in choosing, and seeking for it. This fact of human free-will is taken for granted in all the instructions of the Gospel, through all the articles of the Creed. GOD forces no man into good.

He only provides the way, gives all needful help, presents every impelling motive short of actual coercion, and then leaves man to choose whom he will have for his lord.

JESUS recognizes this inalienable human freedom, and presents Himself as the SAVIOUR of the willing; the bringer of peace to all men of good will; "The Way, The Truth, The Life."

Having become man, He proceeded to do the work necessary for the conquest of sin under which man lay in bondage.

"He suffered under Pontius Pilate, was crucified, dead, and buried."

He thus made "one oblation of Himself, once offered, a full, perfect, and sufficient sacrifice, oblation, and satisfaction for the sins of the whole world." Thus the redemption, made only by JESUS, extended to all mankind. There is no limit to its efficacy, and it becomes efficient to every human person that does not shut himself out from its influence. Neglect or refusal of the means of grace every free man may be guilty of. Whoever accepts and uses the means of grace provided in the Gospel, being within the scope of redemption, is himself saved through the satisfaction for sins made by the GOD-man through His willing sacrifice of Himself on the cross.

"He descended into Hell,"—*i.e.*, into Hades, the place and state wherein the spirits of the departed await the final judgment. What He did there is only partly revealed. He preached to "the spirits in prison," but what He preached is not revealed.

This clause was not in the earliest form of the Apostles' Creed; but has been in use since early in the fifth century.

"And the third day He rose again, according to the Scriptures."

The resurrection of JESUS was the burden of the preaching, and the warrant of the mission of the Apostles. They bore personal testimony to the fact. They saw and touched Him, ate and drank with Him, heard for forty days His instructions concerning the kingdom of heaven. It was their specific mission to set up this kingdom on earth. JESUS breathed on them, bestowing the HOLY GHOST, and gave them thus that grace of ordination which in obedience to His will has been transmitted through them and their successors even to our own times, and will be continued according to promise until the end of the world. He Himself, on bestowing this ordination, promised to be with His Apostles and their successors until the end of the world. The immediate successors of the Apostles took up their testimony, joined to it the link of their own witness, and handed on the chain to their own successors, and thus an unbroken line of witnesses to the fact of the resurrection of JESUS have kept the light of the Gospel shining mid the world-darkness of sin throughout the Christian generations. This conquest over death was made by the GOD-man JESUS as the completion of His work of justification. It stands yet, not only as the ground of assured hope, but as the victorious act of the "last Adam," through which death itself is stripped of its power over all those who place their trust on JESUS.

"He ascended into Heaven." The GOD-man thus ascended. The very humanity of our LORD, now and evermore indissolubly joined to the Divine nature in the person of the Only-Begotten, ascended into heaven, and sitteth at the right hand of GOD. He bore with Himself all the offices He had received, when the FATHER made Him the CHRIST, the Anointed one. He was anointed High-Priest of the new, perfected Tabernacle. In the very presence of GOD He exercises now the office of His High-Priesthood. "He ever liveth to make intercession for us." The worship offered throughout His kingdom on earth—the living Church everywhere—centres in the memorial of His sacrifice; as do also both the public and private devotions of His faithful disciples. He is present on earth in a mystical manner, and makes all His appointed means of grace efficient specifically by His power through the operation of the HOLY GHOST. Yet He remaineth ever at the right hand of GOD, exercising His priesthood in mediation. He takes upon Himself the penalty of all sin, and procures pardons for penitents, grace and help for the needy, assurance of hope with the peace that passeth understanding for all the faithful.

"From thence He shall come to judge the quick and the dead: Whose Kingdom shall have no end."

The Apostles evidently expected the speedy return of our LORD after they saw Him ascending into heaven. The Church, in all the ages since, has had the same expectation. No man, however, knoweth the time of His return. The point in which the Apostles, especially St. John, the last of them, were definitely agreed, was, that JESUS should return in His own personality, "in like manner as He was seen to go into heaven;" that He would then judge the world in righteousness, appoint due awards finally to all mankind, and set up His kingdom visibly in the universe. This continues to be the expectation of Christians. They are looking for this consummation daily. The long delay, as it seems, to those whose experience is bounded by mortal lifetime, is only a purifying trial of faith. The closing words of revelation ring yet in the ears of the saints: "He which testifieth these things says, Surely I come quickly." The hearts of the hopeful, who are waiting for Him on earth and in Hades, respond now, "Amen! Even so, come, LORD JESUS."

His "Kingdom without end" is to be universal. "At the name of JESUS every knee shall bow, of things in heaven, and in earth and under the earth." At the name of JESUS, the GOD-man, the very Divine Human indissoluble person, who was incarnate, dead, buried, risen, ascended! Hence this final universal kingdom shall be visibly presided over, and ruled forever, by GOD incarnate. Our own very human nature shall thus rule forever, in personal union with the Divine nature. This is an unrivaled promise, carrying with it every conceivable honor, distinction, blessing, comfort, and glory which can be conceived of as external to man. In addition, however, it is further revealed that this great final universal LORD shall so take His beloved into union that they, being in Him and He in them, they shall be His friends forever, as well as kings and priests unto GOD.

"And in the HOLY GHOST."

The Nicene Creed closed with these words. What follows to the end was added by the first Council of Constantinople, 381 A.D.:

"I, We believe in the HOLY GHOST, the LORD and Giver of life, Who proceedeth from the FATHER [and the SON]."

This completes the revelation of the mode of the Divine existence, and declares that the one GOD is, not merely appears, but is, from and for all eternity, Three Persons. The specific work of the HOLY GHOST is that of LORD and Giver of life. In operation the FATHER originally wills, the SON forms, and the HOLY GHOST vivifies. In the language of philosophy, the first is the Cause, the second the Formal Cause, while the third is the Efficient Cause of all existence. Their union is substantial. Their distinction is personal. They are one in nature, distinct in relations and office. They are distinct objects of devotion. Either may be addressed in prayer or thanksgiving. All join in the love which is of the Divine essence. All equally possess the Divine attributes. Their relations are real, though they act always in unison. Each executes His specific office. All join in common operation. Whoever is the "friend" of one is the friend of all. Salvation is the work of all. Saved men become the adopted children of the loving FATHER, the brethren of the GOD-man, the Only-Begotten SON, and the communicants in and with the HOLY GHOST.

The clause given above in brackets, "and the SON," was not in the original Creed of Constantinople. It was inserted by the Papal Church, under the influence of the Emperor Charlemagne, and has never been accepted by the Oriental Church. Indeed, the insertion of this clause was and is one of the grounds of the lamentable schism between the Church of the East and that of the West. They who in the West are disturbed by this addition to the old form of the Creed, and yet use it, explain it as the setting forth of the mission and not the nature of the personal HOLY GHOST. His procession from the FATHER they confess in the old form, but add that He proceedeth from the SON in accordance with the words of JESUS: "I will send Him unto you." Others accepting the doctrine of the "double procession," still would rather return to the old form, because it is the old form. Practically, the point does not disturb devotion. It belongs to the domain of metaphysics, and demands the most attenuated use of that philosophy for even understanding its statement.

"Who spake by the Prophets."

This work of the HOLY GHOST belongs to the department of inspiration. He it is who breathes into the men, chosen in the different ages to reveal GOD and His will, the true Word of GOD. The FATHER wills, the SON forms, the HOLY GHOST proclaims the Word of the LORD. Angels have been sometimes chosen as the messengers of revelation. Men, however, have been usually chosen in all generations. Prophets are of two kinds. Original prophets are those to whom the Word was first revealed. The anointed and appointed preachers of righteousness, in all ages, are secondary prophets. The HOLY GHOST inbreathes all. The first He causes to utter the truth, be they willing or unwilling. The latter are not always so compelled. They may mingle the truth of GOD with their own inventions. The words of the first are to be received as the Word of GOD. Those of the latter must be judged of by the hearer. Yet the HOLY GHOST is present in and with all preachers of the Word. The hearers, therefore, are under Divine obligation to heed what they hear, while the preacher is under like obligation "to rightly divide the Word of truth."

The clear apprehension and full reception of the doctrine of the Holy Trinity gives much clearness of understanding for the study of the Word of GOD: while the fact, practically considered, appeals with both tenderness and force to the heart. Those conscious of sin find strength for their love of the FATHER in the personal assurance of the grace of the SON, while the communion of the HOLY GHOST works, in their own perceiving spirits, that perception of pardon and peace in which GOD is the one central power, manifested in beauty, sweetness, and comfort.

The whole Creed to this point treats of the Divine side of the Gospel. It sets forth GOD in His Trinity, distinct as three persons, yet united in substance and co-operation. It is necessary to be believed, because every fact touches human salvation, and pervades all real means of grace. The FATHER, the SON, and the HOLY GHOST all act divinely; but each, in His own chosen sphere, primarily acts and operates. They conjoin but never supersede one another.

We come next to the human instrumentality; set up indeed by Divine wisdom, imbued with Divine authority, and pervaded by the Divine presence with constant grace and help, but still human in its constitution, because composed of human members and organized according to human needs.

"I, We believe one Holy, Catholic and Apostolic Church."

As the belief necessary to the guidance and salvation of one man is the same that is necessary for all men, so are the means of grace the same for one and all. These means are comprised in the Constitution of the Church. Not only is the Church the appointed teacher of truth, but she is the custodian and dispenser of the sacraments, one of which joins every partaker in personal union with the GOD-man, and the other nourishes him with "the bread of heaven." The sacraments not only present truth in the form of doctrine to the mind, and move the heart with solemn memories, but they convey specific graces, corresponding to natural birth and nutrition. In one that new birth is effected in the faithful which makes them very members of CHRIST; and in the other they are "nourished up into everlasting life." They are generally necessary to salvation,—i.e., necessary for one and all where they can be had. The ministration of these visible means of grace supposes and requires the existence of one visible body, the Church. Hence the Gospel appeared at first as a regularly constituted organization It was one and the same in all the early ages. The Apostles, as one college, first administered the affairs of the whole Church. Very soon, however, they took each a specific sphere. St. James took his See in Jerusalem. Paul and Barnabas became missionaries to the Gentiles, and St. Peter to those of the Circumcision. Paul made Timothy and Titus Apostles, and set the first in Ephesus and the other in Crete with Episcopal jurisdiction, as his Epistles to either clearly show. This was followed throughout the Church. From the very dawn of Church history Bishops appear, everywhere, exercising the Apostolic authority, while Presbyters and Deacons are always found working with and under them. Indeed, every national Church of which any record is found, for fifteen hundred years, had its hierarchy composed always of Bishops, Priests, and Deacons. Although the term Bishop, during the historic period of the New Testament, represented only a function—viz., an overseership—and was applied even to some Presbyters, yet the proper office of the Bishop was in the hands of Apostles, including the Eleven, with Matthias and Paul. Afterwards the name Apostle was confined, as a memorial of reverence, to the first receivers of the Episcopal office, and the term Bishop was given to their successors. From that time to the present a Bishop has been and is not merely an overseer, but all that an Apostle ever was in official authority and power within the Church. True Bishops are now successors of the Apostles, by unbroken lines of ordination, and possess the dignity, office, and mission which CHRIST gave to the Twelve, and in which He promised to sustain them by His own presence with them until the end of the world.

The unity of the Church is a fact, because "He is the head of the Church, which is His body, the fullness of Him that filleth all in all." It is holy, because it is His Body, and dispenses all the means of grace, by word, sacrament, and discipline, through which holiness is promoted and preserved. It is Catholic, or universal, because it is one, operating alike for every man and for all. It is Apostolic, because it is founded upon the Apostles and prophets, JESUS CHRIST Himself being the chief corner-stone.

Thus the Gospel is not merely a code of laws, or congeries of doctrines, but is a veritable organism also, divine in origin, and perpetuated by the indwelling presence of the Word of GOD, by the providence and grace and truth which JESUS dispenses by the SPIRIT, through and by means of His own sure though unseen presence.

The Church, though divine thus in origin and perpetuity, is also human; because men, women, and children, in all the generations, constitute her membership. She is the chosen visible witness of GOD on the earth. Her primary mission is to keep alight and glowing this witness in every age, and hand it on to succeeding generations. Besides this specific work for the honor of GOD, she has that of calling the world to repentance, of receiving into the Divine household the "children of adoption," and of keeping that which is committed to her against that day.

While human in constitution, she is not of man's making. Man can no more make a church than he can originally create a living person. He may make images in likeness of the living, but GOD only can breathe in the breath of life and give power to be fruitful and multiply and replenish the earth.

The clause in the Apostles' Creed which is joined with this article—"the Communion of the Saints"—is not found it its earliest forms. It was inserted, no one knows exactly how and when, but has been in common use for about thirteen centuries. It is simply a definite expression of a point included in the original article. The Holy Catholic Church is of course the communion of the saints, because it is the Body of CHRIST; and the communion of all holy persons is with one another through their common union with CHRIST. The thought in this clause includes past, present, and future. All those who are departed in the true faith of the Most Holy Name are at rest in JESUS; not dissevered from the living, but only separated in vision by the curtain of the grave; while all the saved in coming generations will enter the same one body, and join in the one communion. However the clause came in, it is sanctioned by long usage, and sanctified by holiest associations. On every occasion of its utterance it gives sweet and strong expression to that sense of both brotherly and organic common membership in the family and Church of the living GOD, which space and time cannot diminish, which death itself cannot dissever, and which shall continue ever brightening but ever the same through time into eternity.

"I, We acknowledge one Baptism for the remission of sins."

The sins of all those who are joined in communion with CHRIST are remitted. The sentence of pardon to the penitent is declared by those who are ordained to this authority; but the actual impartation of remission is in and through grafting into Him who is the life of the world. This portion of the Creed is in exact accordance, and most perfect harmony, with the pervading idea, or rather essence of the Gospel. The Gospel is more than a system of theology or code of law, or rule of fitness, order, and beauty; it is a veritable organism. It operates beneath the understanding, or will, or affections, even upon the central essence of personality. It takes position in the very being of self, and there joins the faithful to CHRIST. Hence, as CHRIST Himself ingrafts His own chosen branches into Himself, He is the one Baptizer. As St. John says, i. 34, οὑτός ἐστιν ὁ βαπτίζων ἐν Πνεύματι ἁγίῳ, He is the Baptizer with the HOLY GHOST.

His Apostles, with their successors, including all to whom authority to baptize is transmitted, receive into the Church by baptizing with water "into the name of the FATHER, and of the SON, and of the HOLY GHOST." But the promise of Jesus given with this mission, "Lo, I am with you alway," is most sure warrant that He is present when the outward visible form is fulfilled, and that He it is who then and there baptizes with the HOLY GHOST. This makes baptism complete in both visible order and spiritual grace. The question of the possibility of a bar against this spiritual baptism, made by the recipient consciously or unconsciously, is not now under consideration. The point is, that every real baptism is perfected by the one Baptizer; and that it effects such organic union of the baptized person with CHRIST that the remission of sin is secured and conveyed. He who is truly baptized hath "put on CHRIST," and "there is therefore now no condemnation to them that are in CHRIST JESUS."

Hence the terms of the Creed are explicit. It declares the perfectness of remission in baptism. It makes no reservation. Baptism is "generally necessary to salvation," because it is the ordinary and appointed means of effecting that organic union with CHRIST, which is salvation. The person baptized is made one with CHRIST, by the specific operation of the LORD and Giver of life, and CHRIST only imparts this gift of the HOLY GHOST.

"The resurrection of the body." "I, We look for the resurrection of the dead."

This is an exclusively Christian doctrine. It is quite different from the old heathen notion of the immortality of the soul, and unlike all conceptions of a future life held and taught in other forms of religion. Its point is, that the very body of the dead human person is as truly and perfectly his own body as was the body of the dead CHRIST His while it lay in the tomb. There is no conflict between this fact and the equally sure facts of bodily dissolution. We believe the natural decay, disintegration, and possible wide diffusion, through earth, water, or air, of the material substance in which the living human body is manifested in mortal life. It is evidently not the material substance which constitutes the body. It makes itself manifest in this life by means of material substance, though the very particles themselves are continually changing. In what the very essence of body dwells is not known. All we are sure of is that every body is distinct from every other body; that every person has his own body. This body may die, but can never be destroyed. It may be laid in the grave, as seed may be covered in the ground. GOD, however, will raise it up at the last day. As He giveth to every germinating and growing seed His own body, so shall the body of the very person who died in its own identity be recalled to life. St. Paul says, "It is sown a natural body,"—i.e., a psychical or soul body,—"It shall be raised a spiritual body." This teaches us nothing about the substance in which the immortal body shall manifest itself. All it does clearly teach is that as the mortal body is an instrument of the soul, so also shall the immortal body be a fitting instrument for the uses of the spirit. This tripartite constitution of man, in body, soul, and spirit, is thus shown to be essential, and therefore indestructible. Death is only a temporary disruption of the threefold unity of every human person. When death shall be finally conquered, every one of the faithful shall dwell in his completely restored tripartite constitution, in the open presence of the unveiled Trinity.

"The life everlasting." "The life of the world to come."

It will be best always to consider carefully that the Creed is the symbol of faith for all true believers in Christianity. It sets forth exclusively the positive facts and grounds of faith and hope. It is silent of threatenings. Its silence, however, is no evidence that the supplementary contrasts to its assertions are not real and sure. It says nothing of the second death. It leaves that and all similar warnings and threatenings to be made known as they are commanded to be proclaimed. It is like a shout of victory and song of triumph. It is occupied alone with the glories of the saints. They shall enter into "life everlasting." It will be essentially the same as the "eternal life," which GOD hath given to His beloved, and which they enjoy on earth according to their measure. This life is the personal communion of the saints with the person GOD, who is love, light, life. They dwell with Him. Even during mortality He takes up His abode in them. The future life everlasting will be the same reciprocal personal communion, but in the midst of a new environment. Not earth-darkness, sin, sorrow, and toil will then surround the loving ones who are "the friends of GOD," but rest, peace, purity, joy uninterrupted and unceasing will be theirs. Their spiritual bodies will dwell with Him, who human as they are forever, is yet GOD-man, ever continuing "Head over all things to the Church, which is His body." The details of the heavenly environment are not given. Something is either taught literally or suggested in gorgeously figurative description in the Bible, especially in "the book of the Revelation;" but the essential fact that is made known is simply that we shall be like CHRIST. Now CHRIST, in His Divine Manhood, is LORD over all things forever. This, then, is what Christians must surely believe of the life everlasting, viz.: that it will be passed with the reciprocal, loving companionship of all saints, in the very open presence of GOD, where, "all things being subdued unto Him," nothing shall by any means hurt "the sons of GOD," but, through the LORD of All, everything good shall be for the use of those whom JESUS shall finally present to the FATHER and confess before GOD and the angels.

"Amen." The original meaning of this word is verily, or truly. Its frequent use by JESUS during His life on earth, with the manner of that use, gives to it a peculiar solemnity. It is the preface to His most solemn and significant declarations. His assurance of union with the FATHER, His most glorious promises and most fearful denunciations, are begun often with Amen, verily. It is therefore a formula of direct appeal to the GOD of Truth. In this sense it seals the whole Creed, and becomes a solemn declaration, as in the sight of GOD, that this is the very sum and substance of that faith in which the saints live and labor, and into which they hope to enter finally at the perfect consummation.

REV. B. FRANKLIN, D.D.

Criticism. The passing a judgment on any subject. It is a department of study which has been applied, with destructive consequences to the faith of many, to the examination of the books of Holy Scripture. It is subdivided into several parts: I. Philological criticism, testing the genuineness of a document by the style and the words used, determining whether they were at the date assigned to the document in common use, or whether they were of earlier or later date. II. Internal criticism, the examination of the contents of the document, determining whether the subjects discussed were in truth those current at the assigned date, or were earlier or later, or whether the whole document coheres throughout, or contains matter that properly betrays interpolation. III. Criticism based upon external history. Devoutly used these are very great helps to a proper understanding of the different books of the Canon of Scripture, and we have to use with caution and discrimination the instruments it puts into our hands. There are three sources for the popular confusion of ideas about the books of Scripture and their contents: The perfectly just and defensible habit of quoting indifferently side by side texts from all parts of the Bible, though historically Genesis is separated from Revelation by at least fifteen centuries. The carelessness common in giving due instruction about their purposes and contents and upon the doctrine of inspiration. The want of due heed in using and arguing from the contents of the several books of the Bible. When some startling assertion is made, with an array of apparent learning contrary to the vague ideas current as to the date, history, and contents of a book, it is popularly supposed that the book or books in question are not genuine or not authentic. Criticism has done very much to rouse up an intelligent study of Holy Scripture, and with all the sad consequences to some, we must be very thankful for the firm foundation it has proven for the genuineness of the Bible. Attack has not only developed complete defense upon all important points, but it has cleared away a great deal of confused incorrect teaching, as a siege against an impregnable fortress clears away much underbrush which has gathered without the defenses but is itself conducted with much pomp, parade, and noise. And it may be that the obscuring smoke of the attack may hang long over the citadel. The books of the Old Testament have had a great deal of light thrown upon their purpose and contents, while the traditional dates of their composition have been in general established, and wherever modified, only in an unimportant way. The war of criticism has raged chiefly round three points,—the Pentateuch, Isaiah, and Daniel. All other controversies are subordinate to these, and these have been most successfully maintained in their integrity. That after the Captivity explanatory phrases, *e.g.*, " as it is this day," were probably inserted by some authority, as Ezra, is true. That documents were used and rearranged by Moses, documents of their early history preserved carefully among the B'nai, does not at all affect the fact of his inspiration. The minute accuracy of his books has been amply proven at all points. So, too, of Isaiah. Whether there were " two Isaiahs" living at different times, but having their separate writings bound up into one, or a later writer borrowing the name of the earlier genuine Isaiah, depends upon the single fact whether there is such a gift as prophecy or not. If GOD does permit the future to be foretold, then there was but one Isaiah,—the son of Amoz, —who prophesied " in the days of Uzziah, Jotham, Ahaz, and Hezekiah, kings of Judah" (Isa. i. 1). The defense of Daniel has been most ably made by Dr. Pusey in his exhaustive lectures, and by others also.

In the New Testament the authenticity of the Gospel of St. John, of the Apocalypse, of several of St. Paul's Epistles, has been attacked, but the contest now is nearly over; the main battle over the fourth Gospel has been successfully won.

That there has been *no* change in the view in which these books must be held is not asserted, but that there has been any essential change, or that their authenticity, authority, and inspiration has suffered in the slightest, is not true. Their authority is higher than ever, because more intelligently and clearly apprehended.

In this article there is no attempt to recount the canons of criticism, which critics, principally those in Germany, have laid down as inviolable, and have deliberately broken whenever it suited their purpose; to point out how, denying the clear sequence of facts, they have selected such isolated ones as fitted in best with their preconceived theories and absolutely despotically rejected the rest, or to note how often they have built up—as substitutes for plain recitals of easily comprehended narratives, which were thoroughly coherent internally and fitted with the external surrounding, because they were true—vague, wild guesses, that were utterly baseless, and asserted these to be genuine and veracious. The result was that these critics refuted each in turn his predecessor, and substituted for facts his own baseless ideas of what the facts should be, by their own disagreements defeating their purpose. The outcome, though we have not yet seen the end of the whole controversy, has been so far, and will eventually terminate in, the complete vindication of the Inspired Scriptures of the Church of GOD.

Crosier. The pastoral staff of the Archbishop. The pastoral staff is of very early use. It has been claimed as coming to the Church from the staff held by heathen priests. It may probably have been taken from the shepherd's crook, since that was a most appropriate symbol, often used in the Old Testament. Still, the staff as a badge of office, and of use also, was one so universally employed that almost any explanation of its original introduction into the Church's ritual would have some mark of truth, and only tend to show that it was used very early. The crook was later assigned to the Bishop,—the plain pastoral staff; the crosier, *i.e.*, the cross alone, to the Archbishop. The Patriarch was given a staff with two cross-bars.

Cross. Once the instrument of unutterable torture and shame, now the badge of the Christian religion. It is used as an ornament in Churches. It is worn on the person; it is worked into the vestments of the services. It furnishes the plan for many sacred edifices. It was used once universally as a gesture of benediction. It is used in the Church officially at the reception of the infant or adult after baptism into the Christian Church. Its shadow falls upon many a grave. So thoroughly has it passed from an instrument or sign of shame to a badge of the Christian. The true sense of the use of the sign of the cross in baptism is well given by Dr. Burgess's explanation, accepted by King James, and affirmed by Archbishop

Bancroft to be the sense of the Church: " I understand it not as any sacramental, or operative, or efficacious sign, bringing any virtue to baptism or the baptized. When the book says, 'and so sign him with the sign of the cross in token,' etc., I understand the book not to mean that the sign of the cross has any virtue in it to effect or further this duly, but only to intimate and express by that ceremony, by which the ancients did avow their profession of CHRIST crucified, what the congregation hopeth and expecteth hereafter from the infant, namely, that he shall not be ashamed to profess the faith of CHRIST crucified into which he was even now baptized."

Crusades. The expeditions of Christian armies to Palestine and Egypt for the recovery of the Holy Land from the possession of the Saracens. They were called Crusades both because they were undertaken to recover Jerusalem and the so-called Holy Cross, and because the soldiers wore a cross on their clothes and had one upon their standards. There were in all eight crusades, extending over a period of nearly two hundred and seventy years. The causes of the crusades lay farther back than the immediate motives for them. They were begun and continued under religious enthusiasm, intermittent indeed, but sufficiently strong to lead to the enormous sacrifices of means and life which they involved.

The first crusade—the result of the preaching of Peter the Hermit and of the urgings of the Greek emperor and the Patriarch of Jerusalem—was at first a disorganized rabble, under the lead of Peter, was organized by the princes that shared in it, and finally was led by them, at the head of the several columns, formed without much concert, towards Constantinople. Godfrey of Bouillon was the first to reach that city at the head of eighty thousand troops. He at once pushed into Asia Minor and besieged Nice, which he took in six weeks (1097 A.D.). Antioch was captured a year after, and after a siege Jerusalem fell, and was barbarously sacked, and the Jews were burnt in the synagogue and the infidels massacred, it is said, to the number of seventy thousand. Godfrey was chosen king and was crowned, and soon after, upon the crushing defeat of the soldan of Egypt on the plain of Ascalon, the princes disbanded and returned home.

The second crusade was, in 1144 A.D., led by the Emperor Conrad III. and Louis VII., but it proved abortive. The Greek emperor fearing its successes quite as much as he did the Saracens, practically betrayed the German army by misleading it in the defiles of Asia Minor. The French army too was mismanaged, and when at last the remnants of the army were placed in position before Damascus, disease and want and dissensions destroyed its efficiency, and the expedition soon came to an end. It was a most discouraging defeat to all of Europe at the time.

The third crusade was preceded like the first by eager, enthusiastic rabbles, which pressed forward to their destruction. Jerusalem had fallen before Saladin in 1187 A.D. Acre was invested by Guy de Lusignan, and the wastes of the siege repaired by the multitudes who pushed into the siege from Europe. Frederick Barbarossa was drowned after defeating the soldan of Iconium, and his troops were wasted at Antioch. Philip Augustus and Richard I. at last successively reached the plains about Acre. Dissensions broke out, and there was little real concert of action, but Acre finally capitulated. But dissension and the retreat of Leopold and of Philip left Richard alone. A victory over Saladin at Ascalon brought on a truce, and the third crusade ended, 1192 A.D.

Since Jerusalem had not been recovered from the Saracens, a fourth crusade was preached 1198 A.D., but it was not organized till 1202 A.D., but it was diverted from its destination. It captured Zara for the Venetians and Constantinople for Alexis and his father Isaac, but feuds, dissensions, open war with friends and allies, marked its steps, 1203-4 A.D. At last the few who reached Palestine were defeated. No crusade had such excellent chances of success, and not another wasted them so ignorantly (1204 A.D.).

The fifth crusade was undertaken by Hungarian Crusaders in 1217 A.D., and was joined in by Germans, Italians, English, and French under the Duke of Austria. After Andrew of Hungary withdrew, it made an expedition into Egypt, where, upon its successes, peace was asked for by the Egyptian soldans at the price of the cession of Jerusalem. This was refused through the cupidity of the papal legate, and finally the Crusaders were compelled to withdraw, after having lost everything. The Christians still held Acre. Frederick of Germany now headed the crusade, but he was at feud with the Pope (1228 A.D.), and, without attempting military operations, succeeded through negotiation in obtaining free access to Jerusalem and a peace for ten years. He went to Jerusalem and there crowned himself, and then returned to Europe (1228 A.D.).

The seventh crusade, begun 1238 A.D., was likewise formed of separate expeditions. One was led from France, and was wrecked in the defeat at Gaza. The second, which recovered Jerusalem, was led by the Earl of Cornwall, and accomplished its work without a battle. Jerusalem was held till 1242 A.D., when it was recaptured by the Chawarazmian Moguls, who defeated the Templars and the Moslem, and overran all of Palestine. Acre was the sole port left to the Christians. Louis the Pious now undertook to repair these losses, and planned to attack Egypt (1248 A.D.). The same fatality,—wasted time, lost opportunities, and ill-planned battles which were fruitless victories, ended at last in the capture of the king (1250 A.D.) near Cairo. Damietta was surrendered in exchange for him. He remained four years longer at Acre, but at last returned home only to prepare for the last crusade. In 1270 A.D. he led the last crusade, which proceeded against Tunis, but died before the city was captured. A truce was made for ten years, and some liberties for Christians were stipulated in the treaty. Edward of England made an expedition with three hundred knights into Syria, but was compelled to return by the death of his father and his own consequent accession to the throne. So ended the crusades. Acre was captured by the Moslem in 1291 A.D., and they were for centuries left in an undisturbed possession of the Holy Land.

The social and political results of the crusades were in the end beneficial, but never before or since have treasure, lives, and time been so lavishly wasted as in these ill-planned and worse-executed assaults upon Syria.

Crypt. (Hidden place.) A subterranean vault under any portion of the church. It was sometimes used as a place of burial. In very ancient churches it is the surest indication of what were the original plan and dimensions of the church.

Culdees. Probably a corruption of Colidei, *i.e.*, Servi Dei. An order of ascetic monks originally established in Ireland (792 A.D.), and apparently imitators of the rule of Chrodegan of Metz. They existed in Ireland, but in connection with later Cathedral Chapters, till the Reformation, and the name survived till 1628 A.D. But the name and history of these secular ascetics attracted more notice in Scotland, in which country they appeared about 800 A.D. Their peculiar habits differing from other monastic orders, and the fact that they were very frequently married, and that their place in the body was hereditary, that they were governed sometimes by lay Abbots, drew attention to them. They continued to exist as separate both from the old orders of St. Columba and the foreign orders, as the Benedictines, brought into Scotland about two hundred years later. As secular in habits, with clerical ordination, they were an anomaly, which was at last gotten rid of by attaching them, as in Ireland, to some Cathedral Chapter. The name and probably the rule of the body survived for a long time, but they were brought under diocesan rule. Their origin and government, both in Ireland and Scotland, were most probably the outcome of the tendencies and development of their age, and not properly borrowed from any foreign example.

Cup. The chalice used in the administration of the Holy Communion. It is the term used by the translators of the New Testament. "The cup which we bless, is it not the communion of the Blood of CHRIST?" (1 Cor. x. 16.) Its form as a vessel varied according to convenience or means; but at first sometimes of wood, it was usually of silver, gold, glass, more seldom of baser metal.

Doctrinally, the cup is the communicating to the devout recipient all the blessings that the shedding of CHRIST's Blood upon the cross have obtained for us. "Most humbly beseeching Thee to grant that by the merits and death of Thy SON JESUS CHRIST and through faith in His blood, we, and all Thy whole Church, may obtain remission of our sins and all other benefits of His Passion," and so throughout this Prayer of Oblation. It is the reception, how or by what mode we may not now know (St. John xiii. 7, a principle announced by our LORD applicable to all mysteries) of the Blood of CHRIST (St. John vi. 55, 56), to be by us received "in remembrance of His meritorious Cross and Passion, whereby alone we obtain remission of our sins and are made partakers of the kingdom of heaven."

To withhold the cup, then, from the laity upon any imagined principle whatever, practical or doctrinal, is to act contrary to the express command of our LORD and of His Apostles, and to administer a maimed and imperfect sacrament. For any layman, upon any pretext, to withdraw after receiving the Body is to do an insult to the Giver of the Feast, the LORD JESUS CHRIST.

Curate. One who has the cure of souls, under the direction of another. It properly belonged to the Deacon, but was, and is, extended to any Priest who is serving in the parish of another. The term is not known in this country, where the Priest or Deacon is properly—according to rubric and Canon—called the Assistant Minister, though only a Priest can be *instituted* as assistant in a parish.

Cure of Souls. The work of the ministry. The Bishop of the Diocese has an unlimited cure in his jurisdiction, since he is the responsible head of the Diocese, and is the angel of his Church (*cf.* Rev. ii. and iii.). The Priest and Deacon are his subordinates, having limited jurisdiction,—*i.e.*, within the parishes to which they are sent and over which they are to have charge. Offices not in use in this country, as Archdeacons, have elsewhere jurisdiction of supervision and partially of discipline, being the Commissaries of the Bishop. The charge to the Priest at his ordination (*vide* ORDINATION OF PRIESTS) and to the Bishop (*vide* CONSECRATION OF BISHOPS), together with the questions put to each, show plainly the extent and the limit of the cure of souls, and the great responsibilities laid upon each.

D.

Dakota. *Vide* NEBRASKA AND DAKOTA.

Dalmatica. Originally a secular dress, a tunic with either short or no sleeves, belonging to persons of the upper class, and, later, worn only by sovereigns at their coronation. The earliest mention known is in the account of Cyprian's martyrdom (if the MSS. be genuine) (256 B.C.). The martyr took off first his outer cloak, then his dalmatica, which he gave to his Deacons, and stood in his linen under-garment. It was worn by Bishops, and then permitted to Priests, and finally it became the distinctive vestment for Deacons at the celebration of the Holy Communion.

Damnation. The New Testament word for which this is the translation is used indiscriminately both of the sentence and the execution, but there is no detail of the nature of the punishment inflicted implied in the word. Its application (*a*) to the judgment of the wicked at the last day, and (*b*) to the punishment that follows, is to be gathered from the context, not from the word itself. It can only be by comparison that we can determine those passages which bear mainly upon the point of the condition of the lost. Upon this point the Church has never passed any œcumenical teaching, though the certainty of damnation has always been assumed. The materialistic views of some of the earlier teachers soon passed over into the immaterialized spiritual torments held by later doctors. As to the duration of that torment, there has again been no dogmatic teaching by the whole Church, though Origen's ideas of a final remission were condemned. In fact, wherever Scripture is silent, leaving a fact as a mystery to be solved hereafter, the Church has been providentially kept from making a formal statement. But as the weight of Holy Scripture leans to the doctrine of everlasting punishment, so does the mind of the Holy Church. All theorizing about material or spiritual torments and when these are to be fulfilled, all vain interpolations of purgatorial pains, and all theories of final restoration, find no place in her teaching. What her LORD has told she believes, what He has concealed she does not presume to know.

But this word damnation is used in two places which have given rise to much misunderstanding, or rather the second place (in the exhortation to the communicants) is a quotation from the first place (1 Cor. xi. 29). As the word damnation—*krima*—does not in itself determine the nature, degree, or extent of the punishment, it is really a vague term. But the next verse shows the lingering, suspended sentence giving room for its withdrawal; for though the contents of the sentence refer to an actual epidemic, it bears for us a spiritual sense also, and the whole refers to the disciplinary, not the punitive nature of GOD'S sentences upon us here. Therefore it is a morbid straining and an infusion of more than it will bear, to give the word "damnation" in these places the extreme signification often forced upon it.

Daniel. (GOD'S judge, or GOD is my judge.) The name of either three or four different persons mentioned in the Old Testament: (1) 1 Chron. iii. 1; (2) Ezra viii. 2; (3) Neh. x. 6. But it was also borne by the last of "the four greater prophets." According to Dan. i. he was one of a small body of captives carried from Jerusalem to Babylon by Nebuchadnezzar in the third year of Jehoiakim (604 B.C.). Nebuchadnezzar is called "king of Babylon," but his father, Nebupolassar, was still on the throne, as we learn from Jer. xxv. 1, that the *first* year of Nebuchadnezzar coincided with the *fourth* of Jehoiakim, and from Dan. ii. 1, that the *second* year of Nebuchadnezzar was in the third year of Daniel's captivity. All these dates fall into harmony on the natural supposition that Nebuchadnezzar would have been called *king* by the Jews, while actually only his father's viceroy intrusted with the command of their affairs. From these captives a number were selected of royal or of noble family, distinguished alike by their physical and mental characteristics and by their education, to be especially trained for the king's service. Among these were Daniel and his three companions, and of these Daniel was the most distinguished. The name of *Belteshazzar* (the prince of Bel), given to him at Babylon, was doubtless intended as the equivalent of his Hebrew name. His training at the court of Nebuchadnezzar was but just completed when he recalled and explained, by means of the wisdom divinely given, the famous dream of the king when all the wise men of the realm had failed. This at once gave him rank and position, and he was made "ruler over the whole province of Babylon" (Dan. ii. 48). In this position he must have had the opportunity, and have used it, to be of great service to his countrymen who were carried into captivity somewhat later, and he must have become personally acquainted with Ezekiel, the great prophet among them. Later on he explained the second dream of Nebuchadnezzar (Dan. iv.), and in consequence secured from the king a decree declaring his sense of the power of the GOD of the Jews. This must have tended to ameliorate their condition, and they seem to have believed that Daniel's influence with the king could avert the threatened destruction of their city and temple. Hence it became necessary for Ezekiel, in proclaiming that judgment, to say that even his intercession, like that of Noah and Job, would prove unavailing (Ezek. xiv. 14–20). Under the immediate successors of Nebuchadnezzar he appears to have been forgotten, but in the extremity of Belshazzar he was again called forth, and interpreted the handwriting upon the wall pronouncing the doom of the king and the kingdom. At the accession of Darius he was made the first of the "three presidents" of the whole kingdom, and still higher honor was intended (Dan. vi. 1-4), when, by the intrigues of the courtiers, he was thrown into the den of lions. From this he was delivered and restored to honor, and he continued to prosper under the reign of Cyrus, in whose third year his last recorded vision is dated (Dan. x. 1). He must have been now extremely advanced in age, and, notwithstanding some untrustworthy Mohammedan traditions, it is unlikely that he ever returned to his native land. Besides Ezekiel's mention of Daniel already spoken of, he again refers to him (ch. xxviii. 3) as a distinguished example of wisdom. Critics have found difficulty in such mention by the prophet of a man still living and still in the prime of life; but it is plain that Daniel's wisdom was very remarkable, and stood out in public and known superiority to all the famous wisdom of the Chaldeans. His fellow-countrymen in captivity must have looked up to him almost as a superior being, and no higher example of wisdom could have been presented to them.

Daniel, The Book of, is placed in our Canon as the last of the four greater prophets, but in the Hebrew Bible it stands among the *Hagiographa*, or Holy Writings, either between Esther and Ezra or immediately before Esther. Various reasons have been given for this position, such as, that one-half the book being in Chaldee instead of in Hebrew, it was thought it should be separated from the other prophets; or that it was distinguished from them by the fact that all its prophecies were communicated by dreams and visions and not by a direct "Thus saith the LORD;" but the true reason seems to have been a regard to the apocalyptic character of the book and a recognition of the distinction between the functions of the prophet and the seer.

At chapter ii. 4, the language changes from Hebrew to Chaldee when recording the answer of the Chaldeans to the king in their own language (Syriac-Aramaic); and this language continues to the close of chapter vii., when the Hebrew is resumed for the rest of the book. As nearly as may be, therefore, the book is evenly divided between these languages. This change of language is often explained by saying that the half of the book of especial interest to the Chaldeans, and mostly concerned with the dreams and the acts of their kings, is written in their language, while the half more particularly designed for the Church is in the sacred language. This is generally true, but must be supplemented by the statement that the seventh chapter is probably put into Chaldee on account of the vision being substantially the same as the dream of Nebuchadnezzar and its interpretation in chapter ii., which was already in Chaldee. Moreover, there seems no reason why the first chapter, which is simply historical, should have been in Hebrew unless the Jewish tradition be accepted, which states that the several prophecies were written separately and independently, and were collected by the elders of the people, who prefixed this chapter as a needed introduction. If this tradition be accepted, there remains no difficulty in the terms in which Daniel is spoken of, and thus the objection sometimes brought on this ground against his authorship of this book is entirely removed. There is no reason why such a merely historical introduction should not have been prefixed by any competent and authorized person. The Chaldee of the book is of an earlier type than that of the Targums, while the Hebrew is of a late character, resembling that of Ezekiel and Habakkuk, though purer than the former. So far as the language is concerned therefore, a date is indicated for the book in the time of the captivity when the Jews were gradually exchanging their own language for the Aramaic. The same indication is furnished by the few Greek words found in the book. These are all technical names of musical instruments, doubtless brought with the instruments themselves from foreign sources, and naturally result from the commercial intercourse already established between Greece and Babylon. If, as some critics maintain, the book had been written in the closing years of the reign of Antiochus Epiphanes, it is inconceivable that it should not bear the impress of the Greek literature and culture of that period, when Hebrew appears to have become almost entirely a dead language.

After the first introductory chapter, the contents of the book are as follows: chapter ii. contains an account of a forgotten dream of Nebuchadnezzar which he required to have recalled and interpreted. All the wise men of the kingdom having failed, Daniel, through prayer and the intercession of his friends with GOD, was enabled to do this, and showed the king the succession of four great kingdoms, of which his own was the first, all terminating in the universal and everlasting reign of GOD. The circumstances attending the interpretation of this dream must have given it publicity, and Nebuchadnezzar may have feared its effect upon the permanency of his empire. At all events, it is recorded in chapter iii. that he set up a great image, having not only the head but the body also of gold, and sought to unite his whole empire in its worship.

Any one of his officers who should refuse to worship was to be cast into a furnace. The description of the officers summoned seems to have been purposely arranged so as not to include Daniel himself; but his three friends were involved, and refusing the required worship, were at once cast into the furnace. Nebuchadnezzar saw them walking there unharmed with a fourth glorious form "like the SON of GOD," and commanded their release. It is quite in character with the clearness and strength of his mind that, having thus recognized a power greater than his own, he should have issued a decree in honor of the greatness of that Power. A feeble mind might have obstinately persisted in the contest, but he was a man of sufficient sagacity to recognize the utter folly of such a course. Chapter iv. is entirely occupied with a royal decree, recounting a dream and its interpretation by Daniel, the king's temporary insanity, his recovery, and consequent recognition of the power of the Most High. The recently discovered monuments of Babylon afford proof of a period in Nebuchadnezzar's reign in which, according to his own inscription, there was a suspension of all his great works on his temples, and palaces, and canals of irrigation, as well as of his worship and offerings. Herodotus also ascribes to a queen several of the important works which others attribute to Nebuchadnezzar. No other explanation can well be suggested for these remarkable facts than the temporary insanity (technically *Lycanthropy*) which is recorded in this chapter. That an Oriental kingdom should have been preserved to its monarch through such an eclipse is remarkable; but in this case there were strong and peculiar reasons. The heir apparent, Evil Merodach, was a very undesirable ruler; Nebuchadnezzar himself had been a mighty conqueror, and his name was a tower of strength; from the notice of her works by Herodotus, the queen, who acted as regent, seems to have been an excellent ruler; and above all, the internal administration of the empire was largely in the hands of the wise and able Daniel. Chapter v. gives an account of the feast of Belshazzar, in the midst of which came the handwriting upon the wall, interpreted by Daniel, of the death of that monarch, and of the reception of the kingdom by Darius. Much objection was made at one time to this account because Berosus and Herodotus state that the last king of Babylon was Nabonnedus or Labynetus, and that he was not killed at the capture of the city. But the monuments have solved the difficulty by furnishing an inscription in which Nabonnedus addresses his son Belshazzar with royal titles, showing that he had associated him with himself upon the throne, and therefore Belshazzar was naturally left in command of the city when his father had taken the field. Xenophon concurs with Daniel in the statement that the last king of Babylon was slain in the capture of the city. There still remains a question in regard to Darius. Various theories have been proposed, but further information must be obtained from the monuments before he can be certainly identified. In the sixth chapter an account is given of the intrigues of the courtiers, and of the decree obtained from Darius, and of Daniel's being thrown into the den of lions in consequence of his disobedience to this decree. Chapter vii. goes back chronologically to the first year of Belshazzar, and records the extremely important vision, parallel to chapter ii., of the four beasts, representing four world-empires succeeding one another, and all ending in the universal and eternal divine government. The chief controversies concerning the book turn upon the interpretation of this prophecy. To enter into these varying interpretations would occupy too much space. Suffice it to say that the best supported interpretation, and the one, until lately, almost universally received, understands the first kingdom of the Babylonian of which Nebuchadnezzar was head, the second of the Medo-Persian, the third of the Greek rule of Alexander and his successors, and the fourth of the Roman. All the other interpretations, though varying in their methods, concur in making the fourth kingdom that of Alexander or of his successors. These views have been ably refuted in Pusey's work on Daniel. Chapter viii. gives further details in regard to Alexander and his successors, especially concerning Antiochus Epiphanes, and the interpretation is so plainly given in connection with the vision itself that no room is left for doubt. The ninth chapter is chiefly occupied with the prayer of Daniel concerning the close of the captivity, and closes with the wonderful prophecy of the seventy weeks to elapse before the coming of the MESSIAH. Much learning and ingenuity have been expended in seeking to find some other meaning for this prophecy, but none of the varying interpretations thus proposed commend themselves as having either internal probability or the support of any external evidence; and they all rest on the assumption that the writer, living in a later age, did not recognize the historic fact of the fulfillment of Jeremiah's prophecy in the return of the Jews from their captivity. The remainder of the book is one continuous prophecy, given in the third year of Cyrus, and is occupied with the story of the struggles between the Seleucidæ (the kings of the north) and the Ptolemies (the kings of the south, or of Egypt), in the course of which the chosen people suffered greatly, the whole closing with references to the future, which have been variously understood as referring either (1) to the spiritual resurrection of many of the people after their great struggle with the power of the heathen, or (2) to the literal resurrection of the last great day.

The book of Daniel, as a whole, thus stands out as giving more than any other prophecies world-wide and comprehensive views of the providence of GOD in the government of the world, and more definite indication than any other of the exact *time* of the coming of the MESSIAH. Besides the disputed points in its interpretation already specified, mention must be made of "the little horn" of chapter xi., which has been and still continues to be variously understood. Of the genuineness and authenticity of the book there appears never to have been any doubt until the time of Porphyry. It is contained (with apocryphal additions) in the LXX. and other Greek translations of the Old Testament, although in the volume of the LXX. the translation of Theodotion was afterwards substituted for that originally made, probably through the influence of Origen. It is recognized in the books of Maccabees (1 ch. ii. 59, 60, and in its Greek translation, 1 ch. i. 54), and, according to Josephus (Ant., xi. 8, ⅔ 5), its prophecies were shown to Alexander. When we reach the time of the New Testament, it is distinctly quoted as Daniel's by our LORD Himself (Matt. xxiv. 15), and its miracles are alluded to in Heb. xi. 33. It has always been received both in the Jewish and the Christian Church.

Most of the objections made to it have already been considered. One other must be noticed. Porphyry († cir. 305 A.D.), in his zeal against Christianity, objected to this book that its prophecies were minute and exact to the close of the reign of Antiochus Epiphanes, and beyond were vague and untrue; hence the book must have been written at that time. This objection has been taken up in modern days, and forms the whole gist of the argument against the book. On any fair interpretation of the four empires, and of the seventy weeks, this objection utterly falls to the ground, because these prophecies are sufficiently definite, reach far beyond the reign of Antiochus, and have been accurately fulfilled as far as the vision of the prophet has yet been unrolled in the course of time. It remains, however, that there is a certain degree of truth in the objection, in that, in chapter xi., the struggles of the kings of the north and the south are depicted with unusual minuteness through the reign of Antiochus, the great persecutor of the Church, and after that point become only very general. For this, however, there is an obvious and satisfactory reason. In the providence of GOD the voice of prophecy was to be hushed soon after the time of Daniel, and yet the Church under Antiochus was to be called to pass through a terrible ordeal. It was exceedingly important that it should be, as it was, sustained in that trial by these prophecies, and that object having been accomplished, there was no reason why the course of history should be traced further. No other great trial was in store for the Church until the time of the coming of its LORD.

REV. PROF. F. GARDINER, D.D.

DAVID

David is the national hero of Israel. And by name and in character "beloved," the shepherd-king, the soldier who never lost a battle, the impartial judge, the statesman-king, the poet and prophet of GOD, the organizer of the worship of JEHOVAH in forms that are fresh after three thousand years of use, above all, the progenitor and type of CHRIST. His claim to pre-eminent honor is unquestioned.

His story reads like a romance, though it is very simply told. He was the youngest of eight sons of Jesse of Bethlehem. The family was of some local dignity, but not prominent in the tribe or nation. David's name, "beloved," reminds us of another "son of his father's old age" (Gen. xxxvii.), who was born in this same neighborhood, and who was envied and hated of his brethren, both on account of his father's love and "for his dreams and for his words." Perhaps the same reasons explain the humble position in which David is found at the beginning of the story, his father's hesitating answer to Samuel's inquiry (1 Sam. xvi. 11), and his elder brother's insulting language to him before the army. They are jealous, the old father is afraid of them, and he is too gentle and brave to put himself forward without "a cause." He is first brought into notice when Samuel, the prophet and judge, to their surprise and terror, appears in the little town and summons the people, and especially the family of Jesse, to the sacrifice. The youngest son is missing, and they wait for him. When he comes in, "ruddy and of a beautiful countenance, and goodly to look to," the prophet recognizes the object of his mission and anoints him before them all. We are not told that the prophet explained to them, or to David, the meaning of his act, though his former course with regard to Saul would lead us to infer that he made it known to David, and as much and more is implied in the story. But whatever he knew, he continues to sing his psalms with the sheep for listeners, and fight his battles with the lions and the bears, till his fame gets abroad, and he is sent for to play before the king when the attacks of his strange malady come upon him; and for a time he becomes the constant companion of Saul and greatly loved by him.

His next appearance in the narrative is in the fight with the Philistine. There is a difficulty in reconciling the narratives of 1 Sam. xvi. 23, and xvii. 58, which ought not to be passed over, but which need not be made too much of. The Septuagint unites xvii. 12-32, and xvii. 55-xviii. 6. No solution yet proposed is entirely satisfactory, and we must wait for more light for one that is. The general outline of the story would indicate that David returned for a time from the court to his shepherd-life, from which he was summoned by his father to go to the camp of Saul. The description of his personal appearance when the Philistine "disdained him" is the same as on the former occasion, but the narrative brings out more of his personal character, his whole-hearted trust in GOD, and his simple, contagious fearlessness. When he goes forth to the fight, neither Saul nor we have any more doubt what will be the result than he has himself.

He is without fear and yet he takes every precaution. When honors begin to be heaped upon him he is not dazzled by them. He becomes at once the delight and hope of the people and of the army. He is the close friend of Saul's son, and he is loved by Saul's daughter, and at first by Saul himself. But then to Saul's other malady is added the madness of jealousy as he saw in David the heir, and suspected in him the aspirant, to the kingdom. First by violence and then by treachery he tried to get rid of him, nor was his enmity lessened when he was obliged to keep his promise and receive David as his son-in-law. His conduct at length became so violent that David was driven from the court, and fled first to Samuel's protection in Ramah, and then to the court of the king of Gath, whence he only escaped by feigning madness. From the court of Achish (or Abimelech, Ps. xxxiv., title) he fled to the cave of Adullam, and here he began the life which continued till the death of Saul. First his own family came to him, and then others, discontented, in debt, outlaws, and fugitives from society, and he found himself at the head of a constantly increasing band of freebooters, whom, however, he kept in such strict control, that he was more than once betrayed by his neighbors. He was regarded generally by the inhabitants as a protector, and one to whom they gladly paid a kind of tribute. Saul pursued him, and drove him from place to place, until at length, after twice generously sparing the life of his foe, and finding Saul still implacable and false, David saw that there was no safety for him but in flight, and he passed on and took service with Achish, king of Gath, who gave him Ziklag for a residence. Here he remained for a year and four months, until the final battle and defeat on Mount Gilboa, when Saul and his sons were slain and the army of Israel routed and scattered.

The immediate consequence of that great disaster was to advance the Philistines into the very heart of the kingdom and practically to cut it in two. At the same time the force at David's disposal was so increased by the addition of portions of the defeated army that when he came at the call of the tribes to Hebron to be made king over the southern portion of the kingdom, he already had a strong army at his command. For seven years and a half he reigned at Hebron, while the feeble son of Saul maintained a rival throne at Mahanaim. But the desertion and treacherous murder of Abner, his only dependence, was followed by the murder of Ishbosheth, and David was anointed king 'over all Israel and Judah.''

Then began a reign of thirty-three years more, than which none is more glorious. One of David's first exploits was the capture of the Jebusite stronghold of Jerusalem, which he fortified and made the royal city. Thither, with great pomp, he brought up the Ark of the LORD, and made Jerusalem the centre of worship. Then he proceeded to strengthen and enlarge his kingdom. He formed alliances with the kings of Tyre and Hamath. He fought against the Philistines, Ammon, Moab, Edom, and the Syrians, and always with success. In his time and his son's the promise to Abraham was literally fulfilled,—" from the river of Egypt to the great river, the river Euphrates" (Gen. xv. 18). He reorganized the army; he personally administered the kingdom through a department of "judgment and justice;" while the reorganized army, the system of police, the records, and the finances were made separate departments, under appointed chiefs. Nor this alone. He reorganized the system of worship and gave to it his minutest attention, arranging the orders of Priests and Levites, arranging the choirs, and even inventing instruments of music for their use (Amos vi. 5). One great desire of his heart he was not permitted to accomplish, but only to see it afar off. The building of the Temple was reserved for his son, but David did what he could to make preparation for it, and for the project of the Temple and gathering of materials for its erection the honor is due to David.

But the glory of David's reign was tarnished by a great sin. The adultery with Bathsheba was followed by the foul murder of her brave husband, and the sin was visited upon him in consequences of death and shame that never departed from his house. The crime of Amnon's incest was followed by his murder at the hands of his brother Absalom, and Absalom's rebellion drove the old king from his home and throne only to be restored by Absalom's death. His last years were peaceful, and he saw Solomon securely seated on the throne, but the seeds of division were already planted in the kingdom. The other sin, which brought upon his people the visitation of a plague which destroyed seventy thousand, viz., the taking of a census of the people, is one of which we cannot appreciate the heinousness, partly perhaps because we know so little of the circumstances.

But the story of David's life to be appreciated must be read with the Psalms for a commentary. Of the one hundred and fifty psalms he is the author of about one-half, and the rest are built on his foundation. Many of David's Psalms were written for the worship of the sanctuary, of many others the occasions belong to his life, and they partake of his personal character and are full of allusions to his circumstances. The sheepfold (xxiii.), the battle (viii.), the victory (xviii.), the cave (xxxi.), the wilderness (lxiii.), the storm (xxix.), the siege (lx.), and above all his repentance (xxxii., li.), furnish occasion and give form to the words in which the Psalmist pours out his heart to GOD, and it is hardly possible to understand the Psalm without understanding something of his circumstances.

But, besides this personal element in the Psalms, there is another which is also personal, and yet which distinguishes them from other poems and confessions, and even from other hymns of praise. David's wholehearted devotion singled him out as a man fitted for the work which he had to do, and there is a peculiar force in the repeated mention of the *heart* of GOD and of man in his story. He is the " man after GOD'S own heart," and the LORD chose him who " looketh on the heart." His heart was for a time turned away and he fell into sin, but it was never hardened against GOD, and his prayer of repentance is a prayer for a " new and clean heart," the " offering of a broken and contrite heart" to GOD. The key to Abraham's character is his faith; to David's, his love. He loved GOD and GOD loved him, and men loved him, and his Psalms speak to the hearts of all men as his words " bowed the hearts of the men of Judah as the heart of one man."

But not even this deep truthfulness of love is sufficient to account for the fact that the Psalms of David have entered so largely into the worship and life of the Church. David was a prophet, and his words are inspired, but he was a prophet of a peculiar kind. In him prophecy took a new departure, and not only his words but his person and his kingdom were prophetic. More than any other man David was the type of CHRIST. The promise made to Eve in the Garden of Eden and repeated to Abraham, is made more definite still when GOD promised that " of the fruit of his loins He would raise up CHRIST to sit on his throne." Such a promise of GOD must be regarded as the key to David's life. It must be understood to be always present with him, even when its presence has the effect to deepen his penitence for his sin. Accordingly from this time forward the MESSIAS is foretold and expected as the son of David, and even as David (Jer. xxx. 9; Hosea iii. 5). When CHRIST came He was saluted as the son of David, and He came fulfilling in His person and in His Church the kingdom of David.

Here, then, we have the key to the peculiarly Christian character of the Psalms of David. In them the Psalmist speaks as the type of CHRIST and CHRIST speaks by him, and there is that wonderful blending and union of the personal and human element with the Divine which makes them so dear and so true to the disciples and members of the body of the GOD-man. And therefore it is that it has always been the mind of the Church to find CHRIST in them, not only in those which are called " MESSIANIC" (*e.g.*, ii., cx.), and in the single verses which are quoted as such by sacred writers (*e.g.*, xvi.-lxxxix., **xl.**), or by our LORD Himself (*e.g.*, xxii.), but in all of them. Therefore, too, they are so perfectly adapted and so universally used in Christian worship. CHRIST speaks in them, and we Christians speak to Him by them. They tell us of the Throne and Kingdom of the CHRIST, the Anointed, of His law, His enemies, His righteous sceptre, His Divine Sonship, His exalted nature, His death and resurrection, His universal dominion, His everlasting reign. It is David who speaks, but it is not only David the man, the Psalmist, and the king, but David the prophet, David the type of Him who is " David's Son and David's LORD." And his words "are ours because we are CHRIST'S." REV. L. W. GIBSON.

Day. The word, simple and plain as it is, a cycle including a period of darkness and one of light, both together twenty-four hours long, has been the subject of much discussion in connection with the record in the first chapter of Genesis. The geologist, claiming that the term is figurative, as it has been used elsewhere, *e.g.*, the Day of the LORD, the Day of vengeance, insists upon vast ages as included in each successive day. Whatever explanation may be given, or whatever duration may be assigned to the term, the controversy cannot affect the inspiration, and therefore absolute accuracy of the whole passage. The successions of creative work, as there recorded, are in exact accordance with what science has taught us, and the occasional discrepancies alleged are found to disappear as a closer investigation brings out the true facts. There is no clashing to suppose that the " Day" of the Mosaic record may have marked long ages of present time, and till some positive evidence, beyond the demands of theory, however certainly based upon actual facts, shall be found to decide the question, it is not necessary to treat it otherwise than as a postulate in geologic science. It cannot affect the truth or accuracy of the revealed story, for it may be that we interpret words by our ideas of what they *ought* to mean for us. The word is often used for an indefinite time. " Abraham saw my day and was glad." " In that day" is often in the prophets. This use of it is perfectly clear.

Deacon. A minister. So far as the record shows, this was the first office created by the Apostles. They themselves were appointed by the LORD. The account of the election and ordination (Acts vi. 1-6) of the seven Deacons is the model for all succeeding ordinations. It is conjectured that the seventy disciples whom the LORD had sent forth were before this recognized as officers, but it is mere conjecture, and we read of the young men who buried Ananias and Sapphira. But the Deacon had his special duties to do. It is said that of the seven at once two began to preach, but this is perfectly compatible with the duties of a Church officer. In fact, in the first proclamation of the Gospel every man had this laid upon him; but when theological accuracy was required, then trained men, of course, could alone be recognized; these were generally the prophets of the New Testament. (*Vide* PROPHESYING.) That the Deacon should, having the natural gift therefor, preach, and that as evangelist as St. Philip immediately after appears (Acts viii.; *cf.* xxi. 9), he should not only proclaim the Gospel, but also baptize. There is nothing incompatible in having the offices joined in one person. The office of Deacon is not clearly described in either the Acts or in St. Paul's first Epistle to Timothy. It is left very vague indeed. The later development of the office in the Church retained its primary office to look after the finances and details of the parish, but also joined to it the authority to baptize and to preach. To it was secluded, too, the authority to assist in the Holy Communion by the delivery of the cup. Thus they were the stewards and almoners of the Church, the ministers to the poor, sick, and imprisoned. They were specially attached to the personal attendance upon the Bishop, executing his orders and representing him to the people. They were called his hands, ears, mouth, and eyes. They kept the congregation in order, and waited upon the priest at the Holy Communion; in times of stress they could even reconcile a penitent. They were attached to the parish to which the Bishop assigned them. These very nearly correspond to the present position of the order. They cannot remove from a parish but by order of the Bishop. They can administer baptism only when no priest is at hand. They cannot absolve, or bless, or celebrate the Holy Communion. They can preach when thereto licensed by the Bishop. They are to minister to the poor, sick, and needy, to discover them and report their needs to the priest. The exigency of the times has made this office but the stepping-stone to the priesthood, and in the majority of cases has forced the Deacon into the execution of functions for which it was supposed he was imperfectly prepared. The Deacon is forbidden to absolve, bless, or celebrate the Communion, three acts which are within the capacity simply as official acts of any one fit for the Diaconate. This is proper, as not within the scope of that share in the stewardship committed to him. But ability to preach, and the requisite learning to qualify him for the priesthood, are demanded of him, and are exercised by him long before he usually is prepared for the "good degree." The necessities of the Church have forced ill-qualified Deacons to assume duties which ought to require long and patient training, while their office does not permit them to discharge those official priestly acts from which they are debarred by their lower rank, yet for want of which the parish committed to their charge is suffering,—an anomaly in the work which the pressing needs of the Church in her mission work can alone justify. The question is asked, Why are there not permanent Deacons? It is really a question of finance. If the salaries and income of the Diocese were poured into one common treasury, and administered by a financial officer, then Deacons could be maintained for work in their proper sphere; but, since comparatively few parishes can support more persons than the Rector, the office of a Deacon cannot be made more than a step preceding the priesthood. As it now stands, permanent Deacons are almost an impossibility.

Deaconess. A female ministrant in the Apostolic Church. St. Paul (Rom. xvi. 1) commends Phœbe, the servant (Deaconess) of the Church in Cenchrea to the Roman Christians. The older commentators on 1 Tim. iii. 11 (even so must [*their*] wives [*Greek*, women] be grave, not slanderers, sober, faithful in all things) held from the general connection of the passage that, whether these women were the wives of Deacons or not, they were admitted to the order of Deaconesses. Virgins who were formed into an order were also admitted, but so generally were widows, that the term to enter into the widowhood was often synonymous with being made a Deaconess. There are many references to them both in the Fathers and in the Canons from the time of Ignatius (107 A.D.) to the tenth century, though after the fifth century they began to decline in the West. In the East they lasted till at least after the Council in Trullo, 692 A.D. The office was appointed to aid in the Church's work under the existing customs of that age, when women could better minister in many ways to these sisters in the faith, in giving them instruction under circumstances when it would be either impossible or not proper for the Priest or Deacon to do so; to prepare them for the rite of baptism; to minister to the sick and needy; to venture into the prisons to the confesors and martyrs there, when it would be too dangerous for the Priest to go unnecessarily; to exercise some supervision over the order of virgins and widows not in this office. The setting apart with imposition of hands which they received was clearly understood to convey or to imply the gift of no sacerdotal functions. They could not baptize or discharge any part of the public worship which was the part of men to do. As long as the Church work demanded their aid they were useful, but under the changed conditions of a Christianized empire, and when afterwards so many of their active duties could be discharged by the then better controlled order of nuns, their office was dropped, and their work transferred to the rival order. (*Vide* Smith's Dict. of Chr. Ant., Wordsworth on Acts xviii. 18, and on 1 Tim. iii. 2, Bingham, ii. § xxii.)

The order has been revived and used to quite an extent in the Church in late years. Using the term in a wide sense, excluding from it the sisterhoods strictly living under rigid rule, but including some not strictly Diaconal, the outline history of the movement is somewhat thus: In 1845 A.D., Dr. Wm. A. Muhlenberg organized the Sisterhood of the Holy Communion, which was thus the first association of women in the Anglican Church. In 1855 A.D. the Bishop of Maryland instituted the order of Deaconesses in connection with St. Andrew's Parish in Baltimore. The General Convention of 1859 A.D. roused much interest in this work, which was checked at first by the civil war, but this ultimately afforded a practical training for future workers, and furnished a mass of very valuable experience. In 1864 A.D. a very able report, with a large mass of suggestive facts and useful hints, was presented to the Convention of the Diocese of Pennsylvania. Out of it grew the Bishop Potter Memorial House. In the same year Bishop Wilmer, of Alabama, instituted the order of Deaconesses in Mobile. In 1872 A.D. the Bishop of Long Island set apart seven "godly and well-tried women to the office of Deaconess." The order is also at work in Louisiana, and associate members of these Deaconesses are employed in other Dioceses. There are such orders now in five Dioceses in England. Space does not permit us to do more than give, in Dr. Howson's words, the general principles of the order: "(a) *Definition of a Deaconess.* A Deaconess is a woman set apart by a Bishop under that title for service in the Church. (b) *Relation of a Deaconess to a Bishop.* (1) No Deaconess or Deaconess institution shall officially accept or resign work in a Diocese without the express authority of the Bishop of that Diocese, which authority may at any time be withdrawn. (2) A Deaconess shall be at liberty to resign her commission as Deaconess, or may be deprived of it by the Bishop of the Diocese in which she is working. (c) *Relation of a Deaconess to an incumbent.* No Deaconess shall officially accept work (except it be in some non-parochial position, as in a hospital or the like) without the express authority of the incumbent of that parish, which authority may at any time be withdrawn. (d) *Relation of a Deaconess to a Deaconess institution.* In all matters not connected with the parochial or other system under which she is summoned to work, a Deaconess may, if belonging to a Deaconess institution, act in harmony with the general rules of such institution." And six English Bishops signed these suggested rules. "(a) *Probation.* It is essential that none be admitted as a Deaconess without careful previous preparation, both technical and religious. (b) *Dress.* A Deaconess should wear a dress which is at once simple and distinctive. (c) *Religious knowledge.* It is essential to the efficiency of a Deaconess that she should maintain her habit of prayer and meditation, and aim at continual progress in religious knowledge. (d) *Designation and signature.* It is desirable that a Deaconess should not drop the use of her surname, and with this end in view it is suggested that her official designation should be 'Deaconess A. B.' (Christian and surname), and her official signature should be 'A. B., Deaconess.' P.S.—It is desirable that each Deaconess institution have a body of associates attached to it, for the purpose of general counsel and co-operation." This paper, taken from the "Report on Woman's Work," read before the Board of Missions in 1871 A.D., contains many suggestions which are well worth careful study. As we have seen, the order has been tentatively employed in the Church with excellent results. But its relation to the Church has not yet been fairly defined. It is of course fully within the Bishop's power to institute it and to have it as a recognized association in his Diocese, but an effort has been made to obtain for it a wider recognition. In 1880 A.D. a committee reported to the General Convention a Canon, which was laid aside, and a Canon presented by the Bishop of Massachusetts was accepted by a large vote in the House of Bishops; but, owing to the late date of the session when it was sent to the Lower House, there was no time to consider it, and the subject, owing to the press of other business, was not considered at the Convention of 1883 A.D. But this proposed Canon may be given as the deliberate opinion of a majority of the Bishops: "*Resolved*, The House of Deputies concurring, that the following Canon be enacted, to be entitled Canon vi. of Title III., '*Of Organized Religious Societies within the Church.*'"

§ I. All organized Religious Bodies in this Church, of which the avowed object is the increase of holy living and of good works, and of which the members are in any manner set apart and specially devoted to such service of GOD in His Church, as orderly co-operation with CHRIST's ministers, the edifying of His Body, the Christian education of youth, and the promotion of works of mercy and charity, are hereby declared to owe allegiance to the doctrine and ritual of the Protestant Episcopal Church, whose professed representatives and agents they become; and also due recognition of, and obedience to, its constituted authorities. And without such allegiance and obedient recognition such organized bodies may not claim the sanction of this Church.

§ II. (1) Women of devout character and approved fitness may be set apart by any Bishop of this Church for the work of a Deaconess, according to such form as may be authorized by the House of Bishops, or, in default thereof, by such form as may be set forth by the Bishop of the Diocese.

(2) The duties of a Deaconess are declared to be the care of Our LORD's poor and sick, the education of the young, the religious instruction of the neglected, the reclaiming of the fallen, and other works of Christian charity.

(3) No woman shall be set apart for the

work of a Deaconess until she be twenty-five (25) years of age, unless the Bishop, for special reasons, shall determine otherwise, but in no case shall the age be less than twenty-one (21) years. The Bishop shall also satisfy himself that the candidate has had an adequate preparation for work, both technical and religious, which preparation shall have covered the period of at least one (1) year.

(4) No Deaconess shall work officially in a Diocese without the express authority in writing of the Bishop of the Diocese, nor in any parish without the permission of the Rector or Minister thereof.

(5) Deaconesses may be transferred from one Diocese to another by proper letters dimissory, at the request of the Bishop to whose jurisdiction they are to be so transferred.

(6) If a Deaconess should at any time resign her office, she shall not be restored thereto unless in the judgment of the Bishop such resignation was for weighty cause. And no Deaconess shall be removed from office by the Bishop except with the consent of two-thirds of the members of the Standing Committee of the Diocese duly convened.

(7) The Constitution and Rules for the government of any institution for the training of Deaconesses, or of any community in which such Deaconesses are associated, must have the sanction in writing of the Bishop of the Diocese in which such institution or community exists. All formularies of common worship used in such institution or community must have the like sanction, and shall be in harmony with the usage of this Church, and like the principles of the Book of Common Prayer.

§ III. (1) Devout women desirous of living in community, under rule, with sanction of the ecclesiastical authority, for the increase of self-consecration to GOD, and the better performance of the works of faith enjoined in the Gospel, may be formed into Societies with the consent of the Bishop; and such Societies, under the conditions named below, shall be recognized as Sisterhoods in this Church.

(2) The Constitutions and Rules of such Societies, prescribing their organic structure, the qualifications for entrance, the regulations for the common life, and the scope and methods of their work, must have the written approval of the Bishop then exercising jurisdiction in the Diocese; and the said Constitution and Rules, so far as thus approved, shall be unalterable by the same Bishop or by the Sisterhood within his Diocese, except by their joint act and agreement.

(3) The form and order for entrance into such Sisterhood shall be drawn up and prescribed by the Bishop of the Diocese, unless otherwise provided for by the House of Bishops.

(4) The Bishop shall have Episcopal supervision and canonical authority over Sisterhoods within his jurisdiction, and may act as Visitor thereof.

(5) Every such Sisterhood may have its Chaplain or Pastor, who shall be nominated by the Society within the Diocese, and approved by the Bishop; and who shall be a clergyman in Priest's Orders, canonically subject to the Bishop.

(6) In matters concerning only the Christian walk and conversation of the Sisters as individuals,—their personal concerns and private devotional life,—Sisters are free to govern themselves in the sight of GOD, so that all be done in the spirit and methods commended by this Church. But the formularies of common worship in a Sisterhood, and all devotional practices in such worship (other than as usual in this Church), and the books of devotion or religious instruction used in ministering to others, shall be subject to the examination and approval of the Bishop, and shall be in harmony with the usage of this Church and principles of the Book of Common Prayer.

(7) No Sisterhood shall send any of its members to another Diocese to work there except on the request of the Bishop of that Diocese, and with the consent of its own Bishop; nor shall any member of a Sisterhood work officially among the people of any parish of this Church without the consent of the Rector or Minister thereof.

Dean. The title of an ancient office in the Western Church, but only recently becoming current here, though the bearer of the title here is not properly a Dean. (*Vide* CONVOCATION.) The Canon Law recognizes four officials having a right to the title. The Dean, who has a Chapter of Prebendaries or Canons subordinate to the Bishop, as a council assistant to him in matters of religion and in matters temporal relating to his Bishopric. (Burn's Eccl. Law, vol. ii., *sub voce* Dean; *vide* also the article CATHEDRAL.) The second is held by a single person, the Dean of Battel, the abbey William the Norman founded to commemorate the battle of Hastings (1066 A.D.). It is presentative, has cure of souls, but has no Chapter. The third has attached no cure of souls, is a donative, and, having jurisdiction therefore, holds a court, and has a peculiar,—*i.e.*, is amenable only to royal or Archiepiscopal—visitation, as the Dean of Arches in London is exempt from the Bishop of London's jurisdiction, but under the Archbishop of Canterbury. The fourth office is that of the Rural Dean. Probably this last order really has a right to the title (*vide* RURAL DEAN), for "the spiritual governors, the Bishops, divided each diocese into deanries (decenaries, or tithings), each of which was the district of ten parishes or churches; and over every such district they appointed a dean, which in cities or large towns was called the dean of the city or town, and in the country had the appellation of rural dean." (Burn's Eccl. Law.) This principle of governing by tens passed into the monastic rule, and so was transferred to the colleges and universities. (*Vide* Coke on Lit., lib. ii. c. 134 and note.)

Death. The act of the separation of the soul from the body; the death of the soul; eternal death. It is the inevitable doom of all before the moment of the blast of the Trumpet. These shall have some change pass upon them, but all others shall first pass under the law. Death is the contrast to life. But two men in all human history have been exempted, Enoch and Elijah. It has always had a terror for the human mind; the unknown hereafter, the agony itself, the separation from all things we love, make it a dreadful act to many who are yet strengthened by the Christian's faith. The Scriptures represent and record these fears most faithfully, and give as the reason—Sin.

There are three kinds of death: the death of the body, which we can see; the death of the soul,—spiritual death; and the second, or eternal death. The death of the body as the result of sin is a merciful provision of the CREATOR, by which the consequences of sin might be checked, to those who place themselves within the Law of Grace and Life in CHRIST. Spiritual death, the death of the soul, does take place here by a voluntary self-deprivation of all the means of grace, by impenitence, and by the sin against the HOLY GHOST; in fine, by persistence in that state of trespasses and sins into which we are born by nature. Eternal death, the second death, the privation of blessedness in GOD'S presence, the outer darkness of our LORD'S Parable. Death is to be destroyed as it has been already conquered by CHRIST (1 Cor. xv. 26; Heb. ii. 14; Col. ii. 15), as indeed its power must cease when there are no more victims. He has taken away the true fear of death that lies in sin, yet He shrunk naturally as perfect man from the act of death, for it should have no power over Him except as He willed or submitted voluntarily to it.

Death of Christ. It was a real, true, not a phantasmic death. His soul left His body and went into the prison of departed spirits, but His divine nature, being incomprehensible, did not leave either soul or body. It was voluntary, 1st, because He foretold that it should be so, and upon the cross. He bowed his head and said, It is finished; 2d, because it was in a certain degree miraculous. He hung upon the cross alive but six hours, whereas the victim usually lingers three days; and His death He, as it were, announced by the loud cry, by His commendatory prayer, by bowing His head. It was a very and true death, and for us, that He might taste death for every man, that in soul and body He might know all that we undergo, even after death. Therefore it is most useful that His death as well as His passion, and His burial, are placed in the Creed as parts of our Christian Confession.

Decalogue. The ten words (the Hebrew title, also Ex. xxxiv. 28), title of the Ten Commandments; the covenant which was given to Moses on Mount Sinai by GOD Himself. The history of GOD's giving it to Moses and the form and contents are given in Exod. xx. It is repeated in Deut. v. There is but a single discrepancy between the two records. The fourth commandment is based in Exodus upon GOD'S rest after creation; in Deuteronomy it is based upon the deliverance from Egypt. There is no discrepancy in reality, since Moses is reciting them with a different purpose in Deuteronomy. Also, it may be noted that in the last commandment the clauses, Thou shalt not covet thy neighbor's house; thou shalt not covet thy neighbor's wife, are reversed in order in Deuteronomy, and also "his field" is inserted after house. The authoritative form is in Exodus. The division of the commandments into ten has been the subject of some controversy. The Church of England follows the division to which Philo (30 A.D.) gave currency; in this the Calvinistic bodies follow her, but the Lutherans do not. The Romanist joins the first and second commandments into one, and divides the last into two. If the covenant as given in Exodus is the authoritative form, and the one in Deuteronomy is only a repetition of it, then the division which the English Church uses is the most natural, and, for several reasons, the only one possible. The so-called preface is an independent command: "I am the LORD thy GOD. . . . Thou shalt have none other gods but me." A basis for the other commandments from which they flow naturally. In the second, on idolatry, the forbidding of the making of images is followed by prohibiting the worship of them, with a statement of the grounds for this prohibition. As for the last, the inversion of the clauses as noticed above shows that it is but one command. In fact, all other divisions do more or less violence to the sequence of the commandments.

There is some doubt as to how these were arranged upon the two Tables. Again, the grouping which we usually follow commends itself to us, since St. Paul throws the fifth commandment into the second division, though its contents make it a link binding the two groups together. The first four clearly relate to our duties to GOD. The fifth one, by the light thrown upon it by the Proverbs, where "father" and "mother" stand for GOD and the Church, makes a natural transition. Then, too, the family relation lying at the base of the Hebrew polity, it should properly make the first of the second sphere of duties,—to our neighbor. It is not the place here to go into it at any length, but the true foundation for all obedience was LOVE (Deut. vii. 9; Rom. xiii. 8 *sq.*). But the clear apprehension of this was denied by resting upon the other saying, "And it shall be our righteousness if we observe to do all these commandments before the LORD our GOD, as He hath commanded us."

But the covenant enacted for the Israelite extends to all as well, because its root is in the truest aspirations of our nature, and because practically our LORD, by commenting upon it in His sermon on the mount, made it binding upon us, as by the assumption both by St. Paul and by St. James that it is always in force. Therefore in its precise terms it is the covenant by which we are bound at our baptism, interpreted, it is true, by the love which our LORD threw over it. Its recital each Sunday in the service is therefore strictly in the line of instruction which the Church has followed,—the Creed, the LORD'S Prayer, the Ten Commandments put before us constantly, for they are *our* part of the baptismal covenant.

In reciting the Law at the point of the service where it is ordered, the English Church has added to the old Liturgical usage. There is no precedent for it in any of the ancient services which have come down to us. It is not the less a most excellent addition to the service, and forms an outline for instruction, that self-examination which is urged upon us in the exhortations to the Communion office.

At the close of each commandment as it is proclaimed to us (for that is the true office of the minister at that moment), there is placed the familiar response, "LORD have mercy upon us and incline our hearts to keep this law;" (and after the last one) "LORD have mercy upon us and write all Thy laws in our hearts, we beseech Thee." The first words are the ancient Kyrie eleison,—which is not so freely used in the English as in the Oriental services,—and a petition fitted for the commandments appended to it. The whole of this part of the ante-communion is a noble addition to the Liturgic services which the English Church has inherited.

Decree. Holy Scripture speaks of GOD'S purposes or decrees as being eternal, and clearly intimates that events are not fortuitous and accidental, but are known and foreordained by infinite wisdom. But this does not interfere with our perfect freedom to choose our line of action. The controversy is with those who hold to a strict predestination theory,—for, in our ignorance of His essential nature, theory only it must be, since as Bishop Butler acutely remarks, that though necessity may logically be, yet in practice we must act as though it did not exist. This controversy has been popularly overlaid with questions and side issues which do not belong to it, and there results a confusion as to the proper limits of true freedom. Putting aside for a moment our inability to conceive of GOD beyond what He has chosen to reveal to us, we may say that the leading consequences of any act—not the primal act itself—are unavoidable and irrevocable by us; that the general laws of nature and the limitations of our powers by the conditions of our creation and nature, bear also consequences which we cannot escape. Then the inferences and mutual oppositions which form separate and independent lines of action also must be thrown out. All of these belong to GOD'S foreknowledge; as, too, the secret springs of our character, the logical outcome of influences of which we may be unconscious, the heredity of certain tendencies, the limitation of education, which again depends upon the circumstances and conditions of a past not in our hands, and the proper sequences of those interposing acts, whether of mercy or of justice, which He in His infinite wisdom has seen fit to place at conjunctures in the history of our race. All these, too, are foreknown and must enter into His decrees, yet must be thrown out by us when discussing, what is really the gist of the whole controversy, the decree of election or rejection of each separate individual soul; we can only narrow down, not solve, the mystery. In throwing out these things above enumerated, we are only eliminating facts which, however complex they may seem to us, follow out the law of cause and effect. We do not thereby mean to overlook GOD'S presence in them, or His use of them. Their complexity is our puzzle, not His whose knowledge is infinite, and they do not properly fall within the popular conception of His will towards each separate soul of His creation. But it is clear that while we have left ample room for the play of our limited wills, we have taken out of the question much that has confused it. Now at this point GOD'S mercy is declared. He hath no pleasure in the death of a sinner. He willeth that all men shall be saved. He willeth that all men shall come to a knowledge of the truth, yet by the law of second causes and of consequences our minds are dulled, our perceptions and capacities are stunted. However secret and immutable His decrees are, they are founded upon His attributes, in His own perfect nature, and are involved in His foreknowledge and purposes to man in CHRIST JESUS. Yet they amply allow for the responsible use, through our will, of the faculties, capacities, and opportunities GOD has given to us in this our lifetime. The reconcilement of the two statements in Holy Scripture constitutes the mystery unfathomable to us in the present state of our powers. That it is reconciled must be believed, since truth is a fundamental concept of GOD.

Decretals. (I.) The False Decretals. The title of a compilation of Canons and Epistles from various sources, the larger part of which are wholly fictitious. The Papal Epistles, beginning with Siricius, are nearly all genuine; those preceding Siricius are forged. The Canons of the Provincial and Œcumenical Councils, as generally received, are genuine, but there are a large number of fictitious Synods included. The whole mass of both forged and authentic documents was put forth under the name of Isidore, Archbishop of Seville, but was put together probably near Rheims about the year 843–847 A.D. It was intended to meet the troubles and confusions in the Empire at that date. These troubles arose from the ambition of the Prelates, the covetousness of the nobles, and the general ignorance which lay over the mass of the people, many of whom had been but in comparatively recent times brought into the Church. Charlemagne's strong hand repressed these troubles, but his son Louis the Pious was unequal to the task he inherited. The forger thought that by an appeal to a distant power, which yet should have a spiritual authority, he could obtain the solution of the problem. So he made an appeal to Rome the final decision of all quarrels, and introduced the Papacy as the ultimate authority on Church law. This fatal basis brought in the doctrine of the Roman supremacy, hitherto disallowed and often disavowed by the Western Churches. But as his collection was admitted to have the highest authority its teachings were accepted, and so upon a forgery and a falsehood was founded the extension of those arrogant papal pretensions which led to the schism between the Eastern and Western Churches,—those superstitions and malpractices of the Middle Ages which brought on the Reformation and the innumerable sects, schisms, and heresies which have plagued the Church since. The authorship of the book is unknown, but it is probably the work of the same person who had already issued two collections of Capitularies, and was a partisan of the able Ebo of Rheims, whose troubles and deposition may have suggested the redresses, and the authority necessary to enforce them, which are taught in the False Decretals.

(II.) Decretals of the Popes, collected first by Raymond of Peñaflor, under Gregory IX., and afterwards enlarged by the addition of successive books,— *Decretales Epistolæ*, Gregory IX., *Liber Sextus, Clementinæ, Extravagantes Joanni, Extravagantes Communes, Liber Septimus*. Together with the *Decretum* of Gratian (which had been formed out of the labors and collections of previous Canonists since the time of the False Decretals), the whole collection forms the *Corpus Juris Canonum* of the Roman Church.

Dedication. Nearly equivalent to consecration in popular use. But there is a deep distinction. To dedicate is to set apart, as given to GOD. Tithes and offerings are dedicated. Samuel was dedicated to the LORD. To consecrate is to solemnly set apart, with an implied curse against sacrilege, a person, house, or thing to sacred and hallowed uses. Often a thing dedicated is perishable, a thing consecrated is permanent.

Degradation. Deprivation of an office. Really, to deprive of a step or degree of rank or honor. The Bishop, Priest, or Deacon is degraded for cause,—*i.e.*, his degree of office in the Church is taken from him. It varied in the proportion of the offense, as from temporary suspension to total deprivation. For the inferior orders the Bishop was the proper judge and executive officer. But finally the Synod of the Province became the proper tribunal. The crimes for which a clergyman could be deposed were (besides immorality, such as would exclude a layman) offenses against discipline, against doctrine, against the Church and its Ritual. The *form* used doubtless varied, but was accompanied with some significant rites, as depriving the offender of his robes, the vessels used in his office, and ending by scraping his thumb and hand, which had been anointed at his ordination. The act of the Church at this day is very simple. The causes for degradation (deprivation and displacing are its synonyms) are those recited above, and renunciation of the ministry. This deposition is an entire rejection from all office, not from a higher to a lower. Sentence is pronounced whether the offender be present or not, at some service appointed by the Bishop, and due notice must be given to every minister and vestry in the Diocese, and to all the Bishops and to the Standing Committee of any vacant Diocese; the notice specifying under what Canon the said minister has been deposed The Canons on deposition, Tit. ii., Can. ii., ¿ 2, Can. v., ¿ 1, Can. vi., ¿ 2, Can. viii., Can. x., ¿ 2, Can. xi., ¿ 2.

Degrees. (I.) Steps. "The Song of Degrees," the title to Ps. cxx.-cxxxiv. Either hymns sung by the Pilgrims to the Passover at Jerusalem, on their journey thither, or they may have been chanted upon the fifteen steps leading from the women's to the men's court in the Temple. The first explanation of the title is the most likely.

(II.) Steps of kinship. The law of nature forbids marriage within certain degrees. The law of morality, civil regard for social good, and the Church's regard for both, forbid still more remote degrees.

The Canon of the American Church is indefinite, simply forbidding that marriage which the law of GOD disallows. This may be made wider or narrower without further definition. For, *e.g.*, there is no law forbidding the marriage of a deceased wife's sister, yet it is prohibited by the construction of the English Canon law upon the Mosaic table of forbidden marriages (Lev. xviii.), and a bill to repeal it was recently defeated in the English House of Lords. The English Law of Prohibited Degrees is founded upon two rules of interpretation: (*a*) The term degree ascends as well as descends, and so all marriage in an ascending line, as well as in a descending line, must be prohibited; what is held of father or mother is true of grandfather or grandmother. (*b*) What degree is forbidden to the one sex is forbidden to the other also by parity of reason. If a woman is forbidden to marry her husband's brother, then the man is forbidden to marry his wife's sister, the degree of relationship being the same in both cases. Upon these two rules the English Law of

Marriage and Prohibited Degrees is framed. (*Vide* MATRIMONY, where the table of prohibited degrees is placed.)

Deification. This bold term, founded on 2 Peter i. 4, has been used by the Fathers occasionally to express the ultimate perfect union with CHRIST. CHRIST became man that we might be deified (St. Athan. or. De Incar., liv.). It is certainly implied in the common saying, The SON of GOD became the Son of Man that the sons of men might become the Sons of GOD.

Deipara. She who bore GOD, *i.e.*, the Virgin Mary, who was the mother of Him who is Eternal GOD, even the GOD-man JESUS CHRIST our LORD.

Deism is a term sometimes used to include all belief in a Divine Being, but this use of the word is incorrect. Deism is best defined by negatives, and strictly designates a form not of belief, but of unbelief. A Deist is one who, beginning from the position of Christian faith, has cast off everything that is peculiar to that faith, and holds only the belief in one GOD. He holds less than the faith of Israel even, who had the promise and miracles, and a history and sacrifices, and the Scriptures, and symbolizes with Mohammedanism, with which it also agrees historically, inasmuch as it was also in its origin a heresy and departure from Christianity.

At the same time it must be remembered that the Deists of the eighteenth century were never organized into a sect, had no creed or form of worship, recognized no leader, and were constantly shifting their ground, and even denying that they were anything but Christians. So that it is impossible to include them strictly under any definition. That which has been given is as near a definition as possible. Deism is what is left of Christianity after casting off everything that is peculiar to it. The Deist is one who denies the Divinity, the Incarnation, and the Atonement of CHRIST, and the work of the HOLY GHOST; who denies the GOD of Israel, and believes in the GOD of nature.

In dealing with the Christian religion the Deist, therefore, in the first place, puts aside as idle sentiment all that influence of the HOLY SPIRIT upon and within men which is expressed in the Scriptures by the terms " the new birth," " conversion," " the fruits of the Spirit," the " witness of the Spirit," and the like. Pentecost and all that it represents and commences is " unhistorical." Then next the Divinity and worship of our LORD is questioned and set aside for the time, if not absolutely, and he strikes off at once, professedly as a seeker after truth, but really in the spirit of an enemy, what we reckon as the " evidences of Christianity,"—miracles, prophecy, morality. It is easy to see how unfair such a course is, and how far from friendly or honest inquiry is such criticism, and also at what a disadvantage we put ourselves when we consent to such an arrangement of forces. We are really putting the main body of our forces into camp, and leaving the fortress and the leader to accept battle in the rearguard and among the baggage. For the miracles are not mere wonder-works, and the prophecies are not mere foretellings and extraordinary guesses, and the morality of the Old Testament or the wisdom of the New are not abstractions. But all have their key and source in CHRIST our LORD, without whom they are what sunlight would be without the sun. They all spring from Him, and are to be understood by Him and by faith in Him. They are evidences indeed, but they are the necessary and natural results of His presence; proofs certainly, but better seen as consequences. When unbelief makes its attack upon them, therefore, it must be fought off, and the battle with Deism in the eighteenth century ended in its confessed defeat. But the ground was not fairly chosen. The victory on the field of reason was won, but it was won as by soldiers who, at their enemy's challenge, laid aside the shield of faith and the sword of the Spirit.

The unbelief which sprang into life in England in the seventeenth century, and flourished and decayed in the first half of the eighteenth century, had its opportunity in the religious wars, the divisions of Christendom, and the weak divorce of culture from religion, which was one of the prevailing faults of Protestantism, while, on the other hand, the age was one of great intellectual activity and strongly disposed to free inquiry, and a time of great advance in natural science. In England all these causes were strongly at work, and the Church had need of all her strength to stem and direct the current into proper channels. But instead of being at her strongest, first the contest with Rome during and after the Reformation of the sixteenth century, and then the long and bloody struggle with Puritanism in the seventeenth, left the Church weakened, and prepared for almost any settlement which gave promise of peace. The bondage of the Puritans prepared for the rebound of wild license under Charles. A bitter spirit of controversy had been developed and was not laid. The people were determined upon one thing,—that the Church as established should not be disturbed. But from the time when English Church and English State alike were able to find no way of escape from their perplexities save by calling in William of Orange, an alien to both, and in his own eyes the conqueror of both, spiritual religion in England seemed to have fallen into a condition of decay. The people hated popery, and they hated whatever threatened to disturb Church or State, but religious life was at a low ebb, and unless men looked deeply enough into the matter to see in the Church something better than politicians and Erastian divines did see, the tendency of earnest thought was away from her rather than towards her. And out of these seething elements, and in no small part the result of them, arose the Deism of the eighteenth century.

The real Deists, that is, the writers who are known by the name, are only some twelve or fifteen in number, and there is hardly one of them who as a writer deserves a high place. But they were important for their representative character, as they evidently expressed the sentiments of a larger class, and said what many were only thinking, and as they represented a dangerous tendency of the age. And also for their effect upon the Church, in rousing Churchmen to a sense of the danger, and in bringing to the front a host of writers in defense of religion, chief among them Bishop Butler; and also for the effect of their writings in other countries, for from England went the teaching which through Voltaire went over into France, and from France into Germany, and developed into French atheism and German rationalism.

The first writer who can be reckoned as a Deist was one who made his attack upon Christianity long before the name of Deist had its special application,—Lord Herbert, of Cherbury (1581-1648 A.D.), the brother of the Christian poet and divine George Herbert. His argument was (1) that Christianity was not needed, natural religion was sufficient, and (2) that it could not be proved. But he included under natural religion a large part of Christianity,—the being of GOD, and His worship, morality, repentance, and future rewards and punishments. And he relates of himself that when he was in doubt whether to publish his work, he prayed for a sign from heaven, and suddenly it thundered. Hobbes (1581-1679 A.D.), the secretary of Lord Bacon, and the friend of Ben Jonson and Lord Herbert, was a materialist. His principal work is the "Leviathan," and the principles of his system selfishness and despotism. But in his earlier writings his ground was very much the same as that of the later Deists.

The first whose writings made any great noise in the world as a distinct attack upon Christianity was John Toland (1696-1722 A.D.), a convert from the Roman Catholic Church to dissent, whose first book was called "Christianity not Mysterious." He was in fact a pantheist, and went on from his first pretended defense of Christianity against its corrupters to open scorn of all religion and denial of a personal GOD. After him Collins (1713 A.D.) led in the attack upon prophecy in his "Discourse on Freethinking," which called out among others a crushing reply from Bentley, as Toland had brought out Stillingfleet. It is, by the way, a curious illustration of the result of controversy and of the inconsistent course of unbelief, that in his rejection of Daniel and his prophecies Collins takes the ground of denying all Messianic expectation, while later unbelief, e.g., Strauss, not only concedes such expectation, but makes our LORD to have taken constant advantage of it, and to have adapted His conduct to its demands. Woolston (1667-1703 A.D.) represents the assaults upon miracles, attacking them as incredible and absurd. He is distinguished by being probably the only man of all the infidel writers of England who ever suffered for his opinions at the hands of law. His blasphemies were such as to shock and scandalize all decent Christian people, and if ever blasphemy deserved punishment, his is such a case, though he better deserved a lunatic asylum than a prison. His story curiously illustrates one point of his and other infidel attacks in the conflict of evidence with regard to the place of his death; some witnesses certifying that he died in prison, others speaking of him as dying "in his own house." The two conflicting testimonies are reconciled by the fact that he purchased "the liberty of the King's Bench," and lived and died in his own hired house within the precincts of the prison. In Tindal (1656-1733 A.D.) Deism reached its climax. His book, "Christianity as Old as the Creation," in which his ground is that if Christianity has any truth in it as old as creation, if it adds to that old original truth it is an impostor and an upstart, brought out some one hundred and fifty answers, among them Conybeare, Leland, Foster, and, above all, Butler. Conybeare shows that Tindal confounded the Light of nature with the Law of nature, which men learn gradually and require aids to learn, and therefore the ground of a perfect knowledge is taken away. Butler met him with an argument of which J. S. Mill says, "from its own point of view it is conclusive. The Christian religion is open to no objections which do not apply at least equally to the common theory of Deism."

Chubb (1715-1747 A.D.) differs from other Deistic writers in making his attacks upon the New Testament, the Church, and the clergy from the ground of a working-man. At first he allowed revelation and a future judgment and held a high Unitarian view of the divinity of CHRIST; but he developed into denial of miracles, and even doubts about the sinlessness of our LORD and the wisdom of His teaching. Lord Shaftesbury (1713 A.D.) was regarded by his contemporaries as among the bitter enemies of Christianity, but he so veils his rancor under a pretense of playful irony that some have even claimed him as the friend of religion. Thomas Morgan (1743 A.D.) is noticeable for his attack upon the Old Testament, and his denial that JESUS ever accepted the part of MESSIAS in any sense. Morgan's sympathies are all with Solomon in his "tolerant old age," and with Jezebel as against the zealots of the law, while for Moses and the prophets and the Jews as a people he has nothing but scorn and contempt. His book ("The Moral Philosopher") appeared about the same time as Warburton's "Divine Legation of Moses." Dodwell, in his "Christianity not founded on Argument" (1742 A.D.), professes to speak as a Christian, and as such to cast aside reason and to depend on an irresistible light for his convictions; but he really casts scorn on all belief in the operation of the Spirit of GOD in the soul of man, and denies His operation in enlightening reason, and adding evidence which is above reason, but not against reason.

Dodwell therefore represents rather the skepticism which was the position of Bolingbroke (1678–1751 A.D.) and Hume (1700–1776 A.D.) and Gibbon (1737–1794 A.D.). Other writers are claimed on the same side, as, for example, Alexander Pope, whose sympathies were evidently with those who held Deistic views. But those which have been named were the principal ones, and with them and the replies to them the Deistic controversy in England came to an end, leaving the victory confessedly on the side of Christian faith. Of the Deistic writers there is no one who has deserved to be reckoned among England's great writers. Deism failed in England because it wanted enthusiasm, and because it had neither creed, polity, worship, nor accepted leaders; but also for another reason,—because it had opposed to it a Church which had all these, and which only needed rousing from its slumbers to make good use of them. Deism in England was never popular, and it never showed any *constructive* strength nor any ability to adapt the materials which it found at hand.

In France, on the other hand, when Voltaire went back from his residence in England and his friendship with Bolingbroke and opened the campaign of Deism, he found religion weakened not only by superstition and secret unbelief and open immorality, but bound by state despotism and darkened by ignorance of the Scriptures. The French infidels were brilliant and popular writers besides, and Voltaire was a practical reformer. He represents Deism and then skepticism, and later, in spite of his dying declarations, perhaps atheism. Rousseau comes nearer the position of Arianism or high Unitarianism. Helvetius, La Mettrie, Diderot, D'Holbach, were atheists; and against none of them did the Gallican Church or French Protestantism lift up a voice in reply. French unbelief had the field of literature all to itself.

Deism was introduced from England into Germany, and was fostered, and in its French form perhaps introduced, by Voltaire; and here the movement arose not out of grievances, but out of want of faith, was carried on within the Christian body, and resulted in a compromise that was, in fact, the victory of unbelief. It even took a definite name and called itself Naturalism, or Neology, or Rationalism, and, like New England Unitarianism, claimed to be a form of Christian doctrine. Unbelief in Germany is more learned, less irreverent, and develops towards pantheism and atheism less rapidly than elsewhere. Its spread among the people is more critical, more concerned with morals, and therefore less logical than French or even English unbelief.

The unbelief of the nineteenth century has in it very little of the Deistic form. It is more determined to get rid of the supernatural, and leave no room for faith of any kind, and so is more openly atheistic or pantheistic. This is equally the result of scientific research on one side and the distinct advance of the Church on the other, especially in England. And at the same time unbelief, in the nineteenth century has been compelled to change its ground with regard to the Church, and compelled to find an explanation for the manifest *facts* of Christianity, which it tries to do on natural principles. Of this form of unbelief Strauss is the best exponent in Germany, Renan in France, Mill in England.

Authorities: Abby and Overton, English Church of the Eighteenth Century, Cairn's Unbelief in the Eighteenth Century, Aids to Faith.

REV. L. W. GIBSON.

Delaware. The first services in this Diocese were held by Swedes (*vide* PENNSYLVANIA) in a church within Fort Christina (Wilmington) 1638 A.D., nearly fifty years before the founding of Philadelphia. The first missionary was Rev. Rocus Torkillus. In 1667 A.D. Crane Hook Church was built, a mile and a half from the fort. In 1697 A.D., Rev. Ericus Biorck writes: "Their unworthy minister, clad in my surplice, delivered my first discourse to them in JESUS' name." In 1699 A.D., Trinity Church (Old Swedes') was consecrated. It is still used for service. There was intercommunion between the English and Swedish Churches, the English clergy being missionaries of the Propagation Society. Trinity Church owned five hundred acres where Wilmington stands, but the property was given out in interminable leases. In 1749 A.D., Rev. Israel Acrelius, who wrote a history of the Swedish congregations in America, was rector of Trinity Church. After the Revolution, in 1791 A.D., Provost Girelius, then in charge of Trinity Church, returned to Sweden. The Swedish Archbishop, Uno von Toerl, writes affectionately to the Swedish congregations in America concerning their separation from the mother-country, which was now to take place. He expresses the good wishes of the king, and adds his own prayer for GOD's blessing on "the members of the congregations, and that the Gospel light, which, under Divine Providence, was first kindled in these parts by the tender affection of Swedish kings and the zealous endeavors of Swedish teachers, may there, while days are numbered, shine in perfect brightness, and bring forth fruit to everlasting life." With such loving messages closed the work of the Swedish Church, and the parish naturally fell into the care of the Episcopal Church. A debt of gratitude is due to Sweden for these early foundations, built by laborious and self-denying missionaries in this foreign country. In 1792 A.D., Rev. Jos. Clarkson was elected rector of Trinity Church. To go back to the missions of the English Church in Delaware: In 1703 A.D., Gov. Nicholson, of Virginia, who had built churches in several colonies, was building a church in New Castle (Immanuel). In 1704 A.D., Rev. Thos. Crawford was sent to Dover by the Propagation Society. "The glebe lands were presented by Col. Jno. French of New Castle, a devout member of the Church." In 1705 A.D. Rev. Geo. Ross was missionary at New Castle. This year St. Ann's, Appoquinimink, or Middletown, was built. In 1708 A.D. the first church in Dover was finished. This year Rev. Mr. Jenkins died, after only five months of successful work in Appoquinimink. In 1716 A.D., Mr. Richard Halliwell bequeathed to Immanuel Church, New Castle, sixty pounds and his marsh and plantation for the use of the ministers of the parish. In 1716–17 A.D., St. James' Church, White Clay Creek, was built,—Mr. Jas. Robinson gave a few acres of land as a glebe. In 1717–18 A.D., Rev. Geo. Ross, with Gov. Keith, visited Lewes, and Kent and Sussex Counties, "preaching and baptizing large numbers." In 1721 A.D., Rev. Wm. Beckett was appointed for Lewes and adjacent parts. In 1729 A.D., Rev. Walter Hackett was at Middletown. He died in 1733 A.D. "He had been a very laborious missionary." In 1742 A.D., "Rev. Wm. Beckett speaks of his four churches in Sussex as being filled on Sundays and holy-days." In 1749 A.D., Rev. Hugh Neill was missionary at Dover. He catechised a class of one hundred negroes on Sunday evenings, and baptized one hundred and nine adult negroes. Rev. Geo. Ross died in 1749 A.D., aged seventy-five years, having "labored most zealously" in New Castle and through the three counties. In 1757 A.D., Rev. A. Cleveland, lately appointed to New Castle, died at the house of Benjamin Franklin. Franklin's newspaper contained an article highly commending the good man. In 1758 A.D., Eneas Ross, son of Geo. Ross, is settled in New Castle. In 1759 A.D., Rev. Chas. Inglis takes charge of Dover. In six years he baptized in Dover and its vicinity seven hundred and fifty-six children and twenty-three adults, and the communicants increased from forty-nine to one hundred and fourteen. He afterwards became Rector of Trinity Church, New York, and at a later period Bishop of Nova Scotia. The year 1766 A.D. was memorable for the loss by shipwreck of Rev. Messrs. Giles and Wilson, who were returning from England to assume the missions at Dover and Mispillion. In 1782 A.D. the Revolution closed the work of the Propagation Society, which had so long blessed these shores. The first Diocesan Convention met in Dover in 1791 A.D. In 1793 A.D., Bishop White confirmed sixty-three in Trinity Church, Wilmington. In 1803, Bishop Claggett confirmed in the same church. In 1822 A.D., Bishop White, assisted by Bishop Kemp, consecrated Immanuel Church, New Castle. Rev. Robert Clay resigned this parish in 1824 A.D., after a rectorship of thirty-six years. St. Andrew's, Wilmington, was consecrated by Bishop White in 1829 A.D. Bishop H. U. Onderdonk consecrated Trinity Chapel, Wilmington, in 1830 A.D. St. Andrew's Church was burned in 1840 A.D., but rebuilt the same year. On May 26, 1841 A.D., Rev. Alfred Lee was elected Bishop.* After visiting the parishes, he accepted the election, which was unanimous. On October 12 of this year, during General Convention, he was consecrated in St. Paul's Church, New York, Bishop Griswold acting as presiding Bishop. By this act Delaware was withdrawn from the care of the Bishops of Pennsylvania. One of the first tokens of new life was the repairing and reopening of "Old Swedes' Church" in 1842 A.D. In 1843 A.D. St. Luke's, Seaford, was finished and consecrated, and St. John's, Little Hill (Greenville), was repaired and consecrated. St. Paul's, Georgetown, was consecrated in 1844 A.D., and St. Thomas', Newark, the next year. In 1847 A.D. the Chapel of the Comforter, Long Neck, was consecrated, and the same year St. Ann's, Appoquinimink, was repaired and consecrated. The next year St. Mark's, Millsborough, was consecrated, and in 1850 A.D. St. Philip's Chapel, Laurel, received consecration. 1853 A.D., May 20, Grace Church, Baltimore Mills, consecrated. 1854 A.D., September 14, Church of the Ascension, Claymont, consecrated, under the rectorship of Rev. Dr. J. B. Clemson. 1855 A.D., January 14, St. Andrew's, Wilmington, enlarged and reopened. The Bishop is the Rector of this church. 1856 A.D., Christ Church, Christiana Hundred, opened. The chief projector and founder of this church was Alexis I. Du Pont. He died in 1857

---

* The Right Rev. Alfred Lee, D.D., D.C.L., was born in Cambridge, Mass., September 9. 1807 A.D. Graduated at Harvard 1827 A.D. He studied law and was admitted to the Bar in New London, Conn., where he practiced two years. Graduated from General Theological Seminary, New York, 1837 A.D. Ordered Deacon May 21, 1837 A.D. Ordained Priest June 12, 1838 A.D. Officiated a few months in St. James', Poquetonnuck, Conn., in 1838 A.D. In September, 1838 A.D., became rector of Calvary, Rockdale, Pa., where he remained until his elevation to the Episcopate. Received degree of S.T.D. from Trinity, Hartford, 1841 A.D., and from Hobart, Geneva, same year. In 1860 A.D. received same degree from Harvard, and in 1877 A.D. that of LL.D. from Delaware College, Newark. Consecrated first Bishop of Delaware, in St. Paul's Chapel, New York, October 12, 1841 A.D., by the Right Rev. Alexander Viets Griswold, S.T.D., the Right Rev. Richard Channing Moore, D.D., the Right Rev. Philander Chase, S.T.D., the Right Rev. Thomas Church Brownell, S.T.D., the Right Rev. Henry Ustick Onderdonk, S.T.D., the Right Rev. William Meade, D.D., and the Right Rev. Charles Pettit McIlvaine, S.T.D. In 1842 A.D. became rector of St. Andrew's, Wilmington, which position he still holds.—(*Living Church Annual.*)

A.D., having first founded St. John's Church, Wilmington. Christ Church, Delaware City, was consecrated in 1857 A.D. The succeeding year witnessed the consecration of St. Mark's Church, Little Creek. 1858 A.D. St. Peter's, Lewes, consecrated. St. John's, Wilmington, consecrated after the death of its founder, A. T. Du Pont, 1860 A.D. Christ Church, Dover, renewed, and consecrated. 1863 A.D., Calvary Church, Brandywine Hundred, consecrated. Christ Church, Milford, was rebuilt, during the rectorship of Rev. J. Leighton McKim, in 1866 A.D. St. James' Church, Newport, under the rectorship of Rev. W. D. Hanson, was opened October 23, 1875 A.D., and St. John Baptist, Milton, in 1877 A.D. The new Grace Church, Brandywine Hundred, was opened July 4, 1875 A.D. June 1, 1880 A.D., St. Andrew's, Ellis's Grove, was opened under the care of Rev. G. W. Johnson. St. Paul's, Georgtown, having been rebuilt, under the rectorship of Rev. B. T. Douglas, was opened in 1881 A.D. In 1882 A.D. the new Trinity Chapel, Wilmington, was opened, having been built in the rectorship of Henry B. Martin, M.D.

The only General Convention which ever met in Delaware assembled in 1786 A.D. in Wilmington. It had ten clerical and twelve lay deputies from six States. The call for the first Diocesan Convention came from Rev. John Bissett, Appoquinimink, and the vestry of Christ Church, Dover. Several years before a summons had been issued, but there is no evidence of the assembling of a Convention. In 1803 A.D., in Convention, Rev. William Pryce was commissioned to attend the Maryland Convention, and propose the election of a Bishop for Delaware and the Eastern Shore of Maryland. The Maryland Convention deemed this "inexpedient." In 1821 A.D., Rev. Richard D. Hall, of Trinity Church, Wilmington, reports two confirmations by Bishop White, the whole number confirmed being one hundred and sixty-three. In 1838 A.D., Bishop Onderdonk ordained three Presbyters in St. Ann's, Appoquinimink,— Rev. John Linn McKim, Rev. William Nelson Pendleton, and the Rev. William James Clark. When the first Diocesan Convention met in 1791 A.D., it had but three clergymen in it, viz., Rev. Messrs. Thorne, Bissett, and Skelly. Bishop Lee speaks highly of the work of the early clergy in Delaware, from the beginning of its history, and their work in . connection with the laborers of after-years, under GOD, shows an improving state of things to-day, as the following statistics will make evident. The Bishop has prepared a table extending from 1841 to 1881 A.D. Churches. consecrated, 23; built, 24; enlarged, 8; baptisms, 10,082; confirmed, 4327; ordained Deacons, 35; Presbyters, 31; parishes, 27; churches and chapels, 36; ministers canonically resident, 29; candidates, 2; Sunday-school teachers, 290; scholars, 2500.

Statistics for 1886 A.D.: Clergy, 29; parishes, 27; missions, 11; ordination, pr., 1; baptisms, 265; conf., 162; com., 2282; contr., $44,328.78.   REV. S. F. HOTCHKIN.

Demiurge. The Gnostic imaginary Disposer of the Order of the Universe. The title was used by Plato, was transferred by Philo as a sub-title descriptive of the CREATOR, was taken up by the New Platonists, and so was transferred by the Oriental fancies of the Gnostics to their wild theories. The Gnostic (vide ÆON) imagined a Supreme Being from whom, by successive emanations (in some 365 degrees), at last wisdom was reached, from whom sprung the Demiurge, the shaper of the universe.

Demoniacs. Whenever, in the English Authorized Version of the Old Testament, the word "devil" occurs, and in two-thirds of the cases in the New Testament, it signifies not Satan, of whose name it is the equivalent, and to whom it, by rights, should have been restricted, but one of those subordinate spirits of whom he is the "prince," and instead of "devil" we should read "demon." Of the "woman who had a spirit of infirmity" the LORD said, "Satan hath bound her" (St Luke xiii. 11), and certain sufferers are said to be "oppressed of the devil" (Acts), but no man is ever said to "have" or be "possessed by" Satan, always by a "demon," or "demons" (Acts), by "evil" and "unclean spirits," the "angels of the devil."

The history of the word is significant. In the Hebrew Scriptures, on several occasions objects of false worship are mentioned, and always in terms of contempt, but sometimes by names which perhaps really indicated the idol form, sometimes the regard in which the heathen held them (Lev. xvii. 7; 2 Chron. xi. 15; Isa. xiii. 21), sometimes apparently by the titles which their worshipers gave them,—"goats" or "satyrs," "idols" or "images,"—lords" (Ps. xcv. 5; Deut. xxxii. 17; Ps. cvi. 37). Among the Greeks daimon was a general term by which to designate all spiritual authority. It was applied to the gods, to the deified heroes, to guardian spirits. It included also all evil powers; but the term was one suggestive in the mind of the heathen of neither evil nor dishonor. (Vide Acts xvii. 18, 22.) Nor probably would any one of the titles used by the Hebrew writers have been objected to by a heathen. But to the mind of an Israelite believing in the one GOD, holding that idols were abominations, and the deities of the heathen, spirits of evil, intercourse with whom ("familiar spirits") (Lev. xx. 27; 1 Sam. xxviii. 8) was deadly sin, every one of these titles involved the idea of evil. And when he used the word daimon or daimonion he meant a wicked spirit, a "lying spirit" like him that spoke in the prophets of Ahab, an "evil angel" such as the LORD sent to punish Israel (1 Kings xxii. 22; Ps. lxxviii. 49); albeit he did not speak of these as demons unless they became objects of worship. It is in this special sense that St.

Paul uses the word when he tells the Christians of Corinth that the heathen sacrifices to idols are " sacrifices to demons and not to GOD, and ye cannot drink the cup of the LORD and the cup of demons : ye cannot be partakers of the LORD's table and of the table of demons" (1 Cor. x. 20, 21), while that which he cast out of the damsel at Philippi is entitled not a demon, but a "spirit of pytho," or " of divination" (Acts xix. 19). The use of the term in Tobit is more general (Tob. vi. 7, 17), but not like that with which we are familiar in the Gospels.

The difference in respect to the use of the term in its different forms is very marked. The revelation of the truth about Satan and his angels, the kingdom of darkness, is part of the revelation of the truth in CHRIST, and it comes upon us with a burst of light. The state of things into which we are introduced by the Gospels, when the "possession by demons," "having unclean spirits," was a common and recognized form of affliction, and so dealt with by our LORD that there is no possibility of doubt upon the subject without denying His truthfulness,— this state of things is in respect of the knowledge and acknowledgment peculiar. It seems not unreasonable that the powers of evil should have been given a special license just at this time in order that at their very worst they might be met by Him and overthrown ; but certainly one great difference between that time and the times before and after, lay in the great flood of light which poured in upon it with the SAVIOUR's presence.

It is noteworthy that St. John in his Gospel rarely names Satan, and any form of *daimon* only occurs when the enemies of the LORD bring the charge and He repels it, that He "hath a demon." Nor does he once in his Gospel refer to any "spirit" that is unclean or evil, and only once in his first Epistle (1 John iv. 3), where he repeats almost the very words of St. Paul concerning spiritual gifts (1 Cor. xii. 1, 3). Writing later and for a generation which always had the other three Gospels, his record took the form rather of a complement than of a repetition of the others. But in the earlier Gospels the dealing of our LORD with the demons and with those who were possessed by them occupies a prominent place. St. Matthew records how at the beginning of our LORD's ministry "they brought unto Him all sick people that were taken with divers diseases and torments, and those which were possessed with devils, and those which were lunatick, and those that had the palsy" (St. Matt. iv. 24). " They brought unto Him many that were possessed with devils, and He cast out the spirits with His word, and healed all that were sick" (St. Mark i. 34).

In the synagogue at Capernaum there was a man " who had a spirit of an unclean devil, and he cried out, Let us alone ; what have we to do with thee, JESUS of Nazareth ? I know Thee, who Thou art; the Holy One of GOD" (St. Luke iv. 34), and he was one of many whom He rebuked and suffered not to speak, because they knew that He was CHRIST. " In the country of the Gergesenes there met Him one possessed of devils," " who came and worshiped Him, crying out and saying, What have we to do with Thee, JESUS, Thou SON of GOD ? Art Thou come hither to torment us before the time ?" (" The devils believe, and tremble," St. James says, ch. ii. 19). "And JESUS asked him, what is thy name ? And he said, Legion, for we are many. And they besought Him that He would not send them out into the abyss." And at the command of JESUS " the unclean spirits went out and entered into the swine, and the herd (of about two thousand) ran violently down a steep place into the sea." And " the man out of whom the devils were departed was found sitting at the feet of JESUS, clothed, and in his right mind" (St. Matt. viii. 28 ; St. Mark v. 1; St. Luke viii. 26). "They brought to Him a dumb man possessed of a devil, and when the devil was cast out the dumb spake" (St. Matt. ix. 32). He cast out " an unclean dumb and deaf spirit that had possessed one from a child," so that he was lunatic and sore vexed" (St. Luke ix. 42), "and rent him when he came out of him, so that they said, He is dead" (St. Matt. xvii. 18) : " out of Mary Magdalene seven devils" (St. Mark xvi. 9) : out of the daughter of the Syro-Phœnician woman a devil, " an unclean spirit" (St. Mark vii. 26). But not only did CHRIST Himself exercise this power over unclean spirits. He committed it to His disciples, and " even the devils were subject to them in His name" (St. Luke x. 17). Nay, He foretold that men should " in His name cast out devils" whom He "never knew" (St. Matt. vii. 22). Some form of exorcism was indeed practiced among the Jews during our LORD's ministry, which He recognized by His question, " By whom do your sons cast them out?" (St. Luke xi. 19), as, on the other hand, they recognized His power by their charge, "He casteth out devils through Beelzebub, the prince of the devils" (St. Matt. xii. 24, 27). His promise of power was fulfilled when in Samaria, at the word of St. Philip, "unclean spirits, crying with loud voice, came out of many that were possessed" (Acts viii. 7). Afterwards in Philippi, at the word of St. Paul, the "damsel possessed with a spirit of divination" was healed (Acts xvi. 16). And later still, when at Ephesus evil spirits were cast out by the hands of the Apostle, who resisted the authority of the Jewish exorcists (Acts xix. 12). In one of his latest epistles the Apostle warns against "seducing spirits and doctrines of devils" (1 Tim. iv. 1). " Worship of devils," to be misled by "the spirits of devils," is a sin of the last times ; to be " the habitation of devils," the fate of Babylon fallen (Rev. ix. 20 ; xvi. 14; xviii. 2).

Briefly to recapitulate the main points gathered from these passages. The active working of demons—angels and agents of Satan—is recognized in the Old Testament. But their greatest activity was shown in the time of our LORD'S manifestation on the earth. Then they took "possession" of the souls and bodies of men. The "having" or being "possessed by a demon" was a condition to be recognized by certain signs, and though it produced disorder of mind and body, it was clearly and positively distinguished from ordinary physical and even mental disorders. The demoniac might be dumb or lunatic, but all dumb and lunatics are not demoniacs. Our LORD recognizes the fact by the plainest words and the plainest conduct. To question it is to impute to Him shameless falsehood. We do not know what in any case induced the affliction. It has been conjectured that it was prepared for by some habitual vice which weakened the will, and opened the way for the evil and unclean spirit to take captive the soul and body of the sufferer, but we have no reason to suppose that the demoniac was the most wicked of men. "Not the most wicked, but the most unhappy."

Nor is there anything in the condition which restricts it to those times. The work of evil spirits goes on and will. It is less open, but not less real. It may very possibly be that there are cases now in which persistent evil habit has put the will into the power of the evil spirit, and the man is driven into strange and evil ways in spite of himself (2 Tim. ii. 26). If there are such cases, they are very sad, and to human power hopeless. But if there is an evil power in the world, there is also a SON of Man, who "still hath power on earth." The hope of such must be not in ordinary human means, but added to them, in the religion, in the prayers which are offered, and the means of grace which are received "in His name," who most assuredly did not limit to one generation the promise, "in My name they shall cast out devils."

REV. L. W. GIBSON.

Deposition. *Vide* DEGRADATION.

Descent into Hell. (*Vide* CREED.) Our LORD'S descent into the place of departed spirits is an article of faith, inasmuch as it involves the fact that in human soul and body He was in all respects as we are, sin only excepted, and that He was touched with all our infirmities, and went to the confines of all that can befall the soul upon which the law of separation from the body has passed, and from which He returned victorious (Col. i. 15; Eph. iv. 8, 9; Heb. ii. 14). But the space of time during which His soul was there was filled with the work St. Peter describes (1 Pet. iii. 18–20). This very-much-debated passage can really be taken only in its plain, common-sense meaning. There is no difficulty in recognizing the power of Him who is over all to do as He will with all souls. That souls can and do know, remember, and reason is admitted. Why these souls in prison were selected of all others we need not too curiously inquire, since His infinite wisdom is too abundantly proved for us to doubt the perfect justice and mercy of this act. The doctrine in question has been explained away chiefly on two grounds, both apparently well founded, but both untenable. First, it implies the power of repenting after death. The reply is, that the impossibility of repentance beyond the grave is rather a just and equitable deduction, by applying our present condition to what is told us of the future, than an express dogma of Holy Scripture, and therefore its limits are not really known to us; but, that in this case, if this conclusion were drawn, it would be determined only for those who were sometime disobedient, when once the long-suffering of GOD waited in the days of Noah; and, secondly, it is urged that it gives some countenance to the doctrine of purgatory. Rather, it expressly does *not*, for the underlying principle of purgatory is that it is a place of cleansing and purification by fire, or other disciplinary pain, and there is not the slightest ground for this in the text of St. Peter. Rather, for these souls, the tone of the eighty-eighth Psalm should be the one for us to feel in interpreting so difficult a passage.

The article was placed in the Creed probably about the middle of the fourth century. It probably owes its prominence to the Apollinarian controversy (*vide* APOLLINARIANS), when it was necessary to strongly assert the existence of our LORD'S soul as distinct from His divine nature.

The Third of the XXXIX. Articles had originally a clause in addition. As it now runs we have it, "As CHRIST died for us, and was buried, so also it is to be believed that He went down into Hell." It continued thus: "for the Body lay in the sepulchre until the Resurrection, but His Ghost departing from Him was with the hosts that were in prison or in Hell, and did preach to the same, as the place in St. Peter doth testify." (Browne on the XXXIX. Articles.)

Desk. The "pulpit or pew" from which the prayers are said in many churches, which still retain the furniture common forty years ago. It was an innovation which, beginning in the minor contentions in the latter years of Edward VI., was given way to gradually till James I.'s time, when it became universal. It is now generally disappearing, and the older, more sightly, and reverent stalls are taking its place.

Deuteronomy. The second giving of the Law upon the "plains of Moab this side Jordan." The wanderings of the people had now drawn to a close. The forty years were almost ended, and Moses, knowing that he could not cross over into "that good land," recapitulated to the Israelites a rapid outline of the history of their life in the wilderness from the giving of the Law to that moment. It included a repetition (with additions) of the legal and ritual directions and a series of solemn warnings, closing both with an awful prophecy, which was fulfilled in the final destruction of Jerusalem, and with a song of triumph and thanksgiving. The last verses were added of course by some later hand. Before giving the analysis of the book, we will add that though its Mosaic authorship has been denied, this denial would seem to come out of a mere spirit of contradiction. The natural, even necessary, change of style from the historical to the rhetorical has been alleged as a proof that it could not be by Moses. The apparent discrepancies of statement are inevitable when the chronicler in his record sets down leading facts, but when reciting the same general series of events before an audience familiar with the history, nay, actors in it, he naturally neglects the full account of the leading events and mentions secondary facts connected with them. To the audience, there would be no discrepancies, but to us, unable to harmonize the allusions, they seem contradictory. So far as a close examination of the various theories against the Mosaic authorship can be made, it may be confidently denied that they have the slightest ground. A minute criticism, gathering many little seeming contradictory facts, may construct a theory but cannot present a formal case. (*Vide* PENTATEUCH.)

There are three main discourses, in which the history of the people and the legal, religious, and ceremonial laws are repeated.

I. The first discourse (ch. iv. 43) is mainly historical, and rapidly recites the events from the giving of the Law to that moment, mentioning incidentally the contests with the various tribes and peoples in the course of their wanderings. It is rapid, easy, connected, but very concise, and has some allusions which are not recorded in the fuller history.

II. The second discourse (ch. iv. 44; xxvi. 19) recapitulates the various enactments yet with modifications and additions, and is full of zeal and ardent enthusiasm. It lifts up the obedience of the people into a higher plane. It supposes that the discipline of the wilderness, the death of the disobedient by the way, the proofs of GOD'S love, and the abiding presence of the pillar of light and cloud had warmed and inflamed their hearts. Warned that they were obstinate in character, they were urged to love and obey because of GOD'S love and mercy. The laws originally given as for a wandering people, are here and there modified a little to suit their settlement in Canaan. Altogether it is difficult to conceive how a man of the mighty ability and the vast experience of Moses, one who had been the agent of GOD in such wondrous miracles, who had intrusted to him the training of the infancy of a nation, could speak to them with any less fervor when he was about to be separated from them. Filled with the HOLY GHOST, burning with zeal and love for the people, surely language was too poor to convey all he would pour forth out of a full heart, now that he was to be separated from them. Every law that is recited to them has behind it, and pulsing through the words which contain it, the overflowing heart of the Lawgiver. The ten commandments, the religious law; the fear of idolatry, the need of obedience; the ritual law of feasts and (naturally) the flesh allowed in them; their tithes and offering; the seventh year and the Jubilee; the feasts of the Passover, the Pentecost, and the Tabernacle,—form the section on the religious law. The rules for judges and the administration of justice, the regulation for a future king, the inheritance of the Levites, the prophecy of CHRIST the Prophet, the cities of refuge and the law of the avenger of blood, the law on perjury, on war, on homicides, on divorces, on the malefactor not to remain hanging all night, from the section on the political and criminal law. Then the social laws follow (ch. xxii.-xxvi.)

III. Then Moses associated the elders with him, and recited to the people the solemn forms of blessing and cursing which were to be recited upon Mount Gerizim and Mount Ebal. Then followed that awful passage beginning with the promise of abundant blessing, and passing on to the prophecy (the more terrible because we know how fifteen centuries later it was literally fulfilled) of the final punishment of their disobedience, and the destruction of Jerusalem. This discourse closed with a fervent appeal to the people to love and to obey. This is the last formal discourse of instruction, but there remained much more to do. The final arrangements for the leadership of the people, and the placing of the books of the Law in the side of the Ark, and His song and His blessing, were yet to be made and recorded (ch. xxxi.-xxxiii.). And Moses went up to the top of Pisgah, thence saw by the vision GOD gave him the extent of the promised land, and then (as the Jewish tradition beautifully phrased it) GOD kissed him, and so he died and the LORD buried him.

Devil. *Vide* SATAN.

Diatessaron. The Greek name for the harmony of the four Gospels. Tatian, it is said, introduced this mode of arranging the sacred narrative of our LORD'S life. (*Vide* HARMONY OF THE GOSPELS.)

Diet. The Assembly of the Estates in Germany. It had at one time in German history, during the Reformation, an active influence in public, especially in religious affairs. For details, the reader is referred to the Histories of the Reformation on the Continent; the dates only of the more notable ones are here given.

Diet of Worms, 1521 A.D. To which Luther was summoned, and to which he came under the safeguard of the Emperor. In this Diet he appealed to the Holy Scripture.

Diet of Nuremberg (I.), 1523 A.D. At which the *Centum gravamena* were presented, and where the idea of calling a Council was first agitated.

Diet of Nuremberg (II.), 1524 A.D. Where the proposition of the Council was further agitated by the Lutherans.

Diet of Spires (I.), 1526 A.D. Under the Archduke Ferdinand, in behalf of Charles V. The Lutheran Princes led in the debates. They succeeded in directing that every one was to have liberty of conscience, till a General or National Council could be summoned in Germany.

Diet of Spires (II.), 1529 A.D. The work of the Lutherans was undone; the states which had become Lutheran could remain so, but no other of the states could change. The preaching against Roman doctrine was prohibited, the Anabaptists were to be put to death. This undid so much of the work of the first Diet, that six of the Lutheran Princes and the deputies of fourteen imperial cities protested, in writing, against the decree, which they would not obey, and appealed to a General Council, to the Emperor, and to any other unprejudiced judge. Hence they were called from this solemn protestation PROTESTANTS, which the Lutherans first took and afterwards the Calvinistic bodies, and then it became a general term.

Diet of Augsburg (I.), 1530 A.D. Charles V. tried to reunite the Princes in the discussions on religion, and to combine the resources of the Empire against the Turk. Here the Elector of Saxony, with his confederates in religion, offered the famous Augsburg Confession. The general result was the resolve to wait for a General Council.

Diet of Augsburg (II.), 1547 A.D. The decisions of the Council of Trent, then in interrupted session, produced some dissensions, but the whole decision was left to the Emperor, but the Council decrees were acceded to.

Diet of Augsburg (III.), 1548 A.D. The Diet at which the *Interim* was drawn up.

Diet of Augsburg (IV.), 1550 A.D. The Emperor complained of the non-observance of the *Interim*, but the reply was that the Lutheran deputies were not admitted to the Council of Trent as had been agreed, nor was the compact that the Pope should not preside observed.

Diet of Ratisbon (I.), 1541 A.D. Held to effect a reconciliation between the Protestants and the Romanists. After much disputation nothing was effected. Five or six articles out of twenty-two were decided on, but the Diet came to no real decision.

Diet of Ratisbon (II.), 1546 A.D. None of the Protestant powers appeared. The Council of Trent was accepted in its sessions thus far held, and action was taken which led to a war with the Protestants.

Diet of Ratisbon (III.), 1557 A.D. A conference was attempted between the Roman and Lutheran divines, but it soon broke up.

Dignitary. One who holds an office or preferment in the Church, to which jurisdiction is attached.

Dilapidation. In the English Church the Archdeacon has full authority as to deciding upon the needs of repairing churches and the extent of the dilapidations. His monition, or that of the Bishop, is directed to the incumbent, who shall thereupon take steps to have the church or houses of the benefice properly repaired; and to this end he was to expend all proper moneys raised or given upon the Bishop's consent and approval.

Diocese. This is the name now commonly given to the territory over which one Diocesan Bishop's jurisdiction extends. When the Bishop is a Missionary Bishop, not elected by his own clergy and people, the territory under him is called a Missionary Jurisdiction. Until about the end of the third century the common term for a Bishop's jurisdiction was παροικία, or, as we now say, *parish*. Under Constantine the word "Diocese" meant a large aggregation of Provinces,—the same that was afterwards called an *Exarchate*, and still later a *Patriarchate*. The original Parish or Diocese grew out of the Bishop, who commonly began his labors in the chief city of the region. As he multiplied his clergy they naturally lived together with him, working from a common centre. When one building would no longer accommodate all, other buildings were erected, but—as is proved by the Bishop's throne occupying the same position in *each* of the ancient Basilicas—the Bishop was equally the head of each and all. The other clergy were sent by him, and continued to be under his constant direction,—the Bishop himself when present in any church being the usual celebrant, preacher, and minister of adult Baptism, as well as of peculiarly Episcopal functions. Some of the old Canons seem to make his position that of a real father, his clergy being his family. When separate Church buildings became so numerous that the family feeling was outgrown, and when churches became more frequent in the remoter country parts, then there gradually came what is now known as "the parish system." At first all the churches would be served by clergy sent from the Bishop's house, in some order of rotation fixed by him,—all the churches belonging equally to the Bishop. Alexandria was the first city where a separate Presbyter was attached to each church, in something like the modern relation of a rector of a parish. In process of time, it was found that this insured more thorough knowledge of individuals and a closer application of pastoral care, and eventually the separate parishes acquired separate funds and rights of their own; and the parish system—now more than a thousand years old—became in most respects what it is at present.

In this country the process of practical development was precisely the opposite. Instead of Bishops coming first and parishes long afterwards, the parishes came first, some of them being in existence more than an hundred years before there was a Bishop in the country. As a natural result, the position of parishes is much more clearly defined with us than the inherent rights of the Bishops. Before the Revolutionary war there was no "Diocese" in the country, the whole thirteen colonies—by a monstrosity of perversion and abuse—being considered a *part* of the "Diocese" of London, in England. After the war was over, the first attempt at organization was simply among the parishes that happened to be within the territory of any one "State." Nor did the parishes in any State, thus organizing, at first call themselves a "Diocese." They were simply "the Church in the State of Pennsylvania," or in the "State of New York," etc. This is the language of the Constitution as originally adopted in 1789 A.D., in which the word "Diocese" is only once used, and then as synonymous with "district." This is in Art. 4: "And every Bishop of this Church shall confine the exercise of his Episcopal office to his proper Diocese or district, unless requested to ordain, or confirm, or perform any other act of the Episcopal office, by any Church destitute of a Bishop." This formal style was maintained until the subdivision of New York into two Dioceses, in 1838 A.D., gave occasion for a change; and in that same year, in the Constitution the word "States" was struck out in every place except where it follows the word "United," and the word "Dioceses" took its place. There is, to the present day, no law of our Church regulating the organization of a Diocese in any State or Territory. The original Constitution provided that "A Protestant Episcopal Church in any of the United States not now represented may, at any time hereafter, be admitted on acceding to this Constitution." The Churches in *nine* of the States were represented at that General Convention of 1789 A.D.,—Connecticut, Massachusetts, New York, New Jersey, Pennsylvania, Delaware, Maryland, Virginia, and South Carolina. The Constitution also provided that "The Church in each State *shall be entitled* to a representation of both the clergy and the laity." There was no requirement fixing the number of clergy or parishes; but "A Church" in any "State" of the Union not then represented was to be admitted "on acceding to this Constitution." The proof of this "acceding," and of the election of the deputies appearing, was all. Not even a *vote of admission* was thought necessary. In this way Rhode Island made its appearance in General Convention in 1792 A.D., Vermont in 1811 A.D., New Hampshire in 1817 A.D., and others subsequently. At length there grew up the custom of "admitting" by vote of both Houses; but this vote *always* was favorable on proof of "acceding to this Constitution." Nothing else was required.

Meanwhile, the Constitution was changed so as to permit the organization of a Diocese in a Territory as well as in a State. There is absolutely no limit as to numbers either of clergy or laity in a State or Territory at the time of organization. Vermont was admitted when there were only two clergymen in the State, one of them being a Deacon, and *both* came to the General Convention of 1811 A.D., and were admitted without even a vote. Though any two or more clergy and parishes in a State or Territory may thus organize themselves into a Diocese, accede to the Constitution, and claim the right to be admitted into the General Convention, there is a canonical restriction in regard to the election of a Bishop of their own. This they cannot do until there shall have been, for a year before such election, at least six Presbyters settled over parishes, and qualified to vote for a Bishop; and six or more parishes represented in the lay order in the Convention electing. But this is the *only* restriction in the case of a new Diocese organized out of a State or Territory.

The case is entirely different, however, when the new Diocese is formed by subdividing an existing Diocese. This cannot be done without *first* getting the consent of the Bishop and Convention of the Diocese to be divided, and afterwards the consent of the General Convention. And the consent of the General Convention "shall not be given"—so says the Constitution—"until it has satisfactory assurance of a suitable provision for the support of the Episcopate in the contemplated new Diocese." When this phrase became law, its advocates said that it did not mean an endowment or Episcopal Fund; but it would be enough if the Bishop were to be the rector of a parish, or president or professor of a college, or was supported by assessments; and West Virginia and Southern Ohio were both admitted without one dollar of endowment, both these Dioceses supporting their Bishops by assessments. But there are still other restrictions: "No *such* new Diocese shall be formed which shall contain less than six parishes, or less than six Presbyters who have been for at least one year canonically resident within the bounds of such new Diocese, regularly settled in a parish or congregation, and qualified to vote for a Bishop. Nor shall such new Diocese be formed if thereby any existing Diocese shall be so reduced as to contain less than twelve parishes, or less than twelve Presbyters who have been residing therein and settled and qualified as above mentioned." And it is also declared that "No city shall form more than one Diocese." Nor is even this the whole. The Bishop may choose which of the Dioceses he will, the new or the old, and that shall be thenceforth his Diocese. If there be an Assistant Bishop, he may take as his own Diocese that which is not chosen by the Bishop, or he may choose to continue with the Bishop as his Assistant, with right to succeed him. Moreover, the Constitution and Canons of the old Diocese continue to be those of the new (except as local circumstances may prevent) until they may be duly altered by the Convention. There are several other restrictions besides, but not of so much importance as the above.

An American Diocese, as represented in its Convention or Diocesan Synod, consists of its Bishop (and Assistant Bishop, if there be one), who always presides when present; it includes also nearly all the clergy, and lay delegates from each parish. Some Dioceses restrict their clerical membership by excluding all who have not been in residence for six months or a year, as well as all who are not in active clerical duty, or whose parishes are not in union with the Convention. The Diocesan Convention elects its own Bishop, by a separate vote of both orders. It elects also a Secretary and Treasurer, as well as a Standing Committee, who are the Bishop's constant Council of Advice, and without their consent he can do no official act of much importance. The clergy and laity also elect their own deputies to General Convention, and their own Board of Diocesan Missions, who, with the Bishop at their head, conduct the business of Church extension within the bounds of the Diocese itself. At the Convention the Bishop is required to present a full account of his Episcopal work for the year preceding, and he suggests any matters which he may think expedient for the action of his Convention. A Diocese has no reserved rights which it can defend as against legislation by the General Convention. But its Constitution and Canons, though subordinate to those of General Convention, are binding, so that a clergyman of the Diocese is liable to presentment and trial for violating them. The Dioceses are by the Constitution required to provide the mode of trying Presbyters and Deacons. The vote by orders is found in all the Dioceses, so that neither clergy nor laity can infringe upon one another's rights. But very few of the Dioceses give to the Bishop a separate vote in legislation. He commonly votes as one of the clergy. But his influence is generally as strong as his veto would be. The Standing Committee is "the ecclesiastical authority" during the vacancy of a Diocese for all those parts of a Bishop's administrative duty which do not require Episcopal consecration for their validity. They have power to invite any Bishop to perform these Episcopal acts; or the Convention may put the Diocese provisionally under the charge of any Bishop. It is very common for Dioceses of any extent to be subdivided into Convocations, Deaneries, or Archdeaconries; which are chiefly of use in ascertaining, by actual experience, what may be the most convenient lines for future subdivision into smaller Dioceses.

A Missionary Jurisdiction does not elect its own Bishop, nor elect a Standing Committee, nor legislate for itself, nor send a full deputation to General Convention. In many respects its position is analogous to that of a Territory, as compared with a State, in our national political system.

REV. J. H. HOPKINS, D.D.

Diptychs. The tablets from which the roll of the names of the dead were read at the celebration of the Holy Communion. It was probably borrowed from the consular registers of magistrates. There was a class of Diptychs in which the register of the orthodox Bishops who had ruled the See was read. Exclusion from this list was often a punishment. St. Cyprian directs that one of the Bishops subject to Carthage should have his name dropped because of an infringement of Church Law. The better-known class of Diptychs was the roll of names of living and dead benefactors of the Church. These Diptychs became the basis for the Martyrologies. A prayer in the Mozarabic Liturgy is called Post Nomina, —*i.e.*, the prayer after the recitation of the names.

Directory. A book explaining and regulating Church ceremonials.

Disciple. The name borne by the followers of CHRIST in His lifetime. It included more than the Twelve Apostles. The name continued to be given till at last the title the Antiocheans bestowed upon them, of Christians, replaced it.

Discipline. In its fundamental principles the discipline of the Church in the United States is based on the few general directions contained in the New Testament and the primitive practices. In the application of those principles and in the use of particular methods there has been a considerable departure from early customs. The difference is due to many causes. At first the Christian Church stood surrounded by the customs, institutions, and especially the corrupting games and diversions of a heathen society. To these fascinating and seductive immoralities is due the rigid and precise system of ecclesiastical penalties and purgations well known to the student of Church history. The whole social constitution and manners being changed, the Church has resorted to different measures for preserving its honor and its purity. While diverse views are held as to the expediency of enforcing the obligations of upright and holy living by imposing penalties and disabilities, it is admitted on all sides that the spirit, tone, and convictions of the modern world are such as to render the infliction of ecclesiastical penalties extremely difficult. Theologians and divines differ widely on the question how far such penalties actually promote Christian truth and righteousness, even when they are practicable.

The discipline of the clergy is provided for in detail by the Canons. Reference to them shows that the object mainly sought is the maintenance of the character of the Christian ministry and the prevention of scandal and disorder in the Church through

DISCIPLINE   235   DISPENSATION

moral transgression. As with the laity, the discipline is rather corrective than punitive, seeking the welfare of the whole body rather than to measure out a proportionate pain to the transgressor. The law for the arraignment and trial of any clergyman or Bishop, with a specification of offenses, is drawn up with great particularity, and may be found in the "Digest." The offenses may be in doctrine or in practice. Trials for heresy are perhaps as rare as those for immorality, but proceedings are much oftener initiated for the latter than for the former. On confession or by default, clergymen suspended or deposed every year by Bishops. The rule prevails that a man shall be tried by his peers. The information and the court are found among the Clergy, who are supposed to guard both their own rights in their orders and their integrity. Minute precautions are appointed for the protection of the accused and the securing of justice in the sentence. Essentially the Bishop's function is judicial, though to some extent he has the powers of the grand jury, and the initiation or arrest of proceedings is largely at his discretion. Both from penalties for false teaching and bad living there may be restoration on a well-tested reformation or recantation. Thus far the efforts made in General Convention to establish Appellate Courts have not been successful, the best jurists not appearing to favor them. The public opinion of the Church and generally of the community sufficiently supports the judicial decisions of the Episcopate.

For the laity disciplinary authority is found in the few rather general directions on the subject (already referred to) scattered through the New Testament and in the Rubrics of the Prayer-Book, chiefly in those pertaining to the Office of the Holy Communion. As the highest privilege of the believer, and as the chief visible mark of his standing in the body, the LORD'S Supper naturally becomes a criterion of fidelity to the Head of the Kingdom. Admission to it is a kind of certificate of the individual disciple's continuance in faith and obedience. Rejection from it is both the deprivation of a benefit and to some extent a public mark of chastisement or rebuke. Laymen are not brought before a Church tribunal. There is no trial by "brethren." Under the responsibility of the power of the Keys, guided by the grace of ordination and by the wise and loving judgment of the Shepherds of the Flock, the Priesthood admits or rejects. While the voluntary non-communicant can hardly be said to suffer disgrace by not participating, after once being lawfully received, to be prohibited or suspended brings reproach and must be felt as a privation. In each case the Priest depends for his knowledge on all such means of inquiry and evidence as may be within his reach. From flagrant injustice he is restrained by the civil law of the land. His duties being extremely delicate and often extremely difficult, allowance has to be made for possible errors, especially where the case in hand is one where the law of the Church and the law of the State are not agreed, as happens frequently in the States as respects divorce and the relations of the sexes. Not seldom the legal complication prevents action where action ought to be taken. By a vast proportion the instances of moral dereliction unnoticed exceed those of hasty or unjust or excessive punishment. Looking simply at the question of probable good or evil resulting, thoughtful clergymen pause even when a *prima facie* case of guilt is made out. That the fear of what is sometimes called excommunication does hold in check a multitude of people of inferior moral and spiritual sensibility is indisputable; it hardly needs to be said that temporary suspensions at the private suggestion or requirement of the clergy are frequent. Church law allows all persons aggrieved in a sense of unmerited restraint to appeal to the Bishop of the Diocese, who, on inquiry and a full statement from the clergyman exercising discipline, may modify or remit the penalty. Such revisions and restorations are not very common. A laxer discipline than that which now exists would tend to lower the standard at least of outward piety without much raising the standard of charity. A discipline more rigorous and more active would require a catalogue of clearly-defined and universally-recognized moral offenses, apart from the Decalogue and the letter of the New Testament, which at present is not supplied.

RT. REV. F. D. HUNTINGTON, S.T.D.,
Bishop of Central New York.

Dispensation. The word has two distinct uses. The first describes the economies under which GOD has dealt with men, as the Patriarchal, the Mosaic, and now the Christian Dispensation. These have had clear covenant limits, and under the last every man is living, and by it Christians are bound. It is the dispensing to us of the rights, privileges, and blessings obtained for us by CHRIST, which He gives through His Church (Eph. iv. 7, 16). In a subsidiary sense the word is used to mean some particular act or event recognized as coming from GOD,—an act of Providence, or a dispensation of Providence.

The second use is the right—useful at times, and belonging to each Bishop—to relax for cause the rigidity of ecclesiastical discipline. Its force does not go beyond the act and for the cause specified, and is not to be taken as a precedent overthrowing the law, but as a precedent governing the limits under which future dispensations may be granted, and it ceases when the causes which justified it cease. But this right was arrogated to himself by the Bishop of Rome, who made a traffic of his dispensations, which was checked in England by various statutes, chiefly that of

Provisors (Edward III.). In this country and under our Canón Laws dispensations are not needed.

Dissenters. A title given to those who dissent from the Established Church of England. This dissent is twofold: the dissent from her government; the dissent from her doctrines. But it is worthy of all consideration that the avowed principles on which such dissent is based, *e.g.*, the proclamation of a slighted truth, is really the principle of disruption of all bonds. The Church of England does not break the principle of Apostolic unity. Neither her history nor her conduct at any time have laid her open to that charge. But the throwing off the Apostolic government and the magnifying of any one doctrine out of all proportion to the rest of the doctrines of the Faith, really breaks the net knotted of discipline and of truth. Again, it is to be insisted on, with the fullest proof at hand, that there is no doctrine proven to be in the Scriptures but is fully held in the Church in its due place in the frame-work of the Faith. The doctrine of Predestination held and urged by the Presbyterian is taught in *its place* in the scheme. It is not disproportionately extolled. The doctrine of the Methodist, of Free-will, is held within those true limitations that save it from Pelagianism. And so it is a truth that each dissenter will find the truths most dear to him, held, taught, enforced, but not out of its due position, in the joining together of those doctrines left by our LORD, and taught by His Apostles as needful for salvation. (This whole subject is most admirably treated in the Bampton Lecture for 1871, by Dr. G. H. Curteis, " Dissent in its Relations to the Church of England.")

Divinity of Christ. *Vide* JESUS.

Divorce. *Vide* MATRIMONY.

Dogma. A theological principle. The term belongs, strictly, to a positive statement of doctrine derived immediately or by derivation from Divine Revelation, and enunciated by the Church through a General Council. In a looser sense it is applied to the special tenets of particular Churches, or even of sects, if put forth by an authority recognized by them. Dogma presupposes substantial proof which is generally and in the ordinary sense of an historical or logical kind; but it must be remembered that we have reached the highest possible kind of evidence when it is proved that any particular statement has come from GOD. There can be no real opposition between dogma and history, or dogma and logic, so long as these principles are kept in view. But it must be remembered that there are some subjects in theology, especially such as relate to GOD Himself, which are beyond the province of history or of mere logical derivation, for they are dogmas which are known only from His revelation of them (Blunt's Dict. of Hist. Theology). The dogmas of the faith are summed up in the Creeds, and are taught every person. But there is a popular dislike to listen to any direct teaching of dogma as such. This arises partly from the want of skill in the teachers in presenting the dogmatic teaching, and partly from a prevalent idea that dogma is exclusive, and now the desire to break down all barriers and to construct an inclusive body of doctrine, or rather to throw away doctrine altogether is the leading thought. It is an era of reaction against overstrained statements and misapplied dogmatic truths; but dogma can never be cast aside, it is the very constitution of the truth itself.

Dominical Letter. The Sunday letter for the year. (*Vide* CALENDAR.)

Donative. A spiritual preferment in the free gift of a patron, and without admission, institution, or induction by any mandate from the Bishop or other. But the donee may by the patron, or by any other authorized by the patron, be put into possession.

Dossel. A piece of embroidered needlework, stiff silk or cloth of gold, hung at the back of a throne or altar, but more particularly the latter.

Doubles. It may happen that the service of the Sunday and that of a Saint's day coincide. The question then occurs, Which is the service proper to the day? The ancient Sarum rule (which has not been changed by authority in the Anglican communion) is that the Saint's day service should take the place of the Sunday. So, unless that Sunday be a High-Feast day, or in Advent or Lent, the Lessons, Collect, Epistle, and Gospel of the Saint's day replace those of the Sunday. In some places the Collect for the Sunday has been read immediately after the Saint's day Collect, but this does not appear proper.

Doubt. In derivation the word doubt is related to the Latin word *duo*, two. The very word indicates an anxiety and trouble of mind which is painful. A man standing where two roads meet, uncertain which to take, represents the doubter.

" Man knows some things and is ignorant of many things, while he is in *doubt* as to other things. *Doubt* is that state of mind in which we hesitate as to two contradictory conclusions,—having no preponderance of evidence in favor of either." (Krauth's Fleming's Vocabulary of Philosophy.)

' Doubt is some degree of belief, along with the consciousness of ignorance, in regard to a proposition. Absolute *disbelief* implies knowledge; it is the knowledge that such or such a thing is not true. If the mind admits a proposition without any desire for knowledge concerning it, this is *credulity*. If it is open to receive the proposition, but feels ignorance concerning it, this is *doubt*. In proportion as knowledge increases *doubt* diminishes, and belief or disbelief strengthens." (Taylor, Elements of Thought, quoted in the work last named.)

In religion painful doubts are caused by a

defective religious life and by improper views of God. "Fluctuations of religious experience" and "relapses into sin" help to increase them. Doubt is often the result of a natural temperament of mind. Religion is a habit, as well as a belief; and constant private and public prayer, the reading of the Holy Scriptures and good books, a dwelling on God's promises, and a consideration of His goodness, with a due observance of God's laws, and a frequent faithful reception of the Holy Communion, will do much to banish doubt from the mind. A constant fellowship with devout people, that is, the Communion of Saints, is a great help to constancy in faith.

"If any man will do His will, he shall know of the doctrine" (St. John vii. 17), are the words of the Master. An active missionary who had once doubted, when at work said, "I have no time for doubts." Even Moses and the Apostles were at times in doubt by reason of human weakness, but God gave them means of putting away their doubts. Some persons are given great power to assist others in such difficulties. Daniel, the prophet, is spoken of as having the power of "dissolving of doubts" (Dan. v. 12, 16).

Our Lord's rebuke to the sinking Peter was, "O thou of little faith, wherefore didst thou doubt?" (St. Matt. xiv. 31). This is applicable to all. With regard to bodily wants Christ says, "Neither be ye of doubtful mind" (St. Luke xii. 29).

St. Paul declares that the weak brother is to be received, "but not to doubtful disputations" (Rom. xiv. 1).

Faith is natural to man. Children only learn to doubt by the deceptions that are practiced on them, and our Saviour makes a child the pattern of Christian life, and demands from all who would enter the kingdom of heaven a childlike character.

Unbelief and doubt of God's words were the sins by which the devil at first sought to cast men down. The doubt in paradise has propagated itself through all the descendants of Adam and Eve, and can only be dispelled by listening to those Divine words of the Blessed Son of God, "Have faith in God" (St. Mark xi. 22).

Newman's expression, that a hundred difficulties need not produce a single doubt, is strictly true, for in worldly matters difficulties surround men on every side, and yet they act promptly. The farmer, in faith, sows a crop which may never ripen, or which may be gathered after he is dead.

See the faith of men in the future of new countries, in building railroads at vast cost and planning public improvements, notwithstanding a host of obstacles. A nation of doubters would be a stagnant nation.

This is especially the case in religion; as Aubrey de Vere says, the skeptic contracts his being.

Colton, in "Lacon" (cxlvi.), in speaking of doubt uses these words: "He is at once the richest and poorest of potentates, for he has locked up immense treasures, but he cannot find the key." Still this strong man armed may not keep his palace in peace, for the "strong Son of God" comes to the humblest believers with the promise, "Fear not, little flock, for it is your Father's good pleasure to give you the Kingdom" (St. Luke xii. 32).

"Suppose a person deeply perplexed about the state of his soul, continually fluctuating between hope and fear, and overwhelmed with grief were to repeatedly utter this wish: 'O that I certainly knew that I should be able to persevere!' He might be answered thus: 'And what wouldst thou do if this certain knowledge were bestowed upon thee? Do now that which thou wouldst do and rest secure of thy perseverance.'" (Thomas à Kempis, The Imitation of Christ, ch. xxiii.) This thought occurs in Ps. xxxvii. 3: "Trust in the Lord, and do good, so shalt thou dwell in the land and be fed."

Bishop Butler, in the "Analogy" (Part ii. chap. vi.), affirms that even if a man doubts he ought to act: "because the apprehension that religion may be true does as really lay men under obligations as a full conviction that it is true. It gives occasions and motives to consider further the important subject; to preserve attentively upon their minds a general implicit sense that they may be under divine moral government, an awful solicitude about religion, whether natural or revealed. Such apprehension ought to turn men's eyes to every degree of new light which may be had, from whatever side it comes, and induce them to refrain, in the mean time, from all immoralities, and live in the conscientious practice of every common virtue. Especially are they bound to keep at the greatest distance from all dissolute profaneness; for this the very nature of the case forbids; and to treat with highest reverence a matter upon which their own whole interest and being and the fate of nature depends."

Authorities: Spectator, No. 191, Buck's Theological Dictionary, Lange's Commentary on Genesis, Subjective Difficulties in Religion (Answered). Aubrey de Vere, in the Nineteenth Century Review, May, 1883 A.D. Rev. S. F. Hotchkin.

Doxology. An ascription of glory and praise to God. These Doxologies are frequent in the Old Testament, especially in the Psalms, and in the New Testament also. The Doxology closing the form of the Lord's Prayer in St. Matt. (vi. 13) is held by many textualists to be interpolated from the Liturgies, and not to belong to its original delivery (cf. St. Luke xi. 4). St. Paul has several fervent Doxologies in his Epistles, e.g., Rom. xvi. 25-27; Eph. iii. 20, 21; Phil. iv. 20; 1 Timothy vi. 15, 16; so 1 St. Pet. iv. 11; v. 11. But the Revelation is replete with Doxologies both of creatures on earth and spirits in heaven. Rev. i. 5, 6;

iv. 11; v. 9, 12, 13; vii. 10, 12; xv. 3; xvi. 5, 7; xix. 1, 6. The Liturgical Doxologies in the American Prayer-Book are the *Gloria Patri*, the *Gloria in Excelsis*.

Dulia. A term used in Roman Theology to designate the reverence due to the Saints or to any worthy creature of GOD. But the root of the word *doulos*, and the verb *douleuo*, are used of servantship, service, and worship of GOD. St. Paul calls himself the *doulos* of CHRIST. He speaks of serving (*douleuon*) the LORD. *Dulia*, is used of the slavery of corruption in Romans viii. 21. In no place is *douleia* used in a good sense in the New Testament, though its cognates *doulos* and *douleuo*, are. The interior meaning of the word is to serve as a servant bought with a price. Even if the theory of reverence to a creature were tenable, this term is most unhappily chosen, since no saint or angel has redeemed us. The doctrine itself savors of idolatry.

E.

Eagle. In Scripture, symbolic of GOD (Ex. xix. 4; Deut. xxxii. 11.); also the mysterious creatures seen in vision by Ezekiel and St. John. There these Living Creatures appear in fourfold form. In Ezekiel "they four." Apparently each of the four had the face of a man, the face of a lion on the right side, the face of an ox on the left side, and the face of an eagle. In St. John's vision the first Living Creature was like a lion, the second like a calf (ox), the third had a face as a man, and the fourth was like a flying eagle. The symbolism has been variously explained, and that upon which St. John's vision has been most generally received is that they are symbols of the four Gospels. The lion has been connected with St. Mark's Gospel, as setting forth our LORD as the Lion of the tribe of Judah; the ox with St. Luke's Gospel, as setting forth our LORD'S sacrificial and intercessory acts; the man with St. Matthew, as setting forth our LORD as the MESSIAH, the man acquainted with sorrows; the eagle with St. John, as setting forth the Divinity of our LORD in His Incarnation. It is often used as a symbol placed beside the figure of St. John to distinguish him from the other Evangelists, since he has been permitted to soar upward into the Divine Presence as the eagle mounts upward to the sun.

The eagle has been used as a lectern to support the Bible in the Church, and has been made a very effective part of the Church furniture.

Easter. A Saxon word, Eostre, a heathen goddess whose festival fell in the spring. But the Feast of the Resurrection falling at the spring-tide, the name was transferred to the Christian feast. (*Vide* FESTIVALS and FEASTS.) The Church, as soon as the repression caused by persecution permitted her, celebrated this feast with peculiar rejoicings; not only the day itself, but the week following was kept with great pomp. In the Saxon Church it was a festal week. It was called the Queen of Festivals, the Royal Day of Days. It was the day of Light, and in the Eastern Churches from the midnight of Easter-eve till day the churches have ever been illuminated as brilliantly as possible, and the solemn services were celebrated with great magnificence. The catechumens who had just been baptized were admitted to their first Communion then. Every act that could testify to the glad reception of all that the Resurrection can mean was done. It is in truth the key, doctrinally, to our Faith; liturgically, to our worship; practically, to our life; and must be kept with a joyous heart by every Christian. The date of the feast, year by year, was a cause of great solicitude. For several centuries it was the privilege of the See of Alexandria to announce to the Christian world the right date of Easter-Sunday, till at last perfect tables enabled the other Churches to arrive at the same result; and, too, the schisms and quarrels of the Church interfered with and broke up the custom. But the festal epistles of several Patriarchs of Alexandria are of great value. The controversy upon the date which divided many of the Eastern Church from the West (*vide* QUARTODECIMAN) was an evidence of the importance placed upon it everywhere. (Upon the rule for finding Easter-day, *vide* CALENDAR.)

It is one of the days upon which the Church requires all her members to commune. The Epistle and Gospel for Easter-day is apparently a change from the older English use (Col. iii. 1, and St. John xx. 1, for 1 Cor. v. 7, and St. Mark xvi. 1). But the Prayer-Book of 1549 A.D. ordered two celebrations, and gave two sets of Epistles and Gospels. In the revision of 1552 A.D., the older missal set was dropped and the later Epistle and Gospel kept. The Collect dates from 496 A D.

Eastern Churches, The. No intelligent Christian can read the history of the Eastern Churches without emotion, or study their present condition and circumstances without the deepest interest. When we hear of the Church of Jerusalem, we remember that "out of Zion went forth the law and the word of GOD from Jerusalem," so that that Church may well be esteemed the mother of all Churches. We cannot forget that "the disciples were called Christians first in Antioch." What associations cling to the names of Bethlehem and Nazareth, Smyrna and Ephesus, Athens and Corinth, Nicæa and Chalcedon, Alexandria, renowned for its learning, Constantinople, the imperial city! To Eastern Christians, with scarce an exception, were addressed the Epistles of the New Testament, for them primarily, we may say, were the Gospels written, and in a large part of Eastern Christendom the Gospels and Epistles are still read and understood—so little has this language changed—in the inspired original. "The humblest peasant," says Stanley,* "who reads his . . . Greek Testament in his own mother-tongue on the hills of Bœotia, may proudly feel that he has an access to the original oracles of Divine truth which Pope and Cardinal reach by a barbarous and imperfect translation."

The Eastern Churches, properly so called, are divisible into two groups: (1) the Orthodox Churches; (2) the Armenian, the Syrian,† the Coptic, and the Assyrian. Beside these, there are a number of Eastern Christians who, retaining in part, at least, their ancient rites, have come under the dominion of the Church of Rome. Not only are their ecclesiastical relations with the West, but seven-eighths of them live in the West, in Austro-Hungary.

Let us consider first of the Orthodox Churches. The Holy Orthodox Eastern Churches are commonly designated, when taken collectively, as "The Eastern Church," "The Oriental Church," "The Greek Church." They not only outnumber the second group ten to one, but they are the truest representatives of the Church as first planted in those lands. Their special claim to the title *Orthodox* is from this, that they have carefully held to the doctrines set forth in the undisputed General Councils, whilst the other Eastern Churches have refused, as we shall see farther on, to accept the decrees of, however it may be as to the doctrines asserted in, the Councils which have been throughout the Church accepted as œcumenical. One can hardly speak of an *Eastern* or *Western* Church as existing as such before the founding of Constantinople, and the division of the Roman Empire into Eastern and Western, which soon followed thereupon. Whilst the Gospel was soon carried into all lands, it would seem to have met with a more speedy reception in those lands where it was first proclaimed. And, as Milman* well says, "For some considerable (it cannot but be an indefinable) part of the first three centuries the Church of Rome, and most, if not all, the Churches of the West, were, if we may so speak, Greek religious colonies. Their language was Greek, their organization Greek, their writers Greek, their Scriptures Greek, and many vestiges and traditions show that their ritual, their Liturgy, was Greek. . . . So, too, was it in Gaul: there the first Christians were settled, chiefly in the Greek cities which owned Marseilles as their parent, and which retained the use of Greek as their vernacular tongue."‡ The chief theological writers of the first Christian centuries were Easterns, or men of Eastern training. The earliest writer of Latin theological literature dates from the close of the second century. In the words of Dr. von Döllinger, "The Eastern portion of the Church for a long time enjoyed a complete intellectual supremacy; the Western had to learn from their Greek co-religionists, and to receive from them their ecclesiastical and theological education. All Latin theological literature before St. Augustine is, in substance, the application or imitation of Greek models."§ And the present Bishop of Lincoln calls attention to a catalogue of ecclesiastical authors, drawn up by St. Jerome in 392 A.D., in these words: "The catalogue (containing one hundred and thirty-five names) begins with St. Peter, and it is remarkable as a proof of the lack of theological learning at Rome, that Jerome, who had been a secretary of a Pope, and had the best opportunity in this respect, could only enumerate four other Bishops of Rome—Clemens, Victor, Cornelius, and Damasus—in this long list of ecclesiastical writers." ‖

Ages of persecution were not times for perfected organization. We find, however, the 6th Canon of the Council of Nicæa beginning with the words, "Let the ancient customs prevail," and then going on to direct that the metropolitical authority which the Bishops of Alexandria and of Antioch had exercised through long custom over the respectively neighboring Bishops should be continued to them by law. And the 7th Canon of the same Council directs that the honors which usage and ancient tradition had accorded to the Bishop of Jerusalem, then called Ælia, should still be preserved to it.

It was but natural that the Imperial City, Constantinople, should have ecclesiastical as well as political pre-eminence, and in the 3d Canon of the first General Council held in that city, it was decreed that the Bishop of Constantinople should take precedence next after the Bishop of Rome, because Constantinople was New Rome." This precedence

---
* History of the Eastern Churches, Amer. edit., p. 101.
† The Syrian is often called the *Jacobite* Church, and the Assyrian the *Nestorian* Church. The "Christians of St. Thomas," in India, are a dependency of the Syrian Church, and the Abyssinian bears a title relative to the Coptic.

‡ History of Latin Christianity, i. 32.
§ Lectures on the Reunion of the Churches, p. 39.
‖ Bishop Wordsworth's Church History, iii. 202.

seems at first to have been chiefly honorary. But the 29th Canon of the Council of Chalcedon confirmed and extended the privileges of Constantinople, and made that See second, and scarcely second, to Rome in honor and in authority. At Chalcedon, also, the Bishop of Jerusalem acquired for his See patriarchal privileges, having previously held a position of marked honor, and with little authority.

In the early part of the seventh century Antioch, Jerusalem, and Alexandria fell under the power of the Moslem. The Churches in Patriarchates of which these were the Sees were wellnigh crushed, the Christians were subject to men of another race and of alien faith, who oft made them feel the insolence of their conquerors. Constantinople had, as we have seen, a pre-eminence; it now became the only great Christian city of the East. The title of *Œcumenical Patriarch*, given at times in early days to the Bishop of the Imperial City, seemed not to ill befit one of so unrivaled influence in the Eastern Church, and ere long came to be recognized as his proper title.

From time to time difficulties and misunderstandings arose between the Eastern and the Western Churches, but the temporary divisions which thence occurred, "however much they diminished the glory of the Church, did not altogether destroy the principle of Christian charity. It was still universally held that the Church formed but one spiritual fraternity, that all Christians were members of the same body, and that it was their duty to hold communion with each other. When divisions arose, excommunication consisted generally in a simple withdrawal of communion. . . . These withdrawals of communion were intended to procure the reformation of the offending party, and the divided Churches . . . sincerely endeavored to be reunited to their brethren in CHRIST."*

At length the time came when there was to be a lasting separation. In regard to this lamentable division there was fault on both sides. Nevertheless, to use the words of Dr. von Döllinger, "No one acquainted with history can doubt that by far the greater share of the blame rests with the West. An imperious despotism, attended by the fear that the sight of the free Eastern Church might produce an unfavorable feeling towards the Papal monarchy in the West, an evil ignorance of Papal antiquity, and especially of Greek tradition and ecclesiastical literature, on the part of the Westerns, *these* were the real causes of the schism."† The separation, which some have dated from the time of Photius, in 880 A.D., and others from that of Cerularius, in 1054 A.D., each of these being Patriarchs of Constantinople, was not consummated until the taking of the Imperial City by the Latins in 1204 A.D., and then, "above all, by the part which Innocent III. took throughout by supporting the acts of violence"‡ connected with the taking of Constantinople, "with the whole weight of his authority and power, and openly forwarding the subjugation and Latinization of the Eastern Church," setting Latin Bishops over Greek Sees, and so declaring the Eastern in a state of heresy and schism. Attempts were made at Lyons in 1274 A.D., and at Florence in 1438 A.D., to bring about a reunion. But the Popes demanded an admission of their autocratic power, which the Easterns would not give, and so the negotiations were fruitless.

At the time of the separation of the Eastern and the Western Churches there is reason to think that, in number of Bishops and of the faithful, East and West were as nearly as might be on an equality. Palmer, in his "Treatise on the Church of Christ,"§ gives the data for believing there were in each about one thousand and twenty Bishops. A large part of the Patriarchate of Constantinople having already fallen under the power of the Turk, that city itself was taken by them in 1453 A.D. But while the ancient seats of the Eastern Church were fallen into the hands of the infidel, a hardy race of the north received the seeds of Christian enlightenment from the East. There is a tradition that St. Andrew preached the Gospel within the bounds of what is now called Russia. But it is about the middle of the ninth century before we have historic mention of Christianity in connection with Russia,—and shortly before the year 1000 A.D., that Russia, largely through the influence of Vladimir, its first Christian prince, adopted the religion of CHRIST.

The Holy Orthodox Church of the East is made up at this time of ten independent Churches, in full communion with each other, and fully agreeing as to doctrine, while varying to some extent in discipline. These Churches, including in all about 80,000,000 of the faithful, are the Churches in the Patriarchates of Constantinople, Alexandria, Antioch, and Jerusalem, the Church of Russia, of Cyprus, the Orthodox Church of Austro-Hungary, the Church of Montenegro, of Greece, and of Servia. Roumania having been set free from Turkey at the same time with Servia, its Church claims a like independence with that of the Servian Church from the Patriarch of Constantinople, but this claim has not yet been allowed. The Bulgarian Church also claims an autonomy, which has not yet been conceded. There seems to be a difference of opinion among the Eastern Churches as regards the claims of these two Churches, which the Patriarch of Constantinople accounts as still subject to his jurisdiction. It is to be hoped that a satisfactory arrangement may soon be arrived at.

---

* Palmer's Church History, American edit., p. 67.
† Report of the Bonn Conference in 1874, p. 23.
‡ Dr. von Döllinger, Report of Bonn Conference, 1874 p. 25.
§ American edition, i. 198.

Let us take a survey of these various autonomous Churches in their order.

1. *The Patriarchate of Constantinople.*— "The Most Holy Archbishop of Constantinople, New Rome, and Œcumenical Patriarch," Joachim III., has under his jurisdiction in Turkey in Europe, and part of Turkey in Asia, including the Roumanian Church and the Bulgarians, about 11,500,000 of the faithful; seventy Metropolitans, two Archbishops, and twenty-five Bishops in active service, six Metropolitans and eight Bishops who have retired from active duty, and seventeen other Bishops without Sees, but for the most part engaged in assisting other Bishops. In all one hundred and twenty-eight Bishops, of various degree, own him as their ecclesiastical superior. It should be said here that, throughout the East, the titles of *Metropolitan* and *Archbishop* are, for the most part, honorary distinctions. In many cases, when the titles were first bestowed, they were most fitting. The Metropolitan of Ephesus, for instance, had once nearly as many suffragans as there are days in the year, now he has but four. It does not seem unreasonable that the title held of old should be continued to the present occupant of so venerable a See.

The Patriarch of Constantinople has a precedence among his brother Patriarchs, but claims no authority over them. As the chief representative of the Greeks in Turkey, he has a position which often exposes him to great annoyance, and not seldom to real danger. Faithfulness in the discharge of his duties has frequently led to his removal from office, by the more or less direct influence of the Turkish government. Cyril Lucar, two hundred and fifty years ago, was four times removed from his office as Patriarch, and when Patriarch the fifth time was basely murdered. Nor are such vicissitudes things quite of the past. Within a very few years there were living at one time five ex-Patriarchs of Constantinople. And no longer ago than 1821 A.D., the Patriarch Gregory, over fourscore years of age, with three of his Bishops and eight Priests, were hung on Easter-day, by the Grand Vizier's order, at the door of the church in which they had just been celebrating the Paschal Feast. The present Patriarch is in the prime of life, and a man of zeal and enlightenment.

2. *The Patriarchate of Alexandria.*— The early Patriarchs of Alexandria held a position not only of great dignity, but of authority and influence equally great. But Sophronius, "the Most Holy Pope and Patriarch of the Great City Alexandria, Libya, Pentapolis, and Ethiopia, and of all the land of Egypt; Father of Fathers, Pastor of Pastors, Archpriest of Archpriests, Thirteenth Apostle, and Universal Judge," has under him at this time but one Bishop in active service, and 5000 of the faithful. When the Saracens took Alexandria, in 641 A.D., the Greeks in Egypt for the most part lost their lives or left the country. The native Egyptians of the ancient race, who met with fitful favor from the conqueror, had previously become, as their descendants still remain, members of what is known as the Coptic Church, of which a brief account is given below.

3. *The Patriarchate of Antioch.*— "The Most Blessed and Holy Patriarch of the Divine City Antioch, Syria, Arabia, Cilicia, Iberia, Mesopotamia, and all the East; Father of Fathers and Pastor of Pastors," Hierotheus, resides chiefly in Damascus, the provincial city in this Patriarchate. The Christians owning his authority number about 100,000. He has under him eleven Metropolitans and three Bishops, the latter having no Sees. When, in 658 A.D., Antioch was captured by the Saracens, the throne of the successors of Alexander, the seat of the Roman government in the East, which had been decorated by Cæsar with the title of free, and holy, and inviolate, was degraded under the yoke of the Caliph to the secondary rank of a principal town.* The Crusaders, who held Antioch for many years, were scarcely less inimical to Eastern Christians than were the Saracens. Taken from the Latins, in 1268 A.D., by the Sultan of Egypt, its inhabitants were put to the sword or sent into captivity; and for hundreds of years, indeed, until the beginning of this century, believers in CHRIST were almost absolutely excluded from the place where the disciples were first called Christians. The few Orthodox Christians there, until very recently, had no proper church, but worshiped in a grotto in the mountain-side.

4. *The Patriarchate of Jerusalem.*— "The Most Blessed and Holy Patriarch of the Holy City Jerusalem, and all Palestine, Syria, Arabia beyond Jordan, Cana of Galilee, and Holy Sion," has under him five Metropolitans, four Archbishops, and about 20,000 of the faithful. After a vacancy of more than a year, Nicodemus, Archbishop of Mount Tabor, has just been chosen Patriarch, but when these pages went to press had not entered upon his high office.

Until the destruction of Jerusalem, it was regarded not only as the metropolis of Palestine, but in one sense of the whole Christian world. On its overthow, Cæsarea, the civil metropolis of Palestine, became the seat of the Metropolitan, though, from the the remembrance of what Jerusalem had been, its Bishops ranked next after the Metropolitan among the Bishops of the province. Jerusalem attaining a degree of prosperity under Constantine and his successors, its Bishop acquired in the fifth century, as has been already mentioned, the Patriarchal dignity. From Persian, Saracen, Crusader, and Turk Jerusalem suffered like vicissitudes with Antioch. An object

---

* Gibbon, Decline and Fall, li.

of deepest interest to all Christians, it has not seldom given occasion to strifes, civil and ecclesiastical.

"O pray for the peace of Jerusalem!"

5. *The Church of Russia.*—We now come from the consideration of ancient Patriarchates, depressed by long ages of subjection to the infidel, to study a daughter Church, the Church of a vast empire, by far the largest of National Churches; numbering among its members about 64,000,000, or more than three-fourths of Eastern Christendom, and among its prelates three Metropolitans, fourteen Archbishops, thirty-six Diocesan Bishops, twenty-eight Vicars, or Assistant Bishops in active service.

If, as tradition states, St. Andrew first preached the Gospel within the bounds of the Russian Empire, little, if any, visible fruit of his teachings remained when Queen Olga, about the middle of the tenth century, and her grandson, Vladimir, just before its close, embraced Christianity,—his conversion being followed by that of a large portion of his subjects. Vladimir asked that a Bishop might be sent from Constantinople to his capital city, Kieff, which for many years remained the ecclesiastical metropolis of Russia. Then Vladimir became the Metropolitical See, and in 1320 A.D. Moscow. Much of this time the Church of Russia was strictly dependent upon Constantinople. While Russia was overrun by the Tartars, and Constantinople retained its freedom, this arrangement had its advantages; but when the situation was reversed, and Russia was freed from the Tartars, while Constantinople was subjected to the Turks, the Russian Church became virtually self-governed. In 1583 A.D. a Patriarchate was established at Moscow. Ten Patriarchs in succession presided over the Church of Russia, the last of them dying in 1701 A.D. It is considered that the Russian Patriarchate is still in existence, though, for a number of years, it was in charge of one of the Bishops, and since 1721 A.D. it has been administered by the Holy Governing Synod. This Synod now consists of the Metropolitans of St. Petersburg, Kieff, and Moscow, the Exarch of Georgia, two or more other Bishops chosen for two years at a time, and two priests, one the chief chaplain of the Emperor, the other the chaplain general of the forces. The Ober-Procurator represents the lay element in the Church. In matters of practical administration he has an influential voice, but none at all in questions of doctrine.

Much has been done of late years to improve the position of the Russian clergy. Great attention is paid to their education, and for this purpose admirable institutions of learning are provided. A revised translation of the Bible has recently been published, by authority, and steps have been taken to have it widely circulated. No little interest has been manifested lately in missions among the heathen, both within the Empire, in Siberia, and without it, in Japan. The Russian Church is one in which there are manifest and abundant signs of life and influence.

6. *The Church in Cyprus.*—The story of the first planting of Christianity in Cyprus is no doubtful tradition, but is recorded by St. Luke in the Acts of the Apostles (ch. xi. 19-26; xiii. 4-13; xv. 36-41). Cyprus being reckoned from the time of Hadrian a part of the civil prefecture of the East, the Patriarch of Antioch claimed authority over the Church in that island. This claim was stoutly resisted, and the question being brought before the Council of Ephesus in 431 A.D., it was decided that the Church in Cyprus should retain the independent character it had had from the first. Cyprus has had its full share of trials from Saracen, Crusader, and Turk. It is now in the hands of the English. The Orthodox Christians of Cyprus number about 90,000. "The Most Blessed and Holy Archbishop of Nova-Justiniana, and all Cyprus," Sophronius, has under him three Bishops.

7. *The Orthodox Church in Austria.*—In Austro-Hungary there are about 3,500,000 members of the Orthodox Church, under three Metropolitans, entitled respectively "Metropolitan of all the Servians in the Austrian Empire," "Metropolitan of all the Roumanians in the Austrian Empire," "Metropolitan of the Buckovine and Dalmatia." There are also ten Bishops.

8. *The Church in Montenegro.*—"The Metropolitan of Scanderia and the seacoast, Archbishop of Tsettin, Exarch of the Holy Throne of Pek, Vladika of Montenegro and Berda," Bessarion Lubitch, is the only Bishop in Montenegro, that brave little country which has for so many years withstood the Turk. Until about thirty years since, the Metropolitan of Montenegro was also its ruling prince. A second See has lately been set up in the territory recently regained from Turkey. But it appears that the new Diocese has at present no Bishop of its own. The inhabitants of Montenegro, with hardly an exception members of the Orthodox Church, number about 300,000.

9. *The Church in the Greek Kingdom.*— When Greece became independent of Turkey, the Church of Greece, which had hitherto been a dependency of Constantinople, naturally desired to be self-governed, and there were many reasons why it was best this should be the case. The Patriarch of Constantinople was often placed in a false position towards them,—kindly disposed himself, but forced by the Turkish government into a position of antagonism. A National Synod was held at Nauplia in July, 1833 A.D., when it was declared, (1) "That the Eastern Orthodox and Apostolic Church of Greece, which spiritually owns no Head but the Head of the Christian Faith, JESUS CHRIST our LORD, is dependent on no

external authority, while she preserves unshaken dogmatic unity with all the Eastern Ortbodox Churches. . . . (2) A permanent Synod shall be established, consisting entirely of Archbishops and Bishops, appointed by the King, to be the highest ecclesiastical authority, after the model of the Russian Church." The Metropolitan of Athens is always the President of the Holy Synod. With scarcely an exception, the people of Greece, numbering something over 1,600,000, belong to the Orthodox Church.

10. *The Servian Church.*—When the Servians became Christians, they acknowledged a sort of primacy over them as belonging to the Patriarch of Constantinople, but as they aspired to civil freedom so also they sought for ecclesiastical autonomy,—each being attained in the fourteenth century, when Stephen Dushan took the title of " the Macedonian Czar" and Joannicius was chosen Patriarch of Servia. The Servian kingdom lasted but a short time, but the Patriarchate continued. In 1689 A.D. the Patriarch Arsenius took part with the emperor of Austria against the Ottoman power, and when the movement proved a failure, with about 200,000 of his people took refuge in Austria, where he was made Metropolitan of Carlovitz, retaining, as do his successors in the office, the title Patriarch of Servia. Since 1838 A.D. the Archbishop of Belgrade has been recognized as the head of the Servian Church. While Servia remained a dependency of Turkey, the Servian Church had a dependence, little more than nominal, upon Constantinople. Since Servia has become independent, the autonomy of its Church has been recognized. The Servian Church numbers about 1,600,000, under an Archbishop and four Bishops.

Beside the ten Churches which have a recognized position among the Orthodox Eastern Churches, there are two others, the Roumanian and the Bulgarian Churches. *The Roumanian Church* numbers about 4,500,000, under two Metropolitans and six Bishops. When Roumania was set free from Turkey, its Church naturally claimed to be independent. But this independence is not recognized at Constantinople. It seems probable that the differences between the *Roumanian Church* and the Patriarchate will soon be settled by a compromise. In regard to the Bulgarian Church, the difficulties and the antagonisms are greater. It is to be hoped, however, that some means of settling these differences also may soon be devised, since the interests of religion are suffering, and a Romish propaganda has taken advantage of a time of discord to make proselytes. As has been said, the Bulgarian Bishops are not recognized by the Patriarchs. They number in all 16, viz.: Exarch, 1; Metropolitans, 8; Bishops, 2; Vicar Bishops, 2; retired Bishops, 2.

To summarize the information given, according to the best authorities, the Orthodox Christians number :

1. In the Patriarchate of Constantinople:		
Greeks, etc.	3,500,000	
Bulgarian	3,500,000	
Roumanian	4,500,000	11,500,000
2. In the Patriarchate of Alexandria		5,000
3. In the Patriarchate of Antioch		100,000
4. In the Patriarchate of Jerusalem		20,000
5. In the Russian Empire		64,000,000
6. In the Island of Cyprus		90,000
7. In the Austrian Empire		3,500,000
8. In Montenegro		300,000
9. In the kingdom of Greece		1,600,000
10. In the kingdom of Servia		1,600,000
		82,715,000

(For list of Sees, *vide* EPISCOPATE, LIST OF.)

DOCTRINE, DISCIPLINE, AND WORSHIP OF THE ORTHODOX EASTERN CHURCHES.—The Orthodox Eastern Churches and the Anglican alike recognize that " The only pure and all-sufficient source of the doctrine of Faith is the revealed word of GOD contained in the Holy Scriptures ; that " Everything necessary to salvation is stated in the Holy Scriptures, with such clearness that every one reading them with a sincere desire to be enlightened can understand them ;" that " Holy Scripture, being the word of GOD Himself, is the only supreme judge in controversies," so that " No Council whatever can set up an article of faith which cannot be proved from the Holy Scriptures."*

The Eastern Orthodox Churches are not afraid of an appeal " to the Law and to the testimony." Philaret, in the work just quoted, says, " Every one has not only a right, but it is his bounden duty, to read the Holy Scriptures in a language which he understands, and edify himself thereby." And Methodius, Archbishop of Syros and Tenos, in a Pastoral Letter addressed to his people, in June, 1882 A.D., uses, with other like words, this language : " Lay hold upon this Book of Life, the Book of Light, the Book of the world's salvation. Study the Holy Gospel, meditate upon it day and night, regulate your lives by its holy teachings, and happy will you be."

The Anglican and the Eastern Orthodox Churches holding like views as to the supreme authority of Holy Scripture, and as to the principles of its interpretation, we are prepared to find that, as to matters of chief importance, they are in essential agreement, and that in other cases, where there seem to be differences, such differences may for the most part be shown to be rather in appearance than in reality. There is a seeming difference as to the number of the Sacraments. The Anglican Churches defining a Sacrament as " An outward and visible sign of an inward and spiritual grace given unto us, *ordained by*

---

* These extracts are from " A Comparative Statement of Russo-Greek and Roman Catholic Doctrines," by Philaret, Metropolitan of Moscow ; published in an English translation in Paper No. IV. of the Russo-Greek Committee. Philaret, one of the leading prelates of this century, died November, 1867, after an Episcopate of over fifty years.

CHRIST *Himself*," acknowledge *two* Sacraments; the Eastern Orthodox Churches defining a *Mystery* (the word they use instead of our word *Sacrament*) as "A visible sign of invisible grace," sometimes say that "their number is indefinite, but that they are not all necessary to salvation. There are two Sacraments necessary to every man, namely, Baptism and the Holy Eucharist."* Sometimes to the two which they and we esteem the *chief* Mysteries they add five others, as coming next after these in importance, namely, Confirmation, Penitence, Ordination, Matrimony, and Prayer Oil. In regard to Prayer Oil, which is not to be confounded with the Extreme Unction of the Romish Church, administered only to the dying, the Easterns follow literally the injunction of the Apostle (St. James v. 14, 15), and anoint the sick for their recovery. To them we seem to be neglecting a plain command of GOD'S Word. The Eastern Orthodox Churches have not attempted to define the mode of our LORD'S Presence in the Holy Communion, believing it, in the words of a distinguished Metropolitan of the Russian Church, to be "A Mystery to be apprehended by faith, and not a matter to be speculated and dogmatized upon, or reasoned about." "All definitions, or pretended explanations," continues this learned divine, "such as the use of the word 'Transubstantiation,' are but attempts to penetrate the mystery, and in so far tend to overthrow the very nature of the Sacrament."† In the Eastern Churches the Holy Communion is always given in *both kinds*, according to our LORD'S commandment. The Eastern Orthodox Churches believe neither in Purgatory nor in works of supererogation. In the words of Philaret of Moscow, "The condition of a man's soul after death is fixed by his internal state, and there is no such thing as Purgatory, in which souls have to pass through fiery torments in order to prepare them for blessedness." . . "There is no need of any other kind of purification, when 'the blood of JESUS CHRIST cleanseth us from all sin.'" "Works of supererogation in the saints are impossible, as they themselves are only saved by grace."‡

It is well known that there has long been a difference between the Churches of the East and of the West in regard to what is commonly called the Nicene Creed. The Orthodox Eastern Churches have adhered to the original form of the Creed, while in the West, by steps which it is not always easy to trace, the words "and the SON" long since made their way into the Creed at the end of the clause, "And I believe in the HOLY GHOST, the LORD and Giver of Life, who proceedeth from the FATHER." From this addition to the Creed arose the "Filioque Controversy" (the added word in Latin being *filioque*). The Greeks were right in claiming that what had been established in a General Council should not be altered by any lesser authority, but they have often gone further than this, to find in the added words an heretical meaning. At the Conferences held at Bonn in 1874 and 1875 A.D., under the presidency of Dr. von Döllinger, between members of the Eastern Orthodox, the Anglican, and the Old Catholic Churches, it was freely admitted by all that "the addition of the *Filioque* to the Creed was not made in a canonical manner;" but after a full discussion, a statement as to the Procession of the HOLY GHOST was drawn up, in which the members of these three communions could cordially unite, showing that whilst it might be difficult, at this day, to restore the Nicene Creed in the West to its earlier form, so far as concerned Anglicans and Old Catholics, there was no doctrinal difference between them and the Eastern Orthodox.

We should find in no Orthodox Eastern Church *sculptured* representations of our LORD or of the saints, it being believed that such may have an ill influence. But sacred pictures abound in churches and in private houses, and much honor is paid to these *icons*, as they are called, as serving "to remind us of the works of GOD and of His servants, to the intent that we, by looking upon them, may be stirred up to the imitation of holiness." Perhaps, at times, among the more ignorant, the honor paid to the *icons* goes beyond what the Church would approve, and has a character of superstition.

A clergyman of the American Church conversing with a learned Russian priest, expressed the objection that we should have to the manner in which the Virgin and other saints are addressed in hymns and prayers. The reply was that, "to understand these properly, we should interpret them in the Oriental sense, regarding them as poetical apostrophe and pious ejaculations, in accordance with the fervid imagination which characterizes the Orientals, rather than as set prayers, in the literal matter-of-fact way of people of the West." "Translated into English," he went on to say, "and taken in the sense in which you use such language, I should object to many expressions no less than you do; but to understand us as using these expressions in your sense is quite to misunderstand us."§ There is much force in this answer. We would ourselves wish to be judged, not by the meaning that might be given to our words, but by our intent in using them. The language of many of the prayers we use, expressing the deepest emotions of our

---

* The Archbishop of Syros and Tenos, quoted in the Appendix to the Report of the Russo-Greek Committee, 1871.

† Quoted in Paper No. III. of the Russo-Greek Committee.

‡ Quoted in Paper No. IV. of the Russo-Greek Committee.

§ Quoted in Paper No. III. of the Russo-Greek Committee.

hearts, would doubtless seem very cold to an Oriental.

The Orthodox Eastern Churches wish to offer to GOD a reasonable service, and so the Liturgy is celebrated in not less than ten different languages. In Greece and Russia more ancient forms of the language than that in common use are employed in Divine service, but the difference between ancient and modern Greek, between Sclavonic, or old Russian, and modern Russian, is less than is often imagined. We are thankful not to have *too* modern English in our Bibles and Prayer-Books.

So far are the Eastern Churches from enforcing clerical celibacy that parish Priests among them *must* be married men.

The Armenian, the Syrian, the Coptic, and the Assyrian Churches.—Besides the Orthodox Eastern Churches, there are in the East several other Churches, occupying an abnormal position. They have been accounted heretical in regard to so important a matter as the Incarnation of Our Blessed LORD. The first three of these Churches reject the Council of Chalcedon, in which was condemned the error of those who confounded in CHRIST's Person those natures which they should have distinguished. The Assyrian Church has refused to accept the Council of Ephesus, condemning the error of dividing CHRIST into two persons. But although these Churches have erred in not acknowledging Councils owned as General by the Church Catholic, it is not certain that in the case of any one of them is there a real departure from the Faith as set forth in those Councils.

In regard to all of them we need fuller and more definite information than we have. In the brief sketches of these Churches which follow, the facts are given according to those statements which seem best authenticated.

The *Armenian Church* is the largest and most important of these Churches at this time. When the Council of Chalcedon met, in 451 A.D., the Armenians, being at war with the Persians and hard pressed by them, were not represented at the Council. The reports of what was done at Chalcedon were either erroneous in themselves, or were misunderstood by them, and so the Armenian Church denounced the Council of Chalcedon, while, as there is good reason for saying, holding substantially the Faith as there established. Time and again has it seemed that the division between the Eastern Orthodox and the Armenians was on the point of being healed, but political or race feeling has thus far always prevented. A well-informed theologian of the Russian Church states that "it is quite certain that the Armenian Church separated from the Church Catholic, in the fifth century, in consequence of a misunderstanding, and that it is quite orthodox in the Faith. . . . If a union is possible between any two Churches, it is between the Eastern Orthodox and the Armenian, since they are only kept apart by external circumstances."*

The Armenian Church numbers at this time about 4,000,000, and is presided over by a *Catholicos*, or Supreme Patriarch, at Etchmiadzin, at the foot of Mount Ararat; three Patriarchs, at Constantinople, Sis, and Jerusalem; twelve Archbishops, and thirty-two Bishops. About forty Sees are vacant, and in charge of Vicars.

The *Syrian*, commonly called the *Jacobite Church*, after the name of Jacobus Baradæus, an early leader among them, would seem, like the Armenian Church, to have at once rejected the *Council* of Chalcedon and to have held fast to its *teachings*. There is much in regard to the history of this Church which is not clear, but its authorities disavow at present, and in behalf also of their predecessors, erroneous doctrines which, as they say, have been falsely ascribed to them. The parent body of the Syrian Church numbers at this time about 125,000 souls, under the care of a Patriarch residing at the convent of Der Zafran, near Mardin, in Mesopotamia, and eleven *Metrans*, or Metropolitans.

In India a branch of this Syrian Church exists, numbering about 120,000, with one Metran. These Syrians of India are often called "The Christians of St. Thomas," they having a tradition that their ancestors were converted to the faith by the preaching of the Apostle St. Thomas. For many years they formed part of the Assyrian (or "Nestorian") Church, of which we shall speak presently. At the close of the sixteenth century the Portuguese made efforts, by force and guile, to bring them into communion with Rome. After nearly one hundred years of subjection, a large part of them threw off the Roman yoke, and, obtaining a Bishop from the Syrian Church, considered themselves henceforth as forming part of it.

The *Coptic Church* of Egypt is in full agreement and communion with the Syrian Church. Dioscorus, Patriarch of Alexandria, was, as his people thought, unjustly condemned at Chalcedon. They took sides with him, and henceforth the Copts, the descendants of the ancient inhabitants of Egypt, have been in a state of formal separation from the Church Catholic. The few members of the Orthodox Church in Egypt have been almost entirely of the Greek race. An "Association for the Furtherance of Christianity in Egypt" has recently been formed in England, one of whose chief aims is to promote education among the Copts. It is believed by many who have given the matter attention that, whatever may have been their case in the past, the Copts at the present day are not averse to the true Faith. The Coptic Church has a Patriarch, three Metropolitans, and ten Bishops at this time, and numbers about 200,000.

The *Abyssinian* Church is part of the Coptic. It numbers not less, it is believed,

---

* L'Union Chretienne, December 2, 1866.

than 1,500,000, and has at present an Archbishop and two Bishops.

The *Assyrian*, often called the *Nestorian Church*, was in early days distinguished for its missionary zeal. In the eloquent words of Gibbon, "From the conquest of Persia they carried their spiritual arms to the north, the east, and the south. In the sixth century . . . Christianity was successfully preached to the Bactrians, the Huns, the Persians, the Indians, the Pers-Armenians, the Medes, and the Elamites; the barbaric Churches from the Gulf of Persia to the Caspian Sea were almost infinite. . . . The pepper coast of Malabar, and the isles of the sea, Socotra and Ceylon, were peopled with an increasing number of Christians. . . . In a subsequent age, the zeal of the Nestorians overleaped the limits which confined the ambition and curiosity both of the Greeks and Persians. . . . In their progress by sea and land, the Nestorians entered China by the port of Canton, and the northern residence of Sigan. . . . Under the reign of the Caliphs, the Nestorian Church was diffused from China to Jerusalem and Cyprus, and their numbers, with those of the Jacobites, were computed to surpass the Greek and Latin communities."* The Assyrian Church now is reduced to little, if any, over 75,000, under a Patriarch at Kochanes, in Kurdistan, and twelve Metropolitans.

In regard to the orthodoxy of the Assyrian Church, these words of the learned Bishop of Maryland, Bishop Whittingham, are most weighty: "Since there is reason to doubt whether the doctrine condemned by the Council of Ephesus, and, in consequence, by the whole Church throughout the world, was held by Nestorius; since it is certain that it is not now held by the Churches known as Nestorian; . . . since the Churches called Nestorian have constantly denied that they held the error they have been called on to forsake; since they profess their faith in the Catholic Creed, conformably with that of the Catholic Church, they are not lightly to be rejected from the number of the Churches of CHRIST, but rather to be regarded as brethren long alienated, not without some fault on both sides."†

Romanized, or so-called "*United*" *Eastern* Christians. Of these there are about 4,000,000 of the Greek Rite, chiefly in Austria, 120,000 of the Armenian Rite, 15,000 of the Syrian Rite in Turkey, and 120,000 in India, about 5000 of the Coptic Rite, 20,000 of the Chaldee Rite, and about 150,000 Maronites. These, while they have been allowed to keep many of their ancient ways, are members of the Church of Rome, and do not constitute, in any real sense, "Eastern Churches."

REV. C. R. HALE, S.T.D.

* Decline and Fall, chap. iv.
† In a note to Palmer on the Church, Amer. edit., vol. i. p. 388.

Easton, Diocese of. The Diocese of Easton comprises that portion of the State of Maryland, known as the "Eastern Shore," lying east of the Chesapeake Bay and the Susquehanna River; it is composed of the counties of Cecil, Kent, Queen Anne, Talbot, Caroline, Dorchester, Wicomico, Somerset, and Worcester. The Diocese of Maryland, of which Easton was originally a part, is the oldest Diocese but one in the American Church. Connecticut was organized in April, 1783 A.D., and Maryland in August of the same year. The history of the Church in Maryland, however, goes back to a much earlier date than that. It was in the year 1629 A.D. that a colony of about one hundred persons, composed of members of the Church of England, made a settlement on Kent Island. We learn from the scant records of that settlement that provision was made for the maintenance of religious services, and we know that a clergyman of the Church of England officiated on Kent Island for some years prior to 1637 A.D. Our space forbids us to enter into the early history of the Church in Maryland, so we will pass at once to the history of the Diocese of Easton. Soon after his consecration Bishop Whittingham declared that "The time would soon come when the interests of the Church would be furthered by a division of the Diocese." He had always been an advocate of small Dioceses, and while a Presbyter in the Diocese of New York had published an article in defense of his views upon that subject, which had great weight in causing the first division of the Diocese of New York, and which has since done good service in promoting the same good work in other Dioceses. Though the Bishop gave expression to his views so soon after his consecration, they do not seem to have had any effect until the year 1867 A.D. At the Diocesan Convention of that year a memorial was presented, asking "for the erection of the Eastern Shore into a separate and distinct Diocese." The memorial was referred to a committee, who recommended that the request be granted. Acting upon this recommendation, the Convention voted to grant the request, the Bishop gave his consent, and there the matter rested until the General Convention of 1868 A.D., when that body ratified the action of the Diocese of Maryland. The Bishop of Maryland called a Convention of the clergy and laity of the Eastern Shore to meet in Christ Church, Easton, on Thursday, the 19th day of November, 1868 A.D., "then and there to assemble and organize as a new Diocese."

The Convention met on the day appointed. The opening sermon was preached by the Rev. John O. Barton. The Rev. John Crosdale was elected President, and the Rev. James L. Bryan, M.D., Secretary. Twenty-one clergymen and twenty-eight lay delegates, representing thirty-two incorporated parishes and congregations, were found to be present. "Easton" was the name given to the new Diocese, and the assent of the Bishop and Standing Committee of Maryland to this name was announced. After the transaction of certain routine business, the Convention proceeded to the election of a Bishop, and the Rt. Rev. Henry C. Lay, D.D., LL.D., Missionary Bishop of Arkansas and the Indian Territory, was chosen. The Rev. Henry M. Mason, D.D., who had taken an active interest in the division of the Diocese, had entered into rest before this meeting, and the Convention adopted resolutions of regret at his decease. The Constitution of the Diocese of Maryland was so amended as to adapt it to the use of the new Diocese, and resolutions respecting the separation from the Bishop and Diocese of Maryland were adopted and ordered to be spread upon the journal. The Episcopal fund was reported as pledged or paid to the amount of $41,845, and the Bishop's salary was fixed at $2500 per annum. After the transaction of some other business, Christ Church, Easton, was chosen as the place of meeting for the next Convention, and 26th of May, 1869 A.D., appointed as the time. Upon the day appointed the clergy and laity assembled, but owing to the absence of the Bishop and the Standing Committee, in accordance with an informal arrangement previously made, the Convention adjourned until the 9th of the following June. The Convention met pursuant to this adjournment. The opening sermon was preached by the Bishop. Sixteen clergymen and twenty-four lay delegates were in attendance. The Bishop in his address gave a detailed account of his Episcopal labors from the 1st of April, when he surrendered his missionary jurisdiction of Arkansas. The address closed with specific recommendations under the following heads: "Review of the Diocese," "The Diocese of Maryland," "The Diocesan Convention," "Convocations," "Church Work in the Future," and "Specific Recommendations." Under the latter head the Bishop urged the attempt to sustain missionaries in every county, and the appropriation of offerings at Episcopal visitations to Diocesan missions. The Diocese was divided into three Convocations: the northern, comprising the counties of Cecil and Kent, containing seven clergymen; the middle, comprising Queen Anne, Caroline, Talbot, and Dorchester, containing thirteen clergymen; and the southern, comprising Wicomico, Somerset, and Worcester, with seven clergymen. These Convocations were made the subordinate missionary organization of the Diocese, and were to be composed of the rectors and assistant ministers of the counties contained in the Convocation, with two lay delegates from each parish. They were to meet at least three times a year. And at each meeting there was to be a mission service, and an offering made for Diocesan missions.

Having traced the history of the Diocese from the preliminary steps taken towards its separation from the old Diocese to its organization, we have but little else to add. It has gone on quietly doing its appointed work, and those who have been identified with it from the beginning are satisfied with its quiet and steady progress, and feel that they have reason to thank GOD and take courage. If our space permitted, we would like to speak more in detail of the men who, under GOD, were the means of securing for us a separate Diocesan organization. Of John Crosdale, the faithful priest and missionary, who spent his entire ministry in an obscure country parish in order to strengthen the things that remained and that were ready to die; of the faithful rector of St. Michael's Parish, who canvassed the Diocese and raised the Episcopal fund, and of others whose labors in the same good cause were none the less zealous or effective. But we can only say of them all that they did their work well; some of them still survive to see the good results of their labors, and the names of those who have fallen asleep will be held in everlasting remembrance. In conclusion, it may be said that, in spite of the declaration made in certain quarters that the Diocese of Easton is a failure, those who are familiar with her affairs are quite satisfied with the result of division, and see no reason for discouragement. While the growth of the Diocese has not been startling, it has been real, and the following statement by the Bishop of what has been accomplished during the first twelve years of her existence, while it proves that the growth of the Diocese has been steady and marked, will serve as a sufficient answer to the statements of those who, from an insufficient knowledge of the facts in the case, were led to take a different view of the matter:

"The nine counties on the Eastern Shore of Maryland were made a Diocese by reason of a geographical necessity. As a matter of fact and experience, it had proved impossible for the Bishop of Maryland, with the superior claims of the Western Shore, and the intervention of Chesapeake Bay, to render the necessary offices to the less significant region. It does not at all follow that the like course should be pursued where there is no like necessity, and where nobody is neglected in the Episcopal ministrations.

"Furthermore, I suppose that none of our people anticipated that our Diocese would be a splendid example to others. It is peninsular, no tide of travel or emigration flowing through. It has no cities, no towns of more than 3000 inhabitants. It has no extensive manufactures, no foreign trade. In a word, it is emphatically a rural Diocese, made up of farms of moderate extent and of the villages necessary to supply the local trade. As for population, it has 157,000, which is less (according to late estimates) than that of the one city of Washing-ten in the old Diocese from which it was taken.

"Reasonable people must see that we cannot vie with Dioceses of large numbers and resources, having the centralized wealth of a city to sustain Diocesan institutions. . . .

"So far as we ourselves are concerned, we are not at all discomposed, and would not care to make reply. But inasmuch as our example is imported into the general question, it seems right to demur to this disparagement. It has occurred to me that the fairest test of success or failure would be to take the roll of the parishes as I found it at the first Convention over which I presided (viz., that of 1869 A.D.), and to state in each instance the gain or loss, if any, in those particulars which can be computed and measured. I freely grant that success and failure in the highest and truest sense cannot be thus computed. Yet a certain significance attaches to the outward manifestations of zeal and enterprise. Let us, then, go over in order the list of the parishes. I omit none,—not even those which exist only on paper. What are the changes within the last twelve years?

"1. *St. John's, Caroline.*—A new church builded at Greensboro', and rectory improved. Increase, $3000.

"2. *St. Mary's, Whitechapel.* — Revived after a vacancy in the rectorship of a century. Chapel building at Denton. Increase, $1500.

"3. *Augustine.*—Nominal. No change.

"4. *North Elk.*—Divided into two. Two churches builded in Port Deposit and on the fishing shore, and one rectory purchased. Increase, $10,000.

"5. *North Sassafras.* — Parish church rebuilded. Church builded at Cecilton. Increase, $10,000.

"6. *Trinity, Elkton.*—Rectory purchased. Increase, $3000.

"7. *Dorchester.*—New church on Taylor's Island. Increase, $3000.

"8. *East New Market.*—No change.

"9. *Great Choptank.* — Chapel at Maple Dam; other churches restored. Increase, $2000.

"10. *Vienna.*—No change.

"11. *Chester.*—Parish church rebuilt and other improvements. Increase, $6000.

"12. *I. U. Parish.*—No change.

"13. *North Kent.*—New church at Millington. Rectory added. Increase, $6000.

"14. *St. Paul's, Kent.*—No change.

"15. *Shrewsbury.* — Parish church restored. New church at Galena. Increase, $6000.

"16. *Kent Island.*—New chapel. Increase, $1500.

"17. *St. Luke's, Queen Anne.* — Parish church restored. New church at Sudlersville. Increase, $5000.

"18. *St. Paul's, Queen Anne.*—No change, except the establishment of an excellent parish school and some restorations of church.

"19. *Wye.*—No change.

"20. *Coventry.*— Rectory builded. Increase, $2000.

"21. *Somerset.*—New church at Monie. Increase, $3000.

"22. *Wicomico.*—Nominal. No change.

"23. *Pocomoke.* — Rectory purchased. New church at Naswaddux. Increase, $2500.

"24. *St. Michael's.* — Divided into three self-supporting parishes. Parish church rebuilded. Two new churches at Cleburne and Longwoods. Rectory builded. Increase, $20,000.

"25. *St. Peter's, Talbot.*—Parish church enlarged and restored at a cost of $10,000. New congregation formed under the Bishop, with two chapels (shanties, to be sure). Rectory builded. Orphanage established. Increase, $25,000. This includes partial endowment of Home for Friendless Children.

"26. *Holy Trinity, Oxford.* — Nominal. Served from Whitemarsh.

"27. *Whitemarsh.* — Chapel builded at Oxford. Increase, $1500.

"28. *St. Matthew's.* — Nominal. No change.

"29. *Spring Hill.*—Divided into two parishes.

"30. *Stepney.*—Nominal. No change.

"31. *All Hallows.*—No change, except restorations. Increase, $1000.

"32. *Worcester.*—New church at Ocean City. Increase, $1000.

"To sum up these 'simple annals of the poor,' *nowhere has there been any loss.* A few parishes on the list are nominal. A few others exhibit no material gain. In all the rest there has been substantial advance. During the twelve years the communicants have increased one-half; the parochial clergy one-third. The missionary expenditure is three or four times as much as before division. No stated pecuniary aid has come from without.

"I respectfully submit that if the prosperity of the whole can be measured by the prosperity of its parts, the Diocese of Easton is *not* a failure, to be held up as a warning to others.

"The clergy tell me that my estimates are below the mark. I may add that out of sixty-one churches and chapels, fifty-eight have all the seats free.

"I have endeavored to emancipate myself from the influence of imagination, 'that delusive faculty ever obtruding beyond its sphere.' I have purposely weakened my statement by including a number of parishes which have no real existence.

"The facts may readily be verified."

Statistics for 1886 A.D.: Clergy, 31; parishes, 38; churches and chapels, 62; lay readers, 6; candidates for holy orders, 1; baptisms, infants, 427, adults, 18, total, 445; confirmed, 172; communicants, 2727; Sunday-school teachers, 251; Sunday-school scholars, 1788; contributions, $36,813.97.

Rev. J. Worral Larmour.

Ecclesiastes. One of the books written by Solomon. It contains many difficulties which have proved to be a great puzzle to commentators. So much so that though its inspiration and Canonical authority have been admitted, yet it has been denied that it was written by Solomon. The internal difficulties are confessedly very great; but objections can readily be mustered against any theory of interpretation, so that it may very well have been the genuine work of Solomon the Preacher, the Son of David, king in Jerusalem. It has been alleged that the Aramaisms (words and phrases from one of the dialects of Babylonia) number one hundred, and show a late date,—later by four hundred years and more than Solomon's time,—probably *after* the return from the Babylonian exile. The reply reduces the number of Aramaisms to eight, and denies that they and the style are out of harmony with Solomon's reign, for the Hebrew was a singularly poor language, and was better fitted for sententious, pithy aphorisms than for any diffuse discourse. It is alleged that the tone is not such as Solomon could have felt, but so far from that, it is directly in the line of thought a man who had a large share of insight and keenness would feel after having blunted his spiritual perceptions and then have repented. The first tender devoutness is lost, the trustful innocence has disappeared, and the conclusion is that of a man who, having tried everything in his reach of human joys and earthly excesses, at last finds the sum of the whole matter to be, Fear God and keep His commandments. It is, however, a result in words identical with, but in tone dissimilar to, the trustful, "The Fear of God is the beginning of wisdom, a good understanding have they that do thereafter, the praise of it endureth forever." It is a shock to our ideas of truthfulness to suppose that a book written under the name of Solomon, by a later writer, could be admitted into the Canon without a comment or note explanatory of it. It might be defended in ordinary literary work, but it is absolutely opposed to any right conception of the fact that the Canon of Scripture was formed by men, but by the defending and guiding influence of the Holy Ghost.

The truest appreciation of the book is found in considering it the Confessions, in a kind of mental debate, of one who, having had wisdom for spiritual things given him, debased it to searching the depths of earthly happiness; and is in accord with what one in Solomon's position—having wealth, yet corruptions in the state and society destroying his pleasure; having royal power, yet seeing it thwarted; enjoying life keenly, yet having its cup dashed from his lips—would acknowledge to be the sum of his experience. In fact, the objections are more ingenious and plausible than really sound; since we know that conclusions drawn from internal evidence not buttressed by external facts are very treacherous, as they are based upon arbitrary assumptions that may be wholly out of accord with the real contents of the book. The Salomonic authorship may be considered as established.

Ecclesiasticus. A book of the Apocrypha, written by Jesus, the son of Sirach, 190–170 B.C., and translated from the Hebrew by his grandson (130 B.C.). The book was composed at Jerusalem, and was translated in Egypt. It is based upon and imitates the Proverbs, and was evidently the work of a very devout and earnest student of the Scriptures. It is well worth reading and study, since it is full of practical wisdom. It was considered Canonical by a few writers, and was quoted by them freely,—Clement of Alexandria, Origen, Cyprian. It is quoted by Augustine and Jerome, but as useful, excellent, but not in the Canon.

Economist. An officer in some Irish Cathedrals, who is appointed to manage the common Cathedral fund, to see to necessary repairs, to pay Church officers, etc.

Economy. The management of a household by a steward, but used to mean a dispensation, as the Christian Economy administered by the Son of God. It was so used by the Apostle St. Paul (Eph. i. 10): "That in the dispensation of the fullness of times he might gather together in one all things in Christ." It also was used to signify the Apostolic office: "I have intrusted to me a dispensation" (as a steward) (1 Cor. ix. 17). "For His body's sake, which is the Church whereof I am made a minister, according to the dispensation of God" (Col. i. 25). But the Fathers generally keep it to refer to the administration of redemption by the Son of God. St. Athanasius speaks of the Economy of the Cross, of His blood-shedding, of His human nature. St. Basil of the Economy of our God and Saviour in man's behalf, which is the calling from falling and the restoration to the household of God. So, too, Gregory Nazianzen: "But when we speak of God as saving, avenging, justifying, as the God of peace, of Abraham, of Isaac, and of Jacob, or of all Israel, as spiritual and seeing God, these phrases are used of the Economy." Such a term could also readily fall into Gnostic phraseology very readily, and was so misused. But there was another use of the word too. It was used to express the plan by which the Catechist limited (or was limited by the Church) the amount of instruction which would be intrusted to the catechumens. They were intrusted "according to the stewardship," with varying degrees of knowledge in Christian doctrine. It lost this sense with the disappearance of the catechetical classes. It has been very seriously debated how far this concealment was carried, and whether the catechumens were purposely misled or had unfairly withheld from them the proportion of the Faith. To us now it is by no means so important, still, in a lesser degree, it is a very important question how far a teacher, having to attract those ignorant of Church doctrine to receive it, should ignore differences, and dwell upon the agreements and harmonies of the truths held in common. So Clement of Alexandria dwells upon the apparent agreement of Platonic philosophy with Christian truth. St. Paul's speeches at Lystra and at Athens give the fundamental rule to be followed. What we need is a deeper study of irenics, not of polemics; there has been too much of that.

The word Economy has returned into use, latterly, in its older theological sense.

Edification. A building up; a growth in grace, in love, in faith, in all Christian virtues by the help of the HOLY GHOST. It is not identical with sanctification, which has a larger meaning. It is rather applied to individual than to communal development and growth, though this sense is very frequent in Holy Scripture. It includes the idea of instruction, and this has often been wrongly made the exclusive import of the word. Edification refers for its primal force to house-building. Hence this word is used, *oikodomé*, by St. Paul in 1 Cor. iii., to describe a spiritual building, and often elsewhere. *Oikodomos* is used in Acts iv. 11 as a builder, an edifier. And this term wherever used implies man's co-operation. So the discipline of the Church is for edifying, "building up" the Church. The teaching in the Church is for edification, Apostles, Prophets, Evangelists, Pastors, Teachers,—*i.e.*, government and instruction for the same end, "till we all come into the unity of the Faith and of the knowledge of the SON of GOD, . . . may grow up unto Him in all things which is the Head, even CHRIST, from whom the whole body fitly joined together and compacted by that which every joint supplieth according to the effectual working in the measure of every part maketh increase of the body unto the edifying of itself in love." The growth in all virtuous and godly living, the example of patience, courage, love, of all the Christian virtues, is edifying,—*i.e.*, it builds up others, who see it and who are influenced by our conduct. Therefore edification comes by the indwelling of the HOLY GHOST, and is in a sort the work of confirmation, which builds us as consecrated stones into GOD'S Temple, and by which we are built up in our most holy Faith, and through the gifts thus come to us by it are edifying others in the truth. The unity of the Church and our own union with it in the power and grace of the HOLY GHOST are the means of our receiving edification and contributing to the edification of others. The compactest building is best built. The closest communion in the Church is the truest edification, for it is most deeply bound up in the graces of the SPIRIT.

Elder. In Holy Scripture, the office of the Presbyter (from which the word Priest is formed by contraction), who exercised a spiritual function. In scriptural usage and in Church history such a person as a *lay* Elder is an impossible person; the words contradict each other. The first hint of such an officer was given by Calvin.

Election. I. The title of the XVII. "Article of Religion" is, "Of Predestination and Election." The words are used as though they were synonymous, and the first sentence is a definition of their meaning. "Predestination to life is the everlasting purpose of GOD, whereby (before the foundations of the world were laid) He hath constantly decreed by His counsel, secret to us, to deliver from curse and damnation those whom He hath chosen (*elegit*) in CHRIST out of mankind, and to bring them by CHRIST to everlasting salvation." After enlarging upon the last clause of this sentence, the Article goes on to state the comfort and the danger which attend the consideration of the doctrine, and closes with an appeal to the general (*generaliter*—universally) promises of GOD as set forth in Holy Scripture. The word "elect" occurs also in the Collect for All-Saints' day. In the English Prayer-Book it is also found in the Office for Baptism, "Thy faithful and elect children;" and in the Catechism, "me and all the elect people of GOD." The natural question is, how these different uses of the term agree with each other and with the doctrine of Holy Scripture. For as the terms, and therefore the doctrines of predestination and election, occur in the Scriptures, all Christians must hold some "doctrine" upon the subject, and the question for us is, whether what we hold is the doctrine of Holy Scripture.

In the first place, however, it is well to remember that questions about fate and foreknowledge, providence and free-will, are not confined to any time or class of men. "The Essenes among the Jews, Zeno and the Stoics, and the followers of Mohammed were all rigid predestinarians, believing that all the affairs of the world and the actions of the human race were ordered by an eternal and inexorable decree." St. Augustine, in the fourth century, was the great exponent of the doctrine in the Church. Owing to his authority and influence, it was the more general doctrine of the Western Church. After St. Augustine, its great expounder was St. Thomas Aquinas. It was the doctrine of Zwinglius and John Calvin. It is natural that the questions which it involves should arise whenever men think at all, but it is certain that when they depend entirely upon their own reason and knowledge they will fall into one of two errors. Reasoning from the sovereignty of GOD they exclude the freedom of man, which they cannot reconcile with it, and are led into fatalism. Reasoning from the freedom of man, they are led to deny the sovereignty of GOD.

II. The Christian faith does not explain to us the problems which we discover in nature and in ourselves, but it reveals to us Him in whom GOD and man are reconciled, and by whom evil is conquered and man delivered from it. It does not remove the darkness, but it throws light upon us and around us to guide us. It does not explain GOD'S eternal purposes, but it declares to us one purpose and one "decree," the coming of the SON of GOD for man's salvation. "I will declare the decree. Thou art my SON. This day have I begotten Thee" (Ps. ii. 7). If we are to understand the meaning of "the election" of GOD, we must begin from the ground of Christian faith, and not narrow that faith by some preconceived notion of the doctrine.

Another principle is as necessary. The Old Testament and the New are one, and the union of them is in CHRIST. The Old foretells Him and prepares for Him. The New reveals Him. The New is the fulfillment of the Old. The faith of the Old Testament is the faith of expectation, believing the promises of GOD, looking for CHRIST. The faith of the New Testament is the faith of possession, having CHRIST. The Old and the New will use the same words even, and their meaning will unite in CHRIST.

III. We find this word election, or choice, in frequent use in the Old Testament. It is perhaps unfortunate that the more frequent word in the authorized version of the Old Testament is choose, chosen; and elect is rare, while in the New elect is used in a large proportion of cases. But it will help to clear our view if we fix it in mind that the words are translations of the same word. The chosen are the elect. Election is choice.

In the Old Testament the choice or election of GOD falls upon men, cities, peoples, inanimate things. He chooses "a place to set His name there" (Neh. i. 9), one man for a king (Deut. xvii. 15), a people to be His people (Deut. vii. 6, 7), a tribe to be His priests (Deut. xxi. 5), a family to be High-Priests (Ps. cv. 26). Israel is His chosen generation (Ex. xix. 5, 6), Abraham His servant, David His servant (Ps. lxxviii. 70), Israel His elect (Isa. xlv. 4). GOD has a purpose, and with that purpose in view He chooses men to carry it out, while as regards that purpose He passes by and puts aside others. That purpose becomes more and more clear as time goes on. It is the purpose which was indicated by the promise made in the Garden of Eden, and repeated to Abraham, and again to David. Abraham is chosen with reference to that purpose, and after him the people Israel. Israel was therefore elect " according to the purpose" of GOD, and for that purpose elect to special privileges. Pharaoh stood in the way of that purpose and went down before it. Esau was set aside and set himself aside, and in comparison with his brother and with reference to this special purpose of GOD is "hated" (Rom. ix. 14). This, therefore, is election or choice in the Old Testament, the choice of the people Israel, and of men and things belonging to them for the carrying out of GOD'S one purpose of blessing the world "in CHRIST." In the way of that purpose their choice to special blessings; a choice which was indicated by GOD and claimed by them in the rite of circumcision. By which rite they entered upon an inheritance not only of temporal but of spiritual and eternal blessings,—unless indeed they forfeited them.

IV. The purpose of GOD with Israel was fulfilled when " of them CHRIST came, who is over all GOD blessed forever." That purpose was His eternal purpose, and had been declared before Abraham in the Garden. It entered "the parenthesis of the Law" (Rom. v. 20) with Abraham and passed out through the "broken wall of partition" (Eph. ii. 14) into its fulfillment in CHRIST. The Kingdom of Israel is fulfilled in the Kingdom of CHRIST, the law in the Gospel "preached to every creature," the election of Israel in the Church of CHRIST, "which is His body, the fullness of Him that filleth all in all." The same principles underlie the old dispensation and the new. The relation of one to the other throughout is defined in our LORD'S words, "I am not come to destroy but to fulfill" (St. Matt. v. 17).

Two of St. Paul's Epistles may be said to deal especially with this subject of the election and eternal purpose of GOD. The Epistle to the Romans is often appealed to as though it taught the narrowest doctrine of individual election. If we will remind ourselves that it was manifestly written to rebuke the narrowness and exclusiveness of those Jewish Christians who would have claimed the Church as the special heritage of Judaism, and to show how GOD'S purpose reached out towards all who would believe in Him, we will agree with the early Church, which read it as though it breathed the spirit directly opposed to exclusiveness and narrowness, the very spirit of liberty and liberality. It sets before us the purpose of GOD and the election of GOD according to that purpose, but it shows us how that purpose extended to *all* men, and how it is being accomplished in its fullness by CHRIST. Love and hate, honor and dishonor, calling, glory, and mercy, and hardening and casting off and destruction are defined by this purpose of GOD and explain the relation of men to it (Rom. ix.).

Next after the Epistle to the Romans St. Paul wrote that to the Ephesians, and the two are closely connected by common words and thoughts. In both he bases his argument on the eternal purpose of GOD as it is revealed in CHRIST, but in Ephesians he advances a step in the development of the thought which he had sketched in the Romans, and the subject of the Epistle is, the Church as the Body of CHRIST and the body of the elect, " whom GOD hath chosen in Him before the foundation of the world, that we should be holy and blameless before Him in love, having predestinated us to adoption by JESUS CHRIST to Himself, according to the good purpose of His will, to the praise of the giory of His grace" (i. 7), "being predestinated according to His purpose, who worketh all things according to the council of His will" (i. 11). If we use the Epistle to the Galatians as a preface to the Romans, we will therefore have in these three a chain of thought like this,—first, in Galatians, the setting aside of the old system of the law; then, in Romans, the transition stage, the transfer of the rights of the old election to the new; and last, in Ephesians, the full purpose of GOD being fully accomplished in the sight of angels and of men by the Church.

The Epistle to the Ephesians is perhaps the most systematic and complete treatise of any of the Epistles. The thoughts and arguments can be arranged without violence in a kind of concentric circles, of which the centre and sun of the system is CHRIST. "In Him" all things are summed up in heaven and in earth, past, present, and to come. In Him the purpose of GOD is revealed and in Him accomplished. From Him the influence goes out and fills the circle of the Church, which is "His fullness," by which His "wisdom is made known to the powers in heavenly places," which, "with all saints," as a body comprehends His surpassing love, and in which and by which the glory that goes out from Him is returned to Him. Then that circle widens into another, of the members of that body who are made members of it by the one baptism, hold the one faith, belong to the one LORD, worship one GOD the FATHER. By that union by our baptism GOD'S predestination of us is manifested and His election effected. The reason and final cause of His choice of us is "the good pleasure of His will." The fact of our election is proved by His act of calling and receiving us. Then this circle widens again into the practical lessons of the duties which belong to them that are members of the body of CHRIST and elect of GOD. If we bear in mind and add to all this the further thought that GOD is "the living GOD" and "the GOD of the living," and that therefore whatever is His "hath eternal life," so that, as the purpose of GOD is from eternity, so it goes on through eternity, we will have a fair idea of this wonderful Epistle, and of what St. Paul meant by *election*. The Church of GOD is the body of the elect. Election is the choice of men according to the will of GOD to special privileges for the carrying out of His eternal purpose, and with the purpose included of their present and eternal blessing.

One fact will show us how true the view is which identifies the Church with the body of the elect, viz.: that the Apostles constantly address the whole body of the Christians as elect and holy. St. John addresses them as "in Him that is true." St. Peter salutes them as "elect according to the foreknowledge of GOD," and addresses them as "a chosen generation, a royal priesthood," quoting the very words addressed to the Church in the wilderness, and bids them "make their calling and election sure." And the idea of all St. Paul's Epistles is the same, as can be seen by reading the salutations to them. They are addressed as a body. There is no if or hesitation. They have these rights and privileges. The one question is not whether they are sanctified and elect of GOD, but whether they live accordingly.

Otherwise, unless they "work out their salvation," and "make their calling and election sure," their present gifts shall become their condemnation, and they "become castaways," even as "all our fathers were baptized into Moses, and ate the same spiritual food and drank the same spiritual drink. For they drank of that spiritual Rock that followed them, and that Rock was CHRIST. But with many of them GOD was not well pleased: for they were overthrown in the wilderness. Wherefore let him that thinketh he standeth take heed lest he fall" (1 Cor. x.). But, on the other hand, "by their fruits ye shall know them." "The fruits of the Spirit are in all goodness, and righteousness, and truth." And by them "the Spirit witnesseth with our spirit that we are the children of GOD. And if children then heirs. Heirs of GOD and joint heirs with CHRIST." So when "the LORD shall present unto Himself a glorious Church," "an entrance shall be ministered unto you abundantly into the everlasting Kingdom of our LORD and SAVIOUR JESUS CHRIST" (2 Pet. i. 11).

V. This view of election leaves many questions unanswered of which we would be glad to know the answers, but which we do not and cannot, because they have not been revealed. But it has this advantage,—that it does not profess to be wise above what is written; and this also,—that it does not need to explain away anything that is written either in the Old Testament or the New. It was the view which was accepted in the Church before St. Augustine, and is now the generally accepted view in the Church of England and in our own Church. It will not satisfy those who are determined to have a logical theology, even though they come to conclusions like those of Calvin when he said of his own dogma, "It is a horrible decree indeed." But it will satisfy Christian faith.

It only remains to inquire whether this view of election, which identifies the body of the elect with the Church of CHRIST, agrees with the doctrines and formularies of the Church. The view which would give a Calvinistic meaning to the XVII. Article is negatived by the fact that the language of that article is of Lutheran and not of Calvinistic origin, and was drawn up before the Calvinistic system had made any headway in England, by the fact that thorough-going Calvinists have never been satisfied with its language, and at one time made serious efforts to change it. But the strongest argument is that the Calvinistic interpretation cannot be made to harmonize with other articles even, and still less with other formularies. In the Collect for All-Saints' day, and in the Church of England offices for Baptism and the Catechism, "the elect" is synonymous with "the baptized," and though the word is omitted in our office, the idea is the same throughout,—that by baptism this child " is made the member of CHRIST, the child of GOD, and an inheritor of the Kingdom of Heaven," by GOD'S "good will towards him." And in the Holy Communion, " CHRIST died for thee" is asserted to each communicant. And throughout the services of the Church the same idea prevails and underlies them all,—that those who believe and are baptized are numbered with the elect and are in the ark of salvation. Now let them see to it that they "make their calling and election sure."

Authorities: Wordsworth on Epistles, Browne, Burnet, Forbes, on Articles, Faber on Election.   REV. L. W. GIBSON.

Elements. The outward and visible signs in the Sacraments, so called both because water, wine, and bread are simple substances, and because they are of the very essentials of a complete Sacrament. They are the channel of conveyance, the sign and the seal of the Sacrament. How GOD chooses to use them we cannot tell. It is a mystery; but that He does so use them He has repeatedly taught us, and we have but to use them as He appoints: water to the mystical washing away of sin, bread and wine for giving us the Body and Blood of our risen LORD, " whereby He does assure us of His favor and goodness towards us; and that we are very members incorporate in the mystical Body of His SON, . . . and are also heirs through hope of His everlasting kingdom." No baptism can be administered otherwise than by water, nor the Holy Communion otherwise than with bread and wine. These are elementary to the administration of the Sacraments.

Elements; human and divine in Holy Scripture. In the discussions so rife at present about all parts of religion, there is a singular omission to weigh well the different elements which make it up. It is of GOD, and so divine. It is for man, and so must suit, and sympathize with, his nature at all points. It is lived in and assumed by man, and so there is mingled in it a human element. As a document perfect and flawless when it issues from the author's pen, by repeated and careless copying becomes filled with errors and varying readings, and sometimes with perversions, which yet do not destroy, though may nominally impair their own authenticity, and which all point by their varying errors to the true text, so is religion. Its Divine authorship is overlaid or perverted in minute things which amount to real errors, if they do not compensate each other or are not eliminated with care by the human elements. This mixture of the human and Divine is most completely exhibited in the Church, which is the Body of CHRIST and yet is made up of men, and in the Holy Scriptures, which are inspired by GOD and yet were intrusted to men to write and to transmit. Indeed, we bear about in our body the same wonderful commixtion,—our souls the Breath of GOD, our bodies of dust.

Inspiration takes and uses men for its purposes, as heralds, declarers, accurate recorders, and mouth-pieces for its messages. It does not destroy, but it sanctifies and greatly magnifies the powers of such men. Isaiah inspired by the same HOLY SPIRIT did not speak as did Jeremiah or Daniel. Balaam divinely directed by the same HOLY GHOST was not more willing to bless the People than the High-Priest was to prophesy of the death of CHRIST as a blessing for all men. David sang by the HOLY GHOST, but so did Isaiah. And they were preserved from error in any way; their own natural idiom He used to accurately convey His messages, whether of mercy or of warning, of love, and of peace, or His revelations. There was the human element. Each man, with his capacities and devout or indevout temper, his command of language, peculiarly his own,—this man with all his traits of character was chosen and used by that one and eternal SPIRIT of GOD.

The Church receives the inspired record, but is herself founded upon the Resurrection of CHRIST, each member being united to Him by baptism, and bound up with his brother by the double bond of a natural and spiritual brotherhood. The Head, CHRIST, is immortal, the members of CHRIST are now mortal. He is sinless, they are struggling with sin. He is ever present, and educates, feeds, and reconciles us, yet we are restless, oblivious, willful, and ungrateful, still the bond is never broken between the Head and His body, which is to grow in holiness.

The omission to comprehend these two apparently conflicting yet actually ever-present facts both in inspiration, the Church of GOD, and our own nature leads many into fundamental errors upon religion and the soul's relation to GOD, and through Him to his neighbor.

Elevation. The elements of bread and wine in Canon of the Mass in the Roman Church, after consecration, and for the purpose of adoring them. It was an innovation introduced in the twelfth century, and afterwards defined by a rubric in 1271 A.D. by Gregory X., enjoining the celebrant and people to kneel and adore. There was an elevation of the elements in the earliest Liturgies, also after consecration, which was made with the words " Holy things for holy places" (according to Archdeacon Freeman). Neither the later nor the earlier elevations are sanctioned in the Prayer-Book; nor are they consonant with the leading feeling of our Liturgy. The Article XXVIII. closes with this sentence: " The sacrament of the LORD'S Supper was not by

CHRIST'S ordinance reserved, carried about, lifted up, or worshiped." It was a mere deduction of common logic from the previous rejection, in the Article, of the Roman figment of transubstantiation.

Elohim. GOD. One of the names by which He was known to the Jew, and the first name used by Moses. "In the beginning ELOHIM made the heavens and the earth." It is a plural noun, and when used in Hebrew with a singular verb always refers to the CREATOR; with a plural verb it may refer to the false gods and idols. It is translated GOD, while JEHOVAH (JAH) is translated by the word LORD. The word ELOHIM means mighty one, strong one (and is referred to the MESSIAH in Isaiah ix. 5), while the root of JEHOVAH is JAH, the Living One. The plural form, ELOHIM, then wraps up the doctrine of the HOLY TRINITY, while the singular, JEHOVAH, sets forth the self-existence of GOD. The use of the name GOD thus in the first chapter of Genesis is very significant when compared with the first verses of St. John's Gospel, and we can understand why these words, "let us make man in our image;" "behold, the man is become as one of us, to know good and evil," could be used by Moses, whose language is ever supposed to teach the unity of GOD in person as well as in nature; but he does teach really the Unity and the Trinity in the famous *Shema:* "Hear, oh Israel, the JEHOVAH ELOHIM is one ELOHIM." Keeping these facts in mind we can easily see why Moses could use both names, and we shall have a ready answer to those who observe only that Moses did use these names separately, and so conclude that he compiled his first book out of two separate documents, one in which the name ELOHIM was used, and a second in which the name JEHOVAH was used, but who refuse also to observe that he uses the words interchangeably or together. These hypercritics are compelled, to be consistent, to divide sentences into two parts in order to show where, according to their theory, Moses wove two distinct documents into one narrative. The absurdity of the criticism is made glaring by such an effort. That ELOHIM and JEHOVAH were names of their fathers' GOD, well known to the Jews, and that Moses used these names not by direct inspiration and revelation, but from the very religion he was taught, is true. But his use of each name, separately in some places and together in others, is based upon the inner meaning of those passages, and when duly considered will give them a depth which they had not before for the student. To take but the Decalogue: 'in the first commandment, "Thou shalt have no other ELOHIM but me." In the second commandment, against graven images, "For I, JEHOVAH, thy ELOHIM, am a jealous ELOHIM," where all the names are used with the deepest meaning of the Christian religion. In the fourth,—"For in six days JEHOVAH made heaven and earth, the sea, and all that in them is, and rested the seventh day, wherefore JEHOVAH blessed the sabbath day and hallowed it"—the unity of the Divine nature of GOD and His self-existence is appropriately used, setting forth His awful, perfect omnipotence over all His works. In the fifth, "that thy days may be long in the land which JEHOVAH, thy ELOHIM, giveth thee," brings out the deeper meaning of the words land,—in the land of the living (*i.e.*, in heaven,—and they desire a better country, that is, a heavenly), and at once JEHOVAH ELOHIM acquires a wonderful richness of reference to the life and immortality which JEHOVAH, by His CHRIST, has brought to light for us. The absurd criticism has the use of developing the deeper hidden meanings of the sacred text.

Elvira. The Council of Elvira (or Illiberis), in Spain, was held early in the fourth century. Some place it in the year 300 A.D., others as late as 309 A.D., both being influenced by doctrinal views probably to fix it either before or after the date of Constantine's edict of toleration to Christians in Spain (306 A.D.). The occasion of the Council appears to have been troubles in the Church arising out of persecution and oppression by the heathen. There were present at it Hosius, Bishop of Cordova, and eighteen other Bishops; while twenty-six Priests and certain Deacons took part in the deliberations. A large number of strict Canons were passed relating to discipline, some of the chief ones being as follows: Those who had voluntarily sacrificed to idols were to be finally excommunicated; those who had not gone beyond offering a present to an idol might be received into communion again, after penance, at the point of death; the use of marriages was forbidden to the clergy; pictures ought not to be allowed in churches; and severe penalties were enacted in detail against adultery, prostitution, murder, false swearing, and slander.

Authorities: Landon, Robertson.

Emanation. A Gnostic theory, which was worked out in Alexandria, of the creation. It was founded upon the Zoroastrian doctrine of Light,—as the type of the Divine nature, and so that the higher we ascend the nearer we are to the true source of all matter and spirit,—conjoined to the Platonic theory of the Archetypal idea, that is the self-existent Being,—Plato's idea,—and the absolute light of the Persian coincided, for as the thought and as the substance receded from the central light and self-existence, so it became more attenuated, and the fullness (*cf.* Col. i. 19; Eph. i. 23) became emptiness when the limit was reached. This was worked up into the Gnostic doctrine of æons (*vide* ÆON), and probably, as the Gnostic taught successions, emanations, and generations of œons, it was against their wild vagary of "the fullness" St. Paul used the phrase as referred to above, and against these generations of æons that he warned St.

Timothy "neither to give heed to fables and endless genealogies which minister questions." Emanation appears to have been an early form of the now so-called doctrine of evolution.

Ember-days. The derivation of the word *ember* is very doubtful. It has been derived from ember,—ashes, *i.e.*, of each of the four seasons, which is not at all a probable derivation; from a corruption and contraction of the Latin *jejunia quatuor temporum;* German, *Quatember;* Dutch, *Quartertemper;* Danish, *Kratember;* or from the Saxon *Ymbren*,—a revolution or circuit, which, as these are recurrent days in the Church's year, seems to be the most likely. They are three days of fasting in the four seasons, which have been specially observed, to intercede for GOD's mercy on each of these four divisions of the year. The Wednesday, Friday, and Saturday after the first Sunday in Lent, the Feast of Pentecost, September 14 and December 13. The date of the establishment of these fasts lies probably between the Council of Nice and the time of Pope Leo I., 440 A.D. Four fasts were observed, according to Philastrius, after 325 A.D., but they were not the ember fasts, though it is likely that the ember fasts grew out of them. In Leo I.'s time we have a clear description of them, and from that time on there is a continuous notice of them. But they were of Italian origin. The Gallican Church did not receive them much before the ninth century. The African and the Milanese Churches could not have observed them, at least in Leo's time. They were accepted in Spain in the seventh century. In the East they have received no observance. From the beginning of their appointment, it is probable that they were connected, though not canonically till later, with the ordinations of the clergy, a connection which has ever since been maintained with more or less laxness. There are two prayers appointed for those to be ordained, either one of which is to be read at these seasons. They should be used on the Sunday previous and throughout the week, ending with the Sunday after the Ember Saturday. The first of the two prayers is probably by Bishop Cosin, a remarkably beautiful prayer, and the second is from the Collects appointed for the ordination of Priests and Deacons, which is an imitation rather than a translation of the older Salisbury Collects in the like offices.

Emblem. A symbol, or typical representation of some spiritual thing. Under some symbol a solemn Christian truth may be suggested, as the Anchor represents Hope; the Circle and the Triangle within it represents the Mystery of the TRINITY; a Dove symbolizes the descent of the HOLY GHOST. These and many others, as the Cross with the Crown, the Fish (which was an ancient emblem), the Ship, the Chalice, the Emblems of the four Evangelists, the Lily, and others which are in common use. These are natural and proper, and may be fitly used as suggestions of the great truths of Christianity, being themselves alluded to in Scripture (as the Anchor, the Ship) in metaphor or in parable.

Embolismus. An intercalated prayer,— *i.e.*, a prayer added after the petition "Lead us not into temptation, but deliver us from evil," and before the doxology, "For Thine," etc. It was a universal custom at one time, but has left scarcely a trace in the Western Church. A single petition is all that is left, "Deliver us, LORD, we beseech Thee, from all evil," in the West. But in the early Eastern Liturgies this Embolismus holds a very important place, and is often of extreme beauty. It was as it were an expansion of the last petition, uttered in passionate entreaty, as is finely exemplified in this example from the Liturgy of St. Mark : " Even so LORD, LORD, lead us not into temptation, but deliver us from the evil one; for Thy long-suffering knoweth that we through our great infirmity are unable to resist him, but make with the temptation also a way to escape, that we may be able to bear it; for Thou hast given power to tread on serpents and scorpions and on all the might of the enemy ; *(aloud)* for Thine," etc. The deep fervor of this prayer is well expressed. Possibly it may be some such feeling of desiring to expand the perfect compression in the LORD's Prayer that has placed as a *preface* to it in the Mozarabic and Gallican Liturgies a short, humble petition which varies with the season. This is for Christmas-day from the Mozarabic Liturgy : " That which the WORD showed us to follow, that which the Life taught us to speak, that which the Truth instructed us to hold, to Thee, FATHER ALMIGHTY, let us pronounce from on earth with fear and trembling, OUR FATHER," etc. It is after this example, though probably not consciously following it, that in the Institution office the Collect, Direct us, O LORD, precedes and is joined to the LORD's Prayer with the words, " who hath taught us to pray unto Thee, O ALMIGHTY FATHER, in His prevailing Name and words, OUR FATHER."

Encœnia. The anniversary festival of the dedication of a Church. The word means the "renewal,"—*i.e.*, the remembrancer; hence, the Feast of the Dedication. This feast was also kept on the anniversary of the day on which a city was founded.

Encyclical. Originally meant a letter sent by a Bishop or by the officers in authority to other Dioceses for certain purposes. The letter from the Church in Smyrna, recounting the noble martyrdom of St. Polycarp, was an encyclical. The Bishops who deposed Paul of Samosata sent an encyclical to other Dioceses declaring their act and the reasons for it, and warning them of the heresy. The Festal Epistles of the Patriarch of Alexandria were also Encyclicals announcing to all the

Churches of the East and of the West the true date of Easter-day. A Primate would send an Encyclical to his suffragans. But though they do not bear this title, it may help us to appreciate better the Catholic Epistles of St. James, St. Peter, and St. John, to consider them (what they were) Encyclicals. So too, as many copies of the Epistles to the Ephesians do not contain the words "in Ephesus," it has been supposed that this was an Encyclical Epistle from St. Paul to that and the neighboring Churches. But the term now is used solely of a circular letter from the Pope to the Bishops and Churches which acknowledge his authority.

England, Church of. Under the title BRITISH CHURCH will be found an outline of Early English Church History preceding the Reformation. Under this last title will be found a sketch of the work of Henry VIII. In the rapid sketch which follows only the most salient points can be cited.

Edward VI. succeeded his father in 1547 A.D. A council of sixteen, by his father's will, formed a Regency. In this Regency the reformers, led by the Lord Protector and Cranmer, were balanced by the Chancellor and Bishop Tonstal. The strong hand of Henry being removed, confusion was imminent, especially as the lay lords were greedy for Church lands. Much violent preaching was common. A royal visitation was ordered (1547 A.D.). Injunctions were issued, and a book of Homilies, chiefly by Cranmer, was left for the use of each Church. Resistance was made by Gardiner, Bonner, and a remonstrance came from the Princess Mary. Gardiner apparently had legal grounds, since the Homilies were without Parliamentary and Convocational sanction; for this he was imprisoned. Bonner protested but yielded. Serious alterations of the law were initiated; the Bishops were to be appointed by Letters Patent, not by a congé d'élire; the clergy were to administer the Communion in both kinds; the treason acts of the late reign were repealed; the charities, hospitals, and guilds were despoiled of their endowments. Convocation relieved of the penalties threatened by the Six Article Act, demanded a revision of the Canon law, representation in Parliament, a review of the remodeled services to be acted on by them, but their demands were disregarded. A new Communion office was set forth (March, 1548 A.D.) upon the sole authority of the Privy Council, but it was not unanimously received. The many proclamations which were issued show how disturbed the state was with fanatical and imprudent preaching and disputation. Sacrilege was rife, for the Councillors themselves set the example. But by the close of this year the draft of the first Prayer-Book of Edward VI. was submitted to Convocation (November), and was approved by the Commons (December) and, after some opposition by eight of the non-reforming Bishops, by the Lords (January, 1549 A.D.). Its use was legally enjoined by Whitsunday, but many Churches began its use on Easter (April 21). It was generally received, but there was some disturbance, especially in the Devonshire rising. Many who disliked the change made it as nearly like the Romish ceremonial as they could. Its tone and spirit were thoroughly Anglican, and as such it won its way quite as much as for its simplicity, rhythm, and devoutness. In 1549 A.D. the act permitting the marriage of the clergy was passed. In the fall, the efforts to assimilate the Prayer-Book to the "Popish Mass" was checked by a second royal visitation. Bonner, for encouraging such attempts and for his unsatisfactory apologetic sermon at Paul's Cross, was tried, but refusing to admit the authority of the Commission appointed, was imprisoned. When Somerset was replaced by Warwick (1549 A.D.), the reforming policy was still carried on. Old service-books were called in and destroyed. A Commission was ordered to revise the Canon Law. The Ordinal was drawn up and approved (February, 1550 A.D.). Cranmer now desired to form a sort of bond of union among the English and Continental Reformers against the Council of Trent, and so admitted them to a partial influence in English Church affairs. This brought Hooper to the front as Calvin's friend. He was offered the Bishopric of Gloucester (July, 1550 A.D.), but he refused to be consecrated in the prescribed vesture. Since he would not yield to argument, he was sent to the Fleet. After two months, rather than lose the power of the proffered office, he withdrew his objection and was consecrated March 8, 1551 A.D. Ridley, Bishop of London, so wise in all else, removed the altars and ordered Communion-tables. This introduced unseemly contentions, which have not since been wholly quieted. Cranmer was now busy drawing a series of articles, and was also occupied with a review of the Prayer-Book. It is said that Bucer and Peter Martyr influenced the formation of the second Prayer-Book. But their objections were not as many as the English Divines themselves admitted, nor were the corrections made as they wished. Peter Martyr had seriously influenced Cranmer upon the doctrine of the Eucharist, and indirectly it effected a great deal, as was apparent when the second Prayer-Book was issued (November, 1552 A.D.). This book made some alterations for the better, but it sacrificed much which was worth retaining. A revision of the Ordinal was also made, and some symbolic ceremonies dropped. Cranmer now reverted to the articles he was drawing up. These were rapidly drawn up and submitted to the King, who had them reviewed, and then they were laid before the Council. They were ratified (May, 1553 A.D.) by Convocation and signed by the King; with them was bound up Poynet's Catechism,—the basis of Nowel's Catechism later. This work, which could not be undone, was a great gain. Still, in other ways much evil had been done. Church furniture and vessels had been embezzled; Church lands were appropriated; parishes were defrauded and wasted by the lay lords in office. The King alone seemed to see the evil, by trying to apply the money to Church uses. From his care two hospitals, once monastic houses, are now in London, and he founded twenty-two Grammar Schools. His death (July 6, 1553 A.D.) delayed reform. The cruel use made of the Lady Jane Grey only deepened Queen Mary's avowed purpose of restoring Romanism. Out of sympathy with the temper of her subjects, ready to make every sacrifice, deeply attached to Philip of Spain, and therefore under the lead of Spanish policy, had it not been for Bishop Gardiner's wise advice she would have acted in a more headlong fashion. Cranmer, who could have escaped, Latimer, Holgate of York, and Ridley, were imprisoned together in the Tower. Rogers, Saunders, and Taylor and Bishop Hooper were the first martyrs (February, 1555 A.D.). This fatal policy, due to secret Spanish influence, horrified all England. Gardiner withdrew from the work. Meantime, the Parliament refused to repeal the statutes against the Papal supremacy and to be reconciled to Rome until the Pope had confirmed the titles to the holders of the monastic lands. Reluctantly the Pope sent Cardinal Pole as Legate to England, with a Bull empowering him to "give, aliene, and transfer" all Church property to its present holders.

On St. Andrew's day (November 30, 1554 A.D.) the assembled Parliament at Lambeth were solemnly absolved and the nation reconciled to Rome. Later (December 6) he absolved and reconciled the clergy in Convocation, and (December 24) confirmed the lay titles to all Church property.

Farrar, Bishop of St. Davids, was burned at Carmarthen (March 30, 1565 A.D.). The horror at these executions brought on a pause, till the Queen's Council urged the civil magistrates to present cases to the Commission. But the greatest cruelties were principally in three Dioceses,—London, Canterbury, and Norwich; in these in three years one hundred and eighty-nine persons suffered. In fourteen other Dioceses, ninety-seven, and in six none were burnt. But now it did not avail to recant. The persecution descended to the lower classes, and many poor persons were burned. After much disputing and delay, Cranmer, Ridley, and Latimer were tried and condemned at Oxford. Ridley and Latimer lighted "that candle which by GOD's grace in England shall never be put out" on October 16, 1555 A.D. Cranmer wavered and signed several recantations (which would not have saved him), but suddenly he cast off all fear and publicly denounced his past vacillation, though he supposed he was pardoned, and was burnt March 21, 1556 A.D. The next day Cardinal Pole was consecrated Archbishop of Canterbury.

The civil magistrates now shrank back, and a list of twenty laymen was added to the ecclesiastical commission to proceed to extremes. The Pope, who was opposed to Spain and was prejudiced against Pole, revoked his legantine commission, but the Queen wrote to him that it was her pleasure that Pole should continue legate, and the Pope finally yielded. The Convocation took advantage of the loss of Calais, and the consequent demand on them for a war subsidy, to urge the continuance, in another shape, of some of the practical reforms already gained; but before these could be properly presented the Queen died (November 17, 1558 A.D.); Cardinal Pole died the next day. The check which this reign placed on the Reformation brought in the seeds of future trouble from the Continent, but the persecutions thoroughly alienated the nation from Romanism.

Elizabeth was received enthusiastically. The exiles flocked home and began to act in a violent manner, and to introduce the unchurchly principles they had learned abroad. The Roman See, of course, tried to hamper her. The violent language of Paul IV. caused the cessation of all intercourse, which has never been renewed. It influenced some of the clergy who had conformed, but none as yet renounced their mother-Church to set up a foreign schism. The Queen, herself of wide statesmanlike purposes, and her advisers sought to unify and conciliate all parties; but the excesses of the returned exiles alienated her sympathy. The Prayer-Book of 1552 A.D. was put into revision. Meantime, the English Litany and Ante-Communion and the Mass as it was in use were ordered, till Parliament (1559 A.D.) restored to the Crown its ancient jurisdiction of power to visit in causes ecclesiastical. It was a broad and dangerous power. The Queen would accept only the title of "Supreme Governor" of the Church on earth. The Bishops were to be nominated by the Crown to the Cathedral Chapters. In opposition to the Queen's known wishes the revising committee adopted the Prayer-Book of 1552 A.D. It was sanctioned by Parliament, but apparently the Queen had among other things the now vexed Ornaments Rubric inserted after the act was passed. By the Act of Uniformity the use of the Book was made binding from June 24, 1559 A.D. The Marian Bishops, except Landaff, manfully refused to take the oath under the Act of Supremacy and were deprived. All but one hundred and eighty-nine clergy yielded. The Queen now issued a series of Injunctions and Articles of Inquiry. Pius IV. tried a conciliatory policy, and it is said offered to recognize the Prayer-Book and her right to the throne if the Queen would return to the Roman obedience. But her reply was to forbid the Nuncio to set foot in England. Dr. Parker was consecrated Archbishop of Canterbury

(December 17, 1559 A.D.) by Bishops Barlow, Scory, Coverdale, and Hodgkin. In January, Parker consecrated ten Bishops for vacant Sees. They found much to set right. The parishes were badly served, and few fit men came forward for orders. There was needed a new translation of the Scriptures. Ecclesiastical Courts needed reform. Fanatical preachers gave much trouble. It was difficult to enforce a decent rubrical use of the Prayer-Book. Parker had a difficult course to steer, but he had much tact and resource.

The Convocation of 1563 A.D. arranged and agreed to the XXXIX. Articles, but the Queen quietly interpolated the opening clause of Article XX. before ratifying them. The rejection of all holy-days and a lowering of ritual was barely defeated, and the second Book of Homilies was ordered. Parliament, to meet disorders, passed a second, more stringent Act of Supremacy. It was tendered by Bishop Horne to Bonner, who was in his charge. Bonner raised some questions upon the Ordinal, which led to an act re-establishing the legal (not the spiritual, for that was undoubted) authority of the Ordinal of Edward VI. These acts, yielding to neither Pope nor Puritan, offended both, and both now strove to destroy the English Church.

To enforce the rubrical use of the Prayer-Book, Parker issued his Book of Advertisements. It enjoined a minimum of ritual with the use of surplice, or of alb and chasuble. But it was now decided to force conformity, and scruples against the surplice led to a formal schism 1566 A.D. Four years later the rash act of excommunication by Pius V. caused many, under a mistaken notion, to withdraw from the Church and set up a Roman schism, adding to the troubles and intrigues of the time. England's reply was to make the presence of a Roman priest in England a capital offense. Conspiracies followed rapidly, making the position of the Roman party uncomfortable and adding violence to the Puritan faction. The Queen, misled by those lay councillors who looked to profit by the troubles, would not aid the Bishops, but urged them to unpopular policy which they would have avoided. This added fuel to troubles, which led to Parliament requiring the clergy to subscribe to the Supremacy, the Articles, and the Book of Common Prayer, with a recantation of past rubrical disobedience.

Political plots fomented by Rome, and hard measures almost compelled by zealots at home, made England a scene of great turmoil. Parker died in 1575 A.D. Wise, firm, tolerant, had he been thoroughly backed by the Queen he could have added much to the great work he did. Grindal, a Marian exile, was translated to Canterbury from York, to the joy of those who sided with him. But his acts were restrained by the Queen. He tried to enforce discipline, and established a plan of prophesyings resembling a modern Methodist class-meeting. The Queen ordered him to withdraw it. This order he resisted as an interference, and wrote a very admirable letter to her. The Queen suspended him, and had the prophesyings suppressed; but his suspension did not interfere with his proper Episcopal functions, as many acts could be in the name of his subordinates. It lasted for five years, when he made a partial submission. The next year he died. Whitgift (1583 A.D.) was a man prompt and ready with resources. Cartwright and Travers, the leaders of the nonconformists, hoped to defeat his measures. Travers was nominated to the Mastership of the Temple by the lay advisers of the Queen. But Whitgift succeeded by a compromise to place Hooker there. He also protected the Church property from overvaluation. 1587 A.D. was marked by the scurrilous Mar-Prelate libels. The controversy with Travers set Hooker to produce his splendid Ecclesiastical Polity. The effort to silence the libels led to recourse to the Queen's Bench, and this drove out of the country many of the libelers. Whitgift's Calvinistic leaning led him to draw up the famous Lambeth Articles, but they were afterwards quietly withdrawn. After a glorious but troubled reign, Queen Elizabeth died 1603 A.D.

James showed his leaning at the Hampton Court Conference when he had the Dissenters and Bishops confer upon some of the chief objections to the Church. Whitgift was succeeded by Bancroft (1604 A.D.). In the interval between the two Primates the Canons of 1603/4 A.D. were passed, which are the chief English Church Law, and which bear upon our own polity, and may be really in force with us.

Bancroft tried to push the Test Oath, but the courts interfered, with the result that many emigrated to Holland and to this country. The absurd Gunpowder-plot and the conspiracies of the Jesuits made the position of the Romanists still more uncomfortable, and led to the, to us indefensible, act compelling Popish recusants to receive yearly the Eucharist at the Parish Church. Yet James, a little later, was negotiating a Spanish alliance for his son Charles. The glory of the reign was the translation of the Bible. James had projected it soon after his accession. It was discussed in 1604 A.D., resolved on 1607 A.D., and completed 1611 A.D. The king tried to introduce Episcopacy into Scotland (1607-1610 A.D.), and had three Bishops consecrated. Abbot succeeded Bancroft (1610 A.D.), and was as lax as Bancroft had been vigorous. What with his inattention and James's intermeddling, chiefly by the notorious Book of Sports, trouble and nonconformity were stirred up afresh. Court intrigues and change of policy led indirectly to Dr. Laud's advancement to the Bishopric of St. Davids, 1621 A.D. The negotiations with Spain had led to such relaxation of the laws against recusants that Abbot remonstrated.

Charles succeeded his father (1625 A.D.) and to his principles as well. His main misfortune was in having Laud as an adviser. Laud was honest, conscientious, but inflexible, and with no sympathy for those who differed from him. Brave, imprudent, and gifted with power to influence friends by his sincere singleness of purpose, he could not conciliate opponents.

He had a minute mind that descended to details, yet he saw and initiated remedies for greater evils. He tried to protect the poorer clergy and the Church from spoliation, and he made a strong effort to restore ritual, which bore fruit in happier times, in more decent setting of the furniture, and the seemlier celebration of Divine service. Toleration was not known to either side, it was not thought of by friend or foe. His action drove many to New England, where they enforced the like intolerance. The laxness of the past had taken the fancy of influential laymen, and the attack upon Laud was partly from the desire to do as they pleased. The wish for a moderate Episcopacy was only apparent. His inflexible conduct, and abetting the conduct of others in the Council, led to his arrest in 1641 A.D. He was kept in the Tower for three years, his papers were seized and misused, and finally he was tried upon the monstrous principle that petty infractions by cumulation constitute a treason, and was martyred 1645 A.D. The King was powerless to save him, hampered by his own troubles. He was beheaded in 1649 A.D. The Church was beaten down, the Bishops driven off, the clergy ejected, the use of the Prayer-Book made a crime; and the country for ten years was given over to swarms of sectaries. At the Restoration (1660-85 A.D.) Charles promised full liberty to religious opinion, but he held that later political events absolved him from the pledge, and by harshness towards Dissenters tried to hide his Roman intrigues. The Savoy Conference between the Bishops and leading Dissenters did no direct good, but led to the Revision of the Prayer-Book (1662 A.D.). The State now led the Church into painful blunders. The Divine right of kings, held by a majority, led to difficulties in resisting James II., and a reaction as a Latitudinarian party sprang up, which led to Arian views in some influential men in Queen Anne's reign. The false political principles misled James as to what he could hope to effect. His effort to coerce the Church in the famous case of the "Seven Bishops" was a part of the many acts which led to his expulsion. Those of the Bishops and clergy who could not give up their absolutism became non-jurors, refusing the oath of allegiance to William and Mary (1688-1702 A.D.) The men now at the head of affairs sought to carry out a "scheme of comprehension," but the clergy in Convocation saved the Church by refusing to be lowered to the grade of Dissenting bodies, and be numbered as one of several holding the "Protestant religion." A Toleration Act was passed, a tardy and imperfect accordance of right to Dissenters. The devout and lofty tone of the non-jurors measurably counteracted the lowering ideas of such men as Tillotson and Tennison. Guilds, associations, and societies for Church instruction were very numerous. Queen Anne's reign (1702-1714 A.D.) was mainly marked by contests between the upper and lower Houses of Convocation, and by the notorious Sacheverell trial. The influence and hold of the Church on the nation was at its height. She was active and doing good work, and her services were full, and frequent and decorous.

The importance of what followed later, the Bangorean controversy with its disastrous influences, the depressing effect of the Georgian reigns, the laxness and deadness because of the change in the character of the body of the clergy, the rise of the Wesleys and the form it resulted in of Methodism, the giving the Episcopate to the American Church, the lethargy of the early decades of this century, and the wonderful awakening of the past forty-five years, demand a space and a fullness of treatment, bearing as they do upon our own development and conduct, which cannot be afforded. In fact, this history has yet to be written.

Enthronization. In England, after a Bishop has been consecrated, he is solemnly admitted to the Cathedral of his See and placed on the Throne by the Dean and Chapter, thus taking possession of his See. So too the Archbishop is enthroned in his Archiepiscopal Throne.

Enthusiasm. However much this term is misused, the feeling is a real and a deep motive-power in the Church of GOD. Enthusiasm as we generally see it displayed is fitful, wanting depth and wanting stability. For this cause sober men are afraid of any manifestation of an enthusiastic spirit. Enthusiasm is generally connected in our minds with the system of Revivals, and with prearranged efforts to produce an excitement. This must be rejected as a spurious form. But a truer understanding of this feeling, and an appreciation of the fact that it requires not little tact and some wisdom to guide it, will lead us to see that GOD puts into our hands an instrument of great power. It was enthusiasm in this sense that enabled the first converts to not only endure persecution and to suffer with joy, but to go forth upon the work of evangelizing the world. St. Paul is one of the most wonderful examples of true, sustained, and well-controlled enthusiasm. Enthusiasm really underlies all great movements, and so far from suppressing or rejecting it, it should be fostered and developed and guided. It can take the shape of energetic guilds, brotherhoods, co-operative work in the Parish work, or any form that the religious earnestness of each Christian can display itself in readiness and zeal for work. If the test of obedience be applied and can be endured, the person is really enthusiastic. For this reason, every member in a Parish should have some of its work intrusted to him to do faithfully, and as proof of his love to GOD in return for the love shown him. This impression of enthusiasm is one of the oversights we have been too long guilty of committing, and have consequently lost the valuable work of many who would be ready to labor faithfully. The cultivation of a true, holy, persevering enthusiasm develops greater depth and spiritual power. It does more to strengthen the character than any other thing. It helps to form holy habits, and to grave them indelibly upon the soul. It gives intensity to our convictions of the reality of the unseen, under the guidance of the HOLY GHOST. It was enthusiasm which led to the efforts and work of the missionaries of the Primitive Church. It was such an enthusiasm which gave power to the martyrs to endure. It was such an enthusiasm which drove men into the desert to escape the pollutions around them. It is such an enthusiasm now in this generation which is filling the souls of the many engaged in developing the Church's work here. It will be such an enthusiasm which will attempt to solve the problems given us to work out for this nation. It has been well said, "Most religions have sprung from an enthusiast and a band of disciples; but no religion save Christianity has been revived from time to time by a succession of enthusiasts." "One thing is certain, that no community save that against which 'the gates of hell shall not prevail' has shown so wondrous a power of self-repair from within, of renewing by the spontaneous ardor of its own members the vigor of a religious sentiment which has been tending to dissolution.'" "When we see that the light which enthusiasm has kindled in men's minds, however fitful and delusive, has yet cast its rays into the darkest corners of the world,— that its fervor, however morbid and unreal, has often given a healthy glow to the chilled heart of Christendom, we ought to conclude that it too comes from the FATHER of Lights, and that we should attempt wisely to direct rather than sternly to resist its manifestations, 'lest haply we be found to fight against GOD.'"

It is an instrument for good within, and a weapon of attack upon the world which we are slow to use as we well can.

Epact. *Vide* CALENDAR.

Ephesians, Epistle to. This Epistle— one of the noblest of the Pauline Epistles— was written during St. Paul's first imprisonment at Rome (61–63 A.D.), probably in the spring of 62 A.D. There was, so far as appears now, no cause beyond that care of the Churches that lay upon the Apostle's heart to move him to write this Letter. It was quite likely that it was written to several of the Churches in Asia Minor, and that the copy we have was the one directed to Ephesus, for the words "at Ephesus" are not found in some of the best manuscripts, but are yet too well attested to doubt their genuineness. Then there is another fact: the Ephesians were to exchange this with the Laodiceans, who had received a letter from him. The title may have been readily dropped out of the copy of a letter sent to a neighboring Church. But there can be no doubt at all that this is a letter from the great Apostle which was intended for and received by Ephesus, even if we suppose that it was to be sent to other Churches. But the contents of this Epistle are as remarkable, its enunciation of revealed truth as profound, as any in the whole number of St. Paul's letters. It is chiefly occupied with the unity of the Church of CHRIST; with the gracious gifts which are given by it; and it has been well said that a thorough study of the Epistle to the Ephesians, with prayer, together with a devout use of the Litany, would bring any fair-minded man into the Church. Its arguments are so clearly put, its declarations of GOD'S revelation are so cogently worded, that the conclusions from them are irresistible. The contents may be divided into two parts,—the doctrinal portion and the hortatory.

The doctrinal (ch. i.), beginning immediately after the salutation, recites in a long sentence, reaching from the 3d to the 14th verse, the outline of the redemption, the Atonement of CHRIST, their faith in the Gospel, which involved Baptism and Confirmation. A second similar sentence (15–33) declares to us that wonderful outpouring of the Love of the FATHER to us through CHRIST in the gifts of wisdom and knowledge of the inheritance of His glory, that we may be in Him whom He raised from the dead, and under whom He put all things and made Him head over all things to the Church, which is His body, the fullness of Him that filleth all in all. But as we, forgiven, washed, accepted, are in Him, He hath raised us to heavenly places (ch. ii. 1–10) in CHRIST JESUS, and created us in Him for good works, which GOD prepared that we should walk in them. Thence the Apostle declares the unity of the Church for both Jew and Gentile in a magnificent passage, which, beginning with "He is our Peace," goes on to show the breaking down of the partition between them, the reconciliation in one body, the gift of the one Spirit, the membership in the household of GOD, upon the Apostolic foundation, the sanctification of our bodies by being temples of the HOLY GHOST. And (ch. iii.) the mystery of the Church of GOD founded in CHRIST, with its gifts, its inclusion of all men, was now revealed through the Church itself to the principalities and powers of heaven. The chapter closes with a prayer that strengthening and increased wisdom should be given to the Ephesians, and a beautiful ascription of praise. In the fourth chapter the Apostle gathers up into one all the practical results of the doctrinal foundation. "As we have the vocation, let us with all Christian grace use it. Endeavoring to keep the unity of the Spirit in the bond of peace. There is one body and one Spirit, even as ye are called in one hope of your calling; one LORD, one Faith, one Baptism, one GOD and Father of all, who is above all, and through all, and in you all." On His ascension our LORD bestowed the manifold gifts which He had received upon His Church, in Apostles, in Prophets, in Evangelists, in Pastors and Teachers for our perfect training in the body of CHRIST, which is His Church. Within the remainder of the Epistle are contained, under practical directions to a holy life, allusions to Baptism (ch. iv. 24; compare with Rom. vi. 4), to Confirmation (vs. 30 and Acts xix. 6), and the use of music in the Eucharist (giving of thanks, ch. v. 18–21) antiphonally in psalms, hymns, and spiritual songs. Their unity in the Church under the type of marriage is again taught (ch. v. 23–33). The spiritual warfare, the reality of the unseen and supernatural, is grandly described (ch. vi. 10–20). If we may reverently say so of a Book wherein all is given by the wisdom of the HOLY GHOST, this Epistle is one of the most valuable at this day for the Church in the series of Pauline Epistles. Its study will prove to the devout reader the Divine origin, the Apostolic continuity of the Church, its mysterious supernatural relations to the unseen world around us and to our LORD at the right hand of the throne on high, and the need of the constant use of His gifts through the HOLY SPIRIT for our spiritual life. We need no better devotional and doctrinal manual could we enter into the depths of its revelations.

Epiphanies. Manifestations (*vide* ANGELS and THEOPHANY) of a spiritual messenger sent from GOD to His people.

Epiphany. The "*manifestation*" of CHRIST. The word is not confined merely to the Feast-day, for which it stands usually, but it is also used to mean (2 Thess. ii. 8) the Second Advent, and (*vide* EPIPHANIES) the manifestation of CHRIST to His Prophets as the JEHOVAH ANGEL. But we generally mean by Epiphany the Feast-day on the 6th of January. On it we in the West celebrate the manifestation of CHRIST to the Gentiles, who were guided to His cradle at the inn in Bethlehem by the miraculous star. The Eastern Church commemorated His birth and His baptism on this day as representing the natural birth of our LORD, and also the LORD'S baptism, which was a prophecy in act of our own mystical second birth. Upon it fell one of the three solemn seasons at which baptism was administered. But, except in Spain, this was not the custom of the West.

It is not necessary to seek for astronomical explanations of the wonderful star which led the magi to the Infant JESUS. Ignatius (Ep. to the Eph., 19) speaks of it as a wondrous phenomenon. The Evangelist records that the star led them, moved, and "went before them till it came and stood over where the young child was." All of which forces us to accept the account as it stands, that it was a miraculous star, or to reject it altogether.

The Feast in the West has always commemorated this visit of the wise men. All the homilies and liturgical services of this part of the Church's year have reference to this fact, and all make some spiritual or figurative explanation of it. The worship of the wise men, as representatives for the whole Gentile world, was offered Him. Their gifts of gold in honor of His kingly birth, were laid at His feet. The frankincense, as due to Him as Eternal GOD, worshiped forever more, was given to Him. The myrrh, signifying by its bitterness the sorrows of His coming human life, and by its perfume the spicery of His burial, was presented, too. And so, at the outset of that wondrous life, were typical gifts given by wise men, themselves miraculously led by the star of Jacob to Him whose true humanity and perfectly sinless life were to be the most precious gifts ever given to man, and these given to us by miracles.

Episcopacy. The form of polity of the Church Catholic as represented by the succession of her Bishops from the Apostles, who were themselves the Divinely-appointed ἐπίσκοποι from whom all others since derive their authority and commission. In *sacramental form*, this transmission, known as the Apostolic succession, is conveyed through the "laying on of hands" by three or more Bishops, as set forth by Canon in the Council of Nice. In *spiritual efficacy* the succession is transmitted by the HOLY GHOST, who gives His seal to the external act of the laying on of hands for the continuation of the Apostolic ministry, the conservation of the Apostolic faith, and the perpetual witness to the Resurrection.

The word itself is accommodated from the Greek, and signifies overseership. In the New Testament the title ἐπίσκοπος is applied interchangeably to Bishops and Presbyters; but as, when the last of the original twelve had passed away, the name Apostle, signifying any one who had been sent, was thenceforth confined to those who had first borne it under CHRIST, in like manner ἐπίσκοποι, or Bishops, came to designate those only who were the Apostles' successors in rank and order. Episcopacy is thus the Apostolic regimen, which was formally instituted by our LORD when He gave to the first ministry its commission in the words, accompanied by solemn action, "Receive ye the HOLY GHOST. As my FATHER hath sent Me, so send I you." That this commission was not intended by Him to be limited to those on whom it was originally conferred, but was to be extended to their successors, is seen by the promise which accompanied it: "Lo, I am with you always, even unto the end of the world."

Although Episcopacy was thus constituted, in its original membership, in one order, it was invested by its Divine Author (as appeared soon by Apostolic sanction and practice) not only with the power of self-perpetuation, but of setting apart other orders of clergy inferior in spiritual power and dignity to itself. Hence by Episcopacy is understood generally the threefold ministry of Bishops, Priests, and Deacons, derived by an unbroken succession from the Apostles.

From the oneness of this threefold ministry, always existing from age to age and inhering in its original and highest order, comes, as a corollary, the primitive principle of the Church's concrete unity.

Thus St. Ignatius (circa 106 A.D.) writes to the Philadelphians: "Take ye heed to have but one Eucharist. For there is one flesh of our Lord JESUS CHRIST, and one cup to show the unity of His blood; one altar; as there is one Bishop, along with the Presbytery and Deacons."

This threefold ministry in the Christian Church was held by many in ancient times to harmonize with, and even to fulfill in a completed and more highly spiritual and perfect form and function, the ancient Levitical institution of the priesthood. Some of the earliest writers do not scruple to apply the title of High-Priest to the Bishop, and of Levite to the Deacon. To this Hooker seems to refer approvingly when he says, "Bishops are *now* as High-Priests were *then* in regard to power over other Priests; and in respect of subjection unto High-Priests, what Priests were then the same now Presbyters are, by reason of their place under Bishops."

Against the Papal or Italian theory of Episcopacy, viz., that all other Bishops are by Divine appointment made inferior in spiritual authority and order to him who is the alleged successor of St. Peter; and that our LORD conferred on St. Peter a primacy and spiritual principality which made the throne of his successors for all time the Divinely recognized centre of unity and fountain of authority for the Universal Church, the Anglican Communion utters her protest. She maintains, with the ancient Church, the absolute *Unity of the Episcopate*, and the consequent equality of all Bishops in respect of spiritual order and function. She adopts the rule of St. Cyprian (circa 240 A.D.) as her own: "*Episcopatus unus est; Cujus a singulis in solidum pars tenetur*,"—"The Episcopate is one; each part of which is held by each member for the substantial whole." From this principle springs her rule of the independence of National Churches, whose independence of any one central human authority, except that of a General Council, which she accepts and appeals to, does not, therefore, make them judges of doctrine, but rather custodians of a doctrine once for all received; each sharing in this regard with the others a common responsibility. The Anglican Communion does indeed accept for convenience' sake and as a Catholic tradition, the ancient arrangement of Provinces, with their Archbishops and Metropolitans, and is not unwilling to accede even to a Primacy which shall be founded upon universal consent claiming no Divine prescription in its favor. But the principle, which she maintains as inherited from the Fathers, of the Unity of the Episcopate, forbids her acceptance of the sovereignty of one Bishop over the rest founded on pretensions of Divine right and superior order which were unknown, as she is firmly persuaded, to primitive times.

As the Apostolate or Episcopate first called and then Divinely commissioned "to send out other faithful men" was the norm of the original Christian ministry, and, as continued in Episcopacy, it has been its alone fountain since, it follows that validity of orders is dependent upon Episcopal consecration, and that no true Episcopacy can exist which has not historic continuity. "It is evident unto all men diligently reading Holy Scripture and ancient authors (says the preface to the Ordinal), "that from the Apostles' time there have been these orders of ministers in CHRIST'S Church, Bishops, Priests, and Deacons." From this fact, simply considered as such, it results, by stress of necessary inference, that the continuity of the faith, sacraments, and discipline of the Church must be in historic connection with the same order of men who have from the first administered them. Accordingly the preface to the Ordinal first referred to continues: "No man shall be accounted or taken to be a lawful Bishop, Priest, or Deacon in this Church, or suffered to execute any of the said functions, except he be called, tried, examined, and admitted thereunto according to the form hereafter following (*i.e.*, the forms for making Bishops, Priests, and Deacons), or hath had Episcopal consecration or ordination." In this rule the English Church and our own do but echo what St. Ignatius, in the second century, wrote to the Smyrnaeans: "Let that (says St. Ignatius) be deemed a proper Eucharist which is administered either by the Bishop or by one to whom he has intrusted it." And again: "Wherever the Bishop shall appear, there let the multitude of the people also be."

The objection then that is commonly brought against Episcopacy as necessarily "unchurching" all who do not receive it, has no value or force as an argument against it. Those who hold such are not responsible for inferences that may be drawn from it. But aside from this consideration, this Church maintains that all who are baptized are made in baptism "members of CHRIST," and she declines to dogmatize upon the question of GOD'S sovereign will and power, or to affix limits to the operations of His grace

On the human side Episcopacy is largely paternal. While it does more than reflect in its spiritual character, rather while it supplies, and in a higher sense fulfills the mission and significance of the Levitical, it is at the same time comprehensive even of the Patriarchal Priesthood. Ruling with such authority as CHRIST'S law gives, it should blend with its rule the love, forbearance, and mercifulness of a genuine fatherhood; and as every Bishop is, in Hooker's sense, High-Priest and ruler, so he should be father also over that portion of GOD'S family committed to his care. But *Episcopatus unus est;* and as Episcopacy viewed as a whole does on its spiritual side *symbolize,* so should it on the human side, *i.e.,* in the persons of its members, *illustrate* the Fatherhood of GOD.

Episcopacy, thus broad in its comprehensiveness, strong in its unity, and paternal in its character and spirit, offers the best remedy for the distractions of the day, in being able to reconcile fidelity to ancient and Catholic truth with the diversities of opinion which, on minor points, reflect the enlarged intelligence of the age and the consequent demands of a greater mental freedom. While on the one hand the rigor of a central and despotic spiritual rule and headship either enfeebles the will or drives it into rebellion, and on the other hand the unchecked license of private judgment dethrones authority and substitutes, in the end, the reign of rationalism for that of faith; primitive and Catholic Episcopacy, as illustrated in the branches of the Church which maintain it, knows how to reconcile faith with a reasonable exercise of private judgment. "*Quod semper ubique et ad omnibus,*" is with them but the complement of another truth which underlies the entire spirit of their teaching: "In essentials unity, in non-essentials liberty, in all things charity."

Episcopacy is not affected in its spiritual character by the varying civil conditions under which it is found existing in the world. In the Empire, while it remained heathen, it was marked by a greater simplicity than when Christian Rome rebuilt its churches and endowed its Bishoprics. In England, where alliance with the State gives prestige to the clergy and baronial privileges to the Bishops, it wields a greater influence than in the colonies or in this country, where it is unendowed and free from the honors as from the trammels of the State. But everywhere, and in all times, when not overridden by a despotic ruler, civil or ecclesiastical, Episcopacy has been, to the extent of its ability and the measure of its light, the conservator of ancient law and the promoter of present and reasonable liberty. It suffers to-day, in this land, from many popular encroachments, as in the past it has suffered from usurpations of another and very different kind. But it is destined to endure. It has the Divine promise, "Lo, I am with you always, even unto the end of the world.

RT. REV. THOS. A. STARKEY, D.D.,
Northern New Jersey.

Episcopate, List of the Anglican and Eastern.

The Essential Unity of the Church of Christ, for which every Christian should pray, for which our LORD pleaded in the night in which He was betrayed, is ever presented before Him in the Church's service.

"We humbly beseech Thee . . . to inspire continually the Universal Church with the spirit of truth, unity, and concord; and grant that all those who do confess Thy Holy Name may agree in the truth of Thy Holy Word, and live in unity and godly love."

"They are one in their One Original from which they continually and unchangeably derive their being. They adore GOD, the FATHER, SON, and HOLY GHOST, with the same new song of the Gospel; they confess Him in the same words of Apostolic Faith; they offer to Him the same incense of praise, and the same Holy Offering whereof Malachi foretold, 'from the rising of the sun even unto the going down of the same,' pleading on earth to the Eternal FATHER that One Sacrifice as presented in heaven; they receive the same 'Bread which came down from Heaven to give life to the world.' Unknown in face, in place separate, different in language, opposed, alas! in some things to one another, still before the throne of GOD they are One Holy Catholic Apostolic Church; each several portion praying for itself and for the rest, united in the prayers and oblation which it offers for all, by the One Bread and the One Spirit which dwelleth in all."— *Dr. Pusey.*

In the following list of the Anglican and Eastern Communions, the first place is given to the Anglican Churches, than which we believe that, to say the least, none come nearer, in all essential respects, to the Primitive Church. Then come the "Old Catholic" Churches, professing, as do the Anglican, to hold fast all Catholic doctrine, while, and *therefore,* rejecting the innovations of later days. In grouping these Churches together, it is not meant to be implied that they all carry out to like extent their good purpose. The Eastern Orthodox Churches have, in good degree, preserved the Christian traditions of the first ages. Among those set down as "Other Churches" are some whose doctrinal position has been questioned, others the validity of whose orders has been disputed. It may well be that, with fuller information on points of which we know too little, some at least of these objections may be found to have come from misconceptions.

In the list of the Anglican Episcopate, care has been taken as to the due arrangement in Ecclesiastical Provinces.

THE ANGLICAN COMMUNION.

I. THE CHURCH OF ENGLAND.

Canterbury.—The Archbishop of Canterbury is "Primate of all England and Metropolitan." Under him are the Bishops of
London,
Winchester,
Norwich,
Bangor,
Worcester,
Gloucester and Bristol,
St. Albans,
Hereford,
Peterborough,
Lincoln,
Salisbury,
Bath and Wells,
Exeter,
Oxford,
Chichester,
St. Asaph,
Ely,
St. Davids,
Rochester,
Lichfield,
Llandaff,
Truro.

Besides these, there are in the Dioceses of Canterbury, London, Lincoln, and St. Albans, respectively, the Suffragan Bishops of Dover, of Bedford, of Nottingham, and of Colchester; and three Retired Colonial Bishops assist in the Dioceses of London, Winchester, and Peterborough.

York.—The Archbishop of York is "Primate of England and Metropolitan." In his Province there are the Bishops of
Durham,
Ripon,
Chester,
Carlisle,
Manchester,
Sodor and Man,
Liverpool,
Newcastle.

A Retired Colonial Bishop assists in the Diocese of Huron.

II. THE CHURCH OF IRELAND.

Armagh and Clogher.—The Archbishop of Armagh is "Primate of all Ireland and Metropolitan." In his Province there are the Bishops of
Meath,
Down, Connor, and Achonry,
Derry and Raphoe,
Kilmore, Elphin, and Ardagh.

Dublin, Glendelagh, and Kildare.—The Archbishop of Dublin is "Primate of Ireland and Metropolitan." In his Province are the Bishops of
Limerick, Ardfert, and Aghadoe,
Cashel, Emly, Waterford, and Lismore,
Cork, Cloyne, and Ross,
Ossory, Ferns, and Leighlin,
Killaloe, Kilfenora, Clonfert, and Kilmacduagh.

III. THE SCOTTISH CHURCH.

Bishops.

Moray, Ross, and Caithness.—The present Bishop is "*Primus* of the Scottish Church," by election.
St. Andrews, Dunkeld, and Dunblane,
Edinburgh,
Glasgow and Gallouay,
Brechin,
Aberdeen and Orkney,
Argyle and the Isles.

IV. THE AMERICAN CHURCH.

(*a*) *Bishops of organized Dioceses.*

Kentucky.—The present Bishop is "Presiding Bishop" of the American Church by seniority.

Delaware,
Mississippi,
Connecticut,
California,
New York,
Rhode Island,
Texas,
Ohio,
Minnesota,
Easton,
Pennsylvania,
Alabama,
The Province of Illinois,
Kansas,
Western New York,
Tennessee,
Nebraska,
Maine,
Florida,
Georgia,
Virginia,
Vermont,
Missouri,
Long Island,
Albany,
Central New York,
Arkansas,
New Hampshire,
South Carolina,
Central Pennsylvania,
Massachusetts,
North Carolina,
Wisconsin,
New Jersey,
Western Michigan,
Southern Ohio,
{ Illinois,
Quincy,
Springfield,
Fond du Lac,
Iowa,
West Virginia,
Michigan,
Northern New Jersey,
Louisiana,
Pittsburg,
Indiana,
East Carolina,
Maryland.

(*b*) *Assistant Bishops.*

Of these there are four, in the Dioceses of Kentucky, Mississippi, New York, and Virginia.

(*c*) *Bishops in Charge of Missionary Jurisdictions within the United States.*

Idaho and Utah,
Oregon,
Nevada,
South Dakota,
Western Texas,
Northern California,
Northern Texas,
Arizona and New Mexico,
Montana,
Colorado and Wyoming,
Washington Territory,
North Dakota.

(*d*) *Bishops in Charge of Missionary Jurisdictions outside the United States.*

Yeddo (Japan).
(The Missionary Episcopates of Cape Palmas (Africa) and Shanghai (China) are vacant, January 1, 1884.)

(*e*) *Bishops retired from their Sees.*

There are five such, January 1, 1884.

V. THE CHURCH IN THE ENGLISH COLONIES.

(*a*) *The Church in India.*

Calcutta.—The Bishop of Calcutta is Metropolitan of the Church in India and Ceylon. In this Province there are also the Bishops of
Madras,
Colombo,
Bombay,
Lahore,
Travancore and Cochin,
Rangoon.

There are also two Suffragan Bishops in the Diocese of Madras.

(*b*) *The Church in the Province of South Africa.*

Capetown.—The Bishop of Capetown is "Metropolitan of the Church in the Province of South Africa." In this Province there are also the Bishops of

St. Helena,	Pretoria,
Maritzburg,	Zululand,
Grahamstown,	Bloemfontein.
St. John's Kaffraria,	

(c) *The Church in Australia and Tasmania.*

Sydney.—The Bishop of Sydney is "Primate of the Church in Australia and Tasmania." In this Province there are also the Bishops of

Brisbane,	Ballaarat,
Goulburn,	Melbourne,
Perth,	North Queensland,
Grafton and Armidale,	Newcastle,
	Adelaide,
Bathurst,	Tasmania.

(d) *The Church in New Zealand.*

Christ Church.—The Bishop is "Primate of the Church in New Zealand." In this Province there are the Bishops of

Nelson,	Dunedin,
Auckland,	Waiapu,
Wellington,	Melanesia.

(e) *The Church in the Province of Canada.*

Fredericton.—The Bishop of Fredericton is "Metropolitan of Canada" by election. In this Province there are also the Bishops of

Nova Scotia,	Montreal,
Ontario,	Toronto,
Quebec,	Algoma,
Niagara,	Huron.

There is a Coadjutor Bishop in the Diocese of Fredericton.

(f) *The Church in the Province of Rupert's Land.*

Rupert's Land.—The Bishop is "Metropolitan of the Church in the Province of Rupert's Land."

Moosonee,	Athabasca.
Saskatchewan,	

(g) *The Church in the West Indies.*

Guiana.—The Bishop of Guiana is "Primate of the Church in the West Indies" by election. There are also in this province the Bishops of

Antigua,	Nassau,
Trinidad,	Jamaica,
Barbadoes and Windward Islands.	

The Diocese of British Honduras is in charge of the Bishop of Jamaica. There is a Coadjutor Bishop in the Diocese of Antigua.

(h) *Bishops of Dioceses not yet organized into Ecclesiastical Provinces.*

Gibraltar,	Central Africa,
Victoria (China),	The Niger,
North China,	Newfoundland,
Mid China,	Columbia,
Japan,	Caledonia,
Singapore, Labuan, and Sarawak,	New Westminster, British Honduras,
Mauritius,	Falkland Islands,
Madagascar,	Honolulu.

(i) *Bishops retired from their Sees*

There were nineteen such Bishops January 1, 1884.

THE OLD CATHOLIC CHURCHES.

There is in *Holland* an Archbishop (of Utrecht) and two Bishops (of Haarlem and of Deventer) of the Old Catholic Church (often called "the *Jansenis*" Church). There is in *Germany* a Bishop of the *Old Catholic* Church. There is in *Switzerland* a Bishop of the *Christian Catholic* Church. There is in *Hayti* a Bishop of the *Orthodox Apostolic* Church.

THE ORTHODOX EASTERN CHURCHES.

I. THE PATRIARCHATE OF CONSTANTINOPLE.

Presided over by "The Archbishop of Constantinople, New Rome, and Œcumenical Patriarch." In this Patriarchate are the Metropolitans of

Cæsarea in Cappadocia,	Anchialus,
	Varna,
Ephesus,	Maronea,
Heraclæa and Rhædestum,	Silivri,
	Sozoagathopolis,
Cyzicum,	Xanthia,
Nicomedia,	Ganus and Khora,
Nicæa,	Chios,
Chalcedon,	Lemnos,
Dercus,	Imbros,
Thessalonica,	Dyrrachium,
Tirnova,	Scopia,
Adrianople,	Castorea,
Amasæa,	Rasca-Prisrend,
Joannina,	Bodeno,
Brusa,	Coritza,
Pelagonia,	Belegrad,
Necæsarea and Enea,	Castentil and Stipium,
Iconium,	
Berrhæa,	Strumnitza and Tiberopolis,
Pisidia,	
Crete,	Grebeno,
Trapezus,	Sisanium and Siatest,
Nicopolis,	Mogleno,
Philippopolis,	Presper and Ochrida,
Rhodes,	Debri,
Serræ,	Cassandria,
Drama,	Chaldæa and Cheriana,
Smyrna,	
Mitylene,	Elasson,
Didymotichus,	Præconnesus,
Ancyra,	Drynopolis and Debrino,
Philadelphia,	
Melenicus,	Cos,
Enos,	Lititza,
Methymne,	Aleppo,
Mesembria,	Carpathus and Caxus,
Samos and Icaria,	Serbia and Cozania.
Bizya and Midia,	

The Archbishops of

Discate,	Neurocopion.

The Bishops of

Heliopolis and Thyatira,	Callopolis and Madytus,
Crene and Anæa,	Metra and Athyra,

Myriophytum and Peristasis,
Citras,
Campania,
Poliana and Bardasium,
Petra,
Ardamerium,
Hierissus and Monte Santo,
Paramithia,
Bella,
Nicopolis,
Arcadia,
Rhithymene and Aulipotamus,
Petra,
Cydonia,
Cheronesus,
Hiera and Sitea,
Cissamus and Selimus,
Lampe,
Leros,
Moschonesus.

The Titular Bishops of
Cariopolis,
Irenopolis,
Pamphylia,
Supelum,
Myrina,
Erythræa,
Synada,
Meletopolis,
Troas,
Abydos,
Leontopolis,
Chrystopolis,
Poristera,
Argyropolis,
Lite,

There are in this Patriarchate fourteen Bishops retired from their Sees.

II. THE PATRIARCHATE OF ALEXANDRIA.

Presided over by "The Pope and Patriarch of the Great City Alexandria, Libya, Pantapolis, and Ethiopia, and of all the land of Egypt." The seven Sees in this Patriarchate are all vacant at this time. The Patriarch is assisted by a Vicar Bishop with the title of Bishop Xanthopolis. There is also a retired Patriarch of Alexandria, and a retired Metropolitan (of Pelusium).

III. THE PATRIARCHATE OF ANTIOCH.

Presided over by "The Patriarch of the Divine City Antioch, Syria, Arabia, Cilicia, Iberia, Mesopotamia, and all the East." In this Patriarchate there are the Metropolitans of
Seleucia,
Epiphania,
Tripoli,
Theodosiopolis,
Arcadia,
Laodicea,
Edessa,
Tyre and Sidon,
Amida,
Tarsus and Adana,
Berytus,

and the Bishops of
Irenapolis,
Palmyra,
The Hauran.

IV. THE PATRIARCHATE OF JERUSALEM.

Presided over by "The Patriarch of the Holy City Jerusalem, and all Palestine, Syria, Arabia beyond Jordan, Cana of Galilee, and Holy Sion."

In this Patriarchate there are the Metropolitans of
Scythopolis,
Petra,
Ptolemais,
Bethlehem,
Nazareth,

and the Archbishops of
Lydda,
Mount Tabor,
Gaza
The Jordan,
Mount Sinai.

V. RUSSIA.

In Russia there are the Metropolitans of Novgorod, St. Petersburg, Finland, Kieff and Galicia, Moscow and Kolomna.

The Archbishops of
Kherson and Odessa,
Voronej and Zadonsk,
Penza and Saransk,
Yakoutsk and Viluis,
Orloff and Sievsk,
Riazan and Zaraisk,
Archangel and Kholmogor,
Kamchatka, the Kouriles and Blagovashensky,
Astrachan and Enotaevsk,
Koursk and Bielgorod,
Oufa and Menzelinsk,
Tamboff and Shatz,
Tchernigoff and Nijni,
Podolia and Bratslaff,
Pskoff and Porkhoff,
Tobolsk and Siberia,
The Taurida and Simpheropol,
Polotsk and Vitebsk,
Minsk and Touroff,
Yenisee and Krasnoairsk,
Calouga and Boroff,
Simbirsk and Syzran,
Turkestan and Tashkend,
Smolensk and Dorogobouge,
Kharkoff and Akhtyr,
Saratoff and Tsaritsin,
Mogileff and Mstislav,
Riga and Mittau,
Orenburg and the Ural,
Kholm and Warsaw,
Toula and Bieleff,
Lithuania and Vilna,
Poltava and Periaslav,
Irkutsk and Nerchinsk
The Don and Novocherkask,
Kisheneff and Khotinsk,
Tver and Kashin,
Viatka and Slobodsk,
Kazan and Sviajsk,
Volhynia and Jitomir.

The Bishops of
Tomsk and Semipalatinsk,
Vologda and Oustiog,
Olonetz and Petrozavodsk,
Nijni Novgorod and Arsamas,
Jaroslav and Rostov,
Samara and Stauropol,
Vladimir and Souzdal,
Ekaterinoslav and Taganrog,
Perm and Verchotour,
Kostromo and Galitz,
Caucasia and Ekaterinodar.

In Georgia there are "The Exarch of Georgia, Archbishop of Kartalenia and Cachetia," and the Bishops of Imerctia and Gouri.

In America there is the Bishop of the Aleutian Islands and Alaska (vacant January 1, 1884 A.D.).

Assisting in the various Dioceses, there are the Vicar (or Suffragan) Bishops of
Staria Russa,
Ladoga,
Viborg,
Tchigirin,

Ouman,
Dmitroff,
Mojaisk,
Novomirgorod,
Elizabethgrad,
Ostrog,
Ostrogod,
Lublin,
Kovno,
Brest,
Selenginsk,
Aksaisk,
Akkerman,
Tcheboksar,
Sarapoul,
Staritz,
Michaeloff,
Biisk,
Totma,
Ekaterinburg,
Mourom,
Kineshma,
Balachna,
Mozdok,
Novgorod-Sieversk,
Kozloff,
Soumsk,
Beresoff,
Revel,
Balta,
Gori,
Vladikavkas,
Mingrelia.

There are in Russia three Archbishops and eight Bishops retired from their Sees.

VI. CYPRUS.

The "Archbishop of Nova-Justiniana and all Cyprus" has under him the Metropolitans of
Paphos,
Citium.
Cyrene.

VII. AUSTRIA.

"The Patriarch of Servia, Metropolitan of all the Servians residing in the Austrian Empire, Archbishop of Carlovitz," has under him the Bishops of
Bats and Szegedin,
Buda, St. Andrew's, Pesth, Stuhl-Weissemburg, Moshacs, Segesed,
Verschatz, Lugos, and Orsova,
Temesvar, Lippa, Nagy-Beckserk and Panosova,
Pakrats, Slavonia, Posega, and all the Generalate of Warasdin,
Carlstadt, Costanitza, Corbava, and the seacoast towns of Trieste, Rick, and Segni.

"The Metropolitan of all the Roumanian nation in the Austrian Empire, Archbishop of Transylvania," has under him the Bishops of
Arad, Grosswardim, Yenopolsk, and Chalmatosh,
Caran-Sebesh.

"The Metropolitan of the Buckovine and Dalmatia" has under him the Bishops of
Dalmatia,
Bocca di Cattaro, Dulrovnikick, and Spitz.

VIII. MONTENEGRO.

"The Metropolitan of Scanderia and the Sea-Coast, Archbishop of Tsettin, Exarch of the Holy Throne of Pek, Vladika of Montenegro" has *no* Suffragan.

IX. GREECE.

In Greece there are the Metropolitans of
Athens,
Arta,
Larissa,
Phanarium and Pharsalus,
Demetris and Zagorium.

The Metropolitans of
Mantinea and Cynouria,
Acarnania and Ætolia,
Leucadia,
Zacynthus,
Chalcis,
Messania,
Syros and Tenos,
Cythera,
Phthiotis,
Corinth,

The Bishops of
Thebes and Livadia,
Carystia,
Phocis,
Andros and Cea,
Ithaca,
Stagon,
Tricca,
Thaumacus,
Calavryta and Ægialia,
Œtylon,
Gytheum,
Monembasia and Sparta,
Cephalonia,
Corcyra.

Platamon,
Gardicium,
Thera,
Hydra,
Triphylia and Olympia,
Paros and Naxos,
Naupactus and Eurytania,
Gortyna and Megalopolis,
Paxos.

X. THE SERVIAN CHURCH.

"The Archbishop of Belgrade, Metropolitan of all Servia," having under him the Bishops of
Negotin,
Uschidze,
Shabatz,
Nissa.

XI. THE ROUMANIAN CHURCH.

In this Church are the "Metropolitans of Hungro-Wallachia, Primate of all Roumania," and the "Metropolitan of Moldavia and Suceava."
The Bishops of
Roman,
Rimnik on the Alouta,
Bizya,
Chotza,
Ardjetsch,
Stratonicia.

THE BULGARIAN CHURCH.

(This Church is not recognized as in communion with Constantinople.) "The Exarch of Bulgaria," having under him the Metropolitans of
Widdin,
Varna-Prestilava,
Samocab,
Castentil,
Sophia,
Dorostolo-Tchervlen,
Lophitzus,
Tirnova,
Bratch,
Philippopolis,
Slivno,
Adrianople.

There are also two Vicar Bishops and two Bishops retired from their Sees.

THE ARMENIAN CHURCH.*

"The Supreme Catholicos of all the Armenians, exercising special jurisdiction in Russia and Persia," has under him the Archbishops of
Erivan,
Tiflis,
Karabagh,
Zhirvan,
Astrachan,
Bessarabia and New Nakikheran,
Tabriz,
Ispahan and Calcutta,

together with an Archbishop and five Bishops without Sees, residing at Etchmiadzin as members of the Holy Synod.

---

* The Armenian, Syrian, Coptic, Abyssinian, and Assyrian Churches have long been thought to have departed widely in essential matters from the Catholic faith. It would appear, however, that their doctrines are, to say the least, much less erroneous than has been supposed. Further information in regard to them is much to be desired.

The Patriarch of Constantinople has under him the Archbishops of
Brousa, Van.
The Bishops of
Adrianople, Moosh,
Sivas, Balekissar,
Cæsarea, Trebizond,
Urho, or Edessa, The Convent of Armash,
Harpoot,
Smyrna, The Convent of Surp Daniel,
Arapkir,
Erzinguian, The Convent of Maghapayetzolz-Vank.
Rhodosto,
The following Sees in the Patriarchate are vacant, and in charge of Vicars: Aguen, Amasea-Marzuan, Angora, Aphion, Kara-Hissar, Arghen, Babert, Babylon, Bagdad, Bayazid, Biledjig, Bitlis, Charsandjak, Chenkoosh, Diarbekir, Djanig, Egypt and Alexandria, Erzeroum, Givindj-Moosh, Gurin, Hassan-Kale, Kars, Keghi, Kemack, Kutahia, Moldo-Wallachia, Nicomedia, Palu, Papert, Shaborn, Kara-Hissar, Siourt, Tertchan, Themesyadzak, Tokat, Varna.
The Patriarch of Jerusalem.
The Patriarch of Sis, having under him the Bishops of
Hadjin, Yozghad,
Malatia, Zeitoun.
Adana,
The following Sees in this Patriarchate are vacant, and in charge of Vicars: Aintab, Aleppo, Antioch, Behesne, Derende, Divringhi, Gurium, Halys, Husnimansur, Marash.
The Patriarch of Akhtamar, having under him the Bishops of
Limm-Anabat, Guedontz-Anabat.

THE SYRIAN CHURCH.

(Commonly called the *Jacobite* Church.) "The Patriarch of Antioch (resides at the Convent of Zaaferan, near Mardin), having under him the Metropolitans of
Jerusalem, Damascus,
Mosul, Constantinople,
The Convent of Mar Egypt (the Convent of
  Mattai near Mosul,   Mar Behnam),
Jezirah, Boudgia,
Nisibis, Bishirii,
Midyat, Aleppo,
Diarbekir, Adana,
Harpoot, Malabar (in India).
Oorfa,

THE COPTIC CHURCH.

"The Patriarch of Egypt, Jerusalem the Holy City, Nubia, Abyssinia, the five Western Cities (*i.e.* the Pentapolis), and all the Preaching of St. Mark," having under him the Metropolitans of
Cairo, Kouds (the Holy City,
Lower Egypt,   Jerusalem),
    Menouf (Memphis),
and the Bishops of
Fayoum and Beh- Abuteg,
  mase, Aschumin,
Miniyeh, Kos,
Kuskam, Esna and Luxor.
Manfalout, Khartoum and Nubia.
Siout,

THE ABYSSINIAN CHURCH.

The Metropolitan of the Abyssinian Church is called "The *Abouna.*" The office is now vacant, and the Church is in charge of an Archbishop and two Bishops.

THE ASSYRIAN CHURCH.

(Commonly called the *Nestorian Church.*) "The Patriarch of the Chaldeans and of the East." (Resides at Kochanes.)
He has under him at
Be Sheems Ood-Deen, 4 Metropolitans
Ooromiah, 3 "
Berwari, 2 "
Jelu, 1 Metropolitan.
Gawar, 1 "
Doori, 1 "

THE CHURCH OF SWEDEN.*

Upsala.—The Archbishop of Upsala, Primate of Sweden. Under him are the Bishops of
Linkoping, Lund,
Skara, Gothemburg,
Strengas, Calmar,
Westeras, Hermosand,
Wexio, Wisby.

THE CHURCH IN FINLAND.

Abo.—The Archbishop of Abo. Under him are the Bishops of
Borgo, Kuefico.

THE MORAVIAN CHURCH.*

This Church has no Diocesan Bishop. In the German Province it has five Bishops, in the British three Bishops, in the American four Bishops, in the West India Mission Province one Bishop.

REV. C. R. HALE, S.T.D.

Epistle. 1. A letter. Chiefly the Epistles of St. Paul, St. James, St. Peter, St. Jude, and St. John in the New Testament. These were letters called forth by various circumstances, which were addressed by the writers to the several Churches or persons needing the teaching, advice, or warning contained in them. St. Paul's fourteen Epistles cover nearly all the ground of Christian doctrine and practice. Each of them has some special doctrinal subject except that to Philemon, while some of them are more largely hortatory than others. In doctrine we may group together Romans, Galatians and the three Epistles of the Roman imprisonment, Ephesians, Philippians, and Colossians, and the Epistle to the Hebrews. The two to the Thessalonians and the two to the Corinthians may be classed as hortatory and minatory. The two to Timothy and that to Titus are upon Church government, but both doctrinal and hortatory topics are included. While that to Philemon is an intercession in behalf of Onesimus. The Catholic (or Encyclical) Epistles of St.

---

* The *Orders* of these Churches, fully believed in by some, are seriously questioned by others, who have examined into their validity.

James, St. Peter, St. John, and St. Jude are chiefly hortatory upon the principles of Christian life, as works (St. James), practical duties (St. Peter), minatory (St. Jude), love (St. John). There is but little certainty as to the year in which either of these Epistles in the New Testament were written, except in the date of the Epistle to the Romans, but we know with certainty enough within what limits of the Apostolic age they must have been written. The approximate dates of the Epistles are as follows:

1 Thessalonians	53 A.D.
2 Thessalonians	54 A.D.
1 Corinthians	57 A.D.
2 Corinthians	57 A.D.
Galatians	57 A.D.
Romans	58 A.D.
Ephesians	62 A.D.
Colossians	63 A.D.
Philippians	63 A.D.
St. James	62 A.D.
Philemon	63 A.D.
1 Peter	64 A.D.
Jude	65 A.D.
2 Peter	65 A.D.
Hebrews, 1 Timothy, Titus, 2 Timothy.	66 to 68 A.D.
St. John's Epistles, after	98 A.D.

These dates are, after all, but approximations, except in the case of the Epistle to the Romans, whose date is so nearly ascertained that it forms one of the points from which the other data of the Apostle's life may be fixed. The dates of St. John's Epistles are wholly conjectural. The other dates have an approximate and a very probable accuracy.

II. But this title, Epistle, is used to designate that portion of Scripture (usually from the Epistles of the New Testament) which is read before the Gospel for each Sunday, holy, or fast-day in the Church's year. It is so called because it is very generally taken from the Epistles.

This selection of sections of the Epistles for each Sunday, holy-day, saints' day, and fast-day must have, in principle at least, been an early custom. The Epistles and Gospels, arranged nearly as we now use them for the Sundays, are found in the book attributed to St. Jerome,—the Comes (vide COMES). But there must have been an earlier use, though it probably varied in different Dioceses. Basil the Great (389 A.D.) comments on Matt. ii. 1–12 as the Gospel for the Feast of the Epiphany; Gregory Nozianzen on Acts ii. 1–13 as Epistle for Whit-Sunday. Ambrose refers to portions of Scripture selected for Christmas-day and Feast of the Epiphany and St. John's day, which are identical with our own. These show a concurrent usage before the year 400 A.D. If the Comes *is* St. Jerome's work and brought to us from Gaul, as seems likely, then our Epistles and Gospels now are of ancient British use and were found here by Augustine the Monk in 596 A.D.

As the Epistle was taken usually from some portion of the Apostolic writing, the Liturgies called it "the Apostle."

The Epistles and Gospels were chosen with very great care to illustrate, first, the two great divisions of the Christian year,— the Sundays from Advent to Trinity-Sunday, and then the Sundays after Trinity; and, second, and more in detail, to fit in with the glorious recital of our LORD'S redemptive acts from Advent to Pentecost. His acts are presented with an inspired fitness in the selections of the Gospels, and the Epistles are the practical comment upon the history or parable in the Gospel. The original idea of the harmony between the two Scriptures in the mind of the persons who arranged them is not in all cases very clear at first sight to us now. But a little study will often show that there does exist such a special fitness between the two.

These Epistles are not always selected from the Apostolic writings; but some are taken from other books of the Bible, according to their fitness for the lesson to be given on the days for which they are appointed.

The Epistles for these two Sundays are taken from other Scriptures:

Whit-Sunday, Acts ii. 1;
Trinity-Sunday, Rev. iv. 1.

The Epistles on Fast-days from other Scriptures are:

Ash-Wednesday, Joel ii. 12; Monday before Easter, Is. lxiii. 1; Tuesday, Is. l. 5.

The Epistles for Holy-days from other Scriptures are:

Monday in Easter-week, Acts x. 34; Tuesday, Acts xiii. 26; Ascension-day, Acts i. 1; Monday in Whitsun-week, Acts x. 34; Tuesday, Acts viii. 14.

The Epistles for Saints' days, taken from other Scriptures, are:

St. Stephen, Acts vii. 55; Innocents, Rev. xiv. 1; Conversion of St. Paul, Acts ix. 1; Purification, Mal. iii. 1; St. Matthias, Acts i. 15; Annunciation, Is. vii. 10; St. Barnabas, Acts xi. 22; St. John Baptist, Is. xl. 1; St Peter, Acts xii. 1; St. James, Acts xi. 27; St. Bartholomew, Acts v. 12; St. Michael and All-Angels', Rev. xii. 7; All-Saints', Rev. vii. 2. Also in the Ordinal for Deacons, Acts vi. 2 may be read in the Ordinal for Bishops; the alternate Epistle is from Acts xx. 17. The Puritans at the Savoy Conference objected to the heading as it then stood, "the Epistle, Acts," etc., for the Acts and the Prophets were not Epistolary Scriptures at all, and charged that it was a falsehood to say here beginneth the Epistle written in Acts or in other Scripture than an actual Epistle; so, to remove all objection, the heading in such places was changed to "For the Epistle," and the rubric in the Communion office was changed also to agree with this alteration.

Epistoler. The Priest or Deacon who reads the Epistle. Where there are two clergymen present at a service, the one who reads the Epistle should stand on the south side of the Holy Table, while the Gospeler stands on the north side. An old custom was when there was but one clergyman officiating, that he should read the Epistle from the south side, and then cross to the north side to read the Gospel.

Epoch. An era; a cycle of time, or a series of events having a closer interconnection and sequence than other events forming an era in history. These are variously described by different historians, as each groups historical facts or appreciates the boundaries of the different eras in the world's career. The word epoch is applied almost indifferently with the word era to the same general divisions, but more usually it is used with the date of the creation of the world, according to Archbishop Ussher, and in our Bibles on the margin, B.C. 4004, with the date of the deluge usually given as 2349 B.C. But these epochs are discussed in the article CHRONOLOGY.

Erastianism. Erastus, a physician of Baden (1524-83 A.D.), who asserted the authority of secular legislation over the Church. It was a reaction from the opposite theory of Calvin. It was a favorite principle of the Independents against the Presbyterians, and seems to have been taken as a refuge from the natural claim of Divine authority set up by each dominant sect. It really destroys all true conception of the foundation and functions of the Church, making it a creature of the State, and reducing its work to one but little more important than that of doing a sort of moral police duty. Erastianism will always exist as a reaction against extravagant and bigoted conceptions of Divine authority in the Church; but especially, whenever any sect obtains a controlling power, it will be held by opponents. The Church of England, because of the aid it receives from the State to enforce its Canons, has become at times deeply tinged with Erastian notions, especially among the statesmen who give their aid or influence to her work. But it is not true to charge the Church with countenancing any such principle in any way. In this country, with the utter separation between Church and State, it would seem impossible that such ideas could become at all prevalent, yet the current view of those outside of the Church is practically an Erastian view.

Eschatology. The Revelation concerning the Last Things, and the doctrines and conclusions drawn from it. These "Last Things" are Second Advent, Judgment, Death, Hell, Resurrection, Heaven, State of Souls in the future world, and the Millennium. *Purgatory* and other "fond things vainly invented" concerning the Last Things cannot be discussed here. To us as we are living in time, the eternal world around us, but beyond our spiritual grasp or comprehension, must be in the future. So however present in GOD'S Presence all things are, yet the Judgment, Heaven, and our eternal Condition must be treated by us as of the "Last Things." Since Death is not only a physical act, but involves spiritual acts and conditions, that must be the starting-point for us in considering the end of all things. What lies beyond? Revelation has really given us central facts and has added but few details. As these several facts can here be only enumerated, and will be discussed under their several titles more fully, it will be only necessary to give the definition of each here, and it is hardly needed to load the page with texts familiar to every Christian.

I. *The Place of Departed Spirits.* The Greek translations of the Old Testament and the Evangelists call it by its heathen name *Hades*. It is unfortunately (now by the drift of language principally) translated Hell in King James's Version. Hades (A. V. *grave*) in the Old Testament is for the Hebrew *Sheol*. It is in the New Testament also called (1 Pet. iii. 19) a guard-house (prison A. V.). It is divided into two, (*a*) Abraham's bosom, or Paradise. (*b*) That side parted off by an impassable gulf,—the place of sorrow and torment, or Tartarus (2 Pet. ii. 4), the lowest abyss of pain and despair.

II. *The Second Advent.* The revelation is clear and emphatic. It is the sole prophecy embodied in the Creed: "He shall come to judge the quick and the dead."

III. *The Millennium.* So many commentators differ upon the place of the Millennium, whether before or after the Second Advent, that it is best to refer the discussion of it all to that title.

IV. *The Resurrection*, involved in and consequent upon the Second Advent.

V. *Judgment.* The immediate purpose of the Resurrection.

VI. *Heaven.* The award to those who die in the LORD given at the Bar of Judgment.

VII. *Hell.* The sentence passed upon the wicked at the same time.

VIII. A further discussion which involves the last two topics, but must be noticed under a different title, is the *States of Heaven and of Hell.*

Several minor topics, Angels of Judgment, the physical, mental, and spiritual nature of the joys or pains in the future of the Soul after Judgment, the seat of Heaven or of Hell, are really speculative topics. But it is to be clearly noted that there is no final conciliar declaration by the Church defining what CHRIST has chosen to leave so indefinitely described. The Resurrection and the Life of the world to come, in the Creeds, is the nearest definition. She has chosen to declare upon this whole class of subjects, and upon these her words are clear and positive.

Esdras. The Apocryphal books numbered 1 and 2 Books of Esdras. They were very generally rejected in the Primitive Church, though they were quoted by some with approval. Jerome, however, rejected them with decision. The absurdities, the contradictions, not only of the Canonical

Scriptures, but of the facts as recorded in profane history, are such as to destroy their claim to any historical value. The first Book seems to be a rearrangement, according to the compiler's idea of the sequence of events, of the sacred history from the last two chapthers of 2 Chronicles to the close of the books of Ezra and Nehemiah, whose contents he has altered and mistaken. Its facts may have had some basis as isolated occurrences, but the book is worthless historically. The second Book of Esdras is quite as valueless historically, though it is a record of Jewish dreams and anticipations at the period of its composition. The precise date is not known, but it lies about 25 B.C. and 110 A.D. It is influenced in its numerous interpolations, and, if it be by different writers, in later editions by the Christian Scriptures. (An excellent account of these two books is to be found in Smith's Bible Dictionary.)

Espousals. The Betrothal. There is a distinction between Marriage and Espousals. Espousals were binding indeed, but preceded the Marriage ceremony often for years. The ancient Canon Law recognized this and acted upon it. But its basis was to be found in the Old Testament (*e.g.*, Jeremiah ii. 2; Hosea ii. 19, 20), where it is used typically of GOD binding His Church to Himself, and in the New Testament, where St. Paul tells the Corinthians that as a bridesman he has espoused them to CHRIST (2 Cor. xi. 2). There are only passing references to the espousals or betrothal, in the Law, as a fact, *e.g.*, "a betrothed damsel." But Eleazar, Abraham's steward, betrothed Rebecca for Isaac with formal presents, jewelry, and raiment (Gen. xxiv.). The forms of betrothal are only dwelt upon by the prophets, and then in a very slight and allusive manner, most fully, however, in Ezek. xvi. 10-13; compare Rev. xxi. 2.

Established Church. The idea of the "Established Church" is misunderstood very often. It is not that any government ever imagined the absurdity that it could establish the Church, but that religion being necessary to the well-being of the State, the Church was recognized, protected, and allied to the State by law. Its officers received political recognition, and part of the revenues of the State went to its support. Its canons and discipline were enforced by civil enactments, and in time the State had great influence in the affairs of the Church. This joining of Church and State began in the time of Constantine (320-350 A.D.). The alliance was not at all at variance with the notions then current. It was inherited from the protection pagan religions received by becoming State religions, and in their ideas of religion it was an indifferent matter whether they worshiped Jupiter, or Serapis, or Astarte. These notions being current, to divorce Church and State would have seemed to them an unnatural proceeding. That this alliance should ever have been formed, and that the Church ever should be recognized as the religion of the State established by law, is to us quite as unnatural. Yet it was inherited from the Jewish Church, and in it was involved the popular idea of orthodoxy. In fact, the Church and State, both in New England and in the other colonies, was a constitutional fact, and the final severance of the State from religious affairs was effected, *e.g.*, in Massachusetts in the early decades of this century. The perverted idea that the State created the Church only shows how little attention is paid to history.

Esther. The Queen of Ahasuerus,—a very remarkable character. Noble, lovely, deeply devout, obedient even in the king's harem to the traditions of her race, she was probably not raised to the rank of the Queens of Persia, but was chief among the royal concubines, whose state was within that of a real marriage, who yet had no political rank. Her patriotism and wisdom were of the greatest use to her people in their dire need. Her grace and loveliness and exquisite charms are told in such simple language, that we see how holily she bore her honors in the midst of a licentious court. She is to be judged by the ideas and manners of her age and surroundings, and under this test she is one of the fairest characters in Holy Scripture.

Book of Esther.—Its author is not known, but may have been Mordecai, the Queen's uncle. The minute details given, both historical, social, and personal, make this conjecture quite probable. The book of Esther was brought from Babylon and placed in the Canon by Ezra, and put afterwards under the (later) arrangement of the Hagiographa (which see). The simple, straightforward flow of the narrative is strongly marked, while the strangeness of the incidents and the picture of the manners of the sensual despot, the audacity and superstition of Haman, the passive, proud bearing of the Jew, are all fully borne out by what is well authenticated of that time. That Ahasuerus is the Xerxes of the Grecian war is quite clear, and gives to this book almost the appearance of touching upon profane history. In another way, too, this coincidence of time has a curious relation to its contents. The name of GOD does not occur in it, though fasting, prayer, and weeping attest the devoutness of the Jews in their danger. But we have a book placed in the inspired Canon which does not draw aside the veil, as is done in so many other books, and does not show us the presiding care and watchful Providence, but leaves that to be surely inferred from the events of the history itself. In this respect it is to be most highly valued. The translation of Esther in the Septuagint is interpolated, and contains some items which were very likely traditional.

Latter Chapters of (Apocrypha).—These chapters contain a supposed dream of Mordecai, in which Esther is likened to a little fountain which became a river, an account of the conspiracy against the king, and Mordecai's revelation of it, the king's letters to destroy the Jews, and the prayers of Mordecai and Esther to the GOD of Israel. There is also a description of Esther's intercession with the king, and of the king's mercy to her people. Mordecai's pedigree is also given. These apocryphal additions may have arisen in part on account of the desire of the Jews "to dwell upon the events of the Babylonish captivity, and especially upon the Divine interpositions in their behalf." Traditions would be rife. The most popular, or most historical, or those by the most eminent authors, or the most ancient stories, and those which fed the love of national greatness, might obtain special authority. The deliverance of the Jews by Mordecai and Esther would be a favorite subject. The chapters in the Apocrypha are not found in the Hebrew or Chaldee. They were written in Greek, translated into Latin, and were a "part of the Italic, or old Latin version in use before the time of Jerome." They are thought by Horne to be "evidently the production of an Hellenistic Jew."

Authorities: Archdeacon Hervey, in Wm. Smith's Dictionary of the Bible, Horne's Introduction.   REV. S. F. HOTCHKIN.

Eternity. In a strict sense, and as it relates to GOD, eternity has neither beginning nor end. As regards human beings, it has a beginning but no end. "One day is with the LORD as a thousand years, and a thousand years as one day" (2 St. Pet. iii. 8). As Estius "expresses it, all eternity is one day." (Liddon's Bampton Lectures on our LORD'S Divinity, p. 301, note.) Ages are lost in eternity. No human being can grasp the idea fully, because he measures things by comparing them with the finite things about him.

Addison (Spectator, No. 590) calls eternity a line which has neither beginning nor end. The present time he says has been wisely compared to an isthmus in the midst of an ocean. He allows the division into an eternity past and an eternity to come. While this is not strictly scientific, it is convenient, and desirable as a help in grasping the subject.

The incessant anticipation of the human mind has been adduced as a proof that it is fitted for future endless existence. Cato calls it, "This longing after immortality." Time, like a constantly flowing stream, ever rolls on, but it empties into the ocean of eternity.

Eternity is constantly spoken of as future, but we are already in it. Aubrey de Vere (The Subjective Difficulties in Religion) uses this illustration. Eternity is not a prolongation of time, but a vaster sphere clasping a smaller one, and reaching with its penetrating influences to beings at once inclosed within both.

Still time, as but a piece of eternity, so to speak, is transient. Thucydides may speak of a possession for eternity, and Keats of the "joy forever" that springs from "a thing of beauty," but nothing earthly can abide, and outward adorning must perish, as the earth itself, which hastens on to destruction.

In striving to catch an idea of eternity by means of time, astronomy comes to our aid. The thought of heavenly bodies which have kept their appointed courses for thousands of years, while men and nations have vanished from the earth like forest leaves, is a step towards the knowledge of that infinite duration which none can perfectly search out. The idea of Huygenius, that there may be stars whose light has not reached us since creation, is one of the vastest that may be imagined.

When it is considered that time is measured by the revolutions of the heavenly bodies, and yet that the period during which they have revolved in space since the creation is as nothing in comparison with an eternity past, the subject assumes a majestic and overpowering aspect. A spectacle of the starry heavens belittles man in his own estimation, as David expresses it in the eighth Psalm: "When I consider Thy heavens, the work of Thy fingers, the moon and the stars, which Thou hast ordained; what is man, that Thou art mindful of him? and the son of man, that Thou visitest him?" But he fails not to add, "For Thou hast made him a little lower than the angels, and hast crowned him with glory and honor." When the Blessed SAVIOUR declares that the very hairs of our head are numbered, GOD's peculiar care is evident over apparent creatures of a day, who are, however, only waiting on the threshold of eternity.

As character can never change in a future state of existence, the "ornament of a meek and quiet spirit," which may be attained in this life, will beautify the next; the charity, which never faileth hereafter, is to be learned and practiced here. In the eternal loss of earthly things by death are foreshadowed the irrecoverable losses met with during life by reason of wastefulness, forfeiture, dishonor, robbery, or defective title. When men daily see the fearful effect of improper actions on this present life, what can be said of the supreme folly and utter madness of those who treat the passing hour as if it were given them merely for pleasure, or sin, and even crime, careless as to the conditions of a future state commensurate with the existence of GOD, in which they are to continue to be the same persons essentially as they have been on earth? "'For evermore!'" (Rev. i. 18.) "Words easily uttered, but in comprehension vaster than human thought can grasp, till man, entering upon eternity, shall rise to faculties fitted for the scene! 'For evermore'; for an existence to which the age of the earth, of the starry heavens, of the whole vast universe is less than a morning dream; for a life which, after the reiteration of millions of centuries, shall begin the endless race with the freshness of infancy, and all the eagerness that welcomes enjoyments ever new. The blight of all our earthly pleasures is decay; our suns have scarcely risen when they set; we have but just persuaded ourselves that we are happy when the happiness is vanished. Pining after something that will endure, we are not to be forever disappointed; born for eternity, eternity shall surely be ours. But, oh!—horrible thought!—if all this tendency to the eternal, this longing for everlasting mansions, be to any of us but the prophetic twilight, the forecast shadow of unending darkness! oh! agony insufferable, if the eternal life of CHRIST—the Christian's warrant of justification, of sanctity, of happiness—be but the guarantee of a death as everlasting as His everlasting life; if the prolongation of His divine existence be but the seal and surety of that never-dying death which, by a dread union of opposites, seems described as protracting dissolution itself into immortality!" (Archer Butler's Sermons, First Series, Sermon x.)

When Christianity, with its "life and immortality," presented itself to the notice of Edwin, the Saxon King of the North of England, he held a consultation about it, and a nobleman remarked that he had seen a swallow flying through the king's house, entering one door and passing out of another, while the king sat at supper in the hall, and the fire was burning on the hearth, and a tempest of rain or snow raging without. The bird felt the temporary warmth, and escaped. Such he declared was the life of man without Christianity, buried in darkness as to what preceded or followed it. Hence he advised a consideration of the new doctrine.

On the dark future Christianity sheds its light. While it tells of coming years more numerous than the sands on the sea-shore, it declares that they may all be happy if time is spent in preparation for eternity.

See Buck's Theological Dictionary, and Illustrations of the Catechism of the P. E. Church, by an English clergyman, revised by Rev. W. W. Spear, D.D., and Addison's Essay in The Spectator, No. 565.

REV. S. F. HOTCHKIN.

Ethics, Christian. In order to get a distinct idea of Christian Ethics we must consider it in relation to "the Law." In St. Paul's Epistle to the Romans, he contrasts "the Law" very sharply with the Gospel, or with the grace which came by JESUS CHRIST (Rom. iii. to v.). There can be no doubt but that St. Paul in this discussion had in view chiefly the Jewish Law. But the Law of the Jews, the laws or religions of all other nations, and the Law of nature as indicated in Natural Theology and in Moral Philosophy were viewed in common, so that what St. Paul says of the one is applicable with certain modifications and with greater force to all the others.

Moral Philosophy tries to find from a study of man's nature the circumstances under which he lives, the ideal of perfection at which he ought to aim, and the laws and rules of life and duty for men. It appeals to the ideal as a motive, and often doing what it can to excite and cultivate the best motives, it leaves the result to depend on will force, upon the power or the weakness, as it may happen to be, of each one's own will,—his power of self-control and of personal exertion. Its rule is justice,—a law of equality or of rights. It has no idea of forbearance, of pardon, of mercy, or of help from above. Its tendency is therefore to produce rather a sternness of character than the more amiable disposition and that softness of character at which Christianity aims. It tends to puff one up with pride, self-reliance, in view of what he has attained or done for himself, rather than make him humble and self-denying, in view of what has been done for him.

All heathen religions were alike in this very important respect; their ideal of life was not very high; and although they taught and inculcated some form of worship to the gods in which they believed, they did not ascribe to their gods the very highest excellence of character; nor did they teach their devotees to look to their gods for *spiritual* help. The heathens prayed to their gods and worshiped them with sacrifices, but the help they sought was deliverance from some present evil or some future impending calamity of a temporal or purely physical and bodily nature. For purity of heart, and inward strength to resist temptation and to do right, they relied on themselves, so far as they had any thought or care for such things. They did not expect nor seek for any help from the gods in which they believed, or from their religion, in this direction. Hence their religion can hardly be regarded as a help to their morality, or to their efforts at moral purity and moral excellence. And in many cases its influence was quite the reverse. Their religion often led and even compelled them to acts which the very instincts of their nature abhorred, and it familiarized their minds with such vices by ascribing them to their gods.

The Jewish religion, while it was unmeasurably superior to all the others in most respects, was much like them in the one that we have chiefly in view now. It was a religion of law and not of grace. It did indeed inculcate the idea of GOD's moral excellence, not only His power, but His purity, His goodness, and His righteousness and justice in all things. This idea exerted a most powerful influence for good on the Jewish mind. It was a help *upward* and not a debasing influence, tending *downward*, as did all the heathen religions. And, too, the Jewish system of sacrifices was intended as a help and served that end. It inculcated the idea of sin as constituting personal ill desert on the part of the offender, and that all our unhappiness and misfortunes in this world come either *directly* from our own faults and sins, or *indirectly* from the sins and transgressions of GOD'S most righteous laws by others with whom we are most intimately connected. It recognized the impossibility of ever living up to the perfect standard, and of fulfilling all the requirements of the Law. In view of this fact, it made a fuller and clearer revelation of that Law, in order that the people might better understand what to do, but more especially, and above all in importance, for our present purpose, it provided sacrifices of such a nature that there was no one who could not provide the victim that was required, and have it offered for him as an atonement or expiation for his sins and shortcomings. There was thus a help to the performance of duty, and a means of escape from the penalty and punishment which this view of the Divine justice could not but force upon them as a consequence of their transgressions and the failures in duty, which, after they had done their very best, would sometimes occur; but this was rather a help by way of escape from deserved punishment than a means or help to greater purity and holiness of heart or life. Immeasurably superior therefore as the Jewish religion was to all others, in these two respects it falls, nevertheless, far below the Christian religion, in the one respect of inward help and grace.

It does not come within our present purpose to discuss the matter of the Jewish sacrifices and contrast them with the one Sacrifice of our LORD, in reference to their efficiency in securing forgiveness of sins and Divine favor. The contrast which we wish now to pursue is of a different nature. The Jewish religion put into the foreground the Law to be fulfilled. It presented all rites and sacrifices of this religion as a help, a means to either fulfilling the Law or making amends and atonement for its non-fulfillment. The Christian religion, on the other hand, put into the foreground, and in the most conspicuous position, "the grace" that is to help us. This is indeed a fuller disclosure of the love of GOD and the more attractive attributes of His character, if we may properly so speak of them. There is also a fuller revelation of the future life and of what depends there upon our conduct here. But all these things serve only to strengthen motives. Over and above this there is a fuller exhibition of the efficiency and the sufficiency of the sacrifice which GOD has provided for us, and the assurance of Divine help by the inward operations of the HOLY GHOST in the heart of every one that truly believes and will submit himself to that holy influence. And this, what the Law, the natural law of morality, or the Jewish Law, with rites and sacrifices, could not do, through no fault of its own, but on account of the weakness of the flesh, CHRIST hath done for us through grace.

Nor is this all. CHRIST has added to all the motives we had before, and, in addition to the clearer views and brighter hopes of the future life, a motive still stronger and more efficacious in His own example and suffering for us. He said of Himself, signifying what death He should die, " And I, if I be lifted up from the earth, will draw all men unto me." This has been found in all experience to be the strongest motive if measured by its influence upon the human heart. Men are touched and drawn by the simple story of the SAVIOUR's life and death for us as they are by no other motive, and often when all other considerations have failed to reach them.

No life on earth was ever so beautiful, no death so tragic as His. The thought of it when truly presented softens and wins the heart and makes one's sins and ingratitude seem too odious to be any longer persisted in. Men and women are melted and won to repentance and newness of life by the consideration of what CHRIST has done and endured for them, when they could not be reached or touched by any consideration of their own imperfections considered as a mere matter of morality and of " law," or by any estimate or apprehension of the consequences of their own guilt as seen merely in the light of nature or of reason. We have, then, as constituting the Christian Ethics, clearer light, stronger motives, and Divine help, the immediate influences of the HOLY GHOST, and the result is, accordingly, a type of Christian character which is peculiar and unlike everything else ever seen anywhere else. The doctrine of the Atonement, of our dependence for salvation upon *such* a Sacrifice, upon the suffering of *such* a Person, is well calculated to take away all the pride of self-sufficiency, and to produce a disposition to do and to endure in all humility and submission whatever GOD's will may require or appoint for us. Then, too, in the promised help we have our trust, and thus accomplish what we might otherwise fail even to undertake through want of confidence and hope of being able to accomplish anything.

Another important peculiarity of Christian Ethics is the fact that the attraction is so much fixed on the motives, and the assurance that right *motives* are more important than right *actions* whenever there is, or can be, any doubt about our having both. Our LORD made this contrast very conspicuous in His Sermon on the Mount, by putting three cases in which He contrasted His teaching and the character of His Gospel with the law: "Ye have heard that it was said to them of old time, Thou shalt not kill, . . . but I say unto you, That whosoever is angry with his brother without a cause shall be in danger of the judgment: and whosoever shall say to his brother, Raca, shall be in danger of the council: but whosoever shall say Thou fool, shall be in danger of hell-fire" (St. Matt. v. 21, 22). So likewise with the other two examples that are given in the same connection, the design of our Lord was evidently to impress on His hearers and followers the doctrine that the greatest evil, in the evil of each case, was the motive, the condition of the heart from which the evil act proceeds. Law seeks to prevent wrong acts by prohibiting them and by punishing the offender. The Gospel, on the other hand, while disapproving of the wrong acts not less severely than the Law does, aims rather at making the heart right first,—the tree good that the fruit may be good also. And in the Epistles, especially those of St. Paul, are the doctrines brought out, that we are saved or depend for our salvation rather upon the state of the heart, upon faith, than upon the perfection or merit of any works we can perform.

In fact, in the Christian view there can be no merit properly so called. In the estimation of mere Law merit is possible. The Law prescribes a duty, and the extent to which we are obliged to perform the duty, and, of course, it implies also a limit beyond which we are not to go, or need not go. But the Gospel, by summing all duty in the Ten Commandments, love to God and love to man, removes all these limits; and then by representing an excess of love as impossible it removes all possibility of any limit to obedience. Whatever may be done must be; nor can it ever be regarded as more than duty or as work of supererogation. We may easily come short of Divine requirement, but we can by no possibility and in no conceivable way go beyond it; so that, do what we may, we still have reason to consider ourselves but "unprofitable servants," and, feeling so, to continue to recognize our dependence on Divine grace.

But while Christianity thus directs the attention of the believer to his motives,—the state of his heart, as if that were the most important thing, if not the only thing to be kept in mind,—it clearly recognizes the possibility of self-deception, and of our mistaking or misdirecting our motives. Here it refers to the acts that our motives lead us to perform as the best and only infallible test by which to judge of our motives. "By their fruits ye shall know them" is His statement. And our Lord urges the fact that "A good tree cannot bring forth corrupt fruit, nor a corrupt tree bring forth good fruit." "Men do not gather grapes of thorns, nor figs of thistles." Any system of mere "law" is defective also in another very important point. Such a system can lay down general rules, but it cannot go into the thousand details and "small cases" that will arise in the practical affairs of life. Here for any system of moral rules prescribed as a mere matter of morality there must be a department of "Casuistry," consisting of rules to enable us to decide such questions when they arise. These rules look only to the decision of what we *ought* to do. And they might be all-sufficient if only we could always be able to decide by means of them when we are really in doubt. But that is impossible as a mere matter of intellect or judgment; we are often still in doubt after we have done all we can. Besides that, there is always the very great danger that we shall be misled by feelings and self-interest in the case.

To meet this difficulty our Lord prepared His "Golden Rule," as it has been called. "All things whatsoever ye would that men should do unto you, do ye the same unto them." Now it is not supposed that this rule will guide us to the exact knowledge of right actions and to what ought to be done in all cases, irrespective of motives, but it is a plain and practical guide for us to what it is, in a spiritual point of view, always *best for us* to do in the circumstances. Considered as a principle of mere morality or moral philosophy, the rule is open to criticism, and quite fairly. But as we come short of our duty mainly from either self-indulgence or self-love, or from deficiency of love towards our neighbors,—while it may not be best for us always in a selfish or worldly point of view to do to others as we would like to have them do to us or for us,—it is better always in a spiritual point of view to err, if we must err at all, on the side or in the direction of self-denial rather than in the direction of self-indulgence, and on the side of generosity towards others than in the direction of selfishness. We had better go beyond the rule,—the mere requirements of Law in the direction of self-denial and generosity,—rather than run any risk of sinning and injuring our own souls by indulging our ease or our pleasures, or pursuing our own private or personal ends to the detriment of others. Whatever we may lose of the things of this life and its enjoyments, honors, or possessions, this we gain in and for the world that is to come. Nor is this all. Even in this life it is seldom the recollection of an occasion of self-indulgence or an act of selfishness affords us any pleasure; but the recollection of generosity or self-denial for the good of others is a never-failing source of enjoyment.

Rev. W. D. Wilson, D.D.

Eucharist. *Vide* Lord's Supper.

Euchologion. A service book of the Greek Church, containing the offices, rites, and ceremonies of that Church, and corresponding to our own book of Common Prayer. It is *the* Ritual book for all the greater offices, as the Anthologion contains the hymns and festal offices.

Evangel. The Gospel. The glad tidings of salvation through our Lord. The word is used with the greatest latitude. It may mean but the glad tidings of the Resurrection, or it may embrace the Four Gospels. Any central fact of the whole extent of the Redemptive work of Christ may be called an Evangel.

Evangelist. An office in the Apostolic Church,—mentioned three times in the New

Testament. St. Philip the Evangelist (Acts xxi. 8) is the only one spoken of as actually exercising it. St. Timothy, who held another office, was bidden to do the work of an Evangelist (2 Tim. iv. 5); and it is enumerated by St. Paul in the passage in the Epistle to the Ephesians (iv. 11), together with other divinely-appointed orders. "And He gave some (to be) Apostles, and some Evangelists, and some prophets," etc. It was not an order in the Church, as were the Apostle, the Presbyter, and the Deacon, but an office connected with them, and exercised by any one who had the proper gift. So St. Philip is one of the seven Deacons, St. Timothy is an Apostle; St. Paul saying of himself and Silvanus and Timothy, "*We* might have been burdensome as the Apostles of CHRIST" (1 Thess. ii. 6); but they have a special gift,—that of preaching the Gospel, as Evangelists.

The "work of an Evangelist," as the mission intrusted to special men, has been revived in the Church of late years. It is practically an itinerancy. The Evangelist has certain limits assigned him, within which he visits those places where the Church has not yet been preached and searches out those church-members who have been cut off from their privileges and opportunities. Very efficient work has been done by these Evangelists.

Eve. The day before a festival. If a fast is appointed for that day it is a Vigil, if it is not a fast-day it is called an Eve. There are but two Eves observed in the American Church,—Easter-Even and New Year's Eve. The Vigils have been dropped out of our Prayer-Book. According to the old rule, all festivals are preceded by an Eve or a Vigil, including Sundays. All martyrs have Vigils, except those which fall upon Christmas-, Easter-, and Whitsuntide. The other feasts are preceded by Eves. The Collect for the day is said, according to English rule then, on the evening service before, if it be an Eve, but if it be a Vigil, the Collect for the week is recited, and then the Collect of the Feast-day of the morrow.

Eve. The woman whom GOD formed of a rib from Adam's side. Her name is taken from the Hebrew "Havah," living, for she was the mother of all living. Her temptation and fall, and her own tempting Adam in turn, with the fatal results, are most intimately woven into our history, and form the sufficient motive for our redemption. To her was given the promise of the MESSIAH, the restorer, in very enigmatic language, yet she certainly knew somewhat of its import, for she named her first-born Cain,—Acquired, Gotten,—for she said, "I have gotten a man from JEHOVAH." Then when at the birth of her second child she thought herself disappointed, she named him Abel,—Vanity. After Abel's murder, when Seth was given her, she named him so in her gladness. "For GOD hath appointed me another seed instead of Abel whom Cain slew." It is, of course, impossible to say how far she comprehended the promise of the REDEEMER, but that she must have known something of its meaning is but reasonable, both from the names she gave her children and from the use of sacrifice, of the meaning of which she must have been aware. The history about her closes with her joyous naming of Seth (Gen. iv. 25).

Everlasting. *Vide* ETERNITY.

Everlasting Punishment. *Vide* HELL.

Evidences, Christian. In its ordinary and natural significance this expression means any evidence by which Christianity comes to human knowledge, whether in the facts of its origin or in the material of its doctrines; or by act, in these facts and doctrines, it is proved a revelation of Divine truth. Technically, its meaning is more restricted, and has reference more predominately to such evidence defensively exhibited,—evidences of Christianity, called forth in view of objections and difficulties urged against it, misconceptions of friendly inquiries, misrepresentations of enemies. At the same time, from the very nature of the case, and manifested in every great period of conflict, the defense, as part of a successful defensive movement, becomes an assault; such assault involving the positive exhibition of Christianity, by contrast, and as superior to the opposing, and all other systems. Even in such case, however, the expression "Evidences of Christianity," or "Apologetics," its more recent equivalent, carries with it predominantly to ordinary readers its technical and more restricted meaning. Thus taken we recognize the necessity for such Christian evidences, or evidential defense, in its first contact with Jewish and Heathen feeling and thought, in their respective communities. While to a large portion of what afterwards became the Jewish discipleship, there was no existing prejudice, nor even specific knowledge of the person and ministry of JESUS, and the task of the Apostolic teacher, as with Philip to the Eunuch, was simply to show from the Old Testament Scriptures that "this JESUS was the CHRIST," yet with others there was a very different condition of things. Many of them, and this more peculiarly the case with Palestinian Judaism, were full of bitter animosity against Christian doctrine. Looking upon Christianity as a system of imposture, upon its object of loyalty and devotion as a teacher of falsehood, a blasphemous claimant of Messianic and Divine honors, they were not only indisposed to any reception of its claims, but were ready to use all means to arrest its progress. Saul of Tarsus was the type of a class by no means small or insignificant. This class it was by which he himself was so bitterly opposed during his subsequent career. And in his defenses of himself, as a preacher of Christianity, first to the multitude after his rescue by Lysias, and afterwards before Festus, and again before Agrippa, we have the earliest forms of defensive Christian evidence, the first specimens of Christian Apologetics, as addressed to the removal of Jewish prejudice and misrepresentation. But the Apostle never forgot to address himself to the removal of Jewish prejudice. This must have been especially the case in that last recorded interview of the Apostle with his Jewish countrymen, soon after his arrival at Rome. The lengthened argument, "from morning until evening, out of the law of Moses and the Prophets," failing with some but successful with others, while directed to the main conclusion that JESUS was the CHRIST, was also directed, as it began and went on, to the removal of existing specific prejudices and misconceptions against the sect of the Nazarenes, that is, His disciples and followers "everywhere spoken against." Such existing prejudice and odium against Christianity, "this new sect," is given by the Roman Jews as a reason for their desire to hear more fully about it from the Apostle. In other words, to put the matter in later form of expression, they asked of him an exhibition of the "evidences of Christianity." A request with which he promptly complied,—in that compliance removing the prejudices and securing the conviction of at least a portion of his hearers. "Some believed."

So too, as to the necessity of such defensive and explanatory evidence, as passing outside of the circle of Judaism, Christianity was preached and made its converts among the heathen. It thus came in contact with heathen thought and feeling, not only in the persons of its converts, but of those with whom they were in daily association. As both new and diverse from existing forms of worship, it soon called forth not only attention, but prejudice and opposition. Such prejudice would, of course, be intensified as the character of Christianity became manifest. While, unlike Judaism, a world religion, it was, like it, an exclusive one. Its undertaking was to overthrow idolatry in all its forms, to absorb anything that might be good in them, to throw off what was evil, and eventually to supplant them. In the very terms of its existence and progress, it demanded unconditional surrender,—a surrender of systems as of individuals. At first, however, regarded as a Jewish sect, and therefore a form of religion sanctioned by imperial legislation, a "*religio licita*," there was no interference with it by the Heathen authorities. Persecuted by Judaism during the first forty years of its existence, it was, by its supposed Jewish character, saved from that of the Heathen magistracy. But when Judaism passed away, in its terrible overthrow, it was found that Christianity was something different. Here was a new religion, with its converts in every city in the Empire, rapidly spreading, antagonistic to existing religions, itself a "*religio illicita*," having, under imperial sanction, no legal existence, and, therefore, demanding either repression or specific legal toleration and freedom of exercise. This latter it fully obtained (after a long struggle) during the first quarter of the fourth century. In the mean time, effort was made to repress it. These efforts of legal repression were usually local; the repression of lawful authority to local prejudice and feeling, finding expression in distinct accusations. Sometimes, doubtless, they originated in the personal animosity of particular officials; and in some few cases, by direction or instruction from the imperial centre.

But these efforts in the way of legal repression, as showing prejudice and misconception, called forth very soon its response in the Apologies,—the defensive Christian evidences of the second and third centuries. This, indeed, is the characteristic of the Christian writings of that age. The new religion was on trial. The question at issue was, shall it be extirpated or shall it be tolerated? The argument of the Christian apologists was for the latter, for freedom of religious opinion and belief. Such argument was occupied with prevalent impressions against Christianity, and to show that they were unfounded. It went on to exhibit its real character and teaching, and then, still further, its superiority to existing systems of belief and practice. There were other Christian writings during this period. Even those who are specifically known as writers of Apologies wrote on other subjects, sometimes on practical or controversial questions. Still, this is peculiarly the characteristic of this period, and it enters even into the writings of those who are not usually classed with the Apologists. Of these latter some are known only by their names, others by fragments of their writings; with others, again, their works have been preserved to our times nearly complete. Those of Quadratus, Aristides, Herminus, and Melito are but fragments. Those of Justin, Tatian, Athenagoras, and Theophilus are still extant. That of Tatian was addressed to the Greeks, that of Theophilus to a private individual, and the other two to the Emperor. The probability is that they all had reference to this last destination. They are defenses rather of Christians as individuals, Christians accused or under suspicion, than of Christianity as a doctrine.

Of course, in such effort, they would deal with the accusations upon which these persecutions proceeded. When a man confessed that he was a Christian and was condemned, it was not merely for practicing an unlicensed religion, but for the supposed character of that religion. These accusations may be comprehended under three main charges: first, atheism; secondly, gross immorality; and, thirdly, cannibalism. The first of these accusations seems to have found its origin in the spiritual nature of Christianity itself; for in their places of worship, as in their abodes, there were none of the visible representations of Deity. In this new religion there were none of what seemed the great realities to heathen worshipers. The Christians were never seen to bow before the image of a god. They had no sacrificing priests. They offered no sacrifices, having no temples. The inference to a heathen mind was inevitable that the Christians had no gods, no belief in beings of a superior power, were atheists; and, as such, outside of the circle of human sympathy and of human confidence, the proper objects of universal execration.

This impression was naturally connected with the two others,—indiscriminate licentiousness, and the eating of human flesh. In both of these, as in the charge of atheism, there was something real in which these charges originated. The absence, as we have seen, of the only sort of religion which polytheists could understand or appreciate led to the charge of no religion at all, that is, atheism. So, too, the freedom of Christian association of the sexes, an immediate result of Christian teaching and practice as to the sacredness of marriage, and as to the law of purity in all its bearings; the meeting together of the sexes in Christian worship, as in the reception of the LORD's Supper; the ties of love among believers were interpreted to show the very opposite of what they really meant.

The other of these charges, that of eating human flesh, in all probability originated in the celebration of the LORD's Supper, the symbolical eating by faith of the body and blood of the ascended Master, and expressions in regard to it perverted and misunderstood to mean a literal eating of human flesh and blood. Whatever its origin and however perpetuated, as first making its appearance in heathen opinion, it tended to increase the odium against the new religion. Atheists, grossly licentious, unnatural feeders on human flesh, what else could be done with them than hurry them out of the world as speedily as possible?

To these charges the Apologists address themselves. This they do by positive denial of the supposed opinions upon which those facts were asserted of the facts. They further appealed to maxims and principles (the opposite to everything of this kind in the teaching of the Master); to the lives of Christians as in accordance with this teaching. They demanded of the Emperors that the case of persons accused of any of these crimes should be determined upon its own merit; not that the fact of a man's being a Christian should be accepted prior to all proof, and in absence of all proof, that he was a civil and social outlaw.

But these defenses proceed further. It was scarcely possible for men, under these circumstances, to indicate their characters without a positive defense of their faith, of Christianity itself. This would necessitate comparison with that of their accusers, that from which they themselves had departed. They had grown up Heathens and became Christians. Their reason was the abominable evils of polytheism, social and moral, and the purity, the holiness of Christianity. This defense of Christianity involved an assault upon Heathenism.

Thus it was during the earlier period of the Apologists. At a later period, as other points of attack were made, the defenses were constructed to meet them. Still further, as this new religion spread, and its facts and doctrines were promulgated, there were positive attacks upon it by the heathen philosophers and *literati*. To all these forms of obstruction and misconception there was the response of Christian argument, exhibition of its evidences. Among the writings of this class may be mentioned those of the North African school, Tertullian, Minucius, Felix, and at a later period Arnobius and Lactantius; of the Alexandrian school, Clement and Origen. The characteristics of these writers and their peculiar modes of argument we have no space for exhibiting. The necessity of works of this character, so far as protests or protectives against legal persecution, ceased to exist with the triumph of Christianity under Constantine. With the great majority, after this change, the successful argument for Christianity was a prosperous Christendom, the Church under the protection of imperial power. With the exceptionally brief retrogression under Julian,—his attack upon Christianity and the reply to it of Cyril; the work of Eusebius in his reply to Hierocles, his *Evangelica Preparatio* and *Evangelica Demonstratio* (the first written against the philosophers, the second to heathen readers in general, and the last to Jewish readers and inquirers); the still later writings of Augustine, intended to meet the difficulties and objections still lingering in the heathen mind against the Gospel;—with these exceptions, the intellect and scholarship of Christendom were absorbed in a different undertaking: dogmatics, the settlement and definition among Christians themselves of doctrinal issues and points of internal controversy. So far, too, as regarded the call for works of specific defensive evidences, this continued the case during most of the interval until the Reformation. A series of Jewish writers defending their own system and attacking CHRIST, moving on from the twelfth to the sixteenth century, called forth replies from Christian authors. As to the Mohammedans, it has been said the Apologetics of the crusades dealt with these difficulties. Occasional hints occur in mediæval writers of objections by Jews and Mohammedans to the doctrine of the TRINITY,—also of their attacks upon the worship of saints and images. It is to be said, that in the last, the Jews and Mohammedans were really occupying the Christian position; and the professedly Christian defenders of the faith had gotten back upon the old ground of polytheism.

To one form of Christian evidence, however, it is to be recognized that this mediæval period made a large contribution: that evidence of the truth and Divine origin of Christianity as it is seen in the clear exhibition of its truths, in their systematic connections and relations of interdependence, in the rationality of their existence and applications. Those same skeptical tendencies in Christian thought, represented by such men as Duns Seotus and Abelard; and it thus became necessary for such men as Anselm and Aquinas consecutively to neutralize this by their constructive theology. This was, of course, imperfect, and much of it has had to be, and will have to be, done over again. But it is, after all, the ultimate and satisfactory form in which Christian evidence will receive its final statement; the truth, shining in its own clear light, the lesser as well as the greater truths recognized in their proper position perfecting the illumination.

With the revival of literature in the Western Church and the general awakening of intellectual activity there were germinant elements of skepticism and positive unbelief, and with these the occasion for a manifestation of Christian evidences. Christianity had been so corrupted and caricatured by its accredited representatives, that the world outside—heathen, Jewish, and Mohammedan, as well as the great mass of nominal believers—needed to know its real character. As with the average Frenchman or Spaniard now, the Christianity of the average layman of the first quarter of the sixteenth century was that of the Papal system, with its manifest and manifold abominations. When such men were awakened to intellectual activity in the humanist movement, these abuses and the accepted system of which they formed part became their point of attack. But there were two powerfully restraining influences modifying the power of such attack,—prevention of avowed unbelief, open assault upon Christianity. One of these was the risk and personal danger involved; in other words, the Church process of answering heretics and unbelievers. Mere philosophical and literary skeptics make very poor martyrs. It is pleasanter to doubt or philosophize in private than to burn or hang in public. The machinery of ecclesiastical repression was so effectively worked that nothing short of genuine religious conviction ventured to tamper with it. Then again, a great deal of the literary and philosophical skepticism and rejuvenated Heathenism of this period was in the Church itself or among ecclesiastics of the highest order. There was great necessity for an exhibition of Christianity in its reality and its power; of the evidence within of its Divine origin.

This necessity was met in the movements of the Reformation. In that great movement, and the fundamental issues with which it was occupied, all others were absorbed. The triflers were swept aside. The reactive effect of Protestantism, even upon the old system, was to its awakening and purification, saving it from the cancer of skepticism with which it was threatened. Its result and mode of working resembled much those of Methodism in England during the last century. Men thoroughly and religiously in earnest have no time and less taste for theories of skepticism.

But this spirit of earnestness, which had thus put in abeyance the rising skepticism of the new culture, was itself subject to deteriorating influences. The mere division of outward Christianity, and its interference in men's minds with the idea of its essential unity; the divisions and bitter controversies among Protestants and the religious wars of the sixteenth and seventeenth centuries; produced a condition of things in which unbelief could make itself manifest. The forms of this unbelief are more fully developed at a later period. These have been divided into three classes: first, the Deistic, with its two types, the one more spiritualist, represented by Lord Herbert of Cherbury, the other more materialist, represented by Hobbes; secondly, the Pantheistic, represented by Spinosa; and, thirdly, the Skeptical, represented by Bayle. The object of Herbert of Cherbury was to get rid of revelation, by attempting to show its uselessness, and incapability of being proved. The object of Hobbes was to deny and do away with all moral obligations in ethics and politics, in the ordinary sense of those words, and, of course, to sap the foundations of religion. The result, whatever the intent of Spinosa, was to absorb the world in Deity, to destroy alike the personality of Creator and creature, and, of course, with the latter, all personal responsibility. The representative of the last of these divisions, the skeptical, Bayle, was not like these others a system builder to replace or put aside that of the existing faith, but a universal critic, skeptical in his spirit as in the result of investigations. The position of these writers is not, by themselves, closely and consistently defined. They write and express themselves, at times, as approving of the existing system. But it was not very long before their position was recognized.

These, however, were merely precursive to something more clearly and positively defined, the Deistic contest of the next century. "The principal phases of this period of the maturity of Deism, which we shall now successively mention, are four:

"First, what may be called the intellectually rationalistic, that of Toland and Collins. This involved an examination of the first principles of religion, doctrinally, asserting the supremacy of reason, and, of course, its sufficiency to interpret all mysteries. What reason could not thus interpret was not rational, was irrational, and to be rejected.*

---

* Farrar's History of Free Thought, p. 125.

"Secondly, what may be called the ethically rationalistic, that of Lord Shaftesbury. This involved the examination of religion morally; and it asserted the supremacy of natural morality as a rule of conduct, denying the propriety of motives of reward or punishment.

"Thirdly, as following upon the two former, and for which they had prepared the way, was the more direct attack upon the specific Christian evidences, that by Collins of the prophecies of the Old Testament, and that by Wollaston of the miracles of the New.

"Fourth, a combination of all these, in different proportions, by Tindal, Morgan, and Chubb. This effort with each, while destructive, was also constructive. The destructive part was to show that all of Christianity, plus natural religion and natural morality, was irrational and to be rejected, so far as, in accord with them, it demands acceptance. And they undertook to show, upon these principles, how much of Christianity may be rationally accepted as true."

Of the three other noted English writers of this century, Bolingbroke really added very little to his predecessors; Hume, exercising influence in his day through his argument on miracles, is now more influential through his philosophical speculations; and Gibbon, with his natural explanations of the success of Christianity, and his halting defense of heathenism and its persecutions, has lost his power of mischief. His own testimony to the power of Christianity, and the magnitude of its effects upon the world, is to be found everywhere in his volumes.

But to all of these forms of assault there were numberless replies of great power, some of them even by anticipation, others as the unbelieving scheme was put forth.

Two of the most important during the seventeenth century were the *De Veritate Religionis Christianæ* of Grotius and the *Pensées* of Pascal on the Continent, while in England the names of Bacon, Cudworth, Locke, Boyle, Tillotson, Burnet, Leslie, Littleton, Bentley, Clarke, Butler, Warburton, Sherlock, Jennings, Leland, Paley, with many others, met the various issues. Hume's argument against miracles received various replies, the most noted of that century being those of Campbell and Paley, while Gibbon and Paine, coming in rather later, were answered by Bishop Watson. The assault (to use the language of Principal Cairns) "was a failure. The assaults of Deism had been repelled, and the ammunition shot away, and nothing remained but to raise the siege. Churchmen forgot their party differences, and Nonconformists fought by the side of Churchmen against the common enemy. The best works of their antagonists, after the replies to them, look poor and shallow, and hardly anything remains in Christianity to be struck at but the external difficulties of reason and of theology." Connected, however, with these monuments of skeptical and infidel thought in England, and receiving largely their impulses from them, were those of similar character in France and Germany. The character of the French infidelity, taking its tone largely from Voltaire, was more bitter and scoffing than that of the English Deists. At the same time, there was a large infusion (through Rousseau and his imitators) into it of sentimentalism. And with these, through the writings of Diderot, Helvetius, and D'Holbach, were the combinations of Atheistic materialism. Their practical result was the worst excesses of the French Revolution. For, while it may be recognized that the materials had been long in gathering, yet this was the spark to the actual conflagration, and heightened its fury. There were various replies of the Romish clergy. But there was not spiritual life nor intellectual power in the French Church fully to meet these various attacks, and its reconstruction under Napoleon was rather a matter of State policy. Later works from French Protestant and Romish writers of an effective character have appeared. But the spirit of unbelief largely predominates. Renan's legendary theory of the Gospels has perhaps had a wider circulation than any work of a similar character. As a matter of argument, it goes back to the oft-refuted position of Paine and his lame school of English Deists, that of conscious deception. De Pressensé gave an effective reply to it, which has been followed by many others.

In Germany the principles of English Deism passed into what has been called the Rationalistic, or Naturalistic, movement. The peculiarity in this was that its leaders, represented by Paulus and Semler, were clergymen and theological professors, advocates and defenders of supernatural revelation, undertaking to show that there was nothing really supernatural in it.

Coming back to English unbelief and that of this country, we find in the beginning of this century, in England, first the positive effects of a revived Christianity through the movements of Wesley and Whitefield, extending in its influence to the Established Church. Still further, in the revulsion from the infidelity of the French Revolution there was called forth a strong popular sentiment in favor of Christianity. To some degree the same facts had exerted a like influence in this country,—modified, however, by sympathy with France as a people, and especially in view of her assistance rendered during the Revolutionary struggle. There was introduced a great deal of the infidelity of French principles, as that embodied in Paine's "Age of Reason." The religious movements of the first two decades of the century checked a great deal of this, and it was, moreover, met in specific replies and works on Christian evidences. The arguments, as directed to the nature of the objections, were largely historical, reproductions in a more popular form of the materials of such writers as Lardner and Paley. At the same time the internal, moral, and experimental evidences received more specific attention. The work of Hartwell Horne contains a full exhibition of these evidences of this period, say the first forty years of this century. Those of Bishop Williams and of Doctor Chalmers, in Great Britain, and those of Doctor Alexander, Bishop McIlvaine, and President Hopkins, in this country, present them in briefer compass and better adapted to popular use. The great work of Butler, also, was used, with those of the Rationalists, showing the necessity of Christianity.

It remains that we briefly indicate the necessities of Christian evidences at present, and in view of recent tendencies, as of those of the last quarter of a century. There are, first, those claiming to be philosophical, Positivism, Agnosticism, Materialism, including in the latter Material Evolutionism. Secondly, those in the domain of science, antagonizing Science and Theology or depreciating the latter as a ground of rational belief or action. Thirdly, those in the domain of Criticism, the old rationalistic movement largely revived in its spirit and processes, and reducing to its minimum in Scripture the element of the supernatural. And, fourthly, those in the sphere of moral life; the Pantheism which absorbs personal life and personal accountability in a material or ideal universe; the Pessimism which finds this universe with a plan and purpose indeed, but one that is evil. And, last of all, in the sphere of Comparative Religion, the effort of unbelievers (in this) to make Christianity one of the natural religions of the world, a little better in some respects than other theories, not so good, perhaps, in others, but at the best, a religion of the past, to be superseded by a, or the, religion of the future, and that by its future of human development, and so on indefinitely. Against each of these powers of unbelieving thought, the Christian apologist needs to present his defenses and urge his attack. And it is to be said that the ability and scholarship of Christian writers have nobly responded to this demand. "The assault," to use the expression of Professor H. B. Smith, "has been along the whole line." But such assault, at whatever point made, has found defenders inside. And these defenders, repelling the attack, have gone out of their lines for aggressive movement. These different forms of unbelief, in their respective fields of investigation, have been met by the researches and replies of Christian scholarship. Over against the objections and asserted difficulties, for instance, of physical science, made by infidel and atheistic scientists, are the replies of Christian scientists of equal scientific reputations,—such men, for instance, as Whewell, Brewster, Forbes, the Duke of Argyle, Dawson, Dana, Hopkins, and Chadbourne. The efforts, again, of skeptical comparative religionists, have found their answers in the labors and conclusions of Christian scholars and investigators, such men. as Hardwicke, Moffett, De Pressensé, Rawlinson. Then, again, in the department of metaphysics and moral science, the assertions of Positivism, Agnosticism, Materialism, Pessimism, are finding their answers with almost every weekly issue of the press,—in the works of such men as Flint, Caird, McCosh, Harris, Fisher, and Pasteur. What, again, claims to be the higher criticism which disposes of Scripture alike in its inspired and its historical claims, has been met by a thorough investigation, in a profoundly reverential spirit and by conclusions of an opposite character,—in the labors of Lightfoot, Dean Smith, Pusey, Westcott, Brett, Delitsch, Green, Fisher, Wright, and Leathes. These are but samples in each department. Connected too with these may be mentioned Christian reviews and journals in which these items receive discussion, and also regular endowment lectures, the Boyle and Bampton and Hulsean and Warburtonian in England, with several of a similar character in this country. Even the coarse reproduction of some infidel materials, in the efforts of Ingersoll and those of his kind, have not passed without replies,—those of Judge Black and Thurlow Weed fully meeting them. Whenever the demand has been made on Christian ability or scholarship, it has been promptly and effectively met. In each form of contest, too, as in the past, the result has been not only a repulse to falsehood, but a clear gain to the truth of religious conviction and assurance. There has never been a time in which Christianity had such a hold upon the intellect and heart of the world. There has never been a time in which it has had as many and able defenders; when so many, even of its enemies, have felt and confessed its power, and are endeavoring, if not to destroy it, to solve the problem of its origin. Finally, two positive results may be mentioned in connection with these assaults and repulses of unbelief and faith in the last quarter of a century. The quickening of interest and the enlargement of the area of investigation and study in rational theology; the position and prominence given to the person of CHRIST in specific Christian thought as in Christian evidences. The two grand issues are over these points: Is there a LORD in nature? How has He revealed Himself in CHRIST? As these are rightly answered, all others fall into their proper position. And the drift of human thought as of Christian evidence is to bring man to a practical decision. As the contest works on in these various departments of human thought and investigation, that final point of decision, with its alternative, becomes more clear and manifest,—out and out Christianity or out and out Atheism

REV. C. WALKER, D.D.

Evil. Evil differs from sin in that sin refers more to the act and its consequences, while evil refers more to the state and its conditions. But the two terms are used so often interchangeably that this distinction is not clearly kept in view. The Evil One made an evil suggestion to Eve, and she sinned and caused Adam to sin, and so brought evil into our life. Yet this distinction is not preserved in the translation of the Bible, —*e.g.*, in Ps. li. 4: " Against Thee only have I sinned, and done this evil in Thy sight."

But the great question that has overshadowed all other questions upon sin and evil is, Why is it permitted and whence is it? There can be no complete reply, since our spiritual nature is not known to us, nor is the future life so known that we can certainly reply to minor objections. Created beings must be so far (as a higher limit) imperfect, and from that limit there is a descending scale into sin. The sinless angels are charged with folly and the heavens are not clean in His sight, perfect and glorious and lovely as they are. The vanity St. Paul urges we are subject to is the defect whereby we are open to sin. But as law for us implies obedience and its opposite, and these two imply a choice of either course, as obedience and disobedience are moral qualities, we have not the absolute reason, but the relative conditions upon which sin could and did enter into the world. Freedom of will, is a proper reply to the question why it is, for it implies the power, not the necessity nor the willing desire to sin, but that power to act which the will holds as of its own essence; a power it exercises for good or for evil whenever motives and persuasions, sufficiently enticing, are presented to it in either direction. The effects of evil in the soul, of course, affect the intellect, and therefore the body; consequently physical evil and pain, with sorrow, suffering, and natural defects, follow. These mould our whole earthly life. It is to be noted that while the guilt of sin is pardoned and a counter-remedy given, the effects of evil in the system, spiritual and natural, are not removed. Our probation is founded upon the principle that we accept the forgiveness, use the remedy offered as faithfully as possible, and endure the consequences of sin patiently, till the law of restitution in CHRIST shall gain its full power. As sin and its evil consequences work their effect slowly, so the undoing of these effects must be slow. The same wisdom which permitted evil must guide the elimination of evil, and as its inscrutable purposes in permitting it overshadow us, so the like mysterious plans of freeing us must be taken and used in faith. It is for this purpose the Church was founded,—the hospital for sin-sick souls wherein CHRIST the physician has left a perfect remedy, were we but to use it as He has directed and would submit to the guidance of those who are empowered to administer it.

But evil, a poison in the spiritual system, is properly foreign to it, and since its effects are so loathsome and hideous, the conscience exclaims against it. This is the key to St. Paul's passionate self-analysis, and with its triumphant hope of victory (Rom. vii.): "O wretched man that I am! who shall deliver me from the body of this death? I thank GOD through JESUS CHRIST our LORD. So then with the mind I myself serve the law of GOD; but with the flesh the law of sin. "There is therefore now no condemnation to them which are in CHRIST JESUS, who walk not after the flesh, but after the Spirit."

These facts are, then, clearly within our grasp, and these only. We cannot now know why sin was permitted or whence it came, only we know GOD cannot be its author. We can know how it has power over us, because of our (*a*) imperfection, because we are finite, because of our (*b*) freedom of choice, which is a law of our being and the basis of all probation. We know that (*c*) all spiritual, intellectual, and physical defects, sins, and suffering flow from it. We know that (*d*) it is a poison deeply seated, needing the medicine of a Divine healer. We know (*e*) that its consequences are continuous, recurring, and were it not for the constant presence of GOD, would be fatal in every respect. We know (*f*) that while the guilt of evil can be forgiven its temporal consequences are not removed, but that the mode in which these are used or submitted to forms an important part in our training. Further than this, upon the mystery of our future restoration, upon the effect of our individual conduct, upon our future condition, we know nothing. We can trace but cannot fully comprehend the reason why evil in the soul should cause the ruin which befell the material nature around us. There is but one thing open to us for our own good, to feel deeply the evil and to use faithfully the remedy in CHRIST.

Examination for Holy Orders. In the early subapostolic Church this examination must have been rather one in the candidate's moral fitness and general acquaintance with the Scriptures, and varied with the circumstances both of the time and the person. That it was public and well known, according to the Apostolic injunction, "having a good report of them which are without," we have the singular testimony of the Emperor Severus, who ordered that in appointing a new governor inquiry should be made about his character, adding that this was the manner of both Jews and Christians in selecting their priests. There is no minute canonical law such as we have now, at least no mention is made of any, but doubtless the Bishop was the responsible person. The candidates were selected probably by the clergy, and were then presented for acceptance to the Bishop. They were often men of great culture (as Tertullian), and well acquainted with the literature of the day, but the larger number were not so well trained. There are numerous minor canons in the Western Canon Law against too deep a study of the classics, but this was under the influence of Jerome and of Augustine, who in his confessions records his delight in the beauties of Virgil. The examination of a Bishop was rather dependent, as to its extent, upon his fame, and therefore the inquiry into his holding the right faith upon the Creeds would vary very much. With the Middle Ages and the era of Bishops holding political preferment came a general laxness. Yet the learning of the day was almost wholly with the ecclesiastics. Every age, even the darkest, had some bright lights,—men who often were not above the superstitions of their times, but who were nevertheless men of marked ability. Such were Gregory of Tours (573 A.D.), Isidore of Seville (595 A.D.), Cassiodorus (539 A.D.). Later Boniface (730 A.D.), the Apostle of Germany, led in ability, though not in learning. Under Charlemagne many notable scholars were trained, Agobard, Haymo, Rabanus Maurus. Later, Hincmar proved that the line of able and learned Bishops had not died out, and much care in those troublous times to keep up the schools was taken. So too in the East, Photius, Michael Psellus, and others show that diligent care was taken according to their opportunities to see that their priests were trained. Theophylact's Commentary is still valuable. These facts show us that, though we do not know how stringent the examinations were, yet, with whatever ease men were admitted to Holy Orders, their training was not wholly overlooked.

In England the examination for orders is upon the lines of the Divinity studied in the University, though each Bishop has his examining Chaplains. According to the English Canons, the candidate must be a graduate of one of the Universities, or else show his learning by a thesis in Latin upon the XXXIX. Articles, defended by Scripture proof. He must bring certificates of good life and conversation for the "three years next before." The Bishop is himself to examine him in the presence of those ministers who are to assist him in the imposition of hands. Lawful impediments are to be inquired into, Canons 34, 35. Subscription *ex animo* is to be made, I. To the acknowledgment of the Royal Supremacy in matters Spiritual and Ecclesiastical, as well as Temporal, and the acknowledgment in the same subscription to the denial that any "Foreign Prince, Person, Prelate, State, or Potentate hath, or ought to have, any Jurisdiction, Power, Superiority, Pre-eminence, or Authority, Ecclesiastical or Spiritual," in England and its dependencies. II. To a declaration that "the Book of Common Prayer contains nothing contrary to the Word of GOD," and that he will use it exclusively. III. To the XXXIX. Articles and their Ratification.

The American Church is equally careful to have her ministers properly trained, and for this purpose there are numerous theological schools in different parts of the United States. The Canon (Title i., Can. iv.) is full and precise in its directions for the examination of the postulant or the candidate.

Each Diocese shall have two or more examining Chaplains, who shall examine the postulant or candidate in his literary qualifications and report to the Bishop. If the candidate is a graduate of a college, this examination is usually omitted. If he be a candidate for Deacon's orders only, he shall be examined thoroughly in the Holy Scriptures and in the Prayer-Book in all its parts and adjuncts and in the Book of Articles ; in his reverent and edifying performance of the service of the Church and of his diaconal duties. If the candidate has been an ordained or licensed minister in any other denomination of Christians, then he is to be examined specially upon his soundness upon the points of difference. The Bishop may or may not be present, at his pleasure. The candidate for Priest's orders shall pass through three examinations, which, except for extraordinary reasons, shall not be held on the same day, but on three separate days. Each must be both oral and written, and the special subjects may or may not be given previously to the candidate. At each examination he shall read a sermon upon an assigned text and hand in two others composed on texts of his own choice; and he shall be examined upon the reverent conduct of the services and upon his knowledge of his duties; and if he comes to the Church from any denomination, he shall be examined upon his soundness upon the points of difference. No examinations in a theological seminary shall supersede these examinations, which can by no means be dispensed with. These three are: I. On Holy Scripture, its history, and on the Hebrew and the Greek ; though these two may, for sufficient cause, be dispensed with. II. On the evidences of Christianity, Christian Ethics, and Systematic Divinity. III. Church History, Ecclesiastical Polity, and the history and contents of the Book of Common Prayer, and on the Constitution and Canons of the Church.

The Bishop may, as he chooses, preside or not, and he may invite the Presbyter, who shall present the candidate at the ordination, to take part in the examination but the Bishop must take part in one of these examinations at least, or else examine him beside in a fourth examination. If the candidate be of a vacant Diocese, the Bishop who shall ordain him must hold this fourth examination.

Since a candidate for Deacon's orders may be also a candidate for Priest's orders, the first examination for the Priesthood shall be sufficient for the Diaconate examination, but the examination on the Prayer-Book for the Diaconate must be repeated for the Priesthood at the third examination. Signed certificates are required after each examination for either office, and violation of above provisions for examination shall disqualify the candidate and subject the other party concerned to canonical procedure and censure; and the candidate for Priest's orders must apply for his first and second examinations within three years, and for his third within five years, after his admission, and, unless he can give sufficient reasons for this neglect, if he fail to fulfill these enactments he shall be stricken from the list of candidates after due warning from the Bishop.

The conditions are not at all difficult to fulfill, but they are to be stringently enforced.

Examination, Self-. It has been well said that self-examination is forestalling, by devout repentance, the decision of the day of Judgment, when all secrets not blotted out of His Book of Remembrance will be revealed. It is of the greatest importance to the soul, both here in moulding the life, the principles, the conduct, and hereafter as its lessons teach the earnest soul wherein repentance and amendment is necessary, and so it aids to avert the condemnation of the Judgment-day. To be an examination at all it must honestly be carried into the motives, secret or unconscious, until thought upon or avowed; into the thoughts cherished and habitually entertained, to be tested by Christian law and morality; into the words, to be weighed according to the rule both of the Psalmist (Ps. xxxix.) and of CHRIST (Matt. xii. 36); and into the actions, to be tried by the Law of GOD and by the earnestness with which the soul sought the guidance of the HOLY GHOST. By implication the Ten Commandments, placed at the beginning of the Communion Service, and prefaced by a prayer for purity, are the guides the Church would have her children follow in their hearty self-examination. They should question themselves as to the spiritual as well as temporal obedience they yield to these positive laws. Almost from the earliest writings of the Fathers onward, the Church possesses a vast number of most useful manuals, directions, and counsels upon this duty. Every age has special manuals, which have been prepared by devout men upon self-examination into the current sins and temptations of that time, and many outlines have been put forth which meet the needs of the soul in all ages.

Excommunication. The cutting off from the communion of the Church a faithless, evil member. Suspension from privileges is not excommunication, which deprives a person of all spiritual communion with the faithful and of all the spiritual gifts in the Church of CHRIST. It is the delivering the guilty person unto the power of Satan (1 Tim. i. 20). Excommunication is not intended to be perpetual unless the guilty person continues impenitent and so prevents its removal, and besides, its true purpose is disciplinary, not punitive. Like the consequences of sin, which we may make disciplinary if humbly submitted to in faith, so excommunication may be used. The LORD instructed the Apostles about this matter of discipline (St. Matt. xviii. 15–18), and repeated this, with the direct gift of the proper authority (St. John xx. 23), after His Resurrection. The Apostles used it, as did St. Paul in the matter of the incestuous Corinthian (1 Cor. v. 4) and of Hymenæus and Alexander (1 Tim. i. 20). But as baptism confers the birth into CHRIST'S Church, and as excommunication is a disinheriting inflicted with greater or less severity, it is not such a final expulsion that it annuls the baptism. There are two kinds of excommunication, the lesser and greater; both are apparently recognized in the Apostolic Canons, which are the earliest form of Church Law extant. The lesser was called Aphoresis, the greater Catharesis. The Bishop and Clergy together were the party sentencing. No other but the Bishop could try a case occurring in his Diocese. But if he neglected it, his Primate could summon both parties before the Provincial Synod, and could suspend the negligent Bishop, who could only be restored to communion by the Synod.

In mediæval times wild and fearful precations were used in the forms of excommunication. These varied in fullness in different places, and in different times, but were framed upon the curses recorded by Moses in Deuteronomy. The secular arm was called in to uphold the ecclesiastical power, and the sentence was made to involve civil disabilities also.

The forms which accompanied the sentence were made as scenically terrible as possible. The bell was tolled. The Presbyters surrounding their Bishop, as he pronounced out of the Book the sentence, each extinguished a lighted candle he held in his hand. Thence came the saying to excommunicate with Bell, Book, and Candle. The older English Law upon *ipso facto* excommunications has been much modified since time and the development of society has changed the older condition of things, and it is confined only to definitive sentences and decrees pronounced as spiritual censures for offenses of ecclesiastical cognizance.

The Lesser Excommunication deprived a person of the Sacraments. The Greater Excommunication deprived him of all rights and privileges. Certain disobediences of Canon and Ecclesiastical Law, by their commission (technically "*ipso facto*") placed the guilty clerk under excommunication. So, too, certain offenses, as robbing churches, placed the laymen under the same ban. According to the gravity of the office, it was either the lesser or the greater ban. Many of the offenses for which it is inflicted could not occur in this country. Deposition, deprivation, and degradation are used to express one and the same severer punishment for an offending clergyman. Suspension is the lesser sentence. With regard to the laity, the Rubric in the front of the Office for the Holy Communion is the only law in general force. The Paragraph 3 of Section ii., Can. xii. of Title ii., provides for a future enactment for trying the laity, but in the meanwhile recognizes the jurisdiction of the Diocesan Conventions.

Exedra. A building, such as a baptistery, which was not attached to the church, and yet was within the grounds attached to the church.

Exegesis. *Vide* HERMENEUTICS.

Exemption. Many Monasteries and Convents were in their later stage exempted from the rule of the Bishop in whose Diocese they were built. The abuse was protested against by St. Bernard (1163 A.D.), but it went on till a large number of Monasteries and Abbey Churches were under the protection of the Pope or the King, and so were withdrawn from Episcopal visitation. The Abbey of Westminster is a Peculiar, that is, an Exempted Church, amenable not to the Bishop of London, in whose Diocese it is situated, but to the Queen.

Exhortation. A sermon or address, but technically it is the name for the several addresses to the congregation in the Common Prayer-Book. There are traces of such exhortations in the Mozarabic or Spanish Liturgy. Besides the familiar one of the daily service and the four incorporated into the Communion office, there are four apiece in the two Baptismal offices. An exhortation occurs in each of the offices for Confirmation, Marriage, and The Sick. Two are in the Visitation of Prisoners, and a very solemn one in the Ordering of Priests, and one in the Form of Consecration of a Church or Chapel. They are, in fact, short, clear, forcible sermons, which the Church authoritatively provides for the instruction of her children in the offices in which she has placed them. It proves her very great care to have her members well instructed.

Exodus is the continuation of Genesis, with which it is linked most closely; indeed, it may be almost accounted as a part of the same work. The facts narrated have been often called in question, but never with success. The remains of Egyptian customs and the notices of Egyptian history all bear out the minutest accuracy of the work, and would of themselves nearly fix the date of the Exodus. In this book, as well as in Genesis, the two pretended documents, the Elohistic and the Jehovistic, are asserted to exist, but the same difficulty of proof confutes their existence here as well as in Genesis. An analysis of the book will set before us clearly its purpose. For now it is the history of GOD'S deliverance of the family He had chosen for Himself out of all nations. He had placed them while yet feeble in Egypt, in the most fertile country of the globe, and had given them its best portion,—Goshen,—and there in the two hundred and fifteen years of their sojourn they had increased wondrously, and were an element of danger to the Egyptian polity. Not quite eight generations, allowing a fourfold increase to each generation, which is not too extravagant, would raise the number to upward of two and a half millions out of the fifty-six pairs usually supposed to have gone down into Egypt in Jacob's family. These had been protected by the Pharaohs till about the time of Moses' birth, when the policy of the Egyptian rulers changed. Alarmed at the vast increase, they attempted to check it by destroying the male children It was at this point that the history opens, or, to speak more accurately, the most remarkable autobiography in literary history. The book may be divided into two parts,—the autobiographical and the ritual. The autobiographical extends from chapter i. to chapter xviii. 27; the ritual from chapter xix. to the end. This part, however, has much historical matter interspersed.

I. *The Autobiographical.*—The historical circumstances preceding the birth of Moses are recounted in chapter i. The parentage and birth of Moses and his adoption by Pharaoh's daughter are given in chapter ii. to verse 11. Then follow the events of the homicide of the Egyptian who was beating a Hebrew, his flight into Midian, where he became an inmate of the family of Reuel, the priest of Midian, and married his daughter. Chapters iii. and iv. to verse 18, contain the calling of Moses and his mission. Chapter iv. 24, contains an incident full of mystical import. Moses had neglected to circumcise his son, and the LORD met him at the inn and "sought to kill him," when Zipporah circumcised their son, "so He let him go." Moses and Aaron now proceed to execute their commission by delivering the message to Pharaoh (ch. v.) which only resulted in the placing of heavier burdens upon the Israelites. The first threat delivered to Pharaoh (ch. vi.), was accompanied with the sign of Aaron's rod becoming a serpent. The Magicians did the same, not by a miracle, but by a sleight of hand, but Aaron's rod swallowed them up. The first plague of turning the water into blood (ch. vii. 17–22), the second of the frogs (ch. viii. 5–15) were not difficult to imitate; but of the third plague, that of lice (ch. viii. 16–19), they had to confess this is the finger of GOD, and did not try their enchantments any more. St. Paul (2 Tim. iii. 8) has preserved to us the names of Jannes and Jambres, the leaders of the order of Magicians. From this plague on (ch. viii. 21) there followed in quick succession the plague of flies, the murrain of beasts, the plague of boils and blains, of hail, of locusts, and of darkness, and then Moses was finally driven from Pharaoh's presence. The king was obstinate and impolitic and hardened. It would lead us too far from our subject to point out more than that Pharaoh hardened his own heart, and because he had gone too far GOD used him for His judgments upon Egypt. Moses now saw Pharaoh's face no more (ch. x. 29), but proclaimed the last plague, the most terrible of all, the death of the firstborn. But the passover was instituted, the lamb was chosen and the preparations were made and the blood was sprinkled, that His People might be protected when that last fearsome shock should fall upon Egypt. On the appointed night, when the angel of the LORD went forth, there was a great cry in Egypt, for there was not a house where there was not one dead (ch. xi., xii.). Then followed the expulsion, the flight, the pursuit, and the wonderful deliverance at the Red Sea (ch. xiii., xiv.); and Moses' magnificent song of triumph (ch. xv.); the journey to Sinai and the giving of the Law (ch. xvi.-xx. 21.) We have called this autobiographical simply because it is Moses' record, so simple, direct, modest, of the mighty deeds he was directed to do. Throughout it is Moses who is the actor, for GOD chose then as later to deliver men by a man.

II. *The Ritual.*—Though there is some historical matter interspersed,—as the sealing of the covenant with the sprinkling of blood, the founding of the molten calf, the second fast of forty days and nights,—still by far the larger part of the matter of this section is occupied with the details of ritual,—the making an altar. The offering for the tabernacle, the form and size of the tabernacle, the appointment of Aaron and his sons, the sacrifices and their ceremonies, the details of the altar of incense, of the holy oil of the ark, and the mercy-seat overshadowed by the Cherubim, the brazen altar and the brazen laver,—all these, with many minute directions, form the principal part of this portion of the book. Only one legislative section is given here. But throughout the whole book is most consistent, and is full of instruction to him who will read it aright. Like Genesis, it has a miraculous element running through it, but not always recognized. The Deluge would have been attributed to natural causes. Pharaoh doubtless thought that Moses was simply a mightier magician than those he had about him. Men were not then any more than now willing to admit the power of GOD behind them, using, guiding, overruling them and their wishes and plans. And when they would have submitted if they had consented to it, they were smitten for their obstinacy and hardness. Not only Pharaoh, but the Israelites themselves were afterwards guilty of this blindness, which was far more culpable in them, and would have been fatal but for Moses' powerful intercession. True, GOD chose to use human means or natural instruments, but the results were not the less mighty and of Divine power. The book of Exodus is a work that, humanly speaking, could only have been written by the actor himself in the mighty deeds which GOD had commissioned him to do. To destroy the authenticity of its contents and the fact that Moses was really its author, would be to overthrow the Christian religion. Again, it is well worthy of remark that we have here the weaving of religion into the national life. In heathen thought any form of religion sat easily upon them, and it did not cling so closely but that it could be and was materially modified. But in the history of Israel, it is not a nation unless it is a religious nation. This is the cause of its existence. It is to be a royal priesthood. In its after-history it prospered as it carried out the law; it declined and perished as it violated this law. And here in Exodus we have recorded for us the Covenant GOD made with the people, and the giving of that typical ritual which made them not only His in a peculiar sense, but also the prophecy of the people of CHRIST and of His spiritual kingdom.

Exorcism, Exorcists. There was in the Apostolic Church, following our LORD's first conference of spiritual powers upon both the Twelve and upon the Seventy, an order of Exorcists who had power to cast out unclean spirits. The Apostles themselves exercised it, and St. Philip, the deacon, cast out unclean spirits (Acts viii. 7; xvi. 18). It was a power which was used by some of the Jews themselves, as our LORD's argument against them (Matt. xii. 27) shows. This office was necessarily temporary, since, as the spiritual conditions of the world changed after the Resurrection, the needs for such officers in the Church would disappear gradually. (For the subject of *Demoniacs* see that article.) The Exorcists and Exorcism are first mentioned by Justin Martyr and in the Apostolic Constitutions; the Apostolic Constitutions saying that they were not ordained, as their power was a free gift by the grace of GOD through CHRIST, and that whoever had this gift would be made manifest by exercising it. But any one having this power was not thereby debarred from receiving Holy Orders.

That the power was a continuation of the gift given by our LORD to His Apostles, and was one of the weapons for their aggressive warfare, must be acknowledged by every Christian. How long it was retained we do not know. It could not have been an authority used at the mere will of the exorcist, since that was contrary to the economy under which the LORD's power was exhibited. It is probable that the order survived its actual need, and we know that it was organized into one of the minor orders, with a solemn setting apart of the person by giving him a written book of forms, with the sentence, "Take and commit to memory and receive power to lay hands on energumens, whether baptized or catechumens." His work was therefore confined to those over whom the Church had some authority. The forms of exorcism were at first a mere command, as in our LORD's own act and in the act of St. Paul (Acts xvi. 18). But from a hint our LORD gives ("This kind can come forth by nothing but prayer and fasting"), it is more than probable that they to whom this wonderful power was given had to keep themselves in a state of spiritual preparation for their conflict. Indeed, this is the best interpretation to be put upon Tertullian's apparent implication that all Christians possessed this power. But from the realizing sense of these spiritual battles, they then felt that their prayers did have power. As time went on and all work fell into grooves, there were ritual forms; and as the Church brought the possessed into the public services and had public prayers for them, those who had charge of them would naturally have formulas ready for use. Such forms are still extant.* But the principle that each person was possessed by an evil spirit was acted on in the form of exorcism (by breathing on the hair and by the sign of the Cross) used over each postulant for admission to the rank of catechumens. It was also connected with the rites immediately preliminary to the administration of baptism. And such a prayer of exorcism was retained in the English office books till the second Prayer-Book of Edward VI. (1552 A.D.).

Expectation Week. The name given to the ten days from the Ascension-day to Whit-Sunday,—in memory of the waiting of the Apostles till the gift should be given them of the HOLY GHOST.

Expiation. The purgation from sin, whether performed by the sinner or by some one for him. So our LORD offered an expiation for our sins. Its meaning is not so extensive as that of ATONEMENT, but Expiation, together with Propitiation, cover the same ground. Sacrifice included both meanings, and this term expresses all of our LORD'S atoning acts.

Extravagants. Extravagantes, a collection of Papal Decretals and decisions which Pope John XXII. (1315 A.D.) edited under the title of *Extravagantes seu Constitutiones Viginti*, to which were added five books more of *Extravagantes Communes*, edited by several Popes after Pope Sextus IV. (1478 A.D.).

Ezekiel, whose name means "whom GOD will strengthen; or, the strength of GOD," was the great prophet of the Babylonish Captivity. He was a priest, and therefore of the family of Aaron, in the tribe of Levi; his father's name being Buzi, of whom nothing else is known; though it may be inferred that he was careful and conscientious in educating his son. It is probable too that he belonged to the higher class (2 Kings xxiv. 14). Of the birthplace of Ezekiel nothing is known (most likely it was not far from Jerusalem); but we are told by the prophet himself that he dwelt among the captives on the river Chebar (at Tel-Abib?), where he lived with his wife in a house of his own. He was carried into captivity 597 B.C., eleven years before the destruction of Jerusalem, yet a young man (a boy according to Josephus); and as the call to the prophetical office came to him 595 B.C., and, as some infer (from Ezek. i. 1), in the thirtieth year of his age, he must have been born about 625 B.C. Tradition relates many things concerning Ezekiel, to which, however, not much authority can be attached. He is reputed to have performed various miracles; and while some have tried to identify him with Zoroaster, others have thought him to be the same with a poet of Jewish tragedy, one Ezekiel who lived about 40 B.C. Perhaps the most probable of such traditions is that Ezekiel is the same with Nazaratus, the Assyrian instructor of Pythagoras. As already said, Ezekiel dwelt among the Jewish captives at Tel-Abib, on the Chebar; a stream once confidently identified with the Khabour, a tributary of the Euphrates, but now thought by many to be the great canal of Nebuchadnezzar; and there, in the thirtieth year, the call to prophesy came to him (Ezek. i. 1). It is not easy to determine what date is intended by the thirtieth year; but of all suggestions and opinions the most reasonable appears that which makes it the thirtieth year of Nabopolassar, whose reign began 625 B.C.; and this would place the beginning of Ezekiel's prophecy in 595 B.C.; so agreeing with the fifth year of Jehoiachin's captivity, according to the second note of time given by the prophet (Ezek. i. 2). From this time onward the word of the LORD came often to Ezekiel to warn and rebuke, to counsel and encourage the captive Israelites, and to foretell the future of the nations. No prophet is more varied in the style of his writings; visions and symbolic actions, parables, proverbs, and poems, allegories and direct prophecies abound; and in them all are displayed much varied knowledge and learning, great vigor of style and eloquence. Of Ezekiel, Bishop Lowth says, he "is much inferior to Jeremiah in elegance; in sublimity he is not even excelled by Isaiah; but his sublimity is of a totally different kind. He is deep, vehement, tragical; the only sensation he affects to excite is the terrible; his sentiments are elevated, fervid, full of fire, indignant; his imagery is crowded, magnificent, terrific, sometimes almost to disgust; his language is solemn, pompous, austere, rough, and at times unpolished; he employs frequent repetitions, not for the sake of grace or elegance, but from the vehemence of passion and indignation. . . . In many respects he is perhaps excelled by the other prophets; but in that species of composition to which he seems by nature adapted, the forcible, the impetuous, the great and solemn, not one of the sacred writers is superior to him." Critics have made two chief divisions of the prophecy of Ezekiel, the first consisting of the prophecies given

---

* The writer possesses a paper manuscript of the fourteenth century with such exorcisms written out in full.

EZEKIEL

before the destruction of the Temple in Jerusalem (ch. i.-xxiv.), the second of those spoken after that event (ch. xxv.-xlviii.). These divisions are again arranged in various sections as distinguished by their dates or superscriptions. The following synopsis is that of Hävernick: "I. Ezekiel's call, i.-iii. 15. II. The general carrying out of the commission, iii. 16-vii. III. The rejection of the people, because of their idolatrous worship, viii.-xi. IV. The sins of the age rebuked in detail, xii.-xix. V. The nature of the judgment, and the guilt which caused it, xx.-xxiii. VI. The meaning of the now commencing punishment, xxiv. VII. GOD'S judgment denounced on seven heathen nations (Ammon xxv. 1-7; Moab 8-14; the Philistines 15-17; Tyre xxvi.-xxviii. 19; Sidon, 20-24; Egypt, xxix.-xxxii.). VIII. Prophecies, after the destruction of Jerusalem, concerning the future condition of Israel, xxxiii.-xxxix. IX. The glorious consummation, xl.-xlviii." (Smith's Dict. of the Bible.) A chronological order is followed throughout, though it is interrupted in several places, especially in the prophecies against the heathen nations; and a general unity of subject is obvious in the whole book, which is thought to have been studiously arranged by Ezekiel himself. Owing to a passage of Josephus, who speaks of two books of Ezekiel, it has been thought that there was a second volume of prophecies, of which no trace has been found for ages; but it seems more probable that there is some error about the passage of Josephus, or better still, that the single book of Ezekiel may have been at one time divided into two, perhaps at chapter xl. Though there are no direct quotations of Ezekiel in the New Testament, no one can read this prophet and the book of the Revelation without being impressed by the parallels and allusions contained in the latter; and it is not in language only that Ezekiel and St. John are to be associated together, for while the prophet, " writing before the old dispensation had passed away, is guided to represent the perfection of worship under the form of a renewed and more complete ritual, the Christian seer, writing under the new dispensation, represents to us the true character of the worship of GOD, foretold by Our LORD Himself, 'not in Jerusalem, nor in this mountain, but everywhere, in spirit and in truth,' by the striking announcement, ' I saw no temple therein; for the LORD GOD Almighty and the Lamb are the temple thereof' (Rev. xxi. 22)." (Bible Commentary, Introd. to Ezek.). Ezekiel is said to have been murdered by some Jewish prince, whom he had convicted of idolatry, and to have been buried in the tomb of Shem and Arphaxad on the banks of the Euphrates, where a town built by Jehoiachin was pointed out for many centuries as the resting-place of the prophet.

Authorities: Gray's Introduction, Bible Commentary, Lowth, Smith's Bible Dictionary.

EZRA, BOOK OF

Ezra. One of the most useful of the men GOD raised up to restore the nation to rebuild the Temple and prepare the way for CHRIST. The period of his activity begins about fifty years after the decree of Cyrus, which (Ezra i.-vi.) had been suspended by the political opposition of the Samaritans, and renewed by Darius, and now with the influence he had given him in the Persian court he is permitted to go to Jerusalem with the second band of exiles, with full power from the king, Artaxerxes. As a descendant of Aaron he had kept a full register of the priestly descents, a most necessary record for the legal discharge of the Temple worship. When he reached Jerusalem with his company (ch. viii.) he was stricken with intense sorrow at the dissoluteness of the Jews of the first company, who had intermarried with the people around them, and his first care was to separate them from these foreign wives (chs. ix., x.). In this he succeeded, but not entirely (Neh. xiii. 28). It was left to Nehemiah to record how he restored the law (Neh. viii.). His influence was very great. The Jews have many tales of the grace that was in him. It is most probably to his recension and additions that we owe the present condition of the Hebrew Canon, with, of course, the exception of Malachi, the last of the prophets. The tale that he restored the whole of the Canon of the Old Testament is, of course, an idle one, but shows in what reverence he was held, and may have had its source in the fact that he wrote the book of the Chronicles, which, in its genealogies, ascends to Adam. Undoubtedly his influence in the restoration of the Temple, in the reviving the national life, in the work of instructing the people in the law, and his influence in the Persian court is not readily to be estimated. It is said, too, that he was president of the first Sanhedrim, which arranged the Canon. The tradition that he died at an advanced age is probably well founded. Altogether, without the brilliant genius of Daniel or the executive ability of Nehemiah, his learning, devoutness, noble descent, and his great capacity made him a most worthy instrument in the restoration.

Ezra, Book of. The work of the man of GOD to whom it has always been ascribed. Ezra, however, put together much material to which he had access, and which gave a connected outline of the events from the decree of Cyrus to his own visit to Jerusalem, from 536 B.C. to 456 B.C. The first part of the book is made up of the copy of the text of the decree to rebuild Jerusalem and to lay the foundation of the Temple, and a list of those who formed the earliest company of the Return under Zerubbabel and Joshua, with their first efforts to restore the Mosaic ritual (ch. i.-iii. 8). The list of those who went back first is repeated in Nehemiah, as he found it in Jerusalem when he made his visit, but it very properly belongs here. Ezra placed next the account of the laying of the foundations of the Temple, which was probably written by some eye-witness. It is conjectured that it was Haggai. In the narrative Ezra inserts the correspondence from the archives upon the interruption of the work of rebuilding and its resumption (ch. iii. 9; vi. 12). From thence to the end is the account of Ezra's own share in the effort to restore the observance of the moral and religious precepts of the law. He was a man of vast personal influence, for "he had prepared his heart to seek the law of the LORD and to do it, and to teach in Israel His statutes and judgments." Artaxerxes, the son of the famous Xerxes, in 457 B.C., sent him, with ample powers, to regulate the executive and administrative department of the restored people. He carried with him a second company, who carried the offering of the king for the worship at Jerusalem. The great reform which he records as his own effort, was to break up the marriages which the Jews had already made with the people of the country about them. It was a transgression of the law, a source of danger to the weak colony, and destructive of any effort to rouse and intensify that exclusive national jealousy which, however wrong *now*, was then the strongest means of preserving the nation from being absorbed into the surrounding population. His delicate task he effected with great skill. It would seem that this was all he could do independently. When, thirteen years later, Nehemiah came to finish the work, Ezra was an important aider, but what he did in the interval we are not informed. The book ends abruptly with the list of those who had put away their stranger wives. (*Vide* Smith's Bible Dictionary, Speaker's Commentary.)

F.

Faculties. In its technical sense a faculty means a special body of men who teach certain sciences, as a college faculty, which is really a body of teachers formed by the combined faculties of the separate departments,—*e.g.*, the faculties of law or of philosophy. But it also came to mean a transference of the power of canonical or ecclesiastical jurisdiction. In this sense it passed into use as a commission to perform acts, not involving spiritual power, for the Bishop by a Presbyter. It was the office of a Commissary in fact. But then it passed into a dispensation for a Bishop to perform acts for his Primate. Then the Papacy gave the faculty to the Nuncio, and as this produced trouble with the Bishops, the Bishops themselves took faculties from the Pope,—*i.e.*, powers defined and determined by these faculties for the administration of their Dioceses. This last form arose after the Council of Trent, since the Nuncios were multiplied in order to give greater enforcement to the Council's decrees, and to foster the efforts to recover lost ground in Germany. The faculties were usually given for only five years. This consequence has followed: the Council practically determined that the Bishop of Rome was the sole Bishop, and that all others received their mission from him. Then these faculties are really the mission each Bishop receives from him, and when they expire they must be renewed, or his rights over his Diocese are forfeited. This is also the purpose of the promise in the oath the Bishop under the Roman obedience takes, that he will visit the See of Peter every five years unless canonically excused or hindered (for nearer Sees three or four years is the time). It is one of the most serious perversions and extensions of a power which was but a simple right with really definite limits belonging to every Bishop. It destroys all true conception of the solidarity of the Episcopate, all constitutional rights, and overthrows the authority of the Church by giving all ultimate disciplinary power to one man. The truer canonical exercise of this power of granting faculties is yet used in England, where a faculty must be obtained to do anything or to have any alteration effected without the limits of the Canons, but not contrary to them. There is a special Court of Faculties, under a Master of Faculties. It can give license to marry without the previous proclamation of banns. It can license any change in the ornamentation of a church, as a faculty for placing a reredos in a certain position. It can grant a dispensation permitting a Deacon to be ordained under age, or a benefice to be succeeded to by a clergyman's son.

Faith denotes, both in Scripture and in common usage, several distinct, though inter-related things. In its broadest use it means that belief, more or less lofty, in GOD, His justice, love, and mercy, which leads to the adherence to principles and to actions which avow it. It may be merely an intellectual, or it may be an intensely practical, faith. It may mean a trust in, and devotion to, the person of CHRIST our LORD. It may mean the Church as the teaching body, or again, the body of Doctrines, or also the Creed, as the sum of the Faith. Each of these senses is used more or less freely in Holy Scripture, and they all pass into daily use. But we are not careful to use them accurately, the rather since they are derived the one from the other. To point out briefly each of these senses and to show that they are severally necessary to a full knowledge and use of what our Heavenly FATHER has done for us through the grace of our LORD JESUS CHRIST, and by the sanctification of the HOLY GHOST, we must dwell first on Faith in its widest sense.

I. GOD does not require of us any act which is not within our capacity, nor any belief that is not reasonable, nor any principle which does not lift up and ennoble our natures. Our ability or capacity may be lessened, or weakened, or blurred, or even blotted out either by inheritance (Rom. v. 13), or by defect or default in ourselves; it is our failure and loss individually, not that of the race, and above all GOD has foreseen it and provided for it. It is His right to demand of us belief and performance of acts upon this belief, which is above our sinful present level, but to which we can rise, while He is ready to give, yea, has prepared help and means. To require Faith in Him, then, is nothing but His right; to yield it is our true natural power with which we were endowed. A lower, defective form of this Faith we give each other in the belief, credit, and trust which is the bond of all society. On it all science, all government, all commerce, all covenants of daily intercourse are based. Without it, the fairest share of all our work, and certainly all our happiness, would vanish. We trust each other rightly by our nature, despite so many disappointments. Through this capacity religion is founded. GOD bids us believe upon sufficient evidence which He supplies, yet such as calls for trust and sacrifice on our part. By the very structure of our moral being we must believe, and upon the evidence He has given in other lives, He requires us to frame our life. And this course of conduct is not concerning the things of time, but, accepting and using this present probation, it looks forward to a future reward. Abraham believed GOD, and it was counted unto him for righteousness. An intellectual act, passing through and lifting up the moral powers, it becomes a spiritual act. It elevates, ennobles every capacity of our nature, and must show itself in overt acts that bind body and soul to obedience to GOD. "Out of the abundance of the heart the mouth speaketh." It is a primal gift of GOD, as every ability is; but when we are co-workers with Him an increased ability is given us. Our response obtains the gift of greater strength through often increased tests of this Faith, and the trust of our love and faith obtains the blessing of being allowed to worship Him, serve Him in daily act, and kindles a burning desire to prove at all cost our Faith by a still deeper devotion. An increasing power of insight into GOD's dealing with us is also a gift as a part of Faith, which in turn adds still to our Faith and brings forth greater fruit. In this He shows the firmness of His promise, "I will never leave thee nor forsake thee."

II. This Faith in GOD must be through a Faith in His SON JESUS CHRIST. For the Faith that our Heavenly FATHER requires is taught us by His SON, and this SON requires Faith in Himself. "Ye believe in GOD; believe also in Me." No man cometh to the FATHER but by Him. Through Him we both have access by one Spirit to the FATHER. In Him we are builded together for an habitation of GOD through the Spirit. Would we come to GOD.—He is the Way; would we receive the Truth,—He is the Truth; would we live forever,—He is the Life. "Whosoever believeth in Him shall never die." Since GOD was in CHRIST, reconciling the world by Him, there can be no other way. He stands forth before us and is our bondsman. The covenants of life are in Him. Life and all everlasting gifts pass through Him. He stands for us and pleads our cause. He hides our life in Himself. He is our peace. We cannot come to GOD therefore but by Him. Faith in GOD must be equally Faith in CHRIST as a Person having eternal and co-equal power with His FATHER our GOD. And claims our Faith. It is this Man whom the Apostolic Christianity preaches as the one who, having made an atonement as victim, and by His Resurrection received consecration to plead as High-Priest and kingly authority, He is set forth as the interceding and offering Person upon whom our hopes must rest, and through whom alone the FATHER will receive us. It is reasonable, for the exceeding love of the SON, so wondrously shown forth. The passionate words of St. Paul are but sober fact: "If any man love not the Lord JESUS CHRIST let him be anathema." Faith in Him is a deeper act yet, and the New Testament supposes this Faith to proceed to Baptism and Confirmation and Holy Communion. For He demands of those who love Him (and to love demands Faith, and Faith involves something of love) to keep His commandments. Therefore the members of the Church are called the *Believers* and the *Faithful*. And a moment's thought proves that mere Faith without such bands as these is but a feeble grasp, easily lost, and is purposeless, a slight mental act and struggle, without the slightest adequate result.

III. Thence the Church is sometimes said to be the Faith, the Household of Faith, since within it we are fellow-citizens with the saints, and are of the Household of GOD, and have obtained the like precious Faith with the Apostles. For the spiritual Faith leads to using the Sacraments under which CHRIST gives Himself, and these Sacraments make us one with CHRIST. Therefore we recognize that this Faith leads to touch Him, and that touch is in the unity of the Church. So that, as we are taught that there is one LORD, one Faith, one Baptism, so there is but one hope of our calling, which can be found only in that Church which He bought with His blood, loved, sanctified, and adorned for Himself. The whole Epistle to the Ephesians is but an exposition of the Church as the result of Faith, the means of Faith, the strengthener of Faith, and therefore of the unity of the Church as a living body capable of giving those gifts which such an organization has intrusted to it by its Founder to dispense, in the order which He has directed and under the conditions He requires. And as a result, since we may not fully know how His gifts bear upon our eternal life, nor why He has chosen them and none others, it is also an act of Faith to receive them and use them, since we know in whom we have trusted, and that what we are receiving will have a power upon our future eternal glory. It follows, then, that this belief in GOD through CHRIST, and received in the Church with a full honest love, gives us another meaning to the word Faith, for

IV. The Faith refers also to the deposit of doctrine, full and entire, which is given to the Church, and which each faithful member of CHRIST is bound to receive. Analyzing the contents of this deposit of doctrine, we find it based upon the Faith in the TRINITY, which is involved in the words with which we are baptized: In the name of the FATHER, and of the SON, and of the HOLY GHOST. Upon this outline is framed the Creed, which is evidently an expansion of the baptismal formula. The revelations which illustrate and set forth this are summed up in the Creed. In its widest sense the deposit of the Faith is in the Holy Scripture, but its elements are stated in compressed form in the Creeds. The Faith means a belief in GOD as the Framer of the seen and unseen works of nature, of power, and glory. In the eternal nature, and in the several parts of His acts for our redemption. In the work of the HOLY GHOST, in and by the visible office of the Church for our salvation. So by a comparison of the several sermons preached by St. Peter (*e.g.*, Acts iii. and v. and x.) with St. Paul's sermon (Acts xiii.) and the sermon in Heb. vi., we would see how largely the Creed reproduces them, and would be convinced that it was the form of sound words which St. Paul ordered St. Timothy to hold fast (*cf.* Rev. ii. 24, 25), or that it was the proportion of the Faith according to which the prophet was to prophesy (Rom. xii. 6). It was the Faith which St. Timothy was to hold, of which some made shipwreck, which heresies overthrow, which the Apostle had kept in fighting the good fight (*vide* Ep. to Tim.). Faith then, in a word, is applied to the whole range of beliefs and of applications of that belief, sanctified and purified by being from GOD the Friend and offered to GOD the FATHER, and bound up in GOD the SON, and sanctified by the HOLY GHOST. And the Faith in its several parts and in its unity is required of us rightly, because GOD *is* our GOD, and fairly, because we have the ability by nature, by His gift, by our use of it to yield it to Him.

Faithful. The Faithful, the very ancient name for the communicants of the Church. Every person baptized was immediately confirmed and was a communicant at once. He then was called one of the Faithful. It meant this in the New Testament, in Ephesians i. 1, "To the saints which are in Ephesus, and to the faithful in CHRIST JESUS." 2 Cor. vi. 15, "What part hath a believer with an unbeliever?" So too 1 Tim. iv. 3, 10, 12; v. 16. Where the Revised translation makes a phrase out of an adjective used as a noun, *e.g.*, iv. 12, "be thou an ensample to them that believe in word, in manner of life, in love, in faith, in purity," the Authorized Version has "to the believers." It is literally "to the faithful." We have given so different a meaning to the word "believer" that it has lost its synonymous technical signification of "communicant" rightly belonging to it in many places in the New Testament. It was so used in the Liturgies and in Clemens' Rom. Epistles (A.D. 97) and in Ignatius' Epistles (A.D. 107), and thence in the Apostolic Canons, after which time it is not necessary to quote examples.

Faldistory was a low armless folding-chair in which a Bishop sat at the altar after his enthronization or on other solemn occasions. It was a portable chair, and probably would be the proper description of what we now call the Bishop's chair. But since the Bishop's chair strictly can be only in his Cathedral Church, it seems that the present chair, though something more, is really the old faldistory. The name is found in the Capitulary in the inventory of the Monastery and Church at Staffelsee (812 A.D.). The faldistory is probably the Bishop's chair ordered in the Rubrics of the Ordinal.

Faldstool. A Litany stool placed in the Choir from which the Litany is recited. It should be a low desk, merely high enough to kneel at. It was placed in the midst of the Choir, facing eastward. It was retained at Canterbury, York, Lincoln, and Exeter Cathedrals, and is used in St. Paul's. It is becoming much more common, and is frequently found in many Parish Churches.

Fall. There is no real difficulty in receiving the narrative in Genesis iii. as literally true. The condition of all nature and its relations to man were materially different then from what they became through the Fall. Therefore, admitting that sin did come into the world by the disobedience, there can be no disproof alleged of the truth of the details recorded of the act of the sin drawn from our present fallen state, wherein the relation of man to the lower creation is in a disrupted antagonizing condition from that one act. Then there was no fear, there was thorough subjection of all creatures to Adam, and there well could be an intercourse between man and the creation below him which has been practically lost; though even now some wonderful examples occur of man's intercourse with animals. There is, therefore, no reason to be drawn from the history that leads us to reject its literal truth. The three main results of the conscious willful disobedience are, (1) The change of man's relation to GOD. (2) The loss of his original holiness and of the special gifts it contained. (3) The impulse downward in all his desires and passions, and therefore a greater alienation from GOD.

Familiars. Officers of the Inquisition, who arrested obnoxious or suspected persons. These Familiars were often of excellent families, who from special privileges given them, both by the order and by the king, were induced to lend themselves to its iniquitous work. The Order of Inquisition lent its Familiars its protection under all circumstances, for as often as a legal process for any offense was issued against any one of the members, the process was transferred in some way to the Inquisition, who could thereupon stop proceedings.

Fanaticism. A mistaken and senseless misuse of enthusiasm and zeal, chiefly in a religious cause. It is a violation of all the laws of Christian charity, and the fanatic is guilty of a great sin.

Fanon. A term which has several meanings. I. A head-dress worn by the Pope when he celebrated mass pontifically. It was a veil of four colors, like the Mosaic ephod, put upon the head after the Pope was vested with the alb. It was tied round the neck, forming a kind of hood, and the tiara was put on above it. When the Pope performs the ceremony of washing the feet, on Maunday-Thursday, he is to wear the fanon without the mitre. II. The napkin or handkerchief which the priest used to wipe away the perspiration from his face during service. III. In later times, the white linen cloth in which the laity made their oblations of bread and wine at the altar. IV. A still later use of the word is that of Church-banners used in processions. (Smith's Dictionary of Christian Antiquities.)

Farse. A stuffing out (*farcio*); a practice, before the Reformation, of adding, as each verse was recited, in Latin, an interpretation in the common tongue for the benefit of the people. This was not a common practice, yet some singular examples of it may be seen in Neale's "Essays in Liturgiology."

Fasting. To fast for a longer or shorter time or over a stated period has been from earliest ages a means of showing grief, of proving sorrow, of gaining self-mastery, of bearing a spiritual discipline and practice. It was not enjoined by the Law, as extensively as it was afterwards carried out by the people. There was only one fast, that of the Day of Atonement, appointed by the Law, but during, and after, the Captivity, four fasts were kept, the fast of the fourth, fifth, seventh, and tenth months. In the details of Jewish history we find fasts proclaimed for the people or ordered for some sudden occasion. Fasting was acknowledged by GOD Himself. It delayed Ahab's punishment; it prevented the immediate destruction of Nineveh. Our LORD assumed the use of fasts as of ordinary spiritual use in the Sermon on the Mount. He set us the great example in His own practice. He said that some spirits were only quelled by fasting and prayer. When St. Peter was sent to baptize Cornelius it was when he was fasting, and Cornelius received the grace of baptism because of his fasts, alms, and prayers. When Barnabas and Saul were sent forth, it was with fasting as well as prayer. St. Paul was constant in it as a means of spiritual discipline. Fasting is, then, a weapon in our spiritual warfare and an exercise in our spiritual training, one which should be laid aside for no light reason. But one or two principles must be kept in mind : (*a*) Fasting, unless with a distinct spiritual purpose or from a habitual use of it as in obedience to the Church's rule, is not worth anything. (*b*) Fasting without prayer is shorn of its power, and if alms are neglected also, it is of but little advantage, but with prayer and alms it is mighty in the inner soul life.

It would seem that in our heedlessness we overlook the fact that fasting is something more than a sorrow, or than a half restitution, but it should be used only for more than that. To too many this use of fasting is a necessary practice, but it is seldom done, whereas it should be used as a prayerful self-discipline by which we may draw nearer to GOD; so the Church intends it shall be, when she orders that Friday shall always be accounted a Fast, with the single exception when Christmas-day falls upon it; and the forty days of Lent, the Fasts at the Ember seasons, and on the Rogation days, are all intended for that use. Indeed, she has ordered an hundred and four fasting days in the year, and the number is still further increased if Advent be accounted as a lesser Lent. It is necessary, then, to give more heed to what she teaches us upon this duty, which was needful even for the sinless human nature of our LORD that He might learn obedience (Heb. v. 7, 10; *cf.* St. Mark ix. 28, 29), and may not with safety be neglected by us. Our Church has laid down no positive rule as to the extent of our fasting, leaving it to each one to exercise it according to his ability and to his opportunity. Certain classes are exempt,—convalescents, children of tender years, and women about to become mothers or with young infants. Those on whose bodily strength depends the maintenance of a family should carefully regulate their fasting. Those who are aged should be careful. It is not intended that fasting should injure the health and usefulness of the person. But this should by no means be made a cloak for a general excuse. Few there are but could fast oftener and more to their own and others' profit than now do so. Fasting may be a total abstinence from food for a certain time, or it may be a partial abstinence for a longer period, or it may take the form of a giving up for a given time all pleasant food and all ordinary and extraordinary social pleasures. The Church expects an abstinence in greater or less strictness from us on her appointed days other than two, on which she looks for a total abstinence from each of her children, Ash-Wednesday and Good-Friday. Whatever rules we may lay down for ourselves for the other days in Lent, we should on these two days—the one the Church's call to her children to sorrow and self-examination, the other the solemn commemoration of the sacrifice made for all sin—fast with absolute strictness. A reason for the difficulty in carrying out a purpose to fast which some find as a hindrance, is that they plunge into a season of fasting without any previous training. The Lenten fast is to many not as spiritually profitable as it should be, because they have not practiced the lesser abstinence of the weekly Friday fast; a loss to them in their weekly devotional life and a hindrance to them in their larger efforts to gain it.

Fasts, Table of. A table of Fasts in the tables prefixed to the Book of Common Prayer, is part of the tables and rules for the movable and unmovable Feasts, together with the days of Fasting and Abstinence through the whole year. The Fasts which are absolutely strict are the two, Ash-Wednesday and Good-Friday. Of these, Ash-Wednesday is as ordered by the Church, and is only by her express authority made a strict fast, while Good-Friday has yet higher force as universal observance is added to the command of the Church. Indeed, Christmas-day, Good-Friday, and Easter-day—the Birth, Sacrifice, and Resurrection of our dear LORD—compel from the devout Christian an observance which he cannot conscientiously pretermit.

"Other days of Fasting on which the Church requires such a measure of Abstinence, as is more especially suited to extraordinary Acts and Exercises of Devotion:

"1. The Forty days of Lent.

"2. The Ember-days at the four seasons, being the Wednesday, Friday, and Saturday after the first Sunday in Lent, the Fast of Pentecost, September 14, and December 13.

"3. The three Rogation days, being the Monday, Tuesday, and Wednesday before Holy Thursday, or the Ascension of our LORD.

"4. All the Fridays in the year except Christmas-day."

These several fasting days are noted in their proper places in the Cyclopædia, but it is proper to note one or two things in the table. The Church requires, and as good children we should use, such measure of abstinence, not of full fasts, but of self-denial that helps to self-control, that will regulate the pleasures of the palate and be ready to forego pleasant meats, that the mind may be less under the power of self-indulgence. It is not required of us to fast, but to abstain, and, too, no rigid rule is fixed. We should abstain from everything to which we are too much attached; whatever pleasant meats delight us lay these aside. There are ninety-seven such days of abstinence. And if they were devoutly observed, as we are in common duty bound and as our love to the Church should urge us, the devoutness of our spiritual life would be much heightened. What we should abstain from must be left to the circumstances and condition of each person.

Fatalism. "What has been decreed cannot be revoked" is the fundamental idea of the Fatalist. It was the necessity of the Greek, the Fate of the Latin, and is the Fatalism of the Christian who perverts the true doctrine of Predestination. Fatalism is the practical creed of those who overlook the fact that predestination is not taught of individuals but of the Church, in the Bible. GOD raised up certain men, both for honor and, as they chose, for dishonor (*e.g.*, Balaam, who was a prophet and sank to a petty demagogue under Balak's temptation), but this is not the basis of Predestination. But when the stern, narrow logic of later ideas of Predestination is applied to life and to individuals, Fatalism is the unavoidable conclusion. Mohammed brought this forward and made it the Creed of Islam. " Ye cannot will except the LORD willeth" (Korân, Sura 81). It led to wild fanaticism on the field of battle, it leads now to political supineness, and will be one of the final elements in working the destruction of Islamism. But the Spinozism which fashions too much the current of predestination thought, is itself a fatalistic system. Education and the freedom of thought, and the power to reason and also to use the insight of relativity, will be the best corrective to its influence, apart from the deeper devout study of the Scriptures. Fatalism was made indirectly a part of Luther's theology (De Servo Arbitrio), though he afterwards changed it very much. Zwingli also held it, by teaching that the elect were so by the determinate decree of GOD, the correlative of which proposition must follow.

Father. The distinguishing note of the Christian dispensation is the doctrine of the Fatherhood of GOD, through the revelation of His only-begotten SON JESUS CHRIST our LORD. The FATHER is confessed in the Creeds. "I believe in ONE GOD, the

Father Almighty, Maker of heaven and earth, and of all things visible and invisible," is the Confession of the Nicene Creed. "I believe in GOD the Father Almighty, Maker of heaven and earth," is the Confession of the Apostles' Creed. In the records of the earlier dispensation, in which the revelation was mainly of the Unity of the Godhead, this is not so distinctly traced; but, nevertheless, it is taught, and still oftener implied. The FATHER is Himself the source and self-existent Essence of the Divine Nature, and is properly a Father in that He hath an only-begotten Son, the eternal WORD (Ps. ii. 7; Heb. i. 5). Therefore, in the highest, most proper sense, HE is the FATHER of the WORD, and holds and displays in the Divine perfectness all the relations and attributes which belong to the FATHER towards His Son (St. John v. 19, 20, and vs. 17). He grants to His Son all the privileges, and demands for Him all the honors which belong to Him as His Son (St. John v. 21-23). He gives of His own to His Son (St. John xvi. 15). In the Unity of the Divine Essence the Son is all that the FATHER is, in Majesty, Glory, Power, Eternity, and Incomprehensibility, save in that which belongeth to GOD as the FATHER (St. John x. 30; xvii. 5, 21, 22). But, as He is FATHER of the eternal nature, so that Son is no less His Son when by the HOLY GHOST He took upon Himself flesh, and was born of the Virgin Mary, and became man. "For GOD so loved the world that He gave His only-begotten Son, that whosoever believeth in Him should not perish, but have everlasting life" (St. John iii. 16). This only-begotten Son, born of the Virgin, and called then the Son of GOD (St. Luke i. 35) was testified to by the Voice from heaven, "This is my beloved Son, in whom I am well pleased" (St. Matt. iii. 17). By the eternal Son of GOD, who in His human nature, being the Son of Adam, was also the Son of GOD, we become immortal sons of GOD in partaking His nature, putting Him on us as becoming man. He became the Son of GOD, as we are, by creation. He was glorified openly by His FATHER. He was confessed by the Devils (St. Mark iii. 11). He gave to them that received Him power to become the sons of GOD, even to them that believe on His name, which were born, not of blood, nor of the will of the flesh, nor of the will of man, but of GOD. Through His revelation and gift we have GOD to our Father in the highest sense, for He is not ashamed to call us brethren. But in the Christian Church this is only attainable. "For as many as are led by the Spirit of GOD, they are the sons of GOD; . . . ye have received the Spirit of adoption, whereby we cry ABBA, FATHER" (Rom. viii. 14, 15; *cf.* Gal. iv. 5, and St. Mark xiv. 36). So the LORD'S Prayer, "Our FATHER," etc., sets forth the crowning act of our right as sons of GOD; and the first imploration of the Litany but repeats it. Yet this Son of GOD was born a Jew, according to the flesh, and in this dispensation the FATHER'S love is shown, for the Psalmist cried, "Like as a father pitieth his children, even so the LORD pitieth them that fear Him." They that remember the LORD shall be spared, "as a man spareth his own son that serveth him" (Mal. iii. 7). In the first chapter of Proverbs the Fatherhood of GOD is brought out, for the Father and the Mother are GOD and the Church. Moses exclaimed in his song, "Is not He thy Father that hath bought thee?" GOD sent His message by Moses to Pharaoh concerning the people in their bondage. Israel is my son, my first-born. Wider cry yet cometh from the Gentiles through the Prophet Isaiah: "Doubtless Thou art our Father, though Abraham be ignorant of us, and Israel acknowledge us not: Thou, O LORD, art our Father, our Redeemer; from everlasting is Thy name" (Is. lxiii. 16). And these who so stretch out their beseeching hands to GOD are the sons of Adam, who is the son of GOD. Therefore, in the Creeds, in the LORD'S Prayer, in every address to Him as the FATHER, we approach Him by the right of creation in Adam, of revelation in the Jew, of sonship through His Son, who standeth evermore at the right hand of the FATHER, to receive our prayers and to give us access, as He has said, "No man cometh unto the Father but by Me."

Fathers, The. The crudest notions are entertained by the antagonists of Episcopalians respecting their estimation of the Christian Fathers. They look upon us as regarding the Fathers like a secondary sort of Evangelists or Apostles; as though their assertions ranked next to Scriptural ones, if not quite equal to them. They fancy we treat them as St. John would fain have treated the Angel in the Apocalypse, and give them reverential homage if not downright worship.

It is really hard to impress upon them the simple but essential distinction that the Fathers, like many other authors, sustain a twofold character,—that of *divines* and that of *witnesses*. As divines, they may have peculiar and personal opinions. St. Augustine, for example, is supposed by multitudes to have been what would now be called a Calvinist, because he talked so freely of predestination; albeit, his idea of predestination was a predestination to grace in this life, and not a predestination to glory or perdition in the next. St. Jerome was monkish, and Tertullian what we might call somewhat of a Quaker. But, as divines, we receive any peculiarity in their opinions as we receive the opinions of divines now living, for what they are worth, and not as authoritative or directive because of the men who entertained them.

It is as *witnesses* to Christian history, and especially as witnesses to a general or Catholic interpretation of Scripture, that we chiefly value them. They lived near the times when the Christian Scriptures were written;

and of course could tell us how primitive Christians had received their signification, as handed down by the Apostles and their contemporaries. This sort of interpretation in relation to ancient documents, and documents whose signification has been a matter of serious dispute, is of the very highest authority, common sense and common law teach us this; for we find one of the established maxims of courts to be, "*Contemporanea expositio est optima et fortissima in lege,*"—"A contemporaneous exposition is the best and strongest in law." (Wharton's Legal Maxims, p. 57.) This is the exposition which a judge upon the bench esteems above any mere opinion, or grammatical criticism, of the present day. A man's genuine meaning, in anything he says or writes, is what he *intends* by that which he says or writes. The dictionary and grammar may make a man's apparent intention, in his last will and testament, quite unlike his real and actual intention. And therefore a surrogate, or judge of probate, cares much less for the dictionary and grammar than for the genuine *intention* of the testator, if he can reach it without them. And the same rule should govern if the question respected the signification of a Constitution, a Statute, a Treaty, or a Contract. We want the aim, the design, the inward resolve of the authors of a Constitution, a Statute, a Treaty, or a Contract as a key, and the best of keys, to their actual and permanent signification.

Now it is under the influence of such sentiments that we go to the Fathers for the proper construction of the Scriptures and primitive Christian History. They are the persons to tell us what was the contemporaneous exposition of the Bible, what construction the Primitive Church put upon the Bible, because they are the best *witnesses* in the case we can possibly obtain. They were nearest the minds of the Apostles among all in the old Christian world. They were conspicuous and trustworthy persons. As witnesses, they could hardly be mistaken concerning the books which the Primitive Church gathered into a volume, which it called the Bible. They could also tell what sort of a Church had come down from Apostolic times, what rites it cherished, what officers governed it, and how it perpetuated its own existence.

Where else could we go (if we neglected or discarded such witnesses) when the drift of the Bible about such matters is called in question? The Bible does not attest its own Canon, or the construction of its disputed passages. It is a Latin Church book, or a Greek Church book; an Episcopal book, or a Presbyterian book; a Baptist book, or a Congregationalist book; a Methodist book, or a Quaker book; a Unitarian book, or a Free Church book; or, finally, a Rationalistic book; as denominations, or schools, or self-satisfied thinkers choose to account it. We must go outside of it for contemporaneous interpretation, or we must dispute and wrangle to the world's last day.

"We hold, and say we prove, from Scripture plain,
That CHRIST is GOD; the bold Socinian,
From the same Scripture, urges he's but *man.*
Now what appeal shall end the important suit?
Both parts talk loudly, but the rule is mute."

Even such a mind as Dryden's, layman if he were, could see this issue by an act of intuition, and put it to his fellows in a most characteristic way. (Works, 12mo ed., pp. 146, 147.)

True, he put it in the shape of poetry. But Dryden is said to have reasoned better in poetry than in prose; and certainly there is unmistakable and fruitful logic in his quoted lines.

The Church of Rome once saw, and insisted triumphantly, that the Scriptures must be interpreted according to the *unanimous* sense of the Fathers. Well, this test was applied to one of her most favorite authorities,—the text in Matthew, so often appealed to as establishing the Pope's supremacy. The *unanimous* consent of the Fathers, however, did not sustain her. Cardinal Newman saw this at a glance, and so he broached his theory of Development, which finds the germs of Romanism in the Bible, but not its full-blown dogmas.

But suppose the question to have been, Did the Primitive Church acknowledge a Trinity in the Godhead, or an Episcopacy in Church Government?—and we can find even a Gibbon acknowledging that such things were notorious down to the sixteenth century. And this leads us to say that the general, the all but unanimous, testimony of history respecting *chief matters,* fundamental matters, is singularly uniform. The Church Catholic, to this very day, believes in such points with all but consolidated unanimity. And if the Church Catholic would take the two points instanced and make them a basis of a *Concordat,* she would be a consolidated unity still, and the Communion of Saints exist no longer as a mere article of a creed. They are sufficient for the basis of a Concordat which would render all Christendom essentially and harmoniously one. And this is not spoken without book. When the American Episcopal Church first sent a Bishop to the East, he was charged by our Presiding Bishop to offer Christian communion, the fellowship of Christianity, to all who would receive it on the basis of the Nicene Creed for doctrine, and Apostolic Episcopacy for discipline, leaving form of worship and liturgies out of the question, as matters which might be conformed to national customs and educated tastes. The offer was listened to, and proved enough for Greek Christians and Oriental Christians generally.

But Rome, on the one hand, and anti-Episcopalians on the other, will not accept such a basis for a *Concordat.* By no means. There must be a Pope on this side, or ministerial parity on the other side, or the hand of brotherhood cannot cross the chasm and give the clasp of consanguinity. Who, then, are the hinderers, who the schism-makers, if the Church of CHRIST is still divided, and not likely to be one for centuries?

Doubtless we Episcopalians are considered a very exclusive and a very uncharitable people; but we have asked of our tallest Churchmen again and again, and of the most intelligent among them, too, if the Nicene Creed for doctrine, and Apostolic Episcopacy for discipline, would not be enough to start from, for a *Concordat*, with any body of Christians under heaven. And the invariable and cheerful answer has been that it would be. And is not this enough to show that, while we continually deprecate "false doctrine, heresy, and schism" in our Litany, our prayers are as continually answered, and that we are as free from "all uncharitableness" as any body of Christians beneath the sun,—as near a primitive standard as any other Christian body,—and that the Bible, interpreted according to the unanimous consent of the Fathers, is our true profession and our filial inheritance?

REV. T. W. COIT, D.D.

Feast. It is a principle in natural religion to seek by some joyous observance to express our religious feelings of happiness or thankfulness. This natural readiness, shown in innumerable heathen festivals and holidays, was used by Divine Providence for the teaching of His religion and for training mankind in His Life. He used it for the Israelites, beginning with the Passover. "And this day shall be unto you for a memorial; and ye shall keep it a feast to the LORD throughout your generations: ye shall keep it a feast by an ordinance forever" (Ex. xii. 14). And so of the other Feasts, of Pentecost, of Tabernacles, of Trumpets, the weekly sabbath, the seventh year, the year of Jubilee. Thrice a year each male was to appear before the LORD. It is not the place here to do more than note the binding unifying effect of such feasts as these. Since, then, the demands of natural devoutness and GOD's command conjoin to make Feasts a necessity, the Church has followed this principle; in fact, the Passover has become our Easter, Pentecost is Whit-Sunday, and by the guidance of the Spirit the Sabbath of the Jew has been transferred to the LORD's day,—Sunday. These are Feasts commemorating redemptive acts by, and enabling gifts from, our LORD; the round is completed by the joyful celebration of Christmas-day. The Christian year falls into two distinct parts, (I.) the Sundays from Advent to Whit-Sunday, in which the Life, Work, Passion, Crucifixion, Death, and Resurrection, Ascension of CHRIST, and His sending to us the all-containing gift of the HOLY GHOST are commemorated; and (II.) the Sundays extending from Trinity-Sunday on till Advent is reached again. All Sundays are minor Feasts of the Resurrection, but with this they as well as certain week-days have an added teaching and memorial joyfulness. Christmas-day and Epiphany generally, and Ascension-day always, fall upon a week-day, but all other Feasts founded on His work fall on Sunday. Feasts are divided into movable and immovable. Those are movable which depend upon Easter, which Feast depends upon the full moon on or after the 21st of March, giving a latitude of a month (from March 22 to April 25). Upon Easter depend the number of Sundays after the Epiphany, the date of the Ascension-day, Whit-Sunday, and Trinity-Sunday, as these fall at fixed spaces before or after Easter. Those which are immovable are the Feasts which fall on days of the month. Thus Christmas-day is always the 25th of December, and may fall on any day of the week, and Epiphany is the 6th of January, and also may fall on any day of the week.

The Act of Edward VI. (5 and 6, c. 3, s. 1) so clearly sets forth these reasons, is the foundation of our Table of Feasts, and shows Cranmer's hand so plainly, that the first section is here given:

"For as much as men at all times be not so mindful to laud and praise GOD, so ready to resort and hear GOD's holy word, and to come to the Holy Communion and other laudable rites which are to be observed in every Christian congregation as their bounden duty doth require; therefore, to call men to remembrance of their duty, and to help their infirmity, it hath been wholesomely provided, that there should be some certain times and days appointed wherein Christians should cease from all other kinds of labors, and should apply themselves only and wholly unto the aforesaid holy works properly pertaining unto true religion; the which times and days specially appointed for the same are called holidays, not for the matter or nature either of the time or day, nor for any of the saints' sake whose memories are had on those days (for so all days and times considered are GOD's creatures and all of like holiness), but for the nature and condition of those godly and holy works wherein only GOD is to be honored and the congregation to be edified, whereunto such times and days are sanctified and hallowed, that is to say, separated from all profane uses, and dedicated and appointed not unto saint and creature, but only unto GOD and His true worship; neither is it to be thought that there is any certain times or definite number of days prescribed in Holy Scripture, but that the appointment both of the time and also of the number of days is left by the authority of GOD's word to the liberty of CHRIST's Church, to be determined and assigned orderly in every country by the discretion of the rulers and ministers thereof as they shall judge most expedient, to the true setting forth of GOD's glory and the edification of their people; it is, therefore, enacted that all the days hereinafter mentioned shall be kept and commanded to be kept holidays and none other; that is to say, all Sundays in the year, the days of the Feast of the Circumcision of our LORD JESUS CHRIST, of the Epiphany, of the Purification of the Blessed Virgin, of St. Matthias the Apostle, of the Annunciation of the Blessed Virgin, of St. Mark the Evangelist, of St. Philip and Jacob the Apostles, of the Ascension of our LORD JESUS CHRIST, of the nativity of St. John the Baptist, of St. Peter the Apostle, of St. James the Apostle, of St. Bartholomew the Apostle, of St. Matthew the Apostle, of St. Michael the Archangel, of St. Luke the Evangelist, of St. Simon and Jude the Apostles, of All-Saints', of St. Andrew the Apostle, of St. Thomas the Apostle, of the Nativity of our LORD, of St. Stephen the Martyr, of St. John the Evangelist, of the Holy Innocents, Monday and Tuesday in Easter-week, and Monday and Tuesday in Whitsun-week; and that none other day shall be kept and commanded to be kept holy, or to abstain from lawful bodily labor." It will be observed that the Feast of the conversion of St. Paul and the Feast of St. Barnabas were omitted in the act, but their names are inserted properly in the Table of Feasts.

We have here the rules clearly laid down upon which the Churches of England and of these United States have acted in these matters, and from which their practice has never swerved. The office for Thanksgiving-day is a movable one, being the only link which connects the Church's offices with the authority of the State in the appointment of national holidays.

To close with Hooker's noble words: "Well to celebrate these religious and sacred days is to spend the flower of our time happily. They are the splendor and outward dignity of our Religion; forcible witnesses of ancient truth, provocations to the exercise of all piety, shadows of our endless felicity in Heaven, on earth everlasting records and memorials; wherein they which cannot be drawn to hearken unto that we teach may, only by looking upon that we do, in a manner read whatsoever we believe." (Hooker, Eccl. Pol., v., sect. 71, ad fin.)

Festival. The main difference between the words Feast and Festival seems to be that Feast is more often applied to the sacred Feasts which commemorate our LORD's life, while the Festival is applied to the days commemorative of GOD's Saints. And here we may remark that wherever in the calendar there is a Feast of our LORD's life falling on a week-day there should be a celebration of the Holy Communion. The Epistle and Gospel are ordered in all cases for both classes of Feast-days as well as for Sundays for such a celebration. This is their purpose. But at the least, the Feasts not only of Christmas and Ascension, but also of the Circumcision and the Epiphany, should be so kept. It is a growing custom to commemorate the Saints' days by that celebration which the Church intends should be had, by providing the Liturgic Scriptures of the Epistle and Gospel, for it is the sign of our unity in the Body of CHRIST which is His Church, and we profess the Faith once given to the saints as unchanged and unchangeable.

It may be asked, Why not commemorate the Saints of the Old Testament as well as those of the New? Hooker's reply is complete when he remarks that "we are content to imagine, it may be perhaps true, that the least in the Kingdom of CHRIST is greater than the greatest of all the Prophets of GOD that have gone before." (Eccl. Pol., v., sect. 71.) We thank GOD for their examples, praying that we may walk in their holy footsteps, and we desire to be made partakers of that blessedness He has given them, and we acknowledge thereby the deep bond of a common brotherhood in CHRIST our LORD, and note wherein we too can tread in those holy ways which He has prepared for us to walk in.

Filioque. In the controversies which raged in Spain between the Orthodox and the Arians (580 A.D.) the procession of the HOLY GHOST from the SON as well as from the FATHER was a powerful argument against the heretics. The third Council of Toledo (589 A.D.) directed that in the Creed, the clause upon the procession of the HOLY GHOST should read, *Qui, ex Patre, Filioque, procedit.* It was accepted in the Spanish and Gallican Churches. It was noticed as an interpolation by the Greek ambassadors at the Council of Gentilly (767 A.D.). Popes Adrian I. (790 A.D.) and Leo III. (806 A.D.) declined to sanction it, though it was persistently used in Gaul. But Nicolas I. (866 A.D.) found it convenient to use it in his controversy with Photius, the intruding Patriarch of Constantinople. Photius expressed the general denunciation of the East against it, and it continued to be the subject of sharp contentions between the Greek and the Latin Churches till the final rent (1054 A.D.). A conference upon it was held at Nice (1234 A.D.) and a Council at Nymphæa without fruit. So, too, it was discussed at Lyons (1274 A.D.). A reluctant assent to it was wrung from the Greek envoys at Florence (1439 A.D.), which was immediately repudiated by the Oriental Churches. The only discussion of any value since, was at Bonn (1874 A.D.), where its insertion was declared to be illegal, and an effort for its removal was urged. Repeated efforts both in the English Convocations and in our General Convention have been made to have it removed. But it was felt that the reception was so general in the West that it would be well, in view of the apparent course of events, to have it done by a larger portion and more representative of the Western Church than by merely the Anglican Communion acting alone, however needful the removal of the offending clause may be. The objection of the Eastern theologians is that it may be made to teach a dual source of procession, for the FATHER as self-existing is the sole source of the procession of the SPIRIT, the mission to us being through the SON. The interpolation was also bitterly condemned as wholly *extra vires*, as incurring the anathema of the Council of Chalcedon against all tampering with the Creed, and as necessarily forcing a schism in the body of CHRIST. This is a continued protest, and will so remain till the Filioque is cast out. It must be added that these objections do not lie against the imploration in the Litany. There the words are liturgically used, to Him who proceedeth by His mission from the SON to teach us how to pray aright.

Finance, Church. First, the Basis. The ministrations of public worship and of Christian charity cannot be sustained without a large outlay of money. But in our LORD'S teaching the Kingdom of GOD is that thing which a man is "first" to "seek." For one's self, therefore, and for one's family, when one is making up the table of the very necessaries of life, nothing can take higher rank on that list of things indispensable than the ministrations of religion. Nothing can more reasonably expect for itself adequate provision. This is the mere prudence of a wise man in taking care for himself and for his own household.

But the Church is the Representative of that CHRIST who came to this world upon a Foreign Mission, and who both took to Himself a human nature and went about doing good, healing men's bodies, enlightening men's minds, lifting burdens from human souls. The precept is, "Let this mind be in you which was also in CHRIST JESUS." The Church that is His must be a missionary Church. Hospitals, likewise Asylums, Homes for the Aged and for the Orphans, Training Schools of Nurses, and seminaries of good learning spring up wherever this Church has gone.

Reason commends the stern words written in Scripture of him "that doeth the work of the LORD negligently." Here, if anywhere, low maxims and loose practices must be shunned. Titles to Church property and insurance of buildings require honest, that is, scrupulous attention. It ought to be clearly understood that rashly to incur debt in the building of churches is just as reprehensible as to do it in other relations. To leave the rector's salary unpaid a week after it falls due is the same thing as to let a note lie dishonored at the bank. Those clergymen, held in esteem of their people, who have distinctly declared at the first that they should instantly resign the charge if ever the salary was one hour behind in the payment, have done good service in toning up the lazy flocks. And, in all the undertakings of Christian beneficence, the business parts require the same sound principles, wise methods, and careful attention for which men look in secular affairs.

Second. The methods of securing moneys and of disbursing them, and the tenure of Church property.

The Diocese, the real churchly unit as distinguished from the parish, both carries on works within itself and aids works without itself; within the Diocese, the local (parochial) and the more general.

Provision for parochial needs in self-sustaining parishes and the management of their finances the Diocese now leaves almost wholly with the parish. Through the parish the Church fixes the rector's salary and provides for its payment. In this way all parochial needs are met, with few canonical regulations or restrictions, provided the canonical requirements regarding offerings for specified Diocesan objects without the parish be not set aside.

Parochial Needs, the rector's salary, the parish's portion of the Bishop's salary, and other current local expenses are met in various methods. The chief source of revenue are Pew-rentals, Subscriptions, Pledged Weekly Offerings, Unpledged Weekly Offerings, and Endowment Funds.

From Rental of Pews very many large and important parishes derive their income. Among these must be counted many that are most liberal in contributions to Missions and to all works of love. Taking men with their inherited views and habits, in the average strong city parish probably so large and so steady an income for parochial uses as comes through the Pew-rental will not at first be yielded in any other way. It is also true that the system of renting pews for revenue is often so charitably adjusted to individual cases, and is so guarded otherwise, as to be free from the worst evils that accompany it when it is severely carried through. But to large numbers of Churchmen it seems a grave evil that privileges in GOD'S House should be sold for money, an evil that would become a wrong if perpetrated after it can reasonably be brought to an end. So profound has this feeling become with the more vivid apprehension of what is meant by our LORD'S Incarnation, that other methods have been sought out for the maintenance of the LORD'S House more in harmony with primitive practice, and involving no special privileges accorded to wealth in sacred things.

Probably in every Diocese churches will now be found in which no pews are rented. In several more than half the congregation do not resort to Pew-rentals. A few Bishops no longer deem it right to consecrate to Almighty GOD a House afterwards to be sold in parcels, and never do it. "Tolerate no restriction at the door, by pride or tax, which can bar out any child of the FATHER," are the earnest words of the House of Bishops in their Pastoral Letter of 1883 A.D. Wherever Pew-rentals are not had, the aim is to bring the parishioners to contribute each according to his ability to meet the parochial expenses, for these plainly must be met in some way.

Pledged Weekly Offerings have frequently been introduced. If their introduction have been intelligently followed and preceded, not by mendicant appeals, but with rich, generous instruction out of CHRIST'S Gospel, and if the pledges and their fulfillment have been so attended to that every family is reached, and that it is known to the proper person whether the pledge received at the year's beginning is weekly made good, the results have almost invariably been satisfactory. In a large class of parishes, especially in manufacturing towns, but elsewhere as well, this "Envelope Plan" (as it is named) of pledged weekly offerings, has succeeded in a marked degree.

The Weekly Offering Unpledged is in other instances the reliance. This is in several respects the best of all. But for its permanent success the congregation must be of some intelligence and substantial character, and self-respecting. It must be composed of persons who have the mental and the moral power to sit down and quietly decide what they ought to do, and then to hold themselves steadily, year after year, to the doing of it. To the writer of this paragraph a self-supporting parish is known which with neither pledge nor account kept with individuals, in the Sunday offering has nigh a score of years contributed for parochial uses hundreds of dollars annually more than the vestry formerly secured by Pew-rentals. Nor were contributions to objects without the parish suffered to fall off, as they do and will fall off if care be not taken and if some preventive system be not adopted where the offering replaces the Pew-rental. But by and with the change missionary contributions can even be increased, save among folk of the narrowest vision, if the clergyman himself be a man wise, vigilant, and of large heart.

By this method the parish cannot know at the year's beginning precisely upon what income they can rely. To set over against this inconvenience is the pecuniary advantage which the Plan of Offerings, whether pledged or unpledged, every Sunday possesses, that a considerable sum is sure to be received from strangers who happen to be in church, and from other persons who would not "hire a pew." And they whose wages are paid weekly, and many others, find it less difficult to bring weekly their money, some part of which would otherwise, perhaps, have been needlessly spent, than to go on to the quarter's end and then to find a large sum due at one time. And St. Paul's "order" to the Churches in Galatia and in Corinth, on "the first day of the week" carefully to "lay by," as GOD had prospered them, is helpful likewise in these days.

Upon Subscriptions a few parishes largely in rural, agricultural regions principally depend. The Subscription is made yearly to a collector, and the sums are commonly paid to him quarterly. In some places, particularly among farmers whose money comes in at one season of the year, or at two or three seasons, the times of full payment are apt to be determined partly by this fact. In an increasing number of parishes that rely on Subscriptions, the money subscribed is, the first Sunday in each Quarter, placed by the individual contributor in the alms-basin in church, with the person's name. This is done both for spiritual reasons and to save much of the labor of "collecting."

Parochial Endowments, also, have been made in some parishes, by which part of the yearly wants are supplied. The general opinion in the Church is, that if there be considerable Funds belonging to a parish, the parishioners are likely to do less than their own duty in giving, and that in such parishes they have actually done less. For rector's salary and the ordinary expenditures vigorous, healthy, substantial parishes usually deem it best to rely on themselves to furnish, year by year, what is requisite. But even these parishes could often enlarge themselves, and add much to their usefulness, if they were enabled to improve their services and to multiply their ministrations of worship, charity, or instruction.

One sees at this time an evident tendency to encourage the new energies by endowing those particular things in the parish in which the individual benefactor feels the deepest interest. Funds are now established more and more in parishes of all kinds, to secure a large and well-taught choir, to meet the cost of more frequent Services on week-days, for the better Christian instruction of the children, for parochial Homes and Hospitals, and for the poor of the parish. Repair Funds, Rectory Funds, Chapel Funds, and the like are slowly multiplying on every hand, greatly to the glory of GOD. Gifts for special purposes, parochial like these, are thankfully welcomed. For its more ordinary expenses the strong parish does best with few funds or with none.

Three classes of parishes are recognized as forming exceptions, and as calling very urgently for Endowments to furnish a part of that which the ordinary expenses require. First is the parish in sparsely-populated regions, the decaying hill parish it may be. From many a place like this, to which it can hardly be expected that missionary aid will cheerfully go forever, the light of GOD'S Church would have gone out were it not for the permanent Funds which thoughtful piety has supplied.

These Funds are established by a devout parishioner at his departure from this life or before, or by some generous man or woman reared in that parish, or by the son or daughter of one whose native parish it was. With the assistance thus lovingly given for all time, and perhaps, in addition, by the combining of two such cures, the ministrations of our holy religion go on. The dead are buried with words of hope, and the young grow up in GOD'S fear. And from just these Christian rural homes hundreds of young men go forth to stand among the country's most distinguished men, and to be the Church's stanchest sons. The strength and value of the men who have grown up in these rural hill towns is probably out of all proportion to their numbers. So far as one can see, the parishes in townships which have a stationary or a diminishing population will not be continued in existence, and remote rural homes will not be kept Christian without the aid of Parochial Endowments.

The larger manufacturing towns, in the second place, not seldom present congregations of working people in numbers that require the expenditure which pertains to a large church. Yet not one person of any wealth at all may be found; and the congregations are ever changing, with discouraging rapidity. These people are second to none in liberality. Yet it is fast coming to be evident that in such congregations a portion of the yearly needs ought to be assured by Endowments, and Endowments to this end are (alas! too slowly) multiplying.

The third class needing and gradually receiving large permanent Funds for the general ordinary uses of the parish comprises but few, but these have peculiar importance, and ought to be recognized as presenting very exceptional claims. They are the parishes by the side of large Colleges and Universities in villages in which the Church people are neither many nor rich. Perceiving that these people, with the help of the small contributions of students, cannot hope to maintain Divine service respectably as it ought there to be maintained, it is obvious that Endowments are the one thing upon which the Church in these College towns that are small towns must, under God, depend.

This is equally true of villages that are the seat of powerful Academies and other important Schools. Endowments for this blessed work have been built up and are now building, and must go on in building, through gifts of those students who chance to be at once wealthy and thoughtful, and of their friends, through gifts of prosperous persons once students in these institutions, and gifts of any others whose discernment is sufficient to show them how wide-reaching and far-reaching are all strong influences about these centres of learning.

To these three sets of parishes which, it is agreed, ought to look much to Endowments, and which ought to rely greatly thereon, it may be fit to add that some observing men are watching to see in the more populous cities a few large churches, free churches, centrally placed and well appointed in all things, and amply endowed. But of results actually reached in this direction, next to nothing can be recorded.

Parochial moneys are expended by the Vestry (the Rector, Wardens, and Vestrymen in many places the legal title is) The single exception is the Communion Alms. These are wholly at the Rector's discretion. For greater delicacy in dealing with the poor, it is customary for a Rector to submit his account to only one person, usually a Warden. Even this he does only for his own protection.

The title to the church edifice and to the parsonage in most Dioceses is vested in the corporation of the parish. Need has lately been felt of some better guarantee than is thus furnished of the permanent keeping to its original intent of the parish property, that the pious purposes of the donors may not be frustrated. And the Dioceses are rapidly coming to have each a Central Corporation (e.g., the "Trustees of the Protestant Episcopal Church in New Hampshire"). This Corporation is empowered to hold Funds for any religious or charitable object designated by the donor, and in accordance therewith to disburse the income. It also holds in trust for that congregation the title-deeds of the church or parsonage belonging to any parish that may request these trustees to do it. The parishes not quite certain of the future availing themselves of this stronger security are already many. The movement sprang mainly from the laity. It is warmly favored by the Bishops and the other clergy as prudent for a large proportion of the parishes, which being Religious Societies have a corporate existence, and which ask no missionary aid.

In Missions within a Diocese, that which was only useful in the case of a parish becomes more nearly a necessity. Parishes are not now organized at so early a stage of the mission's existence as once they were. Land commonly must be purchased, and the church erected perhaps, before there is in fact a legally constituted society (parish) to hold the Title. The deed, therefore, is very likely to run to these trustees of the Diocese, in trust for this congregation. Rarely is it found that when organized into a parish the congregation desires to withdraw the trust. This Diocesan Corporation is composed of laymen chosen by the Convention, with sometimes a Presbyter or two, and has the Bishop for President.

A Corporator-sole consisting of the Bishop, a device which has been urged by a few writers, to hold and administer the permanent Funds, seems to accord well neither with American usages and ideas nor with the spiritual functions of the Bishop, and it meets with scant favor.

Missions within a Diocese secure that part of the missionary's salary and of the amount for other current expenses which they by agreement undertake to furnish by the methods in vogue in parishes. But Pew-rentals in missions are wellnigh unknown, and Sales and special exertions to add to the income are in missions of more frequent occurrence. This last fact calls for a few words touching the Church's attitude towards what are called "Church Fairs."

An honest Sale, at their real value, of

articles that are the handiwork of good people, the expression of their skill and the gift of love, and that are unduly urged upon no one, is wholly free from objection in principle, and is in every view to be commended. Without this zeal, akin to what was manifested at the making of the Tabernacle in Israel, many a mission would have fared hardly or come to naught. Of Suppers and merry-making Entertainments, innocent and altogether proper at a Parish Festival, the Church generally does not very heartily approve as a means of "raising money." Still less are these well received if repeated year after year, and taken up as a permanent part of parochial or missionary usage.

Church lotteries, rafflings, and this whole brood of unholy doings the Church abhors; and they are coming to be not so much as named among us. There are Dioceses in which a mission that should persist in resorting to these sinful, vulgar practices would speedily find its stipend from the Diocesan Board discontinued. For while the Church desires to build churches, she desires to build only Christian churches; and she knows that it is futile for men to fear the LORD and serve their own gods.

The pecuniary assistance given by a Diocese to its missions comes usually through a Diocesan Board of Missions, and it is distributed as to the amounts by the Board. This Board consists of the Bishop and a number of Presbyters, and an equal number of laymen, elected annually by the Convention. The treasury of the Diocesan Board of Missions is, in a few Dioceses, partially endowed, but it trusts oftener to contributions from all the congregations, made quarterly or at times fixed by Canon. These are sometimes unpledged offerings, presented to GOD in church at the stated days. Sometimes the contributions are individually pledged beforehand, and are gathered each quarter by persons appointed for the business.

Besides parishes and missions, each Diocese has certain more general works and institutions. The Fund for the Support of the Episcopate is designed, in some Dioceses, to furnish the entire salary of the Bishop; in others the Fund yields a part of the salary, and the rest is made up by assessments on the several parishes, laid yearly by the Convention. This Fund, which comes through personal gifts, through offerings in churches, and through bequests, is usually held and invested by the Trustees of the Protestant Episcopal Church in the particular Diocese, if they be a legal corporation.

Diocesan Church Hospitals, Homes for the Aged, and Homes for Orphans, maintained by contributions of individuals and of congregations throughout the Diocese, rest for much of their efficiency on permanent funds which piety bestows in CHRIST'S name. These institutions are usually corporations, holding their own property and administering their own finances. So, also, are colleges and seminaries, and Diocesan schools for girls and for boys.

Of Institutions of Christian learning endowments are the principal support, and ought to be, and with precisely the same fitness in the incorporated school as in the college or university. For the Church school, if it demanded from each pupil the full cost of residence and of tuition, a thing which the college never thinks of demanding, could be the school of only the very rich, and the Church would not lay hold of the people. But the school cannot, like a Home for the Destitute, be always suing for alms and seeking offerings in churches. If churches, schools, and colleges are to be of the best, and within the people's reach, there has been found in this age but one provision possible. That provision is endowments, varied and abundant endowments. Experience has already made manifest the wisdom of those men who have laid foundations of endowments, and of those who have built thereupon.

Outside of the Diocese, General Missions among Indians and colored people, and in the new settlements of the West, and in foreign lands, are conducted, as to their finances, by a General Board of Managers elected by the General Convention. The office of the Treasurer of this General Board is in New York City, and the legal title of the Corporation is the "Domestic and Foreign Missionary Society of the Protestant Episcopal Church."

All parishes in all Dioceses are expected to send regular contributions, received through stated offerings in church, or systematically collected upon pledged subscriptions, to the General Missionary Treasury. Small confidence is felt in endowments for this purpose, and hope is set chiefly on fresh and constant streams of supply. By the Managers a sum is yearly voted to each Missionary Diocese and Jurisdiction, and of the amount the Bishop of the jurisdiction is notified. The Bishop then designates to the Managers the mission stations to be helped, and gives the names of the missionaries and the portion of the entire allowance for his jurisdiction to be devoted to each missionary. The Board, no weighty reason appearing to the contrary, then assigns the several stipends for the year in accordance with the Bishop's nomination.

A few remarks may be added here.

The TITHE is not accepted for the foundation of our financial system. Many sober members of the Church believe the principle of one-Tenth of our income strictly belonging to GOD, and to be employed lawfully only for religious uses, to be permanently binding, and to be a part of our holy religion. This belief is sufficiently prevalent to increase very materially the aggregate of contributions. In the more common view the Tithe, literally applied, would lay unreasonable exactions upon laboring folk, and, if not carefully distinguished from voluntary offerings, would release the rich from obligations, upon their payment of a sum unfairly small. The teachings in the Church most frequently point to the Tithe as an intimation from our heavenly FATHER of what is, with prosperous children of His, accounted right, as the lowest, for them to set aside to the ministries of religion; and that, our spiritual blessings being so much richer than were those of the Jews, the argument is, *a fortiori*,—the Tenth at the least from all those whose daily business GOD has blessed.

They who have most carefully observed the financial side of things in the Church will say, that if the Church in the country despises missions to the heathen in foreign lands, the Diocese will speedily care not for works outside herself, and the parish will neglect the general interests of the Diocese, and the individual parishioner will concern himself little with the parish, and will lock up his heart and will lock up his treasures. But invariably those parishes and those Dioceses whose hearts are enlarged and opened to a practical sympathy with all earnest works everywhere, take best care of their own parish and of their own Diocese. They who most gladly contribute to missions and general charities of the Church are the very parishes and Dioceses that in the long course of years best help themselves. Love flows out and contributions flow in. A narrow spirit in things pertaining to CHRIST, the Gift and the Giver, is the poorest possible financial equipment. There is wealth enough, if hearts be opened, minds informed, and habits systematized.

Do Churchmen give to the General Treasuries, or to specific works and places? To both. Interest in particular places, works, and persons springs from our best nature, and is Divine. An intelligent guiding principle also which leads the Christian man steadily to sustain the general missions and works, though he knows personally little of each, to sustain them through the General Treasury for CHRIST'S love, with no designating of particular objects, this, too, is most Christian, and is withal necessary if we are to have any systematic work. These two things, piety and pity, are not to be brought in contrast. If the Special has in administration at any time been set above the General want, or if the General have ever been hostile to Specials, the entire work has suffered. The Church's policy is to encourage gifts to all worthy objects, and in all right ways. In the end and upon the whole this policy has vindicated itself.

Help towards self-help the Church aims to give, that the mission may be stimulated, not fed in idleness.

Church institutions of charity and of reverent learning receive a large part of these endowments, by which they are enabled to bless mankind and to glorify GOD, through bequests. The clergy, while most grateful for wise and frequent legacies to the setting forward of GOD'S kingdom among men, abstain from much meddling with individuals. They trust rather to sound principles taught in church and to clear information kept before the people touching worthy objects and pressing wants. The Church always discourages bequests to the best of objects if made without due regard to all rights of family and to the needs of near kindred.

In general, the Church, in her Financial System, recognizes that varied interests and various methods are legitimate. She would have contributions cheerful, intelligent, and therefore systematic, a grateful response to the Divine goodness to us, and a conscientious representation in amount of a man's personal ability; not a tax, but a privilege; not a piece of worldly business only, but a reverent transaction with the ALMIGHTY GIVER; not less a luxury than a necessity. Direct methods the instinct of the Church strongly prefers. She knows that financial evils will be cured when her sons and daughters, taught of the HOLY GHOST, shall have come to such ripeness of knowledge as to perceive that the "Kingdom of GOD" is really the "first" thing, and to such ripeness of love as shall make real to each the sacred word, "It is more blessed to give than to receive." Just three things are needed: Love, knowledge, system. Let these three things abound, and the spiritual motive-power will rapidly fill itself to the full, and the machinery will more smoothly move. General treasuries will be richly stored, and special needs quickly supplied. And the Church's GOD and GOD's Church will be held in honor.

RT. REV. W. WOODRUFF NILES, D.D.,
Bishop of New Hampshire.

First Fruits. The first fruits offered to GOD (Ex. xxii. 29; xxiii. 19, etc) and given to the Priests suggested to the Papacy the claim of the first year's income of every Benefice, Bishopric, and Primacy, from the Clerk, Bishop, or Primate-elect, before he could be confirmed in his Benefice or See. The claim for first fruits was made in John's reign, but it was reduced to a form, and a valuation of all livings and Bishoprics was made in 1292 A.D., which lasted till Henry VIII. ordered a new one to be made. Henry VIII. diverted these first fruits into the State treasury, but Queen Anne (1712 A.D.) restored them to the Church, but not by releasing the Sees. They were given by charter to form the fund for the augmentation of small livings.

Flagon. The vessel or cruet containing the wine to be used at the Consecration in the Holy Communion. After pouring out some into the cup, as it may be convenient to consecrate more than the cup can hold, the Celebrant is ordered at the proper moment to "lay his hand upon every vessel in which there is any wine to be consecrated." The Flagon, therefore, may be used for con taining wine in the act of consecration, after the cup has been consecrated.

Flentes. The first order of those who were under the Church's strict discipline. These flentes were placed either in the Porch or in the Vestibule (*Narthex*). Here they besought the prayers of the Faithful as they entered the church. Tertullian (De Pudicit; c. 4) urges repentance of monstrous lusts not merely on the threshold but in the church itself.

Florida, Diocese of. The Diocese of Florida was organized in St. John's Church, Tallahassee, on the 8th day of February, 1838 A.D. The first Anglican missionaries within the limits of the State were sent out from England. "The Society for the Propagation of the Gospel in Foreign Parts," on the 5th of May, 1764 A.D., commissioned and sent out, licensed by the Bishop of London, as Missionary to St. Augustine, the Rev. John Forbes; and on the same date the Rev. Samuel Hart, as Missionary to Mobile, West Florida. The Rev. John Fraser was licensed March 23, 1769 A.D., the Rev. John Leadbetter, November 8, 1773 A.D., both for St. Augustine, and the Rev. John Kinnedy, for St. Mark's, December 24, 1776 A.D. Following Mr. Hart, in West Florida, were the Rev. William Gordon, licensed August 8, 1767 A.D.; the Rev. Nathaniel Colton, March 2, 1768 A.D; and the Rev. George Chapman, licensed for Pensacola, May 3, 1773 A.D. Of these, the Rev. Mr. Forbes is spoken of as residing at St. Augustine in 1771 A.D., filling the places of "Parson, Judge of Admiralty, and Counsellor," and Mr. Fraser as "Parson at Mosquito."

When the province was ceded to Spain by Great Britain, in 1783 A.D., there was an immediate cessation of all Protestant worship. The English church was torn down and its material used in the erection of a Roman Catholic church. A German church at a place called Tolmato shared the same fate. But there still remained individuals and families who adhered to the Liturgy of the English Church, and it is stated on good authority that in one instance the "Morning Prayer" of the Church was maintained in one family regularly for forty-five years.

In July, 1821 A.D., the province was ceded to the United States. In October of the same year the Rev. Andrew Fowler, of South Carolina, under appointment as a Missionary from that Diocese, entered on his duties at St. Augustine, and was succeeded in May, 1823 A.D., by the Rev. M. J. Mott.

"The Domestic and Foreign Missionary Society" of the Church in the United States soon after its organization took an earnest interest in this field, and in 1827 A.D. sent out the Rev. Rolf Williston to Tallahassee. He organized this year the Parish of Christ Church, Pensacola, and the year following St. John's, Tallahassee. In 1830 A.D., under the ministry of the Rev. Alphonse Henderson, Trinity Church, St. Augustine, built of stone, and the oldest church edifice now standing in the Diocese, was erected, and in 1833 A.D. was consecrated by the Rt. Rev. Nathaniel Bowen, D.D., Bishop of South Carolina, to which Diocese Florida gratefully acknowledges her obligation for nursing care in her early days. For some years the Bishop of South Carolina, and afterwards Bishop Stephen Elliott, of Georgia, held jurisdiction in Florida.

October 15, 1851 A.D., the Rev. Francis Huger Rutledge, D.D., was consecrated the first Bishop of the Diocese. At the time of his election he was Rector of Trinity Church, St. Augustine. He died November 6, 1866 A.D. The Rt. Rev. John Freeman Young, S.T.D., was consecrated as the second Bishop of the Diocese, in Trinity Church, New York, on the 25th day of July, 1867 A.D. At the time of his election he was an assistant minister of Trinity Church.

The statistics of the Diocese as reported in 1883 A.D. are as follows:

Clergy, 31; parishes and missions, 42; families, 1076; baptisms, 295; confirmed, 108; communicants, 1642; contributions, $36,212.03. All the churches and chapels in the Diocese are free, and depend on the Offertory for revenue.

Statistics for 1886 A.D.: Clergy, 36; parishes and missions, 45; lay readers, 26; baptisms, 402; confirmed, 65; communicants, 1931; contributions, $45,442.84.

REV. R. H. WELLER, D.D.

Flowers. The Primitive Christians did not make use of flowers, since the Heathen used them in their sacrifices and at their feasts, when heathen rites often polluted the garlands (Clem. Alex., Pæd. ii. c. 8). But when heathenism was on the wane the natural love for flowers and their fitness for adorning the church was admitted and their use gradually permitted (St. Jerome to Nepotian). "These things were trifling in themselves; but a pious mind devoted to CHRIST is intent upon small things, and neglects nothing that pertains even to the meanest office of the Church." The custom, though objected to by some, is one against which no valid objection can be made, and which has become wellnigh universal. The rule should be to employ none but natural flowers in the ornamentation.

Fond du Lac, The Diocese of. At the Annual Convention of the Diocese of Wisconsin, in 1866 A.D., immediately after the election of the Rev. William Edmond Armitage as Assistant Bishop, on motion of Winfield Smith, Esq., the following resolution was adopted:

"*Resolved*, That this Convention is unanimously in favor of the division of this Diocese, and that, therefore, the Bishop of the Diocese be respectfully requested to give his consent to the division of the same, and to place his consent upon the records of this Convention."

The Bishop promptly gave his assent, as follows:

"In accordance with the unanimous request of the Convention of this Diocese, and with my own convictions, repeatedly expressed, I, Jackson Kemper, D.D., by the grace of GOD Bishop of the Diocese of Wisconsin, do hereby declare and place on record my assent and consent to the division of this Diocese, and the erection of a new Episcopal See therein, now, or as soon as practicable hereafter.

(Signed) "JACKSON KEMPER.
"June 14, 1866, A.D."

No further steps seem to have been taken until 1872 A.D., when Bishop Armitage, in his address to the Annual Convention, used the following words:

"I earnestly invoke the aid of the whole Diocese in bringing about this necessary division. We shall never do thorough work in Wisconsin until we have at least four Dioceses within our bounds, and I see not why we may not set off one Convocation after another at successive General Conventions, beginning with the Northeastern in 1874."

Bishop Armitage did not live to see his desire gratified. The General Convention of 1874 A.D., however, consented to, and ratified the formation of, a new Diocese in Wisconsin, to consist of nineteen counties, to wit: Marathon, Oconto, Shawano, Door, Kewaunee, Brown, Outagamie, Waupaca, Portage, Wood, Adams, Waushara, Winnebago, Calumet, Manitowoc, Sheboygan, Fond du Lac, Green Lake, and Marquette, and also such portion of Dodge County as may be necessary to include in the limits of the new Diocese the village of Wampum, such division to take effect on the first day of December, 1874 A.D. The provision made for the support of a Bishop was the sum of fifteen thousand dollars (of which ten thousand dollars were in promissory notes and five thousand dollars in cash securities), the interest of which, and an annual assessment of one thousand dollars and an Episcopal residence, were considered a sufficient compliance with the requirement of Article 5 of the Constitution.

The Primary Council of the new Diocese was convened at St. Paul's Church, Fond du Lac, January 7, 1875 A.D. The Right Reverend E. R. Welles, S.T.D., Bishop of the Diocese of Wisconsin, presided. The Rev. Martin V. Averill was elected Secretary, and Mr. James B. Perry was elected Treasurer. Sixteen clergymen and the representatives of fourteen parishes were present. Fond du Lac was chosen as the name of the Diocese. A Constitution of seventeen articles was adopted. The Bishop of the Diocese of Wisconsin announced that he had chosen the Diocese of Wisconsin as his See. He was requested by the Council to take Episcopal charge of the new Diocese until the election and consecration of its Bishop. The Council then proceeded to the election of a Bishop. On the thirteenth ballot the Rev. Leighton Coleman, of Toledo, Ohio, was elected Bishop. The whole number of clergymen belonging to the Diocese at the time of its organization was nineteen; of communicants, there were reported twelve hundred and eighty-four. The first Annual Council of the Diocese was held June 8, 1875 A.D., at St. Paul's Church, Fond du Lac. Bishop Welles presided. Seventeen clergymen and the representatives of twelve parishes were present. A body of Canons was adopted. The Rev. Leighton Coleman having declined to serve as Bishop, the Council proceeded to a new election. On the third ballot the Rev. Jacob S. Shipman, of Lexington, Kentucky, was chosen. The Rev. Mr. Shipman having declined the Episcopate, a Special Council was assembled at Christ's Church, Green Bay, Wednesday, September 15, 1875 A.D. The Rev. William Dafter presided. On the third ballot for Bishop the choice fell on the Rev. John Henry Hobart Brown, S.T.D., rector of St. John's Church, Cohoes, Diocese of Albany. Dr. Brown accepted the election, and was duly consecrated at St. John's Church, Cohoes, Wednesday, December 15, 1875 A.D., by the Right Reverend Horatio Potter, D.D., LL.D., Bishop of New York, the Right Reverend William Crosswell Doane, S.T.D., Bishop of Albany, the Right Reverend Benjamin H. Paddock, D.D., Bishop of Massachusetts, assisted by the Bishops of Vermont, New Hampshire, Wisconsin, and New Jersey.

In 1880 A.D. the limits of the Diocese of Fond du Lac were enlarged so as to include portions of the counties of Bayfield, Ashland, and Chippewa, and the whole of Taylor and Clark. The present area of the Diocese is about that of one-half of the State, 27,000 square miles. Its population in 1880 A.D. was 442,221. The summary of Diocesan statistics in 1884 is, clergymen, 28; families, 1382; individuals, 6306; communicants, 2390; parishes, 20; organized missions, 30. The Diocese has many advantages of soil and climate, and at some future time will be populous. Its mineral deposits are undoubtedly large, but as yet little developed. The northern portion of the Diocese is heavily wooded. The climate is salubrious, but somewhat cold in winter. The soil generally is good, and in the southern part of the Diocese very productive. The population is formed of an unusual variety of nationalities.

The American settlers are mostly from the New England and Middle States. Germans are next in number. Then follow Norwegians, Swedes, Danes, Poles, Belgians, Bohemians, Hollanders, Welsh, English, French, Canadians, Scotch, Irish, Finns, and Icelanders. There are several reservations of Indians, chiefly of Chippewas, Menominees, and Oneidas. The Winnebagoes have a little land of their own, but some of these and of the Pottawatomies wander about the country in bands and companies. A few of the Stockbridges and Brothertown Indians survive. A portion of the Oneida tribe is settled in Brown County. At Hobart Church, Oneida, about nine hundred of them are baptized, and are under the pastoral charge of the Rev. E. A. Goodnough. About three hundred are communicants. In view of the missionary character of the work the erection of this Diocese was a bold movement, reflecting much credit on the faith and courage of the clergy and people that sustained it.

Statistics for 1886 A.D.: Clergy, 29; parishes, 19; missions, 29; candidates for H. O., 5; ordinations, D. 2, P. 2; baptisms, 399; confirmed, 236; com., 2592; S. S. teachers, 161; S. S. scholars, 1687; contr., $33,644.64.

RT. REV. J. H. H. BROWN, D.D.,
Bishop of Fond du Lac.

Font. The vessel containing the water wherewith the Sacrament of Baptism is administered. It was, as we have seen (*vide* BAPTISTERY), placed in earlier churches in a separate building, but it was later transferred into the church. The Western Church used usually a stone Font, but it might be of any convenient material, and it was to be used for the baptism alone. The Font in the Eastern Church is movable, of wood or metal, and is seldom or never possessed of any beauty. The shape of it in the West was generally octagonal, though a fanciful mysticism occasionally gave it the form of a sepulchre or of a cross. The Font in the Baptistery was surrounded with a low wall, entered by steps, usually seven, three without, three within, excluding the top step. It was placed in the English Church near the west door or the southwestern porch,—a reminiscence of the Eastern practice of the Baptistery. In the act of Baptism the water is not to be placed in the Font before the Priest comes with the child or person to be baptized to the Font. (*Vide* rubric to Office of Public Baptism.) The invocation over the water is one of the most ancient rites in this most ancient office. St. Basil (De Sp. Sanc., c. 27) says that it is one of the Liturgical traditions handed down to us before the Liturgies were committed to writing. But the first direct mention of the benediction of the water is in Tertullian (De Bap., c. 4). Compare the earliest form (of 300 A.D.) with our own prayer, "Look down from heaven and sanctify this water, and grant grace and power that he who is baptized according to the command of Thy CHRIST may with Him be crucified and die and be buried and rise again to the adoption which is in Him, by dying unto sin but living unto righteousness." (Ap. Const., vii. 43.)

The early English use (and so in the first Prayer-Book) was to put water into the Font once a month, and blessing that, to have it ready for the baptisms; but this was changed and the prayer placed where it now stands in the second Prayer-Book of Edward

VI., 1552 A.D. The benediction of the water is not held to be essential, but it is a very old and solemn setting apart of the outward and visible sign of that Sacrament which regenerates us.

Formatæ Literæ. There were several kinds of Formatæ Literæ, or Commendatory Letters. The word formatæ has an obscure origin, but probably means sealed letters. Such we know to have been used in the Apostolic times (2 Thess. ii. 2; 2 Cor. iii. 1). They were both a necessity to the Christian traveler, that he might receive hospitality and relief from the brethren whom he might meet, and a protection and assurance to those who should give him the entertainment due to a brother. It was, too, a bond between the different Churches. It was an unanswerable argument against the Donatists, that their letters were not received outside their own Churches, and therefore that they were a sect. Later these letters, without which a person could not be received, formed a check upon the desire to rove from Diocese to Diocese, and were something like Letters Commendatory. It was under penalty of excommunication that any one received a stranger coming without such a letter, and even then he was subjected to scrutiny. For the abuse had grown up in the letters of confessors and in the letters of peace of not inserting the name of the bearer, so that the letter could be used by any one who held it at the time. This was repressed by refusing such letters any credit, and no cleric was allowed to officiate in a strange city without letters from his Bishop. Later on these letters took special forms. A special mode of signing such letters as were sent by Bishops was agreed upon,—letters asking material aid, letters recommending to communion, and letters dimissory, transferring the bearer to the jurisdiction of another Bishop.

We have retained two forms of these letters. The Canon (Tit. ii., c. 12, ₴ 2) requires that every layman removing from one parish to another should carry with him a letter certifying that he is a Communicant in good standing, and the rector of the parish to which he removes "shall not be required to receive him as a Communicant until such letter be produced." The second form of letter is the Letter Dimissory of the clergyman removing from one Diocese to another. In order to gain canonical residence within the second Diocese he must present to the Ecclesiastical Authority a testimonial from the Ecclesiastical Authority of the Diocese he has left, which shall set forth his true standing and character. The testimonial may be in the following words: "I hereby certify that A. B., who has signified to me his desire to be transferred to the Ecclesiastical Authority of ——, is a Presbyter (or Deacon) of —— in regular standing, and has not, so far as I know or believe, been justly liable to evil report for error in religion or viciousness of life for three years last past." The person presenting is not transferred till it has been accepted by the Ecclesiastical Authority of the Diocese to which he removes. He is allowed six months in which to present this letter. If it is not presented in three months, it *may* be considered void by the Authority that gave it; if not in six months, it shall be considered void. He must be received, unless there are such rumors against him as would justify an investigation in the Diocese he has left, in which case the Ecclesiastical Authority is not permitted to receive him. (*Vide* LETTERS.)

Forms. Forms are necessary, in all important matters at least. Forms are constantly used in all legal instruments, and in very many other matters of business, as much for guidance as for the correct execution of the matter in hand. These forms, so necessary elsewhere, are most necessary in Public Worship, since as the Congregation worship as well as the clergyman, there must be a form to guide them in their common acts, and as these acts of Worship are of the most important man can engage in, forms also furnish the correct conduct and wording of these acts. Indeed, there is no worship at all without some forms, whether bare and insufficient, or full and sufficing. This must be admitted. Then that there must be matter in these forms is shown by our LORD giving us a Prayer with the injunction, "After this manner, therefore, pray ye." The fullness and propriety of the forms used is another part of the subject of forms. Not only outlines of action or successions of procedure in the worship, but the words of the prayers were given in certain cases by GOD Himself (Deut. xxvi. 5–10; xxi. 7, 8; Ps. xc.; Joel ii. 17; Hosea xiv. 2, 3). With such a warranty for our action, the example of our LORD and the use of the Apostles (Acts iv. 24–30, "with one accord" they lifted up their voice to GOD, which could not be unless it were a wellknown prayer), the Church everywhere has ever used forms of prayer. Till the Reformation there was no body of Christians that was without a Liturgy. Such a thing was not dreamt of as possible; indeed, one of the perplexities of those who traveled out of their own country was in the variety of the Liturgical forms they met with, and the customs which were practiced abroad. It was in part the result of the ancient authority each Bishop held to alter the Liturgic forms in his own Diocese, which authority, however, was afterwards exercised by the Primate of the Archprovince that greater unity of Liturgic forms might be obtained. In this matter of forms there should be a proper flexible mean kept between laxness and straitness.

Then the Church in each country has the right to arrange its forms of worship on the general outline of the ancient Liturgic forms, but adapting them to the needs of the people with whom she has to deal. It is wisdom in adaptation, and judgment in using our privileges, and a true valuation of the rich heritage of the forms and sanctified prayers of the Ancient Churches, that will solve the problems of fitting and using our Book of Common Prayer for the need of the Church in this country. Forms of Prayer have been added from time to time, and special prayers are issued by our Bishops whenever there is need, as in the case of war, or of an epidemic, or of a national fast-day.

Formularies. These may be of Worship, as the Book of Common Prayer, or of Faith, as the Creeds, and later, the documents like the Confession of Augsburg, containing formal statements on controverted points of the Faith. A Formulary of worship, as has been shown, has always been found in the possession of every Church, and incorporated in its structure there was always the recitation of the Creed (generally the Nicene). The Formularies of the Creed have been touched upon in the article upon the Creed, but it may be well to add a word upon the formation of the Creed. The Apostles' Creed most probably was a commonly received form, built upon the Baptismal Formula, "In the name of the FATHER, of the SON, and of the HOLY GHOST." Of the FATHER, we believe that He is GOD, Almighty, maker of heaven and earth, a clause which sums up the main articles upon the First Person of the Trinity. Of the SON, we believe that He is the only SON of GOD, and our LORD, and then we recite the outline of His human life, and confess His future coming. Of the HOLY GHOST, we believe that His work abiding in us is the Holy Catholic Church, the Communion of Saints, the forgiveness of sins, the resurrection of the body, and the life everlasting, the sum of what Holy Scripture teaches of His work, and yet bearing internal evidence that it was also a doctrine in the Church concurrent with the Scriptures. This Creed was taught orally to the catechumens at first in substance, not in words, and finally, just before their baptism was intrusted to them in its compact, concise wording. That this formulary should have varied slightly in the different parts of the Church, extending from India to the Atlantic, is not to be wondered at; the wonder is that there were not greater variations even within the just limits of the one Faith; but as a matter of fact, the variations were not material in any respect except that the Article "He descended into hell" was a later addition (about 400 A.D.). The Nicene Creed was set forth by the Fathers at the Council of Nicæa in 325 A.D. It was the result of the comparison of the forms of the Creed held throughout the Church, and had clauses added to meet the Arian heresy. It was structurally the same as the Apostles' Creed, and, as has been well said, it is the Creed upon which all of Christendom will unite. The formula called the Athanasian

Creed is properly a doctrinal hymn, and is called in the English Prayer-Book the Psalm Quicunque vult, from the first words, "Whosoever will be saved." It is not formed upon the same lines precisely as the two Creeds proper, but is rather a full theological statement by assertion and negation of the Doctrine of the TRINITY. It is warmly objected to for the so-called anathemas it contains, but it may be replied with complete force that these damnatory clauses are from the Scriptures, and that, besides, not to believe on the Persons of the Holy Trinity is to believe on some other than GOD. "To believe of CHRIST wrongly is to substitute a figment more or less nearly approaching Him, and therefore to believe wrongly is to fail of salvation. Therefore it is no want of Christian Charity to say, whosoever will be saved before all things it is necessary that he hold the Catholic Faith, which Faith, except every one do keep whole and undefiled, without doubt he shall perish everlastingly. . . . This is the Catholic Faith, which except a man believe faithfully he cannot be saved." These are no stronger than what our LORD said, "He that believeth and is baptized shall be saved, but he that believeth not shall be damned" (St. Mark xvi. 16).

Fraction, of the bread in celebrating the Holy Communion. The rubric orders that the Priest to take the Paten into his hands, at these words "He brake it, and gave it to His disciples, saying, Take, eat," and as he continues, "this is My Body which is given for you," he is to lay his hands upon all the bread. It is this solemn imitation of our LORD'S act that constitutes the consecration of the bread to be for us (to use Justin Martyr's words) no longer common bread but heavenly bread. This "breaking of bread" is the title given to the Eucharist in several places in the New Testament (Acts ii. 42; xx. 7; 1 Cor. x. 16). A second fraction is made usually, when the ordinary wheaten bread is used, when the faithful are communicated.

Frankfort. A Council was held at Frankfort, 794 A.D., under the presidency of the Emperor Charlemagne, being in fact both a Diet of the Empire and an Ecclesiastical Synod. The most important points touched upon by the assembly as a Church Council were the doctrine of Adoptionism and the Worship of Images. The first of these is treated in the first Canon; and the Bishops Felix, of Urgel, in Catalonia, and Elipand, of Toledo, defenders of the heresy, were condemned.

The second Canon discusses the Worship of Images. The Church in the East had for many years been disturbed by the violence of two parties, one in favor of images, the other, the Iconoclasts, bitterly opposed to their use in any way. The Iconoclasts had prevailed for some time, and even in 754 A.D. had procured the condemnation of images by a Synod of Bishops. But when Leo IV. died, after a brief reign, his widow Irene, who ruled as guardian for her son Constantine VI., reversed the policy of the government and the decision of the Synod. Accordingly, a Council was assembled at Nicæa (reckoned the Seventh General Council), in which it was determined that images, or at least paintings or mosaics, "are to be set up for kissing and honorable reverence, but not for that real service which belongs to the Divine Nature alone." The acts of this Council were sanctioned by Pope Adrian, who sent a copy of them to Charlemagne; Charlemagne, however, so far from receiving them without hesitation, employed Alcuin to controvert them; and further gathered as many as three hundred Bishops, with two Legates from Rome, at Frankfort, where the Eastern Synod was condemned, and "both adoration and service of all kinds to images" was refused. But Adrian, notwithstanding this serious difference of opinion, still remained on friendly terms with Charlemagne.

Free-Will. There are ever apparently opposing principles in this visible nature, in our human nature, in the Divine nature. In nature we accept and act upon them because we cannot avoid them, but can combine and use them, or else restrain and avert their consequences. In the Divine nature we see mercy and justice apparently, it may be rashly alleged, in opposition, but reverence and the acknowledgment of an eternal wisdom keep us from misconstruing either, or pushing our conceptions of the one to the denial of the other. But in dealing with our own capacities and GOD-given qualities we argue very frequently without due consideration. What are the limits of necessity, and within what limits does freedom of will act? If these can be practically determined we can let subtle disquisitions pass. Necessity is, first, in the finite bounds of our mortal nature as living only in time, bound to earth, able to employ only natural material instruments, though enjoying the widest range of thought; and again, in the sphere of thought, the limitation of being able to properly conceive of and systematize those facts, spiritual, logical, and material, which pertain to our human nature, for we cannot conceive of any consistent theory upon the nature of angels, and we know only so much of GOD's nature as is revealed to us by Him through His SON. The sin-taint is another mysterious limitation we inherit, and we have a further limit in having to use agents, and to combine special means in accordance with known laws in the short space of each one's mortal life. The resulting forces and influences are complex and varying, being enforced, set free, or enforced by varying combinations not in human power to control, but only to guide and use. But within these limitations we have a freedom of will which makes us each a responsible agent. To be in His image we must have something, sin-stained, yet something of His will in whose image we are

It is this responsibility of being permitted to act for ourselves, to choose what we shall do, how we shall use the life, the capacities, the time, the education, the position, the religion He covers us with, the enjoyments as well as the ills, the stern duties as well as the softer pleasures; it is how we shall choose to use these and their like that makes us accountable beings to GOD, to our fellow-men, to our own conscience here in life, and at the bar of judgment hereafter, for we are all subject to GOD'S Law, order, and harmony; and liberty and free-will are not anarchy and disobedience, though sin has so injured them that many men so miscall and therefore misuse them. Bishop Butler acutely remarks that though men may theoretically assert a preordained necessity, yet practically they must act as though such necessity did not exist. And it must be so, or all Law would cease, for no one could be justly held accountable if he were not free. Choice in human agents implies a moral obligation. So no action, in itself indifferent, but may be made the means of a good or bad result. Through our sin-taint all our acts are stained with this evil, despite a longing to do better. In this we feel our short-coming and our feebleness. The freedom of the will may, does in many, become the means of the worst slavery, a lawless willfulness. To free us from this, first by example, and then by His direct help, and by taking us into Himself, our LORD came upon earth, made His atonement, effected His resurrection, founded His Church, gave His sacraments. His free human will was subordinated to His Divine will, and made perfectly consonant with it. At all times and in all points CHRIST, the LORD of nature, submitted to the limitations of our nature and the action of those laws which constrain us, and through this obedience made Himself acquainted with our griefs and bore our infirmities. And at every point He taught that he was submitting His will to His FATHER'S will. "In the volume of the book it is written of me I delight to do Thy will, O my GOD; yea, Thy Law is within my heart" (Ps. xl. 7, 8). It was of His own free-will He suffered, was crucified, dead, and buried. Of His own free-will He took up our human life, His human life, again and made it immortal. He calls for a willing, a free obedience, full of love and loyalty to Him, for He can make us free indeed, as redeeming us from the bondage to sin. A consecrated freedom of will, then, in CHRIST is the true liberty wherewith CHRIST has made us free. And this freedom of the will is joyous and full of life, taking the ills that befall as disciplinary and rising above them, using the things of this world and not abusing them, living in the gifts of CHRIST'S Church, the means of grace, the sacraments, and the inner meditation and conscious, conscientious effort to subdue the carnal will and to bring it into a loving subjection to the will of CHRIST. GOD the FATHER created us in His own image by His will, and we must by this have been at first created as free within our finite sphere as He in His boundless power. GOD the SON has redeemed us from the slavery of sin, and has made us free in Himself, with restored rights and privileges. GOD the HOLY GHOST is that Spirit of the LORD, that Spirit of Liberty, overshadowing, pleading with, and leading us, given to us at our Confirmation to abide with us, sanctifying us with the perfect law of liberty. So St. Paul, in the very Epistle quoted often to destroy the Christian liberty, urges as his conclusion from his argument, "I beseech you, therefore, brethren, by the mercies of GOD, that ye present your bodies a living sacrifice, holy, acceptable unto GOD, which is your reasonable service" (Rom. xii. 1, 2). Our truest exercise of free-will is in using, in this life, the fullness of our Christian rights for our eternal life hereafter. (Browne on XXXIX. Articles, Art. X.)

Friday. Good-Friday, the day upon which the Atonement for the sins of the whole world was made, has left its impress upon each Friday of the year as the Resurrection has carried the Law of worship on the Sabbath to the first day of the week, and has made every Sunday a commemoration of its glorious victory. Friday has from time immemorial been a weekly fast-day for this reason. But Good-Friday has been the central fast-day of the Christian year. It was strictly observed. Lent had its beginning from the fast of forty hours, which began on Good-Friday and lasted till midnight of Easter-even. The kiss of peace was not given; the Holy Communion was not celebrated; the penitents were reconciled. At one time there was no sermon on that day, but a Council of Toledo (633 A.D.) ordered that there should be a sermon on the Passion on that day. The later ceremonials, added during the mediæval times, were sometimes very significant and solemn. Our own Office for Good-Friday, throwing aside the "Office of the Presanctified" elements of the Holy Communion, has, by assigning an Epistle and Gospel for the day, given us the right to have a celebration on that day.

Funerals. (*Vide* BURIAL.) In all the details connected with a funeral, simplicity and reverent decency should be considered, and all display of any kind suppressed. The Jewish law of utter simplicity is an excellent one to follow. Still more so should be the feeling impressed upon all who assist in showing the last respect due to the mortal remains of the hope of a future resurrection the certainty of the promise. The early Christians bore their dead to the grave with glad hymns and with everything that could mark their faith in CHRIST. This principle should rule in all the arrangements which the rank and position of the departed demand should be made, and it must be the rule for all the preparations at the church.

G.

Galatians. Of all St. Paul's Epistles, except those to the Corinthians, this Epistle is the most vivid, direct, and personal. From it we learn much of the earlier movements of St. Paul after his conversion and before he appears as a participant in the active missionary work of the Church. But beside this it has a great doctrinal value, and is in its contents connected with the Epistle to the Romans, though this last is addressed to readers of a widely different character. The Galatians, a mixed population of the old Phrygian people, dominated by a Celtic conquering tribe, and this further mingled with the settlers from Rome, and Greece, and Judea, who settled there for purposes of trade or other business, were eager, rash, fickle, and easily persuaded. This will explain the astonished exclamations of the Apostle: "O foolish Galatians, who hath bewitched you?" (ch. iii.). "I marvel that ye are so soon removed from Him that called you into the grace of CHRIST unto another Gospel" (i. 6). Their fickleness brought the gain to the Church of this Epistle, which stands forth of untold value in New Testament history, and in the development of the revelation and doctrine of the great Apostle. The chapters we must remember are late and arbitrary divisions, more for convenience than anything else, so that the argument really passes on beyond our present grouping, and arranges itself somewhat differently from what we would suppose it, were we to cling to the chapters only. The Epistle naturally subdivides itself into four great groups.

I. The salutation. The Apostle declares his independent appointment by our LORD to establish his authority and the authenticity of the Gospel he preached. After expressing his surprise that they should change from what he taught, he goes into personal details, extending to the end of the second chapter, in which he proves his independent call, the fullness of the report of the Faith from CHRIST Himself, and the acknowledgment of it by the other Apostles, the chiefest of whom he withstood and rebuked openly upon the very false doctrinal grounds which had now misled the Galatians.

II. But these Galatians were deceived by some who claimed to preach the Gospel (but it was only a perversion), and who persuaded them that they must be circumcised and keep Moses' Law. This was contrary to his preaching. They were not Jews, they were not bound by the Law. They were heirs of Abraham, but not under the covenant of circumcision, but were justified through the like faith he had before he received this covenant, by the promise of the Gospel; they inherited as heirs through the faith of Abraham, yet uncircumcised, under the promise of the CHRIST to come. Their heirship is through the baptism into atonement of CHRIST, and they have by it the freedom of the Gospel (ch. ii. and iii.).

III. But this heirship leads him to speak of the difference of the two covenants, and the bondage of the one contrasted with the life of the second under which they inherit. They inherit by the righteousness, that is, by the Faith of CHRIST. They are not bound by Judaic days, and times, and seasons. This freedom of CHRIST gives them no right to do evil, to live after the flesh in its lusts, but calls them to the love, joy, and glorious sanctifying works of the Spirit. If we live in the Spirit—by it we cry Abba, Father—let us walk in the Spirit (ch. iv. and v.).

IV. The last part is taken up with advice so throughly earnest and full of the Apostle's energy, that the Epistle appears to end abruptly. He reverts to his warning against false teachers, and claims for himself the highest authority: "From henceforth let no man trouble me, for I bear in my body the marks of the LORD JESUS."

Its date may be placed as between 57 and 58 A.D. It is doctrinally valuable for the exposition it gives of the Justification by Faith (ch. ii. 16, and iii.). Historically it is valuable because of the incidental proof it gives of the equality of the Apostles and the disproof it furnishes of the Peterian claims of the Roman See (ch. ii. 11-21). It is one of the most ardent personal and expostulatory of the Pauline Epistles, exhibiting the large heart of the great Apostle.

Gehenna. Literally, the valley of Hinnom, south of Jerusalem. The valley where all filth and carrion of every kind was cast; polluted at first by fires to Moloch, and then by the carcasses cast there; and in it were continual fires kept up. It became the type of the place of everlasting punishment among the Jews before our LORD's coming, and so was fitly used by Him and by St. James, iii. 6, as the name of that dread place. The term Hell, equivalent to Gehenna, is used in Matt. v. 29, 30; x. 28; xxiii. 15, 33; Mark ix. 43, 45; Luke xii. 5; and Hell-fire or fire of Gehenna in Matt. v. 22; xviii. 9; Mark ix. 47; and Jas. iii. 6. It is a narrow and trifling mode of escaping the full sense of Our LORD's words now to give the term Gehenna the local meaning it may have had *before* the Jews themselves had used it as a figure of the dread place of unending woe, for no Jew in Jerusalem could then have so understood it, when our LORD called the future abode of the wicked Gehenna.

General Convention. The name of the representative body having supreme legislative jurisdiction in the system of federated Dioceses, known as the Protestant Episcopal Church in the United States of America, and in the dependencies thereof.

In giving an account of the General Convention it is proposed to speak,—

I. Of its origin and nature.

II. Of its form and method of operation as prescribed by the written Constitution adopted by the several Dioceses.

III. Of the nature and limitations of its constitutional powers.

IV. Of changes in its form, jurisdiction, and constituency resulting from its own action.

I. *Origin and Nature.*—At the close of the Revolutionary war in this country the Church existed in each State as an independent body. This body was actually connected with the original Church of CHRIST by virtue of the participation of its members in the faith and sacraments of His appointment and their relation to the Ministry of His commission, but it was in each case imperfect. It lacked the crown and completion essential to the perfection of every particular Church, and to be supplied by Episcopal authority. Prior to the Revolution the Church, in each colony, had been under the jurisdiction of the English Episcopate. During the Revolution that jurisdiction was incapable of being exercised, and was in abeyance. After the Revolution it was still incapable of being exercised, and all claim to it was abandoned. Practically the Church in each State was in the position of a Diocese temporarily deprived of its Diocesan. The Church in any State was free to seek its own completion in the Episcopate, and to continue its existence with or without combination with the Church in other States. Supposing that the Church in each State had obtained a Bishop of its own, there would have been among them all unity and cohesion resulting from their common dependence upon Episcopal government. Had they chosen to pursue this course their right to do so would have been unquestionable. And their right to proceed to the formation of a common organization and to the adoption of certain principles to which they mutually bound themselves—provided that they did not thereby cut themselves off from that dependence upon Episcopal jurisdiction which was essential to the continuance of their legitimate connection with the Church of CHRIST—must be allowed to be equally unquestionable.

In point of fact the right to move in both these directions not only existed, but was recognized and exercised. The course pursued by the Church in the several States, although not the same in each, was in all such as to establish the conclusion that each one was, and regarded itself as, an independent body so far as the others were concerned. In Connecticut the Church sought first to complete itself by procuring a Bishop. In some of the other States the Church sought first to procure a common organization and union, and afterwards to procure Bishops for the several members of that union. But that union was not effected by those who sought it without the consent of the representatives of the Church in each State represented; nor was the consent of those representatives given without the express permission of their constituency; nor, again, was either the Constitution which was adopted by that consent, or the authority of the General Convention which was established by that Constitution, regarded as binding upon the Church in such States as were not represented, or had not consented although they were represented.

The two great movements for the organization of the Church in this country, which resulted in the establishment of the body which we are now considering, may be called the Episcopal and the Conventional. The success of both stamped upon our Ecclesiastical system the complex character which is original with and peculiar to itself. The combination of Episcopal government, recognized as deriving its authority from the Divine source of CHRIST'S commission to His Apostles and their successors, with the government of delegates, deriving their authority from the commission of the people, or of the body of the Church, composed of the laity and of the subordinate orders of the clergy, was the result of these two movements which in the course of Divine Providence began to take form about the same time. To the Church in Connecticut must be attributed the honor of the Episcopal—to the Church in Pennsylvania that of the Conventional—movement. The movement in Connecticut antedates that in Pennsylvania by a month or more, if we look to the formal beginnings; but the Connecticut movement leads to the possession of a complete Church organization in that State some four years before the Pennsylvania movement attains the accomplishment of its purpose by the complete organization of a Convention duly authorized to act for the Churches which in that and other States had joined in it.

The election of a Bishop took place in Connecticut on the 25th of March, 1783 A.D.; the consecration of that Bishop on the 14th of November, 1784 A.D., and his reception by the Diocese, on his return from the place where he had been consecrated, on the 3d of August, 1785 A.D. It is important to bear in mind these dates in comparison with those which now follow.

The first step towards the formation of an Ecclesiastical Union in the different States was taken at a meeting in May, 1784 A.D., at Philadelphia, of several members of the Church in that city, which appointed "a Standing Committee of the Episcopal Church in this State," and authorized that Committee to "correspond and confer with representatives from the Episcopal Church in the other States, or any of them, and assist in framing an Ecclesiastical government." (Bishop White's Memoirs, p. 72.) At this meeting, which, of course, was purely voluntary, certain propositions were agreed upon which were to be regarded in the proposed correspondence and conference as fundamental principles. In this statement of fundamental principles appears the germ afterwards developed into the General Convention,—a representative body of clergy and laity which should have the sole power to make Canons and laws. The Bishops were anticipated as a future accession to the orders of the ministry then in the country, but they were, like the rest of the clergy, to be under law, and law was to be enacted only by the representative body of clergy and laity jointly. The whole scheme is unformed, but the idea of a representative body of Clergy and laity with supreme powers of legislation is plainly apparent.

In the same month of May, 1784 A.D., a meeting of clergymen in New Brunswick, N. J., discussed the project of Ecclesiastical union, but adjourned after receiving information from one of their number of the action already taken in the Church in Connecticut. Another meeting of clergy from several States assembled at the call of the Standing Committee above mentioned, in New York, in October, 1784 A.D. This meeting was, like the others, purely voluntary, there having been, as Bishop White observes, " no authorities from the Churches in the several States even in the appointments of the members, which were made from the congregations to which they respectively belonged, except of Mr. Parker, from Massachusetts, of Mr. Marshall, from Connecticut, and of those who attended from Pennsylvania. Even from these States there was no further authority than to deliberate and propose; accordingly the acts of the body were in the form of recommendation and proposal." (Bishop White's Memoirs, pp. 80, 81.)

At this meeting it was proposed that there should be a *General Convention* of the Episcopal Church in the United States of America, to which the Episcopal Church in each State was to send deputies, although associated congregations in two or more States might send deputies jointly, and that this General Convention should be composed of clergy and laity, deliberating in one body, but voting separately, the concurrence of both being necessary to give validity to every measure. The first meeting of this Convention, it was further proposed, should be at Philadelphia, the Tuesday before the next feast of St. Michael, " to which it is hoped and earnestly desired that the Episcopal Churches in the United States will send their clerical and lay deputies, duly instructed and authorized to proceed in the necessary business herein proposed for their deliberation."

On the 27th of September, 1785 A.D., according to this recommendation, assembled in Philadelphia a Convention of clerical and lay deputies from seven of the thirteen States, viz., from New York to Virginia, inclusive, with the addition of South Carolina. (Bishop White's Memoirs, p. 22.) At this Convention there was adopted a General Ecclesiastical Constitution, which may be considered as the first draft of that which was finally established in 1789 A.D. At the next Convention of delegates from the same seven States, held at Philadelphia, in June, 1786 A.D., this draft was revised, and the following resolution was adopted: " *Resolved,* That it be recommended to the Conventions of this Church in the several States represented in this Convention that they authorize and empower their deputies to the next General Convention, after we shall have obtained a Bishop or Bishops in our Church, to confirm and ratify a general Constitution respecting both the doctrine and discipline of the Protestant Episcopal Church in the United States of America." This Convention adjourned, subject to the call of its Committee of Correspondence (awaiting a communication from the English Bishops), pursuant to which call it met again at Wilmington, Delaware, October 20, 1786 A.D. This Convention at Wilmington, on a question put, made the following significant decision, viz. : that it had " no authority to admit as members persons deriving their appointment not from a State Convention, but from a particular parish or parishes only." (Bioren's General Convention Journal, p. 39.)

In view of the foregoing, it appears that the General Convention, as projected, was to be a representative body of clergy and laity, including Bishops among the former, constituted of delegates not from parishes as congregations, but from Conventions of Churches in the several States, and having legislative jurisdiction over the members of the Churches which should duly authorize deputies to ratify the general Constitution. It further appears that up to and including the year 1786 A.D. there was in existence no General Convention, properly so called, understanding by that term a body representing and authorized to give law to the Church in all the States. The want of an entire representation, the absence of any claim on the part of such Churches as were represented over those which were not represented, the limited power of the delegates, which prevented their action from being of any authority over the Churches from which they came,—these facts, taken in connection with the fact that the only representation required or recognized was the representation not of congregations but of State Conventions, establish with certainty the position that the Churches in the States were the independent factors of the union which was ultimately established, and as representative of which the General

Convention came into existence. And the evidence shows that prior to 1789 A.D. there was no common authority recognized by these Churches. Agreeable to this is the remark of Bishop White, "that the few general principles recommended by the meeting of 1784 A.D., and adopted by that of 1785 A.D., became a bond of union, and the only one acted under until the year 1789 A.D. For as to the General Constitution framed at the period now before us (1785 A.D.), it stood on recommendation only, and was of no use except in helping to convince those who were attached to that mode of transacting business that it was very idle to bring gentlemen together from different States for the purpose of such inconclusive proceedings." (Memoirs, p. 96.)

On the 28th of July, 1789 A.D., however, representatives from the seven States which had sent delegates in 1786 A.D. were assembled at Philadelphia. The deputies at this Convention were at the beginning of the session called upon to declare their powers relative to the object of the resolution which had been adopted in 1786 A.D., recommending the Conventions of the Church in the several States represented to authorize and empower their deputies to confirm and ratify a general Constitution respecting both doctrine and discipline; and in response to this call "gave information that they came fully authorized to ratify a Book of Common Prayer, etc., for the use of the Church." (Bioren, 48.)

The Constitution which had been proposed in 1786 A.D. was at this session considered and adopted as amended, and by virtue of such adoption became binding upon the Churches in the seven States whose representatives had been empowered to that end. The concluding act of this session was the appointment of a committee for the purpose, among other things, of forwarding its minutes and proceedings " to the Eastern and other Churches *not included in this Union*, to notify to them the time and place to which this Convention shall adjourn, and request their attendance at the same for the good purposes of union and general government." (Bioren, 64.)

At the adjourned meeting of this Convention held in Philadelphia, September 29, 1789 A.D., the Constitution adopted at the last session having been amended in respect to the distribution of powers to be exercised by the General Convention, was adopted as amended, not only by the deputies of the seven States previously represented, but also by the representatives of the Churches in Connecticut, Massachusetts, and New Hampshire, who were present and duly authorized for such adoption. Thus the Churches of ten of the States, by virtue of the voluntary assent of each, declared by representatives duly authorized for the purpose, established the General Convention and placed themselves under its government, vesting it with certain powers, and confirming those powers by the charter of a written Constitution. This Constitution, and by consequence the jurisdiction of the General Convention, then extended to those Churches only which had up to that time acceded to that instrument. But provision was made for the extension of the jurisdiction of the General Convention by the constitutional declaration that a Protestant Episcopal Church in any of the United States not now represented might at any time thereafter be admitted on acceding to the Constitution. In pursuance of which the Church in every State of the Civil Union afterwards became (at greater or less intervals respectively) a member of the Ecclesiastical Union; sending its representatives to the General Convention, and conforming to the laws of its enactment; the extension of the jurisdiction of that body thus keeping even pace with the expansion of its constituency.

Thus the idea conceived, and in substance formulated, so far back as 1784 A.D. was through progressive steps extending over a period of five years, at last brought into effect. The supreme legislative authority over the members of such Churches in the States as consented to the General Constitution was vested in a representative body of clergy and laity, and provision was made for the extension of that authority throughout the Civil Union as soon as the Churches in all the States should be willing to submit themselves to it.

And it is desirable here to note that the Church in each State subsequently acceding to the Constitution bore the same relation to the Ecclesiastical Union, and to the General Convention, as if it had been one of the original seven or ten; and that the Church in each State being the equivalent of the Diocese (*i.e.*, the field or jurisdiction of the single Bishop), the Ecclesiastical Union is a union of Dioceses; and that each Diocese, though it be (as in some cases it has since been) only a part of the Church within a State, holds, the Constitution having been acceded to, the same relation to the Ecclesiastical Union and the General Convention as if it were one of such original members.

That the Ecclesiastical body in each State was independent on all the others was the result of the independent position of the States themselves. That these States were, in Confederate Union, working out under difficulties the problem of their ultimate nationality, made it altogether natural that the Churches should be drawn together in the effort to unite themselves under a common Ecclesiastical government. That the Churches should move slowly and with difficulty was not surprising in view of the varying views of its members in different places, some thinking that the original Constitution of the Church already provided sufficiently for the working together of neighboring Churches under a common Episcopate, and some thinking that Episcopal government was only another name for foreign interference and perhaps domestic tyranny, and that a system of popular representation was essential to the preservation of popular liberties. And beside these differences there was the difference which was obvious in the political contests of the day; some standing for the principle of the self-government of the States as the preservative against the dangers of centralization of power, and some dwelling more upon the idea of the substantial unity of the whole country, resulting from the unity of its inhabitants as being in the main of one blood and one inheritance of civil freedom. There was, moreover, during the first part of the incubation of this scheme of Ecclesiastical Union a very serious uncertainty as to two points: 1st, whether the application to the English Bishops for consecration was to succeed; and, 2d, whether the Civil Union was to continue to be a mere confederacy or was to be established on the basis of a real Nationality. Neither of these doubts was set at rest until after the Convention of 1786 A.D. But with the consecration of Bishops for New York and Pennsylvania in 1787 A.D., and the adoption of the Constitution of the United States in the same year, the promoters of the Ecclesiastical Union found themselves on firmer ground, and neither the accomplishment of that Union nor the form in which it shaped itself were uninfluenced by these events. In the two years which followed the minds of men were prepared to receive with greater unanimity the ideas that the working system of Church government should be co-extensive with the operation of the civil system, and that legislative authority in the Church should not be exercised apart from the official sanction of the Episcopal order. Neither of these ideas then had its full effect, but they were both then put in the way of attaining that universal recognition which they have since received.

II. *Constitutional Form and Method of Operation.*—The General Convention, as may be inferred from what has been said, has passed through several phases.

In what may be regarded as the incipient stages of its growth it appears as an assembly of clergymen and laymen coming from the Church in several States, deliberating together, and voting by States; each State having one vote. This form continues from 1785 A.D. to 1789 A.D. It next appears as an assembly of the same sort, deliberating in the same way, but voting by clergy and laity, each State having in fact two votes, but the preponderance being given to a majority of the States represented in one order concurring with a majority of the States represented in the other order. This form and method are incorporated into the Constitution of August, 1789 A.D., which also provides for a change contingent upon the acquisition of three or more Bishops in the number of the States represented. The contemplated change was the deliberation of the General Convention in two separate Houses, the one composed, as before, of clergy and laity, and voting as before; the other composed of Bishops only, which latter was to be a House of Revision, having power to revise and reject acts proposed by the clergy and laity, who had, however, the power to overrule the rejection by a three-fifths vote of their House.

The next phase is that of a body composed of a House of Bishops and a House of Clerical and Lay Deputies, each having power to originate and propose acts, and the concurrence of both being requisite to constitute the act of the body, but with the provision that the negative of the House of Bishops might be overruled by the vote of four-fifths of the Lower House. This form and method appear in the Constitution of October, 1789 A.D., and continue until 1808 A.D., when by an amendment of the Constitution the power of the Lower House to overrule the negative of the Upper House disappears and both Houses are recognized as co-ordinate branches of one Supreme Legislature, the concurrence of both being necessary to constitute the act of the body, and each having an absolute negative on the acts of the other; the House of Bishops being, however, required to signify their approbation or disapprobation of the acts of the Lower House (the latter with their reasons in writing) within three days.

It appears, then, that by the Constitution the General Convention is a body composed of a House of Bishops and a House of Clerical and Lay Deputies, and that the concurrence of both these is necessary to constitute an act of the body. The method of operation contemplated by the Constitution is that an act proposed in either House, and adopted by it, is to be submitted to the other for its concurrence. If the desired concurrence be yielded, the act is no longer the act of either House, but of the whole body, and without such concurrence no act can become a law. An act adopted by the Lower House and not adopted or rejected by the Upper House it is true becomes law, but that is not because the power of enacting laws belongs, under any circumstances, to the Lower House alone, but because the Upper House, not having signified its disapprobation, as it had power to do, is to be presumed to have approved the proposed measure.

It is observable that the Constitution in prescribing the form and method of the two Houses, is much more explicit in reference to the House of Deputies than in reference to the House of Bishops. This is to be explained by the fact that the House of Deputies was in fact organized before the House of Bishops, and was in a position in the adoption of the Constitution to describe precisely the form and method which it was intended to have, whereas the House of Bishops was yet, in fact, to be established after its legal existence had been recognized.

The clerical and lay delegates from the

States had begun to regard themselves as a General Convention, while they were still a voluntary body, before it was decided whether the application to England for Bishops was to be granted. And when the application was granted, and there were Bishops among the number of those States which were represented, then the representatives proceeded to provide a place for the Bishops as a separate House, by way of addition to the proposed Constitution. The Constitution as proposed in 1786 A.D. provided that in every State where there should be a Bishop duly consecrated and settled, who should have acceded to the Constitution, he should be considered as a member of the Convention *ex officio*, and that a Bishop should always preside if any of the Episcopal order were present. This was before there was a Bishop in the number of the States then represented in the Union. Bishop Seabury had been consecrated in 1784 A.D., but Connecticut was not a member of the Union. In 1789 A.D., however, Bishop White and Bishop Provoost had been consecrated for Pennsylvania and New York, and as there was the anticipation of including Bishop Seabury in the Union, or of having another Bishop consecrated for one of the States actually represented, or of both, it was thought desirable to provide for the session of these, and other Bishops that might be obtained, as a separate House; but the provision was made, as before said, by way of addition or amendment to the plan already incorporated into the Constitution.

In truth, the constitutional provisions for the session of General Convention in two Houses wore every appearance of having been an after-thought; and while explicit directions are given in regard to the Convention which are obviously applicable only to the House of Deputies, the House of Bishops appears to have been recognized, and its organization and arrangement to have been left, with whatever motive, to itself. The extent of this provision as to this House is that the Bishops of this Church, where there shall be three or more in the number of those States which shall have adopted the Constitution, shall form a separate House, that they shall have a right to originate and propose acts, and shall have a negative upon the acts of the House of Deputies as above said. What shall constitute a quorum, for instance, is not specified, and other omissions might be noted.

In directions apparently applicable to the Lower House, however, the provision is that the Church in a majority of the Dioceses which shall have adopted the Constitution shall be represented before the Convention shall proceed to business; that the Church in each Diocese shall be entitled to a representation both of clergy and laity, and that such representation shall consist of not more than four clergymen and four laymen (communicants) residing in, and chosen in the manner prescribed by, the Convention of the Diocese which they respectively represent; and that in all cases, when required by the clerical or lay representation from any Diocese, the vote shall be of a certain kind.

It is important to observe that the method of voting peculiar to the House of Deputies and provided for in Art. ii. of the Constitution is not made obligatory in all cases, but only when required by a clerical or a lay representation from any Diocese. If no such requirement be made, the vote of the House may be taken by acclamation or by division, or even by individual ayes and nays, as usual in other deliberative bodies. But if any clerical or any lay deputation, from any Diocese, require the vote to be taken in the constitutional method, the vote must be so taken; and it is presumable that where the Canons provide that a measure must be adopted by a constitutional majority this method of voting must be pursued by this House.

This method is properly called voting by Dioceses and Orders. It is not a vote by Dioceses alone. It is not a vote by Orders alone. It is a vote by Dioceses and Orders. The manner of voting prior to the constitutional organization of the General Convention in 1789 A.D. was by States. The proposed Constitution of 1786 A.D. expresses what was the practice of that year and of previous years. The vote of the representatives of the Church was taken by States, the Church in each State having one vote, and the majority of suffrages being conclusive. By the Constitution of 1789 A.D. this method of voting was changed; but it was not changed by substituting the vote of the body of clergy and laity present for the vote of the Dioceses which they represented, but by the giving to the Church in each State or Diocese the privilege of two votes instead of one, and requiring that there should be a majority of two kinds corresponding to these two kinds of votes, clerical and lay. The majority, to be conclusive in legislative acts, is not a majority of States or Dioceses having one vote each, but a majority of all Dioceses represented by clergy, concurring with a majority of all Dioceses represented by laity. If a Diocese is represented only in one Order, of course it has only the vote of that Order; but it has the right to be represented by two Orders if it please, and then to have the two votes. If a Diocese be not represented by either clerical or lay delegates it has no vote; but it has the constitutional right to representation, and is therefore concluded by the acts of the body the same as if it had actually consented to them. But the votes of the representatives present are not, in this manner of voting, to be taken in a body. It is not a numerical majority that is conclusive, nor is it a majority of all the clerical representatives present concurring with a majority of all the lay representatives present, but a majority of all the *Dioceses* represented by *clergy*, concurring with a majority of all the *Dioceses* represented by *laity*.

And it is to be observed that this constitutional majority, as it is, on the one hand, not a mere numerical majority, so, on the other hand, is not necessarily identical with the consent of the Church in a majority of Dioceses. For, in fact, a concurrent majority of clerical and lay delegates may be so distributed as to carry a measure when there is no majority of Dioceses, considered as such, and voting in each case as a whole. A majority of clerical representatives of Dioceses counting from the north downward (supposing the case for the sake of example), concurring with a majority of lay representatives of Dioceses counted from the south upward, will carry a measure as well as a majority of Dioceses with solid clerical and lay vote counted from the north downward, or *vice versa*, or distributed anywhere throughout the Union. That the constitutional majority provided for by Art. ii. will generally be equivalent to the expression of the consent of the Church in a majority of Dioceses may be true. Practically there is, perhaps, little probability of the distinction being insisted on. But it is necessary that legal instruments should be understood as providing for possibilities as well as probabilities. And in considering the constitutional prescription for the method of operation of the General Convention in legislative enactments, it is necessary to apprehend exactly what the provision of the Constitution is, and to note that the vote described in Art. ii. is not necessarily identical with the vote of the Church by Dioceses.

III. *Nature and Limitations of Constitutional Powers.*—It might be supposed that a number of independent bodies coming together for the purpose of establishing a common government, and uniting in the adoption of a written Constitution, by the terms of which a common authority was recognized, would agree upon certain specific objects which they desired to put in charge of that common authority, and would be very precise in the designation both of the powers conferred and the powers reserved to themselves. In matters of civil government this course would undoubtedly be pursued. But perhaps it would be too much to expect such strictness in Ecclesiastical concerns, where, indeed, there may be less need for them on some accounts. Under the circumstances attending the constitutional establishment of the General Convention much, no doubt, would be taken for granted. Some defects of arrangement might be overlooked provided that the substantial purpose of union was attained. The feeling that those who were combining their Ecclesiastical interests were all basing their lives upon professed principles of Christian love which would be a safeguard against jealousies, animosities, and mutual exactions, might justly have weight: And the further feeling that, whatever difficulties might be in the way of formal union, and whatever construction might be put upon formal provisions, the members of the Church in the several States were united already, in the one Church of CHRIST's foundation, might account for some want of system. At all events, it is certain that the study of the Constitution will be very disappointing to one who expects to find in it anything approaching to a general statement of Church principles, or of all principles of government applicable to the union of the Churches. And with regard to the powers of the General Convention, remarkable as the fact is in view of the absolute novelty of such an institution, it must be said that they cannot be referred to any specific enumeration contained in the Constitution. The General Convention exists by virtue of the action of the Church in the Dioceses. The Constitution adopted by this Church is the written evidence of its establishment and its authority; but, being in existence, its authority is not specifically declared as to every particular, but is of that general character which belongs to supreme power. Yet, on the other hand, it is not to be inferred that the exercise of this power is arbitrary, either as to the sphere within which it is to operate, or as to the extent of its operation in that sphere.

Those who constituted the General Convention were competent to define and specify its powers, or to constitute it for a certain class of powers and leave it unlimited in the exercise of them; or to constitute it for a certain class of powers, particularly specifying some, and to impose upon it certain limitations in the exercise of its powers. The last of these three courses is what appears to have been chosen. The Constitution contemplates the General Convention as intrusted with the power of legislation. The acts which are adopted by both its Houses are to have the operation of law. But these are limitations imposed by the Constitution upon the exercise of this power. Apart from these limitations, the General Convention appears to possess power to pass laws on any subject as to which a National Church is free to legislate for its members. It can pass any law which the Dioceses together might pass for themselves, supposing them to be able to act together. They do, indeed, act together in all acts which it performs under the Constitution, and not contrary to the limitations which that instrument imposes. It acts for them; they act through it. When such action takes place, it is of superior obligation to the act of the Church in any Diocese. In respect to matters as to which there has been no such common action, the individual Diocese is free to act for itself in its own concerns. And what one Diocese may do for itself, two or more Dioceses may do for themselves in regard to matters of joint interest; subject always to the paramount authority of the General Convention, acting, as before said, under the Constitution and within constitutional limitations. The ability to pass laws obligatory upon the members of all the Dioceses, and irrespective of the consent of individual Dioceses, resulting from the assent of all the Dioceses to the Constitution, is a check upon the power of individual Dioceses. The safety of the individual Diocese from overbearing action on the part of the General Convention lies in the principles of limitation embodied in the Constitution, and only there.

To the Constitution, therefore, we look not for a complete enumeration of the powers and functions of the General Convention, nor for the precise statement of rights referred to the Dioceses, but rather for the evidence of a grant to the common authority of a supremacy including several specified powers, subject to definite limitations by which its action is controlled.

In considering this branch of the subject it will be most convenient to follow the order of the articles of the Constitution, although it is to be remembered that the present purpose is not analysis and explanation of the Constitution, but the ascertainment of the powers and limitations of power of the General Convention as indicated by that instrument. And it would be well for the reader also to bear in mind that, for the sake of brevity in a paper of this sort, it is necessary that, in most cases, conclusions should be stated rather than the grounds upon which these conclusions are based.

1. Things chiefly to be noted in the first article are (a) the establishment of the General Convention as a continuously existing body required to be in session at specified times of regular recurrence, and also authorized to meet at its own discretion in accordance with laws of its own adoption, its personal membership presumably varying, but the body itself not going out of existence. (See Digest, Tit. iii., Can. i, § 1.)

(b) The representative character of the body, and the constituency which is represented. The necessary representation before the General Convention can proceed to business is required to be that of the Church in a majority of the Dioceses which have acceded to the Constitution. The body then is a representative body, and the constituency is the Church in the Dioceses which have acceded to the Constitution.

(c) The provision that the representation from two Dioceses shall be sufficient to adjourn precludes the necessity of a stated session being omitted for the year appointed on account of the delay of the members in coming together. Without this provision, if there were present anything less than a quorum at the day appointed, there would be a necessity of going without a stated meeting for three years, and possibly of resorting to the inconvenient substitute of a special meeting. The expedient gives a sufficient time (and apparently an indefinite time within three years) for the delegates to assemble.

(d) The provision that in all business of the Convention freedom of debate is to be allowed; a provision too well understood and too constantly complied with to require any particular comment.

2. The provisions of Art. ii. of the Constitution have been already considered so far as they relate to the form and method of operation of the General Convention. What is here to be noted is their bearing upon the powers of that body. This article contains the most general grant of power which the representative body has received. The power, however, is not conveyed by the formal statement that the General Convention is authorized to do certain things, or all things of a certain kind; but it is, with equal effect, conferred in a different way; that is, by the abandonment on the part of the Dioceses of any right of objection to acts of the General Convention consummated in a specified way. The article reserves the right of the Church in each Diocese which shall have assented to the Constitution to be represented both by clergy and laity, and by a certain number; all Dioceses being entitled to equal representation. It provides a peculiar method of voting, which makes it impossible for a measure to pass the House of Deputies without the concurrence of a majority of Dioceses represented by clergy with a majority of Dioceses represented by laity, which, in most cases, though not necessarily, is equivalent to the expression of the will of a majority of Dioceses, and leaves it within the power not only of any Diocese, but of any delegation of any Diocese, to force this method of voting upon the rest; and then it precludes any Diocese from refusing to be bound by a measure so passed, not only when it may have voted against it, but even when it may not, in fact, have been represented. If the Church in a Diocese has not been represented, it shall nevertheless be bound by the acts of the Convention. A fuller and more exclusive grant of power it would be difficult to give. And the only limitation upon it, so far as this article is concerned, is that the acts shall be adopted in the method prescribed, if this method is demanded by any delegation, either clerical or lay.

There are, however, other limitations, which, though not stated in this article, are plainly inferable from other articles and from the nature of the case. For (A) the acts by which the Church in each Diocese is to be bound are the acts of the whole body of the General Convention, which, by Art. iii., involve the consent of the House of Bishops, in which each Diocese is represented by its own Bishop; and (B) the acts by which each Diocese is to be bound are acts of a legislative character. This, indeed, is nowhere expressly stated, but it is matter of necessary inference (a) from the expression of Art. iii., that acts of the Lower House proposed to and not acted on in the specified way by the House of Bishops *shall have the operation of law;* (*b*) from the pointed omission in Art. vi. to confer upon the General Convention in matters of trial and discipline any judicial power or anything further than the right to provide the mode of trying Bishops; (*c*) from the requirement (in Art. ix.) of a substantially different method of consent to the alteration of the Constitution from that required for acts of the General Convention.

3. Another constitutional limitation upon the power of the General Convention appears in the recognition and reservation of the right of every Diocese to the choice of its own Bishop. Article iv. provides that the Bishop or Bishops in every Diocese shall be chosen agreeable to such rules as shall be fixed by the Convention of that Diocese. This puts it beyond the power of the General Convention to impose a Bishop of its choice upon any existing Diocese. What the General Convention may do in the way of Canons prescribing certain qualifications and conditions to be complied with before the person chosen by a Diocese shall be consecrated by the Bishops of the Church is another question. The Bishops of the Church cannot be forced to consecrate the person chosen by a Diocese, and they, acting as a House of the General Convention, and concurring with the House of Deputies, may pass laws requiring a person chosen to possess certain qualifications, or to comply with certain conditions, before they will consecrate him. But that is a different thing from interfering with the choice itself.

4. In the matter of the formation of new Dioceses the Constitution confers upon the General Convention certain powers, to which also limitations are annexed.

The question how the General Convention, being created by the Dioceses, could possess power to form new Dioceses might occur to one who had regard only to the origin of the body. But in view of subsequent history the question implies no contradiction. The Dioceses were originally conterminous with the States. Increase of population made division sometimes desirable. New settlements in the Territories and in new States might not be so permanent as in the older communities. Dioceses might sometimes require readjustment. It was not expedient that such changes should be left entirely with the Dioceses particularly interested; but it was desirable, if not necessary, that there should be some common authority in the matter. By amendment to the Constitution this authority is lodged in General Convention.

It is important to observe the distinction between the admission of Dioceses and the formation of new Dioceses by the readjustment of Dioceses already admitted. Art. v. as it stands relates to two entirely distinct classes of cases. (See this distinction elaborately and conclusively maintained by Rev. J. H. Hopkins, D.D., in American Church Review, April, 1881 A.D., p. 135.)

The first part of it provides for the admission of a Protestant Episcopal Church in any of the United States or any Territory thereof on its accession to the Constitution. The second part (by amendment first introduced in 1838 A.D., but afterwards modified) provides for the formation of new Dioceses by the readjustment of those already admitted. At the time of the first introduction of this amendment the words " in any Territory thereof" were introduced into the first part of the Article. Under this, the Church in any State or Territory has the right to admission to the Union upon accession to the Constitution. That fact being certified to the General Convention, it takes its place as a matter of course so far as the Constitution is concerned. The remainder of the article, however, refers to the other class of cases; cases, viz., of Dioceses reformed from a part of a Diocese already admitted, or from parts of two or more such Dioceses.

In such cases the General Convention has constitutional power to act, and without such action no such readjustment can take place. The consent of the General Convention is necessary in order to such readjustment, and that consent the General Convention is forbidden to give unless certain things appear. No new Diocese can be formed within the limits of any other Diocese, nor by the junction of two or more Dioceses, or parts of Dioceses, without the consent of the Bishop and Convention of each of the Dioceses concerned; nor unless General Convention have satisfactory assurance of a suitable provision for the support of the Episcopate in a contemplated new Diocese; nor unless such new Diocese shall contain six parishes and six Presbyters who have been canonically resident and regularly settled for at least a year and qualified to vote for a Bishop; nor if the formation of a new Diocese on such a basis would reduce any existing Diocese to less than twelve parishes and twelve Presbyters; nor if a city would be by the change made to form more than one Diocese. The action contemplated by the Constitution in the case of such changes is the action of Dioceses; the function of the General Convention is that of ratification, the power of ratification being limited by the above-named conditional requirements.

5. The provisions of Art. vi. are worthy of careful attention. They distinctly confer the power of legislation upon General Convention in respect to matters which involve the exercise of judicial power, and pointedly refrain from conferring the judicial power itself. The power of prescribing the mode of exercising judicial power is a high function of legislation. This power is given to the General Convention in a specified class of cases, and in that only. " The mode of trying Bishops shall be provided by the General Convention." This phrase appears to have been understood to involve a power to

prescribe all that relates to the trial of a Bishop, exclusive of the power to conduct the trial itself. Perhaps it does; although so to interpret it is to give rather a wide construction to the word *mode*. Understanding the legislative power in this class of cases, however, to be conferred upon General Convention, that body has the right, in the exercise of this power, to determine the grounds of trial, or what is or is not an offense for which trial may be had; the manner in which accusation shall be formulated, notified to the accused and judicially examined, and the sentence appropriate to offenses proved to have been committed. The judicial function is the determination of the questions whether certain alleged actions constitute an offense; whether allegations are proved; to what penalties certain actions, being proved, are entitled under the law; and, these questions being determined, the actual pronouncement of the sentence. This latter power is by the Constitution reserved to the Bishops in *all* cases of ministerial discipline, and the legislative power of the General Convention which enables it to prescribe the composition of a court for the trial of Bishops is subject to the constitutional limitation that such court shall be composed of Bishops only. The same kind of power is denoted by the expression used in this article in describing the function of the Diocesan Conventions in respect to the trial of subordinate clergy: " In every Diocese the mode of trying Presbyters and Deacons may be instituted by the Convention of the Diocese." This is a constitutional guaranty of a reserved Diocesan right that the trial of the clergy of the Diocese, as distinguished from its Bishop, shall be according to the laws of the Diocese. Or, if that phrase be considered objectionable, it is at least a permission embodied in the Constitution that each Diocese shall possess that right; and while that permission stands the Constitution forbids to the General Convention what it allows to the Dioceses. On what ground, therefore, the General Convention can, as it has done by Canon, determine offenses and penalties in the case of Presbyters and Deacons, or provide a Court of Appeal having jurisdiction over these cases originating in the Dioceses, as it has been often urged to do, is not apparent from the Constitution. That instrument empowers and directs the General Convention to provide the mode of trying Bishops. It limits the power of the General Convention by directing that courts for that purpose shall be composed of Bishops only, and by reserving to the Diocesan Conventions the right to institute the mode of trying Presbyters and Deacons, and by reserving to the Bishops the right to pronounce sentence in every case of ministerial discipline.

The prescribing of qualifications to be possessed, and conditions to be complied with by those who are to be ordained, is an essential function of the office to which the power of ordination belongs. It is therefore in its nature a power of the Episcopate, and is not by the Constitution expressly conferred upon the General Convention. In so far, however, as it is a legislative power, it may be understood to be included in the general grant to that body; and in point of fact appears not to have been exercised by the Bishops in our system, except as composing a part of the General Convention and in concurrence with the House of Clerical and Lay Deputies. The same remark may be made in reference to the prescribing of the terms upon which ministers ordained by one Bishop may be permitted to officiate within the jurisdiction of another. It is, like the other, essentially an Episcopal power. And the provisions of Art. vii. being prohibitions of ordination and license, except under certain conditions, might be considered as constitutional limitations in the power of the Episcopate rather than of the General Convention. But inasmuch as the provisions of this article contemplate the passing of Canons as to these matters, and Canons are not in our system enacted by Bishops alone, but by General Convention, they may be properly considered as limitations of the power of the General Convention. In this view the body is by them precluded from enacting any Canon which will legalize the ordination of any person until he shall have been examined by the Bishop and by two Presbyters, and shall have subscribed the specified declaration of belief in the Holy Scriptures of the Old and New Testaments as being the Word of GOD and containing all things necessary to salvation, and of conformity to the doctrines and worship of the Protestant Episcopal Church in the United States ; and from enacting any Canon permitting a person, ordained by a foreign Bishop, to officiate as a minister of this Church without his subscription of the same declaration.

7. The eighth article of the Constitution devolves upon the General Convention the power of establishing, which involves the power of altering, a Book of Common Prayer, Administration of Sacraments, and other Rites and Ceremonies of the Church, Articles of Religion and Ordinal, providing that such formularies when established by the General Convention shall be used in those Dioceses which have adopted the Constitution. This power conferred by the Constitution of 1789 A.D. upon the General Convention is, however, by amendment of 1811 A.D., subjected to the limitation that no alteration or addition shall be made in these formularies unless the same be proposed in one General Convention, and by a resolve thereof made known to the Convention of every Diocese, and adopted at the subsequent General Convention. The terms of this limitation are very explicit. The alteration which is made in any session of the General Convention must be "the same" as was proposed in the last General

Convention, and by resolve thereof made known to the Convention of every Diocese. An alteration proposed in one General Convention may, of course, be modified or changed in that General Convention. But when it is finally adopted by that General Convention, and by a resolve thereof made known to the Dioceses, it comes up before the next General Convention, not for amendment or modification, but either for adoption or rejection. If it is amended it becomes a new proposition, and in order to adoption must be, by a new resolve, made known to the Dioceses, and must come before the next General Convention as before, either for adoption or rejection.

This strictness was applicable to the Lectionary, or order of reading Holy Scriptures, as to the rest of the Prayer-Book, until 1877 A.D., when the third clause of Art. viii. was added, whereby the General Convention is permitted to alter the Lectionary at any session ("from time to time" are the words used), but on condition that no act for the purpose shall be valid which is not voted for by a majority of all the Bishops entitled to seats in the House of Bishops, and by a majority of all the Dioceses entitled to representation in the House of Deputies. The manner of voting under this article in the House of Deputies is not specified, but the consent required is the consent of a majority of the Dioceses *entitled* to representation. That something more is required in this case than the vote described in Art. ii. appears from the facts, (1) that the vote by Dioceses and Orders does not of necessity signify the consent of a majority of the Dioceses, but may only signify the consent of the clergy of one set of Dioceses concurring with the laity of another set of Dioceses; and (2) that the vote described in Art. ii. need only express the concurrent consent of clergy and laity in a majority of a quorum of Dioceses; and, the quorum being the representation of a majority of Dioceses entitled to representation, the majority of the quorum is less than a majority of the Dioceses. The manner of voting under this amendment to Art. viii. not being prescribed, it seems that the vote may be taken in any manner which will express the required consent. But if the ordinary vote by Dioceses and Orders be used, it must be ascertained that the majority of Dioceses be not merely a majority of the quorum, but a majority of the Dioceses entitled to representation, and that the vote of the clergy and laity be a concurrent vote in each of the Dioceses which constitute the majority. If, however, a Diocese voting on such a question be represented only by clergy or only by laity, it is presumed that it will be bound, under the general rule of Art. ii., by the vote of that delegation by which it is represented.

8. The comments made upon this recent amendment to Art. viii. have prepared the way for the better understanding of Art. ix. This article relates to the amendment of the Constitution itself. It stands precisely as it stood when adopted in 1789 A.D., excepting the substitution of the words "Diocese" and "Diocesan" for "States" and "State." It provides that the Constitution shall be unalterable, unless in General Convention, by the Church, in a majority of the Dioceses which may have adopted the same; and that all alterations shall be first proposed in one General Convention and made known to the several Diocesan Conventions before they shall be finally agreed to or ratified in the ensuing General Convention.

In this process two general principles are to be observed : (1) The alteration must be made *in* General Convention, and (2) it must be *by* the action of the Church in a majority of Dioceses. That is to say, (1) it cannot be made by any Diocese for itself, nor by any joint action of the majority in the whole of the Dioceses other than that taken in the General Convention. But (2) the power which acts in the alteration is not the General Convention as such, but the Church in a majority of the Dioceses which have adopted that Constitution. The Church in a majority of Dioceses is to act, but it is to act in the General Convention. The Church in a Diocese can act in General Convention only by its representatives. Hence the alteration of the Constitution can be constitutionally effected only by the consent of the representatives of a majority of the Dioceses in General Convention. And as the act of alteration is to be the act of the Church in a majority of the Dioceses, the vote by which that act is performed must be a vote which will express the consent of the Church in a majority of the Dioceses. If the usual vote taken by Dioceses and Orders does in fact express that consent, of course there can be no objection to it; but, from what has already been said, it will be apparent (1) that such a vote, when it reveals only the consent of a majority of the number of Dioceses which constitute a quorum of the Lower House, cannot be the vote of a majority of the Dioceses which have adopted the Constitution ; and (2) that if such a vote reveals only the consent of one set of Dioceses represented by clergy, concurring with the consent of another set of Dioceses represented by laity (unless those Dioceses should be respectively represented by a delegation of only one kind), it cannot be the consent of the Church in a majority of the Dioceses which have adopted the Constitution ; and, by consequence, cannot be the consent required by the Constitution.

There is, however, no necessary inclusion of the vote required by Art. ix. within the requirements of Art. ii. The distinction between all questions which can come up for action in the General Convention under a certain fixed Constitution, and a question as to the change of that Constitution itself, is perfectly plain. The Constitution was established by the consent of all the Dioceses, and that consent was given with the stipulation that if the Constitution was changed, it should not be changed without the consent of a majority of them. Nothing less than such consent, ascertain it how we will, can satisfy the stipulation.

And if it be urged that this conclusion would require also the consent of the Bishops of those Dioceses which constitute the majority in the action taken in the Lower House, that does not prove the conclusion to be wrong. When the Constitution, containing this article the same as now, was adopted in October, 1789 A.D., it was signed not only by the representatives of the Dioceses in the Lower House, but also by two out of the three Bishops then in the country. Whence arose the presumption that the Bishops of the Dioceses had no voice as such in the consent of those Dioceses to the alteration of the Constitution? Certainly there is no reason why the Bishops should not have a voice in the action of their Dioceses in General Convention. That such action was not expressly required in concurrence with the action of *elected* representatives is probably due only to the fact already referred to, that the scheme of the Constitution was completed in the conception of a representative body of clergy and laity, without strict regard to, or full understanding of, the proper functions of Bishops, and that their connection with the system of the General Convention was left in some respects unprovided for.

The prevailing impression that the Episcopal consent, required by Art. iii., was practically the same as the consent of a majority of the Bishops of the Dioceses, and that the vote by Dioceses and Orders was equivalent to the vote of the Dioceses, has led to the treatment of questions on constitutional alterations in the same manner as all other questions. This of course has its conveniences, and produces what perhaps is not far from being equivalent to the consent of the Church in a majority of the Dioceses, but it is open to the serious objection, nevertheless, of not being necessarily equivalent to that consent, and of being, in fact, not the action of the Church in a majority of the Dioceses in General Convention, but the action of the General Convention.

IV. *Of Change in Form, Jurisdiction, and Constituency of General Convention, resulting from its own Action.*—The view which has been taken of the General Convention would hardly be complete without the notice of certain changes which have taken place in the form and order of its administration of authority, which are not provided for by the Constitution. The changes to which reference is here made cannot be said to be contrary to the Constitution, but they are, in fact, exterior to it, deriving their authority not from it, but from acts of the General Convention, sustained by the public opinion of that body, of which General Convention is the representative.

There can be no just question that in the beginning of its existence the General Convention had jurisdiction over the members of the Church in those States by whose duly authorized representatives the Constitution had been adopted, and over those only; and that in form it was composed of representatives, Episcopal or elective, of Dioceses only, or of Churches in States equivalent to Dioceses. The expansion of its constituency and the extension of its jurisdiction kept even pace with those accessions to the Constitution which were the precedent conditions of admission to the Union. The Churches in the States were the elements of the combination, the units of the federative system. The Church in any State not acceding to the Constitution remained in its independence, without the privileges or the duties of union. The Church in any State acceding, took its stand on equal terms with those that had already acceded. Churches in Eastern States, feeble in numbers, grouped themselves together under the name of the Eastern Diocese, but the individuality of the Church in these States was not obliterated. The Church in two States, or more than two, might, from paucity of Bishops, or inability to support them, for a time come under a common Episcopate; but the idea that these were individual Churches, practically distinct Dioceses, was not ignored, and the Church in such States was related to the Ecclesiastical Union not as a group, but as several distinct bodies, which individually acceded to the Constitution, and which, ultimately, became actually, as they had before been potentially, single Episcopal jurisdictions.

But although the federation of Dioceses was from the beginning an essential characteristic of this system of Ecclesiastical government, yet the Church was something more than a federation. If the Ecclesiastical Union were desirable at all, it was desirable that it should be extended. If the grouping of Dioceses, existing within the limits of the same civil government, was in conformity with sound Church principle, it was in derogation of sound Church principle that any Diocese should, without the gravest reason touching the very life of the Church, hold itself aloof from that union. And, more than this, if there were scattering members of the same Church in outlying districts which were not States, they could not consistently be left uncared for by the Church, any more than the districts themselves could be regarded as beyond the pale of the protection of the civil authority. In short, as the single Diocese was, in the system, contemplated as the Church in the State, so the Ecclesiastical Union was to be co-extensive with the Civil Union; and, though many a year was to pass before the formulation of the canonical maxim (Digest i. 15; vii. 4) that the jurisdiction of this Church extends in right, though not always in form, to all persons belonging to it within the United States, yet, no sooner was the formal organization complete in the majority of the States than the effort began to be made to reach out beyond the limits of those States. In the second regular General Convention (1792 A.D.) it was resolved, that a joint Committee of both Houses be appointed to report a plan for supporting Missionaries to preach the Gospel on the frontiers of the United States. And in 1808 A.D. a committee was appointed to address the Church in certain districts, with a view (1) to urge Churches represented in General Convention to send regularly a deputation; (2) to invite the Church in every State in which it is organized and which has not acceded to the Constitution to accede to the same; (3) to invite the clergy and some of the most respectable lay members of the Church in the States and Territories, in which the Church has not been organized, to organize and accede to the Constitution; and this Committee was authorized, moreover, to consider and determine on the proper mode of sending a Bishop into said States and Territories, and in case of a reasonable prospect of accomplishing this object, to elect a suitable person to each Episcopacy, any three Bishops being authorized to consecrate such person on the proper certificates; *provided*, that the jurisdiction assigned to him should not interfere with the rights of any State or Diocese which should thereafter adopt the Constitution. (Bioren, p. 252.)

It is, of course, no part of the present purpose to trace the history of the Missionary movement in the Church; but it is necessary to note that the beginnings of that movement, thus early in the working of the Ecclesiastical Union, were based upon principles entirely harmonious with that system, and to call attention to the influence and result of that movement upon the General Convention.

How solicitous the original movers in this direction were, to guide the extension of the Church by missions in conformity with the principles of the system of the Ecclesiastical Union, will appear from Bishop White's account, given to the House of Bishops in 1814 A.D., of his action under a commission of the General Convention of 1811 A.D., "to devise means for supplying the congregations of this Church west of the Alleghany Mountains with the ministrations and worship of the same, and for organizing the Church in the Western States." In consequence of this appointment he, the President, had "begun a correspondence with Bishop Madison; but all further progress was arrested by the decease of the said Right Rev. Brother. This did not hinder the President from submitting to the Convention of this Church in Pennsylvania a proposal, which was complied with, designed so far to meet the desires of some members of this Church in the Western country, as that, in the event of a settlement of a Bishop therein, the congregations in the western counties of the State might be under his superintendence, on such a plan as would not affect the integrity of the Church in the State of Pennsylvania as a component member of the body of this Church throughout our Union, in contrariety to the Constitution." (Bioren, pp. 311, 312.)

The issue of the movement begun on these principles has been not only the growth of the Church, but also its settlement within limits corresponding in the main to the civil divisions of the United States; so that, as the Church in an outlying district was fitted for the position of "a component member of this Church throughout our Union," it became such by acceding to the Constitution according to the provisions of its fifth Article.

But while under this provision of the Constitution the constituency and the jurisdiction of the General Convention might be enlarged by the entrance of new Dioceses into the Ecclesiastical Union, there has been no provision of the Constitution which fixed the status of the Church, organized or not organized, in places where there had been no accession to the Constitution. These places are exterior to the jurisdiction of the General Convention as that jurisdiction is established by the Constitution. That they, or the members of the Church within them, are, in fact, within the jurisdiction of the General Convention, is because the General Convention has by Canon provided for the care and oversight of them, and because they have accepted and assented to the authority thus exercised over them. That this was a natural course of events consequent upon the going out of members of the Church in settled Dioceses, who were, as such, under the authority of the General Convention; and their settling, and seeking to establish the Church, in districts where that authority was unknown, probably no one will dispute. Whether the proper method of extending the authority of General Convention over such districts was not by amendment of the Constitution authorizing the passage of Canons necessary to the end in view is, perhaps, a speculative question, and, certainly, one upon which men may differ. The point of importance is, that, as a matter of fact, there is a whole system of dependencies in the outlying and missionary districts which are and ought to be regarded as parts of the Church under the jurisdiction of the General Convention, but which, really, are a growth or accretion upon the original system.

The dependencies of the Church which has, by accession of its component parts to the Constitution, placed itself under the authority of General Convention, are of three classes, and composed respectively (1) of the members of the Church in outlying districts of the territory of the United States, where such organization of the Church as there may be has never acceded to the Constitution; (2) of members of the Church in foreign countries, who are engaged in the conversion of the heathen, or who have themselves been there converted from heathenism; and (3) of members of this Church residing or sojourning in foreign countries, where there is an organization of some part of the Church of CHRIST, with which this Church has, on account of the divisions of Christendom, no intercommunion.

In these three classes of cases there are large bodies of members of this Church which are not organized into what are technically called Dioceses, but which are under the government of the General Convention, and take their law from its action.

Thus the jurisdiction of the General Convention extends, in fact, not only to the members of the Church in the Dioceses which have acceded to the Constitution, but also to the dependencies of that Church situated in the Territories of the United States and in foreign countries. In the exercise of such jurisdiction the General Convention has, by Canon, organized " The Domestic and Foreign Missionary Society" (Digest, Tit. iii., Can. viii.) has provided for the appointment of Domestic Missionary Bishops (Tit. i., Can. xv., ₰ 7), and of Foreign Missionary Bishops (ib., ₰ 8), and for the organization and regulation of congregations in foreign countries other than Great Britain and Ireland and the colonies and dependencies thereof, and not within the limits of any Foreign Missionary Bishop of this Church, placing them under the Episcopal government and jurisdiction of the Presiding Bishop in the Church in the United States for the time being. (Tit. iii., Can. iv., ₰ 3, et seq.)

And as, in fact, there has been thus an extension of the jurisdiction of the General Convention, so there has been an increase of its constituency, and to some extent, as in equity there should be, an enlargement of its representation. It is true the members of the Church in these several classes are not, under the terms of the Constitution, entitled to send delegates to General Convention; but then, on the other hand, it is also true that these classes are not in any way recognized in the Constitution. The system which provides for them is an accretion upon the original system provided by the Constitution. The new has grown up alongside of the old, and, by custom and canonical regulation, has been grafted upon it, and become part and parcel of it; and on the general principles of its construction, is equitably entitled to some representation. Two additions have been made to the General Convention which have been representative of these classes,—one, recently, by the admission, under resolution of the House of Deputies, of delegates from the Churches in Territories in the United States, who are permitted to attend and speak in reference to the interests of their constituents, though not to have a vote in the body; the other, by Canon, making the Domestic and Foreign Missionary Bishops members of the House of Bishops, and as such presumptively, as they are actually, entitled not only to a voice in the councils of the Church, but also to a vote. And, unless the idea of representation be dwarfed to the notion of elected deputation, these districts are, by this latter connection, a part of the constituency of that representative body which exercises jurisdiction over them. According to the popular, and perhaps it might be said American, notion of representation, those only are representative who are chosen and sent by those whom they represent. But this certainly is not the measure of the Church idea of representation; for representation in a true sense may exist independently of the choice of the persons represented, if they are legitimately under the care and government of those who act for them. The Bishops in the ancient Councils may justly be said to have represented in those Councils the Churches over which they presided. And these bodies of Churchmen have, in fact, a representation of the same kind in General Convention. The Domestic and Foreign Missionary Bishops sit by virtue of their office in the House of Bishops, and as such are members of the General Convention; and the congregations under what are called foreign chaplains, for whom no Bishop has been especially consecrated, are formally placed under the care of a Bishop who is a member of the General Convention, and as such is able to represent them in that body.

REV. PROF. WILLIAM J. SEABURY, D.D.

Generation, Eternal, of the Word. "The Divinity of JESUS CHRIST." Much will be found bearing upon this subject in other articles, but here it is proper to dwell upon it in its aspect as setting forth the consubstantial nature of the SON with the FATHER. The Word of GOD, begotten of the FATHER, must partake of the nature of His FATHER. He, therefore, must be a SON by an Eternal Generation. For infinity of nature belongs to GOD the FATHER, and must, therefore, be shared by the SON, as He partakes, as SON, of the majesty and eternal glory and omniscience and omnipotence of His FATHER. " In the beginning" the SON already was, but this beginning is for us in time. For us this Eternal Generation is set forth in the magnificent description of Wisdom in the eighth chapter of Proverbs. Its glories are hidden in that vastness of worship and adoration paid to Him of which He emptied Himself when He became man (Phil. ii. 7, where the A. V. renders it made Himself of no reputation). Revelation sets Him forth as the brightness of the FATHER'S glory, and the express Image of His Person and the Upholder of all things by the Word of His Power. With these facts of His pre-existent glory we must rest content. No more is revealed to us save that He is the Lamb of GOD, as it had been slain from the foundation of the world. It was this eternal pre-existence of CHRIST which was the central point of the Arian controversy. The Arian claimed that He was the first of all created beings, of the highest rank, but denied that He was truly begotten. In Him the name of GOD might be placed, but the Arian denied that it was inherent. The struggle in the Council of Nice was upon this consubstantial nature of the SON of GOD, which was bound up in the doctrine of His being not only the first, but also the only-begotten SON of GOD in the full sense of the word. His sharing of the nature of the FATHER involving essentially an eternal generation, and so the ancient creed of Nicæa declared this doctrine with great insistence. It ran thus: "We believe in one GOD, the FATHER Almighty, the Maker of all things, visible and invisible, and in one LORD JESUS CHRIST, Begotten of His FATHER the only-begotten, that is of the substance of the FATHER, GOD of GOD, Light of Light, Very GOD of Very GOD. Begotten, not made, being of one substance (*omo-ousios*) with the FATHER, by Whom all things both in heaven and on earth were made; Who for us men and for our salvation came down, and was incarnate, and was made man; suffered, and rose the third day: ascended into the heavens; shall come to judge the quick and the dead.

"And in the HOLY SPIRIT.

"And those who say that there was a time when the SON of GOD was not, and that before He was begotten He was not, and that He was born out of the things which exist not, or assert that He is of another nature or substance, or that He is mutable or subject to change, the Holy Catholic or Apostolic Church holdeth accursed." The repetition in several forms of the assertion of this Eternal Generation is very marked. It was then as now the central Truth in the power of the Incarnation and the Atonement. For under no other conclusion can we possibly believe that Our LORD is Eternal Life. The Word not only was with GOD as the wisdom of GOD, but the Word was GOD, the only-begotten, co-eternal with His FATHER (St. John i. 1-4, 14; 1 John v. 11-13, 20).

Genesis. The first book of the Bible, and the oldest surviving book in the world. Unproven claims have recently been put forth for papyri from Egypt and for some alleged Chinese records, but they have neither been substantiated, nor do their contents, which are merely catalogues, it is said, justify their claims to be considered *books* in any real sense of the word. The oldest book now in existence is rightly the inspired tome which contains the record of the creation, and much more. It is not merely the narrative of the creation of the world for man and the placing of man in it, but a history upon a divine plan, tracing a divine purpose, recording a divine mercy towards erring man. The contents of the book may be divided into five great parts—the Creation, the Fall, the secular history to the time of Abraham, the choice of the Hebrew family to become the Israelitish nation. It is not the place here to decide upon the congruity of shifting and constantly modified scientific speculations with the revelation of GOD. So far no scientific fact, properly established, has been found to clash in any way with the Mosaic outline of the order of creation. It has been always in accord with whatever science has proven so far, and the more deeply the Mosaic record is studied, the more scientifically accurate the terms used are found to be. But another theory, by a different class of assailants, has been alleged, viz.,—that Moses did not write this book from direct revelation, but had used earlier family chronicles and memoranda; and the documents which he used, it is pretended, can be separated, and that, in fact, some editor (whether Moses or some one later) has fused the whole so that they are interlaced in the very structure of the sentences. This may be so far a fact, that for some things Moses was divinely directed to put on record, with absolute precision, facts which had been distorted by tradition, and remnants of which tradition have survived to our day; but that he used them and other documents as the compilers of the books of Kings and of Chronicles did the state records is refuted by the very fact that they who assert these things cannot agree on the documents. These documents are called the Elohistic and Jehovistic, but the terms Elohim (GOD) and Jehovah (LORD) are so interchangeably used and at times so conjoined as to upset any such parceling out of the text, that is, if any credit is to be given to the book at all. (*Vide* PENTATEUCH.)

I. The Creation. It is contained in Gen. i., ii. 3.

II. For a distinct purpose,—to set forth the position of man in the created world,—the second chapter relates with greater fullness the preparation made for him, and his charge. It is not a repetition, not a different document, but after the general introduction the record now goes on to the special purpose of this part of the Book,—the place and relation of man under GOD to the visible creation. Lordship is given to him, and a companion created for him (Gen. ii. 4 to end).

III. The Fall, the sentence, the expulsion, and the placing of the sentinel Cherubim are recited in the third chapter.

IV. The secular history to the time of Abraham (ch. iv.-xi. 27). This period is divided into two portions by the great cataclysm of the Deluge (which in the usual grouping, in fact, forms the close of one of the great sections). The first portion (ch. iv.-vi.) contains names and ages of the antediluvian Patriarchs from Adam to Noah, with short incidental notices of one or two of them, and then the account of the building of the Ark and the preparation for the preservation of Noah and his family and of such living things as GOD had appointed (ch. vii.-viii.). In the ninth chapter the blessing and covenant with all flesh through Noah, and the curse of Ham and the blessing of Shem and Japhet, are recorded. The tenth chapter is probably of the greatest ethnological value. Only to it and no farther back have ethnologists been able to trace the history of nations. The eleventh chapter narrates the confusion of languages at the tower in the land of Shinar, where, with remarkable accuracy, Moses speaks of the confusion as of lip, and therefore of language (*vide* marginal reading). From this point the history changes, and narrows down from the peopling of the earth to the record of a single family,—that of Shem, whose descendants are briefly named,—till we reach Terah, the father of Abram. So far the slight connecting links of the general history Moses has given have in no way been successfully impugned.

V. The call of Abram and the history of his descendants till they were placed in the land of Egypt, and then increased till the land was ready for them to take possession of. The history has been hitherto rather secular than distinctly religious, though throughout GOD'S dealings with men are narrated to us, especially in the history of Noah. But now Abram is chosen, and responds to the choice by his faith, and by wondrous interpositions he is made the father of a son who was to be the type of the greater joy of the whole world. Isaac's son, Jacob, is chosen, and from him come the twelve patriarchs, the heads of large families who grew into tribes, which Moses was commissioned to mould into a nation.

Under the several names Abraham, Isaac, Jacob, and Joseph will be found some accounts of each, and of their history as typical of CHRIST. The Book of Genesis closes with the migration of the Israel and his family of seventy souls into Egypt. The Chronology of Genesis is a difficult subject, and of which many schemes have been made. It would seem that a longer time than that usually placed on the margin of our Bibles is necessary, and while not pretending to decide so perplexing a subject, the table subjoined gives the most satisfactory solution to it:

Creation	0
Flood	2262
Birth of Peleg	401
Departure of Abram from Haran	616
From Abram's departure to Jacob's going down to Egypt	215
	3494

This is a longer computation than the one usually given. It is that of the Septuagint. (*Vide* Smith's Dict., Chronology.) But it best accords with what we know of external history and the need of allowing more time for contemporary secular history. (The subject is, however, too intricate to be discussed here, and the student is referred to the larger Commentaries, the Speaker's, Lange, Smith's Dictionary of Chronology, and similar works. Browne's Ordo Sæclum.)

Georgia, Diocese of. Georgia was the child of philanthropy. It is the only colony planted by disinterested trustees, who received neither fee nor reward for their undertaking. It was the only colony where broad principles of Christian benevolence gathered within its sheltering arms the indigent, the forsaken, the persecuted of various nations and creeds, and gave them a common home and protection. The Church of England entered warmly into the scheme of the twenty-one noblemen and gentlemen who constituted its first Board of Trustees. Nearly a fourth of its trustees were clergymen, and over a hundred ministers received, at their own request, commissions to take up collections in behalf of the colony of Georgia, while the Archbishop of Canterbury, Bishops, Archdeacons, Deans, Chapters, Collegiate and Parochial Clergy contributed to its treasury. General Oglethorpe and Rev. Dr. Herbert sailed with the first emigrants. This clergyman offered his services gratuitously.

The trustees sent a petition to the Society for the Propagation of the Gospel, stating that they had appropriated a site for a church, and a sufficient glebe for the minister, and asking for the usual allowance for a missionary. The Rev. Samuel Quincy was appointed, and reached there four months after the sailing of the first emigrants. In December, 1735 A.D., John and Charles Wesley and Benjamin Ingham came out, full of zeal for the conversion of the Indians. Through no intentional error of the Wesleys they only remained a short time, and left under charges, of which all we can say is they are very remarkable, considering the views with which they are usually identified.

As John Wesley entered the Downs on his return, he passed the ship in which Whitefield sailed for Georgia. After remaining in Savannah a short time he returned to England to be ordained Priest, and raise money for an orphan asylum. He was received with especial favor by the trustees, who appointed him rector of Christ Church, Savannah, and gave him five hundred acres of land for his orphan asylum. In six months he had raised five thousand dollars, and on the 25th of March the first brick of the asylum was laid at a spot nine miles from Savannah, called Bethesda, where he began his asylum. It was burned by lightning, and the property sold. In the good providence of GOD the property was again purchased for the purpose, and to-day a flourishing orphan asylum is liberally supported by the people of Savannah.

The Church was maintained in Savannah sometimes by ministers worthy to follow Wesley and Whitefield, and, again, by others of whom the less we say the better.

The church in Savannah was ordered to be built in 1740 A.D., and a few loads of stone were brought and laid down upon the spot. But little or no progress was made towards its completion.

The governor, in 1746 A.D., wrote, "The roof of it is covered with shingles, but the sides and ends remain a skeleton." In 1750 A.D. the church was completed, and is described as large, beautiful, and commodious. It was burnt in 1796 A.D. It was burnt again, and the present church was rebuilt on the same spot.

Fifty years before Robert Raikes originated his scheme of a Sunday-school in England, Mr. Wesley established a Sunday-school in Christ Church.

In 1748 A.D. the inhabitants of Savannah numbered six hundred and thirteen, of whom three hundred and eighty-eight were dissenters. The number of communicants of Christ Church was sixty-three. The only minister of the Church of England in the colony, though its population was over three thousand, was Rev. Bartholomew Zouberbubler, rector of Christ Church, under whose faithful ministry, and principally by his pastoral work, the Church increased in numbers and influence.

The inhabitants of Augusta, in 1750 A.D., memorialized the Society for the Propagation of the Gospel for a missionary, stating that a handsome and convenient church had been built under the guns of the fort. A minister was sent them, who arrived in December, 1750 A.D., but could find neither glebe nor parsonage promised. He labored on alone, amidst constant alarms of Indian incursions, separated one hundred and thirty miles from his nearest clerical neighbor with but little to cheer him, till 1756 A.D.

In 1758 A.D. the Assembly divided Georgia into parishes, and appropriated twenty-five pounds to the clergyman officiating in each parish. Yet clergymen were not to be had.

Of two of the clergymen sent to Augusta, it is stated that one was grossly immoral, drunk, profane. Of the other, that he behaved in an unchristian and ungentlemanly way, and doing all he could to bring discredit on the Church and religion. It is painful to add no cause did more to keep down the Church in colonial times than the unworthy conduct of many sent here as missionaries. There were noble exceptions, but there were many who were the very off-scourings of the Church; men who were a disgrace not to religion only, but to their country. These men, virtually banished from England, pressed hither, drifted from parish to parish, ravening as hungry wolves upon the unprotected sheep, while there was no authority to bring them to discipline, or purge the Church of such unworthy ministers. The wonder is the Church survived such an influx of wickedness in those who were sent as teachers.

In 1767 A.D., Rev. Edward Ellington was appointed to St. Paul's, Augusta, and from the records of his travels and his labors, he seems to have deserved the title given by the historian of the colonial Church, as being "the most distinguished of Georgia Missionaries."

Missionaries were, for a time, located in Burke and Sunbury, Liberty County. Owing to the troubles growing out of the Revolution, but little could be done by the missionaries. One was barred out of his Church, another driven from his parish and forced to support his family by teaching.

The effect of the Revolutionary war upon the Church in Georgia, as well as elsewhere, was very distressing. The clergy had, at their ordination, taken the oath of allegiance to the Crown, and were mobbed and ill-treated because they could not break their ordination vows. The only wonder is the Church survived. (Bishop Stevens's Semi-Centennial Sermon before the Convention of Georgia is authority for the above.)

In 1811 A.D., we learn from the Journal of the General Convention of that year that Rev. Mr. Barton presented a certificate of his appointment to attend the Convention, signed by the Wardens and Vestry of the Episcopal Church in the city of Savannah, State of Georgia, whereupon, "*Resolved*, That the Protestant Episcopal Church in the State of Georgia not being organized, and not having, in Conventions, acceded to the Constitution of the Protestant Episcopal Church in the United States, Rev. Mr. Barton cannot be admitted a member of this House, but that he be allowed the privilege of an honorary seat."

It was not till 1815 A.D. that a Bishop of the Church visited the State. In the spring of that year Bishop Dehon, of South Carolina, came to Savannah to consecrate the new building and hold the first confirmation, and confirmed sixty persons presented by the rector, Rev. Mr. Cranston.

On the 24th of February, 1823 A.D., three clergymen, Rev. Abiel Carter, rector of Christ Church, Savannah, Rev. Hugh Smith, rector of St. Paul's, Augusta, and Rev. Edward Matthews, rector of Christ Church, St. Simon's Island, and three laymen from Christ Church, Savannah, and three from St. Paul's, Augusta, met in St. Paul's, Augusta, to organize the Diocese of Georgia. They adopted a Constitution and Canons and acceded to the Constitution of the Church in the United States, and requested the Bishop of South Carolina, Rt. Rev. Nathaniel Bowen, to take the oversight of the Diocese. They adopted an address to the people in the State, and elected deputies to the General Convention. Two of these deputies took their seats in the General Convention which met the following May. Thus the Diocese of Georgia became an integral part of the Church in the United States.

Of the strength of the parishes at that time we have no information. From the report to the following Convention, May, 1824 A.D., we learn that there were in Christ

Church, Savannah, 26 baptisms, 3 of them colored, 84 confirmations, 80 communicants, and Sunday-school very flourishing. St. Paul's, Augusta, baptisms, 27, of which 3 were colored; confirmations, 18; communicants, 51.

Christ Church, Macon, was admitted at the next Convention, and its rector, Rev. Lot Jones, reported a number of points at which he found encouragement to commence services.

At the fourth Annual Convention Bishop Bowen presided, and made an address, in which he said he would give them a statement of all Episcopal transactions affecting Georgia of which he had knowledge, and which were nowhere recorded. Bishop Smith, of South Carolina, from 1798 A.D. till his death in 1802 A.D. had endeavored by correspondence to cherish and preserve the Church in Georgia in a sound state. Through the Rev. Mr. Strong, of Oglethorpe County, he became acquainted with the merits of James Hamilton Ray as candidate for holy orders. In 1801 A.D., Mr. Ray was ordained Deacon and Priest. He lived an honored minister in Greene County, and died in 1805 A.D., greatly lamented as a faithful and able pastor of a numerous flock.*

No one can fail, in reading the journals of the Convention, to be impressed that the great defect in the organization of the Church was the want of a Bishop. Had the change made in 1835 A.D. been in operation at any period from the time of the Wesleys, who can even conceive of the growth of the Church? But from that time till the close of the Revolution the colonies could not obtain Episcopal Orders. From that time till 1835 A.D. no Bishop could be elected, except there were in the Diocese so many clergymen and so many parishes. Georgia fully recognized the fact, and was constantly laying plans to procure a Bishop. In 1836 A.D. the Diocese asked that the House of Bishops would appoint a Bishop, and named the Rev. Edward Neufville as a suitable person. He at once peremptorily declined.

At the following Convention a resolution was adopted, "that as the Diocese would soon be in a condition to elect its own Bishop, no action under it was expected."

At the following Convention a memorial was adopted asking the appointment of a Missionary Bishop, who might take charge of Dioceses without Bishops.

The following year the proposition of the Diocese of Florida, that Florida, Alabama, and Georgia should unite and elect a Bishop was made. This Diocese gladly assented to the plan.

The following year, May, 1840 A.D , the Annual Convention met in Clarksville, and having now reached the point where she was entitled to choose her own Bishop, unanimously elected Rev. Stephen Elliott, Professor of Sacred Literature in the College of South Carolina.

Of the President of that Convention and of the Bishop they elected I can only quote Bishop Stevens. Of the first (Dr. Neufville, he says, "Never have I heard our Liturgy read with more unction and effectiveness than by him, while his reading of the Bible was like an illuminated exposition of it, so exquisite were his modulations, so sweet and musical was his voice, and so just and well rendered his emphasis."

"To him the Church in Georgia owes a great debt. He was President of the Standing Committee for many years before his death, and he it was who brought forward the name of Stephen Elliott as a fit person to be the first Bishop of Georgia, thus modestly waiving his own personal claims of no ordinary character in favor of one whom he believed to be better fitted than himself for the high office." So said Bishop Elliott in the sermon preached at Dr. Neufville's funeral in Christ Church. It is known to persons now living that on the occasion of the first sermon preached by Bishop Elliott, in Savannah, when as yet Bishop Elliott was only a Deacon, Dr. Neufville said at its close, "There is the man for the first Bishop of Georgia," and he never altered that opinion.

Of Bishop Elliott, Bishop Stevens said, "But how shall I speak of the first Bishop of Georgia, Stephen Elliott? His character, like his body, was majestic and symmetrical, with manly strength and glory; it was the noble temple of a noble soul. His mind was of large calibre and cultivated with sedulous care. His eloquence was the outburst of a well-stored, well-trained intellect, pouring itself through lips not wet merely with Castalia's dew, but touched as by angel hands with coals from off the altar."

On the 28th of February, 1841 A.D., the Rt. Rev. Stephen Elliott, D.D., was consecrated the first Bishop of Georgia, in Christ Church, Savannah, by the Rt. Rev. William Meade, D.D., Bishop of Virginia, Rt. Rev. L. Silliman Ives, D.D., Bishop of North Carolina, and Rt. Rev. Christopher Gadsden, D.D., Bishop of South Carolina.

At the time of the election of Bishop Elliott there were in the Diocese 8 clergymen, 7 parishes, and 323 communicants, of which number 150 were communicants of Christ Church, Savannah.

The immediate effect of the consecration of Bishop Elliott, as we look back upon it, seems wonderful. In two years parishes were relieved from debt, seven new parishes admitted to the Convention, the number of communicants nearly doubled, four Deacons ordained, and a Church school endowed by a gentleman not of our communion. Of the four ordained, two are men of such high character and commanding talents that

---

* When the writer was candidate for orders the late Rev. Mr. Okeson came across a pamphlet copy of the life and services of this gentleman. It was a wonderful story of a life of labor and self-sacrifice and success. From that day to this the writer has tried in vain to get a copy of the pamphlet.

the Church called them to the office of Bishop in the Church of GOD.*

To give some idea of the state of things, I will mention that the Bishop arrived in Marietta, and first one and then another called on him, and stated that he was the only Churchman in the place. At the close of the services, the Bishop invited those who were friendly to the organization of an Episcopal Church in the place to remain. The amazement at the discovery of so many Churchmen may be imagined, it cannot be described. A Church was organized, and under the admirable management of Colonel C. F. M. Garnett, Chief Engineer of the State Road, a neat stone church (until recently the only one in the Diocese) was erected, for an amount not exceeding the cost of a wooden church.

All the bright hopes of that day have not been realized, notably in the Church school. But the Church learned to know the self-denying devotion of her Bishop, and if the people had realized the fact, what a blessing it might have been to the Diocese; as it is, every year of the Bishop's life gave new proof of the good it had done.

He lived to bury the four leading clergymen that he found in the Diocese. Each died rector of the parish in which he found him,—Dr. Neufville, of Savannah, Dr. Ford, of Augusta, Mr. Caanes, of Columbus, and Mr. Bragg, of Macon. He has left on record his tribute of love to their memories, and then, on the 21st of December, 1866 A.D., he was snatched away by death.

In 1861 A.D. the number of the clergy was 29; parishes, 23; number of communicants, 2184.

In 1867 A.D.: Clergy, 31; parishes, 28; communicants, 2141.

Let it be borne in mind that between these two dates Georgia had been desolated by war, churches burned or desecrated, congregations scattered, then recall the condition in which Bishop Elliott found the Diocese,—surely it shows how faithfully he had labored.

On the 9th of May following the Convention met in Macon, and elected Rev. John H. Beckwith, D D., rector of Trinity Church, New Orleans, his successor.

Statistics for 1886 A.D.: Clergy, 39; parishes, 35; missions, 25; candidates for H. O., 1; ordinations, D. 1, P. 1; baptisms, 475; con., 330; com., 4822; contr., $188,031.11.

REV. W. C. WILLIAMS, D.D.

Ghost. The old English word for spirit, retained chiefly now in the title of the third person of the HOLY TRINITY,—the HOLY GHOST; the adverb "ghostly" occurs in the prayer for those to be confirmed,—" the spirit of counsel and ghostly strength." (*Vide* HOLY GHOST.)

Girdle. This convenient part of the Eastern dress was also a part of the Jewish priestly dress. The High-Priest was girded with a "curious girdle," while the Priests wore a simple linen girdle, edged with wool. The Prophets also wore a girdle of leather, as that of Elijah (2 Kings i. 8) and St. John Baptist (Matt. iii. 4), or linen (Jer. xiii. 1). The girdle for the ordinary dress was not in the same style as these, which were badges of office. The girdle was not used distinctively as a badge of office in the Church till somewhat late, and long after monachism became common. Then it was part of the monkish dress. It became a part of the vestments for the minister about the eighth century. It was used by the Bishop as part of his dress about 1202 A.D. In the Eastern Church the girdle is worn by the Priest and Bishop over the sticharion or alb, and the orarium or stole, and confines them both.

Glebe. Land given to the Church for a parson's use and for the use of the Church. According to the old English law every Church of common right is entitled to house and glebe, and the assigning of these at the first was of such absolute necessity that without them no church could be regularly consecrated. (Burn's Eccl. Law, *sub voc.*) After he is inducted, the freehold of the glebe is in the parson, but with these limitations: (1) He may not alienate nor exchange but upon the conditions set forth in the statutes. (2) He may not commit waste by selling wood. If the glebe has a mine on it, it may be opened, and also a true and full terrier (map) of all the glebe lands in the Diocese must be laid up in the Bishop's registry. When this country was settled, the Church, wherever it was established (as in New York and the Provinces south of it), obtained its glebes, but after the Revolution they were confiscated by the State, as in Virginia, or were lost through the weakness or carelessness of the Church, so that comparatively few parishes now retain their old glebes. But since then, to quite a number of churches have been given glebes and parsonages. It would be well that the Church should see to it in every Diocese that each parish had a parsonage, and, if possible, land attached, as a condition precedent to consecrating the church, and, too, that these glebes and parsonages were properly secured to the Church, and by Canon protected from all wastage or loss. In this matter the laity are as much interested as the clergy, since if properly and generously done it will eventually lighten the burden of support and will secure the comfort of the rector.

Gloria. The first word of two of the ascriptions used in the Prayer-Book, the *Gloria Patri* and the *Gloria in Excelsis.*

The *Gloria Patri* emerges first in the Arian controversy (325-384 A.D.). It was common in the East, but not in the West, and did not at first have the concluding clause, "As it was," etc. It also varied in the preposition. St. Basil used the form Glory be to the FATHER and to the SON

---

*One Bishop Scott, of Oregon, the other Bishop Stevens, of Pennsylvania.

with the HOLY GHOST. It ran also "in the SON" and "by the SON." Basil claims Clement of Rome, Irenæus, the Dionysii of Rome and of Alexandria, Eusebius of Cæsarea, Origen, Africanus, Gregory Thaumaturgus, Firmilian, and Melito as using it in an orthodox sense. This array of names proves its Eastern origin and use. It usually ran "Glory be," but also "Glory and might" was a current form. The West received it slowly. The Council of Vaison (529 A.D.) urges the use of "As it was in the beginning," not only because the Apostolic See used it, but because the East, Africa, and Italy so used it, and, too, to meet Arian blasphemy. Practically, this Gloria was from Apostolic times. St. Polycarp's last words were, "With Whom, to Thee and the HOLY GHOST be glory now and forever. Amen" (169 A.D.). It was a most natural doxology, but its theologic bearing was not dreamt of till Arianism brought it forth to bolster up its specious reasoning, and so brought it into prominence.

The second part dates, probably, from the middle of the fifth century. When it was used first as the Rubric now permits, after each Psalm, cannot be certainly determined, but it was at least urged upon the Gallican Church as early as 847 A.D., for about that date the false decretals contain a forged letter from Jerome to Pope Damasus, saying that the Gloria Patri in the East was sung at the end of every Psalm. However late this use might be, it soon after became the rule, and so passed into the English Prayer-Book. In the American Prayer-Book the rubric orders it only for the end of the Psalter for the day, but permits it at the end of each Psalm, and of the *Venite*, the *Benedicite*, and the other anthems of the Morning and Evening Prayer. Use has probably made it imperative at the end of the anthems. It is an antiphon which marks as it were the teaching, that however Jewish the history of each Psalm may be, yet its contents are spiritually for the whole Church throughout all time.

The *Gloria in Excelsis* has a similar history. Springing from the angelic hymn (St. Luke ii. 14), it grew into general use, and received additions and variation. In St. James' Liturgy only the angelic versicle is used. In nearly our present form it is found in the Alexandrine Codex of the Scripture after the Psalms, and is entitled the Morning Hymn. The only variation is in the last clause, which runs thus in the Cod. Alex.: "Thou only art holy, Thou only art the LORD JESUS CHRIST, to the glory of GOD the FATHER. Amen." A much more variant form is found at the end of the seventh Book of the Apostolic Constitutions, which may well have been current about the year 300 A.D. This has these words: "We worship Thee through the Great High-Priest, Thee who art one GOD, unbegotten, alone, unapproachable," and also, "O LORD, only-begotten Son JESUS CHRIST and HOLY SPIRIT." It closes as does the Alexandrine Version. It is not necessary here to trace the later Latin Versions. They all vary slightly. The Mozarabic Version omits the second, "Thou that takest away the sins of the world, have mercy upon us." When it was used first in the Eucharistic services it would be difficult to determine precisely, but it was before the fourth Council of Toledo (633 A.D.), which in its twelfth Canon replies to objectors.

The *Gloria in Excelsis* is not used in the Morning or Evening Prayer, but only in the Eucharistic service. In the American Prayer-Book it is allowed as an alternate for the *Gloria Patri*.

God. The Being and attributes of GOD is a subject that lies at the foundation of all religion, of all effective morality, and of all social order and prosperity among mankind. We may study this Being and His attributes in these displays or modes of manifestation which He has been pleased to make of Himself for our instruction and benefit, 1, in the Revelation in the Holy Scriptures; 2, in the Person of His SON our LORD JESUS CHRIST; and, 3, in Nature. This is the order in which we will pursue these topics, although in many respects the order should be somewhat different. For *all* persons the works of GOD are manifest in nature (Rom. i. 19, 20), even to those to whom CHRIST has not been preached and to whom no revelation has been given; and to many the Person of CHRIST and the knowledge of GOD in Him is first made known by such human agency as parents and sponsors and the ministry of the Church, and for those who cannot read this is, and must be, their main dependence. But for those who can read, the Bible itself is a source and means of knowledge which nothing else can replace, and whose place nothing else as a substitute can fill.

Turning to the Bible, and taking up its disclosures in the chronological or historical order, we find GOD first presented to us as the "Creator of all things." The narrative represents GOD as existing without beginning of days, and as having created all things out of nothing. The narrative was incidentally intended for a moral and religious rather than for any merely scientific purpose. And yet its coincidence with the results of modern, even the latest scientific, researches into the primitive condition of this material universe and its progressive development or "evolution," as some persons prefer to call it, is such as to constitute one of the most satisfactory proofs of the inspiration of its author. And very much the same remark should be made with regard to all the subsequent history in the Old Testament. It was designed rather to illustrate the nature of man and the character of GOD and "GOD'S dealings with man," than to give such a history of man and of the world as men who study history from merely a human and scientific point of view would desire. And yet the recent discoveries in the valley of the Nile, in Mesopotamia, and elsewhere, wherever old monuments have been found and all old languages and inscriptions deciphered, not only confirm and illustrate the Bible statements, but derive from these statements such light and illustration as that without the Bible they would hardly be intelligible at all. And here again we have another wonderful confirmation of the facts that the Bible statements were not only written at the time they claim to have been written, but also that they were written by men who were guided in the selection of their facts and in the way of presenting them by a wisdom that was higher than their own.

But besides the fact of the oneness of GOD, —which excludes all idea of a polytheism,— and the representation of GOD as the Creator of all things, the Bible of the Old Testament seems to have been written with special reference to an exhibition of the presence of GOD in the world as the chief Cause and Agent of its physical affairs,—the course of nature,—and as a Moral Governor having regard always to the acts and to the moral character of men. The Jews knew but very little of what is taught in these days as "science;" they had not learned to ascribe phenomena to the agency of "laws" and "nature," "force" and "evolution," that can work without a GOD. They believed, on the other hand, and their Scriptures seemed designed to encourage the belief, that GOD is the chief agent, the ever-present cause in them all. He "makes the sun to rise," He "sends the rain," and He it is that causes "the fruitful seasons, filling the hearts of His people with joy and gladness." And hence the Scriptures, while precluding any worship of nature and natural phenomena, taught the people to see GOD in all the phenomena of nature, and to be grateful to Him for whatever should come in the way of the products of the earth, of wealth, and of worldly prosperity. Nor was GOD represented as only a personal agent, ever at work producing these results which we now ascribe to nature, but He was represented as directing them, to some extent, with reference to the character of the people who lived in the land. It is indeed true that it is said "He maketh His sun to rise on the evil and on the good, and sendeth His rain on the just and on the unjust." There is some law and uniformity with disregard of character to some extent, but yet He is often spoken of as sending the caterpillar and the locust, as shutting up the windows of heaven so that there should be no rain, of sending the frost or of withholding the dew, of giving health or sending pestilence; so that there could be no occasion or excuse for men's forgetting that GOD is the One "from whom cometh every good and perfect gift," all the blessings we enjoy or can hope for. The passage just cited from the Sermon on the Mount was, of course, of a later date than the teachings of the Old Testament. It was after men had observed something of the uniformity of nature, and seems to have been said by way of meeting objections to the teaching of the Bible, which may have even then grown up out of such observations, and of too hasty generalizations from what had been observed. We shall recur to this topic farther on in this article.

But the higher object in treating of the subject was doubtless the character of GOD as the Moral Governor of the world. Here we find impressed upon the Jewish mind the idea of sin as something wrong in itself, and something offensive to GOD; not merely as displeasing to Him on personal grounds,— if we may so speak of it,—but as offensive because it is wrong, unjust, and inconsistent with the character of men and the nature of things. The Old Testament represents GOD as holy and righteous in all His ways, so that if men had offended or displeased Him it was because they had done wrong,—had done something that was intrinsically wrong, something that He had forbidden *because* it was wrong; and, as a consequence, they felt, when they suffered remorse, the loss of happiness and of prosperity, not only that they had lost His favor, but that the fault was wholly their own. He was, in their estimation, none the less, but rather the more, righteous because He was angry at their sins and punished them, if not as their demerits deserved, yet so as to impress them with a sense of the awful and all-destroying nature of sin and transgression. So far did this go that it seemed to them that there could be no extreme of folly and of wickedness beyond that of the "condemnation" of GOD which was implied in any attempt to justify themselves, or to proclaim that they were innocent while they were suffering from what was apparently a chastisement from Him (Job xl. 8–10).

If, therefore, there is any one thing which is set forward in the Old Testament with more emphasis and variety of iteration than any other as exhibiting the attributes of GOD, after representing Him as Creator, it would seem to be the presentation of His character as Moral Governor. Even in nature, the inanimate world, He is represented as "ordering all things for good to them that love Him," so far as it is possible without destroying all sense of uniformity and ground of dependence on the constitution of nature; without, in short, taking away all ground and basis for scientific knowledge. But in the moral world there is no such limit or necessity for limitation. In the heart and consciousness of each, one GOD can deal with justice and in accordance with the ends of the individual himself. He can send remorse or can give relief,—a sense and assurance of forgiveness and favor as to Him shall seem best for the spiritual good of His creatures. And if we are shown that GOD can and does guide His faithful servants with special inward manifestations of His will, guiding them to the thing they should do if they would do His will, we see, also, that He can overrule the acts and purposes of the wicked to accomplish His designs. We see many examples of this in the Old Testament. The envy of Joseph's brethren was made by the overruling providence of GOD the means of providing for the posterity of Jacob in Egypt. The obstinacy and cruelty of Pharaoh were used as a means of uniting the chosen people and making so strong their determination to go where alone they could be settled, as a means of accomplishing the far-off purpose of the birth in Bethlehem. But we have in the words of the Prophet Isaiah the fullest disclosure of this attribute of GOD. The Jews had greatly departed from GOD, and He warns them, "What will ye do in the day of visitation, and in the desolation that shall come upon you?" Then He refers to the King of Assyria, and says, "I will send him against a hypocritical nation, and against the people of My wrath. . . . Howbeit he meaneth not so, neither doth his heart think so; but it is in his heart to destroy and cut off nations not a few" (Is. x. 3–8).

In all the Old Testament the justice of GOD is made more conspicuous than His love and compassion, though these latter attributes are by no means overlooked and concealed. It was necessary for man to feel first and to learn first to regard GOD as just—a Being who would by no means allow the guilty to go unpunished—before they would appreciate His mercy and forbearance, when in the exercise of this love He should show these favors to men.

Another view of GOD's character is disclosed in the Old Testament. Although represented as perfectly holy, He is represented as exercising forbearance towards some of the evil institutions of man, so that the deeper principles of his moral government might take a deeper root and work a more complete renovation of human nature. Of this we see illustrations in His dealings with two of the institutions that have prevailed so extensively in human history, as to show their deep seat in the passions and propensities of the human heart. Human slavery had existed in some form in nearly, if not quite every, branch of the human family before history began, or historic records and monuments were left to show what transpires in the earliest ages of man's existence. Another great evil had an early origin, and has shown great tenacity in its grasp upon society,—polygamy. It is usually attended with easy divorce, on the part of the husband at least. The whole tenor of the Jewish Dispensation and legislation is such as to show that in GOD's esteem these institutions are both wrong and of evil tendency. But while prohibiting peremptorily idolatry and the unbelief in other gods than the one eternal JEHOVAH, and such gross sins as intemperance and adultery, GOD did tolerate and allow slavery and easy divorce among His ancient covenant people. He had taught principles and instituted a spiritual discipline that would inevitably outroot them in the course of time,—principles and a discipline that would lead the people to see and realize that they were evil and wrong, and abandon or abolish them voluntarily. Easy divorce and polygamy were peremptorily prohibited in the Christian Dispensation; and we have seen only in these latter days the sentiment of a Christian world making its last struggles against the other.

In all this GOD seems to have acted upon the policy which we often express in the words " we must take men as we find them," adding thereto the other principle without which the one just stated becomes a means of demoralization and may be used as a justification of anything however bad,—namely, that while we must *take* them as we find them, we must also adopt our policy and method of dealing with them so as to make them, in due time, what we would have them to be. This policy adopted and persisted in as the dealings of GOD with man as manifested in both Testaments, shows what was so explicitly affirmed of our LORD in the New Testament, "He knew what was in man." Man cannot be made holy off-hand, nor by miracle, nor by GOD's working alone in his nature; only by man's own efforts, each one for himself co-operating with the Divine influences. To this end GOD has revealed truths and doctrines for them. He has commanded duties and He has instituted ordinances, in the observance of which they would grow in grace and in conformity to the will of GOD.

But in the New Testament we have a fuller exhibition of the attributes of GOD, and more especially of His love. St. John says, "The Law came by MOSES,—grace and truth came by JESUS CHRIST" (ch. i. 17), and, more fully, "GOD so loved the world, that He gave His only-begotten SON, that whosoever believeth in Him should not perish, but have everlasting life" (iii. 16).

The mystery of the Incarnation no finite mind may expect to fully understand. But this is a declaration of our LORD to His disciples that is so fully to our present purpose, that it must form the basis for the teaching upon this part of our subject. In the fourteenth chapter of St. John's Gospel our LORD saith, "Let not your heart be troubled; ye believe in GOD, believe also in Me." These words were uttered in view of His departure from them by His crucifixion, and when their faith would be subjected thereby to the severest test. Our LORD assumes their abiding and unquenchable faith in GOD the FATHER, and encourages them to continue to have faith in Him, notwithstanding the adverse events about to occur. But Philip seems to have had some doubt about the FATHER as well, and said to the LORD, "Show us the FATHER and it sufficeth us." If we could only see GOD it would all be well. We could feel sure that however adverse the indications for the future, all would come out right in the end. Our LORD's reply is worthy of special notice. "JESUS saith unto him, Have I been so long time with you, and yet hast thou not known Me, Philip? He that hath seen Me hath seen the FATHER; and how sayest thou then, Show us the FATHER? Believest thou not that I am in the FATHER and the FATHER in me? The words that I speak unto you, I speak not of Myself: but the FATHER that dwelleth in Me, He doeth the works. Believe Me that I am in the Father, and the Father in Me."

As we have said, the mystery of the Incarnation no one can pretend to understand and comprehend so as to say how these things may be; but still we have the fullest and most emphatic assurance that we may take our LORD, His words, and His works, as the fullest exhibition of the attributes of GOD that we can possibly have. GOD we cannot *see*. He is like the wind; it bloweth where it listeth and we hear the sound thereof, but the wind itself we cannot see. We look at the trees and the grain bowing, and we know that the wind is blowing. And so in nature, the more closely we scan its phenomena and study into its secret processes, the more surely we see that GOD is there, although Him we see not nor can see. Philip, therefore, while asking a perfectly natural question, must be regarded as having asked a privilege that cannot be granted in the sense in which he hoped it might be, and in which the skeptic and unbelieving mind is always asking to have GOD's existence and presence made manifest to him. But for all practical purposes of faith, of holy living, he that hath seen the SON hath seen the FATHER also. For the FATHER was in the SON, spake by Him, acted in Him, and was in Him reconciling the world unto Himself (2 Cor. v. 19).

For all the purposes of faith, of obedience, of love, of trust, it sufficeth us, therefore, to know and study the words of CHRIST, the SON of GOD. We have, then, several groups of works and words that may be considered as each teaching something of the attributes of GOD. We may take the miracles of (1) turning the water into wine (St. John ii. 6 *sq*.), (2) that of feeding the multitudes by a miraculous increase of the loaves and fishes (St. Matt. xiv. 17; xv. 34; xvi. 9, 10; St. Mark vi. 52; St. John vi. 9 *sq*.); (3) that of stilling the waves (St. Matt. viii. 23-27; St. Mark iv. 39), as showing His presence in and power over the phenomena of nature as taught in the Old Testament. These miracles are enough to show that He can and does, in fact, so control the elements and the phenomena of nature that He can give fruitful seasons and avert the pestilence when it pleases Him so to do; enough to show that we can place the most implicit confidence in Him in regard to all our worldly affairs, and go on in the way of duty which He has laid down,—not in the way we may have chosen as that of duty regardless of His commands,—and leave results to Him. If we turn to consider another group of the miracles, we find another truth equally assuring to our faith. We refer to the miracles of healing. Disease and infirmity were then, as they are now, when rightly considered, regarded as results of the fall of man and the transgressions of GOD's laws; although, as our LORD has taught us, we must not in all cases consider disease or misfortune as a result of some transgression by the sufferer. We inherit the consequences of the sins of our ancestors, and often the child is sickly, blind, dumb, or idiotic because of inherited disease from some ancestral sin. Now, our LORD came especially to be a Divine deliverer from sin and its consequences. Hence in these miracles of healing He showed His power to do what He claimed to have come into the world to do. Not only could He forgive sins and restore peace to the troubled conscience, but He wrought miracles expressly, as He Himself assures us, that we might know that the Son of Man hath power on earth to forgive sins (St. Matt. ix. 6; St. Mark ii. 10; St. Luke v. 24), and we read, "the multitudes saw it and glorified GOD that He had given such power unto men," or perhaps we might render it, "such power to be exercised among men."

Another group of miracles, "the casting out of devils," raises a question which we need not discuss. There is a tendency in modern times to regard these "possessions" as only forms of epilepsy or insanity. But in any view, their cure was a manifestation of GOD's power over all the influences of evil to which man may be subjected, of whatever nature they may be. And, finally, in the raising of the dead, of which we have several examples, we have a manifestation of His power to deliver us from all the evil that men can do to our bodies, even from the embrace and sleep of death. And His own resurrection, after His crucifixion and sleep of three days in the grave, carries this exhibition of His powers and purpose to the very highest point,—a manifestation of self-inherent powers of the highest kind, of a power that makes all things else powerless in the comparison.

As a manifestation of GOD's love for man, though a most conspicuous and important part of our LORD's acts, we shall say but little. The whole is summed up in the words of St. John (iii. 16), "GOD so loved the world that He gave His only-begotten Son, that whosoever believeth in Him should not perish, but have everlasting life." And the intensity of this love and what it cost to exercise it and make it effectual for man is shown in the history of the betrayal, the agony of Gethsemane, the shame of the Judgment Hall, and the ignominy and suffering of Calvary. These are enough to show that there is nothing that Wisdom can invent, Love suggest, or Power execute that GOD will not do for the welfare and salvation of man. They show, indeed, as does also the whole tenor of Scripture, that there is something that man must do himself and for himself, or GOD can do nothing for him; but they show that there is nothing that can be done that GOD will not do (1) to guide us in the right way if we will consent to be guided by Him; (2) to save us from pain if we will do what we can to avoid the sin that brings pain and woe to men; (3) to deliver us from the punishment which we deserve, if we will only repent of the evil ways and deeds that have made us deserving of punishment; and (4) to raise us to a higher life in this world and to eternal life in the next if we will only accept the guidance which He has provided for us in His Church,—guidance by the HOLY SPIRIT within and guidance by His Word in our hands; guidance by His ministry, with whom He has promised to be always, even unto the end of the world, and the helps of sacraments, holy meditations, prayer and worship, fellowship and co-operating sympathy which come from membership in His Church, which is His Body and organized means of regenerating the world, when we become co-workers and fellow-helpers with Him in bringing men to see the truth and to be transformed and conformed to His glorious image and spotless character.

But there is a disposition in these latter days to doubt or deny the miracles. Without the miracles CHRIST could be no manifestation of GOD. A wise teacher and a good, earnest friend He might indeed be, but without the miracles He could be no manifestation of the presence and attributes of GOD. We have the Gospels written at the time and by the men who saw Him in person, heard His words, words which He spake as never man spake (St. John vii. 46), —this was the admission of His enemies,— and did works no man could do except GOD were with him (St. John iii. 2), which was the admission of a doubter. It was indeed a credulous and an uncritical age, in which the belief in miracles and impostures of all kinds was prevalent, but there was something about our LORD's miracles that took them out of the common run of extraordinary and unexplainable acts. Not all the persons who saw or knew of His miracles were inclined to believe in Him or in them. His miracles were peculiar and had a meaning that would not allow them to pass unnoticed or unchallenged. If they were true, He was GOD, the very LORD of heaven and of earth, and all must obey Him or perish beneath His displeasure. There was no middle ground and no possibility of compromise in the case. All persons saw and felt the emergency and the necessity of giving heed to what was being done. They saw that if what He said was true, and if the works He performed were really performed, there could be no doubting that His words were true. They saw that not only were they great sinners and in danger of GOD's wrath, but they feared that if they let Him alone and allowed Him to go on in the performance of such works, He would draw all the people after Him, and "the Romans would come and take away their place and nation" (St. John ix. 48). They saw the full import of His miracles,—they foresaw all that they portended,—and they jealously scrutinized them. When our LORD had given sight to one born blind, "the neighbors and they which had known him that had been healed" came together to inquire into the miracle. They could not deny it, nor could they explain it. The Pharisees accused Him of breaking the Sabbath, and the Jews regarded Him as a "sinner," and threatened to cast both JESUS and the man out of the synagogue. But after the closest scrutiny they could not deny the miracle, and the young man, though he could not tell how it was done, insisted that "since the world began it was not heard that any mere man opened the eyes of one that had been born blind." Miracles and wonders doubtless had been wrought in great profusion, but the opening of the eyes of one that had been born blind, by a mere man, had never been heard of,— "therefore, if this man were not of GOD, He could do no such thing" (St. John ix. 33). They could not answer Him on this point, except by saying, "Thou was altogether born in sins, and dost thou presume to dictate to us? and they cast him out."

We have another notable and very instructive instance in the Acts of the Apostles (ch. iii.). SS. Peter and John had healed a man that was lame from his birth; the matter came before the great Council—the Sanhedrin—for investigation. After all that could be done by way of scrutiny and with the most earnest desire to deny the miracle if they could, they were at a loss what to do; but they admitted "that indeed a notable miracle had been wrought is manifest to all them that dwell in Jerusalem, and we cannot deny it" (Acts iv. 16). But they clearly foresaw the consequences of these miracles, in the influence they would exert on the opinions and actions of the people.

We have proof, however, that the miracles were wrought by our LORD and His Apostles outside of, and totally independent of, the Holy Scriptures. We have in the remains of the first century of Christianity fragments of the works that were written by the enemies of Christianity. The Christian writers claimed miracles, and therefore did not deny that miracles had been wrought. Their line of argument was to deny that they were proof of the Divine presence and powers of CHRIST.

Let us examine for a moment the one great miracle,—the Resurrection of our LORD. That the Apostles and the hundreds of others who had seen him after His resurrection believed in its occurrence admits of no doubt. But did the unbelievers deny the fact? Let us look into the Scriptures themselves and see how they treated the matter. First we have them betraying their fear that He would rise. As soon as they were sure that He was dead they went unto Pilate and said, "Sir, we remember that that deceiver said while He was yet alive, After three days I will arise again" (St. Matt. xxvii. 63). And they secured a guard to protect the tomb "lest His disciples come by night and steal Him away and say that He is risen." But after the resurrection we do not find them denying or attempting to deny the fact. But they do persuade the soldiers to lie about it; they gave them large money to say "that His disciples had come by night and stolen Him away" (St. Matt. xxviii. 12, 13). Again, after the great forty days, the matter came up once more for investigation and scrutiny. Our LORD had appeared on several occasions after His resurrection. He had even ascended into heaven in the presence of a great multitude; the lie of the soldiers had proved ineffectual; the Apostles and other believers proclaimed the fact, and "the authorities," who saw that for them everything for this world and for the next was at stake, if the Gospel were true and should be believed, were stimulated to their utmost. Denial did not occur to them as possible, that was out of the question. And so that it should spread no farther among the people they straitly threatened the Apostles. They called the Apostles Peter and John, and commanded them not to speak or teach at all in the name of JESUS or about His doctrine and resurrection (Acts iv. 17 *sq.*). But the Apostles still continued with great power to give witness to the resurrection. But there was no denial or attempt, so far as we are informed, at denial, and there and then, the very best thing possible, if possible at all,—the denial of the fact of the miracles, and of the greatest of them all—the Resurrection—the enemies of the Gospel did not venture to do. The miracles were, indeed, "notable," known to all men, and they as they confessed could not deny it.

What occurred in the Apostolic age, and is recorded for us in Holy Scripture, was continued for several centuries, until unbelievers outside the Church had ceased to exist. We have many fragments—no whole treatise—of these deniers and unbelievers; fragments preserved in the writings of the Christians who wrote to answer the objections and vindicate Christianity from their attacks and objections. But nowhere and never does there appear a denial of the fact that the miracles were wrought as represented and claimed in the Gospels. We cite but one example out of many and show how the apologists treated this branch of their subject. We cite what is known as "The Recognitions of Clement." It is a work of an early date, but of unknown authorship. It was written in Greek, but soon was translated into Latin, and was, perhaps, more extensively read and more widely influential in the earliest centuries than any other book. It purports to give an account of St. Peter as preaching the Gospel and meeting the objections of unbelievers and adversaries. The account purports to have been given by the Clement who is spoken of by St. Paul (Phil. iv. 3), and who afterwards became the first Bishop of Rome. Of course it is a picture, and nobody supposes it to have been intended to be anything else. It was intended to represent St. Peter as he was then understood to have been as a preacher of the Gospel,—as a modern novelist writes his work of fiction to illustrate parts of history,—and the way and the extent to which it was received and the estimation in which it was held at that early period is a sure proof of its trustworthiness in the matter for which we cite it; that is, we do not suppose that any such scene occurred or that the very words were actually used by St. Peter, but only that such was the way in which it was understood at the time that he would have treated the subject. And it was on the whole the way in which the apologists of that day did treat it.

One Nicetas asks St. Peter how he was to discriminate the true miracle from the false; how to distinguish between those wrought by our LORD and His Apostles and those that were wrought by such persons as Simon Magus; and why he should believe Christianity on account of the miracles and not accede to the claims of the impostors. St. Peter says, as his starting-point, that this is an instinct or insight in all good men, who want to distinguish between truth and falsehood, right or wrong, which enables them to do so, and that this applies to the true and the false miracles as well as to anything else (ch. iii.). But often, he says, the false miracles are senseless and do no good to anybody, such as "showing statues walking, dogs of brass or stone barking, mountains dancing, of flying through the air, and such like things." But "those miracles which were wrought by the good One are directed to the benefit of men, such as those performed by our dear LORD, who gave sight to the blind and hearing to the deaf, raised up the feeble and the lame, and drove away sickness, cast out demons and raised the dead, and did such others like things as you see we do" (ch. ix.). Here is no intimation of a doubt that the miracles were performed, but only a question as to the proper view or explanation of them, which were claimed to have been performed by persons who had no divine mission and were laboring to no good end. But it is claimed that the miracles if they were indeed wrought as claimed are no proof of the truth of Christianity. Says Matthew Arnold, "I do not see how the fact that I could perform the miracle of converting the pen with which I am writing into paper would prove the truth of what I am writing." But we may answer, it depends very much on what you are writing. If you are saying that pens can be converted into paper, and claiming that you can perform the miracle of so transforming them, the act of so transforming your pen into paper would be the best proof you could give of the truth of what you are teaching, and of your power to do what you claim to be able to do. So precisely with our LORD and His miracles. He claimed to be the SAVIOUR of the world and the Deliverer of men. He wrought miracles of deliverance and salvation. He promised to raise men from death and the grave, and He not only raised others but He raised Himself. His miracles might not prove a truth of Mathematics or of Natural Science. But they did prove Him to be what He claimed to be, a SAVIOUR, the SAVIOUR of men; "mighty" and able to save. They showed Him to be GOD, as doing that which GOD alone can do, thus giving us our highest ideal of perfect or infinite wisdom and power, and of infinite goodness as well. Considering, then, our LORD as an incarnation of GOD, the infinite and Eternal Being, who is without beginning of days, or end of years, to whom all things are present and all thoughts are known, the eternal and One who because of His very nature as infinite and eternal can speak in the present tense of whatever was, is, or is to come, in relation to men and the events of time, we have a manifestation of GOD, one in whom dwelt "all the fullness of GOD," a complete manifestation of His character and attributes.

But in these latter days there are those who doubt whether the miracles were performed, and who in consequence would reduce our LORD to be a mere man. For without the miracles, and especially the greatest,—the Incarnation and the Resurrection,—we have in Him no such manifestation of the Divine nature and attributes as will enable us to accept them without question and verification by comparison with something else. If GOD was in Him, spake in His words and acted in His acts, then we have GOD by these words and acts as we know any one of our fellow-men by what he says and does. Words and acts manifest the mind, the man that is in the body. The attitude of men towards the miracles in these latter days is, however, reversed from what it was at first. Our LORD could say, " believe Me for the very work's sake." He made miracles the ground of faith and of belief, and on this ground the Apostles and first preachers of Christianity challenged the belief of those whom they addressed, and by so doing they converted the world to CHRIST and Christianity. But in these days men doubt the miracles, and there is an important sense in which they believe not Christianity for the sake of the miracles, but the miracles (if they believe them at all) for the sake of Christianity. That is, Christianity so commends itself to our judgments, and has wrought such good in the world, that we are ready to regard it as having had an origin that is above anything that is merely human, and as worthy of a Divine origin and the interposition of GOD by miracles. Nothing but the worthiness of the occasion can induce us to believe in any such extraordinary occurrences.

Nor can it be doubted that the great amount of attention that has been given to the natural sciences has done much to render men skeptical in regard to the reality and the possibility of miracles, and to make them disinclined to believe that any have been wrought. A deeper view of nature will be sure to dispel this illusion. There is no comprehending nature without the recognition of GOD as a miracle-worker. This world and all the material universe, so far as we know it, is undergoing a change,—is in process of evolution or development, which must have begun in time, and which, therefore, points to a time when it was not. If even matter existed then, it was in a diffused gaseous state, without chemical combinations or organizations, and the masses that now constitute the sun and stars, our earth and its moon included, sustained no such relation to each other as they do now, and have sustained for a few millions of years past. Who or what was before this? It may, indeed, be a piece of mechanism, like a watch which now runs of itself. But there was a time when the brass, steel, and gold of the watch did not exist in their present relation, and even now it is no example of perpetual motion. The watch runs and keeps time only as it is wound up by a power that is not a mere piece of mechanism,—something totally unlike mechanism,—by some intelligent person. Evolution—a theory that is now in great favor—is but a process. It is no adequate explanation of anything. It had a beginning; it must come to an end. It has a subject-matter to work upon that it did not create and cannot destroy. It had a beginning which it did not originate, and it is under a law which it did not ordain, and it will come to an end, when whatever is eternal in its nature will continue on as though evolution had never begun ; to an end when all that is in its course or compass must either be wound up again like a watch or stand still in an endless condemnation of matter forever. But with GOD as its Author and Creator of its subject-matter, with His will as its limit and its law, and His purpose as the explanation of whatever has been, now is, or shall be in the course of mundane affairs, all is intelligible. But GOD as the Beginner was a miracle-worker, and every interposition of His power to produce a new order of things or to originate a new era is a miracle. Of such interventions we can mention several that no scientific man can doubt. There was a beginning of chemical action, of condensation, and of motion. At a time not far in the past, comparatively, there was another interposition, when some of the elements became living matter,—plants and animals,—with the hitherto unknown phenomena of growth and reproduction of decay and death. And so, too, all researches have thus far failed to find any way to account for the introduction of the new *species* of plants and animals which have followed each other in the successions of geological time, until at last, and quite recently, man made his appearance, without special Divine interposition in each case. In the present state of our scientific knowledge they are as undeniable as they are unexplainable without a recognition of Divine interposition,—which is as miraculous in its nature as the introduction of Christianity, including the Incarnation and the Resurrection with all the miracles that are ascribed to our LORD. Science justifies our belief in the miracles of Revelation. This clear justification must be urged, since great efforts are made to find a theory of evolution or development that shall explain all without a recognition of Divine power. And thus nature and its interpreted science justifies and vindicates our acceptance of the Bible as the Word of GOD,—as a manifestation of His nature and attributes.

Having once proved from mere inanimate nature, from the nature of matter that there must have been, and must still be, something that is above nature, something that is spiritual in its nature, nay, something that is a Personal Agent and Creator, the phenomena of the material universe become a manifestation of the attributes and will of GOD. Not only does nature, considered as the work of His hands, show His wisdom in planning it and His power and omnipresence in executing His plans and in carrying on its course of events, its evolutions, but its phenomena everywhere show His purpose as well as by the principle of what we call final causes. Thus a watch or any other piece of mechanism shows not only the skill and physical strength of the maker, but it shows also that he had a purpose, a design, a final cause in planning and making the mechanism. As we consider the movements of the hands and study its internal structure, we cannot doubt that the maker of a watch designed that by the continuance and regularity of its movements it should indicate the passage of time as truly as the sun and the stars indicate the same fact by their motions, and far more conveniently for our use. In this view, any fact or phenomena of nature, every law or truth of science, is an expression of GOD'S will and purpose in nature, as truly as any fact of sacred history and any command of duty is an indication of His will and purpose in history and in the affairs of man. Whatever occurs in nature or in history, in the phenomena of the natural world or in the life of man, is indicative of the way in which He would have things done by man, and those creatures of His hand who can understand His laws and choose for themselves what they will do, and whether they will do right or wrong. Even whatever is painful and adverse to our wishes must be regarded as a proof of those remedial measures by which He would either prevent wrong-doing or obviate its evil consequences. Hence not only the more striking and remarkable indications of design and adaptation of means to ends, but the more uniform and regular of natural phenomena are indications of the way in which He would have things done, and proofs of His wisdom and power. And the more perfectly regular and uniform they are, the better do they indicate His wisdom and power, just as in human works the perfection of the machinery and the completeness and the certainty with which it accomplishes what it was designed for, the greater skill does it show in the designer and maker of the machine. The law of gravity explains GOD'S will in the universe of matter as truly as the law of love expresses that will in the world of social being, and the fact that they fall—atoms and masses—proves His presence and agency as truly, though not as strikingly, as the miracles that are recorded in the New Testament. It is worthy of note that in nature the two attributes of wisdom and power are more conspicuously manifested. Love, benevolence, or goodness, are indeed the predominance of happiness over misery and suffering. But the extent and amount of suffering has led some persons to doubt whether nature alone, and by itself, shows that His goodness or love is infinite, or without limit, or admixture of some feeling of a different nature. "We cannot," say the objectors, "see why there should be suffering at all, or if any, why there should be so much, or why it should be seen so often when there can be no offense in the sufferer to occasion it, nor any apparent benefit to make it a means of greater happiness." But we must remember that we can at best understand the matter only imperfectly; and especially that, to judge of GOD'S dealings and of His works as indicative of His attributes, we must not neglect to take into account what He has done by way of Revelation, and especially by sending His SON to be a way and a means of salvation. This is a part of His work, and is necessary to a full manifestation of His attributes of goodness, love, and mercy, and they do manifest them as no other acts of His have done or can do.

The "New Philosophy," as it is sometimes called, has helped our natural theology in several ways. While there are, indeed, some men of peculiarly constituted minds who have taken extreme views and thought that nature was comprehensible without GOD, the general tendency has been—and the final result will be—to give greater distinction and sharper outlines to the facts and principles of science which make the presence and agency of GOD more manifest and incapable of doubt or denial than it was before. We know now more precisely what we can ascribe to matter and the forces of nature, and just where the agency of GOD comes in, than we did a few years ago. He must have begun the present "evolution," and He must have interposed specially and by way of miracle many times since; and even the "forces of nature," to which as to second causes we are accustomed to ascribe the phenomena of nature, are seen to be nothing without Him. We have seen that "evolution" cannot be eternal, and a world of mere matter without GOD could no more go on forever through a series of successive evolutions than a watch could run forever without being repeatedly wound up.

We have alluded to the flood of light the recent attainments in science have thrown upon the concise and rather obscure statements in the first chapter of Genesis. But there are many other statements and profound principles in the Bible which these illustrate, and to which they give a new meaning or a fullness of meaning which had not before been recognized. We have been accustomed to regard GOD's action in nature as ending on the "sixth day." But our LORD said, "My FATHER worketh hitherto, and I work (St. John v. 17). Hitherto, "until now," GOD worked in creating, until the appearance of man. He worked in history and in providence from this creation until the birth of CHRIST, and He in CHRIST works now, and has wrought ever since the Incarnation, " in the regeneration" (St. Matt. xix. 18). In this stage of His work, and to accomplish it, the WORD became incarnate, suffered on the Cross, instituted His Church, with its Worship and Sacraments, its Ministry and Discipline, and for this He sent the HOLY GHOST to lead His disciples and His people "unto all truth," and for this and by way of carrying it on, He from that day to this has called and sent holy men as ministers, evangelists, and missionaries of His word. (Eph. iv. 12, 13.) Again, the students of nature and natural science claim to have found as one of GOD's Laws what they call "the struggle for life, with survival of the fittest." In view of this Law, anything in nature is considered as having a desire to prolong its existence, and laboring under the necessity, in order to do so, of continued exertion and of avoiding the enemies which otherwise would terminate its existence. And if we suppose any change in circumstances or environment, the one that has the greatest capacity or willingness to adapt itself to the new conditions is most likely to live, is "fittest to survive" under the circumstances. And in both these ways, it is held, the natural species are undergoing changes which are, on the whole, with few exceptions, in the direction of improvement and advance towards a higher type or a higher mode of life. In this way it is held that one branch of the human family, by migrations from the original centres and encountering on its way new environments and new climates, has become red like the Mongolians, another black like the negroes, while in Europe the race has advanced in stature, size of brain, and other physical conditions which give opportunity for a higher civilization. Now our LORD in the Sermon on the Mount announced this law as pertaining to nations, religions, and institutions, of society and of civilization, under the symbol of trees: good trees bringing forth good fruit, and bad trees that cannot bring forth good fruit, but are hewn down and cast into the fire (St. Matt. vii.). This is but history. Whatever is doing the will of GOD and is accomplishing His purposes is spared, and is a success so long as it is needed and does His work. But success does not always imply godliness. The worst of men and the most ferocious of tyrants have sometimes been successful. But they were executing the will of GOD upon those who were not doing His will or regardful of His laws. They are made to clear away the obstacles to the accomplishment of His plans, to bury the dead, remove the offal, and consign to oblivion the institutions of evil. Our LORD could not have been betrayed and crucified—as it was foretold He should be, and as it was needful for the shedding of His most precious blood that taketh away the sin of the world—if there had not been a heartless traitor and a still more heartless rabble to execute the purpose. It is doubtful whether the early converts to Christianity would have been sufficiently impressed with the nature and value of Christianity if it had not been for the violence of its persecutors, giving occasion for confession and for martyrdom. Judaism and the Jewish nation lasted as long as it and they were preparing for the coming of CHRIST. But when they failed to do GOD's work they became an evil tree, —and the Romans, who certainly were no better in most respects than the Jews, did GOD's work, drove them from their homes and destroyed their city. They live, although scattered, despised, and persecuted, because they are doing one part of GOD's work as no other people or agency could do it.

But the other people of that age who did not accept the Gospel have passed away, and all their religious and their political institutions, their philosophies, and whatever else was a means of influencing the lives of men. Within a few centuries after the introduction of Christianity there were no heathen or unconverted peoples or families within the domain of what was then the civilized world. Fix your attention upon any family, village, or neighborhood of people as it was then, and ask yourself what has become of their posterity, and you will find that many were converted and brought into the Church, and the rest of them, if indeed any were not converted, became extinct, leaving neither name nor descendants. So with doctrines, usages, and institutions within the Church, whether good or bad, they come in when there is occasion for them or work for them to do stay as long as they are needed for their work, and that is forever if they are intrinsically good, but if they are or become bad, they are like the evil tree that no longer bringing forth good fruit, is cut down and cast into the fire. The matter is sometimes treated as though our LORD in these words was giving a test for the characters of men. But this can hardly have been His purpose. The context clearly shows that He had something else in mind, and the view we have taken of it points to history as a manifestation of GOD's purposes and attributes, no less than the phenomena of nature. And in fact history exhibits some of His attributes—His benevolence, His love, His personality—better than mere inanimate nature or even the animal creation can do. In mere nature there is nothing to resist or to counteract His will; hence with infinite wisdom and power there may be, as we see that there is, perfect uniformity, and this observed uniformity has been urged by objectors and skeptics as a reason for denying the personality of GOD. But in history we have human beings with a power of choice of their own. And here it is that we find GOD apparently changing His purposes,—changing at any rate His means,—His more immediate purposes to suit man's wants and condition. When man repents GOD relents. Under the Old Dispensation He allowed many things on account of the hardness of their hearts which He absolutely prohibited in the New. Thus animal sacrifices and bloody offerings were not merely accepted, they were commanded; they served a transient purpose; when the atonement was "once made for the sins of the whole world," all forms of bloody offerings passed away and gave place to something far more spiritual,—something adapted to a higher state of civilization, a more elevated phase of life and habit of thought. For the same reason many things that seem cruel, harsh, even unjust, appear to have been allowed and approved by GOD in the earlier days of humanity, which are now seen to be inconsistent with Christianity, if they are not expressly forbidden in the New Testament Scriptures. In all this we see how it is that GOD may be a being of perfect holiness and yet tolerate, and for a while appear to approve what we can now see to be wrong. His holiness will appear in the end to all men.

It is indeed quite true that we find in the Bible many statements with regard to GOD which we cannot take literally or regard as adapted to the higher views which the more cultivated minds of modern times are able to accept. But we must remember that GOD deals with men as they are and according to their needs. He takes them as they are in order to secure the acceptance of the means that are necessary to make them what He would have them to be. We must remember that He is a Person incomprehensible in His nature and modes of existence, but yet we are so made in His image that we can in a measure understand Him although we do not and cannot conceive of Him under forms and modes that are, more or less, inadequate, because they are too much like those of men. But in this respect all men are essentially alike, we differ in degree only. From the feeblest infancy of the lisping child up to the broadest powers of comprehension ever attained by saint or scientist we think of Him to some extent as acting under limitations of time and space, of human weakness and infirmity which we can readily show can have no place in the Divine Nature. Something of this kind is necessary in GOD's dealings with man in order to give a sense of reality to our ideas of Him and to make His name a power upon our thoughts and feelings. Abstractly, the Personality of GOD is incomprehensible to us, and practically it is a different thing for each individual because of our infirmity, so that no one can understand or comprehend Him perfectly. Let us begin by regarding Him as wise and good and holy, and as we progress in wisdom and holiness our ideas of Him and His attributes will advance towards that fuller comprehension of His Being which we may always approach but never fully reach unto. But in all stages of our culture we may know that He is not only GOD and Creator, but Father and Friend as well. A Father and a Friend who never slumbers, nor sleeps, who faints not and is never weary, and whose mercies never fail.

REV. PROF. W. D. WILSON, D.D.

God-Father. *Vide* SPONSORS.

Good-Friday. *Vide* FRIDAY.

Gospels. The word itself means good tidings, "godspell," and in its comprehensiveness includes the several parts of the Redemptive Acts of our LORD. "Behold, I bring you good tidings of great joy, which shall be to all people," was the Gospel of the Incarnation of CHRIST. Again, St. Paul (Rom. x. 9-15) connects the good tidings with the belief in and confession of the Resurrection. The LORD Himself makes the Gospel to lie in a belief in the Kingdom of GOD (St. Mark i. 15). Each of the main facts of the Gospel in its fullness can become the central point which may bear the title belonging to the whole. The Gospel, then, is the message of the Church, the teaching of Christianity, the redemption in and by CHRIST JESUS, the only-begotten Son of GOD, offered to all mankind. But it is the title of the four biographies of the LORD JESUS by four separate writers, two of whom were Apostles, two others companions and fellow-workers with other Apostles of the LORD. But the title is again suggestive. It is the "Gospel—the glad tidings of salvation according to" St. Matthew, St. Mark, St. Luke, or St. John. And as the Gospel is bound up in the very life of CHRIST, His biography and the record of His acts, and the proclamation of what He has to offer the soul, are all gathered into the single word, "The Gospel."

Again, the word is used to mean that part of the record of His life, teaching, and actions which is selected to be read on each Sunday, holiday, or fast-day. There are, then, three uses made of the one word,—the Gospel for the whole doctrine of Christianity in the salvation offered by the SON of GOD; the four several accounts of His life; the short passages read in the Eucharistic Scriptures.

The accounts of the several Gospels will be given under the names of the several writers (*Vide* ST. MATTHEW, ST. MARK, ST. LUKE, ST. JOHN), but here it will be well to consider them as grouped together in a common work,—*i.e.*, to set forth the glorious Gospel of the SON of GOD. The first three are generally spoken of as the Synoptists,—*i.e.*, those who give an abbreviated account, a synopsis of the LORD'S Life. The Gospel of St. John has received, in recent discussions, the title of the Fourth Gospel. Indeed, the three Synoptists have much more in common with each other than they have with the Gospel of St. John. The dates of the composition of their Gospels are closer together. St. John's Gospel is nearly half a century apart from them. They wrote before heresies and internal dissensions had to any extent disturbed the Church, which was girded up to meet her early foes. St. John's Gospel was written when heresies had begun; when they who were once within, but not of, the Church had gone out. Theirs was an intensely practical realization of His work. A man among men as well as the Son of GOD. The anointed JESUS who was King of Israel. The great High-Priest, and the Sacrifice for the sins of the whole world. His was as intense a realization of the work of CHRIST, but it was from its doctrinal aspects that the disciple whom JESUS loved grasped it. The Gospel in its divine side, in its theology, not in its anthropology, or its soteriology, so prominently as in the others, is dwelt upon. Nor must it be for a moment admitted that the view that either one of the four makes the prominent characteristic is ignored by the others. Only that each dwells upon that characteristic of the LORD'S life and Person which he had grasped more completely.

The three Synoptists have certain points of agreement, certain points of independence, and a certain order of chronology peculiar to each. They bear witness in their own way as independent eye-witnesses, with variations even in those cases where all four agree, which show them to be thoroughly truthful. The apparent contradictions are real confirmations of their truth. Without wasting space to demonstrate this, we will indicate those passages in which the three agree, premising that they all agree together in recounting only nineteen facts which St. John records also, which could be reduced in part by avoiding a subdivision of leading events. The four agree in, I. St. John Baptist's Ministry. II. Baptism of JESUS CHRIST. III. John Baptist in Prison. IV. CHRIST'S return to Galilee. V. Feeding of the Five Thousand. VI. Peter's Profession of Faith. So far, the leading events; but from hence onward the Passion of our LORD must of course present many points of coincidence, and yet the accounts are thoroughly independent. VII. Anointing by Mary. VIII. CHRIST enters Jerusalem. IX. Paschal Supper. X. Peter's fall foretold. XI. Gethsemane. XII. The Betrayal. XIII. Before Caiaphas, Peter's denial. XIV. Before Pilate. XV. Accusation. XVI. Crucifixion. XVII. The Death. XVIII. The Burial. XIX The Resurrection. The three Synoptists agree in forty-four facts besides those in which they agree with St. John: I. The Temptation. II. The four Apostles called. III. Simon's wife's mother healed. IV. Circuit round Galilee. V. Healing a leper. VI. Stilling the Storm. VII. Demoniacs at Gadara. VIII. Jairus's daughter, and the woman healed. IX. Healing the paralytic. X. Matthew the Publican. XI. "Thy Disciples fast not." XII. Plucking ears of corn on the Sabbath. XIII. The withered Hand, Miracles. XIV. The Twelve. XV. Parable of the Sower. XVI. Grain of mustard-seed. XVII. His Mother and His brethren. XVIII. Sending forth the Twelve. XIX. Herod's opinion of JESUS. XX. Passion foretold. XXI. Transfiguration. XXII. Lunatic healed. XXIII. Passion again foretold. XXIV. The little child. XXV. Offenses. XXVI. The grain of mustard-seed. XXVII. Infants brought to JESUS. XXVIII. The rich young man. XXIX. Promises to the Disciples. XXX. Death foretold. XXXI. Blind men at Jericho. XXXII. "By what authority doest thou?" XXXIII. Parable of the Wicked Husbandman. XXXIV. The tribute money. XXXV. The state of the risen. XXXVI. David's Son and David's LORD. XXXVII. Against the Pharisees. XXXVIII. CHRIST'S second coming. XXXIX. Last Passover. XL. Judas Iscariot. XLI. Before the Sanhedrim. XLII. The mockings and railings. XLIII. Darkness and other Portents. XLIV. The Bystanders. The Synoptists agree in testifying to forty-four separate events, acts, or teachings of CHRIST where St. John has no parallel fact recorded. We have four witnesses to maintain main facts; three to forty-four other facts. These facts include the central facts of His Baptism, A specially important Miracle, The Confession that He is the SON of GOD, The Paschal Supper, Gethsemane, Betrayal, Trial, Crucifixion, Resurrection. The more important facts to which the three Synoptists only testify are The choice of the Twelve and their Mission, The Passion foretold thrice, The Transfiguration, Judas, Mocking, Darkness, and Bystanders. As our object is one of general comparison, and to show the amount of concurrent testimony the Gospels contain, we will add a list of the facts in which two of the Evangelists agree, without pausing to distinguish which two, since we are only trying to illustrate the truth of the rule "that in the mouth of two or three witnesses every word may be established." I. The birth of our LORD. II. The two Genealogies. III. Flight into Egypt. IV. The Centurion's Servant. V. Messengers of John. VI. Parable of Candle under a bushel. VII. Of the Leaven. VIII. On teaching by Parables. IX. Reception at Nazareth. X. Third circuit around Galilee. XI. Death of John Baptist. XII. The washen hands. XIII. The Syrophœnician Woman. XIV. Miracles of healing. XV. Feeding the Four Thousand. XVI. The sign from heaven. XVII. The Leaven of the Pharisees. XVIII. Elijah. XIX. One casting out Devils. XX. The lost sheep. XXI. Journey to Jerusalem. XXII. Answers to Disciples. XXIII. The LORD'S Prayer. XXIV. Prayer effectual. XXV. The unclean spirit. XXVI. The sign of Jonah. XXVII. The light of the body. XXVIII. The Pharisees. XXIX. What to fear. XXX. Covetousness. XXXI. The Leaven. XXXII. O Jerusalem, Jerusalem! XXXIII. Parable of the Great Supper. XXXIV. Following CHRIST with the Cross. XXXV. Offenses. XXXVI. Faith and Merit. XXXVII. Divorce. XXXVIII. Request of James and John. XXXIX. Parable of the Ten Talents. XL. The barren Fig-tree. XLI. Pray and forgive. XLII. The Parable of the Wedding Garment. XLIII. The great Commandment. XLIV. The Widow's mite. XLV. Parable of the Talents. XLVI. Disciples going to Emmaus. XLVII. Appearances in Jerusalem. XLVIII. Ascension. The central points of great importance are, the human birth, the mysterious law of teaching by parables, the disciples going to Emmaus, the appearances in Jerusalem, and the Ascension.

We have one hundred and eight acts or teachings out of two hundred and seventeen different topics, and the larger number of the remaining one hundred and nine (except St. Luke's circumstantial account of the birth of our LORD), is made up of discourses reported by one or other of the Evangelists alone,—discourses most valuable, but not needing the concurrent testimony the other facts have received. We have, then, the evidence of the legal number of witnesses to His Birth, His Baptism, His Temptation, His Preaching, His Miracles, His Transfiguration, His prophecy of His own death, His prophecy concerning Jerusalem, His institution of the Last Supper, His Passion, Betrayal, Trial, Crucifixion, Death, Burial, and Ascension. These are the outlines of His Gospel. The details that have filled up this outline were the original matter which each could furnish, under the guidance of the HOLY GHOST, out of the abundant stores of his own memory. But there is a theory which has been broached, and has found much favor. It is that there was a document already in circulation, from which the three Synoptists drew such material as they deemed best for their purposes; that St. Mark adhered most closely to this document, and that the other two departed from it at will; and an effort has been made to restore out of the three a supposed text which would represent the contents of this imaginary fourth and earlier authority. Apart from the absurdity of supposing such a document to have utterly disappeared without leaving even a tradition behind it, and of imagining that the Evangelists—if this document were of any worth—would have superseded it by their own narratives without any acknowledgment in some way; apart, too, from the indirect denial of the inspiration of our Gospels which such a theory involves, the whole is baseless, because wherever we find the Evangelists departing from each other we must imagine an altered copy. Therefore this supposed original document has to be supplemented by four other documents altered from the first,—two St. Matthew, one St. Luke, one St. Mark, used in Eichhorn's theory, while Bishop Marsh has to conjecture the use of eight. This, as will be seen, is fatal to the whole conjecture. One good result is that this minute study of the verbal differences existing between their accounts has established the complete independence of the three Evangelists, and has purged the text of interpolations. Another conjecture has been made, that as the Apostles taught the same things, there was an *oral narrative* from which the Evangelists drew. The Apostles would, in their preaching, proclaim the same facts, and, it is very natural to suppose, in as nearly as possible the very same words. There, then, would grow up a skeleton outline on which the three Evangelists could most naturally place their own separate accounts.

This theory would account for the use of the same language and for many coincidences; but it would break down upon the independent order of events on which each Evangelist arranged his narrative. St. Luke is on the whole more nearly chronologically accurate, but all three follow no fixed plan of dates, but group certain classes of teachings or certain series of miracles together, which most probably were taught or performed on very different occasions. This they did to place in one view the leading conception each had formed of the MASTER, His work and His purpose, and this fits best with the inspiration of the HOLY GHOST, leading them to set forth the many-sidedness, the perfect human sympathies, the loving condescensions of the LORD JESUS in far better way, giving room for a better showing of His Divine nature and wondrous power than any other form could supply. A close study of the Gospels will show from their very structure that they in this way only, humanly speaking, could set before us the two natures in the one perfect sinless Person of CHRIST the LORD ; that in this way they link their contents to the contents, and their form to the form of the Inspired Scriptures of the Old Covenant. The Gospel of St. Matthew begins with the genealogy of JESUS CHRIST, the son of David, the son of Abraham, narrating His miraculous birth, and appeals to the prophecy of Isaiah for a proof that He who was according to the flesh the son of Abraham, was also because of this birth the Emmanuel as well as the Joshua of the people. The whole Gospel rests upon the foundation of prophecy. So St. Mark opens with startling abruptness, "The beginning of the Gospel of JESUS CHRIST the SON of GOD as it is written in the prophets. Behold, I send my messenger before Thy face, which shall prepare Thy way before Thee; the voice of one crying in the wilderness, Prepare ye the way of the LORD, make His paths straight," and at once points to this messenger St. John Baptist, who by *his* fulfillment of the prophecy proved that JESUS CHRIST was the MESSIAH of prophecy. St. Luke's Gospel is much more elaborate, and details more at length the birth of the messenger, and then that of the CHRIST. Yet not only the visions and messages of the angels are in strict parallelism to the visions and promises of the Old Covenant, but the Hymns of thanksgiving are thoroughly Hebrew in every way, and as soon as the events require it appeal is at once made to the prophets. St John's Gospel seems (as at first did St. Luke's) to break this law of conjoining to the old prophecies, but it really does so in a far more wondrous way. "In the beginning GOD *made* the heavens and the earth," but also, "In the beginning *was* the Word, and the Word was with GOD and the Word was GOD. The same was in the beginning with GOD." Upon this basis is built the whole superstructure of that glorious Gospel. With less direct quotation from the older Scriptures there is framed into the texture of his Gospel as profound an application of the prophets as in the other three.

Each writer has his method. Each writer has his own individuality, and is enthused by his own characteristic devotion or love, or self-negation, yet is as completely inspired by the HOLY GHOST, kept from error in recording what he knew by the ordinary means of obtaining information, given insight to record accurately the true worth, in just wording of each event or discourse, had revealed to him those doctrines which human wit could not fathom, but which were necessary for our salvation. So St. John (to take but one) recorded with absolute accuracy all he knew, from his own first interview with our LORD, and the many facts of which he was an eye-witness, till he saw the water and the blood flow from the spear-pierced side, saw the risen LORD in that upper chamber, and again upon the shore of Galilee, and heard His triple restoration of the recreant Apostle. It was with greater fullness of the same Spirit, who had given him inerrancy, in fact, that he could divine the true meaning of the High-Priest's unwilling prophecy, or recorded our LORD'S discourses. And the same HOLY GHOST gave to him the revelation of the JESUS CHRIST, the Word of GOD, who was with GOD, and was GOD.

It was not in mortal man to dare to make that statement, which yet is the corner-stone of our salvation. And this in a less prominent way, but not the less truly is the fact with each of the others. It is only their own characteristic temperament making them what they were that gives its form to their record. The fire burns as hotly, but the crust of character is different. The Publican naturally would not feel precisely as, though not less deeply than, the more polished Physician, who was the constant companion of the fervid Apostle Paul. Here we may remark upon the persons who were divinely chosen. St. Matthew, the sober, earnest, devout man, the business man, who, without hesitation, gave up his earthly business for a heavenly traffic, looking at his Master as the man of men, the Son of David, and believing with a daily growing, developing power, that He was the CHRIST, the SON of the Living GOD, in his very quiet shows as intense an enthusiasm as did St. John after sixty-six years of toil for the same Master. Two only of the Apostles were directed to write a narrative of what they knew of that Word of life whom they had seen, handled, followed, loved, ate with, watched with, and for whom they were ready to lay down their lives. It was directed that two others, whose narrative shows them to have been eye-witnesses to some things, and to have received ample, accurate, and undeniable information upon other facts, should write the other two biographies. It is the unbroken tradition that St. Mark wrote his Gospel for the converts of St. Peter, and that St. Luke wrote his for the Churches that St. Paul established; that each wrote under the directions and with the oversight of his Apostolic leader. Here, again, is another proof that the same Spirit who selected the prophets of old from the husbandmen, the shepherds, the plowmen, as well as from the priests and learned families, selected men whom man's judgment would have passed over.

(The contents of each Gospel and the characteristics of each Evangelist will be discussed under the several names MATTHEW, MARK, LUKE, JOHN.)

There was another use made of the Gospels which brought in a third sense. The portion of Scripture from the life of our LORD, appointed for the lessons in connection with the Holy Communion, was called the Gospel. It was a carrying out in the Scriptures of the New Testament the older parallel usage in the synagogue worship. The Law and the Prophets were divided into fifty-four portions each, and appointed to be read through the year. Since these would certainly not be neglected in Christian assemblies, we can well see that at the earliest possible moment the acknowledged Christian Scriptures would be so used. We have a record of the point before which these Scriptures were not so read. The ancient Liturgy of St. James contains this Rubric: "Then are read at large the Sacred Scriptures of the Old Covenant, and of the Prophets, and the Incarnation of the Son of GOD is set forth, His sufferings and His Resurrection, the Ascension into heaven, and His second coming again with glory. And this takes place daily in the sacred and divine ministration." Here the Law and the Prophets are *read* and the Gospel is *set forth*, *i.e.*, recited orally. But this, then, shows the Liturgy to be in its frame-work older than 140 A.D., for Justin Martyr tells us that the memorials (*i.e.*, Gospels) of the Apostles and the writings of the Prophets are read. It is inferred that the Gospel for the day was read as early. It is rather a hasty inference to push it to a conclusion that there was a series of Gospels selected and set forth as ours are. But it is fair to conclude that the Gospel-lections were then customarily introduced. The evidence between that date and that of St. Ambrose is too slight to be adduced to prove more than Justin's words do. But by that time Gospels and Epistles were in regular use. The Council of Laodicea (365 A.D.) ordered the Gospels to be read with the other Scriptures on the Saturday also. To omit other details the Comes of St. Jerome, from which it is probable our Epistles and Gospels come, gives the Gospels for over two hundred days. The use was probably determined by the Bishop of the Diocese, and so we may account for the many variations remarked as occurring at different times. The Comes gives the number cited above, the Mozarabic adds an Epistle and Gospel for the Wednesdays and Fridays in Lent, but there was no such use in Gaul. The Irish Sacramentary provides but one Epistle and Gospel for the whole year; the Epistle is 1 Cor. xi., the Gospel St. John vi. The Eastern Church reads them in order. Again, the use varied as to who should read the Gospel. St. Cyprian had the lector or reader do this, but elsewhere the Deacon, and this became universal. But in some places the Bishop only read it, in other places it was the Priest's office; but this was local. In the American Church the Deacon, if he be alone, reads it, the Priest if he be present, and the Bishop if he choose to do so, when he is present, though there is no rule about it. The rule should be to read the Gospel from the north front of the Holy Table. If there is an Epistoler, he should read from the south front of the Holy Table. But more important is the rule to listen to the Gospel reverently standing. This was very ancient, being directed by the Apostolic Constitutions, and historians who note the infringement of this rule do so with surprise. The Doxology, Glory be to Thee, O LORD, was likewise very old. It was an Eastern custom, and spread thence over to Gaul.

Grace. The word originally meant the *free gift*, favor, or benefit. Then it received the technical meaning it has now in the semi-theologic language of the pulpit. It is one of the most important of all the terms used, for the Grace of our Lord JESUS CHRIST, the free gift He bestows of everlasting life, the free gift of the HOLY GHOST and all the blessings that attend His presence, the favors and benefits that the practice of the Christian virtues procures in our daily life, are all comprehended under that one all-embracing word. The Sacraments are called the means of grace, and not these only, but every outward act, as prayer, alms-giving, fasting, self-denial, are such means. We may truly say that the work of the Second and Third Persons of the HOLY TRINITY is summed up in that single word. Let us, then, keep clearly in mind that the great source of all spiritual graces is the free gift of CHRIST from the FATHER. He gave His only-begotten SON. The basis of Grace is love. The love of GOD to us procured the Atonement, the Absolution, the Gift of Everlasting Life, the hope of Glory. These are of the Grace of CHRIST. When He ascended upon high He led captivity captive, and gave gifts to men, yea, even to His enemies, that the Lord GOD might dwell among them. All spiritual gifts are accompanied with some outward pledge of the reality of the gift. Therefore the gift of the SPIRIT in Confirmation, the gift of Absolution in Baptism and the Holy Communion, the blessings which crown a true repentance, a living faith, a hearty and loving zeal in the Christian life, the reply to prayer, to alms, to all acts of Christian self-control, all of which are so beautifully summed up in the general thanksgiving: "We, Thine unworthy servants, do give Thee most humble and hearty thanks for all Thy goodness and loving kindness to us and to all men. We bless Thee for our creation, preservation, and all the blessings of this life; but, above all, for Thine inestimable love in the redemption of the world by our Lord JESUS CHRIST, for the means of Grace and for the hope of Glory." But there is another side of the subject, upon which we must bestow a few words. The whole Gospel is filled with the Grace of our LORD; but how about ourselves? It must be laid down as an axiom that GOD gives us no gift that is not in sympathy with and in the full reach of our true nature. In fact, so far as we can see, each gift is only a restoration in such part of the original holiness in Paradise. There is in us capacity to hold whatever His Grace bestows. The first part of His work must have been that the Cross of CHRIST put all men into a condition of capacity for salvation, but there is also, more or less strongly, in us each an ability to lay hold of this Grace, otherwise the gift of salvation were beyond our nature, and a new creation of faculties, to enable us to receive His mercy, would have to be made. This ability is, indeed, of the weakest and faintest, and therefore we need help and strength. This He supplies; but as GOD gives us no gift that is not apt to our nature, so He asks us to receive nothing which we are not able to perceive ourselves when once it is put rightly before us. (Hence the lament of CHRIST over Jerusalem: "If thou hadst known, even thou at least in this thy day, the things which belong unto thy peace, but now they are hid from thine eyes.") But our weakness paralyzes all our efforts. The X. Article puts this clearly. "The condition of man after the fall of Adam is such that he cannot turn and prepare himself by his own natural strength and good works to faith and calling upon GOD. Wherefore we have no power to do good works, pleasant and acceptable to GOD, without the Grace of GOD, by CHRIST preventing us, that we may have a good will, and working with us when we have that good will."

The miracle of the paralytic man is a type of our capacity, aptness, disability by sin and weakness, and of GOD'S prevenient grace. He was borne of four into CHRIST'S presence. He was disabled and could do nothing, yet he was a man in body and mind, capable of, fit for, that natural health which lawfully should be his. He was healed,—"thy sins be forgiven thee," which was the free prevenient grace of the LORD, and he took up his bed and departed to his own house. So St. Paul declares, "work out your own salvation with fear and trembling, for it is GOD which worketh in you both to *will*, and to *do*, of His good pleasure." So our LORD, "no man can come unto Me except the FATHER, which hath sent Me, draw him." But we are to beware of what is called irresistible grace. An irresistible grace supplants the responsibility of the will. We can well believe in the urgings and pleadings of the Spirit, the quickening of the conscience, the persuasions of a lively love, and desire for holiness, but all Scriptures point to the Law that the will must choose finally. Grace is all-sufficient for whatever we can do or can desire, but it does *not* remove our true self and take its place. Co-operating grace may so work in us as to help us, possibly insensibly, to yield ourselves and our members servants to righteousness unto holiness. His Grace is sufficient for us all, in the moments of our greatest weakness, to give those who yield to His gifts all-sufficient strength. And while our state continues probationary, and therefore involves trial from GOD and temptation from Satan, GOD is faithful, and by His grace in His own wisdom will make a way to escape before the pressure is too great for our faith or our strength,—*i.e.*, beyond the limit which the flesh can attain of obedience. But our obedience is demanded up to that point. Therefore St. Paul blames the Hebrew Christians for that with the grace given them "they had not yet resisted unto blood." Co-operating grace is the sanctifying work of the HOLY GHOST in the willing and ready heart. But the heart must be ready and self-sacrificing, "For let the Spirit be never so prompt, if labor and exercise slacken we fail. The fruits of the Spirit do not follow men, as the shadows doth the body, of their own accord. If the grace of sanctification did so work, what should the grace of exhortation need? It were even as superfluous and vain to stir men up into good, as to request them when they walk abroad not to lose their shadows. Grace is not given us to abandon labor, but labor required lest our sluggishness should make the grace of GOD improbable." (Hooker, vol. ii., Ap. to Book v., p. 697.) But there are certain means of grace also,—the Sacraments; of these Hooker thus speaks: "Touching Sacraments whether many or few in number, their doctrine is that ours both signify and cause grace; but what grace and in what manner? By grace we always understand, as the Word of GOD teacheth, first, His favor and undeserved mercy towards us; secondly, the bestowing of His HOLY SPIRIT, which inwardly worketh; thirdly, the effects of that Spirit whatsoever, but especially saving virtues, such as are *faith*, *charity*, and *hope*; lastly, the free and full remission of all our sins. This is the grace which *sacraments* yield, and whereby we are all justified. To be justified is to be made righteous. Because, therefore, righteousness doth imply, first, remission of sins; and, secondly, a sanctified life; the name is sometimes applied severally to the former, sometimes jointly it comprehendeth both. . . . For sacraments with us are signs effectual; they are the instruments of GOD whereby to bestow grace; howbeit grace not proceeding from the visible sign, but from His invisible power. . . . Were they not as good, to say briefly, that GOD'S omnipotence, will, causeth grace, that the outward sign doth show His will, and that sacraments implying both are thereby termed both signs and causes, which is the self-same that we say?" (Ib., pp. 700, 703, 705.) The XXV. Article teaches this: "Sacraments ordained of CHRIST be not only badges or tokens of Christian men's Profession; *but rather* they be certain sure witnesses and effectual signs of grace and GOD'S good will towards us, by the which He doth work invisibly in us, and doth not only quicken, but also strengthen and confirm our faith in him. . . . And in such only as worthily receive the same they have a wholesome effect or operation; but they that receive them unworthily purchase to themselves damnation as St. Paul saith." To sum up, Grace is GOD'S free gift to us. It is in the Life, Death, Resurrection of JESUS CHRIST, of which we obtain the benefits and in which we share. Herein Sacraments become the conveying and the visible signs of such sharing. The LORD receiveth and giveth to us the Gift of the HOLY GHOST, pervading our life and sanctifying it, and using every action and habit as a channel by which to convey to us more grace. But we must yield ourselves heart, soul, and body to His influence, and work with Him lovingly, obediently, unflaggingly. Grace is the atmosphere of the Church by which we walk in the Light of the Gospel of CHRIST. It pervades all, it is the proof of the presence of the blessed Trinity.

A *Thanksgiving at Meals.*—The Jew used it. Our LORD sanctioned and sanctified it by using it as an element in His working the miracles of feeding the multitudes, and crowned its power by using it at the institution of the Holy Communion. The Apostles taught it. Meats " were created to be received with thanksgiving of them which believe and know the truth" (1 Tim. iv. 3–5). The Fathers are full of references to it. The directories and sacramentaries contain forms of Grace before and after meals. This is probably the oldest form now surviving : " Blessed art thou, O LORD, who feedest me from my youth up, who givest food to all flesh. Fill our hearts with joy and gladness; that always having a sufficiency, we may abound unto every good work in CHRIST JESUS our LORD, through whom be glory and honor and power unto the world without end. Amen." (Apost. Const., l. vii. c. 49.)

Gradual. Often in Old English Grayl or Grail. An anthem sung after the Epistle. In Africa it was a whole Psalm. It was early sung from the step (gradus) or place where the Epistle was read. The music was often very florid. The service-book which contained the anthem or Psalm, was called the Gradual or Grayl.

Grave. The pit properly prepared in which the coffin containing the corpse is placed. In the early Church, certain persons often associated into a guild, and called Fossores, had charge of the graves and their details. The cemeteries were carefully cared for, and the graves of the dead were looked after with a great deal of loving care.

Greek Church. *Vide* EASTERN CHURCH.

Gregorian Chant. *Vide* MUSIC.

Growth of the Church. Many and valuable statistics have been yearly published to exhibit the rapid growth of the Church, which has been at an average yearly rate of seven per cent., or of twenty per cent. from one triennial report to the General Convention to another. They all tend to show that she is gradually gaining that position which, with her notes of Unity, Apostolicity, and Catholicity, will win men to her holy ways. Wherever the full, plain Doctrines, Constitution, and Liturgy of the Church are set forth as the Canon directs (Tit. i., Can. xxi.), there men will be drawn to her. It must be so, for, aside from the mere changes involved in an altered civilization, she reproduces for the present day the doctrine and the polity of the Church as the New Testament exhibits it, and in her Liturgy she goes back to originals which sprang from the Church at Ephesus. But this growth from seven dioceses and one hundred and ninety clergy in 1790 A.D. to forty-nine confederated Dioceses and fifteen missionary jurisdictions, with seventy-one Bishops and three thousand six hundred and eighty-nine clergy, from twelve thousand communicants in 1800 A.D. to four hundred and twenty-two thousand six hundred and forty-nine in 1886 A.D., and devoting ten millions of dollars annually to religious work, is full proof that GOD is prospering us, that we are under the guidance of the Captain of our salvation. But if the number of communicants form two-thirds of our congregations—and this is an overestimate, as statistics show—the Church reaches a total of five hundred and sixty thousand adults. She draws into her Sunday-schools three hundred and twenty-seven thousand children. In other words, she is directly in contact with more than fifty-five per cent. of the population, teaching, training, influencing them. In the year 1800 she reached but one in four hundred and twenty. These statistics show a most wonderful blessing resting upon us. It is just to record here the report of the Committee on the State of the Church to the General Convention of 1883 A.D.:

"An hundred years ago the English branch of the historic Church of CHRIST in this land was wrenched from the mother-country, and the mother-Church was left in fragments on these shores. On the 11th of May, 1784 A.D., ten clergymen and six laymen sitting in New Brunswick, N. J., as the 'Corporation for the Relief of Widows and Orphans of Deceased Clergymen,' resolved themselves into a ' Voluntary Convention,' and took preliminary steps, which resulted in the October following in a representative assemblage of some eight States in the city of New York, which agreed as a 'first principle' that ' there shall be a General Convention of the Episcopal Church in the United States of America.'

"The next October that General Convention met in this city of Philadelphia. ' A general ecclesiastical constitution' was agreed to; the Book of Common Prayer of the Church of England was revised, to make it consistent with the American Revolution ; and a plan was reported for obtaining the consecration of Bishops in England. It was the season of Michaelmas when these great things were done, and the collect for ' All Angels' was signally answered. Here was a branch of the Apostolic Church, united and free, occupying a position unprecedented since the Christian era,—neither patronized nor persecuted by the civil powers. We have but to contrast that initial convention, less in number than many of the convocations of our rural deaneries, with the great legislative assembly here present,—one of the largest representative religious bodies in the world,—to exclaim, 'What hath GOD wrought!' We have now, in this year of grace 1883 A.D., 48 confederated Dioceses and 15 Missionary Jurisdictions, with 67 Bishops, more than 3500 other clergy, 3000 organized Parishes (not including missionary stations), and nearly 375,000 communicants, using the same Liturgy, and yielding obedience to the Canons enacted by the General Convention. One of the most noteworthy and gratifying facts connected with this council was the presence, at its opening service to give the absolution, and later in the session to pronounce the benediction, of that patriarchal man of GOD, the Right Rev. Benjamin B. Smith, D.D., LL.D., our Presiding Bishop, now in the ninetieth year of his age and the fifty-first of his Episcopate, whose seniority in both respects antedates every Bishop of the Anglican Communion throughout the world. The year of our LORD 1832 A.D., when, with three others,—long since gone to their reward,—he was consecrated to his high office, will forever mark an epoch in the American Church. Perhaps the most touching incident in the sessions of this body was the appearance in the House of Deputies on the fifteenth day of its deliberations of the Right Rev. Dr. William Mercer Green, the venerable Bishop of Mississippi, 'whose praise is in all the churches,' who came to say 'farewell,' and to tell us, with deep emotion, that he was the sole survivor, Clerical or Lay, of the General Convention of 1823 A.D., just sixty years ago, and that when he took Holy Orders there were but nine Bishops in the United States of America."

We now quote from the report of 1886 A.D.:

"Since the last General Convention several of our more venerable dioceses have observed the centennials of their erection with special solemnities of gratitude and joyful eucharists, with sermons and addresses which vividly recalled their history not only since the existence of the United States of North America, but the long period before when the Apostles' doctrine and fellowship flourished on this soil as the Church of England in the American colonies. . . .

"The dioceses heretofore known as Illinois, Northern New Jersey and Wisconsin, by their own action, confirmed by the action of the present General Convention, have substituted for their territorial designations the See names of Chicago, Newark and Milwaukee. Your Committee commend this change as a recognition of principles of apostolic precedent and primitive practice. . . .

"The increase, growth and prosperity of parishes and missions as a rule has been very marked. Candidates for Confirmation have been more carefully instructed. Church debts have been paid or liquidated, and in some instances efforts have been made 'that they who preach the gospel may live of the gospel.' But in general the salaries of the clergy are inadequate to their respectable maintenance. The remedy is in the hands of the laity, and the Church in her conciliar wisdom should devise some method for assuring the sustenance of her spiritual pastors. Provision should be made for them in their declining years, as in the army and navy, as well as for their widows and orphans. To this end your Committee call attention to the Clergyman's Retiring Fund, and to the various funds for the widows and orphans of deceased clergymen. Until such things are settled the Church cannot expect any great accessions to the ranks of her clergy. . . . Indeed the most discouraging feature in the state of the Church to-day is the decline in the number of candidates for holy orders. From all parts of the land only 344 are reported—a smaller number than at any time since 1868. From that year till now the number of communicants has been augmented from 195,835 to about 423,000—an increase of 17 per cent. in the last three years—a larger ratio than any in the last twelve years; and according to this there should be at least 730 candidates for the ministry. In view of these facts your Committee urgently appeal to all the members of the Church that boys and young men and devout men in business pursuits be alike exhorted to this holy work. . . .

"The Girls' Friendly Society, originating in 1877, enlists the interest, sympathy and aid of experienced Church women in behalf of their younger and inexperienced sisters. It has now 90 branches in 28 Dioceses, and four diocesan organizations, comprising 3000 members and 1100 associates. By its efficient instrumentality many have been kept interested in the Church in their own localities, while by its system of careful transfer, members removing, who might otherwise have been overlooked, have been at once introduced, cared for and retained in the Church.

"The Brotherhood of St. Andrew, inaugurated in this city of Chicago in 1883, not quite three years ago, has already become a prominent agency for the extension of CHRIST'S Kingdom among young men. It meets a want universally acknowledged, and with its two features of prayer and effort now has 30 chapters in 12 Dioceses. When the laity in general, men as well as women, are imbued with the like spirit of personal responsibility and personal exertion the day will be hastened when multitudes shall be brought 'to the knowledge and obedience of the Truth.'

"The Church Temperance Society, established five years ago, has now among its vice-presidents 50 Bishops, that already has organizations in thirty-five dioceses. It publishes a monthly paper, and has created a temperance literature on Scriptural principles. No other fact need be given in defense of this movement than that in our own country $900,000,000 are annually spent for strong drink against $505,000,000 for bread.

"The White Cross Society, begun in England in 1883, in less than a year had a branch in this country, and has since spread very widely. It is based upon the Seventh Commandment and baptismal vow 'to renounce all the sinful lusts of the flesh.' Its aim is personal and social purity in its highest and strictest sense. It is both a 'movement' and a 'work.' The twin monsters of evil which are sapping our homes and people are intemperance and impurity, and these can only be conquered by the help of GOD.

"This Church, Catholic, Apostolic and American, presents her corporate life, her ministry, her institutions, her charities to all the people of this land, irrespective of race, color or antecedents. For thirty years at least, more than half of those annually confirmed have been not of churchly parentage. Absorption has gone beyond the power of assimilation, yet this Church so longs for organic Christian unity and the re-union of Christendom that she has at this General Convention shown herself willing to make any overtures which do not compromise essentials in furtherance of the prayer of Him who is 'Head over all things to the Church which is His Body,' that His people may be 'made perfect in one.'"

Summary of Statistics reported to the General Convention of 1886. (From the Journal of the General Convention.)

Number of Dioceses	49
Number of Missionary Jurisdictions	15
Lay Readers in 47 Dioceses and 10 Missionary Jurisdictions	1,203
Candidates for Holy Orders in 49 Dioceses and 12 Missionary Jurisdictions	344
Deacons Ordained in 46 Dioceses and 11 Missionary Jurisdictions	398
Deacons in 45 Dioceses and 11 Missionary Jurisdictions	287
Priests Ordained in 47 Dioceses and 7 Missionary Jurisdictions	391
Priests in 48 Dioceses and 15 Missionary Jurisdictions	3,356
Whole number of Clergy in 48 Dioceses and 15 Missionary Jurisdictions	3,760
Parishes in 49 Dioceses and 9 Missionary Jurisdictions	2,939
Missions in 44 Dioceses and 14 Missionary Jurisdictions	2,072
Corner-stones laid in 38 Dioceses and 7 Missionary Jurisdictions	177
Churches Consecrated in 44 Dioceses and 10 Missionary Jurisdictions	257
Churches and Chapels in 47 Dioceses and 15 Missionary Jurisdictions	4,338
Free Churches and Chapels in 25 Dioceses and 12 Missionary Jurisdictions	1,466
Rectories in 45 Dioceses and 13 Missionary Jurisdictions	1,288
Families in 36 Dioceses and 6 Missionary Jurisdictions	148,994
Number of Souls in 30 Dioceses and 7 Missionary Jurisdictions	446,356
Baptisms { Infants in 47 Dioceses and 15 Missionary Jurisdictions	124,970
Adults in 47 Dioceses and 15 Missionary Jurisdictions	26,246
Total	156,425
Confirmations in 49 Dioceses and 15 Missionary Jurisdictions	93,049
Marriages in 47 Dioceses and 15 Missionary Jurisdictions	41,580
Burials in 46 Dioceses and 15 Missionary Jurisdictions	76,406
Communicants added in 36 Dioceses and 7 Missionary Jurisdictions	82,428
Communicants died in 33 Dioceses and 6 Missionary Jurisdictions	11,290
Communicants in 49 Dioceses and 15 Missionary Jurisdictions	424,424
Sunday-School Teachers in 47 Dioceses and 11 Missionary Jurisdictions	35,150
Sunday-School Scholars in 47 Dioceses and 14 Missionary Jurisdictions	327,272
Parish-School Teachers in 24 Dioceses and 5 Missionary Jurisdictions	745
Parish-School Scholars in 24 Dioceses and 6 Missionary Jurisdictions	13,308
Church Hospitals in 29 Dioceses and 8 Missionary Jurisdictions	54
Church Orphan Asylums in 28 Dioceses and 2 Missionary Jurisdictions	52
Church Homes in 21 Dioceses	37
Academic Institutions in 33 Dioceses and 8 Missionary Jurisdictions	101
Collegiate Institutions in 11 Dioceses and 2 Missionary Jurisdictions	13
Theological Institutions in 14 Dioceses and 2 Missionary Jurisdictions	16
Other Institutions in 12 Dioceses and 3 Missionary Jurisdictions	29
Communion Alms in 40 Dioceses and 6 Missionary Jurisdictions	$855,623.40
Episcopal Fund, Total Income in 43 Dioceses and 2 Missionary Jurisdictions	455,895.55
Diocesan Expenditures, Convention, etc., in 45 Dioceses and 5 Missionary Jurisdictions	292,028.85
Offerings for Diocesan Missions in 46 Dioceses and 7 Missionary Jurisdictions	809,213.75
Offerings for Domestic Missions (of which, in 20 Dioceses and 1 Missionary Jurisdiction, $25,847.05 were specified for Missions for the Colored People; and in 16 Dioceses and 1 Missionary Jurisdiction $31,755.38 were specified for Indian Missions) in 47 Dioceses and 9 Missionary Jurisdictions	649,291.66
Offerings for Foreign Missions in 47 Dioceses and 9 Missionary Jurisdictions	323,584,88
Offerings for Education for the Ministry in 33 Dioceses	81,223.64
Offerings for Aged and Infirm Clergy in 39 Dioceses and 3 Missionary Jurisdictions	186,647.93
Offerings for Widows and Orphans of Clergy in 15 Dioceses	79,005.93
Offerings for other and Miscellaneous Charities in 27 Dioceses and 5 Missionary Jurisdictions	592,891.80
Total of Charitable Offerings and Income in 37 Dioceses and 4 Missionary Jurisdictions	9,872,551.11
Total of Salaries and Parochial Expenses in 46 Dioceses and 6 Missionary Jurisdictions	16,527,491.35
Total Offerings for Religious Purposes in 49 Dioceses and 13 Missionary Jurisdictions	30,783,052.28
Parishes not reporting in 25 Dioceses	206

Guilds, Church. A Guild is a society organized for some common object. The name is said to be derived from the Old English "gild," the payment which each one was bound to make, or as others say, from the Welsh "gouil," a holiday. Guilds have a secular as well as a religious history, extending, it is claimed, far back into heathen times and countries.

I. *Theory.*—Guilds seem to arise out of the associative instinct in man. In the Church, they are an instance of the power of the Incarnation applying itself to the natural principles and tendencies of men to complete and exalt them. The taking of the manhood into GOD magnifies and ennobles men in general, gives each one a new value in the eyes of all the rest, and then laying hold of the spirit of association presents to us the Communion of Saints as the highest form of associate life. Baptism, therefore, being the impartation of the incarnate life, and the admission in consequence into the fellowship of that life, creates a new fraternity. The baptized, as members one of another, with lives knitted together and interests interwoven, engaged in mutual labor and devotion, reciprocating services, interchanging gifts, sharing in the benefits of each other's good works, suffering together, rejoicing together, constitute an organism in which each has his own place, his own office, and in his own degree acts on all the others.

A Guild is an endeavor to realize more intensely and practically this organic relation of the members of CHRIST one to another, and to bring it to bear on specific objects. It is an emphatic avowal and expression of the fact of the Communion of Saints. Its motive being, therefore, a supernatural one, it looks for its sustaining force to the Grace of GOD bestowed through sacraments and prayer. As a Guild has a common aim, so is it distinguished by a common devotional life, being mindful of the promise that "if two shall agree on earth as touching anything that they shall ask, it shall be done for them of MY FATHER, which is in Heaven."

II. *Organization and Management.*—The Guild method will answer a variety of purposes. Any class of works capable of concerted and differentiated activity, pertaining either to the outward, visible, and more material side of religion, or to the spiritual life more directly,—works of mercy, charity, and benevolence, works of sacred art, no less than efforts to strengthen personal holiness,—may be promoted in this way. It is said that immediate neighborhood is an element of the Guild idea. This renders Guilds most meet and apt for parochial use.

The fundamental qualification for admission to all Guild organizations should be baptism. When this is taken to constitute eligibility for Guild work, Christian work is dignified greatly. It appears then in its true light as a privilege and a right inherent in that brotherhood in CHRIST, which results from baptism. The *responsibility* of the members of CHRIST of sharing in the labor of the body is brought home by the Guild system. It affords a plan for securing efficient and disciplined Lay co-operation. The due prosperity of a parish demands the action of every head and heart and hand. Without general occupation our common life stagnates. Without order, and the consideration of fitness in the allotment of work, confusion ensues. Things left to be the business of everybody at once become the business of nobody. The Guild, after calling attention to responsibility, defines, distributes, and fixes it according to aptitude. It increases labor,—not so as to make heavier burdens for some, but, by increasing the laborers, that results may be multiplied and obtained from all. To do this, the various talents and capacities, which form the common store of a band of people, diverse in character and taste, with different degrees of inclination and leisure to devote themselves to church work, must be called out, and made to contribute each in its own way to the one purpose. A system is called for which shall allow the fullest and the freest play of the peculiar gifts and abilities of each. The Parish Guild may operate as such an agency. Its natural and proper head is the parish priest, styled, according to the traditional nomenclature, Master, Warden, Superior, or Provost. It should be entirely under his control and oversight.

Members should require his approbation, and the assignment to work should be his. In this kind of Guild, designed to unify, employ, and interest parishioners in general in the combined work of the parish, membership should be within the spiritual limitation mentioned above, as comprehensive as possible of both sexes, and of all ages. It can then be subdivided into wards, chapters, or committees, each with its own head. The care of the altar and vestments, the poor, the sick, strangers, missions, teaching, sponsorship, church literature, music, decoration, are phases of activity, some or all of which present the opportunity for useful thoughtful care in every congregation. These subordinate departments may have their own ordering of their own work, and at some appointed time, once a month or less often, a meeting of the whole Guild may be held, at which the different wards can report to the Master the condition and progress of the particular work intrusted to their charge. Meanwhile, there goes up from every member the special prayer which has been set forth as the daily intercession for the Guild and its intentions. The united offering of the same supplication should be accounted an indispensable means of attaining success.

Experience has widely shown how largely parochial earnestness may be augmented, and new lines of good discovered, by thus judiciously arranging and disposing of the time and abilities of those of the Faithful who have a mind to work.

Another very desirable and beneficial form of Guild organization is that which has spiritual improvement in view. Guilds of this kind are best composed of the same sex, and restricted to certain specified ages. The object proposed in these Guilds is the maintenance of the spiritual life, fidelity to religious obligations, and deepening of devotion. Boys and girls, young men and young women, are most simply and easily influenced and retained in attachment to the Church through instrumentalities of this sort. When the period of adolescence is reached, it is often found difficult, especially in the case of boys, to keep them true to their religious duties. Here the spiritual Guild comes in, and through the sanctified power of association supplies a very timely agency to fortify young persons against worldly and evil companionships, and to invigorate their constancy to GOD and Holy Church. It reinforces moral courage at that uncertain age when it is most prone to falter. It facilitates and expedites the work of a pastor, because it organizes. Without at all dispensing him from the necessity of direct personal intercourse with individuals, it places him in a position to reach individuals more effectually. Instead of his attempting to look after a large number of scattered individuals, one by one, it brings them under his eye and hand, partaking of, and supported by, the enthusiasm of their numbers, so that he can collectively sway and guide, while at the same time it puts him in the way of becoming more intimately and personally acquainted with the needs and circumstances of each one, and of winning their confidence to counsel, advise, and help them. In these Guilds, the framing of a Rule of Life is one of the first things to be considered. Members are either all communicants, or they include the unconfirmed as well. In case there are these two grades of members in the same Guild, it will be necessary to adapt the Rule to each. In the construction of a Rule, pains should be taken to make it as concise and brief as possible. It should cover the chief obligations of worship and holy living, and guard against the temptations which are most likely to assail and beset the lives of those who are to keep it. Private prayer, attendance at Church, grace before and after meals, observance of the prescribed Days of Fasting and Abstinence, self-examination, the avoidance of evil company, and refraining from bad and impure language, are among the points which may be usually incorporated. Another feature, which has been found to be exceedingly profitable and salutary, is for the Guild to receive the Holy Communion in a body once during the month. This will secure at least one communion a month, where, in many cases, it might be otherwise neglected or forgotten. More thorough and reverent preparation for communion may be thus cultivated. The pious pastor may lead his youth to approach the altar with regularity, with contrition, with fervor, and with fruit. A generous and right-minded emulation will be roused among them, and they will naturally vie with each other in the exercise of self-sacrifice, and in solicitude to perform their sacred duties well. It will be found easy, by the adoption of this Common Rule, to lead them to communicate at an early hour, fasting, and with searched and purified consciences. And if, after the celebration, the Guild remain for a few minutes to say together an office of Thanksgiving, it will be found most conducive to the advancement of their spiritual character.

Meetings may be held twice a month, or oftener. These afford the priest in charge opportunity for instructions in religion, and should be marked by the seemly recitation of some stated office of Devotion. The office of Compline is well suited for a Guild which meets in the evening. For Guild-meetings held in the daytime, some one of the earlier Day-Hour Offices might be selected. In the conduct and management of Spiritual Guilds, the idea should be firmly adhered to of forming habits by the performance of distinct acts of devotion, and by the regular exercise of the devotional faculties.

These Guilds, if properly and wisely administered, may be developed in such a manner as to be a substantial strength to the Church. They may be made to do a more positive and pronounced work than can possibly be expected from the miscellaneous and fragmentary constitution of Sunday-schools. The Guild will put nerve and sinew into Sunday-school work, and standing ready, will take boys and girls and mould and shape them as the Sunday-school from its nature can hardly do. It will impress boys and girls of any age, and especially at that restless period when young persons begin to feel that they have outgrown the ordinary Sunday class, and when they need something more bracing and definite, something that will be more felt in their daily life than the Sunday-school can give them. Guilds will supply in many cases the lack of home influence. They may be made to afford sympathy, elevating companionship, instruction, and wholesome recreation. The *esprit de corps* which they awaken is most valuable if directed aright. Guilds may be the means of raising up in Parishes a band of persons, trained and devout, burning with zeal and energy, foremost in good works for the souls and bodies of men,—powerful as an influence and example, a body-guard to pastors, and a glory to the Church.

Church Guilds, in the ages of their fullest development, always seemed to flourish, especially in England. They are, therefore, a part of the traditional life of the Anglican Communion. And the atmosphere of American society and institutions would seem to be wonderfully adapted to perpetuate this tradition.

Subjoined is a specimen of the Constitution and Rule of Life of a Spiritual Guild.

GUILD OF ST. STEPHEN THE MARTYR.

Object.—To help and encourage young men and boys to lead a Godly and a Christian Life, and to unite them in the fellowship of the Church.

CONSTITUTION.

I.

The Guild shall be called the Guild of St. Stephen the Martyr.

II.

The Guild shall consist, first, of companions, who shall be communicants. Second, of probationers, who shall be baptized boys, twelve years old and upwards.

III.

The Rector of the Parish shall be, *ex officio*, Supervisor of the Guild, and either he or some Priest appointed by him shall be its Director. A Warden, or Wardens, shall be appointed by the Rector. The Secretary and Treasurer shall be elected at the Annual Chapter of the Guild on St. Stephen's day of each year.

IV.

Any person wishing to join the Guild must be proposed at one meeting, elected at a following one, and receive the approbation of the superior.

V.

Members shall contribute monthly such specified sum as shall from time to time be fixed by the Guild.

VI.

On general questions, probationers shall be entitled to one-half a full vote. On admission of members, companions shall be elected by their own order, probationers by the entire Guild.

RULE OF LIFE FOR COMPANIONS.

I.

To pray regularly every morning and evening, devoutly kneeling.

II.

To be present, if possible, at a celebration of the Holy Communion, on all Sundays, and greater festivals of the Church.

III.

To communicate with the other members of the Guild on the fourth Sunday of every month, always fasting, and to make a careful preparation before, and thanksgiving after, Communion.

IV.

To practice daily self-examination.

V.

To say grace before and after meals.

VI.

To observe the fast-days of the Church, by one act of self-denial at least.

VII.

To say daily the prayer for the Guild.

VIII.

To say prayers before and after each service in Church.

IX.

Never to talk lightly of holy things, nor to quote Scripture irreverently.

X.

To avoid the company of bad boys and men, and all places likely to be the means of tempting to sin.

XI.

Not, except for some good reason, to attend any place of worship or Sunday-school not belonging to the Anglican Church.

XII.

To try to do some special work for GOD and His Church, under the direction of the Parish Priest.

RULE OF LIFE FOR PROBATIONERS.

I.

To say one's private prayers morning and evening daily, devoutly kneeling.

II.

To attend, every Sunday, a service of the Church.

III.

To abstain from swearing, bad and impure language, and all bad company.

IV.

To behave reverently at all times in GOD's house.

V.

To say the prayer for the Guild daily.

VI.

Never, except for some good reason, to attend any place of worship or Sunday-school not belonging to the Anglican Church.

REV. GEO. MCCLELLAN FISKE.

H.

Habakkuk. The eighth of the minor Prophets, of whom we have no accurate information. Arguments which are rather ingenious than fully convincing place him in the first year's reign of Josiah (630 B.C.). It is well to read the prophecy through as a single connected composition, and not as several disconnected ones. The bitter wars the Chaldeans would bring upon Judah are the great burden of his prophecy, and the need of a purging of the nation before Him who cannot look upon iniquity. That Judah should survive the scourge he does not doubt, but the woes and calamities that shall fall upon his people because of their sins is not lessened by the knowledge that the instruments of purging, the Chaldeans, shall suffer still more fearfully. He closes with a prayer which is one of the sublimest of all the noble poems that the Hebrew Prophets have given us by the grace of the HOLY SPIRIT. The leading thought of the Prophet is the trust in GOD despite all discouragements. His "the just shall live by faith" is quoted thrice by St. Paul. The seventeenth verse of the third chapter was the text that furnished Hooker the subject for his sermon on Justification by Faith. (*Vide* Smith's Bible Dictionary, Pusey on the Minor Prophets.)

Hades. The place where the souls freed from the body remain till the Resurrection. It was confused in the translation of 1611 A.D. by the use of the word Hell with the place of torment. The term Hades is used by our LORD in St. Matt. xi. 23; xvi. 18; St. Luke x. 15; xvi. 23. St. Peter uses it in Acts ii. 27, 31. In one reading of 1 Cor. xv. 55, it is used (if the reading be the true one) by St. Paul. St. John uses it in Rev. i. 18; vi. 8; xx. 13, 14 (St. Peter uses a participial form, *tartarosas*, from the noun *tartarus*, in his second Epistle, ch. ii. 4, "thrust down to tartarus," which was a part of Hades in the pagan teaching). The equivalent in the Old Testament was Sheol, usually translated the grave, but sometimes Hell, and with the same evil results as befell the confusion in translating Hades by Hell. Jacob will go down to Sheol, the place of departed spirits (A. V. down to the grave), mourning for Joseph. David saith GOD will redeem my soul from the power of Sheol (A. V. grave) for He shall receive me, and just before, "Like sheep are they laid in Sheol (A.V. grave), death shall feed on them, and the upright shall have dominion over them in the morning, their beauty shall consume away in Sheol (A.V. grave) from their dwelling." Isaiah, in one of the most magnificent of his descriptions, "When the King of Babylon dieth (xiv. 9) Sheol from beneath is moved to meet thee. It stirreth up the dead for thee, even all the chief ones of the earth; it hath raised up from their thrones all the kings of the nations. . . . Thy pomp is brought down to Sheol (A. V. grave), and the noise of thy viols." Enough is given to show that the Hebrew knowledge of Sheol was identical with the New Testament teaching upon Hades. Many speculations have been made about the condition of the dead. In the parable (or, as many Fathers hold, the history) of the rich man and Lazarus, there is the declaration that a great gulf is fixed between those in "Abraham's bosom" and those "in torments." It teaches us that we retain feeling, memory, reason, and that then we have a foretaste of the state after judgment. That this would follow from the liberated state of the soul is a natural conclusion which even the heathen held, and which is confirmed by the translation given by some of St. Peter's declaration that our LORD was quickened in His soul, by His death, a translation the Greek will naturally bear, and therefore that the act of death *here* is an added power of existence, whether for joy, as in the case of Lazarus, or of pain and agony, as in the case of the rich man.

Haggai. A name meaning festive or festival. He was the first to prophesy after the captivity of Judah, being called to speak in the Name of the LORD in the year 520 B.C. (Haggai i. 1). It does not appear that he had any claim to the title of prophet before this time, either by call or by family descent; for concerning his parentage nothing is certainly known, though tradition relates that he was born in Babylon. Yet some conjecture that he may have witnessed the destruction of the first Temple (Haggai ii. 3), and so have been contemporary with Jeremiah and Ezekiel. However this may be, it is very probable that he was among the exiles who returned to Jerusalem under the edict of Cyrus (536 B.C.) and witnessed the setting up of the altar of GOD in Jerusalem (Ezra iii. 2). Besides being the author of the book which goes by his name, he is thought to have composed a considerable portion of the Book of Ezra (Ezra iii. 2, to the end of chapter vi., with some omissions), and tradition assigns not a few Psalms to him, with Zachariah, but whether as authors or editors cannot be determined (Ps. cxi., cxxv., cxxvi., cxxxvii., cxlv.–cxlviii.).

The events referred to in the prophecy of Haggai are recorded in the portion of Ezra just mentioned, the prophecy being a message from GOD to ruler, priest, and people relative to the rebuilding of the Temple.

An examination of the book shows that it may be analyzed into four parts, nearly corresponding to the times when they were spoken. The first division, spoken in the second year of Darius, the sixth month and first day (Haggai i.), is a message to Zerubbabel, Governor of Judah, and Joshua, the High-Priest, reproaching rulers and people for apathy in the work of rebuilding the Temple, and threatening a drought and famine, followed by a word of encouragement upon their rousing up to renewed energy in that work.

The second division, spoken in the seventh month and twentieth day (Haggai ii. 1-9), was designed to encourage those who felt the contrast between the former Temple and that then building, and ends with the well-known prophecy of the glory of the latter house being greater than that of the former, fulfilled in due time by the visible presence of our LORD in it. The third division, spoken in the ninth month and twenty-fourth day (Haggai ii. 10-19), is a warning to the priests and people on the folly of offering a divided service to GOD, and the promise of a blessing upon the prosecution of the work on the Temple (see ch. ii. 18).

The fourth and last division, spoken the same day (Haggai ii. 20-23), while a special prophecy to Zerubbabel of the overthrow of the power of his enemies, is also a declaration to him, as the Prince of Judah, the lineal ancestor of our LORD, of the breaking down of the kingdom of sin, Satan, and death, and the establishment of the power of GOD and the kingdom of His CHRIST.

Hagiographa. I. A division of the Old Testament, which included the Psalms, the Proverbs, Job, the Song of Solomon, Ruth, Lamentations, Ecclesiastes, Esther, Daniel, Ezra, Nehemiah, Chronicles. This division our LORD Himself recognized after His resurrection: "These are the words which I spake unto you, while I was yet with you, that all things must be fulfilled, which were written in the Law of Moses, and in the Prophets, and in the Psalms, concerning me" (St. Luke xxiv. 44). In these holy writings the Jews included the historical books of Esther, Ezra, Nehemiah, and the two books of the Chronicles and the Prophet Daniel, whose book is so largely historical. The reference there made by our LORD was not solely to the Psalms alone, but to all Messianic references in the collections of these holy writings.

Hallel. The Psalms so called are the six, cxiii.-cxviii., and are so called from the first word of the first Psalm of the series, Hallelujah. They were used at the three solemn Feasts of the Passover, Pentecost, and Tabernacles, and on the Feast of the New Moon. They were used on these three feasts in the Temple service. The series was divided into two parts, the first part ending at the close of Psalm cxiv., the other ending with the cxviii. It was the festal hymn of the Passover feast, and was so used by our LORD. The hymn that was sung by Him and by His Apostles was doubtless the cxviii. This last Psalm was used antiphonally, as will be seen by noting its construction. It was probably used processionally. It was to this Psalm that our LORD made two formal allusions during the last six days preceding His crucifixion: "Did ye never read in the Scripture, The stone which the builders rejected the same is become the head of the corner; this is the LORD's doing, and it is marvelous in our eyes?" And again, "I say unto you ye shall not see me henceforth until ye shall say, Blessed is He that cometh in the name of the LORD." The six Psalms form *the* Hallel; another series of Psalms from the cxviii. (or cxx. or cxxxv. 4), and ending with the cxxxvi. Psalm, was called the great Hallel. But the Hallel of the Feasts was composed of the above six Psalms.

Harmony of the Gospels. (*Vide* DIATESSARON.) The effort to place the events and incidents of our LORD's life in a chronological order was made at an early date after the Gospels were in circulation. It was very natural that this attempt should be made. The attempt has always had its peculiar difficulties, arising both from the Person and the reverence due to Him and from the scantiness of material. The gaps in the narratives, the lack of any chronological order continuously observed, the possibility, nay, probability, that the same discourses and parables were repeated at different times before different audiences, the possible likeness in incident in really different miraculous cures, are against the complete success of any attempt to make such a harmony as shall be of proof against any objections. The main incidents of our LORD's life, the greater stepping-stones from one phase of His ministry to another, can be put beyond an honest objection. Again, it is not every one who will make the trial who has the true reverent tone of mind. And the same is true of those who study the labors of others in this department of New Testament investigations. To some it is a most vivid picture of the marvelous life, and gives to them an insight they could not otherwise obtain. In others there is an irreverence and failure to appreciate these gains, a caviling, questioning spirit, which wastes itself upon petty questions. Tatian, whose work is lost, was the first who made the attempt, and apparently without any judgment and with some daring changes of the text. It was therefore suppressed. Ammonius took St. Matthew's Gospel as the basis, and comparing the others with it, made up a scheme of parallel places which he placed by its side. These Ammonian sections are often found in the cursive manuscripts of the Gospels. Eusebius of Cæsarea (340 A.D.) arranged these into ten sections, showing where all four agreed, when three agreed, then wherein

St. Matthew and St. Mark agreed, where St. Matthew and St. Luke, where St. Luke and St. Mark, and wherein each had some separate event not recorded by the others. The system was an intricate one, but it has been digested into order by Bishop Wordsworth in his Greek Testament. In recent times many valuable Harmonies have been issued, such as that which accompanies Williams's "Devotional Commentary on the Gospels," in which the arrangement enables us to determine when the Evangelists used the same words and phrases. These are so readily accessible that it is needless to place here a synopsis of Harmony. As has been said above, no arrangement can be made which will not be open to some objection, and probably it is best that it is so. The research thus stimulated and the minute study of the details of usage and allusion has proved to be of immense service in establishing the credibility of the Gospels, in bringing out the inner meaning of many passages, in showing the impossibility that the Gospels could be forgeries, for they are bound by many slight and delicate ties to the time, the place, and the surroundings of the date claimed for them, ties which no forger, no matter how skillful, could have formed with the history and complex social relations which he would necessarily introduce into his work. In this way vast service has been done, despite the difficulties and disappointments which must surround every Harmony.

Head. The head, as the seat of thought and reason, was the type of Lordship. So our LORD is the Head of the Body, His Church. So the husband is the head of the wife, the chief, the responsible person of the household. So covering the head was a token of subjection. Anointing the head a ceremony (*a*) of conferring kingship, (*b*) of consecrating to the High-Priesthood, (*d*) to the Prophetical office, (*e*) as a joyful festal act, (*f*) for recovery from sickness (Jas. v. 14). The LORD was anointed for His burial. But there was and is the spiritual anointing which we share with our LORD, the unction of the HOLY GHOST (1 John ii. 20, 27).

Heart. In Scripture the ideal seat of emotions and affections, as of joy and sorrow, of longing and satisfaction, of envy and of hatred, of love and peace; of the intellectual operations, as of thought and of reason, of understanding and of meditation; of will and desire, as of lust and evil imaginations, of duplicity and folly, of honesty and goodness; of the internal state, "as he thinketh in his heart so is he; eat and drink saith he to thee, but his heart is not with thee." A heart so constituted is indeed the battle-ground for opposing forces, and needs every aid. Keep thine heart with diligence, for out of it are the issues of life. Many images are used to express the Divine desire to control man's heart: "My son, give me thine heart." "With the heart man believeth unto righteousness." Love is poured into our hearts, "He trieth the heart and the reins," He soweth His seed in man's heart. Scripture is full of both the workings of the natural emotions and of the Divine influence upon the heart of man.

Heathen. All tribes who were not either by descent, or by admission into the Covenant by circumcision, into the family of the Chosen People. The word *Goim* is translated as heathen, Gentiles, nations, and refers to nations with whom the Israelites were surrounded, as the seven nations of Canaan, and the more distant people with whom they came into contact later. They were separated from them by strict enactments. They could buy or sell of the Gentiles man-servants and maid-servants. The Moabite was excluded to the tenth generation. The Edomite could be admitted into the nation in the third generation. A deep demarcation was established by the Law, and after repeated scourgings and punishments was at last accepted by the people, between themselves and the heathen. But they were to be the missionaries and teachers of these heathen. Jonah was sent on such a work. The Jews were scattered as dew upon the grass among the nations, to spread the doctrine of the oneness of GOD preparatory for Christianity. The Gentiles were to have the good tidings preached to them also, and at last when Israel turned away from its MESSIAH, the heathen were to become the chosen people, and to be grafted into the stock of the olive. It is our own glory and responsibility that as Gentiles no longer heathen in faith, but of the nations that are afar off, we have been gathered into the spiritual Israel. In us is fulfilled the prophecy of Noah: "GOD shall enlarge Japhet, and he shall dwell in the tents of Shem."

Heaven. As a material part, so to speak, of the universe, the Mosaic record gives very distinct and definite description. The firmament dividing the waters from the waters. The expanse, with its part in the economy of the world, is apparently spoken of in such hard, definite language, that it has been one of the objections made by modern science to his description, and yet it has been shown (Dawson, Science and the Bible) that the words do really describe appearances accurately, and that they bear a perfectly fair scientific interpretation. But it is not necessary here to speak of the heavens in their natural aspect, nor of the classification into the seven heavens of the Rabbins. The language of St. Paul, of his being caught up into the third heaven, has far more weight than we can attach to any other enumeration, but even this tells us nothing beyond the bare fact. Origen says, with eminent good sense, the Christian Scriptures tell us nothing of these subdivisions. But we use this term in a theologic and mystic manner. Heaven, then, the Scriptures tell us, is the abode of GOD. The heavens are His throne, the earth is His footstool. To localize the presence of an omnipresent GOD is difficult, but the Scriptures are certainly full and explicit. Isaiah saw Him on His throne, high and lifted up. Ezekiel saw His glory round His throne, which throne was as the appearance of a sapphire stone. St. Stephen saw the heavens open and the LORD JESUS standing on the right hand of GOD. St. John had a vision of the throne set in heaven. However these and innumerable other texts might be singly interpreted, in their general consent they point to the heavens as the presence chamber of GOD. Perhaps Coleridge's saying, that it is not so much "that GOD is everywhere present, but that everything everywhere is present to GOD," transferring the centre of observation from ourselves to the presence of GOD, has the germ of the truth in it. We cannot comprehend the laws of a self-existent Spirit, so that it is useless to speculate, and we can only receive and believe. It is not contrary to what nature and our own powers tell us, though it is far above all our ability to understand, to hold that the Creator of the universe hath all things laid open in His presence and yet hath His throne whereon He sitteth evermore, and yet to hold that the heavens and the heaven of heavens cannot contain Heaven. This Heaven and Presence Chamber of GOD is the abode of the ministrant spirits, the Archangels Cherubim and Seraphim, the angels and living creatures, the thousand thousands and the ten thousand times ten thousand which stand before Him and who are made messengers and ministers to the heirs of salvation. From this presence Michael was sent to Daniel; from this presence Gabriel was sent to the Blessed Virgin Mary. In this abode of glory and unapproachable splendor of light is the future happy home of the Christian. The Scriptures bid us look up to heaven. The SON of GOD came down from heaven, and up into heaven He was received when He ascended to His FATHER and our FATHER to His GOD and our GOD.

Hebrews. It has been earnestly debated whether the Epistle to the Hebrews is or is not from the pen of St. Paul, and Apollos, St. Luke, and St. Clement have each been suggested with more or less of plausibility as being the author of the Epistle, which the instinct of the Church has ever ascribed to St. Paul. It is not intended to enter into this discussion, which cannot be settled, but it is well to abide by the general voice or silent assent of the Church. And surely the weighty doctrines and the spiritual insight displayed in the Epistle are fully consonant with the noble genius of the Apostle to the Gentiles. It opens with no uncertain blast of the Apostolic trumpet. "GOD, who at sundry times and in divers manners spake in time past unto the fathers by the prophets, hath in these last days spoken unto us by His Son," can well take its place beside the sublime opening of St. John's Gospel,—"In the beginning was the Word, and the Word was with GOD, and the Word was GOD,"—and is the continuation of it in a manner. The date of the Epistle must be placed some time soon after the Apostle's first imprisonment, while he was in Italy, and most probably about 64 A.D. It has hardly an equal in the whole range of the Pauline Epistles for sustained loftiness of tone. There is a sweep of rhetoric in some passages, begining with the first chapter and culminating in the grand roll-call of the heroes of Faith, which are unmistakably the outpouring of St. Paul's mind. Who but he could have penned the argument of the chapters vii.–x.? Who but St. Paul of all the known writers of the Apostolic age could have written the tender, devout passages descriptive of our LORD as the sympathetic High-Priest (ch. ii. 14–18; iv. 12–16; vi. 17–20), or could have composed the twelfth chapter? A careful comparison of the marginal references will show how St. Paul, though writing to a wholly different audience, the Christian Jew of Palestine, yet wove into his argument so much that he had written to the mingled congregations or to the purely Gentile Churches of his own founding. It is but the outpouring of that zeal and love which filled his heart. "Brethren, my heart's desire and prayer to GOD for Israel is, that they might be saved" (Rom. x. 1).

The argument of this Epistle can be best understood if the Apostle's doctrine of Justification be presupposed, and faith, practical living faith in the Atonement, be taken as the proper subject, and that it is an expansion of the doctrine contained in the 24th, 25th, and 26th verses of the third chapter of Romans, and that this expansion is made purposely for the Hebrew Christians, and so that the Priesthood of our LORD is brought out most prominently.

This is shown by rapid analysis somewhat as follows:

Ch. i. and ii. GOD'S Son (*a*) by nature above Angels. (*b*) Passed by the Angels, became man, submitted to humiliation and death that He might become the captain of our salvation, sanctify us, and be our merciful and faithful High-Priest.

Ch. iii. and iv. As captain—*i.e.*, leader— He is compared with Moses, and ourselves are warned by the example of the Israelites in the wilderness. And He is again set forth as our High-Priest.

Ch. v. But a Priest must make an Atonement. So JESUS is a Priest forever. (*a*) As GOD'S only-begotten Son. (*b*) By Consecration of the Father.

Ch. vi. The Apostle characteristically pauses to set forth Christian doctrine, and our steadfastness upon the foundation of GOD'S oath.

Ch. vii. CHRIST is an Eternal Priest, for a provision for the transference of the Priesthood according to the Gospel was made in Abraham. And the Levitical

Priesthood was only bound up with the Law, and was repealed by the Oath, "Thou art a Priest forever after the order of Melchisedec." Therefore the Covenant and Priesthood in CHRIST JESUS is of the Gospel to Abraham, and the Law was an intercalation, and so this statement of facts also brings us to JESUS as our High-Priest.

Ch. viii. The Apostle develops these correlated facts of the Covenant and Priesthood as better than the shadows of the Levitical Covenant and Sacrifices and Priesthood, and adds the mediatorial consequence of this better Covenant.

Ch. ix. Still pursues the types of the Levitical service, and carries on the thoughts of the continuous intercession of our LORD.

Ch. x. Sums up as it were in different phrases the vanishing imperfect nature of the Levitical sacrifices, the perfect offering of one in His own Body, in which, raised from the dead, He is King as well as Priest and Mediator. Then the short preceding appeals to Faith and the access through Him to the FATHER are resumed, with a repetition of the substance of the solemn warning given in the sixth chapter, but now from a new position; and a reference to the past courageous martyrdom of the Hebrew Christians.

Ch. xi. Is wholly after the Apostolic manner, and is a glorious roll-call of the victorious heroes of the Faith, closing with the revelation that they without us will not receive the reward of faith, but are kept waiting that we should be perfected together.

Ch. xii. Makes a practical application of the need of Faith in the dangers of that day, and contains an appeal of wondrous force and beauty, which has so liturgical a tone that it has been claimed as quoted from the Liturgy of St. James, in which it also occurs.

Ch. xiii. Carries on the application of this Faith unto our daily life, and closes with one of those Pauline benedictions which are a peculiar feature of St. Paul's Epistles. Imperfect as the outline is, we can see clearly the doctrine of the Incarnation stated as leading up to this Priesthood, the fullness of the Atonement and its application to us through His eternal Priesthood, and the necessity of Faith in us by which we may lay hold of the hope anchored with JESUS the High-Priest forever after the order of Melchisedec. The Apostle " has provided in this Epistle an exhaustless supply of hope, comfort, peace, and joy for every Christian soul looking to the Cross of CHRIST, and then raising its eyes to Heaven and beholding Him seated as our King at GOD's right hand, ever living as our Priest to make intercession for us, and coming hereafter in His glorious majesty to judge the quick and the dead and to put all enemies under His feet, and to reward all true Israelites who believe in Him, obey Him, and suffer for Him, and who regard Him with the eye of Faith as no other than GOD of GOD, Light of Light, Very GOD of Very GOD, of one substance with the Father, existing before the world, creating and sustaining all things with His Power, and to welcome them to the everlasting mansion of the only continuing city, the Heavenly Jerusalem, whose builder and maker is GOD." (Wordsworth's Introduction to Epistle to the Hebrews.)

Hell. (*Vide* GEHENNA.) It was by a sad confusion that the translation of 1611 A.D., following earlier ones, used the same word Hell for Hades and Gehenna. It obscured two of the most important doctrines upon eschatology,—the doctrine of the intermediate state and the doctrine of future punishment. (In the sense of the abode of the soul before the Resurrection, the reader should consult the articles on ESCHATOLOGY, HADES; also GEHENNA.) As a place of punishment it is under other terms spoken of by the Prophet Isaiah (lxvi. 24): "for their worm shall not die, neither shall their fire be quenched," a phrase which our LORD uses thrice in St. Mark ix. 44, 46, 48. So, too, in Daniel it is written that some shall rise to everlasting life and some to everlasting shame; a contrast our LORD also uses in His parable of the sheep and the goats, "and these shall go away into everlasting punishment, but the righteous into life eternal," where "æonian" is the descriptive adjective in both clauses, as it is in the LXX. translation of Daniel. Where it is we know not, but a terrible hint is given in Isaiah (lxvi. 24): "And they shall go forth, and look upon the carcasses of the men that have transgressed against Me: for their worm shall not die, neither shall their fire be quenched," which will compare with Revelation (xiv. 10): "and he shall be tormented with fire and brimstone in the presence of the holy angels, and in the presence of the LAMB." The sorrows of that dread abode are described in phrases which may bear a metaphorical sense, but literally seem very material. It is not profitable to speculate upon these things, and it is far better to receive what is told us with sorrow that sin has made it so certain.

Hellenist. A Jew who was brought up in a foreign country, and had imbibed more or less of the foreign influence and the current language of his place of residence. The word occurs thrice in the New Testament (Acts vi. 1; ix. 29; xi. 20). The term was applied also to the proselytes of Greek or other Gentile parentage. But since the Hellenic dialect of the Greek was the most widely spread and best understood, the term was applied to all proselytes, of whatever descent. These Hellenists were of the greatest service to the spread of the Gospel, both indirectly and directly. Indirectly, because they already prepared the way by holding and more or less boldly teaching the unity of GOD among the Gentiles, and because by the translation of the Hebrew Scripture into

23

the Hellenic Greek they placed a most serviceable instrument in the hands of Christian teachers. Directly, because many of them, already affected by the Gentile influences, or being proselytes, were ready to accept the Gospel when it was presented to them. It was to these the Dispersion, the strangers scattered in the provinces of Asia Minor, that St. Peter addressed his first Epistle. Among these St. Paul often found the most cordial reception.

Their most lasting service to the Gospel was the preparation, by the translation of the Old Testament into the Hellenic Greek, of a language of the Gospel. (*Vide* SEPTUAGINT.) The work done among them was individual, and often, so far as we can trace, but temporary; the work done through them had most important and permanent results for the Gentile Christians.

Heresiarch. The founder of a heresy, an arch-heretic. As heresy is very largely at first an intellectual error, sometimes a revolt from an overstraining of orthodox doctrine, its moral results are not at once very evident. And a leader in a heresy may be apparently a most estimable man in every relation of life, and by that very goodness of character commend doctrines which without his personal influence would be rejected. Arius was said to be a very devout man. Nestorius practiced great asceticism. St. Augustine spoke of Faustus, his Manichæan teacher, as one who by his life commended his heretical doctrines. So at the present day, since moral sequences stand at some distance along the line of cause and effect, from intellectual and perverted religious teaching. Many strange and absurd notions are disseminated by men of pure lives. The term heresiarch cannot be applied to them as Founders, but in the sense of Leadership it can be applied to them as Leaders in false doctrine.

Heresy. The word had at first a good meaning,—a choice, a profession, a business; then a party, or school of thought, as Josephus says he was brought up in the Pharasaic heresy. But soon in ecclesiastical language in the New Testament it meant the holding of a doctrine persistently contrary to the authoritative statements of it, a choice in error, and that a persistent choice. It is not an infidelity which denies the Faith, but a perversion, more or less extensive, of the Faith. It is overthrowing the foundation by the consequences. It is this which makes it so dangerous. Nestorius, apparently, was most reverent, and in the minds of very many now was much misused; but had his doctrine been allowed to stand, it would have overthrown Christianity as surely as would Arianism have done it. Heresy involves perverse doctrine; schism is separation on points of Episcopal government. St. Paul lays down the rule with regard to the treatment of a heretic. "A man that is an heretic after the first and second admonition, reject." And he excommunicated Hymenæus and Alexander for their false teaching. Heresy is exceedingly subtle in its disguises, though it is thoroughly Antichristian. It professes an insight and a wisdom which speaketh great things. Yet the Church has ever been very careful not to charge heresy but upon sure grounds. This will explain why so many men were apparently dealt with very gently at first and harshly afterwards, for she must, as a net cast into the sea, include all and afterwards select. The earliest heresies, so far as we can now judge of them, were in some degree Gnostic in matter and in form, and became glaring at an early point of their growth, and so were easily dealt with. But it was much more difficult to deal with men like Paul of Samosata, or Beryllus, or Praxeas, since theirs were errors much more logical in form and their defenders often able to hold a catholic doctrine in words, but in a very heretical sense. It was for this reason that the very word over which the Nicene battle was fought and won had been a century before rejected by the Church as capable of an unsound signification—the Homöousion. The heresies of the Cerinthians, Valentinians, and Montanists, of Paul of Samosata, and of Sabellius were mere skirmishes to the gigantic struggles into which Arianism and the secondary heresies which were derived from it plunged the Church. But out of it there came a series of definitions of the Faith which by their affirmation brands every counter-statement as heretical. The Nicene Creed really contains them by deduction. But the special definitions on Nestorianism, Eutychianism, Monothelitism buttress its articles against every wind of doctrine.

These, then, we must accept, and must test every new presented doctrine by them. Upon the definitions of the six Œcumenical Councils the Church must plant herself and defend the one Faith. There is another part, however, of this subject which it is well to speak of. These doctrines we have spoken of above are "of the Faith." But it may be asked, Is there not another series of dogmas which you stamp as heretical? You reject Mariolatry, Transubstantiation, the Immaculate Conception, and Infallibility as clearly as you reject the Pelagianism that is revived in a modern fashion. It is true, and herein, until there is an Œcumenical Council to pronounce them heretical, we only deny that they can endure the test of Holy Scripture and the harmony with the undoubted definitions of the Faith, and use the right belonging to the Church in each country to protect itself by forbidding them to be taught, till they are judged and passed upon by the whole Church in Council assembled. As we have never anathematized either the Eastern or the Latin Churches, we simply hold our accredited teachers to those doctrines taught in the first six centuries, and to none else. English Parliamentary Acts are not binding upon us, but these sentences from an act in the first year of Queen Elizabeth state concisely our position: "but only such as heretofore have been adjudged to be heresy by the authority of the Canonical Scriptures, or by some of the first four General Councils, or by any other Council wherein the same was declared heresy by the express and plain words of the said Canonical Scriptures."

The separate bodies of those who profess and call themselves Christians and show a zealous love towards our LORD are in schism, or in opposition to the external government of the Church, but may practically hold the Faith in all essentials. Still, an examination of many of their writings shows a laxity and that want of accuracy which is perilous. A person may hold heretical doctrine unwittingly, or through excess of zeal may be misled into it, but he is not to be accounted heretical unless so pronounced by the Church. Hooker's note on the title-leaf of the "Christian Letter" expresses the temper of every-one who has authority to teach: "All things written in the books I humbly and meekly submit to the censure of the grave and reverend Prelates within this land, and to the judgment of learned men and the sober consideration of all others, wherein I may happely err as others before me have done, but an heretike, by the help of ALMIGHTY GOD, I will never be." The "Christian Letter" was an attack upon his Ecclesiastical Polity, and his (unpublished) replies were scribbled on the margins.

Apart from the earlier heresies of the Ebionites, Gnostics, Manichæans, Priscillians, which were offshoots of the same tendency to revolt, we must note the false doctrines of Sabellius (240 A.D.), who taught that the TRINITY was but the manifestation in three forms at different times of one and the same Divine Being, and the similar ones of Paul of Samosata; those of Arius, who denied the eternal sonship of CHRIST, and of the modifications in the Semiarian and Eusebian forms of it. Those of Pelagius, who held that man had the capacity still left in him to earn immortal life without grace. Nestorius was led by his zeal against subordinate errors to assert that the Blessed Virgin Mary had given birth only to CHRIST, but not to GOD, meaning thereby that there was not continuously a perfect union of the two natures in the one Person of our LORD. He did not deny the indwelling of the Divine in the human nature, but he would not hold to the perfect union of the two, as the body and soul together subsisting in perfect union make the one man. This heresy brought out its opposites, the Monophysite and the Monothelite heresies. Eutyches, in his fervor against Nestorius, maintained the single nature in CHRIST,—the Divine nature was so united to the human as to form but one nature, as silver fused with gold forms but one alloy. To escape this error (condemned by the Council of Chalcedon, 451 A.D.), Sergius, the Patriarch of Constantinople (630 A.D.), put forth the Monothelite error, in which, acknowledging the two natures, yet the Divine will absorbed the human will, and there was but one will and one energy in the Person of our LORD. These heresies appear to have exhausted all forms of false teaching against the Person of our LORD from within; of course the denial of His Divinity is an assault from without.

Hermeneutics signify the principles of Biblical interpretation, as Exegesis refers to the practical use of these principles. The early writers on Scripture tried to classify these principles and to lay down some fixed rules upon which to apply them. Though they accomplished much, their many subdivisions have in this later age been rejected with perhaps too much scorn. For a guide in researches into the hidden senses of Scripture, a thorough and devout study of the text is itself imperatively necessary. It was this study, in which he spent three years of unrelaxed labor, which gave Chrysostom his almost unrivaled power of exposition, and his great common sense kept him from misapplying his knowledge. Hermeneutics means really the principles of common sense used in the Exegesis of the Bible,—*i.e.*, every department of human investigation must be governed by its own laws, as the physiologist investigates the deeper mysteries of our human system by the facts he has already gained, and his sagacity, common sense, and power to combine these facts skillfully lead to still greater results, but his sagacity and common sense would fail him if he were to apply them without previous special training to some other science, as, for instance, the Law. The Patristic expositors divided the science into from three to twelve or fourteen subdivisions, thereby defeating the establishment of any true system. It is perfectly defensible to lay down these three divisions: (*a*) The Principle that a book (or a text) should be studied in itself,—*i.e.*, the connected form of its contents and their purpose, the surroundings because of which the book was written, and their bearing upon the contents. This may be called the Grammatical method. (*b*) Since each book has claimed for it the authority of Inspiration, it follows that its contents, which historically are local, can also have wider and later applications. This is specially true of special sections in the book,—*e.g.*, our LORD's Parables had usually a historical application at the time they were uttered, but He intended that they should have an application to us in each successive age, and their wonderful wording gives them such a truth for each generation. (*c*) Then within the limits of that common sense spoken of above there is also what is, for want of a more accurate term, called the Principle of allegorizing, of interpreting passages so as to give them their true sense, yet one not on the surface. Such was our LORD's use of the words which He as the

Eternal WORD had used to Moses: "I am the GOD of Abraham, and the GOD of Isaac, and the GOD of Jacob." The perfectly legitimate conclusion our LORD drew from it, that He was not the GOD of the dead but of the living, was not upon the surface nor apparently within the purpose of the words when first uttered. So St. Paul compares Hagar to the Jerusalem that now is, and Sarah to the New Jerusalem, the mother of us all. It was this principle misused and pushed to extremes that brought the whole study of Hermeneutics into disrepute, but it was a very sound one in itself, and gave to the Patristic Exegesis very much of that power which it will never lose.

Hermits. (*Vide* ASCETICS.) The hermit life seems to have originated in the Eastern idea that matter was evil, and that by despising the body the soul might be elevated. The celibate Therapeutæ, clad in white garments, praying at sunrise with their faces to the sun, and with their allegorical rendering of Scripture, were hermits. They lived a life of contemplation, while the Essenes practiced agriculture and the arts, and lived together, and assisted others. The Therapeutæ gave their property to relatives before entering the brotherhood, while the Essenes had a "common treasure." The Therapeutæ lived separately in cells and were ignorant of the outer world, recruiting their ranks from boys brought up by themselves, while the Essenes only accepted adults as members. Banus the Pharisee, with whom Josephus lived, led a life of stern self-mortification, clothed in woven leaves and feeding on roots.

In the first two centuries of the Christian Church, while persecution raged, it was indeed a "church militant," and the great Decian persecution may have driven Christian men into the desert away from heathen cities, and excited a martyr spirit, as in New Testament times (Heb. xi. 38), when Christians "wandered in deserts." When Christianity grew worldly, those who desired to observe a very strict life naturally fell into the ascetic idea. Paul was the author, and Antony the encourager, of hermit life among Christians, and Hilarion and St. Jerome in his Bethlehem community were famed as promoters of it. At first scattered individuals practiced a life of asceticism in the Egyptian deserts, where Paul and Antony had performed their austerities in the third and fourth centuries. Pachomius, in the peaceable reign of Constantine, caused monasteries to be built in Thebais in Egypt, and thence monastic life has spread throughout the world.

While the Church uttered its protest against anything unholy in matter, condemning the abhorrence of things innocent, she approved asceticism in the so-called "Apostolical Canons" as a useful discipline. (Euseb. H. E., v. 3.)

In ancient times the pillar-saint, Simeon Stylites, who for years exposed himself to the weather, standing on pillars of various heights, is pre-eminent as a specimen of ascetic life. He would not leave his post even to embrace his mother, who visited him, although she died at his place of mortification.

St. Patrick in Ireland, St. Columba in Scotland, and St. Martin, Bishop of Tours, in France, have left illustrious names behind them.

In modern times the Russian monks have been remarkable hermits. In Dean Stanley's "Eastern Church" (Lect. x. pp. 393-94) we find the following extract from Fletcher's "Russian Commonwealth": "In the dark forest of Muscovy, in the frozen waters of Archangel, is carried out the same rigid system, at least in outward form, that was born and nurtured in the burning desert of the Thebaid." These Russian monks are very influential. They are called "The Black Clergy." In the sixteenth century they used to go nearly naked, with flowing hair. Many had an iron collar or chain about their necks even in the extremity of winter.

In some rare cases they are considered as prophets, and can rebuke whom they will. One of them checked and rebuked an emperor when he was intent on massacring the town of Plescon. (Stanley, pp. 396-97.)

Some conception of the vast numbers of early monks may be formed from the fact that Cassian speaks of a monastery with five thousand monks in it. The monasteries in deserts had their churches and officiating clergy. St. Jerome describes the effect of the daily sermon of the Abbot at evening prayer as seen in the tears of the brethren, and when the kingdom of CHRIST and heaven were the topics, "then one may observe how each of them, with a moderate sigh and eyes lift up to heaven, says within himself, 'Oh that I had wings like a dove, for then would I flee away and be at rest!'" He also commends the life of the monks of his beloved Bethlehem, where "one could not go into the field but he should hear the plowman singing his hallelujahs, and the vine-dresser tuning David's Psalms." It is of such a life that Geikie speaks, in the "lawless Middle Ages, when the cloister was like a speck of blue in a heaven of storm." Still, extreme asceticism sometimes produces a reaction of excessive laxity, and fleeing from the world to challenge Satan in the wilderness is not as heroic as the struggle with the world, and perhaps the life among others rightly lived may be less dangerous than solitary life.

Authorities: T. Gregory Smith in Smith & Cheetham's Dictionary of Christian Antiquities, Chambers's Library of Universal Knowledge, Schaff-Herzog, Encyclopædia of Religious Knowledge, Bingham's Antiquities, Farrar's and Geikie's Lives of Christ, Prideaux's Connections, Kingsley's Hermits, Euseb. H. E., ii. 17, Sozomen, H. E., i. 13.

REV. S. F. HOTCHKIN.

Hierarchy. The divinely instituted governing order in the Church. It really, both by New Testament evidence and by the testimony of history, comprises three orders,— the Bishop, the Presbyter (contracted into Priest), and the Deacon. By this Hierarchy every historical Church has been and is governed. Since the Reformation the disastrous attempt has been made and is now continued of deriving the government of the Church from the will of the congregation, not from the Divine commission. But the three orders have each been enlarged by a separation of details of government in each order. Thus the development of the Church work and multiplication of Dioceses required at an early date the arrangement of some rule of precedence, and the Episcopal authority held "in solidum" as a common right and power by all Bishops was subdivided by arranging the precedency, with presiding and appellate rights of the Bishop in the chief See of a Province with the title of Metropolitan. As the work grew and the difficulty of meeting all cases, both of government, of discipline, and of faith, which came up, the offices of Patriarch for the whole Province, which was usually coterminous with the civil province, of Metropolitan, and of Archbishop, for the subdivisions of the Province, were created, and under them the small Dioceses, whose territory was arbitrarily determined by the conditions of the Church there and of the work to be done, though it could not be enlarged or diminished at pleasure. But the Bishop of the smallest, poorest Diocese was invested by his office with all the spiritual authority the Patriarch could wield. This gradation of rank within the limits of the order was made gradually, for the sake of order, government, and decent conduct of the work. So too the office of the Priest was enlarged by appointing Archpresbyters and Deans, both which, however, changed their names; the Archpresbyter later took the title Archdeacon, and the Dean became attached to a Cathedral, while his place was taken by a Rural Dean. This was done that the interests of the clergy might be attended to while the Bishop, whose representatives they were, was busied about other important duties. So too the Deacons had an Archdeacon, usually the senior Deacon, set over them, who, when he received Priest's orders, ceased to be Archdeacon, but later the Archpriest took his title and exercised jurisdiction over both orders. It was to meet necessities as they arose, to fulfill the demands the growth of the Church made upon the clergy, to prevent clashing of interests, that these subdivisions of jurisdiction and of rank took place in the three orders of the ministry. Whether they continued to fulfill the needs which gave them existence is another thing. Whether they are needed at present by the extension of our work, and whether the machinery they involve is suited to our state here, is a problem now engaging the attention of the most active minds in the Church. Without intending to assert that they, as they existed in the early Church or are now with their functions defined by the growth of centuries in the English Church, should be transferred to our usages and interpolated into our methods, it is proper to insist that there is a need for some such reorganization of our Diocesan work. There is a shrinking in many minds from the introduction of titles and of such subdivisions of work and of appointing supervisors of it, but the necessity for it is shown by the attempts to meet it in the discussions of the Provincial system in the General Convention; the organizations of the local clergy into Convocations; the use of Church Congresses to discuss such subjects among many others. There is a real difficulty in selecting the names. The offices could be well discharged and are sometimes unconsciously filled by clergy who have a natural talent for leadership and for organization. But in this country we shrink from creating officers to whom we must apparently give the titles of Archdeacon, and Dean, and Provost. This is being met by the common, but usually unofficial, use of the title Dean for the presiding officer of the Convocation. It lies a good deal in the good sense of the clergy and their readiness to organize into a working body, having a system of missionary work which shall be faithfully carried out under such officers, whether titled or not, whom the Bishop may choose to recognize. In a few Dioceses these officers are already recognized and provided by Canon, but in by far the greater part of the Church there is only a semi-official recognition by the Bishop.

In the Hierarchy, then, upon the unalterable foundations of Bishop, Priest, and Deacon, there were developed as need demanded within, in these ranks which grew out of the Episcopate. (I.) The PATRIARCH, who was at first called Archbishop, and the ARCHBISHOP, who was at one time called the Metropolitan. The Patriarch exercising supreme executive jurisdiction over the Archbishops, and the Archbishops under him exercising such authority over the Bishops of their Provinces. (*Vide* also EXARCHS and PRIMATES.) Within the Presbyterial office were developed (II.) the Archdeacons and the Deans. The so-called minor orders did not give any spiritual power, but were the systematized lay co-operation formally recognized by a public setting the person apart for his work by the laying on of hands.

High-Priest. The officer holding the highest office in the Jewish worship. He was to be only of the House of Aaron, to which the Priesthood was confined. It was to belong to the Aaronic family by a perpetual statute. The High-Priest had peculiar functions given him, which were typical of the eternal Priesthood of CHRIST. To him alone once a year it appertained to go into the Holy of Holies, to sprinkle the blood of the sin-offering upon the mercy-seat, and to burn incense within the veil. He could do this only in the proper robes of his office. A type of the robe of our Humanity our LORD wears, entering with it with His own blood of atonement and offering the incense of our Prayers. During his lifetime the homicide who had taken sanctuary in one of the cities of refuge could not leave it. Again, a type of the protection given to the soul by the very life of our High-Priest. Other functions of a judicial and an organizing character which he exercised were rather temporary, and depended more upon the ability and influence than the ecclesiastical office of the High-Priest. As did Eli, he might permit abuses to grow up around him unchecked if not without protest, or he might as Azariah oppose the royal power, or as Jehoiada institute large repairs. In these things the energy or the diffidence of his character was shown. In the service of the office, if the High-Priest were incapacitated by sickness or some defilement, the next of kin could discharge it for him. It must have been for some such reason that Zecharias, the father of St. John Baptist, was in the Holy of Holies offering incense when the Angel appeared to him with his message. Again, in the later political troubles under the Seleucidæ, and under the Romans, one High-Priest was often removed and another put in his place, and as this was done from policy, without the slightest regard to Jewish Law, the people while they submitted to the High-Priest in office paid great reverence to the legal High-Priest. Therefore St. Luke (ch. iii. 2) wrote, "Annas and Caiaphas being High-Priests;" noting the two, Annas the true High-Priest, and Caiaphas his son-in-law, being the one thrust in. Here we can see why Caiaphas, being High-Priest that year, should prophesy "that it is expedient for us that one man should die for the people, and that the whole nation perish not," and why our LORD should be carried first before Annas, and then before Caiaphas.

Holy-day. *Vide* FESTIVALS.

Holy Ghost. The Third Person of the blessed TRINITY, to whom the third imploration of the Litany is addressed. "O GOD the HOLY GHOST, proceeding from the FATHER and the SON, have mercy upon us miserable sinners." And of whom is set forth in the V. Article the true faith we must hold. The HOLY GHOST, proceeding from the FATHER and the SON, is of one substance, majesty, and glory with the FATHER and the SON, very and eternal GOD, and is so confessed in the Creeds. In the Apostles' Creed, "I believe in the HOLY GHOST," and then the remainder of the Creed is a declaration of His work (as much as the preceding parts are each a declaration of the nature and the work of the FATHER and of the SON): "The Holy Catholic Church, The Communion of Saints, The Forgiveness of Sins, The Resurrection of the body, And the Life everlasting." More fully is His Person shown in the Nicene Creed: "I believe in the HOLY GHOST, the LORD and Giver of Life, Who proceedeth from the FATHER [and the SON], Who with the FATHER and the SON together is worshiped and glorified, Who spake by the Prophets." In this Creed also is His work set forth, but the circumstances under which this part of the Nicene Creed was enlarged at the Council of Constantinople (381 A.D.) did not lead the Fathers there to give it the form which shows it, but the answer in our Catechism does this: "Thirdly, in the HOLY GHOST, who sanctifieth me and all the people of GOD." The true faith, then, of the Christian concerning the HOLY GHOST is that He is a Person of the Substance, Power, and Majesty of the GODHEAD, proceeding from the FATHER and the SON. Sent by the FATHER and the SON and received by us, He is a Person, since He is sent by the FATHER. "And I will pray the FATHER, and He shall give you another Comforter, that He may abide with you forever" (St. John xiv. 16). "But the Comforter, which is the HOLY GHOST, whom the FATHER will send in My name. He shall teach you all things and bring all things to your remembrance whatsoever I have said unto you" (id. 26). He is sent by the SON also. "It is expedient for you that I go away, for if I go not away the Comforter will not come unto you, but if I depart I will send Him unto you" (xvi. 7; *cf.* xiv. 17; xv. 26; xvi. 13-15; Acts i. 5, 8). With this proof of His being a Person, we can understand the sentence, "And the SPIRIT OF GOD moved upon the face of the waters" (Gen. i. 2). "My SPIRIT shall not always strive with man" (vi. 3). And, to pass by many other passages, Ps. li., "Take not Thy HOLY SPIRIT from me." St. Peter declared that He was the promise of the FATHER to the SON, and quoted the Prophet Joel (ii. 28-32). But He hath notes and marks as becometh a Person. He is HOLY. It must be His by nature, and it is an inseparable part of His Name—the HOLY GHOST. He is the LORD. "Now the LORD is that SPIRIT, and where the SPIRIT of the LORD is there is liberty" (2 Cor. iii. 17). He is the Giver of Life,— "The Spirit of Life." . . . "But if the Spirit of Him that raised up JESUS from the dead dwell in you, He that raised up JESUS from the dead shall also quicken your mortal bodies by His Spirit that dwelleth in you" (Rom. viii. 2-11). He proceedeth from the FATHER and is sent by the SON. (*Vide* PROCESSION OF THE HOLY GHOST and FILIOQUE.) He, with the FATHER and the SON together, is worshiped and glorified. "GOD is a Spirit, and they that worship Him must worship Him in Spirit and in Truth" (St. John iv. 24). He spake by the Prophets. "For the prophecy came not in old time by the will of man, but holy men of GOD spake as they were moved by the HOLY GHOST" (1 Pet. i. 21).

He is sent to abide forever in the Church;

and therefore He is the informing, guiding Spirit in the Visible Church, which is Holy and Catholic. He is the Instrument of the Forgiveness of sins. "He breathed on them and saith unto them, Receive ye the HOLY GHOST. Whose soever sins ye remit, they are remitted unto them, and whose soever sins ye retain, they are retained" (St. John xx. 22, 23). He is the Instrument, too, of our Resurrection. "Not that we would be unclothed, but clothed upon, that mortality might be swallowed up of life. Now He that wrought us for the self-same thing is GOD, who also hath given unto us the earnest of the SPIRIT" (2 Cor. v. 4, 5). "And grieve not the HOLY SPIRIT of GOD, whereby ye are sealed unto the day of redemption" (Eph. iv. 30). "But if the Spirit of Him that raised up JESUS from the dead dwell in you, He that raised up CHRIST from the dead shall also quicken your mortal bodies by His Spirit that dwelleth in you" (Rom. viii. 11). In Bapti-m He is the regenerating Spirit. "Except a man be born of water and the Spirit, he cannot enter into the Kingdom of Heaven" (St. John iii. 5). In Confirmation He giveth His sevenfold gifts. "And the Spirit of the LORD shall rest upon him, the Spirit of wisdom and understanding, the Spirit of counsel and might, the Spirit of knowledge and of the fear of the LORD, and shall make him of quick understanding in the fear of the LORD" (Is. xi. 2, 3; cf. Collect in Confirmation Office); and makes us Temples of GOD (1 Cor. iii. 16; vi. 19). We are renewed by Him (Tit. iii. 5; cf. Rom. xiv. 2). In Him we bear fruit (Gal. v. 22, 23; cf. St. John xv. 16); and we have all joy and peace in believing (Rom. xv. 13).

"By the HOLY GHOST is given the restoration of Paradise, the return into the kingdom of heaven, the restoration of the adoption of sons, the confidence of calling GOD our FATHER, the communion of the grace of CHRIST, the appellation of sons of light, the participation of eternal glory; in a word, the plenitude of benediction, both in the present time and in the future, of good things prepared for us." (St. Basil on the Holy Spirit, ch. xv.; Browne on XXXIX. Articles; Bishop Forbes on the Nicene Creed; Hare's Mission of the Comforter.)

Holy Table. The name used generally in the Prayer-Book for the synonymous titles, Altar and LORD'S Table. In this the English Church follows the practice of the Eastern Church, where the word "Altar" is seldom used, while the word "Holy Table" is far more usual. But the term Communion-Table is used twice in the Prayer-Book in the Form of Consecration of a Church or Chapel. It seems to be an inadvertence, since the LORD'S Table, the Holy Table, to which we are invited to feast, is not our table,—not the Communicant's Table. (*Vide* ALTAR.)

Holy Week. The eight days from Palm-Sunday to Easter-Sunday have, in all ages of the Church, been observed with great solemnity and devotion. Palm-Sunday, the commemoration of the LORD'S triumphal entry into Jerusalem; Holy-Thursday, the Institution of the LORD'S Supper; and Good-Friday, His Passion. The observance of this week as of universal obligation is spoken of in a Festal Letter in 260 A.D. Tertullian, who lived seventy-five years before, speaks of the continuous fasts during this week. The Gospel narrative of the Passion was read during this week from day to day in the Gospels, the book of Jonah being also read at this time. The fast was as strictly observed as possible. Many privileges were claimed and used during this week. Debtors were released from prison, actions at law were suspended for the week preceding and the week following, slaves were often freed in this week, and a cessation from all business and from unnecessary labor marked it. The several days had each their special name,—Palm-Sunday (also called earlier Indulgence Sunday), Monday in Holy Week, Tuesday in Holy Week, Wednesday in Holy Week, Maundy-Thursday, or "Dies Mandati," the day on which the New Commandment was given, "that ye love one another," Good-Friday, and Easter-Even. The services in the Prayer-Book are only marked by the special Epistle and Gospel, the Palm-Sunday Collect serving till Good-Friday. In this as in several other places the services lose something of that marked character which they should bear, but doubtless the difficulties which beset the steps of the Reformers did not permit them to retain all that they would have wished. However we may regret this, yet by extraordinary acts of devotion and of abstinence and an observance of all the services given with conscientious fidelity and with earnest self-examination, the layman has it in his power to make Holy Week as truly a week of devout penitence as if it were overlaid with rubrical ordinances.

Homiousion. "Of a like or similar substance" with the FATHER, a term devised after the rise of the Arian heresy as a middle term between the Homoousion of the Catholic doctrine and the extreme position of Arius, who taught that the WORD was not of the same substance as the FATHER, but a mere created being, before all other created beings, and above them, but still created.

Homoousion. Of the same substance with the FATHER. The word was previously rejected in the controversy with Sabellius, as implying a trinity incompatible with the true Personality of each of the Three Persons of the TRINITY, but in the controversies with Arius its proper force was determined, and it was made the test word in the Council of Nice and was incorporated into the Creed. It was to express the reality of our LORD'S sonship as being of the same eternal incomprehensible nature as His FATHER, which Arius denied.

Hood. A cap or cowl fastened to the cloak or outer garment and drawn at will over the head to protect it from sun or rain. It became the covering for the head the monks wore. It was afterwards worn in the Church service. As now used in England and in Ireland, it is simply an ornamental fold hanging down the back of a graduate to mark his degree. Therefore it varies considerably both in the universities the one from the other, and, too, as marking the wearer's academical degree, except that in all three universities the Doctor's hood is of scarlet. The English graduate is ordered to wear his hood upon his surplice.

Hosanna. "Save now." It was the processional refrain when our LORD made His entry into Jerusalem. "Hosanna to the Son of David!" It was chiefly used in the services of the Feast of the Tabernacle; on the last day specially, with branches waving and with Psalms, the Jews went seven times around the Altar, saying "Hosanna." The children were expected to take part in these services. Hence "the children crying in the Temple, Hosanna to the Son of David." Compare the Hallel Psalm cxviii. 24, with Ps. xx. 9 (Hebrew 10 verse).

Hosea, the first of the Minor Prophets according to the order of books in the Bible, prophesied in the days of Uzziah, Jotham, Ahaz, and Hezekiah, Kings of Judah, and of Jeroboam II., King of Israel (Hosea i.), and his date must accordingly be between 810 and 698 B.C. His name is the same as that of Hoshea, King of Israel, and in meaning is equivalent to Joshua, or Jesus,— *i.e., Salvation*. Of the prophet personally there is nothing to say besides that he was the son of Beeri, whom some, without reason, would identify with Beerah of the tribe of Reuben (1 Chron. v. 6). There is, however, a late tradition that he was of the tribe of Issachar, which is not improbable; for it is in some measure confirmed by expressions and allusions in his prophecy, which warrant the conclusion that he was a native of the Northern Kingdom.

The period during which Hosea prophesied has been the subject of much dispute; and objections have been raised on the ground of its great length. For if we reckon from the first of Uzziah to the last of Hezekiah (810 to 698 B.C.), we have an interval of one hundred and twelve years; or even if we stop at the sixth year of Hezekiah (and it seems unlikely that Hosea prophesied later than that, otherwise he would have appealed to the fulfillment of his own prophecy (Hosea xiii. 16) in that year), we still have ninety years (the Hebrew reckoning), which is an unusually long ministry. But it is not necessary to begin to reckon Hosea's ministry earlier than the last year of Jeroboam II., King of Israel, and contemporary of Uzziah, nor to continue it later than the first of Hezekiah; a reckoning which gives a period of fifty-eight years (784 to 726 B.C.), which is not improbably long. Hence objections to Hosea on chronological grounds may be disregarded, because the first verse of the prophecy does not require for its truth an interval of more than fifty-eight years, and there are abundant instances of men whose public life has been much longer than that.

It is believed that Hosea himself compiled his prophecies as now arranged after they were all delivered; yet there is no date nor connection by which their chronological order can be determined with certainty. But it is easy to divide the book into two chief portions: the first part consisting of the first three chapters; the second part of the rest of the book; when, however, the analysis and subdivision of these parts are attempted great difficulties arise, so that to give any account of the work of different critics would require much time and space, and it must suffice to say that the first part has been divided into three poems, corresponding nearly to the chapters (ch. iii. is the first poem); and the second part into five sections, with reference to the five contemporary kings; or by some into thirteen sections, according to the subject-matter. But the analysis and arrangement of this prophecy, both from obscure brevity and apparent confusion of order, is so full of difficulty, that Bishop Lowth has not inaptly compared it with the scattered leaves of the Sibyl. Not less difficult, also, has proved the interpretation of the first three chapters of Hosea and the prophet's relation with *Gomer*. Many have understood them literally, but in modern times the tendency of opinion seems to be towards an allegorical interpretation. The design, however, of this part of Hosea, whether taken literally or figuratively, as well as that of the second part, is sufficiently clear. The prophet declaims against the sins of Israel, exposes in the strongest terms the spiritual adultery of the idolatrous worship at Bethel, and denounces GOD'S righteous judgment upon it, in prophecies, some of which were fulfilled in the near future; at the same time there is an accompanying strain of Messianic prediction of future blessings and redemption calculated to animate and encourage those who should heed the rebukes and turn to the cultivation of righteousness. It is on this account that Hosea has been so often quoted in the New Testament.

The importance of Hosea as a witness to the rest of Scripture is very marked; for the book furnishes abundant references and allusions to the Pentateuch, and the historical books of Joshua, Judges, and Samuel; and shows that that portion of the Bible as we read it now was the same before the destruction of the Temple and the captivity of Israel and Judah, in the ninth century before CHRIST. Still further, the state of affairs implied in Hosea is in strict accord with the contemporary history in the books of Kings; and many points of resemblance, allusions, and even quotations are traced between Hosea and contemporary or later prophets. (*Vide* Smith's Bible Dictionary, Bible Commentary, and Gray's Introduction.)

Hospital. The word is derived from the Latin *hospes*, a guest, through *hospitium* a guest-house, then *hospitalis* (domus), *hospitale* (cubiculum). The other word, hospitium, retained its meaning, but hospitale was used in later French and then in English to mean the apartments or the buildings set apart for the sick. We have no traces of any such establishments till after the Church began her LORD'S work. It was His charge to heal the sick, to visit and relieve the poor, sick, needy, and imprisoned. In many places one-third, in others one-fourth, of the income of the Diocese was set apart for the poor and sick and needy. Since there was a careful supervision and no waste was allowed, the moiety, at least, of this sum went to the sick. At what date buildings were set apart for this work we do not certainly know, but we find them as soon as property could be securely held by Christian corporations; as, for instance, Basil the Great (about 350 and 390 A.D.) founded a hospital which lasted for some time. A century before this the brave conduct of the Christians in the epidemic in Carthage and in the plague in Alexandria won for the Church a great influence. To care for the sick, and to see that hospitals were erected for them in his See, was one of the duties of the Bishop. Chrysostom used all the surplus of the income of his Patriarchate in these works. Dwelling only on salient facts, we find when the monasteries were organized not only a large hospitality, but a special care of the sick was also organized, and from the portion of the monastic buildings set apart for this purpose we get the name Hospital. But the work was not necessarily monastic. Lanfranc founded a hospital for lepers and one for ordinary diseases in 1081 A.D. These are the earliest foundations recorded in England.

The Monastic Rule was eminently fitted for such work, and it responded nobly to the demand. Many of the arrangements of the infirmary are worthy of study yet, and have not been improved on since.

At the dissolution of the monasteries, the Monastery of St. Bartholomew was handed over to the citizens of London in 1547 A.D. for a hospital; that of St. Thomas was bought by the mayor and citizens in 1551 A.D. for this use; Henry VIII., in 1547 A.D., gave the Bethlehem (Bedlam) for an asylum for lunatics; Bridewell was first used as a hospital, but became a house of correction; and Christ's Hospital became a school. About 1719 A.D. the work of founding hospitals received a great impulse, and in seventy-eight years no less than fifty were founded in England and Ireland. Many more have since been erected in Great Britain. In this country very much has yet to be done. The last statistics give 45 Church Hospitals in 22 Dioceses and 6 Missionary Jurisdictions for 1883 A.D. The increase is large and direct, but it is by no means the exhibit of such charity work as it should be. No Diocese should be without one or more such institutions, and there should be one in each town of sufficient size in the Diocese, and an Infirmary and Dispensary in lesser towns. It is not merely the Bishop's care that such hospitals are established. It pertains to the Laity also to look to it that they aid in establishing and securing endowments for such institutions. They are the stewards of the ministry of the silver and the gold. Their business training enables them to attend to this financial work, and to see to it that it is based on commonsense business principles. Their secular habits give them a knowledge of men which is invaluable in selecting the proper officers for it. From them the many grateful gifts of necessaries must come. From them the aid, sympathy, and encouragement which the workers need must largely come. In lesser towns, in feebler institutions, when the trained nurses are suddenly occupied with some special cases, or an epidemic breaks out, the Guild and Brotherhoods which should belong to every Parish would relieve much by taking the watching and care of the less dangerously ill patients as their special work.

Spiritual oversight and aid belong to the clergy. They minister to the sin-sick soul, to the diseased mind. But the physician to the body, the tender nurse, the gentle night watcher, the sympathetic assistant, are also doing CHRIST'S characteristic work of love and sympathy. They exercise a part of their royal Priesthood. A hospital has a just demand upon the means of each member of CHRIST, and upon the treasury of the wealthy, second only to the claim which the support of the Priesthood makes upon them. Though the care and oversight of the hospital should be most largely under lay care, yet it must be remembered it is possible only because our LORD instituted His Apostolic Ministry. It is perhaps fairly a matter of regret, which time will doubtless remedy, that there exists in this country no Church Hospital vigorous enough to establish a Church Nursing School, and this for two reasons: I. The nurse approaches more nearly the individuality of any given sick person than others, save it may be the priest of GOD and the physician, ever can; to the nurse most frequently will come the opportunity for a gentle word of comfort or suggestion, while each act done in the body's service is one more invitation to pray for the soul which it hides from view. II. Wherever and whenever a Church Hospital is founded, *experienced* and *trained* nurses are needed, but can seldom be obtained; over and over we read the same depressing, everpathetic history. In prayerful spirit and earnest zeal some priest, or layman, secures a house or a few rooms, gives thereto the name of some saint of old, secures the services of physician and surgeon, appeals to the Church's children for substantial aid, throws open the doors to the wounded and sick of any creed and nation, and puts in charge of the daily life such workers as can be found; these, in most instances, are incompetent, though devoted. They struggle on, some for a few months only, when one by one they fall, discouraged, out of line; others, with stronger brain and more enduring purpose, labor for years, and at last come out into the clear light shed by knowledge. But they reach their goal, in most cases, with broken health and mental vigor scarcely sufficient to enable them to transmit to others any part of the fruit of their dear-bought experience, while these in turn go over the same rough ground with practically the same results. That this state of affairs has so long continued unremedied, wellnigh unnoticed, argues a weak spot somewhere in the Church's plan of work. It cannot be denied that each generation of workers in Church Hospitals leaves some sort of inheritance to its successor. But how small and meagre does it seem when compared with the investments made of devotion, health, talent, culture, money! And how rarely does aught of gain fall to one institution from another! The need is sore of a centre whence may be sent out women who have been taught, with that steadiness and slowness which are the sole guarantee of safe and good issues, how to serve the sick. When the day comes for its establishment,—and come it will,—it is to be hoped that special care will be given to teaching how to teach. In England and elsewhere some work has long been done in this department, but here it is wholly neglected in most secular nursing schools, and is but superficially and ill done in those which give any attention to it.

The popular idea that any one can impart to another that which he himself knows is wholly erroneous. The teaching power is as clearly a special gift as is an aptitude for languages, etc. Occasionally a person is met with who entirely lacks it; but most people possess it in some degree, and in all these it may be developed by judicious and quiet manipulation. The waste of physical strength and of time in Church Hospitals would startle Church folk outside, and even the workers within, could it be lucidly and fully set forth. The one great principle, economic yet wise use of material, which should underlie the system and work of a Church (or any) Hospital, has rare recognition even among Sisters.

For in planning work or in grappling with one and another of its petty details, few remember that effort should primarily be directed to the solution of this problem: How can be done the largest possible amount of work in the best possible manner with the least possible expenditure of time and strength? The charge is sometimes made against Church Hospitals that their size is in inverse ratio to the trouble of running them and the expense *per capita*. This is perfectly true. It is also true that there are two other facts which may counterbalance this one.

All Church Hospitals *may* grow, and some doubtless *will* grow; further, in a country so sparsely settled over the greater part of its area as this country is, the need of many small hospitals is obvious. But he who would start a hospital, as the saying runs, should be sure it is needed in the spot where he would put it. Often it would be far better merely to open some avenue, to feed some institution already existing, bringing all his influence to bear to this end. This is specially applicable in and near cities where, even when amalgamation is inexpedient, different hospitals might so affiliate themselves and their interests as to be mutually enlarged and strengthened. For example, a hospital for convalescents or one for chronic cases might connect itself with an ordinary general hospital, or a nursery or a children's hospital with one for childbirth cases. In a few instances such a plan has been tried here, meeting fair success, but it has obtained abroad to a far larger extent. Church Hospitals are at once too exclusive and too introspective. That is to say, those who do their work know too little, and ofttimes care not to know more, of sister institutions to win the help which comparisons afford, while absorption in details makes them forget the advantages to be derived from a "bird's-eye view." And the hospital walls are allowed to press upon them until shortened vision and stiffened muscles supervene. Perhaps a Church Hospital Association, by promoting discussion of principles and methods of work and by the free use of the interrogation point, would be the most effective antidote to this. In point of fact, the whole great question of Hospitals needs study, and it would seem that Church people *as such* have given slender attention to it. A valuable factor in its adjustment would probably be the deputing an intelligent Churchman with some knowledge of interior hospital life to study the whole system here and abroad, and then to publish a paper which should be at once philosophical and practical. The inventive instinct of man's nature ever runs a neck and neck race with his tendency to slide along in a groove. In art, in mechanics, in music, in business, in science, and in other forms of human interest it wins. Why should it not so do when the matter in hand is the prolongation of earthly life? since these words only constitute a synonym for a little longer space wherein the threefold forces of men may be developed for the life eternal.

When, after patient study, and after a just appreciation, both of the difficulties to be encountered and the discouragements to be overcome, and the imperfect instruments to be employed, it is resolved to open a hospital, still very much has to be done. A building, otherwise suitable, may not be properly located. In a city, to be of real use, it should be where the class it is to minister to should find it most accessible. Again, so many details have to be arranged in a house already constructed for other purposes,—for it usually happens that these ventures of faith have to prove their right to the attempt, not by a first outlay in erecting a proper building, but in running the risk of utter failure by hiring a house which was never intended nor is now fitted for such use. In all such instances remodeling has to be made to a large extent, and even then many inconveniences, especially in drainage and in easy access to the several suites of apartments,—wards they can hardly be called. It is not till success in its mission of mercy has won for it regard and confidence that a Hospital can really command the means to have a suitable building. But when a munificent layman is willing, or a number who can will contribute to consecrate of their abundance to such a work, then a building can be erected upon some such plan as will be now described.

The buildings should be arranged in accordance with the strictest requirements of sanitary science. It is now generally admitted that it is not well to gather a number of invalids under one roof, when several are in one room. The least cubic space for each patient should be about four thousand feet, or a floor space of ten feet each way for the bed, and twelve feet to the ceiling, and thorough ventilation should be secured, so as to remove all foul air as rapidly as can be done without creating a draught. The most approved form for hospitals is that of pavilion wards; that is, entirely distinct structures connected by corridors. Every hospital, however small, should have two wards, one for medical and one for surgical cases, and, if possible, a third should be added for infectious diseases. If this is impossible, one end of the medical pavilion should be cut off by a wall and provided with a separate entrance as the best substitute for a totally isolated building. A good model is the shape of the letter H; the wards on each side the offices for the staff, kitchen and domestic apartments in the middle. The chapelry should be so arranged that it can open into the wards on either side, that the patients may, if proper, enjoy the soothing influences of the Church services and prayers. But of equal importance with the building itself is the proper organization of the *Board of Managers*, the *Superintendent* (or *Matron*), the *Medical Staff*, and the corps of *Nurses*. They should all, from the chief to the lowest subordinate, be wholly unselfish. For in a hospital the first consideration (indeed, it is the reason for the existence of the hospital) should be, *What will most benefit the patients?* and all rules, etc., should be made with this end in view. Therefore everything that is self-seeking on the part of managers, doctors, superintendent, or nurses must be put aside in any well-managed hospital. Many of the troubles that have arisen from time to time in institutions have come from losing sight of this end.

Rules and regulations, or constitutions for the board, would vary for different institutions, of course, but the fundamental rule should always be that the Board of Managers should have entire control of the Hospital, and be responsible for its well-being.

The *Medical Staff* should have *professional* care of the patients. They elect fresh members at the meetings (subject to the Board of Managers), arrange their visits and work, and order what is necessary for the care of the patients.

The *Superintendent* (or *Matron*) of the Hospital should have the entire care of it, and be responsible for such care to the Board of Managers. Devoutness, tact, knowledge of men are necessary. The duties of the Superintendent are:

(*a*) Engaging and discharging nurses and servants.

(*b*) Controlling expenses.

(*c*) Providing stores, etc.

(*d*) Overseeing the proper care of each department.

In fact, he is responsible for the order and economy of the Hospital. In matters that refer directly to the professional care of the patients, he (or she) is subject to the Medical Staff. Matters that affect the order of the Hospital, and are of sufficient importance, should be at once taken to the Superintendent,—this does not refer to petty matters that are easily settled by the head of each department. Should the matter be of such importance, the Superintendent should bring it to the notice of the Board, or to such of them as may be appointed as Executive Committee. But on all occasions the Superintendent should, before acting, inquire into the matter from the person in charge of whatever Department in which the disorder may have arisen. Of course tact and discretion are necessary in a person holding the position of Superintendent; and it is equally necessary that he or she must have the confidence and support of the Managers.

The Nurses.—In training-schools for nurses, experience has proved that women between the ages of twenty-three and thirty are most fitted for nursing. This does not so much matter when the Hospital work is among children, but as a rule, women who enter under twenty-three years of age are apt to break down in health after a few years of nursing.

Some very necessary qualifications for a nurse are good health, good spirits, good temper, neatness, quietness, and self-possession. A nurse should be fairly well educated, and as intelligent and observant as possible. Care should be taken that the food provided for the nurse should be *simple, good*, and *well cooked*. The sleeping-rooms should not be near the wards, and should be light and well aired. These things are absolutely necessary if a nurse is to do her duty and keep her health. It cannot be too earnestly insisted upon that each nurse should be provided with a room to herself. Her spiritual well-being depends upon it almost as much as her physical comfort. Solitude at times is absolutely essential to every one, and more particularly to those who live under a great strain of mind and body. Any extra expense that may be incurred in this will be more than repaid by the increased service she will be able to render.

A nurse should pay strict attention to personal neatness. Her dress should be as simple as possible, and of washing material. A nurse should never repeat any story or gossip about the Hospital patients or Doctors. While care should be taken to instruct her in every detail, she must remember that she is not to supply the Doctor's place, but faithfully to obey his orders. After a nurse has been instructed a few times in the sweeping and cleaning of a room, it is quite unnecessary for her to spend her strength upon this work. All she needs to know is how this work should be done when her time may come to give like instruction. Anything more than this is, as a rule, a waste of her powers. The airing of beds, bedding, patients' rooms, wards, and cleanliness of everything about her patients is very necessary and quite the duty of a nurse, but sweeping and scrubbing unfits her for the time for waiting on her patients, as no nurse can, while doing this kind of work, be ready to wait upon them. But there is yet another qualification. The nurse should be a woman who comes to the work, if not from a love to it, yet from a love for her LORD and a desire to step in His footsteps. She should be prepared to bear, with unfailing patience and gentleness, the trying exactions of sick persons. She is with the patient always, and can speak many a word of comfort or warning, if once confidence is established between them. She can give practical lessons in forbearance, and long-suffering, and love unfeigned which will bear fruit when she least expects it. She can wisely find many opportunities of giving religious comfort, and often a short prayer or a verse of a psalm may be most soothing to a patient who may feel shy or be too sick to ask even for these. Even when this is not the case, much can be quietly done that will not cause excitement or alarm to the patient. Of course, in the case of a dying person, the course of every Christian woman is quite clear. In training-schools rules differ slightly, but these things are quite essential in all,—wise, strict discipline, prompt obedience to orders, and punctuality in being at her post.

The *Chaplain* should, if possible, in every Hospital, and certainly in every one of size, reside in the Hospital. He is then at hand to seize upon a favorable change in the condition of a patient. A short prayer, a few words from the Bible, can sometimes be listened to in an interval of ease, when an hour earlier or later it would be impossible to gain the attention. For in illness the thoughts turn instinctively to spiritual matters, and if the sufferer be within reach of his ministration he can be touched and influenced far more easily than in health. In all cases of doubt the Chaplain should be guided (*a*) by the Physician's judgment; (*b*) by the desire of the patient himself. Only in the case of the dying can the Chaplain act on his own authority.

A few additional words may be permitted upon details.

The *Furniture* may be, as simple or as elaborate as the means of the Institution permit; but whatever economy be practiced in a room or ward, good air, plenty of sunlight, soft coloring upon the walls and on window-shades, quiet and cheerfulness in the apartment are absolutely necessary. The beds should be comfortable, on wire-woven mattresses, and an ample supply of linen and blankets should be on hand.

The *Food* should be prepared by an experienced cook, and no food should be taken to a patient that is not tempting as well as nourishing. Everything provided should be on the dietary arranged by the Medical Staff, and should always be the best of its kind. There should be a dining-room for convalescents at the end of each ward, and it is desirable to have a cheerful sitting-room as well.

The *Laundry.* The washing should, if possible, be done outside the limits of the establishment, and every article well aired before it is returned.

One word more. Larger extension of her hospital work is fast becoming essential for the Church. The Missionary Jurisdictions and the Foreign Missions have, under their Bishops, nobly led the way. But the true success is equally in the hands of the Laity, who should see that sufficient incomes be provided for such Institutions, whether by endowments or by connecting them with regular parochial Institutions. To undertake the establishment of a Home or Hospital for the sick is a venture of faith,—to carry it on a great burden,—but it is CHRIST-like; and if, after a careful weighing of all the surroundings,—the obstacles, the necessary conditions for success, and the favorable circumstances that ought to justify it,—for ordinary human foresight must be used as well as prayer, and faith, and vows,—the work be resolved on in CHRIST'S name, those who so resolve should never falter.

REV. A. C. A. HALL.

Host, from *hostia*, a victim. The term applied in the Roman Church to the consecrated Bread in the Holy Communion. Originally both the Bread and the Wine when consecrated were offered as one Host, and correctly, for both Bread and Wine together are the Sacrament. At the same date the thanksgivings, prayers, and oblations are called a Host. But when the error of Transubstantiation came into practice, the Bread was called the Host, and worship was addressed to it. " Therefore there is no room left for doubting that all the faithful of CHRIST .... do in their worship render to this most holy Sacrament the *cultus* of *Latria*, which is due to the true GOD." (Council of Trent, Session xiii., De Euch. cap. v.)

Hours of Prayer. The older Church of the Jews had stated times of Prayer. Thrice a day, seven times a day, are spoken of in the Psalms. Daniel observed the hour of Prayer. So too St. Peter and St. John " went up together unto the temple at the Hour of Prayer, being the ninth hour." As the day, no matter what its real length was, was divided into twelve hours, the early use of the devout was to set apart a certain hour for these devotions. The first three hours were called together the third hour, the next three ended at noon; were called sexts, or the sixth hour, then the interval ending at three o'clock was called the ninth, or nones, and then at sunset came the duodecima. These intervals of three hours each had special services assigned, which were generally of Prayers and Psalms and Lessons. Archdeacon Freeman concludes that these Hours and services, though neither of Apostolic nor early post-Apostolic date as Church services, had nevertheless probably existed in a rudimentary form, as private or household devotions, from a very early period, and had been received into the number of reorganized public formularies previous to the reorganization of the Western ritual after the Eastern model. (Principles of Divine Service, p. 219.) It was from the services of these Hours, which were probably of Gallican introduction into England, that the Reformers compiled the Morning and Evening Prayer, with valuable additions and some marked emendations. The Seven Canonical Services (beginning with a service before dawn and ending with a compline service at nine at night) had been reduced to three practically by aggregating the services,—*i.e.*, reciting two or three Hours at once,—but the Reformers condensed them instead. The Services for the antelucan, the first, and the third hours were thrown into one for the Morning Prayer. The earlier Prayer-Books of 1549 A.D. began with "Our FATHER"; but in 1552 A.D. the sentences, confession, and absolution were prefixed. The Psalms were read in course,—which was a change for the better from the arbitrary selections before in use,—and the service compressed into the form we now use it. The same process was used to construct the Evening Prayer. So that in a separate and modified form we use daily the services which came over from Gaul into England and were in use before the Norman Conquest.

Housel. The Holy Communion. A Saxon term, chiefly used to mean the administration of the Communion. So as late as Shakespeare we read " Unhouseled, disappointed, unaneled" (Ham., act i., sc. 5).

Hymn. A hymn, according to St. Augustine, must be praise to GOD in the form of song. Properly, this definition should be extended to lyrical *prayers*. In popular acceptance the term includes "spiritual songs" not directly addressed to the DEITY, as " GOD moves in a mysterious way," " From Greenland's icy mountains," and large portions of the Psalms in any version. Ground has been taken for the exclusion of this class from manuals of worship, but neither past usage nor present opinion justify so sweeping a measure, though the form of praise and prayer is to be preferred.

The word *hymn* occurs four times in the New Testament. In St. Matt. xxvi. 30, and St. Mark xiv. 26, it refers to Psalms cxv.–cxviii., the latter part of the Great Hallel, chanted by the Jews during and after the Paschal Supper. Eph. v. 19, and Col. iii. 16, mention the three apparent classes of " psalms, hymns, and spiritual songs" to be used for instruction and admonition as well as worship. By that time probably devout verses other than those of Scripture were composed and sung among the early Christians, and their use rapidly increased. Pliny, when governor of Bithynia, in his famous letter to Trajan, 106 or 107 A.D., says that the believers of that province, on the testimony of some who had left them, "were accustomed on a stated day to meet before daylight and to repeat among themselves a hymn to CHRIST as to a god." Three centuries later St. Jerome says hymns were sung everywhere, by the plowman in the field and by the workman at his bench. Tertullian, in his "Apology" (c. 200 A.D.), says, " As every one is able he is invited to sing in public to GOD out of the Scriptures, or from his own composition," and it was not till the Council of Laodicea, about 370 A.D., that these private productions were forbidden to be used in public worship.

The Gloria in Excelsis and the Te Deum are merely the most illustrious of many early hymns which were produced in Greek, Latin, Syriac, and probably in every language wherein Christian worship was conducted. (See Mrs. Charles's The Voice of Christian Life in Song, 1858 A.D.) In Latin St. Ambrose (397 A.D.) founded a memorable school, whose productions are marked by severe simplicity. He was followed by Prudentius (d. about 413 A.D.), St. Gregory (d. 604 A.D.), Venantius Fortunatus, and others. The mediæval hymns are of richer and freer type. The great names here are St. Bernard (d. 1153 A.D.), Peter Damiani (d. 1072 A.D.), Hildebert (d. 1133 A.D.), Adam of St. Victor (d. 1192 A.D.), and Thomas Aquinas (d. 1274 A.D.). Several single poems by other writers of this age are of great fame and merit, as " Dies Iræ,"

"Stabat Mater," "Veni Creator Spiritus," "Veni Sancte Spiritus," and the "De Contemptu Mundi" of Bernard of Cluny. A few modern writers, as the brothers Santeuil (d. 1684-1697 A.D.) and Charles Coffin (d. 1749 A.D.), have done good work of this kind. (For the Latin hymns in general see the Breviaries, Daniel's Thesaurus Hymnologicus, and Mone's Hymni Latini Medii Ævi; and in translations, Newman's Poems, Chandler's Hymns of the Primitive Church, 1837 A.D.; Bishop Mant's Ancient Hymns, 1837 A.D.; Isaac Williams's Hymns of the Parisian Breviary, 1839 A.D.; Copeland's Hymns for the Week and Seasons, 1847 A.D.; Caswall's Lyra Catholica, 1849 A.D., and Hymns and Poems, 1873 A.D.; Chambers's Lauda Syon, 1857-66 A.D.; Dr. J. M. Neale's Mediæval Hymns, 1851-63 A.D.; Hymnal Noted, 1851 A.D.; Rhythm of St. Bernard, 1858 A.D., etc.) There were also sundry Greek writers of merit, 400-1000 A.D., some of whose lyrics were rendered with wonderful success in Dr. Neale's "Hymns of the Eastern Church," 1862 A.D. (See also Mrs. Browning's Greek Christian Poets, 1842-63 A.D.)

At the Reformation hymns began to be written in the vernacular in the lands most affected by that movement, and chiefly in Germany, where, under Luther's leadership, an immense and valuable body of hymns began to be produced. Very many writers, from that day to this, have taken part in the work, the greatest of them being Paul Gerhardt (1606-76 A.D.). (See Knapp's Liederschatz, a collection of 3000 lyrics; Koch's Geschichte des Deutschen Kirchenlieds, 7 vols.; and in English, Kubler's Historical Notes to the Lyra Germanica, 1865 A.D.; and Miss Winkworth's Christian Singers of Germany, 1869 A.D.) Many of the German hymns have been translated by John Wesley, 1737-40 A D.; Jacobi and Haberkorn, 1722-60 A.D.; the Moravians, 1754 A.D., etc.; Francis E. Cox, 1841-64 A.D.; A. T. Russell, 1851 A D.; R. Massie, 1854-60-64 A.D.; Jane Borthwick (Hymns from the Land of Luther), 1854-62 A.D.; and others, but especially by Catherine Winkworth, whose Lyra Germanica, 1855-58 A.D., and Chorale Book for England, 1862 A.D., are of great merit and value. Sweden, Denmark, France, and even Italy have hymns of their own, but in less quantity, and have contributed little to our stock, though Cowper's renderings (1782 A.D.) from Madame Guion (d. 1717 A.D.) have been valued, and sometimes used.

In England psalmody, rather than hymnody, was the use for two centuries. Myles Coverdale, who was Bishop of Exeter under Edward VI., issued in 153- A.D. forty *Ghostly Psalmes and Spirituall Songes*, partly from the German; but it is not known that they were ever used. Sternhold's *Psalms*, 1549 A.D., completed 1562 A.D. by Hopkins and others, were as popular as Clement Marot's for a time in France; and though their style was soon antiquated, were used in some churches well into the present century, long contesting the ground with Tate and Brady's *New Version*, 1696 A.D. These two were the only versions authorized or used entire in the Church of England; and the often quoted passage from Queen Elizabeth's Injunctions to the Clergy, "that in the beginning or in the end of Common Prayer, either at morning or evening, there may be sung a *Hymn*, or such like *Song*, to the praise of ALMIGHTY GOD," seems to have been applied to them alone or chiefly for one hundred and fifty years or more. James I. did indeed confer special privileges on Wither's *Hymns and Songs of the Church*, 1623 A.D., as "esteemed worthy and profitable to be inserted in convenient manner and due place into every English Psalm-Book in metre," but nothing came of it. England in that century had no lack of noble sacred poets,—Herbert, Quarles, Milton, Vaughan, Crashaw, etc.,—and a few of their lyrics have since been used as hymns, as have been some professedly such by Jeremy Taylor, 1655 A.D.; John Austin, 1668 A.D.; R. Baxter, 1681 A.D.; John Mason, 1683 A.D. But it was then supposed on all hands that only versions from Scripture, and as literal as might be, were fit for public worship. Meantime, the Scotch Kirk and some English Puritans used Francis Rous's version of the Psalms, 1645 A.D., as revised and allowed 1649 A.D.

The making and using of hymns on a large scale began with Dr. Isaac Watts, whose *Horæ Lyricæ* appeared 1705-9 A.D., his *Hymns* 1707 A.D., and his *Psalms* 1719 A.D. His fame and success were at first among his fellow-dissenters; indeed, the Established Church, for a century after these dates, rarely admitted anything metrical, except the Old and New Versions, into her worship. But indirectly and by degrees his influence, and that of the school which he established, were felt by Churchmen, and when they came to make hymn-books of their own, most of the material was necessarily drawn either from Nonconformists or from Methodists (Arminian or Calvinistic), who were within the Church, but had received their ruling principles and spiritual impulse chiefly from other sources. The state of things which prevailed through the eighteenth century was widely different from that which exists now: Churchmen of the sober average type neither wrote hymns nor cared to use them, and with a few exceptions, as Ken, Addison, Pope, Byrom, and Merrick, the tide of lyric devotion flowed from the two great sources supplied by Watts and Wesley. Every one else followed one or other of these, or wrote under their joint influence; so that all but a few dozen of the many thousand English hymns produced between 1700 A.D. and 1800 A.D. belong in matter, style, and spirit to one or other of these three schools, the last being composite.

Dr. Watts (1674–1748 A.D.), who is still considered by many, and probably by a majority, as the greatest of English hymnists, was a good man, who had read much, but (like all his followers) lacked the culture of the great universities. His claim to poetic talent, sometimes denied of late, was valid, though the talent was of no very high order; but his taste was the worst that ever afflicted a poet. With some grand lines and many vigorous lyrics he mingled much wretched bathos and a vast deal of commonplace verse, easy but ignoble. The descent from Vaughan, or even from Mason, to him is "from the mountain to the plain." His theology is average Calvinism; though softened by his amiability, it is sometimes rudely and offensively put. Such as he was, he suited his time completely; their very plainness and frequent vulgarity commended his *Psalms* and *Hymns* to most Britons who desired such provision; they were "laid level to the meanest comprehension," yet had a directness and occasional force unknown in previous compositions of the kind; finer work could not have attained the same success. For over a century "Watts entire" was used by many Dissenting congregations; as late as 1836 A.D. a "Supplement" to him was put forth by the Congregational Union of England and Wales. He is still the largest contributor to every Calvinistic hymnal, and was till lately one of the largest to Church collections. Thus he has done an incalculable amount of good, and of harm, for it is doing harm to keep a low standard when a higher one is obtainable. The gain in refinement and of feeling, in propriety of thought and expression, has been great since his day, and not more than a very small proportion of his verses is now fitted to guide the devotions of Churchmen.

His followers in this field were, like himself, devout and estimable persons, and mostly Dissenting ministers. Their work is usually neither so good nor so bad as his; and their many volumes show a somewhat tame uniformity of views and feelings, broken by little originality of thought or vehemence of temper; they are solid, sober, and often dull. Dr. Doddridge, the greatest of them, is (through a few favorite and indispensable pieces) almost as well known to Churchmen as Dr. Watts: his three hundred and seventy-four hymns, published after his death in 1755 A.D., have a "mild and human tone," and "shine in the beauty of holiness." Anne Steele (1760 A.D.), whose somewhat "feeble elegance" was more valued fifty years ago than now, ranked next to Watts and Doddridge in the Prayer-Book Collection of 1827 A.D., but from seventeen hymns is reduced to eleven in the present Hymnal. Beddome, Fawcett, and S. Stennett were Baptists. Simon Browne Dr. Gibbons, Needham, T. and E. Scott, Mrs. Barbauld, and the Scotch Paraphrasers have each given lyrics to general use.

A new school and era opened with Charles Wesley (1708–88 A.D.), the most fertile, fluent, and highly gifted of sacred lyric poets. With his brother John he began in 1738 A.D. the brilliant series of publications which continued till his death, including with what he left in manuscript some six thousand pieces. Their *Poetical Works*, collected in thirteen volumes, 1868–72 A.D., cover near six thousand pages; of this vast quantity John probably wrote but some forty or fifty, nearly all free versions from the German. C. Wesley had the best culture of his time, and a style of unsurpassed elegance; the grace, fire, and fervency of his muse made imitation hopeless. But he could neither condense, nor always control, his torrent of eloquent song; and his intense emotionalism, which often transcends all bounds, has little in common with that "sober standard of feeling" which Churchmen have generally maintained, and which Keble placed "next to a sound rule of faith." Though a genuine poet, he is pre-eminently "the poet of Methodism," and in proportion as his strains are invaluable to that sect, they are invalidated for Christians of quieter views and habits. It is from excess, and not from defect of qualities that these splendid lyrics so largely fail of general usefulness; their vehemence of feeling and expression is such that we cannot repeat them without insincerity. Thus no poet needs to be so carefully gleaned from as he; and inadvertent compilers have often forced his verses celebrating "sinless perfection" and the like on flocks which heard no such doctrine from the pulpit. Yet some of his best hymns, comparatively free from these excesses, have usually adorned our hymnals, and will long be prized in those of every communion.

C. Wesley could not be closely followed like Dr. Watts, and few have attempted it. Cennick, a man of some talent, little taste or judgment, and great enthusiasm, issued three remarkable volumes, 1741–45 A.D. Hammond (1745 A.D.) and Seagrave (1742 A.D.) were of better education but similar spirit. Toplady (1759–76 A.D.) had original force; an earnest devotee and a fierce bigot, he wrote the greatest hymn (Rock of Ages) and several of the most beautiful of that age, and some of the worst of controversial tracts; one with the Wesleys in everything but the Divine Decrees, their difference from him on that point seemed to him the unpardonable sin. W. Williams, R. Robinson, Olivers, and Bakewell produced each one or two good hymns in the trochaic measures never employed by Watts.

Of those who wrote under the joint influence of Watts and Wesley, the most important are Newton and Cowper, whose tender, faithful friendship gave birth to the famous "Olney Hymns," 1779 A.D. This book was almost a manual for the Evangelical party within and without the English Church; and never were the tenets of that school presented in a more attractive light. The romantic and tragic story of John Newton's earlier life, the mellow sincerity of his after piety, his modest and manly character, all had their due effect; the man is seen on every page, lending a charm to what is often little more than doggerel. His hymns are full of personal experience and wholly void of pretense, while of Cowper's, hardly distinguishable from Newton's, some are utterly unworthy of his then unproved powers, and others fully equal to any of his later poems. Minor but not unimportant writers were Medley and Ryland (Baptists), and Haweis, rector of Aldwinkle: the distinction between Churchmen (of this school) and Dissenters was at that time mainly nominal. Joseph Hart (1759-62 A.D.) may almost be said to have founded a school of his own. A blunt Briton and vehement dogmatist, his rude but vigorous lyrics have become especially dear to advanced Calvinistic sects, and have impressed themselves quite sufficiently upon English-speaking Christendom at large.

Such were the materials which supplied the hymnals of the eighteenth century. These collections were comparatively few, and almost wholly by and for Dissenters, or by Churchmen of the Methodistic, evangelizing type, for the use of their "societies." Of the former class, though later in time, the most important book is Dr. Rippon's Appendix to Watts, 1787 A.D.; this gathered up much of the best work of writers of the old school and of some others, and long exerted an immense influence far beyond Baptist bounds. Of the other class, whose ecclesiasticism is so unobtrusive as often to be invisible, the leading representatives are Whitefield's, about 1755 A.D.; Madan's, 1760 A.D.; Lady Huntingdon's, 1764 A.D.; and John Wesley's, 1779-80 A.D. The last, a production then and long after incomparable for literary excellence, is still the manual of the English Wesleyans, and has been the basis of every other Methodist collection.

Towards the end of the last century Churchmen, probably of the moderate Evangelical type, began to issue selections of metrical psalms, chiefly or wholly from Tate and Sternhold, with slight additions of familiar hymns. This practice grew apace, the number of hymns increased, and B. Woodd and others ventured on psalm renderings of their own. But the legality of all this was doubted, and in 1820 A.D. a suit was brought in the Consistory Court at York against Thomas Cotterill for having introduced a *Selection* of his own (1819 A.D.) into his parish at Sheffield: "its declared object was to prevent the use of any other metrical compositions than the Old or New Version of the Psalms." After a long hearing, the matter was referred to the Archbishop of York, who compromised it by preparing a selection of his own, and presenting copies in quantity to the aggrieved parishes, which seems to have quieted the malcontents. Thereafter collections were freely made, with or without the Bishop's sanction. None of them to this day have had in England more than Diocesan authority, and the voluntary principle was long since established, whereby each parish priest practically uses whatever hymnal he prefers, or makes and brings in one of his own.

Meantime the Church of England, or some of her members, were awaking to the fact that she ought to have hymns suited to her own spirit and services. A few by Heber and Sir Robert Grant, of an elegance anticipated by the Wesleys and Toplady alone, appeared in the *Christian Observer*, 1806, 1811 A.D., etc. Some others, as Gisborne, Cawood, and G. T. Noel, wrote with equal intention if less talent. Cotterill filled his short-lived book with originals that were eagerly copied into others: of modest literary merit, they took a place unfilled before, and held it worthily till most of them gave way to others of higher quality but in the same vein. By these aids Anglican hymnals became in some degree (though as yet very imperfectly) recognizable as such, apart from their title-pages. When, in 1827, appeared Bishop Heber's *Hymns written and adapted to the Weekly Church Service of the Year*, and Keble's *Christian Year*, the English Church had proved her claim to the possession of some lyric life.

Two eminent writers had meantime arisen outside her pale, though one of them was on the boundary line. James Montgomery was a Moravian and a poet, and produced many hymns which were fit to be used anywhere. His main landmarks were Cotterill's *Selection* (1819 A.D.), in which he helped largely, and his own *Songs of Zion* (1822 A.D.) and *Christian Psalmist* (1825 A.D.). Living to collect his three hundred and fifty-five *Original Hymns* in 1853 A.D., he left a saintly and venerable name, to which Churchmen are as much indebted as any others. Thomas Kelly was an Irishman of humble capacity and of singularly naive and childlike style, from which his considerable learning would never be suspected. He was fond of missionary themes and of trochaic measures. Beginning to publish in 1804 A.D., his *Hymns* reached an eighth edition (miscalled on the title-page the seventh) in 1853 A.D., then numbering seven hundred and sixty-five. The best of these are among the earlier: many of them have had an immense currency and a wide popularity, and a few of them are likely to live. Covering the same period of time, Josiah Conder, a Congregational layman of literary culture and churchly spirit, wrote with some force and much grace, giving us, among others, one of our best Communion hymns, which was objected to in the General Convention of 1870 A.D. for its too lofty doctrine Edmeston, Collyer, Raffles, and A. Reed produced some good hymns; and Sir John Bowring, a devout Unitarian, eminent in various fields of labor, wrote many, of which we might well use more than one. Of very recent Dissenters the most eminent is Dr. Bonar, without some of whose lyrics no collection is complete. After him came G. Rawson and Mrs. S. F. Adams.

But for the last half-century the hymnic life of England has been chiefly in the English Church. The way was prepared, as has been shown, by Cotterill, Keble, and Heber, the last of whom had the accomplished and successful co-operation of Dean Milman. Harriet Auber's *Spirit of the Psalms* (1829 A.D.) anticipated both in character and title the work of Lyte (1834 A.D.), whose exquisite "Abide with me" is much later. Bathurst, Mant, Osler, Charlotte Elliott, J. H. Gurney, Dean Alford, and others have made important additions to our stock. The Oxford movement of 1833 A.D. gave a mighty impulse to the development of metrical provision for the Church's wants, and resulted in a genuine revival of sacred song. Newman, Caswall, Bridges, and Faber did their work mainly or wholly after their perversion to Rome; but many loyal adherents of the Anglican Establishment have been as busy on similar lines. Original hymns suited to her teachings and usages have been produced in abundance by Bishop Wordsworth, Dr. Monsell, Sir H. W. Baker, Mrs. C. F. Alexander, Bishop How, J. Ellerton, W. C. Dix, and translations from the Latin, Greek, and German, as mentioned above. The *clarum et venerabile nomen* of this period is that of a great scholar and saint, Dr. John Mason Neale. The leading Hymnals of to-day differ widely from those of forty years ago. In some respects and cases the change has no doubt been overdone, but in the main the improvement in taste and fitness is obvious and great. "Hymns Ancient and Modern" (1861; Appendix, 1868; Revised and Enlarged Edition, 1874 A.D.) was prepared with unusual care and skill, and as estimated by the sale of copies, long ago counted by millions, has attained a success probably unrivaled by any collection in any language.

In America comparatively little has been done or needed, the supplies of England being at command. Above two hundred writers have furnished more than one thousand hymns, which are or recently have been used in home collections; some of these are well known across the ocean, and a few of them are of high rank. The chief names outside our own communion are Thomas Hastings, Dr. Ray Palmer, and Dr. S. F. Smith. Native writers, apart from those admitted to the Prayer-Book collection of 1827 A.D., are little represented in our present Hymnal.

The history of our Episcopal hymnody is brief and simple. In 1789 A.D. the "New Version" of Psalms by Tate and Brady was adopted, with twenty-seven hymns, to which thirty were added in 1808 A.D. Of these fifty-seven, seventeen were from Watts, ten from Steele, and nine from Doddridge; not more than twenty were by Churchmen. In 1827 A.D. the two hundred and twelve hymns appeared, Watts, Doddridge, Steele, C. Wesley, Montgomery, and the Scotch Paraphrasers being the chief contributors; but seventeen new lyrics, some of them of great value, were furnished by Drs. Onderdonk, Muhlenberg, and Doane. In 1833 A.D. the one hundred and twenty-four selected psalms, all but fourteen being from Tate and Brady, displaced their entire version. This meagre provision served exclusively for our public worship for near half a century, though several collections by Dr. Andrews and others were prepared for week-night services and the like. In 1866 A.D. sixty-five Additional Hymns were sent forth by the House of Bishops, and from that time the English "Hymns Ancient and Modern" were allowed in several Dioceses. The present Hymnal appeared in 1871 A.D., and was slightly revised and enlarged 1874 A.D. Little attention had been given to hymnology among our clergy or people, and the Committee could hardly command adequate facilities for such a task; but the result, though not to be compared with the best English collections, is a great improvement on what we had before. It contains an abundant, if not an excessive, supply of psalm versions; some sixty—or half the precious assortment, in number if not in length—being taken from Tate and Brady. Where the use of metrical psalms, standing by themselves as such, is abandoned (as is the nearly universal practice now), there seems no adequate reason for retaining more of them among other hymns than may deserve that rank by intrinsic merit. Then come Dr. Watts with thirty-seven lyrics, C. Wesley with twenty-eight, Montgomery with twenty-six, Doddridge with nineteen, and Newton, Heber, and Steele with eleven each. If the origin of all the five hundred and thirty-two hymns be noted, Dissent appears at length to be somewhat in the minority. Of translations from the Latin there are thirty-seven, from the German sixteen, from the Greek seven; of these together Dr. Neale supplies twenty-one, his originals being somewhat slighted.

Our Church people have cared less for hymns than other Protestants, and been less dependent on them, having the service. To non-liturgical bodies the hymn-book is the only ritual, and its contents take the place of chants, glorias, psalter, and largely of common prayer. But even with us metrical hymns are not to be despised, especially since the growing taste for music causes them to be sung in many parishes at the opening of service, as well as in the old time-honored places in its course. Their possible, and doubtless in many cases their actual, influence is incalculable for good or ill. They reach multitudes who know little of canons, rubrics, or articles. "A verse may find him who a sermon flies," and songs have a power long recognized as beyond that of laws or learning. They sink into the mind in youth, and color its ideas of doctrine, devotion, and duty. They have been repeatedly the solace of poverty and age, the support of the sick and dying. Backed by the subtle charm of melody, they appeal to our emotional even more than to our intellectual nature. As authorized and employed by the Church, they bear an essential part in that constant education which her members are unconsciously receiving at every service. Their place in divine worship is as high as any; for, whether metrical or not, they afford the most fit and natural means of praising GOD. In singing them, as St. Paul has it, we are "speaking to ourselves" and to the LORD. Lack of care and skill in selecting and using them is therefore irreverent and injurious. They carry a double message, and both the human and the divine direction they take deserve and demand our best.

The qualities needed in hymns, individually or collectively, are obvious. They should harmonize with the beliefs and principles of those who use them, or else they promote insincerity. They should not, for common occasions, go beyond the range of ordinary Christian experience, or, at most, imagination. There is a large and varied class of *unreal* hymns, the utterance of which involves falsehood, as " I want to be an angel," which is impossible and against nature. They should not tend to excited and strained feeling. On this account, as has been shown, many of Charles Wesley's most beautiful lyrics, besides many of inferior quality but equal currency by other writers, are not available. They should voice, adequately and genuinely, human penitence, need, and aspiration. They should represent us at our best, holding up a standard which we may follow, so that the worshiper be raised, and not (as may too easily be the case) lowered, by their means. They should, in most cases, be direct addresses to the object of worship. Versified moralities, arguments, and exhortations are out of place and out of date here. We are supposed to sing, not at each other, but to the LORD. Effusions like Hymns 384 and 381 should be relegated to Gospel meetings.

So much for the substance. As to the form, a hymn should be poetical and lyrical, and not merely "prose tagged with rhyme;" however excellent the sentiment, it fails of any real value for its purpose if wooden or mechanical It must be smooth and singable, and it should, like any other literary product, have unity, compactness, and completeness. Abrupt beginnings, as in 111, and endings, as in 110, mar the effect, though the latter may in part be mended by affixing a " Gloria Patri." But when a piece has the true lyric inspiration and hymnic fire, grave faults in its structure may be condoned. No one questions that " Rock of Ages" is a genuine hymn, though some of its lines have always needed and received emendation.

Textual changes have sometimes been sweepingly condemned, and the ground taken that a hymn should be used as its author left it, or not at all : but probably no collection was ever made for public use, or could have been, upon this principle. The practice of "tinkering," *i.e.*, taking needless and wanton liberties with the text (of which there are too many examples), is scandalous, but in many cases some alteration either is necessary, or will produce obvious improvement. To know when these changes are requisite or desirable, and to make or adopt them with a sparing and judicious hand, is part of a compiler's business,—for which, indeed, many of them were not well qualified. Abridgment is a simple matter. Often a hymn is too long, or unequal in the merit of its stanzas, and may be improved by omitting some of them. " Abide with me," and " Sun of my soul," as now everywhere used, are faultless hymns, full of tender and noble life, though only parts of the original poems.

The value of hymns cannot in every case be precisely determined by universal canons, for much depends on position and association. Some that are precious to us may be useless to our brethren of other names, and *vice versa*. Still, the rules of criticism apply here; a hymn has a literary character, though not that alone. In proportion to the culture of those who use them, stress must be laid upon this point. It should be remembered that the end does not sanction the means, and that charitable intent cannot cover intellectual or literary sin All hymns, we may suppose, were piously meant, yet multitudes of them are worthless except as curiosities. Many are dull and lifeless; many more have an unhealthy life in them, being coarse, ignorant, narrow, or heretical. The more accurate taste of our time condemns as gross or ranting not a few that were useful to former generations. The services and methods of the Church, as happily fixed long since, are no less admirable for their æsthetic than for their spiritual character. " The beauty of holiness" shines in her course of Festivals, Fasts, and Seasons, and in her order for public worship. The Prayer-Book is a study in English style, as well as in grave devotion. With its tenor should agree our rendering of the whole, and those musical appurtenances which were so long dreaded or undervalued, but are now firmly established and vastly enjoyed. There is nothing in rhyme and metre to excuse their contradicting, or falling far below, the tone of Morning Prayer, Litany, and Communion office. The spirit which forbids all " light and unseemly music" should exclude unworthiness of whatever sort in hymns as well. In this particular we have been too easy, too negligent. Yet any sound and cultivated judgment, applied here with the same fidelity it bestows on other important subjects, should be able to see what sacred songs are best fitted to edify Christians, and to be offered as incense to the ALL-WISE. There is no lack of models; our most approved and blameless hymns might serve as tests of others. "GOD," says Toplady, in the preface to his Collection of 1776 A.D., " is the GOD of Truth, of Holiness, and of Elegance. Whoever, therefore, has the honor to compose, or to compile (we may add, or to employ) anything that may constitute a part of His worship, should keep those three particulars constantly in view."

REV. PROF. FREDERIC M. BIRD.

Hyperdulia. The second of the three imaginary grades of worship which the Romanist is taught to consider allowable. The first is Dulia, which may be paid to a saint; a worship implying service. (*Vide* DULIA.) The second is Hyperdulia; and the third and highest, the Latria, due to the HOLY TRINITY. Hyperdulia is paid to the Blessed Virgin because of Her privilege in being the Mother of our LORD, but it is claimed that this hyperdulia is as distant from Latria as the creature is from the Uncreated. But it is a feat of imagination to place any difference so vast between these two prayers: " We fly to thy patronage, O holy Mother of GOD! Despise not our petitions in our necessities, but deliver us from all our dangers, O thou ever-glorious and blessed Virgin" (Catholic Piety, p. 35), and these words of the Collect: "O LORD, we beseech Thee mercifully to hear us, and grant that we to whom Thou hast given a hearty desire to pray, may by Thy mighty aid be defended and comforted in all dangers and adversities through JESUS CHRIST our LORD." In fact, the words of the Hyperdulic prayer to the Virgin are stronger than the words of the Collect, which dates as far back as the sacramentary of Gregory, 600 A.D.

Hypostasis. A term used very frequently in theology, in discussions upon the Holy *Trinity*, but one which is not always clearly apprehended by those who use it so freely. It expresses, primarily, "reality," and from this the real identity of nature in the Three Persons, thus showing that the oneness of nature proves that there is but One GOD, but the sharing of this reality of nature in the SON from the FATHER, and in the HOLY GHOST proceeding from the Father, there is a separation of the persons. This union is called the Hypostatical Union. Probably Hooker expresses it as tersely and plainly as any one can: "The substance of GOD, with this property *to be of none,* doth make the Person of the FATHER; the very selfsame substance in number, with this property *to be of the* FATHER, maketh the Person of the SON; the same substance having added to it the property *of proceeding from the other two,* maketh the HOLY GHOST. So that in every Person there is implied both the substance of GOD, which is one, and also that property which causeth the same Person to be really, and truly to differ from the other two. Every Person hath His own subsistence, which no other besides hath, although there be others which have the same substance." (Eccl., v. 51.) The last two sentences contain especially the true notion of the word Hypostasis,—the unity of substance in the reality of each Person, by which in One GODHEAD there is yet the subsistence of the Persons. With such a poor language as we have for expressing the delicate shades of thought and the distinctions necessary in theology, we naturally are unable to express it by a single word.

Hypothetical. *Vide* BAPTISM.

I.

Ichthus (ΙΧΘΥΣ). The initial letters of the Greek words Ιησους Χριστος Θεου Υιος Σωτηρ—JESUS CHRIST, the SON of GOD, the SAVIOUR—made the word ΙΧΘΥΣ, which means "fish." The mystical enthusiasm of the early Christians caught at this in connection with the Parable of the Net and with the Miracles of the Fishes, and to St. Paul's allusion, "I have caught you with guile." The image of a fish appears very often in Christian Art. Tertullian (180 A.D.) refers to it. Clement of Alexandria allows the fish as a device on a seal or ring proper for Christians to wear and use, as itself fitting, and as, too, the heathen would not perceive its mystical connection with the Christian doctrine, as they would if a cross were worn.

Idaho, Missionary Jurisdiction of. *Vide* UTAH.

Ides. In the English Calendar the month retains the triple division—the Calends, Nones, and Ides—of the old Roman use. The Ides begin in March, May, July, and October on the eighth day, and in all other months on the sixth day, and run on for eight days.

Idiotæ. Private persons; laymen. It is the word used by St. Paul (1 Cor. xiv. 16) when speaking of the Eucharistic Service, and the responses of the congregation. The translation in the A. V. "unlearned," is still worse translated in the margin of the revised translation, "him that is without gifts," since the Greek commentators, as Chrysostom, make it to mean the Laity (*cf.*

Wordsworth's Greek Testament, *l. c.*) It means "unprofessional" in 2 Cor. xi. 6, and so too in Acts iv. 13, where the Apostles are said to be "unlearned."

Idolatry. The worship of idols. It is not necessary that the idol should be an image of man or of beast. Idolatry can also be rendered to relics. It is rendered often to any passion or pursuit that overshadows the spiritual life and leads the soul away from the love and worship due to GOD before all else. It is giving to another the glory that is due to GOD (Is. xlviii. 11), and is directly in opposition to the Second Commandment.

It was most sternly repressed by the early Christians in every one received from paganism, since every Christian made a special renunciation. It crept in when men were received more freely after Christianity became dominant. The old superstitions were not so readily thrown off, and the edicts of Emperors and Penitentials of Bishops are filled with penalties inflicted upon those who practiced strange and revolting rites and sacrifices to demons. These Canons begin from the time of the Spanish Council of Elvira, go on to the close of missionary efforts in Europe, a space of over six hundred years. The tendency to superstition and idolatrous practices took a more dangerous form when, under the specious form of reverence for relics, it entered into the Church and tainted her worship, under the cloak of a pretended but uncalled for reverence. The open idolatry of the pagan is harshly reprobated though he knows no better; but the idolatry that is defended under the specious names of dulia and of hyperdulia—words that are barbarously twisted out of their true sense—deserves deeper condemnation; the idolatry that offers the Latria, due, as even the iconolatrous Council of Nicæa asserted, to the Divine nature only, to the *Elements* of the sacrament.

Illinois, Diocese of. The Diocese of Illinois was organized at Peoria, on the 8th day of March, 1835 A.D. There were present, three Presbyters and laymen representing three parishes. The Rt. Rev. Philander Chase, D.D., was chosen Bishop. Dr. Chase, being one of the first to introduce the Church west of the Alleghany Mountains, was elected Bishop of Ohio in the year 1818 A.D. He had founded Kenyon College and was its president. Because of misunderstandings and complications growing out of the administration of the institution he had resigned not only the presidency of the college, but also the Bishopric of Ohio. On his retirement he had removed with his family to Michigan, and was residing on a farm when the call to "come over and help" the new Diocese of Illinois reached him. He accepted the election in the following words: "As I had no agency direct or indirect in producing this important event, I cannot but regard it as entirely providential, and as such implying a command from the great Head of the Church to enter anew in the discharge of my Episcopal duties, so solemnly enjoined in my consecration, and lately so painfully, for conscience' sake, remitted. . . . In accepting the appointment to the Episcopate of Illinois I cannot refrain from mingling with a deep sense I have of the honor they have done me the melancholy reflection that the days of my strength and ability to bear the fatigues of planting churches in the new and pathless sections of our country, widely spread and illy provided with temporal comforts, *are forever past.*"

The resignation of the Diocese of Ohio by Bishop Chase and his election to the Diocese of Illinois, and his acceptance of the same, were without the sanction of Canonical law and without precedent. But the General Convention, recognizing the emergency, admitted the Diocese of Illinois into union with Bishop Chase at its head. The Committee of the House of Bishops to whom were referred the documents from the Convention of Illinois, made the following report:

"The Committee have examined the Constitution and Canons adopted by the Convention and find them not to be inconsistent with those of the General Convention. The Church of Illinois presents herself for admission into union with the General Convention with a Bishop at its head. By recurring to the journal, there appear to be some circumstances in regard to this appointment which may be thought not entirely in consonance with the regulations of the Church, yet the Committee do not deem them of such vital importance as to invalidate his election, and the Committee feel disposed to regard them with the more indulgence, as the case was unprovided for by the Canons of the Church. . . . The Committee therefore recommend the adoption of the following resolution:

"*Resolved*, That the Church of Illinois, under the Episcopal superintendence of the Rt. Rev. Philander Chase, D.D., be, and hereby is, received and acknowledged as a Diocese in union with the General Convention of the Protestant Episcopal Church of the United States.

"All of which is respectfully submitted.
"THOMAS C. BROWNELL,
"BENJAMIN T. ONDERDONK,
"WILLIAM MEADE."

Bishop Chase at once conceived the plan of founding a collegiate institution and a Theological Seminary in his Diocese; and with the intention of securing funds for this purpose went to England. On his return he bought land in Peoria County, and on the 3d day of April, 1839 A.D., laid the corner-stone of Jubilee College. Near the college he made his home, living for years in a comfortable log house, which he called "Robin's Nest," filled in with mud and sticks, and within which was a family of children. In time the college grew in usefulness, and became one of the best known and most successful institutions in the West. But many adverse circumstances have arisen to thwart the well-laid plans of the noble founder.

Bishop Chase was far advanced in years when he came to Illinois; still, notwithstanding the difficulties of traveling in that early day, he visited with promptness and regularity his great Diocese,—great in the extent of its territory, in its trials and its hardships. New towns were springing up; new parishes were formed; new missionary stations were appointed. The Bishop felt that the Diocese required more Episcopal oversight than he was able to give it, and he therefore asked the Convention, which met at Alton in 1847 A.D., to elect an Assistant Bishop. In response to this request the Convention elected the Rev. James Brittain, a Presbyter of the Diocese of Ohio. But the General Convention, which met soon after, refused to confirm the choice. It is due to the memory of the gentleman thus rejected to say that this action of the General Convention was not personal to himself. The opposition to him and his final rejection was due to the heated temper of the times,—to the party spirit that was so violent in the Church.

But the great increase in the growth of the Church, and the physical infirmities of the Bishop, made it necessary that another effort should be made to secure the aid of an Assistant Bishop. Accordingly a special Convention was held at Pekin in September, 1851 A.D., which elected the Rev. Henry John Whitehouse, D.D., rector of St. Thomas' Church, New York. Bishop Chase died September 20, 1852 A.D. Few men in the Church have been more laborious and self-sacrificing than Bishop Chase. He was the pioneer Bishop of the great West. Ohio and Illinois bear evidence of his faithfulness and devotion to the Church and its Divine Head.

To Bishop Whitehouse is due the credit of courage and wisdom in adopting a Cathedral system adapted to the condition of the Church in this country. Like all new projects, it at first met with great opposition; and this opposition retarded for ten years the beginning of the undertaking. The Bishop though discouraged was not cast down, and in time he saw some of his cherished purposes put to practical use. The Bishop's plans for a commencement were very modest. He intended that the Bishop should have a church of which he should have control, and whose sittings should be forever free. Connected with this church there should be a staff of clergy to conduct daily and other services, to educate the young, to prepare candidates for the ministry, and to do a certain kind of missionary work in Chicago and its suburbs. He never supposed that all this could or would be accomplished in his lifetime. He wished to lay the foundation as a wise, far-seeing master-builder, and let others as years passed build thereon. He selected the chief city of his Diocese in which to build this Bishop's church, and hoped that coming generations would recognize its power and help to enhance its usefulness.

His Episcopate convinced him of the impossibility of any man administering with satisfaction to himself or as the Church expected a Diocese so great as the State of Illinois. He had, therefore, recommended a division of the Diocese, and some preliminary steps had been taken to that end; but no definite plans had been adopted at the time of his death, which occurred on the 10th day of August, 1874 A.D. Twenty-two years of active work had brought with them cares, then troubles, and then disappointments; and when clouds were lifting and a clearer sky was appearing, the aged Bishop, though strong in body and intellect, was suddenly called from his labors.

The regular Convention, which met in the Cathedral, Chicago, in September, 1874 A.D., elected the Rev. George T. Seymour, Dean of the General Theological Seminary, Bishop. But the General Convention failing to confirm the election, a special Convention was called, which chose the Rev. James DeKoven, Warden of Racine College, Bishop. Dr. DeKoven not receiving the consent of a majority of the Standing Committees, the Annual Convention, which met September, 1875 A.D., elected the Rev William Edward McLaren, rector of Trinity Church, Cleveland, Bishop, who was consecrated in the Cathedral, Chicago, December 8, 1875 A.D.

Bishop McLaren brought to the Diocese a large knowledge of men and of affairs, a strong intellect, a sound judgment, a warm heart, and a catholic spirit. At once all the elements of discord, and dissensions and variances, the election to the Episcopate of two most worthy gentlemen and their rejection had engendered, were allayed. The Diocese united with its new Bishop in the hearty desire to forget the past, to strengthen and develop the things that remained, and to plan wisely and hopefully for the future.

Bishop McLaren recommended to his first Convention a division of the Diocese. This was followed in 1877 A D. by the organization of the Dioceses of Quincy and Springfield. Bishop McLaren selected the Diocese of Illinois in which to exercise the duties of his office, as the Canon permitted him to do. The Diocese has now 63 clergymen, 46 parishes, and 32 organized and unorganized missions. Communicants, 7467; amount of contributions for the Conventional year ending Easter, 1883 A.D., $309,102.79.

In 1877 A.D., Bishop McLaren, when recommending, suggested the propriety of forming a Federate Council, under Canon viii, Title iii., of the General Convention. In 1880 A.D. the three Dioceses within the limits of the State of Illinois met and organized, under the name of "The Federate Council of the Province of Illinois." This Council meets annually, and is composed of the Bishops and four clergymen and four laymen from each of the three Dioceses. Its objects are:

"The organization and administering an Appellate Court for adjudicating cases brought before it by appeal from the courts of the Dioceses within the limits of the State of Illinois, etc.

"The charge and care of such educational and charitable institutions as it may canonically establish, or as may be established under its jurisdiction.

"The charge and conduct of matters pertaining to the extension of the Church, so far as these matters may be intrusted to it.

"The acceptance and administration of all funds and donations of any kind which may be given or intrusted to it, and legislation upon subjects of common interest to the several Dioceses."

Statistics for 1886 A.D.: Clergy, 73 ; par., 41 ; miss., 35 ; C. for H. O., 2 ; ord., D. 2, P. 3 ; bap., 1318 ; con., 853 ; com., 9581 ; contr., $260,249.96. Rev. T. N. Morrison.

Illumination. The spiritual enlargement of the understanding and the conscience that cometh from the gift of the Holy Ghost and of the indwelling of Christ, " the Light of the World." Baptism bore the name of the Enlightenment. When received, the adults, the newly baptized walked in the new light they had received. Traces of this application of the term illumination appear in St. Paul, as to the Hebrews (x. 32), he writes bidding them remember how "after they were enlightened" they endured a great fight of afflictions; and in vi. 4, occurs that terrible passage which begins, "For it is impossible for those who were once enlightened, and have tasted of the heavenly gift." Not so clearly applicable to baptism, but to its effects as making us new creatures in Christ Jesus, are the several passages wherein he speaks of Christians as the children of the light (Eph. v. 8; 1 Thess. v. 5); also St. Peter uses the same language to the Christian Jews whom Christ had called "into His marvelous light" (1 Pet. ii. 9), and St. John saith that "he that loveth his brother (a new commandment I give unto you, That ye love one another. . . . By this shall all men know that ye are My disciples) abideth in the light." So, from sub-apostolic times, those who had just received baptism were called the Illuminated. But this gift of light flowing from Christ the true Light which lighteth every man, is also by the grace of the Holy Ghost, who lightens the reason, quickens the conscience, fills out the ability, and gives the several gifts fitted for our capacities. By His light in our hearts we can confess Christ (1 Cor. xii. 3), and by His light as by a candle (Prob. xx. 27) are our inward parts searched out and known. and from His presence we cannot escape. So by the gift of the Comforter, which includes all other gifts, for from Him is every grace and gift, we receive that illumination that is for our spiritual growth (cf. 1 Cor. xii. 1–16). The prayer in the Confirmation office shows this His office when the Bishop pleads that we may receive His sevenfold gifts, all of which are for spiritual insight and ghostly strength to walk upon the path of light. "In His Light we shall see light." By humble and lowly use of His illumination can we see both to use aright the graces He bestows, to use the opportunities for growth in holiness, and to use the spiritual knowledge that comes by study of the Word of God and of strict self-examination. These as instruments touch the inmost life. These as habits stir up the moral perceptions. These as dwelt in quicken the spiritual insight, that it can rejoice in the knowledge of God's overshadowing Presence and guidance. He that by prayer and meditation, and by active use of what he has thus learned, will try to draw day by day nearer to God, has received and lives in that light which Christ hath shed from Himself into the world to lighten every soul.

Image of God. No subject has exercised the devout speculation of the greatest theologians with as little tangible result as this question, Wherein doth the Image of God in us consist? It is positively taught in Holy Scripture; we are told of the ruin of this Image, the redemption in Christ, and its restoration to us is the Gospel. The Resurrection-day shall see us redeemed, reclothed with it. It shall be the complete satisfaction of the soul, yet nowhere is it explicitly taught us wherein this Image lies. If in the Body, strictly, then, we are led to anthropomorphic conclusions about the Divine Nature. If in the soul, it is in the spiritual life, yet the soul of man is the breath of God, and it cannot be said that this Image is concluded in that only. If in gifts that were conferred, and which we sum up in the phrase " Original righteousness," then it was not strictly in the creation, but in the gifts crowning that creation, that our likeness to God lieth. We cannot certainly know here, but we shall know hereafter; this is the sum of all our speculations, which involve the conceptions we form of the functions of the Church as His restoring Body for us, and of the work of the Holy Ghost in us, and of the Resurrection Body hereafter. Yet it is not wasted time, since whatever the outcome of our investigations, if we remember that He has chosen to conceal these things, and yet to tell us that they exist, we will be drawn nearer to Him, for we will have something surer from our own research than blind reliance on others' thoughts. There are collected below the chief tests which apply to the main questions raised in the inquiry, subdivided into, I. The creation of man in God's likeness. II. The wearing by the Son of God of the Image of God in man. III. The restoration of the Image of God in man by all the means offered.

I. And GOD said, "Let us make man in our Image, after our Likeness: and let them have dominion over the fish of the sea, and over the fowl of the air, and over the cattle, and over every creeping thing that creepeth upon the earth. So GOD created man in His own Image, in the Image of GOD created He him: male and female created He them" (Gen. i. 26, 27). "In the day that GOD created man, in the likeness of GOD made He him; male and female created He them; and blessed them, and called their name Adam, in the day when He created them" (Gen. v. 1, 2). "Whoso sheddeth man's blood, by man shall his blood be shed: for in the Image of GOD made He man" (Gen. ix. 6). "For a man indeed ought not to cover his head, forasmuch as he is the Image and glory of GOD; but the woman is the glory of the man" (1 Cor. xi. 7). "Therewith [the tongue] bless we GOD, even the FATHER; and therewith curse we men, which are made after the similitude of GOD" (Jas. iii. 9). These *directly* state the bare fact that we are in GOD's Likeness. St. Paul throws upon it a significant side light by adding the word "glory," and asserting that woman (made out of man) is the glory of the man. This, however, cannot here be expanded. The second division of the subject is the fact that the Word of GOD became truly man. Here must be omitted the texts of the Old Testament of the One like to the SON of GOD or in the "similitude of the sons of men."

II. "JESUS Himself, . . . which was the son of Adam which was the Son of GOD" (St. Luke iii. 23–38). "GOD . . . hath in these last days spoken unto us by His SON, . . . who being the brightness of His glory, and the express image of His person, and upholding all things by the word of His power (Heb. i. 1–3), took on Him the seed of Abraham" (Heb. ii. 16). "GOD sending His SON in the likeness of sinful flesh" (Rom. viii. 3). "For whom He did foreknow, He also did predestinate to be conformed to the image of His SON, that He might be the first-born among many brethren" (Rom. viii. 29). "Let this mind be in you which was also in CHRIST JESUS, who being in the form of GOD, . . . was made in the likeness of men, and being found in fashion as a man, He humbled Himself and became obedient unto death, even the death of the Cross" (Phil. ii. 5–8). "So it is written, The first man Adam was made a living soul; the last Adam was made a quickening spirit" (1 Cor. xv. 45).

This class of texts can be expanded indefinitely, but they indicate that the word of GOD, the brightness of His glory (*cf.* "the glory of GOD" above), and the express Image of His Person, could wear fittingly, for our salvation, the likeness of GOD corrupted through sin, and wore it because He was to restore all things. Under the third division of texts this is very directly taught.

III. "Forasmuch then as the children are partakers of flesh and blood, He also Himself likewise took part in the same; that through death He might destroy Him that hath the power of death, that is, the devil; and deliver them who through fear of death were all their lifetime subject to bondage" (Heb. ii. 14, 15). "For our conversation is in heaven; from whence also we look for the Saviour, the LORD JESUS CHRIST: who shall change our vile body, that it may be fashioned like unto His glorious body, according to the working whereby He is able to subdue all things unto Himself" (Phil. iii. 20, 21). "For as in Adam all die, even so in CHRIST shall all be made alive. But every man in his own order. . . . As we have borne the image of the earthy, we shall also bear the image of the heavenly" (1 Cor. xv.). "Beloved, now are we the sons of GOD, and it doth not yet appear what we shall be; but we know that, when He shall appear, we shall be like Him, for we shall see Him as He is" (1 John iii. 2).

Here again these leading texts constantly point to other and less vividly worded texts, binding the whole history of man from the time in which he stood forth the sinless Image of GOD in the Paradise of Eden, throughout his sinful corrupted course, till in the Resurrection-day, redeemed through the second Adam, he shall be restored to the Paradise of GOD.

But as was said above, the lost gifts and faculties have been classified in the most opposite ways. The true clue to the maze is to be found in whatever the LORD JESUS has to bestow, to restore to us. Putting aside forgiveness, because that must be preliminary to any restoration whatever, we see that all His gifts are summed up in the HOLY GHOST. Therefore, in whatever way He reaches into and satisfies and crowns our nature, in these things we can recover the lost traces of our original likeness. To recount these is to recount the strengthening, the glory, the indwelling, the sanctification of the HOLY GHOST, and to describe the work He doth, sent by CHRIST to abide in His Church, in and through the Church and all the restorations she has to give to us. Thus the earthly image of GOD shall, through the eternal Image, be restored to its original state.

Images. The use of images in the heathen world was of course largely, if not wholly, for idolatrous purposes. In the first days of Christianity the use of images at all was forbidden, and the artisan who had made his living thereby was, when converted, compelled to seek some other employment. With the daily sight of their worship, it was not possible that the Church could permit them to appear in the comparatively few places of worship she owned. Her earliest teachers, Tertullian, Clement of Alexandria, Origen, Minutius Felix. Lactantius, Arnobius, all denounce the sculptor's art in more or less measured terms. There is a thorough consensus of the writers down to 350 A.D., testifying that such a thing as an image of CHRIST in a church was abhorrent to the Christian. This included painting also. But after this date we find the churches begin to be ornamented with paintings of historical scenes from the Bible. Already a simple monogram, and then a figure of a lamb or a vine, and then of figures of the Good Shepherd, had appeared in the catacombs, and upon the chalice of the Eucharistic vessels the Good Shepherd had been chased. But it had gone no further. But henceforth we begin to find traces, first of paintings, then of images proper, placed in the churches for adornment and instruction. Epiphanius tells how in one of the churches of Palestine he found a veil with a figure of CHRIST upon it. He tore it down and ordered that it should be used to shroud some poor man, and paid the price of the veil into the Church treasury. But the adornment of the churches had begun and went on apace. The next generation saw with complacency this beautifying of the House of GOD, and justified it on the ground that it was the most convenient way to teach the unlettered in the congregation. The future evil was by no means apparent as yet. But by the year 600 A.D. it began to show itself. Serenus of Marseilles had to remove and destroy all the statues in his Diocese, for the reason that adoration was paid to them, for which Gregory the Great blames him, as destroying what was useful for instruction. In both East and West superstitious ideas were connected from this time on with images, paintings, and relics, and Gregory himself sets the example of recording absurd tales of miracles performed by the relics of saints. The struggle in the East to purify the Church of such a sin gave occasion to the famous Iconoclastic Controversy.

In England, the Saxon Prelates tried to follow the lead of the Council of Frankfort, to which they had informally assented through King Offa. There are abundant proofs that they were fully alive to the danger. But with the Norman conquest came in the later Gallican practice, and soon it passed over the whole kingdom. Though, as in the mandate of William Grenefeld, Archbishop of York (1313 A.D.), there was an effort made to stem the evil.

The Reformation in England put an end to this use of images, with greater zeal than knowledge, for in destroying the images and defacing the shrines much wanton destruction was also committed. The Homily on the Peril of Idolatry was the Church's declaration against one of the crying sins of the day.

What is the true feeling of the Church upon this subject? Probably it may be accurately expressed in this paragraph from Blunt's "Dictionary of Doctrinal and Historical Theology": "There is no rule respecting the use of images given to us in the New Testament. It may be concluded therefore that the Church is left (I.) to that in the Old Testament, which is of perpetual obligation; (II.) to the rules of reason, enlightened by the principles of a complete revelation; (III.) to the measures of a spiritual prudence. Thus (I.) the severity of the Mosaic Law, by which GOD forbade the making images of visible creatures, was only of temporary reason, from the singular proneness of the people to idolatry; the precept of Deut. iv. 15, 16 (comp. Acts xvii. 29), giving a natural reason for a natural duty, is binding on Christians; (II.) reason points out the instruction which may thus be given to the ignorant, the stimulus to a devout imagination, the aid to the memory, the suggestions which may holily minister to faith, while (III.) spiritual prudence remembers that the more ignorance there is the more proneness to superstition, and reminds us that we must be ever on the watch lest faith should become dependent on sight, lest the body should overweight the mind, lest any innate or proper holiness should be attached to the image, and the mind instead of being helped to pass beyond the image, should rest upon it, as an object of worship. Upon such general principles the Church has a lawful use of images." Our appeal being to the use as well as doctrine of the first six centuries as warrant for our customs, there is nothing in which we can more safely follow them than in the limit the Fathers and Bishops in those ages put upon the adornments of the House of GOD, and in the strictness with which they sacrificed these ornaments when they found that they tended to superstitious veneration. It is better to be far within limits than to dare to exceed them.

Immaculate Conception. The dogma that the Virgin Mary was herself conceived without sin, which was made an Article of Faith in the Roman Church December 8, 1854 A.D., and which must be believed by every Romanist on pain of excommunication. It is, of course, utterly contrary to what Scripture has revealed. It is contrary to all the principles of theology to draw any such deduction. It was a suggestion which was scouted by St. Bernard in 1130 A.D. in memorable words. He did not deny that to her, as to Jeremiah and to St. John Baptist, there was a sanctity before birth. But to assert sinlessness of the Blessed Virgin was to go beyond reason and revelation. "What if another should assert that festal honors should be paid to each of her parents? But then the same could be urged for similar reason for her grandparents, and her great-grandparents, and therefore it would go on infinitely, and there would be no end of Feasts. . . . Though it is given to a few of the sons of men to receive sanctity before they receive birth, yet it is not given to be conceived without sin. To one the prerogative of a sinless conception was given who should sanctify all others, and Himself coming without sin, might purge us of our sins." (Letter to the Canons of Lyons, Ep. 174.) It was resisted by a long series of theologians, and curiously, all were forbidden finally by Pope Gregory XV. (1622 A.D.) to discuss it except the Dominican Order, who had always opposed it! But under the influence of the Jesuits the heresy, for it is no less, was promulgated by Pius IX., and made binding upon the Faith and Conscience of all Romanists.

Immanuel. The name prophesied by Isaiah as the name of Him whom the Virgin should bear, and which was given by the Evangelist St. Matthew to the son of the Virgin. The two passages should be compared together.

Isaiah vii. 10–16: "Moreover the LORD spake again unto Ahaz, saying, Ask thee a sign of the LORD thy GOD; ask it either in the depth, or in the height above. But Ahaz said, I will not ask, neither will I tempt the LORD. And He said, Hear ye now, O house of David: Is it a small thing for you to weary men, but will ye weary my GOD also? Therefore the LORD Himself shall give you a sign: Behold, a Virgin shall conceive and bear a son, and shall call His name IMMANUEL. Butter and honey shall He eat, that He may know to refuse the evil, and choose the good. For before the child shall know to refuse the evil, and choose the good, the land that thou abhorrest shall be forsaken of both her kings."

With this compare St. Matt. i. 22, 23: "Now all this was done, that it might be fulfilled which was spoken of the LORD by the prophet, saying, Behold, a Virgin shall be with child, and shall bring forth a son, and they shall call His name EMMANUEL, which being interpreted is, GOD with us."

The Church has always held the prophecy in Isaiah to be fulfilled as the Evangelist by the HOLY GHOST has recorded, and Immanuel is one of the titles of our Blessed SAVIOUR which declares to us His Divinity and the certainty of our redemption. Late neology has tried to attack the prophecy mainly on the ground of the latter part: "Butter and honey shall He eat, that He may know to refuse the evil, and choose the good. For before the child shall know to refuse the evil, and choose the good, the land that thou abhorrest shall be forsaken of both her kings." It is claimed that there must have been a local fulfillment. It is now admitted that Almah can only mean a pure virgin. It is also conceded that prophecy commingles the present and the future in a mode that makes it difficult to separate the one from the other till *after* the event has given us the clue to the interpretation. Here we have a double intermingling, for the Child (who should not be born, in fact, till seven hundred and forty years after) should not know to distinguish between pleasant and unpleasant food before the allies Pekah, King of Israel, and Rezin, King of Syria, should be defeated, Rezin killed, and Pekah deprived of half his dominions. The obscurity lies in the assertion to Ahaz, that this should be a sign then, within a definite time, whereas its proper fulfillment was in CHRIST. There is undoubtedly a reference to some detail which is not recorded, while this special prophecy is bound up with the other clear reference to CHRIST, " For unto us a child is born" (Is. ix. 6). And that IMMANUEL was the name of the child of the distant future is clear, " And he shall pass (*i.e.*, the Assyrian king, as Sennacherib and Nebuchadnezzar) through Judah; he shall overflow and go over; he shall reach even to the neck; and the stretching out of his wings shall fill the breadth of thy land, O IMMANUEL."

Immersion. *Vide* BAPTISM.

Impannation. *Vide* CONSUBSTANTIATION

Implicit Faith. A childlike dispositior to receive doctrine or demands on obedience without question. But it is not the right of our free-will to surrender this Faith to any series of statements or to any doctrine, or to render such personal obedience save to those propounded to us by Him who has all-infallible authority. Therefore GOD alone is the Person to whom implicit faith can be yielded. Such a faith Abraham apparently yielded to GOD thrice. Such a faith the father of the lunatic child prayed for: "LORD, I believe; help Thou mine unbelief."

Imposition of Hands. A ceremony in blessing, ordaining, and in consecrating, which is of the earliest use in the Jewish and in the Christian Church. So the Patriarchs blessed their sons. Isaac blessed Jacob, Jacob blessed Joseph's two sons, so our LORD blessed the children brought to Him. So too the sick had His Hands and the hands of His Apostles laid upon them. So Ananias laid his hands on the blinded Saul. So in confirmation this Imposition was and is essential (Acts viii. 17; Heb. vi. 2). In ordination the Hands of the Apostle gave authority (2 Tim. i. 6; 1 Tim. v. 22). So in consecration, Joshua had Moses' hands laid upon him. So the Bishops lay hands on Bishops for consecration. As Moses laid his hands upon Joshua, so they give of their honor and rank to the Bishop elect.

Impropriation. Ecclesiastical property whose profits have passed into lay hands. Appropriation is when a college receives such profits. Henry VIII. gave monastic property to lay favorites. Archbishop Laud endeavored to redeem such Impropriations.

Imputed Righteousness. It has been terribly perverted so as to be made to mean that CHRIST's Righteousness is so given to us that no sin after that is laid to the charge of the believer. In other words, as one (Dr. Crisp) wrote over two hundred years ago, "Though a believer, after he be a believer, doth sin often, yet GOD no longer stands offended and displeased with him when he hath once received CHRIST," or

Hervey, "Notorious or confessed transgressors in themselves, they have a sinless obedience in CHRIST." Now this is wholly opposed to all the teaching of Holy Scripture. It denies the force of what is taught in Heb. vi. 4–6; x. 29, of innumerable other places which are scattered throughout the Epistles of St. Paul. But there is an imputed righteousness to the baptized person which is clearly taught in Holy Scripture, which yet teaches us that we can forfeit it. This imputed righteousness is set forth by St. Paul most emphatically, in his Epistle to the Philippians iii. 8–11: 'Yea, doubtless, and I count all things but loss for the excellency of the knowledge of JESUS CHRIST my Lord: for whom I have suffered the loss of all things, and do count them but dung, that I may win CHRIST, and be found in Him, not having mine own righteousness, which is of the law, but that which is through the faith of CHRIST, the righteousness which is of GOD by faith; that I may *know Him*, and the *power of His Resurrection*, and the *fellowship of His sufferings*, being *made conformable unto His death*; if by any means I might attain unto the resurrection of the dead." Here it is all dependent upon CHRIST'S righteousness found in the believer, yet that believer must be risen with CHRIST, suffering with CHRIST, conforming to His death, and, in the hope of the future resurrection of the dead, with a clinging, working dependence upon CHRIST. Also we are taught that in Baptism we put on CHRIST and are brought into a Holy BODY, His Church, and are called to be saints, and there is given to us a share in that Holiness, a right to the privileges of CHRIST'S Church. As an adopted son claims the rank and honor of the family that adopts him, and is shielded by its power and influence and shares its privileges in the face of the world, so CHRIST grants these to him, though he may not live in all things up to the lofty standard required. But should he throw away or misuse these advantages given to him and allowed before all the world, surely the Head of the House who adopts may also deprive him and finally disinherit him of those grants his adoption bestowed on him. In these respects we have CHRIST'S righteousness imputed to us, that we may retain it and grow in it. Grace and the Sacraments are given us, and we are urged to live after the SPIRIT. Our dear LORD gives freely, but He demands a hearty, faithful use of what He so lovingly gives, and we may not dare trespass willfully upon His forbearance.

Incarnation, The. This central doctrine of all Christian faith in GOD the FATHER and in our LORD JESUS CHRIST is so freely discussed or used in other articles (*vide* CREED, GOD, JESUS CHRIST), that it is only necessary to make a somewhat more compact and formal statement of the Church's doctrine upon this momentous fact.

The Incarnation was provided for in the eternal counsels of GOD. St. John saw our LORD as the Lamb of GOD as it had been slain from the foundation of the world (Rev. xiii. 8). It was promised at the Fall, it was foretold with ever-increasing fullness in succeeding ages, till Malachi closed the long series with the herald cry that the Angel of the Covenant was at hand (Mal. iii. 1). In the fullness of times the Word of GOD the SON from everlasting took upon Himself flesh,—not the nature of angels, but our flesh,—of the seed of Abraham in the royal line of David; took upon Himself our flesh, —not a phantasmic garb of human form. He was conceived by the operation of the HOLY GHOST in the pure womb of the Blessed Virgin Mary, and was made truly man. He took no body that could be inhabited by another soul. But the body prepared for Him (Ps. xl. 6; Heb. x. 5) He so united to Himself, being the WORD from everlasting, that in the several stages of its conception, development, birth, and growth to full manhood He was ever present in it, filled it as our soul fills our body and is enrobed by it and dwells in it as our personality. He being two Natures, eternal WORD and Perfect Man, became but one Person, JESUS CHRIST. And so He truly united Himself with us, taking body and soul to Himself, entered into and became a part of the vast stream of human beings who are born unto and live in sin, toil, and are disciplined in this world of ours. So He stooped to enter into time, emptied Himself of the glory He had in His FATHER'S courts, took our flesh, became man, suffered pain and hunger and thirst most truly; was sorrowful, and wept and watched and prayed and fasted, as we should; loved His disciples and friends, sympathized with all in sorrow, need, sickness, and affliction, and compassionated the sin-sick, repentant souls; taught as man to fellow-men the wondrous facts about themselves, and of Himself and His purposes, and, making atonement, died as truly as ever man died, and as truly raised Himself the third day, and became, as before, subject to mortal change, so now immortal and above all mortal change.

This but prepares the way for the fuller effect of His Incarnation upon our nature and history. It is a fundamental law that when men realize GOD'S presence and power they acknowledge a duty of service and worship. Were CHRIST but a sinless, perfect, yet mere man, none would feel this duty, but being GOD-man, at once all own a bounden service and worship to Him, and a desire to be overshadowed by His mercy and share in His love, to be bound by His laws, to come into His covenant; and this is intensified by our instinctive recognition of the compassion and wondrous wisdom of His Incarnation, of the fact that it touches our deepest common humanity; that His manhood is related to the poorest and the highest at once in as true and perfect a sense (and with a healing efficacy superadded) as is Adam's. "The first man Adam was made a living soul, the last Adam (is) a quickening spirit. . . . The first man (was) of the earth earthy, the second man is the LORD from heaven." The first Adam died, the last Adam liveth forever; death hath no more dominion over Him. He has arranged the instrumentalities by which we enter into His human nature, are fed and nourished and grow therein,—not simply are in mystical covenant relations, but are made thereby as truly partakers of the Divine Na- 'ure (2 Pet. i. 4) as we by human birth are made, and only so made, sharers in the dead Adam's human nature. Therefore the Incarnation of our LORD JESUS CHRIST was, and is, not only the pivotal fact of our history, but it is the restoring and perfecting act of our most loving Father, whereby our sins are forgiven, ourselves are restored,— nay, more, are immortally set in the eternal throne of JESUS CHRIST, His SON (Eph. ii. 6; Rev. iii. 21, 22).

Incense. Its ritual use, while enjoined in the Old Testament and used in the sacred visions of St. John's Revelation in the New Testament, was not known in the early ages of the Christian Church. How early it was used in the East it is not easy to determine, but after 380 A.D. and before 594 A.D. In the West, it did not become general in Europe till after 850 A.D. and before 1000 A.D., while in Italy it was introduced probably about 700 A.D. All the references to incense that have been quoted to prove its possibly early use can be very fairly interpreted mystically, and a great many passages in the same Fathers cannot be reconciled with any fact of its actual use. Strongly objected to by the early Christians probably because incense was used at heathen altars, and introduced late and very gradually into general ritual use, it became general only by about 950 A.D. In the English Church after the Reformation it gradually passed out of use, though cases are to be noted here and there of its continuance. And its later revival has partaken too much of the partisan spirit. There is no canon or enactment against it, but the tone of the Anglican Church is against its use.

Incomprehensible. In its theological use, means limitless, unbounded. The term is so used in the Athanasian Creed. "The FATHER incomprehensible, the SON incomprehensible, and the HOLY GHOST incomprehensible. . . . As also there are not three incomprehensibles . . . but one incomprehensible." It is the translation of the Latin *immensus*, which means omnipresent. The earlier rendering was immeasurable, which is nearer the sense of the Creed, though the word incomprehensible did not then bear it. The fact of the Incomprehensibility of the Divine Nature is asserted (as elsewhere also) in the very familiar verse, "If I climb up into heaven, Thou art there: if I go down to hell, Thou art there also: if I take the wings of the morning and remain in the uttermost parts of the sea—even there also Thy hand shall lead me, and Thy right hand shall hold me" (Ps. cxxxix. 8, 9). Yet it may well be said that to the human mind GOD is Incomprehensible.

Incumbent. The holder of a Benefice at a given time.

Indefectibility of the Church. I. "And the gates of Hades shall not prevail against it" (St. Matt. xvi. 18). "Lo, I am with you alway, even unto the end of the world" (St. Matt. xxviii. 20. So too, Is. lxi. 8, 9; Dan. ii. 44; John xiv. 16, 17). In these passages we have pledged to us that GOD's Church shall not fail as a whole. Branches of the Church may forfeit their participation in the promise. So Laodicea, Ephesus, Pergamos, and Thyatira have vanished. So any part may be found wanting and have its candlestick removed. Faith may fail. Heresy may—nay, does infect parts of the Catholic Church. Yet the promise is sure that till the end shall come His Church shall surely survive.

II. Inerrant, indefectible in Doctrine. That she should finally fail to teach the truth, the whole truth, and nothing but the truth, it is impossible to believe. Our LORD's promise covers in its perfect language the doctrine of the Church's inerrancy: "And I will pray the FATHER, and He shall give you another Comforter, that He may abide with you forever. Even the SPIRIT of Truth. . . . But the Comforter, which is the HOLY GHOST, whom the FATHER will send in my name, He shall teach you all things, and bring all things to your remembrance, whatsoever I have said unto you. . . . He will guide you into all Truth, for He shall not speak of Himself, but whatsoever He shall hear that shall He speak, and He will shew you things to come" (St. John xiv. 16, 17, 26; xvi. 13; comp. 1 John ii. 27). In this is traced the very outline of the Church's course upon her teaching. She has Him as her guide, her abiding Leader, the Advocate pleading in her and through her. But as He is her guide, she may stray and falter in following His leadership, but as He is to abide in her forever, she cannot fail to return and to receive of Him the full truth, and through Him to teach it to all. The XIX. and XX. Articles practically set forth this doctrine in teaching that some Churches have erred, not only in life and ritual, but in the Articles of the Faith, and the XX. Article notes that the Holy Scripture is the only source from which she draws her Articles of Faith. She teaches and acts as a judge who must abide by the Law, not as a Lawgiver, for that it is from CHRIST by the HOLY GHOST. Therefore the Church is inerrant. Yet as in a court, the case must be made up, to be tried, so evil doctrine may infest the Church for a long time before it so shapes itself that it can be tested and repudiated. But we have every pledge that when she does decide it will be by the grace of the HOLY GHOST, who will keep her from error and lead her into all truth. It is, however, proper to remark that there are two modes in which error, false doctrine, and heresy can arise. Either from additions to the Faith (Mariolatry, Infallibility, Immaculate Conception), or by denials, or imperfect analysis, of the Articles of the Creed (Arianism, Nestorianism, Monothelitism, Monophysitism). It is hardly probable that there can be any more heresies upon the dogmas in the Creed. But additions to the Faith may be infinite. To these, as they come up for the judgment of the Church, must be applied the test of Scripture, and each part of the Church must use this test rigorously till it shall be, in the course of Providence, possible to hold a true General Council. It is in this position that the Churches of England and America hold themselves.

Indefectible Grace. A doctrine which logically inheres with the Calvinistic theory. But as has been elsewhere shown that Grace is given to us all to use, but that we can lose it. It is not irresistible, robbing us of our free-will, but filling out, strengthening, and sanctifying our will, and therefore if not irresistible, then it is not indefectible. We can fall from grace, and can be restored. Such is the teaching of the XV. Article: "After we have received the HOLY GHOST we may depart from grace given, and fall into sin. And by the grace of GOD we may arise again and amend our lives. And therefore they are to be condemned which say they can no more sin as long as they live here, or deny the peace of forgiveness to such as truly repent."

Indiana, Diocese of. The State of Indiana had among its early settlers many persons who had been baptized and trained in the Episcopal Church. It was at rare intervals that they received its ministrations by visiting clergymen, who on some weekday or Sunday held service in a court-house or in a borrowed house of worship. Curiosity, of course, attracted many outsiders, who wanted to see what kind of religion these "Episcopals" had, who, when they saw the black gown and bands, and heard prayers read from a book, went away shaking their pious heads. These adverse influences caused many, no doubt, to drift with the popular current into other persuasions, as they were called in those days.

In the year 1835 A.D. the General Convention elected as its first Missionary Bishop the Rev. Jackson Kemper, S.T.D., then Rector of St. Paul's Church, Norwalk, Conn. He was consecrated on the 25th day of September of the same year, in the forty-sixth year of his age, and at once set out for his assigned field of labor in Indiana and Missouri. He began his work along the Ohio river towns at Madison, Jeffersonville, New Albany, and Evansville, and also visited Vincennes and Terre Haute on the Wabash. In the summer and fall of 1836 A D. he revisited the towns on the Ohio. In January, 1837 A.D., he visited Indianapolis, Richmond, and Crawfordsville, and in the fall of that year, in company, with Rev. Samuel R. Johnson, Missionary at Lafayette, he made a tour of the northern part of the State, taking in Logansport, Michigan City, Laporte, South Bend, Mishawaka, Lima, and Fort Wayne, and thence descending the Wabash Valley he visited Delphi, Americus, and Lafayette.

It thus took two years for the Bishop to do a work which could now be done in two months. Indiana roads were almost impassable for six months in the year. The mud wagon, drawn by four horses, was the only conveyance that could be pulled through the mire or that was safe in fording swollen rivers and creeks. Bishop Kemper was often in great peril by land and water, but Providence had given him a short and compact body, a vigorous constitution, and a cheerful disposition with which to endure the hardships of travel.

At a Convocation of the clergy of Indiana, summoned by the Missionary Bishop, which met at Evansville on the 9th of June, 1838 A.D., it was resolved to hold a Convention at Madison on the 24th of August following, for the purpose of organizing a Diocese. At the time appointed the following delegates assembled, viz.: Rev. Ashbel Steele, Missionary at New Albany; Rev. Melancthon Hoyt, Missionary at Crawfordsville; Rev. James B. Britton, Missionary at Indianapolis; Rev. Geo. Fiske, Missionary at Richmond; Rev. Archibald H. Lamon, Missionary at Evansville; and Rev. Samuel R. Johnson, Rector of St. John's Church, Lafayette. The lay delegates were James W. Borden, of Richmond; Thomas P. Baldwin, of New Albany; Isaac C. Lea, John Creagh, Joseph L. White, Matthew Temperley, N. C. Brace, John McIntire, and James Sidall, of Madison; and James Morrison, of Indianapolis. The other clergy officiating in Indiana but not present were Rev. Henry Caswell, of Madison; Rev. D. V. M. Johnson, of Michigan City; and Rev. Robt. Ash, of Jeffersonville.

The following parishes were reported as organized: St. Paul's, New Albany; Christ Church, Madison; Christ Church, Indianapolis; St. John's, Lafayette; St. Paul's, Evansville; St. John's, Crawfordsville; St. Paul's, Jeffersonville; St. Paul's, Richmond; and Trinity, Michigan City.

The Diocese as organized was received into union with the General Convention held at Philadelphia in September, 1838 A D., and was represented in that body by Rev. James B. Britton, Rev. Henry Caswall, Rev. Saml. R. Johnson, and Rev. Melancthon Hoyt; and by Messrs. Horace Thurston, James Morrison, Geo. W. Leonard, and E. T. Turner.

At the fourth Annual Convention the

Rt. Rev. Jackson Kemper was elected Bishop of the Diocese, but declined, as it interfered with his missionary duties in other States and Territories.

At a special Convention held at Indianapolis, September 29, 1843 A.D., the Rev. Thomas Atkinson, Rector of St. Peter's Church, Baltimore, Md., was elected Bishop of the Diocese, but he declined the office. The same gentleman was again elected the Bishop at the ninth Annual Convention, held at Indianapolis, July 9, 1846 A.D., and again declined the office.

At the tenth Annual Convention, held at Delphi, July 15, 1847 A.D., the Rev. Saml. Bowman, D.D., Rector of St. James' Church, Lancaster, Pa., was elected the Bishop of the Diocese, but declined the office.

At the eleventh Annual Convention, held at Lafayette, June 1, 1848 A.D., the Rev. Francis Vinton, Rector of Emmanuel Church, Brooklyn, N. Y., was elected the Bishop of the Diocese, but declined the office.

At the twelfth Annual Convention, held at Indianapolis, June 28, 1849 A.D., the Rev. George Upfold, D.D., Rector of Trinity Church, Pittsburg, was elected the Bishop of the Diocese. He accepted the office, and was consecrated in Christ Church, Indianapolis, December 16, 1849 A.D., by the Rt. Rev. Benjamin Bosworth Smith, D.D., Bishop of Kentucky, assisted by the Rt. Rev. Charles Pettit McIlvaine, D.D., Bishop of Ohio; the Rt. Rev. Jackson Kemper, D.D., Missionary Bishop of the Northwest; and the Rt. Rev. Cicero Stephen Hawks, D.D., Bishop of Missouri; and thus became the first Bishop of the Diocese of Indiana.

He was born in Shenley Green, near Guilford, Surrey, England, on the 7th day of May, 1796 A.D. In 1804 A.D. his parents removed to the United States, and settled in Albany, N. Y. He graduated at Union College, Schenectady, N. Y., in 1814 A.D., and at the College of Physicians and Surgeons, in New York City, received his degree of M.D. in 1816 A.D. In 1817 A.D. he took up the study of Theology under Bishop Hobart, who ordained him Deacon in Trinity Church, New York, in October, 1818 A.D., and Priest in July, 1820 A.D. He became Rector of St. Luke's Church, New York, in 1822 A.D. In 1830 A.D. he became Rector of St. Thomas' Church in the same city, and in 1831 A.D. became Rector of Trinity Church, Pittsburg. Bishop Upfold received the degree of Doctor of Sacred Theology from Columbia College, New York, in 1831 A.D.; that of Doctor of Laws from the Western University of Pennsylvania, in 1856 A.D.

Bishop Upfold entered immediately upon the duties of his office, and upon the evening of the day of his Consecration administered the rite of Confirmation in Christ Church, Indianapolis. He resigned the rectorship of Trinity Church, Pittsburg, January 1, 1850 A.D., removed his family to Lafayette, Ind., having for additional support accepted the rectorship of St. John's Church in that city, which he held for one year, and in March, 1857 A.D., removed his residence to Indianapolis.

Bishop Upfold died at Indianapolis, August 26, 1872 A.D., having been for seven years totally disabled from work by neuralgic rheumatism.

The Rt. Rev. Joseph Cruikshank Talbot, D.D., LL.D., the second Bishop of Indiana, was born on the 5th day of September, 1816 A.D., in Alexandria, Va. He was educated in Piermont Academy of that city, and in 1835 A.D. removed to Louisville, Ky., where he was engaged in business for several years. He was baptized and confirmed in 1837 A.D., ordered Deacon on his thirtieth birthday, and on the 6th day of September, 1848 A.D., was ordained Priest by the Bishop of Kentucky. He organized St. John's Church, Louisville, while in Deacon's orders, and upon his ordination to the Priesthood became its Rector. In 1853 A.D. he became Rector of Christ Church, Indianapolis.

He received the degree of Doctor of Divinity from the Western University of Pennsylvania, Pittsburg, 1854 A.D., and that of Doctor of Laws from the University of Cambridge, England, 1867 A.D.

In 1859 A.D. the General Convention assembled at Richmond, Va., elected him Missionary Bishop of the Northwest, a jurisdiction embracing the Territories of Nebraska, Dakota, Wyoming, Colorado, New Mexico, Arizona, Utah, Montana, and Idaho. His consecration took place in Christ Church, Indianapolis, February 15, 1860 A.D., by the Rt. Rev. Jackson Kemper, S.T.D., assisted by the Rt. Rev. Benjamin Bosworth Smith, S.T.D., the Rt. Rev. Cicero Stephen Hawks, D.D., the Rt. Rev. George Upfold, S.T.D., and the Rt. Rev. Gregory Thurston Bedell, D.D.

After five years' active labor in his extensive missionary jurisdiction, he was elected Assistant Bishop of Indiana, and was translated to that Diocese October, 1865 A.D. Upon the death of Bishop Upfold he became the Bishop of Indiana.

Bishop Talbot was stricken with partial paralysis in 1880 A.D., which finally terminated in his death at Indianapolis, January 15, 1883 A.D.

At a special Convention of the Diocese March 6, 1883 A.D., the Rev. Isaac Lee Nicholson, D.D., Rector of St. Mark's Church, Philadelphia, was elected Bishop of the Diocese, but he declined the office.

At the forty-sixth Annual Convention of the Diocese, held at Indianapolis, June 5, 1883 A.D., the Rev. David Buell Knickerbacker, D.D., Rector of Gethsemane Church, Minneapolis, Minn., was elected Bishop of the Diocese. His Consecration took place in St. Mark's Church, Philadelphia, Sunday, October 14, 1883 A.D., by the Rt. Rev. A.

C. Coxe, Bishop of Western New York, assisted by Rt. Rev. Theo. B. Lyman; the Most Rev. J. Medley, Lord Bishop of Fredericton and Metropolitan of Canada; the Rt. Rev. H. B. Whipple, Bishop of Minnesota; Rt. Rev. Wm. W. Niles, Bishop of New Hampshire; Rt. Rev. George D. Gillespie, Bishop of Western Michigan; Rt. Rev. John Scarborough, Bishop of New Jersey; and Rt. Rev. George F. Seymour, Bishop of Springfield.

Bishop Knickerbacker was born in Schaghticoke, N. Y., February 24, 1833 A.D. Graduated at Trinity College, Hartford, Conn., 1853 A.D., and from the General Theological Seminary 1856 A.D. Ordered Deacon 1856 A.D. Ordained Priest July 12, 1857 A.D., and spent his whole clerical life in Minneapolis. Received the degree of D.D. from Trinity College in 1873 A.D. Entered upon his work as Bishop November 1, 1883 A.D.

The statistics reported in 1886 A.D. are as follows: Clergy, 37; parishes, 41; missions, 9; families, 2118; candidates for H. O., 1; ordination, P. 1; baptisms, infants, 502, adults, 184, total, 686; confirmed, 874; communicants, 4812; Sunday-school teachers, 341; Sunday-school scholars, 3074; contributions, $71,556.18.

HON. ISAAC H. KIERSTED.

Induction. The form by which, in the English Church, a clergyman is put in possession of the church to which he is presented, the glebe land belonging to it, and other temporalities. The usual method of induction is by virtue of a mandate under the seal of the Bishop to the Archdeacon of the place, who either himself, or by his warrant to all clergymen within his Archdeaconry, inducts the new incumbent by taking his hand, laying it on the key of the church in the door, and pronouncing these words: "I induct you into the real and actual possession of the rectory or vicarage of H——, with all its profits and appurtenances." Then he opens the door of the church and puts the person in possession of it, who enters to offer his devotions, which done, he tolls a bell to summon his parishioners. Compare the office of Institution in our American Prayer-Book. (*Vide* Hook's Church Dictionary.)

Inerrancy. *Vide* INDEFECTIBILITY.

Infallibility. There is a marked gradation in the meaning of the words Inerrancy, Indefectibility, and Infallibility. The first two are GOD'S gifts to His Church, the last is His own prerogative. In practical application the first may be defined as having, as the point from which they issue, His bestowal of them on the Church, but Infallibility may be defined as an inherent attribute.

Therefore to assert as an article of Faith the dogma that in any one person resides an infallibility, no matter how hedged in that infallibility may be by canonical or theological definitions, is to impute to mere man an attribute belonging to GOD, and therefore to fulfill the warning prophecy of the Apostle, that foretells that the "man of sin is the son of perdition who opposeth and exalteth himself above all that is called GOD, or that is worshiped, so that He as GOD sitteth in the temple of GOD, showing Himself that He is GOD" (2 Thess. ii. 3, 4).

Infant Baptism. *Vide* BAPTISM.

Infidel. He who is faithless to a cause to which he was pledged. It is very often improperly used to mean an Atheist. An Infidel is usually an Atheist, but an Atheist may have never been a Christian, while an Infidel must necessarily have been so to bear the name at all correctly. Such were those who went out from the Church (1 John ii. 18, 19). Such is the man who not providing for his own "*hath denied the* faith, and is worse than an unbeliever" (1 Tim. v. 8 R. V.).

Infinite. Boundless, whether in space or in time. (*Vide* PREDESTINATION.)

Initiation. The early term applied to the baptized, as intrusted with all knowledge of Christian verities. When the Church's doctrines were taught only to the baptized, and were carefully hidden from all others, it was frequently the case that the preacher to a congregation would say, "The initiated know what I mean." It occurs, *e.g.*, in the Catechetical Lectures of St. Cyril of Jerusalem (370-90 A.D.).

Inquisition. A tribunal erected in Papal countries, and once very formidable. It was established by the Popes for the examination and punishment of heretics. An engine of terrible cruelty, it was used with ruthless energy. It was one of the means of reducing Spain to Roman obedience, and the political result was disastrous. So, too, in Italy and Portugal. While it had sway in other states (as, during their occupation by the Spaniards, in the Netherlands), in France and Austria its violence and power were a great deal curbed. Its history has never yet been fully written.

Inspiration, or, as the word itself signifies, inbreathing, is an unseen and spiritual operation. The inspiration of the Holy Scriptures proceeded from an influence by the HOLY GHOST bearing upon the minds and wills of the writers, and compelling them to declare specific facts or doctrines in words that accurately expressed them. The inspired person may have been willing or unwilling; but he could not, while under inspiration, say or write anything but the truth.

In the economy of the Gospel the department of planning was and is the FATHER'S; that of forming or organizing belongs to the SON; while that of giving vitality and efficiency is the specific work of the HOLY GHOST. These departments coincide with, and in some respects overlie, each other; but their centres lie each in the three distinct persons of the HOLY TRINITY. The unity of every divine action is, therefore, always threefold. Creation itself, planned by the All-wise FATHER, was put into form by the WORD, while life was inbreathed by the HOLY GHOST.

Inspiration belongs to the special function of the SPIRIT, who is "the LORD and Giver of Life." The inspiration of the Holy Scriptures was according to the will of the FATHER, through His Only-begotten SON, The Word, by the HOLY GHOST.

Revelation is distinct from inspiration, as subject is from method. Revelation flows through inspiration, as the waters of a river down its bed and between its banks, or as force develops from energy. Inspiration thus controls the bounds of revelation, keeping it within the limits of truth. It also supplies the efficiency necessary for its accurate inception and full deliverance.

Revelation was progressive. It began with GOD'S first intercourse with man, and proceeded until the Christian dispensation was first formally completed by CHRIST, and then efficiently spiritualized by the full outpouring of the HOLY GHOST. Inspiration took its due position towards revelation at the first, and continued with it until the whole Gospel was organized, as the Church or Body of CHRIST, with ministry, sacraments, and word, received its mission, and had its Scriptures completed.

Inspiration is twofold,—miraculous and ordinary. Miraculous inspiration is that operation of the SPIRIT which was needful to effect a true and complete revelation. The ordinary inspiration is that operation of the SPIRIT which disposes and helps "men of good will" to know the truth and do the right. The latter was, is, and ever will continue active, through all human progress on earth and in the world to come. It is not confined to the men of good will, for there are calls of the SPIRIT which even the unwilling may hear. He acts wherever GOD'S love reaches. The world, which GOD so loved as to send to it His SON, is the field of the ordinary operations of the inspiring SPIRIT. The Church, which is the organized kingdom and specifically ordered household of the LORD, is the constant home of the inspiring SPIRIT. He presides in her councils, acts through her sacraments, imbues with grace her utterances of devotion, and waits to bless the word read or preached to willing priests and people.

This kind of inspiration is mingled with much human weakness and sin. We cannot separate often the one element from the other. We cannot know, for instance, what is divine and what human in any specific instruction, exhortation, or advice which may reach our ears from "those who are over us in the LORD." Still, the assurance of the ever-presence of the HOLY GHOST in the living Church is designed to make us take heed how we hear," and to ponder devoutly whatever words touch or pierce the conscience. Although the usual channel of this form of inspiration is the Church, acting through worship, administration of holy things, and preaching, yet the brooding SPIRIT does not neglect the chaos of the darkened "world lying in sin." This fact is the warrant and encouragement which sustains evangelic missions, and animates all good works for the bodies and souls of those who know not CHRIST.

Miraculous inspiration was granted as a merciful boon from the forbearing GOD of love to men who had wandered so far from original righteousness that they could no longer of themselves find out the way of Truth. Its recorded beginning was the Divine call, which Abraham was the first fully to heed and follow. Hence the history of the Divine Covenant, evolving through the Patriarchal, National, and Catholic Church, is coterminal with the history of this inspiration. It is miraculous in the sense of being a distinct, peculiar, and specific operation of the HOLY GHOST; made for the definite purpose of clearly setting forth the way and will of GOD in dealing with an elected people; to whom was committed the noble work and high honor of bearing visible witness to His name in the world. The means of grace were associated with this commission of witness, so that the way of salvation for fallen men covered the same path which preserved alive the knowledge and worship of the true GOD. These two conjunct objects of the Divine Covenant are to be carefully considered, in order to obtain a clear and accurate view of miraculous inspiration by the HOLY GHOST. By nature He gives ordinary inspiration. By grace He bestows extraordinary inspiration. Yet the two never conflict. They so work together indeed as to appear often in conjunction. Where the latter is sufficient the former is never resorted to. What even the inspired prophets and teachers could know through ordinary means, they were left to record by human wisdom. The HOLY GHOST, however, supervised even the original narratives of those who declared what they saw and heard, and brought to remembrance clearly the facts recorded. When existing documents were to be elevated to a place in the Scriptures of GOD, the HOLY GHOST supplemented the human talents and knowledge of the writers, and enabled them to eliminate errors and corruptions. An eminent instance of this is seen in the two records of the creation which Moses has given in Genesis. They are sometimes given by him in detached portions, and sometimes mingled together; but these were evidently two original records, out of which he selected the truth, and set it forth in the Book written by Divine command, under the inspiration of the SPIRIT. The "Elohistic" record dealt mainly with the relations of man to nature, while the "Jehovistic" record had for its leading idea and chief point the personal relations of man to the personal GOD. Usually, in the English Bible, the word GOD is used in the Elohistic narrative, and the word LORD in the Jehovistic. Both are none the less Holy Scriptures, because they were originally written before Moses. They became Holy Scripture by means of Moses, who put them in the book GOD commanded him to prepare, and which the HOLY GHOST inspired him to write with accuracy. This fact links the new dispensation, which began with Abraham, with all the old dealings of the Merciful FATHER with His beloved human creatures from the beginning, and shows that the GOD of nature and of grace is one GOD.

The resemblances between the Bible and some of the earliest writings held sacred in old heathen nations only strengthens the evidence of the miraculous inspiration of the Bible. It is entirely free from all those corrupt morals and wild mythical fancies which stain here and there the best books of heathenism. It gives, again, the true knowledge of the true GOD, which they had evidently lost, through the mere nature worship which evolved the various forms of heathen mythology. The sun, the stars, the elements, the forces of nature, which the heathen worshiped, and which they personified and called by various names, as well as the energies of good or evil, to which they also assigned names and functions, often in rivalry or opposition to one another, were all swept away by Moses, while only what was true in their records of facts, of statements of morals, and doctrine was retained. The inspiration of the HOLY GHOST appears in the perfectness and completeness of this redaction.

After Moses, when other writers of Scripture came on in due time, the same SPIRIT continued His inspiring aid. What the writers could record through ordinary knowledge they did evidently in their own way. Hence peculiarities of style distinguish the different books. They comprise together one book, the Bible, or Holy Scriptures, not because every word and form of expression was enforced by the Divine afflatus, but because the facts and doctrines contained were kept exact and true by the watchful Inspirer.

Under this continued influence the Divine revelation grew in volume. It, however, always kept even pace with the development of that visible kingdom, which was made formally complete when the Christian Church was established, being "built upon the foundation of the Apostles and Prophets, JESUS CHRIST Himself being the chief corner stone."

The Patriarchs were inspired in accordance to the measure of revelation they were required to record, and under which they were to live and serve GOD. The revelations given to them are the word of GOD.

The Prophets were called personally. They appeared from time to time, and acted, spoke, or wrote as they were sent and commissioned. Hence their revelations also are the word of GOD.

The Old Testament as a whole is the word of GOD, in accordance with the sense and meaning we have given of the inspiration of the HOLY GHOST. Not everything that is recorded is the word of GOD, for many acts of the otherwise holy men of old were obviously wrong and sinful, and many words they said were evidently erroneous, while some were partially or wholly wise only in the human sense. When, however, the definite "Thus saith the LORD" appears, or whenever the circumstances show that the LORD was giving His word, then the true revelation may be perceived. Still, the inspiration reaches even beyond the revelation, and assures the accuracy of narrative, even where the thing narrated was neither inspired nor approved of GOD.

Throughout the Old Testament the inspiration of the HOLY GHOST continues subservient to the Law. Gleams now and then appear both of the spirit and the facts of the Gospel. These, however, were foreshadowings or foretellings of things to come; not enough to lay open the future, but enough to show, when that future became present, the essential unity of the great divisions in the one developing Divine dispensation. One and the same spirit appears all along, from Abram to St. John the Evangelist. A marked and wonderful community of truth runs like a gleam of light through Holy Scripture from beginning to end, and binds all together in one golden chain of many links. The Divine element appears in every part, while the perfect correspondence of the parts stamps unity upon the whole, making it and showing it to be the very one Holy Scripture, or word of GOD.

Both Testaments are of course open to criticism. No attempt should be made to exempt them from any fair form of investigation, or to place them beyond the reach of any legitimate tests. Mere scholarship, even when skeptical, should be met by Christian scholarship. GOD in His providence has hitherto provided the human wisdom and learning necessary for the defense and elucidation of the Bible upon merely scholastic grounds. Deep understanding of the word of GOD is, however, only possible to those whose own spirits are in harmony with the DIVINE SPIRIT. Spiritual things are spiritually discerned. This point should be duly considered and weighed not only in scholastic criticism, but in practical use of the Bible.

Every writer in the books of the Bible was inspired, whether he were historian, psalmist, moral or religious instructor, warner, foreteller of future events, or speaker or actor in the advancing work of the developing church, kingdom, and household of GOD. The human and peculiarly personal characteristics of each one give, indeed, variety of form to their styles and modes, but the essence of all remains Divine and therefore infallible truth.

Although the stream of authentic revelation lay hidden for four hundred years after

Malachi—the last prophet of the Old Testament—spake and wrote, yet the ever-present inspiring SPIRIT doubtless continued "still to strive with man." The books that were written in this interval preceding the coming of CHRIST were evidently not inspired as were those of the Old Testament. Still, because of the SPIRIT'S presence ever with the chosen people, even the Apocrypha "the Church doth read for example of life and instruction of manners; but yet doth it not apply them to establish any doctrine." (Art. VI.)

The inspiration of the New Testament is essentially the same with that of the Old Testament. The revelations of the latter coincide with, while they supplement those of, the former. Together they constitute the whole Holy Scripture. Similar characteristics mark both. The four Gospels give narratives of the life of CHRIST; but they are evidently the work of writers who each viewed CHRIST from their own natural standpoints. Hence the true humanity of JESUS is the central and pervading idea of the Gospel of St. Matthew; His royalty fills the mind of St. Mark; His sacrificial offering and work of atonement imbues St. Luke; while His light of truth, on earth and in heaven, is the chief theme of St. John. The inspiration which guided and controlled each writer acted in and through his personal character and peculiar circumstances, while the result is a record of the mortal life and work of JESUS that coincides in all essential particulars, and yet gives a whole presentation such as no one man could have delineated and recorded.

The Acts, the Epistles, and the Apocalypse exhibit these same characteristics. St. Paul sets forth the Church, with the word, prominently on its Catholic side. He emphatically pronounces it to be the one Body into which Jews and Gentiles are called and admitted on equal terms. St. James holds on to the Law. While making that prominent, he still presents the Gospel as the fulfillment of the Law. St. Peter's chief mission was to those of the circumcision, and his writings turn upon the unity of the new and old dispensations. The writer of the Epistle to the Hebrews was some one who, to natural eloquence and high rhetorical culture, added a full knowledge of the facts and principles of the Jewish worship. Hence that epistle is full of the essential unity of the offerings and priesthood of the Temple with those of the Catholic Church; while their conjunction in the One High-Priest and full, perfect, and sufficient sacrifice—JESUS—is distinctly detailed and clearly shown. The Revelation of St. John the Divine is the effect of a Divine afflatus, poured through an Apostle, evidently the same as that with which Ezekiel and other old prophets were inspired.

The fact of the inspiration of the Holy Scriptures by the HOLY GHOST fits into the necessities of the whole case, and thus shows the unity of all the acts of the GOD of nature and of grace Could men have recovered the lost knowledge of GOD, and restored the personal communion with Him which sin had broken, they would have been left to their natural powers. Because they could not do this, and because the patient mercy of the loving JEHOVAH sought to restore man, therefore the HOLY GHOST inspired the revelation of the way of salvation. He did this, however, step by step, as the organization of the one Divine family was developing towards the completed unity of the visible Body of CHRIST. He did it also in conjunction with human talents and attainments, and in accordance with the concurrent environments of political, social, and ecclesiastical progress, and of knowledge. Divine facts, and precepts, and doctrines He revealed. Mundane facts, and opinions, and views He permitted to be recorded as contemporary wisdom and learning regarded them; only preserving from corruptions and error the moral and doctrinal instruction they were interwoven with. Hence science and philosophy were not inspired. When they appear therefore in the Bible, they are open as elsewhere to criticism. Only the Divine truth, embalmed in them or illustrated by them, was inspired by the HOLY GHOST; and this Divine truth stands now as hitherto, and as it ever will continue, the very word of the very GOD, infallible, sure, ever living, the foundation truth. The written word of GOD is so one with the person distinguished by name as "The Word of GOD" that they are true as He is "The Truth."

REV. BENJAMIN FRANKLIN, D.D.

Installation. The act of giving a Prebend or Canon possession of his seat by placing him in his stall. So too it is the placing of a Bishop in his Episcopal throne in his Cathedral church.

Institution. I. "Institution of a Christian Man," a book issued in the later years of Henry VIII.'s reign, which contained instruction in the Christian religion. It is of value as giving the position and views permitted to Cranmer and his colleagues at that time, and as throwing light upon the advance that the Reformation had made in England. The book is called the Bishop's Book, since the Bishops dedicated it to the king, while a later modification of the same book was entitled "A Necessary Doctrine and Erudition for any Christian Man, set forth by the King's Majesty of England," etc., 1543 A.D., and so called the King's Book. There are marked variations between the two books, and in some things a retrogression.

II. The act in the English Church by which the Bishop commits the cure of a church to the clergyman who is nominated. To this the Office of Institution in our Prayer-Book is nearly the equivalent. (*Vide* MINOR OFFICES.)

Institutions of the Church. There must be, from the nature of the case, a difference in the relations which the several Institutions, Organizations, and Associations hold to the Church in the United States, or to the several Dioceses. Some Institutions are under the direct control of the General Convention and received their Constitution from it, and their corporators are chosen according to its directions, or as it has made provision in the rules it has given. It is of these Institutions that this article briefly treats. Other institutions are Diocesan, or are general voluntary organizations which are not confined to one city or Diocese, but have some common aim or purpose, which attracts members to it in other States, such as the Church Temperance Society.

The first of the General Institutions of the Church in date of formation and second to none in importance to the Church is *The General Theological Seminary*. It was established by the General Convention May 27, 1817 A.D. Its plan was drawn up in 1818 A.D., by Bishops White and Hobart. The present location, in the then country village of Chelsea, a suburb of New York, was the munificent gift of Dr. Clement C. Moore. Its earliest Professors were the Rev. Drs. Jarvis and Turner. In May, 1819 A.D., it began with six students, who recited first in a room attached to St. Paul's Chapel, then in the vestry-room of St. John's Chapel, and afterwards in a building on the corner of Broadway and Cedar Street. Its financial straits were so great that in 1820 A.D. it was removed to New Haven, but in 1822 A.D. the Sherred legacy of $60,000 brought it back to New York. The corner-stone of the east building was laid in 1826 A.D. From that time on the seminary remained in New York, despite many efforts to have it removed. Active efforts were made to secure endowments and gifts for scholarships, and the Dioceses of New York, New Jersey, Massachusetts, Pennsylvania, Maryland, North Carolina, and South Carolina now hold scholarships upon the basis of their gifts to the Seminary Funds. Its Professors and teachers have always numbered among them men of great ability and mastery in their several chairs. To name but three, Drs. Turner, Johnson, and Mahan, worthily carried forward the reputation of their departments won by their predecessors, and their successors have not failed to maintain the lofty standard they established. Recent efforts to increase the endowments and to restore and refit the building have been highly successful under its present Dean, Rev. Dr. E. A. Hoffman.

The second institution under the supervision of the General Convention is

The Domestic and Foreign Missionary Society.—The sketch of the operations of this Society is given in full in the article of the MISSIONS OF THE CHURCH, and here it will be only necessary to refer to such outlines of its history as are fitting. In the General Convention of 1820 A.D. "there was proposed by the House of Clerical and Lay Deputies, and concurred in by the Bishops, a Constitution of a Missionary Society for Foreign and Domestic Missions, which became inefficient from an irregularity in the choice of Trustees. The Society was located in the city of Philadelphia, and the members there resident, after frequent consultations, did not think themselves authorized to proceed. The error resulted from the press of business on the last day of the session." (Bp. White's Mem.)

At a special meeting of the General Convention, 1821 A.D., the oversight was repaired and a Constitution was adopted. It worked under the Constitution till 1835 A.D., when the great alteration in its Constitution was made. It was recommended by the Society that the Church herself, in dependence on her Divine Head, and for the promotion of His glory, undertake and carry on in her character as the Church, and as "The Domestic and Foreign Missionary Society of the Protestant Episcopal Church in the United States of America," the work of Christian Missions. The change was at once made; the Church recognized her true missionary character, and instead of appointing a Society, resolved itself into that Society, as in truth it is, and appointed two committees to carry on its work, one for Domestic and one for Foreign Missions. The two committees were kept apart, and at the close of the late war a Commission on the Colored Work was added as an appendage to the work of the Domestic Committee, but in 1871 and 1877 A.D. it was merged with the other committees into one General Management of a Board of Missions with a Board of Managers. The members of the Board of Missions are all the Bishops and the Deputies of the General Convention, and the Delegates from the Missionary Jurisdiction. But the Board of Managers is an elective body, not necessarily drawn from the General Convention. It exercises the powers of the Domestic and Foreign Missionary Society, and appoints from its own members the two committees and such other committees as it may deem desirable, and appoints the officers necessary for its work. These committees now are the Committee for Domestic Missions; the Committee for Foreign Missions; the noble Women's Auxiliary to the Board of Missions; and the Church Society for Promoting Christianity among the Jews. In the Domestic Department, 14 Bishops and 470 Missionaries, of which are employed among white people 372; colored, 55 (23 colored clergymen); Indians, 57 (13 native clergymen and 15 native catechists). In the Foreign Department—Ordained clergy, Africa, 13; China, 18; Japan, 9; Hayti, 3; Mexico, 12; total, 65. Unordained workers, 201; candidates for orders and postulants, 26; communicants reported, 2668.

The third organization, which is under the General Convention, is

The American Church Building Fund

Commission.—The Commission was established October 25, 1880 A.D., by the Board of Missions, comprising in its membership both Houses of the General Convention. It consists of all the Bishops, of one clergyman and one layman from each Diocese and Missionary Jurisdiction, and of twenty members at large appointed by the Presiding Bishop. Its object is to create, by an annual offering from every congregation for three years, and by individual gifts, a fund of one million dollars, the income of which shall be given, and portions of the principal of which may be loaned, to aid the building of new churches.

And lastly, one of the most deserving of all, which ought to be thoroughly endowed indeed,

The Fund for the Relief of Widows and Orphans of Deceased Clergymen, and of Aged, Infirm, and Disabled Clergymen.—Its present resources are a royalty upon the Hymnal, and such collections and legacies as may come into its scanty treasury.

These organizations were formed by and are under the control of the General Convention, and belong to the whole Church, have a claim upon it, and owe to it a faithful discharge of their various trusts.

Intention. The motives which lie behind the act and impel the doer to commit it have a modifying effect upon the moral value of the act. For no act can be committed which does not have more or less distinctly a moral value. The time, the place, the opportunity, all affect it so, therefore still more the intention which precedes the act and is its efficient cause. In this lies a large measure of the responsibilities which attach to the person, because of the act and its consequences,—though apart from the intention, the actor is held responsible for much that flows from it. Both in morals and at law it is only equitable to allow due force to the motive, so in a notable class of moral and legal acts, the rule must be that intention makes marriage, and intention makes murder.

Still, while intention has so much influence in determining the status of an act, intention can have no power to affect the validity of acts directed in behalf of others. A witness signing a deed,—his intention not to witness it cannot affect the validity of the signature. A magistrate executing his official duty cannot alter the authority of his acts by merely intending that they shall be of no effect. Therefore the declaration of the Council of Trent, " If any one shall say that in ministers, whilst they effect and confer the sacraments, there is not required the intention at least of doing what the Church does, let him be anathema" (Sess. vii., Can. xi.), is invalid and absurd, for if the validity of baptism depends upon the *intention* of the administrator, it is then impossible for the recipient to be assured that he is baptized, and, consequently, to be assured that he is a Christian at all, and the same is true of the Holy Communion. Indeed, were the doctrine even a remote fact, the possibility of there being no Church of GOD is, to say the very least, strongly suggested to the skeptic, and a powerful weapon is put into the hands of the atheist. A sacrament may be *parodied* by impious or by unauthorized men, and *therefore* invalid, but beyond this, the intention of the proper administrator cannot affect the efficiency of the sacrament if the several parts of that sacrament are duly administered.

Intercession of Christ. The doctrine of the Mediatorship of our LORD must, as one of the offices of a Mediator, involve that of Intercession. Our LORD pledged Himself to His Apostles to do this : " I will pray the FATHER, and He shall give you another *Comforter.*" " Wherefore He is able also to save them to the uttermost that come unto GOD by Him, seeing that He ever liveth to make intercession for them" (Heb. vii. 26). " If any man sin, we have an advocate with the FATHER, JESUS CHRIST the righteous" (1 John ii. 1). It is, therefore, His work in His cession " at the right hand of GOD the FATHER Almighty," as we confess in the Creed. It is part of His priestly office as it was constituted. St. Paul's argument, that He is a Priest forever after the order of Melchizedek, that His is an unchangeable Priesthood, has this fact of His intercession given as the conclusion. It is of the essence of the priestly office to intercede, and to intercede with an offering, therefore St. Paul's argument requires that " this man, after He had made one offering for sins, forever sat down on the right hand of GOD." For " CHRIST being come a high-priest of good things to come, . . . by His own blood He entered in once into the Holy Place, having obtained eternal redemption for us." And since He remaineth in the Holy of Holies till the consummation of all time, it follows that He offers and pleads His one sacrifice continually. " Intercessions and giving of thanks be made for all men ; for kings, and for all that are in authority ; that we may lead a quiet and a peaceable life in all godliness and honesty. For this is good and acceptable in the sight of GOD our SAVIOUR; who will have all men to be saved, and to come unto the knowledge of the truth" (1 Tim. ii. 1–4). This intercession underlies the structure of the Eucharistic office,—appearing in the " Prayer for the whole State of CHRIST'S Church Militant," and in the Invocation. It is the act binding the subordinate derivative office of His Church with CHRIST'S own High-Priestly office of Intercessor, and therefore is second in far-reaching consequences only to the atonement the LORD hath made. But it is to be noted that as our LORD'S coming brought divisions, a sword and a fire, so it is said that the angel who offered the prayers of the saints put fire from the altar into the censer wherein the prayers were placed, and cast the censer thus inflamed upon the earth, and there were voices, and thunderings, and lightnings, and an earthquake. Prayer and intercession is at first a disturbing power, that afterwards procureth peace, light, and glory.

Intercession of Saints. It is a pious opinion that the saints in Paradise, as they with us have learnt the duty and preciousness of intercession, should continue it there. But since they cannot hear us, or know of us and our condition from any prayer, or words, or thoughts, of ours, it is merest superstition to call upon them to pray for us; therefore it was but common sense in the Church of England and in our own to sweep away all such prayers, collects, or litanies from her service-books.

Interdict. An ecclesiastical censure frequent in the eleventh, twelfth, and thirteenth centuries, said to have been used first in France. Lyndwood defines it as an ecclesiastical censure, inflicted as a penalty on contumacy or offenses whereby people are prohibited from receiving the sacraments. It could be general or personal. The first instance of its being fulminated against a people was the interdict pronounced by Gregory VII. against Poland, 1073 A.D. For details of the more famous interdicts,— *e.g.*, of England by Innocent III.,—see the Histories of England, France, Germany, and Venice. "This censure hath been long disused, and nothing of it appeareth in the laws of Church or State since the Reformation." (Burns, Eccl. Law, sub voc.)

Intermediate State. The place where all souls are gathered and kept till the resurrection. (*Vide* HADES, HELL, PARADISE.) The language of Scripture, which, however, should not be pressed too far, implies that it is within the earth. "He also descended first into the lower parts of the earth" (Eph. iv. 9). So other places. But without concerning ourselves *where*, we may concern ourselves *how* souls are there. In a former article (Hades) we have seen that there is a great gulf therein dividing it into two parts (St. Luke xvi. 26). In these there is a foretaste of the natural consequences of the facts of our past human life, and of our already formed characters. It would seem that however much consequences may be suspended or avoided here, there there is no interference or suspension. It is useless to speculate upon details, but the feeling, at least of the early Church, was clear upon the felicity of those who died in the true faith of our LORD JESUS CHRIST (*vide* PRAYERS FOR THE DEAD), as is seen from the language of one of the oldest Liturgies which has come down to us: "Remember LORD, the GOD of the Spirits and of all flesh, the orthodox whom we have commemorated and whom we have not commemorated, from righteous Abel unto this day. Give them rest there in the land of the living, in Thy Kingdom in the delight of Paradise, in the bosom of Abraham, Isaac, and Jacob, our holy Fathers, whence pain, sorrow, and groaning is exiled, where the light of Thy Countenance looks down and always shines. And direct LORD, O LORD, in peace the ends of our lives, so as to be Christians, and well pleasing to Thee, and blameless, collecting us under the feet of Thine Elect when Thou wilt, and as Thou wilt, only without shame, and offense, through Thine Only-Begotten SON, our LORD and GOD and SAVIOUR JESUS CHRIST, for He alone hath appeared on the earth without sin." (St. James' Liturgy.) This intermediate state of anticipative felicity was called the Beatific Vision, the Bosom of Abraham, the Paradise of Pleasure.

Interpretation of Scripture. It includes both Hermeneutics, the principles of Interpretation, and Exegesis, the detailed interpretation. It is clear that since the inspired penmen wrote under the direction of the HOLY GHOST, their writings cannot in every respect be subjected to the same mode of interpretation as that applied to ordinary writings; of course the time at which, the conditions under which the books were written, the surroundings of the national polity, or the spiritual development of the Church, whether Jewish or Christian, must be considered, and the historical sense must be placed first with the grammatical construction, but if the guidance and inspiration of the HOLY SPIRIT be admitted, there must be also added to these principles of interpretation, the allowance of a further and deeper sense, which comparison with other Scriptures or which time would explain. The admission that a large part of the Scriptures are prophetical, and that under another large part there is an ethical application that cannot be narrowed by the letter of some special case (*e.g.*, eating meats offered to idols, or the various senses in which Faith is taken), modifies the use of the broad principles of both Hermeneutics and Exegesis. The Fathers finding CHRIST everywhere, made His presence the basis of their principles of interpretation, and so developed a noble system of Exegesis, marred indeed in places by a fanciful or an imperfect appreciation, and sometimes by a prepossession in favor of some topic, but above all devout, sincere, and having an insight that comes only from prayerful and prolonged study of the Word. The real defect of the Patristic Exegesis was the defect of a sound criticism. This, however, was not their fault; it was the fault or want of the whole space of time from St. Clement to the Reformation. Those who drew nearest to its principles were Chrysostom and Theodoret. Origen had it, but his Alexandrian education and his own devout enthused fancy prevented him from using it, and in this critical faculty too, whenever he did use it, as in the Hexapla, he was too far in advance of his day.

The Fathers distinguished between the (*a*) grammatical, (*b*) the historical and logical, and (*c*) the mystical senses of Scripture; and this last underlying sense they subdivided still further into spiritual, figurative, allegorical. It will be seen that these subdivisions may be carried still further, and some ancient expositors advocated as many as ten or twelve forms. St. Augustine says we must look for things that are eternal, that have been done, that must be done, that are future, and therefore hold to three, historical, moral, mystical.

Modern interpreters, though often disclaiming any such subdivision, are forced, often unconsciously, to use this; otherwise there could be no possible profit to us in a very large part of what has been written for our learning. It is too large a subject to be treated of in this work, but the reader may be referred to the very devout work of Williams on the Study of the Gospels, and to Blunt's and Wordsworth's introductions to their several editions of the Bible.

Intonation. (*Vide* MUSIC.) The notes which introduce the chant or hymn. The Gregorian Tones have this intonation regularly prescribed for the first words of each Psalm.

Intoning. The improper term for the musical rendering, on a monotone and inflected closes, of the service by the officiating minister.

Introit. The hymn or anthem sung by the choir when the officiating minister goes up from the stalls to the sanctuary to begin the ante-communion service. This is his entering into the chancel. The word occurs as early as in St. Mark's Liturgy. The Introit, therefore, was used very early in the East. It was probably introduced from Spain, which used many Eastern rites, so far as the West used it. The Spanish introit varied very much, but probably was at first the xciii. Psalm. The first book of Edward VI. (1549 A.D.) gave the Introits for the several Sundays' Feasts and Fasts throughout the year. The use of the Introit is so ancient and so significant, that it were well to select the hymn upon some principle of continuous reference to the Church's season.

Invitatory. The xcv. Psalm is called the invitatory Psalm, from the spirit of the first verse, O come, let us sing unto the LORD. It was in very early use, having been, as Archdeacon Freeman shows, imbedded, as it were, into the structure of the morning services from the earliest notices of them that have survived. The Psalm was daily used in Jewish worship, which was probably the reason why it was so markedly referred to in the Epistle to the Hebrews (ch. iii.). St. Augustine tells us in a sermon that it was so used: "We have chanted the Psalm, exhorting one another with one voice, with one heart, saying, O come, let us adore Him and fall down before Him, and weep before the LORD who made us." But the invitatory of mediæval usage was different. A sentence that varied according to the season was interpolated at the close of each verse, and was sung after one verse entire and after another only in part, but always entirely at the close of the Venite, before the Gloria Patri. This was done away when the Prayer-Book was arranged.

An invitatory anthem is substituted for the Venite at Easter (from 1 Cor. v. 7; Rom. vi. 9; and 1 Cor. xv. 20).

The Invocation. The invoking of the grace and Presence of the HOLY GHOST upon any special act or undertaking.

It is technically the name of the second part of that noble prayer which follows the words of Institution in the Scotch and American Prayer-Books. It is strictly in the spirit, and very nearly in the language, of the prayers of Oblation and Invocation in use in all the Eastern Liturgies. While there is a maimed and dislocated oblation in the English Liturgy, and a mere fragment of it in the Roman use, and in other now disused Western Liturgies, there is no Prayer for the blessing of the Elements by the HOLY GHOST. It was in the Scotch Prayer-Book of 1764 A.D., which was a revival of the book of 1637 A.D., and revised under the influence of the Non-jurors. From this Bishop Seabury succeeded in having it transferred to our own Prayer-Book in 1789 A.D., the only changes being that for the direct words, "that they may become the Body and Blood of Thy most dearly-beloved SON JESUS CHRIST," there were substituted, "that we receiving them according to Thy SON our Saviour JESUS CHRIST's holy institution, in remembrance of His Death and Passion, may be partakers of His most blessed Body and Blood." There was an insertion of the word "humbly" before "beseeching."

The Western Church always held that the words of Institution were all-sufficient, but the Eastern Theologians taught that whatsoever the HOLY GHOST touched is sanctified and changed (St. Cyril, Catechetical Lectures). This is the concurrent teaching of the Eastern Doctors: That as CHRIST offered Himself by the ETERNAL SPIRIT a full, sufficient, and perfect Sacrifice, so the Invocation of the HOLY GHOST in the act of Consecration is necessary in the Eucharist, the Memorial pleading that one Sacrifice. For this prayer, then, we cannot be too thankful, as it makes our office so perfect.

Invocation of Saints. A practice wholly without warrant in Holy Scripture, and removed from the Offices of the English and American Church. (*Vide* INTERMEDIATE STATE, INTERCESSION OF SAINTS.)

Iowa, Diocese of. In July, 1853 A.D., the Rt. Rev. Jackson Kemper, D.D., the venerable Missionary Bishop of the Northwest, issued an invitation to the clergy and representatives of all organized Church congregations in the State of Iowa to meet him at Muscatine on Wednesday, August 17, at six o'clock P.M. In accordance with this invitation the parties designated assembled at the time appointed, in the chapel of Trinity Church, Muscatine.

The Bishop being absent, the meeting was presided over by the Rev. Alfred Louderback, Rector of Trinity Church, Davenport. By this Convention a Constitution and Canons for the Diocese of Iowa were unanimously adopted, and the following memorial appears on the last page of the journal as a fitting tribute to this Apostolic man, whose remarkable zeal, wisdom, and virtue were chiefly instrumental in planting the Church in the Northwest:

"The Clergy and Laity of the Protestant Episcopal Church in the Diocese of Iowa, in separating the canonical connection between them and the Rt. Rev. Jackson Kemper, D.D., cannot allow this occasion to pass without expressing their deep sense of obligation to him for services rendered to the Church in this State. We shall ever hold in grateful remembrance his untiring zeal and unwearied labors in behalf of the Church in this Diocese; and although our canonical connection is dissolved, we hereby unanimously invite him to continue his Episcopal supervision of this Diocese until we are provided with a Bishop of our own."

Upon the day appointed by the Primary Convention, May 31, 1854 A.D., the first Convention of the Diocese of Iowa was called to order by Bishop Kemper. The place of meeting was Davenport. At the close of his report the Bishop thus addressed the assembled Clergy and Lay delegates:

"As you are now fully organized you will be anxious to enjoy every privilege, and at the earliest possible day to secure to yourselves a Diocesan. I will cordially cooperate with you in such efforts, and will rejoice to welcome another Bishop in the West. Seek out a man of GOD; one who is earnest and simple-hearted, one who is patient of fatigue, ready to endure hardship with a cheerful spirit for the REDEEMER'S sake, and who will consecrate all his energies to the work before him, which unquestionably will be the building up of the Diocese in strength and holiness."

The choice of the Diocese fell upon a man whose future work made most justly applicable to him the words of the good Bishop. The Rev. Henry Washington Lee, D.D., Rector of St. Luke's Church, Rochester, N. Y., having been duly elected, accepted the position, and was consecrated in his parish church, October 18, 1854 A.D., as the first Bishop of Iowa. Bishop Lee preached in his Diocese for the first time October 29, in St. John's Church, Dubuque, of which the Rev. R. D. Brooke was rector. Among Iowa's pioneer missionaries none was more earnest and worthy than the Rector of St. John's, Dubuque, and his parish had the honor of being the first in the new Diocese voluntarily to relinquish missionary aid. The first confirmation by Bishop Lee in Iowa took place November 5, in Trinity Church, Davenport.

The second Annual Convention convened May 30, 1855 A.D., in Christ Church, Burlington, and at its opening service Bishop Lee held his first ordination, admitting to priest's orders the Rev. George William Watson, who remained for many years one of Iowa's most respected, able, and successful Presbyters.

Bishop Lee's first effort in behalf of the material interests of his Diocese was the formation of the "Iowa Episcopate Fund," in which effort he was most successful. Through the liberality, chiefly of Eastern Churchmen, he obtained means for the purchase of six thousand acres of land in Iowa, which land was held until, through increase in value, sales became desirable, thus securing a constantly increasing capital. A wise investment of this has already furnished means for the erection of an elegant and commodious house for the Bishop's residence, besides contributing materially to his support.

On the 1st day of August, 1856 A.D., Bishop Lee having completed the purchase of the property in Davenport known as the "Iowa College," the Diocese took possession, giving it the name of the venerable Bishop Griswold. On the 12th of December following, the Preparatory Department of this Institution was opened, under the charge of the Rev. F. Emerson Judd, who is still one of Iowa's working parochial clergy.

In May, 1863 A.D., the College property, for which was paid $36,000, was in the hands of the Trustees, free from incumbrance. During the year 1864 the Trustees purchased a building in Dubuque for a girls' school, which in September, 1865 A.D., was opened as the "Bishop Lee Seminary for Young Ladies." The following year the Rev. F. Emerson Judd became the principal of this Institution, and held that position until May 1, 1871 A.D., at which time the work was discontinued.

In June, 1866 A.D., by the generosity of David J. Ely, Esq., of Chicago, the "Ely Professorship of Ecclesiastical History" in the Theological Department of Griswold College was endowed, and the Rev. Willis H. Barris was appointed its first Professor, a position which he still holds, being the oldest resident Presbyter in the Diocese. The "Ely Professor" occupies a beautiful residence, erected upon the College grounds by the liberality of Mrs. Ely, who after her husband's death thus supplemented his most valuable gift; simultaneous with Mr. Ely's donation was one of $10,000 towards the endowment of an "Anthon Professorship" by a lady in New York.

The Trustees of the College having authorized the erection of a Diocesan Church edifice upon the centre of the east block of their beautiful grounds, on the 27th of June, 1868 A.D., the corner-stone was laid by Bishop Lee, with most impressive ceremonies. This expensive and very handsome building having been completed, with the exception of the tower and spire, was duly consecrated as "Grace Cathedral," June 18, 1873 A.D., by Bishop Lee, assisted by the Bishops of Nebraska and Minnesota, the Bishop of Minnesota preaching the consecration sermon. In elegance of structure and beauty of situation Grace Cathedral is unsurpassed by any Church edifice in the West. The "Bishop's House," built by the Trustees of the "Iowa Episcopate Fund," was completed before the consecration, and at that time was the pleasant home of the Bishop's family. But this happy home was soon to become the scene of an unexpected and sore bereavement. The good Bishop, although realizing that his health was seriously impaired, yet gave to his friends no indications of immediate danger; therefore his death, which occurred on the 26th day of September, 1874 A.D., after only a few days of alarming illness, both shocked and deeply grieved the entire Diocese. On the 29th his funeral services in Grace Cathedral were attended not only by a very large concourse of the citizens of Davenport, but by lay representatives from parishes throughout the State, by the mass of the clergy of Iowa, and by numerous friends, both lay and clerical, from neighboring and other Dioceses. The services were conducted by the Rt. Rev. Bishops Whipple, of Minnesota, Robertson, of Missouri, and Vail, of Kansas. The sermon was preached by Bishop Vail. The ceremonies at the grave were participated in by all the Bishops, and thus the first Bishop of Iowa was laid to his rest. At a special Convention held in Grace Cathedral December 9, 1874 A.D., a sermon commemorative of the late Bishop was delivered by the Rev. F. Emerson Judd from Romans xiv. 7. In this sermon the preacher paid to the memory of his late Diocesan the following tribute, which met with a hearty response throughout the State of Iowa: "In Iowa the foundations of the American Catholic Church have been wisely laid, broad and deep. No narrow bigotry and no effort of intolerance have ever found encouragement in the policy of the large-minded and large-hearted man, whose comprehensive views and charitable rule for twenty years have guided the development of our youthful Diocese. All of Bishop Lee's writings, his letters, his sermons, his Convention addresses, his pastorals and triennial charges, bear unmistakably the impress of CHRIST's character and teaching. . . . . And if Bishop Lee was eminently catholic in his official position, he was eminently Christian in the various relations of private life. As a husband and father, tenderly thoughtful and affectionate. As a friend, considerate and true. As an acquaintance and neighbor, most sociable and charitable. His cheerful manners and entertaining conversation rendered his society unusually attractive, his words of cheer and deeds of unostentatious, but judicious benevolence, quieted many an anxious heart and gladdened many a needy home." The Church-men of Iowa who knew him will most tenderly cherish the memory of their first Bishop so long as life shall be theirs; and through all time the Church will gratefully acknowledge the strength of the foundation which, amid the changes and excitements of a youthful but giant State, he with so much foresight and toil laid for her future welfare.

The special Convention elected first the Rev. Henry C. Potter, D.D., Rector of Grace Church, New York, who declined the position. The Rev. Wm. R. Huntington, S.T.D., was then duly chosen, and the Convention adjourned. Dr. Huntington also having declined, at the twenty-second Annual Convention, held in Grace Church, Cedar Rapids, May 25, 1875 A.D., the Rev. James Houston Eccleston, D.D., of Philadelphia, was declared by the President duly elected; but he, in consequence of opposition and alleged informality in the matter of his election, declined consideration of the subject. The twenty-third Annual Convention, held in St. Paul's Church, Des Moines, May, 1876 A.D., unanimously elected the Rev. William Stevens Perry, D.D., of Geneva, N. Y., who accepted the position, and became, by his consecration in his parish church, September 10, 1876 A.D., the second Bishop of Iowa.

During the interval, a few days less than two years, between the death of Bishop Lee and the consecration of Bishop Perry, the Rev. F. Emerson Judd, having been appointed "General Missionary" by the Diocesan Board, was instrumental in keeping alive the interest in vacant parishes and unsupplied mission stations, and the excellent Bishop Talbot, of Indiana, kindly made Episcopal visitations to the parishes having classes for confirmation.

Bishop Perry, already widely known through the important positions held in the Church's General Council, and in his pastoral and collegiate relations, received a most hearty welcome throughout the entire Diocese. He found in his new field three very valuable monuments of his predecessor's wise foresight, prudent effort, and untiring energy. The Iowa Episcopate Fund was represented by an elegant mansion, the "Bishop's House," upon which had been expended $21,165.38, also by 1762 54-100 acres of valuable land in the State of Iowa, and investments to the amount of $20,063.60, all of which was drawing interest at the rate of ten per cent. per annum.

Griswold College was in possession of a handsome stone edifice for collegiate purposes, a convenient boarding-house, a chapel, and a commodious residence for the President, all situated in a commanding and very beautiful location in the city of Davenport. Two Professorships were permanently endowed, the "Ely" fully, and the "Anthon" partially. The Cathedral occupying the centre of the east block of the college grounds, and adjoining the lot upon which stands the "Bishop's House," was completed with the exception of the towers and spire, and had been consecrated by Bishop Lee as being "free from incumbrance." But with the two latter of these advantages were associated very grave responsibilities and many serious difficulties. The college and theological schools were to be reorganized, and an adequate support secured, and a suitable cathedral system was to be inaugurated. To the accomplishment of both these objects Bishop Perry was singularly adapted, having had peculiar advantages in connection with both educational and Diocesan institutions. As was to be expected, therefore, under his wise administration and successful efforts, both college and cathedral were soon put in a position to do good and permanent work. Also at a Conference held in Davenport by the eight Bishops whose Sees and Jurisdictions lie between the Mississippi and the Rocky Mountains, it was decided "to unite on Seabury and Griswold as Theological School and College for the great West stretching from the Mississippi to the Pacific slope."

But the extent of the Diocese might well have appalled the stoutest of heart and the strongest in effort. "Larger than all England, or than the five Dioceses of New York, with Connecticut besides," and embracing nearly half a million of souls, it was no wonder that the Diocese of Iowa compelled her second Bishop to say, "We are unable to do this work. It can be no experiment to seek the up-building of a future See." The huge Diocese remains undivided, and its one hundred counties still look to Bishop Perry for Episcopal care, nor do they look in vain. The older parishes, with scarcely an exception, are progressing most favorably, many new ones are springing up, and everywhere the Church is rapidly gaining in favor.

The Diocese was most materially benefited by the bequests of a very estimable lady, who was one of the most efficient Church-workers in Iowa when under the jurisdiction of Bishop Kemper. Of this truly good woman Bishop Perry, in his Convention address of 1879, thus speaks: "In the decease of Mrs. Clarissa C. Cook, widow of the late Hon. Ebenezer Cook, the Church in Iowa has lost one of her members whom generations yet to come will rise up to call blessed. During her years of widowhood she had devised and executed a noble charity,—the building of Trinity Church and School in memory of her husband, and at her death she gave back to GOD most of the wealth He had permitted her to acquire. With a thoughtful care for those who must ever be a care to others, this devoted Churchwoman devised nearly half of her estate to the founding of a 'Home for the Friendless' in the city of Davenport, while a sum second only to this bequest was given for the support of the indigent clergymen and the widows and orphans of deceased clergymen of the Diocese of Iowa. The Board of Missions and the weaker parishes within our bounds were kindly remembered, while the gifts to her parish church and to the congregation of Christ's Church, and to other Church charities outside of the Diocese, attested the interest of this excellent woman in the work of the Church at home and abroad." From Mrs. Cook the Diocese received for Missions $10,000, for weak parishes $10,000, and $5000 placed under the direction of the Bishop. The "Old Clergy Fund" received a direct bequest of $10,000, and was also made the recipient of half of the "rest and residue" of the estate after all legacies had been paid. As residuary legatee the Fund has received thus far $65,000. In the Bishop's address to the Convention of 1882 A.D. is found the following most encouraging statement:

"From the Convention journals it appears that the increase of permanent values of Church property, exclusive of stipends, salaries, subscriptions for current expenses, and offerings for local or general Church work, and inclusive only of moneys paid to redeem Church property from indebtedness; for the erection or purchase of churches, chapels, and rectories, and endowments for Church purposes raised in Iowa and from the Diocese alone, has been at the rate of upwards of one thousand dollars per week for the nearly six years of the present Episcopate. If to this large sum we add the gifts from outside to our college and churches and Church work in various forms, and the appreciation of Church property in Iowa during the last six years, we can estimate the increase of Church property in Iowa during the last six years as nearly or quite half a million,—a sum equal to the permanent acquisitions of the preceding quarter of a century. Gratefully do we record these proofs of a material prosperity. In spiritual things the blessing has not been withheld. The net increase of communicants alone during this period has been fifty per cent. For all these tokens of His power to GOD alone be the praise."

The Diocese when organized in 1853 A.D. numbered ten places, in which services were held with seven clergy and sixty-five communicants. In 1883 A.D., thirty years after, the number of parishes and stations reported in the journal is one hundred and eleven, while the number of clergymen canonically connected with the Diocese is fifty-eight. The communicants reported number four thousand two hundred and forty-seven, and the individuals under pastoral care twelve thousand four hundred and eighty-nine. This paper cannot perhaps find a better conclusion than in quotations from Bishop Perry's last Convention address (1883 A.D.): "It is of little moment the number of clergy and congregations in Iowa has increased tenfold, that the number of communicants has multiplied in far greater proportion, even an hundredfold;

that we have more than ten times the number of churches, chapels, and rectories that we possessed in 1853 A.D.; that we have acquired a noble property in endowments for the Episcopate, for the college, for the Theological School, for our indigent, disabled clergy, for the widows of deceased clergy, for feeble parishes, for missions, and for various educational, eleemosynary, and parochial purposes,—what has been accomplished is only to be regarded as a beginning. Foundations have been laid. We are to build thereupon. . . . It is not our privilege as a Church to boast of numbers in comparison with the religious bodies about us. It will be enough if we abound in good works, if we take the lead in good deeds, if, like the Master, we care for the bodies as well as the souls of our fellow-man. There have been noble beginnings in this direction. The establishment and endowment of Homes for the Friendless by the late Hon. J. M. Griffith, at Dubuque, and the late Mrs. Cook, of Davenport, and the successful founding of the more distinctively Church charity at Des Moines, the Cottage Hospital, are each and all steps in the right direction."

Statistics for 1886 A.D.: Clergy, 51; parishes, 53; missions, 25; candidates for H. O., 2; ordinations, D. 1, P. 1; baptisms, 497; con., 431; com., 5004; contr., $129,986.28.

REV. F. E. JUDD.

Ireland, Church of. Though some of the Irish had probably received Christianity from the British at some earlier date, yet the conversion of Ireland is attributed to Palladius, who (410 A.D.) was consecrated Bishop for the Irish by Pope Celestine, but it is nearly certain that he never reached Ireland. The work of conversion was really effected by St. Patrick, whose whole history was very romantic. His knowledge of men, his good common sense, energy, and courage gave him great influence, and he was able to effect the conversion of a large part of the Irish clans. But he fashioned the methods of Church work to suit the wild people with whom he dealt. The principle was a monastic one of the simplest mode. Bishops were very numerous, and were probably engaged without Dioceses in Missionary work, or were Bishops in charge of a monastery, or working in a clan as tribe Bishop, with the honors which belong to the chief of a tribe. Pagan customs would naturally long survive, though the exiled British, fleeing from the Saxons, helped somewhat to elevate the Irish.

The energy that had been expended in piracy and clan feuds now took a missionary form, and the active Irish, hardy, bold, enthusiastic youths, were the pioneer missionaries among the Picts, and among the tribes of Northern and Central Europe, whose work was garnered by men carrying a stronger plan of organization. St. Aidan's mission from Lindisfarne to the northern Saxons was in truth the firmest and most enduring of the missions in England. This simple flexible mode of work broke down before the later organized methods, when the people were prepared for them, but not before. The Christianity avowed moulded but slowly the character of the tribes, but it produced many noble Christian men and women.

As they rose into more regular system the Irish Archbishops obtained consecration from England. The Archbishop of Dublin was consecrated by Lanfranc 1079 A.D. But in 1155 A.D., Hadrian IV. granted Ireland to Henry II. This led to the Norman invasion (1170 A.D.). From this date the island was the theatre of guerrilla wars and raidings. The conquered possessions, whose limits varied with the political fortunes of the colony, were called the English Pale. The clans in the more difficult parts of the island long remained unbroken. The native Irish Church was at a great disadvantage, and disabilities were declared against the native clergy. The Church of history is practically the Norman-English establishment. The Councils, as of Cashel (1172 A.D.), Dublin (1217 A.D.), of Nova Villa (1216 A.D.), when Paparo, the Legate, presided, were under Anglo-Norman rule. Gradually, however, there was more amalgamation, and some time before the date of the Reformation the Norman influence had re-moulded the Irish Church, and Diocesan Episcopacy ruled the Irish Church. Abuses had arisen. Papal aggrandizement had gone forward since it could act as a mediator between the two parties.

Henry VIII. easily dissolved the monasteries, but some escaped his ruthless rapacity, and the Reformation he had begun in England but proceeded to the same point in Ireland, and more laxly, for Bishops nominated at Rome were not refused their Sees. Edward's Prayer-Book was accepted by the Archbishop of Dublin, but was rejected by the Archbishop of Armagh. Mary's accession drove out the Bishops inclined to Reform. But Elizabeth's supremacy and the English ritual were accepted in a Parliament in 1560 A.D., where there were three Archbishops and seventeen Bishops out of twenty-six. The records are doubtful, but as only two Bishops were a little later deprived of their Sees (and these were intruded under Mary), it is very fair to assert that the rest followed the example of the Archbishop of Dublin and conformed to the reform introduced by Elizabeth. But Roman intrigues obtained a representation at Trent in 1563 A.D. The unhappy antagonisms of the races which were in the island gave a powerful opportunity to the Jesuits to set the two parties at greater variance, and to establish a schism which has included by far the greater part of the Celtic population and has paralyzed all efforts for raising it to a higher level.

The political disturbances were too often fomented by the Priests, and the unfortunate Irish have been used as tools f r designing men. There is no space here for detailing the guerrilla wars in Elizabeth's and the Stewart reigns. In the iron rule of Cromwell Irish representatives sat in Parliament in London. James II. made his only stand in Ireland. From that time on Ireland was a banned country, misunderstood, restive, misruled. After the insurrection of 1798 A.D., the Act of Union joined the two countries and the two Churches together politically.

But the gift of emancipation from political disabilities granted to the Romanists in 1829 A.D. led to further concessions, till at last the Irish Church was disestablished, its revenues seized, its incomes commuted. It was enacted in 1869 A.D., but went into effect in 1871 A.D.

By it the Irish Church was freed from dependence on the Crown. It confined ecclesiastical Law only to the members of the Church. It confiscated to public uses, but subject to life interests, revenues to the amount of £581,000. The Irish Church had to organize anew its work. It declared its sisterhood with the English Church in a General Convention in 1870 A.D. (February), and took preliminary steps for organization.

The General Synod was finally shaped, and became the Church Council. The governing arrangement for the Church is as follows: It consists of the House of Bishops, consisting of two Archbishops and twelve Bishops, and the House of Representatives, consisting of two hundred and eight Clergy and four hundred and sixteen Laity; but, except for special reasons, the two houses sit together. They are presided over by the Archbishop of Armagh by ancient right. The Diocesan Synod consists of the Bishop, Clergy of the Diocese, and Synodsmen sent by the Vestries. There is a Diocesan Court for cases arising in the Diocese, and a Court of General Synod to hear appeals and to try greater causes. The ancient offices of Dean, Archdeacons, and Canons are retained. The Archbishop of Armagh is elected by the Bishops, but the Archbishop of Dublin is elected in Diocesan Synod, as are also the other Bishops.

The present Clergy by law are entitled to an annuity from the Government, for which they may *commute*, by transferring the capital sum it represents to the Governing Body, the corporation in the Church which controls the property; and a *composition* also may be effected, by which a clergyman may compound his right to this annuity by resigning his liability to duty, and receiving a reduced share according to an established scale, varying with age, etc. Vigorous efforts were made to raise the endowments needed and to fund the capital received from Government: the result is a capital of over $35,000,000. The Irish Church has about 640,000 members out of a total population of 5,200,000, or forms one-eighth of the whole. There are 1218 parishes in the twelve Dioceses

It will be seen that as a historical fact the two parties into which the Old Irish Church has been divided by political and race antagonisms have changed sides. So long as the Anglo-Roman Church was in the Papal obedience the old Irish Church, while holding the same doctrines, was in opposition. As soon as the Anglo-Irish Church initiated reform, the Celtic Irish Church threw itself eagerly into the Roman obedience.

Irregularity. A canonical impediment; an incapacity for holding a benefice for some act requiring punishment. It also means the impediments to the reception of Holy Orders, such as occurred by a personal blemish, as under the Jewish law, or under some disability, as being slaves or serfs, or illegitimate, or having received baptism on a sick-bed, or as guilty of some crime which rendered them notorious. The 113th Canon of 1603 A.D. threatened the clergyman revealing "any crime or offense committed to his trust and secrecy" in confession with the "pain of irregularity." It involved the loss of his benefice, if the clergyman had one, or else incapacitated him for holding one if he had not.

Isaac. The incidents of a life which has such momentous lessons in it are strangely few. The child of a promise made to Abraham in consequence of his faith, he had from his youth ever before him the memory of that act of still greater faith in which he was a participant, even though in a subordinate mode. His character seems to have been ever quiet, thoughtful, reserved, and deeply devout. His mother seems to have resented for him the jealous ridicule of Ishmael. When a youth, certainly old enough to know something of the transaction, he was offered up by his father, who received him again in a figure from the dead. It would seem that this solemn action shadowed his life ever after. His father procured for him his wife Rebecca when he was forty, and he was childless for twenty years. Fifteen years later he buried his father. By a famine he was forced to leave Lahai-Roi and go to Gerar. Here GOD renewed His covenant with him. The same timidity which influenced his father led him to deny that Rebecca was his wife to Abimelech, the Philistine king. In this quiet life lay, too, the capacities for something greater, for he increased in wealth and in importance till he roused the jealousy of the Philistines, whose herdsmen contended with his servants for the wells. The deceit of Jacob, in wrongfully claiming what GOD would have given him openly, broke into Isaac's domestic peace, and by Rebecca's persuasion he sent him to Laban, in Padan Aram. His life is now for us a blank till we read that Jacob returned with a large family and considerable property, in time to see his father before his death. "And the days of Isaac were a hundred and fourscore years, . . . and his sons Esau and Jacob buried him." The quiet patience and the peaceableness of his character are the leading traits, which seem to be CHRIST-like, but in one great point he stands the sole, the pre-eminent type of our LORD. In the act of sacrifice by which Abraham placed him upon the altar of wood and was about to slay him, he was the type of the atonement. It was the prefigurement in action of the one great sacrifice on the same mount nineteen centuries later, by his descendant according to the flesh, JESUS CHRIST. It was a figure, a type, and a prophecy of the death and the resurrection of CHRIST, and if larger teaching were given to him as to its meaning, he may well have loved to meditate upon it ever after.

Isaiah (Heb. *Geshayahu,*—JEHOVAH *is helper*), a name in its abbreviated English form found only in connection with the earliest of the four greater prophets, but in its fuller Hebrew form occurring also as the name of certain Levites in the time of David (1 Chron. xxv. 3; xxvi. 25). The prophet was the son of Amos, of whom nothing is known except that he is not the same with the prophet Amos, the two names being very different in Hebrew, though written alike in the Greek of the Septuagint. Of his personal history almost nothing has been preserved except the few incidental notices in the course of his prophecies. In 2 Chron. xxvi. 22, we are told that he was the historian of Uzziah's reign. There is a tradition that he lived to the reign of Manasseh, and was put to death under that monarch by being "sawn asunder," to which Heb. xi. 37, is supposed to allude; but this tradition is very doubtful. We only know that he prophesied "in the days of Uzziah, Jotham, Ahaz, and Hezekiah, kings of Judah" (Isa. i. 1), and that he was still actively engaged in his duties in the fourteenth year of the last reign (Isa. xxxvi. 1; xxxvii.-xxxix.). Supposing his prophecies to have begun in the last year of Uzziah (comp. Isa. vi. 1), they must have extended over a period of at least forty-seven years, and as neither the beginning nor the end of them is fixed, they may have covered a considerably longer period. Isaiah is shown by his prophecies to have been a man of high culture and of great eloquence. He was the counselor of kings, an eminent patriot, and a wise statesman. He was evidently much esteemed by Hezekiah (Isa. xxxvii. 2; xxxviii. 1; xxxix. 3-8).

Isaiah, Book of. This, in point of time and of the order of the Canon, is the first, as it is in many respects the most important, of the "Greater Prophets." The author lived in Judah before, during, and after the captivity of the kingdom of the ten tribes, which took place in the sixth year of Hezekiah (2 Kings xviii. 9-12). Its prophecies are mainly addressed to Judah, although, as in the other prophets, there are burdens in relation to other nations occupying xiii.-xxiii., and some other utterances not especially relating to Judah, as xxviii.

Isaiah's prophecies are the centre of a large prophetic activity. Amos also prophesied under Uzziah, and Hosea and Micah were strictly contemporaries of Isaiah, while Joel is referred by many writers to the same period. It was a great crisis in the history of Israel, when the northern kingdom was carried into captivity and the southern also was threatened with the same fate. At no other period in the history of the ancient Church was there such an outburst of prophetic teaching, except at the still darker time of the captivity of Judah.

The period was one of great political vicissitudes, and to understand the prophecies of Isaiah it is necessary to take into consideration the great political events of the several reigns under which he lived. Uzziah was a wise and good monarch, succeeding to the throne at the age of sixteen, after the assassination of his father, and reigning fifty-two years. His long, wise, and pious reign brought about a state of great comparative prosperity. He subdued the Edomites and other lesser tribes of that part of Arabia, and took Elath, which he fortified as a commercial port at the head of the east branch of the Red Sea. He extended his sway over the Ammonites and Moabites on the east of the Jordan valley and the Dead Sea. They had hitherto been tributary to Israel; he made them tributary to Judah. On the west also he was successful against the Philistines, and razed their principal cities and built new fortified towns in their territory. He also strengthened Jerusalem, and brought a large army into a high state of efficiency, and thoroughly equipped them according to the fashion of the times. His internal administration was equally good. He loved agriculture, dug many wells, and built towns for the protection of the flocks in the parts of the wilderness fitted for pasturage, and he cultivated vineyards and orchards for himself. He was under the influence of a certain prophet Zechariah (not the later Zechariah of the Canon, 2 Chron. xxvi. 5), and never fell away from the worship of JEHOVAH. But towards the close of his reign his prosperity was too much for him; he became inflated with pride and insisted on taking upon himself the priest's office of burning incense (ch. xxvi, 16-21). The High-Priest remonstrated with him in vain, and he was smitten with leprosy. In consequence of this he was obliged to live apart the rest of his life and govern the kingdom through his son Jotham (2 Kings xv. 5). The only prophecy of Isaiah distinctly dated in this reign is chapter vi., in its last year; but the previous chapters may probably be considered as belonging to its closing years, except chapter i., which is rather a general introduction to the whole book. It was, however, under the state of things brought about by this reign that Isaiah's earlier prophecies were uttered.

Jotham succeeded his father at the age of twenty-five years and reigned sixteen years. He does not appear to have been a man of the same force of character, but followed his father's policy as far as he was able. He further strengthened Jerusalem, and built various fortifications in Judah. He also subdued a revolt of the Ammonites. Near the end of his reign the confederacy between Pekah, King of Israel, and Rezin, King of Damascus, against Judah, began to assume threatening proportions. There are none of Isaiah's prophecies dated as belonging to this reign.

Jotham was succeeded by Ahaz at the age of twenty. He reigned also sixteen years, and was both a weak and wicked king. The league of Israel and Syria for the utter destruction of the kingdom of Judah now came into active operation. They invaded the territories of Judah, and finally laid siege to Jerusalem. They failed in the latter attempt, but carried off vast spoil and an immense number of captives. The latter were given up at the instance of the prophet Oded (2 Kings xvi.; 2 Chron. xxviii.); but the kingdom of Judah was otherwise greatly crippled. The allies took the port of Elath, and, as they had no use for it themselves, they restored it to the Edomites; they laid waste the eastern part of Judah and gave an opportunity to the Philistines to invade the south and west. Ahaz, in his distress, and thus encompassed with enemies on every side, sought the assistance of Tiglath-Pileser, the king of Assyria. He helped him just so far as suited his own purposes, conquering and annexing to his own dominions Syria and the trans-Jordanic and northern parts of Israel; but he impoverished Ahaz by the enormous tribute laid upon him. He also led (or probably forced) him to introduce the worship of his own gods into Judah. During this reign Isaiah appears as a patriot prophet, and probably the saving of Jerusalem was largely due to his energy and influence. The prophecies of chapters vii.-ix. belong to this reign, and probably also those of x.-xii. The difficulties in the interpretation of the former are largely removed by remembering that the purpose of Pekah and Rezin was nothing less than the utter and permanent destruction of the kingdom of Judah, and that the promise of the MESSIAH was a proof that this purpose must fail.

Hezekiah, the best of the kings of Judah, succeeded Ahaz, and reigned twenty-nine years (2 Kings xviii. 5, 6). He restored the temple and its worship, and destroyed the "high places." He also destroyed the brazen serpent which had been preserved from the time of Moses, but which had become an object of idolatrous worship. After the fall of the kingdom of Israel, which occurred in his sixth year, he invited the remnants of those tribes to join in his great celebration of the Passover. His invitation was generally ridiculed (2 Chron. xxx. 10), yet was finally accepted by "many of Ephraim, and Manasseh, Issachar, and Zebulun" (ch. xxx., 18), and probably by smaller numbers of other tribes. From this time the remnants of all the tribes seem to have looked upon Judah as their head, and gradually becoming incorporated with it, the continuity of the whole nation was thus kept up. This fact is of some importance in understanding those later passages of the Old Testament, and especially those of the New, in which the existing nation is considered as representing the whole "twelve tribes." Hezekiah attacked the Philistines, retook the lost cities and gained others; he also refused the payment of tribute to Assyria. Shalmaneser (successor to Tiglath-Pileser) marched against him, but was detained five years by the unsuccessful siege of Tyre. Meanwhile Hezekiah strengthened Jerusalem, and the people were prevented by the efforts of Isaiah from forming an alliance with Egypt. Shalmaneser was succeeded by Sargon, who invaded Judah twice. His first attack had no important results, and is merely alluded to in the history; in the second he took large numbers of the cities of Judah. Hezekiah at this time (in his fourteenth year) was very ill, and in answer to his earnest prayer received the promise of the prolongation of his life for fifteen years, the going back of the shadow upon the sun-dial of Ahaz being given him as an assurance of the promise (Isa. xxxviii. 1-8). The report of his sickness and recovery reached Babylon, and the king sent him an embassy of congratulation. There is every reason to suppose that this embassy covered a political purpose, and the suggestion of an alliance between Judah and Babylon against their common oppressor, Assyria. It was doubtless to prove the value of his alliance that Hezekiah ostentatiously showed to the ambassadors all his possessions, especially his treasures and "the house of his armor." In consequence of this, Isaiah pronounced the doom that all these things, together with the descendants of Hezekiah himself, should be carried away to Babylon, —a prophecy which in the existing state of empires seemed impossible of accomplishment, but which was accurately fulfilled after the conquest of Nineveh by Babylon. Sennacharib succeeded Sargon and twice invaded Judah. Hezekiah paid him three hundred talents of silver and thirty of gold, and suffered the loss of part of his dominions, which were given to the Philistines. Egypt also was terribly defeated by Sennacharib. His second attack on Judah was most contemptuous of the GOD of Israel, and was miraculously defeated. Whenever the people relied on Egypt, they suffered; when such aid was out of the question, they were delivered. Hezekiah survived this last invasion only one year.

In the opening of the book he describes his prophecies as "the vision of Isaiah." This word is here evidently to be taken in the general sense of the revelation communicated to him. Of "vision" in the stricter sense, as used by several of the other prophets, there is but a single instance (ch. vi.)

in the whole book. The style of Isaiah has been generally recognized by critics as of the highest order. He has been truly described as the most complete and many-sided of all the prophets, and passages of surpassing eloquence may be selected from almost any part of his writings. He is often called "the Evangelical Prophet," from the clearness and fullness of his Messianic predictions, and especially from the distinctness with which he foretells our LORD'S vicarious suffering for our sins (lii. 13–liii.).

During the last century the integrity of the book has been very earnestly called in question. The book naturally falls into two great parts, chapter i.–xxxix. and chapter xl.–lxvi., the latter forming one complete and closely connected prophecy, while the former is made up of a great number of shorter and more or less disconnected prophecies, and includes some historical matter. The first suspicion that the whole was not the work of Isaiah was suggested by Koppe, about 1780 A.D., and related only to a different authorship of these two parts. His views were taken up and extended by many German writers, until now the supposition of a "Deutero-Isaiah" has become the prevailing one among German scholars. There have been, however, all along, earnest defenders of the integrity of the book among German scholars. Of these, during the present century, may be mentioned Jahn (1802 A.D.), Möller (1825 A.D.), Kleinert (1829 A.D.), Henstenberg and Hävernick (1849 A.D.), Stier (1850 A.D.), Keil (1853 A.D.), and Nägelsbach (1877 A.D.). The last is translated in the large commentary edited by Schaff. In the course of the controversy it became evident to both parties that the arguments relied on to disprove Isaiah's authorship of the last twenty-seven chapters were of equal force against many in the earlier part. The critics were therefore compelled to dismember that also, and reject Isaiah's authorship of (as stated by Ewald) chapters xii. 2; xiv. 23; xxi. 1–10; xxiv.–xxvii.; xxxiv.; xxxv., or about one-quarter of the whole. Other critics differ in regard to several of these passages, and would deny Isaiah's authorship of other passages. Many subsidiary reasons have been urged against the integrity of the book, but these have been amply met, and confessedly are only of secondary importance. The chief argument, and the only one on which much reliance is placed, is that the author of the second part takes his stand-point at the close of the Babylonian captivity and thence looks forward to the subsequent future.

It is urged, with reason, that the date of an author must be determined from his own description of the times in which he lived and in which he places himself. This principle may be fully accepted, and on it may be constructed the strongest argument for the unity of Isaiah. The question is simply whether the author of the disputed portions actually lived in the time of the close of the captivity; or whether, living at an earlier date, he merely transported himself in prophetic thought to that period. Now, if we are willing to set aside entirely the unquestioned tradition of all the previous centuries, and the opinions of all students of the Bible in the ages before us; and if we can explain away the citations in the New Testament from the latter part of the book under Isaiah's name (St. Matt. iii. 3 and parallels; xii. 17–21; St. Luke iv. 17–19; St. John xii. 38; Acts viii. 30, 32; Rom. x. 16; x. 20, 21); if we can set aside the express statement of Josephus (Ant., xi. 1, § 2) that Cyrus read in the book which the prophet Isaiah had left behind him the prophecies concerning himself; if we can forget the unity of design connecting the last part with what has gone before, and attach no weight to the unity of diction pervading both parts; if we could account for the fading out from history of the name of the author of such magnificent and important prophecies, and their being falsely attributed to Isaiah;—if all these things, on which there is not here space to enlarge, could be set aside, there yet remain conclusive reasons why the second part of Isaiah cannot be assigned to the period of the close of the captivity. (1) There is in this second part a recognition of the sacrificial worship of the Jews as actually going on in the time of the writer. Chapter xl. 16 seems to imply this, but lxvi. 3 is a distinct recognition of it. Now we know that all such worship was entirely suspended during the exile. (2) The denunciations of the bold and open idolatry of the people occupy no inconsiderable portion of this second part (xl. 13–20; xlviii. 5; lvii. 5–8; lxv. 2–4, 11; lxvi. 17). But it is well known that they were finally weaned from idolatry by the exile, and that even the little practiced by them at the first of it was, as appears from Ezekiel, of an entirely secret character. The critics endeavor to parry the force of this evidence by supposing these passages to have been written for the idolatrous remnant who continued to live in Judæa. History, however, shows that there was no such remnant. The people who were not carried off by Nebuchadnezzar sought refuge from him in Egypt, and on the return from the captivity there is no recognition of any Israelites as remaining in the land. (3) Throughout this entire part the *prediction* of Cyrus and of the things belonging to the close of the captivity are claimed as proofs of the *foreknowledge* of GOD, and therefore of His rightful claim to the allegiance of His people. (See, *e.g.*, xliv. 24–xlv. 6; xlv. 19–21; xlvi. 8–13; xlviii. 5–8.) It is inconceivable that any prophet could have used such arguments except he were writing so long before the events that they were not yet within the scope of human sagacity. The internal evidence of the book is therefore entirely in accordance with the unbroken tradition of its unity.

REV. PROF. FREDERIC GARDINER, D.D.

J.

Jacob. The grandson of Abraham. His father Isaac was fifty-nine years old when the twins Esau and Jacob were born. It was foretold to his mother Rebecca that Jacob's descendant should rule his brothers. From this Rebecca endeavored, on at least one memorable occasion, to push his interests forward at his brother's expense. The two young men were brought up together sharing their father's wandering life. Esau was loved by Isaac, Jacob by his mother. It was characteristic of Jacob that he should take advantage of his brother's faintness after a long chase, and buy of him the coveted birthright foretold to be his. Esau probably thought little of the sale of it for a mess of pottage, but Jacob treasured it up, and was the more ready to lend himself to his mother's instigation to perpetrate the well-known deceit upon his father. He obtained the blessing by fraud and it brought its own punishment, in the hatred of his brother and his own flight from home. Rebecca's influence over Isaac was great enough to persuade him to send Jacob to seek a wife in his kinsman Laban's family. On this journey was renewed to him at Bethel the covenant, which JEHOVAH had made with Abraham and Isaac, in the vision of the ladder reaching down to earth. The fraud which he had practiced was repaid him by Laban, who betrothed to him Rachel, the younger daughter, but on the marriage night substituted Leah, the older. Jacob was indignant, but Laban bestowed on him his other daughter also, and gave to each a handmaid. Leah bore to Jacob, Reuben, Simeon, Levi, Judah; Bilhah, Rachel's maid, bore him Dan and Naphtali; Zilpah, Leah's maid, Gad and Asher; Leah gave him Issachar and Zebulun and Rachel, Joseph and Benjamin. The wary, observant character of Jacob was shown in the management of Laban's flocks. It was while he was serving Laban, and before Rachel's death, that Joseph, a lad of seventeen, was sold by his brethren into slavery. His early sin was sorely visited upon him by Laban's fraud, the turbulence of his sons, and the loss of Joseph. After twenty-one years' absence, finding Laban very jealous because of his success in caring for his own flocks, he set out to return home to his father. His journey home was marked by three dangers,—the angry pursuit of Laban, whom GOD warned not to speak either good or bad to Jacob; the meeting with his angry brother Esau, whom he propitiated with a present, which, however, Esau would not accept; on the night before, when in anxious sorrow he sent his caravan forward and paused at the brook Jabbok, the Angel of the LORD, the Jehovah-Angel, wrestled with him. In that mysterious contest, which was typical of the religious earnestness and perseverance of the Patriarch, there is much significance, both of the weakness and the strength of the people. Both the contest, the halting, and the blessing have rested together with the name upon Israel. Jacob rested at Shechem, where occurred the disgrace of his daughter Dinah and the vengeance which Simeon and Levi exacted of the Shechemites. Here Divine interposition took him to Bethel, where he purged his family of the idols they had learned to use in Padan-aram, and renewed his covenant with GOD. Apparently he reached his father not long before Isaac's death. Jacob is left here by the sacred narrative, and the acts of Judah are next recorded and the history of Joseph is given. Jacob went down to Egypt to his son Joseph when he was an hundred and thirty years old.

The life of Jacob is marked in the sacred history. He was a type of CHRIST, as a supplanter; the second Adam, not casting out, but supplanting the first Adam with a better life. In this view his fraud is not to be considered as at all justified. The blessing would have been given him could he have waited GOD's time. His after-career was a just sequel to the deceit, while with it were mingled many Divine comforts and blessings. His character was undoubtedly formed in reality by his life and struggles under Laban's jealous and repressive treatment, and but for his own shrewdness he would have fared badly under his kinsman; thrice were his wages changed. His patience was tested and developed; he felt the power of GOD ever about him; his deep religiousness was ever quickened. His dream on the plain; the meeting of the angels at Mahanaim; the wrestling with the Man at Peniel; his renewed covenant with GOD at Bethel, and throughout his whole career his vow of the tenth which could only be offered as a sacrifice, educated him in the life hid with GOD. In two points was his life a type of our LORD's: he was the one who should be a substitute offering a better, holier life; he was a type of CHRIST in that he prevailed in his wrestling. So our LORD's human trials and temptations and prayers and strong cry prevailed, and He, as the Patriarch of old (Gen. xlix.), has left a perpetual blessing behind Him on all who believe on Him who is the GOD of Abraham, the GOD of Isaac, and the GOD of Jacob.

James, St., usually surnamed the Great, the brother of John the beloved disciple. The notices of him in the Gospels are very few. With his brother he was a fisherman, working in his father Zebedee's boat, when he was called by JESUS to follow Him. He was one of the Twelve, and of these he was the second of the three who stood nearest our LORD. ("And He taketh with Him Peter, James, and John.") He with the other two went into the death-chamber of Jairus' daughter. With them he was on the Mount of Transfiguration. His zeal procured him the surname Boanerges,—Son of Thunder. It brought upon him the rebuke of the LORD. For him and his brother his mother preferred her petition that they might sit, the one on the right hand, the other on the left, in His Kingdom. He was one of the four who questioned the Master about the last days. He was one of the three at the Agony in the Garden. Except the record of his name in the list in Acts i. 13, he is not mentioned till we read that Herod killed James, the brother of John, with sword (A.D. 44), when he drank of his Master's cup and received his Master's baptism. Every notice of him by the Evangelists, slight as it is, leaves the impression that there was a nobleness and loveliness in his character. That he and his brother were chosen to be our LORD'S most intimate earthly companions proves their sympathy with Him, if not the insight, which they afterwards assuredly received, into His nature. Even their ambitions tended to better things. Of his labors we know nothing. Everything that is told of him outside the Gospels and Acts is purely legendary. His mission to Spain (of which he is the patron saint) is wholly mythical. His twelve years of work in Jerusalem were not wasted we may be sure, but it is one of the mysterious acts of Providence that he should have been killed just when, humanly speaking, he could have been most usefully employed.

James, St., the Less, properly the Little, the son of Alphæus, is another instance where the life of one chosen to do the LORD'S work has left no earthly record save the name. Their work we know is not forgotten in the Book of Remembrance, and here it was merged into the sum of the labor necessary for founding the Church; but except his title, the son of Alphæus, and his own name in the list of the Apostles, we know nothing about him. It is here assumed that he is *not* the same as the James to whom the LORD appeared at His Resurrection (1 Cor. xv. 7), who presided at the Council at Jerusalem, and who wrote the Epistle. There is considerable difficulty upon either hypothesis, but upon a review of the whole evidence it is more probable that James the Little was not James the brother of the LORD.

James the Just, the brother of the LORD. It is claimed that this James was really the cousin of our LORD, and the son of Alphæus, or Clopas, names which can be shown to be identical, for the title Brother, often meant Cousin, as Son is often "descendant;" that when it is said, "neither did His brethren believe on Him," it does not necessarily include all His brethren; that the omission of the title Brethren of the LORD from the names of James the Little and Jude, his brother, does not prove that they were not His brethren; that it is strange that our LORD should have intrusted His mother to St. John, when there were those whose duty it was to care for her, had there been any brethren according to the Flesh. The reply is that "brother," denoting a kinship, is always used accurately in the New Testament, that the LORD'S brethren appear separately in the Gospel; that the LORD'S brethren are separated from the Apostles in 1 Cor. ix. 5; that James was called a pillar and distinguished from the Apostles by St. Paul (Gal. ii. 9, and Gal. i. 9). The arguments can be seen in full for the identity of the two in Smith's "Dictionary of the Bible;" for the view that they are separate persons, see Professor Plumptre's Introduction to Epistle of St. James, in the Cambridge Bible for Schools.

Assuming, then, that James, the brother of the LORD, was a separate person, the recorded facts of his life are almost as meagre as those in the life of St. James the Greater. His brethren did not believe on Him during his life. "A prophet," said our LORD, "is not without honor but in his own country and among his own kin and in his own house." They, with His mother and sisters, seek Him out, desiring to speak with Him to withdraw Him from His course. They were at the last feast of Tabernacles that preceded His Passion. They were, or at any rate James was, at Jerusalem at the time of His Passion, for the risen LORD was seen first of Cephas, then of the Twelve, then of the five hundred brethren at once, then of James, then of all the Apostles (1 Cor. xv. 5–7). The brethren were present with the Twelve at the election of St. Matthias. Then James appears as the pillar of the Church at Jerusalem when St. Paul goes up thither, then he is the presiding Apostle at the Council (Acts xv.). Then he receives St. Paul upon his last visit to Jerusalem. There is nothing more recorded in the sacred narrative. His Epistle is his great work. That tells us more of his character than anything else we have. The account of his death as given by Eusebius (E.H., ii. 23) out of Hegesipus fits into the current of events and is marked with the traits implied in his Epistle so as to bear at least the air of the truth. "Noted for his asceticism—a Nazarite—he had gained great influence with the people, whom he taught concerning JESUS the Door. He bore the title of Oblias, the bulwark of the people, and the Righteous or Just. He frequented the sanctuary in constant prayer for the people, so that his knees became callous. He was urged to stay those who had gone astray after JESUS, and for this purpose was put upon the pinnacle of the Temple and called upon to proclaim from thence, ' What is the door of JESUS?' 'And he answered with a loud voice, Why ask ye me concerning JESUS the SON of Man? He hath sat down in heaven on the right hand of the GREAT POWER, and is about to come in the clouds of heaven.' Upon this many believed and cried 'Hosanna to the son of David.' But the Scribes and Pharisees who had set him upon the pinnacle were filled with wrath and cast him down, and the people in the court stoned him, and a fuller beat out his brains while, like St. Stephen, he was praying for his murderers." Such is the bare outline of the beautiful narrative Eusebius quotes in full. In it there is nothing improbable, but rather it falls in with all we know of the state of mind among the Jews then.

It is difficult to fix the *date* of the death of St. James. If the Epistle to the Hebrews be St. Paul's, is there a reference to St. James in chapter xiii. 7, 8 ; "Remember them which have the rule over you, who have spoken unto you the word of GOD : considering the end of their conversation : JESUS CHRIST the same yesterday, to-day, and forever." If so, then, as the Epistle was written about 64 A.D., the martyrdom occurred later. In fact, Hegesippus (Eusebius, E. H.) says, and straightway Vespasian began the siege, placing it then about 70 A.D. His EPISTLE has been questioned, rejected, and when received has been the subject of countless controversies. The Church has always received it, though it was classed for a time with the doubtful Epistles. This hesitation most likely was because it was imperfectly circulated, being addressed to the Jewish converts. At the time of the Reformation it was violently discussed, and by some rejected because of its teaching, which seemed so opposed to that of St. Paul. The date of the Epistle has much to do with considering the extent of that alleged antagonism. If (with the Cambridge Editor Plumptre) it is dated before the Council of Jerusalem, it must be placed before 51 A.D. As our space only permits us to give the results, not the details by which this conclusion is reached, we will accept as proven this date in place of the later one of 61 A.D.

The contents of the Epistle have caused great debates, it being claimed that he was opposed to St. Paul. There is no foundation whatever for this in the inspired narrative. Its real source is in the perversions of the heretical romance of the Recognitions and the Homilies of the pseudo-Clement, used with critical skill and infidel principles by the German critics. This, then, is summarily dismissed, for James the Just was not the man to give the right hand of fellowship to a man to whom he was opposed. Let us look at the contents of the Epistle, and then we will be able to judge of the relation of St. James' doctrine of Works to St. Paul's doctrine of Faith. There are many parallelisms of thought and of teaching in this Epistle to that of St. John Baptist. Of these are James i. 22-27 with St. Matt. iii. ; James ii. 15, 16, with St. Luke iii. 11 ; James ii. 19, 20; St. Matt. iii. 9 ; James v. 1-6 ; St. Matt. iii. 10-12. There are others to the Sermon on the Mount (*e.g.*, James ii. 14 ; St. Matt. vii. 21-23 ; James v. 2 to St. Matt. vi. 19). The Jewish cast of thought, the references to the Old Testament history (to Abraham, Job, Rahab, and Elijah), the probable influence of the Wisdom of the son of Sirach, make this a peculiar Epistle. It is more intense than the Epistles of St. Peter, and in this respect is like the First Epistle of St. John. Its ascetic tone, its practical teaching, its stern reproofs, all mark it. But its doctrine of the relation of Faith to Works gives it a special prominence relative to St. Paul's Epistles to the Romans and Galatians. St. Paul asserts Faith without Works alone can save. St. James teaches, " I will show thee my Faith by my Works." St. Paul condemns dead works. St. James condemns a dead Faith. St. Paul adduces Abraham's obedience before circumcision as the obedience of Faith, " and it was counted unto him for righteousness." St. James adduces the obedience of Abraham in offering up Isaac as the righteousness by works. "Seest thou how Faith wrought with his works, and by works was Faith made perfect (ch. ii. 22). Is there any antagonism between these two Apostles, both zealous for their Master, both of the straitest sect, both eager to teach the whole truth ? It is impossible to believe this. The Apostle to the Gentiles was writing to the Gentiles as well as to the Jews, and he adduces one part of Abraham's life, the beginning of his wonderful career. Faith in him must be precedent to action, and all have their blessed significance from his faith. St. James the Just, the unceasing pleader for his people, the Bishop in the Holy City, argues with the faithful of the Dispersion, from the crowning act of faith in Abraham, when his act in its sublimity proved his faith. There is no antagonism, but, rather, both taught the very same truth. For in one of those grand outpourings of his enthusiasm, St. Paul longs that he may " be found in Him," not having mine own righteousness, which is of the Law, but that which is through the faith of CHRIST, the righteousness which is of GOD by faith, that I may know Him, and the power of His resurrection, and the fellowship of His sufferings, being made conformable to His death if by any means I might attain to the resurrection of the dead." It is impossible to exclude work, life-long work, sanctified by Faith, from these words. The fellowship of His suffering, the conformation to His death, the capacity for having the power of His resurrection unto life resting upon him, demand a preceding and continuing presence of Faith shown in and by works. It is noticeable that St. James does not appeal to the Law, " which was four hundred years after," but to the life of Abraham to establish his position. So doth St. Paul, but St. Paul contrasts it for the Gentiles with the mere literal outward obedience to the Law, while St. James in all his teaching which refers to the Law is writing to those Christians who yet felt the binding authority of the Law, and urges the true law of liberty. It is the fact that a similar use of the Law is made by the writer of the Epistle to the Hebrews that indicates that St. Paul must be its author. It is a caviling spirit, or one which, too curiously contrasting the two Apostles, does not mark their agreement, and overlooks the fact that they were addressing Christian audiences differently trained, that can now insist that St. James and St. Paul are in opposition to each other.

The Epistle is not written upon any fixed plan. It deals just with the unsettled, tempted, self-indulgent, self-excusing man. Then it passes to practicing the duty of caring in every way for the poor as a matter of practical faith. Then St. James reproves his readers for sins of the tongue; roused by this, the next chapter (iv.) and part of the fifth are filled with warning and invective against the careless, the rich, the worldly-minded. The pause is sudden, the return to a gentle tone is quite remarkable after so vehement an outburst, and with earnest suggestions upon patience and prayer, he closes with an abruptness that occurs in no other book in the New Testament. It is in perfect keeping with the character of one who was filled with noble, devout asceticism, who was a keen observer and a fearless denouncer of sin, who though not having a polished education was a master of the learning which maketh wise unto salvation, who deserved pre-eminently the title of the Righteous.

Jehovah. The glorious name of GOD. In the English Version it is always translated LORD, as Elohim is translated GOD. It occurs in its simplest form JAH in the lxviii. Psalm, 4 v., and is transferred without translation in Ex. vi. 3; Ps. lxxxiii. 18; Is. xii. 2 (JAH JEHOVAH) xxvi. 4 (JAH JEHOVAH), and in compound names several times. It was the ineffable name, the Tetragrammaton, the name of four letters, and its true pronunciation is said to be lost. Its formal announcement to the nation (for it was known before) was itself a step up for the chosen people. Its meaning, the self-existent ONE, the living GOD (*vide* ELOHIM), involved a doctrine which was the greatest revelation that the Israelite had yet received, and one which of itself separated him from the heathen. It was held to be wrong to pronounce it (Lev. xxiv. 16), and other vowels were attached to the four consonants, so that it is claimed that its true pronunciation is lost, but from the law of the formation of words in Hebrew its true pronunciation was Jahaveh or Jahveh. Its meaning from the Hebrew verb " to be" is I Am that I Am.

He has the attribute of self-existence, and therefore of eternity. " I am Jahveh, I alter not" (Mal. iii. 6). Again, in Joshua (xxii. 22) and in Psalm l. 1, the three titles EL, ELOHIM, JAHVEH follow in ascending intensity of meaning. " The Mighty, The Mighty Ones, The Self-Existent," hath spoken, or knoweth. It implies, then, personality in the strictest sense, and gives the true Israelite a knowledge of Him, a knowledge which revelation can alone establish, that is beyond all the speculations of men. The distinction between EL (and ELOHIM) as GOD known from nature, and JEHOVAH as known by His revelation of Himself, will give a clue to the reason why GOD—Elohim is used at times, LORD—Jehovah at others, and why again both names are combined. A study of these will reveal to him who will undertake it devoutly the marvelous depth and accurate language of Holy Scripture even when it apparently is most arbitrary.

Jeremiah. The prophet whose life and prophetic work was spent in protests against those sins of his people, both political, ecclesiastical, and social, which led to the captivity and to the burning of the Temple by Nebuchadnezzar.

He was the son of Hilkiah, who may have been the Hilkiah the High-Priest, who discovered the Book of the Law in the House of the LORD (2 Kings xxii. 8). He was sanctified for his work from his mother's womb, ordained a prophet unto the nations. His birthplace was in the priestly city of Anathoth. He was called to his life-work quite early. Just at that date Egypt and Nineveh were the upper and lower millstones between which Judah feared she would be ground, and was wavering between alliances with either power, and finally chose to side with Egypt. The people still hankered for the old idolatries, the Ashera (A. V. groves), Astaroth and Moloch. They were guilty of open adultery, false swearing, and murder, and claimed that they were given over to do these abominations; and withal punctually performed the offices of the Temple. Whatever training Jeremiah as the son of a Priest and marked out for a prophet's work received, it had as its basis a deep study of the Law and a grasp of its true spiritual meaning. He prophesied in the last eighteen years of Josiah's reign (629 or 627 B.C. ?), and through the reigns of Jehoahaz (three months), of Jehoiakim of eleven years, and of Jehoiachin (three months), and of Zedekiah of eleven years, in all, his prophecies were uttered during a period of forty years. It was a career full of sorrow and of misunderstanding and gainsaying. He was exposed to reproach and derision, his fellow-townsmen of Anathoth sought his life, his brethren dealt treacherously with him. He was smitten by a fellow-priest, and put in the stocks because of his prophecies. The roll of his prophecies was burnt in the king's presence. Though many of his prophecies had been fulfilled and political events were rapidly hurrying to the final catastrophe which he foretold, yet he met with but little attention, and when he tried to leave the now nearly beleaguered city to attend to his private affairs at Anathoth, he was arrested as a deserter and put into ward under Jonathan the scribe in the prison till Zedekiah sent for him. Jeremiah told him plainly his coming fate and asked for better treatment. The king remanded him to prison, but ordered bread for him. But his political opponents obtained him from the king and cast him into a pit in the prison court, where Jeremiah sank in the mire. From this he was saved by Ebed Melech. Another interview, first with the feeble-minded King and then with Pashur and with Zephaniah, proved useless.

In the eleventh year of Zedekiah the city was stormed, the Temple burnt, Zedekiah captured, his sons slain, and then himself blinded. But Jeremiah himself was cared for by Nebuzaradan, the captain of the guard, who had a special order about him. He settled at Mizpah till Gedeliah, the governor under Nebuchadnezzar, was murdered by Ishmael and the refugees at Mizpah carried away captive. Jeremiah was rescued by Johanan, who, despite Jeremiah's prophecy of evil attendant on such a step, carried the whole company down into Egypt, where the prophet ended his days. The noble form of Jeremiah, the greatest of all the historical and literary prophets, fades from our sight together with the monarchy. In misery and continual peril of death he witnessed the fall of the state and the destruction of Jerusalem; he survived it, but found his tomb in an alien land. His was a rare courage, yet he was of a quiet, retiring disposition, shrinking under the great weight of responsibility laid upon him, despairing because so misunderstood and hated; alone, and sustained only by divine comfort. He speaks plainly, simply, honestly; he makes no pretensions to great literary polish, and does not hesitate to repeat phrases and images and the same thoughts over and often, yet there is such intensity in his purpose that it is no mere repetition, but rather a Divine insistence. He falls back upon the Law and upon earlier predictions. His prophecies do not only relate to the Jews but also to the heathen, for whom also he was ordained a prophet. He bears the cup of fury to the Jews and to the Gentiles from the petty kings of Palestine to the kings of Egypt and Babylon (Sheshak). The burden of woe passed upon Egypt, Philistia, Moab, Ammon, Edom, Damascus, Kedar and Hazor, Elam and Babylon (ch. xlvi.-li.).

The prophecies, as they are now arranged, are evidently not in the order in which they were uttered. It is probable that when the prophet added many more like words to the new roll, which Baruch wrote at his mouth, he made the nucleus of the present work, but that it took a new shape. There are transpositions, and the whole order bespeaks haste and oversight such as would most naturally happen to one who was so hated, imprisoned, maltreated, and forced into a foreign land to die there a sorrowful death. The transpositions that are often dwelt upon as against the authenticity of the book are, in fact, the best internal proof of its genuineness. The later prophecies, inserted in the midst of certainly much earlier matter, show that the prophet had no opportunity to arrange the transcripts of prophecies uttered in so troubled a time. It is probable that the last chapter was added by another hand, possibly by Baruch. Chapter xli. ends, " thus far are the words of Jeremiah." The next chapter contains material found in Jer. xxxix. and in 2 Kings xxiv. 8; xxv. 30; but it also contains other matter besides, and records some things Jeremiah probably did not live to see,—the liberation of Jehoiachin, and the placing him at the royal table.

Jeremiah, in some respects, is himself a type of CHRIST. A parallelism runs through their lives. Not only does he prophesy of CHRIST as the righteous Branch, the LORD our Righteousness, and utter other allusions to the Messianic kingdom, but in his own person there are analogies. In both there is the same early manifestation of the consciousness of a Divine mission; the persecution which drove the prophet from Anathoth had its counterpart in the enmity of the men of Nazareth. His protests against the priests and prophets are the types of the woes against the Pharisee, the scribe, and the lawyer. His lamentations over the coming miseries of his country are as the weeping of the SON of Man over Jerusalem. His sufferings, of those of the whole army of martyrs, come nearest to those of the Teacher against whom princes and priests and elders and people were gathered together. He saw, more clearly than others, that new covenant, with all its gifts of spiritual life and power, which was proclaimed and ratified in the death upon the cross.

Jesus Christ. I. *Divinity of.*—Our LORD asked, " Whom do men say that I the SON of MAN am?" Simon Peter replied, " Thou art the CHRIST, the SON of the Living GOD" (St. Matt. xvi. 13, 16). The SAVIOUR then blesses him and declares that GOD the FATHER has revealed this important doctrine of CHRIST's Divinity to Him (v. 17). Still the Manhood of CHRIST is constantly kept in view in Scripture. " The Word was made flesh"(John i. 14). As " the Angel of the LORD," CHRIST appears to Abraham at Mamre (Gen. xviii. 22, and xix. 1), to Hagar (Gen. xvi. 11), to Jacob (Gen. xxxii. 1 and 30), to Moses at the bush (Ex. iii. 1, 2), to Joshua (Josh. v. 14), to Gideon (Judges vi.11 and 22), and to Manoah and his wife (Judges xiii. 3-24). Our LORD declared that the Old Testament testified of Him (John v. 39), and the Theophanies add their testimony to prophecy, " No man hath seen GOD".(John i. 18) the FATHER, hence " the only-begotten SON" is the One who "hath declared Him." Our LORD'S plan to form a world-wide spiritual Kingdom was a Divine one, and its execution implied Divine aid. Without human greatness and position JESUS CHRIST leaps in a moment beyond the widest view of the greatest emperor. The Kingdom of CHRIST still advances, though its moral requirements are high. The miracles were the work of GOD. The SON claims "absolute Oneness of Essence" with the FATHER, in St. John x. 30: "I and my FATHER are one." He asserts pre-existence thus: "Before Abraham was, I am" (St. John viii. 58). He has life in Himself (see St. John v. 26). He is "the true Light" (St. John i. 9). He is "the Way, the Truth, and the Life" (xiv. 6). The love of GOD shines out in the death of CHRIST (I John iii. 16). Life, Love, and Light meet in GOD and in CHRIST. The title "Son of GOD" is given freely to JESUS in the highest sense, and GOD'S voice from heaven calls Him "Beloved SON" (St. John iii. 17). St. John, the closest companion of our LORD, is the one who most strongly and constantly asserts His Divinity. In the sermon of St. Peter on the Day of Pentecost, and in St. Paul's discourses and writings, it is the assertion of CHRIST'S Divinity that gives the power by the co-working of the HOLY GHOST. Creative power is claimed for JESUS CHRIST. "All things were made by Him" (St. John i. 3; compare Col. i. 16). "Faith in CHRIST" as Divine is St. Paul's frequent theme (see Col. ii. 5; Phil. i. 29; Rom. x. 14; Philem. 5). JESUS CHRIST has been adored as GOD from the beginning of Christianity. St. Thomas addresses Him as "my LORD and my GOD" (St. John xx. 28). When St. John sees Him in glory he falls "at His feet as dead" till he feels the touch of His right hand, and hears the comforting words "Fear not" (Rev. i. 17). The worship of JESUS CHRIST, begun by the Wise Men and repeated by those who had experienced the benefit of His miracles, and by the holy women after the Resurrection (St. Matt. xxviii. 9), and by the early Christians described by Pliny, who at their morning service sang responsive hymns to CHRIST as GOD, has continued and increased on earth, and will continue and increase till "at the name of JESUS every knee" shall bow and "every tongue" . . . "confess that JESUS CHRIST is LORD, to the glory of GOD the FATHER"(Phil. ii. 10, 11). Heaven itself shall continue the song of praise to the Divine CHRIST, "for the LORD GOD ALMIGHTY and the LAMB are the temple of it" (Rev. xxi. 22).

II. *Life of.*—Our Blessed LORD and SAVIOUR JESUS CHRIST, both GOD and man, was born in Bethlehem in Judæa, of the Blessed Virgin Mary, by the power of the HOLY GHOST. The Incarnation of JESUS CHRIST is the foundation-stone of Christianity. To it the prophets looked forward as seamen peer in darkness for a light-house; those who lived in CHRIST'S day could rejoice in His light as those who are opposite the lighthouse. We now look back upon it, but with like rejoicing. The heathen themselves longed for it, and had their dim prophecies of it. Every heathen idol in human form was but a blind groping after the GOD-man. JESUS came as a child to sanctify childhood. He came in poverty to teach contempt of mere worldly riches. The Collect for the second Sunday after Easter shows the double purpose of the Incarnation as "both a sacrifice for sin, and also an ensample of godly life," and it prays that through His grace we may strive "to follow the blessed steps of His most holy life." The example of humility presents itself at every step. The retirement and obedience of His childhood are a pattern for the young. The early visit to the temple at Jerusalem is a lesson of confirmation. The toil of the Carpenter (St. Mark vi. 3) has given dignity to labor. In early manhood the CHRIST comes into public life. The Baptism teaches His followers to imitate Him in this sacred act. The presence at the wedding feast, and the miracle there performed, indicate the sanctity of domestic life. The whole social intercourse of our LORD is an example to the Christian. The halt, the maimed, and the blind were as near to Him as the rich and the great. He entered the dark and humble dwellings of Jewish peasants, and conversed with them as an "Elder Brother." Wherever sickness or sorrow met His eye He strove at once to lighten or remove the load. The unselfishness of this Divine, yet human life, has never had a parallel. The many miracles recorded, and implied, were not acts of display, but means of healing and blessing poor suffering humanity.

Our LORD sought in every way to instruct men in the Divine life. The Parables forced all nature into service, and the growing grain, and the singing bird, or the innocent lamb were used to inculcate the highest lessons.

While the blessed self-denying work of healing and teaching advanced, Satan instigated men to take the life of the Redeemer of men. The SAVIOUR sees the dark cloud approaching, but meets hatred and persecution with love. That His work may be continued on earth, He founds His Holy Church, and appoints the Apostles as Bishops of it. He institutes the Holy Communion, and commands its observation. In agony He prays for relief from the approaching struggle with the powers of evil, but submits meekly to the FATHER'S will. He dies on the cross, but in dying prays for His murderers and pardons a dying penitent. He rises from the tomb, and for a time teaches His wondering disciples. He then ascends heavenward, and now the man CHRIST JESUS, in His life of glory, rules and guides His Church on earth and aids His saints, that when their earthly life is ended, they may be with Him and behold His glory (St. John xvii. 24). The "sacrifice for sin" was the object of this earthly life. It all looked forward to the cross, and now the world looks back to it. "I, if I be lifted up from the earth, will draw all men unto Me" (St. John xii. 32). The tree of scorn is now the tree of glory, and no monarch's crown compares with the cross of CHRIST. Keble asks,—

"Is it not strange . . . .
That to the Cross the mourner's eye should turn
Sooner than where the stars of Christmas burn?"

So it is the sin-sick have looked for centuries to that cross as their only hope, and from it have heard the words of pardon and forgiveness, "Thy faith hath saved thee," and, " Go, and sin no more." To that cross the eyes of the dying have been turned in faith, and, like the stricken Israelites bitten by serpents in the desert, they have found new life. The character and work of our LORD JESUS CHRIST stand alone in the world's history. Such grandeur and humility, such purity, charity, and forgiveness, never appear in any other record. Such wisdom was never before heard on earth. It was the officers sent to apprehend Him who exclaimed, " Never man spake like this Man" (St. John vii. 32). It was a soldier who watched Him, who cried, " Truly this Man was the SON OF GOD" (St. Mark xv. 39). It is remarkable that sinful men and women constantly seek this " Sinless Sufferer," while they fear to confess their faults even to their wicked fellow-mortals. But the LORD'S life teaches that pity is a Divine attribute, and that the LORD GOD, the " lover of souls" (Wisdom xi. 26), is more merciful than man. The work of JESUS CHRIST the SON of GOD, and the Son of man, was not intended merely to excite wonder; it is intensely practical. " He appeared to put away sin by the sacrifice of Himself. And as it is appointed unto men once to die, but after this the judgment: so CHRIST was once offered to bear the sins of many; and unto them that look for Him shall He appear the second time without sin unto salvation" (Heb. ix. 26-28). He who reads this wonderful life is to make the example and the sacrifice influential in his own life-pilgrimage, and to strive by faith to learn the full meaning of those words, which show CHRIST'S life repeated in every believing heart, " CHRIST in you, the hope of glory" (Col. i. 27).

Authority: Liddon's Bampton Lectures on " The Divinity of our Lord and Saviour Jesus Christ." REV. S. F. HOTCHKIN.

Jew. It was not known as a separate name till after the ten tribes revolted, and was not in current use till the tribal distinctions were lost at the Captivity and the Tribe of Judah overshadowed the others. It then became common, partly as this tribe was the largest and most powerful, and partly because of the Temple; and all the religious associations connected with it were, together with the Priesthood, within the territory of Judah. After the Captivity, Judæan (Jew) was the usual term for the Israelites of whatever descent. In the synoptic Gospels the terms are, the People, the Pharisees, Herodians, Sadducees, till the Passion of our LORD is recited. St. Matt. (ch. ii. 2) alone uses it elsewhere. But St. John uses it often, and distinguishes between the people, the Galileans, and the dwellers at Jerusalem. As a restored nation after the Captivity they were ruled first by the Persians (536-333 B.C.), by the Seleucidæ (333-167 B.C.), by their own Asmonæan Princes (167-63 B.C.), and by the Idumæan Herods (63 B.C.-70 A.D.), till the Temple was burnt, Jerusalem razed, millions slain or sold into captivity, and the remnant wanderers upon the earth. But their history of six hundred years had a great effect both upon them and upon the Christian Church, for the training in obedience to a holy law and a ritual, the lessons in faith, the fact forced upon them that the Spiritual Kingdom was separate from the temporal, all were impressed upon the early Christians who were cradled in the very midst of these teachings. The Christian owes the Jew a debt of love and compassion, and desires to bring him to the knowledge of the MESSIAH, a reunion which shall be the glory of the Jew and Gentile together (Rom. x., xi.).

Jewry. Of Judah. It occurs once in the Old Testament (Dan. v. 13), and once in the Prayer-Book (Ps. lxxvi. 1). In the Continental cities, and in Oxford, London, and elsewhere in England, the Jews' quarter was and is known as the Jewry.

Job. This book upon the man of Uz, recording his afflictions and his patience, is filled with some of the most magnificent thoughts and most sublime imagery ever given to men. The endless theories of adverse critics upon its genuineness and antiquity are so mutually destructive that they need no refutation. As Ezekiel (ch. xiv. 14, 20) and St. James (ch. v. 11) both refer to him as a real personage, surely we cannot doubt the truthfulness of the work. Job's riches, patriarchal influence, devout and noble character, are not merely proverbial. They stand forth as characteristics of the devout rich man. It is beyond the plan of this Cyclopædia to discuss the many questions its contents suggest upon the law of our trials and the extent of Satan's permitted power, upon the scope of the arguments of a natural theology so strongly stated in it, upon the knowledge Job had of a Redeemer and a Resurrection, and of the power of intercessional prayer, or upon the invisible and supernatural facts it reveals to us. His patience is proverbial, yet it is full of self-respect. He confesses humbly his sinfulness, and the justice of GOD towards him in this affliction. Yet he is conscious of no willful sin; and he defends himself against the insinuations or open attacks of his three friends. "Though He slay me yet will I trust in Him, but I will maintain mine own ways before Him" (ch. xiii. 15), well expresses the tone of his defense before the three friends. And his humility when GOD speaks displays his devout submission. His losses were doubly repaid when GOD restored him to his health. When so much is, at least at present, conjecture, the opinion that Moses either obtained a copy of the book or himself wrote down the narrative when he was in Midian is the most consonant with the style of the book, and that Job lived about the time of Joseph is most consonant with its contents. (*Vide* Smith's Dictionary of the Bible, and Canon Mozley's analysis of the book in the Christian Remembrancer of 1863 A.D.).

Joel. The second in the order of the minor prophets. He is called the son of Pethuel, but beyond this we know nothing of him. His prophetic work was in Judæa. It was the distress of a public calamity that seems to have given occasion to his prophecy, but only the occasion. Its scope is as vast as the judgments JEHOVAH has revealed. It uses the immediate event as a type for the greater events that lie in GOD'S future. The plague of the locusts is probably merely figurative, as the prophet uses it as the type of the terrible scourge of stern, disciplined armies passing through the land. His calls to repentance and to intercession and prayer are most sublime, and his promise of restoration and blessing and increase and the pouring out of the Spirit so gloriously fulfilled on the day of Pentecost, are full of spiritual beauty and force. But his prophecy passes swiftly farther than that great day, and under the type of the gathering of all people in the valley of Jehoshaphat he pictures the valley of this world, the time of the long-suffering and forbearance of GOD in this valley of decision, over which the day of the LORD hangs as a cloud either of mercy or of judgment. The world is ripe for the sickle of the angelic harvesters (Rev. xiv. 14–20), and then will come the Day of Judgment. The prophet closes with a picture of ineffable peace and joy and plenty. In his prophecy are the germ phrases for the revelations only outlined by him, but more fully given to other later prophets to develop. He uses the term "great and terrible day of the LORD," which means for us the Day of Judgment. The intercessions dictated by him have passed into our Litany. The ingathering of the Gentiles is implied by him (Joel ii. 32). His imagery is probably more freely used in the Apocalypse than that of any other single prophet. (*Vide* Smith's Bible Dictionary, The Speaker's Commentary, Pusey on Joel, in Minor Prophets.)

John, St. The beloved disciple, to whom the English-speaking people owe more than to any other of the Apostles, since from him they have received that Apostolic succession to which they appeal at once for their Apostolicity, Catholicity, and proper independence. The sons of Zebedee seem to have drawn more of their disposition from their mother Salome than from their father. John appears as a devout young man, energetic as his friend Simon, but better balanced, as fervent and as active. Doubtless the four, Simon and Andrew, James and John, had often spoken together of the hopes of Israel then filling every heart. He and Andrew knew the Baptist, though apparently not among his disciples, and were present with him when JESUS walked in Bethabara beyond Jordan, when St. John pointed Him out to them with the words, "Behold the Lamb of GOD" (St. John i. 35–39). They immediately followed JESUS, and abode with Him that night. Then began that love, that attachment to the Person of the LORD, which seems to distinguish St. John and St. Peter from the others. Zebedee did not hinder his sons from following the new Master. They were with Him as yet informally, yet as disciples in Jerusalem when He purged the Temple the first time, and at Cana when He manifested His glory and they were confirmed in their faith. When called, they left all and went with Him. Afterwards chosen into the band of Apostles, John and his brother James, with Simon, are taken more closely into our LORD'S confidence. It is noticeable that St. John in his Gospel does not speak of the band as Apostles, but as *Disciples*. Going in and out with Him, seeing His miracles, listening to His gracious words, wondering at His love, forbearance, patience, the disciples were trained for their future work. Yet, how dull they were! How slowly the truth, brought back to their memory, was afterwards understood! The character he developed, his zeal, his love, his readiness, all endeared him to his LORD. He was not devoid of ambition, as is shown by the request which the disciples, or their mother on their behalf, preferred to our LORD, to sit the one on the right hand, the other on the left, in His Kingdom. Our LORD at once questions: "Ye would have this; can ye pay its price? Are ye able to drink of the cup that I shall drink, and to be baptized with the baptism that I am baptized with? They say unto Him, We are able." His reply was afterwards fulfilled, when this baptism was of blood for the one and of long toil and martyrdom for the other.

The Apostle's zealous energy, that gained for him and his brother the appellation of "the Sons of Thunder," was shown in the request to punish the inhospitable Samaritans with fire, and in forbidding one who did a miracle in CHRIST'S name. With Simon and his brother James he was chosen to witness the Transfiguration, and was afterwards taken to watch at Gethsemane. Though after joining in the avowal of readiness to die with the Master he fled in the tumult of the arrest, yet he came back and gained an entrance with Simon Peter into the court-yard of the High-Priest's palace, and it would seem that his courage rose, for he followed to the Cross, and was with the Holy women as they stood by, and he received the charge of caring for the Virgin Mary from her Divine SON, and apparently was present at the taking down of the Sacred Body. He was first at the Sepulchre on the morning of the Resurrection, was present when the LORD appeared to the disciples that even, and afterwards was the first to recognize Him when He stood on the shore of the Sea of Tiberias and called to them. "Therefore that disciple whom JESUS loved saith unto Peter, It is the LORD!" Of him from the LORD'S words, "If I will that he tarry till I come," the report went out that he would not die. In the Acts we find him (ch. i.) after the Resurrection in the upper chamber with the little company of the faithful when St. Peter proposed that one should be selected to fill the place of the traitor Judas. He was a constant attendant upon the Temple worship, with St. Peter he was taken before the Sanhedrim, with St. Peter he is sent to confirm the Samaritans. Later he also, with St. James the LORD'S Brother, and St. Peter, welcomes Barnabas and Paul into the Apostolic fellowship. Where he labored during this time, whether in Jerusalem or elsewhere, we cannot know. He has no place in the record of the Acts when the Apostle whom he so cordially welcomed into the Apostolic brotherhood came forward. His Epistles, written before the Revelation, and the Gospel, written after it, are the precious legacy the SPIRIT has given us through him. From the Revelation we can gather only these facts : that he was banished to Patmos for the testimony of JESUS CHRIST. It has been conjectured with some truth that he had exercised Apostolic oversight over the seven Churches of Asia Minor to whom CHRIST sends His messages of warning and forbearing love. An early tradition says that upon the death of Domitian (97 A.D.) he was released from Patmos and went to Ephesus, where the Presbyters of that Church, since St. Timothy was dead, prayed him to take the oversight of it. There at their request he wrote the Fourth Gospel, and the last written of the books finally accepted as inspired. He must have attained a great age. The cup of sorrow, and of loneliness, of pain, because of the defection of those who should have proved faithful, because of the denial of the LORD, was his to drink to the dregs. Yet what solace was his! From the little company of one hundred and twenty names to so vast an ingathering! He who was wrapt in the horror of the great darkness of the Crucifixion was permitted to stand in the white light of the Presence of Presences. He who in sorrow had committed to him the care of the Virgin Mother of CHRIST, saw in joy the Church, the New Jerusalem, the Bride of CHRIST, descending from heaven.

His intense, energetic, enthusiastic love, fused every power and capacity into its own great heat, and made him use words that smote with their strength, that could brook nothing less than utter devotion to the Person of Him who so loved us, suffered for us, died a death of shame for us, and rose again for us. This love, strong and overbearing, makes St. John the Son of Thunder for the Church, in the writings he has left it.

His Feast is well placed (December 27) two days after the Nativity of his Master.

John, St., Gospel of. It has always till recently been claimed as the last written of the Canonical books of the New Testament, and has usually been placed after the Revelation, which was dated as about 95 A.D., making the date of the Gospel about 98 A.D. But recent conjectures make the banishment to Patmos earlier and under Nero, and place the writing of the Gospel between the destruction of Jerusalem, 72 A.D., and 95 A.D. This is not the place to enter into elaborate discussions, and while giving these later dates, it is well here to assign to the Gospel the latest date of 98 A.D. It is more generally admitted that it was written at the request of the Ephesian Presbyters. The destruction of Jerusalem, and so the severing of the direct tie that bound the Church to Judaism, the expansion of the work among the Gentiles, had made a restatement of the Apostolic teaching of JESUS CHRIST eminently proper. St. Paul's writings and the use of doctrinal terms had now paved the way for it,—e.g., the use of the word Logos (Word) as applied to our LORD'S eternal nature was growing (Heb. iv. 12; Tit. i. 3), the regeneration which St. Paul had taught (Tit. iii. 5), the Faith in the Person of the LORD, which the doctrine of the Justification by Faith had brought forward, these and the growing errors which might break into heresies within the Church and the heresies without, all demanded a final restatement of the Truth. These facts led the Apostle to compose the glorious Fourth Gospel. It has no statement which cannot be found in the germ in the other three, except the statements of the sixth chapter, but it expands some things and adds some facts not in the others, though it repeats but few of the incidents they record. The fibres that bind it to the other three are many and subtle, but they are no less real. There are sentences in the others that seem as if they were from St. John himself, while again many statements they make are found in his Gospel. A rapid analysis of his Gospel is annexed, but first it may be well to say a few words respecting the controversy about the genuineness of this the Fourth Gospel. It was not suspected at all till within the last century. A fierce attack has been made upon it from rationalistic writers, and it is to be feared from some who sought for notoriety more than for the truth. The objections are, that it comes into prominence only sixty years after the alleged date of its composition; that it contains allusions that are not compatible with the Apostolic age, and combats later heresies; that it is different in style from the other acknowledged Apostolic writings, that it belonged to a much later date, and every year from 116 to 150 A.D. has been assigned for the date of its composition. But the truth is that it is either quoted or alluded to in unmistakable ways by Ignatius. The early written, but not genuine Epistle of Barnabas, Justin Martyr, Polycarp, refers to the First Epistle, and as the Gospel is admitted to be from the same hand, the quotations establish the Gospel also. This catena of Christian doctors is strengthened by the use the heretic Basilides made of it. These all wrote between 107–150 A.D. Beyond the last date it is needless to go. But the internal evidence that it was written by an Apostle who companied with JESUS from the beginning is still clearer. He says at the outset "we beheld His glory" (ch. i. 14). The narrative differing in so many things from the Synoptic Gospels, implies an eye-witness, and this the writer claims to be. "This is the disciple who witnesseth concerning these things, and who wrote these things, and we know his writing is true" (xxi. 24). "He that hath seen hath borne witness, and his writing is true" (xix. 35). None but an eye-witness could have given such life-like descriptions or reported discourses as that of the sixth chapter. He was an Apostle, for he is intrusted with the motives and wishes of his Master,—e.g., xiii. 1-2; xix. 27–28.

That it combats later errors is no more than what all the Gospels are now doing and will do so long as error exists. Who is it that has not noted with apparent surprise that a single word written eighteen centuries ago seems to have its full force only now, and with reference to some current modern error?

But too imperfect as this outline is, it is needless to go further into a controversy which only serves to bring out still more clearly the wonderful truth of this Fourth Gospel. The plan of the Gospel is clear, distinct, and straightforward; the main outlines (Cambridge Bible for Schools, vol. on St. John) may be given somewhat thus:

I. *The Prologue* (i. 1–18).—1, The Word in His own nature (1–5); 2, His Revelation to men and rejection by them (6–18); 3, His Revelation of the FATHER (14–18).

II. *First Main Division, Christ's Ministry, or His Revelation of Himself to the World* (i. 19; xii. 50).—(*a*) The Testimony. 1, of John the Baptist (i. 19–37); 2, of the Disciples (38–51); 3, of the first sign (ii. 1–11). (*b*) The Work. 1, among the Jews (ii. 13; iii. 36); 2, among the Samaritans (iv. 1–42); 3, among the Galileans (iv. 43–54); (the work has become a conflict) 4, among mixed multitudes (v.–xi.). (*c*) The Judgment. 1, of men (xii. 1–36); 2, of the Evangelist (37–43); 3, of CHRIST (44–50); close of CHRIST's public ministry.

III. *Second Main Division, Issues of Christ's Ministry, or His Revelation of Himself to His Disciples.*—(*d*) The inner Glorification in His last Discourses. 1, His love in Humiliation (xiiii. 1–30); 2, His love to His own (xiii. 31; xv. 27); 3, the promise of the Comforter and of His return (xvi.). (*e*) The outer Glorification of His Passion. 1, the betrayal (xvii. 1–11); 2, the ecclesiastical and civil trials (xviii. 12; xix. 16); 3, the crucifixion and burial (xix. 17–42). (*f*) The Resurrection. 1, The manifestation to Mary Magdalene (xx. 1–18); 2, the manifestation to the Ten (xx. 19–23); 3, the manifestation to Thomas with the Ten (xx. 24–29); 4, the Conclusion (xx. 30–31).

IV. *The Epilogue or Appendix.*

There is no one of the other Gospels which is so rich in spiritual insight. All the Evangelists have this more or less, but none so fully, for neither of the other three had that ripe experience, that conviction from long trial, that thorough habit of spiritual apprehension that characterizes St. John's writing. It was a glorious gift, and lightly purchased by the cross he had to bear after his Master, and he has transmitted it to us. To a mind so richly stored with deep knowledge both of the things of CHRIST and of men's character, and so filled with the HOLY SPIRIT and with love, there was no difficulty in selecting those things which should meet the needs of men, and comfort and strengthen their minds for all time to come.

Epistles of.—The three Epistles, together with those of St. Peter, St. James, and St. Jude, are called the Catholic Epistles, since they are not addressed to any one Church by name, but are, as it were, universal, catholic, in their use and purpose. But in these Epistles which were written by the Holy Apostle we find combined the same characteristics which gave him both the surname of the Son of Thunder and the far gentler title of the Disciple whom JESUS loved. There is the same energy and zeal and sternness, an uncompromising trait, yet there is throughout a tenderness and an outpouring of love. It would seem at first sight that these are incompatible, but if we consider the Person on whom his love was poured, and the deep reality of the consequences of either loving or hating that Person, which he felt in all their intensity, and know that his whole Epistles are but a comment upon St. Paul's passionate utterance, "If any man love not the Lord JESUS CHRIST let him be anathema," we can see that they are not merely compatible, but they are the proper and true outcome of such a strong nature as we have seen St. John to have possessed. The evils which pressed upon the Church at the time he wrote, the solitariness of the Apostle, the need for a strong, positive proclamation of the love of GOD, and that it was not a sentiment, but a law of life or of death to men; the pain of seeing those in the Church worldly, of seeing those who misunderstood and perverted the truth leaving it, to their own destruction, branding themselves as anti-CHRISTS,—all these things enter into the Epistle which the HOLY SPIRIT moved the Apostle to write. Its contents may be summarized thus: (A) A declaration of our LORD'S Incarnation as the Word of Life, of whose real human subsistence the Apostle solemnly affirms, and the claim that those who would share in the gift of Life eternal must be in the Apostolic fellowship, which is bound up in the FATHER and the SON, in which fellowship lies the forgiveness of sin, by the blood of JESUS CHRIST, who is our Advocate and the Propitiation for our sins (ch. i.-ii. 3). (B) This forgiveness from Him claims our love, but our love to HIM implies love to our brother and a renunciation of the world (ch. ii. 4, vs. 20). (C) A second positive statement of the Sonship of CHRIST follows, with a further reference to the gift (anointing) of the HOLY GHOST in Confirmation (ch. ii. 20-29). (D) A magnificent appeal, based upon GOD'S love to us and our hope of a resurrection by our union in His SON, to love one another, and to put away all hatred, and to show all compassion (ch. iii.). (E) Chapter iv. implies some partial withdrawal of the gift of prophecy, as the Church needed it less, but it was not the less influential and pronounced in power whenever given and used to proclaim the Sonship of our LORD. Again the Apostle reverts to the topic of brotherly love, which he mingles with short, clear enunciations of doctrine. And as his Epistle draws to an end he puts forward again the absolute need of unity with Him. "Little children, keep yourselves from idols. Amen. And we know that the SON of GOD is come, and hath given us an understanding that we may know Him that is true, and we are in Him that is true, even in His SON, JESUS CHRIST. This is the true GOD and Eternal Life." So ends the first Epistle of the greatest Apostle of the original Twelve.

The second Epistle has been doubted, but its contents are so similar to those of the first, in fact principally restatements, in so concise a form that no forger would care to give himself so much risk for so little result, and the tone of the letter is unmistakably that of St. John. Who the elect lady was, whether a phrase for the Church or some influential lady within St. John's jurisdiction, has been questioned, but the personal allusions make this latter supposition the only really tenable one; her children are spoken of in the first verse and her sister's children in the last verse. The subject of the Epistle is a restatement of the main topic of the first Epistle, the doctrine of CHRIST come in the flesh and a warning against deceivers.

The third Epistle, though much the shortest, has one or two points of great interest in it. It is written to Gaius, whose hospitality and zeal he commends. But he then speaks of a certain Diotrephes who rejected his authority and would not receive those whom St. John sent, but cast them out. St. John threatens to discipline him. The Apostle also commends Demetrius as bearing a good report from all men. Who was Diotrephes? It has been generally assumed that it was some turbulent Presbyter who rejected St. John's authority. But one in that order would scarcely have dared to do so. Nor would any attention have been paid to him had he held only that office, while one in the Apostolic office holding the same relation to St. John that St. Timothy, or Titus, or Silas did to St. Paul, might endeavor to shake off the inconvenient restraint St. John held over his ambition. This is much more likely than that an Elder would act in so authoritative a manner as to reject those whom St. John had sent, and discipline those fellow-Presbyters who would receive them, since he would be in no position to do so, nor could he criticise and speak maliciously of St. John. Altogether it would seem that Diotrephes held a higher office, and one in which it needed St. John's presence as his sole superior to restrain and chastise him. In this letter to Gaius he reiterates some of his positive sentences found in the first Epistle.

Jonah, though the sixth in order of the Minor Prophets, is generally considered the earliest of all the prophets, whose writings are extant. The reason for this opinion is based on 2 Kings xiv. 25, where it is stated that Jeroboam II. "restored the coast of Israel from the entering of Hamath unto the sea of the plain, according to the word of the LORD, which He spake by the hand of his servant Jonah the son of Amittai, which was of Gath-Hepher." Now Jeroboam began to reign 825 B.C., and on the supposition that Jonah made the prophecy some time before his accession, the prophet's date is fixed about the middle of the ninth century B.C., or as given in the Bible, 862 B.C.; but Canon Rawlinson prefers a later date. (*Vide* Five Great Monarchies.) As already stated, Jonah was the son of Amittai, of Gath-Hepher in Galilee, from which, therefore, a prophet did arise contrary to the proverb of the Pharisees. His personal history is entirely drawn from the Book of Jonah, which is an account of his mission to Nineveh. It was perhaps after prophesying to Israel (for Jonah begins in the Hebrew with "and the word of the LORD," etc.) that the prophet was bidden to go to Nineveh and prophesy against it. But Jonah shrank from the task, probably from timidity (for Jonah means *a dove*), though other motives are suggested, such as a desire that Nineveh might be destroyed in the interest of Israel. So he sought to flee from the presence of the LORD,—*i.e.*, from discharging this mission before the LORD,—and he took ship at Joppa, now Jaffa, for Tarshish, which may have been Tarsus in Cilicia, or Tartessus in Spain. This attempt to escape duty proved of no avail, for such a storm arose as to imperil the ship; and when lots were cast to see who was the guilty cause of it, the lot fell upon

Jonah, who bade the mariners cast him into the sea, "For I know that for my sake this tempest is upon you." The men being unwilling to do it, strove hard to row to land, from which it should appear that they could not have gone far from port. "But they could not, so they took up Jonah and cast him forth into the sea, and the sea ceased from raging." But the LORD had prepared a great fish to swallow up Jonah; and Jonah was in the belly of the fish three days and three nights. To this miracle great objection has been made, and some have affirmed that the book of Jonah is merely allegorical, others that it is purely fabulous, or a little history highly ornamented with fable. Of course, with those who deny the possibility of miracles at all, there can be no discussion; but others who find a difficulty in believing this experience of Jonah, should observe that one miracle is as easy to accept as any other, and that there is especial reason for believing this particular one, because it was a type of our LORD'S entombment and resurrection, and referred to by Him as such; and those who believe the greater miracle of the Resurrection cannot object reasonably to the lesser one which foreshadowed it.

These difficulties on the ground of natural history are sufficiently met by the fact that there *are* fish large enough to swallow a man whole, though it may be a mistake to call such fish whales, as the translators have in St. Matt. xii. 40; it is simply a great fish in Jonah. At the end of the three days Jonah repented and humbled himself before GOD, and "the Lord spake unto the fish, and it vomited out Jonah upon the dry land." When the command to preach unto Nineveh came a second time it was obeyed, and Jonah came to Nineveh, an exceeding great city of three days' journey, and began to enter into the city a day's journey, and cried and said, "Yet forty days and Nineveh shall be overthrown." However these expressions of the day's journey be understood, they indicate a place of immense extent, and these indications are fully corroborated by modern explorations and discoveries. (*Vide* Five Great Monarchies.) Word of this strange message came to the king, who proclaimed a strict fast even for beast as well as man, and ordered intercessions, in the hope that GOD would repent and turn away from His fierce anger; and so it came about, for GOD saw their works and deferred the evil threatened to them. Now Jonah had already withdrawn from the city to watch and see what would become of it, and when the forty days were expired and the city was not destroyed, it displeased him exceedingly that his prophecy was not fulfilled, and he wished that he might die; but the LORD condescended to reason with him, in words and by the parable of a gourd (Palma Christi), which grew up suddenly and was a comfort to the prophet by reason of its shade and pleasing form. But no sooner had Jonah realized its worth to him than it was destroyed by a worm, and again he wished he might die. Then the LORD said to Jonah, "Doest thou well to be angry for the gourd? And he said, I do well to be angry, even unto death. Then said the LORD, Thou hast had pity on the gourd, for the which thou hast not labored, neither madest it grow; which came up in a night, and perished in a night; and should not I spare Nineveh, that great city, wherein are more than sixscore thousand persons that cannot discern between their right hand and their left hand; and also much cattle?" Here the book of Jonah ends. It may be that some fail to see in what respect Jonah is a prophet of any but near events, whose interest ended with their fulfillment; but such persons may learn to find a deeper meaning in the book if they will observe that its subject is not so much the mission to Nineveh as the spiritual instruction of Jonah—and the world,—that in every nation he that feareth GOD and worketh righteousness is accepted by Him, and that GOD has a tender compassionate care for every man, whether he be a King of Nineveh or a Phœnician sailor.

Further, the book, as already stated, is a prophecy by types of the death, burial, and resurrection of our LORD, as is shown not only by our LORD Himself in His references to it (St. Matt. xii. 40; xvi. 4; St. Luke xi. 30; xxiv. 46), but also by St. Paul, whose allusion in 1 Cor. xv. 4, is understood to mean the Book of Jonah.

Authorities: Smith's Bible Dictionary, Five Ancient Monarchies, Gray's Introduction, Bible Commentary.

Joseph I. The oldest son of Rachel, the well-loved wife of Jacob. The history of his life is one of the most beautiful passages in the book of Genesis. It is stamped with a naturalness and an inwoven truthfulness that make the objections to it appear as they are, pitiful and but the merest wantonness of hypercriticism. His father's love for him, his own gentle goodness, yet the vanity which was the result of Jacob's treatment; the rough turbulence of shepherd sons, his elder brethren, who lived a hardy, roving, out-of-door life, filled with free, undisciplined willfulnesses; the jealousies that arose, which were the scourge of Jacob's own former deceit; the robe, probably a white tunic embroidered or edged with purple, the gift of a father's love, and the petty cause of hatred; the dreams of the boy and the wonder and hatred they elicited; the cruel sale, the career in Egypt, —all these, so well known, are chiefly dwelt upon as links in the Providential preparations made for the preservation of the chosen people. But while this is true, there is something more. The patriarch was chosen, in and by the very means that his brethren sought to destroy him, to become the deliverer of Egypt for the sake of his father's house, and so to aid in further and larger political events which flowed to all the world from his conduct and statesmanship. Remembering these things, to the Christian his career is a type of CHRIST in its outlines. As was remarked in the article on Jonah, we must carefully separate the human channels from the Divine purpose that flows through them, the human earthiness from the divine gold mingled in it. Jacob's love for Joseph is a type of GOD'S love for His SON. The sale of Joseph for the price of a slave typified the sale of the LORD for the same price. His courage, obedience, and his disgrace while yet finding favor in the eyes of his enemies, are a type of the far lovelier character of CHRIST. His deliverance and his Lordship, and the provision he thus made, both for Egypt and for his father's house, is a type of both the Resurrection and the untiring, loving care of CHRIST over all men, willing that none should be lost, and providing still better things for the household of faith. These are salient points in his life that make him an especial type, but a close study of the incidents will develop other and beautiful suggestions. His coat of many colors the royal robe, the type of the robe of righteousness. His prospering in all things committed to his care as steward. His resisting evil suggestions, the patience with which he bore the discipline (Heb. v. 7-9), and other points of resemblance which would lead us too far afield to trace here. In these, and in the blessings which were bestowed upon him by his father and upon his two sons, and later upon the ten thousands of Ephraim and the thousands of Manasseh, he is pre-eminently a type of JESUS the CHRIST. His history is recorded in Gen. xxx. 22-24; xxxvii., xxxix. to the end of the book. The blessing of Moses upon the two half-tribes, Ephraim and Manasseh (Deut. xxxiii. 13-17). For a full discussion of the history see Geike's Hours with the Bible, and Smith's Bible Dictionary. The date of Joseph's birth is placed there at 1906 B.C. Since the date of the Pharaoh of Joseph's famine cannot be certainly identified as yet, this is the approximate date.

Joseph II. The husband of the Blessed Virgin Mary, who was most probably of the family of Nathan, the son of David. But little is told us of him. A just man, of the house and lineage of David, and thoughtful and kind. He lived in Nazareth, a carpenter by occupation, betrothed to the Virgin, probably his cousin, and whom, upon the direction of the Angel, he took to wife. He carried the Virgin Mary to Bethlehem, there to be enrolled with himself as of the royal house of David, where her son was born. He carried the mother and the young child into the Temple, was present when the wise men offered their homage; he fled to Egypt, and remained there until he was divinely bidden to return, and finally settled in Nazareth, where he continued to care for the wondrous child growing up into a favored, loved youth. When JESUS was twelve years old, Joseph and Mary took Him up to the Temple to keep the Passover, and when they returned to Nazareth, the Child continued to be obedient to His parents, increasing in wisdom and stature, and in favor with GOD and man. Here our knowledge of him ends, for there is no further record of him in the Gospel history.

Joshua. The Son of Nun, one of Israel's great generals. He appears first most suddenly at the battle of Rephidim: "And Moses said unto Joshua, Choose us out men, and go out, fight with Amalek" (Ex. xvii. 9). In 1 Chron. vii. 27 his descent from Ephraim is given, giving thus some ground for the blessing Moses put upon the tribes of Joseph: "His glory the firstling of his bullocks, and his horns the horns of unicorns; with them he shall push the people together to the end of the land,"—*i.e.*, Canaan (Deut. xxxiii. 17). Joshua's instincts are military. The attendant upon Moses what time the Leader went up into the cloudy top of Sinai, when Moses came down at GOD'S bidding to quell the apostasy of Israel, Joshua, as they turned to go down to the riotous people, exclaimed, "There is a noise of war in the camp!" He is annoyed at the irregularity of Eldad and Medad's prophesying in the camp unbidden. Apparently it seemed to him a breach of discipline,—an act without proper commission. Next he appears as one of the spies who traversed the promised land. Of all the band he and Caleb alone insisted that the people could take possession of the land at once. He drops out of mention till Moses is ready to lay down his burdensome charge. Most probably he resumed that attendance upon the tabernacle which apparently fell to him when the tabernacle was first erected (Ex. xxxiii. 11). But upon the plain of Moab, this side Jordan, he has the commission given him to lead the people over the river to take possession of the Land, by the laying on of Moses' hands, before Eleazar the priest and the whole congregation, and by a special charge (Numb. xxvii. 14; Deut. xxxi. 14, 23). After Moses' death Joshua sent out spies to Jericho, crossed the Jordan, and at Gilgal circumcised all the males; and had a vision of the Captain of the LORD'S Host. Jericho fell by a miracle; Ai was taken after Achan's sin had been purged; the Law was recited upon Mount Ebal; the treaty was heedlessly made with the Gibeonites; the victory at Makkedah, won by Divine aid, opened Canaan up to Kadesh-Barnea and Gaza; that at the waters of Merom broke the Canaanitish kingdoms of the north under Jabin, King of Hazor. "So Joshua took all that land, the hills, and all the south country, and all the land of Goshen, and the valley, and the plain, and the mountain of

Israel, and the valley of the same; even from the Mount Halak, that goeth up to Seir, even unto Baal-gad in the valley of Lebanon, under Mount Hermon: and all their kings he took, and smote them and slew them. Joshua made war long time with all those kings" (Josh. xi. 16–18). In six years he broke the power of the Canaanite, destroyed the Anakim, and established Israel firmly in the territory which GOD gave them; but he did not utterly dispossess them. It was expressly ordered that they should not be utterly destroyed; though against some, as against Amalek, the decree of extermination was finally carried out. There is no space here to point out the strategy and skillful planning of Joshua, which was the more noticeable that the composition of the army he led must have made any combined operations nearly impossible. Fearless, straightforward, enthused by his grand mission, noble and kindly, his was indeed a royal nature, born to lead and to command. Devout and unselfish, for he was trained by Moses, he showed the strength of the Israelitish character at its best. His book, which records his campaigns and the division of the land by lot to the tribes, was written either by himself or by an eye-witness in close relation to him. In the account of the division, when we remember that land was allotted to the several tribes which had not yet been fairly conquered and occupied, many alleged discrepancies will disappear. For instance, in chapter xiii. 3, it is stated that Ekron was yet to be taken; but in chapter xv. 45, it is assigned to Judah. Ekron was in the limits of the lot which fell to Judah, but Ekron was in the hands of the Philistines except for the period of the Judges; so of Gaza and Askelon, which remained finally as Philistine cities. Joshua's history is a clear, terse account of GOD'S dealings in behalf of His people by the hand of Joshua, in fulfilling His promise to Abraham regarding the land. It falls into three sections: I. The Conquest. II. The Division. III. The Charge and Warning of the aged, war-worn Captain. There is not sufficient proof of it, but the indirect evidence goes to show that Joshua himself wrote the book. Not only Jewish tradition, but the minute notes of the transactions, the words of conversations, the phrases, point to Joshua's pen. Of course the closing paragraphs were added by another, probably contemporary, pen. But we must add the main points in which he was a type of JESUS. As Moses was His type as Lawgiver, so in name and in act Joshua was the type of JESUS the Captain of our salvation. Joshua began his life in Egypt, and, despite his protest to the people, wandered with them in the wilderness; so CHRIST our JESUS was with us in our Egypt of sin, and has borne with us in our life here. At Jordan Joshua crossed over; at the same stream JESUS was baptized and received His consecration for His work. At Gilgal Joshua rolled away the reproach of Egypt from the people; at Golgotha JESUS rolled away the reproach of the spiritual Egypt from His people. Joshua, by command of the Captain of the LORD'S host, began his work; but the Captain Himself has begun the conquest for us. Joshua mastered Canaan, and gave all its strategic points and many of its strongholds into the people's hands, and broke the Canaanitish power and exterminated the vilest of the nations; so JESUS hath spoiled the strong man, and bound him, and given us his high places, but hath left to us to complete the conquest under His care by His might, with the armor He has furnished. And as Joshua at the first gathering of the people, so JESUS before His Passion; and as Joshua at Shechem at the second gathering, so JESUS after His Resurrection gave a solemn charge, and renewed the Covenant, and left a witness of it.

Jubilate. The anthem after the second lesson. It was adopted in the Prayer-Book of 1552 A.D., but is said to have been in use after the Gospel in some Gallican Churches as early as 450 A.D. It is a joyful anthem of praise to the Good Shepherd. Its continuous use should fall during the Sundays after Trinity.

Jubilee. The year of release, the fiftieth year, in which all lands by the Mosaic law reverted to their original owners, or their heirs. All debts were released, all Hebrew servants sold for debt were set free, unless they chose to remain in bondage. It was a placing upon a common footing, so far as it was possible in their original condition, all the relations of property and its dependencies. This idea of the Jubilee was taken up in mediæval times, and a general indulgence and release ordered by the Pope, and certain privileges granted to those who made pilgrimages, especially to Rome and its holy places.

Jude, or Judas. There were four who bore this name,—Judas, Judas Iscariot, Judas, surnamed Barsabas, who went with Silas to bear the Encyclical letter to Antioch together with St. Paul and Barnabas, and Jude the brother of James. The name Jude or Judas occurs beside as borne by others, but they are not at all prominent.

Jude, St., who wrote the Epistle. It is difficult in the clash of contending views to arrive at any definite conclusion as to whether the Jude the brother of James was the Jude who was the Apostle, or the Jude the LORD'S brother. This last is the most probable conjecture, though it is not without difficulties. If so, then there were but three Judes. Of this Jude we know nothing. Eusebius says that his two grandsons were seized by Domitian's orders and carried to Rome and examined. But when he saw that they were poor laboring illiterate men, and listened to their description of the spiritual kingdom of JESUS the King of the Jews, Domitian dismissed them with contempt, and stopped the persecution of the

Church. They were sent home to Jerusalem, and there were influential as being of the LORD's family and confessors.

Jude, St., Epistle of. It was held as one of the doubtful Epistles, not that it was a forgery, but, since it was so brief and as its contents were found elsewhere, it was questioned whether its author was of weight enough to have it placed in the Canon. As it came more into circulation this objection disappeared, and it was received into the Canon. It is in style so like the second Epistle of St. Peter that it is a question which was the earlier of the two. For the later writer was acquainted with the earlier work and used it with some freedom. If so, it is more likely that the shorter Epistle would be the earlier, as it was more probable that it would be incorporated into a longer one than that the shorter would be excerpted out of the longer, and, too, the difficult phrases in the Epistle of St. Jude would be eliminated from St. Peter's Epistle. It contains a couple of references found nowhere else: "Yet Michael the Archangel, when contending with the devil he disputed about the body of Moses, durst not bring against him a railing accusation, but said, The LORD rebuke thee," a quotation which has not been traced. "And Enoch also, the seventh from Adam, prophesied of these, saying, Behold, the LORD cometh with ten thousands of His Saints to execute judgment upon all, and to convince all that are ungodly among them of all their ungodly deeds which they have ungodly committed, and of all their hard speeches which ungodly sources have spoken against Him," a translation from the Apocryphal Book of Enoch, which had been written about 40 B.C. The Epistle of St. Jude is characterized by warmth and energy: The purity of the Faith once delivered to the saints is earnestly defended, and its corrupters are denounced with vehemence in one of the shortest of all the writings in the sacred Canon. The zeal of St. Jude in behalf of the Faith has left us a tracing of the trials and the discipline which the Church then as now had to undergo. The kinsman of the LORD JESUS, the brother of James, himself not of the original Twelve (vide v. 17), could not but be zealous, and this zeal was reflected in the later Epistle of St. Peter (2 Peter).

Judges. From the conquest of Canaan by Joshua to the Judgeship of Samuel were three hundred and fifty years. During this long period the record of the book of Judges is filled with the fragmentary details of the confusion, disobedience, and scourgings of the people. Throughout the greatest disturbances and under the sternest tyrants who subjugated them, they neither lost their nationality nor were they driven out, nor with all their departure from the Law did they lose their knowledge of JEHOVAH. He did not wholly forsake them, but bore with them while disciplining them severely. The books of Joshua and Judges, the one as it were the counterpart of the other in the Israelitish history, would correspond to the position of the Acts in the New Testament. It is divided into three parts: The introduction (i.-iii. 7). The condition of Israel under Joshua. The era of the Judges (iii. 8; xvi.). Incidents detailing the moral and social ills of the time (xvii.-xxi.). It is difficult to compress into a few paragraphs the discussions of events that have so much bearing upon Israel's future history. All that we can do here is to point out the faith, i.e., full trust in GOD, the Judges severally showed. Their personal shortcomings of duty and the deliverances they wrought would require too much space. The introduction is occupied with recording the prosecution of the conquest after Joshua's death; Caleb's capture of the possession assigned him; the sloth of the other tribes compared with the activity of Judah and Simeon; the intermarriages which led to idolatry, and then the mysterious visit of the Angel of the LORD at Bochim, and their temporary repentance; lastly, their lapse into such evil that they were given into the hand of Cushan-rishathaim. The era of the Judges is parted into four groups: The deliverances and judgeships of Othniel (forty years), of Ehud (after eighteen years' oppression by the Moabites, for eighty years), of Deborah's deliverance (of forty years after Jabin's oppression of twenty years). Then follows the era of Gideon and his son Abimelech, whose resistance to Midian, after seven years' servitude, reached to forty-three years. Then as a transition group come Tola and Jair, who judged and defended Israel, the first twenty-three and the second twenty-two years.

The third group are, after eighteen years under the Ammonites, the Judges, Jepthah, Ibzan, Elon, and Abdon, a period of thirty-one years. Lastly comes Samson, whose wonderful birth, preparation, work, and fate are the most remarkable of all the histories in the book; he judged Israel twenty years. The story of the Benjaminites and their terrible punishment is to be placed as occurring just after Joshua's death (ch. xx. 28), and the story of Micah and the Danites is probably but little later, perhaps before the first oppression by Cushan-rishathaim. Various theories have been held as to the writer of the book. It is most likely that it was drawn up from documents which were put together before Samuel's time, and that the last part was added in David's time. But it is mere conjecture. Nathan and Gad both composed histories, and if this were by either one of these prophets, we would have the date of the work in David's reign. This, however, does not affect either the inspiration of the writer or the true place of the book in the Canon of Scripture. It is recorded for our learning, that we may see the result of religious disunity. Their service of JEHOVAH was the national bond of Israel, and whenever that was broken, every man did as seemed good in his eyes; each fell in with the superstitions of the

Canaanitish communities about them, intermarried, forgot their national obligations, and were given over into the hand of successive oppressors. It is notable that each oppressor whose yoke was thrown off never renewed it. So first the Mesopotamian king, then Moab, then Jabin, then the Midianites, then the Philistines, whose power was shaken by the last slaughter by Samson. Some of these people fought with and successfully invaded Israel again and again, as did the Philistines and Moabites, but not in the sense of the oppressions during the eras of the Judges. Of all the Judges Samson was the leading type of CHRIST in many remarkable points, but for this we must refer to the article on Samson.

Judgment-Day. The doctrine of a judgment after death has always been associated with the idea of man's immortality. It is maintained on the ground of responsibility, and on the absence of a due proportion of rewards and punishments in human actions in this life. The ancient Egyptians passed judgment on the acts of men after their death. In Holy Scripture earthly judgments forecast future ones (Eccl. xi. 9; Heb. ix. 27; Joel iii. 1, etc.; Amos v. 18, etc.; Isa. iii. 14, xxxiv. 1, lxvi. 15, and Dan. vii. 22). They explicitly declare that there will be a Day of Judgment, when, in great solemnity, before the universe, the LORD JESUS CHRIST is to appear in glory as Judge at the resurrection of the dead, when they that have done good shall be partakers of the resurrection of life, and they that have done evil of the resurrection of damnation (St. John v. 21–29; 1 Cor. xv. 22; Rev. xx. 11; St. John vi. 39, 40; xi. 24; 1 Thess. iv. 15). It is declared that the Judgment-Day shall be ushered in by the sound of a trumpet, as the Jewish assemblies were called together. This trump of GOD shall resound through the earth and call all men before His throne (1 Cor. xv. 52, and 1 Thess. iv. 16). (See Ebrard in Schaff-Herzog's Encyclopædia, and Chambers's Library of Universal Knowledge.)

Bishop Pearson, in his work on the Creed, thus expresses the necessity of a future judgment: "Nothing more certain than that in this life rewards are not correspondent to the virtues, punishment not proportionable to the sins, of men. Which consideration will enforce one of these conclusions,—either that there is no judge of the actions of mankind, or if there be a judge, and that judge be just, then there is a judgment in another world, and the effects thereof concern another life. Being, then, we must acknowledge that there is a judge, which judgeth the earth; being we cannot deny but GOD is that judge, and all must confess that GOD is most just; being the rewards and punishments of this life are no way answerable to so exact a justice as that which is divine must be; it followeth that there is a judgment yet to come, in which GOD will show a perfect demonstration of His justice, and to which every man shall in his own bosom carry an undeniable witness of all his actions." So the Church teaches the worshiper to say in the Creed of CHRIST, "From thence He shall come to judge the quick and the dead." The feeling with which men look forward to that judgment is shown in that old Latin hymn, "Dies Iræ." Theodoret observes, that if the loud sound of the trumpet at the giving of the law from Sinai was so dreadful to the Jews that they said to Moses, "Let not the LORD speak to us lest we die," how terrible must the sound be of the trumpet which calls all men to final judgment! De Quincey refers to a person in danger of death seeing "in a moment her whole life in its minutest incidents arrayed before her simultaneously, as in a mirror," and applies the thought to the judgment, saying that things are never forgotten, but disappear like stars. Rev. Dr. H. C. McCook likens the records of the heart to things written with invisible ink, which may be brought out by holding the paper to the fire.

Our Blessed LORD constantly kept the thought of a final judgment before His hearers, and showed the happiness and the misery of a future life of endless duration. The parables continually teach this lesson. See "The Unjust Steward" (St. Luke xvi. 1), "The Marriage of the King's Son" (St. Matt. xxii. 13), with joy within and darkness without, "The Vineyard, with the destruction of the rebels" (St. Matt. xx. 16), "The Wheat and the Tares" (St. Matt. xiii. 42), with the "furnace of fire" to destroy the wicked, while the righteous shine forth as the sun in the Kingdom of GOD. In the same chapter the parable of the Net teaches the same lesson of the "wailing" of the wicked. But the angels, and not men, are to separate the good and bad. "Judge nothing before the time" (1 Cor. iv. 5) is the command for the present life. While the wicked receive punishment the righteous are rewarded. It is declared by CHRIST Himself that the cup of cold water shall not be forgotten by GOD, and that he who feasts the poor, the maimed, the lame, and the blind shall be recompensed at the resurrection of the just (St. Luke xiv. 13, 14). He who neglected the Christian teaching was left in a worse condition than the inhabitants of Sodom and Gomorrah as regarded the Day of Judgment (St. Matt. x. 15). If the Apostles shook off the dust of their feet in leaving a neglectful house or city, they were in danger of perdition. While our LORD came not to judge the world, premonitions of His final work are shown in His woes uttered against the Scribes and Pharisees (St. Matt. xxiii. 13–39). What a foretaste of the last day in verse 33!—"Ye serpents, ye generation of vipers, how can ye escape the damnation of hell?" The judgments of Cain and of Pharaoh in the Old Testament and of Judas Iscariot and Ananias and Sapphira in the New are of the final work of judgment.

"If such was the splendor of His appearance then, and such its effects, what will they be when He comes hereafter in His glorious Majesty to judge the quick and dead?" (Bishop Wordsworth on Acts xxvi. 13.)

"Hannibal is said, after the subjection of Carthage by Rome, to have walked through the city, and as he saw the tears, and heard the wailing of the people who groaned under the terrible burden imposed upon them by the conquerors, to have laughed. Then, when his fellow-citizens rose up against him in indignation, he replied, 'I laugh not from joy to see your bondage, but I laugh at your tears, now too late, now in vain; for had you in proper time fought as men, now you would not be weeping as women.'" (S. Baring Gould's Post-Mediæval Preachers.)

REV. S. F. HOTCHKIN.

Jurisdiction. The sphere of law, whether spiritual, temporal, or territorial, and the limits under which the executive of the law can act. Thus a Bishop has jurisdiction territorially over his Diocese, and spiritually in the Church, holding a common authority with his brethren in the sphere of his duty and office. The LORD gave the Apostles jurisdiction. "All power is given unto me in heaven and in earth. . . . Go ye, therefore" (St. Matt. xxviii. 18, 19). This is the conjoint jurisdiction, but as local order demands that there should be a subdivision, diocesan divisions followed, and an assignment of territorial authority. This led to Churches in the several parts of the civilized world, and to the principle of Sees. The temporal jurisdiction is the Patriarchal. Temporal, for it is the result of the needs of the time, and is only so far territorial as the Patriarch is limited by the bounds of his Province, but is not so as using a mere local authority belonging to the Bishops of the Dioceses in the Province, and his jurisdiction is disciplinary and appellative. There are, then, for the Episcopal jurisdiction three forms historically: I. The Apostolic mission of CHRIST. II. The diocesan distribution for the sake of order, work, and development. III. The Provincial or Patriarchal jurisdiction for the sake of discipline and unification of Church work. But under this of the Apostolic there is also the priestly jurisdiction committed by the Bishop to the Priest as rector or pastor in the parish to be "Messengers, watchmen, and stewards of the LORD, to teach and to premonish, to feed and provide for the LORD'S family, to seek for CHRIST'S sheep that are dispersed abroad, and for His children who are in the midst of this naughty world, that they may be saved through CHRIST forever." This subordinate jurisdiction definitely committed to the Priest by the words of ordination (vide Ordering of Priests in the Prayer-Book) is the most important in the Diocese under the Bishop, and should be clearly understood both in its responsibilities and in its limitations, since the layman's covenant relation to GOD is made through the agency of the Priest in and by the Sacraments. Its responsibilities are well set forth in the charge given to the candidate for that holy order as set forth in the office. It is wholly subordinate to the Bishop, and its holder is properly the Bishop's representative, performing for him the functions committed to that order. Its limitations, then, are first in the nature of a limited agency having defined duties to discharge, and in the bounds set by the Canons, and by the conditions of the cure which he is to discharge, and by the canonical limits of the parochial work he is to do.

Justification. Much needless confusion has been imported into the definitions upon this most wholesome and comfortable doctrine. Luther, who brought the doctrine into prominence during the controversies of the Reformation, did much towards confirming it by his vehement assertions, which savor of a solifidianism that he would have repudiated. Again, terms which only partly state the doctrine have been introduced and sharply debated, such as forensic justification and inherent righteousness. And the words righteousness and justification represent the same Greek word, and are in some degree interchangeable, but as "justification" and "to justify" refer to GOD'S acts to us, restoring us, there has necessarily been added a further meaning to the word. This is not so much an addition to, as it is an extension of, its meaning, if we can so speak of a word which denoting GOD'S perfect righteousness descends also to imply His righteousness in us upon our forgiveness and our being taken into the membership of His SON. It is also difficult in so short an article to sharply define the transition to, and yet the later continuous parallelism with, sanctification. And, again, the formal statement of the doctrine of justification is hardly needed for one who spiritually apprehends the force of our adoption and the reality of our being made partakers of the Divine nature, and our growth in that participation by a continual living in the grace of our dear LORD.

It must be borne in mind that the root idea in the word *righteous* or in the word *just* must be the giving to each one who has a claim upon us his rights, whether it be to GOD, to self, or to our brother. Therefore St. John (1 John iii. 7) writes, "He that doeth righteousness is righteous, even as He is righteous." But this yielding to each his right is a complex act, as GOD'S rights from us are Obedience, Love, Worship, and Works, with all that these imply; our brother's rights are all that we can give of love, forbearance, and aid; the rights due to ourselves are the life and holy happiness, which were ours by creation, and are offered and urged by GOD'S mercy. It is equally true that we are impotent through sinful weakness to render to each party his rights, while we have a capacity with no true abillty. External aid is needed to enable us; a preliminary act of forgiveness, of freeing from the punishment due to sin, and a restoration to that position wherein we may, under covenanted grounds begin to fulfill the duties bounden upon us. Herein lie the facts of our LORD's Atonement and the power of His Resurrection, and the gift of these acts conveyed to us in the Sacraments. "He saw that there was no man, and wondered that there was no intercessor," so He wrought our righteousness for us, fulfilling the Law for us. So He was made under the Law as well as born of a woman, therefore St. Paul declares that by the deeds of the Law there shall be no man justified in His sight (Rom. iii. 20).

Since without holiness no man can see GOD, and we cannot be or become holy by our own strength, GOD gave His only SON to become our righteousness, our holiness, our justification (1 Cor. i. 30; Rom. iv. 25; 1 Pet. i. 15). He by His fulfilling the Law for us, His brethren, to His Father, to Himself, and to us, obtained for us that He could become our bondsman, His righteousness be accepted for us, and we, under the covenant of CHRIST, be restored, adopted, and sanctified. Therefore GOD was in CHRIST reconciling the word unto Himself. GOD receives us because of JESUS CHRIST the righteous, who is the propitiation for our sins (1 John ii. 2).

The mode of restoration is prepared, the means and instruments on GOD's part are all ready. It remains for us to lay hold of them to make them ours, to use them, to grow in them, to become transformed by the renewing of our minds by the power of the HOLY GHOST. This latter part of our Christian life and estate towards our FATHER is more properly discussed under the title SANCTIFICATION. The means whereby we lay hold of those gifts and mercies of GOD are the two hands of the soul which we can stretch up to Him,—Repentance and Faith. Justification, then, the accounting us righteous because of, and solely through, the righteousness of CHRIST, is made ours by the forms and ways by which we lay hold of and secure it to ourselves. We are said very truly to be justified by repentance (St. Luke xviii. 14). Yet repentance cannot be repentance without faith. We are justified by the free gift of GOD, i.e., by grace, but we lay hold of the grace by faith. We are justified by works, but works to be works at all in any Christian sense must be done in faith. In fact, our justification has many sides, is applied in many ways, can be approached by many paths, but all of these have the common element of Faith mingled in them. As our LORD is called a Vine, a Lamb, a Fount, a Door, a Rock, that by these He may show His sympathy with all forms of the human mind, and may be to each what he needs, and yet He is the one JESUS CHRIST, so His righteousness is laid hold of in many ways, yet so that Faith is the infusing and controlling power. We lay hold of His justification by our repentance, but how can we repent unless we believe in a loving LORD, whom we have wronged, and also believe that He will restore us? Therefore the Fathers called Repentance and Faith the two hands we can stretch out to GOD. By these we receive His gift in Baptism, the adoption into the citizenship of the Kingdom of His dear SON, the new birth into a new creation in GOD, and into life. For as in Adam (by natural birth) all die, even so (by baptism) in CHRIST shall all be made alive. But this life is by the righteousness which we have in Him. His righteousness, as we are under covenant through Him, is ours, as He has purchased our redemption by His blood, and accounted righteous in Him by mercy, we must use this grace, grow in it, make it our second nature, and so grow in sanctification as we more completely assimilate our life to our LORD in habit and in principle, through the channels by which He pours His holy life into our hearts. It is not easy to avoid reverting to the original statements, but in so complex an act as this of our justification, which rests upon the several parts of our LORD's redemption, we have to go back in order to follow up another of its many applications.

Righteousness in us rests upon the forgiveness given us in CHRIST. Then, as redemption through His blood is conveyed to us upon our faithful reception of this forgiveness, it follows that Absolution and the Holy Communion are to the faithful so many means of laying hold of that righteousness that is from Him, and thus are approaches to our FATHER, who justifieth us in CHRIST. Baptism, then, conveys to us His justification, and the Sacrament of the LORD's Supper continues us in this state, and helps us to grow in it. "If any man sin, we have an advocate with the FATHER, JESUS CHRIST the righteous, and He is the propitiation for our sins, and not for ours only, but for the sins of the whole world." And it is with the same true, lively faith we lay hold on CHRIST, and receive Him and His righteousness in this solemn renewal of our covenant. But, again, as we are justified by repentance and by faith, and have it freely conveyed to us in the first Sacrament and renewed in the second, so we are also justified by works. "But works without faith are not pleasant unto GOD, as they spring not of faith in JESUS CHRIST, but they have the nature of sin. Therefore works which are the fruits of faith, and follow after justification, are pleasing and acceptable to GOD in CHRIST, and do spring necessarily out of a true and lively faith, insomuch that by them a lively faith may be as evidently known as a tree discerned by the fruit." By works we show forth, and also intensify and strengthen, our faith, and stamp upon our characters so far the justification which GOD giveth to our faith. Works react upon faith, and aid it by their consequents, proving GOD'S mercy and love, and that there is no unrighteousness in Him. What has been said is included in the wonderfully comprehensive language of St. Paul in three several passages, which are placed together, not that they should be torn out of their connection, but that they may be conveniently examined. The first is from Rom. iii. 21:

"But now the righteousness of GOD without the law is manifested, being witnessed by the law and the prophets; even the righteousness of GOD which is by faith of JESUS CHRIST unto all and upon all them that believe: for there is no difference: for all have sinned, and come short of the glory of GOD; being justified freely by His grace through the redemption that is in CHRIST JESUS, whom GOD hath set forth to be a propitiation through faith in His blood, to declare His righteousness for the remission of sins that are past, through the forbearance of GOD. To declare, I say, at this time His righteousness; that He might be just, and the justifier of him which believeth in JESUS." In this it must be noted (a) that the Apostle could not suppose that any one could believe and not at once receive baptism; and (b) that St. Paul uses the word propitiation, referring to our redemption in CHRIST (the sprinkling of blood on the mercy-seat), and the Church gives a Eucharistic interpretation to it by using, among the comfortable words of the Communion Service, the parallel passage from St. John's Epistle.

The second passage is from 1 Cor. vi. 11: "But ye are washed, but ye are sanctified, but ye are justified in the name of the LORD JESUS, and by the Spirit of our GOD." Here, again, it must be remarked, name means power and authority, and may most properly be connected with the threefold name in which we are baptized; but this verse is an outline of the Christian life.

The third passage is from Titus iii. 4–9: "But after that the kindness and love of GOD our SAVIOUR toward man appeared, not by works of righteousness which we have done, but according to His mercy He saved us, by the washing of regeneration and renewing of the HOLY GHOST; which He shed on us abundantly through JESUS CHRIST our SAVIOUR; that being justified by His grace, we should be made heirs according to the hope of eternal life."

These passages are in the main the basis of the XI. Article of Religion. "We are accounted righteous before GOD only for the merit of our LORD and SAVIOUR JESUS CHRIST by Faith, and not for our own works or deservings, wherefore that we are justified by Faith only as a most wholesome doctrine and very full of comfort, as is more largely expressed in the Homily of Justification."

This article while in the general line of the confession of Augsburg and agreeing with Luther and Melancthon's teachings, at the same time is on a very distinct and independent footing, rather following out the general ancient teaching than making such positive and exclusive statements as are elsewhere found, which give a narrowness to the all-embracing doctrine of justification.

In this outline no attempt has been made to give any sketch of the controversies, or to quote formal statements, or even to refer to all the texts which bear upon this doctrine. To do so at all adequately would far exceed our limits. But the "Introduction to the Epistles to the Romans and Galatians," by Bishop Wordsworth, the comment upon the IX. Article in Bishop Browne's work upon the XXXIX. Articles, and Hooker's famous sermon on Justification, refuting the Romish doctrine of an inherent Righteousness, are to be consulted and studied.

K.

Kansas, Diocese of. The organic act of Congress under which the Territory of Kansas was thrown open to settlement was approved on the 30th day of May, 1854 A.D. The Constitution of the State was adopted by the Constitutional Convention on the 29th day of July, 1859 A.D., and was ratified and adopted by the people of the State at an election held on the 4th day of October, 1859 A.D. The State was admitted into the Union by an Act of Congress, approved on the 20th day of May, 1861 A.D. Between the organic act and the act of admission population came into the Territory, and the organization of Churches of different denominations went on side by side with other developments in the opening of a new country.

The first missionary of the Protestant Episcopal Church appointed for Kansas was sent by the Domestic Committee in 1854 A.D., —the Rev. John McNamara, now D.D., and the head of Nebraska College. He had served for two or three years before in Western Missouri, at Weston and St. Joseph. His appointment in Kansas was for Leavenworth. He struggled on for a time, but was soon compelled to withdraw, for those were troublous times of intense political and partisan contest. His experiences are graphically described by him in his very readable book, entitled "Three Years on the Kansas Border."

The first Episcopal missionary who secured a footing and a home was the Rev. Hiram Stone, whose ministry was at Leavenworth, which city, then containing about two thousand people, he entered on November 24, 1856 A.D., and where he organized a parish on December 10 of the same year. In the course of the next three years parishes were formed in Atchison, Fort Scott, Junction City, Lawrence, Manhattan, Topeka, Troy, and Wyandotte. The Territory was a part of the Jurisdiction of Bishop Kemper, the Missionary Bishop of the Northwest, the first and only Missionary Bishop then in the Church.

In 1859 A.D. the few Churches at that time existing constituted themselves into a Diocese, at a Primary Convention at Wyandotte, on the 11th and 12th days of August, under the Presidency of Bishop Kemper, who, on the 26th of the previous July, had summoned the Convention for this purpose. There were at that time in the Territory ten clergymen,—the Rev. Messrs. Callaway, Clarkson, Drummond, Henderson, Nash, Preston, Reynolds, Ryan, Staudenmayer, and Stone. The Diocese was received into union with the General Convention at its Triennial Session in the October following.

At a special Convention held April 11 and 12, 1860 A.D., an attempt was made to elect a Bishop. Eight clergymen were present, and eight parishes were represented. On the twelfth ballot the Rev. Heman Dyer, D.D., of New York, was elected by the clergy, and their choice was confirmed by the laity. But a question arose as to the validity of the election, under the limitations prescribed by the General Canon "of Bishops." The incipient controversy was silenced by the prompt action of the Bishop-elect, who declined the election. That action of the Rev. Dr. Dyer was a happy thing for the Church, in so far as it retained him in that most important and commanding position in the centre of our Church work in the United States, which he has so long occupied in the city of New York.

At the Annual Convention in the September following, the Rt. Rev. Henry W. Lee, Bishop of Iowa, was invited to take the Episcopal charge of the Diocese until the Diocese should elect its own Bishop. The invitation was accepted, and Bishop Lee continued this provisional charge until the election of the present Diocesan, in September, 1864 A.D.

As a *Territory* Kansas included not only all the country now within its prescribed limits, but also so much of Colorado as extended through the three degrees of the width of the State from north to south, thence westward to the top of the Rocky Mountains, including and far beyond Denver,—a district known as Arrapahoe County, and almost as large as all the rest of the State. Kansas became a Diocese while it was a Territory, and *as such* was admitted into union with the General Convention, and had the right to remain so with all the domain which then belonged to it. Ecclesiastical divisions are entirely independent of the civil, as we may have, and have had, Dioceses made of parts of several States, or several Dioceses in one State. The parties concerned could alone remedy the trouble. Bishop Talbot, Missionary Bishop of the Northwest, consented to receive Arrapahoe County as a part of his jurisdiction; the Diocese of Kansas in its Convention, and the Bishop in charge of it, assented to the change, and the case was then finally referred to the General Convention of 1862 A.D., which ratified the change proposed, and made the *Diocese* coterminous with the *State* of Kansas.

During the four years of Bishop Lee's charge he made three visitations, confirming in the few parishes on the Missouri River, and once going into the interior as far as Lawrence and Topeka. West of these there were only about four nominal parishes, and these very small and feeble. The number of persons confirmed in these four years hardly exceeded a couple of dozen. Two Deacons, the Rev. Messrs. Henderson and Hickcox, were ordained by him to the Priesthood. One corner-stone was laid by him, which was found a few years later, by careful measurement and digging, when a fine stone church was built upon it. His work was during the long Civil War, when the wonder is that the Church in this new and border State was not entirely obliterated. But his happy influence in his brief visitations in Kansas, taken out of his crowding labors in his own large Diocese, was to keep alive "the things that remained," in expectation of the brighter day which came with the return of peace. The Diocese is under lasting obligations to this wise overseer.

At the Annual Convention in Atchison, at which Bishop Lee presided, on the 14th and 15th days of September, 1864 A.D., the Diocese, on the recommendation of the Bishop in charge, proceeded to the election of a Bishop. The Rev. William H. Hickcox was the Secretary. Six clergymen answered to their names,—the Rev. Messrs. Egar, Hickcox, Nash, Preston, Ryan, and Stone. Seven parishes were represented,—Atchison, Burlington, Leavenworth, Manhattan, Topeka, Troy and Wyandotte. The Rev. Thomas H. Vail, D.D., Rector of Trinity Church, Muscatine, Iowa, was unanimously elected by the clergy, and their election was unanimously confirmed by the laity. The Rev. R. W. Oliver, Rector of Trinity Church, Lawrence, who arrived just as the election had been concluded, by permission added his suffrage to the electing vote.

The consecration of the Bishop-elect took place at Muscatine, on December 15, 1864 A.D. The Bishops present were Bishop Kemper, the first Missionary Bishop of the Northwest, and at the time of this service Bishop of Wisconsin, the Presiding Consecrator; Bishop Lee, of Iowa, who preached the sermon; and Bishop Bedell (assistant), of Ohio, and Bishop Whitehouse, of Illinois, who together presented the Bishop-elect. On the 1st of January, 1865 A.D., Bishop Vail started for his new field. On the 15th of December, 1883 A.D., he entered upon the twentieth year of his Episcopate.

When he came to the State there were *three* little churches in it in use, at Lawrence, at Leavenworth, and at Wyandotte, and *four* others had been commenced, at Fort Scott, Junction City, Manhattan, and Topeka. Larger churches have taken the place of the first three. The four then commenced have been finished or rebuilt, and *twenty-five* entirely new churches have been added to the previous number. So that now, in December, 1883 A.D., there are 32 churches built and paid for. In connection with these there are also 15 parsonages. In addition to the organized parishes there are some 30 or more missions and preaching stations, so that now there are about seventy points in the Diocese where the services of the Church are held by regular appointment at longer or shorter intervals. Every church which has been built in the Diocese has been aided by or through the Bishop, in amounts varying from $350 to $2500 each. The present rate of aid is from $300 to $500 each. There are now 32 clergymen on the clerical roll.

There is in the Diocese but one benevolent institution in the strict sense, Christ's Hospital in Topeka, arranged on the pavilion plan. The grounds, 10 acres in extent, in the form of a parallelogram, 600 feet wide by 727 feet long, cost $5000, and were presented by Mrs. Vail and the Bishop to the Board of Trustees. There is as yet but one building completed, 160 feet long. The administration end is 40 by 60 feet, and of three stories. The ward is attached of one story, 100 feet long by 28 feet wide, and 16 feet high in the clear. This ward is subdivided into two half-wards of 42 feet long, and each of these again into two quarter-wards of 21 feet in length. Between these half-wards is a reception-room 16 feet long, for receiving patients. Each quarter-ward will hold six or (in an emergency) nine beds, the entire ward holding a total of twenty-four or thirty-six beds. $5500 were raised for the building by voluntary contributions in Topeka, and $5500 were given by friends outside of Topeka through the Bishop. The total cost so far has been $16,000, all of which is paid.

Of educational institutions, besides two or three parochial schools, there is properly but one, the College of the Sisters of Bethany, exclusively for girls, the only one of the sort under any Protestant oversight in the State of Kansas, and for an immense country south and southwest from Kansas. This institution has proved a great success. For eighteen years it has been growing into favor as its facilities have been more and more extended. It now embraces four scholastic departments,—the Kindergarten, the Primary, the Preparatory, and the Collegiate. Girls may enter at a very tender age, and may graduate at eighteen or twenty, with an education about parallel with that of young men who receive their A.B. at other colleges. In connection with these studies, the ornamental branches of music, vocal, choral, and instrumental, and of art in the several grades and varieties of drawing, painting, and sketching in oil and water colors, designing, decorating on ceramics, silks, etc., are thoroughly taught. In the last year 153 pupils were trained in music, and 55 in art.

In addition to the chaplain, who is headmaster, and the choir-master or precentor, and to the bursar, house-mother, matron, and health-matron, twenty lady teachers are employed in the College.

Statistics for 1886 A.D.: Clergy, 37; parishes, 22; missions, 26; ordinations, D. 1; baptisms, 288; con., 187; com., 2258; contr., $36,567.71. RT. REV. THOS. H. VAIL, D.D.,
Bishop of Kansas.

Kentucky, The History of the Church in. Kentucky, as a State, was admitted into union with the nation June 1, 1792 A.D.; as a Diocese in the Church's federation, 1829 A.D.

Ante-Diocesan History.—Christ Church, Lexington, was organized July 3, 1809 A.D. Down to the first Convention in 1829 A.D., *twelve* clergymen can be named who, through "good or evil report," kept the work and name of the Church alive. Among these was the Rev. Mr. Lythe, Chaplain of the first Proprietary Legislature, which met at Harrodsburg in 1795 A.D., and who distinguished himself as a member of that body by offering a bill "To prevent Profane Swearing and Sabbath-breaking." Lythe was the first priest, as he was also *the first minister of any kind or name, to offer up the sacrifice of prayer and praise to the Living* GOD *in Kentucky;* and this, under the shade of an elm-tree, on the first Sunday after this Legislature assembled. Humphrey Marshall, in his "History of Kentucky," published 1824 A.D., writes of 1792 A.D.: "There were in the country, and chiefly from Virginia, many Episcopalians, but who had formed no Church, there being no parson to take charge of it at the period of separation from Virginia in 1792 A.D. It might have been hazarded as a public conjecture that no Episcopalian Church could ever be erected in Kentucky. There is, however (1824 A.D.), one pastor who has a church in Lexington. Education is with this fraternity a necessary qualification for administering the affairs of both Church and State. The forms of their worship are highly decorous, and their discipline calculated to make good citizens."

The Rev. Mr. Moore, educated for the Presbyterian ministry, and chosen President of the Transylvania University, was admitted into holy orders by Bishop Madison, 1794–98 A.D. He was the first clergyman who ministered to the Churchmen of Lexington, and was the means of erecting the first building. "The Rev. Mr. Kavanaugh came to the Diocese in 1802, and ministered generally that year, then removed to Henderson, where he died, respected and lamented, and followed by many good works, in 1806." Record is found of a Rev. Mr. Eliot, who had temporary charge of Christ Church, Lexington, in 1813 A.D. The Rev. Mr. Ward succeeded Mr. Moore in this parish; after him the Rev. Mr. Burgee, who was ordained by Bishop Chase, at Worthington, Ohio, June 16, 1819 A.D., who died shortly after, and then the Rev. Dr. Chapman, which brings us down to Diocesan times. It should be mentioned here that *six of these twelve clergymen* crossed the sea to receive holy orders. They were Sebastian, Gantt, Chambers, Johnson, Eliot, and Crawford. On their return the first named blossomed into a politician and a judge, and of the rest silence shall reign.

On the 8th day of July, 1829 A.D., the Primary Convention assembled in Christ Church, Lexington. Two Priests, one Deacon, with nine Laymen, representing the Parishes of Lexington, Danville, and Louisville, composed the body. To the Rev. Dr. Chapman is due the honor of organizing the Diocese. He was the sole rector in it. Anticipating the General Convention of 1829 A.D., in the spring of that year he issued public notices, visited Danville, organized Trinity Parish, which appointed delegates, and from thence to Louisville, arousing general interest. He was chosen President, and rightfully. He was a man of zeal, power, and learning; and all these virtues are attested, too, by his volume of sermons on the "Distinctive Principles of the Church," a book which was highly commended by Bishop Brownell and by Freeman, historiographer of Kentucky, as "having done more in all parts of the country to disseminate sound knowledge concerning the Church, and bring converts into her Fold, than any work since 'Daubeny's Guide,' which our Fathers put in circulation." To this latter testimony this Diocese can attest that all her larger and more permanent churchly life is due. The Rev. B. O. Peers was chosen Secretary. He was then the Principal of the Pestallozi Academy, Lexington, and afterwards became prominent in Diocesan affairs, "not only for his devotion to the cause of Christian education, but for his learning and ardent piety." He was the fifth President of the Transylvania University, which institution was largely controlled by Churchmen from its beginning to its close,—from Moore to Coit, to Peers, to Holley. Peers was untiring. He spent time, labor, and money, and is the *father of common-school education* in the State. He was a writer of considerable merit, his chief literary work being that on "Christian Education," although in Church circles he was better known in his connection with the old Sunday-School Union. He died at Louisville in 1842 A.D.

The Rev. John Ward, the other clerical member, was principal of a girls' school at Lexington. After the Convention had been organized, it was moved "That the Rev. Samuel Johnston, Rector of St. Paul's Church, Cincinnati, being present, be recognized as a member of this Convention," and he took his seat accordingly.

Kentucky owes much of her growth to the fact of the character of her devoted lay members. They have for the most part been unflinching in contending for the "faith once delivered." Notably in this first Convention we find Dr. J. Esten Cooke, a prominent citizen and a physician, learned and beloved, in Lexington. He was a convert from Methodism, "the most profound medical philosopher of his time," and wrote a masterly work on the "Invalidity of Presbyterian Ordination,"—which "attained a remarkable celebrity in England as well as America." Richard Barnes, "a man in moderate circumstances, but the moving spirit of Christ Church, Louisville." John Bustard, who afterwards endowed the Female Orphan Asylum of that city. From Danville that great physician, Ephraim McDowell, "Father of Ovariotomy," and whose memory is honored by his profession with the erection of a public monument in the city of Danville. H. J. Cowan, who lives in his devoted sons, and Frederick Yeiser. Resolutions were offered in this Convention for the "employment of lay readers in congregations destitute of clerical services," and that "it be recommended to all families of the Church in the Diocese to have daily family worship." It was at this Convention that Dr. Chapman learned that Bishop Ravenscroft, "that noble Cœur de Lion of the Church," was in Nashville, and an invitation was extended him to visit the Diocese; he willingly responded by appearing in Lexington on the 25th of July, and confirmed ninety-one persons. Near the close of the year Bishop Brownell, of Connecticut, visited the Diocese. From his "private note-book" and the manuscripts of his "itinerary" the fullest information is afforded, here briefly summed up. "Arrived at Louisville November 29;" "found the Parish in a cold and depressed state owing to its having been for fifteen months without a clergyman, and to the divisions which had taken place in regard to Mr. Shaw, the last Rector." During the Bishop's visit the new rector, Mr. Paige, arrives, and he departs from Louisville for Frankfort, leaving all things in the most hopeful state in that Parish, predicting that it will become "the most flourishing in the

Diocese." "On board the boat we had a motley company,—several members of the Legislature, half a dozen *blacklegs*, and a couple of actors and actresses,—*the latter the best behaved of the company*. Constant gambling on board and much gross profanity. The members of the Legislature had been introduced to us in Louisville and treated us with great attention." " Lexington is the Athens of the West. A fine medical school, excellent buildings, and an able faculty, and two hundred students. Academical department has one hundred and thirty-six students, eighty of them collegians, the rest in the grammar school. The country the finest in the world; the society highly intelligent, yet plain and simple in their manners. Dr. Chapman's congregation embraces the most valuable part of it. Leaving Lexington, arrive at Frankfort December 7. Next morning call on Governor Metcalfe, and receive a visit from Mr. John J. Crittenden, the most eloquent lawyer in the State. Went with the Governor and Mr. Hanna to the House of Representatives, thence to the Senate, where we heard speeches from Mr. Wicliffe and Mr. Hardin, the two most distinguished members. Took boat for Louisville; this is the great mart of the commerce of Kentucky. Kentucky is a noble State,—fertile soil; fine race of men." The official acts of the Bishop on this visitation were as follows: He consecrated Christ Church, Lexington, and confirmed three. He consecrated Christ Church, Louisville, baptized four adults and eleven infants, and confirmed thirty-one. Stirred up a great interest in Church work " by the dignity and suavity of his manners and the elevation of his piety."

The first recorded statistics of the Church are found in the fragmentary journal of the second Convention, held at Danville, May, 1830 A.D. Population, 687,917; number of parishes, 3; number of clergy, 4; baptisms, infants, 32, adults, 6; marriages, 3; burials, 10. At this Convention an invitation was extended to the Right Reverend W. Meade, Assistant Bishop of Virginia. He came into the Diocese on the 19th of May, 1831 A.D., and began his visitation at Maysville. This was general, extending over the State, and ending at Hopkinsville, June 20. The results were, consecration of Trinity Church, Danville; ordination in Christ Church, Louisville, to the Priesthood of Revs. Messrs. Ash, Deacon, and Giddinge, and at two confirmations fifty-four confirmed.

At the third Annual Convention, the Rev. B. B. Smith, the newly elected Rector of Christ Church, Lexington, was chosen Bishop, but by reason of some informality in the election he declined. At the following Convention, June 11, 1832 A.D., held at Hopkinsville, he was again elected unanimously. He was consecrated in St. Paul's Chapel, New York, on the 31st day of October, 1832 A.D. He was born at Bristol, Rhode Island, June 13, 1794 A.D.; graduated at Brown University, 1816 A.D.; made Deacon, 1817 A.D.; ordained Priest, 1818 A.D. " For more than twenty years the offerings in the Diocese did not exceed the Bishop's traveling expenses to and from the General Convention." When he came to Kentucky not a parish had a set of communion vessels, and but one had either bell or organ. Thomas H. Quinlan, L. H. Van Doren, and D. H. Deacon were the first candidates for holy orders. The first Presbyter ordained was the Rev. S. S. Lewis, and the first Deacon was Erastus Burr, both in 1833 A.D.

In 1834 A.D. the cholera prevailed in Lexington, necessitating the postponement of the Convention to October following, when a Day of Humiliation was fitly observed. In this scourge two Presbyters, three candidates for holy orders, and fifty communicants of the Diocese—one-fourth of its whole strength—had been carried away. In this calamity the Bishop had borne himself with a courage never excelled. He was the only servant of GOD in Lexington, save his Roman Catholic brother, who reported for service. After the cholera, and in this same year, the Diocese also lost largely by emigration to Illinois and Missouri. The Bishop, on May 25, consecrated Christ Church, St. Louis, and confirmed twenty-six, and also laid the first corner-stone in Illinois. Name of place not found.

The Theological Seminary was incorporated February 24, 1834 A.D. A building and two acres of ground were purchased at a cost of $9000. The institution opened with three professors, nine students, and a library of 3500 volumes. In 1835 A.D. the Bishop secured $14,000 for the Theological Fund. Among works undertaken by the students of the Seminary was a Sunday-school for colored children, numbering seventy-five, but going further than oral instruction, the mayor of the city requested its discontinuance. In 1836 A.D. there were eighteen students in the Seminary. Of the number receiving instruction within its walls there were twenty-five received ordination. In 1844 A.D. the building and ground were sold for $11,500, and the library was transferred to Shelby College. *The Church Advocate* was the first Diocesan paper, with Caswall as editor. Its existence was brief.

Shelby College was organized in 1836 A.D. and transferred to the Diocese in 1840 A.D. The Rev. Mr. Drane was its first President. Under the Presidency of Rev. W. J. Waller, covering a period of many years, over $40,000 were spent in improvements on the property, etc. After varying fortunes and many embarrassments the Diocese, on the 20th day of August, 1870 A.D., surrendered the property to the Trustees of the town of Shelbyville.

At the Convention of 1863 A.D., Bishop Smith had reached the seventieth year of his age and the thirtieth year of his Episcopate. The baptisms had been, from 1832 to

1862 A.D., 7470, confirmations 3402, and the communicants 1821.

On Friday, June 1, 1866 A.D., the Rev. George David Cummins, D.D., was chosen by the Convention as Assistant Bishop of Kentucky. Consecrated in Christ Church, Louisville, November 16, 1866 A.D. He was born December 11, 1832 A.D , in Kent, Del. In 1873 A.D. he sent his resignation to the presiding Bishop. Died June 26, 1876 A.D. In this decade the baptisms were 6219, confirmations 4805, and the communicants 3328.

Institutions.—The Protestant Episcopal Female Orphan Asylum, Louisville, organized October 6, 1835 A.D., has an endowment fund of $35,400, good building and grounds, and has accommodation for forty inmates.

Orphanage of the Good Shepherd, for boys, Louisville, organized 1869 A.D. Has a fine building, two acres of ground, and an endowment fund of $1000. Supported by voluntary offerings. Inmates are taught trades, and there is a fine printing-house connected with the building. The Diocesan paper, the *Kentucky Church Chronicle*, is issued from this press.

The Home of the Innocents, Louisville, was founded in 1879 A.D. Its work has so far been done in rented buildings. It provides for sick and destitute children under six years of age, and has also been reasonably successful in aiding fallen women. The work has received general sympathy since its inception.

Church Home for Females and Infirmary for the Sick of both Sexes, Louisville. Ground on which this building stands cost $6000, the structure itself $100,000. The charter was obtained in 1872 A.D , but the work was not begun until 1882 A.D. So far this has been the work of one man. Is not yet opened for patients.

The John N. Norton Memorial Infirmary, Louisville, 1882 A.D. Has a fine building, not yet completed. Cost to date $45,000. Will probably be opened within the present year (1884 A.D.).

Since the year 1872 A.D. the Bishop of the Diocese has, by permission, resided without its limits, save that he made a final visitation, and presided at the Annual Convention, May, 1874 A.D. At a Special Convention held in Louisville, November 11 and 12, 1874 A.D., the Rev. Thomas Underwood Dudley, D.D., was chosen as Assistant Bishop, and was consecrated in Christ Church, Baltimore, January 27, 1875 A.D. He was born in Richmond, Va., September 26, 1837 A.D. Graduated at the University of Virginia, 1858 A.D. Made Deacon 1867 A.D. Ordered Priest 1868 A.D. In the last decade the baptisms have been 5375, confirmations 3447, communicants 4382.

The statistics for the year ending 1886 A.D. are as follows: Clergy, 50; parishes, 34; missions, 14; candidates for H. O., 2; ordinations, D. 2, P. 2; baptisms, 650; confirmed, 485; communicants, 5215; Sunday-school teachers, 465; Sunday-school scholars, 4299; churches consecrated, 1; lay readers, 27; families, 1667; individuals, 6784; contributions, $118,251.85.

REV. L. P. TSCHIFFELY.

Keys. Power of the KEYS. There is constant danger of emptying Holy Scripture of all meaning, and an equal danger of putting far more meaning into it than it can bear. This danger is further increased by the drift of language, and by the fact that when a doctrine has been understated stronger language is needed to restore the fuller form of the truth. This is the fact with the Doctrines of Absolution and Excommunication, or the "*Power of the Keys.*" The term Key, in the Old Testament, means a power or stewardship conferred. The Key of the House of David (Is. xxii. 22) surely means something, when its possessor opens and no man shuts, and he shuts and no man opens,—a power CHRIST hath. Then to say that it was a mere formula, meaning nothing when the LORD gave it to St. Peter, and then to all the Apostles together (St. Matt. xvi. 19; xviii. 18), is to do a wrong to truth. To say that it was a gift to the Apostles alone, and to cease with them, is to take from the Human Agency CHRIST established, by which to confer on His Visible Church the very power to admit or to reject, the sole power which it was to exercise. The Key to open is to admit; the Key to shut is to reject. And these are of the essence of discipline. It follows that the power of the Keys must be an everliving gift in the Church, and is the pledge of His presence in and through His Apostles. But the real question is, having these Keys, how far are they in the power of the human agent, the proper officer? For it is evident that the admission into the Kingdom is by Baptism, and the Deacon being authorised to baptize, then can admit, and the rejection, before baptism, is also in his hands, and after baptism, in the Bishop's hands finally. Putting aside the refusal to baptize those who are evidently unfit,—the impenitent or the hypocritical,—the power of admission, the opening Key, is and can be very seldom refused. It is CHRIST Himself who is the Baptizer, as the Church has ever held. It is He who confers admission, and therefore, upon any reasonable evidence of a real though imperfect faith and repentance, no minister in the Church can refuse admission, and if in doubt, can always appeal to, and abide by, the sentence of the Bishop. The reality of the Power of this Key is identical with the reality and power of the gifts of Baptism. But the power of discipline, the Key to shut out, to reject, is not in any other hands but those of the Bishop. If the Deacon or Priest refuse Baptism to the applicant, he can lay his case before the Bishop. If after Baptism the Priest refuse the Holy Communion, the person so denied must be reported to the Bishop, and the wrong, if it be one, must be decided by him. As the Bishop holds the final authority from the LORD, and as each sentence must be decided by him under revisal finally by the MASTER, this Key of shutting is and will be very carefully wielded, for, after all, as the ministry is a stewardship of the mysteries and gifts of CHRIST, and as a strict account of these stewardships will be exacted, the LORD Himself will revise and repair wrongs. The discipline of the Church must be exercised and enforced, but in a large and loving mode, and with a constant reference to the grace and guidance of the HOLY GHOST and the personal superintendence of the LORD JESUS, who has promised to be always with His Apostles to the end of the world. Then the reply to the question, Does the man who holds these Keys act on his own reponsibility? is this, No more and no less than an officer of the law has to do so in execution of his trust. Errors occur, even wrongs are willfully committed, but because of these facts no one would abolish the office, but would direct the officer to be admonished for not observing the limitations of his trust whenever there is error, and to be punished for wilful misuse of the power committed to him. But the law must be executed, and this execution must be effected by man.

Kings, 1 and 2. It is very probable that Judges, 1 and 2 Samuel, and these two books made one continuous history. In fact, the book of Kings was divided into two portions (1st and 2d) by the Bomberg Rabbinical edition (Venice, 1525 A.D.), after the example of the Septuagint. It was very probably composed by Jeremiah, since many phrases in Jeremiah appear in the Kings. The captives enumerated in 2 Kings xxiv. 14, correspond with Jer. xxiv. 1. The reference to the vessels of the Temple in the one fits in with the other,—2 Kings xxv. 13 sq. compared with Jer. xxvii. 19–22. The fate of Seraiah and Zephaniah and the other under officers enumerated in ch. xxiv. 18–21, is foretold in Jer. xxi. 1-7; xxix. 20 sq., and so of many minor points of resemblance and interconnection. The historical accounts of the books are thoroughly corroborated by the remarkable discoveries at Babylon and Nineveh, even in very minute particulars, where different statements might yet relate truly to the same facts. The names of Omri, Jehu, Menahem, Hezekiah are found in the Assyrian inscriptions, as also Tiglath-Peleser, Sargon, Sennacherib, and Esarhaddon. But the chronology of the period covered by these two books—a period of 427 years—is filled with difficulties that point to the probability that some late Jewish writer had inserted the dates, since in several places the text can fairly be read without the date (e.g., 1 Kings vi. 1, compared with 2 Chron. iii. 2). These lead to discrepancies in synchronizing the reigns of the kings of Judah and of Israel, which amount to some twenty years. These discrepancies may be in part removed by supposing in places an unnoticed interval between the death of a king and the accession of his successor, and in counting current unfinished years—regnal years—as complete. Still the remaining differences are too great, especially as the main periods are noted in the text; as the simultaneous accession of Jeroboam over Israel and Rehoboam over Judah; the simultaneous deaths of Jehoram and Ahaziah; the fifteenth year of Amaziah, which was the first year of Jeroboam II.; the first three years of Ahaz, which synchronize with the last three years of Pekah; and the sixth year of Hezekiah, which fell on the ninth of Hoshea. These undoubted points of synchronization show that the attempted dates are interpolations. In scope the books of the Kings record the events which befell Israel from the accession of Solomon to the destruction of the Temple, a period of 427 years, ending 588 B.C., with a supplemental notice of Jehoiachin's better treatment twenty-six years later,—a period filled in with the most varied events for good and for evil: a Solomon, a Jehoshaphat, and a Hezekiah and a Josiah, with an Ahab, an Ahaz, a Manasseh, and an Ammon. The corruption in religion and in government; the weakness through apostasy; the slow but sure punishment that followed in the path of sin; the perfectly impartial statement of both good and evil acts; the constant reference to JEHOVAH's ever-superintending care; the prominence given to the prophets, as Elijah, Elisha, Isaiah, Abijah; notices of others, as Jonah; the glory of the Temple and its worship, and the profanation of it by Ahaz, and the surrender of its treasures for tribute by Asa and by Hezekiah; the retribution for the blood of Naboth upon Ahab and upon Jezebel; the rise of the flood of sin year by year, till the blood which had filled Jerusalem cried for retribution, and Nebuchadnezzar, with his bands of Chaldeans and his confederates, the Syrians, Moabites, and Ammonites, but executed the commandment of the LORD upon Judah.

"But it is for their deep religious teaching and for the insight which they give us into GOD's providential and moral government of the world, that they are above all valuable. The books which describe the glory of Solomon and yet record his fall; which make us acquainted with the painful ministry of Elijah and his translation into heaven; and which tell us how the most magnificent temple ever built for GOD's glory and of which He vouchsafed to take possession by a visible symbol of His Presence, was consigned to the flames and to desolation for the sins of those who worshiped in it, read us such lessons concerning both GOD and man as are the best evidence of their divine origin, and make them the richest treasure to every Christian man." (See for a full discussion of the critical questions concerning these books Lord Arthur

Hervey's article in Smith's Dictionary of the Bible.)

Kiss of Peace. A salutation mentioned frequently in the Old and the New Testaments. In the latter it has also a ritual significance, since in the celebration of the Divine Offices the Kiss of Peace was exchanged between the communicants, at first exchanged with all of both sexes, but later it was only given by the men to each other, and by the women to their female fellow-communicants. It was a part of every act of Christian worship, but it was especially used at the Holy Communion. In the Eastern Church this salutation comes after the dismissal of the non-communicants and the Oblation. In the West its place varied. In the Churches which were derived from the East, as the Mozarabic and the Gallican, the Kiss came before the Preface. But in the Churches derived from Italy, as the African, it comes directly after the Consecration and before Communion. The Kiss is still used in the Oriental Church. The Kiss was given at Baptism, at Ordination, at Espousals, and to the dying; and the "voice of nature was listened to and a final kiss was given to the corpse before actual interment." (*Vide* Kiss in Smith's Dictionary of Christian Antiquities.)

Kneeling, as a posture in divine worship, has seemed most natural and fit for a suppliant, in all ages and nations, probably from the time "that men began first to call upon the name of the LORD." In the Western Church the practice has always formed a part of the services, and has been enforced by the Bishops and Councils. It is not only a voluntary act of personal humility and reverence, but also one that is required of every person as an individual, forming part of a large congregation, and to neglect it is to omit a duty imposed upon us by the customs of the Church in the worship of Almighty GOD. The Rubric in the Prayer-Book for the proper observance of Public Worship directs that all persons then present shall reverently kneel upon their knees when the General Confession, Litany, and other prayers are read. In the rite of Confirmation all those who receive the Laying on of Hands are to kneel, and in the Marriage Service, the Nuptial Benediction on the newly-married couple is received kneeling.

In the administration of the LORD's Supper the communicants are to receive the same kneeling, as a signification of our humble and grateful thanks for the benefits of CHRIST'S passion therein given to all worthy receivers, and for the avoiding any profanation or unseemly disorder that might otherwise ensue.

In the Eastern Church the practice is dissimilar to ours. Kneeling is not observed, but the whole congregation stand throughout the entire service, with heads bowed low in reverence during the prayers. Even in receiving the Holy Mysteries they do not kneel, esteeming that our human nature has been so exalted by the union with the Divine in the Person of our LORD, and that so lowly a posture does not comport with so joyful and comforting a service. Once only in the year do the people kneel in the service of the Greek Church, and that is on Whitsunday, or the descent of the HOLY GHOST.

Kyrie Eleison (*Greek*, LORD, have mercy). The oldest, the most sorrowful plea of all obsecrations offered to GOD. It is the plea in the Psalms often repeated. It is the cry of the Prophets. It was the prayer of the publican, of the lepers, of blind Bartimæus. It has passed into the continuous solemn Litanies of the Church. LORD, have mercy upon us, CHRIST, have mercy upon us, has risen from the Church continually. It is retained in the Greek words in all Liturgies but our own, and there it is translated upon the general principle that the compilers of the Prayer-Book set for themselves. So Halleluia is translated " Praise ye the LORD." The Kyrie is used in the second part of the Litany, and forms the first portion of the responses to the Commandments: " LORD, have mercy upon us, and incline our hearts to keep this Law." In many offices in the Greek Church, and in the older Western offices, it was repeated successively quite a number of times. In one of the monastic offices it is ordered to be said thirty times at one point in the service. In its use in the responses to the Commandments we imitate closely the publican, who, for his transgressions of the Law, would not lift up so much as his eyes to heaven, but smote on his breast, saying, "GOD be merciful to me a sinner."

L.

Laity. The people of the Christian Church as distinguished from the clergy. In several relations they have different names,—the congregation as gathered into the separate Churches or Parishes, the Laity as a single body, Christians in relation to their Faith. The Laity, as distinguished from the clergy, have had their rights and duties duly noted from the earliest notices of Church history. In the New Testament they are called the Brethren,—though this title was not theirs exclusively,—the Faithful, and the Saints. As the recipients of the grace offered by the Embassadors of CHRIST, they are the governed in the Ecclesia or Church; but since the governed have rights and duties as well as the governors, the laity have had an influence, sometimes a controlling one, either for good or for evil, as saith the prophet, "and my people love to have it so." The responsibility in either case lies not wholly, but largely, with the Laity. The recognition of the Laity as such in the Church goes as far back as the Epistles of Clement (96 A.D.), and from that time on more or less frequent notice of them and their position is made by the Church writers. Their presence is necessary to the proper celebration of all acts of worship and for the due administration of all rites and sacraments, since our LORD'S rule holds universally, "where two or three are gathered together in my name, there am I in the midst of them" (St. Matt. xviii. 20). So Baptism, while it may not be refused because of the failure to have them, should yet be administered before witnesses. The Holy Communion is not a Communion (*i.e.*, fellowship) in the ordinary usage of the word without communicants beside the celebrant. Marriage is before "a company." The Morning and Evening Prayer is in the presence of the dearly beloved brethren, and so every office either presupposes or demands their presence. This is, then, the duty which the Layman owes the Church as the visible Body of CHRIST, that he should be punctual and strict in attendance on her rites to receive her gifts and blessings. In her is the discharge of his Covenant with GOD, and therefore it is a matter of obligation as well as reverence to GOD to attend upon all her services. Being themselves so important a part of all services, the Laity have a right to demand all the services the Church can give them. Morning and Evening Prayer cannot be refused to any sufficient number of the congregation demanding it; nor can the Holy Communion if there be cause. With regard to the Diocese, the Laity have a representation in the Council or Convention, a voice in the management of Diocesan affairs, and their vote should be refused only on doctrinal definitions, but is theirs of right in all questions of local discipline and polity. They usually confirm the nomination for a Bishop made by the vote of the clergy. The reverse should be the case, and was so in the earlier elections. The Laity nominated, the clergy accepted and presented to the Metropolitan, though there were frequent exceptions to this rule.

The Laity having the purse have this duty and sacrifice as part of their Priesthood: "To do good and to distribute forget not: for with such sacrifices GOD is well pleased" (Heb. xiii. 16). But as the covenant is between GOD and them by His Embassadors, and He has ordered His Embassadors to live of the Gospel, it is a part of the layman's bounden duty to contribute liberally to the livelihood of the ministry. "Let him that is taught in the word communicate unto him that teacheth all good things. Be not deceived; GOD is not mocked: for whatsoever a man soweth, that shall he also reap. For he that soweth to his flesh shall of the flesh reap corruption; but he that soweth to the Spirit shall of the Spirit reap life everlasting. . . . As we have therefore opportunity, let us do good unto all men, especially unto them who are of the household of faith" (Gal. vi. 6–8, 10). And this support must not be limited to the Parish dues, but to the larger needs of the Diocese also. The true principle is in the old rule of a *Common Diocesan Fund*, out of which the needs of Bishop, clergy, and poor were supplied; the present Parochial system is later by a thousand years and more. The Layman, as a member of the congregation and a communicant, has a right, under the Canons of each Diocese, to a voice and a vote at all congregational meetings in the elections of the vestry and wardens, who are his chosen representatives for all legal ecclesiastical purposes, and in some Dioceses votes for the lay delegates to the Council or Convention of the Diocese. He has also a sharing in the Priesthood belonging to the whole Church, certain offices to which he may be eligible. His inherent Priesthood is discharged by his presence at all services and by his sharing in all acts of worship. But as lay-reader, and therefore as representative for the congregation in all prayer and supplication, he exercises this; so also as chorister in the worship of song. He should share in the general work of the Parish, such as aiding in visiting the sick, in distributing, under the direction of the Rector, proper tracts, doing his share of work in the Sunday-school, helping to form guilds or brotherhoods, and zealously aiding in sustaining them and in giving them efficiency.

These are duties and privileges which belong to his order in the Church, functions not less important, not inferior in their place, to the functions of the ministry appointed to serve him in all the gifts, graces, and blessings which the LORD has left in His Church for His people. Beyond these limits the Layman trenches on the sin of Korah; below these limits he fails of his duty to GOD and his SAVIOUR and to the Church he should so dearly love for the sake of his LORD.

Whenever the Layman takes an active interest in the parish work the parish will grow, and as his life is moulded by his active Church work, so will his own influence extend, and so will the Church's influence be deepened and broadened. It needs but little consideration to perceive clearly that there is really less, proportionately to their position, in the eloquence and popularity of the Rector than there is in the true, earnest zeal and in the devout moral courage of the Layman, that develops the healthy growth and influence of the Parish. Too frequently a Parish languishes because of the selfish carelessness of the congregation, who think that they have done all when they have only attended the ordinary services with convenient regularity. The devout Layman owes it to his own spiritual welfare and to his loving LORD and to the Church to spend a part at least of that energy he gives to his daily toil in her service, for he thereby exercises his ministry also.

Lamentations of Jeremiah. They were written by the Prophet probably immediately after the fall of the city into the hands of the Chaldeans. The book is written in a rhythmic style. The verses of the first, second, and fourth chapters begin with a successive letter of the alphabet. In the third chapter three verses in succession begin so. " Further, if we take the four alphabetical poems separately, we find the first three of each of the xxii. parts (or verses, but note in chapter iii. each part equals *three* English verses), may itself as a rule be subdivided into three, in chapter iv. into two only, while in the third chapter each of these subdivisions begins with the same letter, and is itself divisible into two. In chapter v., although the number of the verses is the same, the alphabetical order is dropped." " The subject, as we have noted, is the capture of the city under Nebuchadnezzar, and the sorrow and suffering thereby entailed. Herewith are united both the confession that this has come upon the people on account of their sins, and entreaties for deliverance. Taking the poems severally, chapter i. dwells upon the solitary condition and grief of the city. Chapter ii. sets forth the destruction that has come upon her, and acknowledges that it is the result of sin. Chapter iii., which, although framed for the most part in the singular number, yet includes the nation throughout, complains of the bitter cup which GOD's people have to drink, and yet acknowledges that the trials which are come upon them are inflicted by a FATHER's hand. Chapter iv. describes the reverses in fortune that have been brought about by recent events, and again acknowledges sin. Chapter v. recapitulates the pitiful details of their condition, and ends by an earnest prayer for deliverance. 'There are few portions of the Old Testament, perhaps, which appear to have done the work they were meant to do more effectually than this.' It has not been connected with the theological or ecclesiastical disputes of any age, while it has supplied the earnest Christian of all times with words in which to confess his sins and shortcomings, as well as with a picture of Him who bore our sins and carried our sorrows, on whom was 'laid the iniquity of us all.'" The book is annually read among the Jews to commemorate the burning of the Temple. The first and a part of the third are read on Quinquagesima Sunday in the Lessons.

Lammas-day. The observation of this day (August 1) as a feast of thanksgiving for the first fruits of the corn dates from Saxon times, in which it was called Hlafmaesse, or Loaf-mass, from the offering of bread made of new corn. Hence Lam-mass.

Laodicea. A Council was held at Laodicea some time in the fourth century, various dates being assigned, as follows: 314, 363, 365, 372, and 399 A.D. Thirty-two Bishops are recorded as present, and a large number (sixty) of Canons were passed, which, though the tone of the Council was semi-Arian at the least, have gained reception in the code of the whole Church. They are almost all prohibitory, and refer to discipline; some prescribe a proper and becoming order of services; the 57th forbids the placing of Bishops in villages and country places, establishing in their stead Visitors, corresponding nearly to Archdeacons or Rural Deans; and the 60th gives a list of the Canonical Scriptures, in which none of the Apocryphal books are found, nor the Revelation.

Lapsed. These were those Christians who had not strength to encounter persecution, who complied in some form or other with the demands of the heathen magistrates to take part in idol worship,—" they which for a while believed, but in time of temptation fell away." As the persecution ceased the greater part of those who had lapsed would seek reconciliation with the Church. In the first ages such penitents were, upon their confession, readmitted by imposition of hands, and confessors interceding for them often obtained a too speedy reconciliation for these penitents. It became a serious hindrance to the administration of discipline, and it was a lowering of the intensity of repentance in those who sought to be restored. St. Cyprian had both the courage and the tact to break the power of so dangerous an influence. He very wisely insisted upon strict discipline in time of rest, but when a fresh storm of persecution was at hand, he permitted the restoration of all the earnest penitents, believing that they would be stronger in the coming trial. This practice of the Church is a comment upon the modern teaching of some upon the impossibility of the restoration of those who have fallen. Compare the XVI. Article, which gives the true doctrine of Holy Scripture.

Lateran I. A Council was held in Rome in 649 A.D. by Pope Martin, " which, from having met in the ' Basilica of Constantine,' the great patriarchal church adjoining the Lateran Palace, is known as the first Lateran Council." As many as one hundred and five Bishops were in attendance, among whom was Stephen, Bishop of Dor, who had received a special charge from Sophronius, Patriarch of Jerusalem, to maintain the struggle against Monothelism. The decisions of the Synod were against this heresy, and in condemnation of the Ecthesis and the Type (edicts of the emperors favorable to it), and in opposition to them this positive dogma was published : " that there are in the SAVIOUR two natural wills and operations, the Divine and the human, the same LORD JESUS CHRIST, willing and working our salvation both as GOD and man." (*Vide* SIXTH GENERAL COUNCIL.) In retaliation for this reflection upon the Imperial edicts, Martin was dragged to Constantinople, subjected to various examinations concerning alleged political offenses, treated with cruelty as a condemned criminal, and finally banished to the Chersonesus to die in want and destitution, a veritable martyr to the truth. Much the same treatment was meted out to Maximus, a learned Abbot, and one of the most persevering opponents of Monothelism of his day.

Authorities: Robertson's Church History, Landon's Manual of Councils.

Lateran IV. A Council was announced in 1213 A.D. by Pope Innocent III. with the avowed object of correcting the evils of the Church and the depravity of morals. It finally assembled in 1215 A.D. in Rome, and is by some styled the twelfth Œcumenical Council, and by others the fourth General Council of the Lateran. There were present 77 Primates and Metropolitans, 412 Bishops, and 800 Abbots, who, with the various embassadors and others entitled to seats, made a total of more than 2000 members. But it does not appear that this imposing assembly did very much as a Council, for the Pope presented certain chapters of his own preparation which were not debated, and received consent only by the silence of the Bishops. In fact, they were quoted as the decrees of Innocent, rather than of the Council, for a long period after. Arrangements were made for a crusade, which, however, was never carried out; and the English troubles between King John and his barons were meddled with, not to mention interference in French affairs. " But the fourth Lateran Council is chiefly memorable for two Canons, relating to matters of doctrine and discipline respectively; the first, which for the first time laid down, by the authority of the whole Western Church, the doctrine of transubstantiation in the Eucharist; and the twenty-first, which prescribed for every Catholic Christian the duty of confessing once a year, at least, to his own parish priest, and of yearly receiving the Holy Eucharist at Easter.

Authorities: Robertson's Church History, Gieseler, Hardwick, Hagenbach's History of Doctrines, Landon's Manual of Councils.

Latitudinarianism. A school of thought in the Church,—now generally represented by the term Broad-Churchmanship, which dwelling upon the Church of GOD and the gifts therein, does not yet set forth, as fully as might be insisted upon, " the power of CHRIST'S Resurrection and the fellowship of His sufferings" as a principal portion of our spiritual life. It is an undervaluing of the necessity of strong dogmatical teaching. The school of Latitudinarians as an influence in the Church has closed since the days of Dr. S. Clarke (1720 A.D.), but much of its teaching was later reproduced in Coleridge's " Aids to Reflection." Under the vague name of Broad Church, which, however, does not by any means yield as much as did the older Latitudinarian, it has included many very able and influential men.

Latria. Worship of GOD. The word is used exclusively for the service and worship of the Holy and Blessed TRINITY. If given to any other, or if the so-called hyperdulia trenches on the Latria or adoring worship, it is idolatry. Latria is, then, the generic term to describe all acts of worship that are or can be offered to JEHOVAH by every worshiper, and it includes the simplest and merest act and reaches to the highest and most solemn. But it should be noted also that this worship includes some idea of sacrifice more or less distinctly connected with it, and that it is offered under a covenant. " Gather My saints together unto Me, those that have made a covenant with Me by sacrifice."

Lauds. The daybreak service of the English Church before the Reformation, and a part of which was incorporated into the Morning Prayer. The Benedictus and the 1st and 2d Collect were specially drawn from it.

Laura. The name given to a collection of little cells at some distance from each other, in which the hermits of ancient times lived together in a wilderness. There was no community life here, each hermit providing for himself. The most celebrated Lauras were in Palestine and in Egypt. (*Vide* Kingsley's " Hermits.")

Lavipedum. The washing of feet after the example of our LORD (St. John xiii.): It was observed yearly in the churches on Maundy-Thursday, and has been continued in many places, as in Jerusalem, Constantinople, Milan, Rome. Bishops and sovereigns have performed this act. Queen Elizabeth, in 1572 A.D., washed the feet of thirty-nine poor people, that being the number of years of her age. The last English sovereign who used this service was James II., but the lord high almoners continued it till 1731 A.D., and perhaps later. A trace of it is still retained, in the service for Maundy-Thursday, at Whitehall, the almoner and his assistants being girt with linen towels during the service.

Law of Christ. The Gospel and the principles of it developed and applied by the Epistles. CHRIST'S Law is the binding of the precepts of the moral Law to His spiritual life and raising them, illuminating them, and giving them a sanctifying influence. It includes the influence of His revelation upon human life, moulding it anew, since He has brought to light life and immortality. It gives a new stand-point, CHRIST Himself the chief foundation, a fresh motive, love to Him, for obedience, a new end to be attained, everlasting life. But to apply CHRIST'S Law by the inspiring motive of love to Him leads to new arrangements of the details of our life. It brings out our moral courage and tests it in many ways. It shows the intensity of our purpose, the steadfastness of our will, the depth of our self-denial; therefore our LORD said, "He that endureth to the end shall be saved." This has introduced the whole subject of casuistry (*vide* CASUISTRY), or cases of conscience. It is the elevation and consent of the heart which quickeneth both the doctrine of faith and manners. These wise words of Bishop Taylor are well worthy careful thought: "There is no other positive measure of a Christian duty but that which can have no measure itself, and that is love. He that loves will think everything too little; and he that thinks so will endeavor to do more and to do it better. We are for the present children of GOD by adoption, sealed with His Spirit, renewed by regeneration, justified by His grace, and invited forward by most glorious promises greater than we can understand. Now he that considers this state of things and hopes for that state of blessings, will proceed in duty and love together toward the perfections of GOD, never giving over till he partake of the purities of GOD and His utmost glories." The Law of CHRIST is to imitate Him, for His life, and therefore all the part of it, is our example. When He gives no precept but leaves an example therein we have our Law.

Lay Co-operation. In order to obtain a correct and definite idea of the proper work of laymen in the Church and the best methods of performing it we must first clearly understand the relative positions of clergy and laity. Under the Roman, or Hierarchical, idea of the constitution of the Church the laity have by right neither voice nor office in her. The clergy are the Church, and they only are the working element, except in so far as they may assign certain duties to her lay members, which are to be performed entirely under clerical control and direction. Under what may be termed "the Congregational" idea, on the other hand, the laity are the Church, and form the authoritative and working element, the clergy being selected and set apart by them for the duties of preaching and of various public and private ministrations. Under both these systems of organization an immense work has been done and is doing for the cause of religion and the extension of its influences. But for a true test of the correctness of these ideas we must look not to their practical results in this direction, but to the position in which, respectively, they place the clerical order, as compared with the position held by that order in the Apostolic and Post-Apostolic Church. By such comparison we find that the clergy are in the first case unduly exalted over the laity, and in the second unduly degraded, and that consequently in both cases the proper balance of co-operative effort is destroyed and the efficiency of such effort necessarily impaired. Hence neither of these ideas can be correct, and just in proportion to the influence and direction given by either to lay co-operation its practical usefulness must be lessened. In the organization of the Church as displayed in the New Testament we find that clergy and laity are essential, inseparable, integrant parts of an organism, possessing functions, rights, and responsibilities, some in common and some distinct and peculiar, but all necessarily co-operative to a common end, namely, the manifestation of "the Truth as it is in JESUS" and the salvation of mankind through its instrumentality. All baptized Christians who are not Apostles, Presbyters, or Deacons constitute the lay element, and are recognized by the Apostolic writers as co-workers with them towards the objects of the Church's organization. Under the Anglican system these principles are distinctly and prominently recognized, and they are the underlying and directing principles of all efficient and correct methods of lay co-operation.

The Church being an organization as well as an organism, of course organization is essential to the full efficiency of all her work, but we must remember that a most valuable and practical work can be done by laymen acting as individuals and upon the conviction of individual Christian responsibility. If this responsibility, which rests upon all baptized persons, were more generally recognized the labors of the clergy would not, perhaps, be lightened, but would certainly be immensely more fruitful. Nothing can be more obstructive to the extension of the Church's work and the accomplishment of her great mission than the idea that the laity are merely the receivers of benefits which she brings, and on the other hand nothing could more effectively increase her efficiency than the practical recognition of the fact that membership in her entails the obligation to work. The field for this kind of lay co-operation is almost without limit in every parish, and extends over almost every relation of life. The careful teaching of children and servants, the quiet effort to lead others to confirmation or to attendance on public worship, systematic attention to the poor and to strangers, the habit of giving to the clergy all information which may be useful in directing their labors,—these and innumerable other methods which will suggest themselves come under the class of unorganized lay co-operation. But while all these things are helpful and necessary, their efficiency may be vastly increased and strengthened by proper organization, and this organization should extend through the whole system of the Church. We find it exemplified first in the General Convention, where the laity form a most important element in the legislative authority, as well as in matters pertaining to general financial administration. While ecclesiastical law is a distinct system, differing from civil law in its application and details, yet the same general principles underlie all law, and it is of the utmost importance that minds thoroughly formed by legal training and experience, and proved by the test of success, should take part in the framing of a legal system which is to be enforced upon and for the benefit of laymen as well as clergymen. Hence the careful study of Canon Law by earnest laymen of legal knowledge and experience opens up a most useful field of co-operation. Again, in all business affairs the laity can render most efficient service, as well in the Diocese and Parish as in the General Church. Apart entirely from spiritual concerns, but absolutely necessary to the maintenance of that organization by which they are administered, there is a great amount of business detail which the clergyman, however competent, cannot attend to without serious hindrance to his more peculiar work. These details are exactly the same which pertain to all secular business, and must be conducted with the same accuracy, promptness, and fidelity, and upon precisely the same principles. Vestries especially may co-operate with their rectors most efficiently by observing the same business habits and rules in connection with parish matters as they do in those of banking or commercial houses, or of any other business corporations. Their meetings should be regular and conducted by parliamentary usage and law. The income and expenditure of the parish should be collected and disbursed with the most jealously accurate care, and the books of the treasurer should show the same exactness as those of the cashier of a bank. All parish property should be kept fully insured and in good repair and order. All subscriptions and pew-rents should be promptly collected, and all salaries promptly paid. No debt should be incurred unless provision be made beforehand for its proper payment when due. Vestrymen and parish officers should be selected solely upon the ground of their active interest in the Church and their thorough fitness for the duties to be performed, and should be required to perform diligently all that they undertake.

Without such administration behind him a clergyman is as helpless as the captain of a vessel whose crew and engineers are incompetent or negligent of their duties, and there is no form or method of lay co-operation which is more practical or more essential to the progress and welfare of the Church. But to reach this point of efficiency a vestry must be truly representative of the congregation, and that can be the case only where the members of the congregation maintain an active interest in the parish as work for which they are responsible, keeping themselves informed of its affairs and using their right of suffrage with the same diligence which they would exercise in regard to a bank or railroad in which they might be stockholders. A parish so conducted, with an active and earnest rector at its head, supported and upheld by his laity, and encouraged by the assurance of their cheerful and hearty co-operation, will surely illustrate all the possibilities open to it for the performance of the LORD's work. Then the Sunday-school should be conducted entirely by lay-work under the supervision and direction of the rector. The superintendent should be always a communicant of influence and high standing, commanding the confidence of the parishioners and the rector, and the respect of the teachers and pupils. It is his place to relieve the rector, while acting entirely with his advice and approval, of every duty and care in the organization, management, and discipline of the school not necessarily and properly pertaining to the clerical office. The teachers should be selected and should perform their duties with the same conscientious diligence which they would exhibit as salaried assistants in a secular academy, so that the rector will always feel assured of the proper and systematic management of the school as well in his absence as when present, and of the careful and certain carrying out of all his plans and directions. It is hard to estimate the value of this branch of lay co-operation, since upon it depends the character of the future laity of the Church, not only as to religious instruction, but no less as to thorough grounding in all churchly knowledge and habits. Lay-reading is another co-operative duty to which special attention has of late been directed. There should be in every parish several men of high standing in the congregation and community who have been regularly licensed by the Bishop to read the services in the absence of the minister, or to assist him therein when present. Not only are the labors of a clergyman greatly relieved by such assistance, but he is often enabled to bestow his services upon some point where a promising opening is presented for implanting the Church. The lay-reader himself may often pave the way to such openings by gathering a few people around him and giving them the service, and many instances might be cited of flourishing parishes growing out of such beginnings. In England it has become quite customary for such lay-readers to preach sermons of their own composition under the Bishop's license, but they have always a wide choice in selecting from published discourses. Parish Guilds and Brotherhoods form another very important and efficient arm of the service of lay co-operation. So various are the modes of organizing these associations and so many the methods of operation, that it will be sufficient only to point out the principle upon which they should be formed, and to suggest some of the means which may be used through them. The rector should always be the president or chairman, and the memberships should comprise all the active men in the parish, old and young. Woman's work is most efficient when separately organized, and although her active zeal forms a most important part of lay co-operation, such organizations may be best treated under a different heading. The Guild should have regular and frequent times of meeting, and a code of by-laws suited to its special needs and objects. The work to be done should be systematically assigned to various committees, each of which should be composed of members specially qualified for the duties expected of them, the rector being *ex-officio* chairman of each committee, the object being to interest all in Church work by giving each some of it to do, the heavier tasks being laid upon the more earnest, and the less thoughtful made to realize that they are of some use in and to the Church. (*Vide* GUILD.)

Thus there should be committees on "Charities," on "Sunday-School," on "Visiting," on "Music," on "Finances," on "Hospitality," on "Amusements," etc. Those who will do nothing else will often consent to act as ushers in regular turn. Wherever practicable a hall or room should be furnished, and supplied with a library, periodicals, newspapers, chess- and checker-tables, etc., and if possible, a gymnasium attached. Many useful hints may be obtained from the "Christian Associations," where all these things are utilized in the cause of religion. A most important branch of lay co-operation is found in associations of laymen in every Diocese for the relief of aged and infirm clergymen, and the families of deceased clergymen. These associations should be regularly organized and have stated meetings. By a very small expenditure they may keep the life of the rector insured in some reliable company or society. On the death of a clergyman of the Diocese each member should pay a stipulated assessment for the benefit of his family, and a similar assessment may be made to relieve the aged or indigent. The best form of organization is a board of twelve directors, who shall manage all details, and a contributing membership as large as can be obtained in the Diocese. The regular contributions should go to form a permanent Relief Fund and a Widows' and Orphans' Benefit Fund, which, as soon as they begin to assume important proportions, may be readily increased by bequests, gifts, special offertories, and other like methods.

REV. R. WILSON, D.D.

Lectionary (Lat. *lectionarium*, from *legere*, to read) is a word used to designate the Table of Lessons from the Holy Scripture appointed to be read in the public service of the Church. These Lessons are to be distinguished from the Epistles and Gospels. The latter are (1) *short* passages of Scripture (except in Holy Week); (2) are part of the Communion office, and (3) are appointed only for Sundays and the greater holidays.

The practice of reading portions of Holy Scripture in public worship is very ancient, and existed, in fact, before the coming of our SAVIOUR (Nehem. viii. 8; see also St. Luke iv. 7, for the custom during the time of our LORD). The Apostolic Church seems to have adopted the practice which the Synagogue had made familiar. And St. Paul charges the Thessalonians that his Epistle should be read unto "all the holy brethren" (1 Thess. v. 27). In early times there was probably no fixed Lectionary, though some traces of appointed Lessons are found in writers of the fourth century. In the following century, unquestionably, Lectionaries were in use, and one is still extant which is more than twelve hundred years old. (Daniel on the Prayer-Book, p. 114.)

At the Reformation the Lectionary was revised in the English Church so that the Old Testament should be read nearly through once a year, and the New Testament thrice a year. The Apocrypha was retained and read during a part of the year. The books of Chronicles were omitted because to a great extent they covered the same period of history as the books of Kings. The Song of Solomon, large portions of Ezekiel and the Apocalypse, were omitted because it was thought that their obscurity rendered them unfit for reading in public worship. Isaiah was read in Advent because his prophecies refer so largely to the coming of the MESSIAH. The old Lectionary of the English Prayer-Book continued until 1871 A.D. to be the only one permitted. In that year a new one was put forth, though the use of the old was allowed until January 1, 1879 A.D.

In the United States the Lectionary was revised when the new American Prayer-Book was issued, in 1785 A.D. The Lessons were considerably shortened, more appropriate chapters were chosen for the Sundays, and, contrary to the English practice, special Second Lessons were appointed from the New Testament on Sundays, both for the morning and afternoon. The chapters from the Apocrypha were much diminished in number, and these were taken from the Sapiential Books.

At the General Convention of 1883 A.D. a new American Lectionary was adopted, which included a special Table of Lessons for Lent. Many features of our new Lectionary closely resemble the English Lectionary of 1871 A.D., which is generally considered to be in many respects a decided improvement upon the old one. It was not introduced, however, without sharp criticism from several divines, among whom may be particularly mentioned Bishop Wordsworth, of Lincoln, Dean Burgon, and Dean Goulburn.

The following remarks on the New English Lectionary (of 1871 A.D.) are taken from Daniel on the Prayer-Book. They apply to a very large extent to the New American Lectionary. One important difference in the American Table is that special *Second* Lessons are appointed for Sundays, whereas even in the new English Lectionary the New Testament is read through in course, and the Second Lesson for Sunday is the one appointed in the Calendar for the month.

"The chief respects," says the Rev. Evan Daniel, "in which the New Lectionary differs from the old are the following:

"1. The week-day Lessons have been considerably shortened, and are no longer coincident with the present unsatisfactory division of the Bible into chapters, which often obscures the sense by separating premises from conclusion (see Heb. xi., xii.), or an exhortation from the grounds on which it is based (see Heb. iv. v.)." (The second of these instances is corrected in our American Lectionary, but the former remains.)

"2. The New Testament is read through twice in the year instead of thrice." (This change had been previously introduced into the American Lectionary 1785 A.D.)

"3. The Second Lessons in the morning, on ordinary days, are no longer taken exclusively from the Gospels and the Acts of the Apostles, nor the Second Lessons in the evening from the Epistles; but the Lessons are so arranged that when the Gospels are read in the morning the Epistles are read in the evening, and *vice versa*; so that persons who are able to attend divine service daily, either at matins or even-song, have an opportunity of hearing the whole of the New Testament, with the exception of portions of the Apocalypse, read through in the course of the year.

"4. The Lessons for Festivals and Holydays have in some cases been changed for passages more appropriate to the occasion." (As an example, compare the new Lessons for St. James' day (July 25) with the old.)

"5. More portions of the Books of Chronicles, which supplement the Books of Kings, are now read. . . . It will be observed," continues Mr. Daniel, "that the new Lectionary is cast in the same mould as the Old, and only deviates from it for the purpose of carrying out more thoroughly the principles on which the Old Lessons were selected.

Persons unable to attend Church, except on Sundays, may now follow a course of Lessons embracing all the most important passages in the Bible; and persons unable to attend Church more than once a day, instead of hearing, as formerly, the same portions of the New Testament read over and over again, while others were never heard at all, may now hear nearly the whole of the New Testament read through in the course of the year. In the Lessons for Holy-days the relations between type and anti-type are more frequently indicated, prophecies are brought into juxtaposition with their fulfillment, and incidents from the New Testament are instinctively paralleled from the Old."

In the American Lectionary, as has been mentioned, there is a special table of Lessons for the Forty Days of Lent. The three rules following were adopted by the General Convention of 1883 A.D.:

"If in any Church, upon a Sunday or Holy Day, both Morning and Evening Prayer be not said, the minister may read the Lessons appointed either for Morning or Evening Prayer.

"At Evening Prayer on Sunday, the minister may read the Lesson from the Gospels appointed for that day of the month in place of the second Lesson for the Sunday.

"Upon any day for which no Proper Lessons are provided, the Lessons appointed in the Calendar for any day in the same week may be read in place of the Lessons for the day."

The following rules for determining the Lessons in certain doubtful cases are taken from the well-known volume entitled "The Prayer-Book Interleaved" (London, 1866 A.D., 2d edit., p. 29):

1. "A Proper Lesson always takes precedence of a Calendar Lesson. . . .
2. "A Lesson from the Canonical books always (?) takes precedence of a Lesson from the Apocryphal.
4. "The Lessons for the first and fourth Sundays in Advent, for the first Sunday after Christmas, for the first and fifth Sundays in Lent, for the Sunday next before Easter, for Easter-day, for the first Sunday after Easter, for Whitsunday, for Trinity-Sunday, take precedence of the Lessons appointed for any Saints' Days which may occur on those Sundays.
3. "The Lessons for the Circumcision, the Epiphany, St. John Baptist, St. Michael, St. Simon, and St. Jude take precedence of the Lessons for any Sunday on which they occur."

The above rules on a disputed question have the authority which may belong to the excellent manual from which they are taken, and which may be derived from extensive usage among clergymen. They are, of course, not binding in law. Any country clergyman, for example, who is unable to hold services on Saints' Days, may well avail himself, if he see fit, of the concurrence of a Saint's Day with a Sunday to let his congregation hear a fine chapter from the Sapiential books of the Apocrypha; for, owing to the sale of Bibles without the Apocrypha, very many persons are hardly aware of the existence of those books, much less of the wisdom and beauty to be found in them. REV. HALL HARRISON.

Lectern. *Vide* ARCHITECTURE.

Legate. A person sent or deputed by another to act in his stead. The name is now confined to such as are deputed by the Pope to act in his stead in all matters to be negotiated, administered, or arranged in the different Churches which yield to his headship. Before the Reformation Legates could only enter the kingdom by Royal permission, or English Bishops appointed as Legates could only so act by Royal consent. After the Reformation they were not admitted into England. Cardinal Pole was the last Legate to the English Church. Queen Elizabeth forbade the Papal Agents sent by Pius IV. to set foot in England.

Legend. Anything to be read, hence a passage, either of Scripture or of the Fathers, or of history which was read aloud out of a book generally at Divine Service, but often in the refectory while the monks were at meals. The word Legend (*legenda*) became a synonym for all that is told as marvelous, and is absurd and improbable. The word Legend is now often used for traditional tales, orally transmitted, and has thus suffered a slight deflection from its original meaning.

Lent. A fast before Easter has been observed from the earliest Christian times; but the period of its duration varied in different countries and ages down to the seventh century. Of these variations Irenæus wrote in his Epistle to Victor, Bishop of Rome, about the close of the second century, when (speaking of the varying rules about Easter) he says, "For the difference of opinion is not about the day alone, but about the manner of fasting; for some think they are to fast one day, some two, some more; some measure their day as forty hours of the day and night." Tertullian, a few years later, speaks of the practice of the Church as founded upon that passage of the Gospel in which those days were appointed for fasting during which the Bridegroom was taken away; implying a fast extending from Good-Friday morning to the night before Easter. Some few years later, however, towards the middle of the third century, Origen speaks of forty days being consecrated to fasting before Easter. And at the Council of Nicæa this period was taken for granted as if long in use.

But however early the extension of the Lenten fast to forty days may have been, it is certain that the time was counted in several different ways, though always immediately preceding Easter. By various Churches the forty days were distributed over periods of nine, eight, and seven weeks (*i.e.*, from Septuagesima, Sexagesima, or Quinquagesima to Easter), by the omission of Sundays, Thursdays, and Saturdays, of Saturdays and Sundays, or of Sundays alone, from the number of fast-days, and it would appear that Lent was sometimes called by the three names now confined to the three Sundays preceding, as well as by the name of Quadrigesima.

St. Gregory, A.D. 600, introduced our present mode of observance, or sanctioned it with his authority, at the end of the sixth century, by excluding Sundays from the number of fasting days and making the thirty-six days left of the forty-two immediately preceding Easter into an exact forty by beginning the Fast on the Wednesday before Quadrigesima Sunday instead of on the Monday following it. This rule seems to have been very readily accepted in the West, but in the East Lent begins on the Monday after Quinquagesima, and the rule of fasting is so strict, that although some slight relaxation of its rigor is allowed on Sundays and Saturdays, not even the former are wholly excluded from the number of fasting days. The primary object of the institution of a fast before Easter was doubtless that of perpetuating in the hearts of every generation of Christians the sorrow and mourning which the Apostles and Disciples felt during the time the Bridegroom was taken away from them. This sorrow had indeed been turned into joy by the Resurrection, yet no Easter joys could erase from the mind of the Church the memory of the awful forty hours of blank and desolation which followed the last sufferings of her LORD; and she lives over year by year, the time from the morning of Good-Friday to the morning of Easter-day, by a representation of CHRIST, evidently set forth crucified among us (Gal. iii. 1). This was probably the earliest idea of a fast before Easter. But sorrow for CHRIST'S death should be accompanied by sorrow concerning the cause of that death, and hence the Lenten fast became a period of self-discipline, and was so probably from its first institution in Apostolic times. And according to the literal habit which the early Church had of looking up to the pattern of her Divine Master, the forty days of His fasting in the wilderness while He was undergoing Temptation became the gauge of the servants' Lent, deriving still the more force as an example from the typical prophecy of it, which was so evident in the case of Moses and Elijah.

St. Chrysostom speaks of great strictness in fasting on the part of many in his day, such as is still found in the Eastern Church. "There are those," he says, "who rival one another in fasting and show a marvelous emulation in it; some indeed who spend two whole days without food, and others who rejecting from their tables not only the use of wine and of oil but of every dish, and taking only bread and water, persevere in this practice during the whole of Lent"

Lent was in the early Church the principal time for preparing the catechumens for Baptism, and a large portion of St. Cyril's Catechetical Lectures were delivered at this season. There were also constant daily sermons at the services. Public shows were more or less strictly forbidden, and works of charity were engaged in by all who could undertake them. It was a time when sinners were called upon to do outward penance as a sign of inward contrition, that they might be received back to Communion at Easter. Lent was in fact a season of humiliation, abstinence from pleasure, fasting, prayer, penitence, and general depression of tone on account of sin, and was marked on every side with the sombre token of mourning.

The Churches of England and of America have not expressly defined any rule on the subject of Fasting. But so far as any intimation of its use is of worth, the Homily on Fasting in the Book of Homilies, whose teaching is recognized as of authority (*vide* Art. XXXV.), has urged the example of the early Church, as if intending it to be followed with a considerable amount of strictness. The work that is set before most persons, in the Providence of GOD, at the present day makes it quite impossible, however, for those who have to do it to fast every day throughout Lent. But conscientious desire to do our duty to ourselves demands that we shall use fasting and abstinence. We can fast at stated times and use due abstinence at all other times in the Lenten season as becomes the faithful of the Church. It is impossible to lay down any general law as to the amount of abstinence from food which is compatible with individual duties, nor can any one except a person possessed of much physiological acumen determine what is to be the rule for another. But the general rules may be laid down: I. That it is possible for all to diminish in some degree the quantity of their food on fasting days without harm resulting. II. That many can safely abstain from animal food altogether for some days in the week. III. That food should be taken on fasting days as a necessity, and its quality so regulated that it shall not be a luxury. IV. That all can deny themselves delicacies on fast-days which may be very properly used at other times.

Lessons. *Vide* LECTIONARY.

Letter of Orders. The letters of orders given to each Priest or Deacon upon his ordination may, in the use of the several Bishops, differ. There is no form fixed by canon law; this that follows is one in use in Pennsylvania:

"LETTER OF ORDERS.

"*Be it known by these Presents*,

"That on the   day of   , in the year of our LORD one thousand eight hundred and   , in   Church, in the   and Diocese of   , our beloved in CHRIST A. B. was by me rightly and canonically ordained and made a   , I being well assured of his virtuous and pious life, and conversation, and competent learning and knowledge in the Holy Scriptures; and he having, in my presence, freely and voluntarily declared that he believes the Holy Scriptures of the Old and New Testaments to be the word of GOD, and to contain all things necessary to salvation, and having also solemnly engaged to conform to the doctrines and worship of the Protestant Episcopal Church in the United States of America.

"In testimony whereof I have hereunto set my hand and seal at   , this said   day of   , in the year of our LORD one thousand   and in the year of my consecration."

Leviticus. The third book of Moses. It was also called the "Law of the Priests" and the "Law of Offerings," from its contents. It can be divided into seven heads: (*a*) Laws on Sacrifices (ch. i.–vii.). (*b*) A historical section on the consecration of Aaron and his sons (ch. viii.); his offering for himself and the people (ch. ix.); the death by fire of his sons Nadab and Abihu for offering strange fire before the LORD (ch. x.). (*c*) Laws on purity and purification of impurity (ch. xv., xvi.). (*d*) Laws chiefly intended to mark the separation between Israel and the heathen (ch. xvii.–xx.). (*e*) Laws for priests (ch. xxi.); holy-days and festivals (ch. xxiii.); the episode of the blasphemer (ch. xxiv.) and the law about blasphemy (ch. xxvi. 2). (*f*) Promises and threats (ch. xxvi. 2–46). (*g*) An appendix of the law of vows.

This book is linked to Exodus by the latter closing with the completion of the tabernacle, and its consecration by the descent of the cloud upon it. "From the tabernacle, thus rendered glorious by the Divine presence, issues the legislation contained in the book of Leviticus. At first GOD spake to the people out of the thunder and lightning of Sinai, and gave them His holy commandments by the hand of a mediator. But henceforth His presence is to dwell not on the secret top of Sinai but in the midst of His people, both in their wanderings through the wilderness, and afterwards in the land of Promise. Hence the first directions which Moses received after the work is finished have reference to the offerings which were to be brought to the door of the Tabernacle. As JEHOVAH draws near to the people in the Tabernacle so the people draw near to JEHOVAH in the offering. The regulations respecting sacrifices fall into three groups, and each of these groups again consists of a decalogue of instructions. Bertheau has observed that this principle runs through all the laws of Moses. They are all modeled after the pattern of the Ten Commandments, so that each distinct subject of legislation is always treated of under ten several enactments or provisions."

Objections asserted against other books of Moses seem to be in a great measure abandoned as regards this book. Its archaic form, the bold simplicity of its formulas, give disproof to any assertion of a late date; and if those who urge that the historical books of Moses were the work of the palmy days of Israelitish history, can only say that Leviticus must be not later than the times of the Judges, we can safely challenge them to show why it does not belong to the period of the Exodus.

The discussion on the groups of the laws in Leviticus is too intricate for the present work. "But we must not quit this book without a word on what may be called its spiritual meaning; that so elaborate a ritual looked beyond itself we cannot doubt. It was a prophecy of things to come; a shadow whereof the substance was CHRIST and His Kingdom. Of many things we may be sure that they belonged only to the nation to whom they were given, containing no prophetic significance, but serving as witnesses and signs to them of GOD's covenant of grace. We may hesitate to pronounce with Jerome that 'every sacrifice, nay, almost every syllable,—the garments of Aaron and the whole Levitical system,—breathe of heavenly mysteries.' But we cannot read the Epistle to the Hebrews and not acknowledge that the Levitical priests 'served the pattern and type of heavenly things;' that the sacrifices of the Law pointed to and found their interpretation the Lamb of GOD; that the ordinances of outward purification signified the true inner cleansing of the heart and conscience from dead works to serve the living GOD. One idea, moreover, penetrates the whole vast and burdensome ceremonial, and gives it a real glory even apart from any prophetic significance. Holiness is its end. Holiness is its character. The tabernacle is holy; the vessels are holy; the offerings are most holy unto JEHOVAH; the garments of the priests are holy; all who approach Him whose name is 'HOLY,' whether priests who minister unto Him, or people who worship Him, must be holy. It would seem as if amid the camp and dwellings of Israel was ever to be heard an echo of that solemn strain which fills the courts above, where the Seraphim cry one unto another, 'Holy, Holy, Holy.'" (Smith's Dictionary of the Bible, sub voc.)

Libertines. The synagogue of the Libertines is mentioned in Acts vi. 9. Most probably the libertines were the Jews who had been taken and sold into slavery by Pompey and other Roman generals, and had afterwards been emancipated and had settled in Jerusalem or were there for the feasts. The larger part of the Jews in Rome were in the condition of "freedmen" and had a quarter in the Trans-Tiber, but were banished by Tiberius about 19 A.D. Probably many of these had found their way back to Jerusalem, and would become zealous defenders of the law.

Liberty. It would be out of place to do more than to hint at one or two points of Christian Liberty. True liberty is to be distinguished from false liberty, the equivalent for license and anarchy, by the submission to law, by the means used,—*i.e.*, whether selfish and only for self-gratification, whether guided by a pure conscience or by a narrow prejudice substituted for a conscience; and also by the end proposed,—whether terminating in self alone. The truest liberty is always relative towards others, since our life is conditioned by so many antagonizing claims. It must be founded upon a practical compromise. But within ourselves the liberty we claim is that of sole accountability to GOD in the use of the laws, physical, mental, and spiritual, under which we display this triple activity of being. Yet no man is at liberty to harbor or believe in a wrong thought, since wrong antagonizes right and is destructive of all right liberty. Again, the Church permits the utmost liberty of mere opinion compatible with a hearty acceptance of the Apostolic Creed and an honest, sincere use of her formularies. She allows the broadest scope to the play of those faculties which mark individual minds whenever, to use Hooker's phrase, her members do not by their speculations "deny the foundation by the consequents." In these things there is the true Catholicity, for it is founded upon a firm adherence to the truths of the Faith. We must beware that the so-called liberty of conscience be not mistaken for a liberty to entertain prejudice, for conscience cannot claim to judge till it knows, and if it judges before it is properly informed it is no longer a true conscience, but a prejudging self-will.

Life. The creative gift of GOD to man. It is a complex gift, and is so recognized by Moses: "And GOD breathed into his nostrils the breath of life, and man became a living soul," when the Hebrew (and the margin) read "the breath of lives." It was not only a fact recorded by Moses, but it was also a part of that belief which belonged to the purer faith of patriarchal ages. "The breath of the ALMIGHTY hath given me life" (Job xxxiii.). It is therefore but a sequence to this truth that though modern science can trace out the adjuncts and manifestations of the physical life, it cannot touch the life itself,—the vital power that converts, combines, and employs all material presented to it for its use. Heat, light, electricity, nervous force, are intimately associated with the physical part of this complex power; respiration and other functions are intimately woven into its manifestation,—they are the conditions which it uses, by which it remains a tenant of this body of dust. But physical life in man provides also a mental or intellectual life. And since these are the gift of a beneficent CREATOR, and are of His breath, there is also the spiritual life added. Then it follows that in some as yet unrevealed way our LORD, in whom was Life, is intimately concerned in the restoration not only of a spiritual sense, but of actual living power, lost by the fall, heightening the lower forms of this life or living soul by this restoration. For as the FATHER hath life in Himself, so hath He given to the SON to have

28

life in Himself,—"the dead shall hear the voice of the SON of GOD, and they that hear shall live" (St. John v. 25). Compare the teaching that "The first man Adam *was made* a living soul; the last Adam *was made* a quickening spirit."

Therefore we find the fact that "in Him we live and move and have our being" includes all forms of our life, however manifested, and binds them to Him. His own words, "I am the Life," are true in the widest sense; and as He has given certain physical functions as the conditions under which the body retains the physical life, so there are certain spiritual functions also necessary for us to foster and develop. His quickening, reinforcing presence is felt in this our spiritual life. Our souls are the breath of lives which He gave, and which return to Him, not losing their individuality thereby, but ever most truly existing in Him with whom is the fountain of life, and in whose light we see light.

Life is a most sacred gift, hedged about with many defenses, and protected by direct command of GOD. Life is His, for His very Name JEHOVAH means He that *is*. Therefore there can be nothing more sacred to us than life itself, and being restored by regeneration in the SON of GOD who is the Life, and sanctified by the HOLY GHOST who is the LORD and Giver of life, it must be looked upon as the holiest, as it is the basis of all else we can have,—the first of the talents committed to us.

Light. The gift to the world made on the first day of creation. It is typical of the spiritual light vouchsafed to the soul, "and in Thy light shall we see light." So our LORD was to be the Light that lighteneth the Gentiles, and of Himself He said, "I am the Light of the world."

Light has always been the attendant on whatever visible manifestations GOD has chosen to give us of His presence.

It was the "burning lamp" of Abraham's covenant, the burning bush which spake with Moses, the pillar of fire, the glory as of a devouring fire upon Mount Sinai, which also filled the Feast of the Tabernacle at its consecration, so that Moses could not enter. And again, at the dedication of the Temple the glory of the LORD so filled the Holy of Holies and the House of the LORD that the priests could not stand to minister because of the cloud. It was the infolding fire Ezekiel saw; the light of burning coals at His feet of Habakkuk's vision. These revelations all sum up in the glory of the Sun of rightousness, and who is the Light and Sun of His holy Temple. As soon as the Church ritual had developed, soon after the cessation of persecution, light was used symbolically, for the lights were burned at the reading of the Gospel and at other services, as at baptism (when a lighted taper was sometimes put into the hand of the catechumen), and at the celebration of the Holy Communion. Lights were used freely at different festivals and at funeral rites; but while the practice was general, the usages and times at which the lights were used varied very much in the Western Church in the different provinces. The ritual use of lights in the English and American Churches is not at all usual.

Limbus. A word of rather late introduction (*i.e.*, after 1150 A.D.), and one which in the form "limbo" is so perverted by still later misuse that it cannot be employed for any theological purposes. It was invented to describe the place in Hades which the righteous heathen and unbaptized infants and those who lived before the Advent of CHRIST occupy. It was taught in a vague way by the early Church Fathers, but was more dwelt upon by the schoolmen, and received form from them. Every writer of the early Fathers who has occasion to dwell upon the state of the departed in general, had something to say of those who are "un der the uncovenanted mercies of GOD." But their teaching was perfectly distinct from even the thought of a Purgatory.

Litany. A supplicatory prayer restricted to a responsive form of intercession between priest and people. It was used in processions. The Litany received its greatest development in France about the fifth and sixth centuries. It passed into English usage in 747 A.D., though the first vernacular Litany was published in 1544 A.D. by Henry VIII. It was the earliest part of the English Prayer-Book that was published, for the Creed, Commandments, and LORD'S Prayer (1536 A.D.) were for general instruction. It was placed in the Prayer-Book of 1549 A.D., to be said before the Communion Office on Wednesdays and Fridays, but in 1552 A.D. it was ordered as now for Sundays, Wednesdays, and Fridays. It is a compilation from many sources, which Cranmer used freely, removing from them all objectionable phrases, but it is an incomparably perfect form of intercession for all estates of men. It may be divided into five main divisions:

I. The obsecrations offered to the HOLY TRINITY. II. The intercessions offered to our LORD, which take two forms of response: the first reciting petitions for special deliverances and pleading His redemptive acts, the second offering general intercessions for all estates. III. The Kyrie eleisons. IV. The prayers interspersed with responsive versicles. V. The closing prayers, which are enlarged in our American Prayer-Book by placing before the final collect the beautiful General Thanksgiving, which in a slightly different form (with space for special prayers for those who desired the prayers of the congregation) was in English occasional prayers. The practice which omits the versicle "Let us pray" loses the use of the ancient call to increased fervor in prayer, uttered by the Deacon at certain points in the old Liturgies.

Litany-Desk. *Vide* FALDSTOOL.

Liturgy. The classical use of λειτουργία, "a public work" or "duty" was transferred in the Septuagint and New Testament alike to the ministration of public worship; at first, and for several centuries A.D., including the offices of worship generally, but gradually restricted in ecclesiastical language to the Holy Communion. In popular use at the present day, the older and wider meaning reappears of any precomposed form of public prayer; but we treat here only of those forms for the celebration of the Holy Communion found in all ages of Christianity.

The divinely prescribed ceremonial of the Passover was, in its essential features, observed by our LORD at the Institution of the Holy Communion; and His own acts and words on that occasion became the frame-work of all Christian Liturgies. Beyond these,—i.e., the breaking of the bread, the taking of the cup, the blessing or giving thanks (*Eucharist*), the words of institution, and perhaps the LORD'S Prayer and a hymn (or psalm),—there was probably no *original* form of Liturgy from which later ones have been derived. In other words, each church, community, or Diocese had its own way of filling in this outline. But as the earliest centres of Church life and work grew into metropolitan and patriarchal Sees, their use or ritual became naturally that of the lesser Dioceses around them, and crystallized, so to speak, in fixed form as it extended its circle of observance. This was especially the case with the chief Apostolic Sees, afterwards the great Patriarchates of the East and West, —Jerusalem, Alexandria, Antioch, and Rome, and in later days Constantinople; and the Liturgies of these Churches, together with that of Ephesus, have been undoubtedly the sources of all modern Eucharistic offices.

1. Aside from the well-known mention of Christian worship in Pliny's letter to Trajan, where he appears to refer to the Eucharist, the earliest account of a Liturgy is given us by Justin Martyr; probably that of Antioch, about 150 A.D. St. Cyril, of Jerusalem (347 A.D.), in his last Catechetical Lecture, describes the Liturgical use of his day and place, and St. Chrysostom, a little later, that of Antioch, in terms from which it would appear that all these three were of the same family, and essentially the same as the so-called Liturgy of St. James, still in use in its Syriac version by the Jacobites (or Monophysites) of the East, though its Greek or orthodox form has long been disused. With them all may be compared the Greek Liturgy given in the Eighth Book of the Apostolical Constitutions, undoubtedly of or near the age of Chrysostom, and the most complete in all its parts which has come down to us from that day, though we have no proof that it exactly represents any Eucharistic service in actual use. A tabular view, taking the Liturgy of the Apostolical Constitutions as a standard, shows concisely the parts and order of each of these ancient services. All were preceded by Epistle, Gospel, sermon, and prayers for those not yet admitted to Communion,—in other words, a *Missa Catechumenorum*, or ante-communion service.

	Apostolical Constitutions.	Justin Martyr.	Jerusalem (St. Cyril).	St. James (St. Chrysostom).
First Intercessory Prayers for the Faithful	1	1	...	1
Pax ("The Peace of GOD") and Kiss of Peace	2	2	2	4
Priest's Ablution of Hands	3	...	1	...
First Oblation of the Elements (and offerings in kind or money)	4	3	...	5
Priest's Preparatory Prayer and Vesting	5	...	...	2
Apostolic Benediction	6	...	...	3
Sursum Corda ("Lift up your hearts")	7	...	3	6
Preface (variable or constant) and Sanctus	8	4	4	7
Consecration and Second Oblation (of the Consecrated Elements)	9	5	5	8
Intercession for the Living and the Departed	10	...	6	9
Pax (second time)	11	...	...	...
Sancta Sanctis ("Holy things for the holy")	12	...	8	11
Gloria in Excelsis	13	...	...	13
Communion	14	6	10	15
Thanksgiving and Prayer	15	...	11	16
Benediction	16	...	...	...
Not in (The LORD'S Prayer	...	...	7	10
Apost. { *Gustate* ("O taste and see how gracious")	...	...	9	12
Const. (Breaking of Bread (for Distribution)	...	...	...	14

It is highly probable, however, that the LORD'S Prayer was used in every form of Liturgy, though not always mentioned in the above accounts.

2. We come next to the *Alexandrian* family of Liturgies, the service of Egypt and Ethiopia; comprising the Greek of "St. Mark" and Coptic of "St. Cyril" (two most closely related), two others, each in Coptic, Arabic, and Greek, by name (and by name only) those of "St. Basil" and "St. Gregory," and the "Ethiopic Canon." Here again the points of agreement are many, the differences mostly in order of parts, which, however, is invariable for the "ante-communion" or preparation (where it is given), *Sursum Corda*, Preface, Sanctus, and Consecration. In St. Mark and St. Cyril the Second Oblation both precedes and follows the Words of Institution (Consecration); and here occur liturgical phrases (intercessions) identical with those found in St. Clement of Rome,—a curious proof of early communion between Egypt and Rome. All have the LORD'S Prayer after Consecration; the Ethiopic Canon alone after Communion (as in the English Liturgy), and this only does not mention either *Sursum Corda* or the reading of the "Diptychs," which, or some corresponding mention of the living and the departed, was undoubtedly a feature of every primitive Liturgy. It may be

noted here that there is no trace of the *Creed* in any form in the Eucharistic Service before the sixth century; while, as is well known, it was an important part of the Baptismal Office.

3. The Liturgy of *Cæsarea*, commonly known as that of St. Basil (and rightly, as belonging to his Episcopate, and in part, no doubt, composed by him), with that of *Constantinople*, called St. Chrysostom's, but probably several centuries later, are in use throughout most parts of the Eastern Church at this day, but with many modern interpolations. We have both, however, in a comparatively early and incorrupt form, in MSS. of the close of the ninth century, at Rome. Both add to the earlier Liturgies, above noticed, the Creed; and in both, as in some of the Egyptian Liturgies, the Intercessions for the living and the dead *follow* the Consecration and Second Oblation.

4. Passing over three *Nestorian* Liturgies in Syriac, still preserved and used by the Christians of Mesopotamia (of "The Apostles," "Theodore the Interpreter," and "Nestorius"), and presenting no ancient characteristics of special note, we come to the Latin Liturgy of *Carthage*, no longer extant, but described quite fully by Tertullian, St. Cyprian, and St. Augustine. It differs from the Greek order chiefly, perhaps solely, in the introduction of the *Pax* and Kiss of Peace immediately after the Consecration and Second Oblation; and the Intercession for the Living and the Dead, not only before but after the Communion.

5. The next variation of importance is found in the early Liturgies of *Spain* (including the *Mozarabic*, preserved by the Christians of Granada after the conquest by the Moors) and *France*, long since superseded in both countries by the Roman, but having distinct traces of an independent *Eastern* origin, apparently from the Church of Ephesus; and this family has a special interest for us, as the principal, immediate source of the present English Liturgy. This type of Liturgy, although ascribed traditionally to St. John (as would naturally be the case from his late residence at Ephesus), may be supposed with much probability to have originated with St. Paul. (See Freeman, Principles of Divine Service, ii. 399, 404.) Like the Eastern Liturgies before noted, it is preceded by Lessons from the Old Testament, Epistle, and Gospel; the Offertory is accompanied by a Trisagion (in Greek); then comes the Apostolic Benediction, Kiss of Peace, *Sursum Corda*, Preface, Sanctus, etc.; the words of Institution begin as in Greek, "In the night in which He was betrayed," not, as in other Latin Liturgies, "the day before;" the "*Sanctus Sanctis*" and "*Gustate*" are given. The marked characteristics were the constantly varying Prefaces, and the *Embolismus*, or expansion of the LORD'S Prayer, with variable introduction, in Spain before, in France after, Communion. Both the living and the dead are mentioned by name in the Intercessions. Before the Gospel was sung *Benedicite*, and after it was a Sermon, followed in the Spanish and Mozarabic, at least, by the Creed of Constantinople. In all there is a special *Symbolical* Fraction (not mentioned in other Eastern Liturgies) with minute rites, perhaps not as ancient as the substance of these Liturgies. Manuscripts and records of the Spanish and French Liturgies go back to the seventh century; but the original features of the Mozarabic only appear from their correspondence with those of the Eastern Church. The Gallican, with all its Eastern peculiarities, was undoubtedly the type introduced into England by St. Augustine of Canterbury, and many features of it were preserved in the Uses of York, Sarum, and Hereford, down to the Reformation,— *e.g.*, the Hymn *Veni Creator*; the first Oblation after the Introit, of Bread and Wine simultaneously; the entire omission of Adoration *after* Consecration. All these seem to indicate a fusion, to some extent, not only of the Gallican, but of the ancient British and Irish forms observed at the planting of Christianity in Britain with the later general type derived from Rome.

6. The *Roman* Liturgy, through the influence of the Apostolic See, superseded in course of time all other Liturgies in the West. Special features of it can be traced with some certainty to the latter part of the fifth century; but in this instance we must distinguish carefully between the *Sacramentary* (*Libri Sacramentorum*) or variable portion of the service,—*i.e.*, the Collect, Epistle, Gospel, *Secreta* (silent prayer before the Oblation), Preface, Thanksgiving, and Benediction, which is still extant, as arranged by (probably even before) Pope Gelasius (495 A.D.),—and the "Canon of the Mass," which in its earliest existing form is that of St. Gregory the Great, a century later. The earlier Sacramentary and later Canon were certainly long combined, and much of Gelasius's work is probably still included in the Roman Missal. The first part, or *Ordo Missæ*, in the Gregorian Sacramentary, consists of the Introit, *Kyrie*, *Gloria in Excelsis*, Collect, Epistle, Gradual (or Alleluia), Gospel, Offertory, and First Oblation (of the Elements); and the Canon begins with the last words of the prayer *Super Oblata* (the same as the *Secreta* of Gelasius) said aloud, and followed immediately by *Dominus Vobiscum*, *Sursum Corda*, Preface ("It is very meet," etc., as in the English Liturgy, followed by the Proper of the Day), Sanctus, Intercession for the Living, Consecration, and Second Oblation, Commemoration of, and Intercession for, the Departed, Lord's Prayer (with a brief Embolismus), *Pax* (substituted for the more ancient Kiss of Peace), and Benediction. The actual Communion following the *Pax* has no mention in the *Canon*, whose *rubrics*, it must be noticed, are of more modern date. Nor does the Creed occur in the *Ordo*,

though from the sixth or seventh century its Eucharistic use after the Gospel became common in the Western Church.

7. The Church of *Milan* retained its own independent *Ambrosian* Liturgy, in spite of all the efforts of the Roman See, till our own day, varying from the Gregorian in the introduction of a Lesson from the Prophets, Antiphon, or short Anthem, and *Benedictus* with *Alleluia*, between Collect and Epistle; *Gloria in Excelsis* and Benediction *before* the Gospel; *Kyrie* and Antiphon after the Gospel; the First Oblation brought in to the Priest by ten aged men and as many women; Hymns and Prefaces in great number, and many parts of the Canon differing considerably from the Roman Missal.

8. The above represent in a general way all the Liturgies of early Christianity in the East and West. All, it will be noted, show both an essential agreement, in doctrinal teaching, and material differences from the modern uses of Rome and Constantinople.

Intercessions for the living and the departed appear in every account from Tertullian down, but neither separated (by placing the latter after the Consecration, as now in the Roman Missal), nor supplemented by Invocations of the Saints until the sixth or seventh century. Both the First Oblation (bringing of the Elements) and the Second (after Consecration), with the doctrine of the Eucharistic Sacrifice, are recognized by Justin Martyr (the latter in his " Dialogue with Trypho"), and by every Liturgy after his day. The *Epiclesis*, or Invocation of the HOLY SPIRIT, follows the Consecration in all Liturgies of Eastern origin (including the Spanish and Gallican), but not in those of the West. The dismissal of the catechumens (or non-communicants) and actual Communion of the faithful present, are obvious instances of differences between ancient and modern Roman use.

9. To these we add a brief notice of some modern forms of the Liturgy.

(*a*) The Church of *England* set forth in 1549 A.D. a translation and revision of her ancient Liturgy (in what is known as the "First Book of Edward VI."), following closely, in most respects, the Gregorian *Ordo* and *Canon;* omitting its Invocations of Saints, but retaining its Invocation of the HOLY GHOST, Commemoration of the Saints, Second Oblation, Intercessions for the Departed (restoring these to their ancient place *before* the Consecration), and Words of Delivery ("the Body of our LORD," etc.); all of which, together with the rubrics for Eucharistic Vestments, dismissal of non-communicants, bringing in of the Elements, and action of Consecration, were left out, or greatly changed three years later, by the "Second Book," under the influence of the German Reformers Bucer and Martyr. Subsequent revisions in 1562, 1604, and 1662 A.D., especially the latter, have restored the Commemoration, Second Oblation (optional, indeed, and *after* Communion), Words of Delivery (prefixed to those of the Second Book), and rubrics for the bringing in of the Elements and Consecration, adding others for reverent presentation of Alms and covering and consumption of Elements remaining. The LORD'S Prayer and *Gloria in Excelsis* are placed *after* Communion (contrary to all ancient use as well as to the Gregorian Canon), and, on the other hand, the ancient vestments appear to be restored by the present rubrics, though this is questioned.

(*b*) The Liturgy of the *Scottish* Church, 1718 A.D., superseding one set forth by Archbishop Laud in 1637 A.D., now optional in Scotland with the English Liturgy, has been closely followed in most points by (*c*) the *American* Liturgy of 1789 A.D. In both, the Second Oblation and Invocation of the HOLY SPIRIT are restored to their ancient place immediately after Consecration, the American inserting in the Oblation the significant words, "which we now offer unto Thee;" and in some less important details these resemble, more nearly than the English, the First Book of Edward VI. A revision of the American Liturgy, not affecting its doctrinal teaching, is now (1883–86 A.D.) in progress. (*d*) The *Old Catholic* Liturgy of 1880 A.D., and (*e*) the Liturgy of *Sweden* (Evangelical Lutheran), are translations and revisions of the Roman Missal, differing, however, very widely, the former following the Gregorian Canon even more closely than does the first English Liturgy, with which the Old Catholic service is doctrinally identical; the latter a somewhat bald abridgment, wanting many characteristic features of the ancient Eucharistic services. (Both, with the Roman Liturgy, may be found in the *American Church Review*, Jan., 1881 A.D., and June, 1883 A.D. See also Dict. of Chr. Antiquities, of whose full and valuable articles this is little more than a condensation, and references there given.)

Consult also Neale's Holy Eastern Church, Daniel's Codex Liturgicus, Rev. C. R. Hale's Translation of the Mozarabic Liturgy, Blunt's Annotated Book of Common Prayer.

REV. C. W. HAYES.

Lollards. The followers of Wycklif, who took up many of his teachings. Lollardism became a movement about 1380 A.D., and continued on, more as a political movement among the people, till about 1550 A.D. It was to repress Lollardism that the statute "on burning heretics" was passed in the first year of Henry IV.

Long Island, Diocese of, extending from east to west one hundred and twenty miles, with an average width of fifteen miles, embracing an area of 1682 square miles, and including the counties of Kings, Queens, and Suffolk, was set off from the Diocese of New York on the 15th of November, 1868 A.D. The Primary Convention was held in the city of Brooklyn on the 18th and 19th insts. following, when the new Diocese was formally organized, and the Rev. Abram Newkirk Littlejohn, D.D., Rector of the Church of the Holy Trinity, Brooklyn, was elected Bishop. The number of clergy belonging to the Diocese was eighty-five, of whom sixty-nine were entitled to act as depuries; and of organized parishes in union with Convention, fifty-five. There were at this time 9014 communicants, and for the conventional year preceding, 1691 baptisms, 725 confirmations, 503 marriages, 951 burials ; Sunday-school teachers, 1230, and scholars, 10,677 ; and offerings for all purposes, $204,720.62. Dr. Littlejohn was consecrated on the 27th of January, 1869 A.D., the Rt. Rev. Horatio Potter, D.D., of New York, being Consecrator, assisted by the Bishops of New Jersey, Virginia, Western New York, Nebraska and Dakota, Colorado, Pittsburg, Maine, and Oregon and Washington Territories. Bishop Littlejohn was born on the 13th of December, 1824 A D.; graduated at Union College, 1845 A.D.; admitted to the Diaconate on the 19th of March, 1848 A.D., by Bishop De Lancey ; and to the Priesthood on the 12th of June, 1849 A.D., by Bishop Brownell. After officiating for brief periods at St. Ann's Church, Amsterdam, N. Y.; St. Andrew's, Meriden, Conn. ; and Christ Church, Springfield, Mass., he became, in June, 1851 A.D., Rector of St. Paul's, New Haven, and served also for seven years as lecturer on Pastoral Theology in the Berkeley Divinity School. In 1860 A.D. he removed to Brooklyn, L. I., having accepted the rectorship of the Church of the Holy Trinity, which he held until his elevation to the Episcopate. In 1874 A.D. he was appointed by the Presiding Bishop to take charge of the American Episcopal Churches on the Continent of Europe. Besides various charges and occasional sermons, he has contributed numerous critiques, essays, and reviews to the current literature of the day, and published the following volumes: "Conciones ad Clerum," 1879–80 A.D.; "Individualism, its Growth and Tendencies;" Sermons delivered before the University of Cambridge, England, in November, 1880 A.D.; "The Priesthood in the latter part of the Nineteenth Century ;" lectures on the Bishop-Paddock Foundation, 1884 A.D.

At the end of the first decade of Bishop Littlejohn's active Episcopate the following statistics show the healthful growth of the Diocese. There had been over 20,000 baptisms; confirmations, 12,763 ; number of communicants, 14,587 ; Sunday-school teachers, 2033, and scholars, 15,508 ; Deaconesses admitted, 19 ; candidates for Orders, 53 ; Priests ordained, 46 ; Deacons, 41 ; Communion alms, $149,167.99 ; contributions to missions, $303,182.99 ; education for the ministry, $36,430.99 ; Parochial, Diocesan, and general purposes, $4,640,032.82; to which should be added several items not appearing in the summary of the parochial reports, viz. : benefactions to the Church Charity Foundation, liquidation of church debts, increase of several Diocesan funds, purchase of the Episcopal residence, $40,000; donations of property held by the trustees of the estate belonging to the Diocese, $100,000, forming an aggregate for the first ten years of over five millions of dollars.

Besides the development of parochial and missionary work, especial attention has been given to the establishment and building up of charitable institutions and church schools. The Church Charity Foundation, with its several buildings, located on Atlantic Avenue, Brooklyn, and covering an area of forty-five city lots, comprises a Home for Aged Indigent Women, Aged Men, and Aged Married Couples; an Orphan House and School, with a Printing Establishment known as the "Orphans' Press ;" and St. John's Hospital, organized in June, 1871 A.D., with a Memorial Chapel for the accommodation of the several houses, which are under the charge of the Deaconesses of the Diocese and a resident Chaplain,—the whole constituting a property valued at over $300,000, with an endowment fund of $100,000, the income of which, together with the contributions of the churches throughout the Diocese, defrays the current expenses of the beneficiaries. There are also in Brooklyn the Atlantic Avenue Dispensary for the gratuitous treatment of the poor; the Sheltering Arms Nursery, with its Infirmary ; St. Phebe's Mission, for special work in the public institutions; and a Deaconesses' House, on Washington Avenue, owned by the Order. In the latter, with its adjoining capacious school-house, is located St. Catherine's Hall, a boarding and day school for girls, under the management of the Sisters of St. John. Several of the city churches also have parochial and industrial schools.

In 1877 A.D. the Diocese accepted the munificent offer of Mrs. A. T. Stewart to erect a Cathedral at Garden City, with an Episcopal residence and Cathedral Schools, in memory of her husband, Alexander T. Stewart; and, accordingly, the corner-stone of the Cathedral of the Incarnation was laid on the 28th of June, 1877 A.D., and on the 19th of September following, St. Paul's School for Boys, and St. Mary's for Girls, were opened. On the 18th of June, 1879 A.D., the corner-stone was laid of the large and permanent building for St. Paul's School, which was finished and occupied in September, 1883 A.D., and is regarded as one of the most complete edifices for educational purposes in this country, having a façade 300 feet in length, with three wings, each 180 feet deep, comprising a chapel, school-rooms, library, and parlors, dining-hall, gymnasium, laboratory, infirmary, dormitories, bath-rooms, kitchens, etc. The Episcopal residence is also an ornate and commodious building, situated in the extensive park surrounding the Cathedral. Seven years were occupied in the erection of the Cathedral, which is Early English in style, and is constructed of Bellville stone elaborately wrought, consisting of nave and aisles, transepts, choir and chancel, baptistery, tower and spire, with a crypt, sacristy, chantry, and mausoleum. The total length is 190 feet; of choir and chancel, 60 feet; width of transepts, which have aisles, 80 feet; of nave 52 feet, and height of spire 221 feet. The organ is one of the largest ever constructed, and consists of six separate portions located in different parts of the edifice, connected by electric wires and played from one key-box, as are also the chime of bells, thirteen in number. The rich and beautiful design, and its solid and substantial materials and workmanship; the delicately chiseled stone and marbles in the baptistery, rood-screen, and mausoleum; the elegant font and altar; the exquisitely carved organ-cases, Episcopal throne and sedilia; the superb pictorial glass, with the admirable proportions and decorations of the structure everywhere, combine to render this an imposing memorial of the founder of Garden City, and a most worthy and appropriate ecclesiastical edifice and official centre for the Bishop of the Diocese. At the time of writing the Diocese numbers: Clergy, 111; parishes and missions, 107 churches; families, 13,719; individuals, 63,465; baptisms, infants, 2139; adults, 298; total, 2437; confirmed, 1495; communicants, 18,138; marriages, 692; burials, 1553; Sunday-school teachers, 1800; scholars, 16,727; contributions, $571,135.40. The census of 1880 A.D. gives the population of Kings County as 599,549; of Queens, 90,547; and of Suffolk, 53,926; total, 744,022.

REV. T. S. DROWNE, D.D.

Lord. The word used to translate the Hebrew JEHOVAH. It is used freely with the other title, GOD, Elohim (*vide* ELOHIM); so that the hypercritical attempt to distinguish between what are called the Elohistic and the Jehovistic documents falls to pieces. LORD as the self-existent One, the source of Life to all others, is the most secret name revealed to us. This LORDSHIP belongs to the FATHER, to the SON, and to the HOLY GHOST by the unity of the Divine principle. As in the SON dwells the fullness of the FATHER, and as the FATHER communicates to the SON of His own nature and giveth to Him to have life in Himself, LORDSHIP must belong to the SON. So since the HOLY GHOST proceeds from the FATHER and is sent by the SON, so to Him too belongs the title of LORD. But in relation to ourselves, the WORD of GOD, the eternal SON, is both LORD and CHRIST. For the FATHER put all power into His Hands, has made Him Judge as well as Redeemer, and because He has taken our nature and has made Atonement for us He is our High-Priest, and so our LORD and our CHRIST. This LORDSHIP is given to Him in and through His Resurrection. (*Vide* RESURRECTION.)

Lord's Day. *Vide* SUNDAY.

Lord's Prayer was given on two separate occasions, first upon the preaching of the Sermon on the Mount, and secondly when His disciples came to Him to ask Him to teach them how to pray (St. Luke xi. 2-4). In the Sermon on the Mount He set it as the model of all. "After this manner therefore pray ye," was the charge then. But as the sum of all prayer it was given privately,— "When ye pray, say." The Church seems to make something of this use in the twofold use of it in the Holy Communion, placing it as the very first prayer, and apparently to the minister only,—"And the Minister standing at the right side of the Table, or where Morning and Evening Prayer are appointed to be said, shall say the LORD'S Prayer and the Collect following, the People kneeling." But at the close of the Celebration the People are to repeat with him the LORD'S Prayer. It was taught to the catechumens just before baptism as one of the sacred trusts of doctrine. It was used especially in the Liturgies, where it was frequently followed by a special prayer founded upon the last petition. It was incorporated into every public office, and is an integral part of every separate office in the Prayer-Book. It has passed into the constant private devotions of every Christian.

The effort has been made to show that its petitions had been in some form in use before our LORD taught this prayer. It is true that such ideas as are therein used are common to all prayers, but not so compacted and pregnant with multifold meanings. And whenever any apparent parallels have been produced, it has always followed that they are of a date later than the Gospel. There is a slight variation in the petition for daily bread. St. Matthew has "this day," St. Luke has "day by day," but these are proper to the two separate occasions on which they were given.

Lord's Supper. One of the two great Sacraments of the Church, ordained by Christ Himself. (*Vide* SACRAMENT.) Baptism being the Sacrament of admission into, the LORD'S Supper that of continuance in, His Church.

In this article will be considered regarding this Rite, (A) The names by which it has been called, as throwing light upon the meanings attached to it. (B) Its History. (C) Its Nature. (*Vide* also PRIEST and REAL PRESENCE.)

(A) THE NAMES GIVEN TO THIS SACRAMENT.

(1) *The Lord's Supper.*—It is so called by St. Paul (1 Cor. xi. 20), doubtless from the fact of its institution during the Paschal Supper, and it is called by this name by several early writers. It appears to have been at first celebrated in connection with the Love-Feast (*Agapé*), the abuse of which

the Apostle in the above passage is condemning. As that gradually was disused and the time of administering the sacrament was changed from evening to early morning, so this name drifted out of frequent use, for it seemed less used, though found in all the early writers. It is one of the names given it in the Prayer-Book.

(2) *Eucharist.*—This was the most common name for this Sacrament; the giving-of-thanks, or Eucharism, being a prominent feature of the institution of our LORD. St. Paul is supposed to allude to this when he asks, " How shall he that occupieth the room of the unlearned say Amen at Thy giving of thanks?" literally, " at Thy Eucharising" (1 Cor. xiv. 16). It was applied to the Sacrament from the earliest times. Ignatius, Justin Martyr, Irenæus, Origen, Clemens Alexandrinus, all use it. Thus Justin Martyr, 140 A.D., says, after describing the celebration, "And this food-taking is called among us the Eucharist." Clemens writes, " Melchisedec gave bread and wine, consecrated food, as a type of the Eucharist." (Scudamore, Notitia Eucharistica, p. 7.)

(3) *Holy Communion.*—This is also a Scriptural name. "The cup of blessing which we bless, is it not the Communion (or partaking) of the blood of CHRIST? The bread which we break, is it not the Communion of the body of CHRIST?" (1 Cor. x. 16.) The context shows that the Apostle also refers to the Communion or fellowship Christians have one with another as members of CHRIST's body, by the joint partaking of this spiritual food : " For we *being* many are one bread, *and* one body; for we are all partakers of that one bread." So that the word had a double meaning, of the Communing with CHRIST and through Him with one another ; hence is very appropriate. It was not, however, so generally used of the Sacrament as were some other names, being more frequently used to express Church membership. It is the other name used in the Prayer-Book.

(4) *The Breaking of the Bread.*—It is generally agreed that this Sacrament is intended in Acts ii. 42: " They continued steadfastly in the Apostles' doctrine and fellowship, and in the breaking of the bread and the prayers." Also in Acts xx. 7: "And upon the first day of the week, when the disciples came together to break bread," the Holy Communion is meant. This name, however, never came into very general use.

(5) *The Oblation, or Offering.*—This name at first was given because of the various offerings of alms, in kind or money, for the poor, and for the support of the ministry, and also of bread and wine for the celebration itself, which were made at the time of the Eucharist ; also because of the spiritual oblation in the commemoration of the Sacrifice of CHRIST. Gradually the term came to be used chiefly of this last, and so of the Communion itself, and " to partake of the holy oblation" meant to receive. In our own service the bread and wine placed upon the Holy Table are called oblations, and after the words of consecration are offered to the Divine Majesty, as the memorial the SON has commanded us to make; which in the margin is called *The Oblation.*

(6) Analogous to this is the term *Sacrifice*, which from very early days is found used of this Sacrament, though not in the New Testament. It was first used for the material offerings of the alms and of the Bread and Wine, and afterwards of the Commemoration of the Sacrifice of the death of CHRIST. Thus Justin Martyr says, that " the Sacrifices" which Christians offer, as CHRIST commanded, " that is, in the Eucharist of the Bread and of the cup," are pleasing to GOD as foretold by the Prophet Malachi. " Which sacrifices only," he further says, " Christians have undertaken to make ; and in the remembrance also of their food, both dry and liquid, in which also there is a memory of the suffering of the SON of GOD which he endured for them" (Dial. with Trypho, 117). Irenæus and Tertullian both use it in the same way. But gradually the word came to be used chiefly of the Commemoration of CHRIST's Sacrifice, and by the end of the third century the Eucharist was commonly called " The Sacrifice," but always as a commemoration. Thus St. Chrysostom : " We offer, indeed, but making a remembrance of this death. . . . We offer not another sacrifice, like the High-Priest of old, but always the same,—or rather we perform a commemoration of a sacrifice." (Scudamore, p. 16. The reader is referred to the word PRIEST for the view the Church holds.)

(7) *The Mass.*—We have left this name for the last, because though now widely used, especially in the Roman Communion, it was the latest used of all, and there is less authority for it than for any of the others. The word is from the Latin *missa*, and simply means dismissal. It was used by the Deacons to announce the termination of certain portions of the service, and the release of those who were not entitled to remain for the Eucharistic service ; the Deacons proclaiming to the catechumens and others, *Ite ; missa est*,—Depart ; it is the dismissal. And as this was the signal for the beginning of the Liturgy proper, the name *missa* came to be applied to the office which followed it. St. Ambrose, 385 A.D., is said to be the first who so used it, but it did not come into general use until the end of the sixth century. (Scudamore, p. 1.) The English Church, on the final revision of the Prayer-Book, rejected it because of many superstitions which had connected themselves with the word. Traces of its former use remain in such words as Christ-mas, Candle-mas, Lam-mas.

Each of the names by which it has been called throws some light upon the history and meaning of this Holy Sacrament, viz. :

the first and fourth tell of its institution, the second, fifth, and sixth of its nature, Eucharistic and commemorative to GOD and man, the third of the union with CHRIST and through Him with one another, and the seventh of its being for believers only.

(B) THE HISTORY.

It was the night of the Passover, the night in which He was betrayed and given up to be the true Paschal Lamb, that our Blessed LORD instituted this Holy Sacrament. These facts are to be borne in mind when striving to obtain a true idea of its nature and object. We have in the New Testament four accounts of the institution, which are here given in parallel columns:

Matt. xxvi. 26–28.	Mark xiv. 22–24.	Luke xxii. 19, 20.	1 Cor. xi. 23–29.
And as they were eating, JESUS took bread, and blessed *it*, and brake *it*, and gave it to the disciples, and said, Take, eat; this is My Body	And as they did eat, JESUS took bread, and blessed, and brake *it*, and gave to them, and said, Take, eat: this is My Body.	And He took bread, and gave thanks, and brake *it*, and gave unto them, saying, This is My Body, which is given for you: this do in remembrance of Me.	The LORD JESUS the same night in which He was betrayed took bread: And when He had given thanks, He brake it, and said, Take, eat: this is My Body, which is broken for you: this do in remembrance of Me.
And He took the cup, and gave thanks, and gave it to them, saying, Drink ye all of it; For this is my blood of the new testament, which is shed for many for the remission of sins.	And He took the cup, and when He had given thanks, He gave *it* to them: and they all drank of it. And He said unto them, This is my blood of the new testament, which is shed for many.	Also the cup after supper, saying, This cup *is* the new testament in my blood, which is shed for you.	After the same manner also He took the cup, when He had supped, saying, This cup is the new testament in my blood: this do ye, as oft as ye drink it, in remembrance of Me. For as oft as ye eat this bread, and drink this cup, ye do shew the LORD'S death till He come. Wherefore whosoever shall eat this bread, and drink this cup unworthily, shall be guilty of the body and blood of the LORD. . . For he that eateth and drinketh unworthily, eateth and drinketh damnation (or rather condemnation) to himself, not discerning the LORD'S body.

Add these following, and we have all the direct references to the Eucharist to be found in the New Testament:

The cup of blessing which we bless, is it not the Communion of the blood of CHRIST? The bread which we break, is it not the Communion of the body of CHRIST? (1 Cor. x. 16.)

CHRIST our Passover is sacrificed for us; therefore let us keep the feast. (1 Cor. v. 7.)

We have an altar, whereof they have no right to eat which serve the tabernacle. (Heb. xiii. 10.)

From these words of Holy Scripture we gather the following regarding the Sacrament: (1) *Its Institution*. It was instituted while our LORD and His disciples were eating the Passover, with materials then upon the table, viz., bread, probably unleavened, and wine, probably mingled with water. That Passover, as all others had been, was a type of Him, and His disciples in future instead of feeding on the lamb, etc., were to feed on that which He then gave them, the bread which was the Communion of the Body of CHRIST, the cup which was the Communion of His blood. This was to be for a remembrance of Him; and was for the remission of sin, for the showing forth His death, and they who received unworthily condemned themselves, because failing to discriminate the LORD'S body. Also that this is to be partaken as a feeding on the Peace-offering of the Christian Church. (2) *Its Administration*. This consisted of the taking of the bread; the blessing and giving thanks; the breaking, the distribution, the command to eat; the calling it His body. The taking the cup; the giving thanks; the giving to drink; the calling it His blood. The command to continue to do all this, in remembrance of Him. It must be noticed that the eating and drinking are just as essential parts of the Institution as the breaking and thanksgiving.

These simple rites have ever since been considered essential to the due administration of the LORD'S Supper. And however after-ages in love and devotion, and sometimes perhaps in superstition, may have added to them adornments of music and pomp of ceremonies, these have ever remained the great central and unchanged features of the consecration. It was continued in the first ages in its beautiful simplicity just as CHRIST instituted it. Justin Martyr's account describing it to the Emperor Antoninus Pius, the earliest we have, shows how it was administered about 150 A.D. He says that "on the day called Sunday" they meet together, and instruction in Scripture is given and prayer offered. Then " when our prayer is ended, bread and wine and water are brought, and the president in like manner offers prayers and thanksgivings according to his ability, and the people assent, saying Amen; and there is a distribution to each, and a participation of that over which thanks have been given, and to those who are absent a portion is sent by the Deacons" (Apol., Book 1, lxvii.). "This food is called among us Eucharistia." This is not the place to trace the ritual additions which later ages made to the simple rite of CHRIST'S institution. They will be found under the head of LITURGIES.

(C) THE NATURE OF THE SACRAMENT.

It is unnecessary to dwell upon the outward visible sign; that has been already sufficiently shown to be, as the Catechism declares, "Bread and wine which the LORD hath commanded to be received." We therefore proceed at once to a consideration of the "inward part, or thing signified." This we are taught is "The Body and Blood of CHRIST, which are spiritually taken and received by the faithful in the LORD'S Supper" (the English Catechism has, "verily taken and received"). And we are also taught that the benefits we receive thereby are "The strengthening and refreshing of our souls by the Body and Blood of CHRIST, as our bodies are by the bread and wine." Thus the Church teaches that the grace of the Sacrament, *i.e.*, that which we receive by its means, and of which it is a pledge, is the body and blood of CHRIST, spiritually taken and received, and it is for "the strengthening and refreshing of our souls."

We shall understand this better if we refer to the saying of our LORD to the Jews in Capernaum, when they sought Him after the miracle of the loaves and fishes (St. John vi. 26, etc.). In the discourse to Nicodemus (*vide* BAPTISMAL REGENERATION), our LORD foretells of entering the new life by the birth of water and of the Spirit, and afterwards appoints Baptism as the Sacrament of this new birth; so here He tells the Jews of the necessity of heavenly food to keep alive and nourish this new life, even as their Fathers were received out of Egypt, baptized "in the cloud and in the sea," and then sustained in the wilderness by miraculous food and drink, viz., the manna, the bread from heaven, and the water from the rock. And when they ask, "LORD, evermore give us this bread," He declares Himself to be the bread of life, and proclaims, "the bread that I will give is my flesh, which I will give for the life of the world." And when the Jews murmured, "saying, How can this man give us His flesh to eat," He explains not, but declares even more emphatically, "Except ye eat the flesh of the SON of Man, and drink His blood, ye have no life in you." "He that eateth my flesh, and drinketh my blood, hath eternal life, . . . dwelleth in me, and I in him." These words must have made a deep impression on the disciples; they could not understand them and "said, This is an hard saying; who can hear it?" and though He gives some clue to His deep spiritual meaning by adding, "It is the SPIRIT that quickeneth; the flesh profiteth nothing," showing that His words were to be taken not of that carnal body then with them; still we read that in consequence "many of His disciples went back and walked no more with Him." The strong faith of Peter and his companions retained them in their allegiance to Him as the MESSIAH, but we can well understand that the question must often have been in their minds, if not privately discussed among themselves: "How can this man give us His flesh to eat?" Now, in less than a year comes the last Passover, with the institution we have described. When the LORD gave them the bread broken and the cup filled, saying, "Take, eat; this is my body, which is given for you." "Drink ye all of it; this is my blood which is shed for you," their minds must have gone back to that discourse at Capernaum; to the promise of eternal life through eating and drinking the flesh and blood of the SON of Man, and they would immediately have thought, Here in His mercy the Master gives us the means of doing that which to us seemed impossible; He must mean that by eating this bread and drinking this wine we in some mysterious manner become partakers of Himself.

Of course they could not understand how it was; the Spiritual Body was not yet revealed. But in faith they accepted, and in the discourse recorded by St. John which followed, the LORD told them of His presence with them in the HOLY GHOST, who would teach them all it was needed they should know. And so they came to know and believe, as St. Paul was taught by revelation. The bread which we break is the Communion of the Body of CHRIST. The cup of blessing which we bless is the Communion of the Blood of CHRIST. After-ages bringing the wit of man to the attempt to explain divine mysteries, argued about the how and the when, and the nature, still asking and puzzling themselves with the old question, "How can this man give us His flesh to eat?" and so fell into various errors and superstitions in the attempt to explain the inexplicable. The simple childlike faith of the Apostles and earliest Christians was satisfied with the Divine Word, and "not intruding into those things which they had not seen," "thankfully received that His inestimable benefit." It is wise to follow their example, and in the words of one who long years after has inherited their spirit say, "What the word doth make it, that I believe and take it."

But there is yet another point to be considered before we can rightly understand the full nature and purpose of this Sacrament. It was instituted during the Paschal Feast, that was a commemoration of the deliverance from Egypt. The Paschal lamb, by whose blood they were marked as GOD'S people, was then being consumed. When CHRIST said, "Take, eat; this is my Body which is given for you; this do in remembrance of me;" "This is my Blood which is shed for the remission of sins;" they could not fail to perceive the connection between the two. They must have understood that as the lamb and unleavened bread were offered in remembrance of their deliverance from slavery and their union under the Old Covenant, as GOD'S people, so this rite of the New Covenant, this taking, blessing, and eating of the Bread and Wine was to be in place of the former, as a perpetual showing forth of their deliverance through CHRIST from bondage to sin and their union together as CHRIST'S Body. Not that at the time they clearly saw all this, but it must have come to their minds as they reflected upon it, and it was revealed to them afterwards by the HOLY SPIRIT. Even as St. Paul was taught to say, "CHRIST our Passover is sacrificed for us, therefore let us keep the feast;" and St. Peter writes, that we are redeemed "with the precious blood of CHRIST, as of a lamb without blemish and without spot" (1 Pet. i. 19).

There is one more thought that must have presented itself to the minds of the better instructed of the Apostles, viz., the analogy between this new rite and the peace-offering of the Old Covenant. That, as is shown in another place (*vide* PRIEST), was a thank-offering, and a feeding on that offering, so the great feature of the act of CHRIST, in taking the bread and cup, was the blessing, the giving thanks, and the distributing for feasting. It was of a sacrificial nature. The bread and wine taken in the hands of HIM the great HIGH-PRIEST, and by Him blessed, broken, and given for feasting, was to take the place of that sacrifice, and be so continued by His Priests until He should come again. It was to be in reality that which the other was only in type, a lasting, solemn thank-offering to GOD, and a feeding none the less real, because spiritual, on that offering. Not, again, that we need think that all this occurred at the time clearly to the minds of the Apostles; they came afterwards to see it as the true nature of the feast was revealed to them. To this the Apostle doubtless alludes when he writes, "We have an altar, whereof they have no right to eat which serve the tabernacle" (Heb. xiii. 10).

Thus we find set forth in the LORD'S Supper, under the consecration and offering of the bread and wine, and the reception of them, the twofold meaning of the redemption from sin through the death of CHRIST, and the union with Him by the reception of Himself into our souls, and through Him with GOD. There is, in the proper sense of the words, a sacrifice and a feeding on the sacrifice as truly as in the Passover and in the thank-offering.

We have not space here to give quotations from the Fathers or from our own divines, and from the Liturgy of our Church in corroboration of what has been said. Such proof will be found under the words PRIEST and REAL PRESENCE. Let one suffice, taken from the Apology of Justin Martyr. We quote from him because he is one of the earliest writers, and because there is no dispute about the authenticity of his book, and also because he cannot be accused of putting forth what are called very high views of Church doctrine. Not being himself a Priest, he taught what was generally received among Christians. Writing of the Communion, he says, "This food is called among us *Eucharistia*. . . . For not as common bread and common drink do we receive these; but in like manner as JESUS CHRIST our SAVIOUR, having been made flesh by the word of GOD, had both flesh and blood for our salvation, so likewise have we been taught that the food which is blessed by the prayer of His word, and from which our blood and flesh by transmutation are nourished, is the flesh and blood of that JESUS who was made flesh." (1 Apol., lxvi.)

Non-Communicating Attendance. — The Romish Church has made a separation between the two features of the Eucharist, allowing that Christians may assist at the sacrifice, and receive the full benefit of it, for the remission of sins, without partaking of the Consecrated Elements, *i.e.*, Communing. And there has been a disposition shown of late among some of the Anglican Communion to teach the same thing. If what has been said above be correct as to the fulfillment in the LORD'S Supper of the discourse in Capernaum, and as to the analogy between the Passover and the Thank-offerings in the LORD'S Supper,—and they who hold the above views will not be likely to deny this,—then it would seem that such a separation is untenable. The Passover required the eating of the lamb, the Peace-offering also must be eaten. The Scriptures are very plain on this point. So also of the LORD'S Supper: "Take, *eat;*" "*drink* ye all of it," said our LORD. "As oft as ye *eat* this bread and *drink* this cup ye do show forth the LORD'S death till He Come." The Altar is one whereof we *eat*. The early Church knew no such doctrine; many passages might be quoted to show this, did space permit; let these suffice. St. Chrysostom, who will not be considered as taking a low view of the Holy Sacrament, reproves those who are present without communicating in strong language. "It was better that they should be absent, for they did but affront Him that invited them, whilst they stayed to sing the Hymn, professing themselves to be of the number of the worthy, whilst they did not recede with the unworthy. How could you stay and not partake of the table? I am unworthy, say you. If so, you are unworthy to communicate in prayers also." The Apostolic Canons, which are very early, command, "If any Bishop, Presbyter, or Deacon, or any other of the clergy, does not communicate when the oblation is offered, let him show cause why he does not." (Bingham.)

COMMUNION IN BOTH KINDS.

There is no dispute that this was the universal custom of the Early Church; following therein the LORD's example, who gave both the Bread and the Cup to all present. It was not until the twelfth century that any mention can be found of the denial of the cup to the Laity. The reason given at first was the danger of spilling any of the consecrated wine. Afterwards, when the doctrine of Transubstantiation was taught, it was withheld as unnecessary, inasmuch as each particle of the consecrated Bread contained the whole CHRIST, therefore the Blood as well as the Body. This was one of the grievances removed by the Reformation, and the Church rightly orders that the elements in both kinds shall be given to each Communicant. In the Greek Church both are given, but at the same time, the elements being mingled, the bread steeped in the wine, and so together placed with a spoon in the mouth of the recipient. It is defended on the ground of greater reverence in handling the sacred elements. But it is not in accordance with the original institution, and with proper care there is no danger of spilling the consecrated wine.

REV. E. B. BOGGS, D.D.

Louisiana, Diocese of. The history of the Church in the State of Louisiana presents her very largely in those ways that mark her at once as the banner-bearer of Protestantism, and the comprehensive organization of the Catholic Church must be of necessity.

The territory of Louisiana was acquired from France in 1804 A.D., and the transfer of sovereignty meant freedom from the restraint of public worship to the prescriptions of the Roman rite.

The Protestants of New Orleans met for consultation and organization June 2, 1805 A.D., at the boarding-house of Madame Fourage, on Bourbon Street. Among those present were such noted men as Benjamin Morgan, James M. Bradford, Richard Relf, John McDonough, James Brown, and Edward Livingston. On the 16th of June a vote was taken "to determine the religious denomination of the clergyman to be invited," and while forty-five votes were cast for an Episcopalian, only seven were given for a Presbyterian, and one for a Methodist.

For many years a French-speaking congregation of Huguenot extraction was in union with the Diocese.

The second Rector of Christ Church, New Orleans, was a Presbyterian minister when invited to that charge, and was ordained a Deacon two years thereafter.

Unfortunately, in after-years this important position was lost,—what was considered the inflexible rule of uniformity compelled the Bishop to permit the French congregation to drift away to the Presbyterians. The lack of sympathy in a period of distress on the part of more favored Dioceses turned the conflict from one of conquest to a losing struggle for existence.

Organization.—The Church in Louisiana, although planted as early as 1805 A.D., was not fully organized in its Diocesan character until 1841 A.D., or thirty-six years thereafter.

In this interval there was but small growth. Christ Church, New Orleans, was organized, as already stated, in 1805 A.D. Fifteen years later the Rev. William Bowman organized Grace Church, St. Francisville. A parish, St. James' Church, was incorporated at Baton Rouge in 1820 A.D., but the congregation were without a rector until 1839 A.D. In 1838 A.D. St. Paul's Church, New Orleans, was organized. These were the only churches, and they numbered together but one hundred and fifty communicants.

The first attempted Diocesan organization was in 1830 A.D., when a Convention was held for that purpose in New Orleans, under the presidency of the Rt. Rev. Dr. Brownell, Bishop of Connecticut. It was composed of the Rev. Messrs. Hull, Bowman, and Fox, and lay delegates from the churches in New Orleans and St. Francisville.

Before the General Convention met, however, in 1832 A.D., the organization was abandoned, and no application for admission was made. Provision for Episcopal government and services for the churches in Louisiana was, however, taken into consideration by that body, and a Canon enacted which authorized these churches to associate with the Dioceses of Mississippi and Alabama in the election of a Bishop.

A Convention was held under this Canon in New Orleans, March 4 and 5, 1835 A.D., in which the Dioceses of Mississippi and Alabama were properly represented, but Louisiana sent only lay representatives from Christ Church, New Orleans. This Convention organized a "Southwestern Diocese," and elected the Rev. Dr. Francis Lister Hawks Bishop.

The Bishop-elect declined, and no further Convention of this provincial organization was assembled.

Prior to its meeting, however, a Convention had met, January 20, 1835 A.D., composed of all the clergymen resident in Louisiana, and lay delegates from the churches in New Orleans and St. Francisville. This Convention organized a Diocese of Louisiana and made application for recognition to the General Convention. This, however, that body saw proper to refuse on the score, as stated, of the "divided counsels" that prevailed. This reference was undoubtedly to the election by the vestry of Christ Church, New Orleans, of delegates to the Convention that organized the Diocese of Louisiana, and then subsequently of others to that of the Southwestern Diocese, and thus there was a danger in the admission of Louisiana at that time of the presentation to the Church of two Bishops-elect with largely identical jurisdiction, to wit, the State of Louisiana.

Three years after this, April 28, 1838 A.D., another Convention met in New Orleans and organized a Diocese. This was the Primary Convention of the present Diocese. The members of it were the Rev. Dr. Wheaton, Rev. R. H. Ranney, Messrs. Richard Relf, Lucius Campbell Duncan, Thomas Butler, William D. Boyle, and William F. Brand.

The Diocese was admitted to union with the General Convention September 7, 1838 A.D. The Diocesan Convention of 1839 A.D. placed the Diocese under the Episcopal charge of the Rt. Rev. Dr. Polk, who had a few months previously been consecrated Missionary Bishop of Arkansas.

The Diocese delegated to the General Convention of 1841 A.D. the election of a Diocesan, and that body thus empowered made choice of Bishop Polk.

The Episcopate of Bishop Polk.—The next chapter would sketch the history of twenty years, the term of the Episcopate of the first Bishop. And yet it may not be written in the few words that the limits of this article demand. Let it, then, suffice to summarize some of the results that those twenty fruitful years produced.

The Bishop found in Louisiana in 1841 A.D. four clergymen, of whom one was an instructor of youth, and two hundred and twenty-two communicants. He left a Diocese of forty parishes, six mission stations, and upwards of twenty other congregations under the ministry of his clergy, thirty-one clergymen and eighteen hundred and sixty-nine communicants.

During his Episcopate twenty-eight churches and a number of rectories were built, two thousand eight hundred and eighteen persons were baptized and three thousand one hundred and ninety-four confirmed, upwards of half a million dollars were contributed to Church purposes, and the ratio of communicants to total of population was raised from one in every fourteen hundred and eighty to one in every three hundred and seventy-nine.

The days of prosperity had an end. In 1861 A.D. the clouds of war lowered in all the heavens of the Southland, and ominous sounds alarmed even the dullest ears. The call that came to the Bishop of Louisiana seemed to him as the very voice of the Chief Shepherd of all summoning him to defend the flock, no longer by pen and voice, but by the strength of his arm,—a commission in the army was tendered him, and he accepted it. Whatever opinion may be held by any one in respect to the propriety of such action, this much justice and a sense of right demand should be made of record, —in the acceptance of that commission Bishop Polk believed as firmly as he did of any other one act of his life that he was performing a solemn duty that he owed to his Diocese and to GOD.

We would not here extenuate our or his reasonings, but let the curtain drop upon the dreary thoughts as abruptly as the life of the Bishop ended when the cannon-ball rent his breast at Lone Mountain, Georgia, June 14, 1864 A.D.

We must, ere we close this chapter, however, look but once upon the face of the stricken Diocese. All scarred and torn she lay,—the clergy exiled by military order, the temples in many, many instances desecrated or most wantonly destroyed. She lay all cold and almost dead. Five years passed, and no Convention met or could meet. But succor came; kindly and fraternal hands lifted her up; aid came from those who had felt it a duty to crush her, as well as from those whose hearts had throbbed with her in a common cause, and she was bidden to live again.

The Episcopate of the Second Bishop.— The Convention of 1866 A.D. met May 16. The report showed but twenty-two parishes maintaining regular services, twenty clergymen, and 1556 communicants.

This Convention elected the Rev. Joseph Pere Bell Wilmer, D.D., Bishop, and he was consecrated the 7th of the following November.

Bishop Wilmer was the Diocesan for twelve years. During this time twenty-seven churches were built or purchased, five thousand persons were confirmed, twenty-one Deacons and twenty-two Priests were ordained, over nine thousand were baptized. The number of communicants was doubled, and upwards of eight hundred thousand dollars was given to Church purposes.

All this was accomplished with a very inadequate staff of clergy, and among a very poor people. Had the Bishop had his hands held up by a liberal support by the Church, there is little reason to doubt that the growth of the Diocese would have been phenomenal. The good, the wise, the faithful Bishop rested from his labors December 2, 1878 A.D.

The third and Present Episcopate.—The Diocesan Council having chosen the Rev. John Nicholas Galleher, S.T.D., Bishop, he was consecrated February 5, 1880 A.D. The result of his labors and that of his co-laborers may best be told in our concluding chapter, as that is to be of the present state of the Diocese.

A General Summary.—From the organization of the Diocese in 1838 A.D. to the meeting of the last Council, that of 1883 A.D., there have been reported 16,499 baptisms and 10,044 confirmations, and $1,676,-711.10 contributed. The ratio of communicants to population was, in 1841 A.D., one to one thousand four hundred and eighty; in 1861 A.D., one to three hundred and seventy-nine; and in 1881 A.D., one to two hundred and sixty-four.

Among the clergy who have labored in Louisiana as Priests have been Bishops Philander Chase, Young, Pearce, Beckwith, Adams, Galleher, Harris, and Thompson; the Rev. Drs. Wheaton, Hawks, Wm. R. Nicholson, Neville, Crane, Fulton, Currie, and Lawson.

Among the laity prominent in her Councils have been many prominent in secular life,—John L. Lobdell, George S. Guion, William M. Goodrich, Dr. Wm. Newton Mercer, Dr. J. P. Davidson, James Saul (now a Priest), James Grimshaw, Henry Johnson, Lucius Campbell Duncan, Greer Brown Duncan, James McConnell, J. K. Dennett, Henry V. Ogden, General L. D. DeRussey, General Braxton Bragg, D. S. Cage, George Williamson, Jules A. Blanc, W. W. Howe, Robert Mott, Joseph P. Horner, Carleton Hunt, and George W. Race.

The Present State of the Diocese.—The Diocese now (1883 A.D.) has forty-three Parishes, seventeen Missions, and twelve Chapel congregations. There are fifty-one church edifices and sixteen rectories There is an Orphans' Home under a Sisterhood. The estimated value of church property is $624,250.

There are thirty-four clergymen, one Bishop, thirty Priests, and three Deacons, of whom six are without cure. There are 3946 communicants, and 2911 pupils in the Sunday-schools.

The baptisms for the three years last past have averaged 609; the confirmations, 399; the marriages, 164; the funerals, 309; and the contributions, $79,469.66.

There is but one Diocesan eleemosynary institution, the Children's Home of New Orleans.

The principal of invested funds of the Diocese amounts on account of support of the Episcopate to $18,540; superannuated clergy, $6740; and a small sum for widows and orphans of clergymen.

With the exception of four or five churches in New Orleans, that at Alexandria, and that at Shreveport, the Parishes are small, and most of them very feeble.

Probably in no better way could the condition of the Church in Louisiana be illustrated than by a reference to the average number of communicants, and the average amount of contributions for all purposes, and to clergy having cures in Louisiana and in the country at large respectively. In Louisiana there are on the average 146 communicants to each clergyman, and $2943.11 is contributed; while in the country generally the average is 124 communicants and $7905.92.

The clergy of Louisiana are noted, with very few exceptions, as earnest, faithful, successful men; but their number is altogether inadequate to the work required to be done. The above statistics furnish a hint, and of the unequaled burden that is put on them, and the truth of the assertion that the Diocese is waging a losing fight is clearly proven by the large number of doors of our churches closed, and the still greater number of the suspended and abandoned Missions. Fifteen Parishes vacant, nine Missions suspended, and fully as many abandoned! In the sugar-producing portion of the State the ground is being fairly well held for the Church, but not so in the pineries of the Florida Parishes, or in the territory north of the Red River.

The constant gains of the Church in all those portions of the State where her services are maintained, and the ever-increasing ratio of communicants to population, are eloquent prophecies of the possibilities of the Diocese being some day comprehensive, not only as it once was in respect to Protestantism, but also comprehensive in respect to those others who are now commonly called Catholics.

Statistics for 1886 A.D: Clergy, 33; parishes, 41; missions, 33; candidates for H. O., 2; ordinations, P. 1; baptisms, 678; con., 481; com., 4339; contr., $76,114.07.

REV. H. C. DUNCAN.

Low Sunday. This first Sunday after Easter, properly the octave or the first Sunday after Easter, is called Low Sunday, as it was an old custom to hold a second celebration of the solemnities of Easter-day. It was also called the *Dominica in albis*, for on this day those baptized on Easter-day laid aside their baptismal robes of white.

Luke, St., the beloved physician, the Evangelist and historian of the Apostolic Church. What his personal history was apart from the slight notices in St. Paul's Epistles and the inferences to be drawn from his own writings is wholly unknown. But what he has done for the Church in his Gospel and his book of the Acts is most invaluable. Tradition says he was a native of Antioch. Study of his style has led a recent student of his works to infer that he was employed as ship surgeon on some of the crowded merchantmen of the Levant, from his accurate and yet unprofessional use of nautical terms. He seems to come forward suddenly in the history of St. Paul, in Acts xvi. 10, where he begins to use the pronoun "we"; of course this implies a previous acquaintance with St. Paul. He was (if the use of "we" is a sure indication of it) with the Apostle at Troas, and passed with him into Macedonia. Here he was probably left behind, since onward the record of the remainder of St. Paul's work in this journey is in the third person plural, "they." He rejoined him apparently at Philippi, where he had been left seven years before. Thenceforth he is the Apostle's constant companion. Is he the brother whose praise is in the Gospel throughout all the Churches? If so, he is sent by St. Paul on an errand to Corinth with Titus, because he had already shown his ability in evangelizing work. He was most probably with the Apostle to the end. His skill as physician was doubtless invaluable to the wearied Paul, the aged. This is really all we know of the holy Evangelist. He does not name himself in either of his two works. It is only the Apostle who speaks of him, "Only Luke is with me," "Luke, the beloved physician."

Luke, St., Gospel of. This Gospel is undoubtedly his, if any faith can be put in consentient tradition. It is beyond question that the author of the Acts must be the writer of the Gospel also. The connection between the two books, the Gospel beginning and the Acts continuing the history of what JESUS both began to do and to teach, the similarity of style, the accuracy and simplicity, and purity of diction all prove this. The Gospel is first certainly quoted by Justin Martyr (before 168 A.D.) in the Muratorian Fragment on the Canon (170 A.D.). It was used and mutilated by Marcion (140 A.D.). Later references to it need not be referred to. "St. Luke wrote in Greece for the Hellenic world. In style this Gospel is the purest, in order the most artistic and historical. It forms the first half of a great narrative, which traced the advance of Christianity from Jerusalem to Antioch, to Macedonia, to Achaia, to Ephesus, to Rome. Hence it neither leans to the learnings of the past, nor is it absorbed in the glories of the present, but is written with special reference to the aspirations of the future. It sets forth JESUS to us neither as the Messiah of the Jews only nor as the Universal Ruler, but as *the Saviour of sinners.* It is a Gospel not national but cosmopolitan, not regal but human. It is the Gospel for the world: it connects Christianity with man. Hence the genealogy of JESUS is traced not only to David and to Abraham, but to Adam and to GOD." (Farrar's St. Luke, Cam. Bible for Schools.) It is the first *Christian hymnology,* for it contains the *Gloria in Excelsis,* the *Benedictus,* the *Magnificat,* the *Nunc Dimittis.* It is the Gospel of *Thanksgiving,* seven times is "glorifying GOD" mentioned. It is the Gospel of *Prayer,* not only the LORD's Prayer, but six occasions on which He prayed are recorded, and the words in three cases,—in the Garden, when nailed to the Cross, upon the Cross. It is the Gospel of the *Good Tidings* of pity, and pardon, and grace. It is the Gospel of the *outcast,* the publican, harlot, prodigal, and Samaritan. It is the Gospel of *tolerance.* (Condensed from Farrar.) It contains much not found in the other Gospels, as six miracles and eleven parables, besides many slight but notable incidental remarks, and some facts in the history of our LORD's Passion. It is an inspired record of *facts,* not of theories or tendencies. It was written before the destruction of Jerusalem, and before the Acts also, which probably were composed while St. Luke was with St. Paul in his own hired house in Rome. If any interval lies between the dates of the two writings, then it is probable that the Gospel was written at Cæsarea during St. Paul's imprisonment there (58–60 A.D.), and then the old tradition that it was written for the use of the converts St. Paul made has much truth in it. The Evangelist describes things and places in Judæa which a Gentile could not well know about. And too, the universality of the Gospel would come well from one who was St. Paul's attendant and companion.

M.

Maccabees, Books of. The record of the noble defense which the great-grandsons of Chasmon, of the noble priestly family of Jehoiarib, maintained against the Seleucidæ. It began in a resistance made by Mattathias to the effort of Antiochus Epiphanes to force idolatrous sacrifices upon the Jews. Mattathias slew two men who consented to sacrifice, fled to the mountains, and from thence began a successful guerrilla warfare. The struggle was taken up on a larger scale by his sons, who in this order took the leadership: Judas, his third son, "THE MACCABEE," who so extended his resources and won such important victories that finally he was able to strengthen himself with an alliance with the Romans. He fell in the passes of Eleasa, and Jonathan, the fifth son, took the command. His wary conduct, and skill and diplomacy, gave him the title of Apphæs (wary), but he too fell, but by treachery, and after imprisonment. Simon, the second son, placed himself at the head of the patriot party. He was able by allying himself to Demetrius II. to gain the recognition of the independence of the Jews, which led to his full occupation of Jerusalem. His death was through treachery, but his son, Johannes Hyrcanus, displayed the same genius for government his father possessed, and maintained the kingly power the father had won. They began with a handful of patriots, they left a nation welded together by bitter reverse and by glorious victory. They gave that form and character to the Jewish people that they showed in our LORD's day. Their work in relation to the later form of Jewish polity was as important as the work of Samuel, of Saul, and of David. The Books which are almost our sole record for this noble achievement are, chronologically, the III., II.

IV., I. But they frequently are imperfect in details and incorrect in formal facts, and the third book is most probably a rhetorical "adaptation" of some fact. It is hardly historical. But despite these drawbacks the books are very valuable for the Jewish history after Malachi. The Books are not canonical, though the first two being in the Vulgate are so received by the Roman Church. But if the test of absolute literal accuracy be applied to them as to the inspired books, they must be rejected.

Macedonians. A heretical party which denied the divinity of the HOLY GHOST. It was propagated by Macedonius, who had been violently placed in the See of Constantinople. Macedonius was a semi-Arian, and so rejected by the Church, but the Emperor Constantine placed him in the office (343 A.D.), but (in 350 A.D.) Macedonius seemed willing to accept the Nicene definition, but started the error of denying the Divine Nature of the HOLY GHOST. It was to meet this heresy that the latter clauses were added to the Nicene Creed, after the words and I believe in the HOLY GHOST, "the LORD and Giver of life, who proceedeth from the FATHER, who with the FATHER and the SON together is worshiped and glorified, who spake by the prophets." They had been already in local use, but were now added to the Creed (381 A.D.). The denial that the HOLY GHOST was of the Divine Substance, and therefore Very GOD, was held with many varying shades of opinion, but however that might be among themselves, the Macedonians, holding to their error, went out of the Church.

Magi. The wise men who appeared at Jerusalem at the birth of our LORD (St. Matt. ii. 1). It was the name given by the Greeks to the priests of the Zoroastrian doctrine, which taught a pure Monotheism. It occurs as a word in the name Rab-*mag* in the Old Testament, and it was of probably the order of men who bore it that Daniel was made a fellow and afterwards the master (Dan. ii. 2, 13, 48), though the word is not applied to them. They could not have been teachers of directly false doctrine, or Daniel would not have interceded for them, nor would he have consented to become a member of their body. The straightforward simplicity and directness of the narrative in St. Matthew stamps it with the truthfulness that must belong to the inspired narrative. The representatives of the ancient Monotheism of the Gentiles come to do homage to the SON of GOD, born king of the Jews. It may be that there was also a survival among them of the prophecy of Balaam: "There shall come a star out of Jacob, and a sceptre shall rise out of Israel." A loving study of the symbolism of the threefold gifts these wise men presented finds in the offering of gold the acknowledgment of His Royalty; in that of frankincense, the acknowledgment of His Divine Nature; and in that of myrrh, so often used at funerals, the type of the bitterness of human life, and the acknowledgment that He is as yet born a mortal. They stand forth for the Gentiles in owning Him as their King, and as suddenly vanish as Melchisedec emerges, the Gentile Priest and king before GOD, who as suddenly sinks back into the silence of Scripture. When the Magi made their visit—whether, as the narrative in St. Matthew naturally leads us to believe, immediately after His birth or later—we cannot certainly know.

Magnificat. The Hymn of the Blessed Virgin (St. Luke i. 46) upon the occasion of her visit to her cousin Elizabeth. It is appointed to be sung as the alternate anthem after the Second Lesson at Evening Prayer in the English Prayer-Book, and is allowed as an anthem for our own American Service.

Maine. The first service of the Church of England in what is now the State of Maine was celebrated on St. George's Island and in the Kennebec, on Sunday, August 9, 1607 (O.S.), by the Rev. Richard Seymour, Chaplain of the Popham Colony of that year.* In October following, a church was built on the mainland near by; but all ended with the failure of the colony in the following year.

With the Proprietary Government of Sir Ferdinando Gorges in 1636 A.D., at Winter Harbor on the Saco River, came the second Church clergyman, the Rev. Richard Gibson, who fixed his residence at Richmond's Island, off Cape Elizabeth, but officiated also at Saco, and Portsmouth, N. H. A church was built in each of these places, and that on Richmond's Island was supplied with altar-plate and other requisites by the proprietor Robert Trelawny, of Plymouth, England. At Saco the "minister's rates" amounted to £31 15s. quarterly, or nearly $600 a year, a large sum for the time and place. Mr. Gibson, who is described as "a good scholar,† and highly esteemed as a minister," fell under the censure of Puritan Massachusetts in 1642 A.D., for officiating within her pretended jurisdiction; as did his successor, the Rev. Robert Jordan, who from 1640 A.D. till his death, in 1679 A.D., contended nearly single-handed against the growing power of that colony, officiating at Saco, Scarboro', and Falmouth (now Portland), in all which places the early colonists were Churchmen; and three times at least committed to prison for baptizing and marrying without Puritan license.‡ From his time, under Massachusetts rule, the services of the Church were suspended for eighty years, except that we find

---

* Strachey, "Historie of Travaile into Virginia," c. ix., Maine Hist. Coll., iii. 297. Weymouth erected a cross at this same place in 1605 A.D., and held some religious service, but of what kind does not appear. The Sieur du Mont,—under Henri IV. of France, built a chapel on Neutral Island in the St. Croix in 1604 A.D.
† He was of Magdalen College, Oxford, 1636 A.D.
‡ His curious baptismal font of brass has been presented by his descendants to the Maine Historical Society.

a lay-reader at the garrison at Pemaquid in 1683-88 A.D.

In 1756 A.D. the Society for the Propagation of the Gospel in Foreign Parts sent out their first missionary, the Rev. Mr. MacClenachan, to Fort Richmond on the Kennebec. He remained but two years, and was succeeded in 1760 A.D. by the Rev. Jacob Bailey (of Harvard, 1755 A.D.), who ten years later had a church and parsonage built at Pownalboro', but officiated from the first not only there, but at Sheepscot, Harpswell, Damariscotta, and Georgetown, until relieved of part of his wide field by the Rev. Willard Wheeler, appointed to Georgetown in 1768 A.D. Churches were built at this place (now Bath) and Kittery, and, it is said, at Gardiner. A number of the inhabitants of Falmouth had meanwhile, in 1764 A.D., organized St. Paul's Church, whose first minister, the Rev. John Wiswall (Harvard, 1749 A.D.), received an aid of £20 from the S. P. G. The Revolution drove away all these missionaries, and it was not until 1793 A.D. that services were resumed in Gardiner by the Rev. Joseph Warren, succeeded in 1796 A.D. by the Rev. James Bowers, in 1803 A.D. by the Rev. Samuel Haskell, and in 1817 A.D., after eight years' vacancy, by the Rev. Gideon W. Olney. At Portland, Edward Oxuard was lay-reader for some years; Mr. Warren took charge in 1796 A.D., removing from Gardiner; the Rev. Timothy Hilliard in 1803 A.D., for three years, and the Rev. Petrus S. Ten Broeck in 1819 A.D. Maine was included in the Diocese of Massachusetts at its organization in 1790 A.D., and represented in its Convention in 1791 and 1796 A.D., but had no Episcopal visitation earlier than about 1814 A.D., and no officiating clergyman for some years before 1817 A.D.

In 1820 A.D. the "District of Maine" became a State, and immediate steps were taken by Bishop Griswold to organize the present Diocese, whose first Convention of two clergymen and lay deputies from two Parishes met at Brunswick, May 3, 1820 A.D. Simon Greenleaf, Robert H. Gardiner, and Dr. John Merrill were the leading members of this Convention, and for many years the leading laymen of the Diocese; the two former, with the Rev. Messrs. Olney and Ten Broeck, were the first Standing Committee, and Dr. Merrill the first Secretary. Maine remained a part of the New England Confederation known as "the Eastern Diocese" until Bishop Griswold's death, in 1843 A.D., from which time to 1847 A.D. it was under the jurisdiction of Bishop Henshaw, of Rhode Island. At the organization the State had a population of 298,335, of whom there were probably not one hundred communicants of the Church.

In 1824 A.D. was formed the "Maine Episcopal Missionary Society," which, incorporated in 1835 A.D. and 1875 A.D., has directed all the missionary work of the Diocese to this time. Its first effort was the founding of Trinity Church, Saco, in 1827 A.D., the third Parish in the State; and its first missionary was the late Rev. Dr. E. M. P. Wells, of Boston, "at a stipend not exceeding eight dollars a week." But the first "settled minister" of Saco was the present Bishop of New York, Horatio Potter, 1827-28 A.D. St. Mark's Church, Augusta, and St. John's, Bangor, were organized in 1834 A.D.; St. Paul's, Brunswick, in 1844 A.D.; and St. James', Oldtown, in 1847 A.D.; and these, with St. Paul's (reorganized in 1839 A.D. as St. Stephen's), Portland, Christ Church, Gardiner,* and Trinity, Saco, were the seven parishes which, with their seven Priests and a Deacon residing in Massachusetts, met and unanimously elected George Burgess, then Rector of Christ Church, Hartford, Conn., as the first Bishop of Maine.

With his consecration, October 31, 1847 A.D., began a new era for the Diocese. Bishop Burgess was a man of rare intellectual and spiritual gifts; and in energy, patience, prudence, and gentleness singularly adapted to the great work of his Episcopate, the removal of the wall of prejudice with which centuries of Puritanism had hedged round the Church, and the making an opening for its entrance and growth where it had been up to this time utterly unknown. Under his leadership the parishes of the Diocese increased to 19, the clergy to 17, communicants to 1600, missionary offerings to $1571; and throughout the State the Church had become more or less known, and respected wherever it was known. In the small band of able and faithful clergymen who shared his labors were such as Bishops Southgate, Paddock, Armitage, Perry, Niles, and Alexander Burgess, Drs. Gardiner, Goodwin, Haskins, Cotton Smith, D. C. Weston, R. S. and H. R. Howard, and Ballard.

Bishop Burgess died April 23, 1866 A.D., and the Diocese elected as his successor the Rev. Henry Adams Neely, D.D., of New York (b. 1830 A.D.; Hobart College, 1849 A.D.), who was consecrated in Trinity Chapel, January 25, 1867 A.D., and took up his residence at Portland, becoming Rector of St. Luke's Church. In the same year the corner-stone of a Cathedral church was laid (August 15); the nave, aisles, and chancel, of stone, 130 feet by 60, were completed and occupied on Christmas-day, 1868 A.D.; and on St. Luke's day, 1877 A.D., the whole cost of the structure thus far ($125,000) having been paid by the congregation, largely aided by Churchmen in other Dioceses, the Cathedral was consecrated with imposing services, in which nine Bishops and clergymen from twenty-five Dioceses took

---

* Whose fine old stone church was erected by Robert H. Gardiner in 1820 A.D. Bishop Burgess was rector of this parish during his Episcopate. There was no fund for the support of a Bishop, and his nominal salary from the Diocese ($200) was bequeathed by him, with an additional sum, making $7000 in all, for this purpose.

part. The church, one of the noblest and most substantial in New England, is the property of the Diocese, held by the "Cathedral Chapter," incorporated by the Legislature; forever *free*, with daily service and weekly communion, and a simple but dignified and impressive ritual; the Bishop being *ex-officio* Rector and Dean, assisted by resident Canons* elected by the people, and honorary Canons chosen by the Diocese, both on his nomination. It is yearly more and more a centre for all Diocesan work, and a most important instrument in the extension of the Church throughout the State. A substantial Bishop's House, also the property of the Diocese and adjoining the Cathedral, was erected in 1869 A.D., and there is also an Episcopate fund of about $16,000.

Bishop Neely's Episcopate has been noted thus far, first, for the extension of the Church in the vast thinly settled northern and eastern parts of the State, by means of missions with a simple organization, but not incorporated as Parishes, being thus wholly under the control of the Diocese. These now constitute nearly one-half of the congregations, and have much more than doubled the places of regular or frequent services. A remarkable missionary work has been done in Aroostook (a county nearly as large as Massachusetts) by the Rev. W. H. Washburn, who has since built a noble stone church at the great manufacturing centre of Lewiston. Like all poor and frontier Dioceses, Maine suffers from constant changes among its clergy; but one now antedating Bishop Neely's time, Mr. Dalton, of Portland, and three others (Canons Washburn, Leffingwell, and Pyne) of ten years' residence. The Diocese now numbers 26 clergy, 37 Parishes and missions, and about 2200 communicants, having gained in these last *twelvefold* on the population of the State since 1820 A.D. Growth is and must always be slow; but it has maintained an honorable record under its present Bishop in the zeal, unity, and efficiency of its clergy,† and the earnestness and liberality of many of its laity. For many years a nominally "Low-Church" Diocese, it became strong in Church principles before Bishop Burgess's death, and has grown since in every element of Churchly character.

The second notable feature of Bishop Neely's Episcopate is the successful establishment of an excellent Diocesan school for girls, St. Catharine's Hall, Augusta, in 1868 A.D., which has done a great work already in spreading a knowledge and love of Church teaching. Statistics for 1886 A.D.: Clergy, 28; parishes, 23; missions, 14; candidates for H. O., 2; ordinations, D. 1, P. 1;

baptisms, 348; con., 168; com., 2649; contr., $57,673.95.   REV. C. W. HAYES.

Malachi. The Prophet whose book closes the Canon of the Old Testament. Since his name means "My Messenger," some eminent later commentators have doubted whether there was any man who bore this name, and translate, "The burden of the word of the LORD to Israel by My Messenger" (*cf.* ch. iii. 1), since there is no mention of his father's name. But this mode of giving only the name occurs also in the case of Obadiah. Some early commentators, as well as the Septuagint translators, have supposed that it was a record by an angel; and some Jewish writers, admitting that Malachi was not a name, but should be translated My Messenger, claimed the work for Ezra. But these assertions are worthless, and arise from pushing the allegorizing of Holy Scripture to extremity. The contents of the book show that it was the work of a prophet whose mission was to aid in the reforms of the second governorship of Nehemiah (Neh. xiii. 15; 29; *cf.* Mal. ii. 8, and Neh. xiii. 23-27; Mal. ii. 10, and Neh. xiii. 10; Mal. iii. 7-10, the subjects being identical).

It is a short prophecy of only four sections, the first section extending from i. 1 to vs. 5; the second from i. 6 to ii. 9; the third from ii. 10 to vs. 16; the fourth, ii. 17 to end. Its form is peculiar, each section being opened with an assertion of a claim by GOD through His Prophet and a reply: How have we refused this claim? with the Prophet's answer. It contains one of the most distinct Messianic prophecies in ch. iii. 1, and in ch. iv. 2, and a prophecy of St. John Baptist in ch. iii. 1, and in ch. iv. 5. The book closes with this prophecy of the Forerunner of CHRIST.

Man. The peculiar constitution of man as the only member of the animal creation endowed with religious sense and moral responsibility, his unique and complex relations on the one hand to GOD and on the other to the lower animals, and the overwhelming importance of the mere fact of his being combine to make the study of all that pertains to him a matter of the most absorbing interest. That he is the head and crown of a regular series of life-possessing and sentient creatures, rising in a steadily developing ascent from the simplest conceivable forms, is clearly evident; but it is equally evident that he is something more, since however nearly he is approached in physical and mental constitution by the higher groups of this series, he exhibits, even in his lowest developments, the evidences of a totally different nature of which they show no trace. The recognition of this fact and its significance is the simple solution of all the difficulties surrounding the subject. Possessing this dual nature, and bearing a double relationship to the life of this world and to another life beyond it, we cannot expect either nature or revelation alone to open to us his whole history, for nature can

---

* The Rev. Charles W. Hayes, 1867-80 A.D.; the Rev. Charles M. Sills from 1880 A.D.

† Among whom Canons Upjohn (1868-83 A.D.), Alger (1866-80 A.D.) and Leffingwell (1869 A.D.) and the Rev. H. P. Nichols (1877-83 A.D.), are entitled to special mention; only one of the four now remaining in the Diocese, Canon Root, and the Rev. Messrs. Price and Marsden, died in the Diocese after long and faithful service.

teach us only that part of it which belongs to nature, and revelation treats only of those facts and truths which nature cannot possibly make known. The scientist who refuses to study revelation must of necessity know man only as a higher animal, while the believer who seeks all his knowledge from the Bible must also reach only partial results. From these mistakes have arisen all the confusion and mutual misunderstanding, deepened by the frequent confounding of Miltonic fancies with Bible teachings and by interpretations of Scriptural statements equally unwarrantable and untenable. A brief examination and summing up of these two lines of investigation is all that can be given here. Science discovers that all vertebrate animals are constructed physically upon the same model, every part being represented and performing an analogous function in each, but better adapted to the needs of the creature as the scale rises, until in man the nearest approach to perfection is reached. Every organ, tissue, function, and appetite has its analogue throughout the series, and these analogies are traceable to a great extent even far into the vegetable kingdom.

The same progressive series is observable in mental constitution, certain instincts being always present, as, *e.g.*, self-preservation, self-nourishment, and reproduction. In the higher anthropoid apes the resemblance to man in these particulars is startling, and yet between the highest of these forms and the lowest development of humanity the differences are so essential that no bone of a chimpanzee could possibly be mistaken for that of a man, while no lower animal has ever articulated language or used fire. Still, the approach is so suggestive that geological researches have been prosecuted with a special view to discovering a missing link between the brute and human forms. This search has at length been undoubtedly rewarded by the recent discovery of fossil human remains at Abbeville and Mentone in France, the bone-caves of England and elsewhere. Flint implements and weapons have also been found belonging, probably, to the quaternary period. But all with this remarkable result, that the man who was contemporary with the mammoth and other long extinct creatures in Europe was even *more human* in his type than the man of to-day. Thus the skeleton discovered at Mentone exhibits more distinctive human characteristics than the bones of modern man. There were gigantic and diminutive tribes exactly as now, and under similar circumstances. Thus the four-feet skeletons found in France are associated with remains of the reindeer, just as the dwarfish Lapps are to-day. Man then also practiced rude arts and used fire, implements and charred bones being found. This is absolutely all that science has discovered. Man was undoubtedly on earth long before the beginning assigned him by the *accepted* Bible chronology, and the earliest man was a higher type, physically and intellectually, than the Bushman or Papuan of to-day. Now let us look at the Scripture record. In the first chapter of Genesis we find a general statement of the fact of the creation by GOD of the earth and all that live upon it, including man. It is a brief and condensed but complete record, with no hint even as to chronology, or as to the *method* of creation.

In reference to all the lower animals, "Let the earth bring forth" is the formula. The only *fact* insisted on is the creation by GOD. But in the case of man there is a significant difference. The formula is omitted. He is created by special purpose and "in the image of GOD," and he is created "male and female." He is also invested with controlling power and authority. All this is conjoined and much light cast on it by the above-mentioned scientific discoveries. In the second chapter we are told how something was *superadded* to his mere animal nature,— *i.e.*, "the breath of life," and he "*became* a living soul." Then follows a condensed history, to be gathered out of the Scripture narrative, wonderfully according with scientific discovery and historic observation, of his progressive development. Language begins as with the child, by naming objects. The institution of Marriage originates the Family. Man first appears naked, and clothes himself as his mind develops; his first religious ideas are anthropomorphic. Animal sacrifice and the use (apparently) of fire come only with the second generation. So with building. Prayer is mentioned (Seth) still farther on. In the second chapter man eats what the earth naturally produces; in the third chapter he tills the ground; in the fourth chapter he adopts the pastoral life and becomes a rude artificer; in the sixth chapter the deluge develops rude but efficient ideas of navigation, and religion has assumed a very high form; in the ninth chapter man becomes a skilled husbandman, cultivates the vine and discovers the use of wine; in the tenth and eleventh chapters he becomes a hunter, language differentiates and nations begin to organize. Thence on we learn all of his religious life, his immortal nature and destiny. St. Paul (1 Thess. v. 23) alludes to man's tripartite constitution,— "pneuma," life or spirit; "psyche," soul; "soma," body. He is the highest of the animal kingdom, with "soul," the "breath of GOD," superadded. He is the last and best of the earthly series of living creatures, and as such only can science deal with him. But he is the first and lowest of a heavenly series, and as such we must study him by the light of GOD's word. But there is more even than this. His lower nature, that of body and spirit, was made from the dust of the earth which "brought forth," at GOD's command, all his earthly fellow-creatures; but his higher nature is of Divine origin, "the breath of life" breathed into his bodily frame by GOD Himself. Thus early was his being differentiated from all the lower orders of creation, and later on the Divine character of that higher nature was made complete by its indissoluble union with GOD in the Incarnation of the CHRIST. No one who believes this has ever questioned its retroactive efficacy. "For as in Adam all die, even so in CHRIST shall *all* be made alive." So would it be, then, with the inbreathing of. the breath of life, if man had existed for a time as a living, but soulless creature.

We have thus briefly seen how the dual revelation of nature and Holy Scripture is at harmony in itself. It is but one Truth of GOD, the parts of which cannot antagonize each other. The history of man as given in the Bible must be studied with the help of all practicable scientific investigation, and the discoveries of science must be supplemented by the teaching of GOD's word, and thus alone can be obtained a full, accurate, and complete knowledge of the origin, history, nature, and destiny of man and his status in the scale of GOD's creation.

REV. ROBERT WILSON, D.D.

Manasseh, Prayer of. In the Apocrypha there is a short composition of fifteen verses called by the name of the evil king of Judah, whose prayer on his repentance is referred to in 2 Chron. xxxiii. 11-13: "Wherefore the LORD brought upon them the captains of the Host of the King of Assyria, which took Manasseh among the thorns, and bound him with fetters, and carried him to Babylon. And when he was in affliction, he besought the LORD his GOD, and humbled himself greatly before the GOD of his fathers, and prayed unto Him; and He was entreated of him, and heard his supplication, and brought him again to Jerusalem into his kingdom. Then Manasseh knew that the LORD He was GOD." The prayer in the Apocrypha is of course spurious, though it is itself filled with a touching supplicatory tone. The deep repentance in it implies a knowledge of the true spirit of sorrow that worketh life. It was probably the work of some devout Alexandrian Jew of the same school with the son of Sirach,—though probably living nearer the time of Philo.

Maniple. Properly, a handkerchief. It was hung upon the left arm of the priest, and used to wipe away the perspiration from his face. But it soon began to be enriched with broidery and a fringe which unfitted it for its true purpose and made it a mere ornament.

Manse. The old name for the ecclesiastical residence (*mansio*). It is still retained in Scotland and in some places in this country as the name for the rectory.

Maranatha. A word added by St. Paul (1 Cor. xvi. 22) to the word Anathema. It means the "LORD COMETH," and makes the preceding word anathema emphatic. The word has been, however, disconnected from the adjoining phrase by some, and made to have the force of a watch-word that St. Paul gave the Corinthians.

Mark, St., the Evangelist. His mother's name was Mary, who had a house in Jerusalem (Acts xii. 12). He was cousin to St. Barnabas, and was probably from the first intimate with St. Peter (Acts xii. 12). The next notice of him is (Acts xii. 25) where he is the companion of SS. Barnabas and Paul, in their return from Jerusalem to Antioch. He was their attendant on their first missionary journey (48 A.D.), was present at the conversion of Paulus Sergius, and went with the Apostles as far as Perga in Pamphylia (Acts xiii. 13), but shrunk from the further perils of their journey. His shrinking, from whatever cause, led afterwards (51 A.D.), to the sharp contention between the two Apostles, and Barnabas took Mark with him to Cyprus, while St. Paul went with Silas on his visit to the Churches of Syria and Cilicia (Acts xv. 39-41). But the Apostle's harsh judgment of him was softened, for we find him mentioned thrice by St. Paul. He was one of the few fellow-workers unto the Kingdom of GOD who had been a comfort to the Apostle,—and he was now with him in his first imprisonment (61-63 A.D.). He is mentioned twice again by the Apostle, once in his letter to Philemon, and in the Second Epistle to Timothy, where St. Paul says that he was "profitable to him for the ministry" (2 Tim. iv. 11). In the interval between these two notices St. Mark had probably joined St. Peter in his work at Babylon. (*Vide* ST. PETER.) In 1 Pet. v. 13, St. Peter writes, "The Church which is at Babylon, elected together with you, saluteth you; and so doth Marcus my son." These are the only notices we can gather from Holy Scripture. The tradition of the Church affirms that St. Mark visited Egypt and founded the Church at Alexandria, where he was martyred. All other notices are untrustworthy, and often mutually destructive.

Mark, St., Gospel of. St. Mark's Gospel has been the field for much singular speculation. St. Matthew's and St. Luke's Gospels are, like this, more rigidly narratives. The three have many points, both of facts and in language, in common, while there are also marked dissimilarities. It has, therefore, been claimed that one, and most probably St. Mark's Gospel, was the original, and that the others followed it, and broidered upon it such other facts as they witnessed or were accurately cognizant of. An attempt has been made even to reconstruct the original (?) Gospel, which refutes itself by its absurdity. But a short statement of the contents of this Gospel will best show its real independence. The date is uncertain, but probably not before 63 A.D., and, since it predicts the fall of Jerusalem, not later than 70 A.D. The tradition of the Church and the contents of the Gospel show that it was intended for Roman Gentile converts, for it does not quote the Jewish Law; it explains Syrian and Hebrew words and Jewish usages, and it uses Grecized Latin terms. It would, therefore, be most naturally written in Greek, as the most universally known language. As the kinsman of St. Barnabas, and the son of that Mary to whose house St. Peter went as to an accustomed home, when delivered from prison by the Angel, St. Mark was naturally in the reach of authentic information; but, besides, he seems to have been an eye-witness, not merely the recorder or amanuensis for St. Peter, as has been inferred from the tradition that he was the interpreter for St. Peter. Doubtless some of the vivid descriptions came from the Apostle, but there are phrases used which imply a personal knowledge. The Evangelist strikes at once and boldly the opening chord, "The beginning of the Gospel of JESUS CHRIST, the Son of GOD." No genealogy, no details of His human birth. The next verse binds the Gospel, as the fulfilled conclusion, to the prophecy of eight full centuries before. It begins then to bring forward repentance, baptism, and daily trial, culminating in the Passion, and then the Immortal life of the Eternal SON of GOD. It is characteristic of St. Mark that he brings forward the true manliness of our LORD. Not that the other Evangelists do not do it also, but hardly in so prominent a way; for it is true that each presents all the traits of the wonderful Life, but selects naturally those by which he would himself be attracted. Our LORD'S love, pity, compassion, wonder, anger, indignation, St. Mark dwells upon in his own emphatic way. So, too, he brings our LORD'S person vividly before us in His looking round upon the multitude, His taking little children in His arms, putting His hands upon them and blessing them. He goes before the disciples, and they follow in amazement. His very words, as, for example, Boanerges, Talitha-cumi, Ephphatha, are recorded in special cases. St. Mark, too, notes the awe and the wonder of both multitudes and disciples, and their eagerness to be about their LORD. He is minute in noting time, place, person, and number. His details are those that would come from a person who was on the spot. He mentions the hired servants in Zebedee's employ; the LORD'S resting asleep on a *pillow* in the storm; the green grass whereon the multitude sat; the running of the rich young man; the name of the blind Bartimæus; the place where the two disciples who were sent found the colt tied; the young man in the garden at the arrest. These things, and they might be largely increased, not only show how minute and accurate, but how independent a writer St. Mark was, though he often reproduces the same language that St. Matthew used. That he repeated what others had said is not against his own veracity or real independence. "Repetition is by no means derogatory to the dignity of the HOLY SPIRIT. On the contrary, it is one of the characteristics of inspiration." (Wordsworth, Intro. St. Mark.) The last verses of the Gospel (ch. xvi. 9–19) have been rejected recently by many scholars, chiefly because they are wanting in the Vatican and the Sinaitic MSS. But they are found in three of the four Uncial MSS. (A, C, D), and are quoted without suspicion by Irenæus. Their genuineness is defended by many equally skilled scholars and cannot be reasonably doubted, since the weight of evidence is in their favor.

Marriage. *Vide* MATRIMONY.

Martinmas. A festival in honor of the famous Martin, Bishop of Tours. He was a native of Pannonia and bred a soldier, but entering the Church, he was made Bishop 374 A.D., and after a very active and munificent Episcopate, distinguished for his zeal in destroying the heathen altars still remaining, he died 400 A.D. His name was held in great reverence in France. The feast was appointed upon the 11th of November. (See the Calendar of the English Prayer-Book.)

Martyr. A witness; then a witness to the Christian faith, and then one who seals his faith with his death. This witness was in a sense official, as every one who bears the Christian name ought to bear witness to the truth of the Faith he professes. It at first did not necessarily imply that death was a part of this act, but soon this distinction was drawn between the Martyr and the Confessor; but the mode or the circumstances of this suffering did not affect the title,—*e.g.*, whether the Martyr suffered in a riot or by form of heathen Law. From this generally admitted rule was derived another claim to the name of Martyr for those who died from the indirect consequences of Persecution. The Church did not at all encourage the headlong zeal of those who would rush into danger, and looked with kindness on those who justly and fairly avoided martyrdom, proving their constancy in other ways. So St. Cyprian retired from Carthage in two Persecutions, for the Church needed him, but at a third Persecution he surrendered himself, and the Church has always commended his conduct. Hence those who sought martyrdom, or who rashly incurred danger, as by breaking idols or by vehement conduct, were refused the name, though they may have suffered bravely. The Church was exceedingly careful that the honor of martyrdom should not be carelessly attributed to those whose conduct was in any way blamable. There were dangers enough without adding this peril, since the Christian religion was legally forbidden.

It may be well to add that in its essential point of bearing witness, Martyrdom can never cease so long as evil exists and there are men to mock, sneer, and flout at things sacred. Not only is Augustine's sentence true, "You will go hence a Martyr if you have overcome all temptations of the devil" (Serm. iv., c. 4), but there is a patient courage, a readiness to bear our witness against evil, and for the truth and the whole truth needed, which is as truly a martyrdom as though it were borne amid bodily tortures, and one which demands a yet finer and more enduring courage.

Martyrology. The List containing the names of the Martyrs, whether of a city or of a Diocese. The earliest traces of such lists are found in allusions to them in Tertullian (De Corona, ₰ 13), in Cyprian (Ep. 39, al. 34). A century later we find a singular Calendar which contains the Dominical and Nundinal letters, a cycle for Easter, and, among other matter of a pagan and secular character, a List of the funeral days of the Popes of the past century, and a List of the funeral days of the Martyrs. Its date is 354 A.D. The study of the various Martyrologies (which differed in the several localities to which they belonged) is of considerable interest and value for determining dates of lesser importance. The more valuable Martyrologies were The Syriac, which was dated as early as 412 A.D.; The Hieronymian, attributed to St. Jerome, and certainly earlier than 596 A.D., but most probably founded upon other and widely differing materials; The Lesser Roman Martyrology, which probably belonged to about 700 A.D., and was found in Ravenna 850 A.D. Later works than these Martyrologies are not so trustworthy (and in fact these have many interpolations), but become more numerous as the calendars of the Churches were changed or reformed. Besides, there are several metrical Martyrologies in imitation of the Greek menologies. The English Church while it has noble martyrs has no Martyrology. Bede's Calendar is the basis, with many modifications, of what scanty remains of Black-letter Saints' days the Reformers chose to retain of the fuller and not always authentic festivals of the Pre-reformation period.

Mary. A name borne by five women in the New Testament,—*i.e.*, Mary (the wife of) Cleophas, Mary Magdalene, Mary the mother of Mark, Mary a helper of St. Paul (Rom. xvi. 6), and the Blessed Virgin Mary, or as she is called in the Prayer-Book, St. Mary the Virgin. The name is the same as the Hebrew Miriam. The only authentic notices of her are those in the New Testament, all beside is purely legendary. She appears suddenly without any previous hint about her in the Gospels. Whether she was a cousin of her husband Joseph, and her genealogy that given by St. Luke, as has been conjectured with but little ground for credence, cannot be proven. We know that she was of the tribe of Judah, and that she was a cousin of Elizabeth, the mother of St. John the Baptist, and was a resident at Nazareth, when she was the betrothed of St. Joseph.

It was in the year 5 B.C. (according to undoubted correction of the current date) that the Angel Gabriel appeared before her, and with a salutation akin to the salutation given to holy women before, but which had a far deeper meaning for the whole human race, he announced to her the glorious grace reserved for her,—to become the Mother of the MESSIAH. Her humble reverent acceptance, " Behold the hand-maiden of the LORD, be it unto me according to thy word," is a key to her whole character. She visited her cousin Elizabeth soon after, and upon that occasion uttered the beautiful hymn—the Magnificat—which, whether uttered without premeditation or precomposed, shows an intimate knowledge of the sacred writings of the Old Testament, for some of its phrases, and its tone certainly, are drawn from the older historical books, and in form, rhythm, and phrase it is founded upon the Psalms. Suspected of unchastity, but defended by the Vision to St. Joseph, she is taken by her husband to Bethlehem, the seat of the House of David, when he went up to be taxed. There she bore, in the stable of an inn, the SAVIOUR of the world and laid Him in a manger. The visit of the shepherds; the circumcision; adoration of the Wise men; the Presentation of the Holy Infant in the Temple; the touching poverty of her offering for her Son the LORD of the world; the flight into Egypt,—all these bring her forward, and yet so modestly and simply.

She next appears as sorrowfully looking for her SON and finding Him in the Temple. When our LORD's ministry begins she is almost wholly withdrawn. She is with Him at the marriage in Cana. More than eighteen months after, she with His brethren seek to see Him, to persuade Him to relax His ministerial work, when He gave the reply to the messenger, " Who is my mother, and who are my brethren? And He stretched forth His hand towards His disciples and said, Behold my mother and my brethren! For whosoever shall do the will of my FATHER which is in heaven, the same is my brother, and sister, and mother." She is at the foot of the cross suffering the fullest fulfillment of the aged Simeon's words, " And a sword shall pass through thine own soul also." There is something sublime in the words, " Woman, behold thy Son!" when He gave her into the care of His beloved disciple. St. Ambrose considers that He lovingly put away from Himself all human ties when He was about to complete our Redemption. He needed no aider for the redemption of all, He received the love of His mother, but He sought no help of man. Nothing is told us of her hopes, fears, faith, and sorrow, and joy. She is simply counted among the women who were with the Apostles after the Ascension in that upper room. And so she disappears from the sacred history. It is in thorough accord with the lofty aim of the sacred narrative. Her work, for which all rise up to call her blessed, was to bear for us in the Flesh truly man of body and soul subsisting, the eternal SON of GOD. When this was accomplished and her care and love must not interfere with His work, she is gently put aside by our LORD with words implying slight reproof whenever she endeavors to come forward. "Woman, what have I to do with thee?" and, "Who is my mother, and who are my brethren?" have the tone of a separation in purpose and in work from His past life at Nazareth. Her perpetual virginity, a devout suggestion, can be urged on no historical grounds, however much we may hold it. The early Church was singularly silent about her, and treated her name as it did those of the holiest of the older Saints of the Old Testament, commemorating her as it did them in the Holy Communion. So, too, we find in one of the beautiful prefaces of the Mozarabic Liturgy a singularly beautiful contrast between the Virgin as the Mother of our LORD'S human nature and the glorious work in us of our Mother the Church; one which draws sharply the distinction, while it gives her all due honor. The worship now paid her by the Roman Church is not earlier than the sixth century. Earlier, worship was offered by the Collyridian heretics.

Maryland, Diocese of. Maryland, one of the thirteen original States of the Union, lies south of Pennsylvania, from which it is separated by Mason and Dixon's Line, so famous in American politics. Its total area is about twelve thousand square miles, of which about two thousand three hundred are covered by water. The most notable geographical feature (which has had its decided influence on the *diocesan*, as well as on the political, history of Maryland) is the Chesapeake Bay, the largest inlet in the United States, which divides the entire State into two portions, known as the Eastern and Western Shores. These two divisions are unequal in extent, and very dissimilar in their physical characteristics. The Eastern Shore is the smaller and is very level, while large parts of the other side of the bay are hilly and mountainous. Maryland is now divided into twenty-three counties and the corporation of Baltimore City. Of these counties, *nine*, viz.: Cecil, Kent, Queen Anne, Talbot, Caroline, Dorchester, Wicomico, Somerset, and Worcester, lie east of the Chesapeake Bay, and in the year 1868 A.D. were organized into a new Diocese, by the name of the Diocese of Easton. The Western Shore, together with the District of Columbia, is now known as the Diocese of Maryland. The population of the Diocese, including, of course, the District of Columbia, is estimated at about 755,502; the total population of the State, without the District, was, in 1880 A.D., 934,943, and of these no less than 210,250 were colored people.

The charter of Maryland was granted by King Charles I., on June 20, 1632, to Cecilius Calvert, the second Lord Baltimore, and the colony was named in honor of Queen Henrietta Maria. In the following year Lord Baltimore dispatched a company under command of his brother, Leonard Calvert, to colonize the new territory; they landed at St. Mary's on the 27th of March, 1634 A.D.

Before this, however, in 1629 A.D., under the authority of Virginia, which colony claimed the territory under a previous grant, a trading station had been established on Kent Island in the Chesapeake by William Claiborne, or Clayborn, whose name figures frequently in early contests and disturbances, until he was finally expelled by the followers of Lord Baltimore. Among Claiborne's associates and settlers was a clergyman of the English Church, the Rev. Richard James, who deserves mention as the first Christian minister who set foot on the territory of Maryland. Passing by the ecclesiastical history of the colonial period, we can barely mention that after the revolution of 1688 A.D. the Church of England was "established" in Maryland, and disabilities were imposed upon Roman Catholics and dissenters. The counties were divided into parishes, with metes and bounds after the English custom, and under names which remain to this day and attest the history of their formation. In 1779 A.D. the Legislature passed an act to establish Vestries, and vested in them, as trustees, all the property that had belonged to their respective parishes while they were part of the "Church of England." This elaborate act, as somewhat modified in 1798 A.D. and subsequent years, is still in force in the Dioceses of Maryland and Easton, and it puts the relations between Church and State and the tenure of religious property on a somewhat different footing from that which prevails in most other States and Dioceses of the Union.

The Diocese of Maryland, as distinguished from the Church of the colonial period, dates from the year 1783 A.D. On the 13th of August in that year a Convention was held at Annapolis, in which was adopted an important document entitled "A Declaration of certain fundamental *Rights* and *Liberties* of the *Protestant Episcopal Church* of Maryland." "This," says Bishop Whittingham in the margin of his copy of Dr. Hawks's Narrative, "is, so far as I can discover, *the first time that title is used.*" The Declaration furnishes conclusive evidence, says Dr. Hawks, that the Church of Maryland, like that of Virginia, claimed to have a distinct, independent existence, without reference to any connection with the Church in any other colony. The most serious need was that of a Bishop, for the Declaration of Rights had declared that an Episcopal ordination and commission were necessary to the valid administration of the Sacraments and the "due exercise of the ministerial functions in the said Church." This need was supplied by the consecration, on the 17th of September, 1792 A.D., in Trinity Church, New York, of the Rev. Thomas John Clagett, D.D., who had been chosen unanimously by both orders of clergy and laity to be Bishop of

Maryland. All the four American Bishops, Seabury, Provoost, White, and Madison, united in this first consecration in America. Bishop Provoost, of New York, contrary to the wish of Maryland, insisted upon acting as Presiding Bishop on the occasion in place of Bishop Seabury, who by seniority of consecration should rightfully have officiated in that capacity.

Bishop Clagett, 1792–1816 A.D.—The Diocese, which had before been without a head, prospered under its new Bishop, though there was unfortunately considerable strife between the so-called Evangelical, or Low-Church party, and those who were called High-Churchmen. This culminated in 1814 A.D., when the Rev. James Kemp, D.D., was elected Suffragan Bishop of Maryland, —the Eastern Shore being assigned as his special jurisdiction. The leader of the Evangelical party, the Rev. G. J. Dashiell, Rector of St. Peter's, Baltimore, caused Bishop Clagett and the Church no little trouble by his turbulent conduct. Chagrined, as Dr. Hawks thinks, that the choice of the Diocese for Bishop had not fallen upon himself in place of Dr. Kemp, he finally seceded from the Church and attempted to establish a sect and schism of his own. After having greatly disturbed the peace of the Diocese, he was at length deposed from the sacred ministry by Bishop Clagett.

Bishop Kemp, 1816–1827 A.D.—Upon the death of Bishop Clagett in 1816 A.D., Bishop Kemp succeeded to the full Episcopate. His character was amiable without being weak, and his administration was earnest and vigorous. He lived down the ill feeling which party spirit had aroused at the time of his consecration, and died, much beloved and lamented, from the upsetting of a stage-coach in the year 1827 A.D.

Bishop Stone, 1830–1838 A.D.—It is painful to record that for nearly three years after the death of Bishop Kemp, Maryland was again the scene of discord and strife, so violent that the Diocese obtained an unenviable notoriety in the Church at large. At length the Convention united in electing the Rev. William Murray Stone, D.D., a man of amiable temper, and not very closely allied to either of the parties which still divided the Diocese. After a quiet and peaceful Episcopate of eight years he died on the 26th of February, 1838 A.D.

Bishop Whittingham, 1840–1879 A.D.— Again there was serious difficulty in choosing a Bishop. Neither the Rev. Dr. W. E. Wyatt nor the Rev. Dr. John Johns, each of whom had a nearly equal following, could obtain a constitutional majority (which in Maryland was, and still is, two-thirds of each order). The Rev. Dr. Eastburn, the Rt. Rev. Bishop Kemper, and the Rev. Dr. Dorr were each successively elected, and each declined to accept the office. Finally the Rev. Dr. William Rollinson Whittingham, Professor of Ecclesiastical History in the General Theological Seminary in New York, was elected, and consecrated in St. Paul's Church, Baltimore, on the 17th of September, 1840 A.D. The Convention Journal of 1841 A.D. gives the following statistics, which furnish some idea of the condition of the Diocese at the beginning of Bishop Whittingham's Episcopate: Clergy, 75; parishes, 58; separate congregations, 20; places of worship, 106; communicants, 3881; baptisms, 1293; confirmed, 337; contributions, $15,402.07. In 1837 A.D., the last Convention at which Bishop Stone was present, the confirmations were reported 67, and the contributions $6837.63. Bishop Whittingham was well known as one of the most learned and vigorous of American Bishops, and during his long and stirring Episcopate the Church made much progress and Maryland became a strong Diocese Many new churches were built in Baltimore and Washington, and also in the rural districts. The College of St. James, under the Rev. Dr. Kerfoot, and other schools of learning were founded, and did good service in the cause of education. In 1868 A.D., the year in which the Diocese was divided, and the counties of the Eastern Shore organized as the Diocese of Easton, Maryland contained 162 clergy, and 139 parishes and congregations. The communicants were 12,269; contributions (*not* including salaries of clergymen), $145,348. In 1870 A.D., the Bishop's increasing infirmities caused him to apply for an assistant Bishop, and the Rev. William Pinkney, D.D., was elected by a large majority on the second ballot. The election was notable as indicating an entire subsidence of the old party contentions. Dr. Pinkney was consecrated in the city of Washington on October 6, 1870 A.D Bishop Whittingham's health becoming more and more feeble, the visitation of the parishes devolved almost entirely upon the assistant Bishop, who became very dear both to clergy and laity. But the labors of Bishop Whittingham in his study, and in all business which did not require locomotion, were still, as always, most assiduous. In 1879 A.D. he transmitted to the Convention from his sick-chamber a copy of his official journal, which showed that, ill as he had been, he had given to his Diocese from five to fifteen hours of work per diem. Bishop Whittingham died in Orange, N. J., on the 17th of October, 1879 A.D., having bequeathed to his Diocese his most valuable property, the large theological library which he had been all his life accumulating. He was buried from St. Mark's Church, Orange, of which in early life he had been rector, his funeral being attended by a large concourse of Bishops, clergy, and laity.

Bishop Pinkney, 1879–1883 A.D.—Under Bishop Pinkney the progress of the Diocese continued, and the Bishop was, as he had always been, indefatigable in his labors. With characteristic generosity he requested the family of Bishop Whittingham to continue to occupy the Episcopal residence in Baltimore, and with his approbation the

Bishop's daughter was made *Librarian* and custodian of the literary treasures which it had been her father's joy and pride to collect. In 1883 A.D., the one hundredth anniversary of the founding of the Diocese was celebrated in Baltimore, the Diocese of Easton joining with Maryland in brotherly commemoration of an event in which they were equally interested, and in which, one hundred years ago, their ancestors had had so large and so distinguished a share. The various proceedings were published in a pamphlet, which is an interesting memorial of the occasion. Shortly after participating in this joyous celebration Bishop Pinkney died suddenly, on the 4th of July, 1883 A.D., while holding a visitation in Sherwood Parish, Baltimore County. The feelings of the bereaved Diocese are well expressed on the last page of the Centennial Pamphlet, above mentioned, which was passing through the press when the Bishop suddenly ended his earthly career. "The loving heart which ever warmed to others, but never spared itself, grew still while the voice of its last earnest message was yet lingering in our ears. Zealous and brave, and true to the high trust committed to him, he died as such soldiers of the Great Captain ever wish to die,—at the front, and in the very act of duty."

Authorities: Dr. Hawks's Narrative of Events; Bishop Wilberforce's History of the American Church, London, 1846 A.D.; and above all, the valuable and complete Life of Bishop Whittingham, by William Francis Brand, 2 vols. 8vo, New York, 1883 A.D.

Statistics for 1886 A.D.: Clergy, 164; parishes and missions, 138; ordinations, D. 2, P. 3; baptisms, 2796; confirmed, 2064; com., 24,926; contr., $509,288.30.

REV. H. HARRISON.

Masorah. The Masorah is the arrangement and proper preservation of the text of Holy Scripture by Jewish Doctors, which they gathered from tradition, both the oral and that in the Talmud. It was busied with the verses, words, and letters of the sacred text. The Masoretic Doctors of the school at Tiberias were the great masters of this department of Biblical research, and, which was their most generally useful invention, probably arranged the vowel points and pauses, which later developed into the system now in use. But the Masorah, "The Tradition," was the result of their and others' labors. Not merely the verses, words, and letters were noted, but they recorded the various readings,—the K'ri, what should be read for the Chetheb, also the actual word in the text; and words interpolated. Their minute records of such apparently trifling details were of use in settling the value of various readings, though of little real use, as amid the multiplicity of various families of manuscripts the text would vary, and the number of letters or words or verses would be uncertain,—*e. g.*, the Bomberg Bible, 1518 A.D., contains 1171, and the Plantin, 1566 A.D., only 793 K'ris, while Elias Levita could reckon but 848, after twenty years' study of the Masorah. Nearly every Hebrew Bible contains not only the different readings at the foot of the page, but also some Masoretic technical notes and remarks at the end of the volume.

Mass. The ordinary name for the Communion Service or Liturgy of the Latin Churches. It is a corruption of the words of dismissal: "*Ite, missa est.*" The name appears also in the First Book of King Edward VI. in the heading over the Communion Service: "The Supper of the LORD and the Holy Communion commonly called the Mass." But this was dropped, and it is no proper term for the Liturgy of the English Church. It is divided into two principal parts, the Ordinary of the Mass and the Canon of the Mass, which latter begins with the intercessions preceding the words of Consecration.

Mass, Sacrifice of. *Vide* EUCHARIST.

Massachusetts, The Diocese of. The popular impression is that the Pilgrims at Plymouth and the Puritans of the Massachusetts Bay Colony were the first to celebrate the worship of GOD on the New England shores. The truth is that over forty years before the Pilgrims landed the voice of a clergyman of the Church of England had been heard along the shores of Maine and the Provinces, celebrating the rites of religion with the voyagers of Frobisher's expedition, which he accompanied as chaplain, in 1577 A.D.

In 1605 A.D. an English expedition, in search of a Northwest passage, sailed up the Penobscot River, in Maine, and planted a cross on its banks.

In 1607 A.D. a settlement was made on the coast of Maine by a company made up principally of members of the Church of England, who brought with them a Church clergyman, the Rev. Richard Seymour. The colony, in that year, built fifty houses and a church, and observed with great regularity the ordinances of religion according to the usages of the mother-Church. It was not a successful colony, however, and was finally abandoned on account of the severity of the climate and their inexperience of the conditions of the new land. This settlement is usually known as "Popham's Colony," after the name of its first president. The royal letters of instruction directed that the religion of the Church of England should be established, and it is certain that thirteen years before the coming of the Pilgrims to Plymouth the hallowed ritual of the Church was heard on the shores of Atkins' Bay.

The settlement at Saco, in Maine, was the first permanent English colony in this region in which the rites of the English Church were celebrated.

In 1636 A.D. William Gorges came out as Governor of the territory out of which the present State of Maine has been formed. The patent of this territory established the

Church of England as the religion of the colony, and gave the right of nominating clergymen to the patentee.

The first regularly settled clergyman was the Rev. Richard Gibson, who came in 1637 A.D., and spent about seven years in Saco. He extended his labors to the settlers at Richmond Island, the Isle of Shoals, and Portsmouth. He was a good scholar, a popular speaker, and highly esteemed.

The Rev. Robert Jordan was one of the earliest of the Church clergymen, serving as an itinerant whenever he had opportunity. He sometimes held the position of judge in the Province, but never laid aside his ministerial character. He died at New Castle, in Maine, in 1679 A.D., being sixty-eight years old.

In 1641 A.D. a report was made to Governor Winthrop, of Massachusetts, that the people of Saco, in Maine, " were much addicted to Episcopacy." In fact, a large proportion of the settlers in Maine were Church people. What would have been the result had not these early settlements been disturbed by the strong hand of the rising power of the Massachusetts colony we can only conjecture. The territory of Maine passed by purchase into the possession of Massachusetts in 1677 A.D., and thenceforth the religious teachers encouraged in the Province were Puritans. Notwithstanding all that was done to crush out Episcopacy it continued, and some existing parishes trace their history back to those trying days.

It was a difficult matter to plant the Church in any place over which the Puritan held rule. In fact, he had come here to avoid the Church, and to set up one of his own. He was unwilling to tolerate any rival, and especially to permit the English Church to gain any foothold.

The first English Church clergyman to settle in the bounds of Massachusetts was the Rev. William Blackstone, who established himself on the promontory on which Boston was subsequently built. He came here before the Puritans, and shortly after the Pilgrims reached Plymouth. He was a man of means, and managed a large farm, on which he built a substantial house and other buildings. The Puritans went first to Dorchester and to Charlestown, and were in these places a year before they concluded to move to the edge of the bay, where they founded Boston. They had numerous interviews of an unsatisfactory character with Blackstone, but they finally bought his buildings and lands, and he gladly moved away to Rhode Island. It is not known that he ever publicly officiated here, except to a congregation made up of his family and servants.

The Church clergyman who appears next in the annals of Massachusetts is the Rev. William Morrell, who came with Gorges in 1623 A.D., having a commission from the English Church to exercise a kind of superintendence over the parishes which might be established in New England.

Morrell collected some information, but was regarded as an intruder, and finally went back to England baffled and discouraged.

"Thus," as one says, "the Church of England found herself shorn of her strength at the very moment when a door seemed opened for her extension in the New World. Her children, whom she had thrust out, stood with scowling brows and sturdy arms ready to repel her from the shores which they had made their refuge."

It must not be thought, however, that there were no friends of the old Church among the Puritan colonists, for in Salem there were at least three whose good deeds make them worthy of special honor. They were Francis Higginson, John and Samuel Brown. It was expected that they would stand high in the colony, but their love for the old Church brought them into sorrows. They were denounced as ringleaders of a faction, and were sent off home. When Charles II. was restored to the throne of England an order was issued "that such as desired to use the Common Prayer should do so, without incurring any penalty, reproach, or disadvantage."

In 1688 A.D. the Rev. Robert Ratcliffe came over, and held services in the townhouse in Boston. He struggled against many difficulties for two years, but before he returned to England he secured the erection of a place of worship where King's Chapel was subsequently built.

About this time there was considerable earnestness in forming parishes. The work was greatly aided by the Missionary Society formed in England in 1649 A.D., whose scope was enlarged in 1661 A.D., and which in 1701 A.D. was incorporated as "The Society for the Propagation of the Gospel in Foreign Parts." They sent out chaplains, missionaries, and schoolmasters for the conversion of the Indians and for the welfare of the white settlers.

There were not many favorable openings for the agents of this Society, but they did their work with courage and vigor, and were rewarded in the growth of parishes, mission stations, and schools. The wonder grows as we look at these efforts that opposition could be so bitter, and that their courage to meet it was so great. In no section of the country did the Church find so hard a field as in Massachusetts.

Some of the early proposals to secure the Episcopate were met here by ridicule and invective. A Bishop was to many of the Puritans the symbol of all that was hateful. Caricatures are preserved to this day which show how antagonistic was the popular feeling towards Episcopacy, especially as the colonial troubles grew. The two causes which led to this feeling were their inherited hatred of the Church of England, and their fear that the introduction of Episcopacy would overturn what was really the State religion of Massachusetts, and which continued until as late as 1830 A.D. It was indeed only in this year that Congregationalism ceased to be the religion established by law in this State.

The history of some of the old parishes in this State is full of interest, particularly in such parishes as Marblehead, Newburyport, King's Chapel, and others, but they cannot be given here.

The position of the Massachusetts clergy during the events leading up to the Revolution and during that long period was particularly trying. They had never been in much favor here, and when the Revolution was inaugurated they were almost all subjected to severe penalties or to popular censure, which cost them friends and positions. Some of them, however, cast themselves into the movement for breaking loose from England, others tried to maintain a neutral position, but many relinquished their parishes and moved away or were driven away.

We can hardly understand the peculiar hardships of many of the most kindly spirits who lived in those times. Loyal to the Church of England, loving peace, deprecating the wrongs visited upon this country, hoping redress by means other than armed revolt, they waited in agony some settlement of the difficulties, and when war actually came, found themselves treated as enemies and scorned by the people in general. Some of them waiting until they saw no hope of England's doing justice to her colonies, and still others looking ahead with the forecast of patriots, joined in the movement. It was a dreary period for the Church here for many years.

When the independence of this country was established, a meeting of the clergy of Massachusetts was held in Boston, in 1784 A.D., at which resolutions were passed embodying the principles deemed proper to be made prominent in organizing the Church in this country.

In 1789 A.D. the clergy of Massachusetts met again, and concluded to elect a Bishop of their own. Accordingly, on the 4th of June, 1789 A.D., they elected Edward Bass, of Newburyport, Bishop of Massachusetts and New Hampshire; but there were difficulties in the way of his consecration, mainly the unwillingness of some to have Bishop Seabury, who had been consecrated by the Scotch Bishops, take part in the perpetuation of the Episcopate in America.

The consecration of Bishop Seabury was declared valid by our General Convention, but in the mean time Dr. Bass resigned his election In 1796 A.D. he was re-elected, and on the 7th of May, 1797 A.D., was consecrated in Philadelphia. In May, 1798 A.D., he met the Massachusetts Convention in old Trinity Church, Boston, and presided over its deliberations as its Bishop. It was a small body then. There were only five clerical and seven lay deputies present. The clergy were Drs. Walker and Parker, the Rev. Messrs. Montague, Harris, and Burhaus.

Trinity and Christ Churches were the only two parishes in Boston in 1797 A.D. King's Chapel had been appropriated by the Unitarians shortly after the Revolution.

Bishop Bass continued to perform the duties of Rector of St. Paul's Church, Newburyport, after he became Bishop, the demands for Episcopal services not being very great in that time of the Church's weakness. He was a courteous, dignified gentleman, amiable and benevolent; his religious character was serious, practical, and stable. He discharged his duties with great fidelity. He died September 13, 1803 A.D. Massachusetts has had five Bishops,—Bass, Parker, Griswold, Eastburn, and Paddock.

In May, 1810 A.D., a Convention of the clergy and representatives of the New England States, except Connecticut, was held in Boston to form a union under the title of *The Eastern Diocese.*

The territory was a large one, but the Church was weak. In 1811 A.D. there were in all this territory only twenty-two parishes and sixteen officiating clergymen. Of these parishes only a few had any numerical or financial strength; in fact, but three, Trinity, Boston; St. John's, Providence; and Trinity, Newport, could be called strong parishes. At this Convention in 1810 A.D. the Rev. A. V. Griswold, of Bristol, R. I., was elected Bishop. He was consecrated in May, 1811 A.D., in New York.

He was born April 22, 1766 A.D., and died February 15, 1843 A.D., being seventy-seven years old, and having been a Bishop for thirty-two years. Part of the time he served as Rector of St. Peter's Church, Salem. The thirty-two years of his Episcopate witnessed marvelous growth of the Church in New England, so much so that one by one the associated Dioceses became strong enough to have a Bishop each for itself, and five Bishops were selected to take charge of the work which was originally placed in one man's hands.

Bishop Griswold's increasing infirmities compelled him to ask for an assistant, and Dr. Manton Eastburn, a native of England, but a resident of this country from childhood, and at the time of his election rector of the Church of the Ascension, New York, was elected in 1842 A.D., and was consecrated in December of that year. Bishop Griswold died the February following, and Bishop Eastburn became Bishop. The Diocese increased at first slowly, but yet surely, in strength and in numbers. The clergy were active, energetic, filled with a missionary zeal, and faithfully sowed the sacred seed of Church doctrine which is now yielding a most abundant harvest. The Bishop repeatedly recorded in his several reports, both to the Diocese and to the General Convention, a description of the peculiar difficulties under which the Church toiled.

"Planted amidst untractable elements —

by the side of institutions which are, on system, impatient of all distinctive claims,— and obliged either to use, or to oppose, traits of character which, though venerable and pious, are not of her own producing, our Church yet holds her difficult progress;" and later, "We *wait* for the salvation of the LORD, and have the most decided tokens that we shall not wait in vain." Later statistics show that this confident faith was fully justified.

In 1843 A.D., when the Bishop had fairly taken possession of his See, the clergy numbered 52; in 1872 A.D. they were 121; in 1883 A.D. they were 168. In 1843 A.D. there were 4118 communicants; in 1872 A.D. there were 11,706; in 1883 A.D. there were 18,582. In 1843 A.D. the contributions were $22,847; in 1872 A.D. they amounted to $330,381.67; in 1883 A.D. they reached $518,665.86. The Bishop, after thirty years of earnest and faithful toil throughout a large and rapidly increasing Diocese, passed to his rest September 12, 1872 A.D.

His successor, the Rt. Rev. Benjamin H. Paddock, S.T.D., a native of Norwich, Conn., born February 29, 1828 A.D., was elected by the Annual Convention May 6, and was consecrated the following 17th of September, 1873 A.D. The Diocese had emerged from its earlier difficulties and had now become a power in that Commonwealth which had once made it almost a crime to belong to her Communion.

Its great size, numerous parishes, and rapidly widening work, which would require all the energies and tax the strength of any man, receive from him earnest, watchful, fostering care. This is well shown by the carefully-drawn and wisely-planned Canon on Deaconesses and Sisterhoods, which was offered by him and passed the House of Bishops in 1880 A.D. It was too late in the session to obtain the passage of it in the House of Deputies, and being laid over to the last General Convention, the consideration of it was necessarily deferred there from the pressure of other business. A comparison of the statistics given above shows how the Diocese has grown under his Episcopal oversight.

The following statistics are taken from the Convention Journal of 1883 A.D. They are made up from the Parochial Reports, and inasmuch as some six or more parishes failed to report, and a number of others made defective reports, it is safe to assume that the correct totals are really larger than are here given.

Contributions for purposes outside the Parishes..	$78,774.42
Contributions for purposes within the Parishes..	439,891.44
Total.................................	$518,665.86
Baptisms...	2,261
Confirmed...	1,055
Communicants...	18,582
Teachers in Sunday-schools...........................	1,229
Pupils " " "	16,848

Statistics for 1886 A.D.: Clergy, 178; parishes, 110; missions, 62; candidates for H. O., 14; ordinations, D. 8, P. 11; baptisms, 2969; confirmed, 1650; communicants, 22,268; S. S. teachers, 1920; S. S. scholars, 17,000; contributions. $684,258.68.

REV. G. W. SHINN.

Master. A title or designation for the heads of various Guilds, Orders, Institutions, Colleges, or Hospitals.

Matins. The ancient name for the daybreak service of the reformation offices of the English Church. This Matin service, together with that of Prime and Tierce, was compressed into our present Morning Prayer. In it are remnants of the very ancient Gallican system of daily prayer, which contains elements which are probably Eastern in their origin. Indeed, of our services it may be said that there are embedded in them in versicle, rubric, or prayer, phrases or ritual directions which belong to a very early Eastern system of daily services.

Matrimony (Latin, *matrimonium*), or marriage, signifies the nuptial state, that is, the relation of husband and wife, a relation which imposes obligations and creates rights, which are regulated by divine, and also, as to many details, by human law. "Marriage" (says Hugh Davey Evans, in his work on "The Christian Doctrine of Marriage") "is a civil contract, and as such subject to the jurisdiction of the State and the law of the land; but it is also a divine institution, and as such, not under their authority. GOD Himself instituted the appropriation of one woman to one man, and subjected it to certain laws, which the State ought to enforce, but which she may at her peril refuse to enforce. If she refuse, there are no means of compelling her, for she has no human superior; but the divine laws are not less binding. The State ought to enforce the divine laws, because they would promote the temporal welfare of her citizens; but if she be of a different opinion, it only remains that Christians should obey them, and endure whatever inconveniences may arise from their not being enforced upon others. In this country the State declines to enforce them, and it is the more necessary that Christian men and women should be familiar with them" (p. 91). In this article marriage will be treated chiefly as a divine institution, subject to the regulation of the Church, which is guided in this, as in all matters, by what she believes to be the "Word of GOD." The best account of the character and objects of Christian marriage is to be found in the Service of the English Church. The passage is worthy of being quoted here, because it was unaccountably omitted by the American revisers of the Prayer-Book in 1789 A.D. In the face of the admitted looseness of doctrine and practice prevalent in our country in regard to marriage, it can hardly be maintained that we have gained anything by the omission of this plain-spoken, admirable exhortation. In the English Church, every married couple and the assembled congregation are solemnly informed that holy matrimony " is an honorable estate, instituted of GOD in the time of man's innocency, signifying unto us the mystical union that is betwixt CHRIST and His Church; which holy estate CHRIST adorned and beautified with His presence, and first miracle that He wrought in Cana of Galilee; and is commended of Saint Paul to be honorable among all men; and therefore is not by any to be enterprised nor taken in hand, unadvisedly, lightly, or wantonly to satisfy man's carnal lusts and appetites, like brute beasts that have no understanding; but reverently, discreetly, advisedly, soberly, and in the fear of GOD; duly considering the causes for which Matrimony was ordained.

"First, It was ordained for the procreation of children, to be brought up in the fear and nurture of the LORD, and to praise His Holy Name.

"Secondly, It was ordained for a remedy against sin, and to avoid fornication; that such persons as have not the gift of continency might marry, and keep themselves undefiled members of CHRIST's body.

"Thirdly, It was ordained for the mutual society, help, and comfort, that the one ought to have of the other, both in prosperity and adversity."

The persons to be married are then charged both in the English service and in our own, that " if either of them know any impediment why they may not lawfully be joined together in matrimony, they should confess it for if any persons are joined together otherwise than as GOD's Word doth allow, their marriage is not lawful."

This is a plain intimation, in the very service itself, that whenever, as in this country the State refuses to be guided and bound in its legislation by GOD's Word, Christian men and women cannot be content with simply obeying the State. In other words, the State may and does allow some marriages to be contracted which the Church deems unlawful, and permits others to be dissolved for causes which the Church cannot allow to be valid. Difficult questions and troublesome cases of conscience may arise, but collisions between Church and State in this country are not very likely to occur. The State may permit what the Church forbids, but members of the Church are not forced by the State to avail themselves of the permission which is given. A correct understanding of the relations of Church and State, and of the duties that Christian men and women owe to both of those divine institutions, lies at the bottom of this whole question. The subject has been so lucidly expounded by Hugh Davey Evans, in his elaborate " Treatise on the Christian Doctrine of Marriage," that the reader will pardon an extended quotation from that learned author.

" When a question arises whether the law of the land conflicts with the law of GOD, it cannot be decided by the law of the land, which is of inferior authority to the law of GOD. The law of GOD, which is the higher law, must be the rule, and conscience the judge to apply that rule. Every one who is called upon to act upon the question must decide it for himself, as every one who is called to act upon any question must decide it for himself. The private man must decide it according to his conscience. The officer of the Church who is called to advise, direct, or judge the conduct of the private Christian must decide according to his private conscience, unless the Church has furnished him with a rule. The Church herself, in her legislative capacity, must be governed by what may be called her aggregate or public conscience.

" If the two laws do not conflict, every one, including the authorities of the Church, must obey both. If one permit what the other forbids, men should respect the prohibition. If one command what the other forbids, we must obey GOD rather than man. Suppose a man should apply to be received into the communion of the Church who had married after a civil divorce which was contrary to GOD's law. How ought the rector of the parish to act? Public opinion would perhaps say that the twice-married man should be received, because he had done nothing not allowed by the law of the land. But the true question is, Has he done an act contrary to the law of GOD? The law of the land, which is, at best, an interpretation of the law of GOD, made by temporal rulers for temporal purposes, has nothing to do with spiritual questions" (pp. 33, 34).

" With respect to marriages which the law of the land allows, but which the law of GOD forbids, no one ought to enter into them or to continue in them. The parties to them have not been joined by GOD, and man ought to put them asunder. In some cases the civil courts undertake to dissolve marriages which were originally valid, for causes for which the law of GOD does not allow them to be dissolved. No Christian can consider a marriage which was once valid as dissolved by any power whatever, except only in the case in which our LORD has permitted such dissolution. No Christian can intermarry with any one who has been released from a valid marriage for a reason which was scripturally insufficient—for any cause 'saving the cause of fornication'—without being guilty of adultery. By following these few rules a private Christian may avoid being mixed up with the unchristian laws which have been adopted in America. He can thus keep a conscience void of offense in this matter before GOD and man.

" But the clergy may sometimes meet with embarrassing cases. They will come in one of two forms. A clergyman may be called on to solemnize a marriage which the law of the land allows, and the law of GOD forbids. There is no reason for believing that such a marriage can receive the Divine blessing, or possess the sanctity and unity of marriage. A clergyman should refuse to solemnize such a marriage, at whatever cost or risk to himself. Happily, an American clergyman can incur no danger from the State; for there is no law of the land which requires him to solemnize any marriage whatever. The only danger is that of giving offense to the public and to his parishioners. This is sometimes an important consideration; but we ought to obey GOD rather than men. At other times the question may present itself in the shape of a case of lay discipline, when a person who is living in a sinful marriage desires to be admitted to the Holy Communion. In the Primitive Church, such a person would have been rejected until he or she separated from his or her partner in guilt. Whether a modern clergyman is called upon to revive this discipline by his own authority and upon his own responsibility is a grave and difficult question which every clergyman must decide for himself, with the aid and counsel of his Bishop. It may be observed that the power of rejecting or suspending a communicant is very much limited by the first rubric of the Communion service. It seems to require that the evil life for which a communicant may be suspended or rejected should be such as to give offense to the congregation" (pp. 249, 250).

What remains to be said may be arranged under three heads. I. Duties of husbands and wives. II. The "impediments" which the Church service refers to, and which make the marriage unlawful. III. Divorce.

I. *Duties of Husbands and Wives.*—What is usually called the marriage vow is the promise which the parties mutually make to each other. It is a promise of the most solemn character, witnessed before GOD and the congregation. Both husband and wife promise, each to the other, that the contract shall be life-long and indissoluble, each using the solemn words, "till death us do part." "The parties by this vow engage their personal fidelity, expressly and specifically; they engage likewise to consult and promote each other's happiness; the wife, moreover, promises *obedience* to her husband. Nature may have made and left the sexes of the human species nearly equal in their faculties, and perfectly so in their rights; but to guard against those competitions which equality, or a contested superiority, is almost sure to produce, the Christian Scriptures enjoin upon the wife that obedience which she here promises, and in terms so peremptory and absolute that it seems to extend to everything not criminal, or not entirely inconsistent with the woman's happiness. 'Let the wife,' says St. Paul, 'be subject to her own husband in everything.' 'The ornament of a meek and quiet spirit,' says the Apostle Peter, speaking of the duty of wives, 'is, in the sight of GOD, of great price' No words ever expressed the true merit of the female character so well as these." The above quotation is from Paley, who adds, that "the marriage vow is violated, 1, by adultery; 2, by any behavior which, knowingly, renders the life of the other miserable; as desertion, neglect, prodigality, drunkenness, peevishness, penuriousness, jealousy, or any levity of conduct which administers occasion of jealousy."

II. *Impediments to Marriage.*—The consent of the parties and the blessing of GOD are the formative elements of Christian marriage. "But where no consent has been given, or where the marriage is in direct violation of a divine law, and the absence of the consent and the unlawfulness can be shown by provable facts, man may separate those whom GOD hath not joined. . . . There are, then, some things which make an outward marriage unlawful and void. They are called impediments to marriage, and are of two classes. The first are facts which prove that there has been no consent. The others are facts which prove that the marriage is of a class not allowed ' by GOD's Word.'" (H. D. E., ch. xiii. § 2.) The subject is intricate, and the cases of conscience that arise are sometimes perplexing. Perhaps no recent writer has treated the matter from a Christian stand-point more elaborately and learnedly than Dr. Evans, and to his treatise and other works of the kind the reader is referred for more extended discussion. Both the State and the Church have erred in creating impediments which are not really such. The State may forbid certain persons to intermarry, and the law would bind the consciences of her citizens. But if a really valid marriage took place, the State could not make it void, except so far as it relates to the civil effects of marriage. The Church, however, during the Middle Ages erred far more grievously than the State, by creating many frivolous canonical impediments. Among these was the rule which made marriage between a godparent and his or her god-child unlawful. Still more curious and unreasonable was the prohibition of marriage between persons who had been sponsors for the same person, and who were regarded as spiritual brothers and sisters. The evils resulting were remedied to some extent by a system of dispensations, which at the same time served to increase the revenue and the power of the Popes. The practical consequence was that the Divine law that marriage cannot be dissolved was virtually made of none effect, and while divorce was not allowed, many valid marriages were annulled when money and other influences were brought to bear.

The Roman casuists distinguish two kinds of impediments, *impedimenta impedientia,* and *impedimenta dirimentia.* Under the first class are included impediments which render the marriage illicit, *aut impediunt usum,* until the impediment be removed. Such, for example, according to their rules, would be a marriage at a forbidden time, as in Advent, or in Lent. In the other class are comprised impediments which render the marriage absolutely null and void. These latter only require any particular mention, and by impediments, in the probable sense of the marriage service, must therefore be understood not considerations which might make a marriage undesirable or improper, but facts which, when proved, would justify the so-called marriage being pronounced by a court as null and void *ab initio*.

Of these impediments it is sufficient to mention here the following: (1) Existing marriage of either party. (2) Bodily or mental impotence. (3) Tender age, below the period allowed by law, which makes consent doubtful or impossible. (4) Being within the forbidden degrees of consanguinity and affinity. The last head involves many difficult questions, one of the most troublesome of which is the lawfulness of marriage with a deceased wife's sister. All that can be said in this place on the subject is, that such marriages are contrary to the inherited traditions of the English Church, and the general sentiment of English-speaking people. This is plainly shown by the very word sister-*in-law*, which means that a woman who is not really a man's sister is his sister *in law*, and therefore, like his own sister by blood, is to be regarded and treated as a woman whom he cannot marry. The term which embodies this tradition is still used in America, although in this country a wife's sister is not the husband's sister *in law*, because according to the law of most or all of our States, he may marry her. The General Convention has not positively decided the question for Churchmen, though the House of Bishops, in 1808 A.D., declared that in their opinion *The Table of Degrees*, appended to the English Prayer-Book, was binding in this Church. The subject is fully discussed, with his usual learning, by the author so often quoted in this article (ch. xiv., on the Doctrine of Incest). Dr. Evans approves the decision of the House of Bishops, and considers such marriages unlawful. It must, however, in fairness be added, that every part of this vexed question is involved in doubt and difficulty. The meaning of the text (Levit. xviii. 18), and the bearing of verse 16 on this subject, are disputed by Hebrew scholars and eminent commentators, and whether or not the whole body of the Levitical prohibitions in regard to marriage forms part of the moral law, so as to be binding upon Christians, is a further question of no little intricacy. Notwithstanding Dr. Evans's learned, painstaking, and apparently impartial support of the traditional doctrine, candor requires the admission that the prevailing sentiment of American Churchmen and scholars is favorable to marriage with a deceased wife's sister, while the opposition of English divines and of English society to the validity of such a union (beginning with Archbishop Whateley in 1851 A.D.) is perceptibly weakening, and, as the recent debates in Parliament have disclosed, is less and less based upon any Scriptural prohibition. It is proper to append, for reference, the table of which mention has been made.

"A TABLE OF KINDRED AND AFFINITY,.

Wherein whosoever are related are forbidden in Scripture and our laws to marry together.

" A man may not marry his grandmother, grandfather's wife, wife's grandmother, father's sister, mother's sister, father's brother's wife, mother's brother's wife, wife's father's sister, wife's mother's sister, mother, step-mother, wife's mother, daughter, wife's daughter, son's wife, sister, wife's sister, brother's wife, son's daughter, daughter's daughter, son's son's wife, daughter's son's wife, wife's son's daughter, wife's daughter's daughter, brother's daughter, sister's daughter, brother's son's wife, sister's son's wife, wife's brother's daughter, wife's sister's daughter.

"A woman may not marry with her grandfather, grandmother's husband, husband's grandfather, father's brother, mother's brother, father's sister's husband, mother's sister's husband, husband's father's brother, husband's mother's brother, father, stepfather, husband's father, son, husband's son, daughter's husband, brother, husband's brother, sister's husband, son's son, daughter's son, son's daughter's husband, daughter's daughter's husband, husband's son's son, husband's daughter's son, brother's son, sister's son, brother's daughter's husband, sister's daughter's husband, husband's brother's son, husband's sister's son." (Divorce, p. 18.)

III. *Divorce.*—By divorce is properly understood a dissolution of the marriage *bond*, so that one or both of the parties may lawfully contract a second marriage. Under certain circumstances it may be advisable or necessary that married persons should live apart, and that such separation should be protected by law. The practice is to call such legal separations *divorces a mensa et toro* (from bed and board), while the dissolution of the bond itself is called *divorce a vinculo matrimonii*. It is only this latter species of divorce that calls for any discussion.

Marriage, as has been said, is a life-long union between one man and one woman. Each promises to take the other "till death us do part, according to GOD'S holy ordinance," and over the union are pronounced the solemn words of our SAVIOUR, "Those whom GOD hath joined together, let no man put asunder." Indissolubleness, therefore, is the *rule* of Christian marriage. The rule, however, is subject to one exception, stated by our LORD Himself in these words: "Whosoever shall put away his wife, except it be for fornication, and shall marry another, committeth adultery; and whoso marrieth her which is put away, doth commit adultery" (St. Matt. xix. 9).

The parallel passages in the Gospel are St. Matt. v. 32; St. Mark x. 11 ; St. Luke xvi. 18. The latter verse is as follows : " Whosoever putteth away his wife, and marrieth another, committeth adultery ; and whosoever marrieth her that is put away from her husband committeth adultery."

In this passage in St. Luke, and also in St. Mark, the exception mentioned by St. Matthew is omitted, and an absolute prohibition to marry a divorced woman under any circumstances seems to be laid down. It is well known that there are not to be found in the whole New Testament any texts whose interpretation has been more earnestly disputed, even from early times, than these which touch upon divorce. It may be well to quote the cautious and modest opinion of Hugo Grotius, one of the greatest of modern expositors. He concludes his long and elaborate note on St. Matt. v. 32, with the following words : " Sed hæc, quæ de divortiis dixi, eo dixi animo, ut piis et eruditis occasionem darem rei diligentius excutiendæ. Nihil definio, nihil certi pronuntio. Valeat in dubio ea sententia quæ quam maxime sanctam et inconcussam vult esse matrimonii fidem ; ne temere rumpamus vinculum a DEO institutum." That is to say, " What I have said about divorce, I have said with the view of leading good and learned men to examine more carefully into the subject. I give no definite, positive opinion. I pronounce nothing as absolutely certain. In a doubtful case of conscience, it is best that that opinion should prevail which regards the marriage troth, as far as it is possible, as a thing holy and inviolable; lest, in our rashness, we should break a bond instituted by GOD Himself." In a work like the present nothing can be done but to state fairly the conflicting opinions and authorities, and then to add the Canons and regulations which the Church has provided for the guidance of her clergy and laity.

(1) The doctrine of the Church of Rome is that divorce *a vinculo matrimonii* is never, under any circumstances, lawful. That Church, therefore, holds that the exception mentioned by St. Matthew refers to divorce *a mensa et toro*, which gives no permission to either party to contract a second marriage while a husband or wife is still living. " Hic est perpetuus ecclesiæ usus, sensus et praxis," says Cornelius a Lapide (Comment. on St. Matt., v. 32). This teaching, seemingly strict, became in practice very lax by reason of the doctrine of impediments already mentioned, of which her casuists mention no less than fifteen, some of which are of the most frivolous character. (See Alphonsus de Liguori, Homo Apostolicus, Tract xviii., § 60, De Impedimentis Dirimentibus, tom. ii. p. 229, Paris, 1834.)

The same doctrine of absolute indissolubility has been held by a large body of learned English divines, among whom may be mentioned Bishop Andrewes, Keble, Canon Liddon.

Canon Liddon also maintains the opinion of the eminent Dr. Döllinger, that the word rendered fornication in St. Matt. v. 32, and xix. 9, does not mean adultery, but that our LORD was referring to Deut. xxii. 13-21, and was speaking of ante-nuptial sins, which, as implying fraud on the part of the woman, freed the husband without, however, giving the guilty woman liberty to marry again. He further holds that our LORD meant this teaching (though found in the Sermon on the Mount) to apply to the Jews only. (See Liddon's University Sermons, 2d series, Sermon xvi., " Christ and Human Law.")

(2) Bishop Wordsworth, of Lincoln, Alford, and the majority of modern commentators (not Roman Catholic) hold that our LORD's exception, recorded in two places in St. Matthew, must be understood in St. Mark and St. Luke also; and that the effect of the exception is to permit the innocent party to remarry. A wife divorced for adultery, they hold, cannot marry again according to the Gospels. This interpretation makes the bond—*vinculum*—binding upon one partner and not upon the other.

(3) Dr. Hugh Davey Evans, whose examination of this difficult question is more elaborate and exhaustive than any other part of his treatise, holds that the adultery of the wife is the one exception made by our blessed LORD Himself, to the rule of the indissolubleness of marriage, and that when a legitimate divorce has been obtained, *both* parties are absolutely at liberty, and may marry.

Whether the privilege allowed to the husband in the saving clause extends to the wife—*i.e.*, whether a marriage can be divorced for the adultery of the husband— Dr. Evans considers a doubtful and difficult question. " English divines," he says, " have generally taken the negative side of the question ; in this country their view is sometimes spoken of as absurd. It may be erroneous, but it is not absurd. It may not be easy to show that it is erroneous" (p. 240). . . . " Upon the whole it may be said that the one text on the subject (St. Mark x. 11, 12) is plain against a woman putting away her husband and being married to another. The exception is not plain. It is therefore safest for all Christians to act as though divorce for the adultery of the husband were not lawful" (p. 243).

With regard to the great question whether the exception, "saving for the cause of fornication," found in St. Matthew, is to be understood and read into St. Mark and St. Luke, the conclusion which Hugh Davey Evans arrives at, and the reasons for it, cannot be more concisely expressed than in the words of Archbishop Manners Sutton, of Canterbury, in the British House of Lords, in 1820 A.D. The Archbishop said, " I admit that the passages in Matthew are not in

Mark, nor in Luke; but in Matthew the exception is given, and Mark and Luke have the general institution without the exception. Now, I conceive that the passages in which the exception is omitted ought to be measured by the passage in which it is expressed; for it is impossible to believe that that was not intended which was expressed, though that which was not actually expressed might yet be intended." (Quoted by H. D. E., p. 193, from Jebb " On Adultery and Divorce," pp. 111, 112.)

The opinion of Hugh Davey Evans (which has been severely condemned, though never yet refuted) receives confirmation of no little value from one of the latest and best known of English Commentaries (Bishop Ellicott's New Testament Commentary for English Readers). The author of the Commentary on the first three Gospels in that work, who is the well-known Dean of Wells, Dr. Plumptre, writes as follows on St. Matt. v. 32:

"*Whosoever shall marry her that is divorced.* The Greek is less definite, and may be rendered either ' a woman who has been put away,' or better, ' her when she has been put away.' Those who take the former construction, infer from it the absolute unlawfulness of marriage with a divorced woman under any circumstances whatever; some holding that the husband is under the same restrictions, *i.e.*, that the *vinculum matrimonii* is absolutely indissoluble; while others teach that in the excepted case, both the husband and the wife gain the right to contract a second marriage. The Romish Church, in theory, takes the former view, the Greek and most Reformed Churches the latter; while some codes of law, like that now recognized in England, go back to the looser interpretation of Deut. xxiv. 1, and allow the divorce *a vinculo* for many lesser causes than incontinence. Of these contending views, that which is intermediate between the two extremes seems to be most in harmony with the true meaning of our LORD's words. The words 'put away' would necessarily convey to His Jewish hearers the idea of an entire dissolution of the marriage union, leaving both parties free to contract a fresh marriage; and if it were not so, then the case in which He specially permits that dissolution would stand on the same level as the others. The injured husband would still be bound to the wife who had broken the vow which was of the essence of the marriage-contract. But if *he* was free to marry again, then the guilt of *adultery* could not possibly attach to *her* subsequent marriage with another. The context, therefore, requires us to restrict that guilt to the case of a wife divorced for other reasons. The injured husband would still be bound to the unfaithful wife. This, then, seems the true law of divorce for the Church of CHRIST as such to recognize. The question how far national legislation may permit divorce for other causes, such as cruelty or desertion, seems to stand on a different footing, and must be discussed on different grounds. In proportion as the ' hardness of heart,' which made the wider license the least of two evils, prevails now, it may be not only expedient, but right and necessary, though it implies a standard of morals lower than the law of CHRIST, to meet it, as it was met of old, by a like reluctant permission."

It is not, of course, denied that the Church or the State has the right to inflict a penalty upon the guilty party, and this penalty might take the form of a prohibition to marry again. This view of the case may have influenced the General Convention, as we know it did influence some members of it, in passing the present Canon (see below), which permits marriage only to the innocent party in such a divorce. The real question is the more difficult one, whether, *if* such a marriage were contracted irregularly, and contrary to the Church's prohibition, the Church would have the right to declare such marriage *void*. Dr. Evans, following the most widely accepted interpretation of our LORD's words in St. Matthew, maintains that the effect of the exception is to make such a marriage valid. He argues that the Church, in permitting the innocent party to marry, must thereby logically hold that the marriage has been dissolved; otherwise marrying the woman would now be " adultery," and the *innocent* man who remarried would also become an adulterer, because he would still have a wife living,— an adulterous wife, it is true,—but still his *wife*, unless the *vinculum matrimonii* has been dissolved.

In the face of this diversity of opinion among such noted Biblical scholars, the following propositions will hardly be disputed:

(1) That any one contemplating a second marriage with a divorced wife or husband, while the other partner is still living, has a difficult question of conscience to decide, and is treading upon dangerous ground, in which the lax laws of the State are no sufficient guide to those " who profess and call themselves Christians."

(2) That no clergyman can be forced to solemnize any marriage which he honestly believes to be forbidden by "GOD's Word," even if he feels bound to take the strictest and narrowest of the above interpretations.

(3) That no clergyman, on the other hand, is justified in questions of discipline and admission to the Sacraments of the Church, in going beyond the precise directions which the Church, whereof he is a minister, has chosen to give him in the premises.

(4) That it is the duty of the Church to give by Canon explicit directions, so far as may be necessary, to her Bishops and other clergy, in a matter which so deeply concerns morality and religion.

The only rule which the Protestant Episcopal Church has given upon the matter will be found in the Canon passed by the General Convention of 1877 A.D., which is added here for convenience of reference, as well as to complete such treatment of this difficult topic as seemed suitable for a work like the present one.

"CANON XIII.

"OF MARRIAGE AND DIVORCE.

"*Marriage, except as God's Word doth allow, not lawful.* (Digest, Title ii.)

"SECTION 1. If any persons be joined together otherwise than as GOD'S Word does allow, their marriage is not lawful.

"*No Minister shall unite in marriage those divorced, save for the cause of adultery.*

"SEC. 2. No Minister, knowingly, after due inquiry, shall solemnize the marriage of any person who has a divorced husband or wife still living, if such husband or wife has been put away for any cause arising after marriage; but this Canon shall not be held to apply to the innocent party in a divorce for the cause of adultery, or to parties once divorced seeking to be united again.

"*The Sacraments to be withheld from persons married otherwise than as God's Word doth allow, save to a penitent person in danger of death.*

"SEC. 3. If any Minister of this Church shall have reasonable cause to doubt whether a person desirous of being admitted to Holy Baptism, or to Confirmation, or to the Holy Communion, has been married otherwise than as the Word of GOD and discipline of this Church allow, such Minister, before receiving such person to these ordinances, shall refer the case to the Bishop for his godly judgment thereupon. *Provided, however,* That no Minister shall, in any case, refuse the Sacraments to a penitent person in imminent danger of death.

"*Questions to be referred to the Bishop.*

"SEC. 4. Questions touching the facts of any case arising under Section 2 of this Canon shall be referred to the Bishop of the Diocese or Missionary Jurisdiction in which the same may occur; or, if there be no Bishop of such Diocese or Missionary Jurisdiction, then to some Bishop to be designated by the Standing Committee; and the Bishop to whom such questions have been so referred shall thereupon make inquiry in such manner as he shall deem expedient, and shall deliver his judgment in the premises.

"*The Penalties under this Canon limited.*

"SEC. 5. This Canon, so far as it affixes penalties, does not apply to cases occurring before it takes effect, according to Canon iv., Title iv."

(In the above article, though many books have been consulted, Hugh Davey Evans has been closely followed, even in parts where quotation marks were not inserted. The full title of his invaluable work is as follows: "A Treatise on the Christian Doctrine of Marriage," by Hugh Davey Evans, LL.D., with a biographical sketch of the author, and an appendix containing Bishop Andrewes's "Discourse Against Second Marriage," etc., New York, Hurd & Houghton, 1870 A.D. Out of the vast literature on the subject the following may be named as specially interesting to Churchmen, and easy to be obtained: "The Laws of Marriage," by John Fulton, D.D., LL.D., New York, 1883 A.D. This work treats specially of impediments and of divorce, and presents a mass of useful material. "Liddon's University Sermons," second series, New York, 1880 A.D.; "Keble's Argument against Repealing the Laws which treat Marriage as Indissoluble," Oxford, 1857 A.D.; Wordsworth, "Occasional Sermons in Westminster Abbey;" an article in the *Quarterly Review* in the year 1857 A.D., by the Rt. Hon. W. E. Gladstone, reprinted in the sixth volume of his "Gleanings of Past Years;" Wolsey, "Divorce and Divorce Legislation," New York, 1882 A.D. (second edition); Baum, "The Rights and Duties of Rectors, Church-wardens, and Vestrymen," Philadelphia, 1879 A.D.)

REV. H. HARRISON.

Matthew, St. The Apostle and Evangelist, also called Levi, the son of Alphæus. Of the details of his life we are wholly ignorant. He must have had some property, as he gave a feast at his own house on the occasion of his call. He was a publican, a person who either farmed the public taxes, or an inferior officer who attended to the collection of them. Probably St. Matthew was of this order, since he was sitting at the receipt of custom when our LORD was passing by and called him. His prompt obedience shows that he had already a devout character, and was looking for the Hope of Israel, and further, that he, too, had heard of JESUS with the spiritual ear. The feast which he gave led to the lessons on humility which our LORD gave, while He practically illustrated them. These St. Matthew never forgot, for in his Gospel he gives himself the hated name of "the publican," a name the other two Evangelists never apply to him. What became of him after our LORD'S Ascension, where he wrote his Gospel, and what were the special circumstances that led him to do this work, we cannot now know. The sublime reticence of Holy Scripture, the Divine parsimony that wastes no words, records no needless facts, but teaches us that GOD'S servants only need to be remembered by their Master when and as He wills. He is commemorated upon the 21st of September.

Matthew, St., Gospel of. The witness of all Christian antiquity is unvarying in attributing this Gospel to the Apostle and Evangelist. We cannot ascertain the precise date when the Gospel was written, but we can reach an approximate date. It was the first written, and could only have been written within a few years after the Ascension. It was written for Jewish converts. Since general tradition states that the Apostles were in Jerusalem, as a centre of work for some years, preaching at the Passover to the multitudes who gathered there, the Gospel may well have been written for the use of those who were converted there and who needed such a record for their instruction. Be that as it may, the Gospel is distinctively Hebrew in cast. It is national, retrospective, and through those very facts which might make it seem narrow, its intensity makes it most universal. It quotes prophecy freely. It appeals to the fulfillment of history in CHRIST. It speaks most sharply of the sins of the Jews and their rulers. It refers to the Law, as in the Sermon on the Mount. It traces our LORD'S descent through David to Abraham. It brings out the spiritual turn to the intensely Jewish hope of a restored kingdom,—a heavenly kingdom. He brings out this at many points of the narrative, in the parables he records, in the declarations of our LORD at His Passion. In these we see the earnest, hopeful Jew, whose national longings found their truest realization in the spiritual kingdom of His Master, and the eye-witness who writes in sober honesty those things of which he was personally cognizant. Whether he wrote in Hebrew (Aramaic) or in Greek is a question which may be probably answered in the affirmative, but cannot now be settled. At any rate the Greek must be attributed to him, and must be equally authentic as any Hebrew form of it could possibly be. He preserves for us two miracles,—healing of two blind men and the tribute money,—ten parables, nine discourses, and some fourteen incidents—these last chiefly in connection with our LORD'S Passion—which are not recorded by the other three Evangelists. The contents of this Gospel may be classified in seven parts : I. The birth and childhood of JESUS the King of Israel. II. The founding of the kingdom, beginning with the heralding by His forerunner and His first victory in the temptation. III. The works and signs of the kingdom, in His declaration of its fundamental Laws, in His royal power shown in miracles, in His teaching about His kingdom. IV. Preparations for the final conflict, by the confession of St. Peter, by predicting His Passion, by His parables. V. The triumphs of the King, His entry into Jerusalem. VI. His final warfare, in His Passion and death. VII. The perfected victory, in His Resurrection.

Though St. Matthew does not follow strictly the chronological order in his Gospel, yet he does not violate the proper sequence of the main events, and there is an internal coherence of thought and a grouping together of facts which have a subtle interconnection, which is of more importance to us than the historical order, where it has been broken. To St. Matthew's purpose it was essential to set forth the Son of GOD as the looked-for MESSIAH, the King of both the historical and the spiritual Israel, and as the perfect Man.

Matthias, St. The Apostle who was elected to take the place of the traitor Judas. It is a probable conjecture that he was one of the seventy disciples. "Different opinions have prevailed as to the manner of the election of Matthias ; the most natural construction of the words of Scripture seems to be this. After the address of St. Peter the whole assembled body of the brethren, amounting in number to about one hundred and twenty, proceeded to nominate two, namely, Joseph surnamed Barsabas and Matthias, who answered the requirements of the Apostle ; the subsequent selection between the two was referred in prayer to Him who, knowing the hearts of men, knew which of them was the fitter to be His witness and Apostle. The brethren then, under the heavenly guidance which they had invoked, proceeded to give forth their lots, probably each by writing the name of one of the candidates on a tablet and casting it into an urn. The urn was then shaken, and the name that first came out decided the election." (Smith's Dict. of the Bible, sub voc., p. 1839.) It was a solemn act of referring the decision to GOD alone.

The Apostle is commemorated upon the 25th of February.

Maundy - Thursday. Thursday in Holy Week. It derives its name from the antiphon sung at the service, "Mandatum novum do vobis ut diligatis invicem" (St. John xiii. 34),—"A new commandment give I unto you, That ye should love one another." But this day, long before it received this name of Maundy, had many important services celebrated upon it. On it the catechumens who were ready for baptism were taught the Creed. On it penitents who had passed their probation were publicly absolved and restored. On it the chrism, the consecrated oil for anointing the newly baptized, was consecrated. On it, at least in the African Church, the Holy Communion was celebrated at night. It was excepted from the general rule which was enforced early after persecution ceased. But this practice was looked upon with disfavor and it gradually fell into disuse. As a day of preparation for the fast of Good-Friday, and in view of our LORD'S acts upon this day, it has always held a very important position in the holy services of Passion-week.

Mediation. *Vide* MEDIATOR.

Mediator. Bishop Butler in his Analogy draws attention to the fact that living creatures are brought into the world and preserved by the instrumentality of others as mediators, and hence to the fact that a "Mediator between GOD and man" is accordant with nature (1 Tim. ii. 5). He also speaks of the bad consequences of our follies being prevented by the assistance of others, as being analogous to the act of GOD in giving His only-begotten SON for wicked men (St. John iii. 16), and of CHRIST being the author of eternal salvation to the obedient, after His suffering (Heb. v. 8, 9). We see a human mediator in Moses, refraining from his food in a long fast because of the sin of the people (Deut. ix. 18), in his prayer for Aaron (v. 20), and for his people (v. 26). The Jewish writer Philo describes the Word as "an intercessor for mortal man to the immortal GOD, and an ambassador from the King to His subjects." The sacrifice of CHRIST is intended to deliver man both from the power and the punishment of sin. Abraham, as a relative mediator, pleading for Sodom (Gen. xviii. 23–32), points to CHRIST as the absolute Mediator. Noah with his family in the ark, and Lot with his household, spared from Sodom, may represent CHRIST as the SAVIOUR of His Church. The Jews called the MESSIAH the Middle One, as standing between GOD and man. Job longed for a daysman, that is, an arbitrator on the day of trial (Job ix. 33). This umpire who lays his hand on the GODHEAD and on manhood is found in JESUS CHRIST. Heathen mythology groped after this truth; Christianity declares it in giving the only Name whereby we may be saved (Acts iv. 12), and by which we may come unto the FATHER (St. John xiv. 6). Those who were enemies of GOD are reconciled by CHRIST'S death (Col. i. 21, 22). CHRIST by obeying the law of GOD and satisfying justice brought His people into the favor of GOD (Eph. ii. 18). As Man, He was related to the sinner, and in human nature could make the reconciliation and obey the law (Gal. iv. 4; Rom. v. 19). As Man, CHRIST could shed His blood for man (Heb. ii. 10, 15, and vii. 3–5). As Man, He became a sympathizing High-Priest (Heb. ii. 17, 18, and iv. 15). The Mediator must be holy and without spot (Heb. vii. 26, and ix. 14, and 1 John iii. v.). He must be GOD to perform a work which men and angels could not do. As GOD-man we hope in CHRIST. His Manhood brings Him near to our affections. "Mercy and truth are met together; righteousness and peace have kissed each other" (Ps. lxxxv. 10). CHRIST is the only Mediator (1 Tim. ii. 5), to the exclusion of saints and angels. He is Mediator for Jews and Gentiles, and of saints in the Old and New Testaments (Eph. ii. 11–22). He is the Propitiation for the sins of "the whole world" (1 John ii. 2). "He is a suitable, constant, willing, and prevalent Mediator; and His mediation always succeeds, and is infallible." "He is able also to save them to the uttermost that come unto GOD by Him, seeing He ever liveth to make intercession for them" (Heb. vii. 25). May all thus come to Him and find eternal salvation. He who rejects the king's son slights the king.

Authorities: Buck's Theological Dictionary, Whitby on 1 Tim. ii. 5, McKnight on the Epistles, Essay vii., Lange's Genesis.

REV. S. F. HOTCHKIN.

Means of Grace. Since "Grace" has as its root idea the free gift out of good will, the means of grace are all those instruments for our growth in holiness which GOD of His love has given to each of us to use. From the Sacraments, in their place, down to the ordinary and usual Christian graces of a daily holy life, every part and act has its place under the collective title of the means of grace. In whatever channel He conveys graces to us, and in whatever degree He intrusts us with a share of that holiness without which no man can see GOD, so far we receive and use the means of grace. The Sacraments do ordinarily convey grace to us, in the limited sense we now use that word, and they are essential to our salvation because they are "*the means.*" But, since our LORD by His ascension gave *given gifts* to men, we may, nay, must, include all the instruments whereby He chooses to convey both the results of His atonement and strength for our spiritual growth. Every gift of spiritual grace is a proof that He knows that His grace is sufficient for us. In this would be included, as indeed St. Paul does (Eph. iv. 7–16), the Apostolic office and the assisting officers. The peace and harmony of the Church, the steadfastness in the Faith, the growth in nearness to our LORD, to whom all grace was given without measure, and who divides through the HOLY GHOST severally to every man as He wills. In this sense the largeness of that thanksgiving for our redemption and for the means of grace and for the hope of glory come out prominently. It is in no narrow application to merely the Sacraments, principal means as they are, but in a breadth, fullness of appreciation of the fact that she is the appointed visible conveyer of these gifts, and the guide of the soul to Him who can bestow abundantly the more secret and special graces we each need according to our station that the Church uses this wonderfully pregnant phrase, "for the means of grace," in the prayer of thanksgiving she gives her children.

Menaia. These are the office-books of the Greek Church, which contain the variable parts of the offices for fixed festivals.

Mendicancy. A danger in the dispensation of Church charities is the encouragement of those who would idly live on the charity of others,—a danger which needs to be guarded against, and which has led to various organizations and methods by which such impostors may be detected and rejected. While this can never be wholly checked, and much must be given to undeserving objects,—and let us remember that so our LORD must have bestowed His gracious aid,—yet the principle of requiring every applicant for aid to do something in return, and if possible to fairly earn it, is the best way, both of bestowing charity and of detecting those who would live upon others' bounty. To this end, Guilds and Brotherhoods in the Church or Parish could very well aid in organizing work and in distributing it properly and equitably. But the danger is greater in large cities than in small towns or villages. Still, the duty of giving involves the duty also of giving, or rather of distributing, the alms, relief, or aid to those who really deserve it, and therefore of administering the alms with Christian justice and charity, and so some recognized arrangement, even if informal, should exist in every parish, by which the rector could be aided in distinguishing the deserving poor from the mere mendicant.

Mercy. The act of GOD towards the sinner, whereby He offers His forgiveness and forbearance and the atonement of His SON. His mercy, is also a term gathering into one the facts of His love as well as His forbearance, His gracious gifts of life and abundant love and protection, as well as His forgiveness. "His tender mercies are over all His works," includes all creation. "GOD who is rich in mercy, for His great love, wherewith He hath loved us, even when we were dead in sins, hath quickened us together with CHRIST," declares His life-giving love and mercy towards us. Therefore practically our LORD teaches, " Blessed are the merciful, for they shall obtain mercy."

Messiah. *Vide* TITLES OF OUR LORD.

Metaphors. A form of expression that spiritualizes what is tangible, as, " Ye are the salt of the earth," is a metaphor, a substitution of one expression for another. Metaphors of this sort are frequent. "I am the light of the world," and, " I am the bread which came down from heaven," are metaphors our LORD uses, descriptive of Himself, so " I am the Good Shepherd," I am the Vine," " I am the Door." St. Paul uses such metaphors with great effect.

Metropolitan. The Bishop of the See in the metropolis of a Province. The title indicating a rank in the Episcopate is first found in the Nicene Canons. The Metropolitan was the Chief Bishop in the Province, holding the See of the capital of the Province, and so is identical with the Archbishop. A Metropolitan was not to have less than three Bishops under him. It is his duty to ordain the Bishops of his Province, to convoke Provincial Councils, to exercise a general disciplinary power over the Bishops; and clergy within the Province can appeal to him against their Bishops if aggrieved.

Micah (Who as JEHOVAH?), the Morasthite, stands the sixth in the order of the Minor Prophets as they are arranged in our Bibles. He was cotemporary with Hosea and Amos and Isaiah (Jer. xxvi. 18; Micah i. 1). His prophecies may be grouped into three sections. The first, which is in the first two chapters, recites in splendid language the coming of JEHOVAH to judge His people and His sore chastisements, but it closes the promise of restoration with a verse which the Fathers often applied to the Resurrection: " The Breaker is come up before them : they have broken up, and have passed through the gate, and are gone out by it: and their King shall pass before them, and the LORD on the head of them ;" the second section begins with the third and ends with the close of the fifth chapter. Again the judgments and chastisements of the LORD are foretold, but now they are tempered with the promise of the ingathering of the heathen and of the birth of the " King of the Jews" (Matt. ii. 1-6). The last two chapters form the third portion. They are filled with GOD'S visitation for the sins of the people, and yet in the midst of threatening, mercy and love and forgiveness are promised. Its last verse is taken up as fulfilled triumphantly in the birth of CHRIST " Thou will perform the truth to Jacob and the mercy to Abraham which Thou hast sworn unto our fathers from the days of old," was incorporated by Zacharias into his hymn upon the birth of his son, St. John. The love of his people and his grief at what will befall them, his energetic warnings of the sins of Judah and of Israel, and above all his clear prophecies upon our LORD, which the chief priests and the scribes themselves quoted, make him one of the most notable of the Minor Prophets.

Michael, St. The name of one of the Archangels. In Daniel (x. and xii. 1) he is called a chief prince of the people. In Jude he is called the Archangel. He is the warrior prince of the heavenly host; the prince warring for the people of GOD; the caster out of Satan and his angels from heaven, yet not arrogating any power to himself. When contending with the devil he disputed about the body of Moses, he durst not bring against him a railing accusation, but said, " The LORD rebuke thee" (compare the passage in Zechariah (iii. 1), where the " Angel of JEHOVAH" said unto Satan, " JEHOVAH rebuke thee, O Satan"). The Rabbins invented many tales about the Archangel, which, however, are but capricious inventions built on perhaps single words in Holy Scripture, and frequently not even on so slight a foundation. GOD'S use, in His purposes, of angelic ministrations in their wondrous orders is commemorated in the festival of St. Michael and all angels on September 29.

Michigan. As Michigan was originally a part of the French province of Canada, there were no English settlers before the conquest of 1765 A.D. Even after that date English inhabitants were few, and many of them married into French families. Church of England services were held in the British garrison, but so far as certain knowledge extends, only one regular chaplain visited Detroit during the British rule. " It appears that the Rev. Chaplain Turring, of the Fifty-third Regiment, performed the marriage ceremony for Dr. George Christian Anthon in 1770 A.D., the father of the distinguished brothers, Henry, John, and Charles."

The commanding officer and the surgeon acted as chaplains when there was no clergyman. During the British occupation, which ended in 1796 A.D., the services were mostly by lay-readers, who were officers. Towards the end of the Revolutionary war the excellent David Zeisberger and other Moravian clergy established a colony about twenty-five miles from Detroit, near Mount Clemens, "and Zeisberger officiated occasionally at Detroit. They left Michigan in 1785 A.D. Thereafter there was no resident Episcopal clergyman for a long time, but Rev. Richard Pollard, an English missionary of the venerable Society for the Propagation of the Gospel in Foreign Parts, came to Western Canada, and frequently officiated in Detroit. Lay-reading seems to have been conducted with some regularity, chiefly by Dr. Wm. McDowell Scott, up to the war of 1812 A.D. In 1821 A.D., Rev. Alanson W. Welton, who had been a missionary in Western New York under Bishop Hobart, came to Detroit as a teacher, and officiated for a time. He died within a year of his arrival. At this time Michigan included Wisconsin, Iowa, and Minnesota."

Through the instrumentality of Bishop Hobart, the Church Missionary Society appointed Rev. Richard F. Cadle to the work in Detroit. He was a man of learning and piety and meekness, and of a conciliating temper. He at once drew to him the sympathies of "the feeble band of Churchmen." He was twelve days in going from New York to Detroit. He found three or four communicants and about forty persons inclined towards the Church. A small stone building, used as an Indian council-house, and for the courts and public meetings, was the place of service, being cleaned up on Saturday nights. Here was the germ of the Church in Michigan from which so many strong parishes have sprung. Now there are six Dioceses in the Territory then known as Michigan. Mr. Cadle's first missionary report was made in July, 1824 A.D. In December of that year the three communicants had increased to nine. In November of this year St. Paul's Parish was organized, and Mr. Cadle was chosen rector; the salary was one hundred and fifty dollars,—the Missionary Board added the same sum. In 1826 A.D. the worshipers had grown in numbers to sixty, and the communicants to twenty. In 1827 A.D. there is a notice of a Sunday-school with three teachers and twenty pupils. It was determined to build a church, and aid was asked from the East. A brick building, forty by sixty feet, "was, after much tribulation, completed." The building was afterwards improved in 1834 A.D., under the supervision of Judge Elliott, and an addition was made to it, and a tower built. Bishop Hobart, in 1827 A.D., laid the corner-stone and confirmed a large class. The next year he consecrated the building.

The history of one such parish is the history of many. The early missionaries in Michigan lacked the aids to travel which now abound. St. Andrew's, Ann Arbor, was incorporated in 1824 A.D. by Rev. Mr. Cadle. The point is now important as the seat of a University. St. John's, Troy, was incorporated in 1829 A.D. by Mr. Cadle, also the Church in Green Bay, Wisconsin, where he had an Indian Mission. We cannot leave this pioneer missionary without a further notice. He toiled faithfully to the last. He died in 1858 A.D., while rector of St. Luke's Church, Seaford, Delaware, having worked on in illness. Bishop Lee styles him "the beloved and venerated Cadle," and "an earnest minister of CHRIST."

St. Luke's, Ypsilanti, was incorporated in 1830 A.D., by Rev. Silas C. Freeman; Trinity, Monroe, in 1831 A.D., by Rev. Richard Bury; and St. Peter's, Tecumseh, in 1832 A.D., by Rev. Silas C. Freeman.

On September 10, 1832 A.D., delegates met at Detroit from Detroit, Monroe, Dexter, Ypsilanti, Tecumseh, and Troy, and organized a Diocese. Michigan Territory then extended from the Canada line to the Mississippi River. Rev. Richard Bury, rector of St. Paul's, Detroit, was one of the leaders in this action. He lived long to see the fruit of his work. At the time of this Convention, Bishop P. Chase lived in the southern part of Michigan Territory, and "at and near Green Bay were Rev. Mr. Cadle, Rev. Daniel L. Brown, and Rev. Eleazer Williams. Mr. Cadle endeavored to get delegates sent by his vestry, but the time was too short to convene them before the steamer left." Mr. Bury was a delegate to the General Convention, and was instrumental in securing the admission of the Diocese of Michigan. The Constitution provided, at that time, only for State Conventions. As Michigan was a Territory, one committee disagreed as to its admission, a second viewed the matter more favorably. Of this subject Judge Campbell gives the following explanation: "The treaty being within the articles of compact contained in the ordinance of 1787 A.D. (passed before the adoption of the United States Constitution) was considered by jurists as having an absolute right to become a State on attaining a certain amount of population, and the analogy was therefore closer than it might have been otherwise to a State of the Union."

A Standing Committee was elected. The Rev. Mr. Bury, Rev. Silas C. Freeman, and Rev. John O'Brien were the clerical members; and Messrs. Henry Whiting, Elon Farnsworth, Henry M. Campbell, Charles C. Trowbridge, and Seneca Allen the lay members. Mr. Trowbridge, the last survivor, was re-elected every year until 1883 A.D., when he died.

The Diocese the year after its formation placed itself under the spiritual jurisdiction of Bishop McIlvaine, of Ohio, and in May 1834 A.D., he made visitations in Detroit

Tecumseh, and Monroe, "confirming the churches." Sickness prevented him from visiting Green Bay (now in Wisconsin), as he had intended. He presided in the Convention at Monroe, and urged the Diocese to choose a Bishop. In the next year the Convention at Tecumseh elected Rev. Dr. H. J. Whitehouse, of Rochester, N. Y. (afterward Bishop of Illinois). He declined to accept the election. At the election there were but six Presbyters in the Diocese, the minimum number for such a purpose; one afterward withdrew; but the General Convention, by a Canon, authorized the House of Bishops, in such an emergency, to elect a Bishop upon the request of a Diocese. In 1836 A.D., by this arrangement, Rev. Samuel A. McCoskry, D.D., was consecrated as Bishop. The election of Bishop McCoskry was Bishop White's last official act. It was understood that the Bishop could be supported only by being rector of St. Paul's, Detroit, but neither parish nor Diocese nominated or suggested who should be Bishop.

The new Bishop entered on his work at a period when fearful financial difficulties were about to afflict the country at large. Speculation had affected even the wise men and professional and business leaders. Western land ventures were rife, and New York and New England were interested in them. The Michigan people felt wealthy, but it was a paper wealth, and would soon flee away. St. Paul's Parish relied on annual subscriptions. The Bishop arrived in 1836 A.D. He brought with him two missionaries, Rev. Samuel Marks and Rev. Henry F. Whiteside. The Bishop, accompanied by Mr. Trowbridge, a lay member of the Standing Committee, and warden of St. Paul's, Detroit, visited the populated part of his Diocese, "traveling about five hundred miles, over horrid roads, passing several weeks, preaching every day or evening, in the small school-houses, reading prayers by the light of a tallow dip, sometimes held by a village magnate."

An Episcopal Fund was begun, founded on profits of uncertain ventures.

In 1837 A.D. the revulsion came. Failures were incessant throughout the whole country. Specie payments were suspended; distress followed and continued till 1844 A.D. It was feared that the clergy would be forced to give up their work, but their "courage and devotion" endured the test, and the noble men remained, though it was nearly ten years before there was any considerable addition to the number of the clergy. All Church enterprises languished. An effort to establish a Diocesan paper failed.

The Episcopal Fund, valued at $8000 in 1838 A.D., came to nothing.

A charter was, at a later period, obtained by Rev. Dr. F. H. Cuming for a Church college to be located at Grand Rapids, and to be called St. Mark's. In 1850 A.D. it was opened under the presidency of Rev. Charles C. Taylor, and one hundred and ninety pupils attended, but the effort was abandoned. There were other similar attempts and similar failures.

In 1874 A.D. the division of the Diocese was effected, and the once feeble Church became two bands.

The indefatigable labors of the clergy resulted in gradual Church growth. The communicants increased one-third, the Sunday-schools four-tenths.

In 1878 A.D., Bishop McCoskry resigned his jurisdiction.

In 1879 A.D., Rev. Dr. Samuel Smith Harris, Rector of St. James' Church, Chicago, was elected Bishop. His acceptance was received with joy, and his work has been successful. Among the foreign population pouring into his Diocese "he has found a goodly portion who are attached to this household of faith." New churches and chapels have been consecrated, and others are being erected; from the older parishes the stigma of Church debt has been removed; everything betokens thorough work." The Episcopal Fund has been increased from $32,000 to $86,500, "besides the Episcopal residence, valued at $20,000. Three years were allotted to the committee in which to obtain this increase. It was perfected in six weeks."

Diocesan Missions early engaged the attention of the Diocese. In 1850 A.D. the system of annual pledges from parishes and individuals was adopted. The collections for Diocesan Missions under this system, "from 1851 to 1874 A.D. inclusive, the year of the division, amounted to $64,103.82; from 1874 to 1883 A.D. inclusive, $31,217.47; for Domestic and Foreign Missions, 1857 to 1874 A.D, $37,157.84; 1875 to 1883 A.D. inclusive, $28,766.78."

From 1861 to 1883 A.D. inclusive, "the contributions for church building, aid to feeble churches, alms for the poor, help to aged and infirm clergymen, St. Luke's Hospital and Church Home, Society for the Increase of the Ministry, Indian and Freedmen's Missions, excluding missions and parish expenses, were $1,930,771.02." The clergy in 1883 A.D. numbered 66, lay-readers 25, communicants 8472, Sunday-school teachers and officers 943, scholars 8249; value of church property, $1,230,000; total number of church sittings, 23,000, about one-half of which are free. There are completed edifices at seventy-nine points, with appended chapels to several of them. There are twenty-three rectories."

"The revenue from the Episcopal Funds is supplemented by annual assessments upon the parishes to make up the yearly expenses of the Diocese. Annual collections are made for the Fund for the Relief of Aged and Infirm Clergymen, and the Widows of Deceased Clergymen. This fund, in the old Diocese, is now $7000, and is constantly increasing."

The principal Diocesan institution is the Church Association, a corporation including leading laymen of different parishes. It holds and executes trusts, titles to land, for church sites and bequests. It had excellent legal aid in its formation, and has received grants of land, and been nominated trustee in wills. "It has been instrumental in building several churches and chapels." "It acts from love to souls. No salaries or fees are paid to any of its officers."

St. Luke's Hospital and Church Home, Detroit, is supported by the Detroit parishes. It is not a Diocesan institution. It can accommodate forty patients and aged infirm people; but large additions are in contemplation in the near future. It owns ten acres of ground. "A chapel on the grounds in memory of Mrs. Catherine W. S. Trowbridge, was consecrated on the 27th of February, 1881 A.D." Mr. Trowbridge closes the sketch, from which these details are drawn, in these words: "Summing up the facts here briefly related, and looking back to July, 1824 A.D., when the meek Cadle gave the bread of life to three or four communicants; to the little flock of forty hearers, some of whom probably were curious to know 'what this babbler would say;' to the dirty little Indian council-house; to the salary of one hundred and fifty dollars; to 1827 A.D., and the Sunday-school of three teachers and twenty pupils, ought not the members of this branch of CHRIST'S earthly kingdom to bow with humble gratitude, and to show forth their thankfulness by renewed efforts to extend that kingdom?" The faithful layman who wrote these words, and the devoted clergyman whom he describes, rest together in the Paradise of GOD, and rejoice together that they were permitted to work for CHRIST in the wilds of Michigan.

Statistics for 1886 A.D.: Clergy, 75; parishes, 64; missions, 63; candidates for H. O., 2; ordinations, D. 4, P. 2; baptisms, 1558; con., 841; com., 10,488; S. S. teachers, 1177; S. S. scholars, 9961; contributions, $196,406.99.

REV. S. F. HOTCHKIN.

Militant. The Church as the army of CHRIST here on earth is called the Church Militant. Its true mission is to be aggressive, or rather progressive in fulfilling the work committed to it. Its members must not only war against the world, the flesh, and the devil for their own spiritual life, but they must contend earnestly for the faith once committed to the saints, speaking the truth in love, pushing on all organized labor, aiding in sustaining Mission work, whenever possible sharing in the active work, as in Vestries, in Guilds, Brotherhoods, Sunday-schools, and other such works. Each member of the Church is able to take his place in the ranks as a faithful soldier, and is vowed to do all this faithfully, without fear, without shame. But as a body the Church must be Militant or it is dead. It must use the whole armor of GOD, and every weapon of holy warfare which the Captain has furnished that he may fulfill His commission. To keep this important fact ever before us is a chief use of the bidding sentence at the head of that Prayer in the Communion Service.

Millennium. The thousand years' reign of CHRIST upon the earth (Rev. xx. 6, 7). The views and interpretations upon this most difficult prophecy are as various and numerous as there are commentators to pen them. It is an intricate and obscure passage, and while it is revealed for a purpose, it will be for the greater confirmation of the Faithful in the time of future trial than for any present use, but it will be ever a subject of deepest interest, as all prophecy must be, and especially that which relates to the future of the Christian religion. In the special interpretation of the prophecy we find that there are two schools, the one accepting literally the Presence of our LORD, however obscured, the other giving it a mystical interpretation. The first class of interpreters also receive literally the preceding "first resurrection." The second class apply this to the spiritual resurrection (St. John v. 24, 25).

Vagaries which sprang up in the Church from the introduction of Judaic notions, led to a misapplication of the passage in the Revelation, and so to a depreciation of the book itself, and for a while it was undeservedly classed among the doubtful books. But when the grotesque notions of the Chiliasts lost their influence in the Church the Revelation was restored to its true place in the as yet undefined Canon. (*Vide* CANON OF SCRIPTURE.) These gross views passed into the doctrinal schemes of several heretical bodies, as the Montanists or Marcionites, but a far more refined and intellectual view was current among some of the Fathers of the earlier Church. Still, it did not come prominently forward in public instruction, though there were always many earnest men who held and often urged a realistic explanation, without countenancing any of the whimsical deductions formerly attached to it. But the Anabaptists (1530 A.D.) by their vile and abominable excesses prevented any cool discussions upon the doctrine. They produced such a reaction that the Augustan Confession contained an Anathema against it. It, however, appears in the Catechism Edward VI. (Liturgies, Parker Society) published in 1553 A.D. The doctrine was put forward a few years ago in this country and gained at one time a large adherence, since its propagators set a time for its fulfillment, which date is now past. But it is fading away, and those who hold it do so rather as adhering to the organization than from the cause which first gathered them together, the certainty of a fixed date for its fulfillment. The late Dean Alford, in his Commentary, records his deliberate acceptance of a literal fulfillment. "If the first resurrection is spiritual then so is the second; . . . but if the second be literal then so is the first, which in common with the whole Primitive Church, and many of the best modern expositors, I do maintain and receive as an article of faith and hope." (Note to Rev. xx. 4-6.)

Minnesota, History of the Protestant Episcopal Church in. The territory included in the Diocese of Minnesota originally formed a part of the missionary jurisdiction of the Rt. Rev. Jackson Kemper, D.D., Missionary Bishop of the Northwest. In the year 1859 A.D. the present Bishop, the Rt. Rev. Henry Benjamin Whipple, D.D., was elected and entered upon the duties of his office.

The first clergyman of the Protestant Episcopal Church in Minnesota of whom we have any record was the Rev. E. G. Gear, D.D., who was appointed Chaplain at Fort Snelling in 1839 A.D. He also established the services of the Episcopal Church in St. Paul at an early day.

In 1850 A.D. the Rev. Messrs. J. Lloyd Breck, Timothy Wilcoxson, and J. Austen Merrick established an Associate Mission at St. Paul for missionary and educational work. The Mission opened a school and had in training one candidate for the ministry. The clergy held services in the different settlements of the Territory, extending their labors as far as La Crosse in Wisconsin.

Soon after their arrival the corner-stone of Christ Church, St. Paul, was laid, and before the close of the year another church edifice was begun at the Falls of St. Anthony. The Mission had in view theological training, church building, the endowment of the Episcopate, the purchase of land for parish glebes, and mission buildings wherever needed. The same year the lands now held in trust by the corporation organized in 1857 A.D., and known as the Minnesota Church Foundation, were purchased. The present value of this property is $50,000.

The record of the first year's work shows 50 baptisms and 8000 miles traveled by the clergy, mostly on foot. Bishop Kemper visited 14 stations in charge of the Mission and consecrated Christ Church, St. Paul. Thirteen persons were confirmed at this visitation. The number of communicants in St. Paul in 1852 A.D. was 26. Offerings the first year, $600. At the close of the year 1852 A.D. there were three churches,—one at St. Paul, and one at St. Anthony Falls and Stillwater.

In the year 1852 A.D., application having been made by the Chippewas for a teacher, a mission was established by Dr. Breck at Gull Lake, which was also greatly aided by the Rev. Solon W. Manney, who had lately been appointed Chaplain at Fort Ripley. A church was soon built, and the Indians began to adopt the habits of civilized life. In 1853 A.D. another mission was begun at Leech Lake. In 1854 A.D. over 30 Indians had been received into the Christian fold. Three Indians and one white youth were in training for the ministry. The work continued to prosper until the middle of 1857 A.D., when the Indians at Leech Lake, in consequence of the sale of whisky, became hostile, and the missionaries were obliged to flee for safety. For a time the work was abandoned. More than 100 Indians had been baptized and 22 prepared for confirmation, 400 were working during some part of the year, and an offering had been made by them for theological training at Nashota, Wis., of $59.90. Dr. Breck had received application for a teacher from seven different stations.

The discouraging aspect of the Indian field turned the attention of Dr. Breck to the educational work, for which more especially he had come to Minnesota. His associate, however, the Rev. E. Steele Peake, and Enmegahbowh resumed the work under great discouragements. After his consecration in 1859 A.D., Bishop Whipple became warmly interested in the welfare of the Indians. By his untiring efforts the work revived. At present (1883 A.D.) there are 1500 Indians at White Earth living as civilized men; a beautiful church has been erected this year with 600 sittings, and over 200 communicants in charge of two Indian clergymen. There are two Indian churches at White Rice River, two at Red Lake, one at Leech Lake, in charge of native pastors, with from 20 to 60 communicants each. There is a hospital with 20 beds in charge of a government physician. The entire work is under the superintendence of Rev. J. A. Gilfillan.

In 1856 A.D. the Rev. D. B. Knickerbacker, D.D., began to hold services in Minneapolis, in Gethsemane, the mother-parish of the city. By his labors, aided by the generous gifts and co-operation of the laity, the Church has rapidly increased in numbers. In 1883 A.D. there were nine church edifices.

In 1857 A.D., Messrs. Breck and Manney selected Faribault as the location of a school, which was opened the following year by Dr. Breck and the Rev. D. P. Sanford, D.D. Three candidates for the ministry and three postulants were connected with the Mission. This was a continuation of the Associate Mission founded by Dr. Breck at St. Paul in 1850 A.D., and included the mission to the Chippewas. It was supported by contributions through the correspondence of Dr. Breck.

In 1857 A.D. a Primary Convention was held in St. Paul, at which a Constitution and Canons were adopted. Fifteen clergy besides Bishop Kemper were present.

At the First Annual Convention, in 1858 A.D., the number of clergy belonging to the Diocese was 22. There were 12 parishes, besides mission stations. This year St. Paul's Parish began to worship in their new church. This parish was founded by Rev. A. B. Paterson, D.D., and has been distinguished for its large charities.

In 1859 A.D. the Rev. H. B. Whipple was elected Bishop of the Diocese, and consecrated at Richmond, Va., October 13, following. In the spring of 1860 A.D. he decided to make Faribault the Episcopal residence, where Drs. Breck and Manney were in charge of the work of the Associate Mission.

The following decade saw a large growth in Church work in the rural districts. In 1867 A.D. there were 37 clergy, 17 candidates for holy orders, 1720 communicants, and 396 confirmations. A large number of stations were cared for. The parishes in St. Paul, Minneapolis, and Red Wing were centres of wide influence. The latter, under the charge of Rev. E. R. Welles, D.D., the present Bishop of Wisconsin, had one Deacon besides lay-helpers, a parish school, and several stations in the country, where regular services were maintained by the Rector and his assistants.

In the year 1860 A.D. a Mission was begun by the Rev. S. D. Hinman at the Red Wood Agency, among the Sioux, which prospered until the outbreak in 1862 A.D. Numbers of the Christian Indians were loyal to the whites. This Mission was removed in 1867 A.D. to the missionary jurisdiction of Nebraska.

In the second decade of Bishop Whipple's Episcopate the schools at Faribault reached their present flourishing condition. By his efforts Shattuck School, named in honor of Dr. George C. Shattuck, of Boston, the Seabury Divinity School, and St. Mary's Hall have been provided with commodious buildings. The Divinity School has 8 professors, 25 students, 56 Alumni, and a library of 5000 volumes. Shattuck School, a military school for boys, is the outgrowth of the Parish School opened by Dr. Breck in 1858 A.D. It has accommodations for one hundred and twelve boarding pupils, with nine teachers. The present Rector, Rev. James Dobbin, succeeded Dr. Breck on his retiring from the Mission in 1867 A.D. St. Mary's Hall, a boarding-school for young ladies, was opened by the Bishop in 1866 A.D. It has accommodations for one hundred boarders. The first principal was Miss S. P. Darlington. The Cathedral at Faribault has seven hundred sittings, and is held in trust by the Bishop. Seabury Mission, incorporated in 1860 A.D., is under the care of the Bishop, and is occupied by the schools and parish for divine service.

Other schools under the auspices of the Protestant Episcopal Church are the Bishop Whipple School at Moorhead, founded by the Rev. T. E. Dickey in 1882 A.D., with accommodations for ninety boarders, and St. Catherine's School, for young ladies, at St. Paul, of which Rev. E. S. Thomas is Rector.

Eleemosynary institutions are located as follows: St. Barnabas' Hospital at Minneapolis, with accommodations for fifty patients; the Sheltering Arms, an orphanage, with accommodations for fifty children, also in Minneapolis; there is a hospital in St. Paul, and also one at Duluth, with fifty beds.

Table showing the Growth of the Protestant Episcopal Church in Minnesota.

Date.	Churches.	Sittings.	Clergy.	Candidates for Orders.	Communicants.	Souls.	Offerings.
1850			4	1	3		
1860	17	2,500	20	5	583		
1870	45		41	12	2,533	7,575	$65,709
1880	85	13,412	73	12	4,836	14,165	80,149
1883	106	14,000	79	11	5,021	16,379	137,558
1886	150		79	9	6,832		185,799.74

REV. GEORGE C. TANNER.

Miracles. The Almighty, in His dealings with men, has usually chosen to act through certain agencies, and upon certain principles which He has laid down. When these have been inadequate to produce special desired results, He has brought in, for the occasion, some power or agency, unexerted, and, in His ordinary government of us, needless, and yet perfectly in harmony with all previously ordained laws. A miracle is not a violation of nature; it is a special exercise of power above and beyond nature. If GOD controls the world at all, He can, as in the whole history of the Jewish nation, bring in any number of agencies otherwise unknown to His creatures, whenever He judges best. But revelation does not demand of us belief of Divine interposition in every strange circumstance. Misunderstanding of Scripture has resulted from magnifying into miracles many events only a little out of the order of daily occurrence. But it is weak to underrate miracles because of such mistaken zeal; because we cannot comprehend them; or because they are not accomplished under those laws which, on account of their regularity, we claim to understand. What we call the laws of nature are, for us, only our deductions from our observations of the regularity with which the GOD of nature continues His unwearied support of what He has made. And until we know all of those laws, and comprehend them fully, we cannot assume that that which occurs occasionally is any contradiction of what occurs every day. The Supreme Maker has a right to exert special powers, at times, in His own world; and why should He not alter what we call the course of nature, or intensify the power which He usually exerts, as well as retain His power always in equal measure? And as He rules the moral as well as the physical world, and cares more for its moral good than for its mere physical order, it is certain that the laws of nature may well yield occasionally, at His will, to laws governing the moral world. So far from there being anything contradictory in this, with a GOD so accurate and beneficent, extraordinary Divine interpositions are only what a reasonable mind might expect; and none should be so credulous as to suppose that the vast universe could go on without the intervention of its all-wise Creator, or be so foolish as to attempt to explain miracles, so as to make them comprehensible by such limited capacities as ours, or correspondent with ordinary laws; for this virtually disposes of the miracle altogether. Miracles have been accorded to us to solve all doubts respecting the authority of the Bible. They prove its inspiration. "As the existence of power is demonstrated by its operations, so the possession of *surpernatural knowledge* is proved by *supernatural works*, or miracles."

Dr. Kitto distinguishes the Old Testament miracles as of three classes: 1. Miracles of *Fact*, events different from the ordinary course of nature, as dividing the sea, raising the dead, and causing the shadow to go back. 2. Miracles of *Time*, or *Prophecy-Miracles*, events foretold as to occur at a particular time, and which did accordingly occur. 3. Miracles of *Circumstance*, or the application of ordinary circumstances to bring about ends so special and determinate as to manifest Divine interposition. In the Old Testament we may recognize as miracles all those wonders wherein the circumstances clearly indicate that a miracle was necessary,—*i.e.*, when natural agencies, through which GOD generally chooses to act, were inadequate to produce His special required end. Many were wrought to typify the miraculous advent of the promised REDEEMER, or some circumstance connected with it. The magicians of Egypt wrought "enchantments," but with the bold design of retarding truth; and these bore the same relation to miracles as does the counterfeit to the coin. Their only value is to prove the fact that there *were* real miracles, which otherwise they could not have attempted to counterfeit.

In the New Testament we are distinctly told that CHRIST wrought miracles and gave His disciples power to do so. Their design was both to mark Divine interposition in the affairs of men, and, among extraordinary difficulties, to establish the all-essential claims of the world's REDEEMER. Possessing requisite characters to indicate their truth, we accept them as manifesting Him as indeed the long prophesied MESSIAH. The six criteria of Horne (Introduction, ch. iv. sec. 2) to test a miracle apply to His. These, condensed, are: 1. A fact given as miraculous should have an important design worthy of its author. 2. It must be instantaneously and publicly performed. 3. It must be such that men can judge of it. 4. It must be independent of second causes. 5. Memorials and observances must be performed in memory of it. 6. These must have been instituted at the time when it took place, and never have been interrupted. The miracles of CHRIST and of those whom He empowered combined all these criteria, and were all wrought with one kind, noble design. Unlike the imitations of Simon Magus, to deceive, or those of pagan pretenders, merely to astonish or uphold superstition, they were all to urge a helpful and elevating doctrine. Each was "in small, and upon one side or another, a partial and transient realization of the great work for which He came, that in the end He might accomplish it perfectly and forever." Each was part of His redemptive work, not a "gratuitous and barren wonder," but at once an illustration and argument to receive that spiritual benefit of which the outward kind act was but a figure. Leprosy was the type of sin, and His miraculous cure of it taught CHRIST's power and readiness to cleanse from sin. Restored eyesight enforced the need of help from Him who "lighteth every man that cometh into the world," if they would see GOD. Raising from the dead taught a great spiritual and bodily redemption. And so each miracle was both a temporal mercy and an illustration of spiritual succor.

Even the Jews of His time, or the heathen, never denied the reality of CHRIST's miracles. Jews, in malignity, attributed them to the supernatural power of the evil one, and reproached Him with inability to save Himself although confessing that He had power to save others. And the heathen attributed them to magic, but freely admitted their reality. But, no matter to what cause all might assign them, their consent to their reality was the involuntary confession of enemies of their supernatural origin.

The crowning miracle of all was CHRIST's Resurrection. Upon the truth of that depends the whole Christian faith, with all its hopes and promises. The Christian who questions miracles casts a doubt upon this miracle; and if he have a flaw in his faith in this, he surrenders all hope of rescue from the condition of condemnation into which his natural birth brought him. "If CHRIST be not raised, . . . ye are yet in your sins" (1 Cor. xv. 17). And the reason is, that CHRIST founded everything upon this. Upon no prediction did he lay such stress. Disciples and enemies alike were told to look for it. It was as if He had said, "I am the long-promised Divine MESSIAH. I will pay the price of men's sins with my life and save them; and, if I am what I claim to be, then look, upon the third day after my death, and you will see that I have done what I say that I can and will do, and will raise myself from death; and this will be to you my overwhelming proof of the truth of all that I have promised, for only GOD could work such a miracle, and if I am GOD, then it must be beyond all question that everything that I have told you that I would do for you can only be truth." So apprehensive were His enemies lest men be persuaded that He would accomplish this most important and conclusive miracle, which would be indeed the utter conquest over them, that they used every possible means to prevent it, and even prepared a falsehood beforehand to hinder men from giving credit to it when it should take place.

And so necessary was this miracle for the salvation of men, that ten times did JESUS supply evidence of its achievement, five hundred persons at one time seeing Him, of whom the greater number were alive to corroborate the accounts of it when published to the world, or deny or question it, had it not taken place.

And this Resurrection-miracle bears the six tests proposed to prove all miracles : 1. Its important design—our eternal happiness and the praise of the Eternal Trinity—is worthy of its merciful and loving Author. 2. It was instantaneously performed, and was publicly proved. 3. Men—even a doubting Apostle and enemies—had ample opportunities to judge of it ; and confessed, or dared not attempt to controvert it. 4. It was wholly independent of second causes, as He had power not only to lay down His life, but proved His own power to take it again (St. John x. 18). 5. Memorials and observances of it have been continued to the present day. 6. And these were instituted at the very time, Easter becoming early an important day in the Church, which has continued to regard the day as "the queen of festivals," the Resurrection being the corner-stone of the whole edifice, nations and generations hanging, as for life, upon that as their one hope of their own resurrection ; their only hope of rescue from death eternal ; their one, only hope that soul and body may be redeemed in heaven.

If any is tempted from his steadfast faith in miracles by the subtle, plausible, stealthy propensity of the day to explain away GOD'S power and His gracious will to interpose kindly in men's affairs for their good, or would endeavor to drag these supernatural works within the little circle of weak human comprehension, let him remember that he belittles them to his peril. For, if there be an ALMIGHTY, He can work miracles ; if He be "Love," He will work them readily for those whom He loves ; if He has devised an all-wise plan for saving men, and gives proof to convince and win them, even such as the Resurrection of the SON of GOD, telling us that this is part, and the consummating part, of that plan, and as the first-fruits, the pledge of our eternal garnering, then woe to him who, Pharisee-like, is willing enough to be saved by a greater than his own human strength, but regards himself superior to all that is amazing in the amazing scheme, and keeps himself down within the government of mere nature's laws, laws under which he was only born in sin and weakness, and which can do nothing to deliver him from death. Evil, brought into the world by a supernatural seducer, has been met by an infinite supernatural Power, and miraculously conquered.

And, beyond the advantage to us, GOD may have many unknown designs for other portions of His great universe, in the marvelous wonders which He has performed, and is daily performing.

Authorities : Goodhugh and Taylor's Pictorial Dictionary of the Bible, Trench on Miracles, Kitto's Palestine, Smith's Dictionary of the Bible, Horne's Introduction, Calmet's Dictionary, etc.

REV. T. GARDINER LITTELL.

Mission. The sending forth to preach the Gospel. As our LORD at the first sent forth the Apostles and the seventy, and distinctly declared that His sending gave them power, and then after His resurrection gave them their commission as based on His own ("As my Father hath sent Me, *even so* send I you"), the mission or the authority to preach, properly given, is essential to the validity of a ministry. It involves the right as well as the power. Power (or ability) to exercise Priestly duties and functions is inherent in the office, but the field in which this power is to be wielded constitutes mission. Our LORD sent the Apostles into all the world, but they parted the field between themselves at first on the broadest lines, as when St. Peter and St. Paul divided their jurisdictions into preaching, the one to the Circumcision, the other to the Uncircumcision. And then St. Paul exercised his Apostolic authority by sending Titus to Crete, Timothy to Ephesus, and others of his companions on separate missionary expeditions, as Crescens to Galatia. When our present diocesan system was developed (*Vide* DIOCESE), mission meant jurisdiction over and in only that Diocese, and any Bishop who intruded became thereby, and so far, guilty of schismatical acts, for he had no mission therein. In a certain sense as depending upon Church enactment, mission is an ecclesiastical arrangement, but it really is much more than that, for it is based upon the Divine Law of order and harmonious working in the Church ; "for GOD is not the author of confusion, but of peace, as in all Churches of the Saints" (1 Cor. xiv. 33). For this reason no Bishop can be consecrated as Bishop at large, as it were. He must have a field assigned him, and that field he must retain till wholly disabled or removed. Therefore the resignation of a Bishop must be reluctantly accepted, and only for good cause. From this it follows that mission cannot be conferred at will, but according to the fundamental law of the Church, and in consonance with Ecclesiastical and Canon law. A consecration or an ordination, therefore, which does not include also a mission, must be irregular, though it may be in itself a valid consecration. But it is conferring a power and granting a commission without also granting the jurisdiction in which to use it, and therefore it contains an element of discord and so of schism.

The recognition of this principle is contained clearly in five several places in the Gospels : (*a*) The appointed chief of the nation had a right to ask of St. John Baptist, "Who art thou ? Art thou Elias ? Art thou that prophet ?" and in reply he gave his mission, "I am the Voice of one crying in the wilderness." His mission had been determined for him by the HOLY GHOST speaking by Isaiah. (b) Nicodemus acknowledged CHRIST'S mission: "Rabbi, we know that thou art a teacher come from GOD, for no man can do these miracles that thou doest except GOD be with him." (c) The chief Priests had a right to ask Him, "By what authority doest thou these things, and who gave Thee this authority?" only they forfeited the right to a reply by the spirit in which they asked it. (d) Our LORD twice enforces this, first, "Ye have not chosen Me, but I have chosen you, and ordained you that ye should *go and bring forth fruit ;*" (e) and, secondly, after the Resurrection it was formally conferred: "As My FATHER hath sent Me, even so send I you." The Apostles recognized it by sending SS. Peter and John on a special mission to Samaria, and in the cases of SS. Paul and Barnabas.

With reverence be it said, but Holy Scripture shows to us these principles of mission and jurisdiction in the eternal counsels of the TRINITY. Our LORD is the Apostle, sent with a special mission and a universal jurisdiction. The HOLY GHOST is sent by our LORD, and is the ever-present Apostle, conferring Apostolic grace and mission upon His visible agents, and so for us having a special jurisdiction in the work of our salvation.

Missionary. One sent upon a mission; a clergyman who is doing the work of an Evangelist in preaching the Gospel to men, whether in missionary work at home or abroad.

Missions. The Church has never forgotten her missionary character, but has at all times, with varying zeal and energy, carried on her work. From the first she has been mindful of her LORD'S command, and has gone out into all lands, so that now there are few places on the face of the earth where the Gospel either has not been preached or whither efforts are not in preparation to carry it. The following very compressed outline of her work from the earliest time can give but a faint idea of what has been done.

From Jerusalem her work was borne to Samaria, and then the centre of missionary activity was transferred to Antioch. From this point the fervid zeal of St. Paul carried the Gospel into Asia Minor, and over into Macedonia, Thessaly, and Greece. The Gospel was preached and the Church established from Babylon on the Euphrates to Spain by the time of his martyrdom, and by that time, or very soon after, Africa, Gaul, and Britain had been pressed by the feet of Apostolic missionaries, or rather of Christians who made this a necessary duty, for as yet there were no organized missionary efforts in the modern sense of the word, and indeed persecution would seriously interfere with the success of any such combined efforts. But even before peace came to the Church we find that Pantænus had been sent on a mission to India. Origen had done some mission work in Arabia. Frumentius was doing good work in Abyssinia. But soon after the Council of Nicæa, Ulphilas, himself a Goth, set himself to work among his countrymen, translating the Gospels into their tongue, so that his praise is literally in the Gospels. Eusebius of Vercelli, 370 A.D., made his Cathedral the centre of a wide mission work. But to St. Chrysostom is due the honor of organizing such work by starting a training school for Gothic missionaries, and, when in exile, soliciting funds for mission work. The example was not immediately followed, but the monastic institutions which were becoming popular were to become, after a season, centres of missionary work. The wars with the barbaric invaders destroyed very much of the power to conduct mission work, and only here and there was it kept up. From the islet of Lerins (410 A.D.), in the roadstead of Toulon, the work went forth into southern Gaul. But the distractions of the succeeding age hindered again the work. It was taken up by strange hands. From the almost forgotten isle of Britain and Ireland there went forth men who had been providentially trained for the task. St. Patrick had established Christianity in Ireland and had given it an impulse which lasted for ages after. This zeal had produced many monks and ascetics, such as Columba, the Apostle to the Scots and Picts, Aidan, the Apostle to the Northumbrian Saxons, Columbanus, the Apostle to the Burgundians, Gallus to the Swiss, Killian to the Thuringians, Virgilius to the Carinthians, and many more, who flung themselves into the struggle with inspired zeal and faith. But during the greater part of this era the Saxons were conquering England, and they at the first received the light of the Gospel, not from the British Christians who had cooped up in Wales, but from Augustine, the monk sent by Gregory the Great. His chief work, and that of his Latin followers, was to break the way, for nearly all the permanent work was accomplished by the Celtic and Welsh missionaries working from the north and west. The two lines of authority met in the gentle St. Chad. But the Anglo-Saxons were themselves ready to plunge into the strife as soon as they had received the faith. Christianity, though dominant, had not fairly exterminated paganism out of England before Wilfrid of York, wrecked on Friesland coasts, began to teach the men on the sea-coast. This was taken up by Willibrod. The brothers Hewald sealed their mission to the continental Saxons with their blood. Swithbert and a goodly company toiled on the shores of the German Ocean and the Baltic, while soon after Winfrith, or Boniface, led the way for the conversion of the Germans. With only the barest necessaries, a staff, a scrip, and a leathern bottle, a case for his service books and vessels, ready to build a booth and sleep on the ground under it, the Celtic monk laid the foundations of an enduring work, for it was built upon Faith. Rigid in discipline, self-denying, and eager to proclaim his message, he made a deep impression on the heathen, who listened to him under their forest oaks. His chapel was rudely built, and his hut was a poor protection. To him succeeded the Benedictine monk, who changed the active guerrilla mode of warfare into the well-planned system of centrally placed monasteries. A grant of wild waste wood or fell from the overlord was the first step, and from that, as the monks proved worthy by their earnestness, gifts, aid, additional members flowed in, till the monasteries became centres of education, and sometimes were turned into influential Sees. As rapidly as possible a native clergy was gathered and trained. It was the generosity of Charlemagne and of his sons that laid most securely the power of these already established centres. It was a long toil, but the laborers were ready to bear the burden and heat of the day. As yet (826 A.D.) the Northman had not been reached. Ebbo, the versatile Archbishop of Rheims, planned a mission to the Swedes, which fell to the lot of Ansgar to execute. His work was nearly lost, when the Danish King Canute, of England, sent missionaries thither. And later, Olaf the king, himself a convert, established Christianity there. The Peninsula owes its Faith to Englishmen. There came a pause in aggressive work, which was not broken, save by a few futile efforts of single enthusiasts among the Moors of Africa and the Saracens of the East, till the discovery of America. In the carrying the witness of Christianity to the Indians of this country the Roman Church took the lead, organizing missions, erecting sees, establishing churches; but its work has been ever a shifting one, wherever the Spaniard or the Frenchman did not also establish a state. Most noted were the French missions in Canada, and adown the Mississippi River. The ruthless conduct of the Spaniards in Mexico and South America forced a Christianity upon the southern Indian, which he can hardly understand to this day. These efforts led to the establishment and proper equipment of the Congregation of the Propaganda at Rome. While the work of the first missions in this country was germinating, the romantic mission of the famous St. Francis Xavier (1542–1551 A.D.) in India, Ceylon, and Japan was executed. The establishment of the English Church here will be found recounted in the sketch of the American Church. After the Revolution and the gift of the Episcopate to the Churchmen in these United States, Mr. Pitt consented to erect a See in Nova Scotia, and Dr. Inglis was consecrated to it in 1787 A.D. Six years later Quebec was made a Bishopric, and since that time the missionary efforts of the Church of England have never relaxed. To Dr. Bray's efforts, after his residence as Commissary for the Bishop of London in this country, are due two of the English organizations, the Christian Knowledge Society and the Society for the Propagation of the Gospel in Foreign Parts. By the aid of these and of their offshoot, the Church Missionary Society, the English missions have deepened and widened, till now the world is girded round with more than an hundred and twenty Bishoprics, which owe their mission to the Mother-Church of England, and all have been established within a century.

Missions of the American Church. The planting of the Church in America and its maintenance for nearly two centuries, feebly and grudgingly as the work was done, was genuine missionary work. The Church here was a mission of the Church of England. After the establishment of the Society for the Propagation of the Gospel in 1704 A.D., the Church acted more understandingly in her missionary character, and, outside of Maryland and Virginia, the clergy were supported by that society. The Revolutionary war deprived them of this source of revenue, and from that time down to, say 1820 A.D., the American Church was engaged in the struggle for existence. That question once settled, in the face of a bitter and persistent opposition, another came up for its answer, —whether the Church which had been adapted to England was adapted to America, whether this Church of Bishops and Liturgy, which suited the cultivated few, could adapt itself to the new forms of rude and fast Western life, and whether it had the heart in it to go down and out to meet the wants of the poor, the ignorant, the degraded of this and of other lands. And this is the question which has been getting its answer from that time. The earliest action of the Church on the subject of missions of which we have notice was taken at the General Convention of 1792 A.D., when the Church counted some two hundred clergy. At that time a joint committee was appointed "for preparing a plan of supporting missionaries to preach the Gospel on the frontiers of the United States," who reported an "Act" accordingly, in which it was recommended that every minister preach a sermon and take a collection on the first Sunday in September of each year for this purpose. But in 1811 A.D. the effort to obtain funds for the support of a Missionary Bishop had proved so far a failure. At the Convention of 1820 A.D. the formation of a Missionary Society of the Church was attempted, but in such a way that the scheme came to naught." It was not till 1821 A.D. that the Constitution of the Missionary Society of the Church was perfected.

In the address prepared by Bishop White after the organization of the Domestic and Foreign Missionary Society in 1821 A.D., he appeals to the good work done in this country by the Church of England through the Society for the Propagation of the Gospel. "We stand in a relation to our brethren in the new States not unlike to that which before the Revolution the Episcopal population in the Atlantic provinces stood to their parent Church in England. Then she extended her fostering care to her sons, and organized a society in which the prelates took the lead, without whose aid all traces of our Apostolic Church in many of the provinces would have been lost. The time is come for us to repay the benefit, not to them, but to those who migrated from us, as our fathers did from the land of their nativity." Bishop Griswold, in 1815 A.D., had already called the attention of the Church to the duty of those who "professed a purer faith and a more ardent zeal for the Gospel of CHRIST, not to deserve the reproach of indifference to missionary labors."

Two missionary societies had been already formed in Philadelphia, one in 1812 A.D., for work within the borders of Pennsylvania, and the other (1816 A.D.) for work beyond the borders. In 1820 A.D. this last society issued a report, which was credited to the Rev. Messrs. Kemper, Muhlenberg, and Boyd, in which they urge the formation of a general missionary society of the American Episcopal Church, to labor in the two fields of Foreign and Domestic Missions. And at the General Convention of 1820 A.D. an effort was made, which failed through mismanagement, to form such a society. In 1821 A.D., however, the Committee adopted "the Constitution of the Domestic and Foreign Missionary Society of the Protestant Episcopal Church," composed of the Bishops and Deputies of General Convention, represented by a Board of Directors, and working by an Executive Committee of eight. An address was prepared by Bishop White, the president, which has been already quoted, which also sets forth the claims of the Foreign Missionary work. It dwells upon the successful efforts made in early times to preach the Gospel to the heathen, and also more recently in Asia and Africa and among the savage inhabitants of our Western wilderness. "There has lately appeared in various countries a zeal for missionary labors beyond anything of the same spirit since the age of the first preaching of the Gospel." At their meeting in 1822 A.D. the Executive Committee report the formation of eleven auxiliary societies, of which eight were Female Auxiliary Missionary Societies, and of the whole eleven, eight were in Pennsylvania. Others were formed in other Dioceses in the following years, so that in 1826 A.D. there were thirty-two auxiliaries reported. It is to be noticed by the way that the limits of the two fields were not defined as they are at present, for at that time by "Foreign" missions were meant all missions to the heathen, including the aborigines of our own country, whereas now the "Domestic" field covers all our country, and includes these and other heathen in its limits. These were in the eyes of our fathers those in whom they "took a more immediate interest," and the mission at Green Bay is named in the report of 1826 A.D. as one of peculiar promise. Before the next General Convention, owing to wild mismanagement, that mission had proved a mortifying failure. In 1827 A.D. the Board resolved that they would always feel themselves bound to give a preference to domestic demands, but that at the same time they welcomed benefactions for foreign missions, and especially on the western coast of Africa, and among the aborigines. In 1828 A.D., on motion of Bishop Hobart, it was "resolved, that the Bishops and the ecclesiastical authorities be requested to recommend to the clergy and congregations to make an annual collection in favor of this society."

In 1829 A.D., Dr. Wainwright told them that "Domestic and Foreign Missions, though they may be distinct in name, yet the cause itself is one and indivisible. That which makes them Foreign and Domestic is the difference of our civil relations, but what has the Gospel of CHRIST to do with boundaries of kingdoms?" "As we are a Church professing primitive faith and Apostolic discipline, let us also exhibit primitive zeal and Apostolic devotion. He has promised to be with us 'to the end of the world,'—provided we preach the Gospel to every creature."

In 1830 A.D., while the Board of Directors were not assured of the expediency of extending their foreign operations, they listened with deep interest to Bishop Brownell's report of his journey in the West, and were "deeply impressed with the wants of the immense population which is filling up the Valley of the Mississippi and which make a powerful appeal to the sympathy and beneficence of the Church." "Up to this moment," says a writer in 1829 A.D., "we have but one small infant station among the heathen, and that chiefly for the purposes of education, and not a single foreign missionary on any distant shore." In the Green Bay Mission the Rev. Eleazer Williams had been employed as Missionary to the Oneidas at Fox River, and later the Rev. Richard Cadle had been appointed Missionary and Superintendent. The Rev. Mr. Oson, appointed to Liberia, died before he was able to sail for Africa. The Rev. Lot Jones, appointed to Buenos Ayres, was delayed, and "made other arrangements." When this pamphlet was written Messrs. Robertson and Hill had not sailed for their field of labor.

In 1833 A.D. the Board were greatly encouraged with the prospect, and recommended the appointment of twenty additional missionaries in the domestic field, and of two to Africa as soon as suitable persons could be found.

In 1835 A.D. the Board was reorganized, to include henceforth the Bishops and thirty elected members, working through two committees, for Domestic and Foreign Missions respectively. In connection with this rearrangement the committees, of which Bishop Doane was chairman, in their report lay down certain general principles for the future direction of the Board, that the missionary field is always to be regarded as one,—THE WORLD,—the terms Domestic and Foreign being understood as terms of locality, adopted for convenience. The appeal of the Church is made expressly to all baptized persons as such, and on the ground of their baptismal vows, and to each parish as a missionary association.

It has been said already that up to at least 1820 A.D. the Church was engaged in the struggle for existence. It was not till this action of 1835 A.D. that she formally took action in her missionary capacity, but it would be grossly unjust to ignore the fact that every new Diocese "organized" and admitted into Convention—and in 1830 A.D. there were twenty such organizations—meant a distinct advance of the Church into new fields and of the same kind, with the addition of Missionary Bishoprics in later times. In one respect the later times have the advantage,—the Missionary Bishop goes out with encouragement and an assured living. The Bishop of a new Diocese depended on his rectorship for his living, or perhaps on his farm or his school. Bishop Chase, at the end of his first five years in Illinois, declared that neither as Bishop, Rector, nor Missionary had he received but twenty dollars.

The work of missions,—that is, the work of preaching the Gospel and making disciples of all nations,—as to any Church of any nation, naturally divides itself into two parts, which may for convenience be very well designated by the terms "Domestic" and "Foreign," meaning those people who are near and those who are farther off. At first, as has been noticed, the Church's "Foreign missions" included missions to the aborigines of our own country, but after a few years the more convenient distinction became common between those who were within and those without the limits of the United States. Taking this last division as accurate, and looking out from the ground which was occupied by the Church in America in 1821 A.D. or in 1883 A.D., here is a very large field included under the term *Domestic*. Here is a territory of more than twice the extent of the Roman Empire at its period of greatest extent, inhabited and being rapidly filled up with portions of all the nations of Europe, having in its southern portions several millions of the African race, on its western coast a large number of Chinese, and in its western portion the remnants of the aborigines, and each portion bringing with it its own form of religion or of unbelief. In this wilderness of nations and tongues and languages and creeds and sects and unbeliefs the Voice that cries before the coming LORD would seem to have a mission and a work to do without going very far from home. And the Church which occupies such a field to the extent of preaching the Gospel, even to a very limited extent, has its hands full. If to preach the Gospel of CHRIST means something more than to kindle an unregulated blaze, and if the Church of CHRIST is something more than a cold form, even the embodied Gospel, and if to preach the Gospel and to extend the Church are one and the same thing, then the special mission of this Church of ours is set for her as plainly as was the mission of the Church of the Roman Empire when the flood of the barbarians poured over it. The indications of Providence may point and lead to this or that special distant "foreign" field, but it is not necessary for us to fly to the ends of the earth for a field. Until we have made a strong "beginning at Jerusalem," to seek a foreign field is to pass by our wounded neighbor.

The work of "Domestic Missions" comprises work not only among all varieties of a foreign population speaking all the languages of Europe, but also among the Indians, among the negroes, and among the Chinese of our Western coast. And all this must be understood as included when we speak of our "Domestic Missions." Some of our Western Bishops include in their jurisdiction Indian missions, others Chinese missions, one lives among the Mormons, and all the Southern Bishops are engaged in African missions, while in many Eastern Dioceses services are held in the different languages of Europe.

The missionary work of the Church in the United States, even if there were no other reasons for standing by it, has proved its worthiness by its fruits. The missionaries have been the pioneers of the Church, the Missionary Jurisdictions have developed into Dioceses, and the whole Church has reason to be grateful and proud of the work which they have done. But neither that work nor its fruits, nor its needs and claims, can be understood by any one who does not understand very distinctly that the work of the Church in the new parts of our country is a purely missionary work, as the work in Africa or China. In the new West it is a rare thing to find Churchmen where there is no church,—a seeming paradox which is easily explained. Any Churchman moving into a new country with a choice of locations before him, inquires, the very first thing, where there is a church, and selects accordingly. The missionary and the church must go first, therefore, and must be planted and sustained independently, until other Churchmen come in, and until he has had time to extend his influence and gather in the people. To ask or expect a missionary to be supported at the outset of his work by the restless, shifting people of our new Territories, and people, besides, to whom, even if they have time for any attention to religion, the Church is a novelty, is as absurd as it would be to expect the natives of Africa to do the same thing. It is to impose a task on those who are working not for themselves, but as the agents of the whole Church, which is as much ours as theirs, and when they fail the failure is ours, who have not held up their hands.

In one respect our Episcopal system compels us to follow the dictates of sound wisdom. We choose good strong men as Bishops of the new jurisdictions, they understand that they are to be chief missionaries, and we give them, if not a liberal, at least a sufficient salary. Every missionary jurisdiction is sure of having one strong and settled missionary, and he gives the Church a position at once in the eyes of the people which the ordinary starveling dependent missionary could only secure for it by long years of labor and sacrifice, if he ever did. And neither they nor the Church lose anything in the eyes of the people by the fact that such men devote time and talents to the traveling and preaching and teaching and other labors which occupy the time and abilities of a Missionary Bishop, or by the fact that they are decently supported.

The story of the missions of the Church is in fact best told by a list of names and dates. They belong together, "Domestic" and "Foreign." And it is only to be understood when we read it, not as a list of Bishops, but as a list of chief missionaries, of men who were taken from prominent and honorable positions in the Church and sent out to preach in school-houses, and teach schools, and travel from place to place among scattered families, and do work that when it is told of seems very petty drudgery for such men to be engaged in. But such is all missionary work.

KEMPER, 1835 A.D., Missouri and Indiana; 1854, Wisconsin. BOONE, 1844 A.D., China. FREEMAN, 1844 A.D., Arkansas. SOUTHGATE, 1844 A.D., Turkey; resigned, 1850 A.D. PAYNE, 1851 A.D., Africa; resigned, 1871 A.D., KIP, 1853 A.D., California. LAY, 1859 A.D., Arkansas; 1869 A.D., Easton. TALBOT, 1860 A.D., Northwest; 1865 A.D., Indiana. CLARKSON, 1865 A.D., Nebraska and Dakota. RANDALL, 1865 A.D., Colorado. WILLIAMS, 1866 A.D., China and Japan. TUTTLE, 1867 A.D., Montana and Utah. MORRIS, 1868 A.D., Oregon and Washington. WHITAKER, 1869 A.D., Nevada and Arizona. PIERCE, 1870 A.D., Arkansas and Indian Territory. HARE, 1873 A.D., Niobrara. AUER, 1873 A.D., Africa. SPALDING, 1873 A.D., Colorado. ELLIOTT, 1874 A.D., Western Texas. WINGFIELD, 1874 A.D., Northern California. GARRETT, 1874 A.D., Northern Texas. ADAMS, 1875 A.D., New Mexico; resigned, 1875 A D. PENICK, 1877 A.D., Africa; resigned, 1883 A.D. SCHERESCHEWSKY, 1877 A.D., Shanghai. DUNLOP, 1880 A.D., New Mexico. BREWER, 1880 A.D., Montana. PADDOCK, 1880 A.D., Washington. WALKER, 1883 A.D., Dakota.

Besides these Bishops and the clergy working under them, it must be remembered that in a number of the Dioceses are missionaries at work, and by them and the Bishops much purely missionary work is done. It would not be possible, for instance, to pass over the work which has been done among the Indians by Bishops and clergy of the Church, and yet when we have named Hobart and Williams, Breck and Whipple and Hare, we have done all that our space and the line which we have indicated for ourselves permits.

From this list and from the reports of General Convention and other, it appears that though efforts were made previously to send out Missionary Bishops, it was not till 1835 A.D. that one was actually sent. At that most important Convention the leading spirit was Bishop Doane, and it was largely owing to him that the new Constitution of the Board was established, based on the principle that every baptized person was by the fact of his baptism a member of the missionary organization, and pledging the Church as a Missionary Church Two Missionary Bishops were elected, but Dr. Hawks was not consecrated. The man who was made Bishop was a host in himself, and the field of "the Northwest" was not too large for him,—a man of tact and energy, pure, loving, and holy, a true saint and apostle of the Church. In the mean time, besides the election of Bishops Freeman for Arkansas and Kip for California, a number of "Dioceses" had been organized, which were little more than missionary jurisdictions, and in 1859 A.D., by the election of Bishop Talbot for Nebraska and the Northwest, and Bishop Lay for Arkansas and the Southwest, it might be said with some truth that the "Episcopate of the American Church was at length co-extensive with the boundaries of the United States." As an evidence that the hand of GOD had been with the Church, and that the Church was at least and at last recognizing her duty and her right to occupy the whole land, the occasion was one to justify the "Gloria in Excelsis" with which the Convention received the announcement. It falls strictly into line under this subject to notice the action of the General Convention of 1865 A.D. in accepting the resolutions of the Committee of Missions, "that there never was a time when the demand for missionary effort was so great, and calling upon the ecclesiastical authorities to institute a system of itineracy, and urging the appointment of lay-readers, and the maintenance of family worship and home instruction in the Catechism and offices of the Church by those who are cut off from stated worship." In 1865 A.D. the Secretaries of the two Houses were selected on the spot for Colorado and Nebraska and Dakota. Bishop Randall died in 1873 A.D. Bishop Clarkson lived to make Nebraska an independent Diocese, while he resigned and handed over Dakota to two successors. In 1867 A.D., Bishop Tuttle was elected to Montana, Idaho, and Utah, which jurisdiction was divided in 1880 A.D., and Montana given to Bishop Brewer, while Bishop Tuttle's work goes nobly on in the midst of "the ignorance and error of the odious heresy of Mormonism."

In 1868 A.D., Bishop Morris was elected to Oregon and Washington, which latter Territory he handed over in 1880 A.D. to Bishop Paddock. Other changes are indicated by the list-divisions which are multiplications in Texas and California, as well as in those that have been named, and which indicate a much greater growth in actual numbers and influence, so that there are some six Bishops at work within what was included in Bishop Talbot's jurisdiction of "the Northwest" in 1859 A.D. It would require a larger number to include the successors of Bishop Kemper in his field of "the Northwest" in 1835 A.D. A very important action was taken at the Convention of 1877 A.D., in amending and enlarging the Constitution of the Domestic and Foreign Missionary Society, so that the General Convention is made for the time being the Board of Missions, representing the whole Church, every member of which is a member of the Missionary Society; and meeting during the session of the General Convention, so that the General Convention is henceforth the great missionary meeting of the Church. The consequence of this action was seen in the Conventions of 1880 and 1883 A.D., when the subject of Missions was beyond all others the subject of the occasion, and in 1880 A.D. three new Missionary Bishops were elected, and one in 1883 A.D.

The interest in Domestic Missions for the last twenty years has been largely owing to the zeal and tact of one man, the Rev. Alvi T. Twing, D.D., who, after having acted for several years as "General Agent" of the Board, from 1866 to 1882 A.D., the year of his death, was "Secretary" of the Board. The change is manifest by a comparison of the receipts. In 1863 A.D. the gross receipts for Domestic Missions were $37,458, in 1882 A.D. $228,875. When he became Secretary there were but four Missionary Bishops and ninety-nine Missionaries in the Domestic field. At the date of his death the corps had increased to thirteen Missionary Bishops and three hundred and forty-six clergymen.

The growth of both the country and the Church is well set forth in Bishop Morris's address in 1883 A.D. "Chicago with half a million of people occupies the site of what was in 1812 A.D. an abandoned military post, and Illinois has a population of three millions, and contains the Sees of three Bishops and the cures of a hundred and forty clergymen When the Bishop of Nebraska was ordained in 1847 A.D., Nebraska was an unknown region. When the Bishop of Colorado was ordained in 1857 A.D., Colorado was the home of the buffalo. When the Bishop of California was ordained in 1835 A.D., San Francisco was a small trading-post. The year that the Bishop of Oregon was ordained Oregon and Washington passed by treaty into the hands of the United States. Where in 1856 A.D. there was not a white settler, now four Bishops and over fifty clergymen are laboring." The country has grown enormously, and the Church has also extended her work in proportion. There is nothing to boast of in such a retrospect, but enough to show us that, in her special field of the United States at least, this Church of ours has not altogether neglected her duty as a Missionary Church.

In 1829 A.D. the resolution was adopted to add to the missionary stations "some suitable place or places in Greece." The world was filled with the story of the noble struggle of the Greeks for independence, and this country was wild with sympathy for them. The Rev. Mr. Robertson first went out to Greece, and at his second departure in 1830 A.D., the Rev. John H. Hill accompanied him. As these were the first "foreign missionaries" who were ever sent out by the American Church, it will accord with our purpose to trace at this point a brief outline of the history of their mission.

The party consisted of the two missionaries, their wives, and Mr. Solomon Bingham. Their "instructions" indicate "their schools and their press" as the effective agencies through which they are to conciliate the favor of the people, and while they are to do nothing which may cause the impression that they are endeavoring "to establish another Church," but instead to make known the many points of agreement between the two sister Churches, and avoid making even errors "matters of direct attack or sweeping censure," to direct their attention to the education of the people in the truths of the Gospel, and their restoration to its holy simplicity and glorious purity. The missionaries were men competent to carry out these singularly wise instructions. They established themselves as soon as possible in Athens. Mr. Robertson took charge especially of the printing and publishing work, while Mr. Hill devoted himself to the work of education. The fruits of their persevering and self-sacrificing labors among the priesthood and the people generally were abundant, but no part of their work has been in apparent results equal to the girls' school which Mrs. Hill took in hand, aided by her sister, Miss Mulligan, and succeeded by Miss Muir. In the words of a Greek, that school has been "a central university shedding forth the light of education through the whole of free Greece, and beyond its borders." When, in 1882 A.D., the venerable missionary died at the age of ninety-one, his funeral was attended by great numbers and with all honor.

In 1835 A.D. the Rev. George Benton, then a student in the General Theological Seminary, offered himself for the mission work, and in 1836 A.D. was sent to Crete, where he established two schools, which were kept in successful operation till 1844 A.D.

when the mission was abandoned and he returned to the United States.

The first who offered himself for the Foreign missionary work of the Church was the Rev. Joseph R. Andrus of the Eastern Diocese, who went out, in 1820 A.D., "as a missionary and agent of the Colonization Society" to Liberia, but died the next year. The Executive Committee in 1828 A.D. made mention of the "unanimous voice of the General Convention of 1826 A.D., that measures should be taken for establishing missions at Liberia and at Buenos Ayres," and report that they had since then nominated Mr. Jacob Oson, a man of color, a missionary for Africa, so soon as he should obtain holy orders, and also that Mr. Oson had been recently ordained by Bishop Brownell, and was ready to sail for Liberia as soon as a passage could be procured for him. But the message that the vessel was about to sail found Mr. Oson on his death-bed. The same report of 1829 A.D. which announces Mr. Oson's death mentions an "African Mission School which had been established the previous year at Hartford, Conn., to prepare young men of color for usefulness in the Colony of Liberia," and the Convention repeated their former action of "advising the sending of a missionary to Liberia."

It was not, however, till 1836 A.D that the first white missionaries landed, viz., the Rev. Messrs. Savage, Payne, and Minor. In 1841 A.D., Dr. Vaughan was elected Bishop at Cape Palmas, but declined. In 1844 A.D. the Rev. Alexander Glennis was elected, but declined. In 1850 A.D. the Rev. John Payne was elected, and consecrated in 1851 A.D. After his resignation, in 1872 A.D., the Rev. Jacob Auer was made Bishop, and after his death the Rev. Clifton Penick, who resigned his jurisdiction at the Convention of 1883 A.D. on the ground of ill health. At that time there were reported in the African Mission thirty-four stations, twelve clergymen (of whom one is white and eight Liberians and three natives), five foreign ladies, four lay-readers, two business agents, and sixteen catechists and teachers. The report for 1881–82 A.D. gives as the "average attendance upon public worship 1036; baptisms, adults, 30, infants, 53; confirmations, 46; and communicants, 567." The reports of the Bishop and missionaries tell us of the special difficulties in the African climate and the African character, which encompass the steps of the missionary in Africa, and which account for the slow progress of the Church.

The mission to China owes its beginning to the devotion of Augustus Foster Lyde, a youth who died in 1834 A.D. at the age of twenty-one. "It was in his heart to preach the Gospel to the Chinese, and for this service he had offered himself to GOD and the Church, but it pleased his Heavenly FATHER to call him early home." So reads the slab in St. Peter's Church-yard in Philadelphia. In 1835 A.D. the necessary funds were obtained, and the Rev. Messrs. Hanson and Lockwood sailed for China. The beginning of teaching Chinese children was made in Java, and the missionaries moved up the coast until they reached Shanghai, in 1845 A.D., where the station and missionary jurisdiction was founded. Bishop Boone was consecrated in 1844 A.D. and died in 1864 A.D. From that time to 1877 A.D. the China Mission was included in the jurisdiction of Bishop Williams. In 1877 A.D., Bishop Schereschewsky was consecrated, but was compelled by ill health to re-ign in 1883 A.D. The purpose of Bishop Boone was to establish schools of a high order for both boys and girls, in which he was ably seconded by the clergy and teachers, both foreign and native, but the work was interrupted by the American civil war, in the midst of which Bishop Boone died. Mr. Schereschewsky went out to China in 1859 A.D., and at Pekin undertook and accomplished the work—aided of course by others, but himself the principal—of translating the Prayer-Book and the whole Scriptures into the mandarin dialect. "The greatness of this work in itself, and the toil and study which it required, are beyond our ability to understand. The importance of it is beyond our arithmetic to compute." His efforts were mainly directed to carry on and enlarge the scheme of Bishop Boone, by establishing a Missionary College which should give native young men the highest education and train up a native ministry. It is a large and noble undertaking to establish an agency for reaching such a people. China is destined to play a great part in the world. The question is whether it shall play that part as a heathen or a Christian nation. There are at this time in China seventeen clergymen, three missionary physicians, eleven foreign teachers, one trained nurse, and fifty-nine catechists, teachers, and Bible-readers. The number of communicants is two hundred and sixty-seven, of whom all but twenty are natives. Besides the station at Shanghai, the principal missionary stations are the Wu-Chang and Hankow Stations, six hundred miles up the Yang-tze-Kiang.

Both in China and in Japan one very important branch of the missionary work is the work of the medical missionaries. The physicians of China and Japan are ignorant of anatomy and physiology, and know comparatively little of the nature of disease. The field for the educated Christian physician is a very wide one, and the reports show how much is being done. The cases of all kinds treated at the different points in China and Japan during one year, by the four missionary physicians and their assistants, numbered many thousand. The mission to Japan dates from 1859 A.D., and is an offshoot of the China Mission. Since the persecution of Christians, which culminated in the dreadful massacre of 1636 A.D., when it was said that more than two hundred thousand were put to death, the Christian religion had been proscribed, and no Christian permitted to set foot within the Empire. But the opening of the two ports in 1854 A.D. made it possible to build churches and teach Christian doctrine. And in 1859 A.D. the Rev. John Liggins, of the China Mission, and the Rev. Channing Moore Williams were appointed missionaries to Japan. The return of those who had been associated with him left Mr. Williams for some time alone, and in 1865 A.D., when he was made Bishop to succeed Bishop Boone as Missionary Bishop to China and Japan, he for a time resided in China. But in 1869 A.D. he returned to Japan, where the persecution of native converts still continued, and which did not cease until 1872 A.D. That year and the following year several additions were made to the missionary force, the school at Osaka numbered some fifty pupils, and the little chapel was enlarged. In 1874 A.D. the Bishop removed to Tokio, and twenty converts were baptized and confirmed. The year 1876 A.D. was marked by a serious disaster, the burning of the mission chapel and school-room and the Bishop's house in a great fire which destroyed some ten thousand houses. In 1877 A.D. the first native of Japan was ordained,—Mr. Isaac K. Yokoyama. In 1878 A.D. the Divinity Training School at Tokio contained thirteen students, and encouraging reports are made of the other schools at Osaka and Tokio. But in 1880 A.D., Mr. Yokoyama was deposed at his own request, and the same year the Bishop's house was again consumed in a great fire. The schools, however, continued to do good work. In 1882 A.D. there were seven chapels in Tokio. In 1883 A.D. there were, besides the Bishop (who since 1877 A.D. had been relieved of the Chinese Mission by the appointment of Bishop Schereschewsky), eight clergymen, one missionary physician, nine foreign lay-workers, and twenty-five catechists, preachers, lay-readers, and Bible-readers. The number of native communicants is eighty-four. The population of Japan is estimated at some thirty-five millions, intelligent and impressionable, who have cast off their old religion, and are in danger of drifting into atheism, and who cannot understand how there can be different and hostile kinds of Christianity. Between such a mass and the less than a corporal's guard of missionaries the disproportion is very great, and it is not to be wondered at that the devoted few have not accomplished more.

The mission in Haiti was undertaken in 1861 A.D. Mr. James Theodore Holly, a young man of African descent, who had visited Haiti in 1855 A.D., as the agent of the Foreign Committee, sailed in 1861 A.D. with a missionary colony numbering one hundred and eleven persons, chiefly from Connecticut. The colony was greatly weakened by removal and death, but the Rev. Mr. Holly remained. In 1863 A.D., Bishop Lee visited the island, and administered the rite of confirmation. In 1866 A.D., Bishop Burgess made a visitation, and ordained one Deacon and one Priest, and administered confirmation. He died suddenly on the return voyage, and the church which he promised was sent as a memorial of him. In 1873 A.D., Bishop Coxe made a visitation to the churches on the island, and acting on his advice and report, Mr. Holly was elected and consecrated Bishop of the Haitian Church in 1874 A.D. There are reported at present " in the Haitian Church," besides the Bishop, twelve clergymen, twenty-seven lay-readers, catechists, and teachers, and four hundred and one communicants.

The Mexican Mission must be mentioned, but it can only be mentioned with sorrow and shame. Bishop Riley was consecrated in 1879 A.D., and requested to resign in 1883 A.D. There are reported eleven clergymen, three foreign lay-workers, forty-one native workers, fourteen hundred and eighty communicants. It is believed that in the mission schools, and perhaps elsewhere, good work has been done. It is a pity that our summary of missions, bald as it is, must close with such an instance of incompetence and failure, for even this summary is enough to show us that missionary work has been and is, even under all disadvantages of weakness and error, the very opposite of failure.

But while there is enough to encourage every Christian man in the story of missionary work, there is another side to the picture. Our advances have been late and slow. We have missed a thousand opportunities. The real work has been done by a few. If it had been done earlier, or if there had been more hands at work, how much more might have been done! Why has it not been done? Our missionaries have been very few, and they have been miserably supported. As a rule, among our Domestic Missionaries, the Bishops have been the only ones who have had a decent living support. The income which would fairly support one has been divided among three or four, and with the natural consequences. The excuse for this course is the lack of means. There is a feeling that the work ought to be done, and at whatever cost. But at such cost it is doubtful whether it is not too costly. Certainly we have no right to demand such sacrifices. If men are willing to go as our representatives into the mission field, the least that we can do is to insure them a decent support, and not to look on them as beggars when they ask us for money to build churches in which they have no more interest than we have. This is a matter which is coming more and more before the laity, and which depends on them. If they can be roused up and will give the money, then the more missionaries the better, and the higher salaries they can have the better,—there is no danger of their getting too much. But there are those who have had experience in the field who believe that it would be better policy, as it would certainly be the more honorable course towards our missionaries, to send out only one-third of the number and give that third a reasonable support. Said one, " Nobody will believe what our missionaries endure until one of them starves to death." Our Church in the West has been planted by such laborers, and the story is not an honorable one for the laity of the Church. Before we congratulate ourselves on the "rapid growth of the Church" let each one ask himself, What has been my part in the work? What will be my sentence in the day when the LORD shall say, "I was an hungered"? Are we among those who "did it to Him," or among those who "did it not"? For with money and means the growth would be more rapid, and the cost would be distributed and not all laid on the few, whom we selfish idlers blame because they have not done more. REV. L. W. GIBSON.

Mississippi. " On the 17th of May, 1826 A.D., clergy and lay delegates met in Trinity Church, Natchez, for the purpose of organizing a Diocese of the Protestant Episcopal Church in the State of Mississippi. The Rev. James Pilmore preached the opening sermon. The Rev. Albert A. Muller was chosen President. Besides these clergymen there were present the Rev. James A. Fox and the Rev. John W. Cloud. The Rev. Adam Cloud, residing in the State, did not attend. Delegates, eleven in number and representing four Parishes,—those at Natchez, Woodville, Port Gibson, and Christ Church, Jefferson County,—were present, one of them being the Hon. Joshua G. Clarke, the Chancellor of the State. The Convention formally acceded to the Constitution and Canons of the Church in the United States. A Constitution and Canons were adopted. The Committee on the State of the Church reported the details of individual parochial work in the various Parishes. A committee was appointed to correspond with the Domestic and Foreign Missionary Society ' on subjects concerning the present state of the Church in this Diocese.' The clergy were earnestly requested to visit the Parishes destitute of ministers. Two hundred and fifty copies of the journal were ordered to be printed. Diocesan officers and delegates to the General Convention were appointed. Thus was inaugurated the Diocese of Mississippi."

The Diocese was for a time in charge of the Rt. Rev. Leonidas Polk, D.D., as Missionary Bishop. He and the Rt. Rev. James Hervey Otey, D.D., Bishop of Tennessee, were Provisional Bishops. The Rt. Rev. William Mercer Green, D.D., LL.D., was consecrated as Bishop of Mississippi in St. Andrew's Church, Jackson, February 24, 1850 A.D., by Bishops Otey, Polk, Cobbs, and Freeman. Bishop Green was "born in Wilmington, N. C., May 2, 1798 A.D. Graduated at the University of North Carolina, Chapel Hill, 1818 A.D. Ordered Deacon April 29, 1821 A.D. Ordained Priest April 20, 1823 A.D. Rector of St. John's, Williamsboro'. N. C., four years. Then became Rector of St. Matthew's, Hillsboro', where he remained until 1837 A.D., when he was made Professor of Belles-Lettres and Rhetoric in the University, Chapel Hill, which position he occupied until his elevation to the Episcopate. Received degree of D.D. from University of Pennsylvania, 1845 A.D."

" The forty-second Annual Convention met in St. Peter's Church, Oxford, on the 28th of April, 1869 A.D. The Bishop's address reported more ordinations to the Diaconate and Priesthood than for several previous years, and noticed that there were now eleven candidates for holy orders, several of them men of age and experience. The name 'Convention' was changed to 'Council.' The establishment of Convocations was approved, and serious consideration was given to the revival of the Primitive Diaconate."

" The forty-third Annual Council met in St. Andrew's Parish, Jackson, on the 27th and 29th of April, 1870 A.D. The Parish of the Holy Trinity, Vicksburg, was admitted into union. The Bishop in his address reported the ordination of three to the Diaconate, and the same number to the Priesthood. One church had been consecrated and five parishes organized. There were eleven candidates for Orders. The number of clergy was twenty-eight. The University of the South, the system of Convocations, the *Church Calendar* newspaper, the Society for the Increase of the Ministry, and the Domestic Missionary Committee received the commendation of the Bishop. The Treasurer of the Episcopal Fund reported the fund as amounting to $8271.64, and advised the sale of the Church property for the purpose of discharging the diocesan indebtedness, and the provision of a permanent residence for the Bishop of the Diocese. A resolution reported by the Committee on the State of the Church, advising the election of an assistant Bishop, was, after discussion, laid on the table."

" The clergy, through the senior Presbyter, the Rev. James A. Fox, presented the Bishop with 'a pastoral staff' as an emblem of his office, and as a token of their affection and confidence. The Committee on the State of the Church reported 'the Church in this Diocese largely on the increase, true, not only of 'outward material growth, but of a deep, spiritual interest. Bishop Green, in his report to the General Convention of 1874 A.D., speaks of the poverty of his Diocese and the depression of the Church in outward things at least, as corresponding with that of the country. Promising fields were uncared for, as fit laborers could not be supported, hence useful clergy had removed from long established Parishes. Notwithstanding the ordinations, the clergy list was below that of former periods." " Notwithstanding this, it is believed that there are signs of increased fervor and spirituality, and an increased devotion of the substance to the LORD, which, when He shall send us again prosperity, will exhibit the glad fruit of many good works." In several Parishes there had been efforts made to recover the hold of the Church on the African race. "In St. Andrew's, Jackson, a very large colored Sunday-school has been for some years successfully kept up, superintended, and in great part instructed by the zealous wife of the rector. In the Church of the Good Shepherd, Terry, the school under the care of Miss Wharton has had eminent success. At Dry Grove a colored candidate for orders has been educated, and is now at work as a Deacon, while a large school is instructed by the candidates for orders at that place. A number of other Sunday-schools are maintained at no little self-sacrifice by loving members of the Church living at points distant from organized parishes. The efficiency of these is somewhat impaired by the inability to supply them with books and other aids to instruction." To assist in providing clergy a Mission Training School had been organized at Dry Grove. There were six candidates and postulants residing there, while two Priests and the colored Deacon named above were "laboring in their stations as the first fruits of this enterprise." Experience had shown the necessity of "a home training" for at least a part of the candidates for orders. Lay cooperation was "receiving much attention." In St. Andrew's, Jackson, a Guild of young men had labored earnestly and successfully in the public institutions of the State capital, and the Daughters of St. Andrew had "devoted themselves with equally blessed results to 'Woman's Work.'" The Bishop closes his report thus: " May our weary and painful passage through the wilderness bring us, in GOD'S good time, to the joyful feast of fat things, when the ransomed of the LORD shall return, and come to Zion with songs and everlasting joy upon their heads, when they shall obtain joy and gladness, and sorrow and sighing shall flee away." In the report of the Committee on the State of the Church to the General Convention of 1883 A.D., by the Rev. Dr. George M. Hills, Chairman, the following well-merited tribute occurs: " Perhaps the most touching incident in the sessions of this body was the appearance in the House of Deputies, on the 15th day of its deliberations, of the Rt. Rev. Dr. William Mercer Green, the venerable Bishop of Mississippi, 'whose praise is in all the Churches,' who came to say 'farewell,' and to tell us with deep emotion, that he was the sole survivor, clerical or lay, of the General Convention of 1823 A.D., just sixty years ago, and that when he took Holy Orders there were but nine Bishops in the United States of America." In 1883 A.D. the Rev Hugh Miller Thompson, D.D., was consecrated as Assistant Bishop in Trinity Church, New Orleans. He was born in County Londonderry, Ireland, and graduated at Nashotah, where he served in after-years as Professor of Ecclesiastical History. He was at one time rector of St. James' Church, Chicago, and also of Christ Church, New York. At the time of his election he was rector of Trinity Church, New Orleans. He is the author of "First Principles," "Copy," and of various tracts and pamphlets. Bishop Adams, having resigned the jurisdiction of New Mexico, is Rector of Holy Trinity Church, Vicksburg. He is one of the examining chaplains, being associated with Rev. Drs. Sansom and Harris, and Rev. Alex. Marks. Statistics from "Living Church Annual" of 1886 A.D.: Clergy, 36; parishes, 36; missions, 15; candidates for H. O., 4; baptisms, 370; con., 297; com., 2311; S. S. teachers, 200; S. S. scholars, 1500; contr., $44,877.24.

Authorities: Bishop Perry's Churchman's Year-Book, 1870 and 1871 A.D., and Living Church Annual, 1884 A.D.

REV. S. F. HOTCHKIN.

Missouri, History of the Diocese of. The earliest settlers of the State came largely from Kentucky and Tennessee, where the most of them had for a time lived; they or their ancestors having previously emigrated from Virginia and Maryland. It was from these States that most of the earlier Church people came, and the first ministrations were secured. The first parish west of the Mississippi River was established in St. Louis by the Rev. John Ward, of Lexington, Ky., in the autumn of 1819 A.D. The first regular service was held on October 24, in a one-story frame building, occasionally used as a court-house and a dancing-hall. Six persons composed the congregation. This was the first public service by a clergyman of the Episcopal Church west of the Mississippi, of which we have any record. Christ Church, St. Louis, was organized November 1, 1819 A.D. There were long intervals during which no services were held, and the first building was not completed for use until November 10, 1829 A.D., and consecrated May 25, 1884 A.D., by Bishop Smith, of Kentucky. He also at the same time administered the first confirmation.

So soon as Bishop Kemper was, in September, 1835 A.D., consecrated Missionary Bishop of the Northwest, he was called to the rectorship of Christ Church. At his coming began the growth of the Church in the State outside of St. Louis. The time at his disposal for explorations in the State, and for the establishing of churches, was restricted, from the fact that for nearly five years he held the rectorship of Christ Church, St. Louis, the only organized parish at the time of his coming; and that his duties included Indiana, and subsequently, as the country filled up, Wisconsin, Iowa, Kansas, and Minnesota.

The settlements were mainly along the rivers, and here the first parishes were formed. The Bishop soon saw that one of the great needs for his work was a better supply of clergymen. In 1836 A.D. he started the plan of Kemper College, and in twenty working days secured in the East $20,000 for the project. One hundred and twenty-five acres were bought within five miles of the city limits of St. Louis, buildings were erected, and very soon a considerable number of boys and young men were gathered, from among whom several clergymen were afterwards ordained.

In the latter part of 1836 A.D. and the beginning of 1837 A.D. services were begun at St. Charles, Boonville, and Fayette, on or near the Missouri River, and at Palmyra, near the Mississippi River. Shortly after this, in 1840 A.D., the parish at Jefferson City, the capital of the State, was organized. It was not until 1844 A.D. that the work was carried farther up the Missouri River, and services held in Brunswick, Lexington, and Independence. At this time the Indians were yet in the newly-acquired Platte Purchase in the western part of the State, and Independence was within fourteen miles of the Indian Territory.

In the mean time, on the 16th of November, 1840 A.D., the Diocese of Missouri was organized, there being at that time eight clergymen in the Diocese, and four parishes represented. The Diocese placed itself under the Episcopal supervision of Bishop Kemper, and was received into union with the General Convention in 1841 A.D. Bishop Kemper found very great difficulty in keeping the missions that he had established supplied with ministers. He could persuade but few to come west of the Mississippi River, and many of those who came seemed to be ill adapted to the hard conditions of the work, and did not remain long. In 1835 A.D., when he first came West, the Bishop wrote to his friend, Bishop Chase, of Illinois, in view of the possibilities, that he was afraid he had come too late to that fair inheritance of the LORD. In 1843 A.D. he says that, while he does not despair, a number of places in which work had started had to be abandoned because of the lack of ministers, and the impossibility of inducing them to go beyond the Mississippi.

In 1843 A.D., Bishop Kemper resigned his jurisdiction in Missouri and removed to Wisconsin. The Diocese in Convention, September 23, 1843 A.D., nominated to the General Convention the Rev. Cicero S. Hawks, Rector of Trinity Church, Buffalo, N. Y., as Bishop, he having also been elected Rector of Christ Church, St. Louis. There were at that time but seven clergymen in the Diocese, of whom two had no parochial charge, and there were but three parishes represented in Convention, two clergymen engaged in duty outside of St. Louis. The only support to which the Bishop could look was that which he would receive as Rector of Christ Church. Mr. Hawks was at this time only thirty-one years of age. He assumed the rectorship of Christ Church January 1, 1844 A.D., and was consecrated to the Episcopate in New York on the 20th of October following.

The young Bishop found on his accession to office that all of the churches were in debt, his own parish church owing $17,000, and that Kemper College was in desperate straits with a debt of $16,000 incurred in the erection of buildings. The Bishop went East in the summer of 1845 A.D., to endeavor to secure means with which to save the property, but in vain, and in November, 1845 A.D., a property belonging to the Church, which Bishop Kemper had secured with the most anxious effort, and intended to be the best monument of his Episcopate, was sold for a debt of $16,000. It is now within the city, and is worth nearly half a million dollars. This was one of the greatest calamities which the Church in the West has ever received, and Bishop Kemper to the end of his life could never speak of its loss without tears in his eyes.

The Bishop's opportunities for more general work throughout the Diocese were restricted by his rectorship in St. Louis, which he held until February 1, 1854 A.D., when the parish pledged itself to contribute a sufficient sum annually for five years to secure him a salary of $2500. The Church's work was extended farther up the Missouri River, to Weston and St. Joseph; but it was not until 1857 A.D. that the first services were held in Kansas City, which is now the second city in the Diocese, with seventy-five thousand inhabitants. One of the missionaries writing in 1843 A.D., declares his belief that Missouri had then proved the hardest soil in the United States to plant the Church upon. He finds the reason of this in the adverse antecedents of the most of those who had come to the State, and the relative absence of the English element, which in many places forms a nucleus for the Church. He thinks, therefore, that the whole of that generation must pass away before Church institutions could make much impression on the popular mind.

At first, outside of the travel by steamboat, the Bishop had to take long journeys on land by stage-coach and otherwise in his vast Diocese.

The growth of the Diocese, which had been steady, received a severe shock during the period of the civil war. Being one of the border States, it was successively overrun by both of the opposing armies. Outside of St. Louis religious services for three or four years were almost entirely suspended; and for some time after the people could do little for religion because of the impoverishment and desolation caused by the war. Immigration, however, soon began to pour into the State, and its rate of increase has since been very great.

In 1867 A.D., Bishop Hawks began to show signs of the disease which, on the 19th of April of the next year, caused his death. At this time there were 24 clergymen and 32 parishes in the Diocese, 18 church buildings, and about 2100 communicants reported.

At the Convention, May 29, 1868 A.D., the Rt. Rev. D. S. Tuttle, D.D., Missionary Bishop of Montana and Utah, was elected Bishop of the Diocese. He declined the duty, and at an adjourned Convention, September 3, 1868 A.D., the Rev. Charles F. Robertson, D.D., Rector of St. James' Church, Batavia, Western New York, was elected. He was born in New York City in 1835 A.D., and was thus in his thirty-fourth year. He was consecrated October 25, 1868 A.D., in Grace Church, New York, and took up his abode soon after in the Episcopal residence, which had just been purchased.

The growth of the State and of the Diocese has of late years been rapid. There are now (1883 A.D.) 62 clergymen and 5385 communicants reported in the Diocese. There are 73 churches, 12 chapels, and 12 rectories. The estimated value of the church property is $1,154,375, on which there is indebtedness only to the amount of $39,500. The amount raised during the last year for Church purposes was $132,662.36, and for the past three years $362,742.77.

In 1846 A.D. the institution that subsequently became St. Paul's College, Palmyra, was begun under the care of the Rev. Dr. Corbyn. It prospered very greatly until the time of the civil war, when it became involved in debt and was sold. It was purchased by the Diocese again in 1869 A.D., but did not attain the numbers which it previously had, and suspended its operations in 1882 A.D.; its location, in the changes of population and communication, not being any longer sufficiently central.

In 1867 A.D. St. James' Academy, Macon City, was established by the Rev. E. Talbot. It has secured a fine property, and has now six teachers and over one hundred pupils.

In 1871 A.D. the Sisterhood of the Good Shepherd transferred its work from Baltimore to St. Louis, and at first took charge of the internal management of the Orphans' Home and St. Luke's Hospital. Two years after, however, they relinquished the former duty, in order to begin a school for girls, which has had each year increasing numbers and good results.

In 1848 A.D. the Orphans' Home was established in St. Louis, at first as a part of the work of St. John's Church. Shortly after it came under the care of all the St. Louis parishes. The present building was erected in 1873 A.D., at a cost of $40,000, exclusive of the land. During the last year it has taken care of 108 children, with an income of $6239.80. It has an endowment amounting to $37,360.

In 1866 A.D. St. Luke's Hospital was established in St. Louis. Its building, on the corner of Washington Avenue and Twenty-third Street, was finished in 1882 A.D., at a cost of $43,000, exclusive of the cost of the land. It gave its care last year to 350 patients, beside its dispensary work, and had an income, beside the amount derived from patients, of $5729.32. Its internal care is in the hands of the Sisterhood of the Good Shepherd.

The Diocese has in it 67,380 square miles, and, according to the census of 1880 A.D., a population of 2,168,804 inhabitants. It is as large in area as the five New York and five of the New England Dioceses, and has a larger population than any other Diocese.

Statistics for 1886 A.D.: Clergy, 58; parishes, 52; missions, 33; ordinations diac., 1; pr., 2; candidates for H. O., 3; baptisms, 607; confirmed, 336; communicants, 6596; contributions, $126,080.65.

RT. REV. C. F. ROBERTSON, D. D.,
Bishop of Missouri.

Mitre.

Monarchia. It is the statement of the true interrelation of the Three Persons in the Unity of the Blessed TRINITY. The self-existent nature of GOD demands our faith in His UNITY. But He has also revealed to us the Trinity in this Unity. (*Vide* TRINITY.) But since by Eternal Generation for the SON and by Eternal Procession for the HOLY GHOST there is a subordination in authority and in order, there comes out the monarchia of the FATHER as the Fount or Source in the TRINITY. The SON is subordinate to the FATHER, but not in His nature, being GOD of GOD, for He is GOD and LORD equally with the FATHER, and therefore very GOD of very GOD. So, too, the HOLY GHOST proceedeth from the FATHER, and is sent by the SON, showing a coequality in origin and rank, but a subordination relatively in the work of the Ever-Blessed TRINITY.

Monophysites. *Vide* COUNCILS, ŒCUMENICAL.

Monothelites. *Vide* COUNCILS, ŒCUMENICAL.

Montana. The House of Bishops, in special session, on October 4, 1866 A.D., in rearranging the missionary field in the Northwest, constituted the Territories of Montana, Utah, and Idaho the jurisdiction of a Missionary Bishop. Previously, Montana and Idaho had been attached to the missionary jurisdiction of Colorado, and Utah to that of Nevada. The Bishop of the new missionary jurisdiction was designated the Missionary Bishop of Montana, with jurisdiction in Utah and Idaho. On October 5 the Rev. D. S. Tuttle was accordingly elected Missionary Bishop of Montana. For fourteen years this arrangement continued, until, on the 9th of October, 1880 A.D., the House of Bishops divided the Missionary District of Montana, Idaho, and Utah into two Missionary Districts, Utah and Idaho to constitute one, and Montana the other. The missionary jurisdiction (or District) of Montana consists of the Territory of Montana. Its area is nearly 146,000 (145,776) square miles, divided by natural landmarks into three sections, Eastern, Middle, and Western. The Eastern section is the Valley of the Yellowstone River; the Middle, the Valley of the Upper Missouri and its tributaries; the Western, on the Pacific side of the Rocky Mountains, the valley of the head-waters of Clark's Fork of the Columbia River. The Territory is traversed by the main range of the Rocky Mountains, running irregularly from southwest to northwest, and by numerous subordinate ranges. It is thus cut up into many comparatively small valleys, isolated in differing degrees by intervening mountains. It is crossed from east to west by the Northern Pacific Railway, while the Utah and Northern Branch of the Union Pacific enters at the southwest and runs northeasterly to a junction with the Northern Pacific.

The population of Montana in 1880 A.D. was 39,157; it is now (January, 1884 A.D.) nearly double. It is attractive to immigrants by reason of two prominent industries, mining and agriculture. The many mountain ranges by which it is cut up abound in the precious metals, while the numerous valleys are very fertile, well watered, and fitted for the growth of the cereals especially.

Its history as connected with the Protestant Episcopal Church in the United States perhaps begins with Christmas, 1865 A.D., when lay-services were begun at Virginia City, in the southwestern part of the Territory, and continued for a few weeks. These services were conducted by Professor T. J. Dimsdale, an Englishman residing in the place, and were the first services according to the Book of Common Prayer in the present District of Montana. But its ecclesiastical history proper begins with the action of the House of Bishops in 1866 A.D. Being before that time attached to Colorado, one thousand miles away, it was necessarily outside the sphere of that Church's active work. Bishop Tuttle was consecrated May, 1867 A.D., and reached Montana in July of the same year, accompanied by the Rev. E. N. Goddard. An organization had been made at Virginia City the March preceding, under the name of St. Paul's Church. In August a mission was organized in Helena, now the capital of the Territory, when the Bishop returned to Virginia City and assumed pastoral charge, Mr. Goddard remaining in charge of St. Peter's Mission, Helena. The Bishop purchased at Virginia City an unfinished building, begun by the Methodists, remodeled and completed it, and it was opened for services on the Sunday after Ascension, May 24, 1868 A.D. For several years it was the only church building we had in Montana. The third mission organized was St. James', Deer Lodge, of which the Rev. W. H. Stoy was the first minister. In 1876 A.D. another organization was effected at Bozeman; a building erected by the Good Templars was purchased and refitted for Church uses during 1876-77 A.D., which was named St. James' Church, the second of our churches in the Territory. In 1877 A.D. the Mission of St. James, Deer Lodge, began the erection of a stone church, and the Mission of the Holy Spirit was organized at Missoula, the Rev. Geo. Stewart taking charge of it. In 1878 A.D. the church at Deer Lodge was completed and consecrated, and St. Peter's Church, Helena, of stone was begun, being completed the year following. In 1879 A.D. resident ministers were placed at Butte and Fort Benton. St. Paul's Church, Fort Benton, of brick, was built during the years 1880-81 A.D.; St. John's, Butte, a stone edifice, in 1881 A.D.; St. James', Dillon, of wood, 1881-82 A.D.; St. Paul's Chapel, Miles City, of wood, in 1883 A.D.; and the church of the Holy Spirit, Missoula, of brick, is now (1884 A.D.) in process of erection. Numerous outlying missions attached to the larger ones have been established from time to time, and worked according to the available force. There is one Parish, organized as such, St. Peter's, Helena; the parochial organization having been effected in 1880 A.D. All other stations are missions, the minister and other officers being appointed by the Bishop.

Statistics for 1886 A.D.: Clergy, 12; missions, 22; ordinations, P. 1; baptisms, 139; con., 58; com., 927; S. S. teachers, 78; S. S. scholars, 680; contr., $20,975.37.

REV. E. GREGORY PROUT.

Moral Philosophy is the Philosophy of Moral Action. In it we treat more of rational and accountable beings.

We shall get our best idea of moral action by first considering the nature of physical or natural action.

Throughout nature there is a regularity, a conformity, and a certainty of action that we do not find in human conduct. Mere matter is inert, while in man there is a power of spontaneity, or a freedom of choice and origination of action.

The inertia of matter we express in the following principles or laws: (1) Any mass or particle of matter being in a state of rest or of inactivity cannot, of *itself*, change from that state; but in order to a change from it, the matter, whether particle or mass, must be acted on by something else to set in motion or put it into a state of activity. (2) The second law is, that whenever any piece of matter is in motion, or action, it cannot, of *itself*, change the intensity or rate of action,—but it must keep on forever, unless it is acted upon by something else besides, and outside of itself. Thus, if a stone is lying on the ground before me, it will lie there forever unless something acts upon it to move it, whereas a human being can start and move on at will or as he chooses to do. And if I pick up the stone and throw it into the air, it moves on until the attraction of the earth brings it down. If, however, there were nothing else acting upon it except the impulse which I gave it, it would move on in a straight line forever. But when a man is in motion, he can walk on or stop as he pleases. He can also slacken his pace or move on faster, start off in a run or turn and go in the opposite direction as he chooses.

This is enough to show that man is, in part of his activity at least, totally different from mere inanimate or lifeless matter. And this part of man forms so large an element in his constitution, as to make it necessary that *Moral* Philosophy should be a science totally distinct from *Natural* Philosophy.

There are, indeed, those who deny this difference and hold, that as the material objects around us by the forces of nature, so man is moved by his " emotions;" always acting in accordance with the strongest motive. But the difficulty arises, How will we decide which motive is the strongest? Do we say, " by the result"? this is begging the whole question. You say a man is moved by the strongest motives, and then we decide that a certain motive *is* the strongest because he is moved by it or acts in accordance with it.

A very simple illustration will show the fallacy of this argument. Suppose there is something on the floor that ought not to be there, and is offensive to me. This fact produces in me a motive to pick it up and toss it out of the window; I stoop to do so, supposing it to be very light,—to weigh perhaps an ounce or so,—but it is much heavier than I had supposed, and does not come with the first effort I make; I increase the effort, and continue to do so until I accomplish my object. But meanwhile the object has become no more offensive than it was before, and consequently the motive has grown no stronger. But *I have increased the effort.* Now this is just what no inanimate object, no piece of mere matter, can do. And it shows, too, the essential difference between the forces which act in nature and upon mere matter and the motives by which man is supposed to be actuated.

Motives, like the forces in nature, are of two kinds in reference to their influence upon our actions. The one class act suddenly and on the impulses of the moment, and the other act with less intensity *at any given moment;* but they continue to act for a long time, perhaps forever. And on this difference we find an illustration and an explanation of some of the most important phenomena and laws of moral action.

We have a good illustration of this difference in the forces of nature in the case of a stone thrown upwards into the air. The hand that throws it is the stronger force for the moment, for if it were not the stone would not go up. But gravity is a *continuous* force and acts always, and will prove itself the stronger *in the end;* so that however fast the stone may move at first, it will soon come back to the earth.

Now this illustrates the difference between the two classes of human motives upon which so much of our experience in life, and so many of the principles of moral philosophy, and, we may add, so many of the precepts of Christianity depend. All the appetites, or "lusts of the flesh," are of the *impulsive* kind. Many of the affections, such as anger, hate, etc., are also of this kind; they are strong at first, and in many cases they are exhausted by indulgence,— exhausted for the moment at least. No man is hungry after he has "eaten enough." But the higher principles of morality, those of conscience and religion, are of the other kind. They seldom or never become "passions," they are not apt to be so strong *for the moment* as the appetites and passions. And herein is temptation and the danger of temptation. We yield and sin and forever after suffer remorse, shame, and self-reproach for the act.

I have thus pointed out one great difference between us and the object in nature constituting the difference between natural and moral philosophy. This, however, is but the beginning and starting-point of other and broader differences.

(1) Man suffers in consequence of his actions as the object in nature cannot. If a piece of matter is dropped it may be broken and spoiled, but it suffers no pain. But if a man falls and breaks a limb he is disabled for a time and suffers great pain in consequence. And so with every wrong action that man performs, or can perform. He is liable to pain of some kind as a consequence of his act.

(2) The second great difference is that man can understand the laws of nature, and, to some extent, foresee the consequence of his acts, and vary his actions accordingly. Here comes in the exercise of his moral freedom or power of device. Philosophers have speculated a great deal about the nature of this power, and some of them have denied the reality of its existence. But no one of them has ever acted as though he did not believe in its reality. Of themselves they forecast the consequences of their acts, and avoid, as far as they can, those that will produce undesirable results, and in reference to others they blame them for what they consider wrong-doing, as though they fully believed that they were capable of choosing and doing differently.

(3) The third point of difference is more important, though it cannot exist without the other two: it is the power which man has, by the formation of habits, himself to change his own character. In fact, every act we perform does something towards making us either better or worse. As we know very well, a strong man may corrupt and debase his nature by sensual indulgence, and produce and develop in himself appetites and passions that had no previous existence, which, however, may become so strong as to be nearly if not quite uncontrollable. Perhaps the most frequent case of this kind is the appetite for intoxicating drinks, which is the cause of ruin to so many young persons. But in the other direction

every good act performed is one step towards a *habit* of performing such acts,—the habit may be persevered in until it comes to be an instinct, a sort of second nature. I am inclined to think that this is what Holy Scripture refers to when it speaks of the laws of God being in the hearts of men (Jer. xxxi. 31, 32; Heb. viii. 10).

Now it is the business of the writer on Moral Philosophy to describe the various classes of motives and the rules of action that man ought to follow, with the consequences to himself of his keeping or violating these rules. The best that can come as a result is the eradication of evil passions, propensities, and appetites, and the formation of a character conformed to the highest ideal we can form; and the worst that can come is the complete enslavement of the man, soul and body, to the appetites of the lower or animal nature, making man in that respect worse than the beasts, for with them lust and ferocity are passing emotions, and not, as with debased man, a perpetual state or condition. Moral Philosophy can, of course, look for no help to man outside of himself in the transformation of his nature for the better. The help must all come from within, from conviction and force of will. Or, if there is anything in addition to this, it is the influence of friends and external surroundings. It is the characteristic excellence of Christianity that it offers Divine aid,—a supernatural help. The belief in the existence of GOD, of a righteous moral government in this world, and of a state of final rewards and punishments in the world to come, is of itself a great stimulus and a powerful influence. But Christianity proffers something more. And I think we may regard it as one of the items of proof of the truth and supernatural origin of Christianity, that it has never failed to accomplish what it thus promises when its precepts are complied with.

The rules of morality are derived from these subjects of consideration: (1) In the first place, man's actions and the motives or feelings he indulges always have *an effect on himself*. Not only do they make or mar his happiness, they do something for him by way of changing his character and his inward self. They make him either better or worse. Voluntary actions become by repetition habits, and habits are of the nature of instincts,—a kind of second or acquired nature. Hence any motive indulged, or any action performed which tends to debase a man or make him worse, is wrong and contrary to the principles of morality, no matter how much pleasure the act may bring him. Morality regards moral excellencies as far superior to mere enjoyment,—any enjoyment, or any kind or form of happiness which can come from any act or form of indulgence that tends to degrade him in the scale of moral excellencies.

(2) In the second place, man is a social being. He is born into society,—the society of parents and friends at least,—and he must live in society as long as he lives. But society is made up of human beings like himself, and of persons who have the same right to whatever belongs to humanity in general as he has; their influence on him is very great for good or for evil. And this influence upon each in promoting the happiness and higher moral or spiritual welfare on both is very great. Sometimes their entire happiness is dependent on him. Hence he can have no right to act towards them in such a way as to make them unhappy, unless and except as they have done wrong or are in the wrong to such an extent that he cannot enjoy or pursue his natural rights without constraining their wishes. It then becomes a question of casuistry how far one is bound in duty to forego his rights and pleasures out of regard to the happiness and welfare or wishes of others.

And here Christianity comes in with a light which mere reason and morality could never supply, although they may approve it. It not only teaches us in the golden rule to love others as we love ourselves, and to do to others all things that we would have them do unto us, but it teaches that in yielding to others so far as we can without doing wrong to ourselves we are doing the very best thing we can do for ourselves in a spiritual point of view: we are losing our life that we may gain it. It teaches that every sacrifice we can make, without violating some principle of faith or of duty, for the sake of peace and the happiness of others will turn finally to our gain.

(3) We must not only consider what man is and what are the several relations and circumstances by which he is surrounded. We must also consider what *he ought to be*. We must have our ideal standard at which each one should be aiming, and with which we must compare him. This ideal standard for man is, in the estimation of moral philosophy, the highest good at which he can aim or which he can hope to realize. Not only is it a character of moral excellence, but it is supposed to imply in its possession the highest happiness that man can have. If it does not include all forms of enjoyment, it does imply so much enjoyment of other and higher kinds that the want of the lower pleasures will not be felt. On the contrary, it will be regarded as a blessedness not to wish for them.

Many questions of duty and the right or wrong of actions can be determined only by reference to the standard, what the perfect man *will* not do, and will not wish to do, the imperfect man *ought* not to be willing to do. Moral philosophy, then, tries to discover and develop the rules of right and wrong action merely from the light of nature, from such objects and sources as each one may see, consult, and study for himself. These are moral law. It sets before us also higher motives to action, but law is a rule which we must strive to conform to by force of conviction and will. The appetites are often at variance with the laws of duty, and urge us with all their force in their own direction. When we resist them we do it by will force, a force of our own, in which we are unaided, and can look for no aid outside of ourselves, so far as mere moral philosophy can teach us, and so far as can be certainly known by any mere light of nature and without a revelation from GOD. This is also true of all forms of heathen and natural religion. They teach a sort of belief in GOD and prayer, but it is for material deliverance, seldom or never to overcome sinful passions. Nor do they attempt to reveal the help sinful man needs. What St. Paul says mainly of the Jewish law holds good with mere moral law. "What the Law could not do in that it was weak through the flesh, GOD, sending His own SON in the likeness of sinful flesh, and for sin, condemned sin in the flesh that the righteousness of the Law might be fulfilled in us," and did accomplish, or has enabled us, " who walk not after the flesh but after the Spirit," to accomplish in the communion and fellowship of His Church.

REV. PROF. W. D. WILSON, D.D.

Mortal Sin. The early Fathers, Tertullian, Cyprian, and after them Augustine and others, made a distinction between mortal and venial sin. While all sin is deadly to the soul, some sins are, to use St. Augustine's phrase, fatal " by reason of their number" (cf. Ps. xl. 12), others are so grievous that they kill the soul, as the sin against the HOLY GHOST. All sin is of its own nature fatal to spiritual life, but there must be distinctions in degree, distinctions which lie in the fact of our complex relations to GOD, to our neighbor, to ourselves. It is evident that an angry word may not have the same guilt attached to it, nor the same consequences, as an angry blow, and this too may not have the same consequences as a fatal stab, though the angry word may be in intimate connection with the fatal stab. Those sins which are prohibited by positive enactment must be considered more heinous than those fretting carelessnesses which indeed eat into the soul life as moths fretting a garment, but which are incident to our daily life. Idolatry in any form, the gross idolatry of the heathen, or the subtle idolatry of self; murder, adultery, lying, theft, covetousness, pollution of the LORD's day, the dishonor of parents, the hatred of one's brother, all are deadly sins. "Venial sin is a transgression against the end of some divine law through inadvertence or carelessness or indulgence." The mortal sins are usually reckoned seven in number,—Pride, Envy, Sloth, Luxury, Covetousness, Anger, Gluttony; but it is evident that these are general terms for many fatal forms of sin that may be traced to their sources, as covetousness, which may show itself not only in an open coveting, but in withholding alms from GOD's messengers for them, in a pitiless temper, in discontent. So anger may hold murder (St. Matt. v. 21, 22). So our LORD sanctions this form of classifying sins (cf. 1 John iii. 14–17). All sin is hateful to GOD and must be hateful to us (Ps. cxxxix. 21–24). It is liable to His penalties each in its degree, and so must receive forgiveness only by His mercy. But some require direct and avowed confession. Others are of infirmity and are unwittingly done, and since we know them not, for these a general acknowledgment and a prayer for better self-knowledge, and a deeper love, and more watchfulness is needful, and a supplication for renewed grace.

Mortification. Positive teaching upon it is in Holy Scripture, but the word "to mortify" occurs only twice in our translation (Rom. viii. 13; Col. iii. 5). It is a strong word, setting forth the death unto sin and the life unto righteousness which forms the Christian's struggle. A practice of mortification must form some part of every Christian life. It is a part of that self-mastery which is beyond mere self-control or temperance, and it must take a very prominent place in the inner CHRIST life of the soul. It is the crucifixion to the world that we must make of self. But the very force of the term has always imported into it ascetic ideas, and the general conception of ordinary acts of mortification includes extraordinary practices. It does imply earnest self-examination, a strict carrying out of any rule of self-discipline without shrinking from publicity if that should follow. It does mean true fasting and prayer, and a putting aside of everything but the proper necessaries of life. Such a mortification is within the reach of any one who would, for the love of CHRIST and for his own soul's sake, mortify the lusts which reign in our "members which are upon the earth." Were it practiced more generally it would give strength, and teach a sympathy with others who do not have force of will enough to withstand the general laxness of spiritual training so common.

Mortuaries. Payments, whether by gift by way of fee or by custom made, in behalf of a dead person for recompense of personal tithes omitted during his lifetime. It seems to have been originally an oblation made at a person's death, at first voluntary, then often by will.

Moses. Of all those who were in their life or office types of CHRIST, no one is more remarkable than Moses, the Lawgiver, the Leader, to whom it was given to receive charge of a tribe and to discipline it into a nation. A faithful servant, a patient, thoughtful, provident ruler, modest, self-sacrificing, bearing his people's burden with utter trust in GOD, none of mortal men can compare with him before the coming of his Master. The youngest of the three children of Amram, the grandson of Levi, he was a goodly child, a proper child, a child fair to GOD (Acts vii. 20, margin), so that his mother made every effort to conceal him, and successfully so for three months; then when he could no longer be hidden, she made the ark of bulrushes and laid him in it and hid him in the flags on the river-brink. The touching story of Pharaoh's daughter finding him is told with such lovely simplicity. The cry of the babe stirred her pity, and by the same feeling she committed it to its mother to nurse for her. The adopted son of Pharaoh's daughter, he was trained in all the learning of the Egyptians, and was mighty in words and deeds. His subsequent ability as an organizer and administrator shows that he had received a training fitting him for the office he was afterwards to fill. No Egyptian training, however, destroyed his love for his own people. "Moses, when he was come to years, refused to be called the son of Pharaoh's daughter; choosing rather to suffer affliction with the people of GOD than to enjoy the pleasures of sin for a season; esteeming the reproach of CHRIST greater riches than the treasures of Egypt" (Heb. xi. 24–26). It was this love for his oppressed people that led him to slay the Egyptian maltreating a Hebrew, and that afterwards made him a peace-maker among them. Their rejection of his appeal, and their accusing him of the homicide, showed him his danger, and he fled to Arabia, there for forty years to be a silent, patient shepherd. There he married Zipporah, the daughter of Jethro, the Priest of Midian, who had hospitably received him. It has been conjectured, but it is little more than conjecture, that during the latter part of his sojourn Moses was concerting a joint uprising of the Hebrews and of the recently expelled shepherd tribes of Arabs. But the narrative that Moses has left is too meagre to lend any proof or disproof of such a conjecture. At the close of the forty years he was commissioned to his future work by the Voice speaking from the Burning Bush, despite his plea to be released from it. His diffidence led to putting his brother forward as chief speaker, but the final authority remained with him. So close the two periods of his trial and training. Meek, ready to withdraw from view, he is yet equal to the vast burden laid upon him, for he knew in whom he trusted. Henceforth he belongs to the spiritual history of the world. He is commissioned with power to work signs and wonders. The shepherd's rod becomes mightier than the imperial sceptre. His word effects wonders no other human speech has ever wrought. He stands before the Pharaoh,—the scattered dust becomes lice when smiten by Aaron's rod; the ashes scattered by Moses and Aaron become boils. He spake the word for JEHOVAH, and all manner of flies and frogs appeared over the land. Moses stands forth the wonderful man of GOD.

It is not necessary to dwell upon the history of the Ten Plagues; but these remarks may not be amiss. The first three wonders were imitated, evidently by sleight of hand, by the magicians, nor was it impossible to do so on a very small scale, while those which Moses wrought affected the whole land. But when the plague of lice smote them they confessed that this (the third plague) was of GOD. Then natural phenomena, supernaturally used and combined, marked the next six plagues. They were miraculous because of their vastness, their completeness, their falling in rapid succession, out of all dependence upon seasons, upon the whole land, the field of Zoan,—i.e., the Delta,—while yet the land of Goshen was exempted. The last final terrible stroke fell from the scourge of the LORD Himself. They were warnings, disciplines, and then judgments upon Pharaoh and his people. At last Moses led the people out,—a hurried, anxious multitude, guarded by the six hundred thousand men at arms, who were apparently in a state of efficient discipline. So far in Moses' career we have seen a developed ability, patriotism, and a modest, retiring character that yet showed courage and constancy, and through it all unshaken faith. But he was to be yet more sorely tried. His faith obeyed the command to go down the banks of the Red Sea, and there his rod wrought GOD's deliverance. But now his patience, his ability as an organizer, his love for a stiff-necked, undisciplined multitude, his constant intercession, his untiring toil, all were to be developed in the wanderings in the wilderness. No less courage was needed then than before in this man of eighty, who was to spend the next forty years in disciplining a congeries of tribes into a nation fit to take possession of the land GOD would give them. He needed all the converse, all the revelations, all the directions he received, and yet he nearly sank under the burden. Their idolatries, their rebellious temper, their disobedience, must have sorely grieved him, yet he never swerved in his love, not when GOD offered to replace them with his own family. And in this connection it may be noted that his sons Gershom and Eliezer scarcely appear in the sacred history at all. As general, he displayed a capacity for strategy in the two chief campaigns against Sihon and Og. So for forty years he led them, divinely guided and supported, yet himself nobly equipped by capacity and education for the office. One other point in his character. He has been called the meekest man. If patient endurance shows it he truly was so. But he also showed a hasty temper under much provocation, but this meekness was more truly a sympathy for others, and an appreciation of their feelings and a desire to aid and to plead for them. But his hasty words deprived him of the right to enter the promised land. The details of the wanderings in the wilderness can find no place here, for we must use the history mainly to show how he as the faithful servant in the house was a type of the SON, and he is of that house. In patience, forbearance, love for his people, and his self-restraint, his abandoning all for their sakes, Moses becomes a type of our LORD, who became of none effect for us.

Again, Moses, though a full-born Israelite, is an alien trained by a stranger, and an outcast from his people. So in this he is a type of our LORD, trained in this world at the carpenter's work-bench, and when he would come to them, rejected by His people. Again, Moses, as Leader and Lawgiver, is more directly the type of our LORD in His ascended work as the Captain of our salvation. As Leader he brings the people to the border of the Promised land, and leaves them there to enter in, being refused himself for their sakes, and in this the type would seem to fail. Yet in a deeper sense was he the type of CHRIST in all that constitutes a Leader. Every quality he displayed or developed, even to minute matters, contains a reference to our LORD,—His foresight, His organization, His gracious love, as Lawgiver. Moses' Law was largely one of ritual, yet it was the shadow of good things to come, and so a revelation of what was the direction of GOD's will. In many matters of internal economy it was what Christian States are now beginning to recognize as truest law. Its basis, the Decalogue, was re-enacted, developed, and sanctified by our LORD Himself in His Sermon on the Mount, and was presupposed by the Apostles as binding upon all men. Our LORD's new commandment lay concealed in the old commandment if men would but see it. For love is the fulfilling of the Law. But in the highest office Moses held, as Prophet, was he specially the type of CHRIST. His actual predictions were but few, and the chiefest was that on the destruction of Jerusalem. But so it was with our LORD; He exercised the predictive part of the Prophetic office only in the like subject, transferring its terrors as a type to the still greater terrors of the Day of Judgment. It was in action, in the whole round of his life, that he was like his LORD, at that distance which separates the servant from the master, in his life he exercised the highest predictive office. And again, as the messenger bearing the revelation of the loftiest title of GOD, JEHOVAH, I AM THAT I AM, he did not so much teach an utterly new fact as bring forward and establish it forever, making it the corner-stone of Jewish polity. So our LORD, declaring the Doctrine of the TRINITY, more indeed by the consequence of His teaching than by any direct assertion, forever made it the last and chiefest revelation, and built upon it the whole superstructure of Christianity. Yet as in the name of Moses' mother, Jochebed, lay the holy name JAH, and so showed it was not unknown to the tribes of Israel, so in the Old Testament lies embedded this doctrine of our LORD, which he brought forward, not as new, but as now to be chiefly taught. As Prophet, Leader, Lawgiver, as the creator of a nation, the founder of a theocracy, Moses is the type of our LORD, in some single points perhaps more brilliantly surpassed by others, but in the grandeur of his life, his faith, his work, the foremost man who has ever lived. And our LORD ever refers to him as the highest authority preceding Himself. Moses gave the Law and prepared the way for the Gospel.

Motet. *Vide* MUSIC.

Movable Feasts. Those which depend upon Easter for the time of their celebration. The calendar in the Prayer-Book contains rules for finding Easter-day, but generally it lays down this rule: "Easter-Day, on which the rest depend, is always the first Sunday after the Full Moon, which happens upon or next after the Twenty-first Day of March; and if the Full Moon happen upon a Sunday, Easter-Day is the Sunday after.

"Advent-Sunday is always the nearest Sunday to the Feast of St. Andrew, whether before or after.

Septuagesima) (Nine)
Sexagesima } Sund. { Eight } weeks before Easter.
Quinquagesima } is { Seven }
Quadragesima.) (Six)
Rogation-Sunday is Five Weeks }
Ascension-Day " Forty Days } after Easter."
Whit-Sunday " Seven Weeks }
Trinity-Sunday " Eight Weeks)

Music. The harp and the organ were invented by Jubal long before the Flood, and since then mankind has never been without musical instruments. It would seem from Gen. xxxi. 27, that family celebrations were gladdened "with songs, with tabret, and with harp." The religious use of music is first mentioned after the destruction of Pharaoh and his host in the Red Sea, when Moses and the children of Israel sang unto the LORD that glorious song, which is mentioned again in Rev. xv. 3: "the song of Moses the servant of GOD, and the song of the Lamb."

Not only did Moses and the men of Israel lead in this glorious song, but Miriam and all the women answered them, with timbrels and with dances, repeating the triumphant chorus probably many times over. There is no hint that this was now first invented or devised, but the mention of it looks rather like an outburst of that with which they were all familiar. We have, then, vocal and instrumental music, the men choir and the women choir, the recitative and the great chorus, all in full use already. When, under David and Solomon, the ritual of the Temple received its most splendid development, it seems to have exceeded anything else recorded in history in that line. Of the 38,000 Levites, 4000 were appointed to praise GOD with the instruments which David made; and it would seem that he wrote them certain tunes or chants, as well as the words of psalms, both of which were used for ages after. There was a further division among the singers, for greater variety and skill, and that the service should not be too burdensome; for there were no less than twenty-four different courses, each containing twelve men; and under these 288 the rest were trained. the great Festivals, it is probable, bringing all the 4000 together. The three great families of the Levites all had part in this remarkable organization,—Heman representing the Kohathites, Asaph the Gershonites, and Ethan (or Jeduthun) the Merarites. The glory and beauty of this musical service seems to have been preserved and perpetuated through all the subsequent corruption of the Nation, and was famous through all the countries round about. Even in their captivity, those who had led them away captive required them to "sing one of the songs of Zion." At the restoration, the musical service and the courses of the singers were lovingly restored, and were maintained—with few and brief interruptions—until the destruction of the city by Titus.

When we look at the Psalms, we find that almost every one of them has its proper musical inscription, showing that they were *intended* from the first to be sung, and with instrumental accompaniment besides. When we look a little further, we find that this wonderful system of music was, with singular tenacity, maintained on the Temple site for more than a thousand years. We see how intensely the nation was attached to a musical inheritance, the like of which no other nation ever had. We know that the Psalter at least—to say nothing of other parts of Divine Service—has been sung in all ages, over all Christendom, as it was among the Jews. We know that the Jewish Church and the Christian Church overlapped one another for forty years, the Christians in Jerusalem during all that time frequenting the Temple service, and continuing undiminished their familiarity with the Temple music. We find a peculiar kind of music—*Chanting*—everywhere used for the Psalter; and all ecclesiastical tradition tells us that it was derived from the East. Under these circumstances, the idea that the Temple music suddenly disappeared, —became absolutely unknown; and that an entirely new system of music was with equal suddenness invented by nobody knows whom, and nobody knows where; and that this new style should have had vitality enough to endure to our own day: this is inherently *absurd*. The only rational idea is, that the music traditionally derived from the East, and which has been as tenacious of its existence since as well as before, *must* be, in its main features at least, the old Temple music. In the East, antiphonal chanting was already established, under St. Ignatius of Antioch, within twenty years after the death of St. John. In the West, the ancient chant was domiciled at Milan by the great St. Ambrose in the fifth century. The purity of his modes was restored by St. Gregory the Great, Bishop of Rome, in the seventh century; and his arrangement has been so permanent that the name "Gregorian" is attached to that entire style of music to this day. From time to time it has become grievously corrupted by ignorance, vanity, and bad taste. These caprices of musicians had so overloaded the sacred words at the time of the Reformation, that the Council of Trent actually had it under consideration to exclude music entirely from Divine Service. An exquisitely simple and dignified Mass by Palæstrina, which was composed for the purpose, and performed before the Council, alone prevented the entire banishment of music. No Liturgy has ever been set forth with any *authorized* music, other than the Gregorian; and after all its periods of corruption, it has had, like religion itself, its seasons of revival and a return to primitive purity. It is now more zealously cultivated, both in the Anglican and in the Roman Communion, than at any other time for the past five hundred years: having come up afresh in the great Catholic Revival of our own day.

It is not easy to give any idea of the variety and richness and religious depth of Gregorian music to those who have been educated only in the mechanical shallowness of modern music. This modern music has only two modes, *major* and *minor*. The striking difference in *character* between these two is due to the fact that the two semitones occur in different places of the scale. In the *major* mode (ascending) the semitones occur between the third and fourth, and between the seventh and eighth notes of the scale; in the *minor* mode, between the second and third, and between the fifth and sixth notes of the scale. But these are the *only* two varieties. No matter what the *key* may be, major is major, and minor is minor: these are the only two *modes*. Moreover, these two modes know but one *dominant*, and that is a fifth above the tonic. Now, in the Church Modes, of which there are *eight* (some would make them *fourteen*), there are no two of them in which the semitones occur in the same places of the scale; or if any two scales are alike in that, the mode of harmonizing them makes them entirely different. The impression produced upon the ordinary mind is, that in Church music the major and minor seem to be mingled together in perpetually changing proportions and relations. There are four of these modes called "*authentic*," and four "*plagal*." To get the scale of the four authentic, the easiest way is to go to a piano-forte or organ, and use only the white keys, omitting the black altogether. Then the scale of an octave from D to D will give the scale of the *Dorian* mode; that from E to E, the *Phrygian*; that from F to F, the *Lydian*; that from G to G, the *Mixolydian*. All these have as their *tonic* the note on which their scale begins and ends. The four *plagal* modes are related to these four in the following way: For the scale of the *Hypodorian*, begin *one-fourth below* the tonic of the *Dorian*, and close with the octave *above* the note on which you start, that is to say, from A to A; but this is to be harmonized so that the final chord is that of D,—the same as the *Dorian*. The other three plagal modes—the *Hypophrygian, Hypolydian,* and *Hypomixolydian*—are formed in precisely the same manner from their corresponding authentic modes.

The famous Gregorian Tones are eight in number, and are founded on these eight modes. The root principle of these glorious old Chants is, that the *recitative* note shall be the *same note* in each half of the Chant; and it must be taken at such a pitch as shall be easily sustained by all manner of voices in unison, say not lower than F natural nor higher than B flat. The *Tonus Peregrinus* (irregular) is the only one where there is a different note for the recitative, and there the difference is only one tone. In the strictest notation, no one of the Gregorian tones extends its melody beyond a range of six consecutive notes of the scale. Within these narrow limits *every* voice can join, without straining, or fatigue, or danger of flatting; and when a whole congregation has been trained to take their part, the majestic deep river of unison rolls onward with resistless strength, the organ accompaniment to this *canto firmo* varying with every verse, yet never for an instant confusing the solid power of the melody. Besides the variety of harmonic relations inseparable from the eight different modes, there is a further variety in the fact that the Gregorians have not—like the Anglican Chants—a fixed length and uniform rhythm. Sometimes there is one note, with one accent, in the mediation, sometimes more; and the cadences are even more varied than the mediations. Moreover, they may be used with the intonation (each Tone having its own characteristic intonation), or without it. And still further, each Tone has a festal form, as well as a ferial form. And nearly all the Tones have a great variety of endings, some complete, some incomplete: the former ending on the tonic of the Mode, the latter having some other final note in the melody. The Modes are also used for Hymn melodies and Anthems, as well as for Chants, though commonly with rather more freedom. Nor is Gregorian music ever written in *strict time*, like modern music. It has only three different notes, one of which is long, another short, and the third may be called medium: but their length is relative only, and not an exact double. The words used therewith regulate the actual length, so that the flexibility of Gregorian music is like the flexibility of the skin upon the living body. The spirit of Gregorian music is very strongly infused into the earlier German *chorales*, and the earlier Cathedral Music of the Church of England, but becomes less perceptible as we approach modern days. The English Cathedrals have kept up, with wonderful tenacity, through degenerate days, the grand old traditions of the Choral service. Anciently, the *entire* service was musically rendered, the Scriptures having their own peculiar intonation and inflections (as with the Jews when reading the Hebrew Scriptures); and the conversational or ordinary tone being excluded altogether. The *Cantus Scripturarum*, however, is now generally disused.

The chanting of the Psalms has always been maintained in Cathedrals and in many parish churches, and is becoming daily more and more common. Anthems (both *word* and *thing* having been developed, by free changes, from the old *Antiphon*) have always been popular, and are authorized by the declaration of the House of Bishops in 1814 A.D., that " Anthems taken from Scripture, and judiciously arranged, may, according to the known allowance of this Church, be sung in congregations, at the discretion of their respective Ministers." Metrical hymns, however, are the most easily learned, and therefore the most popular kind of music in most of our congregations. Unfortunately, they are too largely, both in words and music, deficient in churchliness of tone, though there is a gradual and very perceptible improvement slowly going on among us. The choral service, and surpliced choirs of male voices, are spreading from year to year, with general acceptance wherever they are tried.

There are *three* parts of Church music, taking that term in its fullest sense: 1, that of the congregation; 2, that of the trained choir; 3, that of instruments. As to the first, it must be confessed that general Church practice has rather discouraged the singing of the entire congregation, and the most ancient Canon (Laodicea, xv.) on the subject provides expressly that "No others shall sing in the church, save only the canonical singers, who go up into the Ambo and sing from a book." But where musical education is becoming daily more general, there will be an increasing number of those who are able, and ought to be willing, to join in the simpler kinds of music. It should always be insisted on that *some* part of what is sung should be simple enough for all to join in. The *Venite* and Psalter (sung to Gregorians, in unison), and the Hymns, should be of this description, and also the versicles and responses, the Litany, and the *Amens*, to the prayers. But where there is a trained choir, a considerable portion of the music should be left to them. They have a *right*—as they spend so much of time, trouble, and musical skill in preparing for their public service—to offer to the LORD *of their best:* and their best will necessarily be too elaborate to permit the joining of those who do not practice at all. As to instrumental music, the support of the organ is very valuable, in preventing the flatting of the singers, as well as in adding dignity, majesty, and power to the general effect. It is becoming more common, also, to reinforce the organ with one or more orchestral instruments, especially on high festivals.

At the beginning of this century and for some time after, it was taken for granted that furnishing the music in church was a wholly secular business, not needing that those who took part in it should be members of the Church. The organ-gallery was commonly as far as possible from the chancel, high up above the body of the congregation, and with curtains drawn in front, behind which the choir might do as they pleased until the time came tor them to sing. The abuses growing out of this state of things became intolerable. The other theory is now recognized as the true one, which makes those who lead the worship of the sanctuary to be a *part of the ministry*, and therefore clothes them in cassocks and surplices, gives them seats in the chancel (or as near it as may be), has them enter and depart with the clergy, and inducts them into office with an appropriate special service, training them to that devoutness and reverence which ought to characterize such holy work. Of course none but baptized members of the Church should be admitted to this honorable service, and as many as are competent should be confirmed and communicants also. The boy choir has several great advantages. It is composed of those who are yet "under authority," and there is far less likelihood of factious friction developing "unpleasantnesses" in the choir. There is constant change in the *personnel*, as the boys' voices cannot last many years before "breaking." This is troublesome, but it has its compensations. It prevents the settling down of dear old barnacles in the choir, who have served for so many years that nobody can think of hurting their feelings by telling them that they ought to retire. It is continually sending forth youths who have been well trained in Church music, and drawing in fresh subjects for the same training, thus steadily adding to the numbers of those who are *able* to serve acceptably, whether in the choir or out of it. And last, not least, it is a valuable means of interesting the *hearts* of the young in the sacred beauty of God's House, to such a degree that not a few of them eventually study for holy Orders. Moreover, such choirs are always more numerous than quartette choirs, and as each boy has his own circle of relatives and friends who take a deep interest in seeing him surpliced and hearing him sing, it furnishes a permanent element of attraction to the public services of the Church. It is no wonder, then, that, with some local exceptions from accidental causes, the establishment of boy choirs, surpliced, has been almost uniformly successful, and is steadily and rapidly increasing in all parts of the Church. And, with them, there always comes a more solid, substantial, and Churchly tone in the music of the Sanctuary. Rev. J. H. Hopkins, D.D.

Mystery. Something into which one must be initiated. Some fact, principle, or doctrine, whether of the world, of nature, of intellect, or of religion, that is not yet understood, but can be, either by a future combination of what we now know, or by direct revelation. So our Lord, "to you it is given to know the mysteries of the kingdom of heaven" (St. Matt. xiii. 11). Again, the mysteries of God are those things which the ministers of God have as stewards for Him to give to His people (1 Cor. iv. 2). The Gospel is a mystery now revealed. The change that shall come upon our mortal bodies is a mystery (1 Cor. xv. 51). The whole revelation of Christ is a mystery of Godliness (1 Tim. iii. 16). In Greek theology the term has always been used as the equivalent of the Latin *Sacramentum*. But both terms were in the earlier theology used with far more width of application than a later and more rigidly formulated theology would admit. They were used, as in the New Testament, to stand for anything relating to God, and to the Church, and to our Life which can be, though it may not yet be, within the scope of our knowledge. So the mystery of the Incarnation, not wholly explained yet, is far better understood than it could have been by the Jews, who only could have held it through revelation as a fact yet to be,— still, a mystery to be put within the range of our powers. Not perhaps here shall we be able to understand all mysteries; but we will hereafter, when we shall know even as we are known. Mysteries are an exercise of our faith, and we can accept and act upon them as we do accept and act upon as great mysteries in their kind in the world of physical nature, or in the sphere of human nature. They need give us no more trouble; but the mysteries of our Christian faith demand an equal obedience and faithful use.

N.

Nag's Head Consecration Story. Matthew Parker, who in the reign of Queen Elizabeth succeeded Cardinal Pole as Archbishop of Canterbury, was duly consecrated in the chapel at Lambeth, December 17, 1559 A.D. All the official documents, civil as well as ecclesiastical, relating to this consecration are on record. Forty-five years afterwards, viz., in 1604 A.D., a noted and unscrupulous controversialist, who, by order of James I., had been banished from England, Christopher Holywood, a Jesuit, published at Antwerp, in a violent book of his, the story of a mock consecration of Parker and other Bishops at the Nag's Head tavern, Cheapside, London. This story, utterly without foundation, but intended to cast discredit upon the line of succession through Parker and his coadjutors, was eagerly seized upon by Romish polemical writers, and repeated by them with various additions. Its first appearance in print nearly half a century after it was said to have occurred, when, had it had the slightest element of truth about it, it must have been known long before by the enemies of the Church of England, and would have been as gladly used by them then as it was subsequently, has not tended to its acceptance at the present day. Indeed, all fair-minded and intelligent writers of the Roman Obedience have long since abandoned this weak and vindictive invention of Holywood's. A very thorough sifting of the story will be found in Haddan's Apostolical Succession in the Church of England, and in the third volume of Archbishop Bramhall's Works, Oxford, 1844 A.D. REV. T. C. YARNALL, D.D.

Nahum. Nahum the Elkoshite is the seventh in order of the Minor Prophets. The epithet Elkoshite is thought to indicate the place of the prophet's birth or residence rather than his descent, and for many centuries it was believed that he was a native of Elkosh, a village said to be in Galilee; but in modern times another tradition represents Nahum as a native of Alkush, near Mosul, on the Tigris, where a tomb is pointed out to this day as his. Very little authority is to be attached to either tradition, or to the statement that he was of the tribe of Simeon; but it is considered probable from expressions used by the prophet, that he was familiar with the scenery of Palestine, and most likely a resident of Judah, when his prophecy was delivered; yet Ewald argues for the same reasons that Nahum must have been an eye-witness of the destruction of Nineveh. Nearly as much uncertainty exists about the prophet's date as about his birth and residence. The date 713 B.C. is given in our Bibles, and with this the best critics agree, though some incline to an earlier one, while others would place Nahum nearly a hundred years later. The prevailing opinion is that he was a younger contemporary of Isaiah, and possibly of Hosea and Micah. The Book of the Vision of Nahum the Elkoshite, is the Burden of Nineveh, and is wholly a prophecy of the destruction of that city. The three chapters into which it is divided form a continuous whole, in which, in lofty and poetical language, the prophet unfolds the woe denounced upon the chief city and mistress of the world. So literally was this prophecy fulfilled that for twenty centuries the very site of Nineveh was disputed, and only within the present generation has it been determined by discoveries which illustrate in the most remarkable manner the predictions of Nahum and his fellow-prophets. (*Vide* Nineveh in Smith's Dict. of Bible.) The elevated style and poetical beauty of Nahum are evident to any reader; and the opinion of Bishop Lowth, though spoken of the original, will readily be accepted by those who know the translation only : "None of the Minor Prophets seem to equal Nahum in boldness, ardor, and sublimity. His prophecy forms a regular and perfect poem ; the exordium is not merely magnificent, it is truly majestic ; the preparation for the destruction of Nineveh, and the description of its downfall and desolation, are expressed in the most vivid colors, and are bold and luminous in the highest degree." Nahum signifies Consolation.

Authorities: Bible Commentary, Smith's Bible Dictionary, Lowth, Gray.

Name. The name; Christian name. The name is the most necessary of all words in a language. Adam received his name from GOD, and he in turn, in token of Lordship, named all living things. It was the great and glorious name of JEHOVAH which was the subject of the most important revelation before the Incarnation, and it was the revelation of the names FATHER, SON, and HOLY GHOST which was a part of His Gospel. We have these names pronounced upon us at our baptism, and are named thenceforth Christians, and we have our names written in the Lamb's Book of Life. The name, then, which we bear is a most solemn reminder of our duty and our vows, which bind us to GOD and give us a brotherhood in CHRIST and a fellowship with the Saints. It is a badge or token to be highly esteemed, since we share the name of Him whose name is above every name, and at which every knee should bow.

Narthex. The long, narrow vestibule which ran across the front of the church.

The term also included the outer porch, as well as the inner vestibule. It had two doors, and in it were placed those who were under discipline and the energumens. Near, but beyond it, in the body of the church, the mixed congregation of the hearers and the heathen were placed, while the faithful alone sat or stood farther within, and occupied the nave proper.

Natural Religion. Whatever subordinate ideas may be attached to the conception of Religion, yet, whether primal, natural, or based on revelation, religion includes the acknowledgment of some supreme power and of our relation to it as owing a duty and service in return for life and continuance, and is the debt of worship by some outward acts of reverence and prayer. A religion to be such *must* assume the existence of a GOD, so we are here precluded from discussing whether the intuitions of our nature afford sufficient grounds for such a belief. It is enough for us to claim such a knowledge, no matter how crude or debasing, if it is distinctly a knowledge of a Power outside the limits of our own human capacities. The Fetich of the Negro, the Good Spirit of the Indian, are the base of their ideas of GOD as much as our better knowledge from Revelation, and it is so far a religion. But does natural religion simply become the sum of those concepts which are left after we have carefully removed, if it be possible for us to do so, all that Revelation has imported into our knowledge? or is it not rather the sum of those and conceptions of the human mind which increase as observation, experience, and religious emotions expand and react till at last their sum shapes itself almost, if not quite, into a system of religion? This last appears to be the natural course which the religious ideas within the range of mere human capacity would take.

There is, then, but developed in varying degrees, a natural religion. It is based upon the longings that belong to human nature. It seizes hold of any conception of a power that can give its helplessness aid. It acknowledges a dependence. It offers a payment of duty, obedience, worship. This may be but slightly understood, but it is understood and yielded. Besides this, there appears another conception, itself a speculation, but subtly bound up in the first. It is that as the man owes a service to GOD, why should GOD so treat him? Why should his soul perish, or where does GOD bestow it after death? There can be no clearer proof of the immortality of the soul than there can be of the existence of GOD. But as the conception of true religion develops, so does the belief of immortality and future happiness of the soul develop. They are both parts of that natural religion which is implanted in our nature. What natural religion cannot do is, it cannot show to us the Resurrection. That is a distinct Revelation. It is on the truest instincts of such natural religion, and not in any conflict with them, that GOD's revelation bases itself and claims our assent. But natural religion is not strong enough to put any restraints upon our passions. It is not able to give sufficient motives for self-control. It cannot supply the objective aims of religion vividly enough; and its chief appeal is to the weaker side of a merely human moral law, based upon an undefined good,—undefined, that is, as sharply as the conscience recognizes it when presented through Revelation. For any man thus to rest only upon natural religion, though carried up to Theistic or Deistic notion, when he has the light of Revelation, is a mere subterfuge,—a paltering with his conscience in the endeavor to avoid the responsibilities of the greater knowledge Revelation gives us. In a Christian land we may appeal to the dictates of natural religion, but as a proof that even in our human nature GOD has not left us without proofs of what is more clearly known to be His will, and to show that our Faith is in consonance with and glorifies the rudimentary ideas, which are really simply indications of our natural capacity for all the gifts He has given us in His SON. We have avoided complicating this statement with other subordinate ideas, or with any analysis of Fetichism Polytheistic notions, or with a nature-worship which has been carried out by some nations (as the Sabeans) into a system of some perfectness. But for us here in this Christian country, natural religion should hold the same relation to our spiritual life that our elemental childish ideas on any secular subject hold to our better and riper knowledge. A subject of inquiry as helping us better to comprehend the working of our minds.

Nature. That which exists, whether it be self-existent, as in the Divine Nature, or derivative and dependent, as in all else which has being, whether visible to us or not. But existence implies some kind of organization, and organization implies Law; for that chaos which can be conceived by us must be made up of nature, and it would be hard to conceive of the ultimate particles of matter without some organization, though the congeries of such matter might have no cohesion. This being true, we then can conceive of all nature whatever as governed by law and the expression of law.

Nature, Divine. *Vide* GOD.

Nature, Laws of. The modes by which the complex parts and elements of Nature work together, each having the modes of its existence, and so co-ordinated and so limited that they work together harmoniously, or whenever they clash there is a compensation offered in some way. It is not in the limits of this work to dwell upon these laws, but to rather point out the power that is given to man to use directly or to combine for his purposes the several laws of Nature. We are constantly doing this with each extension of our knowledge of the working of, and results effected by, these laws. All arts and sciences, the conveniences of life, these all depend upon our combining with more or less skill the elemental laws of Nature which we have discovered, and whenever we more perfectly understand the extent and the limits of each of these laws we apply them to new uses, and attain new and wonderful results with them. But it is well to point out, that man to effect his ends has to combine several of these natural laws, and to limit the one by the other, but the Divine wisdom in many ways reverses this; each one of His Laws is made to have multiform applications, and to effect His purposes with a simplicity and an ease that we do not perceive as we ought, living as we do in the midst of their operation. So silent, so sure, so perfect is their work, and their compensations in large results so complete, that men have been deceived and have said that Law was GOD, and we had no need of a Personal God, that the Universe was self-restoring. We can but see His will behind ordering all things in a perfect constitution thoroughly harmonious with His own Perfections.

Nave. *Vide* ARCHITECTURE.

Navicula. A ship or ark; a vessel which was used to pour out the frankincense into the censer. It was used in Bishop Andrews' Chapel and in Queen Elizabeth's.

Nazarenes. A name which Christians once bore because of their LORD. They were of the "sect of the Nazarenes" (Acts xxiv. 25). But it was later the name for a sect of heretics who took up a mixture of both Christian and Jewish tenets. They used circumcision and kept the Sabbath, and observed the Mosaic Law, but also received Baptism and observed the Christian Law. They could be traced back apparently to those Christians who retired from Jerusalem when the last siege was threatened, and who probably kept up observances which were elsewhere abandoned as soon as the Jewish nationality was destroyed. Possibly against the traditions they kept up were directed the Canons against the Judaizers in the Apostolical Canons. They kept up their organization for four hundred years or more.

Nebraska and Dakota, Missionary Jurisdiction of. The missionary jurisdiction of Nebraska and Dakota was erected by the House of Bishops in 1865 A.D.

The Rev. Robert Harper Clarkson, D.D., Rector of St. James' Church, Chicago, was elected the first Bishop of the jurisdiction by the General Convention of 1865 A.D. He was consecrated on the 15th day of November in the church of which he was Rector, in the city of Chicago, by Bishop Hopkins, who was then the Presiding Bishop of the Church.

These two Territories, Nebraska and Dakota, had previously been part of the great missionary jurisdiction of Bishop Talbot, which embraced nearly all of the country west of the Missouri River to the Rocky Mountains. Nebraska is twice the size of the State of New York, and Dakota is double the size of Nebraska. When Bishop Clarkson entered upon his work there were seven clergy connected with the jurisdiction and four small churches, located at Nebraska City, Omaha, Decatur, and Nemaha City. The white population of the entire jurisdiction was at this time (1865 A.D.) above 90,000, nearly seven-eighths of which was in the Territory of Nebraska. There were then above 30,000 Indians in the jurisdiction, chiefly in the Territory of Dakota. Missions were established among these Indians in 1866 A.D.

The Bishop took up his residence first at Nebraska City, and commenced a Boys' School (Talbot Hall) there in 1866 A.D., which has since grown into Nebraska College, now under the charge of the Rev. Dr. McNamara.

In 1867 A.D. the Bishop removed his residence to Omaha, and about this time the present Brownell Hall building for the Diocesan Girls' School was erected in that town. The Institution had been organized a few years previously by Bishop Talbot, and was located in the country, three miles from Omaha. This excellent Institution, which has been doing a noble work in the education and teaching of young women for nearly twenty years, needs very much at this time (1884 A.D.) new and larger buildings. The Bishop is endeavoring now to raise a fund of $15,000 for the purpose, and he feels sure that the same amount of money cannot be more judiciously expended for Church work anywhere in the country.

Very soon after Bishop Clarkson commenced his duties in Nebraska and Dakota, the tide of population began to flow into these new Territories. New and large towns sprung up with great rapidity throughout the jurisdiction. The population at this time (1884 A.D.) cannot be less than 600,000 in Nebraska and 300,000 in Dakota. In 1868 A.D. Nebraska became a State, and was erected into a Diocese, and admitted into union with the General Convention.

Among the first efforts of the new Diocese was the commencement of an Episcopal Fund. An assessment for this purpose was made upon every parish and mission, and collected and invested every year. Other means were also taken to increase the fund, which was carefully managed, until now it amounts to $36,000.

Bishop Clarkson was chosen unanimously the Diocesan of the new Diocese of Nebraska in 1870 A.D., and accepted the same, retaining his charge of Dakota as Missionary Bishop. He declined to accept the salary offered to him by the Diocese of Nebraska as long as he remained Missionary Bishop, but allowed the amount to be added every year to the permanent Episcopal Fund of the Diocese.

In 1871 A.D. the missionary jurisdiction of Niobrara was erected out of that of Nebraska and Dakota, it being chiefly that portion which contained the Indian missions;

and in 1872 A.D., Bishop Hare was called to the oversight of this new jurisdiction.

In 1883 A.D. the missionary jurisdiction of North Dakota was erected out of Dakota, and the Rev. W. D. Walker consecrated as Bishop of the same. And at the same time the boundaries of the jurisdiction of Niobrara were enlarged, and the name changed to South Dakota. So that there are now (in 1884 A.D.) three jurisdictions in the original one assigned to Bishop Clarkson in 1865 A.D., with 3 Bishops, 60 churches, 60 clergy, and about 4500 communicants in them all.

In 1872 A.D. the Bishop of Nebraska commenced to collect funds in the city of Omaha for the erection of a Cathedral church in that city. In the spring of 1880 A.D. the corner-stone of the Cathedral was laid in the presence of six Bishops and thirty clergy and a very large concourse of people. The work went slowly onward as fast as the money could be procured for the purpose, no debt being allowed to be incurred in the erection of the edifice.

On the 15th day of November, 1883 A.D., being the eighteenth anniversary of the consecration of the Bishop, the fine Cathedral was consecrated to the worship of ALMIGHTY GOD. The Rt. Rev. Dr. Garrett, the Bishop of Northern Texas, preached the sermon on the occasion, and the Lord Bishop of Toronto, the Rt. Rev. Dr. Sweatman, and the Rt. Rev. Bishop Burgess, of Quincy, were present and participated in the services of the consecration. The Cathedral is entirely finished except the tower and the chapter-house, and it cost as it stands, with its furniture and appointments, above $70 - 000, the larger part of which was contributed by the Churchmen and citizens of Omaha.

A noticeable feature of the Cathedral is its wealth of memorials. Every window and every article of furniture and adornment is a memorial gift.

In connection with the Cathedral, and adjoining it, is an Episcopal residence built in 1881 A.D., and a large and beautiful Childs' Hospital and Home built in 1883 A.D.

Through the efforts of the Rev. Dr. Oliver a valuable property has been secured in Nebraska City, named Shoenberger Hall, originally designed for a Divinity school. It is now used for primary educational purposes. There is an endowment for a Theological Professorship, which is now utilized for the support of a General Diocesan Missionary.

A legacy of $5000 left to the Diocese by the late Mrs. Clarissa Cooke has been funded, and the interest is used every year, at the discretion of the Bishop, to aid struggling parishes in erecting churches. A church is built by the aid of this legacy every year.

A legacy of $10,000 left to the Diocese by Mrs. Fiske, of Ithaca, New York, was added to the Episcopal Fund. It is the settled purpose of the Bishop and the trustees of the property of the Diocese to fund all legacies and use only the interest of the same.

At the General Convention of 1883 A.D. the Bishop of Nebraska resigned his charge of Dakota, on the ground that Dakota needed a Bishop of its own, and that Nebraska alone was more than enough for any one Bishop properly to look after and care for.

In doing so the Bishop used this language: "I am happy to be able to report that Nebraska is able henceforth to support her own Bishop. She has now 36 clergy, 35 churches, and 2200 communicants, two excellent institutions of learning, a hospital, a Cathedral, a Bishop's residence, a moderate Episcopal endowment, and, what is better than all, a body of as earnest, united, and faithful clergy as ever a Bishop was blessed with."

Statistics.—Clergy, 36; parishes and missions, 118; families, 1230; individuals, 4920; baptisms, 286; adults, 80; total, 366; confirmed, 187; communicants, 2200; marriages, 84; burials, 122; Sunday-schools, teachers, 177; scholars, 1793; contributions, $34,682.69.

Statistics for 1886 A.D.: Clergy, 33; parishes and missions, 75; baptisms, 336; confirmed, 228; communicants, 2215; Sunday-school teachers, 164; Sunday-school scholars, 1489; contributions, $35,678.93.

RT. REV. R. H. CLARKSON, D.D.,
Bishop of Nebraska.

Necessity. (*Ne* and *cesso*, that which cannot cease.) "I have one thing to observe of the several kinds of necessity, that the idea of some sort of firm connection runs through them all; and that is the proper, general import of the name necessity. Connection of mental or verbal propositions, or of their respective parts, makes up the idea of logical necessity; connection of end and means makes up the idea of moral necessity; connection of causes and effects is physical necessity; and connection of existence and essence is metaphysical necessity." (Waterland, Works, vol. iv. p. 432, in Krauth's Fleming's Vocab. of Philos.)

Nehemiah. The son of Hachaliah, and chosen to be one of the cup-bearers before King Artaxerxes, who was divinely appointed to administer the judicial authority in the restored nation. He found such favor in the sight of the King that he had his prayer for leave to go to Jerusalem granted, and received authority to procure all that was needful for the rebuilding of both the Temple and the walls of the Holy City. He set about this on the fourth day after his arrival, and the work was speedily pushed on amid many difficulties and much opposition from Sanballat the Samaritan. He finished the building and aided in organizing the internal administration of the city, put down usury and its consequence,—slavery,—acted with Ezra in breaking up marriages with those without the people, and displayed a great administrative and military capacity. His book is useful in giving invaluable details of the places in Jerusalem, and of the circuit of the walls, and it contains the first record of a written compact and covenant.

A part of it has been supposed to be an interpolation by another hand, principally of genealogies, letters, and documents. But while this may be true of the genealogies, since Ezra arranged the Canon, it may well be that Nehemiah had placed them there himself as documents relative to the whole plan of restoration.

Nehemiah was a patriot, willing to sacrifice everything to the restoration of his people; disinterested, self-denying, with much political sagacity, and of so lofty a character that he was able to convince so suspicious a King as Artaxerxes of his perfect integrity and trustworthiness. He had, as indeed was a necessary part of one in his position, considerable skill in organizing and in obtaining the hearty co-operation of those with whom he was joined in his work of restoration.

Neology. The later deistical Theology which sprang up in Germany about ninety years ago. It was richer and in many respects higher than the Deism of the English Infidel school, from which it really was derived, and it also stood on a higher plane, in so far as it accepted somewhat more of the Scriptures. Though the neologians were at variance among themselves how far they should receive the Scripture, they rejected at will whatever was at variance with their own theories, and kept whatever suited them with but little regard to the true nexus of the sacred text. A lower time-bounded view of the worth and work of religion and of morals seems to have pervaded their writings. Whatever was utilitarian, that they retained; whatever did not comport with their ideas of such utility they rejected. Upon such principles the most arbitrary canons of criticism were announced and ruthlessly applied to the Gospels and Epistles. To the neologic school we owe the fierce controversy about St. John's Gospel and the destructive criticism applied to St. Paul's Epistles, and the theories about the prophet Isaiah and the attacks upon the Book of Daniel. Indirectly they have done much service, in helping to clear away much untenable matter that had gathered about the several books of the Bible, and in bringing forward defenders of the Book and in giving a great impetus to its study; but it is rather the good that comes out of evil than the good that flows from another holy act. Their researches have brought out a vast amount of critical material which will be hereafter very useful. But they have succeeded in shipwrecking the faith of many.

Neophyte. A new convert; a person newly baptized. St. Paul uses it in limiting the class of persons from whom a Bishop should be selected,—"not a novice." The margin reads, "not newly come to the faith." But the full sense is "one newly planted." The limitation was perfectly correct. For one newly brought into the Faith needs the training of growing up into the holiness of the Faith and a familiarity with the facts of the Faith which one newly planted can scarcely claim.

Nevada was erected into a Missionary Jurisdiction at the General Convention of 1868 A.D.

The present jurisdiction embraced also at the date of its erection, and till 1874 A.D., the Territory of Arizona, when it was separated. (*Vide* NEW MEXICO AND ARIZONA.) The first services of the Church in Nevada were held by the Rev. Mr. Smeathman, of California, in the months from August to October, 1861 A.D., while officiating for the Territorial Legislature of Nevada as its Secretary in its sessions in Virginia City, and again from October to December 31 at Carson, to which place the Legislature was removed. From this beginning, twenty-three years ago, the work has gone on slowly but surely. In 1863 A.D. the present Bishop went out immediately upon his ordination, and took charge of St. John's, Gold Hill. After nearly two years' work he returned East, but was recalled in 1867 A.D. to St. Paul's, Virginia City, elected Missionary Bishop of Nevada by the General Convention in 1868 A.D., and consecrated to his office in St. George's Church, New York (October 13, 1869 A.D.). The history of the Diocese is very largely the record of his personal efforts. With one clergyman to aid him, he bravely began his work. Arizona could not be attended to at first without too much loss of valuable time, so he concentrated his work upon Nevada. With one clergyman and with one hundred and sixty-nine communicants, scarce a fourth of which were males, he entered upon the toilsome Episcopal duty, which, from the very conditions of the Territory and the mode in which it was settled, was very discouraging. Mining towns are proverbially uncertain. A community gathered in a few months by the thousands over some rich deposit may upon the sudden failure of the mine as suddenly disappear, scattered forever. Work done for such towns will bear fruit in individual lives, but cannot be proven to be effective when measured by statistics. A floating, restless, adventurous population, ever seeking new scenes, careless of spiritual things, desecrating in utter heedlessness what should be held most sacred, needs constant, redoubled work, an itinerating ministry which can follow from place to place with the least possible sacrifice of material, and with the greatest amount of adaptation to existing conditions. It was amidst such discouragements that the Bishop began his work. The clergy were increased to five by 1871 A.D. The communicants were one hundred and ninety-four, and over $14,000 had been contributed. In 1874 A.D. the report showed eight clergy at work at nine parishes and two mission stations, and an aggregate of two hundred and sixty-nine communicants. The total of the contributions for the three years was $43,000. It was at this time that the Bishop planned his girls' school at Reno which, by help from Eastern funds, was gotten to work in 1876 A.D. It had to incur a debt of about $8000, which has been steadily reduced, and is nearly, if not now quite, extinguished. The reports from year to year show great fluctuation, and the uncertainty of the work is shown by the fact that with all the immigration into the Territory, yet the confirmations (about six hundred) are nearly the whole number of the communicants, six hundred and eighty-six. The contributions rose at one triennial report to over $73,000, and then fell off to $33,000 at the last report.

Bishop Whitaker's retrospect (Spirit of Missions, November–December 1880 A.D.) of ten years' work is so pertinent that it is necessary to quote it here:

"In the good providence of GOD, I am permitted to see the end of ten years of missionary work in Nevada.

"They have been years of almost unremitting labor, much of which has been attended with manifold discouragements and apparently meagre results. The continual change which is taking place in the population of our towns, and the almost universal disregard of Sunday as a day of rest and worship have everywhere combined to retard the progress which it should seem the Church ought to have made during this time. If the people of Nevada were attached to the places in which they live, instead of constantly pushing for a removal, it would be much easier for them to become identified with Church work; and if they could be persuaded to relax their labors for one day of the week, a much larger attendance upon Sunday services could be easily secured. Whether this will ever be, in this generation, is very doubtful. It is certain that but little progress has been made in this direction in the last ten years.

"Still, with all these discouragements there has been much which should call forth my devoutest gratitude to GOD; much which leads me to believe that this work has not been done in vain.

"Personally, I have had almost everything to be thankful for. No one could receive kinder or more considerate treatment from any people than I have uniformly received from the people of this State. I feel identified with them, and am entirely content to labor with and for them so long as GOD gives me strength to labor in His service.

"And contrasting the present condition of the Church in Nevada with what it was ten years ago, there are to be found evidences not only of much work performed by the Clergy, but also of liberal giving by the people, and of substantial growth in all the elements of Church strength.

"When I entered upon the performance of my duties as Missionary Bishop there was but one clergyman belonging to the Jurisdiction; now there are seven. There were then three churches; now there are ten. There were then two rectories; now there are eight. There were then one hundred communicants; there are now three hundred and forty. There were then thirty Sunday-school teachers and three hundred and twenty scholars; there are now ninety-three teachers and one thousand two hundred and forty-two scholars.

"During this time there have been one thousand one hundred and ninety-nine infants baptized, and one hundred and forty-five adults. Three hundred and sixty-eight persons have been confirmed; five hundred and eighty-nine marriages have been solemnized. The number of burials has been one thousand one hundred and twenty-nine.

"The total value of Church property in Nevada ten years ago was $36,400; it is now $125,000. In making up this valuation I have deducted $10,000 from the actual cost, on account of depreciation in the actual value. But were all the Church property to be destroyed it could not be restored to its present condition for less than $125,000."

The report to the General Convention of 1883 A.D. showed the condition of the Diocese, while not gaining very materially, certainly held its own, and was deepening and strengthening what it had gained in the past.

The General Convention of 1886 A.D. has put Nevada with Utah under one Bishop. Bishop Whitaker has been translated as Assistant Bishop for Pennsylvania.

Statistics for 1886 A.D.: Clergy, 13; parishes and missions, 31; candidates for H. O., 3; postulants, 3; baptisms, 278; confirmed, 115; communicants, 900; contributions, $33,141.80.

These (from the "Living Church Annual") contain the statistics of Utah also.

New Creation. In Holy Scripture we meet constantly an assertion of a new creation, a new heavens, a new earth, a new order, the old to pass away, all things to become new (Is. lxv. 17; lxvi. 22; 1 Pet. iii. 10; Rev. xxi. 1, 5; 2 Cor. v. 17). And in these places it is evident that a material change in nature is taught as to take place, a renovation of the physical nature around us. There is a renewal, a restoration, a new creation of our spiritual life in the psychical nature, but this is to be also a material restoration. St. Paul points to the connection of the two natures in, "For we know that the whole creation groaneth and travaileth in pain together until now. And not only they, but ourselves also, which have the first-fruits of the Spirit, even we ourselves groan within ourselves waiting for the adoption, to wit, the redemption of our body" (Rom. viii. 22, 23). Then there is a plain prophecy that there will be a new creation of this earth, and it is to be symmetrical with the new creation of our souls, for he who is baptized is in CHRIST JESUS, and he who is in CHRIST JESUS is a new creature, and he who is a new creature here is renewed by the HOLY GHOST, and transformed (the same word in St. Luke is "transfigured"), and passes from glory to glory. The object is clear. It is to present us in His Church holy, spotless, unrebukable, that His Bride may be in His universe, "That He might present it to Himself a glorious Church, not having spot, or wrinkle, or any such thing; but that it should be holy and without blemish" (Eph. v. 27). And in this we must have a share, therefore we are not to be unclothed, but clothed upon. We, as inheritors, will be changed and redeemed and sanctified. We are to live on a sinless earth. We may not speculate further as to the conditions of our existence. Whether the Paradisaic state, as sketched for us in Genesis, will be restored, or whether lifted to heavenly places, seated in our LORD's Throne, made kings and priests unto GOD and His FATHER we shall be endued with faculties glorified; or whether our rank in the scale of created beings there will not be beyond all Angelic essences. It is rash to intrude into the unseen. It is safe merely to say, how these things shall be we do not know; when, in His good time; where, as He may please; but this we do know, that all things in that New Creation will be far more glorious than mortal eye now can look upon, mortal ear can now hear, mortal heart can now understand.

New Hampshire, Diocese of. I. The history of the Church in New Hampshire begins with that of the colony itself, the first settlers (1623 A.D.) being Churchmen. By 1638 A.D. a church and parsonage had been built in Portsmouth (then Passataquack), fifty acres of land given as endowment, and the Rev. Richard Gibson, a missionary in Maine, called as rector. In 1642 A.D., however, when New Hampshire had fallen under the authority of Massachusetts, Mr. Gibson was banished by the Puritan authorities of Boston, having confessed the only offenses charged against him, that he had "defamed the government,"—*i.e.*, protested against their usurpation,—and had performed marriages and baptisms at the Isles of Shoals. A Puritan congregation voted themselves the Church property, and for the next ninety years the Church had here no history. In 1732 A.D. a parish was organized, and Queen's Chapel begun. It took nearly three years to finish a small building, and two years of tedious correspondence (partly with officers of the S. P. G. in London) to secure a rector, the Rev. Arthur Browne. Of six hundred families in Portsmouth in 1741 A.D. less than sixty conformed to the Church, but all the Churchmen in New Hampshire were his parishioners, and he administered the charge with faithful diligence from 1736 A.D. till his death in 1773 A.D. He was helped in the itinerancy by his son Marmaduke (1755-62 A.D.) and by the Rev. Moses Badger (1767-74 A.D.), the latter reporting the number of souls under his care in 1768 A.D. as eleven hundred and thirty-two, "which at his first coming did not exceed seven hundred and forty."

A second parish was organized in 1773 A.D. at Claremont, settled by Churchmen from Connecticut. The building then begun still stands as Union Church, West Claremont. The Rev. Ranna Cossit was the first rector (1773-85 A.D.).

The storm of the Revolution fell heavily upon the two parishes. Mr. Cossit narrowly escaped death at the hands of an armed mob in 1774 A.D., and was for several years a prisoner within the town limits. A British officer writing in 1778 A.D. says, "Rev. Dr. Wheelock (President of Dartmouth College, in New Hampshire), in conjunction with Deacon Bayley, Mr. Morey, and Mr. Hurd, all justices of the peace, put an end to the Church of England in this State as early as 1775 A.D." In April of that year Portsmouth had called the Rev. Matthew Byles from Boston. He could not go. In October, 1776 A.D., it was still "utterly impracticable," and he wrote to the S. P. G., "if government should not be reestablished, I am well convinced that no Episcopal Church will be tolerated in New England."

Nevertheless, the war-clouds broke, and the Church was seen to be stronger than before. In Claremont, twenty-seven families became forty-three. The S. P. G. hears in 1781 A.D. that "the Episcopal congregations in Massachusetts and New Hampshire have greatly increased, even where they have had no ministry." In Claremont, again, thirty families of the Congregational Society conformed to the Church in a body in 1790 A.D. We hear much of hurt done to the Church by its tory clergy, but there are two sides even to that story. A letter to the S. P. G. in 1778 A.D. shows that even "rebels" could respect a clergy sensitively faithful to their peculiar obligations. "The Church in Portsmouth is in a ruinous condition, the windows broken and many of the pews shattered. There are several good families which belong to the Church still. A clergyman who was supposed to have abjured the king offered to preach there. The warden, who was a rebel general and commissary of the province, refused him, saying the doors of the church should never be opened till they could have somebody else to enter and officiate besides those perjured villains, who had broken their oaths of allegiance and their promises at ordination." Again, the S. P. G. report of 1782-83 A.D. speaks of "the clergy themselves increasing in esteem for their steady conduct, in diligently attending to the duties of their calling, and preaching the Gospel, unmixed with the politics of the day."

The war over, the need of organization began to be much felt. Valuable property was at stake, over forty thousand acres of land having been reserved for the endowment of future parishes and of the S. P. G. in the lay-out of towns by the elder Governor Wentworth. A small company met accordingly at Hanover, in August, 1785 A.D., and signed the following Declaration: "We, Whose Names are hereafter subscribed, Do meet and form ourselves into an appiscopalian Body in order for a church with full power and authority to act as such." Unfortunately, this bold assertion had no effect. It may be added here that the larger part of the land endowment was ultimately lost. A small amount has gone to help the Diocesan missionary work, and something to the support of the Bishop, but most of that which was recovered fell into the hands of two of the least needy parishes, being now partly represented by specially heavy assessments paid by those parishes for Diocesan expenses.

In 1789 A D. New Hampshire was represented at a meeting of six clergymen in Salem, Mass., when Dr. (afterwards Bishop) Bass was elected Bishop of the two States, application being made to the General Convention for his consecration, 1789 A.D. Deputies of New Hampshire and Massachusetts signed the Constitution, October 2, when the matter seems to have dropped.

Meanwhile, Portsmouth, for thirteen years without clerical services, had obtained a rector, the Rev. John C. Ogden (1786-93 A.D.), and a third parish had been formed, at Holderness, in the centre of the State. Here again the Church was first in the field. Judge Livermore, the chief proprietor, was a Churchman, and the Rev. Robert Fowle, who held that charge for more than fifty-eight years (1789-1847 A.D.), shepherded the flock without a rival till 1814 A.D. A fourth parish sprang into being in 1798 A.D. in Cornish, near Claremont. Cornish contained no Churchmen, apparently, till Philander Chase, a student in Dartmouth College, became one, and the carrying over of nearly a whole township to Episcopacy may probably be ascribed to the sole influence of the future Missionary Bishop. The meeting-house built by the town was voted an Episcopal Church, and Mr. Ogden ministered for a time as rector, though living in Hartland, Vermont, and supplying five towns with regular services, and ten or twelve others occasionally. In 1795 A.D. Cornish voted to purchase a Bible and a copy of Bishop Seabury's Sermons, being evidently reduced to lay-reading, but the end of the century finds four parishes and three clergymen in the State.

II. The Diocesan history proper begins with the meeting (in Concord, August 25, 1802 A.D.) of the first Convention, the rectors of Portsmouth, Claremont, and Holderness, and two Lay Delegates each from Portsmouth, Holderness, and Cornish. The Rev. Joseph Willard, of Portsmouth, presiding, and the three clergymen being made a Committee to draw up a Constitution, reported one the same day, which was signed by all present except the Rev. Daniel Barber, of Claremont. That remarkable man, able, ambitious, unwise, had already, a year before, accomplished the organization of another Convention, of the Churches in the Connecticut Valley (Western New Hampshire and Eastern Vermont), and having obtained from the General Convention a dispensation allowing such a union of parts of two States, he would not give up his scheme. He had brought to this Convention a proposal from the Valley Convention looking to a union of all New Hampshire and Vermont in one Diocese, but the Concord gathering declared themselves not authorized to act on such a business, and Claremont held quite aloof till the General Convention of 1808 A.D., at the earnest request of the Convention of New Hampshire, rescinded the harmful dispensation. The Valley Convention met no more after 1808 A.D., and Mr. Barber appeared in the New Hampshire Convention of 1809 A.D.

Meanwhile, the Diocese had been wholly without Episcopal care. Bishop Bass was invited to take charge of it in 1808 A.D., but died within a few weeks. In 1810 A.D. the Convention declines to take part in the election of a Bishop for Massachusetts, but promises to receive the person chosen, and accedes to the Constitution of the Eastern Diocese. In 1812 A.D., Bishop Griswold presided in the Convention for the first time, and began the first Episcopal visitation of this region. For thirty years the Church in New Hampshire enjoyed his superintendence, and made slow but fairly steady gains in numbers and in popular respect. Hopkinton had been added to the number of parishes in 1803 A.D., and Plainfield in 1804 A.D., and to these were now joined Drewsville, Charlestown, Concord, Dover, and Manchester, besides the building of a church in the prosperous village of Claremont, far from the old church in the "west part." Parochial reports began to be made in 1810 A.D. The number of communicants reported in that year was 151; in 1820 A.D., 198; in 1840 A.D., 394.

III. The need of a separate Bishop had been suggested occasionally, but even after the death of Bishop Griswold the feeble, scattered churches of New Hampshire hesitated to undertake such a responsibility. At a special Convention, October 4, 1843 A.D., the motion to elect barely prevailed. But that point settled, the Convention was unanimous in the choice of the Rev. Carlton Chase, of Bellows Falls, Vermont. He was consecrated in October, 1844 A D., and served the Diocese faithfully and wisely to his death, in January, 1870 A.D. He had to be rector of Trinity Church Claremont, till June, 1863 A.D., and when the Diocese did assume his support, his salary was $900, ill paid. But he left 23 parishes instead of 12,

21 clergymen for 11, and about 1350 communicants for 500. Far greater was his work of making the Church respected in a community full of bitter prejudice. Of such work, sinking strong foundations through a quicksand till they reach a solid bed, Bishop Chase and his clergy did very much which cannot now be reckoned, but which makes possible the work of to-day.

St. Paul's School, Concord, also deserves honorable mention here. It gathers most of its pupils from other States; but its high success has won honor for the Church which it represents, and in this way and by many gifts and helps, it has been a powerful promoter of the Church's good in New Hampshire. It was begun in 1856 A.D. Located near St. Paul's School, due to its rector, and greatly helped by it, the Diocesan Orphans' Home is another blessing of this period.

In May, 1870 A.D., the Convention elected as successor to Bishop Chase the Rev. Wm. W. Niles, Professor of Latin in Trinity College, Hartford, and he was consecrated at Concord, September 21.

In twelve years since the Diocese has grown to have 22 parishes and 13 mission stations, including (most properly) the chapel of St. Paul's School. In 1882 A.D. the number of clergy (besides the Bishop) was 31, communicants, 2062, this, a gain in a nearly stationary population. The contributions for all purposes, which in 1870 A.D. were under $10,000, were nearly $25,000 in 1882 A.D.

The "Holderness School for Boys" was opened in 1879 A.D. as a Diocesan school in the old mansion of the Livermores, and the venerable church now serves as its chapel. Destroyed by fire in March, 1882 A.D., the historic homestead has given place to new buildings specially adapted to the school work. The number of pupils is about 50, and the school has prospered every way beyond hope. The charges—$200 a year for New Hampshire boys and $250 for all others—suggest what is aimed at, a school thoroughly good yet cheap. A committee is already considering the possibility of a similar school for girls.

Another Orphanage, the "Chase Home for Children," was founded in 1879 A.D. in Portsmouth, and has now eighteen children in residence.

This is a day of small things, but the future seems bright. A greatly loved and honored Bishop, a zealous, active, brotherly clergy, a population slow to receive new truth, but serious and tenacious withal when they do receive it, make up in part our promise for the coming years, while old systems are failing and leaving an unfilled gap.

Statistics.—Clergy, 33; parishes and missions, 34; families, 1605; individuals, 8025; baptisms, infants, 131; adults, 48; total, 179; confirmed, 140; communicants, 2173; marriages, 71; burials, 126; Sunday-schools, teachers, 163; scholars, 1177; contributions, $52,133.13   REV. L. WATERMAN.

New Jersey, Diocese of. New Jersey, in its early colonial days, was chiefly under Presbyterian and Quaker influence; and its people were so nearly cut off from the ministrations of the Church of England, that Bray, in his memorials, describes them as being "wholly left to themselves, without priest or altar."

But in the reign of Queen Anne the proprietary government was resigned to the sovereign; and the Good Queen was a "nursing mother" to the Church, generously bestowing money grants and gifts of books, Communion silver and bells. In 1701 A.D. the two Jerseys contained about 15,000 inhabitants, of which not above 600 frequented the Church, nor hardly more than 200 communicants.

George Keith, a convert from Quakerism, and John Talbot, were among the first and the most efficient missionaries of the venerable Society for the Propagation of the Gospel (1702 A.D.). Talbot became Rector of St. Mary's, Burlington, but continued to make extensive circuits. Dr. Hawks said of him, "the society never had, at least in our view, a more honest, fearless, and laborious missionary." In 1722 A.D. he received Episcopal orders at the hands of non-juring Bishops in England, and was thereupon dismissed from the society's service. It is not known that he ever performed Episcopal acts. His death took place November 30, 1727 A.D., at Burlington, and it is believed that he was buried under the old church. Keith returned to England in 1704 A.D. Vaughan and Chandler at Elizabethtown, and Beach at New Brunswick, were leading Presbyters, and these two towns, with Burlington and Shrewsbury, were strong Church centres before the Revolution.

Several ecclesiastical movements, of national importance, had their beginnings within the borders of New Jersey. The first memorial from American Churchmen, petitioning the English Archbishops and Bishops to send a Bishop to America, was signed in Burlington, November 2, 1705 A.D., the petitioners being fourteen clergymen of New York, New Jersey, and Pennsylvania.

Of the four colonial Bishoprics proposed by the S. P. G., two for the islands, and two for the Continent of America, one was to have its See at Williamsburg, Va., another at Burlington. Mr. Talbot wrote, in 1709 A.D., "I have got possession of the best house in America for a Bishop's seat." The house and land were long held for this purpose, but ultimately conveyed to the parish church of St. Mary's.

A more successful measure was begun eighty years later, and is thus described in Bishop White's Memoirs: "The first step towards the forming of a collective body of the Episcopal Church in the United States was taken through the medium of the Rev. Abraham Beach, at a meeting of a few clergymen of New York, New Jersey, and Pennsylvania at New Brunswick, N. J., on the 13th and 14th of May, 1784 A.D. The first day was chiefly taken up with discussing principles of ecclesiastical union. The next morning (in consequence of new information received) it was agreed that nothing should be urged further on the subject at present. But before the clergy parted it was determined to procure a larger meeting on the 5th of the ensuing October, in New York, to confer and agree on some general principles of a union of the Episcopal Church throughout the States."

The Diocese was organized—so far as it could be without a Bishop—in 1785 A.D., the first session of its Convention being held in Christ Church, New Brunswick, July 6 of that year; when four clergymen and six laymen were elected to represent the Diocese at the General Convention, in Philadelphia, the following September. These delegates were empowered " to accede, on the part of this Convention, to the fundamental principles published by the Convention of the Protestant Episcopal Church held in New York on the 6th and 7th of October, 1784 A.D., and to adopt such measures as the said General Convention may deem necessary for the utility of the said Church, not repugnant to the aforesaid principles."

But its adhesion was not without discrimination. The next year it unanimously approved the political alterations in the Prayer-Book, made by the General Convention, as well as the address to the Archbishops and Bishops; and a Diocesan Committee was appointed to correspond with the English Bishops. But the "further alterations" proposed and the proposed Constitution were *not approved*. Again, in 1787 A.D., it voted approval of the *Old Liturgy*.

Some other of its early acts are worthy of notice. In 1786 A.D. it was resolved to vote by congregations; clergy and laity to deliberate together, but to vote separately, a concurrence being necessary to give validity to any measure. Every clergyman, of whatever order, duly settled in a congregation, should be a member of Convention *ex officio*: when a Bishop should be regularly settled, he should be President *ex officio*. In 1787 A.D. it resolved that no one should be a Church officer, or delegate to General or State Convention, who does not openly declare himself a member of the Church, and profess belief that the Ordinal and the threefold ministry, as used in this Church, are most agreeable to the Word of GOD. In 1790 A.D. it appointed a Standing Committee, five clergymen and five laymen, " for the recommendation of Candidates for Holy Orders;" and for a number of years following this appears to be the only duty devolved upon the Standing Committee, that continued to be elected annually, with variations as to the numbers and constitution of its membership. In this year, 1790 A.D., it declared "the Convention and Church in this State bound by the proceedings of the General Convention in establishing the Constitution, Canons, and Prayer-Book." In 1794 A.D. it made Baptism and "good character" necessary to office. It also directed its Treasurer to pay to the Treasurer of the General Convention certain contributions " for supporting missionaries on the frontiers" of the United States. In 1795 A.D. it resolved, that this Convention agree to vest the House of Bishops with a full negative on the proceedings of the House of Deputies in the General Convention.

Bishops of the neighboring Dioceses, generally Bishop White and Bishop Hobart, performed Episcopal acts in New Jersey, as they were requested by the Standing Committee, until the consecration of Bishop Croes in 1815 A.D.

In August, 1796 A.D., the Rev. Uzal Ogden, D.D., Rector of Trinity Church, Newark, was elected Bishop, but the General Convention hesitated to confirm the election, on the ground of alleged irregularity. A special Convention, in October, 1799 A.D., resolved that the election had been " orderly," and addressed the several Standing Committees a circular asking their ratification. It was never given, and New Jersey probably had no reason to regret the denial. For, on May 9, 1805 A.D., its Standing Committee, as authorized by a special Convention in the December preceding, " and with the aid and consent of the Rt. Rev. Dr. Moore, Bishop of New York, unanimously resolved to suspend the Rev. Dr. Ogden from the exercise of any ministerial duties within this State, and he is hereby suspended accordingly." The retired Rector declared his withdrawal from the Protestant Episcopal Church, and his purpose to be Rector still, by virtue of his English orders and allegiance.

There have been four Diocesan Bishops hitherto, as follows: John Croes, consecrated November 19, 1815 A.D., died July 30, 1832 A.D.; George Washington Doane, consecrated October 31, 1832 A.D., died April 27, 1859 A.D.; William Henry Odenheimer, consecrated October 13, 1859 A.D., selected the new Diocese of Northern New Jersey November 12, 1874 A.D., died August 14, 1879 A.D.; John Scarborough, consecrated February 2, 1875 A.D.

Bishop Croes was also Rector of Christ Church, New Brunswick, and there resided thoughout his Episcopate.

Bishop Doane making Burlington his " temporary residence," and having actually accepted " an invitation from the Rector, wardens, and vestry of Trinity Church, Newark, to establish himself in that place," on terms of great generosity, leaving him " free from parochial responsibility," the death of Dr. Wharton, Rector of St. Mary's Church, and the peculiar circumstances of the parish, presented a conflicting duty. The result was that he remained permanently at Burlington, discharging the duties of Rector of St. Mary's during all his Episcopate. He occupied the old parsonage until the erection of his own house, "Riverside," which, by his deed of gift, became the property of the Diocese at his death.

Bishop Odenheimer lived at Riverside until his removal to the Northern Diocese, and by a gracious Providence it was again made his home during the year of great physical suffering with which his life closed.

Bishop Scarborough removed the See to Trenton, and in 1878 A.D. a property in that city was presented by Samuel K. Wilson, Esq., to the Diocese, and deeded to the Trustees of the Episcopal Fund to be the Episcopal residence.

Bishop Doane founded two Church schools, for girls and boys respectively, St. Mary's Hall, in 1837 A.D., Burlington College, in 1846 A.D., placing them upon the Delaware, on the right and on the left of Riverside. Of these schools the Bishop of New Jersey is *ex-officio* president. Both are under one Board, the Trustees of Burlington College, which has a charter from the State. The Hall for nearly fifty years has sent forth annually a class of well-instructed Churchwomen, whose influence for good became, long since, a proverb in the Church and in the country. The success of this first venture induced many to follow the example, till nearly every Diocese has its Hall, and St. Mary's is the acknowledged and revered mother of Church schools for girls the land over.

Burlington College, between 1850 and 1860 A.D., graduated in Arts ten classes. After that date, there being no endowment, it was found necessary to suspend the College classes, and for the next sixteen years it was carried on in its Preparatory Department. Since 1879 A.D. it has been leased by the Trustees to the Rev. Messrs. Reilly, who have there the older boys of St. John's Academy, Haddonfield. St. Agnes' Hall is a Church school for girls, under the same management, at Haddonfield.

Financial embarrassment and failure have been the penalty paid by several American Bishops, who, in advance of their age, with excess of zeal or lack of worldly prudence, heroically founded Christian schools. Bishop Doane's case was not to be an exception. Two sentences of his own will almost tell the story : " A perfect confidence that continued success would insure ultimate relief encouraged exertion, and made trials tolerable, for the work's sake, which no personal interest would have sustained one week." "The provision was made, and the children were collected. And he, who with GOD's blessing had accomplished these things, after two most dangerous attacks of illness, which confined him for nearly five months, having exhausted, in his enterprise for Christian education, his means and his credit, was left with two most prosperous institutions, whose annual receipts were not less than $70,000, and with an unmanageable debt."

In March, 1849 A.D., the Bishop "made an assignment of all his property for the benefit of all his creditors," and committed the business department of the schools to committees of trusted friends. Financial aid was now generously contributed in all parts of the Diocese, and there was no more pecuniary embarrassment. But the troubles were not over. Nearly three years elapsed, and then four laymen preferred charges of dishonesty, with numerous specifications ; and three Bishops were induced to make a presentment of the Bishop of New Jersey for trial by his peers. The Diocesan Convention vindicated their Bishop, and claimed the primary right of presentment, and when the Court of Bishops met, in October, 1852 A.D., asked that Court to dismiss the case, pledging the readiness of the Diocese "to investigate any charges against its Bishop that may be presented from any responsible source." On the eighth day of the session, it was "*Ordered*, that this Court, relying upon the said pledge, do not now proceed to any further action in the premises." A second presentment was made notwithstanding, and a second Court summoned, in September, 1853 A.D. To a committee of this Court the Bishop respondent, while asserting perfect integrity of purpose, acknowledged "That, in the course of all these transactions, human infirmity may have led him into many errors he deeply feels." "After prolonged consideration, and the utmost delicacy towards every one concerned, the Court came to the unanimous decision to dismiss the case. The decision has brought peace to a whole Diocese, and, we may add, peace to the Church." (Extract from Rep. of Comm. to Dioc. Conv., May, 1854 A.D.)

The missionary work of the Diocese is carried on, under the Bishop, by the two Convocations of Burlington and New Brunswick, each Convocation having a Dean, Secretary, Treasurer, and Executive Committee.

The Convention elects a Registrar, to conserve its store of printed documents. The Bishop, with the concurrence of the Standing Committee, appoints a Chancellor of the Diocese, who is the legal adviser of the Bishop and Standing Committee. He has a seat and voice in the Convention, but no vote. In each Convocation three examining Chaplains are appointed, yearly, by the Bishop.

The Diocesan Institutions are *The Corporation for the Relief of Widows and Orphans of Deceased Clergymen*, *The Christian Knowledge Society*, and *The Trustees of the Episcopal Fund*, empowered to hold property in trust for any ecclesiastical, charitable, or educational objects, under the control of the Convention or other Diocesan authority. There are also a *Fund for Aged and Infirm Clergymen*, *The Conover Fund*, and *The Bishop's Trust Fund*, wherewith " to meet emergencies, and to confer benefits in a quiet way upon those who would not ask alms of the Church." The New Jersey Branch of the Woman's Auxiliary and Board of Missions reported last year an aggregate amount, in money and work, of $13,845.

The *Episcopal Infant School for Orphans and Half Orphans of the Diocese*, at South Amboy, founded and endowed by Mr. John Stevens, trains girls for service, and finds them homes in Christian families.

A great deficiency in the Diocese is the want of parish schools. Burlington, Princeton, and South Amboy alone report them.

The *Choir Guild*, composed of the men and boy choirs of the Diocese, was formed in 1880 A.D., to introduce a higher standard of Church music, and greater uniformity in its selection and rendering. It includes now six choirs and one hundred and fifty singers.

The following statistics will show the growth of the Diocese during the last six decades: 1823 A.D., 13 clergy, 25 churches, 740 communicants; 1832 A.D., 18 clergy, 900 communicants; 1843 A.D., 48 clergy, 45 parishes, 2150 communicants; 1853 A.D., 67 clergy, 64 parishes, 3570 communicants; 1863 A.D., 106 clergy, 107 parishes, 6376 communicants; 1873 A.D., 142 clergy, 124 parishes, 11,310 communicants. (In 1874 the Diocese was divided, the seven northern counties being erected into the new Diocese of Northern New Jersey, with rather more than one-half the ecclesiastical strength of the entire State.) 1883 A.D., 97 clergy, 115 congregations, and 8381 communicants; candidates and postulants for Holy Orders, 14; lay-readers, 41.

All debts on church property, whether parochial or diocesan, are extinguished with two or three exceptions.

The sea-side churches form a remarkable feature of the Diocese. From the mother-church at Shrewsbury to Cape May more than twenty churches and chapels line the Atlantic coast; some of them open only during "the season," but the larger number —and more each year—assuming the form of regular parishes.

Authorities: Anderson's History of the Colonial Church, Journals of the Diocese, Bishop Doane's Addresses.

Statistics for 1886 A.D.: Clergy, 102; parishes, 74; missions, 41; ordinations, D. 1, P. 2; candidates for H. O., 7; baptisms, 1369; con., 707; com., 9781; contr., $241,301.08.

REV. ELVIN K. SMITH.

New Mexico and Arizona, the Missionary Jurisdiction of, was created at the General Convention of 1874 A.D., the Bishop of Colorado being relieved from the oversight of New Mexico, and Arizona being separated from Nevada.

The Rev. Wm. F. Adams, Rector of St. Paul's Church, New Orleans, Louisiana, was elected first Bishop of the new Jurisdiction. He was consecrated in his Parish church, January, 17, 1875 A.D., by the Bishop of Mississippi, the Rt. Rev. Wm. M. Green, D.D., LL.D., assisted by Bishop Wilmer, of Louisiana, and Bishop Beckwith, of Georgia.

On Saturday, February 6, 1875 A.Y., Bishop Adams, accompanied by the Rev. Henry Forrester, reached Santa Fé, New Mexico's ancient capital, after a stage-ride of seventy-six hours from Pueblo, Colorado. He was very ill the next night from the fatigue of the journey, and for several days thereafter was confined to his room; being unable to officiate in the Church services till Friday, the 12th inst.

On the 1st day of March the Bishop started on a visitation of Southern New Mexico and Arizona. He was accompanied as far as Albuquerque by Mr. Forrester, and there, on the 4th of the same month, the Hon. Hezekiah S. Johnson, Judge of the Second Judicial District of New Mexico, was ordained to the restricted Diaconate. Very few Americans were then in Albuquerque, and the Judge himself had a Mexican wife. The service was held in a room of the Exchange Hotel, and the congregation consisted of only nine persons. This ordination gave the new Jurisdiction all the orders of the ministry,—one Bishop, one Priest, and one Deacon. There was another Priest somewhere in Arizona, but he was on his way out of the country, and therefore could not be counted. The new Deacon died in May, 1876 A.D., having been able to render but little service.

Bishop Adams continued his journey by stage to Southern New Mexico, stopping at Fort Selden, Las Cruces, Mesilla, and, finally, Silver City. From the last he started by buckboard to Tucson, Arizona, two hundred miles distant, but became ill on the road and had to stop. He then returned to Silver City, and from there to Mesilla, and was then called to his family, which was still in New Orleans, on account of the serious illness of two of his children. He went through Texas, staging several days and nights before reaching a railroad, and arrived at home utterly exhausted. He had a very severe attack of the illness that had twice prostrated him in New Mexico, and his physicians positively forbade his return until his strength should be entirely restored.

Under these circumstances Mr. Forrester, who had removed his family to Santa Fé, and was temporarily in charge of the Parish there, took up the general missionary work, acting, as far as possible, as the Bishop's representative. In the autumn of 1875 A.D. he visited Las Vegas, Cimarron, Socorro, the Magdalena mines, Las Cruces, Mesilla, Silver City, Georgetown, the Mimbres Reduction Works, and Forts Craig, Selden, and Bayard. At Mesilla, which was then the principal place in Southern New Mexico, a large house, containing sufficient room for a residence and also a chapel, was secured for the Church at a very low price. The property was paid for by the Rev. Dr.

James Saul, of Philadelphia, and was deeded to him and the Rev. Dr. Twing, as Trustees for the Domestic and Foreign Missionary Society of the Protestant Episcopal Church. In the spring of 1876 A.D. nearly all the points in Southern New Mexico were visited again, the missionary residing still at Santa Fé, and officiating there when not traveling. At this time there was no railroad in the Jurisdiction, traveling being done by stage, or by buckboard, or by private conveyance. It took three days and nights to go from Santa Fé to Mesilla, stopping only long enough to change horses and get meals. Bishop Adams, having finally come to the conclusion that he was permanently incapacitated for the work in his jurisdiction, sent his resignation to the Presiding Bishop in the summer of 1876 A.D. As soon as this became known in New Mexico, a petition was framed requesting the House of Bishops to send out another Bishop as soon as possible. This petition was signed by a number of the most prominent gentlemen in the Territory, including the Secretary of State and the Commanding Officer of the Military District. It was presented to the Bishops at their meeting in Philadelphia in October of the same year. They preferred, however, not to accept the resignation of Bishop Adams at this time, and action was deferred for another year. In the mean time, Mr. Forrester continued to reside at Santa Fé and to do the general missionary work as circumstances required and opportunity was afforded.

In the spring of 1877 A.D., by the help of friends in the East, the chapel at Mesilla was neatly furnished. A school had been started, at the earnest request of the people, in the autumn of 1876 A.D., but it was never self-supporting, and was finally abandoned. The mission, in the absence of the missionary in charge, was placed under the care of Mr. George D. Bowman, lay-reader, who has continued, and still continues, to render most faithful and acceptable service.

A school was opened at Santa Fé also, and succeeded very well. When the Congregationalists introduced their system of Academies into the Territory, beginning at Santa Fé, it was deemed best to suspend the Church school, that a combined effort might be made to secure the advantages offered by them.

At the General Convention of 1877 A.D., Bishop Adams's resignation was accepted by the House of Bishops, and the Rev. D. B. Knickerbacker, who afterwards became Bishop of Indiana, was elected to fill the vacancy. After the adjournment of the Convention Dr. Knickerbacker declined to be consecrated, so the Episcopate was left vacant, and, under the Canons, the oversight of it fell to the Presiding Bishop. In calling a meeting of the Bishops for August, 1878 A.D., to consider the case of the Bishop of Michigan, the Presiding Bishop included, as part of the business to come before them, the election of a Bishop for New Mexico and Arizona. It was found, however, that there was a canonical obstacle in the way of action at this time, and so the Jurisdiction was placed by the Presiding Bishop under the care of Bishop Spalding, of Colorado, who consented to take it until the next General Convention.

The Rev. J. A. M. La Tourrette, Chaplain U.S.A., having come to Fort Union, New Mexico, was now transferred to the Jurisdiction, and Bishop Spalding appointed the first Standing Committee as follows: The Rev. J. A. M. La Tourrette, President; the Rev. H. Forrester, Secretary; Col. J. P. Willard, U.S.A., and Mr. George D. Bowman.

In 1879 A.D., as the A. T. & S. F. R. R. came southward from Colorado and approached Las Vegas, New Mexico, services were begun there, and Bishop Spalding visited the place in August. While there, he secured lots for Church purposes, and on the 9th of the following November the Bishop made a second visit, and opened St. Paul's Chapel for divine service. The same month the missionary moved from Santa Fé to Las Vegas, making his residence there temporarily. In December the Rev. D. A. Sanford was sent by Bishop Spalding to assist in the work, and regular services were thereafter held at Albuquerque, where there had been several visits made during the preceding six months. Occasional services were held at Santa Fé also, and Mesilla was still visited as opportunity offered.

In May, 1880 A.D., the Primary Convocation of the Jurisdiction was held at Albuquerque, under the presidency of Bishop Spalding. The members were Bishop Spalding, the Revs. J. A. M. La Tourrette, H. Forrester, and D. A. Sanford, and, from Sante Fé, Mr. L. Bradford Prince; from Mesilla, Mr. W. H. Cobb; from Las Vegas, Mr. Chas. Wheelock; and from Albuquerque, Messrs. W. C. Hazledine, W. K. P. Wilson, and R. C. Vose.

The officers of the Jurisdiction were appointed or elected as follows: Standing Committee, Rev. J. A. M. La Tourrette, President; Rev. H. Forrester, Secretary; Hon. W. C. Hazledine, Mr. H. C. Baldwin. Chancellor, Hon. L. Bradford Prince. Treasurer, Mr. W. W. Griffin. Registrar, Rev. H. Forrester. Examining Chaplains, Rev. J. A. M. La Tourrette, Rev. H. Forrester. Delegates to General Convention, Rev. H. Forrester, Col. J. P. Willard, U.S.A.; Alternates, Rev. J. A. M. La Tourrette, Hon. W. C. Hazledine. Trustees of Church Property, the Bishop exercising Jurisdiction, the Members of the Standing Committee, the Chancellor and the Treasurer.

The Officers and Committees of the Convocation were: Secretary, Rev. H. Forrester; Treasurer, Mr. W. K. P. Wilson; Committee on Constitution, Order of Proceedings, and Rules of Order, the Bishop exercising Jurisdiction, Rev. J. A. M. La Tourrette, Rev. H. Forrester, Hon. L. B. Prince, Hon. W. C. Hazledine; Committee on Common Fund for Church Work, Rev. H. Forrester, Rev. J. A. M. La Tourrette, Hon. W. C. Hazledine, Mr. W. T. Guyer.

At the second Convention, held under the presidency of the new Bishop, at Santa Fé, in July, 1881 A.D., the latter Committee reported, affirming the Common Treasury system to be the true Christian system, and urging that its underlying principle should by all means be preserved. It also recommended a plan to be used in the Jurisdiction providing for this end. The resolutions offered by the Committee were unanimously adopted, and thus the Missionary Jurisdiction of New Mexico and Arizona was the first Episcopal jurisdiction in the United States to declare, by its representative body, its acceptance of the financial system of the Primitive Church.

At the General Convention of 1880 A.D., the Rev. George K. Dunlop, Rector of Grace Church, Kirkwood, Mo., was elected to the vacant Episcopate. He was consecrated November 21 of the same year, in Christ Church, St. Louis, the Bishop of Minnesota being Consecrator, assisted by the Bishops of Missouri, Iowa, Quincy, and Springfield. The new Bishop reached Las Vegas, on his first visitation, December 2 following, and from there went on to Santa Fé, Albuquerque, and Mesilla. He took up his residence, with his family, at Santa Fé, March 31, 1881 A.D. After building a handsome stone church there, he moved to Las Vegas, where he still resides.

The progress of Church work during Bishop Dunlop's administration has been very encouraging. Churches have been built at Albuquerque, Tombstone, and Santa Fé, and rectories at Las Vegas and Tombstone. The value of Church property has increased from five thousand to forty thousand dollars. Confirmations have about doubled every succeeding year, and the increase in the number of Communicants has been in much higher ratio.

Statistics for 1886 A.D.: Clergy, 6; missions, 21; lay readers, 5; baptisms, 47; con., 32; com., 181; contr., $6721.

REV. H. FORRESTER.

New York, Diocese of. The first Convention of the Diocese of New York was held Wednesday, June 22, 1785 A.D. Up to the time New Amsterdam was ceded by the Dutch, its original owners, at the treaty of Breda, to the English, there was no service of any kind held in the English language. The change of ownership which took place transferred at once the garrison chapel to the English, and they forthwith introduced the services of their Church. Within these narrow walls it was limited for many years, until in 1696 A.D. a considerable number of the inhabitants met together and determined to have the worship of the Church of England settled among them. The result was the organization of the parish of Trinity Church, and the election of the Rev. Dr. Vesey as its first Rector. The new parish found zealous supporters in Governor Fletcher, by whom it was endowed temporarily, and in Lord Cornbury, his successor, who assigned it the freehold of a neighboring property, known as the King's Farm. The influence of the Church of England began now to increase in many towns, but especially in New York City. This was in a great measure owing to the Rev. Mr. Vesey, who by his conduct completely won the affections of the people. Outside of the city the Church was greatly indebted to the fostering care of the venerable Society for the Propagation of the Gospel in Foreign Parts. In 1702 A.D. the Rev. Mr. Barton became the missionary of the Society in Westchester, "a small town upon the seacoast," a few miles above New York, and made occasional journeys to New Rochelle, East Chester, Rye, Mamaroneck, and Bedford. The chief obstacle, however, in the way of the Church's progress was the lack of the Episcopate. All her spiritual children who were born here were growing up without the valued benefit of confirmation. Not one edifice for public worship had been consecrated. Our clergy and our parishes were destitute of that superintendence which is the very life of our Church government. Every candidate upon our shores who would be admitted to holy orders was compelled to seek ordination in the far-distant mother-country. A great gulf lay between,—an ocean of three thousand miles. No less than a fifth part of our young men who were destined for the LORD's service in the sanctuary—being exposed to various "perils in the sea"—paid with their lives the cost of the severe ecclesiastical requisition of the Church of England. Roman Catholics in North America had a Bishop, Francis Laval, as early as 1659 A.D., and the Moravians had four Bishops previous to the year 1750 A.D., but for the Church of England here there was not provided one spiritual Father to take "the oversight thereof." Queen Anne, in 1714 A.D., was propitious to the design, and but for her death it would soon have been accomplished. The first George also appeared favorable, but a dangerous rebellion concentrated all his thoughts and feelings on another object, and then "it was not time to attend to the subject of American Bishops." Thus the matter dragged slowly along until our national liberty gave it a new form.

It was several years after our civil independence when the plan of a General American Church, with an independent American Episcopate, was formed. Incipient measures for the organization of the Protestant Episcopal Church in the United States were first adopted by the Church in Pennsylvania. The earliest general meeting called expressly to consider this subject was at New York, in October, 1784 A.D., when clerical and lay deputies from the States of

Massachusetts, Rhode Island, Connecticut, New York, New Jersey, Pennsylvania, Delaware, and Maryland first took counsel together concerning the peculiar exigencies of the Church. A more numerous Convention of the deputies from several States, held at Philadelphia in September of the next year (1785 A.D.), prepared an address to the Archbishops and Bishops of the Church of England, requesting them to confer Episcopal consecration on such persons as might be recommended by the Church in the United States. The consent of the Archbishops and Bishops was obtained in 1786 A.D. Without delay the Rev. Dr. White, Bishop-elect of Pennsylvania, and the Rev. Dr. Provoost, Bishop-elect of New York, who had been chosen at the second Annual Convention of the Diocese, set sail for England. On their arrival they were consecrated in the chapel of the Archiepiscopal palace at Lambeth by the Archbishop of Canterbury, assisted by the Archbishop of York, the Bishop of Bath and Wells, and the Bishop of Peterboro', on Sunday, February 4, 1787 A.D. The new prelates soon set sail from England, and after a "very tedious and boisterous passage," during which Dr. Provoost was "so ill that it was feared he would not live," they reached New York, April 8, 1787 A.D., on Easter-Sunday.

The Diocese of New York could now rejoice in its first Bishop. The result was seen at once in the impetus given to the Church's growth. It is true the new Diocesan was not a man of magnetic character or a very ardent worker, but the Church in New York at last had found its proper head, and, in spite of adverse circumstances, continued to increase in power and public favor. Bishop Provoost remained for fourteen years in charge of the Diocese. At last, overwhelmed by the heart-rending loss of his wife in August, 1799 A.D., by the heart-rending death of his youngest and favorite son in the July following, and by many painful domestic and embarrassing official cares, he resigned the rectorship of Trinity Church in September, 1800 A.D., and his Episcopal jurisdiction at a meeting of the Convention in the year 1801 A.D. He was succeeded by the Rev. Dr. Benjamin Moore, who was chosen in December, 1800 A.D., Rector of Trinity Church, and Bishop of New York on the day after the first Bishop's resignation of the crosier. He was consecrated at Trenton, N. J., September 11, 1801 A.D. The Rt. Rev. Dr. White officiated as Presiding Bishop, and Bishops Clagget and Jarvis aided him in the performance of the primitive solemnity.

Of the second Bishop of New York it can be said, "He rose to public confidence and respect, and to general esteem solely by the force of talents and worth. His love for the Church was the paramount principle that animated him. He entered on her service in the time of trouble. Steady in his principles, yet mild and prudent in advocating them, he never sacrificed consistency,—he never provoked resentment. In proportion as adversity pressed upon the Church was the firmness of the affection with which he clung to her. And he lived until he saw her, in no inconsiderable degree by his counsel and exertions, raised from the dust and putting on the garments of glory and beauty. It was this affection for the Church which animated his Episcopal labors; which led him to leave that family whom he so tenderly loved, and that retirement which was so dear to him, and where he found while he conferred enjoyment, and to seek in remote parts of the Diocese for the sheep of CHRIST's fold." In 1811 A.D., his health having become greatly impaired, he suggested to the Convention the propriety and the necessity of an Assistant Bishop, and the request meeting with unanimous approval, the Rev. John Henry Hobart, one of the assistant ministers of Trinity Church, was elected upon the first ballot. The consecration of the Bishop-elect took place in Trinity Church, May 29, Bishop White officiating as Presiding Bishop, with Bishops Provoost and Jarvis as his assistants in the ceremonial. This was the turning-point in the history of the American Church. The war of the Revolution had made her unpopular with the multitude, who looked with disfavor upon her because of her British origin. Bare toleration was only accorded her, for no one, up to this time, had thought of claiming honor for her because of her Apostolic descent. In this state Bishop Hobart found matters, but their continuance in this state he would not endure. Trained in a Presbyterian college, he was a Churchman in the fullest conviction of his reason. He early declared his own principles to run up in brief into these two: "We are saved from the guilt and dominion of sin by the Divine merits and grace of a Crucified REDEEMER, and that the merits and grace of this REDEEMER are applied to the soul of the believer by humble and devout participation in the ordinances of the Church administered by a priesthood who derive their authority by regular transmission from the CHRIST, the Divine Head of the Church and the source of all the power in it."

As was to be expected, the enunciation and the enforcement of such sound views was followed by a marked increase of Church life. The Church began to be honored, because men for the first time found out that she was worthy of honor. Bishop Hobart, on the death of Bishop Moore, in 1812 A.D., became Diocesan of New York. From this time on his labors became more incessant to build up the Church of CHRIST in her ministry, in her ordinances, and her most holy faith; this was the great object which awakened his solicitude and called forth his incessant and untiring efforts. For several years before he was compelled to intermit his activities he recorded in his anniversary addresses seldom less than thirty and sometimes more than forty visitations of parishes widely separated. Added to this onerous toil were the charges which he delivered to the clergy of his Diocese, the various publications which he prepared for the press, the educational and beneficent institutions which he organized and watched over with unflagging interest. As was to be expected, his efforts were too exhaustive to be endured even by his vigorous frame. His health declined, and while making a visitation at Auburn he died, September 12, 1830 A.D., being fifty-five years of age. At a Convention of the Diocese held in the same month, the Rev. Benjamin Tredwell Onderdonk, one of the assistant ministers of Trinity Church, was elected as his successor. His consecration took place November 26, 1830 A.D. In 1838 A.D. the Diocese had attained such vast proportions that it became evident that one Bishop could not properly attend to it, and the result was the formation of the Western Diocese, Bishop Onderdonk retaining the eastern portion. Charges affecting the moral character of the Bishop having been made, he was tried in December, 1844 A.D., by the House of Bishops acting as a court, and after a long and searching investigation the court decided (eight voting for deposition and nine for suspension) that he be suspended from the office and functions of the ministry (January 3, 1845 A.D.). The Bishop never acknowledged himself to be guilty of the offenses imputed to him, and urgent efforts were made by his friends for the removal of the suspension.

After much delay the General Convention passed a Canon allowing a provisional Bishop to be chosen. The choice fell upon Jonathan Mayhew Wainwright, an assistant minister of Trinity Church, who was consecrated November 10, 1852 A.D. The arduous duties of the Episcopate, greatly enhanced by the long period the Diocese had been without an acting head, proved to be too great for the new Diocesan. He died in New York, September 21, 1854 A.D. At the next Convention Horatio Potter, Rector of St. Peter's Church, Albany, was elected to the vacant Episcopate, and consecrated November 22, 1854 A.D. During Bishop Potter's long and wise administration the Church in New York has seen its most prosperous years. Parishes have multiplied; the number of the clergy has increased sixty- and a hundred-fold; educational institutions, hospitals, orphan asylums have been established; vast sums of money for foreign and domestic missions and other charitable purposes have been contributed. In 1868 A.D. the Church had become so unwieldy from its vast growth that the new Dioceses of Albany and Long Island were set off. In 1883 A.D., the health of Bishop Potter having become impaired, the Convention at his request consented to the election of an assistant Bishop, and Henry Codman Potter, a nephew of the Diocesan, and Rector of Grace Church, New York, was chosen with singular unanimity

to fill the place. The assistant Bishop-elect was consecrated in Grace Church, October 20, 1883 A.D., in the presence of a vast assemblage of the clergy and laity, by the venerable Presiding Bishop, Dr. Smith, of Kentucky.

Statistics for 1886 A.D.: Clergy, 331; parishes and chapels, 200; candidates for H. O., 40; ordination, D. 18, P. 15; baptisms, 6480; con., 3895; com., 44,728; contributions, $2,721,964.60.

REV. E. GUILBERT, D.D.

Niobrara. (*Vide* SOUTH DAKOTA.) The Rev. William Hobart Hare, D.D., was consecrated in 1873 A.D. as a Bishop having special charge of work among the Indians. Bishop Hare, in his report of 1880 A.D., states that he had traveled during his spring and summer visitations 2000 miles in his wagon, besides not a little stage-coaching. He found most of the Indian tribes friendly, and a number had presented themselves for confirmation. In the seven and a half years of his mission there had been 4 boarding-schools established, in which 115 children were cared for, and 10 new congregations gathered "among the wilder and remoter tribes." Eleven mission residences and 10 churches had been built and paid for. The Bishop considers the Indians like other people in character, and thinks that they have been treated too much in a special way "as a strange people." The report announces the death of the faithful missionary, the Rev. E. J. K. Lessell, who had been a pioneer in the Black Hills. The Bishop gratefully acknowledges the aid of the female missionaries, as well as the wives of the clergy in his field, and the ladies' associations who had sent aid for the work. There had been 120 confirmations in Niobrara.

In the Santee Mission, Rev. W. W. Fowler and his wife had taken six lads into their house to be taught English and trained in Christian life, and to assist on the Mission farm. The Yankton Mission had been under the care of the veteran missionary, Rev. Jos. W. Cook. Sister Julia had done a merciful work in the homes of the people in this mission as a Deaconess, and in Emmanuel House, under her charge, in which "were persons recovering from severe surgical operations, and sick women and children who could not be cared for in their own miserable homes." In the Yanktonnais Mission a number of the Indians, led by the Lay-reader and two or three Christian Indians, had formed themselves into a Co-operative Farmers' Association, to encourage each other in farming and building houses. Most of them had been heathen, but at the Bishop's visitation they enrolled themselves as catechumens. When the Bishop, the evening before their admission, gave an outline of the Christian religion and the duties of civilized life, he asked with regard to each duty, "'Will you try to do it?' their earnest answers (writes the Bishop), 'How' (or yes) were only less impressive than the scene when we closed our interview by all standing up and repeating, they after me, the Apostles' Creed." After Baptism and Confirmation the Bishop "celebrated with the native congregation in the Eucharist the death of Him who gathers together in one the children of GOD who are scattered abroad."

The Lower Brule Mission had been faithfully and patiently conducted by the native Presbyter, Rev. Luke C. Walker, and his assistants. The Cheyenne Agency Mission was under the charge of the Rev. H. Swift, the tribes being under the "admirable management of Captain Schwan, U.S.A., Acting Agent." The people had progressed, and the Church had grown. The Indians were inclined to settle on farms, and Mr. Swift had planted himself on the Missouri River, where the conditions were favorable to farm life. A church and parsonage had been built near by, and paid for by friends in Connecticut. One of the chiefs here wrote the Bishop, "Let all our friends hear these words. We long for life. Help us more and more." Upper Brule Mission was under Rev. W. J. Cleveland. A number of white men who had married among the Sioux were identified with this Mission, and helpful in it. The congregation was large and the worship hearty; they took pride in their church building, and gave liberally towards its embellishment. In the Ogalala, or Pine Ridge Mission, likewise under Mr. Cleveland, Mrs. J. J. Astor had given a church, which was soon to be completed. The Bishop urges the need of constant Christian care over Indians giving up their wild life and striving after civilization. The work of the Church in this case must be tireless and incessant.

Most of the clergy have now learned the language of the Indians, and the Prayer-Book, a Hymn-Book, the King's Highway, and the Calvary Catechism have been translated into their tongue by them, while others have given the natives the Bible in the vernacular. "No words can express too emphatically the blessing these versions have been." "The secret of any success the Missionaries in Niobrara have had lies largely in the fact that they have taken up their homes among the people, and made them hear in their own tongues wherein they were born the wonderful works of GOD." Still, the Bishop has thought it best to press the study of the English language in the schools. He has striven to break down "the middle wall of partition" between whites and Indians.

In the District of Niobrara in 1883 A.D. the Bishop baptized 26 adults and 15 infants, and confirmed 117 persons. Then he visited the Chapel of the Redeemer in a farming population, where in a heavy rain 70 assembled from their scattered houses and 36 "participated in the celebration of the Holy Communion." Of the Rev. Mr. Cook's work in the Yankton Mission the Bishop says, "This Mission was begun in the year 1869 A.D. by Rev. Paul Mazakute. In 1870 A.D. the Rev. J. W. Cook took charge. He has seen the whole people pass from tent to log house life, and has presented 293 persons for confirmation." There is a central church, which serves as the Bishop's church, and two chapels, each fifteen miles distant. Mrs. Fox, assisted by Angelique Gayton, had done an excellent work in Emmanuel House, though a sacred duty of paramount importance had called her away, causing a suspension in the special work until a successor could be secured. The Yanktonnais (Crow Creek) Mission is under Rev. H. Burt. Springfield Mission is supervised by W. J. Wicks, Catechist and Layreader. Hope School is located there. In the Black Hills Mission, Deadwood, there has been a vacancy since the death of Rev. Dr. Pennell, in May, 1882 A.D. In his Boarding-School work, Bishop Hare has followed "the plan of having small schools (none exceeding 36 scholars), that family life, as contrasted with that of an institution, may be preserved, and that the personal contact of the officers with each individual scholar may be frequent and familiar." These schools are at four different points, that the "centres of heat and light may be distributed as much as possible." For Hope School, Springfield, he has secured a superb site and subscriptions of $4000. In reviewing the Mission's history the Bishop finds much cheer. The "fantastic gear of the savage" and "the hideous orgies of heathen dances" have given place to "25 congregations of decently dressed worshipers, aggregating an *average* attendance of 1160 Indians, who gather every Sunday and offer in prayers and spiritual songs their homage to Almighty GOD, as revealed in His love and holiness in His beloved SON." Churches and chapels dot the wilderness, with comfortable parsonages at their side. During the three years preceding the report of 1883 A.D. there had been 864 infants and 468 adults baptized. During the preceding ten years nearly 900 had been confirmed.

Statistics for 1886 A.D. (including South Dakota): Clergy, 29; parishes and missions, 65; candidates for H. O., 3; ordinations diac., 1; pr., 2; baptisms, 660; con., 167; com., 1314; contr., $11,246.23.

REV. S. F. HOTCHKIN.

Noah, whose name signifies "rest," was the tenth from Adam in the line of Seth At his birth, his father Lamech, in choosing a name, and expressing a hope for the child, uttered (possibly unconsciously) a prophecy of his future office and function. "And he called his name Noah, saying, This same shall comfort us concerning our work and toil of our hands, because of the ground which the LORD hath cursed" (Gen. v. 29). "Clearly there is an almost prophetic feeling in the name which he gives his son, and hence some Christian writers have seen in the language a prophecy of the MESSIAH, and have supposed that as Eve was mistaken on the birth of Cain, so Lamech in like manner was deceived in his hope of Noah. But there is no reason to infer from the language of the narrative that the hopes of either were of so definite a nature." When Noah was about five hundred years old the wickedness of man had become such that the LORD resolved upon the destruction of the human race, still allowing a respite of one hundred and twenty years for repentance. It must have been during this interval that Noah became a "preacher of righteousness," if in no other way, by his upright conduct, whereby he found grace in the eyes of the LORD, and by his obedience to the command to build an ark and prepare for the threatened flood. The very interesting questions called up by the name of Noah, relative to the wickedness of the antediluvians, the building of the ark, the extent of the flood, etc., are here passed over in silence, it being intended only to say so much as will show how Noah was a type of CHRIST, and his whole story a great prophetic forepicturing of salvation of the world from a flood of sin by CHRIST and in the Church of CHRIST. We may see this in his name, which means rest; in his office of a preacher of righteousness; and in his preparation of an ark of salvation for his sons who believed him; all these clearly foreshadow Him who has prepared a rest which remaineth for the people of GOD; whose Gospel is preached as the word of life to them that receive it; and whose Church is the sole ark and refuge of safety from the flood of sin which threatens to overwhelm the soul of man in eternal death.

Authorities: Bible Commentary, Dictionary of the Bible.

Nocturns. Services held anciently during the night. The night was divided into three parts and an office recited at each, while lauds was recited at dawn. But finally the three nocturn services were said together with lauds at a single office. The Psalter was divided so as to form certain portions, the first of fourteen, the second of three, and the third of three Psalms, and then when the nocturns were dropped the Psalms, with their nocturn titles, passed into the matin office. So it is also a name for a portion of the Psalter.

Nominalism (*nomen*, a name) is the doctrine that general notions, such as the notion of a tree, have no realities corresponding to them, and have no existence but as names or words. The doctrine directly opposed to it is Realism. "The Nominalists were called Terminists about the time of the Reformation." "The Terminists, among whom I was, are so called because they speak of a thing in its own proper words, and do not apply them after a strange sort. They are also called Occamists, from Ockham, their founder. He was an able and a sensible man." (Luther's Table-Talk, Krauth's Fleming's Vocab. of Philos.; see also Cousin's Hist. Mod. Philos. on Nominalism and Realism.)

Nomination. In the English Church it is the naming of a clerk to the Patron, who has the right to present to the Bishop the name of the clergyman to whom he would present the living. The right to nominate and to present may be in one person, or each may be vested in separate persons; and if either person misuse his right, the right is forfeited to the Queen. But in our own Church all this is done away. Not but that the right to nominate exists, and is constantly exercised in connection with the right to present, though neither right bears such a title. A clergyman is usually nominated by some one to the Vestry, and they elect, and often without reference to the Bishop, whose consent is assumed (or the need of such consent is disregarded or overlooked); they present to the accepting clergyman, who accepts with perhaps as little reference to the Ordinary. It is an informality which should not be allowed, and to correct which was evidently the purpose of the Office of Institution. The Vestry is the presenting body, and rightly so, but it also arrogates to itself the right of induction, which (if the Institution office is of obligation) can belong only to the Bishop.

Nonconformity. The refusal to conform to the rites, ceremonies, or tenets of the National Church. In every era of her history as parted into National Churches there have been Nonconformists. Nor is it necessary to suppose that they really held in all cases unorthodox or heretical doctrines. A Nonconformist is one who does not yield that conformity to the observances and ritual of the Church of his nationality; but he may be very orthodox in his creed. The modern idea of nonconformity begins with the Puritan troubles in Queen Elizabeth's times. Nonconformists passed easily into Separatists (can. ix. of 1603 A.D.), and this became their title till it was replaced by the more recent name Dissenter. (*Vide* DISSENTER.) It was because the Church and State were identical in interest, and in fact the theory of both the parties, that Nonconformity was dangerous to the State, as the Rebellion of 1640 A.D. proved. There was then no conception that there could be any severance between Church and State. That is an idea of modern times, and practically carried out in this country. Here there can be no such thing as Dissent in the sense in which it is used in England. Nonconformity here is upon a wholly different footing, and can only be thought of as existing for those who do not admit the claims of the Church upon them, and is therefore merely a relative term between two separate organizations. The same objection lies against the use of the term Dissenter. The Church is here in the position of dissent (and very rightly) towards the religious bodies around her, as well as they towards her. It is only upon the deeper and surer ground of a (willing or unwilling) schism from her organization and of revolt from her rightful claims that here we can apply the terms of Nonconformity, or Separation, or Dissent to those who may be as zealous as ourselves. The position of religious bodies in this country renders the union on important matters hereafter much easier than elsewhere. The real division has ever lain in the totally different conception of the nature and Divine authority of the Church. When there is unity on this, a broad Catholic Conformity will be more than possible.

Nones. A word used in the English Calendar, derived from the ancient Roman Kalendars. The nones were the fifth day of each month (except March, May, July, October, when the nones fell on the seventh day). They were so called as they were the ninth day before the Ides, on which time, in the older lunar months, the full moon appeared. So the nones fell on the completion of the first quarter and the ides on the second quarter.

Non-Jurors. Those who in the revolution of 1688 A.D. refused the oath of allegiance to William and Mary. The oaths were tendered to be taken by the 1st of August upon pain of suspension, and deprivation was to follow if the refusal to take them was persisted in.

Archbishop Sancroft and eight Bishops refused. But two of them died before being suspended, and one other before deprivation was enforced. About four hundred clergy followed their example and were deprived of their benefices. The non-jurors acted conscientiously upon the well-known principles of passive obedience, though but a few years before, in the conflict between King James II. and the Church, seven of the Bishops, and Ken the chiefest of them, preferred imprisonment to yielding to the King. But that was yet only a passive resistance. It was a civil question indeed, and they were deprived uncanonically and by force of the civil power. They were in a troubled position indeed, and under all the circumstances bore themselves very nobly. Still, they acted in one important matter in a way that has been condemned. Three had died, Ken and Frampton stood aloof, but Archbishop Sancroft decided that it was right to consecrate a new Bishop to preserve the Apostolical succession, since in the confusions of the moment it seemed to them very doubtful if King William would continue the present connection of the Church and the State, and Presbyterianism might obtain political and ecclesiastical ascendency. He died, however, before the consecration of Dr. Hickes, which took place under his sanction 1693 A.D. Other consecrations followed, but beyond this first step their act becomes indefensible, since afterwards the Church's future was established beyond doubt. One of the last of those consecrated by the non-jurors to keep up their line, Taylor (consecrated 1721 A.D.), visited this country afterwards. But the non-jurors were in every respect men of great ability. The studies of Bret and Nelson in the history and the uses of our Prayer-Book are of the highest value. Dodwell, Collier, and Carte in history, Kettlewell, Spinkes, Law, and Nelson in devotional theology, Lawrence, Law, and Leslie in controversial theology, are mighty names even yet, and their influence was and is very great. The schism, for such it became, slowly died out, and at last, in 1799 A.D., the last non-juring Bishop quietly renounced his schism and was received into communion in the English National Church.

Norman. *Vide* ARCHITECTURE.

North Carolina, Diocese of. This Diocese, as at present constituted, embraces the entire State of North Carolina, with its 52,286 square miles. The civil divisions of the State are into ninety-six counties; the total population, including a few Indians, is 1,399,750 by the census of 1880 A.D.

The ecclesisastical divisions of the Diocese are into six Missionary Convocations, viz.: of Edenton, of Newbern, of Wilmington, of Raleigh, of Charlotte, and of Morganton. The Convocations at present organized and in operation are those of Edenton, of Raleigh, of Charlotte, and of Morganton. The other subdivisions of the Diocese are Parishes and Mission Stations, the latter being entirely under the Bishop's control, and being entitled to one delegate in the Convention, but not to a vote.

History of the Church in North Carolina. —The first services of the Church in the territory now constituting the United States were on the coast of North Carolina. Raleigh's first expedition landed at Roanoke Island in July, 1584 A.D. August 13, 1587 A.D., Manteo, an Indian chief, was baptized at Roanoke Island, the first Indian convert; and a few days after, Virginia Dare, the first white child born in America of English parents. In Harriot's Narrative, 1586 A.D., we have an interesting account of the efforts of that distinguished scientist to convey to the minds of the aborigines some knowledge of the facts and doctrines of the Christian religion.

No permanent settlement, however, was effected until about 1662 A.D., and for many years after that date the Province was destitute of religious services. In 1701 A.D. the Assembly passed an act for the support of the Church, but it came to nothing. About 1702 A.D. a church was built, probably near where the town of Edenton now stands. In the same year Dr. Blay, Commissary of the Bishop of London, sent the first minister of the Church into the Province, Daniel Brett (who officiated only a few months), and with him a small collection of books, which were kept at Bath, and constituted the first public library in North Carolina.

In 1704 A.D. the Society for the Propagation of the Gospel in Foreign Parts sent its first missionary, the Rev. Mr. Blair, and others from time to time, until in 1770 A.D.

there seem to have been eighteen ministers regularly settled in as many parishes, mostly east of Hillsboro; Salisbury being the only place farther west which had a minister. The western counties were settled chiefly by Presbyterians, with a good many German Lutherans, and a flourishing colony of Moravians about Salem. But the Church never had any really healthy existence during this period. It suffered the disadvantages of a State connection without enjoying the supposed compensating benefits. The laws in its favor could not be enforced where its adherents were not a majority of the freeholders, and when enforced they were insufficient to effect their purpose, while they served to check individual effort. But the annals of this period are not altogether barren. The names of Clement Hall, Thomas Burgess, Nathaniel Blount, and other faithful missionaries are preserved in honor for their works' sake. And the true remedy for the low condition of Church life was plain to some of the prominent laymen. Governor Dobbs writes once and again to the Society urging the absolute necessity of sending Bishops to America, and Governor Tryon, in a letter of July 31, 1765 A.D., presses upon the Society the importance of a larger number of ministers, saying that a majority of the whole population remained attached to the Church, although almost entirely deprived of her ministrations. It was probably owing to the efforts of Governor Tryon that the number of ministers in the Province rose from five in 1765 A.D. to eighteen in 1770 A.D.

The results of the Revolution seemed altogether disastrous to the Church. Most of her congregations were deprived of their ministers, and a very bitter popular prejudice arose against her. Her churches and chapels were deserted, her property fell into the hands of others, who in some instances still retain it, and her voice was hardly heard in the land.

In 1790 A.D., at the suggestion of Bishop White, an effort was made to revive the Church in North Carolina. Meetings of clergy and laity were held in Tarboro' in June and November, 1790 A.D., in November, 1793 A.D., and in May, 1794 A.D. At this last meeting six clergymen (including one in Lutheran orders) and a small number of prominent laymen were present. A Constitution was adopted, Deputies to the General Convention and a Standing Committee were appointed, and the Rev. Charles Pettigrew was chosen Bishop. Mr. Pettigrew set out to attend the General Convention of 1795 A.D., but was providentially prevented from accomplishing his journey, and seems never to have felt able to undertake the work afterwards. Thus this attempt to organize the Church failed. The Colonial Church was an infant which never learned to walk alone, and by 1800 A.D. seemed to be dead beyond hope of resurrection.

In November, 1816 A.D., the Rev. Bethel Judd, of Connecticut, and the Rev. Adam Empie, of New York, traveling for their health, met in the city of Wilmington. Finding a church and a congregation, they began to officiate regularly. In January, 1817 A.D., the Rev. Jehu Curtis Clay became Rector of the Church in Newbern. On Easter-Monday, 1817 A.D., Mr. Judd organized a Church in Fayetteville. These three clergymen, with delegates from their several parishes, and with one layman also from the Church in Edenton, met in Newbern, April 2, 1817 A.D., and organized the Diocese of North Carolina, requesting Bishop Moore, of Virginia, to take Episcopal oversight thereof. He consented to do so, and in 1819, 1820, 1821, and 1822 A.D. made brief visitations to the chief places in the Diocese and presided in the Annual Conventions.

In 1823 A.D. the clergy numbered seven, and the communicants four hundred and eighty. The Convention resolved to elect a Bishop. It was felt that a man must be found who should be able to assert with boldness, and to maintain with power, the true position and doctrines of the Church, then but little appreciated among many of her professed children. Providence had provided such a man. In the very month in which the Diocese was organized, April, 1817 A.D., a Virginia planter, forty-five years of age, John Stark Ravenscroft, had been ordained Deacon by Bishop Moore. Six years later, when the Church in North Carolina came to choose a Bishop, the youngest of her Priests, William M. Green, at present Bishop of Mississippi, rose in the Convention, and told his brethren what he had seen of the work of this laborer, who, although called so late into the vineyard, seemed by his zeal and strength to be "*earning more than his penny.*" Mr. Ravenscroft was personally known to no other member of the Convention, but he was elected unanimously by both orders on the first ballot, April 12, 1823 A.D. He was consecrated May 22 following. He found in the Diocese only seven clergymen (one of whom soon after withdrew from the Church), and a few weak and scattered congregations. As he is said to have expressed his work, "he could only assert the true position and claims of the Church, and strike dismay to the hearts of her adversaries." But the world instinctively knows greatness, and he became at once a power in the State. He fed his flock with a faithful and true heart, and ruled them prudently with all his power until his death, March 5, 1830 A.D., and he left an impression upon his Diocese which time has not effaced.

The Rev. Levi Silliman Ives was chosen Bishop of North Carolina by an all but unanimous vote, May 21, 1831 A.D., and was consecrated September 22 following. He found in the Diocese, clergy, fifteen; communicants, eight hundred and nine. The history of his active and, in its earlier stages, most effective Episcopate cannot be properly summarized in the space at command. His successor found forty clergy and over two thousand communicants in the Diocese. Besides inspiring his clergy with self-denying missionary zeal, and setting them an example of earnest missionary work, he struggled nobly to establish permanent institutions for religious and secular instruction. The Episcopal School at Raleigh, Trinity School, and the School at Valle Crucis failed, but the necessities of the Church to-day emphasize the wisdom of those attempts. St. Mary's School is founded on the failure of the Episcopal School, although the Church has entirely lost the beautiful property and the large sums of money invested in it.

It was very largely by reason of practices and teachings said to prevail in the school at Valle Crucis that suspicions of the Bishop's faithfulness to the Church began to be widely entertained throughout the Diocese, as is noticed in the report of the Committee on the State of the Church to the Convention of 1849 A.D. After several years of doubt and distress to the Diocese, and of painful vacillation on the part of the Bishop, he obtained leave of absence, and six months' salary in advance, in September, 1852 A.D., for the ostensible purpose of traveling for his own and his wife's health. He went abroad soon after, and on the 22d of the following December addressed a letter from Rome to the Convention of the Diocese, announcing his abandonment of the Church and his intended submission to the Pope of Rome.

May 28, 1853 A.D., the Rev. Thomas Atkinson, D.D., Rector of Grace Church, Baltimore, was chosen Bishop, and was consecrated October 18 following. His administration secured at once the perfect confidence of his people, and prevented any of those disastrous consequences which might have been feared from the defection of his predecessor.

The civil war which broke out in 1861 A.D. necessitated the organization of the Church in the Confederate States, with its General and Diocesan *Councils*; and all the energies of the Church in North Carolina were called out to supply the spiritual wants of her people at home and in the field. Prayer-Books and Testaments were imported from England; Catechisms and Tracts were printed at home; and a fund was begun for the establishment of a Diocesan Divinity and Training School. Some of the ablest and most zealous of the clergy became Chaplains of regiments, and many of those who retained charge of their parishes followed the example of the Bishop in giving part of their time and attention to the soldiers, in camp or in the hospitals.

It was in the wreck which followed the overthrow of the Confederacy in 1865 A.D. that the character of Bishop Atkinson appeared in its true greatness. His wisdom, firmness, and simple devotion to duty, guided by an enlightened appreciation of true Church principles, were of lasting service to the Church at large. It is now admitted that the presence of Bishop Atkinson with his full delegation of clergy and laity (this being the only Southern Diocese so represented) at the General Council of 1865 A.D., and especially the wisdom and firmness with which he met the delicate issues of that critical time, made the immediate and perfectly harmonious reunion of the Northern and Southern Dioceses possible. Their presence secured from their Northern brethren not only perfect fairness, which might have been expected in any case, but the most delicate courtesy in all the proceedings relative to the separation and to the terms of reunion, and so made it morally impossible for the Southern Dioceses to refuse to return.

Another most important question Bishop Atkinson and his Diocese settled at once by taking the true churchly position in the face of much popular prejudice. There has never been any distinction made in the Conventions since 1865 A.D. between white and colored ministers or members of the Church. All meet in the Councils of the Church on common ground. In the interest of the colored people, and especially to supply them with competent teachers of their own race, St. Augustine's Normal School and Collegiate Institute was founded in 1867 A.D., chiefly by the efforts of the Rev. J. Brinton Smith, its first principal. To this has been added a Theological department, for the education of colored candidates for orders.

The Ravenscroft Associate Mission and Training School, at Asheville, was founded by Bishop Atkinson for the evangelizing of the mountain regions, and for the training of candidates for orders of this Diocese.

Soon after the war the Bishop began to find the care of so extensive a Diocese too much for one man; and from 1867 to 1873 A.D. he advocated the division of the Diocese at the earliest practicable moment. In the latter year, May 30, the Rev. Theodore Benedict Lyman, D.D., of San Francisco, was elected Assistant Bishop, and was consecrated December 11 following. Bishop Atkinson died January 4, 1881 A.D., and Bishop Lyman became Bishop of the Diocese.

The movement for division, begun by Bishop Atkinson in 1867 A.D., was never allowed to drop altogether. It was renewed from time to time, and at the last Convention, May, 1883 A.D., was carried by a very large majority of both orders. By the action of the General Convention, a new Diocese was erected in the eastern part of the State, comprising the counties of Hertford, Bertie, Martin, Pitt, Green, Wayne, Sampson, Cumberland, and Robeson, with all that portion of the State lying between the said counties and the Atlantic Ocean. The new Diocese has taken the name of East Carolina, and has elected Rev. A. A. Watson, D.D., to be its first Bishop.

Statistics from the Journal of 1883.—
Bishop, 1; Priests, 53; Deacons, 22; total,
76. Candidates for orders (including 11 of
the above Deacons, who are candidates for
Priest's orders), 22; postulants, 11; total,
33. Parishes, 87; mission stations, 30;
total, 117. Communicants, 5889. Total
contributions reported, $61,817.69.
REV. J. B. CHESHIRE, JR.

North Dakota. This new jurisdiction,
formed by the General Convention of 1883,
comprises the portion of Dakota Territory
north of the 46th parallel. Its population
in 1880 was 100,000, but emigration is flowing
into Dakota with wonderful rapidity. The
jurisdiction contains 50,000 square miles.
It had been under the care of Bishop Clarkson,
of Nebraska. The Rev. Wm. D.
Walker having been elected as Missionary
Bishop, was consecrated in Calvary Church,
New York, December 20, 1883. He was
"born in New York City in 1840. Graduated
from Trinity School and Columbia
College, New York. Ordered Deacon in
1862. He was at once appointed minister in
charge of Calvary Chapel, New York, and
this charge he retained up to his elevation
to the Episcopate."

Statistics.—Baptized, 117; confirmations,
85; Sunday-school scholars, 600; total of
contributions, $15,386.10.

The fifteenth Annual Convocation will
meet at the call of the Bishop.

Authorities: Whittaker's Prot. Epis.
Almanac and the Living Church Almanac.

North Side. Some years ago the position
of the celebrant in the Holy Communion
was seriously debated, the determination of
it depending upon the meaning of the term
in the rubric,—" Standing at the north side
of the Table." In ordinary terms the meaning
would be clearly that side of the table
standing at which the Priest faces south
when celebrating. But the term in the rubric
was really taken from the older rubrics
of the Latin service-books in the English
use; there it clearly means the northern side
of that edge next the congregation, and not
the northern end of the Holy Table. It is
really a matter of rubrical conformity and
obedience. And the principle of interpretation
chosen should be as naturally the
meaning that belonged to the words, which
were transferred from the older use into the
English Prayer-Book.

Northern California, Missionary Jurisdiction of. Bishop Kip in 1871 A.D., and again
in 1873 A.D., urged upon his clergy the need
of relief from the increasing burdens of his
growing Diocese, which was of too great an
extent for his powers. The suggestion was
acted upon, and the Convention seriously
took up the consideration of the division of
the Diocese, and in two successive Conventions
received reports upon it, which took
finally this shape at the Convention of
1874 A.D.

"This proposed *Missionary Diocese* contains
twenty-five (25) counties, or all the
territory north of the southern boundaries
of Sonoma, Napa, Sacramento, Amador, El
Dorado Counties. This section is remarkable
for its varied characteristics and solid
capacity for the sustenance of a dense population.
The Sacramento Valley is noted for
its immense crops of wheat, barley, oats,
fruits, and vegetables. The timber is without
practical limit. The gold, silver, and
quicksilver mines of California are chiefly
in this northern section of the State, and,
in the opinions of scientific men, their richest
points have not yet been touched. At no
very distant day the fisheries of Northern
California will realize vast sums of money."
It was anticipated that a large population
would soon fill up this section. In the imagination
of the Committee there existed
"the healthy germ of a magnificent Diocese."
They spoke to the General Convention
of *nine self-sustaining* parishes, 600
communicants, and 17 Presbyters; of the
offerings for that year being $20,000 (twenty
thousand dollars), and of a population of
210,000 people. They also assured the
General Convention that 20 missionary
stations could be started at once, and they
closed their petition thus: "In the name of
the neglected souls for whom CHRIST died,
and for the sake of the *millions* who will
soon be pressing to these shores, we beg," etc.
With such a presentation and plea, with
such a prospect for the Church, there was
nothing left for the House of Bishops to do
but accede to the pleading of the Diocese of
California, and accordingly on the 28th day
of October, the House of Bishops then in
session in New York City, the General Convention
elected for Bishop of Northern California,
the Rev. John Henry Ducachet
Wingfield, D.D., LL.D., Rector of St.
Paul's Church, Petersburg, Va. On the
29th of October the nomination was unanimously
confirmed.

The Rev. Dr. Wingfield was consecrated
on the 2d of December, 1874 A.D., in St.
Paul's Church, Petersburg, Va.

In 1870 A.D. the jurisdiction covered a
territory of 52,000 square miles, with an accredited
population of 214,000. The census
of 1875 A.D. estimated that there were 2464
Indians and 24,980 Chinese. Thus the Diocese
was inaugurated without anything being
guaranteed towards the support of the
Bishop. And what the Committee would
understand by "only a temporary charge,"
when it asked the General Church for this
division, we cannot conjecture. There is but
one town of any size, Sacramento, which
has a population of 25,000, and which, however,
finds a difficulty in supporting the
parish. It was so when the division was
made. The report of the Committee certainly
leaves a false impression with one who
is unacquainted with the jurisdiction. It
raises hopes with Eastern Churchmen, which
not being realized, bring upon the Bishop
and his missionaries their severe criticisms.
If there is such an opportunity for the Church

to grow,—" the germ of a magnificent Diocese,"—why does it not discover itself? The question is naturally asked, and not unkindly. The Bishop is expected with such *proposed* materials to accomplish a great deal. And if he does not, then the censures fall upon him. He, and the General Convention also, was influenced by this imaginary portrayal. There was nothing for him to do which could not have been done by the Bishop of California, or by an Assistant Bishop. And even supposing that there were these *prospects* for a Diocese, the migratory habits of the people are such as to forbid any reliance being placed upon them. And this Committee seemed to place great importance upon these districts.

The *Primary* Convocation was held in Grace Church, Sacramento, May, 1875 A.D. There were fourteen clergymen connected with the jurisdiction, eight of whom were present, with fourteen laymen. There were eighteen parishes and missions from which reports were received.

The Convocation, with the consent of the Bishop, placed itself under the Canons of California.

Bishop Wingfield said in his first address to his clergy and laity, " One thing must be established in the minds and hearts of the people,—that the Jurisdiction of Northern California is most emphatically a Missionary District. There is not, so far as I know, any point where the Church supports herself after the Apostolic pattern. There is scarcely a congregation which is legitimately independent. There is not a clergyman whose support is guaranteed by the even and regular contributions of the people. There is scarcely a Church building unencumbered by debt."

The first year's work of the Bishop shows: services at which he had officiated, 405; sermons preached, 104; lectures and addresses, 74; baptisms, 43; confirmations, 214; Church buildings consecrated, 1; lots for Church secured, 3; holy communions, 28.

Thus he was busily engaged daily about the Master's work, and no one but himself knows how great the strain upon him, and the discomfort, disappointment, absolute distress and fatigue he endured in this first year's work. There was no enthusiasm, no defined Churchmanship, no hearty greeting to meet him in his work. He had not found the nine self-sustaining parishes of which the Committee had spoken, nor had he crossed the tidal wave of immigration to which it alluded. There was much work for the Church, but he had left as important work for this. It was not of sufficient importance *per se* to claim a Bishop's sole and undivided attention. There is an air of sadness in this peroration of his second address: " I sympathize with you in all your trials, and earnestly pray for your success in winning souls. I know that the tongue of the ungodly is always ready to blame your most faithful efforts, and perhaps to praise what may not be pleasing to your Heavenly FATHER. Let us strengthen ourselves in the sublime Faith of Him who was unmoved by earthly approval or disapproval. Let us make little of human censure and less of human praise, and, fixing our eyes on the Master, think of His judgment, of His strict scrutiny, and of His just rewards."

It remains that we speak of the institutions which give character to the jurisdiction.

The College of St. Augustine was founded May, 1867 A.D., by Dr. J. L. Breck, who came from the Indian Mission, and is located at Benecia.

Bishop Wingfield took charge of the College, June, 1875 A.D. It was not ready-made by any means when he took charge; it was a burden he should have been spared, and is almost too much for a Bishop in whose Diocese neither learning nor religion are regarded as of the supremest importance. " The College of St. Augustine," he says to the Convocation in 1878 A.D., " has received much of my immediate and personal attention since my last report, the hard times rendering it necessary to husband finances in order to meet obligations. This is a sad and weary work for me, and more especially because I have grave doubts as to its compatibility with the duties of my office as a Bishop of the Church of GOD. Alone, unaided, and meeting opposition at all points, I feel that my cross is sometimes too heavy indeed for me to carry." From this time the College received his personal oversight. In 1880 A.D. it was indebted to him for the sum of nearly $17,000. The Board of Trustees had determined to rent or sell the property to meet the mortgages, amounting to $20,000. Failing in this, Bishop Wingfield, desiring to save the College and the Church, determined to assume the whole debt of $38,490.20.

Another feature in the Diocesan work of the jurisdiction which marks its life is *St. Mary of the Pacific*. The property had been purchased by Dr. Breck with money raised in the East, a large contributor being William H. Aspinwall, and in his will it was to be under a Board of Trustees chosen from both Dioceses. Dr. Breck had mortgaged the property to a bank in San Francisco. The interest on the debt had not been paid during his lifetime, and at his death the Trustees were called upon for both interest and principal. The Board was unwilling to assume the obligations, and the property was ordered to be sold. On the 12th of June, 1877 A.D., it was sold at public auction, Bishop Wingfield being the highest bidder. He thus came to the rescue, hoping that Churchmen would at least assist him in its payment. Instead of which, on the 1st of January, 1878 A.D., he found himself responsible for the sum of $18,411.20, bearing interest at the rate of ten per cent. per annum.

He says, "I have regretted my well-meant action at the auction sale in San Francisco, and been sometimes tempted to despair."

Another burden, through the sloth and indifference of Churchmen, is added to his shoulders. Now he has two schools for which he is personally responsible. In 1879 A.D. he placed *St. Mary of the Pacific* under the charge of the Rev. L. D. Mansfield, who has continued his work to the present year. Mr. Mansfield was to pay a nominal rent of $500 for the year ending June 1, 1880 A.D. This sum being below the interest on $23,000 would not justify the Bishop in accepting it beyond the first year.

In 1881 A.D., Bishop Wingfield thus speaks of St. Augustine's and St. Mary's: "The two Boards of Trustees have abandoned all thought of the Institutions over whose interests they were appointed by the Churchmen of the whole State, and have thrown all the burden of debt and stigma of failure on the shoulders of one man, and he a Missionary Bishop of the Church, with a Parish to look after, and having the care of all the churches besides. But he is not discouraged. Abandoned by the parent Diocese, unsustained by his own Jurisdiction, without a dollar of endowment, overwhelmed with debt, without a word of encouragement from the millionaires of this State, who are rolling in wealth, which they are hoarding for selfish ends, unrepresented by a single layman of our Church,—he will continue to stand by his work to the last."

And the future will tell that he has acted wisely. His work is improving, and a Blessing will rest upon so unselfish an undertaking to which he has given, amidst the sneering smiles of indifferent Church people, his worldly substance. This sacrifice will possess a savor which GOD will recognize and accept.

During the last four years Bishop Wingfield has been called to the older and stronger and larger Dioceses of Louisiana and Mississippi; and while we recognize the assurance of their trust in him as an able administrator, we must not fail to award him all praise for the manliness shown in declining the tempting offers, and settling down to a residence among the rocks and hills of Northern California. The last year's work shows a total of eight parishes, twenty missions, eight hundred and sixty-seven communicants, two hundred and eight baptisms, ninety-eight confirmations; offerings, including all moneys raised, twenty-one thousand two hundred and fifty-seven dollars and nine cents. The clergy list sums up eighteen.

REV. W. LEACOCK.

Northern New Jersey, Diocese of. This Diocese consists of the counties of Essex, Hudson, Bergen, Passaic, Morris, Warren, and Sussex, and of the township of Summit, Union County, in the State of New Jersey, and was organized in 1874 A.D.

At the Annual Convention of the Diocese of New Jersey, held in 1871 A.D., a resolution was offered by the Rev. Joseph H. Smith for the appointment of a committee to consider and report upon the propriety and feasibility of dividing the Diocese. The consideration of this resolution was postponed until the next Convention. In 1872 A.D. Bishop Odenheimer called attention to the subject, and a committee of thirteen was appointed, who reported the following year in favor of "the formation of a new Diocese within the limits of the present Diocese of New Jersey." The resolutions appended to the report of the committee were adopted by the Convention, and Bishop Odenheimer gave his constitutional consent to the erection of the proposed new Diocese.

At the Annual Convention of 1874 A.D., the question came up again, and to satisfy all parties as to the real wishes of the clergy and laity, the vote was taken by orders, and the division of the Diocese on the lines reported by the committee was agreed to by an overwhelming majority. At the General Convention which met in October of the same year the formation of the new Diocese was consented to and ratified, and Bishop Odenheimer issued his call the same day for the meeting of the Primary Convention, and announced his intention of electing the new Diocese as his future jurisdiction.

The Primary Convention met at Grace Church, Newark, November 12, 1874 A.D., Bishop Odenheimer presiding, and the sermon was preached by the Rev. Dr. Farrington from the text, "Love the Brotherhood." It was decided that the Diocese should be called NORTHERN NEW JERSEY, and the following officers were duly elected: Secretary, the Rev. William G. Farrington, D.D. Standing Committee, the Revs. James A. Williams, D.D., Robert N. Merritt, George Z. Gray, and E. B. Boggs, D.D., and Messrs. D. Dodd, A. Mills, H. Meigs, and J. Edgar. Treasurer, Mr. Henry Hayes. Registrar, the Rev. Samuel W. Sayres.

Bishop Odenheimer departed this life August 14, 1879 A.D., full of honors and sincerely lamented, and a special Convention was called to elect his successor. This Convention was held at Trinity Church, Newark, October 28, 1879 A.D., and on the seventh ballot the Rev. Thomas Alfred Starkey, D.D., Rector of St. Paul's Church, Paterson, N. J., was duly elected Bishop. His consecration took place January 8, 1880 A.D., at Grace Church, Newark, the Rt. Rev. the Bishop of Rhode Island presiding, and he has just completed the fourth year of a successful Episcopate.

The Diocese contains 2800 square miles, or a little more than one-third of the area of the State of New Jersey, and has a population of over 600,000 souls. Since its formation it has steadily increased in the elements of strength, and already *ranks* three-fourths of the Dioceses which compose the American Church. Its Episcopal Fund amounts, in Parish bonds and other securities, to $56,000, and its Aged and Infirm Clergy Fund to

$14,700. It has two Church Hospitals, viz.: St. Barnabas, Newark, and Christ, Jersey City; both of which are doing a noble work in ministering to the souls and bodies of men, and are prosperous.

The situation of the Diocese, between the Delaware and Hudson Rivers, and by the side of one of the world's great centres of commerce, its iron roads crossing every county, its rich ore-beds, its thriving manufacturing cities of Newark and Paterson, its growing towns and villages, many of them "beautiful for situation," all point to the continued and increasing material prosperity of this portion of the State, and this assured prosperity and the encouraging statistics given at the end of this article justify the prediction that a bright future is in store for the Church in this goodly jurisdiction.

The statistics for the last Conventional year (ending May 1, 1883 A.D.) are as follows: clergy, 82; parishes and missions, 79; candidates for holy orders, 9; baptisms, 1549; confirmed, 828; communicants, 9273; marriages, 311; burials, 829; Sunday-school teachers, 923; Sunday-school scholars, 8565; offerings and contributions, $270,769.

REV. WILLIAM G. FARRINGTON, D.D.

Northern Texas, Missionary Jurisdiction of. No better introduction to the Historical Sketch of this Missionary Jurisdiction can be given than that which the venerable Bishop of Texas has furnished in the history of his Diocese:

"In 1874 A.D., at the Convention in Jefferson, May 28, final action was taken upon the important subject of the reduction of the Diocese, which had been considered in previous Conventions and by the General Convention at its last session, the matter of making canonical provision being then considered. On this occasion a special committee reported in accordance with the recommendation of the Bishop,—proposing the cutting off large portions of the State (or Diocese) to be formed into the Missionary Districts of Northern and Western Texas, according to the lines suggested by the Bishop, and that the General Convention be petitioned to provide for and ratify the same. This was done notwithstanding the grave difficulty that no legal provision had been made for such a mode of relief. The Rev. Alex. C. Garrett, D.D., was elected Missionary Bishop of Northern Texas, and was consecrated at Omaha, Nebraska, 20th of the following December."

The area thus set off was 100,000 square miles, containing at that time about 400,000 inhabitants. There were five clergymen and thirteen parishes and stations in the jurisdiction. The new Bishop undertook his arduous task in a brave spirit, and began to set in order the means which the new Diocese afforded for the task. He at once began to have schools established and a Cathedral planned. Dallas became his residence, and there he placed the Cathedral of St. Matthew. There was great need both of means and laborers, and both were but slowly supplied. The care of the scattered parishes few and feeble, and the visits to new fields and the efforts to arouse and stimulate workers to greater exertions necessitated constant traveling, much of which was done in an open buggy. By 1878 A.D. three more clergy had been added and parishes had increased to nine, with five organized missions; and twenty-three other mission points had been opened. There were 968 communicants, and the contributions amounted to $14,275.21. Perhaps the greatest trial was, and will be for some time to come, the difficulty in retaining men for the work in a State whose population, so constantly increasing and so bent upon the most material things, cannot patiently listen to the Gospel. Too many workers lose heart.

"The population is cosmopolitan. Every degree of refinement and the reverse, of knowledge and its opposite, of religionism and agnosticism, may find here many representatives. The tongues of Europe, the dialects of England, the sounds peculiar to the lands of Burns and of Moore, mingle in our streets with those which may be heard in Boston or New Orleans. The sentiment of these people is as various as their nativity.

"The problem of civilization, politics, and the Church is the same,—to blend these heterogeneous elements in common language, nationality, and religion. With the last of these only have we any present concern.

"If any one will examine the few brief sentences traced above, the following observations will seem to be of weight:

"1. Speculation is excessive. Every owner of real estate gives it a fictitious value, while every owner of capital seeks investment with a view to speedy and extravagant returns.

"2. Investment rather than assured income is the normal condition of almost all the capital at present available for legitimate business purposes. Merchants and corporations and companies are all alike expending in hope of future benefit, but as yet have hardly begun to realize any profits upon the outlay.

"3. These circumstances and the peculiarities of our population above alluded to render the work of the Church, both in the erection of buildings and the maintenance of the Ministry, a work of extreme difficulty. To allay the prejudices of early training and association, overcome varieties of language and nationality, break the power of atheism and infidelity, and subdue the bitterness of sectarian animosity, would be a hard thing to do if original sin had been eradicated from the human heart; but while mankind is constituted as we find it, the bravest might well shrink from so great a task. This may, perhaps, account in some degree for the frequent changes among the Clergy. Men quite equal to the average, if not above it, as is proved by the good positions they have occupied elsewhere, have found it impossible to continue with us long. Some of them have plainly stated that the strain occasioned by the cosmopolitan character of the population, and its consequent lack of co-operation and cohesion, was too much for their powers. If this be so in the sphere of spiritual things, it will require no labored argument to prove a still greater difficulty in that of temporal things. Comparatively few have received any training in the Church. Of these, again, only a few have been trained to habits of systematic liberality in the cause of GOD. Hence gifts are seldom made or services rendered for the honor and glory of GOD, but rather to serve some lower purpose of a personal nature.

"To these facts we must add one more,—the fluctuating character of our population. The losses by 'removal' are so severe as to have almost extinguished some of our most promising Missions. This is an evil against which no foresight can guard. Restlessness is characteristic of the age, and especially of new settlements. Sudden changes of value, caused by a new railroad or town, shift the centre of population of a district or county, and the plans and labor of years are scattered to the winds."

By 1880 A.D. the organized missions had increased to eight, and the mission points which the Bishop himself mainly visited were now twenty-four. The calls for more laborers and for men who could move easily from point to point are ever urgent in such a jurisdiction as that of Northern Texas. But the disastrous seasons had injured very much the ability of the people to aid in the support of a clergyman, and it is difficult to obtain men who are not more or less encumbered. The last report of the Bishop (1883 A.D.) shows a marked increase. The communicants are 1112, eighteen parishes and organized missions, and twenty-six points at which more or less services are held during the year. Here as everywhere else schools are specially needed for the training of the young, and for the dissemination through them of the sound principles of the Church. There is no section of the South which needs to receive more aid in this than does Northern Texas. Three or four Church schools well founded and in successful operation in the three Dioceses would be capital and work wisely expended for the future of the Church. If means were given to the Northern and Western Missionary Jurisdictions of Texas, there would soon be great advance in growth in the Church.

Statistics for 1886 A.D: Clergy, 16; parishes, 12; missions, 20; candidates for H. O., 2; ordinations, D. 1, P. 3; baptisms, 235; con., 204; com., 1639; contr., $25,463.51.

Notes of the Church. *Vide* CATHOLIC, APOSTOLIC SUCCESSION, UNITY.

Novice. *Vide* NEOPHYTES.

Numbers. The Book of Numbers. The third of the five books of Moses, so called because it contains the two numberings of the people, the one when they left Sinai, the second when they were on "the plains of Moab by Jordan near Jericho." The book may be divided into four main divisions: I. The leaving Sinai (chs. i.-x. 10). II. Journey to Paran (x. 11; xiv. 45). III. Sojourn there and wanderings (cxv., xix.). IV. The last year of their wandering to the plains of Moab (xx., xxxvi.). The book is evidently the memoranda of the more notable events which befell the Israelites, the sore judgments they brought upon themselves by their conduct, and yet GOD'S wondrous protection over them. The time had come for them to take possession of Canaan. The people in covenant with JEHOVAH, with the sanctity of His presence, now set forward in solemn march to fulfill their mission, thoroughly organized and after some sort of discipline, and with the Ark in the midst and the pledge of His presence, and with the Pillar of Cloud and of Fire leading them.

The second division contains the narrative of their march, the discipline GOD inflicted because of their murmurings at Taberah, and at Kibroth-hattaavah, and their arrival at Hazeroth. In this journey the people wearied of the manna, and were surfeited with quails, but with their willfulness came the penalty too. At Hazeroth the spies were sent out, and brought back an evil report, which led the people, despite the remonstrances of Joshua and Caleb, to refuse "to go up to possess the land." Then when GOD condemned them to the forty years in the wilderness they repented as suddenly, and were tempted to make a rash attack upon the Amalekites in the endeavor to force a way into Canaan. The third division (from ch. xv.-xx.) records their wanderings for thirty-seven years; the notable events which befell them, as the rebellion of Korah, Dathan, and Abiram, and the budding of Aaron's rod, together with various Laws. Fourth, the account of what occurred (ch. xx.) at the camp in Kadesh. Miriam dies here. Moses and Aaron, for speaking unadvisedly with their lips, are forbidden the promised land. From thence, after vainly asking for a passage through Edom, they pass down southward. At Hor Aaron dies and is buried. On the journey thence the people murmur and are bitten with serpents. To heal them, Moses, by GOD'S direction, made a brazen serpent and put it upon a pole. "But it came to pass, that if a serpent had bitten any man, when he beheld the serpent of brass, he lived." They asked a passage of Sihon, King of the Amorites, who, for reply, attacked them. But he was utterly defeated and his kingdom taken from him. The fear this produced in Moab led to the messages to Balaam, and his unwilling blessing, and to the plots he advised, which led to the destruction of Moab and Midian, and at last they reach the plains of Moab and encamp, preparatory to their crossing over. Here Moses makes the final dispositions and directions, gives the last Laws which are to be observed, and prepares for his death. It was in this interval that he read to the people the Book of Deuteronomy. The work has been often attacked, but none of the objections advanced can stand the severe criticism that they are arbitrary, willful, and inconsistent, and are based first on conjecture, and then that this conjecture is proven fact, a process that would establish any proposition that can be invented. Gaps do occur, but those incident to a record of notable facts, and special laws whose record covers a period of thirty-eight or nine years. The book is acknowledged to be, whenever traced, an accurate itinerary, jotted down by one who was an eye-witness. In the book we have several fragments of popular poetry, or of battle-hymns, most naturally, if briefly, introduced, and the three noble rhythms,—the chant when the people began their march, and the chant when they went into camp, and the threefold blessing of JEHOVAH, which was to rest, evening by evening, upon His people. In the very difficulties picked out or imagined we have a proof of the integrity of the book. The writer heeded nothing of apparent inconsistency. The several facts were true. He did not think of any imaginary discrepancy that might be fancied at a later date.

(*Vide* Smith's Bible Dict., Schaff-Hertzog Dict., Stephen's Book of Common Prayer.)

Numerals. In Holy Scriptures there are certain recurring numbers, either integrally or as factors of larger numbers, as Three, Seven, Ten, Thirteen, Forty, Fifty, and Seventy. The recurrence of these, and the fact that the periods assigned in many prophecies are products of such factors, have led many early interpreters to put a good deal of stress upon the numbers and the "arithmetic" of Scripture. It must be freely conceded that the prophetic cycles do have a roundness that shows a purpose, that seven is used mystically, as also forty, and that the seventy weeks of Daniel's prophecy do represent a period which accurately included the midst of the week when the MESSIAH was cut off, and was terminated when Jerusalem was sacked and the Temple burnt. There is no doubt of the interrelation of the numbers used typically, and the times and seasons which GOD hath appointed, but which He keeps in His own hand. Nor can we doubt but even in names were concealed numbers which made the names highly significant, for the letters of the alphabet were anciently used as numerals. No more than we can suppose for a moment that it was by accident that the birthplace of our LORD received its name, "the house of bread," or that it was not with an inner relation to His being the bread of Life that He was born there, though chiefly because it was the ancient home of the House of David. But it is only in accomplished predictions based upon periods of time that we can be certain that the results are correct, and such results too are useful to us now. A harmony thus appears which shows a definite purpose, a premeditation in the prophecy that utterly removes it from the rash objection that it was possibly a clever guess based upon political insight. No clever guess could have given to Jeremiah's prophecy its accuracy; nor to the far greater prophecy of Daniel, which so strangely compresses in its phrases tangled skeins of after-history, which were to help forward the unification of the once shattered Jewish nation and to give it the characteristics it bore when the MESSIAH did come.

These numbers in Scripture have a great value then, but a study of them becomes so fascinating that it tends to mislead. It was discredited because of the absurd theories built upon systems arbitrarily using the numerals given us. But it is not necessary to discredit a truth because it has been misapplied. And it surely is a misapplication to endeavor to force not only out of names but out of texts results which possibly might be wholly upset were a different reading to be established. It is a valuable auxiliary in proving the perfect accuracy of fulfilled predictions, but a dangerous one by which to try to solve future mysteries.

Nunc Dimittis. Simeon's Hymn of Thanksgiving when he took the infant SAVIOUR in his arms at the time the Virgin Mary presented Him in the Temple. It has been used for about thirteen centuries in the Services of the Church.

The American revisers omitted it in 1787 A.D., but within the past few years there has grown up a use of it after the Communion service has ended, and there is also a frequent use of it as an anthem. The proposed revision of the Prayer-Book has replaced it in the Evening Service.

O.

Oath. An oath is a most solemn asseveration. GOD Himself is spoken of as thus asserting the truth to man (Heb. vi. 16, 17). Punishment for oath-breaking is denounced (2 Chron. xxxvi. 13; Ezek. xvii. 13, 18). Inviolability of an oath is declared in Num. xxx. 2. "Shall swear by the GOD of truth" (Isa. lxv. 16). Cicero (De Officiis, iii. 29) styles an oath a religious affirmation. It is commonly used on solemn or legal occasions. It is usual to object to all oaths whatever, from our LORD'S own words and from St. James' Swear not, but in St. Matt. xxvi. 63, 64, our LORD does not disallow the adjuration of the magistrate; though He Himself does not originate the oath, He answers it. The Church then understood our LORD'S prohibition as directed against profane and careless swearing, not against the serious and judicial form.

An oath is taken as in the special presence of GOD. "Abram said to the King of Sodom, I have lift up mine hand unto the LORD, the most high GOD, the possessor of heaven and earth" (Gen. xiv. 22).

In oaths GOD is called upon as witness and judge, and their violation brings on, after conviction, the severe punishment meted out to perjury, which is considered as aggravated falsehood. "Love no false oath: for all these are things that I hate, saith the LORD" (Zech. viii. 17). "I will be a swift witness against false swearers, saith the LORD of hosts" (Mal. iii. 5).

In taking either an oath or affirmation one should think and speak as not only before GOD, but as conscious of His special presence, as when kissing His Holy Word, the prayer is said with due solemnity, "so help me GOD." After such a prayer, "the truth, the whole truth, and nothing but the truth" should follow. After such an oath there should be great care in making statements.

There are Oaths of Testimony, Oaths of Promise or Engagement, somewhat like the Jewish vows, and Oaths of Office for civil officers, and even for the King. In ancient times the soldiers took a military oath, and the oath of allegiance is a part of monarchical institutions. This oath is noticed in Ecclesiastes viii. 2: "I counsel thee to keep the King's commandment, and that in regard of the oath of GOD."

The King, or Queen, of Great Britain on assuming the regal office takes a coronation oath. Members of the English Parliament either take oaths or make affirmation. Certain English officers are required to take oaths of allegiance and the official oath. In the United States, when the President assumes his position he swears or affirms that he "will faithfully execute the office."

For the most part in this country oaths are made use of in courts of justice, and in the execution of legal documents. That their solemnity may be preserved it is desirable that they be not used on light and trifling occasions.

Authorities: Wm. Smith's Dict. of the Bible, which contains numerous Scripture references, Bingham's Antiq., Whewell's Elements of Morality, Constitution of the United States, Chambers's Library of Universal Knowledge.

REV. S. F. HOTCHKIN.

Obadiah. Of Obadiah, the fourth of the Minor Prophets, we know nothing with certainty except what is to be learned from his prophecy, though there is a tradition that he was of the tribe of Ephraim, and some relate that he was carried a captive to Babylon, while others affirm that he died in Samaria. There are as many as twelve persons called by the name of Obadiah in the Old Testament, of whom there is hardly one who has not been thought to be the same as the prophet, but this very difference of opinion shows on how little ground these identifications are based, and while, on this account, they call for no attention, they are besides unnecessary, for Obadiah, meaning *Servant of the Lord*, was probably a very common name among the Hebrews. The date of the prophecy of Obadiah is determined according to the interpretation of the 11th verse, which speaks of a capture of Jerusalem. If this is understood to mean the captivity by Nebuchadnezzar, then Obadiah would have spoken after 588 B.C., and as the same monarch made a conquest of Edom in 583 B.C., these two dates are commonly assigned as the limits within which the prophecy must be fixed. This conclusion would probably be looked upon as final were it not that the book of Obadiah is arranged between Amos and Jonah, two of the very earliest prophets, and it is asked, Why was Obadiah put next to them if he were not contemporary with them, or nearly so? An answer has been suggested that there is a close connection in subject between the last few verses of Amos and the prophecy of Obadiah, such that the latter is, as it were, an expansion of the former. The similarity between the opening verses of Obadiah and Jeremiah xlix. 7 (as well as passages in Lamentations) make it probable that one of these prophets had the words of the other in mind when he spoke, which might very well be, for if the date assigned to Obadiah is correct, they were contemporaries; but it is held that Obadiah was the first to utter his prophecy. The book consists of a rebuke of Edom for taking part in the sack of Jerusalem, and cutting off the fugitives from the city (v. 12 to v. 14), and of a prophecy of judgment upon the Edomites for so doing (v. 15 and 16). "Remember the children of Edom, O LORD, in the day of Jerusalem, how they said, Down with it, down with it, even to the ground" (Ps. cxxxvii. 7). The prophecy concludes with a vision of the restoration of the captivity of Zion (v. 17 to v. 21). It is held that the words of Obadiah have been fulfilled (1) in the conquest of Edom by Nebuchadnezzar; (2) in the reduction of the Idumæans by the Maccabees; and (3) that the restoration of Zion has been accomplished in the return from the Babylonish captivity. But a fuller realization of this prophecy is yet to be looked for in the deliverance of Zion from Edom; in the triumph of the Church of CHRIST over the powers of darkness. For the curious interpretations of Obadiah made by the modern Jews, reference may be made to Smith's Dictionary of the Bible.

Authorities: Gray's Introduction, Bible Commentary, Dictionary of the Bible.

Obit. At present a memorial service on the anniversary of the death of a founder or benefactor. Originally it was a funeral service in the church apart, apparently, from the burial service. "In many of the English Colleges the *Obit*, or anniversary of the death of the founder, is piously observed. . . . The *Obit Sundays* (once a quarter) at St. George's, at Windsor, were celebrated formerly with great magnificence, and are, to a certain degree, still." (Hook, Church Dictionary sub voc.)

This commemoration is sometimes instituted in this country, but the instances are rare. "Commemorations" are more frequent.

Oblation. In Canon law the term "oblation" means an offering of any kind, whether of movable or immovable property devoted to pious and hallowed uses; but it is now usually taken to describe the offering of the Bread and Wine, which is placed upon the Holy Table at the offering of the Prayer for "the whole State of CHRIST's Church militant." It was originally selected from the offerings of the people for the support of the ministry, and every one offered in the supposition that of his offering at least some part of the oblation would be taken. And it was a reproach uttered by St. Cyprian that a certain rich woman did not offer, but partook of the offering of a poor person. And St. Augustine writes, "The Priest receives from thee that which he may offer for thee." Later the gifts of bread and wine for the general use of the Church ceased, and alms in money was substituted for them. The oblation of the Bread survived for some time. At the Reformation it was ordered that each house in the parish in turn should be at charges for the celebration in its turn, and should offer, since the Priest generally provided the loaf, "the just valour and price of the holy loaf, with all such money and other things as were wont to be offered with the same, . . . and that the house that offered should at that time communicate with the Priest" (First Book Edw. VI.). But in the Second Book, the rubric at the end directed that "The bread and wine for the Communion shall be provided by the Curate and the Church-wardens at the charges of the Parish, and the Parish shall be discharged of such sums of money or other duties which hitherto they have paid for the same, by order of their houses every Sunday." It is then, if not bounden upon the Wardens, at least in strict accordance with their duties, to provide in the name of the Congregation out of the devotions of the Congregation the Bread and the Wine as a formal act. The oblation is a formal one itself, and should be very solemnly valued by the Communicants. For the oblation thus received from them by the Priest is used in the most solemn act of our holy religion, and for the most sacred use for our own selves. Its preparation, and the placing of it upon the Credence-Table, should be done by the Priest or his assistant, and not carelessly left to other hands, as has been too often the case. The act of oblation is formally made by the Priest in the words of the Prayer, "We humbly beseech Thee most mercifully to accept our alms and oblations, and to receive these our prayers, which we offer to Thy Divine Majesty." Wherein there is a threefold offering of Alms, Oblations, and Prayers.

Octave. The eighth day after a festival. It was in honor of the festival, which was always one of the first order. It was an early Western use, based upon Jewish usage. For it was held that whatever was commanded the Jews was an intimation of what was acceptable to the Divine will, and so, if it could be justly used in principle in the Christian Dispensation, it should be received and carried out. As there were several Jewish feasts which were celebrated through seven days, and one—the feast of Tabernacles—which was observed for eight days after, the Church in the West observed the principle in regard to the feasts of Christmas, Easter, Whitsunday, and perhaps in places the feast of the Epiphany also, though this was probably done when it was observed as identical with Christmas. The American Church has received from her English Mother, and has formally retained only the octave on all feasts, except that of Trinity Sunday, for which she has provided a proper Preface,—*i. e.*, Christmas-day, Easter, Ascension, and Whitsunday.

Offertory. It is commonly applied to the act of receiving the alms and other devotions of the people, and of humbly presenting and placing them upon the Holy Table. But accurately the term means the sentence or sentences recited by the Priest. "After which the minister shall return to the LORD's Table and begin the offertory, saying one or more of these sentences following, as he thinketh most convenient." The anthem these sentences represent was introduced in St. Augustine's time (400 A.D. circ). Again, Raban Maurus (850 A.D.). "After this the oblations are offered by the people, and the offertory is sung by the clergy, which took its name from that very cause, being, as it were, the song of the offerers." The custom is now growing by which the minister recites a single sentence and the choir then sing an anthem. If it is done at all, the anthem should be strictly one of the sentences appointed for the offertory, and *not* anything selected at will. But taking the word offertory in its common use, the privilege of giving in the Church was confined anciently only to the communicants. None else were permitted to offer then and there, and any one under censure was not permitted to offer any gift. The privilege of giving is a very sacred one, and is indeed a grace which we should most highly value, for it is a consecration of a part of our goods which we hold in trust as stewards. It is a very important part of our worship. And our gifts are humbly presented and placed upon the LORD'S Table as our acknowledgment of His Lordship, and of our holding only at His will and long-suffering. It is a part of our sacrifice of self and all we have. Notice that we offer the sacrifice of reverence of our bodies, the offering of prayer and praise, and then with our oblations the sacrifice of our goods. So that no part of our whole self is left not represented in some way.

Office. One of the three proper words for the several Services, as the Office of Burial, or the Funeral Office, the Visitation Office. It is used of the Infant and Adult baptismal forms in the rubric at the close of the form of Adult Baptism. It is the title of the Institution Office. The term ORDER is given to the Offices of Morning and Evening Prayer, Communion, Baptism, Confirmation, Visitation of the Sick, and Burial. FORM is applied to the Offices of Marriage, Prayers at Sea, Visitation of Prisoners, Thanksgiving, Family Prayer, Ordination and Consecration, and the Consecration of Churches. The term OFFICE is used once of the Institution Office as a heading, but it occurs in several places, notably in a rubric at the end of the Order of Adult Baptism. Service is a term used generally in the rubrics of all the offices. But chiefly the ancient use of the word was in reference to the Daily Service, which were named the Holy Office, the Divine Office. We now employ the word in a broad use for all the offices and forms provided in the Prayer-Book. Appended are the notices of the minor offices of the Prayer-Book.

Office for the Burial of the Dead.—All right feeling would prompt us to bury the dead with decent rites, but now that life and immortality are brought to light through the Gospel, the bodies of the dead in CHRIST are laid away in the hope of the resurrection. The Church has always taken especial care of the dead bodies of her children, and has committed them to their rest with confidence in the power of Him who is the resurrection and the life.

The Burial Office is forbidden in the case of unbaptized adults, excommunicate persons, and suicides. The reason for this prohibition is that adults unbaptized and excommunicate are not members of the Church. This service is for her members. In the case of suicides, no words of hope can be spoken if they have rushed unbidden into the presence of their Maker. The charitable instincts of our day prompt us to suggest insanity as generally preceding suicide.

The Burial Office consists of the following parts: 1. Passages from the Scriptures. 2. The Burial Anthem, taken from the 39th and 90th Psalms. 3. The Lesson, from 1 Cor. xv. 4. The Meditation and Prayers at the grave. 5. The Committal Sentence. 6. The words from Rev. xiv. 7. The LORD'S Prayer, other Prayers, and the Benediction. All parts of this service are appropriate, and as a whole it is one of singular beauty and significance. The Committal Sentence, uttered at a time when hearts are heavy and when the remains of loved ones are to be hidden from sight, brings to view the sure coming of the LORD JESUS, and when the bodies of those who sleep in Him shall be changed and be made incorruptible.

The main objection made to this service is, that it speaks hopefully alike of all over whom it is used. The answer is:

1. It is to be used over those who, having been baptized, are thus in the membership of the Church.

2. We are never to judge what is the spiritual state of the departed. They have gone beyond all human tribunals. We do not know what their inner experiences have been before they left us. Shall we publicly condemn any? The service sets forth the words proper to be used over the Christian departed. The tone of the service shows what should have been the character of the departed, and we must err upon the side of charity if at all.

Office for the Churching of Women.—The other title for this office indicates its object, "The Thanksgiving of Women after Childbirth." It consists of an exhortation to the woman to give thanks, the recitation of a Psalm, the LORD'S Prayer, some versicles, and a thanksgiving prayer. It is to be regarded as a most appropriate way in which a mother may acknowledge GOD'S goodness to her, and may supplicate the continuance of His mercy.

The substance of this office has come to us from the Sarum use. A service for mothers after childbirth was in use in the early Christian centuries. It is mentioned in old records as far back as 460 and 610 A.D.

There are two important points in the rubric at the end of the office. One is that the woman should make a thank-offering, to be applied to the relief of distressed women in childbed. The second is that the person receive the Holy Communion, if it is then administered.

Two words occur in this office which are worthy of special notice. The word "*Ordinary*" and the word "*convenient.*" The first means the person who orders, rules, or directs. Usually it refers to the Bishop of the Diocese. Here it may refer to the Dean or some one acting for the Bishop. The word "convenient" has the old significance of proper, seemly, most befitting.

Permission is given the clergy to use either the whole office or only the concluding prayer. Usually the latter is preferred in this country, but in other countries the whole office is frequently used.

The Confirmation Office.—The Rite of Confirmation, or the laying on of hands, has come down to us from the days of the Apostles. It is mentioned in Heb. vi. 2, as one of the first principles of the Christian faith. As a rite it is alluded to in Acts viii. 14–17; xix. 6.

It is administered to baptized persons for three reasons:

1. To enable them to renew their baptismal vows.
2. To assure them of GOD's favor and good will.
3. To convey to them the gifts of the HOLY SPIRIT.

The essential points in Confirmation are:
1. It is to be administered by the Bishop.
2. The candidates must previously have received baptism.
3. They must have reached years of discretion.
4. They must have a sufficient knowledge of the elementary truths of religion.
5. They must have a sincere purpose, with GOD's help, to live a Christian life.

The significance of the reply "I do," which the candidates make to the Bishop's question, extends to a renunciation of evil, the acceptance of the Christian faith, and a determination to live piously and soberly henceforth.

The benefits of Confirmation are numerous:

1. It gives opportunity for those baptized in infancy to make confession of CHRIST before the world.
2. It enables persons trained in other religious bodies, where this rite is not preserved, to conform to an Apostolic usage and to come into accord with our Apostolic Church.
3. It brings the persons into the most favorable condition for receiving the strengthening gifts of the HOLY GHOST.
4. It is a step forward to a reception of the Sacrament of the Body and Blood of CHRIST.

Office for the Consecration of a Church or Chapel.—The Consecration Office was set forth in 1799 A.D. by the American Church.

It is eminently proper that there should be some formal setting apart a church or chapel to its holy uses.

The service begins by the recitation of words from the 24th Psalm by the Bishop and clergy. Then are read any papers containing the record of the gift or endowment of the building. This is followed by the Bishop's address, in which he calls upon the congregation to beg the Divine blessing upon the present undertaking. Then follow the Consecration Prayers, in which the building is set apart to the honor of GOD, and dedicated to His service for the reading of His Holy Word, celebrating His Sacraments, for offering prayer and praise, and for the performance of other holy offices.

The Bishop then, turning to the people, who remain kneeling, continues the prayers, reciting the various purposes for which the building may be used, and imploring GOD's blessing upon those who use it for these purposes.

Baptism, Confirmation, Holy Communion, Reading and Preaching the Word of GOD, and Holy Matrimony are each specified. The concluding prayer of this part follows the outline of the exhortation used in the daily service.

The Sentence of Consecration is next read. This is a document set forth by the Bishop declaring the purposes for which the building has been erected, and its solemn dedication, and its separation from all unhallowed and worldly uses.

At the end of the reading of this Sentence the Order for the Morning Prayer follows:

The first Lesson is the story of the dedication of the Temple. The second is that part of the Epistle to the Hebrews in which we are taught that we may now, through the blood of JESUS, have access to the Holy of Holies, and that He is the High-Priest over the House of GOD.

The Epistle tells us that we are the temples of GOD through the indwelling of His Spirit, and the Gospel tells of the cleansing of the Temple by Him who would not have it made a house of merchandise or a den of thieves.

The Office for the Institution of Ministers.—This is the last office added to our Prayer-Book. Its date is 1808 A.D. The institution of a minister is his formal recognition by the Bishop and the congregation as the rector or assistant minister of the parish. It furnishes opportunity for the offering of especial supplications for the blessing of GOD upon the work of the new incumbent. The use of this office, although it does not necessarily secure permanence to the minister's relation to his parish, serves to set forth the fact that the tie is not to be broken lightly, and makes it necessary that the proposal to terminate it shall be referred to the Bishop.

The Institution Office itself is very simple. There has to be, first of all, a certificate from the vestry of the election of the minister. When this is received by the

Bishop he grants his letter of institution, which is read after the Morning Prayer has been said.

At Morning Prayer the institutor (who may be the Bishop or some one appointed by him), the new minister, and the attending clergy enter the church together. The wardens take their place outside the chancel-railing to the right and left, the senior warden holding the keys of the church. The Morning Prayer proceeds as usual, except that special Lessons and Psalms are appointed. When it is ended the institutor announces the object before them and demands if there be any impediment. If no impediment is urged, the Bishop's letter is next read. The senior warden then delivers the keys to the new minister with words of recognition of him as the rector of the church or parish. The minister, receiving the keys, promises, in the name of the TRINITY, to be a faithful shepherd.

After the prayers which follow, the institutor receives the incumbent within the rails, and presents him the Bible, the Prayer-Book, the Books of Canons of the General and Diocesan Conventions, charging him to let them be the rule of his conduct in dispensing the Divine word, in leading the devotions of the people, and in exercising the discipline of the Church, and exhorts him to be a pattern to the flock. An Anthem and special prayers are next in order. After the benediction which here follows, the instituted minister kneels at the altar and uses prayers for himself and for his people. These two prayers are very full and pointed summaries of the needs of a clergyman and his congregation. The Communion must be celebrated by the incumbent himself on this occasion, as is eminently proper.

At the close of the whole service the wardens, the vestry, and others are directed to salute the instituted minister and welcome him, bidding him GOD-speed.

The Office for the Solemnization of Matrimony.—Marriage is not a mere civil contract between two persons, but it is a holy estate, which is to be entered into soberly, advisedly, and in the fear of GOD. The Church has done much to preserve correct views as to the sanctity of marriage by setting forth an office which is admirable in its simplicity, and full and clear in the essential truths. The service is made up of two old forms, viz., the *Betrothal* and the *Marriage* proper.

It was once the custom to have a formal betrothal or engagement of the parties made in public before the marriage, with some religious rites. These rites were known as the service of Betrothal. In our present office the essential parts of this old service of betrothal are prefixed to the regular marriage service. The office may be analyzed as follows:

1. Exhortations to the friends and to the parties.
2. The Betrothal.
3. The Giving Away of the Bride.
4. The Vows of Affection and Fidelity.
5. The Endowment.
6. The Prayer.
7. The Formal Declaration.
8. The Benediction.

There are impediments to marriage which the law recognizes, such as an existing wife or husband, certain nearness of blood relationship, and immaturity of age, but beside these the Church forbids marriage to divorced persons, except that the innocent one of a divorced couple may remarry, and persons under the legal age must have the consent of parents.

The Church's aim is to set forth marriage as a most solemn and binding covenant, which no caprice or temptation or change of feeling should be allowed to break. For one cause only may it be annulled, and that is the offense mentioned by CHRIST Himself as the one offense for which the bond may be canceled. The position of the Church and the position of the State are in antagonism upon the question of divorce, but while the State grants divorces upon grounds other than adultery, nothing can compel the clergy to marry persons who have been separated for these reasons, and they can decline solemnizing the marriages of persons whom the civil magistrate or the less conscientious minister may unite.

The Office for Prayer in Families.—The forms of Morning and Evening Prayer to be used in families were composed for the Book of 1789 A.D.

They were probably suggested by the difficulty which many had in attending the daily service of the Church, and also by the fact that owing to the scarcity of clergymen and the changed habits of modern life but few churches were open daily.

Family Prayer has many reasons to commend its use. GOD is thus honored, the household is bound together more closely, and the members are trained in habits of devotion.

The simple services which are set forth in the Prayer-Book occupy each but a few minutes, but are very comprehensive.

After reading a portion of the Scriptures, the LORD'S Prayer is said, and then in the morning an acknowledgment is made of GOD'S mercy in keeping us through the night, and we dedicate ourselves to Him anew, and grace is asked to guide and keep us through the day and to bless our work.

In the evening we confess our sins, ask grace to amend our lives, intercede for others, thank GOD for His goodness, and beg His protection for the night.

Offices to be used at Sea.—We derived our American Prayer-Book from the English Book, and as England is a great naval nation it is to be expected that provision would be made for services to be used upon her ships at sea. These forms were composed and adopted in 1661 A.D., and their author is probably Bishop Sanderson. There being no established Church in this country, and few of the government chaplains being ministers of our Church, these offices are comparatively seldom used in the navy as they are here set forth.

The first rubric directs that the Daily Morning and Evening Prayer shall be said, and then some special Collects are appointed for use in ships of war. These are followed by special prayers in time of a storm and before an engagement.

Some appropriate prayers for individuals when they cannot join with the others are given.

Special Prayers "with respect to the enemy," and "in respect of a storm," follow.

When the danger is very great, the direction is given that as many as can be assembled shall come together to confess their sins to GOD, and to hear the absolution which the Priest, if any be present, is to repeat.

Thanksgiving services are provided with their special Psalms and Collects, and the office ends with a modification of the Burial Office to suit an interment at sea.

In many American merchant vessels no provision whatever is made for holding services, and a sailor's life becomes one of peculiar deprivation of the means of grace,—not only so, but the temptations in port are of such a character that it is especially difficult for the seamen to live religiously.

The establishment of Seamen's Bethels in various ports, the distribution of Prayer-Books and religious literature, has of late enlisted the sympathy of many Churchmen, so that the disgrace of leaving those men so utterly unprovided with facilities of knowing the Gospel is to some slight extent removed, but the destitution is still most lamentable.

Office of Prayer and Thanksgiving for the Fruits of the Earth.—In the Preface to the Proposed Book of 1785 A.D. it is stated that "whereas it hath been the practice in the Church of England to set apart certain days of thanksgiving to ALMIGHTY GOD for signal mercies vouchsafed to the Church and nation, it hath best also been considered as conducive to godliness that there be two annual solemn days of prayer and thanksgiving to ALMIGHTY GOD set apart, viz., the fourth day of July, commemorative of the blessings of civil and religious liberty in the land wherein we live, and the first Thursday in November, for the fruits of the earth, in order that we may thereby be stirred up to a more particular remembrance of the signal mercies of GOD towards us; the neglect of which might otherwise be the occasion of licentiousness, civil miseries, and punishments."

When the Prayer-Book of 1789 A.D. was adopted this part of the Preface was omitted, as was also the service for the Fourth of July, but the Thanksgiving service was retained. Three additional sentences from Scripture were prefixed to the service as first set forth in the Proposed Book.

When proclamations calling upon the people to keep a day of Thanksgiving and Prayer are now issued by the civil authorities, the order for the observance of the first Thursday in November is of course modified to suit. Inasmuch, however, as the season is late when this fraternal Thanksgiving is appointed in some places, a *Harvest Home Festival* is celebrated earlier, usually at the close of the summer or early in the autumn. The origin of the formal united thanksgiving for the fruits of the earth is set forth in the first Lesson read on this day, Deut. viii., and it is in accordance with such scriptural precepts as 1 Thess. v. 18; Eph. v. 20.

The service appointed follows the order of the Morning Prayer, except that special sentences are read at the opening, the Venite gives place to appropriate jubilant verses from other Psalms; a special thanksgiving follows the General Thanksgiving, and a special Collect is given for the Communion.

Common usage on this day devotes the offerings to the relief of the poor, the sick in hospitals, and those who have been deprived of temporal blessings.

Office for the Visitation of Prisoners.—One main object to be attained by the detention of prisoners in jail is the reformation of their vicious lives, and hence the propriety of bringing to bear upon them the teachings of religion. In some of our large prisons chaplains are appointed, but in others all the religious instruction the prisoners receive is from the volunteer efforts of unofficial visitors.

When the Morning or Evening Prayer is used in a jail the 130th Psalm is substituted for the Venite, and special collects are provided.

A form for the visitation of a prisoner confined for some great or capital crime is given. It includes versicles, prayers, exhortations, and the like, with directions for the examination of the prisoner by the minister as to his repentance for sins and his being in charity with men. Especial admonitions are to be given him respecting the crimes of which he is charged, and he is to free his mind preparatory to the reception of the Communion. The purpose of this form of visitation is to bring the prisoner to repentance, confession, and amendment.

When the prisoner has been sentenced to death a form of visitation for one in his condition is provided, containing special prayers, exhortations, and examinations. Part of this form and the Commendatory Prayer may be used at the time of the execution. When the Communion is administered a special Collect, Epistle, and Gospel are appointed.

A curious form of prayer occurs at the end of this office, viz., a Prayer for Imprisoned Debtors, it once being the custom to imprison men for debt. The laws under this head being abolished, the prayer is now no longer used in this country. The sufferings of imprisoned debtors in old times appealed strongly to the sympathies of prayerful men, and hence this prayer.

This office is important as setting before the clergy their duty to visit the prisoner and him that is appointed unto death, and also for the clear statements of the Church's teaching. The exhortations are remarkably exact, and are full of suggestive truths which may well be pondered in other connections.

There is no such office in the English Prayer-Book. Part of it appears to have been taken from the Irish Prayer-Book, and part was composed by our American Fathers.

The Office for the Visitation of the Sick.— Our mother, the Church, follows her children with holy words and solemn rites throughout all the circumstances of their lives. Inasmuch as sickness makes up, or is likely to make up, part of our experience here, she has provided an Office for the Visitation of the Sick, which includes suitable prayers, exhortations, and Scriptures.

The office in its complete form is probably seldom used now, but it stands as a most instructive service, and suggests proper modes of ministering to those who are overcome by illness. Although the full office is now but seldom used, its prayers and exhortations, its responsive versicles, and its Scriptures are always ready for use as circumstances permit. The commendatory Prayer, the Prayer for all present, have become especially hallowed. The rubrics in this office are worthy of study, inasmuch as they set forth duties which are too often neglected. One of them requires that notice of sickness shall be given to the minister. Usually the minister has to find it out in some way for himself. Another requires the minister to examine the sick person as to his repentance and charity, and to exhort him to settle his temporal affairs.

With reference to the latter point, there is usually the utmost diffidence felt by the minister in speaking of making wills, paying debts, etc., and he prefers to fall back upon that other part of the rubric which declares that men while in health should be put in mind of the duty of settling their temporal affairs. Unfortunately, but few direct reminders are given to men in health about these matters.

This Visitation Office is particularly important as declaring the Church's Faith concerning what a proper preparation for death consists of. It emphasizes the need of repentance for sins and faith in the LORD JESUS, and declares with utmost solemnity that there is no other name under heaven given to man in whom and through whom health and salvation may be received.

The Visitation Office shows very clearly that the Church expects her ministers to aim at the spiritual profit of her children when they are visited, and also that just what is required at the commencement of a religious life is required at its close, viz., repentance, faith, and charity.

Office for the Communion of the Sick.— It ought to be considered a high duty and privilege to partake of the Communion while in health, and particularly when we are likely to be exposed to especial peril.

In the rubric before this office the Church reminds us of this fact, and warns us to be prepared always for death. To be a devout communicant is to be ready for death, inasmuch as no one can be a devout communicant unless he repent of sin, have a lively and steadfast faith in CHRIST, and be in charity with all men. Repentance, Faith, and Charity,—these are the needful prerequisites for a departure hence in peace and in the favor of GOD. When it is desirable to administer this Sacrament to a sick person there is a special order provided. Another rubric requires the administration to the sick person last. This is to prevent the spread of contagion, and for other good and sufficient reasons which are obvious.

The Collect used in this office gives us an idea of what a proper prayer for the sick is. It is not an absolute petition for his recovery, but if it be GOD'S will. Patience is asked for, and, in the event of the sickness being unto death, that the departing soul may be made clean through the LORD JESUS. The Epistle and Gospel bring out the two truths that the sick person is in the hands of a loving LORD, and that eternal life is through His dear SON; but the general form of service is the same as that used in the church, some parts being omitted. There must usually be others present beside the minister and the sick person, and the presence of these others is stated in the old service-books to be "a singular great comfort to the sick person and a mark of their charity or good will towards him."

Provision is made by a special rubric for the comfort of a man in circumstances where it is impossible to administer this Sacrament to him. The minister is told to instruct him that he may eat and drink the Body and Blood of CHRIST profitably, although he do not receive the Sacrament with his mouth. If he repent of his sins, and firmly and thankfully believes in CHRIST and what He has done for him, he thus may receive CHRIST profitably to his soul's health.

REV. G. W. SHINN.

Ohio, Diocese of. That portion of the great Northwestern Territory which has become the great State of Ohio was, at the close of the last century, but little more than a wilderness.

In 1796 A.D. the estimated population of the entire Territory was fifteen thousand, including men, women, and children. Settlements were small, and Church services only occasionally held.

The first clergyman of the Protestant Episcopal Church who is known to have officiated in Ohio was the Rev. Joseph Doddridge, M.D. His home was upon the Virginia side of the Ohio River, but he gladly extended his Christian labors into the new territory beyond.

Dr. Doddridge was the first Christian minister who officiated in what is now the city of Steubenville. It was in May, 1796 A.D. Services were held in an upper room, reached by log steps on the outside of the building. In the year 1800 A.D., Dr. Doddridge commenced forming a congregation in what is now Jefferson County. So far as is known, this was the earliest attempt at Church organization.

In the year 1804 A.D. fifty-six persons in Worthington formed themselves into a religious society, by the name of "St. John's Church in Worthington and parts adjacent," expressing their agreement in the faith, worship, and doctrines of the Protestant Episcopal Church, and beginning preparations for the establishment of Church services.

In the year 1809 A.D. certain inhabitants in the towns of Boardman, Canfield, and Poland, in Trumbull County, met, organized a "regular Episcopal Society," and sought incorporation and counsel from the Bishop of New York. They also made an effort to secure the services of a clergyman. In September, 1814 A.D., they were visited by the Rev. Jackson Kemper, afterwards Bishop Kemper, then acting as missionary from the Society of the Protestant Episcopal Church for the Advancement of Christianity in Pennsylvania. During his visit Mr. Kemper baptized twenty-nine persons.

In other places throughout the State many Churchmen remembered the Church of their fathers, and maintained its services by lay-reading. Bishop Wilberforce, of England, in his history of the American Church, pays a deserved tribute to these faithful pioneers, making special mention of the work of Mr. Samuel Gunn, the founder of the Church in Portsmouth.

The earliest organized parishes in Ohio were St. James', Cross Creek; St. Thomas', St. Clairsville; St. Peter's, Morristown; St. James', Zanesville,—all formed under the ministry of Dr. Doddridge in 1816 A.D. At the head of the roll of the clergy who have labored in Ohio must be placed the name of the Rev. Joseph Doddridge, M.D.

After him comes the Rev. Roger Searle, who in January, 1817 A.D., left a well-established parish in Connecticut that he might seek for CHRIST's sheep that were scattered abroad. He gave as his reasons for journeying to Ohio,—

1st. Its increasing population, in 1800 A.D. 45,000, in 1817 A.D. 400,000,—a population with the best elements of strength.

2d. It was represented to him that as many as one-eighth of this number had been trained as Episcopalians.

3d. Many of them were from Connecticut, and personally well known to him.

4th. He was an elected member of the General Convention soon to assemble. He might visit this missionary field, study its needs, and report to the governing body of the Church.

Mr. Searle reached Ohio on the morning of the 16th of February. At the line he knelt and offered a fervent prayer. His first visit was to Ashtabula, where he organized St. Peter's Church. He afterwards organized successively Trinity, Cleveland; St. John's, Liverpool; St. Mark's, Columbia; St. Paul's, Medina; St. Luke's, Ravenna; St. James', Boardman.

While Mr. Searle was thus officiating in Ohio, the mind of another clergyman was earnestly turned towards the great Western field.

Philander Chase was then Rector of Christ Church, Hartford. Many men would have remained at ease in such a position. But Philander Chase was of heroic mould, and besides, he felt within him the call of the DIVINE SPIRIT to push towards the regions beyond. He left Hartford on the 2d of March, 1817 A.D., and two weeks later preached his first sermon in Ohio, at Conneaut Creek, now the town of Salem. At Windsor he organized Christ Church, and there he met the Rev. Mr. Searle and some prominent laymen, who were connected with the Church throughout the Western Reserve. It was agreed that a Convention of all the parishes in Ohio should be held in Worthington during the following January. Both Mr. Searle and Mr. Chase then journeyed throughout the State, laboring to do their Master's work.

Mr. Searle reported to the General Convention, which met in New York in May, what he had seen and heard of the Church "in the West." It was received as most gratifying intelligence, and measures were adopted looking "to the speedy organization of the Church, as well as to the sending of missionaries to the Western country." Dr. Horace Reed, of Zanesville, was admitted to an honorary seat in this General Convention.

The Primary Convention of the Church in Ohio was held in January, 1818 A.D., at the house of Dr. Goodale, in Columbus. This Convention adopted a Constitution for the government of the Church in Ohio, signified its union with the Church in the United States, and, having appointed a committee upon the support of the Episcopate, adjourned to meet in Worthington in June.

On the 3d of June, 1818 A.D., was held the first Annual Convention of the Church in Ohio. Four Ohio clergymen were present, and laymen representing ten parishes. Rev. Dr. Doddridge was also present. The chief matter transacted by the Convention was the election of the Rev. Philander Chase as Bishop. He was afterwards consecrated on the 11th of February, 1819 A.D., in St. James's Church, Philadelphia, by Bishop White, assisted by Bishops Hobart, Kemp, and Croes.

Bishop Chase remained Bishop of Ohio for more than twelve years. During his administration the clergy list increased from four to sixteen. The growth in the number and strength of the parishes was correspondingly great.

The chief work of Bishop Chase's administration was the establishment of the Theological Seminary of the Diocese of Ohio and Kenyon College. It was strongly felt that "sons of the soil" were needed for Western work. Men sent to the East for training were likely to linger there. Besides, it was thought that men trained at home would do better work. After various efforts of one kind and another, Bishop Chase determined to ask aid from the mother-Church of England. He was opposed by influences in the American Church which were commanding, but he was resolute; he fought a hard battle and finally won the day. Subscriptions were received from hundreds of men and women, aggregating in all nearly thirty thousand dollars.

Eight thousand acres of land were bought in Knox County, in the midst of a well-nigh untrodden forest. For a time the students lived in log houses, and the institution owned two mills, a printing-office, a hotel, a carpenter's and a shoemaker's shop, with houses for professors and for workmen to dwell in. It was a monopoly, and carried on business of various kinds. The pioneer Bishop's first resources were soon exhausted. But he tried again. He first petitioned Congress for a grant of land, and spent a winter in Washington "lobbying." His bill passed the United States Senate, but was not reached by the lower house. Then he bethought himself of a small sum from many friends, and asked for *one dollar* each. The request was then a novel one, and brought success.

Through Mrs. Chase's wisdom and efficiency, and Bishop Chase's untiring labors, Kenyon College was for a time very prosperous. There was a strong corps of professors, headed by Dr. William Sparrow, and more students than could be well accommodated. But troubles came. Bishop Chase had dreamed of a patriarchal institution.

"Kenyon College," he wrote at the time, "is like other colleges in some respects, and unlike all in many other respects. The fundamental principle in which it differs from all others is, that the whole institution is patriarchal. Like Abraham on the plains of Mamre, it hath pitched its tent under the trees of Gambier hill, it hath its flocks and its herds, and its different families of teachers, scholars, mechanics, and laborers, all united under one head, pursuing one common interest, and receiving their maintenance and food from one common source, the funds and farms of the college." The picture, it must be confessed, is not without its beauties, though the coloring is certainly more Occidental than Oriental.

Accurately drawn, it would have shown Western workmen ready to cry "independence," a Western faculty to question the limits of authority, and Western Young America to cheer them on. Pecuniary troubles added to the embarrassments of the situation. So, on the 9th of September, 1831 A.D., Bishop Chase resigned the Presidency of the college and the Episcopate of Ohio. The next day he mounted "Cincinnatus," and rode sorrowfully away, and Gambier saw his face no more. He was afterwards elected Bishop of Illinois, and died at "Robin's Nest," where he had founded Jubilee College.

Bishop Chase has been well described as "that toilsome, way-worn soldier of the Cross who was perpetually laboring while others entered into his labor, who was incessantly sowing while others reaped the fruits of his toil, who was ever moving Westward with the wave of emigration, having nowhere at times to lay his head, no rest for the soles of his feet. But he knew when he commenced his work what were the wages of a Christian hero, and that he looked for, that he reaped in rich abundance."

When he died, the language adopted by the Convention of Ohio was this: "Whatever alienation once existed on the part of the Convention of this Diocese from that great and good man has long since passed away, and we believe that throughout the Diocese of Ohio but one feeling is prevalent, and that is, reverence for his memory."

Charles Pettit McIlvaine was elected the second Bishop of Ohio, and was consecrated in St. Paul's Church, New York, on the 31st of October, 1832 A.D.

Bishop McIlvaine remained Bishop of Ohio for more than forty years. He died March 12, 1873 A.D.

For some years he acted as President of the Theological Seminary and Kenyon College. He lived indeed in Gambier till 1846 A.D., when he removed to Clifton, Cincinnati.

During the early years of his administration the growth of the Diocese was rapid. In five years the number of the clergy increased from 17 to 53. At the time of his death the number had risen to 108. The list of communicants grew from 900 to 10,000. The yearly charities of the Diocese, as reported, increased from $770 to $205,000.

In 1859 A.D. the health of Bishop McIlvaine had become so impaired that it was deemed wise to elect an Assistant Bishop. With great unanimity the choice fell upon the Rev. Gregory Thurston Bedell, D.D., then Rector of the Church of the Ascension, New York. He was consecrated in St. Paul's Church, Richmond, Va., on the 13th of October, 1859 A.D. For thirteen years he continued to labor with Bishop McIlvaine "harmoniously, easily, lovingly, without a jar or jealousy."

He too girded on his armor to labor for

the Theological Seminary and Kenyon College. In addition to more than a hundred thousand dollars obtained by him for the endowment of professorships, he was enabled to build (through the generosity of his former parishioners in New York, aided by his own never-failing benefactions and those of Mrs. Bedell) the Church of the Holy Spirit, which is one of the most beautiful and attractive churches ever erected to the glory of GOD. The lover of art might well make a pilgrimage to Gambier for the sole purpose of beholding this "poem in stone and mortar," this temple that tells of the worship of the living GOD.

In 1874 A.D. the Diocese of Ohio was divided, Bishop Bedell electing the northern half of the State, which retains the old name of the Diocese of Ohio. The division has been a blessing. For ten years now Bishop Bedell has gently led his flock as sole Diocesan. The gray hairs have come to him, but his influence for good increases as the years go by. His step is still vigorous. May he continue for many years to tell the story which he knows so well how to tell with magic power, of the love of CHRIST, and to illustrate by his life the sanctifying power of the HOLY SPIRIT.

Statistics for 1886 A.D.: Clergy, 66; parishes, 71; missions, 18; candidates for holy orders, 4; ordinations, D. 4, P. 1; baptisms, 1111; confirmed, 716; communicants, 7801; Sunday-school teachers, 812; Sunday-school scholars, 7074; contributions, $161,835.03.

REV. WM. B. BODINE, D.D.

Oratory. It was used to mean a stool, and also a shrine of costly materials, in which were placed relics of saints, but chiefly and now principally it means a small chapel attached to some house, as either a Church, or a Monastery, or a Hospital, or a College, in which services were held for convenience or other cause.

Orders, or more generally Holy Orders, is the term used to designate the three classes of the Ministry of the Church collectively, and the character conferred by Ordination, or the Laying on of Hands. Three Orders of Ministers are recognized in the Church, viz., Bishops, Priests or Presbyters, and Deacons. These are men set apart and authorized to minister holy things, in the functions of their respective degrees, by the laying on of the hands of the Bishop with prayer, Priests uniting with him in the act in the case of Ordination to the Priesthood. A Deacon is said to be " in Orders ;" when *advanced* to the Priesthood he is " in full Orders." A Bishop is a priest " consecrated" to the highest degree, and invested with authority to transmit Orders to others, and to bear rule over other ordered men within an assigned jurisdiction. The authority of Orders is derived through the Bishop in unbroken official succession from the Apostles, and it can be derived in no other way. Because no man can have authority to minister divine things except by receiving it from some one himself authorized to confer such authority. But the only source of such authorization must be CHRIST, the Divine Founder of the Church. Hence no such authority can exist unless miraculously conferred, or derived in unbroken series from CHRIST Himself. The *fact* of such unbroken succession through the Bishops is abundantly proven by the historic records of the Church. The character conferred by Orders is indelible. An ordained man may be deprived for cause and by due process of law of the right to exercise the functions of his ministry, either irrevocably by deposition, or temporarily by suspension; but if restored to that right, he may not be re-ordained, having never lost the character impressed upon him. In England no ordered man may sit in the House of Commons, and in some of the United States, as Maryland, no "Minister of the Gospel" is eligible to the General Assembly. The *functions* bestowed by Orders vary with each degree, but are progressive. Thus a Deacon may minister in public worship and in pastoral duties. He may baptize, bury the dead, and celebrate matrimony; but he may not preach, unless specially licensed by the Bishop to do so, and he may not even by license pronounce the benediction or consecrate the elements in the LORD'S Supper. A Priest may do all these things, and have the cure of souls by virtue of his Orders. A Bishop may exercise all the functions of the Priesthood, and in addition may administer the Laying on of Hands in Confirmation and Ordination. The method of conferring Holy Orders is that instituted and practiced by the Apostles (Acts xiii. 2, 3; 1 Tim. iv. 14, v. 22; 2 Tim. i. 6; Heb. vi. 2), and used uninterruptedly by the Church since their day. In the Greek and Roman Churches Orders is ranked among the Sacraments, but in Churches of the Anglican Communion that term is restricted to Baptism and the LORD'S Supper, the definition of the Catechism excluding Orders which possess no "outward and visible," *i.e.*, material, "sign," as water, bread, or wine, of the "inward and spiritual grace" conveyed, and which lack scriptural record of having been "ordained by CHRIST Himself."

What are known as the " Minor Orders" in the Greek and Roman Churches are not esteemed by them as "Holy Orders," and are not in use in any Churches of the Anglican Communion. It should be noted that the various offices held by Bishops, Priests, and Deacons, such as Cardinals, Archbishops, Archdeacons, Deans, etc., are not to be regarded as Orders of the Ministry, but only as official distinctions belonging to different forms of ecclesiastical administration. It should also be observed that the three Orders as found in the Apostolic Church were Apostles, Presbyters, and Deacons, the term "Episcopus" or Bishop being applied in the New Testament to

Presbyters or Elders. In the post-Apostolic Church the same Orders have been maintained, but the term Apostle fell early into disuse, and the term Bishop was transferred from the second to the first degree. In reminding Timothy of his ordination, St. Paul says, "Neglect not the gift that is in thee, which was given thee by prophecy, with the laying on of the hands of the presbytery" (1 Tim. iv. 14), but in 2 Tim. i. 6, he adds, "I put thee in remembrance that thou stir up the gift of GOD which is in thee by the putting on of my hands." This is exactly the custom of the Church in conferring Orders. St. Paul was miraculously called to the Apostolate, and preached for years before the other Apostles received him. But he and Barnabas are not called Apostles until they had been separated for the work by the laying on of hands (Acts xiii. 2, 3; xiv. 14). REV. R. WILSON, D.D.

Ordinances of the Church are not only those Rites and Sacraments which are of Divine obligation, but are also those greater rules and disciplinary matters which are by the appointment of the Church herself. The Liturgy is in use by an ordinance of the Church. Feasts, Fasts, and Order of Services, morning and evening, are ordinances. The Sunday was substituted for the Jewish Sabbath, and the holy observance of the day was and is by an ordinance of the Church. But their obligation is not as clearly felt as it should be. As the Church acts in her collective capacity under the guidance of the HOLY GHOST, her ordinances are needful corollaries drawn from the essential propositions of the Faith in the Creeds, and are for the easier and more fruitful use of these greater Sacraments and Sacramental rites which are of direct Divine institution. Our CREATOR did not disdain to dictate for the chosen people a minute ritual. Without needing to claim for such minutiæ, in the Church, the like observance, yet she must claim of every member a due obedience for his own sake of her broader ordinances.

Ordinary. The Bishop of the Diocese. The term ordinary, "ordinarius (which is a word we have received from the civil law), is he who hath the proper and regular jurisdiction, as of course and of common right, in opposition to persons who are extraordinarily appointed." The Bishop is called the ordinary, "and so he is at common law, as having ordinary jurisdiction in causes ecclesiastical; albeit, in a more general acceptation the word *ordinary* signifieth any judge authorized to take cognizance of causes in his own proper right, as he is a magistrate, and not by way of deputation or delegation" (Burn's Eccl. Law, sub voc., vol. ii. p. 39.)

Ordination. Part of this subject has been discussed under ORDERS (which see). But there are one or two points with reference to the three Orders which it may be proper to discuss here. It is a state to which a man is advanced by his ordination, and in one sense an irrevocable step. For it is an act done in GOD'S name in His behalf. Now, since it is in His name and by His power committed to the Church, it confers a rank and a jurisdiction which cannot be revoked by any one less than GOD, as in Baptism, it is CHRIST who is the baptizer, the minister being His agent; and so none but CHRIST, at the last day, can deprive us of our birthright, though our mother, the Church, can discipline us. So, though the exercise of the powers conferred by ordination can be resigned by him, or they can be restrained or prevented by the discipline of the Church, whether acting justly or unjustly, still the ordination itself and its powers can never be annulled and the man revert to his lay estate. He may act as a layman and live in that estate, and be prevented from doing his office, but he is not a layman really. Again, the three Orders of Bishop, Priest, and Deacon are distinct orders. The Bishop's office *contains* all others and *retains* as solely its own Ordination, Confirmation, and Jurisdiction,—this latter can be delegated to lower officials, not so of the other two. The Bishop commits to the Order of the Priesthood the power to celebrate the LORD'S Supper, Absolution, and Benediction, with power, if so commissioned, to exercise special or extraordinary jurisdiction. The Diaconate receives the power to Baptize and to minister to the Priest in the divine service and at the Holy Communion, and to take a care in Parish work. The authority to preach is official in the Bishop, and committed by him, as a usual part of his jurisdiction, to the Priest, and specially trusted to the Deacon by license. But all of these several divisions of the stewardship committed to the Apostolate are by the grace of GOD for the gifts and graces to be conveyed to the people in the Covenant of Baptism. Ordination is, then, itself an indelible character; it is a grace from GOD in itself, and it is to authorize men to be the conveyers of His Graces to the Elect, and to be the Embassadors for our reconcilement to GOD. While, therefore, Ordination is not properly a Sacrament, it has a sacramental grace in it.

Oregon, Missionary Jurisdiction of. The following account of the history of the Church in Oregon is drawn from the excellent report of Rev. J. W. Sellwood to the Centennial Commissioners in 1876 A.D. It was kindly furnished by Bishop Morris. This general acknowledgment of authority will be deemed sufficient.

The first Episcopal clergyman who visited Oregon was Rev. St. M. Fackler, who in 1847 A.D. went there in search of health. The first Church services recorded were held by him in Oregon City in 1848 A.D., at the house of Mr. McKinlay. He found a few members of the Church there desirous of services, but, as his health was poor, he did not attempt to organize a parish. In 1851 A.D., Rev. William Richmond, of the Diocese of New York, was appointed by the Board of Domestic Missions the first Missionary to Oregon.

Mr. Richmond reached Portland on May 11, 1851 A.D. His first service was held in the Methodist house of worship. He was assisted by Mr. Fackler, and baptized the infant daughter of that clergyman. Portland and Oregon City were chosen for central work, while Columbia City, the Dalles, Milwaukee, and Salem were selected as Mission stations. The Rev. Mr. Fackler's health improved, and he was appointed a Missionary. The newness of the country and the hardships to be endured are displayed in the following extract of a letter written by Mr. Richmond: "I occupy a room in a shanty, merely clapboards, quite open to the air, with a rough, unplaned, ungrooved floor; no carpets, no plastering, no ceiling. For this I pay twelve dollars a month, three dollars (fifteen was the price) having been deducted by the landlord on account of my Mission. I also do my own cooking, and gather my own wood out of the forest behind me, and yet my expenses will be as great as in a good boarding-house in New York."

In the fall of 1852 A.D., Rev. Jas. A. Woodward, of Pennsylvania, going to Oregon for health, was quite restored. He, by the courtesy of the Congregationalists, used their building for services in Oregon City till a room was prepared.

In 1853 A.D., Rev. Jno. McCarty, D.D., came as chaplain in the army to Fort Vancouver, Washington Territory. He took charge of Trinity Church, Portland.

The clergy and laity, at a meeting, requested a Missionary Bishop for Oregon and Washington, and the General Convention elected Rev. Thos. Fielding Scott, of Georgia, to that office. He was consecrated June 8, 1854 A.D. Bishop Scott was occupied from February 19 to April 22 in going from New York to Portland. A Convocation was held, when the Bishop, Dr. McCarty, Rev. Mr. Fackler, and lay delegates from Portland, Oregon City, and Champoeg were present. On September 24, Trinity Church, Portland, was consecrated. This was the first church consecrated in Oregon, but St. John's, Milwaukee, was the first Church building.

The Bishop was encouraged by the admission of Mr. Jas. L. Daly as a candidate for Holy Orders.

In 1855 A.D. churches were consecrated at Milwaukee and Salem. In the fall Rev. Johnstone McCormac reached the field.

In 1856 A.D., Rev. John and Rev. Jas. R. W. Sellwood promised to engage in mission work, but John Sellwood was wounded in a massacre at Panama, so that he could not enter upon work at once. This year a boys' boarding-school was opened at Oswego, under Mr. Bernard Cornelius, nearly seventy acres of land, with a house, beautifully located on the Willamette River, having been bought for the purpose.

The ordination of Mr. Daly increased the clerical force this year, a gain being made of two Deacons and one Presbyter.

Bishop Scott's work is compared by Mr. Sellwood to that of the officers of an army, who should see the depredations of Indians and yet have no men to station at needed posts. The Bishop says, "Since my return I have been continually on the tramp,—calling occasionally to spend a few days with my wife; northward to Vancouver's Island, and southward nearly to the head of the Willamette Valley; eastward to the Dalles, and westward to the Pacific. And yet, alas! in all this how little have I *done!* I can say little else of each point than *veni, vidi, discessi*. Were there a faithful clergyman at each point thus visited how different were the work, how different were the fruit, how different the retrospection!"

In 1859 A.D. St. Mary's Church, Eugene City, was consecrated.

In 1860 A.D. the Bishop was cheered by the arrival of five clergymen, viz., Rev. Messrs. Carlton P. Maples, T. A. Hyland, D. E. Willes, W. F. B. Jackson, and P. E. Hyland. Two, however, soon returned East, and one went to Washington Territory.

In 1861 A.D. the Bishop opened a school for girls at Spencer Hall, Milwaukee. It received a good patronage. This year the first number of the *Oregon Churchman* appeared. It was a monthly.

In 1862 A.D., John W. Sellwood was ordained Deacon. The Mission this year cheered the Bishop, as the parishes, schools, and Church paper seemed to promise growth.

In 1863 A.D. St. Stephen's Chapel, Portland, was opened, giving two places for Church services in that town.

In 1865 A.D., Rev. Messrs. Roberts and Stoy arrived, and the Bishop was encouraged by the ordination of Rev. John W. Sellwood to the Priesthood, as he was the first fruit of efforts to raise up men on the soil for missionary work.

In 1866 A.D. the Bishop was much discouraged by the closing of the Diocesan schools. He began to wish that some younger man should be appointed to the charge of his Mission field. In 1867 A.D. the Convocation met in Portland preparatory to the Bishop's return East for his wife's health, which was precarious. His address proved to be a farewell one. He detailed his thirteen years of toilsome labor for CHRIST and His holy Church. He says, "At no time have there been more than ten engaged in the work." Twelve churches had been set apart for sacred use, though one was not quite finished. They were free from debt. The greater part of those confirmed by the Bishop had removed to other parts of the country. "Shortly after Convocation the Bishop left for the East, and had only been in New York three days when he was called home to enter upon that rest which remaineth for all the people of GOD. When the sad intelligence of his death flashed across the wires it produced a feeling of deepest sadness, not only over the whole Church, but also over the whole State. His genial manners, and his marked ability as a preacher, won for him the affection and commanded the respect of all who had ever heard him preach, or been personally acquainted with him, so that not only did his children in the Church weep at the loss of their Reverend Father in God, but also all who had ever known him."

Oregon struggled on without a Bishop until the Rt. Rev. B. Wistar Morris, D.D., 'of St. Luke's Church, Germantown, Phila., arrived to take up the work, in June, 1869 A.D. His friend and companion in the Diocese of Pennsylvania, Rev. C. R. Bonnell, preceded him, and took charge of the Church at Salem. The coming of Bishop Morris marks a new era. In addition to a hearty zeal he is possessed of a sound common sense, and has business qualifications which lead men to follow his plans, believing that every dollar given will do its exact and appropriated work, if the Bishop can possibly make it do it. A school for girls was immediately planned by this wise master-builder. He was familiar with Bishop Doane's plans, as carried out in St. Mary's Hall, Burlington, N. J., and was accompanied by those who were also familiar with that school, and so its counterpart arose in St. Helen's Hall. Nearly a block of land was purchased in Portland for the school, and it opened with fifty pupils. In 1870 A.D. it was enlarged, and had one hundred and twenty pupils.

The Bishop at once began those journeyings of visitation and exploration which he has so faithfully continued.

In 1870 A.D. the Bishop Scott Grammar and Divinity School was opened as a boys' boarding-school with forty-six pupils. A large tract of land, beautifully situated, was secured for this purpose in the Couch addition to Portland. This year a church was commenced in East Portland, and a church and school at Corvallis commenced and nearly completed. Rev. John Rosenberg was added to the mission staff this year. Lots were obtained for the erection of churches. The Convocation of 1871 A.D. notes that the *Oregon Churchman* was revived as a monthly, and that there were many marks of improvement in the parishes. Two clergymen had been added to the clerical list.

In 1872 A.D., Rev. R. D. Nevius, D.D., and Rev. John H. Babcock arrived in Oregon. Trinity Parish, Portland, built a handsome new church, the Bishop Scott Grammar School was enlarged, and a Chinese school was opened in Portland. In 1873 A.D. there is a note of encouragement in the number confirmed, especially in Eastern Oregon, where the field was white for the harvest. At La Grande, Baker City, Union, and the Cove services were held at intervals by Rev. Mr. Wells, of Walla Walla. In 1874 A.D. two clergy were added. The corner-stones of five churches were laid, and ground broke for two others. The Bishop bought ground in Portland for the Good Samaritan Hospital and Orphanage. On Ascension-Day its corner-stone was laid. In 1874 A.D. the people offered to God $20,010.80. In 1875 A.D. the hospital and orphanage was formally opened. Six children had been previously admitted, and within twenty-four hours after its opening a patient was received into the hospital department. Mr. George Boyd was Superintendent, and Mrs. Cornelius, Matron.

The Sunday-school has been found a valuable help in Church advancement in Oregon, and Women's Guilds have done much good.

In Bishop Morris's report for 1883 A.D., we find that sixteen clergy are under his care. The Bishop's visitations disclose new Church families to be cared for, and he endeavors to exercise a sort of parochial oversight over those who, in their dispersion, are still without settled rectors, and yet who show by their offerings their interest in the Church. A church building has been secured in Oakland, and St. Paul's, Salem, and the Church of the Redeemer, Pendleton, and St. David's, East Portland, have been enlarged. Rectories have been built at St. Matthew's, Portland, and at La Grande, and one has been purchased at Canyon City. There are fourteen rectories. Lots for a church have been donated in Sellwood, a district of Portland. The Episcopal residence is valued, with the adjoining ground, at $20,000. There is a small Episcopal fund. Samuel G. French lately bequeathed a beautiful property of one hundred acres for a girls' school, which the Bishop styles the Cove School, from its situation on a cove. St. Helen's Hall and the Bishop Scott School proper have had, together, in the past year two hundred and thirty-one pupils. Pupils have been received from Connecticut, British Columbia, and Honolulu. The Bishop considers the schools "the right arm" of his work. St. Helen's Hall has purchased a large block of ground for new buildings. The Bishop Scott School needs aid sadly on account of expensive street improvements made and contemplated. The Good Samaritan Hospital has cared for two hundred and sixty-five patients, and needs a women's and children's ward. Contributions of the Diocese reported to the Convocation, $25,244; communicants, 800.

The development of Oregon makes new demands on the Church at large. The Northern Pacific Railroad has taken much Eastern money for worldly purposes, the East should make it a highway for God by sending over it Bibles, Prayer-Books, Missionaries, and rich contributions to the Western Church. The advance in Church life under the present hard-working Bishop is shown in the fact that the report states that the number of clergy in Oregon alone is only one less than "the largest number ever reported when Oregon and Washington Territory made one jurisdiction." The work is, however, yet a scattered one, as is indicated by the fact that the Rev. Reese P. Kendall's ministrations extend for a distance of over sixty miles. In considering the lumber, coal, and grain interests of Oregon, it may be well to remember that this magnificent country was saved to the United States, when England was about to purchase it of our Government, by the heroic self-denial and fatiguing journey of the missionary Whitman, who, by returning to the East, succeeded in informing those in power that the district was too valuable to be lost. Let us honor this man, though he was not of our body, for showing even business men the value of missions. This narrative naturally notes the work of Bishops as leaders, but they would be the first to say that the history could never have been written had it not been for the constant help of faithful missionaries. Their deeds are recorded in Heaven.

Statistics for 1886 A.D.: Clergy, 18; missions, 25; ordinations, P. 1; baptisms, 205; con., 117; com., 1217; S. S. teachers, 109; S. S. scholars, 1089; contr., $29,497.00.

REV. S. F. HOTCHKIN.

Organizations in the Church. It is needless here to point out the need of co-operation and thorough organization to accomplish any purpose which may claim the energy and work of more than a single mind. Skill, thoroughness, and adaptability or flexibility in the plan of organization are as necessary as persistent, zealous labor in a given cause. In the Catholicity of the Church there is warrant for the widest scope for the full play of all aims in harmony with the broad lines of her fundamental polity,—no petty narrowness or restraint within the bounds of loyalty to the Faith, the Government, and Discipline of the Church. She must, to be really all things to all men, be ready to use all the varied energies of the men for whose sake she was founded, and to whom she ministers. So organizations apparently clashing, really representing those schools of thought which must be side by side in her borders, are to be found in the Church. The ancient Templum of the old divination was the open sky, meted out in its several parts by arbitrary mystic lines; in the spiritual Templum the metes and bounds may have different aspects, but they are in the beams of the sun of righteousness, and those who seek to work in one quarter, may be as much guided by the LORD of true Liberty, who wills that all should be in the sweetness and light and glory of a holy order, as those who work in another. The organizations which are sketched below are placed more as representatives than from any arbitrary selection, and certainly no invidious choice has led to the omission of other organizations quite as equally deserving of a place here.

The American Church Missionary Society was organized by Bishops, other Clergy, and Laity of the Church, May 9, 1860 A.D., and incorporated April 13, 1861 A.D. In the words of its constitution, "The object of this Society shall be to extend and build up the Kingdom of our LORD JESUS CHRIST in accordance with the principles and doctrines of the Protestant Episcopal Church." Its plan of organization is the same as that of the Church Missionary Society of the English Church, and known as "The Voluntary Principle." Its work is a national one, embracing the Missionary Jurisdictions and many of the Dioceses of the Church. It has been largely instrumental in aiding the formation of such missionary fields as Kansas, Iowa, Nevada, Colorado, Minnesota, and Dakota.

One of its ablest advocates, the late Rev. Dr. John Cotton Smith, thus presented its special mission: "The real purpose and object of this Society js not to preach the gospel upon the basis of the principles of the Protestant Episcopal Church in the broad acceptation of these terms, according to the understanding which any one may have of their meaning, but it is to preach the gospel in what is known as the evangelical understanding of it, upon the basis of the moderate and liberal principles of our Church; this is the object of this Society, and the only reason of its being."

In addition to its work of Domestic Missions, it has founded the work in Hayti, and for five years sustained that in Mexico, sending to the latter country more than $85,000. During the twenty-three years of its history it has sustained hundreds of missionaries, built churches in very many places in the West and South, and expended more than half a million of dollars. It is also the trustee of large amounts intended to promote, in perpetuity, the evangelical interests of the Church in colleges, missionary foundations, and special parish work. Its President is always a layman.

WILLIAM A. NEWBOLD,
General Secretary.

The New York Bible and Common Prayer-Book Society was organized in the city of New York in the year 1809 A.D., and from that date to the present time has been engaged in the circulation of Bibles and Prayer-Books.

It now distributes yearly from 40 to 50,000 volumes, valued at from $7000 to $8000. Its income is from interest on invested funds, church collections, and individual donations. The aim of the Society is mainly to furnish Prayer-Books to Missionary Stations scattered throughout the United States. Thus far its work has been found most useful and beneficial, and its importance most generally acknowledged. Without an agency of this kind the growth of the Church would be much retarded.

The Protestant Episcopal Tract Society is an institution in the city of New York organized for the purpose of distributing Church books and tracts. Its means are limited. Its publications are confined to those relating to the distinctive teaching of the Episcopal Church.

It distributes yearly from 700,000 to 1,000,000 pages of tracts. JAS. POTT.

The Protestant Episcopal Society for the Promotion of Evangelical Knowledge.—This Society was organized in the city of New York during the sessions of the General Convention in 1847 A.D. The occasion of its organization was the prevalence of opinions and teachings in the Episcopal Church which were regarded by many as unscriptural, and hostile to the acknowledged standard of said Church and opposed to its best interests. What was popularly known as the Oxford or Tractarian movement in the Church of England was quickly and widely felt in this country, and awakened no little anxiety on the part of many of the Bishops, Clergy, and Laity. To counteract what were considered the Romeward and dangerous tendencies of this movement the Society was established. It was at first located in the city of Philadelphia, and was under the management of a President, Vice-Presidents, Board of Directors, Executive Committee, Secretary, and Treasurer. The Rt. Rev. Bishop Meade, of Virginia, was its first President. Among its Vice-Presidents were Bishops Smith, of Kentucky, McIlvaine, of Ohio, Elliott, of Georgia, Eastburn, of Massachusetts, Lee, of Delaware, Johns, of Virginia, and several other Bishops. A few years later the Society was removed to the city of New York and located at the Bible House. The Rev. John S. Stone, D.D., was its first Editor and General Secretary. He was succeeded by the Rev. C. W. Andrews, D.D., of Virginia. When the war broke up the relations between the North and the South, the Rev. H. Dyer, D.D., who had been for some time the Corresponding Secretary and General Agent, was made the Editor and General Manager of the Society affairs. The chief work of the Society was the preparation and distribution of books, tracts, and periodicals bearing upon the issues agitating the Church. The growth of the Society was rapid and remarkable. Commencing with nothing, it soon had quite an extensive catalogue of its own and selected publications, suited to parochial, Sunday-school, and family use. Within a few years it had an income from the sale of publications, and from contributions, of from *forty to fifty thousand dollars* a year. It was not long before its own publications amounted to some six hundred in number. Many of them were good-sized volumes. It published and widely circulated the *Parish Visitor*, designed for use in parishes and families, and *The Standard Bearer* for Sunday-schools.

The Society is still doing an important work. Upon the death of Bishop Meade, its first President, Bishop McIlvaine, of Ohio, was elected as his successor, and upon the death of the Bishop of Ohio, the Bishop of Delaware, the Rt. Rev. Alfred Lee, D.D., was elected to the office.

REV. H. DYER, D.D.

Bishop White Prayer-Book Society.—This Society has just completed its fiftieth anniversary. The history of its establishment in brief is as follows: "The Rt. Rev. J. H. Otey, D.D., having been invited by the Executive Committee of the Domestic and Foreign Missionary Society of the Protestant Episcopal Church to make some statements relative to the condition and prospects of the Church in Tennessee, a meeting was held for that purpose in St. James' Church on the evening of his consecration, January 14, 1834 A.D. Among the remarks to which his statement gave rise, the importance of a Prayer-Book as a means of promoting the cause of religion and the Church was adverted to, and the Rev. Dr. Delancy made some observations on the good which might be effected by a Society for its distribution as a *tract*. The Rev. Dr. Bedell expressed himself as much pleased with the idea, which, he said, had not before occurred to him, and it was very favorably received by all present." It so happened that four laymen occupied a pew in a remote part of the church, and to each of them the thought suggested itself that he would make an effort for the foundation of a Society. When the services were over they were pleased to find that a common spirit animated them all, and on the 6th of February, 1834 A.D., the preparatory steps having been taken, a meeting was held at the house of Mr. W. H. Newbold, to whom the society is chiefly indebted for its formation, when the following persons were present: "the Rt. Rev. Bishop Onderdonk, Rev. Messrs. Boyd, James, and Morton, Messrs. William Musgrave, James M. Aertsen, John Welsh, William H. Wayne, W. H. Newbold, and Dr. S. Littell.[*] On the 13th of February another meeting was held, at which the work previously begun was completed, and on the 18th of February, 1834 A.D., a public meeting was held in Christ Church, Bishop White presiding, with Bishops Onderdonk and Doane in the chancel, when the Society was organized. James S. Smith, Esq., Chairman of the Committee, presented and read the Constitution, and when he read the title, "The Bishop White Prayer-Book Society," Bishop White, in an audible and somewhat excited voice, exclaimed, "No, no, no!" but the audience were unmoved by his protest, and the name of that eminent and revered father of the Protestant Episcopal Church in the United States was then given to the Society, and in these days so given to changes the hope may be expressed that it will ever continue to be known by it. The Society has during these fifty years distributed a total of 328,631 Prayer-Books and 65,665 Hymn-

---

[*] Extracted from the records of Mr. Jas. M. Aertsen

als. The total receipts into the Treasury have been $100,322.02. What the Society will do in the next half-century is known only to Him alone in whose service it is engaged. We can only utter the prayer that its humble work may be blessed, and that its usefulness may be increased with each passing year. (From the Fiftieth Annual Report of the Society.)

The *Evangelical Educational Society* of the Protestant Episcopal Church was organized in the City of Philadelphia by Bishop Alonzo Potter, November 3, 1862 A.D., as *The Divinity Students' Aid Society.*

It was at first Diocesan, but subsequently made general, and incorporated November 1, 1869 A.D., under its present name. It is governed by a Board of Managers, consisting of President, Secretary, Treasurer, and twenty-two other gentlemen, who represent the Church in different sections of the country, and are elected annually at the public meeting of the Society, which consists of those who have contributed to its treasury within the year. During the twenty-one years of the Society's work it has raised directly over five hundred thousand dollars to aid young men who are preparing for the ministry of the Episcopal Church, and a very large additional sum for the endowment of theological seminaries, colleges, and schools. It has sent into the ministry more than three hundred men, distributed thousands of books and tracts, and given considerable aid to aged, sick, and infirm clergymen, and the widows and orphans of the clergy.   * REV. R. C. MATLACK, D.D.

The Church Society for promoting Christianity among the Jews.—This most useful Society was incorporated in 1878 A.D. Its purpose is surely one which appeals most earnestly to our aid as well as prayers and sympathy. To the Jew we owe every authentic revelation of GOD's love and mercy. Salvation comes to us from them. The Church was first sent to them. For a thousand years, but in ever-dwindling numbers, they entered the Church. It is indeed true that there has always been some one of that chosen race ministering at her altars. Some have risen to the Episcopate. But for a century and a half the old Judaism of the Talmud has been breaking down. The Jew has lost his hope of the MESSIAH, and in some of their catechisms even they have taught that the career of the nation is the fulfillment of the prophecy of the MESSIAH. They tend now to rationalism more than to any Faith. Yet by Faith comes their inheritance to them, and more than are willing to confess it are secret believers in the CHRIST. (*Vide* JEW.) Within this century more than twenty thousand have embraced Christianity. It is the holy purpose of this Society to aid in so glorious a work, which is, in fact, an endeavor reverently to forward GOD's declared purposes towards the people He has so loved. It has established work among the Jews in thirty-four Dioceses and in ten Missionary Jurisdictions. It aids largely the clergy in their parochial work by contributing Bibles, Prayer-Books, and Messianic and Christian publications. Its work is purely spiritual, no temporal aid being given to proselytes.

Free and Open Church Association.—The objects of the Association are: 1. To maintain, as a principle, the freedom of all seats in Churches.

2. To promote the abandonment of the sale and rental of pews and sittings, and in place thereof, the adoption of the principle of systematic free-will offerings by all the worshipers in our Churches, according to their ability.

3. To promote the recognition of the Offertory as an act of Christian worship, and as a Scriptural means of raising money for pious and charitable uses.

4. To promote the practice of keeping Churches open throughout every day of the week for private prayer.

The following are the means employed: The printing and dissemination of Tracts and Papers; the holding of Public Meetings; the Preaching of Sermons; Discussions in the Public Press; and the promotion of needful Legislation.

The Council is always ready to assist in the organization of Public or Private Meetings in reference to particular localities and Churches, so that friends who wish to influence the public opinion of their neighborhood may obtain not only tracts and pamphlets, but speakers to help them, by applying to the Secretary.

The Council is also prepared to afford legal advice on questions connected with the movement.

The Association is entirely free from party character.

It has thirty Bishops as its patrons. As only a partial result of its work, out of a total of 1859 parishes in twenty-seven Dioceses from which comparatively full returns have been received, 1179 are made free and open to all who enter the Church doors. Nearly all the Churches in the Missionary Jurisdictions have been established as free Churches.

The Society for the increase of the Ministry (founded 1857 A.D., incorporated 1859 A.D.). —As an exposition of the motives which have led to the formation of this Society, an extract from the report of the Corresponding Secretary to its second annual meeting is here given:

"The need of such a movement as this has long existed, and has been deeply felt. Those who are at all familiar with the affairs of our Church, need not be told that for several years past, and even from the beginning of her history in this country, her progress has been greatly retarded by the want of clergymen. At no time and in no part of the land, not even in those sections where she has been longest established, has the supply been sufficient for her actual wants. But the deficiency at the present time is greater and more alarming than at any previous period. The facts which official statistics reveal in regard to this matter are truly startling. They show that, while the population of the country is increasing with unexampled rapidity, and while new and promising fields, at home and abroad, are continually opening to the Church, the supply of laborers, so far from keeping pace with this growing demand, is scarcely increasing in any sense; that the yearly ordinations but little more than make good the annual losses by death and other causes; and that the number of candidates for orders now is not much larger than it was fifteen years ago. It appears that there was a gradual falling off from 1844 to 1850 A.D.; and while the reports to the General Convention show a gradual increase from 1850 to 1856 A.D., from 1856 A.D. to the present time there has been another falling off, so that there are not as many candidates now (1859 A.D.) as there were when the last General Convention met, though in the mean time there has been an absolute gain of about nine thousand communicants and two hundred parishes.

"The whole number of our clergy is about the same as the number of our parishes. But the number of those who, though occupying various stations of usefulness in the Church, are without parochial charge, together with the infirm and superannuated, must amount to at least three hundred and fifty, and thus that number, or more than one-sixth of our parishes, must be without pastors, or if supplied at all, only by lay-readers and occasional services of clergymen. It is no wonder, in view of such a state of things, that those who have the interests of the Church at heart, especially those to whom the oversight and administration of its affairs are intrusted, should feel so much anxiety on this subject as they have manifested, nor that it should have been dwelt upon so frequently and earnestly in our Conventions and journals, in the addresses of our Bishops and sermons of our clergy, and in the reports and appeals of our missionaries and Missionary Boards."

It is important that the character and plan of the Society should be thoroughly understood. It is a general association, intended to cover every Diocese, and to include every member of the Church throughout the country. It knows no sectional objects or party purposes, but is organized as an institution of the whole and nothing less than the whole Church. At the same time, it acknowledges itself to be a voluntary organization, without the right to exclude other organizations, and with no design of interfering with local societies engaged in the same or a similar enterprise. It seeks to establish itself on a permanent basis, to deserve and to secure the confidence of the Church as something more than a temporary association, and so to conduct its affairs and discharge its responsibilities, as to be everywhere regarded in the light of a carefully, economically, and effectively administered institution. Whatever funds it may obtain will be devoted wholly to the great object which it professes to serve, subject to the smallest possible charges for expenses, and without any deductions for percentages or salaries.

The Society proposes a twofold course. In the first place, it undertakes to find suitable candidates for holy orders, not waiting for candidates to present themselves, but searching after them, encouraging them, and sustaining them, provided they prove deserving, in their earliest aspirations towards the ministry. In the second place, the Society desires to furnish the necessary instruction for such candidates as it may find to be entirely worthy of assistance, at the school, the college, and the Theological school, through either or all of which, according to individual cases, it is the intention of the Society to carry its beneficiaries.

The constitution admits as members all persons paying a yearly subscription of not less than three dollars. Clergymen may make the same payment, or they may take up a collection, or raise a subscription every year; or they may do both,—that is, subscribe for themselves and obtain contributions from others. Laymen, likewise, may serve the Society by raising subscriptions among their friends and fellow-parishioners, or within their respective Dioceses. Women may contribute to it through their sewing societies and similar associations, and Sunday-school children may aid the cause by devoting to it their offerings.

The disbursements of the Society will be proportioned to the contributions which it receives. It seeks for beneficiaries among parishes as well as for subscribers. Every Sunday-school, every secular school, every college or university, ought to be kept in view as likely to furnish some youth fitted for the ministry, and yet hesitating, perhaps unable, to prepare for it. It would urge parents to bring the obligation of the ministry before their children.

The society has aided 629 clergy in their studies, besides helping 111 sons of the clergy, not ordained. It has raised $577,279.72.

Original Sin, otherwise Birth Sin, is the infection or corruption inherent in human nature through inheritance from Adam, by which every man born into the world is in a state of condemnation without reference to the commission of actual sin; which infection so depraves the moral nature of man as to produce a constant tendency to evil and prevent any disposition to good. This doctrine makes it necessary not only that man must be restrained from the evil and incited to the good by the external help of God's grace, but that he must in some way be relieved from the condemnation due to Original Sin before he can be received into God's favor. It will at once be seen that a doctrine involving such subtile distinctions, and dealing with so obscure a subject, must have led to much controversy and diversity of explanation, and such is the fact. The denial of any such taint as Original Sin is known as Pelagianism, from Pelagius, who first taught it in the fourth century. The Council of Carthage condemned the doctrines of Pelagius as heresy. Denying the existence of Original Sin, there still remained the fact, proved by all experience, of man's tendency to evil, and this the followers of Pelagius account for by supposing an inherited *weakness* of will, through which all men sin after the similitude of Adam. This is known as Semipelagianism, and is condemned in the IX. Article of Religion of the Book of Common Prayer. The variety of views held in regard to Original Sin has been almost infinite, even within the limits of orthodoxy. Of these the harshest and most uncompromising are those of St. Augustine of Hippo and of the Westminster Confession. These teach the absolute opposition of the natural human will to GOD, and its utter indisposition to all good, disability to perform it, and entire inclination to evil. This is the result of the sin of our first parents, the guilt of which is imputed to all their descendants, and the infection of which is transmitted to them by ordinary generation. This extreme view, known as the doctrine of Total Depravity, was certainly unknown to the earliest Christian Fathers, such as Clement of Alexandria and Irenæus. In a modified form it was taught by Tertullian, but was fully developed and formulated by Augustine, under the polemical heat of his controversy with Pelagius. At the time of the Reformation a similar reason operated to fix it deeply in the Lutheran system and in that of Calvin, it being a powerful weapon in the disputes of the Reformers with Rome upon the doctrine of merit by good works. The influence of Erasmus is probably seen in the milder teaching of the Anglican Articles of Religion, which hold (IX. Art.) that "it is the fault and corruption of the nature of every man that naturally is engendered of the offspring of Adam, whereby man is very far gone from original righteousness, and is of his own nature inclined to evil, so that the flesh lusteth always contrary to the Spirit; and therefore in every person born into this world, it deserveth GOD'S wrath and damnation." There is here a careful avoidance of the Tertullian doctrine of the natural heredity of Original Sin, as well as of the Augustinian view of total depravity of the will. The infection remains, however, even in those who are regenerated. Baptism, therefore, does not absolutely cleanse away Original Sin, but only secures its pardon through the merits of CHRIST, and insures the help of the HOLY GHOST to overcome its influences. From all this it is evident that the Scriptural teachings on the subject must be extremely obscure, and unquestionably they are so. The doctrine of St. Paul of the Second Adam seems to throw the most light upon this difficult and much-vexed problem.

Adam is not only the natural progenitor, but the typal representative and federal head of the human race unregenerated. The moral taint and its condemnation which he incurred fell through him upon the whole race of men: "By one man sin entered into the world, and death by sin; and so death passed upon all men, for that all have sinned (Rom. v. 12). "Death reigned from Adam to Moses, even over them that had not sinned after the similitude of Adam's transgression" (v. 14). But in the Incarnation, CHRIST, of whom Adam was in this respect the type, became the typal Representative and federal Head of Regenerated Humanity: "For as by one man's disobedience many were made sinners, so by the obedience of One shall many be made righteous" (Rom. v. 19). All men are naturally members of Adam. But in Baptism all men (baptized) are made members of CHRIST; because they are made members of the Church which is His body, and the members of the body must be members of the Head. All, therefore, who are thus made partakers of the nature redeemed and glorified by the Incarnation become the lawful inheritors of that release from the power and consequences of their natural moral infection which was won by the sinless life of CHRIST. "For as in Adam all die, even so in CHRIST shall all be made alive." But as the nature inherited from Adam was only redeemed, not changed, by the Incarnation, its taint of Original Sin was not removed, but only antagonized by the infusion of the Christ-Life, the indwelling of CHRIST'S Spirit, CHRIST Himself in His own Person being alone without sin. Hence the dual nature of which St. Paul is conscious, the evil constantly warring against the good and struggling for the mastery of the will; and hence, also, his attributing all his tendency to good, not to himself, but to the Spirit of CHRIST within him. "All his sufficiency is of CHRIST." But as this inheritance from the Second Adam is not by natural descent and concerns only man's moral nature, so we may reasonably infer that the evil nature inherited from the first Adam, which also concerns only man's moral life, is derived federally, rather than by natural descent; supposing, therefore, that it could be proven that Adam was not the natural progenitor of all men, it would in no way disturb the fact of the universality of either Original Sin or its remedy in the Atonement.

The subject of Original Sin has not been left entirely in the hands of theologians, but has been vigorously discussed by such philosophers as Kant, Schelling, and Hegel. Perhaps the most appropriate closing of the consideration of such a topic is that of Bishop Burnet's treatise on the subject: "One great and constant rule to be observed is to represent men's opinions candidly, and to judge as favorably both of them and their opinions as may be; to bear with one another and not to disturb the peace and union of the Church by insisting too much and too peremptorily upon matters of such doubtful disputation, but willingly to leave them to all that liberty to which the Church has left them and which she still allows them."

REV. ROBERT WILSON, D.D.

Ornaments. It is needless to show at length that by Divine command there were rich and costly ornaments provided for His service, and that this Law holds, since our LORD enacted that the Law should not pass away till it was fulfilled, nor that He obeyed the Law and fulfilled its bloody sacrifices and took them away. But the Epistle to the Hebrews proceeds upon an interpretation of the Law of ritual, which makes it apparent that the beauty, decency, and order of service were not abrogated. The earliest Liturgies exhibit an elaborate ornament both of furniture and of vestment. Eusebius gives the tradition that St. John wore a *petalon*, or mitre, like the High-Priest. So coming on down, we find the ornaments in the Church's service as beautiful as the circumstances of each Diocese or parish permitted.

Ornaments, in the legal sense of the word, are the necessary furniture and vessels for the due celebration of Divine service, especially the Holy Communion, and the necessary and uniform vesture of the Priest that shall execute the holy ministry. And the definitions concerning these several ornaments have in recent years formed the subject of several famous Judgments in English Ecclesiastical Courts. It has been a moot question whether, and if so, how far, the English Ecclesiastical Law holds in this country. This has never been decided; but the soundest legal opinion inclines clearly to the view that it stands with regard to the Church as the Common Law of England does to the Law of nearly all of the United States or the Civil Law to the Law of Louisiana. The Common Law of the times before 1776 A.D. is in force wherever it has not been directly abrogated by Statute Law. So the English Canon Law, as it was up to 1784–87 A.D., holds for the Church under common sense limitations, except where it is abrogated by our own Canon Law. It is limited by utter change of circumstances in some things, by the different relations of Bishops, Priest, and people in other things. In all else it holds. So, then, the famous Ornaments rubric of Edward VI.'s First Prayer-Book is deemed by many to be in force. The question is, in many points of view, to be considered as still open, and probably it is much more in the Bishop's power to decide it than is usually supposed, since by ancient rule it was an inherent part of the Bishop's office to regulate the Liturgy of his Diocese. This is ceded to the Province or to the National Church, but belongs to the House of Bishops properly. The Ornaments rubrics are as follows,—they rest for their force on the rubric of 1662 A.D. in these terms: "The Morning and Evening Prayer shall be used in the accustomed place of the Church, Chapel, or Chancel, except it shall be otherwise determined by the Ordinary of the Place; and the Chancels shall remain as they have done in times past. And here it is to be noted that such ornaments of the Church, and of the ministers thereof, at all times of their ministrations shall be retained and be in use as were in this Church of *England*, by the authority of Parliament, in the second year of the reign of King *Edward* the Sixth." The Rubric for the Vestments for Daily Prayer runs thus: "In the saying or singing of Matins or Even-song, Baptising and Burying, the minister in parish churches, and chapels annexed to the same, shall use a Surplice." Then follows a clause as to dignitaries and graduates of colleges wearing the hood of their several degrees. "And whensoever a Bishop shall celebrate the holy communion in the church, or execute any other public ministration, he shall have upon him, beside his rochette, a Surplice or alb, and a cope or vestment (*i.e.*, chasuble), and also his pastoral staff in his hand or else borne or holden by his Chaplain." The Rubric for the Vestments at the celebration of the Holy Communion runs thus: "Upon the day, and at the time appointed for the ministration of the holy Communion, the Priest that shall execute the holy ministry shall put upon him the vesture appointed for that ministration, that is to say, a white Alb, plain, with a vestment or Cope. And where there be many Priests or Deacons, there so many shall be ready to help the Priest in the ministration as shall be requisite, and shall have upon them likewise the vestures appointed for the ministry, that is to say, Albs with tunicles."

The furniture and vessels used in Edward VI.'s second year have given rise to the greatest controversies, and even to differing and sometimes opposing Judgments. The only plan followed seems to have been to discover what was in use then by the lists and inventories, which have been transmitted to us. The list given here is merely what was considered legal in the Purchas Judgment of 1871 A.D. 1. A cross, but not on the Communion-Table, or attached to it. 2. A Credence-Table as made necessary by the rubric concerning the elements. 3. The plain linen cloth covering the Table at the time of the ministration. 4. The "carpet" of silk or decent stuff, ordered by the Canon of 1603 A.D., to cover the Table during Divine Service, other than at the Communion, might be changed, and be of various colors and ornamentation, subject to the discretion of the Ordinary. 5. The Organ.

With regard to vestments, the surplice is most nearly what we know of the vestments of the first four or five centuries of the Christian history. The vestments ordered by Edward's First Prayer-Book, if white is the dominant color, is nearly corresponding to the dress of the ministry from about 500 A.D. to 900 A.D. Vestments later than these are the inventions which were introduced at the worst period of the Church's History (900 A.D. to 1100 A.D.).

Authorities: Rev. Chas. Marriott's Vestments, Hoffman's Ritual Law, Stephen's Sealed Books, with legal notes, Prayer-Book Interleaved, Blunt's C. P. Annotated, Smith's Dictionary of Christian Antiquities.

Orthodoxy. The holding the true interpretation of "the Faith once committed to the Saints." The acceptance of the Doctrines of the Catholic Faith. The test of orthodoxy must be the general consensus of the Teachers of the Church. What was the true sense of the Doctrines given in the New Testament has produced the department of Theology, and the discussion of these Doctrines results in a general consent, which is acknowledged to give the orthodox interpretation. In the Fathers we find the earlier orthodox teaching. In the Councils we have the dogmatic definitions of the Articles of the Faith. In the Creeds we have the Rule of Faith. So he holds the orthodox faith who holds (a) the Creed, (b) the definitions of the four general Councils, (c) the interpretation of those definitions in the line of general teaching of the Church. But while this is true, it must be added that without surrendering it he also submits his private judgment upon Scripture, its contents and its inspiration, to the definitions and authoritative interpretation of the Church.

P.

Pædobaptism. Infant baptism. For argument and proof in behalf of infant baptism, see BAPTISM.

Pagans. "The worshipers of many gods, the heathen, who were so called by the Christians because, when Constantine and his successors forbade the worship of the heathen deities in the cities, its adherents retired to the villages (*pagi*, hence *pagani*, countrymen), where they could practice their ceremonies in secrecy and safety. In the Middle Ages this name was given to all who were not Jews or Christians, theirs being considered the only true religion and divine revelations; but in more modern times Mohammedans, who worship the one supreme GOD of the Jews and Christians, are not called *Pagans.*" (Encyc. Amer.) As Christianity had its first great success in cities, the Epistles in the New Testament are largely directed to them, as Rome, Corinth, etc. The term heathen means dwellers on a heath, and refers to those who dwelt in the country. In the city men congregate in masses, and are more easily influenced together than in quiet country districts. REV. S. F. HOTCHKIN.

Pall. From Pallium, a cloak thrown over the shoulders. It was originally an article of dress. It was in use as the coarse outer garment of the monks. From a cloak it became reduced to a long stole-like ornament, with a hole in the centre to put over the neck. At first it was given to Bishops by the Emperors as a mark of honor and privilege, as Anthimus of Constantinople received it from the Emperor Justinian, and when he was expelled of his See he returned the Pall to the Emperor. Later the Pall became more common in the East under the name Omophorion, and is worn by Bishops and Patriarchs. But in the West it was reserved as a special mark of honor given by the Pope to such Archbishops as he would honor, or upon whom he would confer certain vicarial powers.

But the word is used in another sense also. It is the cloth which is thrown over the coffin at a funeral. When used, it should be of black or of violet cloth with a cross of white upon it, the cross to extend across the whole of the Pall.

It is sometimes used to mean the Veils which should be put over the Cup and the Paten to prevent insects from falling upon the Elements, and sometimes the single Veil of the Cup. This Pall should be of fine linen about a foot square.

Palm-Sunday. The Sunday next before Easter. This is a very usual name for it, but it has dropped out of use in the English Prayer-Book, and has lost many of the ceremonies which from the tenth century were in use upon this Sunday, which ushers in the solemnities of Holy Week.

These ceremonies of blessing the palm branches, which were then distributed and borne in procession through the church, are of mediæval date. But the Sunday bore this name of Palm-Sunday fourteen centuries ago. The Collect expresses the tender love of GOD in the humiliation of His SON for our sakes, and the prayers for the gift of humility. The Epistle taken from the Epistle to the Philippians sets forth both the equality of the SON of GOD, His humiliation and His exaltation, and the worship due to Him; while the Gospel begins the wonderful recital of that passion and death by which our souls are redeemed.

Pantheism. A subtle and very attractive form of religious belief. It was very ancient, occupying the thoughts of acute reasoners in India. In its relation to Christianity it appeared through Egyptian influence in the Gnostic theories, after having fallen with the Gnostics. After several centuries of comparative abeyance it reappeared in the midst of the Christian Faith, under the influence of the famous John Erigena (850 A.D.). It passed into Spain, and was in vogue among the Arabs. Its latest authoritative expounder was Spinoza, and from him it has passed into much of modern thought, especially in late German speculation. For its history the reader must go to the Histories of Philosophy (*cf.* Schwegler, Morrell, and Tenneman). "It deifies the universe, it amalgamates together the notions of the Finite and Infinite, unity and universal substance. The system is a necessary result of the negation of the two received points of Christian Faith: that the world is created and that truth has been revealed to man from heaven. The old crux, *ex nihilo nihil fit*, is repeated. The universe, as it is now, is stated to have existed from all eternity; if, then, the world has had a necessary existence without a beginning, it is a necessary condition of the Divine substance as being co-eternal with it. Again, a direct revelation of the truth is denied. It is not questioned that man may possess the truth, but that he can gain a knowledge of it from any other source than the energy of human reason. He works it out for himself. Therefore the Divine substance and the Divine truth are identified with the spirit of man. Moreover, since human reason is a variable, changeful element, self-consistent at one while, self-contradictory at another, it is therefore a finite intelligence, but the Divine intelligence is infinite; nevertheless the finite and the infinite are also one, of which later the finite is only a particular mode. And further, since a divinely revealed system of truth is devised, and human reason is declared to be the only source of truth; since also there is no such thing for man as absolute truth, but only such modes of it as are discoverable by his finite intelligence; therefore all opinions stand upon the same level, whether they affect religion, philosophy, or political principle. They may be expected to wax and wane, to ebb and flow, like everything else in this world. Truth, like time, is in a state of perpetual flux." (Blunt's Dict. of Hist. and Doc. Theol., sub voc.) This concise statement of the main doctrine of Pantheism, opposed, as is pointed out, to two prime facts asserted by Christianity, the Personality of GOD and the fact of a Revelation, carries its own refutation with it to every Christian mind. The identification of Deity with the universe leads practically to the most degrading Nature worship; the denial that absolute truth lies without man and is imparted to him by some revelation leads to the practical destruction of all social ethics. It is by these things that the true value of a doctrine is to be set. The true question to be asked is, What does its teaching result in, in practice? not, What is the intellectual setting forth of its fundamental propositions? Valued in this way, we can easily see what the theory of Pantheism is worth to the human race, despite its subtility and apparent philosophy.

Papa. Derived from the Greek πάππας, a word which passed into common use, and has so continued, as the name for the Presbyters of the Greek Church. It was early used so in the West, but became restricted to the Bishops and Abbots, and finally was confined to the Pope, who claimed it as his special title at or about the middle of the fifth century. (*Vide* POPE.)

Parables. In teaching children comparisons are constantly used, because they must be taught what they know not by reference to what they know.

Men are children in religious matters, and what "eye hath not seen nor ear heard" (1 Cor. ii. 9) must be learned by what eye hath seen and what ear has heard. The use of parables was common among the Jews. The comparison of the death of children to the plucking of rosebuds to bloom in heaven is a Jewish parable. This mode of instruction was in vogue among the Persians and Arabians, and in this country the North American Indians are noted for their figurative speech. Says Bacon, "As hieroglyphics preceded letters, so parables preceded arguments; and the force of parables ever was and will be great, as being clearer than arguments, and more apposite than real examples." The Scriptures are loaded with figurative language. When Nathan would rebuke David, he does it by the parable of the ewe lamb (2 Sam. xii.). When the wise woman of Tekoah would help Absalom, she uses similar means to gain her end (2 Sam. xiv.). Of our LORD's teaching it is written (Matt. xiii. 34), "Without a parable spake He not unto them." So the Great Supper, the Prodigal Son, the Shepherd, the Figtree, or the Lily, yield lessons at His command, and "the common people heard Him gladly." A woman once said, "The parts of the Bible I like best are the likes." The best preachers and Sunday-school teachers must imitate our LORD in this respect. Arguments have been styled the pillars of a discourse, and illustrations the windows. The Holy Scriptures form a book of rich pictures. Palestine held in a small compass, hardly possible in other lands, rock, tower, stream, forest, desert, gulf, sea, watchman, vine-dresser, robber, and beast of prey. All could give religious lessons. The gentle dove told of the HOLY SPIRIT, and the viewless wind of the new birth of the soul.

It has been supposed that some of our SAVIOUR's parables narrate real events; in any case the ideas are true for humanity, if not related in regard to any special person. Our LORD'S parables secured attention as being attractive stories and touching sensible objects, and giving occupation to the mind in seeking their meaning. (For beautiful expositions of these parables, see Wordsworth's Introd. to St. Luke, on the Good Samaritan and the Prodigal Son, and Farrar's Life of CHRIST, on " The Sower," and Trench's Parables.) The " various reception" of the Gospel is shown in the Sower, the " mingled results" in the Tares and the Net; the "priceless value" in the Treasure and the Pearl; and its "slow, gradual extension" in the Mustard-Seed, the Leaven, and "the Springing Corn." As to the vividness and picturesqueness of the parables of our LORD, Geikie writes as follows: '" Analogies hitherto unsuspected between familiar natural facts and spiritual phenomena; lessons of duty enforced by some simple imaginary narrative or incident; striking parallels and comparisons, which made the homeliest trifles symbols of the highest truths, abound in all the discourses of JESUS." " Nothing was henceforth left unused. The light, the darkness, the houses around, the games of childhood, the sightless wayside beggar, the foxes of the hills, the leathern bottles hung up from every rafter, the patched or new garment, and even the noisy hen amidst her chickens, served, in turn, to illustrate some lofty truth. The sower on the hill-side at hand, the flaming weeds among the corn, the common mustard plant, the leaven in the woman's dough, the treasure disclosed by the passing plowshare, the pearl brought by the traveling merchant from distant lands for sale at Bethsaida or Tiberias,—at Philip's court or that of Antipas,—the draw-net seen daily on the lake, the pitiless servant, the laborers in the vineyards around, any detail of every-day life, was elevated, as occasion demanded, to be the vehicle of the sublimest lessons. Others have uttered parables, but JESUS so far transcends them that He may justly be called the creator of this mode of instruction."

Sometimes, as Westcott shows, the parables in St. John's Gospel are transformed into words and acts. According to a figure daily and hourly before men, CHRIST is "the Door" (St. John x. 9), the True Vine (ch. xv.). The "corn of wheat" preaches of the resurrection (ch. xii. 24). Our LORD in taking a towel and girding Himself and washing His disciples' feet acted out a parable of humility (ch. xiii.). John the Baptist gives a short parable in likening himself to " the friend of the bridegroom" (ch. iii. 29). Compare our LORD'S saying in Matt. ix. 15: " Can the children of the bridechamber mourn as long as the bridegroom is with them ?"

To the devout soul in its Heavenly FATHER'S house even here on earth all things are reminders of GOD.

Authorities: Trench on Parables, Bacon's Advancement of Learning, Rev. Dr. H. C. McCook's Scripture Object Lessons, E. H. Plumptre in William Smith's Dictionary of the Bible, Foster's Cyclopædia of Illustrations, Illustrations of the Catechism of the Protestant Episcopal Church, Thompson's Land and Book, Farrar's and Geikie's Lives of CHRIST, Westcott's Introduction to the Gospels, Rev. Dr. H. Tullidge's Triumphs of the Bible, " L. P. H." in Kitto's Cyclopædia of Bible Literature.

REV. S. F. HOTCHKIN.

Paraclete. The name given to the HOLY SPIRIT by our LORD in HIS discourse in the last chapter of St. John's Gospel. It is there somewhat strainedly translated Comforter, but its chief meaning is ADVOCATE. It is a title of one of the offices of our LORD, and is properly translated Advocate in the text, "We have an advocate with the FATHER, JESUS CHRIST the righteous" (1 John ii. 1). It is one of the special offices of the HOLY GHOST to be the Advocate, the Pleader of the Truth, before the bar of our conscience, our will, and our reason. He is our guide, our leader into all truth, as we heed His pleading with our souls. And thence, in a secondary sense, He becomes our Consoler, our Comforter, as He by His very pleading for and presentation of the Faith comforts us in our feebleness, and consoles us in our shrinking because of our sins. But the early English meaning of the title Comforter was Strengthener, or Supporter, which was more nearly the general use of the word Paraclete in our LORD'S discourse. But his office of Advocate is also set forth by St. Paul: " The SPIRIT itself beareth witness with our spirit, that we are the children of GOD" (Rom. viii. 16). Nor is His office of Advocate confined to pleading with us, but He is also our pleader, making intercession for us, as well as helping our infirmities. The title Paraclete, then, while given to CHRIST, is also, and chiefly, given to the HOLY GHOST, describing His office towards us and His work in us as Advocate, and as Strengthener and Consoler.

Paradise. This word seems to come from the Sanscrit, *parrdêça*, a region of surpassing beauty, and the Armenian *pardes*, a garden or park. It is a place planted with trees, or pleasure-grounds (Solomon's Song iv. 13; Neh. ii. 8; Eccl. ii. 5). In the Septuagint it is used for the Garden of Eden (Gen. ii. 8). Xenophon makes use of the word for the pleasure-gardens of Persia. In the New Testament the word advances to signify the region in Hades—the invisible world—where faithful souls await their perfect bliss. "Their (the Jews') meaning, therefore, was this: that as paradise, or the Garden of Eden, was a place of great beauty, pleasure, and tranquillity, so the state of separate souls was a state of peace and excellent delights" (J. Taylor). " To-day," said our LORD to the penitent thief, "shalt thou be with Me in Paradise" (St

Luke xxiii. 43). But the word goes higher than this inferior Paradise, and also means "The Paradise of God" (Rev. ii. 7), that is, "the third heaven" (2 Cor. xii. 2, 4). St. Paul, by using "paradise" and "third heaven" here as of the same meaning, indicates the place where the spirits of the blessed dwell with God. The imagery in Rev. ii. 7, is drawn from Gen. ii. 8, and so Old and New Testament combine. The Jews spoke of the upper and under paradises. So the word grows from "any garden of delight" to the Garden of Eden, and then to the joyful resting-place of souls, and lastly to Heaven, so revealed religion exalts a word "from glory to glory" (2 Cor. iii. 18). In the inferior Paradise the souls of the righteous enjoy a foretaste of future bliss and await the Resurrection and Day of Judgment, when they will be reunited to their bodies, and "be admitted to the infinite and everlasting glory of Heaven." In St. Luke xvi. 23, our Lord represents Lazarus as being in Abraham's bosom, as if reclining joyfully at a feast. He adopted a Jewish expression for Paradise. Christ's body was laid in a garden (St. John xix. 41, 42), and his faithful ones shall find the grave a garden of Paradise, and they shall be like "the dew of herbs, and the earth shall cast out the dead" (Isa. xxvii. 19).

Whatever may be concluded, of St. Paul's vision or visions, the general and proper ancient idea of Paradise is that it is, as W. Archer Butler styles it, "the antechamber of Heaven," where the eye may be prepared for "the luminous Presence of the Ineffable One, a gentle twilight between the Night of this life and the Morning of Immortality." In the mystical imagery of Henry Suso, Paradise is painted as "the meadows of the bright May, the true valley of delight" where the martyrs shine "in their robes red like roses," and the confessors in "splendid beauty" and the virgins "in angelic purity." But this and much more Suso himself regarded as an image, and he thought that true happiness consisted in union with God. Happiness lies in character rather than place. Paradise is the home of divine life; the Rabbis rightly called it "the land of life." Such life is opposed to sin, which is the soul's death. Sin drove man from the Paradise of Eden ; the Second Adam, Christ Jesus, opens the door of a new and better Paradise.

The right view of Paradise is a great help to the toiling soul in this world. A thin veil divides it from a place of rest and felicity, where streams of living water shall quench its thirst. While the paradise or park is not the Great King's Palace, it lies on the way to it, and is a preparation for it. As the dead in Christ pass away one by one, Christian mourners sorrow not as those who "have no hope" (1 Thess. iv. 13), but can think of the departed as in a state of great happiness, and freed from all pain.

" 'Tis sweet, as year by year we lose
Friends out of sight, in faith to muse
How grows in Paradise our store."
Keble on the Burial of the Dead.

Paradise is not a mere theory, but a place where the reader may be to-morrow.

Authorities: Gesenius's Heb. and Eng. Lexicon, Robinson's Gr. and Eng. Lex. of the N. T., Trench on the Epistles to the Seven Churches, Commentaries of Wordsworth, Whitby, A. Clarke, and Bloomfield, McKnight on the Epistles, Hagenbach's Hist. of Doctrines, Wm. Archer Butler's Sermons, Fairbairn's Typology of Scripture.

Rev. S. F. Hotchkin.

Paraphrase. The word is used to signify the enlarging of a text by the interpolation of descriptive words, or by putting the same ideas into more diffuse and clearer language. The Targums, the Chaldee translations of some of the books of the Bible, are paraphrases also, and give the interpretation of the text current at that time among the Jews. At whatever date the Targums may be placed, still they contain remarkable paraphrases, which show that the Jews before our Lord's coming held the clue to the true meaning of the prophecies concerning Him. Paraphrases of the Gospels became more common in the mediæval ages, and several very valuable commentaries have been published upon this plan. The danger of interpolating a meaning not cognate to the text, or of doing something worse, makes the value of such works really very uncertain.

Parclose. Screens separating chapels, especially those at the east end of the aisles, from the body of the church, are called *parcloses*.

Pardon. *Vide* Absolution.

Parish. The English Parish in America.—The word parish is derived through the French and Latin from the Greek παροικια, which originally meant either a collection of men not enjoying full rights of Greek citizenship, or a class distinct from the rest of the people. In the latter sense the word was the designation of a body of Christians living in a city and its neighborhood, to distinguish them from the other inhabitants. Gradually, as Christianity spread over Western Europe, and the Church organization became more determined, it adjusted itself to the civil and military divisions existing under the Roman provincial system, and the *parochia* obtained a territorial meaning, and was applied to the district under the care of a Bishop. Under the Roman system any organization such as the present parish would have been almost impossible, and would have been prevented also by the centring of things ecclesiastical and lay in the hands of the Priests, and through them in the Bishop. It is not known positively when the *parochia* was introduced into England, but Gildas, writing about the sixth century, used it to denote the territory under the jurisdiction of the Bishop in Wales. The local divisions introduced into the island by the English were but reproductions and developments of the conquerors' organization in Germany, and they were but little, if in any degree, affected by the Romano-Celtic institutions which they supplanted. Christianity was reintroduced into England from two directions, and by different methods. The policy of the Roman missionaries was to convert the ruler and to organize downward. The practice of Aidan and his successors in the North was to labor among the people, establishing mission stations here and there, and to work up to the king.

The two methods, modified by each other, resulted in the Priest's being naturally confined in his ministrations to the territory of the township, or of a number of townships united, while the Bishop superintended the religious work of the shire or kingdom. Thus the civil and ecclesiastical organizations, with no apparent intention of so doing, were developing side by side, and the Englishman's duties to Church and State were becoming more nearly related, and it is probable that the laity began to claim a share in directing church affairs. The tendency to coalesce was greatly increased, though modified, by the unifying work of Theodore of Tarsus, the traditional founder of the English parish in its restricted sense. But, according to Pearson, *parochia* in England meant, up to the time of the Norman Conquest, the Bishop's province, and it is found with this meaning in the writings of Lanfranc, Anselm, and other ecclesiastics, although the smaller district, with its civil and religious organization, must have been in existence. One result of the Conquest was the conferring upon lords of land the right to found churches on their lands, which corresponded frequently in extent with the old township, and by the end of the twelfth century "the Parochial system, with all its legal apparatus, advowson, presentation, institution, induction, sequestration, etc.," had begun to displace the diocesan system. From that time the parish may be considered as the ecclesiastical form of the township, for the boundaries of the parishes and of the original units were identical, and in later days the personality of the older institution was in many instances absorbed into that of the younger. When the people of the township assembled to consider the affairs of the Church, the meeting was called a Vestry, from the place of meeting, originally the *vestiarium*, or apartment for the clerical garments. Many of the powers and duties of the township were bestowed upon the courts and officers of the manor, and the vestry had to attend to all business, civil and ecclesiastical, that did not come under the jurisdiction of the manor.

This rule brought about a confusion of the terms parish, vill, and town, though the word parish was used generally in referring to Church matters. From its beginning the ecclesiastical side of the parish was inclined to supersede the civil side, and this was the condition of affairs at the time of the first English settlements in America. The various classes and kinds of colonists may be, for convenience, considered as having been divided into two main streams, the first formed of those who settled New England, whose doctrines and practices have moulded the ideas of what to-day is known as the North; the second consisting of the first English dwellers in the region south of the present Mason and Dixon's Line, who influenced the life of the South. Massachusetts may be taken as representing the former, Virginia as a type of the latter. The men who founded Virginia and exercised the formative influence upon her institutions were in perfect accord with the pretensions of royalty and faithful adherents of the Church of England, and it can be safely said that in the golden age of the colony the predominant features of the customs and laws of the English at home were reproduced in Virginia. There it was that the parish, as it existed in England, was instituted, although, on account of the peculiar circumstances of the young estate, it was, as a local unit, preceded in time of organization by the military and civil divisions, and, in consequence, never possessed civil powers entirely equal to those of the same institution in the mother-country. On the other hand, the colonists of Massachusetts, originally members of the English Church, either came to America out of sympathy with the Establishment, or in their new home learned to cherish another form of church polity. The political unit in the colony was the township. But Parker wrote: "They founded a civil State upon a basis which should support the worship of GOD according to their conscientious convictions of duty; and an ecclesiastical State combined with it, which should sustain and be in harmony with the civil government, excluding what was antagonistic to the welfare of either."

In the union of the State and the Church there was produced an ecclesiastical government which was a combination of Independency and Presbyterianism, and which developed in course of time into Congregationalism. Such terms as "Church and Town," and "Members of the Church and inhabitants of the Town," did not signify, therefore, an English parish, but an English township, with provisions for the support of religion. The word parish was used in New England to denote the township from the ecclesiastical point of view as well as a portion of a township not possessing town rights, —but this was not the true English parish. The township of New England was the parish of England shorn of its ecclesiastical powers, and the Virginia parish was the English parish stripped of some of its civil functions. In Virginia the parish, both as a territorial division and as an institution, was a development, and in this respect differed from the same institution in Maryland, the Carolinas, and Georgia, which was fastened upon the body politic almost full grown and influenced by, if not modeled directed upon, that in Virginia. Its beginning may be seen in the order of the Assembly in 1624 A.D., that every plantation should have a place set apart for worship, and that "there should be in every parish a publick garnary" where should be stored by every person over eighteen years of age, within a year after his arrival in the colony, a bushel of corn, which was to "be disposed for the public uses of every parish by the major part of the freemen." The parishes in Virginia were at first co-extensive with the plantations, which lay along the rivers, and which afterwards became counties. Later the limits of county and parish were often the same. To meet the requirements of an increased population the original parish was divided, and smaller parishes thus formed became in a few years the bases for new counties. In Maryland and South Carolina parishes were originally divisions of the counties, and in the former province the hundred, which seems to have been laid out according to nature's bounds, was the basis for the new division, although not an integral part of the parish, but of the county. Some parishes, such as those lying between the rivers James and York, were very small, containing perhaps not more than thirty-six square miles, but some, on the contrary, were very large, for Augusta Parish in Virginia extended from the Blue Ridge to the Mississippi River, and many in Maryland contained over five hundred square miles. The consent of the Assembly had to be given before a new parish could be formed, and the inhabitants of the new parish paid all debts due the old one before they were legally organized. To meet the wants of all, chapels of easement were erected in very large parishes, and services were held in them when the mother-church was closed.

Governor Johnson, of South Carolina, was instructed about the year 1730 A.D. to lay out in the province eleven towns, each containing 20,000 square acres. Each of these towns were to be erected into a parish, which was to extend several miles around the town, and when one hundred heads of families had settled in the parish, it was to enjoy all the privileges of any other parish. This last provision was not carried out, at least for several years, for in a pamphlet description of South Carolina, printed in 1761 A.D., it was stated that "some towns which by the King's instructions have a right to be erected into Parishes, and to send two Members, are not allowed to send any." By a law of 1720 A.D. the South Carolina parishes became the election districts for representatives in the lower house of the Assembly, and they continued to send their delegates after they had changed from ecclesiastical to secular divisions. The same right, in somewhat modified form, was enjoyed by the Virginians, but experience soon limited it to cases in which the parish had some special measures to bring before the Assembly, and before the eighteenth century the practice had ceased. The parishes could make by-laws when no general law was applicable to certain circumstances. This arrangement did not work well, so it was changed to the right of electing two representatives of the parish to be assessors to the justices of the county court in making by-laws for the county. The first person in the parish was the minister. The Bishop of London *ex officio* had the general supervision of the Church in the American colonies, and in theory he sent over ministers to be presented by vacant parishes, and they were inducted by the governor. In practice, however, things were quite different. In South Carolina, by law, the parishioners were empowered to elect their rector, which was the same idea as that represented by the Massachusetts town-meetings choosing its minister, or by the poll-parish of Pennsylvania selecting the candidate of the "Society for the Propagation of the Gospel in Foreign Parts." The Churchmen of Maryland recognized as a rule the governor's right of induction, but there were instances when this right was strongly disputed, the opposition being carried to such ends as locking the unwelcome minister out of the church, and threatening him with physical force. In Virginia, the matter was in dispute from 1662 A.D. until the Revolution, when it was settled by the institution of the voluntary system. The vestries acknowledged that the governor could induct a minister into a parish that had remained vacant over twelve successive months, but they evaded this right by employing their rectors by the year, and if, after some time, all were satisfied, the vestry would present the minister to the governor for induction. A great deal of the trouble arose no doubt from a confusion of the terms induction and presentation, but so strong was the feeling of the people against what they believed an invasion of their rights, that they submitted to the makeshift of lay-reading, although the vestries were thereby brought sometimes under suspicion of misappropriating parish funds that should have been devoted to the support of a rector. Matters came to such a crisis that an appeal was taken to England, and Sir Edward Northey delivered an opinion which the Virginia authorities construed against the vestries, and the governors foolishly tried not only to induct but also to present ministers to parishes, but the vestries stoutly maintained their position. There were, however, exceptions on both sides, some governors refusing to urge their claims, some vestries accepting whomsoever the governors sent.

Ministers were supported in Maryland for a few years by private subscriptions, and then by an annual poll-tax on every taxable of forty pounds, afterwards thirty pounds, of tobacco; in South Carolina their salary was made up by money from the Society, by private contributions, and by State aid; the ministers of Virginia at first were paid from the results of an annual levy of ten pounds of tobacco and a bushel of corn for every ground-tiller. This salary was increased until, in 1696 A.D., it was fixed at not less than sixteen thousand pounds of tobacco a year. In the colonies, especially in Maryland, parochial libraries for the use of the rectors were provided through the untiring efforts of the Rev. Dr. Thomas Bray, the first commissary sent to Maryland. There was generally in each parish a glebe for the use and support of the rector, who was also assisted by occasional fees for a baptism, wedding, or funeral. To the minister was joined a clerk, who in the incumbent's absence could perform all the Church services, except matrimony and the two sacraments. He published banns, read the responses, for Prayer-Books were scarce in the colonies, and set the tunes until the introduction of organs at quite a later date. He was sometimes the vestry clerk, and acted as collector of the tithes, similar in many respects to the town rates of New England. The church door, in accordance with an old English custom, and for convenience, was the place for advertising matters of all kinds,— the lists of taxed bachelors, notices of persons leaving the country, the extent of patrol districts, and the crying of boats or hogs that had been found or caught. The parish affairs were administered by select vestries, varying in different colonies in numbers, in powers, in the length of their tenure of office, and in minor points. The select vestries, which found their parallel in the selectmen and assessors of a New England town, were probably suggested by the select committees of the English vestry, and were adopted in America because of the impossibility of gathering together all the parishioners for the transaction of business. The minister, when present, was the presiding officer, though it was not unusual for the church-warden to occupy the position. In Virginia as early as 1615 A.D., the minister and four most religious men looked after the moral and spiritual welfare of the people, besides keeping the church in repair and fit for the worship of GOD. In this body one writer sees a resemblance to a Dutch consistory, but its prototype is more likely to be found in the " reeve and four best men," who represented the town or parish in the hundred-court and shire-moot of England. A somewhat similar idea found expression in Maryland, where, during the absence of an incumbent, the principal, i.e., the eldest, vestryman, with four of the next oldest vestrymen, had to account to the governor for the expenditures of the parish poll-tax. In 1643 A.D. the Virginia Assembly made a law requiring a vestry to be held in every parish, and " that the most sufficient and selected men be chosen and joined to the minister and church-wardens to be of that Vestrie," for the care of the church, laying of levies, etc. There does not seem to have been any limit to the number of vestrymen until 1660 A.D., when it was found that twelve would be sufficient, although in the eighteenth century there were still some irregularities, arising, no doubt, from misunderstandings. At the time of the Bacon rebellion in 1676 A.D., an unsuccessful attempt was made to restrict the term of office to three years at one time. When once elected, the vestry filled vacancies in its body; but vacancies rarely existed, except on account of death, removal from the parish, or old age, unless for incapability or misdemeanors the whole vestry was dissolved by act of Assembly.

The Church of England was established, and parishes were organized, in Maryland by an act of 1692 A.D., and in the vestry were combined features which had already appeared or were afterwards prominent in similar bodies in other provinces. Six vestrymen were chosen at the first election by the legal voters of the parish. On each succeeding Easter-Monday the two eldest vestrymen were voted out, and the vacancies filled by two others elected in the same way. Neither of the ex-vestrymen were liable to serve during the next three years. Everywhere the qualifications of vestrymen were nearly the same. They were to be sober and discreet, and not members of the Church of Rome, and they were often men of good repute and occupying places of honor and trust in the community. Governors, members of the Council, and other high functionaries held the office, and many made it a step to political preferment. In the Virginia Convention of 1776 A.D. there were not three who were not or had not been vestrymen. When elected they took the oath of allegiance, supremacy, abjuration, the test, etc., varying according to the times. Although church-wardens existed in Virginia before vestries, yet after the latter had been created they chose annually from their own body two church-wardens, sometimes re-electing one to be a sort of adviser to the new appointee. In the proceedings of the first representative legislative assembly in America, held at Jamestown in 1619 A.D., the minister and church-wardens are mentioned as being the proper ones to bring offenders against the moral code to justice. In Maryland and South Carolina the wardens were elected annually in the same manner as the vestrymen. The vestry of a Virginia parish met at least twice a year at some convenient place, generally a small vestry-house, though a court-house or dwelling had to serve the purpose. The vestry-house represented a peculiarity of the Church, quite different from the idea of the New England meeting-house, which was used not only for religious services, or for assemblies for Church purposes, but also for the transaction of secular business. The Easter meeting was for the purpose of electing the new wardens and of examining the accounts of the retiring ones. At the fall meeting was apportioned the annual levy. This was done by adding the parish expenses, such as minister's salary, provision for the poor, etc., and dividing the whole amount by the number of tithables, which determined how much each had to pay. Ministers and poor or infirm persons were excused from paying tithes or poll-tax, which was collected by a sheriff, constable, or special collector. In Maryland vestries met generally once a month, and in some parishes refreshments were prepared for the members, who had traveled, perhaps, the whole morning through the forests. Eleven o'clock forenoon was the legal hour for the meeting, at which were discussed matters relating to the welfare of the parish, or in lieu of anything else absent members were fined, though the fines were remitted at the next meeting. Proceedings of vestries were chronicled in the vestry-book by the clerk or register, who kept also a record of births, marriages, and deaths. The clerk gave notices of vestry meetings, presented the claims or wishes of the vestry to the county courts, and attended to minor matters.

The guardianship of parish property and the censorship of parish morals were confided to the vestry, who had also charge of the building or repair of churches, the inspection of parochial libraries, the nomination in South Carolina of overseers of the poor the sending of laborers for making and keeping highways in order, and the employment of the sexton. In Virginia, once in four years the vestry divided the parish into precincts, and appointed two persons in each of them to "procession" the lands. The surveyors in company with neighbors examined and renewed the boundary-marks by blazing trees or planting stones, and the results were recorded in the parish books. This custom, rendered necessary by the nature of the country and the fewness of fences, was nothing else than the old English system of perambulations, which still obtains. The name is preserved in the "processioners" of Georgia, men who are liable to be called on at any time to fix disputed boundaries. The vestries had to concern themselves about the decent maintenance of the indigent. In the palmy days of the colony, after the first bitter experiences and before so much land had been occupied, the few paupers in private houses and the expenses incurred by the householder were paid from the parish funds. When a pauper wandered from one parish to another, he was brought back by a constable. Poor children were apprenticed to people who promised to give them religious instruction and to teach them some art or trade, while, on the other hand, the children were obliged to endeavor to help their masters as much as possible and to keep out the company of evil companions. But poverty increased with the growth of the colony, so in 1755 A.D. a law was passed for the erecting in parishes of workhouses. The vestries had power to make laws for the government of these workhouses, and offenders against them were to be soundly thrashed. It was also enacted that the inmates should "upon the shoulder of the right sleeve of his or her uppermost garment, in an open and visible manner, wear a badge with the name of the parish to which he or she belongs, cut either in blue, red, or green cloth." With few exceptions this law of workhouses seems to have remained inoperative. Certain fines in Maryland were appropriated for the help of the needy, but the parish was concerned as a rule only with such poor persons as were members of the congregation. To endowed public schools the vestry sent a limited number of charity scholars. Rev. Thomas Bacon, an energetic rector, managed, with the aid of collections on communion Sundays and of private subscriptions, to found a charity working school, where even negroes could be taught reading, writing, and reverence to GOD, at no expense other than the cost of their living. Similar treatment of the poor prevailed in South Carolina after parishes had been introduced by a law of 1704 A.D., where overseers of the poor nominated yearly by the vestry were empowered to act with the church-wardens. As the tobacco crops were the chief sources of parish revenues, it was of the greatest importance to the vestries that the value of the staple should not be lessened. The parish was divided into precincts, in each of which two tellers or counters were appointed by the vestry to prevent the growth of too much or trashy tobacco, and vestrymen and church-wardens could arrest persons who tried to "run" tobacco, that is, smuggle it from the province. The counter's office was after a time discontinued, and the duties with some changes fell to the lot of inspectors, who were nominated by the vestry and appointed by the governor. Marriages within certain degrees of consanguinity or relationship were forbidden, and vestries in Maryland and South Carolina had to place in the parish church a table of such unlawful unions, and summoned those who infringed the law to appear before them. If the guilty parties could make no explanation, they were handed over to the clerk, who had to present their names to the clerk of indictments of the county court. At stated times during the year the minister or clerk had to read in church the laws against adultery, fornication, etc. Persons suspected of immorality were summoned to a hearing before the vestry, who caused them to leave each other or to marry. Negro women guilty of adultery were whipped. If the summons was not heeded, offenders were reprimanded by the rector or some members of the vestry, and if they still persisted in their evil ways, were presented to the county court.

Men who were profane in the presence of

a minister, church-warden, or vestryman were liable to a fine; and if they refused to pay, any of the church officers could commit them to the stocks, or appoint a deputy constable to whip them. After Braddock's terrible defeat it was found necessary to increase the militia. To pay for this a tax was laid upon bachelors over a certain age, and the vestry prepared for the use of the sheriff a complete list of such delinquents. In Virginia, the minister and the church-wardens, or the church-wardens alone, were intrusted with the checking of immoral practices. When elected, wardens were required to take the following oath, which is a clear outline of their duties: "You shall sweare that you shall make presentments of all such persons as shall lead a prophayne or ungodlie life, of such as shall be common swearers, drunkards, or blasphemers, that shall ordinarilie profane the saboth dayes or contemne GOD's holy word or sacraments. You shall also present all adulterers or fornicators, or such as shall abuse their neighbors by slanderinge, tale carryinge, or back bitinge, or such as shall not behave themselves orderlie and soberlie in the church duringe devyne servise. Likewise they shall present such maysters and mistrisses as shall be delinquent in the catechisinge the youth and ignorant persons. So helpe you GOD!!!" Fines for drunkenness, Sabbath-breaking, neglect to have children baptized, and absence from church were collected by the church-wardens, and it was their duty to see that in church every one had a seat commensurate with his wealth or position as in the New England meeting-house, and to remove from the church and place in the stocks all disorderly persons. For adultery and slander penance was done, though such an act did not always relieve the offender from liability to prosecution by the civil authorities.

Unnecessary journeys, hunting, card-playing, gatherings for non-religious purposes, on Sundays, were prohibited, and the duty of preventing or correcting such offenses and of compelling attendance upon service, which had once belonged to the captain of the watch during the military régime, was transferred to the church-warden, whose office in this and in many other respects differed but little from that of tithingman or sabbath-warden in Georgia and New England.

Foundlings and bastards were bound out by the churchman, and who also could sell for a service of five years a woman convicted of bastardy, if she refused to pay her fine, while the father had to protect the parish from any loss likely to arise from the care of his child. They were the guardians of the pulpit to prevent all but regularly qualified clergymen from officiating, and they had charge of the church decorations, linen, and vessels for the Sacrament. They provided at the cost of the parish the bread and wine for Communion, which was adminis-tered at least three times a year. The church-wardens in Maryland, when they attended the visitation of the commissary, were compelled to make reports concerning the conduct and character of the rectors, the condition of parish property, and offenses coming under the penal laws. They saw that means were provided for the burial of paupers, looked up the infirm poor and paid for their accommodation in private houses, and sent some to the workhouse. By the workhouse act in Virginia, of 1755 A.D., the church-wardens had authority to commit a vagrant to the workhouse, and they were to keep a register of the poor in the parish. The last official in the parish was the sexton, having about the same duties as the present. Such was the parish in Southern colonies, in which were reproduced, as occasion required, with new features to suit different surroundings, the laws and customs of old England. But there grew up in the Northern colonies, from Pennsylvania to Maine, where there was opposition to a Church of England establishment, a system of Episcopal societies or congregations known as poll parishes, which meant either a body of Churchmen under one rector, somewhat resembling the ancient παροικια, or this body with their estates. There was a partial exception in the province of New York, where at the same time were both poll and territorial parishes, and even in Philadelphia there was a tendency towards the idea of a territorial division. For when St. Paul's Church was struggling for existence, it was written by Rev. Hugh Neill, that "All the Town Clergy had one point in view, and that was either to anihalate the Church, or bring them under the dominion of Christ Church Vestry; as it seems to be an established maxim among them, that if Philadelphia was fifty Miles Square and had two hundred Churches in it, they must be all subject to one Rector and one Vestry."

These organizations originated either in a number of Churchmen of the same neighborhood sending to England for a rector, or in the small congregation that some missionary of the Society for the Propagation of the Gospel in Foreign Parts had succeeded in gathering about him. The temporal affairs of such parishes were in the hands of church-wardens and vestrymen, whose number and mode of appointment differed widely in various sections. The general rule, however, was for the parishioners to elect them, annually, though sometimes the rector appointed one of the wardens. The church-wardens were the agents or executive officers of the vestry, whose meetings they called. In the early part of the eighteenth century there was held a Convention of clergymen from New York, New Jersey, and Pennsylvania, who proposed to do without vestries, but this did not meet with approval, and vestries continued to exist. They were of two kinds, one composed of the church-wardens and congregation, the other of church-wardens and vestrymen, in number ranging from twenty to two. Their duties were only such as related to Church affairs and were quite similar to those of present vestries. Occasionally vestrymen were appointed to civil offices, not as vestrymen, however, but as representative members of the Church of England. The minister was necessary to the complete organization of a parish, and to accomplish this the Bishop of London was made the first rector of Trinity Church Parish, New York. The ministers were supported by stipends from the government, by funds of the Society, or by private subscriptions. In the New England colonies Churchmen gained gradually the right of exemption from town rates. By a law of 1735 A.D., town treasurers in Massachusetts were obliged to pay to the minister of the Church of England the taxes collected from such of his parishioners as could prove that they were regular in their attendance upon his services. In the Declaration of Rights, in Maryland, made in 1776 A.D., there was a like provision. No one sect alone could be aided by the State, but the Legislature could impose a tax for the support of religion, and each person could designate to whom his quota should be paid. Rectors were either chosen by the vestries, appointed as in New York by the governor, or inducted by the vestries after presentation to the Bishop of London. In induction were without doubt the germs of the later office of institution. The vestry sent a deputy to the Bishop of London to recommend a desirable person for the rectorship. If all things were agreeable the Bishop gave to the minister a certificate and license, which were read to the vestry and congregation. All then left the church, the senior warden at the door giving the key to the minister, who locked himself in, tolled the bell, and, throwing open the door, welcomed his parishioners. But the American Revolution, which had been fomenting in vestry and town-meeting, checked the growth of the Church of England in America. The de-establishment of religion, the departure to England of many loyal clergymen for conscientious reasons, the rise of Methodism, and the general apathy if not hatred shown for the Church as such, produced disastrous results that at this day can hardly be appreciated. In those regions especially where the minister's support had depended upon taxes imposed by government, there seemed to be little hope of any kind of reorganization, and the churches in the North were strongly inclined to Congregationalism.

In some States the property of the Church remained in her possession, in others it was confiscated. As soon as the struggle was over, active movements were started for its organization upon an Episcopal basis. Conventions of the clergy had been held at intervals before the Revolution in some sections of New England annually. The idea was revived and extended to all the seaboard States, and lay representation from parishes was developed. With the American Episcopate the Diocesan system was introduced, and in combining into Dioceses parishes had to relinquish certain privileges, and in time the civil duties of vestries were taken from them. To-day they exist for ecclesiastical purposes, controlled by Diocesan canons, and as civil corporations governed by State laws. The word parish is used, in rather a loose way, to designate the territorial parish, the poll parish, and the congregation, which is nearly the same as the poll parish. It is a recognized law or custom in some territorial parishes, that no new congregations within them can be admitted into union with the Diocesan Convention without asking the rector's consent. Parish affairs are controlled in some instances for special reasons by trustees, but generally by the "Rector, Church-wardens, and Vestrymen," who, as a corporate body, can make and enforce by-laws. But wide differences as to qualifications, number, and rights of vestries exist not only among different Dioceses, but among the parishes of single Dioceses. The General Convention of 1877 A.D. recognized this fact, and appointed a committee, who made an exhaustive report before the next General Convention on the "functions of Rectors, Wardens, and Vestrymen." In this report is shown with regret the prevailing want of uniformity, and suggestions are made which have been and should continue the ideal of parish organization in all Dioceses. To avoid unpleasant relations between rectors and vestries it was proposed that the Bishop should have something to say in the selection of a rector, for "according to the present laws of the Church, he has no right to say a word in reference to bringing into his Diocese, of which he is the sole custodian, and into his ecclesiastical family, of which he is the spiritual father, any minister who may be asked by a vestry to come into that Diocese, and take a place in that clerical family over which the Bishop presides." The opinions of the committee in regard to the functions of rector, wardens, and vestry may be summarized as follows: The rector being the ecclesiastical head of the parish, is president of the vestry, has control for parochial purposes of Church buildings, and, as a minister, is answerable to the authorized head of the Diocese only. The vestries and their representatives, the wardens, are guardians of the property and rights of the corporate parish, they can elect their rectors, whom they are bound to support, and to aid him as far as possible. A majority, if not all, of these officers ought to be communicants in the Church. If these suggestions were carried out faithfully there would be a unity in Church organization which would result in greater spirituality and increased usefulness.

EDWARD INGLE.

WORK IN A CITY PARISH.—We do not propose under this heading to say anything concerning the organization of a parish, its vestry, wardens, and other officers. Such matters are ruled by the Canons of each Diocese, or, failing these, by the Canons of the whole Church in the United States. Information upon such points must be sought from the Diocesan or other authorities. Our intention is to assume the existence of a parish such as may be found in any of our large cities, to consider the manner in which the work of such a parish is usually conducted, and perhaps to offer some suggestions for the better and more efficient management of the same. And first of—

The Church.—The church building is the centre of the life and work of the parish. It ought to be emphatically the Religious House of the people. In the older countries of Europe, and perhaps especially in rural districts, this is much more the case than is generally to be found among ourselves. There the Church has stood in the midst of the homes of the people perhaps for many hundreds of years, and has gathered around it a mass of history, tradition, and association, making it very dear to their hearts. The more fixed habits of the people, and the different character of parish organizations, have no doubt much to do with this. The parish there is a territory lying all around the church building, and every resident within its circumference has a right, whether he exercises it or not, to speak of "my parish," "my parish church." Many an emigrant, driven by necessity to seek our shores, has felt that the hardest wrench of all in leaving his native land was the separation from his church. In it he and all his family had been baptized, there he had been married, around it in the quiet church-yard lay the remains of many generations of his forefathers, in it he had many a time received words of cheer for daily troubles, and in the clergyman he had always found a kind friend and sympathetic adviser. It is much to be desired that the church should hold a larger place in the lives and hearts of American Church people than now it does.

The church should be worthy of its place in the parish. Pleasant, bright, and attractive, for the sake of the people; stately and richly furnished as may be, for the glory of GOD.

There should be in it all to teach by eye and influence as well as by words spoken. Children should feel instinctively that it is no common house into which they have come, and should be early taught habits of reverence. The emblems of salvation upon walls and altar should remind "How dreadful is this place, this is none other than the House of GOD, this is the gate of Heaven."

To be the home of the people the Church must be open all day that they may come in at any time and say a prayer, and feel a hallowing influence touching the weary and commonplace every-day life. It is well, too, that they should be able to find their clergyman there in vestry or parish room, either at stated times or by frequent appointments, that in any difficulty or sorrow they may know where they will be sure to find a friend.

In addition to the main building of the Church, with its chancel, transepts, nave, and vestries, there need to be for its efficient working suitable parish rooms, where parish business may be transacted, charities dispensed, and Bible-classes or other classes for instruction held. And further, there must be one or more large rooms for Sunday-school purposes or large gatherings of the parishioners on social and business occasions. Many Churches have such rooms now, and often call them mistakenly *chapels*. We say mistakenly, for a chapel is but a small church, and should have its altar and other church-like fittings, and should only be used for sacred purposes, as the Church itself. Magic-lanterns, Christmas-trees, and social gatherings are as much out of place in the Chapel as they are in the Church itself; while they have their appropriate place in school-room or lecture-room, and are useful agencies in parochial work.

Clergy.—It is impossible that a City Parish, if it has any large number of communicants and is to have any number of good works or organizations connected with it, and still more if it is to be a missionary work towards the neighboring population, can be worked efficiently by one clergyman alone. Two, or still better, three, are needed.

If these men are single, they should live together in a clergy-house in the neighborhood of the Church, even though that neighborhood is poor and unattractive. A clergyman living away from his Church, for whatever reason, is sure more or less to fail in his work.

If, as is generally the case, the Rector of the parish is married, the assistants will probably not be, and they can live together in some suitable house. The strength that comes from sharing work with another and feeling mutual sympathy in all cares and labors cannot be measured.

Where three or more men are working together thus, the assistants may be chosen for special gifts. We are getting to expect too much of our clergy. It is not reasonable to expect to find in every clergyman a man who is at once a deep theologian, an eloquent preacher, a good financier, a skillful organizer, a discreet spiritual guide, an accomplished musician to superintend the choir, and of great and acceptable social gifts. All these qualities may well be found and efficiently used for the service of the Church where several men are living and working together.

The power of a parish is marvelously increased when it is felt that whatever the hour, whatever the need, whether among its own people or strangers, at their church or clergy-house, a clergyman can always be found ready and willing to aid.

Lay-Helpers.—But even where there are many clergy they must not be left to do all the work, the laity have their share.

Foremost, perhaps, among Lay-helpers are Sisters of Charity. We say advisedly *Sisters,* not a *Sisterhood.* A Sisterhood is no part of parish work. It is something altogether outside and independent of ordinary parochial work. It is autonomous, electing its own Superior and making its own rules, taking in and dismissing its own members, and directing and controlling its own work. By *Sisters* we mean a small company, or two or more Sisters, sent out from some Sisterhood to do work in some parish. In their own house, which must be near the Church and distinctly set apart for them, they keep their own rule of life, but in all their work they are directed by the clergyman of the parish. It were well that the number thus working should not be less than three, so that a change of one might be made from time to time, as there was occasion for one or another to return to her community, without disturbing the general work they were engaged in.

Such Sisters, associating other ladies with themselves, would visit the poor and sick in their homes, administering necessary comforts of life, thus securing greater efficiency in the work by wise direction, and saving much time to the clergy. The sick and poor will often receive their words of spiritual counsel and help which hardly reach them from other lips.

Sisters will naturally gather girls around them, moulding them for good and raising their moral tone by such associations. Guilds and confraternities for girls of all ages may well be carried on under their direction. In many places their work has been very powerful among lads and young men, who, turning aside from other men and keeping away in timidity from the clergymen, are won in true, manly, and chivalrous feeling by the gentle influence of a high-minded, tender-hearted, and religious woman. The ladies working with the Sisters cannot but be helped themselves. Indeed, there seems no limit to the influence for good in a city parish that may be exercised by such a little company of devoted Sisters.

Other methods of lay-help will be what we have just hinted at, the visiting of the poor and sick by others than the Sisters. This work, generally delegated to women, may well be shared in by men. Indeed, in many cases, the work may be far better done by men whose business habits, trained minds, and strong resolution can hardly be more usefully exercised than for the benefit of the poor and sick.

The Sunday-school calls for lay-help, the choir also, and the workingmen's club and reading-room, if such there be.

Sunday-schools are too large a topic to be spoken of here. This much may be said,— the Sunday-school must be under the eye and direction of one of the clergy. Let one of the assistants have it as a special care. Let him appoint every superintendent and teacher. Let him know every child by face and name, and be able to greet all with an appropriate word. Let him direct the lessons and catechise the children. When the Sunday-school is thus worked there ought to be a school in which the children feel themselves at home, and that their Church loves and cares for them; in which the teachers may feel that theirs is a real work for GOD; in which teachers, children, and clergy alike are banded together and go forward lovingly in devotion to GOD and faithful service to His Church.

The choir, too, should be ruled on a similar plan. Let one of the clergy be in charge and have the general direction of the music. He need not train the choir, but be the friend of all. Let every man and boy feel that he is known and has a share in his clergyman's interest, and a high tone of life as well as of singing may be maintained. The choir should never be a singing party, or club, apart from the clergy. Every adult member should be a regular communicant, and every boy baptized and looking forward to his confirmation. No unbaptized person should ever be allowed to take an official part in the services of the Church, nor any person outside the fold, unless in some exceptional instance where one is earnestly seeking and preparing for admission.

Enough here has been said to indicate the tone that ought to be maintained in the choir, the subject is large enough to receive separate treatment. It may be added that it is better that none of the adult members of a choir be paid, but that they should give their services a free-will offering to the glory of GOD. Some small payment may be made to boys as insuring greater regularity at practices and more sustained interest.

Other forms of lay-help will occur, but too much stress cannot be laid upon the importance of the work of *men* in visiting the poor, and in teaching in the Sunday-school.

Services.—The hours of service must be suited to the habits and residences of the people, with some limitations. The great distance at which many parishioners live is a hindrance to church-going. It would be well if the lay-people would take this a little more into consideration when selecting a locality for their home.

Services must be frequent. The Daily Morning and Evening Prayer of the Church should be said in the principal church building of the parish, or in the chapel attached to it. In most city parishes it will be found well to have one or two early celebrations of Holy Communion during the week, looking forward to the time when they will be daily. This is a matter of real convenience when many members of a family are communicants and all cannot well leave home together on a Sunday morning. It also enables some to keep their birthdays or other anniversaries in the highest Christian method.

While an afternoon hour will generally be found most convenient for the Evening Prayer, some later services should be provided during the week for those whose hours of labor occupy them all the day. Such late evening services may be accompanied by sermon, lecture, or instruction, while the afternoon service may well be preceded or followed by a public Bible-class or meditation intended more especially for persons of inferior education; of course all Festivals of the Church and all Saints' Days will be observed by the celebration of Holy Communion and other services. It is sometimes found well to have a service with address on the evening before a Festival. The minds of the people are thus led on to think more of such days and give more heed to their observance.

In every well-worked city parish there will be at least one celebration of Holy Communion on every LORD's Day, generally there will be two, one early in the morning and one at a later hour. Probably 7 30 A.M. is the most convenient hour for the general communicants, but there may well be an occasional earlier service for servants, nurses, mothers of families, or others whose avocations employ them on Sundays as well as week-days.

The morning service at 10.30 or 11 A.M. is generally the best attended, and care should be taken to make the sermons and teaching of an educational as well as hortatory character. Sunday morning church-goers are oftentimes those to whom church-going is a mere habit, and who have little appreciation of the great spiritual realities that underlie the teachings and practices of the Church.

The afternoon service may well be devoted to children. If the Sunday-school meets at 2.30 or 3 P.M., a bright service in Church at 3.30 will be found very attractive. In our opinion the forms of service given in most Service-books for children are very objectionable. Let the older children be taught to attend the regular services of the Church, and to use their Prayer-Books, but at the children's service, which is intended distinctly for the young, let the Service be as simple as possible.

A processional Hymn, the Creed, a Metrical Litany, sung kneeling, followed by the Lord's Prayer and a Collect, is sufficient. Then let there be a short lesson from Scripture, another Hymn, and after that a bright address or catechising of not more than fifteen minutes, ending with another Hymn, a Collect, and the Blessing. The service will be about forty minutes, and the children's interest sustained throughout. Children get very fond of a service intended for themselves. Such service should not be limited to the children of the Sunday-school, but all parents belonging to the Parish may be invited to bring or send their little ones.

In some city parishes it will be found well to have the Evening Prayer on Sunday at 4.30 or 5 P.M., either with or without a sermon, and then to have a later service, when the office will be less formal and liturgical and the preaching of a character more adapted to mission work.

With regard to the time for Communion, the practice of receiving in the middle of the day is very much a matter of habit, and a little instruction will show the more intelligent of our Church people the better way of rising early, even at the cost of a little self-denial, to receive the Bread of Life. As we write, a parish occurs to us, where out of 520 communicants on an Easter-day, 470 received before 8.30 A.M. There were on that day celebrations at 6, 7, and 8 A.M., as well as at the 10.30 service.

Sermons.—The sermon is a most important factor in the life of the parish. Without exalting preaching above praying, this must be distinctly recognized. The majority of people do not read much, either in the Bible or in books of religious instruction. For the greater number their teaching comes altogether from the lips of the preacher.

Preachers need to remember this, and to make their preaching *instructive.* They must not think that the people in general know all that they ought to do, and the reasons why such things should be done, and only need to be moved to action by impassioned appeals. It is not really so, and many an earnest appeal is made in vain because the doctrines, or Scripture facts, upon which the appeal is founded are unknown.

For this reason instructive sermons are needed, and also instructions in addition to sermons. It is most useful to have set times for instruction, pure and simple, apart from homiletics and exhortation. Such instructions may well follow sermons on Sunday evenings, as they do in the course of Parochial Missions; or they may be given in connection with a week-day afternoon or evening service.

So much has been said by all sorts of teachers upon the subject of preaching that little need be said here, but the foregoing hints will be found useful and practical in working in a city parish.

Mission Chapels.—Subsidiary to the church building, in which the chief services of the Parish are conducted, and round which its life centres, may be small mission rooms, or mission chapels.

These may be located in the poorest localities of the city, being made out of some store or stable, clean, simply colored, and made bright with pictures. Here may be gathered a little Sunday-school of shabbily-dressed children, and on Sunday evenings a miscellaneous company, including many who could not be got within a church door. The Sunday-school may be worked entirely by Laymen, young or old, and so also may the evening service, if a really competent man can be found to speak. Written sermons in such places are worse than useless, but it will be well for the Rector or one of the assistants to go round from time to time with words of kindly interest. No Sacraments will be administered in such rooms, but the people will be led on to the Parish Church. It is not proposed that such places shall become in time parishes, but that they shall always retain their missionary character as feeders to the central church. As one family or individual after another is raised in religious, and therefore social life, or is prepared to receive Sacraments, he will be handed on to the parish itself, though he may still remain attached to the mission room as a helper for the sake of his influence upon others. Many a soul now in Paradise praises GOD for the work of conversion begun in some such simple room.

Societies.—There is much to be said for and against the multiplication of Societies within the Parish. Some we must have, and they are useful in organizing work and employing workers, but it is easy to have too much machinery.

Some that seem the most useful may be mentioned. A Temperance Society with both adult and juvenile branches. It is better that this should be a branch of the Church Temperance Society on its comprehensive basis, than a merely local organization.

A society for young girls, such as the Girls' Friendly Society, is a real need, and also some similar Guild or Society for boys.

It is extremely doubtful if large, mixed Parochial Guilds and Societies do good in proportion to the amount of labor they involve, and whether they do not really hinder work. All parishioners ought to be working in some way or another, whereas the existence of a Guild or Rector's Aid Society may hurt the workers, those not belonging to it giving that as a reason why they need not work.

An organization for distinctly spiritual purposes may be really valuable, in which, for instance, all the members undertake to keep a spiritual rule of life. An association for intercessory prayer, in which the obligation is to give a certain time to this work every day, and also meet together from time to time for united intercessions, is of great use in building up the true spiritual life of the parish.

An Altar Society is also desirable, not for the purpose of raising money, but to bind together in work and with a Rule of Prayer those who have leisure to care personally for the sanctuary and its furniture, or can occupy themselves in the necessary needle-work, embroidery, or washing of linen, etc.

In working among the poor advantage should be taken of any societies existing in the city, whether connected with the Church or not. In many places, as Philadelphia, Buffalo, Boston, and New York, there are Charity Organization Societies of various kinds. Clergy and visitors among the poor will do wisely to work in harmony with all such, and will find their own labors lightened thereby. It does not seem well to have a distinct society in the parish for the care of the poor, but still such work must be done methodically and under direction. If there are Sisters of Charity connected with the parish, it will naturally fall under their care. If none such can be had, individual visitors should be asked to care for individual cases, meeting together occasionally for mutual counsel and advice. Such meetings might be held weekly and be presided over by one of the clergy, or better still, by some competent layman.

Foreign and Domestic Missions must not be omitted, but this ought not to be a matter for personal solicitation and collections. It is the duty of Christians to give for such purposes, and such duty should form part of the regular instruction of the people, so that when the offerings are made at stated times the contributions of the parishioners may be forthcoming as a matter of course.

Finances.—Finances generally need a few words. The Scriptural mode of dealing with the matter is that the Church shall be free to all, and that all expenses be met by the free-will offerings of the people laying up as GOD has prospered them. Where this plan has been tried in faith and prayer it has not failed.

To win the young, the timid, and the poor, the Church must be free. Such are willing to come, and will give of their means to support the Church and its works, but they are not equal to the effort involved in taking a pew. Many, too, will come to free churches who would feel themselves pledged or compromised by taking a seat before they at all see their way to come out on the side of GOD and of His Church.

In free churches the envelope system is often tried, whereby persons pledge themselves to give certain amounts weekly or monthly through the year. By this means a fixed sum is guaranteed, and the wardens do not live in any anticipation that they will not be able to meet their liabilities. This plan has its advantages, though to some it may seem rather to take away the freedom of giving. Of course, however, where this plan is adopted, any person can add at will to his or her weekly contribution.

Permanence.—As we write a continually recurring thought is, But all this takes time to work out, and much of this work and these plans can only be tested by years of patient labor; and we live in an age of restlessness and change. People move, clergy move, there is little fixity at present in any of our Church work.

This is, unfortunately, true, and it is a reason why our city parishes will hardly ever reach that high state of efficient organization and work which may be seen by visitors to London and other great English cities. The people there are much more fixed in their homes and habits, while the Rector is almost an absolute permanency.

Whether the English plan by which a Rector once installed settles down and accepts the parish as his life-work, as by far the greater number of Rectors do, there being no power to displace him so long as he observes ecclesiastical law, could ever be naturalized in our country, or would work well if it were so naturalized, is a question. We do, however, need more stability. Clergy ought to be more content with their positions, and not be continually looking upon them as simply steps to something better. Parishioners, too, should be content with their Rector as he grows in years. He may, perhaps, lose something of brightness and freshness, but this is more than compensated for by the added experience and knowledge of his people. A younger assistant can always be found to meet the thoughts and wishes of younger people. A continual succession of young, inexperienced men is fatal to any spiritual growth in the parish.

So, too, with residences. We do change too much. And when we change we think far too little about our Church. It is not creditable that so many Church people, after they have secured a home and are comfortably settled, suddenly finding themselves far removed from any Church, should say, " I never thought of asking about the Church." No Christian has a right for mere purposes of comfort or money-getting to exile himself from the means of grace.

If the Rector remains at his post and gives time and energy to know and work among his people, and his people loyally and faithfully stand by him, all bearing and forbearing with one another, and all heart and soul in the work to which GOD calls each, a growing interest will be created, and the parish will increase in strength, efficiency, and spiritual life, and be fruitful not only in good works, but in a harvest of souls to the glory of GOD.

REV. EDWARD OSBORNE.

HOW TO ESTABLISH A COUNTRY CONGREGATION.—In establishing a country parish, the first requirement is a Rectory. The presence of the minister should be a fixed and recognized fact, and he should be secured against landlords and rivalry. In preparing to build, every one should be asked to have a share, thus enlisting interest. Many small offerings from many persons are far preferable to one of even greater amount from a single giver. And a score of churches could be built while congregations of men of small means are waiting for some rich and generous person to do all for them. Happily, for spiritual good and education in sustaining parishes afterwards, such events are comparatively rare. As the whole cost seems large to people who, really or in fancy, will always be " poor," write down each article needed, windows, furniture, etc., with its price, and many will agree with alacrity to place their names opposite as pledged workers, and will raise the small sum in a few months, who could not be aroused to the seemingly hopeless task of "helping to build a church." Scores can be found who will readily give one cent a day, who would be regarded liberal if, at the end of a year, they gave a dollar, who yet, by system, cards, and collectors, will even more cheerfully in the year give much more, and feel it less. It is marvelous how rapidly the whole amount thus accumulates. If all will thus give, there will be less disposition to engage in fairs and other expedients often more hurtful than leaving the church unbuilt, and hindering to the necessary acquirement of learning how to give from principle. As a matter of economy, whatever furniture is procured should be handsome and of the kind needed for the church. As soon as a room can be had, let the minister open a Sunday-school. If good teachers of sufficient number cannot be obtained, the minister should teach for a short time, and then drill in a part of the Church service. As Evening Prayer is the shorter of the two, it would be well, as soon as the children have learned two or three chants and hymns, to have regular Evening Service, with the scholars as the choir; this to be followed by catechising in place of a sermon, and enriched by anecdotes, but especially Bible stories. Brief catechising every Sunday should be a matter of course. Let the first books used be Prayer-Books and Church Hymnals. The "Nursery of the Church" should not drill for the Church in substitutes or imitations of her Liturgy, nor can we afford to expend brief time and limited opportunity in teaching hymns, good or bad, which have no place in her services. How to take their place in our worship is the lesson for our scholars, and they will delight as much in using the Prayer-Book and Hymnal, as in the ephemeral Liturgies and books of song which do nothing towards instructing in the Church. This will do much to solve the problem, "How to retain the older scholars in the Church." Each class should engage in work for some article of furniture.

The organization of a vestry should be deferred for a year or two, and until the men understand something of the Church's system and their peculiar duties. In some Dioceses the property can be vested in the Bishop. A treasurer, if desired, could be appointed by the minister. Two or three trustees could act for a year or two, when a vestry could be elected, and the organization effected.

Faithful visiting, avoidance of controversy, cottage meetings, spirited services, preaching, good common sense, and a loving spirit will commend the Church anywhere. We want no better "plan" or "system." Give the Church its opportunity, which it has not always enjoyed, without diluting or laying aside what we have for seemingly successful experiments, and we have all we need to plant the Church even in villages or country where others have failed.

REV. T. G. LITTELL.

Parochial Missions. We use the phrase "Parochial Missions" advisedly that we may at once clearly distinguish for our readers the nature of that of which we speak. We do not speak of "Missions" in the sense of mission stations permanently established with a view to future churches and parishes; nor yet of missions to the heathen, whether foreign or domestic, conducted by the Central or any Diocesan Board. We speak of missions of and the kind comparatively new and untried in the American branch of the Church Catholic.

By a Parochial Mission we understand a special effort made in a parish already existing and having a corporate life, lasting during a limited period, and intended to build up the parish in its life and work, to deepen the spiritual life of the individual members, and to draw others in the town or neighborhood within hearing of the Gospel, that they may also become partakers of the spiritual blessings held out to them in the Church of CHRIST.

I. A Parochial Mission implies a parish and a clergyman in charge of it. It involves much labor in preparation, and more still in carrying on the works that may result from the mission, and harvesting fruit from the seed sown.

A mission is not a substitute for the ordinary labors of a parish, such as services, sermons, house to house visiting, and the like. It is something added to all the organization and work of a parish, to fill these with new spirit and energy, and to supplement them by accomplishing that which they are not intended or are unable to do.

We can imagine a parish, long settled and solvent, with a church in good repair and well attended; a congregation drawn in average proportion from various walks of life; a fair number of communicants, the greater number of whom, however, are women; Lent and other Church seasons observed by somewhat more frequent services; the charities of the parish sustained; the Sunday-school in good order; a good feeling existing between clergyman and people, the former having been in the parish some years and knowing his flock and feeling himself at home with them. Such a parish might be accounted by some a model parish.

And yet the clergyman has a feeling, shared with him by some of the more devout lay-people, that all is not just as it ought to be. Perhaps the feeling is hard to describe. He is conscious of a want. He takes pains with his sermons, but there is a want of result; the words seem to have become familiar and to have lost their power with the people. The number of Eucharists may be increased with the increase of the parish, but the number of Communions made by individuals does not grow. Even the young people coming forward for Confirmation seem to do it in a formal way without the earnestness he desires to see. The parish works go on, as Guilds and other societies, but there is a lack of zeal. Besides this, there seems to be a cessation of the power of the parish as a missionary centre. Outsiders do not come, the people of the neighborhood are not affected by it, there are many, it may be living close by the Church, either poor or of the well-to-do classes, who disregard the Church and her services, who never heed the LORD's Day, who practically, though so near the Church, are living without GOD in the world.

Here is the exact field for a Parochial Mission. "We want stirring up." "We want a revival, only we can't have that in the Church." "We want deepening in some way." "What is to be done?" A Parochial Mission is the answer.

II. For a Parochial Mission is a Church Revival, a time of awakening and stirring up, a "time of refreshing from the presence of the LORD."

It is a special and earnest attempt to bring all the agencies the Church has at command to bear upon those both within and without her fold, an attempt carried on vigorously for from seven to fourteen days, and, if possible, for a longer time, with many services, sermons, and instructions at different hours and suited to different classes of persons. There will be Eucharists at which many can be present and pray. There will be spiritual instructions adapted to those who have made some advance in spiritual things, and more elementary addresses to beginners. There will also be opportunities for intercession by those who have learned to pray, and rousing sermons with burning words appealing to those who never have bent the knee, or have given up the good habits of their childhood. The children of the parish, too, will not be forgotten, but have some opportunities provided when suitable words may be spoken to them, for though the mission is mainly for adults, still the young ones of the flock are capable of being interested and drawn nearer to GOD; through them, too, some of the parents may be reached. Special addresses will also be given to men and women separately, bearing upon their own special difficulties, temptations, and sins. Something may also be done for the young men and women just growing into manhood and womanhood, with life and its joys and temptations opening before them.

It will be seen at once that a mission in the Church differs from an ordinary Methodist revival in this great characteristic,—it is not simply a call to the unconverted, but while it is that, it is also a call to the converted and faithful members of the Church to a higher and closer walk with GOD, to more faithful and devoted lives in His service.

III. It may be fitting to say a word here of the origin of Parochial Missions. Like very many other things which mark the revived life of the English Church, and of our own branch of it, they had their origin in France.

St. Vincent de Paul, when chaplain to the De Gondi family, was called to minister to a dying peasant. He found to his horror that this man, though using the sacraments of the Church and living an outwardly respectable life, was yet in a state of most grievous sin which he had neither confessed nor attempted to overcome. Impressed with the thought that there were probably many others in the same condition, he preached on the Feast of the conversion of St. Paul, 1617 A.D., on the subject of a general confession. The effect of this sermon was so great that he had to send to Amiens for other clergy to help him in ministering to the people whose consciences were aroused. So encouraging were the results of this his first mission, that it was determined to set on foot others in other villages and towns, and to secure suitable preachers for the work. From this arose the Congregation of Mission Priests, or Lazarists, as they are sometimes called, an order of Priests in the French Church dedicated to this special work. Other religious orders, as the Dominicans, Passionists, and Redemptionists, have also engaged in it, and Parochial Missions have now become a recognized part of the system of the Roman branch of the Church.

John Wesley and others had long seen the need of some such work in the Church of England, but it was not until about 1869 A.D. that their thoughts and wishes took shape. In that year a mission was organized in the city of London, in which some sixty churches took part. The success of this effort and the many blessings following it caused Parochial Missions to be fully accepted in the Church of England. In 1874 A.D. the Bishop of London, Rochester, and Winchester organized another mission for London, in which nearly three hundred churches shared, and now a third is planned to take place in 1884 A.D., only, owing to the magnitude of the city, it has been determined to divide it into two sections and hold a mission for each section at different seasons.

From London the influence spread, until every large city and town in England has had its united mission, and many a small village and parish besides. It would not be easy to say how many of the thousands of parishes of the Church of England either have had, or are looking forward to, the time when in the near future they will have the benefit of Parochial Missions.

The need of men fitted for the work has been felt in England just as it was in France, and in several of the Dioceses Missionary Brotherhoods have been formed whose members are Priests, and in the Dioceses of Lichfield and Oxford laymen also, set apart for the special undertaking of preaching Parochial Missions.

In our own Church a beginning has also been made. The city of Baltimore stands alone, as far as we know, in having had a general mission in which the greater number of the churches of the city took part, but there have been a considerable number of missions in separate parishes in other cities and towns; Boston, Newark, N. J., Hoboken, Chicago, Cleveland, O., Utica, N. Y., Philadelphia, St. Louis, Springfield, O., Tilton, N. H., Louisville, Ky., Nashua, N. H., Kansas City, and others come into our mind as we write. Many missions have also been preached in Canada, as, for instance, in Toronto, Halifax, Montreal, Quebec, St. John, and other smaller places.

IV. It may be asked, What is the nature of the preaching, and what are the subjects of instruction, during such a mission? Perhaps the best answer will be to subjoin a full list of Sermons and Instructions given in a mission in Trinity Church, Utica, N. Y., in Advent, 1882 A.D., taken from the *Earnest Worker*, the parish paper.

Sermons.

Amos. iv. 12. The will of GOD the end of man.

Hag. vii. 5-7. The unsatisfying character of all earthly things.

Hag. vii. 5-7. Sin leading away from GOD.

St. Luke xv. 11-13. The beginning of sin.

2 Cor. v. 10. The judgment after death.

St. John xi. 28. The call of death.

1 John iv. 9. The Love of GOD in the Incarnation.

1 Cor. vi. 20. The Love of GOD in the Passion.

1 Cor. iv. 5. The coming of CHRIST the time of approval.

Rev. iv. 1. The call to Heaven.

Phil. i. 21. Spiritual life in CHRIST.

Rev. xxi. 1. Heaven.

Each sermon, except on Sunday mornings, was followed by an Instruction, the subjects being, What is a Mission? On making the Mission profitable. Conversion. Self-examination. Repentance. Confession of Sin. Pardon of Sin. Mission Resolutions. The Blessed Sacrament. Perseverance.

Addresses were given at mid-day upon Prayer, and at 4 P.M. on each week-day there was a Bible-class upon the life of St. John Baptist. Four special services for children were held. Two addresses were given to men on "The Image of GOD in Man by Creation" and "The Restoration of the Image of GOD in the Incarnation." One address was given to young women, and a Temperance Meeting was also held, at which a Branch of the Church Temperance Society was organized. On the first day there was an address to Church-Workers, and on the first Saturday night a Prayer-Meeting. The opening address of the Mission was given by the Bishop of the Diocese, who commended the Mission Preacher to the prayers and attention of the people. The Mission began on Friday evening and lasted until the morning of the Wednesday week following. In addition to the sermons, etc., the Holy Eucharist was celebrated on each morning, and Matins and Even-song were also said.

Where so many sermons or instructions are given in so short a space of time (forty-eight in eleven days at the above Mission), there must be some course of teaching to avoid mere repetition. In this the power of a Mission comes out. One thought can be taken and fully dwelt upon, and then before it is forgotten or the effect has passed from the mind of the hearers another is brought forward, bearing upon the former and enforcing it, and the soul is by this roused to attention and stirred to action.

This result is also attained by the use in many instances of what are sometimes known as "after-meetings." Generally an Instruction on some point of Christian Faith or Practice follows the evening sermon, but this is occasionally omitted, and an after-meeting either in the church or some adjacent room substituted. At such meetings the speaking is of a more personal and experimental character, the Missioner going round the room and addressing himself to one after another with the invitations of the Gospel. Several prayers are offered, either extempore or in the form of a Litany. Others engage in the work, conversing with individuals and endeavoring to lead them to repentance or faith in the LORD JESUS. Such workers are either men or women, Sisters of Charity, or simply private persons. The results of such after-meetings are often remarkably great and happy.

It will be understood from the foregoing that the *Services* at the time of the Mission are of the simplest character, without the ordinary formality. Matins and Even-song are generally said on week-days unaccompanied by any sermon or address. At the Mission Services proper there will generally be a Hymn, a few verses of Scripture, the LORD'S Prayer, and a few Collects, followed by the Sermon; after the Sermon a few more Collects will be said, or perhaps some words of extempore prayer. A form of Confession from the Prayer-Book or the opening sentences of the Litany are profitably used, or a penitential Psalm. Anything in the way of a musical service or choral singing would be entirely inappropriate. For this reason a volunteer choir is often better than the usual choir of the Church, whom it is difficult to move out of their accustomed manner of choral praise.

Much, or elaborate, music would destroy the penitential character of the work of the Mission. All deepening of spiritual influences must be accompanied by deepening penitence, and everything in the services should conduce to this end. In churches where variously-colored altar-cloths and hangings are used, violet is that chosen for the season of a Mission.

The last service of the Mission will generally be of a more joyful character; indeed, the TE DEUM is often sung as an appropriate thanksgiving to Almighty GOD that He has allowed the work to be brought to a successful issue.

V. In addition to the public teaching, there will be the fullest opportunity afforded for free intercourse between the preacher and those of his hearers desiring explanation, instruction, or spiritual help in their own lives. Such intercourse may be simply in the way of conversation over special needs and difficulties, or in the way of more formal use of the confession and absolution provided by the Church for souls burdened with a sense of sin.

It has always been found that this personal intercourse is the most important part of the work. There are many who find it difficult to speak to their own Pastor, meeting him frequently in daily life, who will open their hearts readily to a stranger; and many, who have long wished to speak to some clergyman upon spiritual matters, but to whom the right moment seems never to have come, are glad to avail themselves of the special opportunity which the Mission affords. Half the benefit of sermons is lost because the impression made is allowed to pass away. A few moments alone with the clergyman, with heartfelt words of counsel and an earnest prayer and blessing, will many a time save that which is most precious.

VI. Of course such a work as we have described needs preparation to make it really effectual. The preparation should in no case be less than three months.

The earnest communicants of the Parish should be asked to remember the proposed mission in their prayers, and especially at the time of the Eucharist. Bands of workers may be organized who will distribute tracts or papers inviting to the mission. The young people should be sought, and all those who, having been confirmed and become communicants, are known to have fallen away; the opportunity of a return to means of grace will be urged upon them. The clergyman and his workers will be careful to visit all persons living in the neighborhood of the church, whether attendants or not at any place of worship, and invite them to be present. Curiosity may bring some who will stay for better reasons, and there are in every community anxious souls who will be thankful to hear of such a work and occasion, on which mayhap they will obtain that which they are longing for.

A volunteer choir should be formed to supplement or take the place of the ordinary choir, and bright, stirring hymns be well rehearsed, that the singing throughout the Mission may be hearty and congregational.

A weekly or fortnightly Prayer-Meeting for special intercession will be found most helpful, persons being invited to send in special cases to be prayed for.

All such preparation carefully and thoughtfully made will tend to create a feeling of reality in the minds and hearts of the people. A great opportunity is really coming, a message to which they must give heed, a voice from GOD in their midst, a call to change their lives in some way; all this and more will come to them and prepare them to cry out and seek for the blessing of GOD upon themselves, their parish, and all those around.

VII. After the mission much remains to be done. At the closing services of the mission "Resolution Papers" are given away, that those who have received benefit may write upon them some good resolution by which the impression made may be fixed and become lasting, obtaining the signature of the Mission Preacher as a witness. It is for the parish clergyman to help such to keep their resolutions. Some will need instruction for Baptism, Confirmation, or Holy Communion, and for these classes must be formed without delay. Others who have been deeply moved desire to learn more of spiritual things that they may go forward. For these it is well to have one or more Bible-classes,—if none exist to which they can be invited. Special instructions upon various matters of doctrine or practice which have been brought prominently forward by the Mission may be usefully given at convenient times. In some cases it is well to organize a Parish Guild, or a Guild for some special class in the parish,—*e. g.*, boys or young men. A Temperance Society may also be begun, or a branch of the Girls' Friendly Society. Nothing better can be used than a meeting for prayer and intercession. To this many will gladly come, and brief spiritual instruction on the deeper things of the Christian life may well be joined with it.

VIII. The results of the mission must be left until the Day of the Revelation of JESUS CHRIST. Some things will be seen, as increased attendance at church and at Holy Communion, an increasing number of candidates for Confirmation, more liberal offerings for Church purposes, perhaps the clearing off of some debt, a greater desire on the part of individuals to take an active part in the work of the parish, a distinct increase in the attendance at church of men; all these may be thankfully noted. But the mission preacher and the parish clergyman must often be content to labor and leave other men to enter into their labors.

It is not to be expected that all the parishioners will be benefited, nor that all will approve. Many careless ones will dislike to be aroused. Many staid, old-fashioned people may object because a mission is something new and, in their judgment, sensational. Possibly there may be some opposition to be overcome and much prejudice to be encountered in a spirit of faith and prayer.

In connection with the matter of prejudice, it is to be observed that these Parochial Missions have been adopted by every section of the Church, and have been prepared for, and also preached by, men of very varying shades of theological opinion and belief. Of course in every case the parish clergyman will be careful to secure the services of a preacher who is in full sympathy with himself and whom he can fully trust in every respect.

IX. This brings us to the last, and for some reasons hardest, part of our subject. Who is to preach such a mission? Where are the men to be found who are capable of giving from forty to fifty sermons or addresses on ten or more consecutive days, keeping up and deepening the interest of the hearers? Where are the men who have sufficient experience in dealing with spiritual things to be able to meet and deal well and wisely with the many souls who may come to them for counsel and help during the course of a mission?

Such men are greatly needed in the Church. We need Orders of men trained for the work. Men with no parochial ties, who can go from place to place as they are needed, at the invitation of the parish clergyman or Bishop of the Diocese. The number needed is large, for the work is growing, and where it is possible two preachers should always go together.

We have already the Society of St. John the Evangelist, with its houses in Boston and Philadelphia, and the more recently organized Society of the Holy Cross in New York, but these only represent one section of the Church's thought and teaching, and are but few in number. We have heard that in some Dioceses an effort has been made under the direction of the Bishop to associate together men adapted for the work. Where there is a Cathedral with staff of clergy, some of the Canons might well be set apart for this distinctive form of labor.

Meantime, the help of the parochial clergy must be sought by their brethren. The number of sermons, etc., does not seem so great and overwhelming when it is remembered that they are arranged in courses and are preached to strangers, and not to those among whom the clergyman is daily visiting. Many clergymen who have had the benefit of Missions in their own parishes might, from the experience there gained, be able to go forth to aid their brethren.

Still there is a need, and a growing one, of men for the work. We cannot doubt that as the need is felt GOD will be pleased to raise up men to supply it. For this it would become all Churchmen interested in the true spiritual growth of their Church to pray.

X. The last word must be a financial one. Of course the Mission Preacher receives nothing for his services, but is put to no expense for traveling or board. The expense for tracts and papers will be from twenty-five to fifty dollars, according to the size of the parish and number required. This and the necessary expenses of the preacher or preachers will readily be met by a collection on the last day of the Mission only (there should be none on the other days), supplemented by the free-will offerings of some of the wealthier parishioners. The expense should not be allowed to fall upon the clergyman of the parish.

REV. EDWARD OSBORNE.

Parson. The Priest set over a congregation is called a Parson (from the Latin *Persona*), because he is the representative of the Church, representing her in that Parish, and having certain legal rights, and too, certain responsibilities in the eye of the law. He is the holder of all the rights, temporal and spiritual, belonging to his office in relation to the Parish over which he is placed, and he is also answerable for all the affairs of the Parish which fall within the purview of his office. But the title does not occur in the Canons of the American Church. The titles used to describe this office are Rector or Minister in charge of a congregation. We have dropped the titles Curate and Parson from our Canons, and in fact the word Parson is retained only in common parlance. The canonical terms for those in holy orders (besides the three names Bishop, Priest, and Deacon) are Presbyter, Clergyman, Rector and Minister, and Assistant Minister. Vicar, Parson, and Curate have dropped out of our canonical usage. (*Vide* RECTOR.)

Parsonage. The house which should be provided by every parish as a residence for the Rector.

Paschal. Relating to Easter, or more correctly, to Easter through the Jewish Passover. It is the title of our LORD as the true *Paschal* Lamb. The Paschal Letters were letters written by Patriarchs and Archbishops to the Bishops within their jurisdiction, and by Canonical right, the letters written by the Pope of Alexandria to his brother Patriarchs to give the due notice of the true day on which Easter was to be observed in their several jurisdictions. There was also a famous controversy called the Paschal Controversy, which was set at rest by the Nicene Council, 325 A.D. Some claimed that Easter should be observed according to the Jewish rule, on the third day after the fourteenth day of the month Nisan, irrespective of the day of the week upon which it would fall,—the fourteenth of Nisan being the very day upon which our LORD'S Passion and Death took place. This was a very early custom of the Asiatic Churches. But the Church at large followed the present rule of observing as Easter-day the Sunday after the fourteenth of Nisan. The controversy dates as early as the days of Polycarp (160 A.D.), and was carried to that pitch that Victor, Bishop of Rome, attempted to excommunicate those Asiatic Churches which followed the rule they claimed came to them from St. John.

Traces of these practices are found in the usage of the British Churches, which show the Ephesine origin of their foundation.

Easter is sometimes called the Paschal Feast.

Passing Bell. A bell which was tolled when any one was dying. The sixty-seventh Canon of 1603 A.D. enjoins, "When any is passing out of this life a bell shall be tolled, and the minister shall not then slack to do his last duty; and after the party's death (if it so fall out) there shall be rung no more but one short peal, and one other before the Burial and one other after the Burial."

Passion. The very and real suffering of our LORD, from His agony in the garden on through His trial, scourging, and revilings to its consummation in the parting of His soul from His body in a true and real death. That to a pure nature as His the jarring and clash of sinful men with evil passion was a suffering is very true. That a man so perfect should shrink in inexpressible pain from our pains, and suffer by coming in contact with them, is as true. But in neither of these senses do we generally speak of our LORD'S Passion. To measure its love at all requires from every man earnest and true meditation. Its extent cannot be felt, its power will be unknown to us, its love a misty conception unless we will try to consider it in its several aspects towards ourselves and our needs, so great and pressing in His sight that for love of us He willingly did that from which He as naturally shrank. To give directions upon this is beyond the limits of this work, but there are many books of devotion which give much excellent direction for such profitable meditation.

Our LORD'S Passion was in a certain sense necessary to show Him perfectly human as well as perfectly sinless,—its agony showed Him sinless, its reality showed Him human. It was in its beginning the fit step preparatory to the Atonement, which He completed by His death. As it passed from point to point of shame and pain, it was something far more than a most lovely example, it had a bearing upon the inner life of all His followers, and was a test for them. In its culmination upon the Cross He was made the victim and accomplished an act of redemption which we could not share in, but of whose inestimable benefits every baptized person becomes a partaker, and through the Christian indirectly but really all mankind, since CHRIST died for all men. It is noticeable that Plato should have pointed out that the good men must suffer shame and even death; but his was only a heathen idea, which could not conceive that GOD should take upon Himself perfect and pure flesh, and in it, by suffering all that hatred and malice could heap upon Him, wrest from His enemies the very instrument by which forgiveness could be proffered to them and to all. In this the Passion of our LORD is wonderful and beyond reach.

Passion-Week. (*Vide* HOLY WEEK.) To enforce upon us so far as she can the necessary meditation upon the marvelous work of redemption in its last steps, the Church has from very early times appointed the days before Easter at first only from Good-Friday, then prefixing to these the preceding days, till now Passion-Week, or Holy Week, extends from Palm-Sunday to Easter-even. For usages and ceremonies, see HOLY WEEK. But here it may not be amiss to add, that whatever worth the solemn services have for our souls, and whatever impression is made upon us, it must come from our own endeavor, both as individuals and as congregations, to realize the verities set forth, the facts commemorated, by meditation and by prayer.

Passover. "It is the sacrifice of the LORD'S Passover, who passed over the houses of the children of Israel in Egypt when he smote the Egyptians and delivered our houses." The relation of this central Feast of the Mosaic worship to our LORD and to ourselves is so great that it must find a place in every work that relates to His Person and Life. While historically it was the commemoration of the deliverance of the Israelites, it was also a prophecy of the wider deliverance of GOD'S people throughout all time, and over the whole earth, through the Blood of JESUS. Its observance was kept with a solemnity and care that marked its place in the National Life. The leaven carefully removed, the garnishing of the houses, the preparation of a guest-chamber for visiting Jews, the pure water brought to the house from a living stream, the ushering in of the solemn Feast with the blast of trumpets, the choice lambs taken to the Temple and there slain, and the offerers having the blood of the lamb poured out at the foot of the altar, and the kidneys and fat burnt with incense on the great altar,—all these made the public solemnity one of surpassing importance, while the worship at home by their families and the joyful feast which followed, was of incalculable use in preserving the household religion aflame in the Jewish home. Then the tale of their deliverance, so beyond all hope and human power, was the chief point with their children, which roused their pride in, and stimulated research into, their national history, and kept them up to the rigid observance of this Feast. But its historical value overshadowed its prophetic value, and the Jew was not prepared to admit that it prefigured anything else than this wondrous redemption. But with the Christian the Passover was a type of the greater passing of GOD'S Judgments over those who have been sprinkled with the Blood of the Lamb upon those who have not. The fulfillment of the type in the sacrifice of CHRIST our Passover is very remarkable. It was at the time of the daily evening sacrifice, which was now offered earlier in the evening to allow space for the slaying of the Paschal Lambs, that the darkness covered all the land, and the evening sacrifice was interrupted, and as the light returned and our LORD yielded up the ghost, the true Paschal Lamb had shed His blood to be the deliverance of the children of GOD. CHRIST'S Atonement, then, is that blood of the Passover that protects GOD'S people. Its sprinkling upon the lintel and door-post of our life, our bodies and their senses, the gateways whereby our soul goes out to the world and through which it can return within itself, is by baptism, which is the application to our bodies and souls of the Blood of the LAMB. The Passover, then, is full of prophetic significance, and has not only a historic value and was a most important rite in the national religion, and was bound up in the political life of Israel, but it has a doctrinal significance to the baptized Christian. As the Israelite was, so is he of GOD'S elect, and that Judgment which falls upon the world falls not on him. Yet as the Israelite, in the face of all that he had seen and shared in of GOD'S holy deliverances, could sin and was destroyed of the destroyer, and fell by the way, so the Christian must feel that his deliverance is from the Judgments that fall on the world, but not from the discipline needful for him, or from the destruction which his disobedience may have brought upon him. Yet the relation of this Passover to ourselves must enter as completely into our religion, into our Christian citizenship, be as rigidly observed and as joyfully celebrated. Its spiritual application must but intensify its power over our lives and educate us to a better realization of the unseen.

Pastor. The word Pastor, or Shepherd, is an appropriate designation for a clergyman in charge of his spiritual flock, and it is to be regretted that it is not more in common use in this country. In Germany it is a familiar word, and when one reads of such a man as Oberlin he may consider it rightly given. Such names as Heber and Keble in England at once call up the thought implied in the word. In France, Archbishop Fénelon, sitting on the grass, and talking with the people about their affairs, and about religion, entering cottages, and eating with the poor, as a brother, or father, and even driving home a peasant's lost cow on a dark night, was a beautiful example of a pastor. The word is frequently used in Holy Scripture. The shepherd's duty was to feed his flock, and to watch them, lest wild beasts should tear them; and even to spend the cold night, if need be, in the oversight of his charge. In the xxiii. Psalm, ALMIGHTY GOD Himself is the Shepherd who provides "green pastures" and "still waters" for His flock, and guides them through "the valley of the shadow of death." CHRIST is "The Good Shepherd" who gives "His life for the sheep" (St. John x. 11), and who still from Heaven watches over them. Jeremiah styles spiritual teachers "pastors" (Jer. iii. 15).

After Christ's Ascension, "He gave some pastors" (Eph. iv. 11). David was a shepherd (1 Sam. xvii. 34). It was necessary that the shepherd should be tender towards the young and feeble (Isa. xl. 11, and Gen. xxxiii. 13). King Cyrus is called God's shepherd, and Homer speaks of the king as the shepherd of the people. In Heb. xiii. 20, the risen Christ is the "great Shepherd." In 1 Pet. ii. 25, He is "the Shepherd and Bishop of your souls." Did St. Peter in writing these words think of our Lord's direction to him, "Feed my sheep"? (St. John xxi. 15-17.) As Christ is "the chief Shepherd" (1 Pet. v. 4), His ministers are under-shepherds, seeking " a crown of glory" in His service. The term pastor is personal, while rector and priest are official. The clergyman is by his office somewhat isolated, and in giving social confidence to his people he needs to have it returned from them. Like the Good Shepherd he should know his flock by name, and they should gladly follow his lead. Geikie draws attention to the close relation that subsisted between the shepherd and the sheep as they found companionship on the lonely mountain. They shared common dangers, and the leader's voice was known as the call of safety. So has Christ drawn near to His people in His own figure, and so should His clergy feel that the words shepherd, watchman, overseer, and steward imply an acquaintance with individual wants, and a proper distribution of needed benefits. Bishop Andrews engraved on his Episcopal seal the words of St. Paul, " Who is sufficient for these things ?" (2 Cor. ii. 16.) The Holy Spirit answered St. Paul, and he answered himself, " our sufficiency is of God." Again, in trouble, this faithful pastor is cheered by the divine message, " My grace is sufficient for thee: for my strength is made perfect in weakness." As Matthew Henry says, the clergyman should "study Christ, preach Christ, live Christ."

Christian art delights to keep up the pastoral idea in the pictures of Christ bearing the lost sheep in His arms, which has been engraved even on the Sacred Vessels of the Holy Communion; and it is seen also in the pastoral staff of the Bishop. One of the best exemplifications of what a Christian pastor should be is found in the life of George Herbert, the saintly rector of Bemerton. The secret of his success is shown in his delightful book, " A Priest to the Temple ; or, The Country Parson." Chap. i. is entitled " Of a Pastor." He begins with this definition : " A pastor is the deputy of Christ, for the reducing of man to the obedience of God." He demands a holy life of the Country Parson, and learning, especially in Holy Scripture. He should be devout in public prayer, earnest in preaching, a peace-maker, and a comforter of the sick. He should be courteous and charitable, and a visitor and counselor " from house to house" (Acts xx. 20). He must watch as a sentinel. He is a faithful catechiser, and wisely and reverently administers the Holy Sacraments. Chap. xxxvi is on " The Parson Blessing ;" and as he treats of the proper assurance and power of that benediction through God's authority, we can feel that Herbert's blessing was no common one, and it blessed the giver as well as the receiver, so that the Christian world sanctions Isaac Walton's description of him as " that pattern of primitive piety."

Authorities : Upham's Life of Madame Guyon, Walton's Lives, Geikie's Life of Christ, Bridges on the Christian Ministry, Heber's Memoir, prefixed to Poems, T. Woodward's Memoir of W. Archer Butler, prefixed to Sermons.

Rev. S. F. Hotchkin.

Pastoral Letter. A letter or an instruction issued by one who holds a Pastoral relation to a congregation or to a Diocese. But chiefly it refers to the triennial letter issued by the House of Bishops at the close of the sessions of the General Convention. It is read there for the first time, and afterwards at the earliest convenient time to each congregation by its rector. The Bishop of a Diocese also may issue a Pastoral to his Diocese or to any separate members of it, as to the laity or to the clergy alone. In many parishes it is a custom for the rector to have to issue a letter to his congregation upon some pressing subject, calling their attention to or urging their action upon it. It has often proved of service, and may be made by the rector an effective way of appealing to his flock in some really important conjuncture.

Pastoral Staff. *Vide* Crosier.

Paten. The *Patena* (Latin), a wide and shallow dish, most usually and correctly made of metal, gold or silver, in which the bread for the Holy Communion is placed when offered as the oblation, and on which it is consecrated. Ancient patens were of large size, as some of them were said to be very weighty, but those of modern use are much smaller. The paten used to be made with a foot beneath it, but it is now more usual that it should have no foot, and the bed be only of a size to fit upon the rim of the cup or chalice. The brim of the paten is often very broad and has some inscription upon it. The old paten was shaped like an ordinary plate, but made of silver. Gold patens are frequently presented by devout donors.

Patriarchs. The word Patriarch is found only in the New Testament, in Acts vii. 8, and then applied to the twelve sons of Jacob. Our common usage transfers the title first to Noah (though sometimes also to the antediluvians), and then to Shem, Abraham, Isaac, and Jacob, but generally withholds it from the sons of Jacob. In strictness, however, it should be extended not only to them but to the chiefs of great houses, as to Jesse. But the title has acquired in the Church another application. It was given to the Bishops of the five centres of Christendom, and thence to other important Sees. But originally there were only Antioch for Asia, Alexandria for Africa, Rome for Europe, and Jerusalem as the Mother City. Constantinople was added when it became the seat of the Empire. These, except Constantinople, were Apostolical Churches, as being founded by Apostles. But since political importance was the guide in arranging church precedence, Constantinople was raised to the second rank by the decree of the Council of Chalcedon (451 A.D.), an act which was not submitted to by the See of Rome for some time. But in the earliest usage, Primate and Patriarch were synonymous, and in fact the title was used rather in a general than in an official sense for some time after it was recognized as the proper designation of these five Sees. Their Patriarchal rank was acknowledged as early as the Council of Nice (325 A.D.), but the name was not exclusively used of them till about the time of Charlemagne. Besides these, other Sees were ranked as Patriarchal, and some of them still survive with this title, but, of course, do not rank with the Patriarchates as above recited. These are Canterbury, Toledo, Vienne, Lyons, Venice, Aquileia. The Church in this country has properly the extent of a Patriarchate, and were there an Appellate Court properly established, it would contain one of the chief notes of a Patriarchate. But as its Synod, the General Convention, is now organized and the precedence of its Bishops not placed upon any provincial system (*vide* PROVINCE), it is an inchoate Patriarchate.

The authority of the Patriarch is thus described (Blunt's Dict. Hist. and Doct. Theol.): "Their authority consisted in ordaining Metropolitans, confirming them or imposing of hands, in giving the pall, in convening patriarchal synods and in presiding in them, in pronouncing sentence according to the plurality of votes when metropolitical synods were insufficient to decide some important difference, and in some honorary privileges, such as the acclamation of the Bishops to them at the end of a general council."

The exercise of Patriarchal power is not refused, by every Churchman at all acquainted with Church history, to each Patriarch. But the exercise of such power without his jurisdiction has always been forbidden, and the Patriarch of Rome assuming to himself an uncanonical Supremacy, has suffered the consequences of a revolt from his communion of so many parts of Christendom. At a General Council his place in the rank of Patriarchs would not be refused him; his arrogated supreme powers alone would be excepted to and denied him. The Archbishop of Canterbury exercises practically Patriarchal powers in England, and his right to preside in all formal gatherings of the Bishops of the Anglican and American Communions is acknowledged. Two such gatherings, for they were not Synods and had no conciliar authority, have been held (the first in 1867 A.D., the second in 1877 A.D.) at Canterbury.

Patrimony. A name by which the estates and revenues of the Church were described. The most famous was the "Patrimony of St. Peter." The older Churches had estates given them in different parts of the Empire. Thus both the Sees of Ravenna and Milan had estates in Sicily. And Rome had large estates left to the See for various purposes,— the poor, the clergy, the church-furnishing,—*e.g.*, one in Lombardy was for keeping the lamps alight in St. Peter's Church. It is eminently proper that some of the Church's permanent work should be independent of what is called the voluntary system. In this class should be put the support of the Episcopate, and the establishment of schools and hospitals. They should have a patrimony for their proper maintenance, and this patrimony should be so secured that it could not be wasted, alienated, or forfeited. It deserves the best attention of the laity, since to them is committed the ministry of the temporals of the Church, and upon them rests in the largest proportion the regulation of those matters of finance which should place the work of the Church and the discharge of her responsibilities upon a secure basis. This duty has been discussed under the head of FINANCE.

Patron. "The person who has the right to present to a benefice. The greatest part of the benefices in England are presentative: the thanes or lords who built and endowed churches having first agreed with the Bishops that they should have the privilege of presenting fit clerks to serve and receive the profits of the churches founded by them. This was a modification of the older system that built the churches at common charge and by which the right of presentation lay in the congregation. It was, however, the outcome of the needs of the times, and its use was the cause of many disputes between the wealthy founders and the Bishops. There is as yet in this country no departure from the primitive mode, but should there arise any imitation of this custom (which began about 400 A.D.), the limitations and the rights established elsewhere would form a sufficiently authoritative guide for the settlement of any disputes. These disputes, it may be added, have at times led to results far different from those involved in them at their inception. For example, the refusal of the Bishop of Exeter to induct the Rev. Mr. Gorham into the vicarage of St. Just in Cornwall, upon the presentation of Lord Lyndhurst, because of alleged unsoundness in the Faith, led to the famous "Gorham case." (*Vide* Hook's Ch. Dict., Stephen's Book of Common Prayer, Philimore's ed. of Burn's Eccl. Law.)

Paul, St. "Saul, who is also called Paul," was born at Tarsus, the capital of the province of Cilicia, and one of the three great Academies (Athens, Alexandria, Tarsus) of the classic world. His father was a Jew, a Benjamite, one of the great orthodox-patriotic party of the Pharisees; a "Hebrew," in the special sense of a maintainer of Hebrew customs and of the use (within his own household) of the Aramaic language, and, finally, a known citizen. This citizenship was no result of the "freedom" of Tarsus; for civic "freedom" under the Empire implied no more at the most than municipal self-government and exemption from public taxation. Saul's father may have been the freedman of a Roman noble, or he may have received citizenship in reward for political services during the great civil wars; or, just possibly, he may have bought the privilege. His name, as that of his wife, is unknown to us. We gather (2 Tim. i. 3) that they were sincerely pious. They had, besides Saul, at least one child, a daughter (Acts xxiii. 16). Saul's circumcision-name was perhaps common in his tribe, in memory of the First King. His other and, to us, far more familiar name, *Paul* (Paulus), was probably given him also in infancy for use in the Gentile world, just as Jewish children in England now have a Hebrew home-name as well as an English (or otherwise European) name for exterior use. If his father was in any sense a dependent of the Æmilian family, the choice of Paulus is easily explained, for Paulus was a common cognomen of the Æmilii. But it was used also by the Sergii and other families. The name first occurs, Acts xiii. 9. The marked mention of it there is sufficiently explained by the fact that the Gentile name was, just then, in the Apostle's life, necessarily coming to be the more usual name of the two, and that the first distinguished Gentile before whom he spoke for CHRIST was himself, by a coincidence, a Paulus. The exact date of Saul's birth is quite uncertain, but it must lie within the few years before and the few years after the common (or Dionysian?) date of the birth of CHRIST. When Stephen died Saul was still a "young man" (in the then recognized sense of the words); that is, he was not more than forty years old. And the date of Stephen's death must probably be placed in, or very near, 30 A.D. Quite early, perhaps as early as his ninth or tenth year, Saul was transferred, as a student of the Law, to Jerusalem, where the great Pharisaic teacher of the day was Gamaliel, grandson of Hillel. Gamaliel was an orthodox "Hebrew," but also a student of Gentile literature, and Saul, under his influence, not only matured into the best Rabbinist of his generation (Gal. i. 14), but also gained an acquaintance, traceable in his Epistles and Discourses, with at least a few Greek authors and with the then prevalent Greek philosophies. Under Gamaliel, too, he would not be discouraged from using (along with the original Scriptures) the "Septuagint" (lxx.) Greek Version.

His quotations from the Old Testament indicate an equal familiarity, or nearly so, with the Original and the Version. He quotes in Greek much as an English Hebraist, with the authorized Version in his memory, might quote in English. Whether Saul dwelt continuously at Jerusalem till his first recorded public acts is uncertain. Acts xxvi. 4, 5, suggests a residence continuous on the whole; but, on the other hand, St. Paul's silence is sufficient proof that our LORD during His earthly life was unknown to him by sight. This suggests a break of residence, an absence (in Cilicia or at Alexandria) during about the period of our LORD's ministry; after which, perhaps, a return to Jerusalem was prompted by the sudden prominence of the *Nazarene heresy*. At the date of Stephen's work Saul was perhaps a member (as a Scribe) of the Great Sanhedrim. But more probably his election into it (which seems to be proved by Acts xxvi. 10, "I gave my *vote* against them") was due to his display at that great crisis (for such it was both for the Church and the Synagogue) of intense and energetic zeal. He now became a regular delegated inquisitor for the Sanhedrim, and, among other places (Acts xxvi. 11), visited Damascus, of whose 50,000 Jews, as of all the Jews of the Dispersion, the High-Priest (under certain imperial grants) was not only the spiritual head, but also in some respects the civil *patronus*. His delegate thus carried the power of arrest. Under King Aretas of Petra (a vassal of the Empire), who was just then lord of Damascus, the Jews there had a governor (*ethnarch*, 2 Cor. xi. 32) of their own, to whom Saul would show his commission, but who was soon to set guards at the city gates to bar the renegade's escape. On the ever-memorable conversion we only remark here that the appearance then granted was, in the convert's own life-long belief, radically different from what is commonly called a vision. It was truly, though mysteriously, *corporeal*, for St. Paul (1 Cor. xv. 8) bases upon it his claim to count among the witnesses of our LORD's corporeal Resurrection. We do not dwell on the absolute and perfectly permanent change in the intense purpose of Saul's life which then and there took place; it is best read in the Scripture pages. We only suggest the study of its two contrasted yet harmonious aspects,—the *supernatural* aspect, in that it was wrought by an objective Divine act which was the issue of a Divine purpose (Gal. i. 15), and the first step in a life-long experience of Divine inspiration; and the *natural* aspect, in that it left the frame-work of character unchanged, preserved unimpaired the balance of intellectual judgment, or rather gave a vastly greater expansion to its legitimate use; and far from leading Saul impatiently to reject old beliefs as such, left him quite as fixedly as ever, and far more deeply than ever, sure of the entire and eternal truth of the prophetic Scriptures and of the Divine meaning of the very Ritual which had once seemed to him irreconcilably to contradict the teaching of the Nazarenes.

After baptism, and some intercourse with the Damascene disciples (Acts ix. 19), and then a withdrawal from the city (Gal. 1. 17) for some weeks or months, Saul began at Damascus the new work of his life. His withdrawal had secured for him, probably, the mysterious preparation of supernatural intercourse with his Master in the solitudes of Arabia,—perhaps in the peculiarly congenial solitudes of "Sinai in Arabia." After three years (at most) he left Damascus, to avoid arrest or murder, and made his way to Jerusalem, where Barnabas, his friend and perhaps once fellow-student, introduced him to the still hesitating Apostles. He became St. Peter's guest; but after a fortnight of discussions with the Hellenists of Jerusalem he was again compelled, by plots of assassination, to retire to the coast of Syria, and thence to his native Tarsus (38 or 39 A.D.). From Tarsus, no doubt, he now worked as the evangelist of Cilicia, and so spent at least three years. At length he was summoned by Barnabas to the Syrian Antioch, the scene of wholly new developments; for in it first the "Greeks" or heathen Gentiles (Acts xi. 20) had now been freely welcomed to the covenant of the MESSIAH.

At Antioch he labored with Barnabas for "a whole year," about 43 A.D., probably a year memorable as the birthtime of the *Christian* name (Acts xi. 26); and then visited Jerusalem to carry relief there during (or just before) one of the great dearths which marked the reign (41–54 A.D.) of Claudius. The martyrdom of St. James, the son of Zebedee, and the seizure and deliverance of St. Peter, occurred while Saul and Barnabas were in or near Jerusalem. This brief and troubled visit is scarcely (it would appear from the words of Gal. ii. 1) to be reckoned as a visit to the Apostles at all. Now followed, at Antioch, another period of work for Saul and Barnabas. It is a period not easy to date: some reckonings close it 45 A.D., some as late as 49 A.D. It lasted, however, till a Divine oracle called Saul and Barnabas to embark on their great missionary tour. They began with Cyprus, where at Paphos the Proconsul Paulus became, we may hope, a true convert to the Gospel through the work and word of the Tarsian Jew who bore his name. They then passed to the Pamphylian shore, and thence to the inner uplands of Pisidia and Lycaonia, including the Isaurian fastnesses where Derbe stood. At length they approached, from the west, the Cilician border, and then returned on their footsteps to the port of Attalia, and so by sea to the Syrian Antioch.

We attempt no details of this memorable circuit,—crowded as its story is both with Divine instruction and with innumerable notes of historic accuracy and reality. At Antioch they remained "a long time,"—probably till 50 or 51 A.D. And now a disturbance of extreme gravity broke in upon the work in this great centre of Gentile Christianity. The *Judaic* party in the Christian Church, retaining and intensifying the exclusive views which had once clouded even St. Peter's mind (Acts x. 34), and which degenerated afterwards into manifold heretical divergences, now intruded on the field of St. Paul. Jerusalem, where by this time the LORD's brother was what we may fairly call the Bishop, was recognized as the metropolis of the Gospel, and the dispute was referred thither,—a Divine oracle (Gal. ii. 2) concurring with, or prompting, the resolve of the Church. The result was in some sort a compromise, though it was a compromise divinely sanctioned (Acts xv. 28); but it was at least so solemn a statement of the covenant equality of Gentile Christians, and thus so real a victory for St. Paul, that it secured to him for life the bitter and restless opposition of the Judaic party,—an opposition curiously developed in somewhat later days in the heretical literature falsely inscribed with the name of Clement of Rome, and in which St. Paul is covertly assailed as the grand corrupter of the *primeval Gospel*. The undiminished energy of the Judaists, even just after the decision at Jerusalem against their main principle, appears from the successful pressure they put upon St. Peter himself, and that at Antioch (to which he appears to have followed St. Paul), to act for the moment as a separatist (Gal. ii. 11–21). From this crisis, then, St. Paul came forth as more than ever a recognized Apostle, co-ordinate with the Twelve, and also more than ever the object of intense hatred with a powerful party. He had returned to Antioch with Barnabas, and accompanied by the newcomers from Jerusalem, Judas and Silas (Silvanus); and now, after a residence there of "some days," he proposed to Barnabas a second circuit. But a personal difference led to their separation, and St. Paul set out with Silas (say 51 A.D.) on an independent track. This time he went by land; revisited his plantings in Syria, Cilicia, and Lycaonia; joined the young Timotheus to his company in what proved to be a life-long connection; broke new ground in Phrygia and the "Galatian region," where (it seems from Gal. iv. 13) he was detained among the Celtic inhabitants by illness,—a detention overruled to a large and enthusiastic acceptance of the Gospel, soon, however, to be marred by Judaic intruders; and then attempted other districts of Asia Minor. But Divine commands, perhaps in the form of "prophesying," closed all avenues, and at last guided St. Paul across the Ægæan to Europe. Here he landed in Macedonia, perhaps 52 A.D.; made his first converts, now in peace, now amidst cruelties and terrors, at Philippi; passed southward to Thessalonica, a Jewish centre and a busy trading-place, where he planted a vigorous Church; then, southward still, to *Berea*, still followed by Jewish violence, but also by Divine blessing; and at last, for safety's sake, to Athens. Silas and Timotheus were left at Berea, with orders to follow in due time. At Athens he took advantage of the ways of the place, and opened discussion with the students and *dilettanti* who frequented the walks of the Agora; and at length (whether formally or informally, seriously or in irony, who shall say?) he was brought up to answer for his strange doctrine before (or at least in) the sacred Court of Areopagus. His address indicates familiarity with Stoicism. Before long he left Athens for Corinth, the seat of the Roman government of Achaia (*i.e.*, the Southern Greek Province). Here a scene of mingled activity and vice made both peculiar difficulties and peculiar opportunities for St. Paul. Early in 52 A.D., Claudius, by a severe but soon canceled edict, banished from Rome its multitude of Jews. Of these, one married pair, Aquila and Prisca (or Priscilla), settled or rested at Corinth. They were work-people, hair-cloth-workers, and thus plied the trade which long before (according to Rabbinic precepts, by which every Rabbi was to learn a handicraft against a time of need) had been taught to the boy Saul, and this trade was now standing St. Paul, the Christian Rabbi, in good stead; and thus, perhaps at first in the way of business, he fell in with Aquila and Priscilla. Whether he found them Christians, or (under GOD) made them such, we shall never know, but it is more probable that they were already believers,—for otherwise we should certainly expect some distinct allusion in the Acts or the Epistles to so important a conversion. But doubtless they owed their first direct apostolic teaching to St. Paul, to whom now they were bound for life in a holy friendship. We have thus in Aquila and Priscilla, very probably, an example of what is antecedently likely,—the arrival already of the Gospel at Rome; the first facts and doctrines may have reached the city soon after the Pentecostal preaching (see Acts ii. 10), and there they would find rather easy audience than otherwise. At Rome a peculiar weariness of paganism was manifest in many directions. The East was, in a certain sense, in fashion; Judaism had attracted abundant notice; and the prophecies must have been at least superficially known to a multitude of proselytes or semi-proselytes.

But no organized Church seems as yet to have arisen at Rome. Indeed, there is no clear token of any Christian organization west of the *Ægæan* before St. Paul's arrival at Philippi. At Corinth St. Paul spent eighteen months. This time was marked by the writing of his earliest Apostolic Letters,—the two *Epistles to the Thessalonians*. These must be dated in, or near, 53 A.D., certainly not earlier. Great opposition and great success marked the beginnings of the great Corinthian Church, with the "outstations" (in modern missionary language), which, doubtless, then sprung up at the port of Cenchreæ and other neighboring towns. Probably the assistants of St. Paul carried the Gospel through the whole Achaian province at this time, or very soon after (2 Cor. i. 1). About this stage of St. Paul's life Nero succeeded Claudius, October, 54 A.D.

After scenes of outrage which the Proconsul Gallio treated with impartial indifference, St. Paul at last left Corinth for Syria, say some time in 54 A.D. He touched at Ephesus; left Aquila there with his wife, perhaps to be the organizer of a regular community, and himself departed for *Cæsarea* and Jerusalem. There he was perhaps in time to keep, as he had intended, one of the great Festivals; but all that is certain is that he "saluted the Church" of St. James, and then soon left for Antioch, where again he spent "some time" (Acts xviii.). Now followed a missionary tour in the "upper coasts,"—*i.e.*, the inland regions, of Asia Minor. It must have been long and laborious; but it is dismissed by St. Luke with a brief allusion. At length St. Paul reached the shore, at Ephesus, some time (say) in 55 A.D. Here an eminent Alexandrian Hellenist convert, Apollos, had meanwhile arrived; had held intercourse with the more advanced and instructed Aquila and Priscilla, and had crossed to Corinth; there to do much good (Acts xviii. 27, 28), but also, probably, by his more ornate and philosophically-worded preaching, to raise prejudices, unwittingly, against St. Paul. The Apostle spent about three years at Ephesus in ceaseless Christian labors; and during this time his assistants traveled, it seems, to Colossæ, and Laodicea, and other places in proconsular Asia which he could not reach (Col. ii. 1). At length the tumult of Demetrius, perhaps at the festival of the Ephesia, hastened St. Paul's already-planned departure for the European side. Very shortly before this departure (spring, 57 A.D.) he had written and sent the *First Epistle to the Corinthians*,—occasioned by distressing reports from Corinth as well as by questions raised by the Church there. To give the Epistle time to do its work, he resolved to reach Corinth by a long circuit round the head of the *Ægæan*, and so southward through Macedonia. Titus went before, to ascertain the state of the Corinthians, and to report to St. Paul, if possible, in Asia Minor; but this proved impracticable, and St. Paul's intense anxiety was not relieved by the longed-for tidings until he entered Macedonia (2 Cor. ii. 12, 13). Thence he wrote the *Second Epistle to the Corinthians*,—a wonderful mosaic of serene revelations of eternal truth and outpourings of personal anxiety and affection.

He was now free to visit Macedonian churches and to evangelize new districts.

Here we may probably place his westward tour (Rom. xv. 19) as far as the Adriatic sea-board. Now also he effected throughout Macedonia (*i.e.*, in the then sense of that term, the Northern Grecian Province) the ingathering of a fund, already organized, for the poor Christians at Jerusalem (Rom. xv. 25, 26; 2 Cor. viii. 1–4; ix. 1, 2); a task which was not only a tangible proof of deep sympathy with the work of St. James, but also an expression of St. Paul's own heart's love for his fellow-Jews. (See Rom. xv. 27.) But the most lastingly important effort of this period (for to this period it surely belongs) was the *Epistle to the Galatians*,— the result of news of the inroads of Judaic propaganda in that well-loved, but already troubled, scene of his earlier labors. At length he reached Corinth; there found (as we have good cause to think) happy results of his two messages of warning and instruction, and there also collected the Achaian gifts for the Jerusalem Fund, which he now (Rom. xv. 25) prepared to carry to St. James. This stay at Corinth lasted only three months. But it was made memorable forever by the writing of our great Epistle, —the *Epistle to the Romans*. The Epistle was evidently written not under pressure of anxiety, but with calm deliberation. It was composed, apparently, in the house of a Corinthian Christian, Gaius or Caius, dictated by St. Paul, and written down by one Tertius. Would that we could call up the scene in the Corinthian chamber! The three months at Corinth over, he left Achaia for Macedonia, spent Passover at Philippi, crossed to Asia Minor, addressed the Ephesian Presbyters at Miletus, sailed to Tyre, and at length (amidst prophecies of danger) reached Jerusalem, perhaps in May, 58 A.D., —not long after an Egyptian impostor, at the head of a huge gang of the zealot *Sicarii* (Assassins), had seriously threatened the Roman authorities of Palestine.

In the act of a last effort to conciliate the Judaic party, St. Paul was almost murdered in the Temple by the Jews; rescued by the Roman commandant, but under the belief that the victim of the mob was the Egyptian rebel; allowed to defend himself on the spot before the multitude, and the next day before the Sanhedrim, and then, for safety, conveyed as a prisoner to Cæsarea. There, within a fortnight of his arrival at Jerusalem, he was heard before the Procurator Felix, who lingered, however, over the case, and at last, two years after, when recalled on a serious charge (summer of 60 A.D.), left St. Paul a prisoner still. Of these two years of St. Paul's life we know almost nothing. Some critics assign to them the writing of the Epistles to the Ephesians, Colossians, and Philemon. But these are certainly to be dated later, and from Rome. At length, before Porcius Festus, the Apostle was heard again; but even this far better judge hesitated to do him full justice, and he appealed in due form, as a citizen to the Emperor's own hearing. He was, ere long, shipped for Italy; but off the Cretan coast, perhaps early in October, a typhoon struck the ship, which soon was a drifting wreck, and was at last run aground at Malta. There the rescued company wintered, and not till the early spring of 61 A.D. (the year of Boadicea's revolt in Britain) did St. Paul at last see Rome. At some distance from the city, in detached parties, at two different spots, the representatives of the Church (now for nearly three years in possession of the great Epistle) met the captive Saint, and cheered his anxious and weary spirit by their loyal sympathy. In the city he was permitted to occupy a hired lodging, perhaps a story of one of the lofty Roman *tabernæ*. Here, a few days after his arrival, he made a last, long effort to convince the leaders of the Roman Jews of the Messiahship of JESUS; and here, under military custody, but otherwise unmolested, he spent "two whole years," full, no doubt, of immense mental and spiritual labor, and holy influence, and marked forever by the writing of the four Epistles (probably in this order), Colossians, Philemon, Ephesians, Philippians. This Roman residence closed in the course of 62 A.D., probably in the summer. The question *how* it closed—whether with condemnation to death or acquittal—is a famous one. Its discussion would be out of place here, but our undoubting conviction is that the result was St. Paul's acquittal; that he was set free, and once more undertook missionary labors; that he visited Western and Eastern Europe and Asia Minor; and that, late in this last stage of his life, he wrote the Pastoral Epistles,—in the order, 1 Timothy, Titus, 2 Timothy.

This last most affecting letter is dated once more from a prison, and from Rome. It is our only relic of St. Paul's *second* Roman captivity, which ended in his martyrdom,— probably 66 A.D., the year of the Great Fire and of the Neronian Persecution, though perhaps the date of the martyrdom must be placed one or two years later. Probably soon before St. Paul's execution, and probably also at Rome, St. Peter had suffered his predicted death. And (if 66 A.D. is the true date) the Jewish war had already begun a few months when St. Paul died,—to close four years later with the Fall of Jerusalem. The one question within our scope here, connected with this last period of St. Paul's life, is the question of a visit to Spain. Was the hope of Rom. xv. 24, 28, at length fulfilled? There seems to be good evidence that it was. In the Epistle to the Corinthians, written by St. Paul's own follower, St. Clement of Rome, we find it stated (ch. v.) as a familiar fact that St. Paul, before his "departure from this world to the holy place," "went to the end of the West." It has been pleaded against the theory of a Spanish journey, that this may mean only *Italy*, as viewed from the locality of St. Clement's correspondents at *Corinth*. But the then centre of the world could not possibly be so described, and above all not by a writer dating from Rome, however he might care to put himself in his reader's geographical position. And there is direct evidence besides that such a phrase as "the end of the West" would have a familiar connection, at that time, with Spain. (See Bishop Lightfoot's St. Clement of Rome, p. 49–51.)

This witness, certainly genuine and quite contemporary, is fairly conclusive. St. Clement cannot have been mistaken or ignorant on so leading a fact of his great master's latest labors as the westward limit of those labors. The only serious difficulty in the theory of the Spanish visit (once granting the theory, necessary to the genuineness of the Pastorals, of St. Paul's release and second Roman imprisonment) is that there is no traditional trace whatever of any work of St. Paul's in Spain. But this is equally true of other districts (as Illyricum), in which, however, we have St. Paul's own word for his labors.

We take it, then, for certain that St. Paul, some time after the spring or summer of 62 A.D., and probably before the spring of 66 A.D., visited the Western Peninsula,—whose present name, España, is said to be an aboriginal word, meaning "The Land's End." The belief that he landed in Britain possesses, in Bishop Lightfoot's words (St. Clement of Rome, quoted above), "neither evidence nor probability."

It is impossible not to wish to know something of St. Paul's personal appearance. Mr. Lewin (in his Life and Epistles of St. Paul, vol. ii. ch. xi.) has collected all that approaches to information in this matter; and in this one case at least tradition appears to be something better than mere fancy. It seems to be certain that St. Paul's stature was short, if not diminutive; that his head was bald and his face bearded; and that his expression, even if deformed in some measure by *ophthalmia* (which is one of the many conjectural explanations of the "thorn in the flesh"), yet reflected something of his soul. A medallion, dating perhaps from the generation next to St. Paul's own, is engraved by Mr. Lewin (vol. ii. p. 411): it gives the profiles of St. Paul and St. Peter; and that of St. Paul expresses, or seems to do so, all the elevation and intensity both of thought and feeling which still, as we read the Epistles, touch us with the touch of life. The character and labors of St. Paul have been so often eulogized, and are so inimitably described in a thousand unconscious touches by his own pen, that it would be vain in this brief summary to attempt another portrait.

We will only quote the words of but one of the many existing delineations.

"Amidst the circumstances of his apostolic work he developed a force and play of spirit, a keenness, depth, clearness, and cogency of thought, a purity and firmness of purpose, an intensity of feeling, a holy audacity of effort, a wisdom of deportment, a precision and delicacy of practical skill, a strength and liberty of faith, a fire and mastery of eloquence, a heroism in danger, a love, and self-forgetfulness, and patience, and humility, and altogether a sublime power and richness of endowment, which have secured for this chosen Implement of CHRIST the reverence and wonder of all time." (Meyer, Brief an die Komer, Einleitung, p. 7. From Rev. H. C. G. Moule's Intro. to his Comment. on St. Paul's Epistle to the Romans.)

Peculiars. They were parishes or monasteries which, for some reason or cause, were exempted from the jurisdiction of the Bishop in whose Diocese they were situated. During the Middle Ages there were many such exemptions granted upon one or other cause. Nearly all of those which lay in England were swept away at the Reformation; but some were retained, notably the famous Westminster Abbey, which is subject to visitation from the Queen only.

Pelagianism. This heresy, though it takes its name from Pelagius, "does not so much represent single notions of a single man as a complete moral and religious system," its peculiar tenets being concerned with original sin, freedom of the will, Divine grace, and predestination.

Differing opinions concerning these matters were entertained, and more or less clearly expressed, from the earliest times; but it was not until the fifth century that they were so developed as to claim general attention and merit the decision of Councils. In the beginning of this century there appeared, among others, two who seem to have been chief in formulating that system which has been rejected and condemned by the Church, Celestius, a monk of Rome, and Pelagius, a British monk, from whom the heresy has taken its name—Pelagianism.

They were bitterly opposed by St. Jerome, and with less asperity by St. Augustine, whose writings contain the orthodox doctrines on the disputed points. The following seven heads are given by Hagenbach as St. Augustine's summary of the Errors of Pelagius:

1. Adam was created mortal, so that he would have died whether he had sinned or not.

2. Adam's sin has only affected himself, and not the human race.

3. New-born infants are in the same condition in which Adam was previous to the fall.

4. The whole human race dies neither in consequence of Adam's death, nor of his transgression; nor does it rise from the dead in consequence of CHRIST's resurrection.

5. Infants obtain eternal life though they should not be baptized.

6. The Law is as good a means of Salvation as the Gospel.

7. There were some men, even before the appearance of CHRIST, who did not commit sin.

It is probable that some of these propositions would have been universally condemned by the earlier theologians, while upon others there would have been some differences of opinion. But the contrast between Pelagianism and orthodoxy may be best exhibited by comparing what each taught on the chief points of difference. Pelagius appears to have held that there is no other connection between the sin of Adam and the sin of his posterity than that which exists between example and voluntary imitation. Hence infants are in the same condition in which Adam was prior to the fall, and are free to develop sin or virtue as they choose, and are alone responsible for what they do. In opposition to this St. Augustine taught, "As all men have sinned in Adam they are justly exposed to the vengeance of GOD, because of this hereditary sin, and guilt of sin."

As regards liberty and grace Pelagius held that man stands in need of Divine aid, which he spoke of as the grace of GOD, assisting the imperfections of man; but this was something external, added to the efforts put forth by the free-will of man, and even merited by virtuous inclinations.

Augustine, on the other hand, taught that grace was "the creative principle of life, which produces out of itself the liberty of the will, which is entirely lost in the natural man." Out of this position follows as a logical consequence the whole doctrine of predestination, from whose harsh conclusions Augustine himself seems to have shrunk, seeking to soften them by practical cautions, though he combated the views of the Semi-Pelagians, who proposed a middle course between Pelagianism and Augustinism. The following summary may serve to illustrate this subject:

"The motto of Pelagius was free-will; that of Augustine efficacious grace. The former held that, notwithstanding the fall, the human will was perfectly free to choose at any time between good and evil; the latter that, in consequence of the fall, the will is in a state of moral bondage, from which it can only be freed by Divine grace. With the British monk election is suspended on the decision of man's will; human nature is still as pure as it came originally from the hands of the CREATOR; CHRIST died equally for all men, and as the result of His death, a general grace is granted to all mankind, which any may comply with, but which all may finally forfeit. With the African Bishop election is absolute. We are predestinated, not from foreseen holiness, but that we might be holy; all men are lying under the guilt or penal obligation of the first sin, and in a state of spiritual helplessness and corruption; the sacrifice of CHRIST was, in point of destination, offered for the elect, though, in point of exhibition, it is offered to all; and the saints obtain the gift of perseverance in holiness to the end." (Historical Introduction to Pascal's Provincial Letters, by Rev. Thomas McCrie.)

Pelagianism was condemned in the person of its teachers, Celestius and Pelagius, in a series of Councils from 412 A.D., the chief of which were held in Carthage in 417 and 418 A.D.; and in particular our own Church has condemned the doctrines of Pelagius in the IX., X., and XVII. Articles of Religion; not without reason, for the heresy is still held by many, though never at any time have Pelagianists formed a distinct sect. It is extremely probable that many of the sects would defend his doctrines, and in particular it may be shown that the Jesuits in their controversy with the Jansenists have probably fallen into this error.

In pursuit of this subject the reader is referred to Hagenbach's History of Doctrines, Blunt's Dictionary of Theology, Pascal's Provincial Letters, and Burnet and Browne on the Articles.

Penance. The outward expression of the inner repentance of the heart. This was required in the early Church, where the heathen civil law did not take cognizance of many offenses against the moral law. He who was guilty of some offense whereby the congregation was offended and injured was suspended from Communion, and was required before readmission to testify and prove in some public way his repentance. It was the protection that the Church then demanded for her purity, and from it arose the penitential discipline of the Primitive Church. It was natural, since the fault was more or less public, that the reparation of it should be as public. It was, moreover, a defense, and a hindrance to those who might be tempted to sin, were there no penalty. It was the expression, too, of the inward contrition of the soul. The publican in the Temple abased his eyes, beat upon his breast, and stood apart. In our own day, since there are legal penalties for nearly all overt infringements of ordinary morality, there is no public expression of contrition demanded of offenders, except in the cases of evil living or of a quarrel between communicants, as recited in the rubrics before the "Order for the Administration of the LORD'S Supper;" nor is there at this place any order for any penitential act in any other sense than the acknowledgment of the fault or sin, and the vow of amendment. The ancient penitential system required something more than this. There was a definite penalty assigned for every breaking of the moral law, and the person who submitted to the Church's censures had to undergo it. If he were contumacious it but increased the severity when he finally did submit. "The theory of penitential discipline was this: that the Church was an organized body with an outward and visible form of government; that all who were outside of her boundaries were outside the means of grace; that she had a command laid upon her and authority given to her to gather men into her fellowship by the ceremony of baptism; but as some of those who were admitted proved unworthy of her calling, she had also the right by the power of the keys to deprive them temporarily or absolutely of the privilege of communion with her, and on their amendment to restore them once more to Church membership. . . . It was a purely spiritual jurisdiction. It obtained its hold over the minds of men from the belief, universal in the Catholic Church of the early ages, that he who was expelled from her pale was expelled also from the way of salvation, and that the sentence which was pronounced by GOD'S Church on earth was ratified by Him in heaven." (Smith's Dict. of Chr. Antiq., sub voc.) Penitence has at once its origin and sanction in the New Testament, and primarily in the promise of CHRIST Himself (St. Matt. xviii. 18). There is room only for a mere mention here of the several orders of Penitents in the Primitive Church. In the earliest records we find the duration of the penance, as of fasting and weeping and prayer, quite short,—from two to seven weeks. This was gradually lengthened, and after the close of the second century we find years substituted for weeks, though the judgment of the Bishops and the circumstances of the case, as well as the dangers from persistence, often led to a shortening of the time. But the concession of the privilege of being restored was also granted. For with the shorter time was also held the greater depth of humiliation and the greater strictness of life after restoration. So it came to pass that the longer period, with all its sharp discipline, led to no greater strictness afterwards. But about 260 A.D., Gregory Thaumaturgus arranged an order of restoration, which was as follows: The *Flentes* were without the door of the church, where the sinner can beg the prayers of those who go in. The *Audientes* stood in the vestibule (Narthex), where they were to stand till the Catechumens were dismissed, as only worthy to hear the Scripture and the Instruction, but not to hear the prayers. The *Substratentes* stood within the Church, after the Catechumens were dismissed. The *Consistentes* were mingled with the Faithful, and did not leave with the Catechumens. This was in practical use, but still the Bishops could curtail it, and very often did so shorten or omit entering one or other of the steps.

The arrangement, too, varied in different parts of the Church, as however rigid the discipline was, it was yet adapted to the character of the people for whose correction it was inflicted. Besides, sackcloth was worn, sometimes continuously, but necessarily at some step in the restoration, also ashes were sprinkled upon the head. The restoration, when at last it did take place, was with public prayer and with imposition of the hands of the Bishop. If a penitent were in a mortal sickness the Priest could restore him at once, and if it happened that the penitent recovered, the remainder of the sentence was thereby remitted. But later on he was required to resume and complete it. It is foreign to our plan to go farther in this sketch, which applies only to those ages of the Church when penance, penitence, and repentance were more clearly understood, and the Church's work was to see that her spiritual power was enforced. Nor can we enter into any details of the English system of Church discipline, which is outlined in the Canons of 1603 A.D., and which is carried out in Archidiaconal and Episcopal courts.

In our own Church in this matter of penance, there is no enforcement of a public penalty in the Church, at least in the case of laymen. Suspension from the Communion is almost the sole penalty, and practically a layman conscious of having offended excommunicates himself by absenting himself therefrom. Nor under the Rubric can any notice be taken of scandals, unless they become notorious and the congregation be thereby offended. In, however, this matter of observation and presentment, the vestry who can have much of the public opinion of the congregation in their hands, can be of material aid in presenting scandalous persons in such a way to the clergyman that he can act. For it is a hardship which now hinders the clergyman, in his effort to control his parish and admonish his flock, to present to himself as judge, an offender, and to be jury and witness both, and further, to execute the sentence. Yet practically this is the case, for the Bishop leaves it to him to do all that is needful. Happily, the notorious cases are but few, and there are some compensations in the consciences of offenders that keep them from urging an impudent claim for spiritual gifts; a private admonition generally is all that is needed. (*Vide* REPENTANCE and DISCIPLINE.)

Penitence. The preceding article has touched upon so much of what properly belongs to this, that but little more will be needed. A penitent mind continues in the state of repentance. It is a frame of life, so to speak, that holds over itself the discipline that a "godly sorrow that worketh a repentance to salvation not to be repented of" will constantly exercise. "My sin is ever before me" was David's repentant admission. It is the energetic display of sorrow for which St. Paul commended the Corinthians (2 Cor. vii. 11).

Penitential. A book of discipline containing the lists of crimes, offenses against, and infractions of the moral and ecclesiastical Law. The first books were probably digests of disciplinary canons, which were very numerous in the Church in Central and Western Europe. They were also the enactments of local authorities, and sometimes were in conflict with the canonical discipline. Probably this was owing to the attempt to apply to the people a relaxed form of the monastic discipline. Its attempt to classify sins, and to give a penalty rather than a remedy for it, had a bad effect. The chief Penitentials were that of Theodore, Archbishop of Canterbury, who, however, was not the actual author, that of the Venerable Bede, and that of Egbert of York. On these were based many other Penitentials, of which the chief was that of Halitgar's Collection of Canons. This effort at discipline was intended to impress the newly converted tribes of Upper Europe with the heinousness of vice and the need of compensation. It took hold of their ideas of fines and compensations, and through these endeavored to enforce the morality of a Christian life by the power of the Church wielded in a way that they could understand.

Penitential Psalms. The penitential Psalms were very early picked out and called by this name. In the West their use, especially in penitential systems, was much more marked than in the East. They are the sixth, thirty-second, thirty-eighth, fifty-first, one hundred and second, one hundred and thirtieth, and one hundred and forty-third. These have been appointed for the Service on Ash-Wednesday, but in rearranging our service, by oversight the fifty-first Psalm was omitted in the enumeration, since it was printed at length instead of being referred to by number in the English Commination Office, from which our Intercessions before the General Thanksgiving are taken. Their repetition was often imposed as a penance upon penitents, and thus they became by far the most familiar portions of Holy Scripture.

Pennsylvania. The Swedish Church is an Episcopal Church, and Bishop Morris therefore begins his sketch of this Diocese in "The Churchman's Calendar," with an account of the establishment of Swedish services. Pleasant relations subsisted in provincial days between the Swedish and English missionaries, and when the Swedish mission was given up by the mother-country, the parishes fell into the ranks of the American Episcopal Church. Wicaco (Gloria Dei), and Kingsessing (St. James'), and Upper Merion (Christ Church), Bridgeport, lay in Pennsylvania. During Dr. Nicholas Collin's long rectorship these Churches were Swedish, until 1831 A.D., when Rev. J. C. Clay, D.D., became rector of the united parishes, as a clergyman of the American Church. Dr. Collin used the Prayer-Book, and his assistants for forty-five years were American Episcopal clergymen. The Swedish Governor, Printz, brought Rev. John Campanius with him, and settled at Tinicum. There he built a church, near the Lazaretto, in 1646 A.D. The church and burying-ground were dedicated by Campanius. This was the first church in Pennsylvania, and this clergyman of the Catholic and Apostolic Church was at work nearly forty years before William Penn's arrival. Campanius "translated Luther's Catechism into the Indian language." In 1677 A.D. the "Block-house" at Wicaco was "first used as a place of worship." It had loop-holes as windows, and the congregation came with fire-arms, through fear of a surprise by Indians. In 1697 A.D., Rev. Andreas Rudman arrived as pastor. In 1700 A.D. the present brick church (Gloria Dei) was built, and dedicated July 2. Rev. Andrew Rudman was the founder of this church. He afterwards officiated for the Dutch in New York, and at Oxford and Christ Churches, Philadelphia, where he died in 1798 A.D. Rev. Nicholas Collin, of Upsal, was appointed to the Wicaco Church in 1786 A.D., and died in 1831 A.D. In William Penn's charter (1681 A.D.) it was, by the desire of the Bishop of London, stipulated that if twenty persons in the Province should apply to the Bishop for a clergyman, that he might "reside within the Province, without any denial or molestation whatsoever." In 1695 A.D. Christ Church erected its first house of worship. It was "a goodly structure for those days, and of brick, with galleries large enough to accommodate more than five hundred persons." (Dr. Dorr's Historical Account.) "The cost was more than six hundred pounds." In 1697 A.D., Governor Nicholson is thanked by the members of the Church for his liberal assistance. In 1695 A.D., Rev. Thomas Clayton is appointed first minister by the Bishop of London. In 1699 A.D. he died of yellow fever, "caught in visiting the sick." In 1700 A.D., Rev. Evan Evans was sent as a missionary by Bishop Compton. William Penn writes of him, that he "appears a man sober and of a mild disposition." On November 8, 1702 A.D., Rev. George Keith and Rev. John Talbot, on a missionary tour, preached in Christ Church. They were missionaries of the Propagation Society. Keith notes that services were held at Christ Church on Wednesdays and Fridays, and holy-days. This year a bell was presented to Christ Church. It is now in St. Peter's. The Communion service of Christ Church was presented by Queen Anne in 1708 A.D. In 1711 A.D. Christ Church was enlarged. While it was closed, for three Sundays, the congregation worshiped with the Swedes at Wicaco. To denote their fellowship and unity, a Swedish hymn was sung at the English service. In "1721 A.D. the Propagation Society acknowledged the services of Swedish ministers in preaching to the vacant English Churches, and made an appropriation of ten pounds per annum for such services." Mr. Evans held Christ Church eighteen years, and in 1717 A.D. resigned and moved to Maryland. He was "a faithful missionary, and had proved a great instrument toward settling religion and the Church of England in these wild countries." In 1724 A.D., Rev. Dr. Richard Welton took charge of Christ Church. He had been consecrated a Bishop in England by a non-juring Bishop. He was recalled to England "for having exercised Episcopal functions in this country," but he went to Portugal, where he shortly died. In 1728 A.D. Christ Church bought an organ, cos ing two hundred pounds. In 1739 A D., Whitefield preached in this Church. In 1754 A D. a chime of bells, cast by Lester & Pack, of London, for Christ Church arrived. Now Thomas Makin's "*Descriptio Pensilvaniæ,*" 1729 A.D., may be recalled in its reference to this church:

"A lofty tower is founded on this ground,
For future bells to make a distant sound."

In 1750 A.D., Christopher Gist, while exploring Western Pennsylvania, on Christmas-day read Prayers and a Homily to the Indians and traders, on, or near, what is now the town of Coshocton. In 1754 A.D., Col. Washington conducted public prayers in Fort Necessity, and in 1755 A.D. he read the Burial Service at the funeral of General Braddock. In 1758 A.D., Rev. Thos. Barton, Missionary of the Propagation Society, held service in presence of Col. Washington, and many officers and soldiers, at Raystown, (now Bedford). On May 2, 1760 A.D., "a voluntary Convention" of Episcopal clergy in Christ Church heard "a sermon by Dr. Smith on the conversion of the 'Heathen Americans.'" In 1761 A.D. St. Peter's Church, and also St. Paul's Church, Philadelphia, were opened. In December of 1770 A.D., Wm. White was ordained Deacon by Bishop Young, of Norwich, in the Royal Chapel at London. In April, 1772 A D., he was ordained priest by the Bishop of London. In November of this year he was elected Assistant Minister of Christ Church and St. Peter's, Philadelphia. In 1772 A.D., Dr. Jno. Kearsley, architect of Christ Church, died. He left a large part of his property to found Christ Church Hospital. He was a vestryman for fifty-three years. In 1774 A.D., on September 7, Rev. Mr. Duché, an Assistant Minister of Christ Church, read Prayers for the First Continental Congress, in Carpenters' Hall, Chestnut St., Philadelphia. The Psalter included Psalm xxxv. Jno. Adams wrote, "It seems as if Heaven had ordained that Psalm to be read on that morning." In 1775 A.D., Mr. Duché was elected Rector of Christ Church. On July 20 of this year, being a Fast-day appointed by the Continental Congress, the Congress attended service at Christ Church. On July 4, 1776 A D., the Vestry of Christ Church and St. Peter's resolved to omit the prayer in the Liturgy for "the king of Great Britain." In 1775 A.D., Rev. Wm. White was elected chaplain to Congress, then sitting in Baltimore, but there is no evidence that he then entered on the duties of the office. In 1776 A.D., Rev. Mr. Duché was appointed chaplain. In 1777 A.D., Rev. Wm. White was elected chaplain to Congress, in connection with Rev. Mr. Duffield, a Presbyterian. The Congress, on account of British success, had left Philadelphia for York, Pa. Bishop White had removed temporarily to Maryland. Being on a journey, a courier met him, and announced his appointment. It was a very gloomy period in American affairs, but with his usual decision, he turned his horses' heads, and went to the Congress. In a like spirit, when the Bishop, on taking the oath of allegiance to the new Republic, was warned of his danger by a gesture from an acquaintance, after having taken the oath, he acknowledged to the gentleman that he knew it to be dangerous, but that he trusted in Providence, believing the American cause just. In 1779 A D., Rev. Wm. White was elected Rector of Christ Church and St. Peter's. In 1785 A.D. the Protestant Episcopal Academy was opened in Philadelphia. A meeting in New Brunswick in reference to the corporation for the Relief of Widows and Children of Deceased Clergy led to the call of a General Meeting in New York, which meeting provided for a call for a General Convention in Philadelphia, September 27, 1785 A.D. In this year the Primary Convention of the Church in Pennsylvania met at Christ Church. The clergy were Dr. White, Robt. Blackwell, Jos. Hutchins, and Samuel Magaw. There were twenty-one laymen. Sixteen Churches were represented. Dr. White was chairman. In 1785 A.D. the first *proper* Diocesan Convention of Pennsylvania met in Christ Church "Of the first twenty-nine Annual Diocesan Conventions, all but one were held in Christ Church."

At the close of the Revolution the Pennsylvania country parishes had been scattered and their pastors driven away. The missionaries of the Propagation Society could no longer pursue their faithful work. Bishop Perry refers to the second volume of the "Historical Collections of the American Colonial Church," and to Bishop White's Memoirs of the Church, for the sad story. Bishop White took steps, however, for organization. In 1784 A.D. a meeting was held at his house, composed of persons delegated by the vestries of Christ Church, and St. Peter's and St. Paul's. They asked for a conference with the Episcopalians from the country, who were then in Philadelphia, and some Churchmen were members of the House of Assembly in session there. A circular letter was sent out to the churches in the State, calling a meeting of clergy and laity in Philadelphia. On May 24, 1784 A.D., this meeting took place in Christ Church. At this time and on the following day delegates were present from Christ Church and St. Peter's, Philadelphia; St. Paul's, Philadelphia; St. James', Bristol; Trinity, Oxford; All-Saints', Pennapecka (Torresdale); St. Paul's, Chester; St. David's, Radnor; St. Peter's, in the Valley; St. Martin's, Marcus Hook; St James', Lancaster; St. James', Perkiomring; St. John's, New London, and Huntingdon Church, York County; and St. Mary's, Reading, and St. Gabriel's, Marlatton, Berks County. A Standing Committee of clergymen and laymen was appointed to confer with representatives from the Church in other States, "and assist in framing an ecclesiastical government." The committee delegated their powers to certain persons of their own number, together with Samuel Powel and Richard Peters, Esqs., who attended a meeting held in New York. At a meeting February 7, 1785 A.D., it was resolved, that there should "be sent to every clergyman and congregation in the State an account of the proceedings of the Committee, in concurrence with sundry clergymen and others at a meeting in the city of New York, on the 6th and 7th days of October last," and that a Convention should meet in Christ Church, Philadelphia, on May 23, "to organize the Episcopal Church in this State, agreeably to the intentions of the body assembled in New York, as aforesaid." This resulted in "An Act of Association." It was determined that there should be a Diocesan Convention, composed of clergy and laity, each congregation having one vote. The Orders were to vote separately, and their concurrence was needed to make a measure valid. The Convention of Pennsylvania should have power to admit clergy or deputies desiring seats from any adjoining State or States. The Act of Association was signed by the Deputies on May 24, 1785 A.D. Bishop White was a leader in the idea of lay representation, and it has been generally acceptable in this country, though the Diocese of Connecticut, for a time, insisted on clerical representation alone in its own Convention, but it soon gave way. The meeting chose deputies, "in accordance with the recommendation of the preliminary Convention at New York, for the meeting in Philadelphia, in September, 1785 A.D." This first General Convention met in historical Christ Church. "There were clerical and lay deputies from seven of the thirteen States, viz., from New York to Virginia inclusive, with the addition of South Carolina." What a small body compared to the General Convention which met in 1883 A.D. in the same church for its opening service! "What hath GOD wrought!" still, let us not boast, when so much remains undone on this vast Continent.

A special Diocesan Convention elected Rev. Dr. Wm. White as Bishop, September 14, 1786 A.D. He was consecrated at Lambeth together with Bishop Provoost, of New York, on February 4, 1787 A.D., by the Archbishop of Canterbury, assisted by the Archbishop of York, and the Bishops of Bath and Wells, and Peterborough. In 1809 A.D., Bishop White confirmed in Trinity Church, Swedesborough, N. J., 251 persons. The Episcopal Fund began this year by receipt of a bequest of $2000 of Mr. Andrew Doz. St. James', Philadelphia, was consecrated this year. In 1812 A.D. the Advancement Society was organized. In 1816 A.D. the Episcopal Missionary Society of Philadelphia was formed, which was the germ of the General Foreign and Domestic Society. In 1823 A.D. St. Stephen's, Wilkesbarre, was consecrated. In 1825 A.D. Trinity Church, Pittsburg, was consecrated, and 135 persons confirmed there. Rev. Jos. Pilmore, D.D., died this year. In 1826 A.D. an attempt was made to elect an Assistant Bishop; Rev. Wm. Meade (afterwards Bishop of Virginia) had 27 clerical votes, and Rev. Bird Wilson 26. There being 54 entitled to vote and one not voting, there was no election. This year the corner-stone of St. Stephen's, Harrisburg, was laid, Rev. Messrs. Bedell, Clarkson, Piggot, and Clemson assisting. In 1827 A.D., Rev. H. U. Onderdonk was elected Assistant Bishop. He was consecrated this year in Christ Church, Philadelphia. In 1828 A D. St. James' Church, Philadelphia, was separated from Christ Church and St. Peter's, but Bishop White remained Rector of the three parishes. In 1831 A D., Rev. H. J. Morton was elected Assistant Minister to Bishop White at St. James' Church, Philadelphia. In 1832 A.D. Christ Church and St. Peter's were separated as corporations, but Bishop White was still Rector of both. In 1834 A.D. the Bishop White Prayer-Book Society was organized. Bishop White died July 17, 1836 A.D., in the eighty-ninth year of his age, having been Bishop nearly fifty years. Prefixed to Bishop Stevens's sermon, "Then and Now," is a fac-simile of the certificate of the ordination of Bishop White to Deacon's orders in 1770 A.D. by the Bishop of Norwich. Little did the English Bishop, or the young American deacon, afterwards to be Presiding Bishop, dream of the history that should follow. A lady, who was a playmate of the future prelate, declared that "Billy White was born a Bishop," as he would always be playing Church in his childhood. Dr. Morton speaks of his youthful wisdom. In old age his venerable form impressed all. The universal regret at his death showed his wide influence. He was buried in a vault adjoining Christ Church, but in 1870 A.D. the remains were moved to the Chancel of that Church. At one time Bishop White (as a Presbyter) was the only Episcopal clergyman in Pennsylvania. At the Convention next before his death, that of 1836 A.D., there were 86 clergy and 91 congregations. It was a blessing to this Diocese that it was so long guided by a Bishop so judicious and godly. The advance in Church life has continued under other wise Bishops. Dr. Buchanan, in the Convention Sermon of 1876 A.D., recalls his memory of the small Convention of 1834 A.D. as compared with that one, though the Diocese then contained but five counties, instead of the whole State. The State now has three Dioceses.

In 1841 A D. the Christmas Fund for Disabled Clergymen was created by the Convention. Rev. Dr. Abercrombie died this year. "Up to this year the Diocese of Delaware had been under the care of the Bishop of Pennsylvania." In May Rev. A. Lee was elected Bishop of Delaware, and consecrated at the General Convention in St. Paul's, New York, October 12.

In 1842 A.D., Bishop, Mar Johannan, of Persia, was introduced into the chancel by Bishop Onderdonk at Convention. In 1844 A.D. a special Convention received the resignation of Bishop Onderdonk. In 1845 A.D., Bishops Kemper, Lee, and Gadsden performed various Episcopal services. This year Rev. Alonzo Potter, D.D., was chosen Bishop. He was consecrated in Christ Church, Philadelphia, September 23. In 1847 A.D., Bishop Potter requested offerings for sufferers by famine in Ireland, and nearly nine thousand dollars were raised. In 1849 A.D. there were one hundred and forty-four clergy and one hundred and forty-three organized congregations in the Diocese. The floating church for seamen was consecrated this year. Now (1884 A.D.) the mission has a beautiful stone church on land not far from the Delaware River.

The Clergy Daughters' Fund was established in 1849 A.D. In 1850 A.D., Bishop Potter, in his Convention address, commended the Bible Society. In 1858 A.D., Bishop Onderdonk died. This year Rev. Samuel Bowman, D.D., was elected Assistant Bishop. He was consecrated in Christ Church, Philadelphia, on August 25. The missionary work of the Diocese was, in 1859 A.D., committed by the Convention to the Diocesan Board of Missions. The corner-stone of the new building of the Episcopal Hospital was laid by Bishop Potter, in presence of members of the Convention, in 1860 A.D. This noble institution is largely indebted to Bishop Potter for its existence. In 1861 A.D. (August 3) "Bishop Bowman fell dead while walking beside the Alleghany Railroad, about twenty miles from Pittsburg," while on a visitation. Thus closed a saintly life. In 1861 A.D., Rev. William Bacon Stevens, D.D., was elected Assistant Bishop. In 1862 A.D. the Philadelphia Divinity School was organized, with Bishop A. Potter as President. Bishop Stevens was consecrated in St. Andrew's Church, Philadelphia, where he had long been rector, on January 2, 1862 A.D. On the 23d of May in this year the chapel of the Episcopal Hospital was consecrated during the session of the Convention. In 1864 A.D., the Convention was held in St. Peter's and Trinity Churches, Pittsburg. In 1865 A.D. the Convention consented to the division of the Diocese. On Tuesday, July 4 of this year, "Bishop Potter died on board the steamship Colorado, in the harbor of San Francisco, California." So passed away a wise master-builder in the Church of CHRIST. In 1869 A.D., Bishop Stevens, in his Convention address, spoke of the necessity of a further division of the Diocese. The Diocese of Pittsburg had been set off by the General Convention in 1865 A.D., and had held its first Convention in Pittsburg November 15 of that year, and elected Rev. Dr. J. B. Kerfoot, President of Trinity College, as Bishop. He was consecrated January 25 (St. Paul's Day), 1866 A.D. In 1869 A.D., Bishop Stevens recommended to the parishes the insurance on the lives of their clergy. The Committee on the Episcopal Residence reported its purchase, the amount needed ($35,000) having been procured. The Christmas Fund for Disabled Clergy, and the Widows and Orphans of Deceased Clergy had received over $5000. Ten churches were admitted into the Convention. A committee recommended the free opening of the churches for "at least one service on every Sunday." In 1870 A.D. the Bishop in his address to Convention noted the death of the venerable Dr. Dorr, rector of Christ Church. Mr. John Welsh's gift of $18,000 to the Episcopal Hospital was named. The Bishop outlined the plan of the City Mission, with a Superintendent, all the missionaries being appointed by the Bishop, and responsible to him. He also desired lay-workers to assist the missionaries. The benevolent and reformatory institutions of the city needed religious instruction, and it was thought best thus to secure it. The Bishop consented to the second division of the Diocese, stipulating that there should be left "in the Diocese of Pennsylvania not less than the five counties of Philadelphia, Montgomery, Delaware, Chester, and Bucks." The Committee on Parochial History had received sketches of twenty-nine parishes, and accumulated numerous "books, pamphlets, and files of Church papers,—some of them rare and important." The Convention consented to the formation of another new Diocese. Eight churches were admitted into union with the Convention.

Rev. Dr. M. A. De W. Howe having been elected Bishop of Central Pennsylvania, was consecrated in St. Luke's Church, Philadelphia, of which parish he had been rector, on December 28, 1871 A.D. The Diocese of Pennsylvania, thus diminished greatly in size by two divisions, in 1883 A.D. had 20 candidates for orders, 200 clergy, and 120 parishes, including 2 not in union with the Convention. There were 9 corner-stones laid and 9 consecrations. The whole number of churches is 120, and chapels 27. There are 61 parsonages. There were over 10,000 baptisms, and 5583 persons received confirmation. The value of Church property, including parsonages, cemeteries, school buildings, and endowments, hospitals, etc., was $8,700,000. The Bishop, in his address in 1883 A.D., spoke of the death of Rev. Dr. Suddards, who ministered "for nearly half a century" in Grace Church, Philadelphia. There are in Philadelphia Italian and Spanish Missions, and a Chinese Mission. Faith Home, for crippled children, has lately been opened, as a venture of faith, by a Christian

37

lady. The Hospital of the Good Shepherd, for children, at Rosemont, is a similar institution, which has been doing loving and faithful work for years. There is also a Home for the Homeless. The Episcopal Hospital does a CHRIST-like work. The Burd Orphan Asylum, the Church Home for Children, the Lincoln Institution, must not be forgotten. There is also a Mission work among Deaf-Mutes, conducted by Rev. H. W. Syle. If the early Church people, who for a few Sundays in 1711 A.D., during the enlargement of Christ Church, walked along the river-shore to Gloria Dei to worship with their Swedish friends, could see the wharves and residences and places of business that now cover the green fields of their day, and could behold the churches and charitable institutions of Philadelphia at this time, they might realize the importance of the good work which they began, and which the children of GOD have continued. May the blessed work still prosper and advance to the glory of CHRIST.

Authorities: For the most part, Bishop Morris's Sketch in the Churchman's Calendar of 1866 and 1867 A.D. Bishop Morris refers to Clay's Annals of the Swedes, Smith's History of Delaware County, Colonial Records, Dorr's History of Christ Church, Humphries's History of Propagation Society, Hazard's Annals, and Convention Journals. The author of this article has also received aid from Bishop Perry's Churchman's Year-Book, 1870 and 1871 A.D.

Statistics for 1886 A.D.: Clergy, 215; parishes, 120; missions, 31; churches consecrated, 5; guild and societies members, 17,500; families, 13,250; candidates for H. O., 18; ordinations diac., 5; pr., 5; baptisms, 3880; confirmed, 2257; communicants, 31,580; contributions, $896,704.59.

REV. S. F. HOTCHKIN.

Pentateuch. The writer of this article has availed himself largely of Bishop Harold Browne's Introduction to the Pentateuch in the first volume of the Bible Commentary, and of "Moses and the Prophets" by Professor W. H. Green, D.D., of Princeton Theological Seminary, in addition to other works.

The Pentateuch, the name given to the first five books of the Old Testament, is a Greek word, signifying the fivefold volume. It is derived from the Septuagint translation, and some authors attribute to those translators the division into separate books. The Jews, however, recognized this arrangement, but distinguished the different portions by the initial word of each. The whole was called by them "The Law" (Torah), or "The Law of Moses."

In the Pentateuch are contained the annals, civil and religious institutions of the people of Israel, and a record of the Divine dealings with them until the eve of their entrance into the land of Canaan. This national history is prefaced with an account of the creation of the world the formation of man and his lapse from a state of original righteousness, the growing corruption of the human race, the judgment of Almighty GOD consequent thereupon, bringing upon the earth a deluge of water, the saving of Noah and his family from the common doom, the repeopling of the earth by his posterity, and very interesting notices of kingdoms founded in the region of Mesopotamia and ancient cities built there. Then the historian passes to the call of Abraham, the great progenitor of the Hebrew people, from the midst of idolatry to the knowledge and worship of JEHOVAH, the true and living GOD, and his removal from Chaldea to Canaan. The incidents of his life are related, as well as those of Isaac, his son, and Jacob, his grandson, and with much particularity the circumstances which brought the sons of Jacob, ancestors of the twelve tribes, to become dwellers in Egypt.

The Book of Genesis is evidently introductory. It accounts for the sojourning of the Israelites in the land of Egypt, narrates their ancestral traditions, and explains their inherited faith. Without it much of the subsequent history would be unintelligible. While we are by no means compelled to maintain that every portion and word were written by the author of the remaining books, there is clear indication of one mind directing and arranging the whole work.

In the Book of Exodus are fully related the bondage, deliverance, and departure of the Israelites from Egypt through direct intervention of JEHOVAH. The plagues sent upon the Egyptians, the passage through the Red Sea, and many incidents of their wanderings in the desert are graphically described. Miracles are interwoven with the whole narrative, and especially was the giving of the Law upon Mount Sinai accompanied with awe-inspiring manifestations of the majesty of GOD. The writer sets forth an array of wonders which he evidently believes, and would have his readers believe, accompanied a theophany. For his legislation, and for the religious system and worship which he enjoined, he constantly and confidently claimed Divine warrant and direction. The Law came by Moses, but he himself being witness, the Lawgiver was JEHOVAH.

In the remainder of the Book of Exodus, and in that of Numbers, the wanderings of the twelve tribes for the space of forty years are related, and the most noteworthy events occurring during this long period.

The Book of Leviticus contains the ceremonial law, the ordinances of priesthood and sacrifice, and whatever pertains to Divine worship.

Deuteronomy is hortatory, didactic, and prophetic. The great legislator, before laying down his office and his life, seeks to impress, with earnest reiteration, the duties bound upon a people so distinguished from other nations, and with whom the ALMIGHTY had condescended to enter into a special covenant relation. The book is full of allusions to past events in their history, appeals to miracles wrought in their behalf as well-known facts, and contains prophetic announcements of the rewards that would follow their obedience and the severe punishments that would be sure to follow disobedience and apostasy. As Genesis is a preface to the whole work, so Deuteronomy is an appropriate conclusion, such a summary of facts and duties, such a recapitulation and practical enforcement of the lessons of the past, as became the author upon the point of resigning his great charge. Such a man as Moses, at such a period, might well speak in just this manner to the people over whom for so many years he had been so faithful a shepherd. The Pentateuch, therefore, is a unit—a single coherent work, following out a great purpose from beginning to end. The attempt to break it up into fragments and assign different portions to different authors is doing violence to a well-arranged and complete whole. Of the skeptical tendency inspiring and underlying the criticism which so boldly gainsays the integrity and unity of the work, there will be occasion to remark.

We have spoken of Moses as the author of the Pentateuch in accordance with the concurrent testimony of Hebrew and Christian antiquity. This is a vital point, and upon this mainly hinges the controversy between the maintainers and impugners of the Divine inspiration of the work and the reality of the supernatural interpositions. Denial of the supernatural is the true source and meaning of the destructive criticism that has been of late so radical and positive. If the authorship of Moses be conceded, then the account of the signs and wonders therein described was the work of an eye-witness and principal actor. It was credited by the generation then living. Laws, rites, ceremonies, and observances commemorated them. The miracles and the institutions were coeval. Of course it would have been impossible to persuade a whole people that they saw with their own eyes what they never had seen, experienced deliverances and chastisements which they had never known, and were observing ceremonies in testimony of events which had never occurred.

Then there is that in their later history which closely corresponds with warnings and denunciations contained in the book, especially in Deuteronomy. If really written by the hand of Moses, it is difficult to deny his prophetic inspiration. He uttered, through the HOLY SPIRIT, Divine oracles. The only escape from this conclusion is to deny that these supposed prophecies were penned by Moses. To this recourse those critics are driven who admit no such thing as Divine inspiration. With them it is a foregone conclusion that miracles and prophecies are incredible. The histories embodying them, therefore, were the production of subsequent ages. Old myths and legends were converted into historical facts. Ingenious forgers palmed upon their credulous contemporaries compositions written after the events referred to had taken place, as if they had come down from remote antiquity. Moses being a heroic character in the nation's infancy, was the most attractive name to be affixed to these fables. Policy and priestcraft combined to persuade the people into the acceptance of these fictitious writings as if they were genuine works of the venerated lawgiver of Israel. Thus laws, doctrines, ceremonies, tributes, were imposed upon the nation, and this mainly from religious and patriotic motives. According to these critics the Pentateuch is largely a pious fraud.

Encountered by such bold denials, we turn to the reasons for the opinion once so universally prevalent. Upon what grounds do we believe Moses to be the author of the Pentateuch?

In maintaining this view we are not obliged to contend that every word was penned by his own hand or written from his mouth. For historical works to contain documents of an earlier age, public or private record, and genealogies, fragments from ancient annalists is not unprecedented or uncommon. If some of the narratives embodied in the Pentateuch, especially in the Book of Genesis, are of this nature, it does not at all invalidate the claim to Mosaic authorship. There is no necessity for solving perplexing questions as to whether the use of the words Jehovah and Elohim indicate different sources, nor to draw the lines between the respective positions of each. We can readily grant that the accounts of the creation, the fall, the antediluvian patriarchs, the deluge, etc., had been preserved by tradition, and were transmitted by Noah to his descendants. The similarity of these primeval annals to records preserved by the most ancient nations, especially by Egypt and Babylonia, point to a common origin. The traditions of these people bear a striking resemblance to the Biblical narratives, although often distorted and intermingled with heathen fables. If Moses selected certain accounts, of the truthfulness of which he was well assured, and inserted them in his book, this detracts nothing from his authorship of the work or from overruling Divine inspiration. This will satisfactorily explain peculiarities of style upon which great stress has been laid by skeptical critics.

So also, at a subsequent period, explanatory notes may have been introduced by learned men, like Ezra, who reviewed the work, and perhaps the Old Testament Canon. The account of the death of Moses was of course so written, and some geographical and historical annotations. To this source might be ascribed personal allusions, like Exodus xi. 3, and Numbers xii. 3, although there is no urgent necessity for admitting this. The objection that Moses could not have spoken of himself is a petty cavil, unworthy of scholars who have read Cæsar's Commentaries.

In support of the genuineness of the Pentateuch appeal is first made to its own testimony. This is *prima facie* evidence, and of great weight unless it can be set aside by convincing arguments. Moses repeatedly represents himself as the writer. Exodus xvii. 14, "And the LORD said unto Moses, Write this for a memorial in a book,"—where instead of a "a book" read "the book," reference being to a well-known register. Exodus xxxiv. 27, "And the LORD said unto Moses, Write thou these words: for after the tenor of these words I have made a covenant with thee and with Israel." Moses makes express mention of his doing what was thus enjoined. Exodus xxiv. 3, 4, "And Moses came and told the people all the words of the LORD, and all the judgments: and all the people answered with one voice, and said, All the words which the LORD hath said will we do. And Moses wrote all the words of the LORD." So he recorded the history of the wanderings of Israel in the desert, specifying the stages of their journeys. Numbers xxxiii. 2, "And Moses wrote their goings out, according to their journeys by the commandment of the LORD."

Towards the close of the book (Deut. xxxi. 9-12) we read, "And Moses wrote this Law, and delivered it unto the priests the sons of Levi, which bare the ark of the covenant of the LORD, and unto all the elders of Israel. And Moses commanded them, saying, At the end of every seven years, in the solemnity of the year of release, in the feast of tabernacles, when all Israel is come to appear before the LORD thy GOD in the place which the LORD shall choose, thou shalt read this Law before all Israel in their hearing. Gather the people together, men, and women, and children, and thy stranger that is within thy gates, that they may hear, and that they may learn, and fear the LORD your GOD, and observe to do all the words of this Law." Deut. xxxi. 24-26, "And it came to pass, when Moses had made an end of writing the words of this Law in a book, until they were finished, that Moses commanded the Levites, which bare the ark of the covenant of the LORD, saying, Take this book of the Law, and put it in the side of the ark of the covenant of the LORD your GOD, that it may be there for a witness against thee."

This mention of the writing of the book of the Law by Moses himself may have applied only to Deuteronomy. Granting this detracts not from the weight of the arguments already adduced in behalf of the preceding books. Deuteronomy, moreover, has been the special object of assault by recent critics, who while assigning this book to the reign of Josiah, or to a still later period, have been willing to allow to Moses considerable portions of the others.

While reading the majestic flowing sentences of this grand composition, glowing with intense feeling and breathing sentiments so elevated, it is difficult to repress some emotions of indignation, if not contempt, for men who, whatever the extent of their erudition, can see nothing here but an artful invention of priestcraft. The impress of a noble spirit, far above dishonest arts and base imposture, is stamped upon the whole. And what forger would venture so to speak in the name of JEHOVAH, and use such solemn language of warning against any attempts to tamper with the oracles he was commissioned to deliver? Deut. iv. 2, "Ye shall not add unto the word which I command you, neither shall ye diminish aught from it, that ye may keep the commandments of the LORD your GOD."

Moses was perfectly competent to compose such a work as the Pentateuch. It is impossible to deny eminent* ability and intellectual power to the man who led a multitude of serfs out of Egypt, formed them into a compact, well-ordered nation, and impressed himself so deeply upon their institutions and traditions. For this we have the concurrent testimony of both secular and sacred history. Moses is indisputably a historical character, and the transfer of the Jewish people from Egypt to Israel is established from other sources than the Scriptures. That such a man should have superior knowledge and mental training is a necessity.

When Stephen affirmed that "Moses was learned in all the wisdom of the Egyptians and was mighty in words and in deeds," he uttered what was not only the universal belief of his people, but an unavoidable inference from his public life and acts. Even the most carping and destructive critics concede the Decalogue to Moses, and the man who can be believed capable of producing such a code cannot surely be pronounced incompetent to compose the entire Pentateuch. That the art of writing was then well known in Egypt is abundantly proved. Papyri of dates several hundred years earlier than the Exodus have been brought to light.

Moses being certainly capable of such a performance would naturally desire to effect it. He would not, we may be confident, have been willing to abandon the memory of events so important to the uncertainties of oral tradition, or that laws and religious rites should lack a sure and trustworthy method of transmission. Coming generations had as deep a stake in the truths and ordinances delivered as that which was then living. The solicitude of the great lawgiver for the future welfare of his people is everywhere apparent. His patriotism was profound and fervent. For the preservation of their national existence and prosperity he

---

* Bishop Browne's Introduction, The Bible Commentary, vol. i. p. 2.

was ready to make any personal sacrifice. He was always looking forward to the future destinies of the nation, most anxious for its loyalty to JEHOVAH and faithful observance of the covenant. He felt his own mission to be very much preparatory. He was moulding and shaping a nation for the great part it was to perform in another land and through many ages. Knowing how much depended upon the Israelites' keeping in mind the eventful beginnings of their history, he would certainly not have neglected to put these things in permanent shape. Without overweening self-estimate, Moses knew that no subsequent leader or legislator could give institutions better adapted to the wants of the people than his own, or speak with anything like his authority.

For such a work, moreover, he had time and opportunity during the long sojourn of Israel in the wilderness. During these weary waitings and wanderings, Moses was profitably occupied in composing records of such deep interest and vital consequence to the welfare of his people.

The historical, political, and geographical allusions found in the Pentateuch are in perfect harmony with the theory of its Mosaic authorship. The writer shows especial familiarity with Egypt and Arabia. The recent highly-interesting disclosures of old Egyptian life in no way contradict, and often strikingly confirm, his references thereto. The royalty and priesthood of Egypt as described in this book, the labors imposed upon bond-servants, the congruity of the plagues, with phenomena of the region and features of the prevalent idolatry, sepulchral rites, proficiency in the arts of embalming, engraving, and embroidery, and occasional words and phrases, accord with modern discoveries. It is scarce conceivable that writers of a later age and different nationality and education should manifest such familiarity with the customs of Egypt, or that a fabricator should introduce so many local allusions and never betray himself by anachronism or misstatement.

The wilderness has left its impress on the work. Many passages breathe the air of the desert and tell of a nomad people dwelling in tents. The nation could be readily assembled. Each tribe had its position in the encampment and in the order of march. The unclean and lepers were to remain without the camp, and thither was the sin-offering to be carried and consumed. The phraseology thus originated was of lasting continuance. "To your tents, O Israel," was the watch-word of sedition. The Hebrew Christians were reminded that JESUS, as a sin-offering, "suffered without the gate," and were exhorted to "go forth to him without the camp." The tabernacle, so conspicuous a feature in their religious institutions, was a movable tent, and precise directions are given concerning the mode of its transportation. Could such numerous, often slight and incidental, allusions have proceeded from a forger and have been designedly scattered throughout the work?

The consensus of later books of the Old Testament corroborates the Mosaic authorship of the Pentateuch. From Joshua to Chronicles and Malachi there are numerous quotations from the Pentateuch, or allusions to events and precepts there recorded, and nowhere the least doubt expressed or implied. The Law of Moses is the constant standard of appeal. Obedience or disobedience thereto is the test of character, the key of Divine blessings or judgments. Those who reverence it are commended. Those who neglect or scorn it are threatened and condemned. The constitution, laws, and rites represented as obligatory correspond with the legislation and ordinances of the Pentateuch. The Priesthood is continued in the family of Aaron. To the tribe of Levi is assigned the performance of various ministries connected with divine service. The ark is regarded with peculiar veneration, as the depository of the tables of the ten commandments, and associated with the manifestation of the Divine glory. There is constant mention of circumcision, the Passover, the sacrifices, as well known to those addressed. Now, is it credible that this minute, onerous, and expensive ritual could be foisted upon generations which had not grown up under it, and that they could be made to believe that they had received it from those before them as divinely communicated through Moses? It would seem that one who could persuade himself of this had little cause to sneer at the credulity of believers, who reverently accept as trustworthy the account of those miracles and the early date of the prophetic portions.

So cogent is this argument that the impugners of the Mosaic authorship are compelled to deal in like manner with the later books. Inasmuch as the Book of Joshua is so closely connected with the Pentateuch, that also must be discredited. The allegation of forgery is a short and easy method of disposing of this troublesome witness. And so the process is continued. Either whole books or intractable passages must be swept away by this bold assumption. Historians, judges, and prophets, unless they confirm the theories of rationalizing critics, are summarily thrust aside. Verily, according to the theories of these intrepid arguers, we have in the Old Testament a most amazing series of literary impositions. The attempts of later ages in this line fade into insignificance. For unscrupulous, plausible, and successful fictions these ancient prophets and scribes must be allowed the palm. Wonderfully have they deceived after-ages as well as their own, the learned as well as the ignorant, teachers as well as the multitude, Christian Apostles as well as Jewish Rabbis, and we cannot avoid adding (with reverence) JESUS CHRIST Himself. And what was to be gained by these stupendous frauds?

According to some critics the imposition of the Levitical sacrificial and ritual system was to be a proof of priestly power and a support of monotheism. Others charitably impute such devices to zeal for promoting the moral and religious improvement of the nation, and suggest that through these means it was better prepared for the acceptance of the gospel. It is even piously intimated that the hand of GOD may be recognized in this preparation. It is difficult to decide whether such theories are the more preposterous or dishonorable to the GOD of truth.

And who were the astute and crafty men, of intellects so acute and of morality so defective, who successfully essayed this great imposture? To what age and to what agents shall it be attributed? Here the critics are much at variance among themselves. Each propounder of a new interpretation begins by demolishing that of his predecessor. Whether successful or not in establishing his own hypothesis, he is fairly so in overthrowing structures already reared. "The most effectual reply to these various hypotheses often is to set them over against each other and exhibit their mutual contrariety."* Samuel, Hilkiah, Jeremiah, Ezekiel, and Ezra have been named in turn as probable achievers of this marvelous deception. Dr. Robertson Smith maintains that Deuteronomy first appeared in the reign of Josiah, and that the Levitical Law was not in existence before the time of Ezra. Great stress is laid upon the finding of the book of the Law, in repairing the Temple, and the effect produced upon the king, as recorded in 2 Kings xxii. 8. Hence it is argued that previously to this presumed occurrence the law could have had no existence. The finding of the Bible by Luther in the library of the convent at Erfurth, produced upon his mind an impression as profound as that ascribed in the passage referred to upon King Josiah. This would be as valid an argument to prove the non-existence of the entire sacred volume before Luther's day. The constant references to the Law in earlier writings cannot be dismissed in this summary way. During the reigns of Josiah's predecessors who favored idolatry, especially Manasseh, whose reign was of such long continuance, there would be no disposition to bring into prominent notice a testimony so strong against prevailing evil practices. The rolls of the Law would be treated, as the holy volume has been often treated since, thrust out of sight and out of mind. Copies must have been rare, and it is not improbable that some were purposely destroyed. But Hezekiah's attempted reform recognized the obligation of this Law a century before. It was "the testimony" given to Jehoash at his coronation (2 Kings xi. 12). Solomon appealed to it in his prayer at the dedication of the Temple (1 Kings viii.). The Book of the Law found in the Temple was very possibly the autograph directed by Moses to be deposited in the side of the ark. If from the circumstances of his education Josiah had only a partial acquaintance with the words of the Torah, the complete work, so remarkably brought to light, would naturally agitate a mind so open to religious impression and render him more zealous for the national reformation.

Ingenious attempts are made to disprove the Mosaic authorship by adducing passages showing the neglect and disregard of many of the injunctions contained in the Pentateuch in subsequent ages. If infraction of a Law proves its non-existence, Christianity is likely to suffer as well as Judaism, the New Testament is as open to attack as the Old, and the existence of the LORD JESUS CHRIST as an actual living person might be called in question. In truth, the perverse heart of man is continually struggling to escape from the holy commandments of GOD. "Why call ye me LORD, LORD, and do not the things which I command?" The disobedience of the recipients of Divine revelations is their own sin and loss, no disproof of the revelation itself. This is a sufficient answer to objections drawn from irregularities of worship, as well as from moral disobedience.

That there were periods when the prescribed ritual was not fully carried out, nay, fell into extreme neglect, and when corrupt practices widely prevailed, is freely conceded. Of this degeneracy we have frequent instance, during the periods embraced in the Book of Judges, and until the establishment of Divine worship as it had been appointed in the reign of David. It is hence argued that the provisions restricting sacrifice to one appointed place could not have been then enacted, and so the early date of the Pentateuch is discredited.

But wherever GOD manifested His glorious presence it was lawful to erect an altar and offer sacrifice. This is sufficient explanation of the sacrifices offered at Bochim (Judges ii. 1–5), by Gideon (Judges vi. 20), by Manoah (Judges xiii. 16), and by David at the threshing-floor of Araunah (2 Sam xxiv.). In the Book of Judges the Tabernacle at Shiloh, containing the ark, is recognized as the house of the LORD until the ark was carried into captivity by the Philistines. This was a Divine judgment. GOD'S people had broken their covenant with Him, and were no longer entitled to retain the symbol of His presence. Shiloh then lost its peculiar sacredness, and was deserted by JEHOVAH (Jer. vii. 12, 14). Afterwards Samuel, as GOD'S prophet, exercised a general religious superintendence. During the interval between the capture of the ark and its solemn restoration by David, the regular performance of the Levitical service was suspended. Upon solemn occasions Samuel, the LORD'S prophet, exercising gen-

---

* Green, Moses and the Prophets, page 20.

eral religious superintendence, offered sacrifices. But while the ark was in the hands of the Philistines God had no sanctuary in Israel. And when first returned by its captors, the ark became a source of terror and alarm. No priest or Levite ministered before it. From the time the ark was laid up at Kirjath-Jearim till David removed it to Zion there is scarcely a recorded instance of sacrifice where Samuel was not present, except Saul's rash and unhappy act. Samuel is plainly the centre of the religious life of this period. (Green, pp. 101–105.)

To argue, therefore, from the record of sacrifices offered elsewhere than at Shiloh, during this season of disorder, while ordinary service was intermitted, against the existence of the Levitical directory, is to base grave conclusions upon very slight premises. Can such reasoning overthrow conclusions founded upon clear and cogent proofs which have carried conviction to the minds of thousands of thorough Biblical scholars? Is the veritable historian and lawgiver of ancient Israel to be thrust aside and mighty miracles converted into myths and fables by cavils of this sort?

So, also, if the prophets in their zeal for true religion, genuine faith, and godliness sometimes use very strong language in condemnation of formalism and hypocrisy, are we to understand them as meaning to deny that the ceremonies and sacrifices of the Law were actually given as set forth in the Pentateuch? For instance, we read in Jeremiah (vii. 22, 23), "I spake not unto your fathers, nor commanded them in the day that I brought them out of the land of Egypt, concerning burnt-offerings or sacrifices. But this thing commanded I them, Obey my voice, and I will be your God, and ye shall be my people: and walk ye in all the ways that I have commanded you, that it may be well with you." Can it be seriously maintained that the prophet here denies the enactment of the Ceremonial Law? Or can a like inference be drawn from penitential confessions, such as those of David? (Ps. li. 16, 17.) Who that is familiar with Scripture style cannot turn to numerous instances of similar phraseology? Is Samuel controverting the Divine appointment of altar-service when he says to Saul, "Hath the Lord as great delight in burnt-offerings and sacrifices as in obeying the voice of the Lord? Behold, to obey is better than sacrifice, and to hearken than the fat of rams." The spiritual requirements of the Law coexisted with the outward ordinances, and the mission of the prophets was mainly directed to arouse the national conscience, and turn the hearts of the people to God in repentance, submission, and holiness of life.

Arguments against the Mosaic authorship of the Pentateuch have also been sought in its phraseology. It has been urged that the style is too much like that of later books of the Old Testament to warrant the opinion that so long a period of time intervened. But to this it is answered that there is not in Semitic languages the tendency to change which exists in modern European tongues. Scholars attest that the Arabic of the Koran does not differ materially from that of the present day, although quite as long a duration has elapsed as that between Moses and Ezra. The Syriac of later times is said not to vary from that of the Peshito version. Egyptian papyri much more widely separated from each other in age are the same in style. The work of Moses, moreover, like the translations of Tyndall and Luther, would strongly tend to fix the national style and become the standard of language as well as of religion. The sacred books were mainly the literature (τα γραμματα) of the people.

Biblical scholars, however, do find archaisms in the Pentateuch and peculiar phrases to fully as great extent as could be reasonably expected.

Another objection, somewhat dissimilar, has been drawn from alleged variations of style between Deuteronomy and the preceding books. But when the respective circumstances under which they were composed are considered and the design of the author, this is no more than might be looked for, and is rather a confirmation than a difficulty. An interval of nearly forty years separates them. Probably the earlier books were written, from time to time, in detached portions. In Deuteronomy, the venerable lawgiver in a connected discourse reviews the past, pours out his heart in affectionate exhortations, solemn prophecies, and fervent praises. The prophetic spirit burned within him. His eye penetrated into the hidden future, his soul was wrapt in holy ecstasy, and his great loving heart yearned over the people whom he had watched over for so many years, and from whom he was now about to be removed. A more elevated, diffuse, and impassioned style would fittingly clothe his farewell utterances.

The theory of the later date of the Pentateuch involves far greater inconsistencies and difficulties than are encountered by those who accept its early composition. According to this interpretation laws are promulgated which have no meaning or fitness. What object in the reign of Josiah to issue injunctions forbidding peace with the Amalekites, who had long since disappeared? Or to prohibit foreign conquests, when the urgent question was whether Judæa could maintain its own existence against powerful and warlike neighbors? A law discriminating against Ammon and Moab in favor of Edom had its warrant in the Mosaic period, but not in the times of the later kings, when Edom was to the prophets the representative foe of the people of God. Would an injunction to show no unfriendliness to Egyptians be found in a code composed by the prophets, who were striving with all their might to dissuade the people from alliance or association with Egypt? And what necessity for the requirement that, when the kingdom was established, the King should be a native and not a foreigner, when for ages the succession to the throne in the family of David had been undisputed? (Green, pp. 62-66.) On the post exilian theory there is a ritual arrangement, full and particular, framed at a time when no cultus existed, an exhaustive description of the tabernacle and all its parts as if it were a reality, when according to this assumption it was an imaginary structure, great prominence given to the ark and all that pertained to it, although the ark perished in the destruction of the first Temple, and was never subsequently renewed. (Green, pp. 62, 67.) Such are specimens of the absurdities and incongruities continually confronting the acceptors of this pretentious criticism, which claims to disabuse us of old and vulgar errors.

The great schism, which was never afterwards healed, took place in the reign of Rehoboam, about 975 A.C. It was the policy of Jeroboam to deepen and perpetuate the alienation between Israel and Judæa. With this end he discountenanced any participation of his subjects in the prescribed Temple worship at Jerusalem, and established shrines of an idolatrous character at Dan and Bethel. The prophets who testified in Israel against these corruptions constantly appeal to the Law of Moses as the standard of religious truth. The correspondence of many passages in Hosea, Amos, Micah, with events described and laws contained in the Pentateuch show unmistakable reference thereto. Now it would have been a manifest impossibility, after the separation, to have palmed upon the Northern Kingdom a fictitious work containing such strong condemnation of their own practices. There is no way of accounting for the reverence in which the Pentateuch was then held but upon the fact of its having been the sacred book of the whole nation prior to the severance. Jereboam and his counselors tried to prevent the subjects of his kingdom from going to Jerusalem to worship, but did not venture to question the Divine mission of Moses or the genuineness of the received sacred books. The books, therefore, were existent, and their holy character recognized prior to the revolt of the ten tribes. This is of itself a sufficient answer to all pretenses of a subsequent fabrication.

As illustrative of references in the prophets, compare

Hosea ix. 10 with Numb. xxv. ;
Hosea xi. 8 with Deut. xxix. 23 ;
Amos iv. 9, 10 with Deut. xxviii. 27, 60 ;
Micah vi. 5 with Numb. xxii., etc.,

and very many similar correspondences.

The date of the Samaritan Pentateuch is disputed, but there is reason for assigning it to an age as early as that of Ezra, if not earlier. Indeed, there is much to favor the supposition that the priest sent by the King of Assyria to teach the Samaritans the manner of the GOD of the land, and who taught them how they should fear JEHOVAH, then gave them the Torah (2 Kings xvii. 26-28). This book, differing not materially from the Jewish text, has been held in the highest veneration by the Samaritans. Jealous as they were of their Jewish neighbors, it is incredible that they could have accorded to the volume implicit faith unless its claims and character, as communicated by GOD through Moses, were considered indisputable.

There remains another branch of confirmatory evidence, that derived from the New Testament, than which none can be more conclusive to the believer in the LORD JESUS CHRIST. The Scriptures of the Old Testament, just as we have them now, were in the hands of the Jewish people at the time of our SAVIOUR'S appearance. In His intercourse with that people the import and meaning of these books were a subject of constant discussion. With those who accept JESUS as the SON of GOD, the light of the world, the great revealer of grace and truth, there can be no question as to His knowledge of the grounds upon which the belief of the nation rested, and whether or not their reliance was justified. If JESUS knew that they were laboring under an error in believing Moses to have been the author of the books attributed to him, would He not have sought to undeceive them? Would He have taken advantage of their mistakes and availed Himself of falsehood? Yet, so far from uttering a syllable to that effect, He consents entirely to their exalted estimate of the Scriptures, and appeals to their testimony in support of His Messianic claims. He argues therefrom to expose and condemn the corrupt glosses of the Scribes and traditions of the Rabbins, as from a standard fixed and incontrovertible.

When the Pharisees question Him upon the subject of divorce and adduce the permission given by Moses (Deut. xxiv. 1), He makes no question of the permission having proceeded from Moses, nay, expressly admits it, but assigns the reason for his legislation, "Moses because of your hardness of heart suffered you to put away your wives" (Matt. xix. 8). When the Sadducees hoped to entangle Him by pretended perplexities touching the resurrection, connected with the provision in Deut. xxv. 5, He does not gainsay their assertion that the injunction came from Moses, but rising to a loftiness far above their wretched cavils, He charges them with ignorance of the very Scriptures upon which they rely. "Do ye not therefore err, because ye know not the Scriptures, nor the power of GOD?" And in proof of the doctrine of the resurrection He educes great meaning, unsuspected by His hearers, from a passage in the book of Exodus, "Have ye not read in the book of Moses, in *the place concerning* the bush, how GOD spake unto him, saying, I am the GOD of Abraham, and the GOD of Isaac, and the GOD of Jacob? He is not the GOD of the dead, but of the living" (St. Mark xii. 18-27). Here our LORD recognizes not only the authorship of Moses, but his Divine mission, taking the words quoted as undoubtedly the words of GOD. In St. John iii. 14, CHRIST recognizes the genuineness, as well as historical accuracy, of the Book of Numbers in the reference to the brazen serpent. In St. John vi. 32, the miraculous supply of manna is argued from as a historical fact. So far from our LORD making any attempt to weaken the popular faith in the writings of Moses, He rests His own title to acceptance upon the words of the great lawgiver rightly interpreted. "Had ye believed Moses, ye would have believed me; for he wrote of me. But if ye believe not his writings, how shall ye believe my words?" (St. John v. 46, 47.)

In the converse of the risen Saviour with His disciples there is express and conclusive attestation to the genuineness and inspiration of the Scriptures, classified, as the Jews were wont, in a threefold division. "And he said unto them, These are my words which I spake unto you, while I was yet with you, how that all things must needs be fulfilled, which were written in the Law of Moses, and the prophets, and in the Psalms, concerning me" (St. Luke xxiv. 44). That the first division, the Law of Moses, consisted of the five portions of the Pentateuch, is undeniable. We could not have a more decided and conclusive attestation. The entire fivefold volume is stamped with the seal of the world's Redeemer. Questions of minor importance, to which allusion has been made, are not so determined as to preclude examination and discussion, but the language of JESUS leaves no room for doubt that He accredits the Pentateuch as a whole, and confirms the Divine mission of Moses.

The Apostles deal with the Scriptures with the same reverence, and appeal to the volume as ultimate authority, nowhere intimating the slightest doubt as to the authenticity and credibility of the different books. The words ascribed to Moses are relied upon as his veritable utterances, and decisive upon the points in dispute (Acts iii. 22; vii. 1-41; xiii. 39; xv. 21; xxvi. 22; xxviii. 23; Rom. x. 5; 1 Cor. x. 1-11; 2 Cor. iii. 7-16). The reasoning of the Epistle to the Hebrews supposes throughout the Divine institution of the Levitical law and ceremonial, and the Apocalypse authenticates the song of Moses.

It is no satisfactory answer to these citations to say that the age was not a critical one, and that JESUS and His Apostles adopted the current opinions of the day. JESUS is Himself "the Truth." He can neither be deceived Himself nor mislead others. "Every one that is of the truth heareth His voice." We are not indeed by our faith in CHRIST compelled to discourage critical inquiry, or shut our eyes to evidence, or to decline discussion. The studies and investigations of learned and judicious men are to be welcomed. The purity of the text and the elucidation of obscurities are to be diligently sought. Words may be changed, other readings may be vindicated as of superior authority, and some portions traced with more or less probability to other sources. But to suppose that a stupendous fabrication was imposed upon the Jewish people, that the oracles esteemed by them as of GOD were the invention of priestcraft, and that JESUS CHRIST was either imposed upon, or knowingly countenanced a fraud, is too monstrous a supposition to be admitted for a moment. He knew whereof He affirmed, and we know that His witness is true. And the theories and objections of skeptical critics, were they vastly more able, ingenious, and alarming than they are, will not shake this conviction, and need occasion no anxiety to the sincere, albeit unlearned follower of the LORD JESUS CHRIST.

RT. REV. ALFRED LEE, D.D.,
Bishop of Delaware.

Pentecost. The Feast of weeks. It was a single, solemn feast-day when the harvest was completed,—the fiftieth day from the great Sabbath of the Passover, when the unleavened bread was put away and the Paschal Lamb was prepared. The feast of the Pentecost was the offering of the harvest sheaf and the two loaves of leavened bread, the unleavened bread of the first feast typifying the pure nature (1 Cor. v. 6-8) of our LORD which He offered for us, the leavened bread our own human nature. For at this Feast the HOLY GHOST was given to the Apostles, according to the most true promise of our LORD (Acts ii.) when the "HOLY GHOST came down from heaven with a sudden great sound, as it had been a mighty wind, in the likeness of fiery tongues lighting upon the Apostles to teach them, and to lead them into all truth, giving them both the gift of divers languages, and also boldness with fervent zeal constantly to preach the Gospel unto all nations, whereby we have been brought out of darkness and error into the clear light and true knowledge" of GOD and of His SON JESUS CHRIST (Preface for Whitsunday). Its real meaning and power is summed up in the prophetic verse of the lxviii. Psalm, so appropriately used on the Feast-day: "Thou hast ascended on high; Thou hast led captivity captive; Thou hast received gifts for men, yea, for the rebellious also, that the LORD GOD might dwell among them." It is that Gift that includes all other gifts, the Gift of the abiding of the HOLY GHOST in the Church of the SON of GOD. It was the filling of the mystical body of CHRIST with His Spirit, which should lead that body into all truth, and should preserve it despite all its failures and falterings from utter loss. It is this aspect of the celebration of this day, which has passed with all its pomp and significance from the Jewish into the Christian ritual. The

Church administered baptism to the classes of the catechumens who had been preparing, and received them at the font clad in white array. It was a day of solemn celebration of worship and of thanksgiving, and was observed with all due honor. It is a type of our own confirmation when we receive from the Bishop's hands that gift of the HOLY GHOST which St. Peter preached was the special gift of that day,—" and ye shall receive the HOLY GHOST. For the promise is unto you and to your children, and to all that are afar off, even as many as the LORD our GOD shall call" (Acts ii. 38, 39).

Pentecostals, otherwise called Whitsun farthings, took their name from the payment due at the Feast of Pentecost. It appears that Pentecostals were oblations, and as the inhabitants of chapelries were bound on some certain festival or festivals to repair to the Mother-Church and make their oblation there in token of subjection and dependence, so, as it seems, were the inhabitants of the Diocese obliged to repair to the Cathedral (as the Mother-Church of the whole Diocese) at the Feast of Pentecost. These oblations grew by degrees into fixed and certain payments from every parish and house in it. These are still paid in a few Dioceses, being now only a charge upon particular Churches where by custom they have been paid. (Burn's Eccl. Law.)

Perambulation. An old custom, now nearly fallen into disuse, in England. The Parson, the Church-wardens, and parishioners went in solemn procession round the bounds of the parish once every year, in or about Ascension-tide. There is a homily to be read on this occasion, extant in the Book of Homilies. Queen Elizabeth's injunctions appointed the cxii. and civ. Psalms to be recited during the procession. The custom was also used in this country in colonial days.

Pernoctations. Vigils. It was a custom among the early Christians upon certain feasts and fasts to watch all the night previous.

Perpetual Curate. When the revenues of an English parish are in the hands of a lay impropriator and there is neither spiritual rector nor vicar, the curate who does duty under the impropriator is called a perpetual curate. It can be held with a benefice, and is revokable if the impropriator so choose. The title "perpetual" seems to mean that the impropriator is compelled to have a curate in charge continually, but not that particular curate to whom he may have given it. But Acts of Parliament, however, provided for some cases.

Perpetual Virginity of St. Mary the Virgin. *Vide* MARY.

Persecution. It is the suffering of what malice, hatred, and violence, whether legally or irresponsibly, can inflict upon a person because of his religious convictions. Persecution means, generally, physical pains and more than mere threats to compel a surrender of opinion. In this Persecution, by whomsoever used, is an evil, and has always proved to be a most dangerous weapon in the hands of those who use it, and it should be remembered that persecution cannot be used in behalf of a righteous cause. Truth must be intolerant of error, the two are incompatible, but we must speak the truth, the whole truth, in love, and we must use all such influences as are holy and right to lead others into the truth. There is a holy compulsion that lies within the power and influence of a holy life, but this is the sole compulsion we should use. The Church's compulsion is the earnest prayer she uses. It is the loving setting forth of the doctrine of our LORD JESUS CHRIST, and a trust that if she is faithful to her trust He will not fail in His answer to her intercessions. But the rulers of the Church have not always taken this view, and because of some chance expressions of the Fathers, notably of St. Augustine, upon force to be used with those who will not believe aright, the power to inflict temporal penalties for spiritual offenses has been assumed, as by the Roman Church. But again, since Church and State were joined together and overt acts against the religion established by law would lead, as was foreseen, to the attack upon political institutions, the English State persecuted religious opinions after the Reformation. The history of Persecution is divided naturally into two parts. The first is the Persecutions she suffered, at the hands of the Jews as a sect subversive of Judaism, and at the hands of the heathen as being a *religio illicita;* and, secondly, the Persecutions which were taken up by the Church and State in later times. It is impossible to give more than an outline of either of these. In their attempts at persecution the Jews either prosecuted the Christians by their own officers (as when Saul, yet breathing out threatenings and slaughter, went to the high-priest and desired of him letters to Damascus to the Synagogue, that if he found any of this way, whether they were men or women, he might bring them bound unto Jerusalem), or raised a riot (as Acts xiii. 50; xiv. 2), or used the prefects and governors for the same end (Acts xvii. 4-9). But when Christianity outgrew this limit it was ranked as treason against the State, and therefore was proceeded against by imperial edicts and by legal enactments. In consequence there was a constant persecution going on all the world over, till the conversion of Constantine, 315 A.D. But the formal persecutions inaugurated, sometimes by the policy of the Emperor, sometimes by some conjuncture, were reckoned as ten in number. Not counting that of Nero, 64 A.D., they are: I. Domitian's, 95 A.D. II. Trajan's, 102 A.D. III. Marcus Antoninus's, 167-177 A.D. IV. Severus's, 202 A.D. V. Maximin's, 235-237 A.D. VI. Decius's, 250 A.D. VII. Valerian's, 257 A.D. VIII. Gallienus's, 260 A.D. IX. Diocletian's, 303 A.D. X. Maximin's, 311 A.D. For the next ten years the political troubles and the struggles for the purple make it difficult to distinguish into formal persecution the edicts issued and then modified and then partially enforced by Gallerius, Maximin, Maxentius, and Heraclius, together or in turn. Persecutions which occurred later, as in Persia, and the martyrdoms of such great men as Boniface, the Anglo-Saxon Apostle to Germany, are not within our limits. But we now turn to the persecutions of heretical bodies in Europe. The most notable are the war against the Albigenses, ordered by Innocent III., 1209 A.D.; the continuous persecutions of the Inquisition, an organization which sprang out of this war against the Albigenses; and the persecution of the Spanish Jews, 1391 A.D. The war of the Hussites was a successful resistance to persecution. The Inquisition was one continuous act of persecution of both Jews and heretics, which was pushed forward with the vigor of a relentness organization. Kings were made its executioners, since the Church could shed no blood. The Reformation was the real culmination of persecution. In England there had been a persecution of the Lollards, but when Mary Tudor ascended the Throne (1554 A.D.) she began, contrary to the advice of her soundest Councillors, that persecution which only established the Anglican Church more firmly under the rule of Elizabeth.

The English Church was also guilty of persecution later. (The execution of the Jesuits and of the seminary priests who suffered under Elizabeth was not a persecution, it was Elizabeth's counter-stroke to the excommunication and forfeiture of her kingdom issued against her in her excommunication by the Pope.) The dissenters, who were fined and imprisoned for opinion's sake, suffered persecution. But as was pointed out at first, there was in men's minds then no such idea as we have now of religious liberty, and to attack the Church was in the conception of the statesmen of those days to injure the majesty of the State. This principle was used quite as freely by the Presbyterians and Independents when they obtained power (1642-1656 A.D.). Toleration was not thought of as a Christian duty till after the Revolution, and there was no complete announcement of religious liberty. Indeed, Toleration is only a half-step. In Maryland, the nearest approach to civil liberty was granted by Charles I. to Lord Baltimore. But persecution in one sense never ceases. So long as the world lies in hatred and enmity, so long must persecution in one or other shape exist. It is an exercise of faith, it is the patience in which the Christian must possess his soul, and it is not the less a persecution if it comes from one's own household,—the division of homes our LORD foretold His Doctrine would bring about.

Person. Person, in theological language, refers to the (*a*) Personality of GOD as being a SPIRIT, sole, self-existent, governing all things, and apart from them. Here we can only speak of the Nature of the HOLY TRINITY. GOD has revealed to us the Unity of His Substance and the TRINITY of Persons. For ourselves the Unity can be readily conceived of, and that He can act through the many powers of nature. That so men did mislead themselves into Polytheism, is also a historic fact. But that the Divine Substance consists in Three Persons is a mystery that we cannot now, comprehend. But if GOD be not a Personality in the highest sense, our noblest instincts are at fault. We seek for the impersonation in some form or other of all abstract moral and religious ideas; they must become facts, and must be related either as essential or as attributive to some living sentient Being. We cannot merely or consistently worship an abstraction. So far can we go, but here we must stop. GOD must be a Being. Revelation, then, shows us that these apparently abstract ideas, the longings of the soul, are indeed indissolubly bound up in the Essence of GOD. GOD is love, GOD is truth, GOD is Justice. The Being whose law of Being involves these. The Persons, then, of the HOLY TRINITY most certainly contain these as facts, as essential laws. "I am the Light of the World" saith our LORD, "I am the Bread of Life," "I am the way, the truth, and the Life." Holiness is of the essence, Perfectness is of the nature, of the HOLY GHOST.

(*b*) As for the Person of our LORD, His humanity is so infolded with His Divine Nature, that from the moment it began to be in the virgin womb it was perfectly His own, as it grew, was perfected, and entered into our life. He had our nature interpenetrated with His own eternal nature, so that the two not being commingled yet thoroughly cohering together, were but one Person,—the GOD-man, CHRIST JESUS. This, while an unfathomable mystery, because on a higher plane, is yet quite within the range of our acceptance by the analogy of our dual nature while we are yet single Persons. In this Person our hopes are bound up, and all our realization of what our GOD has done and is doing for us. Through Him we receive that partaking of the Divine Nature which it is His prerogative to bestow upon us. Therefore to us the Person, JESUS CHRIST, is *the* man.

(*c*) As for the HOLY GHOST, He must be a Person, for He is sent from the FATHER by the SON. He searches the deep things of GOD, He gives the gifts CHRIST hath received for us, He reveals, He sanctifies, He guides, He leads into all Truth. No abstract idea can do these things, only a Person can possibly execute them.

It is not necessary for us to picture to ourselves aught beyond these facts, but it is necessary to conceive of and acknowledge with all our power the fact of the Persons of the Holy Trinity and their relation to us, that our religion may have its rightful power over our lives, and that our worship may be fervently paid, not to a holy idea, but to the living GOD.

Persona. *Vide* PARSON.

Peter's Pence. Offa, King of Mercia (793 A.D.), made a pilgrimage to Rome, where he granted to the English school a silver penny from every family in his dominions as a yearly income for its maintenance. It was claimed as a tax later, and continued to be paid, not without remonstrance (see Hart's Eccl. Records), and not without many interruptions, till Henry VIII. forbade it altogether.

Peter, St. The notices in the New Testament of St. Peter's life are very scanty, but there is a coherence in them which enables us to restore in a measure the great Apostle's characteristic traits. When we leave the New Testament, however, we are without any trusty guide; on the contrary, we are wholly misled by tradition, which is too late to be of any value. Simon, son of Jona, was a native of the village of Bethsaida, on the Sea of Galilee; a fisherman in partnership with his brother and his friends, the brothers John and James, the sons of Zebedee. His brother Andrew and another (doubtless John) had been attending upon the ministry of St. John the Baptist, who pointed out to them JESUS the Lamb of GOD; they at once followed Him; abode with Him that night; and the next day Andrew sought his brother Simon and brought him to JESUS. The LORD addressed him with the memorable words, "Thou art Simon the son of Jona: thou shalt be called Cephas, which is by interpretation 'A stone' (Peter)." Henceforth he bears this name also, being sometimes called in the Gospels Simon, often Simon Peter, but generally Peter. Simon returned to his work till CHRIST was ready to call him from it to be trained to catch men. As JESUS was preaching on the seaside the people so pressed on Him that He entered Simon Peter's boat, and from thence taught them. His sermon finished, He would reward the owners of the boat. The miracle of the large draught of fish follows, and the consequent call to him and to the two brothers to leave all and follow Him. As yet for some months the Twelve were not chosen, but our LORD was gathering around Him the band. Peter was present at some of His miracles, and was present when Levi was called; and with James and John was present at the raising of Jairus' daughter. When the LORD chose the Twelve, St. Peter seems to have been the leader. He stands first in all the lists. He is spokesman for the rest. He shows his love and zeal for our LORD promptly, almost to rashness. When, after the discourse at Capernaum, the LORD turned to the Twelve and asked, "Will ye also go away?" St. Peter at once replied for them all, "LORD, to whom shall we go? thou hast the words of eternal life. And we believe and are sure that Thou art the CHRIST, the Son of the living GOD" (St. John vi. 66-69). Here this Confession was indeed the same as the one made afterwards at Cæsarea Philippi. But it was not so much that personal conviction now, which it was at the later Confession.

With the others, two and two, he is sent forth by our LORD when He had given them special supernatural gifts by which they were to attract notice to, and prove the authority of, the preaching He gave them, to cast out evil spirits, to heal the sick, to raise the dead, to cleanse the lepers (St. Matt. x. 8). Nothing is recorded of their work. They seem to have, however, little insight into the spiritual character of their work. It was to them a power to be wielded, not a training, which they had received. In these things St. Peter shows the defects of his character as well as its salient strong points. Ready to begin, bold, forward, trained in the hardy work of a fisherman on a dangerous lake, loving, devoted, zealous, yet he is easily daunted, and passes from one extreme to the other. This he displayed at the several crises of his training from our LORD. When he made his great Confession and received for it the famous promise, it would seem that he was so elated with spiritual pride, that when soon after the LORD showed to His disciples His future humiliation, St. Peter took Him and began to rebuke Him, saying, "Far be it from Thee, LORD, this shall not be unto Thee." Then, again, when before this the LORD appeared to the disciples at near dawn, walking on the sea, St. Peter asked, "LORD, if it be Thou, bid me come unto Thee on the water. And He said, Come. And when Peter was come down out of the ship, he walked on the water, to go to JESUS. But when he saw the wind boisterous, he was afraid, and beginning to sink, he cried, LORD, save me. And immediately JESUS stretched forth His hand, and caught him, and said unto him, O thou of little Faith, wherefore didst thou doubt?" The disciples here too worshiped our LORD, confessing Him to be the Son of GOD. Again, this characteristic of St. Peter, in failing to completely apprehend spiritual things, is shown by his reply, so wide of the meaning of the scene when on the Mount of Transfiguration. After seeing the wondrous change in the Master's person, and hearing the converse of Moses and Elias, he could only say, Master, it is good for us to be here: and let us make three Tabernacles: one for Thee, and one for Moses, and one for Elias. For he wist not what to say; for they were sore afraid" (St. Mark ix. 5, 6).

But these characteristics came out most strongly on that sorrowful night; how he shrank at first from the Master's humble service! how he vowed devotion to death! how poor a guard he kept with the two while the LORD underwent His agony! how rashly he smote with the sword, and yet how readily he fled! how he timidly crept into the Court of the High-Priest and there denied his Master! well might he go out and weep bitterly. It was so wholly in keeping with all we have been told, the loving, bold, yet easily daunted heart, ready to go to either extreme. Even at the Tomb, St. Peter, outstripped by St. John in running to see if indeed the Sepulchre were empty, enters in when St. John shrinks back at first. So too after the Resurrection, when they go to their fishing on the Lake. St. John exclaimed to St. Peter as he looked on the shore, "It is the LORD!" then St. Peter plunged into the water and hastened to the LORD. It was then that the threefold restoration for his triple denial took place. St. Peter's answers show how utterly devoted he was to his LORD: "LORD, Thou knowest all things: Thou knowest that I love Thee," and yet the old temperament made him ask of the fate of his brother Apostle: "LORD, and what shall this man do?" to receive the check again: "If I will that he tarry till I come, what is that to thee? follow thou Me." So too, St. Peter leads in the election of St. Matthias, and his sermon is chosen as typical of the sermons preached at Pentecost. He is foremost in the steadfast confession the Apostles made before the Sanhedrim. He administers the discipline of the Church, as in the case of Ananias and Sapphira. He is sent with St. John to Samaria by the College of Apostles to confirm those baptized by the Evangelist St. Philip. He afterwards spent some time in the villages near, goes to Lydda and to Joppa. Here again came a crisis in his life. He was at Joppa, in the house of Simon the tanner. While fasting there was given him the thrice repeated vision of the great sheet knit at the four corners, and filled with all manner of beasts of the earth and wild beasts and creeping things and fowls of the air. While wondering at the vision the messengers from Cornelius the Centurion came seeking him, and the Spirit bade him go with them nothing doubting, for He had sent them. The Baptism of Cornelius was the fulfillment of the LORD's promise that he should be a foundation-stone of the Church. Attacked by the stricter brethren, he defended himself by reciting to the Apostles the Divine authority by which he acted.

The next record of him is his imprisonment by Herod (Easter, 44 A.D.), and his deliverance by the Angel. His work in the interval is not given us, but he appears in Jerusalem at the council which was summoned under the presidency of St. James to decide the question of circumcising the Gentile converts. After much debate, St. Peter clearly and concisely stated his position in the question, urging that it was too heavy a yoke for the Gentiles to bear. SS. Barnabas and Paul then recounted their mission work, and St. James summed up the question and gave the final decision. The last time St. Peter comes before us is most characteristic. When at Antioch, first he had eaten with the Gentile converts, yet from fear of the censure of those who came thither from St. James, he withdrew and separated himself from his Gentile brethren, and influenced many Jews to do this, and even Barnabas was carried away with their dissimulation. Therefore St. Paul withstood him to the face, because he was to be blamed. Apparently St. Paul did not take a hasty step, nor too soon, since St. Peter's vacillation had affected so many who should have known better. This is the last authentic notice of him in the New Testament history, save (what we may note in his Epistle) that he was at Babylon (65 A.D.). Legend has given us minute accounts of his life, which may be briefly dismissed by saying that they are too late to be authentic. The tradition that he died at Rome is not sufficiently early to be free from much doubt. We have passed rapidly over his career, and omitted many slighter details—if aught in the Gospels could be called slight—to obtain space to discuss one or two points of special importance in his career, and of the claims founded upon them by the Roman See. The Promise given to him upon his Confession at Cæsarea Philippi. His confession, "Thou art the CHRIST, the Son of the Living GOD," procured for him the blessing, "Blessed art thou, Simon Bar-Jona: for flesh and blood hath not revealed it unto thee, but My FATHER which is in heaven. And I say unto thee, That thou art Peter, and upon this Rock I will build My Church; and the gates of hell (Hades) shall not prevail against it. And I will give unto thee the keys of the kingdom of heaven: and whatsoever thou shalt bind on earth shall be bound in heaven: and whatsoever thou shalt loose on earth shall be loosed in heaven." (St. Matt. xvi. 17-19.)

The Roman theologians claim that this gives to St. Peter a transmissible headship over the Visible Church, which belongs now to the See of Rome. The reply is clear, concise, convincing. (*a*) That the words Peter, or stone, and Rock, are two different things, and are to be determined by their use in the New Testament; now St. Paul uses the word Rock to refer to CHRIST: "For they drank of that spiritual Rock that followed them, and that Rock was CHRIST" (1 Cor. x. 4). (*b*) That St. Peter's relation to the foundation of the Church is settled by St. Paul's words: "Now therefore ye are no longer strangers and foreigners, but fellow-citizens with the saints, and of the Household of GOD; and are built upon the foundation of the Apostles and Prophets, JESUS CHRIST Himself being the chief corner-stone" (Eph. ii. 19, 20), and by St. John's words of the Vision of the New Jerusalem, "And the city had twelve foundations, and in them the names of the twelve Apostles of the Lamb" (Rev. xxi. 14). (*c*) Again, St. Peter received the privilege of being the leading Apostle. This was undoubtedly a prerogative of leadership, but certainly not of supremacy. In no official act after the Resurrection did he lead, save in one,—the election of St. Matthias. In this he did take the directing part. As for his Sermon at Pentecost, it was not the only Sermon preached, but his was the only one reported. He passed sentence upon Ananias and Sapphira, but this was a momentary disciplinary act, involving no leadership. He was by natural temperament chief spokesman before the Sanhedrim. But he is sent by the College of Apostles to Samaria (Acts viii. 14). He was questioned before the Apostles by some of the brethren (Acts xi. 1-18). When miraculously escaping from prison he sends word to St. James (Acts xii. 17). He is a chief debater only in the Council at Jerusalem (Acts xv.). It is very evident from these facts that he was the foremost and the influential Apostle, but not the Governor. But in a still more marked way we find this to be his true position when we contrast him with St. Paul. St. Paul gives very positively their relation to each other (Gal. i. 18, 19; ii.). In this narration he declares his independence. He and St. Barnabas received the right hand of fellowship from SS. James, Cephas, and John (notice the order). His own gifts were equal with St. Peter's. They parted the mission work between them, and this at Jerusalem, where St. Peter's influence would be paramount. At Antioch St. Paul rebuked St. Peter openly, and apparently St. Peter made no defense. In another place St. Paul is not behind the chiefest Apostles. At every point, by undeniable facts, we find St. Peter acknowledged a leader, but by no means a master.

Turning to the claim that St. Peter established his supremacy in and transmitted it through the Roman See, the facts prove to be still weaker. The passages which refer to his going there at all are at the best a full century after the alleged event. The "Clementines," a heretical work, rejected by Rome herself, first assigns to St. Peter a visit to Rome. But Dionysius of Corinth (170 A.D.) refers to it in an Epistle to Rome. Irenæus (177 A.D.) repeats it. Tertullian (180 A.D.) speaks of it; and Caius of Rome, 200 A.D. The tradition, of course, was more widely received as time went on. St. Cyprian (250 A.D.) takes it for granted, and argues from it. Firmilian, 250 A.D., says that it was urged in Rome very strenuously. But this visit and martyrdom, not testified to by any earlier writer than Dionysius, had grown to a residence and a government of twenty-five years by the thirteenth century. In the light of these facts, while a martyrdom in Rome may be admitted, there is not the shadow of proof that he exercised any Episcopal right. Nay, if any did so, it must have been St. Paul, who was there in his own hired house two whole years at his first imprisonment. Of the legends which surround his life, but one is really worth the quoting. It is said that on the night before his martyrdom he succeeded in escaping from prison. As he was passing the city walls he met his MASTER coming, and exclaimed, *Domine quo Vadis*, —MASTER, whither goest Thou? The reply was, To suffer in place of my servant. St. Peter at once returned to his cell, and was crucified the next day,—some later writers say head downward, as not worthy to suffer as did his LORD.

Epistles of.—The First Epistle of St. Peter, addressed to the Christian Jews of the dispersion, was received at once and without dispute. As we read that Silvanus (St. Paul's companion) was with the Apostle at the time, and since those addressed were partly churches which St. Paul had founded, we see at once the kindly relationship which existed between the two chief Apostles. It is most probable that the Apostle wrote from the Babylon upon the Euphrates and as the Apostle to the Circumcision. That he knew of St. Paul's Epistles to these Churches is shown by the similarity of thought in the Epistle to those of St. Paul to the Ephesians, Romans, Colossians, Corinthians, and Thessalonians. These are not in any sense quotations, but certain coincidences, which prove that each of the two Apostles was aware of the teachings of the other. St. Peter's practical character is shown in his Epistle. Earnest, straightforward, zealous, he has not the genius of St. Paul, but a soberness seems to run through what he writes. There is mingled a strain of reminiscences and allusions to our LORD'S life and the incidents at which St Peter was present which give a vividness to some of his sentences. He begins with an allusion to their inheritance in CHRIST'S Kingdom, of which they had a most certain hope, based upon a faith which, indeed, had not seen the LORD, but rejoicingly accepted Him. He exhorts them to be steadfast in holiness and purity, seeing by whom they were redeemed, and at what a price. As innocent children live in purity and truthfulness founded upon CHRIST JESUS and in Him act as a royal priesthood, a peculiar people. Then (ch. ii. 11 *sq.*) he urges them to greater purity of life, since their Christianity makes them, as it were, public, submitting to the Law and to the Administrator of it. Servants are exhorted to bear and to forbear, as CHRIST did, wives to be obedient, husbands to honor their wives. The love towards each other, the keeping a good conscience, the reference to the baptismal vow (the answer of a good conscience is the replies to the questions in a good conscience) which makes us subject to CHRIST, our ascended LORD, are used as urgent reasons for a greater use of their opportunities for patience, for prayer, for suffering joyfully for the LORD'S sake, committing themselves to Him in all things. The Apostle closes with an exhortation to the Presbyterate to rule CHRIST'S flock as ensamples to the flock, and with a prayer for their firmer establishment in the Faith.

The Second Epistle at an early date had

suffered from doubts of its genuineness. It had some points of resemblance to the Epistle of St. Jude, and was consequently quite different in style from the first and undoubted Epistle. The question is closed for us, since the canon is received by the Church, and, admitting the guidance of the HOLY GHOST, and the inspiration of Scripture, not to preserve the identity of style, but to reveal and to teach, there is no reason for us to doubt of its genuineness. It contains the doctrine of the "last things," conveyed in a style different from those of any other Epistle. It reads more as the production of the headlong zeal of the disciple who smote off the ear of the servant of the High-Priest than of the calm courage of the Apostle before the High-Priest. It has very much of the tone of St. Jude. In these very objections we see that very character of the Apostle which both the Gospel and the Acts bring before us. He is calm and courageous at one time, at another he shrinks, and again he is forward through zeal. This Epistle may well have been suggested by St. Jude's Epistle, as probably the first Epistle was written because of the visit of Silvanus, St. Paul's companion. Its contents may be summarized thus: (A) The first chapter is very similar in every respect to the parallel passage in the first Epistle, the salutation, the reminders to them of their calling, and of the Christian virtues they should cultivate, of their redemption, of the value of prophecy. (B) With the second chapter he begins his denunciation of false teachers deceiving the members of the Church. The warning is vehement and couched in energetic style, condemning their evil life, which is intimately bound up in their false doctrines. The third chapter closes the Epistle, with a passage which seems written for the scientific opposition of the present day upon the end of all things. "If these things are true, and their consummation is largely in your own hands, hasting unto the coming of that day by your prayers and conduct, be diligent, that ye may be found of Him in peace without spot and blameless."

Pews. Anciently the ground floor of a church was open. The chancel contained stalls for the officiating clergy and musicians. Standing and kneeling space was free to all, and the worshiper had no special place assigned to him. The founder of an English church and his family often retained a part of the building for their use, one side of the church, or the east end of an aisle. Here they buried their dead, and the place in church descended to the heirs. Sometimes a person added a chapel or aisle to a church. In the fourteenth or fifteenth century, benches were occasionally placed in the nave or aisles of the churches; considerably later they were supplied throughout the building. In a few old English churches a stone bench ran around the inner, and even almost as often the outer, part of the edifice, and in one case round each pillar.

In the greater part of Europe the churches are still without fixed seats, except a bench or so.

In old times stools seem to have been used, according to antique pictures, as early as the fourteenth century. The earliest example of regular benching Hailes met with in the nave of the cathedral at Soest, Westphalia. The word "pew" is used in the diary of Pepys in the seventeenth century. In 1454 A.D. there is a record of Swaffham Church having been pewed by "Thomas Styward and Cecily his wyf" previously. In one version of Pier's "Plowman's Vision," in the fourteenth century the word "pues" occurs. Accounts of St. Michael's, Cornhill, London, 1457 A.D. and onward, contain references to pews, and I am sorry to say, refer to doors and "a lok." From the beginning of the sixteenth century there is a frequent mention of pews. The Church accounts contain entries concerning mending and making them. It is probable that the churches were only fitted in part with pews, and especially in country places their use was not universal until long afterwards. Seats in the church and choir were given to kings and distinguished persons. Anciently, women occupied one side of the church and men the other. In the sixteenth and seventeenth centuries, young women were separated from matrons in some English churches. In St. Margaret's, Westminster, in the seventeenth century, expenses about old and new pews are noted in the accounts. In the early part of the sixteenth century payment for use of pews is recorded in that parish, before pews were common in that church. It seems to be a rare case at the time. In England there were corporation pews and a mayor's pew. Up to the middle of the sixteenth century there does not appear to have been a payment for a pew-rent, except at St Margaret's, Westminster. St. Matthew's, Friday Street, London, has accounts which show that the pews were numbered in 1569-70 A.D., where payment is made for painting the numbers. Spelman, 1641 A.D., refers to the sale, but not the renting of pews. A motion against locks was issued by Bishop Neile, of Winchester, 1631 A.D.

Pepys, in 1661 A.D., was obliged to stay at the door of his pew during "a good sermon by Mr. Mills," because the sexton had not unlocked it. Galleries, or lofts or scaffolds, as then called, were built because the general allotment of pews required larger accommodation. The early pews were benches, with backs and ends, not square pews. A pew at St. John's, Winchester, is thought to be as old as the third quarter of the fourteenth century. Doors were used as early as 1457 A.D. in St. Michael's, Cornhill. The benches at Bishop's Hull, Somerset, had a bar across them for a door. While Gothic architecture prevailed the seats were rows of single benches, which seem always to have faced the East, though possibly some examples might be found of their facing North or South. Practice did not allow the congregation to sit with their backs to the altar. Afterwards seats were made approaching a square in form; the earliest is dated 1601 A.D., at Barking, Suffolk. In 1612 A.D. a pew is named five feet high. At Cholderton, Wiltshire, is a pew six feet high, with glass windows in the door to enable the occupants to see the preacher, and other windows in the side to permit them to survey the congregation, all being fitted with sliding shutters. At Branksea, Dorsetshire, there is a pew as large as a drawing-room, magnificently furnished, having a fire-place, and windows, and blinds to secure privacy. In Little Bemingham Church, Norfolk, a pew was built by a shepherd for strangers and wedding parties. On it is a skeleton carved in wood, and an inscription warning the passer-by to "Remember Death."

In Central and Southern France chairs are used in church. In Spain and Italy the cathedrals and churches are free and unappropriated, and the Eastern Church, including Russia and Greece, keeps up its old traditions, and has a clear and free area for all worshipers. The noble and peasant may kneel together before GOD, who "is no respecter of persons" (Acts x. 34). "The rich and the poor meet together: the LORD is the Maker of them all" (Prov. xxii. 2). The Church of GOD should be as free as His blessed sunlight, and reviving air, and refreshing water. In giving a church to GOD, let us not keep "back a part of the price." Pews should be low, so as not to be obstructions, and doors, and locks, and waiting for seats should be unknown. It is the plain duty of the Church to return to the custom of primitive times, and to make the house of GOD free. Can she not hear her Master's cry as it comes down loud and clear through the ages, "Make not my FATHER'S house an house of merchandise"? (St. John ii. 16.) The "man with a gold ring in goodly apparel" and the "poor man in vile raiment" (James ii. 2) are to be equally cared for in the Christian "assembly." We may not say to him of the "gay clothing," "Sit thou here in a good place;" and to "the poor, Stand thou there, or sit here under my footstool;" if so, we become "partial" and "judges of evil thoughts" (ver. 4).

Pew-rents are declared by some to be necessary for the expenses of the parish, but quite half of our parishes are free. The offering on the LORD'S day is the old Apostolic plan of church support (1 Cor. xvi. 2). New dioceses and new parishes can correct old faults. The desirability of seating families together is urged for the pew-rent system, but in many cases by early attendance that could be secured, and the principle of church freedom would not be violated. Free churches imply a deep and constant interest in all, but if a tithe of the money spent in fine houses, rich dress, jewelry, and travel could find its way to the altar of GOD, not only could the church be free, but also open daily for public and private prayer. May GOD hasten the good day that this may be a reality. The facts of this article are drawn from the valuable work of Alfred Heales, F.S.A., Proctor in Doctor's Commons, on the "History and Law of Church Seats or Pews," 2 vols. That author refers to Rev. Jno. Mason Neale's "History of Pews," and to works by Billings, Oliphant, Fowler, and Rogers, as well as many others, and to various church records. The second volume has references to cases in law with regard to ownership in church seats, which lawsuits should never have been possible, for no man should have the slightest right to call a church a gift to GOD, and then to claim any part of it for himself.

REV. S. F. HOTCHKIN.

Pharisees. The leading party or school of theology among the Jews in our LORD'S day. Their name meant separated. By a minute analysis of the Law, and by petty regulations they had formalized, as well as formulated, the precepts of Moses, and by these means had constructed a system which went counter to the spirit and often to the very letter of the Law they professed to obey. Now our LORD at once opposed this, for it created a party and a sect of pretentious saints; it also separated the people from the obedience to the law,—these were, to the Pharisee, ignorant of the Law, and so cursed. It was, therefore, in defense of the Law our LORD opposed them; in defense of the rights of the people He denounced them; in defense of all true interpretation of the Law He wittingly broke through their maxims. What of truth they taught that He did but commend, "these ought ye to have done and not to leave the other undone." They held to the resurrection of the dead and to the duty of constant prayer, which two doctrines are not enjoined in the Law at all. They trained their nation in that exclusiveness which is even yet so marked a characteristic, and when their wretched troubles unified the Jewish nation, if indeed it needed this after the Babylonish Captivity, most Jews were Pharisees in doctrine. It has been only lately that this yoke has been really broken. But this formalism trained the Pharisee in a hypocrisy which our LORD most bitterly denounced. It was an ostentatious, sinful observance of the letter of religion, the long prayer, the parade of gifts and of natural formalities, the niceties of dress and of meats, and with it was a disregard of an inner morality. This party had yet noble men in it, Nicodemus, Joseph of Arimathea, Saul. Many fled from it into Christianity, as the refuge that could satisfy them, as is shown by the mysterious hints given in the Talmud, of the influence of the hated sect of Christians. Both by their evil traits, by their organization, and by the good that was in them, for they upheld the law, and the prophets, and were conservators of the main doctrine (the resurrection), and the chief practice (prayer) of Christianity, both for good and for evil they stamped their form of Judaism upon the Nation, which shrunk from the epicurean scorn of the Sadducee.

Philemon. The Epistle St. Paul wrote to his friend Philemon at Colosse, commending to his pardon and favor the slave Onesimus, who had run away and whom St. Paul had found and recovered at Rome. It was written at the same time that the Epistle to the Colossians was written. It is replete with all the love and tenderness and friendship that the Apostle's large heart felt. Onesimus was reclaimed no longer a faithless runaway slave, but a Christian in the same bonds of Faith as his master. Onesimus was St. Paul's son in the Faith, and he pleads for him as for a son. It is of importance both as having a relation to the Apostle's life and work, and as having beneath it the divine will upon the relation of master and servant, the true principle upon which emancipation from slavery can be soundly instituted and as from which emancipation will surely follow.

Philip, St., the Apostle. Philip of Bethsaida, the fellow-townsman of SS. Andrew and Peter, was the first to whom our Lord said, "Follow me." Of his life we have only the scanty notices in the Gospels. From his finding Nathaniel and bringing him to Jesus, and from his intimacy with St. Andrew, we may conjecture that these had before been bound together in a common communion upon the highest of all the hopes of the Jew,—the coming of the Messiah. It is a lovely trait that is pictured to us. John and Andrew follow Jesus and abide with Him; they bring Simon to the Messiah; Jesus seeks their fellow-townsman and attaches him to Himself; but as he obeys the call Philip brings another, Nathaniel, the guileless Israelite, to the Lord. It may well have been the bond of a longing common to them that brought them to that height of faith which fitted them to be His Apostles. After our Lord began His fuller ministry after the imprisonment of St. John the Baptist He called anew the band He had selected. When our Lord set them apart for the Apostolate he in the lists stands fifth. At the head of the second group of four, and closely joined to him is Bartholomew (who was most probably also the Nathaniel of St. John i. 45 fin.). That Philip was most devotedly attached to the Master is shown in the very few notices of him in the Gospels. Clement of Alexandria assumes as a well-known fact that Philip was the one who pleaded to the command to follow Him, "Suffer me first to go and bury my father," and received the reply, "Let the dead bury their dead, follow thou me." It was to Philip that our Lord addressed the question, "Whence shall we buy bread that these may eat?" when He paused in His instruction to the people. How little he could yet trust the Divine power, how little he could forecast his own future duty of feeding the hungry multitudes with spiritual food is shown by his reply, "Two hundred pennyworth of bread is not sufficient for them that every one may take a little." This spiritual dullness was not his peculiarity; the other Apostles shared it, yet it was compatible with loving zeal. It was to him the Greek proselytes came, asking to see Jesus. Again he goes to his friend Andrew, and the two bring the Greek seekers to Jesus. Once more Philip comes forward. He has listened to our Lord's discourse, He is going to the Father, those who know Him know His Father also. The eager Philip exclaims, Lord, show us the Father and it sufficeth us. His faith is yet with dimmed spiritual eyes, and our Lord gently pleads, "Have I been so long time with you, and yet hast thou not known me, Philip?" The Apostle afterwards undoubtedly understood the tenderness of the appeal when it was his duty by his Apostolic labors to make others see Jesus as he had seen Him, and to know Him as he had known Him. This is the last incident in which he appears. All beyond is either doubtful tradition, or it is so apocryphal as to be beyond belief. He is said to have married and not to have refused his daughters in marriage, and also it is stated that he died a natural death, but this again is contradicted.

Philip, the Evangelist. The notices of the Evangelist are all confined to the Acts of the Apostles. He appears as one of the seven men of good report selected for the work of serving tables, and is ordained deacon. When upon the death of Stephen the disciples were scattered, St. Philip proved to be a most active Evangelist. He went to Samaria and then among the proselytes, converted and baptized very many; tidings of his success came to the Apostles (who still remained in Jerusalem), and they sent SS. Peter and John to confirm the new converts. St. Philip was not permitted to remain longer in Samaria, but the Holy Ghost selected him to convert the Ethiopian Eunuch, the treasurer of Queen Candace. This is a marked record, since it gives us the terms of admission (repentance implied), and Faith in Christ as the Son of God. It gives us the rule for the Church as to the proper procedure when compared with the direction of our Lord, just to baptize them, to teach them all things whatsoever He had commanded the Apostles to instruct the Church in. Then he was sent to the villages of the old Philistine country. Finally he came to Cæsarea. There we find him in his own house, the centre of many, journeying to and coming from Jerusalem. He has a family, four daughters, who were endowed with the gift of prophecy. He is the entertainer of St. Paul on his way to Jerusalem, the last journey the Apostle made of his own freewill, for thenceforth he journeyed as a prisoner of the State. "At such a place as Cæsarea the work of such a man must have helped to bridge over the ever-widening gap which threatened to separate the Jewish and the Gentile Churches. One who had preached CHRIST to the hated Samaritan, the swarthy African, the despised Philistine, the men of all nations who passed through the seaport of Palestine, might well welcome the arrival of the Apostle of the Gentiles." (Smith's Dict. of Bible.) Here we lose sight of the Evangelist. His future, whether he died at Cæsarea or whether he really became Bishop of the Trallians, cannot be known in this present life.

Philippians, Epistle to. This is usually considered the last of the Epistles of the first Imprisonment. It has been assigned to the Apostle's imprisonment under Felix, but this is to do violence to all the indications of the chronology of St. Paul's life contained in the Acts and in the Epistle itself. It is far more natural to suppose that it is the last of the series, Ephesians, Colossians, Philemon, and Philippians. The contents of the Epistle are so within the scope of the Apostle's time and the order of his work that no rational commentator can doubt its authenticity, and Dean Alford has well branded the doubts of recent German Commentators as the insanity of hypercriticism. The Epistle must have been near the close of his imprisonment, for Epaphroditus' sickness being known to the Philippians implies at least four journeys, back and forth, between St. Paul's arrival in Rome and the date of his letter. First the news that he had reached Rome, then Epaphroditus' journey, then the report of his sickness, and, lastly, the return account of the anxiety at Philippi, before St. Paul indites this letter. Besides, the tone of his letter shows that his present condition and future acquittal were very doubtful at the time he wrote. This places the date of the Epistle near the time of his trial, which took place probably in 63 A.D.

The contents of the Epistle are chiefly notable for two things : (*a*) That there are none of the warnings against some besetting sins that were current in the other cities, as in Corinth, or in Ephesus, or in Colosse, as is shown by the other letters. Here his exhortations are general, and imply a faith and general purity which call rather for his commendation ; and indeed an **exhortation to Euodias and to Syntyche to unity is the** only hint at any failure of charity from his pen. (*b*) The contents of the Epistle are grouped around two central points. The inscription, so different from the others by the omission of his official position as Apostle, introduces his urging to greater love and confidence and forbearance in the midst of affliction and persecution, culminating at last in the noble passage declaring the Divinity, the manhood, the humiliation and exaltation of the LORD JESUS CHRIST (a passage the Church reads most fitly upon the Sunday next before Easter), followed by a loving exhortation to a blameless life. The passage is on its surface wholly dissimilar, yet withal underneath very like the parallel exhortation in St. Peter's first Epistle upon the meekness of CHRIST. A comparison of the two is very instructive. With this thought of meekness and longsuffering in his mind, the Apostle is next led to speak of those temporal advantages which he had joyfully cast away for CHRIST'S sake, and thus adds a noble practical declaration of the righteousness which cometh by the Faith of CHRIST and his longing for that resurrection in Him ; to gain this he urges the pressing forward to the mark of our high calling of GOD in CHRIST JESUS, and closes with that magnificent image of the Politeia we have in our Mother-City in heaven of which we are colonists, by whose laws we are governed here, and from which we look for our Judge, who will refashion us into His own perfect and glorious body. The glow of love, tenderness, enthusiasm, eager longing for his LORD'S presence, and the exhortations scattered through the whole Epistle, not as in others placed at the end, make it, apart from its great doctrinal value, one of the most delightful of all the Apostle's letters. We seem to be on different terms with him. He is not the Lawyer holding a weighty brief, as in the Epistle to the Romans, not a vehement expostulator, as in the Galatian and Corinthian Epistles, nor setting forth the unity of the Church, as in the other two Epistles of the Imprisonment, but here, as in the short Epistle to Philemon, apparently pouring out his enthusiastic heart to loving friends in the joy of their faith.

Pilgrim. The word pilgrim means a wanderer or traveler, and it is generally used to designate those who visit some sacred place. Sometimes the term has a general sense, as in Purchas's "Pilgrimages, or Relations of the World." In Bunyan's "Pilgrim's Progress" the Christian is represented as journeying through earth to his heavenly home.

Pilgrimages. There is a natural desire among men to behold places which have been made famous by the residence of those who were esteemed great or holy. The looking on the scenes which gratified the eyes of heroes and the treading on the ground where they have trod seems to bring them nearer to us. The idea attains its height in respect to our LORD and SAVIOUR. It is, then, little wonder that hundreds of thousands through the Christian centuries should have thronged to look on the abode of CHRIST. As one stands on the Lake of Galilee he can almost hear again the Divine words which resounded over it when the SON of GOD taught men there, and can in imagination see the waiting crowds who heard them.

Pilgrimages were common among the Jews. Jerusalem, their central place of worship, called them to its sacred services thrice a year, and with glad Psalms they approached it in vast crowds. "Our feet shall stand within thy gates, O Jerusalem" (Ps. cxxii. 2), was the burden of their song, and the city is described as the place "whither the tribes go up, the tribes of the LORD, unto the testimony of Israel, to give thanks unto the name of the LORD" (ver. 4).

In Christian times Jerusalem again became a centre of pilgrimages. The Church historians, Socrates and Theodoret, relate that Helena, the mother of Constantine the Great, was instructed by a dream to go to Jerusalem, and believed that she had found there the cross on which our Blessed LORD was crucified. Thus she "seems to have been the first who gave the signal for these religious journeys." Many went to be baptized in the Jordan, which was the desire of Constantine, and they were also "attracted by the marvelous and the love of relics." Even the very dust of the Holy Land was thought of great value, and was carried home by pilgrims.

"Chrysostom says that from all quarters of the earth men flock to see the place where CHRIST was born, where He suffered and was buried." He also declares that "the memory of Job drew many pilgrims to Arabia to see the dung-heap and to kiss the earth on which the man of GOD had suffered with such resignation." It seemed to Chrysostom a remarkable thing that places sanctioned by religion should be sought after for thousands of years in preference to "monuments of earthly glory," and he speaks of the profit from such sacred recollections. The trouble was that the impression was too often a fleeting one. It is easier to trust in the outward than to seek inward grace, and hence we find St. Jerome declaring that "the places of the crucifixion and of the resurrection of CHRIST profited those only who bore their own cross, and rose each day with CHRIST, but those who said 'The temple of the LORD, the temple of the LORD,' should hearken to the Apostle, 'Ye are the temple of the LORD, the HOLY SPIRIT dwells within you.' Heaven stands open to us in Britain as well as in Jerusalem; the kingdom of GOD should be within ourselves." He states that the venerable monk Hilarion, in Palestine, had visited the holy places but once, though near them, that he might not countenance the exaggerated veneration of them.

Gregory of Nyssa said, "Change of place brings GOD no nearer. Wherever thou art, GOD will visit thee, if the mansion of thy soul is found to be such that He can dwell and rule in thee. But if thou hast thy inner man full of wicked thoughts, then, whether thou art on Golgotha, on the Mount of Olives, or at the monument of the Crucifixion, thou art still as far from having received CHRIST into thy heart as if thou hadst never confessed Him." In after-years the Council of Chalons (813 A.D.) found it necessary to denounce the false confidence of some in the merit of pilgrimages to Rome and the church of St. Martin at Tours, without a holy life, being "so foolish as to believe that by the mere sight of a holy place they should be cleansed from their sins." The pilgrimages were thought commendable which proceeded from sincere piety, and aimed at amendment of life. Alcuin wrote to a nun troubled in conscience on account of inability to finish a pilgrimage which she had begun: "This was no great harm; for GOD had chosen some better thing for her; she had now only to expend in supporting the poor what she had appropriated to so long a journey." The English pilgrimages to Rome in the eighth century, though often morally injurious, helped to transplant a needed culture to rude Britain, and were the means of bringing Bibles and other good books to her shores, as well as "the elements of many of the arts."

As the ages passed on an undue reverence for the tombs of martyrs caused many to make superstitious pilgrimages to them. People who should have remembered that their own bodies were temples "of the HOLY GHOST" (1 Cor. vi. 19) began to reverence the bones of dead saints, who if they could have spoken from Paradise would have rebuked such action, as Barnabas and Paul did the heathen priest at Lystra, who "would have done sacrifice with the people" to "men of like passions" with themselves (Acts xiv. 13, 15). They warned the people to turn "unto the living GOD."

The Crusades, those strange mixtures of war and devotion, were pilgrimages, and Peter the Hermit and others excited vast numbers of people to throng to the Holy Land to redeem the sepulchre of CHRIST from the hand of the Turks. Perhaps the most remarkable feature of these times was the children's crusade, whereby thousands of innocents were drawn from their homes, many of whom perished miserably.

While merit is not to be sought in pilgrimages, Christian hearts will always long to behold the scenes of CHRIST's earthly work, and crucifixion, and burial, and resurrection, and ascension. Dr. Johnson, with his usual good sense, in "Rasselas," makes distinctions between proper and improper pilgrimages. He calls them "reasonable or superstitious according to the principles upon which they are performed."

In short, instead of leaning on sacred places or sacred people to make us holy, we must be ourselves "perfecting holiness in the fear of God" (2 Cor. vii. 1). St. Peter's exhortation (1 Pet. ii. 11) is, "Dearly beloved, I beseech you as strangers and pilgrims, abstain from fleshly lusts, which war against the soul." Life is the real pilgrimage, Heaven is the true goal. The aged Jacob speaks of his still more aged fathers, "in the days of their pilgrimage" (Gen. iv. 7 9). Earthly life to the patriarchs was as an inn or a tent, a sojourning place. Their steps tended towards the "city which hath foundations," the "Jerusalem which is above." "From the ends of the earth do I cry unto Thee" (from this distant earth, this remote and foreign land); "O that I might dwell in Thy tabernacle of the eternities. O that I might find shelter under the covert of Thy wings, in the secret place of Thy Presence" (Ps. lxi.). In Ps. cxix. 54, the statutes of GOD are the "songs of the Psalmist in the house of his pilgrimage." In the eleventh chapter of Hebrews, the ancient worthies, who "died in faith, confessed that they were strangers and pilgrims on the earth" (ver. 13). Philo says that "All the wise men are introduced by Moses as strangers, their souls coming from heaven to travel here on earth, looking upon heaven as the city where they dwell, and the earth in which they travel as their place of pilgrimage." The philosophers taught that to die was to go into our country, "to the true country whence we came." Abraham and David call themselves strangers and sojourners (Gen. xxiii. 4; Ps. xxxix. 12). So of the Jewish nation (2 Chron. xxix. 15, and Lev. xxv. 23). The rest for the pilgrim and the stranger comes hereafter, and the best pilgrimage is that which ends in Abraham's bosom, the Paradise of GOD.

Authorities: Mosheim's, Gieseler's, and Neander's Church Histories, Illustrations of the Catechism of the Prot. Epis. Ch., Buck's Theological Dict., Encyc. Amer., Note of Tayler Lewis, in Lange's Genesis, on Chap. xlvii., Whitby, Com. on Heb. xi. 13.   REV. S. F. HOTCHKIN.

Pittsburg, Diocese of. The Diocese of Pittsburg is formed out of that part of the old Diocese of Pennsylvania lying west of the Alleghany Mountains, and comprises twenty-four counties of the State; the Eastern boundary being formed by the Eastern lines of McKean, Cameron, Clearfield, Cambria, and Somerset Counties. According to the last census the population of these counties is about 1,300,000. The first movement towards setting apart this territory a separate Missionary Jurisdiction was made in the early part of the century. The consent of Bishop White was readily obtained, and the preparatory steps were taken in General Convention; but nothing practical came of it. The project was not revived until some fifty years later, and it then took the form of a proposal to form a new *Diocese.* The application to the Convention of the Diocese of Pennsylvania was made at nearly every annual meeting; but for a long time was vehemently opposed and consent refused. At length, in the Convention of 1865 A.D., a resolution was passed permitting the formation of the new Diocese, coupled, however, with the condition that the consent of the Bishop should not be asked until the sum of at least $30,000 should be raised and safely invested, as a fund for the support of the new Bishop. A larger amount than was demanded was very soon secured, and the Bishop of the Diocese of Pennsylvania gave the required consent. This action of the Diocesan Convention and the Bishop was ratified by the General Convention at its session held in Philadelphia, October, 1865 A.D., to take effect November 1, 1865 A.D. It is worthy of note that this was the first instance of the division of a Diocese since the formation of the Diocese of Western New York in 1836 A.D. It is also to be remarked that the Diocese of Pittsburg was the first to adopt as its ecclesiastical title the name of the leading city within its bounds, and the consent of the Bishop in charge was given only with the public declaration that "the name adopted is open to very grave objections."

The Primary Convention was held in Trinity Church, Pittsburg, November 15, 1865 A.D. All the clergy entitled to seats, 28 in number, were present, and 28 parishes were represented by lay delegates. The Rt. Rev. Wm. Bacon Stevens, of Pennsylvania, the Bishop in charge, preached the sermon at the opening service and presided over the sessions. The preliminary business having been disposed of, on the second day the President announced the order of the day to be the election of a Bishop. The Rev. Mr. Swope, Rector of Trinity Church, Pittsburg, nominated the Rev. John Barrett Kerfoot, D.D., President of Trinity College, Hartford, Conn., and the Rev. Dr. Page, of Christ Church, Alleghany, nominated the Rev. Frederic Dan Huntington, D.D., Rector of Emmanuel Church, Boston. The election was suspended in order to fix the salary of the Bishop who should be elected, which was, upon the motion of Mr. John H. Shoenberger, made $4500 per annum.

The election then proceeded, and on the first ballot Dr. Kerfoot was "duly nominated and supported by the order of the clergy" by a vote of 19 to 9. The election was confirmed by the laity; 19 Parishes voting for approval, 8 for disapproval, and 1 being divided.

Dr. Kerfoot accepted the election, and was consecrated in Trinity Church, Pittsburg, St. Paul's Day, January 25, 1866 A.D. The Presiding Bishop, the Rt. Rev. John Henry Hopkins, D.D., of Vermont, Bishops McIlvaine, Whittingham, Williams, Talbot, Coxe, and Clarkson took part in the consecration.

Bishop Kerfoot's Episcopate extended over fifteen years, though for nearly eighteen months before his death he was disabled by sickness from performing his accustomed duties. He died, after a long illness, at Meyersdale, Somerset Co., July 10, 1881 A.D. During his administration the Diocese developed both strength and growth. The effects of closer supervision and more frequent Episcopal services were speedily felt. At the end of two years, in his Convention address of 1868 A.D., he was able to report that the amount raised for Diocesan and City Missions was six times as great as before

Division, i.e., $6000; that the Clergy had increased from 33 to 49; that the number of Communicants had grown 50 per cent. (from 2000 to 3000), and that the Confirmations had increased threefold. Besides, $100,000 had been expended in Church building.

Again, in 1871 A.D., he summarizes the growth of the Diocese for the six years of separate Church life and the six years previous to the Division for comparison, showing the increase in offerings for Diocesan Missions was in the ratio of 6 to 1; in Communicants of 5 to 3; in Confirmations of 5 to 2. Up to that time there had been at least $500,000 spent in Church building; and during the same period of six years 22 new churches had been built, 17 of them being entirely new organizations. The amount of labor which Bishop Kerfoot performed can be appreciated only by an examination of his yearly journal.

The progress of the Diocese may be estimated by the following comparison of statistics for the first year of Diocesan life, 1866-67 A.D., with those of the last Convention year, 1881-83 A.D.:

	1866.	1883.
Baptisms	712	1012
Communicants	2629	6206
Confirmations	404	506
Sunday-School Teachers and Scholars	3679	6200
Contributions	$130,500	$191,250
Clergy	49	53
Parishes	44	58

The Church Institutions were, 1. The Church Home, having as inmates 5 aged women and 71 children. 2. The Bishop Bowman Institute, a Church School for Girls. 3. The Bishop Kerfoot Library, bequeathed by the first Bishop of the Diocese for the use of the clergy. There is also a flourishing Boys' School, Trinity Hall, at Washington, Pa., under Church, but not Diocesan, control. After Bishop Kerfoot's death, a special Convention was called to meet at Trinity Church, Pittsburg, October 19, 1881 A.D., to elect a successor. At this Convention, on the fifth ballot, the Rev. Cortlandt Whitehead, D.D., Rector of the Church of the Nativity, South Bethlehem, Pa., was elected by the clergy, and the next day confirmed by a vote of the Parishes.

Dr. Whitehead accepted the election, and was consecrated St. Paul's Day, January 25, 1882 A.D., in Trinity Church, Pittsburg. Under his care the Diocese has kept up its previous progress.

Statistics for 1886 A.D: Clergy, 63; parishes, 59; missions, 34; candidates for H. O., 4; ordination, D. 1, P. 6; baptisms, 1202; con., 780; com., 7298; contr., $179,088.08.

REV. M. BYLLESBY.

Plurality. The holding of one or more benefices. It was an abuse that grew up in the Middle Ages, and has been productive of much evil, since a clergyman sometimes obtained a very large income from the holding of several Parishes the duty for which he had to remit to curates, at insufficient salaries, while he received all the profits without doing the work for them. In this country, however, at present the stipend in many parishes is so small that it is a matter of necessity for a clergyman to undertake the care of more than one to eke out a support.

Polygamy. The marriage by one man of several wives at one time. This was a custom of very early existence. The first instance we have is in Genesis iv. 19, where Lamech took two wives. The reverse also occurs among some rude tribes, where one woman had several husbands. The Law allowed the marriage of several wives. Before this Abraham, Jacob, Esau, and Ishmael had married several wives. Before the coming of our LORD there seems to have been no positive precept against polygamy. It was not only allowed, but in the case of King David taking Saul's wives it was a State act, implying that he had become seized of all the property of his predecessor. So Absalom defiled his father's wives for a like reason. Yet with all this practice the tendency of the Jewish Scriptures was against polygamy. Solomon, with his three hundred wives and seven hundred concubines, yet does not allude to polygamy in his writings. Its evils were then as many and as great as we now see them to be in the modern cases of the Turk and of the Mormon. The moral and the legal consequences are all bad, and must always be so. But beyond this the home life, which is so very important, is injured, if not practically destroyed. After the Captivity the Jews appear to have dropped polygamy. No case is recorded among them in the Evangelists. Our LORD did not have to forbid it directly, since it was not at all common in His day. He assumed that there was but one wife. So too St. Paul. He assumes that there is but one wife. He does not seem to suppose that such a thing is allowable. "Let every man have his own wife, and every woman her own husband," is the rule. His comparison of CHRIST and the Church is upon the ground of the single wife. The Roman civil Law also made polygamy an offense. The heathen Greeks were far laxer. The early Fathers are very clear and pointed, both in stating the prevalence of it, its absolute prohibition by the Church, and the strict enforcement of monogamy.

The evils which are produced by polygamy are destructive of morals, as it ministers to the debasing lusts and passions of our nature. It is based essentially upon them. The average man rises no higher than his moral level, and if by the indulgence of the lower appetites, not only lust, but selfishness, and, together with other and correlated evil habits, a man's character is thus hampered, the development of pure social ethics is also hampered. But not only private morals, but also the legal rights of the offspring are affected by it. The tenure of property, the right of succession, the relation of kindred, and the descent of families would all be affected by it in our present state of complex civilization. And the very source of all the purity and honor of the state, the domestic life, would be polluted by it.

Pontifical. The Pontifical is a book containing the offices peculiar to a Bishop. In the Latin and Greek Churches there are several offices which a Bishop celebrates which are not retained in the Anglican Church. In the Anglican Church the Pontifical is that part of our Prayer-Book (however, not an integral part of it) which contains the form and manner of making, ordaining, and consecrating Deacons, Priests, and Bishops, the Litany and the Communion Service, the Form of Consecration of a Church or Chapel, and the Office of Institution of Ministers. Its offices can only be performed by a Bishop, except the last, which by delegation from the Bishop can be discharged by a Priest. In this Pontifical is not included one other office which pertains to the Bishop, the order of Confirmation, but this office was probably placed where it is to set forth the succession of spiritual acts directly connected with each man's life, and by which offices he receives the gifts the Church has to give him.

Pope (Latin *Papa* "Father"), was originally the title of all Bishops. There is no evidence that St. Peter was ever Bishop of Rome; in fact, the Roman Church in the year 96 A.D. appears to have had only a college of presbyters at its head. The earliest lists of the Roman Bishops, by Irenæus (202 A.D.), contain names only, no numbers; and the numbers added in the fourth century by Eusebius, Jerome, and the Liberian catalogue of Popes, are contradictory and therefore of little if any value. Various circumstances combined at length to favor the pre-eminence of the Bishops of Rome: the labors and martyrdom of St. Paul at Rome; his epistle addressed to the Roman Christians; the prominence of the city as the metropolis of the world, etc. The first Roman Bishop who claimed authority beyond the confines of his own particular Church was Victor (189 A.D.). In a dispute concerning the time of observing Easter he peremptorily demanded a council to judge the Asiatic Bishops, and threatened or actually pronounced a disruption of all communion with those who opposed his views in the matter. Eusebius (H. E., v. 24) says, "Victor, the Bishop of the Church of Rome, forthwith endeavored to cut off the churches of all Asia, together with the neighboring churches, as heterodox, from the common unity. And he publishes abroad by letter, and proclaims, that all the brethren there are wholly excommunicated."

Leo I. may be regarded as the first Pope, viewed from the stand-point of a later realization of the papal idea in the history of Latin Christianity. Rome had been the capital of the world; her Bishop was the head of the universal Church, and the successor of the chief of the Apostles. As such, he ruled with Apostolic authority, inheriting from St. Peter supreme power. Leo condemned all heretics, and was especially severe towards the Manicheans. In the affair of a sentence pronounced by Hilarius of Arles against the Bishop of Besançon, he addressed a letter to the bishops of the province of Vienne, denouncing the resistance of Hilarius to the authority of St. Peter, and releasing them from allegiance to the See of Arles. Instigated by Leo, the Emperor Valentinian III. promulgated an edict condemning the contumacy of Hilarius "against the primacy of the Apostolic throne, confirmed alike by the merits of St. Peter, the chief of the Apostolic order, by the majesty of the Roman city, and by the decree of a holy council." Through Leo's influence an order proceeded from the same emperor, to the effect that any bishop who refused to attend the tribunal of the Pope, when summoned, should be compelled to do so by the governor of his province. The primacy of St. Peter was boldly asserted as perpetual, the Bishop of Rome being the successor of that apostle through all time. The collected sermons of Leo are the first preserved to us from a Roman Bishop, and besides these discourses, ninety-six in number, we have from him many epistles.

Gregory I., also called "the Great" (590–604 A.D.), while destitute of real scholastic acquirements, was nevertheless the author of numerous writings,—more than any other pope, with perhaps a single exception. He was a rigid ascetic, yet an exceedingly ambitious and persevering prelate, and something of a politician as well. Conspicuous among his productions is his Exposition of the Book of Job,—the work of a devout mind rather than of a profound theologian. His liturgical labors are also worthy of note, as under him the ritual of the Church was greatly improved. The authority assumed to be inherent in the successors of St. Peter, and by so much wanting in the Episcopate, was not only most decidedly claimed by him, but was practically illustrated. He revived the appellate jurisdiction of the Roman see,—*e.g.*, a deposed Spanish bishop appealed to Rome, and Gregory commissioned a legate of his to examine the case and render a decision accordingly. Also, the bishops of France were requested by him, whenever any contention arose, to obey Virgilius of Arles as his authorized representative. The Council of Sardica (347 A.D.), composed of 100 Western bishops, and 73 bishops from the East,—Hosius of Cordova presiding,—had adopted a canon whereby an appellate jurisdiction was conceded to the Bishop of Rome. While yet a monk, Gregory's attention was directed to Britain as a promising field for missionary effort, and after succeeding to the pontifical chair he sent Augustine, a monk, to that country with some thirty assistants,—afterwards increased in France to forty—ostensibly for the purpose of converting the pagans there. Gregory was doubtless actuated by a measure of the same missionary spirit which he manifested earlier, yet there is sufficient evidence of a determination on his part to advance the jurisdiction of the Holy See. The familiar story of his seeing a number of fair captive boys from the distant isle in the market-place of Rome, and thereupon expressing a desire for the conversion of their countrymen,—indulging at the same time in a fanciful play upon words, —should probably be relegated to the legendary. Though according to him considerable missionary zeal, we are compelled to regard in him a degree of ambition for the furtherance of his patriarchal jurisdiction. Augustine was consecrated the first Archbishop of Canterbury by Virgilius, Bishop of Arles, and in due time received the *Pallium* from Gregory, whereby the primacy of the Pope over the Frankish bishops was asserted. In a conference with the British bishops, Augustine proposed that they should conform to the Roman customs in the celebration of Easter; also, in the rite of Baptism, etc. Replying thereto, they declared that they were "obedient subjects of the Church of GOD, and to the Pope of Rome, and to every godly Christian, to love every one in his degree, in perfect charity, and to help every one of them, by word and deed, to be the children of GOD. And other obedience than this we do not know to be due to him whom you name to be Pope, nor to be father of fathers; and this obedience we are ready to give, and to pay to him and to every Christian continually." Besides, they were "under the government of the Bishop of Caerleon-upon-Usk," the old Welsh archbishopric. In short, the whole history of Augustine's establishment in Britain represents Gregory in the attitude of attempting to destroy the autonomy of an independent Apostolic Episcopate.

For the next hundred years or more the successors of Gregory I. appear to have gained no considerable increase of their ecclesiastical power. Honorius I. (625–38 A.D.) having declared himself a Monotholite, was condemned as a heretic by the sixth General Synod, convoked by Constantine Pogonatus at Constantinople, 680 A.D. He was not therefore regarded as an *infallible* Pope. Gregory III. (731–41 A.D.) appealed to Charles Martel (Mayor of the Palace) for protection against the powerful invading Lombards, who, said the Pope, were "ravaging by fire and sword the last remains of the property of the Church, which no longer suffices for the sustenance of the poor, or to provide lights for the daily service" (740 A.D.). The keys of the tomb of St. Peter had already been sent to the mighty Frank as a symbol of allegiance. Stephen II. (752 A.D.) crossed the Alps, visited Pepin in person, and implored his interposition to restore the domain of St. Peter. The king promised the desired aid, and was afterwards anointed by the Pope. After Stephen's return he sent letters to Pepin beseeching him to save the beloved city of Rome from the unceasingly hostile and thoroughly hated Lombards. A similar request was made by Hadrian I. (772–95 A.D.) to Charlemagne, who having conquered the king of the Lombards visited the Holy City, did homage to the throne of St. Peter, and ratified the donation of Pepin, which is said to have embraced the whole of Italy, the Exarchate of Ravenna, from Istria to the frontier of Naples, including the island of Corsica. Hadrian's death occurred in 795 A.D., and his successor, Leo III., hastened to recognize the supremacy of Charles by sending to him the keys of the city of Rome, and those of the sepulchre of St. Peter. Charles was subsequently crowned by Hadrian and proclaimed Cæsar Augustus. Thus all Western Christendom became consolidated under one monarchy. During this period the lustre of the Popes was greatly increased by the Frankish alliance, by the munificent donation to the head of the Church, and by the acceptance of the imperial crown from the hands of the pontiff. Charlemagne could doubtless have subjected the papacy to the State had he desired to do so, but he preferred evidently to have an ally in the Pope, such in fact was the position of the latter at this time.

During several centuries it was undecided as to which of the two powers—the secular or the spiritual—should have the supremacy. At length, however, a contest arose which settled the question: a nearly complete victory was gained for the spiritual power, and a full realization of the essential idea of the papacy was the result. Yet this was in substance no new phenomenon if the fundamental principle of the papacy be considered; for long before this it was declared that the Bishop of Rome was the supreme guide and governor, as of the clergy so also in affairs secular. The Pseudo-Isidorian Decretals, which appeared about the end of the eighth century, purported to be the productions of the early Bishops of Rome. According to these false decretals every Bishop was amenable to the immediate tribunal of the Pope, and to that only. To the Church was accorded so exalted a position that to subordinate her to the state seemed highly improper and inadmissible. The spiritual power was to be perfectly untrammeled; but in that the secular and the spiritual could not be definitely separated, and everything secular has its spiritual side, it was natural that to the spiritual power should be given the pre-eminence. Immediately after the death of Pope Alexander II., Hildebrand, an archdeacon, while conducting the funeral ceremonies in the Lateran Church, was proclaimed Pope (1073 A.D.), and was enthroned in the chair of St. Peter as Gregory VII According to a decree of Nicolas II. (the second Lateran Council, 1059 A.D.), after the nomination of a Pope by the cardinals, and the ratification of the same by the clergy and the people of Rome, it was necessary to obtain the assent of the Emperor. Henry IV. of Germany was now appealed to for such assent, but he dispatched a messenger to inquire why the Romans had proceeded to an election without consulting him. However, his assent was subsequently given. Gregory began at once a vigorous warfare against simony and the marriage of the clergy. "He was no infant Hercules," says Milman; "but the mature ecclesiastical Hercules would begin his career by strangling these two serpents; the brood, as he esteemed them, and parents of all evil." The decree of a Synod held in Rome within the first year of his pontificate declared invalid all sacraments administered by simoniacal or married priests. To Philip I., king of France, he wrote a letter reproving him for oppressing the Church. "Either let the king repudiate this base traffic of simony, and allow fit persons to be promoted to bishoprics, or the Franks, unless apostates from Christianity, will be struck with the sword of excommunication," and the bishops were instructed to excommunicate him in case he failed to obey their admonitions. Gregory's first intercourse with England was in the form of an arbitrary letter to Archbishop Lanfranc respecting the Abbey of St. Edmondsbury, over which he claimed jurisdiction. In a letter to William the Conqueror he asserted his right to the levying of Peter's pence throughout the kingdom. The claim was admitted, but to the demand of fealty William replied, "I have not, nor will I swear fealty, which was never sworn by any of my predecessors to yours." The kings of Spain were told by the Pope that their entire realm was not only within the spiritual jurisdiction of the Holy See, but was her property. It was with the Empire that Gregory pressed his most significant and far-reaching contest. He exacted a ready acquiescence, on the part of the temporal power, in the prerogative of the cardinals to elect a Pope; and all claims on the investiture of the prelates and other clergy were to be abandoned. Moreover, the Pope was to have and to exercise the right of dictating in matters of State whenever in his opinion there should be cause for his interference. Gregory admonished Henry IV. to rule more wisely, to abstain from simoniacal presentation of benefices, and to render obedience to his spiritual superior. These monitions were well received, and the clemency of the pontiff was sought.

At a Council held in Rome, 1075 A.D., Gregory abrogated the right of investiture by the temporal ruler, and at a Synod held in Mentz, the papal legate displayed the mandate of the Apostolic See requiring the Bishops to compel their clergy either to renounce their wives or to cease from exercising the functions of the ministry. Henry IV. was afterwards summoned to Rome to answer to the charges against him; on the other hand, the king called an assembly of Bishops at Worms, and it was there decided that Gregory should be no longer obeyed as Pope. This was followed by the convening of a Council in the Lateran palace, at which Henry was excommunicated and deprived of his kingdoms,—of Germany and Italy. After this he sought absolution from the Pope, but his military successes strengthened his position, and he was crowned by the antipope Guibert. Subsequently, Gregory repaired to Salerno, where he died an exile. The controlling principle in the pontificate of Gregory was the total submission of the secular power to the spiritual.

The metropolitans, who had been required by the Council of Frankfort (742 A.D.) to seek the pallium at the hand of the Pope, promising obedience to his commands, had now to take an oath of fealty to him as the universal Bishop.

During the pontificate of Paschal II. (1099 –1118 A.D.) the question of investiture was especially prominent, and was the cause of a bitter contest between the papacy and the temporal power. Paschal excommunicated Henry IV., who had already been under the ban of Gregory VII. and Urban II. (1088-99 A.D.). Henry's son intrigued against him at the head of a considerable party, and refused to submit unless the Emperor would become reconciled with the Church. No reconciliation was, however, effected, and Henry died excommunicate. At several Synods held by Paschal, investiture by lay hands was condemned. An attempt was subsequently made to settle the question by a treaty, according to which Henry V. on the day of his consecration was to concede the investiture of all the churches, while, on the other hand, the Church was to surrender possession of the royalties conferred by the empire. The Prince Bishops of Germany objected strenuously to this, and Paschal was compelled to yield,—as he said, to save the city of Rome. A Council at Vienna (1112 A.D.) excommunicated the Emperor, condemning at the same time investiture by lay hands, and Paschal ratified the decrees. Henry afterwards advanced upon Rome, and the Pope died in exile (1118 A.D.). Under Calixtus II. (1122 A.D.) a compromise was arranged in the form of a concordat, whereby the Emperor resigned forever the investiture by the ring and crosier, and recognized the liberty of elections. In return it was agreed that elections should take place in his presence or that of his representatives, and that the new Bishop should receive his temporalities from the Emperor by the sceptre. (See Hallam, Mid. Ages, chap. vii. 1.)

Hadrian IV., Nicholas Breakspeare (1154- 1159 A.D.) was the only Englishman elevated to the papal chair, the dignity of which he maintained with the boldness and courage of a Hildebrand. To Henry II. of England he granted the kingdom of Ireland, at the same time holding that all islands when Christianized belonged to the jurisdiction of the Roman Pontiff. In return for this grant Hadrian exacted Peter's pence. The Emperor, Frederick Barbarossa, was solemnly crowned by him at Rome, yet the Pope's imperious attitude towards this warlike and powerful sovereign induced the latter to put forth an edict forbidding the clergy from all intercourse with the Apostolic See. A reconciliation was effected, but it was soon followed by further quarrels. At length Hadrian addressed a paternal and very condescending letter to Frederick, accusing him of irreverence and a disregard of the fealty he had sworn to St. Peter. The strife continued until ended by the death of Hadrian, as he was preparing for more decisive measures, including the excommunication of Frederick.

Innocent III. (1198–1216 A.D.) was one of the greatest of the Popes, second only to Gregory VII., than whom he certainly seems to have been more successful. In his inauguration discourse he said, " Ye see what manner of servant that is whom the LORD hath set over His people; no other than the vicegerent of CHRIST, the successor of Peter. He stands in the midst between GOD and man; below GOD, above man; less than GOD, more than man." Innocent entered vigorously upon the restoration of Italy from the domination of the Germans, and the regaining of the papal territories. In the long, and at times sanguinary, conflict relative to the imperial throne, he interposed as supreme arbiter. He said, "It belongs to the Apostolic See to pass judgment on the election of the Emperor, both in the first and last resort; in the first because by her aid and on her account the empire was transplanted from Constantinople; by her as the sole authority for this transplanting, on her behalf and for her better protection; in the last resort because the emperor receives the final confirmation of his dignity from the Pope; is consecrated, crowned, invested in the imperial dignity by him." Otho IV. became the undisputed Emperor, and was crowned by Innocent in St. Peter's Church, Rome. His subsequent course was, however, such that the Pope excommunicated him, and required the Archbishops of Ravenna, Milan, and Genoa, and all the Bishops of Italy to publish the ban. A fierce and fateful contest was waged by Innocent and Philip Augustus, King of France, who had married Ingeburga, the sister of Canute IV. of Denmark, and had speedily rejected her, taking another for his wife. The matter had been brought before Pope Cœlestine, but he had not the courage to deal with it. Innocent, his successor, threatened now to place the realm of Philip Augustus under an interdict—suspending all sacred offices, except the baptism of infants and absolution by the clergy—if he refused to submit to the monitions of the papal legate. The command was unheeded, whereupon the papal legate summoned a council at Dijon, which pronounced the king and his territories to be under the ban,—all religious offices from that time ceasing. Thus, by the imperative order of Innocent thousands of souls were deprived of the means of grace,—to such an extent had the disciplinary power of the Popes been developed. Finally the King was compelled to yield to the demand of Innocent, and several prelates who had favored the obstinate ruler were obliged to seek absolution at the feet of the haughty and resolute pontiff. The arbitrary and fearless spirit of the Hildebrandian type of the Papacy was here displayed. The Church ruled the State.

Gregory IX. (1227–41 A.D.) had a new compilation made of the Papal Decretals, and promulgated them as the great statute law of the Universal Church. Also, for neglecting to undertake a crusade to Palestine, thus to fulfill a condition upon which the imperial crown was bestowed (by Honorius III.), the Emperor of Germany, Frederick II., was excommunicated by the Pope, and his subjects were absolved from their allegiance. Within the next year the Emperor sailed for the Holy Land, but as he was excommunicate, the movement was regarded by Gregory as the profanation of a crusade. In all his quarrels with Frederick the authority of the pontiff was boldly asserted; there was again a fierce conflict, in which the absolute sovereignty of the Church was the governing principle on the side of the successor of St. Peter. Not only did the Popes usurp the rights of bishops, metropolitans, and princes, but they claimed the prerogative of convoking Councils and confirming their decrees. None of the passages from the letters of the Pontiffs and from conciliar acts usually adduced by Roman Catholic writers in evidence of the participation of the Roman See in the calling of the *general* synods of Christian antiquity are, however, found to stand the test of a thorough examination.* Consequently this favorite theory with the Roman Church turns out to be entirely groundless, and that it is so can excite no surprise when its origin is considered. It originated in the sixteenth century, and essentially in opposition to the Protestantism of that time. Certain Protestants pointing to the calling of the early councils by the emperors disputed the right of the Popes to convoke them. Bellarmine, in his Disputations, endeavored to show that their convocation belonged in fact not to the Emperor but to the Pope, and though some councils had been called by the former, on the other hand several had been convened by the latter; at all events, that no general council had been announced *a solo imperatore*, that is, without the consent and authority of the Roman Pontiffs; that although the first five general synods in particular

---

* A remarkable monograph on this subject appeared recently from the pen of Prof. Dr. Francis Xavier Funk, of the Roman Catholic faculty of the University of Tübingen, a translation of which, made by the author of this article, was published in the *Church Eclectic* for May and June, 1883 A.D.

had been announced by the Emperors, yet it was only *ex pontificum sententia et consensu*. In a later period the theory of the participation of the Popes in the calling of synods was invested in somewhat different language only; but its origin certainly does not commend it. It owes its existence to partisan polemics, and to an almost equally partisan apology. True, Bellarmine's procedure is intelligible from the adverse position of Protestantism, but it is not the less without foundation. Instead of simply rejecting the conclusion which the Protestants drew from certain facts, he denied the facts themselves, or at least, endeavored to render them of doubtful authority. Therefore the most of his arguments were rightly abandoned even by those who maintained essentially his view. The other arguments from which support in this regard is usually derived— whether produced by Bellarmine or later writers—are fundamentally unreliable. As evidence that approbation or confirmation has been conferred by the Popes various passages are appealed to, in which no more is really said than that the Roman See accepted the councils. In this wise could the Popes speak, though they had consented to the councils through their legates only. In the same way could all the rest of the Bishops speak, and must indeed have spoken, if they were so situated as to be able to express themselves with regard to their position towards a synod; and as little as we may now be disposed to take the word relative thereto in the sense of a *confirmation* so little may the latter have occurred. With expressions of this sort neither more nor less is to be shown than that the Roman See simply accepted, that is, did not reject. Non-rejection is, however, very far from being identical with approbation. In short, of the testimony which is commonly brought forward in behalf of the Papal Confirmation of the general councils, nothing can be found which will bear a critical examination. On the contrary, several synods so expressed themselves with reference to their relation to Rome as directly to exclude papal approbation. REV. H. H. LORING.

Post-Communion. That portion of the Communion Office which follows the reception of the elements. It includes the prayer of thanksgiving, the *Gloria in Excelsis*, the Collects (when they are used), and the benediction. The early Liturgies also dismissed the faithful with an office of prayer, often one of great beauty. But the later the Liturgy the more likely it is that the Post-Communion has been made more ornate. A strict construction of the rubric probably would not authorize the present use of the Collects appended to the Communion Office.

Postil. Homilies, or short expositions, upon the Gospels principally. The word came from the words *post illa verba*, as the comment followed after the passage of Scripture selected. There were a good many Postils published, some of which are quite valuable. Tavener, a writer of the signet in Henry VIII.'s time, published a volume of them, out of which were taken the Homilies for Good-Friday and Easter-day found in the Book of Homilies. Nicholas de Lyra (1320 A.D.) wrote two series of Postils, which deservedly had great influence. They were printed first about 1471 A.D.

Praise. The bounties of GOD'S Providence and the wonders of His grace call for a return in ceaseless praise. "All Thy works shall praise Thee, O LORD; and Thy saints shall bless Thee" (Ps. cxlv. 10).

Heaven is a place of ceaseless praise. The seraphim of Isaiah's vision, and the living creatures beheld by St. John, were constantly crying "Holy, holy, holy," before GOD. Though centuries had passed since the Prophet's sight of Heaven, the evangelist hears the same music. The Church on earth joins with angels and archangels in this blessed work. In Psalms and Hymns, in *Te Deum* and *Benedicite*, and *Gloria in Excelsis*, she imitates the heavenly host. The Prayer-Book is a book of praise, and layman as well as clergyman is bidden to honor GOD with heart and voice. The Family Morning Prayer begs "that we may fervently join in the prayers and praises of Thy Church." Praise is the daughter of gladness. When Creation was finished "the morning stars sang together, and all the sons of GOD shouted for joy" (Job xxxviii. 7). When CHRIST was born the angels sang. When the Wise Men saw the star over CHRIST'S cradle "they rejoiced with exceeding great joy" (St. Matt. ii. 10). There must be no thought of self in praise. The song of man to GOD must be full and free, like that of the bird. It must be universal, as in Ps. cxlviii. 12, 13, "Young men and maidens; old men and children," are exhorted to "praise the name of the LORD." The thought culminates in the one hundred and fiftieth, or closing Psalm, where in six verses the word praise is repeated thirteen times and ten instruments of music are called for, as Bishop Patrick notes. But the last verse widens the command to everything that hath breath, and then makes its application, "Praise ye the LORD."

St. Francis de Sales speaks of the larks who sing louder as they soar higher, so the human soul needs to rise from this earthly atmosphere to lose itself in beholding the glory of GOD. Even martyrs, dying in agony, have learned to praise GOD in the fires of affliction, as the tortured Euplius, torn by the cruel rack, could still exclaim to him who attempted to persuade him to abjure Christianity, "I adore CHRIST." Even under the torture he cried, "Thanks be to Thee, O CHRIST. Help me, O CHRIST. For Thee do I suffer thus, O CHRIST." As strength failed he repeated these or other exclamations with his lips, when his voice could no longer utter them. Surely there was a glad burst of praise when that voice was regained in Paradise.

The doxology ascribed to Polycarp as among his last words is another evidence of how the thought of GOD'S glory may overcome human trials. It reads thus: "For this, and for all things else, I praise Thee, I bless Thee, I glorify Thee, by the eternal and heavenly High-Priest, JESUS CHRIST, Thy beloved SON, with whom, to Thee, and the HOLY GHOST be glory, both now and to all succeeding ages. Amen." He who would thus be ready to praise GOD, even in a painful death, must make his "daily life a psalm." To such this life will be too short to declare all the praises of GOD.

REV. S. F. HOTCHKIN.

Prayer has always been universally recognized and required as an essential part, and, indeed, the most prominent part, of Divine worship. It is the first suggestion of a sense of GOD'S power and man's dependence on Him, and thus we find that every form and system of religion, however low and imperfect its conception of GOD may be, makes prayer a necessary feature of all its acts of worship. We must be careful to remember that prayer means a great deal more than the mere asking for something that we want. This is its leading idea, but is really neither the whole nor the highest part of prayer. In fact, the obtaining of our requests must necessarily not be the principal object of prayer, for the reason that there can be no true prayer without a spirit of submission to the wisdom and beneficence of GOD, which leaves it with Him to grant or refuse our petitions as may be most for our good. If we study our LORD'S example, we may from that obtain the clearest and truest perception of what prayer is. We find Him habitually spending much of His time in prayer as a means of communication with His FATHER, asking at times for that which He knew must be His, as when He prays that GOD would glorify Him with the glory which He had with Him before the world was (John xvii. 5), and again asking in an agony of supplication for that which He knew could not be granted, and which it was not His will to receive, as when He prayed in Gethsemane that the cup of suffering might pass from Him. That these were prayers of His human nature does not alter the fact, since the submission of that nature to His FATHER'S will was the object of His assuming it. Hence we learn that one great object of prayer is to bring the human mind into direct communication with GOD, without reference to the granting of its petitions. Nor must the subjective influence of such an act be allowed to pass out of view, the elevating and calming effects of such august intercourse being one of the most important and valuable objects of prayer. Apart from any direct answer and from any objective influences of the HOLY GHOST, we have thus a most efficient means of cultivating Faith, Humility, Love, Reverence, and many other mental and emotional conditions essential to religious life. Again, prayer is in itself the direct acknowledgment, and the only direct acknowledgment possible to man, of the sovereignty of GOD, and therefore it is due to Him as an act of homage. It must include praise and even sacrifice, because the very act of offering these to the sovereign implies the request that He will permit and accept them. But necessary as is this aspect of prayer, the whole character of Christianity would be changed if prayer were only homage. The Christian prays as a child to his FATHER, upon whose personal love he relies, and with whom he has no other means of communication. He asks for the rain and the sunshine, which GOD sends freely to the just and the unjust, the unthankful and the evil alike, because he does not wish to receive them as either the unjust or the unthankful, but as his FATHER'S child. He has been taught by his Master to ask GOD for his daily bread, although he must earn it by his own efforts, because he cannot live like the lower animals on food taken where it is found at the promptings of instinct, but must resort to complex processes dependent upon many laws which he recognizes as made and administered by his heavenly FATHER, whom he recognizes as the source and Giver of even that sustenance which the lower creatures unthoughtfully enjoy. This filial character of prayer is not derived, however, from the broad sense of spirit of GOD'S fatherhood as the Creator or the Sovereign, but from the special sonship which comes of union with GOD'S well-beloved and only-begotten SON. Hence all Christian prayer is made in the name and for the sake of JESUS CHRIST our LORD.

The question of how Prayer can be efficacious,—how the will of man can influence that of GOD, sometimes causes a great deal of unnecessary trouble and confusion. That there is a psychic force through which one human mind comes *en rapport* with another and influences its action is probably true, and this as yet only suspected law may in some way concern the *method* by which Prayer is conveyed to GOD. But the truth is that this is a matter with which we have nothing whatever to do. We know and can know absolutely nothing of GOD except through His revelation in Holy Scripture. There we find Him revealed as the Hearer of Prayer, and we find Prayer prescribed by Him as an Ordinance, together with His promise to answer it. This puts all such questions upon precisely the same footing as all other revealed Truth, and we might as well attempt to explain the eternity of GOD or the mystery of the Trinity. The Christian believes Prayer to be efficacious because he believes the Bible to be GOD'S word, and upon all such points he cannot argue with an infidel objector or meet his questions, because they move in entirely different planes. It is this fact which makes absurd and disingenuous all challenges to test the efficacy of Prayer by scientific experiments. "Take," says one, "two wards in the same hospital. Pray for the patients in one, but not for those in the other, and abide by the result." We might as well attempt to measure distance by weight, or test the soundness of a logical proposition by the laws of applied chemistry. Prayer lies entirely outside of science, and has no conceivable connection with its laws and methods. To ask such a test is to demand a manifest impossibility, for the promise of answer is to *believing* Prayer. " Whatsoever ye shall ask in prayer, *believing*, ye shall receive" (Matt. xxi. 22). Prayer, therefore, cannot, from its very nature, be made matter of experiment. But if it is said, " We ask only Elijah's test," the answer is, " These are not Elijah's days, and Elijah is not here." The question of Special and Direct Answers to Prayer is of far greater practical interest. Are we to expect such, or not? We see at once that this involves the question of Special Providences, and in reply it is sufficient to say that true Christian faith is as far removed from superstitious credulity as from skepticism. A broad-minded heathen poet has said, " I have learned that not every wonder worked by nature is sent from high heaven by the angry gods" (Hor. Sat. i., vi. 102–3), nor does any reasonable Christian believe that the daily bread which he prays for comes as a direct gift from GOD. But Christianity and reason alike teach the direct personal oversight and administration by GOD of His own laws and His personal care for the wants of His creatures. No one can expect miracles to be wrought at his request, nor petitions to be granted the consequences of which to others he could not possibly foresee. But no faithful praying man can fail to have experienced the prompt responses which so often come through perfectly natural, though unexpected means, producing the desired result. He asks in full recognition of the element of uncertainty involved, in submission to GOD's wisdom, and obtaining his desire he gratefully acknowledges it as from his FATHER's hand. But what, it may be asked, of unanswered Prayer, in view of the many and positive promises which the Scriptures contain assuring a certain response? The reply is very simple. GOD has certainly promised to grant all things which are asked in trusting faith, but He has not promised when or how He will grant them. Times and compensations are alike reserved by Him to be settled by His own wisdom and beneficence, nor must it be forgotten that Prayer belongs essentially to that life which is not limited by time or mortality. As a father may withhold what a son requests in order that his inheritance may be the greater, so GOD may refuse the perishable good which we ask of Him only to insure a richer heritage of blessing in the life hereafter.

REV. ROBERT WILSON, D.D.

Prayer for the Dead. There is a vast difference between prayer *to* the dead and prayer *for* the dead. It was found in all the Liturgies from the earliest date. It was not a prayer for a change from a state of condemnation to one of pardon. There is no intimation that such a change could be effected after death. As the tree falleth so must it lie, but it *was* believed that living and dead were in one communion, that death was a quickening of the soul into greater life, that the soul could pass from glory to glory, and that it had not wholly dissevered its participation in those gifts which were imparted to it here. So at the solemn celebration of the Holy Communion there was a commemoration of the dead, and a prayer that they might be in the refreshment of joy and bliss, and that they might be sharers in the glory of Abraham, Isaac, and Jacob. Specially in each Diocese, the chief of those who had died, the more noted martyrs, the late Bishops, and then special individuals were named from a roll, and a prayer offered for them and for the whole body of those who had died in the true Faith.

The practice has been defended on very insufficient Scriptural grounds, and many passages have been adduced as indirectly sanctioning it from the New Testament. But the fact that it was used from the first, that there is no intimation in any way that it was doubted as proper, that to be left out of the diptychs was one of the penalties used against some who broke the Church's discipline, all point to the *consensus* that brings its use up to sub-Apostolic times. It could hardly be called an abuse or an innovation. It must have for its basis, then, something in our own nature. It proclaims that death is not a severance of ties. It is, to say the very least, a pious and comforting use. It is admitted in principle by the closing petitions in the Prayer for the whole state of CHRIST's Church militant, " And we also bless Thy Holy Name, for all Thy servants departed this Life in Thy faith and fear, beseeching Thee to give us grace so to follow their good examples that with them we may be partakers of Thy heavenly kingdom." In the Prayer-Book of 1549 A.D. this passage closed thus: "We commend unto Thy mercy (O LORDE) all other Thy servauntes which are departed hence from us with the signe of faithe, and now do reste in the slepe of peace. Graunte unto them, we beseeche Thee, Thy mercy and everlastyng peace, and that at the daie of the general resurreccion we and all thy which be of the mistical body of Thy Sonne, may altogether bee set on His right hand and hear that His most joyful voice, 'Come unto me, O ye that be blessed of my FATHER, and possesse the kingdome whiche is prepared for you from the begining of the worlde.' " This was dropped out (together with some sentences just preceding, which are not here quoted) in 1552 A.D., and the words now in use were substituted only in 1662 A.D. These words, it will be noted, strike the same tone which the closing prayer in the burial service utters, showing that the Church has not lost (if for many reasons she has hitherto chosen to partly lay aside) this ancient custom.

Prayer-Book, The American. It is not the purpose of this article to treat of the sources or the history of the Prayer-Book of the Church of England; it must be confined to an outline of the history of the service-book of the American Church. Until the Revolution, the services used were those of the English Books, and it would appear that very strict conformity to them was practiced, for we read of some who had scruples as to reading the closing exhortation in the office for the Baptism of Infants, on the ground that it was almost an impossibility that the sponsors would ever be able to bring the child to a Bishop to be confirmed. When the war of Independence broke out, some of the clergy persisted in the use of the State prayers until their services were possibly stopped; others omitted them altogether, and others adapted them to the case of the new civil authority, the people sometimes insisting, as did those at New London, Conn., "that no person be permitted to enter the Church, and as a pastor to it, unless he openly prays for Congress and the free and independent States of America, and their prosperity by sea and land." But no other changes were favored in any quarter. In Virginia, where the Church was established by law, the Prayer-Book was altered by the State Convention, on the 5th of July, 1776 A.D., "to accommodate it to the change in affairs," but no other alterations were allowed. Things remained in this condition at the close of the war. An informal convention of delegates from eight different States which met in New York in October, 1784 A.D., agreed to certain "fundamental principles," one of which declared that the Episcopal Church in the United States of America should "adhere to the liturgy of the said Church [of England] as far as shall be consistent with the American Revolution and the constitutions of the respective States;" and it was agreed that a formal convention should be held in September of the next year. Before that time Bishop Seabury had returned from Scotland, where he had received consecration to the Episcopate. He met his clergy at Middletown on the 2d day of August, 1785 A.D., and on the 5th a committee, consisting of the Rev. Messrs. Bowden and Jarvis, of Connecticut, and the Rev. Mr. Parker, of Boston, was appointed to act with the Bishop in proposing such changes in the Prayer-Book as should be thought necessary. Certain alterations were agreed upon, and those relating to the State prayers were published by Bishop Seabury on the 12th day of August. The others were to be reported to the clergy of Connecticut, and also to the conventions of Massachusetts, Rhode Island, and New Hampshire; in September the latter body adopted most of the proposed changes, with a few others, but voted that their use should be postponed till it should be seen what the Churchmen in the other States were likely to do; and at last, July 20, 1786 A.D., it was left to the discretion of the parishes to adopt the changes or to keep to the old liturgy. It is sufficient to say of these alterations that they were "in most respects identical with those contained in the 'Proposed Book,'" which will presently be mentioned. The Connecticut clergy were found to be averse to any changes, and apparently they took no action on the proposed amendments. The convention which met at Philadelphia, September 27, 1785 A.D., contained representatives of seven States to the south of New England. The minds of many of the delegates had been turned to the question of revision, and some of them were practically agreed upon the form which it should take. The Rev. Dr. (afterwards Bishop) White presided; but the chief part in the work of revision was taken by the Rev. Dr. William Smith, of Maryland. The convention adjourned on the 7th of October, after attending a service at which "the liturgy, as altered, was read." Yet the changes were not formally adopted, and probably the convention felt that it had no authority in the matter; they were only "proposed and recommended;" and it was left to a committee to edit and print the book. In the following spring (the prothonotary's certificate bears date April 1, 1786 A.D.) the book was published, it being plainly stated on its title-pages that it was "the Book of Common Prayer as revised and proposed to the use of the Protestant Episcopal Church." This is the book now known as the "Proposed Book," though many English authorities—it having appeared in two reprints—quote it as the American Book. It has no more right to the name than that of 1637 A.D. has to be called the Scotch Book, or that of 1689 A.D. the English Book.

Besides alterations made necessary by the change in the form of civil government, and certain verbal amendments, the most important differences from the English book were the following: the Absolution in the daily service was headed, "A declaration concerning the forgiveness of sins;" the *Benedicte* was omitted, except for discretionary use on the 31st day of the month; the Nicene Creed and the Athanasian were omitted, and the clause "He descended into Hell," was omitted from the Apostles' Creed; the *Gloria in Excelsis* was permitted to be used at the end of the Psalter for the day; parents were allowed to act as sponsors; the sign of the Cross might be omitted in baptism, if desired; the word "regenerate" was omitted from the latter part of the baptismal office; the marriage service was shortened, as in our present book; the form of committal to the ground in the burial service was altered to nearly its present form; the absolution in the visitation of the sick was given in the same words as in the communion office; a form for the visitation of prisoners was taken from the Irish Book of 1711 A.D.; the answer to the second question in the Catechism was changed to these words: "I received it in Baptism, whereby I became a member of the Christian Church;" the Commination service on Ash-Wednesday was discontinued, and its prayers ordered to be said after the Litany; and selections were made from the Psalms for daily use, omitting (with others) the so-called "damnatory clauses." No sooner was this proposed book published than "it was evident," as Bishop White said, "that, in regard to the liturgy, the labors of the convention had not reached their object." Though some of the Diocesan Conventions approved it nearly as it stood, New York and New Jersey did not accept it; and the English bishops, to whom application had been made for the Episcopate, wrote objecting, with grief, to the omission of two of the creeds, and the excision of a clause from the other. Moreover, the book was very unsatisfactory to the Churchmen in Connecticut. When the convocation of that diocese met on the 22d of September, Bishop Seabury, in his charge, besides expressing an opinion adverse to the merit of the changes in the services, called attention to the fact that they had been made without waiting till action could be had with the concurrence of bishops, as a thing unprecedented in the Church; and he "set forth and recommended" to the use of his people a Communion Office almost identical with that in use by the Scotch bishops, from whom he had received his consecration. A General Convention of the (so-called) Southern dioceses met in October, 1786 A.D., but nothing was done with the proposed book, except to obviate the objections of the English bishops, by restoring the omitted clause of the Apostles' Creed, and inserting the Nicene Creed. At last, October 2, 1789 A. D., the Church in this country was united in one Convention, with the Bishops as a separate house. Action was at once taken in regard to the Prayer-Book. The Bishops (Drs. Seabury and White alone were present) entered upon their work as proposing alterations in the English book. The lower house in theory considered itself as framing an entirely new book; but practically there was no difference in the matter. The Proposed Book was ignored, at least in its objectionable features. The bishops originated the review of some offices, and the lower house that of others; and all was arranged to the decided satisfaction of all concerned. And it is to be remembered that nothing was admitted into the book of 1789 A.D. which was not approved by both Bishop Seabury and Bishop White.

Almost all the changes made show that they were not adopted without consideration; those which were brought over from the Proposed Book seem to have been such as must have appeared to the minds of most men necessary to the times; and many apparently minor matters, such, for instance, as the accurate use of the words "minister" and "priest," witness to much thought before the convention and much carefulness at the time. It is not necessary to note here all the changes from the English Book. The state prayers were, of course, modified; many repetitions were omitted; verbal alterations were made in numerous places; and selections of Psalms were set forth, chiefly, as it would appear, for the relief of those who did not like to use the damnatory psalms in public worship. An alternative absolution was introduced into the daily offices; the *Venite* was made up of parts of two psalms; the *Benedictus* was shortened; substitutes for the *Magnificat* and the *Nunc Dimittis* were formed from the Psalter; the use of the Nicene Creed was made discretionary with that of the Apostles' Creed, and the Athanasian Creed was omitted; the mediæval form of absolution was omitted from the visitation of the sick, our LORD's summary of the Law was allowed to be read after the commandments in the Communion office; and an alternative Preface was allowed for Trinity-Sunday. Bishop Taylor's works furnished the revisers with the five special prayers which follow that to be used "in time of great sickness and mortality," and with the three last prayers in the office for the visitation of the sick. The service for the visitation of prisoners was taken, as in the Proposed Book, from the Irish service of 1711 A.D.; that for Thanksgiving-day, from the Proposed Book itself; the Family Prayers from some which had been drawn up by Bishop Gibson, of London. But by far the most important change was that introduced through the influence of Bishop Seabury, the adoption of the Scotch form of the Prayer of Consecration in the Communion office, with a verbal modification, which was doubtless proposed by the delegates from Maryland. This form, which differs from any ever used by the Church of England, has a distinct and formal Oblation and Invocation following the words of Institution,—the primitive order, first appearing in English in Stephens's service about 1700 A.D., adopted by the Non-Jurors in 1718 A.D., and taken from them by the Scotch Church. Bishop White readily assented to the insertion of this form, and it was accepted by the house of deputies "without opposition, and in silence if not in reverence." It should be noted, perhaps, that there was a misunderstanding as to the printing of the words in the Apostles' Creed about which there had been so much discussion, but it was settled by a vote of the Convention of 1792 A.D. The new book went into use October 1, 1790 A.D. Its standard edition was established by Canon in 1820 A.D., another in 1838 A.D., another in 1844 A.D., after a most careful and valuable report from the pen of the Rev. Dr. T. W. Coit, and another in 1871 A.D., having a large number of minute changes from the former standards. Provision has been made for translations of the book into several modern languages; but the Church cannot yet be said to have a standard edition except in English.

At the Convention of 1792 A.D. an Ordinal was adopted, differing from the English chiefly in having the Litany printed by itself and also the Communion office added, with the word "Bishop" instead of "Priest" in the rubrics, and in the provision of an alternative form in the ordination of priests. In 1799 A.D., the form of consecration of a Church was added to the Prayer-Book, the service being adapted from that drawn up by Bishop Andrewes in 1620 A.D. The Articles were set out in 1801 A.D. In 1804 A.D., the office of Institution (then called Induction) was adopted, being substantially one drawn up by the Rev. Dr. William Smith, of Connecticut, and accepted by the clergy of that Diocese in 1799 A.D. The form of prayer to be used at the meetings of conventions, put into its present place in 1835 A.D., was taken in great part from a paragraph in the homily for Whitsunday. Also, in 1835 A.D., the word "right" was substituted for the word "north" in the last rubric before the Communion Service. The Bishops have from time to time, either of their own motion or at the request of the house of deputies, expressed their opinion as to the meaning of rubrics or the proper method of conducting the service. Thus, in 1821 A.D., they gave, as their interpretation of the last rubric in the Communion office, that the preaching of a sermon did not remove the obligation to read the Ante-Communion service; in 1832 A.D., they gave their opinion as to the proper postures for priest and people in the Communion office; in 1835 A.D., they advised that the customary Collect and Lord's Prayer before the sermon be omitted, that the General Confession be said by the people with, and not after, the minister; and in 1865 A.D. a committee of their house proposed a rule as to postures in the offices for baptism and confirmation; in 1868 A.D., a like committee recommended that on Sundays being also holy-days, both Collects should be read, with the epistle and the gospel for the Sunday. The first movement in the way of securing shortened services was made by the house of bishops, on motion of Bishop Hobart, in 1826 A.D. The proposed plan was approved by the house of deputies of that year, but it was so strongly opposed throughout the Church, that the next Convention dismissed the consideration of the subject. The memorial of the Rev. Dr. Muhlenberg and others to the Bishops in 1853 A.D. asked for a relaxation for the rubrics in certain cases, and led to a declaration by that house in 1856 A.D., that the Morning Prayer, the Litany, and the Communion Service were separate services, that on special occasions the clergy might use such parts of the Prayer-Book and such lessons of Scripture as they judged to tend most to edification, and that the several Bishops might provide special services for peculiar cases. The memorial, however, led to no legislation on the subject.

In 1868 A.D., the Bishops, in reply to another memorial for greater latitude in the use of the Prayer-Book, unanimously voted that "such latitude" as was asked "could not be allowed with safety, or with proper regard to the rights of our congregations." The matter of shortened services was again discussed in 1877 A.D., and led to the proposal by the next Convention that the ratification of the Book of Common Prayer should be so amended as to give the desired liberty; but the proposal failed of adoption in 1883 A.D. Meanwhile, in 1880 A.D., a committee of seven Bishops, seven Presbyters, and seven laymen, was appointed to consider the question of alterations in the Prayer-Book "in the direction of liturgical enrichment and increased flexibility of use." The report of this committee, embodied in the "Book Annexed," was discussed in 1883 A.D., and as amended then is to come for action before the Convention of 1886 A.D. Into the details of this proposed revision it is beyond the scope of this paper to enter.

A word should be added as to the tables of lessons. Those in the Proposed Book were quite different from those in the English Book, and appear to have been proposed by Bishop White. In 1789 A.D. a new table was adopted for Sundays, but the others were taken with few changes from the Proposed Book. In 1877 A.D., the constitution having been so amended as to allow a single Convention, under certain restrictions, to make changes in the "Lectionary," permission was given to use the table of lessons adopted by the English Church in 1871 A.D., and also during Lent, a specially prepared table of lessons; in 1880 A.D., a joint committee prepared new tables both for Sundays and holy-days, and for the general calendar, the use of which was made discretionary; and in 1883 A.D., these tables, with certain amendments, were adopted in place of those of 1789 A.D.

It may be added that the provision in the Constitution, that any change in the Book of Common Prayer (the Lectionary being now excepted) shall have the approval of two successive General Conventions, having been submitted to the Dioceses in the intervening years, dates from 1811 A.D.

Authorities: Journals of Conventions, Bishop White's Memoirs of the Church, Bishop Perry's Hand-Book of the General Convention and Introduction to the American Edition of Procter's History of the Book of Common Prayer, Bishop Seabury's Communion Office, Bishop Brownell's Family Prayer-Book.

REV. PROF. S. HART.

Prayer, Family. There is no duty which should be more faithfully discharged than this of household prayer It lies at the root of all household religion. And the home is divinely intended to be the true training-place in devout and holy life. No excuse, then, of inconvenience, and of hurry, and preoccupation should be allowed, but of all the duties the head of a family discharges, this of gathering the members of the household around the home altar should be most rigidly discharged. Its influence upon the household life is very marked, the extent of its sanctifying work can never be known. It sanctifies the head of the House as discharging his priestly office. It consecrates those under him. Every man is a priest in his own house was the true remark of one of our Bishops when he directed his host, a Layman, to fulfill this holy duty. It teaches the children by example and by act to believe that they are bound together in GOD'S household. It conveys to them a part at least of the godly instruction they should receive. So careful is the Church to have this attended to that there was included in our American Prayer-Book an admirable form of Family Prayer, abridged from the Prayers composed by Dr. Gibson, Bishop of London, the famous Canonist. It should be made a conscientious duty in every household of the Church to have family prayer with all due regularity. A blessing rests upon the household whose custom it is.

Preaching. The chief public work of the clergyman as GOD'S embassador and His Herald. Its outward form may vary as circumstances and the needs of the times vary. But it remains as a permanent duty upon the Herald to declare the will and the offers of the Great King, and it is equally a duty upon the citizens to listen to that will and to heed the offers made to them. There is a good deal of confused and imperfect information about preaching which could be readily placed in right order if we but heeded two or three facts. The right, the duty of the Bishop and the Priest, and by special commission the Deacon also, is inalienable and it is imperative. "For though I preach the gospel, I have nothing to glory of: for necessity is laid upon me; yea, woe is unto me, if I preach not the gospel" (1 Cor. ix. 16). This duty was at first exercised by the Bishop, and later by him committed to the Priest, but the responsibility was with him. It was not till much later that the Deacon was licensed to preach. But this duty considered with regard to the Laity places upon them the need of hearing, and being instructed in, the will of GOD, and also their right to claim this instruction. We have so placed the sermon, which is the usual form which preaching takes, at the close of the service, that its importance is overlooked.

The sermon is no part of the service proper unless there is a celebration. Anciently, while it occupied the same place relatively to the Holy Communion, it preceded all but the reading of Scripture and the few collects which were used for the mixed congregation. Then it was not preceded by a long service. It would be well that some rearrangement could be effected by which the sermon could be separated from the service and be delivered to the congregation as with all authority,—a message to them or a comment upon some part of that message. There is also another consideration: custom has compelled a sermon a Sunday and often a couple of lectures a week. While no Priest should be allowed to shirk his duty, and he would not conscientiously do so, there are frequently so great demands made upon his time and energy by Parochial work that he has no time to prepare himself fitly to deliver the message intrusted to him. Yet it is demanded of him "to say something" when he has had no opportunity to prepare "something to say." The dignity of his office, the respect due to the congregation, the honor of Him whose embassador he is, demand that he shall take all due diligence to prepare and deliver his proclamation with the effectiveness it deserves. Apart from mere personal ability, the vast difference in the modes with which the same topics are preached to the people lies chiefly in the unreadiness of the preacher. We do not make enough of preaching, and yet we so place it that we belittle it as an office, and its effectiveness does not depend upon the nobleness proper to it as an act, but to the cleverness or ability of the speaker. There should be an effort for a better balancing o. the two. This is very much in the hands of the laity, since they can, if they choose, readily have the long service dissevered from the sermon and the sermon placed in the afternoon, leaving a short exhortation—a practical "*postil*"—for the morning, and so permitting the clergyman to give to each service the proper tone. The accidents of the time may often make it necessary to preach a sermon upon some topic whose proper treatment may be wholly different from the tenor of the service for the day. The effect of a joyous festival service may be neutralized by the delivery of a practical sermon whose drift may be penitential. This, however, is not so generally marked. But when the Priest has to deliver a message and to enforce its commands and only half an hour to do this in, his message can hardly be delivered with full effect. The separation of the two would therefore give more time for a thorough discharge of this duty. Again, it is a matter of great importance that the layman should understand his duty in listening to sermons. At the baptism of a child the charge is to the sponsor, "and chiefly ye shall take care that he shall hear sermons." It is considered a valuable part of the instruction which the Church provides. Our LORD has also given a hint upon this duty of attending to sermons: "Take heed what ye hear. With what measure ye mete it shall be measured to you, and unto you that hear shall more be given." Our spiritual knowledge and, too, our discernment cometh from the heed we give to our instructors. But it should also be compared with St. Paul's warning upon this very duty of preaching. Urging St. Timothy to greater zeal and thoroughness in preaching, the Apostle goes on: "For the time will come when they will not endure sound doctrine; but after their own lusts shall they heap to themselves teachers, having itching ears; and they shall turn away their ears from the truth, and shall be turned unto fables" (2 Tim. iv. 3, 4). An examination of the passage will throw much light upon the Church's principles, which involve both the questions how sermons should be listened to and what teachers should be heard. The Church's law upon this topic is set forth in the XXIII. Article: "It is not lawful for any man to take upon him the office of *public preaching* or ministering the sacraments in the congregation before he be lawfully called and sent to execute the same, and those we ought to judge lawfully called and sent which be chosen and called to this work by men who have public authority given unto them in the congregation to call and send ministers into the LORD's vineyard." And the convocation of 1571 A.D. enjoined: "In the first place, let preachers take care that they never teach anything in the way of preaching, which they wish to be retained religiously and believed by the people, except what is agreeable to the doctrine of the Old and New Testaments, and what the Catholic Fathers and ancient Bishops have collected from that same doctrine."

Prebendary (Lat. *præbenda*). A clergyman attached to a cathedral or collegiate Church, who enjoys a prebend in consideration of his rendering stated services. His stall is a prebend's stall, and differs from a canonry in that a canon has a right as a proper officer of the Church to share in its government. But a prebend receives an income for certain duties he is to discharge in the Church. He is appointed by the Bishop generally, but the Queen has also prebends in her gift. (*Vide* CATHEDRAL.)

Predestination. Election, foreknowledge, and fore-ordination are words which occur very frequently in the writings and speculations of theologians; and the subjects which they denote must occur in some form or other to every one who diligently studies his Bible or thinks on "the ways of GOD with man." The Bible speaks of GOD as foreseeing the events of history and showing, to some extent at least, the end from the beginning. It represents Him as determining certain things long before they come to pass. In some cases He has promised what was not to come about for many centuries. At other times the Bible represents Him as threatening certain evils,—as calamities or punishments that are not to be realized for many generations. All this clearly implies foreknowledge, and a purpose with power to contrast events so far and in such a way as to be able to accomplish that which He has promised or threatened. On the other hand, the writers always address men as free agents,—as choosing, or as able to choose, what they will do; they also represent them as held responsible by GOD for the consequences of their own acts, and this accords with the belief and consciousness of mankind. Every one feels that he can choose how he will act, can choose the right and avoid the evil, to a large extent. And whether he is able to do in all cases what he sees to be right, and chooses to do, or would choose to do, if he could do it or not, yet he feels responsible for his choice, and experiences remorse or a sense of shame and regret for what he has done that is wrong. And in this way it comes about that there seems to be a contradiction between a doctrine of Revelation and a fact of experience, which fact is also in harmony with much of the most explicit and most emphatic teaching of Holy Scripture.

A moment's consideration must satisfy us that the subject is, in some respects at least, beyond human comprehension. GOD is a Being of infinite intelligence, and His "thoughts" must in many respects "be far above, out of our sight." He has Himself warned us of the danger of attempting or expecting to comprehend all of His ways, and His reasons for them. Thus He says (Isa. lv. 8, 9), "My thoughts are not your thoughts, neither are your ways My ways. For as the heavens are higher than the earth, so are My ways higher than your ways, and My thoughts than your thoughts." We see an illustration of the principle, enough both to understand it and to conceive of its truth, in the comparison we can make at any time between ourselves and the children that we have under our care. With immature and undeveloped minds, their intelligence is far below our own. We understand many things that are mysterious and entirely incomprehensible to them. We know the reason for many things that must for them rest entirely upon authority and positive command. We see and know how many things are accomplished that are quite incomprehensible, and some altogether impossible to them. But we must remember that while they are as yet far below us in intelligence and power of comprehension, we ourselves are but as children in comparison of that infinite Mind who ordains and comprehends all things. If we acknowledge GOD to be infinite in wisdom and in power, we must admit that He has plans, and ways, and means for accomplishing them incomprehensible to us. Hence when speaking of our phase or aspect of them, it must be expected that He will say what is perfectly comprehensible to us, when we look at that aspect of the subject only. While, nevertheless, when speaking of the subject from some other point or with reference to some other phase of it, whether of doctrine or duty, He will say what, though perfectly intelligible and credible in itself, does seem inconsistent with what He had said before or on another occasion with reference to the same facts.

What we are thus expressing in our relations to GOD and in our study of His word, our children are constantly expressing in our dealings with them. Let us listen to them and study their thoughts and we shall be able, if not to understand the mysteries of His Providence, to reconcile ourselves to the need of walking by faith and trusting that GOD in His own time and way will make the mystery and seeming contradiction entirely plain. At all events, the study will satisfy us, if we are reasonable in our demands and expectations, that so long as GOD is in Heaven and we on earth, as He is infinite and we finite in our powers and intelligence, there must be points and statements in His revelations and commands to us that we cannot comprehend, and that if we would walk in the way that leads to GOD and to Heaven, we must walk in faith and wait for a fuller development and more maturity of our faculties before we can comprehend all the relations and reasons of that rule of life and way of salvation that GOD has provided for us. There are also several important facts that may be of use to us in our meditations and speculations on this subject. In the first place, mere knowledge of what one is doing is no interference with the liberty of the person who does it. I am writing now, and some one is standing by and sees me doing so. I intend to do something to-morrow, and my friend not merely knows this, but the very way in which the act will be done. But in neither case does his knowledge interfere with my freedom to act or not. But it is said, the future act is not certain. Whereas in the future which GOD predicts the acts must be certain, and so the freedom of the agent or agents that are to co-operate is so far limited. But by way of obviating this objection two things must be considered. In the first place, it would seem as though the infinity of GOD would preclude the element of time which comes in to embarrass the speculation as we entertain it. To illustrate what we mean, consider for a moment that each one of us is finite, we see all objects from the point where we are; one thing is on the right, and then on the left, one is before us, another is behind. But now, suppose that GOD is infinite and everywhere present. He will see all those objects that are around us and which appear to be around us, because we can see them from one point only, from all points at one and the same time. In relation to Him there can be no left, no right; nothing is afore another: all are embraced in His omnipresence. So too with thoughts: we are finite, we have one thought now; we had one a little while ago, and another will follow the present one. We can entertain but one thought in our minds at a time. But for the infinite mind this must be otherwise. All thoughts (for it takes up all thoughts to make up omniscience) are and must be present to His Mind at all times and all at the same time for Him. Whatever is past, present, or future to us must be present in thought or as idea at all times, and the matter of time, and time relations involving *fore*knowledge, *pre*destination, prediction, and such like phenomena, must be very different in their relations to GOD from what they are to us, and very different from anything we can conceive or comprehend. Must not their *fore*knowledge in reference to GOD be the same as knowledge is in reference to us? We simply ask the question. It does not become us to dogmatize or to assert positively in a matter of this kind. It must be conceded to be one of "the secret things that belong unto GOD, while only those that are revealed belong unto us" (Deut. xxix. 29).

The second consideration is the fact that in the course of GOD'S Providence He is often seen to work results by means which seem to us most unlikely, and (so far as human purposes and intentions are concerned) by those acts of men which were intended to produce a very different result. Of this the history of the world, as well as our own experience, are full of illustrations. We have the declaration of the Bible that this was the case in regard to the sale of Joseph into Egypt by his brethren. What their motive was we know. But Joseph says (Gen. xlv. 5), "GOD did send me before you to preserve life." Again, GOD is represented in Isaiah (x. 5 *sq.*) as saying of the King of Assyria, he is the "rod of Mine anger, and the staff in their hand is Mine indignation. I will send him against an hypocritical nation, and against the people of my wrath will I give him a charge. . . . Howbeit, he meaneth not so, neither doth his heart think so; but it is in his heart to destroy and to cut off nations not a few." In the case of Judas, the betrayer, and those who conspired with him to produce the Crucifixion of our LORD, we have another example. Without something of the kind the atonement would hardly have been made. But at all events, the result was far from what those who took part in it expected or desired. So, too, when at the time of our LORD'S rising from the grave, the enemies of His religion bribed the soldiers that watched the grave to deny that He had risen, and afterwards straitly charged the Apostles not to preach His resurrection. They did the best they could, considering who and what they were, to put the certainty of these facts and the foundation on which the Gospel rests on a sure basis and beyond the possibility of a reasonable suspicion. We may reasonably doubt whether there could anything have been better arranged to unify the testimony of every one in and about Jerusalem in behalf of the fact of the Resurrection,—the testimony of friends and of confessed believers, and those of His avowed enemies, bent to put a speedy end to the proclamation of the Gospel. What has been actually accomplished is to make the basis of testimony on which it rests unassailable; the most certain and the most indisputable of all events that have occurred in human history or in human experience. And yet there was clearly no interposition to change the intentions of the men or to interfere with their freedom of choice; but GOD did use these acts for His purposes, to further the accomplishment of that which He had foreordained should come to pass.

In nature GOD works. From a religious point of view we must regard all its phenomena as the works of His hand, the manifestations of His will and power. He causes the sun to shine, He moves the stars in their courses and the planets in their orbits. He makes the rain to fall and the plants to grow. But in this sphere there is no freedom, no power of choice; all is foreordination. Here we can learn what will take place, and in calling it *Science* we may obscure, ignore, or deny the fact that it is GOD'S work. But in this domain there is no conflict between what we regard as foreordination and foreknowledge; or we seem to understand it is impossible because of fore-ordination, because all things are predestined in the very constitution of physical nature. But with man and in the sphere of human action we meet with freedom and the power of choice. And it seems to us that if there is freedom or power of choice, there can be no precise foreknowledge of the act we shall choose to perform. But I think we have seen that GOD has and exercises a power over the consequences of our acts so He can bring out of them results that are very far from, and very unlike, what we had foreseen or intended they should effect. Shall we say, then, that there is no foreknowledge of the specific acts we shall perform? But only such a foreknowledge of whatever and of all that man does not perform and cannot control that He can foresee, be sure of, and predestinate results and events that make up the prominent and the controlling facts of history, as well as the prominent phenomena of human life. We can hardly venture to do this. Whenever we attempt or ask a complete solution of these questions we are assuming a power of comprehending them which a moment's consideration must show us that we do not possess. It is enough for us to know, and it is perhaps all that we can know, that GOD worketh all things according to His will, and that in doing this He often bringeth the counsel of princes to nought and maketh the wrath of man work to promote His praise. REV. W. D. WILSON, D.D.

Pre-Existence of Christ. *Vide* ETERNAL GENERATION.

Preface. The Preface is usually restricted to describe the offering of thanks that precedes the SANCTUS. But it should also include the preceding portions. In the earlier Liturgies the portion extending from the Versicle "Lift up your hearts" (Sursum Corda) to the words "Holy, Holy, Holy," bore the name of the Preface. Taking this extension as then correct, the Versicles are preparatory steps that lift the souls of the worshipers as up the ascent of a glorious temple till the Priest begins the solemn words, "It is very meet and right and our bounden duty,"—the form in use in the East and the West. The Eastern form of the Preface is longer and more rhetorical, and it is invariable in each Liturgy. But the Western form is very short, compact, and stately, and there is a varying Proper Preface for the several great Festivals. These are in the Mozarabic Liturgy very numerous, and often of exceeding beauty; in the other Liturgies, as of Milan and Gaul, they were not so numerous nor so fine. The English Church has only retained five out of the many which originally were in her Missals, and which about the end of the twelfth century were reduced to ten. Three of these five are taken derivatively from the ancient sacramentaries of Gelasius (490 A.D.) and Gregory (596 A.D.), but directly from the Salisbury Missal, the most popular and the best of the Liturgies in use in England before the Reformation,—the Prefaces for Easter-day, Ascension-day, and Trinity-Sunday. In our American Book we have an alternate Preface besides. The Christmas and Whitsunday Prefaces appear to have been written at the time of the Reformation. The alternate form in our Prayer-Book seems also to belong to our American Fathers. They are noble compositions, containing manifold meanings in their pregnant phrases, and replete with the very loftiest spirit of prayer. None can be conceived of as better fitted to be uttered before the glorious words, 'Therefore with Angels and Archangels, and with all the company of heaven, we laud and magnify Thy glorious name, evermore praising Thee and saying." Properly, and according to ancient rule, the Priest alone should make this grand oblation of praise, and then at this point the People should make their offering conjointly with him, " Holy, Holy, Holy."

Prelate. A term meaning the office of one having jurisdiction over others. The word now is synonymous with Bishop, but it is not accurate to confine it to this sense. For the authority of a BISHOP, see the word.

Presanctified, Liturgy of. In some parts of the early Church it was not permitted to consecrate the Eucharist in Lent save on Saturday and Sunday. Therefore, as frequent communions through the week were usual, the consecrated elements were reserved, and hence the name for the service when there was a Communion: the Liturgy of the præsanctified,—that is, a Liturgic form in which the actual consecration of the elements is omitted, since this had already been effected, but in which there is the proper offering of worship, praise, and reception of the elements by the Communicants. The modern Latin practice is to omit only on Good-Friday a proper celebration. But the Greeks continue the older rule.

Presbyter. In the English Version of the New Testament it is always translated Elder. It was used by the Septuagint translators to designate the chiefs of the people, whether of the families, or of the tribe, or of the nation; they also so named the Elders who received the gift of prophecy. The word then passed into New Testament usage. One tradition says that the seventy sent forth by our LORD became the elders under the Apostles. At any rate, the institution of this rank is not recorded as is that of the deacons, but is assumed. They were placed by SS. Barnabas and Paul in every city where they gathered converts. The name Presbyter is literally "the elder;" hence one whose age invests him with respect, thence an officer, because of his experience and wisdom. The word *Presbeuo* meant to be an embassador (2 Cor. v. 20; Eph. vi. 20); hence the august and weighty officer of an embassador is attached to the Eldership. It is not that the Presbyter is chosen for his gravity or worth merely, but as fit to share in the noble embassy which CHRIST has given His Apostles, and so to share in their mission. The Presbyter had also in the New Testament usage a second title, *Episcopos*, which was afterwards transferred and made to denote the Apostolic office of the successors of the Apostles. But there is a glory added to the title, for in the Vision of St. John's Revelation the four-and-twenty Elders crowned and enthroned are sharers with the heavenly multitude in the heavenly worship, and themselves offer a special thanksgiving, as well as join in the praises of the redeemed, and the angels to Him who sitteth upon the Throne and to the Lamb of GOD. This honor belongs to the order whose title is so glorified. It is by a fit instinct, then, that the word PRESBYTER is retained throughout the Church to denote the officer appointed by the Apostles to aid in their work. It has been contracted into the word Priest (*vide* PRIEST), but both words are in common use side by side. (*Vide* ELDER.)

Authorities: Bishop Onderdonk's Episcopacy tested by Scripture, Marshall's Notes on Episcopacy.

Presbyterium. The part in the church occupied by the Presbytery. The earliest arrangement placed the Bishop's throne against the Eastern wall and behind the altar, which was placed farther out. On each side were the seats for the Presbyters. But when this arrangement was abandoned in the West,—if indeed it ever largely obtained at all there,—the Presbyterium was a part of the choir, or beyond the choir and part of the sanctuary. But in the East it must refer to the part behind the altar.

Presence of Christ The Presence of CHRIST is manifold. He is in the Presence of Presences, the Holy of Holies, as our Intercessor, and there is His proper seat and presence. But He has promised to be in the midst of the two or three who are gathered together in His name, to be present with His Apostles to the end of the world. He is in His Church as its Head, and is in each member of the Church. In these respects He is present mystically. He is present as the giver of baptism, and as the gift of baptism. For as many as have been baptized into CHRIST have put on CHRIST. There is, then, a presence in this sacramental gift of CHRIST.

Again, He has said, this is my Body, this is my Blood, of the consecrated elements of Bread and Wine in the Holy Communion, and here, in whatsoever way He may be present, it is sacramentally. Then we may define the Presence of CHRIST to be threefold: His Proper Presence, as the SON of GOD, and as Mediator and Intercessor, at the right hand of His FATHER. His mystical presence in His Church, His Apostles, and His members. And His presence in the sacraments. (*Vide* REAL PRESENCE.)

Presentation of Christ in the Temple. A Feast-day, usually called the Feast of the Purification (February 2); but this is wrong, since the Feast was instituted in honor of our LORD, and so the Greek Church understands it, the title for the feast meaning the meeting, —*i.e.*, of Simeon and Anna with the Virgin Mother and her SON. It was probably instituted by the Emperor Justinian, about 526 A.D., and was received throughout the whole Church. The Collect is from the Gregorian sacramentary, and is worthy of study as presenting so compactly the purpose of the feast. As the Epistle and Gospel are those appointed in the ancient Lectionary, the Church of England has clung closely to the old use. The Scripture for the Epistle is according to the Western use, but the Gospel (practically the same everywhere) follows the Eastern use in reading a longer portion. The change of the title from that of the "Presentation" to that of the Purification may most probably be due to the leading thought of the Purifying that our LORD has instituted here, as set forth both in the Epistle from Malachi and in the words of Simeon. (*Vide* CANDLEMAS.)

Presentation to a Cure. The right of the Patron, or of the person who has purchased that right, to present a clerk to the Bishop to be instituted in a cure. As parishes are founded very differently in this country, this right resides in the vestry or in those persons of a parish who may be delegated to exercise it. It cannot be too often reiterated that the Office of Institution is the fundamental law, and the proper inferences to be drawn from it, and the circumstances it presupposes, should dictate to the vestry the mode of procedure, which is too often overlooked in the usual way a rector is called and received in a parish.

Priest. It is proposed, in this article, to consider whether the Christian Church has a true Priesthood, not figurative, but real, and whether that Priesthood has sacrifices, in the proper sense of the word, to offer, and if so, what their nature. The two hang together, and must be considered together. A Priest must have somewhat to offer; a sacrifice necessitates some one to make the offering. In order, therefore, fully to present the subject we shall here say something first of the nature of sacrifice, and then of the Priesthood.

I. OF SACRIFICES.

A sacrifice is literally that which is made holy or dedicated to GOD. There is also always implied the idea of thereby pleasing GOD or propitiating His favor. It would be aside from our purpose to give any history of sacrifice outside of the Jewish and Christian dispensations, even the former briefly, as helping to understand the latter.

The Mosaic Sacrifices.—The "gifts and sacrifices" offered by the Mosaic priesthood were divinely appointed types of the one great sacrifice of the SON of GOD, to be once for all offered in the fullness of the time. They were both animal (*zebach*), therefore bloody, and vegetable (*mincha*), unbloody, and may all be classed under three heads, viz.:

A. { The Sin-offering (*chattath*). } EXPIATORY.
   { The Trespass-offering (*asham*). }
B. The Whole-Burnt-offering (*'olah*). DEDICATORY.
C. The Peace-offering (*shelem*). { bloody } EUCHARISTIC.
                                  { vegetable }

And used in connection with the others:

D. Incense (*ketoreth*). INTERCESSORY.

Briefly of each:

(A) The great features of the *sin* and *trespass-offerings* were (1) The offering the victim to the LORD by the laying on of the hands of the offerer, with, in some cases, confession of sins. (2) The sprinkling of the blood before the Divine Presence. (3) The partial burning on the great Brazen Altar. (4) The carrying outside of the camp in the skin, and the complete burning of the remains. None of it was to be eaten by the offerer (Lev. vi. 30).

It stood forth as EXPIATORY. In it was remission by "the blood of sprinkling." Therefore, on the great Day of Atonement, it preceded all others, preparing the way for them. Through it alone Priest and People were made worthy to approach the Divine Presence, as pardoned sinners.

(B) *The Burnt-offering* was as follows: (1) The victim was to be presented by the laying on of the hand of the offerer, by whom it was then to be slain; (2) the blood was sprinkled by the Priest about the brazen altar; (3) the carcass was properly cut up "according to the manner;" (4) the whole was to be consumed by fire upon the altar. The blood was not to be taken within the Sanctuary, none of the flesh was to be eaten. This sacrifice was a *Whole-offering*, dedicated entirely to GOD, and represented the dedication of the offerer himself to GOD.

(C) The *Peace-offering*, sometimes called the *Meat-offering*, differed essentially from the others. This consisted of either an animal or a vegetable offering, generally of both. (1) The animal was offered and slain; (2) the blood was sprinkled upon the altar; (3) certain portions only, as the fat and liver, were burnt upon the altar; (4) the rest was eaten by the Priest and the offerer with their friends, as a *Holy Feast of Thanksgiving*, for which the sin- and burnt-offerings—the atonement and dedication—had prepared the way. With the animal of this Peace-offering, as an essential part, *sometimes even brought by itself alone*, were the vegetable offerings of Frankincense and of Fine Flour, with beaten Oil and Wine. A handful of these last, with all the incense, was to be burned, together with the parts of the victim, on the altar, "as a memorial;" the rest was baked and eaten with the flesh, or roasted or boiled, as being part of the Peace-offering; a solemn act of *Thanksgiving* and a *Memorial* before the LORD.

With all these sacrifices incense was to be offered, as a separate act, representing the intercessory prayer of the Priest for himself and people.

The sacrifices, then, present three features: the *Propitiatory*, the *Dedicatory*, and the *Thanksgiving*; the latter involving, also, communion with GOD, in the eating together by Priest and people of that which had been offered to GOD; and as such may be considered that for which the others prepared the way, therefore the highest act of worship.

It must be noticed, also, that one thing is common to all, death by the shedding of blood, or in the case of the vegetable offering, by destruction; the wheat being ground into fine flour, the oil and wine crushed from the fruit, and all consumed by fire or eating.

Now these complex ceremonies did not owe the efficacy they possessed to any value in themselves, but solely to something they as types or shadows represented. The Epistle to the Hebrews clearly sets this forth (Heb. x. 1), and St. Paul thus puts it: "They were the shadow of things to come, but the body is of CHRIST" (Col. ii. 17). He was truly the sin-, the burnt-, and the peace-offering. His blood, shed on the cross, atones for sin; He gave Himself, and with Himself His people, a willing offering entirely to GOD; "He is our peace," and gives Himself to be feasted on, as the true bread of life, the wine of GOD; and His intercessions are the true incense offered before the Mercy-seat on High. He is also the true High-Priest, called of GOD; and as man and in man's behalf offering Himself the victim for man; and taking His body wounded and pierced into heaven before GOD, presenting it for man in atonement for sin, and therefore He is revealed in heaven as "a Lamb, as it had been slain" (Rev. v. 6). In Him, therefore, all these Mosaic sacrifices find their fulfillment and end. There is no more, *i.e.*, no further sacrifice for sin. None other can be needed. "This man after He had offered one sacrifice for sins forever, sat down on the right hand of GOD." "By His one offering He hath perfected forever them that are sanctified." "Through the offering of the body of JESUS CHRIST once for all." Not once for all men, but ἐφάπαξ once only "denoting the absolute cessation of an act under the idea that it has been perfectly performed" (Heb. x. *passim*). In the words of the Prayer-Book: "His one oblation of Himself once offered, was a full, perfect, and sufficient sacrifice, oblation, and satisfaction for the sins of the whole world." The substance being come the figures are done away, the old Mosaic sacrifices are ended; they are to us of value as teaching of the true sacrifice.

II. THE PRIESTHOOD.

CHRIST is not only the sacrifice, but also the true High-Priest, "who is set on the right hand of the throne of the Majesty in the heavens; a minister of the sanctuary, and of the true tabernacle, which the LORD pitched, and not man" (Heb. viii. 1, 2), "where He ever liveth to make intercession for us." In Him the Aaronic Priesthood is, if we may so say, absorbed. It came in Him to an end, for when no more such sacrifices are required, no such Priesthood is needed. But CHRIST'S Priesthood is everlasting. In heaven He is the sin-offering, the whole-offering, the thank-offering, ever presented for man, and which cannot be repeated. The benefits thereof of pardon, acceptance, and communion He as High-Priest ever sent down to man by the HOLY SPIRIT. But His Priesthood is not that of the old, but of the new covenant, or rather it includes the two. "He does all that the old Priesthood could not do for the weakness and unprofitableness thereof." He adds to this the Priesthood of the better covenant in His blood, of which He is the surety; even the eternal Priesthood "after the order of Melchisedec" (Heb. vii. 21, 22), thus described: "This is the covenant that I will make with them after those days, saith the LORD; I will put my laws into their hearts, and in their minds will I write them; and their sins and iniquities will I remember no more. Now where remission of these is, there is no more offering for sin" (Heb. x. 16, 17). CHRIST, then, is the High-Priest of the Church which is called by His name and is His body. By virtue of His one sacrifice He obtains for it remission of sins. Making it one with Himself, He offers it to GOD, to do His will. The true peace-offering, He gives it His own Body and Blood, to sustain its new life by this communion with Himself, as He said to His disciples, "He that eateth My flesh, and drinketh My blood, dwelleth in Me, and I in him" (St. John vi. 56).

But in accordance with GOD'S dealings with man, in pity to his weakness, to strengthen his faith and enable him to apply for all these benefits, CHRIST has been pleased in the New Covenant, as under the Old, to appoint means of grace, outward visible signs and proofs of that which He does for us. A Priesthood was needed to minister these on CHRIST'S behalf to man, and to act for man towards Himself. A Priesthood, not like that of Aaron, which was fulfilled in CHRIST, but like His own, after the order of Melchisedec. A ministry of Reconciliation, Blessing, and Peace. None the less a real Priesthood because spiritual; therefore, indeed, of a higher order than the old, with real offerings, more real and valuable than those of Aaron, because not shadows of good things to come; retaining such features of the Old Covenant as under the New are needed.

(I.) It is a REAL PRIESTHOOD. "As my Father hath sent me, even so send I you," is its commission (St. John xx. 21). Writes St. Paul: "GOD hath given to us the ministry of reconciliation. Now, then, we are Ambassadors for CHRIST" (2 Cor. v. 18, 20). And to the Romans he writes: "That I should be the minister of JESUS CHRIST to the Gentiles, ministering the gospel of GOD, that the offering up of the Gentiles might be acceptable, being sanctified by the HOLY GHOST" (Rom. xv. 16). On which Dr. Bloomfield, in his note, remarks, that he describes his ministry to the Gentiles in "formula derived from the Jewish religion, in order the more strongly to impress on the Jewish Christians the dignity of his Apostleship; calling himself, not διάκονος, a *minister*, but λειτουργὸς, a *sacred* minister; and saying his office is, not κηρύσσειν, to preach, but ἱερουργεῖν τὸ εὐαγγέλιον, —*i.e.*, to preach the Gospel as a *Priest* of the *New Covenant* (literally, ministering as a Priest the Gospel). So προσφορα and ἡγιασμένη, *sacrificing* and *sanctified*, a little after, are likewise terms borrowed from the Temple service."

As Ambassadors for CHRIST, called by the HOLY GHOST, His ministers represent and act for Him; as taken from among men, and chosen by men, they act for men, and thus are as truly Priests as were the Aaronic, according to the word, "For every High-Priest taken from among men is ordained for men in things pertaining to GOD" (Heb. v. 1).

(II.) IT OFFERS TRUE SACRIFICES. A priest must have somewhat to offer. What offering does the Christian Priesthood make?

(A) *Remissory; or the Ministry of Reconciliation*.—The Christian Priest makes no typical sacrifice expiatory of sin; nor does he repeat the sacrifice by offering CHRIST to the FATHER in the mass, as the Romanist pretends; but he offers to GOD for and with the people their confession of sins, and he declares to them officially, as from GOD, the remission of sins, through the sacrifice of Calvary, which remission is conveyed by the HOLY GHOST to the individual soul, according to the commission of the risen LORD, "whosoever sins ye remit, they are remitted unto them" (St. John xx. 23). He administers Baptism for the remission of sins. He offers to GOD for the people the memorial of the one great sin-offering, with prayer that thereby they may obtain remission of sins. Surely when the Priest, leading the congregation with penitent hearts and lively faith to the throne of grace, offers a confession of sin, and pleads by the memorial of His Body and Blood which CHRIST has commanded to be made, His one sacrifice of Himself for the sins of the whole world, this memorial and this lifting up of hands and hearts is a Priestly act, a true sacrifice, accepted by GOD for CHRIST'S sake.

(B) *Intercessory.*—The Priest prays for and with the people; this takes the place of the old Incense-burning (Rev. v. 8). CHRIST receives and makes these prayers His own, offering them before the throne. As the frankincense of old accompanied every sacrifice, so the prayer of faith gives value to all Christian ministrations.

(C) *Dedicatory.*—The Christian Priest not only urges men to give themselves up to GOD, through CHRIST, but offers the sacrifice on their behalf and receives it officially on GOD'S. This is an important feature of the sacraments. In Baptism, the minister receives the child or person, dedicates to GOD'S service, and on GOD'S behalf announces remission of sin, and a new birth as GOD'S child; this is repeated in Confirmation, and renewed from time to time in the Holy Communion, in which " we offer and present unto Thee, O LORD, ourselves, our souls and bodies, to be a reasonable, holy, and living sacrifice unto Thee." Which sacrifice, we believe, is accepted by GOD because a voluntary one, and chiefly because presented for us by our great High-Priest in heaven, who has already atoned for its imperfections; and by His intercession makes it worthy to be received. This is a Priestly act of the most solemn nature.

(D) *Eucharistic.*—This is the peculiar feature of the Melchisedician Priesthood to which all others are preparatory, the offering, consecrating, and giving of the Bread and Wine, for His memorial, who said, "Take, eat; this is My Body. Drink ye all of this; for this is My blood of the New Covenant." " Do this in remembrance of Me." This the true Peace- and Meat-Offering, on which we by faith feed, as on Him, the one sacrifice, and so are in communion with GOD. This the true Thank-offering, " our sacrifice of praise and thanksgiving." This unites in itself the four acts of the old ritual, Remission, Intercession, Dedication, and Eucharistic,—feeding for Communion.

(E) But there is a higher feature of the Christian Priesthood peculiar to it, unknown to the Mosaic. It is under the dispensation of the HOLY SPIRIT, obtained for it by its ascended Head, in whom His promise is fulfilled, " Lo, I am with you alway." " Wherever two or three are gathered together in my name, there am I in the midst of them." It is this gives value and efficacy to all their acts. This the special feature of the New Covenant. This is a gift from GOD to man, bestowed ordinarily with or by means of the ministrations of the Christian Priest. " Be baptized for the remission of sins and ye shall receive the gift of the HOLY GHOST." Thus it is connected with baptism. " Through laying on of the Apostles' hands the HOLY GHOST was given" (Acts viii. 18). Thus it is connected with confirmation. And it is in the Holy Communion that we receive CHRIST, through the HOLY SPIRIT, and by that same SPIRIT are sanctified.

It remains to show briefly that what has been said of the Christian Priesthood and Sacrifices is in accordance with the teaching of our Church, as set forth in her Communion Office.

(1) We have the humbly presenting and placing upon the Holy Table " the alms and other Devotions of the People." Then the placing upon the same " the Bread and Wine," with the prayer to GOD " most mercifully *to accept our alms and oblations*, and to receive our prayers." (2) The confession of sins by Priest and People, with the absolution, denoted a Priestly act because to be said by a Priest only. (3) The song Holy, Holy, Holy, offered by all as a sacrifice of Praise. (4) The Prayer of Humble Access, another Incense-burning. (5) The solemn special Priestly function in the solemn repetition of the LORD'S words, " This is my Body," " This is my Blood," and of His acts in the taking, breaking, and blessing of the Bread; and taking and blessing of the Cup, doing this as a memorial of Him, as a showing forth of His death. (6) The oblation or offering of these " holy gifts" thus consecrated to the FATHER, in what we may call sacrificial words, " We, Thy humble servants, do celebrate and make here, before Thy Divine Majesty, with these Thy *holy gifts, which we now offer unto Thee*, the memorial Thy SON hath commanded us to make;" and again, " And we earnestly desire Thy fatherly goodness, mercifully to accept this *our sacrifice* of praise and thanksgiving;" yet again, " And here we offer and present unto Thee, O LORD, ourselves, our souls and bodies, to be a *reasonable, holy, and living sacrifice* unto Thee," "and although we are unworthy, through our manifold sins, to offer unto Thee any sacrifice, yet we beseech Thee to accept this our bounden duty and service." (7) The devout reception by the Priest himself, and then his delivering to the people of the Communion in

both kinds. (8) The solemn Benediction in the name of the Blessed TRINITY.

Here are eight ways in which the Church, following the Ancient Liturgies, sets forth plainly the Priestly character and sacrificial acts of her ministers; uniting thus in one the Prophetic and Priestly functions. And it has been shown that for so doing she "Has most certain warrant of Holy Scripture." We are not wrong, then, in calling our Ministers true Priests, and in saying that they offer sacrifices, not figurative, but real, and none the less so because most truly spiritual. "For if the ministration of death. . . . was glorious, . . . How shall not the ministration of the spirit be rather glorious?" REV. E. B. BOGGS, D.D.

Primate. A synonym for *metropolitan*. It is a term taken from the civil government, but its bounds of power were slowly defined. The primacy was one at first of honor and of seniority, but as the Church grew and Synods became necessarily more frequent, and the presidency over them, and the right of precedence in them, more important, the Primacy which belonged naturally to the civil metropolis attached to the See of that Capital. In Africa the rule of presiding by right of seniority held, and the oldest Bishop, as in our own arrangement, was Primate of the Province. The East had a slightly different arrangement from the West; the Province was under a Metropolitan and the Metropolitans under a Patriarch. But the West later had Patriarchs distributed as numerously as in the East, and so the Metropolitans were the chief Bishops. The Primacy was created under the Carlovingians to supply this defect, and the office became in one sense permanent; but as the Popes who helped to establish it found it in their way, in the matter of appeals, and as the Metropolitans did not like to have any one over them, the Primacy became but little more than titular. In the English Church the title was but little more than titular when, as a settlement of the quarrels between York and Canterbury, the Pope gave to York the Primacy of England, and to Canterbury the Primacy of all England. But latterly this Primacy of Canterbury has given the Archbishop a great deal of weight, both in England and elsewhere, and he is looked up to as the first Clergyman in England, and as having the Presidency in all gatherings of the Bishops of the Anglican Communion. But a Primacy is far different from a Supremacy. So far as the West is concerned the Primacy of the whole Church in the West could be in the Bishop of Rome, but his usurpation of the title and creation of the powers of Pope, and a consequent claim to Supremacy, has led to the forfeiture and loss of his Primacy. Papal Supremacy is inconsistent with and condemned by all the facts of a true Apostolic Primacy.

Prime. The service said at the first hour,—at sunrise. The Monastic service of the English use contributed to the office of Daily Morning Prayer the Creed, the short Litany,—O LORD, shew thy mercy upon us, etc. O LORD, save the King. R. And mercifully hear us when we call upon thee. V. Endue thy ministers with righteousness. R. And make thy chosen people joyful. V. O LORD, save thy people. R. And bless thine inheritance. V. Give peace in our time, O LORD. R. Because there is none other that fighteth for us, but thou only, O LORD. V. O GOD, make clean our hearts within us R., etc. The restoration of the Versicles and Responses here given into our American Service is one of the proposals now before the Church from the Committee on the Enrichment of the Prayer-Book.

Primer. A book of Elementary Instruction. In the history of the Prayer-Book it means an elementary book upon the main points of the Faith. Several such books were published from 1527 A.D. to 1564 A.D. A very early English Primer dates from 1390 A.D., but the first that really entered into the Reformation work was Marshall's, 1535 A.D., which was apparently a private venture. It contained expositions of the Creed, LORD'S Prayer, Commandments, and the Ave Maria. It also contained the offices and Hours, the Seven Penitential Psalms, the Dirige, and the commendations taken from the Roman offices. But the next Primer, "The Godly and Pious Institution of a Christian man," was a step forward, both in contents and in authority (1537 A.D.). It was called the "Bishop's Book," being authorized by the King, and having the signatures of the two Archbishops and 19 Bishops, 8 Archdeacons, and 17 Doctors of Divinity and Law. It went much further than Marshall's, though containing still some matters on Purgatory. The Primer of Bishop Hilsey, though published after his death, in 1539 A.D., had also a by-part in the coming work of preparing a New Use. It gave the basis of our present Calendar of Lessons for Sundays and Holidays, and too, so far as modifications were admitted, for our Epistles and Gospels. The King receded somewhat from the position in the Necessary Doctrine and Erudition for any Christian man (1543 A.D.). But in 1545 A.D. the King's Primer, which incorporated the Litany, which (1544 A.D.) had been ordered in English, though formed upon the model of the previous Primers, was still greater advanced, though much was yet to be effected. In the reign of Edward VI., the King's Primer was reprinted 1547 A.D., and in 1553 A.D. there was a new Primer of Private Prayers issued. This King's Primer was also the basis of Queen Elizabeth's first Primer (1559 A.D.). A second (1566 A.D.) was a good deal changed from this; altogether the Primers had a good deal to do with the instruction and preparation for the work of Reformation. They taught a far more correct doctrine, still, fell short of what was needful, and they put forth what might be called tentative forms, which paved the way for the use of the Prayer-Book. Those of Elizabeth's reign had, of course, not so much influence. After the one put forth in 1571 A.D. no more were issued. This form of instruction has since been done by the very common books of Devotion, which under other names have practically carried on the work begun by Marshall's Primer.

Primitive Church. This phrase, which is rather indeterminate, may be taken to refer to the period from the close of the Apostolic age to the holding of the Sixth General Council, 680 A.D. But in a narrower and more correct sense it may be taken to only include the Council of Chalcedon, 451 A.D. Reference is constantly made to this early period of the Church for several reasons. The government of the Church as then carried out must have been according to the establishment of it by the Apostles. Therefore all the writings of the sub-Apostolic Church are of great value in this respect. What Clement, the companion of St. Paul, and Ignatius, the convert of St. John and friend of SS. Peter and Paul, held and wrote, must much more really reflect the mind of the Apostles, and more accurately report what they did for the organization of the Church, than any inferences we can make from the letter of the New Testament. For Church polity the writings of those who conversed with the Apostles and of those of the second generation must be of far greater value than our speculations at present. Again, in doctrine, the fierce persecutions the first Christians had to endure were of service in making them cling but the more tenaciously to the doctrines of the Faith once delivered to the Saints. So what the ante-Nicene Fathers held (before 325 A.D.), their clear, simple statements and the defense made by the great doctors of the Church down to the Sixth General Council against heresies and false teaching, the writings of the great leaders in the contests of the Church, must be of worth to us in determining how Holy Scripture is to be understood. It is clear, of course, that the Fathers are valuable to us as unbiased, honest witnesses of what was held and taught and defended by them as of vital importance to the Church. They cannot dictate to us their private opinions, some of which were untenable, but wherever they consent together in testifying that such were the doctrines of the Church, they are of great value. Again, in practice, what they concur in testifying to be of Churchly practice in their day is of great importance to us.

Their mention of what the Liturgies were, how they conducted the services, how they observed Feasts, and Fasts, and Holidays, casts a good deal of light upon our own Prayer-Book, and guides us into a better appreciation of that beauty of holy worship which is our inheritance,—a historic inheritance we may not lightly part with. These great facts about the early Church, its government, its faith, its practice, enable us to judge whether what we now hold in government, in faith, in practice, is an innovation, something of a later age, an invention for convenience, or was from the first. For it is clear that any Body of co-religionists to claim to be a part of the Church Catholic must show that it has a historic continuity, that it is descended from the Church our LORD established at His Resurrection. For if it has broken the government He gave to the Apostles, or has lost the Faith He has deposited with them, it has forfeited its claim. Or if it has been formed and organized in these latter days, it is *not* of the ancient Faith. It has no links that bind it to the Cross of CHRIST. It has but a mushroom growth. Its definitions are only upon the basis of modern opinion.

The appeal that the Episcopal Church makes to the New Testament and to the Primitive Church is free and honest. It challenges an examination by them. What does the New Testament teach? How did Clement, and Ignatius, and Polycarp, and Irenæus, and Cyprian, and Athanasius, and Jerome, and Augustine, and Cyril receive and transmit, the one to the other, the Doctrines, and the Government, and the Worship of the Church? Upon their usages, upon their Faith, historically the English, and then her daughter, the American Church, rest their claim to a part, a living, continuous part, in the Holy Catholic Church of CHRIST. What they showed that the Church held then we hold now, what they taught as the Church's doctrine we teach now, and we do not fear the closest scrutiny into our claims by this test.

More, we desire it, we urge it. Those who have thrown away Apostolic government cannot endure it. Those who have added to the Faith shrink from it. Of all bodies of the Christian world now, the Anglican Church and her daughter Communions alone can abide by the test of the Primitive Church. She therefore makes great use of it in her controversies, and she must, upon every legal maxim, demand that Her Organization, and Her History, and Her Standards of Faith be judged by this touchstone.

Procession. It meant generally in the ante-Nicene days the going to church. But later, when Litanies were more common, the procession to the church in solemn state was used. In this the early Christians revived a custom from the pagan processions, which they did not deem contrary to their Faith.

In the church, the clergy always left the vestry in order of rank, and so formed with their attendants a procession into the Sanctuary. But these processions in use in the Church service in the East were at the reading of the Gospel, which was carried in state from the Holy Table through the side chapel round into the Sanctuary again; and also at the bringing in of the oblations which are to be used at the celebration. The Deacon has the paten placed upon his shoulder by the priest, who then takes the cup himself, and so they move out of the side chapel, which corresponds to our Vestry room, and pass through the church into the Sanctuary. In our own Church, processions in the church are directed at the consecration of a church and at the institution of a minister.

Procession of the Holy Ghost. The doctrine of the Third Person of the HOLY TRINITY regarding the mode of His Being. It is well to begin all statements of doctrine upon the HOLY TRINITY by saying that, no matter what deductions may be drawn from what we are taught, the doctrines themselves rest only upon revelation. Antecedently to revelation we can know nothing. Therefore to attempt to explain how the HOLY GHOST from all eternal proceeded from the FATHER is mere folly. "If thou dost curiously inquire how the SON is begotten and how the SPIRIT proceedeth, I will inquire of thee as curiously how the soul and the body are conjoined." (St. Gregory Nazianzen, Orat. xx.) It is a part of the Nicene Creed, being set forth and appended to it by the General Council of Constantinople, 381 A.D.: "Who proceedeth from the FATHER." In a Creed, or rather statement, of doctrine set forth by St. Epiphanius a little earlier, the same words occur: "We, therefore, believe in Him, that He is the HOLY GHOST, the Spirit of GOD, the Perfect Spirit, the Paraclete Spirit, the Creator, proceeding from the FATHER, and received from the SON, and to be believed." Again, the same Father saith, "Always hath the Spirit proceeded from the FATHER and received of the SON; for He is not different from the FATHER and the SON, but is from the same essence, from the same Deity, from the FATHER and the SON, with the FATHER and the SON" (Hær. 62, c. 4). The reverence of these quotations sets forth the spirit in which we must receive the statements of our LORD upon this revelation. "But the Comforter, which is the HOLY GHOST, whom the FATHER will send in My name, He shall teach you all things" (St. John xiv. 26). "But when the Comforter is come, whom I will send unto you from the FATHER, even the Spirit of Truth, which proceedeth from the FATHER, He shall testify of Me" (St. John xv. 26).

In these texts the LORD declares the mode of the subsistence of the HOLY GHOST. But He further declares the work of the HOLY GHOST in the economy of man's redemption. He shall guide you into all truth. He shall receive of mine and show it unto you. And the HOLY GHOST, therefore, is sent by the SON. The doctrine of the Eastern Church, that He proceedeth from the FATHER and is sent by the SON, is more close to Holy Scripture. Though indeed proceeding eternally from the same self-existent FATHER, as the SON is the only-begotten of that FATHER, we may well say that they are consubstantial with the FATHER, and therefore that, as of the same eternal essence, the HOLY GHOST proceedeth from the SON also. Still, this is not so close to the Scriptures, but an inference from them, since He receives of the FATHER and the SON. This, however, does not justify the interpolation of the words "and the SON" in the Creed (*vide* FILIOQUE), though it does make the imploration, "O GOD the HOLY GHOST who proceedeth from the FATHER *and the SON*, have mercy upon us miserable sinners, a most proper and prevailing intercession, since by His mission from the SON He shares in our redemption. The doctrine, then, of the HOLY GHOST proceeding from the FATHER (and, too, in a Divine sense, also from the SON) is of the Faith, and is to be most religiously believed. (*Vide* HOLY GHOST, FILIOQUE, SPIRIT.)

Proctor. (Lat. *Procurator.*) An officer who represents in judgment the parties who empower him (by warrant under their hands, called a *proxy*) to appear for them to explain their rights, to manage and instruct their cause and to demand judgment.

The Proctors of the clergy represent them in Convocation. The Deans, Archdeacons, and Proctors of the several Chapters sat in it *ex officio*, but the Parsons, Vicars, and perpetual Curates in each Diocese, who alone had the right of being represented, chose two Proctors to represent them. This is in the Convocation of Canterbury. But in the Convocation of York two Proctors are sent from each Archdeaconry.

The title Proctor is given also to certain officers of the colleges who have a care over the morals and quiet of the universities.

Procuration. A compounding by a payment of money for the charges due for entertainment of a Bishop when upon a Visitation. The Procuration was not due without an actual Visitation.

Prophecy. The general meaning of the word is the foretelling events by the revelation or inspiration of the HOLY GHOST,— "who spake by the Prophets." Prophecy was a part of the economy of GOD the Father in teaching, first, men in general, then the Patriarchs, then by special Messengers, His chosen People, and, lastly, ourselves by the One great Prophet, JESUS CHRIST. So a prophecy was *given* by GOD Himself of the Deliverer, "Enoch, the seventh from Adam, prophesied" (Jude v. 14). So Noah in his blessing Shem and Japhet and in cursing Ham acted as a prophet. Abraham received direct revelations of Him who should be the Heir of the world. Isaac and Jacob were inspired with the spirit of Prophecy, in delivering their several blessings. The prophetic word was withheld till Moses was endowed with it. But through him it took a wider and deeper tone. The Spirit of prophecy gave present instructions, as in the case of the Seventy, who prophesied, but to him it was reserved to foretell the future. And here, singularly as in our LORD'S own prophecy of the end of the world, Moses' direct prophecy was of the destruction of Jerusalem. With him ceased again the spirit of prophecy till the time of Samuel. In the sense of prophetical teaching there had been no great interruption, but in the higher sense of the word the gift was restored in Samuel. The power of prophecy was a gift which depended wholly upon the wisdom and purposes of the SPIRIT. The subjects of prophecy were the most varied, as may be well supposed of HIM for whose care nothing is too minute and for whose might nought is too great. They were all intended to have one aim, the preparation of the world for the coming of CHRIST, and according to the exigencies of the time in which they were delivered, so were ordered the minor accessories to this main theme.

Egypt, Assyria, Greece, and Rome, the greatest kingdoms, were prophesied of. The Edomite in his stronghold, the Moabite beyond Jordan, were warned in prophecy of their coming fate. The household of the King, the birth of a son, were all included. Wider than these was the prophecy of the last great Kingdom,—the Kingdom of the Messiah and the ingathering of the Gentiles. This we are now aiding to fulfill. The effect of prophecy upon the mind of men is deepened rather than lessened by Christianity. Few prophecies yet remain unfulfilled, but the study of prophecy and its fulfillment has but confirmed our faith in the certainty that those prophecies yet to be accomplished will not fail of a complete and literal fulfillment. The study of the prophecies has also another result. They have been so minutely carried out, even in cases where it was not apparently necessary to do so, that the devout student is led to believe in something more than the mere general inspiration of the prophet. Take Jeremiah's prophecy (Jer. li. 27–58), uttered seventy years before it was fulfilled, of the destruction of Babylon, and read it carefully and compare it with the secular accounts, and the reader will see how literally it was carried out.

The minuteness, too, of the prophecy of Isaiah of Cyrus, who was to fulfill the prophecy of Jeremiah, "That saith of Cyrus. He is my shepherd, and shall perform all my pleasure, even saying to Jerusalem, Thou shalt be built, and to the temple, thy foundations shall be laid,"—for by the decree of Cyrus the work on each went so far,—is remarkable. The subject is too broad for so small a space as is allowed here. But a law of prophecy may be noted at this point—The manifold application of prophecy. The seventy-second psalm was of Solomon, but it passed behind him and depicted the Messiah. Out of Egypt have I called my *Son*, was of Israel in the first place, but of CHRIST afterwards. Of Judah's blessing the full meaning could only enter in the Lawgiver SHILOH, the LORD JESUS CHRIST. And through this predictive element comes the secondary, but no less important, one of establishing our faith in the moral government of GOD, as well as in His ordering all things according to His purposes. For it is one thing to admit His sovereignty, and another to acknowledge the moral law of this sovereignty.

Prophecy ceased with the Revelation of St. John the Divine, and the gift has not been bestowed since upon men, nor is there any real need of it, as there is no real need now of miracles. We are now fulfilling prophecy, aiding in completing it. As our Faith is founded upon a completed prophecy for our strengthening, so for our trial, it involves a yet incomplete prophecy, which is also a part of our prayer. "He shall come to judge the quick and the dead," sums up the limit of prophecy, and the petition, Thy Kingdom come, is essentially the same thing. But there are yet several unfulfilled predictions before this consummation. The conversion of the Jew, the practical unity of the Church and the gathering of all people into it, and, it may be added, the restoration of Jerusalem to the Jew, are main points of prophecy that lie yet in the history of the future. That they may be at hand no one can assert who reads the surface signs of the times, and yet, beneath the outward course of the political and the religious world, we see and feel deeply that there is at work the power of GOD's Spirit, which at any time can bring about their completion. And, too, it must be remembered that He who combines all things to work together for good, doeth it for the greatest good of the greatest number, and, too, knoweth when men's hearts are best prepared to receive His acts. There is a mercy in the very delays in the accomplishment of the prophecies.

Prophesying. In the New Testament this word usually means the public instruction and the worship rather than prediction. There were prophets, of course, in the Apostolic Church endowed with the knowledge of the future. Such was Agabus. It was more nearly our modern idea of preaching than that which we understand by Apostolic preaching. The Apostles were heralds, and so proclaimed the Gospel to all men,—its terms of mercy and its grand inclusiveness. But other subordinate officers could very properly resume these subjects and enforce them in the congregations of the faithful, and could urge the obligations of that holy religious life and the lofty morality of the Gospel. Prophesying was a gift, a charisma, and treated as such, as being especially suited to the needs of a new work. The possessor of it was treated with special consideration, and yet it happened that his conduct would lead to others slighting the usefulness of the charisma. Directions upon this are given very fully by St. Paul in the fourteenth chapter of 1 Corinthians and elsewhere. It is extended by some expositors to include the singing of the worship.

Prophet. The prophets of the Old Testament were nearly all in some way or other prophets of CHRIST. If not in word yet in type, as in the case of Jonah, whose prophecy is yet a history, whose history was a type of our LORD, and whose sole prophecy in the short sentence, "Yet forty days and Nineveh shall be destroyed," led to that repentance on the part of the Ninevites which has become the pattern of all preaching of repentance. Some of the prophets only appear once and then disappear from the sacred record,—a single message apparently, and then the messenger is discharged. Others again, as Elijah, bore a very prominent part in the political history of the nation. Elijah was the type of St. John the Baptist, who came in the power and grand sternness of the older prophet. But it is true that nearly all of those of whom any continuous account is given were in some way instruments in the preparation of the nation for the coming of the MESSIAH. Of these, the leading prophets, Moses, Isaiah, Jeremiah, Ezekiel, and Daniel, are the chief. Isaiah is indeed so full that he is called the Evangelical prophet. Next in extent of the prophecy, but not by any means less important in the contents of his prophecy, comes Daniel, then Jeremiah, and then Ezekiel, and, lastly, Moses. But it is to be understood that this ranging of them is only in the number and extent of their prophecies, for we may note that Moses gave but one principal prophecy of CHRIST, and that one which only describes his prophetic office; and yet so deep was the prophecy fixed in men's memory, that when St. John the Baptist began his preaching he was asked, "Art thou Elijah, art thou *that prophet?*" and of CHRIST, very many rightly believed that He was *that prophet.* They exercised a general advisory power. Ahijah, Elijah, Elisha, Isaiah, Jeremiah, are notable instances of this, and this office of advice, warning, and of authoritative interference was very seldom resented. The career of Elijah was very remarkable, as exercising a singular influence at a marked period of the history of Israel.

Was it necessary that the prophet should know the full extent and importance of his prophecy? That could hardly be. He was but the messenger, and did not need to know the import of his message. It was enough if he delivered it accurately, and in fact, there were many things to prevent his full conception of the prophecy. It was not in the Jew to realize all that was meant by the reception of the Gentile into the Covenant. He could not realize the conditions under which it afterwards became possible and passed into history; as now we cannot realize how the Jew is to be restored, for we cannot forecast accurately the political conditions under which alone it can be effected. All we know is that it surely will be. Again, while the prophets all contributed to the sum of the prophecies on the Messiah, they did not do so in sequence. After the prophecy of the person of the Messiah was clearly established, then each of the prophets had some special trait in His mission or person to describe. One gives one point, another a different one, but they all spake as that one HOLY SPIRIT gave to them, who was at the same time ruling and overruling the political and social development of men. They spake not of their own will, nor proclaimed their message as they pleased, but with a wisdom given from the HOLY GHOST they unfolded for us visions of the things yet to be, speaking only of those things which were revealed to them alone by GOD for our sakes.

The Jews grouped their prophets in the second of the triple division they made of the sacred books, the Law, the Prophets, and the Psalms. It is well worth adding that there can be no parting asunder of these as if they had no bonds. The Law contained prophecies, the Prophets illustrated and enforced the Law. The Psalms, in the service of the Law, repeated the Prophecies and offered them in solemn worship to GOD. Comparing several accounts and only giving central dates, we may suppose that the prophets would fall into something like this order: Hosea, 740 B.C. Joel, 800 B.C. Amos, 787 B.C. Obadiah, 877 B.C. Jonah, 840 B.C. Micah, 722 B.C. Isaiah, 758 B.C. Nahum, 660 B.C. Habbakuk, 630 B.C. Zephaniah, 630 B.C. Jeremiah, 600 B.C. Ezekiel, 580 B.C. Daniel, 580 B.C. Haggai, 520 B.C. Zechariah, 520 B.C. Malachi, 430 B C. This is probably as nearly correct as any arrangement that can now be made of them, since for two or three of them there is not sufficient indication or allusion to enable us to ascertain more than the approximate date at which they prophesied.

We must refer to the Commentaries and to Smith's Bible Dictionary for more extended information upon this most deeply interesting subject, since the questions that could be discussed are too many, and would lead us too far aside our purpose to permit them to be introduced here. (Horne's Introduction, Fairbairn's Prophecy: its Nature, Functions, and Interpretation, Lee on the Inspiration of Holy Scripture, Keith on the Prophecies,—a good book, but needing revision and addition.)

Propitiation. The word occurs but thrice in the English version (Rom. iii. 25; 1 John ii. 3). But the doctrine is of the foundation of our Faith. It means "the price of expiation," the "expiatory offering," and perfectly represents the verse in Hebrews, "He entered in once into the Holy Place, having obtained eternal redemption for us" (Heb. ix. 12). St. John uses the Greek word signifying Propitiation, the act or effective cause of GOD's being appeased, twice: once in the Comfortable words, and again in 1 John iv. 10, putting there the act for the actor, and so identifying, as is often done in Holy Scripture, the responsibility of the actor for the act. But St. Paul uses the word that signifies the mercy-seat, which word is of the same root as the one St. John uses. And St. Paul, by this word official, technical, identifies our LORD'S entrance into the Presence of Presences with the sacrifices of the day of Atonement, and with the entrance of the High-Priest into the Holy of Holies, and the sprinkling of the mercy-seat beneath the Cherubim with the blood of Atonement. In CHRIST is our covenant. His Law of Liberty is the interpretation of the Law on the Tables (2 Cor. iii. 3), and He is our Mercy-seat (*cf.* Rom. iii. 25, with Lev. xvi. 12, 13). Those types, then, that had to be themselves separated were combined by ritual into one act, as Aaron the Priest, with the Blood of the sin-offering, made atonement upon the mercy-seat. All these separate types meet in CHRIST, who is our High-Priest forever, making an atonement with His own blood, and is the Mercy-seat, the Propitiatory from which forgiveness is given to us. All these ceremonies centre upon Him who is our Advocate and our Propitiation.

Prosa. Upon the close of the singing of the Allelujah the voice dwelt upon and prolonged the cadence; this cadence later had words placed to the notes, and hence these were called a Sequence, or a Prosa. This custom dates from the ninth century. The words which were set to these cadences were often very beautiful and noble hymns. The *Veni Creator Spiritus*, *Lauda Sion*, and *Dies iræ*, are Sequences, since they were written to the music of the prolonged cadence of the Alleluia.

Protestant. The word Protestant came from the Protest of those Princes who protested at the II. Diet of Spires (1529 A.D.) against the revocation of a resolution of the I. Diet of Spires (1526 A.D.), which had granted to each Prince authority to regulate the ecclesiastical affairs of his jurisdiction until a General Council could be summoned. They protested against the breaking of the agreement, and warned the Emperor of the troubles which would follow. This is the origin of a term which has been wholly changed in its application to modern Christian bodies. If used simply to declare that the Church protests against error of every sort, it is proper enough. The Church of GOD protests against sin. She protests against heresy. She protests against false doctrine. She protests against usurpation. She protests against innovation. In this sense the Church must be protestant, and in no other. But when the term is made to include all who may be protestants against some doctrine they may fancy is wrong, and who claim it simply because they are not Romanists, then the term is misleading at least. Any body, of those who profess and call themselves Christians, that chooses, may protest against true doctrine, against ancient practices and worship, and claim to be Protestant. The Church cannot permit herself to be herded with these. The word is so extended as to mean principally those who hold mere negations of the Faith. It does not mean now an intelligent repudiation of Roman error and Papal usurpation, and an equally intelligent and earnest defense of the Catholic Faith and the Divine institution and authority of the Church. In these things the Church stands upon essentially different ground from the Protestant bodies around her, and Her position, which is perfectly clear and sound, seems to many even of Her own members to be anomalous and contradictory. It is not so, but it is rather the reverse. Under the title CHURCH the foundation of the Church has been set forth, and to that we refer for information, and it must follow that to be true to Her LORD, to the deposit of the Faith HE has given Her, and to Herself as HIS Body, she must teach positive truth. Therefore, as controversies and attacks upon Her vary, so Her position, ever the same, needs varying defenses. The protest against Rome has given Her Her title; but she as truly protests against the negations, now popular, the paring away of the faith, the shrunken defenses of doctrine, the casting away of ancient rites and worship among those who delight to call themselves Protestants.

Protevangelion. An apocryphal Gospel attributed to St. James. It was brought from the East by Protulus, who translated it from the Greek.

Prothesis. In the Eastern Church, (*a*) the room in which the elements are prepared for the Celebration. It is partly a vestry room and partly a chapelry, and varies in the different churches. In some it is really the Credence-table of the Western. In more costly and magnificent churches it is a chapel.

(*b*) The office of the Prothesis. It appears that the idea of the office was taken from the Tabernacle service, when the Table of the Shewbread was ordained. It is a solemn preparation of the elements in the Chapelry, or at the Side table, in quite a long service, after which the elements are taken in procession through the holy doors to the Altar. This service is of great antiquity, as it is alluded to in St. Cyril's Catechetical Lectures delivered in 380 A.D. in Jerusalem, as if then it was a customary part of the service.

Prothonotary. The chief of the notaries or scribes, the ecclesiastical officers who had various duties connected with collecting and registering the facts of Church affairs, often the recording the acts of the martyrs, the notes to be made of synodal decisions, the transcribing and preserving records, and similar functions. They were chiefly attached to the Church at Constantinople. They often discharged the double function of Registrars and Historiographers.

Prototype. The pattern upon which a thing is formed. Moses received the prototype of the Tabernacle from heaven. But the term has a theological sense, which removes it far above such a material use.

Adam was formed upon the prototype of the image of GOD. It is, then, a very important term, since it relates to our redemption in CHRIST. It has a bearing upon our LORD'S Human Nature, upon our Likeness in soul and body to Him, upon His restoring us, broken and tainted with sin, to His own likeness and righteousness, upon our immortal condition hereafter. How far have we fallen from that form in which we were created? What gulf lies between us and that prototype, the Image of GOD? and has that gulf been bridged by our LORD? The Scriptures are very explicit on some points, but totally silent on others. Man was formed after GOD'S image. But in what way we wear that glorious Image we cannot now know, for GOD is a Spirit, and the conditions and Image of a self-existent Spirit we cannot understand. But as to our restoration in CHRIST the Scriptures are equally explicit, and it was their purpose and office so to be. CHRIST is the very Image of GOD, in the form of GOD, the Image of the Invisible GOD, and took upon Himself the form of a servant for our sakes. He became man, and the prototype became a partaker of the nature of the type, and He by this act bound Himself to us and us to Him for our restoration. He is in us, in a real, true, restoring sense. By our transfiguration (cf. Rom. xii. 2, and St. Matt. xvii. 2) we are restored to that archetype, a restoration which will not be completed till the body and soul shall be re-joined at the resurrection. But the means thereto given us are many, and pertain to every form of our bodily and spiritual life. Our baptism is a new birth. Our confirmation is the sanctification of our bodies and souls as Temples of GOD. Our Services in His House place us in the gleam of His glorious presence. Our absolutions are constant restorations to His favor. Our communions the medicine of the soul and body now, and the food for our future restoration. Our benedictions put His holy name upon us. So that in the Holy Church we have the means and graces given us for a renewing, a remoulding, a transforming of ourselves in heart and will, in soul and body, till we be completely restored to that prototype in the splendor of the Image of GOD in which we were created.

Proverbs. The collection of pithy, wise sentences into a single book. The word proverb has several meanings, of "byword," "sharp saying," often witty, sometimes sarcastic, always containing a practical truth. Some proverbs have grown up among the people, some have been framed as maxims by men having deep insight and knowledge of human nature. Some have been framed of utterances which had originally no connection with proverbial wisdom. The proverb may contain a half truth and so mislead, were it not counterbalanced by some other proverb which contains its correlative.

PROVERBS, the Book of Proverbs, is usually and hastily attributed as a single composition to King Solomon. The express statements in the thirtieth chapter, "The words of the son of Jakeh," and in the thirty-first chapter, "The words of King Lemuel, the prophecy that his mother taught him," at a glance show that it must have received at least these two appendices; but turning to chapter twenty-five we read, "These are also the proverbs of Solomon, which the men of Hezekiah, King of Judah, copied out." And again, the tenth chapter begins briefly the Proverbs of Solomon. We find, then, at least five collections of proverbs, made at different times,—the first (ch. i.-ix. 18) claimed by Solomon; the second (ch. x.-xxiv. 34) briefly headed as his; the third (ch. xxv.-xxix. 27) collected by the men of Hezekiah, and so far the whole bears Solomon's name, but the other two appendices (ch. xxx. and ch. xxxi.) are by different men. Who Agur and King Lemuel were cannot be known, whether mere names placed there by the composer, or whether they were men living later than Hezekiah. But it is far more devout and reasonable to suppose that they were really men, for Holy Scripture does not need to borrow fictitious names to commend its writings. The Rabbins say that these were names of King Solomon. It has also been claimed that only the second section (ch. x.-xxiv.) can be Solomon's, since it is in a different style from the first. But the first verse is decisive of this, and the argument from style is a very doubtful one. There may be such marked disagreements in style that we cannot certainly know that the composition under criticism could have been the work of the alleged author, but there is always something in and under the style itself, the tone of thought, which is determining. Hence from the very variety of the subjects discussed no such criticism can hold good. The Book of Proverbs, then, is principally by King Solomon with these additions. Its contents, then, can be grouped into the five divisions pointed out above. The first is a description of true wisdom, beginning with the precept which runs through the whole of the Bible, "The fear of the LORD is the beginning of knowledge" (Prov.), "of wisdom" (Psalm), and ends with a splendid description of wisdom, which can only have its personification in CHRIST, and points in the closing verses with a terribly significant warning against the strange woman whose guests are in the depths of Sheol. The second section is made up of sententious, pithy verses, short, pointed, and clear, composed in the style of poetry, so common among the Jews, which brings out the antithesis of the thought, for example:

"A wise son maketh a glad father:
But a foolish son is the heaviness of his mother."

These proverbs are so simple and transparent in language that they seem as though they need hardly to be uttered, yet in their very simplicity there is a depth of insight which can only come from one who, however he misused it for himself, yet had received wisdom from on high. There are half truths uttered here and there, but there is always its correlate at hand in an apparently contradictory proverb. As in the well known proverb (Prov. xxvi. 4, 5), "Answer not a fool according to his folly, lest thou be also like unto him;" which is balanced by "Answer a fool according to his folly, lest he be wise in his own conceit." There are other contradictory proverbs, which led some of the Rabbins to doubt if the books were canonical, but the decision was characteristic. "And even the Book of Proverbs they sought to make apocryphal because its words were contradictory the one to the other. And wherefore did they not make it apocryphal? The words of the book Koheleth (Ecclesiastes) are not apocryphal, we have looked and found the sense: here also we must look." It is a mark of the Solomonic writings that they are contradictory. But is not that the result of his strange contradictory career? Wise above all others, and using his divine gift wrongly, plunging into all human knowledge, and so into the depths of the double sins of pride and idolatry, his proverbs must have the same contradictory nature in them. It is objected that some proverbs are those of a man of business, or of a householder, or of an ordinary citizen, of a keen observer of, but not participant in, politics, and surely a king could not so write. The objection is strange, for if there are given proverbs upon all these ranks and businesses, they should be in the true line of the character represented, and one like King Solomon, able to stand apart and criticise himself as in Ecclesiastes, could surely write wise sayings from these several stand-points.

There are about fourteen quotations in the New Testament from this book. Our Lord quotes it once, but in a form which also occurs in the Law; St. Paul seven times, with probable allusions elsewhere. St. James four times; St. Peter four times; St. John once, in his first epistle. For us this establishes the authority of the Book upon indisputable grounds. It was read in the public services of the Church; and in the Calendar of our own Prayer-Book it is read both through the month of August in the daily service, and it is appointed for the Sundays after Trinity, beginning with the twenty-third.

Providence. Providence means foresight. The term is generally used in a religious sense to signify God's care over all things which He has made. The idea was not unknown to the heathen world. We see it in Homer's golden chain reaching from heaven to earth. Cicero speaks of the providence of the gods. While Natural Religion gives some idea of the providence of God, His care, as opposed to blind Fortune and mere accident, is especially shown in the Word of Revelation. God controls all things so as to promote the highest good of the whole. "The Providence of God displays omnipresence, omniscience, omnipotence, holiness, justice, and benevolence." The telescope shows God's wonder-working power in the heavenly bodies, while the microscope discloses new beauties in the vegetable kingdom and "the insect world." If nature could work of herself, then, as Sir Thomas Browne says, "let our hammers rise up and boast that they have built our houses, and our pen receive the honor of our writings." The mechanic preserves the object of his skill, the parent guides the child, so God preserves the universe. "By the word of the Lord were the heavens made" (Ps. xxxiii. 6). "The Lord looketh from heaven; He beholdeth all the sons of men" (ver. 13). The regularity of the seasons shows a governing Mind. In moral life, the blessings of the righteous and the punishments of the wicked display the working of God's hand. The final result will be seen at the Judgment-day. God's care over the preservation of His Sacred Word and His Holy Church, and His dividing the nations of the world according to His will, and then condescending to number the hairs of man's head, and watch the sparrow's fall, and paint the lily, are indications of the extent and minuteness of His Providence. The xci. Psalm narrates how God specially watches over the righteous, and gives them in charge of His angels. In the magnificent civ. Psalm all creation waits upon Him, and He opens His hand, and fills all things with good. In God "we live, and move, and have our being" (Acts xvii. 28). In Hebrews i. 3, we behold God in the Person of Christ, "upholding all things by the word of His power." St. James in his Epistle (chap. i. 17) assures us that "every good gift and every perfect gift is from above." Even afflictive dispensations may be a part of God's providence, and end in good, as seen in the cases of Job, and in the history of Joseph's humiliation and exaltation and in losses by death, where human judgment is puzzled.

Even handicraft is to be traced to God's providence. Bezaleel was filled "with the spirit of God, in wisdom" to do the work of the Tabernacle, as well as his companions (Ex. xxxi. 1-6). Of the plowman it is said that "his God doth instruct him in discretion" in breaking the clods and casting in the wheat (Isa. xxviii. 24–29).

The Christian idea of Providence is that all things, great and small, are under the ceaseless care and guidance of God. That while He calleth the stars by their names (Isa. xi. 26), and hath established the earth (Ps. cxix. 90), still, He humbleth Himself to hear the prayer of every fainting heart, and even the cry of the young raven (Job xxxviii. 41).

If God guides great events, small affairs must be also in His hand, for from apparent trifles great things proceed. The doctrine of a general Providence must imply that of a special one, though man is not always able to trace the "footsteps of GOD marching through time."

Authorities: Rev. James D. Butler, in Kitto's Cyclopædia of Biblical Literature, McCosh on the Divine Government, Chalmer's Astronomical Discourses, Baring-Gould's Post-Mediæval Preachers.

REV. S. F. HOTCHKIN.

Provinces. When our LORD ascended up on high, He did not leave His entire authority with St. Peter, telling all the other Apostles that they should render implicit obedience in all things to him,—which is the Papal theory; but He said, "As My Father hath sent Me, even so send I you" (in the plural); and "Lo, I am with you (plural again) alway, even unto the end of the world." The entire Episcopate, therefore, could it be assembled and speak unitedly, would be to us as the Voice of the HOLY GHOST Himself ("it seemed good to the HOLY GHOST and to us." Acts xv. 28). The definitions of the undisputed General Councils are substantially such utterances, and therefore they are of œcumenical and perpetual authority. Now there are only three possible theories in regard to the exercise of Episcopal power: 1st. That the Pope is the sole real Bishop, the others being only his deputies, and subject to his arbitrary power. 2d. That each individual Bishop has all power within himself, with no liability to correction or restraint from any other; which would make as many Popes as Bishops, and render real unity impossible. 3d. That the power is in the *Order*, the authority of each individual being *inseparable* from that of the Order, and every official action, therefore, being amenable to the superior authority of the *Order*, whenever called in question by any. This is simply St. Cyprian's famous rule: "*Episcopatus unus est, cujus a singulis in solidum pars tenetur.*" In matters of ordinary occurrence it would be entirely impracticable to get the judgment of all the Bishops in the world, and therefore the Catholic Church has, from the earliest antiquity, been subdivided into portions of convenient size, so that, in each, there might easily be joint action in the ordinary administration of Church discipline. In ascertaining the boundaries of these, the Church—having exactly the same reasons as the State for seeking convenience of action—uniformly accepted the State division of *Provinces*, conforming her ecclesiastical organization to the lines laid down by the civil government. Each Province had a number of Bishops and Dioceses,—seldom less than four or five,—often as many as fifteen or twenty. They were numerous enough to continue the Apostolic Succession of the Bishops in case of any vacancy; and, to show their essential equality, it was the rule that whenever there was a vacancy in their chief See, the other Bishops of the Province should unite in consecrating their own Metropolitan.

The chief Bishop of the Province was, almost without exception, the Bishop of the Metropolis, or chief city, and therefore he was styled *Metropolitan*. The assembled Bishops of the Province represented the original College of the Apostles, and there was *no* ecclesiastical matter whatsoever, arising within the Province, which might not be appealed to their decision, from any part of the Province whatsoever. And *no* question could be carried *out* of the Province, to be settled elsewhere, unless perchance it was a question of Faith. Moreover, the assembled Bishops of the Province formed a Provincial Synod, with power to make Canons (subject to those of National or General Councils); and no single Diocese had any power of the kind. Where a nation was of small extent, or few in population, there might not be room for more than one Province within its bounds; and in that case the Province and the National Church were identical. But when the Nation was larger, it was subdivided into two or more Provinces, and all these Provinces, united, formed the National Church. And each National Church was organized under its own Chief Bishop, in accordance with the 34th of the Apostolical Canons:—"It is necessary that the Bishops of every Nation [ἑκάστου ἔθνους] should know who is chief among them, and should recognize him as their head by doing nothing of great moment without his consent," etc. In the Church of Scotland, which is small, there is only one Province, and that Province is therefore the National Church. In England there are two Provinces, Canterbury and York, and it takes both of these, united, to make the National Church. In this country we began, like Scotland, with Church people few and feeble. Our one Province was our National Church. As a Province of the Holy Catholic Church, our Provincial Synod (which we call the GENERAL CONVENTION) has all the powers belonging to the ancient Provincial Synods, which it may choose to exercise. As to Doctrine, it is bound to accept, and does accept, the definitions of the Faith as set forth by the undisputed General Councils. As to Discipline and Worship it inherits, through the English Branch, the entire system of the Holy Catholic Church, with the alteration of such minor details as local circumstances may require; but its decisions on these points are not subject to the revision of any other authority. The erection and subdivision of Dioceses, the election and confirmation and consecration of Bishops, the ordination of Priests and Deacons, the entire legislation on Worship and Discipline,— this, or as much of it as may seem advisable, is *inherently* in the hands of the General Convention, as being a Provincial Synod and a National Church, all in one. Our

Presiding Bishop is recognized as our Chief Bishop, in full accordance with the 34th of the Apostolic Canons.

But as our one Province has grown till it covers the immense territory of the United States, with sixty or seventy Bishops in the Provincial Synod, the conviction is being forced upon the minds of thoughtful men that we *must* have something intermediate between the General Convention and the single Diocese. Parts of the ancient work of a Province have become impossible with us. Anciently, the Provincial Synod was required to meet *twice* a *year*, so as to hear promptly all appeals from any quarter that might be sent up. But our General Convention, having associated large numbers of clergy and laity with the Bishops, for better legislative action, has, from the first, felt itself disqualified for the exercise of Appellate powers, and we have been *without any appeal whatsoever*. Moreover, at first, the territory of an entire State was included in each Diocese. This was in accordance with the general practice of the Catholic Church, in accepting civil divisions as the proper boundaries of Ecclesiastical jurisdictions. But as the larger Dioceses have needed subdivision, this original principle has been unwisely departed from. New York has now five Dioceses, each of which is as independent of the other four as if New York had been subdivided into five separate *States*. The proper remedy for this is, not to abandon the subdivision of our larger Dioceses,—which is becoming more necessary every day,—but to understand that, with a National Church so extensive as ours is now, our original identity of a National Church with one single Province is *outgrown:* and while our General Convention remains as the voice of our National Church, we *must* have the organization of many separate Provinces in subordination to that chief authority. This cannot be done by one sudden, transforming act: it must come by gradual growth. It cannot come by arbitrarily binding together a number of Dioceses, each (from its foundation) embracing an independent State. In their Ecclesiastical arrangements of Provinces (or what occupy the practical position of Provinces) State lines have been ignored by Roman Catholics, Presbyterians, Methodists, and others. But that which is so peculiar and indestructible a feature of our National life *must not* be disregarded by the Church of America. The true remedy, therefore, is to look forward to the time when each *State* (with perhaps two exceptions) will become a *Province*. Illinois, with its three Dioceses of Chicago, Quincy, and Springfield, has already become a Province, name and thing, with its Provincial Synod and Court of Appeal. New York and Pennsylvania show that they are contemplating something of the same sort. In this form the change will be gradual, one State after another coming into line, as it is ready. The easiest way to accomplish the result will be for a State Diocese to subdivide, at the first, into three or four Dioceses, *continuing over* its Diocesan Convention with only one change in its Constitution; and that is, that whenever a question is taken "by Orders" the Order of Bishops—of whom there will then be three or four—shall have a separate and coordinate vote.

The entire power of *legislation* (subordinate to that of General Convention) should eventually be left in the hands of these Provincial Synods. The legislation of one small Diocese is so commonly the reflection of the peculiarities of its own Bishop for the time being, that it cannot win a sufficient solidity for permanent effect. But legislation by a group of Dioceses, all springing from a common source (the original State Diocese), and with a separate approval of the Bishops as an Order, and with a Provincial Court of Appeal to enforce that legislation by a consistent treatment in actual cases : all this would add effectiveness and stability to every part of our Church system. When there was a cheap and easy remedy provided (in the Court of Appeals) for any possible abuse, it would be *safe to trust the Bishops with much more of administrative power*. Until then it would *not* be safe. Let us look ahead a few years, then, and see how a proper Provincial System would appear in action. Each large State (at least) would be a Province, having four or more Dioceses,—some, perhaps, from ten to twenty Dioceses. Each Diocese would have all the rights it has at present, except that of making and altering Constitution and Canons. It would elect its own Bishop, Secretary, Treasurer, Standing Committee, Deputies to General Convention, etc., and conduct its own Diocesan Missions. The Provincial Synod, containing all the Bishops of the Province, and clerical and lay members in proportion to the numbers of clergy and communicants in the Dioceses respectively, would have the sole power of legislation, subordinate to that of General Convention. The support and government of Educational and Charitable Institutions, and some organization by which the weaker parts of the Province might be helped by the stronger in the work of Home Missions, would also form subjects for Provincial action. The Court of Appeals would furnish a ready remedy for any grievance or abuse occurring anywhere in the Province. For all purposes *except* legislation, there might be a *temporary* union of State Dioceses to form a Province. But it should be *essential* to any such temporary arrangement that any State Diocese should, *ipso facto*, become a Province as soon as it had three or four Dioceses of its own. In each Province, the Bishop of the chief city—consecrated by the other Bishops of the Province —would be the Metropolitan or President of the Province ; and when the Dioceses in a State were sufficiently numerous, the rights of confirming and consenting to the election of a Bishop, and the erection of new Sees, now exercised by the entire American Church, should be secured solely to the Province concerned. The General Convention should be *left undisturbed just where it is now*. Once in three years is not too often for it to meet. And *every Bishop* should attend, and *every Diocese* should be represented in both orders. In all probability by that time each Diocese would be content to send only one or two deputies, instead of four of each Order. And the General Convention might, of its own accord, reserve to itself all legislation on intercommunion with other branches of the Church, all decisions on Doctrine, all legislation on the Prayer-Book and Ritual, and some chief points of Discipline, leaving all other matters to the Provincial Synods. But even these possible changes are no necessary part of the Provincial System, which might be carried into effect, leaving General Convention entirely unaffected. The change needed is to be wrought by *elevating the State Dioceses into Provinces*, and not by interfering with General Convention in any way.

REV. J. H. HOPKINS, D.D.

Provision. A usurped intrusion of the Pope upon the right of patronage to Ecclesiastical Benefices in England. It was an arbitrary intrusion, placing Italian clerks into English cures which they never saw, but from which they drew the revenues. It was stoutly resented by the Laity, and the statutes of provisors made under Edward III. (1355 A.D.) and Richard II. (1385 A.D.) followed with some success the ingenious devices for evasion by the Canon lawyers of the Roman Curia. Still, the Pope retained the power to set aside the canonical rights of the Ecclesiastical patrons, and to present to Benefices in their gift *mero motu*. Of course all this was stopped at the Reformation.

Psalms, The. The Psalms are sacred poetry, although they do not have the poetical form usually recognized in modern times. They have the peculiar form of Hebrew poetry, which contained what may be styled "thought rhythm" or "parallelism."

The sentiment is so distributed that, as thought succeeds thought, it is connected with what precedes. Sometimes the links of connection are arbitrary, and sometimes they depend upon the repetition of a word or its antithesis.

The use of poetic imagery is common as in modern poetry, and the language of emotion largely prevails.

The Psalms treat of a great variety of topics. They were written not all at once nor by one author, but during a period of some centuries. They reflect the sentiments of their authors in that they were the outpourings of their hearts. It is this latter quality which makes them so well suited for the expression of our own religious feelings. Love, joy, hope, trust, sorrow for sin, fear, and some others are common, or may be common to all, and hence a man to-day may adopt the expressions used by him who lived many centuries ago.

They are especially valuable now in the expression of Christian experiences, inasmuch as they are the productions of men inspired by the HOLY GHOST, and were designed to be of permanent value and of lasting use. While they were true as the outpouring of the soul's emotions when written by David, or Ethan, or Asaph, they are equally true if they become the soul's expressions to-day. They set forth such and such things as true and in the connections when they were first composed, but beyond this they have a meaning which they were intended to have for later generations of men.

Many versions of the Psalms have been made. The most prominent are the Septuagint, the Vulgate, the English, and the German, besides the translations into all the dialects of men. Vast stores of learning have been used in the elucidation of their meaning, and in the tracing up of their history, and with many a devotional writer they have been the favorite study.

They have helped to quicken the devotions of the private Christian, and to swell the praises of the great congregation. The most earnest and pious students of sacred lore have regarded them as a treasury whence may be gathered precious truths concerning CHRIST and His Church which GOD the HOLY GHOST has inspired. Many holy and learned expositors have striven humbly, but earnestly, and with deep faith to search the Psalms for the things which speak of the Heavenly Bridegroom and His Bride, and have found beneath the references to Israel and David, and the most common things, hidden allusions to One greater than all, and have brought sweetness out of the carcass of the lion slain by the wayside.

Among the many questions of interest which are suggested by the study of the Psalms are those which relate to their Canonical Position and Titles, their Authorship, their Occasions, their Use in the Jewish Service, their Exegesis, their Prophetical Character, their Poetical peculiarities, and the Musical references attached to them.

Of their use in Christian Worship, and their Christian Adaptations, something will be found under the heading "THE PSALTER."

The Psalms may be grouped under six general heads. Below will be found the names of the groups, with some illustrations under each.

1st. *Prayer and Penitence.*—Psalms vi., xxv., xxxii., xxxv., xxxviii., li., lxiii., lxiv., cii., cix., cxl.

2d. *Thanksgiving.*—ix., xviii., xxii., lxxv., cxxiv., cxxix., cxxxv., cxxxvi., cxlix.

3d. *Adoration.*—xxiii., xxxiv., c., civ., cxi., cxxxix., cxlvii., cl.

4th. *Instructive.*—i., v., vii., ix., lxxxiv. cxix., cxxviii., cxxxiii.

5th. *Prophetical.*—ii., xvi., xxii., xl., xlv., lxviii., lxxii., lxxxvii., cx.

6th. *Historical.*—lxxviii., cv., cvi.

Commentaries upon the Psalms are numerous. Among the most valuable are Bishop Horne's, Isaac Williams's, "The Psalms interpreted by CHRIST," and Lange's Commentary. While the scholar will of course study them in the original Hebrew, the English student will find valuable help by comparing the King James' version with the Prayer-Book version; the latter being smooth and expressive, retaining with singular force the meaning of the original. Still further help will be found by examining some of the translations in which the peculiarities of Hebrew poetry are retained by means of Parallelisms, although no translation can preserve fully the distinctive traits of the original poetic form.

REV. G. W. SHINN.

Psalter, The. The common name for the collection of Psalms as they are used in divine service is the *Psalter.* They are frequently spoken of as *The Psalms of David,* because David composed the larger number of them. The other authors to whom some are ascribed are Solomon, Moses, Hezekiah, Ezra, Ethan, and Asaph. The authorship of others is unknown.

Many of them were used in the Temple service of the Jews, while Solomon's Temple was standing, but others came later, after the return from the captivity. All of the 150 were used in divine worship by the Jews during the four centuries preceding the coming of CHRIST, and were at once adopted as part of the ritual of the Christian Church when it was established, and have continued in use in the Church during all these eighteen Christian centuries.

The Psalter was early divided into five parts, as may be seen by the doxologies at the end of the 41st, 72d, 89th, and 106th Psalms, but the principle upon which the division was made by the Jews is not very evident.

In the Christian Church this division was disregarded, and there grew up various modes of using them. In later ages some were appointed for certain days and seasons, and finally, in the English Church, they were distributed through the month for Morning and Evening Prayer, beginning with the first on the first day of the month and ending with the last on the thirtieth day, with special selections for certain seasons. There are various modes of saying or singing them in divine service. Sometimes they are sung as a chorus, by the choir and people, but as often sung antiphonally. In places where they are not sung they are read responsively by the minister and people.

The Prayer-Book version of the Psalter is not the same as the King James' Version as found in our Bibles. It is taken from the first authorized version of our English Bible, put forth in 1540 A.D.

The use of the Psalms in Christian worship has always been a very marked feature. The Psalter is the great Song Book of the Church. There are some general principles worthy of note, and which will show the fitness of the Psalms for use in Christian assemblies. The first of these is the fact that *God designed the Jewish Church to be in many things the type of the Christian Church.*

In the history of the Jewish Church we have accounts of its deliverance from bondage, of its being led through the wilderness, of its crossing the Red Sea and the Jordan, of its settlement in Canaan, of its conflicts with the people of that land, and of the gradual development of its ritual and laws.

In each of these particulars it typified similar things pertaining to the Christian Church. There are deliverances from bondage of sin and the world, wearing marchings through trials, feeding upon food from heaven, conflict with foes, and the growth of the divine life and energy in the souls of believers.

Transfer, then, much of what is said about Israel to the Christian Church, and it will be found to be as true as if written only to-day.

The second principle is that *Moses, David, and Solomon were in some particulars types of Christ* Moses was the leader from bondage, David the founder of the prosperity of the kingdom, and Solomon the wisest of kings and the man of peace.

In whatever there was of excellence in these works, and in the character of the workers, there are contained predictions of Him who is the leader of His people, the Wisdom of GOD, and the Prince of Peace.

The third principle is that *some of the Psalms are direct prophecies of Christ and His Church, and others have a double fulfillment, first in the things near at hand, and then in those under the Christian dispensation.*

This application of the Psalms was made by CHRIST and His Apostles on various occasions. Thus, for example, He predicted the treachery of Judas in words from the 49th Psalm, while on the cross He poured out His lamentation in words from the 22d. When St. Peter spoke of His resurrection he quoted from the 16th Psalm.

The fourth principle is, that *the Psalms are the expression of the religious experiences of men in general.* They are the outpourings of the heart in gladness and in sorrow, in penitence and in faith, in hope and in fear.

A very simple adaptation of the Psalms to Christian uses may be made by transferring mentally the figures used to their present Christian equivalents, thus:

Afflictions of David = Afflictions of CHRIST.

David by name and Character = Type of CHRIST.

Enemies of the King = Enemies of CHRIST.

House of **Aaron** = Christian Ministers.
King's daughter = The Church.
Moab, Edom, and others = Enemies of the Church.
Sanctuary = The Christian Church.
Sacrifices = Christ's one offering.
Sins of Israel = Sins of Christians.

Rev. G. W. Shinn.

Public Worship. The desire to worship pervades the heathen as well as the Christian world. So strong is it that men have adored gold and silver images, the work of their own hands, or even animals and vegetables. The first idea of worship in a proper sense is that of the individual communing with God. Adam in Eden, Moses on Mount Sinai, Abraham in the starry night (Gen. xv.), are examples of primitive religion. The mountain-top, the sea-side, or the arched grove are fitting places to adore the Creator. But men must associate for such a purpose to quicken each other in devotion. They must be sheltered from the weather, and it is desirable that beautiful buildings should be erected to the honor and glory of God. Plutarch says, "It is possible to find cities without walls, without letters, without kings, without wealth, without coin, without schools and theatres, but a city without a temple, or that useth no worship, prayers, and so forth, no one ever saw." He believed that a city might more easily be built without a foundation than a community of men retain any cohesion without religion. The worship of Moses is shared by others when they see God (Ex. xxiv. 9, 10). Common, public worship is a duty and a privilege. The children of God's family come before their Heavenly Father for absolution and benediction, and for receiving spiritual food, and acknowledging benefits received. Public service should be formal and orderly, decent and reverent (1 Cor. xiv. 40). Each one should be early at church, if possible, to get the full benefit of the service. There should be no whispering. A Jewish teacher taught this in a comparison: if a man were presenting a petition to a king he would not be talking to his neighbor, much more should we come reverently before God. Worship implies self-abasement, confession, supplication, contemplation of God, and desire for communion with Him through Christ, by the aid of the Holy Spirit. As frequent taking of bodily food is necessary, so frequent worship is needed to renew spiritual life. It was our Saviour's custom to worship in the Jewish Synagogue (St. Luke iv. 16, 43). On the Mountain of the Transfiguration He prayed with His disciples, (St. Luke ix. 28, 29; see also xi. 1). He promises His presence where two or three worship Him (St. Matt. xviii. 20). The Apostles combined in worship (Acts i. 13, 14, 24, and ii. 1, and St. Luke 24, 53). At Pentecost the Holy Spirit descended among faithful worshipers. Not to forsake assembling ourselves together is a Scripture injunction (Heb. x. 25). St. Paul wills "that men pray everywhere" (1 Tim. ii. 8). Public worship is an open profession of faith in Christ, and love for Him. It keeps up a sense of religion. It is a means of receiving instruction and partaking in worship, and receiving the Holy Sacraments, and it is a good example to others. Proper teaching influences unbelievers to join in Christian worship (1 Cor. xiv. 25). The service should be solemn: God is "greatly to be feared in the assembly of the saints and to be had in reverence" (Ps. lxxxix. 7). Public worship is to be cheerful "with gladness" and "singing" (Ps. c.). It must be spiritual, as "God is a Spirit" (St. John iv. 24). The humble soul is the temple of God (Isa. lvii. 15; 1 Cor. vi. 19). God is to be worshiped "in the beauty of holiness" (1 Chron. xvi. 29; Ps. xxix. 2, and xcix. 9). Gold, and silver, and brass, and stone were marvelously wrought together in the Jewish Temple to make it a suitable place for the worship of the all-glorious God. To it the longing eye of the Jew turned in prayer wherever he might be (1 Kings viii.; Ps. v. 7, and xiii. 8. 2). A picture of united worship before the building of the Temple, but when it has been prepared for, occurs in 1 Chron. xxix. 20. Josephus says that the Jew would sooner cease to breathe than to worship. In the Tabernacle service the thought of a present God was ever before the Israelites, "as at the moving of the ark Moses prayed, Rise up, Lord. . . . And when it rested, he said, Return, O Lord, unto the many thousands of Israel" (Numb. x. 35, 36). In the Jewish worship the children were not forgotten, they heard the prayer of the Tabernacle service, and they also stood in the courts of the sacred Temple. They were "planted in the house of the Lord," and so they flourished "in the courts of our God" (Ps. xcii. 13). So should they "bring forth fruit in old age" (v. 14). Would to God that the children of Christian parents were all to-day found with their fathers and mothers in the Church of God, then might we hope the early habit would breed a life custom, and they would "dwell in the house of the Lord forever" (Ps. xxiii. 6). The great day of early Christian worship was the Lord's day (Acts xx. 7; 1 Cor. xvi. 2). Wednesday and Friday became special Church days, the former in remembrance of Christ's betrayal, and the latter of His crucifixion. Saints' Days keep in remembrance the dead in Christ. Pliny in describing primitive Christians says, "that they affirmed of their worship that they met in the early morning, and sang a hymn by turns to Christ as God." The poor persecuted saints kept up their responsive worship when death stared them in the face. When persecution ceased, the anthem and prayer rose in vast cathedrals, and kings and queens were nursing fathers and mothers to the Church. So the song begun in Eden has floated through ages, and Tabernacle, and Temple, and Synagogue have given way to the Christian Church, and we hope for a time when every knee shall bow to CHRIST, and a redeemed world shall praise Him as GOD.

Such is heaven's worship as seen by St. John. The Lamb of GOD is its centre (Rev. v. 5, 6). An inner circle of worshipers is formed by the four living creatures and the four-and-twenty elders with harps and "golden vials" filled with "the prayers of the saints." They sing the new song to the glorified CHRIST. Outside of this circle is another of thousands of angels, singing "Worthy is the Lamb that was slain to receive power." Beyond these is a "third sphere," containing all created living things "in heaven and on earth, and under the earth, and in the sea," and they join in praising the Lamb of GOD. If such is the occupation of heaven, those who hope to enter that blessed abode should learn the divine song on earth, "When ye exalt Him (GOD), put forth all your strength, and be not weary; for ye can never go far enough" (Ecclesiasticus 43, 30). An ancient writer declares that the responses of the primitive Church sounded like thunder. Bishop White in his lectures on the Catechism (Dissn. 13) shows how favored we are in a service which gives the people so much Scripture reading, and a responsive service, and a proper bodily worship. Let us rightly use our good heritage.

Authorities: Life of Isaac Walton prefixed to Walton's Lives, Buck's Theolog. Dict., John Howe's Living Temple, Gilfillan's Sabbath, Lardner's Introd., Liddon's Bampton Lectures. REV. S. F. HOTCHKIN.

Pulpit. The first mention of a pulpit is in Nehemiah viii. 4, from which Ezra read the book of the Law to the people. In the early Eastern Church the Ambon was the pulpit, at least St. Chrysostom used it so, though the Bishop usually preached sitting in his chair. Later it became more common. The word Pulpit came to the Church from the theatre. It was the stage on which the actors performed their parts. This would indicate to us the raised platform, whether of wood or of stone, which is now in use, is of Western origin; and since the arrangement of the Eastern Churches was so different from those of the Western Basilicas, it is very probable that it was so, the Eastern Church using a movable frame (*analogeion*), which apparently was the proper place for the Epistle and Gospel. Often there were two *analogeia*,—one for each Scripture. The pulpit is usually upon the Gospel side, though not necessarily so.

Purgatory. The Roman figment of a purgatory has had its rise first in an opinion which some of the Fathers held that there was a cleansing from all but mortal sins, either by death itself, or after death, and this was based upon a deep sense of the loathsomeness of sin and our own imperfect efforts at repentance, and upon the obscure words of St. Paul in 1 Cor. iii. 13-15, but it was only an opinion. St. Augustine (398 A.D.) expressed it very cautiously, giving the opinions of some, and goes on to say, "I will not argue about it, for *perhaps* it may be true." He treats it as a mere opinion and no more. St. Chrysostom thinks the fire St. Paul speaks of is of trial and not of cleansing, and so it is destructive. But Gregory I. (590 A.D.), in his dialogues upon the dead, gave form and popularity to the opinion which grew up vaguely in this interval of two hundred years. The opinion never got a foothold in the Eastern Church, and when in 1439 A.D., at Florence, the Greek Bishops in their political distress, being pressed by the Turks, and needing Western aid for their defense, were induced to agree to the doctrine of a purgatory, but had first to ask what it was. The reply, asserting the efficacy of prayers and intercessions for the dead, went on to say, "But whether purgatory is a fire, or a mist, or a whirlwind, or anything else, we do not dispute to." Vague as this was, when the action of the Bishops was called home, it was indignantly repudiated by the whole East, with the other definitions which the Bishops had agreed to. The XXII. Article rightly calls it "a fond thing, vainly invented, and grounded on no warranty of Scripture, but rather repugnant to the word of GOD." (*Vide* Browne, XXXIX. Articles, Tomlin's Elements of Theology, Blunt's Dict. of Doct. and Hist. Theology.)

Purification of Saint Mary the Virgin. *Vide* PRESENTATION OF CHRIST IN THE TEMPLE.

Puritans. The Novatians of the third century were styled Cathari or Puritans, on account of their strict discipline and high requirements as to the excellence of Christians. While such a Purist spirit may be traced in the history of the Church, in modern times the name Puritans has been given to a party in the English Church in the sixteenth and seventeenth centuries which tried to introduce Genevan doctrine and Calvin's discipline in place of the system of the English Reformation. The name was first used about 1564 A.D. (Fuller's Ch. Hist., ix. 63) for a party in the English Church, but afterwards it was applied to the Separatists, who left her fold. These Separatists afterwards took various names, Independents, etc. The Puritan idea was a floating element in the Church of England for two centuries before the name was given. In the latter part of the reign of Henry VIII. the Calvinistic system was arranged. Calvin had some influence in England in the reign of Edward VI., and some of his followers obtained positions in the English Church, viz., Peter Martyr, Martin Bucer, and others. The Puritans desired to overthrow Episcopacy and alter the Prayer-Book. They objected to Church vestments, and sponsors and the sign of the cross in Holy Baptism, and the wedding-ring, and the observance of Festivals or Holy-days, and the Cathedral worship and antiphonal chanting and responsive service and the use of organs and Confirmation. Hooker's great work on Ecclesiastical Polity was drawn out by the Puritan controversy. The Jesuits are said to have officiated as Puritan preachers to sow discord. In the reigns of Queen Elizabeth and the Stuarts the troubles were much mixed with governmental affairs. The Long Parliament abolished the use of the Prayer-Book, but after the Puritan triumph they were broken by Sectarianism into various bands. They highly appreciated their own times, but despised much that was ancient, and destroyed "national heirlooms."

The "joyful noise" and "pleasant harp" of Ps. lxxxi., the praise of "young men, and maidens, old men, and children" (Ps. xiv. 8), and the "trumpet" and "highsounding cymbals" (Ps. cl.), hardly describe a Puritan service. GOD's natural works in the beautiful sky, and varied landscape, the singing birds, the motion and rejoicing of young animals and children show that the CREATOR made a glad world. Joy is to be a ruling power in religion, even in affliction. "Rejoice in the LORD alway, and again I say rejoice" (Phil. iv. 4). While the Church has her Ash-Wednesday and Good-Friday, she must also sing her glad songs on Christmas and Easter. While a system may be condemned noble men in that system must be honored, and Coleridge rightly says, "The diffusion of light and knowledge through this kingdom by the exertions of Bishops and clergy, by Episcopalians and Puritans, from Edward VI. to the restoration was as wonderful as it is praiseworthy, and may be justly placed among the most remarkable facts of history." The stanch Churchman, Dr. Johnson, pronounced all of Baxter's works good, and John Howe, the author of the "Living Temple," has no mean standing in the Christian world to-day. We have reason to thank GOD that in this new world the civil differences in governmental matters have disappeared, and that the descendants of Cavaliers and Puritans are combining to build the walls of the American Church wide and broad. The Dioceses of Massachusetts and Connecticut show that the differences of past ages may be forgotten, and that men of various forms of thought and education may kneel at a common altar, and the union is strong, for the Church's commission is to bring all men into one mind and into one household.

Authorities: Blunt's Dict. of Doc. and Hist. Theology, Staunton's Ecc. Dict. on Novatians, Mosheim's Ecc. Hist., Coleridge's Aids to Reflection. Blunt refers to Fuller's Ch. Hist., Neal's Hist. of the Puritans, The Troubles at Frankfort, and Bishop Bancroft's Dangerous Positions and Proceedings.

REV. S. F. HOTCHKIN.

Pyx. As in the early Church consecration of the elements was made only in the Church, and from thence it was taken or sent to the sick if need be, or was carried to the Hermits and Monks in the desert, reservation of the Consecrated Bread and Wine was common. This necessitated a fit receptacle for their proper conservation. (*Vide* RESERVATION.) Such vessels have been preserved which date back to the fourth century. Their shape was various, as probably some costly carved case made for other purposes was afterwards set apart for this. These were called pyxes, from pyx, a fist. Where there is no reservation allowed, and where consecration of the elements is allowed in a sick-room, there is no need of a Pyx.

Q.

Quadragesima (or Τεσσαρακοστή), meaning forty days, is generally used to signify the whole period of Lent, but often used for the first Sunday in Lent, from analogy with the three Sundays preceding it. As Sundays were omitted from the number of fasting days, the six weeks preceding Easter were reduced to thirty-six days of abstinence, so that to make up the number of forty days, which Origen declares in the third century to have been consecrated to fasting before Easter, four days from the week preceding have been added, and Lent begins on Ash-Wednesday.

Quicunque Vult. The first words of the Psalm which is generally known as the Creed of St. Athanasius. It is rather a strong formula of the Faith than a Creed; and as it is constructed in a series of rhythmic sentences, it has been called a Psalm. It has been claimed for Hilary of Arles (440 A.D.) by Dr. Waterland, but later researches have shown that while some of the terms can be traced to Augustine (400 A.D.), and fragments of it were in use as a theological formula by 700 A.D., yet its present form appears practically about 870 A.D. Its date may be placed as between 813 A.D., when a portion now incorporated into it was used by Paulinus of Aquileia, and 870 A.D., when we find it publicly used. It passed into daily use at one time in England. It must be used on certain special feast-days, Christmas-day, Epiphany, St. Matthias, Easter, Ascension, St. John Baptist, St. James, St. Bartholomew, St. Matthew, St. Simon and St. Jude, St. Andrew, and on Trinity-Sunday. The American Church removed it from the Prayer-Book principally because of the strong clauses with which it begins.

Quincy. The Diocese of Quincy, one of the three constituting the Province of Illinois, is small in area and young in history. It embraces that part of the State lying west of the Illinois River, and south of the counties of Whiteside and Lee. There are 13,700 square miles and a population of 750,000. Up to the year 1877 A.D. it was a part of the Diocese of Illinois. Division of the old Diocese had long been a subject of anxious solicitude on the part of both Bishop and Convention.

At the thirty-third Annual Convention, in 1870 A.D., Bishop Whitehouse pointed out the need for division, and a committee of thirteen was appointed, who presented two resolutions, which were adopted, requiring, first, that two new Dioceses should be erected according to bounds intimated in the Bishop's address, and, secondly, that the matter be referred to the next Convention for the necessary action to accomplish it. Of this committee the Rev. Samuel Chase, D.D., one of the earliest and strongest friends of division, was chairman.

At the next Convention a plan for division was proposed for dividing the State transversely into three Dioceses. These might be called, geographically, northern, middle, and southern.

This action was reported to the General Convention of 1871 A.D., and consent asked. The House of Bishops declined to give their consent, and the request was withdrawn, by permission, from the lower House.

Though no definite action was taken, the subject of division found mention in each succeeding Convention and Bishop's address up to 1874 A.D. In August of this year Bishop Whitehouse died, and the whole attention of the Diocese was turned to the securing of a successor in the Episcopate. In September Dr. McLaren was elected. The same Convention re-expressed the determination of the Diocese for division, and appointed a committee "to prepare plans, or such modifications of existing plans as should seem most expedient."

The Convention of 1876 A.D. continued the committee, reaffirming the old resolutions, with the additional clause, "It is the sense of this Convention that one new jurisdiction should be erected within the present limits of the Diocese at the earliest practicable day."

At the Convention of 1877 A.D. the Committee on Division having reported their inability to come to any satisfactory conclusion, a series of resolutions was offered calling for division into three Dioceses and fixing bounds nearly as at present established. These were readily adopted, and for the second time the Diocese of Illinois had arrived at a definite plan for division.

The chief difficulty all along had been the matter of Episcopal support for the proposed two new Bishops. The difficulty in the Diocese of Quincy was met in this way. In the city of Quincy were two parishes, one of them having a large stone church. These two congregations by formal action bound themselves to furnish $3500 annually to the Bishop and to an assistant clergyman. The congregation of St. John's Church further deeded all their Church property to the Bishop and to his successors for Cathedral purposes. Both congregations also bound themselves to give to the Bishop all their revenues, to be used by him, with the advice of his Chapter, in the furtherance of Church work in the Diocese and city of Quincy.

Following this action in the proposed See-city, a meeting of clergy and laity was held in September at St. Mary's School, Knoxville, and an additional pledge of $1000 made.

When the General Convention of 1877 A.D. met, the proposed new Diocese of Quincy had the following showing to present:

Consent of the Diocese of Illinois and of its Bishop; population, 700,000; communicants, 1300; clergy, 20; Parishes, 15; Missions, 8; average annual assessment for four years, $1131; contributions the last year to Diocesan Missions, $680; pledges for the Episcopate, with a cathedral property $60,000 in value, $3500.

After the case was understood—it was presented for Quincy by the Rev. Dr. Leffingwell, of St. Mary's School—little or no difficulty was encountered. On the 10th day of October, the seventh day of the session, the matter came up for decision. After reading the papers in the case, and the message of the House of Bishops giving their consent to division on the lines imposed, on motion of Mr. Burgwin, of Pittsburg, the lower House concurred; thus the long-sought-for division was at last accomplished.

The Diocese of Springfield was set off at the same time. By this action Illinois was divided according to her original wish into three separate jurisdictions, though with different lines of division from those first proposed; Illinois (Chicago in 1883 A.D.), lying north, Springfield south, and Quincy southwest.

The Bishop of Illinois at once issued a call for a Primary Convention for the new Diocese of Quincy, and on the 11th day of December (in the proposed cathedral and See-city) the Convention met. At the opening service Bishop McLaren celebrated the Holy Communion, and the Rev. Dr. Chase preached the sermon. At the organization thirteen clergy were present, and fifteen parishes represented. The first act was formally to determine the name of the new Diocese; this was declared to be "the Diocese of Quincy." A standing committee was elected, the Diocese placed under the oversight of the Bishop of Illinois, and then the Convention adjourned to the next day with a special order, after opening, for the election of a Bishop. On the following day, by a unanimous vote, the Rev. Dr. Harris, the present Bishop of Michigan, was elected.

Intimately associated with the project of division, all along, had been the idea of the establishment of an Illinois province formed from the jurisdiction contained in the old Diocese. As soon as Dr. Harris had been elected, this first Convention, in its new relations, re-expressed the old conviction as to the desirability of the Province. The Convention then adjourned.

Dr. Harris having declined his election to the Episcopate, a special Convention was called for February 26, 1878 A.D., to elect again.

The Convention met on the day appointed at the Cathedral, Quincy, and the Bishop of Illinois not being present, the Rev. T. N. Benedict was elected President. Dr. Chase had died on the 15th of January. Thirteen clergy were present and 16 parishes represented. Four names were put in nomination, those of the Rev. Dr. Leffingwell, of the Rev. Cyrus F. Knight, Lancaster, Pa., of the Rev. Cortland Whitehead, Bethlehem, Pa., and of the Rev. Dr. Locke, of Grace Church, Chicago.

Twelve ballots were had without result; on the thirteenth the Rev. Mr. Knight was nominated by the clergy. The laity failed to confirm, and after a long series of ineffectual ballots the Convention adjourned to the next day. On reassembling, balloting continued to the forty-fourth ballot, when the Rev. Alex. Burgess, S.T.D., was nominated by the clergy and confirmed by the laity. Resolutions in reference to the death of Dr. Chase were passed, and the Convention adjourned.

Dr. Burgess, in due time, signified his acceptance, and was consecrated first Bishop of Quincy, in Christ Church, Springfield, Mass., May 15, 1878 A.D. •

The first Annual Convention, the new Bishop presiding, was held in the Cathedral, Quincy, on the 28th of May following. Beside the regular routine business the chief matter of record was the appointment of a committee to act with similar committees from the other Dioceses in the State in establishing the proposed Province.

The second Convention, which met on the 27th of May, 1879 A.D., adopted the canon establishing the Province and elected delegates to the preliminary council. At this Convention the organization of the Cathedral and Chapter was also announced.

In the year 1880 A.D. the Rev. T. N. Benedict died. In the fall of this year the General Convention granted most of the powers asked for by the Province of Illinois. In December, at Springfield, Ill., the Diocese of Quincy, through its representatives, entered into full Provincial relations with the other Dioceses in the State. In the three years succeeding the Diocese has gone on with its work. No marvelous things have been done, except as the LORD'S doings are always marvelous. Following is a contrasted statement of statistics and a list of the present officers of the Diocese:

	1877 A.D.	1883 A.D.
Families	476	1000
Communicants	1300	1800
Parishes, 15 } Missions, 8 }	23	33
Clergy	20	30

In Six Years.—Baptisms, 888; confirmed, 813; ordained, 16; churches consecrated, 6; offerings, $210,000.

The Diocese has three institutions: St. Mary's Girls' School, Knoxville; Homewood School for Boys, Jubilee; Lindsey Hospital and Home, Quincy.

Statistics for 1886 A.D.: Clergy, 25; parishes, 26; missions, 16; lay readers, 20; candidates for H. O., 3; ordinations, D. 1, P. 1; baptisms, 237; confirmed, 138; communicants, 2222; Sunday-school teachers, 197; Sunday-school scholars, 1901; contributions, $36,831.10.

REV. E. H. RUDD. B.D.

Quinquagesima Sunday. The Sunday before Ash-Wednesday. How early the three Sundays before Lent were set apart before the time of Gregory the Great (596 A.D.) it would be difficult really to determine, since he reformed the previous practice. The present collect for this Sunday superseded the ancient one in the Salisbury use in 1549 A.D. It is a noble proof of the devout temper of the Reformers and the thorough appreciation they had of what constituted the proper contents of a collect. The Epistle and Gospel are the same as those used universally throughout the Western Church.

R.

Rationalism. One of the most attractive of modern heresies. It is an attempt to account for the supernatural, whether in Revelation, Religion, or natural phenomena, by explanations which debase them to the level of each man's reason. It is the pride of human understanding. In denying revelation or the necessity of it, it practically denies GOD, for such is ordinarily the conclusive result for men, for if GOD does not communicate with us why need to heed Him? It denies religion, for if we are not to believe in the supernatural, of what use is Faith to the mass of men? It denies GOD in nature and makes all things the result of a vast chance, that by chance hit upon a chance law and property of natural things, and so chanced to fall into the chance of some order. Its canons of investigation and criticism are all based upon the fundamental rule that nothing is to be accepted unless it can be reduced to the grasp of the searcher's reasoning power.

And the applications of this law lead to the wildest criticisms and to the vaguest of speculations which in daily life would be called utter folly. If reason alone can furnish us with all knowledge, and revelation is condemned as absurd, yet, rationalism can never be rid of the knowledge which Revelation has given, or of the influences it has introduced, or of the discipline it has given to human capacity. But it is evident that reason cannot reach to subjects not within its sphere, which yet are known to exist beyond and to rest upon a different basis. Rationalism ignores the limitations of the law of reasoning from similars when the elements of the second are indicated, but as parallel only in given points, and claims that there must be either absolute parallelism or there is no existence in the second subject. So far as parallel reasoning can carry us, Revelation is consonant in its proportions. When we cannot reason by comparison, positive revelation tells us what GOD would teach us. Rationalistic criticism having a low, imperfect canon of investigation, becomes but a destructive criticism it cannot replace.

Indirect replies to the assaults of this criticism as applied to the Sacred Canon are given in the introductions to the several books, but a noble defense of Revelation is found in the Letter of the Bishops on Rationalism, issued in 1877 A.D. It is well worth a careful study, as well as are the remarks upon it that are scattered on the pages of other earlier and later Pastorals. The attacks made by it upon the evidences of Christianity and the defenses are rapidly reviewed in that article to which we refer. But Rationalism is not wholly occupied with the Sacred Canon or with evidences. It would drag down to its level the fairest hopes of men which are formed upon the Incarnation and the Revelation that CHRIST our LORD has made. If the restless, ever-inquiring reason could be contented with only the material world, possibly we would be able to avoid all speculations.

But the whole range of topics which attract the reason includes so many which pass beyond the things seen to the unseen, which cannot be shunned, that those which relate to divine things follow by natural sequence from apparently mere material things. No scientist worthy of the name but at once ranges himself either for or against the validity of a revelation with more or less eagerness. It is the result of our very nature, and should be a full refutation of the claims for the sufficiency of mere reason. For if the denial of the fact of a revelation were valid, why should the scientist trouble himself further with the visions of those who believe in divine communications? But rationalism, however speciously veiled, has for its main objects the getting rid of the responsibilities that a revelation and the doctrine of a superintending care of GOD involves, the destruction of the demands of conscience, and the indirect relaxation of those strong social bonds religion makes imperative, and which curb mere willfulness. More or less clearly these results are placed before them as the ultimate result of their work. Its fruits are a ghastly infidelity, which would deny all accountability; a credulity in other things far more absurd to the reason than the objects of faith can possibly appear to it; a crude speculation irresistibly forcing itself into and dictating upon subjects which GOD alone has revealed; a system of philosophy more fatal to human hopes than even the heathen had framed; a creed which has for its main formula, "I do not know."

Honest and sincere inquiry and a reverent spirit must always be welcome. Revelation has nothing to fear from it. More truly it has nought to fear from any speculations whatever, but those who accept it and are bound up in the welfare of those near and dear to them fear for their peace and happiness who are caught in the meshes of such a rationalism. There are many topics in the range of such sacred subjects as involve the gravest consequences by their rejection, upon which a free and searching, but just and reverent inquiry would be very welcome. But hasty and rash conclusions, and immature theories and irreverent and scoffing inquiries, awake but aversion in the mind of the reverent and thoughtful believer. They react healthily upon the mass of thinking men, for there is a deep element of religiousness in us, but they do not serve any good end, but rather destroy unwary souls. Parts of this topic have already been discussed under the heads of AGNOSTICISM, and DOUBT, and PENTATEUCH, and indirectly under numerous other titles throughout this work.

Rate. There is much confusion in the popular mind as to what are meant by the Church rates in England. All property at first had a lien upon it for the repair of the Parish church and the kindred costs under that head. This is also a rebate upon the salable value of that property. It comes, therefore, under the same head as taxes in estimating the value of an estate, therefore a church rate which is publicly assessed after due notice at a public meeting, and is laid by the Church-wardens, is as honest a claim upon it as are the taxes due the town, and the county, and the State. To reclaim against them is simply to seize upon so much additional property, for the estate is valued at a given sum, *less* the principal, of which the rate is the interest; precisely as if men were to refuse to pay taxes and so raise the market value of their estates. The details of the levy for these rates and the different items for which it is raised are of no importance to us here.

Reader. In the early Church the reader was a regular officer in the Church. He was set apart for his office, after a nomination by the congregation testifying to his fitness, by imposition of hands. This was in the hands of the people. The Bishop accepted and set apart the man the congregation chose for themselves. The office is accounted a minor office, not one of holy orders. (*Vide* ORDERS.) In the English Church the public official appointment by the Bishop has been revived in the present day, but while the office has been generally laid aside there, it was never wholly lost. In our own Church the necessities of the time have brought out and established a modification of the office, and it is recognized in the Canons, but there is no public appointment as in the ancient Church, a ceremony which is desirable, since it would give that sanction and authority to the office which really belongs to it, and which is disregarded too much by the congregation. The Canon is very clear and precise as to the Duty of the Lay-reader.

"OF LAY-READERS.

" § i. A Lay Communicant of this Church may receive from the Bishop a written license to conduct the service of the Church in a Congregation convened for public worship as a Lay-Reader; but such license shall not be granted for conducting the service in a Congregation without a minister which is able and has had a reasonable opportunity to secure the services of an ordained minister. Such license may be given by the Bishop of his own motion for service in any vacant Parish, Congregation, or Mission; but where a Rector is in charge, his request and recommendation must have been previously signified to the Bishop. Such license must be given for a definite period, not longer than one year from its date; but may be renewed from time to time by the Bishop's indorsement to that effect. The license of any Lay-Reader may be revoked at the discretion of the Ecclesiastical Authority.

" § ii. A Lay-Reader so licensed shall not act as such in any Diocese other than his own, unless he shall have received another license from the Bishop of the Diocese in which he desires to serve. If he be a student in any Theological Seminary, he shall also obtain the permission of the presiding officer of such institution.

" § iii. Every Lay-Reader shall be subject to such regulation as may be prescribed by the Ecclesiastical Authority. In all matters relating to the conduct of the service and to the Sermons or Homilies to be read, he shall conform to the directions of the minister in charge of the Parish, Congregation, or Mission in which he is serving, or when there is no minister in charge, to the directions of the Bishop. He shall not use the Absolution, nor the Benediction, nor the Offices of the Church, except those for the Burial of the Dead and for the Visitation of the Sick and of Prisoners, omitting in these last the Absolutions and Benedictions. He shall not deliver Sermons of his own composition; but he may deliver addresses, instructions, and exhortations in vacant Parishes, Congregations, or Missions, if he be specially licensed thereto by the Bishop. He shall not assume the dress appropriate to clergymen ministering in the Congregation. He shall not without urgent reason read any part of the Service except the Lessons when a clergyman is present. This Canon shall not prevent students in any college or seminary from reading such parts of the Chapel Services as may be assigned to them from time to time by the Presiding Officer."

The Lay-Reader of the present day is merely intended to serve only under some stress, but anciently the Reader had his appointed place and share in the Services, the Psalms, and Lessons.

Real Presence. A phrase used to express the special Presence of CHRIST in the Holy Communion, in distinction from those who hold that there is no such special Presence, but that the Communion is in memory of the death of CHRIST, who Himself is not present, but is in heaven. Those who hold this view are called Zwinglians from the Reformer of that name, though it is doubtful if Zwinglius so taught.

While the great number of Christians believe in the Real Presence, there is a very wide difference of opinion as to the manner and nature of such Presence. These may all be classed under three divisions.

1. *Transubstantiation.*—The change of the substance of the Bread and Wine into the

natural flesh and blood of CHRIST, the same body that was born of the Virgin Mary. This is the doctrine of the Church of Rome. The term transubstantiation was not used before the twelfth century; and the doctrine it teaches was unknown before the ninth century. About the year 831 A.D. a Monk, Pascnasius Radbert, appears to have been the first writer who taught it. It was violently denied by other writers, especially by Ratram, whose book is still extant. But the doctrine suited the superstitious spirit of the Middle Ages and the metaphysical refinements of the schoolmen, and gradually obtained favor. The term and the full formula of the doctrine were first authoritatively expressed by the Council of Lateran, 1216 A.D., and so became an Article of Faith of that Church; and by the famous Council of Trent was finally set forth in these words:

"If any one shall say that in the very holy sacrament of the eucharist the substance of the bread and of the wine remain together with the body and the blood of our LORD JESUS CHRIST; and denies that wonderful and singular conversion of the whole substance of the bread into the body, and of the whole substance of the wine into the blood, till only the form (or appearance) of bread and wine remaining: which change the Catholic Church very fitly calls transubstantiation, let him be anathema." (Conc. Trid., Sessio. xiii., cap. viii. Canon ii.)

A subtle distinction was made by the schoolmen between the "substance" and the "accidents," by which latter they meant the touch, taste, smell, the "form or appearance," which they held were distinct from the real substance of a thing; so that while the latter might be essentially changed the former might remain the same. Thus they accounted for the undeniable fact: that to the senses, in outward form of taste, touch, look, the bread and wine were unchanged. These they held were mere accidents and could remain the same; while the reality of the substance was truly changed into the corporal body and blood of CHRIST.

This doctrine of Transubstantiation was not held by the early Church, though some figurative expressions of certain writers have been quoted as teaching it, contradicted, however, by other words of the same authors. It was repudiated at the time of the Reformation by the Church of England, and is in Article XXVIII. declared to be "repugnant to the plain words of Scripture, overthroweth the nature of a sacrament, and hath given occasion to many superstitions." This Transubstantiation, then, is not the true doctrine of the Real Presence.

(2) *Consubstantiation.*—This is called the Lutheran doctrine. It denies any change in the substance of the bread and wine, but teaches that with and in these elements are the natural Body and Blood of CHRIST, not spiritually, but corporally present. It was illustrated thus: That as in hot iron there is the nature both of iron and heat, each remaining unchanged, so in the Eucharist there is both the bread and wine and the Body and Blood of our LORD. The objection to this doctrine of the Real Presence is that it makes that presence a corporal one. But the Corporal Body of JESUS ascended to heaven and there remaineth.

(3) *The Spiritual Real Presence.*—This is the teaching of the early Church and of the Church of England and of our own: "The Body of CHRIST is given, taken and eaten, in the Supper, only after a heavenly and spiritual manner, and the mean whereby it is received and eaten in the Supper is faith" (Art. XXVIII.). If "given, taken and eaten," it must be present; that which is absent cannot be "given and taken." In the Communion Service we return thanks that we have been fed "with the spiritual food of the most precious Body and Blood of Thy SON our SAVIOUR, JESUS CHRIST." He must, then, have been present: we could not feed on an absent body and blood; but it is not corporally, but spiritually and sacramentally, i.e., mysteriously, present. None the less real because spiritual; spiritual as not corporal. The promise is, "where two or three are gathered together in my name, there am I in the midst of them" (St. Matt. xviii. 20). This must be especially true when the disciples are gathered together to do that which CHRIST commanded to be done in memory of Himself, and to receive that which He declared to be His Body and His Blood. And this can be nothing less than a true real presence. We believe, then, that there is such a *Real Spiritual Presence* of our blessed LORD at the Holy Communion. But here we reverently pause. We may not pretend to explain the *how*, the *when*, the *where* of that presence, we may not define or localize it as some vainly pretend to do; some holding that the Presence is after consecration on the altar with the Elements, others that it is, as Hooper says, "in the worthy receiver of the Sacrament." The Scriptures, the Early Fathers, our own Liturgy, have not attempted to solve this mystery; let us imitate their wise reserve and confess that it is a holy mystery above our comprehension. We cannot do better than to use the words of Hooker: "What these elements are in themselves it skilleth not, it is enough that to me which take them they are the body and blood of CHRIST, His promise in witness hereof sufficeth, His word He knoweth which way to accomplish; why should any cogitation possess the mind of a faithful communicant but this, O my GOD, Thou are true, O my soul, thou art happy?"

Eucharistic Adoration.—This is a fitting place to speak of what is called Eucharistic Adoration, or the worship of CHRIST as present on the Altar in the Eucharist. There are objections to this way of putting it. That there is with the Holy Communion the highest act of worship may not be doubted. But it is not to be addressed to

CHRIST as then lying on the Altar, for that is nowhere commanded nor taught by Scripture or the Church. When the LORD instituted this Sacrament, He does not say, This is My Body, worship it, or Me in it, but, "Take, eat; this is my Body," and so of the cup. Says St. Paul, "as oft as ye eat this bread, and drink this cup, ye do shew the LORD's death till He come" (1 Cor. xi. 26). They do not say worship, but eat. For CHRIST is present to give Himself to the faithful soul, with all the benefits of His passion. Yet it is very true that, as St. Augustine writes, "No one eats that Flesh except he first adore." Adore the Holy Trinity, not CHRIST alone as locally there present in the flesh, but FATHER, SON, and HOLY GHOST. And it is worthy of special notice how in the Liturgy of our Church, founded as it is on the ancient ones, there is no special adoration addressed to the Presence of the SON. It is all to the FATHER, through the SON, by the HOLY GHOST. A careful examination of the Communion Service is very instructive, as showing how entirely what is called Eucharistic Adoration is avoided. *Sursum Corda*, "Lift up your hearts," is the ancient cry. "We lift them up unto the LORD," is the response. The Tersanctus which follows is addressed "Unto Thee, O LORD, Holy FATHER, Almighty, Everlasting GOD." The Prayer of Humble Access prays the gracious LORD, to grant that we may "eat the flesh of Thy dear SON," etc. The Consecration Prayer is offered to the Heavenly FATHER, and He is invoked to so bless and sanctify with His Word and Holy Spirit, His gifts and creatures of bread and wine, as to make us, receiving them according to His SON's institution, partakers of His most blessed Body and Blood." And finally, after reception, it is GOD we thank for feeding us "with the spiritual food of the most precious Body and Blood of Thy SON, our SAVIOUR, JESUS CHRIST." There is not in the whole service one Act of Adoration or one prayer addressed to CHRIST as being in the elements or present on the Altar. The *Gloria in Excelsis* does, indeed, invoke the SON as the Lamb of GOD; but it is addressed to Him, "Thou that sittest at the right hand of GOD the FATHER." The negative testimony of the Church is very strong, that CHRIST is really spiritually present in the Eucharist to be received; but not to be specially and separately adored.

It may be well to insert here from the English Prayer-Book a part of "The Declaration on Kneeling," or "Black rubric," as it is generally called, because, though not found in our book, it sets forth the doctrine of that Church on this subject; "and this Church is very far from intending to depart from the Church of England in any essential point of doctrine, discipline, or worship" (*Preface to Prayer-Book*). "It is here declared, That thereby (*i.e.*, in receiving the communion kneeling) no adoration is intended, or ought to be done, either unto the Sacramental Bread or Wine there bodily received, or unto any Corporal Presence of CHRIST's natural Flesh and Blood. For the Sacramental Bread and Wine remain still in their very Natural Substances, and therefore may not be adored (for that were Idolatry, to be abhorred of all faithful Christians), and the Natural Body and Blood of our Saviour CHRIST are in heaven, and not here; it being against the truth of CHRIST's Natural Body to be at one time in more places than one."
REV. E. B. BOGGS, D.D.

Realism. "Realism, as opposed to Nominalism, is the doctrine that genus and species are real things, existing independently of our conceptions and expressions; and that, as in the case of singular terms, there is some real individual corresponding to each, so in common terms also, there is something corresponding to each; which is the object of our thoughts, when we employ the term." (Whately, Logic, Bk. iv. ch. v. 71.)

"Realism as opposed to idealism, is the doctrine that in perception there is an immediate or intuitive cognition of the external object, while according to idealism our knowledge of an external world is mediate and representative, *i.e.*, by means of ideas." (Sir Wm. Hamilton, Reid's Works, note C, Edin. Rev., vol. iii. pp. 175–181.)

Vide Krauth's Fleming's Vocabulary of Philosophy, on Nominalism and Realism; see also Cousin's Modern Philosophy.

Recantation. *Vide* ABJURATION.

Reconciliation. In a former article on Atonement, the Justice of GOD, His Truth, the establishment of the Law, and the Powerlessness of man to recover were set forth, the Atonement of our dear LORD as a satisfaction for sin, and the majesty of a broken Law, and as an at-one-ment, between the offended Creator and Sovereign and His disobedient subject, was shown. In speaking of our Heavenly FATHER as an offended Creator we lose sight of the fact, that He so loved the world that He *gave* His only-begotten Son, that whosoever believeth in Him should not perish, but have everlasting life. The eternal Counsel of redemption was framed in love, the execution of it in Mercy and Love. In the Sacrifice upon the Cross, in the Blood of CHRIST shed for our souls, the perfect redemption of the human race was effected in Him who became our second Adam. And the reconciliation, the power for which was granted because of His Atonement, gives to our LORD a direct power of Lordship over those who are His brethren. GOD was in CHRIST reconciling the world unto Himself. Our LORD stands forth as the Second Sinless Adam. And as in the first Adam all die as a race penalty, so by the spiritual birth of baptism into CHRIST all live, for GOD the FATHER doth not impute to them their trespasses; for He hath made Him to be sin for us who knows no sin that we might be made the righteousness of GOD in Him. In this new Covenant our LORD, then, becomes our new head. He is our bondsman. He is the Maker-at-one, and Intercessor. He takes us under His protection, and our reconciliation is made through Him and by Him. To Him we are bound. Therefore our Baptism though in the Name of the HOLY TRINITY yet is in CHRIST. We become new creatures therein. We have put on CHRIST. We are named with the new name of Christians. We are no longer under an attainder, but have the rights of citizenship and the liberty of freemen in Him. No longer strangers, but of the Household of GOD. Not mere servants no matter how fully cared for, but Sons of GOD, and therefore we receive no wages as servants, but as sons we *inherit*. In this first act of reconciliation Our Blessed LORD stands forth as the Reconciler of those who humbly sue for pardon, with the outstretched hands of repentance and Faith, with a loving FATHER whose Justice and Majesty inflicted a righteous penalty for a broken Law, but who was ever ready to receive with outstretched arms, yea more, to plead with us that we His lost sheep might return, and prove that He was more than willing by the sending, the giving of His only SON, our loving LORD. It was with this plea the Apostles went forth to all nations : " We are embassadors for CHRIST, as though GOD did beseech you by us : we pray you in CHRIST'S stead, Be ye reconciled to GOD" (2 Cor. v. 20).

The whole series of acts from the Atonement on the Cross to the Covenant made and sealed by His Resurrection are set forth again in the weighty words of the Apostle in Rom. v. 8-10 "But GOD commendeth His love toward us, in that, while we were yet sinners, CHRIST died for us. Much more, then, being now justified by His blood, we shall be saved from wrath through Him. For if, when we were enemies, we were reconciled to GOD by the death of His SON, much more, being reconciled, we shall be saved by His life." Then our Baptism effects this reconciliation, which is also an adoption (*vide* ADOPTION), and bringing us into this membership of CHRIST, places us in His Kingdom, which is His Church, which He purchased with His precious blood. Our membership in His Church is the pledge of His having effected a reconciliation in our behalf. It is our election which we have to make sure (2 Pet. i. 10). It is this joyful reconcilement that forms the Good News, the Gospel of CHRIST. It was prepared for by the sacrifices given to Adam, to the Patriarchs, to the children of Israel. It was typified and taught in the many acts of GOD to His people, in the rest of the Seventh day, in the presence of His Glory with them, in the cleansing from pollution. It is urged again and again by the Old Testament Prophets as the plea for the return of Israel to their Faith. But this leads to the further consideration : This reconciliation is a permanent fact unless we cast it away ; but its joy (" And not only so, but we joy in GOD through our LORD JESUS CHRIST, by whom we have now received the reconciliation." Rom. v. 11) may be marred, and we become finally estranged by carelessness, willfulness, over-confidence, and the manifold temptations to which we are exposed. To meet this danger our LORD gives us the HOLY GHOST in Confirmation to be His Advocate with us, and our Leader, Guide, and Consolator. He has left the restorations of the Holy Communion, the Absolutions of His Church, and He has also committed to Her the discipline by which we may be reconciled to Him. This danger of breaking this peace, the trials and temptations to which we are exposed, the warnings against the seductions to evil, the examples of the past, the holy virtues to be gained, the grounding of our souls in the faith and love of CHRIST, our being in a constant state of Conversion, all these are the subject of the pleading, the urging, the counsel, the warning of the Apostles, with which they all close their several Epistles, and not only of the Apostles, but of the LORD Himself.

Rector. There is a legal difference in the English Church between a Parson, a Rector, and a Vicar. The Parson is the representative of the Church in her corporate capacity. He performs all spiritual functions in her name ; he can sue and be sued as Parson. He claims all temporalities as Parson. (*Vide* PARSON.) A Vicar " is one who hath a spiritual promotion or living under the Parson, and is so denominated as officiating *vice ejus* in his place or stead, and such promotion or living is called a Vicarage, which is a part or portion of the Parsonage allotted to the Vicar for his maintenance and support." (Burn, Eccl. Law, sub voce.) But a rector appears to be but another name for a Parson. And in this country the assistant minister is somewhat in the position of the Curate or Vicar in the degree of the work in the parish assigned to him. But in the Parish there is only the Rector, and according to Blackstone the title Parson is more honorable, and beneficial, and legal. Our Canons have these titles for the spiritual head of the Parish : Rector, Minister, Stated Minister, but minister is the usual term used there. The title clergyman is also used, but apparently (as is the case with the word minister) to designate one in his spiritual office, and not generally the holder of a Parish.

Recusant. The term used to describe those who refused the ministrations of the Church of England. But it was usually employed to describe the Roman schismatics in England.

Redeemer. The full force of our LORD'S title is lost to us by the secondary use of it, or rather the overlooking of the type of it in the Jewish Polity. The Redeemer had a twofold function. (*a*) He was the redeemer of forfeited family estates, the next of kin who could take when the next heritor declined, as Boaz did for Ruth when the next of kin refused to marry Ruth, that he might hold the estate. (*b*) The same nearest of kin or of blood was also the avenger of blood, according to the early institution which Moses regulated and confined. (Mozley, Ruling Ideas in Early Ages.) This is not the place to carry out the application of this type to our LORD'S redemptive act and the beautiful type of the provision of the City of Refuge, but in these provisions of the Mosaic law we find active energizing powers in the national life, whose term of Redeemer (Goel) kept before the minds of the people that the MESSIAH was the next of kin to redeem us from sin and the avenger of the blood of the Saints and the City of Refuge and the High-Priest who ever liveth and under whom we have an eternal security. (*Vide* JESUS.)

Redemption. It covers the whole series of redemptive acts, but means chiefly the ransom of sinners from the consequences of sin, by the humiliation, sufferings, and death of CHRIST, who is hence called our Redeemer. I. The idea of redemption is therefore that of buying back again from a condition of slavery. That condition has come upon mankind universally by original sin and is perpetuated by actual sin. For both original and actual sin entail ties of obedience to the tempter. "Know ye not, that to whom ye yield yourselves servants to obey, his servants ye are to whom ye obey; whether of sin unto death, or of obedience unto righteousness?" (Rom. vi. 16.) It is from such a bondage that CHRIST has redeemed and is redeeming sinners, REDEMPTION from original sin and pardon from actual sin being each accorded on account of the Ransom which He has paid. II. Hence the idea of redemption contains also that of claim to the service of the redeemed on the part of the Redeemer. "Being then made free from sin, ye became the servants of righteousness" (Rom. vi. 18). He that is called, being free, is the servant of CHRIST. "Ye are bought with a price; be not ye the servants of men" (1 Cor. vii. 23). The Redeemer has not only redeemed us to freedom by His Ransom, but has also bought us for His own Service, that bondage which is perfect freedom. (Blunt's Dict. of Doct. and Hist. Theol., sub voc.)

Reformation, The. The Reformation of the Church of England was not the mere isolated movement of an insular kingdom. It arose from a feeling of abhorrence and of passionate opposition to the frightful corruptions and abuses of the Papacy in the fifteenth century, which pervaded the minds of many holy men in all those countries in Europe which were subject to the Roman obedience. That feeling found energetic and simultaneous expression on the Continent and in England. It was felt as a power in the partial Reformations effected, and the still greater ones attempted in the Councils of Pisa, Constance, Basle, and Florence. It spoke with clear and trumpet tones in the works and the preaching of Miltitz, Conrad of Waldhausen, and John Huss, their disciple, on the Continent, at the same time that the intrepid and gifted Wiclif translated the Bible into English for the people, and dealt his powerful blows against the intolerable domination of the Papacy in England. These "Reformers before the Reformation" did not limit their efforts to the removal of the external evils under which the Church and the kingdom groaned. They labored to promote an inward and spiritual life of love and devotion to GOD as the necessary condition of all moral improvement and reform, and as the only effectual power by which both doctrinal corruptions and practical abuses could be removed. Although they did not discard all the dogmas of Rome which were subsequently rejected by the Reformers in the sixteenth century, nor claim complete exemption from its authority, they had adopted some doctrines whose logical result would be to undermine the whole Papal system.

The corruption of doctrine and discipline, which had been increasing in the Western Church since the transfer of the Papacy to Avignon, culminated at the close of the fifteenth and the beginning of the sixteenth century. It might seem that England, farthest removed from Rome, and with the advantage of occupying an insular position, would have been better able than the other Kingdoms of Europe to resist the encroachments of the Papacy upon her national and ecclesiastical immunities and rights. But in truth, although from time to time her Kings, and some of her best Bishops, lifted loud protests against the exactions of the Pope, no country in Europe came more completely under the Papal domination than England, and in none were the Bishops and clergy more thoroughly secularized. "At this period [the beginning of the sixteenth century] perhaps more than at any other, the clergy in England were completely occupied with secular employments. The Archbishop of Canterbury was Lord Chancellor until relieved of that post by Wolsey. Wolsey held together, or in succession, the sees of Tournai, Lincoln, York, Durham, Winchester, while all the time he was acting simply as a lay statesman. The Bishops of Bath, Worcester, Llandaff, and Hereford were foreigners and non-residents. Fox, Bishop of Winchester, was Lord Treasurer; Ruthall, of Durham, Secretary of State; Tonstal, of London, Master of the Rolls. And among the lower clergy, a great proportion was employed in diplomatic or civil offices. These being for the most part near the source of preferment had accumulated a great number of benefices. A list of twenty-three clergymen of this period had been drawn out, who on an average held eight benefices apiece. In addition to these ecclesiastical abuses, the social state of England at the beginning of the sixteenth century was thoroughly rotten. Executions for robbery were constant, and mendicity prevailed to such an extent that statute after statute of the most terrible severity was needed to check it." (Perry's History of the Church of England from the Reformation, etc., p. 5.)

In the fall of 1511 A.D. a memorable sermon was preached by Dean Colet, of St. Paul's Cathedral, before the Convocation of Canterbury, in which he exposed with great fidelity and earnestness the dreadful abuses which prevailed in the Church, and traced them directly to the faithlessness and vices of the clergy. His own pure and lofty character rescued this representation from the charge of presumption. He warned them plainly that unless a reformation were first wrought in the character and lives of the Bishops and clergy, no increased stringency in applying discipline would avail to remedy the crying evils of the time in Church and State. He presented a vivid picture of the utter and shameless secularity of all orders of the clergy. With unsparing fidelity he exposed their "greediness and appetite for honor and dignity in the Church," their "stately countenance and high looks and lordly living," their devotion " to sports and plays and banquets and hunting and hawking," their absorption in secular pursuits, their nepotism, simony, and non-residence, and the corruption of the Bishops' Courts and the Provincial Councils. In short, in his arraignment of them he seems to describe the presence of all possible clerical vices and the absence of all clerical virtues. Like priest like people! He tells them that they are largely responsible for the prevailing vices of the laity. "Forsooth, if ye keep the laws, and if ye reform first your life to the rules of the Canon laws, then ye shall give us light, that is to say, the light of your good example, and we seeing our fathers so keeping the laws, will gladly follow the steps of our fathers. The clergy and the spiritual part once reformed in the Church then may we with Just order proceed to the reformation of the lay part; which truly will be very easy to do if we be first reformed. For the body followeth the soul; wherefore if the priests who have charge of the souls be good, strait the people will be good. Our goodness shall teach them more clearly to be good than all other teachings and preachings. Our goodness shall compel them into the right way, truly more effectually than all your suspendings and cursings. Wherefore if you would have the lay people to live after your wish and will first live yourselves after the will of GOD, and so (trust me) ye shall get in them whatever ye will." (Blunt's Reformation, vol. i. 14, 17.)

In the early part of the reign of Henry VIII. there were some eminent men who deeply felt that Church and State were in a process of disintegration, through the intolerable corruption and tyranny of the Church of Rome, and that some remedy must be found or anarchy and ruin would ensue. They are sometimes called Reformers, but may more truly be designated as the forerunners of the Reformation. For none of them aimed at the source of the prevailing evils, which was to be found in the constitution of the Papacy, but labored only to check the exorbitancies of her admitted prerogatives and powers, and encroachments upon those national rights in Church and State which were fundamental, and had been claimed and enforced through successive centuries, and had never been officially surrendered by the nation during the darkest period of the Roman domination. Of those forerunners of the Reformation there were several classes. Warham, Archbishop of Canterbury, was a representative of that class of devout prelates who were devoted to the Roman see, and who were at the same time vigilant to check any attempts to reform its doctrines or to repress its practical superstitions, and only anxious to introduce disciplinary reforms, and to bring the administration of the Papal power within limits which would be consistent with the national liberties and rights. There was another class of eminent scholars, called the humanists, devoted to the revival of classical learning and to educational reforms in the curriculum of studies prescribed in the Universities. They were men of great cultivation and refinement, to whom the superstitions of the vulgar, and especially of the monks, were repulsive, because they were gross and offensive to their tastes, rather than shocking to their religious sensibilities. The most celebrated of these were Dean Colet, Erasmus, and Thomas More. Erasmus did immense service to literature, but from his timid and compromising temper rather hindered than helped the more earnest spirits in Germany and England, who were laboring for doctrinal Reform and for the revival of spiritual life and earnestness in the Church. Sir Thomas More in his earlier years, when he wrote the "Utopia," strongly advocated religious toleration; but later in life he became a thorough advocate of the supremacy of the Pope, and died at the stake for maintaining it; and so earnestly did he repent of his youthful speculative toleration that he directed that the following sentence should be engraved upon his monument: *Furibus, homicidis, hereticisque molestus.* Dean Colet, like Erasmus and More, a thorough scholar, was far more earnest in character, and in his lectures upon St. Paul's epistles animadverted so plainly upon the departure of the Church of Rome from the theology of St. Paul as to have incurred suspicion of Lollardism, and to have awakened anxious misgivings in the mind of his friend Warham, the Archbishop of Canterbury.

But the most conspicuous of all those who have been called Educational Reformers was the great Cardinal Wolsey. There can be no doubt that Wolsey, a scholar, a lover of learning and of learned men, was thoroughly in earnest in the work of intellectual reform. But that his zeal in this cause was entirely apart from any intention or expectation or hope that it would influence the doctrine, or curtail the power of the Papacy in England, is equally clear. It was with the eye of a statesman rather than of a theologian that he looked upon the degraded condition of the Church of England. There is no evidence of religious motive in the large foundations and endowments for learning which he established. As the virtual administrator of the government, the abuses that prevailed in the Church seemed a reflection upon his statesmanship, as their removal he knew would be accounted to his honor. He would lift the Church out of intellectual debasement in order that its revived intelligence might be employed in its own vindication. He would cleanse the Church from some of its external defilements, but he would not change its structure. He would allow all the superstitious symbolism and paraphernalia and ceremonialism of the Roman worship to remain, but he would have the dust and cobwebs brushed off from the statues of the saints, and the faded letters of their legends gilded anew, and would give increased pomp to their services and processions, by clothing their priests in new robes of glory and beauty. All this fresh lustre given to the unchanged Church would be reflected upon himself. It is incredible that one whose master-passion was the love of power, and whose plans had been steadily directed to the one object of securing the triple crown, would at the same time labor to limit the abuses which gave it supremacy over all thrones and kingdoms and churches, and made it the highest prize which it was possible for human ambition to obtain.

How much of latent Lollardism survived the persecution of Henry V. and subsequent kings until Henry VIII. it is difficult to judge. From the number of enactments passed against them from the death of Wiclif it is natural to infer that they were numerous. A contemporary chronicler, Knighton, gives decided testimony to their rapid increase after the death of Wiclif. He affirms that "Wiclif's followers were multiplied like suckers from the root of a tree," and "that a man could scarcely meet two people upon the road without one of them being a Wiclifite." "There was a third party in the country," says Mr. Froude, "unconsidered as yet, who had a part to play in the historical drama composed at that time merely of poor men; poor cobblers, weavers, trade apprentices, and humble artisans, men of low birth and low estate, who might be seen at night stealing along the lanes and alleys of London, carrying with them some precious load of books which it was death to have, and giving their lives gladly, if it must be so, for the brief tenure of so dear a treasure." (Froude, vol. i. 168.) It is not from this class that leaders of a religious Reformation could be looked for in a kingdom so aristocratic as England. While it was much less dependent upon the personal passion and will of King Henry than it has been represented by Roman historians to have been, it is no doubt true that the proceedings of the King rallied and extended the latent opposition to the Papacy which had existed in England for the previous two hundred years. And no doubt, also, the Reformation gained ascendency all the sooner because of the King's opposition to the Pope, and because it enlisted the higher and governing classes in its support. In Germany it originated from below and worked its way upward. In England, on the contrary, it originated from above and worked its way downward. Hence, also, we may perceive the reason why in the one case Episcopacy went down and in the other was retained. The hierarchy in Germany, possessing more than anywhere else privileges and temporal immunities and advantages which were dependent in large measure upon the Papacy, threw themselves in opposition to the Reformation. In England, Bishops found it to their interests to adhere to the crown; and a sufficient number of them were found to throw themselves into the Reformation to save the order and perpetuate the succession. (Dr. C. M. Butler, Ecclesiastical History, vol. ii. p. 390.)

Henry VIII. ascended the throne with such personal and political advantages as soon gave him an immense popularity. His political position, through the skilful management of his father, was secure. His title was undisputed. He inherited no wars. He succeeded to the immense treasures accumulated by his penurious father. He had no hatreds, public or private, to gratify, no injuries to avenge, no feuds to cherish, no onerous benefits to repay, no clamorous partisans to satisfy. It is difficult to conceive a more auspicious succession to a crown.

Nor were his personal advantages and his apparent merits less. The brutality of his character in later life makes it difficult to conceive of him as he was in his bright youth. For he seemed to possess all the characteristics and accomplishments which give the promise of a glorious reign. His education was far in advance of most of the princes and nobles of his time. He was but eighteen years of age, a pattern of manly beauty, expert in all athletic exercises, and with a frank and bold address, a ready wit, and a bluff humor, which often passes for goodness of heart, when it may be in fact nothing more than the expression of self-complacency. The Italian and Venetian envoys at his court enlarge with enthusiasm upon the beauty of his person and his varied acquirements. The Venetian ambassador, Giustiniani, writes, "He is not only very expert in arms, but gifted with mental accomplishments of every sort. He speaks

English, French, Spanish, and Latin; understands Italian well; plays on almost every instrument; sings and composes fairly; is prudent and sage, and besides, is so good a friend to the State that we consider it certain that no Italian sovereign ever surpassed him in this respect." We cannot wonder at the high anticipations which were entertained of his future when we read such eulogies from a foreign envoy, whose duty it was to present a faithful portrait to his government of the new king, that they might know precisely what sort of a man he was with whom they would have to deal. "Such was the man," says Geikie, "whom Wolsey at more than double his age had in his hands to make or mar."

But these bright anticipations were soon dispelled. In no true sense was he found to be "sage." He soon squandered the enormous treasures left by his father in every species of luxury and extravagance, and especially in play. He began early to play the part of despot, and recognized no limitations to his power in his Parliament or privy council. They were both regarded as merely his counselors and agents; and by the pressure of his arbitrary will he reduced them in a few years to that position. As neither he nor Wolsey undertook any remedial legislation for the benefit of the people, their condition became, or rather continued to be, deplorable. Henry VII. reached no higher wisdom than that of plundering his subjects under the forms of law; and Wolsey and Henry pursued the same policy of plunder without the sanction of law; and neither of them learned that even if the highest aim of government were to secure large revenues from the people, the surest way to secure this result would be to leave to them at least the instruments by which wealth was to be produced.

The first prominent event of interest in the reign of Henry in the way of Reformation was a bill which was passed in Parliament in 1513 A.D., subjecting all robbers and murderers to the civil power, and exempting from it among the clergy only Bishops, Priests, and Deacons. The bill created the most violent excitement among the clergy. Although it subjected only the four lower orders to the civil law, it was loudly clamored against as a breach of immemorial and legalized clerical privilege. The question was argued before the king and council with great heat on both sides; but no change was made in the provisions of the statute (Burnet, pp. 10, 11.)

It was when this question was angrily discussed that the case of Hunne, a citizen of London, greatly increased the excitement. Hunne was a merchant tailor of London, whose infant child died in the parish of Whitechapel, where it had been put out to nurse, and the priest of that parish and the priest of his own both demanded a "mortuary fee."

This was the name of an oppressive claim for the second best horse or other animal belonging to a dead person, if he had been rich, or the clothes which he had worn, if he had been poor. In the case of an infant the demand was for "the bearing-sheet," and as two were demanded in the present instance, one was justly refused. Being cited to appear before the spiritual court, Hunne sued the priest under the statute of premunire. Upon this, Hunne, who had given expression to violent feelings towards the clergy, was accused of heresy. The Bishop or his Commissary could in a charge of heresy proceed without any previous proof of its probability or certainty, and accordingly he was committed to the Lollard's tower, and was soon after found dead in prison. The finding of the coroner's jury was to the effect that he had been made away with, and afterwards hanged, and that Dr. Horsey, chancellor of the Bishop of London, was accessory to the murder. But the Bishop of London, in contempt of this decision, ordered Hunne's body to be burnt for heresy. Dr. Horsey was put on trial, but as no positive proof was given of his complicity in the crime, he was allowed to escape. But the incident was significant and memorable for the amount of bitter feeling against the clergy which it revealed. An appeal was made by the Bishop of London to Wolsey that the trial might be removed from London to some impartial place, "for assured I am," he adds, "that if any chancellor be tried by any twelve men in London, they be so maliciously set *in favorem hereticæ pravitatis* that they will condemn any clerk though he be as innocent as Abel."

St. Paul's Cross was used as an ecclesiastical rostrum from which sermons having a political bearing were often preached. A similar question arose in reference to the relation of the civil to the ecclesiastical power as that which was involved in the case of Hunne soon after the liberation and acquittal of Dr. Horsey. While Parliament was in session in 1515 A.D., the Abbot of Winchelcome preached a sermon at the Cross, in which he denounced the act by which the four lower orders of the clergy were made amenable to the temporal courts in civil causes. He added that all who had assented to that act had incurred the censures of the Church,—a reckless statement, which involved in his condemnation the King and Lords and House of Commons. The lay members of both houses petitioned the King to repudiate the principle proclaimed by the Abbot. Henry accordingly held a special council at the Blackfriars in order that the subject might be discussed before him and his councillors. Dr. Standish, Warden of the Franciscans in London, contested the position of the Abbot. Some time after this the Convocation was reported to have called Dr. Standish to account for what he had said before the King. It was a rash proceeding, for such communications were always held as privileged, and to question them or reprove them when the King had not done so was regarded as both unbecoming and an infringement of the Royal prerogative. The answer of the Convocation is obscure and equivocal; but in the midst of much subservient verbiage and many protestations of fidelity to the king, it is seen that the Convocation adhere to their contention that "the punishment of clerks should not appertain to secular Judges." Accordingly, the King answered in a formal and stately speech, the purport of which could not be misunderstood. "By the permission and ordinance of GOD we are King of England, and the Kings of England in times past had never any superior but GOD only. Therefore know you well that we will maintain the right of our crown and of our temporal Jurisdiction, as well in this as in all other points, in as ample manner as any of our progenitors have done before our time. And as for your decrees, we are well assured that you of the spirituality go expressly against the words of diverse of them, as hath been showed you by some of our council; and you interpret your decrees at your pleasure, but we will not agree to them more than our progenitors have done in former times." This incident is important as foreshadowing that discussion respecting the Royal prerogative which ended in the clergy's Act of Submission." (Blunt, Ref., vol. i. 395–400.)

It does not appear that up to this period of Henry's reign there was anything in the king's views, or in those of his powerful minister, Wolsey, to incline either of them to measures favorable to Reformation. The former had just won the title of defender of the faith from the Pope for his work against Luther, and the latter was laying his plans with a view to succeed to the Papal chair. Fuller expressed his doubts of the King's giving himself time from his pleasures for so elaborate a production, and attributes the work to Bishop Gardiner. "Some other gardener," he writes, "gathered the flowers, while the King wore the posey." No doubt the King would save himself much of the drudgery of investigation; but that he arranged the materials and constructed the argument has not been questioned. Henry was much gratified with the commendations of the Pope, and boasted that he had called it "a certain admirable doctrine sprinkled with dew of ecclesiastical grace." (Strype's Memorials, vol. i. pt. 1, p. 55; Collier, iv. 31, 88, an abstract of the King's book.)

King Henry's book not only revealed the fact that there was no little Lutheranism in England, but awakened curiosity to read works which had enlisted a Royal antagonist for their confutation. It is evident too that before the writings of Luther were disseminated in England, or were written,—as early indeed as 1511 A.D.,—a number of poor people were called upon to abjure certain opinions as to the necessity of sacraments, the power of the priesthood, the efficacy of pilgrimages, and the worshiping of saints. After the dissemination of Luther's works, Warham writes with much anxiety to Wolsey (1521 A.D.), concerning the spread of Lutheranism in some of the colleges of Oxford. He fears that both the Universities are contaminated. Longland also, the King's confessor, writes earnestly to the Cardinal on the same subject and in the same vein. The Cardinal sends for a certain number of Oxford divines to come to him in London. They agree upon a solemn paper of condemnation of Luther's tenets, and it is affixed on the dial of St. Mary's Church. A more impressive ceremony followed. The Cardinal prepared a solemn holocaust of heretical books, to which he gave every possible accessory of publicity and pomp. Attended by thirty-six abbots, mitred priors, and Bishops, he repaired to St. Paul's and heard a sermon from Fisher, Bishop of Rochester. Then the condemned books were ranged before him in baskets, and a huge fire having been lighted, the baskets were emptied into the flames. But books were not exterminated by fire. They were more multiplied and disseminated than before. Soon was added to them the most valuable of all books, the New Testament, translated by Tyndale, and printed at Worms. Although the price of the book was necessarily high, numbers of the working classes became possessed of it. So that it would seem from these facts that a large number of doctrinal dissentients from the Roman Church in the year 1527 A.D. were to be found in England. The fact is exceedingly important in connection with the statement so often ignorantly or maliciously made, that there would have been no Reformation of England but for the love of Henry for Anne Boleyn. It is perfectly clear that there was a strong, deep, underlying opposition to the Papacy, and an earnest desire for Reformation, long before Henry's feelings were enlisted,—not in the desire to reform the Church, but to break away from thraldom to the Papacy, and become himself in effect Pope in his own dominions.

Into the details of the long and tangled proceedings connected with Henry's separation from Queen Catherine and his marriage with Anne Boleyn, it is not possible, in this brief sketch, to enter. The main facts of the case are well known; but upon their significancy and effect there was at the time, and there still is, much and wide difference of opinion. The undisputed facts are these. After the death of Arthur, King Henry VII.'s eldest son, the marriage of his widow (Catherine of Arragon) to Henry, then in his fourteenth year, was authorized by the Pope. But Henry protested against the marriage, either from the prompting of Archbishop Warham or from his own scruples. But by this proceeding on the part of Henry the way was prepared in advance for the subsequent movement of separation from the Queen. But, notwithstanding these avowed scruples, Henry was married to Catherine, under what influences does not appear, six weeks after his accession to the throne. It was on the occasion of the negotiations for the marriage of the Dauphin of France, and subsequently of the King of France himself, with the princess Mary, that the question of the validity of Henry's marriage was revived; and it was while these negotiations were in progress that his scruples were, or professed to be, renewed. Even if Henry felt no real scruples of conscience, he must have been not a little annoyed by having the question raised whether he had not been living in adultery for nearly a score of years, and whether his only surviving child were not illegitimate. Atrocious and brutal as was the conduct of the King in the progress of the transactions which ended with his marriage to Anne Boleyn, it is but historical justice to admit that it was before he had known her that these scruples, real or feigned, arose. The King himself declared four years after, to Simon Gryneas, that he had entertained these scruples for seven years, and had abstained for three years from conjugal intercourse with his wife. He professed to consider the death of his male children a judgment on him for his marriage with Catherine. He communicated his doubts and scruples to the Pope. But Clement VII., being then virtually a prisoner of Charles V., was not prepared to give an unequivocal answer to the King. After a study of Thomas Aquinas, Henry's doubts, real or assumed, were increased, and he required the Archbishop of Canterbury to obtain the opinion of the Bishops of England as to the lawfulness of his marriage. With the single exception of Fisher, Bishop of Rochester, they all declared that the marriage was unlawful. The King solemnly declared subsequently to the Legatine court that neither Cardinal Wolsey nor Longland had suggested these scruples, but that they had arisen unprompted in his own mind. He had indeed urgent political reasons to wish to have the affair settled and to have a male child. For, if Mary should be married to the French King, then, in case of his death, his Kingdom would revert to France, or become a prize struggled for by the French King and the next heir to the throne, the King of Scotland.

The vacillating conduct of the Pope on this occasion was the result of political rather than of religious considerations. He was trammeled in his relations to the Emperor Charles V., the uncle of Queen Catherine, and favored or discountenanced the divorce according to the varying interests and necessities of his position. There never had been, on moral or religious grounds, any difficulty in obtaining from Popes dispensations to marry within the prohibited degrees, nor even for obtaining divorces for personal or political purposes. At this very time Catherine's sister, Isabel, was wedded to Manuel, King of Portugal, although she had been previously the wife of Don Alphonso, his brother, and although all the parties were within the prohibited degrees. When Clement was a prisoner in the hands of the Imperialists at Rome, he would commit himself to nothing which would seem to favor the cause of Henry. But after his escape to Orvieto he reluctantly consented to appoint a commission to investigate the case. Cardinal Campeggio was sent to England, authorized to decide the question in conjunction with Cardinal Wolsey, also appointed a legate by the Pope for that purpose. Campeggio brought with him a bull to confirm the sentence of the Legates. But it was necessary to proceed with great circumspection with regard to the bull of dispensation by which Henry had been authorized to marry Catherine. It would not do to invalidate the Papal authority in the past by the mode of exercising it anew. Hence it was necessary to make it out to be a case in which the Pope, in granting a dispensation, was taken by surprise, and upon a misapprehension of the facts. The Pope's complications with the Emperor made it necessary for him to prevaricate and delay. Hence, although he had intrusted Campeggio with a bill of divorce, which he was to show to the King and then to destroy, he was in an agony of anxiety until he learned that it had been burned.

The Legatine court for the trial of the case was not opened until the 1st of May, 1529 A.D. After the refusal of the Queen to acknowledge its authority, or to appear before it a second time, it was adjourned until October. The Cardinal Campeggio in vain endeavored to persuade the Queen to retire to a convent. Six months passed away in fruitless consultations, purposely protracted by Campeggio, as to the course that should be pursued. But the King became exceedingly impatient at these delays. He now made no secret of his purpose to wed Anne Boleyn when the divorce or act of separation should be pronounced. His dissatisfaction with Wolsey because he had not succeeded in procuring his divorce led to that great minister's dismissal and disgrace. He was deprived of his chancellorship, and most unjustly subjected to the penalties of the statute of premunire for acting as legate for the Pope, although he accepted that office with the King's consent, and Henry had acknowledged the authority of that court by personally submitting himself to its jurisdiction. After discharging the duties of Archbishop of York for about a year, he was arrested for high treason, and on his journey to London to be committed to the Tower he sickened upon the way and died at Leicester. His memorable saying, "that if he had served GOD as he had the King, he would not have given him over so in his gray hairs," is one of the most impressive testimonies in history to the fact that of guilty greatness the root is rottenness and the blossom dust. He was a man of magnificent talents, of splendid tastes, of large designs, but the attempt to make him out in any true sense a Reformer, and to have been moved in all his grand undertakings by noble and unselfish motives, can be made plausible only by assertions which deny facts, and by omissions which would overwhelmingly confute this new reading of his life. The futility of higher education, to which Wolsey devoted so much energy and such munificent gifts, as a means of moral and spiritual reform was evident, from the fact that the greatest corruptions and abuses prevailed in the highest places among men—and he was the most conspicuous of them all—who were highly endowed and educated.

It was at this period, when all the King's efforts to bring about his separation from Queen Catherine had failed, that Cranmer's agency in the matter was invoked by the King. It seems that Cranmer was employed at Waltham as a tutor to the sons of a Mr. Cressy, when the King was making a progress through the kingdom, and that he paused for a few days at that place. Bishops Fox and Gardiner, in the suite of the King, called upon Cranmer, and the conversation naturally fell upon the subject that was then agitating all England,—the King's divorce. Cranmer suggested that the question should be referred to the foreign universities, and (which was far the most important part of his advice) that it should then *be acted upon and decided by holding a Court in England.* The King was delighted with the suggestion, and sent for Cranmer, and, pleased "with the modesty and learning of the man," ordered him to present his views in writing. This work was done by Cranmer in the house of the Earl of Wiltshire, the father of Anne Boleyn. In that paper Cranmer contended that if the universities and divines should declare in favor of the divorce, the Pope would find it difficult to avoid giving a decision in accordance with that judgment; or if he should still refuse, the marriage would then be proved illegal and void, and could be so pronounced by a national tribunal. It was bold ground to take, for there was involved in it the assumption that the voice of the Church, represented by the universities and the divines, was of higher authority than that of the Pope. When the question was thus referred to the universities, it was found that Oxford, Cambridge, the Sorbonne, and nine other foreign universities, returned a favorable answer, and declared that marriage with a brother's widow was contrary to the law of God, and therefore null from the beginning. It having proved impossible to procure from the Pope a bull annulling the marriage, Henry acted upon the suggestion of Cranmer and the universities, and was married to Anne Boleyn in the autumn of 1532 A.D.

Just at this juncture Archbishop Warham died, and the King at once appointed Cranmer to the vacant see. When he was consecrated he swore obedience to the Pope, with the proviso that this oath should not affect the duty which he owed to his God, and King, and Country, nor prevent him from attempting such a Reformation as it should appear to be his duty to promote. This oath, with these conditions, he solemnly repeated three times,—at the chapter-house of the cathedral, at the high altar, and when he assumed the pall. These conditions were added evidently in view of the measures to which, by the expression of his opinions, he was virtually committed. The sentence of divorce which he pronounced was not without its serious logical difficulties. If the marriage of Catherine had not been null from the beginning, then Henry by his marriage with Anne Boleyn before the divorce was pronounced was guilty of bigamy. If the marriage of Catherine had been null from the beginning, there was no occasion for a decree of divorce.

This oath of Cranmer to the Pope in connection with reservations which seemed to nullify it, has been severely censured. But though it may not be considered in itself a manly and ingenuous proceeding, yet when it is looked at in the light of the circumstances in which the Archbishop was placed, it will appear to be capable of extenuation, if not of complete vindication. At first Cranmer strenuously declared that he would not take the oath. "But," says Burnet, "this having been communicated to some of the Canonists, they found a temper which agreed better with their maxims than with Cranmer's sincerity." This *temper*, or reconciling expedient, was the protest which they persuaded Cranmer to make at the time of taking the oath. Here we see that Cranmer was determined not to take the oath, but that the Canonists and Casuists persuaded him that he might take it with a good conscience if he would accompany it with a protest. We may say truly that he ought not to have taken the oath with the protest, because by the former he assumed obligations which he could not discharge in consistency with the latter. But in estimating the moral quality of the act as performed by him, it must be remembered that he at first refused to take the oath; that he was persuaded by others eminent for their character and knowledge that he could do it with a good conscience; that his age and his studies had familiarized his mind to such casuistical reconciliation of conflicting duties; and that he made not a secret and mental, but an open and emphatic protestation. At the most and worst it was a weakness, and not a baseness nor a crime.

The divorce pronounced by Cranmer constituted a direct rupture with the court of Rome. It was followed by a bill which abolished the supremacy of the Pope and asserted that of the King, and declared that the children of Anne should be heirs to the throne. The title "head of the Church," even with the explanations attached to it, was not granted without some hesitation. When the King demanded a subsidy of the Convocation in 1531 A.D., the document which named the amount which it was proposed to grant to him contained this expression : " of the English Church and clergy of which the King alone is protector and head." This expression was offensive to the Lower House. Their objection was thus expressed : " Lest perchance after a long lapse of time the terms so generally included in the Article might be strained to an obnoxious sense." They begged that the expression might be modified. The King being consulted proposed this form : " He alone is protector and supreme head *after* GOD of the English Church and clergy." The clergy still objected, and at length the King sent down another form : " of the English Church and clergy of which we recognize his Majesty the singular protector, the only and supreme Governor, and, so far as the law of CHRIST permits, the supreme head." This was accepted and adopted. This title, explained by contemporaneous expositions, such as that of " the necessary erudition of a Christian man," goes much further than a mere claim of jurisdiction over spiritual persons and causes in civil cases. The act itself, in direct terms, appears to be a transfer to the King of supreme spiritual authority, and to obliterate all distinction between his civil and spiritual jurisdiction. It is as follows : " The King shall have full power and authority to visit, repress, redress, reform, order, correct, restrain, and amend all such *errors*, *heresies*, abuses, whatsoever they be, which by *any manner of spiritual authority* ought or may be reformed or redressed." It should be added to this statement that by no monarch of Great Britain has a claim like this to full spiritual authority been subsequently made, nor would such a claim have ever been admitted by any divines of the Church of England, except perhaps by a small group in the reign of Charles I.

But the most portentous stretch of power was made by the King, on the suggestion of Cromwell, who had taken the place of Wolsey in the confidence of the King. Cromwell represented to him that the clergy, by accepting Wolsey's acts, had become accessory to them, and thus subjected themselves to the penalties of premunire. By the decision of the judges it was actually decided that all the laity and clergy of the kingdom had forfeited their lands, their goods, their liberties and lives, by their sanction of the proceedings of Wolsey. As the clergy were wholly in the power and at the mercy of the King, the Convocation, at the suggestion of Cromwell, was invited to sue for pardon and offer a composition. The Convocation of Canterbury on the offer of £100,000, and that of York on a compromise of nearly £20,000,—enormous sums for that period—were, by an act of Parliament, called the " Clergy Submission Act," graciously pardoned by the " King's mercy and tenderness." The acknowledgment of the King's supremacy and the offer of this large sum of money secured the King's gracious forgiveness. It was a shameless specimen of rapacity on the most unreal pretenses. For when the clergy acquiesced in the proceedings of Wolsey, in the Legatine court, they did thereby but acquiesce in the will of the King. The King then held all their lives and possessions forfeit for acting in accordance with his own will and after his example. By the principle on which this decision was based Henry himself would have forfeited all his possessions, for no one of his subjects had more distinctly acknowledged the Pope's supremacy than himself. He allowed himself to be arraigned and to have his case pleaded in the court of Campeggio, to the disgust of his subjects for his unkingly self-humiliation. This treatment of the clergy was an act of baseness, tyranny, and hypocrisy which even he himself in his long and cruel reign never surpassed.

"The clergy's Act of Submission" which soon followed (25 Henry VIII., chap. xix., 1533 A.D.), has probably had more influence in placing the clergy in a humiliating position, and in limiting the legitimate power of the Church as an independent national Church, than any other or all others in the long list of the enactments of the British Parliament. While it does not take away the power of the Church in convocation, it enables the King to prevent the exercise of that power. For the convocation can assemble only on the King's writ; it can legislate only on points specified or approved by him; and its canons are void of authority unless they receive the Royal sanction.

After this period, until the adoption of the Six Articles, the King and Kingdom's independence of the Pope continued to be claimed and sustained, although no advance was made in doctrinal reformation. The great Sir Thomas More and the saintly Bishop Fisher were executed because, though willing to acknowledge the King's supremacy, they were unwilling to declare the marriage of Anne legal, and that of Catherine illegal. The effect of this was to make the children of Anne illegitimate and incapable of succession to the throne. Other executions for heresy speedily followed. Bilney, a clergyman of Cambridge, Byfield, a monk, Tewksbury, a citizen of London, and Bainham, a lawyer, were burnt as relapsed heretics. The most distinguished clerical victim to this persecution was Frith, a young man of great learning and piety who had successfully maintained a contest with Sir Thomas More on the doctrine of the Eucharist. The chief resistance to the King's supremacy was on the part of the friars. In consequence of their persistent and outspoken opposition a general visitation of the monasteries was instituted, and Lord Cromwell was appointed at first "Vicar-

General," and afterwards "Lord Vicegerent," to carry out this decision. The King on this occasion acted upon the theory of his absolute spiritual supremacy, which, as we have seen, was proclaimed in the Act. He suspended the exercise of the Episcopal authority of the Bishops during the visitation, and afterwards restored it to them in words of which the following is the purport: "Since all authority, civil and ecclesiastical, flows from the Crown, and since Cromwell, to whom the ecclesiastical part has been committed, is so occupied that he cannot fully execute it, we commit to you the license of ordaining, proving wills, and using other ecclesiastical jurisdiction; and we allow you to hold this authority during our pleasure, as you must answer it to GOD and to us." No King or Queen of England would now use such language; but the warrant for it still remains in the act of supremacy. (Short, ¿ 201.)

During this period there were publications and controversies which proved that the principles of the Reformation and opposition to the doctrines of the Church of Rome were making progress among the people. In the year 1528 A.D , "The Supplication of the Beggars," a violent attack upon the superstitions of the Papacy, and especially of the doctrine of purgatory, appeared in England. It was the production of Simon Fish, a gentleman of Gray's Inn, who had incurred the resentment of Wolsey and taken refuge abroad with Tyndale. It referred to the doctrine of purgatory as that by which the religious houses, monasteries, and chantries were sustained. It aims to be a witty and satirical production, and presents a frightful picture of the licentiousness, drunkenness, and degradation of the clergy and the monks; and its invectives against them are so savage that its attempts at wit are quite stifled by them. Yet its influence on the public mind was so great that it was answered by Sir Thomas More, in a work entitled "The Supplication of Souls." As "The Supplication of Beggars" had represented them as making a lamentable cry for alms, of which they had been defrauded by the monks and clergy, so Sir Thomas makes "the silly souls" in purgatory send forth a lamentable cry lest Christian people should cease to pray and offer alms for them; and thus leave them forever in their dreary and painful prison. Another work, "The Practice of the Papistical Prelates," unfolds the story of the oppressions, worldliness, and impurity of the higher clergy. Other controversies in a more doctrinal vein were carried on by Tyndale and More, and by Cranmer in his "Book of Directions." But this progress of the spirit of doctrinal Reform was offensive to the King. A dreadful example and warning of the danger of holding heretical opinions was given in the trial and execution of fourteen Anabaptists, two of whom were burned at Smithfield, the remaining twelve being sent to be executed in the chief towns in England, to give a striking proof of the orthodoxy of the King and of the fatal results of heresy. Thus did the King press his rebellion against the Pope to its utmost limit, while he attempted to hold the people back from a revolt against the doctrines of the Roman Church.

In addition to Tyndale's translation of the New Testament, the whole Bible, translated by Coverdale, was published in 1535 A.D., and put under his Majesty's protection and allowed to be circulated. In the same year the first Reformed Primer, or book of private devotions, appeared. It contained, besides its implied positive teaching of the truth, a condemnation of some of the superstitions and popular practices of the period.

Something has been said of Cardinal Wolsey's great endowments for the promotion of learning. The dissolution of the minor monasteries in 1525 A.D. furnished him with the means of rendering this, his one great service to the Church and the realm of England. At the close of Henry's reign, chiefly through the agency and example of Wolsey, who began the work, about eleven hundred of the twelve hundred religious houses which were in England at the accession of the King were dissolved. The visitations of these houses revealed a condition of revolting immorality in most of them, the disgusting details of which are recorded in Strype's memorials and Fuller's history. It was the design of Cranmer that the revenues of those houses which were dissolved after the fall of Wolsey should be devoted to the endowment of Bishoprics and free schools of learning; but this design was very imperfectly realized. A large part of these revenues was squandered among the courtiers, and much of them was applied to the current expenses of the government. But that which was accomplished shows how much might have been done if this fund had been sacredly applied to the objects for which it was pledged. Six Bishoprics and fifteen chapters were established and provided for, and several hospitals and twelve colleges were built and endowed. Successive dissolutions of different classes of monasteries were made in 1525, 1535, 1536, 1537, 1540, and 1545 A.D.

It is not practicable in this sketch to describe in detail the remaining events in the reign of Henry; nor is it necessary in order to understand the position of the government, the clergy, and the people in reference to a Reformation of the doctrine and discipline of the Church. The cause of Reformation no doubt met with a blow by the death of Queen Anne. She was first condemned for adultery, and then divorced on the ground of precontract with Lord Percy,—decisions which are contradictory of each other. The almost universal verdict of history upon Queen Anne acquits her of guilt, but not of indiscretion and levity and familiarity with persons of the other sex of high and low degree unbecoming a Queen, or any woman of dignity and virtue. After the King's marriage with Jane Seymour, Parliament passed an act of succession, which made the children of Queens Catherine and Anne illegitimate; but in case of no issue by Lady Jane, left the King at liberty to designate his heir by letters patent or by his will. By the convocation, which met June 9, 1536 A.D., " Articles of Religion were agreed upon, which Fuller calls a draught of twilight religion." In them the Scriptures and Creeds were declared standards of the faith, the operation of saving faith was truly stated, Purgatory and the worship of images and saints were proscribed. "The Pilgrimage of grace" (1536 A.D.) was a formidable insurrection which occurred in the North of England. It professed to be a religious movement, and was excited by Priests in consequence of the Anti-Papal policy of Henry, and especially by the dissolution of the monasteries. The insurgents numbered 20,000, and were with difficulty put down by the Duke of Norfolk. Under the continued reaction of the mind of Henry and the influence of Papistical divines *the Six Articles* were enacted, which reaffirmed all the chief Papal dogmas, except that of the Pope's supremacy. The dogma of transubstantiation was announced in its most stringent form, and the penalty of death denounced against the denial of it. Cranmer refused to sign these Articles, and was protected from suffering the penalty of his refusal by the interposition of the King. And then followed the death of Queen Jane, the marriage of Henry to Anne of Cleves, from whom he was soon separated because she did not please his taste, the fall of Cromwell, because he had brought about this marriage, and the subsequent marriage of the King to Catherine Howard, and her speedy execution because of her previous licentious life; and finally, his union with his last wife, Catherine Parr, who narrowly escaped death for her suspected heresy.

Henry died January 16, 1547 A.D. The chief points of Reformation gained through his reign were: 1. The destruction of the Pope's supremacy. 2. A restraint upon some of the grosser idolatries of the people. 3. The Bible and the Creeds declared to be the rule of faith. 4. The translation of the Bible and its use authorized by the government. 5. The dissolution of the monasteries.

REV. PROF. C. M. BUTLER, D.D.

Regale. The royal privilege in France to enjoy all revenues from vacant Bishoprics, and to present to such cures and dignities as were without an incumbent during such vacancy. This vacancy could occur by conviction of crime as well as by death, and lasted till the new Bishop took the oath of allegiance. If a Bishop were created Cardinal, then, too, his revenues accrued to the King till the new Cardinal repeated the oath of allegiance. Again, this privilege lasted thirty years in the right of patronage, so that if the Bishop appointed to a vacant cure or dignity, yet the King could within that time remove the incumbent and substitute his own nominee, and this was absolute. The regale was finally, after many struggles, curtailed as to the right of patronage.

But as this right was, in the Tridentine Churches, the subject of concordats between the Papacy and Crown, so in England and in all independent Churches it was vested in the Crown, and formed the basis of the royal supremacy. It must be understood that it was the principle, not the detail of French usage, which is here referred to.

Regeneration. A new birth, or being born again, or from on high, which our LORD told Nicodemus, is necessary for entrance into the kingdom of GOD. And He connects it with Baptism as the means, adding, " Except a man be born of water and of the Spirit, he cannot enter into the kingdom of GOD" (St. John iii. 3, 5). Its nature cannot be better set forth than in the words of the Catechism: it is "a death unto sin, and a new birth unto righteousness, for being by nature born in sin, and the children of wrath, we are hereby made the children of grace." By the natural birth we are the children of Adam, inheriting a fallen nature; by the spiritual birth we are made the children of GOD, adopted into His family, brought in His Church under the influence of His Holy SPIRIT, then given us; a new spiritual life begins in us, with the certainty, if it be nourished and rightly developed, that it will grow up in holiness into the life everlasting. Regeneration means, therefore, a change of condition, a being " called to a state of salvation through JESUS CHRIST our SAVIOUR." It is not a moral change, for the sinful nature " doth remain, yea, in them that are regenerated." But it makes man capable of a moral change and spiritual growth in holiness. By it GOD " hath delivered us from the power of darkness, and hath translated us into the kingdom of His dear SON" (Col. i. 13). " Being born again, not of corruptible seed, but of incorruptible, by the word of GOD, which liveth and abideth forever" (1 Pet. i. 23).

Of this new birth, or REGENERATION, Baptism is the Sacrament, for it was " ordained by CHRIST Himself as a means whereby we receive the same, and a pledge to assure us thereof."

That the Church so teaches the quotation from the Catechism, given above, shows. Also, in the Baptismal Office, we are taught to pray for the child or person, that " he coming to Thy holy Baptism, may receive remission of sins by *spiritual regeneration*," " that he may be born again." After the Baptism, the minister is instructed to declare that " this child or person is *regenerate*, and engrafted into the body of CHRIST's Church ;" and to return thanks to the merciful FATHER " that it hath pleased Thee to *regenerate* this infant with Thy HOLY SPIRIT, to receive him for Thine own child by adoption, and to incorporate him into Thy Holy Church." And Article XXVII. declares that "Baptism is a sign of Regeneration or New Birth, whereby, as by an instrument, they that receive Baptism rightly are grafted into the Church; the promises of the forgiveness of sin, and of our adoption to be the sons of GOD by the HOLY GHOST, are visibly signed and sealed."

But is the Church justified in using such language? The word "Regeneration" is found only twice in the New Testament. Once it refers to the second coming of CHRIST (St. Matt. xix. 28); the other is in Titus iii. 5: "Not by works of righteousness which we have done, but according to His mercy He saved us, by the washing (or laver) of regeneration, and renewing of the HOLY GHOST." Here it can mean nothing but Baptism, for there is no other washing with water for remission of sins. But though the exact word be so seldom used, that which it means is frequently expressed in other language in connection with Baptism. Our LORD said to Nicodemus, a man must be born of water and of the SPIRIT. St. Paul writes: "Know ye not, that so many of us as were baptized into JESUS CHRIST were baptized into His death? Therefore we are buried with Him by Baptism into death; that like as CHRIST was raised up from the dead by the glory of the FATHER, even so we also should walk in newness of life" (Rom. vi. 3, 4). "Buried with Him in Baptism, wherein also ye are risen with Him through the faith of the operation of GOD" (Col. ii. 12). "By one SPIRIT are we all baptized into one body;" "Now ye are the body of CHRIST" (1 Cor. i. 12, 27); "As many of you as have been baptized into CHRIST have put on CHRIST;" "For ye are all one in CHRIST JESUS;" "And if ye be CHRIST'S, then are ye Abraham's seed, and heirs according to the promise" (Gal. iii. 27-29). These quotations suffice to show that the LORD and His Apostles regarded Baptism as conveying regeneration. Other passages will be found under the head of BAPTISM.

The testimony of ancient writers is to the same effect. Justin Martyr, one of the earliest of Christian writers, thus describes Baptism in his Apology to the Emperor Trajan. After mentioning the preliminaries of instruction, of faith, of prayer, of fasting, he proceeds: "Then they are taken by us where there is water, and are regenerated after the same manner in which we ourselves were regenerated. For in the Name of GOD, the FATHER and LORD of the universe, and of our SAVIOUR, JESUS CHRIST, and of the HOLY SPIRIT, they then receive the washing with water." (Apol. i., cap. 61.) So Hippolytus, another early writer, says, "Do you see, beloved, how the prophet spake beforetime of the purifying power of baptism? For he who comes down in faith to the laver of regeneration and renounces the Devil, and joins himself to CHRIST, . . . he returns a son of GOD and joint-heir with CHRIST." (Discourse on the Holy Theophany, 10.) It would be easy to give a long list of quotations to the same effect, but these suffice to show that the Prayer-Book re-echoes the voice of Holy Scripture and of the early Church.

It may interest some of our readers to know that the Anglican Church is not the only Reformed communion which teaches this doctrine. The Westminster Confession of Faith, which is the standard of Presbyterians, in chapter xxviii., *Of Baptism*, declares: "Baptism is a Sacrament of the New Testament, ordained by JESUS CHRIST, not only for the solemn admission of the party baptized into the visible Church, but also to be unto him a sign and seal of the covenant of grace, of his ingrafting into CHRIST, of *regeneration*, of remission of sins, and of his giving up unto GOD through JESUS CHRIST, to walk in newness of life." So also the Confession of Faith of the Synod of Dort, which is that of the Reformed (Dutch) Church: "As water washeth away the filth of the body, when poured upon it, and is seen upon the body of the baptized, when sprinkled upon him; so doeth the blood of CHRIST, by the power of the HOLY GHOST, internally sprinkle the soul, cleanse it from its sins, and *regenerate* us from children of wrath unto children of GOD." (Article xxxiv.) And in their Catechism the question is asked, "Why, then, doth the HOLY GHOST call baptism 'the washing of regeneration,' and 'the washing away of sins?'" "*Answer:* GOD speaks thus not without great cause, . . . but especially, that by this divine pledge and sign He may assure us that we are spiritually cleansed from our sins as really as we are externally washed with water." (xxvii.)

But though Scripture and the Church thus testify that this is the proper use of the word regeneration, some good Christians have been greatly offended at it. One great reason for this is, that they understand the word in a different sense from that received by the Church. They confound "regeneration" with renovation, and "Conversion," or "Change of heart," as they call it, and some, even with "Sanctification." But there is a great difference. The new-born child has in him all the faculties of the man, both mental and physical, but unless these are nourished, educated, developed, by the use of the proper means, it would practically be as though he had them not, and the new life would soon die out. So the new spiritual life may be given to the child, but unless nourished by the use of the means of Grace, and if neglected by a renewing through repentance and Conversion, it will avail nothing. To use the words of another, "Regeneration and Conversion are two distinct things. Regeneration is GOD'S act, whereby He takes man out of his merely natural position and places him in a new and spiritual one. Conversion is GOD'S work in the man's soul, whereby he either prepares the man to accept Regeneration, or enables him to preserve the gift when given, or to recover it when the blessed privileges of it have been lost. Conversion is necessary either as the preparation for, or completion of, or restoration to, the state of Regeneration. Regeneration is necessary either as the completion of, or preparation for, Conversion." (T. J. Ball, Commentary on the XXXIX. Articles.)

The Church by no means teaches that all baptized persons are thereby saved, or that the grace of baptism works altogether *ex opere operato*,—*i.e.*, by inherent virtue in it, entirely independent of all co-operation on the part of the recipient. The new birth is indeed entirely the gift of GOD, in which the person has no more efficient part than has the new-born child in its birth. But GOD has chosen to annex to it certain conditions, as of Faith and Repentance, which in the Infant must succeed, in the Adult precede, the Sacred Rite; and unless these be present the life given is, so to speak, dormant, to be called into activity by their exercise. In the case of Infants these are promised for them by their sureties, whose duty it is to nourish and care for this spiritual life, so that as soon as possible the child may itself perform them both, and so receive the full benefit of the divine gift, for which provision is made in CONFIRMATION. But if they neglect to do this, "to work out their own salvation," then the spiritual life will pine away and become almost, though perhaps never entirely, extinct, and Conversion and renewing of the HOLY SPIRIT are necessary to restore its vitality.

In the case of Adults baptized, they previously profess these, repentance and faith, and an intention to lead a new life; and it is on the charitable assumption that they are sincere the Church declares them regenerate. That the Church requires in all her members a true turning of the heart to GOD, a continued repentance, an earnest seeking after holiness, and all in humble dependence on the aid of the HOLY SPIRIT, is shown in numerous passages of the Prayer-Book. Thus the Collect for Ash-Wednesday: "Create and make in us new and contrite hearts," in that for Christmas: "Grant that we being regenerate, and made Thy children by adoption and grace, may daily be renewed by thy HOLY SPIRIT," and again: "Grant us the true circumcision of the Spirit; that our hearts and all our members, being mortified from all worldly and carnal lusts, we may in all things obey Thy blessed will." No one who will study the Prayer-Book can misunderstand the teaching of the Church as to the necessity of a spiritual change of heart in all her members.

The importance of the subject must excuse the length of this article. In conclusion, we repeat, that much false teaching would be avoided by not confusing different terms and by putting things in their proper order. Repentance, Faith, Conversion, may precede or follow Regeneration; Renovation and Sanctification must follow it, and are the proper result of the new life given in Baptism. REV. E. B. BOGGS, D.D.

Register. The keeping of a Parish Register dates back only to the injunction of Lord Cromwell, in 1538 A.D. It was taken up by Edward VI. and Queen Elizabeth, in whose reign each minister at his induction had to make this formal pledge (among others): "I shall keep the Register book according to the Queen's Majesty's injunctions." By late statutes the older statutes have been modified, but the Canon (70th) is still in force. The Register must contain all Christian weddings and burials. It must be kept in a Coffer provided with three locks and three keys, one to be the Rector's, the other two to be given each to the two Church-wardens severally, so that all three have to be present at the opening of the Coffer; and entries were to be made in their presence and subscribed by the three together. The Register has always been of great value as evidence in the Courts. The provision in our own Church is clear and precise, but it is not hedged with a penalty, so that it is but little better than a strong recommendation, though a minister is bound in all honesty by his profession of obedience to obey its instructions. As the country grows in population the value of these registers increases. The Canon is as follows: Tit. i., Can. xiv., § v. "(1) Every minister of the Church shall keep a Register of Baptisms, Confirmations, Communicants, Marriages, and Funerals within his cure, agreeably to such rules as may be provided by the Convention of the Diocese where his cure lies; and if none such be provided, then in such manner as in his discretion he shall think best suited to the uses of such a Register. (2) The intention of the Register of Baptism is hereby declared to be for other good uses, so especially for the proving of the right of the Church membership of those who may have been admitted into this Church by the holy ordinance of Baptism. (3) Every minister of this Church shall make out, and continue as far as practicable, a list of all families and adult persons within his cure, to remain for the use of his successor, to be continued by him and by every future minister in the same Parish." There is a further duty (Tit. i., Can. xvii.) of compiling from the Register and the companion lists and parochial notitia the full statistics of the Parish, to be presented at the next Convention. The different Dioceses supply the blank forms for such lists and reports.

Relics. The remains, or portions of them, of deceased saints, or something which belonged to and was used by them, which were reverently kept at first, but which afterwards were superstitiously reverenced. The early Christians took up the remains of the martyrs, and laid them away with reverent care, and they held their religious meetings in the cemeteries where these bodies were laid. But they did not go beyond this apparently. But after persecution ceased, then a superstitious care for the relics of those who had suffered for the faith sprang up. But it was constantly protested against from St. Augustine's time to our own, and imaginary miracles which were reported added greatly to this evil. Relics soon came to be highly valued, and to be eagerly sought after, and after a while relics were invented to suit the demand. It is too much aside from the plan of this work to do more than mention the subject. The discussion of it has formed a large literature. In nearly every mediæval writer, and in almost every chronicle of any length, some reference to relics and the transference of the remains of saints from their first resting-place to some church is made; and at last it grew to such a pitch that no church was properly equipped unless it had within its precincts the relics of some saint. This led to many impostures and to relic-mongering and to the stealing of them. There is still in the churches under the Roman obedience a great use made of relics.

For curious details, see Smith's Dictionary of Church Antiquities; also Littledale's Plain Reasons against Joining the Church of Rome, where the references give the literature upon the subject.

Religion. It is perhaps best defined by an old definition which is not etymologically correct,—The bond which binds us to GOD. The later and correct derivation,—The pondering on holy things, states only part of the truth. It does not cover the lofty aims of RELIGION. For it is the glory of our manhood to be religious. It is a trust not always recognized. It *is* a right to appear before GOD, which is broken by sin. To repair it is the fruitless act of man, is the merciful gift of GOD, given as a trust, increasing in elevating, ennobling power as its extent and fullness has been added to from the time sacrifices were given to Adam till CHRIST brought in the last and perfected bond in Himself. In the Incarnation of our LORD religion is perfectly restored to us. He is our peace, He is the days-man who stands able to lay His hand upon both. In this view this bond is restored as of original right to every man who is baptized in CHRIST JESUS. The Religion of CHRIST perfects, and so supersedes all other forms of faith towards GOD. Our LORD is not merely our Mediator, not only our Atoner, but as GOD was in Him reconciling the world, so we by being baptized in Him have, as one of the restored rights once forfeited by sin, the right of being bound to GOD, having Him as our protector, and appealing to Him for aid, and endowed with the right to come before Him when we choose. Then Religion involves all the spiritual life, as so referred to GOD. It is the life hid with CHRIST in GOD. It requires of us the careful use of all the means of grace, of all the acts which bring us to GOD, which strengthen our souls, which nourish us in all goodness, since we have not passed from the probationary condition of the present, which involves Freedom of will. Whatever helps to holiness of living, whatever places us into closer relations with our GOD, whatever repairs the sin-frayed life in us which CHRIST has given us, *that* is of religion. All inner spiritual training, all sacramental approaches to GOD, all the outer defenses and guidance that the visible organization of the Church can give, the public services, the sermons and catechising, the exhortations, the receiving of His doctrine and the confession of our faith in Him, all are needed.

For in all these CHRIST appears, in all these we through Him enter upon the joyful and blessed discharge of our religion. In Him it is a perfect act, and as more closely we draw to Him so more perfectly we live in new religion. Then holiness and religiousness are our true and noble condition. We are, then, only rising to the true level of our blessedness in CHRIST. To relax any effort on our part and to reject any part of His teaching or of His work for us and in us, is an injury to our spiritual life. Religion, then, requires the careful development of all the details relating to these three chief points, Sacraments, Inner Life, Public Worship; they are directly interrelated, and the minor details which gather round each may be likened to the complex system of arterial circulation and of muscles and of nerves, which bind brain, heart, and lungs together as the essential points of where life resides and which must be sedulously guarded. Religion gathers into the proper discharge of its function all the powers and capacities of our nature. It receives and distributes to our spiritual wants all the gifts of GOD, manifold, subtle, and varying, from the secret unconsciously felt influence of His Holy Spirit to the public and open ministrations of His sacraments. In these things we live in our LORD, and by these we grow in grace and have our bounden duty and service accepted. It should take away willfulness, repress spiritual pride, stimulate us to greater activity, strengthen us to be mightier athletes in the spiritual contest. It follows that the perfectly religious life is one of intense activity, in the membership of His Visible Church, in the unity of the faith, in the use of the Sacramental Life, which binds us to Him. Less than this is so far defective. More than this is impossible, for the servant cannot reach to his LORD, much less pass beyond Him. But each in his rank and station of life can attain far more of it than we ever have done.

Religious. It once meant all in holy orders,—*i.e.*, vowed to a life of extraordinary religious devotion. But it has lost that breadth of usage in a measure, and refers now only to those under monastic vows in the Roman Church, as monks and nuns, while the clergy not belonging to some order are called secular Priests.

Renovation. As Creation is of the FATHER, Regeneration of the SON, so we can also say Renovation is of the HOLY GHOST. It is the summing up given in the Catechism: "First, I learn to believe in GOD the FATHER, who hath made me and all the world. Secondly, in GOD the SON, who hath redeemed me and all mankind. Thirdly, in GOD the HOLY GHOST, who sanctifieth me and all the people of GOD." So St. Paul writes to Titus: "He saved us by the washing of regeneration and the renewing of the HOLY GHOST." It is again set forth in the Epistle to the Romans (ch. xii. 2): "And be not conformed to this world, but be transformed by the renewing of your minds." It is, then, the daily operation of the HOLY GHOST upon the heart of the regenerate, renewing it by the willing co-operation of the will: "Work out your own salvation with fear and trembling, for it is GOD who worketh in you both to will and to do, of His good pleasure." This renovation proceeds, is checked, or lost, as we will to speed or to hinder or to cast it away, for GOD does not compel salvation, but urges, pleads, waits, and by all means short of taking away the responsibility of our will, brings us to a better estate of grace. Then the renewal is progressive, as growth after birth is progressive. It is of GOD, yet by misuse, by vice, neglect, imprudence, the health of the body is often lost, and the growth and development checked, and death ensues. The case is parallel in the spiritual life. The same heed to the use of means, the same dependence upon the HOLY GHOST, the LORD, and GIVER of Life, the same watchfulness over ourselves, the same care for our souls that we bestow upon the development of our intellect and education of our faculties, would strengthen and develop by the grace of the Spirit that renewed mind. The importance of Confirmation is infinite to the soul. It is the sum of all the gifts that our LORD gave His Church. The Gifts which He obtained for us by His Atonement and Resurrection are given by the HOLY GHOST, and in this connection the latter part of the 18th verse of the lxviii. Psalm is very forcible, when we remember its use by St. Paul: "Thou hast gone up on high, thou hast led captivity captive, and received gifts for men; yea, even for thine enemies, that the LORD GOD (*i.e.*, the HOLY GHOST, whom I will send from the FATHER) might dwell among them." It is, then, bound up in the renewal of our spiritual life, and it is a fatal loss to reject it willfully.

This renewal, as has been shown, we are to share in by our co-operating efforts, and we are to confirm by the use (through the HOLY GHOST) of all the means of grace given to us. It is starving the soul to refuse them. It is destructive of life to reject them, since they are offered by Him who is sent to be our Sanctifier. In this connection occur to the memory the two passages in the Epistle to the Hebrews. I. (ch. vi. 1–6.) In this, as the laying on of hands refers to Confirmation, the public open gift of the HOLY SPIRIT having been made, so the partakers of the HOLY GHOST must refer to it also. The Apostle clearly states that the soul loses the power of renewal to repentance when it deliberately rejects, or rather throws away, the graces offered and once enjoyed. He does not say that there is no hope, but that the soul has lost the power of co-operating by repentance and a living Faith, and it is a distinct act of long-suffering and mercy if the sinner is brought back to a state of repentance. II. (ch. x. 26–29.) Here, again, it culminates in rejection of the Holy Communion, and in doing despite to the SPIRIT of grace. In this also we must remember that willful sin paralyzes the spiritual Life, and so as we go on in the rejection, so we will become more and more dead. For there is a loss of spiritual desire for holy things, though an intellectual appreciation of them may remain in the soul.

But turning away from this too imperfect a hint upon a danger ever overhanging every soul, we revert to what was said before upon renovation. It is a part of the dispensation of our LORD by His gift of the HOLY GHOST for our growth and development here in all spiritual graces, that we may be fit for the spiritual places He has prepared for us. The viii. chapter of Romans, then, sets forth the work and power of the SPIRIT involving our Resurrection by Him. The Epistle to the Galatians sets forth the fruits of the SPIRIT which are consequent upon a walk in the SPIRIT. The iv. chapter of the Second Epistle to the Corinthians declares that "though the outward man perish, yet the inward man is renewed day by day," and this line of thought recurs on through the Epistle.

The Church's doctrine, then, of the renewal of our spiritual Life by the ever-present grace and help of the HOLY GHOST, is but the orderly statement in one form of the many shapes in which the Scriptures teach it. It is correlated to the teaching upon the reconciliation which our LORD has made for us through Himself. For the HOLY GHOST, the Paraclete, *i.e.*, Advocate and Leader and Guide whom He sendeth, is the *One* who keeps our feet from falling. The Collect for Whit-Sunday, the prayer in the Institution Office, and the third prayer in the Visitation of the Sick, together set forth the devotional use we may make to our great profit of this work of the Sanctifying SPIRIT.

Renunciation. A giving up, a renouncing of something that was either believed or practiced before this abandonment of it. The chief renunciation is in the Baptismal Vows. Wherein the Person, or the Sponsors for the Child, if he be an Infant, renounce the devil, the world, the flesh, and promise to serve GOD faithfully all their days. For it is a principle of our nature that if a renunciation leaves a void in our thoughts or habits, there must be a filling up from some other source. Therefore we promise to serve Him for the rest of our life, for the renunciation is to be final, and any reverting to these sins after baptism must be heartily repented of and the life amended. These renunciations are of very great antiquity. They can be traced back to Tertullian's age (177 A.D.), and they are probably alluded to by St. Peter in the text, "The like figure, whereunto even Baptism doth now save us" (not the putting away of the filth of the flesh, but the answer, *i.e.*, the reply to the question, of a good conscience towards GOD), by the resurrection of JESUS CHRIST. Renunciation applies to the abjuration of heretical or schismatical tenets. (*Vide* ABJURATION.) It is also used in the Canons of one who abandons the ministerial office. (Title ii. Canon v.)

Re-Ordination. The receiving of ordination a second time. It is not possible to receive orders a second time, any more than it is possible to receive baptism a second time. Baptism is a spiritual birth, and so cannot be reiterated. Orders convey an indelible character (*vide* CHARACTER), which cannot be taken away. A person can renounce the Ministry, can abjure the Faith, can, for himself, abandon all previous position. But he cannot be rid of the impression upon his life, nor of the authority once committed. The Church has the disciplinary power of depriving a person of *exercising* the powers she has conferred, but only the Giver of these powers, CHRIST Himself, can finally annul the grant. The Church's authority extends only to discipline, not to entire abrogation. Therefore a person, if he has been ordained by Bishops of the Apostolic Succession, cannot be re-ordained. If he has not been so ordained, he has not received the authority which CHRIST left in His Church, and to confer this authority upon one already exercising a ministry is *not* re-ordination. For we must carefully distinguish between the authority a congregation gives to a man to offer prayers and intercessions *for* them and the authority from CHRIST given only by the Apostles and their successors, to minister *to* their congregations in the things appertaining to GOD. Therefore it is not a re-ordination to confer orders upon one not Episcopally set apart for the ministry. But it is re-ordination to do this to one previously so ordained. If it is done at all it is a mockery, and the actors in it are guilty of a profanity. When, therefore, any minister of any one of the Christian bodies without the Church desires to take up the ministerial work, he has to receive ordination. The weighty Preface to the Ordinal sets forth these principles in compact and clear language.

"It is evident unto all men diligently reading Holy Scripture and ancient Authors that from the Apostles' time there have been these Orders of Ministers in CHRIST's Church,—Bishops, Priests, and Deacons; which offices were evermore held in such reverend estimation that no man might presume to execute any of them except he were first called, tried, examined, and known to have such qualities as are requisite for the same; and also by public Prayer, with imposition of Hands, were approved and admitted thereunto by lawful Authority. And therefore, to the intent that these Orders may be continued and reverently used and esteemed in this Church, no man shall be accounted or taken to be a lawful Bishop, Priest, or Deacon in this Church, or suffered to execute any of the said Functions, except he be called, tried, examined, and admitted thereunto according to the Form hereafter following, or hath had Episcopal Consecration or Ordination."

The conclusions that are to be fairly drawn from this quotation are all in accord with the principle of the Nicene Canon on the ordination of those who came to the Church from the bodies who had parted from Him. Those who had no Apostolic orders in their organization were treated differently from those who, separating, yet kept the same orders, though schismatically used.

Repentance. Repentance is called by the Fathers one of the two hands we stretch out to GOD to implore His mercy and to receive His gifts. It presupposes some thing to be repented of. It presupposes a Person having a right to receive repentance and to grant pardon. The whole Christian doctrine upon Sin, its nature and power, and upon GOD's love and mercy in forgiving this sin and removing its power and repairing its consequence, also demands the doctrine of repentance. The heathen did not fairly apprehend the power of sin and the horror of sinfulness, though they knew what was sin, and felt its power; consequently, the words which we have freighted with a deeper meaning had only a surface application to the doctrine. "To change one's mind," "to change one's care," "to change from shame or fear of punishment," were their chief words, and had no exclusive reference to a repentance from sin such as Christian theology has given them. The Greek words come into the Gospels by the Septuagint Version of the Old Testament, which gave them to the writers of the New Testament.

But it is necessary to examine the facts with regard to Repentance. First note that the LORD preached repentance *because* of His Church. "Repent, *for* the Kingdom of Heaven is at hand." This the Twelve and the Seventy were sent forth to preach; for though the word Repent is omitted, yet the order to them to preach that the Kingdom—the Church—was at hand, involved this repentance, as we see by His own words, and the same account in St. Mark. Again, St. Peter proclaiming the Kingdom to the audience on the Day of Pentecost repeated the LORD'S command: "Repent, and be baptized every one of you in the Name of JESUS CHRIST for the remission of sins, and ye shall receive the gift of the HOLY GHOST" (Acts ii. 38). So St. Paul to the Athenians, "but now [GOD] commandeth all men everywhere to repent" (Acts xvii. 30). The contact of the Church with men in heathendom requires of them Repentance. It is evident that this means something more than what we now understand by Repentance, and yet something less. That they should at once comprehend it and discharge it in all its parts, as one within the Church should comprehend it, is not at all likely. It retained, then, its primitive sense more largely. Change the desires of your cares, change the objects filling your minds, the relation to your GOD is changed through the Atonement of CHRIST. The Kingdom of Heaven, the visible Church of GOD, receives you into covenant relations, the assurance of Immortality is held out to you. That He calls you through it, changes all things for you.

That these things would be so a little consideration of the position of the Church to the world, and of relation of Him upon which she is built to the world, will show. So in these public addresses the Apostles did not define the fullness of repentance. But her work here is much confused because, having a mixed multitude in her audiences, now the second kind of repentance is brought more prominently forward, since this is the repentance demanded of a mind aroused, of a conscience quickened, of a soul that grasps something of the vastness of the salvation GOD has prepared in CHRIST. The Repentance of the unbaptized man who is *drawn* to the Church is mingled with an imperfect yet trusty Faith. If not as fully dwelt upon here, yet the truth that a deeper faith is developed step by step with a greater and more earnest repentance is not to be overlooked. For a repentance looketh towards GOD, for he that cometh to GOD must believe that He *is*, and that He is a rewarder of them that diligently seek Him. But to him believing this and received into His Body, there is a shrinking, yet a longing. "Peter fell down at JESUS' knees saying, Depart from me, for I am a sinful man, O LORD." The soul cannot go away, it must come, but it shrinks back and feels its sinfulness in the glorious power of GOD. But what are the steps of the repentance acceptable to GOD ? First is always placed a Fear of consequences and a compunction of conscience. This, indeed, is natural and one that we must feel; a fear of Him is a motive, for if we did not fear we could not be persuaded. Our LORD Himself uses this as an argument for obedience, cleansing of soul, and Faith (Luke xii. 5). This fear is the beginning of wisdom, but it may not pause there. Compunctions of conscience rest in part upon memory, and these recall the past; and sorrow for the evil brings this first step of a true repentance. "The sacrifices of GOD are a broken spirit,—a broken and a contrite heart, oh, GOD, Thou wilt not despise." Fear, then, that is only a sorrow of the world is not a true fear. It must be a sorrow after a godly sort. It worketh carefulness, cleansing of the soul of evil habit, indignation against oneself for being so stained, fear that hath love in it, vehement desire, zeal, revenge against oneself. So far a true contrition has all these mental stages,—more or less eager in different characters, but to be a true contrition equally real and influential, according to the capacity for and insight into spiritual things each soul possesses.

But this contrition is not perfect if it does not renounce evil habits and false principles of action. This renunciation while resolved upon at once is not effected at once. A single resolution, however firm and persistently carried out, cannot undo at one stroke the education of the past, and unloose the habits that have twined themselves into the character, and besides, the evil of some habits lies not so much in the habits themselves as in the consequences they produce, and this is not always evident. Renunciation must, to be rightly carried out, be done with honest self-examination and a right valuing of self before GOD. Again, renunciation must go down into the selfishness of the heart. It must learn the hatefulness not only of actual sin but of sinfulness, and so it must go to the root of the evil. The last step is restitution. It is a giving back to GOD by confession of the fault what we have taken from Him, and also, which is really less costly but far harder to do, a confession of and an effort to restore so far as we can what we have deprived our neighbor of. Restitution is the test of the moral courage of the man, and the measure of the depth of his repentance, and the proof of the power of GOD over his heart and will. These, then, form the parts of a true repentance. Fear, and compunction, and sorrow for the past leading to *Contrition*. Contrition bringing out *Renunciation* and self-examination, and these producing *Confession* and *Restitution*. As was said, the increase of Faith is not dwelt upon, nor, again, the increase of love to GOD through our LORD, and a greater thankfulness as the person learns better what repentance means and how GOD'S mercy and love overshadows all his acts and he knows that the HOLY GHOST is leading, quickening, renewing him in grace. We do not all follow out equally the steps here described, since the protection thrown over some is greater than over others; nor do the complex influences at work always permit every one to apprehend them; and without guidance morbid minds have passed into despondency over their states. Many, too, brought up in godly Christian lives have not that to repent of that stains others' souls. In all these cases, wherever there is earnestness and willingness, we may well believe that the HOLY SPIRIT who divides severally to every man as He wills and who maketh intercession for us will bring each to a peaceful issue. We should remember St. Augustine's prayer that GOD would reveal to him his state that he might repent aright, and lest he should despair, that GOD would reveal His mercy also. But the results of a true repentance for sin must be permanent. Repentance is a principal part of Conversion, and this Conversion is a state so largely in our power. Therefore we should try to live in a repentant state, for so long as we live we are subject to the attacks of sin from the triple forms in which it approaches us. We are ourselves sinful and weak, and therefore stained daily with petty and corrosive frets and failures; these things wear away the spiritual life, and therefore we are taught in the beautiful prayer in the Visitation of the Sick, "Renew in (me), most loving Father, whatsoever hath been decayed by the fraud and malice of the devil, or by (my) own carnal will and frailness." The Services of Daily Prayer, and of the first part of the Communion, and of Ash-Wednesday, are all framed upon the deep and devout apprehension of the doctrine of Repentance. There is a healthiness and honest manliness in them that should show every one how manly and noble an act in CHRIST'S religion Repentance is. And by her constant public use of the Confessions in these offices sets forth two grand facts of the Gospel committed to her: I. The parts of a true Repentance, so that every one of her children shall be instructed in it. II. The state of Repentance and of Faith in which we must each live,— *i.e.*, the true converted life to which the means of grace are life-giving. So her Doctors have ever called these two, Repentance and Faith, the hands of the spiritual life. They are the conditions upon which we are received into the state of grace and by which we can cling to the Cross of CHRIST.

Again, it is necessary to note that though, of course, Remission of sin and restoration is promised by our LORD upon repentance, and is surely given, yet there is no necessary inherent connection between the two; and this is necessary to note, for many have said, "Since pardon is given upon repentance, I will wait and repent later, for I will be sure of forgiveness;"—a fatal error, for this principle defeats any true repentance, and so deludes itself to hope for a pardon that will be denied to a selfish mockery of sorrow.

There are so many books of sermons and of devotion which set forth this whole doctrine of the Gospel upon repentance, that it is needless to give *references*. But, probably, it may be well to refer to Taylor's "Holy Living" and "Holy Dying."

Reprobation. The teaching held by some, that by the eternal council or decree of GOD a part of mankind are given over to all evil and doomed to eternal death. While it is a most sorrowful fact that some will reject His mercy, and, dying unrepentant, will suffer for their sins forever, yet it is against the express words of Revelation to suppose for an instant that this is by a foredoom, but only by a consequent of their action. Compare 2 Pet. iii 9, and Rom. xi. 32, for this.

Reredos. In many churches a screen is raised behind the altar, which is called a reredos. It is frequently carved and adorned with great magnificence. In England there are many very fine examples of the Reredos.

Reservation, Mental. There was at one time, under Jesuitical teaching, a pernicious doctrine of "Mental Reservation;" that is, that a promise, pledge, or other agreement or a statement could be made with a "mental reservation," which would make it, if under oath, tantamount to perjury. This was the teaching of a "mental reservation." If this had gained currency it would have been subversive of all honor and trust. But, happily, it was refuted and exhibited in its true colors. It was condemned in Euripides by even the lax morality of the heathen, and it certainly could not be tolerated in a Christian.

Reservation of the Consecrated Elements of the Holy Communion. It was the custom of the early Church to consecrate only in the church, so the Communion had often to be given to the sick and to others, as martyrs, hermits, and distant members of the Church, who could not be present to receive. Those of the ordinary communicants who desired also could reserve a part of the Holy Bread and carry it home with them. (*Vide* Blunt and Smith's Dicts.) This reservation was a necessity, then, from such a law, but it led to abuses from an at first over-reverent, and next from a superstitious use of the consecrated Bread as an amulet or protection, and latterly because it was carried about in procession. The English Church at the Reformation forbade this reservation. A rule which, as having authority in all rites and ceremonies within her jurisdiction, she had a right to make, and this rule has been perhaps as faithfully observed as any other. And there is no real cause for reservation of the consecrated elements, since she consecrates on any or every day of the year (*vide* PRÆSANCTIFIED), and orders it in private houses for the sick or permits it when otherwise necessary.

Reserve. In the divine communication of the Truth it was always as men could bear it, yet the briefer or more elemental revelation contained within it the ground of the larger and fuller declaration of the same truth. As children are taught the elements of knowledge and these elements in a crude form, yet the child is not mistaught, but prepared for a fuller explication of them and their application in a more developed form. So too our catechism gives the minimum of what the child is to know of Church truths. A larger and fuller statement is taught him as soon as he is able to bear it. We must act upon this law in mission work. In statement of elemental *principles* it is proper and only honest to declare the truth and the whole truth, but we may doubt the propriety of descending to minute particulars which could not be comprehended without previous training. With this law of applying elementary instruction we can compare GOD's dealings with men. Take but the Law of development of the great revelation of the MESSIAH, the central fact of the world's history. Given to Eve in a hidden form, developed still more to Abraham, repeated still more fully to Moses, brought into prominence by the prophets, placed as a part of the confession of faith in the Temple worship by the use of the Psalms, it was only gradually brought forward, till in the ripeness of the time CHRIST came, born of a woman that He might redeem us all. So in our LORD's own teaching He used a wise and just reserve, till the proper time should come to bring it forward. This principle must run through all our teaching, but a wise and well co-ordinated plan of instruction will always permit the clergyman to bring forward and develop some fact or doctrine of the Church of which he had previously given the elementary instruction.

Residence. The requirement that a Parson should live in his Parish, or the cathedral official in the precincts, or the Bishop in his Diocese seems needless, but there have been so many examples of non-residence that the Canons had to take notice of it. From the Council of Sardica (347 A.D.) on this evil has forced itself upon the Church's notice. The English Canon Law is clear and copious upon it. So far in our own Church there is in the Canons but the single enactment (Tit. i., Can. xv. § xii.), "It is the duty of every Bishop of this Church to reside within his Diocese."

Resignation. The surrender of a trust or a charge, in due form, as of a Rector resigning a parish or a Bishop his Diocese. The Rector's resignation should be made both to the Bishop and to the vestry (*vide* charge in the Office of Institution, since the fact that the Office of Institution is in the Prayer-Book should make it in every Diocese where it is used the ruling authority in such a matter). The Ordinary is properly the authority to whom the resignation should be sent first, and then it should be sent to the Vestry. No resignation should take place without good reason on each side, since a hasty, unconsidered resignation may be followed by unforeseen and injurious consequences to either party. But the Church has ever been still more chary in accepting the resignation of a Bishop. It was a mode of describing the indissolubility of the bond into which the Bishop had entered towards the Diocese by saying He has *married* his Diocese. The Canons do not permit him to resign upon his own motion, but upon examination of the circumstances by his brother Bishops. If his resolution has been made during the six months previous to the session of the General Convention he is to submit it to the House of Bishops, who are thereupon to examine the case and to vote upon it. But if not within this time, then he shall inform the Presiding Bishop, who shall convene a majority of the House of Bishops *after* three months' delay, and this majority of the whole house can determine the case, and the Presiding Bishop shall, if the resignation be agreed to, notify each Bishop of the Church of the said resignation. And the Bishop so resigning cannot be chosen to any Diocese, whether an old one or one erected after his resignation, and forfeits his seat in the House of Bishops. But he may perform Episcopal acts under authority of any Bishop who may choose to ask him to act for him in his Diocese. But his resignation does not release him from the authority of the General Convention or from obedience to the Canons.

Responds. The Psalms or portions of Psalms between the lections of the various offices of the Church. They were so called from being antiphonally sung. They were at first sung by single voices, with a response from the whole choir. As these responds became very complicated they were cut off in Edward VI.'s Prayer-Book. The responses to the Commandments are properly responds, and the only ones retained from the old system.

Responses. The public worship of GOD, from the time of Moses, has always been responsive. Miriam's story of triumph upon the shore of the Red Sea was responsive. The system of Psalms and Hymns of the Jewish worship was responsive. It was an integral part of all Liturgic worship, and is, in fact, after the pattern of the Heavenly worship (Is. vi. 3). This Liturgic Law passed into the Christian use from the Jewish services, and must necessarily have done so as soon as the Psalms were taken into public use. But it was very early placed in the Liturgy, especially in the versicles of the Communion Service. "Lift up your hearts." "We lift them up unto the LORD." "Let us give thanks unto the LORD." "It is very meet and right to do so," have an antiquity and sacredness of use which can be traced to the days of those who had seen the Apostles of the LORD. But this Liturgic Law is itself founded upon the priesthood of the Laity. There is a mutual benediction in the versicle and response "The LORD be with you." "And with thy Spirit." There is a common sacrifice of praise in the antiphonal reading of the Psalter. There is a common act of intercessory prayer in the Litany. So that most fully are the people taught that they are priests with the offering from pure lips of holy inspired words. The priestly act of the people being thus acknowledged, used, made the corner-stone of a large part of the worship, and so insisted upon, creates a responsibility that rests upon the congregation to discharge. We are bound, then, as a people with a priesthood, to use the responsive worship of our Prayer-Book. Nowhere else in the whole Church is this so fully recognized and carried out as in the English Communion. So that a congregation in its official capacity, if we may so term it, in its holy relation to our LORD, in its position in the community, by using such intercession, and in its offering of praise, is bound to respond. Responses are not appointed merely for beauty and to heighten our devout feelings, and kindle our enthusiasm, and to keep a congregation ever in a living sense of worshiping, though these are all of them results from its use, but as the worship is presentative of ourselves, souls, and bodies, and representative of the people's office in the community in which they are placed, responses become acts of the highest and most solemn import.

The responses are often divided into four classes: I. Amen. II. The responses to the Versicles. III. The responses in the Litany. IV. The responds to the Commandments.

Restitution. That part of a true repentance which requires probably the highest moral courage to carry out. "Behold, LORD, the half of my goods I give to the poor," was easy compared to the other part of Zaccheus' pledge, "If I have taken anything from any man by false accusation, I restore him fourfold."

Resurrection of Christ. The Vth Article of the Apostles' Creed, "The third day He rose again from the Dead," and the Xth in the Nicene Creed, "And the third day He rose again according to the Scriptures," declare sufficiently the Faith of the Church upon this her challenge to the whole world. For if CHRIST be not raised our faith is vain, we are unforgiven; more, we believe and proclaim a lie, we mortify ourselves and ask others to do so upon a miserable delusion. "But now *is* CHRIST risen from the dead." His Resurrection was in a true sense the inevitable completion of His incarnation as well as the central fact of the world's history. It was the miracle of all miracles, compared with which all others are of less wonder; for all others lead up to it directly or indirectly. It was prepared for by type, though men lost the meaning of the types. It was foretold, though the predictions were misunderstood. It was asserted by Him who was to accomplish it. And in His Person who did so accomplish it, and in the results which follow through all time for all men from this Resurrection, results for good or for evil as men choose. It stands forth pre-eminent. These statements are not perhaps arranged in their historical order, but rather in the order in which we can best apprehend them. It will be the purpose of this brief article to show these five facts.

A. It did complete the purpose of the Incarnation, for blessed as His presence even for the short public ministry of three and a half years was for men, yet it would have been most apparently as aimless, as inconsequent, as those who deny the Resurrection are forced to admit our life to be. To be heralded by prophecy, to be announced by an Angel, to be borne sinless of a pure Virgin, to be welcomed by Angels, to be a wondrous blessing to those about Him, to wield the mighty Power which was His as the eternal Son of GOD and then to die a felon's death,— the very statement of these facts can but compel us to say, that if CHRIST be not risen, then a vast combination, effected by Divine powers upon stubborn wills made to serve for His coming, was for a comparatively petty end. But His Resurrection perfected with immortality the sinless body He had taken and the Human Soul He had joined to His Divine Essence, so that the Human Nature which He assumed and wore and died in, He by His Resurrection made immortal, and so joined indissolubly to His Eternal Nature that it can never more be disjoined, but the Eternal Son of GOD becoming immortal Son of man is now but one sole Person, the LORD JESUS CHRIST. So in a true sense His Resurrection perfected His incarnation.

B. It was the crowning miracle. It was the true answer to the challenge, Physician, heal thyself. He needed no healing, but our nature which He took did, and He healed it by this Resurrection, as well as redeemed us by the Atonement, the Resurrection the Three Persons of the Glorious Trinity shared in. His soul truly leaving His body at His death upon the Cross, went into that place of departed spirits whither we all go, and there remained till the FATHER raised Him again (Gal. i. 1). And, too, "Whom GOD hath raised up, having loosed the pains of death: because it was not possible that He should be holden of it" (Acts ii. 24). He raised Himself as He foretold. "Destroy this Temple and in three days I will raise it up" (St. John ii. 19); and again, "Therefore doth My Father love Me, because I lay down My life that I might take it again" (St. John x. 17). "I have power to take it again" (St. John x. 18). Then the HOLY GHOST is also present in the Act of Resurrection, as St. Paul saith joining our Confirmation to our hope of Resurrection. "But if the Spirit of Him that raised up JESUS from the dead dwell in you, He that raised up CHRIST from the dead shall also quicken your mortal bodies by His SPIRIT that dwelleth in you." Then the HOLY GHOST by whom the Virgin became the Mother of Him who is our GOD, fashioning His mortal body, dwelling in Him, abiding with Him, was also the quickener of the Body of our LORD, "who was quickened by the SPIRIT" (1 Pet. iii. 18). It was the Crown of all miracles, as it surpasses all precedent, not that a dead man should be raised, but that he should raise himself. Other miracles led up to it, as preparatives. Elijah and Elisha restored by prayer the souls to the bodies of children. The corpse that was cast into Elisha's tomb revived upon the touch of the bones of the Prophet. Our LORD not only raised the dead (not merely in the three recorded instances, but in numberless others also), but gave the power to His Apostles when He sent them forth. They prepared men's minds to receive the fact that He did raise Himself from the dead when this action was announced. If we accept this miracle, then we must accept all others If we reject this miracle we more than reject all others, we reject CHRIST, we reject our own future Resurrection; we have no right to believe, but can only imagine the joys of a disembodied existence; we practically reject a judgment, and so reject all future retribution; we live unrepentant, die unforgiven.

C. The Resurrection is not bound up merely in our hopes, but it had a wondrous retrospective power. It was prefigured in type, and so was taught, it may be dimly, still enough to show that they who lived before it were to be participants in it. The Ark of Noah was a type of the Resurrection (1 Pet. iii. 21). The sacrifice of Isaac was an act that not only typified the future giving of GOD'S SON, but also His Resurrection. The release of Joseph from prison and his exaltation, Samson bearing the gates of Gaza, and the miraculous restoration of Jonah were also types. The effects of the sacrifices of the Law were the continuous types of a restoration that was only to be fully realized in the Resurrection of CHRIST. The Fathers, then, before the Incarnation had a living hope in the Resurrection of our LORD. To this end, too, pointed that mysterious preaching to the souls in prison. Not only was He witnessed to before His coming, but these witnesses had a share in the hope for which they testified.

D. It was foretold. It seems strange that Christian Doctors should deny that passages in Holy Writ which can fairly bear such a meaning do not do so because they who uttered them did not so apply them. If this were a true exegesis few passages could be applied to our LORD. But they are all pregnant with meaning concerning Him. Job could say, "I know that my Redeemer liveth, and that He shall stand at the latter day upon the earth" (ch. xix. 25). But we are not allowed to believe that this involves that CHRIST must first rise, for Job may not have known who that avenging next of kin —the Redeemer CHRIST—should be. St. Peter has given the definite interpretation to the words of David: "Thou wilt not leave my soul in hell, neither wilt Thou suffer Thy holy one to see corruption." But we may well claim the words of Micah: "The Breaker is come up before them: they have broken up, and have passed through the gate, and are gone out by it: and their king shall pass before them, and the LORD on the head of them" (Micah ii. 13). And the Psalm that saith, "But GOD will redeem my soul from the power of the grave, for He shall receive me" (Ps. xlix. 15; *cf.* v. 7-9), and the prophecy of Hosea: "I will ransom them from the power of the grave; I will redeem them from death. O death, I will be thy plagues; O grave, I will be thy destruction" (Hos. xiii. 14).

E. It has a very solemn relation to ourselves and our hopes. For since by His Incarnation He became man, by the new creation and the perfecting of His Human nature the Resurrection, He has become the Second Adam, the quickening Spirit in whom we re-live here and shall perfectly live hereafter. He made it the critical test of belief in Him. It was after His Resurrection that no more doubt or questioning was permitted. It has to be accepted or rejected completely. Upon it He has founded His Church. It demands obedience, love, purity, and self-denial. He has not received unless it bear this fruit in the believer. And since the Person who accomplished it demands worship because of it, then it requires faith in Him. This is not upon the mere act, as though because it has been done it will be again, and He is *only* the first fruits; but also because He has power to give this immortal life in and after the Resurrection He offers; and He sends His Heralds to proclaim before all men the conditions, the love, and the mercy of them, and the terrible consequences He cannot avert from those who reject Him and His Act. Therefore the Resurrection of CHRIST JESUS our LORD, on which so many doctrinal truths (as of Justification and Sanctification, Grace and Election) turn, is a Fact accomplished by a Person who is the Eternal Son of GOD and Immortal Son of Man, and who personally bestows the gift of it and its manifold glories upon him who believeth in Him.

Revelation. The one prophetical book of the New Testament. Its history may be shortly stated. It was written by St. John on the Isle of Patmos, when an exile there for the word of GOD and the testimony (*i.e.*, martyrdom for the sake of) of JESUS CHRIST. He was banished there, it is said, by Domitian, probably about 96 A.D. An earlier date has too many difficulties in it to be tenable. Its style, its quiet, unassuming supposition that the writer is so well known as to need no other words of introduction than "His servant John," "John to the seven Churches," "I, John," the position of the writer as one having authority in the Asian Churches, all point to the Apostle St. John as the author. The book was so received and so spoken of generally in the Church, till the wild fantasies of the Gnostics seized upon its prophecy of the thousand years' reign, and distorted it so successfully that some pretext was sought by many to reject its authority; and in the Greek Church many felt towards this book as the Latin Church did towards the Epistle to the

Hebrews,—regarding it as inspired, but not the work of St. John. Its proper place was indicated for it in time, and since the fifth century has never been disturbed till recent critics have tried to attack it on very insufficient grounds.

The Apocalypse is a very mysterious and wonderful volume. It may be roughly divided into two parts. After the introductory verses, the first part is the Vision of the glorified LORD and His message to the seven Churches of Asia, part of the field of the Church where St. John had recently labored, and in which he was the last surviving Apostle. Each Angel of the Church is addressed by our LORD, who gives it some token of Himself with the significant formula, "I know thy works," and then each has his responsibility set forth, and his failure or success in his work pointed out. Of these Angels we can very probably identify two,—Timothy at Ephesus and Polycarp at Smyrna,—and in both cases the admonition sent to each fits in well with what we know of their characters. This first Vision closes very abruptly with the last message, and the second part opens with a vision whose splendor and pomp are only to be paralleled with the Visions of Ezekiel. The Door opens in heaven, and after a glorious revelation of the Throne, and of Him that sat thereon, of the Living Creatures around it in sleepless worship, of the four and twenty elders who adore Him, follow a series of visions of what was to be. The Lamb of GOD as it had been slain, standing in the midst of the glorious service of heaven, can alone unseal the mystic book of seven seals; and as each of the first four seals was opened there went forth a rider upon a horse with a special mission, the first conquering and to conquer, the second to take peace from the earth, the third to bring famine, the fourth wore the dread name of Death, and Hades followed with him.

The fifth seal was a vision of the souls under the Altar. The sixth brought an earthquake. In the long pause that followed the redeemed were gathered. The seventh seal is not described, only an awful silence ensues. Here it is impossible to attempt any interpretation further than to state that these seals extend (according to the soundest interpreters) from the resurrection to the end of time; some having a longer duration than others. The first seal referring to our LORD is not recalled, the other riders had orders given them; they probably were withdrawn with the fall of the Roman empire. The sixth seal refers to the work of the Church and the ingathering of all nations. The subjects of the seventh seal are still hidden. Then followed the vision of the seven trumpets. These are held to be parallel to the seven seals, but not necessarily beginning and ending each with the like seal. They display the history of the Church and the world from another point. Before the seven Angels sound their trumpets (ch. viii.) the Angel at the Altar (CHRIST the LORD) offers up the prayers of the saints in his golden censer, and after this offering, filling the censer with fire from the Altar, He casts it to the earth, and voices and thundering and lightnings and an earthquake follow. In the Trumpets the imagery of the plagues of Egypt are partly used. The blast of the first Trumpet brings hail and fire mingled with blood upon the earth. The second Trumpet is followed by a burning mount cast into the sea, the third part of which became blood. The third Trumpet sounded and the Star Wormwood fell from heaven, embittering the third part of the waters. The fourth Trumpet brings such darkness upon sun, moon, and stars that not a third of the day shone upon the earth. A pause again, that the voice of these woes may be uttered over the earth. Then the fifth Trumpet was blown and a star fell (ch. ix. 1–11), to whom was given the key of the bottomless pit, and the first woe was loosed therefrom, the terrible plague of locusts,—which is generally interpreted of the Mohammedan power. The sixth Trumpet sounded (ch. ix. 12–21), and the four mysterious Angels which were bound in the river Euphrates were loosed, with power to slay the third part of men; a vast army is given to them, and they execute their dread mission, and yet those spared repented not of their sins. Ch. x. places a pause in the series by intercalating these two visions. First, the Angel vociferating the seven thunders, whose utterances St. John recorded and sealed. The little book in the Angel's hand the Apostle was bidden to take and eat.

Next follows the Vision of the Temple which he was directed to measure, and was shown the two witnesses, whose mission, career, and the glorious power given them, and their final triumph, is recorded. In these two visions is included the second woe. And now the peal of the seventh Trumpet is the victorious proclamation that the kingdoms of the world are become the kingdoms of our LORD and His CHRIST. GOD is worshiped by the Elders, and adorations are paid. The temple of GOD opens, and therein is seen the Ark of the Testimony. The series of visions (ch. xii.–xiv.) which follow are upon the Church of GOD and her fate here, the opposing powers that arise, and their final fall. These visions are also in some measure parallel to the Seals and Trumpets already recounted, and to the outpourings of the seven Vials that are to follow immediately after. They exhibit especially the history of the Church as warred against by subtle spiritual powers of evil. The vision of the crowned angel, like to the SON of man, who was bidden to reap the harvest of the Earth, is synchronous with its whole history, till the Angel with the sharp sickle reaps the vintage of judgment. The Seven Angels with the seven cups of GOD'S wrath (ch. xv.) were preparing, but the Apostle has a preparative and comforting vision of the victorious redeemed. To the Seven were given the cups by one of the Living Creatures, and the glory filled the Temple, so that no man could enter in till the plagues were accomplished. These two begin with the other seven, and recount but another side of the spiritual history transacting in the world. The first cup poured a noisome boil upon those who bore the mark of the beast; the second cup turned the waters of the sea into blood; the third also transmuted the waters of the springs and rivers; the fourth cup poured upon it gave scorching power to the sun; the fifth brought darkness, the biting of the tongue with pain upon the unrepentant blasphemers against GOD; the sixth was poured out, and the river Euphrates was dried up, and three unclean spirits having power to work miracles went abroad deceiving and gathering the Kings of the Earth together for the great battle of Armageddon; the seventh cup closed the series with the sound of the great Voice saying, It is done. And now the Vision of Babylon, the counterfeit Church, is unrolled before us (ch. xvii.). Her power to deceive, her vast political power, and her terrible destruction by the horns of the beast upon which she rode. The majority of commentators, both ancient and modern, interpret this of Rome. The fall of Babylon (ch. xviii.) is then recited, with a glowing imagery which recalls the diction of Jeremiah and Ezekiel.

Here the Visions of earthly temporal transactions cease. The next is the Vision of the triumph of CHRIST and the preparation for the marriage of the Lamb, and the glad summons to the wedding. But the Vision of Him that rode forth conquering and to conquer from the first seal is resumed, and the Word of GOD, the King of Kings, the LORD of LORDS, is revealed as leading the Hosts of heaven to the final Victory over all His enemies; the binding of Satan, and the thousand years' reign upon the earth, and destruction of all foes are recounted. Then St. John in the last two chapters (xxi. and xxii.), with a beauty of language and a wondrous tone of love and triumph, recites to us the descent of the Bride of the Lamb from heaven. The holy eternal city is measured, its glory and magnificence are recounted, and in the last chapter he carries us back to the Garden of Eden, from whence four rivers issued, but now one upon whose bank grows the tree of life, of which they who keep the commandments alone can have a right to eat. Then our LORD speaks as at the first, and this strange and wonderful prophecy closes with the words that express the yearning of every Christian heart: "Even so, come, LORD JESUS."

It is difficult to say any more with the scanty space allowed. But it may be added here that it seems strange that any Christian believing that the HOLY SPIRIT speaks as He wills by man, can ever read this book without feeling its thorough inspiration. It cannot be entirely interpreted. Part of its fulfillment we, each in his place, are aiding to bring about now. There may be doubt about the accuracy of some of our interpretations of what we feel must have been fulfilled already. But deeper than these doubts is forced upon us the conviction that its very difficulties are of GOD. Its abrupt transitions, the resumption of, as it were, unfinished visions, the gathering into this book the diction of the Hebrew prophets and using it for nobler prophecies, the testimony of other earlier prophecies woven into this, is beyond human skill. And again, to make so prominent the history of GOD's Church, its struggles, its open humiliations in the world, and, too, its secret triumphs in the souls it gathers in, the spiritual comfort of those in tribulation, the messages from the glorified ascended LORD to His Church by His Apostle, a continually recurring subject until it reaches the culmination in the marriage of the Lamb and His Church, is a proof of its inspiration. As a master-musician who has a solemn hymn, a victorious anthem, and a lament to weave into one symphony, takes these themes, develops them each in part, and as the symphony broadens and deepens, ever recurs to, resumes, and interweaves triumphant fears and sad wailings and glorious adorations into one perfect whole and makes his work of human hopes reach holier aspirations, so there is no note in the scale of human feeling from despair and utter agony to the loftiest and finest raptures that the sanctified heart can feel towards its REDEEMER but the Apostle has been taught by the HOLY SPIRIT to touch it for our comfort and strengthening. The Book is sadly neglected both in public and private reading, yet it is the only book which has a blessed promise to its reader: "Blessed is he that readeth, and they that hear the words of this prophecy, and keep those things which are written therein: for the time is at hand" (Rev. i. 3).

Rhode Island, Diocese of. The history of the Church in Rhode Island naturally divides itself into three periods:

1. The Unorganized Period (nearly coincident with Colonial times), extending from the founding of the first parish, in 1698 A.D., to the first Diocesan Convention, in 1790 A.D.

2. The Incompletely Organized Period, from 1790 A.D. to the election of the first particular Diocesan Bishop, in 1843 A.D.

3. The Completely Organized Period, from 1843 A.D. to the present time.

The Colonial Church.—The advent of Episcopacy in Rhode Island was nearly, if not quite, coincident with the settlement of the State, in 1635 A.D. Probably somewhat previously to the arrival of Roger Williams, the Founder, or certainly not materially later, came the Rev. William Blackstone, a regularly ordained clergyman of the Church of England, and settled on the bank of the river, still bearing his name, a half-dozen miles north of the present city of Providence. It is recorded that he "used frequently to come to Providence to preach the Gospel." But as Mr. Blackstone died in 1675 A.D., leaving no organic result of his labors, we must look to a later date for the true founding of the Church.

The earliest enduring work was that which led to the formation of Trinity Church, Newport, and was begun in 1698 A.D. by the preaching there of the Rev. Mr. Lockyer. The first principal patron and original founder of Trinity, and therefore the one entitled to the honor of being considered the Founder of the Church in Rhode Island, was Sir Francis Nicholson, successively royal governor of New York, Virginia, Maryland, Nova Scotia, and Carolina.

Previously to the close of the seventeenth century there were but two organized bodies of Christians in Newport, the Baptist and the Quaker, the same being substantially true of the other parts of the State. But it was found that the leading gentlemen of the town were favorable to this new undertaking. A considerable parish was soon gathered, and, by the aid of Governor Nicholson, a "handsome, but not beautiful" church was completed, not later than 1702 A.D. While this enterprise was under way, in the year 1701 A.D. was founded, in England, the association since long known as the venerable Society for the Propagation of the Gospel in Foreign Parts, and Trinity Church, Newport, was destined to be apparently the first point in New England to enjoy its fostering care and to become its largest beneficiary within that territory.

On the solicitation of the wardens, through the Bishop of London, recognized as having jurisdiction in the colonies, the Rev. James Honeyman was appointed a missionary and sent over to Newport, in 1704 A.D., being accompanied by a valuable library of the best theological books of the day for the use of the church. Mr. Honeyman lived nearly a half-century as rector of Trinity, and was so fortunate as to see it grow large and flourishing. In 1709 A.D., Queen Anne presented the church a bell. In 1724 A.D. there were about fifty resident communicants. In 1726 A.D. a new church—the one still standing —was completed, "acknowledged by the people of that day to be the most beautiful timber structure in America," and the adherents of the Parish had increased to fourfold the number of the original promoters. In 1729 A.D. came Dean (afterwards Bishop) Berkeley to Newport, where he resided for several years, frequently preaching in Trinity, bestowing upon it several gifts, and, in general, exercising a powerful and salutary influence upon the young Church of Rhode Island. The venerable Society continued its stipend to the rectors of the church in Newport until 1772 A.D., sixty-seven years. From 1698 to 1785 A.D. there were 2722 baptisms, 485 marriages, and 861 burials.

The second foothold of the Church in Rhode Island was gained in what was known as the Narragansett country, in the southwestern portion of the State. Previously to the year 1700 A.D. a number of families attached to the Church of England had settled in the region, and were accustomed to hold occasional worship in private houses. In 1706 A.D. the Rev. Christopher Bridge became their regular pastor, and continued to officiate among them for a year or more. The first church edifice, still standing, although not upon the original site, and not in present use, was erected in 1707 A.D. In 1717 A.D. the Society for the Propagation of the Gospel in Foreign Parts appointed the Rev. William Guy missionary over the Narragansett parish. The most distinguished of all the early ministers of St. Paul's Church was the Rev. James McSparran, settled in Narragansett in 1721 A.D., on the urgent petition of the parish to the venerable Society, and judged to have been "the ablest divine that was sent over to this country" by that body. For thirty-six years he continued to preach the Word and break the Bread of life to this people with great faithfulness and acceptability. During his pastorate he baptized 538 persons, besides admitting to membership in the church a considerable number already baptized. The successor of Dr. McSparran was the Rev. Samuel Fayerweather, who remained until the Revolution.

The third parish founded in what is now Rhode Island, although not so at that date, was St. Michael's, Bristol. Feeble efforts towards the establishment of Episcopal services had been made in the early part of the eighteenth century, but it was not until 1719 A.D. that they became effective. In response to an application to the Bishop of London and the Society for the Propagation of the Gospel in Foreign Parts, the Rev. James Orem was sent out as missionary, and found a comfortable wooden church already nearly completed, at a cost of fourteen hundred pounds.

In the year 1722 A.D. the Society again provided a missionary in the person of the Rev. John Usher, who completed a fruitful ministry of more than a half-century in Bristol, dying there in 1775 A.D.

Mr. Usher baptized 713 persons, officiated in the marriage service 185 times, and attended 274 funerals. In the earlier history of the Bristol church, before the town was set off from Massachusetts to Rhode Island, in 1746 A.D., it is repeatedly recorded that men of the Church of England were imprisoned for refusing to pay towards the support of the Presbyterian pastor of the town.

The fourth and last colonial church of Rhode Island is St. John's, Providence, known previously to 1794 A.D. as King's Church. The Rev. Mr. Honeyman, of Newport, had preached repeatedly in Providence from as early a date as 1720 A.D. to 1722 A.D., when, at one time, "in the open fields," he addressed "more people than he had ever before seen together in America." The erection of the first church was begun upon St. Barnabas' Day, in the latter year. In 1723 A.D. the venerable Society supplied this infant parish with the Rev. George Pigot as a missionary, transferring him from Stratford, Conn. After several short pastorates, in 1739 A.D. the Rev. John Checkley, having just been ordained by the Bishop of Exeter, at the age of fifty-nine, became rector, and so continued until 1753 A.D., being a missionary of the Society for the Propagation of the Gospel in Foreign Parts.

Mr. Checkley was followed by the Rev. John Graves, another missionary of the Society, who remained through the troublesome times of the Revolution, refraining, however, from officiating after the Declaration of Independence, because not permitted to offer prayers for the king.

Services were held, during this period, at several other points, and especially at Cowesett, in Warwick, where the first Newport church was re-erected in 1728 A.D., and remained standing until about 1764 A.D., Dr. McSparran, Mr. Fayerweather, and Mr. John Graves often officiating in it, but no other permanent parish was formed. Among the names to be honored as those of powerful friends and promoters of the Colonial Church is that of the distinguished Huguenot, Gabriel Bernon, the first signer of the petition for Trinity Church, Newport, one on the earliest list of vestrymen of the Narragansett Church, in 1718 A.D., and one of the first wardens of King's Church, Providence.

Another signal benefactor was Nathaniel Ray, Collector of the King's customs at Newport and one of the Vestry of Trinity, as early as 1720 A.D. In addition to liberal gifts during his lifetime, he made large bequests, at his death in 1734 A.D., to that parish, as well as to St. Michael's, Bristol, for the foundation of parochial schools. Although the long withholding of Bishops from America, on the part of England, left the Church in Rhode Island in a grievously imperfect condition, yet it is not to be overlooked that her forced dependence upon the old country for ordination and oversight, and her continued allegiance to the Bishop of London, served to perpetuate a closer intercourse than would otherwise have prevailed between the mother and the daughter.

Nor is it possible to overestimate the value of the aid and sympathy afforded by the venerable Society for the better part of the eighteenth century,—an aid without which the four feeble churches in this embryo Diocese could not have survived. In estimating the influences which prevailed at the birth of the Church of Rhode Island, we should not, likewise, forget the principle of religious liberty on which the State was founded, and by which the Church was to such an extent inspired as never to have violated it in her treatment of other Christians.

The general condition of the Church at the close of the Revolutionary war was most pitiable. Trinity, Newport, was for years without a pastor, her property in a state of dilapidation, her people discouraged, party spirit raging even within the parish, the edifice itself being occupied for several years by a minister of the "Six-Principle-Baptist Society" and his congregation.

The Narragansett Church was unopened for worship for a dozen years or more, being used as a barrack for the American soldiery during the war.

St. Michael's, Bristol, was in ashes, having been burned in 1778 A.D. by a band of the British. King's Church, Providence, after having been served by a number of clergymen and laymen, among them a Baptist minister, was closed against its regular rector, the missionary still paid by the Society, who desired, at the restoration of peace, to resume his public ministrations. To the human eye the Episcopal Church in Rhode Island seemed ready to die, if not already dead.

The Organization of the Diocese.—The natal day of the Diocese of Rhode Island was November 18, 1790 A.D. By that time the parishes had begun to revive from the depression of the war, all having, for several years, enjoyed the services of a rector except Bristol, which, although the church had been already rebuilt, was still served by a lay-reader, the son of the faithful old rector. On the above-mentioned day there met in Newport the first Diocesan Convention, consisting of two clergymen and five laymen, representing all the parishes save St. Paul's, Narragansett. The first business of the Convention was to constitute the new Diocese an integral part of the National Church by a resolution of adherence to the canons passed by the General Convention of 1789 A.D., and by another adopting the Revised Book of Common Prayer, whose use had become obligatory only the preceding month. The Rt. Rev. Samuel Seabury, D.D., Bishop of Connecticut, was, by vote, *declared* Bishop of the Church in Rhode Island. Already, however, had he, soon after his return from his consecration in Scotland, in 1784 A.D., officiated in Rhode Island by an ordination in Newport and a confirmation in Providence. The Diocese continued under Bishop Seabury until his death, in 1796 A.D. In 1798 A.D., Bishop Bass, Diocesan of Massachusetts, was elected Bishop of Rhode Island, accepting the position and holding it until his death, in 1803 A.D. Bishop Benjamin Moore, of New York, was next elected, in 1806 A.D., to the Episcopate of Rhode Island, but whether or not he accepted and exercised the trust does not seem to be recorded. In 1810 A.D. the Convention elected delegates to represent it in the proposed Convention of the Eastern Diocese, and to take part in the election of a Bishop who should have jurisdiction also in Rhode Island. This election resulted in the choice of Alexander

Viets Griswold, at that time rector at Bristol, who was consecrated in 1811 A.D., and continued to exercise the bishopric in a most meek and gentle spirit until his death, in 1843 A.D., having, however, removed to Massachusetts in 1829 A.D.

The first parochial reports of which a record is preserved were presented to the Bishop at the Convention of 1813 A.D. The baptisms in the three parishes, at Bristol, Newport, and Providence, had amounted during the preceding year to 137, and the communicants numbered 312. Although the four Colonial parishes had all been established by the close of 1722 A.D., yet it was not until 1816 A.D. that a fifth (St. Paul's, Pawtucket) was added to the list, if we except the Tower Hill Church, which failed to become a permanent organization. St. Paul's was thus the only parish founded for more than a century,—from the establishment of St. John's, Providence, in 1722 A.D., to that of Grace Church, in the same city, in 1829 A.D. Henceforth, however, for the next ten years, there intervened a period of extraordinary growth, such as the Rhode Island Church never saw before, nor has ever seen since, as far, at least, as the number of new organizations is concerned, averaging three in each two years. At the time of Bishop Griswold's death, in 1843 A.D., there were twenty-one parishes, of which four have since become extinct. In fifteen parishes (two or three of the largest, however, not reporting) the baptisms that year were 233, and the communicants numbered 1276.

The Completely Furnished Diocese under Bishops of its own.—After the decease of Bishop Griswold, it was felt that the time had come when Rhode Island should enjoy the exclusive services of a Bishop. A special Convention was accordingly called to meet at St. Stephen's Church, Providence, on April 6, 1843 A.D., for the election of such an officer. It consisted of 80 members, of whom 21 were clergymen, being nearly twelvefold as many as took part in the first Convention a half-century before. The almost unanimous choice of the Convention fell upon the Rev. John Prentiss Kewley Henshaw, D.D., rector of St. Peter's Church, Baltimore, who was consecrated during the ensuing August. Bishop Henshaw served the Diocese with eminent ability, energy, and devotion until his death, in 1852 A.D. His Episcopate was a period of large missionary interest and activity, many new points, especially in the manufacturing districts, being occupied; not less than six, which grew into parishes, surviving to the present time as permanent stations of the Church.

In addition to his Diocesan duties, Bishop Henshaw was also rector of Grace Church, Providence, an elegant edifice of stone, being one of the first fruits of his labors.

The present Bishop of Rhode Island, the Rt. Rev. Thomas March Clark, D.D., was elected to that office at a special Convention, on September 27, 1854 A.D., there being 21 parishes represented, and 95 members, of whom 24 were clergymen, being present. During his Episcopate the number of parishes in Rhode Island has doubled, and the number of communicants nearly trebled. It has been a period of solid growth, not only in numbers, but in public estimation, until the Episcopal Church in Rhode Island, in influence and dignity, stands second to no other religious body, in marked contrast to its lamentable condition a century since.

Another feature of the present administration has been the marked decline in party spirit in these latter years, and the attainment of a high degree of charity and tranquillity. On the 6th of December, 1879 A.D., there was held in Grace Church, Providence, amidst the most inspiring associations, the Twenty-fifth Anniversary of the consecration of the Bishop. Almost the only element marring the pleasure of the occasion was the reflection that so many of those who participated in the election, a quarter-century before, had already passed from the earth, notably, among the clergy, the Rev. Dr. Crocker, long rector of St. John's Church, Providence, the Rev. Dr. Taft, similarly identified with St. Paul's Church, Pawtucket, the Rev. Dr. Crane, rector of St. Luke's, East Greenwich, and the Rev. Dr. Waterman, rector of St. Stephen's, Providence. Only three out of the twenty-four remained alive and connected with the Diocese. One of the auspicious enterprises of this Episcopate has been the raising of so large an Episcopal fund as now, for several years, to have freed the Bishop from the necessity of serving a parish as rector, and thus enabled him to devote himself exclusively to the prosecution of his proper office. At the Annual Convention of 1854 A.D., the year of Bishop Clark's accession, there were reported, parishes, 23; clergy, 27; baptisms, 228; communicants, 2446; marriages, 141; burials, 291; teachers and scholars in Sunday-school, 2363; offerings and contributions for religious purposes, $6711.31.

The statistics of the last year (1886 A.D.) are: Clergy, 55; parishes, 41; families, 3730; missions, 8; candidates for holy orders, 5; ordinations, D. 1, P. 2; baptisms, infants, 716, adults, 229, total, 945; confirmed, 544; communicants, 7823; Sunday-school teachers, 876; Sunday-school scholars, 7288; contributions, $177,-348.92.

REV. D. GOODWIN.

Righteousness. The Hebrew verb from which the Old Testament idea of righteousness is derived means to be right or straight, "as if spoken of a way." In Ps. xxiii. 3, we have "the paths of righteousness," and in Isa. xxxiii. 15, the good man is "He that walketh righteously and speaketh uprightly." Such an one "shall dwell on high: his place of defense shall be the munitions of rocks: bread shall be given him; his waters shall be sure." His "eyes shall see the King in his beauty" (vs. 16, 17). As righteousness signifies being righteous, it is most naturally an attribute of Almighty GOD. Abraham exclaims, "shall not the Judge of all the earth do right?" (Gen. xviii. 25.) And Elihu says, I "will ascribe righteousness to my Maker" (Job xxxvi. 3). Righteousness in man consists in a proper relation towards GOD, who is the Fountain of Justice. The man who "shall abide" in GOD'S "tabernacle," and "dwell" in His "holy hill," is "he that walketh uprightly, and worketh righteousness, and speaketh the truth in his heart" (Ps. xv. 1, 2. See Isa. lxiv. 5). Of the CHRIST the psalmist sings, "Thou lovest righteousness, and hatest wickedness, therefore GOD, thy GOD, hath anointed thee with the oil of gladness above thy fellows" (Ps. xlv. 7). While GOD commands that "Just balances, just weights, a just ephah, and a just hin" (Lev. xix. 36) shall be used by His people, these things are but outward, and a person may use them from expediency, therefore true righteousness must go deeper than the outward act, and stimulate the soul and direct the motives. Isaiah speaks of the people "in whose hearts is" GOD'S "law" (li. 17). When David hopes to behold GOD'S "face in righteousness" (Ps. xvii. 15), he must refer to something higher than a mere policy of honest living. True righteousness, then, must have relation to GOD. He sits "in the throne judging right" (Ps. ix. 4). "Righteousness and judgment are the habitation of His throne" (Ps. xcvii. 2). If a man is conscious of his obligation to be like a righteous GOD, then his treatment of his neighbor will display a character which naturally results from such a sense of duty. Achish says to David, "Thou hast been upright" (1 Sam. xxix. 6). David's prayer to GOD is, "Judge me, O LORD, according to my righteousness" (Ps. vii. 8). A part of righteousness is to honor father and mother and to love one's neighbor as himself (St. Matt. xix. 19). Man has gone far away from original righteousness, he has broken GOD'S law, and robbed GOD by using his body and his goods contrary to the will of the Giver (Mal. iii. 8). The "tithes and offerings" have been wanting, and the spiritual service which gladly gives the outward offering has been lacking. But in robbing GOD we rob ourselves, for true happiness lies in religion. Not doing our duty towards GOD we are maimed in our feeble attempts to do our duty towards our neighbor, and have not the ability to give rights due to others because we are unrighteous ourselves. The sinfulness of man is, however, to be met and overcome by the sinlessness of CHRIST. "And this is His name whereby He shall be called, THE LORD OUR RIGHTEOUSNESS" (Jer. xxiii. 6). "CHRIST JESUS, who of GOD is made unto us wisdom, and righteousness, and sanctification, and redemption" (1 Cor. i. 30).

Man broke the law of GOD, CHRIST has fulfilled that law, and the second Adam has thus atoned for the sin introduced by the first Adam. CHRIST now stands as our sponsor, and we are accepted in Him and for His sake. "GOD was in CHRIST, reconciling the world unto Himself, not imputing their trespasses unto them" (2 Cor. v. 19). The whole Christian idea of righteousness, therefore, relates to the believer's position towards the SAVIOUR. Jeremiah and St. Paul, guided by the same HOLY SPIRIT, point to one Redeemer, "The LORD our Righteousness." REV. S. F. HOTCHKIN.

Ring. A wedding-ring was made use of by Romans, and to some extent by Jews, and it was adopted by Christians, who, however, in ancient times used it at the espousals, and not at the marriage.

The Hebrew's ring contained his seal, and so the signet-ring was a symbol of authority, as in the case of Joseph (Gen. xli. 42. See also Esther iii. 10; 1 Macc. vi. 15; St. Luke xv. 22; Jer. xxii. 24; Hagg. ii. 23; Eccles. xlix. 11). Rings used by women (Isa. iii. 21). Presented by men and women for the service of the Tabernacle (Ex. xxxv. 22). The signet-ring was worn on the right hand (Jer. xxii. 24). From Ex. xxviii. 11, it is thought "that the rings contained a stone engraven with a device, or with the owner's name." Massive Egyptian rings have been discovered, most of them of gold. The Greeks and Romans had an abundance of rings. They were worn particularly by men.

In St. James ii. 2, the term translated "with a gold ring" means "golden-ringed," implying "the presence of several gold rings."

In the use of a ring in the investiture of a Bishop, it was a symbol of his espousals with his Church in CHRIST'S stead.

Authorities: W. L. Bevan in Smith's Dictionary of the Bible, Bingham's Antiq., Bowden's Greg. VII.

REV. S. F. HOTCHKIN.

Ritual. Modern scientific investigations show more clearly than ever the close connection between the body and the soul of man. It has always been found by experience that each constantly influences the other, but it is only of late years that real scientific proof has been given of the perpetual action and reaction of soul on body, and body on mind and soul. GOD is a Spirit, and is to be worshiped in spirit and in truth; but, since He is the GOD of Nature, and the GOD who, having wrought out salvation through the Incarnation of His SON, now applies the benefits of that salvation to men through the Sacraments, it is not surprising that the worship due to GOD is most effectually rendered by the soul when it is associated with an outward and bodily service; that is, with a certain amount of Ritual.

The details of the Jewish Ritual were all laid down by GOD'S Revelation, but under the free dispensation of the Gospel, the working out of the minutiæ of Christian Ritual has been left to the practical experience and wisdom of the Church, as she speads from one continent to another, from the warm south to the cold north. The ideal of the Church's unity is well shown, not by an iron uniformity in small matters, but by the substantial identity of things important, and a diversity in ceremonial law and usage. The XXXIV. Article well expresses the judgment of the Church that it is not necessary "that Traditions and Ceremonies be in all places one and utterly like, for at all times they have been divers, and may be changed according to the diversity of countries, times, and men's manners, so that nothing be ordained against GOD'S Word."

The Ritual of public worship concerns three things: first, the divisions and arrangements of the church edifice and the character and position of the different articles of church furniture; secondly, the dress of the various ministers and the adornments of the building and its contents; thirdly, the postures of the officiating clergy and of the congregation, the manual acts of the Sacraments, and the proper and orderly rendering of the words appointed for the different services, or the performance of Divine worship as it affects the eye and the ear.

The ritual law as to the "Ornaments" of minister and church will be discussed under the article on VESTMENTS. The divisions and arrangement of the church edifice have varied considerably at different periods, but have in the main always exhibited a threefold division corresponding to the nave, or place for the congregation, the choir, or place for the inferior ministers and for the performance of the less sacred portions of the service, and the Chancel or Sanctuary, where the most solemn portions of the Liturgy, and in particular of the Holy Communion, were celebrated. The questions raised by the third class of things included under the head of Ritual are so numerous and so various that it is obviously impossible to discuss them, except in a very general way, in a work of this description, but for the investigation of any detail certain general principles may be laid down.

In the first place, it may be said that public service is primarily commanded, not so much to benefit men by instruction or prayer as to do homage to GOD by worship and praise, though, of course, the secondary blessing is obtained if the primary duty is rightly performed. All the acts of the officiating clergyman are therefore divided into two great classes: first, those where he stands as the representative of the one great High-Priest, and, secondly, those in which he is the leader of the people in their adorations and devotions. In the celebration of the Eucharist it is evident that the Priest, in the teaching of the Sermon, in the reading of Scripture, in the Epistle and Gospel, the Commandments and Comfortable words, in speaking the words of pardon, in the Absolution and of blessing in the Benediction, stands as the representative of GOD, and so turns towards the people, while during the Collects, the prayers of Consecration, Oblation, and Invocation, the prayers of Intercession, the commemorations of the special and common Prefaces and the Thanksgivings, he stands as the leader of the people, who in their corporate capacity as the Church offer together their prayers and worship to GOD, and that he, therefore, turns his back to the Congregation as an officer turns his back to the men whom he leads into battle.

In the second place, it is easy to see that the rubrics of the American and English Prayer-Books are very far from complete, are very much less complete than those of the Roman Missal or the Greek Liturgy of St. Chrysostom. To take a few simple examples to show this, no directions whatever are given as to the position of the font in the church, the attitude of the congregation during the Epistle, the part of the church where the Confirmation service shall take place, the posture of the Celebrant while he administers the Communion to himself, the time at which the Priest shall return the baptized infant to the parents or godparents, the place where the Litany shall be said or sung, or the taking of the privately baptized child into the Minister's arms when he is publicly signed with the mark of the cross.

If, then, the Prayer-Book is so defective in Ritual directions, where are we to look for information to enable us to carry out the details of divine service properly? In the American Church seven sources of information are open to us:

First. The explicit directions of the rubrics of our own Book of Common Prayer.

Second. The explicit directions of the English rubrics where they have not been obviously and designedly corrected by our own Church.

Third. The *implied* directions of rubrics, as, for example, that contained in the concluding direction of our Communion Office, which commands the reverent consumption of all that remains of the consecrated elements. This rubric, on the one hand, plainly forbids Reservation, and when taken in connection with the known practice of the English Reformation period, and the practical difficulty of consuming all the consecrated wine, implicitly orders the cleansing of the Chalice by the introduction and drinking of a little water.

Fourth. The directions and recommendations of the American Canons, and the English Canons in force at the time of the American Revolution. It is under this authority that we practice the bowing of the head at the mention of our LORD'S name in the Creed.

Fifth. A careful consideration of the historical circumstances under which any given direction was inserted in the rubrics;

a thorough knowledge of the position of the Altar during the time of Charles I. and Charles II. would have prevented all controversy as to the " Eastward position."

Sixth. The rubrics and customs of the Pre-Reformation Liturgies of England, where they have not been corrected or abolished by the successive editions of the reformed Prayer-Book.

Seventh. Continued custom and usage.

It is obvious that these different means of information vary greatly in value, and that to balance the evidence on any point not decided by either the first or second source of information requires extended knowledge, ample time, good judgment, and freedom from prejudice. Church history during the sixteenth century shows repeatedly that a considerable amount of ritual not provided directly by the Prayer-Book was taken for granted, but after the interruptions of the Civil War of the next century, and the long-continued disuse of various customs, it is practically necessary for the ordinary Priest or Layman to accept on any particular point the general judgment of those who have made Ritual a special study. Passing over more technical and unattainable works, an excellent popular manual will be found in the little pamphlet " Ritual Conformity," published by Parker & Co., London, an interpretation of the rubrics drawn up by a conference of some of the best authorities of England, or, as in the case of Vestments, the reader may be referred to Blunt's " Annotated Book of Common Prayer" and other commentaries on the Prayer-Book.

Canon xxii., Title i., of the Digest of our National Canons provides that on the complaint in writing of any two Presbyters of the Diocese that " ceremonies or practices not ordained or authorized in the Book of Common Prayer, and setting forth or symbolizing erroneous or doubtful doctrines, have been introduced by any Minister during the celebration of the Holy Communion, it shall be the duty of the Bishop to summon the Standing Committee as his Council of Advice, and with them to investigate the matter." If this investigation justifies the complaint, the Bishop is directed to admonish the Minister in writing, and, if he disregard this admonition, it shall be the duty of the Standing Committee to cause him to be tried for a breach of his ordination vow."

EDWARD M. PARKER.

Rochet. *Vide* VESTMENTS.

Rogation Days were instituted, it is said, by Mamertus, Bishop of Vienne, in France, 452 A.D., upon the calamities which were said to have befallen his diocese,—an earthquake, fire, and an incursion of wolves. The Bishop set apart the three days before Ascension-day as a solemn fast, during which processions, with Litanies, were to be made throughout the diocese. This custom was taken up by other dioceses, and became common throughout the West. While the old Collect, Epistle, and Gospel for Rogation days were not retained, they were themselves kept in the Calendar as private fasts, and a Homily " for the days of Rogation week" on these fasts is in the Book of Homilies. Hooker, in his " Ecclesiastical Polity," has a fine section (Book v. ¿ 41) upon the whole subject of Litanies and Rogation days.

Romanism. The word " Romanism," when correctly used, designates those erroneous views and practices which the Roman Church has engrafted upon the Catholic Faith.

Sometimes the word is incorrectly employed by ultra-Protestants to indicate views and practices which, however primitive and Catholic, are no longer retained by them. Thus at one time Liturgical worship and Episcopacy were spoken of as parts of " Romanism."

We must therefore be careful to distinguish between the correct and the incorrect use of the word. The best help to ascertaining what are the errors which the Roman Church has engrafted upon the primitive and Catholic Faith is found in the study of the XXXIX. Articles of Religion of our Church.

These Articles were framed to set forth the doctrinal views of the Church in England after the Reformation, when that Church was purged of Roman errors, and restored to the primitive simplicity of the Faith as held in England long before Romanism became dominant.

The Errors protested against in the Articles are as follows:

1st. *That the Church may set forth new Articles of the Faith.* Of late years the dogmas of the immaculate conception of the Virgin Mary, and the infallibility of the Pope " *docens ex cathedra,*" have been set forth. Against all of this this Church protests in her VI. and XX. Articles.

2d. *That the Latin language alone shall be used in public religious services.* Article XXIV. declares that " it is repugnant to the Word of GOD and to the custom of the primitive Church to have public Prayer in the Church, or to minister the Sacraments in a tongue not understood of the people."

3d. *That there are seven sacraments,*— Baptism, the Supper of the Lord, Confirmation, Penance, Orders, Matrimony, and Extreme Unction.

This Church declares that there are only two Sacraments ordained by the LORD,— Baptism and the Supper of the LORD. The five called Sacraments by the Roman Church " are not to be counted Sacraments of the Gospel, they have not like nature with these two, for that they have not any visible sign or ceremony ordained of GOD."

4th. *That the substance of the Bread and Wine in the* LORD'S *Supper are changed into the veritable Body and Blood of* CHRIST. This doctrine of Transubstantiation is denied in Article XXVIII., where it is declared that " the Body of CHRIST is taken and eaten in the Supper only after a heavenly and spiritual manner," and by faith. The same Article *condemns the reservation, carrying about, lifting up, and worshiping the consecrated elements.*

5th. *That the lay-people should not receive the wine in the Sacrament of the* LORD'S *Supper.* Article XXX. declares that both the parts of the LORD'S Sacrament by CHRIST'S ordinance and commandment ought to be ministered to all Christian men alike.

6th. *That in the Mass the priest offers* CHRIST *for the remission of the sins of the living and the dead.* Article XXXI. declares that this is a blasphemous fable and a dangerous deceit, for the one offering of CHRIST on Calvary was a perfect redemption, propitiation, and satisfaction for all sins.

7th. *That the clergy must not marry.* Article XXXII. says that it is allowable for them to marry at their discretion, as they shall judge the same to help them lead godly lives, there being no command in Scripture to marry or to abstain from it.

8th. *That the clergy should not be subject to civil law.* Article XXXVII. declares that the power of the civil magistrate extends to clergy as well as to the laity in all things temporal, but not in things purely spiritual.

9th. (1) *That the souls of the dead are helped through Purgatory by the prayers and gifts of the living; by the intercession of the saints in heaven, and by the sacrifice of the mass.* (2) *That the treasure of merit stored up in the Church may be applied by the Pope to redeem souls from Purgatory and from temporal punishment.* This is usually called the doctrine of Indulgence or Pardons. (3) *That images and relics may be worshiped.* Against all three of these errors Article XXII. is directed, and speaks of them collectively as a "fond thing, vainly invented, and founded upon no warranty of Scripture."

What this Church, then, formally condemns as "Romanism" may be briefly stated as inventing new dogmas, using a tongue which the people do not understand, multiplying Sacraments, Transubstantiation, denying the cup to the laity, declaring that CHRIST is offered in the Sacrifice of the Mass, forbidding the clergy to marry, declaring the clergy free from obedience to civil law, Purgatory, Indulgences, and the adoration of images and relics.

REV. G. W. SHINN.

Romans, Epistle to. It was written in the spring of 58 A.D., when the Apostle deferred his intended visit to carry the alms of the Churches in Macedonia to Jerusalem (Acts xx. 16). It is remarkable for its tact, delicacy of tone, courtesy, and for the great exposition of the doctrines of grace, justification, and election. It was addressed to a congregation which had not yet received the visit of any Apostle; which was composed of a large proportion of Jewish as well as Gentile converts; and which contained several of the Apostle's kinsmen and many personal friends. He knew much of its condition from the constant intercourse which was natural between the Capital and all parts of the Empire, and, too, because of the several expulsions of the Jews who had settled there. These claims upon him led the Apostle to write to the Christians at Rome this noble Epistle. In a Church not founded by any Apostle, but composed of the different Christians who from various causes dwelt there, some of whom were of the three thousand converted at the Pentecostal outpouring of the HOLY GHOST, some of evidently later conversion, Jews, Proselytes, and Gentiles together, there was much that would attract the Apostle, and would call forth his best skill in correcting erroneous doctrines and presenting the truth, especially as he had no authority over them as a founder. He would have to state to both the Jew and the Gentile the meeting-point, and common ground for them in the Gospel. This is done with great ability and without withholding a jot of the whole truth. The analysis of the Epistle which follows is not as close as it would be could more space be devoted to it. The main divisions are six, and extend somewhat as follows:

I. After his salutation the Apostle naturally speaks of his desire to preach the Gospel in Rome, because he is a debtor both to Jew and to Gentile as the Apostle to the Gentiles. This Gospel is one to be received by Faith, since all are guilty before GOD; then follows the most remarkable outline of the great sins of the heathen world traced by a master's hand, truthfully, but with great delicacy. This leads him to show how all are concluded under the sentence of death, conscience proving this, since it proves that we all have sinned whether under the law or without the law. He pauses here—if it be a pause—to show the advantages of the Jew as the chosen of GOD, yet that all have transgressed (ch. i.–iii. 20).

II. He then shows the preparation for restoration in the mercy of GOD through the redemption of CHRIST, and our acceptance by Faith in His Atonement, that GOD might justify all alike through Faith in the Blood of JESUS, excluding the claim of wages for works, for no work can be done acceptable to Him (ch. iii. 21–31). Abraham's example was shown by Faith, not of works; so too David's forgiveness was of GOD's mercy. Abraham's Faith was shown in his trust before circumcision, so that the Gentile too might heir through him (ch. iv.).

III. The Apostle can now come back to the Justification in CHRIST. It is His love, His mercy, to us, "for when we were without strength, in due time CHRIST died for the ungodly." The Atonement is the source of our joy in GOD, and we have peace in CHRIST. For sin from Adam on to ourselves is condoned and forgiven in Him in whom is righteousness unto eternal life (ch. v.). So far the Apostle leads us without any but the most general terms. But now he changes to a narrower but far more personal application. The sixth is the crucial chapter.

IV. This justification by Faith, this righteousness which is granted to faith in the Atoning Sacrifice of CHRIST which gives us life, is conveyed to us by BAPTISM, whereby we die to sin (ch. i.–vi.) and live unto GOD. Dead to the world, risen in CHRIST. This release from sin is as a release from slavery; it is as a woman married to a brutal husband from whose power death has freed her, so that she can be married holily to one who would care for her rightly. So CHRIST has bought us and made us free, so CHRIST has released our souls from sin by destroying it and married us to Himself by BAPTISM (ch. vi.–vii. 6).

V. Yet, as we are in the world, we must be struggling with the power of sinfulness, left as a probation and a discipline. We are, as it were, in the body of this death, from which CHRIST can and does free us (ch. vii. 7–25). But there is aid given.

VI. There is the gift of the Spirit to the Baptized, for CONFIRMATION must follow Baptism. This ch. viii. is one of the most magnificent chapters written by the Apostle. The SANCTIFICATION by the Holy SPIRIT, in whom we have our Resurrection, by whom we can only pray aright, through whom cometh the restoration of all things, by whose working in our hearts is the call, the justification, the sanctifying glory. And here we have a glorious description of our closeness to GOD and His SON through the HOLY GHOST, whereby, more than conquerors in Him, naught of this world can separate us from the love of GOD which is in CHRIST JESUS our LORD (ch. viii.)

Here ends the proper doctrinal part of the Epistle, but St. Paul had in view the congregation he addressed, and he turns to his kinsmen according to the flesh. He would gladly perish for their sakes.

VII. Why is the Jew rejected and the Gentile taken in? It would be enough to reply, GOD according to His sovereignty could choose as He would His instruments, so He can do as His Wisdom overruling and using man's sinfulness may direct. If the chosen seed did not believe in later days, they would be put aside, as preparation had been made by prophecy for such a contingency. Therefore the righteousness by the law failing, the righteousness which is by faith must be accepted. So, then, the Jew is put aside till he will turn, and the Gentile accepted. But the Jew is not wholly cast off, but will be received as soon as he is willing to have the veil removed. The Apostle touches upon the mystery of Predestination, and shows how GOD'S purposes cannot fail, and His instruments must obey Him (ch. ix.–xi.).

VIII. He now leaves off these high themes and proceeds to urge that if these are true and we live by them, then our lives must be a holy sacrifice unto GOD. In a series of very practical suggestions and advice upon the holy life, he introduces maxims and principles which are of universal obligation and apply to all times (ch. xii.–xv. 4).

IX. He closes with a reference to the mingled congregation, not advising, but speaking of their mutual relations, because of the thanksgiving the Gentiles owe to GOD because of His mercy to them. And now, as he is hindered for the present in his purpose to visit them, he alludes again to his Apostolic mission to preach the Gospel to the Gentiles, and beseeches their prayers, that he may be delivered from the dangers he is about to encounter from unbelieving Jews when he returns to Jerusalem (ch. xv. 5–33).

X. The last chapter (xvi.) is filled up with courteous salutations and messages to friends and kinsmen in Rome, and with a beautiful and characteristic ascription to GOD he ends the Epistle.

It is a wonderful composition, whether we consider its grace and skill, or its doctrinal teachings, or the broad sweep of the lofty thoughts and of the revelations given us through the Apostle. It is of value, too, as telling the fact that the Roman Church had no Apostolic founder, and must have been only strengthened by the later presence of St. Paul, and possibly of St. Peter, who at this date was in the East. There are many questions that grow out of side statements of the Apostle, such as were pertinent to, but not involved in, the main links of his argument,—those chiefly relating to election and grace,—which we have not room to discuss, but only mention; thus we may also note that whereas this Epistle is often used now to defend extreme statements upon these topics, the Church used it for a general defense of the doctrine of the freedom of the will, and of the broad and full gifts of GOD'S grace. Much of the matter in this Epistle is related to the arguments in the Epistle to the Galatians.

Authorities: Wordsworth's Epistle of St. Paul, Smith's Dictionary of the Bible, Cambridge Bible for Schools.

Rood. A cross (rod). The Rood was the Cross placed upon the beam or across the arch of the Choir, or surmounted the Screen or lattice-work of the Chancel, which was carried up quite high. This was then called a Rood-Screen, for it was the carved screen-work which was finished by the Cross placed upon it.

Rood-Loft. Often the screen was given more weight, was made of stone, and was turned into a gallery, gained by a well staircase. It still, of course, bore the Cross, carved prominently upon it. It was large enough to be turned into a chapel with an Altar in it in some churches, and is now, wherever it has been preserved, made use of as an organ-loft. It is claimed that there are no instances of the Rood-Screen or Rood-Loft earlier than the twelfth century.

Roof. *Vide* ARCHITECTURE.

Rubric. Literally, a direction or remark written in red letter. The word is borrowed from the phraseology of the old Roman Law-books, in which the titles, remarks, and sometimes the leading decisions were written in red ink. In the same way the regulations for the manner of performing the sacred offices of the Church were called rubrics, and were commonly written in red characters to make them easily distinguishable from the text of the office itself. (Smith's Dict. of Christian Antiquities, sub voc.) The body of the rubrics formed a compilation at first separate from the Liturgy, which contained comparatively few rubrics. There were regulations in force at one time ordering the Priest to report what ceremonial he used in the several offices of the Church. The office-books, however, gradually introduced more rubrics, and they were often so elaborate as to be confusing and contradictory. The mass of rubrics was constantly increasing, and the various Diocesan usages were adding to the confusion. In England, the uses of Bangor, Hertford, Winchester, Lincoln, Durham, and others clashed with the more popular use of Sarum; and the Roman use, though not in force, also was used. So that there was, as the Preface to the First Prayer-Book of Edward VI. declared, "more business to find out what should be read than to read it when it was found out." And one of the ends sought to be accomplished by this Book was that it should be a complete directory. "Furthermore, by this order, the curates shall need but none other books for their public service but this book and the Bible; by means whereof the people shall not be at so great charge for books as in time past they have been."

It was therefore to supersede all other preceding uses. All other rubrics were abrogated, and these only were to be in use. And proper provision was made for the due interpretation of any doubts,—"And forsomuch as nothing can almost be so plainly set forth but doubts may rise in the use and practicing of the same, to appease all such diversity (if any arise), and for the resolution of all such doubts concerning the manner how to understand, do, and execute the things contained in this book, the parties that so doubt or diversely take anything shall always resort to the Bishop of the Diocese, who, by his discretion, shall take order for the quieting and appeasing of the same, so that the same order be not contrary to anything contained in this book." And the Prayer-Book of 1552 A.D adds: "And if the Bishop of the Diocese be in any doubt, then he may send for the resolution thereof to the Archbishop." (Preface to the English Prayer-Book.) This, then, cuts off the authority of all previous orders, ceremonials, or Pontificals, and makes the Prayer-Book the sole source for rubrical information and direction in understanding, doing, and executing the offices of the book. No rubrics from other sources can be introduced. Still, since these rubrics are in nearly every instance either translations or modifications of the older ritual, it follows that, to explain them, recourse must be had to these rituals, but simply as illustrating or correcting our apprehension of the application of our own Rubrics. For Rubrics have a very peculiar position in the great body of Church Law. They are inherited; they cannot be changed without much delay, a thorough sifting, and by constitutional enactment. Other Laws and Canons are applicable only either to certain circumstances, provide for certain contingencies, enact penalties for certain offenses, or supply remedies for certain defects, and therefore receive special attention only upon given occasions. But the Rubrics are of unceasing use and practice in the solemn public and constantly recurring worship of the Church. They are prominently before every congregation in the land. They demand constant observance in what they prescribe, and they presuppose a proper preparation for their fulfillment. They may be classified as (a) those concerning the general but positive directions for the service, e.g., the Rubrics for Morning and Evening Prayer; (b) those of the less frequent offices, or private offices which allow some liberty, e.g., those of the Visitation of the Sick and Prisoners and Family Prayer, Offices at Sea, and (c) those directions which concern the general conduct of the people as members of the Church, e.g., those who shall be admitted to Confirmation and Communion, the disciplinary Rubrics prefacing the order for the Holy Communion: the Rubrics upon the Catechism put at the end of it. Nearly every Rubric will fall under one or other of these divisions. Those concerning the public worship and the administration of the Sacraments and the several offices that may be demanded upon occasion, as those of Confirmation, Institution, Ordination, form upon these respective topics as nearly complete directions as in the nature of the case could be required. There are gaps and deficiencies in the code of Rubrics, it is true, but some of these will be accounted for farther on. (*Vide* also RITUAL.)

It must be here noted that these Rubrics form a complex but beautifully compacted Order of Service upon certain clear and well-defined principles, which set forth through them a harmonious order of worship. They thus form the Law upon the highest spiritual acts which Priest and people can join in, and so are of the strongest obligation. We should feel ourselves bound to carry them out strictly, and to provide such arrangements of the House of GOD, and such furniture and other conveniences that may enable us devoutly and reverently to celebrate our Public Worship according to their directions. Since, then, so many are concerned in their punctual discharge, and they form so much of our spiritual training, their observance or neglect or transgression is keenly felt by most, and in the last two instances is of positive loss and detriment to all concerned. For the minister is under solemn promise to obey them, and the people receive the Prayer-Book as a part of their spiritual inheritance. For us in the American Church the Rubrics are of the revision of 1789 A.D.; but while omission of a rubric in a deliberate revision like this must be equivalent to repeal or abrogation, we can go for explanation of things not supplied, or for illustration or other guidance, to the English Revision of 1662 A.D., and thence to that of 1552 A.D., and thence to the First Prayer-Book of 1549 A.D. These are our guides in the study of our rubrical Law, and for historical data we should apply to the older body of Rubrical Observances in the pre-Reformation period. It is not possible here to go into any full discussion of the Rubrics, but it should be pointed out how materially the care for the proper arrangement of the Church gives point and sense to the Rubric, and how flexible in many regards they really are. The Rubric for the saying of Morning and Evening Prayer does not prescribe, but takes for granted that there is all proper provision of stalls and of seats made (*vide* DESK, LITANY-STOOL, STALL), and of a Lection for the Bible a proper place, whether a pulpit or desk, for the Sermon a credence-table in the chancel, and so of other necessary and accustomed furniture, vessels, and vestments. (*Vide* ORNAMENTS.)

But in every code of Rubrics there is an amount of omission which requires some living authority, which shall decide what things are to be supplied or what are prohibited. In our own case, while the omission of specific Rubrics in the English Prayer-Book amounts to a prohibition, the omission to enumerate what is not enumerated in the English Prayer-Book cannot be construed as a prohibition, but rather the contrary. Again, there is a minimum below which disobedience asserts itself, and a maximum beyond which observance of the Rubric ceases. What these limits are and how far the place, the congregation, and the means for the due conduct of divine service modify use, and what interpretation should be put upon the Rubrics, belong to the Ordinary to decide. But it is by no means within the power of the Bishop to add to or to diminish the Rubric, nor can he set it aside. Again, the right interpretation of the Rubric is parallel to the like interpretation of an ambiguous Canon or an ambiguous Law. The history and scope of the Rubric must be considered. And, as in the matter of godly admonitions (*q. v.*), the Bishop has no right to forbid a practice proven to be strictly rubrical, simply because it does not coincide with what he deems fit and reverent. And again, non-usage or contrary custom cannot stand for a moment against a plain Rubric. But he has a right to enjoin a cessation of practices that are yet in doubt till such doubt is resolved, and to forbid all strange and intrusive practices interpolated into the service and which are injurious to or subversive of the Catholic doctrines of the Church. Obedience to such injunctions is a mark of a true love for CHRIST His Church. The Preface of the English Prayer-Book contains these pregnant words: "And although the keeping or omitting of a ceremony in itself considered is but a small thing, yet the wilful and contemptuous transgression and breaking of a common order and discipline is no small offence before GOD."

The missionary character of the Church in this country and the exigencies of the hour, as well as our colonial history, have affected the tone and spirit of our rubrical observances. When the work is wholly missionary and the services *cannot* be rendered, no rubrical observance is possible. But the instant a congregation is formed the authority of the rubrical Law asserts itself, and the Laity are bound as parties to its observance and as holders of the means therefor, to supply all due and proper furniture, vessels, and vestments for carrying out its provisions in the several services and offices of the Prayer-Book, and for the enforcement of such of its directions as the congregation or the several members thereof can and ought to observe, both in the regular services and in the cautionary and disciplinary Rubrics. In too many instances the Laity have taken no notice of their obligations, and have allowed or even forced usages to arise which are contrary to this part of Church Law and order. A better knowledge and study of the Rubrics will always lead to a better observance of them.

Rule of Faith. By this is meant that measure of indubitable truth by which all statements in religion are to be tested.

There may be opinions, fancies, views, interpretations, but nothing is to be set forth as absolutely essential in religion which is not according to the Rule of Faith.

The principle laid down by Vincentius of Lerins, 434 A.D., is a safe one for all Churchmen. It is this: "We must be peculiarly careful to hold that which hath been believed in all places, at all times and by all the faithful." It is often quoted in its briefer Latin form thus: "*Quod ubique, quod semper, quod ab omnibus creditum est.*" According to this principle we may determine the Rule of Faith by looking for universality, antiquity, and consent.

Whatever thus gained the assent of believers must have been based upon the teachings of the Master, whose command to the Apostles was: "Go ye, therefore, teach all nations, baptizing them in the name of the FATHER, and of the SON, and of the HOLY GHOST; *teaching them to observe all things whatsoever I have commanded you.*"

In the effort to teach others what the LORD had commanded them there grew up of necessity a Creed, not formally set forth, or issued by Apostolic authority formally given, but a form of sound words which in its essential features has been accepted by Christians in all the ages all along as the Rule of Faith in the essential doctrines of Christianity.

Irenæus said, "thus the Church, scattered though it be throughout the whole world, hath received from the Apostles and their disciples faith in one GOD," and then follow the several terms of the Creed, and he adds, "the faith of the Church is in accordance with it, her preaching and instruction and tradition are in harmony with it." Tertullian says the rule of faith is altogether one, it alone is invariable and unalterable, namely, "of faith in one GOD, the Creator of the world," etc., and he goes on to enumerate the other articles of the Creed.

For some years after the establishment of the Church there were no written records such as now constitute the Canon of New Testament Scriptures. The Faith was taught orally from one to another. It may be that the first records were liturgies in which the form of some words was preserved. Fragments of these "liturgical germs," as they may be called, are preserved in the Epistles of the New Testament.

It pleased GOD, the HOLY GHOST, to inspire men to write accounts of the life and sayings of the LORD JESUS, of the planting of the Church, and to compose letters to the Churches. In these various compositions there were preserved the truths which had formerly been taught orally. The Church did not grow out of the Scriptures, nor did it gain its Faith primarily from them. The Church was founded, with its ministry, sacraments, ordinances, and doctrines, before a line of New Testament Scripture was written.

The Canon of the New Testament Scriptures was determined by the application of the simple principle to each book, Does this writing contain what is agreeable to the Faith which the Church has received? The Canon being once established, Holy Scripture was thenceforth to be appealed to as containing whatever was essential in Christian doctrine, and hence our Church in the VI. Article of Religion declares that "whatsoever is not read therein nor may be proved thereby is not to be required of any man that it should be believed as an article of the Faith, or be thought requisite or necessary to salvation." No part of our belief, therefore, is to rest upon mere tradition. We are to appeal to the infinitely superior authority of Scripture, and to make it the only final resort. It is there that we can find the sure means of ascertaining the Rule of Faith, the teaching of CHRIST and His inspired servants.

A division may be made between what is the Rule of Faith with reference to essentials, and what has been the common belief of the majority of Christians in the ages all along with reference to points not essential to salvation.

Sometimes this latter classification is confounded with the former, and points are pressed as included within the Rule of Faith which really do not belong there. They may be agreeable to it, but not included within it, as essentials.

The need of giving attention to this point is shown by considering the position of the Roman Church on the one hand, and modern denominations of Christians on the other. Rome widens the Rule of Faith by adding to the teachings of Scripture the traditions which had their origin in obscurity, and the decisions of Popes whom she declares infallible. Hence the Rule of Faith may be different (according to this view) from age to age.

Modern Christian sects, on the other hand, deny, obscure, belittle, or omit portions of the Faith, and consequently do not present before us that indubitable truth by which all views are to be measured.

It is the glory of our branch of the Christian Church that in its ministry, sacraments, ordinances, creeds, and liturgy it aims to preserve the Rule of Faith as it was received everywhere, by all and in every place before there were divisions in the Body of CHRIST. REV. G. W. SHINN.

Rural Dean was at first the same as the Archpresbyter; but he obtained his title of *Decanus ruralis* about the time of Charlemagne (800 A.D. circ.). The office was introduced into England about 1052 A.D., in the days of Edward the Confessor. Its development into the present office and functions of the English Rural Dean followed as the Church's needs and work developed. The functions of the office are well set forth in the oath of office, which was in some Dioceses anciently administered: "I, A. B., do swear diligently and faithfully to execute the office of Rural Dean within the Deanery of D. First, I will diligently and faithfully execute, or cause to be executed, all such processes as shall be directed unto me, from my Lord Bishop of C., or his officers, or ministers by his authority. Item, I will give diligent attendance by myself or my deputy at every consistory court to be holden by the said reverend father in GOD, or his Chancellor, as well as to return such processes as shall be by me or my deputy executed; as also to receive others there unto me to be directed. Item, I will from time to time during my said office diligently inquire, and true information give, unto the said reverend father in GOD, or his Chancellor, of all the names of all such persons within the said deanery of D. as shall be openly and publicly noted and defamed, or vehemently suspected of any crime or offense as is to be punished or reformed by the authority of the said court. Item, I will diligently inquire, and true information give, of all such persons and their names as do administer any dead man's goods before they have proved the will of the testator or taken letters of administration of the deceased intestates. Item, I will be obedient to the right reverend father in GOD, J., Bishop of C., and his Chancellor, in all honest and lawful commands; neither will I attempt, do, or procure to be done or attempted, anything that shall be prejudicial to his jurisdiction, but will preserve and maintain the same to the uttermost of my power." They convened rural chapters of all the instituted clergy or their curates as proxies for them, and presided as Prolocutors. The office of Rural Dean has only within the last forty years been revived in England. His powers are simply of inspection. It has been partially imitated in several Dioceses in this country by giving this title to the president of Convocation. It has always in its past history been found to be a convenient rather than a necessary office. It has a good deal of interest attached to it, since it appears that at one time the Rural Dean was made a Chorepiscopus—or country bishop—with restraint, but this delegation of Episcopal powers was inhibited by Alexander III., 1089 A.D. But Archbishop Ussher in his scheme for a "Moderate Episcopacy," which he propounded just before the great rebellion (1640 A.D.), proposed to erect the rural Deaneries into Sees. The office, were it generally revived, could be made a very important adjunct to the work of the Church in this country. But in order that it should be efficient and obtain that weight which would make it influential, it should be instituted by a common consent of the Bishops and Dioceses. The observation of the old canonist Lindwood upon Rural Deans in his day was, that they were rather after the custom of the country than founded by Canon Law. (Magis nituntur consuetudini patriæ quam usui communi.) And this will probably belong always to the office. (Burn's Eccl. Law, vol. ii. p. 120.)

Ruth. The short book of Ruth is perhaps one of the loveliest idyls extant in any language, apart from its canonical authority and from its historical importance in the Christology of the Old Testament. It is the record of the heathen ancestress of our LORD introduced into the line of His forefathers after their settlement in Canaan. The migration of Naomi and Elimelech to the land of Moab because of the famine, the marriage of Mahlon to Ruth, his death, and Naomi's desire in her widowhood to return to Judah, all are told with the utmost simplicity and directness. The touching devotion of Ruth, "Whither thou goest I will go, and where thou lodgest I will lodge; thy people shall be my people, and thy GOD my GOD; where thou diest I will die, and there will I be buried. The LORD do so to me and more also if aught but death do part me and thee" (Ruth i. 16, 17), reveals the depth of loving character that fitted her to be taken into the chosen people. The narrative that follows, of Boaz and his generous treatment and protection of the homeless widow and her daughter-in-law, is in perfect keeping with the time, the customs, and usages of the age to which it refers. But still more important is the record of the steps by which, upon the surrender of the nearest of kin, Boaz secured the right of purchase of the inheritance which belonged to the family. It is a type of the Redeemer; the "Goel" which, as Boaz became by the plucking off the shoe, CHRIST became by His redemption. "Over Edom will I cast out my shoe: Philistia, triumph thou because of me" (Ps. lx. 8).

The Book was most probably written during David's lifetime, certainly not earlier than the latter days of Samuel. The customs and slight notes of manner, the absence of any prejudice against a stranger, the straightforward character of the narrative, the slight details that are preserved, all attest to its genuineness.

S.

Sabaoth. A peculiar title of JEHOVAH. The Anglicized word occurs only twice in King James' Version, but it is a frequent appellative of GOD. The LORD of Hosts is His Name. It was the ascription of the Seraphim, Holy, Holy, Holy is the LORD of Hosts. It has become a familiar title from its use in the TE DEUM, but in its translated form it is also in the preface in the Communion Service. The LORD of all the hosts of heaven and of earth, it is our LORD's title, for He whose vesture was dipped in blood, whose name is the Word of GOD, upon whose vesture and thigh is written KING of Kings and LORD of Lords, leads the armies which are in heaven.

Sabbatarians. Those who observe the Sabbath-day because they allege that there is no sufficient proof to them that there is any authority to change from the Sabbath to the first day of the week. They have but little foothold in this country.

Sabbath. The Jewish day of rest. It was peculiarly so called, for it was doubly typical: I. As of the ceasing from the creation of this world. II. As of the day when GOD gave His people rest from their bondage in Egypt. Both of these arguments are given each in the separate forms of the Covenant as recited at Sinai, and as repeated by Moses in the Book of Deuteronomy. It is, then, no light thing for the Church, guided by the HOLY GHOST, to have changed from a day of rest so impressively commanded to the LORD'S day. (*Vide* SUNDAY.) The Sabbath, as a sacredly observed day, was probably, though not certainly, older than the Mosaic age, and came of the Patriarchs. In fact, upon the general ground of regularity in the offering of worship, it becomes very probable, and we know that the period of weeks was used. But the institution of the Sabbath is founded not merely on Jewish needs; it is of the highest human observance also, as it meets the needs of man both in the offering of worship and in the necessity of rest from manual and secular occupations. The name itself gives the reason of its recurrence,—rest. Its place on the Tables of Stone gave it a rank that was beyond other ritual enactments of the Mosaic Law. It was made a part of the Covenant. It was put as an observance ever to be kept in mind. Its pollution was one of the grave charges against the Nation. It was a day far above all but the great feasts in the strictness in which it was to be observed, and the trials of the Maccabean Kingdom stamped its full ritual, even burdensome, observance upon the Nation.

Our LORD'S own observance of the Day and His protests against its abuse, are well known. But all allusion to it ceases in the Epistles. In the Acts we trace a change by the reference to the first day of the week, and in the Apocalypse to the LORD'S day. The tracing of the change will be found in the Article SUNDAY. But here it is noted that Sunday being the equivalent and so accepted of the Sabbath, the covenant to observe the LORD'S day as our LORD has taught us is obligatory upon us. And so as the prosperity of the Jew rested in part upon the sanctity with which he observed the day, so the Christian observance of the day is a part of our national prosperity. It is evidently so, even upon the low ground of the perpetually recurring instruction on that day in morals and in general religious instruction, not to dwell upon the worship due to our GOD. The Sabbath was invaluable as a means of instructing the people who were gathered into the synagogues. But the Sabbath took in a wider range, also founded upon the use of the number seven. The seventh day for rest and worship; the seventh week after the Passover brought the Feast of Pentecost; the seventh year was the year of rest for the ground,—the Sabbatical year—the non-observance of which regulation brought upon the people their seventy years of captivity; then the year of the seven times the Sabbatical year,—the Jubilee, which was the year of release of all hired servants sold for debt, and of release of all estates that had been sold for various reasons. The year of Jubilee was the year of restoration. It was in itself a wise provision, which recent political disturbances, based upon tenure of land, has brought up into discussion. But beyond this thought of its political importance, there is also the spiritual significance as a type of the great day of redemption and of release in the Kingdom of CHRIST. The Sabbath, then, was a part of the Covenant made with men as fundamental. Its change to the Sunday will be traced elsewhere, but its sanctity, so defended and so insisted on, is given as a guide to us for our observance of the LORD'S day. The due observance, which was a blessing in the one, is a blessing in the other also. But it is not proper to give the name of the Jewish Sabbath to the LORD'S day, and Churchmen should be very careful not to confuse the two in ordinary conversation.

Sacrament. A Latin word, not found in the New Testament, meaning a solemn oath, originally a judicial phrase, afterwards applied to the oath taken by soldiers to the government. Ecclesiastical writers used it as a translation of the Greek word μυστηριον, mystery (though it does not seem to express the same idea), and so finally it came to be applied only to certain rites and ceremonies which under some external form set forth spiritual truths. In this sense it had a very wide application, so that nearly every religious act or doctrine was called a sacrament; even the creed was so styled by a Latin writer. (See Smith's Dict. Christian Antiq.) The Church of Rome eventually, by a decree of the Synod of Trent, limited the number to be called Sacraments to seven; viz., Baptism, the LORD'S Supper, Confirmation, Penance, Orders, Matrimony, and Extreme Unction, pronouncing Anathema on those who say there are more or less than these seven. In the lax sense of the word noted above it may be applied to these, but need not be confined to them. The error is in declaring all the seven, as that Council does, to have been instituted by CHRIST Himself, which is not true of five, and also making them all necessary for salvation, which they are not. Article XXV. declares of these, that they "are not to be counted for Sacraments of the Gospel, being such as have grown partly of the corrupt following of the Apostles, partly are states of life allowed in the Scriptures." By the phrase "corrupt following" we are to understand incorrect, mistaken; as, for instance, the putting Confirmation, an Apostolic rite, to be a Sacrament of the Gospel, on the same footing as Baptism and the Eucharist, which were appointed by CHRIST Himself.

To place these, too, in their proper position as distinguished from all others, and superior to them, the Church has given a strict definition of the word Sacrament, limiting its use to these two. In the Catechism it is declared to mean "an outward and visible sign of an inward and spiritual grace given unto us; ordained by CHRIST Himself, as a means whereby we receive the same (*i.e.*, inward and spiritual grace), and a pledge to assure us thereof." Three things, then, are necessary to constitute a Sacrament according to the Church's definition: 1st. The Outward Sign. 2. The Ordinance of CHRIST appointing this to be. 3. The means and pledge of receiving an Inward and Spiritual Grace. And under this definition it is declared there are "two Sacraments only. as generally (*i.e.*, universally) necessary to salvation, that is to say, Baptism and the Supper of the LORD."

The other five, though some of them may partake of a Sacramental character, yet are not by our Church called Sacraments, for they have not visible signs, appointed by CHRIST Himself, to convey the corresponding spiritual grace. *Confirmation* is a complement of Baptism, of Apostolic ordinance, but not appointed by CHRIST Himself. *Penance*, a word not found in the New Testament, if it simply mean repentance, is indeed required, but has no divinely appointed outward sign of remission of sins. *Orders* is not generally necessary, but is only for those specially called by the HOLY GHOST and the Church, nor did our LORD appoint any special outward sign to be used in conferring it. *Matrimony* has been in the world from the creation of man, and is not a special Gospel means of Grace. And as for *Extreme Unction*, for which is quoted the word of St. James, v. 14, it is not now given for the healing of the sick, but to fit the passing soul for death. Our LORD never appointed the use of oil for such purpose, neither indeed did His Apostles.

It is better for all good Churchmen to be guided by the teaching of the Church, and use the word Sacrament, as she does, only of the two appointed by our blessed LORD Himself, viz., of BAPTISM and of the SUPPER OF THE LORD.

"The Sacraments were not ordained of CHRIST to be gazed upon, or to be carried about, but that we should duly use them. And in such only as worthily receive the same, they have a wholesome effect or operation; but they that receive them unworthily, purchase to themselves damnation, as St. Paul saith." (Article XXV.) The Church teaches that the Sacraments do not work like charms or magic, but their efficacy depends upon the state of mind of the recipient. The Inward Grace indeed always accompanies the Sacrament duly administered, but operates savingly only when received in the heart by Faith and Repentance. (*Vide* BAPTISM and LORD'S SUPPER.)   REV. E. B. BOGGS, D.D.

Sacrilege. The sin of sacrilege has a far wider reach than the enumeration of those acts which are classed as sacrilegious. It is as well to avoid too close an enumeration of what might be turned into a sin, but we too may be unconsciously guilty of sin when we do not know it. A sacrilege is the violating a sacred place, or applying to profane and secular uses things which have been set apart for a holy service. Care must be taken, then, to see that we do not so misuse for selfish ends what is GOD's. Much of the old classification of sacrilegious acts is now obsolete, since decency and custom have prevented their recurrence. But to appropriate what has been given to His Church for sacred use is a sacrilege that is sometimes now committed. To use the Church building for secular and unhallowed purposes is a sacrilege. To interfere with and affront the minister in the services is a sacrilege. To plunder graves is a sacrilege. But if to profane anything consecrated is in degree sacrilegious, it is plain that we may be guilty of the sin, though avoiding overt criminal acts. So if we would train ourselves in devout and reverent recognition of what is GOD's, and endeavor not to misuse what is given to Him for His worship and for our honoring Him, we will be exceedingly careful not to fall into this sin.

Sacristan. The treasurer of the vestments, vessels, and other valuables of the Church. He is usually confused in ordinary usage with the Sexton. In the older Churches the sacristan was also a dignitary.

Sacristy. The Vestry-room of the older Churches where the vestments and vessels were placed. Sometimes under other names it was a large room often large enough to hold meetings of the Diocese.

Sadducees. The Sadducees of our LORD's day were a wealthy, powerful party, not very large, but apparently numbering among themselves the family of Aaron. Their truths were apparently to hold as of Faith as little as possible. They rejected all oral tradition outside of the Law; denied the Resurrection and the existence of all created spiritual beings. They were cold, cool, worldly, full of political wisdom, and with little religious enthusiasm. It is to be noted that our LORD was not resisted by them so vehemently and openly as by the Pharisees. It is not therefore recorded in the Gospels that He publicly denounced them, except once, when they joined the Pharisees in asking for a sign (St. Matt. xvi. 6), though they were faulted for their denial of the Resurrection. "Ye do err, not knowing the Scriptures." They lent themselves to the purposes of the Pharisees in the movement against our LORD, but, except as they felt that their power was at stake, they did not seem to care. So after the Resurrection it was because of the courageous, outspoken conduct of the Apostles that the chief priests who were of the sect of the Sadducees began to persecute them. They disappeared as a party after the destruction of Jerusalem.

Saint, from *sanctus*, holy. Hence the name is given to those eminent in holiness, and perhaps the idea of purity in doctrine may be implied. In the early days of Christianity, according to the Epistles of the New Testament, the word seems to have been used in a more general sense than now, and as nearly equal to the term "Christian," or in extraordinary cases to "Reverend." "All that be in Rome" are "called to be saints" (Rom. i. 7). "Without holiness no man shall see the LORD" (Heb. xii. 14). Therefore all must be saints in the widest sense of the word, if they expect to enter Heaven. St. Paul writes "to the saints which are at Ephesus" (Eph. i. 1). In our LORD's day the Essenes and Pharisees were esteemed saints by the Jews. In Ps. cvi. 16, Aaron is styled "the saint of the LORD." (See Dan. viii. 13, and vii. 18, 21, and 27.) "Ten thousands" (Deut. xxxiii. 2); congregation (Ps. lxxxix. 5, 7); bodies of saints arose (St. Matt. xxvii. 52); Saul persecuting saints (Acts ix. 13, and xxvi. 10); collection for saints (1 Cor. xvi. 1); saluted (Rom. xvi. 15); saluting (2 Cor. xiii. 13). The title of saint is given to such of the worthies in the Old and New Testament who have been holy in life and death, or were dedicated to GOD, as the Israelites (congregation of saints), and Christians ("churches of the saints") (1 Cor. xiv. 33); "a peculiar treasure" (Ex. xix. 5, and Ps. cxxxv. 4); "a peculiar people" (Deut. xiv. 2; Tit. ii. 14; 1 Pet. ii. 9), intended for a specially near relation to GOD, the Fountain of holiness. St. John, in the Revelation, applies "saint" almost exclusively to martyrs, and calls CHRIST "the King of Saints" (Rev. xv. 3). In later ages the word was used to designate martyrs. The "Communion of Saints," in the Greek, has a general meaning. Saints' Days were for a Eucharistic commemoration of martyrs; there were so many martyrs that All-Saints' Day was added. Thus, even before CHRIST's second coming, "the King of saints" is "glorified in His saints" (2 Thess. i. 10). Their "virtuous and godly living" is an example, and a "vivid sense is kept up of the 'communion and fellowship' which, in GOD's 'elect,' are 'knit together' in the 'mystical body' of CHRIST." If these blessed examples are followed, the believer may come to the "unspeakable joys" of Heaven. (See Collect for "All-Saints' Day.") While the primitive Church honored saints, it condemned the worshiping of them. The undue elevation of saints occurs especially in dark and ignorant ages. When lights are lit before the evening comes on they attract little notice, but when the darkness closes in they are very conspicuous.

The references in this article are drawn from Blunt's Dict. of Doctrinal and Historical Theology. See also Conybeare and Howson's Life and Epis. of St. Paul, Brownlee's Life of St. Patrick, and Bingham's Antiq., v. i. bk. 13, c. iii.

REV. S. F. HOTCHKIN.

Saints' Days. The days set apart for the commemoration of the several saints of the Christian Church. The principle upon which these Feasts are instituted is that they who by their lives and death illustrated the power of our blessed LORD over the hearts of men, and the purifying and strengthening of the Faith and the might of GOD the HOLY GHOST in the triumph over all foes, should be held in remembrance by us, thanking GOD for their good examples, and evermore ourselves endeavoring to follow in their holy footsteps. It is a very useful and beautiful regulation in the Church, restricted as it is to the commemoration of those only whose sanctity is in the Holy Scripture. While the blessed lives of later holy followers of the saints are not to be doubted, still, as names were formerly added year by year, till the number of those commemorated was vastly larger than the number of days in the year, it was a wise decision which led the English Reformers to drop out all names but those of the holy Apostles, the commemoration of the Holy Innocents, of St. Stephen the Proto-Martyr, of the Evangelists, of St. John Baptist, and of All Saints; with the Feast of St. Michael and All Angels. The day appointed for each was the day of his death or martyrdom, for that was called his proper birthday, as born into everlasting life. It was a point on which great stress was laid by the Primitive Christians to ascertain correctly the day upon which the Martyrs suffered, that they might be remembered yearly at the recurrence of the day in the Holy Communion. It was out of this usage that Saints' days were set apart. The Church of England retains upon her Calendar, but orders no service for, a number of saints whose names are printed therein in "black letter." They were many of them Saints and holy men who lived and labored in Great Britain, but some others are also admitted to the list, as St. Augustine, St. Lawrence, St. Cyprian, and St. Clement of Rome. Their names were kept there partly as being popular and having reference to the history of the Church, and partly in honor of the men themselves, being all eminent doctors or laborers in the Faith, or signalized their devotion by a martyr's death; but there was no service provided, and those only were to be accounted holy-days—*i.e.*, of Legal and Canonical observance—which had respect to our LORD and to His blessed Mother, to the Apostles, to the Evangelists and Martyrs of Holy Scripture.

Salutation. The salutation of the angel to St. Mary the Virgin (St. Luke i. 28): "Hail, thou that art highly favored, the LORD is with thee; blessed art thou among women." This was the salutation to her who was chosen to be the Mother of our LORD.

Salutations, in a Christian sense, involve the principles of either blessing or of praying for a blessing. As the "LORD be with you" is a blessing, so "And with Thy spirit" is as much a blessing, and is so to be considered.

Salvation. The putting a person in a state of safety. It is so used in the Catechism: "And I heartily thank our Heavenly Father that He hath called me to this state of Salvation, and I pray unto GOD to give me His grace, that I may continue in the same unto my life's end." In this place it means the redemption in JESUS CHRIST our LORD. In some places in Holy Scripture the term is used of national deliverance only from foes or calamities, but its usage is generally only in a spiritual sense. And this salvation of man is confessed in the Creed to be the object of the mightiest act ever done on the earth: "I believe in one LORD JESUS CHRIST; . . . Who, for us men, and for our salvation, came down from heaven, And was incarnate by the HOLY GHOST of the Virgin Mary, and was made man." The salvation or deliverance, not only from the evil and the taint of present sin, but also from the terrible end of the second death and to give the blessedness of eternal life, *is* the salvation He offers. It is a double salvation, as it were, that is offered. Therefore our LORD prayed, and "this is eternal life to know Thee, the only true GOD and JESUS CHRIST, whom Thou hast sent" (St. John xvii. 3). For this knowledge "makes us wise unto salvation" (2 Tim. iii. 15). The redemptive acts of our Redeemer are set forth elsewhere, but here we will dwell upon the extent of the salvation. He is the Author and the Captain of our salvation. It is entire and complete;—From sin, for the remembrance of which will be blotted out; from its taint and stain, for that we are washed clean in the blood of the Lamb; from its consequences of second death, for He hath destroyed him who hath the power of death, and He hath put it under His feet. He giveth us life: "I am come that they might have life, and that they might have it more abundantly." Peace: "Peace I leave with you, My peace I give unto you." Joy: "Now the GOD of hope fill you with all joy and peace in believing." It is given to confession of the lips. It is the work of a godly sorrow. It is the end of Faith. It is the free gift for the Christian's work. It is bound up in grace. It is the long-suffering of the LORD. It is the end of His appearing. It is the inheritance of the Saints. It is, then, one of the terms which includes as a result all the acts, gifts, graces, and blessings of the Gospel. And it is of GOD, through GOD, and in GOD. Salvation belongeth unto GOD. Therefore, in the highest sense, GOD is our salvation. The FATHER hath made the SON unto us "Wisdom and Righteousness, and Sanctification and Redemption." And therefore the heavenly hosts ascribe Salvation, as well as Glory and Honor, as among the titles of GOD.

Samaritans. The Samaritans were the descendants of those tribes which Shalmanezer, or Esarhaddon, placed in the depopulated country of Samaria fifty years after he had stripped it of its Israelitish inhabitants. They were heathen, but when they were plagued by the wild beasts which had overrun the long desolated land, the superstitious colonists sent to the King for some priests of JEHOVAH to teach them "the manner of the GOD of the land," that they might be protected from the ravages of the wild beasts. This was taught them by a priest who was sent them, but they still retained their old heathen worship, beside this, persisting in their idolatry. Therefore the Jews, when restored by Cyrus, would have nothing to do with the Samaritans, and utterly refused all intercourse with them. The Samaritans retorted with equal bitterness. It was owing to their influence that the rebuilding of the Temple was hindered. They had a Temple worship on Mount Gerizim, they kept a Passover, they tried to keep the Law. In this state, when every Jewish feeling of national and religious pride was inflamed and the stubborn temper inflamed by the infliction of so much hardship, the Samaritan came in for a full share of hatred and scorn. In our LORD'S time this was not lessened, and to those around Him His conduct must have seemed inexplicable and even disgraceful. His love, care, and tender treatment of them, His abode in their villages, His teaching among them, His healing of the Samaritan leper, seemed so contrary to Jewish self-respect. The noble parable of the good Samaritan was all the more pointed because the chief personage in it was of the hated intruder into the Holy Land. He forbade the Twelve when first sent out (St. Matt. x. 5) to enter into the Samaritan villages, but that had a special significance in their mission work. Afterwards He sketched out for them their widening labors thus: They were to preach first in Judæa, then in Samaria, then to the uttermost parts of the world. The Samaritan may fitly be used as the type of the mixture of modern religious feeling. It is now as it was at first: "They feared the LORD and served their own gods,"—the observance of religious ceremonies and ordinances with the selfish indulgence in all manner of sin.

Samuel. The most remarkable of the prophets after Moses and Elijah. Standing between the two, acting with great sagacity both as a Priest, as a Prophet of GOD, and as a Judge over the people, he was able to restore the Israelitish strength in a great measure. The terrible defeat and the loss of the Ark at the rash battle at Ebenezer had thrown the nation into despair; twenty years of waiting, of grief, and of national stagnation followed, while Samuel was gaining the religious confidence of the nation. At last, as Prophet and Priest unto GOD, he brought the people before JEHOVAH at Mizpah. There he wrought a religious reformation and a civil reorganization. It took some time, at least long enough for the Philistines to gather their forces and to try the conclusions of a battle at Ebenezer, the scene of their old victory. The LORD utterly overthrew them and Israel smote them so that for the rest of Samuel's lifetime they were not able to attack Israel. Against his earnest advice the people, taking his organization as a hint, demanded a king. He was grieved at it, but as he was divinely directed he yielded, and presented to the people Saul of Benjamin. Samuel loved Saul and tried to guide his willfulness. Saul's imperious conduct and his disobedience, both as to the Amalekites and by arrogating to himself the right to offer sacrifice, and consequent forfeiture of the Kingdom, saddened the last days of the Prophet. He had a singular fortune. The child given to earnest prayer, devoted to the LORD, before he could know a mother's love and the sweets of home sent to the Temple, consecrated to GOD's service, growing up in favor with the throngs of worshipers at Shiloh, as the sins of the sons of Eli had horrified them, known to be in the favor of GOD, the chosen messenger to Eli, who had nurtured him, of the doom passed upon his family, the accepted prophet to the people, the religious reformer and civil magistrate, then the anointer first of Saul, then of David, and, finally, after his death summoned by his loved Saul from the rest of Paradise only to pronounce against him the sentence of outlawry from GOD's favor. He was the third in rank of might and the second in influence of the prophets the LORD sent His people. He was the type of our LORD in these things, as patient, self-sacrificing, in favor with GOD and man, and as organizer of a system. It indeed passed out of Samuel's unwilling hands to take a breadth which was not foreseen and to produce results, both for good and for evil, which were beyond all human power to anticipate. Our LORD, on the other hand, committed the organization of the Church to His Apostles to the infinite blessing of the world. His was, as our LORD's own mission, a mission in a time of transition, though we must never forget that Samuel was raised up to meet the emergency; but our LORD came to fulfill His own mission, to complete the past and to mould the future of the whole world.

Samuel, the Books of. The four chief books of Israelitish history are all linked together in so much, that the title given to the first two books, though representing an early division,—in the Septuagint—is not a fair one. The writer of the first book must be unknown. But we may very safely assume that he was the Prophet who would record the main facts of his time, and that the later chapters were added by Gad and Nathan, who most probably wrote the second book. It is a special mark of the historical books of the Old and New Testament that the author never gives his name. Only once is this broken,—Nehemiah names himself as the author. The material was from Samuel's hand at least (1 Chron., ch. xxix. 29). The books were probably compiled out of this earlier material than the separation of Israel into the two kingdoms. The canonical authority of the books has always been admitted, and the references to it in the New Testament by our LORD, St. Peter, St. Stephen, and St. Paul, seal it for us. Its minute historical accuracy is evident upon any fair examination, and shows that the work was compiled from notes by an eyewitness. The first book contains the history of the close of the Theocracy and of the rise of the Monarchy. Samuel, the last Judge, the Prophet of GOD, effects that religious and political reformation which becomes afterwards the basis of the Monarchy. The first seven chapters, then, are a distinct section, giving an account of Samuel, his training, the calamity of Israel, the abeyance of religious observances for twenty years, then his Judgeship. The eighth chapter opens with the sinfulness of Samuel's sons, and the restlessness of the people; then follow (ch. ix.-x.) the election of Saul; Saul's reign till his rejection (xi.-xv.); recounting his military achievements, his unification of the people; his royal character in many things marred by his arrogance, selfishness, and demoniac possession. This brings on the substitution of David for Saul by GOD's appointment (xvi.-xviii. 9). Saul growing jealous of David and seeking his life (xviii. 10-xxvii. 12). Lastly, Saul's death (xxviii.-xxxi.).

The second book is wholly occupied with David's life from the date of Saul's death. This book also parts into two sections. His reign over Judah, and then his reign over the whole kingdom. David did not at first succeed to the whole sovereignty, but the claims of Ishbosheth were maintained by his uncle, Abner. Joab had begun already to wield an interfering power in David's career, and feared that David would be rid of him. When, therefore, Abner abandoned Ishbosheth's cause, and offered to David to bring all Israel under his sway, Joab assassinated him. But David's reign over Israel was itself to be shaken to the foundation by his sin. After the removal of the Ark (ch. v. 17–vii.), and vow to build a temple to JEHOVAH, and the blessing promised him, came his fall in the matter of Bathsheba. This was grievously punished in his family troubles (ch. x.-xix.), by Absalom's rebellion and death, and in Sheba's insurrection. The sword was not to depart from his family. It hung over it, and fell so often for the sins of his descendants. The famine that desolated the land (xxi.), the sin of taking the census (xxiv.), and the plague that followed, show the greatness and the weakness of the King's character.

A King after a right royal sort, David was yet in so many things an undisciplined man. He was a soldier of fearless stuff; a King having political insight and management; a man possessed of magnetic attractiveness; a man full of religious earnestness and enthusiasm, one whom all loved, yet tempted to pride and to sensuality, and by these led to commit acts whose consequence fell not on himself alone, but on his people also. One proof, and no mean one, of the veracity and the authority of the second book of Samuel lies in the fact of the plain, simple statement of facts, without extenuation, or exaggeration, or explanation. Whatever Canonical authority belongs to the first book must also belong to the second, since they were not divided in the Hebrew till after they were translated into the Greek, and were then divided.

See for these two books the Speaker's Commentary, the Cambridge Bible for Schools, Smith's Bible Dictionary, and the authorities cited there.

Sanctification. It is a state or a condition of grace and holiness from the power of the HOLY GHOST in our hearts. We can never too clearly recognize that it comes from Him co-operating in our hearts and with our wills to produce that fruit unto holiness. It must, therefore, be a growth, a state, a condition, and the two co-operating forces are the Spirit of GOD and the will yielding to His guidance. Without holiness we cannot see GOD. This holiness, which is our own co-operating work, must be founded upon the redemption of CHRIST and our baptism in Him, and so our receiving His righteousness (justification, the being made or declared righteous): "but ye are washed, but ye are sanctified, but ye are justified in the name of the LORD JESUS and by the Spirit of our GOD." Sanctification, then, begins with baptism as a part of its manifold gifts, or more truly, as a power of many of its graces it confers. As we put on the LORD JESUS and all grow in that new creation, so we have as the accompanying state holiness, and though holiness is no part of our unregenerate state, since it *was* of the original creation, a growth in holiness is, as it were, a gradual recovery of our original condition, and becomes ours as we work together with the HOLY SPIRIT. It is a restoration to our nature of the first condition. It is, then, as Hooker (Serm. on Justification) states it, inherent. "Concerning the righteousness of sanctification, we deny it not to be inherent; we grant that unless we work we have it not, only we distinguish it as a thing different in nature from the righteousness of justification; we are righteous, the one way by the faith of Abraham, the other way, except we do the works of Abraham, we are *not* righteous. . . . St. Paul doth plainly sever these two parts of Christian righteousness, one from the other, for in the sixth to the Romans thus he writeth: 'Being freed from sin and made servants to GOD, ye have your fruit in holiness and the end everlasting life.' 'Ye are made free from sin and made servants unto GOD,' this is the righteousness of justification. 'Ye have your fruit in holiness,' this is the righteousness of sanctification. By the one we are interested in the right of inheriting, by the other we are brought to the actual possession of eternal bliss, and so the end of both is eternal life." Then as we grow in grace, in spiritual strength, in the use of that knowledge and wisdom given to us by the HOLY GHOST, we grow in Sanctification, and so far as it enters into our life and our character, it is ours.

Our LORD in His Intercessional Prayer (St. John xvii.) prays both for the Apostles, "sanctify them through Thy truth," and of Himself He saith, referring to His perfect humanity and to its discipline, "and for their sakes I sanctify Myself that they also might be sanctified through the truth." Not only the discipline He underwent (Heb. ii. 10, 11), but also as Victim He sanctified Himself. And in the unity of His Holy Body are we made Holy, Sanctified. So we may say that (this having a bearing upon the article of the Creed "the Communion of Saints") He hath sanctified Himself for the Church's sake that He might sanctify Her, that He hath given to Her the Sanctifying Spirit, that as children in the Church growing up into the manhood of the Christian life, we have given to us the Sanctification of the Spirit through JESUS CHRIST. Therefore all the exhortations with which St. Paul closes his Epistles (and more markedly that to the Galatians) are to this end, our Sanctification. The old controversies upon Sanctification and Justification have died out; a deeper, truer sense of the living power of the graces of the HOLY SPIRIT and the need to live and grow in them, has made them needless. We are called to be saints, let us make our calling and election sure. This is our co-operation with the Spirit of Holiness, and in Him we shall surely be Sanctified.

Sanctuary. The word correctly belongs to the Jewish ritual, meaning the Holy Place, which was properly of two parts. I. The Holy of Holies, and then without the veil that concealed its contents from view, II. The Holy Place in which the Priests ministered unto GOD in the Sacrifices. In this Holy Place, the outer Sanctuary, were the ever-burning Lamp, the Shew-Bread, the Altar of Incense. None but the priests trod there, as none but the High-Priest ever entered into the Holy of Holies.

The corresponding place in the Christian Church, the place where the Holy Table or the Altar stood, was also treated with great reverence, as the Screen and the Holy doors before it in the Eastern Church show, but it was not called the Sanctuary till comparatively late. It was, however, always surrounded with a general sense of its holiness. In the West, the Sanctuary is the chancel, though it sometimes also included the choir. It was not, however, so sacredly guarded from intrusion as in the East.

But the Churches had early given to them the right of asylum. It had existed in the Temple. The right of asylum was conceded to heathen temples. It was attached to the Christian temples also as soon as the Emperor Constantine, becoming Christian, recognized and conceded it. The right of asylum at first apparently was intended only to give such delay as would prevent injustice being done to the person obtaining it. This right of asylum, at first belonging only to the Church building, afterwards was extended so as to include the precincts also. But after a while it became an obstruction to justice. In wild times, as during the transition from the Roman civil power through the turbulence of the Middle Ages, it served a very useful purpose, but on the settlement of the peoples into something like order and the proper discharge of justice, this right became an evil. In England it was abolished in the twenty-first year of James I.

Sanhedrim. The Jewish Judicial Court which tried our LORD, and before which, afterwards, the Apostles were brought several times. The date of its origin is uncertain, and, indeed, if it existed before, it does not come prominently forward till the time of the Maccabees. It had then and afterwards the power of Life and Death. Its chief jurisdiction was in minor cases, however. Heresy and blasphemy were the higher subjects upon which it passed sentence. The Sanhedrim was deprived of the power over life by the Romans. Therefore our LORD was taken by the High-Priest and a hastily-gathered part of the Sanhedrim to Pilate. St. Stephen's martyrdom by the Sanhedrim was most probably a sudden, unpremeditated act. But after this the Sanhedrim sat upon the heresy of the sect of the Nazarenes, and used all its influence at home and abroad among the Jews to check its rising power. Therefore St. Paul asked leave of the Jews at Rome to defend himself before them. It arrested St. Peter and St. John. St. Stephen was taken before it. St. Paul was examined by it, and was in danger of his life in the angry debate which followed his appeal upon the hope of the Resurrection. Its later history recounts its wanderings, till at last it was permanently settled at Tiberias, where its labors were upon the Talmud and on the text of Scripture. It finally disappeared, it is said, before 300 A.D.

Sardica. A Council was held at Sardica in the year 347 A.D., though later authorities prefer the date 343–44 A.D. The occasion appears to have been the differences and irregularities arising out of the Arian Schism, and its continuation by the Semi-Arians or Eusebians. As these grew more and more scandalous, the Emperors Constans and Constantius, of the West and East respectively, joined in summoning a Council of the whole Church at Sardica (now Sophia), in Illyricum, on the borders of the two Empires. Bishops assembled from all quarters to the number of 100 from the West and 76 from the East. The venerable Hosius of Cordova presided, and among other noteworthy men present were St. Athanasius, Marcellus of Ancyra, Stephen of Antioch, and Asclepias of Gaza. The Pope, Julius, was represented by two priests and a deacon. The Oriental Bishops at the outset protested against the admission of Athanasius, Marcellus, and other deposed Bishops; but when they found that matters were to be freely discussed, and that no violence would be allowed, they withdrew to Philippopolis, in Thrace, and there held a separate synod under Stephen, Bishop of Antioch, in which they drew up a new creed, deposed the most conspicuous members of the other Council, and forbade communion with many others, and especially Pope Julius. They were accompanied by five Bishops from the West, while two Eastern Bishops remained at Sardica. After the departure of the Easterns, the Council proceeded with its business; they declared it unnecessary to reopen questions of faith, the Nicene Creed being sufficient; they deposed many Bishops of the Easterns; they declared Athanasius and Marcellus innocent of the charges brought against them, and restored them to their Sees, so far as their decision could do it. They addressed a letter to the Emperors invoking them to interfere in behalf of the oppressed, and they wrote to Pope Julius, to the clergy of Alexandria, and to all the Bishops of the Church to urge them to unity and adherence to the faith of Nice. They also passed a number of Canons, some of which became of the greatest importance. These Canons were drawn up in the form of motions put by various members of the Council, and voted on by all.

Canons 1 and 2 forbid the promotion of Bishops from one See to another.

"Canon 3. Hosius made two propositions: first, that no Bishop should be permitted to enter another province unless called to assist at some judgment; and, secondly, that for the honor of St. Peter's memory it be ordered that if a Bishop, condemned in his own province, maintain his innocence, his judges might write to the Bishop of Rome, in order that he might determine whether the Bishop's cause required a fresh hearing; that if he and the judges whom he should nominate agreed in deeming a new trial requisite, it should be entered upon at once; but if not, the original sentence should stand good."

"Canon 4. Bishop Gaudentius submitted to the Council an addition to the last Canon, to the effect that care should be taken that the Bishop so condemned in provincial synod, and appealing to Rome, should not be deprived of his See, nor a successor be appointed, until the cause should be entirely concluded by the Pope."

"Canon 7. Hosius proposed that in the case of a Bishop condemned by the synod of his province and appealing to Rome, if the Bishop of Rome should decide that it was necessary to have a new trial, it should be lawful for him either to delegate the cause to the Bishops bordering upon the diocese of the accused Bishop, or to send delegates to the spot to take cognizance of the question." (Landon's Manual of Councils.)

Canon 5 forbids consecrating Bishops for insignificant places. Canon 8 forbids Bishops going to the Emperor's Court except when called by the Emperor. Canon 13 forbids ordinations *per saltum.* Canons 14 and 15 forbid Bishops absenting themselves from their dioceses. Canon 17 provides for appeals by priests or deacons from the decision of their own Bishop to the other Bishops of their province. It is on Canons 3, 4, and 7 that the claim made by Rome over the other branches of the Church is based; but against this assumption it is argued that the council was a local one; that the limited authority is conferred as a *new thing;* that the Bishop of Rome had no power to evoke a cause from before another tribunal; nor any personal voice in the decision; but could only receive appeals on application of the Councils from which they were made, the power of such appeals being limited to Bishops; and also that the power conferred was temporary and personal, being given to Julius by name, without any reference to his successors. Nevertheless, the Canons of Sardica were received by the whole Church.

Sarum Use. The Liturgy according to the use of the Diocese of Sarum (Salisbury) was one of the most influential and important of the many Uses (*i.e*, Liturgies in use) in England. The Sarum Missal was itself the outcome of Bishop Osmund's reformation of the Older Uses which had obtained and which (from his being a Norman over a Saxon Diocese) he would wish to modify. He composed a Custom-Book which it is claimed became the Sarum Missal (1085 A.D.). The later Sarum Missal, which was so freely used for material and guidance in the formation of the Prayer-Book, probably had by this time received many additions. It was the leading Use in England at the time of the Reformation, though the Dioceses of Lincoln, Hereford, and Bangor had their own, and the province of York had also an Older Use, dating in part from 700 A.D. Durham seems also to have had a separate Use. (*Vide* USE.)

Satan. "The first that sinned against GOD was Satan. And then through Satan's fraudulent instigation man also. They 'kept not their first estate' because 'they stood not in the truth,' from which it may be very probably thought that infidelity through pride was their ruin, the too great admiration of their own excellency having made incredible the truth revealed to them: the truth of that personal conjunction which should be of GOD with men. As also envy maketh them, ever sithence the first moment of their own fall, industrious to work our ruin." (Hooker.) Under the names and titles of Satan ("the Adversary"), the devil ("the accuser"), the Tempter, the Evil One, Beelzebub, the prince of demons, the serpent, there is set before us in the Scriptures, and especially in the New Testament, one whose awful personality only Christian faith can face without flinching. Unbelief has no refuge but to deny his existence. Believing in CHRIST the Saviour from sin, we can without shrinking accept the facts of sin, Satan, and death, and without attempting to be wise above what is written, receive what is written concerning Satan and his work in the world in its literal plain meaning.

The history of mankind has hardly begun, and the first pair are just created and placed upon the earth, righteous, wise, and happy, when there comes upon the scene one who in the form of a serpent, with fair promises and bitter taunts against GOD, induces first the woman and then the man to transgress the one prohibition that had been laid upon them, and fall into sin. So "sin entered into the world, and death by sin" (Rom. v. 12). We accept the record of Genesis iii. as simply and literally true. But it perhaps makes but little difference in the result, as it makes little difference in the "difficulty" of the record, whether we understand that the full meaning of the events recorded in Genesis iii. is hidden under the form of the words or under the form of the acts, if we only understand that what is recorded is essential truth, and that whether Satan is concealed under the form or under the name of the serpent, here is the account—and the only explanation in the world—of the introduction into the world of sin and death. We find later additions, which tell us about him who was the means of the beginning of evil in the world, but here at first is no word to explain how GOD could permit evil in His universe, no word of its origin, but only a simple statement of the facts of the creation and then of the fall, and not even the name of the evil agent is given nor a hint of his high spiritual origin and character. What is made evident is, the subtle personal character of the tempter of men.

It is a serious error that "devil" is in an English authorized version made the translation of two words of entirely distinct meanings, with the natural result of misleading and confusing the ordinary reader One is the word *diabolos,* the Greek equivalent of the Hebrew *Satan,* and of which "devil" is a transfer into English rather than a translation. The other, which under some form occurs about twice as often in the New Testament, the word *daimon,* which the same treatment would render '*demon.*" (*Vide* DEMONIACS.) That is, in the New Testament, when the word "devil' is used, only in one-third of the cases is the reference to Satan himself, in the other cases to his subordinate evil spirits.

As a proper name Satan is found but in three places in the whole Old Testament (1 Chron. xxi. 1, where alone the article is wanting). "Satan stood up against Israel, and provoked David to number Israel" (Zech. iii. 1, 2). "He showed me Joshua the high-priest standing before the angel of the LORD, and Satan standing at his right hand to assist him, and the LORD said unto Satan, The LORD rebuke thee, O Satan" (Job i. 6–9; ii. 1), when Satan "came also to present himself before the LORD," and received permission to afflict Job. In the books called apocryphal, once, the equivalent, "the devil," "through envy of the devil came death" (Wis. ii. 24). But when we enter the field of the New Testament we are conscious of an entire change in this respect. St. Matthew uses the name of Satan three times, once identifying him with "the devil" of the temptation (ch. iv. 10), once with "Beelzebub the prince of demons" (ch. xii. 26), and once recording our LORD'S application of the name to St. Peter. "The devil" he uses six times (ch. xvi. 23), four times of the six in the narrative of the Temptation, once in the Parable of the Sower, and once in the prophecy of the judgment-day. His title of "the evil one" St. Matthew uses several times, notably in the LORD'S Prayer (ch. vi. 13), and the parable of the tares (ch. xiii. 19). St. Mark names him Satan three times (St. Mark i. 13; ii. 23; iv. 15). St. Luke as "the devil" twice, in the Temptation and in the parable of the sower, as Satan four times, "falling from Heaven," the captor of the woman "bowed with a spirit of infirmity," "entering into Judas" (who was "a devil"), "desiring to sift Peter as wheat" (St. Luke iv. 8; x. 18; xiii. 16; xxii. 3, 31). St. John three times as "the devil," two of the three in reference to Judas, once as "the evil one" (St. John vi. 70; viii. 44; xii. 2; xvii. 15), three times, repeating our LORD'S words, as "the prince of this world" who "shall be cast out," who "cometh and hath nothing in me," and who "is judged" (St. John xii. 31; xiv. 30; xvi. 11). In the Acts twice as "the devil,"—"them that were oppressed of the devil," and "thou child of the devil." As "Satan" twice (Acts x. 38; xiii. 10), he filled the heart of Ananias with a lie (Acts v. 3), and it is "from his power" that the Gospel turns men (Acts xxvi. 18). In St. Paul's Epistles repeatedly as "the devil" (Eph. iv. 27), whose opportunity is hoarded anger, his methods of attack wiles (ch. vi. 11), pride the cause of his fall (1 Tim. iii. 6) and his snare (ch. iii. 7); who enslaves the will of his captives (2 Tim. ii. 26); who has the power of death, but this death the Saviour of men (Heb. ii. 14) conquered and spoiled him, "the strong man despoiled by one stronger than he" (St. Luke xi. 22). As Satan whom "GOD shall bruise under our feet shortly" (Rom. xvi. 20), but to whom the Apostle delivers over the incontinent sinner of Corinth "for the destruction of the flesh that the spirit may be saved" (1 Cor. v. 5), who tempts this lust and pride (ch. vii. 5), who transforms himself into an angel of light (2 Cor. xi. 14), who hinders the LORD'S servants in their work (1 Thess. ii. 18), who "works in the lawless one, the man of sin" (2 Thess. ii. 9), to whom near the close of his ministry the Apostle once again "delivers" men "that they may learn not to blaspheme" (1 Tim. i. 20), but apparently, in the case of one of them at least, not with any good result (2 Tim. iv. 14). As "the evil one" "from whom the LORD will guard you" (2 Thess. iii. 3), and whose "darts the shield of faith shall quench" (Eph. vi. 16).

He is "the prince of the power of the air who rules the course of this world, the spirit that now worketh in the children of disobedience" (Eph. ii. 2). He is one who is set over the "principalities, powers, rulers of the darkness of this world, spiritual wickedness in high places, against which we wrestle" (Eph. vi. 12). He is "the power of darkness from which we are delivered" (Col. i.). He is "the god of this world who hath blinded the minds of those that believe not" (2 Cor. iv. 4). St. James bids, "resist the devil and he will flee from you" (St. James iv. 7). St. Peter warns against "your adversary the devil, who goes about seeking whom he may devour" (1 Pet. v. 8). St. John tells us that sin is the business of the devil and the sign of his children, and "for this the SON OF GOD was manifested, that He might destroy the works of the devil." He images them that "have overcome the wicked one," "of whom" was Cain the envious murderer, but who shall not touch the child of GOD to hurt him, albeit "in him the world lieth" (1 John ii. 13; iii. 12; v. 18, 19). St. Jude shows him contending against the archangel about the body of Moses and receiving his rebuke (Jude 9). It is left for the last books to enlarge upon the words of our LORD concerning both the fall and of the destiny of Satan and his angels. "The angels," writes St. Jude, "which kept not their first estate, but left their own habitations, He hath reserved in everlasting chains under darkness unto the judgment of the great day" (Jude 6). And St. Peter, "for GOD spared not the angels that sinned, but cast them down to hell, and delivered them into chains of darkness, to be reserved unto judgment" (2 Pet. ii. 4). In the Letters of the Apocalypse, the contentious Jews are "the synagogue of Satan" (Rev. ii. 9, 13, 24), the dwelling of the Angel of one church is where the throne and dwelling of Satan are, of another, where "the depths of Satan" are the doctrines taught, and "the devil" is about to "cast some of them into prison" for their trial. In the vision (Rev. xii. 7–9), "there was war in heaven: Michael and his angels fought against the dragon; and the dragon fought and his angels, and prevailed not; neither was their place found any more in Heaven. And the great dragon was cast out, that old serpent called the Devil, and Satan, which deceiveth the whole world: he was cast out unto the earth, and his angels were cast out with him." And later on, "I saw an angel come down from Heaven... And he laid hold on the dragon, that old serpent which is the Devil, and

Satan, and bound him a thousand years" (Rev. xx. 2). And then later still, "the devil which deceived them was cast into the lake of fire and brimstone, and shall be tormented day and night for ever and ever" (Rev. xx. 10). Of all the writers of the New Testament St. Paul in his letters is fullest in the instruction which he gives concerning the present work of Satan in the world. It is for others to prophesy concerning his eternal destiny.

From this examination of the teaching of the Scriptures, it is plain that while we are made acquainted with the presence of Satan in the world, with his power and his character from the outset, the Holy Scriptures are satisfied for a long time, and until a certain definite time, to add but little to that knowledge. It is never lost, never questioned, but held in abeyance. When that time does come, the fullness of knowledge concerning the prince of evil, his authority, his wiles, his kingdom, is opened to us all at once. And finally, to the instruction concerning him which is given in the New Testament all the world's wisdom has never added a particle. It has denied him and his work, as it denies the LORD his Conqueror, but it has taught, and has pretended to teach, us nothing positive even in the place of what it has denied. Of the problem of evil it has no solution. The close connection between the world's dealing with these two beliefs—in the LORD and about His enemy—is suggestive, for it is indeed a connection which exists between these two and all that belongs to them respectively from the beginning.

The fall of man through the agency of Satan was closely followed by the promise which was to undo that fall,—"Her seed shall bruise thy head, and thou shalt bruise his heel." From that time, if evil was in the world, there was the knowledge of GOD in the world also, and a definite faith in His promise, a definite expectation of a Deliverer, divine and human. The exclamation of the first mother was, "I have gotten a man, the LORD." The work of evil went on in GOD's world, and prevailed over the good; but the hope and faith was never lost. It was renewed to Abraham and preserved in his family, and repeated and defined. It is the key to the history and prophecy and the whole system of Israel. The LORD was in the world, and the world and His own people were being prepared for the keeping of His promise. When His appointed time came, the promise was kept.

With the coming of CHRIST there is a loosing of Satan and his angels for a time, as appears by the demoniacal possessions which were so frequent just at that time, as well as in the intensified badness of the world, and with the revelation of CHRIST comes a revelation of knowledge of Satan and his works such as had never been made before. The mystery of the eternal purpose of GOD was revealed in CHRIST (Eph. i. 9; 2 Thess. ii. 7), the "mystery of iniquity" had its own revelation in the work of the devil and his angels. The two great enemies met in the Temptation, and the victory over one man in the Garden, was more than reversed. The world is Satan's organized kingdom. In it the LORD planted His kingdom to leaven and absorb it. The angels of GOD are the ministers of CHRIST their LORD. Satan has his angels, the fallen evil spirits. "Of thrones and dominions and principalities and powers CHRIST is head" (Col. i. 16), and "principalities and powers and rulers of darkness, spiritual wickedness in high places," are those against which we wrestle. Men are citizens of one kingdom or the other, servants of one master or the other. The two kingdoms exist side by side and so near that we are "translated out of darkness into the kingdom of His dear SON" (Col. i. 13). While Satan and his emissaries of evil angels and evil men are on the watch to snare and destroy those who err from the right way, and the casting out from the communion of the Church is the "delivering over to Satan." Righteousness is the business of the kingdom of CHRIST. Sin in every form, of the devil and his children. The name of the promised one is JESUS, for He shall save His people from their sins and destroy the works of the devil. In other words, the contrast and opposition which exists between evil and good, right and wrong, sin and righteousness, is no contrast between abstractions, and is not limited to things which we might name by these terms. Evil, like good, is the character of an organized system which extends through all the world, and which has its centre and its king in the person of Satan. The contrast and the contest is between these two kingdoms and between these two kings, a contrast and a contest that goes on whenever anything exists which belongs to either, and will go on till one or the other is destroyed.

Which shall prevail we know. Which is prevailing, and has been ever since the LORD came. Every Christian life that is lived, every act of righteousness and charity that is done, scores a victory. The advance of the Church is a course of victory. And victory on one side means defeat on the other, a lessening of the kingdom of Satan, a binding of him and his power. The end will not be till he is finally cast down. It is not coming as rapidly as we would desire. But it will come, for He has come who came to destroy the works of the devil, and the will of GOD will be done.

REV. L. W. GIBSON.

Satisfaction. The term "satisfaction" is properly a legal term that comes to us from the Roman Law, and as a theological term was not used till St. Anselm of Canterbury employed it, but it has passed into use, but much modified from his teaching. It is probable that from him came the use of the word in the Canon of our Liturgy "who made there (by His one oblation of Himself once offered) a full, perfect, and sufficient sacrifice, oblation, and satisfaction for the sins of the whole world." The doctrine of satisfaction simply for sin by a sacrifice is found in Holy Scripture from the very first. It could have been the only idea attached to Sacrifices before the flood, since none ate flesh then, and the feast upon the Sacrifice was not instituted till Moses ordained it. The Sacrifices offered by Abraham were whole burnt-offerings—*i.e.*, none were reserved at all. So onward, the Sacrifice seems to have had simply the purpose of offering some victim by which GOD was appeased; and here let us note lest the mere offering could appease GOD or could purge the consciences of the worshipers that this was a memorial before Him of the satisfaction yet to be made in CHRIST. The idea of satisfaction by a sacrifice was that it was anticipatory of the proper and only satisfaction to be made afterwards. In this sense only we may say that our heavenly FATHER was appeased. Now, throughout the Mosaic Law the whole burnt-offering alone was the complete sacrifice retaining the principle of satisfaction, but the feast upon the sacrifice for the sin-offering and trespass-offering was the introduction of another principle. In the first was set forth the solitariness of the Atonement of our LORD. He trod the wine-press alone. We only have bestowed on us the results; we could not share in His Atoning act. In this He made the one full, perfect, and sufficient sacrifice, oblation, and satisfaction for the sins of the whole world. It is not necessary to point out here the many texts which teach us how fully He took upon Him the iniquity of us all. How He was wounded for our transgressions, and how His soul made a sin-offering. The fifty-third chapter of Isaiah is both the prophecy and the best exposition of His satisfaction as the sin-offering for the world. It is upon the foundation of the fullness of His satisfaction that the sinner *now* finds acceptance before GOD. It is ascribed to Him in glorious worship of the redeemed. It is the constant ground upon which we can hope for everlasting life. But St. Anselm brought it forward as a debt for sin, which was viewed more as a breaking of GOD'S majesty than as of itself a loathsome taint which needed to be atoned for. There was a harshness in the mode in which the Archbishop put it, and a seeming intention to push forward the thought of the crime of sin more than its present and fatal effect upon the sinner. His use, then, of the term is narrow. This doctrine of satisfaction brings out the love displayed in the Incarnation of the SON of GOD. It shows that for the hour and the agony of the Atonement our blessed LORD came into the world, and that this satisfaction, resting upon that and leading up to His Resurrection and to the gifts flowing from it, also brings forward the facts of our sanctification by the HOLY GHOST. But we must be very careful to separate from this any idea of satisfaction we might dream we could make for ourselves. This is a deduction which by no means follows from the other. The satisfaction of the LORD and our acceptance through Him constitute the grounds upon which the doctrine of good works must be placed, and these can have no wages, but whatever we receive for them is the free gift of GOD through JESUS CHRIST.

Saxon. *Vide* ARCHITECTURE.

Saying and Singing. The rubrics in several places direct there shall be "said or sung" such an Anthem or Psalm. The words have a technical meaning, and are in strictness so to be construed. Saying meant then a recitation of the passage so ordered upon a musical tone, a plain, simple note with little or no inflection or cadence. The English Prayer-Book was published very early by Daye, Merbecke, Tallis, and others musically set. Now, saying is an ordinary reading. Singing meant a more ornate musical recitation. Now, custom has made the word "said" in the rubrics refer to the alternate reading and response of the minister and congregation, and the singing is more of the chant than the anthem music. The places in the rubrics in the Prayer-Book where this phrase "said or sung" is used are for the *Venite*, the *Gloria Patri*, or the *Gloria in Excelsis* after the Psalms; the *Te Deum*, the *Jubilate*, and *Benedictus* in the Morning Prayer; the *Cantate*, *Bonum est*, *Deus Misereatur*, and the *Benedic Anima Mea*, in the Evening Prayer; the Preface and the *Gloria in Excelsis* in the Communion Office; the Sentences and the three Anthems in the Burial Service; the selection of Psalms or other portion of Psalms in the Thanksgiving Office; the *Veni Creator Spiritus* in the Ordinal; the Hundredth Psalm in the Office for the Consecration Office; the anthem *Laudate Nomen* in the Office of Institution. In all of these the rubric permits in strictness a recitation upon a musical note and fuller musical rendering. But except in the *Veni Creator Spiritus* of the Ordinal, there is no direction as to who is to say the particular Anthem or Hymn or Psalm. It might be, for all the rubric could determine, read by the congregation responsively. Custom, which must rule and sometimes overrule in defining rubrics, has of course arranged it, but it is a mark of how much was left to discretion and to the law imposed by preceding usages, by the Reformers, and of how far for many historical causes we have drifted from the old custom. (*Vide* RUBRIC.)

Sceptic. *Vide* DOUBT and AGNOSTICISM.

Schism. DIVISION (and then subdivision) of the Body of the Church. Schism, as a *sin*, is not considered with sufficient care by the Laity. Its open surface evils are acknowledged. The hindrance to the cause of Christianity is freely admitted. The bitterness it engenders are deprecated upon all sides, yet every schismatical body hugs its own schism all the closer. The

Evangelical Alliance is but a compromise between the consciousness of the sin of schism and the need of unity; and though as a mere expedient a failure for unity, yet a clear proof that the knowledge of evil and the sin of schism is gaining ground. First, it is necessary to admit the difficulty of breaking up and reorganizing large organizations simply because they are acknowledged to be on a wrong principle; and, secondly, that every schism, to have any force in it, must be founded upon at least a half truth. And, again, the *zeal*, though of a half-informed knowledge, is gladly granted. But still the great sin remains, not palliated, but rather defined more clearly by these limitations. Then, many of the members of the different denominations are so by descent. They have inherited their Faith, and the change involves a greater struggle than can be easily measured by those who have not passed through it. But it is the great sin of the religious world in this country. The New Testament is very clear upon this subject—this of division. Our LORD warned His disciples against false teachers who should arise, saying, Here is CHRIST, or He is there. He laid down the principle of *unity*, and of love to one another. In His Sermon on the Mount He spoke of false prophets and false teachers, but also of those who would work *lawlessness* (iniquity in the Authorized Version. Matt. vii. 21-24). The Apostles St. Jude, St. Peter, St. John, St. Paul have all something to say about the sin of schism, either in its deeper form involving heresy, or in the form of a mere rending of a united body. But all, at some point in their protests against it, point out that it is a form of willfulness. It would be a willful choice for themselves of what they should accept and believe.

St. Paul, in the First Epistle to the Corinthians, sets schism, division, in its true light,—the rending of the Body of CHRIST. " Is CHRIST divided?" is his vehement exclamation, yet these schisms had not amounted to an open division, only parties *within* the Church. He argues that they all speak the same thing, they all be perfectly joined together in the same mind and in the same judgment. Afterwards his language (ch. xi. 19) shows how he foresaw its result. GOD would permit it, that they who were steadfast and approved of GOD should be made manifest; and as yet there was no open rending, and the point in that place is upon the disorders at the Communion. Again (in ch. xii. 12-31), he compares the Church to the human body, and the unity in it and the work and honor assigned to each. It is on the gifts (Charismata) given, and then he enumerates the offices and helps, from the Apostolic down to the gift of language. It is not the place here to more than point out that if partyism, which might issue in something like our modern schism, could draw out such protests, what is not the position of those in actual willful schism? Passing over St. Peter's and St. Jude's strong words, since these also apply to errors held by men in the Church, we find St. John speaking with sorrowing words of those who had left the Church. How full of suppressed intensity of feeling are these solemn words: "Little children, it is the last time: and as ye have heard that antichrist shall come, even now there are many antichrists; whereby we know that it is the last time. They went out from us, but they were not of us; for if they had been of us, they would no doubt continue with us: but they went out, that they might be made manifest that they were not all of us" (1 John ii. 18, 19). Here schism, in the modern sense of the word, is set forth, and St. John calls those who joined themselves to it antichrists. But the sin of schism is better seen by turning to the doctrine of unity our LORD laid down. First He taught, "He that is not with me is against me." But this being with Him must rest upon Unity in the Faith and in the Covenant, in His Visible Body, for there is none other stated. Pointing out by His comparisons of one Net, one Fold, one Vineyard, one Vine, the unity of Love, the unity of abiding in Him, or we shall be but withered branches fit for the burning, we turn to the Prayer for His Church (St. John xvii.). It is that those the Apostles and those who believe through their word may be one in CHRIST, as He is one with HIS FATHER. Unity He left as a part of the Church's Constitution. But as clearly unity in the Apostolic office. St. Paul's and St. John's arguments would be worthless if the Apostolic office were to fail.

St. Paul insists that unity is necessary, and asserts his authority and claims that fellowship with him is essential. So do St. John (1 John i.), St. Peter, and St. Jude imply it. (*a*) Unity in Apostolic Faith. "If any man preach any other gospel unto you than that ye have received, let him be accursed. . . . I certify you, brethren, that the gospel which was preached of me is not after man. For I neither received it of man, neither was I taught it by man, but by revelation of JESUS CHRIST (Gal. i. 9, 11, 12). So in clearer language St. John in the first chapter of the first Epistle, so Acts ii. 42, and many other places; indeed, the fact that the Epistles were written implies that unity in the Faith is a necessity. (*b*) Unity under Apostolic government (Acts ii. 42, and 1 John i.). Eph. iv. 11-16: "And He gave some, Apostles; and some, prophets; and some, evangelists; and some, pastors and teachers; for the perfecting of the saints, for the work of the ministry, for the edifying of the Body of CHRIST: till we all come in the unity of the faith, and of the knowledge of the SON of GOD, unto a perfect man, unto the measure of the stature of the fullness of CHRIST: that we henceforth be no more children, tossed to and fro, and carried about with every wind of doctrine, by the sleight of men, and cunning craftiness, whereby they lie in wait to deceive; but speaking the truth in love, may grow up into Him in all things, which is the Head, even CHRIST: from whom the whole body fitly joined together and compacted, by that which every joint supplieth, according to the effectual working in the measure of every part, maketh increase of the body unto the edifying of itself in love." In this, the freedom, flexibility, the unity, and the government of the Church, the living Body of CHRIST, is very plainly set forth. The second and third Epistles of St. John are almost entirely upon direction to refuse to commune with those who bring in false doctrines.

We draw these conclusions. That schism, even in the undeveloped state of partyism, is a Sin. That developed schism is based according to our LORD'S words and to St. Paul's warning on lawlessness. That schism divides from the Unity of the Church, that those who are steadfast and approved are made manifest. Therefore that it is so utterly not Apostolic in any way, that it is solemnly protested against by the Apostles as an imminent danger. But the real question now is for those who are charged with schism to decide from what body are we in schism; so many rival bodies claim to be "The Church;" so many pretensions are put forth; so much confusion is brought in by discussion of side issues. Upon the doctrine of the Church we must refer to that article. And for the proofs of the Apostolic Succession to the article upon that subject. And upon the Faith to the article the RULE OF FAITH. But the solution must be the reply that each can give to this question, Can.I claim to be in all respects upon the foundation laid down in the description of the three thousand converted on the Day of Pentecost, "And they continued steadfastly in the *Apostle's doctrine and fellowship, and in breaking of bread, and in* [*the*] *prayers*"? If it was necessary then it is necessary now. It is of the very life of the Christian to be in the Body his LORD created, purchased, loved, and sanctifies. He cannot be sure that he is in union with his LORD unless he is in the Apostolic unity in the Apostolic teaching. He is only certain that he is in his LORD'S presence when he is with those who are gathered by his LORD'S authority. (*Vide* NAME.) That men may be in formal schism who are unwittingly or unwillingly so is true. That Schismatics may have Apostolic Orders is possible, but they have not the other note of Apostolic Unity of doctrine. But there is only certainty when these two are united.

Scotland, Church of. The planting of the Church among the Caledonians is involved in much obscurity. Tertullian claims that in Britain the Gospel was preached where the Roman armies could not penetrate. But whoever first introduced it thither carried it in forms which had no direct connection with the Church of Southern Europe. The old Scotch historians speak of King Donald I. (203 A.D.), probably the chief of some stronger tribe of the Picts, as the first Christian King. Amphibalus, Modocus, Calanus, Carnocus, are traditional names of early preachers of Christianity to them. It is said that Diocletian's persecution (303 A.D.) drove many British Christians into Scotland. The Gospel helped to elevate them, polygamy was repressed, but their wild, warlike life was not so easily laid aside. Ninian, a well-born Briton, said to have been trained in France, has the honor of being the first really historical personage who succeeded in planting the Church effectively among the southern Picts. His holy life, earnest and zealous (412 A.D.), won for him a reverence he well deserved. He founded the Church at Whitehorn and is reputed the first Bishop of Galloway. Paladius, whose mission was originally to the Irish, was diverted from that field to labor with great influence for many years (450 A.D.) among them. He sent the first missionary to the northern Picts. The Bishops seem to have been, as throughout the contemporary history of Britain and Ireland, Tribe-Bishops. Malcolm II. (1010 A.D.) first parted the jurisdiction of the Bishops into Dioceses. This principle of the Tribe-Bishops led to the custom of their living in a monastery with the Monks and of being, as members of the community, subject to the Abbot, a fact which has misled many writers. (*Vide* CULDEES.) The name next of note was that of St. Columba, the great Saint from Ireland, who was gifted with a powerful mind and considerable capacity as a statesman (563 A.D.). From Iona, which from him was afterwards called I-Colum-kill, or Hy of Columb of the Cells, he did his work. His was a singular career. Of a princely family, a soldier, then a monk, he won a greater fame in his strifes for the Gospel than he had gained in the struggles of his clan. After gathering around him men whom he impressed with his own zeal, and having preached in various parts of Scotland, he at last, at seventy-seven years of age, died on his knees before the altar in his little chapel at Iona.

Out of Iona came the gentle and saintly Aidan, who went through South Pictland and North England afoot upon his Episcopal work, teaching, preaching, founding Churches. A successor, Colman (650 A.D.), held the famous controversy with Wilfrid, Archbishop of York, at Whitby, as to what rite—the Old Celtic or the Latin—should prevail. Colman was defeated, and retired from Northumbria to work more exclusively in Scotland.

St. Cuthbert, the laborer among the Cumbrians, also made his work felt north of the Solway by his zeal and energy.

The principal Sees at this date were those of

Man and Galloway. Others appear, but with uncertain bounds. Kenneth (844–860 A.D.), who crushed the Picts, winning the leadership for the Scots, gave greater regularity and more certain bounds to the Dioceses. The See of St. Andrew's was removed from Abernethy, and was made the chief See in Scotland. Gradually as missions were established in different places these Sees were formed, till all the kingdom was under Episcopal oversight. The influence of the Archbishopric of York, which claimed to have all Scotland under its sway, introduced the Roman rites and broke up the older Celtic traditions. Kellach (904 A.D.) went to Rome for confirmation in the See of St. Andrew's. Later the protracted struggle against the marriage of the clergy was begun. It was not readily ended, for we find Canons against their wives (*focariæ*) as late as 1225 A.D. The Scotch Kings striving to break up the dependence of their Bishops upon York, tried to use the quarrels between York and Canterbury (1098 A.D.) to gain this end. Most probably the fact was that consecration was conferred generally by the Bishops within the realm, but that upon occasion, as now, political reasons led to different courses. The claim on the part of York was not given up for a long time, and frequent consecrations were given by its Archbishops to the Scottish Sees. King David (1124 A.D.) endowed some Sees. They were distributed somewhat as follows: St. Andrew's, with a large jurisdiction in Fife, Lothian, Merse (now Berwick), Stirling, Angus, and Mearns; Glasgow in the West; Mortloch (later Aberdeen), Brechin, Dunblane, Ross, Dunkeld. The events in the Scottish Church were varied by visits from Cardinals, who came upon a pretext for reform, but really to extort money, and who were at last forbidden to enter the realm but by the King's license. In the unhappy strifes in the State the Bishops sometimes suffered much at the hands of the reckless lords. When the kingdom was plunged into its lowest state by the attacks of Edward I., the lords appealed to the Pope, who sent a Bull to the English King claiming the kingdom as under him, but this interference Edward fiercely rejected.

The more notable events in the history of the Church were the prosecution against the Templars (1300 A.D.), the erection of St. Andrew's into an Archbishopric (1472 A.D.) by Bulls from Rome. Influenced by petty intrigues, the King inhibited Bishop Graham from publishing them. The Bishop, a gentle man, after a struggle of twelve years, succumbed under his troubles and was succeeded by his bitterest foe, Shevez. The ambition of the Bishop of Glasgow led him to obtain a like advancement for his See (1478 A.D.), though the precedency rested in St. Andrew's. At the time of the Reformation the Archprovince of St. Andrew's included the suffragans of Aberdeen, Brechin, Caithness, Dunblane, Dunkeld, Moray, Orkney, and Ross, while Glasgow had under it Galloway, Argyle, and the Isles. The Scotch Church was infected with the same abuses and evils that had tainted the rest of the Church that acknowledged the Roman obedience. The Lollards began at the beginning of the sixteenth century to disseminate their opinions in Scotland. Some were arrested, but were not punished till Hamilton, the young Abbot of Firme (1527 A.D.), was accused of heresy. His execution did more to stir up the people than many disputations. This martyrdom led to many others. But the effort at Reformation was of a much more mixed character than elsewhere. The wild, reckless character of the nobility, their rapacity, and the peculiar tribal relations, gave the Reformation there a much different tone. The political aspect the struggle soon assumed was one of its marked features. When James V. died (1542 A.D.) the Earl of Arran, a reformer, was regent, but soon the Roman party got influence over him, and the persecuting, repressive efforts were renewed. John Knox, who had returned from a residence in Geneva (1555 A.D.), began to gather a congregation about him in Edinburgh.

The English Reformation had affected those in Scotland so far that the counsel of the English leaders was sought by them, and Edward's Prayer-Book was introduced. In 1558 A.D. the Earls of Argyle, Glencairn, and Morton, and the Lord of Lorne, entered with others into a league together to urge a reformation and to introduce the Book of Common Prayer. Soon followed political excesses, the destruction of the monasteries, the deposition of the Queen regent. Then came the Parliament of 1560 A.D., wherein the Bishops kept silence, and strangely permitted themselves to be overslaughed. Weakness on the one side, hurry and violence on the other; the intrigues and conspiracies which gathered around Queen Mary Stuart for seven years; the dying off of the Bishops, who were allowed to hold the property of their Sees, and the introduction of the Presbyterian discipline, 1572 A.D., and the appointment of the Titular Bishops,—not Bishops by consecration, but only by a political device to hold the seats of the spiritual estate in Parliament, to keep up constitutional forms. When this empty order was attacked (1572-80 A.D.) Presbyterianism prevailed, under the leadership of Andrew Melville. For thirty years this continued, till the accession of James VI. to the English throne (1608 A.D.), when he took measures to restore Episcopacy to the Scotch Church, which were finally carried out in 1610 A.D. There were no commotions nor more trouble than was natural in effecting such a change. Laud endeavored to enforce the use of a Liturgy, and drew up the ill-starred book of 1637 A.D. The troubles which were gathering around Charles I. gave opportunity for the discontented to foment fresh troubles, which grew into riots at Edinburgh. The leaders in Scotch affairs banded together in the famous National Covenant, and took the name of Covenanters. The overthrow of Episcopacy followed upon the death of Charles. The next era in the varied fortunes of the Church extends over twenty-seven years (1661–1688 A.D.). Charles II. upon his restoration promised toleration to all; but so many prominent Presbyterians were so deeply plunged in the treasons against his father, as well as implicated in religious disturbances, that State prosecutions for treason wore the appearance of persecutions. He restored the Scotch Episcopate as soon as possible. Archbishops Sharp and Fairfoul, and Bishops Hamilton and Leighton, were consecrated in Westminster Abbey by Sheldon, Bishop of London, assisted by the Bishops of Worcester, Carlisle, and Llandaff (December 15, 1661 A.D.). They consecrated seven Bishops to fill the old Sees on the 7th of May, and two others on the 1st of June, 1662 A.D. The administration of the Church's affairs was as mild as it could be consistently with its preserving dignity and truthfulness. No Liturgical form was introduced. The right of presentation to benefices lay in the Patrons, and the induction was with the Bishops. The change in the incumbents created some confusion, and the imposition of fines by Act of Parliament upon all who did not attend church added to the difficulties. Continued disaffection and opposition, which could have been overcome by time and patience, was aggravated by legal suppression, which finally found vent in the foul assassination of Archbishop Sharp, after several attempts, 1679 A.D.

The accession of James II. affected the Church in Scotland very seriously. His efforts for the restoration of Romanism in Scotland were resisted by the Bishops in Parliament, and incurred the royal displeasure. However, the adherence of the Bishops to King James and the factious conduct of the Presbyterian leaders effected a second overthrow of Church polity and gave Scotland over to the Presbyterians. These changes showed that there was still a strong Church feeling among many, especially in the north of Scotland. No move was made by the ejected Bishops to continue the succession till 1704–5 A.D., when the death of the Archbishop of St. Andrew's brought this necessity forcibly before them. Two clergymen were selected, Revs. J. Fullarton and J. Sage. This last was a noted and able controversialist; in fact, his Episcopate was chiefly spent in this labor. In truth, the position of the Bishops seemed at this time to revert to the ancient custom in Scotland, for they were in no position to hold Sees. The adherence of the lay members of the Church in Scotland to the Stuarts prevented any practical amelioration of the condition of the clergy. Two other clergymen, Revs. J. Falconer and H. Christie, were consecrated in 1709 A.D. In 1712 A.D. the Bishops adopted the English Book of Common Prayer, and later (1764 A.D.) revised the office of the Holy Communion from materials supplied by the English non-jurors, by adding more especially the Invocation after the prayer of Consecration, which Bishop Seabury introduced into our own American Prayer-Book with some verbal changes. The broken and scattered Church had by this time so consolidated that the clergy could now desire to have a Bishop in settled residence, and Bishop Fullarton was chosen Diocesan and Primus (1720 A.D.). The clergy suffered severely from the government after the insurrection of 1745 A.D. The acts passed against them were severe, and were so denounced by the English Bishops in Parliament. However, obliged to endure much hardship they still kept up their services, and when another clergyman was advanced to the Episcopate it was as Diocesan of Aberdeen. Gradually the Sees were being again filled in a quiet way. So in difficulties and dangers was preserved the Church which was destined to give to the American Church her first Bishop. Bishop Seabury's election, suit to the English Bishops for consecration, and, upon the advice of Dr. Berkeley (the son of Bishop Berkeley) his successful application to the Scotch Bishops, are recorded also in the articles upon the American Church and upon the Church in Connecticut. He received his orders November, 1784 A.D., from Bishops Kilgour (Primus), Petrie, and Skinner. It drew the attention of the English Bishops to the depressed estate of the Scotch Church, and they procured the repeal of the penal statutes of 1746–48 A.D. The debt of our Church to the Scotch Bishops is very great, and must always be gratefully acknowledged. Yet the English Church is after all the real source of the Scotch line. We are not the less practically indebted to them for the Orders given us by our Mother-Church; for the consecration of Bishop Seabury led the English Parliament to relax the stringent act, and to permit the consecration of Bishops White and Provoost. Gradually the Bishops became Diocesans, reviving as far as practicable the old lines and holding several of them as a single jurisdiction. Moray, Ross, and Caithness are held by Bishop Eden, St. Andrew's, Dunkeld, and Dumblane are under Bishop Wordsworth, Edinburgh is under Bishop Cotterell, Glasgow and Galloway are ruled by Bishop Wilson, Brechin by Bishop Jermyn, Aberdeen and Orkney by Bishop Douglass, and Argyle and the Isles by Bishop Chinnery-Haldane. The growth of the Church in Scotland has been slow but sure. It does not exhibit that rapidity of increase which we have here. In 1708 A.D. there were 133 clergy and 79 parishes vacant. In 1838 A.D. there were about 190 clergy. In 1882–83 A.D. there were 252. In this same year 28,144 communicants were reported.

Scriptures. The Holy Books of the Bible were so called very early in the Church from the New Testament usage. Then, of course, the term referred to the Old Testament (*e.g.*, 2 Tim. iii. 15, 16; so Rom. xv. 4; 2 Pet. i. 20). They are called the HOLY Scriptures, the Scriptures of the PROPHETS. The title as given to both Testaments as early as the Epistles of St. Clement. (*Vide* BIBLE.) The Scriptures were from the first read constantly by the Church, both in public and in private. The public reading of them is treated at large in the articles LECTIONARY and LESSONS. We do not now understand how fully they were read in private. It is not probable that the complete copies we have in daily use were generally possessed by any but the rich, and we have numerous MSS. of only parts of the Scriptures; but not only were they read so constantly and largely in the public services that the attentive hearer could become familiar with their contents, but the people were so constantly referred to the books themselves, that the only conclusion was, that the preachers who so referred them were confident that they could easily gain access to them. Clement, Polycarp, Theophilus, Justin Martyr, Tertullian, a series of writers for the first century after the Apostles, imply this (97-190 A.D.). Clement of Alexandria continually refers to the private study of the Scriptures. St. Cyprian made specially collection of Testimonies against the Jews,—*i.e.*, of texts bearing upon the controversies with the Jews. But St. Chrysostom is the one who specially urges, with great persistence and force, the duty, the profit, the delight, in studying the word of GOD. We are very apt to suppose that the study of the Scriptures was laid aside during the period called the Dark Ages; but this is the reverse of the truth. The many copies made by those monks whose affair it was to make them, the reading in order in the daily offices, which latterly, however, became overlaid with other liturgical uses, the numerous comments on the several books of Holy Scripture,—*e.g.*, by Haymo of Halberstadt (840 A.D.),—and especially the many comments on the Apocalypse, attest that the study of it was by no means relaxed. That many in the monasteries were unable to read at all is true, but many of these listened so attentively that they were quite skilled in the text. That the wild, undisciplined Franks and Goths could not read them, did not care for them, is a fact, but when we consider what the Church had to do in educating them, with the difficulties of only MSS. at hand, we can well see that much ignorance may be excused them. Making all allowances for these drawbacks, there was a very large amount of Biblical instruction disseminated under great hindrances. The Emperors and nobles had their choicely prepared MSS. Gospels, the rich had their copies, the Churches had public copies in the church, and there was constant instruction given in different ways.

The true defect was in the substitution, too often, of listening to the public reading in preference to spending much time in private study. But however much the amount of private study varied at different times and in different places, still there were ever some in every age who had reverently studied the Holy Scriptures. In this day we are giving more attention to them than ever; some of the most absorbing controversies of the day are upon portions of the Holy Book, and the recent issue of the Revised translation has given a great impetus to a closer reading of the New Testament. There is no book in the world which has been so constantly printed, of which so many thousands of editions have been published. Yet there is but little intelligent reading of them. They have been read through by course as a stated daily task year after year by a good many, who think themselves students, and who yet have never retained a clear idea of all they have read. The Scriptures have been read, on the other hand, by those who wanted to find the authority for certain private views, others pick out favorite passages and reread these only. There are three rules to be laid down for a profitable reading of the Scriptures. The two first are general and to be constantly used, the third is for gaining a more particular training in their contents. I. Not merely to read with attention, but with that attention which leads to comparison of passages. II. To meditate frequently as we read, and endeavor to find some practical lesson or to receive, with better insight into its meaning, the doctrine taught us. III. After a general training in Holy Scripture by these two rules to then take some chief topic, as the Articles of the Creed, the divinity of our LORD, the Unity of the Church, or the such like, and compare Scripture with Scripture, "comparing Spiritual things with Spiritual." But again, there is a caution ever to be had: not to look for some preconceived idea of what should be there. The error of sectism in the study of Holy Scripture is twofold: it goes to Scripture to bolster up an already formulated doctrine, and reject every text that does not square with this formula; and, secondly, it does not touch large portions of Holy Scripture which set forth truths incompatible with the theory the reader wishes or seeks to uphold. For example, few without the Church spend much time in tracing the office and continuity of the Apostles in the New Testament. The texts upon Absolution are largely overlooked. The full witness to Confirmation is not often noticed. The texts on the Unity of the Church are seldom dwelt upon, for they do not fit in with preconceived notions. Private judgment reads into Holy Scripture much that never was there, and leaves out much that Holy Scripture insists upon. It is a practical mangling of GOD's Word. The full round of Bible Doctrine is seldom studied and mastered. The rule should be, that as the Creeds have defined, so difficult or opposing texts are to be accepted; and that Scripture cannot be quoted against itself. The Scriptures read with the Prayer-Book beside it, and a reference to the way the Church has arranged and selected certain Scriptures, would help very much. The XXXIX. Aticles, though only binding on the clergy, furnish excellent hints upon difficult topics. The use of some special texts in the Services or the Offices, as of the Holy Communion and Baptism, will guide to a better understanding not only of the texts selected, but of others that are connected with them. One rule has been left to the last, the rule of ever reading the Holy Word of GOD with prayer.

Sealed Books, The, of Common Prayer, were the officially-ordered copies of the English Book of Common Prayer, revised by the Commission of 1661 A.D., which were to furnish the standard text for all future editions. Every Cathedral and Collegiate Church had to procure a copy of it, certified under the great seal of England, which Book was to be "kept and preserved by them in safety forever, and to be also produced and showed forth in any Court of Record as often as they shall be thereunto required." The Courts at Westminster and the Tower of London were to receive copies. By these copies all other printed copies of the Prayer-Book were to be compared and corrected, and when properly certified to, these copies were to be received in Law as good records as the "original book" itself. The original MS. was not found for a long while, and not till after the valuable edition by Archibald Stephens, Q.C., was published from the Legal Copies. These Sealed Books are of the utmost importance in criticising the text of our own Prayer-Book, in which many variations (despite all care to prevent them) from the Standard edition, issued in 1847 A.D., have appeared.

Secondaries. The general name for the inferior members of Cathedrals, as vicars choral, etc. The *clerici secundæ formæ, i.e.*, of the second or lower range of stalls. . . . The Priest, Vicars, and Minor Canons were sometimes included in the superior form. Some of the lay-singers at Exeter are so called. Sometimes the term was applied to the assistant priest in course, even though not of the second form. At Hereford the second Vicar who assists in chanting the Litany is the "secondary." (Hook's Ch. Dict.)

Second Advent. The doctrine which is expressed in the confession of a Prophecy yet to be fulfilled: "From thence He shall come to judge the quick and the dead." Our LORD's prophecy (St. Matt. xxiv. 30, 31; St. Mark xiii. 26, 27, and elsewhere), the constant preaching of the Apostles (1 Thess. iv. 16; 2 Thess. i. 7; 1 Pet. i. 7; Heb. ix. 28; Phil. iii. 20, 21), the prophecy of St. John (Rev. i. 7; xxii. 12), are the basis of this Article in the Creed. The Apostles confidently expected it in their day. It has been looked for from age to age, and many holy men have been sure that it was only at the door. It is well to expect it, for we believe it as an assured fact of the future, but it is one of those things which can never be foreseen. Our LORD has clearly put this, that He will come as a thief at an unlooked-for hour, when the times and seasons in His FATHER'S power only are ripe. He has distinctly said that no man, not even Himself, as SON of Man, knoweth that time, but the FATHER only. He has only certified solemnly to that coming to deliver a judgment, which will be His by office and by His Human Nature. In this Second Advent (whether preceded by a millennial reign the future only shall show) He will summon all before Him, the quick and the dead, to give an account of their deeds and words, and to receive a righteous award. The strictness of this inquisition, the laying bare of the secrets not of our lives, but of our thoughts and motives, the double witness both of His book of Remembrance and of our own memory, are all clearly brought in. The awful splendor of that great day, when, with the sign of the SON of Man in mid-air to proclaim His Presence, He shall come with His holy ones, seated in the clouds with the Angels of Judgment, summoning all, from earth and sea, with the blast of the Archangelic trump, He has described in language grand by its very simplicity and by the weight of facts in prophecies. These should be the subject of our meditations. The ends of that Judgment are: The conclusion of that great scheme of probation whereby each child of Adam goes through his trial, and as he fulfills his mission or fails in it, shall be rewarded or punished accordingly. It is the end of all those providences which are connected with the free-will of man. Each man's life is a course of trial, and the end alone shows the result. Now, though as a matter of a particular judgment must needs be passed on each one in the hour of death, to determine his position, yet it needs the solemnity of the final day to declare it.

And next, it is the great means by which the justice of GOD is made manifest. Here we only see the end of the golden chain that hangs between heaven and earth, and there are many providences which we cannot fathom. We see virtue crushed to the earth, and vice triumphing. We see the most total disproportion of the lots of men. Why should the lord have more than the beggar? We see one man carried to the grave after a life of uninterrupted success, another the victim of the frowns of fortune. Why is this? Though GOD occasionally gives us hints of His justice, and shows us just enough to convince us that it is well with the righteous and ill with the wicked even here, yet to mark the Christian dispensation (unlike the earlier times) He has referred the ultimate retribution, both of good and bad, to the future state. And accordingly, when the great day comes, much that is inscrutable to us now will be cleared up. God has revealed to us the judgment, that by the thought of it we should be urged both to piety and patience. " Blessed is that soul, which day and night hath no other care than how, in the great day, when every creature shall stand around the Judge to give an account of their works, she shall be able to relate her life. For whosoever continually places that day and that hour before his eyes, and ever thinks of his defense at that most just tribunal, is likely to commit no sin, or at least very few." Hence, also, St. Chrysostom says, " Let us ever be saying to ourselves and to others, there is a resurrection, and a terrible judgment awaiting us."

Sect. It means a division in the body of Christians. It is a body that itself cuts off from the unity of the holy Church Catholic, for in that body there must be a unity. It is noticeable that a sect has the name of some human leader or founder given to it despite its repudiation of it, thus marking its human origin. This natural law was as old as the parties in the Corinthian Church. " I of Paul," " I of Apollos," " I of Cephas," and lastly and truly, " I of Christ," so St. Paul asks," Is Christ divided?" If, then, we have any name other than that of Christ, both God and man, called upon us, we are guilty of partyism or of sectism. Therefore it was that our Lord warned us, " Neither be ye called masters: for one is your Master, even Christ" (St. Matt. xxiii. 10).

Secularization. The alienation and the application of Church property to secular uses. It has happened repeatedly in the history of the Church that its property has been seized and secularized by the state. There is here no reference to the petty seizures and spoliations of lands and property from which Parishes or Dioceses have suffered more or less in every age, but to the larger acts that affected the real estate of the national Church, or of the richer corporations, which (as, for instance, the Templars, the Jesuits, and other large bodies) were spread throughout the Church. The Templars were prosecuted and suppressed and their property seized by Philip Augustus in 1312 A.D. In England, Henry VIII. seized upon the Monastic property, and though he promised to found Bishoprics with it, either put it into the treasury for his own purposes or gave it to his favorites. In France at the Revolution all Church property was secularized, though much of it has been recovered since. In Spain, in Italy, in Austria, in every country in Europe there has been such secularization of Church property. Even the State of Virginia at the close of the Revolution seized upon the glebes belonging to the Church.

Secular Clergy. The name given to those of the clergy in the Roman Church who do not belong to some one of the Monastic orders.

Sedilia. Seats or stalls, usually three in number, placed within the Chancel on the south side. They are either level or are graduated, following the steps of the altar, the highest seat being nearest the east end. They are intended as seats for the clergy during the sermon.

See. (*Vide* Diocese.) It comes to us from the Latin " *Sedes*" through the French *siege*, a seat. It was the name given to the seat or residence of the Bishop, and so to the city in which he had his Throne. St. Augustine speaks of those cities in which the Apostles formed Churches as the Apostolic Sees, and so they are usually named. It was from this fact, in part, that Rome's opposition came when Constantinople was raised, because of its political importance, to the second place, for Constantinople was not an Apostolic See. Jerusalem, Antioch, Rome, Corinth, and Ephesus were named Apostolic Churches, as having Apostles for their founders.

Semi-Pelagians. As Pelagianism was practically but the assertion that man could save himself, and so was refuted by the Theologians and condemned by the Councils of the Church, so Semi-Pelagianism sought to find a mean between the two. It would not fairly accept the doctrine that man was indeed far gone from original righteousness, and is of his own nature inclined to evil; nor yet could it hold that a man could save himself, and could live without sin and keep the commandments of God perfectly if he willed it. Those who sought an escape from either statement formulated their opinion thus: that the first strivings of repentance can originate and are within the power of the will of man, but that if he would grow in grace at all, he must have and use the grace of the Holy Spirit. This doctrine was very popular in the south of France among the Theologians there, the chief of whom was Cassianus. It has never been fairly dropped, but ever reappears from time to time. Augustine's extreme doctrines were the result of this resistance to Pelagius. The less cautious though correct doctrines of St. John Chrysostom were taken up by the Gallican Doctors, while they resisted Augustine's formulation of doctrine. Augustinianism gradually won its way.

It is not within our plan to dwell upon the controversies which sprang up from time to time upon these questions. The most noted was the contest between the Jesuits and the Jansenists, who followed the Augustinian statements. In the end the laxer Jesuits triumphed. In England the numerous sectaries who sprang up during the Reformation and just after it were more or less tainted with Semi-Pelagianism.

And at this day there is current a large amount of Semi-Pelagian doctrine, chiefly from carelessness and from inaccurate reasoning than from any recognition of it as a theory, and very often probably in utter ignorance that there was ever any school that bore that name. The doctrine of the Church Catholic is properly set forth in the Articles (Articles IX., X.).

Septuagesima. The Sunday which is about seventy (accurately sixty-three) days before Easter. It took its name (Septuagesima) probably from counting back from Quinquagesima Sunday, which is forty-nine days before Easter, and so, roundly, is the fiftieth day from Easter-day. The name is very old, being used in the Sacramentaries as early as Gelasius, 494 A.D. The preparation for Lent is begun in the Epistles and Gospel, which are upon the self-control (1 Cor. ix. 24-27) needed in the Christian race. The Gospel (the parable of the Laborers in the Vineyard) has its interconnection with the Epistle in implying the nature of the toil imposed upon the laborers in the spiritual kingdom, whether of the soul or of the larger field of the Church. The Collect has been traced through the Sarum Missal to Gregory I. (596 A.D.).

Septuagint. The most famous and valuable of all the ancient Versions of the Old Testament. It is called the Septuagint (LXX., or the Seventy) from the legend that King Ptolemy procured from the High-Priest at Jerusalem a company of seventy-two learned Jews, who translated for him the Hebrew Scriptures in seventy-two days. The legend varies in details in different reports. The legend is worthy of credence, so far as it shows Alexandria to have been the place of the translation, and that it was at some time placed in the library there. But the translation itself shows such variations in style and manner that it is impossible to suppose it to have been made by any one set of men, or at one date. The facts, from internal evidence, point to many translators, and perhaps recensions, separated by considerable spaces of time. We may suppose with great likelihood that the collection which we call the Septuagint was the result of the translations made as the needs of the Jews of the dispersion demanded. It was the version universally accepted in the time of our LORD, and was the one which the Hellenic Jews would be most familiar with. So its great value lay in the wide dispersion of copies of it, in the fact that it prepared a language, so to speak, in which the Gospels could be written, for it introduced so many Hebraisms and Jewish forms of thought that the style of the Gospels (written by men Jews by birth and speaking the Aramaic vernacular, yet engaged in original composition) would not grate so harshly upon the Greek ear. Both, of course, used forms of the Hellenic-Greek current after the time of Alexander the Great, but both used the language as an instrument to be tempered anew for their sacred work. This Version was in such current use that St. Paul uses it freely, seldom making any attempt to give a closer rendering of the Hebrew original. And so do the other Apostles, though, of course, to a less extent, since their audiences were not so generally Gentile as were his. "The use made of the LXX. in the New Testament has rendered it very precious to the Church. Of three hundred and fifty direct quotations from the Old Testament, scarcely fourteen per cent. differ from the Septuagint. Of thirty-seven quotations ascribed to our SAVIOUR, thirty-three agree almost verbatim with the LXX. Two follow the Hebrew, and differ from the LXX. One agrees with neither, and another partly with both. In the speech of St. Stephen there are nearly thirty quotations from the LXX. The Ethiopian Eunuch was converted by reading the LXX. All the quotations in the Acts of the Apostles are taken from this version, and wherever the word (graphé) Writing or Scripture occurs, it means the LXX. The Epistles of St. James and St. Peter, being addressed to Hellenists by birth, are fully furnished with quotations from the LXX. St. Paul, the Apostle to the Gentiles, and deeply versed in the Hebrew Scriptures, yet quotes from the LXX. on all occasions. His first and longest address in the synagogue at Pisidia is full of allusions to the LXX. His vocabulary is wholly supplied from the same source, and this is no less true of the immediate successors of the Apostles. Timothy, of Hellenistic parentage, could only have been instructed in the Septuagint Version." (Blunt's Dict. of Hist. and Doct. Theol., sub voc.) But there are one or two things to note as to the Version. Either it was made from a Hebrew text which varies much from our own, accepted from the Jews and certified to, or it takes many liberties with the text. It is no part of the point to be made to attempt to defend any liberties so taken, but the variations are certainly more numerous and wider from the Hebrew text than any modern version could possibly venture upon. Yet the writers of the New Testament did not disdain to use it, with all its imperfections, but incorporated its language into their own Inspired Writings. It was rightly not their mission to retranslate the Version, since they would prejudice the reader against their own work, though they did correct any very glaring defect in the text they chose to quote. Now, is not this case somewhat parallel with that of our authorized Version (with vastly the advantage on the side of the English Version in point of accuracy), as compared with the Revision lately put forth? Again, as it grew and was accepted as the best Version possible for the Hellenistic Jews, it was the accepted Version for the Eastern Church, and from it the Lessons in the Church, the prooftexts in Controversies of the utmost importance, as in the Arian Controversy, the current comment in Sermon and in Lecture, were taken.

There is needed yet an edition of the text worthy of its importance in the History of the Scriptures and the Versions in the Church's keeping.

Sequestration. This is a separating the thing in controversy from the possession of both the contending parties. It is of frequent use in England. When a living becomes void by the death of an incumbent or otherwise, the Bishop sends out his sequestration to have the cure supplied, and to preserve the profits (after the expenses deducted) for the use of his successor. Sometimes a benefice is left under sequestration for many years together, namely, when it is of so small value that no clergyman fit to serve the cure will be at the charge of taking it by institution. In this case sequestration is committed sometimes to the Curate only, sometimes to the Curate and Church-Warden jointly. There are several other kinds of sequestration, as for neglect of duty, and a levy upon the Parson's goods for debt, made through the Bishop. All acts involving sequestration pass through the Bishop. (From Hook's Ch. Dictionary.)

Seraphim. *Vide* ANGELS.

Sermons. The Sermon, or Discourse, has always been a most important part of the work and duty of the Parish Priest, or of the Deacon, " if he be licensed thereto by the Bishop." Originally it was confined to the Bishop as an official act. But this rule was very frequently broken, and laymen were at times allowed to preach or to exhort. In the Apostolic Age the pressing necessities of an active, energetic Apostolate, and the miraculous gifts which were shown by many lay members, led to the use of orders of men who had this authority to preach. And instead of these orders having been dropped, it is far more probable that as spiritual gifts ceased, the offices were held by one and the same person. It must be carefully borne in mind that the preaching of the Apostles and the modern sermon have distinct aims. In the first place, the Apostle had a heathen or a Jewish audience to whom he proclaimed the Faith as a perfectly new thing (hence the Gospel, good news). But when there was a congregation gathered, then it would be a mixed audience, and for these the prophets were appointed (for prophesying was not merely a predictive power, but also it included the wider power to teach), and the prophets in the New Testament were also teachers. Later the Presbyter held this as well as other functions joined to his office, so that it was merged not lost. The Missionary really used the Apostolic authority to preach. The Parish Priest is the Teacher or Prophet in its broader meaning. Our own modern Sermon is much more nearly the older use in the Primitive Church, and it is (as might be expected) a fact that those old Sermons, freed from the mere local and temporary accessories of the age, can be effectively used now as well as then, and the later homilies and expository form of Sermons is but a reverting to the great models which the Fathers have given us. It was and now is meant for direct instruction in the Scriptures. It is said that the power of the pulpit has declined, but this is far from true. The mode of preserving religious truth must be affected by the circumstances about it. It is not given to every man, on whom is laid the duty of preaching, to be an orator. Attractive speaking in this day is equally amusing as in Athens eighteen centuries ago. But it does not always prove most effective. Soundness in teaching will alone last. It is the preacher's duty to make his Sermon interesting, but it is also the hearer's duty to listen heedfully to him who has the care of souls. Our LORD said, " Take heed what ye hear," and St. Paul predicted that " the time will come when they will not endure sound doctrine; but after their own lusts shall they heap to themselves teachers having itching ears, and they shall turn many from the truth" (2 Tim. iv. 3, 4). Here are the Churchman's rules as to whom he will listen to. If they are heedfully examined they will keep him straitly in his own Parish church. There is also the responsibility of hearing aright. A Sermon can be upon only a fragment of the great body of doctrines. It presupposes some acquaintance with the general topic treated, and with its interrelation to the whole teaching of the Faith. Still, it requires close attention on the part of the hearer, with faith (Heb. iv. 2) and prayer. The Sermon is within the lines that the Scripture, the Creeds, the Prayer-Book, and the Articles draw around it, and a serious departure from them would be instinctively felt. So the Congregation have an unnoticed but real defense against wrong doctrine.

Sermons may be roughly divided into Doctrinal, Hortatory, or Expository. Sometimes the Sermon may partake of all three, usually of only one, though every Sermon should be practical in some way. There is a general but wrong objection to doctrinal Sermons. But if they are laid aside the preaching would soon become poor and shrunken. Doctrines are our Faith,—*e.g.*, the Incarnation, the Atonement, the Resurrection, the work of the HOLY GHOST,—the living power of the Church. We rest upon them. We need to hear them explained, enforced, and illustrated. The Church intends that her children shall receive doctrine. Of the three this class of Sermons should be most valued.

Again, there is a tendency with some to undervalue, with others to overvalue, the Sermon in comparison with the worship and service of the Church. In truth, there is no comparison, each is distinct, each is essential. That they are joined together is the result of convenience, of custom, of the rubric enjoining the Sermon when there is a

Communion, of the opportunity to use the lessons of the service to point the instruction to be given. That the Congregation may be attracted most by what costs the least effort is true, for the service is a holy work, a sacrifice; so the Sermon is impatiently looked for and the glorious beauty of worship is obscured. And as by the exigency of the hour the Sermon must be short, it may fail to be as instructive as it should be, because there is not time to develop and enforce any very important topic upon the minds of the hearers. There can be no rubrical reason why the Church could not be opened for the Sermon only with the shortened service at some convenient hour, not the usual hour for service, when full time could be given to the service. There is this serious duty resting upon every Churchman, to take heed what he hears and to whom he listens, to consider for himself, and to urge on others to receive instruction, not seek amusement.

We will not be allowed to plead ignorance of the Law of GOD when we can know, and we should listen carefully to authoritative explanations that we may not transgress it ignorantly.

Service. A general term, including the offices of Morning and Evening Prayer and other most frequently used offices. It is used to describe also separate musical renderings of a part of the Public Service. A "Morning Service" would contain the *Venite*, the *Te Deum*, and *Jubilate*, or *Benedictus*, or the *Benedicite* in place of the *Te Deum*. A "Communion Service" contains the *Responses* to the Commandments, the *Prefaces* and *Sanctus*, and the *Gloria in Excelsis*. The proper musical rendering of the service should also include the Versicles and the Amens. It is not an easy matter to persuade those in charge that there should be more unity of movement and intention in the usual selection of the Chants and Glorias chosen for the regular Sunday service. The Precentor should select the several portions of the music with reference to the general unity of the service. Not, as is so often the case, choose each piece separately because it happens to be pleasing, without regard to the fact whether it is in harmony with what precedes or what may follow it. Such a service properly compiled from churchly music is as much a "service" as though the whole series of Anthems and Canticles had had appropriate music from the pen of a single composer. Such musical settings of the Morning and Evening Prayer and of the Communion Service require a training from those in charge, which makes them an act and a sacrifice of praise which has cost something to prepare and to offer to GOD.

Session of Christ. His sitting on the right hand of His FATHER is a necessary part of that Confession of the Facts of our Redemption which constitute the Creed. The value of this constant confession is less felt than it should be. The Article of His Ascension is properly followed by a declaration of His session at the right hand of GOD the FATHER Almighty. He that liveth and was dead, and, behold, is alive for evermore, has carried our human nature into the Presence of Presences. There our LORD JESUS CHRIST abideth in the full majesty of all that was His as Eternal SON of GOD, and waiteth as our Judge, clothed with plenary power. He is there in that true Human Body (then mortal and passible, but now immortal and impassible), which He took in the Virgin's womb, together with the true Human Soul which belongs to His Human Nature, and which was, during His life on earth, completely joined to His Divine Nature, yet without fusion, and which separated from His body by Death, was reunited to it upon the third day after His Crucifixion, and constituted His true and real Resurrection; and with this He as perfect immortal man, as well as GOD for evermore, has "gone into heaven, and is on the right hand of GOD, angels and authorities and powers being made subject unto Him." By this session at the Right Hand of His FATHER is set forth His Supremacy. But also our LORD being our High-Priest, and having entered into the holiest with His own blood, abideth there to make continual intercession for all who shall come to Him. It is His mediatorial office which He must retain till the fullness of the times shall come. "Sit Thou at my right hand until I make Thine enemies Thy footstool." The facts we confess, then, in this Article of the Creed, are His Immortality, His Presence at the Throne of His FATHER, His Royal Supremacy over all things visible and invisible, His Mediatorial Office, His exercise of this Office continually until the time shall come when He shall appear in the clouds of Heaven as the Supreme Judge of the quick and the dead.

Sexagesima. The Sunday falling on the fifty-sixth day before Easter. As in the case of the Septuagesima Sunday, the name is given from the round number, not from the actual count of days. The Collect, Epistle, and Gospel are from the Sarum Missal, but slightly altered, since there was a reference to St. Paul as a protector, which was removed and a correct phrase substituted. The Epistle has double but distinct lines of allusion to the Gospel: first the notable sower, St. Paul under the guidance of the HOLY GHOST; next the example he gave of endurance, of depth of good ground, and of the abundant harvest his sowing has produced. "I have planted, Apollos watered, but GOD gave the increase" (1 Cor. iii. 6).

Sexton. Segestan, contracted from Sacristan. His duties are not so dignified or responsible as were those of the Sacristan, who had the care of the valuables of the Church. The Sexton has generally charge of the menial offices about the church building. His duties vary in detail as the customs of the several parishes vary, but they generally lie within the limits of caring for the church building, ringing the bell, and looking after such matters as the rector shall direct or require. It is really an office that deserves much more consideration than it receives, being a charge in the care of sacred things. "I had rather be a door-keeper in the house of my GOD, than to dwell in the tents of wickedness," was the Psalmist's impassioned exclamation. Any service rendered for the decency and order and comfort of the worshipers in GOD'S house is accompanied with a blessing.

Shechinah. It may be freely expressed by the Indwelling Presence of GOD. It was a word of later coinage, and was the word by which the Jews expressed the presence of GOD dwelling in the Holy of Holies. It was not the Glory or the Pillar, but it was that abiding presence of which the Glory and the Pillar were the manifestations. He dwelt in the bush in Horeb and it was not consumed. He dwelt between the Cherubim, and thence gave answers to His People. His promise: "Sing and rejoice, O daughter of Zion, for, lo, I come, and I will dwell in the midst of thee, saith the LORD" (Zech. ii. 10), expresses in part the meaning of this Shechinah. It was a word used in explanation of the Targums, not a word of the Inspired writers. It was a preparation as it were for the later coming, teaching of the wondrous indwelling of our LORD among men. We may, therefore, say that what the devout Jew understood and confessed of the indwelling of GOD'S glory among men was fulfilled in our LORD. Wherever the New Testament speaks of the Word being made flesh and dwelling among men, and of His glory (St. John i. 14; iii. 11; Rev. vii. 15; xii. 12; xiii. 6; xxi. 3), the Jew would readily understand the Shechinah of His Presence. But since this is so, the references by our LORD to Himself are so to be understood: "I am the light, the Life of men. Abide in me, and I in you." These refer to His dwelling as a glory and a sanctification in the heart,—a fulfillment of His pledge. "I dwell in the high and holy place, with him also that is of a contrite and humble spirit." "He that dwelleth in the secret place of the most High shall abide under the shadow of the Almighty." We can well understand this as a spiritual reference, but it is something far more than that, it is much nearer what St. Peter expressed by the words "partakers of the divine nature." And the presence of His Glory among us is pledged to us by the promise, "Where two or three are gathered together in My Name, there am I in the midst of them." In these ways this later Jewish word taught by anticipation the truth of His abiding presence, with a fullness which we are likely to lose in this day.

Shew-Bread. The Twelve Loaves which were to be placed upon a table overlaid with fine gold, and which was set in the outer Sanctuary with the Seven-branched Lamp and the Altar of Incense. The twelve loaves were to be placed there fresh every Sabbath with incense upon them, that they may be a memorial, even an offering made by fire, unto the LORD. The loaf of the previous week was the priest's portion to be eaten then in the Holy Place (Ex. xxv. 23-30; Lev. xxiv. 5-9). It was never to fail; it was the bread before the face of the LORD, and so a memorial, to be set before the LORD alway. As the Bread before the Face of GOD. So, to use Bähr's beautiful language (Smith's Bible Dict., sub voc.), "The Bread of the Face is therefore that bread through which GOD is seen, that is, with the participation of which the seeing of GOD is bound up, or through the participation of which man attains the sight of GOD. Whence it follows that we have not to think of bread merely as such, as the means of nourishing the bodily life, but as spiritual food, as a means of appropriating and retaining that life which consists in seeing the face of GOD. Bread is therefore here a symbol, and stands here, as it so generally does in all languages, both for life and nourishment; but by being entitled the Bread of the Face, it becomes a symbol of a life higher than the physical: it is, since it lies on the table, placed in the symbolic heaven, heavenly bread. They who eat of it and satisfy themselves with it see the face of GOD (Bähr, Symbolic). It is to be remembered that the Shew-Bread was taken from the children of Israel by an everlasting covenant, and may therefore be well expected to bear the most solemn meaning." It is the type of Him who was at once the perfect Image of GOD, the one who abides in the Presence of Presences as the Bread of Life, and who also has given us Himself the Bread for the nourishment of the soul (St. John vi. 51).

Shrine. A place where relics or consecrated things are solemnly placed. It is used to designate holy places, as the Holy Shrines at Jerusalem and in the Holy Land, to which pilgrimages used to be made. It may also mean a tomb, since the bodies of saints were placed in costly tombs in the churches.

Shrive. To pronounce the absolution over penitents. It was done publicly once a year during the Holy Week, when all penitents who had faithfully fulfilled the required proofs of a thorough repentance were solemnly absolved and restored to Communion. But it also came to mean the private administration of absolution upon confession.

Shrove-Tuesday. Tuesday before Ash-Wednesday. It obtained its name from the confession and absolution given upon that day in preparation for the Lenten fast.

Sick. Visitation of the Sick. *Vide* MINOR OFFICES.

Sign. The Hebrew word *ôth*, signifying sign, is used in Ex. iii. 12, where it means a token of GOD'S power. Gideon asks for a sign from GOD that it is really His angel who talks with him (Judges vi. 17). The flesh and the unleavened cakes brought by Gideon are consumed by fire at the touch of the staff of the angel (v. 21), and thus the sign is given by a miracle, and Gideon accepts the divine commission to enter on his great work for GOD. In the New Testament the scribes and Pharisees ask for a "sign" from CHRIST (St. Matt. xii. 38, St. Mark viii. 12), but He declines to perform wonders for those who cavil against Him. This craving of the Jews appears again in St. John ii. 18, and vi. 30, and 1 Cor. i. 22: "The Jews require a sign." In 1 Cor. xiv. 22, we read, "Tongues are for a sign not to them that believe, but to them that believe not." In St. Mark xvi. 17, our LORD speaks of the miraculous signs which "shall follow them that believe," and the twentieth verse tells of the fulfillment of the prophecy. In the plural number the word is usually combined with wonders, and denotes GOD'S interventions preternaturally warning men of approaching judgment, and also the miracles wrought by means of GOD'S ministers.

In the XXV. and XXVII. Articles the term sign is used in reference to the Holy Sacraments. In the XXV. Article they are called "effectual signs of grace." In the XXVII. Baptism is called "a sign of Regeneration or New Birth." In the Church Catechism the word Sacrament is defined as "an outward and visible sign of an inward and spiritual grace." In this ecclesiastical sense of the word we learn that both outward acts and inward spiritual life are needed to perfect the Christian. The white garment formerly worn at Baptism was an indication of the purity of life which should follow the reception of that Holy Sacrament. Those who receive the Holy Communion should be so united to CHRIST that they may partake of the heavenly banquet, and be ever "with the LORD" (1 Thess. iv. 17).

St. Paul likens the Christians to the branches of a wild olive-tree grafted into a good tree (Rom. xi. 17). So by the Holy Sacraments believers are engrafted into CHRIST. But the grafts must not simply be bound to the tree; they must also "take hold of the stock," and the budding shows that they have received sap from the root, and "are really united to the tree." Here we have both the "outward and visible sign" and the "inward and spiritual grace."

Authorities: Blunt's Dict. of Doct. and Hist. Theology, Illustrations of the Catechism of the Prot. Epis. Church.

REV. S. F. HOTCHKIN.

Simon, St. The surnames Zelotes and the Canaanite (these two titles, the first given by St. Luke and the other by St. Matthew) are all that we have to mark him or to give us the slightest insight into his character. They both point out that he belonged at one time to the faction of Zealots, which was so noted a party in the last sad scenes of Jewish history. It shows how broad our LORD'S human sympathies were, and how He could by His wondrous influence harmonize the most jarring and conflicting elements, could gather into one body the headlong St. Peter, the energetic yet loving St. John, the calm and stately St. James, and the earnest men like St. Andrew and St. Philip, and those with a fanatical past like St. Simon, and send them forth with the one aim, the one enthusiasm, the one energizing conviction that would give them the victory.

Simony. The sin of simony consists in a willing sale and purchase of spiritual gifts, or of those offices and preferments by which spiritual gifts are conferred. Our LORD had laid down the rule, "freely have ye received, freely give." And St. Peter's indignant rebuke to Simon Magus, "Thy money perish with thee, because thou hast thought that the gift of GOD may be purchased with money." Simony can, it is evident, take many shapes and can find excuses for itself. To check it, it was very early enacted that the buyer and seller of the offices of Bishop, Priest, or Deacon should be cut off from the Church. The Councils, both Diocesan, Provincial, and Œcumenical, repeatedly passed canons against it. Much of the confusion which occurred in ecclesiastical affairs during the Middle Ages was incurred by the effort to suppress it. There must be no fee for baptism, or for the spiritual gifts which Our LORD left to be freely given to His people. Thank-offerings were not to be refused, but no fees were to be charged. But all spiritual preferments must be given only on due examination of the fitness of the person, without bribe or thought of future reward. The Papal extortions which began about 1126 A.D. and were continued on for three centuries, afforded the real foundation for the present legal enactment against simony. They sold offices and Benefices to the highest bidder, and claimed and obtained by means of provisions, reservations, and commendams a large income from those who were willing to pay. The Benefices were valued as annuities are. This state of things led to the numerous and complicated laws in England upon simony, and the simple direct rights of patronage became much confused by the claims and counter-claims between the Papal Court and the Parliament.

The sale of livings which now exists, and is hedged in by law, is felt as a great evil, which from its conditions may not be actual simony, but which brings in all the scandal of it. And steps have been taken during the past years both by the Convocations of Canterbury and York to urge the movement made in Parliament for the removal of the evil. Simony in the Church in this country is not known.

Sin. Among the many and various definitions of sin, there can be no safer or more accurate guide than St. Paul's exhaustive treatise in the Epistle to the Romans. From that we learn clearly that sin is the failure to attain to the standard of GOD'S moral requirement, and is independent of any direct revelation of His will, although that standard is fixed by His revealed moral law. The Greek verb *hamartano*, to sin, means to fall short of the mark, as with a javelin badly thrown: "For all have sinned and come short of the glory of GOD" (Rom. iii. 23). "As many as have sinned without law shall also perish without law." (See also verses 14, 15, of the same chapter.) In general it is the willful transgression of either GOD'S laws or the moral sense as witnessed by conscience. The mere consent of the will without any overt act is sufficient to constitute sin, as our LORD distinctly asserts. Indeed, an action not intrinsically wrong may be sinfully performed or purposed, if its propriety be even doubted, since "Whatsoever is not of faith is sin." From the universality of sin, affecting even angelic natures, it would seem to be a necessary result of the freedom of imperfect will. The origin of sin in the world was coeval with the origin of man. It appeared in the first man with the first temptation which came in his way, and with him it was the deliberate transgression of the Divine command. In what the primal innocence of Adam consisted the Scriptures leave us in doubt, whether it was a willing obedience, or a lack of moral responsibility, or a mere ignorance of right and wrong. The two latter conditions are strongly indicated by the exceedingly low state of civilization and development attributed to him (*vide* MAN), and by the coupling of his disobedience with the sudden awakening to a knowledge of good and evil. The immediate result of sin was the passing of man from a state of mere animal idleness and security to one of labor, sorrow, and the fear of death, which the Scriptures declare to be the direct consequence and punishment of sin. But while this declaration is positive we are not to receive it as definite. Physical death was certainly in the world before man, and therefore before sin. It had swept away generations of living forms before man's creation, and the constitution of numberless creatures contemporary with him made it necessary to their life, if not to his own. Nor is it necessary to raise the physiological and other difficulties incident to the theory of a forfeited immortality in the case of man alone. From its very nature sin concerns only that higher life which was superadded to man's animal nature when he "became a living soul," and can only incidentally affect his animal part. It is the death of that higher life which sin brought into the world, and from that death only, not physical death, did the sacrifice of CHRIST redeem the human race. No change whatever has passed on man's mortality because of the tragedy of the Cross, and therefore if physical death were that curse of sin from which man was to be redeemed by the Atonement, then the Atonement has failed of its purpose and itself become in some sense a "missing of the mark,"— *hamartia*, Sin. This argument alone, the *reductio ad absurdum*, is sufficient to prove the irrelevancy of sin to the question of physical death.

The punishment of sin is of two kinds, viz., that which it brings of itself in this world, as ill health, mental anguish, or social disgrace, and that which GOD will inflict for it hereafter, the death of man's GOD-life, by which he shall become fitted only for the eternal companionship of the fallen angels and deserve a share in the terrible fate reserved for them. Sin is necessarily hostile to true happiness, because its nature is essentially evil, and evil is inconsistent with happiness, which is in itself good. "The pleasures of sin," therefore, cannot be true pleasures, and must eventually result in some development of evil. Since sin is itself evil and the perversion of what should be man's moral nature, and since its inevitable final consequence is moral death, it is the great and universal moral disease which infects man's higher life. The Remedy for sin is the Atonement (*q.v.*) made by the Divine SON of GOD assuming the nature infected by sin, living its life without sin in His own person, and bearing its punishment in behalf of the human race. While this sinless life and death of the GOD-Man does not enable any other man to live a life free from actual transgression, it has yet secured GOD'S pardon for every sinning man upon condition of his believing in JESUS CHRIST and becoming mystically united to Him by Baptism (St. Mark xvi. 16). It also secures to man the help of the HOLY GHOST, the Spirit of CHRIST, to strengthen his will in resisting temptation to sin. Although the effect of sin is to alienate man from GOD and destroy his love for Him, it yet does not alienate GOD'S love from man. Indeed, it was because of GOD'S love for sinners that He sent His Only-Begotten Son into the world to redeem man from sin and its penalty (St. John iii. 16). When sin is the performance, or the mere consent of the will to the performance of some evil act, it is known as sin of *Commission*. When it is the simple failure to obey or to perform some duty, it is sin of *Omission*. Some of our LORD'S severest denunciations are against the latter class of sin (St. Matt. xxv. *passim*). The distinction of venial and deadly sin is made by the Roman Church, but is not generally recognized among Christians. The unpardonable sin, or sin against the HOLY GHOST, has occasioned much dispute and is often a source of great mental anxiety, the belief that it has been committed being a frequent feature of insane hallucinations. The belief in the possibility of such a sin arises from our LORD'S declaration that "All manner of sin and blasphemy shall be forgiven unto men: but the blasphemy against the HOLY GHOST shall not be forgiven unto men, . . . either in this world, either in the world to come" (St. Matt. xii. 31, 32), and also from St. John saying, "There is a sin unto death: I do not say that he shall pray for it" (1 John v. 16). It is generally conceded by the ablest interpreters that the sin here mentioned consists in the deliberate and final rejection of GOD'S grace in CHRIST, as by the Jews rejecting the testimony of the HOLY GHOST to CHRIST'S claims as the Divine MESSIAH, or a sinner dying in willful refusal to accept His redemption. The very obscurity of the subject should be a sufficient safeguard against the despairing fear of the commission of such sin, since so terrible a possibility could not be left in doubt without vitiating every assurance of GOD'S love for man, while no man could possibly commit such a sin who believes in CHRIST sufficiently to fear it. REV. R. WILSON, D.D.

Sisterhoods. Sisters of Mercy, Sisters of Charity, Sisters of the Church, or simply Sisters, as they are variously called, have become an accepted fact in the life and work of our Church. Their power for good has been fully recognized, and the Church now only desires to see more of them coming forward and devoting themselves to GOD. Yet for all this many Churchmen and Churchwomen have but a very vague idea of what a Sister is, of what the life is that she is called to live. It is our purpose in this article to give clear and simple instruction upon this.

A Sister is a woman who is consecrated to Almighty GOD in His Church. It is true that this may be said in a degree of all baptized Christians, but the consecration of a Sister is something more than that to which others are called.

There are some to whom the voice of the Master comes now as it came of old, calling "Follow Me," with a special call involving the leaving of all that the world holds dear, houses, land, friends, father, mother, for His sake. James and John heard and obeyed; and some hear it now. GOD makes Himself known to the soul as the "chiefest among ten thousand and altogether lovely." He reveals to the soul what He has done for it, what He will be to it. The soul sees that there is "none to be desired in comparison with Him," it is filled with gratitude and love at the revelation of what He has done for it, it bows itself before Him in loving, adoring self-surrender. "LORD, what wilt Thou have me to do?" "LORD, I will follow Thee whithersoever Thou goest."

This call of GOD is what is technically called *Vocation*, and it is consecration in obedience to this that underlies and is the foundation of the true Sister's life.

When GOD has thus called the soul and the soul has surrendered herself, He makes clear in the way of His providence what His will is for that particular soul. Sometimes it is long before He does this, and the soul must wait in simple obedience and in a dedicated spirit until the way is clear for a change to be made in the outer life.

This change is made when the one who believes she has this vocation becomes a member of a Religious Community, that is, enters a Sisterhood. Probably she is guided in her choice of a Community by her previous knowledge of some Sisters with whom she has been brought in contact, or by the advice of her clergyman, with whom of course she takes counsel, or by hearing or reading of some works in which Sisters have been engaged. If she is wisely guided she will seek some large, well-organized Community, where she will have the benefit of experienced training, and a well-developed and tried Rule of Life. While it is desirable that the number of Sisters in the Church should be largely increased, it is not well that there should be many little Sisterhoods. A few large Communities will do more to keep up a high ideal of life, and fit and train women for the life to which they are thus called, than little independent societies in separate parishes, struggling on feebly with insufficient discipline, and overweighted with a multitude of parish cares.

It has sometimes happened that an earnest clergyman feeling the need of women's work among the people, and seeing certain devout women apparently fitted for the work, has tried to gather them into a little Sisterhood, under his own care, and for the benefit of his own parish. It would have been better if he had guided such women to some existing Community, where they would have had teaching and training such as it was not in his power to give, and from whence they might possibly return, or others might come in their place, as Mission Sisters, or even as a Branch House of the order they had joined.

When a woman desires to join a Community the question of money naturally arises. It may be well to say here that this is not a matter of real importance. In some Communities it is required that a certain sum be brought as dowry by those seeking admission, or if not required it is thought advisable; but this is not a general rule, and very few Communities would reject any one on this ground if she were otherwise well qualified for admission. If any one is already possessed of money, she is not required to give it to the Community. She may do so if she pleases, or she may distribute it among her friends. The Community would refuse to receive it if she had any relatives who needed assistance and whom it was her duty to help. It is only required that she shall not retain any money for her own use.

In most Communities there are two or more orders of Sisters. The first or higher order are called Choir-Sisters, the others variously Lay, Minor, or Second Order Sisters. The first Order is composed of those of superior education and gifts, and in them the management of the Sisterhood rests, the Superior and other officers being elected by themselves from their own number; they also elect the Chaplain.

To the Lay, Minor, or Second Order Sisters a somewhat subordinate position is given. They keep the same spiritual rule as the others, but they do the lesser works of the Community, the duties of the household and such like, and have no share in its government.

On entering a Sisterhood the *Postulant*, as she is called, being in the position of one seeking admission, remains on trial for some six months, keeping the rule of the Order and being under the direction of the Novice-Mistress, an officer elected or appointed because of her fitness for training others. At the end of this time the Postulant is admitted as a Novice, and wears the dress of the Order and bears also the name of Sister. The Novitiate lasts from two to three years, when the Sisters, if they think her fit and worthy to join the Order, elect her into their number. She is then *professed*, that is to say, she publicly before the Sisters and Chaplain, and in many cases the Bishop of the Diocese also, professes her willingness to give up her whole life to GOD, to remain in this Community and keep its rules as long as she lives, and then vows herself to GOD before His altar. During the time she is Postulant or Novice the Sister may return at any time to her former life in the world, but once professed it is a pledge for life. Before profession also, the Community may dismiss her if they think her wanting in the true spirit of consecration, or in other needful gifts; but after profession she cannot be sent away unless for some grave moral fault, which may GOD forbid.

We have referred to the Rule, or Rule of Life. This varies in different Sisterhoods, but in all it is based upon the three great principles of *Poverty*, *Chastity*, and *Obedience*. Poverty separates the soul from the world; Chastity lifts it up to GOD; Obedience binds it in the Life of the Community and in self-discipline and control under the will of GOD. Something must be said of each separately.

Poverty.—The soul that has heard the call of which we have spoken desires to give up all for Him who has called her. She will not any longer have anything to call her own, and what she has while she continues to live in this world she will use for Him and for His glory. For this reason she gives up everything when she is finally professed. The Sister has nothing, her very clothes belong to the Community, she wears what is given her without question or murmur. All that she needs she must ask for, she may not help herself. Of all that is intrusted to her for use she must give careful account. Of everything she is most sparing as one who is really poor. So the food of the Community, while it is wholesome, is only such as the poor eat, and taken for necessity, not for pleasure. Many things accounted necessary in the world Sisters readily learn to do without. They may not receive any presents for themselves, nor may they receive payment for work done. All that any may wish to give them can only be received for the Community to be shared for the common good. They are called to be poor, and by all possible ways they try in their life to realize this.

Chastity.—The Sister comes to the Community because she has felt the constraining power of the Love of CHRIST. That love takes possession of her soul, and all other loves become subordinate to it. The motive, the inspiration, the power of the life is all in this, "My Beloved is mine, and I am His." Hence the true Sister is willing to leave all other friends and ties and to have and love only as GOD wills her to love. GOD first, and all others for His sake; and this all through her life. The Sisters' life is not for those who have used up all pleasures in the world and found them worthless, or who have been disappointed and perhaps embittered by the treatment they have received in the world; such rarely make good Sisters. The life of a Sister is the life of one who, looking upon the face of JESUS CHRIST, can say, "I have found Him whom my soul loveth," and saying that, can give up all else for Him, and having Him desires nothing else. "CHRIST is all."

Obedience.—The Sister comes to the Sisterhood not only to give up her worldly possessions, moved by the love of GOD, but to do that which is so much harder, to submit her will to the will of GOD. For this she takes the vow of obedience to the Rule of the Community and to all those who shall be set over her. Of course this vow in no way conflicts with conscience and her obedience to the revealed will of GOD. It only affects her life in all those matters in which she is free to choose. She by this vow surrenders her liberty of choice, accepting in its place the voice of the Superior speaking in the name and on behalf of the Community. It would, of course, be impossible to conduct a Sisterhood without such a rule and vow; if all were free to choose their own work and way, there might early be discord and difficulty where all ought to work easily in order and harmony. This, however, is not the chief end of the Vow of Obedience. The chief end is that the highest powers and faculties of the soul may be brought under control and be disciplined, that the soul may learn to lay itself aside, that the will of GOD may be felt in all the details of every-day life.

All the rules and regulations of the Sisterhood are based upon these three great principles, expanding them and applying them variously, according to the genius of each Sisterhood and the works undertaken by its members.

A life under such discipline of course separates those who live it very much from others. It brings a gravity and seriousness into the life, a quietness of deportment, and perhaps a certain sadness. It can hardly be but that those who are drawn near to the Master in close and enduring bonds of love should be drawn to Him in a penitential spirit, sharing in His sorrow over a world lying in sin. The quiet dark habit of the Sisters befittingly sets forth this aspect of their life.

The life comes first, but we must speak also of the work. Of course Sisters will work, and work hard. They are called to be poor, but not to be idle. Church-people are asked to contribute to the maintenance of Sisterhoods and the works of the Sisters, not that the Sisters may do nothing, but that they may have a place in which to live and means to do their work well. Indeed, Sisters work very hard, harder than many who work for the wages of this world, while they only work for the love of GOD.

Their works are of many kinds. They teach the children of the rich and the children of the poor. They take charge of hospitals, orphanages, penitentiaries, and asylums of various kinds. They nurse and visit the sick and poor in their own homes, and carry out missionary works for the good of the Church. In many cases they do embroidery and other needle-work for the sanctuary, by the sale of which they often almost entirely support themselves. Besides these more distinct works, they exert an influence which can hardly be defined or measured. Many a hard and worldly heart has been brought to GOD by the gentle influence of their devoted lives; many a sorrowful, broken-hearted sinner has been cheered and strengthened by the love that came forth from those who in close communion with their LORD had learnt the secret of the love that caused Him to lay down His life for the world.

What is the power that is to hold women up in such a life? The power of GOD alone can do it, and this is only to be obtained by prayer. The Rule of every Community, therefore, implies many hours daily given to prayer and devotion. Seven times a day at least the Sisters come together in their chapel to pray. If possible, the Holy Communion is celebrated daily in their midst. Besides this, every one has her own hours set apart for private prayer and meditation. Without this the Community would soon sink down into a mere society of persons living together for the sake of the work they can do, instead of being a company gathered together in the Church to live in loving devotion to Almighty GOD, irrespective of the work which each member might be able to do. In Prayer and Meditation and the use of all the means of grace the Sisters strive to live near to their LORD, and to drink in of His Spirit, that their own souls being first purified from sin, they may be instruments of His glory, and accomplish the work to which He sends them in the world.

A life of consecration, a life of poverty, a life of earnest self-denial and self-surrender, a life of devoted work,—such is the life of the Sisters of our Church, but more than all, a life of Prayer and of continual communion with Him who said, "If a man love me, he will keep my words, and my FATHER will love him, and we will come unto him, and make our abode with him."

REV. EDWARD OSBORNE.

Solifidians. Those who rest on faith alone for salvation, without any reference to works or to repentance. This pernicious heresy was at one time rampant in England, so much so as to make quite a party. The doctrine, in its evil consequences, is not current, but the extravagant and unguarded language of some popular preaching would lead one to suppose that it is still held.

Son. The doctrine of the Divinity of our LORD is that He is the Eternal SON of GOD; that this Sonship was His whom we confess to be JESUS CHRIST; that it was foretold, and His birth, work, and redemptive acts were in perfect accordance with the prophecy, and that Eternal Word, in whom entered the glory of the FATHER, the Man CHRIST JESUS, is also the Mediator now at the right hand of the FATHER. The Scriptures are full, express, and clear upon this. The confession of it entered into the worship of the Jew, for he sang before GOD the inspired words of the FATHER to the SON, "Thou art my SON; to-day have I begotten Thee. Ask of me, and I shall give Thee the heathen for thine inheritance, and the uttermost parts of the Earth for Thy possession" (Ps. ii. 7, 8).

Again, "Give the King Thy judgments, O GOD, and Thy righteousness unto the King's SON (Ps. lxxii. 1), where the Psalm gives an outline of the offices that can only belong to the SON of GOD. So in the forty-fifth Psalm. These are dwelt on because they were in the public services, and formed part of the National worship and the National Confession of Faith. Nor are these the only places in the Psalms, for there are Ps. lxxxix. 27, and cx., where His Sonship is set forth clearly, and not by inference. The prophecy of Isaiah, "For unto us a child is born, unto us a SON is given," and, "Behold, a Virgin shall conceive and bear a SON, and shall call His name Immanuel" (Is. ix. 6, and vii. 14), can only describe Him whom Nebuchadnezzar saw walking in the midst of the fiery furnace,—"and the form of the fourth is like the SON of GOD" (Dan. iii. 25). Here no attempt is made to show how much more fully the prophecy of the SON of GOD pervades all of Hebrew predictive writings, and there is omitted perhaps the most pointed of all the promises to David, that recorded in 2 Sam. vii., since it would involve a longer discussion than is possible here. Then the prophecy was continuous and accepted, in the History of David's family, in the Worship in the Temple, in the Prophets, that the SON of GOD should come on earth and be born, and take upon Him our flesh. It was fit, then, that the Gospels should begin with this. St. Matthew begins with the descent of JESUS CHRIST, the son of David, the son of Abraham, who is Immanuel,— GOD with us. St. Mark writes, "The beginning of the Gospel of JESUS CHRIST, the SON of GOD." St. Luke records the Annunciation to the Virgin, "He shall be called the SON of the Highest: and the LORD GOD shall give unto him the throne of His father David: and He shall reign over the house of Jacob forever; and of His kingdom there shall be no end." And St. John, "In the beginning was the WORD, and the Word was with GOD, and the Word was GOD. The same was in the beginning with GOD. . . . And we beheld His glory as of the Only-begotten of the Father."

Passing over all other references, we will quote our LORD'S own claim. He had said, "I and My FATHER are one." Nor did He retract when the Jews took up stones to stone Him as a blasphemer, but added, "Say ye of Him whom the FATHER hath sanctified and sent into the world, Thou blasphemest, because I said I am the SON of GOD?" Not only did He claim it, but Satan based one of his temptations upon its being true; and after His victory the demons, whom He dispossessed of men, cried out, "JESUS, Thou SON of GOD." And it was distinctly upon this charge that He was arrested and tried, and when solemnly adjured by the High-Priest, "I adjure Thee by the living GOD that Thou tell us if Thou be the CHRIST, the SON of GOD? JESUS saith unto him, Thou hast said." So, in other terms, do the other Evangelists. And when He was brought before Pilate, and the governor tried to release Him, the Jews charged that He was worthy of death, because He made Himself the SON of GOD. And Pilate was the more afraid, and sought the more eagerly to let Him go; and at last, at the sight of the terrors of that Crucifixion, the Centurion of the Guard was compelled to confess, "Truly this man was the SON of GOD." Our LORD'S claim was repeated by all that came about Him. His Apostles confessed it, His enemies hated Him for it, His judge and His executioners felt its truth; and when He rose from the dead, that held as doctrine was now proven historic fact, for the SON of Man risen with power from the dead could only be the Eternal SON of GOD. It was upon the truth of this Sonship that the Apostles went forth to evangelize the world, and to baptize in His name, and to establish His Church. It was this doctrine that gave them their power. St. Peter, who had the grace given him to be the first to confess it, reminded those to whom he wrote (2 Pet. i. 7), how on the Mount of Transfiguration he heard the "voice from the excellent glory," "This is my beloved SON, in whom I am well pleased." St. John (1 John v. 12), "He that hath the SON hath life, and he that hath not the SON of GOD hath not life." So St. Paul, in innumerable passages, one for its devoted love: "And the life I now live in the flesh, I live by the faith of the SON of GOD, who loved me and gave Himself for me." Therefore the Creed puts into our mouth and teaches our hearts to believe this fact, which is eternal, and which by the Manhood of the Word comes into our lives and begetteth it, "And I believe in JESUS CHRIST His Only SON our LORD." This faith reaches from the Throne of GOD to the depth of our sinfulness,—for "there is joy in the presence of the Angels of GOD" (i.e., on the Throne of GOD) "when one sinner repenteth;" and repentance must be upon the ground of faith that JESUS is the SON of GOD, and is able to save them to the uttermost that come unto GOD by Him, seeing that He ever liveth to make intercession for them.

Son of Man. The related doctrine and fact to the confession of the SON of GOD is the further confession that He became for us the SON of Man. The prophecy that went before of the SON of GOD in some cases, as in those from Isaiah, spoke of that SON of GOD as born a man; the Virgin's SON is a man, but also Immanuel. The man to be born of David's line (2 Sam. xxvi.) was the MESSIAH. So far David knew, and the Psalm he wrote upon this (Ps. lxxxix.) shows that he knew Him also to be the SON of GOD. Isaiah's prophecy of the suffering MESSIAH is too large, too heroic a figure for any mere mortal man. He who could fill out its proportions and bear its awful burdens must be the SON of Man, who is also the SON of GOD. But the prophecy implies this, and can only be understood when it is acknowledged in its fullness. The term Son of Man occurs frequently in the Old Testament, and most often as applied to Ezekiel as the type of CHRIST. The royalty of the SON of Man is set forth in the eighth Psalm. The Judicial office of the SON of Man is set forth in Dan. vii. 13, 14. It was the special name which our LORD gave Himself. The Evangelists do not give it to Him as from others, but it is His name for Himself. It was to identify Himself with the prophecy and to claim His place in the Human race that He did this, we may reverently suppose. On two crucial occasions He uses this title, when He asks His Apostles, "Whom do men say that I, the SON of Man, am?" and St. Peter makes the confession for Him and the rest, "Thou art the MESSIAH, the SON of the living GOD." Again, when the High-Priest adjured Him to confess if He claimed to be the SON of GOD, He replied, "I am, and ye shall see the SON of Man sitting on the right Hand of power, and coming in the clouds of heaven." It was the declaration of His twofold nature, the announcement of Himself as the GOD-Man. It is not necessary here to quote all the texts which set Him forth as the SON of Man in the Gospels. But in this character it was that He lived the wonderful life of His sojourn here.

It was as SON of Man that He humbled Himself, it is as SON of Man that He is exalted; it was as SON of Man, born of a woman, that He was made under the law (Gal. iv. 4), and as SON of Man He was LORD of the Sabbath-day (St. Matt. xii. 8); as SON of Man He suffered for sin (St. Matt. xvii. 12; St. Mark viii. 31), and as SON of Man He has authority on earth to forgive sins (St. Matt. ix. 6). It was as SON of Man that He had not where to lay his head (St. Matt. viii. 20; St. Luke ix. 58), it is as SON of Man that He wears on His head a golden crown (Rev. xiv. 14); it was as SON of Man that He was betrayed into the hands of sinful men, and suffered many things, and was rejected, and condemned, and crucified (see St. Matt. xvii. 22; xx. 18; xxvi. 2, 24; St. Mark viii. 31; ix. 31; x. 33; St. Luke ix. 22, 44; xviii. 31; xxiv. 7), it is as SON of Man that He now sits at the right hand of GOD, and as SON of Man He will come in the clouds of heaven, with power and great glory, in His own glory, and in the glory of His FATHER, and all His holy angels with Him, and it is as SON of Man that will "sit on the throne of His glory" and "before Him will be gathered all nations" (St. Matt. xvi. 27; xxiv. 30; xxv. 31, 32; St. Mark xiv. 62; St. Luke xxi. 27); and He will send forth His angels to gather His elect from the four winds (St. Matt. xxiv. 31), and to root up the tares from out of His field, which is the world (St. Matt. xiii. 38, 41), and to bind them in bundles to burn them, and to gather His wheat into His barn (St. Matt. xiii. 30). It is as SON of Man that He will call all from their graves, and summon them to His judgment-seat, and pronounce their sentence for everlasting bliss or woe; "for *the Father* judgeth no man, but hath committed unto *the Son;* . . . and hath given Him authority to execute judgment also, *because* He is the *Son of Man*" (St. John v. 22, 27). Only "the pure in heart will *see God*" (St. Matt. v. 8; Heb. xii. 14); but the evil as well as the good will see their judge: "*Every eye* shall see Him" (Rev. i. 7). This is fit and equitable; and it is also fit and equitable that He, who as SON of Man was judged by the world, should also judge the world; and that He who was rejected openly, and suffered death for all, should be openly glorified by all, and be exalted in the eyes of all, as King of kings, and LORD of lords. (Smith's Dict. of the Bible.) This is the truth which is so tersely expressed in the Creed. The facts of His life and His death set forth His true manhood, and in that very and true manhood was bound as under a veil, and yet in closest union, the eternal SON of GOD. To confess this with a loving heart, and to live the life such a faith implies, is the true life of the Christian. For it is a strange fact that we cannot speak of or dwell upon the life of JESUS CHRIST without feeling that He has a power over us that compels a love and an obedience or repels the unhappy rejecter. His words are true of every man that hears His words: "He that is not with me is against me, and He that gathereth not with me scattereth." It is an attraction unto life or a repulsion unto death that the SON of Man is wielding over the whole world.

Song of Solomon. This lovely poem by King Solomon, possibly upon his marriage, is a mystical description of CHRIST and His Church (Rev. xxi. 2, 9). It was preceded in date by Ps. xlv. The type is frequent (Isa. liv. 5, 6; lxii. 5; Jer. ii. 2, etc.). The title (vs. 1) is probably not by Solomon. In structure the Song is idyllic; in form, dramatic. It has been divided into VII. sections, to correspond with the seven days of the nuptial feast, but it readily divides into these V. sections. The Persons are the Bride, the Bridegroom and a Chorus of the daughters of Jerusalem. I. The Bride and her Lord and the Chorus, ch. i.–ii. 17. II. Bride addresses Chorus, ch. iii. III. The Bridegroom to the Bride, ch. iv.–v. 1. IV. Bride to the Chorus, ch. v. 2–vi. 3. V. Bridegroom to the Bride, vi. 2–viii. 14. Its strangeness to us is (*a*) because we do not understand the Oriental allusions; (*b*) because the translation does not transfuse the delicacy of thought also. It should be read with the heads ov the chapters. The Fathers were fond of commenting on this book.

Soul. (*Vide* SPIRIT.) The Greek word used in the New Testament for soul originally means breath. It is the vital spirit or life: "This night thy soul shall be required of thee" (St. Luke xiv. 20). The corresponding Hebrew word occurs in Gen. xxxv. 18, Rachel's "soul was in departing." Our SAVIOUR widens the word to include the world beyond the grave in St. John xii. 25: "He that hateth his life in this world shall keep it unto life eternal." In this expression the word "life" or "soul" in the Greek is natural life, while the word "it" gives us a reference to the same word as meaning immortal life. In St. Matt. xvi. 25, 26, JESUS said that he who would save his natural life should lose it, but he who would lose it for His sake should find it, and then asks the weighty question, "For what is a man profited, if he shall gain the whole world, and lose his own soul? or what shall a man give in exchange for his soul?" He adds a warning concerning the judgment-day. In a parallel passage (St. Luke ix. 25) the expression is "lose himself, or be cast away." The soul, then, is the real self.

The word soul sometimes means a departed spirit: "The souls of them that were slain for the word of GOD" (Rev. vi. 9). "The souls of them that were beheaded for the witness of JESUS" (xx. 4). The term soul is used also to designate the seat of the senses and desires, the animal nature. "Spirit, soul, and body," in 1 Thess. v. 23, includes the whole man. Again it refers to the mind, as (2 Pet. ii. 14) "unstable souls." "Heartily" (Col. iii. 23) is in Greek "from the soul." Unanimity (Acts iv. 32) is shown by the phrase "of one soul." The soul of man may include "his spiritual and immortal nature, with all its higher and lower powers, its rational and animal faculties." "Fear not them which kill the body, but are not able to kill the soul; but rather fear Him which is able to destroy both soul and body in hell" (St. Matt. x. 28). "That believe to the saving of the soul" (Heb. x. 39). "They watch for your souls" (xiii. 17). "The engrafted word which is able to save your souls" (James i. 21). "The end of your faith, even the salvation of your souls" (1 Pet. i. 9). "Abstain from fleshly lusts, which war against the soul" (ch. ii. 11). "Shepherd and Bishop of your souls" (v. 25). "Let them that suffer according to the will of GOD commit the keeping of their souls to Him in well-doing, as unto a faithful Creator" (ch. iv. 19).

The word soul is used for a living thing: "The first man Adam was made a living soul" (1 Cor. xv. 45). This is an allusion to Gen. ii. 7. (See Rev. xvi. 3; Gen. i. 24, and ii. 19, and ix. 10, 12, 15.) It is used for man: "Fear came upon every soul" (Acts ii. 43. See iii. 23). "Let every soul be subject unto the higher powers" (Rom. xiii. 1). "Every soul of man" for every man (Rom. ii. 9. See Acts ii. 41, and vii. 14, and xxvii. 37; 1 Pet. iii. 20; Gen. xlvi. 15).

Reasoning is not performed by the body, love is not a bodily act. The soul is affected by moral culture, as the body by exercise. It is injured by sin, and restored by repentance and faith in CHRIST. It progresses in this life, and is thus prepared for a higher future life. While it is perhaps impossible to define fully what the soul is, every reflecting mind may be aware that in man's constitution there is something higher than mere matter, and that a spiritual part dwells within the body and works through it. As it is destined to live through endless ages hereafter, how carefully should it be trained in devotion and obedience to GOD here! This care of the soul concerns all men, and is the one thing needful. It is of the highest importance, involving peace here and blessedness hereafter (St. Luke x. 42; Jer. vi. 16; Heb. xii. 14). If one had a valuable jewel which he wished to bequeath to a friend he would keep it fair and clean, so should he endeavor to present his soul at last before GOD washed by the tears of repentance. Our LORD declares that none can kill the soul; it must live forever (St. Luke xii. 4). It is to endure as long as GOD Himself, for ever and ever. The souls of the righteous enter into joy. Lazarus is in Abraham's bosom. The wicked, as Dives, lie down in sorrow (St. Luke xvi. 22). The penitent thief enters Paradise (ch. xxiii. 43). Those who die in the LORD are blessed (Rev. xiv. 13). The soul of man can find true happiness only in GOD. As the image of the sun in a lake displays its character and beauty, so even on earth a holy man reflects the character of GOD, in whose image he is made, and if he is a partaker "of CHRIST's sufferings" (1 Pet. iv. 13), he may become a partaker "of the divine nature" (2 Pet. i. 4).

The faculties of the soul are not fully developed here. The world cannot satisfy it, and if a man sells his soul for a world it is a fearful loss, because that which is outside of him cannot satisfy his spiritual needs. The dissatisfied soul of man cries after GOD. In weakness it needs a higher Being to trust, and love, and lean upon. This thirst for GOD must have its gratification from that GOD who places on earth the running stream to satisfy the bodily thirst. He cannot give bodily aid and deny spiritual help. The higher men rise in life, often the greater dissatisfaction is experienced. The immortal soul dwells in a body which in Holy Scripture is called a garment or a tabernacle, or house. 2 Pet. i. 13, "As long as I am in this tabernacle." This shows the soul to be distinct from the body.

Authorities: Buck's Theolog. Dict., Wordsworth's Com. on Gr. Test., Robinson's Gr. and Eng. Lex. of the N. Test., A. Clarke's Com. on 2 Pet. i. 13, 15, T. Gataker, in Spencer's Things New and Old, Whewell's Elements of Morality, Hodge's Systematic Theology, Bloomfield's Com. on Gr. Test., 1 Thess. v. 23, Krauth's Fleming's Vocab. of Philosophy. REV. S. F. HOTCHKIN.

South Carolina, Church in. The first attempt to settle the Province of Carolina was in 1660 A.D. The first effectual attempt in 1670 A.D. In 1672 A.D. the present site of Charleston was laid out, and about 1681 or 1682 A.D. the first Episcopal church in Carolina was built in that city. It was built of black cypress, upon a brick foundation, on the site now occupied by St. Michael's Church. It was called St. Philip's Church.

The first clergyman in South Carolina was the Rev. Atkin Williamson. He was there in 1680 A.D. In 1698 A.D. an Act of Assembly was passed "to settle a maintenance on a Minister of the Church of England in Charles Town." It appropriated a salary of £150 per annum to him and his successors forever, and directed that a negro man and woman and four cows and calves be purchased for his use, and paid for out of the public treasury.

In 1698 A.D., Mrs. Affra Coming donated seventeen acres of land, now in the city, and the glebe of St. Philip's Church.

In 1700 A.D. the population of the Province was estimated at 5300, besides Indians and Negroes. But one clergyman of the Church of England was settled out of Charles Town. The Rev. William Corbin officiated among the settlements on Goose Creek.

The Society for the Propagation of the Gospel in Foreign Parts, incorporated in 1701 A.D., appointed their first Missionary to South Carolina, Rev. Samuel Thomas, in 1702 A.D. He was instructed to attempt the conversion of the Yemassee Indians, but the Governor interposed, and his cure was on Cooper River.

In 1704 A.D. an Act of Assembly was passed prescribing oaths, and requiring con formity to the Church of England. It was opposed alike by Churchmen and Dissenters. The Rector of St. Philip's, Rev. Edward Marston, was involved in difficulty by reason of his strong opposition to the Act, and was removed from office by a Lay Commission appointed by the Act itself. The Society for the Propagation of the Gospel determined to send no more Missionaries to Carolina until the section relating to Lay Commissioners should be repealed.

Nine clergymen had been in the Province prior to 1706 A.D., four remaining at that date.

The Church of England was established by law, by Act of Assembly (Nov. 30, 1706 A.D.), known as the Church Act. It established six Parishes outside of Charles Town, in Berkeley County, provided for building six churches and six rectories, and appointed Commissioners to execute these provisions. The Parishes are Christ Church, St. Thomas, St. John, St. James, St. Andrew, and St. Dennis, in a French settlement. It also divided Colleton County into two Parishes—St. Paul's and St. Bartholomew's—and erected the Parish of St. James on Santee. The Act sets forth that "the rector of the Parish, duly appointed, is the body corporate," and provides that the Rector or Minister shall be one of the Vestry. It also affixed penalties upon both the Minister and the parties who should "presume to marry" contrary to the Table of Marriages.

In 1707 A.D. the Rev. Gideon Johnson was appointed Commissary of the Bishop of London in South Carolina, and was elected Rector of St. Philip's Church. In 1711 A.D. the Society for the Propagation of the Gospel established a school in Charles Town, under the charge of Rev. Wm. Guy. There is no Parochial Register of St. Philip's Church before 1719 A.D., nor any Journals of the Vestry before 1732 A.D. On Easter-Monday of that year two Church-Wardens and seven Vestrymen were elected.

In 1711 A.D. an Act of Assembly was passed for building St. Philip's Church of brick on its present site, and another in 1720 A.D. for its completion. It was opened for worship on Easter-Day, 1723 A.D., and finished in 1724 A.D. In 1724 A.D. a letter from the clergy to the Bishop of London represents the Church in the Province as in "a very flourishing and prosperous condition."

In 1726 A.D., Rev. Alexander Garden, Rector of St. Philip's Church, was his Commissary for North and South Carolina and the Bahama Islands. Commissary Johnson died in 1816 A.D. Individual efforts had been made for the conversion of the Negroes, and many had been baptized; but about this time the Clergy addressed a Joint Letter to "the Society" in England on the subject; and Dr. Gibson, Bishop of London, published a Pastoral Letter "to the Masters and Mistresses of families in the Plantations," and another "to the Missionaries," urging it upon them. About the year 1730 A.D. the Society for the Propagation of the Gospel in Foreign Parts had twelve Missionaries in South Carolina.

The Commissary convened the Clergy for the first time (Oct. 20, 1731 A.D.), when they exhibited their Letters of Orders and License. The celebrated George Whitefield first came to Charles Town in 1738 A.D. In 1740 A.D. he was cited to answer before the Commissary "certain articles" touching irregularities and breach of pledges made at Ordination. Mr. Whitefield excepted to the authority of the Court, and appealed. After the expiration of a year and a day proceedings were resumed, and Mr. Whitefield failing to appear or to answer after successive adjournments for that purpose, he was declared suspended from his office.

In 1742, Commissary Garden procured a school-house, to be built by private subscription, for instructing the negroes, and purchased, "at the expense of the Propagation Society, two intelligent negro boys, with the intention of having them prepared in this school for the tuition of others." "These youths received the baptismal names of Harry and Andrew. They continued in the school at Charles Town, and there are colored persons now (1819) living here who were taught by them to read." (Dalcho, p. 149.) In 1744 A.D. upwards of 60 children were instructed in this school daily, of whom "18 read in the Testament well, 20 in the Psalter, and the rest were in the spelling-book."

In 1749 A.D. the Commissary resigned his office, after twenty-three years' service, having held eighteen visitations. Henceforward the Clergy held annual meetings, one object of them being to supply with services the vacant parishes.

Up to the year 1750 A.D. there had been fifty-nine Clergymen in the Province, the average number during the later years being ten or twelve. Seven Parishes had been added to the original ten, and eight others were added between this date and the American Revolution.

In 1751 A.D. the General Assembly provided for the erection of another Parish in Charles Town,—St. Michael's; the church to be built "on or near the place where . . . St. Philip's formerly stood." The church was opened for Divine worship February 1, 1761 A.D. The bells and clock were imported in 1764 A.D. In 1757 A.D. the Rector of St. Philip's reported the Negro School flourishing and full of children, and from its success lamented the want of establishments for the Christian instruction of 50,000 Negroes.

In 1758 A.D. Chief-Justice Pinckney, who died that year, founded *The Pinckneyan Lecture*, charging his estate with the payment of "five guineas yearly and forever to a lecturer appointed . . . to preach two sermons a year on the greatness and goodness of GOD." The fulfilment of his purpose was delayed until the "breaking out of the war; but his son, General Charles Cotesworth Pinckney, established the Lectures in 1810 A.D., and they were regularly delivered until interrupted by the breaking out of another war, in 1861 A.D."

In 1759 A.D., Rev. Robert Smith, afterwards first Bishop of South Carolina, succeeded to the Rectorship of St. Philip's Church. He had come over from England as its Assistant Minister in 1757 A.D. In 1762 A.D. "The Society for the Relief of the Widows and Children of the Clergy" was founded by the Clergy, but made slow progress until 1771 A.D., when Laymen applied to be admitted. In 1818 A.D. its funds amounted to $45,461.11, and continued to increase until 1860 A.D. In 1766 A.D. the Society for the Propagation of the Gospel discontinued their appropriations, having aided the Church in South Carolina during sixty-four years.

The last "Annual Meeting" of the Clergy on record before the Revolution was in 1770 A.D. Nine clergymen were present and six absent. The largest number in any previous year was twenty.

One hundred and twenty-eight clergymen, in all, had been in the Province since its settlement, but the sojourn of many was very brief,—of the larger number, only two or three years.

In 1774 A.D. the Assistant Minister of St. Michael's gave offense to many of his congregation by a sermon bearing upon political questions, and was compelled to leave the Parish. Five of the Clergy out of twenty adhered to Great Britain and left the country. The late Bishop Smith was banished by the British to Philadelphia. Rev. H. Purcell was Chaplain in the Army and Deputy Judge-Advocate-General. Of the twenty-five Parishes existing prior to the Revolution, twenty are still in union with the Convention, the other five are virtually extinct.

In consequence of proposals for a General Convention, at a meeting held on the 12th of July, 1785 A.D., at which eight Churches were represented, five Deputies thereto were chosen; one of them being a Clergyman.

In 1786 A.D. a committee was appointed to form a constitution for the "Associated Churches," and six "Fundamental Articles" were adopted. In 1790 A.D. the Constitution and Canons adopted by the General Convention, and also "The Liturgy," were unanimously agreed to. Also, a Standing Committee was provided. In 1795 A.D. the Rev. Robert Smith, D.D., long time Rector of St. Philip's Church, Charleston, was unanimously elected Bishop. He was consecrated in Christ Church, Philadelphia, on the 13th of September of the same year, and died October 21, 1801 A.D. To the Convention which elected Bishop Smith testimonials were presented in behalf of Mr. Milward Pogson, the first candidate for Holy Orders in the Diocese on record.

No Diocesan Convention met from 1798 to 1801 A.D. That year one assembled, and the Rev. Edward Jenkins, D.D., was unanimously elected Bishop. Dr. Jenkins declined the office because of advanced age and inability. In 1806 A.D. "Rules and Regulations for the government of the Churches" were, for the first time, adopted. In 1810 A.D. the first Parochial Reports were made to the Convention. The same year was incorporated "The Protestant Episcopal Society for the Advancement of Christianity in South Carolina," which for many years was the missionary agent of the Church in the Diocese.

In 1812 A.D. the Rev. Theodore Dehon was elected the second Bishop, and was consecrated on the 15th of October. During his brief Episcopate an impulse was given to the Church in South Carolina. In 1813 A.D. he delivered the first Episcopal Address, and reported the first church consecrated in the Diocese; also the first new congregations organized. The next year he reported the first Confirmations; the aggregate number being 516. He departed this life August 6, 1817 A.D., universally lamented.

The following year the Rev. Nathaniel Bowen, D.D., was unanimously elected Bishop, and consecrated on the 8th of October. His judicious, conservative administration extended over a period of twenty-one years, until 1839 A.D., when he died on the 25th of August.

The Rev. Christopher Edwards Gadsden, D.D., was elected Bishop on the 14th of February, 1840 A.D., and consecrated on the 21st of June of that year. He zealously and earnestly discharged the duties of the office until 1852 A.D., when he entered into rest on the 23d of June.

Rev. Thomas Frederick Davis was elected Bishop at the ensuing Convention, on the 6th of May, 1853 A.D. He was consecrated October 17. About the year 1860 A.D. Bishop Davis was stricken with blindness, but continued to discharge the duties of his office with wonderful energy. The effects of civil war produced a great change in the condition of the Diocese during his administration. Some of the results are given by committees appointed to ascertain them, thus:

Ten churches burnt; three have disappeared; twenty-two Parishes suspended; eleven parsonages burnt; the Society for Relief of the Widows and Orphans of the Clergy lost $100,000; the Society for Advancement of Christianity in South Carolina lost $56,000; the Bishop's Fund lost $18,000.

Amid all these depressing conditions the blind Bishop labored on until 1871 A.D., when he was constrained to ask for help, and in response thereto the Rev. W. B. W. Howe was elected Assistant Bishop on the 14th of May of that year. Bishop Howe was consecrated in Baltimore on the 8th of October, and on the decease of Bishop Davis in

December of the same year became the Diocesan.

Total Parishes in South Carolina up to 1790 A.D.... 25
(Statistics not to be procured.)

1810 A.D. Clergy entitled to seats in Convention...		11
Parishes		25
Communicants, white..................	439	
Communicants, colored	199	
		638
1821 A.D. Clergy entitled to seats		23
Parishes...		28
Communicants, white..................	996	
Communicants, colored.................	394	
		1390
1830 A.D. Clergy		34
Parishes...		30
Organized Congregations.........................		3
Communicants, white..................	1490	
Communicants, colored................	521	
		2011
1840 A.D. Clergy		46
Parishes and Congregations...................		37
Communicants, white.........	1963	
Communicants, colored.................	973	
		2936
1850 A.D. Clergy		71
Parishes, 50 ; Congregations, 3..............		53
Communicants, white..................	2669	
Communicants, colored.................	2247	
		4916
1860 A.D. Clergy		69
Parishes, 67 ; Congregations, 3..............		70
Communicants, white..................	3166	
Communicants, colored.................	2960	
		6126
Offerings, etc.................................	$50,209.69	
1870 A.D. Clergy		53
Parishes and Congregations...................		60
Communicants, white..................	2633	
Communicants, colored	328	
		2961
Offerings, etc.................................	$46,119.23	
1880 A.D. Clergy		47
Parishes and Congregations...................		59
Communicants, white..................	3932	
Communicants, colored.................	619	
		4551
Offerings, etc.................................	$66,239.84	
1883 A.D. Clergy		49
Parishes and Congregations...................		59
Missions..		18
Communicants, white..................	4306	
Communicants, colored	701	
		5007
Offerings, etc.................................	$81,882.68	

Statistics for 1886 A.D.: Clergy, 48; parishes, 53; missions, 23; candidates for H. O., 5; ordination, D. 2, P. 1; baptisms, 518; con., 424; com., 5142; contr., $80,839.30.

REV. J. D. McCULLOUGH.

South Dakota. (*Vide* NIOBRARA and NORTH DAKOTA.) In the General Convention of 1883 A.D., Bishop Clarkson, retaining the Diocese of Nebraska, resigned his position as Missionary Bishop of Dakota, and the Territory was divided into two jurisdictions, North and South Dakota. South Dakota was put in charge of Rt. Rev. W. H. Hare, D.D., who had been Missionary Bishop of Niobrara. His field includes the part of the Territory south of the forty-sixth parallel, with the Santee Indian Reservation in Nebraska. Bishop Hare estimates the white population at 200,000, and thinks their interests linked with those of the Indians. The immigration for sixty or eighty days last spring was at the rate of 3000 to 6000 each day. Over 100 new post-offices were opened in the past year, more than were opened during the same period in all the other Territories together.

The new-comers are largely Americans, and favorable to the Church. Towns grow as if by magic. Churches are needed, and an itinerating clergy. The towns demanding occupation are numerous, and the need for work is urgent, and the Bishop calls earnestly on the Church to hold up his hands in this interesting and wonderfully promising field. (See his statements in the *Spirit of Missions*, January and February, 1884 A.D.) Institutions: St. Paul's School, Yankton Agency, D. T., a Normal and Divinity School for Indians; St. Mary's School, Santee Agency, Neb., a boarding-school for Indian girls; Hope School, Springfield, D. T., a boarding-school for Indian boys and girls; St. John's School, Cheyenne Agency, D. T., a boarding-school for girls. REV. S. F. HOTCHKIN.

Southern Ohio. The question of dividing the Diocese of Ohio was agitated many years before that measure went into effect. In fact, the subject was brought before the Convention as early as 1850 A.D. The State embraces an area of nearly forty thousand square miles. Its average length north and south is two hundred and twenty miles; its average breadth is nearly the same. Parishes lay upon the extremes, as well as in interior and central parts. To visit them required an amount of travel and fatigue quite beyond the strength of any one man. But the measure proposed was not at that time deemed expedient. Soon thereafter, however, it became evident that the health and strength of Bishop McIlvaine, the then incumbent, was fast giving way under his accumulated and still increasing burdens. The question of an Assistant Bishop, in preference to a division of the Diocese, was now agitated. In 1859 A.D. this measure was adopted, and the Rev. Gregory T. Bedell, Rector of the Church of the Ascension, of New York, was elected to that office.

In the year 1873 A.D., Bishop McIlvaine died, after a laborious and distinguished Episcopate of forty-one years. Bishop Bedell now succeeding to the entire charge of the Diocese, it soon became evident that some way must be found to relieve him of a portion of his labors. The old question of division came up for consideration. The Bishop himself proposed this measure, and it seemed to be generally preferred. Accordingly, the Convention at its Annual Session at Gambier, in June, 1874 A.D., passed a resolution for the division of the Diocese by a line running east and west along the southern boundary of the following counties, to wit: Mercer, Shelby, Logan, Union, Morrow, Knox, Coshocton, Tuscarawas, Harrison, and Jefferson. The northern portion, by the same resolution, was to be called "The Diocese of Ohio," the southern portion "The Diocese of Southern Ohio." In determining the name which the northern Diocese should bear, compliance was required with a provision of the Constitution of the Theological Seminary, which made it indispensable that the Bishop of the Diocese of Ohio should be, *ex officio*, President of its Board of Trustees, and as the line of division agreed upon left that Institution in the northern part, that name was accordingly adopted. The action of the Convention was confirmed by the General Convention at its session in New York in October of the same year.

By this division forty of the eighty-eight counties comprising the State were left in the new, or Southern, Diocese. These counties included a little more than half the population of the State, although somewhat less than half its area. The number of parishes left by this division in the Diocese of Ohio was seventy-five; the number of clergy seventy-four. The number of parishes in the Southern Diocese was forty-four; the number of clergy thirty-nine.

Bishop Bedell having, in accordance with his privilege under the Constitution, chosen the Diocese of Ohio as his jurisdiction, called a Primary Convention of the new Diocese for the organization of the same and for the election of a Bishop, to be held in Trinity Church, Columbus, on the 13th day of January, 1875 A.D. This action was in conformity with the requirements of Canon vi., Title iii., of the General Convention; and Articles v. and xi. of the Constitution of the Diocese of Ohio.

The Convention met pursuant to this call; twenty-eight clergymen entitled to seats being in attendance, and eighty-three lay-delegates representing thirty-five parishes. The new Diocese was duly organized and a Bishop elected. The lot fell upon the Rev. Thomas Augustus Jaggar, D.D., Rector of the Church of the Holy Trinity, Philadelphia, Pa. His consecration took place in the church of which he was Rector on the 28th day of April, 1875 A.D. Bishop Jaggar entered upon the duties of his Episcopate in the following month. He was present and presided at the first Annual Convention of his Diocese, which was held in St. Paul's Church, Cincinnati, on the 19th, 20th, and 21st of that month (May). The Convention Sermon was preached by the Bishop. It gave great satisfaction by its clear and forcible presentation of Gospel truth and requirement. This, together with his cordial manners, his manly bearing, and his hearty engagement in his new work, drew to him the confidence and respect of his Diocese. That confidence and respect greatly increased as time went on, and has continued to the present. His administration, extending now over eight years, has been characterized by wisdom, prudence, and earnest devotion to the interests of the Church. During this time the number of the clergy has increased to forty-eight; the number of parishes, including missionary stations, to sixty-five. The policy of the Diocese, under the advice of the Bishop, has been to discourage the full organization of parishes until such time as they should be able to be self-supporting. It is provided by Canon that missionary stations may have a provisional organization, by virtue of which they are entitled to a representation in the Convention, and are thus brought into close relations to the Diocese. In pursuance of this policy a large number of *quasi*-parishes are held back from full canonical organization, and hence the number of parishes, as such, does not represent the actual strength of the Diocese.

The number of communicants has increased since the Diocese was constituted from 4171 to 5651, the number reported this present year (1883 A.D.). The contributions of the Diocese for all purposes during this period have been as follows, to wit: in 1875 A.D., so far as reported, $62,884 (report very imperfect); in 1876 A.D.; $118,554; in 1883 A.D., $147,663.

The number of church buildings and chapels in the Diocese is 57; the number of rectories 13.

A "Woman's Auxiliary Society to the Board of Missions" was formed in 1876 A.D., which, under an energetic and judicious directorship, has done good service in the Diocese and in the General Missions of the Church. The result of its last year's work is the sum of $7765.95.

At the last Convention (1883 A.D.), Bishop Jaggar delivered a "Charge" on "The Duty of the Clergy in Relation to Modern Skepticism." It was an able, affectionate, and timely admonition on that subject, and produced a deep impression. A brief extract from the concluding portion will indicate, in a general way, the treatment of the subject:

"I have tried to show you that your duty in relation to the prevailing skepticism is determined by the nature of your office, and of the truth committed to you.

"Your office being a *stewardship*, your duty is to preach positively that which is committed to you.

"The trust committed to you being *personal*, a trust in JESUS, your duty is to set Him forth in all the fullness of His person and work; to let Him be your strong fortress and tower of defense against unbelief; to make it your aim to bring men up to the faith of personal loyalty to Him; above all, to keep yourselves personally in the truth, letting the love of CHRIST constrain you.

"The truth being essentially *supernatural*, your duty is to understand clearly the meaning of the supernatural, to stand firmly in the historic fact of the resurrection which verifies it, to attempt no compromises with the spirit which would eliminate it.

"The truth being *self-manifesting*, commending itself to every man's conscience, your duty is to the conscience, depending upon and keeping yourself in the line of the quickening and awakening power of the HOLY SPIRIT."

The prospects of the Diocese of Southern Ohio for the future may be regarded as in a large degree favorable. All her machinery, so to speak, is in good working order; no serious differences, either in doctrine or in the conduct of worship, prevail. Harmony in an unusual degree marks her Conventional proceedings. Her Liturgy is now appreciated in places where, at no distant period, it was an offense. Her festivals and fasts are coming into favor, and to some extent into observance, by those without, instead of being regarded as old superstitions. The claims of her ministry, as derived through Episcopal authority, are better understood and more indulgently allowed. And the time seems near at hand when, under Divine favor and blessing, and faithfulness on the part of her people, a large degree of prosperity will mark her advancement.

Among the hinderances which have hitherto retarded the advance of the Church in Ohio (both north and south) has been the large and constant drain upon the number of her clergy for the supply of regions farther West. This probably was due to the geographical position of the State, as being in what was formerly considered as the West, and adjacent to the rapidly forming new Dioceses and Missionary Jurisdictions. These naturally called for help to those nearest at hand, and Ohio suffered greatly from this cause. The same may be said in respect to her Laity. Of these, very large numbers have removed farther West. In this manner many parishes have suffered great loss, and some have been wellnigh depleted. It is likely that, as means of travel and communication between all parts of the country have now become easy and rapid, these hinderances will in a measure disappear.

In the division of the Diocese of Ohio, although the line of separation adopted left her Theological and Literary Institutions in the Northern Diocese, yet careful regard was observed that each division should have a joint and equal share in the interests and rights of these Institutions. Only in one or two particulars is it otherwise. By the terms of the Constitution (Art. viii.) adopted when the Institutions were founded, it was made an essential condition that the "Bishop of Ohio" should be forever, *ex officio*, President of the Board of Trustees, and by Art. ix. the Theological Seminary is put under his immediate charge and supervision. It is to be understood that the Board of Trustees is the corporate authority of all the Institutions, and, as such, has control of all the property held for their support, whether used for the Seminary proper, or for Kenyon College, or for Preparatory Schools, the corporate name being "The Board of Trustees of the Theological Seminary of the Diocese of Ohio."

Except in the particulars above specified the Southern Diocese possesses equal rights and powers in the Institutions, being entitled to an equal number of representatives in the Board, and consequently to an equal share in their government. Dioceses contiguous to Ohio are also given an interest in these Institutions. They are entitled to a representation in the Board. They may each send two Trustees, one clerical and one lay, with rights co-ordinate with those of the other members of that body. And as soon as certain measures, recently initiated, can be perfected by the assent of other authorities, the Bishops of the aforementioned contiguous Dioceses will also be entitled to seats in the Board.

It is a matter of no small congratulation that the plans adopted for the equal co-working of both Dioceses, and for enlisting the interest and aid of the adjacent Dioceses, in these Institutions have resulted most favorably. The utmost harmony has prevailed, and great good is anticipated from these wise and liberal adjustments. Gambier, the seat of these noble Foundations, is in a county (Knox) adjoining the Southern Diocese, and but a few miles from the dividing line. It is very near also to the geographical centre of the State. It is beautiful for situation and natural scenery, and beautiful also from improvements in buildings, parks, and grounds. It is unsurpassed for healthfulness.

Statistics for 1886 A.D.: Clergy, 52; parishes, 46; missions, 14; candidates for H. O., 3; ordinations diac., 3; pr., 2; baptisms, 671; confirmed, 626; communicants, 6722; contributions, $150,620.79.

REV. ERASTUS BURR, D.D.

Spirit. *Vide* HOLY GHOST, SOUL.

Sponsors. Persons who make vows for others are called "Sponsors." They are also in the Church called "God-fathers" and "God-mothers." The persons who stand with adult candidates for baptism are spoken of in the rubric as God-fathers and God-mothers, but in the body of the service they are called "Witnesses."

The "Witnesses" make no vows for the adult person, but they assent to the injunction to put him in mind of his vow, promise, and profession, and to see that he is rightly instructed in GOD'S Word. The Witnesses in adult baptism may be spoken of as Sponsors, but that use of the word is not entirely correct, inasmuch as they make no vows for the person baptized.

The word Sponsors is correctly applied, whereas, in the case of infants and persons not having reached years of discretion, some others stand forward and make vows for those who are admitted to the membership of the Church by Baptism.

The office of Sponsor is of ancient authority. It is mentioned by the early Fathers as existing in their time, and has always continued in the Anglican Church. The qualifications for the position, while never having been authoritatively defined, may be gathered from the Baptismal Office itself, where such duties are specified for the Sponsor that no one but a devout person can properly engage to perform them. How can one engage to renounce all evil for the child if he is the slave of sin himself? How can he say that the child shall be taught to believe the Articles of the Christian Faith if he does not believe them himself? How can he promise that the child will obey GOD's commands if he is living in disobedience himself?

Consistency demands that the sponsor should be a practical believer. It is not required that he be eminent for saintliness, but he should be a sincere Christian. The neglect of duty on the part of sponsors shows that too often the office is entered upon without any real understanding of what it involves, and with no true desire to do what is best for the child's welfare.

It is an absolute perversion of the sponsorial office to think of it as a mere formal appendage to a naming ceremony. If a sponsor think of himself as merely witnessing the giving a name to the child, and regards his work as ending there, he has not understood the matter at all. He is to be the child's religious friend, watching over him as opportunity will permit, seeing that he is taught and trained in a Christian way, and is finally brought to the Bishop to be confirmed. The relationship of the sponsor to the child ought always to be such that the latter may confidently look upon him as a safe teacher and a reliable guide, and expect from him a full measure of Christian sympathy and help. REV. G. W. SHINN.

Springfield, the Diocese of. The Diocese of Springfield is composed of all that part of the State of Illinois lying south of the counties of Woodford, Ford, Livingston, and Iroquois, and east of the Illinois River. It has an area of 30,000 square miles, and had in 1880 a population of 1,300,000 persons.

The consent of the Bishop and Convention of Illinois to the organization of this new Diocese was given in September, 1877 A.D. The consent of the General Convention having been obtained at its session in October of the same year, the Diocese was formally organized at the Primary Convention, held in Springfield (December 18, 1877 A.D.).

The division of the Diocese of Illinois was suggested by Bishop Whitehouse, in the 33d Annual Convention in 1870 A.D., when the matter was referred to a committee of six clergymen and six laymen, with the Bishop. It was proposed to divide the Diocese into three, but the proposed action failed to receive the consent of the General Convention of 1871. The subject of division was considered in each of the Conventions of 1872, 1873, and 1874 A.D. The decease of Bishop Whitehouse, in 1874 A.D., prevented, for the time, any further action on the subject. Bishop McLaren, the successor of Bishop Whitehouse, in his address to the Diocesan Convention of 1876 A.D., intimated his willingness to consent to such a division of the Diocese as would secure the consent of the General Convention. The first definite step towards securing such compliance with canonical requirements as would render the division of the Diocese practicable was taken on the 23d of April, by the Churchmen of Quincy, who conveyed all the property of the two parishes in Quincy to the Bishop of Illinois in trust, to be reconveyed to the Bishop of Quincy, when such person should exist, and pledged the sum of $3500 annually for the support of the Bishop and an assistant clergyman. The lines at first proposed for the new Diocese of Quincy not meeting the approval of a majority of those concerned, they were modified so as to include the existing limits of the Diocese. At the meeting of the Diocesan Convention of 1877 A.D., arrangements were perfected for the division of the Diocese into three on the lines since adopted.

While this division was being carried out for the purpose of obtaining increased Episcopal supervision, the idea was steadily kept in view that *division* was not necessarily *separation*. The plan of a federation of the Dioceses within the State, as authorized by the General Convention, was contemplated from the first.

At the Primary Convention for the organization of the Diocese of Springfield, held in the city of Springfield on the 18th of December, 1877 A.D., 17 clergymen were entitled to seats, and 19 parishes to representation. Of these, 16 clergymen and the representatives of 15 parishes were actually present. On the first ballot for Bishop, the Rev. Geo. F. Seymour, S.T.D., Dean of the General Theological Seminary, was unanimously elected by the concurrent votes of the clergy and laity. When the consent of a majority of the Standing Committees had been obtained, Dr. Seymour, acting under the advice of his Bishop and the members of the Standing Committee of the Seminary, declined the election. At the first Annual Convention, held on the 28th day of May, 1878 A.D., 15 clergymen were entitled to seats, of whom 14 were present, together with the representatives of 12 parishes. The Rev. Dr. Seymour was unanimously requested to withdraw his declination. He consented to do so, and was consecrated as first Bishop of Springfield, in Trinity Church, New York, on St. Barnabas' day, 1878 A.D. Ten Bishops united in the laying on of hands, among whom was one of the English Colonial Bishops, thus again uniting the two lines of succession.

The harmony of the Diocese, thus happily begun, has continued to the present time. No party issue has ever been raised or party vote cast in the Convention. The Diocese has grown, as shown by its statistics, with unexampled rapidity. The number of clergy has risen from 16 in 1878 A.D. to 42 in 1883 A.D.; the number of parishes and missions from 21 to 47; the communicants have increased from 1425 to 2129; the amount of contributions from $22,685 to $38,884. An orphanage, supported by the general offerings of the Diocese, and a school of high grade for girls, are in successful operation in Springfield, and five grammar schools for boys, under the patronage and supervision of the Bishop, have been organized in as many places. The beginning of a Diocesan Library, about 500 volumes, has been made.

The Diocese has been the first to introduce into the Church in America the office of Archdeacon, as it exists in the Church of England. The duty of this officer is specially to look after the real estate and other property of the Church in the Diocese, the security of titles, and the proper care of church buildings, plate, and vestments. There are at present three Archdeaconries, those of Springfield, Alton, and Cairo. The ancient office of Rural Dean is also recognized and adopted by the Diocese. There are six Rural Deaneries.

In the legislation of the Diocese, the inherent rights of the Episcopate are recognized by the provision that no change in the Constitution or Canons shall be made without the consent of the Bishop. An important change was made in 1882 in the time of holding parish meetings for the election of vestries. In every other Diocese, so far as known, these meetings are held on Easter-Monday, thus bringing an election which is often a fruitful source of contention immediately after the solemnities of Holy Week. In this Diocese parish meetings are held on the Monday before Advent. In the year 1882 A.D. the name Convention was changed to Synod, and the word "male" was stricken from the description of qualified voters at parish elections.

Statistics for 1886 A.D.: Clergy, 40; parishes, 21; missions, 27; candidates for H. O., 9; ordinations, D. 1, P. 1; baptisms, infants, 306, adults, 101, total, 434; confirmed, 338; communicants, 3031; Sunday-school teachers, 206; Sunday school scholars, 1822; contributions, $28,100 46.

REV. J. D. EASTER, D.D.

Stalls. (*Vide* SEDILIA.) To say that a person has a stall is only another way of saying that he has an office in that Church.

Standing. The rubric directs standing at certain times in the service. We stand at the opening of the service as an act of reverence. So in acts of Praise, as in the Anthems and the Hymns, and as showing reverence when the Gospel is read, and when notice of the Communion is given. Standing in prayer was a Jewish custom as well as kneeling. Solomon knelt, so also Daniel. The Pharisee stood. Standing is now the posture of the Easterns in the Sunday services, except for the fifty days of Pentecost. At Baptism the congregation should stand till after the baptism is administered. The adult at Baptism should also stand when receiving that sacrament. Those to be joined in matrimony should stand till the benediction, when they should kneel. Indeed, the rule may be held universal that the congregation should not kneel till so directed in the rubric. As for those to be married, kneeling even at the benediction is not ordered, but only it is a proper posture. But the Priest stands in token of authority at the Absolution, in reading the Commandments, in reading the Prayer for the whole estate of CHRIST'S Church Militant, at the Consecration of the Elements, and at the Benediction when all the congregation are still kneeling. The decency and reverence of these rules is evident to all who consider that the worship of GOD is more than a mere form, and has a meaning and is directed to an Infinite Person.

Stations, were the assembling of the congregations at certain services which were protracted, so that the days on which these services occurred were called stated days, and the assembly a station, and it was held as a fast. The station or fast was explained "as an encampment, which protects us from the attacks of the devil" (St. Ambrose, Sermon 25). The congregations on the Sunday later acquired that name. The processions called stations were of later origin, but the "stations" of Passion-Week are of quite a later date, and had a close connection with image worship.

Stephen, St. The first martyr of the Church, the first witness to the Faith of CHRIST who sealed it with his blood, the leader of the noble army of martyrs. A man full of Faith and of the HOLY GHOST, filled with wisdom, grace, and power. He was chosen with six others to be the first deacons of the Church. By his faith and power he did such great wonders and miracles among the people, and then disputed with such wondrous force, that he overbore all opposition. He was arrested upon a charge which, in the evil sense the Jews placed on his words, was probably correctly quoted, but in the fact and the intention with which it was preferred wholly false;—that he had spoken blasphemous words against Moses and against GOD, which they made out from his assertion that JESUS of Nazareth would destroy the Temple and remove the Law. Before the Sanhedrim he rose equal to the trial. His face was as it had been the face of an Angel. So far from retracting, he only placed in a clearer light the facts. GOD is not bound to any one place as holy. Horeb was holy. Sinai was holy, as well as the Temple. Then he suddenly broke out into a vehement invective, seeing his words made no impression upon his audience, and in his ecstasy the heavens opened and he rapturously exclaimed, "I see the heavens opened, and the Son of Man standing on the Right hand of GOD." It was this that maddened them beyond endurance, and they who were stately judges transformed themselves into angry executioners. They hurried him out of the city, and casting their garments at the feet of a "young man whose name was Saul," they stoned him. Calling upon GOD and saying, "LORD JESUS, receive my spirit," he kneeled down and cried with a loud voice, "LORD, lay not this sin to their charge," and when he had said this he fell asleep. The worth in which he was held and the might of his character were shown by the devout men who, in the midst of a dangerous persecution, could bury him with that state which is implied by the words, "they together bore him to his burial and made great lamentation over him." His must have been a most glorious character. Energy, knowledge, power, steadfastness, unflinching courage, a loveliness of mind that transfigured his face to angelic beauty, all concentred upon this, one of the mightiest of the early converts to Christianity. Of the depth of the impression he made upon those of his own day we have the best proof in that by the direction of the HOLY SPIRIT St. Luke, who may well have been an eye-witness of it, records the history proportionally more fully than any other single part of his record. St. Stephen's speech, in the ease and readiness, in the freedom and force of his arguments, stands forth as a model. Its criticism Dean Stanley shows is natural and just. It differs from the record of the Hebrew, where we may well suppose tradition would supplement the concise statements of Holy Writ. These have provoked much discussion, into which we cannot enter, but the result has always been to show how accurate the different writers of the New Testament really were, and that there is no necessary disagreement if the statements are fairly valued. St. Stephen's day falls upon the 26th of December. In art he is represented with a mural crown.

Stipendiaries. Members of choirs and other officers who were paid salaries were usually called Stipendiaries, in distinction from others who were supported from the Fund or Endowment.

Stole. *Vide* VESTMENTS.

Subcantor. (*Vide* SUCCENTOR.) As subchanter he was the representative for the Precentor, and to him was assigned the duty of arranging the musical services of the feasts of the second class.

Subdeacon. An office which had an early existence in the Church, but which the English Church dropped at the Reformation, together with the other minor orders, Acolytes, Exorcists, Readers, and Door-keepers. It is not in use in the Anglican Church at all now, while it is still in use in the Eastern and Latin Churches. The name was given from the duties which appertained to the office,—to serve the deacon in filling his ministry.

Sublapsarian. They who hold that GOD foreknew but did not predestine Adam's fall. But that the decree of Predestination did take effect immediately upon all of Adam's descendants. This mode of attempting to avoid the logical consequences of the supralapsarian theory—for both can be but theories—cannot relieve the difficulties by merely removing their action a step lower. The consequences of the decree of Predestination, whether before the fall or after it, do not change the terrible, logical inference that GOD is the author of sin, nor do they the less render the Scriptures of none effect, which distinctly teach us that GOD willeth that all men should repent and be saved, by the mere change of the point at which the supposed decree of Predestination was operative. The consequences must necessarily be the same to us. It is only, therefore, a mere nominal escape from the doctrines which flow from an extreme statement of Predestination, which excludes the apparently but not really opposed fact of freedom of will. (*Vide* PREDESTINATION.)

Substance. It is the "Being," existence. We are of the substance of our parents, different in person, but of the same substance, limited by the same conditions, having the same general capacities. The unity of our human nature, which we all feel but cannot readily express, is the common substance, as it were, of our nature. We as individuals with varying abilities are yet tied down to the common limits which time and mortal nature and the opportunities of the hour furnish. By using these as instruments with those abilities which belong to us, controlled by and controlling events, we advance or retard development of our powers, but we cannot go beyond. Our substance is created. But of the Supreme Being we cannot limit our conceptions to these things. GOD is a Spirit and self-existent. Of the conditions of His self-existence we cannot conceive. But we know Him to be a substance, unbegotten, eternal. The substance of GOD is ONE, SOLE, SELF-EXISTENT; subject to nothing that can affect any other being in the universe. We confess to be in the three Persons of the TRINITY,—The FATHER, Eternal, Unbegotten, the SON of One substance with the FATHER, the HOLY GHOST proceeding from the Substance of the FATHER and through the SON sent to us. It is a mystery incomprehensible to finite minds, not contradictory of our other knowledge of divine things, but above our reach and known only by revelation, but not solvable by reason alone. As our substance is common to many individuals, it is not beyond this analogy to confess the Unity and the circuminsession in the substance of GOD,—of the Three Persons, the FATHER, the SON, and the HOLY GHOST.

Succentor. The leader of the second choir, as St. Augustine explains the use of the Psalms antiphonally, or he was the leader of the chorus, as St. Basil seems to imply in explaining the singing of the Psalms in his day..

Suffragan. The Bishops in a province under an Archbishop or Metropolitan are called Suffragans. So the Archbishop of Canterbury has twenty-two Suffragan-Bishops in his Province of Canterbury. The Archbishop of York has eight in his Province of York. But besides the use of the title there is another, which forms a part in the compound title, Suffragan-Bishop. Anciently the Chorepiscopi, or country Bishops (vide CHOREPISCOPI), were doing a missionary work subordinate to the Bishop of the See. His was a city, they were in the country in some sort as his commissaries, with equal spiritual prerogatives, which they exercised under him. The order was removed after a long struggle (when its missionary work had made the Church a national one) in the several countries in Europe, and so it disappeared from England. But in the spoliation of the monasteries it was intended to endow twenty-six Sees, to be practically chorepiscopates under the title of Suffragan-Bishoprics. Of these, one was actually filled by Hodgkin at Parker's consecration. The Act of Henry VIII. ordering the Suffragan-Bishoprics fell into desuetude, but it was held could be revived at any time. It has been so revived in England that three, Dover, Bedford, and Colchester, are filled, and it is proposed that the Isle of Wight shall be also filled.

Suffrages. The votes of assent and of approbation; and hence the assenting petitions of the people in the Litany are called the suffrages, and the versicles and responses after the Creed in the Morning and Evening Prayer, in the Visitation of the Sick and of Prisoners, and Offices of the Prayers at Sea. These suffrages are very ancient in substance, and there is sufficient similarity to the prayers called the Ectene in the Eastern Church to lead the masters in Liturgies to suppose a common origin for them. The suffrages for some of the Lenten offices in the Mozarabic Liturgy are of great beauty.

Sunday. GOD, from the first, set apart one day in seven for His service. This was the seventh day, because He is said to have "rested" on that day from His work. The sanctification of it by the Jews was their acknowledgment that they were worshipers of Him as their only Creator; and also their proclamation of Him as peculiarly their Redeemer from the bondage of Egypt; and their deliverance on that day at the Red Sea was Moses' argument with them to keep the Sabbath. But this rescue of Israel by Moses was only a type and pledge of a spiritual deliverance by CHRIST. Therefore the shadow must give place to the substance, and GOD is now to be worshiped as the One who has fulfilled the promise; and the Christian, after six days of work, also sanctifies a day, to acknowledge the same obligation to his Creator, and to his Redeemer, who, on the first day of the week, by rising from the dead, delivered him from death.

The change from the seventh day to the first was made by the earliest Christians with sufficient reason; for if the Jews sanctified the seventh day in gratitude for temporal deliverance, which was only a pledge of a spiritual, surely the Christian has more cogent reason to sanctify that day on which the pledge was fulfilled by CHRIST'S rising, and He was delivered from spiritual captivity, His enemies overwhelmed, and He led, not to an earthly Canaan, but to an inheritance incorruptible in heaven. And we have abundant testimony of Scripture that the first day of the week, or Sunday, has always been the day which Christians have consecrated to GOD's service: "Upon the first day of the week" "the disciples came together to break bread" (Acts xx. 7), etc., etc. And GOD approved it, for it was upon this day that the HOLY GHOST came down visibly upon the Apostles, to qualify them for their ministry in the evangelization of the world. This change continued, and Ignatius emphasizes the fact, when he urges the Magnesians "not to sabbatize with the Jews, but to lead a life agreeable to the LORD'S day, on which our life was raised from the dead by Him" (i.e., CHRIST) "and by His death."

It is called the LORD's day in Scripture; "I was in the Spirit on the LORD's day" (Rev. i. 10).

It is called Sunday by many early writers, as Ignatius, Justin Martyr, Tertullian, and others. It was originally the day dedicated by the heathen to the sun, and early Christian apologists in speaking of the Church to heathen governors, used the name with which they were familiar. In the edicts of the first Christian emperors it is almost always called Sunday. The name is appropriately retained, because Christians dedicate it to the SAVIOUR, whom Malachi called the Sun of Righteousness (ch. iv. 2).

It is only recently that this day has been called the Sabbath. In a sense it may be so spoken of, since it is a day of rest; but Scripture and all primitive ecclesiastical writers apply the term Sabbath only to Saturday, the Jewish sacred day.

Chrysostom says that it was sometimes called The Day of Bread, because of the general custom in the primitive Church of meeting for "the breaking of bread" on every Sunday throughout the year.

Pliny, a heathen magistrate soon after St. John's death, learned from some Christians that their custom was to meet together early in the morning before light, on a certain fixed day (which Ignatius explains was Sunday), to sing hymns to CHRIST as their GOD, and bind themselves with a sacrament to do no evil, and afterwards to partake of a common feast.

To secure proper observance of Sunday, it was ordered by Constantine that all proceedings at law be suspended on that day, except in cases of absolute necessity, or when there was opportunity for some eminent charity; and all Christian laws forbade the frequenting of games or sports on that day. In time the Jews grew careless in observance of their Sabbath, spending it in idleness and indulgence, and heathen practices were continually tending to divert Christians, and therefore the fourth Council of

Carthage decreed, "That if any one forsook the solemn assembly of the Church on the LORD'S day to go to a public show, he should be excommunicated." Persons were liable also to excommunication who absented themselves for three LORD'S days from the public assembly without good reason, if they went to the games at any time on that day, left the church while the Bishop was preaching, refused to join in the prayers or receive the Holy Communion, or held or frequented a separate assembly.

Recreations and relaxations for health, or to promote the more proper observance of the holy day, were permitted. Therefore, strict as the early Church was in observing fasts, yet no fast was ever allowed upon Sunday, not even in Lent; but these, in honor of the risen LORD, were made days of refreshment, recreation, and religious rejoicing. Tertullian says that they regarded it a crime to fast on that day. St. Ambrose condemns the Manichees for fasting on Sunday, because they thus in effect denied the LORD'S resurrection. The fourth Council of Carthage reckons him no Catholic who fasts upon that day; and the first council of Braga particularly anathematized a number of sects because they persevered in this custom.

So eager were the early Christians to attend Divine worship, that nothing but sickness or great necessity, such as imprisonment or banishment, could detain them from it; and they did not regard persecution as an excuse for forsaking the assembling of themselves together (Heb. x. 25), and when they could not meet by day, did so at night. Their zeal for the observance of Sunday showed itself in long vigils preceding the day, begun of necessity in times of persecution, but continued afterwards as useful exercises of piety. They usually had sermons twice on that day. But where there was no sermon in the evening, they still had evening prayer, which they considered themselves obliged to attend as a necessary part of public worship and observance of the day. In obedience to St. Paul's injunction, "on the first day of the week" they made liberal offerings for the poor and for religious purposes.

The enforcement of the observance of Sunday throughout mediæval times was a very important factor in the process of disciplining and Christianizing the wild tribes whom the Church had to evangelize. And while we find constant laxness of observance, beside this, we find as persistent, urgent teaching and canonical enactment upon its being kept as a holy day. It was, it is, emphatically a holy day: "This is the day the LORD hath made: we will rejoice and be glad in it." The neglect of it is a pollution, and, without any exaggeration, it may be asserted, that wherever this day is publicly desecrated, then trouble, social and political, has brooded over the country. The LORD'S day is a blessing we should zealously guard as a protection to our land. Not in a narrow, pharisaical spirit, but in the broader and holier ground of a thankful, rejoicing spirit. To better preserve it, the Church has enacted this Canon, conceived and issued in this spirit (Tit. i., Can. xx.): "All persons within this Church shall celebrate and keep the LORD'S Day, commonly called Sunday, in hearing the Word of GOD read and taught, in private and public prayer, in other exercises of devotion, and in acts of charity, using all godly and sober conversation."

Like other monuments, the continued observance of this day, as a matter of course, by nations widely distant, not only perpetuates the memory, but demonstrates the historical fact of CHRIST'S Resurrection. And nations have been thankful to cling to the observance of that which, for nearly two thousand years, has borne silent testimony to that greatest of events upon which all of man's hopes for eternity depend.

Authorities: Bingham's Antiquities, Chapin's Primitive Ch., Wheatley on the Book of Common Prayer, Nelson's Festivals and Fasts. See also Smith's Dict. of Christian Antiquities, Hessey's Bampton Lecture, Sunday.

REV. T. G. LITTELL.

Sunday-School Work in the Church. The relationship of the Sunday-School to the Church is determined by two principles which have always been held, and which must always be maintained.

The first is that *every child should be baptized*, and thus brought into covenant relations with GOD. The second is that *every baptized child is to be taught by parents, sponsors, and pastor* the truths of the Christian Faith; should be trained to live a Christian life; and should be encouraged to seek help in the use of the means of grace.

These two principles make the Christian nurture of the young so vitally important that nothing can ever be regarded as a substitute for the personal work of pastor, parent, and sponsor.

Other agencies may become helps, but never can they be substitutes.

The Sunday-School is a helping agency. It supplements the work which is to be done by those who are directly responsible for the child's welfare, and it supplies some training where there is neglect on the part of any of the three classes of responsible parties before mentioned.

In no case, however, can the Sunday-School relieve pastor, or parent, or sponsor of the duty of imparting that instruction and training which are needed by the baptized child to enable him to understand the terms of the covenant under which he is to GOD, and to perform the practical duties growing out of it.

There will always be the need of home training in the ways of godliness, always the need of that watchfulness and sympathy which a sponsor should manifest, and always the need of that fidelity in teaching and guiding which a pastor should exercise.

The Sunday-School, therefore, *cannot be thought of as an independent organization*, or as *having a mission separate from the Church*, or as *working in lines and by methods which are not under the supervision of the clergyman* who is the spiritual guide of all in his parish, of the young as well as of the old.

The baptized child is already a member of the Church of Christ. His baptism was not a mere ceremony in which he received a name, but a sacrament in which he became "a member of CHRIST, a child of GOD, and an inheritor of the Kingdom of Heaven."

There is contemplated the period when the baptized child, after faithful teaching and training, will realize the relationship in which he stands to the LORD, will turn to Him with sorrow for sin and faith in CHRIST, and will take upon himself his baptismal vows, seeking in the Apostolic Rite of Confirmation the gift of the HOLY SPIRIT to be a faithful disciple of the LORD JESUS. His confirmation admits him to the Holy Communion, in which Sacrament he is taught not only to remember the love of his divine Master, but also to feed spiritually upon Him. From Baptism to Confirmation, from Confirmation to Communion, and from Communion to a life of personal fidelity and usefulness,—these are the well-marked lines of growth in the history of a Christian child properly trained according to the Church's ways.

Very prominent, then, among the means to be used for this training is *the catechising by the pastor*. It is hardly to be thought that the spirit of the Church's provision for the catechising of the children is complied with in the hard, dry, technical recitation of the Church Catechism sometimes in vogue.

While this summary of the things "which a Christian ought to know and to believe" should be committed to memory, its mere recitation is not sufficient. It should be regarded as the ground-work, the outline of the range of truth which is to be taught and illustrated; the convenient series of hooks and pegs on which to hang the many topics included in a religious education.

Catechising the children openly in the church is required of the clergy and is faithfully performed by many of them, although in varying methods, some calling the children together for a Children's Service, others going regularly into their Sunday-Schools, and others meeting the spirit of the requirement in ways which their own judgment finds most effectual.

The children come especially under the pastor's training as they approach that age when they reach the period of discretion, that is, when they are old enough for Confirmation.

To meet their needs, and to enable them to come to that Apostolic Rite properly prepared, it is the usage to form a *Confirmation Class* in the parish, where for a length of time they receive the clergyman's especial instructions. These instructions cover quite a range of topics, including a review of the elementary principles of religion, the practical duties of the Christian life, the history and meaning of Confirmation, and the nature and benefits of the Holy Communion.

The Confirmation class, or rather the Confirmation instruction, holds a most important part in this Church in the whole matter of the religious training of the young. Although no definite form has been given to it, it is felt by almost all to be one of the most important of the pastor's duties.

This brief summary of some of the things the Church expects the clergy to do in the way of teaching the young leads us on now to consider *the work of the Sunday-School.*

Regarding the Sunday-School as a help in teaching and training the young, and regarding the Church Catechism as containing the summary of the things to be taught, we think first of *the organization of the Sunday-School.* The school should not be mob-like. If it is not organized it defeats its own purposes, but its organization should be simple. Not many rules are needed, and not many officers. No matter how large the number of scholars, the machinery of the school should never be elaborate or cumbersome.

Some one must be at its head; some one else is to record attendance, and attend to various like details; some one is needed to change library-books, and a sufficient number of teachers are required to permit the scholars to be grouped into departments, or else to be divided into classes.

A Superintendent, Secretary, Librarian, and Teachers are the usual working force, but to these may be added a Treasurer and a Chorister or Organist.

Very much of the efficiency of a school depends upon the kind of a superintendent it has. If he is an active, faithful, and pious man, with a fair share of tact and earnestness, and disposed to co-operate with the rector, he will find his position one of great usefulness, and he can do much towards making the school what it ought to be.

On the other hand, an indolent, neglectful, and blundering man, or one who cannot work with the clergyman, is manifestly incompetent to have charge of the Sunday-School.

Whether the clergyman himself should act as superintendent is often debated. It is certainly helpful if a good layman can be found to attend to the many details which the position involves, so that the rector may have more time and opportunity for religious instruction.

Some of the clergy find it a very good plan to put the opening services and various matters of detail in charge of the superintendent, but they, the clergy, make it a point to be present some ten or fifteen minutes before the session closes to catechise the children upon the lessons for the day.

It is hardly necessary to speak here of the duties of the other officers, except to remark that one of the most useful persons in a school is the chorister, who can teach the children to sing.

There ought always to be some one with sufficient musical ability, and also with that necessary enthusiasm to teach new hymns, chants, and carols, from time to time, and to lead the singing at the regular sessions.

A good chorister is a treasure in the Sunday-School. Something should be said here on the general subject of the music and hymns suitable for children. We have, on the one hand, a great mass of light trifling melodies attached to very silly and sometimes very erroneous words. On the other, we have heavy harmonies with very little melody, and words that may suit the piety of adult years, but which are not at all suitable for children.

The number of really good hymns and tunes for children is very small. They have to be searched for. It is certainly desirable to avoid the trashy, sensational music so persistently advertised, and equally desirable to avoid the heavy sort which children cannot and should not use. Where the hymns in the Hymnal are suitable, and where the music is within the power of the children, it is manifestly proper that they should be made familiar with them, as likewise with the Canticles in the Prayer-Book. Nowhere, however, are more care and judgment needed than in the selection of hymns and tunes for the Sunday-School.

Passing on to *the qualifications needed to make one a good teacher*, we are met by the fact that many of the persons who are available as teachers have had very little training, and do not always have the right conception of the work before them.

It is a pity that more of the older persons, the fathers and mothers, do not take classes. Too often this work is handed over to young men and young women, who, whatever may be their zeal, do not always have sound judgment in dealing with the children. But given the average teacher, the person who wants to be useful, and who is willing to go to some trouble to accomplish a good result, much may be done by the rector or superintendent in the way of *Teachers' Meetings for the study of the Lessons.*

In many places the Teachers' Meeting is regularly held each week, and the lesson appointed for the following Sunday is gone over with great care, so that each one goes to his class with some fair understanding of what is to be taught. There are few expedients so helpful to the same teachers as these meetings, where the lesson is talked over, discussed, and illustrated, but others prefer the more quiet opportunities which their own homes, with the aid of Commentaries, Teachers' Helps, and the like, provide.

It matters not how the preparation is attained so that *the teacher comes to the class full of the topic* of the lesson. And no teacher should ever come empty. It is a dreadful waste of time to pretend to teach when one has nothing to impart. The children soon perceive a teacher's ignorance, and are not slow to comment upon it. Not only should a teacher come well prepared upon the lesson for the day, but *he should come punctually and regularly.* His irregularities in this regard tell badly upon the class, and lead to most deplorable results, sometimes to the breaking up of the class altogether. If he has to be away he should provide a substitute, or if unable to do this, should notify the superintendent.

Then, too, the teacher should feel that *his presence with his class is for a definite purpose.* He is not to appear to them as if he did not know what he had come for, nor is he to waste his time and theirs by chatting upon miscellaneous topics. They have come to be taught something in religion, and he is there to teach them.

Above all else *the teacher should be a religious man.* No others should teach in Sunday-School. It is better to have a few good teachers than a score of those whose lives negative all their words. A man need not be perfect before he take a class, but he must be sincere. He must be interested in personal religion to that extent that he will do his utmost to teach his pupils to revere GOD's truth, and to aim at serving Him in a Christian life. After all, the religious faculty in children is reached not so much through the intellect as through the affections. Indeed, it seems to be awakened and stimulated in ways that we cannot describe other than to say that a sympathetic soul comes into the presence of others, and their spiritual faculties become active. It is very wonderful, this awakening of the spiritual faculties of others. Eloquence, learning, and earnestness fail to accomplish that which sincerity and straightforward simplicity will secure. The one qualification which every teacher should have and may have is this personal piety, which in itself is the best of all agencies for awakening a responsive interest on the part of those who are taught.

The three divisions of the Sunday-School which are usually found most convenient are the Infant Department, the Main School, and the Bible-Classes. The first is intended for the children who are to receive oral instruction, the second for those who are able to read, and the third for the older scholars of a more advanced standing.

It is well to have the three departments brought together for the opening and the closing exercises, and especially in the latter, that they may all have the benefit of the review of the lesson and the catechising.

The Subjects of Study in the Sunday-School next engage our attention. They may be divided into five classes:

1. The Sacred Scriptures. 2. The Catechism. 3. The Prayer-Book. 4. The History of the Church. 5. The Practical Duties of the Christian Life.

Although thus separated here for the purposes of our consideration, we are not to think of them as being always distinct. Thus any study of the Scriptures means gaining some knowledge of the practical duties of Christian life, and any study of the Prayer-Book involves some study of Church History. What is meant is that, in the usual order, the infant becomes *familiar first with the Bible Stories, then with parts of the Catechism, then with the Gospels,* afterwards he gains some knowledge of the Prayer-Book as he grows old enough to use it, of the History of the Church, and finally of the many things a Christian ought to do. There is afterwards the going back over ground previously trodden, to examine it more fully, and then widening out on either side.

Among the earliest parts of a child's religious education, and one of the most helpful, is *telling him Bible Stories.* The story-telling ability of the teacher should be so cultivated that he will be able to impress the stories of the Bible indelibly upon the youthful memory. These old stories are the most interesting, and the freshest in the world, and they carry with them their unmistakable lessons. They show the struggle between good and evil, and reveal what style of character GOD approves. There is no more effective mode of teaching than that of being able to tell the Bible Stories in simple but striking language adapted to the comprehension of children.

Passing on from story-telling, the teacher then begins to *employ the child's memory in parts of the Catechism,* especially in the Creed, the LORD'S Prayer, and the Ten Commandments.

Following closely upon this will come *some explanation of the Church's year,* so that as the child begins to note the coming and going of days and weeks, he may be able to associate them with the facts and doctrines which the Church commemorates.

A child has received a good start when he knows the principal Bible Stories, can recite the leading parts of the Catechism, and understands what the principal divisions of the Church's year commemorate. But now he has learned to read the Scriptures for himself, and his knowledge widens out. How much there is now for him to learn! The narratives of Holy Writ, the Words of the LORD JESUS, the doctrines in the Epistles, the planting of the Church, the daily duties of the daily life,—there never need be any lack of topics for the teacher's teaching.

Without enlarging upon these, it seems proper to add that *the children of the Church are to be taught as children of the Church.* Our Church has a definite system of truth, clear and simple. It covers a few points of doctrine, and that system of truth should be adhered to. Our Church has an orderly form of worship, her children should be taught to love it and to unite in it.

Our Church makes demands upon the personal service and loyalty of her children. They should be taught to give willing adhesion. In a word, the children ought to be so trained in Sunday-School that as they grow up they will become loyal members of this Church. It is not enough to make them mildly acquiesce in her ways. They should become thoroughly in love with them. This is not to make them bigots and uncharitable, but to give them tone and fibre whereby they will go out into the world and be of some positive use in the world.

First sincere Christians, then loyal Churchmen,—who can doubt that children trained to be thus will develop noble characters and find their work for CHRIST and His Church?

And that is the object of the Sunday-School. It offers to aid parents, sponsors, and pastors in developing the religious life of the young, in filling their minds with the truths of our Most Holy Faith, and in training them to serve GOD faithfully in their day and generation. Whatever its defects of administration, this is its aim.

REV. G. W. SHINN.

Supererogation. Works which it is claimed may be done over and above what is commanded us to do. The XIV. Article is very express in disproving this: "Voluntary works, besides over and above GOD'S commandments, which they call works of supererogation cannot be taught without arrogancy and impiety: for by them men do declare that they do not only render unto GOD as much as they are bound to do, but that they do more for His sake than of bounden duty is required; where, as CHRIST saith plainly, 'When ye have done all that are commanded you say, We are all unprofitable servants.'" That some advice in Holy Scriptures is given which may be lawfully chosen or declined, as celibacy, yet it is equally plain that it demands all our willingness to obey the motions of the HOLY SPIRIT only to do what is commanded us. The choice of doing or not doing certain things is of expediency. If one sells all that he has and gives to the poor he is doing well, but it may be inexpedient in another, or he may not choose to do this, using the uncertain riches to obtain a treasure hereafter. The young man who kept all the commandments (in his own estimation) yet owned he lacked something that he was told could be supplied by his selling all and following the LORD, this touched the defect not only in his conduct, but in his character too. He lacked self-denial in its best form. But we are taught in Holy Scripture that we can do no good thing of ourselves, that if we say we have no sin we deceive ourselves, that in many things we offend all. Then there can be no power of ourselves to do more than what is commanded. If we but consider that the very best we could do would be but the mere measure of our duty, and we can add nothing more, we cannot overpass that, we could not dream for an instant that there were works of an obedience more than is required of us. The choice in the counsel is not an *addition* to a sufficient goodness, it is a voluntary selection of a certain form of obedience left to us to choose. Then as we are taught in Scripture, we can merit nothing, but all is of grace and of His gift. It follows, then, that there can be no treasury of good works which we can help to fill with those things over and above what we do as sufficient for ourselves, which treasured good words may be passed, as it were, to the blessing of those who are disobedient and erring; an error which is too glaring for any one seriously thinking of his own duty to fall into. Our life in CHRIST is not a task or a business. So much to be done for so much wages. Such obedience only required, and the rest of our work as we choose. This was one form of Pharisaic hypocrisy. It is a life, and to be a healthy spiritual life requires all our own energy, work, and labor from an humble sense of our own unworthiness and a deep, earnest love to Him who loved us and gave Himself for us. He learned obedience in the days of His sinless flesh, with pain, and tears, and strong crying. And we who are sinful can never with wailing, and tears, and prayers ever gain in this mortal life HIS sanctity. It is of His worthiness, and His mercy, by His eternal power that the treasury of His atoning acts is sufficient for us.

Supernatural. The word supernatural is popularly opposed to natural, being that which is beyond the experience and knowledge of man. Its more exact use is to express the higher region of system, the lower region being that of things and events in ordinary experience and knowledge. Supernatural things are not opposed to order and law, but form "the higher portion of an universal order, and are the subjects of an unknown, but not unknowable law." The idea of mystery varies in different generations according to their degree of information, but it always will exist. But in what is mysterious the devout and thoughtful mind still finds that "Order is Heaven's first law." Even the miracle may fall under law. Man can interrupt the action of gravity by stopping the fall of a descending body, so GOD can interrupt the course of nature without a violation of law. The law of resistance is as much a law as the law of gravitation. "The veil of the supernatural is lifted by a miracle for a moment, and it is then evident that nature is not to be limited by our experience, but extends into a region ordinarily unseen, and forms one great system of order, of which the supernatural is but the higher atmosphere."

In primitive ages men were freely inclined to believe in the supernatural, as is evident in the religions of Egypt, Greece, and Rome. They believed "in fates and furies, nymphs and graces." The Sophists tried to resolve mythic tales into "facts and powers of nature." The Sadducees acted similarly in CHRIST'S day. The supernatural is, however, a necessary part in the system of GOD. "He is before all things, and by (or in) Him all things consist" (Col. i. 17). This shows that Christianity was not an after-thought of GOD, but a fore-thought, and that CHRIST existed before the natural world, "before all things," and created "all things" (v. 16). He is "the Lamb slain from the foundation of the world" (Rev. xiii. 8). The world was made to include Christianity. By or in CHRIST all things con-sist, stand together, as many parts coalesce in a whole. "All things were made by Him, and without Him was not anything made that was made" (St. John i. 3). A personal loving relation to GOD in CHRIST is the key which unlocks mysteries. "Every one that loveth is born of GOD, and knoweth GOD" (1 John iv. 7). "The whole life of faith is an experience and spiritual discovery of GOD." It was to CHRIST'S own disciples that He said, "it is given unto you to know the mysteries of the kingdom of heaven" (St. Matt. xiii. 11). Says Archbishop Benson, "The countless tribes which broke up the old civilizations were governed by an absolute naturalism in feeling and in action, and she (the Church) overcame it." The introduction of the supernatural was an unanswerable argument. The natural conclusion from the marvels wrought by JESUS was, "no man can do these miracles that thou doest, except GOD be with him" (St. John iii. 2). "Since the world began was it not heard that any man opened the eyes of one that was born blind. If this man were not of GOD, he could do nothing" (St. John ix. 32, 33).

In the Old Testament the fact of the supernatural is constantly present. It meets us in the account of the creation: "By the Word of the LORD were the heavens made; and all the host of them by the breath of His mouth" (Ps. xxxiii. 6), "the utterance of His mouth, that is, the originating Word." "The heavens declare the glory of GOD" (Ps. xix. 1). "Thou hast established the earth, and it abideth" (Ps. cxix. 90). The lightnings obey GOD (Job xxxviii. 35). "He appointed the moon for seasons; the sun knoweth His going down" (Ps. civ. 19). What a mighty and yet peculiar care of the world is displayed in Job xxviii. 25, 26, where GOD is represented as making "the weight for the winds," and weighing "the waters by measure," and making "a decree for the rain"! In Jeremiah xxxiii. 20, we read of GOD'S "covenant of the day," and His "covenant of the night," that they should preserve their order. The rainbow was made "the symbol of nature's constancy."

"The true notion of the natural cannot be held without the complementary idea of the supernatural, since nature can have no beginning in itself (the thought involving a contradiction), and therefore demands a power older than itself, beyond and above itself." Even the magicians of Pharaoh acknowledged "the finger of GOD" in His miraculous work (Ex. viii. 19). The tables of the law were "written with the finger of GOD" (Ex. xxxi. 18, and Deut. ix. 10). Our SAVIOUR speaks of casting out devils "with the finger of GOD" (St. Luke xi. 20). Of the volcano the Psalmist says of GOD, "He toucheth the hills and they smoke" (Ps. civ. 32), "the lightness of the effort implying the mightiness of the power." In the Old Testament the supernatural is seen at the creation, in the passage of the Red Sea and other miracles, the wonders of Sinai, and the smitten rock in the Wilderness. In the book of Job the natural appears in the thunder and storm, and in animal life. In Ps. xxix. the voice of GOD is represented as dividing "the flames of fire," and shaking "the wilderness." The natural and supernatural are mingled in the account of the Flood, the crossing of the Red Sea, the Egyptian plagues, and the providing of food in the Wilderness. "Again, the great natural is so described in Job and the Psalms, that the awe of the supernatural is upon us, and we receive the impression of a divine presence as distinctly as though it had been all miracle." Both at the creation and at the present time we are to think of the natural and supernatural as constantly mingled, and as being alike the work of GOD. The earth bringing forth at the creation was obeying GOD, and creation and growth are named together, so each harvest is a repetition of the work of the Author of the world, who opens His hand daily to fill his waiting creatures with good (Ps. civ. 27, 28).

Authorities: Blunt's Dict. of Doct. and Hist. Theology, McCosh on the Supernatural in Relation to the Natural, Bushnell's Nature and the Supernatural, Schaff's Introd. to Gen. i. in Lange's Genesis, Sir Joshua Reynolds in Pycroft's Course of English Reading.

REV. S. F. HOTCHKIN.

Supplication. The act of offering an humble request and a pleading that it may be granted, whether it be for ourselves or for others, as did Daniel in his intercession. It is usually in the form of a litany. The *preces*, or prayers, these supplicatory forms, were the people's part, therefore they were responsive. The supplications in the Litany are properly the first four of the *preces*. The rest of the Litany is addressed to our LORD. The term is by no means to be confined merely to mean responsive prayers, for St. Paul directs supplications to be offered for all men. So in the Collect at the end of the Communion Office, "Assist us mercifully, O LORD, in these our supplications and prayers."

Supremacy. Lordship, whether natural, as GOD's supremacy, or given as man's lordship over the lower creation or constitutional, as that of Rulers both in Church and State, either according to Law or usurped, in Church or State.

GOD's supremacy is part of natural religion, and is universally received by all who believe in Him. Our LORD's supremacy is part of our Christian Faith. His Supremacy is by direct grant from GOD the FATHER. He hath given all things, all power in heaven and in earth, into the hands of the SON. So also is man's supremacy over the lower creation (Ps. viii.). The Bishops, as the successors in office, have the supreme government in the Church by a grant from CHRIST: "As my FATHER hath sent me, even so send I you." And by Constitutional enactment for government the different ranks of precedence or appellant power are arranged. There is also a usurped supremacy in the Church, as that of the Pope. This supremacy was not from the beginning. The Bishop of Rome had a Patriarchal sway over the Province of Rome, the suburbicarian Dioceses near Rome, and an advisory right in the Western Church. Against anything but this advisory right the Spanish Bishops protested, in St. Cyprian's time. They did not admit his patriarchal right. This was all that was held till after the year 606 A.D. The Sardican Decree (347 A.D.) was passed only by the Western Bishops after the Council had partly broken up. It gave an appellate jurisdiction to the then Bishop of Rome, Julius (347 A.D.), and Valentinian III. made it absolute (445 A.D.). But it was very slowly accepted in the West through an hundred and fifty years. It interfered very seriously with the government of the Metropolitans over their Provinces, and affected the trials of cases. It was admitted at times, and again resisted, as short-sighted self-interest and the political state of things varied. The Popes gradually stretched this power towards supremacy, first by an extension of the general right to hear appeals, next by decretal letters interfering and ordering changes, next by assuming the right to confer jurisdiction. But these alterations of Church Constitution, vast as they were, received an immense impetus from the Pseudo-Isidorean Decretals. These forged documents formulated the floating, shapeless ideas of the time, and fixed them in favor of Roman Supremacy by the usual appeal to the "Thou art Peter," and by a series of daring inventions. The Papacy gladly seized upon them, and by the skillful use of only three or four little sentences, embodying a new principle, were enabled to overturn the whole fabric of the Church Constitution.

From the acceptance of the Pseudo-Isidore on to the Reformation, the encroachments of the Papacy were unceasing. The resistance was disconnected, dependent upon the political expediency of the moment. Yet strangely, the semblance of power universal in the West, which seemed to be within the Papal grasp, ever eluded it at the critical moment. The arrogance of Gregory VII. crushed the Emperor Henry IV., because of the irregularly controlled abilities of that great Emperor; and just as Gregory deemed himself successful he died, with the knowledge that he had failed to complete his purpose. So, too, Innocent III. held England as a papal fief for a moment, but exasperated the English and irritated the French, and was powerless to prevent the Magna Charta, the instrument which helped to make England free. His reign marked the highest point which Roman absolutism ever reached. Boniface VIII. overreached himself by his violence, and this led to the Avignonese residence of the Popes under French influence. Then came the line of the great Councils of Constance, Pisa, and Basle, which further weakened the Roman prestige, which at last was to incline the different provinces to act in either direction. The next step was to make the Metropolitans the holders of delegated power from Rome. This was a usurpation based upon an assumption of false principles. (*a*) That the See of St. Peter was supreme in the Church, a doctrine which the Roman Bishops persistently taught everywhere. (*b*) That the Appellate jurisdiction which Valentinian III. had conferred could overset and supplant the ancient liberties of the Metropolitans. Both principles were contrary to fact and to history, but self-interest in petty contests among the Metropolitans, and a steady adherence to a fixed policy on the part of the Roman Bishops, gave the desired opportunities to establish them both. The violations of the ancient canon law were always made with a protest that either they were in direct line with the spirit of the Canon law, or because St. Peter's See had plenary authority, or because the exigencies of the time demanded that a lesser evil should be done to avoid a greater; but throughout, the value of a convenient precedent was always appreciated. This course continued down to the year 860 A.D. Numberless cases could be adduced, did space allow, to show that this encroachment was resisted in the West. The East as yet knew nothing of the assertions of the Pope as meaning anything more than a magnifying of his office. The resistance in the West, as in the case of the Priest Apianus of Carthage, who appealed to the Pope against his Bishop, and in the case of Hilary of Poictiers, was by appeal to the Canons, but there was no concerted resistance. The gift of the Pallium, which was at first a mark of favor, became a yoke of obedience to the Roman See, and was so accepted by the Franco-German Bishops under the lead of Boniface, the English apostle of Germany. But Pope Zachary complains that some of the Bishops did not care to receive it. But this Pall or cloak as investing with Metropolitan dignity, came to mean the grant of Metropolitan Jurisdiction,—a further step in encroachments.

To trace the Constitutions of Clarendon and the earlier articles of Louis IX., and the Concordats drawn up with the several governments of Europe, and the political diplomacy used by the Popes, and their waste of diplomatic sagacity in endeavoring to control Italy to the aggrandizement of their several families, would be too long. But the facts are irrefutable that a Patriarchate extending at first only to the suburbicarian provinces, and an advisory position as Bishop of the once capital of the world, a skillful use of political events upon a steadily adhered to line of policy, and a claim to preside, either directly or by proxy, at the Councils of the Church, were ably used to make a Primacy of honor, the supremacy of a power so destructive of all constitutional rights in the Church, so thoroughly a despotism, so glaring in its usurpations, that it could not be endured. The wounds it inflicted upon the Church have not been healed, but it has been fettered and hampered in every way possible. This Supremacy yet claimed, urged, and lately fortified with a decree of Infallibility, is a thing of the past. It can never return again, but this does not repair the breaches, nor does it remove the present ill consequences to the Body of CHRIST.

Authorities: Barrow on the Supremacy, and all Eccl. Histories worth the name.

Surplice. The usual form of the Alb, which was anciently much less loose, with closer sleeves, than in the present Surplice. It is a corruption of the word superpelliceum. Its present form goes back to the twelfth century. (*Vide* VESTMENTS.)

Surrogate. The deputy for a Chancellor, Commissary, Archdeacon, or official, who had to hold a benefice near the place where the Court was held, be in good repute, and skilled in both civil and ecclesiastical Law. He could hold such Courts as his principal, could issue the like licenses and mandates. Usually he issued licenses to marry, for he was the deputy of the Bishop who could dispense with the banns and give a license. He also admitted wills to probate.

Sursum Corda. The versicle "Lift up your hearts," with the response "We lift them up unto the LORD." It is the part of the Preface which formerly began with a benediction, but now in our own Prayer-Book forms the introduction. Its antiquity is very great. It was the usual versicle at this point of the Liturgy in the time of St. Cyprian (252 A.D.), and was then quoted as the common form. That it should not have been quoted oftener and earlier is not surprising when we consider the secrecy with which all celebrations of the Communion were made. The next writer who quotes it is St. Cyril (380 A.D.) of Jerusalem, who speaks of it in his lectures to the Catechumens. After that the references are quite frequent. But the *Sursum Corda* includes also the remaining versicles and responses. "Let us give thanks unto our LORD GOD. It is meet and right so to do. It is very meet, right, and our bounden duty that we should at all time and in all places," etc. The Preface extends from the Lift up your hearts to the first words of the *Sanctus.* After the prayer of Humble Access, the Canon or rule of the Holy Communion begins and goes on to the Hymn.

Susanna, Book of (Apocrypha). The name Susanna means a lily. The Book containing the story of this Jewish woman is a part of the Apocryphal Additions to Daniel. It was called "The History of Susanna (or the Judgment of Daniel)." There is no evidence that it ever formed a part of the Hebrew text. It is thought that it may have been the work of an Alexandrine writer. The story, whether true or not, is intended to teach the excellence of virtue, and the punishment of a lying tongue and an unclean heart. "To Christian commentators Susanna appeared as a type of the true Church tempted to infidelity by Jewish and Pagan adversaries, and lifting up her voice to GOD in the midst of persecution." In the Septuagint this history of Susanna is placed at the beginning of the Book of Daniel, while in the Vulgate it forms the thirteenth chapter. That the account of Susanna was written originally in Greek instead of Hebrew or Chaldee is shown by the fact that when Daniel is represented as declaring what would be the punishment of the wicked men who were making a false accusation to shield themselves, he makes use of a paranomasia, or play upon words, which could only hold good in the Greek language. The Hebraisms show that the addition to Daniel was written by a Hebrew in Greek. As the elders were judges, Calmet concludes that the Jews had judges during the captivity, though it may be doubted whether they had power to put to death Jewish writers thought that the punishment was inflicted by Nebuchadnezzar. St. Bernard and St. Chrysostom compare the persecuted matron to an innocent lamb, and the wicked judges to ravenous wolves, but their prey was taken from them; and so the narrative ends with an account of the pride of husband and parents and kindred in the noble Susanna and of Daniel's great reputation in the sight of the people.

Authorities: B. F. Wescott in William Smith's Dic. of the Bible. He refers to Hippel, "In Susann." Arnald's Comm. in Patrick, Lowth, and Whitby, Horne's Introduction, Prideaux's Connections.

REV. S. F. HOTCHKIN.

Suspension. The penalty of suspending a layman from communion or a person in orders from any or all his official functions is not a final, and may be a temporary, deprivation.

A clergyman may for cause be suspended from the office of preaching alone, or he may be suspended from holding a Parish, or from all his functions, as the gravity of the offense may require. According to the Canons of the General Convention, there are three grades of punishment for five different classes of offenses—viz., admonition, suspension, or degradation—either of which is to be inflicted according to the Canons of the Diocese in which the trial takes place, until otherwise provided for by the General Convention. Suspension is also inflicted upon a clergyman absenting himself for five years from his Diocese without proper reason or excuse, satisfactory to his Bishop, which shall only terminate when he gives in writing sufficient reason, or when he returns to reside in the Diocese, or renounces the ministry. Suspension or degradation is also the penalty for a contumacious non-appearance in the Court if the clergyman is on trial for any offense. But there can be no suspension pronounced against a Bishop, Priest, or Deacon which does not specify what terms or at what time the penalty shall cease.

For the layman, suspension from the Holy Communion is the only penalty known in our Canon Law, and this cannot be pronounced and enforced but by consent of the Bishop, to whom every case of discipline requiring such suspension must be referred. Restoration may be, generally is, granted upon sufficient proof of amendment of life. According to the ancient Canon Law, admonition should precede Suspension, unless the case was such as required immediate action. And if suspension in ordinary cases was not preceded by an admonition, there would be cause for an appeal.

Symbol. It was early used to mean the CREED. The reason for this cannot be satisfactorily traced. But the Symbols of our Faith are the Creeds,—the Nicene and the Apostolic. The word, however, latterly, is not confined to the Creeds, but is applied to all confessions of Faith by different Churches, Denominations, or Religious Societies. In this it takes a wider range than should be permitted to so technical a term. But the word is used to mean the representation of something by another by which it can be suggested, as a letter for a sound, a type for a reality, or a hieroglyph for a word or concrete idea, and thence passing into the Christian ritual and decorative art. Symbolism has taken a very important part in the development of certain Christian ideas. The Cross, the A and Ω, and the ☧ are common symbols of our LORD. The ☧ imagery of the Revelation has passed into decorative symbolism in the forms of the Four living creatures taken as symbols of the Four Evangelists, and the Cherubs of the Hebrew temple have been imagined and reproduced with other angelic forms. These and the like have passed into allowed decorative symbolism, but it has ever been a difficulty to draw the line between what is perfectly allowable, what is doubtful, and what must be absolutely rejected, as, for instance, the attempt to represent the Supreme Being. To us the Crucifix, or the representation of the Virgin Mother and the Holy Infant, have both ideas behind them that make their use most doubtful, if they do not condemn them. A deeper and better symbolism is carried out in the proper plan and construction of a church. There from the great door to the Eastern window all can be symbolically arranged, in gradations, as we find them carried out in the Temple of the Courts, of the Gentiles, Women, Men, Priests, and the Sanctuary, and the Holy of Holies. The Narthex, the Nave, the Choir, the Sanctuary, had their appropriate positions. The Cruciform plan, the Arch of triumph over the choir, the lights of the Eastern window, all were marked with a beauty of symbolism, which was the more deep and enduring because it places the worshiper into the centre of its types, and existed for him and his service made use of it. Of all the plans of constructive symbolism the Eastern Church is the most complete; from crypt to dome it was originally intended to have a significance, to tell a fact, to symbolize the doctrine of the Faith. It was so considered, and the explanations and allegorical descriptions which appear so puerile to those who do not admit the value of symbolism, are full of meaning to the student. Take, for example, the work of St Simon of Thessalonica, which was written in 1430 A.D. How trifling it seems to the one, how devout to the other! One more part of symbolism is to be noticed. That which the Divine wisdom of our LORD has attached to certain acts. The pouring of the water in the act of Baptism, the breaking of the Bread and the taking of the Cup in the Holy Communion, are by His example. The raising of the hands to bless, and the kneeling in prayer and bowing as a worship, are religious acts which are common to all religions and to all Faiths. The white robes of the ministers of GOD are noted as the symbol of righteousness. In fact, no doctrine of religion can take form in outward act without the use of some symbolism or other.

Symphony. The harmony of voices and instruments, or again, the concert of many instruments together. There is no room in the service for a symphony.

Synod. Speaking broadly, Synod is the Eastern word for Council (the Western word), for the assembly of the Bishops and Clergy and Delegates, who have a right to meet and to enact Canons, to hear cases, and to decide upon the work of the Church, whether it be of a Diocese or Province, or a National Church, or whether it be an Œcumenical Council. It has not taken root in the Western Church, *Council* being the usual term employed. Under their respective titles will be found the outlines of the more important Councils held at different times in various parts of the Church. It may be noted here that Synod was the more usual name for the Anglo-Saxon Councils till the Norman influence, beginning with Edward the Confessor, supplanted it by the term Council,—not so but that Synod was used later, and two Councils before that, but in each time less commonly than the other term.

Synodals. Payments made by the Clergy to the Bishop at the time of their attendance at the Synod. But it was distinctly urged that this payment was made then from convenience. The payment was due to the Bishop, but was not a fee for permission to attend a Synod which was of his own summoning.

The decisions of Provincial and Diocesan Synods also received this name occasionally, and ordered to be read to the Parishes throughout the Province or Diocese wherein they were to be enforced.

"**Systematic Divinity**" is a sublime designation. Some, perhaps, may think it is one step from the sublime. It is certainly one or the other. If the revelation of GOD can be reduced to a system, he must have a capacious understanding who can take it all in; and a wonderfully analytical and synthetical mind who can distinguish all its parts, and put them together, in due relations of order and reciprocal support, into a system.

The designation is not very old. Some of the early Christian Fathers were voluminous writers upon divinity. They were mighty philosophers as well. But they were content to deal with portions of the doctrine of the Faith. Being often controversialists, they were eminently successful in supporting the point of truth that was assailed, and in showing its vital importance towards preserving the integrity of the whole. They do not appear, however,—any one or any class of them,—to have attempted to put all the truth, or as the phrase now is, all the *essential* truth, into one complete system. Even the "Apologists for Christianity" appear to have aimed rather at showing its superiority to heathenism, and its accordance with sound philosophy, than at exhaustive statements and elucidations of all the truth it taught. Later writers, including even the voluminous schoolmen, remained also content with treating of portions of the faith. Very comprehensive many of them were, but none ventured the attempt to put the whole into a system.

The sixteenth century invented systematic divinity. It produced several systems indeed. It was remarkable as the era of systems. Every eminent reformer had his own system. It accorded with his peculiar germinal ideas, and was developed according to his conception of some general principle. For example, Calvin took the sovereignty of GOD for both principle and germinal idea. Putting aside whatever conflicted, as he thought, with it, and not recognizing a "duality," much less a "manifoldness," in truth, he simply followed out deductively, with hard logic, his one chosen principle. The whole systematic divinity of Calvinism flowed from this postulate. The universality of his first "logical" term being accepted, it followed of course that the Almighty Sovereign, as He knew, so also ordered all things from beginning to end. He not only "foreknew"—more accurately, was ever, eternally knowing—whatever occurred, how every man would live and act, but He actually decreed the destiny of every man from his birth. It mattered not to Calvin that every man knew himself to be free. This he treated as a general delusion. He accepted the Divine Humanity of JESUS, preached the atonement, but he brought that also within the close circuit of the single, irresistible, self-evolution, all-embracing will of the ALMIGHTY. It mattered not to him that, if the will of GOD was all, the Sacrifice was unnecessary and therefore unreal. It was GOD'S will that CHRIST should die for our sins. That was enough. GOD'S consistency was not a point for man's reason to inquire into. Submission was the single duty of the reason, as it was the sole practicability for the human person as a whole.

It will be observed that Calvinism and Romanism meet at their respective extremes. Neither has room for personal, free man. The immense, accumulated piles of Roman theology or divinity, all fall together into a system, whose practical principle is submission to one central authority, or rather usurpation. The authority of the Church—which is a fact and, within its scope, legitimate—was, under Romanism, made, first to crush the individual into one homogeneous mass, and then to put the efficient work of his salvation into the partly directing and partly ministering hands of the priesthood. This system of divinity completes itself in the infallible headship of the Pope. The whole system of Romanism stands upon a half-truth; which, like all half-truths when developed, has become a hideous distortion of the Catholic faith.

The systematic divinity of Calvin was a thoroughly logical devolution. Its fault lay in its major premise or postulate. It is true that GOD is sovereign, but it does not necessarily follow that He will, much less that He must, act purely and simply after the evolution of Almighty power. GOD is something besides the ALMIGHTY. He may have made a creature after His own image, and have endued that creature with liberty of choice, and may then have dealt with that creature according as he should exercise his granted freedom. This He clearly did. Hence Calvinism fails in its postulate, and consequently fails throughout.

Arminius was the opponent of Calvin. He took for his postulate the liberty of man. He or his followers, in the exasperation of controversy, and because of the blinding influence of his own half-truth, perhaps did seem to deny or rather diminish the Divine Sovereignty; certainly they were charged with it.

The Arminians have always accepted the doctrine of the Atonement. They have been chiefly remarkable for a system of divinity which placed the whole efficient work of salvation within the soul of the individual man. They agree with Calvinism in this respect. They differ in that they regard personal "conversion," "change of heart," or "experience of religion," not as a single operation of irresistible grace, but as an operation of grace in which the man's own will co-operates, and which may be lost and won not only once, but many times. The systematic divinity of Arminianism, having for its postulate human free-will, has developed in the direct line of opposition to Calvinism. Both, within their scope, are completed systems of divinity. Either is comparatively easy of understanding, and not difficult in evolution and practical application. Both postulates being true, and either without the other being only a half-truth, it follows that their systems, being both one-sided, are both erroneous.

Lutheranism has its systematic divinity, which differs from both Calvinism and Arminianism. It is more comprehensive than either. Lutheranism has, however, always been remarkable for its adherence to the State. Luther contended against the Pope with the aid of princes. The Emperor favored the Pope, but did not simply follow his behests. He dealt with Luther as with a political agitator. Hence proceeded a mingled religious reformation and political revolution. The two ideas reciprocally affected each other. They remain yet united. Protestant Germany has state churches, Presbyterian in form, Erastian in spirit.

The systematic, doctrinal divinity of Lutheranism is deduced from two fundamental principles,—personal spiritual liberty under direct responsibility to GOD, with the right of "private judgment," and the sufficiency in and by itself of Holy Scripture. Of course these principles entered into the whole Protestant Reformation, but in Lutheranism they were received pure and simple. They constituted its original germ and energy, and have since evolved themselves by natural development. Luther rejected not only papal usurpations, but all church authority. Nothing remained, therefore, but such lines of theological invention as proceeded from private judgment of the Written Word. Luther, his associates, and his near successors, were not exempt from the influence of traditional doctrine, and did not, therefore, wander entirely off from the primitive faith. Having dropped, however, the principle that "the Church hath authority in matters of faith," there was nothing to limit the widest application of "private judgment." His followers have not failed to use "private judgment" both in Scriptural interpretation itself, as well as in criticism, at every point and in every way, of Scripture itself. Hence the two principles so came into conflict that one had to yield. Private judgment was not the one to yield. The result was what is known as "destructive criticism," and the consequence is that the Word of GOD itself—bereft of its rightful interpreter, the primitive Church, and taken away from its appointed keeper, the living Church—is accepted, notably in Germany and by Lutherans generally, according to current knowledge, prevalent philosophy, and the critical private judgment of the day.

The chief doctrinal peculiarity of Lutheranism is solifidianism, or justification by faith only.

"Indulgences" were on sale openly. It was asserted that the "saints" had done so many more good works than were needed for their own salvation that the "Church" had a vast accumulation in its spiritual treasury, out of which it could make sales of purgatorial exemptions to those whose good works were deficient or even wholly wanting.

Luther, in his fierce opposition to such uses of "good works," naturally drifted to the opposite extreme. While Faith, or personal trust in CHRIST, is to those capable of it the sure intelligent ground for the hope of salvation, yet, as St. James shows, "faith without works is dead." Luther, in the fervor of his Protestantism, separated faith from works, leaped the barrier of the Epistle of St. James by calling it an "epistle of straw," and invented the phrase "justification by faith only." The Antinomians soon pushed this doctrine to its extreme consequences, and taught boldly that the moral law was no longer binding upon the justified in CHRIST. Luther does not appear to have liked this consequence of his own doctrine, but nevertheless held on to it, as have many of his followers since, both in and out of Lutheranism.

In fact, the distinguishing points of Lutheranism, out of which grew its whole systematic divinity, were every one true, but every one also only half the truth. Hence the system, on the whole, is one-sided; and its drift, far away from the concrete Church and doctrine of CHRIST, has been rapid, perhaps fatal.

Modern Lutheranism has drifted far off the position held by Luther and Melancthon. While it still possesses learned and able scholars, who defend the Scriptures, it has many more who apply "destructive criticism" to them. The result is a systematic divinity and prevalent theology, going by the name of Lutheranism, which holds little in common with Luther except "the right of private judgment."

The Anglican Reformation retained not only the primitive order and unbroken continuity of the Church, but asserted, even rather more strongly than did the Continental Reformers, the dignity of man, his indefeasible liberty, and direct personal responsibility to GOD, in virtue of his original creation after the Divine image, and because of his right and duty to accept for himself individually the benefits and consequent obligations of the redemption. These two points have therefore distinguished the systematic divinity of Anglicanism,—the authority of the Church and the personal liberty of man. They have been acknowledged principles from the first, and remain still living energies in both life and doctrine. Voluminous writings of able, learned, and devout theologians have already grown into a vast catalogue of Anglo-Catholic theology. It has been particularly rich in Church history. It has shown through history not only the unbroken continuity of the organic Church in England with the primitive Catholic Church, but her strict adherence also to the primitive "faith once for all delivered to the saints." Some of her divines have leaned most to the side of Church authority, and have elucidated most fully and earnestly such points as the Apostolicity of Episcopacy, the efficacy of Sacraments, and the blessed reality of the organic communion of the Saints, living and dead, in the one Body of CHRIST, in which He everywhere and always dwells, bestowing the grace of the Spirit, who Himself as "LORD and giver of Life" inspires the chosen Household of GOD, and guards His temple.

On the other hand, another able, zealous and devotional body of English divines have written largely upon Christian doctrine and practice, as they relate to personal man under the personal GOD,—FATHER, SON, and SPIRIT. With earnest orthodox zeal, they have distinguished the persons in the substantial Trinity of the One GOD; have applied all the old established doctrines of the unchanging One Faith to the mind, heart, and conscience of the individual man; have set forth clearly and strongly penitence, faith, and holy obedience, and have promoted earnestly the reproduction in living disciples of CHRIST'S example, by teaching the duty of resting on Him alone for pardon and grace, vouchsafed for His sake by the loving FATHER, and made efficient by the light and power of the HOLY GHOST.

These two classes of divines, one looking in the direction of organic Church life, and the other in the direction of individual salvation and personal immortal growth, have not always, as is natural, fully appreciated each other. Sharp and protracted theological controversies have been waged between them, within the bosom of the English Church. Their systems of divinity have been thought by many to be irreconcilable. But the English Church has remained without schism, and both schools are now at last perceiving that each holds one wing in the united citadel of the faith, and that both are joined together and made one in the common centre and Head,—CHRIST.

Divinity or theology, so far as it can be systematic, has in England a dual system. The organic principle is as essential to the unity of the Truth, as that of the indefeasible personal dignity and responsibility of man is to "the liberty wherewith CHRIST hath made us free." The form of the point of junction between these two principles is incapable of definition, because it lies hidden in the GOD-manifest, who is both the personal Saviour of every man that believeth, and the "Head over all things to His Church, which is His Body."

Such contributions as have been made to systematic divinity in America have followed very much after English examples. A more open and clearer field, however, is found in America, for a deeper exposition and wider application of the principles of manly dignity and independence. In social and political life, this principle has already developed a specifically American type. It has in these directions developed strength, force, and a prevalent confidence of power. Nor has it wholly failed in a gentle refinement, one in which self-assertion is more and more felt to be needless.

American Christianity is thrown into this current of far occidental feeling, thought, and force of evolving progress. The Church in America intrusts to her divines the work of setting her forth, clearly and definitely, amid this American development. Without the prestige enjoyed by the English Church, she cannot, even if she would, begin by claiming authority and demanding reverence. She is not helped by such social conditions as the English Church enjoys. The American people are not habitually reverent. Before they pay respect even, they wish to understand on what grounds it is claimed.

Here, then, is a new field for the Church; out of which must grow a somewhat peculiar—not new essentially, but new in order and form—systematic divinity. There is a chapter in the great book of all Catholic theology which England has commenced but never can finish. Its principle is the glorious manhood of the image of GOD, with its resplendent development through membership in CHRIST. The Church in America has to grow into the American Church. She can only do so as she absorbs into herself and sanctifies the irrepressible, because natural and providential, American instinct. The systematic divinity of the future will be that which honors and conserves man's free personality, and shows his Person, all the larger and more free, in the organic communion of the Living Church.

The GOD-man is the perfect type of humanity. He is His Church, as a body. He is "the light that lighteth every man that cometh into the world." The Americans, that will learn and know the truth, need not step outside the line of their progress. There is a nobler manliness and a larger liberty in the Church than can possibly be in the world.

Upon the whole, it is apparent that systematic divinity never can be a single treatise, nor indeed a single line of treatises, embracing the whole formal instruction in Christianity. It is contained in many books, with many chapters; some dusty and forgotten, some venerable but not now efficient, some old yet ever young, some in course of writing, some yet to be written. The subject of all, however, is the "one faith" "once for all delivered to the saints," embodied in the historic Church and manifested by the ever Living Body of CHRIST. Systems of divinity come and go; but the truth, as it is in JESUS, ever remaineth ever liveth, and goeth on forever.

REV. B. FRANKLIN, D.D.

T.

Tabernacle. The symbol of GOD's presence. The Tabernacle was the type of His Presence with His People. It was complex in its symbolism. The gradation from the outer broad admittance to all, on to the solitary entrance once a year of the High-Priest into the Holy of Holies, was a lesson upon the inner life. The Sacrifices, varying yet all upon a consulted plan, inculcating the true doctrine of sin as GOD sees it, were types of a mode of access to Him. The constant offerings taught the necessity of prayer. The ministrations of the priests in their appointed order and rank; the giving by them of the Blessing of Peace; the services of the Psalms and Hymns,—all trained the people in a conception of holiness and of the abiding presence of GOD, which should have raised them into a higher and nobler character. It did do so, but Holy Scripture ever records the sins as well as the virtues of the chosen People so impartially, that we do not feel that they were, as they really became, far above the nations around them. This teaching by rite and by symbol reached farther than the training of the people. It was the pattern of the things GOD showed Moses in the mount, with the charge to carry them out strictly. They were the shadows of the reality in CHRIST JESUS, and they even had a preventing grace, an anticipatory character, and so were to teach the great truth of the Atonement for sin. They were a declaration of GOD's will and purpose upon the law of worship, which we are to offer willingly, as it is in Psalms of the new birth of the Church in CHRIST: "In the day of Thy power shall the people offer Thee free-will offering with an holy worship: the dew of Thy birth is of the womb of the morning." It is but following out the comment of the Epistle to the Hebrews, as illustrated by the Vision of the Revelation, to hold that the Mosaic ritual, a shadow of the good things to come, is a guide to us in reverently seeking the Divine will as to worship in the freedom and the liberty of the glorious Gospel of CHRIST.

Te Deum. The noblest of the uninspired hymns, if indeed it can be truly said that it is not inspired. Its origin is very dim. The story that it was a responsive improvisation in the enthusiasm of the moment by St. Ambrose and St. Augustine when the latter was baptized is only a beautiful legend. Its material was most probably gathered from many devotional sources. St. Cyprian's tract, "De Mortalitate," closes with a strain very like "the glorious company of the Apostles praise Thee:" "*There* is the glorious company of the Apostles. *There* is the number of exulting prophets. There is the innumerable multitude of the martyrs." The passages in the hymns at the end of St. Clement of Alexandria's works are evidently the source of much of the *Te Deum*. Other material may yet be forthcoming; and it may well have been sung, not in its present state, but in some fragmentary form, at St. Augustine's baptism. It was most evidently a growth that has become perfected by the joyful use in the public worship of innumerable holy hearts. The earliest notice of it is in the rule of Cæsarius (527 A.D.). From that time it passed into more and more frequent use. It is often chanted after a victory or a great deliverance. The famous *Te Deum* which Handel wrote was upon the victory at Dettingen. The constant use in daily worship passed into the English Prayer-Book of Edward VI. (1549 A.D.). Its permissory use outside of the daily service is in the Forms of Prayer to be used at Sea, when it may be used, after the anthem appointed to be used after a Victory. In Edward's first Prayer-Book it was not to be used in Lent, but the *Benedicite* was to be substituted for it, but this direction was omitted afterwards.

Temple. The first Temple vowed, and prepared for, by King David, and built from his plans and with the treasure he had accumulated by his son Solomon, upon Mount Zion. It was seven years in building, and so faithfully were the plans of the architects carried out and the varied parts so well prepared, that when the Temple was erected there was neither hammer, nor axe, nor any tool of iron heard in the house while it was building. The cost of the work was immense. The total sum (supposing money to have been worth sixteen times as much then as now) exceeded three hundred millions of dollars. Its equipments for worship were complete, and perhaps the most splendid, as they certainly were the most extensive, ever made. The Temple on its completion was consecrated with magnificent pomp and a profusion of sacrifices which are unparalleled. But it must be noticed that these ceremonies followed, did not precede the offer of the Temple to JEHOVAH.

When the ark was put into its place, then the glory of the LORD descended, and by its insupportable presence drove the priests into the outer court, where they made their offerings. After this Solomon uttered the grand prayer of dedication. In its relation to the Tabernacle, the Temple was the type of the Christian dispensation in its relation to the Mosaic. It completed, set in order, and celebrated with a greater splendor the typical ritual of the Law which could not be so carried out, and was in fact intermittently used for many years. It is used also in relation to the Christian life as a type of the indwelling of the HOLY GHOST. "What!" exclaims St. Paul, "know ye not that ye are the Temple of GOD?" "that your body is the Temple of the HOLY GHOST which is in you, which ye have of GOD, and ye are not your own?" (1 Cor. iii. 16; vi. 19.) Again, the service of GOD in the Temple was the home of the Christian Liturgy. There is a parallelism in the two, which shows that the one was the pattern for the other. Its choral character impressed itself on the Christian worship. Its responsive structure has been taken up and enlarged. Its intercessory services are re-impleaded with the one, full, perfect, and sufficient sacrifice through which all our pleadings are offered. The great festivals, so significantly carried out in the Temple worship, were transferred under a more spiritual meaning into the Christian worship. Looked at in every way, the Temple in its glory is the type and the earlier pattern of so much which belongs to the Church of GOD. It is probable that the Temple worship did not always retain such stately splendor. Only in Solomon's day, in the reformation of Hezekiah, and at the restoration of Josiah, was there a full realization of it. In the Second Temple and in Herod's Temple there were wanting several things which especially belonged to the Solomonic Temple. The ark had perished. The glory did not rest upon either one. The perfect appointments of vessels and of minor details were wanting. As in so many other of GOD's dealings, His gifts are not recognized. The presence of CHRIST in the Second Temple, which was indeed its greater glory, was not acknowledged, but His people drove out and gave up to be crucified Him who was at once the Presence and the Priest.

Temptation. This word has been and is used so confusedly, that it is difficult to force on men's minds the real meaning of the word in the several places where it may occur. The intention under the word at the place in which it is used, affects its force very seriously. Properly and in a good sense, it is but the trial under which a superior always places an inferior as a test of his trustiness. This is always admitted as being perfectly fair in our daily life. So GOD tried, tempted, tested Abraham. So every opportunity that is put in our hands is a trial, a test, a temptation. But it has an evil sense, when we turn what was a test to evil ends; so GOD's fair tests may by our evil take a worse turn, and we yield, either by our own carnal will, or by suggestion of the devil, to the evil side of the trial. So Adam was justly tempted by GOD, but was ignorantly tempted by Eve, who was herself evilly tempted by the devil. A third sense still lower, and the usual one, is when the devil tempts us to sin; in this case we use most commonly the word in its worst meaning. The devil tempted Eve with wicked intention, Eve tempted Adam ignorantly; out of these comes a fourth form, when men tempt each other to sin, whether wittingly or unwittingly. And lastly, when men tempt themselves; for it is a wonderful power in our human nature that a man can, as it were, go outside of himself and tempt himself to sin, as if he were a second person.

This life, which should be a holy probation, is by our sinfulness and by the combinations of causes beyond us, a time of temptation, which descends from the trial which fits for heaven through every step to the sin that destroys the soul. And a single probation from GOD, by the interference of men and the secret temptations of the fiend, and by our own weakness, either from habit or from carelessness, may become a temptation. The petition in the LORD's Prayer, "Lead us not into temptation," while one of the most difficult to explain, yet is one of the most needful of its petitions. It is the cry of the trembling soul to a merciful CREATOR to lighten its trial, to relieve and to strengthen it in the mortal struggle, to open the WAY of escape. Temptation is the sin-tainted form for GOD's holy probation. In every way our LORD's temptations are an example for ourselves to use, and in themselves are the Victory that He must win that we may be more than conquerors in Him. His temptations were not only the ones which assailed Him after His fast, nor were they those that His enemies put upon Him; but the temptations He speaks of when He saith, "Ye are they that have continued with me in my temptations," are those trials which as the SON of Man, tempted in all points like as we are, He had to endure,—the jarring against His perfect nature by the weak and faithless, the ignorant and unbelieving. His temptations conclude all that was necessary to make Him master of our weaknesses, failings, and temptations. For this cause He is not ashamed to call us brethren. The extent and subtlety of temptation, the power to resist it, the power granted to Satan to tempt, the relation so wonderful of our LORD's sympathy with the tempted, and His ever-present help, are all subjects that need a far longer discussion than space allows, and to indicate without developing each of these would be to do harm rather than good. Every Commentary should supply some light upon these questions, and the innumerable sermons upon it published, and which are easily accessible, would give more instruction than could be given in a few sentences here.

Tennessee, History of the Protestant Episcopal Church in. Unlike those of some of the older States, its records do not extend far into the past, only dating from 1829 A.D. Five or six years before this period, Bishop Otey emigrated to Tennessee, and preached to congregations at Franklin, and Columbia, and Nashville, at which latter place the Episcopal Church in Tennessee, July 1, 1829 A.D., was first regularly organized. Upon this occasion a meeting was held, and a Constitution and Canons for the government and regulation of the Protestant Episcopal Church in Tennessee were adopted. At this meeting there were present only three clergymen, Rev. Daniel Stephens, Rev. James H. Otey, and the Rev. John Davis, and nine laymen. Bishops Ravenscroft and Mead visited Tennessee, the former presiding at the first Convention of the Church in Tennessee. On the 29th of June, 1833 A.D., the Rev. James H. Otey was elected Bishop of Tennessee, and immediately after his consecration, January 14, 1834 A.D., he entered upon the duties of the Episcopate, and for nearly thirty years, not only as the Bishop of Tennessee, but also as Missionary Bishop of Arkansas, Louisiana, Mississippi, and Florida, most faithfully dispensed the word of life. The coadjutors of Bishop Otey were not many, but their interest in the Church never diminished. After the election of Bishop Otey the prospects of the Church were encouraging. The Book of Common Prayer was sought after, books explanatory of our doctrines and worship were read, Sunday-schools, Missionary Societies, and institutions of learning were established.

The progress of the Church was seriously impeded by the civil war. Some of the churches were without clergymen, her people scattered, and the perils of the times seemed to extinguish the zeal of the freeness of the Church. At the close of the war a special Convention was held at Nashville, at which Rev. C. T. Quintard was elected Bishop, and from that time the Church has gradually progressed. Churches were organized in many places: in Memphis 3, Bolivar 1, Jackson 1, Cleveland 1, Chattanooga 1, Cumberland Furnace 1, Sewanee 1, Trenton 1, Tullahoma 1, Edgefield 1, Knoxville 2, Greenville 1, Mason 1, Brownsville 1, Pulaski 1, Covington 1, Winchester 1

Shelbyville 1, Nashville 2, besides many missionary stations. Sewanee is the University of the South. At Columbia is a flourishing female school, and also one in Bolivar.

Statistics for 1886 A.D.: Clergy, 45; parishes, 29; missions, 38; candidates for H. O., 3; ordinations diac., 2; pr., 3; baptisms, 620; confirmed, 415; communicants, 4031; contributions, $83,194.58.

REV. GEO. WHITE, D.D.

Tenure of Church Property. The property with which this article has to do consists mainly in Houses of Worship, Rectories, buildings devoted to eleemosynary, hospital, or educational purposes, and their appurtenant grounds. From the nature of the case it is apparent that the tenure by which this property is held must of necessity be fiduciary in its character. It is, therefore, of the first importance that the legal title, in whomsoever vested, be firmly impressed with the trust which it is intended to subserve, and that this trust be so clearly defined and securely guarded as to be protected, beyond peradventure, against diversion or misuse. Not only is this precaution important in order to secure the benefits intended to flow from the property of the Church already in possession, but additionally so in respect of encouraging gifts, bequests, and devises, which for want of it might be withheld.

The General Convention of 1880 A.D. having had its attention drawn to the subject of Church incorporations and the methods of tenure of Church property by the Deputies in that body from the Diocese of Minnesota, took action in the matter by the appointment of a Commission to inquire into and report upon the subject. The report of that Commission made to the General Convention of 1883 A.D. so fully and ably presents the whole matter, that we shall content ourself with adopting and reproducing here its principal parts.

In a communication published under date of February 6, 1881 A.D., the Chairman of the Commission, the Right Rev. the Bishop of Central New York, set forth the objects sought to be attained by the appointment of the Commission, and the importance to the Church of close attention to the practical bearing of the subject.

Attention was called to the frequent loss of gifts, bequests, and property through defects or irregularity in legal forms, and to the "waste in Dioceses, Parishes, and public charities for the want of duly constituted and qualified trust corporations empowered to receive and manage the endowments."

Reference was made to facts then already brought to the attention of the Commission, showing the disaster resulting from imperfect legislation, fiduciary negligence, and the ignorance of testators.

A request was made for facts, opinions, and suggestions; and the following recommendations were made to all Dioceses in the United States where such action had not already been taken:

1. To consider the expediency of obtaining, if possible, from the legislative authority in each State or Territory, an Act making the Diocese itself, or its Convention or Council, a legal corporation, qualified to receive and hold in trust any Church property designed for religious, benevolent, or educational purposes, under suitable conditions.

2. To appoint, from time to time, a committee to examine the state, title, and securities of all funds or investments or real property having a Diocesan character.

3. To require every parish to report to the Diocesan Convention or Council whether there is good ground to believe that its right to receive and hold property is good under the provisions of the common or statute law.

As a result of this action, the subject was drawn under consideration in several of the Diocesan Conventions; and with respect to what has already been done, both before and since the appointment of the Commission, it may fairly be said that there has been a good beginning, and some progress in the direction indicated in the suggestions made.

In August last a circular letter was prepared, containing ten questions intended to elicit information upon the whole subject; and copies were sent to the Bishops, and also to the Secretaries of the Diocesan Conventions.

To this letter from only nineteen Dioceses have answers been received containing information of some value, but not full enough to furnish the material for such a report as the Commission desired to make, nor to offer a basis for the compilation of statistics, either comprehensive or exact.

Enough has been ascertained, however, to warrant the estimate that the aggregate value of property held by the Church, for various uses, cannot be less than thirty millions of dollars, not including the large properties controlled by Trinity Parish in New York. The control of this large interest is distributed among more than three thousand corporations in different States, with different powers, subject to different trusts; and it is to be feared, at the very least, more than half of it not impressed with the trusts to which it is intended to be applied in such manner as to insure the protection of the law.

It will, in the judgment of the Commission, be impossible for any candid mind to apply itself to even a superficial examination of this subject without being duly impressed with the lack of system, uncertainty, and ineffectiveness with which these great property interests are secured to the future use and benefit of the Church. And, in most of the Dioceses, there are now possibilities of loss, which by greater legal precision, and the adoption of accurate forms of conveyance, well-considered corporate supervision, and attention to the clear and legal definition of trusts, might be reduced to a minimum, if not absolutely avoided.

It might be presumed that, with respect to the Church buildings and Rectories, the interest of the individual Parishes would be strong enough to afford adequate protection. We venture, however, to hazard the assertion that, in Dioceses where this subject has not been especially and carefully considered and acted upon, it will be found to be the rule that there is no barrier which could, in case of necessity, be interposed to prevent the diversion of the property from its legitimate use, or its being hopelessly encumbered by any Vestry which might, by accident or otherwise, find itself in the control of it. The Canon upon the subject of the alienation and incumbrance of Church property affords no legal protection whatever, as has been demonstrated in several notable cases arising in the courts of law.

Such, generally stated, being the condition of affairs, it is apparent that the subject demands the most careful consideration and serious attention of the Church. The remedy for these evils, however, cannot be furnished or applied through the General Convention, but must be sought in and through the several Dioceses.

It is very important that it be clearly understood that the subject cannot be covered by Canonical legislation, either general or Diocesan, but must be controlled by the statute law of the respective States. The provisions of Canon 24, Title I., have, of themselves, only moral, not legal, force, to prevent alienation or incumbrance contrary to its provisions. The effect of the existing Canon has probably been misleading in creating a false impression of security. What is needed is, not a provision depending upon voluntary action, but one which will restrain a Vestry which does not consider itself bound by the Canon, and makes the Church property useless to a purchaser, because available for no other use than that to which it has been consecrated.

If there is to be a Canon on the subject, it would seem to be desirable to so frame it as to secure the execution of its provisions *ex vi termini*. And it is practicable to require by General Canon, that for the future, the title to real estate for Church buildings, Chapels, and Rectories shall be taken only under conveyances expressly defining a trust, the general terms of which might possibly be set forth. The Commission have not considered it within the proper scope of the present report to suggest any Canonical legislation. If, upon consideration, the Committees on Canons should deem such legislation advisable, it would not be difficult to frame such amendments as would accomplish what is intended by the present Canon, at least wherever the common-law doctrine of uses and trusts is in force.

Beyond this point legislation by the General Convention could not go; since the title to real property must be acquired and held under such diverse systems of law as, were there no other reason, to forbid any attempt to furnish unvarying forms and methods.

It was, nevertheless, a timely measure of prudence for the General Convention to direct attention to a subject so vital in its relation to the future welfare and prosperity of the Church. Already its action has led, in more than one instance, to Diocesan action; and it is believed that, if the present interest be not suffered to abate, few, if any, Dioceses will fail to make proper provision for the future security of their property.

Entertaining these views, the Commission has not considered the scope of its authority—conferred by the somewhat indefinite resolution under which it was appointed—to go beyond the collection of information, and the suggestion of such general principles of action as might be safely recommended.

While it is to be regretted that the information obtained has been so meagre, it is yet sufficient to show the necessity for prompt and energetic action to secure permanence in the tenure of Church property, and the creation of suitable Church corporations with such powers as to make them available for all present or future necessities of a Diocese.

Without entering into or attempting to prescribe details, except for the purpose of illustration, the Commission desire most earnestly to direct attention to these vital points:

1. It is of the utmost importance that, upon the *title* of every separate property dedicated to the uses of the Church, there be impressed a trust which will be so clear and well defined as to secure it for all time against diversion, and to protect it against the contingency of being alienated from its legitimate use, either directly or through the medium of incumbrances, even by the action, or with the assent, of those who happen, for the time being, to be entitled to its use.

With proper attention to legal forms the end may be secured, whether the legal title to the property be vested in the Parochial or in a Diocesan corporation.

It is not within the province of the Commission to decide between the two systems; but it may be permitted to suggest some of the advantages which accrue from an adequate Diocesan provision for the separation of the legal from the equitable title.

The former may be vested in such corporations as are hereafter recommended, as a dry trust, which in certain contingencies— as, for example, the failure of the Parish organization — would become an active trust, subject to proper limitations to be prescribed in each case. The use may, in such case, be vested absolutely in the Parish, and subject to its control for every legitimate end as fully as under an absolute conveyance to it. If there be objection in any quarter to the application of this system to existing Parishes, it may be made compulsory only for the future, and voluntary as to others. If the admirable features of this system are understood, it may, when that is desired by a Diocesan Convention, be safely left to work its own way to popular favor, when the necessary machinery is provided to make it practicable.

What is termed, for convenience, the Diocesan system, has the additional advantage of providing a proper custodian of the property when, from any cause, there ceases to be a local Parish or organization to use and to protect it. The provision of a corporation of the Diocese, to hold the legal title to real estate held for Parochial as well as Diocesan purposes, also furnishes the necessary machinery hereafter recommended for the convenient administration of trusts of every species of property, whether the amount be large or small, and secures its application to the purpose designated by the donor.

It is a fact well understood, that the want of security and certainty for the future restrains many pious and benevolent persons from making gifts, devises, or bequests, which would otherwise be secured to some one of the many objects for which the Church is constantly appealing for pecuniary aid.

The frequent changes in the Vestries, the composition of very many of them, and the confessed impossibility of present improvement in this respect, together with the fact that they are intrusted with the care of the property interests which were never intended to be at the disposal of any one generation, —all demonstrate the impropriety of having these important interests at the mercy of so unstable and accidental a guardian.

It is to be remembered, on the other hand, that care must be taken, where titles are vested in the Diocesan corporation, that nothing shall be done to weaken the sense of responsibility of the Parishes and local authorities for maintaining the services of the Church, and doing their work to the extent of their ability. The suggestion of the Diocesan system does not affect the relation of the Parish to its property, since upon it must rest the entire responsibility and actual control as heretofore.

Another measure, already adopted in some States, for the protection of Church buildings and real estate of kindred character, is a statutory provision forbidding the alienation of such property without the prior approval of a competent court of equity. The publicity attending applications to the court under such laws insures an opportunity for all interested parties to be heard; and, if these laws should be extended to embrace mortgages as well as absolute conveyances, they would probably afford adequate protection. Where, under the practice of a Diocese, the title is vested in the Parochial corporation or local trustees, the passage of such a law would be a valuable safeguard; and even where the legal title is vested in a Diocesan body, though the necessity is less pressing, it is still an additional security if alienation and incumbrance of the Church building, at least, be only permitted under the direction of the court. Such laws exist in the States of Virginia and Ohio, and possibly in others not reported to the Commission.

2. This naturally suggests the other branch of inquiry included in the resolution under which the Commission was appointed.

The necessity of a comprehensive Diocesan corporation, capable in law of holding any species of property upon any trust which may be ingrafted upon it, is apparent, and now becoming so generally recognized as to require statement only, and not discussion.

Such a corporation may be comprehensive enough to administer any and every trust within the Diocese, whether its object be Diocesan or Parochial, and whether it be strictly ecclesiastical, or one of those eleemosynary, educational, or benevolent foundations which are already frequent, and, as the real spirit of the Divine Master more thoroughly permeates the Church, will the more abound if the creation of proper Diocesan agencies insures fidelity in their execution and reasonable certainty in their future safe-keeping.

Such corporations, responsible to the Diocesan Convention or Council, are annually subjected to the scrutiny which business considerations render necessary; and embarrassments to the trust by death or resignation of trustees, and the lapse or loss of trust property, are thus guarded against with absolute certainty.

Such corporations appear, from the reports made to the Convention, to have been already provided in several Dioceses; and the number of them is increasing. Some of those already created are very comprehensive, and will afford satisfactory precedents for similar legislation for Dioceses which have not yet acted upon the subject.

3. In order to secure both or either of these points, it will be essential for each Diocesan Convention to provide, as early as is practicable, for the thorough examination of the condition of its titles, and the tenure of its property; and to obtain from the legislature such enactments as shall be found necessary to secure adequate protection for the future. At the same time, the creation of such Diocesan corporate bodies as may be required should be secured.

Where, as is done in some cases, the Diocese is itself incorporated, there should be provision in the charter for the administration of trusts and property interests by a board of trustees with some degree of permanence, rather than by so transitory a body as the Diocesan Convention. The trustees may be elected by the Convention for fixed terms, or may be named in the Act of Incorporation, with provision for filling vacancies by vote of the Convention or otherwise.

The Commission recommend that this subject be presented to the attention of the several Dioceses more effectually than will be accomplished by the publication of this Report in the Journal. If it be deemed advisable, provision may also be made for the continuance of this Joint Commission, to be charged with the duty of assisting, when such assistance shall be requested, in the formulation of Diocesan and legislative action, suggesting well-considered forms of conveyance and the collection of information, to be reported to the next General Convention.

The passage of the following resolutions is respectfully recommended:

1. *Resolved* (the House of Bishops concurring), That it is recommended to each Diocese to obtain, without delay, such legislation as may be found necessary with respect to the existing laws of the State, for the protection of its property, real and personal, and whether held for Diocesan or Parochial uses.

2. *Resolved* (the House of Bishops concurring), That all real estate held in any Diocese, for Diocesan or Parochial purposes, should have the use for which it is held impressed upon its title.

3. *Resolved* (the House of Bishops concurring), That a form of conveyance should be provided, under which churches shall acquire title to real estate, with proper limitations in trust.

4. *Resolved* (the House of Bishops concurring), That the Committees on Canons be, and they are hereby, requested to consider and report if, in their judgment, Canon 24, Title I., should be amended so as to require that title to real estate for Churches, Chapels, or Rectories shall be so taken as that the trusts under which they are held shall be limited in the conveyance.

5. *Resolved* (the House of Bishops concurring), That a permanent board of trustees, with proper provision for filling vacancies, should be legally incorporated in each Diocese, to take charge of and control all such property of the Diocese or of its Parishes as may be intrusted to it. When the Diocese is itself incorporated, the Act of Incorporation should provide for the exercise of its corporate powers in the care of property, and the administration of trusts, by a board of trustees having some permanence of organization, rather than directly by the Diocesan Convention.

6. *Resolved* (the House of Bishops concurring), That the joint commission upon Church Incorporations and the Tenure of Church Property be, and the same is hereby, continued for the purpose of assisting, when requested, in the formulation of Diocesan and legislative action, suggesting forms of conveyance, and the collection of further information to be reported to the next General Convention.

Ter Sanctus. The Hymn which Isaiah heard in his vision in the Temple (Isa. vi. 1-4), and which has been ever used in the Celebration of the Holy Communion. The Preface at the ordinary celebration or the Proper one for the Feast having been recited, the Priest begins the Ascription alone:

"Therefore with Angels and Archangels, and with all the company of heaven, we laud and magnify Thy glorious Name; evermore praising Thee, and saying—"

Then the Priest and people together chant:

"Holy, holy, holy, LORD GOD of Hosts, Heaven and Earth are full of the Majesty of Thy Glory. Glory be to Thee, O LORD most High. Amen."

This is a shorter form (both in the immediate Preface and in the *Ter Sanctus*) than in other Liturgies. The Sanctus in the form usual elsewhere ended with the words, "Hosanna in the highest, Blessed is he that cometh in the name of the LORD. Hosanna in the Highest." There seems to be no assignable reason for the change from a venerable form. In the preceding words, "Therefore," etc., the form was different in every Western Liturgy, and was probably made variable from a very early date, while the Eastern Liturgies clung to a single unvarying Preface. (*Vide* PREFACE.)

Testament. The word for Testament is also the one for Covenant, but the translators of the English Bible have not always observed this, and have used the word indifferently, but to our loss, as in Heb. ix. 19, 20, where it must mean Covenant, as it is correctly translated in Gal. iii. 15, and this mistranslation has passed into the Words of Institution in the Communion office when the Priest recites the words, "This is my blood of the New Testament," in place of the New Covenant, which was our LORD'S full meaning. (*Vide* COVENANT.) But the word is now usually used of the New Testament, and when the whole Bible is referred to by it, it is customary to use the phrase, "the Old and New Testaments."

Testament, Old.—The Old Testament, as a volume, begins with an inspired account of the creation of the world in Genesis, and closes in Malachi with a prophecy of the coming of CHRIST. It comprises Divine accounts of history, and sacred laws, and prophecies, and Psalms and Proverbs. An ancient division of the entire book made three parts—the Law, the Prophets, and the Hagiographa, or Holy Writings. "The Law" included the Pentateuch,—that is, the first five books of Scripture. "The Prophets" contained Joshua, Judges, Ruth, Samuel, Kings, Isaiah, Jeremiah, Lamentations, Ezekiel, Daniel, the twelve Minor Prophets, Job, Ezra, Nehemiah, and Esther. The Hagiographa embraced the Psalms, the Proverbs, Ecclesiastes, and the Song of Solomon. Afterwards the Jews made a different division. The Jewish historian, Josephus, who was contemporary with the Apostles, divides the Old Testament into the Law, the Prophets, and "Hymns and Instructions for Men's Lives." There is a similar division in Philo. Our LORD'S words are, "that all things must be fulfilled which were written in the law of Moses, and in the Prophets, and in the Psalms concerning Me" (St. Luke xxiv. 44). In this phrase the Hagiographa are styled Psalms. The Pentateuch or Law was divided into sections, to be read as lessons in the synagogues on the Sabbath-Day, as we now read Scripture lessons in church. In the dispersion of the Jews, the synagogues, with their Scripture readings and teachings, prepared the way for Christianity. One of the most striking scenes in the New Testament relates the blending of the old and new dispensations in a Jewish synagogue. Our Blessed LORD in Nazareth, "as His custom was,"—a lesson of worship for mortals,— "went into the synagogue on the Sabbath-Day," and read and commented on the outpouring of GOD'S Spirit of blessing described in Isaiah, and declared the prophecy fulfilled in Himself (St. Luke iv. 16-22). The ancient Book of GOD in the hands of the SON of GOD is a sublime picture (see also Acts xv. 21, and xiii. 15). The Jews kept the Holy Scriptures in a sacred chest, and thrice a week they were read in the synagogues. Every seven years, at the Feast of Tabernacles, when all Israel were assembled before the LORD, the law of the LORD was read (Josh. viii. 35). The sacredness of the five books of the Law is seen in the fact that they were, by the command of Moses, deposited by the Ark of the Covenant, within the Holy of Holies, on which the Divine Presence rested (Deut. xxxi. 9, 26). Sometimes the phrase "the Law and the Prophets" includes the whole Old Testament. Both in the Old and New Testaments a prophet means not simply one who predicts, but also "any one sent by GOD." See St. Luke xxiv. 27, where CHRIST speaks of " Moses and all the prophets," and immediately the words " all the Scriptures" follow. In St. Matt. xxii. 40, " All the law and the prophets" appears to include all the Old Testament, as in St. Matt. vii. 12, and xi. 13. So highly did the Jews reverence their sacred Scriptures that they were ready to die, if necessary, for "the Oracles of GOD."

One interesting fact which meets us in beginning the Old Testament is the great age which was then granted to men. Methuselah lived from Adam to Noah, Shem conversed with Noah and Abraham. Isaac conversed with Abraham and Joseph, from whom traditions might have been easily conveyed to Moses by Amram, "who lived long enough with Joseph." "When first revelation was given to man, men's lives were so long, that there was little danger lest the light of truth should be lost; Adam, Seth, Enoch, Methuselah, Noah, were in fact all but contemporaries. Seth, the son of Adam, lived to within fifteen years of the birth of Noah. Tradition, therefore, may have sufficed for them; and yet we have reason to believe that, even then, the faith was much corrupted." (Browne on the Articles.) Hence various Revelations have been needed, and GOD has given them from the days of Moses to the time of St. John. The Old Testament is a Covenant between GOD and man (Ex. xxiv. 3-12; Deut. v. 2; Gen. xv.; Ex. xxiv.; Jer. xxxii. 22). The Mosaic Covenant or Testament was an agreement which engaged the Hebrews to worship GOD alone, while in return GOD promised that they should be His chosen people. The Christian religion is a New Testament or Covenant (St. Matt. xxvi. 28). Hence St. Paul speaks of "the two Covenants" (Gal. iv. 24) The Covenant of Sinai and the Covenant of Calvary are alike parts of GOD'S plan for man's redemption. The New Covenant is that of forgiveness through faith in CHRIST. The Old Testament looks forward to CHRIST. He asserts that they testify of Him (St. John v. 39). The New Testament is the key to the Old. The Seed of the woman is promised in Eden, and born in Bethlehem. Our LORD in the Sermon on the Mount shows "how deep is the moral teaching implied in its letter." The prophecies foretold CHRIST. In Isa. liii. the crucifixion is plainly foreshadowed. As the Jewish Church was under a Theocracy, so is the Church under CHRIST. "The Law was our schoolmaster to bring us unto CHRIST" (Gal. iii. 24).

The promise to Abraham concerning his seed, and to David about his son, and the types of passover and scape-goat, and the sacrifices on the Day of Atonement, and the consecration of the High-Priest, all point to CHRIST. St. Paul speaks of the Jews as eating "spiritual meat" and drinking " spiritual drink: for they drank of that spiritual Rock that followed them : and that Rock was CHRIST" (1 Cor. x. 3, 4). The same Spirit is needed and promised to those who seek to know the Scriptures now (St. Luke xi. 13). The Church has been commissioned to hand the Scriptures down to us, as the Samaritan woman brought her townspeople to CHRIST. The liturgical use of Scripture in Lessons and Psalms has kept it before the people, and so the Church has been the keeper of Holy Writ. To speak of the various books of the Old Testament: Genesis signifies generation, or production, and tells of the generation of all things. Exodus is the departure of the Israelites from Egypt. Leviticus contains the Laws of Sacrifices and the Institution of the Priesthood. Numbers has an account of the numbering of the Israelites, with a part of their history. Deuteronomy means the second law, or the law repeated. It also gives a history of Moses. Joshua gives name to a book which contains his acts. Judges gives the administration of thirteen Judges from Joshua's death to the time of Eli. The book of Ruth is generally considered as an appendix to the book of Judges and an introduction to that of Samuel.

Ruth was an ancestress of David, and so of CHRIST. This Moabitish damsel's history is thought to be an intimation of the reception of the Gentiles into the Christian Church. It also shows GOD'S providential care over those who fear Him. The greater part of 1 Samuel is supposed to have been written by Samuel. The names and characters of Samuel, Eli, Saul, and David are mingled with Jewish history in 1 and 2 Samuel. In the books of Kings, Solomon and his successors appear, and the division of the kingdom occurs, and finally the tribes go into captivity. The Chronicles contain Genealogical Tables and Histories. The book of Ezra harmonizes with, and illustrates the prophecies of Haggai and Zechariah; it shows GOD'S Fatherly care over His people. Nehemiah narrates the rebuilding of the walls of Jerusalem by his oversight, and the two reformations accomplished by him. The noble Queen Esther deservedly gives name to the book which records her pious deed of self-sacrifice for her nation. The Poetical Books are Job, Psalms, Proverbs, Ecclesiastes, and the Song of Solomon. In Job we see the patriarchal doctrines, and a prophecy of resurrection, and a delineation of final retribution. The Psalms the Hebrews styled the Book of Hymns, or praises; they were to be sung with the voice, accompanied with instruments of music. As to the name, see St. Luke xx. 42. The use of the Psalter in the Church Services keeps up an echo of the Temple worship through the centuries. They are often termed the Psalms of David, because he was the chief author. Many of them refer to CHRIST, "Great David's Greater Son." "The book of Proverbs has always been ascribed to Solomon," though it has been doubted whether he wrote every maxim. It instructs men in the mysteries of wisdom and understanding, the perfection of which is the knowledge and fear of GOD. The Apostles frequently quote it. Ecclesiastes signifies a Preacher. The book is ascribed to Solomon. As for the title, see chap. i. 1, 12. The object of the book is to display the vanity of earth, and to draw men to communion with GOD, as the "only permanent good," and to teach that happiness must be sought "beyond the grave." The "vanity of vanities" (ch. i. 2) rings through the book until "the conclusion of the whole matter: Fear GOD, and keep His commandments: for this is the whole duty of man" (ch. xii. 18). The Song of Solomon is generally deemed "a mystical poem, or allegory." It is full of Oriental figures. Scott considers it as intended "to describe the state of his (the Christian's) heart at different times, and to excite admiring, adoring, grateful love to GOD our Saviour." The Prophetical Books are chiefly prophecy, though history and doctrine are also to be found in them. They are sixteen in number, the Lamentations being considered an appendix to Jeremiah. The Greater Prophets are Isaiah, Jeremiah, Ezekiel, and Daniel, so designated from the size of their books. The Minor Prophets are Hosea, Joel, Amos, Jonah, Obadiah, Micah, Nahum, Habakkuk, Zephaniah, Haggai, Zechariah, and Malachi. This "Goodly Fellowship of the Prophets," as the *Te Deum* styles them, all point to the coming CHRIST: "To Him give all the prophets witness" (Acts x. 43). In reading the Two Testaments, or Covenants, we should reflect that a proper Covenant implies the agreement of two parties, and if GOD gives miracles and prophecies, and sends His Blessed SON to die for man, man must on his part in faith accept the benefits. "He that hath the SON hath life; and he that hath not the SON of GOD hath not life" (1 John v. 12). "Now the GOD of hope fill you with all joy and peace in believing, that ye may abound in hope, through the power of the HOLY GHOST" (Rom. xv. 13).

Authorities: Browne on the Articles, Chr. Wordsworth on the Canon, and Com. on the Gr. Test., Encyc. Amer., Jos. Francis Thrupp in Wm. Smith's Dict. of the Bible, Horne's Introduction. As to Ruth and the Gentile world, see Lange in Van Oosterzee's Christian Dogmatics.

Testament, New.—The New Testament, as a complete book, consists of four Gospels, the Acts of the Apostles, twenty-one Epistles, and the prophetic book of the Revelation of St. John the divine. The life and teaching of Our Saviour JESUS CHRIST form the topic of the New Testament. It begins with the events which preceded the birth of JESUS, and ends with a picture of the "same JESUS" in glory, and a declaration that He who came once in humility will come again in power to judgment. The crucifixion and atonement—the act of CHRIST'S death, and its blessed effects—are the central points in this volume. As the Old Testament in the Prophets and Psalms testified of the coming CHRIST, the New Testament declares that He has come. A connecting link throughout this varied book is found in St. John, the beloved disciple. He commences his Gospel by saying, "In the beginning was the Word" (compare Gen. i. 1). He ends the Revelation with a prayer for CHRIST'S second advent, and the blessing through CHRIST. His great age permitted him to see the working of the Church after CHRIST'S Ascension, and to complete the Gospels. His personal association with our LORD gives deep interest to all his teachings. In the endearment of love he never loses the thought of his LORD'S divinity. Well did the ancients make the soaring eagle an emblem of St. John The zeal of St. Peter and the logic of St. Paul supplemented the work of St. John. The Epistles show much human feeling, as especially the wide-hearted salutations of St. Paul in Rom. xvi. The description of the earthly life of CHRIST is closed in the beginning of the book of Acts. The lives and acts of CHRIST'S disciples, and the doctrines they taught, through the guiding of the HOLY SPIRIT, form the rest of the New Testament. In their teachings these men of GOD, like their Master, constantly appealed to the Old Testament, so that the quotations from that book are numerous. The teaching is intensely personal and practical. CHRIST is represented as a Person, and man's relation to Him here and hereafter is to be the incentive to Christian living.

St. Paul was "in Christ" (2 Cor. xii. 2). Believers were "baptized into JESUS CHRIST" (Rom. vi. 3). St. Paul is "crucified with CHRIST." "CHRIST liveth in" him (Gal. ii. 20). Hence "to live is CHRIST, and to die is gain." (Phil. i. 21). Then the New Testament is not a mere story. It is the tremendous announcement of the saving work of the SON of GOD, not to be debated over, but to be reverently received, as the starving man grasps at food. The Collect for the second Sunday in Advent teaches how it is to be digested. The early Church saw in the Four Gospels a representation of the Cherubim seen by Ezekiel (ch. i. 5–26, and x. 1–22). Like them they bear GOD "on a winged throne into all lands," moving by the Spirit's guidance. Like them they are "joined together," are "full of eyes," and sparkle with heavenly light. Like them, they sweep from heaven to earth, and from earth to heaven, and fly with lightning's speed, and with the noise of many waters. Their sound is gone out into all lands, and their words unto the end of the world" (Ps. xix. 4). St. John sees these Four Living Creatures in heaven, and they cry, "Holy, holy, holy, LORD GOD Almighty, which was and is, and is to come" (Rev. iv. 4–11). Each Evangelist has his particular mode of displaying CHRIST. St. Augustine shows that St. Matthew more fully declares CHRIST's Kingly character. His genealogy is from David the King, by a line of Kings, and the wise men do homage to the "King of the Jews." St. Luke dilates on the Priestly character of our LORD, and describes the sacrificial offerings made for the infant CHRIST (St. Luke ii. 22–24). He oftener reveals CHRIST in his mediatorial office in prayer, ever living "to make intercession for us" (Heb. vii. 25). St. Luke was the Evangelist of the Gentiles. He taught the inefficiency of the Mosaic law, and the "saving efficacy of CHRIST's Sacrifice, and the blessedness of the Atonement made by Him on the Cross, and justification by Faith in His Blood." This justification he makes a "practical principle," and "the root of Christian virtue." As our LORD says in the parable of the Good Samaritan, "Go and do thou likewise." "All who would be saved by His death must imitate His life." The lion is referred as an emblem to St. Matthew (see Rev. iv. 7), because he is the king of beasts, and our LORD is called "The Lion of the tribe of Juda" (Rev. v. 5). St. Mark relating what CHRIST did in His Human Nature is symbolized as the Man in adapting (Rev. iv. 7). The Ox, the Sacrificial Victim, is ascribed to St. Luke. St. John with his eye fixed on the Light of CHRIST is the Eagle. St. John teaches that "the contemplation of the Truth and the sweetness of Love" must go together.

The book of Acts is the first history of the Christian Church. It has been called the Gospel of the HOLY GHOST, as it represents the wonderful work of the Spirit from the day of Pentecost onward. The character of the primitive Church is shown in chap. ii. 46 : "They, continuing daily with one accord in the temple, and breaking bread from house to house, did eat their meat with gladness and singleness of heart." Here was the constant prayer and the communion of saints. No wonder that the next verse adds that the "LORD added to the Church daily such as should be saved." As the little Church thus grew it made its home in various places, and Pastoral Letters were needed from its Bishops; hence came the Epistles, which are for the most part addressed to Churches or to Christians in general. A few are directed to individuals. By these inspired Epistles Church order and true doctrine were inculcated, so that the new converts were "built upon the foundation of the Apostles and Prophets, JESUS CHRIST Himself being the chief corner-stone" (Eph. ii. 20). A pleasant connection between an Epistle and a Gospel occurs in Col. iv. 14 : "Luke, the beloved physician, and Demas, greet you." A touching motive for writing is given by St. Peter (2 Ep. i. 15) : "I will endeavor that ye may be able after my decease to have these things always in remembrance." He also connects the Epistle with the Gospel accounts in speaking of the Transfiguration (vs. 16–18). The Epistles are a continuation and amplification of the Gospels (Gal. i. 11). While the Acts describe the planting of the Church, the Epistles give an account of its training. St. Paul, as a missionary, founded Churches, and when he could, revisited them, and in cases where he could not do this, he wrote to them, answering their letters and messages, and comforting and strengthening them. Hemsterhusius says that St. Paul's Epistles "seem to have been written under an almost celestial excitement of mind." Jerome remarks that his "words are thunder-bolts." Tholuck gives "power, fullness, and warmth" as the distinguishing marks of St. Paul.

St. Chrysostom calls St. Paul's Epistles "an adamantine wall to the Church through-out the world." The Epistle of St. James was to give fortitude to the Jewish Christians, and enforce the practice of the Gospel. Of St. Peter's first Epistle, Alford says that it follows out our LORD's "command to its writer, 'And thou, when thou art converted, strengthen thy brethren'" (St. Luke xxii. 32). The second Epistle is distinguished by the sublime description of the destruction of the earth by fire, and should move in every reader's heart a prayer for mercy through CHRIST in the "Day of the LORD" (ch. iii. 8–13). The Epistles of St. John abounding in love recall the legend that "the Apostle of love" in the feebleness of age used to utter the brief sermon, "Little children, love one another." St. Jude's Epistle is an earnest exhortation to "contend for the faith which was once delivered unto the saints" (v. 3). The prophetic book of the Revelation, with its magnificent description of Heaven, fitly closes the Sacred Volume: "Blessed is he that readeth, and they that hear the words of this prophecy, and keep those things which are written therein" (Rev. i. 3). With so many topics and such various writers the unity of the New Testament denotes the work of the Spirit of GOD. Furthermore, the Old and New Testaments are in wondrous agreement. The Fathers called them "the perfect and well-tuned organ of GOD," "from differing sounds" giving "one saving voice to those who are willing to learn." Justin Martyr says, "What else is the Law but the Gospel foreshadowed? What other the Gospel than the Law fulfilled?" St. Augustine compares things in the Old Testament to such as are under a shadow, the New Testament brings them into the open sun. The Old and New Testaments have been likened to the lower and upper millstones, which together grind the wheat.

Authorities: Bishop Chr. Wordsworth's Introd. to the Four Gospels, McWhorter's Hand-Book of the New Test., Whitby's Pref. to Gospels and Acts, Trench's Star of the Wise Men. REV. S. F. HOTCHKIN.

Testimonials. The certificates of good character and of proper qualifications which the Canons demand must be presented in behalf of a postulant or candidate for holy orders, that he may be duly received as such by the Bishop. The testimonials are demanded at every step taken in the premises, that the Church may be sufficiently protected against the admission of unworthy applicants. Despite all the care taken, it does occur that unworthy men are admitted to holy orders. A great responsibility lies upon those who are asked to sign these testimonials and certificates, for a heavy duty towards GOD and the Church is placed upon them, and there is no room for courteous or kindly intentions, or for any wish to spare the feelings of the applicant, no matter how well intentioned he may be. Archbishop Dolben, of York, charged his clergy with these solemn words: "Not to impose upon him by signing the testimonials which they did not know to be true, as they would answer it to Him at the dreadful day of judgment." It should be well weighed with the laity, for with them lies much of the responsibility, by avenues of information practically closed to a clergyman. If, then, by laxness, heedlessness, or other insufficient cause, testimonials are signed for a man known not to be fit for the ministry and harm to the flock of CHRIST come thereby, then those who aided his admission must bear their share. Reasonable doubt should weigh, not a prejudice nor a past life which has been heartily repented of, and sufficient personal knowledge should in all cases be the basis for any consent to sign such testimonials.

Texas, the Protestant Episcopal Church in. A sketch of the Church in Texas, within the limits prescribed for this article, must be very brief, and so far unsatisfactory. Only a general and meagre outline can be given. Its first planting goes back about forty-six years. In 1838 A.D. the Rev. Caleb S. Ives came to Texas as the first Missionary, under the auspices of the Foreign Committee of the Board of Missions of the Church in the United States. He settled in Matagorda, an old Spanish town, near the mouth of the Colorado River, and the outlet of a fertile agricultural region. It was then one of the most flourishing points in the infant Republic. By his godly life, earnest zeal, and faithful teaching he soon won his way to the hearts and confidence of the people, and laid deep and lasting the foundations of the Church, organizing a Parish which has retained its churchly and loyal character amid all subsequent changes, and the general decline in latter years of that region. He collected funds both in the North and South for a church building. It was framed and shipped from New York in 1839 A.D., a neat and commodious edifice, and sufficiently advanced towards completion to be used for service the same year. In 1844 A.D it was consecrated by Bishop Polk, of Louisiana. Mr. Ives was at this time, and for years previous and subsequent, the most Southern and Southwestern Episcopal Minister in North America. After abundant labors, he died in the latter part of 1849 A.D., beloved as few have ever been in the Church.

His successor was the Rev. S. D. Dennison, so prominently connected with the General Missionary work in after-years. Seeking temporary relief from Parish labors in a voyage to the South, he arrived in Texas in December, 1849 A.D., having been appointed a Missionary to Matagorda. He entered on the work and was elected Rector of the Parish, but resigned the following October. The Rev. D. D. Flower, of Alabama, was called in the spring of 1851 A.D., and accepted, but remained only a short time. The Rev. H. N. Pierce (the present Bishop of Arkansas) followed Mr. Flower, and remained until his removal to New Orleans. He was succeeded by the Rev. S. R. Wright, of Alabama. On the eve of his departure for this field, in October, 1854 A.D., Matagorda was wellnigh destroyed by one of the most terrific tornadoes that ever swept the coast of the United States. The church building shared in the general wreck. The vestry, deeply despondent, offered to release Mr. Wright from the engagement, but this devoted man of GOD would not decline. He officiated for a few weeks, and then went

North and East to raise funds for another church building. His efforts were crowned with success, and a most comely structure was reared, the pride of the town and county, the first and most conspicuous object seen by the traveler on his approach, many miles away on the prairie. In a destructive storm of 1875 A.D. it was partially destroyed, but fitted up, to be used, it is hoped, for many years to come. Mr. Wright soon after, 28th of January, 1857 A.D., was called to his rest, taken ill in his vestry room while preparing for a funeral, and surviving but a few hours. A succession of faithful men followed him in the Parish, among the most prominent of whom was the Rev. John Owen, who died during the epidemic in Galveston, 1867 A.D, one, like the saintly Wright, "whose praise was in all the Churches."

The name of the Rev. R. M. Chapman stands next to that of Mr. Ives as a Missionary to Texas. He was appointed by the "Foreign Committee" from the "Eastern Diocese," and sailed from New York, October 31, 1838 A.D., for Houston. He came with the purpose of supporting himself in part by teaching. In March, 1839 A.D., subscriptions were made of about $5000 for a church building. On the 1st of April a Parish was organized, and wardens and vestrymen were elected. Whether discouraged by surrounding circumstances, or impaired in health by the climate, is not known, but Mr. Chapman left the following summer. In April, 1840 A.D., Church officers were again elected, and on the 21st of that month the Rev. Henry B. Goodwyn, of Maryland, then in Houston on a visit, was elected Rector, but remained only a few months. During the previous year the first Episcopal Visitation was made to this then distant field. In the latter part of 1888 A.D. the Right Rev. Leonidas Polk, Bishop of Louisiana, was requested by the Foreign Committee of the Board of Missions "to visit Texas with reference to the Missions of the Episcopal Church to be established in that country." The Bishop came the following spring, and in his report to the Board, dated Houston, May 17, 1839 A.D., says, "There is a Presbyterian congregation organized here, and also one of our own Church. Four or five thousand dollars have been subscribed for erecting an Episcopal church." This visitation to Houston and other places was doubtless most encouraging to the few and scattered members in this remote field. For that noble man and Bishop never failed to leave behind him the enduring impress of his godly character, his genial spirit, and commanding presence as he journeyed in his Apostolic office among the Churches.

Houston and the adjacent region were not left long without a Minister. The Rev. Benjamin Eaton arrived January 14, 1841 A.D., his appointment having been previously communicated by the Secretary of the Board of Missions to the Wardens at Houston. Mr. Eaton began his work here. He also visited Galveston, soon after organized a Parish there, and was called to the Rectorship, which he accepted. His first intention was to divide his time between Galveston and Houston, but after doing so for three months he concluded to confine his labors to the former, although he found there "only four persons who professed any attachment to the Church, while at Houston there were seventeen Communicants, the majority males." In a letter written some years afterwards, May, 1858 A.D., Mr. Eaton says, "I commenced the building of the church here six months after my arrival, having by that time collected a large congregation. The church was opened in June, 1842 A.D. It was blown from its foundations and greatly injured the following September, which obliged me to make a second begging expedition. The liberality of friends abroad enabled me to repair and again open it in about six months. The corner-stone of the present building was laid under very discouraging circumstances on Thanksgiving-Day, 1855 A.D., and the church opened November 1, 1857 A.D. The extreme exterior length is 154 feet, and the width 66. It has seats for 750 persons, and is generally well filled. Whenever necessary, it can be made to accommodate 1500." Of Mr. Eaton's long rectorship of thirty years, his varied gifts, his faithful labors, and his tragic death,—falling at the desk where he had so long preached the unsearchable riches of CHRIST, carried by weeping friends along the aisle and to the rectory, where he breathed his last after a few hours of unconsciousness,—the Church has been generally informed. His reward is with him, and, "being dead, he yet speaketh."

Next came the Rev. Charles Gillette, long an active and prominent clergyman of Texas. He set sail from New York for Galveston January 12, 1843 A.D. For several months before, under the direction of the Board of Missions, he had been engaged in making collections for the rebuilding of the church in Galveston, which was blown down the September previous, and raised about $1000. He was instructed by the Board to select his own field of labor, and went first to Washington, as probably the most eligible point, it being then the seat of government. He found the opening, however, better at Houston, and, returning there, continued his ministrations as Rector for a time in that place. In June, 1844 A.D., he visited the North, seeking aid in the erection of a church building, and secured $1800. The building was completed and opened for service Easter-Day, April 4, 1847 A.D. In September, 1845 A.D., with Mr. Eaton, he made a tour through Middle and Western Texas, among other places visiting Brenham, Independence, Austin, and San Antonio. In September, 1847 A.D., by request of certain citizens there, Mr. Gillette again visited Austin, held a series of services, and organized a Parish, under the name of Christ Church. The second Episcopal visitation to Texas was made by Bishop Polk in February, 1844 A.D. He confirmed some persons in Houston. Accompanied by Mr. Gillette, the Bishop proceeded through the country to Matagorda, and thence, with Mr. Ives also, returned along the coast to Galveston.

Prior to this, in May, 1843 A.D., Messrs. Eaton, Gillette, and Ives met at Matagorda for the purpose of organizing the Diocese of Texas, but owing to adverse causes the project was defeated.

The two visitations of Bishop Polk already mentioned were necessarily hurried, and made with a long interval between. The need for more frequent, indeed, constant Episcopal supervision was more and more sorely felt. To meet this need the following memorial was prepared, to be presented at the ensuing General Convention:

"GALVESTON, March 13, 1844 A.D.

"The undersigned, Presbyters of the Dioceses of Alabama, Missouri, and Virginia, Missionaries in the Republic of Texas, feeling the urgent necessity of constant Episcopal supervision for the welfare of the Church in this Republic, and being satisfied of the kind intention of the Church in the United States, manifested hitherto by her fostering care, are encouraged to ask such assistance as may early supply our necessities. And we would respectfully solicit such action by the General Convention of the Episcopal Church in the United States at their approaching meeting as shall provide us with such Episcopal supervision as is enjoyed by Missionary Districts in the United States.

"CALEB S. IVES,
Rector Christ Church, Matagorda.
"BENJAMIN EATON,
Rector Trinity Church, Galveston.
"CHARLES GILLETTE,
Rector Christ Church, Houston."

To provide for the expected consecration of a Bishop for Texas, then a foreign power, a "Promise of Conformity to the Doctrine, Discipline, and Worship of the Church in the United States" was drawn up by the House of Bishops, when a Bishop for Texas should be elected. This soon followed. On the 22d of October, 1844 A.D., the House of Bishops nominated to the House of Deputies the Rev. Geo. W. Freeman, Rector of Emmanuel Church, New Castle, Delaware, as Missionary Bishop of this Church, to exercise Episcopal functions in the State of Arkansas and in the Indian Territory, south of the 36½ parallel of latitude, and to exercise Episcopal supervision over the Missions of this Church in the Republic of Texas." The Deputies concurred, and Dr. Freeman was duly elected, and consecrated without delay. In his first triennial Report to the General Convention October, 1847 A.D., he says, "Leaving the place of his former residence 17th of February, 1845 A.D., he proceeded on his first visitations, which from the lateness of the season when it was commenced was somewhat hurried, and confined chiefly to the Missionary Stations already existing, and was completed in the latter part of the month of June." "In the three years which have elapsed since his consecration, besides visiting the Churches and Missionary Stations within his jurisdiction thrice, he has visited Columbia and Brazina, in Brazina County, Texas, twice, and Richmond and Velasco in the same State once. The number of Communicants within his jurisdiction he reports to be, as nearly as he has been able to ascertain, 200 in Texas and 70 in Arkansas; whole number, 270." This was in October, 1847 A.D. He also says, "In Texas the congregations in the three established Parishes have been steadily growing, at Houston the number of Communicants is about 80; the church recently completed and consecrated is already found too small to accommodate the increasing congregation, and notwithstanding the large Confirmation (35 persons) lately held there, the worthy Rector reports that he has already a large class of additional candidates for that holy rite. At Galveston the congregation is large, and still increasing; the number of Communicants is 62, and the erection of a new church is seriously spoken of, although the present building is the largest belonging to our Communion in the State. At Matagorda, too, the Church is prospering, though, of late, there have come in some who 'rise up and speak against her.' The faithful Missionary is doing good service, both by his pastoral labors and his schools, which are becoming important nurseries for the Church; and although his field is apparently circumscribed by the limits of a small town, the whole population of which does not exceed three or four hundred, the circle of his influence for good is far more extensive, and may be considered as embracing the country around for many miles. The number of Communicants is 38. In various other parts of the State there is a manifestly growing interest in religious things in general, and a decided bias towards the Church, and nothing appears to be wanting, with the blessing of GOD, but a band of faithful and efficient Missionaries to insure a glorious ingathering of the faithful into the fold of CHRIST. To earnest, devoted, and self-denying men, capable of 'enduring hardness' in the cause of CHRIST, there is scarcely a more promising field in the whole range of our Missionary operations than that presented by Texas."

The next important step, contemplated for some years past, was the organization of the Diocese of Texas. Bishop Freeman called a meeting of the Clergy and Laity at Matagorda, August 1, 1849 A.D. They assembled as members of the Church of the

United States living in Texas. The Bishop presided at this primary Convention, and the same day the organization was completed.

It was ordered that the next meeting of the Convention should be held in Houston, on the second Wednesday in December of the same year, unless the Bishop, who was authorized to change the time, should see fit to so do. It was changed, and the meeting was held in Christ Church, Houston, May 9, 1850 A.D. Five Clergymen were in attendance, with the Bishop, and delegates from three Parishes. Four new Parishes were admitted into union with the Convention, viz.: Trinity Church, San Antonio; St. Peter's, Brenham; St Paul's, Washington; and St. Paul's, Polk County. The Bishop reported the ordination of two Deacons to the Priesthood,—the Rev. H. N. Pierce and the Rev. Henry Sansom. There were also reported 10 organized Parishes, and, since the previous Convention, 211 Baptisms, and 80 Confirmations. In 6 Parishes, 262 Communicants, and in 3 Parishes, Sunday-School Teachers, 33; and Scholars, 211. Action was taken for the establishment of a Mission, or Church School, and a Committee appointed to take the necessary steps for raising means, the selection of a location, providing Teachers, and to report to the next Convention. By resolution, the Bishop was earnestly requested to make his home at some central and convenient point within the Diocese.

At the succeeding Convention in Galveston, March 1, 1851 A.D., the Bishop, in his address, urged as absolutely essential to the welfare and progress of the Church that they should have a Bishop exclusively their own. The matter was referred to a Committee, which strongly indorsed the Bishop's views, and recommended it to the serious consideration of the next Convention. Further action was taken as to the Diocesan School, and the Rev. C. Gillette was requested to undertake, under the direction and advice of the Bishop, the raising of funds, providing for Teachers, and putting the said school in operation.

At the Convention of 1852 A.D., May 13, in St. Luke's Church, Chapel Hill, 7 Clergymen were present and delegates from 6 Parishes. Three new Parishes were admitted into union with the Convention, viz.: the Church of the Epiphany, Austin; Redeemer, Anderson; and All Faith Church, Liberty.

The Bishop again urged the necessity for a resident Episcopal head, the wisdom of at once making provision for his support, and preparing for his election at no distant day, intimating " that, in view of advancing age, his mind had been much inclined to the thought of resigning his present Episcopal charge altogether." A report was made in accordance with the recommendation, and the Convention decided to proceed to the election of a Bishop. On the first ballot, Bishop Freeman was unanimously chosen. He stated in reply that " he had neither anticipated nor cherished such a result, and was not prepared at present to respond, and asked time for consideration."

The Diocesan School was reported to have been located at Anderson, Grimes County, and put in operation the 1st of January preceding. Mr. Gillette also reported the commencement of a Female School, distinct from the other, for which he had been obliged to become personally responsible.

The Diocesan School soon after took the name of St. Paul's College, and was so incorporated. There were reported in 10 Parishes 176 Baptisms, 261 Communicants, and 52 Confirmations during the year; contributions for Church purposes in 4 Parishes, $1744.28.

At the next Convention, May 5, 1853 A.D., in Austin, assessments were laid on the Parishes, amounting to $500, towards the support of a resident Bishop; and the Deputies to the General Convention were requested to solicit the Board of Missions to grant Bishop Freeman a fixed income per annum, should he accept the Episcopate of Texas. From 13 Parishes 510 Communicants were reported.

In 1854 A.D., Bishop Freeman informed the Convention " that the circumstances of his family relations, and other matters, rendered it impossible for him to remove into the Diocese without greater sacrifices than he felt able or willing to make;" that without such removal the permanent Diocesan charge would be of no material advantage, and would scarcely be desired; and he therefore felt constrained to decline it. No action was then taken as to another election. In the Convention of 1855 A.D., at Seguin, after favorable and adverse reports, and much discussion, it was decided not to go into the election of a Bishop, and not until the succeeding Convention, 1856 A.D., at Galveston, was a choice made. The Rev. Arthur Cleveland Coxe, of Baltimore, was elected, but declined, and so the Diocese continued without a resident head. The following year, at Austin, May 21, 1857 A.D., a letter was read from Dr. Coxe, of March 25, offering, if the Diocese would raise $1000 annually for three years, he would pledge, with the co-operation of sundry clergymen in New York, Philadelphia, and Baltimore, the additional sum of $1500 per annum, three years, for the person who might be elected their Bishop, with his expenses of travel, that so he might be exempt from all incumbrance of parochial work or other sort, for the entire devotion of his time and talents to the Episcopal work. A committee was appointed to secure, if possible, the required amount on the part of the Diocese. The Rev. Alex. H. Vinton, D.D., was elected Bishop. The next day Bishop Freeman, assured, as he said, now of a favorable result, and regarding the question as to the permanent Bishopric settled, resigned his provisional charge. Dr. Vinton, however, declined the call for weighty and conclusive reasons, in a letter marked by propriety and good sense.

At the following Convention, April 15, 1858 A.D., in Houston, Rev. Benjamin Eaton presiding, the Rev. Sullivan H. Weston was elected, and again the Diocese was doomed to disappointment, Mr. Weston declining. A few days after the adjournment of this Convention, Bishop Freeman died in Little Rock, Ark., April 29, 1858 A.D. The next Convention adopted a report, paying the following tribute to the departed Prelate: "Ever firm, faithful, and conscientious in the discharge of duty, and at the same time kind and conciliatory, he did much to lay a firm and broad foundation for the Church in Texas. He labored faithfully as a Bishop in the Church of GOD; and rests from his labors, and his works do follow him." The statistics for the previous year showed no marked advance except in the increase of Sunday-School teachers and scholars, and contributions for Church objects, amounting to $26,437.47. St. Paul's College had passed already through a troublous financial history. The Rev. C. Gillette had taken charge of Christ Church, Austin. The Rev. Mr. Platt, a worthy and devoted man, succeeded Mr. Gillette, but the decline continued; and in the early part of 1860 A.D. the school was no longer in existence, the Parish at Anderson retained little more than a nominal existence, and only one or two buildings remained to tell the story of the failure.

The tenth Annual Convention was held in Galveston, May 5, 6, 1859 A.D. The Rev. Alexander Gregg, Rector of St. David's Church, Cheraw, S. C., was elected Bishop. His acceptance was in due time made known, and his consecration took place in the Monumental Church, Richmond, Va., October 13. The Bishop began a brief Visitation at Galveston, December 11, going thence to Brenham, Austin, San Antonio, Gonzalez, Columbus, Richmond, and Houston. He returned from South Carolina with his family the middle of February, 1860 A.D., and took up his residence at Austin. The first Convention after his coming was held in Matagorda, April 13. The statistics from nine Parishes were: of Baptisms, 165; Confirmations, 114; Communicants, 456; Candidates for Orders, 3; Clergy, 14; Contributions for Church purposes, $10,689.50.

The following year the war began, but notwithstanding the unfavorable influences and spiritual drawbacks of such a protracted civil strife, the Church continued to advance, as was shown by the statistics reported at the Convention in Houston, June 15-17, 1865 A.D., viz.: "Baptisms, 278; Confirmations, 271; Communicants, 962; Contributions, $12,387; Clergy, 19." In 1874 A.D., nine years after, at the Convention in Jefferson, May 28, there were reported: "Clergy, including the Bishop, 34; Candidates for Orders, 7; Lay-Readers, 21; Parishes organized, 3; Missions, 6; Baptisms, 466; Confirmations, 290; Communicants, 2567; Sunday-School Teachers, 203; Scholars, 1362; total Contributions, $53,096.34; Value of Churches, Rectory, Schoolhouses, etc., $127,050." At this meeting final action was taken on the important subject of the reduction of the Diocese, which had been considered in previous Conventions, and by the General Convention, at its last session, the matter of making Canonical provision being then considered. On this occasion a special Committee reported, in accordance with the recommendation of the Bishop, proposing the cutting off large portions of the State (or Diocese), to be formed into the Missionary Districts of Northern and Western Texas, according to the lines suggested by the Bishop, and that the General Convention be petitioned to provide for and ratify the same. This was done, notwithstanding the grave difficulty that no legal provision had been made for such a mode of relief. The Rev. Alexander C. Garrett, D.D., was elected Missionary Bishop of Northern Texas, and was consecrated at Omaha, Neb., 20th of the following December. The Rev. R. W. B. Elliott, D.D., was elected Missionary Bishop of Western Texas, and consecrated at Atlanta, Ga., 15th of November. The territory of Northern Texas embraced an area of 100,000, and Western Texas 110,000, square miles, leaving the Diocese with 59,694, the population being more unequally distributed. The total population of the State was estimated at 1,200,000. The Diocese, as reduced, contained nearly 600,000; Northern Texas, 400,000; and Western Texas, a little over 200,000. The State embraced 167 counties, 57 of which were in the Diocese, and 55 each in the Missionary Jurisdictions.

The Diocese as it was then reported 39 Parishes, 34 Missions, and 32 Clergymen. Of these it retained 26 Parishes, 15 Missions, and 20 Clergymen, Northern Texas having 4 Parishes, 9 Missions, and 5 Clergymen, and Western Texas 9 Parishes, 9 Missions, and 7 Clergymen. The progress of the Church throughout this vast territory since has been encouraging, and the wisdom of the action taken in October, 1874 A.D., abundantly justified by the results. In October, 1883 A.D., at the last General Convention, the statistics reported for the Diocese were: Clergy, 20; Parishes and Missions, 57; families, 1200; individuals, 5600; Baptisms the previous year, 335; Confirmations, 146; Communicants, 2400; Sunday-School Teachers, 183; Scholars, 1748; Contributions, $47,600. For Northern Texas: Clergy, 9; Parishes, 9; Missions, 15; Baptisms, 107; Confirmations, 50; Communicants, 1134; Sunday-School Teachers, 88; Scholars, 715; Contributions, $9736.36. Western Texas: Clergy, 15; Parishes, 12; Missions, 18; Baptisms, 143; Confirmations, 79; Communicants, 1153;

Sunday-School Teachers, 124; Scholars, 888; Contributions, $14,155.16.

By the close of another decade it is not to be doubted but that the growth of the Church will be found to have kept pace with that of population.

Statistics for 1886 A.D.: Clergy, 26; parishes, 31; missions, 30; baptisms, 473; confirmed, 269; communicants, 2782; contributions, $45,569.74.

Rt. Rev. Alexander Gregg, D.D.,
Bishop of Texas.

Text. The letter of the Holy Scripture. Usually the word applied to the verse or verses upon which a set discourse is delivered. But it is also the letter of the Scriptures, whether in the Greek or Hebrew, or in some particular version under examination. The Old Testament text was settled by the Jewish doctors (the Masorites, *vide* Masorah) fifteen hundred years ago. It is now in the state in which they placed it. Earlier MSS. in point of time do not exist, but some MSS. represent copies of the Old Testament which were transcribed before this recension, and also the Masorites themselves distinguished between a reading which they did not displace, but which was wrong, and the reading they recommended (the K'ri and the K'theb, "what should be read" and "what is in the text." The text was providentially preserved to us intact, for though human weaknesses intervene to prevent us from a positive certainty that we have every letter as it came from the pens of the inspired writers, yet we are sure that we have a very accurate copy of the work. The vast labors of Scholars, Jewish and Christian, have not touched the integrity of the Masoretic Text, though emendations may be suggested. So, too, of the New Testament. The text of the Greek of the New Testament was arranged by a famous printer in Paris, Robert Stephens, in 1546 A.D. (and later 1549 A.D., and the Regia, 1550 A.D.), from confessedly imperfect MSS. but with remarkable freedom from essential defects. The labors of a long line of eminent scholars since then have produced a purer text, yet of the thirty thousand variations in MSS. collated and arranged not three affect doctrine or the essentials of the text, and but few omit any of the important words. The passages affected are 1 John v. 7, which is generally supposed to be a late insertion; and St. John viii. 2-11, which is most probably genuine, and has very strong authority. The third is a various reading of Who for God in 1 Tim. iii. 16, a variation which does not affect the doctrinal statement. A good idea of general variations in the text made by modern criticism may be obtained by a comparison of the marginal notes in the recent Revised Translation upon what is left out or what is considered doubtful, with the parallel passages in the Authorized Version. By far the larger number of variations are to the ordinary reader nearly valueless, being variations in tense or mood or a change of particles. But very few out of so large a number change the words of a text. In still fewer instances a sentence evidently inadvertently repeated from another suggestive or parallel passage has been left out. The Textus Receptus, as the text of Stephens of Paris is called, will probably remain practically the text of our New Testaments, though critical editions are imperatively necessary for the Biblical Scholar and the Theologian. Such have been recently published, foremost of which is Westcott's Text of the New Testament.

This very imperfect notice of the Text of the originals should be supplemented by the information to be found in Smith's Dictionary of the Bible. For a notice of the Authorized Version of the Bible and Revised Version of the New Testament, see Versions.

Thanksgiving. If it is a plain duty and an act of common politeness to thank any one for a favor, much more is it an obligation laid on every human being to heartily thank God for the countless undeserved blessings received at His hand. "Every creature of God is good, and nothing to be refused, if it be received with thanksgiving" (1 Tim. iv. 4). Cruden defines Thanksgiving thus: "An acknowledging and confessing with gladness the benefits and mercies which God bestows either upon ourselves or others." Thanksgiving naturally forms a part of the Church services. The Jew had a "sacrifice of thanksgiving" (Lev. vii. 12, 15). There were psalms of thanksgiving (Neh. xii. 8, 46). "Offer unto God thanksgiving" (Ps. l. 14). "Let us come before His presence with thanksgiving" (Ps. xcv. 2). "Enter into His gates with thanksgiving" (Ps. c. 4). St. Paul exhorts that "giving of thanks be made for all men" (1 Tim. ii. 1). Prayer is to be "with thanksgiving" (Phil. iv. 6). Public thanksgivings are given for public mercies, as the song of triumph after the miraculous passage of the Red Sea (Ex. xv.), and in the Prayer-Book the hymns and prayers after deliverance from tempest, or after a victory. Special acknowledgments occur in Scripture for special mercies, for "wisdom" (Dan. ii. 23), for the faith of Christian believers (Rom. i. 8), "for the grace of God" given by Jesus Christ" (1 Cor. i. 4). The four and twenty elders thank God for the enlargement of Christ's kingdom (Rev. xi. 16, 17). Anna, the prophetess, "gave thanks unto the Lord" for the infant Christ (St. Luke ii. 36, 38). This spirit of general and particular thankfulness to God finds proper expression in the Prayer-Book. The " General Thanksgiving" for bodily and spiritual mercies and redemption through Christ is placed in the Morning and the Evening Prayer. Various Thanksgivings for personal and national mercies of providence and grace are found in the Occasional Prayers. In the " Family Prayer" for the " Evening" is a beautiful and comprehensive form for acknowledging the daily benefits received from GOD. In thanking the LORD for " our reason" in this prayer it may be well to remember the question of the insane man to a London merchant, as to whether he ever thanked GOD for his reason. The merchant said that he never after offered thanks to GOD without thinking of gratitude for reason and right mind. A much neglected occasional prayer is the Thanksgiving " for a Recovery from Sickness." The prayer " For a Sick Person" is often called for, but when GOD blesses the invalid, too often, like the nine ungrateful lepers, he does not return thanks. Dr. Samuel Johnson writes, " I am so far recovered that on the 21st I went to church to return thanks, after a confinement of more than four long months." The word " Eucharist" means thanksgiving, and after recovery from sickness it is most desirable to draw near to GOD in this Holy Feast. Indeed, the Holy Communion is the great act of Christian thanksgiving, and stands pre-eminent in this respect.

The Prayer-Book contains " A Form of Prayer and Thanksgiving to Almighty GOD for the fruits of the earth, and all the other blessings of His merciful Providence." In the United States this festival often very properly combines the idea of a Harvest-home and a family reunion. The " Midlenting" or " Mothering" of English sons visiting the family abode corresponds to the social part of this festival. It is a pleasant custom to deck the church with the fruits of the earth, and then give them to the poor, and a large offering for some worthy object should on such a glad day be placed thankfully on GOD'S altar. The Law declared that bread was not to be eaten before an offering was made to GOD (Lev. xxiii. 14). In Deut. xxvi. 1-11, is an account of the offering of first fruits, and when the American thinks of his nation's advancement, and how the " few" have become " a nation, great, mighty, and populous" (v. 5), like the descendants of the Syrian Jacob, he should freely return to GOD a part of what he has so freely received. Grace at table is a private thanksgiving in accordance with this public one. " When thou hast eaten, and art full, then thou shalt bless the LORD thy GOD, for the good land which He hath given thee" (Deut. viii. 10). If the Jew blessed GOD when he smelled a flower, much more should we bless Him at the daily meal, spread by His bounty.

When the spirit of thanksgiving shows itself in an offering to GOD, it is desirable to sing, as the offering is presented at the altar, the words of David, " All things come of Thee, and of Thine own have we given Thee" (1 Chron. xxix. ' '). If thanksgiving is a proper employment for GOD'S people on earth, it is also the work of angels in heaven, as they fall " before the throne on their faces and" worship GOD, " Saying, Amen : Blessing, and glory, and wisdom, and thanksgiving, and honor, and power, and might, be unto our GOD for ever and ever. Amen" (Rev. vii. 12).

REV. S. F. HOTCHKIN.

Theandric Operation. A word compounded of *Theos* and *Andros*, of GOD and man. We use frequently a similar compound, JESUS CHRIST, the GOD-man, to intimate the complete, interrelated union without fusion of our LORD'S two natures in His one Person. The theandric operation also denotes the complete harmonious, subordinated work of His human will under His divine will. The word was of late introduction (640 A.D.), and is comparatively unused.

Theology is the philosophy of the Faith. In so far as it is of the Faith it is fixed and unchangeable, because the Faith was once for all delivered to the saints. So far as its philosophical element reaches, Theology is subject to the laws of human reason, and is affected by the progress or retrogression of knowledge. Hence Theology changes from time to time. Its changes are causes of conflict. Those who defend the old theologic forms of expression and modes of argument think they are contending for the faith itself, while those who assail these old forms and modes may declare themselves the more strongly attached to the Faith, and possessors of the more confidence in it, for the very reason that it can be shown to stand firmly even while the Theology generally received as expressing it is found no longer consistent with advanced knowledge or with improved logical methods. Every one will recollect the standard illustration of this point. The Word of GOD was as true, and the Faith it enshrines as sure, after Galileo proved that the earth moved round the sun, as they were before. In our own period, too, the true faith respecting creation is only more fully set forth and elucidated by the fact that Theology requires some reconstruction in order to fit it into the unfolding facts of geological science. No one now thinks of the six days, of the progressive creation of the world, as fixed temporal quantities of twenty-four hours each.

Skeptics, of course, exult when they make a breach in old walls of theologic opinions and prove untenable some forms of its expression. Many timid saints, also, tremble for the stability of the " building of GOD." But the Faith is never shaken. The Church sacraments and doctrine as given or sealed by CHRIST and the HOLY GHOST are immutable, because they rest on the Corner-Stone, the Rock, the Word of GOD, GOD with us, the Truth, in whom dwelleth all the fullness of GOD.

Thus it is seen that the Faith is that sum of fact which rests in and on CHRIST, which cannot, therefore, be prevailed against, which will remain the one Faith forever.

Theology is not to be underrated, because it never can stand on the clear ground of certainty. It is more or less probable, and therefore, when well used and duly esteemed, becomes a great help towards understanding and applying the Truth. Human reason is just as much a GOD-given faculty as the faculty of faith itself. Within its own limits, men should esteem, value, and follow it. Reason may fairly test the foundation of the Faith. Then the man must take what rests on that foundation into his faculty of faith. From this, as a second starting-point, reason may proceed according to both its methods. It may deduce, from facts of the Faith, just consequences and conclusions; and, if its deductions are sound, its results will carry the obligation to believe, follow, and obey. It may lay points of the Faith alongside other points, and mingle them even with philosophic or scientific truth; and, upon induction from the whole, draw out a theological conclusion, or even a chain of doctrine and law. If this induction be fair, full, and faithful, the whole theological conclusion becomes binding upon the minds and consciences of those who receive or ought to receive it.

Hence Theology is a thing of weight, a power given from on high, a means of wide instruction, a legitimate basis of exhortation. Sermons are generally theological discourses. They are designed to apply points of the "one Faith" to the specific needs of hearers. Though not infallible, they may be true. In so far as they are true they are spoken of GOD, because spoken according to His will by those sent by Him, His own chosen prophets or teachers. Hearers are not bound by every theological instruction or exhortation they may hear; they are, however, bound to take heed how they hear. They may not innocently reject or neglect what they hear, merely because the human element in the discourse takes away its whole infallibility; because whatever of truth there is remains GOD'S truth still, and hence binding on conscience and obligatory to the will.

The Theology of the past embalms much of the history of man. Christian theology has run side by side with the currents of human progress. Mankind are very much indebted to it for mental, moral, social, and political advancement. The Western human tidal flood of progress has been impelled always by strong theological forces. Indeed, its recuperative and evolving forms of civilization have been, and yet are, imbued with power that proceeds from Christian theology. While not overvaluing, one must also take heed lest he undervalue, that great energy of Divine-human Theology, through and by which GOD works in, into, over, and around mankind.

REV. BENJAMIN FRANKLIN, D.D.

Theophany. It refers to the anticipative manifestations of GOD the Word as the JEHOVAH Angel, in the Old Testament. In the following list only those which are admitted as undoubted Theophanies are given. Excluding first the free intercourse of GOD with yet sinless man, and the expostulations of GOD with Cain, and the communications to Noah, there is the appearance of the Angel of the LORD to Hagar when first driven from Abraham's tent (Gen. xvi. 7-13); the visit of the three Angels which appeared to Abraham on the plains of Mamre and one of whom was the LORD (Gen. xviii.); the Angel of the LORD appearing to Abraham at the offering of Isaac (Gen. xxii. 11 *sq.*). Passing by the earlier appearances to Jacob in visions, there was the mysterious wrestling with the Angel at the ford Jabbok (Gen. xxxii. 24-30). Jacob devoutly acknowledged His presence and guiding care when he blessed Joseph's sons: "The Angel which redeemed me from all evil bless the lads" (Gen. xlviii. 16). The Angel of JEHOVAH in the Burning Bush (Ex. iii.-iv. 17). The Angel of GOD in the Pillar of Fire (Ex. xiv. 19). The Angel in whom is the Name of GOD and who led the People through the wilderness (Ex. xxiii. 20-23). This is the Angel that appeared to Balaam (Num. xxii.), to Joshua at the siege of Jericho (Josh. v. 13), to the People at Bochim (Judges ii. 1), to Gideon (Judges vi. 11), to Manoah (Judges xiii. 3), over Jerusalem with drawn sword (2 Sam. xxiv. 16). He chose to withdraw Himself and to reach His People by other channels. But in visions He was seen by His Prophets, as when Isaiah saw His glory, and heard His Worship sung by the Seraphim, and when Zechariah in a vision saw Him beside the High-Priest, Joshua, to protect him from Satan (Zech. iii. 1, 2). It was this Angel of the Covenant who should appear suddenly (Mal. iii. 1). These are the chief and undenied Theophanies of the WORD, who was from the beginning with GOD and was GOD, and this Word of GOD is JESUS our LORD.

Theophori. A name the Christians often gave themselves. Bearers of GOD in their hearts. It is said that St. Ignatius gave himself this name when questioned by Trajan.

Theosophy. Wisdom concerning GOD. It was principally applied to the grotesque speculations of Jacob Boehm, the philosophic shoemaker of Görlitz (1575-1624 A.D.), but it has also been given to the speculations of metaphysical Brahmins. The system of Jacob Boehm is a most quaint farrago of deep spiritual and mystic speculations, written in a style that resembles strongly the Rosicrucian and Alchemic jargon. It was translated by William Law, the famous non-juror, who wrote against Bishop Hoadly. Law was himself a man of remarkable power and of deep devoutness, but apparently unbalanced in those speculations in which he was not forced by controversy to be precise and accurate. In these speculations he gave reins to his mystical tendency.

Thessalonians, First Epistle. By a series of just inferences from St. Paul's movements in his second missionary journey, we may fairly infer that this Epistle was written some months after he had established the Church in Thessalonica, 52–53 A.D. St. Timothy had been sent to revisit them, as the Apostle could not do so himself, and his report was so encouraging to the Apostle that he wrote his letter to them in a spirit of commendation which is also found in the Epistle to the other Macedonian city, Philippi. In this First Epistle, which was also the first of the grand letters which St. Paul wrote, he dwells, as is natural, upon the central truth of the Faith, and chiefly upon the Second Advent. As yet there had been but little antagonism to the Apostle which would bring out a written enunciation of the teaching he afterwards recorded. Faith and works and justification are not named indeed, but they are thoroughly implied. He dwells naturally upon the comfort of the hope of the Future Life and the preparation to meet our LORD, and implies that there had been a persecution, in which the Christian Thessalonians had stood firm. He warns them against the besetting sins of the day, and bids them be patient. It is not that St. Paul's own teachings were elemental, but rather that as yet the difficulties in the Church did not demand of him a full record of what he taught orally. The general plan of the Epistle is wholly characteristic of the Apostle.

I. Ch. i. He recalls his mission and preaching and then conversion.

Ch. ii. He reminds them how he lived among them disinterested and blameless.

Ch. iii. He speaks of his anxiety for them and of Timothy's report, and offers a very earnest prayer for their increase in the Faith.

II. Ch. iv. He exhorts them to purity, brotherly love, and honest life, comforting those whose friends had died with the certainty of the Resurrection, and (ch. v.) assuring them that though he looked for it in his day, yet it was in the determination of GOD. The Epistle ends with practical suggestions and warnings.

In its construction we see a larger reference to the articles of the Creed, dwelling so pointedly upon our LORD'S passion, death, resurrection, and coming to judgment, and founding his exhortation upon it.

THE SECOND EPISTLE must have followed the first quite soon, as St. Paul appears to have found that he was misrepresented in some way, and he writes repeating what he had said of the LORD'S coming, but dwelling upon the hindrances which must be removed before that could take place. His language here has been used controversially in an endeavor to fix the person of the man of sin, and so has given a prominence to this Epistle. It is very markedly in the same line of teaching as the previous one. As full of fervent zeal, of delicate suggestion, and warning, as earnest in declaring the Faith, and in urging that suffering is a condition of entering into the Kingdom of Heaven, and a reiteration of the coming of the SON of Man to judge the world, it is well to give this outline of the Epistle:

I. The Apostle's joy in their faith and exhortation to suffer gladly for the LORD'S sake, that they may receive double at His hand when He shall come to judgment (ch. ii.). But that Coming is hindered by many things, some of which were political, and, too, that characters might be developed, and that those who are His be proven.

II. Ch. iii. A practical suggestion or two upon the holy life and upon discipline of unworthy members, so delicately and so mercifully worded that the Apostle's tenderness and sympathy are well displayed. This Epistle is better known because of the polemical use made of it, but throughout, the devoted zeal of the Apostle, his earnestness and love, are so characteristic that these form the true worth of the Epistle apart from that enunciation of the Gospel which he makes in it. It as full of love expressed in St. Paul's manner as are St. John's Epistles; love to his LORD and love to the Christians at Thessalonia because of his LORD'S love to him.

Thomas, St., in the list given of the twelve Apostles by three of the Evangelists, is the seventh in place. St. John, who has recorded no list of the Apostles' names, seems to have had a personal knowledge of St. Thomas, as he alone (note the name Thomas is Syriac, and means a twin) mentions him as Didymus, or a twin. He also seems to have understood his character better, as he both heard and recorded the four remarkable sentences uttered by St. Thomas. When called to be an Apostle, he is supposed to have been like St. John and St. Philip, a young man, a Galilean, and a fisherman. His character, to judge from the account of him in St. John's Gospel, was ardent and affectionate, bold and courageous, but possessed of a degree of caution that made it difficult for him to receive any truth that was not fully explained to him, and rendered him unwilling to believe in his LORD'S reappearance after the Resurrection on the testimony of others. It made him boldly declare, "Except I shall see in His hands the print of the nails, and put my finger in the print of the nails, and thrust my hand into His side, *I will not believe.*" This proof had already been given to the other Apostles, and why should he not demand it also? How those eight days of doubt were passed by him we can only conjecture; but when the first day was come again, and the disciples were assembled together, Thomas was with them, and then the doors being shut, JESUS stood in the midst and said, "Peace be unto you." Then addressing Thomas by name, He said, "Reach hither thy finger and behold my hands, and reach hither thy hand and thrust it into my side, and be not faithless, but believing." In ecstasy and devotion, St. Thomas made use of the wonderful exclamation, "My LORD and my GOD."

The festival of St. Thomas is of ancient date, having been observed in the time of St. Gregory; it falls on the 21st day of December. The Collect has the leading idea, drawn from a Homily of St. Gregory when he says, "that by this *doubting* of St. Thomas we are more confirmed in our belief than by the faith of the other Apostles." It is recorded by Eusebius that after the day of Pentecost and the gift of tongues the Apostles were scattered abroad, and that St. Thomas was sent to the Parthians, Medes, Persians, and Chaldeans, founding churches among them till he penetrated into India. The Christians of St. Thomas, a remarkable religious community, still bear witness to his labors in that distant land; they are settled along the Malabar coast of the Indian peninsula. To the north also there seem to be relics of the Christian faith preached by St. Thomas mixed with the strange religion of Thibet. St. Thomas was martyred at a place called Taprobane. Having been at first assailed with stones, he was at last killed by the thrust of a spear, thus offering a comparison to the words of our LORD to him: "Reach hither thy hand and thrust it into my side." It was not granted to St. Thomas to have his courageous aspiration fulfilled to die with CHRIST, but to die for His cause. It is related that the Portuguese found an ancient inscription in Meliapore, purporting that St. Thomas had been pierced with a lance at the foot of a cross which he had erected in that city, and that in 1523 A.D. his body was found there and transported to Goa. It would appear that St. Thomas traveled farther than any of the Apostles, and preached to various nations of different languages, showing that as his incredulity was great, so was his faith great in proportion.

In Sacred and Legendary art St. Thomas finds a conspicuous place. "The Incredulity of Thomas" has been variously treated by different painters, but by none more successfully than by Rubens, whose picture is in the gallery of Antwerp. In purely Legendary painting he is the subject of many beautiful fancies. When painted alone or with the other Apostles, his attribute is always a builder's rule or square, and for this reason he is called the patron of architects and builders. This attribute must be sought for in a popular legend of which he is the subject. He was sent by our LORD, so says the legend, to an Indian king who was seeking architects to build him a palace. Being pleased with the appearance of St. Thomas, the king gave him large sums of gold and silver, bidding him build a palace finer than the emperor's at Rome. The king then went into a distant land for two years. St. Thomas meanwhile, instead of building the palace distributed all the treasure among the poor and sick. The king on his return was full of anger, and cast St. Thomas into prison, intending to torture him to death; but he was shown in a vision a beautiful palace in heaven, which the Angel told him St. Thomas had built for him. The king ran to the prison to deliver the Apostle, who said, "Know, O king, that I have laid up thy treasures in heaven."

Throne. The Bishop's chair in his Cathedral. It is often so called, but properly the title Throne describes the rank of the Patriarch, but the Bishop's chair is a *Cathedra*. It is placed generally beyond the stalls, and is raised. Its position in the ancient Church was beyond the Holy Table, which was placed nearly in the centre of the Chancel, and this arrangement is carried out in some Cathedrals. This was once the position of the Marble Chair of the Archbishop of Canterbury, which may well be called a *Throne*. The Patriarchal Sees are called Thrones.

Tiara. The mitre, surrounded with a triple crown, which the Pope wears upon certain State occasions. The Tiara was a comparatively late ornament added to the Pontifical dress. It was a round cap at first. John XIII. placed upon it the first crown. Boniface VIII. added the second, and Benedict XIII. a third. (*Vide* Hook's Church Dictionary.)

Tiles. (*Vide* ARCHITECTURE.) The glazed brick of various colors used in Church Architecture, which is now extensively used, especially for floors in churches.

Timothy. The best beloved of all of St. Paul's companions. To him probably more than to any one else St. Paul confided the thoughts of his great soul. Timothy was born of holy parentage. His mother and grandmother were faithful, earnest Jewish women, living either at Derbe or at Lystra. His temperament, as we may gather from what St. Paul alludes to in the two Epistles to him, shows him an earnest, zealous youth, devoutly trained by a loving mother and grandmother, accepting with them the Gospel, and proceeding in all godliness, so that it were easy that Prophets in the Church should point him out as a fit person to rule in the Church. At St. Paul's second visit he was set apart to do the work of an Evangelist. He then was circumcised, since, being half an Israelite, that the covenant of his forefathers remained uncompleted would be a scandal to Jewish converts. He was henceforth the Apostle's constant companion, leaving him only upon imperative need. He was at Berea and Athens; he goes on a mission to Thessalonica. For the next five years he is not noticed, but probably actively serving St. Paul. Then he is sent to Macedonia and Achaia, when the Apostle plans his third Missionary Journey. His relations to Corinth are those of the most kindly nature. A large circle of friends scattered throughout the Church receive greetings from him in St. Paul's Epistles, or hear from St. Paul of his labors. How often he left the Apostle's side or when he returned to it from some special mission we cannot now determine. From the letter to the Romans in which he sends a salutation till the Apostle is a prisoner there we lose sight of him. But now he becomes the Apostle's constant messenger. He is arrested, and witnesses a good Confession. St. Paul, after he is released, leaves him at Ephesus to regulate and correct disorders. He is set over men older than himself, and has to see to the many and various duties which fall to a Bishop now. Ordination, Discipline, Finance, Preaching, and Personal Conduct as a public man are all set before him as proper to his office. He is to fight a steadfast warfare. But the Apostle is arrested a second time, and is in prison at Rome again. How long an interval lies between the first Epistle and the second we cannot know accurately. Timothy is still at Ephesus, and now St. Paul needs him, and writes to him one of the most touching of all the Epistles he had yet written. In it the master calls the servitor to come to him, and it is probable that Timothy is now at the last scene of St. Paul's eventful life. What his future career was we do not certainly know, but there is very much probability in the conjecture that he is the Angel of the Church warned and appealed to by our LORD in St. John's Apocalypse (Rev. ii. 1-7). That this was certainly so of course cannot be proven, but it is very likely the warning of the Angel's faults and the commendations of his zeal suit very well the temperament of St. Paul's beloved companion, and there is nothing at all more likely than that when St. Paul laid down his life Timothy would return to Ephesus, where his work was already planned out, and where his office and authority were not only known, but were established: probability would point that way. But whether this was so or not, Timothy's charge, which he received from St. Paul, only establishes the more clearly the continuance of the Apostolic office and the extent and limitations of its authority. In Ephesus is a well-established Christian community, and has Elders set over it already. If Elders could ordain Elders, then why should Timothy be imposed upon them with a higher office of ordination as well as discipline? But if (as St. Paul calls him when writing to the Thessalonians, 1 Thess. i. 1, compared with ii. 6) he is an Apostle in office, then the whole of his duty falls in at once with the lines that the Epistles lay down. Any other supposition compels us to do violence to some part or other of the Sacred record. In this, which is led up to by the general facts of the New Testament, the Apostolic nature of his authority, and the linking of his name with the Angel of the Church of the Apocalyptic Message, are clear, natural, and within the lines of the office as our LORD established it and as St. Paul instructed Timothy to wield it.

Timothy, Epistles to. The two Epistles to Timothy which we receive have been fiercely assaulted as spurious. But the refutation is complete and decisive. Style, purpose, date, and contents all are unmistakably St. Paul's, and Timothy's relation to him and the missions upon which he was sent all prove that they are genuine. The first Epistle was written after the first imprisonment, at some place from Macedonia probably, but under what surroundings we do not know. Timothy is left at Ephesus (*a*) to teach sound doctrine and to discipline those who teach false doctrine as the Apostle had, Hymenæus and Alexander. (*b*) He is to set in order the Liturgy (giving of thanks is "the Eucharist's"). (*c*) To ordain fit persons for the Diaconate and Presbyterate. (*d*) The Apostle recurs to false teaching again. (*e*) He outlines the practical government to be exercised both over the Ministry and the Laity, and intermingles personal directions and exhortations to him, and gives him the topic upon which he is to warn those committed to his charge. The Epistle closes with a most earnest personal appeal and a magnificent doxology, and then most characteristically with an addition of warnings,—as if Timothy in his own loving sympathetic nature might be tempted to relax that strictness which so difficult a position as that at Ephesus demanded. The second Epistle, which was written at the second imprisonment, almost with the gleam of the sword above him, is full of St. Paul's marked style. It is intensely personal; his own prayers, the tenderness of St. Timothy, the kindness of friends who were not ashamed of his chain, the dispersion of his companions upon missions, his loneliness, his fear that Timothy may be confused by babbling heretics, the salutations of his friend, his sermons to St. Timothy to come with speed, all are so direct, so personal, that we may almost see the chained Apostle in his cell striving to dictate to an amanuensis (probably St. Luke) his message of love and warning and summons to his best beloved son in the Faith. Its contents may be summarized somewhat thus: (*a*) A personal appeal and mingled reminiscences, with a compact restatement of the gospel whereof he is appointed a preacher and an Apostle and a teacher to the Gentiles. (*b*) The holding fast to and transmission of the form of sound words, and the steadfastness in confessing and insisting upon them. On this he quotes from a Christian hymn, and closes with a warning to teach and preach meekly. (*c*) A prophecy of the last times, and an urging Timothy again by his own example to be courageous and to preach the Word constantly, despite the sectaries that would oppose themselves. (*d*) The summons to come to Rome as soon as he can, with mingled warnings against certain opposers, and a statement of his lonely state and salutations to friends at Ephesus.

These Epistles and that to Titus are called pastoral Epistles, since they give directions upon the Pastoral office, and are written to men in Apostolic office that they may know how they ought to behave themselves in the house of GOD, which is the Church of the living GOD, the pillar and ground of the Truth. By these Epistles, and by the just inferences to be drawn from them, the Bishops, Pastors, and Teachers of the Flock of CHRIST have been guided in all matters pertaining to Ordination, to Discipline of the Clergy, and instruction and government of the Laity.

Tippets were hoods of some black material, which must not be silk, which were worn on the shoulders of such ministers as were not graduates of any University, to distinguish them from those who wore the robe and colored hood pertaining to their order.

Tithes. The tenth part, paid by Divine command, by the Jew for the maintenance of the Levites and the worship at the Tabernacle, and kept up as long as the Jews retained any national organization. The principle of the tithe was universally acknowledged by the Gentile, the Patriarch, and the Jew. The Carthaginians paid tithes not only to their deities, but to the deities of other countries. The nations in Asia Minor had such a custom. It was vowed to their deities by the Romans on the eve of battle. The Greeks acknowledged it. It must not, however, be supposed that this was regularly observed. The law of the tithe was broken constantly. But the principle was confessed and often acted upon. Abraham paid tithes to Melchisedec. Jacob vowed the tithe at Bethel. GOD ordered it in the Mosaic Law as a regular and fixed charge upon the income of the Jew. It was a tithe upon all the income,—produce and flocks alike. This did not include the free-will- and thank-offerings and first-fruits. Then, at the end of every third year, the increase was to be tithed also, and a public festival was to be held at some central place for each locality. And the Jew was to invite the widow, the fatherless, and the stranger, and he was to offer a solemn prayer, declaring that he had offered to the LORD all that he was commanded to do by the Law. The Jew, then, who fulfilled his duty, paid the tithe of the increase, and made his offerings with a glad heart, offered nearly twenty-five per cent. of his income as a holy thing to JEHOVAH, and this was a bounden duty. His prosperity depended upon it; and so long as he paid it he was blessed in his store, in his basket, in his flock, and in his field. It seems that it was intended to stamp upon the religious mind the necessity of offering tithes as a condition of grace, and then it was to be left to the conscience and free-will of the offerer. But tithes were not commanded under the Christian dispensation, while their principle is evidently presupposed in the Sermon on the Mount. As in so many other points the will of GOD having been sufficiently declared and the precedent having been set, the Christian Church was left at liberty to act as circumstances should direct. The Church was to be as flexible and have as large a power of adaptability as was possible. Yet the precedent of the Mosaic Law was not to be lost sight of in the larger liberty of the Gospel. In the first century of Apostolic work we know from the New Testament what the freedom of the Gospel led men to do,—sell houses and lands to give all to their poor. They gave of their ability each one severally as he would. So in the second century we find but little allusion to this, yet the Fathers taught that as the principle of the commandments was carried further back than the letter of the law, so our LORD intended to remove the restraint of the tenth that we might give more joyfully and freely. Again, in the third century we find this gladsome giving urged; and we know that immediately after a severe persecution St Cyprian was able out of the Church treasury to send quite a large sum for the ransom of some Christian captives carried off by plundering Numidian marauders. The tithe so far from being the maximum was not even set as the minimum. There was no real limit, for every one was expected to do all he could freely. The suggestion of tithes was later; the law of tithes was first alluded to in the Apostolic Constitutions, which, since it was a kind of Directorium, was probably a work that grew in successive editions, as would be natural. The idea was further suggested by St. Ambrose's saying that the Christian Priest succeeded to the position of the Levitical. Thence this idea of the tithe was introduced and became the principle of giving; but as this which had been the minimum before now became the maximum, it was enacted by the various provincial synods from about Charlemagne's time that tithes were the first property of the Church, and this demand was enforced by civil enactments. From this time on, tithes took their place in the regular income and was a charge upon the estates. It is not necessary for us to trace this further, since tithes are only a voluntary act, but indeed as really binding upon a man, if offered by vow or promise, as if made compulsory.

But it is a very serious duty for every one in the receipt of any income, whether by daily toil or from any other source whatever, to consider his dependence upon the merciful compassion of the LORD of the Universe, and to ask himself if a tithe is not the least that he can offer in return for what he has received from GOD. The remarks of the earlier Fathers in connection with this subject, that our LORD bade His disciples see to it that their righteousness should exceed the righteousness of the Scribes and Pharisees, taught the duty of alms-giving, and so far from condemning, commended the paying of the tithe of mint, anise, and cummin, and are worth more than a passing thought. They suggested that the Christian should do more than the Jew. Nor is it too much to say that tithes honestly paid with a glad heart bring prosperity and contentment. It is a trust from GOD that enables us to have anything to give, and it is a grace of the HOLY GHOST in the heart that enables the devout giver to give joyfully and to prove that he is fit to be trusted with more. Tithes were held to be the minimum. Free-will-offerings, Gifts, Thank-offerings, were also poured into the treasury of the Church. St. Cyprian upon his taking orders, after providing for his sister, gave all his goods to the Church in Carthage, among other real estate some gardens which he owned. So others upon coming into the Church gave freely. Were the tithes and the ancient system of a common treasury for each Diocese faithfully carried out, the work of the Church in Missions and other responsibilities would be well supplied with all things needful.

Title. The ancient Canon law provided that no one could receive holy orders unless he were appointed to serve some Parish church or some Priest in a Parish. An exception was made in favor of those who were to serve in a Cathedral and those who were officers in a College. Under this principle the Canons require that no one can receive Priest's orders who cannot produce to the Bishop a satisfactory certificate that he is engaged to serve some Church, Parish, or Congregation, or is an agent for some Missionary Society recognized by the General Convention, or is a Tutor, Professor, or Instructor of youth in some incorporated educational Institution, or is to serve as Chaplain in the Army or Navy (Tit. i., Can. viii., § iii.). It is eminently proper, or many could receive orders in the Ministry with no field in which to minister their office.

Titles, the, of the Holy Trinity. The first Person of the Ever-Blessed TRINITY is in Holy Scripture styled a "CREATOR" (Ecc. xii. 1; Isa. xi. 28; Rom. i. 25; 1 Pet. iv. 19). The endearing term "FATHER" is applied to Him (Deut. xxxii. 6; 1 Cor. viii. 6); "FATHER of all" (Eph. iv. 6); "One FATHER" (Mal. ii. 10); "Our FATHER" in the LORD'S Prayer (St. Matt. vi. 9). Our SAVIOUR addresses Him as "FATHER" (St. John xvii. 1), and "the only true GOD" (v. 3); "Holy FATHER" (v. 11); "Righteous FATHER" (v. 25); "LORD of heaven and earth" (St. Matt. xi. 25). In the fourth verse of the sixty-eighth Psalm GOD is called "JAH," and in the next verse, "A Father of the fatherless and a Judge of the widows." "Maker," "Husband," "Holy One of Israel," and "GOD of the whole earth" (Isa. liv. 5). The Spirit of adoption teaches men to "cry, Abba, Father" (Rom. viii. 15). The idea of the Fatherhood of GOD expresses a still closer relation in the term, "The Father of our LORD JESUS CHRIST" (Rom. xv. 6; 2 Cor. xi. 31; and Eph. i. 3). The majesty of GOD is shown in Ps. xxiv. 7, by the expression "King of glory," and St. Paul calls GOD "The Blessed and only Potentate; the King of kings, and Lord of lords" (1 Tim. vi. 15). In Abraham's prayer for Sodom he pleads with GOD as "the Judge of all the earth" (Gen. xviii. 25). He is represented as a "Lawgiver" (Isa. xxxiii. 22; James iv. 12). The glorious orb of day furnishes an emblem of the beneficence of GOD: "The LORD GOD is a sun" (Ps. lxxxiv. 11). The same verse indicates His protective power by the word "shield." "GOD is our Refuge and strength" (Ps. xlvi. 1). The stability of GOD draws from David the figure of a "Rock" and "Fortress" (Ps. xxxi. 3). The word rock is a favorite one in the Psalms in this connection: "Lead me to the Rock that is higher than I" (Ps. lxi. 2). The song of Moses refers to this comparison: "For their rock is not as our Rock, even our enemies themselves being judges" (Deut. xxxii. 31).

David also speaks of GOD as his "Light," and "salvation," and "the strength of his life" (Ps. xxvii. 1). The unlimited power of GOD the FATHER displays itself in His address to Abram: "I am the Almighty GOD" (Gen. xvii. 1). The Hebrew Name JEHOVAH, from the verb to be, relates to the fact that GOD exists of Himself, and that He has existed from all eternity, and that He will forever exist (Ex. vi. 3). "I AM hath sent me unto you" (Ex. iii. 14). The troubled Jacob understands that his Maker is "the GOD of Beth-el" (Gen. xxxi. 13). Similar is the oft-repeated expression, "The GOD of Israel" (Ex. xxiv. 10, etc.). The character of GOD shines out in His own description of Himself as "the Holy One" (Hosea xi. 9). The echo of this comes back in our LORD'S words, "Holy FATHER" (St. John xvi. 11). What a comfort in St. Paul's expression, "the GOD of patience and consolation"! (Rom. xv. 5.) The duration of GOD is manifested in the phrase "the eternal GOD" (Deut. xxxiii. 27), and "the everlasting GOD" (Gen. xxi. 33. See Isa. lx. 28). Nebuchadnezzar describes GOD as "the most high GOD" (Dan. iii. 26), Cyrus as "the LORD GOD of heaven" (Ezra i. 2). GOD speaks to Amos as "the LORD, the GOD of hosts" (Amos v. 16). Moses designates Him as "the living GOD" (Deut. v. 26), and Nehemiah (ix. 31) as "a gracious and merciful GOD." In Ps. lxxxix. 8, we find the words "strong LORD." These titles of GOD the FATHER present Him as Creator, Father, King, Judge, and Refuge, and as ever-existing, all-holy, all-powerful, and all-merciful. Thus He is the constant Preserver and the ceaseless Benefactor of the creatures whom His own hand has made.

The Second Person of the Trinity, our LORD and SAVIOUR JESUS CHRIST, appears in prophecy in the beginning of the Old Testament Scriptures as the "Seed" of the woman who should bruise Satan (Gen. iii.

15). He is "the Head-Stone of the corner" (Ps. cxviii. 22); "A precious Corner-stone, a sure Foundation" (Isa. xxviii. 16; *cf.* 1 Pet. ii. 6, and Eph. ii. 20). JESUS CHRIST was "a righteous Branch," and "a King," and should "be called THE LORD OUR RIGHTEOUSNESS" (Jer. xxiii. 5, 6). The High-Priest typified CHRIST (Heb. ii. 17): "A merciful and faithful High-Priest." He was "the Lamb of GOD, which taketh away the sin of the world" (St. John i. 29), and "the Messias" (v. 41), "The SON of GOD," and "the King of Israel" (v. 49; compare St. John v. 19, 23, 25; 1 Cor. xv. 28, and St. Mark xiii. 32). But while our LORD claims the homage of "the SON of GOD," He also humbles Himself to be "the SON of man" (v. 27): "JESUS CHRIST our LORD" (Rom. i. 3); "Thou art my SON" (Ps. ii. 7); "The SON of the living GOD" (St. Matt. xvi. 16); "The CHRIST of GOD" (St. Luke ix. 20). CHRIST means Anointed One, or Messiah: "Alpha and Omega, the beginning and the ending" (Rev. i. 8); "The Door" (St. John x. 7); "The Good Shepherd" (v. 11); "The Sun of righteousness" (Mal. iv. 2); "A Star out of Jacob" (Num. xxiv. 7); "The bright and morning Star" (Rev. xxii. 16); "The true Light which lighteth every man that cometh into the world" (St. John i. 9); "The resurrection and the life" (St. John xi. 25); "A Fountain" (Zech. xiii. 1); "The Rose of Sharon and the Lily of the valleys" (Solomon's Song ii. 1); "The Bread of Life" (St. John vi. 35); "The True Vine" (St. John xv. 1); "First-born" (Ps. lxxxix. 27); "The image of the invisible GOD" (Col i. 15); "The Head of the body, the Church" (v. 18); "A Prince and a Saviour" (Acts v. 31); "Prince of life" (Acts iii. 15); "The Holy One and the Just" (Acts iii. 14); "Heir of all things" (Heb. i. 2); "Brightness of His glory, and the express image of His Person" (v. 3); "The Beginning, the First-born from the dead" (Col. i. 18); "The Way, the Truth, and the Life" (St. John xiv. 6); "My LORD and my GOD" (St. John xx. 28); "The Word" (St. John i. 1); "The Word of GOD" (Rev. xix. 13); "Equal with GOD" (Phil. ii. 6. See, also, St. John v. 17, 18, for our LORD'S own assertion of Sonship, and the natural inference of the Jews); "The only-begotten SON" (St. John i. 18); "The CHRIST" (v. 20); "JESUS of Nazareth" (ver. 45); "JESUS" (St. Matt. i. 21, 25); "The LORD JESUS CHRIST" (1 Cor. viii. 6); "The LORD" (Heb. ii. 3); "Emmanuel, . . . GOD with us" (St. Matt. i. 23, and Isa. vii. 14); "Author of eternal salvation unto all them that obey Him" (Heb. v. 9); "The Author and Finisher of our faith" (Hab. xii. 2); "Wonderful, Counselor, The mighty GOD, The everlasting Father, The Prince of Peace" (Isa. ix. 6); "Our LORD JESUS, that great Shepherd of the sheep" (Heb. xiii. 20); "The chief Shepherd" (1 Pet. v. 4); "The Shepherd and Bishop of your souls" (1 Pet. ii. 25); "CHRIST in you, the hope of glory" (Col. i. 27); "Our LORD and SAVIOUR JESUS CHRIST" (2 Pet. iii. 18); "King of kings, and Lord of lords" (Rev. xix. 16); "A Prophet" (Acts iii. 22); "The LORD of glory" (1 Cor. ii. 8). These titles represent the SON of GOD as a Saviour and Redeemer and Lord, and the manner in which, in Holy Writ, the same terms are used for both the Holy FATHER and the Holy SON teach us, to quote our LORD'S own words, "That all men should honor the SON, even as they honor the FATHER. He that honoreth not the SON, honoreth not the FATHER which hath sent Him" (St. John v. 23); "Search the Scriptures; for in them ye think ye have eternal life, and they are they which testify of Me" (v. 39).

The following names are given to the HOLY SPIRIT, the Third Person of the Holy Trinity: "The Spirit of GOD" (Gen. i. 2, and Job xxxiii. 4). In the reference in Job the phrase is added, "the breath of the Almighty;" "the Comforter" (St. John xiv. 26); "the Eternal Spirit" (Heb. ix. 14); "Free Spirit" (Ps. li. 12); "Spirit of the LORD GOD" (Isa. lxi. 1, and see St. Luke iv. 18); "the Spirit of the LORD;" "the Spirit" (St. Luke iv. 1); "the Spirit of His SON" (Gal. iv. 6); "the Spirit of JESUS CHRIST" (Phil. i. 19); "Spirit of CHRIST" (Rom. viii. 9, and 1 Pet. i. 11); "Spirit of Judgment" and "Spirit of burning" (Isa. iv. 4); "Good Spirit" (Neh. ix. 20; see Ps. cxliii. 10); "the Spirit of our GOD" (1 Cor. vi. 11); "Spirit of the living GOD" (2 Cor. iii 3); "the HOLY GHOST" (Acts ix. 31); "GOD" (Acts v. 4; *cf.* v. 3); "HOLY SPIRIT" (Ps. li. 11, and St. Luke xi. 13); "Holy Spirit of GOD" (Eph. iv. 30); "Holy Spirit of promise" (Eph. i. 13); "the LORD" (2 Cor. iii. 17; compare Nicene Creed); "the Power of the Highest" (St. Luke i. 35); "Spirit of adoption (Rom. viii. 15); "Spirit of Truth" (St. John xv. 26); "the Spirit of Him that raised up JESUS from the dead" (Rom. viii. 11); "the Spirit of His Son" (Gal. iv. 6); "the Spirit of life" (Rom. viii. 2); "the Spirit of your Father" (St. Matt. x. 20); "the Spirit of Grace" (Heb. x. 29); "the Spirit of Prophecy" (Rev. xix 10); "the Spirit of Wisdom and Understanding, the Spirit of Counsel and Might, the Spirit of Knowledge and the Fear of the LORD" (Isa. xi. 2); "the Spirit of Holiness" (Rom. i. 4); "the Spirit of Wisdom and Revelation" (Eph. i. 17); "the Spirit of Glory" (1 Pet. iv. 14); "the Seven Spirits of GOD" (Rev. iii. 1); "Voice of the LORD" (Ps. cvi. 25). The epithet "Holy" indicates the sanctifying power of the Spirit of GOD: "Sanctified by the HOLY GHOST" (Rom. xv. 16). His guiding and leading work is shown in our LORD'S words, "He will guide you into all truth" (St. John xv. 13); "the finger of GOD" (St. Luke xi. 20). In addition to the titles given to the HOLY SPIRIT in Scripture, several emblems are made use of to explain its work.

Water is abundant and free. It cleanses,

purifies, and refreshes, hence the prophet says, taught by the Spirit how to speak of Himself, "I will pour water upon him that is thirsty, and floods upon the dry ground; I will pour my Spirit upon thy seed" (Isa. xliv. 3). Water was naturally used in Holy Baptism, and the SAVIOUR declares that "except a man be born of water and of the Spirit, he cannot enter into the kingdom of GOD" (St. John iii. 5). Spiritual life is "living water" (St. John iv. 10). It is not stagnant, but constantly flowing. Fire enlightens and purifies. The disciples of CHRIST were to be baptized "with the HOLY GHOST, and with fire" (St. Matt. iii. 11). On the Day of Pentecost "there appeared unto them cloven tongues like as of fire, and it sat upon each of them. And they were all filled with the HOLY GHOST" (Acts ii. 3, 4). The Wind is powerful and reviving. The word Spirit means breath or wind, and our LORD says of its unseen work, "So is every one that is born of the Spirit" (St. John iii. 8). Oil heals, and is used for consecrating. The Wise Virgins in the parable were furnished with oil, or spiritual life (St. Matt. xxv. 4). The rain and the dew are gentle and vivifying. Hosea says of GOD, "He shall come unto us as the rain" (ch. v. 3), and, "I will be as the dew unto Israel" (ch. xiv. 5). The dove is an emblem of meekness and innocence. After the baptism of JESUS we read of "the Spirit of GOD descending like a dove, and lighting upon Him" (St Matt. iii. 16). A voice teaches, "If any man hear My voice, and open the door, I will come in to him, and will sup with him, and he with Me" (Rev. iii. 20). A seal impresses and secures: "Ye were sealed with that HOLY SPIRIT of promise" (Eph. i. 13).

The idea of the Holy Trinity embedded in the Scriptures is well compared to that of a cross in the ground plan of a Cathedral. The whole structure shows the design. "And if, too, to him (St. John) this great belief was more than belief, this "light" was also "life"; if he could feel it blessed to acknowledge a Father who is *our* Father, a Son in whom *we* also "are called the sons of GOD," a Holy Spirit who "dwelleth with *us* and shall be in us;" may we also find in the TRINITY the ground of practical devotion, pure and deep, till, quickened by the power of this faith, the Three that bear record in Heaven shall bear their witness in our hearts; and the Trinity shall have become, not the cold conclusion of the intellect, but the priceless treasure of the affections, the blessed foundation, and the perpetual strength of the new and spiritual life!" The mystery of faith is an invaluable treasure, but the vessel that contains it must be clean and undefiled; it must be held in a pure conscience; as the manna, that glorious symbol of the word of faith preached to us by the Gospel, was confined to the tabernacle, and preserved in a vessel of gold.

Authorities: Foster's Cyc. of Illustrations, Cruden's Definitions in his Concordance, Knapp's Theology, Bishop Horne's Ser. on the Trinity, E. H. Bickersteth's Rock of Ages, H. T. Bailey's Liturgy Compared with the Bible, Prof. Butler's Ser. on The Trinity Disclosed in the Structure of St. John's Writings, and Jones on The Trinity.   REV. S. F. HOTCHKIN.

Titus. One of the nearest and dearest of the companions St. Paul took with him. Silas, Timotheus, Titus, Luke, seem to have been his loving associates. "I had no rest in my spirit," wrote St. Paul to the Corinthians, "because I found not Titus, my brother." He is only noticed in the Epistles, but these notices and the missions he is sent upon all imply a man of forcible and upright character, thoroughly to be trusted, and zealous in anything he undertook. St. Paul tells the Galatians that Titus was a Gentile. He sends him to Corinth twice upon a mission which was connected with the discipline of the Church. He left him in Crete to establish the Church there, and the charge he gave him implied that Titus was a man of firmness and nerve. St. Andrew, Archbishop of Crete, describes him as the first founder of the Church in Crete, "the pillar of the Truth, the main stay of the Faith, the unwearied trumpeter of the Evangelical Promises, the lofty utterer as a tongue for St. Paul." The Apostle recalled him from Crete, apparently after his first imprisonment, and was probably with him till the second, when he was sent on a mission to Dalmatia. Here all our really authentic information ends.

Titus, Epistle to. The Apostle writes after his first imprisonment this second of the three Pastoral Epistles to Titus, his own son after the common Faith. The Apostle knowing the difficulties of his position and the character of the Cretans, gives him short, clear, and authoritative counsels for action. The directions are all explicit, and show that Titus was a man of more than ordinary vigor and capable of dealing sharply and promptly, as he probably had proven in his mission to the Corinthians. He is bidden to set the Church in order; to ordain Elders; to rebuke the careless, that they may be sound in the Faith; to see that the men and women conduct themselves soberly and discreetly in all things; to direct the slaves to honest, faithful service; to put them in mind of the rightful authority of the powers that be; to reject heretics. It is evident that age and toil had not lessened the Apostle's sense of authority and responsibility, and that he bade his fellow-workers exercise their commission to the full. There is one argument in favor of the continuance and increase of the Apostolic office drawn from this Epistle of the Apostle. It is impossible to suppose that St. Paul had planted a Church without giving to it Elders. If the Elders (Presbyters) were competent to perpetuate their office, why leave Titus, then, with special instructions about them? If he was an Apostle also, as St. Paul's words elsewhere imply (2 Cor. viii. 23), then all is clear and plain. And, too, Titus is in exactly the same position that Timothy held in Ephesus. Now Timothy is numbered by St. Paul in his first Epistle to the Thessalonians with himself as an Apostle (1 Thess. i. 1): "Paul, and Silvanus, and Timotheus, . . . when we might have been burdensome as the Apostles of CHRIST" (ch. ii. 6). If Silas and Timothy, then Titus too. In fact, St. Paul's company must have consisted of men with Apostolic Commission above the rank of the Presbyters fitted to take the missions upon which St. Paul sent them. He was too skilled an organizer and too delicately appreciative of others' feelings and rights to have made so signal a blunder as would be implied by any other course.

Tobit, Book of. This story of a faithful captive Jew contains many points which are interesting and instructive. It was highly esteemed among the Jews. Tobit's prayer of rejoicing (chap. xiii.) is a hearty rendering of praise to GOD. The doctrine of good and evil spirits is plainly taught by the introduction of the evil Asmodeus, and of "Raphael, one of the seven holy angels, which present the prayers of the saints, and which go in and out before the glory of the Holy One." The miracles are not in keeping with those narrated in historical Scripture. The book may have had a historical basis, but extraordinary details have found place in it. The point is in the good moral lessons, while the incidents are pictures to enliven the story and impress the teaching. It is thought by Ewald that the work may have been written in the East, "towards the close of the Persian period." The way in which Media is spoken of (ch. xiv. 4) would imply the strength of the Persian monarchy at that time. There is much reference to alms-giving, and the burial of the dead, and to the Jerusalem worship. Luther said of this book that it was "a truly beautiful, wholesome, and profitable fiction, the work of a gifted poet. . . . A book useful for Christian reading." Tobit is quoted in the Second Book of Homilies (of Alms-deeds). Three verses are found among the sentences at the offertory, beginning, "Give alms of thy goods," etc. (iv. 7-9). For the reference to the sins of our forefathers in the Litany, see Tobit iii. 3. The book is valuable as a beautiful picture of Jewish domestic life Its works seem to spring from living faith. The alms-giving is loving service (i. 16, 17; ii. 1-7; iv. 7-11, 16). The injunction in the last reference is noteworthy, "let not thine eye be envious when thou givest alms." The tenderness of domestic life displays itself in this book in the weeping of Anna when her son had started on his journey (v. 17) and the father's pious consolation, which pointed to angelic aid, and dried her tears (vs. 20-22). The affection of Raguel and his family (vii. 4-8) is a pleasant touch of Eastern life. Tobit counts the days, impatiently awaiting the return of his son, while the mother neglects her food, and goes out into the way to watch for her child's coming (x. 1-7). The various family relations are painted in simple patriarchal style, as in the happy return of Tobias (ch. xi.). Prayer is highly esteemed (iv. 19). The angel Raphael is represented as a healer by the appointment of GOD (iii. 17), and the one who brought remembrance of faithful prayers "before the Holy One" (xii. 12). The particular incidents and descriptions of this book may show a historical basis. Horne conjectures that it was begun by Tobit, continued by his son Tobias, and finished by some other member of the family. We have lessons of charity and patience in Tobit's ready aid to his distressed brethren, and his pious submission, like that of Job, to captivity, poverty, and blindness. St. Jerome translated this book into Latin in a rapid manner, by the aid of a learned Jew. The closing up of the book is very striking. Tobit ends his praises of GOD, and declares his faith in the prophecy of GOD by Jonah concerning Nineveh. He looks forward to the destruction of idolatry, and the turning of the nations to sacred Jerusalem, and so in faith he dies, an hundred and fifty-eight years old, and receives honorable burial; his wife follows him shortly to the same tomb. The son Tobias grows old with honor, and dies "an hundred and seven and twenty years old."

Authorities: B. F. Westcott in Wm. Smith's Dict. of the Bible, Prideaux's Connections, Arnald's Comm. in Patrick and Lowth and Whitby, Horne's Introduction.

REV. S. F. HOTCHKIN.

Toleration. To bear with those who hold what is not approved of as true is an act in which we imitate the forbearance of our LORD. To tolerate what is wrong or leads to wrong, when we have the responsibility of seeing that it may be amended, or of protesting against it, is contrary to honesty. To tolerate our neighbor's *sins* without trying to urge him to amendment is a wrong to society. But to force him to do as we think right is to interfere with him and to usurp an illegal authority. The duty and the limits of true toleration are not properly understood. In this country, where equal freedom is given to all "to worship GOD according to the dictates of their own conscience," there is no need to use the word with regard to those who form religious bodies separate from our own, and their rights we are bound to respect. But within the limits of the Church there can be no such thing as toleration. The widest liberty is allowed in accord with the truth. The VI. Article lays down this principle: "Holy Scripture containeth all things necessary to salvation: so that whatsoever is not read therein, nor may be proved thereby, is not required of any man, that it should be believed as an Article of the Faith, or be thought requisite or necessary to salvation." There can be no larger liberty possible; no conditions are laid down other than those in Holy Scriptures. But it would be evidently subversive of the very existence of the Church to yield more, and to tolerate any infringement upon these. It would be fatal to permit any doctrine of men to be substituted and enforced. It is but a just defense of the truth which we must ever enforce. It was on this principle that St. Paul resisted the intolerant conduct of those who would fetter the true Faith with their notions (Gal. ii. 4, 5). It was the disciplinary power of the Church which purged it from heretics and false teachers. Toleration in this sense must be necessarily impossible if the principles set forth in the last message of our LORD to the Church (Rev. ii., iii.) are true. There is a forbearance and an expostulation and an admonition which must be used (Tit. iii. 10). There must be an allowance for defects in education and in capacity to understand, but this is another thing. Beyond the point of kindness to the individual, there should be care for the safety of others in the Church, who might be misled. It lies with the Bishops as the responsible Angels of the Church to judge what is the true limit of a toleration, and where kindness and forbearance cease to be rightly and charitably exercised.

Tonsure. It was a practice in the Church from early times to cut the hair of those entering into holy orders; but tonsure or shaving of a portion of the hair of the crown (as in the Western Church), or totally (as in the Eastern), was of comparatively late date. The earliest authentic order upon it is said to be a Canon of the fourth Council of Toledo (633 A.D.). From that time, however, directions about it are more and more common. In the English Church, Tonsure was dropped at the Reformation.

Tradition. The word tradition (a thing or fact or belief handed down, whether by written memoranda or orally) has lost so much of its better meaning that it is difficult to make that just and right use of the word which is demanded by facts. Our LORD condemned the traditions of the Jews, which made the commandments of GOD of none effect. This is probably, in part, the reason why the word has gained with us an evil sense. The other reason is that so many false traditions had grown up in the Church during the Middle Ages that when the English Church purged these away, the word was used to brand them as unworthy of credit; and despite the protest of the XXXIV. Article the popular use of the word has overborne its legitimate use. The Jews, we know, had an Oral Law which, while it merited our LORD'S condemnation in many things, yet contained the true explanation of the prophecies concerning Him, and kept ever clearly before them the doctrine of the resurrection. St. Paul speaks of the traditions which he had given the Thessalonians, and condemns others' teachings. Now while it may be said that these were not traditions as we now use the word, yet the teaching by "word of mouth" was the foundation of tradition. But there were necessarily traditional usages, unwritten customs which could and did vary in different places; and for the years of persecution and trial in the Primitive Church much had to be intrusted to tradition. There then grew up cases and interpretations of practices right in themselves which formed that body of unwritten common law which is called tradition. To this day we must use tradition. No series of rubrics in the Prayer-Book are so closely joined or contain such minute directions but something is left to inherited custom. Such were the directions of St. Paul when protesting against innovation. He practically appealed to the principle of tradition when he wrote, "we have no such custom, neither the Churches of God" (1 Cor. xi. 16). Using the word, then, in its true sense as the handing down correctly of a custom, a usage, or of some unwritten law of the Church, we find the English Church and our own setting forth the just use of tradition in its rites and ceremonies thus: "It is not necessary that Traditions and Ceremonies be in all places one, or utterly like, for at all times they have been divers, and may be changed according to the diversity of countries, times and men's manners, so that nothing be ordained against GOD'S word. Whosoever through his private judgment willingly and purposely doth openly break the traditions and ceremonies of the Church which be not repugnant to the Word of GOD, and be ordained and approved by common authority, ought to be rebuked openly (that others may fear to do the like), as he that offendeth against the common Order of the Church and hurteth the Authority of the Magistrate, and woundeth the consciences of the weak Brethren. Every particular or national Church hath authority to ordain, change, and abolish Ceremonies or Rites of the Church ordained only by man's authority, so that all things be done to edifying." (Art. XXXIV.)

The Consenting witness of the early ages of Christianity is not to be despised. Indeed, much more depends upon it than many have thought. Tradition, in its best sense, and treating of subjects of the highest importance, has preserved for us the proofs of the Apostolic Succession, the genuineness and the Canonical Authority of Holy Scripture, the Apostles' Creed, the observance of the LORD'S Day, the continuity of the Church, the rites of Baptism, the early proof of the use of Infant Baptism. Subjects of less essential importance, but of great value, are the Liturgical observances, the divisions of the Christian year, the arrangement of the great Feasts, the healthy growth of Ritual. The Rubrics of our own Prayer-Book, which were arranged at its compilation, in 1549 A.D., presuppose a tradition and custom which have been but imperfectly transmitted in continuous use from several causes. (*Vide* RUBRICS.) It is one of the efforts made by many to endeavor to recover and to restore these traditions, so far as practicable. But the Article most wisely states that each Church " has authority to ordain, change, or abolish Ceremonies or Rites of the Church ordained only by man's authority, so that all things be done to edifying." It would be a sad loss and a breakage of the finer lines of that cord of continuous discipline and usage and Ritual which holds us to the past and may be in essentials traced to Isapostolic usage and tradition. Still, for overruling cause, for the sake of winning souls, for the preaching of the Gospel, all of these lesser bonds might and should be broken. Let that day never come.

Transfiguration. Feast of Transfiguration (August 6). This feast was one of somewhat late institution. It was introduced into the Greek ritual about 700 A.D., for St. John Damascenus, and Cosmas wrote hymns for the Office. In the West it is claimed that it was observed as early as the time of Leo I., 450 A.D. But Potho of Prum, 1152 A.D., condemned it as a novelty. It was ordered to be universally observed in the West by Calixtus II., 1457 A.D., upon occasion of the defeat of the Turks before Belgrade. The date of its observance is, throughout the Orthodox Greek Churches and the West, August 6. It was dropped from the list of the greater feasts in the English Church. The General Convention, October, 1886 A.D., have restored it, and appointed a Collect, Epistle, and Gospel for it.

It commemorates an act of our LORD which has a deep significance in relation to our spiritual life. He, before His last journey to Jerusalem, took the three chief Apostles with Him into a high mountain, and then as He prayed He was transfigured before them. His raiment became as white as snow, His face shone as the Sun, and Moses and Elias appeared and talked with Him of the decease He should accomplish at Jerusalem. There are several important points to be noted. It was in His human nature that this took place, and after His discipline, which preceded the last of the series of the acts of the Redemption. The glory that shone through that humiliation was now a part of His sinless nature, and it was the consequence of His fasting prayers and doing so perfectly the will of His FATHER. This glory, the Shekinah which was His in His eternal nature, was already manifested in His miracles, in His wondrous powers over nature. It was this by which He awed His opponents. "Never man spake as this man."

Yet the transfiguration was a step more. His humanity was now interfused and perfected in the glory. Henceforth we note a change in our LORD. Acting, teaching, leading with authority always, now He goes forward steadfastly towards Jerusalem. He sends messengers before His face to prepare His way. He, as it were, rules and overrules the acts of others that He should now accomplish His decease, and after that be received up again. The grace and the strength of the Transfiguration were needed (let us say it reverently) for the Cross, as the Baptism and the Dove must precede the temptation. For us, then, St. Paul's language, " be not conformed to this world: but be ye transformed by the removing of your mind, that ye may prove what is that good, and acceptable, and perfect will of GOD," is divinely given us to receive its interpretation from the Transfiguration of our dear LORD.

Translation of a Bishop from one See to another of higher importance and value. It was early practiced in the Church, and gave a good deal of trouble. There were frequent efforts made by ambitious holders of small Sees to obtain promotion, which in many instances were successful, contrary to the regulations. But the later Councils, while forbidding it as a practice, still allowed it under only certain extreme cases; and the irregularity of the act was once made the pretext for removing Gregory Nazianzen from the Patriarchate of Constantinople. In the English Church, translations are quite frequent. In our own Church there have been several instances of translation from Missionary Jurisdictions to Dioceses.

Treasurer. A dignitary to whom was committed the collection and the disbursement of the moneys of the Church or of the Monastery. Now he has the same office in the Parish or in the Diocese. It is the most important of all the offices held in the management of the Temporalties of the Church. It requires much financial tact and skill, and is that office which when properly discharged lessens the friction of the different parts of the Parochial or Diocesan organization. Our peculiar economical arrangements throw very much into the hands of the treasurer, who has with irregularly paid and, too often, scanty moneys to meet the many and varied requisitions made upon him by the needs of the Rector and of the Parish. If he should prove incompetent in skillful management the defect is instantly felt; should he be competent he is hardly known. His office represents the health of the Parish in temporals. And as health of body is assumed and carelessly used, and only valued when lost, so the functions and delicate duties of the treasurer are often only felt and rightly valued when they fail to be properly discharged.

Trent. The great Council of the Roman Church which was held at Trent, in the Tyrol. The progress of the Reformation in Germany, the appeals of the Reformers to a Free General Council, and the demands of the Emperor Charles V. for such a Council, and the promises made by previous Popes, forced Clement VII. to take steps to have a Council summoned in 1534 A.D. But he delayed, threw so many hinderances in the way, that it fell to his successor, Paul III., to convoke it, in 1546 A.D. Its history, of its prorogations and delays, of the intrigues and trickeries used, of the dissensions which threatened to dissolve it, of the political questions which influenced it, and of the political causes which reversed the conduct of the Embassadors present at it, the principles upon which its policy was based, are too intricate and involve the recital of too many concurrent secular events to permit any lengthened notice of it.

It was summoned in 1545 A.D. (December 13). It was removed to Bologna, where it was prorogued in 1547 A.D., after holding ten sessions in all. It was again convened at Trent in 1551 A.D., and held six more sessions, when, in 1552 A.D., it was again prorogued for two years, but this was extended to ten years. When its seventeenth session was held, January, 1562 A D., nine more sessions were rapidly held, and then, after reciting and confirming the acts of its earlier convocations, it dissolved. Clement VII. prepared the steps, Paul III. summoned it, Julius III. reconvened it, Paul IV. refused to end its prorogation, and finally Pius IV. ordered its last sessions. Its acts are divided into two series: (a) on Faith, (b) on Reformation, and on both it failed to meet the demands made upon it. Many things were ignored and others produced much dissension. The strongest arguments against the Papacy were urged, and it required all the address and diplomacy of the Italian legates, and all the political influence they could command, to avoid decisions upon some dangerous topics. The results of the Council were not adequate to the needs of the time, and the Popes congratulated themselves when they succeeded in proroguing it, and Pius IV. was relieved when it was dissolved. It refused relief on some doctrinal questions. It made the least possible concession on reform. It crystallized popular Roman doctrine and made some decrees that are absolutely at variance with all facts. It neutralized all important concessions by the phrase "reserving the rights of the holy See." Its claims to be a General Council are worthless; neither the Eastern nor the English Bishops were represented in it. Its decrees were protested against from time to time by the French or Spanish Embassadors. It was not free, but was constantly under the control of the Pope, who prorogued it whenever it threatened to become unmanageable. Its decrees are received in France, but not in name. It failed to meet the true issues upon the questions for which it was summoned. Its whole effect was to solidify into one form the unformed floating opinions and doctrines of the Roman obedience, to bind more firmly the abuses of the Roman Curia, to enable the Pope to formulate an appendix to the Nicene Creed which made the decrees of that Council as binding upon every Bishop and Priest as the Articles of the Faith in the Creed.

A good, impartial history of the Council is yet needed, but the necessary documents are not all, even yet, collected, and the mass of papers now in reach have not been collected and put into proper order. Fra Paolo Sarpi in 1629 A.D. published a history of the Council, which exhibited its defects with great wit and sarcasm. A reply was attempted by Cardinal Pallavicini, 1660 A.D., but, except that it supplied some documents of value, it is not to be compared to Sarpi's attack. The genuine acts of the Council have only lately been published at Prague, by Father Thenier.

Authorities: Brent's translation of Sarpi's History, Mendham's Council of Trent, Pallavicini's History in Migne's Library, Paris, and numberless minor histories and defenses which are readily accessible.

Trine Baptism. The immersion of, or the pouring of water upon, the person baptized thrice,—once in the name of each Person of the HOLY TRINITY. It is an ancient custom, and of so early a date that it may be derived from Apostolic usage, as is shown in the recently discovered "Teaching of the Twelve Apostles," which is dated 120–160 A.D. The earliest mention of the details of the administration of the Sacrament gives this as the practice, and the Apostolic canons, which probably represent the rules which obtained before 325 A.D., direct that the Bishop or Priest who does not so administer baptism shall be deposed. It is something more than a devout practice, for at the least it makes it certain that the immersion or the affusion had been performed, which were it done but once and hastily might be doubted.

Trinity. It is the full all-containing revelation, the declaration of which our LORD came to complete. It was shadowed out in the Old Testament from the very first. The Names by which GOD chose to reveal Himself in His unity also included the TRINITY. (Vide ELOHIM and JEHOVAH.) The Name JEHOVAH was the name by which our LORD was addressed and received worship, and is now adored in heaven and in earth. ("Therefore let all the house of Israel know assuredly, that GOD hath made that same JESUS, whom ye have crucified, both LORD and CHRIST." Acts ii. 36.) He revealed the Unity of Nature in the One GODHEAD and the TRINITY of Persons: "I and My FATHER are One." "But when the Comforter is come whom I well send unto you from the FATHER, even the Spirit of Truth which proceedeth from the FATHER, He shall testify of Me." The Baptismal words also must imply whatever we believe of the Name of the FATHER, that also is the power of the Name of the SON, and of the Name of the HOLY GHOST. Not Three Names but one Name,—i.e., Power, Majesty, and Glory. Co-equal honor, worship, and obedience are due to the Three Persons in the Oneness of the Substance of GOD.

This doctrine of the TRINITY makes us Christians, for we must believe that CHRIST is the very and only-begotten SON of GOD, according to the summary of the Revelation in the Nicene Creed, or CHRIST has not the claim He makes and we yield for our worship and obedience. It is the foundation of our Confession. It is woven into our worship. It is in the front of all doctrinal statements. Passing by the Nicene Creed referred to, the first four obsecrations of the Litany express it: "O GOD the FATHER *of heaven; have mercy upon us miserable sinners.* O GOD the SON, *Redeemer of the world; have mercy upon us miserable sinners.* O GOD the HOLY GHOST, *proceeding from the FATHER and the* SON; *have mercy upon us miserable sinners. O holy, blessed, and glorious Trinity, Three Persons and One* GOD; *have mercy upon us miserable sinners.*"

Beside the other Liturgic offerings of prayer founded upon this Truth, as in the Invocation in the Communion office, and in the several offices of the Church and in the Collects, such as the slightest examination of the Prayer-Book will reveal, the first of the XXXIX. Articles puts forth this formal statement of the Doctrine: "There is but one living and true GOD, everlasting, without body, parts, or passions; of infinite power, wisdom, and goodness; the Maker and Preserver of all things, both visible and invisible. And in unity of this GODHEAD there be Three PERSONS, of one substance, power, and eternity; the FATHER, the SON, and the HOLY GHOST." Full expositions of this Article are so readily accessible that a full discussion here is unadvisable. But it may be well to note that the Fathers, before 325 A.D., having to combat varied local and temporary heresies, used often in defense phrases which, in view of subtler attacks (which they could not anticipate), appear now incautious; but throughout there is a wonderful consensus of teaching, remarkable, when the difficulties of interchange of thought and of agreement upon lines of defense between the leaders in any sudden emergency are considered. It only proves how full and complete the original deposit of the doctrine was, and how universally it was received. We owe the *term* TRINITY to the genius of Tertullian (who, however, did not use it in his controversy with Praxeas), when he gives this statement: "The union of the FATHER in the SON, and of the SON in the PARACLETE, implies Three conjoined, which Three are one Thing, not one Person." The most famous defender of the Doctrine of the TRINITY was St. Gregory Nazianzen, whose Five Theological Orations have placed him foremost, and to which we must go for subtle and thorough statements of this fundamental Article of the Faith.

"If the Christian faith concerning the TRINITY consist in admitting three Persons really distinct in a numerical unity of essence, it follows that these Persons must be co-eternal, co-equal, and consubstantial with each other; that the One must proceed from the other, the SON from the FATHER by eternal generation; the HOLY SPIRIT by way of procession from the FATHER and the SON as from one principle. And being convinced that the Three Persons are mysteriously united in one nature from all eternity, the believer is able to give a consistent account of the other truths of Christianity. He can consistently, with this belief, assert that one Person of the ever-blessed Trinity took upon Him our nature and remained undivided from GOD, retaining His nature as GOD, and His distinct personality while He took the Manhood into GOD. By saying this he neither divides the substance of GOD, by saying that part of Him became incarnate instead of saying that one Person of the GODHEAD took upon Him our nature; nor confounds the Person by calling them only three different manifestations of the same Person. By believing a Trinity of Persons he is relieved from the necessity of the blasphemy of the disceptibility of GOD, and, by believing in a Unity of nature, from the folly of dividing the essence of the Infinite. And when he asserts that one Person of the all-glorious Trinity took upon Him our nature, he does not thereby assert His unchangeable, divine nature to be subject to our passions or diminish aught from His eternal perfections, but that through His divine nature made flesh to be divine, seeing He did not destroy His body, but took it up to heaven, where it now ministers to the Christian's good in divers ways. To believe Him to have taken into GOD our nature is easier than to believe that He is the soul of the world; and to believe that there are distinct Persons in the GODHEAD than that He separated all creatures from His own essence; to believe that He has now a human body in heaven to which He will liken the bodies of the saints at last, according to His mighty working, is an easier task than that our bodies and all matter in the universe are an unreality." (Bishop Forbes's Nicene Creed, pp. 77, 78.)

Consult the Commentaries upon proof-texts, and Brown on the Trinity, Graves on the XXXIX. Articles, Blunt's Dict. of Hist. and Doct. Theol., Hook's Church Dict.

Trinity-Sunday. The Sunday following Whit-Sunday, and by which the Church completes the declaration of all the Doctrines of the holy Faith upon fixed days. It is one of the most valued of our Festival Sundays. It gathers up into one service an outline of all the revelations upon the Nature of GOD and our relation to Him as set forth in the Holy Scriptures, and closes the series of Articles of the Christian Faith. Its observance by name is peculiar to the English Church. Trinity-Sunday has the Epistle and Gospel which were assigned to the Sunday of the Octave of Pentecost in the Comes of St. Jerome, and its Collect is the one assigned in the Sacramentary of St. Gregory (596 A.D.). The retention of the name is a proof of the independence of the British

Church, since its offices, though lost now, influenced markedly the Earlier Saxon, which in turn moulded the Norman English Offices, so that the English Liturgic rule has ever retained its own distinctive marks. Our Feast of the HOLY TRINITY is, then, a most valuable one in many ways. Doctrinally, as training the members of the Church in all truth. Liturgically, as completing the cycle of worship and commemoration assigned to the Sundays of the year. Historically, (a) as teaching us (in the world's history) our relation to GOD in its lesson (Gen. i.), and (b) in its observance in the Church the true apostolic primitive independence of our Mother-Church of England.

Trisagion. A form of the *Ter Sanctus* which has obtained in the East and is used there: "Holy GOD, Holy and Mighty, Holy and Immortal, have mercy upon us." It is assigned to the time of St. Proclus of Constantinople (434 A.D.), but Freeman traces its elements to the Eighteen Prayers of the Synagogue, which were in use before our LORD'S day, and in which He joined in the Synagogue worship. It passed into Greek Liturgic use, and is of doctrinal importance. When Peter the Fuller (485 A.D.), Patriarch of Antioch, added "who wast crucified for us," the words, as either transferring its application from the Holy Trinity to our LORD alone, or as savoring of heresy, created great disturbances. Its use in the Latin Church of the West is limited only to Good-Friday, and it was dropped by the English Church.

Tropology. That use of a text which gives it a moral significance apart from, or rather folded within, the external and temporary meaning of the text.

Truth. We all, by the constitution of our nature, demand the truth. No question is harder to answer than Pilate's, "What is truth?" when we turn to the human side; none more readily answered when we accept our LORD'S declaration, "I am the Truth." Truth is largely relative, and only in the case of *facts*, and of these as facts, can absolute truth be obtained. There is nothing harder to get at than the "Truth, the whole truth, and nothing but the truth." The reason for this is plain when we pass behind the mere surface. The taint of sin destroys the perfect harmony of our intercourse with each other, and we, from selfishness and sin, act towards each other in half-truths. It has so fatally destroyed the intercourse with GOD, the source of all truth, that He alone can restore it, and only as we are willing can we receive His truth, from which all subordinate truths receive their true relation. Truth, then, as a thing to be acquired, possessed, is the desire of every heart, but it is so dislocated and distorted that we cannot get it as fully as we would, nor do we accept it as fully as we profess it. Again, the Truth of GOD, as a possession, is not of our creation. We do not make it, but we must make it our own by accepting it. In the dealings of man with man, whether with a superior, equal, or inferior, truthfulness is our professed principle of action, but it is only half acted upon, and we live with each other more or less on terms of semi-concealment and of implied generally unconscious falsehood. This is the case in business relations, and it decidedly affects our social relations. If, then, we are so trained by daily habits, how shall we be able to accept GOD'S truth fairly and with a pure heart?

Again, in receiving truth, we take it upon evidence. But in most cases the evidence is received and examined by the few, and is reported upon, and the mass accept and act upon this report. Leading masterful intellects, then, whether competent or not to weigh evidence, fashion much of the truth which is generally received. Again, from the nature of some kinds, and these the most important truths, the evidence in their behalf must be most imperfect. In religious truths we are as children learning the alphabet, and have not the ability to comprehend the tithe of the actual evidence direct and circumstantial which is placed within our reach. Glimpses of it and of the extent to which GOD has actually given it are vouchsafed us, but the spiritual mind alone can enter into its meaning. With these facts before us, we can see why men so often reject some truths which are most vital, and substitute for them fair-seeming provisions, and why, with the plain, full statements of the Gospel before them, many men reject the Truth, more half accept it, and reject what they do not care to examine, and but few accept the whole truth. It is therefore true that because they will not choose to hear it the whole Truth is a sealed book to multitudes. For all men have not the Faith,—*i.e.*, that belief in GOD which enables them to willingly accept it and follow it to its true consequences. And many shrink from their own convictions of what the truth really is. Let us leave mere secular truth out of the discussion and only treat of Divine truth, and so apply the principles laid down. Holding, then, as we must, that nothing can endure for a day that has not some truth in it, and that the more of truth a person or a body of men can accept the longer they can endure, but that the falsehood (as does a disease in the body) will finally prove fatal if there be not enough of truth held to overcome it, and lastly, that the full truth is held only in the Holy Church Catholic, we can readily see the relations which men hold to the truth. Truth requires sacrifice of all prejudgments, of all preconceptions, of all wishes. Truth, as it is revealed in the SON of GOD, requires an obedience and an acceptance of the appointed Teachers. These are:

I. The HOLY GHOST, who shall lead the willing mind into all truth. II. The Apostolic teachers, whom alone our LORD sent to teach the world, and by believing their word shall we share in our LORD's earnest Prayer: "Sanctify them through THY truth: THY word is truth. As Thou hast sent me into the world, even so have I also sent them into the world. And for their sakes I sanctify myself, that they also may be sanctified through the truth. Neither pray I for these alone, but for them also which shall believe on Me through their word; that they all may be one; as Thou, FATHER, art in Me, and I in Thee, that they may be one in us: that the world may believe that Thou hast sent Me" (St. John xvii. 17–21). This, then, is the crown of our acceptance of the Truth, to receive it in and by the Apostolic office which our LORD has blest, which alone is commissioned to deliver the Truth to the whole world. But as the Truth is more or less completely received by those within the Apostolic Unity, so it produces more or less fully those fruits which it should. What wonder, then, that it should not exhibit all its true power equally upon all men? But again, the full Truth of the Gospel, owing to the defects in men's capacity to grasp the interrelation of Truths and their proper subordination the one to the other, cannot be held in its entireness. Taking the statements of the Apostles' Creed, it is safe to assert that though gladly received with an honest intention by the Christian, yet few do really understand their sequence and yet their separate importance. Therefore one portion of the Truth is exaggerated and taken out of its proper place, and so dislocated as it were. And it may be perfectly true that this grasp of the helm is not an exaggeration of it in its separate value, but it results in a depression of other interrelated Truths. And as the heat of a fever is the result and reaction from some unhealthy depression of the system, so some truths too greatly depressed have received a reaction as much too great in their favor, and this has resulted in heresy, or at least in schism. The balance of Truth committed to us has been disturbed, and a breaking of Unity is the consequence. Nearly every schism or heresy has come from an imperfect or heedless holding of the Truth by those who have had its keeping. And at the rate in which those who created the schism, upon a distorted idea of the value of the particular Truth they defend, have retained a measure of the other interrelated Truths, so far will they have the power to continue. It is a fact that we to whom so much has been committed have to at once rejoice in and to deplore. Assuredly St. Paul did not rejoice that CHRIST was preached, of contention by some, to add to his bonds, but he did rejoice that CHRIST was preached and prayed that they who believed might come to the fullness of the Truth. There is yet another point to which the thoughtful mind should be directed, and this is, that as the Truths of Nature are so much nearer our powers than spiritual Truths, which can be only held as such by spiritual men, it is easier for men to say that they will believe only what they can test, and then add that they conscientiously reject Christianity because they cannot test it. If they applied as searching and patient examination into the Truths of Christianity they might have some show of pleading a conscientiousness, which is but another name for a prejudgment. It is forgotten that GOD has proclaimed Himself as He that hideth Himself, and that His Truth must be humbly searched for; and, too, that our LORD rejoiced that these things which so many desire to see have been hidden from the wise and prudent and have been revealed to the lowly hearts. The Laws of Nature cannot be applied to solving the Laws of Spiritual Truth, but the common sense which bids the student in the one to study the conditions of his experiments should bid him study the true conditions of the Laws of GOD's Truth.

Tunicle, among Ecclesiastical garments, is the outer vestment worn by the Episteler at the Holy Eucharist, also called, as worn by the Deacon or Gospeller, Dalmatic (Στοιχοριον, in the Greek Church, of the Deacon). It is a kind of loose coat or garment, reaching below the knees, partially open at the sides; it has full but not large sleeves; in material and color it should correspond to the chasuble. The Deacon's dalmatic was usually somewhat more ornamented than the Tunicle worn by the Subdeacon or Episteler. From Inventories made of church vestments in the sixteenth century, it appears that Dalmatics, or Tunicles, were made of rich materials, silk, satin, or velvet, and of every variety of color. That a desire has long existed and increases to adopt a greater variety of color in the ornaments and vestments of the Church, and especially in the coverings of the Altar, is plain from what has already been accomplished; the object assigned for this variety is the useful one of distinguishing, and so teaching by outward tokens, the changes of Church seasons and the occurrence of Ecclesiastical Holidays.

Type. The image or the likeness of something substantial but not present, and having to be represented for certain sufficient reasons, or to attain certain ends. The Type was not only a memorial of what was yet to be revealed, but in some one or more ways was a precise prefigurement of the actual thing or person so foreshadowed. Types may be grouped (*a*) as in Rite or Ceremonial, (*b*) as in some historical fact, (*c*) in the lives of some persons whose whole career or whose culminating acts were typical of what was yet to be. So, in Rite, the sacrifices prefigured the sacrifice of CHRIST centrally and collectively in the shedding of blood; severally as He is the sin-offering, or our Peace-offering. As we severally plead His atonement for ourselves, or as He offers the Atonement as the whole burnt-offering He made for the sins of the whole world. So the Paschal Lamb was a type of the Lamb of GOD slain from the foundation of the world. So the heave-offering was a type of His Ascension. The Tabernacle, and still more the Temple, planned by divine inspiration were the types of the perfect Heavenly Temple and the glorious worship of the redeemed and of the heavenly Hosts. In these things the history of the ritual of Israel is the record of the types of the worship before JEHOVAH. (d) In history we find the Ark the type of the Church and of baptism; the passage of the Red Sea also a type of baptism; the wandering in the wilderness a type of the discipline of the Christian life; the descending of the glory upon the Temple at its dedication the type of the gift of the HOLY GHOST making men living Temples. (e) The life of men and their actions, whether continuously in their career here, or in some single or crowning act of their life. So Abraham by his Faith and by the solitariness of his religious life was the type of CHRIST. Melchisedec was the type of our LORD'S eternal Priesthood, as Aaron was the impersonation of his Priestly acts and typified His one great sacrifice. Joseph in his humiliation and exaltation was a type of our LORD. Moses, as Lawgiver, was the greatest of the prophets; as having the greatest self-denial, the greatest forbearance, he was an eminent type of our LORD. So Samson, as Nazarite, Judge, and Deliverer, foreshadowed His mighty acts of redemption. David, Elijah, Jonah, St. John the Baptist, all were in their lives, in some great striking fact, or in their careers to typify Him.

The study of these types is important, for they show Him as the Second Adam, as touching ourselves at every point wherein GOD chooses to reach, teach, and sanctify our lives by His interference. Again, these types are of the very texture of the Sacred history, they cannot be denied in the Mosaic ritual, yet they spoke of the MESSIAH; this was their prophetic use. The facts of history cannot be destroyed, but they taught of His deliverance which was yet to be. The biographies of the saints cannot be disproved, yet these men by their Faith and Works spake more emphatically than by words of Him who was to justify us by Faith and to make us a people zealous of good works. In the attacks upon Holy Scripture so common now, prophecy may be torn out of its historic place, and with a short-lived triumph be held up as a forgery, an interpolation, a record of an eager wish that anticipated a fortunate reality. Prophecy can defend itself in the end. But the types cannot be so treated; they are historic, they take their places in the proper sequences of the world's records, they are woven into the texture of the religion of the people of GOD. To deny them is to brand as fable the whole history of the past, and to preclude every way of accounting for the present of either civilization or of religion. The type in Holy Scripture is of the very fullness of proof, which He has multiplied on every side, in disproof of the complaint that He desires Faith and gives insufficient grounds. In type, in Prophecy, in History, in men's lives, He has carved a record of His truths far more conspicuous to the world than if they were carved in marble and placed in every market-place, for we bear about in our lives the consequences of such records.

U.

Unction. Anointing persons and places by pouring oil upon them is frequently mentioned in Holy Scripture. Jacob, after his wondrous vision of the heavenly ladder, poured oil on the stone which had been his pillow, and named the place Bethel (Gen. xxviii. 18, 19; cf. xxxi. 13). In setting one apart to an office, anointing was used to signify the endowment of the "gifts and graces of the HOLY SPIRIT." In Rev. iii. 18, the term refers to spiritual blindness, which is to be removed by the "ointment of CHRIST." (Compare St. John ix. 6, 11, as to the blind man's healing.) Our Blessed LORD, as Prophet, Priest, and King, and as being filled with the HOLY SPIRIT beyond measure (St. John iii. 34), was styled the Anointed or Messiah, which has the same meaning (Ps. ii. 2, and xlv 7; Acts iv. 27). "The anointed of the LORD" (Sam. iv. 20) is the King. The olive oil poured upon the head of a person represented the gift of the HOLY GHOST. The Jews were accustomed to the practice of anointing their bodies (Deut. xxviii. 40, and Micah vi. 15). To abstain from anointing was a sign of mourning (2 Sam. xiv. 2; Dan. x. 3; St. Matt. vi. 17). Anointing signifies joy (Ps. xcii. 10; Eccl. ix. 8). Sometimes a host seems to have anointed the head of his guest with oil or ointment, in token of respect. Our LORD says to Simon, "My head with oil thou didst not anoint" (Luke vii. 46). As to unction for special offices, Elijah is commanded by GOD to anoint Jehu as king and Elisha as prophet (1 Kings xix. 16). At the institution of the Levitical priesthood, priests were all anointed, "the sons of Aaron as well as

Aaron himself" (Ex. xl. 15; Num. iii. 3). Afterwards anointing seems to have been reserved especially for the high-priest (Ex. xxix. 29; Lev. xvi. 32). The idea of anointing a king is found in Jotham's parable (Judges ix. 8, 15) before the Jewish monarchy was established. The ceremony was the " principal and divinely-appointed one" in the inauguration of the Jewish kings. Samuel anoints Saul (1 Sam. ix. 16, and x. 1), Zadok anoints Solomon (1 Kings i. 34, 39). The LORD'S anointed was a common appellation for a theocratic king (1 Sam. xii. 3, 5; 2 Sam. i. 14, 16). David was anointed king three times: privately by Samuel (1 Sam. xvi. 1, 13); in this case it is added, "the Spirit of the LORD came upon David from that day forward" (v. 13). He is again anointed over Judah at Hebron (2 Sam. ii. 3, 4), and lastly he is anointed king over all the nation (2 Sam. v. 3). When two kingdoms arose, the kings both of Judah and Israel seem still to have been anointed (2 Kings ix. 3; xi. 12). In addition to the anointing of king, prophet, and priest, we find that the tabernacle itself, with all its furniture, was anointed (Ex. xxx. 26–28).

With respect to anointing persons, JESUS CHRIST, as the Prophet, Priest, and King, is especially the Anointed, or the Messiah (Ps. ii. 2; Dan. ix. 25, 26). He is anointed with "The Spirit of the LORD GOD" (Isa. lxi. 1), and Himself refers to this prophecy in St. Luke's Gospel (ch. iv. 18). As oil made the "face to shine" (Ps. civ. 15), spiritual unction was the "oil of gladness" (Ps. xlv. 7; Heb. i. 9). JESUS of Nazareth is declared to be the Messiah, or CHRIST, or Anointed in the New Testament (St. John i. 41; Acts ix. 22; xvii. 2, 3; and xviii. 5, 28). The fact of CHRIST'S anointing is narrated in the descent of the Spirit (St. John i. 32, 33; cf. Acts iv. 27; x. 38). Spiritual unction with the HOLY GHOST is conferred also upon Christians by GOD (2 Cor. i. 21), and they are described as having "an unction from the Holy One," by which they "know all things" (1 John ii. 20, 27). The word unction has a special sense thus defined by Johnson: "That fervor and tenderness of address which excites piety and devotion."

Anointing, or unction, was used in ancient times before baptism, but this is not mentioned by Justin Martyr or Tertullian. While Tertullian speaks of unction, it was that which followed baptism in confirmation, accompanied with the laying on of hands. Therefore Daille and Bingham think this custom arose after the time of Tertullian. In after-ages there was an unction before baptism called "the unction of the mystical oil," and another after baptism called "the unction of chrism." These unctions were consecrated by the Bishop. The author of the Apostolical Constitutions gives a form of consecration for the sanctifying oil used before baptism. The same author calls this ' mystical oil," and that used before confirmation " mystical chrism," and gives a distinct form for the consecration of each. The first was administered before the person went into the water, the other after he came out. Cyril of Jerusalem speaks of the first unction as making men " partakers of the true olive-tree, JESUS CHRIST." "St. Ambrose compares it to the anointing of wrestlers before they enter their combat." The unction was a ceremony not essential to baptism, and, if oil was wanting, it could be omitted; but in all these ceremonies may we not see a craving after spiritual help?

Extreme Unction is the anointing the sick with oil as practiced by the Church of Rome. A foundation for this custom is claimed in St. James (v. 14, 15), but that anointing was for healing, and it is said, " the LORD shall raise him up" (v. 15), while Romanists use it as the last sacred act before death. It is an abuse of the text. When the Apostles were sent out by CHRIST they "anointed with oil many that were sick, and healed them" (St. Mark vi. 13). The passage in St. James appears to refer to such miraculous acts as were vouchsafed in the beginning of the Christian Church. As extreme unction is claimed as one of the seven Sacraments, the XXV. Article denies the claim, and the English and American Churches do not deem it an ordinance, much less a Sacrament. In extreme unction the oil having been blessed is applied "to the five senses of the dying man." "It is administered when all hope of recovery is gone, and generally no food is permitted to be taken after it." Roman Catholic writers cannot trace their present custom to an earlier date than the fifth century, and even then it seems to have been a matter of question. Extreme unction is supposed by Romanists to give "the final pardon," "in the last agony," as Bishop Burnet says, and he adds, " Here is, then, an institution that, if warranted, is matter of great comfort; and if not warranted, is matter of as great presumption."

Authorities: T. T. Perowne in William Smith's Dict. of the Bible, Bingham's Antiq., Buck's Theologl. Dict., Staunton's Eccles. Dict., Browne on the XXXIX. Articles, Burnet on the XXXIX. Articles.

REV. S. F. HOTCHKIN.

Uniformity. Refers specially to the Act of Uniformity prefixed to the English Prayer-Book. It was intended to produce a uniform use throughout the English Church. In the time previous to the Reformation there were a variety of uses in the celebration of the Services of the Church. There had been originally the custom of each Bishop arranging the Services and the Rubrics as he chose. The jarring that this produced and the violent changes that were made were so great, that about the fifth century it was arranged that each Province should have but one use. This to a great extent unified the services, but it did not change minor customs. In England, apparently the various uses belonged not to the Provinces, but to separate Sees, and point to the continuance of the earlier Episcopal privilege. This was broken up by the introduction of the Prayer-Book of Edward VI., 1549 A.D., and subsequently, as there was yet much diversity of minor usages, Elizabeth repealed Mary Tudor's acts and restored those of Edward VI. A statute of Uniformity of Common Prayer was enacted (1 Eliz., c. 2), and again a statute for Uniformity of Public Prayer (14 Charles II.). Upon these two rest the binding observance of the Prayer-Book and the general Uniformity of Ritual. The variations which have occurred in rubrical observance and usages recently in England do not affect the actual obedience which all render to use the service, the controversies turn upon the meaning of various rubrics within the use of the Prayer-Book. Mere Uniformity is in itself a very great gain, but when at the expense of adaptability and of gaining souls to the Church it is a loss. The ordination vow, and the pledge to conform to the Doctrine and Discipline of the Church, binds every conscientious clergyman to scrupulously carry out all the service. Still, in missionary work it has often occurred that, under sanction of the Bishop, the service has often to be much modified as circumstances direct. No mere fancy or covert of this sort can be admitted when the Church services can be carried out. And no layman living in a secluded or place remote from the Church but can aid, if he heartily tries, in having the services celebrated in a proper and seemly way. They exhibit the Beauty of Holiness so well, that an explanation of them given forth with a kindly spirit would gain from almost all such congregations a co-operation which (as a result of their use) will make a deep and devout impression upon them. Uniformity is GOD'S Law, but this uniformity must be deeper than outward conformity.

Union, Hypostatical. The complete union in one Person of the two Natures of CHRIST. Hooker has nobly translated two passages, one from Hilary upon the HOLY TRINITY (lix. § 3): "He which in Himself was appointed a Mediator to save His Church, and for performance of that mystery of mediation between GOD and man, is become GOD and man, doth now, being but one, consist of both those natures united; neither hath he through the union of both incurred the damage or loss of either, lest by being born a man we should think He hath given over to be GOD, or that because He continueth GOD therefore He cannot be called man; also, whereas the true belief which maketh a man happy proclaimeth jointly GOD and man, confesseth the Word and flesh together." "Cyril more plainly, 'His two natures have knit themselves the one to the other, and are in that nearness as uncapable of confusion as of distraction. Their coherence hath not taken away the difference between them. Flesh is not become GOD, but doth continue flesh, although it be now the flesh of GOD.' 'Yea,' saith Leo, 'the properties are all preserved and kept safe.'" (Hooker, v. liii. § 2.) And this interposition without confusion, this union which is a glorifying of our Flesh, is so complete that our LORD may be said to have enrobed Himself with our assumed nature so that it cleaveth to His Divinity indissolubly by His resurrection; so that St. Paul did truly say (because of the co-operation of His two natures in His one work of Redemption) that the Church was purchased by the blood of GOD (Acts xx. 28). And then our union in Him by Baptism is so close that as by descent we are sons of the first Adam, from whom are our living souls, so from the second Adam by the New Birth we become quickened spirits. So that joined to Him, of His flesh and of His bones (Eph. v. 30), we become partakers of the divine nature. Therefore, though we cannot by the absolute nature of the conditions be joined to Him, as He, being the WORD, has joined our nature to Himself, yet by this His very Hypostatical Union of the two natures in the one person, He has placed us within the shadow of His own eternal nature. As He hath said, "To him that overcometh will I grant to sit with Me in My throne, even as I also overcame, and am set down with My FATHER in His Throne" (Rev. iii. 21).

Unity. Oneness. This Law of unity in complexity has been brought out very clearly by modern speculative and natural philosophy. Its results illustrate the divine Law of unity, yet complexity in the spiritual things. But there is only one side of the topic which can be dwelt upon here,— the Unity of the Church.

The Unity of the Church must follow because that the nature to be saved by CHRIST being one, and the means He uses but one, there cannot be many churches, but one Church. Then, too, the LORD accomplishing one Act of Redemption, and not several for several races, has unified all races into one. This is His purpose. It was the One Fold, One Shepherd, One Net, One House, One Vine, One Vineyard, One City, One King, One Redeemer. His prayer was: "Neither pray I for these alone, but for them also which shall believe on their word; that they all may be one; as Thou, FATHER, art in Me, and I in Thee, that they also may be one in us: that the world may believe that Thou hast sent Me. And the glory which Thou gavest Me have I given them; that they may be one, even as we are one: I in them, and Thou in Me, that they may be made perfect in one; and that the world may know that Thou hast sent Me, and hast loved them, as Thou hast loved Me" (St. John xvii. 20–23). Unity involves glory, perfectness, and love from the FATHER through the SON. This Unity is a real Unity, or else there is no truth in the words of our LORD. It is this Unity, by the means He has given us, which is made as real as the kinship in a family. But this unity grapples us as with hooks of steel to the unity of CHRIST.

To effect this He chose twelve Apostles, for His Church was to be of living men gathered into it by living men, not merely the assent of a faith that comes from study. It is evident that working under His One Supreme command, the Churches thus established were equal in rank and in a common unity with the Head. However wide apart these might be established they were co-equal, and united to CHRIST by the same bonds. And it is also evident that time cannot weaken the fact that they are on the same foundation. So that though a Church in Spain might be unknown to a Church in Abyssinia, yet it would be in the unity of the Church, being of Apostolic foundation; and, as our LORD prayed for all those who should believe through the Apostolic preaching, the missionary expansion of each Apostolic Church would give the same unity to the daughter Churches. But they must continue in that unity. But Apostolic foundation is not all that is needed. Our LORD gave as means of union with Him also the necessity of believing in Him. That is much more than believing about Him, but so believing in Him that we put our whole trust in Him and follow His commands, and so trust in Him that whatever He may direct will be our law, and we gladly abide His time and His will, and confess His doctrine and live the life of self-denial He demands of us. And this belief, and the basis of it in the facts of His life, is given to us in the Apostles' Creed. It was not written by the Apostles, but it was the sum of their teachings, and it was everywhere received by the Churches of Apostolic foundation, and so is historically a proof of the unity of their teaching, and of the oneness of the Faith everywhere received. And it is a recital of facts and not of theories. It is a compressed statement of foundations for and of the acts themselves of our redemption. Therefore the Creed is a part of the means of unity, for we in it and by it profess the same thing.

But Apostolic foundation and Apostolic teaching are not by any means all that our LORD gave as bonds of unity with Him. He gave, as it were, instruments whereby to bind men to Himself. He gave the Sacrament of Baptism, which He ordained to be a new Birth into Him, whereby he that is baptized becomes a member of CHRIST united to Him, having put Him on, translated from the darkness of sin into the Kingdom of CHRIST, of Light, of Heaven. And then this birth implying life and this life requiring nourishment, He has given a second Sacrament, the Holy Communion, which He has ordained for the food of the soul (St. John vi. 47–58). By these two, while we receive them by the Apostles, *i.e.*, Messengers He has sent us, and so from those who have authority, we are in direct, continually received unity with Him, and continue in that outward, visible unity, which must be from the fact of there being a visible outward formal organization.

But besides these two standing intermediate and, as it were, the link for them, stood a third ordinance, that of Confirmation. It is not a Sacrament, yet something of Sacramental in its nature. As in Baptism we put on CHRIST, so He gives His HOLY SPIRIT, whereby we receive the sanctification and renewing. It was to send us this HOLY GHOST, the anointing which is of GOD, that He ascended up on high and sends us the STRENGTHENER, CONSOLER, COMFORTER, the Sanctifier of our lives and of our hearts. It is the gift of the Spirit, whereby we become something more than we were before. Members of CHRIST by Baptism, by Confirmation we become Temples of the HOLY GHOST, and receive of Him the power to be renewed, the gift of a true, constant, repentant state, whereby we grow in grace. These are the bonds that tie us to CHRIST in our lives. But there is another part of the unity which remains to be considered. Summing up what has just been stated, that by Apostolic men, by the Apostolic creed, with Sacraments given to us by which to receive life, union, and grace in our LORD, we are brought into a Body of Men having the like organization, governed by these Commissioned Officers, and being at Unity of intercommunion. The Unity of the Church resides in the Sacraments delivered us by those having authority to do so. And this government must be Episcopal the world over, otherwise it is not in the Historical Body of CHRIST. Now we see this visible unity of intercommunion broken at the moment. It has been severed for a thousand years. This has been permitted in GOD's providence because of the transgression of this law of Apostolic equality in two directions; the first was a usurpation to itself (from a false notion of unity) by one Apostolic See of the liberties and authority which were the rights of the Bishops in common. This usurpation of rights, breaking the unity in complexity, brought on the reacting transgression of the law by a denial that the Apostolic office was a necessity for unity at all. On the one side is the Papacy, with its autocratic theories and its practice destructive of Unity by a cast-iron uniformity, and on the other extreme are the many bodies of co-religionists who claim a freedom to determine their own government, and to create for themselves the right to administer at will those bonds of unity with CHRIST for the giving of which He created and commissioned a special body. Between these two the ancient Apostolic Bodies of the East and of the English and American Churches, though formally apart, acknowledging each other in the unity of the one body, hold to the proper liberty and authority of all Bishops in the Apostolic Commission. This unity of outward visible communion is daily acknowledged more and more by all earnest Christian men of all bodies to be a necessity to the Conversion of the world, the special mission of GOD'S Church. And till this unity be effected the work is either stopped or held in abeyance. This desire for unity which is daily growing is of GOD, who can heal all our dissension, in answer to our prayers for the oneness of His Holy Church. It is of His wisdom that the evils of Separation and Schism and Heresy are permitted to infest the Visible Body of our LORD. But as He has so permitted them, we can have but one duty for ourselves and one towards those without this unity. The one for ourselves is to be assured, as indeed we are, of our holding on fast to the Head, JESUS CHRIST. "For we are partakers of CHRIST if we hold the beginning of our confidence steadfast to the end." The doctrine of unity is a settled and fundamental one, closed, and on which we build. The second duty is earnest prayer.

We are in Christian love towards others, to pray more especially for CHRIST'S Holy Church Universal "that it may be so guided and governed by His good Spirit that all who profess and call themselves Christians may be led into the way of truth, and hold the faith in unity of spirit, in the bond of peace, and in righteousness of life." Nor has the Church forgotten to teach us this in her prayers. It is one of the intercessions of the Litany. It is in her daily prayers; in the Institution of her Priests in their parishes; it is in the supplications for Good-Friday. As the Apostles' Creed is the Confession of a one Faith, so this unity must come upon the reception of the Nicene Creed by all Christians alike,—"I believe in one, Holy, Catholic, and Apostolic Church."

This unity of the Church should be dear to us all, as touching the honor and glory of our LORD'S visible Body, and as setting forward the work which His blessed Passion and Death and glorious Resurrection began. That it will be in vain of course is impossible, but we may not by our carelessness share that blessedness of helping to heal the divisions, dissensions, schisms, and perversions that now hinder the conversion of the world. (*Vide* CHURCH, CATHOLIC, APOSTOLIC SUCCESSION.)

Universal Redemption. One of the clearest of all the statements in the Holy Scriptures, repeated continually in some shape or other, is the truth that redemption is fully, freely offered to all men; that GOD desireth not the death of a sinner; that He willeth that all men should repent and be saved; that as in Adam all die, so in CHRIST shall all be made alive. These and such like statements pervade Holy Scripture, often in the Old Testament, but, as is natural, more frequently in the New Testament. It was, it is, the Gospel of CHRIST which was made from the first. This is a faithful saying, and worthy of all acceptance, that "CHRIST JESUS came into the world to save sinners." GOD "hath given to us the ministry of reconciliation,—to wit, that GOD was in CHRIST reconciling the world unto Himself, not imputing their trespasses unto them, and hath committed unto us the word of reconciliation." That this redemption had a retroactive force is shown by that our LORD preached to the souls in prison who had sinned before the flood. It was offered through the Sacrifices of the Law by anticipation. It was, it is offered constantly. Therefore St. John in his Vision saw the Lamb of GOD as it had been slain before the foundation of the world. But as it is full and free and complete, and as it had a power over the past as well as over the future, so we are plainly taught that it is offered upon condition, for (*a*) a man is not saved against his will, and (*b*) the conditions, Faith and Repentance, upon which it is offered are such only as fit the man for the reception of the salvation, since it would be absurd and impossible for a man who disbelieved to receive the salvation he would not admit existed, and it would be equally shocking for a man who did not sorrow over and forsake his sins to receive the purity of CHRIST when he would defile it deliberately and consciously by his own wickedness. Therefore Redemption, though universally offered and efficacious for all souls that ever have or will come into this world, must still, from the very nature of the case, be offered upon conditions not burdensome, but in themselves cleansing and healing,—nay, commending themselves to the common sense of men. Then the restrictions placed upon the power and efficacy of this redemption over men are because of their sinfulness or blindness. The word of GOD is not bound. But we bind it.

GOD is not willing that any should perish, but that all men should come to repentance (2 Pet. iii. 9). "GOD our Saviour, who will have all men to be saved and come to a knowledge of the truth." That all men have not faith, that many refuse to repent, that some will be lost, are sad facts indeed, but they belong to the complex problems of man's sinfulness and willfulness, and not to the truth of the fact, or of its power, that CHRIST died for the whole world. The limits upon His redemption are those interferences from a sinful use of the freedom of our wills. And the study of this fact will help us to feel how fully our LORD has made this atonement, and how lovingly He has provided for its proclamation throughout the world by the machinery and agencies of His Church. It is not possible to point out all the limitations upon the universality of its acceptance, but (*a*) We may consider how the willfulness of men rejects it either by a direct refusal, or by substituting some other plan of their own in place of an humble reception of His terms. (*b*) We can see how education will lead a man to make a final rejection of this redemption. (*c*) How other influences (which perhaps is after all a form of education) may, too, lead a man to act upon his prejudices and not upon his knowledge of the truth. (*d*) Indulgence in sin and evil habit may so become part of character that they prevent the actings of faith, which would be but a mere belief such as the devils have, and repentance be but unavailing remorse. These are practical every-day facts which can be traced in the lives of those around us who reject the offers of salvation.

The ancient Church taught the full efficacy of our LORD'S death. So Ignatius, "Let no one be deceived. Heavenly beings, and the glory of the angels, and the powers visible and invisible all believe in the blood of CHRIST." Justin Martyr, "Cleansing through His blood those who believe on Him." So Irenæus, "The LORD washed us in His blood, gave His life for our life, and His flesh for our flesh." And so many other quotations might be added. So the closing sentence of the XVIII. Article, "For Holy Scripture doth set out unto us only the name of JESUS CHRIST, whereby men must be saved." In Article XXXI., "The offering of CHRIST once made is that perfect redemption, propitiation, and satisfaction for all the sins of the whole world, both original and actual; and there is none other satisfaction for sin but that alone." So, too, in the Catechism we are taught to believe in JESUS CHRIST, "who redeemed me and all mankind." And in the Communion Office this freedom and fullness of redemption is assumed. So in the Collects for Ash-Wednesday and in the General thanksgiving. In all of these places the Church not merely recognizes the fact, but founds her intercessions, her prayers, her thanksgiving upon it.

Use. The different nations had differently arranged Liturgies, following always the same great outlines, but varied to suit the temperament or the customs of the people among whom each was *in Use*. In the article on Uniformity was shown that the Bishops had originally the power to refashion each the Liturgy of his Diocese. But that they generally followed the precedents set them, and that after some time the Provinces had each one use throughout their several jurisdictions. But while we have many indications of this, yet we find that Liturgies can be classified into families, and that these obtained currency in quite large areas, the Ephesine in parts of Asia Minor, the Petrine in Southern Italy, Ambrosian at Milan, Mozarabic in Spain, the Liturgy of St. Mark in Egypt, of St. James in Palestine, till at length the Liturgy of St. Chrysostom is now in general use in the East, with an exceptional use of the Liturgy of St. Basil upon certain days, and that of St. James on his feast-day, in the Churches of Jerusalem and Cyprus. The Roman Missal has expelled the Ambrosian, Gallican, and Mozarabic uses. And the English Prayer-Book has supplanted the many uses of the English Church before the Reformation, as those of Sarum, Hereford, Bangor, Lincoln, York, and Durham. Use, then, has a technical sense, meaning the liturgy in *use* in some particular Church. It is therefore a proper term to use for our own Book of Common Prayer, whose title runs further, thus: "and administration of the Sacraments and other Rites and Ceremonies of the Church according to the USE of the Protestant Episcopal Church in the United States of America." Here we note the proper technical employment of this term USE.

Utah and Idaho, the Missionary Jurisdiction of. The present Missionary Jurisdiction of Utah and Idaho originally belonged to the Jurisdiction of the Northwest, the field assigned by the Church to the Rt. Rev. Joseph C. Talbot, D.D., in the year 1860 A.D. Bishop Talbot never performed any official duty in Utah or Idaho, though he passed through this region on his way to Nevada. In 1865 A.D. he was translated to the Diocese of Indiana, and it was in a great measure owing to his reports and representations of the wants and character of the field that, upon his resignation, the jurisdiction of the "Northwest" was divided into three: Nebraska with Dakota was assigned to the Rt. Rev. R. H. Clarkson, D.D.; Colorado with "parts adjacent," understood to include New Mexico, Wyoming, and Idaho, which then included Montana, was assigned to the Rt. Rev. G. M. Randall, D.D.; the third, Nevada with Arizona, having been declined by the Bishop-elect; a special meeting of the House of Bishops was called October 9, 1856 A.D., and the Missionary Jurisdiction of Montana with Idaho and Utah was erected, and the Rev. D. S. Tuttle elected Missionary Bishop. In 1880 A.D. this jurisdiction was divided, Montana set apart, and Bishop Tuttle became Missionary Bishop of Utah and Idaho.

The Rev. D. S. Tuttle was rector of Zion Church, Morris, N. Y., at the time of his election. He was consecrated Bishop at Trinity Chapel, New York, on the Feast of SS. Philip and James, May 1, 1867 A.D. The consecrators were Bishops Hopkins, Presiding Bishop, H. Potter, Odenheimer, Randall, Kerfoot, and Neely. The Bishop-elect was presented to the Presiding Bishop by the Bishops of New York and Pittsburg. The testimonials were read by the Rev. J. H. Hobart, D.D., and the attending Presbyters were the Rev. S. R. Johnson, D D., and the Rev. Morgan Dix, D.D. The Bishop of Colorado preached the sermon from the words, "Make full proof of thy ministry." In his personal address to the Bishop-elect allusion was made to the fact that he was probably the youngest Bishop in the Catholic Church.

Very soon after the consecration, on May 22, Bishop Tuttle, accompanied by the Rev. E. N. Goddard and the Rev. G. D. B. Miller, started for their field of work. They had been preceded on the 5th of April by the Rev. Geo. W. Foote and the Rev. Thos. W. Haskins. This was in the days before the transcontinental railway, and the stage-journey was tedious and dangerous by reason of Indian troubles and swollen streams. The Bishop's party did not reach Salt Lake City until July 2, having been forty-one days on the journey. Rev. Messrs. Foote and Haskins had already established regular church services, and opened a day school in Independence Hall. The Rev. Mr. Miller was stationed at Boise City, Idaho, and the Rev. Mr. Goddard accompanied the Bishop on his first visitation of Montana. The Bishop and his helpers found absolutely virgin soil as far as Church work is concerned, with the exception of a short visitation of Idaho in 1864 A.D. by Bishop Scott, of Oregon. A small wooden church had been built at Boise City under the supervision of the Rev. S. Michael Fackler, who labored in that vicinity a little more than a year. The population of Idaho in 1867 A.D. was estimated at about twenty thousand, almost exclusively engaged in mining. They gave the Church and its ministers a cordial welcome. Of Utah, the estimated population was one hundred thousand, all Mormons, with the exception of a small body of merchants, tradesmen, and employés of Wells, Fargo & Co., in Salt Lake City. There were also some apostate Mormons of English descent ready to welcome the Church. From the Bishop's first annual report, August 31, 1867 A.D., it is found that the number of communicants in Utah and Idaho was thirty-three, and one hundred and twenty children had been gathered into Sunday-schools. At the end of the first decade, 1877 A.D., there are reported 7 clergymen, 4 church buildings, 400 communicants, 624 Sunday-school pupils, 756 day-school pupils, and church property valued at $124,700. The first confirmation in the jurisdiction was at Salt Lake City, July 14, 1867 A.D.; eleven persons were confirmed. The first ordination occurred September 19, 1869 A.D, at Salt Lake City. The Rev. Thos. W. Haskins was ordained priest. The next week, September 26, the Rev. Henry L. Foote was advanced to the priesthood at Boisé City.

In 1870 A.D. the Rev. J. L. Gillogly began work at Ogden, Utah. The Memorial Church of the Good Shepherd was built in 1874 A.D., at a cost of above $7000, and a substantial building of stone was erected in 1878 A.D., costing $4300, for the School of the Good Shepherd. In the same year a school-house was built at Plain City, an outlying mission of Ogden. Mr. Gillogly did faithful and efficient work until his sudden death in 1881 A.D. All his enterprises had a steady growth from the first. He was succeeded by the Rev. S. Unsworth, who was brought up from a child in Utah, and received his preparatory education at St. Mark's School.

St. Mark's Cathedral, Salt Lake City, was completed in 1871 A.D. It is built of red sandstone from plans by Upjohn, and cost fifty thousand dollars. The Bishop is rector, and the Rev. R. M. Kirby became assistant minister in 1871 A.D. He resigned in 1882 A.D., and was succeeded by the Rev. N. F. Putnam. Under Mr. Kirby's supervision St. Mark's Hospital was opened April 30, 1872 A.D., with thirteen patients. It is mainly supported by the monthly dues of miners in the surrounding region, who are entitled to the benefits of the Hospital if disabled by sickness. The buildings cost $10,000, and the yearly number of patients treated is five hundred and thirty-five, at a current expense of $11,359.

Church work was begun at Logan, Utah, in 1873 A.D., by the Rev. W. H. Stoy, and St. John's School established. The population being almost wholly Mormon, the progress of the work has been slow, but the Church and school are steadily gaining ground, and exerting a beneficial influence upon the community.

In the summer of 1878 A.D. funds were placed at the disposal of the Bishop for a Memorial Church. He decided to place it in Salt Lake City; and St. Paul's Chapel was opened for service in October, 1880 A.D. It is a well-built stone structure, with a seating capacity of three hundred. The chapel is under the administration of the rector and vestry of St. Mark's Cathedral, and is served by one of the assistant ministers.

Parish Schools have been among the most important agencies of Church work in the jurisdiction. St. Mark's School, Salt Lake City, was opened July 2, 1867 A.D., with sixteen pupils, and grew so rapidly that immediate measures had to be taken for the erection of a suitable building. This was completed in 1872 A.D., at a cost of $22,000, and opened with two hundred and fifteen pupils. The number soon rose to nearly four hundred, and the school has had between four and five hundred in constant attendance up till the present. Fully four-fifths of the pupils have been of Mormon antecedents. Rowland Hall, a boarding-school for girls, was opened in 1881 A.D., and has seventeen boarders and sixty day pupils. St. Michael's School, Boisé City, Idaho, was opened in 1867 A.D., and was well sustained until the community became more settled, and the character of the public schools superseded the necessity of its longer continuance. The School of the Good Shepherd, Ogden, with one hundred and twenty pupils, has steadily grown in reputation and numbers, under the management of the Rev. Chas. G. Davis. About one hundred children of Mormon parentage come under the instruction of the Church yearly in St Paul's School, Plain City, and St. John's School, Logan.

At the first Convocation of the jurisdiction, then including Montana, there were seven clergy and eight parishes and organized mission stations on the roll. At the last Convocation, 1883 A.D., of Utah and Idaho, there were eleven clergy and seventeen parishes and organized mission stations. The seventeenth annual report of the Bishop, 1883 A.D., gives the present condition of the field : 11 clergy, 5 church buildings, 728 communicants, 930 Sunday-school pupils, 794 day-school pupils, and church property of the value of $195,150. Idaho now has a population of 38,000, and Utah 147,000.

The Bishop has made an official visitation throughout the jurisdiction every year, reaching as far as possible every town, mining settlement, and hamlet. In Idaho, it is only a question of aggregation of population whether they will have a settled clergyman and the regular ministration of the Church. Any town of a thousand people will take care of itself; but the bulk of the population is in small settlements, and scattered through the valleys on ranches or farms. These can be served only by itinerant missionaries. The parish at Bcisé City is self-supporting, but all the rest of Idaho is purely missionary ground, and the amount of work accomplished depends upon the men and means at the disposal of the ecclesiastical authority. The state of affairs is quite different in Utah. Outside of Salt Lake City and Ogden, little, if any, help or encouragement is given, and the field must be worked on the same principles and by the same methods as the missionary work in foreign lands. While no overt acts of hostility are manifested, the Mormon faith presents a steady, unbroken front of moral opposition to all forms and enterprises of Christian endeavor. Seldom, if ever, is there an instance of an adult Mormon coming directly from Mormonism into the Church. Most of the aggressive work, above unperceived moral influences, has been accomplished through the education of the young, though there has been considerable accession to the Church from apostate Mormons, originally brought up in the Church of England.

REV. G. D. B. MILLER.

V.

Veils. I. In England and in some parishes in this country it is customary that the women and girls who are presented for confirmation wear a light veil. II. Usually the term Veil is given to the covers of very thin light linen fabric which should be provided to protect the bread and the wine from insects before and during consecration, after the "fair white linen cloth" is removed. They should be not more than eight or nine inches square and decently wrought, but as light as possible.

Veni Creator Spiritus. A Hymn used in the Office of Ordination of Priests and Consecration of Bishops. It was attributed to St. Ambrose (380 A.D.), but it is not found anywhere earlier than the ninth century, when it was put into the Ordinal of the Consecration of a Bishop. It is a beautiful hymn addressed to the HOLY GHOST, by whose gift it is that all Apostolic offices are wielded. The translation of the Hymn in the Prayer-Book was made, it is said, by Cranmer.

Venial Sin. Sins may be divided generally into two great divisions, Mortal and Venial. Venial sin is as much a *sin* as a Mortal sin, but not as heinous in degree, as larceny is as much a transgression of the Law as burglary, yet the latter is a felony and the other is a misdemeanor. "There is a sin unto death. All unrighteousness is sin: and there is a sin not unto death" (1 John v. 16, 17). Both Mortal and Venial sins bring penalties, and Venial sin becomes fatal to the soul when its frets and temptations eat away the soul by piece-meal. It is despising small things to our great loss to overlook and neglect the little sins of which we all are guilty. It is a dangerous habit to excuse them. To master these by daily watchfulness is really as great a work as to resist some great temptation. It is a training of the Christian character, and produces that beauty of soul which makes it so lovely. The constant use of self-examination and of the Holy Communion is necessary, that we may be rid of them as noxious weeds that choke the good seed.

Venite. The portions of the xcv. and xcvi. Psalms which are joined into a single anthem, in place of the English use of the single xcv. Psalm. It is an invitatory Psalm, and its choice for this place is peculiarly felicitous. It was used by the Jews in their Synagogue worship, in the earliest Eastern daily service, and in the Western Churches. Its use was either complete, as in the English Service, or partial, as in the Eastern, and with verses from other Psalms, as in our own use. Its responsive (musical) use dates from a very early time, and its hortatory composition makes it specially fit for its present place in public worship. In fact, its use should be, whether musically rendered or not, fully and wholly congregational.

Verger. The name of the officer who

carries a "mace before the dean or canons in a Cathedral or Collegiate Church. In some Cathedrals the dean goes before any member of the Church, whether Capitular or not, unless he leaves his place to perform any part of the service. An officer of a similar title precedes the vice-chancellor in the English universities." (Hook's Church Dict.).

Vermont, Diocese of. The organization of the Protestant Episcopal Church in Vermont was extremely defective until the year 1811 A.D., and not complete till 1832 A.D. But prior to the former date there was an Annual Convention of its Clergy and lay representatives, beginning in the year 1790 A.D.

Before the Revolution the present territory of this State was a part of the Province of New Hampshire. And Governor Wentworth, of that Province, had granted 138 townships within the present limits of Vermont, reserving in each of them a lot of land for the English "Society for the Propagation of the Gospel in Foreign Parts," and a glebe for "the Church of England as by law established," and another share for "the first settled minister" of whatever name. These grants doubtless excited a hope in the minds of Churchmen in Massachusetts and Connecticut of ultimately bettering their religious privileges here, and induced some to settle here. But there seems to have been no concert having this end in view among the settlers as to their location, excepting perhaps in the town of Arlington. Thus in most of the townships the Church settlers were too few and poor to think of immediate organization, or of obtaining regular ministrations of the Gospel according to their faith. In a very few places the Liturgy was said by laymen, and rare occasional visits of clergymen from New Hampshire, Massachusetts, and Connecticut afforded the only opportunities for receiving the Sacraments of the Church.

Before 1790 A.D. only four Church clergymen are known to have rendered any regular service here, and two of these resided without the State, and their service was limited and transient. The other two were residents, who were admitted to holy orders by Bishop Seabury in 1787 A.D. Bethuel Chittenden was the first, and deserves an ever-grateful remembrance. He was a brother of Governor Thos. Chittenden; was an early settler in Tinmouth; had cleared his farm and done other business there; and, at forty-nine years of age, with only the preparation of a clear mind and a very common education, gave himself to the ministry, and spent the remaining twenty-two years of his life largely in visiting the little clusters of Churchmen in the State, and doing what he could to hold them together until a better day. The other was Reuben Garlick, M.D., of Alburg, who received only Deacon's Orders, and combined with his sacred ministrations the practice of medicine and school-teaching. He was respectable and very useful among the rude settlers in thus caring for their threefold nature, but naturally found himself in the background when society was able to employ men that gave themselves to the "one thing," and at length removed to Canada, and died there.

There met at the first Convention (1790 A.D.) two clergymen and eighteen laymen, representing eight so-called parishes. The organization of this Convention was hastened by a well-grounded fear lest they should lose their chartered inheritance if they did not take active measures to keep it. And the same motive urged them to take measures in advance of their ability to complete their organization by obtaining a Bishop.

At the Annual Convention in 1793 A.D., the Rev. Edward Bass, D.D., of Newburyport, Mass., was regularly chosen Bishop of Vermont. This position he finally consented to accept, on the condition that he should not be required to change his residence until the income of the lands should suffice for his support, which was probably as favorable an answer as the Convention had anticipated. But there was no further action upon it. In February of the following year a specious project was devised by men not properly Churchmen, which occasioned a hasty and imperfect call of a Special Convention. At this the engineers of the movement were well represented, and the Church proper but poorly; and then the Rev. Samuel Peters, D.D., formerly of Connecticut, then of London, England, was nominated for Bishop, and at once elected, not without opposition. Several years passed in vain efforts to secure his consecration in England, and, that failing, in the United States.

In the mean time (1794 A.D.) the General Assembly of the State sequestered the lands, both the glebes and those granted to the Society for the Propagation of the Gospel, and applied the avails of them to the support of common schools. On the other hand, late in 1802 A.D., there was a valuable accession to the Clergy, in the person of the Rev. Abraham Bronson, from Rhode Island, who settled in Manchester, officiating also in Arlington, in one or both of which parishes he labored with great usefulness to them and the Diocese for more than thirty years. To him perhaps more than to any other one the Church is indebted for the tenacity which finally recovered a part of her inheritance. At the time of the formation of the Eastern Diocese he was the only Church clergyman in the State. The means being so meagre, of course the Church as a whole, in this region, could not grow; the wonder is that it was not crushed under the weight of prejudice and the oppressive action of the State. From the sequestration of the lands to 1811 A.D. the Annual Conventions comprised an average of less than two clergymen and eleven laymen from less than six parishes. But there were among them men with a keen sense of right respecting both their religious obligations and the Church's claims, and who would neither abandon the one nor surrender the other.

A brighter prospect at length appeared. A proposition of the Church in Massachusetts to the Churches in the other New England States, excepting Connecticut, which had a Bishop of its own, and Maine, which was not yet developed to the desire of one, but which afterwards joined the rest, was adopted, namely, to confederate in the election and maintenance of a Bishop who should have jurisdiction over all; and in a joint Convention, in 1811 A.D., choice was happily made of the Rev. Alexander V. Griswold, D.D., of Rhode Island, for the Bishop. He was consecrated on the 24th of May in that year, and commenced his supervision in the four, afterwards five, States. These had each its own Convention, and all together a Biennial Convention in common.

The war of 1812 A.D. renewed old prejudices, and in various ways hindered for a time the good fruits of this approach to an organization according to the principles of the Church. But the Bishop was so earnest, faithful, wise, and lowly, that in a few years his coming was a time of special interest to almost the whole community. An old Congregationalist expressed the feeling: "He is the best representative of an Apostle that I have ever seen, particularly because he does not know it." The Church visibly increased from about 1816 A.D.

In 1817 A.D. a Power of Attorney was received from the Society for the Propagation of the Gospel by certain persons who had been recommended to the Society for this end, empowering them to act as its agents to take care of its claims in Vermont; it being understood that the Society should be involved in no expense and that the Church here should have the avails of what should be recovered.

After a thorough study of the case a suit was brought, which it was thought would decide all the claims. A favorable decision was rendered, but was carried up to the Supreme Court, and there finally confirmed in 1823 A.D. But litigations continued for some years, the holders of the grants usually finding something peculiar, each in his own case. At length claims which could be clearly traced were recovered. But the glebes of the Church of England have never been recovered, there being here no Church of that name and by law established to make a claim which would be legally binding; though the Protestant Episcopal Church is known to be, to all moral and religious intents, a continuation of that Church in this country.

The Bishop soon came to regard Vermont as the most fertile portion of his wide field, and as early as 1822 A.D. recommended the Diocese to have a Bishop of its own as soon as convenient. But ten more years of evident prosperity elapsed before this was accomplished. It became evident, however, that the unwieldy confederation must soon be dissolved. The Convention of Massachusetts expressed its desire to retain the Bishop. And in 1832 A.D. the Convention of the Church in Vermont, comprising 13 clergymen, and 39 laymen from 19 parishes, having before it the advice of the Bishop, and the consent of the Eastern Diocese, and of its several Diocesan parts, erected itself into a separate jurisdiction. It prepared a most loving parting address to its late Diocesan, and then proceeded to elect one for Vermont.

The Rev. John Henry Hopkins, D.D., of Boston, formerly of Pittsburg, Pa., was its choice. Being consecrated with other Bishops-elect at the close of the General Convention in 1832 A.D., he came at once to Vermont, settling in Burlington. Here he took St. Paul's Church as his parish, a Church recently gathered by the Rev. Geo. T. Chapman, and the consecration of its plain stone edifice was the first Episcopal act of the new Bishop. There were at that time in the Diocese but two other churches built of that material, one in Middlebury and one in Arlington, and they were of like plainness.

The life of Bishop Hopkins is too well known to be dwelt upon here, except as involved in that of the Diocese. While his attainments were remarkably varied, and his personal power and energy great, his natural temperament and modes of action were almost the opposite of those of Bishop Griswold. Some friction inevitably resulted, but was overcome by the earnestness and weight of the Bishop.

The great trial of his Episcopate resulted from his erecting with generous purposes for the Diocese, by his own means and credit, an Academical and Theological Institution, called the Vermont Episcopal Institute. On spacious grounds, admirably located, three noble buildings for the Episcopal residence, the Academy, and the Theological School were completed by 1838 A.D. The Academy had already for a time had a goodly number of boys, and the Theological department a few students. But the expense was too heavy for the Bishop, and he desired at this time to transfer it to the Diocese at cost. He was willing further to solicit aid in other Dioceses and in England for the object. He secured in England and Ireland about $5000, with 400 volumes for the Library, and by this help offered the property to the Diocese for $30,000.

But the Church had few members of wealth. Most of them were poor, and all unaccustomed to large offerings and rapid movements. A financial panic hastened the end. The Diocese did not respond; the Institute was lost to the Church; the Bishop's own property was gone; and a heavy residuum of debt rested upon him. Such an issue of his plans and labors disheartened even his resolute soul, but he accepted the stroke as from the LORD, and engaged himself laboriously in his parochial and Episcopal duties and in writing books. Assisted by his eldest son, a purchase was made of a romantic woodland farm on the shore of the lake and of Burlington Bay, named Rock Point, three miles from the city, where the family together built a plain house with the timber or its avails, where he resided until his death, and where his honored widow still abides.

The growth of the Church was not rapid, but generally constant. The Bishop's parish increased rapidly, and its church was enlarged and adorned under his supervision in 1852 A.D. The next year the Bishop reckoned that within the twenty years of his Episcopate the number of his Clergy and their relative proportion to the population was more than doubled, and that the old disputes of High- and Low-Churchmen had entirely ceased.

In 1854 A.D., fourteen years after the wreck of the former Institute, he proposed another, the scheme comprehending the purchase of the Rock Point farm as the site, and also the removal of his old indebtedness. The Convention approved, and an act of incorporation was obtained. For the better prosecution of the undertaking the Bishop resigned his parochial cure (Easter, 1856 A.D.), and in person solicited, collected, and expended the means, was architect and superintendent of the building, adorned the chapel largely with his own hand, and the result is the valuable Institute at Rock Point, admitted by all to have been economically and skillfully erected, and all free of debt. The Diocese contributed willingly, though not bountifully, the larger part of the cost being met by the generosity of brethren without. The chapel was consecrated in 1860 A.D.

Released from the incubus of debt, and assured of the affection of his Diocese, the Bishop's vast energy was conspicuous in this work and in all that followed. He now proposed the addition of a female department to the Institute, and collected several thousand dollars towards it, but the outburst of civil war deferred its accomplishment. The fund is considerably improved, but not yet applied to that object.

During the war, the Bishop was politically very unpopular in Vermont; but he so thoroughly restrained himself and his Diocese from the introduction of politics into the Sanctuary, that the time passed without a rupture. Three valuable churches of stone were consecrated during this period, two of them being affecting memorials of his varied activity and skill.

By the decease of the late Presiding Bishop the functions of that officer fell to Bishop Hopkins, and added much to his labors. He seems to have been in just his proper element, with work enough, and that diverse, important, and appreciated. In 1867 A.D., St. Paul's, Burlington, became vacant, and he again acted as Rector, and the Church building was again greatly enlarged and beautified under his direction, and the Parish property in other respects greatly improved. He attended the Lambeth Conference in that year, the means being readily provided. On his return in November, most of his clergy assembled to welcome him, and the warmth of their mutual affection was very conspicuous. Almost immediately he entered upon the delayed annual visitation of the Diocese. Twenty-one parishes and missions had been visited, but a service at Plattsburg, N. Y., rendered for the Bishop of that Diocese, in that inclement season with its exposures, brought on pneumonia so severe that his robust constitution could not withstand it. After a very short and painful sickness, heroically and sweetly borne, he entered into his rest January 9, 1868 A.D. A beautiful monument, devised by his eldest son, has been erected by the family and the Diocese to mark his grave at Rock Point.

A special Convention was soon called, and assembled at Burlington on the 11th of March, for the election of his successor. There were present eighteen clergymen and fifty-six laymen from twenty-five parishes. The choice was made of the Rev. William Henry Augustus Bissell, D.D., of Geneva, N. Y., but formerly of Vermont. He was consecrated on the 3d of June, at the Annual Convention, by five Bishops, in the new, beautiful, and costly Christ Church, Montpelier; that church itself having been consecrated the day before by Bishop Williams.

Without presuming to characterize the living, this may be said, after he has gone in and out among the parishes, missions, and places where the Church was before unknown for fifteen and a half years: his loving heart, and easy accessibility, and faithful preaching, and judicious management have made him welcome and useful everywhere and with every class. And the statistics of the Diocese show a more rapid growth than at any former period, notwithstanding the severe depression in business during the larger part of the time. A fine stone church in East Berkshire, the richer and more beautiful church in Bellows Falls, and several handsome churches of other materials have been consecrated by him. Beautiful stone chapels have been erected in Burlington and Rutland. The Missions of the Diocese have been greatly enlarged. The northeastern counties of the State which had no church before have now several. The Diocesan branch of the Woman's Auxiliary to the Board of Missions has been inaugurated, and is doing a great work. The wealth of richer Churchmen flows more freely in sacred channels. A partial endowment ($25,000) of the Episcopate has been secured. An Episcopal residence within the city of Burlington has been presented to the

Diocese by a generous friend in New York. The p,rmanent Missionary Fund has received a handsome endowment.

To appreciate the following statistics the increasing drain of the native population of the State by emigration must be borne in mind. During Bishop Griswold's Episcopate the annual gain in population was 1½ per cent., and that mostly American; during that of Bishop Hopkins, ⅜ per cent., not more than the foreign immigration; during that of Bishop Bissell, less than ⅛ per cent., —a serious loss of population that is now accessible to the Church.

This Statistical Table was prepared for a recent occasion, October 31, 1882 A.D.:

	1811.	1832.	1868.	1882.	Ratio of the present to fifty years ago
Clergy	2	13	26	33	2½ to 1
Active Parishes	7	24	40	48	2 to 1
Communicants	Unknown.	1169	2381	3488	2 4-5 to 1
Ratio of Communicants to whole population		1 to 247	1 to 137½	1 to 95	2 3-5 to 1

Average Annual Confirmations.

By Bishop Griswold in five States, those in Vermont not generally distinguishable	238
By Bishop Hopkins in Vermont alone	127
By Bishop Bissell in Vermont alone	247

	1811.	1832.	1868.	1882.	Ratio of the present to fifty years ago.
Number of Churches	0	14	31	43	3 to 1
Value of Churches	0	$56,000	$250,000	$327,000	Nearly 6 to 1
Number of Rectories	0	1	12	18	18 to 1
Value of Rectories	0	$1,500	$25,000	$49,000	Nearly 33 to 1
Missionary Contributions in the single year specified	0	$125	$1,791	$4,780	39 to 1

Rev. A. H. BAILEY, D.D.

Vernacular. (*Verna*, Latin for slave. Originally indigenous, thence popular or common. Vernacular, a speech that may be understood by the poorest or most ignorant.) It is used now especially of the translations of Holy Scripture and the Liturgic worship in the *language of the people*. It seems very strange that there should be needed any argument in its behalf, yet it is gravely claimed that Latin should be used as the sacred language in which all services of religion must be recited. Even St. Paul assumes the absurdity of it in his expostulation: "How shall he that occupieth the room of the unlearned say Amen at thy giving of thanks (Eucharist), seeing he understandeth not what thou sayest? For thou verily giveth thanks well, but the other is not edified" (1 Cor. xiv. 16, 17). In the case of the Scriptures we have the example of the Targums, which were paraphrases from the Hebrew Scriptures into the Aramaic vernacular, and into the current Greek of the third century before CHRIST. These were in common use; and the Greek translation, with all its defects, some of which might have caused hot controversy, was used by the Evangelists and the Apostles. Nor was there any doubt about the propriety of the translation. The Peschito translation of the New Testament is the Syriac version. There was the old Italic version. Ulphilas, the Apostle to the Goths, translated portions of the New Testament into Mæso-Gothic. In fact, the evidence is overwhelming upon the use of the Vernacular. The only objection, that in cases of controversy there may be a wrong use made of an inaccurate phrase in a popular translation, is met by the constant use of the Greek translation of the Old Testament, which received the silent sanction of being quoted in the New Testament by writers who were perfectly familiar with the Hebrew Scripture, and could and did make an independent translation where it suited their purpose.

But if this be the case with the Sacred Canon of Holy Writ, how much more forcible are the arguments in favor of the use of the Services in the Vernacular. Here, too, the Primitive Church used them in the several dialects necessary. Greek, Latin, Syriac, Coptic, Georgian, Bulgarian Liturgies are preserved, and show fully that as each country was converted the Faithful used the Liturgy in their own tongue. It was in direct obedience to St. Paul's rule, as quoted above. There were causes which led for a while to the universal use of the Latin throughout the West; but these could not endure, and we have proof that the rule was broken through in the baptismal services, and probably in much else that yet has only been preserved in Latin. Surely the plain sermons of St. Boniface to his German converts could not have been of any use to them if they were delivered in the Latin in which we now have them. So, too, of other discourses. But after a while the bondage of the Latin Service in Teutonic countries became too heavy, and it was one of the first things to be removed when the Reformation began. (*Vide* PRIMER.) So now wherever the Papal yoke is thrown off, thereupon the Liturgy is at once given to the people in the Vernacular. It is only common sense to do this. Scripture and Early Church History are full of suggestions which commend themselves to every mind that but considers the great importance that public prayer is to the people. All these facts readily prove the need that every Church should use only the plain, common speech of the people to which it ministers. To this end the Prayer-Book has been translated into French, German, and Swedish, for our own populations, and for the English subjects it has been translated into eight different languages.

Verse. Verses are the short subdivisions of a paragraph, including one or more sentences. The word also means a stanza of a Hymn. In its first meaning it refers to a short sentence in the Bible. The Bible was first reduced to chapters, it is said, by Cardinal Hugo de Sancto Caro, about 1240 A.D. But the chapters were divided into verses for the Old Testament by Rabbi Nathan 1440 A.D., and for the New Testament by Robert Stephens 1551 A.D. A verse is also a short passage of Scripture that is sung, or an anthem is often so called.

Versicles. The short verse and its response are so called whether they be of Benediction, as, "V. The LORD be with you. R. And with Thy Spirit," or of praise, as, "V. Praise ye the LORD. R. The LORD's name be praised," or of precate intercession, as, "V. O LORD open Thou our lips. R. And our mouth shall show forth Thy praise," or of invocation, as, "O CHRIST hear us." In all these versicles and responses the people's share is an important one, as it is an exercise of their priestly office of intercession. These versicles and responds are very old. The principle was taken from the Synagogue worship, and they were at first framed out of the Psalms, as they in fact still are. They were in use at least thirteen hundred years ago.

Versions. The translation of the Old and New Testaments into the Vernacular of the several countries into which Christianity has gone. As for modern versions, either of the whole or a part of the Holy Scriptures which are designed for mission work, the number is upwards of one hundred and fifty and is yearly increasing, as missionaries in new stations find need and acquire facility in the language.

The chief ancient Versions were: The Septuagint (*q.v.*). The old Latin, which may have been made for the North African Church, and a revision of which is called the Itala. The Vulgate of St. Jerome (380-400 A.D.), supplanted the Itala translation, so that only a few fragments beside the Psalter remain. The Peschito of the Syriac Church was a very early translation, probably in the second century. It became gradually obsolete, and was corrected and revised and otherwise changed as time went on. Three Arabic Versions of the Old Testament. A Coptic Version in three forms, which may late from the rise of Monasticism (250 A.D.). An Ethiopic translation, which was made at an uncertain period, probably about the sixth century.

The value of these translations of the New Testament is very great, for they not only throw light upon the meaning of obscure words, but they help to determine the true reading of disputed passages. The student of the New Testament has a task of no small magnitude before him to attempt to co-ordinate and reduce to order the value of the several translations which early Christianity had to make, into the different languages, to take into consideration the general skill of the translator, and to understand the conditions under which he labored. The work also helps to determine the value of some of the MSS. of the Greek text, which may represent in some distant land a very different reading from that in use in another country. The question is a very fascinating one. The history of our modern Versions is much more important. The history of the Authorized Version is one of growth. Translations of parts of the New Testament were early made in the Saxon. The Psalms and parts of the three Gospels, and then that of St. John, by Bede, were made before 735 A.D. King Alfred (890 A.D.) retranslated the Psalms. In the next century Aelfric of York translated parts of the Old Testament, but these efforts went no further for the time. The Norman Conquest disturbed the quiet needed for such work, and it was not till much later that any effort was made; though much Biblical knowledge was within reach (as is shown in the long Poem of Piers Plowman), and some paraphrases were made. Wyckliffe was the first to make a complete translation into English of the whole Bible, but it was taken from the Vulgate. He had two co-workers, Richard Purvey and Nicholas of Hereford; the former of whom revised the work, finishing his revision after Wyckliffe's death, 1384 A.D. Through the studies for successive translations, Wyckliffe's terse English has entered largely into our Authorized Version.

This translation exists in a good many MSS. in England, showing that it had become quite diffused. It contains many obsolete words, and were the uncouth spelling modernized it would still be remarkably near the common language yet to be found in retired places in this country, spoken as it was brought over from England. Tyndale began to translate his Version of the New Testament from the Greek (1502 A.D.) at Oxford, but apparently did not do much till 1522 A.D., when he went to London, but had to leave for the Continent because of his reforming sympathies. He began to print at Cologne, but was driven thence to Worms, where he finished the first edition and issued another, 1525 A.D. He resided probably at Wittenberg while translating parts of the Old Testament,—the books of Moses, and Jonah (1530-1531 A.D.). He was a fugitive during this and succeeding years, but was arrested in 1535 A.D., and martyred 1536 A.D. He laid the foundation for a translation, using Luther, Wyckliffe, and the Vulgate, but working from his own clear judgment. Taking into consideration his difficulties, the translation is a remarkably excellent one. Coverdale, (titular) Bishop of Chalcedon, made a translation of the Bible in 1535 A.D., using the German and the Vulgate. The next edition, for it really was such, of the English Bible (1537 A.D.) was put forth by John Rogers (afterwards the Marian martyr), who placed the name of Thomas Matthew on the title-page. It was a revision of Tyndale and Coverdale, with notes and prefatory matter, which made his edition a valuable one to English readers, especially as it was strongly antipapal. Tavener, a Greek scholar of the same time, also issued (1539 A.D.) an edition of the Bible. His revision of the New Testament showed his knowledge of Greek, and some of his renderings were retained. But for the Old Testament he trusted to the Vulgate. These different editions were not entirely in accordance with the intention of those who were then using the efforts of Cranmer for reform for their own purposes, and the Lord Protector, Cromwell, ordered another revision, which was made by Coverdale, who went to Paris to have the work printed. He used all the latest revisions and translations at hand, and at last (forced by the Inquisition to return to England when his work was finished) he produced what was known as the Great Bible (1539 A.D.). It was from this Bible that the passages of Scripture were taken for the Prayer-Book, some of which, as the Commandments and the Comfortable Words, still remain, though the other portions were made to conform to the King James translation. These different editions had the sanction, more or less fully, of Henry VIII., under the advice of Cromwell or of Cranmer, who of course would willingly go further. The succeeding editions (1540-1541 A.D.) of the Great Bible had prefixed to them a short preface by Cranmer and his coadjutors, Tonstal and Heath. The next revision, for it became a revision now, was made by the Marian Exiles (1555-1560 A.D.) at Geneva, principally by William Whittingham, assisted by Thomas Sampson, Anthony Gilby, and others. They used Tyndale and the Great Bible, and Beza's Latin Version, with much independent work of their own. Its strong antiprelatical leaning, the attempt to introduce the Hebrew and Greek names unchanged, and sometimes a harshness of rendering are the notable points in it. It is also known as the Breeches Bible from the translation of Gen. iii. 7, "And they sewed fig-leaves together and made themselves breeches." It was published in 1560 A.D., at Geneva. It was so much better than the previous translations that Archbishop Parker determined to have the Cranmer Bible revised accordingly. He selected a company of learned men, who made a more pretentious than successful revision.

The Books were rearranged, according to subjects. The chapters to be omitted in public reading were marked. There was some additional matter—as Genealogical tables—added. There were two editions (1568-1572 A.D.). In the mean time the Romanists found it best to prepare an English version also, and after some delay (in 1582 A.D.) they issued at Rheims a translation of the New Testament, which had been prepared by Martin, Allen, and Bristowe.

The Old Testament was published at Douay in 1609 A.D. It was as strongly marked with polemics as the Genevan Version was. Its language was as uncouth and its translations of words as nearly a transference of the original words as possible. These several efforts, over so long a space, 1480-1600 A.D., had leavened the English people with a knowledge and love for their English Bibles, but something yet was wanting in all of these several translations, revisions, and re-editings. After much controversy, a feeling that these should be in some way superseded was very prominent. The Puritans at the Hampton Court Conference (1604 A.D.) wished to have a new translation undertaken. King James was caught with the idea that it would be the glory of his reign to have it effected. He took up the work and had the instructions prepared, which were given to the translators. Fifty-four men eminent for learning and ability were chosen, and the work distributed among them. Three companies were formed, under the direction of six persons,—the two Hebrew and two Greek Regius Professors at Oxford and Cambridge, and Andrews, Dean of Westminster, and Barlow, Dean of Chester. Suggestions were invited from every quarter. The work was begun in 1606 A.D., and was conducted by the separate companies till the work drew near completion. The heads of the companies then were selected for final revision and arrangements for printing, and after much labor and devout toil a task which had no moneyed considerations involved in it was brought to a close in 1611 A.D. Bilson, Bishop of Winchester, wrote the "arguments" prefixed to the several books, and Dr. Miles Smith the dedication and the Preface, which, most unfortunately, has been left out of nearly every edition of the Bible. It should be replaced to the great gain of every careful reader, who would know upon what principles the translation and revision were made. They consulted every accessible version in French, German, Spanish, Italian, Portuguese, and spared no labor to give, as nearly as the state of learning then permitted, the most thorough translation yet produced. And they succeeded. The Version had to work its way into public favor. From the first it was quietly but really accepted, displacing slowly but surely all previous Versions. It was freely criticised, and was objected to at first, but the approval of those who, like Bishop Walton, the Editor of the London Polyglott, knew its value, was much in its favor. It was the work of men who were masters of a noble English style, quite the contemporaries of Shakespeare, Raleigh, Spenser, and of Hooker. No better time could have been chosen, when the English was at a robust strength that could not exist at any other stage. The previous translations were freely used, and the broidery of phrases that can be traced to Wyckliffe, Tyndale, Coverdale, Rogers, Tavener, the

Geneva, the Douay, shows how diligently they compared, corrected, and incorporated all that they found of worth. There is hardly a passage which has not a rhythmic flow which is inimitable. The errors in it of translation are notably few when the state of Hebrew and Greek learning is considered, advanced as it was then. The chronological indices and the dates on the margin were placed there by Bishop Lloyd. The marginal readings are often to be preferred to the reading of the Text.

But the Version which has grown so dear to all Englishmen was charged with having too many obsolete words, mostly mistakes in the transference of proper names, chiefly in geography, and errors in grammar and in archaic expressions. Efforts were made for some years by such able men as Archbishop Trench and Bishop Ellicot and Bishop Lightfoot to get a revision undertaken. In 1870 A.D., in the Convocation of Canterbury, the first steps were taken. Fifty-two men were selected to do the work, and were divided into two companies,—twenty-seven for the Old Testament and twenty-five for the New Testament. Two years later a company of twenty-seven was formed in America,—fourteen for the Old Testament and thirteen for the New Testament. These worked in close correspondence, and compared results constantly with the English Revisers. The New Testament companies were able to issue their Revision in May, 1881 A.D. It has revised the Greek text in some places; has left out one text of more than doubtful genuineness, the seventh verse of the fifth chapter of St. John's first Epistle; the word HE is substituted for the word "GOD" in 1 Timothy iii. 16. Many marginal notes exhibit the result of a comparison of many texts and MSS. The poetical quotations from the Old Testament are printed exhibiting the ancient Hebrew parallelism. The most important doctrinal gain, however, is the substitution of Hades for Hell wherever the place of departed spirits is meant, while Hell is reserved for those passages where everlasting punishment is taught. The Revision has undoubtedly done very great service both in correcting some errors and, much more, in giving a vast impulse to the study of the New Testament among ordinary English readers. But it has not the delicate cadences of the old Version, and it has rudely shocked some prepossessions, while the practical gain on the whole is less than could have been looked for from the amount of toil expended. It will probably not become popular, but will always be a most useful and necessary adjunct to any study of the English Versions. The principles which guided the Revisers are stated very forcibly in the preface to the work.

There have been several French translations, which can only be mentioned here very hastily. The first Protestant Version of the Bible in French was made in 1530 A.D., by Lefèvre d'Étaples. This formed the basis for another translation, by Pierre Robart Olivetan, a kinsman of Calvin, who corrected his work and expressed a great wish to see a new edition put forth. The French Genevan Pastors issued another revised translation under the care of Beza, 1588 A.D. It was a great improvement, but the need of correcting it was felt as Biblical science progressed, but no effort was successful till recently, when, in 1874 A.D., Dr. L. Segond, of Geneva, published a new translation, which was afterwards republished by the University Press of Oxford. In Holland, Van Leesveldt published a complete Dutch translation in 1526 A.D. After the publication of a second edition he was arrested and beheaded for so doing. His edition was afterwards replaced by Van Utenhove's, 1556 A.D., which is still held in esteem. As in so many Versions, as above recited, there was comparatively little original work. Luther's original translation was fully used so far as it had appeared, and was supplemented from other sources. This Version opened the way for another, perhaps the most perfect that has yet been made. This last was a direct translation from the original tongues, but was affected by the leading Versions of other countries. But from the conception of this work by the Pastor, St. Aldegonde (1593 A.D.), besides much previous private preparation, on to the final publication in 1637 A.D., lay an interval of forty years. In it were many political changes and fresh theological disputes, as that between Gomar and Arminius upon Predestination and Free-will, the holding of the Synod of Dort, and the distractions of a part of the Thirty Years' War. The work was done at public expense, and hence the Bible has been called the States' Bible. A recent effort (1854–1867 A.D.) for revision has failed to commend itself to public approval.

The translations in the Italian and Spanish that have been made are all defective in some one point or other. Diodate's translation (1607 A.D.) was the leading Italian translation, and is yet circulated. But Archbishop Martini's Version (1776 A.D.) is said to be more perfect, and is published by the British and Foreign Bible Society. In Spain, the several translations made from 1543 A.D. on to 1794 A.D. have not circulated freely. The translation of Miguel, a Spanish Ecclesiastic, was made in the latter year. This is the best received, and is in circulation through the British and Foreign Bible Society. The Portuguese have two Versions, one made in Amsterdam (1712–1719 A.D.), and a second in Lisbon (1784 A.D.).

The circulation of these Versions varies very much, according to the race. Most freely in the Teutonic, less so in the Celtic, and least in the purely Latin nations.

Vestments. Some have supposed that the Christian vestments were copied from those used by the Jews, but it seems much more probable that they are adaptations of the ordinary dress of well-to-do persons dur ing the time of the Empire. It is impossible to fix the times when the present names and shapes were definitely given to the various vestments, but from an early date we find notices, lists, and canons which refer to one and another of them, and in ancient mosaics Bishops and Priests are pictured as wearing a regular ecclesiastical dress.

Different colors were probably not assigned to different seasons until rather a late date, the first definite mention of them being about the year 1200 A.D.; in early days White was the general color of all vestments, and was taken to signify the bright light of truth and spotless purity. Red, when adopted, typified ardent love; Green, the color of thriving vegetation, typified life; and Violet, compounded of red and black, the union of love and pain in hopeful repentance.

The different Eucharistic vestments are as follows:

The Amice.—This is a broad and oblong piece of linen with two strings to fasten it, and with an ornamented or embroidered strip on the middle of the outer edge. It is the first vestment assumed in preparing for a Celebration, and is placed on the head like a hood, and fastened by passing the strings under tne arms and then round the back until they meet on the chest, where they are tied. After the Alb is put on, the Amice is pushed back from the head on to the shoulders, where it has the appearance of a loose ornamental collar.

The meaning of the various vestments is well shown by the prayers appointed by an old Western Liturgy to be said while assuming them; that used at the putting on of the Amice is, " Place upon my head, O LORD, the helmet of salvation, to drive away all the assaults of the devil."

The Alb.—This is a loose and long garment of white linen coming down to the feet, and having close-fitting sleeves reaching to the hands. It is slipped over the head after the putting on of the Amice, and is fastened by the Girdle, so that it hangs an inch or two from the floor. Prayer: " Cleanse (dealba) me, O LORD, and purify my heart, that cleansed (dealbatus) in the blood of the Lamb, I may attain everlasting joys."

The Girdle.—This needs no detailed description, and its use is given in the preceding paragraph. Prayer: " Gird me, O LORD, with the girdle of purity, and extinguish in my loins the fire of concupiscence, that the grace of temperance and chastity may abide in me."

The Maniple.—This was originally a narrow strip of linen about two and a half feet long, employed to wipe the sacred vessels, or the hands of the Celebrant. Subsequently it became a mere ornament, and as such it is now hung on the left arm of the Priest, and fastened with a loop to the wrist. Prayer: " Grant me, O LORD, to bear the light burden (manipulum) of grief and sorrow, that I may with gladness receive the reward of labor."

The Stole.—This is a strip of silk about three inches wide and eight and a half feet long; it may be either plain or richly ornamented. It is hung around the neck of a Priest, and when celebrating should be crossed on the breast and passed under the girdle. The Deacon should wear it suspended over the left shoulder, crossing the back and breast and fastened on the right hip. Prayer: " Give me again, O LORD, the robe (stolam) of immortality which I lost by the sin of my first parent; and although I unworthily approach Thy Holy Mystery, yet may I attain everlasting joy."

The Chasuble.—This vestment is worn over the Alb. Originally it was nearly circular in shape, having an opening in the centre, through which the head of the wearer passed; at a later period the portions on the arms were reduced, and the general shape became more elliptical, and the extremities more pointed. The English Chasuble resembles the pre-Reformation vestment, while in the modern Roman Chasuble the sleeve portion has been entirely cut away, leaving the arms free, but showing to the eye the unpleasing " fiddle-shaped" stiff back and front, instead of the graceful folds of the older pattern. The back of the Chasuble is frequently ornamented with a Latin cross, but more usually with what is called the Y Orphrey. Prayer: " O LORD, who hast said, My yoke is easy and my burden is light, make me to have strength so to bear it that I may attain Thy grace. Amen."

The other vestments may be more briefly described. The common Surplice and the Bishop's sleeveless linen Rochet are modifications of the Alb. The Tunicle and Dalmatic are different names given to the similar robes of the Epistler and Gospeler. They should resemble the Chasuble of the Celebrant in material and color; in form they are a kind of loose frock or coat reaching below the knees, open partially at the lower part of the sides, with full though not large sleeves. The Cope is a long, full cloak of semicircular shape, reaching to the heels, and open in front. From the top downwards it has a richly-ornamented hood, and is fastened at the throat by a large clasp called the Morse. The Cope is used at litanies and choir services, and, according to the Prayer-Book of 1549 A.D. and the Canons of 1603 A.D., may be worn at Celebrations instead of the Chasuble.

By the first Prayer-Book of Edward VI. the Bishop was to wear at Celebrations beside his Rochet, an Alb or Surplice, and a Cope or Chasuble, and to have in his hand or that of his chaplain a Pastoral Staff. A brass of the date of 1631 A.D. represents a Bishop in Cope, Rochet, and Mitre, with a Pastoral Staff; and the Mitres of Laud, Trelawny, and others are still preserved in England, while that of our own Bishop Seabury can be seen in the Library of Trinity College, Hartford. In the reigns of Henry VIII. and Edward VI. the Bishops often

49

wore their Doctor of Divinity scarlet habits with the Rochet, and in the latter part of the reign of Elizabeth black satin was substituted for the brighter color. The present dress, therefore, consists of the sleeveless Rochet and the Doctor's gown, or black satin Chimere, with lawn sleeves, which properly belong to the Rochet attached to it.

It would occupy too much space to discuss the question of the legality of the different vestments in the United States. Briefly, however, they depend, in the absence of any definite legislation by the General Convention, on the connection of the daughter with the Mother-Church, and the statement in the Preface to our Prayer-Book, that "this Church is far from intending to depart from the Church of England in any essential point of doctrine, discipline, or worship." We are therefore thrown back on the Ornaments Rubric of the English Prayer-Book, which directs "that such Ornaments of the Church and of the Ministers thereof shall be retained and be in use as were in this Church of England, by the authority of Parliament, in the second year of the reign of King Edward the Sixth." For the fuller discussion of this whole subject, the reader is referred to the Introduction and Appendices of Blunt's Annotated Book of Common Prayer.

REV. E. M. PARKER.

Vestry. The Vestry (*Vestiarium*, Wardrobe) was either an apartment, or a distinct building of the Church, in which the vestments, and sometimes also sacred vessels and treasures, of the Church were kept. It was also used as a place of meeting and gave its name to the assembly held therein, hence is derived our use of the words Vestry Room and Vestry.

In the Primitive Church nothing is found corresponding to the modern Vestry; circumstances then existing did not demand nor even permit such a lay adjunct. Later, when fuller organization became practicable, the sacerdotal power absorbed all ecclesiastical control, the lay element was ignored, the entire management of the Church was in the hands of the various ecclesiastical orders. The office of Church-warden may be traced to the later part of the Middle Ages, when the duty of keeping the nave in repair and of providing utensils for the Divine Service was laid upon the laity. To the vestrymen corresponded in some features the ancient Sidesmen (Synodsmen), who at synods reported under oath to the Bishop the moral condition of the Diocese. In the Church of England, parish churches generally have wardens and vestrymen whose functions are regulated by custom and by legislation; on account of the connection of the Church with the State their duties are partly civil and partly ecclesiastical, so that they furnish no precedent nor guide for us, though we inherit from that Church this feature of the parish, and find in their "Select Vestry" that which corresponds to our own.

The relations, rights, and duties of Vestrymen are not defined and determined by generally acknowledged authority, they vary with the canons of the different Dioceses, and with the charters and by-laws of different parishes; this diversity has resulted in much confusion and occasionally in conflicting claims between Bishops, Rectors, and Vestries. Recognizing this defect, and in order to remedy it, the General Convention of 1877 A.D. appointed a Joint Committee of both houses "to consider and report to the next General Convention what are the several functions of Rectors, Wardens, and Vestrymen in the control and administration of the Parishes, ascertaining the right and authority of each in the premises, according to the principles and laws of the Church." By this committee a valuable report was presented to the General Convention of 1880 A.D., and printed in the Journal. The committee again reported in 1883 A.D., when at their own request the committee was enlarged and continued; accordingly they still have the subject under consideration. In their last report they state that they "have found themselves unable as yet to agree upon any substantive measures which would be practically available in meeting the difficulties and settling the important questions involved in the subject. It is, however, one of growing importance, especially in view of the difficulty of avoiding bringing the law of the Church in conflict with the laws of the several States regulating the organization of Church corporations, and the powers and functions of their office. The proper adjustment of these relations will require patient investigation and conference." In the present state of the inquiry this article must be content to accept and to define existing conditions, to deal with general principles. Handbooks and guides have been published which cite and codify such laws as are in force in certain dioceses and parishes, to these reference may be made for details to which no room here can be given. Diocesan canons are passed and Parochial organizations formed for the express purpose of carrying on the avowed mission and legitimate work of the Church, therefore if they conflict with the general principles and laws of the Church they violate the essential principle for which they were created, they are therefore bound to consult and to conform to the will of the Church in so far as it has been expressed. To ascertain this expressed will we must refer to the utterances of the Church, given in the Book of Common Prayer, and made from time to time by legislative bodies.

The time and manner of electing Vestrymen, the number to be elected, and qualifications for the office vary in different Dioceses. Efforts have been made repeatedly to bring the General Convention to require in Vestrymen some guarantee of conformity and loyalty to the Church with the interests of which they are intrusted. In attempting to make such a general law difficulties have been encountered of embarrassing feeble parishes, and of coming into conflict with existing terms of incorporation. The House of Deputies in 1883 A.D., by resolution, "earnestly commends to the Diocesan Conventions the importance of requiring that none but communicants shall be Churchwardens, and of requiring some proper regulations as to the conformity of Vestrymen with the worship and discipline of the Church."

I. To the Bishop the Vestry is related as to the head of the Diocese, its chief ecclesiastical authority, in whom is vested primarily the spiritual care and jurisdiction over all its Rectors and parishes. Accordingly, when a parish becomes vacant it is the duty of the Vestry immediately to give notice thereof to the Bishop. It is the common practice for the Vestry through its Wardens to provide ministerial services for a parish during its vacancy, but some Dioceses provide that this be done by the Bishop, recognizing that to him reverts the spiritual management of a parish while it is without a Rector; this accords with the established polity and avowed principles of the Church. "On the election of a minister into any church or parish, the Vestry shall deliver or cause to be delivered to the Bishop, or where there is no Bishop to the Standing Committee of the Diocese, notice of the same according to the form prescribed" (Title i., Can. xiv., Sect. 1). Not unless the Bishop, or the Standing Committee, which in certain cases represents and acts for a Bishop, is satisfied that the Rector-elect is a qualified minister of the Church and in good standing, is the Rector recognized as such and placed upon the record and list of the clergy which is kept by the Secretary of the Convention. The relations here indicated are still further expressed by the "Office of Institution," which, whether used or not, utters and helps to interpret the law of the Church. In this office the action of the Vestry receives the Bishop's sanction and seal, by him the newly-elected minister is authorized to claim and enjoy all the accustomed temporalities appertaining to the cure; and in any difference between him and his congregation as to a separation, the Bishop is declared to be "the ultimate arbiter and judge."

The canons and the Office of Institution agree in recognizing that the Bishop is the source of ecclesiastical jurisdiction in his Diocese, and that by his permission and under his authority Ministers act as such within his Diocese. Evidently it is the will of the Church and for its peaceful and best administration that the Bishop should have a voice in both the appointment and the removal of Rectors within his Diocese, should counsel and influence, though not control, the Vestries in their choice of those who are to administer the parishes which are under the Bishop's supervision, and for which he ultimately is responsible. The relations of the Vestry to their Diocesan are still further indicated by the canonical requirement that the Wardens and Vestry shall give to the Bishop, at his annual visitation, such information of the state of the Congregation as he may require of them (Title i., Can. xiv., Sect. 5).

II. To the Rector the relations of a Vestry begin with his call to the parish. The practice of requiring or expecting a clergyman to preach on trial as a candidate for the position to be filled has been, and deserves to be, severely censured by representative men of the Church, both clerical and lay. It reverses the original and true relations of minister and people, degrades his office, disturbs the parish, and embarrasses the Vestry, inviting general discussion and expression of opinion, and furnishes no reliable test of his abilities and adaptation to the parish. Full inquiries should be made covering the question of his ability and faithfulness at his last post, he should be seen and heard in his parish, if practicable, his visit to the parish to be filled should follow, not precede a call; then, if on an interview with the parish electing him he should appear to be not adapted to the position, he could decline it, and on learning that this is the desire of the Vestry, he would do so, if worthy to be thought of at all for the position. The call should be made in writing, and should distinctly state the provisions made for the minister's support. The extending and accepting of the call form a legal contract unlimited in continuance, unless limitations be expressly stated. The salary offered is a legal debt recoverable by law, and cannot be either withheld or reduced, except by consent of him to whom it is due. Should the minister neglect or fail to perform his duties, it would be the duty of the Wardens and Vestry to make complaint to the Ecclesiastical Authority of the Diocese. Should serious disagreement arise between the Rector and his Vestry, and a dissolution of the pastoral connection become desirable, relief may be had according to the laws and by methods duly provided (Title i., Can. xiv., Sect 6, and Title ii., Can. iv.). A Rector cannot resign his parish without consent of his Vestry, nor can the Rector be removed against his will except for the causes named and in the manner prescribed in the canons. The Church has carefully provided that the Rector's tenure of his position should be undisputed, undisturbed, and permanent, that the pastoral relation should not be dissolved except for "urgent reason," that the incumbent should be independent of the unstable opinion and preferences of those whom he is to exhort and rebuke, as occasion may require. For his own offenses he is amenable to his ecclesiastical Superior and to the Chief Shepherd and Bishop of souls. His authority as a Minister of

CHRIST is not derived from nor dependent upon the Vestry who call him to a parish, but is conveyed to him in his ordination, as indicated in the words, "Take thou authority to execute the office of a Priest in the Church of GOD, now committed unto thee by the imposition of our hands." The Vestry, in calling him to a parish, recognize this authority, place the parish under his spiritual care and control, and pledge to him that of which they are legal custodians.

The use of the "Office of Institution," if not made obligatory by Diocesan Canons, is left to the option of the Vestry. It confers no new rights or powers upon either Rector or Vestry, but by its strong expressions and significant acts it declares and helps to define the mutual relations into which they have entered, and of which the call made and accepted is sufficient evidence. In conveying to the Rector the "Temporalities" and the "Keys of the Church," the Vestry do not surrender their trust as custodians of the property of the parish and as managers of its revenue. The Rector cannot of his own motion alienate, or make any alteration in any of the property which belongs to the parish, nor can he incur any expense for the Vestry nor involve them in any obligation without their consent. The temporalities to which he is entitled are that portion of the revenue which the vestry has pledged for his support. The "keys" placed in his hands indicate that to him is given the use and control of the church edifice for all purposes of worship and ordinary parochial work; he has the right to enter the church at all times, to open it when and as he may deem proper for worship, or instruction, for all rites and offices of the Church. To him belongs the control and direction of all Sunday-schools, parish schools, associations, or meetings held within the parish for its work or welfare; *ex officio* he holds the first place in all spiritual interests and activities of the parish, in spiritual matters he has no co-ordinate authority in the parish; in temporal affairs he is associated with his Vestry, with it he forms a part of the corporation. In theory the corporation represents three interests or estates, as indicated by the title "Rector, Wardens, and Vestry." In some Dioceses the State law requires that, in order to legally transact business, each of these three must be represented. To mention and to regard the Vestry apart from the Rector is an usage which has grown out of the power and privilege exercised by the Vestry during a vacancy of the Parish Rectorate, but the Rector is or ought to be an integral part of every parish, related to it as a Bishop is to his Diocese, sharing in the care of its temporality, present at the meetings of the Vestry, presiding in them, and taking such part in the proceedings as the laws of the Diocese and the Parish prescribe or permit, acting by virtue of his office as head of the Vestry as well as of the parish. (Hoffman, Law of the Church, pp. 255-56 and 262-66.) The understanding of this subject, and the practical observance of the principles and distinctions here indicated, would promote the order and peace of parishes; would, on the one hand, deter vestrymen from transgressing the limits of their official duties in making themselves judges of spiritual matters and in attempting to control that which the Church has intentionally placed beyond their reach; and, on the other hand, would withhold Rectors from extending their exclusive direction of spiritual things over those matters which are intrusted to the Vestry, and which should be left to its management, or at least not be taken in hand except by its approval and consent.

III. To the congregation the relations sustained by the Vestry have been implied in the statements already made. The Vestrymen are elected by the congregation to represent it in law; to have charge and care of its property; to look after its temporal interests; to collect and disburse its revenue; to elect Delegates who may represent the congregation at Diocesan Conventions; acting for the parishioners, and under the jurisdiction of the Bishop, they choose and call a minister and make provision for his support; in the absence of a Rector they are bound to see that no person ministers to the congregation without sufficient evidence that he is duly qualified to do so. If the Rector prove unworthy, unfaithful, or incompetent, they in the interests of the parishioners make complaint to the Bishop. They provide that all things needful for worship and for the work of the Parish be furnished. Although they act officially as vestrymen only when in Vestry meetings, yet the relations which they hold and the interests with which they are intrusted, should prompt them to be foremost among parishioners in promoting the welfare and growth of the parish, stimulating others, sustaining and aiding the Rector, cheerfully undertaking and faithfully performing such duties as may be assigned to them, and such as the welfare of the Parish may require.

Authorities: Dr. Wm. Smith's Dictionary of Christian Antiquities, Bishop Wilberforce, History of the American Church, Hoffman, Law of the Church, Reports of the Joint Committee of the General Convention, Journals of 1880 and 1883 A.D. Papers prepared by Rev. Dr. Dix and Mr. James Parker, read before and printed by request of the Joint Com. (Pamphlet, 1880 A.D.); Paper by Bishop B. H. Paddock, presented to the House of Bishops, Gen. Convention Journal, 1883 A.D., Appendix x.; Parish Duties, in a Pastoral Letter to the Laity, Bishop Wm. H. De Lancey; Rev. Dr. Thomas Richey, The Churchman's Hand-Book; Rev. H. M. Baum, The Rights and Duties of Rectors, Church-Wardens, and Vestrymen in the American Church.

REV. J. DE WOLFE PERRY.

Via Media. The position of the Church between the extremes of Papal usurpation and of Dissenting rejections has procured for her the name of the "Via Media" (*Middle Way*). It describes her position with tolerable accuracy, but it implies that it is a deliberate compromise. But this is not so. The Truth which lies between extremes of false statement is in itself no compromise. It is simply "the Truth." So the Church in all countries is not the result of compromises but she is the visible Body to whom the proclamation of the facts of the Gospel and their consequent power over our lives is committed. That in some countries too great assumptions are made and the truth overlaid with false tradition, while by reaction others have torn off too much of the truth in ridding themselves of false tradition, does not make the Church, which is affected by neither, a middle way. It is no half-way house between extremes. But there is yet another consideration. In holding all truths the Church must hold them in their proper relative positions, and not exaggerate any one at the expense of others. It is the "proportion of the faith" which the Apostle shows we must set forth: "Having then gifts differing according to the grace that is given to us, whether prophecy (*i.e.*, preaching), let us prophesy according to the proportion of the faith" (Rom. xii. 6). Since the majority of men can only grasp a portion of the truth and hold that with enthusiasm, it requires some balance of mind to see that these may drag all other truths, whether as pendent or independent, out of their true relations, and so may disturb the due proportion of the Faith, *i.e.*, the Articles of the Creed. Here again the "Via Media" is only so because the Church can admit no disproportions in the use of Scripture, and allow no depression of one Article at the expense of the other. No Scripture can be alleged against another, no text interpreted at the expense of another, no meaning of Scripture either minimized or pushed to extreme consequences. For this reason the concurrent tradition (not oral, but recorded) of the Church upon Scripture and upon practice and discipline determine her wise *Politeia*, her statesmanship now under her divine Constitution. The Via Media is popularly and from one view correctly expressed in that name under which her chartered and corporate rights are secured to her by the Civil Law,—Protestant Episcopal. It may cover a higher, nobler right, but it cannot obscure it, and only forces us to bring out more strongly, her right as a part of the Church Catholic and Holy. But Protestant she is against the blunders and excesses or defects of those who heedlessly delight in or abuse the name and misuse its Christian meaning. Episcopal she must be by force of her divine Constitution. In these senses her name in Law is proper. It expresses that balance which is hers to uphold, and which in the end will draw all men to her who are not utterly blinded. The Via Media of her position is not the result of a pitiful shrinking, but the balanced and clear enunciation of the principles of the Faith once committed to the Saints, and which she has to uphold.

Viaticum. (Literally, the provisions for a journey.) It is usually used to mean the Holy Communion administered to a dying person. The spiritual food for the soul upon its last journey. It was a very ancient name for it. Clement of Alexandria (172-206 A.D.) so employs it,—"the provision for the journey to the unseen life;" possibly, in this sense, also, Clement of Rome, a hundred years earlier. From the time of the Council of Nice (325 A.D.) the term was most usually employed to mean this administration of the Eucharist to the dying.

Vicar. A term not occurring often in this country, since in our parish system a Vicar, a *locum tenens*, has no proper existence. It is usually supposed to refer to the same person, who may be called a Rector or a Parson as well indifferently. It was the result of the complications of the English system of Patronage, by the gift of, and the holding of, a Benefice. The Vicar was, in the complex mode of arranging the incomes of the parishes, the stipendiary Curate of the Parson in such cases where the Parson, from some cause, gives the Parish into the Curate's hands and has no cure of the souls in the Parish. "A Vicar (*vicarius*) is one that hath a spiritual promotion or living under the parson, and is so denominated as officiating (*vice ejus*) in his place or stead, and such a promotion or living is called a vicarage, which is part or portion of the parsonage allotted to the Vicar for his maintenance and support." The causes which led to the formation of these Vicarages are rather intricate, and are not of value to us here, but can be found in Burn's Eccl. Law and in Blackstone's Commentaries.

Vicarious Sacrifice. *Vide* SACRIFICE.

Vice. Vice is the habitual characteristic breaking of the moral Law. It is characteristic, and therefore it is one of the most fearful forms of sinfulness. It may be displayed in only a single evil habit, or it may be shown in a thoroughly debased character. It is the fault or defect of the spiritual nature of the man, so that, prone by inherited aptitudes for some form of sinfulness, he does not care to free himself from its power, and so loses that power for a spiritual life which is the true health of the soul. For viciousness is very largely the result of evil education, of sinful thoughts falling on congenial soil, of a blunted or a defective consciousness of sin and the loathsomeness of it, of habits it may be carelessly taken up, but certainly not striven against and not controlled. It was against the vicious of the age that our LORD uttered His severest denunciations, and there is no subtler viciousness than that which cloaks itself under spiritual form. Throughout the Holy Scriptures the sinner from weakness or sudden temptation is tenderly dealt with, but the vicious character is held up to view in the most scathing terms. Our LORD'S denunciations of the vices of His own day, the writings of St. Paul, St Peter, and St. Jude against the sins of the heathen around them, the terrible passages in Hebrews against willful sin under whatever secondary guise it may be shown, are all directed against the root form of viciousness of life. In pagan countries it was far more prominent and unrebuked of course than it is now. And yet it is but too general, too easily found, here and now. The purlieus of our cities, the street corners and lounging-places where lewd fellows of the baser sort do congregate, are places that have a terrible attractiveness for young men who have been but irregularly controlled and are still more irregularly reached by holy influences. Since vice is for a proportion of our population largely the result of an education in it, to root out vice is one of the great ends of the Church's influence, and the purpose of the educational and training agencies which are organized or should be organized in every parish. These are the chief causes for the existence of a parish. It is to supply a better, healthier education to the soul. It must create by its agencies an influence in the community which will raise the starveling soul fed on vice out of the mire of its groveling lusts. As an instrument of living power used by the HOLY GHOST, it must exert itself for good. In co-operation with His ceaseless strivings and pleadings with the heart, the Church's parochial and social influences must be exerted so that those classes may be reached who are now more or less under vicious-living. It is, then, a very important responsibility that rests upon the men in the Church of to-day, in actively using those means and instrumentalities which are almost at hand, and can be organized in every parish, by Guilds, by Brotherhoods, by co-operative associations, which can readily be begun and with tact carried on with success. Were it but a Guild for intercessional prayer it would be an instrument of vast good. And it certainly is one of the simplest that can be instituted. But whatever means may be used in any case, the object must be still the same, to prevent the accession to the ranks of the criminal classes, and to save from their souls' peril, the large floating mass of our young who are by their impressibleness readily attracted in either direction, and whose dimmed sense of sin and of responsibility makes them peculiarly open to temptation. To do this successfully is a problem which needs the lay co-operation in each parish to the utmost extent.

Vigil. The eve of a festival which is kept as a fast-day. An eve is unfasted. A Vigil is observed with a fast. The English Reformers cut off a large number of Evens and Vigils in their rearrangement of the Calendar, but retained sixteen. These are Christmas-day, Purification, Annunciation, Easter-day, Ascension-day, Whit-Sunday, St. Matthias, St. John Baptist, St. Peter, St. James, St. Bartholomew, St. Matthew, SS. Simon and Jude, St. Andrew, St. Thomas, and All-Saints.

As the observance of a Festival begins at the evening service of the day before, and its Collect is properly read then, the fast is for the day till the Evening Prayer if the Feast have a vigil. But Evens are not fasted. We have retained but one of the Evens or Vigils, but we have kept in popular phrase Christmas-Even. Easter-Eve is the only one we have retained in the Liturgy.

Virginia. Rev. T. Grayson Dashiell, D.D., has done a good work for this Diocese in preparing a Digest of its Conventions and Councils. This sketch will be a synopsis of that volume. It is very desirable that every Diocese should have such a compend.

The history of the Church in Virginia is a matter of especial interest to Churchmen, as in that State the first regular services of the Church were celebrated, and as that ancient Diocese has been the mother of Bishops and clergy who have not only gone throughout this land, but also to heathen shores.

In 1607 A.D. the Jamestown colony landed, with good Parson Hunt as their spiritual leader. He was a godly man, a peace-maker, and a cheerer of the colonists in their difficulties. In the reign of Charles II. a charter was drawn up for the erection of a Bishopric in Virginia, making Jamestown a cathedral city.

In beginning an account of Virginia Conventions, it must be noted that those gatherings in old times were not merely business meetings, but they also had a social character. The hospitality of patriarchal and early Christian times was renewed, and the fervent religious services served to knit together CHRIST'S people in love, as Bishop Meade expresses it.

After the Revolution, the Church was greatly depressed, and was robbed of much of her property by wicked legislation, though the Church-people had done much to advance the war, and Washington himself was a Churchman.

The first Convention after the Revolution met in Richmond in 1785 A.D.; Rev. Jas. Madison, D.D., was President, and 36 clergy and 71 laymen assembled. An address was prepared to stir up the wills of the faithful and call forth their aid.

In 1786 A.D., Rev. David Griffith was elected Bishop.

In 1787 A.D. the parishes were exhorted to provide for the expense of educating two youth from their early years for the ministry.

In 1789 A.D., Dr. Griffith relinquished his election to the Episcopate. The Church did not come forward to meet the expense incident to a voyage to England for consecration, and domestic affliction also proved an obstacle. He was an excellent man, and worthy of the position offered him.

In 1790 A.D., Rev. James Madison, D.D., was elected Bishop, and was consecrated the same year in Lambeth. He was President of William and Mary College. Bishop Madison's first address in 1791 A.D. was a forcible exhortation to build up the kingdom of CHRIST. A resolution was adopted looking to the formation of a society for the relief of widows and orphans of clergymen, and the next year a plan presented by Rev. Samuel Shield was adopted.

In 1792 A.D. upwards of 600 were confirmed in 5 parishes.

In 1805 A.D. the vexed question of the right to glebes was before the Convention, as it had been previously under consideration. The trouble continued for many years. Bishop Madison asked for an Assistant Bishop, but the nomination was deferred until the next Convention. Bishop Madison died in 1812 A.D. His addresses show an earnest spirit, but the obstacles before him were great. In the Convention this year a canon concerning itineracy was reaffirmed. Rev. John Bracken, D.D., was elected to fill the vacant Bishopric, but the next year declined the position.

In 1814 A.D., Rev. Richard Channing Moore, D.D., rector of Monumental Church, Richmond, was chosen Bishop. The choice was a happy and blessed one.

In 1815 A.D. a proposition was made by the President of William and Mary College concerning the support of a Theological Professor in that institution, and the Convention considered the object a desirable one.

In 1815 A.D., Bishop Moore made an encouraging report to the Convention.

In 1816 A.D. a Common Prayer-Book and Tract Society was formed. About 730 confirmations were reported.

Up to 1814 A.D. the Conventions met in the Capitol at Richmond, for two years after that date in Monumental Church, Richmond, the next year in the church at Fredericksburg, and then rotation commenced through certain parishes which were selected as proper places of meeting.

In order to supply clergy the ministers were recommended to receive young men into their families, and to make use of them as lay-readers during their preparatory studies. In 1819 A.D. the Convention recommended the organization of a Missionary Society for the benefit of vacant parishes.

In 1823 A.D. over $10,000 were reported as subscriptions to a proposed Theological School. The attempt to educate candidates at William and Mary College was not a success. In 1823 A.D. the funds for the Widows and Orphans of the clergy reported over $5000. Rev. Reuel Keith was appointed a Theological Professor, and the next year it was resolved to locate the young Seminary in Alexandria for the present. In 1825 A.D. there were 21 students and 2 Professors, Mr. Norris being the second one. In 1829 A.D. a property for the Seminary was bought near Alexandria.

In 1829 A.D., Rev. Wm. Meade, D.D., was elected Assistant Bishop.

In 1830 A.D. the number of organized churches was about 100, the clergy being less than half that number.

In 1835 A.D. we find, by Bishop Moore's commendation of the *Southern Churchman* in his address, that the idea of the importance of a Church newspaper was already felt. Rev. William F. Lee was the editor. The paper still does a good work. This year attention was reported to Sunday-schools and Bible-classes, and to the spiritual necessities of the colored people.

In 1838 A.D., Bishop Meade speaks touchingly in his address of the old churches of Virginia. This is one of the most interesting subjects connected with the history of this State. It is very sad to read that some of these buildings had been lost to the Church. Sometimes the materials were ruthlessly taken away to construct other buildings. The grave-yard walls were falling, and the beautiful locations became a grief to the passer-by, as presenting a scene of desolation. The churches in King William County were named after the creeks, and it sounds strangely to hear of Mangohick and Aquinton Churches. Some of the old churches were cruciform. Yeocomico Church was built in 1706 A.D., and it was believed at the time of the Bishop's visitation this year that no new shingle was ever put upon its roof. That these churches were strongly built is shown by the fact that they so long endured the ravages of time when exposed to the weather within as well as without. Any one who has seen Christ Church, Alexandria, or St. Paul's, Norfolk, may have a fair idea of their appearance. The antiquarian may still find much to delight him in these old churches of Virginia, while the Churchman feels deeply moved to think of the alienation, spoliation, and destruction which has been the lot of many of them.

Farnham Church, unused for worship for thirty or forty years, and abused by worldly and improper uses, was consecrated this year, having been refitted, it being believed that the old churches were never consecrated. The Wicomico Church was without doors and windows. Inside the church were the wagon, the plow, and barrels of lime and tar, and lumber. Cattle had free admission, and the slab of marble which covered the body of one of its latest ministers was covered with dirt and rubbish. The old bell, which had called the faithful to worship GOD, lay in a pew near the falling pulpit. Steps had been taken towards repair, though the Bishop was doubtful of the result. A more cheerful view was presented at Christ Church, Lancaster County, which was a fine edifice, built at the expense of Mr

Robin Carter. Bishop Meade passed the ruins of Pope's Creek Church, in which Washington was baptized and attended service in early life. The Bishop loved to hold service in these deserted churches, even when they were in a ruinous condition. His descriptions of them are poetic, and he wails like an ancient prophet over the desolations of Zion. He was deeply moved at the desolate appearance of Pohick Church, near Mount Vernon. Washington selected its location and worshiped in the venerable building. An effort to repair it has since been made. The visitor at Mount Vernon may readily prolong his drive to see this hallowed spot.

In 1841 A.D. the eloquent and loving Bishop Moore died. He was a man with a great heart, loving all, and beloved by all. Bishop Meade speaks of him as being peculiarly amiable and interesting, and venerable in form and countenance and manner.

In 1842 A.D., Rev. John Johns, D.D., was elected as Assistant Bishop.

In 1843 A.D., Bishop Meade reported 31 candidates for holy orders, and that more than 1000 persons had been confirmed by Bishop Johns and himself. The Virginia Conventions at times passed very strong resolutions with regard to Christian morals, protesting against gambling, dancing, theatre-going, intemperance, and the desecration of the LORD'S Day. Both Bishops and Conventions have also constantly protested against changes in the order of worship, and a great simplicity has been observed with regard to ornamentation of churches. The feeling of the Church, like that of the State, has been exceedingly conservative, and everything like novelty or change has been generally discouraged. A scattered country population is not easily moved, and walks readily in the ways of its fathers.

In 1844 A.D. the Bishop gives a report of old churches "repaired and once more rendered vocal with the praises of GOD, after the silence and profanation of many years." In reference to this matter it must be remembered that after the Revolution the number of clergy was greatly lessened, and the Church was fearfully depressed. Even at Bishop Moore's election Bishop Meade states that but seven clergy were present in Convention. When Bishop Meade was ordained Deacon by Bishop Madison, in Williamsburg, on a bright Sunday morning, only about fifteen gentlemen, young and old, and two ladies were present. On the other hand, in 1845 A.D., Bishop Meade, in the same address which records the weakness of the Church in Bishop Madison's day, exclaims, "What hath GOD wrought!" as he notes the full employment of two Bishops in visiting nearly 200 churches and stations, while the Diocese contained 100 clergymen, and 50 persons studying for the ministry. While formerly English clergy served in Virginia, in later years she has sent Missionaries to Europe, Asia, and Africa. Bishop Boone, of China, Bishops Payne and Penick, of Africa, and Bishop Williams, of Japan, were from her Theological Seminary. In addition to her diocesan work the Virginia Church was interested in the Bible and Colonization Societies. In 1860 A.D. the contributions, exclusive of current expenses, were $113,510.57, the largest sum reported up to this time.

Bishop Meade died in 1862 A.D. He was a strong, earnest, godly man, to whom Virginia is deeply indebted. He was uncompromising as to what he considered to be the truth in CHRIST. As an evangelist he gladly endured hardness, and made his visitations faithfully throughout a vast Diocese. In friendship he was kind and sympathetic. At the Convention preceding his death he gave a semi-centennial discourse, humbly giving his experience of a lifetime. Bishop Johns says of this address, "There was impressively evident 'a ripeness and perfectness of age in CHRIST,' which might have advised us that his maturity for Heaven was attained, and 'the time of his departure at hand.'" When we compare the deadness of the Church in Virginia in the beginning of Bishop Meade's clerical work to the life shown in it at the end of his Episcopal work, we can but say that, under GOD, the blessed change was largely due to his untiring labors and constant faith. When even Chief-Justice Marshall, and the General Convention itself, doubted concerning the future of the Virginia Church, Bishop Meade gave little heed to evil forebodings, but toiled on in storm as well as sunshine, and he was blessed in his deed. His remains lie in Hollywood Cemetery, Richmond, and a costly monument has been erected over them by a sorrowing people.

The War separated Virginia from the General Convention for a short period. The Church then found work to do among the Confederate soldiers by means of her chaplains. When peace was restored, Bishop Johns wisely advised the Council to resume its former relations with the North. In reflecting on the terrible devastation suffered by Virginia during the war, he must be blind indeed who cannot see the good hand of our GOD in this action. The address of Bishop Johns was full of love, and not bitterness, and in due time the Church in Virginia again sent her delegates to the General Convention. The return of the Southern Dioceses is one of the fairest pictures in the history of the Church of CHRIST. It is very easy to keep up divisions after they have taken place. If the whole religious world could imbibe the spirit which influenced the Southern Bishops at this juncture, the words sect and schism might be forgotten on earth. May this loving act be a precursor of the time when all the people of GOD shall see eye to eye, and join hand with hand. In 1866 A.D., Cassius F. Lee offered a resolution in favor of resuming connection with the General Convention, which was adopted.

Frequent notices occur in the Conventions of interest in work among the colored people. In 1879 A.D., Bishop Whittle commends the noble work of Mrs. F. E. Buford, and calls attention to the movement guided by her mission in the Zion Union Apostolic Church.

In 1867 A.D., Rev. Francis M. Whittle, rector of St Paul's Church, Louisville, Ky., was elected Assistant Bishop.

In 1870 A.D. it is reported that an Episcopal residence has been purchased in Richmond; Bishop Johns resided near Alexandria. Bishop Johns died in 1876 A.D. Bishop Whittle speaks of his peaceful and triumphant death, after a ministry lacking but one month of fifty-seven years, comprising abundant labors as Assistant Bishop, and Bishop for nearly thirty-three years. He was a Christian teacher, faithful and beloved. The Council made an appropriation towards building a monument for him.

In 1877 A.D. consent was given to the erection of a Diocese in West Virginia. After the loss of West Virginia, in the Council of 1881 A.D. there were 12,778 communicants reported. From 1865 A.D. to 1881 A.D., 119 were ordained as Priests and 136 as Deacons, and 16,174 confirmed. The contributions noted for that period for diocesan and external objects amounted to $2,500,000. The last report of communicants as given in the *Church Almanac* for 1884 A.D. is 14,153.

In 1883 A.D., Rev. Alfred Magill Randolph, D.D., of Emmanuel Church, Baltimore, was consecrated Assistant Bishop. Being a Virginian by birth and a graduate of William and Mary College and the Theological Seminary of Alexandria, he will minister among his own people.

The educational institutions of Virginia are the Theological Seminary and the High School near Alexandria, the Virginia Female Institute, Staunton, and the Episcopal Female Institute, Winchester.

The history of the Church in Virginia would be incomplete without a sketch of the Theological Seminary, which has been in a great measure the means of its revival and increase. Prof. Packard's discourse at its Semi-Centennial gives the following facts: Rev. Dr. Reuel Keith and Rev. Dr. Wm. H. Wilmer were the first Professors; from a small beginning hundreds have now been educated and over thirty have gone as Missionaries to the heathen. Bishop Meade was interested in founding the Seminary before he was advanced to the Episcopate. Dr. Keith was a man of great fervor in devotion, and rendered the Liturgy most impressive by his manner of reading it. Bishop Meade pronounced him the most eloquent preacher he had ever heard. Dr. Wilmer did more than any other man except Bishop Meade to revive the Church in Virginia. The Professors in this Seminary have been men of holy lives, and have done much to infuse a proper spirit into the minds of the students. Rev. Dr. Clemson, in his reminiscence of Seminary life, quoted in the Rev. Philip Slaughter's address on this occasion, speaks of the Rev. Oliver Norris as "a lovely man of the sweetest piety," and adds, "he always reminded me of the Apostle John." Dr. Keith he describes as "a man of fine intellect and attainments. All respected and revered him. The Rev. Dr. Wilmer was a bland, cheerful, companionable man." The amiable Mr. Lippitt and Charles Mann and Dr. Sparrow must not be forgotten as early workers in this field. The Rev. James May, D.D., by his devout life and faithful teaching left a strong impress on this school of the prophets. Over the grave of Bishop Meade is the inscription, "The Founder of the Theological Seminary of Virginia," and certainly the Seminary itself is a noble monument. The Apostolic Bishop Moore was interested in the institution and attended its annual examinations, with "his massive and noble countenance, his long flowing locks, his sonorous voice." A pleasant incident in the Seminary's history is the erection of Aspinwall Hall by the Aspinwalls, at the suggestion of Bishop Bedell. Bohlen Hall was the work of the Bohlen family, and munificent gifts have been received from Anson G. P. Dodge and others. Bishop Griswold's widow gave his library.

Any one who has visited the Seminary must have been struck with its magnificent situation on a hill, which covers a view of great beauty, stretching many miles towards Washington and Georgetown. In such a place, and among such teachers, were domestic and foreign Missionaries trained, and a feeling of social and private piety engendered. From this spot Hanson, Hazlehurst, Hening, Syle, Nelson, Parker, Thompson, and Dr. Hill, with many others, went forth to work in foreign fields. In the graveyard at Cape Palmas five alumni rest,— Minor, Holcomb, Messenger, Robert Smith, and Colden Hoffman. Let us hear the devoted Hoffman from his African grave calling with his dying breath to the American Church, "Tell them by the Crucified One not to hold back their hands." While this Seminary has been distinguished for its foreign missionary work, other Divinity Schools are now learning its lesson of devotion. The General Theological Seminary in New York is a little older than the Alexandria Seminary, though the subject of Theological education was broached in the Virginia Convention some time before the Alexandria Seminary was founded. These two Divinity Schools are our oldest Theological Institutions, and from them a great number of our Bishops and Clergy have graduated, though as the country advances in extent and population, it has been thought necessary to open other schools of this kind. May they long send their healing streams throughout this land and foreign lands,

Statistics for 1886 A.D. : Clergy, 147; parishes, 125; missions, 90; candidates for H. O., 15; ordinations diac., 9; pr. 9; bap., 1495; con., 1397; com., 15,381; contr., $221,357.63.

REV. S. F. HOTCHKIN.

Virginity. While the sanctity of marriage, its honor, and its holy estate are not by any means undervalued in Holy Scripture, and it is commanded of all men to be had in reverence, still the state of virginity is highly commended in Scripture. One of the traditional sayings of our LORD is with reference to it. The Apostle St. Paul commends it. In the Revelation it is a mark of those who alone sing the song of the Lamb. The Virgins, as an order in the Church, probably existed from its first practical organized work. St. Philip the Deacon had four daughters who were Virgins. To merely say that they were unmarried does not convey the full force of the passage. And immediately after the Apostolic age we have constant references to virginity of both sexes. This was an almost inevitable state for those who would escape the fearful pollution of heathen society, and who would live in religious seclusion. It was to be a life-long vow. Those who broke it, either by sin or by marrying, were in many places marked persons, and were in some way made to feel that they had fallen in the Church's estimation. It must have been so marked, since it was a natural and healthy movement *within* the Church and among the Laity. It gave to the Church many earnest, unattached lay-workers, who could be employed by her in undertakings which would have been impossible to married persons. This state of things continued for two hundred years, but the necessity for secluding them into communities led to the formation of religious associations of a more regular and positive rule, and from this grew up the institution of nuns.

Virtues, Theological. Virtue, in the Christian sense, is moral goodness. It arises from love to GOD, and love to man (Phil. iv. 8). "Actions to which we are rightly directed by our Reason are Duties. The Habits and Dispositions by which we perform our Duties are Virtues" (Whewell). "Truth," says Warburton, "and Virtue are twin-born sisters, . . . Truth being speculative Virtue, and Virtue only practical Truth." A truly virtuous man rises above popular opinion, and, as Bacon declares, would be virtuous in a desert. It was a pretty conceit of Plato that if virtue " could be made the object of sight, it would excite in us a wonderful love of wisdom." Hypocrisy is a compliment paid by the wicked to virtue, but it is easier to be virtuous than to feign the appearance of goodness. Swift shows that as health is one thing, but diseases are many, so we may reduce the virtues to a few heads, while vices are without number. The various Christian virtues combined in unity form a Christian life, though no man is perfectly innocent. The three virtues styled Theological are Faith, Hope and Charity (1 Cor. xiii. 13). Faith is placed first, for it is the foundation-stone in the Christian edifice. "Without faith it is impossible to please Him; for he that cometh to GOD must believe that He is, and that He is a rewarder of them that diligently seek Him" (Heb. xi. 6). By faith weak man lays hold on GOD, who is his "refuge and strength." The human garment of rags is replaced by the robe of CHRIST'S righteousness, and guilty man stands acquitted because his Saviour has borne the penalty of his sin. Hence, when in Holy Baptism the person is introduced into CHRIST'S Church, the question is properly asked as to his belief in the Creed, which is the sum of Christianity. In the first prayer in that service the Theological Virtues are welded together thus: "steadfast in faith, joyful through hope, and rooted in charity." With such faith the believer passes safely "the waves of this troublesome world," and comes to CHRIST'S Heavenly Kingdom. The question of our LORD to the man whose blindness He had removed was, "Dost thou believe on the SON of GOD?" And he said, "LORD, I believe. And he worshiped Him" (St. John ix. 35, 38). Such faith accompanied with Christian acts brings salvation.

"If Faith begins the Christian life, Hope continues and supports it. Even the heathen in the myth about Hope remaining in the bottom of the box of Pandora, when a multitude of evils had flown from it, saw its wonderful power. Hope bends over the infant's cradle, and relieves the watcher by the sick-bed. It nerves the laborer's arm, and gives the patriot assistance in oppression. In religion St. Paul tells us that "we are saved by hope" (Rom. viii. 24). Such hope breeds patience (v. 25). It is the "anchor of the soul" "which entereth into that within the veil" (Heb. vi. 19). The hope of an open heaven and a waiting CHRIST, as seen by St. Stephen, brightens the lot of GOD'S children, and in the midst of toil holds out the promise of blessed rest (Heb. iv. 9).

And now follows the crowning grace of Charity. The word comes to us from the Greek, and means love, though in common speech it is often restricted to alms-giving. "GOD is love" (1 John iv. 8). The suffering of CHRIST for man (vs. 9, 10) is the highest manifestation of GOD'S love. St. John brings the duty into practice in saying, "Beloved, if GOD so loved us, we ought also to love one another" (v. 11). Hence the long-suffering, modesty, and endurance of love, as described in 1 Cor. xiii., show how this virtue is the mother of many virtues, and is needed to complete faith and hope. "Love is the fulfilling of the law" (Rom. xiii. 10). On love to GOD and love to man "hang all the law and the prophets" (St. Matt. xxii. 40). A man who loves his neighbor will not rob his goods, or seek his life, or injure his good name, and man's whole duty may be comprehended in this thought of love, or charity. "And now abideth faith, hope, charity, these three; but the greatest of these is charity" (1 Cor. xiii. 13).

The four Cardinal Virtues are Justice, Prudence, Temperance, and Fortitude. Justice is one of GOD's perfections. He is just in His nature and in His acts. "Justice and judgment are the habitation of Thy throne: mercy and truth shall go before Thy face" (Ps. lxxxix. 14). The ruler is to display justice as the agent of GOD. Job says, "My judgment was as a robe and diadem" (Job xxix. 14). See, concerning Abraham, Gen. xviii. 19. Pilate's wife well styles our LORD "that just man" (St. Matt. xxvii. 19), and St. Peter charges on the Jews that they "denied the Holy One and the Just" (Acts iii. 14. See also vii. 52, and xxii. 14, with regard to this term). The true idea of Justice is that of giving each man his own due share in property, position, and in all things. The Golden Rule, given by "the Just One," covers our whole duty in this regard: "As ye would that men should do to you, do ye also to them likewise" (St. Luke vi. 31).

The second Cardinal Virtue is Prudence. It was one of the gifts of Solomon (2 Chron. ii. 12), and he declares that wisdom dwells with prudence (Prov. viii. 12), and that "the prudent man looketh well to his going" (vs. 14, 15). This virtue is seen in Our LORD's life constantly. It is especially to be noted in the case of the tribute money, and in His walking "no more openly among the Jews" (St. John xi. 54) when they plotted His death. St. Joseph's life is held up by F. W. Faber as a model of prudence, as in doubts, and dreams, and perplexities he was quiet and docile, doing all for GOD, leading an interior life, never looking before light and grace were given, but childlike and prompt the moment the divine command came. Bishop Butler, in his "Dissertation of the Nature of Virtue," shows that a due concern of our interest or happiness and a reasonable effort to secure it is praiseworthy. Raise this thought to heavenly things, and reflect on CHRIST's promises of endless joy, and prudence and religion meet, and the foolish man is seen to be the wicked one.

The next Cardinal Virtue is Temperance. This word of late years in this country has been used to signify abstinence from intoxicating drinks. St. Paul uses the word in a much wider sense (Gal. v. 23). It signifies a proper and decent moderation in all things, bodily and mental. True temperance cannot be restricted to the idea of refraining from one particular sin. The temperate man bridles his animal nature, and keeps his body in "subjection" as if it were a well-tamed horse or an adversary whom he was overcoming (1 Cor. ix. 27). Still, he knows that the mind rules the body, and therefore he strives to think temperately, as well as to act temperately. To such a man anger, hatred, and envy are unpleasant, as indications of a lack of that self-restraint imposed by Christianity upon him.

The last of the Cardinal Virtues is Fortitude. As the word virtue is derived from the Latin *vir*, "man," and means manliness, so Fortitude comes to us from the same language, in which *fortis* signifies strong. This is the virtue which helps men to "suffer and to be strong." Locke calls it "the guard and support of the other virtues." Fortitude animated the thousands of martyrs in the early Church who died for CHRIST. St. Ignatius writes in an Epistle to St. Polycarp, "Stand firm and immovable as an anvil when it is beaten upon." Adversity only helps to bring out fortitude. Misery has been called "virtue's whetstone." The highest instance of fortitude is that of our Blessed LORD, in His great agony, crying, as He looked forward to a painful and shameful death, "O my FATHER, if it be possible, let this cup pass from me: nevertheless not as I will, but as Thou wilt" (St. Matt. xxvi. 39).

These various virtues combine to form a Christian and Christlike character. Virtue, knowledge, temperance, patience, godliness, brotherly kindness, and charity are enumerated by St. Peter as Christian virtues, and he adds to his enumeration these words of application: "For if these things be in you, and abound, they make you that ye shall neither be barren nor unfruitful in the knowledge of our LORD JESUS CHRIST" (2 Pet. i. 5-8). By the life he describes men may receive the benefit of the "exceeding great and precious promises," and become "partakers of the divine nature, having escaped the corruption that is in the world through lust" (v. 4). Such a life in CHRIST promises a happy immortality.

"Only a sweet and virtuous soul,
Like seasoned timber, never gives;
But, though the whole world turn to coal,
Then, chiefly lives."

REV. S. F. HOTCHKIN.

Visitation, Episcopal. The visitation of the Bishop is looked forward to in every Parish with a very varying appreciation of its purpose, its blessing, and the power which is implied in the Bishop's right to visit. It is not merely the visit of the Chief Pastor of the Diocese for the purpose of preaching, confirming, and blessing; these are essential parts of his duty. Anciently he was the only one properly intrusted with the power to preach. It is his office to declare and pronounce to the people the forgiveness of sins as well as to bless them. It is a great privilege to receive from his hands the food for the Resurrection (St. John vi. 54) the LORD hath left us. For the Bishop is the representative and living holder of the one sole order of the ministry our LORD commissioned after His resurrection. The Covenant made and executed in the visible Church is through him, though the Priest or Deacon may be the administrator of the action. So in the rite of Confirmation there is a Confession made before him of the binding force of our baptismal vows, and we upon this public acknowledgment receive the grace of the HOLY GHOST. But the powers implied in a visitation reach further. Whether they are used at all, or in part, or in full would depend upon the need, fitness, or expediency the Bishop may wisely see should be used. But he has certain powers further which have been used, and these rights as being disciplinary are a part of his office. He has the right to inquire into and ascertain the true condition of each Parish in his Diocese. It is a part of his office formerly exercised in person, but in after-times delegated to the Archdeacon whose office was created for this use. He may question either Rector or Vestry, or both, as to the strength, resources, and spiritual condition of the parish ; may inquire into the frequency of the services and the zeal of the people in attending upon them; into the proper furniture of, and reverent care for, the Church ; into the sympathy and moral support the people give their rector ; indeed, into all those things which enter into the proper welfare of the Parish as a living part of the Church of GOD, so that he may be enabled to give right counsel, and to correct faults or remedy defects, and, too, that he may be enabled to obtain from the Parish such aid as may materially forward his work in the Diocese.

Whether in all cases it is well to carry out this authority depends upon many local and temporary causes, but it is a right that inheres in the office of a Bishop by virtue of the commission from our LORD. That a right so to visit is a part of the office is seen both by the visitation St. Paul threatened to hold at Corinth (1 Cor. iv. 21; 2 Cor. xiii. 10), and by the directions he gave both SS. Timothy and Titus as to their duties.

Vocation. A calling, or "inward motion by the HOLY GHOST" (Jer. xxiii. 21; Heb. v. 4; Rom. x. 15) to the ecclesiastical state, is marked by right motives in seeking it,—that is, without desire of the glory of this world, or of income, or a pleasant, easy life, but by readiness in enduring pain and labor, and by desire to promote the glory of GOD and the edifying and salvation of man. Bishop Andrews explains to Peter du Moulin, that the words "pastor" and "vocation" in the sense placed upon them by Protestants, that is, with the meaning of ordination and ministers, were innovations of the sixteenth century; as the pastorate of Scripture (1 Pet. ii. 25) and of ecclesiastical writers designates the office of Bishops, and "vocation" has its special meaning. The XXIII. Article is distinct upon this point: "It is not lawful for any man to take upon him the office of public preaching, or ministering the Sacraments in the Congregation (" *Ecclesia*," Lat. vers.) before he be lawfully called, and sent to execute the same. And those we ought to judge lawfully called and sent, which *be chosen and called* to this work by men who have public authority given unto them in the Congregation, to call and send Ministers into the LORD'S vineyard."

"Our Apostles," says St. Clement, "knew, through our LORD JESUS CHRIST, that there should arise contention touching the name of the Episcopate, and for this cause, being endowed with a perfect prescience, they constituted the aforesaid (Bishops and Deacons), and thenceforward laid down a succession, that when they were fallen asleep, then other men approved (of the HOLY SPIRIT) might receive their office and ministry." (Ad Corinth, c. xliv.). The XXXVI. Article further and explicitly asserts that " We decree all such to be rightly, orderly, and lawfully consecrated or ordered" according to the rites of the Ordinal; and in the Preface to the latter it is said, " No man might presume to execute any of them" (the orders of Bishops, Priests, and Deacons), "except he were first called, tried, and examined, and known to have such qualities as are requisite for the same; and also by Public Prayer, with Imposition of Hands, were approved and admitted thereunto by lawful Authority ;" that is, "hath Episcopal consecration or ordination." The candidate is therefore required to state that he "thinks he is *truly called*, according to the will of our LORD JESUS CHRIST and the due order of this realm (Ordering of Deacons, "this United Church of England and Ireland ;" Ordering of Priests and Consecration of Bishops) to the ministry of the Church." (Blunt's Dict. of Doct. and Hist. Theol.)

Vulgate. The famous translation of the Bible which St. Jerome made of the Hebrew into Latin and the Greek. It is called *Vulgate* as being in common use, but the term belonged also to the Septuagint and to the Italic Version upon which St. Jerome worked. The New Testament was first translated. He revised the Psalter twice. The first revision was used in Italy, the second revision was accepted in Europe generally, and was the one from which our Version of the Psalms in the Prayer-Book was made. St. Jerome first translated Samuel and Kings, and after that he worked with zeal and rapidity, but seems to have withheld his translations, except from intimate friends, till he could revise them ; still, though he labored sixteen years at the translation, to the last there was something to revise. It had to work its way against the old Latin translation made before 177 A.D., and against the Itala which was a revision of this latter work made through the Greek text, and which was held to be a very close and faithful rendering.

It mastered all opposition at last by its great superiority, but itself fell into gross inaccuracies from transcribers, so that a revision and correction was called for, and partly effected by Alcuin (800 A.D.), but was not fully done till the art of printing was discovered and successive editions passed through editorial scrutiny. Still, it has not been completely effected even yet. When Sextus V. (1582 A.D.) put forth his edition, he so changed it that "he brought peril on the Church." The Vulgate was, however, again revised after many delays, and the last text which was authoritative was issued 1598 A.D. There is still great room for revision and correction. There is large work yet to be done by a competent scholar in the collation of materials for a proper edition of the Vulgate.

W.

Wafer. The unleavened bread used in the Holy Communion in the Roman Church. Bread, *i.e.*, leavened, was the unchanged practice of the Eastern Church, but unleavened bread was the use of the West generally. It was left as an indifferent matter in the last revision of the Prayer-Book in 1662 A.D. In fact, the leaning in England being generally towards wafer bread, instances of its continued use down to the beginning of the last century can readily be adduced, and its use is partly revived in many English Churches. But the remark of Scudamore upon this is well worthy of careful heed, at least in our own American Church: "Legally we are in the same position as our forefathers; but, looking at the long and general disuse of the wafer bread, we are morally bound, in deciding which kind we ourselves will use, to give unusual weight to every alleged consideration of expediency and charity." For ourselves no *legal*, but all ordinary, moral considerations would prevent our using aught but the finest and best wheaten bread.

Warden. *Vide* VESTRY.

Washington Territory. (*Vide* OREGON.) The history of the Church on the Northwestern coast is to be gathered from pamphlets containing the proceedings of the Convocation of Oregon and Washington, which formed one jurisdiction, having been organized in 1854 A.D. The records of the first meeting were not published in the form of a pamphlet, and those of the ninth session only appeared in brief in the first number of the *Oregon Churchman*. For a list of these rare pamphlets, see Bishop Perry's Churchman's Year-Book, 1870 and 1871 A.D., under "Oregon and Washington Territory." Since Bishop Morris took charge of the jurisdiction, the clergy of Washington Territory have organized a Convocation. St. Helen's Hall and the Bishop Scott School have done good work in educating the children of Washington, as well as Oregon. They have proved a great blessing. Washington was under the charge of Bishop Scott, of Oregon, and afterwards fell under the care of Bishop Morris. He reported to the General Convention of 1874 A.D. that there was an Episcopal Seminary for girls, at Walla Walla, in Washington Territory, with 13 teachers and 120 male and 140 female pupils, having an endowment of $9000. In 1880 A.D. the Rev. T. A. Paddock, D.D., the busy rector of the active St. Peter's Church, Brooklyn, was consecrated as the Bishop of Washington, as Bishop Morris found that his extensive field needed division. In 1882 A.D. the *Living Church Annual* reports a second school, at Spokane Falls, named the Rodney-Morris School. The school was under the charge of the Rev. Dr. Nevins. The population of this Territory in 1880 A.D. was 75,120, and it contains 69,994 square miles. There is a Diocesan Board of Missions, and Episcopal and Disabled Clergy Funds are on the report.

St. Paul's School for Girls, Walla Walla, is now in charge of Rev. H. D. Lathrop, D.D. The Fannie C. Paddock Memorial Hospital at Tacoma is a monument to the Bishop's devoted wife, who died while on the journey to the scene of her husband's labor. Rev. D. H. Lovejoy, M.D., formerly at the Episcopal Hospital, Philadelphia, is chaplain and superintendent. Statistics for year ending June 27, 1883 A.D.: Clergy, 11; confirmed, 22; communicants, 406; scholars in Sunday-schools, 464; contributions, $12,406.47. Bishop Paddock has received some aid from the East in his endeavor to establish Church Schools, and needs and earnestly solicits much more to enable him to lay foundations deep and strong in that new land. Bishop Paddock was born in Norwich, Conn., January 19, 1825. He is the son of an Episcopal clergyman, and his brother is Bishop of Massachusetts. He graduated at Trinity College, Hartford, in 1845 A.D., and from the General Theological Seminary in 1849 A.D. Ordered Deacon July 22, 1849 A.D. Ordained Priest April 30, 1850 A.D. Was Rector of CHRIST Church, Stratford, Conn., for five years, and of St. Peter's, Brooklyn, L.I., from 1855 A.D., to his elevation to the Episcopate. Consecrated Missionary Bishop of Washington Territory in St. Peter's Church, Brooklyn, on December 15, 1880 A.D., by the Rt. Rev.

Benjamin B. Smith, D.D., the Rt. Rev. Alfred Lee, D.D., the Rt. Rev. Benjamin Paddock, D.D., the Rt. Rev. Daniel S. Tuttle, D.D., the Rt. Rev. Horatio Potter, D.D., and the Rt. Rev. George F. Seymour, D.D.

In Bishop Paddock's Report for 1883 A.D. he states that he has baptized three children and eleven adults, and confirmed thirty in the Territory, and one in Idaho at the request of Bishop Tuttle. He had visited the Indian station at Aloh Bay, and baptized five adults of the Makah tribe, instructed by Mr. J. H. Y. Bell, teacher of the Government School, and candidate for holy orders. About sixty are here under instruction. The Bishop writes that as far as he "can learn, these are the first Indian adults who have been baptized by a clergyman of our Church in this northwestern region. We labor and pray that they may be followed by many who shall help to make up the 'great numbers' to be gathered out of 'every kindred, and tongue, and people, and nation.'" At St. Luke's, Vancouver, a sweet-toned bell has been placed in the church tower by an association of young persons belonging to the parish. At Fort Townsend the church had been removed and repaired. St. Peter's Church at Pomeroy had been consecrated, and services were conducted there by Rev. Wm. A. Fair. St. Luke's Memorial Church, New Tacoma, had been consecrated. This is the finest church building on the Pacific coast north of San Francisco. Bishop Morris was present at the consecration of this church, and preached the following day at the ordination of Rev. H. S. Bonnell to the Priesthood. The Memorial Hospital at Tacoma has done a good work "for the healing of the body and the saving of the soul." The Bishop is naturally deeply interested in Christian education, and quotes the report of the Committee on that subject at the General Convention of 1880 A.D. thus: "There is no subject more vital, more closely connected with the well-being, nay, the very life of the Church, than this subject. The whole growth of Christianity and the stability of society depend upon the kind of education which our children are securing." That Convention requested Bishops and clergy to "remind the people of their duty to support and build up our schools and colleges, and to make education, under the auspices of the Church, superior in all respects to that afforded in the institutions." The Church School for Girls at Walla Walla, in the southeastern part of Washington, has done a good work for ten years past. A new building is required. For this the citizens pledged $5000 "if the Bishop would aid." Valuable offers of "land and money" have been made "for a like school at New Tacoma, in the northwestern part of the Territory." The Bishop has received from the Atlantic States $3000 for a chapel at Walla Walla, "and about $25,000 for the school for girls at New Tacoma." The corner-stone of this school was laid August 22, 1883 A.D. This the Bishop is very anxious to secure. "If," he says, "by the expenditure of any time and toil on my part it shall be my privilege to see these institutions for the promotion of sound learning and Christian education established on good foundation, I shall be very thankful, believing that a work will be done that will not only be a blessing to the young now growing up, but for the temporal and eternal good of multitudes in age after age, and for generation after generation."

Statistics for 1886 A.D.: Clergy, 14; missions, 15; families, 550; individuals, 1910; baptisms, infants, 98, adults, 55, total, 153; confirmed, 92; communicants, 582; Sunday-school teachers, 75; Sunday-school scholars, 736; contributions, $12,158.61.

REV. S. F. HOTCHKIN.

Wave-Offering. The wave-offering, together with the heave-offering, was a rite peculiar to the peace-offering. The right shoulder was holy to the LORD, and so was "heaved" and belonged to the priest; the breast was waved before the LORD. Their significance was connected with our LORD'S Ascension and presentation of Himself as the heave-offering and wave-offering of the one sacrifice, holy and perfect, that should belong to the High-Priest by an ordinance of the LORD from the Children of Israel. But another wave-offering, that of the sheaf of the first-fruits, was still more significant. "The type in respect of the day was the waved sheaf in the feast of the first-fruits, concerning which this was the law of GOD by Moses: 'When ye be come into the land which I give unto you, and shall reap the harvest thereof, ye then shall bring a sheaf of the first-fruits of your harvest unto the priest: and he shall wave the sheaf before the LORD, to be accepted for you: on the morrow after the Sabbath the priest shall wave it. And ye shall offer that day when ye wave the sheaf, an he-lamb without blemish of the first year for a burnt-offering unto the LORD' (Lev. xxiii. 10–12). For under the Levitical Law all the fruits of the earth in the land of Canaan were profane; none might eat of them till they were consecrated, and that they were in the feasts of the first-fruits. One sheaf was taken out of the field and brought to the priest, who lifted it up as it were in the name of all the rest, waving it before the LORD, and it was accepted for them, so that all the sheaves in the field were holy, 'the lump also is holy' (Rom. xi. 16). And this was always done the day after the Sabbath, that is, the paschal solemnity, after which the fullness of the harvest followed; by which this much was foretold and represented, that as the sheaf was lifted up and waved, and the lamb was offered on that day by the priest to GOD, so the promised MESSIAS, that immaculate Lamb which was to die, that priest which dying was to offer up Himself to GOD, was upon this day to be lifted up, raised from the dead, or rather to shake and lift up and present Himself to GOD, and so to be accepted for us all, that so our dust might be sanctified, our corruption hallowed, our mortality consecrated to eternity. Thus was the resurrection of the MESSIAS after death typically represented both in the distance and the day." (Pearson on the Creed, p. 391.)

Wednesday. It was observed as a fast, together with Friday, as early as 150 A.D.; it being one of the days for the Christians to gather in their week-day assemblies. The Litany is to be recited on that day as well as on Friday, marking it in our use as a day if not of abstinence, yet a day of penitence. Wednesday in Holy Week in the older pre-reformation offices was marked with solemn recitation of the Tenebræ, an office which was as old as the eighth century, in which the fifteen candles burning at the beginning of the Vesper Service were extinguished one by one, as the choir chanted the fifty-first Psalm, till the church was in utter darkness. This Tenebræ Service was repeated for three days in succession in Holy Week.

Week. However much we may be persuaded that the earliest observance of the week was one of the very earliest ordinances given to man,—as we find a notice of the week in Noah's waiting seven days before the dove was sent forth, and in Laban's bidding Jacob to fulfill Leah's week, and then to marry Rachel,—yet on purely historic grounds, as a sacredly-appointed measure of time, it belongs to the Mosaic Law. Seven was a main factor in the ritually and nationally recurring feasts. It was a very remarkable measure of time, and one which furnishes such a common measure of longer periods at only long-recurring intervals, that its observance must have rested on only divine ordinance. Seven is not the measure of the three hundred and sixty-five days of the year, and by the use of it forces the Sabbath-day or Sunday upon every day of the year in the course of a cycle of nineteen years. It forms, very singularly, the just division of labor and of rest. Other periods have been tried, but they have proved unsatisfactory, as, *e.g.*, the Decade of the French Revolution. After a trial of some years the French were compelled to return to the six days of work and the seventh of rest.

West Virginia, Diocese of. A brief outline showing the creation of the new Diocese of West Virginia.

Political division of the State of Virginia.—The question of a division of the State of Virginia had long been agitated. As early as 1829 A.D., after the call of a Convention to alter and amend the old Constitution which had been the fundamental law for more than forty years, a body of distinguished citizens of the State assembled in the city of Richmond. This Convention, composed as it was of eminent Divines, Jurists, and Statesmen from every section of the State, north and south, east and west, than whom none more distinguished had met in America since the celebrated Convention which framed the Constitution of the United States, the charter of our liberties, now within five years of a century old, that governs us to-day.

At this Convention the rights of the western portion of the State were asserted, and a Constitution framed, which was submitted to the popular vote and ratified. Twenty years more elapsed, when another Convention was called, and met in Richmond, in 1850–51 A.D., and the Constitution again amended and by a vote of the people adopted. In these Conventions of 1829–30 and 1850–51 A.D., the relative condition of the two sections was ably and fully discussed; concessions were made by the east which in a measure pacified and satisfied the claims of the west. The question uppermost in the minds of the people, for a division, was again deferred.

Ten years later, 1860–61 A.D., the late war between the North and the South precipitated events, and the State was divided, or at least so much of the territory of Western Virginia as was occupied by the Federal forces (dividing the State by an unnatural line), was formed into a separate State,—whether wisely or not is not a question for discussion here. Such is the political feature of the division.

Ecclesiastical.—The division of the State has certainly been of very great benefit to the Church. A division of the Diocese of Virginia was first agitated as early as 1821 A.D., over sixty years ago, when we had but 15 Dioceses.

Western Virginia, that portion of the State lying west of the Blue Ridge, was sparsely populated, and at that early period there were not more than three or four self-supporting parishes west of the Alleghany Mountains. The Episcopal Church was scarcely known, and to-day there are large counties where perhaps a minister of the Church has never been seen; at the sight of one clothed in his surplice, or a Bishop in his robes, the people would flee to the woods. But by the blessing of the great head of the Church, our faithful clergy, and able, energetic, efficient Bishop, this state of things will not long continue. We have no records, nor are there any persons living, from which or from whom we can learn what steps were taken in the direction of securing such division. The venerable Bishop Meade was consecrated as Assistant Bishop of Virginia in 1829 A.D.; in the latter part of the summer of that year he first visited Western Virginia, and in his intercourse with the few prominent Episcopalians the subject of a division may have been talked of. And it is understood that he always opposed the measure on the ground of inexpediency, and the impossibility of an adequate support of the Episcopate in a country so destitute of friends and members of the Church as ours was.

The first decided practical move made in the matter was in 1851 A D., at a Convocation of the clergy in Western Virginia, some seven in all, held in Charleston, County of Kanawha. A memorial which had been prepared by the late Rev. James D. McCabe, D.D., at Wheeling, setting forth the wants and the claims of the western portion of the Diocese, and looking to a division, was presented. Bishop Meade was present. The paper was read. The Bishop reiterating his sentiments as often previously expressed, as to our inability to maintain a separate organization, and objecting to the petition going to the Diocesan Convention to assemble the following year, and any further action upon the subject, the paper was withdrawn.

It was doubtless true that the Church west of the mountains was too weak at that day to support an independent Diocese, and we must conclude the Bishop was right.

The Church was very much weakened and its growth retarded in Western Virginia by the war, many parishes were without ministers, and no services at all for four years. Upon the reorganization of St. John's in Charleston, under the Rectorship of the late Rev. W. F. M. Jacobs, at the close of the war this energetic minister revived the question of a division here, while some steps were in progress at Wheeling and at Parkersburg, under the leadership of Rev. W. L. Hyland, now of the Diocese of Maryland. Mr. Jacobs had corresponded with the Clergy and some prominent Laymen of those sections of the State, and a time and place had been agreed upon for a conference with the late Bishop Johns upon the subject. This meeting took place at Clarksburg, in Harrison County, the 24th August, 1865 A.D. It led to no favorable result for the new Diocese, as the Bishop met with no encouragement from the Clergy and Laymen present that an Episcopate could be supported, and he advised the meeting to make no application to a Diocesan Council for a separate organization until they could go up with a guarantee that such support would be given. Thus this effort ended.

By some it was proposed to place West Virginia under a Missionary jurisdiction. This measure was not favored by the wise Bishop, and he would never give his consent. It must be an independent Diocese, on an equal footing with the others, or none at all.

The result has proved the wisdom and foresight of this distinguished and eminent Prelate, and it is a matter of regret that he was not spared to see how signally his views have been verified. He knew the west was not yet ripe for a separation.

During the period that elapsed after the failure in 1865 A.D. to accomplish anything towards effecting a second Diocese, the subject was constantly brought before the people; but no definite action was taken by Clergy or Laymen, vestries or congregations, until seven years later.

At a Convocation held at Charleston the 15th of November, 1872 A.D., for the district south of the South Kanawha River, composed of Clergy and Laymen, the subject of creating a Diocese of the State of West Virginia was introduced. A. T. Laidley, a lay delegate from St. John's Church, Charleston, presented a paper asking the co-operation of the Convocation in measures looking to such organization. Much discussion was elicited. Action was finally taken, and Mr. Laidley was appointed a committee to open a correspondence with vestries upon the subject, and to report to a Convention to be held at Volcano, in the county of Wood, on the 23d day of April, 1873 A.D.

Such correspondence was had, the Convention held, and the response laid before it; but these were so meagre and incomplete, that there was but little for the Convention to act upon. There was opposition to the measure, and but little acquiescence, and nothing was done favorable to the move.

Again, at a meeting of the vestry of St. John's Church, Charleston, held January 19, 1874 A.D., A. T. Laidley made another effort to get a full expression of the people in behalf of the new Diocese. A call was issued for a Convention to be held in the April following. The day was fixed, Clergy and Laymen invited, and vestries urged to send delegates. This met with little favor, —especially was there opposition in the counties in the eastern part of the State. Thus failed again the measure.

Bishop Johns visited the Churches west of the mountains in the autumn of 1875 A.D. (his last visitation). While in Charleston in October of that year, he was approached upon the subject. He told the writer, with great emphasis, that he was in favor of the new Diocese, and that if our people of West Virginia would go earnestly to work, and present to the next Council, to be held in Alexandria in May, 1876 A.D., an assured guaranty that the Episcopate would be supported, he would earnestly recommend the measure, and would give his consent to the division.

This was encouraging to the friends of a new Diocese, and we improved the opportunity thus given us. The important turn in events was imparted to friends of the measure throughout the State; and as the next Convocation was to be held in Wellsburg, in the April following, steps were taken looking to a final effort to be made at the Council in Alexandria. To our great grief and lamentation our venerable Bishop and friend had been called to his reward. With sorrowing hearts in our loss, we went before the Council; and though still meeting with some opposition from brethren in the eastern counties, such action was taken as to assure us that we would succeed at the Council to be held in Staunton the next year.

We had the misfortune to lose an able and efficient advocate in our cause in the death of General J. J. Jackson, a Layman from the Church in Parkersburg, occurring a few months previous to the assembling of the Diocesan Council in May, 1877 A.D.

To this body we repaired with a formidable force of the Clergy and Lay delegates, and presented our claims in a petition. The subject was referred to a Special Committee. The Committee made a favorable report to our claims, and on the 18th of May, 1877 A.D., by an almost unanimous vote of the Council, the report was adopted by which the new Diocese of West Virginia was created, and to embrace within its limits the territory within the boundaries of the State. The Rt. Rev. Bishop of the Diocese gave his consent in the paper following:

"STAUNTON, VA., 18th May, 1877 A.D.

"I hereby signify my consent to the action of the Council of the Diocese of Virginia in cutting off that part of the Diocese included within the State of West Virginia, and erecting it into a separate Diocese.

"FRANCIS M. WHITTLE,
"*Bishop of the Diocese of Virginia.*"

It now remained for the General Convention, which met in Boston in October following, to ratify it. On the 8th of that month the House of Clerical and Lay Deputies passed a resolution adopting the report of the Committee favorable to the creation of the new Diocese, and on the 13th the House of Bishops ratified the act, and thus was the Diocese of Virginia divided and a new one created. The next step was to organize the new Diocese by the election of a Chief Shepherd. Bishop Whittle issued a call dated at Boston, October, 1877 A.D., appointing the 5th day of December, 1877 A.D., as the time, and Charleston as the place, for holding this Convention. This body, composed of the Clergy and Laymen within the Diocesan limits, met and elected the Rev. J. H. Eccleston, D.D., of the Diocese of New Jersey, as Bishop. Dr. Eccleston declined to accept. A second Convention was called to meet at Charleston, in Jefferson County, the 27th February, 1878 A.D. At this Convention Rev. George W. Peterkin, of Baltimore, was elected. This young and eminent divine accepted, and on the 30th of May, 1878 A.D., was consecrated in St. Matthew's Church, Wheeling. He entered upon the discharge of his duties at once. The machinery of a new organization thus completed has worked admirably the past six years, and with the blessings of GOD, to whom we ascribe all the glory, we hope soon to take rank with many of the older and more favored of the great galaxy of the States' vineyards of the LORD. We were once feeble. Within the recollection of a few living witnesses to-day there are parishes where there were but one, two, or three communicants; now they number their hundreds. To show the increase of the Church in the past few years, an abstract of the Bishop's annual address to the Council in June, 1883 A.D., may appropriately be given: "I may properly call attention to the encouraging fact that our little band of communicants has grown from about 1200 to upwards of 2000, the number of confirmations in the five years amounting to 909, our Clergy have increased from 14 to 23, our churches and chapels from 22 to 37, with the prospect of 12 more to be added from one to two years hence, and 10 parsonages have increased to 15, and another in progress; and upon this work our people have expended $100,000. Our Sunday-schools have increased from 878 to about 2000."

I feel that I ought not to omit from this paper a tribute to the memory of those faithful ministers and laymen who so ably and zealously aided in this work of securing to us this Diocese. In this connection I may name the Rev. Wm. Armstrong, so long the Rector of St. Matthew's, and the Rev. Doctor McCabe, then Rector of St. John's, Wheeling, the Rev. W. F. M. Jacobs, Rev. C. M. Calloway, and Rev. Andrew Fisher, of the Clergy, and General Jackson, of Parkersburg. Those have long since passed away, and gone to their reward in Heaven.

There are still living a number of Clergymen and Laymen who actively and energetically participated in efforts to get the measure through.

Statistics for 1886 A.D.: Clergy, 22; parishes, 27; missions, 21; ordinations diac., 4; pr., 1; baptisms, 307; confirmed, 493; communicants, 2485; contributions, $44,136.67.
ALEX. T. LAIDLEY.

Western Michigan. The first motion looking to a division of the Diocese was made in Detroit, in 1871 A.D., at the Convention held there, by Mr. P. R. I. Peirce, of Grand Rapids. It was referred to a Committee to report to the next Convention, but they took no action, as Bishop McCoskry proposed to speak of it in his annual address (1872 A.D.). This he did, and, in consequence of his promise to further whatever decision might be reached, after a thorough investigation it was decided not to proceed further at that Convention, but to issue a circular of information to the several Parishes to enable them to form an intelligent judgment in the matter. The result of this deliberate conduct of the matter, that in the Convention (1873 A.D.) the vote of the 55 Clergy present out of 79 belonging to the whole Diocese was 39 for and 16 against the division. Of those voting *aye*, 24 were from the proposed new Diocese, while 8 from the same section voted *nay*. And of the 53 Laity who voted *aye*, 24 were from this portion, while of those who voted *nay*, only 7 were from it. The decision of the boundary-line was referred to the next Convention. There the line was established as follows:

"*Resolved*, That the Counties of Branch, St. Joseph, Cass, Berrien, Van Buren, Kalamazoo, Calhoun, Eaton, Barry, Allegan, Ottawa, Kent, Ionia, Montcalm, Muskegon, Oceana, Newaygo, Mecosta, Isabella, Clare, Osceola, Lake, Mason, Manistee, Wexford, Missaukee, Kalkaska, Grand Traverse, Benzie, Leelenaw, Antrim, Charlevoix, and Emmet be, and the same are, set apart and erected into a new Diocese (the assent of the Bishop and General Convention being given), under the name of   . And the remainder of the Counties in the Lower Peninsula not above designated, with the Island of Mackinac and the Upper Peninsula, shall constitute the present Diocese of Michigan. And that the General Convention be respectfully requested to grant the request of this Convention for such division, when the Constitution and Canons relative to such cases are complied with."

The Bishop gave his Canonical consent, and the Committee who were intrusted with the details of the necessary papers and the arrangements preliminary to presenting their application to the General Convention were able to secure $34,545 for the endowment. Michigan retained 52 Clergy and 58 Parishes, while the new Diocese received 29 Clergy and 32 Parishes. The House of Bishops decided favorably, while at the same time the applications of Southern Ohio* and Wisconsin were denied, on the ground that they had not made the suitable provision required by the Canon. The new Diocese retained three of the oldest Parishes, —Trinity Church, Niles, 1834 A.D., St. Mark's, Grand Rapids, and Trinity, Marshall, 1838 A.D.

At the Primary Convention (December 2, 1874 A.D.) at St. Mark's, Grand Rapids, 21 Clergy and 49 Lay delegates took their seats. After the necessary rules of procedure were ordered, the name of Western Michigan was, after some discussion, decided upon, and Bishop McCoskry formally chose to remain in the old Diocese of Michigan. The new Diocese was placed temporarily under his charge. The Convention proceeded to elect a Bishop, and upon the seventh ballot Rev. George De Normandie Gillespie was elected. His consecration took place on St. 'Matthias' Day (February 24, 1875 A.D.), in St. Mark's Church, Grand Rapids. Bishop McCoskry was the consecrator. Bishop Littlejohn preached the sermon. Bishops Talbot and Paddock were the presenters, and Bishops Bissell, Robertson, and Welles assisted. In the new Diocese 18 Clergy were canonically resident, but 29 were within its limits; there were 32 Parishes and 12 Mission Stations and Chapels. There were 2588 Communicants. The increase has been slow. The population is one that is found so generally in mining and lumber regions. Church work among them does not make the striking exhibition which can be shown in other and more favored places. Nor can a rich harvest be gathered till the ground has been well prepared. The number of Clergy reported in 1880 A.D. were 29, the Parishes 28, the Mission Stations 30, the Communicants 3068. But in 1883 A.D. the Clergy reported were 23, the Parishes were 28, Missions 21, the Communicants 3111. The shifting population and the changes which occur naturally may account for the apparent loss, but a real gain is proven by the fact that the number of church edifices was increased to 43, and the contributions, which three years before were $143,817.50, were in 1883 A.D. reported as $193,476. These statistics show that this apparent lowering in numbers was due to the exigencies of the times and work. The cords may be shortened, but the stakes are strengthened.

Statistics for 1886 A.D.: Clergy, 27; parishes, 27; missions, 24; baptisms, 292; confirmed, 185; communicants, 3151; contributions, $64,681.11.

Western New York, Diocese of. I. *Colonial History.*—The earliest Christian worship in Western New York was by the French Franciscans Le Caron, Viel, Sagard, and La Roche Dallion, about 1625 A.D., on the southwest shore of Lake Erie and the Niagara River; then in Jesuit missions at Onondaga, Cayuga Lake, and Avon or Geneseo, 1642–69 A.D; then at Fort Niagara by the French chaplain, Père Millet, 1686 A.D., and later; then by the Moravians under Zeisberger, at Onondaga, 1750–76 A.D., and by the Rev. Samuel Kirkland, Congregational missionary to the Oneidas many years, from 1765 A.D. No permanent fruits resulted from any of these missions. Church of England services began in 1759 A.D. with the occupation of Fort Niagara, whose chapel, and Brant's Indian church at Lewiston, 1776 A.D., were her only places of worship before 1797 A.D. A chapel for the Onondagas at Oswego was projected, but not built, and altar-plate sent out, but not used, under Queen Anne; and the early Society for the Propagation of the Gospel in Foreign Parts' missionaries went no farther west than Schenectady and Fort Hunter (near Johnstown).

II. *Diocese of New York.*—The State of New York became a Diocese June 22, 1785 A.D. One-half of it, from Fort Schuyler, or Utica, west, formed in 1788 A D. the town of Whitestown, with a white population of about 200. The "Committee for Propagating the Gospel in the State of New York," constituted in 1796 A.D., appointed in 1797 A.D. the Rev. Robert G. Wetmore their first missionary. He traveled within a few months through Western New York, 2386 miles, on foot and on horseback, baptized 47 adults and 365 children, and preached 107 times. St. Paul's Church, Paris Hill, the first in Western New York, was organized Feb-

---

* Proper provision for support of a Bishop was provided before the General Convention adjourned, and the division was granted in the case of Southern Ohio.

ruary, 1797 A.D., the next year the Rev. Philander (afterwards Bishop) Chase visited many places, organized several churches (only one of which, however, was kept up, St. Luke, Harpersville, 1799 A.D.), baptized 14 adults and 319 infants, preached 213 times, and traveled some 4000 miles. In 1802 A.D. the Rev. Davenport Phelps began a vigorous and successful missionary work throughout Western New York, mostly at Geneva and farther west, ending only with his early death in 1813 A.D. He founded a number of permanent parishes, and made Geneva from 1806 A.D. an important centre of Church work. The Rev. Jonathan Judd and the Rev. Gamaliel Thatcher were missionaries farther east in 1804 A.D., and the Rev. Amos G. Baldwin at Utica, 1806 A.D., when Bishop Moore consecrated Trinity, Utica, the first Episcopal act in Western New York. Most of the early parishes were many years without church buildings or clergymen, and were kept up and nursed into strength by regular lay-reading. The consecration of Bishop Hobart, 1811 A.D., gave a great impetus to Church work in Western New York. In the nineteen years of his Episcopate he made twelve visitations to this distant region (as it was then), promoted the founding of 54 parishes, consecrated 34 churches, added 46 clergymen to the 4 he found in 1811 A.D., confirmed nearly 2000 (among these 200 Indians at the Oneida Mission, afterwards removed to Green Bay), and established Geneva, now Hobart, College, the Christian Knowledge Society of Western New York, the *Gospel Messenger* (which continued for forty-five years as the Church paper of the Diocese), and other instrumentalities of growth. The population of Western New York had increased in that time from 275,168 to 875,016, and the communicants from 240 to 2331, nearly tenfold. Early missionaries of special note were Wm. A. and Orin Clark (brothers), Wm. B. Lacey, Russell Wheeler, Alanson W. Welton, Daniel McDonald, E. G. Gear, Henry U. Onderdonk, Joshua M. Rogers, and Geo. H. Norton. Their stipends, at first $150, were fixed in 1824 A.D. at $125, and so remained forty years. Under Bishop Onderdonk (Bishop Hobart's successor in indefatigable labor, though not in force of intellect) the parishes increased (1830-38 A.D.) to 96, and clergy to 74. The erection of a new See in the now overgrown Diocese was suggested as early as 1830 A.D., recommended by the Bishop in 1834 A.D. (after four years of annual visitations and rapid growth), and completed by the action of the General and Diocesan Conventions, November 1, 1838 A.D.

III. *Diocese of Western New York to* 1868 A.D.—The history of the original Diocese of Western New York is that of the Episcopate of William Heathcote De Lancey, consecrated May 9, 1839 A.D., died April 5, 1865. He found in the new Diocese, with its 75 clergy and 96 congregations (68 of the latter being missionary stations), an Episcopate fund of $35,000, and permanent Missionary fund of $10,000; a college, small, feeble, and without endowments; and the days of rapid growth over. Diocesan missions, no longer sustained by the wealth of New York, became his first and greatest care. The Diocese never asked or received anything from the Church at large. Monthly offerings required by its own canons, for missions both diocesan and general, the distribution of Bibles, Prayer-Books, and Tracts, and Disabled and Infirm Clergy, have met all the demands of its work to this time; though as late as 1865 A.D. there were still 100 missionary parishes out of 160, while communicants and families had increased fourfold, and offerings sixfold. During Bishop De Lancey's Episcopate these offerings were $186,000 for diocesan, and $100,000 for general objects, besides special contributions doubling the original Episcopate Fund, $25,000 for the Diocesan Training School, $8000 for the Permanent Missionary Fund, and some $400,000, including bequests, to Hobart and De Veaux Colleges, in all not less than $750,000.

The Diocese had in its early years the services of clergymen of great ability at important points,—Drs. Proal, Leeds, Matson, and Brandegee in Utica; Whipple (now Bishop) at Rome; Gregory and Ashley at Syracuse; Hale, Bissell (now Bishop), Wilson, and Metcalf at Geneva; Whitehouse and Lee (afterwards Bishops), and Van Ingen at Rochester; Bolles at Batavia; Shelton, Hawks (afterwards Bishop), Ingersoll, and Schuyler at Buffalo,—mostly those who, like their Bishop, had been pupils of Hobart. Under such leadership it maintained a high standard both in Church principles and practical work, and became known as "the Model Diocese." The Bishop, a man of extraordinary energy and system, impressed these characters on all features of his diocesan work. He had the most entire confidence of both clergy and laity, and retained it through all the controversies and agitations in ecclesiastical affairs which marked the early years of his Episcopate, without giving way in the least to the claims of partisans on either side.

Hobart College, without endowments, and sustained up to 1847 A.D. partly by a State grant, had for several years from that time a hard struggle for existence. A considerable endowment, secured in 1860 A.D. mainly by Bishop De Lancey's earnest efforts and since increased to $300,000, has placed it on a firm basis, while from first to last its standard of scholarship, in classics and mathematics especially, has been of the highest. De Veaux College for Orphan and Destitute Children, founded in 1852 A.D. by a bequest of $300,000 from Judge Samuel De Veaux, of Niagara Falls, and the Diocesan Training School, now De Lancey Divinity School, founded in 1861 A.D. by Bishop De Lancey's personal efforts, are the chief, and indeed the only permanent additional educational foundations thus far.

The Bishop's health giving way in 1864 A.D., the Rev. Arthur Cleveland Coxe was chosen Assistant Bishop; consecrated January 4, 1865 A.D., and on the death of Bishop De Lancey succeeded as second Bishop of Western New York, April 5, 1865 A.D. In the following year he recommended the erection of a new See; and in 1867 A.D. the Diocese was divided into two, the western half retaining the former name, and the Bishop remaining in charge.

IV. *Diocese of Western New York*, 1868–84 A.D —The Diocese as thus reduced contained 15 counties, 11,345 square miles, 774,762 inhabitants, 78 parishes (of which 37 only were "self-supporting"), 76 churches, 43 rectories, 82 clergymen, and 8636 communicants, an average of 1 to 90 of the population. Its offerings for 1868 A.D. were, parochial $180,440, diocesan $12,760, general $7801, in all $201,001; and its church property (parochial only), $1,057,643. The Journal of 1883 A.D. reports 90 parishes ("self-supporting" parishes not shown), and 9 missions, 100 churches, 104 clergymen, and 11,142 communicants (1 to 84 of population); offerings, parochial $187,903, diocesan $25,243, general $13,977, in all $227,124; church property, parochial $1,702,509. The fund for the support of the Episcopate is $41,717,* permanent fund for Missions, $28,579; for Disabled Clergymen, and Widows and Orphans of Clergymen, $16,338; for the De Lancey Divinity School, $47,200; other diocesan funds (not including Hobart and De Veaux College property), about $10,000. Church Homes have been founded in Buffalo, Rochester, and Geneva; the two former with substantial buildings and considerable endowments. Forty churches have been consecrated by the present Bishop. Trustees have been incorporated for a future cathedral in Buffalo, and in Rochester a costly and beautiful church, endowed, is held, through individual munificence, for a similar use when needed. The missionary work of the Diocese is directed by the Convocations of the four Deaneries of Buffalo, Batavia, Rochester, and Geneva, each holding quarterly meetings of clergy and lay representatives of parishes; the missionary stipends for 1883 A.D. were $5470.

Statistics for 1886 A.D.: Clergy, 108; parishes, 101; lay readers, 60; candidates for holy orders, 5; ordinations diac., 1; pr. 4; baptisms, 1555; confirmed, 1089; communicants, 12,463; Sunday-school teachers, 3519; Sunday-school scholars, 39,173; contributions, $231,116.99.

REV. C. W. HAYES.

Western Texas, the Missionary District of. The Missionary District of Western Texas is a vast territory of about one hundred and ten square miles, and includes, with the exception of a few counties on and along the Colorado River, all that portion of the State of Texas lying between the said river and the Rio Grande, the Gulf of Mexico, and the thirty-second parallel of northern latitude.

Its surface is varied, low and flat for about fifty miles or more from the coast, where a gradual rise begins, which, with variations of hill and dale, level plains and rolling table-lands, reaches, in the mountain region west and northwest of San Antonio, an elevation of between two and three thousand feet above the gulf, while that at Fort Davis, Presidio County, is four thousand seven hundred feet, and the mountains in its neighborhood and farther west are still higher.

Though the sea-board towns sometimes suffer from yellow fever, which is *always imported*, the climate on the whole is exceedingly salubrious, that of the table-lands and mountain region west and northwest of San Antonio being specially suited to persons suffering from pulmonary diseases. The atmosphere of these portions of Western Texas is pure, dry, tonic, and so transparent that strangers are constantly deceived as to the magnitude and distance of objects.

It has large quantities of coal in its western portions, and also iron and other minerals, while its beautiful but unnavigable streams and rivers would furnish abundant water-power for manufacturing purposes. Though it has a fertile soil, the uncertainty of the rain-fall has confined agriculture chiefly to its eastern counties; but the motto of the rain-belt seems to be Westward Ho! and with its extension goes the farmer, who, should he fail to make a crop one year, is almost sure to make enough the next to compensate him for the labor of both. But, notwithstanding its ever-increasing number of farms, nearly the whole vast region west, southwest, and northwest of San Antonio is still the land and the home of the stockman. Here are those large sheep and cattle ranches of which almost every one has heard, though the small ones far outnumber the large, and men of small means, if *honest* and *industrious*, have as good a chance to make a comfortable living at the business as men of large capital to make fortunes.

Its facilities of travel have greatly increased within the last five or six years. There are over fifteen hundred miles of railroad in it to-day, the chief roads being the Great Northern and International, and the Galveston, Houston, and San Antonio; and other roads and branches of these roads are projected, which, if built, will make travel as easy and expeditious in Western Texas as in any other part of the State. Even now nearly all its important interior towns can be reached by rail, and even some of

---

* Besides the "See House" in Buffalo, the residence of the Bishop, valued at $22,000, held by the Cathedral Corporation, and containing the large and valuable Episcopal or "Cathedral Library," the munificent gift of the Bishop to the Diocese.

those on the coast, as Corpus Christi and Indianola.

The population of the District of Western Texas to-day is fully three hundred thousand. In it nearly all nationalities are represented. But, though the German element is very large in some communities, and also the Mexican along the Rio Grande frontier, the American predominates in the District as a whole, and is gradually increasing by immigration from the Northern and older Southern States. As in nearly all new countries, there is a lawless element in its society, but not as large as is often supposed, nor is it found to any extent in our older settled communities. Though its cow-boys may be wild, and the free use of the whisky-bottle may sometimes make them disorderly and dangerous, since the advent of the railroads and the presence of the State rangers acts of highway robbery and murder have become things of rare occurrence, and property and life are as safe here as they are in any part of the country. The vast majority of its people are law-abiding, peaceable, well-behaved, industrious, hospitable, courteous, and by no people are they surpassed in common sense and natural intelligence. Nor is everything among them of a rough kind or order. In many portions, especially in those that have been longest settled, are pretty towns and villages, beautiful homes, and refined and cultivated people, while even in its more western wilds are to be found, under a rough exterior, men of polished manners, of education, and culture, graduates perhaps of the universities of old England, or of our Northern and Southern colleges. No people set a higher value on education, and their first care is to provide good schools and teachers for their children.

In religious matters as in all others, there has been progress. The various denominations which divide older communities are all represented, and, with few exceptions, have their ministers, churches, and Sunday-schools, except in some of the more western portions, where, in consequence of the sparse population, it is difficult to gather congregations, and to build churches and support them. This is all still purely missionary ground, and the religious wants of the people, if supplied at all, must be supplied to a very large extent by the itinerant. But while there are encouraging features in the religious condition of Western Texas, there are also some that are very discouraging. If the people in certain portions still retain the religious habits which they themselves or their forefathers brought with them, it cannot be denied that in other portions, especially in the cities and larger towns, those habits have been seriously affected by those of the foreign element with which they have socially mingled. Till a few years ago the Rio Grande frontier had been left almost entirely to the missionary of Rome, and we need not wonder that under the influence of a Church which calls her people to mass on Sunday morning, but tolerates the bull- or the cock-fight Sunday afternoon, together with the love of gain which hesitates not, unless restrained, to turn the holy day into a day of worldly traffic, many even of American birth and training and education should have lost all sense of the sacredness of the Sabbath. But a change for the better is already taking place among these people, and no religious body has done more to bring about this change than our own Church, who, in many places at least, has been the pioneer on the Rio Grande.

With this sketch of the Missionary District of Western Texas, we now proceed to the history of the Church in it. There were no doubt among the first settlers in Western Texas a few Episcopalians, but it was not till some time after the independence of Texas had been achieved, and its annexation to the United States, that their number was sufficiently large at any point for mission or parochial organization. As a part of the State of Texas it formed a part of the Missionary District of the Southwest, which was first under the charge of the Rt. Rev. Leonidas Polk, D.D., and then under that of the Rt. Rev. George Washington Freeman, D.D. Bishop Polk visited Texas several times, but it does not appear whether he extended his visits to any points in Western Texas. Bishop Freeman's first visit to Texas was in March, 1845 A.D. If not in this year, he subsequently visited San Antonio, Seguin, and other points in Western Texas where his Episcopal ministrations were needed.

The Diocese of Texas was organized at Matagorda, January 1, 1849 A.D., and by resolution of the Convention was put under the charge of Bishop Freeman as Provisional Bishop. In May, 1852 A.D., Bishop Freeman was elected Bishop of the Diocese, but declined in May, 1854 A.D., preferring to act as Provisional Bishop till other arrangements could be made.

The first parishes in Western Texas that were admitted to the Convention were Trinity, San Antonio (May, 1850 A.D.); Advent, Brownsville (May, 1851 A.D.); Emmanuel, Lockhart, and the Redeemer, Seguin (May, 1854 A.D.). The parish of the Redeemer, Seguin, was organized by the Rev. J. W. Dunn, now deceased, but its name was subsequently, by resolution of the Convention, changed to that of St. Andrew's; while Trinity Parish, San Antonio, which had been organized by the Rev. J. T. Fish, U.S.A., was at length reorganized under the name of St. Mark's, and as such admitted to the Convention in 1858 A.D.

Others of the pioneer clergy of Western Texas were Rev. W. Passmore, who went to Brownsville in August, 1851 A.D.; Rev. C. S. Hedges, who went to Indianola and Lavaca in 1853 A.D.; and Rev. L. H. Jones, who was first in charge at Seguin, and then at San Antonio, where, in December, 1859

A.D., he laid the corner-stone of the church now known as St. Mark's Cathedral. Mr. Hedges still survives, and is now a Presbyter of the Diocese of Louisiana.

After the death of Bishop Freeman several elections to the Bishopric of Texas were made, but declined; but on May 6, 1859 A.D., the Rev. Alexander Gregg, D.D., then a Presbyter of the Diocese of South Carolina, was elected by the Convention, then in session at Galveston, who, having signified his acceptance, was consecrated at Richmond, Va., during the session of the General Convention there, October 13, 1859 A.D. Under this good and godly man, of apostolic zeal and courage, the Church in Texas grew and prospered, Western Texas receiving its full share of the benefit of his labors. But the herculean task of attending to the wants of a Diocese larger in territory than most of the empires of Europe, in which new communities were constantly forming and growing up, with Church people in them asking for his ministrations, was too great for even his indomitable energy and perseverance; so that, after deferring the matter again and again, he was at last, in October, 1874 A.D., compelled to ask relief of the General Convention, then in session in the city of New York. In response, the General Convention set off from the old Diocese of Texas the two Missionary Jurisdictions "ecclesiastically known as Northern and Western Texas."

By the same General Convention the Rev. Robert W. B. Elliott was elected the first Bishop of Western Texas, who, on November 15 of the same year, was consecrated in St. Philip's, Atlanta, Ga., of which parish he had been rector for the last three years preceding.

The new Bishop lost no time in visiting his large and distant jurisdiction, to make himself acquainted with its condition and needs, and to minister at the points where his presence was most needed. His first service was at Luling, December 20, 1874 A.D., where he officiated in a passenger-car, which was kindly loaned for the occasion, and which was well calculated to suggest to him, at the outset of his Episcopal career, new ideas, *if he did not have them before*, of the nature of the work to which he had now devoted himself.

Our young Bishop, young in appearance as well as in years, by his lovable qualities soon endeared himself to the hearts of both clergy and laity, while his ability in the pulpit, his wisdom in council, his resolution, energy, hopefulness, and courage, speedily convinced us that the General Convention had made no mistake in appointing him as our chief standard-bearer in this new, and at that time still, to a vast extent, untried region of country. With his advent began a new era of growth and progress for the Church in Western Texas, the signs and proofs of which, after the lapse of nine years, are seen in almost every part of his vast jurisdiction. New parishes have been organized, new churches built, to a number of which parsonages have been attached, schools and institutions of learning founded and put in successful operation, new missions organized, and new and distant points visited, the Bishop himself being often the pioneer.

At a Missionary meeting held in Christ Church, Hartford, Conn., November 13, Bishop Elliott said, "Since the last General Convention (Convention of 1880 A.D.) one building has been put up for every four months that have passed, and, leaving out Williams' Hall, three-fourths of the money has been given in Western Texas." This progress still continues, and goes on to-day as vigorously as ever. New churches are being built at points where, but a year ago, there was no Protestant worship at all, and new ones will be built at other points where they are as badly needed, as soon as the necessary funds are secured. One of the greatest services which Bishop Elliott has rendered Western Texas has been in finding and raising up for it generous friends abroad, but for whose assistance, not to speak of other things, he could never have kept in the field the staff of clergy by whom, under him, so much of this work has been done.

The Bishop's residence is in San Antonio, the chief city of the District, and the commercial capital of Western Texas. Always an important frontier town, with a large military post attached, since the advent of the railroads it has nearly doubled in size, and now contains a population of about thirty-five thousand. While the stranger may find in the somewhat foreign aspect of the city, its narrow streets, its tortuous river, and the manners and customs of its almost cosmopolitan people, much to excite his curiosity, he will also find there congenial society and many of the material comforts and conveniences which belong to an older civilization. But San Antonio, sunny and warm, and strange and picturesque, and, in some places, beautiful, is the stronghold of Romanism, and also of its twin-sister, Agnosticism; the first affecting a very large portion of its humble and more ignorant people, the other tinging the thought and influencing the lives of a large number of its educated citizens, especially those of foreign birth. As against both of these systems and their influences the Church of GOD must wage unceasing warfare; in no city of our land is aggressive work more urgently needed. The Bishop, with his small band of clergy there, two besides himself, is doing what can be done, with the means in hand, to stem the double current. In the city there are two parishes, St. Mark's and St. Paul's, and two Missions, St. Luke's and St. John's, and one school for girls and young ladies, called St. Mary's Hall. St. Mary's is doing a needed and noble work in keeping our girls from the convent by furnishing an education as good or superior to that which may be had there, and its usefulness could be largely increased by the addition of new buildings for the accommodation of boarders. St. Paul's Parish is without a church, but one is soon to be erected. The church of the parish of St. Mark's is also the Bishop's Cathedral. It has a history of its own. Its corner-stone was laid, as we have seen, by a former rector, Rev. L. H. Jones, December, 1859 A.D., but work was suspended on it during the war, and not resumed till July, 1873 A.D. It is perhaps, with its beautiful and imposing interior, the best specimen of church architecture in Texas, and is an enduring monument to the faith, skill, patience, and perseverance of its present dean, the Rev. W. R. Richardson, and the earnestness and liberality of his people.

The other important towns and villages in the District, where we have churches, are Victoria, Cuero, Goliad, Hallettsville, Gonzales, Seguin, Lockhart, San Marcos, Barne, El Paso, Uvalde, Del Rio, Laredo, Brownsville, Corpus Christi, and Rockport.

At Seguin are Montgomery Institute, and, attached to it, Williams' Hall, for girls and young ladies. The first bears the name of the late Dr. Montgomery, of New York, an old friend of the Bishop, by one of whose generous people, Mrs. S. J. Zabriskie, $500 were given towards its erection; the other, the honored name of the present Bishop of Connecticut, by whose liberal and large-hearted people the funds to build it were entirely contributed. At Seguin is also St. Andrew's Academy, for boys, which, though small, sufficiently answers the purpose intended.

The following is a statistical comparison between 1875 and 1883 A.D., which, though imperfect, is correct as far as it goes:

	1875 A.D.	1883 A.D.
Clergy, including Bishops	10	14
Parishes and Mission Stations	9	30
Church buildings	4	20
Parsonages	1	6
Schools	...	3
Sunday-School Teachers	38	122
Sunday-School Pupils	283	888
Communicants	370	1153

The Church in Western Texas is no longer an experiment. All that is needed now, with the blessing of GOD, are more men to do the work, and more means to sustain them. There is scarcely a clergyman laboring in Western Texas to-day who is not doing the work of two men, and some are doing more. Who will come "to the help of the LORD against the mighty"? Young men who are honestly striving to answer such a question for themselves need have no fear of burying themselves alive by coming to this District. If they have anything in them, this is the land and the people to bring it out. Men of thorough education, strong intelligence, and good sense, as well as of earnest piety, are needed, and by no people on the face of the earth will they be better appreciated.

Statistics for 1886 A.D.: Clergy, 14; parishes, 14; missions, 30; candidates for H. O., 3; ordination, pr., 1; baptisms, 191; confirmed, 119; communicants, 1367; Sunday-school teachers, 138; Sunday-school scholars, 1053; contributions, $22,182.44.

REV. J. T. HUTCHESON.

Whit-Sunday (Pentecost, Ger. Pingsten, Old Ger. Whingsten, Old Eng. Whit-Sun). The fiftieth day from Easter,—the Sunday on which the Church celebrates the outpouring of the HOLY GHOST upon the Apostles, and through them upon His Church, to abide with it forever. It was commemorated in the Primitive Church with festival services. The whole period of fifty days was kept with a festal tone, which was crowned with the Whit-Sun celebrations. It was the completion of the work our LORD came to do. "It is expedient for you that I go away: for if I go not away, the Comforter will not come unto you" (St. John xvi. 7). Therefore this day was always observed with holy solemnities. The Acts were read throughout this season in the East and in the North African Church, as we do now. In our own Service, the Collect is the ancient one, being traced to Gregory's Sacramentary. Our Epistle agrees with the Eastern Epistle (Acts ii. 1–11), and our Gospel is the same as in the Latin use, being the old Sarum use (St. John xiv. 15–31). The Proper Preface is the composition of the framers of the first Prayer-Book of Edward VI., but is singularly like a fine Gallican Preface. Edward's Prayer-Book of 1549 A.D. was appointed to be used for the first time on Whit-Sunday. The account in the Act of its Compilation is very reverent,—"His Highness . . . hath appointed the Archbishop of Canterbury and certain of the most learned and discreet Bishops and other learned men of this Realm" who "should draw and make one convenient and meet Order, Rite, and Fashion of common and open Prayer and Administration of the Sacraments, . . . the which at this Time, by the aid of the HOLY GHOST, with one uniform agreement, is of them concluded, set forth, and delivered. . . . And that all and singular ministers in any Cathedral or Parish in this Realm . . . shall, from and after the Feast of *Pentecost* next coming, be bounden to say and use the Mattens, Even-Song, Celebration of the LORD'S Supper, commonly called the Mass, and administration of each of the Sacraments, and all their common and open prayer, in such Order and Form as is mentioned in this same Book, and none other or otherwise." From that time forth, by the grace of the HOLY SPIRIT, the English-speaking people have had one of the noblest Liturgies any part of the Church Catholic hath ever possessed given to it.

Widow. In the Mosaic dispensation, widows who were friendless were to be aided by the triennial third tithe (Deut. xiv. 29; xxvi. 12). The forgotten sheaf in the harvest-field was to be left "for the stranger for the fatherless, and for the widow." The remaining olives and grapes were to be granted to the same needy persons, that GOD'S blessing might rest upon the work of His benevolent people (Deut. xxiv. 19–21). The widow was to be remembered in religious feasts (Deut. xvi. 11, 14). Her raiment was not to be taken "to pledge" (Deut. xxiv. 17). It is the wicked who take the "widow's ox for a pledge" (Job xxiv. 3). The command was, "Ye shall not afflict any widow" (Ex. xxii. 22). "Plead for the widow" (Isa. i. 17). Our LORD accuses the Scribes and Pharisees of devouring "widows' houses" (St. Matt. xxiii. 14). In the Apostolic Church provision was made for widows by a "daily ministration" to their needs (Acts vi. 1–6). St. Paul directs who are to be rightly admitted into this class (1 Tim. v. 3–16). The aged widow Anna, who gives thanks for the infant CHRIST, is a good representative of the class of holy women who were given to the service of GOD (St. Luke ii. 36–38). The touching petition in the Litany for "fatherless children and widows" may have been prompted by the fact that long after Apostolic times the widow was in a specially weak condition, when women were allowed so little opportunity to gain a subsistence, and the prayer is needful to-day. The widows in the early Church lived under certain rules and performed certain "charitable offices connected with the Church." In Tertullian's day the Deaconesses "were commonly chosen out of the widows of the Church." The Council of Laodicea calls them elderly widows, as the Deaconesses were generally somewhat advanced in years. A canon of the first Council of Orange speaks of a "widow's garment," so that these Church widows had a special dress. It was the duty of the Deaconesses "to be a decent help to the female sex in the time of their Baptism, sickness, affliction, or the like," as Epiphanius states. Virgins and widows, according to a statement of St. Ambrose, had a special place assigned to them in the church building.

Authorities: William Latham Bevan in William Smith's Dict. of the Bible, Bingham's Antiq. of the Christian Ch., C. S. Henry's Christian Antiq.

REV. S. F. HOTCHKIN.

Wisconsin. On the Feast of St. John the Baptist, 1847 A.D., the Clergy in Wisconsin Territory met, with Lay delegates, in St. Paul's, Milwaukee, a call having been issued for the meeting by the Missionary Bishop of the Northwest. The Bishop presided. The Bishop, in his address, noted the ordination of seven Deacons, while five candidates for holy orders were pursuing their studies. He expressed his satisfaction at the presence of Norwegians and Oneidas among the delegates. Rules of Order and "a Constitution for the Diocese, and one for Parishes, were adopted. The Rt. Rev. Jackson Kemper, D.D., LL.D., was unanimously elected Diocesan. Choice was also made of Diocesan officers, and a deputation to the General Convention. It was resolved that there should be Quarterly Collections for Diocesan Missions. Four Oneida Indians being present as Delegates from Hobart Church, Duck Creek, a congratulatory resolution was adopted on this circumstance. The principal Chief of the Nation, Tay-ka-wia-ti-on, through his interpreter, Nisaty-erha, replied. A committee was appointed to apply to the Legislature for the incorporation of the Trustees of the Episcopal Fund. The second Annual Convention was in Trinity Church, Janesville, in June, 1848 A.D. Bishop Kemper presided. The church where the Convention met was consecrated. The Convention sermon was preached by Rev. Frederick W. Hatch. The Bishop spoke of the admission of Wisconsin into union with the General Convention," and reported four ordinations to the Priesthood, three consecrations of churches, one laying of a corner-stone, and seven candidates for holy orders, eight names being added before the Convention adjourned. Bishop Kemper "declined the Diocesan Episcopate, and was requested to take charge of the Diocese as its Provisional Bishop until the Diocese shall be in a condition to support a Diocesan. The act incorporating the Trustees of Church Property was accepted and members of the Board elected." Two Deacons were ordained Priests at the close of the session. The third Convention met in the same church, in June, 1849 A.D. Bishop Kemper reported three ordinations of Deacons, one for the Diocese of Indiana, and one ordination to the Priesthood, and eleven candidates for Holy Orders. He urged on the parishes the duty of becoming self-supporting. "A committee was appointed to confer with the Trustees of Nashotah, 'touching the expediency of placing said school under the supervision and control of the Diocese of Wisconsin.'" The fourth Convention met in St. Matthew's Church, Kenosha, in June, 1850 A.D. The Bishop made report of three ordinations to the Diaconate and two to the Priesthood, thirteen candidates for Holy Orders, and two consecrations of churches. A renewed effort for the increase of the Episcopal Fund was commended. The Missionary Committee urged the importance of "procuring glebes and building sites in all parts of the country." The Trustees of Church Property were instructed to loan the Episcopal Fund only upon unencumbered real estate.

The fifth Annual Convention was in St. Paul's, Milwaukee, in June, 1851 A.D. The Bishop reported the ordination of three Deacons and one Priest, twelve candidates for orders, and commended the Nashotah School. An effort to establish a Female Seminary was indorsed. The Bishop was requested to divide the Diocese into Convocational districts. The sixth Convention met in the same church in June, 1852 A.D.

The Bishops of Indiana and Pennsylvania were present with the Missionary Bishop. The Bishop had ordained seven Deacons and one Priest. Four candidates were studying at Nashotah. Two corner-stones had been laid, and one burying-ground consecrated. One church had been consecrated. Racine College had been established. One church was admitted into union. The seventh Convention, in 1853 A.D., met in the same church. St. Ann's Hall, Milwaukee, Racine College, and Nashotah were commended. The eighth Convention met in the same church, Rev. W. W. Arnett, D.D., preaching the sermon. "Another Female Seminary, St. Mary's Hall, at Janesville, had been established." Bishop Kemper was a second time elected Diocesan, and accepted. A committee for securing glebe land and lots for churches was appointed. At the ninth Convention, in Mineral Point, the Bishop reported the death of Rev. George Thompson, and resolutions were adopted respecting it. Trinity Church, where the Convention was sitting, was consecrated, and there was an ordination to the Priesthood. The tenth Convention met in St. Paul's, Milwaukee, the Rev. Geo. B. Eastman preaching the Convention sermon. A communication was received from the parish in Watertown announcing that it was self-supporting. A resolution strongly urging the support of Church Schools and Colleges was unanimously adopted. "The Board of Missions was requested to raise $12,000 for Diocesan Missions the ensuing year." Bishop Kemper, who is shown in this record as the beloved Bishop of Wisconsin, was born in Dutchess County, N. Y., in 1789 A.D. He graduated from Columbia College, N. Y.; was ordained Deacon in 1811 A.D., and Priest in 1812 A.D., and was for years at St. Peters Church, Philadelphia, and afterwards in Connecticut. He was consecrated as the first Missionary Bishop of Missouri and Indiana in St. Peter's Church, Philadelphia, September 25, 1835 A.D. He was the first Missionary Bishop in the American Church. Missouri, Indiana, Iowa, and Minnesota were all within his original jurisdiction. He was revered throughout his wide field, and as he brought in one Diocese after another to the General Convention, his spiritual children, who were called on thus to part with him, blessed the good providence of GOD, which had given them such a founder. The writer of this sketch once asked him, on one of his many journeys, "Do you ever get tired?" He gave one of his earnest looks, and replied, "Do you get tired of doing your daily duty, sir?" And so the tireless man worked on, exchanging Eastern comforts for his simple Western home, near his much-loved Nashotah, until GOD called him to rest.

In 1866 A.D., Rev. W. E. Armitage became Assistant Bishop. He was born in Brooklyn, educated at Columbia College and the General Theological Seminary, and was Rector of St. John's, Detroit, when elected to the Episcopate. After the faithful work of a few years, he died in 1873 A.D. In 1869 A.D., Bishops Kemper and Armitage were present at the Convention. There were 13 candidates for orders, 618 had been confirmed, 307 of whom had come in from various denominations, 10 having been Roman Catholics. Both Bishops referred to the death of Rev. W. M. Hickox. Associate missions were approved. A plan was reported of raising up an order of self-denying, self-supporting missionaries as "teaching Deacons." At the Council of 1870 A.D., Bishop Kemper's death was officially announced by the Standing Committee: "He fell asleep in JESUS, . . . and now rests in hope on the soil which, for a third of a century, has been consecrated by his prayer and love." "With you who knew him, loved him, and honored him, there needs no prompter of his praise." An appeal was made by Bishop Armitage for the purchase of a girls' school, called Kemper Hall, as a monument to the late Bishop. It was resolved that an early division of the Diocese was desirable, and a committee was appointed on the subject. The Mission Farm at Green Bay was put in charge of Christ Church Parish in that place. Bishop Welles was consecrated in 1874 A.D., in St. Thomas' Church, New York. He is a native of Waterloo, N. Y., and a graduate of Hobart College. He was Rector of Christ Church, Red Wing, Minn., at the time of his election to the Episcopate.

In 1875 A.D. the Diocese of Fond du Lac was set off from Wisconsin. (*Vide* FOND DU LAC.) Nashotah has been the great feeder of the ranks of Wisconsin clergy. Dr. Cole says, "When towards the close of the day, in the autumn of 1842 A.D., the first occupants of the Mission knelt upon a spot covered probably by this chapel (St. Sylvanus', Nashotah), and prayed for a blessing on their endeavors, they had nothing in hand for the morrow. It was a venture of faith. . . . The LORD in whom they trusted opened the hearts and hands of His people. He that fed Elijah by the brook Cherith, that gave manna to Israel in the wilderness, brought help to His servants in the daily mail." Kemper Hall, Kenosha, is under the charge of the Sisters of St. Mary. There is a Day School at the Cathedral in Milwaukee; St. John's Home, Milwaukee, under the chaplaincy of Rev. H. B. St. George, Sr., St. Luke's Hospital, Racine, under the chaplaincy of Rev. Dr. Conover, and St. Luke's Hospital, Chippewa Falls, of which Rev. S. J. Yundt is chaplain, are worthy of mention.

Statistics.—Clergy, 75; Parishes and Missions, 108; Baptisms, 376; Confirmed, 329; Communicants, 4800; Sunday-School Teachers, 264; Scholars, 2189; Contributions, $91,401.46.

Authorities: The Churchman's Calendar, 1868 A.D. The Churchman's Year Book

1870 and 1871 A.D., and the Living Church Annual, 1884 A.D., for Statistics, etc.

REV. S. F. HOTCHKIN.

Witanagemot. Witanagemot—*i.e.*, meeting of the wise men—was an assembly among the Anglo-Saxons, summoned by the King (probably at stated times) for council in all the main acts of government. It consisted of the principal men of the nation,—the aldermen of the shires, the chief ecclesiastics, such as Bishops and Abbots, and perhaps other, both lay and clerical. It lay within its province to settle the laws, to elect, or at least confirm the King, and to choose Bishops. Each kingdom of the Heptarchy had its own Witanagemot; but on the conquest of England by William the whole system was swept away. Some of its features, however, survive in Parliament, such as the Bishops sitting in the House of Lords; yet it cannot be said that the latter assembly is modeled upon the former.

Authorities: Hallam's Middle Ages, Chambers's Cyclopædia, Blunt's Early English Church.

Woman. The position and obligations of woman in the Church are determined, like her place and duties in society, by the object of her creation. which was to be "an helpmeet for man." Simple as this ought to be from the teaching of nature as well as from the statements of Revelation, it has yet always been difficult for man to understand it, and the mistakes of the highest civilization upon this point are quite as great as those of the rudest savagery. There are two distinct and apparently contradictory accounts of her origin in Genesis, which are yet perfectly reconcilable if read aright. In Gen. i. 27, we are told that "GOD created man in His own image; in the image of GOD created He *him*, male and female created He *them*." This is a plain, intelligible statement, involving co-equality of man and woman in their relative positions and giving to neither priority of origin. Its textual connection and its assertion *first* clearly establish it as the purposed revelation of a fact. Man, therefore, is male and female, either part being incomplete without the other. Not man generically, but *the* man needed an helpmeet for him to fulfill the objects of his being, and only in woman could such help be found. Nature teaches the same truth, woman being in every aspect, physical, mental, and even moral, the complement of man. Without woman man, therefore, cannot rightly and fully accomplish his work in the Church any more than in the world. But the converse of this is equally true, and it follows necessarily that there is much to be done in the work of the Church *which it is not woman's place to do*. We can find no better guide to determine the particulars in this respect than the Scriptures of the New Testament. There we always find woman a co-worker with man, active and zealous, not in an inferior position, but in a distinctive line of duty. Only when seeking to go beyond her sphere, as was evidently the case among the Greek converts, do we find her reminded of her subjection—not inferiority—to the stronger sex (1 Cor. ii. 8, 9; 1 Tim. ii. 11, 12). St. Paul distinctly and very emphatically forbids a woman to teach, and we find no instance of any female in holy orders, or intrusted with the public ministrations or administration of the Church. It is, of course, evident that St. Paul's language is not to be accepted literally, at least in any general application, for we should then be deprived of the services of woman as a teacher in schools or mission-fields to her own sex, and as a matter of fact the Apostle speaks approvingly of the instruction received by Timothy himself, to whom he is writing, from his mother Eunice and his grandmother Lois,—for such is the fair interpretation of his language. But enough is clear to condemn as altogether unscriptural the assumption by woman of the office of public preaching or exhorting. Neither is there any scriptural authority for the ordination of women as "Deaconesses," the term applied to Phœbe (Rom. xvi. 1) meaning simply "a servant," as translated in the King James' Version. It may be accepted as a principle, therefore, that woman is debarred by her sex from all strictly masculine employment in the Church, and restricted to work in subjection to and by direction of a higher authority. Her proper sphere is in all those private ministrations which demand especially the gentleness, patience, and watchfulness of her nature, and in the care and oversight of those matters, necessary and abundant, in the working economy of the Church which are analogous to the household duties of domestic life. First among these is the religious instruction of young children. Remembering that the child cannot be taught too early the knowledge of GOD and His Church, and that to woman peculiarly belongs the care of his earliest years, it becomes evident that he must learn this from her or lose the golden opportunity. To teach her children the Holy Scriptures, the Catechism of the Church, and the high value of their birthright therein is a solemn duty and a blessed privilege which no mother may delegate to others. Where this duty is properly realized and performed its influence is marked on the character of the community no less than of the individual. The Sunday-school assumes its proper place as a missionary work and a means of bringing the Rector into close acquaintance with the children of his charge, and in it the younger women and those who have no children of their own find a field to minister instruction to those little ones who are deprived of a mother's training.

Another most useful department of woman's work, in which a field is open to every one who is willing to do personal service, is found in ministering to the physical comfort and spiritual needs of the poor and ignorant. In every neighborhood some object for such ministrations may be found. A visit of inquiry with a few words of kindly sympathy, or a small contribution to the comfort of some poor sister, personally offered is a good work for CHRIST'S sake, which will bring more happiness and blessing than it bestows. A half-hour spent in reading the Bible and Prayer-Book to some sick or aged person who cannot read them for herself is one of the best ways in which a Sunday afternoon can be occupied, and hundreds of women might thus utilize the leisure which hangs heavily upon their hands. There should be in every Parish some organized association for woman's work by means of which the peculiar qualifications and leisure hours, few or many, of all may be turned to account. The regular "Sisterhoods"(q.v.), of which there are at least thirteen in operation in the various Dioceses, are adapted to those only whom circumstances permit to give their entire time to charitable and religious employment. But Parish Guilds may accomplish a great deal without so complete a self-devotion, and indeed without any serious inconvenience to those, even, whose time is largely occupied by the demands of other duties. The Rector will know what are his needs in this direction. Let him organize an association comprising all the active women of his Parish. Visiting Committees of two should be appointed in monthly turns, whose duty should be to inquire for and call upon the poor, the needy sick, or strangers, inviting the latter to church and calling for them on Sunday, and reporting all cases of necessity, illness, or ignorance to the Rector; if need require, nursing for the sick is to be supplied either from the membership or by competent nurses hired and supervised by the association. A very small contribution from each, paid monthly, will, if the membership be general, furnish an ample treasury for all ordinary requirements. As a rule the whole Parish will readily join the list of contributors, and there should be two members appointed monthly to make the collections. Another most admirable form of organization, perfectly practicable in every Parish, is the "Ladies' Church Aid Society." Twelve managers, or fewer, if the Parish be small,—a President, Vice-President, Secretary, and Treasurer form the association. Subscribers for small amounts monthly— five or ten cents—are obtained among the congregation, larger amounts, or semi-annual subscriptions, being accepted. Permanent committees of two, as in the former case, collect these sums monthly, and exercise an active rivalry in gaining new subscribers. The officers never collect. It is wonderful how much is accomplished by this simple machinery, assisted, when some extensive work has been undertaken, by a supplementary Offertory in the church. No Rector who has once experienced the aid and comfort of such an organization will ever willingly be without one in his Parish. The chief aim of the society should be to accomplish each year some important and permanent work in the adornment and furnishing of the church edifice or some similar enterprise, or in giving a tangible shape and practicability to some plan which has seemed beyond the means of the congregation. No church, however poor the people, will remain dingy and shabby or ill equipped in proper appointments for public worship with such an organization at work. Even the building and furnishing of a rectory is not too great a task for it to undertake and push to completion by stirring up the zeal of the congregation to help carry out a determined purpose. The Rector should guide and advise, but leave the managers abundant liberty of choice and action. A definite system should be maintained in the direction of the work, always doing something which no one else is likely to undertake, and avoiding those matters which must be done.

In addition to these objects, the society should take charge of the surplices and altar-linen, the chancel and its furniture, the Christmas and Easter decorations, and all similar matters, assigning each to a special committee of two, and holding the treasury responsible for such slight expenses as their duties involve. An extremely valuable and practical work may be done by such a society in bringing together the members of the congregation who would be otherwise unknown to each other, and thus fostering mutual acquaintance, if not sociability. This may be accomplished in various ways, as circumstances may suggest. The "Parish Sociable" is an excellent method, the members in turn keeping open house for one evening in each month, and personally inviting *all* to be present, the duty thus falling on each less frequently than once a year. Where this is not practicable, the "Garden Party" once or twice a year in summer is an admirable substitute. A suitable place and evening are selected, and the grounds made attractive with torches, Chinese lanterns, and similar devices. Cakes, ices, and lemonade are served from rustic tables, the privilege of purchasing these refreshments relieving constraint and inducing the attendance of many who would otherwise hesitate to come. The boys of the congregation gladly act as waiters under the direction of the committee, while the managers mingle among the guests, introducing and entertaining them. The result is always happy, and the influence for good in thus bringing people together lingers long after the occasion has passed by.

These are a few of the ways in which woman may find an active field for usefulness in the Church without in any way interfering with her domestic and social obligations. The practice of these will itself be suggestive of many others.

REV. R. WILSON, D.D.

Word of God. The title WORD of GOD as applied to the second Person of the Holy Trinity, is derived from the Old Testament to us. That the Jews understood the theological import of the term Word as the Christian understands it is not likely; but that the Apostle took it from any other source than Holy Scripture is not possible. The term was found in the writings of Philo Judæus, a wealthy, influential, and learned Jew of Alexandria in our LORD'S time, and a little later, and his works gave the term LOGOS (WORD), by which he meant a divine influence, an exhibition of the divine mind, but not a Person in the Unity of the Divine Nature. The MESSIAH was indeed in the Targums set forth as the SON of GOD, and so the two parallel teachings prepared the minds of the thoughtful for the reception of the divine revelation that the MESSIAH was the WORD of GOD, and in a far deeper sense than the uninspired paraphrasts and recorders of Jewish interpretation and the speculative platonizing Jew of Alexandria could have fathomed. They cleared the way by using terms in a lower sense than the full truth demanded. But it was given to the disciple whom JESUS loved to declare this full truth. The second Person of the Holy Trinity of the very substance of the FATHER was by the Psalmist declared to be the Word of GOD, by whom the heavens were made, and so, though not knowing its fullness, anticipating the doctrine of St. Paul and the declaration of St. John, that not only the "Word was with GOD and the Word was GOD," but that by Him were all things made, "and without Him was not anything made that was made." St. John's full enunciation was reserved as the last and crowning declaration of our LORD'S Divine Nature, the setting forth of the secret intimate union of His Person with the Person of the FATHER, like as, by a most distant analogy, the Word is most intimately bound up in the power of expressing Himself each Person possesses. That it is a mystery not to be known here is most true, and it is to be devoutly and faithfully accepted. But with this confession we yet may be allowed to speak of this form of His Personality. "For ever, O LORD, Thy Word is settled in Heaven" (Ps. cxix. 89), carries us back to the eternal nature of the WORD, and sets forth the worker before the works. The Word of GOD came to the Prophets, and they spake the mind of CHRIST; the mysterious secret one who in man's appearance, with man's voice, sent the Angel Gabriel to strengthen the fainting prophet (Dan. viii. 15, 16). Already St. Paul had used this term as a title of our LORD, commending the Ephesians to GOD and to the WORD of His grace (Acts xx. 32), and alluding to this commendation in his Epistle to them, in their trust when they heard the Word of Truth (Eph. i. 13); warning the Hebrew Christians that the WORD of GOD is quick and powerful, and sharper than any two-edged sword (Heb. iv. 12), and saluting Titus with a reminder that GOD had manifested His Word through preaching. St. John had already in his Epistles called his Master the Word of Life. And in the vision of the Rider going forth in His righteousness, whose name is called the Word of God (Rev. xix. 13; comp. Ps. xlv. 3, 4). So far had the title been applied to our LORD in even deeper appreciation of its truth, till the Church was prepared to have the full deposit made with her in the sublime words, "In the beginning was the Word, and the Word was with GOD, and the Word was GOD." Now that this is declared, other terms and titles of our LORD, other descriptions of Himself and His work, gain immeasurable importance, — the Wonderful, the One whose name is secret, the numberer of secrets, He that hath a name that no man knoweth. The mystery is not removed, but the Word of GOD must be a Person if these are His titles and are descriptions of Him and His Nature; and again, without this last title we might hold Him to be a Mighty Being, only now we know Him to be intimately GOD of GOD of the One Substance of the FATHER.

WORD of GOD is generally the name given to the Holy Scripture; but while it is perfectly correct for us to use it so now, we must remember that wherever this phrase occurs in Holy Scripture itself, it is to be usually understood of our LORD, since the usual name in the New Testament for the Old Testament Books was the Scripture or Holy Scripture, but not the Word of GOD.

Work, Church, for the Future. When the thoughtful and observant eye looks back over the past century, there is nothing more astonishing than the influence exerted by the Church upon every other variety of Religion in this land. Just after the Revolutionary war, nearly dead,—supposed to be past the possibility of a revival,—despaired of even by some Churchmen, and that for a whole generation after the Episcopate was obtained, who could have expected such a result as we see to-day? Moreover, her claims were, of course, rejected by Rome, and her "Apostolic Succession" and her "prayer by a book" were the scorn of the rest, while her "exclusiveness" made her beyond measure odious to all the Protestant denominations. But now all this is changed, and is still changing. These denominations have all been moving from the ground they occupied half a century ago, and the steady drift of their changes brings them daily nearer to the Church. The uncompromising aspirates of their original sectarian shibboleths are softening down or disappearing. The architecture, the music, the decorations, the liturgical devotions, the reverence for houses used for public worship, the organs, the stained glass, the memorial windows, the use of chanting, the public recital of the Creed, the LORD'S Prayer, and the Ten Commandments, and many other things first known in this country only through the Church, have been creeping into more and more general use among all the Evangelical Denominations, and even among some who are not Evangelical. Christmas and Easter are already well observed; the New York Stock Board adjourns over every Good-Friday on the motion of a Jew; and seventy non-Episcopal ministers of Brooklyn have agreed together this year to keep a part of the season of Lent. The Church element is so strong in all our great cities that the whole social current is largely regulated by the Feasts and Fasts of the Church. The Church of Rome, the hardest to move, is nevertheless moving also. By the operation of the free atmosphere of this country, by the common-school system, and specially by the anxiety of the priests to conciliate Protestants as much as possible by *not* making prominent those things which they know to be most repugnant to the Protestant mind,—by all these things, the quality of Romanism itself is perceptibly changing. Every such change dilutes the intensity of Ultramontanism, gives more and more of an American tone, and thus brings the masses of Romanists gently but inevitably nearer to us. Now, if all this has been accomplished in one century (and nearly all only in the latter half of it), what reasonable man can refrain from looking ahead and anticipating what will be the result of the same changes going on for a hundred years to come? We Churchmen should have coolness and clear-headedness enough to measure the vastness of the responsibility which Providence has placed upon us, and see what practical changes we need to make in our own working system in order to accomplish our task.

We inherited, by tradition from our Mother-Church of England, a cast-iron system, with close union of Church and State (meaning, too often, the undue dominance of the State), a body of Canons largely obsolete, and a Church legislature (the Convocations of Canterbury and York) unable to act at all. The spiritual tone of that Church was at the lowest point it had ever known. We received it in that its lowest, poorest, and coldest shape. Our task has been to accommodate a Church and State system to a country where there could be *no* union between Church and State; to take a cast-iron system and melt it over, and make it more like spring steel; to work out a body of Canons suitable to our own condition, and by a Church legislature deriving no authority from the Civil Power; and to put warmth and heartiness into a worship which was cold and almost dead. This we have done: but much more yet remains. We need to get rid entirely of the pew system, so that no one can secure, by a money payment, a right to a seat in the House of GOD. In a country where all are equal in the eye of the law, it will never answer that there should be more of fraternity in *the law* than in *the Gospel*. The *social* element—which is so strong a binding power among the Denominations—cannot be used with us as with them, for we must include *all* grades of society. But the missing link may here be supplied by the formation of Guilds, Brotherhoods, Sisterhoods, and all manner of organizations for mutual help, grouping them all around the Church as their real Mother. The Sisterhoods devote themselves to hospitals, to out-door nursing of the sick, to teaching, to church embroidery and decoration, etc.; and the Brotherhoods are mainly priests trained for the holding of parochial Missions, although lay Brotherhoods also have accomplished much good. There is a vast field here which has only just begun to be worked, and in which social fellowship, in good works and material help of all sorts, will give the needed practical activity to our parishes and Dioceses. These organizations may be made to supply precisely that want which leads so many into the ranks of the Freemasons, Odd-Fellows, and other Orders of like character.

Among other wants, a Financial System which will have more distributive equality and more spiritual efficacy than our usual corporation of "Rector, Church-wardens, and Vestrymen" supplies, is a need felt more and more deeply by very many among us.

The old rigidity of public worship has already been wonderfully changed for the better. Hardly any two parishes can now be found whose order and manner of worship is exactly the same. And this is like the living variety of Nature, where no two leaves can be found exactly alike on the same tree: while bullets run in the same mould by machinery *can* be made exactly alike, because they are things without life. Even the immovable Prayer-Book has felt the new spirit, and a nearly unanimous vote of General Convention has declared that it *must* acquire both enrichment and flexibility. In music—especially in the establishment of Surpliced Choirs—much has been done, and improvement is going on rapidly. The quartette music of modern shallowness is steadily retreating before a style of more Churchly simplicity, strength, solemnity, and grandeur. Orchestral accompaniments, on great festivals, add still further to the effect. And the variety and freedom of additional services brings with it a freshness and earnestness which are continually deepening and increasing the spiritual magnetism and attractiveness of the Church.

The perfecting of our own traditional organization is one of our most imperative wants. The true theory of Episcopacy does *not* require that a vast territory should be put under one man, which no one man can possibly attend to efficiently. Where population is reasonably dense, a Diocese ought not to be more than from twenty to fifty miles square. Every one of our present States and Territories (except, perhaps, Rhode Island and Delaware) will eventually become a Province containing three or more Dioceses, and some of them are now large enough for six or eight Dioceses, or even more. Not until this subdivision is carried out will it be possible to carry ecclesiastical tilth to the proper point of personal and proper care. Then, also, our Judicial system is wretchedly defective. Each Province should furnish a ready Court of Appeal, where every complaint or grievance could be heard, and nothing that is wrong be left without a possible and practicable remedy. The sooner this part of our machinery is put into good repair, the better it will be for every other branch of the operations of the Church.

The School question is, in this country, one of vast importance and almost insoluble difficulty. The endowment of education by State Governments, the General Government, and private bequests or gifts, is so vast, that in less than a century from now this interest will be the richest that the world has ever seen. Against this overwhelming preponderance of wealth it were vain to expect that Church-people alone should, by voluntary gifts, set up another educational system able to compete with that of the public. The Roman Church is trying to do this, and its efforts have been heroic. But the Roman system enables them really to levy large sums from the pockets of Protestants: and a very small proportion of the public school taxes is paid by their people. In both respects we stand on very different ground from them. And yet with both these advantages, their success is very incomplete. As all the Evangelical denominations, together with the Roman Church and our own, are agreed in professing to accept the Apostles' Creed, the LORD'S Prayer, and the Ten Commandments, it is theoretically possible that they should all combine to have that much, at least, of religious teaching in the public schools. But though theoretically possible, it is not now within reach practically. It may become so by and by, however, as sectarian bitterness and suspiciousness decrease. The most that can be done is to establish Church schools of high grade, for boys and for girls, the advantages of which shall be within the reach of those who are of moderate means. It will be found that, by placing these under the charge of members of some Religious organization, the *best* organization and the highest kind of influence will be secured, with the greatest steadiness of administration, and at the least possible expense. As to Church colleges, those we have are in great need of further endowment, yet without much chance of getting it. Owing to the wide comprehensiveness of the Church, no two Church colleges have exactly the same ecclesiastical tone. Each can appeal, therefore, only to the sympathies of a portion of Churchmen: and no one of them is likely to get anything from outside. In all the older denominational colleges, the denominational spirit has become so unpopular, that all organic guarantees of denominational supremacy have been voluntarily removed. Their growing unsectarianism has drawn rich additional gifts and endowments. The better Church policy will be to establish Halls or Houses for Church undergraduates in connection with every such college. Thus organizing our Church strength will make it far more effective as a leaven for the whole lump. And we can do it the more safely, as there is not another religious body in the country that is likely to make any effort in that direction. This would render all the older and wealthier colleges even *more* useful to the Church than if they were her own: for few will come to a Church college except youths of Church families; while, on the other plan, a definite Church influence will constantly be brought to bear on the larger number of undergraduates who are *not* Churchmen.

There are special fields of Church work, each of which has its own special claims. First in magnitude should be mentioned the colored population, mainly—though not exclusively—to be found in the Southern States. Wherever—as in the larger cities —any appreciable portion of that population has risen to a certain grade of cultivation and comfort, there we always find some congregations of them in the Church. But these are miserably few in proportion to the vast numbers of that race. The Church has shown such phenomenal slowness and want of success in getting hold of this element, that we need to look facts squarely in the face and find out the reasons. The *race* difficulty is the first to meet us. That all men are equal in GOD'S House is a principle that cannot be abandoned. There is neither Jew nor Greek, male or female, Barbarian or Scythian, bond or free; but all are *one* in CHRIST JESUS. Yet generally, in the earliest ages, Jewish congregations had usages of their own, and were separate organizations (or parishes) from the Gentile Christians. This distinction was carried up to the highest point—the Apostolate—when St. Peter was specially commissioned as the Apostle of the Circumcision, and St. Paul as the "Apostle of the Gentiles." Taking human nature as it is, the most of our congregations of white people would not permit any large number of colored people to come in and help run a parish on the same footing as themselves. And the great majority of colored people, who are sufficiently elevated to appreciate the Church and her worship, do not enjoy trying to be members where they feel (whether justly or unjustly) that they are looked on by some as intruders; and they are not really comfortable until they have a church of their own. This does not imply a colored minister; but they like to feel that the place where they meet, the organization to which they belong, is their own Now here is a practical contradiction. The pride of equality with the whites theoretically demands one thing: the actual comfort of a practical working system demands the other. In the supply of the Ministry the same thing is true. The vast majority of the colored race being yet ignorant, it is vain to hope for a competent supply of ministers of their own color, if the high literary requirements of our present Canons are insisted on. Practical common sense would therefore be willing to lower them. But when this was proposed to the last General Convention, a Convention of Colored Clergy and Laity of the Church protested loudly against the indignity of any such color line, and insisted that only those colored men should be ordained priests in the Church who could sustain the full examinations required of the whites. Moreover, the middle and lower classes of colored people are exceedingly clannish, and must be dealt with rather in masses than as individuals. They are bound together by a subtle sympathy, which makes them act together.

In any plans for their improvement this peculiarity must never be lost sight of. The work cannot be thoroughly done among them unless by a Ministry largely, if not wholly, of their own race. Moreover, our liturgical and disciplinary system needs to be seriously modified before it will be able to meet the requirements of the work. With millions, so large a proportion of whom cannot read, it is nonsense to try to teach them to respond all through our regular service, Psalter and all. We must find some mode of worship which will give them quite as much to do, if not more: and yet give it in such a shape as to make it easy for them to do it. This lies ready to our hand in the old original *Antiphon* system, by which *one verse*—as characteristic of the day as possible—was selected, and taught to the people as a burden or chorus, and they introduced it after each verse of Canticle or Psalm. This frequent repetition is what the colored people—who are all singers—greatly delight in. The one hundred and thirty-sixth Psalm, with the burden, to every verse, "for his mercy endureth forever," is an exact model of what we mean. The *Benedicite* is another specimen. It would require one who has an intuitive perception of the simple, the sympathetic, and the striking, together with great natural musical taste and feeling, to revive this feature of ancient Church worship. It was originally invented in order to interest congregations of unlearned people, who had no printed Prayer-Books in their hands: and it would succeed as well now as then. The entire service should be made as musical as possible. Much may also be done in the way of vestments, lights, and other decorations to interest a race whose temperament is decidedly more sensuous than our own. That sensuousness now shows itself in their protracted nocturnal orgies, where shouting, clapping, jumping, dancing, and similar "exercises" are kept up until a physical excitement is produced of a kind wellnigh destructive of true Religion. The orderly and regulated attractiveness of a musical service, with colored vestments, light, and incense, would give elevation and dignity, while yet free from the evils of the other plan. Nature has clothed our dusky brother in mourning anyhow, all over. When only white is combined with black, it is merely another variety of mourning. In nothing does he delight more than in bright and positive colors; and why not let him have them in his Religious services? He is very fond of lights also, and why not let him have them? And of the propriety of incense, few, who have had experience, would doubt. When race peculiarities are in question, things of slightest importance in themselves may be the key to success; and the neglect of them, and attending only to great matters, may insure total failure. The lubricating oil is a very slight item in the outfit of a railway train: but if it be omitted, all the rest will soon come to a stand-still. In ascertaining, by practical experiment, what will be likely to succeed, there must be reasonable freedom from Canonical and rubrical fetters. It is a work for individuals of peculiar gifts and qualifications; and in which legislative bodies, deciding in advance of experience, can only show their impotence for any good.

Of the two very different efforts now attracting great attention in the colored field,—that of St. Mary's Church, Baltimore, and that of Mrs. Buford at Laurenceville, in Virginia,—the former comes the nearest to the suggestions made above. The services are largely choral, and highly "ritualistic;" and the ten-years-old experiment, beginning with nothing, now shows a fine stone church seating over 800 people, with 3 clergy, and a body of Sisters at work. They have an Orphanage with 20 boys, 188 children in the Parish School, and 250 in the Sunday-school. The offerings of the congregation for the last year were $1343.14. Mrs. Buford's work is purely rural, and the peculiar and unaccountable obstacles placed in her way have prevented the development of any settled plan of operations as yet. But her care for the sick and suffering and ignorant has already made her a power in that part of the country. She has a daily school of 260, a hospital with 18 beds, a night-school of 56, and a Home prepared for Sisters to reside in and take charge of part of the work. She has herself stood as sponsor or witness for 425 persons at their Baptism. The remarkable work of the Rev. A. Toomer Porter, D.D., in Charleston, the Rev. G. B. Cooke in Petersburg, the Rev. Dr. J. L. Tucker in Mississippi, and others, as well as the excellent service rendered by St. Augustine's Normal School, Raleigh, N. C., ought not to pass without mention. In coping with the difficulties of the work, it will probably be found that the peculiarities of primitive practice may give still further points worthy of revival; for instance, it is well known how strong an impression is made upon the imagination of the colored people by being *put under the water* by the Baptists.

A similar effect, in a different and more desirable way, might be produced by reviving the ancient chrisom robe, and clothing every person, as soon as he is baptized, and as a part of the service, *with a white garment*. It would be a most impressive way of teaching the baptized person that CHRIST had given him forgiveness of all his sins: and that he must take care to keep this purity unspotted by fresh sins in future. For open and scandalous sins, committed after Baptism, it would also be well to revive the *public penance* of the Primitive days. The childlike immaturity of mind and character, the absence of the personal sensitiveness and high-strung self-respect of the whites, and the intense clannishness of the colored people, all combine to point out *this* as one of the most indispensable means towards the moral elevation of the Race. But it is a very large problem. And its solution will probably be very slow, especially since there is no general agreement as to the direction in which that solution should be sought.

There are other Race problems,—the Indians and the Chinese, for instance. As to the former, much has been done; and no Missions among them have been more successful than those carried on by the Church. The effort has been to advance the whole man, so that the Indian shall become a civilized Christian instead of a savage Pagan. The services of Dr. James Lloyd Breck and of Bishop Whipple in this field have made for both of them national reputations. These efforts cannot fully succeed, however, until the Indian is recognized as a citizen, and is clothed with the legal rights of citizenship. Work has already been begun among the Chinese; but with the rooted antipathy to further immigration, and the legal barriers erected to prevent it, the extension of this work is not a matter of immediate and *growing* pressure.

A much more important subject is the question of foreign nationalities subsisting here in their distinctness of language and religion for several generations, and in large numbers. In Colonial times, the Swedish Churches in and near Philadelphia remained distinct for a long while, with pastors from Sweden, and services in the Swedish language. Eventually, *all* these were absorbed into our Church, and still remain among our parishes, with no distinction as to services or anything else. The Huguenot settlements in and around New York and in the Carolinas, as well as in some other places, have also been largely absorbed into the Church. In the case of the *Église du S. Esprit* in New York, the service is still in French,—a French translation of our Prayer-Book, —in other cases there is now no difference between these and other parishes. The German settlers of Pennsylvania, Georgia, and elsewhere have been more tenacious, keeping up their own services in their own language, and with Lutheran or other religious organizations to preserve and perpetuate their distinctness. From these have arisen the various Lutheran and German Reformed sects, some of whom are the most Churchly in doctrine and worship of all the Evangelical denominations. Among the very large immigrations of Swedes and Norwegians in late years not much has been done, as yet, to draw them Churchwards; but there is a strong probability that the earlier history will repeat itself as soon as the barrier of the foreign language begins to disappear. The true policy, in all these cases, is to relax our rubrical and canonical rigidity somewhat, so that congregations of all these foreign nationalities may be brought into a vital connection with the Church, through an Apostolic ministry, while yet retaining the worship to which they are accustomed, in their own language, and as nearly as possible in the very words which they have always used. Their customs as to parochial organizations should also be followed as closely as may be. All subordinate details should be left unchanged, in order to secure the *one* point of union in a regular ministry and valid sacraments, the Catholic Creeds being the only tests of faith required.

The same principle, expanded, would easily permit of the union of the greater body of English-speaking denominations in this country on the foundation of our Apostolic Church. We began by speaking of the general movement of all these great denominations towards the Church. What will be the natural result of this but *actual union?* The dropping our sectarian name "Protestant Episcopal," and calling ourselves simply "The Church in the United States," would greatly facilitate such a union. And we ought to make this actual union as easy as possible, provided no fundamental principle be violated. It would be enough to require that every such congregation uniting with us should, 1st. Accept the definitions of the Faith as set forth by the undisputed General Councils; 2d. Have a ministry of Apostolic succession, given hypothetically if not absolutely; 3d. Should receive Confirmation at the hands of a Bishop; and, 4th. Should pledge themselves to the use of only valid forms in the administration of the two great Sacraments of Baptism and the Holy Eucharist. Outside of these essentials, *everything* should be left free. On the other side,—that towards Rome,—it must be remembered that, although the Pope excommunicates Anglicans, the Anglican Church has never excommunicated the Pope or any other branch of the One Apostolic Church. The XXXIX. Articles, in which some Romish opinions and practices are condemned, are not a Creed, and are not required of the Laity in any wise. All that is required of the Laity is the Baptismal vow, ratified in Confirmation; and every baptized and confirmed Romanist has complied with those conditions as completely as any of our own people. On our own principles, therefore, we cannot but be ready to admit all Romanists to our communion *now*. The obstacle is on their side,—they are not willing to come. But as they draw nearer and nearer, the time may arrive when they *will* be willing. We should then remember that—whatever may be their errors—their Liturgy contains no heresy that has been condemned as such by the whole Catholic Church. We should, therefore, admit them to union without demanding any change in the form of worship to which they are accustomed, and with no change in Discipline further than is inseparable from the act of union itself. The same principle would apply to congregations of Oriental Christians, or any other branch of the Apostolic Church, should such be found in our country.

And this brings us to the last and greatest of the works which the providence of GOD seems to be laying at *our* doors, although we are the youngest and the weakest of all the Apostolic Churches. The principles which necessarily underlie the attempt to bring together, into one body, all the varieties of Christianity found in this "Home of all Nations" are precisely the same principles which, if carried out, would reunite the sundered communions of Christians everywhere. Historically, those melancholy separations were due more to the unions of Church and State, and complications of worldly politics and national jealousies, than to the *odium theologicum* alone. The Papacy itself—the *fons et origo malorum*—is in its essence a wrong *polity;* and if that wrong polity were reformed, all other evils would soon reform themselves. If the Absolute Despotism of the Papacy were to yield to the ancient Catholic polity of Liberty regulated by Law,—the free Spirit speaking through the organs of the Body,—what more could be asked? Now, owing to the fact of our entire freedom from entanglements with the State, our action cannot be liable to any suspicion of covering up a political purpose. We *can*, therefore, take the initiative, in a way that is *possible* to no other branch of the Church in Christendom. The tendency towards reunion with the Eastern Church was *begun by us* more than half a century ago, when the Rev. Messrs. Hill and Robertson were sent as missionaries to Greece, with instructions which breathed a purely brotherly spirit towards the Greek Church; and that mission has been maintained on the same principle ever since. In 1862 A.D. the appointment of a Russo-Greek Committee by our General Convention marked a new era in the good work, which soon caused the appointment of a similar committee by the Convocation of Canterbury. The impulse thus given went on until it culminated in the Bonn Conference of 1874 A.D., where a formula of agreement was adopted which, logically, ends a controversy that has raged between the East and the West for a thousand years concerning the Procession of the HOLY GHOST. Formal intercommunion has already taken place between the Orientals and the Old Catholics and between the Old Catholics and ourselves. The Lambeth Conference,—the first suggestion of which was made by an American, the first Bishop of Vermont,—at the opening meeting in 1867 A.D., carried its doctrinal requirements for a reunited Christendom no further than the acceptance of the definitions concerning the Faith set forth by the undisputed General Councils.

The position of the Eastern question is giving more and more influence to Russia and England; and neither France nor Austria are as zealous for Papal propagandism in the East as they once were. It looks as if, before many years, all branches of the Anglican and Oriental Churches, together with the Old Catholics, will be in full communion with one another; and *that way* lies the best hope of the peace of Christendom.

In the Roman Communion itself there are numberless brave souls groaning under the evils of their false system, and turning to us with eyes of faith and hope. Campello and Savarese—coming to us from St. Peter's in Rome, and from the immediate service of the Pope in the Vatican—are only samples of thousands of others. As the visible unity consolidates around us, the signs of change for the better will grow stronger even in Rome itself, and thus at last *all* may be One.

Let no narrowness, or coldness, or blindness, or prejudice on our part hinder this greatest of all the works which the wonderful providence of GOD has given us to do.

REV. J. H. HOPKINS, D.D.

Workingmen's Clubs and Institutes. The origin of the associations now known under the general designation of Workingmen's Clubs and Institutes is said to have been the agitation in 1825-30 A.D. in England in favor of Mechanics' Institutes "originated by that true friend of the working classes, Dr. Birkbeck. Then came various unconnected intermittent attempts to provide what were called 'Reading-rooms' for working men, in which the chief element was the supplying a place where time might be innocently passed, but where neither education, social intercourse, nor recreation was offered, except so far as reading a newspaper or book in the same room with other people might be supposed to afford all or either. Next came the formation of Mutual Improvement Societies, which met chiefly in school-rooms, and aimed at classes, discussions, and especially at the preparation

51

of short papers on interesting and improving topics. There was often a good deal of the sociable spirit in these little organizations, but they were seldom long-lived."*

Several somewhat similar organizations were started at about the same time; but the most important was the Brighton Workingmen's Institute, founded by the Rev. F. W. Robertson in 1849 A.D. Then followed in other places the formation of night-schools and societies for promoting adult education. In 1852 A.D. was opened in the Colonnade Clare-market "The Colonnade Workingmen's Club," which undertook to provide amusement and refreshment for the members as well as newspapers and books; and shortly after village clubs were established in many places throughout the United Kingdom. In 1854 A.D. the Rev. F. D. Maurice and his colleagues established the "London Workingmen's College," which has been said to be "one of the greatest, if not *the* greatest impulse yet given in this country [England] to the movement for elevating workingmen in the social scale."† In this "College" were combined both amusement and instruction, and its success was so marked that a general interest was excited, culminating eventually in 1862 A.D. in the formation of "The Workingmen's Club and Institute Union,"—an organization whose object, as stated in a prospectus issued at the time, is that "of helping Workingmen to establish Clubs or Institutes where they can meet for conversation, business, and mental improvement, with the means of recreation and refreshment, free from intoxicating drinks; these clubs at the same time constituting societies for mutual helpfulness in various ways."

From that time to the present (1884 A.D.) the formation of clubs having these objects in view in England has gone on in an increasing ratio, until at present there are at least one thousand such clubs scattered throughout the United Kingdom. In the United States, the initiative in the movement was taken by a number of gentlemen connected with St. Mark's Church, Philadelphia, Pa., in 1871 A.D., and after a few years other clubs, chiefly founded in connection with parish work, were organized in Philadelphia and elsewhere. At present there are, however, in the United States, so far as known to the writer, not more than twenty-five or thirty organizations which strictly come within the designation of "Workingmen's Clubs." In 1883 A.D. there was formed a union called "The Congress of Workingmen's Clubs," whose object is to promote the formation of clubs and to give advice and encouragement whenever practicable. A Workingmen's Club, as now understood in England and in the United States, is an association formed for the purpose of affording to workingmen the means of healthful and innocent amusement and recreation, an opportunity for intellectual cultivation, and the promotion of habits of economy and thrift. It may be connected with other work, as are those clubs formed and managed under the auspices of a particular parish or union of parishes, or it may have no connection of any kind with any other organization, but be wholly autonomous. If founded in connection with parish work, the usual form of government is by a Board of Trustees or Managers, from twelve to twenty-five in number, appointed by the rector of the parish, or if several parishes are united in the undertaking, each rector appoints an equal number. If the club has no necessary connection with church or parish work, it may be governed by a self-constituted Board, which itself fills its own vacancies, or it may be wholly democratic, and the Board of Directors may be annually elected by the members of the club. Sometimes both features are adopted, and one-half of the board is appointed and the other half elected. A workingmen's club is never intended or expected to be a purely charitable undertaking, and in many cases the clubs are wholly self-supporting. The funds are partially contributed, in the case of parish clubs, by the church or churches with which the club is connected, or by any benevolent person who may be interested in the work; but there is generally an initiation fee, and always a monthly payment made by the members. The initiation fee is never in excess of $1, and the monthly payment about 1s. in England, or 25 cents in America. In the English clubs, though not, so far as known to the writer, in any American club, a restaurant connected with the club is often a source of revenue. There are, of course, in addition, various entertainments given by the clubs, which frequently prove very lucrative. In the annual report of the Workingmen's Club and Institute Union, in England, for 1882-83 A.D., it was stated that the answers received to inquiries in regard to club statistics showed that upwards of 73 per cent. of the clubs were reported to be entirely "self-supporting, and without any pecuniary aid from outside friends." This could not be said, however, of the clubs in America, where the proportion of self-supporting clubs is very small, if it really exists at all.

In all clubs there are the two departments of education and amusement, and there is sometimes a third relating to economy. The educational department is of course always represented by a circulating library and reading-room, and no feature of the club work is better calculated to be of service than this. In the reading-room should be at least two or three daily and weekly papers for the current news of the day, and so many magazines and periodicals as the finances of the club will permit, care being taken to select them with reference to the tastes and appreciation of the members. It is usual

---

* Workingmen's Social Clubs and Educational Institutes. Henry Solly, London, 1867 A.D.
† Henry Solly.

also to have at stated intervals, once or twice a month, lectures or "friendly talks" upon subjects of interest, supplemented at times perhaps by occasional readings: to these the members are frequently allowed to bring their friends. In England the local clubs derive much valuable assistance in this respect from the Union, which has for many years circulated books among the smaller clubs, and in some instances even made grants of books which have been presented to it for this purpose. It has also for many years obtained the services of lecturers, but at present this particular branch of its work has been undertaken by "the Social Educational League," formed for this purpose. There are established in connection with many clubs classes for instruction in the elementary branches of learning if the members are of a very humble and uneducated class, or if they are mechanics, and belong to the better educated classes, there are classes in History, Philosophy, or other similar branches of learning. In England the Union fosters this work by offering prizes for papers sent in on various subjects, as well in History as in Poetry, Industrial and Social questions. Not the least useful of all of the educational features of the club is the debating society, which meets once or twice a month, or perhaps weekly, where the members learn not only to think of subjects, which, but for its suggestion they would pass quite unnoticed, but also to think upon their feet and express themselves, so that others may understand them. For debates also the English Union offers annual prizes, and the debates are held in a hall convenient to the purpose, at which the competing clubs attend.

The amusement department of a club depends in large measure upon the local circumstances. If situated in a village or country town, it may have an athletic club, or cricket, foot-ball, or base-ball club, indeed, any outdoor sport that is popular in the neighborhood and feasible for the members. For winter evenings there should always be, however, a game-room for chess, checkers, backgammon, or any other games, if nothing in the nature of gambling is permitted, and where it can be afforded, pool or billiard-tables, or both. The two latter are frequently made a source of revenue by charging a moderate fee for each game. There are also social gatherings of various kinds, concerts and recitations, either by friends or by the members, if they develop any taste or capacity for such work. There is in many clubs a glee-club or singing-class, and perhaps, although not so frequently, an orchestra. If really successful in their efforts, the vocal and instrumental societies by their concerts are sometimes enabled not only to pay their own expenses, but to contribute handsomely to the treasury of the club itself. In all of the club-houses there is a room or hall adapted to lectures and social gatherings, and where the club-house has been built for the purpose, this hall is large enough to accommodate a fair audience, and is usually supplied with a stage, and perhaps with the ordinary curtain and stage scenery, if anything like dramatic performances take place. In the economical department of the club work may be included Beneficial Societies, of which there are two kinds, perpetual and annual; in the former the members continue to pay annually, and so long as they are in good standing are entitled to the benefits of the society; in the latter the society dissolves each year, and whatever balance may be in the treasury is divided *pro rata* among the members, and a new society is then formed, from which are eliminated all those who would be deemed undesirable members if making an original application. The Annual societies seem to be preferred. In some of the Philadelphia clubs there are building-associations, societies until recently peculiar to that city, by which, through a system of contributions and loans, the members are enabled to buy or build their own houses at a great saving of expense and by easy payments. There have also been tried, and with some success, savings-banks or societies, for the purpose of saving pure and simple. Co-operative societies have been established, but so far as known with no great success.

It remains to point out some of the elements of success and failure in the clubs.

The most vital element of success is the co-operation in every club of a minority of well-educated and intelligent men, with a majority whose opportunities have been fewer. The key-note of the whole movement is the brotherhood of all men, and the desire on the part of those who have been highly favored and whose advantages, both in respect to education and amusement, are great, to enable their less-favored neighbors to share in a measure in these blessings. To this end the two classes must mingle in a fraternal spirit, with no patronage on the one hand, or cringing acceptance of favors on the other. The presence of the higher class is essential in directing the various enterprises connected with the club, and in pointing out new fields of interest and profit to their humbler companions, whose experience would quite fail them in this direction; for this reason it is highly important that at least the preponderating influence in every Board of Management should be composed of members of what are called the upper class. In England, at one time, in some clubs two governing bodies were made use of, the one composed of "gentlemen," with whom lay the ultimate control and disposition of everything, while under them was a committee of the club-members proper, but the plan was a signal failure. Not only is it necessary that the Board of Management should be so largely represented by the more educated class, it is equally important that they should be in constant and friendly intercourse with the members, and to this end, as well as for the general purpose of preserving order and giving necessary information, it is customary for the members of a board of management to have one of their number present at the clubhouse every evening, the members serving in rotation for this purpose. By this means the use of the library may frequently be most usefully directed, and important influences for good in other ways be brought to bear. It is equally important that the members themselves, of whatever class they may be, should feel the responsibilities as well as share the privileges of membership. To this end there should be a representation of the workingmen's element, as distinguished from the gentlemen on the governing board, whatever may be the form of government. Judging from the experience of the clubs, it should be the aim of the managers to provide such influences as will enable the members to feel that they have something to gain by continuing their membership besides the mere social pleasure which it affords. Experience has also demonstrated that no one under twenty-one years of age should be admitted as a member. The men who seek the club for study or quiet recreation, which they frequently are unable to obtain in their own homes amid a family of children, do not find themselves benefited in the society of boisterous boys, and many clubs have either actually perished, or nearly done so because of their membership dropping off in consequence of this evil. Another most important rule to be observed is the exclusion from public discussion of religious and even political questions, two topics which unfortunately are very apt to excite ill feeling.

The conditions under which clubs may be successfully carried on in America are not essentially different from those in England, except that perhaps, as the American laboring classes are generally more comfortably housed and fed, the need of the creature comforts of a club may appeal less powerfully to them. But the best of the laboring classes will usually find enough advantages in a well-managed club to more than repay the trifling expense attending membership. On the other hand, republican manners and habits render the intercourse between the various classes much more easy and friendly, and, if approached in the right spirit, to that extent more effective in imparting and receiving information and instruction. For a detailed history of the movement in England, the reader is referred to "Workingmen's Clubs and Educational Institutes," by the Rev. Henry Solly, London, 1867 A.D., published by the Workingmen's Club and Institute Union, and to the occasional papers published by that association, and the *Club and Institute Journal,* published fortnightly by the Union at its office, No. 31 Southampton Street, Strand, London, W.C. The present Secretary is Mr. J. J. Dent, and his address the office of the Union. The Workingmen's Club Congress in America are also prepared to furnish information and suggestions on application to the Corresponding Secretary, John B. Pine, Esq., 41 Pine Street, New York City.

N. DUBOIS MILLER.

Works. Every being must act in some way. It is a condition of life. Every intelligent human being by the powers given him gives some one of these three characters to each act. It is either an act indifferent, or involving moral principles, or involving spiritual principles. It most frequently has two of these characters; it is seldom, when rightly viewed, without some moral force, and often has spiritual power, and always has spiritual consequences. If the sorrowful taint and weakness of sin be in the actor, then all of his acts will be affected by this weakness, will have this taint. And it will make no difference in the act viewed alone whether this weakness was inherited or not. It *does* make a great difference in the responsibility of the actor, but not in the act. It is a distinction to be kept in mind when we consider the consequences of the act to the actor before a just judge. But, since actions are the inevitable concomitants of life, and our life is a complex one, and our acts have a like complex character, it follows that with the best intentions on the part of the doer, yet everything done cannot be perfect, even though the limits placed upon a finite being be not considered. Works, then, done by every child of Adam, no matter how well-intentioned, must be affected by the taint of original sin. So the XIII. Article puts it, "Works done before the grace of CHRIST, and the Inspiration of His Spirit, are not pleasant to GOD, forasmuch as they spring not of faith in JESUS CHRIST; neither do they make men meet to receive grace, or (as the School-authors say) deserve grace of congruity: yea rather, for that they are not done as GOD hath willed and commanded them to be done, we doubt not but they have the nature of sin." But baptism is our adoption into His household as sons, and the gift of all things necessary for a true and filial obedience, for the forgiveness of the guilt of original sin, and for a discipline that shall remove the taint and heal the weakness of the child of GOD, and shall fit him for the higher and better estate of which he is the heritor.

In GOD'S saints the sense of weakness and the strength of a dependence upon Him and upon the inspiration of the HOLY GHOST is ever clearer as they grow in grace, and the imperfection of their works, nay, their uselessness without CHRIST, is much more humbly felt.

So, on the other hand, the rejecting, the unregenerate man can do nothing which can be received, because he refuses this obedience, which must be a condition precedent to redemption. It may be even that the act of the indifferent and disobedient man may be *externally* better than the obedience of the earnest child of GOD. But the difference is clear when we consider that the kind act of a stranger cannot have the characteristic notes of the filial act of a son. It is this obedience of a son that makes the works done in faith acceptable to GOD, and makes the doer of them righteous through CHRIST. It is the indifference with which these acts are done by one who rejects the loving call of his LORD, and willfully does or does not what may be in itself right, together with the weakness proper to the act itself which leads to their rejection. All things not done either directly for His sake and in His name, or by one who is habitually a lover of holiness, are said in Holy Scripture to be done in unrighteousness. A statement relating, indeed, to one extreme form of heathen and Jewish hardness of heart, but to be received in principle as applicable to works, is to be found in the second chapter of 2 Thess. It is the love of the truth that is rejected, and so the truth cannot be believed, and pleasure in unrighteousness follows. As a general proposition (which must be essentially modified we must admit both by the love and mercy in the Redemption, by the changed relation of the person to GOD through CHRIST by his adoption, and by the fact that it is all by gift by grace, as to sons, and not by wages, as to servants), the relation of either party —those who reject the Gospel and those who accept it—to GOD is something of the relation of those who accept employment to the employer. What is the attitude of the employer to those who accept his terms and those who reject them, and yet expect to receive some wages? The answer is ready at once. Put, then, the employed into the relation of a son lovingly received and cared for, yet upon probation and under a disciplinary education, and treated by a wise and loving father according to a plan of training that relates to a higher and more blessed relation, and which the son is directed to obey without hesitation, that he may prove his fitness for a truer companionship with his everlasting FATHER. "Come ye blessed of my FATHER, inherit the kingdom prepared for you from the foundation of the world," is spoken to sons and is founded on works done in love for CHRIST'S sake. Placing the righteousness which is by faith as precedent and essential, the righteousness which is by works upon that faith is equally essential. It is, then, upon this foundation that the XI. and XII. Articles proceed.

"We are accounted righteous before GOD, only for the merit of our LORD and SAVIOUR JESUS CHRIST by Faith, and not for our own works or deservings." "Albeit that Good Works, which are the fruits of Faith, and follow after Justification, cannot put away our sins, and endure the severity of GOD'S judgment; yet are they pleasing and acceptable to GOD in CHRIST, and do spring out necessarily of a true and lively Faith; insomuch that by them a lively Faith may be as evidently known as a tree discerned by the fruit." There are many side issues and discussions which spring out of these statements, but they do not seriously affect our own duty, and not at all the fundamental truth of the statement. The condition of the heathen who have not known GOD, the condition of those who, even in a Christian land, have never been reached by the Gospel by counteracting causes, the relation of intention to the value of the deed, are all questions which may puzzle us, but which can be of no use. The plain, straightforward duty of doing all we can obediently, with the grace of the HOLY GHOST guiding us, and the certainty that our LORD will as lovingly accept our bounden duty and service as it is lovingly done,—this is all we need. If we grasp these facts, we have enough to guide us in the justification by works.

Wrath of God. A declaration often occurring in Holy Scripture. His anger is not as our anger, as His thoughts are not as our thoughts, or His ways as our ways. His wrath is indeed most fearful, but it is so in its calmness, its terrible serenity, if we may be permitted so to word it, in its freedom from menace in any human sense, for He does not threaten as one who hath to take trouble or great exertion to execute, but as one whose threatenings are only the declaration of results which are inevitable from such evil course of conduct. His is a wrath that, since His nature is love, is only the expression of His absolute Justice, and therefore constantly in Holy Scripture He declares His readiness to put it away, to forgive, to restore, to bless a thousandfold. His mercies are ever new; His compassions fail not. His continual warning to the chosen people of His wrath and yet of His purpose to forgive and to restore are prophecies of His wrath towards our sins, and of His forgiveness through His SON and His restoration of men upon their repentance. GOD was in CHRIST reconciling the world unto Himself. It is this that gives the Incarnation of the SON of GOD such glorious yet terrible significance. For our sakes He trod the winepress of the wrath of GOD alone. For our sakes, in our Flesh, as true SON of Man, He made an atonement for our sins. For our sakes, though sinless and pure, He, putting Himself in our place, endured the hiding of His FATHER'S face, and made His soul an offering for sin, and could cry out in agony, *Eli, Eli, lama sabacthani*. His love and the utter unreserved putting of Himself into our place, not merely to be touched with a feeling for our infirmities, but to be stricken and smitten of GOD and afflicted for our transgressions, to be bruised for our iniquities, to make our peace by taking our chastisement, to heal us by His stripes,—all these show us the terribleness of the wrath of GOD. How it is to be displayed hereafter, how sinners who disdain His mercy are to suffer, and what the punishments will be that are to be apportioned, are recorded for us, but in words that by their very weakness reveal the terror and awfulness of the wrath. There are two other points to be noted. This wrath and vengeance is not as human wrath or vengeance; so the FATHER in mercy hath given judgment to the SON, who gives us the revelation of His FATHER'S pity and of His own love, and who is yet to be the upright Judge, and is to impartially award love to them that love Him, and indignation and wrath, tribulation and anguish, upon every soul of man that doeth evil. And the execution of the sentence is committed to the Angels of Judgment, who are appointed for that purpose to gather all from the four corners of the earth and to lead them away to suffer their sentence.

Wyoming. *Vide* COLORADO.

Y.

Year. Not the secular, but the ecclesiastical year is dwelt on here. The Church year is the consecration to GOD of a natural cycle of time in a holy round of services, each separate one offering to Him praise and worship for His own great glory and for the noble and wonderful acts of creation, preservation, and, above all, redemption, with earnest thanksgivings and commemorations of the several acts of Redemption, from the Incarnation to the Gift of the HOLY GHOST, and remembrances thankfully made for the good examples of those who have become His Saints. There is here subject-matter enough for the whole year. If we add to these the penitential acts with which we must constantly discipline ourselves, we will feel that He has given us so much to dwell upon and to study over of His love, mercy, superintending care, and forbearance, that the wonder is why so many should think so little about it, and why others should need to seek for fresh subjects of devotion.

With such abundant cause for rejoicing and for humility before GOD, with the great central acts of our Redemption demanding from the Christian fervent adoration for the mercies in them, it was impossible to avoid making a division of the fifty-two days sacred unto GOD into a full, orderly, and connected cycle of services. The Feasts of Christmas, of Easter, and of Whit-Sunday marked the broader outlines of this holy year, and indeed Easter and Whit-Sunday fell upon times already sanctified unto GOD by His appointment under the Mosaic Law. The Jew, because of his national feasts, could readily accept the Christian Year. The Gentile was trained in religious feasts occurring at stated periods, and found everything to satisfy him. In fact, these probably were larger and more frequent in the earlier history of Christianity than it is usual to suppose. It would readily result from this that the Christian Year, having certain fixed festivals which were universally observed in all national Churches throughout the world, there would be most naturally developed the intermediate festivals and fasts, each according to the needs of the Church locally, and the bent or characteristic temper of the people to which the Church had to minister.

In this way, without interference and clash, there would be the widest room for those services, and those lessons in them, which the Church could select, both for Worship and Adoration from the people to GOD, and of instruction into all Faith and Practice of holy living. These two, Faith and Practice, must be ever brought prominently forward; so we find in the many links of the Liturgic service of the successive Sundays a principle that interweaves a confession of Faith with the substance of the Worship, which serves also as an instruction in the truths, and seizes upon certain secondary facts and acts of our LORD'S Life, and upon the examples of His Apostles, and holds these up for imitation and practice in the holy conduct of life.

The Calendar of our own Prayer-Book exhibits this. The year is divided into two grand divisions: the first, of the Sundays that extend from the first Sunday in Advent to Trinity-Sunday, and the second, from Trinity-Sunday on through the half-year to Advent-Sunday again. The first part is used to teach doctrine, the second, given up to practical instruction, not so exclusively, however, that there is not a free interchange. But from Advent to Christmas the historical facts of the preparation for CHRIST'S Coming and His Advent, and His Second Coming and our preparation therefor, are dwelt upon. And, following an ancient custom, *Isaiah* is the Prophet chosen for this part of the year. From Christmas through Epiphany, with its Sunday, the LORD JESUS is shown by His miracles to be LORD over all nature. Diseases yield, demons are quelled, the storms are laid at His word. Then come the three Sundays of solemn preparation for Lent, when our duty of self-control and of self-renunciation are brought forward, and so we enter into the remembrance and the sad faltering, distant, imitation of our LORD'S great Fast and of His resistance to temptation.

It calls up to our remembrance the reasons why our LORD suffered, it reminds us that for our sins He endured, and so step by step it prepares us for the solemn Fasting Services of the Holy Week, which terminate at last in the great Fast of Good Friday, which is followed by the glories of the Easter-Feast. The Sunday on which the doctrine of the Resurrection is proclaimed, is made the centre around which all the preceding and succeeding Sundays throughout the universal Church arrange themselves. All refer to this as the crowning act of that Incarnation which the whole Church commemorates at Christmas. The period of forty days from Easter to the Ascension, and of ten days from the Ascension on to Whit-Sunday, are taken up with setting forth the doctrine of the Church, and are always counted as a continuous Feast. The doctrines of the Resurrection, of His sitting as Intercessor and Mediator at the Right Hand of His FATHER, and the Descent of the HOLY GHOST to abide forever with the Church, are all Festal facts for our humanity. Trinity-Sunday is peculiar to the Anglo-Saxon race and to those countries of Northern Europe influenced by Anglo-Saxon missionaries. But for the succeeding Sundays the subjects of teaching change. The Historic pivotal facts are not now dwelt upon, but the practical lessons which yet involve doctrine are taken up one by one, and something of the facts of the unseen world about us is taught. What with the unvarying parts of the Liturgy and with the broidery of Scripture and the key-note struck by the Gospel and Epistles, a rich variety, and yet a continual adherence to a fixed system, is the result. In the mediæval Church the several Sundays had their significant names, which served to keep these several lessons in mind. The Eastern Church following the same plan for the first half of the year, varies the latter part of it by having a different series of Epistles and Gospels and formal names for the several Sundays of the year.

But with this variable system the Church has interwoven a series of holy-days upon fixed dates. These are for our LORD'S Life; the Christmas Feast (December 25), Circumcision (January 1), Epiphany (January 6), the Presentation of CHRIST in the Temple (February 2), Annunciation to the Blessed Virgin Mary (March 25), and the Transfiguration (August 6). The Nativity of St. John the Baptist, the commemorations of our LORD'S Apostles, and of the Holy Innocents, and of St. Stephen the First Martyr, and All Saints, and St. Michael and All Angels, form special holy-days. In other portions of the Church Catholic a larger calendar of saints has been in use, but the American Church has wisely kept to the commemoration of those Saints and blessed ones whose names are written not merely in the yet sealed book of life but in GOD'S book here, and has recognized these only as being worthy to publicly thank GOD for, as gifts to His people. And she returns thanks "for all His servants departed this life in His Faith and Fear, beseeching Him to give us grace so to follow their good examples that with them we may be partakers of His heavenly Kingdom" at every celebration of the communion. A study of the wise and comprehensive plan upon which the Church year is arranged does bring out the truths of the Christian Faith, and enforces them upon the attention in a way that no other that can be devised can do. Its flexibility, its unity of purpose, its various teachings, its insistance Sunday by Sunday of the same essential verities, all these make it as nearly an inspiration as an institution which is the outgrowth from the Christian longings and worship can be.

Our Feasts and our Fasts are influencing those devout Christian bodies around us, who draw near our Common LORD in His Spirit. Imitation and concurrent observances are becoming more and more usual, year by year attesting to the vital power over the Christian life, in a Christian community, which a Christian year devoutly planned and consecrated by ages of holy use must wield.

Z.

Zacharias. The Father of St. John the Baptist, who was an aged Priest of the order of Abijah, the eighth in the course of the twenty-four appointed by King David. A righteous man looking for the promise to Israel, blameless of life. It was his by lot to burn incense at the inner altar of incense at the season of the Atonement. While performing his office there was fulfilled to him the promise made when the altar of incense was commanded: "And thou shalt put it before the veil that is by the ark of the Testimony, before the mercy-seat that is over the testimony, where I will meet with thee."

With reverent bowing towards the veil, alone in the sanctuary, he put upon the altar the incense, and there met him an angel, with the message that he was to be the father of the stern Herald of CHRIST. His incredulity so natural, yet strange in one so full of faith as he was, was given a sign which was at once a judgment and a sure token of the fulfillment of the vision. He was stricken dumb, so that he could not put the blessing upon the people when he came forth from the sanctuary. It continued till after the birth of his son, and then the dumbness was removed when he was required to name his son, and he "wrote saying, His name is John." His hymn of praise is a noble prophecy, with the first verses of which we are thoroughly familiar. It is worthy of note that Zacharias speaks first and most fully of the MESSIAH, and only the latter third of his prophecy dwells upon the mission of his son, the greatest born of women, the mightiest of the messengers of GOD. Beyond what is told us in Holy Writ, we know nothing of this blameless Priest.

Zealots. A fanatic sect of the Jews who were in great vogue in the time of our LORD. They claimed to hold in great honor the commandments, but the spirit in which they interpreted these was a distortion of the zeal of Phinehas the High-Priest who slew the sinning Prince of the tribe of Simeon (Numb. xxv.). They were numerous, daring, and resisting not only the civil power, but their spiritual rulers as well. Annas the High-Priest tried to curb them. Of their number at one time was Simon the Apostle. In the last terrible days of the siege of Jerusalem the Zealots were one cause of the miseries suffered, and of the final fall of the Holy City.

Zechariah. Zechariah, the eleventh of the Minor Prophets, calls himself (Zech. i. 1) the son of Berechiah, the son of Iddo the priest; but in the book of Ezra he is called the son of Iddo (Ezra v. 1). This seeming discrepancy may be explained by the Eastern use of the word *son* to mean any descendant; or by the suggestion that Berechiah, the father, died about the time of the birth of his son, and that Iddo discharged a father's duty by his grandson. This Iddo is thought by many to be "Iddo the priest" mentioned in Neh. xii. 4, whose son Zechariah (v. 16), doubtless the prophet himself, was a priest contemporary with Joiakim, the son of Joshua the High-Priest of the return from captivity (Neh. xii.). It is not known where Zechariah was born, nor at what age he began to prophesy; but as he was with his grandfather, among the first of those who returned to Jerusalem, he must have been born in captivity, and have been about thirty years old when called to the office of prophet; and he is related to have lived to a great age, and to have been buried beside Haggai at Jerusalem. Zechariah the prophet has been identified, or rather confounded, with others of the same name, especially with Zechariah the son of Jeberechiah (Isa. viii. 2), and with Zechariah the priest, son of Jehoiada, murdered by Joash (2 Chron. xxiv. 20), owing probably to the text of St. Matt. xxiii. 35. But the date at which Zechariah the prophet lived and prophesied is sufficient to show the impossibility of these suppositions. For it was in the eighth month of the second year of Darius (520 B.C.) that he was called to the office of a prophet; just two months later than Haggai, with whom he was constantly associated in exhorting the Jews to energy in the work of rebuilding the Temple. In the Septuagint titles of the Psalms the following are attributed to Haggai and Zechariah together: cxxxvii., cxiv., cxlvi., cxlvii., cxlviii. The Peschito Version adds cxxxv., cxxxvi.

In making an analysis of the prophecy of Zechariah it is found convenient to divide it into two parts (chap. i. to viii. and ix. to xiv.), and to consider these separately. In the first part, which is admitted by all to be the genuine work of Zechariah the son of Iddo, three sections are distinguished. The first (chap. i. 1–6), which is introductory, consists of an appeal to the people, founded on experience of the truth of GOD, to repent and be energetic in the work on the Temple. The second section (chap. i. 7 to vi. 15) is made up of a series of visions, all seen in one night, "descriptive of all those hopes and anticipations of which the building of the Temple was the pledge and sure foundation." The third section (chap. vii. and viii.), communicated two years later, is an answer to certain questions addressed to the priests and prophets, followed by a prophecy of the glory of Zion, when the LORD shall return to her, and dwell in the midst of Jerusalem. The second part of Zechariah is the subject of much dispute; some denying that it is indeed by Zechariah the son of Iddo, others maintaining that it is his work; so that critics are nearly equally divided in opinion; and still further, there is much dispute over the authorship of the two sections into which the second part is to be divided, viz.: 1 (chap. ix –xi.), a prophecy against Damascus and Tyre, with promises of protection to Jerusalem; and, 2 (chap. xii.–xiv.), "The burden of the word of the LORD for Israel," —*i.e.*, for the whole nation of the Jews. It is impossible to enter into these questions in so limited a space as a short article, and the reader who desires to pursue them further must be referred to fuller works. (Art. Zechariah in Smith's Dictionary of the Bible.) Whatever view he may adopt concerning their authorship, the moral lesson to be gathered from these chapters is the same, "in either case they satisfy the condition, 'To Him give all the prophets witness;' in either case they are GOD's words addressed to the hearts and consciences of mankind." (Bible Commentary, Introd. to Zech.) Zechariah concludes his prophecy with a grand picture of all nations coming up to Jerusalem to worship, in that day when the kingdoms of this world shall become the kingdoms of our LORD and of His CHRIST, and everything shall be sanctified to His Service; the trappings of worldly pomp and pride, " the bells of the horses;" the meanest utensils, " every pot in Jerusalem" shall be inscribed " Holiness unto the LORD." Zechariah is frequently quoted in the New Testament; the prophecy of the progress of the SAVIOUR into Jerusalem riding upon the foal of an ass, and that of the purchase of the potter's field with the thirty pieces of silver, being from his book. The name Zechariah means " whom the LORD remembers."

Authorities: Smith's Dict. of Bible, Bible Commentary, Gray's Introduction.

Zephaniah. Zephaniah, the ninth of the Minor Prophets, announces himself to be the son of Cushi, the son of Gedaliah, the son of Amariah, the son of Hizkiah (Zeph. i. 1). As this name is the same as that of the King Hezekiah, it is thought that the prophet was of the royal house of Judah. But, as the interval between the time of the King and the date of the prophet is rather short to admit of three intermediate generations, others adopt the tradition that Zephaniah was of the tribe of Simeon. His prophecy was delivered in the days of Josiah, King of Judah; probably in the early part of it; as the denunciations, warnings, and promises of Zephaniah would have been a great assistance to the religious reformation effected by Josiah in the eighteenth year of his reign. Some, indeed, find reason for thinking that Zephaniah preceded Jeremiah, who prophesied in the thirteenth year of Josiah's reign, because the latter seems to speak of certain abuses as corrected against which Zephaniah had prophesied (compare Zeph. i. 4, 5, 9. with Jer. ii.). Hence the date of this prophet would be from 642 to 629 B.C.

The book of Zephaniah, which is addressed to Judah and Jerusalem, is short, its chief characteristics " are the unity and harmony of the composition, the grace, energy, and dignity of its style, and the rapid and effective alternations of threats and promises. Its prophetical import is chiefly shown in the accurate predictions of the desolation which has fallen upon each of the nations denounced for their crimes; Ethiopia, which is menaced with a terrible invasion, being alone exempted from the doom of perpetual ruin. The general tone of the last portion is Messianic, but without any specific reference to the person of our LORD." (Art. Zephaniah in Smith's Dict. of the Bible.) The following analysis of the prophecy is given: " In chap. i. the utter desolation of Judah is predicted as a judgment for idolatry and neglect of the LORD, the luxury of the princes, and the violence and deceit of their dependents (3-9). The prosperity, security, and insolence of the people is contrasted with the horrors of the day of wrath (10-18). Chap. ii. contains a call to repentance (1-3), with a prediction of the ruin of the cities of the Philistines and the restoration of the House of Judah after the visitation (4-7). Other enemies of Judah, Moab, and Ammon are threatened with perpetual destruction (8-15). In chap. iii. the prophet addresses Jerusalem, which he reproves sharply for vice and disobedience (1-7). He then concludes with a series of promises (8-20)." (Student's O. T. History, App. i.) The name Zephaniah means " Watcher of the LORD," or as some will have it, " One whom JEHOVAH guards."

Same authorities as for other Minor Prophets.

L'ENVOI.

This CHURCH CYCLOPÆDIA, which is offered to the Laity of the American Church, is intended to convey to the Churchman all necessary instruction upon the History, Doctrine, Worship, and Ritual of his own branch of the Church Catholic. Only such reference is made to other parts of the Church as will explain his own position. Its purpose is to set forth as clearly as possible the Person and Redemptive Acts of our Blessed LORD; the foundation and organization of the Church as His Body; the facts of the historical continuity of the Church in these United States in that Body as a living integral portion of the Church Catholic; the proof that She is the Keeper and Witness for, and defender of, the Integrity, Authority, and Inspiration of Holy Writ; that Her Priests are Stewards of the Mysteries of GOD; that She carries out in our modern civilization the great Nicene principles; and that She boldly meets, and by the grace of the HOLY SPIRIT will solve, the religious problems of the day.

How far the CYCLOPÆDIA has fulfilled this conception others must decide; but the very valuable papers contributed by writers authorized to speak on their several topics will go far to substantiate the claim. All the articles have been written anew for the CYCLOPÆDIA. The Dictionaries of Broughton, Hook, Blunt, and Smith have been freely used. The editor is responsible for all unsigned articles except those upon the COUNCILS and the MINOR PROPHETS, which are from the pen of the Rev. R. A. Benton, of St. Paul's School, and the article upon the Atonement, which is contributed by one recently called to the highest office in the Church. To the Rev. S. F. Hotchkin the editor's hearty thanks are due for valuable aid in procuring Diocesan Histories.

Two contributors have been called to their rest. The grief of the whole Church has burst forth at the loss of one of her foremost Bishops, the Rt. Rev. Robert H. Clarkson, of Nebraska. The like shadow of grief fell no less deeply upon the little circle of those who were bereaved of a beloved mother, summoned most suddenly into the Presence of the LORD.

May He bless the work to which His sainted servants have contributed.

A. A. BENTON.

DELAWARE COLLEGE,
  NEWARK, DELAWARE.